NEW MAY 2002

S0-BAU-360

KEY TO WORLD MAP PAGES

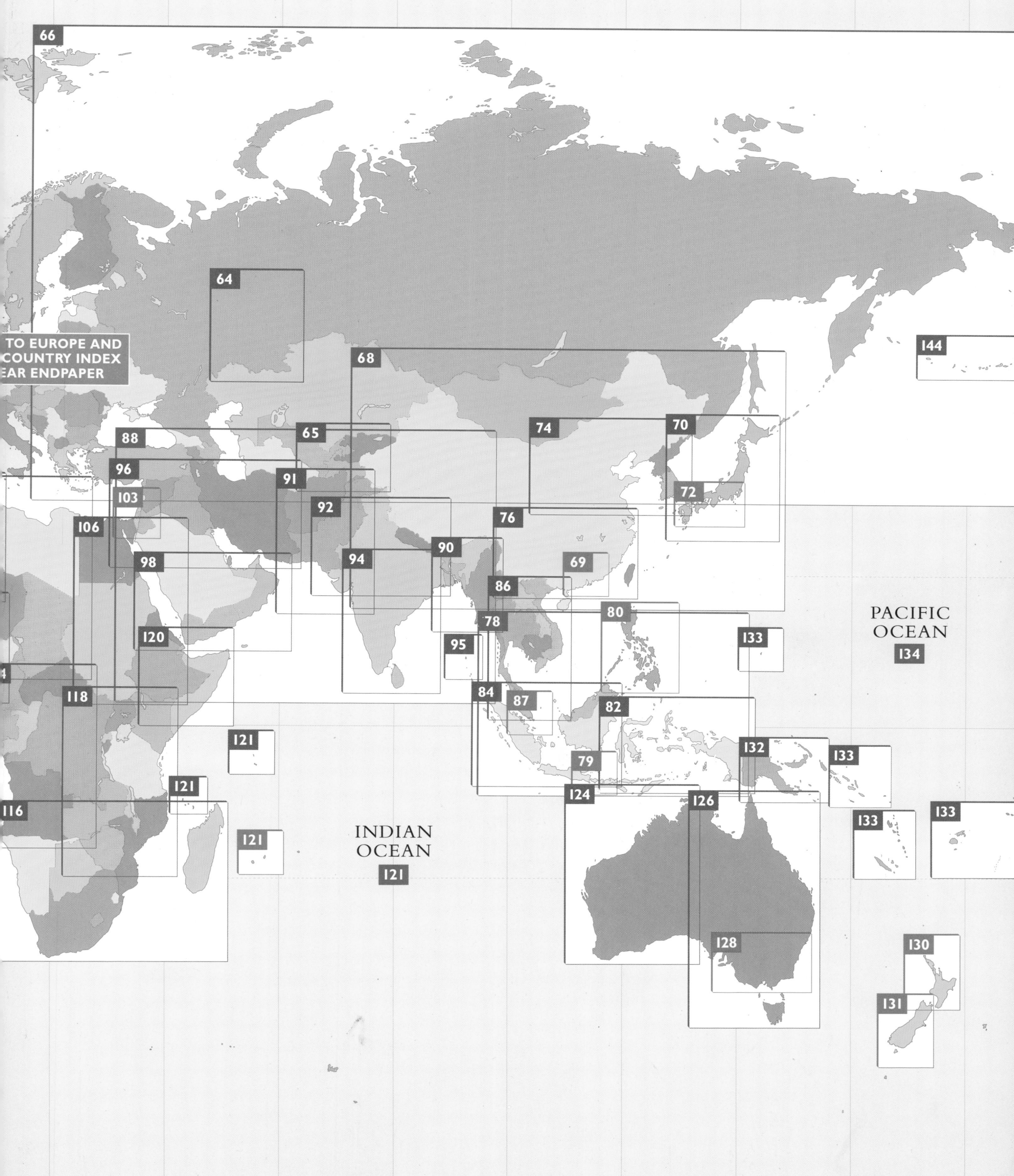

66

64

TO EUROPE AND
COUNTRY INDEX
EAR ENDPAPER

68

88

65

74

70

96

91

103

92

76

72

106

94

90

69

98

86

80

PACIFIC
OCEAN

134

120

78

133

95

116

118

84

87

82

121

132

133

121

79

133

133

124

126

116

121

INDIAN
OCEAN

121

128

130

131

OXFORD

ATLAS
OF THE
WORLD

NINTH EDITION

ACKNOWLEDGEMENTS

IMAGES OF EARTH (PAGES IX–XXIV)
All satellite images in this section courtesy
of NPA Group Limited, Edenbridge, Kent
(www.satmaps.com)

THE GAZETTEER OF NATIONS
TEXT Keith Lye

INTRODUCTION TO WORLD GEOGRAPHY
PICTURE ACKNOWLEDGEMENTS
Courtesy of NPA Group, Edenbridge,
 UK 9, 48
Science Photo Library /Earth Satellite
 Corporation 20, /NOAA 22 bottom left
 and bottom right

ILLUSTRATIONS
Stefan Chabluk, William Donohoe,
Bernard Thornton Artists /Steve Seymour

STAR CHARTS
John Cox and Richard Monkhouse

CARTOGRAPHY BY PHILIP'S

CITY MAPS
PAGE 11, Dublin. Based on Ordnance Survey
Ireland by permission of the Government
Permit No. 7337. © Government of Ireland

PAGE 15, London, and page 11, Edinburgh.
Based upon the Ordnance Survey Maps with
the permission of the Controller of Her
Majesty's Stationery Office. © Crown copyright
2001. All rights reserved. Licence No. 339817

VECTOR DATA: Courtesy of Gräfe and Unser
Verlag GmbH, München, Germany (city
center maps of Bangkok, Beijing, Cape Town,
Jerusalem, Mexico City, Moscow, Singapore,
Sydney, Tokyo and Washington D.C.)

Copyright © 2001 Philip's

Philip's, a division of
Octopus Publishing Group Limited,
2–4 Heron Quays, London E14 4JP

Published in North America by
Oxford University Press, Inc.,
198 Madison Avenue,
New York, N.Y. 10016

www.oup.usa.org/atlas

Oxford is a registered trademark of
Oxford University Press

All rights reserved. No part of this
publication may be reproduced, stored in
a retrieval system, or transmitted in any
form or by any means, electronic, electrical,
chemical, mechanical, optical, photocopying,
recording, or otherwise, without the prior
permission of the Publisher.

*Library of Congress Cataloging-in-Publication
Data available*

ISBN 0–19–521848–5

Printing (last digit): 9 8 7 6 5 4 3 2

Printed in Spain

FOREWORD

A N AUTHORITATIVE AND SERIOUS REFERENCE WORK, the Oxford *Atlas of the World* is one of the finest atlases available anywhere in the world. The atlas incorporates computer-derived maps which have been produced using the very latest in digital cartographic techniques.

The Oxford *Atlas of the World* has been revised and updated with the help of a panel of specialist geography consultants from the United Kingdom and the United States, whose specialties range from the history of cartography, urban and social geography, epidemiology and the European Union to biogeography and applied geomorphology. The result of their valuable input can be seen in the wealth of up-to-date maps and data contained in the "*Introduction to World Geography*" section of this atlas.

HOW TO USE THE ATLAS
The atlas is divided into a number of sections which are explained below.

WORLD STATISTICS AND IMAGES OF EARTH
World statistics on topics such as area and population for every country in the world, and physical dimensions – including the largest islands, lakes and seas, the highest mountains and the longest rivers, by continent. Also included in this section is a selection of detailed, up-to-date maps highlighting regions around the world that are currently in the news, such as the former Yugoslavia and Kosovo, the Near East, India and Kashmir, and the Caucasus region. This section is followed by a beautifully illustrated satellite section showing 16 of the world's major regions and cities in the Americas, Europe, Africa, Asia, and Australasia.

THE GAZETTEER OF NATIONS
A comprehensive A–Z reference providing concise profiles of every country's geography, climate, history, politics and economy, together with ready-reference tables, and illustrated with flags and locator maps.

INTRODUCTION TO WORLD GEOGRAPHY
A richly informative section comprising 48 pages of maps, charts, graphs, and diagrams which explain key themes about the world in which we live. The topics covered include the Solar System, oceans, climate, the environment, energy, and trade. Explanatory text on each spread describes the patterns shown by the data.

CITY MAPS
A detailed selection of maps for 67 urban areas around the world. These are useful for planning trips abroad as well as for comparative studies of cities worldwide. Also included is a 7-page index to the city maps.

WORLD MAPS
An outstanding collection of 176 pages of distinctive Philip's cartography. The highly acclaimed physical world maps combine relief shading with layer-colored contours to give a striking visual picture of the Earth's surface. Roads, railroads, canals, and airports are accurately depicted on the maps, and towns and cities are clearly marked. More information on the key features employed in the construction and presentation of the maps is given on the facing page.

INDEX
The 75,000-name index to the world maps includes geographical features as well as towns and cities, with both latitude/longitude and letter/figure grid references.

SPECIALIST GEOGRAPHY CONSULTANTS

THE EDITORS are grateful to the following people for acting as specialist geography consultants on the '*Introduction to World Geography*' front section:
Professor D. Brunsden Kings College, University of London, UK
Dr C. Clarke Oxford University, UK
Professor P. Haggett University of Bristol, UK
Professor M-L. Hsu University of Minnesota, Minnesota, USA
Professor K. McLachlan Geopolitical and International Boundaries Research Centre, School of Oriental and African Studies, University of London, UK

Professor M. Monmonier Syracuse University, New York, USA
Professor M. J. Tooley University of St Andrews, UK
Dr T. Unwin Royal Holloway, University of London, UK

THE EDITORS would also like to thank:
Keith Lye
Robin Scagell
Dr I. S. Evans Durham University, UK
Dr Andrew Tatham The Royal Geographical Society

WORLD MAPS

The reference maps which form the main body of this atlas have been prepared in accordance with the highest standards of international cartography to provide an accurate and detailed representation of the Earth. The scales and projections used have been carefully chosen to give balanced coverage of the world, while emphasizing the most densely populated and economically significant regions. A hallmark of Philip's mapping is the use of hill shading and relief coloring to create a graphic impression of landforms: this makes the maps exceptionally easy to read. However, knowledge of the key features employed in the construction and presentation of the maps will enable the reader to derive the fullest benefit from the atlas.

MAP SEQUENCE

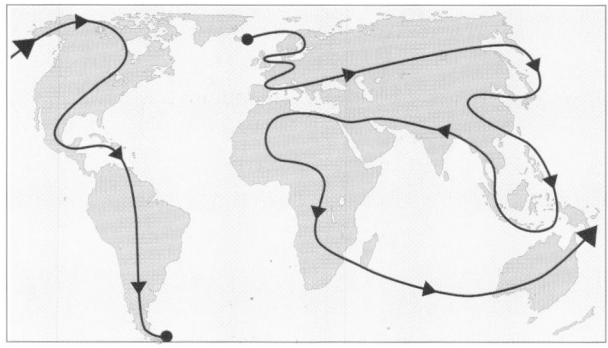

The atlas covers the Earth continent by continent: first Europe; then its land neighbor Asia (mapped north before south, in a clockwise sequence), then Africa, Australia and Oceania, North America and South America. This is the classic arrangement adopted by most cartographers since the 16th century. For each continent, there are maps at a variety of scales. First, physical relief and political maps of the whole continent; then a series of larger-scale maps of the regions within the continent, each followed, where required, by still larger-scale maps of the most important or densely populated areas. The governing principle is that by turning the pages of the atlas, the reader moves steadily from north to south through each continent, with each map overlapping its neighbors. A key map showing this sequence, and the area covered by each map, can be found on the endpapers of the atlas.

MAP PRESENTATION

With very few exceptions (e.g. for the Arctic and Antarctic), the maps are drawn with north at the top, regardless of whether they are presented upright or sideways on the page. In the borders will be found the map title; a locator diagram showing the area covered and the page numbers for maps of adjacent areas; the scale; the projection used; the degrees of latitude and longitude; and the letters and figures used in the index for locating place names and geographical features. Physical relief maps also have a height reference panel identifying the colors used for each layer of contouring.

MAP SYMBOLS

Each map contains a vast amount of detail which can only be conveyed clearly and accurately by the use of symbols. Points and circles of varying sizes locate and identify the relative importance of towns and cities; different styles of type are employed for administrative, geographical and regional place names to aid identification. A variety of pictorial symbols denote landforms such as glaciers, marshes and coral reefs, and man-made structures including roads, railroads, airports and canals. International borders are shown by red lines. Where neighboring countries are in dispute, for example in parts of the Middle East, the maps show the *de facto* boundary between nations, regardless of the legal or historical situation. The

symbols are explained on the first page of the World Maps section of the atlas.

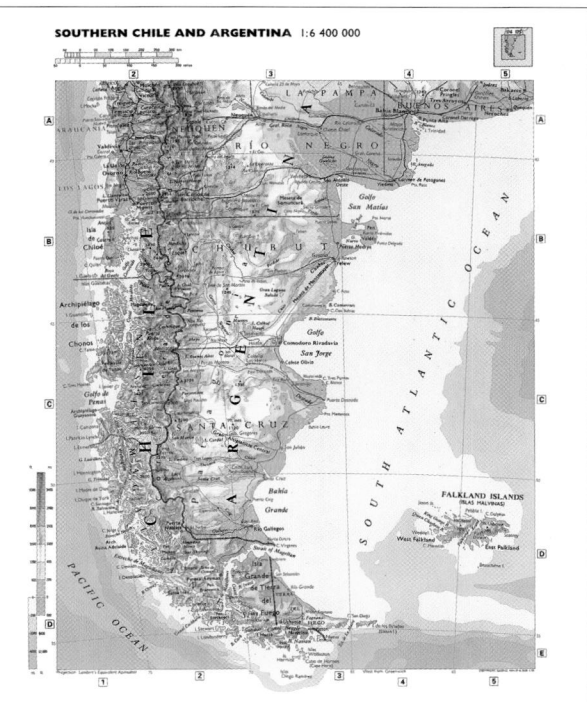

MAP SCALES

1:16 000 000
1 inch = 252 statute miles

The scale of each map is given in the numerical form known as the "representative fraction." The first figure is always one, signifying one unit of distance on the map; the second figure, usually in millions, is the number by which the map unit must be multiplied to give the equivalent distance on the Earth's surface. Calculations can easily be made in centimeters and kilometers, by dividing the Earth units figure by 100 000 (i.e. deleting the last five 0s). Thus 1:1 000 000 means 1 cm = 10 km. The calculation for inches and miles is more laborious, but 1 000 000 divided by 63 360 (the number of inches in a mile) shows that 1:1 000 000 means approximately 1 inch = 16 miles. The table below provides distance equivalents for scales down to 1:50 000 000.

LARGE SCALE		
1:1 000 000	1 cm = 10 km	1 inch = 16 miles
1:2 500 000	1 cm = 25 km	1 inch = 39.5 miles
1:5 000 000	1 cm = 50 km	1 inch = 79 miles
1:6 000 000	1 cm = 60 km	1 inch = 95 miles
1:8 000 000	1 cm = 80 km	1 inch = 126 miles
1:10 000 000	1 cm = 100 km	1 inch = 158 miles
1:15 000 000	1 cm = 150 km	1 inch = 237 miles
1:20 000 000	1 cm = 200 km	1 inch = 316 miles
1:50 000 000	1 cm = 500 km	1 inch = 790 miles
SMALL SCALE		

MEASURING DISTANCES

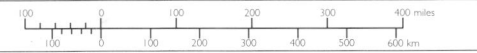

Although each map is accompanied by a scale bar, distances cannot always be measured with confidence because of the distortions involved in portraying the curved surface of the Earth on a flat page. As a general rule, the larger the map scale, the more accurate and reliable will be the distance measured. On small-scale maps such as those of the world and of entire continents, measurement may only be accurate along the "standard parallels," or central axes, and should not be attempted without considering the map projection.

MAP PROJECTIONS

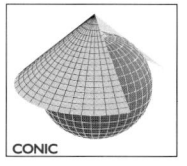

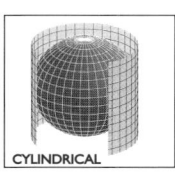

Unlike a globe, no flat map can give a true scale representation of the world in terms of area, shape and position of every region. Each of the numerous systems that have been devised for projecting the curved surface of the Earth on to a flat page involves the sacrifice of accuracy in one or more of these elements. The variations in shape and position of land masses such as Alaska, Greenland and Australia, for example, can be quite dramatic when different projections are compared.

For this atlas, the guiding principle has been to select projections that involve the least distortion of size and distance. The projection used for each map is noted in the border. Most fall into one of three categories – conic, cylindrical or azimuthal – whose basic concepts are shown above. Each involves plotting the forms of the Earth's surface on a grid of latitude and longitude lines, which may be shown as parallels, curves or radiating spokes.

LATITUDE AND LONGITUDE

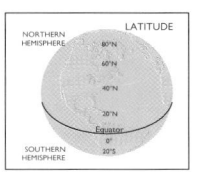
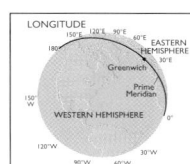
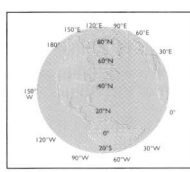

Accurate positioning of individual points on the Earth's surface is made possible by reference to the geometrical system of latitude and longitude. Latitude parallels are drawn west–east around the Earth and numbered by degrees north and south of the Equator, which is designated 0° of latitude. Longitude meridians are drawn north–south and numbered by degrees east and west of the prime meridian, 0° of longitude, which passes through Greenwich in England. By referring to these co-ordinates and their subdivisions of minutes (1/60th of a degree) and seconds (1/60th of a minute), any place on Earth can be located to within a few hundred yards. Latitude and longitude are indicated by blue lines on the maps; they are straight or curved according to the projection employed. Reference to these lines is the easiest way of determining the relative positions of places on different maps, and for plotting compass directions.

NAME FORMS

For ease of reference, both English and local name forms appear in the atlas. Oceans, seas and countries are shown in English throughout the atlas; country names may be abbreviated to their commonly accepted form (e.g. Germany, not The Federal Republic of Germany). Conventional English forms are also used for place names on the smaller-scale maps of the continents. However, local name forms are used on all large-scale and regional maps, with the English form given in brackets only for important cities – the large-scale map of Russia and Central Asia thus shows Moskva (Moscow). For countries which do not use a Roman script, place names have been transcribed according to the systems adopted by the British and US Geographic Names Authorities. For China, the Pin Yin system has been used, with some more widely known forms appearing in brackets, as with Beijing (Peking). Both English and local names appear in the index, the English form being cross-referenced to the local form.

CONTENTS

World Statistics: Countries

This alphabetical list includes all the countries and territories of the world. If a territory is not completely independent, then the country it is associated with is named. The area figures give the total area of land, inland water and ice. Units for areas and populations are thousands. The population figures are 2000 estimates. The annual income is the Gross National Product per capita in US dollars. The figures are the latest available, usually 1999 estimates.

Country/Territory	Area km² Thousands	Area miles² Thousands	Population Thousands	Capital	Annual Income US $
Afghanistan	652	252	26,511	Kabul	800
Albania	28.8	11.1	3,795	Tirana	870
Algeria	2,382	920	32,904	Algiers	1,550
American Samoa (US)	0.20	0.08	39	Pago Pago	2,600
Andorra	0.45	0.17	49	Andorra La Vella	18,000
Angola	1,247	481	13,295	Luanda	220
Anguilla (UK)	0.1	0.04	8	The Valley	6,800
Antigua & Barbuda	0.44	0.17	79	St John's	8,520
Argentina	2,767	1,068	36,238	Buenos Aires	7,600
Armenia	29.8	11.5	3,968	Yerevan	490
Aruba (Netherlands)	0.19	0.07	58	Oranjestad	22,000
Australia	7,687	2,968	18,855	Canberra	20,050
Austria	83.9	32.4	7,613	Vienna	25,970
Azerbaijan	86.6	33.4	8,324	Baku	550
Azores (Portugal)	2.2	0.87	238	Ponta Delgada	–
Bahamas	13.9	5.4	295	Nassau	20,100
Bahrain	0.68	0.26	683	Manama	7,640
Bangladesh	144	56	150,589	Dhaka	370
Barbados	0.43	0.17	265	Bridgetown	7,890
Belarus	207.6	80.1	10,697	Minsk	2,630
Belgium	30.5	11.8	9,832	Brussels	24,510
Belize	23	8.9	230	Belmopan	2,730
Benin	113	43	6,369	Porto-Novo	380
Bermuda (UK)	0.05	0.02	62	Hamilton	35,590
Bhutan	47	18.1	1,906	Thimphu	510
Bolivia	1,099	424	9,724	La Paz/Sucre	1,010
Bosnia-Herzegovina	51	20	4,601	Sarajevo	1,720
Botswana	582	225	1,822	Gaborone	3,240
Brazil	8,512	3,286	179,487	Brasília	4,420
Brunei	5.8	2.2	333	Bandar Seri Begawan	24,630
Bulgaria	111	43	9,071	Sofia	1,380
Burkina Faso	274	106	12,092	Ouagadougou	240
Burma (= Myanmar)	677	261	51,129	Rangoon	1,200
Burundi	27.8	10.7	7,358	Bujumbura	120
Cambodia	181	70	10,046	Phnom Penh	260
Cameroon	475	184	16,701	Yaoundé	580
Canada	9,976	3,852	28,488	Ottawa	19,320
Canary Is. (Spain)	7.3	2.8	1,494	Las Palmas/Santa Cruz	–
Cape Verde Is.	4	1.6	515	Praia	1,330
Cayman Is. (UK)	0.26	0.10	35	George Town	20,000
Central African Republic	623	241	4,074	Bangui	290
Chad	1,284	496	7,337	Ndjaména	200
Chile	757	292	15,272	Santiago	4,740
China	9,597	3,705	1,299,180	Beijing	780
Colombia	1,139	440	39,397	Bogotá	2,250
Comoros	2.2	0.86	670	Moroni	350
Congo	342	132	3,167	Brazzaville	670
Congo (Dem. Rep. of the)	2,345	905	49,190	Kinshasa	110
Cook Is. (NZ)	0.24	0.09	17	Avarua	900
Costa Rica	51.1	19.7	3,711	San José	2,740
Croatia	56.5	21.8	4,960	Zagreb	4,580
Cuba	111	43	11,504	Havana	1,560
Cyprus	9.3	3.6	762	Nicosia	11,960
Czech Republic	78.9	30.4	10,500	Prague	5,060
Denmark	43.1	16.6	5,153	Copenhagen	32,030
Djibouti	23.2	9	552	Djibouti	790
Dominica	0.75	0.29	87	Roseau	3,170
Dominican Republic	48.7	18.8	8,621	Santo Domingo	1,910
Ecuador	284	109	13,319	Quito	1,310
Egypt	1,001	387	64,210	Cairo	1,400
El Salvador	21	8.1	6,739	San Salvador	1,900
Equatorial Guinea	28.1	10.8	455	Malabo	1,170
Eritrea	94	36	4,523	Asmara	200
Estonia	44.7	17.3	1,647	Tallinn	3,480
Ethiopia	1,128	436	61,841	Addis Ababa	100
Faroe Is. (Denmark)	1.4	0.54	49	Tórshavn	16,000
Fiji	18.3	7.1	883	Suva	2,210
Finland	338	131	5,077	Helsinki	23,780
France	552	213	58,145	Paris	23,480
French Guiana (France)	90	34.7	130	Cayenne	6,000
French Polynesia (France)	4	1.5	268	Papeete	18,050
Gabon	268	103	1,612	Libreville	3,350
Gambia, The	11.3	4.4	1,119	Banjul	340
Georgia	69.7	26.9	5,777	Tbilisi	620
Germany	357	138	76,962	Berlin	25,350
Ghana	239	92	20,564	Accra	390
Gibraltar (UK)	0.007	0.003	32	Gibraltar Town	5,000
Greece	132	51	10,193	Athens	11,770
Greenland (Denmark)	2,176	840	60	Nuuk (Godthåb)	16,100
Grenada	0.34	0.13	83	St George's	3,450
Guadeloupe (France)	1.7	0.66	365	Basse-Terre	9,200
Guam (US)	0.55	0.21	128	Agana	19,000
Guatemala	109	42	12,222	Guatemala City	1,660
Guinea	246	95	7,830	Conakry	510
Guinea-Bissau	36.1	13.9	1,197	Bissau	160
Guyana	215	83	891	Georgetown	760
Haiti	27.8	10.7	8,003	Port-au-Prince	460
Honduras	112	43	6,846	Tegucigalpa	760
Hong Kong (China)	1.1	0.40	6,336	–	23,520
Hungary	93	35.9	10,531	Budapest	4,650
Iceland	103	40	274	Reykjavik	29,280
India	3,288	1,269	1,041,543	New Delhi	450
Indonesia	1,905	735	218,661	Jakarta	580
Iran	1,648	636	68,759	Tehran	1,760
Iraq	438	169	26,339	Baghdad	2,400
Ireland	70.3	27.1	4,086	Dublin	19,160
Israel	27	10.3	5,321	Jerusalem	17,450
Italy	301	116	57,195	Rome	19,710
Ivory Coast (Côte d'Ivoire)	322	125	17,600	Yamoussoukro	710
Jamaica	11	4.2	2,735	Kingston	2,330
Japan	378	146	128,470	Tokyo	32,230
Jordan	89.2	34.4	5,558	Amman	1,500
Kazakstan	2,717	1,049	19,006	Astana	1,230
Kenya	580	224	35,060	Nairobi	360
Kiribati	0.72	0.28	72	Tarawa	910
Korea, North	121	47	26,117	Pyŏngyang	1,000
Korea, South	99	38.2	46,403	Seoul	8,490
Kuwait	17.8	6.9	2,639	Kuwait City	22,700
Kyrgyzstan	198.5	76.6	5,403	Bishkek	300
Laos	237	91	5,463	Vientiane	280
Latvia	65	25	2,768	Riga	2,470
Lebanon	10.4	4	3,327	Beirut	3,700
Lesotho	30.4	11.7	2,370	Maseru	550
Liberia	111	43	3,575	Monrovia	1,000
Libya	1,760	679	6,500	Tripoli	6,700
Liechtenstein	0.16	0.06	28	Vaduz	50,000
Lithuania	65.2	25.2	3,935	Vilnius	2,620
Luxembourg	2.6	1	377	Luxembourg	44,640
Macau (China)	0.02	0.006	656	Macau	16,000
Macedonia	25.7	9.9	2,157	Skopje	1,690
Madagascar	587	227	16,627	Antananarivo	250
Madeira (Portugal)	0.81	0.31	253	Funchal	–
Malawi	118	46	12,458	Lilongwe	190
Malaysia	330	127	21,983	Kuala Lumpur	3,400
Maldives	0.30	0.12	283	Malé	1,160
Mali	1,240	479	12,685	Bamako	240
Malta	0.32	0.12	366	Valletta	9,210
Marshall Is.	0.18	0.07	70	Dalap-Uliga-Darrit	1,560
Martinique (France)	1.1	0.42	362	Fort-de-France	10,700
Mauritania	1,030	412	2,702	Nouakchott	380
Mauritius	2.0	0.72	1,201	Port Louis	3,590
Mayotte (France)	0.37	0.14	141	Mamoundzou	1,430
Mexico	1,958	756	107,233	Mexico City	4,400
Micronesia, Fed. States of	0.70	0.27	110	Palikir	1,810
Moldova	33.7	13	4,707	Chişinău	370
Monaco	0.002	0.0001	30	Monaco	25,000
Mongolia	1,567	605	2,847	Ulan Bator	350
Montserrat (UK)	0.10	0.04	13	Plymouth	4,500
Morocco	447	172	31,559	Rabat	1,200
Mozambique	802	309	20,493	Maputo	230
Namibia	825	318	2,437	Windhoek	1,890
Nauru	0.02	0.008	10	Yaren District	10,000
Nepal	141	54	24,084	Katmandu	220
Netherlands	41.5	16	15,829	Amsterdam/The Hague	24,320
Netherlands Antilles (Neths)	0.99	0.38	203	Willemstad	11,500
New Caledonia (France)	18.6	7.2	195	Nouméa	11,400
New Zealand	269	104	3,662	Wellington	13,780
Nicaragua	130	50	5,261	Managua	430
Niger	1,267	489	10,752	Niamey	190
Nigeria	924	357	105,000	Abuja	310
Northern Mariana Is. (US)	0.48	0.18	50	Saipan	11,500
Norway	324	125	4,331	Oslo	32,880
Oman	212	82	2,176	Muscat	7,900
Pakistan	796	307	162,409	Islamabad	470
Palau	0.46	0.18	18	Koror	5,000
Panama	77.1	29.8	2,893	Panama City	3,070
Papua New Guinea	463	179	4,845	Port Moresby	800
Paraguay	407	157	5,538	Asunción	1,580
Peru	1,285	496	26,276	Lima	2,390
Philippines	300	116	77,473	Manila	1,020
Poland	313	121	40,366	Warsaw	3,960
Portugal	92.4	35.7	10,587	Lisbon	10,600
Puerto Rico (US)	9	3.5	3,836	San Juan	8,200
Qatar	11	4.2	499	Doha	17,100
Réunion (France)	2.5	0.97	692	Saint-Denis	4,800
Romania	238	92	24,000	Bucharest	1,520
Russia	17,075	6,592	155,096	Moscow	2,270
Rwanda	26.3	10.2	10,200	Kigali	250
St Kitts & Nevis	0.36	0.14	44	Basseterre	6,420
St Lucia	0.62	0.24	177	Castries	3,770
St Vincent & Grenadines	0.39	0.15	128	Kingstown	2,700
Samoa	2.8	1.1	171	Apia	1,020
San Marino	0.06	0.02	25	San Marino	20,000
São Tomé & Príncipe	0.96	0.37	151	São Tomé	270
Saudi Arabia	2,150	830	20,697	Riyadh	6,910
Senegal	197	76	8,716	Dakar	510
Seychelles	0.46	0.18	75	Victoria	6,540
Sierra Leone	71.7	27.7	5,437	Freetown	130
Singapore	0.62	0.24	3,000	Singapore	29,610
Slovak Republic	49	18.9	5,500	Bratislava	3,590
Slovenia	20.3	7.8	2,055	Ljubljana	9,890
Solomon Is.	28.9	11.2	429	Honiara	750
Somalia	638	246	9,736	Mogadishu	600
South Africa	1,220	471	43,666	C. Town/Pretoria/Bloem.	3,160
Spain	505	195	40,667	Madrid	14,000
Sri Lanka	65.6	25.3	19,416	Colombo	820
Sudan	2,506	967	33,625	Khartoum	330
Surinam	163	63	497	Paramaribo	1,660
Swaziland	17.4	6.7	1,121	Mbabane	1,360
Sweden	450	174	8,560	Stockholm	25,040
Switzerland	41.3	15.9	6,762	Bern	38,350
Syria	185	71	17,826	Damascus	970
Taiwan	36	13.9	22,000	Taipei	12,400
Tajikistan	143.1	55.2	7,041	Dushanbe	290
Tanzania	945	365	39,639	Dodoma	240
Thailand	513	198	63,670	Bangkok	1,960
Togo	56.8	21.9	4,861	Lomé	320
Tonga	0.75	0.29	92	Nuku'alofa	1,720
Trinidad & Tobago	5.1	2	1,484	Port of Spain	4,390
Tunisia	164	63	9,924	Tunis	2,100
Turkey	779	301	66,789	Ankara	2,900
Turkmenistan	488.1	188.5	4,585	Ashkhabad	660
Turks & Caicos Is. (UK)	0.43	0.17	12	Cockburn Town	5,000
Tuvalu	0.03	0.01	11	Fongafale	600
Uganda	236	91	26,958	Kampala	320
Ukraine	603.7	233.1	52,558	Kiev	750
United Arab Emirates	83.6	32.3	1,951	Abu Dhabi	17,870
United Kingdom	243.3	94	58,393	London	22,640
United States of America	9,373	3,619	266,096	Washington, DC	30,600
Uruguay	177	68	3,274	Montevideo	5,900
Uzbekistan	447.4	172.7	26,044	Tashkent	720
Vanuatu	12.2	4.7	206	Port-Vila	1,170
Venezuela	912	352	24,715	Caracas	3,670
Vietnam	332	127	82,427	Hanoi	370
Virgin Is. (UK)	0.15	0.06	15	Road Town	–
Virgin Is. (US)	0.34	0.13	135	Charlotte Amalie	12,500
Wallis & Futuna Is. (France)	0.20	0.08	26	Mata-Utu	–
Western Sahara	266	103	228	El Aaiún	300
Yemen	528	204	13,219	Sana	350
Yugoslavia	102.3	39.5	10,761	Belgrade	2,300
Zambia	753	291	12,267	Lusaka	320
Zimbabwe	391	151	13,123	Harare	520

World Statistics: Physical Dimensions

Each topic list is divided into continents and within a continent the items are listed in order of size. The bottom part of many of the lists is selective in order to give examples from as many different countries as possible. The order of the continents is the same as in the atlas, beginning with Europe and ending with South America. The figures are rounded as appropriate.

World, Continents, Oceans

	km²	miles²	%
The World	509,450,000	196,672,000	–
Land	149,450,000	57,688,000	29.3
Water	360,000,000	138,984,000	70.7
Asia	44,500,000	17,177,000	29.8
Africa	30,302,000	11,697,000	20.3
North America	24,241,000	9,357,000	16.2
South America	17,793,000	6,868,000	11.9
Antarctica	14,100,000	5,443,000	9.4
Europe	9,957,000	3,843,000	6.7
Australia & Oceania	8,557,000	3,303,000	5.7
Pacific Ocean	179,679,000	69,356,000	49.9
Atlantic Ocean	92,373,000	35,657,000	25.7
Indian Ocean	73,917,000	28,532,000	20.5
Arctic Ocean	14,090,000	5,439,000	3.9

Ocean Depths

Atlantic Ocean	m	ft
Puerto Rico (Milwaukee) Deep	9,220	30,249
Cayman Trench	7,680	25,197
Gulf of Mexico	5,203	17,070
Mediterranean Sea	5,121	16,801
Black Sea	2,211	7,254
North Sea	660	2,165

Indian Ocean	m	ft
Java Trench	7,450	24,442
Red Sea	2,635	8,454

Pacific Ocean	m	ft
Mariana Trench	11,022	36,161
Tonga Trench	10,882	35,702
Japan Trench	10,554	34,626
Kuril Trench	10,542	34,587

Arctic Ocean	m	ft
Molloy Deep	5,608	18,399

Mountains

Europe		m	ft
Elbrus	*Russia*	5,642	18,510
Mont Blanc	*France/Italy*	4,807	15,771
Monte Rosa	*Italy/Switzerland*	4,634	15,203
Dom	*Switzerland*	4,545	14,911
Liskamm	*Switzerland*	4,527	14,852
Weisshorn	*Switzerland*	4,505	14,780
Taschorn	*Switzerland*	4,490	14,730
Matterhorn/Cervino	*Italy/Switzerland*	4,478	14,691
Mont Maudit	*France/Italy*	4,465	14,649
Dent Blanche	*Switzerland*	4,356	14,291
Nadelhorn	*Switzerland*	4,327	14,196
Grandes Jorasses	*France/Italy*	4,208	13,806
Jungfrau	*Switzerland*	4,158	13,642
Grossglockner	*Austria*	3,797	12,457
Mulhacén	*Spain*	3,478	11,411
Zugspitze	*Germany*	2,962	9,718
Olympus	*Greece*	2,917	9,570
Triglav	*Slovenia*	2,863	9,393
Gerlachovka	*Slovak Republic*	2,655	8,711
Galdhöpiggen	*Norway*	2,468	8,100
Kebnekaise	*Sweden*	2,117	6,946
Ben Nevis	*UK*	1,343	4,406

Asia		m	ft
Everest	*China/Nepal*	8,850	29,035
K2 (Godwin Austen)	*China/Kashmir*	8,611	28,251
Kanchenjunga	*India/Nepal*	8,598	28,208
Lhotse	*China/Nepal*	8,516	27,939
Makalu	*China/Nepal*	8,481	27,824
Cho Oyu	*China/Nepal*	8,201	26,906
Dhaulagiri	*Nepal*	8,172	26,811
Manaslu	*Nepal*	8,156	26,758
Nanga Parbat	*Kashmir*	8,126	26,660
Annapurna	*Nepal*	8,078	26,502
Gasherbrum	*China/Kashmir*	8,068	26,469
Broad Peak	*China/Kashmir*	8,051	26,414
Xixabangma	*China*	8,012	26,286
Kangbachen	*India/Nepal*	7,902	25,925
Trivor	*Pakistan*	7,720	25,328
Pik Kommunizma	*Tajikistan*	7,495	24,590
Demavend	*Iran*	5,604	18,386
Ararat	*Turkey*	5,165	16,945
Gunong Kinabalu	*Malaysia (Borneo)*	4,101	13,455
Fuji-San	*Japan*	3,776	12,388

Africa		m	ft
Kilimanjaro	*Tanzania*	5,895	19,340
Mt Kenya	*Kenya*	5,199	17,057
Ruwenzori (Margherita)	*Ug./Congo (D.R.)*	5,109	16,762
Ras Dashan	*Ethiopia*	4,620	15,157
Meru	*Tanzania*	4,565	14,977
Karisimbi	*Rwanda/Congo (D.R.)*	4,507	14,787
Mt Elgon	*Kenya/Uganda*	4,321	14,176
Batu	*Ethiopia*	4,307	14,130
Toubkal	*Morocco*	4,165	13,665
Mt Cameroon	*Cameroon*	4,070	13,353

Oceania		m	ft
Puncak Jaya	*Indonesia*	5,029	16,499
Puncak Trikora	*Indonesia*	4,750	15,584
Puncak Mandala	*Indonesia*	4,702	15,427
Mt Wilhelm	*Papua New Guinea*	4,508	14,790
Mauna Kea	*USA (Hawaii)*	4,205	13,796
Mauna Loa	*USA (Hawaii)*	4,169	13,681
Mt Cook (Aoraki)	*New Zealand*	3,753	12,313
Mt Kosciuszko	*Australia*	2,237	7,339

North America		m	ft
Mt McKinley (Denali)	*USA (Alaska)*	6,194	20,321
Mt Logan	*Canada*	5,959	19,551
Citlaltepetl	*Mexico*	5,700	18,701
Mt St Elias	*USA/Canada*	5,489	18,008
Popocatepetl	*Mexico*	5,452	17,887
Mt Foraker	*USA (Alaska)*	5,304	17,401
Ixtaccihuatl	*Mexico*	5,286	17,342
Lucania	*Canada*	5,227	17,149
Mt Steele	*Canada*	5,073	16,644
Mt Bona	*USA (Alaska)*	5,005	16,420
Mt Whitney	*USA*	4,418	14,495
Tajumulco	*Guatemala*	4,220	13,845
Chirripó Grande	*Costa Rica*	3,837	12,589
Pico Duarte	*Dominican Rep.*	3,175	10,417

South America		m	ft
Aconcagua	*Argentina*	6,960	22,834
Bonete	*Argentina*	6,872	22,546
Ojos del Salado	*Argentina/Chile*	6,863	22,516
Pissis	*Argentina*	6,779	22,241
Mercedario	*Argentina/Chile*	6,770	22,211
Huascaran	*Peru*	6,768	22,204
Llullaillaco	*Argentina/Chile*	6,723	22,057
Nudo de Cachi	*Argentina*	6,720	22,047
Yerupaja	*Peru*	6,632	21,758
Sajama	*Bolivia*	6,542	21,463
Chimborazo	*Ecuador*	6,267	20,561
Pico Colon	*Colombia*	5,800	19,029
Pico Bolivar	*Venezuela*	5,007	16,427

Antarctica		m	ft
Vinson Massif		4,897	16,066
Mt Kirkpatrick		4,528	14,855

Rivers

Europe		km	miles
Volga	*Caspian Sea*	3,700	2,300
Danube	*Black Sea*	2,850	1,770
Ural	*Caspian Sea*	2,535	1,575
Dnepr (Dnipro)	*Black Sea*	2,285	1,420
Kama	*Volga*	2,030	1,260
Don	*Black Sea*	1,990	1,240
Petchora	*Arctic Ocean*	1,790	1,110
Oka	*Volga*	1,480	920
Dnister (Dniester)	*Black Sea*	1,400	870
Vyatka	*Kama*	1,370	850
Rhine	*North Sea*	1,320	820
N. Dvina	*Arctic Ocean*	1,290	800
Elbe	*North Sea*	1,145	710

Asia		km	miles
Yangtze	*Pacific Ocean*	6,380	3,960
Yenisey–Angara	*Arctic Ocean*	5,550	3,445
Huang He	*Pacific Ocean*	5,464	3,395
Ob–Irtysh	*Arctic Ocean*	5,410	3,360
Mekong	*Pacific Ocean*	4,500	2,795
Amur	*Pacific Ocean*	4,400	2,730
Lena	*Arctic Ocean*	4,400	2,730
Irtysh	*Ob*	4,250	2,640
Yenisey	*Arctic Ocean*	4,090	2,540
Ob	*Arctic Ocean*	3,680	2,285
Indus	*Indian Ocean*	3,100	1,925
Brahmaputra	*Indian Ocean*	2,900	1,800
Syrdarya	*Aral Sea*	2,860	1,775
Salween	*Indian Ocean*	2,800	1,740
Euphrates	*Indian Ocean*	2,700	1,675
Amudarya	*Aral Sea*	2,540	1,575

Africa		km	miles
Nile	*Mediterranean*	6,670	4,140
Congo	*Atlantic Ocean*	4,670	2,900
Niger	*Atlantic Ocean*	4,180	2,595
Zambezi	*Indian Ocean*	3,540	2,200
Oubangi/Uele	*Congo (D.R.)*	2,250	1,400
Kasai	*Congo (D.R.)*	1,950	1,210
Shaballe	*Indian Ocean*	1,930	1,200
Orange	*Atlantic Ocean*	1,860	1,155
Cubango	*Okavango Swamps*	1,800	1,120
Limpopo	*Indian Ocean*	1,600	995
Senegal	*Atlantic Ocean*	1,600	995

Australia		km	miles
Murray–Darling	*Indian Ocean*	3,750	2,330
Darling	*Murray*	3,070	1,905
Murray	*Indian Ocean*	2,575	1,600
Murrumbidgee	*Murray*	1,690	1,050

North America		km	miles
Mississippi–Missouri	*Gulf of Mexico*	6,020	3,740
Mackenzie	*Arctic Ocean*	4,240	2,630
Mississippi	*Gulf of Mexico*	3,780	2,350
Missouri	*Mississippi*	3,780	2,350
Yukon	*Pacific Ocean*	3,185	1,980
Rio Grande	*Gulf of Mexico*	3,030	1,880
Arkansas	*Mississippi*	2,340	1,450
Colorado	*Pacific Ocean*	2,330	1,445
Red	*Mississippi*	2,040	1,270
Columbia	*Pacific Ocean*	1,950	1,210
Saskatchewan	*Lake Winnipeg*	1,940	1,205

South America		km	miles
Amazon	*Atlantic Ocean*	6,450	4,010
Paraná–Plate	*Atlantic Ocean*	4,500	2,800
Purus	*Amazon*	3,350	2,080
Madeira	*Amazon*	3,200	1,990
São Francisco	*Atlantic Ocean*	2,900	1,800
Paraná	*Plate*	2,800	1,740
Tocantins	*Atlantic Ocean*	2,750	1,710
Paraguay	*Paraná*	2,550	1,580
Orinoco	*Atlantic Ocean*	2,500	1,550
Pilcomayo	*Paraná*	2,500	1,550
Araguaia	*Tocantins*	2,250	1,400

Lakes

Europe		km²	miles²
Lake Ladoga	*Russia*	17,700	6,800
Lake Onega	*Russia*	9,700	3,700
Saimaa system	*Finland*	8,000	3,100
Vänern	*Sweden*	5,500	2,100

Asia		km²	miles²
Caspian Sea	*Asia*	371,800	143,550
Lake Baykal	*Russia*	30,500	11,780
Aral Sea	*Kazakstan/Uzbekistan*	28,687	11,086
Tonlé Sap	*Cambodia*	20,000	7,700
Lake Balqash	*Kazakstan*	18,500	7,100

Africa		km²	miles²
Lake Victoria	*East Africa*	68,000	26,000
Lake Tanganyika	*Central Africa*	33,000	13,000
Lake Malawi/Nyasa	*East Africa*	29,600	11,430
Lake Chad	*Central Africa*	25,000	9,700
Lake Turkana	*Ethiopia/Kenya*	8,500	3,300
Lake Volta	*Ghana*	8,500	3,300

Australia		km²	miles²
Lake Eyre	*Australia*	8,900	3,400
Lake Torrens	*Australia*	5,800	2,200
Lake Gairdner	*Australia*	4,800	1,900

North America		km²	miles²
Lake Superior	*Canada/USA*	82,350	31,800
Lake Huron	*Canada/USA*	59,600	23,010
Lake Michigan	*USA*	58,000	22,400
Great Bear Lake	*Canada*	31,800	12,280
Great Slave Lake	*Canada*	28,500	11,000
Lake Erie	*Canada/USA*	25,700	9,900
Lake Winnipeg	*Canada*	24,400	9,400
Lake Ontario	*Canada/USA*	19,500	7,500
Lake Nicaragua	*Nicaragua*	8,200	3,200

South America		km²	miles²
Lake Titicaca	*Bolivia/Peru*	8,300	3,200
Lake Poopo	*Bolivia*	2,800	1,100

Islands

Europe		km²	miles²
Great Britain	*UK*	229,880	88,700
Iceland	*Atlantic Ocean*	103,000	39,800
Ireland	*Ireland/UK*	84,400	32,600
Novaya Zemlya (N.)	*Russia*	48,200	18,600
Sicily	*Italy*	25,500	9,800
Corsica	*France*	8,700	3,400

Asia		km²	miles²
Borneo	*Southeast Asia*	744,360	287,400
Sumatra	*Indonesia*	473,600	182,860
Honshu	*Japan*	230,500	88,980
Sulawesi (Celebes)	*Indonesia*	189,000	73,000
Java	*Indonesia*	126,700	48,900
Luzon	*Philippines*	104,700	40,400
Hokkaido	*Japan*	78,400	30,300

Africa		km²	miles²
Madagascar	*Indian Ocean*	587,040	226,660
Socotra	*Indian Ocean*	3,600	1,400
Réunion	*Indian Ocean*	2,500	965

Oceania		km²	miles²
New Guinea	*Indonesia/Papua NG*	821,030	317,000
New Zealand (S.)	*Pacific Ocean*	150,500	58,100
New Zealand (N.)	*Pacific Ocean*	114,700	44,300
Tasmania	*Australia*	67,800	26,200
Hawaii	*Pacific Ocean*	10,450	4,000

North America		km²	miles²
Greenland	*Atlantic Ocean*	2,175,600	839,800
Baffin Is.	*Canada*	508,000	196,100
Victoria Is.	*Canada*	212,200	81,900
Ellesmere Is.	*Canada*	212,000	81,800
Cuba	*Caribbean Sea*	110,860	42,800
Hispaniola	*Dominican Rep./Haiti*	76,200	29,400
Jamaica	*Caribbean Sea*	11,400	4,400
Puerto Rico	*Atlantic Ocean*	8,900	3,400

South America		km²	miles²
Tierra del Fuego	*Argentina/Chile*	47,000	18,100
Falkland Is. (E.)	*Atlantic Ocean*	6,800	2,600

WORLD: REGIONS IN THE NEWS

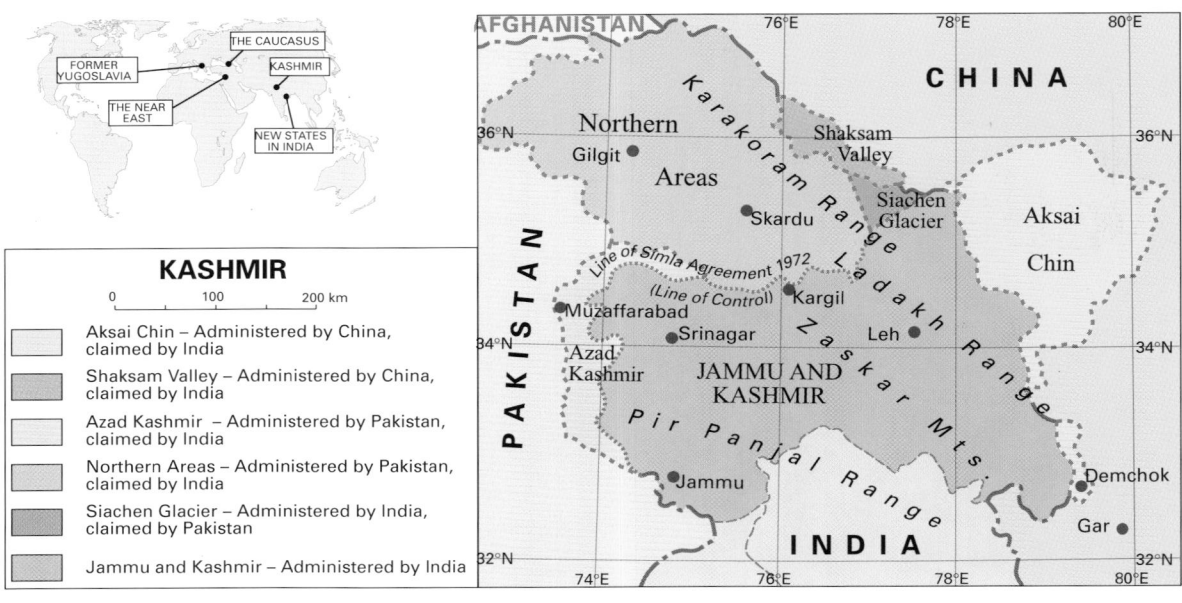

THREE NEW STATES IN INDIA

0   100   200 km

Chhattisgarh: Created 01/11/00 (formerly part of Madhya Pradesh) Population: 17.6 million Capital: Raipur

Uttaranchal: Created 09/11/00 (formerly part of Uttar Pradesh) Population: 7.0 million Provisional capital: Dehra Dun

Jharkhand: Created 15/11/00 (formerly part of Bihar) Population: 26.9 million Capital: Ranchi

KASHMIR

0   100   200 km

Aksai Chin – Administered by China, claimed by India

Shaksam Valley – Administered by China, claimed by India

Azad Kashmir – Administered by Pakistan, claimed by India

Northern Areas – Administered by Pakistan, claimed by India

Siachen Glacier – Administered by India, claimed by Pakistan

Jammu and Kashmir – Administered by India

YUGOSLAVIA

Population 10,761,000
(Serb 62.6%, Albanian 16.5%, Montenegrin 5%, Hungarian 3.3%, Muslim 3.2%)
Serbia Population: 5,799,800
(Serb 87.7%, excluding the provinces of Kosovo and Vojvodina)
Kosovo Population: 2,084,4000
(Albanian 81.6%, Serb 9.9%)
Vojvodena Population: 1,980,800
(Serb 56.8%, Hungarian 16.9%)
Montenegro Population: 635,000
(Montenegrin 61.9%, Muslim 14.6%, Albanian 7%)

CROATIA
Population: 4,960,000
(Croat 78.1%, Serb 12.2%)

SLOVENIA
Population: 2,055,000
(Slovene 88%, Croat 3%, Serb 2%)

MACEDONIA (F. Y. R. O. M.)
Population: 2,157,000
(Macedonian 64%, Albanian 21.7%, Turkish 5%, Romanian 3%, Serb 2%)

BOSNIA-HERZEGOVINA
Population: 4,601,000
(Muslim 49%, Serb 31.2%, Croat 17.2%)

FORMER YUGOSLAVIA

0   100   200 km

- · – · International boundaries
- · – Republic boundaries
- - - Province boundaries
- ■ Capital cities
- Dayton Peace Agreement Boundary
- Muslim–Croat Federation
- Bosnian Serb Republic

THE NEAR EAST

0   25   50 km

- – · – 1949 Armistice Line
- – – 1974 Cease–fire Line
- Palestinian control
- Joint Israeli/ Palestinian control
- *Efrata* ● Main Jewish settlements in the West Bank and Gaza Strip
- Halhul ▫ Main Palestinian Arab towns in the West Bank and Gaza Strip
- Road corridor linking Gaza and West Bank

COUNTRIES AND REPUBLICS OF THE CAUCASUS REGION

RUSSIAN REPUBLICS
North Ossetia (Alania)
Population: 695,000
(Ossetian 53%, Russian 29%, Chechen 5.2%, Armenian 1.9%)

Chechenia Population: 1,308,000
(Chechen and Ingush 70.7%, Russian 23.1%, Armenian 1.2%)

Ingushetia (Split from Chechenia in June 1993)
Population: 250,000

GEORGIA
Population: 5,777,000
(Georgian 70.1%, Armenian 8.1%, Russian 6.3%, Azerbaijani 5.7%, Ossetian 3%, Greek 2%, Abkhazian 2%)

Abkhazia Population: 537,500
(Georgian 45.7%, Abkhazian 17.8%, Armenian 14.6%, Russian 14.3%)

Ajaria Population: 382,000
(Georgian 82.8%, Russian 7.7%, Armenian 4%)

ARMENIA
Population: 3,968,000
(Armenian 93%, Azerbaijani 3%)

Nagorno-Karabakh
Population: 192,400 (Armenian 76.9%, Azerbaijani 21.5%)

AZERBAIJAN
Population: 8,324,000
(Azerbaijani 83%, Russian 6%, Armenian 6%, Lezgin 2%)

Naxçivan Population: 300,400

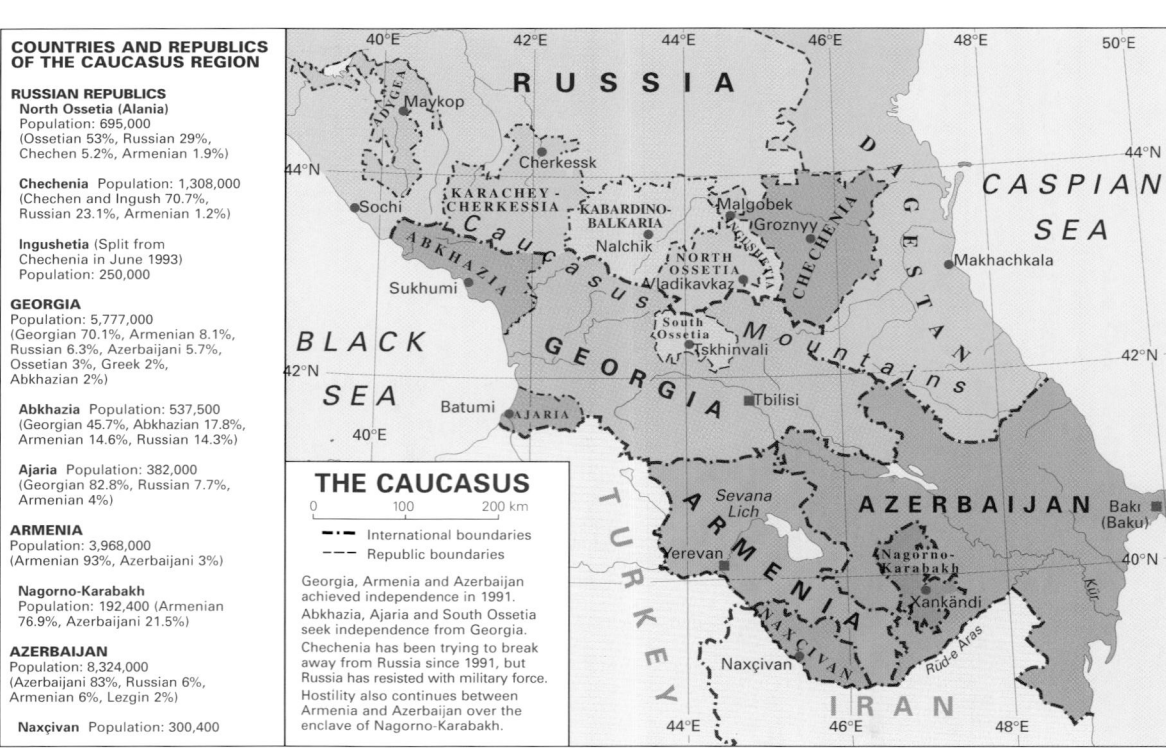

THE CAUCASUS

0   100   200 km

- – · – International boundaries
- – – Republic boundaries

Georgia, Armenia and Azerbaijan achieved independence in 1991. Abkhazia, Ajaria and South Ossetia seek independence from Georgia. Chechenia has been trying to break away from Russia since 1991, but Russia has resisted with military force. Hostility also continues between Armenia and Azerbaijan over the enclave of Nagorno-Karabakh.

ISRAEL
Population: 5,321,000 (inc. East Jerusalem and Jewish settlers in the areas under Israeli administration. Jewish 82%, Arab Muslim 13.8%, Arab Christian 2.5%, Druze 1.7%)

West Bank
Population: 1,122,900 (Palestinian Arabs 97% [of whom Arab Muslim 85%, Jewish 7%, Christian 8%])

Gaza Strip
Population: 748,400 (Arab 98%)

JORDAN
Population: 5,558,000 (Arab 99% [of whom about 50% are Palestinian Arab])

IMAGES OF EARTH

— VANCOUVER, CANADA —

The city of Vancouver grew up around its fine, natural
harbor on the north side of the Fraser River delta,
developing as the western railhead of the Canadian Pacific
Railroad. Just to the south of the delta runs the 49th parallel,
the boundary between Canada and the USA. To the north of
the city lie the Coast Mountains, and to the west, across the
Strait of Georgia, is Vancouver Island with the town of
Victoria visible at the bottom left of the image.

– LOS ANGELES, USA –

The sprawling urban area of Greater LA covers most of the
area to the south of the San Gabriel Mountains, which run
across the top of the image. The population of the whole area
is over 14 million people. Jutting into the left-hand side of
the image, just below center, the darker colors of the eastern
end of the Santa Monica range can be seen; the center of the
city proper is just to the southeast of the end of the range.
On its southern slopes lie Beverly Hills and Hollywood,
with the San Fernando Valley to the north.

– NEW YORK, USA –

This image covers most of the largest urban area in
the USA, which has a population of over 20 million people.
Flowing from the north, the Hudson River divides the two
cities of New York (to the east) and New Jersey (to the west).
Toward its mouth on the east bank lies Manhattan Island,
with Central Park clearly visible. Below this is the end of
Long Island, which is connected by bridge to
Staten Island, to the west.

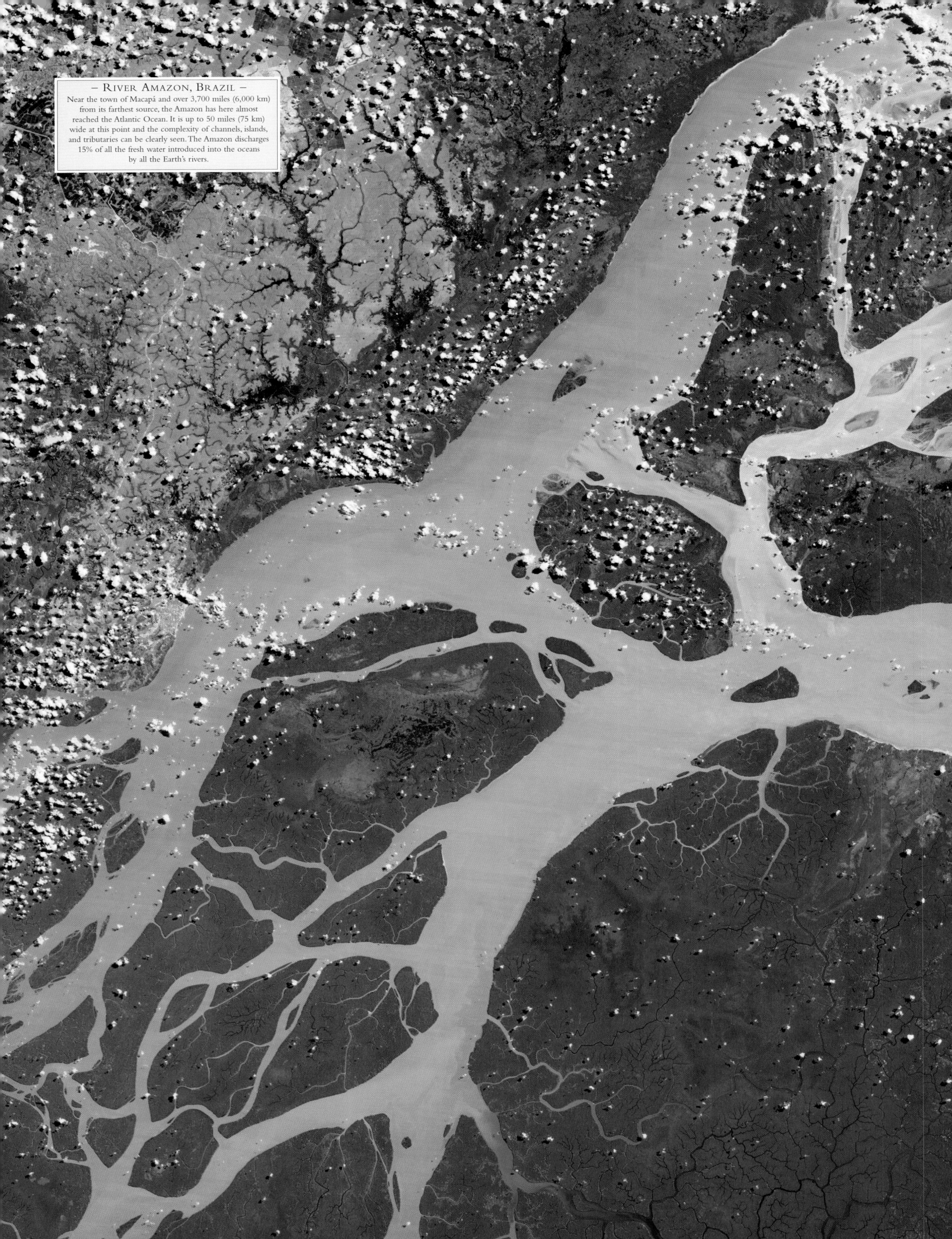

- RIVER AMAZON, BRAZIL -

Near the town of Macapá and over 3,700 miles (6,000 km)
from its farthest source, the Amazon has here almost
reached the Atlantic Ocean. It is up to 50 miles (75 km)
wide at this point and the complexity of channels, islands,
and tributaries can be clearly seen. The Amazon discharges
15% of all the fresh water introduced into the oceans
by all the Earth's rivers.

— SANTIAGO, CHILE —

The Chilean capital city, Santiago, lies in a fertile valley at
the foot of the Andes, some 37 miles (60 km) southeast of the
main port of Valparaíso. To the east the mountains rise to over
20,000 ft (6,000 m). At top right of the image the boundary
with Argentina runs along the watershed. The city expanded
rapidly to its current population of over 5 million inhabitants
and this resulted in air pollution problems in the 1980s,
though measures have since been taken to deal with this.

– LONDON, UNITED KINGDOM –

The whole area of Greater London is shown here, including
Heathrow Airport at far left. The River Thames stands out,
as do the former London docks and the reservoirs in the
River Lea valley to the northeast. Despite having a
population in excess of 8 million people, there are still many
open spaces and parks around the city center.

— IJSSELMEER, NETHERLANDS —

This unique feature was created in the 13th century when
the sea breached a protective sand bar, flooding all the
low-lying land. The remnants of the bar can still be seen
as the chain of Frisian Islands at the top of the image.
Reclamation on a large scale started in 1932 with the
completion of the causeway in the north. Since then four
"polders" have been drained and reclaimed. The city of
Amsterdam is situated at bottom left.

— NAPLES, ITALY —

The city, situated in the northeastern corner of the
Bay of Naples, has a population in excess of 1 million
inhabitants. The cone of the active volcano Vesuvius, 4,200 ft
(1,281 m) high, dominates the bay. Evidence of other
volcanic activity can also be seen to the west of the town
in the area known as the Phlegraean Fields. Pompei, once
buried by its lava, lies near the mountains to the southeast.
On the southern peninsular is the town of Sorrento, and
beyond, the island of Capri.

– STRAIT OF GIBRALTAR –

The strait separates the Mediterranean Sea (to the right) from
the Atlantic Ocean, and the continent of Europe (above)
from Africa. At its narrowest eastern end, shown in the image,
the strait is only 8 miles (13 km) wide. On the Spanish side,
the deep inlet of Algeciras Bay stands out, with the British
naval base at Gibraltar on the tip of its eastern peninsula,
beneath the Rock. The Moroccan port of Tangier is
at the bottom left of the image.

— CAIRO, EGYPT —

The largest city in Africa with almost 10 million inhabitants, Cairo evolved on the eastern bank of the River Nile, near its delta. This image clearly shows the differences between the arid desert areas to the southeast and southwest, the fertile lands of the Nile flood plain, and the urban area itself. The shadows of the Pyramids on the Giza Plateau can be seen on the left-hand edge of the cultivated area, below where the road crosses it.

— WESTERN CAPE, SOUTH AFRICA —
Cape Town sits to the bottom left of this image, with
the Cape Peninsula running southeast to the Cape of
Good Hope. Inland from the fertile coastal plain, where most
of South Africa's wine is produced, is the rugged interior
of the Great Karoo where parallel mountain ranges are
dissected by river valleys.

— TEHRAN, IRAN —

On the sheltered southern slopes of the Elburz (Alborz)
Mountains, the street layout of Tehran, the capital city of
Iran, can be clearly seen toward the bottom left-hand side
of this image. However, it is the dissected parallel ridges
of the mountains and the spectacular snow-covered peak
of Demavend which dominate this scene. At 18,386 ft
(5,604 m), the peak is the highest in the Middle East and
is an extinct volcanic cone with no recorded historic
eruptions, although there are still active hot
springs on its slopes.

— KARACHI, PAKISTAN —

The largest city in Pakistan with over 9 million inhabitants,
Karachi is the administrative headquarters of Sind province
and is also the commercial and industrial capital of the whole
country. To its south lie the mangrove swamps of the vast
delta of the River Indus, 130 miles (210 km) wide where it
flows into the Arabian Sea. To the north and east of the city
are the dry, hot Sind plains, which are subject to a mean
annual rainfall of only 5–10 inches (125–250 mm).

— TOKYO, JAPAN —

At the head of Tokyo Bay, the city, with its satellites of
Kawasaki and Yokohama, forms one of the world's most
densely populated areas with over 26 million people. Owing
to the shortage of space, much development has taken place
on areas reclaimed from the sea. One of these is Haneda
International Airport, whose runway pattern is clearly
visible at the mouth of the Tama River. The Tokyo Bay
bridge/tunnel projects into the Bay from the eastern shore.

— SYDNEY, AUSTRALIA —

Sydney, the largest city in Australia, was founded at the
end of the 18th century on the north shore of Botany Bay,
the southern of the two enclosed bays shown here. The
runways of the international airport project into this, and to
the north, on the south shore of Sydney Harbor, the
shadows of the skyscrapers in the central business district
can be seen, with the Sydney Harbor Bridge beyond.

— CHRISTCHURCH, NEW ZEALAND —

Situated on the east coast of South Island, the city
of Christchurch, with more than 300,000 inhabitants, lies
between the braided River Waimakiriri and the spectacular
Banks Peninsula. The latter was formed by the erosion of two
ancient volcanic cones by glaciers and their subsequent
inundation by the sea to create the two large harbors of
Lyttleton to the north and Akaroa in the south, as well as
numerous flooded valleys. Inland, to the west, lie the
fertile Canterbury Plains, New Zealand's prime
sheep-rearing area.

THE GAZETTEER OF NATIONS

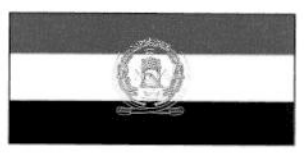

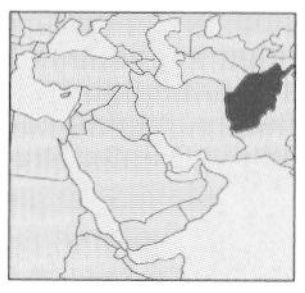

AFGHANISTAN

GEOGRAPHY The Republic of Afghanistan is a landlocked, mountainous country in southern Asia. The central highlands reach a height of more than 22,966 ft [7,000 m] in the east and make up nearly three-quarters of Afghanistan. The main range is the Hindu Kush, which is cut by deep, fertile valleys.

The height of the land and the country's remote position have a great effect on the climate. In winter, northerly winds bring cold, snowy weather to the mountains, but summers are hot and dry.

POLITICS & ECONOMY The modern history of Afghanistan began in 1747, when the various tribes in the area united for the first time. In the 19th century, Russia and Britain struggled for control of the country. Following Britain's withdrawal in 1919, Afghanistan became fully independent. Soviet troops invaded Afghanistan in 1979 to support a socialist regime in Kabul, but, facing fierce opposition from Muslim groups, they withdrew in 1989. However, Muslim factions continued to fight each other. At the start of the 21st century a group called Taliban ("Islamic students") controlled 90% of the country.

Afghanistan is one of the world's poorest countries. About 60% of the people live by farming. Many people are seminomadic herders. Natural gas is produced, together with some coal, copper, gold, precious stones and salt.

AREA 251,772 sq mi [652,090 sq km] **POPULATION** 26,511,000
CAPITAL (POPULATION) Kabul (1,565,000)
GOVERNMENT Islamic republic **ETHNIC GROUPS** Pashtun ("Pathan") 52%, Tajik 20%, Uzbek 9%, Hazara 9%, Chahar 3%, Turkmen 2%, Baluchi 1% **LANGUAGES** Pashto, Dari/Persian (both official), Uzbek **RELIGIONS** Islam (Sunni Muslim 74%, Shiite Muslim 25%)
CURRENCY Afghani = 100 puls

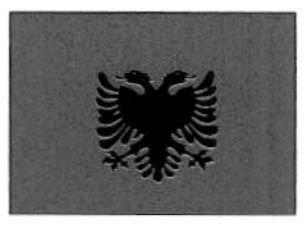

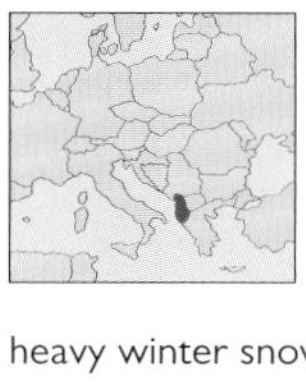

ALBANIA

GEOGRAPHY The Republic of Albania lies in the Balkan peninsula, facing the Adriatic Sea. About 70% of the land is mountainous, but most Albanians live in the west on the coastal lowlands.

The coastal areas of Albania experience a typical Mediterranean climate, with fairly dry, sunny summers and cool, moist winters. The mountains have a severe climate, with heavy winter snowfalls.

POLITICS & ECONOMY Albania is Europe's poorest country. Formerly a Communist regime, Albania introduced a multiparty system in the early 1990s. The change proved difficult. But, following elections in 1997, a socialist government committed to a market system took office. In 2001, the stability of the region was threatened when Albanian-speaking Kosovars, many of whom favored the creation of a "Greater Albania," attacked northwestern Macedonia.

In the early 1990s, agriculture employed 56% of the people. The land was divided into large collective and state farms, but private ownership has been encouraged since 1991. Albania has some minerals and chromite, copper and nickel are exported.

AREA 11,100 sq mi [28,750 sq km] **POPULATION** 3,795,000
CAPITAL (POPULATION) Tirana (251,000) **GOVERNMENT** Multiparty republic **ETHNIC GROUPS** Albanian 98%, Greek 1.8%, Macedonian, Montenegrin, Gypsy **LANGUAGES** Albanian (official) **RELIGIONS** Many people say they are non-believers; of the believers, 65% follow Islam and 33% follow Christianity (Orthodox 20%, Roman Catholic 13%) **CURRENCY** Lek = 100 qindars

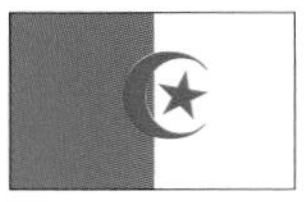

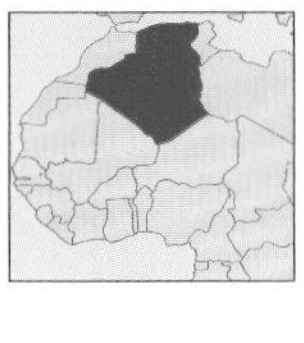

ALGERIA

GEOGRAPHY The People's Democratic Republic of Algeria is Africa's second largest country after Sudan. Most Algerians live in the north, on the fertile coastal plains and hill country bordering the Mediterranean Sea. Four-fifths of Algeria is in the Sahara. The coast has a Mediterranean climate, but the arid Sahara is hot by day and cool at night.

POLITICS & ECONOMY France ruled Algeria from 1830 until 1962, when the socialist FLN (National Liberation Front) formed a one-party government. Following the recognition of opposition parties in 1989, a Muslim group, the FIS (Islamic Salvation Front), won an election in 1991. The FLN canceled the elections and civil conflict broke out. About 100,000 people were killed in the 1990s. In 1999, following the withdrawal of the other candidates who alleged fraud, Abdelaziz Bouteflika, who was assumed to be favored by the army, was elected president. Bouteflika's peace offensive reduced the violence, but sporadic killings continued into 2001.

Algeria is a developing country, whose chief resources are oil and natural gas, which were discovered in the Sahara in 1956. The natural gas reserves are among the world's largest, and gas and oil account for 90% of Algeria's exports. Cement, iron and steel, textiles and vehicles are manufactured. Barley, citrus fruits, dates, potatoes and wheat are the major crops.

AREA 919,590 sq mi [2,381,740 sq km] **POPULATION** 32,904,000
CAPITAL (POPULATION) Algiers (2,168,000)
GOVERNMENT Socialist republic **ETHNIC GROUPS** Arab 83%, Berber 16%
LANGUAGES Arabic (official), Berber, French **RELIGIONS** Sunni Muslim 98% **CURRENCY** Algerian dinar = 100 centimes

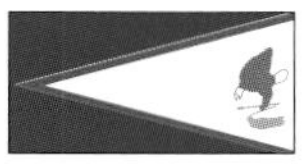

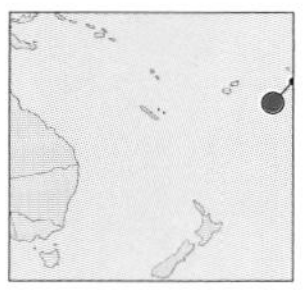

AMERICAN SAMOA

An "unincorporated territory" of the United States, American Samoa lies in the south-central Pacific Ocean.

AREA 77 sq mi [200 sq km]
POPULATION 39,000 **CAPITAL** Pago Pago

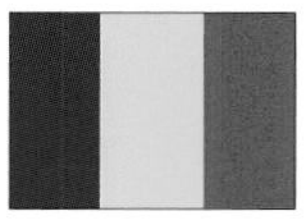

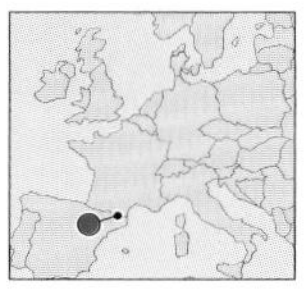

ANDORRA

A mini-state situated in the Pyrenees Mountains, Andorra is a co-principality whose main activity is tourism. Most Andorrans live in the six valleys (the Valls) that drain into the River Valira.

AREA 175 sq mi [453 sq km]
POPULATION 49,000 **CAPITAL** Andorra La Vella

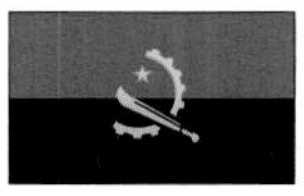

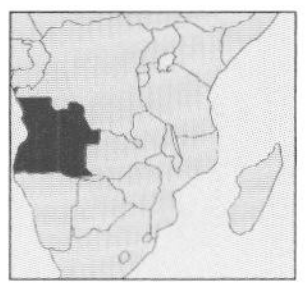

ANGOLA

GEOGRAPHY The Republic of Angola is a large country in southwestern Africa. Much of the country is part of the plateau that forms most of southern Africa, with a narrow coastal plain in the west.

Angola has a tropical climate, with temperatures of over 68°F [20°C] throughout the year, though the highest areas are cooler. The coastal regions are dry, but the rainfall increases to the north and east.

POLITICS & ECONOMY A former Portuguese colony, Angola gained its independence in 1975, after which rival nationalist forces began a struggle for power. A long-running civil war developed, finally ending with a peace treaty in 1994, which led to a coalition government in 1997. However, civil war again broke out in 1999.

Angola is a developing country, where 70% of the people are poor farmers. The main food crops are cassava and maize. Coffee is exported. Angola has much economic potential. It has oil reserves near Luanda and in the Cabinda enclave, which is separated from Angola by a strip of land belonging to Congo (Dem. Rep.). Oil is the leading export. Angola also produces diamonds and has reserves of copper, manganese and phosphates.

AREA 481,351 sq mi [1,246,700 sq km] **POPULATION** 13,295,000
CAPITAL (POPULATION) Luanda (2,418,000)
GOVERNMENT Multiparty republic **ETHNIC GROUPS** Ovimbundu 37%, Mbundu 22%, Kongo 13%, Luimbe-Nganguela 5%, Nyaneka-Humbe 5%, Chokwe, Luvale, Luchazi **LANGUAGES** Portuguese (official), many others **RELIGIONS** Christianity (Roman Catholic 69%, Protestant 20%), traditional beliefs 10%
CURRENCY Kwanza = 100 lwei

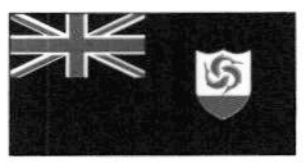

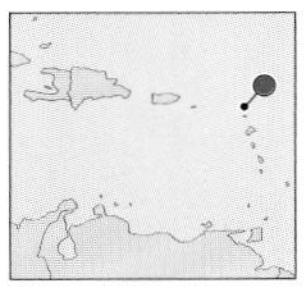

ANGUILLA

Formerly part of St Kitts and Nevis, Anguilla, the most northerly of the Leeward Islands, became a British dependency (now a British overseas territory) in 1980. The main source of revenue is now tourism, although lobster still accounts for half the island's exports.

AREA 37 sq mi [96 sq km] **POPULATION** 8,000
CAPITAL The Valley

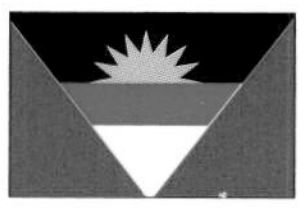

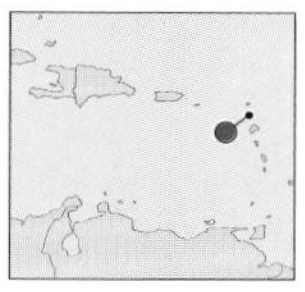

ANTIGUA & BARBUDA

A former British dependency in the Caribbean, Antigua and Barbuda became independent in 1981. Tourism is the main industry, though sugar is an important product.

AREA 170 sq mi [440 sq km]
POPULATION 79,000 **CAPITAL** St John's

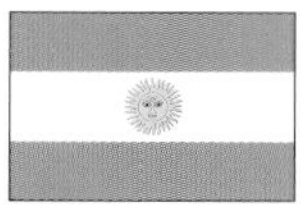

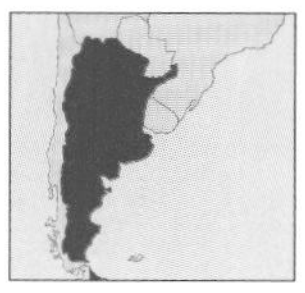

ARGENTINA

GEOGRAPHY The Argentine Republic is South America's second largest and the world's eighth largest country. The high Andes range in the west contains Mount Aconcagua, the highest peak in the Americas. In southern Argentina, the Andes Mountains overlook Patagonia, a plateau region. In east-central Argentina lies a fertile plain called the pampas.

The climate varies from subtropical in the north to temperate in the south. Rainfall is abundant in the northeast, but is lower to the west and south. Patagonia is a dry region, crossed by rivers that rise in the Andes.

POLITICS & ECONOMY Argentina became independent from Spain in the early 19th century, but it later suffered from instability and periods of military rule. In 1982, Argentina invaded the Falkland (Malvinas) Islands, but Britain regained the islands later in the year. Elections were held in 1983 and a new constitution was adopted in 1994.

According to the World Bank, Argentina is an "upper-middle-income" developing country. Large areas are fertile and the main agricultural products are beef, maize and wheat. But about 87% of the people live in cities and towns, where many work in factories that process farm products. Other industries include the manufacture of cars, electrical equipment and textiles. Oil is the leading mineral resource. The leading exports include meat, wheat, maize, vegetable oils, hides and skins, and wool. In 1991, Argentina, Brazil, Paraguay and Uruguay set up Mercosur, an alliance which aimed to create a common market.

AREA 1,068,296 sq mi [2,766,890 sq km] **POPULATION** 36,238,000
CAPITAL (POPULATION) Buenos Aires (11,256,000)
GOVERNMENT Federal republic **ETHNIC GROUPS** European 85%, Mestizo, Amerindian **LANGUAGES** Spanish (official)
RELIGIONS Christianity (Roman Catholic 92%)
CURRENCY Peso = 10,000 australs

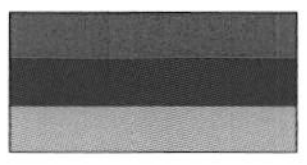

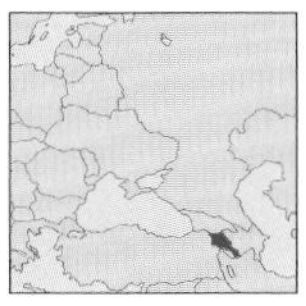

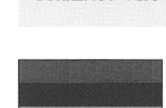

ARMENIA

GEOGRAPHY The Republic of Armenia is a landlocked country in southwestern Asia. Most of Armenia consists of a rugged plateau, criss-crossed by long faults (cracks). Movements along the faults cause earthquakes. The highest point is Mount Aragats, at 13,419 ft [4,090 m] above sea level.

The height of the land, which averages 4,920 ft [1,500 m] above sea level gives rise to severe winters and cool summers. The highest peaks are snow-capped, but the total yearly rainfall is generally low.

POLITICS & ECONOMY In 1920, Armenia became a Communist republic and, in 1922, it became, with Azerbaijan and Georgia, part of the Transcaucasian Republic within the Soviet Union. But the three territories became separate Soviet Socialist Republics in 1936. After the breakup of the Soviet Union in 1991, Armenia became an independent republic. Fighting broke out over Nagorno-Karabakh, an area enclosed by Azerbaijan where the majority of the people are Armenians. In 1992, Armenia occupied the territory between it and Nagorno-Karabakh. A cease-fire agreed in 1994 left Armenia in control of about 20% of Azerbaijan's land area.

The World Bank classifies Armenia as a "lower-middle-income" economy. The conflict has badly damaged the economy, but the government has encouraged free enterprise, selling farmland and government-owned businesses.

AREA 11,506 sq mi [29,800 sq km] **POPULATION** 3,968,000
CAPITAL (POPULATION) Yerevan (1,248,000)
GOVERNMENT Multiparty republic **ETHNIC GROUPS** Armenian 93%, Azerbaijani 3%, Russian, Kurd **LANGUAGES** Armenian (official)
RELIGIONS Christianity (Armenian Apostolic)
CURRENCY Dram = 100 couma

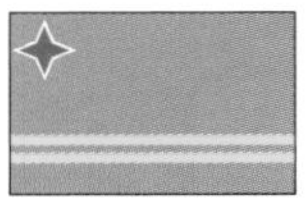

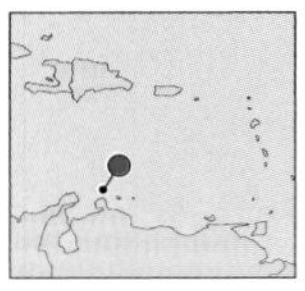

ARUBA

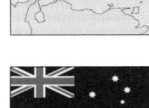

Formerly part of the Netherlands Antilles, Aruba (the most western of the Lesser Antilles) became a separate self-governing Dutch territory in 1986.

AREA 75 sq mi [193 sq km]
POPULATION 58,000 **CAPITAL** Oranjestad

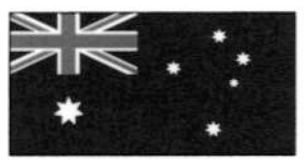

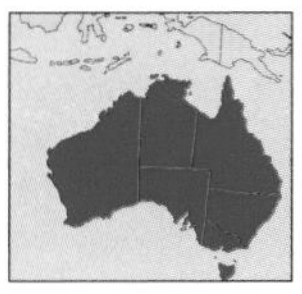

AUSTRALIA

GEOGRAPHY The Commonwealth of Australia, the world's sixth largest country, is also a continent. Australia is the flattest of the continents and the main highland area is in the east. Here the Great Dividing Range separates the eastern coastal plains from the Central Plains. This range extends from the Cape York Peninsula to Victoria in the far south. The longest rivers, the Murray and Darling, drain the southeastern part of the Central Plains. The Western Plateau makes up two-thirds of Australia. A few mountain ranges break the monotony of the generally flat landscape.

Only 10% of Australia has an average yearly rainfall of more than 39 in [1,000 mm]. These areas include the tropical north, where Darwin is situated, the northeast coast, and the southeast, where Sydney is located. The interior is dry, and water is quickly evaporated in the heat.

POLITICS & ECONOMY The Aboriginal people of Australia entered the continent from Southeast Asia more than 50,000 years ago. The first European explorers were Dutch in the 17th century, but they did not settle. In 1770, the British Captain Cook explored the east coast and, in 1788, the first British settlement was established for convicts on the site of what is now Sydney. Australia has strong ties with the British Isles. But in the last 50 years, people from other parts of Europe and, most recently, from Asia have settled in Australia. Ties with Britain were also weakened by Britain's membership of the European Union. Many Australians believe that they should become more involved with the nations of eastern Asia and the Americas rather than with Europe. In 1999, Australia held a referendum on whether the country should become a republic or remain a constitutional monarchy. By a majority of about 55 to 45, the country retained its status as a monarchy.

Australia is a prosperous country. Crops can be grown on only 6% of the land, but dry pasture covers another 58%. Yet the country remains a major producer and exporter of farm products, particularly cattle, wheat and wool. Grapes grown for winemaking are also important. The country is a major producer of minerals, including bauxite, coal, copper, diamonds, gold, iron ore, manganese, nickel, silver, tin, tungsten and zinc. Australia also produces oil and natural gas. Metals, minerals and farm products account for the bulk of exports. Australia's imports are mostly manufactured products, although the country makes many factory products, especially consumer goods, such as foods and household articles. Major imports include machinery.

AREA 2,967,893 sq mi [7,686,850 sq km] **POPULATION** 18,855,000 **CAPITAL (POPULATION)** Canberra (325,000) **GOVERNMENT** Federal constitutional monarchy **ETHNIC GROUPS** White 95%, Aboriginal 1.5%, Asian 1.3% **LANGUAGES** English (official) **RELIGIONS** Christianity (Roman Catholic 26%, Anglican 24%, others 20%), Islam, Buddhism, Judaism **CURRENCY** Australian dollar = 100 cents

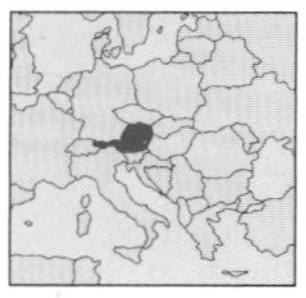

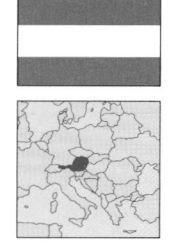

AUSTRIA

GEOGRAPHY Austria is a landlocked country in Europe. Northern Austria contains the valley of the River Danube, which flows from Germany to the Black Sea, and the Vienna basin. Southern Austria contains ranges of the Alps, their highest point at Grossglockner, 12,457 ft [3,797 m] above sea level.

The climate is influenced by westerly and easterly winds. Moist westerly winds bring rain and snow, and moderate temperatures. Dry easterly winds bring cold weather in winter and hot weather in summer.

POLITICS & ECONOMY Formerly part of the monarchy of Austria-Hungary, which collapsed in 1918, Austria was annexed by Germany in 1938. After World War II, the Allies partitioned and occupied the country. In 1955, Austria became a neutral federal republic. It joined the European Union on January 1, 1995, but was a focus of controversy when, in 2000, a coalition government was formed by the right-wing People's Party and the extreme right-wing Freedom Party.

Austria is a prosperous country. It has plenty of hydroelectric power, as well as some oil, gas and coal reserves. The country's leading economic activity is manufacturing metals and metal products. Crops are grown on 18% of the land, and another 24% is pasture. Dairy and livestock farming are the leading activities. Major crops include barley, potatoes, rye, sugar beet and wheat. Tourism is a major activity in this scenic country.

AREA 32,374 sq mi [83,850 sq km] **POPULATION** 7,613,000 **CAPITAL (POPULATION)** Vienna (1,595,000) **GOVERNMENT** Federal republic **ETHNIC GROUPS** Austrian 93%, Yugoslav 2%, Turkish, German **LANGUAGES** German (official) **RELIGIONS** Christianity (Roman Catholic 78%, Protestant 6%), Islam **CURRENCY** Euro; Schilling = 100 Groschen

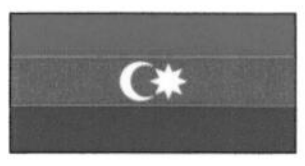

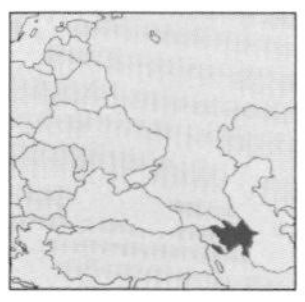

AZERBAIJAN

GEOGRAPHY The Azerbaijani Republic is a country in the southwest of Asia, facing the Caspian Sea to the east. It includes an area called the Naxçivan Autonomous Republic, which is completely cut off from the rest of Azerbaijan by Armenian territory. The Caucasus Mountains border Russia in the north.

Azerbaijan has hot summers and cool winters, with low rainfall on the plains and much higher rainfall in the highlands.

POLITICS & ECONOMY After the Russian Revolution of 1917, attempts were made to form a Transcaucasian Federation made up of Armenia, Azerbaijan and Georgia. When this failed, Azerbaijanis set up an independent state. But Russian forces occupied the area in 1920. In 1922, the Communists set up a Transcaucasian Republic consisting of Armenia, Azerbaijan and Georgia under Russian control. In 1936, the three areas became separate Soviet Socialist Republics within the Soviet Union. In 1991, following the breakup of the Soviet Union, Azerbaijan became an independent nation. After independence, the country's economic progress was slow, partly because of the conflict with Armenia over the enclave of Nagorno-Karabakh, a region in Azerbaijan where the majority of people are Armenians. A cease-fire in 1994 left Armenia in control of about 20% of Azerbaijan's area, including Nagorno-Karabakh.

In the mid-1990s, the World Bank classified Azerbaijan as a "lower-middle-income" economy. Yet by the late 1990s, the enormous oil reserves in the Baku area, on the Caspian Sea and in the sea itself, held out great promise for the future. Oil extraction and manufacturing, including oil refining and the production of chemicals, machinery and textiles, are now the most valuable activities.

AREA 33,436 sq mi [86,600 sq km] **POPULATION** 8,324,000 **CAPITAL (POPULATION)** Baku (1,720,000) **GOVERNMENT** Federal multiparty republic **ETHNIC GROUPS** Azerbaijani 83%, Russian 6%, Armenian 6%, Lezgin, Avar, Ukrainian, Tatar **LANGUAGES** Azerbaijani (official) **RELIGIONS** Islam **CURRENCY** Manat = 100 gopik

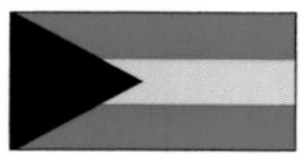

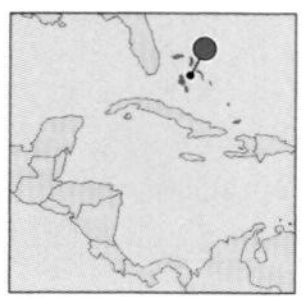

BAHAMAS

A coral-limestone archipelago off the coast of Florida, the Bahamas became independent from Britain in 1973, and has since developed strong ties with the United States. Tourism and banking are major activities.

AREA 5,359 sq mi [13,880 sq km]
POPULATION 295,000 **CAPITAL** Nassau

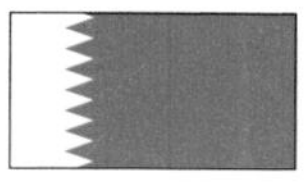

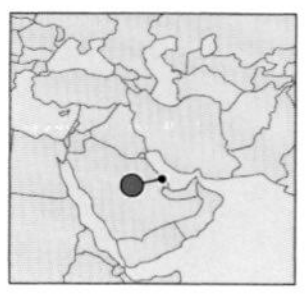

BAHRAIN

The Emirate of Bahrain, an island nation in the Gulf, became independent from the UK in 1971. Oil accounts for 80% of the country's exports.

AREA 262 sq mi [678 sq km]
POPULATION 683,000 **CAPITAL** Manama

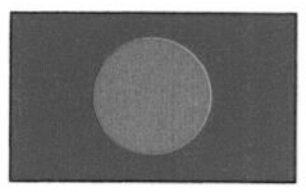

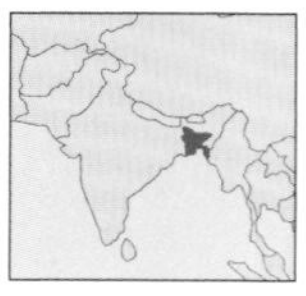

BANGLADESH

GEOGRAPHY The People's Republic of Bangladesh is one of the world's most densely populated countries. Apart from hilly regions in the far northeast and southeast, most of the land is flat and covered by fertile alluvium spread over the land by the Ganges, Brahmaputra and Meghna rivers. These rivers overflow when they are swollen by the annual monsoon rains. Floods also occur along the coast, 357 mi [575 km] long, when cyclones (hurricanes) drive seawater inland. Bangladesh has a tropical monsoon climate. Dry northerly winds blow in winter, but, in summer, moist winds from the south bring monsoon rains. Heavy monsoon rains cause floods. In 1998, about two-thirds of the entire country was submerged, causing great suffering.

POLITICS & ECONOMY In 1947, British India was partitioned between the mainly Hindu India and the Muslim Pakistan. Pakistan consisted of two parts, West and East Pakistan, which were separated by about 1,000 mi [1,600 km] of Indian territory. Differences developed between West and East Pakistan. In 1971, the East Pakistanis rebeled. After a nine-month civil war, they declared East Pakistan to be a separate nation named Bangladesh.

Bangladesh is one of the world's poorest countries. Its economy depends mainly on agriculture, which employs over half the population. Bangladesh is the world's fourth largest producer of rice.

AREA 55,598 sq mi [144,000 sq km] **POPULATION** 150,589,000 **CAPITAL (POPULATION)** Dhaka (6,105,000) **GOVERNMENT** Multiparty republic **ETHNIC GROUPS** Bengali 98%, tribal groups **LANGUAGES** Bengali, English (both official) **RELIGIONS** Islam 87%, Hinduism 12%, Buddhism, Christianity **CURRENCY** Taka = 100 paisas

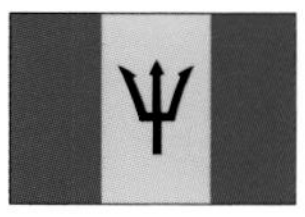

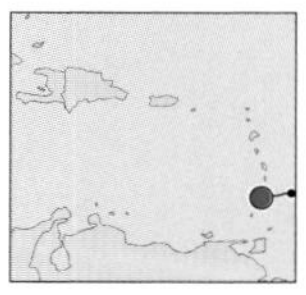

BARBADOS

The most easterly Caribbean country, Barbados became independent from the UK in 1960. A densely populated island, Barbados is prosperous by comparison with most Caribbean countries.

AREA 166 sq mi [430 sq km]
POPULATION 265,000 **CAPITAL** Bridgetown

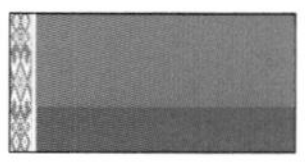

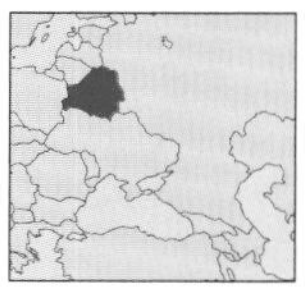

BELARUS

GEOGRAPHY The Republic of Belarus is a landlocked country in Eastern Europe. The land is low-lying and mostly flat. In the south, much of the land is marshy and this area contains Europe's largest marsh and peat bog, the Pripet Marshes.

The climate of Belarus is affected by both the moderating influence of the Baltic Sea and continental conditions to the east. The winters are cold and the summers warm.

POLITICS & ECONOMY In 1918, Belarus (White Russia) became an independent republic, but Russia invaded the country and, in 1919, a Communist state was set up. In 1922, Belarus became a founder republic of the Soviet Union. In 1991, Belarus again became an independent republic, though Belarus continued to support reunification with Russia. In 1998, Belarus and Russia set up a "union state," with plans to have a common currency, a customs union, and common foreign and defense policies. But any surrender of sovereignty was not anticipated. A union treaty aimed at a merger of the two countries, but in reality largely symbolic, was signed in 1999.

The World Bank classifies Belarus as an "upper-middle-income" economy. Like other former republics of the Soviet Union, it faces many problems in turning from Communism to a free-market economy.

AREA 80,154 sq mi [297,600 sq km] **POPULATION** 10,697,000 **CAPITAL (POPULATION)** Minsk (1,700,000) **GOVERNMENT** Multiparty republic **ETHNIC GROUPS** Belarussian 80%, Russian, Polish **LANGUAGES** Belarussian, Russian (both official) **RELIGIONS** Christianity (mainly Belarussian Orthodox, with Roman Catholics in the west) **CURRENCY** Belarussian rouble = 100 kopecks

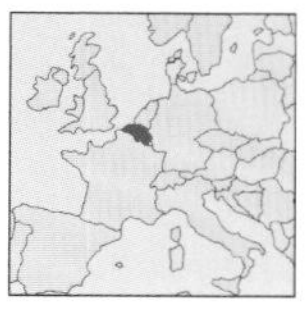

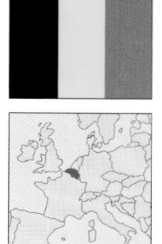

BELGIUM

GEOGRAPHY The Kingdom of Belgium is a densely populated country in western Europe. Behind the coastline on the North Sea, which is 39 mi [63 km] long, lie its coastal plains. Central Belgium consists of low plateaux and the only highland region is the Ardennes in the southeast.

Belgium has a cool, temperate climate. Moist winds from the Atlantic Ocean bring fairly heavy rain, especially in the Ardennes. In January and February much snow falls on the Ardennes.

POLITICS & ECONOMY In 1815, Belgium and the Netherlands united as the "low countries," but Belgium became independent in 1830. Belgium's economy was weakened by the two World

Wars, but, from 1945, the country recovered quickly, first through collaboration with the Netherlands and Luxembourg, which formed a customs union called Benelux, and later through its membership of the European Union.

A central political problem in Belgium has been the tension between the Dutch-speaking Flemings and the French-speaking Walloons. In the 1970s, the government divided the country into three economic regions: Dutch-speaking Flanders, French-speaking Wallonia and bilingual Brussels. In 1993, Belgium adopted a federal system of government. Each of the regions now has its own parliament, which is responsible for local matters. Elections under this system were held in 1995 and 1999.

Belgium is a major trading nation, with a highly developed economy. Most of the materials needed for manufacturing are imported. Its main products include chemicals, processed food and steel. The textile industry is also important and has existed since medieval times in the Belgian province of Flanders.

Agriculture employs only 3% of the people, but Belgian farmers produce most of the food needed by the people. Barley and wheat are the chief crops, followed by flax, hops, potatoes and sugar beet, but the most valuable activities are dairy farming and livestock rearing.

AREA 11,780 sq mi [30,510 sq km] **POPULATION** 9,832,000
CAPITAL (POPULATION) Brussels (948,000)
GOVERNMENT Federal constitutional monarchy
ETHNIC GROUPS Belgian 91% (Fleming 55%, Walloon 32%), Italian, French, Dutch, Turkish, Moroccan
LANGUAGES Dutch, French, German (all official)
RELIGIONS Christianity (Roman Catholic 90%), Islam
CURRENCY Euro; Belgian franc = 100 centimes

BELIZE

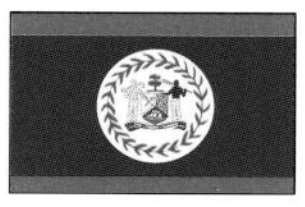
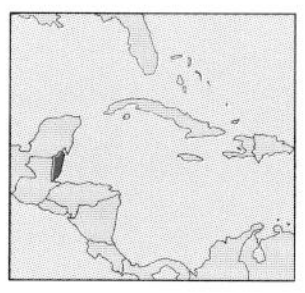

GEOGRAPHY Behind the swampy coastal plain in the south, the land rises to the low Maya Mountains, which reach a height of 3,674 ft [1,120 m] at Victoria Peak. The north is mostly low-lying and swampy.

Belize has a tropical, humid climate. Temperatures are high throughout the year and the average yearly rainfall ranges from 51 in [1,300 mm] in the north to over 150 in [3,800 mm] in the south.

POLITICS & ECONOMY From 1862, Belize (then called British Honduras) was a British colony. Full independence was achieved in 1981, but Guatemala, which had claimed the area since the early 19th century, opposed Belize's independence and British troops remained to prevent a possible invasion. In 1983, Guatemala reduced its claim to the southern fifth of Belize. Improved relations in the early 1990s led Guatemala to recognize Belize's independence and, in 1992, Britain agreed to withdraw its troops from the country.

The World Bank classifies Belize as a "lower-middle-income" developing country. Its economy is based on agriculture and sugarcane is the chief commercial crop and export. Other crops include bananas, beans, citrus fruits, maize and rice. Forestry, fishing and tourism are other important activities.

AREA 8,865 sq mi [22,960 sq km] **POPULATION** 230,000 **CAPITAL (POPULATION)** Belmopan (4,000) **GOVERNMENT** Constitutional monarchy **ETHNIC GROUPS** Mestizo (Spanish-Indian) 44%, Creole (mainly African American) 30%, Mayan Indian 11%, Garifuna (Black-Carib Indian) 7%, White 4%, East Indian 3% **LANGUAGES** English (official), Creole, Spanish **RELIGIONS** Christianity (Roman Catholic 58%), Hinduism **CURRENCY** Belize dollar = 100 cents

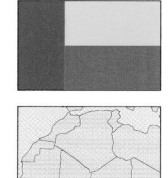

BENIN

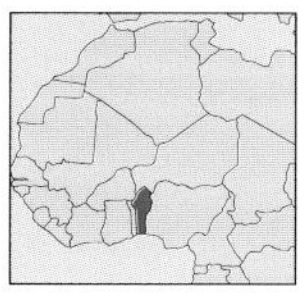

GEOGRAPHY The Republic of Benin is one of Africa's smallest countries. It extends north–south for about 390 mi [620 km]. Lagoons line the short coastline, and the country has no natural harbors.

Benin has a hot, wet climate. The average annual temperature on the coast is about 77°F [25°C], and the average rainfall is about 52 in [1,330 mm]. The inland plains are wetter than the coast.

POLITICS & ECONOMY After slavery was ended in the 19th century, the French began to gain influence in the area. Benin became self-governing in 1958 and fully independent in 1960. After much instability and many changes of government, a military group took over in 1972. The country, renamed Benin in 1975, became a one-party socialist state. Socialism was abandoned in 1989, and multiparty elections were held in 1991, 1996 and 1999.

Benin is a poor developing country. About 70% of the people earn their living by farming, though many remain at subsistence level. The chief exports include cotton, petroleum and palm products. Cocoa, coffee, groundnuts (peanuts), tobacco and shea nuts are also grown for export.

AREA 43,483 sq mi [112,620 sq km] **POPULATION** 6,369,000
CAPITAL (POPULATION) Porto-Novo (179,000)
GOVERNMENT Multiparty republic **ETHNIC GROUPS** Fon, Adja, Bariba, Yoruba, Fulani **LANGUAGES** French (official), Fon, Adja, Yoruba
RELIGIONS Traditional beliefs 60%, Christianity 23%, Islam 15%
CURRENCY CFA franc = 100 centimes

BERMUDA

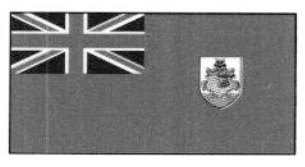
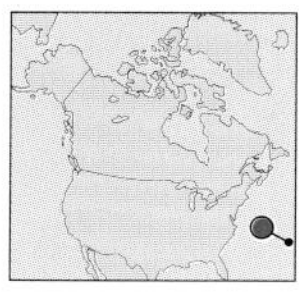

A group of about 150 small islands situated 570 mi [920 km] east of the USA. Bermuda remains Britain's oldest overseas territory, but it has a long tradition of self-government.

AREA 20 sq mi [53 sq km] **POPULATION** 62,000
CAPITAL Hamilton

BHUTAN

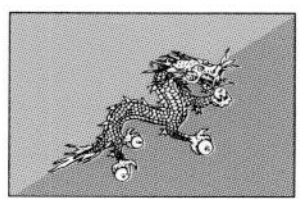
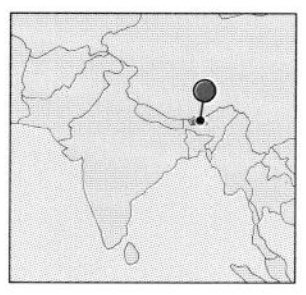

GEOGRAPHY A mountainous, isolated Himalayan country located between India and Tibet. The climate is similar to that of Nepal, being dependent on altitude and affected by monsoonal winds.

POLITICS & ECONOMY The monarch of Bhutan is head of both state and government and this predominantly Buddhist country remains, even in the Asian context, both conservative and poor. Bhutan is the world's most "rural" country, with about 87% of the population dependent on agriculture and only 7% living in towns.

AREA 18,147 sq mi [47,000 sq km] **POPULATION** 1,906,000
CAPITAL (POPULATION) Thimphu (30,000)
GOVERNMENT Constitutional monarchy **ETHNIC GROUPS** Bhutanese, Nepali **LANGUAGES** Dzongkha (official) **RELIGIONS** Buddhism 75%, Hindu **CURRENCY** Ngultrum = 100 chetrum

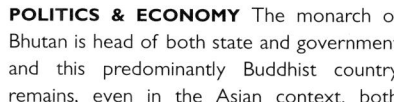

BOLIVIA

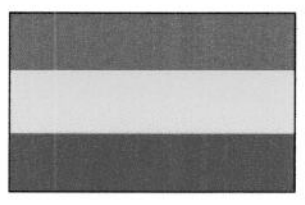
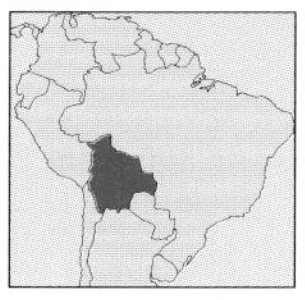

GEOGRAPHY The Republic of Bolivia is a landlocked country which straddles the Andes Mountains in central South America. The Andes rise to a height of 21,464 ft [6,542 m] at Nevado Sajama in the west.

About 40% of Bolivians live on a high plateau called the Altiplano in the Andean region, while the sparsely populated east is essentially a vast lowland plain.

The Bolivian climate is greatly affected by altitude, with the Andean peaks permanently snow-covered, and the eastern plains remaining hot and humid.

POLITICS & ECONOMY American Indians have lived in Bolivia for at least 10,000 years. The main groups today are the Aymara and Quechua people.

In the last 50 years, Bolivia, an independent country since 1825, has been ruled by a succession of civilian and military governments, which violated human rights. Constitutional government was restored in 1982. From the 1980s, Bolivia has pursued economic reforms and free-market policies.

Bolivia is one of the poorest countries in South America. It has several natural resources, including tin, silver and natural gas, but the chief activity is agriculture, which employs 47% of the people. However, experts believe that the main export may be coca, which is used to make the drug cocaine. Coca is exported illegally and the government is trying to stamp out this growing industry.

AREA 424,162 sq mi [1,098,580 sq km] **POPULATION** 9,724,000
CAPITAL (POPULATION) La Paz (1,126,000)
GOVERNMENT Multiparty republic **ETHNIC GROUPS** Mestizo 31%, Quechua 25%, Aymara 17%, White 15%
LANGUAGES Spanish, Aymara, Quechua (all official)
RELIGIONS Christianity (Roman Catholic 94%)
CURRENCY Boliviano = 100 centavos

BOSNIA-HERZEGOVINA

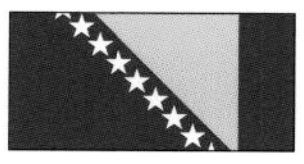
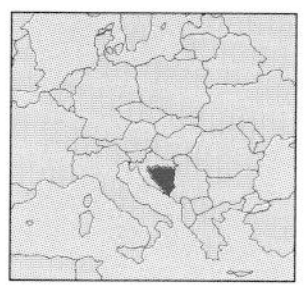

GEOGRAPHY The Republic of Bosnia-Herzegovina is one of the five republics to emerge from the former Federal People's Republic of Yugoslavia. Much of the country is mountainous or hilly, with an arid limestone plateau in the southwest. The River Sava, which forms most of the northern border with Croatia, is a tributary of the River Danube. Because of the country's odd shape, the coastline is limited to a short stretch of 13 mi [20 km] on the Adriatic coast.

A Mediterranean climate, with dry, sunny summers and moist, mild winters, prevails only near the coast. Inland, the weather is more severe, with hot, dry summers and bitterly cold, snowy winters.

POLITICS & ECONOMY In 1918, Bosnia-Herzegovina became part of the Kingdom of the Serbs, Croats and Slovenes, which was renamed Yugoslavia in 1929. Germany occupied the area during World War II (1939–45). From 1945, Communist governments ruled Yugoslavia as a federation containing six republics, one of which was Bosnia-Herzegovina. In the 1980s, the country faced problems as Communist policies proved unsuccessful and differences arose between ethnic groups.

In 1990, free elections were held in Bosnia-Herzegovina and the non-Communists won a majority. A Muslim, Alija Izetbegovic, was elected president. In 1991, Croatia and Slovenia, other parts of the former Yugoslavia, declared themselves independent. In 1992, Bosnia-Herzegovina held a vote on independence. Most Bosnian Serbs boycotted the vote, while the Muslims and Bosnian Croats voted in favor. Many Bosnian Serbs, opposed to independence, started a war against the non-Serbs. They soon occupied more than two-thirds of the land. The Bosnian Serbs were accused of "ethnic cleansing" – that is, the killing or expulsion of other ethnic groups from Serb-occupied areas. The war was later extended when Croat forces seized other parts of the country.

In 1995, the warring parties agreed to a solution to the conflict. This involved keeping the present boundaries of Bosnia-Herzegovina, but dividing it into two self-governing provinces, one Bosnian Serb and the other Muslim-Croat, under a central, unified, multi-ethnic government. Elections were held in 1996 and 1998 under this new arrangement.

The economy of Bosnia-Herzegovina, the least developed of the six republics of the former Yugoslavia apart from Macedonia, was shattered by the war in the early 1990s. Before the war, manufactures were the main exports, including electrical, machinery and transport equipment, and textiles. Farm products include fruits, maize, tobacco, vegetables and wheat, but food has to be imported.

AREA 19,745 sq mi [51,129 sq km] **POPULATION** 4,601,000
CAPITAL (POPULATION) Sarajevo (526,000) **GOVERNMENT** Federal republic **ETHNIC GROUPS** Muslim 49%, Serb 31%, Croat 17%
LANGUAGES Serbo-Croatian **RELIGIONS** Islam 40%, Christianity (Serbian Orthodox 31%, Roman Catholic 15%, Protestant 4%)
CURRENCY Convertible mark = 100 paras

BOTSWANA

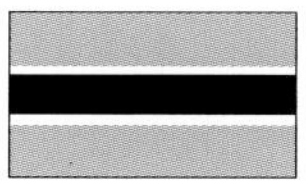
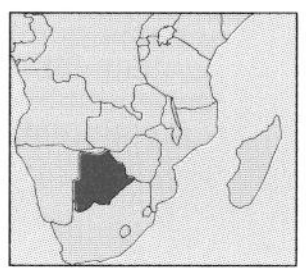

GEOGRAPHY The Republic of Botswana is a landlocked country in southern Africa. The Kalahari, a semidesert area covered mostly by grasses and thorn scrub, covers much of the country. Most of the south has no permanent streams. But large depressions in the north are inland drainage basins. In one of them, the Okavango River, which rises in Angola, forms a large, swampy delta.

Temperatures are high in the summer months (October to April), but the winter months are much cooler. In winter, night-time temperatures sometimes drop below freezing point. The average annual rainfall ranges from over 16 in [400 mm] in the east to less than 8 in [200 mm] in the southwest.

POLITICS & ECONOMY The earliest inhabitants of the region were the San, who are also called Bushmen. They had a nomadic way of life, hunting wild animals and collecting wild plant foods.

Britain ruled the area as the Bechuanaland Protectorate between 1885 and 1966. When the country became independent, it was renamed Botswana. Since then, the country has been a stable, multiparty democracy. However, a major setback occurred in the early 21st century, when health officials announced that around 25% of the people were infected with HIV/AIDS. In 1966, Botswana was extremely poor, depending on meat and live cattle for its exports. But the discovery of minerals, including coal, cobalt, copper, diamonds and nickel, has boosted the economy. About 22% of the people now depend on agriculture, raising cattle and growing crops. Industries include the processing of farm products.

AREA 224,606 SQ MI [581,730 SQ KM] **POPULATION** 1,822,000
CAPITAL (POPULATION) GABORONE (133,000)
GOVERNMENT MULTIPARTY REPUBLIC **ETHNIC GROUPS** TSWANA 75%, SHONA 12%, SAN (BUSHMEN) 3% **LANGUAGES** ENGLISH (OFFICIAL), SETSWANA **RELIGIONS** TRADITIONAL BELIEFS 49%, CHRISTIANITY 50%
CURRENCY PULA = 100 THEBE

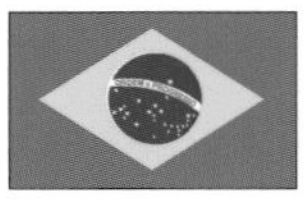

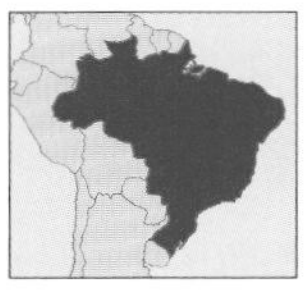

BRAZIL

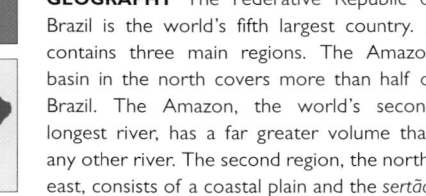

GEOGRAPHY The Federative Republic of Brazil is the world's fifth largest country. It contains three main regions. The Amazon basin in the north covers more than half of Brazil. The Amazon, the world's second longest river, has a far greater volume than any other river. The second region, the northeast, consists of a coastal plain and the *sertão*, which is the name for the inland plateaux and hill country. The main river in this region is the São Francisco.

The third region is made up of the plateaux in the southeast. This region, which covers about a quarter of the country, is the most developed and densely populated part of Brazil. Its main river is the Paraná, which flows south through Argentina.

Manaus has high temperatures all through the year. The rainfall is heavy, though the period from June to September is drier than the rest of the year. The capital, Brasília, and the city Rio de Janeiro also have tropical climates, with much more marked dry seasons than Manaus. The far south has a temperate climate. The northeastern interior is the driest region, with an average annual rainfall of only 10 in [250 mm] in places. The rainfall is also unreliable and severe droughts are common in this region.

POLITICS & ECONOMY The Portuguese explorer Pedro Alvarez Cabral claimed Brazil for Portugal in 1500. With Spain occupied in western South America, the Portuguese began to develop their colony, which was more than 90 times as big as Portugal. To do this, they enslaved many local Amerindian people and introduced about 4 million African slaves. Brazil declared itself an independent empire in 1822 and a republic in 1889. From the 1930s, Brazil faced periods of military rule and widespread corruption. Civilian rule was restored in 1985. Brazil adopted a new constitution in 1988, though it was amended in 1997 to allow presidents to serve for two four-year terms.

The United Nations has described Brazil as a "Rapidly Industrializing Country," or RIC. Its total volume of production is one of the largest in the world. But many people, including poor farmers and residents of the *favelas* (city slums), do not share in the country's fast economic growth. Widespread poverty, together with high inflation and unemployment, cause political problems.

By the early 1990s, industry was the most valuable activity, employing 25% of the people. Brazil is among the world's top producers of bauxite, chrome, diamonds, gold, iron ore, manganese and tin. It is also a major manufacturing country. Its products include aircraft, cars, chemicals, processed food, including raw sugar, iron and steel, paper and textiles.

Brazil is one of the world's leading farming countries and agriculture employs 22% of the people. Coffee is a major export. Other leading products include bananas, citrus fruits, cocoa, maize, rice, soya beans and sugarcane. Brazil is also the top producer of eggs, meat and milk in South America.

Forestry is a major industry, though many people fear that the exploitation of the rain forests, with 1.5% to 4% of Brazil's forest being destroyed every year, is a disaster for the entire world.

AREA 3,286,472 SQ MI [8,511,970 SQ KM] **POPULATION** 179,487,000
CAPITAL (POPULATION) BRASÍLIA (1,821,000)
GOVERNMENT FEDERAL REPUBLIC **ETHNIC GROUPS** WHITE 53%, MULATTO 22%, MESTIZO 12%, AFRICAN AMERICAN 11%, JAPANESE 1%, AMERINDIAN 0.1% **LANGUAGES** PORTUGUESE (OFFICIAL)
RELIGIONS CHRISTIANITY (ROMAN CATHOLIC 88%)
CURRENCY REAL = 100 CENTAVOS

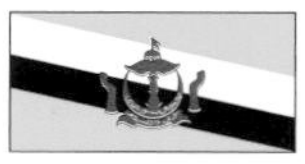

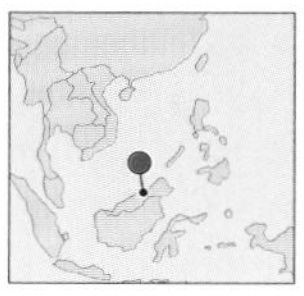

BRUNEI

The Islamic Sultanate of Brunei, a British protectorate until 1984, lies on the north coast of Borneo. The climate is tropical and rain forests cover large areas. Brunei is a prosperous country because of its oil and natural gas production, and the Sultan is said to be among the world's richest men.

AREA 2,228 SQ MI [5,770 SQ KM] **POPULATION** 333,000
CAPITAL BANDAR SERI BEGAWAN

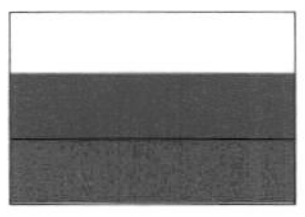

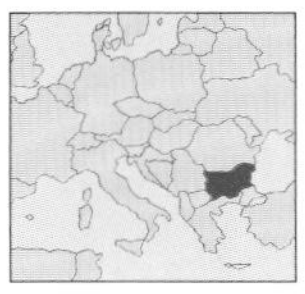

BULGARIA

GEOGRAPHY The Republic of Bulgaria is a country in the Balkan peninsula, facing the Black Sea in the east. The heart of Bulgaria is mountainous. The main ranges are the Balkan Mountains in the center and the Rhodope (or Rhodopi) Mountains in the south.

Summers are hot and winters are cold, though seldom severe. The rainfall is moderate.

POLITICS & ECONOMY Ottoman Turks ruled Bulgaria from 1396 and ethnic Turks still form a sizable minority in the country. In 1879, Bulgaria became a monarchy, and in 1908 it became fully independent. Bulgaria was an ally of Germany in World War I (1914–18) and again in World War II (1939–45). In 1944, Soviet troops invaded Bulgaria and, after the war, the monarchy was abolished and the country became a Communist ally of the Soviet Union. In the late 1980s, reforms in the Soviet Union led Bulgaria's government to introduce a multiparty system in 1990. A non-Communist government was elected in 1991, the first free elections in 44 years. Throughout the 1990s, Bulgaria faced many problems in pursuing its policies of economic reform and, in 2000, the Bulgarian media accused government officials of widespread corruption.

According to the World Bank, Bulgaria in the 1990s was a "lower-middle-income" developing country. Bulgaria has some deposits of minerals, including brown coal, manganese and iron ore. But manufacturing is the leading economic activity, though problems arose in the early 1990s, because much industrial technology is outdated. The main products are chemicals, processed foods, metal products, machinery and textiles. Manufactures are the leading exports. Bulgaria trades mainly with countries in Eastern Europe.

AREA 42,822 SQ MI [110,910 SQ KM] **POPULATION** 9,071,000
CAPITAL (POPULATION) SOFIA (1,116,000) **GOVERNMENT** MULTIPARTY REPUBLIC **ETHNIC GROUPS** BULGARIAN 86%, TURKISH 10%, GYPSY 3%, MACEDONIAN, ARMENIAN, ROMANIAN, GREEK **LANGUAGES** BULGARIAN (OFFICIAL), TURKISH **RELIGIONS** CHRISTIANITY (EASTERN ORTHODOX 87%), ISLAM 13% **CURRENCY** LEV = 100 STOTINKI

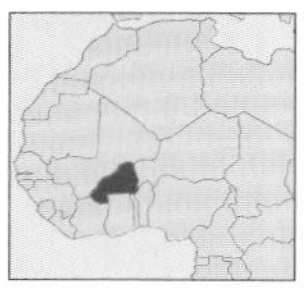

BURKINA FASO

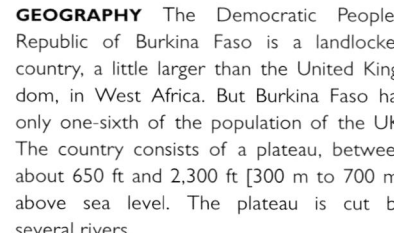

GEOGRAPHY The Democratic People's Republic of Burkina Faso is a landlocked country, a little larger than the United Kingdom, in West Africa. But Burkina Faso has only one-sixth of the population of the UK. The country consists of a plateau, between about 650 ft and 2,300 ft [300 m to 700 m] above sea level. The plateau is cut by several rivers.

The capital city, Ouagadougou, in central Burkina Faso, has high temperatures throughout the year. Most of the rain falls between May and September, but the rainfall is erratic and droughts are common.

POLITICS & ECONOMY The people of Burkina Faso are divided into two main groups. The Voltaic group includes the Mossi, who form the largest single group, and the Bobo. The French conquered the Mossi capital of Ouagadougou in 1897 and they made the area a protectorate. In 1919, the area became a French colony called Upper Volta. After independence in 1960, Upper Volta became a one-party state. But it was unstable – military groups seized power several times and a number of political killings took place.

In 1984, the country's name was changed to Burkina Faso. Elections were held in 1991 – for the first time in more than ten years – but the military kept an important role in the government.

Burkina Faso is one of the world's 20 poorest countries and has become very dependent on foreign aid. Most of Burkina Faso is dry with thin soils. The country's main food crops are beans, maize, millet, rice and sorghum. Cotton, groundnuts and shea nuts, whose seeds produce a fat used to make cooking oil and soap, are grown for sale abroad. Livestock are also an important export.

The country has few resources and manufacturing is on a small scale. There are some deposits of manganese, zinc, lead and nickel in the north of the country, but there is not yet a good enough transport system there. Many young men seek jobs abroad in Ghana and Ivory Coast. The money they send home to their families is important to the country's economy.

AREA 105,869 SQ MI [274,200 SQ KM] **POPULATION** 12,092,000
CAPITAL (POPULATION) OUAGADOUGOU (690,000)
GOVERNMENT MULTIPARTY REPUBLIC **ETHNIC GROUPS** MOSSI 48%, MANDE 9%, FULANI 8%, BOBO 7% **LANGUAGES** FRENCH (OFFICIAL), MOSSI, FULANI **RELIGIONS** TRADITIONAL BELIEFS 45%, ISLAM 43%, CHRISTIANITY 12%
CURRENCY CFA FRANC = 100 CENTIMES

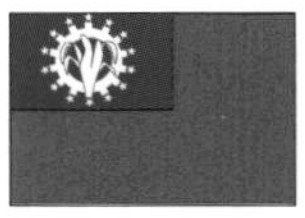

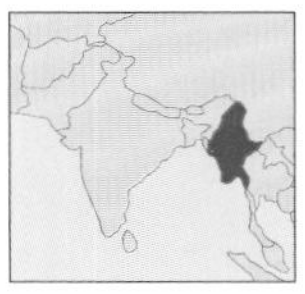

BURMA (MYANMAR)

GEOGRAPHY The Union of Burma is now officially known as the Union of Myanmar; its name was changed in 1989. Mountains border the country in the east and west, with the highest mountains in the north. Burma's highest mountain is Hkakabo Razi, which is 19,294 ft [5,881 m] high. Between these ranges is central Burma, which contains the fertile valleys of the Irrawaddy and Sittang rivers. The Irrawaddy delta on the Bay of Bengal is one of the world's leading rice-growing areas. Burma also includes the long Tenasserim coast in the southeast.

Burma has a tropical monsoon climate. There are three seasons. The rainy season runs from late May to mid-October. A cool, dry season follows, between late October and the middle part of February. The hot season lasts from late February to mid-May, though temperatures remain high during the humid rainy season.

POLITICS & ECONOMY Many groups settled in Burma in ancient times. Some, called the hill peoples, live in remote mountain areas where they have retained their own cultures. The ancestors of the country's main ethnic group today, the Burmese, arrived in the 9th century AD.

Britain conquered Burma in the 19th century and made it a province of British India. But, in 1937, the British granted Burma limited self-government. Japan conquered Burma in 1942, but the Japanese were driven out in 1945. Burma became a fully independent country in 1948.

Revolts by Communists and various hill people led to instability in the 1950s. In 1962, Burma became a military dictatorship and, in 1974, a one-party state. Attempts to control minority liberation movements and the opium trade led to repressive rule. The National League for Democracy led by Aung San Suu Kyi won the elections in 1990, but the military continued their repressive rule throughout the 1990s, earning Burma the reputation for having one of the world's worst human rights records. Burma's internal political problems have helped to make it one of the world's poorest countries. Its admission to ASEAN (Association of Southeast Asian Nations) in 1997 may have implied regional recognition of the regime, but the European Union continues to voice its concern over human rights abuses.

Agriculture is the main activity, employing 64% of the people. The chief crop is rice. Maize, pulses, oilseeds and sugarcane are other major products. Forestry is important. Teak and rice together make up about two-thirds of the total value of the exports. Burma has many mineral resources, though they are mostly undeveloped, but the country is famous for its precious stones, especially rubies. Manufacturing is mostly on a small scale.

AREA 261,228 SQ MI [676,577 SQ KM] **POPULATION** 51,129,000
CAPITAL (POPULATION) RANGOON (2,513,000) **GOVERNMENT** MILITARY REGIME **ETHNIC GROUPS** BURMAN 69%, SHAN 9%, KAREN 6%, RAKHINE 5%, MON 2%, KACHIN 1% **LANGUAGES** BURMESE (OFFICIAL), SHAN, KAREN, RAKHINE, MON, KACHIN, ENGLISH, CHIN **RELIGIONS** BUDDHISM 89%, CHRISTIANITY, ISLAM **CURRENCY** KYAT = 100 PYAS

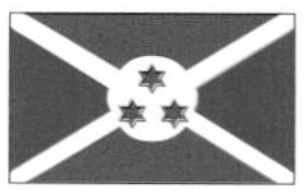

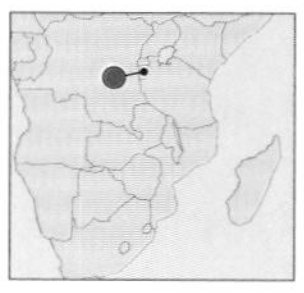

BURUNDI

GEOGRAPHY The Republic of Burundi is the fifth smallest country in mainland Africa. It is also the second most densely populated after its northern neighbor, Rwanda. Part of the Great African Rift Valley, which runs throughout eastern Africa into southwestern Asia, lies in western Burundi. It includes part of Lake Tanganyika.

Bujumbura, the capital city, lies on the shore of Lake Tanganyika. It has a warm climate. A dry season occurs from June to September, but the other months are fairly rainy. The mountains and plateaux to the east are cooler and wetter, but the rainfall generally decreases to the east.

POLITICS & ECONOMY The Twa, a pygmy people, were the first known inhabitants of Burundi. About 1,000 years ago, the Hutu, a people who speak a Bantu language, gradually began to settle the area, pushing the Twa into remote areas.

From the 15th century, the Tutsi, a cattle-owning people from the northeast, gradually took over the country. The Hutu, though greatly outnumbering the Tutsi, were forced to serve the Tutsi overlords.

Germany conquered the area that is now Burundi and Rwanda in the late 1890s. The area, called Ruanda-Urundi, was taken by Belgium during World War I (1914–18). In 1961, the people of Urundi voted to become a monarchy, while the people of Ruanda voted to become a republic. The two territories became fully independent as Burundi and Rwanda in 1962. After 1962, the rivalries between the Hutu and Tutsi led to periodic outbreaks of fighting. The Tutsi monarchy was ended in 1966 and Burundi became a republic. Instability continued with coups in 1976, 1987, 1993 and 1996, with periodic massacres of thousands of people as Tutsis and Hutus fought for power.

Burundi is one of the world's ten poorest countries. About 92% of the people are farmers, who mostly grow little more than they need to feed their own families. The main food crops are beans, cassava, maize and sweet potatoes. Cattle, goats and sheep are raised, while fish are an important supplement to people's diets. However, Burundi has to import food.

AREA 10,745 sq mi [27,830 sq km] **POPULATION** 7,358,000
CAPITAL (POPULATION) Bujumbura (300,000) **GOVERNMENT** Republic
ETHNIC GROUPS Hutu 85%, Tutsi 14%, Twa (pygmy) 1%
LANGUAGES French and Kirundi (both official)
RELIGIONS Christianity 85% (Roman Catholic 78%), traditional beliefs 13% **CURRENCY** Burundi franc = 100 centimes

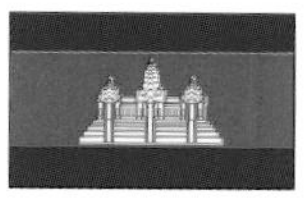
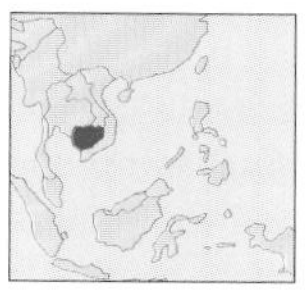

CAMBODIA

GEOGRAPHY The Kingdom of Cambodia is a country in Southeast Asia. Low mountains border the country except in the southeast. But most of Cambodia consists of plains drained by the River Mekong, which enters Cambodia from Laos in the north and exits through Vietnam in the southeast. The northwest contains Tonlé Sap (or Great Lake). In the dry season, this lake drains into the River Mekong. But in the wet season, the level of the Mekong rises and water flows in the opposite direction from the river into Tonlé Sap – the lake then becomes the largest freshwater lake in Asia.

Cambodia has a tropical monsoon climate, with high temperatures throughout the year. The dry season, when winds blow from the north or northeast, runs from November to April. During the rainy season (May to October), moist winds blow from the south or southeast. The high humidity and heat often make conditions unpleasant. Rainfall is heaviest near the coast, and rather lower inland.

POLITICS & ECONOMY From 802 to 1432, the Khmer people ruled a great empire, which reached its peak in the 12th century. The Khmer capital was at Angkor. The Hindu stone temples built there and at nearby Angkor Wat form the world's largest group of religious buildings. France ruled the country between 1863 and 1954, when the country became an independent monarchy. But the monarchy was abolished in 1970 and Cambodia became a republic.

In 1970, US and South Vietnamese troops entered Cambodia but left after destroying North Vietnamese Communist camps in the east. The country became involved in the Vietnamese War, and then in a civil war as Cambodian Communists of the Khmer Rouge organization fought for power. The Khmer Rouge took over Cambodia in 1975 and launched a reign of terror in which between 1 million and 2.5 million people were killed. In 1979, Vietnamese and Cambodian troops overthrew the Khmer Rouge government. But fighting continued between factions. Vietnam withdrew in 1989, and in 1991 Prince Sihanouk was recognized as head of state. Elections were held in May 1993, and in September 1993 the monarchy was restored. Sihanouk again became king. In 1997, the prime minister, Prince Norodom Ranariddh, was deposed, so ending four years of democratic rule. This led to Cambodia's application to join the Association of Southeast Asian Nations to be delayed until 1999.

Cambodia is a poor country whose economy has been wrecked by war. Until the 1970s, the country's farmers produced most of the food needed by the people. But by 1986, it was only able to supply 80% of its needs. Farming is the main activity and rice, rubber and maize are major products. Manufacturing is almost nonexistent, apart from rubber processing and a few factories producing items for sale in Cambodia.

AREA 69,900 sq mi [181,040 sq km] **POPULATION** 10,046,000
CAPITAL (POPULATION) Phnom Penh (920,000)
GOVERNMENT Constitutional monarchy **ETHNIC GROUPS** Khmer 94%, Chinese 3%, Cham 2%, Thai, Lao, Kola, Vietnamese **LANGUAGES** Khmer (official) **RELIGIONS** Buddhism 88%, Islam 2% **CURRENCY** Riel = 100 sen

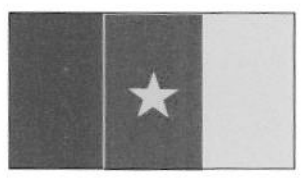
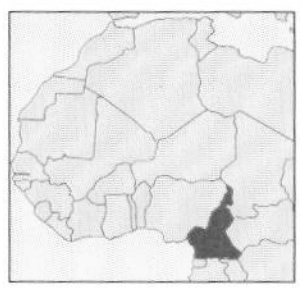

CAMEROON

GEOGRAPHY The Republic of Cameroon in West Africa got its name from the Portuguese word *camarões*, or prawns. This name was used by Portuguese explorers who fished for prawns along the coast. Behind the narrow coastal plains on the Gulf of Guinea, the land rises to a series of plateaux, with a mountainous region in the southwest where the volcano Mount Cameroon is situated. In the north, the land slopes down toward the Lake Chad basin.

The rainfall is heavy, especially in the highlands. The rainiest months near the coast are June to September. The rainfall decreases to the north and the far north has a hot, dry climate. Temperatures are high on the coast, whereas the inland plateaux are cooler.

POLITICS & ECONOMY Germany lost Cameroon during World War I (1914–18). The country was then divided into two parts, one ruled by Britain and the other by France. In 1960, French Cameroon became the independent Cameroon Republic. In 1961, after a vote in British Cameroon, part of the territory joined the Cameroon Republic to become the Federal Republic of Cameroon. The other part joined Nigeria. In 1972, Cameroon became a unitary state called the United Republic of Cameroon. It adopted the name Republic of Cameroon in 1984, but the country had two official languages. In 1995, partly to placate English-speaking people, Cameroon became the 52nd member of the Commonwealth.

Like most countries in tropical Africa, Cameroon's economy is based on agriculture, which employs 73% of the people. The chief food crops include cassava, maize, millet, sweet potatoes and yams. The country also has plantations to produce such crops as cocoa and coffee for export.

Cameroon is fortunate in having some oil, the country's chief export, and bauxite. Although Cameroon has few manufacturing and processing industries, its mineral exports and its self-sufficiency in food production make it one of the better-off countries in tropical Africa.

AREA 183,567 sq mi [475,440 sq km] **POPULATION** 16,701,000
CAPITAL (POPULATION) Yaoundé (800,000) **GOVERNMENT** Multiparty republic **ETHNIC GROUPS** Fang 20%, Bamileke and Bamum 19%, Duala, Luanda and Basa 15%, Fulani 10% **LANGUAGES** French and English (both official) **RELIGIONS** Christianity 53%, traditional beliefs 25%, Islam 22% **CURRENCY** CFA franc = 100 centimes

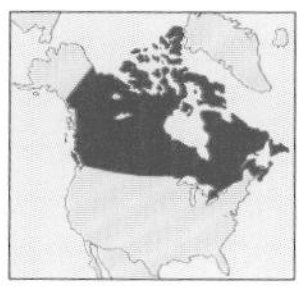

CANADA

GEOGRAPHY Canada is the world's second largest country after Russia. It is thinly populated, however, with much of the land too cold or too mountainous for human settlement. Most Canadians live within 186 mi [300 km] of the southern border.

Western Canada is rugged. It includes the Pacific ranges and the mighty Rocky Mountains. East of the Rockies are the interior plains. In the north lie the bleak Arctic islands, while to the south lie the densely populated lowlands around lakes Erie and Ontario and in the St Lawrence River valley.

Canada has a cold climate. In winter, temperatures fall below freezing point throughout most of Canada. But the southwestern coast has a relatively mild climate. Along the Arctic Circle, mean temperatures are below freezing for seven months a year.

Western and southeastern Canada experience high rainfall, but the prairies are dry with 10 in to 20 in [250 mm to 500 mm] of rain every year.

POLITICS & ECONOMY Canada's first people, the ancestors of the Native Americans, or Indians, arrived in North America from Asia around 40,000 years ago. Later arrivals were the Inuit (Eskimos), who also came from Asia. Europeans reached the Canadian coast in 1497 and a race began between Britain and France for control of the territory.

France gained an initial advantage, and the French founded Québec in 1608. But the British later occupied eastern Canada. In 1867, Britain passed the British North America Act, which set up the Dominion of Canada, which was made up of Québec, Ontario, Nova Scotia and New Brunswick. Other areas were added, the last being Newfoundland in 1949. Canada fought alongside Britain in both World Wars and many Canadians feel close ties with Britain. Canada is a constitutional monarchy, and the British monarch is Canada's head of state.

Rivalries between French- and English-speaking Canadians continue. In 1995, Québeckers voted against a move to make Québec a sovereign state. The majority was less than 1% and this issue seems unlikely to disappear. Another problem concerns the rights of the Aboriginal minorities, who would like to have more say in the running of their own affairs. To this end, in 1999, Canada created a new territory called Nunavut for the Inuit population in the north. Nunavut covers approximately 64% of what was formerly the eastern part of Northwest Territories.

Canada is a highly developed and prosperous country. Although farmland covers only 8% of the country, Canadian farms are highly productive. Canada is one of the world's leading producers of barley, wheat, meat and milk. Forestry and fishing are other important industries. It is rich in natural resources, especially oil and natural gas, and is a major exporter of minerals. The country also produces copper, gold, iron ore, uranium and zinc. Manufacturing is highly developed, especially in the cities where 78% of the people live. Canada has many factories that process farm and mineral products. It also produces cars, chemicals, electronic goods, machinery, paper and timber products.

AREA 3,851,788 sq mi [9,976,140 sq km] **POPULATION** 28,488,000
CAPITAL (POPULATION) Ottawa (1,022,000)
GOVERNMENT Federal multiparty constitutional monarchy
ETHNIC GROUPS British 34%, French 26%, German 4%, Italian 3%, Ukrainian 2%, Native American (Amerindian/Inuit) 1.5%, Chinese
LANGUAGES English and French (both official)
RELIGIONS Christianity (Roman Catholic 47%, Protestant 41%), Judaism, Islam, Hinduism **CURRENCY** Canadian dollar = 100 cents

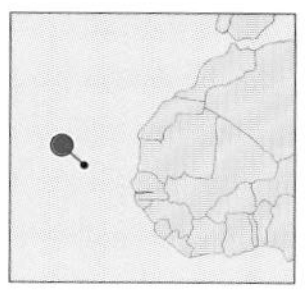

CAPE VERDE

Cape Verde consists of ten large and five small islands, and is situated 350 mi [560 km] west of Dakar in Senegal. The islands have a tropical climate, with high temperatures all year round. Cape Verde became independent from Portugal in 1975 and is rated as a "low-income" developing country by the World Bank.

AREA 1,556 sq mi [4,030 sq km]
POPULATION 515,000 **CAPITAL** Praia

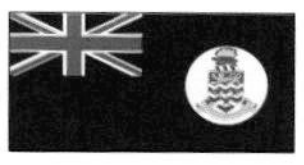
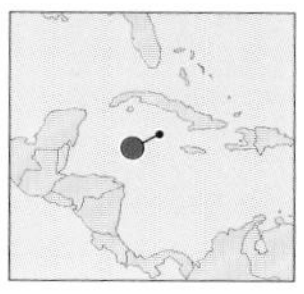

CAYMAN ISLANDS

The Cayman Islands are an overseas territory of the UK, consisting of three low-lying islands. Financial services are the main economic activity and the islands offer a secret tax haven to many companies and banks.

AREA 100 sq mi [259 sq km]
POPULATION 35,000 **CAPITAL** George Town

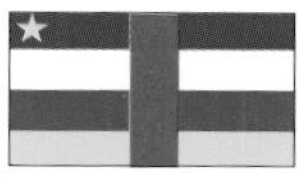
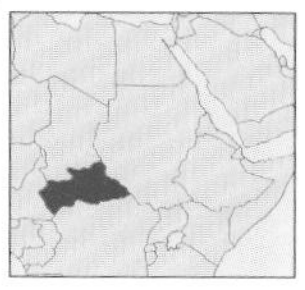

CENTRAL AFRICAN REPUBLIC

GEOGRAPHY The Central African Republic is a remote, landlocked country in the heart of Africa. It consists mostly of a plateau lying between 1,970 ft and 2,620 ft [600 m to 800 m] above sea level. The Ubangi drains the south, while the Chari (or Shari) River flows from the north to the Lake Chad basin.

Bangui, the capital, lies in the southwest of the country on the Ubangi River. The climate is warm throughout the year, with average yearly rainfall totaling 62 in [1,574 mm]. The north is drier, with an average yearly rainfall of about 31 in [800 mm].

POLITICS & ECONOMY France set up an outpost at Bangui in 1899 and ruled the country as a colony from 1894. Known as Ubangi-Shari, the country was ruled by France as part of French Equatorial Africa until it gained independence in 1960.

Central African Republic became a one-party state in 1962, but army officers seized power in 1966. The head of the army, Jean-Bedel Bokassa, made himself emperor in 1976. The country was renamed the Central African Empire, but after a brutal and tyrannical reign, Bokassa was overthrown by a military group in 1979. As a result, the monarchy was abolished and the country again became a republic.

The country adopted a new, multiparty constitution in 1991. Multiparty elections were held in 1993 and 1998. An army rebellion in 1996 was put down in 1997 with help from French troops.

The World Bank classifies Central African Republic as a "low-income" developing country. Over 80% of the people are farmers, and most of them produce little more than they need to feed their families. The main crops are bananas, maize, manioc, millet and yams. Coffee, cotton, timber and tobacco are produced for export, mainly on commercial plantations. The country's development has been impeded by its remote position, its poor transport system and its untrained work force. The country depends heavily on aid, especially from France.

AREA 240,533 sq mi [622,980 sq km] **POPULATION** 4,074,000
CAPITAL (POPULATION) Bangui (553,000) **GOVERNMENT** Multiparty republic **ETHNIC GROUPS** Banda 29%, Baya 25%, Ngbandi 11%, Azande 10%, Sara 7%, Mbaka 4% **LANGUAGES** French (official), Sango **RELIGIONS** Traditional beliefs 57%, Christianity 35%, Islam 8%
CURRENCY CFA franc = 100 centimes

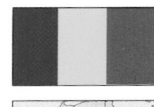

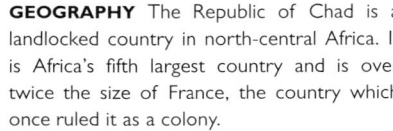

CHAD

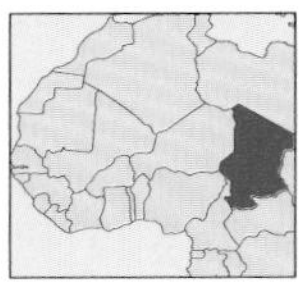

GEOGRAPHY The Republic of Chad is a landlocked country in north-central Africa. It is Africa's fifth largest country and is over twice the size of France, the country which once ruled it as a colony.

Ndjamena in central Chad has a hot, tropical climate, with a marked dry season from November to April. The south of the country is wetter, with an average yearly rainfall of around 39 in [1,000 mm]. The burning-hot desert in the north has an average yearly rainfall of less than 5 in [130 mm].

POLITICS & ECONOMY Chad straddles two worlds. The north is populated by Muslim Arab and Berber peoples, while black Africans, who follow traditional beliefs or who have converted to Christianity, live in the south.

French explorers were active in the area in the late 19th century. France finally made Chad a colony in 1902. After becoming independent in 1960, Chad has been hit by ethnic conflict. The 1970s were marked by civil war and coups. Chad and Libya agreed a truce in 1987 and, in 1994, the International Court of Justice ruled against Libya's claim on the Aozou Strip. Chad enjoyed more stability in the 1990s. A new constitution was adopted in 1997.

Hit by drought and civil war, Chad is one of the world's poorest countries. Farming, fishing and livestock raising employ 83% of the people. Groundnuts, millet, rice and sorghum are major food crops in the wetter south, but the most valuable crop in export terms is cotton. The country has few natural resources and very few manufacturing industries.

AREA 495,752 sq mi [1,284,000 sq km] **POPULATION** 7,337,000
CAPITAL (POPULATION) Ndjamena (530,000)
GOVERNMENT Multiparty republic **ETHNIC GROUPS** Bagirmi, Kreish and Sara 31%, Sudanic Arab 26%, Teda 7%, Mbum 6%
LANGUAGES French and Arabic (both official)
RELIGIONS Islam 40%, Christianity 33%, traditional beliefs 27%
CURRENCY CFA franc = 100 centimes

CHILE

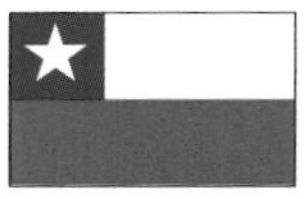
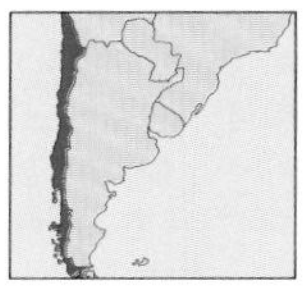

GEOGRAPHY The Republic of Chile stretches about 2,650 mi [4,260 km] from north to south, although the maximum east–west distance is only about 267 mi [430 km]. The high Andes Mountains form Chile's eastern borders with Argentina and Bolivia. To the west are basins and valleys, with coastal uplands overlooking the shore. Most people live in the central valley, where Santiago is situated.

Santiago has a Mediterranean climate, with hot, dry summers from November to March and mild, moist winters from April to October. The Atacama Desert in the north is one of the world's driest places, while southern Chile is cold and stormy.

POLITICS & ECONOMY Amerindian people reached the southern tip of South America 8,000 years ago. In 1520, Portuguese navigator Ferdinand Magellan was the first European to sight Chile. The country became a Spanish colony in the 1540s. Chile became independent in 1818. During a war (1879–83), it gained mineral-rich areas from Peru and Bolivia.

In 1970, Salvador Allende became the first Communist leader to be elected democratically. He was overthrown in 1973 by army officers, who were supported by the CIA. General Augusto Pinochet then ruled as a dictator. A new constitution was introduced in 1981 and elections were held in 1989. Pinochet remained important since he served as commander-in-chief of the armed forces. In 2000, a socialist, Ricardo Lagos, was elected president.

The World Bank classifies Chile as a "lower-middle-income" developing country. Mining is important, especially copper production. Minerals dominate exports. The most valuable activity is manufacturing; products include processed foods, metals, iron and steel, transport equipment and textiles. The chief crop is wheat, while beans, fruits, maize and livestock products are also important. Chile's fishing industry is one of the world's largest.

AREA 292,258 sq mi [756,950 sq km] **POPULATION** 15,272,000
CAPITAL (POPULATION) Santiago (5,067,000)
GOVERNMENT Multiparty republic **ETHNIC GROUPS** Mestizo 92%, Amerindian 7% **LANGUAGES** Spanish (official)
RELIGIONS Christianity (Roman Catholic 81%)
CURRENCY Peso = 100 centavos

CHINA

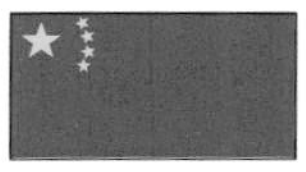
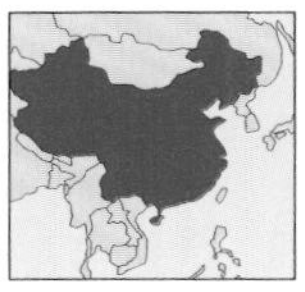

GEOGRAPHY The People's Republic of China is the world's third largest country. It is also the only country with more than 1,000 million people. Most people live in the east – on the coastal plains or in the fertile valleys of the Huang He (Hwang Ho or Yellow River), the Chang Jiang (Yangtze Kiang), which is Asia's longest river at 3,960 mi [6,380 km], and the Xi Jiang (Si Kiang).

Western China is thinly populated. It includes the bleak Tibetan plateau which is bounded by the Himalaya, the world's highest mountain range. Other ranges include the Kunlun Shan, the Altun Shan and the Tian Shan. Deserts include the Gobi Desert along the Mongolian border and the Taklimakan Desert in the far west.

Beijing in northeastern China has cold winters and warm summers, with a moderate rainfall. Shanghai, in the east-central region of China, has milder winters and more rain. The southeast has a wet, subtropical climate. In the west, the climate is severe. Lhasa has very cold winters and a low rainfall.

POLITICS & ECONOMY China is one of the world's oldest civilizations, going back 3,500 years. Under the Han dynasty (202 BC to AD 220), the Chinese empire was as large as the Roman empire. Mongols conquered China in the 13th century, but Chinese rule was restored in 1368. The Manchu people of Mongolia ruled the country from 1644 to 1912, when the country became a republic.

War with Japan (1937–45) was followed by civil war between the nationalists and the Communists. The Communists triumphed in 1949, setting up the People's Republic of China.

In the 1980s, following the death of the revolutionary leader Mao Zedong (Mao Tse-tung) in 1976, China introduced reforms. It encouraged private enterprise and foreign investment, formerly forbidden policies. But the Communist leaders have not permitted political freedom. Opponents of the regime continue to be harshly treated, while attempts to negotiate some degree of autonomy for Tibet were firmly rejected in 1998.

China's economy, which is one of the world's largest, has expanded rapidly since the late 1970s. This is partly the result of the gradual abandonment of some fundamental Communist policies, including the setting up of many private manufacturing industries in the east. China's sheer size, combined with its rapid economic growth, led to predictions in the 1990s that China would become the world's biggest economy "within a generation." This was made more likely by the return of Hong Kong in 1997. China wants to regain the prosperous island of Taiwan, which it regards as a Chinese province, but this seemed unlikely in the early 21st century.

In the early 1990s, agriculture employed about 70% of the people, although only 10% of the land is used for crops. Major products include rice, sweet potatoes, tea and wheat, together with many fruits and vegetables. Livestock farming is also important. Pork is a popular meat and China has more than a third of the world's pigs.

China's resources include coal, oil, iron ore and various other metals. China has huge steel industries and manufactures include cement, chemicals, fertilizers, machinery, telecommunications and recording equipment, and textiles. Consumer goods, such as bicycles and radios, are becoming increasingly important.

AREA 3,705,386 sq mi [9,596,960 sq km]
POPULATION 1,299,180,000 **CAPITAL (POPULATION)** Beijing (12,362,000) **GOVERNMENT** Single-party Communist republic
ETHNIC GROUPS Han Chinese 92%, 55 minority groups
LANGUAGES Mandarin Chinese (official) **RELIGIONS** Atheist 50%, Confucian 20% **CURRENCY** Renminbi yuan = 10 jiao = 100 fen

COLOMBIA

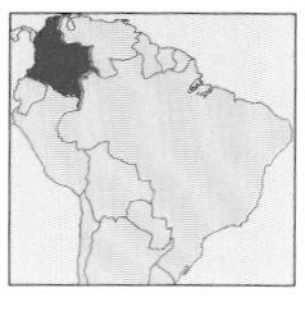

GEOGRAPHY The Republic of Colombia, in northeastern South America, is the only country in the continent to have coastlines on both the Pacific and the Caribbean Sea. Colombia also contains the northernmost ranges of the Andes Mountains.

There is a tropical climate in the lowlands. But the altitude greatly affects the climate of the Andes. The capital, Bogotá, which stands on a plateau in the eastern Andes at about 9,200 ft [2,800 m] above sea level, has mild temperatures throughout the year. The rainfall is heavy, especially on the Pacific coast

POLITICS & ECONOMY Amerindian people have lived in Colombia for thousands of years. But today, only a small proportion of the people are of unmixed Amerindian ancestry. Mestizos (people of mixed white and Amerindian ancestry) form the largest group, followed by whites and mulattos (people of mixed European and African ancestry).

Spaniards opened up the area in the early 16th century. They set up a territory known as the Vice-royalty of the New Kingdom of Granada, including Colombia, Ecuador, Panama and Venezuela. In 1819, the area became independent, but Ecuador and Venezuela soon split away, followed by Panama in 1903. Recent history has been unstable. Rivalries between main political parties led to civil wars in 1899–1902 and 1949–57, when the parties agreed to form a coalition. The coalition government ended in 1986 when the Liberal Party was elected. Colombia faces economic problems, as well as the difficulty of controlling a large illicit drug industry run by violent dealers. In 2000, the United States began to provide military aid to help Colombia fight drug-trafficking. Colombia exports oil, coffee and chemicals.

AREA 439,733 sq mi [1,138,910 sq km] **POPULATION** 39,397,000
CAPITAL (POPULATION) Bogotá (6,004,000) **GOVERNMENT** Multiparty republic **ETHNIC GROUPS** Mestizo 58%, White 20%, Mulatto 14%, Black 4% **LANGUAGES** Spanish (official) **RELIGIONS** Christianity (Roman Catholic 93%) **CURRENCY** Peso = 100 centavos

COMOROS

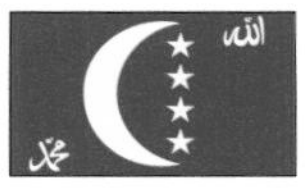
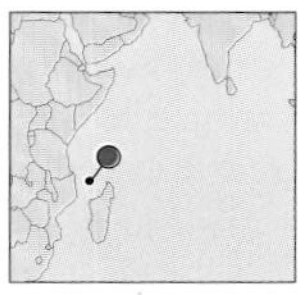

The Federal Islamic Republic of the Comoros consists of three large islands and some smaller ones, lying at the north end of the Mozambique Channel in the Indian Ocean. The country became independent from France in 1974, but the people on a fourth island, Mayotte, voted to remain French. In 1997, secessionists on the island of Anjouan, who favored a return to French rule, defeated forces from Grand Comore and, in 1998, they voted overwhelmingly to break away from the Comoros. Most people are subsistence farmers, although cash crops such as coconuts, coffee, cocoa and spices are also produced. The main exports are cloves, perfume oils and vanilla.

AREA 861 sq mi [2,230 sq km] **POPULATION** 670,000 **CAPITAL** Moroni

CONGO

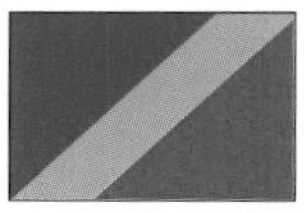
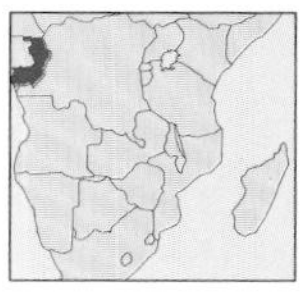

GEOGRAPHY The Republic of Congo is a country on the River Congo in west-central Africa. The Equator runs through the center of the country. Congo has a narrow coastal plain on which its main port, Pointe Noire, stands. Behind the plain are uplands through which the River Niari has carved a fertile valley. Central Congo consists of high plains. The north contains large swampy areas in the valleys of the tributaries of the River Congo.

Congo has a hot, wet equatorial climate. Brazzaville and its environs experience a dry season between June and September. The coastal plain is drier and cooler than the rest of the country because a cold ocean current, the Benguela, flows northward along the coast.

POLITICS & ECONOMY Part of the huge Kongo kingdom between the 15th and 18th centuries, the coast of the Congo later became a center of the European slave trade. The area came under French protection in 1880. It was later governed as part of a larger region called French Equatorial Africa. The country remained under French control until 1960.

Congo became a one-party state in 1964 and a military group took over the government in 1968. In 1970, Congo declared itself a Communist country, though it continued to seek aid from Western countries. The government officially abandoned its Communist policies in 1990. Multiparty elections were held in 1992, but the elected president, Pascal Lissouba, was overthrown in 1997 by former president Denis Sassou-Nguesso. Civil war again occurred in January 1999, but peace was restored.

The World Bank classifies Congo as a "lower-middle-income" developing country. Agriculture is the most important activity, employing more than 60% of the people. But many farmers produce little more than they need to feed their families. Major food crops include bananas, cassava, maize and rice, while the leading cash crops are coffee and cocoa. Congo's main exports are oil (which makes up 70% of the total) and timber. Manufacturing is relatively unimportant at the moment, still hampered by poor transport links, but it is gradually being developed.

AREA 132,046 sq mi [342,000 sq km] **POPULATION** 3,167,000
CAPITAL (POPULATION) Brazzaville (937,000) **GOVERNMENT** Military regime **ETHNIC GROUPS** Kongo 52%, Teke 17%, Mboshi 12%, Mbete 5%
LANGUAGES French (official), Kongo, Teke **RELIGIONS** Christianity (Roman Catholic 54%, Protestant 25%, African Christians 14%
CURRENCY CFA franc = 100 centimes

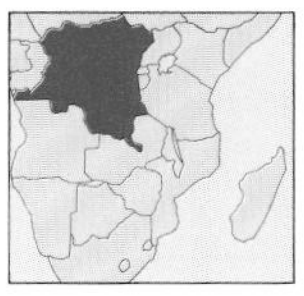

CONGO (DEM. REP. OF THE)

GEOGRAPHY The Democratic Republic of the Congo, formerly known as Zaïre, is the world's 12th largest country. Much of the country lies within the drainage basin of the huge River Congo. The river reaches the sea along the country's coastline, which is 25 mi [40 km] long. Mountains rise in the east, where the country's borders run through lakes Tanganyika, Kivu, Edward and Albert.

The equatorial region has high temperatures and heavy rainfall throughout the year.

POLITICS & ECONOMY Pygmies were the first inhabitants of the region, with Portuguese navigators not reaching the coast until 1482, but the interior was not explored until the late 19th century. In 1885, the country, called Congo Free State, became the personal property of King Léopold II of Belgium. In 1908, the country became a Belgian colony.

The Belgian Congo became independent in 1960 and was renamed Zaïre in 1971. Ethnic rivalries caused instability until 1965, when the country became a one-party state, ruled by President Mobutu. The government allowed the formation of political parties in 1990, but elections were repeatedly postponed. In 1996, fighting broke out in eastern Zaïre, as the Tutsi–Hutu conflict in Burundi and Rwanda spilled over. The rebel leader Laurent Kabila took power in 1997, ousting Mobutu and renaming the country. A rebellion against Kabila broke out in 1998. Rwanda and Uganda supported the rebels, while Angola, Chad, Namibia and Zimbabwe assisted Kabila. A peace treaty was signed in 1999, but the fighting continued. However, hopes for peace were rekindled when Kabila was assassinated in 2001 and succeeded by his son, Major-General Joseph Kabila.

The World Bank classifies the Democratic Republic of the Congo as a "low-income" developing country, despite its reserves of copper, the main export, and other minerals. Agriculture, mainly at subsistence level, employs 71% of the people.

AREA 905,365 sq mi [2,344,885 sq km] **POPULATION** 49,190,000
CAPITAL (POPULATION) Kinshasa (1,655,000)
GOVERNMENT Single-party republic **ETHNIC GROUPS** Luba 18%, Kongo 16%, Mongo 14%, Rwanda 10%, Azande 6%, Bandi and Ngale 6%, Rundi 4%, Teke, Boa, Chokwe, Lugbara, Banda
LANGUAGES French (official), tribal languages
RELIGIONS Christianity (Roman Catholic 48%, Protestant 29%, indigenous Christian churches 17%), traditional beliefs 3%, Islam 1%
CURRENCY Congolese franc

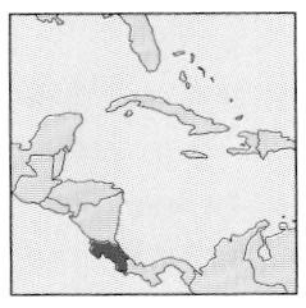

COSTA RICA

GEOGRAPHY The Republic of Costa Rica in Central America has coastlines on both the Pacific Ocean and also on the Caribbean Sea. Central Costa Rica consists of mountain ranges and plateaux with many volcanoes.

The coolest months are December and January. The northeast trade winds bring heavy rain to the Caribbean coast. There is less rainfall in the highlands and on the Pacific coastlands.

POLITICS & ECONOMY Christopher Columbus reached the Caribbean coast in 1502 and rumors of treasure soon attracted many Spaniards to settle in the country. Spain ruled the country until 1821, when Spain's Central American colonies broke away to join Mexico in 1822. In 1823, the Central American states broke with Mexico and set up the Central American Federation. Later, this large union broke up and Costa Rica became fully independent in 1838.

From the late 19th century, Costa Rica experienced a number of revolutions, with periods of dictatorship and periods of democracy. In 1948, following a revolt, the armed forces were abolished. Since 1948, Costa Rica has enjoyed a long period of stable democracy, which many in Latin America admire and envy.

Costa Rica is classified by the World Bank as a "lower-middle-income" developing country and one of the most prosperous countries in Central America. There are high educational standards and a high life expectancy (to an average of 73.5 years). Agriculture employs 20% of the people.

The country's resources include its forests, but it lacks minerals apart from some bauxite and manganese. Manufacturing is increasing. The United States is Costa Rica's chief trading partner. Tourism is a fast-growing industry.

AREA 19,730 sq mi [51,100 sq km] **POPULATION** 3,711,000
CAPITAL (POPULATION) San José (1,220,000)
GOVERNMENT Multiparty republic **ETHNIC GROUPS** White 85%, Mestizo 8%, Black and Mulatto 3%, East Asian (mostly Chinese) 3%
LANGUAGES Spanish (official) **RELIGIONS** Christianity (Roman Catholic 81%) **CURRENCY** Colón = 100 céntimos

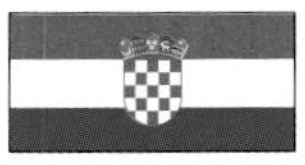

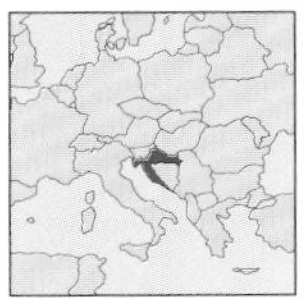

CROATIA

GEOGRAPHY The Republic of Croatia was one of the six republics that made up the former Communist country of Yugoslavia until it became independent in 1991. The region bordering the Adriatic Sea is called Dalmatia. It includes the coastal ranges, which contain large areas of bare limestone. Most of the rest of the country consists of the fertile Pannonian plains.

The coastal area has a typical Mediterranean climate, with hot, dry summers and mild, moist winters. Inland, the climate becomes more continental. Winters are cold, while temperatures often soar to 100°F [38°C] in the summer months.

POLITICS & ECONOMY Slav people settled in the area around 1,400 years ago. In 803, Croatia became part of the Holy Roman empire and the Croats soon adopted Christianity. Croatia was an independent kingdom in the 10th and 11th centuries. In 1102, the king of Hungary also became king of Croatia, creating a union that lasted 800 years. In 1526, part of Croatia came under the Turkish Ottoman empire, while the rest came under the Austrian Habsburgs.

After Austria–Hungary was defeated in World War I (1914–18), Croatia became part of the new Kingdom of the Serbs, Croats and Slovenes. This kingdom was renamed Yugoslavia in 1929. Germany occupied Yugoslavia during World War II (1939–45). Croatia was proclaimed independent, but it was really ruled by the invaders.

After the war, Communists took power with Josip Broz Tito as the country's leader. Despite ethnic differences between the people, Tito held Yugoslavia together until his death in 1980. In the 1980s, economic and ethnic problems, including a deterioration in relations with Serbia, threatened stability. In the 1990s, Yugoslavia split into five nations, one of which was Croatia, which declared itself independent in 1991.

After Serbia supplied arms to Serbs living in Croatia, war broke out between the two republics, causing great damage. Croatia lost more than 30% of its territory. But in 1992, the United Nations sent a peacekeeping force to Croatia, which effectively ended the war with Serbia.

In 1992, when war broke out in Bosnia-Herzegovina, Bosnian Croats occupied parts of the country. But in 1994, Croatia helped to end Croat–Muslim conflict in Bosnia-Herzegovina and, in 1995, after retaking some areas occupied by Serbs, it helped to draw up the Dayton Peace Accord which ended the civil war there.

The wars of the early 1990s disrupted Croatia's economy, though the election of a pro-democratic coalition government in 2000 held out hope for the future, including a revival of the valuable tourist industry. The country has many manufacturing industries and manufactures are the main exports.

AREA 21,824 sq mi [56,538 sq km] **POPULATION** 4,960,000
CAPITAL (POPULATION) Zagreb (931,000) **GOVERNMENT** Multiparty republic **ETHNIC GROUPS** Croat 78%, Serb 12%, Bosnian **LANGUAGES** Serbo-Croatian **RELIGIONS** Christianity (Roman Catholic 77%, Eastern Orthodox 11%), Islam 1% **CURRENCY** Kuna = 100 lipas

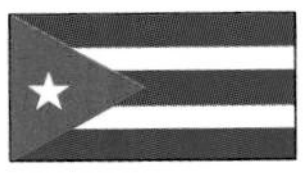

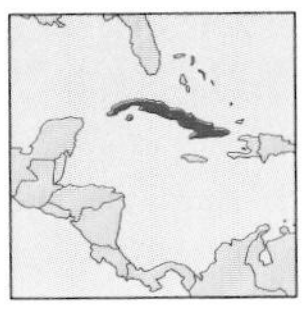

CUBA

GEOGRAPHY The Republic of Cuba is the largest island country in the Caribbean Sea. It consists of one large island, Cuba, the Isle of Youth (Isla de la Juventud) and about 1,600 small islets. Mountains and hills cover about a quarter of Cuba. The highest mountain range, the Sierra Maestra in the southeast, reaches 6,562 ft [2,000 m] above sea level. The rest of the land consists of gently rolling country or coastal plains, crossed by fertile valleys carved by the short, mostly shallow and narrow rivers.

Cuba lies in the tropics. But sea breezes moderate the temperature, warming the land in winter and cooling it in summer.

POLITICS & ECONOMY Christopher Columbus discovered the island in 1492 and Spaniards began to settle there from 1511. Spanish rule ended in 1898, when the United States defeated Spain in the Spanish–American War. American influence in Cuba remained strong until 1959, when revolutionary forces under Fidel Castro overthrew the dictatorial government of Fulgencio Batista.

The United States opposed Castro's policies, when he turned to the Soviet Union for assistance. In 1961, Cuban exiles attempting an invasion were defeated. In 1962, the US learned that nuclear missile bases armed by the Soviet Union had been established in Cuba. The US ordered the Soviet Union to remove the missiles and bases and, after a few days, when many people feared that a world war might break out, the Soviet Union agreed to the American demands.

Cuba's relations with the Soviet Union remained strong until 1991, when the Soviet Union was broken up. The loss of Soviet aid greatly damaged Cuba's economy, but Castro continued the country's left-wing policies. In 2000, the United States lifted its food embargo on Cuba. The ban on travel was also liberalized, though the ban on tourists remained.

The government runs Cuba's economy and owns 70% of the farmland. Agriculture is important and sugar is the chief export, followed by refined nickel ore. Other exports include cigars, citrus fruits, fish, medical products and rum.

Before 1959, US companies owned most of Cuba's manufacturing industries. But under Fidel Castro, they became government property. After the collapse of Communist governments in the Soviet Union and its allies, Cuba worked to increase its trade with Latin America and China.

AREA 42,803 sq mi [110,860 sq km] **POPULATION** 11,504,000
CAPITAL (POPULATION) Havana (2,241,000)
GOVERNMENT Socialist republic **ETHNIC GROUPS** White 66%, Mulatto 22%, Black 12% **LANGUAGES** Spanish (official)
RELIGIONS Christianity (Roman Catholic 40%, Protestant 3%)
CURRENCY Cuban peso = 100 centavos

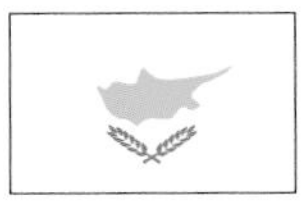

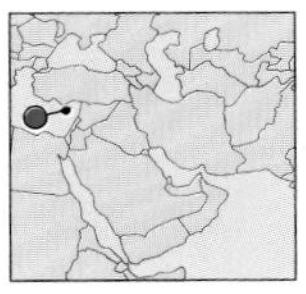

CYPRUS

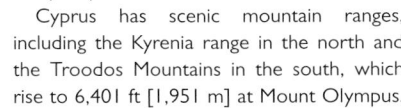

GEOGRAPHY The Republic of Cyprus is an island nation in the northeastern Mediterranean Sea. Geographers regard it as part of Asia, but it resembles southern Europe in many ways.

Cyprus has scenic mountain ranges, including the Kyrenia range in the north and the Troodos Mountains in the south, which rise to 6,401 ft [1,951 m] at Mount Olympus. The island also contains several fertile lowlands, including the broad Mesaoria plain between the Kyrenia and Troodos mountains.

Cyprus has a Mediterranean climate, with hot, dry summers and mild, moist winters. But the summers are hotter than in the western Mediterranean lands; this is because Cyprus lies close to the hot mainland of southwestern Asia.

POLITICS & ECONOMY Greeks settled on Cyprus around 3,200 years ago. From AD 330, the island was part of the Byzantine empire. In the 1570s, Cyprus became part of the Turkish Ottoman empire. Turkish rule continued until 1878 when Cyprus was leased to Britain. Britain annexed the island in 1914 and proclaimed it a colony in 1925.

In the 1950s, Greek Cypriots, who made up four-fifths of the population, began a campaign for *enosis* (union) with Greece. Their leader was the Greek Orthodox Archbishop Makarios. A secret guerrilla force called EOKA attacked the British, who exiled Makarios. Cyprus became an independent country in 1960, although Britain retained two military bases. Independent Cyprus had a constitution which provided for power-sharing between the Greek and Turkish Cypriots. But the constitution proved unworkable and fighting broke out between the two communities. In 1964, the United Nations sent in a peacekeeping force. Communal clashes recurred in 1967.

In 1974, Cypriot forces led by Greek officers overthrew Makarios. This led Turkey to invade northern Cyprus, a territory occupying about 40% of the island. Many Greek Cypriots fled from the north which, in 1979, was proclaimed an independent state called the Turkish Republic of Northern Cyprus. But the United Nations still regarded Cyprus as a single nation under the Greek-Cypriot government in the south. A Turkish proposal to make the island a confederation was rejected by Greek and Cypriot leaders in 1998.

Cyprus got its name from the Greek word *kypros*, meaning copper. But little copper remains and the chief minerals today are asbestos and chromium. However, the most valuable activity in Cyprus is tourism. Manufactures include cement, clothes, footwear, tiles and wine.

In the early 1990s, the United Nations reclassified Cyprus as a developed rather than a developing country. But the economy of the Turkish-Cypriot north lags behind that of the more prosperous Greek-Cypriot south.

AREA 3,571 sq mi [9,250 sq km] **POPULATION** 762,000
CAPITAL (POPULATION) Nicosia (189,000) **GOVERNMENT** Multiparty republic **ETHNIC GROUPS** Greek Cypriot 81%, Turkish Cypriot 19%
LANGUAGES Greek and Turkish (both official)
RELIGIONS Christianity (Greek Orthodox), Islam
CURRENCY Cyprus pound = 100 cents

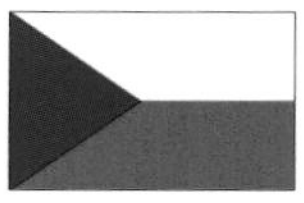

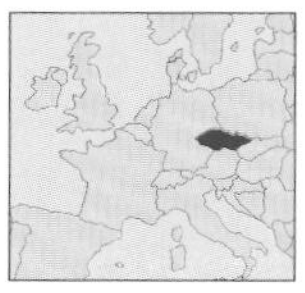

CZECH REPUBLIC

GEOGRAPHY The Czech Republic is the western three-fifths of the former country of Czechoslovakia. It contains two regions: Bohemia in the west and Moravia in the east. Mountains border much of the country in the west. The Bohemian basin in the north-center is a fertile lowland region, with Prague, the capital city, as its main center. Highlands cover much of the center of the country, with lowlands in the southeast.

The climate is influenced by its landlocked position in east-central Europe. Prague has warm, sunny summers and cold winters. The average rainfall is moderate, with 20 in to 30 in [500 mm to 750 mm] every year in lowland areas.

POLITICS & ECONOMY After World War I (1914–18), Czechoslovakia was created. Germany seized the country in World War II (1939–45). In 1948, Communist leaders took power and Czechoslovakia was allied to the Soviet Union. When democratic reforms were introduced in the Soviet Union in the late 1980s, the Czechs also demanded reforms. Free elections were held in 1990, but differences between the Czechs and Slovaks and a resurgence of Slovak nationalism led the government to agree in 1992 to the partitioning of the country on January 1, 1993. The break was peaceful. In 1999, the Czech Republic became a member of NATO.

Under Communist rule the Czech Republic became one of the most industrialized parts of Eastern Europe. The country has deposits of coal, uranium, iron ore, magnesite, tin and zinc. Manufacturing employs about 40% of the Czech Republic's entire work force. Farming is also important. Under Communism, the government owned the land, but private ownership is now being restored. The country was admitted into the OECD in 1995.

AREA 30,449 sq mi [78,864 sq km] **POPULATION** 10,500,000
CAPITAL (POPULATION) Prague (1,209,000) **GOVERNMENT** Multiparty republic **ETHNIC GROUPS** Czech 81%, Moravian 13%, Slovak 3%, Polish, German, Silesian, Gypsy, Hungarian, Ukrainian
LANGUAGES Czech (official), Moravian
RELIGIONS Christianity (Roman Catholic 39%, Protestant 4%)
CURRENCY Czech koruna = 100 haler

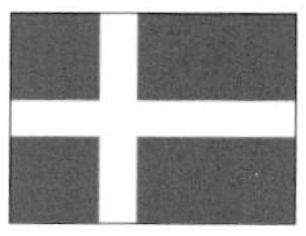

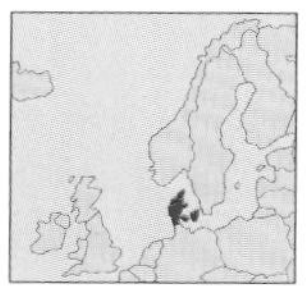

DENMARK

GEOGRAPHY The Kingdom of Denmark is the smallest country in Scandinavia. It consists of a peninsula, called Jutland (or Jylland), which is joined to Germany, and more than 400 islands, 89 of which are inhabited.

The land is flat and mostly covered by rocks dropped there by huge ice sheets during the last Ice Age. The highest point in Denmark is on Jutland. It is only 568 ft [173 m] above sea level.

Denmark has a cool but pleasant climate, except during cold spells in the winter when The Sound between Sjælland and Sweden may freeze over. Summers are warm. Rainfall occurs all through the year.

POLITICS & ECONOMY Danish Vikings terrorized much of Western Europe for about 300 years after AD 800. Danish kings ruled England in the 11th century. In the late 14th century, Denmark formed a union with Norway and Sweden (which included Finland). Sweden broke away in 1523, while Denmark lost Norway to Sweden in 1814.

After 1945, Denmark played an important part in European affairs, becoming a member of the North Atlantic Treaty Organization (NATO). In 1973, Denmark joined the European Union, although it rejected the adoption of the euro in 2000. The Danes now enjoy some of the world's highest living standards, although the extensive social welfare provisions exert a considerable cost.

Denmark has few natural resources apart from some oil and gas from wells deep under the North Sea. But the economy is highly developed. Manufacturing industries, which employ about 17% of all workers, produce a wide variety of products, including furniture, processed food, machinery, television sets and textiles. Farms cover about three-quarters of the land. Farming employs only 4% of the workers, but it is highly scientific and productive. Meat and dairy farming are the chief activities.

AREA 16,629 sq mi [43,070 sq km] **POPULATION** 5,153,000
CAPITAL (POPULATION) Copenhagen (1,362,000)
GOVERNMENT Parliamentary monarchy **ETHNIC GROUPS** Danish 97%
LANGUAGES Danish (official) **RELIGIONS** Christianity (Lutheran 91%, Roman Catholic 1%) **CURRENCY** Krone = 100 øre

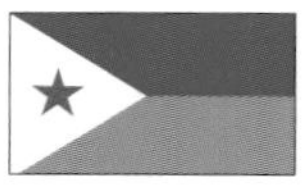

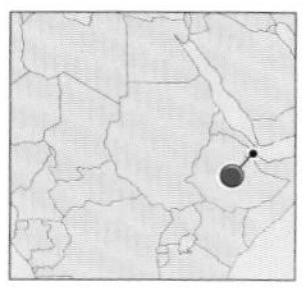

DJIBOUTI

GEOGRAPHY The Republic of Djibouti is a small country in eastern Africa which occupies a strategic position where the Red Sea meets the Gulf of Aden. Behind the coastal plain on the northern side of the Gulf of Tadjoura is a highland region, the Mabla Mountains, rising to 5,850 ft [1,783 m] above sea level. Djibouti also contains Lake Assal, the lowest point on land in Africa.

Djibouti has one of the world's hottest and driest climates. Summer days are very hot with recorded temperatures of more than 112°F [44°C]. On average, it rains on only 26 days every year.

POLITICS & ECONOMY Islam was introduced into the area which is now Djibouti in the 9th century AD. The conversion of the Afars led to conflict between them and the Christian Ethiopians who lived in the interior. By the 19th century, the Issas, who are Somalis, had moved north and occupied much of the traditional grazing land of the Afars. France gained influence in the area in the second half of the 19th century and, in 1888, set up a territory called French Somaliland. The capital of the territory, Djibouti, became important when the Ethiopian emperor, Menelik II, decided to build a railroad to it from Addis Ababa, thus making it the main port handling Ethiopian trade.

In 1967, the people voted to retain their links with France, though most of the Issas favored independence. The country was renamed the French Territory of the Afars and Issas, but it was named Djibouti when it became fully independent in 1977.

Djibouti became a one-party state in 1981, but a new constitution was introduced in 1992, permitting four parties which must maintain a balance between the country's ethnic groups. Conflict between the Afars and Issas flared up in 1992 and 1993, but a peace agreement was signed in 1994. In 1999, Hassan Gouled Aptidon, who had served as president since 1977, stood down and his nephew, Ismail Omar Gueleh, was elected president. Djibouti is a poor country. Its economy is based mainly on the revenue it gets from its port and the railroad to Addis Ababa.

AREA 8,958 sq mi [23,200 sq km] **POPULATION** 552,000
CAPITAL (POPULATION) Djibouti (383,000)
GOVERNMENT Multiparty republic **ETHNIC GROUPS** Issa 47%, Afar 37%, Arab 6% **LANGUAGES** Arabic and French (both official)
RELIGIONS Islam 96%, Christianity 4%
CURRENCY Djibouti franc = 100 centimes

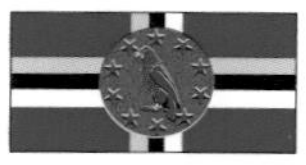

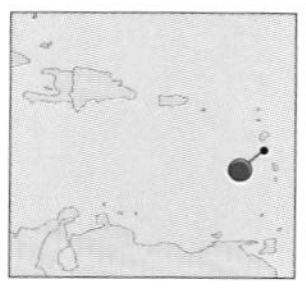

DOMINICA

The Commonwealth of Dominica, a former British colony, became independent in 1978. The island has a mountainous spine and less than 10% of the land is cultivated. Yet agriculture employs more than 60% of the people. The manufacturing of coconut-based soap is important, while mining and tourism are other minor activities.

AREA 290 sq mi [751 sq km] **POPULATION** 87,000
CAPITAL Roseau

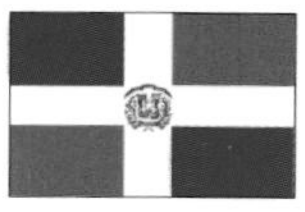

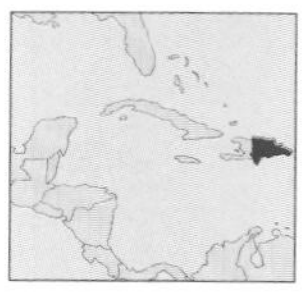

DOMINICAN REPUBLIC

GEOGRAPHY Second largest of the Caribbean nations in both area and population, the Dominican Republic shares the island of Hispaniola with Haiti, with the Dominican Republic occupying the eastern two-thirds. The country is mountainous, and the generally hot and humid climate eases with altitude.

POLITICS & ECONOMY The Dominican Republic has chaotic origins, having been held by Spain, France, Haiti and the USA at various times. Civil war broke out in 1966 but soon ended after US intervention. Joaquín Balaguer, elected president in 1966 under a new constitution, stood down in 1996 and was replaced by Leonel Fernández Reyna.

AREA 18,815 sq mi [48,730 sq km] **POPULATION** 8,621,000
CAPITAL (POPULATION) Santo Domingo (2,135,000)
GOVERNMENT Multiparty republic **ETHNIC GROUPS** Mulatto 73%, White 16%, Black 11% **LANGUAGES** Spanish (official)
RELIGIONS Roman Catholic 93% **CURRENCY** Peso = 100 centavos

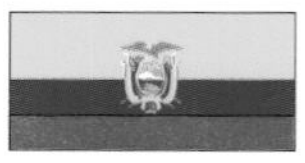

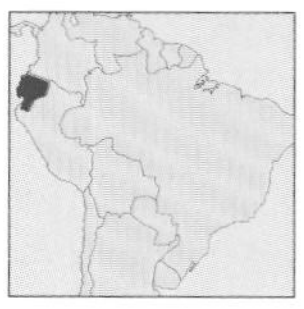

ECUADOR

GEOGRAPHY The Republic of Ecuador straddles the Equator on the west coast of South America. Three ranges of the high Andes Mountains form the backbone of the country. Between the towering, snow-capped peaks of the mountains, some of which are volcanoes, lie a series of high plateaux, or basins. Nearly half of Ecuador's population lives on these plateaux.

The climate in Ecuador depends on the height above sea level. Though the coastline is cooled by the cold Peruvian Current, temperatures are between 73°F and 77°F [23°C to 25°C] all through the year. In Quito, at 8,200 ft [2,500 m] above sea level, temperatures are 57°F to 59°F [14°C to 15°C], though the city is just south of the Equator.

POLITICS & ECONOMY The Inca people of Peru conquered much of what is now Ecuador in the late 15th century. They introduced their language, Quechua, which is widely spoken today. Spanish forces defeated the Incas in 1533 and took control of Ecuador. The country became independent in 1822, following the defeat of a Spanish force in a battle near Quito. In the 19th and 20th centuries, Ecuador suffered from political instability, while successive governments failed to tackle the country's social and economic problems. A war with Peru in 1941 led to a loss of territory. Disputes continued until 1995, but a border agreement was signed in January 1998. Economic crises in the early 21st century led the government to abolish the sucre, its official currency, and replace it with the US dollar.

The World Bank classifies Ecuador as a "lower-middle-income" developing country. Agriculture employs 30% of the people and bananas, cocoa and coffee are all important crops. Fishing, forestry, mining and manufacturing are other activities.

AREA 109,483 sq mi [283,560 sq km] **POPULATION** 13,319,000
CAPITAL (POPULATION) Quito (1,487,000)
GOVERNMENT Multiparty republic **ETHNIC GROUPS** Mestizo (mixed White and Amerindian) 40%, Amerindian 40%, White 15%, Black 5%
LANGUAGES Spanish (official), Quechua **RELIGIONS** Christianity (Roman Catholic 92%) **CURRENCY** US dollar = 100 cents

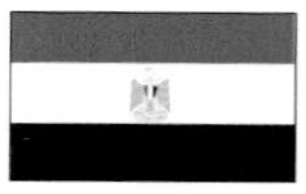

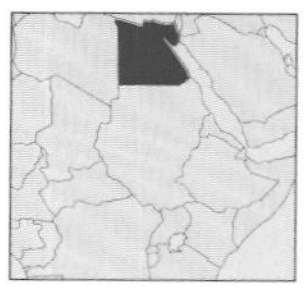

EGYPT

GEOGRAPHY The Arab Republic of Egypt is Africa's second largest country by population after Nigeria, though it ranks 13th in area. Most of Egypt is desert. Almost all the people live either in the Nile Valley and its fertile delta or along the Suez Canal, the artificial waterway between the Mediterranean and Red seas. This canal shortens the sea journey between the United Kingdom and India by 6,027 mi [9,700 km]. Recent attempts have been made to irrigate parts of the western desert and thus redistribute the rapidly growing Egyptian population into previously uninhabited regions.

Apart from the Nile Valley, Egypt has three other main regions. The Western and Eastern deserts are parts of the Sahara. The Sinai peninsula (Es Sina), to the east of the Suez Canal, is a mountainous desert region, geographically within Asia. It contains Egypt's highest peak, Gebel Katherina (8,650 ft [2,637 m]); few people live in this area.

Egypt is a dry country. The low rainfall occurs, if at all, in winter and the country is one of the sunniest places on Earth.

POLITICS & ECONOMY Ancient Egypt, which was founded about 5,000 years ago, was one of the great early civilizations. Throughout the country, pyramids, temples and richly decorated tombs are memorials to its great achievements.

After Ancient Egypt declined, the country came under successive foreign rulers. Arabs occupied Egypt in AD 639–42. They introduced the Arabic language and Islam. Their influence was so great that most Egyptians now regard themselves as Arabs.

Egypt came under British rule in 1882, but it gained partial independence in 1922, becoming a monarchy. The monarchy was abolished in 1952, when Egypt became a republic. The creation of Israel in 1948 led Egypt into a series of wars in 1948–9, 1956, 1967 and 1973. Since the late 1970s, Egypt has sought for peace. In 1979, Egypt signed a peace treaty with Israel and regained the Sinai region which it had lost in a war in 1967. Extremists opposed contacts with Israel and, in 1981, President Sadat, who had signed the treaty, was assassinated.

While Egypt plays a major part in Arab affairs, most of its people are poor. Some Islamic fundamentalists, who dislike Western influences on their way of life, have resorted to violence. In the 1990s, attacks on foreign visitors caused a decline in the valuable tourist industry. In 1999, Hosni Mubarak, president since 1981, was himself attacked by extremists, but he was re-elected to a fourth term in office.

Egypt is Africa's second most industrialized country after South Africa, but it remains a developing country and income levels remain low for the vast majority of Egyptian people. Oil and textiles are the chief exports.

AREA 386,660 sq mi [1,001,450 sq km] **POPULATION** 64,210,000 **CAPITAL (POPULATION)** Cairo (9,900,000) **GOVERNMENT** Republic **ETHNIC GROUPS** Egyptian 99% **LANGUAGES** Arabic (official), French, English **RELIGIONS** Islam (Sunni Muslim 94%), Christianity (mainly Coptic Christian 6%) **CURRENCY** Pound = 100 piastres

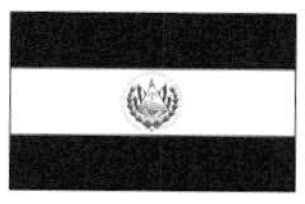

EL SALVADOR

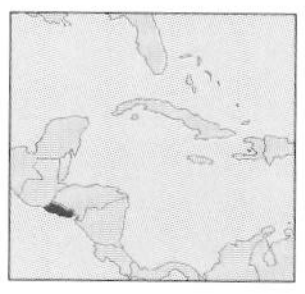

GEOGRAPHY The Republic of El Salvador is the only country in Central America which does not have a coast on the Caribbean Sea. El Salvador has a narrow coastal plain along the Pacific Ocean. Behind the coastal plain, the coastal range is a zone of rugged mountains, including volcanoes, which overlooks a densely populated inland plateau. Beyond the plateau, the land rises to the sparsely populated interior highlands.

The coast has a hot, tropical climate. Inland, the climate is moderated by the altitude. Rain falls on practically every afternoon between May and October.

POLITICS & ECONOMY Amerindians have lived in El Salvador for thousands of years. The ruins of Mayan pyramids built between AD 100 and 1000 are still found in the western part of the country. Spanish soldiers conquered the area in 1524 and 1525, and Spain ruled until 1821. In 1823, all the Central American countries, except for Panama, set up a Central American Federation. But El Salvador withdrew in 1840 and declared its independence in 1841. El Salvador suffered from instability throughout the 19th century. The 20th century saw a more stable government, but from 1931 military dictatorships alternated with elected governments and the country remained poor.

In the 1970s, El Salvador was plagued by conflict as protesters demanded that the government introduce reforms to help the poor. Kidnappings and murders committed by left- and right-wing groups caused instability. A civil war broke out in 1979 between the US-backed, right-wing government forces and left-wing guerrillas in the FMLN (Farabundo Marti National Liberation Front). In 12 years, more than 750,000 people died and hundreds of thousands were made homeless. A cease-fire was agreed on February 1, 1992, and elections were held in 1993 and 1999. With its economy shattered by war, El Salvador remains a "lower-middle-income" economy, according to the World Bank. Farmland and pasture cover about three-quarters of the country. Coffee, grown in the highlands, is the main export, followed by sugar and cotton, which grow on the coastal lowlands. Fishing for lobsters and shrimps is important, but manufacturing is on a small scale.

AREA 8,124 sq mi [21,040 sq km] **POPULATION** 6,739,000 **CAPITAL (POPULATION)** San Salvador (1,522,000) **GOVERNMENT** Republic **ETHNIC GROUPS** Mestizo (mixed White and Amerindian) 89%, Amerindian 10%, White 1% **LANGUAGES** Spanish (official) **RELIGIONS** Christianity (Roman Catholic 94%) **CURRENCY** US dollar; Colón = 100 centavos

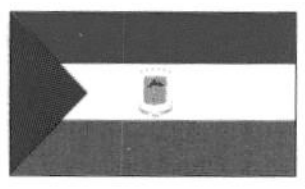

EQUATORIAL GUINEA

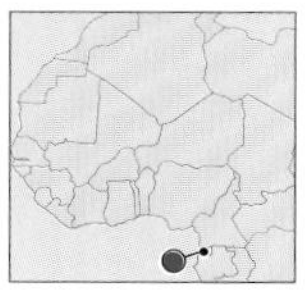

GEOGRAPHY The Republic of Equatorial Guinea is a small republic in west-central Africa. It consists of a mainland territory which makes up 90% of the land area, called Mbini (or Rio Muni), between Cameroon and Gabon, and five offshore islands in the Bight of Bonny, the largest of which is Bioko. The island of Annobon lies 350 mi [560 km] southwest of Mbini. Mbini consists mainly of hills and plateaux behind the coastal plains.

The climate is hot and humid. Bioko is mountainous, with the land rising to 9,869 ft [3,008 m], and hence it is particularly rainy. However, there is a marked dry season between the months of December and February. Mainland Mbini has a similar climate, though the rainfall diminishes inland.

POLITICS & ECONOMY Portuguese navigators reached the area in 1471. In 1778, Portugal granted Bioko, together with rights over Mbini, to Spain.

In 1959, Spain made Bioko and Mbini provinces of overseas Spain and, in 1963, it gave the provinces a degree of self-government. Equatorial Guinea became independent in 1968.

The first president of Equatorial Guinea, Francisco Macias Nguema, proved to be a tyrant. He was overthrown in 1979 and a group of officers, led by Lt-Col. Teodoro Obiang Nguema Mbasogo, set up a Supreme Military Council to rule the country. In 1991, the people voted to set up a multiparty democracy. Elections were held in the 1990s. But the President continued with his semi-dictatorial rule.

Equatorial Guinea is a poor country. Agriculture employs up to 66% of the people. The main food crops are bananas, cassava and sweet potatoes, but the most valuable crop is cocoa, grown on Bioko.

AREA 10,830 sq mi [28,050 sq km] **POPULATION** 455,000 **CAPITAL (POPULATION)** Malabo (35,000) **GOVERNMENT** Multiparty republic (transitional) **ETHNIC GROUPS** Fang 83%, Bubi 10%, Ndowe 4% **LANGUAGES** Spanish (official), Fang, Bubi **RELIGIONS** Christianity 89%, traditional beliefs 5% **CURRENCY** CFA franc = 100 centimes

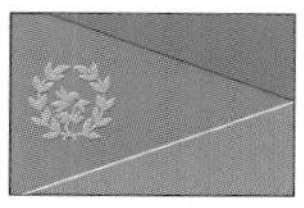

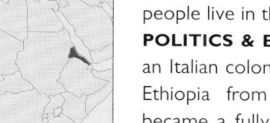

ERITREA

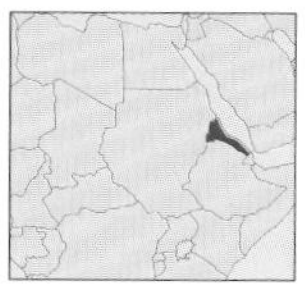

GEOGRAPHY The State of Eritrea consists of a hot, dry coastal plain facing the Red Sea, with a fairly mountainous area in the center. Most people live in the cooler highland area.

POLITICS & ECONOMY Eritrea, which was an Italian colony from the 1880s, was part of Ethiopia from 1952 until 1993, when it became a fully independent nation. National reconstruction was hampered by conflict with Yemen over three islands in the Red Sea, while in 1998–9, border clashes with Ethiopia caused loss of life. However, a peace agreement was signed in 2000. Farming and livestock rearing are the main activities in this war-ravaged territory. Eritrea has few manufacturing industries, based mainly in Asmara.

AREA 36,293 sq mi [94,000 sq km] **POPULATION** 4,523,000 **CAPITAL (POPULATION)** Asmara (367,500) **GOVERNMENT** Transitional government **ETHNIC GROUPS** Tigrinya 49%, Tigre 32%, Afar 4%, Beja 3%, Saho 3%, Kunama 3%, Nara 2% **LANGUAGES** Arabic, English, Tigrinya, Tigre, Saho **RELIGIONS** Coptic Christian 50%, Muslim 50% **CURRENCY** Nakfa

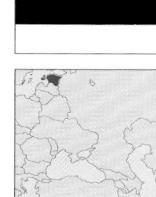

ESTONIA

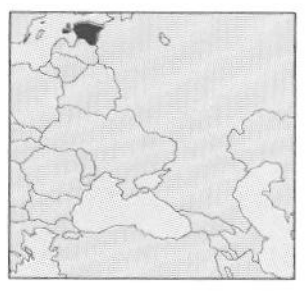

GEOGRAPHY The Republic of Estonia is the smallest of the three states on the Baltic Sea, which were formerly part of the Soviet Union, but which became independent in the early 1990s. Estonia consists of a generally flat plain which was covered by ice sheets during the Ice Age. The land is strewn with moraine (rocks deposited by the ice).

The country is dotted with more than 1,500 small lakes, and water, including the large Lake Peipus (Chudskoye Ozero) and the River Narva makes up much of Estonia's eastern border with Russia. Estonia has more than 800 islands, which together make up about a tenth of the country. The largest island is Saaremaa (Sarema).

Despite its northerly position, Estonia has a fairly mild climate because of its nearness to the sea. This is because sea winds tend to warm the land in winter and cool it in summer.

POLITICS & ECONOMY The ancestors of the Estonians, who are related to the Finns, settled in the area several thousand years ago. German crusaders, known as the Teutonic Knights, introduced Christianity in the early 13th century. By the 16th century, German noblemen owned much of the land in Estonia. In 1561, Sweden took the northern part of the country and Poland the south. From 1625, Sweden controlled the entire country until Sweden handed it over to Russia in 1721.

Estonian nationalists campaigned for their independence from around the mid-19th century. Finally, Estonia was proclaimed independent in 1918. In 1919, the government began to break up the large estates and distribute land among the peasants.

In 1939, Germany and the Soviet Union agreed to take over parts of Eastern Europe. In 1940, Soviet forces occupied Estonia, but they were driven out by the Germans in 1941. Soviet troops returned in 1944 and Estonia became one of the 15 Soviet Socialist Republics of the Soviet Union. The Estonians strongly opposed Soviet rule. Many of them were deported to Siberia.

Political changes in the Soviet Union in the late 1980s led to renewed demands for freedom. In 1990, the Estonian government declared the country independent and, finally, the Soviet Union recognized this act in September 1991, shortly before the Soviet Union was dissolved. Estonia adopted a new constitution in 1992, when multiparty elections were held for a new national assembly. In 1993, Estonia negotiated an agreement with Russia to withdraw its troops.

Under Soviet rule, Estonia was the most prosperous of the three Baltic states. Since 1988, Estonia has begun to change its government-dominated economy to one based on private enterprise, and the country has started to strengthen its links with the rest of Europe. Estonia's resources include oil shale and its forests. Industries produce fertilizers, machinery, petrochemical products, processed food, wood products and textiles. Agriculture and fishing are also important.

AREA 17,300 sq mi [44,700 sq km] **POPULATION** 1,647,000 **CAPITAL (POPULATION)** Tallinn (435,000) **GOVERNMENT** Multiparty republic **ETHNIC GROUPS** Estonian 62%, Russian 30%, Ukrainian 3%, Belarussian 2%, Finnish 1% **LANGUAGES** Estonian (official), Russian **RELIGIONS** Christianity (Lutheran, with Orthodox and Baptist minorities) **CURRENCY** Kroon = 100 sents

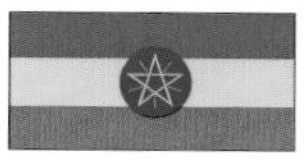

ETHIOPIA

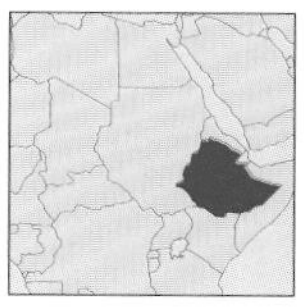

GEOGRAPHY Ethiopia is a landlocked country in northeastern Africa. The land is mainly mountainous, though there are extensive plains in the east, bordering southern Eritrea, and in the south, bordering Somalia. The highlands are divided into two blocks by an arm of the Great Rift Valley which runs throughout eastern Africa. North of the Rift Valley, the land is especially rugged, rising to 15,157 ft [4,620 m] at Ras Dashen. Southeast of Ras Dashen is Lake Tana, source of the River Abay (Blue Nile).

The climate in Ethiopia is greatly affected by the altitude. Addis Ababa, at 8,000 ft [2,450 m], has an average yearly temperature of 68°F [20°C]. The rainfall is generally more than 39 in [1,000 mm]. But the lowlands bordering the Eritrean coast are hot.

POLITICS & ECONOMY Ethiopia was the home of an ancient monarchy, which became Christian in the 4th century. In the 7th century, Muslims gained control of the lowlands, but Christianity survived in the highlands. In the 19th century, Ethiopia resisted attempts to colonize it. Italy invaded Ethiopia in 1935, but Ethiopian and British troops defeated the Italians in 1941.

In 1952, Eritrea, on the Red Sea coast, was federated with Ethiopia. But in 1961, Eritrean nationalists demanded their freedom and began a struggle that ended in their independence in 1993. Clashes along the border with Eritrea occurred in 1998 and 1999, but a peace agreement was signed in 2000. Ethnic diversity in Ethiopia has led to demands by some minorities for self-government. As a result, the government divided Ethiopia into nine provinces in 1995. Each province has its own regional assembly.

Ethiopia is one of the world's poorest countries, particularly in the 1970s and 1980s when it was plagued by civil war and famine caused partly by long droughts. Many richer countries have sent aid (money and food) to help the Ethiopian people. Agriculture remains the leading activity.

AREA 435,521 sq mi [1,128,000 sq km] **POPULATION** 61,841,000 **CAPITAL (POPULATION)** Addis Ababa (2,112,000) **GOVERNMENT** Federation of nine provinces **ETHNIC GROUPS** Amharic 38%, Galla 35%, Tigrinya 9%, Guage 3%, 60 others **LANGUAGES** Amharic (official), 280 others **RELIGIONS** Islam 43%, Christianity 40%, traditional beliefs 11% **CURRENCY** Birr = 100 cents

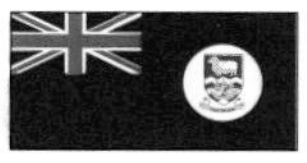

FALKLAND ISLANDS

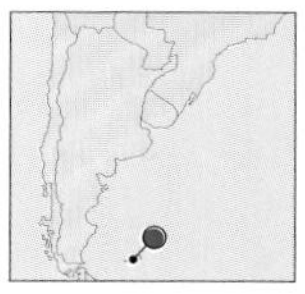

Comprising two main islands and over 200 small islands, the Falkland Islands (or the Islas Malvinas, as they are called in Argentina) lie 300 mi [480 km] from South America. Sheep farming is the main activity, though the search for oil and diamonds holds out hope for the future of this harsh and virtually treeless environment.

AREA 4,699 sq mi [12,170 sq km] **POPULATION** 2,000 **CAPITAL** Stanley

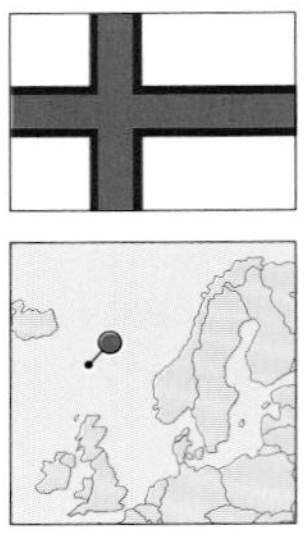

FAROE ISLANDS

The Faroe Islands are a group of 18 volcanic islands and some reefs in the North Atlantic Ocean. The islands have been Danish since the 1380s, but they became largely self-governing in 1948. In 1998, the government of the Faroes announced its intention to become independent of Denmark.

AREA 541 sq mi [1,400 sq km]
POPULATION 49,000 **CAPITAL** Torshávn

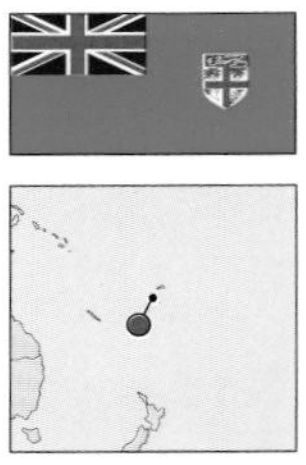

FIJI

The Republic of Fiji comprises more than 800 Melanesian islands, the biggest being Viti Levu and Vanua Levu. The climate is tropical, with southeast trade winds blowing throughout the year. A former British colony, Fiji became independent in 1970. Its recent history has been marred by efforts by ethnic Fijians to impose their rule, stopping members of the ethnic Indian community from holding senior cabinet posts. Their actions have provoked international criticism.

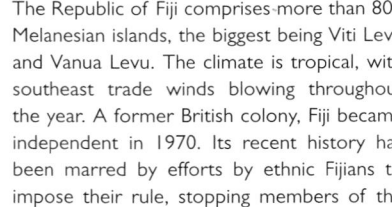

AREA 7,054 sq mi [18,270 sq km] **POPULATION** 883,000 **CAPITAL** Suva

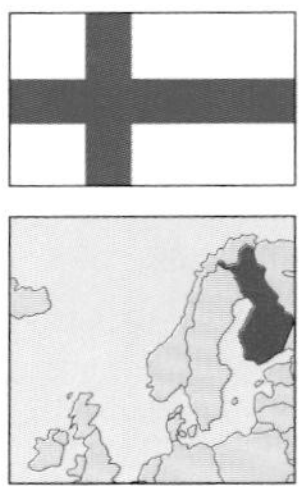

FINLAND

GEOGRAPHY The Republic of Finland is a beautiful country in northern Europe. In the south, behind the coastal lowlands where most Finns live, lies a region of sparkling lakes worn out by ice sheets in the Ice Age. The thinly populated northern uplands cover about two-fifths of the country.

Helsinki, the capital city, has warm summers, but the average temperatures between the months of December and March are below freezing point. Snow covers the land in winter. The north has less precipitation than the south, but it is much colder.

POLITICS & ECONOMY Between 1150 and 1809, Finland was under Swedish rule. The close links between the countries continue today. Swedish remains an official language in Finland and many towns have Swedish as well as Finnish names.

In 1809, Finland became a grand duchy of the Russian empire. It finally declared itself independent in 1917, after the Russian Revolution and the collapse of the Russian empire. But during World War II (1939–45), the Soviet Union declared war on Finland and took part of Finland's territory. Finland allied itself with Germany, but it lost more land to the Soviet Union at the end of the war.

After World War II, Finland became a neutral country and negotiated peace treaties with the Soviet Union. Finland also strengthened its relations with other northern European countries and became an associate member of the European Free Trade Association (EFTA) in 1961. Finland became a full member of EFTA in 1986, but in 1992, along with most of its fellow EFTA members, it applied for membership of the European Union, which it finally achieved on January 1, 1995. On January 1, 1999, it adopted the euro, the single European currency.

Forests are Finland's most valuable resource, and forestry accounts for about 35% of the country's exports. The chief manufactures are wood products, pulp and paper. Since World War II, Finland has set up many other industries, producing such things as machinery and transport equipment. Its economy has expanded rapidly, but there has been a large increase in the number of unemployed people.

AREA 130,552 sq mi [338,130 sq km] **POPULATION** 5,077,000 **CAPITAL (POPULATION)** Helsinki (532,000) **GOVERNMENT** Multiparty republic **ETHNIC GROUPS** Finnish 93%, Swedish 6% **LANGUAGES** Finnish and Swedish (both official) **RELIGIONS** Christianity (Evangelical Lutheran 88%) **CURRENCY** Euro; Markka = 100 penniá

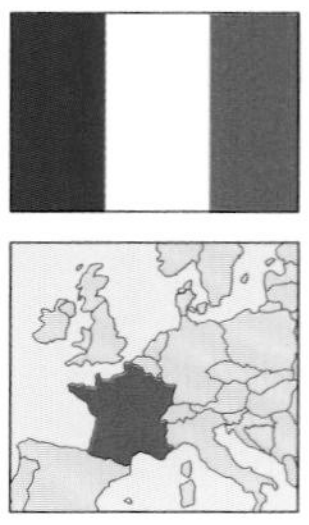

FRANCE

GEOGRAPHY The Republic of France is the largest country in Western Europe. The scenery is extremely varied. The Vosges Mountains overlook the Rhine valley in the northeast, the Jura Mountains and the Alps form the borders with Switzerland and Italy in the southeast, while the Pyrenees straddle France's border with Spain. The only large highland area entirely within France is the Massif Central between the Rhône-Saône valley and the basin of Aquitaine in southern France.

Brittany (Bretagne) and Normandy (Normande) form a scenic hill region. Fertile lowlands cover most of northern France, including the densely populated Paris basin. Another major lowland area, the Aquitanian basin, is in the southwest, while the Rhône-Saône valley and the Mediterranean lowlands are in the southeast.

The climate of France varies from west to east and from north to south. The west comes under the moderating influence of the Atlantic Ocean, giving generally mild weather. To the east, summers are warmer and winters colder. The climate also becomes warmer as one travels from north to south. The Mediterranean Sea coast has hot, dry summers and mild, moist winters. The Alps, Jura and Pyrenees mountains have snowy winters. Winter sports centers are found in all three areas. Large glaciers occupy high valleys in the Alps.

POLITICS & ECONOMY The Romans conquered France (then called Gaul) in the 50s BC. Roman rule began to decline in the fifth century AD and, in 486, the Frankish realm (as France was called) became independent under a Christian king, Clovis. In 800, Charlemagne, who had been king since 768, became emperor of the Romans. He extended France's boundaries, but, in 843, his empire was divided into three parts and the area of France contracted. After the Norman invasion of England in 1066, large areas of France came under English rule, but this was finally ended in 1453.

France later became a powerful monarchy. But the French Revolution (1789–99) ended absolute rule by French kings. In 1799, Napoleon Bonaparte took power and fought a series of brilliant military campaigns before his final defeat in 1815. The monarchy was restored until 1848, when the Second Republic was founded. In 1852, Napoleon's nephew became Napoleon III, but the Third Republic was established in 1875. France was the scene of much fighting during World War I (1914–18) and World War II (1939–45), causing great loss of life and much damage to the economy.

In 1946, France adopted a new constitution, establishing the Fourth Republic. But political instability and costly colonial wars slowed France's post-war recovery. In 1958, Charles de Gaulle was elected president and he introduced a new constitution, giving the president extra powers and inaugurating the Fifth Republic.

Since the 1960s, France has made rapid economic progress, becoming one of the most prosperous nations in the European Union. But France's government faced a number of problems, including unemployment, pollution and the growing number of elderly people, who find it difficult to live when inflation rates are high. One social problem concerns the presence in France of large numbers of immigrants from Africa and southern Europe, many of whom live in poor areas.

A socialist government under Lionel Jospin was elected in 1997. Under Jospin, France adopted the euro, the single European currency, and shortened the working week. The French system of high social security taxes seemed likely to continue, although the economy continued to thrive. In the early 21st century, French politicians were plagued by allegations of corruption and illegal party funding.

France is one of the world's most developed countries. Its natural resources include its fertile soil, together with deposits of bauxite, coal, iron ore, oil and natural gas, and potash. France is also one of the world's top manufacturing nations, and it has often innovated in bold and imaginative ways. The TGV and hypermarkets are typical examples. Paris is a world center of fashion industries, but France has many other industrial towns and cities. Major manufactures include aircraft, cars, chemicals, electronic and metal products, machinery, processed food, steel and textiles.

Agriculture employs about 7% of the people, but France is the largest producer of farm products in Western Europe, producing most of the food it needs. Wheat is the leading crop and livestock farming is of major importance. Fishing and forestry are leading industries, while tourism is a major activity.

AREA 212,934 sq mi [551,500 sq km] **POPULATION** 58,145,000 **CAPITAL (POPULATION)** Paris (9,319,000) **GOVERNMENT** Multiparty republic **ETHNIC GROUPS** French 93%, Arab, German **LANGUAGES** French (official), Breton, Occitan **RELIGIONS** Roman Catholic 86%, Islam 3% **CURRENCY** Euro; Franc = 100 centimes

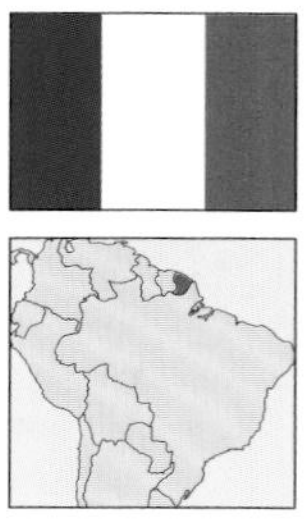

FRENCH GUIANA

GEOGRAPHY French Guiana is the smallest country in mainland South America. The coastal plain is swampy in places, but some dry areas are cultivated. Inland lies a plateau, with the low Tumachumac Mountains in the south. Most of the rivers run north toward the Atlantic Ocean.

French Guiana has a hot, equatorial climate, with high temperatures throughout the year. The rainfall is heavy, especially between December and June, but it is dry between August and October. The northeast trade winds blow constantly across the country.

POLITICS & ECONOMY The first people to live in what is now French Guiana were Amerindians. Today, only a few of them survive in the interior. The first Europeans to explore the coast arrived in 1500, and they were followed by adventurers seeking El Dorado, the mythical city of gold. Cayenne was founded in 1637 by a group of French merchants. The area became a French colony in the late 17th century.

France used the colony as a penal settlement for political prisoners from the times of the French Revolution in the 1790s. From the 1850s to 1945, the country became notorious as a place where prisoners were harshly treated. Many of them died, unable to survive in the tropical conditions.

In 1946, French Guiana became an overseas department of France, and in 1974 it also became an administrative region. An independence movement developed in the 1980s, but most people want to retain their links with France and continue to obtain financial aid to develop their territory.

Although it has rich forest and mineral resources, such as bauxite (aluminum ore), French Guiana is a developing country. It depends greatly on France for money to run its services and the government is the country's biggest employer. Since 1968, Kourou in French Guiana, the European Space Agency's rocket-launching site, has earned money for France by sending communications satellites into space.

AREA 34,749 sq mi [90,000 sq km] **POPULATION** 130,000 **CAPITAL (POPULATION)** Cayenne (42,000) **GOVERNMENT** Overseas department of France **ETHNIC GROUPS** Creole 42%, Chinese 14%, French 10%, Haitian 7% **LANGUAGES** French (official) **RELIGIONS** Christianity (Roman Catholic 80%, Protestant 4%) **CURRENCY** French franc = 100 centimes

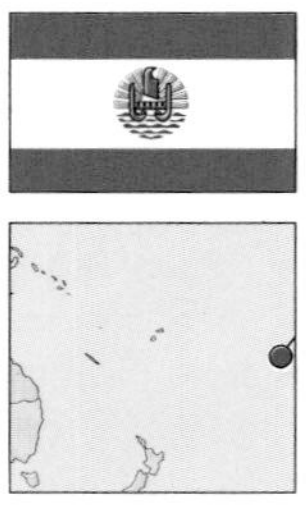

FRENCH POLYNESIA

French Polynesia consists of 130 islands, scattered over 1.5 million sq mi [4 million sq km] of the Pacific Ocean. Tribal chiefs in the area agreed to a French protectorate in 1843. They gained increased autonomy in 1984, but the links with France ensure a high standard of living.

AREA 1,520 sq mi [3,941 sq km]
POPULATION 268,000 **CAPITAL** Papeete

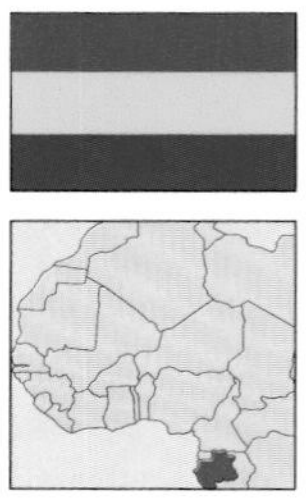

GABON

GEOGRAPHY The Gabonese Republic lies on the Equator in west-central Africa. In area, it is a little larger than the United Kingdom, with a coastline 500 mi [800 km] long. Behind the narrow, partly lagoon-lined coastal plain, the land rises to hills, plateaux and mountains divided by deep valleys carved by the River Ogooué and its tributaries.

Most of Gabon has an equatorial climate, with high temperatures and humidity throughout the year. The rainfall is heavy and the skies are often cloudy.

POLITICS & ECONOMY Gabon became a French colony in the 1880s, but it achieved full independence in 1960. In 1964, an attempted coup was put down when French troops intervened and crushed the revolt. In 1967, Bernard-Albert Bongo, who later renamed himself El Hadj Omar Bongo, became president. He declared Gabon a one-party state in 1968. Opposition parties were legalized in 1991, but Bongo was re-elected president in 1993 and 1998.

Gabon's abundant natural resources include its forests, oil and gas deposits near Port Gentil, together with manganese and uranium. These mineral deposits make Gabon one of Africa's better-off countries. But agriculture still employs about 75% of the population and many farmers produce little more than they need to support their families.

AREA 103,347 sq mi [267,670 sq km] **POPULATION** 1,612,000 **CAPITAL (POPULATION)** Libreville (418,000) **GOVERNMENT** Multiparty republic **ETHNIC GROUPS** Fang 36%, Mpongwe 15%, Mbete 14%, Punu 12% **LANGUAGES** French (official), Bantu languages **RELIGIONS** Christianity (Roman Catholic 65%, Protestant 19%, African churches 12%), traditional beliefs 3%, Islam 2% **CURRENCY** CFA franc = 100 centimes

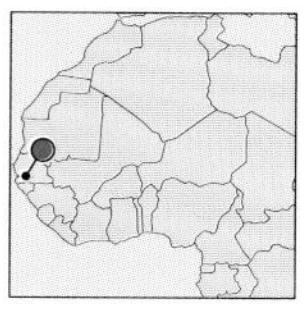

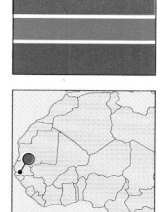

GAMBIA, THE

GEOGRAPHY The Republic of The Gambia is the smallest country in mainland Africa. It consists of a narrow strip of land bordering the River Gambia. The Gambia is almost entirely enclosed by Senegal, except along the short Atlantic coastline.

The Gambia has hot and humid summers, but the winter temperatures (November to May) drop to around 61°F [16°C]. In the summer, moist southwesterlies bring rain, which is heaviest on the coast.

POLITICS & ECONOMY English traders bought rights to trade on the River Gambia in 1588, and in 1664 the English established a settlement on an island in the river estuary. In 1765, the British founded a colony called Senegambia, which included parts of The Gambia and Senegal. In 1783, Britain handed this colony over to France.

In the 1860s and 1870s, Britain and France discussed the exchange of The Gambia for some other French territory. But no agreement was reached and Britain made The Gambia a British colony in 1888. It remained under British rule until it achieved full independence in 1965. In 1970, The Gambia became a republic. Relations between the English-speaking Gambians and the French-speaking Senegalese form a major political issue. In 1981, an attempted coup in The Gambia was put down with the help of Senegalese troops. In 1982, The Gambia and Senegal set up a defense alliance, called the Confederation of Senegambia. But this alliance was dissolved in 1989. In July 1994, a military group overthrew the president, Sir Dawda Jawara, who fled into exile. Captain Yahya Jammeh, who took power, was elected president in 1996.

Agriculture employs more than 80% of the people. The main food crops include cassava, millet and sorghum, but groundnuts and groundnut products are the chief exports. Tourism is a growing industry.

AREA 4,363 sq mi [11,300 sq km] **POPULATION** 1,119,000
CAPITAL (POPULATION) Banjul (171,000)
GOVERNMENT Military regime **ETHNIC GROUPS** Mandinka (also called Mandingo or Malinke) 40%, Fulani (also called Peul) 19%, Wolof 15%, Dyola 10%, Soninke 8%
LANGUAGES English (official), Mandinka, Fula
RELIGIONS Islam 95%, Christianity 4%, traditional beliefs 1%
CURRENCY Dalasi = 100 butut

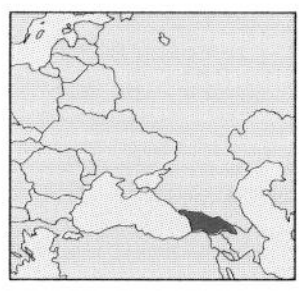

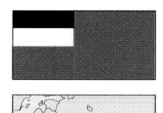

GEORGIA

GEOGRAPHY Georgia is a country on the borders of Europe and Asia, facing the Black Sea. The land is rugged with the Caucasus Mountains forming its northern border. The highest mountain in this range, Mount Elbrus (18,481 ft [5,633 m]), lies over the border in Russia.

The Black Sea plains have hot summers and mild winters, when the temperatures seldom drop below freezing point. The rainfall is heavy, but inland Tbilisi has moderate rainfall, with the heaviest rains in the spring and early summer.

POLITICS & ECONOMY The first Georgian state was set up nearly 2,500 years ago. But for much of its history, the area was ruled by various conquerors. Christianity was introduced in AD 330. Georgia freed itself of foreign rule in the 11th and 12th centuries, but Mongol armies attacked in the 13th century. From the 16th to the 18th centuries, Iran and the Turkish Ottoman empire struggled for control of the area, and in the late 18th century Georgia sought the protection of Russia and, by the early 19th century, Georgia was part of the Russian empire. After the Russian Revolution of 1917, Georgia declared its independence and was recognized by the League of Nations. But Russia invaded the country, making it part of the Soviet regime.

In 1991, following reforms in the Soviet Union, Georgia declared itself independent. It became a separate country when the Soviet Union was dissolved in December 1991.

Georgia contains three regions containing minority peoples: Abkhazia in the northwest, South Ossetia in north-central Georgia, and Adjaria (also spelled Adzharia) in the southwest. Civil war broke out in South Ossetia in the early 1990s, while fierce fighting continued in Abkhazia until the late 1990s. In 2000, Georgia agreed to recognize Adjaria's autonomy in the country's constitution.

Georgia is a developing country. Agriculture is important. Major products include barley, citrus fruits, grapes for winemaking, maize, tea, tobacco and vegetables. Food processing and silk and perfume-making are other important activities. Sheep and cattle are reared.

AREA 26,910 sq mi [69,700 sq km] **POPULATION** 5,777,000
CAPITAL (POPULATION) Tbilisi (1,300,000)
GOVERNMENT Multiparty republic **ETHNIC GROUPS** Georgian 70%, Armenian 8%, Russian 6%, Azerbaijani 6%, Ossetes 3%, Greek 2%, Abkhazian 2%, others 3% **LANGUAGES** Georgian (official)
RELIGIONS Christianity (Georgian Orthodox 65%, Russian Orthodox 10%, Armenian Orthodox 8%), Islam 11%
CURRENCY Lari = 100 tetri

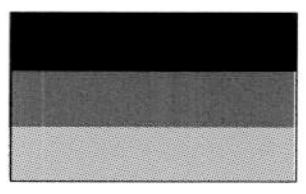
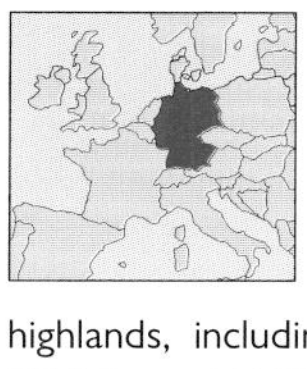

GERMANY

GEOGRAPHY The Federal Republic of Germany is the fourth largest country in Western Europe, after France, Spain and Sweden. The North German plain borders the North Sea in the northwest and the Baltic Sea in the northeast. Major rivers draining the plain include the Weser, Elbe and Oder.

The central highlands contain plateaux and highlands, including the Harz Mountains, the Thuringian Forest (Thüringer Wald), the Ore Mountains (Erzgebirge), and the Bohemian Forest (Böhmerwald) on the Czech border. South Germany is largely hilly, but the land rises in the south to the Bavarian Alps, which contain Germany's highest peak, Zugspitze, at 9,721 ft [2,963 m] above sea level. The scenic Black Forest (Scharzwald) overlooks the River Rhine, which flows through a rift valley in the southwest. The Black Forest contains the source of the River Danube.

Northwestern Germany has a mild climate, but the Baltic coastlands are cooler. To the south, the climate becomes more continental, especially in the highlands. The precipitation is greatest on the uplands, many of which are snow-capped in winter.

POLITICS & ECONOMY Germany and its allies were defeated in World War I (1914–18) and the country became a republic. Adolf Hitler came to power in 1933 and ruled as a dictator. His order to invade Poland led to the start of World War II (1939–45), which ended with Germany in ruins.

In 1945, Germany was divided into four military zones. In 1949, the American, British and French zones were amalgamated to form the Federal Republic of Germany (West Germany), while the Soviet zone became the German Democratic Republic (East Germany), a Communist state. Berlin, which had also been partitioned, became a divided city. West Berlin was part of West Germany, while East Berlin became the capital of East Germany. Bonn was the capital of West Germany.

Tension between East and West mounted during the Cold War, but West Germany rebuilt its economy quickly. In East Germany, the recovery was less rapid. In the late 1980s, reforms in the Soviet Union led to unrest in East Germany. Free elections were held in East Germany in 1990 and, on October 3, 1990, Germany was reunited.

The united Germany adopted West Germany's official name, the Federal Republic of Germany. Elections in December 1990 returned Helmut Kohl, West Germany's Chancellor (head of government) since 1982, to power. His government faced many problems, especially the restructuring of the economy of the former East Germany. Kohl was defeated in elections in 1998 and was succeeded as Chancellor by Social Democrat Gerhard Schröder. In 1999, Germany's parliament moved from Bonn to the reconstructed Reichstag building in Berlin.

West Germany's "economic miracle" after the destruction of World War II was greatly helped by foreign aid. Today, despite all the problems caused by reunification, Germany is one of the world's greatest economic and trading nations.

Manufacturing is the most valuable part of Germany's economy and manufactured goods make up the bulk of the country's exports. Cars and other vehicles, cement, chemicals, computers, electrical equipment, processed food, machinery, scientific instruments, ships, steel, textiles and tools are among the leading manufactures. Germany has some coal, lignite, potash and rock salt deposits. But it imports many of the raw materials needed by its industries.

Germany also imports food. Major agricultural products include fruits, grapes for winemaking, potatoes, sugar beet and vegetables. Beef and dairy cattle are raised, together with many other livestock.

AREA 137,803 sq mi [356,910 sq km] **POPULATION** 76,962,000
CAPITAL (POPULATION) Berlin (3,470,000)
GOVERNMENT Federal multiparty republic **ETHNIC GROUPS** German 93%, Turkish 2%, Yugoslav 1%, Italian 1%, Greek, Polish, Spanish
LANGUAGES German (official) **RELIGIONS** Christianity (Protestant, mainly Lutheran 45%, Roman Catholic 37%), Islam 2%
CURRENCY Euro; Deutschmark = 100 Pfennig

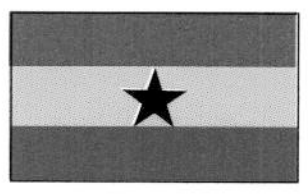
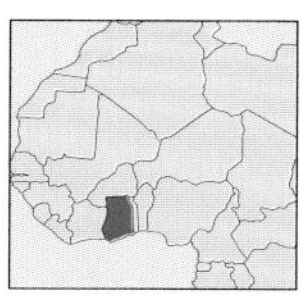

GHANA

GEOGRAPHY The Republic of Ghana faces the Gulf of Guinea in West Africa. This hot country, just north of the Equator, was formerly called the Gold Coast. Behind the thickly populated southern coastal plains, which are lined with lagoons, lies a plateau region in the southwest.

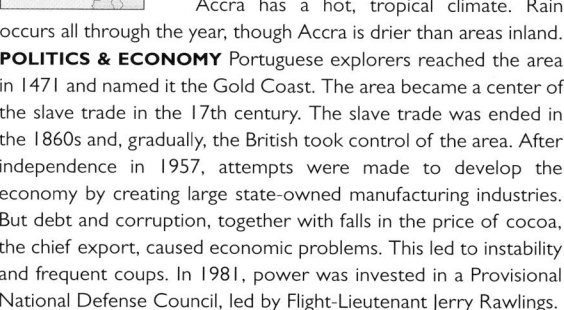

Accra has a hot, tropical climate. Rain occurs all through the year, though Accra is drier than areas inland.

POLITICS & ECONOMY Portuguese explorers reached the area in 1471 and named it the Gold Coast. The area became a center of the slave trade in the 17th century. The slave trade was ended in the 1860s and, gradually, the British took control of the area. After independence in 1957, attempts were made to develop the economy by creating large state-owned manufacturing industries. But debt and corruption, together with falls in the price of cocoa, the chief export, caused economic problems. This led to instability and frequent coups. In 1981, power was invested in a Provisional National Defense Council, led by Flight-Lieutenant Jerry Rawlings.

The government steadied the economy and introduced several new policies, including the relaxation of government controls. In 1992, the government introduced a new constitution, which allowed for multiparty elections. In late 1992 and again in 1996, Rawlings was re-elected president.

The World Bank classifies Ghana as a "low-income" developing country. Most people are poor and farming employs 59% of the population.

AREA 92,100 sq mi [238,540 sq km] **POPULATION** 20,564,000
CAPITAL (POPULATION) Accra (949,000) **GOVERNMENT** Republic
ETHNIC GROUPS Akan 54%, Mossi 16%, Ewe 12%, Ga-Adangame 8%, Gurma 3% **LANGUAGES** English (official), Akan, Mossi
RELIGIONS Christianity 62%, traditional beliefs 21%, Islam 16%
CURRENCY Cedi = 100 pesewas

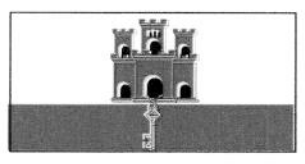
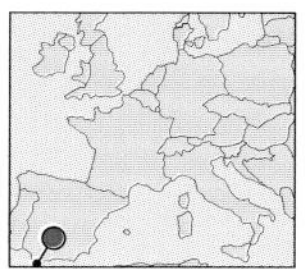

GIBRALTAR

Gibraltar occupies a strategic position on the south coast of Spain where the Mediterranean meets the Atlantic. It was recognized as a British possession in 1713 and, despite Spanish claims, its population has consistently voted to retain its contacts with Britain.

AREA 2.5 sq mi [6.5 sq km] **POPULATION** 32,000
CAPITAL Gibraltar Town

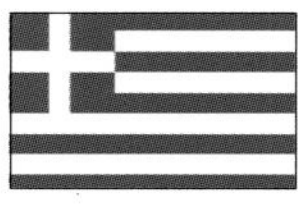
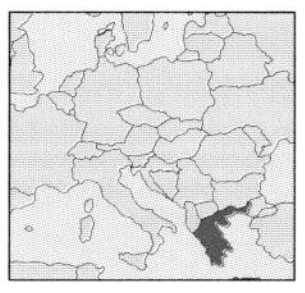

GREECE

GEOGRAPHY The Hellenic Republic, as Greece is officially called, is a rugged country situated at the southern end of the Balkan peninsula. Olympus, at 9,570 ft [2,917 m] is the highest peak. Islands make up about a fifth of the land.

Low-lying areas in Greece have mild, moist winters and hot, dry summers. The east coast has more than 2,700 hours of sunshine a year and only about half of the rainfall of the west. The mountains have a much more severe climate, with snow on the higher slopes in winter.

POLITICS & ECONOMY After World War II (1939–45), when Germany had occupied Greece, a civil war broke out between Communist and nationalist forces. This war ended in 1949. A military dictatorship took power in 1967. The monarchy was abolished in 1973 and democratic government was restored in 1974. Greece joined the European Community (now the EU) in 1981. Despite efforts to develop the economy, Greece remains one of the EU's poorest nations. On January 1, 2000, it adopted the euro, the single European currency.

Manufacturing is important. Products include processed food, cement, chemicals, metal products, textiles and tobacco. Greece also mines lignite (brown coal), bauxite and chromite.

Farmland covers about a third of the country, and grazing land another 40%. Major crops include barley, grapes for winemaking, dried fruits, olives, potatoes, sugar beet and wheat. Poultry, sheep, goats, pigs and cattle are raised. Greece's beaches and ancient ruins make it a major tourist destination.

AREA 50,961 sq mi [131,990 sq km] **POPULATION** 10,193,000
CAPITAL (POPULATION) Athens (3,097,000) **GOVERNMENT** Multiparty republic **ETHNIC GROUPS** Greek 96%, Macedonian 2%, Turkish 1%, Albanian, Slav **LANGUAGES** Greek (official) **RELIGIONS** Christianity (Eastern Orthodox 97%) **CURRENCY** Euro; Drachma = 100 lepta

GREENLAND

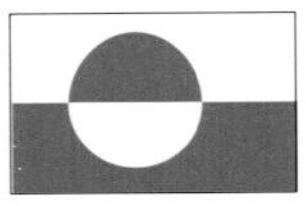

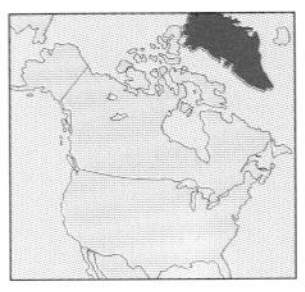

Greenland is the world's largest island. Settlements are confined to the coast, because an ice sheet covers four-fifths of the land. Greenland became a Danish possession in 1380. Full internal self-government was granted in 1981 and, in 1997, Danish place names were superseded by Inuit forms. However, Greenland remains heavily dependent on Danish subsidies.

AREA 838,999 sq mi [2,175,600 sq km] **POPULATION** 60,000
CAPITAL Nuuk (Godthaab)

GRENADA

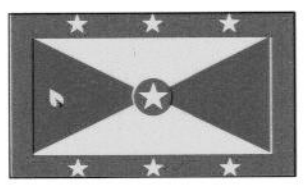

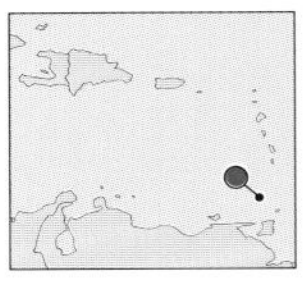

The most southerly of the Windward Islands in the Caribbean Sea, Grenada became independent from the UK in 1974. A military group seized power in 1983, when the prime minister was killed. US troops intervened and restored order and constitutional government.

AREA 133 sq mi [344 sq km]
POPULATION 83,000 **CAPITAL** St George's

GUADELOUPE

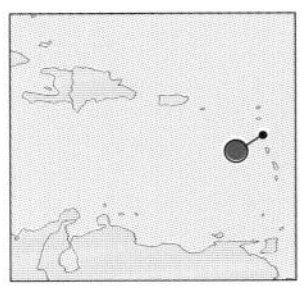

Guadeloupe is a French overseas department which includes seven Caribbean islands, the largest of which is Basse-Terre. French aid has helped to mantain a reasonable standard of living for the people.

AREA 660 sq mi [1,710 sq km]
POPULATION 365,000 **CAPITAL** Basse-Terre

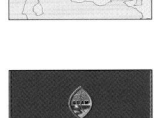

GUAM

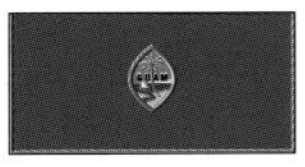

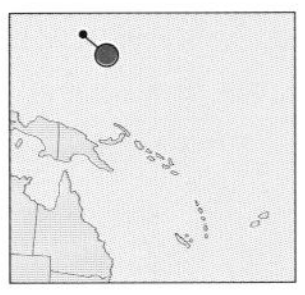

Guam, a strategically important "unincorporated territory" of the USA, is the largest of the Mariana Islands in the Pacific Ocean. It is composed of a coralline limestone plateau.

AREA 209 sq mi [541 sq km]
POPULATION 149,000 **CAPITAL** Agana

GUATEMALA

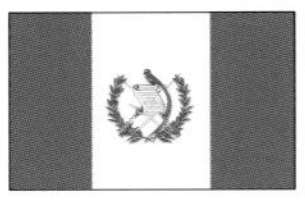

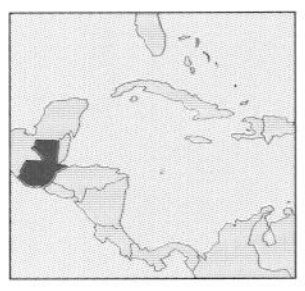

GEOGRAPHY The Republic of Guatemala in Central America contains a thickly populated mountain region, with fertile soils. The mountains, which run in an east–west direction, contain many volcanoes, some of which are active. Volcanic eruptions and earthquakes are common in the highlands. South of the mountains lie the thinly populated Pacific coastlands, while a large inland plain occupies the north.

Guatemala lies in the tropics. The lowlands are hot and rainy, but the central mountain region is cooler and drier. Guatemala City, at about 5,000 ft [1,500 m] above sea level, has a pleasant, warm climate, with a marked dry season between November and April.

POLITICS & ECONOMY In 1823, Guatemala joined the Central American Federation. But it became fully independent in 1839. Since independence, Guatemala has been plagued by instability and periodic violence.

Guatemala has a long-standing claim over Belize, but this was reduced in 1983 to the southern fifth of the country. Violence became widespread in Guatemala from the early 1960s, because of the conflict between left-wing groups, including many Amerindians, and government forces. A peace accord was signed in 1996, ending a war that had lasted 36 years and claimed perhaps 200,000 lives.

The World Bank classifies Guatemala as a "lower-middle-income" developing country. Agriculture employs nearly half of the population and coffee, sugar, bananas and beef are the leading exports. Other important crops include the spice cardamom and cotton, while maize is the chief food crop.

AREA 42,042 sq mi [108,890 sq km] **POPULATION** 12,222,000
CAPITAL (POPULATION) Guatemala City (1,167,000)
GOVERNMENT Republic **ETHNIC GROUPS** Amerindian 45%, Ladino (mixed Hispanic and Amerindian) 45%, White 5%, Black 2%, others including Chinese 3% **LANGUAGES** Spanish (official), Mayan languages
RELIGIONS Christianity (Roman Catholic 75%, Protestant 25%)
CURRENCY US dollar; Quetzal = 100 centavos

GUINEA

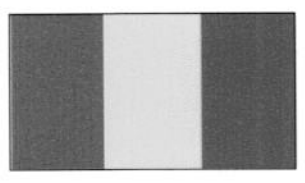

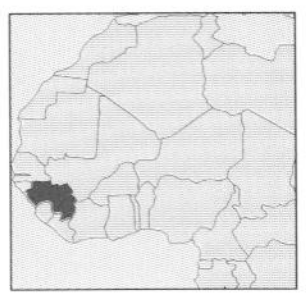

GEOGRAPHY The Republic of Guinea faces the Atlantic Ocean in West Africa. A flat, swampy plain borders the coast. Behind this plain, the land rises to a plateau region called Fouta Djalon. The Upper Niger plains, named after one of Africa's longest rivers, the Niger, which rises there, are in the northeast.

Guinea has a tropical climate and Conakry, on the coast, has heavy rains between May and November. This is also the coolest period in the year. During the dry season, hot, dry harmattan winds blow southwestward from the Sahara Desert.

POLITICS & ECONOMY Guinea became independent in 1958. Its president, Sékou Touré, pursued socialist policies, though he had to resort to repressive policies to hold on to power. After his death in 1984, a military government, under President Lansana Conté, introduced free enterprise policies. In the late 1990s, Guinea faced border problems with its neighbors, Liberia and Sierra Leone, where civil wars had caused much disorder.

The World Bank classifies Guinea as a "low-income" developing country. It has several natural resources, including bauxite (aluminum ore), diamonds, gold, iron ore and uranium. Bauxite and alumina (processed bauxite) account for 90% of the value of the exports. Agriculture, however, employs 78% of the people, many of whom produce little more than they need for their own families. Guinea has some manufacturing industries. Products include alumina, processed food and textiles.

AREA 94,927 sq mi [245,860 sq km] **POPULATION** 7,830,000
CAPITAL (POPULATION) Conakry (1,508,000)
GOVERNMENT Multiparty republic
ETHNIC GROUPS Fulani 40%, Malinke 26%, Susu 11%, Kissi 7%, Kpelle 5% **LANGUAGES** French (official), Fulani, Malinke
RELIGIONS Islam 85%, traditional beliefs 5%
CURRENCY Guinean franc = 100 cauris

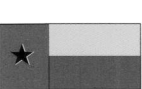

GUINEA-BISSAU

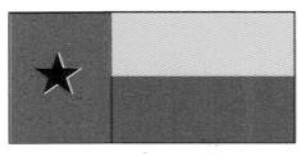

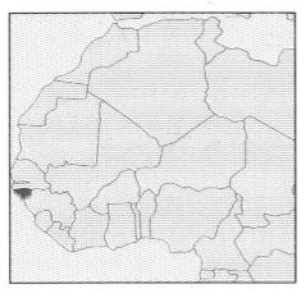

GEOGRAPHY The Republic of Guinea-Bissau, formerly known as Portuguese Guinea, is a small country in West Africa. The land is mostly low-lying, with a broad, swampy coastal plain and many flat offshore islands, including the Bijagós Archipelago.

The country has a tropical climate, with one dry season (December to May) and a rainy season from June to November.

POLITICS & ECONOMY Portugal appointed a governor to administer Guinea-Bissau and the Cape Verde Islands in 1836, but in 1879 the two territories were separated and Guinea-Bissau became a colony, then called Portuguese Guinea. But development was slow, partly because the territory did not attract settlers on the same scale as Portugal's much healthier African colonies of Angola and Mozambique.

In 1956, African nationalists in Portuguese Guinea and Cape Verde founded the African Party for the Independence of Guinea and Cape Verde (PAIGC). Because Portugal seemed determined to hang on to its overseas territories, the PAIGC began a guerrilla war in 1963. By 1968, it held two-thirds of the country. In 1972, a rebel National Assembly, elected by the people in the PAIGC-controlled area, voted to make the country independent as Guinea-Bissau.

In 1974, newly independent Guinea-Bissau faced many problems arising from its under-developed economy and its lack of trained people to work in the administration. One objective of the leaders of Guinea-Bissau was to unite their country with Cape Verde. But, in 1980, army leaders overthrew Guinea-Bissau's government. The Revolutionary Council, which took over, opposed unification with Cape Verde. Guinea-Bissau ceased to be a one-party state in 1991 and multiparty elections were held in 1994. Civil war broke out in 1998 and a military coup occurred in May 1999. In elections in 1999 and 2000, Kumba Ialá was elected president.

Guinea-Bissau is a poor country. Agriculture employs more than 80% of the people, but most farming is at subsistence level. Major crops include beans, coconuts, groundnuts, maize and rice.

AREA 13,946 sq mi [36,120 sq km] **POPULATION** 1,197,000
CAPITAL (POPULATION) Bissau (145,000)
GOVERNMENT "Interim" government
ETHNIC GROUPS Balante, Fulani (or Peul), Malinke, Mandyako, Pepel **LANGUAGES** Portuguese (official), Crioulo
RELIGIONS Traditional beliefs 54%, Islam 38%
CURRENCY CFA franc = 100 centimes

GUYANA

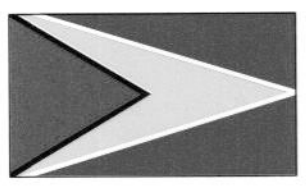

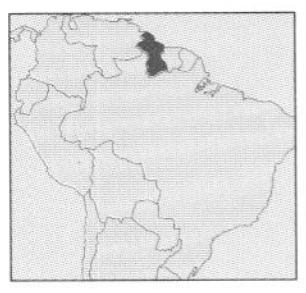

GEOGRAPHY The Cooperative Republic of Guyana is a country facing the Atlantic Ocean in northeastern South America. The coastal plain is flat and much of it is below sea level.

The climate is hot and humid, though the interior highlands are cooler than the coast. The rainfall is heavy, occurring on more than 200 days a year.

POLITICS & ECONOMY British Guiana became independent in 1966. A black lawyer, Forbes Burnham, became the first prime minister. Under a new constitution adopted in 1980, the president's powers were increased. Burnham became president until his death in 1985. He was succeeded by Hugh Desmond Hoyte. Hoyte was defeated in elections in 1993 by an ethnic Indian, Cheddi Jagan. Jagan died in 1997 and was succeeded by his wife, Janet. In 1999, Bharrat Jagdeo was elected president.

Guyana is a poor country. Its resources include gold, bauxite (aluminum ore) and other minerals, forests and fertile soils. sugarcane and rice are leading crops. Electric power is in short supply, although the country has great potential for producing hydroelectricity from its many rivers.

AREA 83,000 sq mi [214,970 sq km] **POPULATION** 891,000
CAPITAL (POPULATION) Georgetown (200,000)
GOVERNMENT Multiparty republic **ETHNIC GROUPS** Asian Indian 49%, Black 36%, Mixed 7%, Amerindian 7%, Portuguese, Chinese
LANGUAGES English (official) **RELIGIONS** Christianity (Protestant 34%, Roman Catholic 18%), Hinduism 34%, Islam 9%
CURRENCY Guyana dollar = 100 cents

HAITI

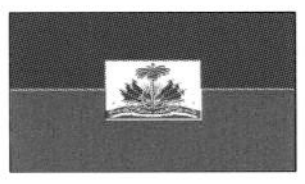

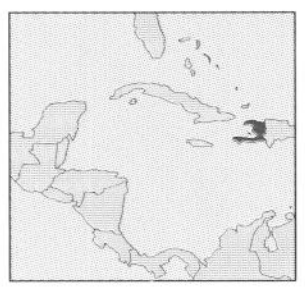

GEOGRAPHY The Republic of Haiti occupies the western third of Hispaniola in the Caribbean. The land is mainly mountainous. The climate is hot and humid, though the northern highlands, with about 79 in [200 mm], have more than twice as much rainfall as the southern coast.

POLITICS & ECONOMY Visited by Christopher Columbus in 1492, Haiti was later developed by the French. The African slaves revolted in 1791 and the country became independent in 1804.

Since independence, Haiti has suffered from instability, violence and dictatorial rule. Elections in 1990 returned Jean-Bertrand Aristide as president, but he was overthrown in 1991. Following US intervention, he returned in 1994. In 1995, René Préval was elected president, but Aristide was again elected president in 2000 amid accusations of vote-rigging.

AREA 10,714 sq mi [27,750 sq km] **POPULATION** 8,003,000
CAPITAL (POPULATION) Port-au-Prince (1,402,000)
GOVERNMENT Multiparty republic **ETHNIC GROUPS** Black 95%, Mulatto 5% **LANGUAGES** French (official), Creole
RELIGIONS Roman Catholic 80%, Voodoo
CURRENCY Gourde = 100 centimes

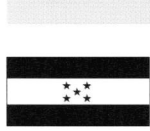

HONDURAS

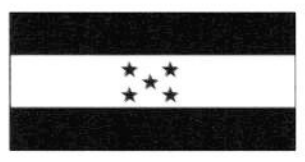

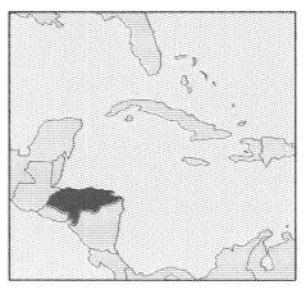

GEOGRAPHY The Republic of Honduras is the second largest country in Central America. The northern coast on the Caribbean Sea extends more than 373 mi [600 km], but the Pacific coast in the southeast is only about 50 mi [80 km] long.

Honduras has a tropical climate, but the highlands, where the capital Tegucigalpa is situated, have a cooler climate than the hot coastal plains. The months between May and November are the rainiest. The north coast is often hit by hurricanes. In 1998, Hurricane Mitch caused the worst destruction in the area in modern times.

POLITICS & ECONOMY In the 1890s, American companies developed plantations in Honduras to grow bananas, which soon became the country's chief source of income. The companies exerted great political influence in Honduras and the country became known as a "banana republic," a name that was later applied to several other Latin American nations. Instability has continued to mar the country's progress. In 1969, Honduras fought the short "Soccer War" with El Salvador. The war was sparked off by the treatment of fans during a World Cup soccer series. But the real reason was that Honduras had forced Salvadoreans in Honduras to give up land. A peace agreement was signed in 1980.

Honduras is a developing country – one of the poorest in the Americas. It has few resources besides some silver, lead and zinc, and agriculture dominates the economy. Bananas and coffee are the leading exports, and maize is the main food crop.

Honduras is the least industrialized country in Central America. Manufactures include processed food, textiles, and a wide variety of wood products.

AREA 43,278 SQ MI [112,090 SQ KM] **POPULATION** 6,846,000
CAPITAL (POPULATION) TEGUCIGALPA (813,000)
GOVERNMENT REPUBLIC **ETHNIC GROUPS** MESTIZO 90%, AMERINDIAN 7%, BLACK (INCLUDING BLACK CARIB) 2%, WHITE 1%
LANGUAGES SPANISH (OFFICIAL) **RELIGIONS** CHRISTIANITY (ROMAN CATHOLIC 85%) **CURRENCY** HONDURAN LEMPIRA = 100 CENTAVOS

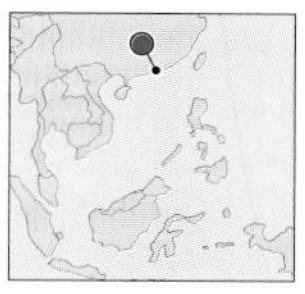

HONG KONG

Hong Kong, or Xianggang as it is known in Chinese, was a British dependency until 1 July 1997. It is now a Special Administrative Region of China. It consists of 236 islands, part of the mainland, and is home to over 6 million people. Hong Kong is a major financial and industrial center, the world's biggest container port, and a major producer of textiles.

AREA 413 SQ MI [1,071 SQ KM] **POPULATION** 6,336,000

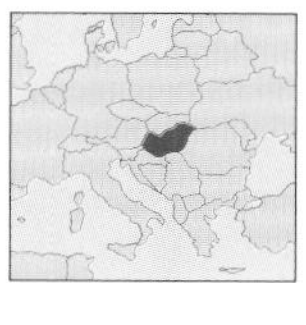

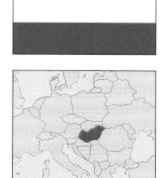

HUNGARY

GEOGRAPHY The Hungarian Republic is a landlocked country in central Europe. The land is mostly low-lying and drained by the Danube (Duna) and its tributary, the Tisza. Most of the land east of the Danube belongs to a region called the Great Plain (Nagyalföld), which covers about half of Hungary.

Hungary lies far from the moderating influence of the sea. As a result, summers are warmer and sunnier, and the winters colder than in Western Europe.

POLITICS & ECONOMY Hungary entered World War II (1939–45) in 1941, as an ally of Germany, but the Germans occupied the country in 1944. The Soviet Union invaded Hungary in 1944 and, in 1946, the country became a republic. The Communists gradually took over the government, taking complete control in 1949. From 1949, Hungary was an ally of the Soviet Union. In 1956, Soviet troops crushed an anti-Communist revolt. But in the 1980s, reforms in the Soviet Union led to the growth of anti-Communist groups in Hungary.

In 1989, Hungary adopted a new constitution making it a multiparty state. Elections held in 1990 led to a victory for the non-Communist Democratic Forum. In 1994, the Hungarian Socialist Party, composed of ex-Communists who had renounced Communism, won a majority in new elections and, in 1999, Hungary became a member of NATO.

Before World War II, Hungary's economy was based mainly on agriculture. But the Communists set up many manufacturing industries. The new factories were owned by the government, as also was most of the land. However, from the late 1980s, the government has worked to increase private ownership. This change of policy caused many problems, including inflation and high rates of unemployment. Manufacturing is the chief activity. Major products include aluminum, chemicals, and electrical and electronic goods.

AREA 35,919 SQ MI [93,030 SQ KM] **POPULATION** 10,531,000
CAPITAL (POPULATION) BUDAPEST (1,885,000)
GOVERNMENT MULTIPARTY REPUBLIC **ETHNIC GROUPS** MAGYAR (HUNGARIAN) 98%, GYPSY, GERMAN, CROAT, ROMANIAN, SLOVAK
LANGUAGES HUNGARIAN (OFFICIAL) **RELIGIONS** CHRISTIANITY (ROMAN CATHOLIC 64%, PROTESTANT 23%, ORTHODOX 1%), JUDAISM 1%
CURRENCY FORINT = 100 FILLÉR

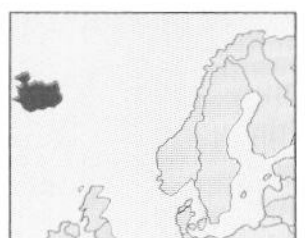
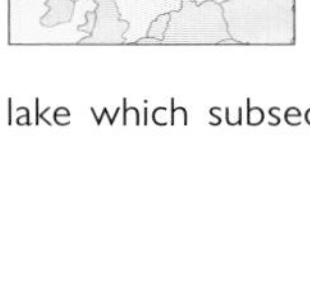

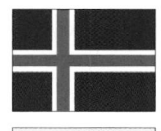

ICELAND

GEOGRAPHY The Republic of Iceland, in the North Atlantic Ocean, is closer to Greenland than Scotland. Iceland sits astride the Mid-Atlantic Ridge. It is slowly getting wider as the ocean is being stretched apart by continental drift.

Iceland has around 200 volcanoes, and eruptions are frequent. An eruption under the Vatnajökull ice cap in 1996 created a subglacial lake which subsequently burst, causing severe flooding. Geysers and hot springs are other common volcanic features. Ice caps and glaciers cover about an eighth of the land. The only habitable regions are the coastal lowlands.

Although it lies far to the north, Iceland's climate is moderated by the warm waters of the Gulf Stream. The port of Reykjavik is ice-free all the year round.

POLITICS & ECONOMY Norwegian Vikings colonized Iceland in AD 874, and in 930 the settlers founded the world's oldest parliament, the Althing.

Iceland united with Norway in 1262. But when Norway united with Denmark in 1380, Iceland came under Danish rule. Iceland became a self-governing kingdom, united with Denmark, in 1918. It became a fully independent republic in 1944, following a referendum in which 97% of the people voted to break their country's ties with Denmark.

Iceland has played an important part in European affairs and is a member of the North Atlantic Treaty Organization. Conflict with Britain over fishing rights have occurred since Iceland extended its territorial waters in the 1970s. Other fishing disputes with Norway, Russia and others continued in the 1990s.

Iceland has few resources besides the fishing grounds which surround it. Fishing and fish processing are major industries which dominate Iceland's overseas trade. Barely 1% of the land is used to grow crops, mainly root vegetables and fodder for livestock, but 23% of the country is used for grazing sheep and cattle. Vegetables and fruits are grown in greenhouses heated by water from hot springs.

AREA 39,768 SQ MI [103,000 SQ KM] **POPULATION** 274,000
CAPITAL (POPULATION) REYKJAVIK (103,000)
GOVERNMENT MULTIPARTY REPUBLIC **ETHNIC GROUPS** ICELANDIC 97%, DANISH 1% **LANGUAGES** ICELANDIC (OFFICIAL)
RELIGIONS CHRISTIANITY (EVANGELICAL LUTHERAN 92%, OTHER LUTHERAN 3%, ROMAN CATHOLIC 1%)
CURRENCY KRÓNA = 100 AURAR

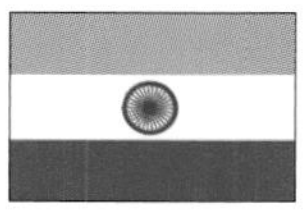
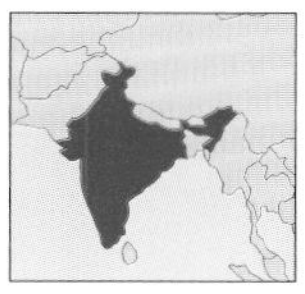

INDIA

GEOGRAPHY The Republic of India is the world's seventh largest country. In population, it ranks second only to China. The north is mountainous, with mountains and foothills of the Himalayan range. Rivers, such as the Brahmaputra and Ganges (Ganga), rise in the Himalaya and flow across the fertile northern plains. Southern India consists of a large plateau, called the Deccan. The Deccan is bordered by two mountain ranges, the Western Ghats and the Eastern Ghats.

India has three main seasons. The cool season runs from October to February. The hot season runs from March to June. The rainy monsoon season starts in the middle of June and continues into September. Delhi has a moderate rainfall, with about 25 in [640 mm] a year. The southwestern coast and the northeast have far more rain. Darjeeling in the northeast has an average annual rainfall of 120 in [3,040 mm]. But parts of the Thar Desert in the northwest have only 2 in [50 mm] of rain per year.

POLITICS & ECONOMY In southern India, most of the people are descendants of the dark-skinned Dravidians, who were among India's earliest people. Most northerners are descendants of lighter-skinned Aryans who arrived around 3,500 years ago.

India was the birthplace of several major religions, including Hinduism, Buddhism and Sikhism. Islam was introduced from about AD 1000. The Muslim Mughal empire was founded in 1526. From the 17th century, Britain began to gain influence. From 1858 to 1947, India was ruled as part of the British empire. Independence in 1947 led to the breakup of British India into India and Muslim Pakistan.

Although India has 15 major languages and hundreds of minor ones, together with many religions, the country remains the world's largest democracy. It has faced many problems, especially with Pakistan, over the disputed territory of Jammu and Kashmir. Tension arose again in 1998 when both India and Pakistan tested nuclear devices. However, India's declaration of a cease-fire at the end of 2000 raised hopes of a settlement of this problem.

Economic development has been a major problem and, according to the World Bank, India is a "low-income" developing country. After socialist policies failed to raise the living standards of the poor, the government introduced private enterprise. Farming employs 64% of the people. The main crops are rice, wheat, millet, sorghum, peas and beans. India has more cattle than any other country. Milk is produced but Hindus do not eat beef. India has reserves of coal, iron ore and oil, and manufacturing has expanded greatly since 1947. Iron and steel, machinery, refined petroleum, textiles and transport equipment are major products. India also imports rough diamonds and exports jewelry.

AREA 1,269,338 SQ MI [3,287,590 SQ KM] **POPULATION** 1,041,543,000
CAPITAL (POPULATION) NEW DELHI (PART OF DELHI, 7,207,000)
GOVERNMENT MULTIPARTY FEDERAL REPUBLIC
ETHNIC GROUPS INDO-ARYAN (CAUCASOID) 72%, DRAVIDIAN (ABORIGINAL) 25%, OTHER (MAINLY MONGOLOID) 3%
LANGUAGES HINDI 30% AND ENGLISH (BOTH OFFICIAL), TELUGU 8%, BENGALI 8%, MARATI 8%, URDU 5%, TAMIL, MANY LOCAL LANGUAGES
RELIGIONS HINDUISM 83%, ISLAM (SUNNI MUSLIM) 11%, CHRISTIANITY 2%, SIKHISM 2%, BUDDHISM 1%
CURRENCY RUPEE = 100 PAISA

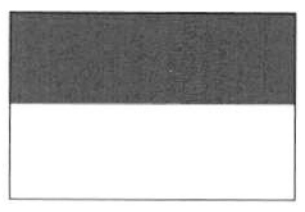
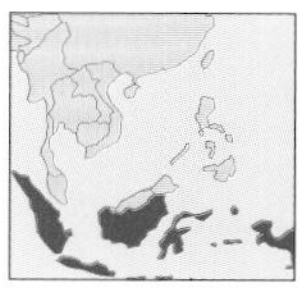

INDONESIA

GEOGRAPHY The Republic of Indonesia is an island nation in Southeast Asia. In all, Indonesia contains about 13,600 islands, less than 6,000 of which are inhabited. Three-quarters of the country is made up of five main areas: the islands of Sumatra, Java and Sulawesi (Celebes), together with Kalimantan (southern Borneo) and Irian Jaya (western New Guinea). The islands are generally mountainous and Indonesia has more active volcanoes than any other country. The larger islands have extensive coastal lowlands.

Indonesia lies on the Equator and temperatures are high throughout the year. The climate is also humid. The rainfall is generally heavy, and only Java and the Sunda Islands have a relatively dry season. The highlands are cooler than the lowlands.

POLITICS & ECONOMY Indonesia is the world's most populous Muslim nation, though Islam was introduced as recently as the 15th century. The Dutch became active in the area in the early 17th century and Indonesia became a Dutch colony in 1799. After a long struggle, the Netherlands recognized Indonesia's independence in 1949. The economy has expanded, but ethnic and religious conflict have slowed down economic progress. In 1999, the people of East (formerly Portuguese) Timor voted for independence amid much violence. Ethnic conflict, together with corruption in the government and army, have led some observers to believe that Indonesia could split up in the 21st century.

Indonesia is a developing country. Its resources include oil, natural gas, tin and other minerals, its fertile volcanic soils and its forests. Oil and gas are major exports. Timber, textiles, rubber, coffee and tea are also exported. The principal food crop is rice. Manufacturing is increasing, particularly on Java.

AREA 735,354 SQ MI [1,904,570 SQ KM] **POPULATION** 218,661,000
CAPITAL (POPULATION) JAKARTA (11,500,000)
GOVERNMENT MULTIPARTY REPUBLIC
ETHNIC GROUPS JAVANESE 39%, SUNDANESE 16%, INDONESIAN (MALAY) 12%, MADURESE 4%, MORE THAN 300 OTHERS
LANGUAGES BAHASA INDONESIAN (OFFICIAL), OTHERS
RELIGIONS ISLAM 87%, CHRISTIANITY 10% (ROMAN CATHOLIC 6%), HINDUISM 2%, BUDDHISM 1%
CURRENCY INDONESIAN RUPIAH = 100 SEN

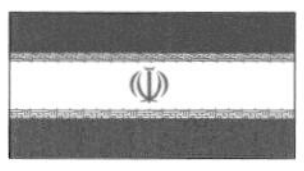
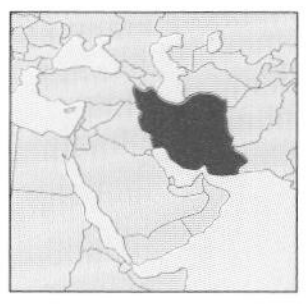

IRAN

GEOGRAPHY The Republic of Iran contains a barren central plateau which covers about half of the country. It includes the Dasht-e-Kavir (Great Salt Desert) and the Dasht-e-Lut (Great Sand Desert). The Elburz Mountains north of the plateau contain Iran's highest peak, Damavand, while narrow lowlands lie between the mountains and the Caspian Sea. West of the plateau are the Zagros Mountains, beyond which the land descends to the plains bordering the Gulf.

Much of Iran has a severe, dry climate, with hot summers and cold winters. In Tehran, rain falls on only about 30 days in the year and the annual temperature range is more than 45°F [25°C]. The climate in the lowlands, however, is generally milder.

POLITICS & ECONOMY Iran was called Persia until 1935. The empire of Ancient Persia flourished between 550 and 350 BC, when it fell to Alexander the Great. Islam was introduced in AD 641.

Britain and Russia competed for influence in the area in the 19th century, and in the early 20th century the British began to develop the country's oil resources. In 1925, the Pahlavi family took power.

Reza Khan became shah (king) and worked to modernize the country. The Pahlavi dynasty was ended in 1979 when a religious leader, Ayatollah Ruhollah Khomeini, made Iran an Islamic republic. In 1980–8, Iran and Iraq fought a war over disputed borders. Khomeini died in 1989, but his fundamentalist views and anti-Western attitudes continued to dominate politics. In 1997, Mohammad Khatami, a liberal, was elected president. His reform policies won support in elections in 2000, but the conservative clerics made actual reform difficult.

Iran's prosperity is based on its oil production and oil accounts for 95% of the country's exports. However, the economy was severely damaged by the Iran–Iraq war in the 1980s. Oil revenues have been used to develop a growing manufacturing sector. Agriculture is important even though farms cover only a tenth of the land. The main crops are wheat and barley. Livestock farming and fishing are other important activities, although Iran has to import much of the food it needs.

AREA 636,293 SQ MI [1,648,000 SQ KM] **POPULATION** 68,759,000
CAPITAL (POPULATION) TEHRAN (6,750,000)
GOVERNMENT ISLAMIC REPUBLIC
ETHNIC GROUPS PERSIAN 46%, AZERBAIJANI 17%, KURDISH 9%, GILAKI 5%, LURI, MAZANDARANI, BALUCHI, ARAB
LANGUAGES FARSI/ PERSIAN (OFFICIAL), KURDISH
RELIGIONS ISLAM 99% **CURRENCY** RIAL = 100 DINARS

IRAQ

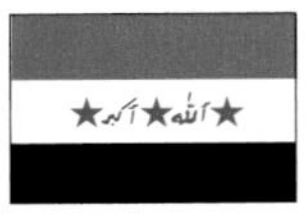

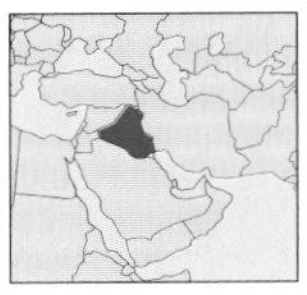

GEOGRAPHY The Republic of Iraq is a southwest Asian country at the head of the Gulf. Rolling deserts cover western and southwestern Iraq, with part of the Zagros Mountains in the northeast, where farming can be practised without irrigation. The northern plains, across which flow the rivers Euphrates (Nahr al Furat) and Tigris (Nahr Dijlah), are dry. But the southern plains, including Mesopotamia, and the delta of the Shatt al Arab, the river formed south of Al Qurnah by the combined Euphrates and Tigris, contain irrigated farmland, together with marshes.

The climate of Iraq varies from temperate in the north to subtropical in the south and east. Baghdad, in central Iraq, has cool winters, with occasional frosts, and hot summers. The rainfall is generally low.

POLITICS & ECONOMY Mesopotamia was the home of several great civilizations, including Sumer, Babylon and Assyria. It later became part of the Persian empire. Islam was introduced in AD 637 and Baghdad became the brilliant capital of the powerful Arab empire. But Mesopotamia declined after the Mongols invaded it in 1258. From 1534, Mesopotamia became part of the Turkish Ottoman empire. Britain invaded the area in 1916. In 1921, Britain renamed the country Iraq and set up an Arab monarchy. Iraq finally became independent in 1932.

By the 1950s, oil dominated Iraq's economy. In 1952, Iraq agreed to take 50% of the profits of the foreign oil companies. This revenue enabled the government to pay for welfare services and development projects. But many Iraqis felt that they should benefit more from their oil.

Since 1958, when army officers killed the king and made Iraq a republic, the country has undergone turbulent times. In the 1960s, the Kurds, who live in northern Iraq and also in Iran, Turkey, Syria and Armenia, asked for self-rule. The government rejected their demands and war broke out. A peace treaty was signed in 1975, but conflict has continued.

In 1979, Saddam Hussein became Iraq's president. Under his leadership, Iraq invaded Iran in 1980, starting an eight-year war. During this war, Iraqi Kurds supported Iran and the Iraqi government attacked Kurdish villages with poison gas.

In 1990, Iraqi troops occupied Kuwait but an international force drove them out in 1991. Since 1991, Iraqi troops have attacked Shiite Marsh Arabs and Kurds. In 1998, Iraq's failure to permit UNSCOM, the United Nations body charged with disposing of Iraq's deadliest weapons, access to all suspect sites, led to Western bombardment of military sites in Iraq. Another major Western offensive against strategic sites was launched in February 2001.

Civil war, war damage, UN sanctions and economic mismanagement have all contributed to economic chaos in the 1990s. Oil remains Iraq's main resource, but a UN trade embargo in 1990 halted oil exports. Farmland, including pasture, covers about a fifth of the land. Products include barley, cotton, dates, fruit, livestock, wheat and wool, but Iraq still has to import food. Industries include oil refining and the manufacture of petrochemicals and consumer goods.

AREA 169,235 SQ MI [438,320 SQ KM] **POPULATION** 26,339,000
CAPITAL (POPULATION) BAGHDAD (3,841,000)
GOVERNMENT REPUBLIC **ETHNIC GROUPS** ARAB 77%, KURDISH 19%, TURKMEN, PERSIAN, ASSYRIAN **LANGUAGES** ARABIC (OFFICIAL), KURDISH (OFFICIAL IN KURDISH AREAS) **RELIGIONS** ISLAM 96%, CHRISTIANITY 4%
CURRENCY IRAQI DINAR = 20 DIRHAMS = 1,000 FILS

IRELAND

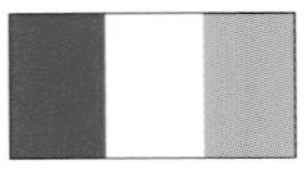

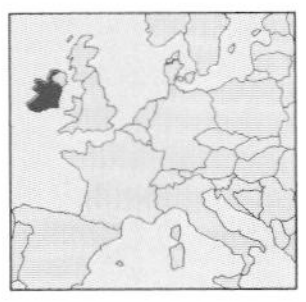

GEOGRAPHY The Republic of Ireland occupies five-sixths of the island of Ireland. The country consists of a large lowland region surrounded by a broken rim of low mountains. The uplands include the Mountains of Kerry where Carrauntoohill, Ireland's highest peak at 3,415 ft [1,041 m], is situated. The River Shannon is the longest in the British Isles. It flows through three large lakes, loughs Allen, Ree and Derg.

Ireland has a mild, damp climate greatly influenced by the warm Gulf Stream current that washes its shores. The effects of the Gulf Stream are greatest in the west. Dublin in the east is cooler than places on the west coast. Rain occurs throughout the year.

POLITICS & ECONOMY In 1801, the Act of Union created the United Kingdom of Great Britain and Ireland. But Irish discontent intensified in the 1840s when a potato blight caused a famine in which a million people died and nearly a million emigrated. Britain was blamed for not having done enough to help. In 1916, an uprising in Dublin was crushed, but between 1919 and 1922 civil war occurred. In 1922, the Irish Free State was created as a Dominion in the British Commonwealth. But Northern Ireland remained part of the UK.

Ireland became a republic in 1949. Since then, Irish governments have sought to develop the economy, and it was for this reason that Ireland joined the European Community in 1973. In 1998, Ireland took part in the negotiations to produce a constitutional settlement in Northern Ireland. As part of the agreement, Ireland agreed to give up its constitutional claim on Northern Ireland.

Major farm products in Ireland include barley, cattle and dairy products, pigs, potatoes, poultry, sheep, sugar beet and wheat, while fishing provides another valuable source of food. Farming is now profitable, aided by European Union grants, but manufacturing is the leading economic sector. Many factories produce food and beverages. Chemicals and pharmaceuticals, electronic equipment, machinery, paper and textiles are also important.

AREA 27,135 SQ MI [70,280 SQ KM] **POPULATION** 4,086,000
CAPITAL (POPULATION) DUBLIN (952,000)
GOVERNMENT MULTIPARTY REPUBLIC **ETHNIC GROUPS** IRISH 94%
LANGUAGES IRISH AND ENGLISH (BOTH OFFICIAL)
RELIGIONS CHRISTIANITY (ROMAN CATHOLIC 93%, PROTESTANT 3%)
CURRENCY EURO; IRISH POUND = 100 NEW PENCE

ISRAEL

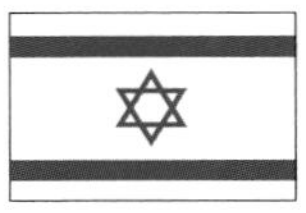

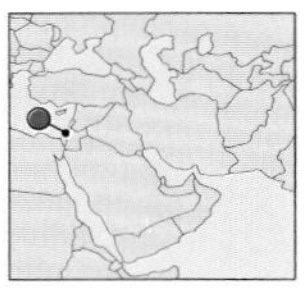

GEOGRAPHY The State of Israel is a small country in the eastern Mediterranean. It includes a fertile coastal plain, where Israel's main industrial cities, Haifa (Hefa) and Tel Aviv-Jaffa are situated. Inland lie the Judaeo-Galilean highlands, which run from northern Israel to the northern tip of the Negev Desert in the south. To the east lies part of the Great Rift Valley which contains the River Jordan, the Sea of Galilee and the Dead Sea.

Israel has hot, dry summers. Winters on the coast are mild and moist, but the rainfall decreases from west to east and from north to south, where the Dead Sea region has only 2.5 in [70 mm] a year.

POLITICS & ECONOMY Israel is part of a region called Palestine. Some Jews have always lived in the area, though most modern Israelis are descendants of immigrants who began to settle there from the 1880s. Britain ruled Palestine from 1917. Large numbers of Jews escaping Nazi persecution arrived in the 1930s, provoking an Arab uprising against British rule. In 1947, the UN agreed to partition Palestine into an Arab and a Jewish state. Fighting broke out after Arabs rejected the plan. The State of Israel came into being in May 1948, but fighting continued into 1949. Other Arab-Israeli wars in 1956, 1967 and 1973 led to land gains for Israel.

In 1978, Israel signed a treaty with Egypt which led to the return of the occupied Sinai peninsula to Egypt in 1979. But conflict continued between Israel and the PLO (Palestine Liberation Organization). In 1993, the PLO and Israel agreed to establish Palestinian self-rule in two areas: the occupied Gaza Strip, and in the town of Jericho in the occupied West Bank. The agreement was extended in 1995 to include more than 30% of the West Bank. Israel's prime minister, Yitzhak Rabin, was assassinated in 1995. In 1996, his successor, Simon Peres, was defeated by the right-wing Benjamin Netanyahu, under whom the peace process stalled. In 1999, the left-wing Ehud Barak defeated Netanyahu and revived the peace process. But, following violence between the Palestinians and Israeli forces, Barak resigned. In 2001, Barak was defeated by the right-wing Ariel Sharon, who demanded an end to violence before further peace talks.

Israel's most valuable activity is manufacturing and the country's products include chemicals, electronic equipment, fertilizers, military equipment, plastics, processed food, scientific instruments and textiles. Fruits and vegetables are leading exports.

AREA 10,290 SQ MI [26,650 SQ KM] **POPULATION** 5,321,000
CAPITAL (POPULATION) JERUSALEM (591,000)
GOVERNMENT MULTIPARTY REPUBLIC **ETHNIC GROUPS** JEWISH 82%, ARAB AND OTHERS 18% **LANGUAGES** HEBREW AND ARABIC (BOTH OFFICIAL)
RELIGIONS JUDAISM 82%, ISLAM 14%, CHRISTIANITY 2%, DRUSE AND OTHERS 2% **CURRENCY** NEW ISRAELI SHEQEL = 100 AGORAT

ITALY

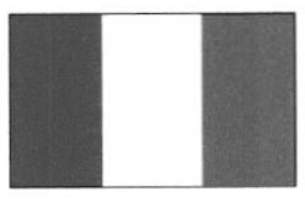

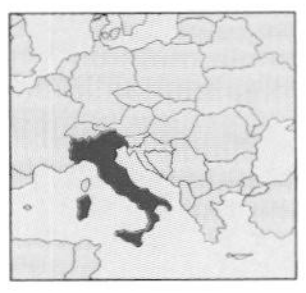

GEOGRAPHY The Republic of Italy is famous for its history and traditions, its art and culture, and its beautiful scenery. Northern Italy is bordered in the north by the high Alps, with their many climbing and skiing resorts. The Alps overlook the northern plains – Italy's most fertile and densely populated region – drained by the River Po. The rugged Apennines form the backbone of southern Italy. Bordering the range are scenic hilly areas and coastal plains.

Southern Italy contains a string of volcanoes, stretching from Vesuvius, near Naples (Nápoli), through the Lipari Islands, toMount Etna on Sicily. Sicily is the largest island in the Mediterranean.

Milan (Milano), in the north, has cold, often snowy winters, but the summer months are warm and sunny. Rainfall is plentiful, with brief but powerful thunderstorms in summer. Southern Italy has mild, moist winters and warm, dry summers.

POLITICS & ECONOMY Magnificent ruins throughout Italy testify to the glories of the ancient Roman Empire, which was founded, according to legend, in 753 BC. It reached its peak in the AD 100s. It finally collapsed in the 400s, although the Eastern Roman empire, also called the Byzantine empire, survived for another 1,000 years.

In the Middle Ages, Italy was split into many tiny states. These states made a great contribution to the revival of art and learning, called the Renaissance, in the 14th to 16th centuries. Beautiful cities, such as Florence (Firenze) and Venice (Venézia), testify to the artistic achievements of this period.

Italy finally became a united kingdom in 1861, although the Papal Territories (a large area ruled by the Roman Catholic Church) was not added until 1870. The Pope and his successors disputed the takeover of the Papal Territories. The dispute was finally resolved in 1929, when the Vatican City was set up in Rome as a fully independent state.

Italy fought in World War I (1914–18) alongside the Allies – Britain, France and Russia. In 1922, the dictator Benito Mussolini, leader of the Fascist party, took power. Under Mussolini, Italy conquered Ethiopia. During World War II (1939–45), Italy at first fought on Germany's side against the Allies. But in late 1943, Italy declared war on Germany. Italy became a republic in 1946. It has played an important part in European affairs. It was a founder member of the North Atlantic Treaty Organization (NATO) in 1949 and also of what has now become the European Union in 1958.

After the setting up of the European Union, Italy's economy developed quickly. But the country faced many problems. For example, much of the economic development was in the north. This forced many people to leave the poor south to find jobs in the north or abroad. Social problems, corruption at high levels of society, and a succession of weak coalition governments all contributed to instability. Elections in 1996 were won by the left-wing Olive Tree alliance led by Romano Prodi, who was replaced in 1998 by an ex-Communist, Massimo D'Alema. D'Alema resigned in April 2000, following right-wing victories in regional elections.

Only 50 years ago, Italy was a mainly agricultural society. But today it is a leading industrial power. It lacks mineral resources, and imports most of the raw materials used in industry. Manufactures include textiles and clothing, processed food, machinery, cars and chemicals. The chief industrial region is in the northwest.

Farmland covers around 42% of the land, pasture 17%, and forest and woodland 22%. Major crops include citrus fruits, grapes which are used to make wine, olive oil, sugar beet and vegetables. Livestock farming is important, though meat is imported.

AREA 116,320 sq mi [301,270 sq km] **POPULATION** 57,195,000
CAPITAL (POPULATION) Rome (2,775,000) **GOVERNMENT** Multiparty republic **ETHNIC GROUPS** Italian 94%, German, French, Albanian, Ladino, Slovenian, Greek **LANGUAGES** Italian 94% (official)
RELIGIONS Christianity (Roman Catholic) 83%
CURRENCY Euro; Lira = 100 centesimi

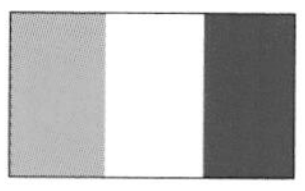
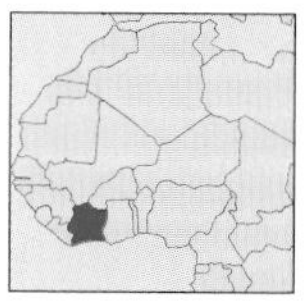

IVORY COAST

GEOGRAPHY The Republic of the Ivory Coast, in West Africa, is officially known as Côte d'Ivoire. The southeast coast is bordered by sand bars that enclose lagoons. The southwest coast is lined by rocky cliffs.

Ivory Coast has a hot and humid tropical climate, with high temperatures all year. The south has two rainy seasons: between May and July, and from October to November. Inland, the rainfall decreases and the north has one dry and one rainy season.

POLITICS & ECONOMY From 1895, Ivory Coast was governed as part of French West Africa, a massive union which also included what are now Benin, Burkina Faso, Guinea, Mali, Mauritania, Niger and Senegal. In 1946, Ivory Coast became a territory in the French Union.

Ivory Coast became fully independent in 1960. Its first president, Félix Houphouët-Boigny, became the longest serving head of state in Africa with an uninterrupted period in office which ended with his death in 1993. Houphouët-Boigny was a paternalistic, pro-Western leader, who made his country a one-party state. In 1983, the National Assembly agreed to make Yamoussoukro, the president's birthplace, the new capital. In 1993, Henri Konan Bédié became president. In 1999, he was overthrown by a military coup led by General Robert Guei. However, in presidential elections in 2000, Guei was defeated by a veteran politician, Laurent Gbagbo.

Agriculture employs about two-thirds of the people, and farm products make up nearly half the value of the exports. Manufacturing has grown in importance since 1960; products include fertilizers, processed food, refined oil, textiles and timber.

AREA 124,502 sq mi [322,460 sq km] **POPULATION** 17,600,000
CAPITAL (POPULATION) Yamoussoukro (120,000)
GOVERNMENT Multiparty republic **ETHNIC GROUPS** Akan 41%, Kru 17%, Voltaic 16%, Malinke 15%, Southern Mande 10%
LANGUAGES French (official), Akan, Voltaic
RELIGIONS Islam 38%, Christianity 28%, traditional beliefs 17%
CURRENCY CFA franc = 100 centimes

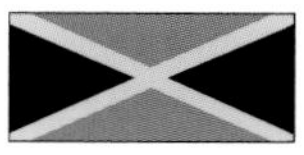
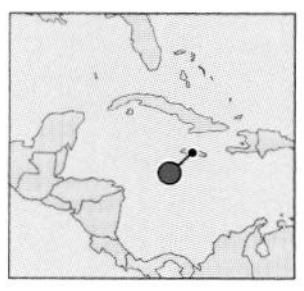

JAMAICA

GEOGRAPHY Third largest of the Caribbean islands, half of Jamaica lies above 1,000 ft [300 m] and moist southeast trade winds bring rain to the central mountain range.

The "cockpit country" in the northwest of the island is an inaccessible limestone area of steep broken ridges and isolated basins.

POLITICS & ECONOMY Britain took Jamaica from Spain in the 17th century, and the island did not gain its independence until 1962. Some economic progress was made by the socialist government in the 1980s, but migration and unemployment remain high. Farming is the leading activity and sugarcane is the main crop, though bauxite production provides much of the country's income. Jamaica has some industries and tourism is a major industry.

AREA 4,243 sq mi [10,990 sq km] **POPULATION** 2,735,000
CAPITAL (POPULATION) Kingston (644,000)
GOVERNMENT Constitutional monarchy
ETHNIC GROUPS Black 76%, Afro-European 15%, East Indian 3%, White 3% **LANGUAGES** English (official), Creole, Hindi, Spanish, Chinese **RELIGIONS** Protestant 70%, Roman Catholic 8%
CURRENCY Dollar = 100 cents

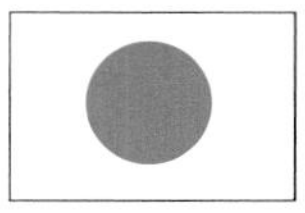
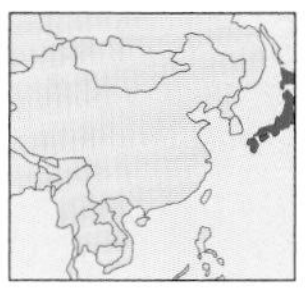

JAPAN

GEOGRAPHY Japan's four largest islands – Honshu, Hokkaido, Kyushu and Shikoku – make up 98% of the country. But Japan contains thousands of small islands. The four largest islands are mainly mountainous, while many of the small islands are the tips of volcanoes. Japan has more than 150 volcanoes, about 60 of which are active. Volcanic eruptions, earthquakes and tsunamis (destructive sea waves triggered by underwater earthquakes and eruptions) are common because the islands lie in an unstable part of our planet, where continental plates are always on the move. One powerful recent earthquake killed more than 5,000 people in Kobe in 1995.

The climate of Japan varies greatly from north to south. Hokkaido in the north has cold, snowy winters. At Sapporo, temperatures below 4°F [–20°C] have been recorded between December and March. But summers are warm, with temperatures sometimes exceeding 86°F [30°C]. Rain falls throughout the year, though Hokkaido is one of the driest parts of Japan.

Tokyo has higher rainfall and temperatures, though frosts may occur as late as April when northwesterly winds are blowing. The southern islands of Shikoku and Kyushu have warm temperate climates. Summers are long and hot. Winters are mild.

POLITICS & ECONOMY In the late 19th century, Japan began a programme of modernization. Under its new imperial leaders, it began to look for lands to conquer. In 1894–5, it fought a war with China and, in 1904–5, it defeated Russia. Soon its overseas empire included Korea and Taiwan. In 1930, Japan invaded Manchuria (northeast China) and, in 1937, it began a war against China. In 1941, Japan launched an attack on the US base at Pearl Harbor in Hawaii. This drew both Japan and the United States into World War II.

Japan surrendered in 1945 when the Americans dropped atomic bombs on two cities, Hiroshima and Nagasaki. The United States occupied Japan until 1952. During this period, Japan adopted a democratic constitution. The emperor, who had previously been regarded as a god, became a constitutional monarch. Power was vested in the prime minister and cabinet, who are chosen from the Diet (elected parliament).

From the 1960s, Japan experienced many changes as the country rapidly built up new industries. By the early 1990s, Japan had become the world's second richest economic power after the US. But economic success has brought problems. For example, the rapid growth of cities has led to housing shortages and pollution. Another problem is that the proportion of people over 65 years of age is steadily increasing.

Japan has the world's second highest gross domestic product (GDP) after the United States. [The GDP is the total value of all goods and services produced in a country in one year.] The most important sector of the economy is industry. Yet Japan has to import most of the raw materials and fuels it needs for its industries. Its success is based on its use of the latest technology, its skilled and hard-working labor force, its vigorous export policies and its comparatively small government spending on defense. Manufactures dominate its exports, which include machinery, electrical and electronic equipment, vehicles and transport equipment, iron and steel, chemicals, textiles and ships.

Japan is one of the world's top fishing nations and fish is an important source of protein. Because the land is so rugged, only 15% of the country can be farmed. Yet Japan produces about 70% of the food it needs. Rice is the chief crop, taking up about half of the total farmland. Other major products include fruits, sugar beet, tea and vegetables. Livestock farming has increased since the 1950s.

AREA 145,869 sq mi [377,800 sq km] **POPULATION** 128,470,000
CAPITAL (POPULATION) Tokyo (26,836,000)
GOVERNMENT Constitutional monarchy **ETHNIC GROUPS** Japanese 99%, Chinese, Korean, Ainu **LANGUAGES** Japanese (official)
RELIGIONS Shintoism 93%, Buddhism 74%, Christianity 1% (most Japanese consider themselves to be both Shinto and Buddhist)
CURRENCY Yen = 100 sen

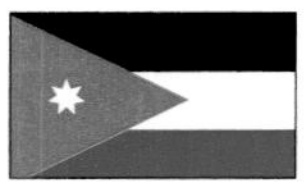
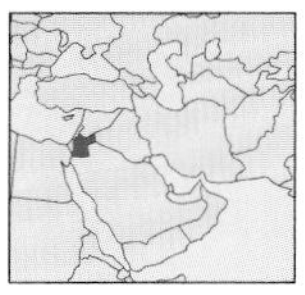

JORDAN

GEOGRAPHY The Hashemite Kingdom of Jordan is an Arab country in southwestern Asia. The Great Rift Valley in the west contains the River Jordan and the Dead Sea, which Jordan shares with Israel. East of the Rift Valley is the Transjordan plateau, where most Jordanians live. To the east and south lie vast areas of desert.

Amman has a much lower rainfall and longer dry season than the Mediterranean lands to the west. The Transjordan plateau, on which Amman stands, is a transition zone between the Mediterranean climate zone to the west and the desert climate to the east.

POLITICS & ECONOMY In 1921, Britain created a territory called Transjordan east of the River Jordan. In 1923, Transjordan became self-governing, but Britain retained control of its defenses, finances and foreign affairs. This territory became fully independent as Jordan in 1946.

Jordan has suffered from instability arising from the Arab–Israeli conflict since the creation of the State of Israel in 1948. After the first Arab–Israeli War in 1948–9, Jordan acquired East Jerusalem and a fertile area called the West Bank. In 1967, Israel occupied this area. In Jordan, the presence of Palestinian refugees led to civil war in 1970–1.

In 1974, Arab leaders declared that the PLO (Palestine Liberation Organization) was the sole representative of the Palestinian people. In 1988, King Hussein of Jordan renounced Jordan's claims to the West Bank and passed responsibility for it to the PLO. Opposition parties were legalized in 1991 and elections were held in 1993. In October 1994, Jordan and Israel signed a peace treaty, ending a state of war that had lasted more than 40 years. Jordan's King Hussein commanded respect for his role in Middle Eastern affairs until his death in 1999. He was succeeded by his eldest son who became Abdullah II.

Jordan lacks natural resources, apart from phosphates and potash, and the economy depends substantially on aid. The World Bank classifies Jordan as a "lower-middle-income" developing country. Because of the dry climate, less than 6% of the land is farmed or used as pasture. Jordan has an oil refinery and manufactures include cement, pharmaceuticals, processed food, fertilizers and textiles.

AREA 34,444 sq mi [89,210 sq km] **POPULATION** 5,558,000
CAPITAL (POPULATION) Amman (1,300,000)
GOVERNMENT Constitutional monarchy
ETHNIC GROUPS Arab 99%, of which Palestinians make up roughly half **LANGUAGES** Arabic (official) **RELIGIONS** Islam 93%, Christianity 5% **CURRENCY** Jordan dinar = 1,000 fils

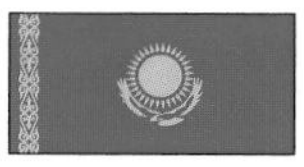
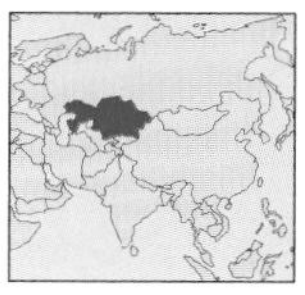

KAZAKSTAN

GEOGRAPHY Kazakstan is a large country in west-central Asia. In the west, the Caspian Sea lowlands include the Karagiye depression, which reaches 433 ft [132 m] below sea level. The lowlands extend eastward through the Aral Sea area. The north contains high plains, but the highest land is along the eastern and southern borders. These areas include parts of the Altai and Tian Shan mountain ranges.

Eastern Kazakstan contains several freshwater lakes, the largest of which is Lake Balkhash. The water in the rivers has been used for irrigation, causing ecological problems. For example, the Aral Sea, deprived of water, shrank from 25,830 sq mi [66,900 sq km] in 1960 to 12,989 sq mi [33,642 sq km] in 1993. Areas which once provided fish have dried up and are now barren desert.

The climate reflects Kazakstan's position in the heart of Asia, far from the moderating influence of the oceans. Winters are cold and snow covers the land for about 100 days, on average, at Almaty. The rainfall is generally low.

POLITICS & ECONOMY After the Russian Revolution of 1917, many Kazaks wanted to make their country independent. But the Communists prevailed and in 1936 Kazakstan became a republic of the Soviet Union, called the Kazak Soviet Socialist Republic. During World War II and also after the war, the Soviet government moved many people from the west into Kazakstan. From the 1950s, people were encouraged to work on a "Virgin Lands" project, which involved bringing large areas of grassland under cultivation.

Reforms in the Soviet Union in the 1980s led to its breakup in December 1991. Kazakstan kept contacts with Russia and most of the other republics in the former Soviet Union by joining the Commonwealth of Independent States (CIS), and in 1995 Kazakstan announced that its army would unite with that of Russia. In 1997, the government moved the capital from Almaty to Aqmola (later renamed Astana), a town in the Russian-dominated north. It was hoped that this move would bring some Kazak identity to the area.

The World Bank classifies Kazakstan as a "lower-middle-income" developing country. Livestock farming, especially sheep and cattle, is an important activity, and major crops include barley, cotton, rice and wheat. The country is rich in mineral resources, including coal and oil reserves, together with bauxite, copper, lead, tungsten and zinc. Manufactures include chemicals, food products, machinery and textiles. Oil is exported via a pipeline through Russia; however, to reduce dependence on Russia, Kazakstan signed an agreement in 1997 to build a new pipeline to China. Other exports include metals, chemicals, grain, wool and meat.

AREA 1,049,150 sq mi [2,717,300 sq km] **POPULATION** 19,006,000
CAPITAL (POPULATION) Astana (280,000) **GOVERNMENT** Multiparty republic **ETHNIC GROUPS** Kazak 40%, Russian 38%, German 6%, Ukrainian 5%, Uzbek, Tatar **LANGUAGES** Kazak (official); Russian, the former official language, is widely spoken **RELIGIONS** Mainly Islam, with a Christian minority **CURRENCY** Tenge

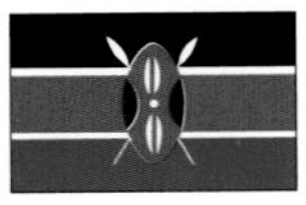

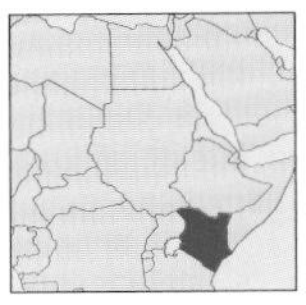

KENYA

GEOGRAPHY The Republic of Kenya is a country in East Africa which straddles the Equator. Behind the narrow coastal plain on the Indian Ocean, the land rises to high plains and highlands, broken by volcanic mountains, including Mount Kenya, the country's highest peak at 17,057 ft [5,199 m]. Crossing the country is an arm of the Great Rift Valley, on the floor of which are several lakes, including Baringo, Magadi, Naivasha, Nakuru and, on the northern frontier, Lake Turkana (formerly Lake Rudolf).

Mombasa on the coast is hot and humid. But inland, the climate is moderated by the height of the land. As a result, Nairobi, in the thickly populated southwestern highlands, has summer temperatures which are 18°F [10°C] lower than Mombasa. Nights can be cool, but temperatures do not fall below freezing. Nairobi's main rainy season is from April to May, with "little rains" in November and December. However, only about 15% of the country has a reliable rainfall of 31 in [800 mm].

POLITICS & ECONOMY The Kenyan coast has been a trading center for more than 2,000 years. Britain took over the coast in 1895 and soon extended its influence inland. In the 1950s, a secret movement, called Mau Mau, launched an armed struggle against British rule. Although Mau Mau was eventually defeated, Kenya became independent in 1963.

Many Kenyans felt that Kenya should have a strong central government, and Kenya was a one-party state for much of the time since 1963. But democracy was restored in the early 1990s and elections were held in 1992 and 1997. In 1999, Kenya, with Tanzania and Uganda, set up an East African Community, which aimed to create a customs union, a common market, a monetary union, and, ultimately a political union.

According to the United Nations, Kenya is a "low-income" developing country. Agriculture employs about 80% of the people, but many Kenyans are subsistence farmers, growing little more than they need to support their families. The chief food crop is maize. The main cash crops and leading exports are coffee and tea. Manufactures include chemicals, leather and footwear, processed food, petroleum products and textiles.

AREA 224,081 sq mi [580,370 sq km] **POPULATION** 35,060,000
CAPITAL (POPULATION) Nairobi (2,000,000)
GOVERNMENT Multiparty republic **ETHNIC GROUPS** Kikuyu 21%, Luhya 14%, Luo 13%, Kamba 11%, Kalenjin 11% **LANGUAGES** Swahili and English (both official) **RELIGIONS** Christianity (Roman Catholic 27%, Protestant 19%, others 27%), traditional beliefs 19%, Islam 6%
CURRENCY Kenya shilling = 100 cents

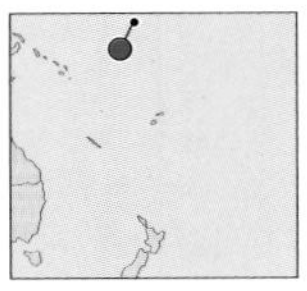

KIRIBATI

The Republic of Kiribati comprises three groups of corall atolls scattered over about 2 million sq mi [5 million sq km]. Kiribati straddles the equator and temperatures are high and the rainfall is abundant.

Formerly part of the British Gilbert and Ellice Islands, Kiribati became independent in 1979. The main export is copra and the country depends heavily on foreign aid.

AREA 281 sq mi [728 sq km] **POPULATION** 72,000 **CAPITAL** Tarawa

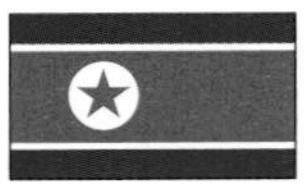

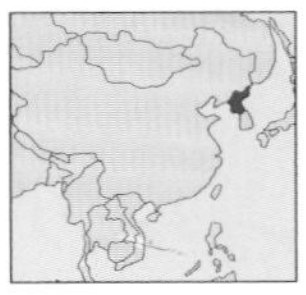

KOREA, NORTH

GEOGRAPHY The Democratic People's Republic of Korea occupies the northern part of the Korean peninsula which extends south from northeastern China. Mountains form the heart of the country, with the highest peak, Paektu-san, reaching 9,003 ft [2,744 m] on the northern border.

North Korea has a fairly severe climate, with bitterly cold winters when winds blow from across central Asia, bringing snow and freezing conditions. In summer, moist winds from the oceans bring rain.

POLITICS & ECONOMY North Korea was created in 1945, when the peninsula, which had been a Japanese colony since 1910, was divided into two parts. Soviet forces occupied the north, with US forces in the south. Soviet occupation led to a Communist government being established in 1948 under the leadership of Kim Il Sung. He initiated a Stalinist regime in which he assumed the role of dictator, and a personality cult developed around him. He was to become the world's most durable Communist leader.

The Korean War began in June 1950 when North Korean troops invaded the south. North Korea, aided by China and the Soviet Union, fought with South Korea, which was supported by troops from the United States and other UN members. The war ended in July 1953. An armistice was signed but no permanent peace treaty was agreed. After the war, North Korea adopted a hostile policy toward South Korea in pursuit of its policy of reunification. At times, the situation grew so tense that it became a matter of international concern.

The ending of the Cold War in the late 1980s eased the situation and both North and South Korea joined the United Nations in 1991. The two countries made several agreements, including one in which they agreed not to use force against each other. However, North Korea remained as isolated as ever.

In 1993, North Korea began a new international crisis by announcing that it was withdrawing from the Nuclear Non-Proliferation Treaty. This led to suspicions that North Korea, which had signed the Treaty in 1985, was developing its own nuclear weapons. Kim Il Sung, who had ruled as a virtual dictator from 1948 until his death in 1994, was succeeded by his son, Kim Jong Il. In the early 2000s, attempts were made to reconcile the two Koreas, though the prospect of reunification seems remote.

North Korea has considerable resources, including coal, copper, iron ore, lead, tin, tungsten and zinc. Under Communism, North Korea has concentrated on developing heavy, state-owned industries. Manufactures include chemicals, iron and steel, machinery, processed food and textiles. Agriculture employs about a third of the people of North Korea and rice is the leading crop. Economic decline and mismanagement, aggravated by three successive crop failures caused by floods in 1995 and 1996 and a drought in 1997, led to famine on a large scale.

AREA 46,540 sq mi [120,540 sq km] **POPULATION** 26,117,000
CAPITAL (POPULATION) Pyŏngyang (2,639,000)
GOVERNMENT Single-party people's republic
ETHNIC GROUPS Korean 99%
LANGUAGES Korean (official) **RELIGIONS** Traditional beliefs 16%, Chondogyo 14%, Buddhism 2%, Christianity 1%
CURRENCY North Korean won = 100 chon

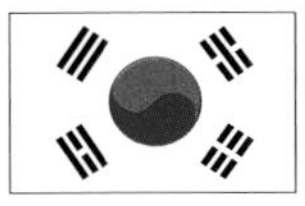

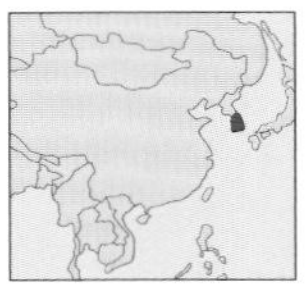

KOREA, SOUTH

GEOGRAPHY The Republic of Korea, as South Korea is officially known, occupies the southern part of the Korean peninsula. Mountains cover much of the country. The southern and western coasts are major farming regions. Many islands are found along the west and south coasts. The largest of these is Cheju-do, which contains South Korea's highest peak, Halla-San, which rises to 6,398 ft [1,950 m].

Like North Korea, South Korea is chilled in winter by cold, dry winds blowing from central Asia. Snow often covers the mountains in the east. The summers are hot and wet, especially in July and August.

POLITICS & ECONOMY After Japan's defeat in World War II (1939–45), North Korea was occupied by troops from the Soviet Union, while South Korea was occupied by United States forces. Attempts to reunify Korea failed and, in 1948, a National Assembly was elected in South Korea. This Assembly created the Republic of Korea, while North Korea became a Communist state. North Korean troops invaded the South in June 1950, sparking off the Korean War (1950–3).

In the 1950s, South Korea had a weak economy, which had been further damaged by the destruction caused by the Korean War. From the 1960s to the 1980s, South Korean governments worked to industrialize the economy. The governments were dominated by military leaders, who often used authoritarian methods and flouted human rights. In 1987, a new constitution was approved, enabling presidential elections to be held every five years. In 1991, South and North Korea became members of the United Nations and they signed agreements, including one in which they agreed not to use force against each other. Tensions continued, though hopes were raised when negotiations between the two countries took place in the early 21st century.

The World Bank classifies South Korea as an "upper-middle-income" developing country. It is also one of the world's fastest growing industrial economies. The country's resources include coal and tungsten, and its main manufactures are processed food and textiles. Since partition, heavy industries have been built up, making chemicals, fertilizers, iron and steel, and ships. South Korea has also developed the production of such things as computers, cars and television sets. In late 1997, however, the dramatic expansion of the economy was halted by a market crash which affected many of the booming economies of Asia. In an effort to negate the economic and social turmoil that resulted, tough reforms were demanded by the International Monetary Fund and an agreement was reached to restructure much of the short-term debt faced by the government.

Farming remains important in South Korea. Rice is the chief crop, together with fruits, grains and vegetables, while fishing provides a major source of protein.

AREA 38,232 sq mi [99,020 sq km] **POPULATION** 46,403,000
CAPITAL (POPULATION) Seoul (11,641,000)
GOVERNMENT Multiparty republic **ETHNIC GROUPS** Korean 99%
LANGUAGES Korean (official) **RELIGIONS** Buddhism 28%, Christianity (Protestant 19%, Roman Catholic 6%)
CURRENCY South Korean won = 100 chon

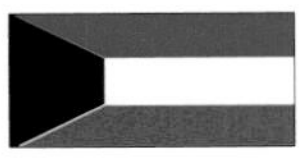

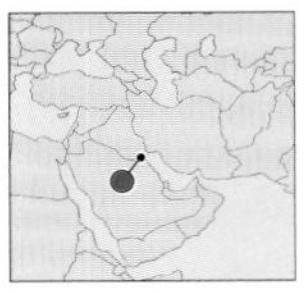

KUWAIT

The State of Kuwait at the north end of the Gulf is largely made up of desert. Temperatures are high and the rainfall low. Kuwait became independent from Britain in 1961 and revenues from its oil wells have made it highly prosperous. Iraq invaded Kuwait in 1990 and much damage was inflicted in the ensuing conflict in 1991 when Kuwait was liberated.

AREA 6,880 sq mi [17,820 sq km] **POPULATION** 2,639,000
CAPITAL Kuwait City

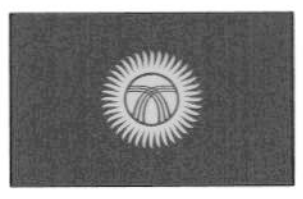

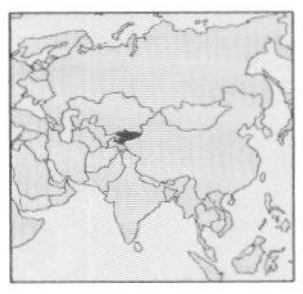

KYRGYZSTAN

GEOGRAPHY The Republic of Kyrgyzstan is a landlocked country between China, Tajikistan, Uzbekistan and Kazakstan. The country is mountainous, with spectacular scenery. The highest mountain, Pik Pobedy in the Tian Shan range, reaches 24,406 ft [7,439 m] in the east.

The lowlands of Kyrgyzstan have warm summers and cold winters. But the altitude influences the climate in the mountains, where the January temperatures plummet to –18°F [–28°C]. Far from any sea, Kyrgyzstan has a low annual rainfall.

POLITICS & ECONOMY In 1876, Kyrgyzstan became a province of Russia and Russian settlement in the area began. In 1916, Russia crushed a rebellion among the Kyrgyz, and many subsequently fled to China. In 1922, the area became an autonomous oblast (self-governing region) of the newly formed Soviet Union but, in 1936, it became one of the Soviet Socialist Republics. Under Communist rule, nomads were forced to work on government-run farms, while local customs and religious worship were suppressed. However, there were concurrent improvements in education and health.

In 1991, Kyrgyzstan became an independent country following the breakup of the Soviet Union. The Communist party was dissolved, but the country maintained ties with Russia through an organization called the Commonwealth of Independent States. Kyrgyzstan adopted a new constitution in 1994 and parliamentary elections were held in 1995.

In the early 1990s, when Kyrgyzstan was working to reform its economy, the World Bank classified it as a "lower-middle-income" developing country. Agriculture, especially livestock rearing, is the chief activity. The chief products include cotton, eggs, fruits, grain, tobacco, vegetables and wool. But food must be imported. Industries are mainly concentrated around the capital Bishkek.

AREA 76,640 sq mi [198,500 sq km] **POPULATION** 5,403,000
CAPITAL (POPULATION) Bishkek (584,000) **GOVERNMENT** Multiparty republic **ETHNIC GROUPS** Kyrgyz 52%, Russian 22%, Uzbek 13%, Ukrainian 3%, German 2%, Tatar 2% **LANGUAGES** Kyrgyz (official), Russian, Uzbek **RELIGIONS** Islam **CURRENCY** Som = 100 tyiyn

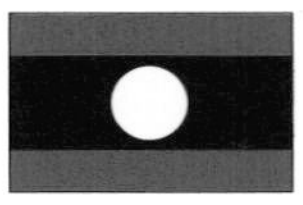

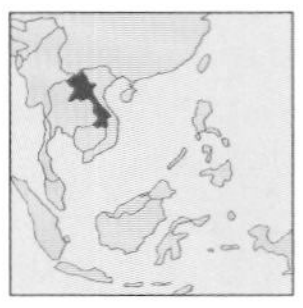

LAOS

GEOGRAPHY The Lao People's Democratic Republic is a landlocked country in Southeast Asia. Mountains and plateaux cover much of the country. Most people live on the plains bordering the River Mekong and its tributaries. This river, one of Asia's longest, forms much of the country's northwestern and south-western borders.

Laos has a tropical monsoon climate.

Winters are dry and sunny, with winds blowing in from the northeast. The temperatures rise until April, when the wind directions are reversed and moist southwesterly winds reach Laos, heralding the start of the wet monsoon season.

POLITICS & ECONOMY France made Laos a protectorate in the late 19th century and ruled it as part of French Indochina, a region which also included Cambodia and Vietnam. Laos became a member of the French Union in 1948 and an independent kingdom in 1954.

After independence, Laos suffered from instability caused by a long power struggle between royalist government forces and a pro-Communist group called the Pathet Lao. A civil war broke out in 1960 and continued into the 1970s. The Pathet Lao took control in 1975 and the king abdicated. Laos then came under the influence of Communist Vietnam, which had used Laos as a supply base during the Vietnam War (1957–75). From the early 1980s, the economy deteriorated and opposition appeared when bombings occurred in Vientiane in 2000. They were attributed to rebels in the minority Hmong tribe or to politicians who wanted faster economic reforms.

Laos is one of the world's poorest countries. Agriculture employs about 76% of the people, compared with 7% in industry and 17% in services. Rice is the main crop, and timber and coffee are both exported. But the most valuable export is electricity, which is produced at hydroelectric power stations on the River Mekong and is exported to Thailand. Laos also produces opium.

AREA 91,428 sq mi [236,800 sq km] **POPULATION** 5,463,000
CAPITAL (POPULATION) Vientiane (449,000)
GOVERNMENT Single-party republic **ETHNIC GROUPS** Lao 67%, Mon-Khmer 17%, Tai 8% **LANGUAGES** Lao (official), Khmer, Tai, Miao
RELIGIONS Buddhism 58%, traditional beliefs 34%, Christianity 2%, Islam 1% **CURRENCY** Kip = 100 at

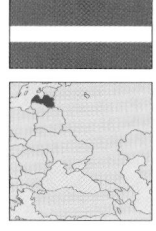

LATVIA

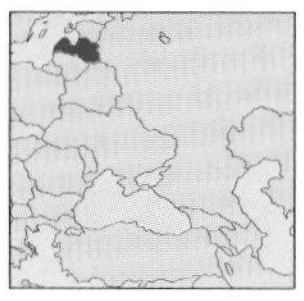

GEOGRAPHY The Republic of Latvia is one of three states on the southeastern corner of the Baltic Sea which were ruled as parts of the Soviet Union between 1940 and 1991. Latvia consists mainly of flat plains separated by low hills, composed of moraine (ice-worn rocks).

Riga has warm summers, but the winter months (from December to March) are subzero. In the winter, the sea often freezes over. The rainfall is moderate and it occurs throughout the year, with light snow in winter.

POLITICS & ECONOMY In 1800, Russia was in control of Latvia, but Latvians declared their independence after World War I. In 1940, under a German-Soviet pact, Soviet troops occupied Latvia, but they were driven out by the Germans in 1941. Soviet troops returned in 1944 and Latvia became part of the Soviet Union. Under Soviet rule, many Russian immigrants settled in Latvia and many Latvians feared that the Russians would become the dominant ethnic group.

In the late 1980s, when reforms were being introduced in the Soviet Union, Latvia's government ended absolute Communist rule and made Latvian the official language. In 1990, it declared the country to be independent, an act which was finally recognized by the Soviet Union in September 1991.

Latvia held its first free elections to its parliament (the Saeima) in 1993. Voting was limited only to citizens of Latvia on 17 June 1940 and their descendants. This meant that about 34% of Latvian residents were unable to vote. In 1994, Latvia restricted the naturalization of non-Latvians, including many Russian settlers, who were not allowed to vote or own land. However, in 1998, the government agreed that all children born since independence should have automatic citizenship regardless of the status of their parents.

The World Bank classifies Latvia as a "lower-middle-income" country and, in the 1990s, it faced many problems in turning its economy into a free-market system. Products include electronic goods, farm machinery, fertilizers, processed food, plastics, radios and vehicles. Latvia produces only about a tenth of the electricity it needs. It imports the rest from Belarus, Russia and Ukraine.

AREA 24,938 sq mi [64,589 sq km] **POPULATION** 2,768,000
CAPITAL (POPULATION) Riga (846,000)
GOVERNMENT Multiparty republic **ETHNIC GROUPS** Latvian 53%, Russian 34%, Belarussian 4%, Ukrainian 3%, Polish 2%, Lithuanian, Jewish **LANGUAGES** Latvian (official), Russian
RELIGIONS Christianity (including Lutheran, Russian Orthodox and Roman Catholic) **CURRENCY** Lats = 10 santimi

LEBANON

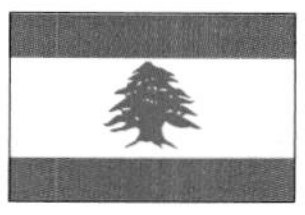

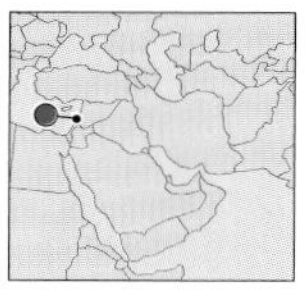

GEOGRAPHY The Republic of Lebanon is a country on the eastern shores of the Mediterranean Sea. Behind the coastal plain are the rugged Lebanon Mountains (Jabal Lubnan), which rise to 10,131 ft [3,088 m]. Another range, the Anti-Lebanon Mountains (Al Jabal Ash Sharqi), form the eastern border with Syria. Between the two ranges is the Bekaa (Beqaa) Valley, a fertile farming region.

The Lebanese coast has the hot, dry summers and mild, wet winters that are typical of many Mediterranean lands. Inland, onshore winds bring heavy rain to the western slopes of the mountains in the winter months, with snow at the higher altitudes.

POLITICS & ECONOMY Lebanon was ruled by Turkey from 1516 until World War I. France ruled the country from 1923, but Lebanon became independent in 1946. After independence, the Muslims and Christians agreed to share power, and Lebanon made rapid economic progress. But from the late 1950s, development was slowed by periodic conflict between Sunni and Shia Muslims, Druze and Christians. The situation was further complicated by the presence of Palestinian refugees who used bases in Lebanon to attack Israel.

In 1975, civil war broke out as private armies representing the many factions struggled for power. This led to intervention by Israel in the south and Syria in the north. UN peacekeeping forces arrived in 1978, but bombings, assassinations and kidnappings became almost everyday events in the 1980s. From 1991, Lebanon enjoyed an uneasy peace. But, Israel continued to occupy an area in the south. In the 1990s, Israel launched several attacks on pro-Iranian Hezbollah guerrillas in Lebanon, but all Israeli troops were withdrawn in May 2000.

Lebanon's civil war almost destroyed valuable trade and financial services that had been Lebanon's chief source of income, together with tourism. Manufacturing, formerly a major activity, was badly hit.

AREA 4,015 sq mi [10,400 sq km] **POPULATION** 3,327,000
CAPITAL (POPULATION) Beirut (1,900,000) **GOVERNMENT** Multiparty republic **ETHNIC GROUPS** Arab (Lebanese 80%, Palestinian 12%), Armenian 5%, Syrian, Kurdish **LANGUAGES** Arabic (official)
RELIGIONS Islam 58%, Christianity 27%, Druse
CURRENCY Lebanese pound = 100 piastres

LESOTHO

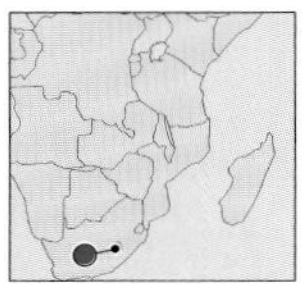

GEOGRAPHY The Kingdom of Lesotho is a landlocked country, completely enclosed by South Africa. The land is mountainous, rising to 11,424 ft [3,482 m] on the northeastern border. The Drakensberg range covers most of the country.

The climate of Lesotho is greatly affected by the altitude, because most of the country lies above 4,921 ft [1,500 m]. Maseru has warm summers, but the temperatures fall below freezing in the winter. The mountains are colder. The rainfall varies, averaging around 28 in [700 mm].

POLITICS & ECONOMY The Basotho nation was founded in the 1820s by King Moshoeshoe I, who united various groups fleeing from tribal wars in southern Africa. Britain made the area a protectorate in 1868 and, in 1871, placed it under the British Cape Colony in South Africa. But in 1884, Basutoland, as the area was called, was reconstituted as a British protectorate, where whites were not allowed to own land.

The country finally became independent in 1966 as the Kingdom of Lesotho, with Moshoeshoe II, great-grandson of Moshoeshoe I, as its king. Since independence, Lesotho has suffered instability. The military seized power in 1986 and stripped Moshoeshoe II of his powers in 1990, installing his son, Letsie III, as monarch. After elections in 1993, Moshoeshoe II was restored to office in 1995. But after his death in a car crash in 1996, Letsie III again became king. In 1998, an army revolt, following an election in which the ruling party won 79 out of the 80 seats, caused much damage to the economy, despite the intervention of a South African force intended to maintain order.

Lesotho is a "low-income" developing country. It lacks natural resources. Agriculture, mainly at subsistence level, light manufacturing and money sent home by Basotho working abroad are the main sources of income.

AREA 11,718 sq mi [30,350 sq km] **POPULATION** 2,370,000
CAPITAL (POPULATION) Maseru (130,000)
GOVERNMENT Constitutional monarchy **ETHNIC GROUPS** Sotho 99%
LANGUAGES Sesotho and English (both official)
RELIGIONS Christianity 93% (Roman Catholic 44%), traditional beliefs 6% **CURRENCY** Loti = 100 lisente

LIBERIA

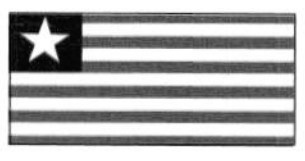

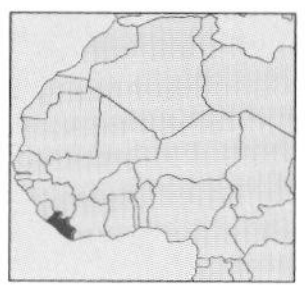

GEOGRAPHY The Republic of Liberia is a country in West Africa. Behind the coastline, 311 mi [500 km] long, lies a narrow coastal plain. Beyond, the land rises to a plateau region, with the highest land along the border with Guinea.

Liberia has a tropical climate with high temperatures and high humidity all through the year. The rainfall is abundant all year round, but there is a particularly wet period from June to November. The rainfall generally increases from east to west.

POLITICS & ECONOMY In the late 18th century, some white Americans in the United States wanted to help freed black slaves to return to Africa. In 1816, they set up the American Colonization Society, which bought land in what is now Liberia.

In 1822, the Society landed former slaves at a settlement on the coast which they named Monrovia. In 1847, Liberia became a fully independent republic with a constitution much like that of the United States. For many years, the Americo-Liberians controlled the country's government. US influence remained strong and the American Firestone Company, which ran Liberia's rubber plantations, was especially influential. Foreign companies were also involved in exploiting Liberia's mineral resources, including its huge iron-ore deposits.

In 1980, a military group composed of people from the local population killed the Americo-Liberian president, William R. Tolbert. An army sergeant, Samuel K. Doe, was made president of Liberia. Elections held in 1985 resulted in victory for Doe.

From 1989, the country was plunged into civil war between various ethnic groups. Doe was assassinated in 1990, but his successor, Amos Sawyer, continued to struggle with rebel groups. Peacekeeping forces from other West African countries arrived in Liberia, but the fighting continued. In 1995, a cease-fire was agreed and a council of state, composed of former warlords, was set up. In 1997, one of the warlords, Charles Taylor, was elected president.

Liberia's civil war devastated its economy. Three out of every four people depend on agriculture, though many of them grow little more than they need to feed their families. The chief food crops include cassava, rice and sugarcane, while rubber, cocoa and coffee are grown for export. But the most valuable export is iron ore.

Liberia also obtains revenue from its "flag of convenience," which is used by about one-sixth of the world's commercial shipping, exploiting low taxes.

AREA 43,000 sq mi [111,370 sq km] **POPULATION** 3,575,000
CAPITAL (POPULATION) Monrovia (490,000)
GOVERNMENT Multiparty republic **ETHNIC GROUPS** Kpelle 19%, Bassa 14%, Grebo 9%, Gio 8%, Kru 7%, Mano 7%
LANGUAGES English (official), Mande, Mel, Kwa
RELIGIONS Christianity 68%, Islam 14%, traditional beliefs and others 18% **CURRENCY** Liberian dollar = 100 cents

LIBYA

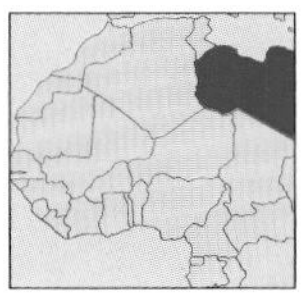

GEOGRAPHY The Socialist People's Libyan Arab Jamahiriya, as Libya is officially called, is a large country in North Africa. Most people live on the coastal plains in the northeast and northwest. The Sahara, the world's largest desert which occupies 95% of Libya, reaches the Mediterranean coast along the Gulf of Sidra (Khalij Surt).

The coastal plains in the northeast and northwest have Mediterranean climates, with hot, dry summers and mild, sometimes wet winters. Inland, the average yearly rainfall drops to 4 in [100 mm] or less.

POLITICS & ECONOMY Italy took over Libya in 1911, but lost it during World War II. Britain and France then jointly ruled Libya until 1951, when the country became an independent kingdom.

In 1969, a military group headed by Colonel Muammar Gaddafi deposed the king and set up a military government. Under Gaddafi, the government took control of the economy and used money from oil exports to finance welfare services and development projects. Gaddafi was criticized for supporting terrorist groups around the world, and Libya became isolated from the mid-1980s. In 1998, he tried to restore Libya's reputation by surrendering for trial two Libyans suspected of planting a bomb on a PanAm plane which exploded over the Scottish town of Lockerbie in 1988. In 2001, one of the Libyans was found guilty and the other acquitted of the bombing. Gaddafi also paid compensation to the family of a British policewoman killed in 1984 by shots fired from the Libyan People's Bureau in London. These actions helped to end Libya's pariah status.

The discovery of oil and natural gas in 1959 led to the transformation of Libya's economy. Once one of the world's poorest countries, it has become Africa's richest in terms of its per capita income. It remains a developing country because of its dependence on oil, which accounts for nearly all of its export revenues.

Agriculture is important, although Libya has to import food. Crops include barley, citrus fruits, dates, olives, potatoes and wheat. Cattle, sheep and poultry are raised. Libya has oil refineries and petrochemical plants. Other manufactures include cement and steel.

AREA 679,358 SQ MI [1,759,540 SQ KM] **POPULATION** 6,500,000
CAPITAL (POPULATION) TRIPOLI (1,083,000)
GOVERNMENT SINGLE-PARTY SOCIALIST STATE **ETHNIC GROUPS** LIBYAN ARAB AND BERBER 89% **LANGUAGES** ARABIC (OFFICIAL), BERBER
RELIGIONS ISLAM **CURRENCY** LIBYAN DINAR = 1,000 DIRHAMS

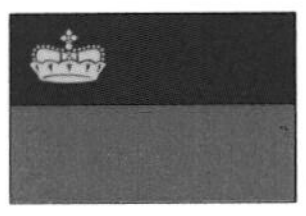
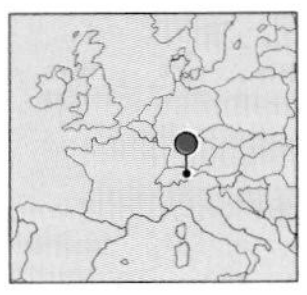

LIECHTENSTEIN

The tiny Principality of Liechtenstein is sandwiched between Switzerland and Austria. The River Rhine flows along its western border, while Alpine peaks rise in the east and south. The climate is relatively mild. Since 1924, Liechtenstein has been in a customs union with Switzerland and, like its neighbor, it is extremely prosperous. Taxation is low and, as a result, the country has become a haven for international companies.

AREA 61 SQ MI [157 SQ KM] **POPULATION** 28,000 **CAPITAL** VADUZ

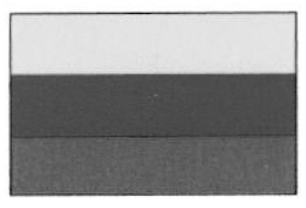
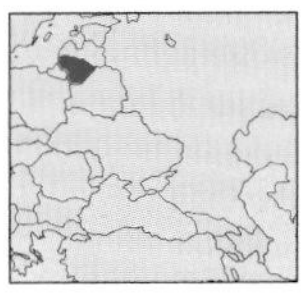

LITHUANIA

GEOGRAPHY The Republic of Lithuania is the southernmost of the three Baltic states which were ruled as part of the Soviet Union between 1940 and 1991. Much of the land is flat or gently rolling, with the highest land in the southeast.

Winters are cold. January's temperatures average 27°F [–3°C] in the west and 21°F [–6°C] in the east. Summers are warm, with average temperatures in July of 63°F [17°C]. The average rainfall in the west is about 25 in [630 mm]. Inland areas are drier.

POLITICS & ECONOMY The Lithuanian people were united into a single nation in the 12th century, and later joined a union with Poland. In 1795, Lithuania came under Russian rule. After World War I (1914–18), Lithuania declared itself independent, and in 1920 it signed a peace treaty with the Russians, though Poland held Vilnius until 1939. In 1940, the Soviet Union occupied Lithuania, but the Germans invaded in 1941. Soviet forces returned in 1944, and Lithuania was integrated into the Soviet Union. In 1988, when the Soviet Union was introducing reforms, the Lithuanians demanded independence. Their language is one of the oldest in the world, and the country was always the most homogenous of the Baltic states, staunchly Catholic and resistant of attempts to suppress their culture. Pro-independence groups won the national elections in 1990 and, in 1991, the Soviet Union recognized Lithuania's independence.

After independence, Lithuania faced many problems as it sought to reform its economy and introduce a private enterprise system. In 1998, Valdas Adamkus, a Lithuanian-American who had fled the country in 1944, was elected president.

The World Bank classifies Lithuania as a "lower-middle-income" developing country. Lithuania lacks natural resources, but manufacturing, based on imported materials, is the most valuable activity.

AREA 25,200 SQ MI [65,200 SQ KM] **POPULATION** 3,935,000
CAPITAL (POPULATION) VILNIUS (580,000) **GOVERNMENT** MULTIPARTY REPUBLIC **ETHNIC GROUPS** LITHUANIAN 80%, RUSSIAN 9%, POLISH 7%, BELARUSSIAN 2% **LANGUAGES** LITHUANIAN (OFFICIAL), RUSSIAN, POLISH
RELIGIONS CHRISTIANITY (MAINLY ROMAN CATHOLIC)
CURRENCY LITAS = 100 CENTAI

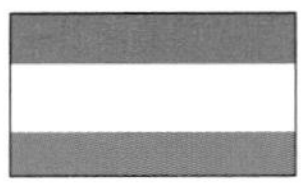
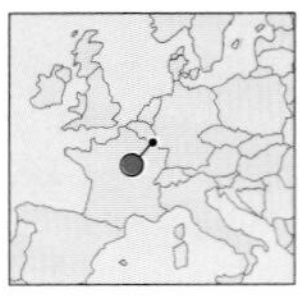

LUXEMBOURG

GEOGRAPHY The Grand Duchy of Luxembourg is one of the smallest and oldest countries in Europe. The north belongs to an upland region which includes the Ardenne in Belgium and Luxembourg, and the Eifel highlands in Germany.

Luxembourg has a temperate climate. The south has warm summers and autumns, when grapes ripen in sheltered southeastern valleys. Winters are sometimes severe, especially in upland areas.

POLITICS & ECONOMY Germany occupied Luxembourg in World Wars I and II. In 1944–5, northern Luxembourg was the scene of the famous Battle of the Bulge. In 1948, Luxembourg joined Belgium and the Netherlands in a union called Benelux and, in the 1950s, it was one of the six founders of what is now the European Union. Luxembourg has played a major role in Europe. Its capital contains the headquarters of several international agencies, including the European Coal and Steel Community and the European Court of Justice. The city is also a major financial center.

Luxembourg has iron-ore reserves and is a major steel producer. It also has many high-technology industries, producing electronic goods and computers. Steel and other manufactures, including chemicals, rubber products, glass and aluminum, dominate the country's exports. Other major activities include tourism and financial services.

AREA 1,000 SQ MI [2,590 SQ KM] **POPULATION** 377,000
CAPITAL (POPULATION) LUXEMBOURG (76,000)
GOVERNMENT CONSTITUTIONAL MONARCHY (GRAND DUCHY)
ETHNIC GROUPS LUXEMBOURGER 71%, PORTUGUESE 10%, ITALIAN 5%, FRENCH 3%, BELGIAN 3% **LANGUAGES** LETZEBURGISH/LUXEMBOURGIAN (OFFICIAL), FRENCH, GERMAN **RELIGIONS** CHRISTIANITY (ROMAN CATHOLIC 95%) **CURRENCY** EURO; LUXEM. FRANC = 100 CENTIMES

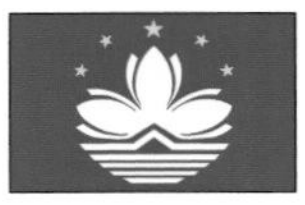
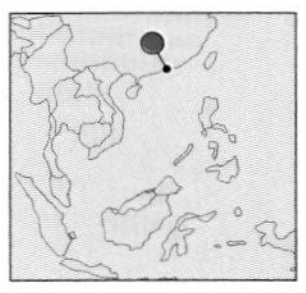

MACAU

Macau is a small peninsula at the head of the Zhu Jiang (Pearl) River, west of Hong Kong. A Portuguese colony since 1557, Macau was returned to China in 1999. Its main industries are textiles, gambling and tourism.

AREA 6 SQ MI [16 SQ KM]
POPULATION 656,000 **CAPITAL** MACAU

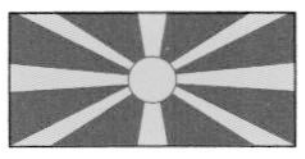
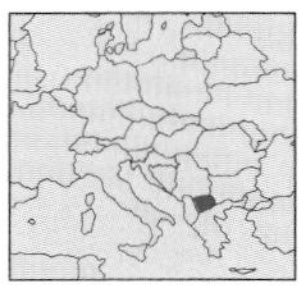

MACEDONIA (FYROM)

GEOGRAPHY The Republic of Macedonia is a country in southeastern Europe, which was once one of the six republics that made up the former Federal People's Republic of Yugoslavia. This landlocked country is largely mountainous or hilly.

Macedonia has hot summers, though highland areas are cooler. Winters are cold and snowfalls are often heavy. The climate is fairly continental in character and rain occurs throughout the year.

POLITICS & ECONOMY Between 1912 and 1913, the area called Macedonia was divided between Serbia, Bulgaria, which took a small area in the east, and Greece, which gained the south. At the end of World War I, Serbian Macedonia became part of the Kingdom of the Serbs, Croats and Slovenes, which was renamed Yugoslavia in 1929. After World War II, Yugoslavia became a Communist regime.

Tito died in 1980 and, in the early 1990s, the country broke up into five separate republics. Macedonia declared its independence in September 1991. Greece objected to this territory using the name Macedonia, which it considered to be a Greek name. It also objected to a symbol on Macedonia's flag and a reference in the constitution to the desire to reunite the three parts of the old Macedonia.

Macedonia adopted a new clause in its constitution rejecting any Macedonian claims on Greek territory and, in 1993, the United Nations accepted the new republic as a member under the name of The Former Yugoslav Republic of Macedonia (FYROM).

By the end of 1993, all the countries of the European Union, except Greece, were establishing diplomatic relations with the FYROM. In 1995, Greece lifted its trade ban, when Macedonia agreed to redesign its flag and remove territorial claims from its constitution. In 2001, fighting along the Kosovo border spilled over into northwestern Macedonia. It was attributed to nationalists who want to create a Greater Albania, including part of Macedonia.

The World Bank describes Macedonia as a "lower-middle-income" developing country. Manufactures dominate the country's exports, Macedonia mines coal, but imports all its oil and natural gas. The country is self-sufficient in its basic food needs.

AREA 9,927 SQ MI [25,710 SQ KM] **POPULATION** 2,157,000
CAPITAL (POPULATION) SKOPJE (541,000) **GOVERNMENT** MULTIPARTY REPUBLIC **ETHNIC GROUPS** MACEDONIAN 65%, ALBANIAN 21%, TURKISH 5%, ROMANIAN 3%, SERB 2% **LANGUAGES** MACEDONIAN (OFFICIAL), ALBANIAN **RELIGIONS** CHRISTIANITY (MAINLY EASTERN ORTHODOX, WITH MACEDONIAN ORTHODOX AND ROMAN CATHOLIC COMMUNITIES), ISLAM
CURRENCY DINAR = 100 PARAS

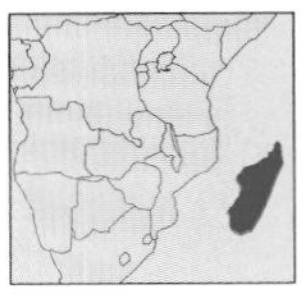

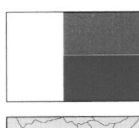

MADAGASCAR

GEOGRAPHY The Democratic Republic of Madagascar, in southeastern Africa, is an island nation, which has a larger area than France. Behind the narrow coastal plains in the east lies a highland zone, mostly between 2,000 ft and 4,000 ft [610 m to 1,220 m] above sea level. Broad plains border the Mozambique Channel in the west.

Temperatures in the highlands are moderated by the altitude. The winters (from April to September) are dry, but heavy rains occur in summer. The eastern coastlands are warm and humid. The west is drier and the south and southwest are hot and dry.

POLITICS & ECONOMY People from Southeast Asia began to settle on Madagascar around 2,000 years ago. Subsequent influxes from Africa and Arabia added to the island's diverse heritage, culture and language.

French troops defeated a Malagasy army in 1895 and Madagascar became a French colony. In 1960, it achieved full independence as the Malagasy Republic. In 1972, army officers seized control and, in 1975, under the leadership of Lt-Commander Didier Ratsiraka, the country was renamed Madagascar. Parliamentary elections were held in 1977, but Ratsiraka remained president of a one-party socialist state. The government resigned in 1991 following huge demonstrations. In 1992–3, Ratsiraka was defeated by opposition leader, Albert Zafy. But Ratsiraka returned to power following presidential elections in 1997.

Madagascar is one of the world's poorest countries. The land has been badly eroded because of the cutting down of the forests and overgrazing of the grasslands. Farming, fishing and forestry employ about 80% of the people. The country's food crops include bananas, cassava, rice and sweet potatoes. Coffee is the leading export.

AREA 226,656 SQ MI [587,040 SQ KM] **POPULATION** 16,627,000
CAPITAL (POPULATION) ANTANANARIVO (1,053,000)
GOVERNMENT REPUBLIC **ETHNIC GROUPS** MERINA 27%, BETSIMISARAKA 15%, BETSILEO 11%, TSIMIHETY 7%, SAKALAVA 6%
LANGUAGES MALAGASY, FRENCH (BOTH OFFICIAL)
RELIGIONS CHRISTIANITY 51%, TRADITIONAL BELIEFS 47%, ISLAM 2% **CURRENCY** MALAGASY FRANC = 100 CENTIMES

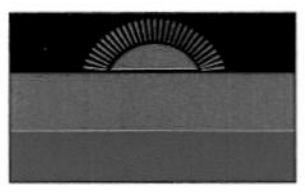
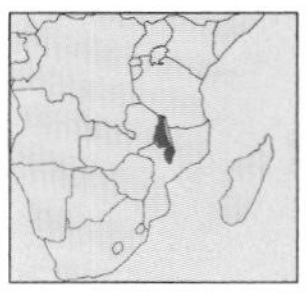

MALAWI

GEOGRAPHY The Republic of Malawi includes part of Lake Malawi, which is drained by the River Shire, a tributary of the River Zambezi. The land is mostly mountainous. The highest peak, Mulanje, reaches 9,843 ft [3,000 m] in the southeast.

While the low-lying areas of Malawi are hot and humid all year round, the uplands have a pleasant climate. Lilongwe, at about 3,609 ft [1,100 m] above sea level, has a warm and sunny climate. Frosts sometimes occur in July and August, in the middle of the long dry season.

POLITICS & ECONOMY Malawi, then called Nyasaland, became a British protectorate in 1891. In 1953, Britain established the Federation of Rhodesia and Nyasaland, which also included what are now Zambia and Zimbabwe. Black African opposition, led in Nyasaland by Dr Hastings Kamuzu Banda, led to the dissolution of the federation in 1963. In 1964, Nyasaland became independent as Malawi, with Banda as prime minister. Banda became president when the country became a republic in 1966 and, in 1971, he was made president for life. Banda ruled autocratically through the only party, the Malawi Congress Party. A multiparty system was restored in 1993. Banda and his party were defeated in elections in 1993. Bakili Muluzi became president and was re-elected in 1999. Banda died in 1997.

Malawi is one of the world's poorest countries. More than 80% of the people are farmers, but many grow little more than they need to feed their families.

AREA 45,745 SQ MI [118,480 SQ KM] **POPULATION** 12,458,000
CAPITAL (POPULATION) LILONGWE (395,000)
GOVERNMENT MULTIPARTY REPUBLIC **ETHNIC GROUPS** MARAVI (CHEWA, NYANJA, TONGA, TUMBUKA) 58%, LOMWE 18%, YAO 13%, NGONI 7% **LANGUAGES** CHICHEWA AND ENGLISH (BOTH OFFICIAL) **RELIGIONS** CHRISTIANITY (PROTESTANT 34%, ROMAN CATHOLIC 28%), TRADITIONAL BELIEFS 21%, ISLAM 16%
CURRENCY KWACHA = 100 TAMBALA

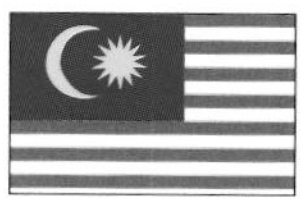
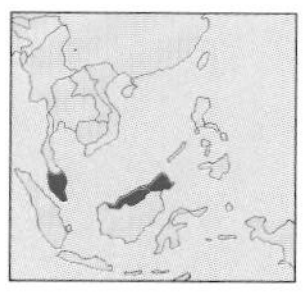

MALAYSIA

GEOGRAPHY The Federation of Malaysia consists of two main parts. Peninsular Malaysia, which is joined to mainland Asia, contains about 80% of the population. The other main regions, Sabah and Sarawak, are in northern Borneo, an island which Malaysia shares with Indonesia. Much of the land is mountainous, with coastal lowlands bordering the rugged interior. The highest peak, Kinabalu, reaches 13,455 ft [4,101 m] in Sabah.

Malaysia has a hot equatorial climate. The temperatures are high all through the year, though the mountains are much cooler than the lowland areas. The rainfall is heavy throughout the year.

POLITICS & ECONOMY Japan occupied what is now Malaysia during World War II, but British rule was re-established in 1945. In the 1940s and 1950s, British troops fought a war against Communist guerrillas, but Peninsular Malaysia (then called Malaya) became independent in 1957. Malaysia was created in 1963, when Malaya, Singapore, Sabah and Sarawak agreed to unite, but Singapore withdrew in 1965.

From the 1970s, Malaysia achieved rapid economic progress and, by the mid-1990s, it was playing a major part in regional affairs, especially through its membership of ASEAN (Association of Southeast Asian Nations). However, together with several other countries in eastern Asia, Malaysia was hit by economic recession in 1997, including a major fall in stock market values. In response to the crisis, the government ordered the repatriation of many temporary foreign workers and initiated a series of austerity measures aimed at restoring confidence and avoiding the chronic debt problems affecting some other Asian countries.

The World Bank classifies Malaysia as an "upper-middle-income" developing country. Malaysia is a leading producer of palm oil, rubber and tin.

Manufacturing now plays a major part in the economy. Manufactures are diverse, including cars, chemicals, a wide range of electronic goods, plastics, textiles, rubber and wood products.

AREA 127,316 SQ MI [329,750 SQ KM] **POPULATION** 21,983,000
CAPITAL (POPULATION) KUALA LUMPUR (1,145,000)
GOVERNMENT FEDERAL CONSTITUTIONAL MONARCHY
ETHNIC GROUPS MALAY AND OTHER INDIGENOUS GROUPS 62%, CHINESE 30%, INDIAN 8% **LANGUAGES** MALAY (OFFICIAL), CHINESE, IBAN **RELIGIONS** ISLAM 53%, BUDDHISM 17%, CHINESE FOLK RELIGIONIST 12%, HINDUISM 7%, CHRISTIANITY 6%
CURRENCY RINGGIT (MALAYSIAN DOLLAR) = 100 CENTS

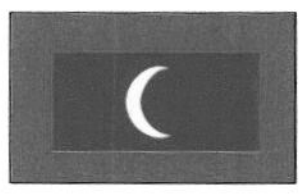
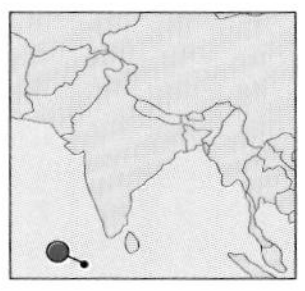

MALDIVES

The Republic of the Maldives consists of about 1,200 low-lying coral islands, south of India. The highest point is 79 ft [24 m], but most of the land is only 6 ft [1.8 m] above sea level. The islands became a British territory in 1887 and independence was achieved in 1965. Tourism and fishing are the main industries.

AREA 115 SQ MI [298 SQ KM] **POPULATION** 283,000 **CAPITAL** MALÉ

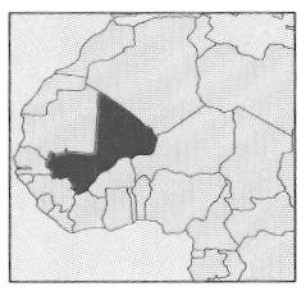

MALI

GEOGRAPHY The Republic of Mali is a landlocked country in northern Africa. The land is generally flat, with the highest land in the Adrar des Iforhas on the border with Algeria.

Northern Mali is part of the Sahara, with a hot, practically rainless climate. But the south has enough rain for farming.

POLITICS & ECONOMY France ruled the area, then known as French Sudan, from 1893 until the country became independent as Mali in 1960.

The first socialist government was overthrown in 1968 by an army group led by Moussa Traoré, but he was ousted in 1991. Multiparty democracy was restored in 1992 and Alpha Oumar Konaré was elected president. The new government agreed a pact providing for a special administration for the Tuareg minority in the north.

Mali is one of the world's poorest countries and 70% of the land is desert or semidesert. Only about 2% of the land is used for growing crops, while 25% is used for grazing animals. Despite this, agriculture employs more than 80% of the people, many of whom still subsist by nomadic livestock rearing.

AREA 478,837 SQ MI [1,240,190 SQ KM] **POPULATION** 12,685,000
CAPITAL (POPULATION) BAMAKO (800,000) **GOVERNMENT** MULTIPARTY REPUBLIC **ETHNIC GROUPS** BAMBARA 32%, FULANI (OR PEUL) 14%, SENUFO 12%, SONINKE 9%, TUAREG 7%, SONGHAI 7%, MALINKE (MANDINGO OR MANDINKE) 7% **LANGUAGES** FRENCH (OFFICIAL), VOLTAIC LANGUAGES
RELIGIONS ISLAM 90%, TRADITIONAL BELIEFS 9%, CHRISTIANITY 1%
CURRENCY CFA FRANC = 100 CENTIMES

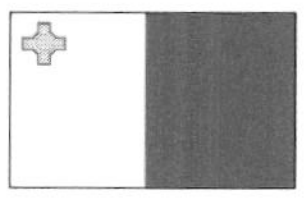
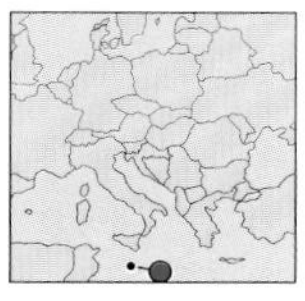

MALTA

GEOGRAPHY The Republic of Malta consists of two main islands, Malta and Gozo, a third, much smaller island called Comino lying between the two large islands, and two tiny islets.

Malta's climate is typically Mediterranean, with hot and dry summers and mild and wet winters. The sirocco, a hot wind that blows from North Africa, may raise temperatures considerably during the spring.

POLITICS & ECONOMY During World War I (1914–18) Malta was an important naval base. In World War II (1939–45), Italian and German aircraft bombed the islands. In recognition of the bravery of the Maltese, the British King George VI awarded the George Cross to Malta in 1942. In 1953, Malta became a base for NATO (North Atlantic Treaty Organization). Malta became independent in 1964, and in 1974 it became a republic. In 1979, Britain's military agreement with Malta expired, and Malta ceased to be a military base when all the British forces withdrew. In the 1980s, the people declared Malta a neutral country. In the 1990s, Malta applied to join the European Union. The application was scrapped when the Labor Party won the elections in 1996, but, following the Labor Party's defeat in elections in 1998, the situation changed yet again.

The World Bank classifies Malta as an "upper-middle-income" developing country. It lacks natural resources, and most people work in the former naval dockyards, which are now used for commercial shipbuilding and repair, in manufacturing industries and in the tourist industry.

Manufactures include chemicals, processed food and chemicals. Farming is difficult, because of the rocky soils. Crops include barley, fruits, potatoes and wheat. Malta also has a small fishing industry.

AREA 122 SQ MI [316 SQ KM] **POPULATION** 366,000
CAPITAL (POPULATION) VALLETTA (102,000)
GOVERNMENT MULTIPARTY REPUBLIC **ETHNIC GROUPS** MALTESE 96%, BRITISH 2% **LANGUAGES** MALTESE AND ENGLISH (BOTH OFFICIAL)
RELIGIONS CHRISTIANITY (ROMAN CATHOLIC 99%)
CURRENCY MALTESE LIRA = 100 CENTS

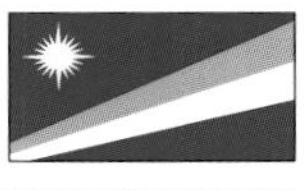
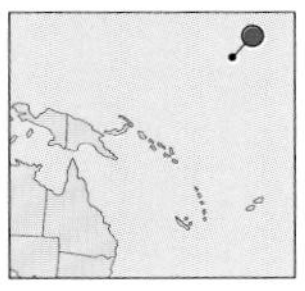

MARSHALL ISLANDS

The Republic of the Marshall Islands, a former US territory, became fully independent in 1991. This island nation, lying north of Kiribati in a region known as Micronesia, is heavily dependent on US aid. The main activities are agriculture and tourism.

AREA 70 SQ MI [181 SQ KM] **POPULATION** 70,000
CAPITAL DALAP-ULIGA-DARRIT, ON MAJURO ISLAND

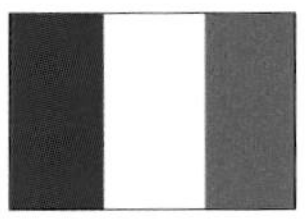
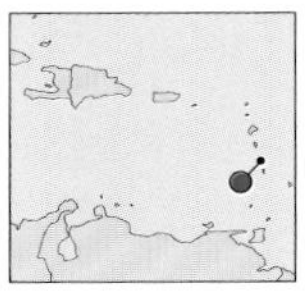

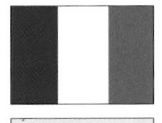

MARTINIQUE

Martinique, a volcanic island nation in the Caribbean, was colonized by France in 1635. It became a French overseas department in 1946. Tourism and agriculture are major activities. About 70% of Martinique's Gross Domestic Product is provided by the French government, allowing for a good standard of living.

AREA 425 SQ MI [1,100 SQ KM]
POPULATION 362,000 **CAPITAL** FORT-DE-FRANCE

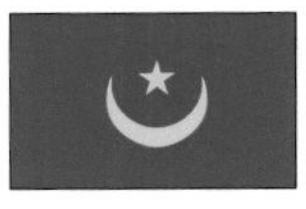
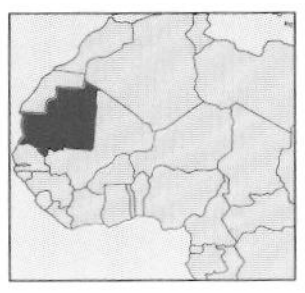

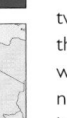

MAURITANIA

GEOGRAPHY The Islamic Republic of Mauritania in northwestern Africa is nearly twice the size of France. But France has more than 28 times as many people. Part of the world's largest desert, the Sahara, covers northern Mauritania and most Mauritanians live in the southwest.

The amount of rainfall and the length of the rainy season increase from north to south. Much of the land is desert, with dry northeast and easterly winds throughout the year. But southwesterly winds bring summer rain to the south.

POLITICS & ECONOMY Originally part of the great African empires of Ghana and Mali, France set up a protectorate in Mauritania in 1903, attempting to exploit the trade in gum arabic. The country became a territory of French West Africa and a French colony in 1920. French West Africa was a huge territory, which included present-day Benin, Burkina Faso, Guinea, Ivory Coast, Mali, Niger and Senegal, as well as Mauritania. In 1958, Mauritania became a self-governing territory in the French Union and it became fully independent in 1960.

In 1976, Spain withdrew from Spanish (now Western) Sahara, a territory bordering Mauritania to the north. Morocco occupied the northern two-thirds of this territory, while Mauritania took the rest. But Saharan guerrillas belonging to POLISARIO (the Popular Front for the Liberation of Saharan Territories) began an armed struggle for independence. In 1979, Mauritania withdrew from the southern part of Western Sahara, which was then occupied by Morocco. In 1991, the country adopted a new constitution when the people voted to create a multiparty government. Multiparty elections were held in 1992 and 1996–7.

The World Bank classifies Mauritania as a "low-income" developing country. Agriculture employs 40% of the people. Some are herders who move around with herds of cattle and sheep, though recent droughts forced many farmers to seek aid in the cities.

AREA 397,953 SQ MI [1,030,700 SQ KM] **POPULATION** 2,702,000
CAPITAL (POPULATION) NOUAKCHOTT (735,000)
GOVERNMENT MULTIPARTY ISLAMIC REPUBLIC
ETHNIC GROUPS MOOR (ARAB-BERBER) 70%, WOLOF 7%, TUKULOR 5%, SONINKE 3%, FULANI 1% **LANGUAGES** ARABIC (OFFICIAL), WOLOF, FRENCH **RELIGIONS** ISLAM 99%
CURRENCY OUGUIYA = 5 KHOUMS

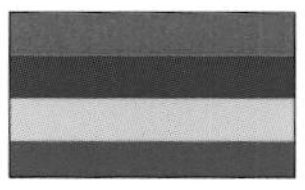
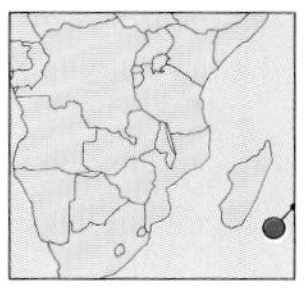

MAURITIUS

The Republic of Mauritius, an Indian Ocean nation lying east of Madagascar, was previously ruled by France and Britain until it achieved independence in 1968. It became a republic in 1992. Sugar production is in decline but tourism is vital to the economy.

AREA 718 SQ MI [1,860 SQ KM]
POPULATION 1,201,000 **CAPITAL** PORT LOUIS

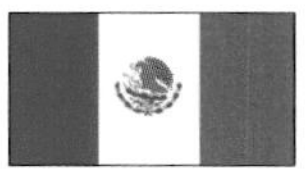
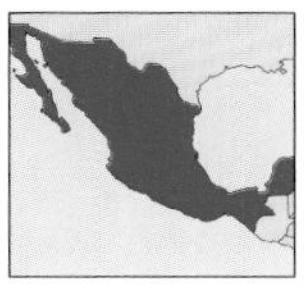

MEXICO

GEOGRAPHY The United Mexican States, as Mexico is officially named, is the world's most populous Spanish-speaking country. Much of the land is mountainous, although most people live on the central plateau. Mexico contains two large peninsulas, Lower (or Baja) California in the northwest and the flat Yucatán peninsula in the southeast.

The climate varies according to the altitude. The resort of Acapulco on the southwest coast has a dry and sunny climate. Mexico City, at about 7,546 ft [2,300 m] above sea level, is much cooler. Most rain occurs between June and September. The rainfall decreases north of Mexico City and northern Mexico is mainly arid.

POLITICS & ECONOMY In the mid-19th century, Mexico lost land to the United States, and between 1910 and 1921 violent revolutions created chaos.

Reforms were introduced in the 1920s and, in 1929, the Institutional Revolutionary Party (PRI) was formed. The PRI ruled Mexico effectively as a one-party state until it was finally defeated in 2001. The new president, Vicente Fox, faced many problems, including unemployment and rapid urbanization especially around Mexico City, demands for indigenous rights by Amerindian groups, and illegal emigration to the United States.

The World Bank classifies Mexico as an "upper-middle-income" developing country. Agriculture is important. Food crops include beans, maize, rice and wheat, while cash crops include coffee, cotton, fruits and vegetables. Beef cattle, dairy cattle and other livestock are raised and fishing is also important.

But oil and oil products are the chief exports, while manufacturing is the most valuable activity. Mexico is the world's leading silver producer, and it also mines copper, gold, lead, zinc and other minerals. Many factories near the northern border assemble goods, such as car parts and electrical products, for US companies. These factories are called *maquiladoras*. Hope for the future lies in increasing economic cooperation with the USA and Canada

through NAFTA (North American Free Trade Association), which came into being on January 1, 1994.

AREA 756,061 sq mi [1,958,200 sq km] **POPULATION** 107,233,000
CAPITAL (POPULATION) Mexico City (15,048,000)
GOVERNMENT Federal republic
ETHNIC GROUPS Mestizo 60%, Amerindian 30%, European 9% **LANGUAGES** Spanish (official)
RELIGIONS Christianity (Roman Catholic 90%, Protestant 5%) **CURRENCY** New peso = 100 centavos

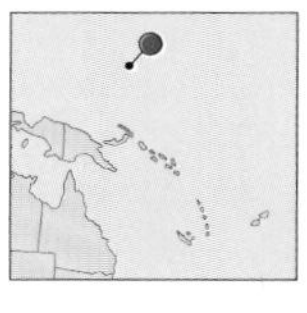

MICRONESIA

The Federated States of Micronesia, a former US territory covering a vast area in the western Pacific Ocean, became fully independent in 1991. The main export is copra. Fishing and tourism are also important.

AREA 272 sq mi [705 sq km]
POPULATION 110,000 **CAPITAL** Palikir

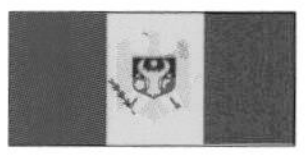
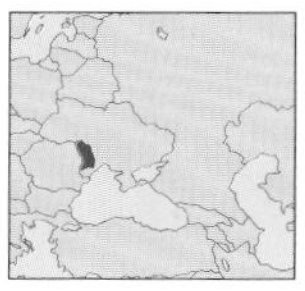

MOLDOVA

GEOGRAPHY The Republic of Moldova is a small country sandwiched between Ukraine and Romania. It was formerly one of the 15 republics that made up the Soviet Union. Much of the land is hilly and the highest areas are near the center of the country.

Moldova has a moderately continental climate, with warm summers and fairly cold winters when temperatures dip below freezing point. Most of the rain comes in the warmer months.

POLITICS & ECONOMY In the 14th century, the Moldavians formed a state called Moldavia. It included part of Romania and Bessarabia (now the modern country of Moldova). The Ottoman Turks took the area in the 16th century, but in 1812 Russia took over Bessarabia. In 1861, Moldavia and Walachia united to form Romania. Russia retook southern Bessarabia in 1878.

After World War I (1914–18), all of Bessarabia was returned to Romania, but the Soviet Union did not recognize this act. From 1944, the Moldovan Soviet Socialist Republic was part of the Soviet Union.

In 1989, the Moldovans asserted their independence and ethnicity by making Romanian the official language and, at the end of 1991, Moldova became an independent country. In 1992, fighting occurred between Moldovans and Russians in Trans-Dniester, a mainly Russian-speaking area east of the River Dniester. The first multiparty elections were held in 1994, when a proposal to unite with Romania was rejected. Economic problems made the government unpopular and, in 2001, Moldova became the first former Soviet state to return the Communist party to power in a general election.

Moldova is a fertile country in which agriculture remains central to the economy. Major products include fruits, maize, tobacco and wine. Moldova has few natural resources and the country imports materials and fuels for its industries. Light industries, such as food processing and the manufacturing of household appliances, are gradually expanding.

AREA 13,010 sq mi [33,700 sq km] **POPULATION** 4,707,000
CAPITAL (POPULATION) Chişinău (700,000)
GOVERNMENT Multiparty republic
ETHNIC GROUPS Moldovan 65%, Ukrainian 14%, Russian 13%, Gagauz 4%, Jewish 2%, Bulgarian
LANGUAGES Moldovan/Romanian (official)
RELIGIONS Christianity (Eastern Orthodox)
CURRENCY Leu = 100 bani

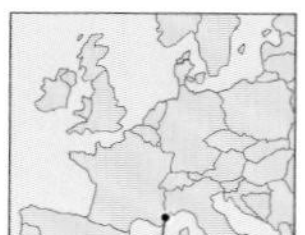
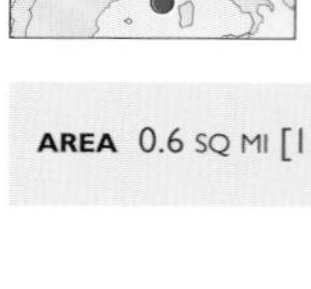

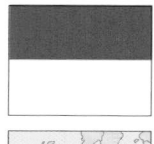

MONACO

The tiny Principality of Monaco consists of a narrow strip of coastline and a rocky peninsula on the French Riviera. Its considerable wealth is derived largely from banking, finance, gambling and tourism. Monaco's citizens do not pay any state tax. Its attractions include the Monte Carlo casino and such sporting events as the Monte Carlo Rally and the Monaco Grand Prix.

AREA 0.6 sq mi [1.5 sq km] **POPULATION** 30,000 **CAPITAL** Monaco

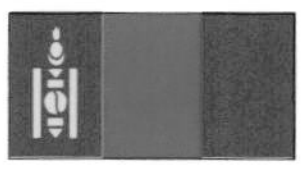
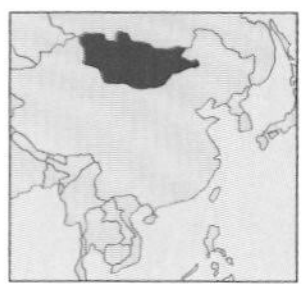

MONGOLIA

GEOGRAPHY The State of Mongolia is the world's largest landlocked country. It consists mainly of high plateaux, with the Gobi Desert in the southeast.

Ulan Bator lies on the northern edge of a desert plateau. It has bitterly cold winters. Summer temperatures are moderated by the altitude.

POLITICS & ECONOMY In the 13th century, Genghis Khan united the Mongolian peoples and built up a great empire. Under his grandson, Kublai Khan, the Mongol empire extended from Korea and China to eastern Europe and present-day Iraq.

The Mongol empire broke up in the late 14th century. In the early 17th century, Inner Mongolia came under Chinese control, and by the late 17th century Outer Mongolia had become a Chinese province. In 1911, the Mongolians drove the Chinese out of Outer Mongolia and made the area a Buddhist kingdom. But in 1924, under Russian influence, the Communist Mongolian People's Republic was set up. From the 1950s, Mongolia supported the Soviet Union in its disputes with China. In 1990, the people demonstrated for more freedom, and free elections in June 1990 resulted in victory for the Mongolian People's Revolutionary Party, which was composed of Communists. Communist rule ended in 1996, when the Democratic Union coalition won power. But the Communists regained power in 2000, though they were expected to continue free-market policies.

The World Bank classifies Mongolia as a "lower-middle-income" developing country. Most people were once nomads, who moved around with their herds of sheep, cattle, goats and horses. Under Communist rule, most people were moved into permanent homes on government-owned farms. But livestock and animal products remain leading exports. The Communists also developed industry, especially the mining of coal, copper, gold, molybdenum, tin and tungsten, and manufacturing. Minerals and fuels now account for around half of Mongolia's exports.

AREA 604,826 sq mi [1,566,500 sq km] **POPULATION** 2,847,000
CAPITAL (POPULATION) Ulan Bator (627,000)
GOVERNMENT Multiparty republic **ETHNIC GROUPS** Khalkha Mongol 79%, Kazak 6% **LANGUAGES** Khalkha Mongolian (official), Kazak
RELIGIONS Tibetan Buddhist (Lamaist)
CURRENCY Tugrik = 100 möngös

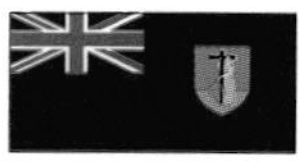
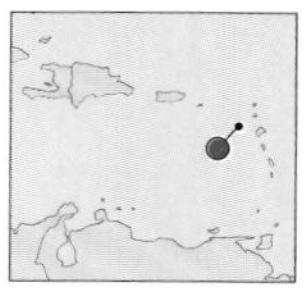

MONTSERRAT

Monserrat is a British overseas territory in the Caribbean Sea. The climate is tropical and hurricanes often cause much damage. Intermittent eruptions of the Soufrière Hills volcano between 1995 and 1998 led to the emigration of many of the inhabitants and the virtual destruction of Plymouth, the capital, in the southern part of the island.

AREA 39 sq mi [1,100 sq km] **POPULATION** (prior to the volcanic activity) 13,000 **CAPITAL** Plymouth

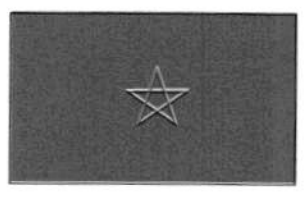
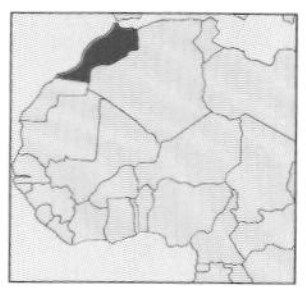

MOROCCO

GEOGRAPHY The Kingdom of Morocco lies in northwestern Africa. Its name comes from the Arabic Maghreb-el-Aksa, meaning "the farthest west." Behind the western coastal plain the land rises to a broad plateau and ranges of the Atlas Mountains. The High (Haut) Atlas contains the highest peak, Djebel Toubkal, at 13,665 ft [4,165 m]. East of the mountains, the land descends to the arid Sahara.

The Atlantic coast of Morocco is cooled by the Canaries Current. Inland, summers are hot and dry. The winters are mild. In winter, between October and April, southwesterly winds from the Atlantic Ocean bring moderate rainfall, and snow often falls on the High Atlas Mountains.

POLITICS & ECONOMY The original people of Morocco were the Berbers. But in the 680s, Arab invaders introduced Islam and the Arabic language. By the early 20th century, France and Spain controlled Morocco, which became an independent kingdom in 1956. Although Morocco is a constitutional monarchy, King Hassan II ruled the country in a generally authoritarian way since his accession to the throne in 1961 to his death in 1999. His son and successor Mohamed VI faced several problems, including the future of Western Sahara which Hassan II had vigorously claimed for Morocco.

Morocco is classified as a "lower-middle-income" developing country. It is the world's third largest producer of phosphate rock, which is used to make fertilizer. One of the reasons why Morocco wants to keep Western Sahara is that it, too, has large phosphate reserves. Farming employs 44% of Moroccans. Chief crops include barley, beans, citrus fruits, maize, olives, sugar beet and wheat. Processed phosphates are exported, but most of Morocco's manufactures are for home consumption. Fishing and tourism are also important.

AREA 172,413 sq mi [446,550 sq km] **POPULATION** 31,559,000
CAPITAL (POPULATION) Rabat (1,344,000)
GOVERNMENT Constitutional monarchy **ETHNIC GROUPS** Arab 70%, Berber 30% **LANGUAGES** Arabic (official), Berber, French
RELIGIONS Islam 99%, Christianity 1%
CURRENCY Moroccan dirham = 100 centimes

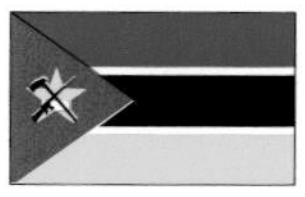
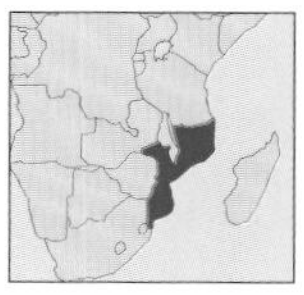

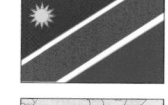

MOZAMBIQUE

GEOGRAPHY The Republic of Mozambique borders the Indian Ocean in southeastern Africa. The coastal plains are narrow in the north but broaden in the south. Inland lie plateaux and hills, which make up another two-fifths of Mozambique.

Mozambique has a mostly tropical climate. The capital Maputo, which lies outside the tropics, has hot and humid summers, though the winters are mild and fairly dry.

POLITICS & ECONOMY In 1885, when the European powers divided Africa, Mozambique was recognized as a Portuguese colony. But black African opposition to European rule gradually increased. In 1961, the Front for the Liberation of Mozambique (FRELIMO) was founded to oppose Portuguese rule. In 1964, FRELIMO launched a guerrilla war, which continued for ten years. Mozambique became independent in 1975.

After independence, Mozambique became a one-party state. Its government aided African nationalists in Rhodesia (now Zimbabwe) and South Africa. But the white governments of these countries helped an opposition group, the Mozambique National Resistance Movement (RENAMO) to lead an armed struggle against Mozambique's government. Civil war, combined with droughts, caused much suffering in the 1980s. In 1989, FRELIMO declared that it had dropped its Communist policies and ended one-party rule. The war ended in 1992 and multiparty elections in 1994 heralded more stable conditions. In 1995 Mozambique became the 53rd member of the Commonwealth.

In the early 1990s, the UN rated Mozambique as one of the world's poorest countries. The second half of the 1990s saw a surge in economic growth, but huge floods in 2000 and 2001 proved to be a major setback. About 80% of the people are poor and agriculture is the main activity. Crops include cassava, cotton, maize, rice and tea.

AREA 309,494 sq mi [801,590 sq km] **POPULATION** 20,493,000
CAPITAL (POPULATION) Maputo (2,000,000)
GOVERNMENT Multiparty republic **ETHNIC GROUPS** Makua 47%, Tsonga 23%, Malawi 12%, Shona 11%, Yao 4%, Swahili 1%, Makonde 1% **LANGUAGES** Portuguese (official), many others
RELIGIONS Traditional beliefs 48%, Christianity (Roman Catholic 31%, others 9%), Islam 13% **CURRENCY** Metical = 100 centavos

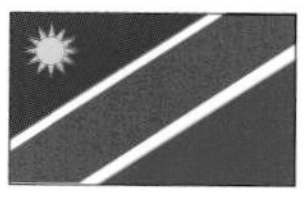
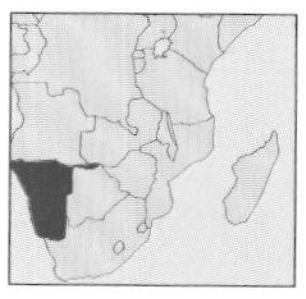

NAMIBIA

GEOGRAPHY The Republic of Namibia was formerly ruled by South Africa, which called it South West Africa. The country became independent in 1990. The coastal region contains the arid Namib Desert, which is virtually uninhabited. Inland is a central plateau, bordered by a rugged spine of mountains stretching north–south. Eastern Namibia contains part of the Kalahari Desert, a semidesert area which extends into Botswana.

Namibia is a warm and arid country. Lying at 5,500 ft [1,700 m] above sea level, Windhoek has an average annual rainfall of about 15 in [370 mm], often occurring during thunderstorms in the hot summer months.

POLITICS & ECONOMY During World War I, South African troops defeated the Germans who ruled what is now Namibia. After World War II, many people challenged South Africa's right to govern the territory and a civil war began in the 1960s between African guerrillas and South African troops. A cease-fire was agreed in 1989 and Namibia became independent in 1990. In the 1990s, the government pursued a policy of "national reconciliation." An enclave on the coast, called Walvis Bay (Walvisbaai), remained part of South Africa until 1994, when it was transferred to Namibia. In 1999, a secessionist group staged an unsuccessful uprising in the Caprivi Strip.

Namibia is rich in mineral reserves, including diamonds, uranium, zinc and copper. Minerals make up 90% of the exports. But farming employs about two out of every five Namibians. Sea fishing is also important, though overfishing has reduced the yields of the country's fishing fleet. The country has few industries, but tourism is increasing.

AREA 318,434 sq mi [825,414 sq km], including Walvis Bay, a former South African territory **POPULATION** 2,437,000
CAPITAL (POPULATION) Windhoek (126,000)
GOVERNMENT Multiparty republic **ETHNIC GROUPS** Ovambo 50%, Kavango 9%, Herero 7%, Damara 7%, White 6%, Nama 5%
LANGUAGES English (official), Ovambo **RELIGIONS** Christianity 90% (Lutheran 51%) **CURRENCY** Namibian dollar = 100 cents

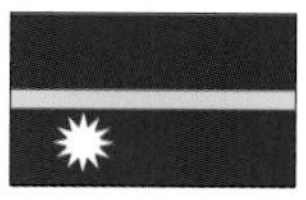
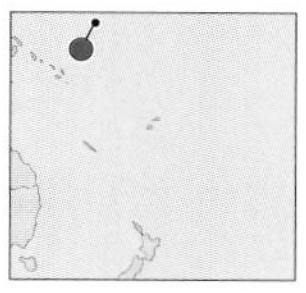

NAURU

Nauru is the world's smallest republic, located in the western Pacific Ocean, close to the equator. Independent since 1968, Nauru's prosperity is based on phosphate mining, but the reserves are running out.

AREA 8 sq mi [21 sq km] **POPULATION** 10,000
CAPITAL Yaren

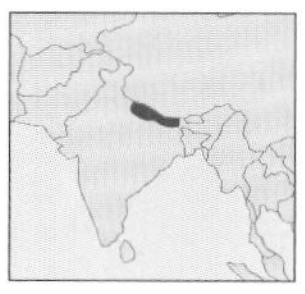

NEPAL

GEOGRAPHY Over three-quarters of Nepal lies in the Himalayan mountain heartland, culminating in the world's highest peak (Mount Everest, or Chomolongma in Nepali) at 29,035 ft [8,850 m].

As a result, there is a wide range of climatic conditions from tropical forest to the permanently glaciated landscape of the high Himalaya.

POLITICS & ECONOMY Nepal was united in the late 18th century, although its complex topography has ensured that it remains a diverse patchwork of peoples. From the mid-19th century to 1951, power was held by the royal Rana family. Attempts to introduce a democratic system in the 1950s failed. The first democratic elections in 32 years were held in 1991, but, by the early 21st century, Nepal faced many problems, including the activities of Maoist guerrillas, corruption and increasing crime.

Agriculture remains the chief activity in this overwhelmingly rural country and the government is heavily dependent on aid. Tourism, centered around the high Himalaya, grows in importance each year, although Nepal was closed to foreigners until 1951. There are also ambitious plans to exploit the hydroelectric potential offered by the ferocious Himalayan rivers.

AREA 54,363 sq mi [140,800 sq km] **POPULATION** 24,084,000
CAPITAL (POPULATION) Katmandu (535,000)
GOVERNMENT Constitutional monarchy **ETHNIC GROUPS** Nepalese 53%, Bihari 18%, Tharu 5%, Tamang 5%, Newar 3%
LANGUAGES Nepali (official), local languages
RELIGIONS Hindu 86%, Buddhist 8%, Muslim 4%
CURRENCY Nepalese rupee = 100 paisa

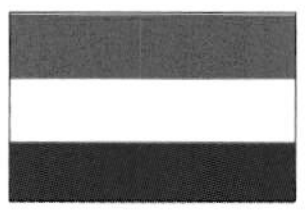
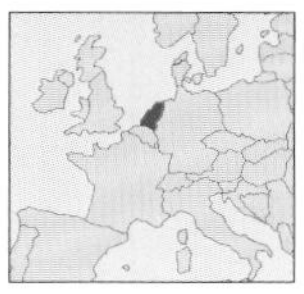

NETHERLANDS

GEOGRAPHY The Netherlands lies at the western end of the North European Plain, which extends to the Ural Mountains in Russia. Except for the far southeastern corner, the Netherlands is flat and about 40% lies below sea level at high tide. To prevent flooding, the Dutch have built dykes (sea walls) to hold back the waves. Large areas which were once under the sea, but which have been reclaimed, are called polders.

Because of its position on the North Sea, the Netherlands has a temperate climate. The winters are mild, with rain coming from the Atlantic depressions which pass over the country. North Sea storms often batter the coasts.

POLITICS & ECONOMY Before the 16th century, the area that is now the Netherlands was under a succession of foreign rulers, including the Romans, the Germanic Franks, the French and the Spanish. The Dutch declared their independence from Spain in 1581 and their status was finally recognized by Spain in 1648. In the 17th century, the Dutch built up a great overseas empire, especially in Southeast Asia. But in the early 18th century, the Dutch lost control of the seas to England.

France controlled the Netherlands from 1795 to 1813. In 1815, the Netherlands, then containing Belgium and Luxembourg, became an independent kingdom. Belgium broke away in 1830 and Luxembourg followed in 1890.

The Netherlands was neutral in World War I (1914–18), but was occupied by Germany in World War II (1939–45). After the war, the Netherlands Indies became independent as Indonesia. The Netherlands became active in West European affairs. With Belgium and Luxembourg, it formed a customs union called Benelux in 1948. In 1949, it joined NATO (the North Atlantic Treaty Organization), and the European Coal and Steel Community (ECSC) in 1953. In 1957, it became a founder member of the European Economic Community (now the European Union), and its economy prospered. On January 1, 1999, the Netherlands became one of the 11 countries in the European Union to adopt the euro, the EU's single currency.

The Netherlands is a highly industrialized country and industry and commerce are the most valuable activities. Its resources include natural gas, some oil, salt and china clay. But the Netherlands imports many of the materials needed by its industries and it is, therefore, a major trading country. Industrial products are wide-ranging, including aircraft, chemicals, electronic equipment, machinery, textiles and vehicles. Agriculture employs only 5% of the people, but scientific methods are used and yields are high. Dairy farming is the leading farming activity. Major products include barley, flowers and bulbs, potatoes, sugar beet and wheat.

AREA 16,033 sq mi [41,526 sq km] **POPULATION** 15,829,000
CAPITAL (POPULATION) Amsterdam (1,101,000)
GOVERNMENT Constitutional monarchy
ETHNIC GROUPS Netherlander 95%, Indonesian, Turkish, Moroccan, German **LANGUAGES** Dutch (official), Frisian
RELIGIONS Christianity (Roman Catholic 34%, Dutch Reformed Church 17%, Calvinist 8%), Islam 3%
CURRENCY Euro; Guilder = 100 cents

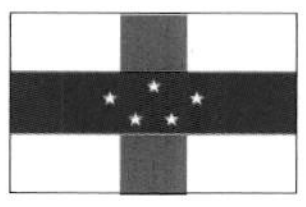
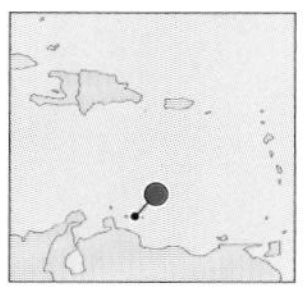

NETHERLANDS ANTILLES

The Netherlands Antilles consists of two different island groups; one off the coast of Venezuela, and the other at the northern end of the Leeward Islands, some 500 mi [800 km] away. They remain a self-governing Dutch territory. The island of Aruba was once part of the territory, but it broke away in 1986. Oil refining and tourism are important activities.

AREA 383 sq mi [993 sq km] **POPULATION** 203,000 **CAPITAL** Willemstad

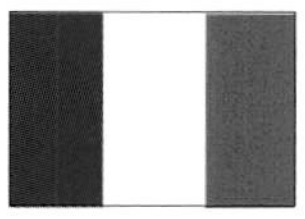
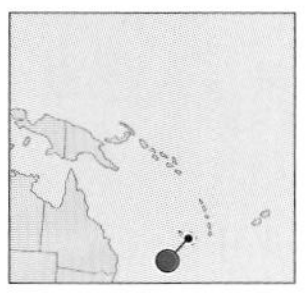

NEW CALEDONIA

New Caledonia is the most southerly of the Melanesian countries in the Pacific. A French possession since 1853 and an Overseas Territory since 1958. In 1998, France announced an agreement with local Melanesians that a vote on independence would be postponed until 2014. The country is rich in mineral resources, especially nickel.

AREA 7,174 sq mi [18,580 sq km] **POPULATION** 195,000 **CAPITAL** Nouméa

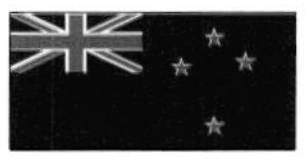
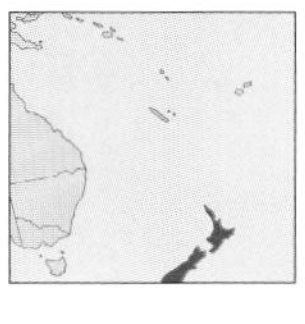

NEW ZEALAND

GEOGRAPHY New Zealand lies about 994 mi [1,600 km] southeast of Australia. It consists of two main islands and several other small ones. Much of North Island is volcanic. Active volcanoes include Ngauruhoe and Ruapehu. Hot springs and geysers are common, and steam from the ground is used to produce electricity. The Southern Alps, which contain the country's highest peak Mount Cook (Aoraki), at 12,313 ft [3,753 m] form the backbone of South Island. The island also has some large, fertile plains.

Auckland in the north has a warm, humid climate throughout the year. Wellington has cooler summers, while in Dunedin, in the southeast, temperatures sometimes dip below freezing in winter. The rainfall is heaviest on the western highlands.

POLITICS & ECONOMY Evidence suggests that early Maori settlers arrived in New Zealand more than 1,000 years ago. The Dutch navigator Abel Tasman reached New Zealand in 1642, but his discovery was not followed up. In 1769, the British Captain James Cook rediscovered the islands. In the early 19th century, British settlers arrived and, in 1840, under the Treaty of Waitangi, Britain took possession of the islands. Clashes occurred with the Maoris in the 1860s but, from the 1870s, the Maoris were gradually integrated into society.

In 1907, New Zealand became a self-governing dominion in the British Commonwealth. The country's economy developed quickly and the people became increasingly prosperous. However, after Britain joined the European Economic Community in 1973, New Zealand's exports to Britain shrank and the country had to reassess its economic and defense strategies and seek new markets. The world economic recession also led the government to cut back on its spending on welfare services in the 1990s. Maori rights and the preservation of Maori culture are other major political issues.

New Zealand's economy has traditionally depended on agriculture, but manufacturing now employs twice as many people as agriculture. Meat and dairy products are the most valuable agricultural products. The country has more than 48 million sheep, 4 million dairy cattle and 5 million beef cattle. Major crops include barley, fruits, potatoes and other vegetables, and wheat. Fishing is also important.

AREA 103,737 sq mi [268,680 sq km] **POPULATION** 3,662,000
CAPITAL (POPULATION) Wellington (329,000)
GOVERNMENT Constitutional monarchy
ETHNIC GROUPS New Zealand European 74%, New Zealand Maori 10%, Polynesian 4% **LANGUAGES** English and Maori (both official) **RELIGIONS** Christianity (Anglican 21%, Presbyterian 16%, Roman Catholic 15%)
CURRENCY New Zealand dollar = 100 cents

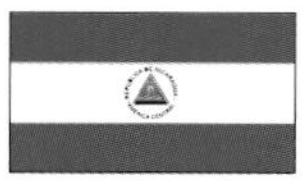
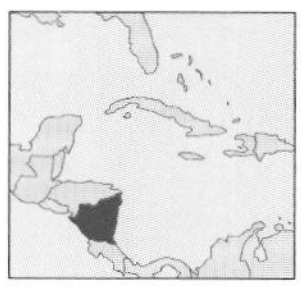

NICARAGUA

GEOGRAPHY The Republic of Nicaragua is a large country in Central America. In the east is a broad plain bordering the Caribbean Sea. The plain is drained by rivers that flow from the Central Highlands. The fertile western Pacific region contains about 40 volcanoes, many of which are active, and earthquakes are common.

Nicaragua has a tropical climate. Managua is hot throughout the year and there is a marked rainy season from May to October. In October 1998, Hurricane Mitch caused great devastation in Nicaragua. The Central Highlands and Caribbean region are cooler and wetter. The wettest region is the humid Caribbean plain.

POLITICS & ECONOMY In 1502, Christopher Columbus claimed the area for Spain, which ruled Nicaragua until 1821. By the early 20th century, the United States had considerable influence in the country and, in 1912, US forces entered Nicaragua to protect US interests. From 1927 to 1933, rebels under General Augusto César Sandino, tried to drive US forces out of the country. In 1933, US marines set up a Nicaraguan army, the National Guard, to help to defeat the rebels. Its leader, Anastasio Somoza Garcia, had Sandino murdered in 1934 and, from 1937, Somoza ruled as a dictator.

In the mid-1970s, many people began to protest against Somoza's rule. Many joined a guerrilla force, called the Sandinista National Liberation Front, named after General Sandino. The rebels defeated the Somoza regime in 1979. In the 1980s, the US-supported forces, called the "Contras," launched a campaign against the Sandinista government. The US government opposed the Sandinista regime, under Daniel José Ortega Saavedra, claiming that it was a Communist dictatorship. A coalition, the National Opposition Union, defeated the Sandinistas in elections in 1990. In 1996, the Sandinistas were again defeated and Arnoldo Alemán, leader of the Liberal Alliance Party, became president.

In the early 1990s, Nicaragua faced many problems in rebuilding its shattered economy. Agriculture is the main activity, employing nearly half of the people. Coffee, cotton, sugar and bananas are grown for export, while rice is the main food crop.

AREA 50,193 sq mi [130,000 sq km] **POPULATION** 5,261,000
CAPITAL (POPULATION) Managua (864,000)
GOVERNMENT Multiparty republic **ETHNIC GROUPS** Mestizo 77%, White 10%, Black 9%, Amerindian 4%
LANGUAGES Spanish (official), Misumalpan
RELIGIONS Christianity (Roman Catholic 91%, others 9%)
CURRENCY Córdoba oro (gold córdoba) = 100 centavos

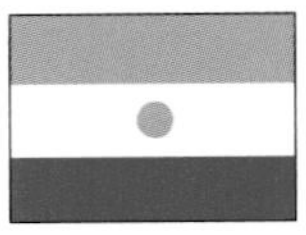
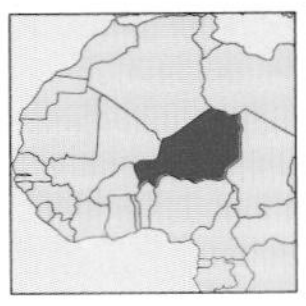

NIGER

GEOGRAPHY The Republic of Niger is a landlocked nation in north-central Africa. The northern plateaux lie in the Sahara Desert, while Central Niger contains the rugged Aïr Mountains. The most fertile, densely populated region is the Niger valley in the southwest.

Niger has a tropical climate and the south has a rainy season between June and September. The north is practically rainless.

POLITICS & ECONOMY Since independence in 1960, Niger, a French territory from 1900, has suffered severe droughts. Food shortages and the collapse of the traditional nomadic way of life of some of Niger's people have caused political instability. After a period of military rule, a multiparty constitution was adopted in 1992, but the military again seized power in 1996. Later that year, the coup leader, Col. Ibrahim Barre Mainassara, was elected president. He was assassinated in 1999, but parliamentary rule was rapidly restored and Tandja Mamadou was elected president in November.

Niger's chief resource is uranium and it is the fourth largest producer in the world. Some tin and tungsten are also mined, although other mineral resources are largely untouched.

Despite its resources, Niger is one of the world's poorest countries. Farming employs 85% of the population, but only 3% of the land can be used for crops and 7% for grazing.

AREA 489,189 sq mi [1,267,000 sq km] **POPULATION** 10,752,000
CAPITAL (POPULATION) Niamey (398,000)
GOVERNMENT Multiparty republic **ETHNIC GROUPS** Hausa 53%, Zerma-Songhai 21%, Tuareg 11%, Fulani (or Peul) 10%
LANGUAGES French (official), Hausa, Songhai
RELIGIONS Islam 98% **CURRENCY** CFA franc = 100 centimes

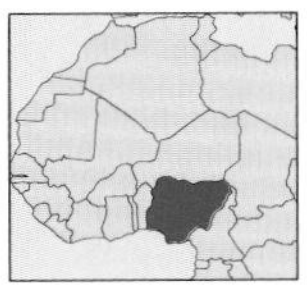

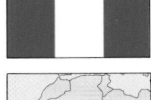

NIGERIA

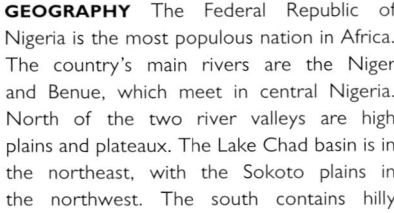

GEOGRAPHY The Federal Republic of Nigeria is the most populous nation in Africa. The country's main rivers are the Niger and Benue, which meet in central Nigeria. North of the two river valleys are high plains and plateaux. The Lake Chad basin is in the northeast, with the Sokoto plains in the northwest. The south contains hilly uplands and coastal plains.

The south has high temperatures and rain throughout the year. The north is drier and often hotter than the south.

POLITICS & ECONOMY Nigeria has a long artistic tradition. Major cultures include the Nok (500 BC to AD 200), the Ife, a major Yoruba culture which developed about 1,000 years ago, and the Benin, which flourished between the 15th and 17th centuries. Britain gradually extended its influence over the area in the second half of the 19th century.

Nigeria became independent in 1960 and a federal republic in 1963. A federal constitution dividing the country into regions was necessary because Nigeria contains more than 250 ethnic and linguistic groups, as well as several religious ones. Local rivalries have long been a threat to national unity, and six new states were created in 1996 in an attempt to overcome this. Civil war occurred between 1967 and 1970, when the people of the southeast attempted unsuccessfully to secede during the Biafran War. Between 1960 and 1998, Nigeria had only nine years of civilian government. However, in 1988–9, Nigeria held elections restoring civilian rule. A former general, Olusegun Obasanjo, was elected president. The new regime faced many problems. In 2000, Muslim–Christian clashes occurred in the north when several states adopted *sharia* (Islamic law).

Nigeria is a developing country with great potential. Its chief natural resource is oil, which accounts for most of its exports. Agriculture employs 43% of the people and the country is a major producer of cocoa, palm oil and palm kernels, groundnuts (peanuts) and rubber. Industry is increasing and manufactures include cement, chemicals, fertilizers, textiles and timber.

AREA 356,668 sq mi [923,770 sq km] **POPULATION** 105,000,000
CAPITAL (POPULATION) Abuja (339,000)
GOVERNMENT Federal multiparty republic
ETHNIC GROUPS Hausa 21%, Yoruba 21%, Ibo (or Igbo) 19%, Fulani 11%, Ibibio 6% **LANGUAGES** English (official), Hausa, Yoruba, Ibo **RELIGIONS** Islam 43%, Christianity 35%, traditional religions 19%, other 3%
CURRENCY Naira = 100 kobo

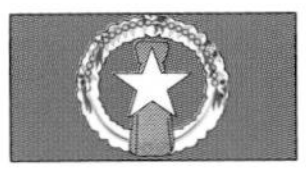
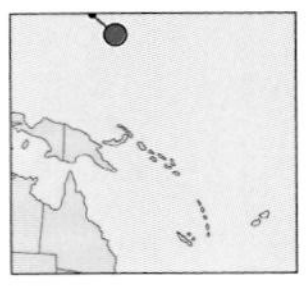

NORTHERN MARIANA ISLANDS

The Commonwealth of the Northern Mariana Islands contains 16 mountainous islands north of Guam in the western Pacific Ocean. In a 1975 plebiscite, the islanders voted for Commonwealth status in union with the USA and, in 1986, they were granted US citizenship.

AREA 184 sq mi [477 sq km] **POPULATION** 50,000 **CAPITAL** Saipan

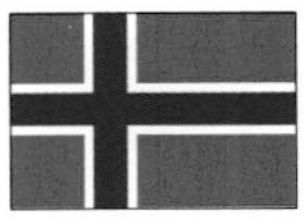
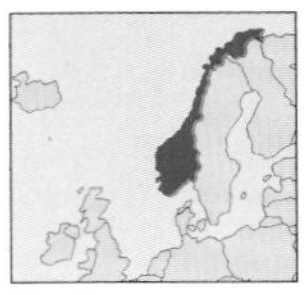

NORWAY

GEOGRAPHY The Kingdom of Norway forms the western part of the rugged Scandinavian peninsula. The deep inlets along the highly indented coastline were worn out by glaciers during the Ice Age.

The warm North Atlantic Drift off the coast of Norway moderates the climate, with mild winters and cool summers. Nearly all the ports are ice-free throughout the year. Inland, winters are colder and snow cover lasts for at least three months a year.

POLITICS & ECONOMY Under a treaty in 1814, Denmark handed Norway over to Sweden, but it kept Norway's colonies – Greenland, Iceland and the Faroe Islands. Norway briefly became independent, but Swedish forces defeated the Norwegians and Norway had to accept Sweden's king as its ruler.

The union between Norway and Sweden ended in 1903. During World War II (1939–45), Germany occupied Norway. Norway's economy developed quickly after the war and the country now enjoys one of the world's highest standards of living. In 1960, Norway, together with six other countries, formed the European Free Trade Association (EFTA). In 1994, the Norwegians voted against joining the EU.

Norway's chief resources and exports are oil and natural gas which come from wells under the North Sea. Farmland covers only 3% of the land. Dairy farming and meat production are important, but Norway has to import food. Norway has many industries powered by cheap hydroelectricity.

AREA 125,050 sq mi [323,900 sq km] **POPULATION** 4,331,000
CAPITAL (POPULATION) Oslo (714,000)
GOVERNMENT Constitutional monarchy
ETHNIC GROUPS Norwegian 97%
LANGUAGES Norwegian (official), Lappish, Finnish
RELIGIONS Christianity (Lutheran 88%)
CURRENCY Krone = 100 ore

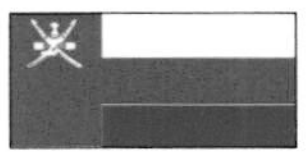
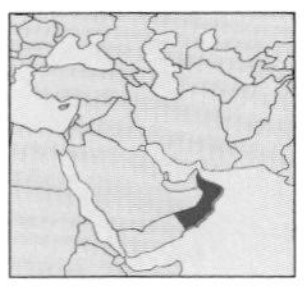

OMAN

GEOGRAPHY The Sultanate of Oman occupies the southeastern corner of the Arabian peninsula. It also includes the tip of the Musandam peninsula, overlooking the strategic Strait of Hormuz.

Oman has a hot tropical climate. In Muscat, temperatures may reach 117°F [47°C] in summer.

POLITICS & ECONOMY British influence in Oman dates back to the end of the 18th century, but the country became fully independent in 1971. Since then, using revenue from oil, which was discovered in 1964, the absolute ruler, Qaboos ibn Said, and his government have sought to modernize the country. However, by 1995, only three out of every five adults was literate, while defense spending was high.

The World Bank classifies Oman as an "upper-middle-income" country. Oil accounts for the bulk of the exports, while huge natural gas deposits were discovered in 1991. However, agriculture remains important. Major crops include alfalfa, bananas, coconuts, dates, limes, tobacco, vegetables and wheat. Some cattle are raised and fishing, especially for sardines, is important. But Oman still has to import food.

AREA 82,031 sq mi [212,460 sq km] **POPULATION** 2,176,000
CAPITAL (POPULATION) Muscat (350,000)
GOVERNMENT Monarchy with consultative council
ETHNIC GROUPS Omani Arab 74%, Pakistani 21%
LANGUAGES Arabic (official), Baluchi, English
RELIGIONS Islam (Ibadiyah) 86%, Hinduism 13%
CURRENCY Omani rial = 100 baizas

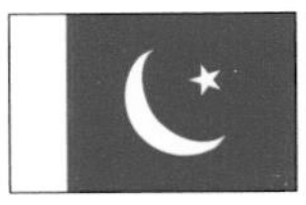
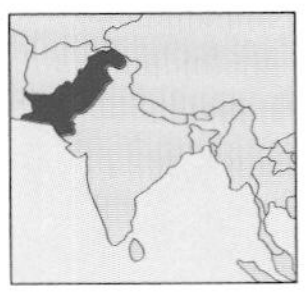

PAKISTAN

GEOGRAPHY The Islamic Republic of Pakistan contains high mountains, fertile plains and rocky deserts. The Karakoram range, which contains K2, the world's second highest peak, lies in the northern part of Jammu and Kashmir, which is occupied by Pakistan but claimed by India. Other mountains rise in the west. Plains, drained by the River Indus and its tributaries, occupy much of eastern Pakistan. The Thar Desert is in the southeast and the dry Baluchistan plateau is in the southwest.

Most of Pakistan has hot summers and mild winters, though the mountains are cold in winter. The rainfall is generally sparse. Most of it comes between July and September, when southwest monsoon winds blow.

POLITICS & ECONOMY Pakistan was the site of the Indus Valley civilization which developed about 4,500 years ago. But Pakistan's modern history dates from 1947, when British India was divided into India and Pakistan. Muslim Pakistan was divided into two parts: East and West Pakistan, but East Pakistan broke away in 1971 to become Bangladesh. In 1948–9, 1965 and 1971, Pakistan and India clashed over the disputed territory of Kashmir. In 1998, Pakistan responded in kind to a series of Indian nuclear weapon tests, provoking global controversy.

Pakistan has been subject to several periods of military rule, but elections in 1988 led to Benazir Bhutto, daughter of former prime minister and president Zulfikar Ali Bhutto, becoming prime minister. She was removed from office in 1990. She again served as prime minister from 1993, but was dismissed in 1996. After elections in 1997, Narwaz Sharif became prime minister, but he was overthrown in 1999 by a coup led by General Pervez Musharraf, who promised to restore democracy in 2002.

According to the World Bank, Pakistan is a "low-income" developing country. The economy is based on farming or rearing goats and sheep. Agriculture employs nearly half the people. Major crops include cotton, fruits, rice, sugarcane and wheat.

AREA 307,374 sq mi [796,100 sq km] **POPULATION** 162,409,000
CAPITAL (POPULATION) Islamabad (204,000)
GOVERNMENT Military regime **ETHNIC GROUPS** Punjabi 60%, Sindhi 12%, Pushtun 13%, Baluch, Muhajir
LANGUAGES Urdu (official), many others
RELIGIONS Islam 97%, Christianity, Hinduism
CURRENCY Pakistan rupee = 100 paisa

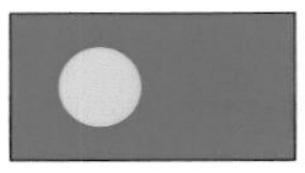
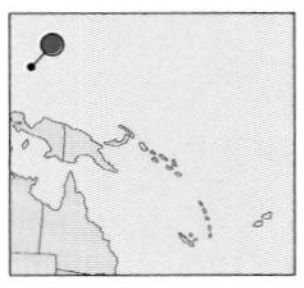

PALAU

The Republic of Palau became fully independent in 1994, after the USA refused to accede to a 1979 referendum that declared this island nation a nuclear-free zone. In December 1994 Palau joined the United Nations. The economy relies heavily on US aid, tourism, fishing and subsistence agriculture. The main crops include cassava, coconuts and copra.

AREA 177 sq mi [458 sq km] **POPULATION** 18,000 **CAPITAL** Koror

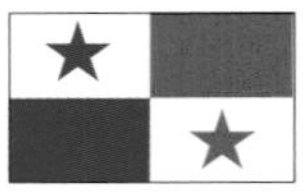
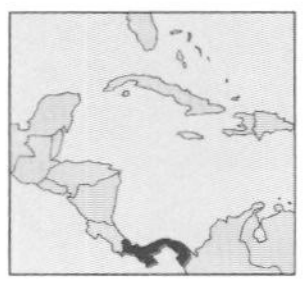

PANAMA

GEOGRAPHY The Republic of Panama forms an isthmus linking Central America to South America. The Panama Canal, which is 50.7 mi [81.6 km] long, cuts across the isthmus. It has made the country a major transport center.

Panama has a tropical climate. Temperatures are high, though the mountains are much cooler than the coastal plains. The main rainy season is between May and December.

POLITICS & ECONOMY Christopher Columbus landed in Panama in 1502 and Spain soon took control of the area. In 1821, Panama became independent from Spain and a province of Colombia.

In 1903, Colombia refused a request by the United States to build a canal. Panama then revolted against Colombia, and became independent. The United States then began to build the canal, which was opened in 1914. The United States administered the Panama Canal Zone, a strip of land along the canal. But many Panamanians resented US influence and, in 1979, the Canal Zone was returned to Panama. Control of the canal itself was handed over by the USA to Panama on December 31, 1999.

Panama's government has changed many times since independence, and there have been periods of military dictatorships. In 1983, General Manuel Antonio Noriega became

Panama's leader. In 1988, two US grand juries in Florida indicted Noriega on charges of drug trafficking. In 1989, Noriega was apparently defeated in a presidential election, but the government declared the election invalid. After the killing of a US marine, US troops entered Panama and arrested Noriega, who was convicted by a Miami court of drug offences in 1992. However, Panama made significant strides in consolidating democracy by holding national elections in 1994 and 1999.

The World Bank classifies Panama as a "lower-middle-income" developing country. The Panama Canal is an important source of revenue and it generates many jobs in commerce, trade, manufacturing and transport. Away from the Canal, the main activity is agriculture, which employs 27% of the people.

AREA 29,761 SQ MI [77,080 SQ KM] **POPULATION** 2,893,000
CAPITAL (POPULATION) PANAMA CITY (452,000) **GOVERNMENT** MULTIPARTY REPUBLIC **ETHNIC GROUPS** MESTIZO 60%, BLACK AND MULATTO 20%, WHITE 10%, AMERINDIAN 8%, ASIAN 2% **LANGUAGES** SPANISH (OFFICIAL) **RELIGIONS** CHRISTIANITY (ROMAN CATHOLIC 84%, PROTESTANT 5%), ISLAM 5% **CURRENCY** US DOLLAR; BALBOA = 100 CENTÉSIMOS

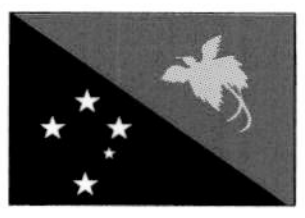

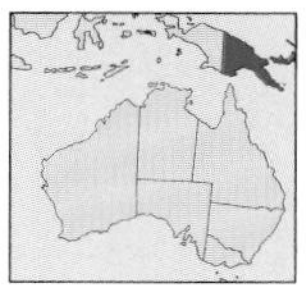

PAPUA NEW GUINEA

GEOGRAPHY Papua New Guinea is an independent country in the Pacific Ocean, north of Australia. It is part of a Pacific island region called Melanesia. Papua New Guinea includes the eastern part of New Guinea, the Bismarck Archipelago, the northern Solomon Islands, the D'Entrecasteaux Islands and the Louisiade Archipelago. The land is largely mountainous.

Papua New Guinea has a tropical climate, with high temperatures throughout the year. Most of the rain occurs during the monsoon season (from December to April), when the northwesterly winds blow. Winds blow from the southeast during the dry season.

POLITICS & ECONOMY The Dutch took western New Guinea (now part of Indonesia) in 1828, but it was not until 1884 that Germany took northeastern New Guinea and Britain took the southeast. In 1906, Britain handed the southeast over to Australia. It then became known as the Territory of Papua. When World War I broke out in 1914, Australia took German New Guinea and, in 1921, the League of Nations gave Australia a mandate to rule the area, which was named the Territory of New Guinea.

Japan invaded New Guinea in 1942, but the Allies reconquered the area in 1944. In 1949, Papua and New Guinea were combined into the Territory of Papua and New Guinea. Papua New Guinea became fully independent in 1975.

Since independence, the government has worked to develop its mineral reserves. One of the most valuable mines was on Bougainville, in the northern Solomon Islands. But the people of Bougainville demanded a larger share in the profits of the mine. Conflict broke out, the mine was closed and the Bougainville Revolutionary Army proclaimed the island independent. But their attempted secession was not recognized internationally. An agreement to end the conflict was signed in 1998 and the island was granted local autonomy in 2000.

The World Bank classifies Papua New Guinea as a "lower-middle-income" developing country. Agriculture employs three out of every four people, many of whom produce little more than they need to feed their families. Minerals, notably copper and gold, are the most valuable exports.

AREA 178,703 SQ MI [462,840 SQ KM] **POPULATION** 4,845,000
CAPITAL (POPULATION) PORT MORESBY (174,000)
GOVERNMENT CONSTITUTIONAL MONARCHY **ETHNIC GROUPS** PAPUAN 84%, MELANESIAN 1% **LANGUAGES** ENGLISH (OFFICIAL), ABOUT 800 OTHERS **RELIGIONS** CHRISTIANITY (PROTESTANT 58%, ROMAN CATHOLIC 33%, ANGLICAN 5%), TRADITIONAL BELIEFS 3% **CURRENCY** KINA = 100 TOEA

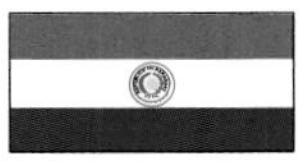

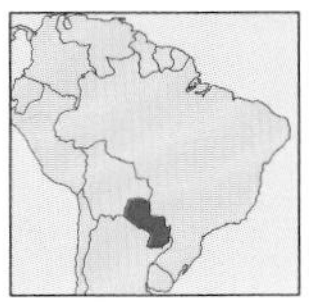

PARAGUAY

GEOGRAPHY The Republic of Paraguay is a landlocked country and rivers, notably the Paraná, Pilcomayo (Brazo Sur) and Paraguay, form most of its borders. A flat region called the Gran Chaco lies in the northwest, while the southeast contains plains, hills and plateaux.

Northern Paraguay lies in the tropics, while the south is subtropical. Most of the country has a warm, humid climate.

POLITICS & ECONOMY In 1776, Paraguay became part of a large colony called the Vice-royalty of La Plata, with Buenos Aires as the capital. Paraguayans opposed this move and the country declared its independence in 1811.

For many years, Paraguay was torn by internal strife and conflict with its neighbors. A war against Brazil, Argentina and Uruguay (1865–70) led to the deaths of more than half of Paraguay's population, and a great loss of territory.

General Alfredo Stroessner took power in 1954 and ruled as a dictator. His government imprisoned many opponents. Stroessner was overthrown in 1989. Free multiparty elections were held in 1993 and 1998. However, the return of democracy frequently seemed precarious because of rivalries between politicians and army leaders.

The World Bank classifies Paraguay as a "lower-middle-income" developing country. Agriculture and forestry are the leading activities, employing 48% of the population. The country has abundant hydroelectricity and it exports power to Argentina and Brazil.

AREA 157,046 SQ MI [406,750 SQ KM] **POPULATION** 5,538,000
CAPITAL (POPULATION) ASUNCIÓN (945,000)
GOVERNMENT MULTIPARTY REPUBLIC **ETHNIC GROUPS** MESTIZO 90%, AMERINDIAN 3% **LANGUAGES** SPANISH AND GUARANÍ (BOTH OFFICIAL) **RELIGIONS** CHRISTIANITY (ROMAN CATHOLIC 96%, PROTESTANT 2%) **CURRENCY** GUARANÍ = 100 CÉNTIMOS

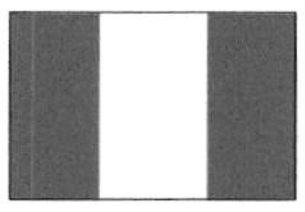

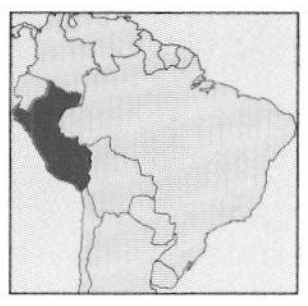

PERU

GEOGRAPHY The Republic of Peru lies in the tropics in western South America. A narrow coastal plain borders the Pacific Ocean in the west. Inland are ranges of the Andes Mountains, which rise to 22,205 ft [6,768 m] at Mount Huascarán, an extinct volcano. East of the Andes lies the Amazon basin.

Lima, on the coastal plain, has an arid climate. The coastal region is chilled by the cold, offshore Humboldt Current. The rainfall increases inland and many mountains in the high Andes are snow-capped.

POLITICS & ECONOMY Spanish conquistadors conquered Peru in the 1530s. In 1820, an Argentinian, José de San Martín, led an army into Peru and declared it independent. But Spain still held large areas. In 1823, the Venezuelan Simon Bolívar led another army into Peru and, in 1824, one of his generals defeated the Spaniards at Ayacucho. The Spaniards surrendered in 1826. Peru suffered much instability throughout the 19th century.

Instability continued in the 20th century. In 1980, when civilian rule was restored, a left-wing group called the Sendero Luminoso, or the "Shining Path," began guerrilla warfare against the government. In 1990, Alberto Fujimori, son of Japanese immigrants, became president. In 1992, he suspended the constitution and dismissed the legislature. The guerrilla leader, Abimael Guzmán, was arrested in 1992, but instability continued. A new constitution in 1993 gave increased power to the president. Following his victory in disputed presidential elections in 2000, Fujimori resigned. Charged with misuse of public funds, he sought sanctuary in Japan.

The World Bank classifies Peru as a "lower-middle-income" developing country. Agriculture employs 35% of the people and major food crops include beans, maize, potatoes and rice. Fish products are exported, but the most valuable export is copper. Peru also produces lead, silver, zinc and iron ore.

AREA 496,223 SQ MI [1,285,220 SQ KM] **POPULATION** 26,276,000
CAPITAL (POPULATION) LIMA (LIMA-CALLAO, 6,601,000)
GOVERNMENT TRANSITIONAL REPUBLIC **ETHNIC GROUPS** QUECHUA 47%, MESTIZO 32%, WHITE 12%, AYMARA 5% **LANGUAGES** SPANISH AND QUECHUA (BOTH OFFICIAL), AYMARA **RELIGIONS** CHRISTIANITY (ROMAN CATHOLIC 93%, PROTESTANT 6%) **CURRENCY** NEW SOL = 100 CENTAVOS

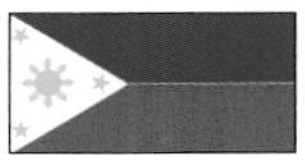

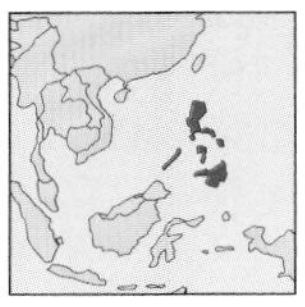

PHILIPPINES

GEOGRAPHY The Republic of the Philippines is an island country in southeastern Asia. It includes about 7,100 islands, of which 2,770 are named and about 1,000 are inhabited. Luzon and Mindanao, the two largest islands, make up more than two-thirds of the country. The land is mainly mountainous.

The country has a tropical climate, with high temperatures all through the year. The dry season runs from December to April. The rest of the year is wet. The high rainfall is associated with typhoons which periodically strike the east coast.

POLITICS & ECONOMY The first European to reach the Philippines was the Portuguese navigator Ferdinand Magellan in 1521. Spanish explorers claimed the region in 1565 when they established a settlement on Cebu. The Spaniards ruled the country until 1898, when the United States took over at the end of the Spanish–American War. Japan invaded the Philippines in 1941, but US forces returned in 1944. The country became fully independent as the Republic of the Philippines in 1946.

Since independence, the country's problems have included armed uprisings by left-wing guerrillas demanding land reform, and Muslim separatist groups, crime, corruption and unemployment. The dominant figure in recent times was Ferdinand Marcos, who ruled in a dictatorial manner from 1965 to 1986. His successors were Corazon Aquino (1986–92), Fidel Ramos (1992–8), and Joseph Estrada, who resigned after massive public protests against his alleged corruption in 2001. He was succeeded by the vice-president, Gloria Macapagal Arroyo.

The Philippines is a developing country which has a "lower-middle-income" economy. Agriculture employs 45% of the people. The main foods are rice and maize, while such crops as bananas, cocoa, coconuts, coffee, sugarcane and tobacco are all grown commercially. Manufacturing now plays an increasingly important role in the economy.

AREA 115,300 SQ MI [300,000 SQ KM] **POPULATION** 77,473,000
CAPITAL (POPULATION) MANILA (METRO MANILA, 9,280,000)
GOVERNMENT MULTIPARTY REPUBLIC **ETHNIC GROUPS** TAGALOG 30%, CEBUANO 24%, ILOCANO 10%, HILIGAYNON ILONGO 9%, BICOL 6% **LANGUAGES** PILIPINO (TAGALOG) AND ENGLISH (BOTH OFFICIAL), SPANISH, MANY OTHERS **RELIGIONS** CHRISTIANITY (ROMAN CATHOLIC 84%, PHILIPPINE INDEPENDENT CHURCH OR AGLIPAYAN 6%, PROTESTANT 4%), ISLAM 4% **CURRENCY** PHILIPPINE PESO = 100 CENTAVOS

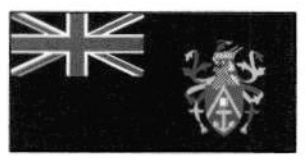

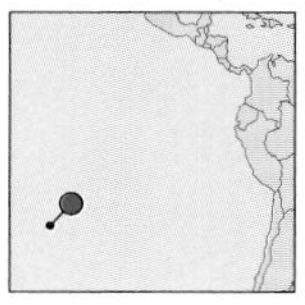

PITCAIRN ISLANDS

Pitcairn Island is a British overseas territory in the Pacific Ocean. Its inhabitants are descendants of the original settlers – nine mutineers from HMS *Bounty* and 18 Tahitians who arrived in 1790.

AREA 19 SQ MI [48 SQ KM] **POPULATION** 60
CAPITAL ADAMSTOWN

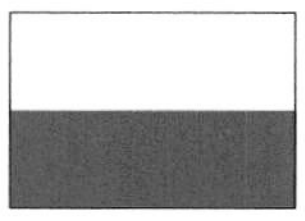

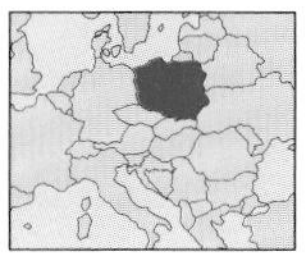

POLAND

GEOGRAPHY The Republic of Poland faces the Baltic Sea and, behind its lagoon-fringed coast, lies a broad plain. A plateau lies in the southeast, while the Sudeten Highlands straddle part of the border with the Czech Republic. Part of the Carpathian Range (the Tatra) lies in the southeast.

Poland's climate is influenced by its position in Europe. Warm, moist air masses come from the west, while cold air masses come from the north and east. Summers are warm, but winters are cold and snowy.

POLITICS & ECONOMY Poland's boundaries have changed several times in the last 200 years, partly as a result of its geographical location between the powers of Germany and Russia. It disappeared from the map in the late 18th century, when a Polish state called the Grand Duchy of Warsaw was set up. But in 1815, the country was partitioned, between Austria, Prussia and Russia. Poland became independent in 1918, but in 1939 it was divided between Germany and the Soviet Union. The country again became independent in 1945, when it lost land to Russia but gained some from Germany. Communists took power in 1948, but opposition mounted and eventually became focused through an organization called Solidarity.

Solidarity was led by a trade unionist, Lech Walesa. A coalition government was formed between Solidarity and the Communists in 1989. In 1990, the Communist party was dissolved and Walesa became president. But Walesa faced many problems in turning Poland toward a market economy. In presidential elections in 1995, Walesa was defeated by ex-Communist Aleksander Kwasniewski. However, Kwasniewski continued to follow westward-looking policies and he was re-elected president in 2000. Poland joined NATO in 1999 and seemed likely to be among the first eastern European countries to join an expanded European Union.

Poland has large reserves of coal and deposits of various minerals which are used in its factories. Manufactures include chemicals, processed food, machinery, ships, steel and textiles.

AREA 120,726 SQ MI [312,680 SQ KM] **POPULATION** 40,366,000
CAPITAL (POPULATION) WARSAW (1,638,000)
GOVERNMENT MULTIPARTY REPUBLIC **ETHNIC GROUPS** POLISH 98%, UKRAINIAN 1%, GERMAN 1% **LANGUAGES** POLISH (OFFICIAL) **RELIGIONS** CHRISTIANITY (ROMAN CATHOLIC 94%, ORTHODOX 2%) **CURRENCY** ZLOTY = 100 GROSZY

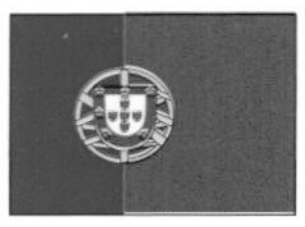

PORTUGAL

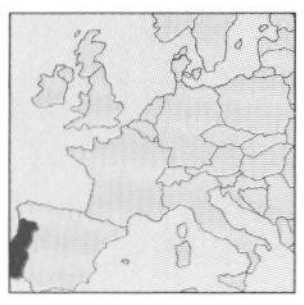

GEOGRAPHY The Republic of Portugal is the most westerly of Europe's mainland countries. The land rises from the coastal plains on the Atlantic Ocean to the western edge of the huge plateau, or Meseta, which occupies most of the Iberian peninsula. Portugal also contains two autonomous regions, the Azores and Madeira island groups.

The climate is moderated by winds blowing from the Atlantic Ocean. Summers are cooler and winters are milder than in other Mediterranean lands.

POLITICS & ECONOMY Portugal became a separate country, independent of Spain, in 1143. In the 15th century, Portugal led the "Age of European Exploration." This led to the growth of a large Portuguese empire, with colonies in Africa, Asia and, most valuable of all, Brazil in South America. Portuguese power began to decline in the 16th century and, between 1580 and 1640, Portugal was ruled by Spain. Portugal lost Brazil in 1822 and, in 1910, Portugal became a republic. Instability hampered progress and army officers seized power in 1926. In 1928, they chose Antonio de Salazar to be minister of finance. He became prime minister in 1932 and ruled as a dictator from 1933.

Salazar ruled until 1968, but his successor, Marcello Caetano, was overthrown in 1974 by a group of army officers. The new government made most of Portugal's remaining colonies independent. Free elections were held in 1978. Portugal joined the European Community (now the European Union) in 1986. Despite its small economy, it adopted the euro, the single currency of the EU, on January 1, 1999.

Agriculture and fishing were the mainstays of the economy until the mid-20th century. However, manufacturing is now the most valuable sector.

AREA 35,670 SQ MI [92,390 SQ KM] **POPULATION** 10,587,000
CAPITAL (POPULATION) LISBON (2,561,000)
GOVERNMENT MULTIPARTY REPUBLIC
ETHNIC GROUPS PORTUGUESE 99%, CAPE VERDEAN, BRAZILIAN, SPANISH, BRITISH **LANGUAGES** PORTUGUESE (OFFICIAL)
RELIGIONS CHRISTIANITY (ROMAN CATHOLIC 95%, OTHER CHRISTIANS 2%) **CURRENCY** EURO; ESCUDO = 100 CENTAVOS

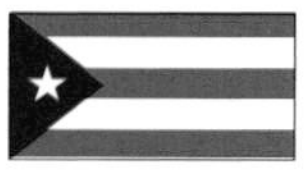

PUERTO RICO

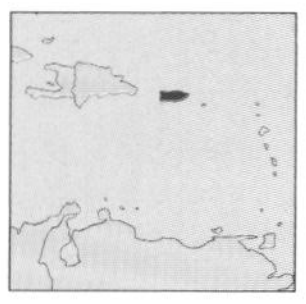

The Commonwealth of Puerto Rico, a mainly mountainous island, is the easternmost of the Greater Antilles chain. The climate is hot and wet. Puerto Rico is a dependent territory of the USA and the people are US citizens. In 1998, 50.2% of the population voted in a referendum on possible statehood to maintain the status quo. Puerto Rico is the most industrialized country in the Caribbean. Tax exemptions attract US companies to the island and manufacturing is expanding. The chief exports are chemicals and chemical products, machinery and food.

AREA 3,436 SQ MI [8,900 SQ KM] **POPULATION** 3,836,000
CAPITAL SAN JUAN

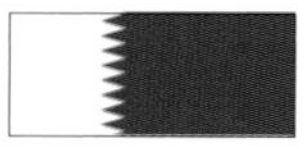

QATAR

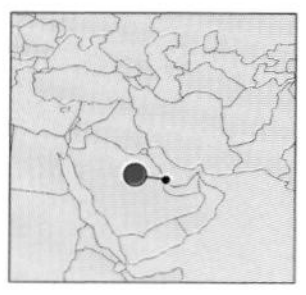

The State of Qatar occupies a low, barren peninsula that extends northward from the Arabian peninsula into the Gulf. The climate is hot and dry. Qatar became a British protectorate in 1916, but it became fully independent in 1971. Oil, first discovered in 1939, is the mainstay of the economy of this prosperous nation.

AREA 4,247 SQ MI [11,000 SQ KM] **POPULATION** 499,000 **CAPITAL** DOHA

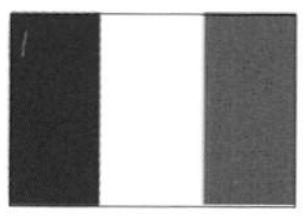

RÉUNION

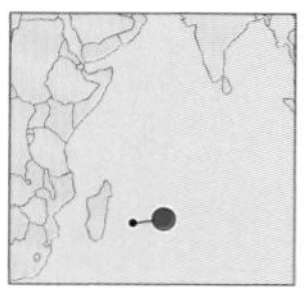

Réunion is a French overseas department in the Indian Ocean. The land is mainly mountainous, though the lowlands are intensely cultivated. Sugar and sugar products are the main exports, but French aid, given to the island in return for its use as a military base, is important to the economy.

AREA 969 SQ MI [2,510 SQ KM]
POPULATION 692,00; **CAPITAL** SAINT-DENIS

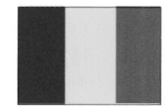

ROMANIA

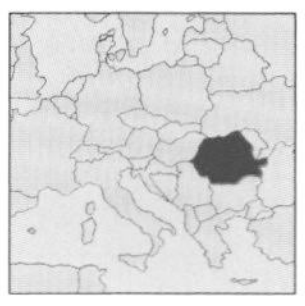

GEOGRAPHY Romania is a country on the Black Sea in eastern Europe. Eastern and southern Romania form part of the Danube river basin. The delta region, near the mouths of the Danube, where the river flows into the Black Sea, is one of Europe's finest wetlands. The southern part of the coast contains several resorts. The heart of the country is called Transylvania. It is ringed in the east, south and west by scenic mountains which are part of the Carpathian mountain system.

Romania has hot summers and cold winters. The rainfall is heaviest in spring and early summer, when thundery showers are common.

POLITICS & ECONOMY From the late 18th century, the Turkish empire began to break up. The modern history of Romania began in 1861 when Walachia and Moldavia united. After World War I (1914–18), Romania, which had fought on the side of the victorious Allies, obtained large areas, including Transylvania, where most people were Romanians. This almost doubled the country's size and population. In 1939, Romania lost territory to Bulgaria, Hungary and the Soviet Union. Romania fought alongside Germany in World War II, and Soviet troops occupied the country in 1944. Hungary returned northern Transylvania to Romania in 1945, but Bulgaria and the Soviet Union kept former Romanian territory. In 1947, Romania officially became a Communist country.

In 1990, Romania held its first free elections since the end of World War II. The National Salvation Front, led by Ion Iliescu and containing many former Communist leaders, won a large majority. A new constitution, approved in 1991, made the country a democratic republic. Elections held under this constitution in 1992 again resulted in victory for Ion Iliescu, whose party was renamed the Party of Social Democracy (PDSR) in 1993. But the government faced many problems. In 1996, the center-right Democratic Convention defeated the PDSR, led by Emil Constantinescu, who became president. He was re-elected in 2000.

According to the World Bank, Romania is a "lower-middle-income" economy. Under Communist rule, industry, including mining and manufacturing, became more important than agriculture.

AREA 91,699 SQ MI [237,500 SQ KM] **POPULATION** 24,000,000
CAPITAL (POPULATION) BUCHAREST (2,060,000)
GOVERNMENT MULTIPARTY REPUBLIC **ETHNIC GROUPS** ROMANIAN 89%, HUNGARIAN 7%, GYPSY 2% **LANGUAGES** ROMANIAN (OFFICIAL), HUNGARIAN **RELIGIONS** CHRISTIANITY (ROMANIAN ORTHODOX 87%, ROMAN CATHOLIC 5%, GREEK ORTHODOX 4%)
CURRENCY ROMANIAN LEU = 100 BANI

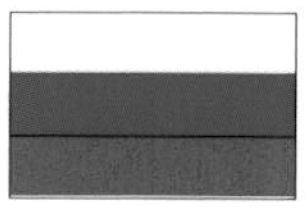

RUSSIA

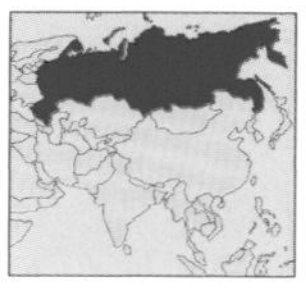

GEOGRAPHY Russia is the world's largest country. About 25% lies west of the Ural Mountains in European Russia, where 80% of the population lives. It is mostly flat or undulating, but the land rises to the Caucasus Mountains in the south, where Russia's highest peak, Elbrus, at 18,481 ft [5,633 m], is found. Asian Russia, or Siberia, contains vast plains and plateaus, with mountains in the east and south. The Kamchatka peninsula in the far east has many active volcanoes. Russia contains many of the world's longest rivers, including the Yenisey-Angara and the Ob-Irtysh. It also includes part of the world's largest inland body of water, the Caspian Sea, and Lake Baikal, the world's deepest lake.

Moscow has a continental climate with cold and snowy winters and warm summers. Krasnoyarsk in south-central Siberia has a harsher, drier climate, but it is not as severe as parts of northern Siberia.

POLITICS & ECONOMY In the 9th century AD, a state called Kievan Rus was formed by a group of people called the East Slavs. Kiev, now capital of Ukraine, became a major trading center, but, in 1237, Mongol armies conquered Russia and destroyed Kiev. Russia was part of the Mongol empire until the late 15th century. Under Mongol rule, Moscow became the leading Russian city.

In the 16th century, Moscow's grand prince was retitled "tsar." The first tsar, Ivan the Terrible, expanded Russian territory. In 1613, after a period of civil war, Michael Romanov became tsar, founding a dynasty which ruled until 1917. In the early 18th century, Tsar Peter the Great began to westernize Russia and, by 1812, when Napoleon failed to conquer the country, Russia was a major European power. But during the 19th century, many Russians demanded reforms and discontent was widespread.

In World War I (1914–18), the Russian people suffered great hardships and, in 1917, Tsar Nicholas II was forced to abdicate. In November 1917, the Bolsheviks seized power under Vladimir Lenin. In 1922, the Bolsheviks set up a new nation, the Union of Soviet Socialist Republics (also called the USSR or the Soviet Union).

From 1924, Joseph Stalin introduced a socialist economic programme, suppressing all opposition. In 1939, the Soviet Union and Germany signed a non-aggression pact, but Germany invaded the Soviet Union in 1941. Soviet forces pushed the Germans back, occupying eastern Europe. They reached Berlin in May 1945. From the late 1940s, tension between the Soviet Union and its allies and Western nations developed into a "Cold War." This continued until 1991, when the Soviet Union was dissolved.

The Soviet Union collapsed because of the failure of its economic policies. From 1991, President Boris Yeltsin introduced democratic and economic reforms. Yeltsin retired in 1999 and, in 2000, was succeeded by Vladimir Putin. Russia maintains contacts with 11 of the republics in the former Soviet Union through the Commonwealth of Independent States. However, fighting in Chechenia in the 1990s and early 21st century showed that Russia's sheer size and diverse population makes national unity difficult to achieve.

Russia's economy was thrown into disarray after the collapse of the Soviet Union, and in the early 1990s the World Bank described Russia as a "lower-middle-income" economy. Russia was admitted to the Council of Europe in 1997, essentially to discourage instability in the Caucasus. More significantly still, Boris Yeltsin was invited to attend the G7 summit in Denver in 1997. The summit became known as "the Summit of the Eight" and it appeared that Russia will now be included in future meetings of the world's most powerful economies. Industry is the most valuable activity, though, under Communist rule, manufacturing was less efficient than in the West, and the emphasis was on heavy industry. Today, light industries producing consumer goods are becoming important. Russia's abundant resources include oil and natural gas, coal, timber, metal ores and hydroelectric power.

Most farmland is still government-owned or run as collectives. Russia is a major producer of farm products, though it imports grains. Major crops include barley, flax, fruits, oats, rye, potatoes, sugar beet, sunflower seeds, vegetables and wheat.

AREA 6,592,800 SQ MI [17,075,000 SQ KM] **POPULATION** 155,096,000
CAPITAL (POPULATION) MOSCOW (9,233,000) **GOVERNMENT** FEDERAL MULTIPARTY REPUBLIC **ETHNIC GROUPS** RUSSIAN 82%, TATAR 4%, UKRAINIAN 3%, CHUVASH 1%, MORE THAN 100 OTHER NATIONALITIES
LANGUAGES RUSSIAN (OFFICIAL), MANY OTHERS **RELIGIONS** CHRISTIANITY (MAINLY RUSSIAN ORTHODOX, WITH ROMAN CATHOLIC AND PROTESTANT MINORITIES), ISLAM, JUDAISM **CURRENCY** RUSSIAN ROUBLE = 100 KOPEKS

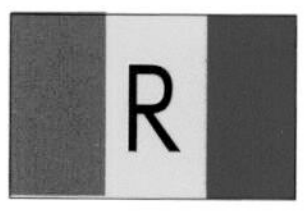

RWANDA

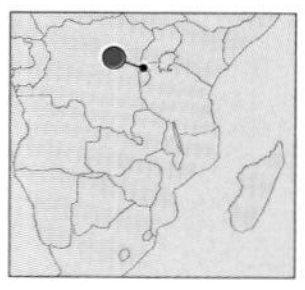

GEOGRAPHY The Republic of Rwanda is a small, landlocked country in east-central Africa. Lake Kivu and the River Ruzizi in the Great African Rift Valley form the country's western border.

Kigali stands on the central plateau of Rwanda. Here, temperatures are moderated by the altitude. The rainfall is abundant, but much heavier rain falls on the western mountains.

POLITICS & ECONOMY Germany conquered the area, called Ruanda-Urundi, in the 1890s. However, Belgium occupied the region during World War I (1914–18) and ruled it until 1961, when the people of Ruanda voted for their country to become a republic, called Rwanda. This decision followed a rebellion by the majority Hutu people against the Tutsi monarchy. About 150,000 deaths resulted from this conflict. Many Tutsis fled to Uganda, where they formed a rebel army. Burundi became independent as a monarchy, though it became a republic in 1966. Relations between Hutus and Tutsis continued to cause friction. Civil war broke out in 1994 and in 1996 the conflict spilled over into Congo (then Zaïre), where Zaïrean Tutsis staged a rebellion. This led to political instability.

According to the World Bank, Rwanda is a "low-income" developing country. Most people are poor farmers. Food crops include bananas, beans, cassava and sorghum. Some cattle are raised.

AREA 10,170 SQ MI [26,340 SQ KM] **POPULATION** 10,200,000
CAPITAL (POPULATION) KIGALI (235,000) **GOVERNMENT** REPUBLIC
ETHNIC GROUPS HUTU 90%, TUTSI 9%, TWA 1% **LANGUAGES** FRENCH, ENGLISH AND KINYARWANDA (ALL OFFICIAL) **RELIGIONS** CHRISTIANITY 74% (ROMAN CATHOLIC 65%), TRADITIONAL BELIEFS 17%, ISLAM 9%
CURRENCY RWANDA FRANC = 100 CENTIMES

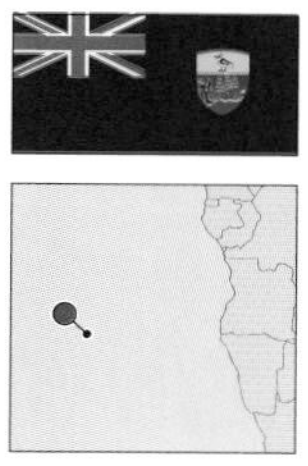

ST HELENA

St Helena, which became a British colony in 1834, is an isolated volcanic island in the south Atlantic Ocean. Now a British overseas territory, it is also the administrative center of Ascension and Tristan da Cunha.

AREA 47 sq mi [122 sq km]
POPULATION 8,200 **CAPITAL** Jamestown

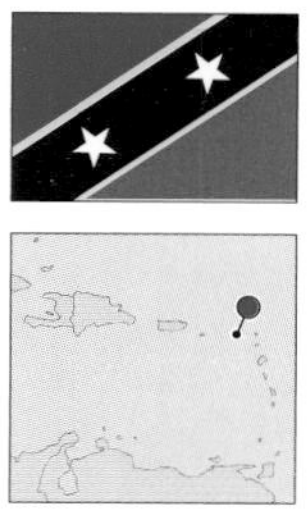

ST KITTS AND NEVIS

The Federation of St Kitts and Nevis became independent from Britain in 1983. In 1998, a vote for the secession of Nevis fell short of the two-thirds required.

AREA 139 sq mi [360 sq km]
POPULATION 44,000 **CAPITAL** Basseterre

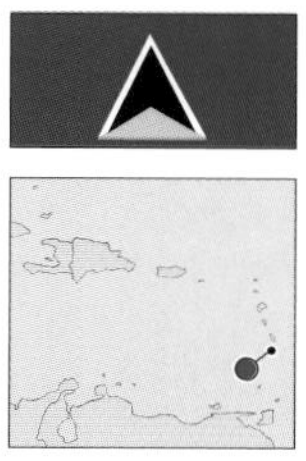

ST LUCIA

St Lucia, which became independent from Britain in 1979, is a mountainous, forested island of extinct volcanoes. It exports bananas and coconuts, and now attracts many tourists.

AREA 236 sq mi [610 sq km]
POPULATION 177,000 **CAPITAL** Castries

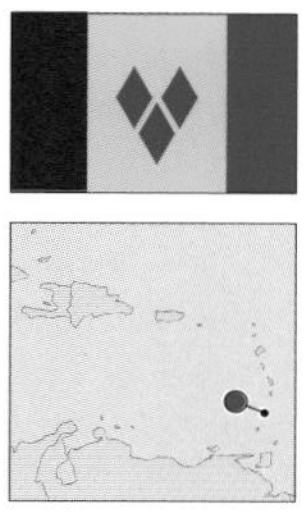

ST VINCENT AND THE GRENADINES

St Vincent and the Grenadines achieved its independence from Britain in 1979. Tourism is growing, but the territory is less prosperous than its neighbors.

AREA 150 sq mi [388 sq km]
POPULATION 128,000 **CAPITAL** Kingstown

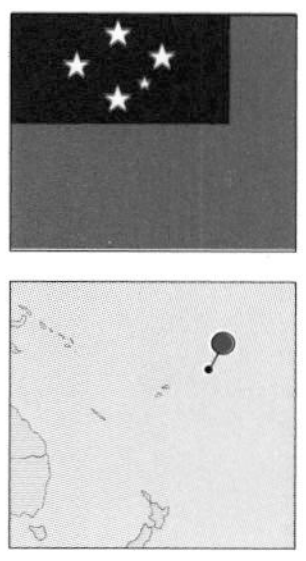

SAMOA

The Independent State of Samoa (formerly Western Samoa) comprises two islands in the South Pacific Ocean. Governed by New Zealand from 1920, the territory became independent in 1962. Exports include coconut cream and beer.

AREA 1,097 sq mi [2,840 sq km]
POPULATION 171,000 **CAPITAL** Apia

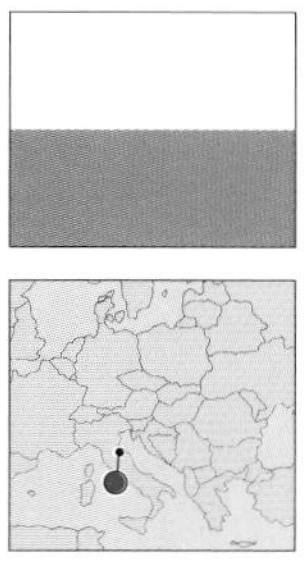

SAN MARINO

San Marino in northern Italy has been independent since 885 and a republic since the 14th century. It is the world's oldest republic.

AREA 24 sq mi [61 sq km] **POPULATION** 25,000
CAPITAL San Marino

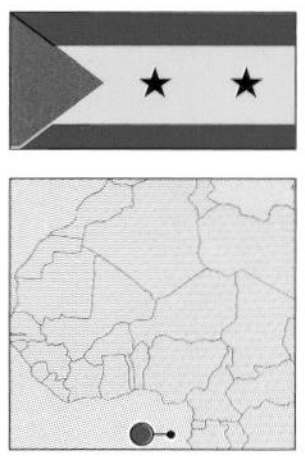

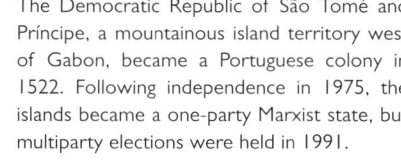

SÃO TOMÉ AND PRÍNCIPE

The Democratic Republic of São Tomé and Príncipe, a mountainous island territory west of Gabon, became a Portuguese colony in 1522. Following independence in 1975, the islands became a one-party Marxist state, but multiparty elections were held in 1991.

AREA 372 sq mi [964 sq km] **POPULATION** 151,000 **CAPITAL** São Tomé

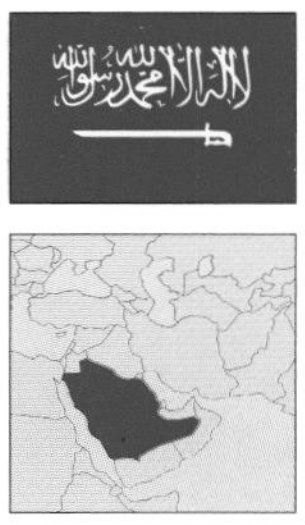

SAUDI ARABIA

GEOGRAPHY The Kingdom of Saudi Arabia occupies about three-quarters of the Arabian peninsula in southwest Asia. Deserts cover most of the land. Mountains border the Red Sea plains in the west. In the north is the sandy Nafud Desert (An Nafud). In the south is the Rub' al Khali (the "Empty Quarter"), one of the world's bleakest deserts.

Saudi Arabia has a hot, dry climate. In the summer months, the temperatures in Riyadh often exceed 104°F [40°C], though the nights are cool.

POLITICS & ECONOMY Saudi Arabia contains the two holiest places in Islam – Mecca (or Makka), the birthplace of the Prophet Muhammad in AD 570, and Medina (Al Madinah) where Muhammad went in 622. These places are visited by many pilgrims.

Saudi Arabia was poor until the oil industry began to operate on the eastern plains in 1933. Oil revenues have been used to develop the country and Saudi Arabia has given aid to poorer Arab nations. The monarch has supreme authority and Saudi Arabia has no formal constitution. In the first Gulf War (1980–8), Saudi Arabia supported Iraq against Iran. But when Iraq invaded Kuwait in 1990, it joined the international alliance to drive Iraq's forces out of Kuwait in 1991.

Saudi Arabia has about 25% of the world's known oil reserves, and oil and oil products make up 85% of its exports. But agriculture still employs 48% of the people, including nomadic herders. Crops grown in the southwestern highlands and at oases include dates, vegetables and wheat. Modern irrigation and desalination schemes have greatly increased crop production. The government is continuing to encourage the development of modern agriculture and new industries to help diversify the economy.

AREA 829,995 sq mi [2,149,690 sq km] **POPULATION** 20,697,000
CAPITAL (POPULATION) Riyadh (1,800,000)
GOVERNMENT Absolute monarchy with consultative assembly
ETHNIC GROUPS Arab (Saudi 82%, Yemeni 10%, other Arab 3%)
LANGUAGES Arabic (official) **RELIGIONS** Islam 99%, Christianity 1%
CURRENCY Saudi riyal = 100 halalas

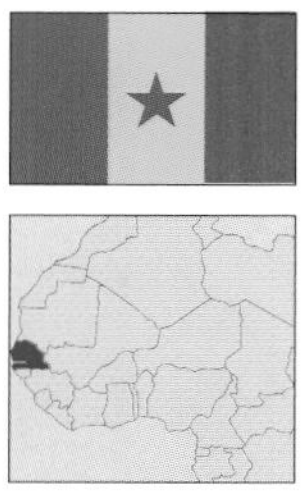

SENEGAL

GEOGRAPHY The Republic of Senegal is on the northwest coast of Africa. The volcanic Cape Verde (Cap Vert), on which Dakar stands, is the most westerly point in Africa. Plains cover most of Senegal, though the land rises gently in the southeast.

Dakar has a tropical climate, with a short rainy season between July and October.

POLITICS & ECONOMY In 1882, Senegal became a French colony, and from 1895 it was ruled as part of French West Africa, the capital of which, Dakar, developed as a major port and city.

In 1959, Senegal joined French Sudan (now Mali) to form the Federation of Mali. But Senegal withdrew in 1960 and became the separate Republic of Senegal. Its first president, Léopold Sédar Senghor, served until 1981, when he was succeeded by Abdou Diouf, who was later made "president for life." However, in 2000, Diouf was defeated in presidential elections by Abdoulaye Wade.

Senegal and The Gambia have always enjoyed close relations despite their differing French and British traditions. In 1981, Senegalese troops put down an attempted coup in The Gambia and, in 1982, the two countries set up a defense alliance, called the Confederation of Senegambia. But this confederation was dissolved in 1989.

According to the World Bank, Senegal is a "lower-middle-income" developing country. It was badly hit in the 1960s and 1970s by droughts, which caused starvation. Agriculture still employs 81% of the population though many farmers produce little more than they need to feed their families. Food crops include groundnuts, millet and rice. Phosphates are the country's chief resource, but Senegal also refines oil which it imports from Gabon and Nigeria. Dakar is a busy port and has many industries.

AREA 75,954 sq mi [196,720 sq km] **POPULATION** 8,716,000
CAPITAL (POPULATION) Dakar (1,571,000)
GOVERNMENT Multiparty republic
ETHNIC GROUPS Wolof 44%, Fulani-Tukulor 24%, Serer 15% **LANGUAGES** French (official), tribal languages
RELIGIONS Islam 94%, Christianity (mainly Roman Catholic) 5%, traditional beliefs and others 1%
CURRENCY CFA franc = 100 centimes

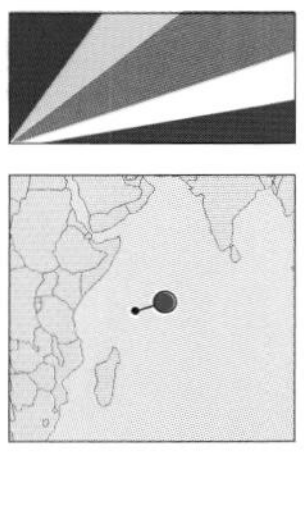

SEYCHELLES

The Republic of Seychelles in the western Indian Ocean achieved independence from Britain in 1976. Coconuts are the main cash crop and fishing and tourism are important.

AREA 176 sq mi [455 sq km]
POPULATION 75,000 **CAPITAL** Victoria

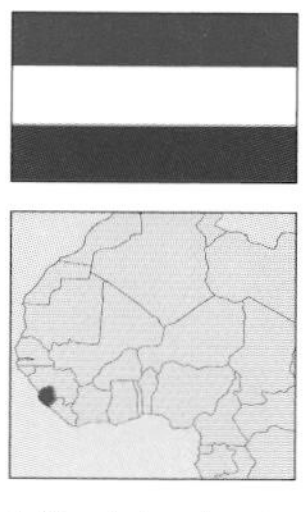

SIERRA LEONE

GEOGRAPHY The Republic of Sierra Leone in West Africa is about the same size as the Republic of Ireland. The coast contains several deep estuaries in the north, with lagoons in the south. The most prominent feature is the mountainous Freetown (or Sierra Leone) peninsula. North of the peninsula is the River Rokel estuary, West Africa's best natural harbor.

Sierra Leone has a tropical climate, with heavy rainfall between April and November.

POLITICS & ECONOMY A former British territory, Sierra Leone became independent in 1961 and a republic in 1971. It became a one-party state in 1978, but, in 1991, the people voted for the restoration of democracy. The military seized power in 1992 and a civil war caused much destruction in 1994–5. Elections in 1996 were followed by another military coup. In 1998, the West African Peace Force restored the deposed President Ahmed Tejan Kabbah. In 1999, a peace agreement followed further conflict. As part of this agreement, Foday Sankoh, one of the rebel leaders, became vice-president. However, in 2000, the peace agreement collapsed and conflict resumed. Sankoh was arrested and charged with war crimes.

The World Bank classifies Sierra Leone among the "low-income" economies. Agriculture provides a living for 70% of the people, though farming is mainly at subsistence level. The most valuable exports are minerals, including diamonds, bauxite and rutile (titanium ore). The country has few manufacturing industries.

AREA 27,699 sq mi [71,740 sq km] **POPULATION** 5,437,000
CAPITAL (POPULATION) Freetown (505,000) **GOVERNMENT** Single-party republic **ETHNIC GROUPS** Mende 35%, Temne 37%
LANGUAGES English (official), Mande, Temne **RELIGIONS** Traditional beliefs 51%, Islam 39% **CURRENCY** Leone = 100 cents

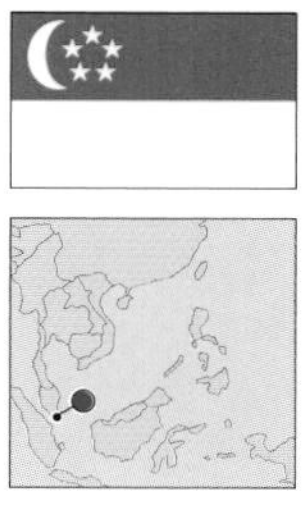

SINGAPORE

GEOGRAPHY The Republic of Singapore is an island country at the southern tip of the Malay peninsula. It consists of the large Singapore Island and 58 small islands, 20 of which are inhabited.

Singapore has a hot, humid climate. Temperatures are high and rainfall is heavy throughout the year.

POLITICS & ECONOMY In 1819, Sir Thomas Stamford Raffles (1781–1826), agent of the British East India Company, made a treaty with the Sultan of Johor allowing the British to build a settlement on Singapore Island. Singapore soon became the leading British trading center in Southeast Asia and it later became a naval base. Japanese forces seized the island in 1942, but British rule was restored in 1945.

In 1963, Singapore became part of the Federation of Malaysia, which also included Malaya and the territories of Sabah and Sarawak on Borneo. In 1965, Singapore broke away and became independent.

The People's Action Party (PAP) has ruled Singapore since 1959. Its leader, Lee Kuan Yew, served as prime minister from 1959 until 1990, when he resigned and was succeeded by Goh Chok Tong. Under the PAP, the economy has expanded rapidly though some consider its rule rather dictatorial.

The World Bank classifies Singapore as a "high-income" economy. A skilled work force has created a fast growing economy, but the recession in 1997–8 was a setback. Trade and finance are leading activities. Manufactures include electronic products, machinery, scientific instruments, textiles and ships. Singapore has a large oil refinery. Petroleum products and manufactures are the main exports.

AREA 239 sq mi [618 sq km] **POPULATION** 3,000,000
CAPITAL (POPULATION) Singapore City (3,104,000)
GOVERNMENT Multiparty republic **ETHNIC GROUPS** Chinese 78%, Malay 14%, Indian 7% **LANGUAGES** Chinese, Malay, Tamil and English (all official) **RELIGIONS** Buddhism, Taoism and other traditional beliefs 54%, Islam 15%, Christianity 13%, Hinduism 4%
CURRENCY Singapore dollar = 100 cents

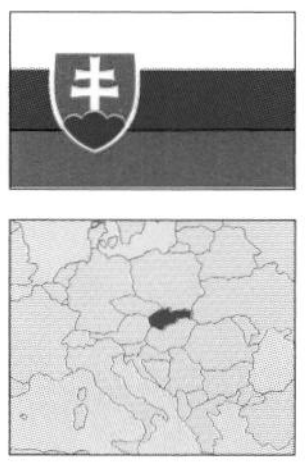

SLOVAK REPUBLIC

GEOGRAPHY The Slovak Republic is a predominantly mountainous country, consisting of part of the Carpathian range. The highest peak is Gerlachovka in the Tatra Mountains, which reaches 8,711 ft [2,655 m]. The south is a fertile lowland.

The Slovak Republic has cold winters and

warm summers. Kosice, in the east, has average temperatures ranging from 27°F [–3°C] in January to 68°F [20°C] in July. The highland areas are much colder. Snow or rain falls throughout the year. Kosice has an average annual rainfall of 24 in [600 mm], the wettest months being July and August.

POLITICS & ECONOMY Slavic peoples settled in the region in the 5th century AD. They were subsequently conquered by Hungary, beginning a millennium of Hungarian rule and suppression of Slovak culture.

In 1867, Hungary and Austria united to form Austria–Hungary, of which the present-day Slovak Republic was a part. Austria–Hungary collapsed at the end of World War I (1914–18). The Czech and Slovak people then united to form a new nation, Czechoslovakia. But Czech domination led to resentment by many Slovaks. In 1939, the Slovak Republic declared itself independent, but Germany occupied the country. At the end of World War II, the Slovak Republic again became part of Czechoslovakia.

The Communist party took control in 1948. In the 1960s, many people sought reform, but they were crushed by the Russians. In the late 1980s, demands for democracy mounted and a non-Communist government took office in 1990. Elections in 1992 led to victory for the Movement for a Democratic Slovakia headed by a former Communist and nationalist, Vladimir Meciar, and the independent Slovak Republic came into existence on January 1, 1993.

Independence raised national aspirations among Slovakia's Magyar-speaking community, but relations with Hungary deteriorated when the Magyars felt that administrative changes under-represented them politically. The government also made Slovak the only official language. The government's autocratic rule and human rights record provoked international criticism. In 1998, Meciar's party was defeated and Mikulas Dzurinda replaced Meciar as prime minister. In 2001, the parliament approved changes to the constitution that would enable Slovakia to become a member of NATO and the European Union.

Before 1948, the Slovak Republic's economy was based on farming, but Communist governments developed manufacturing industries, producing such things as chemicals, machinery, steel and weapons. Since the late 1980s, many state-run businesses have been handed over to private owners.

AREA 18,932 sq mi [49,035 sq km] **POPULATION** 5,500,000
CAPITAL (POPULATION) Bratislava (451,000)
GOVERNMENT Multiparty republic **ETHNIC GROUPS** Slovak, Hungarian, with small groups of Czechs, Germans, Gypsies, Poles, Russians and Ukrainians **LANGUAGES** Slovak (official), Hungarian **RELIGIONS** Christianity (Roman Catholic 60%, Protestant 6%, Orthodox 3%) **CURRENCY** Koruna = 100 halierov

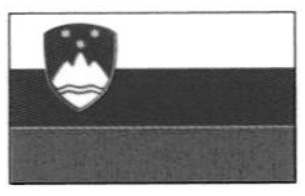

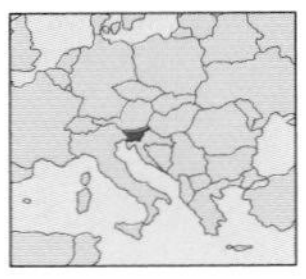

SLOVENIA

GEOGRAPHY The Republic of Slovenia was one of the six republics which made up the former Yugoslavia. Much of the land is mountainous, rising to 9,393 ft [2,863 m] at Mount Triglav in the Julian Alps (Julijske Alpe) in the northwest. Central Slovenia contains the limestone Karst region. The Postojna caves near Ljubljana are among the largest in Europe.

The coast has a mild Mediterranean climate, but inland the climate is more continental. The mountains are snow-capped in winter.

POLITICS & ECONOMY In the last 2,000 years, the Slovene people have been independent as a nation for less than 50 years. The Austrian Habsburgs ruled over the region from the 13th century until World War I. Slovenia became part of the Kingdom of the Serbs, Croats and Slovenes (later called Yugoslavia) in 1918. During World War II, Slovenia was invaded and partitioned between Italy, Germany and Hungary but, after the war, Slovenia again became part of Yugoslavia.

From the late 1960s, some Slovenes demanded independence, but the central government opposed the breakup of the country. In 1990, when Communist governments had collapsed throughout Eastern Europe, elections were held and a non-Communist coalition government was set up. Slovenia then declared itself independent. This led to fighting between Slovenes and the federal army, but Slovenia did not become a battlefield like other parts of the former Yugoslavia. The European Community recognized Slovenia's independence in 1992. The electors returned a coalition led by the Liberal Democrats in 1992, 1996 and again in 2000.

The reform of the economy, formerly run by the government, and the fighting in areas to the south have caused problems for Slovenia, although it remains one of the fastest growing economies in Europe. In 1992, the World Bank classified Slovenia as an "upper-middle-income" developing country, and it is expected to be among the first countries to join an expanded European Union.

Manufacturing is the leading activity and manufactures are the main exports. Manufactures include chemicals, machinery and transport equipment, metal goods and textiles. Slovenia mines some iron ore, lead, lignite and mercury. Agriculture employs 8% of the people. Fruits, maize, potatoes and wheat are major crops, and many farmers raise animals.

AREA 7,817 sq mi [20,251 sq km] **POPULATION** 2,055,000
CAPITAL (POPULATION) Ljubljana (280,000)
GOVERNMENT Multiparty republic
ETHNIC GROUPS Slovene 88%, Croat 3%, Serb 2%, Bosnian 1% **LANGUAGES** Slovene (official), Serbo-Croat
RELIGIONS Christianity (mainly Roman Catholic)
CURRENCY Tolar = 100 stotin

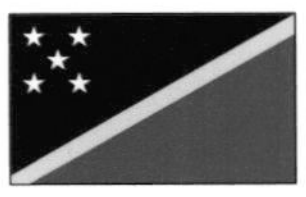

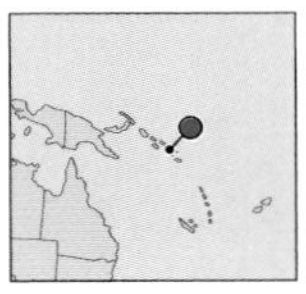

SOLOMON ISLANDS

The Solomon Islands, a chain of mainly volcanic islands in the Pacific Ocean, were a British territory between 1893 and 1978. The chain extends for some 1,400 mi [2,250 km]. They were the scene of fierce fighting during World War II. Most people are Melanesians, and the islands have a young population profile, with half the people aged under 20. Fish, coconuts and cocoa are leading products, though development is hampered by mountainous, forested terrain.

AREA 10,954 sq mi [28,370 sq km] **POPULATION** 429,000
CAPITAL Honiara

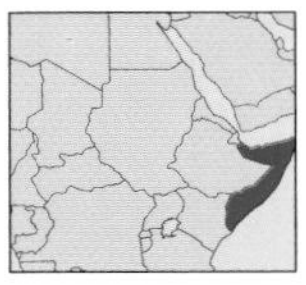

SOMALIA

GEOGRAPHY The Somali Democratic Republic, or Somalia, is in a region known as the "Horn of Africa." It is more than twice the size of Italy, the country which once ruled the southern part of Somalia. The most mountainous part of the country is in the north, behind the narrow coastal plains that border the Gulf of Aden.

Rainfall is light throughout Somalia. The wettest regions are the south and the northern mountains, but droughts often occur. Temperatures are high on the low plateaux and plains.

POLITICS & ECONOMY European powers became interested in the Horn of Africa in the 19th century. In 1884, Britain made the northern part of what is now Somalia a protectorate, while Italy took the south in 1905. The new boundaries divided the Somalis into five areas: the two Somalilands, Djibouti (which was taken by France in the 1880s), Ethiopia and Kenya. Since then, many Somalis have longed for reunification in a Greater Somalia.

Italy entered World War II in 1940 and invaded British Somaliland. But British forces conquered the region in 1941 and ruled both Somalilands until 1950, when the United Nations asked Italy to take over the former Italian Somaliland for ten years. In 1960, both Somalilands became independent and united to become Somalia.

Somalia has faced many problems since independence. Economic problems led a military group to seize power in 1969. In the 1970s, Somalia supported an uprising of Somali-speaking people in the Ogaden region of Ethiopia. But Ethiopian forces prevailed and, in 1988, Somalia signed a peace treaty with Ethiopia. The cost of the fighting weakened Somalia's economy. In the 1990s, Somalia gradually broke apart. In 1991, the people in what was formerly British Somaliland set up the "Somaliland Republic," although it never received international recognition. The northeast, which was called Puntland, also seceded from Somalia, while civil war, based on clan rivalry, raged in the south. US troops sent into the south by the UN in 1993 were forced to withdraw in 1994 and the clan warfare continued. However, hopes of reunification were raised in 2000, when a three-year transitional Assembly was set up in the south, following a peace conference held in Djibouti.

Somalia is a developing country, whose economy has been shattered by drought and war. Catastrophic flooding in late 1997 displaced tens of thousands of people, further damaging the country's infrastructure and destroying hopes of economic recovery.

Many Somalis are nomads who raise livestock. Live animals, meat and hides and skins are major exports, followed by bananas grown in the wetter south. Other crops include citrus fruits, cotton, maize and sugarcane. Mining and manufacturing remain relatively unimportant in the economy.

AREA 246,201 sq mi [637,660 sq km] **POPULATION** 9,736,000
CAPITAL (POPULATION) Mogadishu (1,000,000) **GOVERNMENT** Single-party republic, military dominated **ETHNIC GROUPS** Somali 98%, Arab **LANGUAGES** Somali and Arabic (both official), English, Italian
RELIGIONS Islam 99% **CURRENCY** Somali shilling = 100 cents

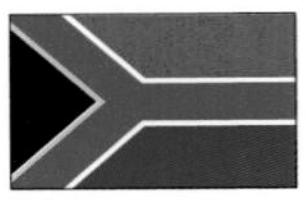

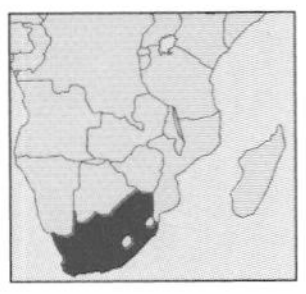

SOUTH AFRICA

GEOGRAPHY The Republic of South Africa is made up largely of the southern part of the huge plateau which makes up most of southern Africa. The highest peaks are in the Drakensberg range, which is formed by the uptilted rim of the plateau. In the southwest lie the folded Cape Mountain ranges. The coastal plains are mostly narrow. The Namib Desert is in the northwest.

Most of South Africa has a mild, sunny climate. Much of the coastal strip, including the city of Cape Town, has warm, dry summers and mild, rainy winters, just like the Mediterranean lands in northern Africa. Inland, large areas are arid.

POLITICS & ECONOMY Early inhabitants in South Africa were the Khoisan. In the last 2,000 years, Bantu-speaking people moved into the area. Their descendants include the Zulu, Xhosa, Sotho and Tswana. The Dutch founded a settlement at the Cape in 1652, but Britain took over in the early 19th century, making the area a colony. The Dutch, called Boers or Afrikaners, resented British rule and moved inland. Rivalry between the groups led to Anglo-Boer Wars in 1880–1 and 1899–1902.

In 1910, the country was united as the Union of South Africa. In 1948, the National Party won power and introduced a policy known as apartheid, under which non-whites had no votes and their human rights were strictly limited. In 1990, Nelson Mandela, leader of the African National Congress (ANC), was released from prison. Multiracial elections were held in 1994 and Mandela became president. After Mandela's retirement in 1999, his successor, Thabo Mbeki, led the ANC to an emphatic victory in the elections.

South Africa is Africa's most developed country. However, most of the black people are poor, with low standards of living. Natural resources include diamonds, gold and many other metals. Mining and manufacturing are the most valuable activities.

AREA 470,566 sq mi [1,219,916 sq km] **POPULATION** 43,666,000
CAPITAL (POPULATION) Cape Town (legislative, 2,350,000); Pretoria (administrative, 1,080,000); Bloemfontein (judiciary, 300,000)
GOVERNMENT Multiparty republic **ETHNIC GROUPS** Black 76%, White 13%, Colored 9%, Asian 2% **LANGUAGES** Afrikaans, English, Ndebele, North Sotho, South Sotho, Swazi, Tsonga, Tswana, Venda, Xhosa, Zulu (all official) **RELIGIONS** Christianity 68%, Hinduism 1%, Islam 1% **CURRENCY** Rand = 100 cents

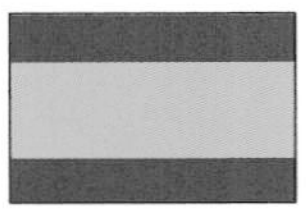

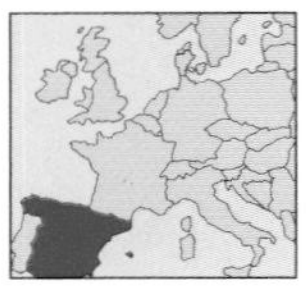

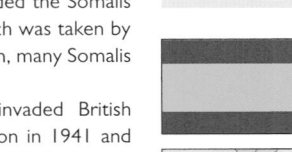

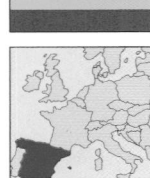

SPAIN

GEOGRAPHY The Kingdom of Spain is the second largest country in Western Europe after France. It shares the Iberian peninsula with Portugal. A large plateau, called the Meseta, covers most of Spain. Much of the Meseta is flat, but it is crossed by several mountain ranges, called sierras.

The northern highlands include the Cantabrian Mountains (Cordillera Cantabrica) and the high Pyrenees, which form Spain's border with France. But Mulhacén, the highest peak on the Spanish mainland, is in the Sierra Nevada in the southeast. Spain also contains fertile coastal plains. Other major lowlands are the Ebro river basin in the northeast and the Guadalquivir river basin in the southwest. Spain also includes the Balearic Islands in the Mediterranean Sea and the Canary Islands off the northwest coast of Africa.

The Meseta has a continental climate, with hot summers and cold winters, when temperatures often fall below freezing point. Snow frequently covers the mountain ranges on the Meseta. The Mediterranean coastal regions also have hot, dry summers, but the winters are mild.

POLITICS & ECONOMY In the 16th century, Spain became a world power. At its peak, it controlled much of Central and South America, parts of Africa and the Philippines in Asia. Spain began to decline in the late 16th century. Its sea power was destroyed by a British fleet in the Battle of Trafalgar (1805). By the 20th century, it was a poor country.

Spain became a republic in 1931, but the republicans were defeated in the Spanish Civil War (1936–9). General Francisco Franco (1892–1975) became the country's dictator, though, technically, it was a monarchy. When Franco died, the monarchy was restored. Prince Juan Carlos became king.

Spain has several groups with their own languages and cultures. Some of these people want to run their own regional affairs. In the northern Basque region, some nationalists have waged a terrorist campaign. A truce in 1998 was ended in 1999 when talks failed to produce results.

Since the late 1970s, a regional parliament with a considerable degree of autonomy has been set up in the Basque Country (called Euskadi in the indigenous tongue and Pais Vasco in Spanish). Similar parliaments have been initiated in Catalonia in the northeast and Galicia in the northwest. All these regions have their own languages.

The revival of Spain's economy, which was shattered by the Civil War, began in the 1950s and 1960s, especially through the growth of tourism and manufacturing. Since the 1950s, Spain has changed from a poor country, dependent on agriculture, to a fairly prosperous industrial nation.

By the early 1990s, agriculture employed 10% of the people, as compared with industry 35% and services, including tourism, 55%. Farmland, including pasture, makes up about two-thirds of the land, with forest making up most of the rest. Major crops include barley, citrus fruits, grapes for winemaking, olives, potatoes and wheat.

Spain has some high-grade iron ore in the north, though otherwise it lacks natural resources. But it has many manufacturing industries. Manufactures include cars, chemicals, clothing, electronics, processed food, metal goods, steel and textiles. The leading manufacturing centers are Barcelona, Bilbao and Madrid.

AREA 194,896 SQ MI [504,780 SQ KM] **POPULATION** 40,667,000
CAPITAL (POPULATION) MADRID (3,029,000)
GOVERNMENT CONSTITUTIONAL MONARCHY
ETHNIC GROUPS CASTILIAN SPANISH 72%, CATALAN 16%, GALICIAN 8%, BASQUE 2% **LANGUAGES** CASTILIAN SPANISH (OFFICIAL), CATALAN, GALICIAN, BASQUE
RELIGIONS CHRISTIANITY (ROMAN CATHOLIC 97%)
CURRENCY EURO; PESETA = 100 CÉNTIMOS

SRI LANKA

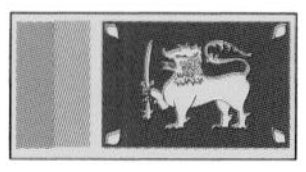

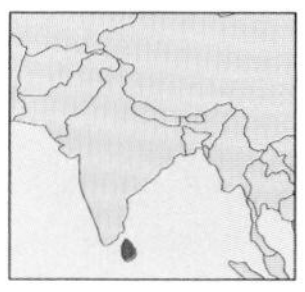

GEOGRAPHY The Democratic Socialist Republic of Sri Lanka is an island nation, separated from the southeast coast of India by the Palk Strait. The land is mostly low-lying, but a mountain region dominates the south-central part of the country.

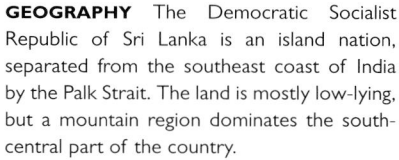

The western part of Sri Lanka has a wet equatorial climate. Temperatures are high and the rainfall is heavy. Eastern Sri Lanka is drier than the west.

POLITICS & ECONOMY From the early 16th century, Ceylon (as Sri Lanka was then known) was ruled successively by the Portuguese, Dutch and British. Independence was achieved in 1948 and the country was renamed Sri Lanka in 1972.

After independence, rivalries between the two main ethnic groups, the Sinhalese and Tamils, marred progress. In the 1950s, the government made Sinhala the official language. Following protests, the prime minister made provisions for Tamil to be used in some areas. In 1959, the prime minister was assassinated by a Sinhalese extremist and he was succeeded by Sirimavo Bandanaraike, who became the world's first woman prime minister.

Conflict between Tamils and Sinhalese continued in the 1970s and 1980s. In 1987, India helped to engineer a cease-fire. Indian troops arrived to enforce the agreement, but withdrew in 1990 after failing to subdue the main guerrilla group, the Tamil Tigers, who wanted to set up an independent Tamil homeland in northern Sri Lanka. In 1993, the country's president was assassinated by a suspected Tamil separatist. Offensives against the Tamil Tigers continued into the 21st century.

The World Bank classifies Sri Lanka as a "low-income" developing country. Agriculture employs half of the work force, and coconuts, rubber and tea are exported. Rice is the chief food crop. Manufacturing is concerned mainly with processing agricultural products and producing textiles.

AREA 25,332 SQ MI [65,610 SQ KM] **POPULATION** 19,416,000
CAPITAL (POPULATION) COLOMBO (1,863,000)
GOVERNMENT MULTIPARTY REPUBLIC
ETHNIC GROUPS SINHALESE 74%, TAMIL 18%, SRI LANKAN MOOR 7% **LANGUAGES** SINHALA AND TAMIL (BOTH OFFICIAL)
RELIGIONS BUDDHISM 69%, HINDUISM 16%, ISLAM 8%, CHRISTIANITY 7%
CURRENCY SRI LANKAN RUPEE = 100 CENTS

SUDAN

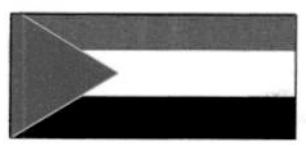

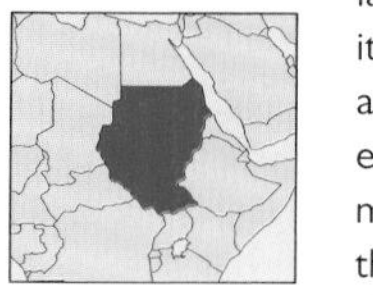

GEOGRAPHY The Republic of Sudan is the largest country in Africa. From north to south, it spans a vast area extending from the arid Sahara in the north to the wet equatorial region in the south. The land is mostly flat, with the highest mountains in the far south. The main physical feature is the River Nile.

The climate of Khartoum represents a transition between the virtually rainless northern deserts and the equatorial lands in the south. Some rain falls in Khartoum in summer.

POLITICS & ECONOMY In the 19th century, Egypt gradually took over Sudan. In 1881, a Muslim religious teacher, the Mahdi ("divinely appointed guide"), led an uprising. Britain and Egypt put the rebellion down in 1898. In 1899, they agreed to rule Sudan jointly as a condominium.

After independence in 1952, the black Africans in the south, who were either Christians or followers of traditional beliefs, feared domination by the Muslim northerners. For example, they objected to the government declaring that Arabic was the only official language. In 1964, civil war broke out and continued until 1972, when the south was given regional self-government, though executive power was still vested in the military government in Khartoum.

In 1983, the government established Islamic law throughout the country. This sparked off further conflict when the Sudan People's Liberation Army in the south launched attacks on government installations. Despite attempts to restore order, the fighting continued into the 21st century. In 1998, the government announced that it accepted the idea of a referendum on the secession of the south, though definitions of the "south" varied. Widespread famine in southern Sudan in 1998 attracted global attention and humanitarian aid.

AREA 967,493 SQ MI [2,505,810 SQ KM] **POPULATION** 33,625,000
CAPITAL (POPULATION) KHARTOUM (925,000) **GOVERNMENT** MILITARY REGIME **ETHNIC GROUPS** SUDANESE ARAB 49%, DINKA 12%, NUBA, BEJA, NUER, AZANDE **LANGUAGES** ARABIC (OFFICIAL), NUBIAN, DINKA
RELIGIONS ISLAM 73%, TRADITIONAL BELIEFS 17%, CHRISTIANITY (ROMAN CATHOLIC 4%, PROTESTANT 2%) **CURRENCY** DINAR = 10 SUDANESE POUNDS

SURINAM

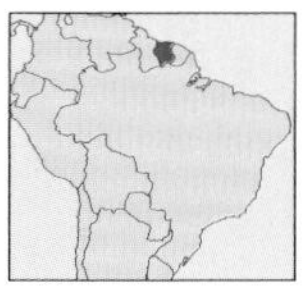

GEOGRAPHY The Republic of Surinam is sandwiched between French Guiana and Guyana in northeastern South America. The narrow coastal plain was once swampy, but it has been drained and now consists mainly of farmland. Inland lie hills and low mountains, which rise to 4,199 ft [1,280 m].

Surinam has a hot, wet and humid climate. Temperatures are high throughout the year.

POLITICS & ECONOMY In 1667, the British handed Surinam to the Dutch in return for New Amsterdam, an area that is now the state of New York. Slave revolts and Dutch neglect hampered development. In the early 19th century, Britain and the Netherlands disputed the ownership of the area. The British gave up their claims in 1813. Slavery was abolished in 1863 and, soon afterward, Indian and Indonesian laborers were introduced to work on the plantations. Surinam became fully independent in 1975, but the economy was weakened when thousands of skilled people emigrated from Surinam to the Netherlands. Following a coup in 1980, Surinam was ruled by a military dictator, Dési Bouterse. The adoption of a new constitution led to the restoration of democracy in 1988, though another military coup occurred in 1990. Elections were held in 1996, but instability, deteriorating relations with the Netherlands and economic problems continued. In 1999, Bouterse was convicted in absentia in the Netherlands of having led a cocaine-trafficking ring during and after his tenure in office.

The World Bank classifies Surinam as an "upper-middle-income" developing country. Its economy is based on mining and metal processing. Surinam is a leading producer of bauxite, from which the metal aluminum is made.

AREA 63,039 SQ MI [163,270 SQ KM] **POPULATION** 497,000
CAPITAL (POPULATION) PARAMARIBO (201,000)
GOVERNMENT MULTIPARTY REPUBLIC **ETHNIC GROUPS** ASIAN INDIAN 37%, CREOLE (MIXED WHITE AND BLACK), 31%, INDONESIAN 14%, BLACK 9%, AMERINDIAN 3%, CHINESE 3%, DUTCH 1% **LANGUAGES** DUTCH (OFFICIAL), SRANANTONGA **RELIGIONS** CHRISTIANITY (ROMAN CATHOLIC 23%, PROTESTANT 19%), HINDUISM 27%, ISLAM 20%
CURRENCY SURINAM GUILDER = 100 CENTS

SWAZILAND

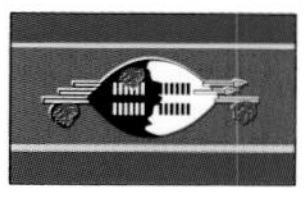

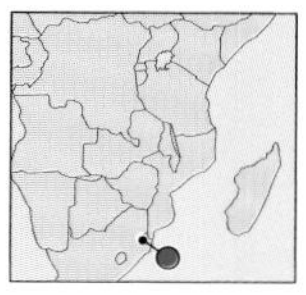

GEOGRAPHY The Kingdom of Swaziland is a small, landlocked country in southern Africa. The country has four regions which run north–south. In the west, the Highveld, with an average height of 3,937 ft [1,200 m], makes up 30% of Swaziland. The Middleveld, between 1,148 ft and 3,281 ft [350 m to 1,000 m], covers 28% of the country. The Lowveld, with an average height of 886 ft [270 m], covers another 33%. Finally, the Lebombo Mountains reach 2,600 ft [800 m] along the eastern border.

The Lowveld is almost tropical, with an average temperature of 72°F [22°C] and low rainfall. The altitude moderates the climate in the west.

POLITICS & ECONOMY In 1894, Britain and the Boers of South Africa agreed to put Swaziland under the control of the South African Republic (the Transvaal). But at the end of the Anglo–Boer War (1899–1902), Britain took control of the country. In 1968, when Swaziland became fully independent as a constitutional monarchy, the head of state was King Sobhuza II. Sobhuza died in 1982 and was succeeded by one of his sons, Prince Makhosetive, who, in 1986, was installed as King Mswati III. Elections in 1993 and 1998, in which political parties were banned, failed to satisfy protesters who opposed the absolute monarchy. But Mswati continued to rule by decree and freedom of speech was severely restricted.

The World Bank classifies Swaziland as a "lower-middle-income" developing country. Agriculture employs 74% of the people, and farm products and processed foods, including soft drink concentrates, sugar, wood pulp, citrus fruits and canned fruit, are the leading exports. Many farmers live at subsistence level, producing little more than they need to feed their own families. Swaziland is heavily dependent on South Africa and the two countries are linked through a customs union.

AREA 6,703 SQ MI [17,360 SQ KM] **POPULATION** 1,121,000
CAPITAL (POPULATION) MBABANE (42,000)
GOVERNMENT MONARCHY **ETHNIC GROUPS** SWAZI 84%, ZULU 10%, TSONGA 2% **LANGUAGES** SISWATI AND ENGLISH (BOTH OFFICIAL)
RELIGIONS CHRISTIANITY 77%, TRADITIONAL BELIEFS
CURRENCY LILANGENI = 100 CENTS

SWEDEN

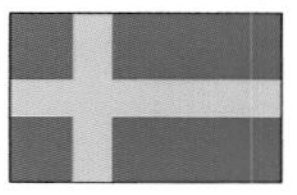

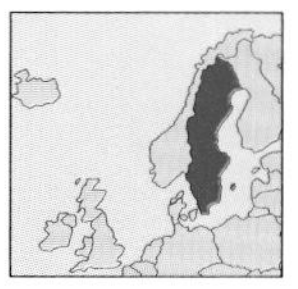

GEOGRAPHY The Kingdom of Sweden is the largest of the countries of Scandinavia in both area and population. It shares the Scandinavian peninsula with Norway. The western part of the country, along the border with Norway, is mountainous. The highest point is Kebnekaise, which reaches 6,946 ft [2,117 m] in the northwest.

The climate of Sweden becomes more severe from south to north. Stockholm has cold winters and cool summers. The far south is much milder.

POLITICS & ECONOMY Swedish Vikings plundered areas to the south and east between the 9th and 11th centuries. Sweden, Denmark and Norway were united in 1397, but Sweden regained its independence in 1523. In 1809, Sweden lost Finland to Russia, but, in 1814, it gained Norway from Denmark. The union between Sweden and Norway was dissolved in 1905. Sweden was neutral in World Wars I and II. Since 1945, Sweden has become a prosperous country. In 1995, it joined the European Union. However, many people were sceptical about the advantages of EU membership and Sweden did not adopt the euro, the single EU currency, in 1999.

Sweden has wide-ranging welfare services. But many people are concerned about the high cost of these services and the high taxes they must pay. In 1991, the Social Democrats, who had built up the welfare state, were defeated. They were re-elected in 1994 and 1998, but they tried to control public spending and expand the economy.

Sweden is a highly developed industrial country. Major products include steel and steel goods. Steel is used in the engineering industry to manufacture aircraft, cars, machinery and ships. Sweden has some of the world's richest iron ore deposits. They are located near Kiruna in the far north. But most of this ore is exported, and Sweden imports most of the materials needed by its industries. Sweden also has a major forestry industry.

Development of hydroelectricity has made up for the lack of oil and coal. In 1996, a decision was taken to decommission all of Sweden's nuclear power stations. This is said to be one of the boldest and most expensive environmental pledges ever made by a government.

Area 173,730 sq mi [449,960 sq km] **Population** 8,560,000
Capital (Population) Stockholm (1,744,000)
Government Constitutional monarchy **Ethnic Groups** Swedish 91%, Finnish 3% **Languages** Swedish (official), Finnish
Religions Christianity (Lutheran 89%, Roman Catholic 2%)
Currency Swedish krona = 100 öre

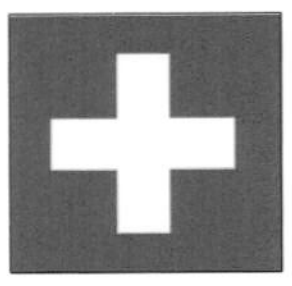
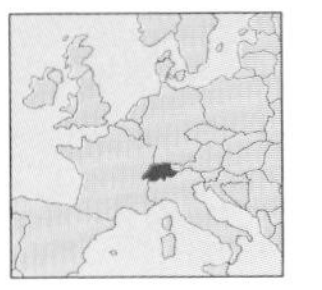

SWITZERLAND

GEOGRAPHY The Swiss Confederation is a landlocked country in Western Europe. Much of the land is mountainous. The Jura Mountains lie along Switzerland's western border with France, while the Swiss Alps make up about 60% of the country in the south and east. Four-fifths of the people of Switzerland live on the fertile Swiss plateau, which contains most of Switzerland's large cities.

The climate of Switzerland varies greatly according to the height of the land. The plateau region has a central European climate with warm summers, but cold and snowy winters. Rain occurs all through the year. The rainiest months are in summer.

POLITICS & ECONOMY In 1291, three small cantons (states) united to defend their freedom against the Habsburg rulers of the Holy Roman Empire. They were Schwyz, Uri and Unterwalden, and they called the confederation they formed "Switzerland." Switzerland expanded and, in the 14th century, defeated Austria in three wars of independence. After a defeat by the French in 1515, the Swiss adopted a policy of neutrality, which they still follow. In 1815, the Congress of Vienna expanded Switzerland to 22 cantons and guaranteed its neutrality. Switzerland's 23rd canton, Jura, was created in 1979 from part of Bern. Neutrality combined with the vigor and independence of its people have made Switzerland prosperous. In 1993 and again in 2001, the Swiss people voted against opening negotiations to join the European Union.

Although lacking in natural resources, Switzerland is a wealthy, industrialized country. Many workers are highly skilled. Major products include chemicals, electrical equipment, machinery and machine tools, precision instruments, processed food, watches and textiles. Farmers produce about three-fifths of the country's food – the rest is imported. Livestock raising, especially dairy farming, is the chief agricultural activity. Crops include fruits, potatoes and wheat. Tourism and banking are also important. Swiss banks attract investors from all over the world.

Area 15,942 sq mi [41,290 sq km] **Population** 6,762,000
Capital (Population) Bern (942,000) **Government** Federal republic **Ethnic Groups** German 64%, French 19%, Italian 8%, Yugoslav 3%, Spanish 2%, Romansch 1% **Languages** French, German, Italian, Romansch (all official) **Religions** Christianity (Roman Catholic 46%, Protestant 40%) **Currency** Swiss franc = 100 centimes

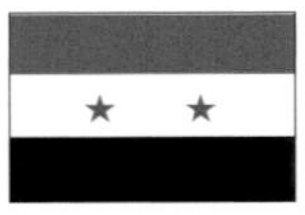
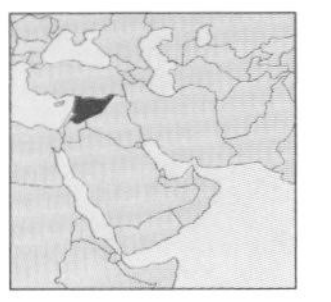

SYRIA

GEOGRAPHY The Syrian Arab Republic is a country in southwestern Asia. The narrow coastal plain is overlooked by a low mountain range which runs north–south. Another range, the Jabal ash Sharqi, runs along the border with Lebanon. South of this range is the Golan Heights, which Israel has occupied since 1967.

The coast has a Mediterranean climate, with dry, warm summers and wet, mild winters. The low mountains cut off Damascus from the sea. It has less rainfall than the coastal areas. To the east, the land becomes drier.

POLITICS & ECONOMY After the collapse of the Turkish Ottoman empire in World War I, Syria was ruled by France. Since independence in 1946, Syria has been involved in the Arab–Israeli wars and, in 1967, it lost a strategic border area, the Golan Heights, to Israel. In 1970, Lieutenant-General Hafez al-Assad took power, establishing a stable but repressive regime. In 1999, Syria had talks with Israel concerning the future of the Golan Heights. These talks formed part of an attempt to establish a peace settlement for the entire east Mediterranean region. Following the death of Assad in 2000, his son, Bashar Assad, was nominated to succeed him.

The World Bank classifies Syria as a "lower-middle-income" developing country. But it has great potential for development. Its main resources are oil, hydroelectricity from the dam at Lake Assad, and fertile land. Oil is the main export; farm products, textiles and phosphates are also important. Agriculture employs about 26% of the work force.

Area 71,498 sq mi [185,180 sq km] **Population** 17,826,000
Capital (Population) Damascus (1,549,000)
Government Multiparty republic
Ethnic Groups Arab 89%, Kurd 6%
Languages Arabic (official) **Religions** Islam 90%, Christianity 9% **Currency** Syrian pound = 100 piastres

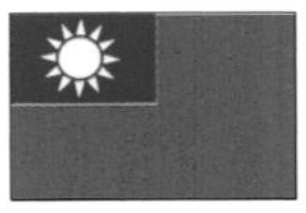
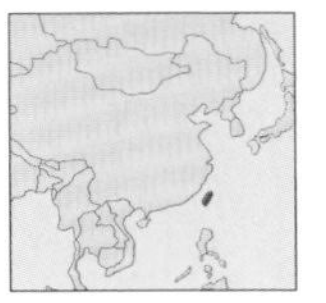

TAIWAN

GEOGRAPHY High mountain ranges run down the length of the island, with dense forest in many areas.

The climate is warm, moist and suitable for agriculture.

POLITICS & ECONOMY Chinese settlers occupied Taiwan from the 7th century. In 1895, Japan seized the territory from the Portuguese, who had named it Isla Formosa, or "beautiful island." China regained the island after World War II. In 1949, it became the refuge of the Nationalists who had been driven out of China by the Communists. They set up the Republic of China, which, with US help, launched an ambitious programme of economic development. Today, it produces a wide range of manufactured goods. Mainland China regards Taiwan as one of its provinces, though reunification seems unlikely in the foreseeable future.

Area 13,900 sq mi [36,000 sq km] **Population** 22,000,000
Capital (Population) Taipei (2,653,000)
Government Unitary multiparty republic
Ethnic Groups Taiwanese (Han Chinese) 84%, mainland Chinese 14% **Languages** Mandarin (official), Min, Hakka **Religions** Buddhist 43%, Taoist & Confucian 49%
Currency New Taiwan dollar = 100 cents

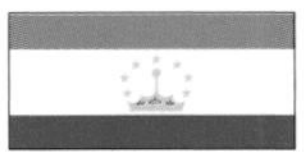
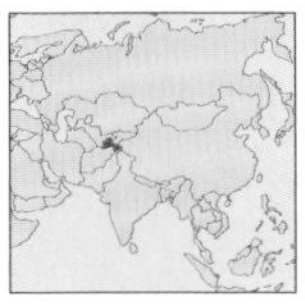

TAJIKISTAN

GEOGRAPHY The Republic of Tajikistan is one of the five central Asian republics that formed part of the former Soviet Union. Only 7% of the land is below 3,280 ft [1,000 m], while almost all of eastern Tajikistan is above 9,840 ft [3,000 m]. The highest point is Communism Peak (Pik Kommunizma), which reaches 24,590 ft [7,495 m]. The main ranges are the westward extension of the Tian Shan Range in the north and the snow-capped Pamirs in the southeast. Earthquakes are common throughout the country.

Tajikistan has a severe continental climate. Summers are hot and dry in the lower valleys, and winters are long and bitterly cold in the mountains.

POLITICS & ECONOMY Russia conquered parts of Tajikistan in the late 19th century and, by 1920, Russia took complete control. In 1924, Tajikistan became part of the Uzbek Soviet Socialist Republic, but, in 1929, it was expanded, taking in some areas populated by Uzbeks, becoming the Tajik Soviet Socialist Republic.

While the Soviet Union began to introduce reforms during the 1980s, many Tajiks demanded freedom. In 1989, the Tajik government made Tajik the official language instead of Russian and, in 1990, it stated that its local laws overruled Soviet laws. Tajikistan became fully independent in 1991, following the breakup of the Soviet Union. As the poorest of the ex-Soviet republics, Tajikistan faced many problems in trying to introduce a free-market system.

In 1992, civil war broke out between the government, which was run by former Communists, and an alliance of democrats and Islamic forces. A cease-fire was agreed in 1996, and in 1997 representatives of the opposition were brought into the government. Presidential elections were held in 1999, followed by parliamentary elections in 2000.

The World Bank classifies Tajikistan as a "low-income" developing country. Agriculture, mainly on irrigated land, is the main activity and cotton is the chief product. Other crops include fruits, grains and vegetables. The country has large hydroelectric power resources and it produces aluminum.

Area 55,520 sq mi [143,100 sq km] **Population** 7,041,000
Capital (Population) Dushanbe (524,000)
Government Transitional democracy
Ethnic Groups Tajik 62%, Uzbek 24%, Russian 8%, Tatar, Kyrgyz, Ukrainian, German
Languages Tajik (official), Uzbek, Russian
Religions Islam **Currency** Tajik rouble = 100 tanga

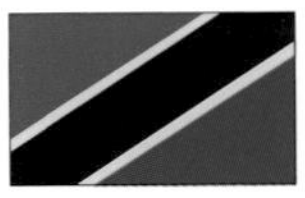
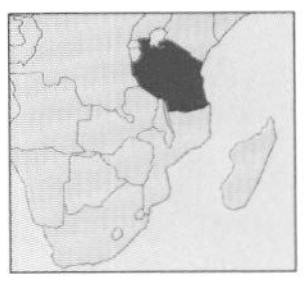

TANZANIA

GEOGRAPHY The United Republic of Tanzania consists of the former mainland country of Tanganyika and the island nation of Zanzibar, which also includes the island of Pemba. Behind a narrow coastal plain, most of Tanzania is a plateau, which is broken by arms of the Great African Rift Valley. In the west, this valley contains lakes Nyasa and Tanganyika. The highest peak is Kilimanjaro, Africa's tallest mountain.

The coast has a hot and humid climate, with the greatest rainfall in April and May. The inland plateaux and mountains are cooler and less humid.

POLITICS & ECONOMY Mainland Tanganyika became a German territory in the 1880s, while Zanzibar and Pemba became a British protectorate in 1890. Following Germany's defeat in World War I, Britain took over Tanganyika, which remained a British territory until its independence in 1961. In 1964, Tanganyika and Zanzibar united to form the United Republic of Tanzania. The country's president, Julius Nyerere, pursued socialist policies of self-help (*ujamaa*) and egalitarianism. Many of its social reforms were successful, though the country failed to make economic progress. Nyerere resigned as president in 1985, although he retained much influence until his death in 1999. His successors, Ali Hassan Mwinyi and, from 1995, Benjamin Mkapa, introduced more liberal economic policies.

Tanzania is one of the world's poorest countries. Crops are grown on only 5% of the land, yet agriculture employs 85% of the people. Food crops include bananas, cassava, maize, millet and rice.

Area 364,899 sq mi [945,090 sq km] **Population** 39,639,000
Capital (Population) Dodoma (204,000)
Government Multiparty republic
Ethnic Groups Nyamwezi and Sukuma 21%, Swahili 9%, Hehet and Bena 7%, Makonde 6%, Haya 6%
Languages Swahili and English (both official)
Religions Christianity (mostly Roman Catholic) 34%, Islam 33% (99% in Zanzibar), traditional beliefs and others 33%
Currency Tanzanian shilling = 100 cents

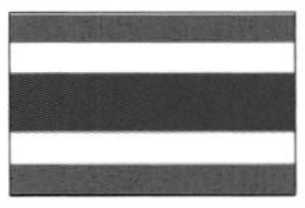
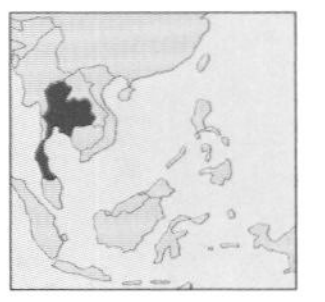

THAILAND

GEOGRAPHY The Kingdom of Thailand is one of the ten countries in Southeast Asia. The highest land is in the north, where Doi Inthanon, the highest peak, reaches 8,514 ft [2,595 m]. The Khorat plateau, in the northeast, makes up about 30% of the country and is the most heavily populated part of Thailand. In the south, Thailand shares the finger-like Malay peninsula with Burma and Malaysia.

Thailand has a tropical climate. Monsoon winds from the southwest bring heavy rains between the months of May and October. The rainfall in Bangkok is lower than in many other parts of South-east Asia, because mountains shelter the central plains from the rain-bearing winds.

POLITICS & ECONOMY The first Thai state was set up in the 13th century. By 1350, it included most of what is now Thailand. European contact began in the early 16th century. But, in the late 17th century, the Thais, fearing interference in their affairs, forced all Europeans to leave. This policy continued for 150 years. In 1782, a Thai General, Chao Phraya Chakkri, became king, founding a dynasty which continues today. The country became known as Siam, and Bangkok became its capital. From the mid-19th century, contacts with the West were restored. In World War I, Siam supported the Allies against Germany and Austria-Hungary. But in 1941, the country was conquered by Japan and became its ally. However, after the end of World War II, it became an ally of the United States.

Since 1967, when Thailand became a member of ASEAN (the Association of Southeast Asian Nations), its economy has grown, especially its manufacturing and service industries. However, in 1997, it suffered recession along with other fast-developing countries in eastern Asia, and its economic policies had to be modified.

The economy still depends on agriculture, which employs more than two-fifths of the people. Rice is the chief crop. Cassava, cotton, maize, rubber, sugarcane and tobacco are also grown. Thailand also mines tin and other minerals. However, the chief exports are manufactures, including food products, machinery, timber products and textiles. Tourism is another major source of income.

AREA 198,116 sq mi [513,120 sq km] **POPULATION** 63,670,000
CAPITAL (POPULATION) Bangkok (5,572,000)
GOVERNMENT Constitutional monarchy
ETHNIC GROUPS Thai 80%, Chinese 12%, Malay 4%, Khmer 3% **LANGUAGES** Thai (official), Chinese, Malay
RELIGIONS Buddhism 94%, Islam 4%, Christianity 1%
CURRENCY Thai baht = 100 satang

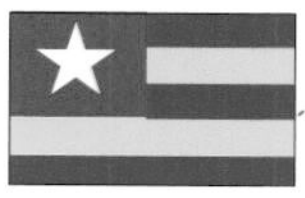
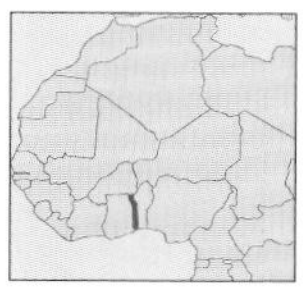

TOGO

GEOGRAPHY The Republic of Togo is a long, narrow country in West Africa. From north to south, it extends about 311 mi [500 km]. Its coastline on the Gulf of Guinea is only 40 mi [64 km] long and it is only 90 mi [145 km] at its widest point.

Togo has high temperatures all through the year. The main wet season is from March to July, with a minor wet season in October and November.

POLITICS & ECONOMY Togo became a German protectorate in 1884 but, in 1919, Britain took over the western third of the territory, while France took over the eastern two-thirds. In 1956, the people of British Togoland voted to join Ghana, while French Togoland became an independent republic in 1960.

A military regime took power in 1963. In 1967, General Gnassingbe Eyadema became head of state and suspended the constitution. Under a new constitution adopted in 1992, multiparty elections were held in 1994. However, in 1998, paramilitary policies stopped the count in the presidential elections when it became clear that Eyadema had been defeated. As a result, the leading opposition parties boycotted the general elections in 1999.

Togo is a poor, developing country. Farming employs 65% of the people and major food crops include cassava, maize, millet and yams. The leading export is phosphate rock, which is used to make fertilizers.

AREA 21,927 sq mi [56,790 sq km] **POPULATION** 4,861,000
CAPITAL (POPULATION) Lomé (590,000)
GOVERNMENT Multiparty republic **ETHNIC GROUPS** Ewe-Adja 43%, Tem-Kabre 26%, Gurma 16% **LANGUAGES** French (official), Ewe, Kabiye
RELIGIONS Traditional beliefs 50%, Christianity 35%, Islam 15%
CURRENCY CFA franc = 100 centimes

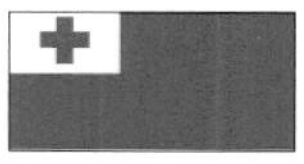
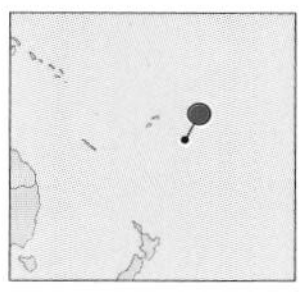

TONGA

The Kingdom of Tonga, a former British protectorate, became independent in 1970. Situated in the South Pacific Ocean, it contains more than 170 islands, 36 of which are inhabited. Agriculture is the main activity; coconuts, copra, fruits and fish are leading products.

AREA 290 sq mi [750 sq km] **POPULATION** 92,000 **CAPITAL** Nuku'alofa

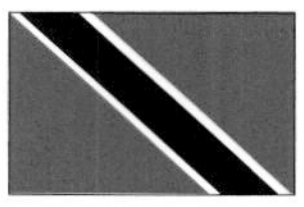
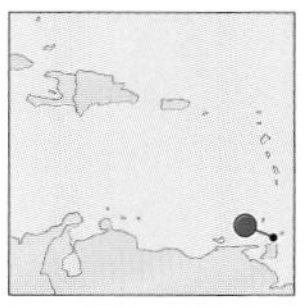

TRINIDAD AND TOBAGO

The Republic of Trinidad and Tobago became independent from Britain in 1962. These tropical islands, populated by people of African, Asian (mainly Indian) and European origin, are hilly and forested, though there are some fertile plains. Oil production is the mainstay of the economy.

AREA 1,981 sq mi [5,130 sq km]
POPULATION 1,484,000 **CAPITAL** Port-of-Spain

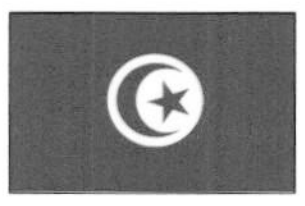
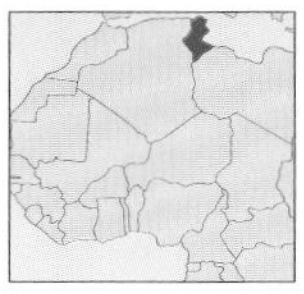

TUNISIA

GEOGRAPHY The Republic of Tunisia is the smallest country in North Africa. The mountains in the north are an eastward and comparatively low extension of the Atlas Mountains. To the north and east of the mountains lie fertile plains, especially between Sfax, Tunis and Bizerte. In the south, low-lying regions contain a vast salt pan, called the Chott Djerid, and part of the Sahara Desert.

Northern Tunisia has a Mediterranean climate, with dry, sunny summers, and mild winters with a moderate rainfall. The average yearly rainfall decreases toward the south.

POLITICS & ECONOMY In 1881, France established a protectorate over Tunisia and ruled the country until 1956. The new parliament abolished the monarchy and declared Tunisia to be a republic in 1957, with the nationalist leader, Habib Bourguiba, as president. His government introduced many reforms, including votes for women, but various problems arose, including unemployment among the middle class and fears that Western values introduced by tourists might undermine Muslim values. In 1987, the prime minister Zine el Abidine Ben Ali removed Bourguiba from office and succeeded him as president. He was elected in 1989 and re-elected in 1994 and 1999.

The World Bank classifies Tunisia as a "middle-income" developing country. The main resources and chief exports are phosphates and oil. Most industries are concerned with food processing. Agriculture employs 22% of the people; major crops being barley, dates, grapes, olives and wheat. Fishing is important, as is tourism.

AREA 63,170 sq mi [163,610 sq km] **POPULATION** 9,924,000
CAPITAL (POPULATION) Tunis (1,827,000) **GOVERNMENT** Multiparty republic **ETHNIC GROUPS** Arab 98%, Berber 1%, French
LANGUAGES Arabic (official), French
RELIGIONS Islam 99% **CURRENCY** Dinar = 1,000 millimes

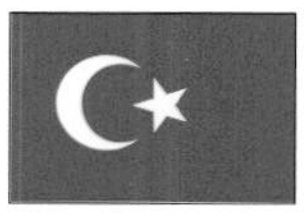
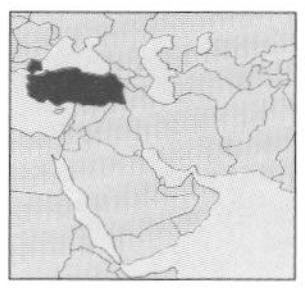

TURKEY

GEOGRAPHY The Republic of Turkey lies in two continents. European Turkey, also called Thrace, lies west of a waterway linking the Mediterranean and Black seas. Most of Asian Turkey consists of plateaux and mountains, which rise to 16,945 ft [5,165 m] at Mount Ararat (Agri Dagi) near the border with Armenia. Earthquakes are common. More than 15,000 people were killed in 1999, when earthquakes struck in the northwest.

Central Turkey has a dry climate, with hot, sunny summers and cold winters. The driest part of the central plateau lies south of the city of Ankara, around Lake Tuz. The west has a Mediterranean climate, but the Black Sea coast has cooler summers.

POLITICS & ECONOMY In AD 330, the Roman empire moved its capital to Byzantium, which it renamed Constantinople. Constantinople became capital of the East Roman (or Byzantine) empire in 395. Muslim Seljuk Turks from central Asia invaded Anatolia in the 11th century. In the 14th century, another group of Turks, the Ottomans, conquered the area. In 1435, the Ottoman Turks took Constantinople, which they called Istanbul.

The Ottoman Turks built up a large empire which finally collapsed during World War I (1914–18). In 1923, Turkey became a republic. Its leader Mustafa Kemal, or Atatürk ("father of the Turks"), launched policies to modernize and secularize the country.

Since the 1940s, Turkey has sought to strengthen its ties with Western powers. It joined NATO (North Atlantic Treaty Organization) in 1951 and it applied to join the European Economic Community in 1987. But Turkey's conflict with Greece, together with its invasion of northern Cyprus in 1974, have led many Europeans to treat Turkey's aspirations with caution. Political instability, military coups, conflict with Kurdish nationalists in eastern Turkey and concern about the country's record on human rights are other problems. Turkey has enjoyed democracy since 1983, though, in 1998, the government banned the Islamist Welfare Party, which it accused of violating secular principles. In 1999, the Muslim Virtue Party (successor to Islamist Welfare Party) lost ground. The largest numbers of parliamentary seats were won by the ruling Democratic Left Party and the far-right National Action Party.

The World Bank classifies Turkey as a "lower-middle-income" developing country. Agriculture employs 37% of the people, and barley, cotton, fruits, maize, tobacco and wheat are major crops. Livestock farming is important and wool is a leading product.

Turkey produces chromium, but manufacturing is the chief activity. Manufactures include processed farm products and textiles, cars, fertilizers, iron and steel, machinery, metal products and paper products. Over 9 million tourists visited Turkey in 1998. But, in 1999, tourism was threatened by Kurdish bombings in Ankara and Istanbul.

AREA 300,946 sq mi [779,450 sq km] **POPULATION** 66,789,000
CAPITAL (POPULATION) Ankara (3,028,000)
GOVERNMENT Multiparty republic **ETHNIC GROUPS** Turkish 86%, Kurdish 11%, Arab 2% **LANGUAGES** Turkish (official), Kurdish
RELIGIONS Islam 99% **CURRENCY** Turkish lira = 100 kurus

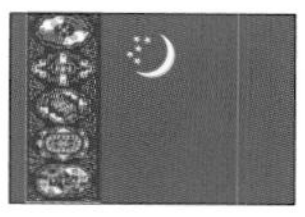
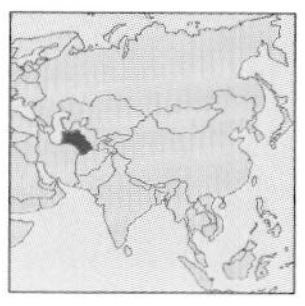

TURKMENISTAN

GEOGRAPHY The Republic of Turkmenistan is one of the five central Asian republics which once formed part of the former Soviet Union. Most of the land is low-lying, with mountains lying on the southern and southwestern borders. In the west lies the salty Caspian Sea. Most of Turkmenistan is arid and the Garagum, Asia's largest sand desert, covers about 80% of the country. Turkmenistan has a continental climate, with average annual rainfall varying from 3 in [80 mm] in the desert to 12 in [300 mm] in the mountains. Summer months are hot but winter temperatures drop well below freezing point.

POLITICS & ECONOMY Just over 1,000 years ago, Turkic people settled in the lands east of the Caspian Sea and the name "Turkmen" comes from this time. Mongol armies conquered the area in the 13th century and Islam was introduced in the 14th century. Russia took over the area in the 1870s and 1880s. After the Russian Revolution of 1917, the area came under Communist rule and, in 1924, it became the Turkmen Soviet Socialist Republic. The Communists strictly controlled all aspects of life and discouraged religion. But they improved such services as education, health, housing and transport.

In the 1980s, when the Soviet Union began to introduce reforms, the Turkmen began to demand more freedom. In 1990, the Turkmen government stated that its laws overruled Soviet laws. In 1991, Turkmenistan became fully independent after the breakup of the Soviet Union. But the country kept ties with Russia through the Commonwealth of Independent States (CIS).

In 1992, Turkmenistan adopted a new constitution, allowing for the setting up of political parties, providing that they were not ethnic or religious in character. But, effectively, Turkmenistan remained a one-party state and, in 1992, Saparmurad Niyazov, the former Communist and now Democratic Party leader, was the only candidate. In 1994, a referendum prolonged Niyazov's term of office to 2002, while, in 1999, the parliament declared him president for life.

Faced with many economic problems, Turkmenistan began to look south rather than to the CIS for support. As part of this policy, it joined the Economic Cooperation Organization which had been set up in 1985 by Iran, Pakistan and Turkey. In 1996, the completion of a rail link from Turkmenistan to the Iranian coast was seen both as a revival of the traditions of the ancient silk road, and as a highly significant step for the future economic development of Central Asia.

Turkmenistan's chief resources are oil and natural gas, but the main activity is agriculture, with cotton, grown on irrigated land, as the main crop. Grain and vegetables are also important. Manufactures include cement, glass, petrochemicals and textiles.

AREA 188,450 sq mi [488,100 sq km] **POPULATION** 4,585,000
CAPITAL (POPULATION) Ashgabat (536,000) **GOVERNMENT** Single-party republic **ETHNIC GROUPS** Turkmen 72%, Russian 10%, Uzbek 9%, Kazak 3%, Tatar **LANGUAGES** Turkmen (official), Russian, Uzbek, Kazak **RELIGIONS** Islam **CURRENCY** Manat = 100 tenesi

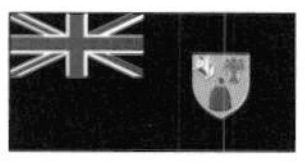
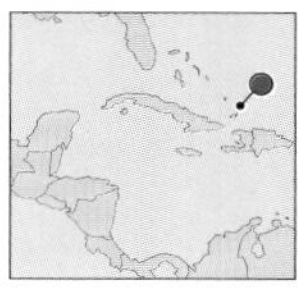

TURKS AND CAICOS ISLANDS

The Turks and Caicos Islands, a British territory in the Caribbean since 1776, are a group of about 30 islands. Fishing and tourism are major activities.

AREA 166 sq mi [430 sq km]
POPULATION 12,000 **CAPITAL** Cockburn Town

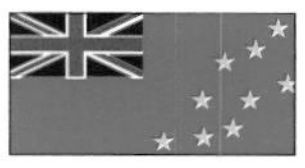
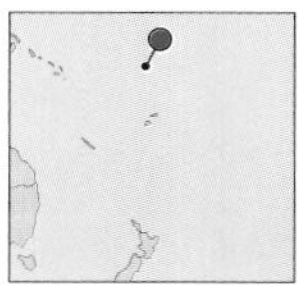

TUVALU

Tuvalu, formerly called the Ellice Islands, was a British territory from the 1890s until it became independent in 1978. It consists of nine low-lying coral atolls in the southern Pacific Ocean. Copra is the chief export.

AREA 9 sq mi [24 sq km] **POPULATION** 11,000
CAPITAL Fongafale

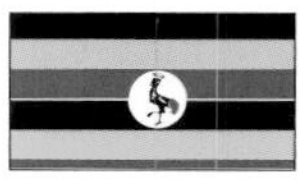
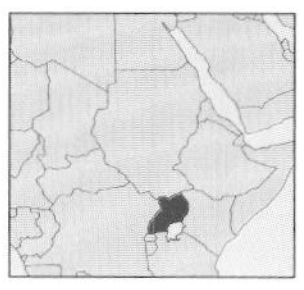

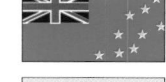

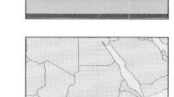

UGANDA

GEOGRAPHY The Republic of Uganda is a landlocked country on the East African plateau. It contains part of Lake Victoria, Africa's largest lake and a source of the River Nile, which occupies a shallow depression in the plateau.

The equator runs through Uganda and the country is warm throughout the year, though the high altitude moderates the temperature. The wettest regions are the lands to the north of Lake Victoria, where Kampala is situated, and the western mountains, especially the high Ruwenzori range.

POLITICS & ECONOMY Little is known of the early history of Uganda. When Europeans first reached the area in the 19th century, many of the people were organized in kingdoms, the most powerful of which was Buganda, the home of the Baganda people. Britain took over the country between 1894 and 1914, and ruled it until independence in 1962.

In 1967, Uganda became a republic and Buganda's Kabaka (king), Sir Edward Mutesa II, was made president. But tensions between the Kabaka and the prime minister, Apollo Milton Obote, led to the dismissal of the Kabaka in 1966. Obote also abolished the traditional kingdoms, including Buganda. Obote was overthrown in 1971 by an army group led by General Idi Amin Dada. Amin ruled as a dictator. He forced most of the Asians who lived in Uganda to leave the country and had many of his opponents killed.

In 1978, a border dispute between Uganda and Tanzania led Tanzanian troops to enter Uganda. With help from Ugandan opponents of Amin, they overthrew Amin's government. In 1980, Obote led his party to victory in national elections. But after charges of fraud, Obote's opponents began guerrilla warfare. A military group overthrew Obote in 1985, though strife continued until 1986, when Yoweri Museveni's National Resistance Movement seized power. In 1993, Museveni restored the traditional kingdoms, including Buganda where a new Kabaka was crowned. Museveni also held elections in 1994 but political parties were not permitted. Museveni was elected president in 1996 and re-elected in 2001.

The strife since the 1960s has greatly damaged the economy, but the economy grew during a period of stability in the 1990s. The situation worsened when Uganda intervened militarily in Congo (then Zaïre) in 1998. Agriculture dominates the economy, employing 86% of the people. The chief export is coffee.

AREA 91,073 sq mi [235,880 sq km] **POPULATION** 26,958,000
CAPITAL (POPULATION) Kampala (773,000)
GOVERNMENT Republic in transition
ETHNIC GROUPS Baganda 18%, Banyoro 14%, Teso 9%, Banyan 8%, Basoga 8%, Bagisu 7%, Bachiga 7%, Lango 6%, Acholi 5%
LANGUAGES English and Swahili (both official)
RELIGIONS Christianity (Roman Catholic 40%, Protestant 29%), traditional beliefs 18%, Islam 7%
CURRENCY Uganda shilling = 100 cents

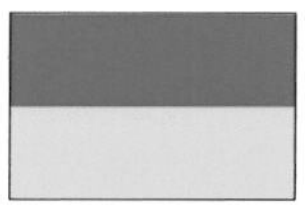

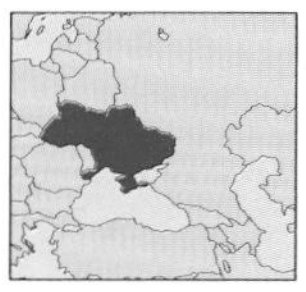

UKRAINE

GEOGRAPHY Ukraine is the second largest country in Europe after Russia. It was formerly part of the Soviet Union, which split apart in 1991. This mostly flat country faces the Black Sea in the south. The Crimean peninsula includes a highland region overlooking Yalta.

Ukraine has warm summers, but the winters are cold, becoming more severe from west to east. In the summer, the east of the country is often warmer than the west. The heaviest rainfall occurs in the summer.

POLITICS & ECONOMY Kiev was the original capital of the early Slavic civilization known as Kievan Rus. In the 17th and 18th centuries, parts of Ukraine came under Polish and Russian rule. But Russia gained most of Ukraine in the late 18th century. In 1918, Ukraine became independent, but in 1922 it became part of the Soviet Union. Millions of people died in the 1930s as a result of Soviet policies, while millions more died during the Nazi occupation (1941–4).

In the 1980s, Ukrainian people demanded more say over their affairs. The country finally became independent when the Soviet Union broke up in 1991. Ukraine continued to work with Russia through the Commonwealth of Independent States. But Ukraine differed with Russia on some issues, including control over Crimea. In 1999, a treaty ratifying Ukraine's present boundaries failed to get the approval of Russia's upper house.

The World Bank classifies Ukraine as a "lower-middle-income" economy. Agriculture is important. Crops include wheat and sugar beet, which are the major exports, together with barley, maize, potatoes, sunflowers and tobacco. Livestock rearing and fishing are also important industries.

Manufacturing is the chief economic activity. Major manufactures include iron and steel, machinery and vehicles. Ukraine has large coalfields. The country imports oil and natural gas, but it has hydroelectric and nuclear power stations. In 1986, an accident at the Chernobyl nuclear power plant caused widespread nuclear radiation.

AREA 233,100 sq mi [603,700 sq km] **POPULATION** 52,558,000
CAPITAL (POPULATION) Kiev (2,630,000)
GOVERNMENT Multiparty republic
ETHNIC GROUPS Ukrainian 73%, Russian 22%, Jewish 1%, Belarussian 1%, Moldovan, Bulgarian, Polish
LANGUAGES Ukrainian (official), Russian
RELIGIONS Christianity (mostly Ukrainian Orthodox)
CURRENCY Hryvna

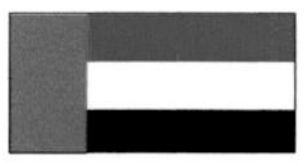

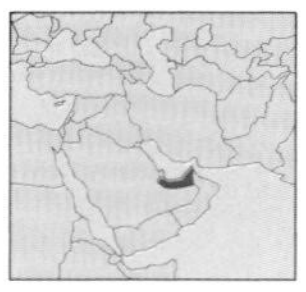

UNITED ARAB EMIRATES

The United Arab Emirates were formed in 1971 when the seven Trucial States of the Gulf (Abu Dhabi, Dubai, Sharjah, Ajman, Umm al Qawayn, Ra's al Khaymah and Al Fujayrah) opted to join together and form an independent country. The economy of this hot and dry country depends on oil production, and oil revenues give the United Arab Emirates one of the highest per capita GNPs in Asia.

AREA 32,278 sq mi [83,600 sq km] **POPULATION** 1,951,000
CAPITAL Abu Dhabi

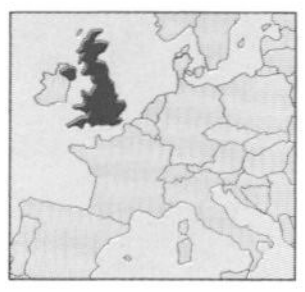

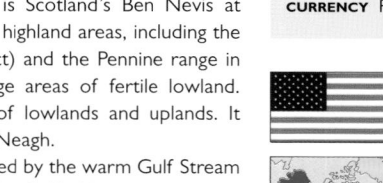

UNITED KINGDOM

GEOGRAPHY The United Kingdom (or UK) is a union of four countries. Three of them – England, Scotland and Wales – make up Great Britain. The fourth country is Northern Ireland. The Isle of Man and the Channel Islands, including Jersey and Guernsey, are not part of the UK. They are self-governing British dependencies.

The land is highly varied. Much of Scotland and Wales is mountainous, and the highest peak is Scotland's Ben Nevis at 4,406 ft [1,343 m]. England has some highland areas, including the Cumbrian Mountains (or Lake District) and the Pennine range in the north. But England also has large areas of fertile lowland. Northern Ireland is also a mixture of lowlands and uplands. It contains the UK's largest lake, Lough Neagh.

The UK has a mild climate, influenced by the warm Gulf Stream which flows across the Atlantic from the Gulf of Mexico, then past the British Isles. Moist winds from the southwest bring rain, but the rainfall decreases from west to east. Winds from the east and north bring cold weather in winter.

POLITICS & ECONOMY In ancient times, Britain was invaded by many peoples, including Iberians, Celts, Romans, Angles, Saxons, Jutes, Norsemen, Danes, and Normans, who arrived in 1066. The evolution of the United Kingdom spanned hundreds of years. The Normans finally overcame Welsh resistance in 1282, when King Edward I annexed Wales and united it with England. Union with Scotland was achieved by the Act of Union of 1707. This created a country known as the United Kingdom of Great Britain.

Ireland came under Norman rule in the 11th century, and much of its later history was concerned with a struggle against English domination. In 1801, Ireland became part of the United Kingdom of Great Britain and Ireland. But in 1921, southern Ireland broke away to become the Irish Free State. Most of the people in the Irish Free State were Roman Catholics. In Northern Ireland, where the majority of the people were Protestants, most people wanted to remain citizens of the United Kingdom. As a result, the country's official name changed to the United Kingdom of Great Britain and Northern Ireland.

The modern history of the UK began in the 18th century when the British empire began to develop, despite the loss in 1783 of its 13 North American colonies which became the core of the modern United States. The other major event occurred in the late 18th century, when the UK became the first country to industrialize its economy.

The British empire broke up after World War II (1939–45), though the UK still administers many small, mainly island, territories around the world. The empire was transformed into the Commonwealth of Nations, a free association of independent countries which numbered 54 in 2001.

But while the UK retained a world role through the Commonwealth and the United Nations, it recognized that its economic future lay within Europe. As a result, it became a member of the European Economic Community (now the European Union) in 1973. In the 1990s, most people accepted the importance of the EU to the UK's economic future. But some feared a loss of British identity should the EU evolve into a political federation. In 1999, Britain did not adopt the euro, the single currency of the EU, but it seemed that the issue of Britain's involvement in the EU would continue to provoke debate in the early 21st century.

The UK is a major industrial and trading nation. It lacks natural resources apart from coal, iron ore, oil and natural gas, and has to import most of the materials it needs for its industries. The UK also has to import food, because it produces only about two-thirds of the food it needs. In the first half of the 20th century, Britain was a major exporter of cars, ships, steel and textiles. But many industries have suffered from competition from other countries, with lower labor costs. Today, industries have to use high-technology in order to compete on the world market.

The UK is one of the world's most urbanized countries, and agriculture employs only 1% of the people. Production is high because of the use of scientific methods and modern machinery. However, in the early 21st century, especially following the outbreak of foot-and-mouth disease in 2001, questions were raised about the future of rural industries. Major crops include barley, potatoes, sugar beet and wheat. Sheep are the leading livestock, but beef and dairy cattle, pigs and poultry are also important. Fishing is another major activity and the UK is one of the largest fishing countries in the EU. Important catches include cod, haddock, plaice and mackerel.

Service industries play a major part in the UK's economy. Financial and insurance services bring in much-needed foreign exchange, while tourism has become a major earner.

AREA 94,202 sq mi [243,368 sq km] **POPULATION** 58,393,000
CAPITAL (POPULATION) London (8,089,000)
GOVERNMENT Constitutional monarchy
ETHNIC GROUPS White 94%, Asian Indian 1%, Pakistani 1%, West Indian 1% **LANGUAGES** English (official), Welsh, Gaelic **RELIGIONS** Christianity (Anglican 57%, Roman Catholic 13%, Presbyterian 7%, Methodist 4%, Baptist 1%), Islam 1%, Judaism, Hinduism, Sikhism
CURRENCY Pound sterling = 100 pence

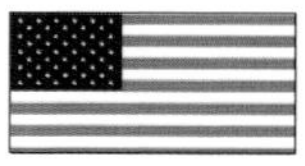

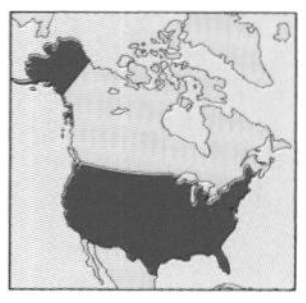

UNITED STATES OF AMERICA

GEOGRAPHY The United States of America is the world's fourth largest country in area and the third largest in population. It contains 50 states, 48 of which lie between Canada and Mexico, plus Alaska in northwestern North America, and Hawaii, a group of volcanic islands in the North Pacific Ocean. Densely populated coastal plains lie to the east and south of the Appalachian Mountains. The central lowlands drained by the Mississippi–Missouri rivers stretch from the Appalachians to the Rocky Mountains in the west. The Pacific region contains fertile valleys, separated by mountain ranges.

The climate varies greatly, ranging from the Arctic cold of Alaska to the intense heat of Death Valley, a bleak desert in California. Of the 48 states between Canada and Mexico, winters are cold and snowy in the north, but mild in the south, a region which is often called the "Sun Belt."

POLITICS & ECONOMY The first people in North America, the ancestors of the Native Americans (or American Indians) arrived perhaps 40,000 years ago from Asia. Although Vikings probably reached North America 1,000 years ago, European exploration proper did not begin until the late 15th century.

The first Europeans to settle in large numbers were the British, who founded settlements on the eastern coast in the early 17th century. British rule ended in the War of ndependence (1775–83). The country expanded in 1803 when a vast territory in the south and west was acquired through the Louisiana Purchase, while the border with Mexico was fixed in the mid-19th century.

The Civil War (1861–5) ended the threat that the nation might split in two parts. It also ended slavery for the country's many African Americans. In the late 19th century, the West was opened up, while immigrants flooded in from Europe and elsewhere.

During the late 19th and early 20th centuries, industrialization led to the United States becoming the world's leading economic superpower and a pioneer in science and technology. Because of its economic strength, it has been able to take on the mantle of the champion of the Western world and of democratic government. The fall of Communism and the subsequent breakup of the Soviet Union left the United States as the world's only real superpower. While this supremacy may well be challenged by China in time, the USA remains the most powerful voice in global politics.

The United States has the world's largest economy in terms of the total value of its production. Although agriculture employs only 2% of the people, farming is highly mechanized and scientific, and the United States leads the world in farm production. Major products include beef and dairy cattle, together with such crops as cotton, fruits, groundnuts, maize, potatoes, soya beans, tobacco and wheat.

The country's natural resources include oil, natural gas and coal. There are also a wide range of metal ores which are used in manufacturing industries, together with timber, especially from the forests of the Pacific northwest. Manufacturing is the single most important activity, employing about 17% of the population. Major products include vehicles, food products, chemicals, machinery, printed goods, metal products and scientific instruments. California is now the leading manufacturing state. Many southern states, petroleum rich and climatically favored, have also become highly prosperous in recent years.

AREA 3,618,765 SQ MI [9,372,610 SQ KM] **POPULATION** 266,096,000
CAPITAL (POPULATION) WASHINGTON, D.C. (4,466,000)
GOVERNMENT FEDERAL REPUBLIC
ETHNIC GROUPS WHITE 80%, AFRICAN AMERICAN 12%, OTHER RACES 8% **LANGUAGES** ENGLISH (OFFICIAL), SPANISH, MORE THAN 30 OTHERS **RELIGIONS** CHRISTIANITY (PROTESTANT 53%, ROMAN CATHOLIC 26%, OTHER CHRISTIAN 8%), ISLAM 2%, JUDAISM 2%
CURRENCY US DOLLAR = 100 CENTS

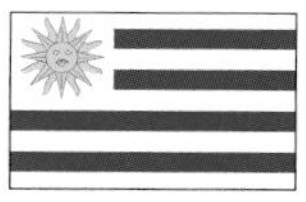
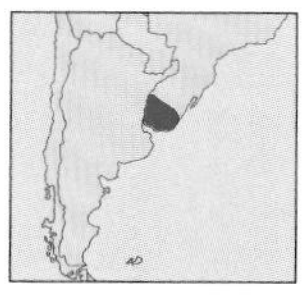

URUGUAY

GEOGRAPHY Uruguay is South America's second smallest independent country after Surinam. The land consists mainly of flat plains and hills. The River Uruguay, which forms the country's western border, flows into the Río de la Plata, a large estuary which leads into the South Atlantic Ocean.

Uruguay has a mild climate, with rain in every month, though droughts sometimes occur. Summers are pleasantly warm, especially near the coast. The weather remains relatively mild throughout the winter.

POLITICS & ECONOMY In 1726, Spanish settlers founded Montevideo in order to halt the Portuguese gaining influence in the area. By the late 18th century, Spaniards had settled in most of the country. Uruguay became part of a colony called the Viceroyalty of La Plata, which also included Argentina, Paraguay, and parts of Bolivia, Brazil and Chile. In 1820 Brazil annexed Uruguay, ending Spanish rule. In 1825, Uruguayans, supported by Argentina, began a struggle for independence. Finally, in 1828, Brazil and Argentina recognized Uruguay as an independent republic. Social and economic developments were slow in the 19th century, but, from 1903, Uruguay became stable and democratic.

From the 1950s, economic problems caused unrest. Terrorist groups, notably the Tupumaros, carried out murders and kidnappings. The army crushed the Tupumaros in 1972, but the army took over the government in 1973. Military rule continued until 1984 when elections were held. Julio Maria Sanguinetti, who led Uruguay back to civilian rule, was re-elected president in 1994. He was succeeded in 2000 by Jorge Batlle of the incumbent Colorado Party.

The World Bank classifies Uruguay as an "upper-middle-income" developing country. Agriculture employs only 5% of the people, but farm products, notably hides and leather goods, beef and wool, are the leading exports, while the leading manufacturing industries process farm products. The main crops include maize, potatoes, wheat and sugar beet. Uruguay depends largely on hydroelectric power for energy and exports electricity to Argentina.

AREA 68,498 SQ MI [177,410 SQ KM] **POPULATION** 3,274,000
CAPITAL (POPULATION) MONTEVIDEO (1,378,000)
GOVERNMENT MULTIPARTY REPUBLIC
ETHNIC GROUPS WHITE 86%, MESTIZO 8%, MULATTO OR BLACK 6%
LANGUAGES SPANISH (OFFICIAL) **RELIGIONS** CHRISTIANITY (ROMAN CATHOLIC 96%, PROTESTANT 2%), JUDAISM 1%
CURRENCY URUGUAY PESO = 100 CENTÉSIMOS

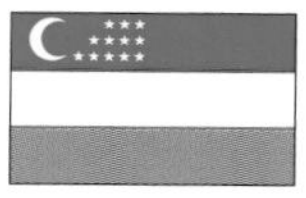
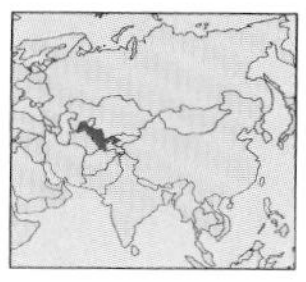

UZBEKISTAN

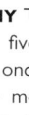

GEOGRAPHY The Republic of Uzbekistan is one of the five republics in Central Asia which were once part of the Soviet Union. Plains cover most of western Uzbekistan, with highlands in the east. The main rivers, the Amu (or Amu Darya) and Syr (or Syr Darya), drain into the Aral Sea. So much water has been taken from these rivers to irrigate the land that the Aral Sea shrank from 25,830 sq mi [66,900 sq km] in 1960 to 12,989 sq mi [33,642 sq km] in 1993. The dried-up lake area has become desert, like much of the rest of the country.

Uzbekistan has a continental climate. The winters are cold, but the temperatures soar in the summer months. The west is extremely arid, with an average annual rainfall of about 8 in [200 mm].

POLITICS & ECONOMY Russia took the area in the 19th century. After the Russian Revolution of 1917, the Communists took over and, in 1924, they set up the Uzbek Soviet Socialist Republic. Under Communism, all aspects of Uzbek life were controlled and religious worship was discouraged. But education, health, housing and transport were improved. In the late 1980s, the people demanded more freedom and, in 1990, the government stated that its laws overruled those of the Soviet Union. Uzbekistan became independent in 1991 when the Soviet Union broke up, but it retained links with Russia through the Commonwealth of Independent States. Islam Karimov, leader of the People's Democratic Party (formerly the Communist Party), was elected president in December 1991. In 1992–3, many opposition leaders were arrested because the government said that they threatened national stability. In 1994–5, the PDP won sweeping victories in national elections and, in 1995, a referendum extended Karimov's term in office until 2000, when he was again re-elected.

The World Bank classifies Uzbekistan as a "lower-middle-income" developing country and the government still controls most economic activity. The country produces coal, copper, gold, oil and natural gas.

AREA 172,740 SQ MI [447,400 SQ KM] **POPULATION** 26,044,000
CAPITAL (POPULATION) TASHKENT (2,107,000)
GOVERNMENT SOCIALIST REPUBLIC **ETHNIC GROUPS** UZBEK 71%, RUSSIAN 8%, TAJIK 5%, KAZAK 4%, TATAR 2%, KARA-KALPAK 2%
LANGUAGES UZBEK (OFFICIAL), SEVERAL OTHERS
RELIGIONS ISLAM **CURRENCY** SOM = 100 TYIYN

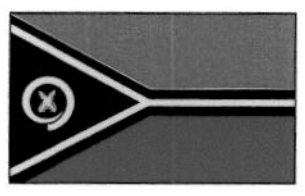
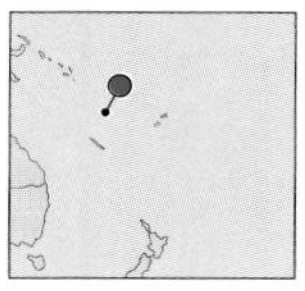

VANUATU

The Republic of Vanuatu, formerly the Anglo-French Condominium of the New Hebrides, became independent in 1980. It consists of a chain of 80 islands in the South Pacific Ocean. Its economy is based on agriculture and it exports copra, beef and veal, timber and cocoa.

AREA 4,707 SQ MI [12,190 SQ KM]
POPULATION 206,000 **CAPITAL** PORT-VILA

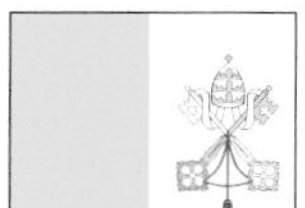
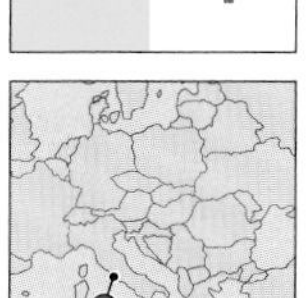

VATICAN CITY

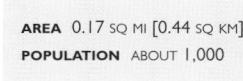

Vatican City State, the world's smallest independent nation, is an enclave on the west bank of the River Tiber in Rome. It forms an independent base for the Holy See, the governing body of the Roman Catholic Church.

AREA 0.17 SQ MI [0.44 SQ KM]
POPULATION ABOUT 1,000

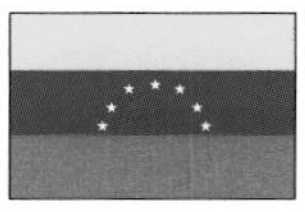
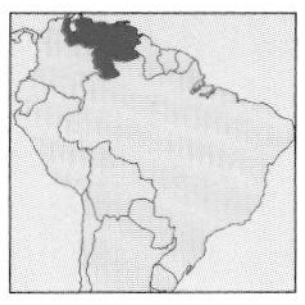

VENEZUELA

GEOGRAPHY The Bolivarian Republic of Venezuela, in northern South America, contains the Maracaibo lowlands around the oil-rich Lake Maracaibo in the west. Andean ranges enclose the lowlands and extend across most of northern Venezuela. The Orinoco river basin, containing tropical grasslands called *llanos*, lies between the northern highlands and the Guiana Highlands in the southeast. The Orinoco is Venezuela's longest river.

Venezuela has a tropical climate. Temperatures are high throughout the year on the lowlands, though the mountains are much cooler. The rainfall is heaviest in the mountains. But much of the country has a marked dry season between December and April.

POLITICS & ECONOMY In the early 19th century, Venezuelans, such as Simón Bolívar and Francisco de Miranda, began a struggle against Spanish rule. Venezuela declared its independence in 1811. But it only became truly independent in 1821, when the Spanish were defeated in a battle near Valencia.

The development of Venezuela in the 19th and the first half of the 20th centuries was marred by instability, violence and periods of harsh dictatorial rule. But Venezuela has had elected governments since 1958. The country has greatly benefited from its oil resources which were first exploited in 1917. In 1960, Venezuela helped to form OPEC (the Organization of Petroleum Exporting Countries) and, in 1976, the government of Venezuela took control of the entire oil industry. In 1999, Hugo Chavez, who had staged an unsuccessful coup in 1992, was elected president and a new constitution, giving the president considerably more power, was adopted. In 1999, the Caribbean coast of Venezuela also suffered disastrous floods and mudflows.

The World Bank classifies Venezuela as an "upper-middle-income" developing country. Oil accounts for 80% of the exports. Other exports include bauxite and aluminum, iron ore and farm products. Agriculture employs 13% of people and cattle ranching is important; dairy cattle and poultry are also raised. Major crops include bananas, cassava, citrus fruits, coffee and rice. The chief industry is petroleum refining. Other manufactures include aluminum, cement, processed food, steel and textiles.

AREA 352,143 SQ MI [912,050 SQ KM] **POPULATION** 24,715,000
CAPITAL (POPULATION) CARACAS (2,784,000)
GOVERNMENT FEDERAL REPUBLIC **ETHNIC GROUPS** MESTIZO 67%, WHITE 21%, BLACK 10%, AMERINDIAN 2%
LANGUAGES SPANISH (OFFICIAL), GOAJIRO **RELIGIONS** CHRISTIANITY (ROMAN CATHOLIC 94%) **CURRENCY** BOLÍVAR = 100 CÉNTIMOS

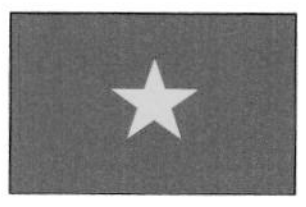
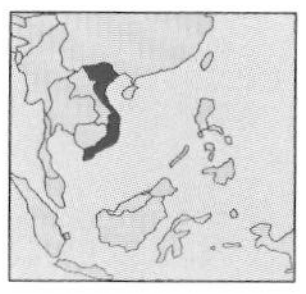

VIETNAM

GEOGRAPHY The Socialist Republic of Vietnam occupies an S-shaped strip of land facing the South China Sea in Southeast Asia. The coastal plains include two densely populated, fertile delta regions: the Red (Hong) delta facing the Gulf of Tonkin in the north, and the Mekong delta in the south.

Vietnam has a tropical climate, though the driest months of January to March are a little cooler than the wet, hot summer months, when monsoon winds blow from the southwest. Typhoons (cyclones) sometimes hit the coast, causing much damage.

POLITICS & ECONOMY China dominated Vietnam for a thousand years before AD 939, when a Vietnamese state was founded. The French took over the area between the 1850s and 1880s. They ruled Vietnam as part of French Indochina, which also included Cambodia and Laos.

Japan conquered Vietnam during World War II (1939–45). In 1946, war broke out between a nationalist group, called the Vietminh, and the French colonial government. France withdrew in 1954 and Vietnam was divided into a Communist North Vietnam, led by the Vietminh leader, Ho Chi Minh, and a non-Communist South.

A force called the Viet Cong rebeled against South Vietnam's government in 1957 and a war began, which gradually increased in intensity. The United States aided the South, but after it withdrew in 1975, South Vietnam surrendered. In 1976, the united Vietnam became a Socialist Republic.

Vietnamese troops intervened in Cambodia in 1978 to defeat the Communist Khmer Rouge government, but it withdrew its troops in 1989. In the 1990s, Vietnam began to introduce reforms. In 1995, the United States opened an embassy in Hanoi and, in 2000, a major trade pact was agreed by the countries.

The World Bank classifies Vietnam as a "low-income" developing country and agriculture employs 67% of the population. The main food crop is rice. The country also produces chromium, oil (which was discovered off the south coast in 1986), phosphates and tin.

AREA 128,065 SQ MI [331,689 SQ KM] **POPULATION** 82,487,000
CAPITAL (POPULATION) HANOI (3,056,000)
GOVERNMENT SOCIALIST REPUBLIC **ETHNIC GROUPS** VIETNAMESE 87%, THO (TAY), CHINESE (HOA), TAI, KHMER, MUONG, NUNG
LANGUAGES VIETNAMESE (OFFICIAL), CHINESE
RELIGIONS BUDDHISM 55%, CHRISTIANITY (ROMAN CATHOLIC 7%)
CURRENCY DONG = 10 HAO = 100 XU

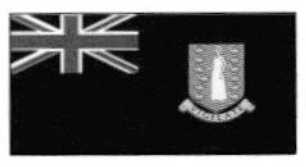
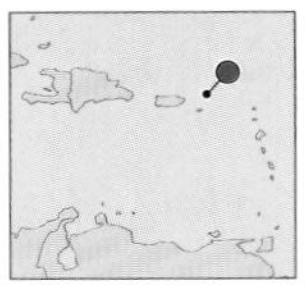

VIRGIN ISLANDS, BRITISH

The British Virgin Islands, the most northerly of the Lesser Antilles, are a British overseas territory, with a substantial measure of self-government.

AREA 59 sq mi [153 sq km]
POPULATION 15,000 **CAPITAL** Road Town

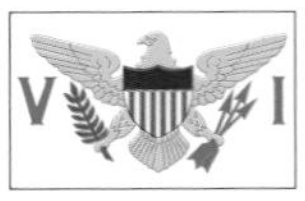
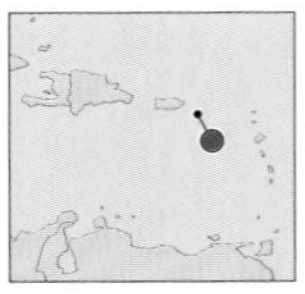

VIRGIN ISLANDS, US

The Virgin Islands of the United States, a group of three islands and 65 small islets, are a self-governing US territory. Purchased from Denmark in 1917, its residents are US citizens and they elect a non-voting delegate to the US House of Representatives.

AREA 130 sq mi [340 sq km]
POPULATION 135,000 **CAPITAL** Charlotte Amalie

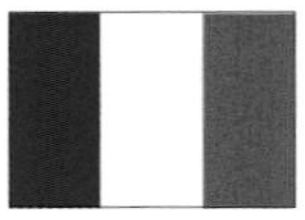
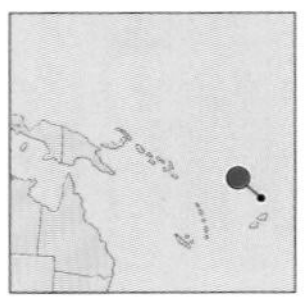

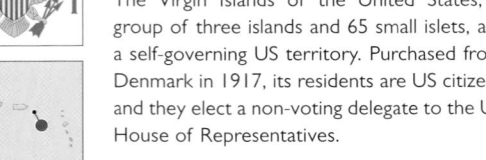

WALLIS AND FUTUNA

Wallis and Futuna, in the South Pacific Ocean, is the smallest and the poorest of France's overseas territories. French aid remains vital to an economy based on subsistence agriculture.

AREA 77 sq mi [200 sq km]
POPULATION 26,000 **CAPITAL** Mata-Utu

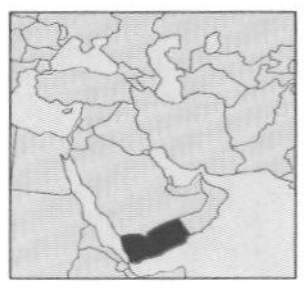

YEMEN

GEOGRAPHY The Republic of Yemen faces the Red Sea and the Gulf of Aden in the southwestern corner of the Arabian peninsula. Behind the narrow coastal plain along the Red Sea, the land rises to a mountain region called High Yemen.

The climate ranges from hot and often humid conditions on the coast to the cooler highlands. Most of the country is arid. The south coasts are particularly hot and humid, especially from June to September.

POLITICS & ECONOMY After World War I, northern Yemen, which had been ruled by Turkey, began to evolve into a separate state from the south, where Britain was in control. Britain with drew in 1967 and a left-wing government took power in the south. In North Yemen, the monarchy was abolished in 1962 and the country became a republic.

Clashes occurred between the traditionalist Yemen Arab Republic in the north and the formerly British Marxist People's Democratic Republic of Yemen but, in 1990, the two Yemens merged to form a single country. Further conflict occurred in 1994, when southern secessionist forces were defeated. In 1998 and 1999, militants in the Aden-Abyan Islamic army sought to destabilize the country, with kidnappings of tourists and bombings.

The World Bank classifies Yemen as a "low-income" developing country. Agriculture employs up to 63% of the people. Herders raise sheep and other animals, while farmers grow such crops as barley, fruits, wheat and vegetables in highland valleys and around oases. Cash crops include coffee and cotton.

Imported oil is refined at Aden and petroleum extraction began in the northwest in the 1980s. Handicrafts, leather goods and textiles are manufactured. Remittances from Yemenis abroad are a major source of revenue.

AREA 203,849 sq mi [527,970 sq km] **POPULATION** 13,219,000 **CAPITAL (POPULATION)** San'a (972,000) **GOVERNMENT** Multiparty republic **ETHNIC GROUPS** Arab 96%, Somali 1% **LANGUAGES** Arabic (official) **RELIGIONS** Islam **CURRENCY** Rial = 100 fils

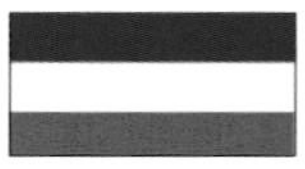
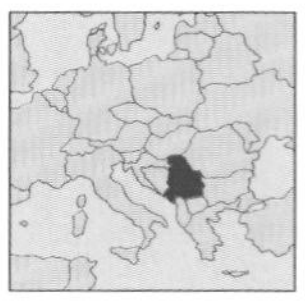

YUGOSLAVIA

GEOGRAPHY The Federal Republic of Yugoslavia consists of Serbia and Montenegro, two of the six republics which made up the former country of Yugoslavia until it broke up in 1991 and 1992. Behind the short coastline along the Adriatic Sea lies a mountainous region, including the Dinaric Alps and part of the Balkan mountains. The Pannonian plains make up northern Yugoslavia. This fertile region is drained by the River Danube and its tributaries. The river enters neighboring Romania through a scenic gorge called the Iron Gate.

The coast has a Mediterranean climate. The interior highlands have bitterly cold winters and cool summers. The wettest season is the summer, but there is also plenty of sunshine.

POLITICS & ECONOMY People who became known as the South Slavs began to move into the region around 1,500 years ago. Each group, including the Serbs and Croats, founded its own state. But, by the 15th century, foreign countries controlled the region. Serbia and Montenegro were under the Turkish Ottoman empire.

In the 19th century, many Slavs worked for independence and Slavic unity. In 1914, Austria-Hungary declared war on Serbia, blaming it for the assassination of Archduke Francis Ferdinand of Austria–Hungary. This led to World War I and the defeat of Austria–Hungary. In 1918, the South Slavs united in the Kingdom of the Serbs, Croats and Slovenes, which consisted of Bosnia-Herzegovina, Croatia, Dalmatia, Montenegro, Serbia and Slovenia. The country was renamed Yugoslavia in 1929. Germany occupied Yugoslavia during World War II, but partisans, including a Communist force led by Josip Broz Tito, fought the invaders.

From 1945, the Communists controlled the country, which was called the Federal People's Republic of Yugoslavia. But after Tito's death in 1980, the country faced many problems. In 1990, non-Communist parties were permitted and non-Communists won majorities in elections in all but Serbia and Montenegro, where Socialists (former Communists) won control. Yugoslavia split apart in 1991–2 with Bosnia-Herzegovina, Croatia, Macedonia and Slovenia proclaiming their independence. The two remaining republics of Serbia and Montenegro became the new Yugoslavia.

Fighting broke out in Croatia and Bosnia-Herzegovina as rival groups struggled for power. In 1992, the United Nations withdrew recognition of Yugoslavia because of its failure to halt atrocities committed by Serbs living in Croatia and Bosnia. In 1995, Yugoslavia was involved in the talks that led to the Dayton Peace Accord, which brought peace to Bosnia-Herzegovina. But the issue of Yugoslav repression of minorities flared up again in 1998 in Kosovo, a province where the majority are ethnic Albanians. In response to Serb ethnic cleansing, NATO forces launched an aerial offensive against Yugoslavia in March 1999. A Serb military withdrawal was agreed in June 1999. Elections in 2000 resulted in defeat for the Yugoslav president, Slobodan Milosevic, whom many regarded as responsible for much of the conflict in the 1980s. He was succeeded by Vojislav Kostunica.

Under Communist rule, manufacturing became increasingly important in Yugoslavia. But in the early 1990s, the World Bank classified Yugoslavia as a "lower-middle-income" economy. Its resources include bauxite, coal, copper and other metals, together with oil and natural gas. Manufactures include aluminum, machinery, plastics, steel, textiles and vehicles. Chief exports are manufactures, but agriculture remains important. Crops include fruits, maize, potatoes, tobacco and wheat. Cattle, pigs and sheep are reared.

AREA 39,449 sq mi [102,170 sq km] **POPULATION** 10,761,000
CAPITAL (POPULATION) Belgrade (1,137,000)
GOVERNMENT Federal republic
ETHNIC GROUPS Serb 62%, Albanian 17%, Montenegrin 5%, Hungarian, Muslim, Croat
LANGUAGES Serbo-Croat (official), Albanian
RELIGIONS Christianity (mainly Serbian Orthodox), Islam
CURRENCY Yugoslav new dinar = 100 paras

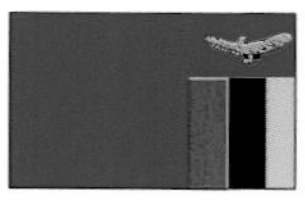
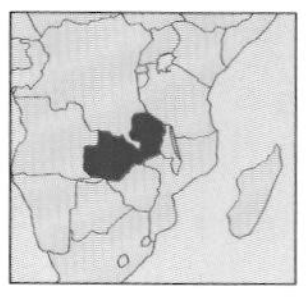

ZAMBIA

GEOGRAPHY The Republic of Zambia is a landlocked country in southern Africa. Zambia lies on the plateau that makes up most of southern Africa. Much of the land is between 2,950 ft and 4,920 ft [900 m to 1,500 m] above sea level. The Muchinga Mountains in the northeast rise above this flat land.

Lakes include Bangweulu, which is entirely within Zambia, together with parts of lakes Mweru and Tanganyika in the north.

Zambia lies in the tropics, but temperatures are moderated by the altitude. The rainy season runs from November to March.

POLITICS & ECONOMY European contact with Zambia began in the 19th century, when the explorer David Livingstone crossed the River Zambezi. In the 1890s, the British South Africa Company, set up by Cecil Rhodes (1853–1902), the British financier and statesman, made treaties with local chiefs and gradually took over the area. In 1911, the Company named the area Northern Rhodesia. In 1924, Britain took over the government of the country.

In 1953, Britain formed a federation of Northern Rhodesia, Southern Rhodesia (now Zimbabwe) and Nyasaland (now Malawi). Because of African opposition, the federation was dissolved in 1963 and Northern Rhodesia became independent as Zambia in 1964. Kenneth Kaunda became president and one-party rule was introduced in 1972. However, a new constitution was adopted in 1990 and, in 1991, Kaunda's party was defeated and Frederick Chiluba became president. Chiluba was re-elected in 1996. A state of emergency was declared in 1997, following an abortive coup, but it was lifted in 1998.

Copper is the main resource, accounting for 80% of Zambia's exports in 1997. Zambia also produces cobalt, lead, zinc and gemstones. Agriculture employs 69% of workers, as compared with 4% in industry and mining. Major food crops include cassava, fruits and vegetables, maize, millet and sorghum, while cash crops include coffee, sugarcane and tobacco. The production of copper products in the leading industrial activity.

AREA 290,586 sq mi [752,614 sq km] **POPULATION** 12,267,000
CAPITAL (POPULATION) Lusaka (982,000)
GOVERNMENT Multiparty republic
ETHNIC GROUPS Bemba 36%, Maravi (Nyanja) 18%, Tonga 15%
LANGUAGES English (official), Bemba, Nyanja
RELIGIONS Christianity 68%, traditional beliefs 27%
CURRENCY Kwacha = 100 ngwee

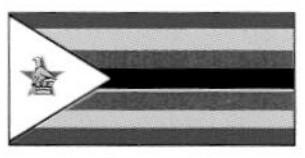
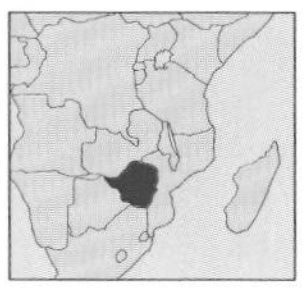

ZIMBABWE

GEOGRAPHY The Republic of Zimbabwe is a landlocked country in southern Africa. Most of the country lies on a high plateau between the Zambezi and Limpopo rivers between 2,950 ft and 4,920 ft [900 m to 1,500 m] above sea level.

From October to March, the weather is hot and wet. But in the winter, daily temperatures can vary greatly. Frosts have been recorded between June and August. The climate varies according to the altitude.

POLITICS & ECONOMY The Shona people became dominant in the region about 1,000 years ago. The British South Africa Company, under the statesman Cecil Rhodes (1853–1902), occupied the area in the 1890s, after obtaining mineral rights from local chiefs. The area was named Rhodesia and later Southern Rhodesia. It became a self-governing British colony in 1923. Between 1953 and 1963, Southern and Northern Rhodesia (now Zambia) were joined to Nyasaland (Malawi) in the Central African Federation.

In 1965, the European government of Southern Rhodesia (then called Rhodesia) declared their country independent but Britain refused to accept this. Finally, after a civil war, the country became legally independent in 1980, though rivalries between the Shona and Ndebele people threatened stability. Order was restored when the Shona prime minister, Robert Mugabe, brought his Ndebele rivals into his government. In 1987, Mugabe became the country's executive president and, in 1991, the government renounced its Marxist ideology. Mugabe was re-elected president in 1990 and 1996. During the late 1990s, Mugabe threatened to seize white-owned farms without paying compensation to the owners. Despite international pressure, including threats by the IMF to withdraw loans to Zimbabwe, landless "war veterans" began to occupy white farms. Following elections in 2000, which resulted in victory for Mugabe's party, the seizure of farms continued and resulted in the murders of several white farmers.

The World Bank classifies Zimbabwe as a "low-income" developing country. The country has valuable mineral resources and mining accounts for a fifth of the country's exports. Agriculture employs 27% of working people. Maize is the chief food crop, while cash crops include cotton, sugar and tobacco. Cattle ranching is another important activity.

AREA 150,873 sq mi [390,579 sq km] **POPULATION** 13,123,000
CAPITAL (POPULATION) Harare (1,189,000)
GOVERNMENT Multiparty republic
ETHNIC GROUPS Shona 71%, Ndebele 16%, other Bantu-speaking Africans 11%, White 2%
LANGUAGES English (official), Shona, Ndebele, Nyanja
RELIGIONS Christianity 45%, traditional beliefs 40%
CURRENCY Zimbabwe dollar = 100 cents

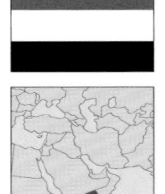

INTRODUCTION TO
WORLD GEOGRAPHY

The Universe

About 15 billion years ago, time and space began with the most colossal explosion in cosmic history: the so-called "Big Bang" that is believed to have initiated the universe. According to current theory, in the first millionth of a second of its existence it expanded from a dimensionless point of infinite mass and density into a fireball about 19 billion miles across; and it has been expanding ever since.

It took almost a million years for the primal fireball to cool enough for atoms to form. They were mostly hydrogen, still the most abundant material in the universe. But the new matter was not evenly distributed around the young universe, and a few billion years later atoms in relatively dense regions began to cling together under the influence of gravity, forming distinct masses of gas separated by vast expanses of empty space. To begin with, these first proto-galaxies were dark places: the universe had cooled. But gravitational attraction continued, condensing matter into coherent lumps inside the galactic gas clouds. About three billion years later, some of these masses had contracted so much that internal pressure produced the high temperatures necessary to bring about nuclear fusion: the first stars were born.

There were several generations of stars, each feeding on the wreckage of its extinct predecessors as well as the original galactic gas swirls. With each new generation, progressively larger atoms were forged in stellar furnaces and the galaxy's range of elements, once restricted to hydrogen, grew larger. About 10 billion years after the Big Bang, a star formed on the outskirts of our galaxy with enough matter left over to create a retinue of planets. Nearly five billion years after that human beings evolved.

The Sun is one of more than 100 billion stars in the home galaxy alone. Our galaxy, in turn, forms part of a local group of approximately 30 similar structures, some much larger than our own; there are at least 100 billion other galaxies in the universe as a whole. The most distant ever observed, a highly energetic galactic core known only as quasar PC 1247 +3406, lies about 12 billion light-years away.

Life of a Star

For most of its existence, a star produces energy by the nuclear fusion of hydrogen into helium at its core. The duration of this hydrogen-burning period – known as the main sequence – depends on the star's mass; the greater the mass, the higher the core temperatures and the sooner the star's supply of hydrogen is exhausted. Dim, dwarf stars consume their hydrogen slowly, eking it out over 1,000 billion years or more. The Sun, like other stars of its mass, should spend about 10 billion years on the main sequence; since it was formed less than five billion years ago, it still has half its life left.

Once all a star's core hydrogen has been fused into helium, nuclear activity moves outward into layers of unconsumed hydrogen. For a time, energy production sharply increases: the star grows hotter and expands enormously, turning into a so-called red giant. Its energy output will increase a thousandfold, and it will swell to a hundred times its present diameter.

After a few hundred million years, helium in the core will become sufficiently compressed to initiate a new cycle of nuclear fusion: from helium to carbon. The star will contract somewhat, before beginning its last expansion, in the Sun's case engulfing the Earth and perhaps Mars. In this bloated condition, the Sun's outer layers will break off into space, leaving a tiny inner core, mainly of carbon, that shrinks progressively under the force of its own gravity: dwarf stars can attain a density more than 10,000 times that of normal matter, with crushing surface gravities to match. Gradually, the nuclear fires will die down, and the Sun will reach its terminal stage: a black dwarf, emitting insignificant amounts of energy.

However, stars more massive than the Sun may undergo another transformation. The additional mass allows gravitational collapse to continue indefinitely: eventually, all the star's remaining matter shrinks to a point, and its density approaches infinity – a state that will not permit even subatomic structures to survive.

The star has become a black hole: an anomalous "singularity" in the fabric of space and time. Although vast coruscations of radiation will be emitted by any matter falling into its grasp, the singularity itself has an escape velocity that exceeds the speed of light, and nothing can ever be released from it. Within the boundaries of the black hole, the laws of physics are suspended, but no physicist can ever observe the extraordinary events that may occur.

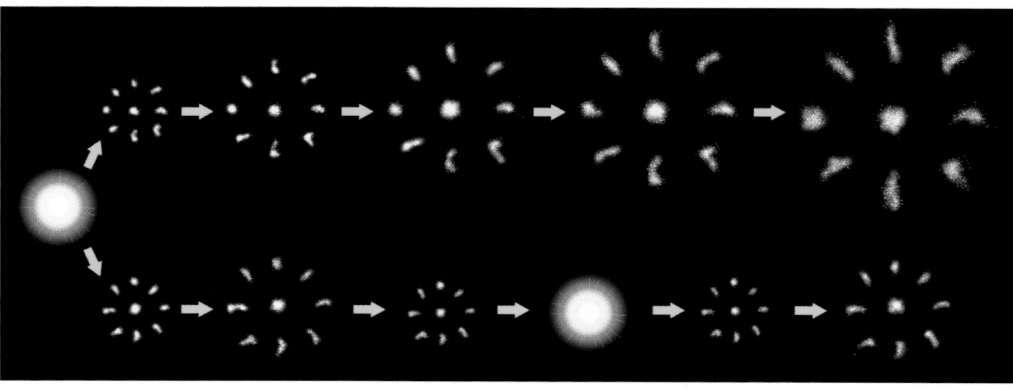

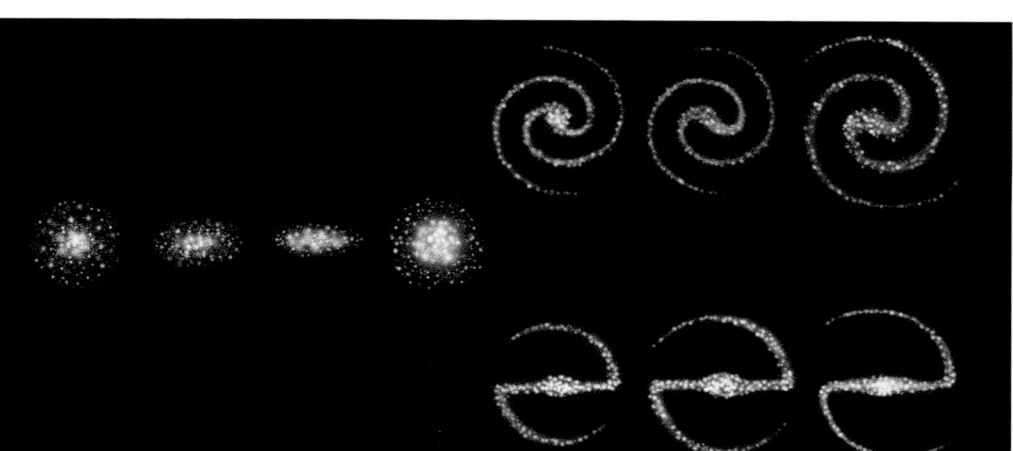

The End of the Universe

The likely fate of the universe is disputed. One theory (top left) dictates that the expansion begun at the time of the Big Bang will continue "indefinitely," with ageing galaxies moving further and further apart in an immense, dark graveyard. Alternatively, gravity may overcome the expansion (bottom left). Galaxies will fall back together until everything is again concentrated at a single point, followed by a new Big Bang and a new expansion, in an endlessly repeated cycle.

The first theory is supported by the amount of visible matter in the universe; the second assumes there is enough dark material to bring about the gravitational collapse.

Galactic Structures

Many of the universe's 100 billion galaxies show clear structural patterns, originally classified by the American astronomer Edwin Hubble in 1925. Spiral galaxies like our own (top row) have a central, almost spherical bulge and a surrounding disk composed of spiral arms. Barred spirals (bottom row) have a central bar of stars across the nucleus, with spiral arms trailing from the ends of the bar. Elliptical galaxies (far left) have a uniform appearance, ranging from a flattened disk to a near sphere. So-called SO galaxies (left row, right) have a central bulge, but no spiral arms. Most galaxies, however, have no obvious structure at all.

Galaxies also vary enormously in size, from dwarfs only 2,000 light-years across to great assemblies of stars 80 or more times larger.

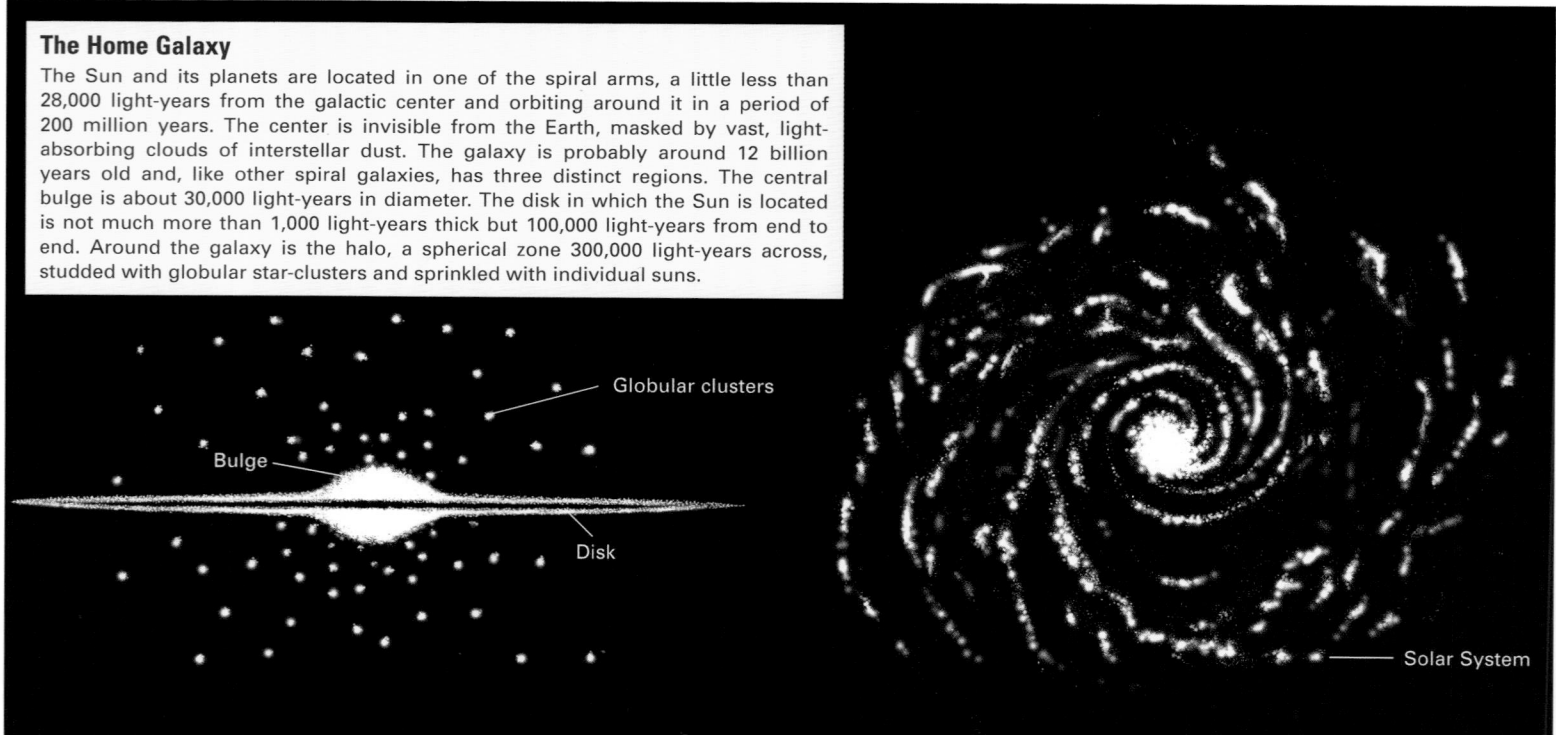

The Home Galaxy

The Sun and its planets are located in one of the spiral arms, a little less than 28,000 light-years from the galactic center and orbiting around it in a period of 200 million years. The center is invisible from the Earth, masked by vast, light-absorbing clouds of interstellar dust. The galaxy is probably around 12 billion years old and, like other spiral galaxies, has three distinct regions. The central bulge is about 30,000 light-years in diameter. The disk in which the Sun is located is not much more than 1,000 light-years thick but 100,000 light-years from end to end. Around the galaxy is the halo, a spherical zone 300,000 light-years across, studded with globular star-clusters and sprinkled with individual suns.

Globular clusters

Bulge

Disk

Solar System

CARTOGRAPHY BY PHILIP'S. COPYRIGHT GEORGE PHILIP LTD

Star charts are drawn as projections of a vast, hollow sphere with the observer in the middle. Each circle below represents slightly more than one hemisphere, centered on the north and south celestial poles respectively – projections of the Earth's poles in the heavens. At the present era, the north pole is marked by the star Polaris; the south pole has no such convenient reference point.

Astronomical coordinates are normally given in terms of "Right Ascension" for longitude and "Declination" for latitude or altitude. Since the stars appear to rotate around the Earth once every 24 hours, Right Ascension is measured eastward – counterclockwise – in hours and minutes and is marked around the edge of the map. One hour is equivalent to 15 angular degrees; zero on the scale is the point at which the Sun crosses the celestial equator at the spring equinox, known to astronomers as the First Point in Aries. Unlike the Sun, stars always rise and set at the same point on the horizon. Declination measures (in degrees) a star's angular distance above or below the celestial equator and is marked on the vertical line.

To use the maps, first choose the one for your hemisphere and hold it with the month at the bottom. The stars in the lower part of the map are then due south (or north, in the southern hemisphere) at about 1 AM local time, not allowing for summer or daylight saving time. Their exact position above the horizon depends on your latitude. The closer to the Equator you live, the higher in the sky these stars will appear. Some additional stars from the map for the other hemisphere will be visible in the lower sky.

Stars near the top of the map will be below the opposite horizon at this date and time but will be visible at other times of the night and year. The sky appears to move counterclockwise around the celestial pole during the course of the day (clockwise in the southern hemisphere), so the same stars will be visible at 11 PM a month earlier.

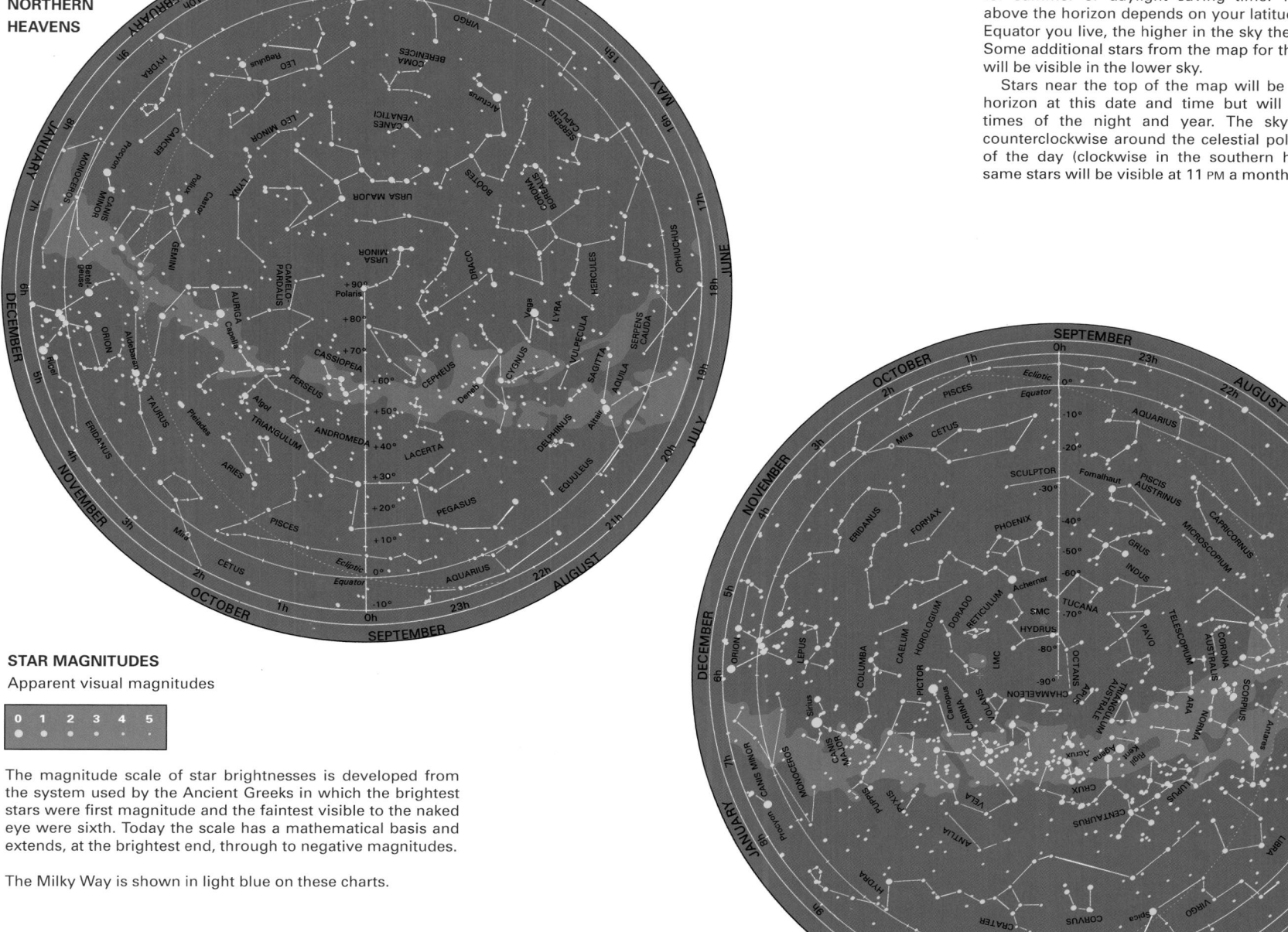

NORTHERN HEAVENS

SOUTHERN HEAVENS

STAR MAGNITUDES
Apparent visual magnitudes

0	1	2	3	4	5

The magnitude scale of star brightnesses is developed from the system used by the Ancient Greeks in which the brightest stars were first magnitude and the faintest visible to the naked eye were sixth. Today the scale has a mathematical basis and extends, at the brightest end, through to negative magnitudes.

The Milky Way is shown in light blue on these charts.

THE NEAREST STARS

The 20 nearest stars, excluding the Sun, with their distance from Earth in light-years*

Proxima Centauri	4.25
Alpha Centauri A	4.3
Alpha Centauri B	4.3
Barnard's Star	6.0
Wolf 359	7.8
Lalande 21185	8.3
Sirius A	8.7
Sirius B	8.7
UV Ceti A	8.7
UV Ceti B	8.7
Ross 154	9.4
Ross 248	10.3
Epsilon Eridani	10.7
Ross 128	10.9
61 Cygni A	11.1
61 Cygni B	11.1
Epsilon Indi	11.2
Groombridge 34A	11.2
Groombridge 34B	11.2
L789-6	11.2
Procyon A	11.4
Procyon B	11.4

Many of the nearest stars, like Alpha Centauri A and B, are doubles, orbiting about the common center of gravity and to all intents and purposes equidistant from Earth. Many of them are dim objects, with no name other than the designation given by the astronomers who investigated them. However, they include Sirius, the brightest star in the sky, and Procyon, the seventh brightest. Both are far larger than the Sun; of the nearest stars, only Epsilon Eridani is similar in size and luminosity.

* A light-year equals approx. 5,900 billion miles

THE CONSTELLATIONS

The constellations and their English names

Andromeda	Andromeda	Circinus	Compasses	Lacerta	Lizard	Piscis Austrinus	Southern Fish
Antlia	Air Pump	Columba	Dove	Leo	Lion	Puppis	Ship's Stern
Apus	Bird of Paradise	Coma Berenices	Berenice's Hair	Leo Minor	Little Lion	Pyxis	Mariner's Compass
Aquarius	Water Carrier	Corona Australis	Southern Crown	Lepus	Hare	Reticulum	Net
Aquila	Eagle	Corona Borealis	Northern Crown	Libra	Scales	Sagitta	Arrow
Ara	Altar	Corvus	Crow	Lupus	Wolf	Sagittarius	Archer
Aries	Ram	Crater	Cup	Lynx	Lynx	Scorpius	Scorpion
Auriga	Charioteer	Crux	Southern Cross	Lyra	Lyre	Sculptor	Sculptor
Boötes	Herdsman	Cygnus	Swan	Mensa	Table	Scutum	Shield
Caelum	Chisel	Delphinus	Dolphin	Microscopium	Microscope	Serpens	Serpent
Camelopardalis	Giraffe	Dorado	Swordfish	Monoceros	Unicorn	Sextans	Sextant
Cancer	Crab	Draco	Dragon	Musca	Fly	Taurus	Bull
Canes Venatici	Hunting Dogs	Equuleus	Little Horse	Norma	Level	Telescopium	Telescope
Canis Major	Great Dog	Eridanus	Eridanus	Octans	Octant	Triangulum	Triangle
Canis Minor	Little Dog	Fornax	Furnace	Ophiuchus	Serpent Bearer	Triangulum Australe	Southern Triangle
Capricornus	Goat	Gemini	Twins	Orion	Orion	Tucana	Toucan
Carina	Keel	Grus	Crane	Pavo	Peacock	Ursa Major	Great Bear
Cassiopeia	Cassiopeia	Hercules	Hercules	Pegasus	Winged Horse	Ursa Minor	Little Bear
Centaurus	Centaur	Horologium	Clock	Perseus	Perseus	Vela	Sails
Cepheus	Cepheus	Hydra	Water Snake	Phoenix	Phoenix	Virgo	Virgin
Cetus	Whale	Hydrus	Sea Serpent	Pictor	Easel	Volans	Flying Fish
Chamaeleon	Chameleon	Indus	Indian	Pisces	Fishes	Vulpecula	Fox

The Solar System

Lying 28,000 light-years from the center of one of billions of galaxies that comprise the observable universe, our Solar System contains nine planets and their moons, innumerable asteroids and comets, and a miscellany of dust and gas, all tethered by the immense gravitational field of the Sun, the middling-sized star whose thermonuclear furnaces provide them all with heat and light. The Solar System was formed about 4.6 billion years ago, when a spinning cloud of gas, mostly hydrogen but seeded with other, heavier elements, condensed enough to ignite a nuclear reaction and create a star. The Sun still accounts for almost 99.9% of the system's total mass; one planet, Jupiter, contains most of the remainder.

By composition as well as distance, the planetary array divides quite neatly in two: an inner system of four small, solid planets, including the Earth, and an outer system, from Jupiter to Neptune, of four much larger planets composed of lighter materials, such as gas, liquid and ice. Between the two groups lies a scattering of rocky asteroids, perhaps as many as 400,000. They may be debris left over from the inner Solar System's formation. The outermost planet, Pluto, may simply be the largest of a number of bodies composed of rock and ice orbiting beyond Neptune, similarly left over from the formation of the outer Solar System.

By the 1990s, however, the Solar System also included some newer anomalies: several thousand spacecraft. Most were in orbit around the Earth, but some had probed far and wide around the system. The valuable information beamed back by these robotic investigators has transformed our knowledge of our celestial environment.

Much of the early history of science is the story of people trying to make sense of the errant points of light that were all they knew of the planets. Now, men have themselves stood on the Earth's Moon; probes have landed on Mars and Venus, and orbiting radars have mapped far distant landscapes with astonishing accuracy. In the 1980s, the US *Voyagers* skimmed all four major planets of the outer system, bringing new revelations with each close approach. Only Pluto, inscrutably distant in an orbit that takes it 50 times the Earth's distance from the Sun, remains unvisited by our messengers.

Orbits of the Planets

The solar planets and their orbits, showing the relative position of each planet at the vernal equinox of 1992.

Orbits are drawn to exact scale, but with the Sun and planets greatly enlarged for clarity. The Solar System is shown from the viewpoint of an observer a few light-hours distant in the direction of the constellation Hercules. Seen from such a position, above the plane of the ecliptic, all the planets revolve about the Sun in a counterclockwise direction. The perspective view exaggerates the elliptical form of all the planetary orbits: only Pluto and Mercury follow paths that deviate noticeably from circularity. Near perihelion – its closest approach to the Sun – Pluto actually passes inside the orbit of Neptune, an event that last occurred in 1983. Pluto did not regain its station as the Sun's outermost planet until February 1999.

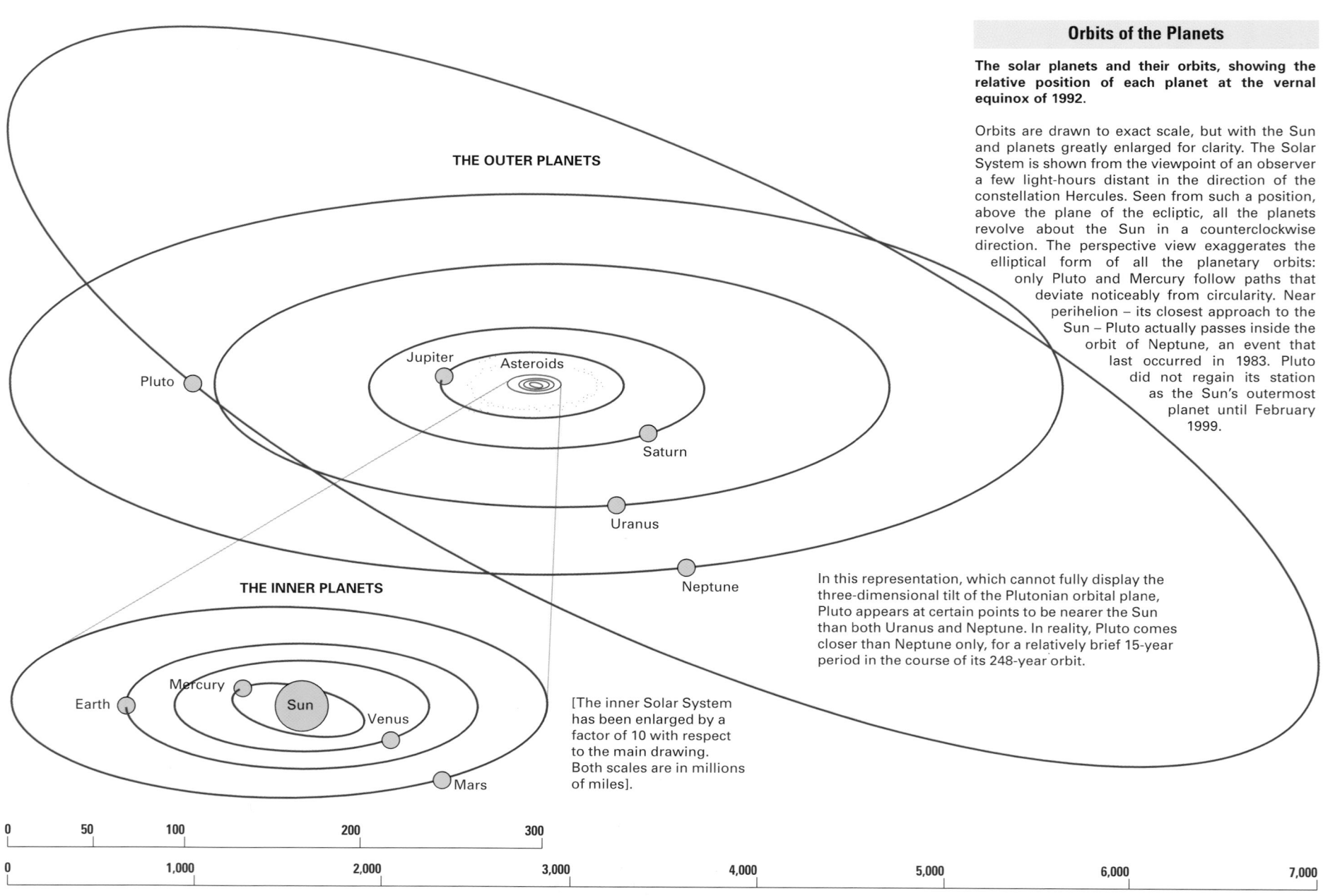

THE OUTER PLANETS

Jupiter

Asteroids

Pluto

Saturn

Uranus

THE INNER PLANETS

Neptune

In this representation, which cannot fully display the three-dimensional tilt of the Plutonian orbital plane, Pluto appears at certain points to be nearer the Sun than both Uranus and Neptune. In reality, Pluto comes closer than Neptune only, for a relatively brief 15-year period in the course of its 248-year orbit.

Mercury

Earth

Sun

Venus

Mars

[The inner Solar System has been enlarged by a factor of 10 with respect to the main drawing. Both scales are in millions of miles].

0	50	100	200	300

0	1,000	2,000	3,000	4,000	5,000	6,000	7,000

Planetary Data

	Mean distance from Sun (million miles)	Mass (Earth = 1)	Period of orbit (Earth years)	Period of rotation (Earth days)	Equatorial diameter (miles)	Average density (water = 1)	Surface gravity (Earth = 1)	Escape velocity (miles/sec)	Number of known satellites
Sun	–	332,946	–	25.38	870,000	1.41	27.9	383.7	–
Mercury	36.0	0.06	0.241	58.67	3,031	5.43	0.38	2.64	0
Venus	67.2	0.8	0.615	243.00	7,519	5.24	0.90	6.44	0
Earth	93.0	1.0	1.00	1.00	7,926	5.52	1.00	6.95	1
Mars	141.6	0.1	1.88	1.02	4,222	3.93	0.38	3.13	2
Jupiter	483.6	317.8	11.86	0.41	88,732	1.33	2.69	37.03	28
Saturn	886.6	95.2	29.46	0.42	74,500	0.706	1.16	22.12	30
Uranus	1,783.0	14.5	84.01	0.45	32,600	1.25	0.93	13.11	21
Neptune	2,793.9	17.1	164.79	0.71	30,100	1.77	1.21	15.29	8
Pluto	3,666.2	0.002	247.7	6.39	1,519	1.40	0.05	0.75	1

Planetary days are given in sidereal time – that is, with respect to the stars rather than the Sun. Most of the information in the table was confirmed by spacecraft and often obtained from photographs and other data transmitted back to the Earth. In the case of Pluto, however, only earthbound observations have been made, and no spacecraft will encounter it until well into the 21st century. Given the planet's small size and great distance, figures for its diameter and rotation period have only recently been confirmed.

Pluto is not massive enough to account for the perturbations in the orbits of Uranus and Neptune that led to its 1930 discovery, but it is now widely believed that these perturbations can be explained away as observational errors made by the earlier observers.

CARTOGRAPHY BY PHILIP'S. COPYRIGHT GEORGE PHILIP LTD

The Planets

Mercury is the closest planet to the Sun and hence the fastest-moving. It is very hot with a cratered, wrinkled surface very similar to that of Earth's Moon. It is small and has no gravity, hence there is no significant atmosphere.

Venus has much the same physical dimensions as Earth. Its dense atmosphere is composed of 97% CO_2 resulting in a runaway greenhouse effect that makes the Venusian surface, at 890°F, the hottest of all the planets in the Solar System. Radar mapping shows relatively level land with volcanic regions whose sulfurous discharges explain the sulfuric acid rains reported by soft-landing space probes before they succumbed to Venus' fierce climate.

Earth seen from space is easily the most beautiful of the inner planets; it is also, and more objectively, the largest, as well as the only home of known life. Living things are the main reason why the Earth is able to retain a substantial proportion of corrosive and highly reactive oxygen in its atmosphere, a state of affairs that contradicts the laws of chemical equilibrium; the oxygen in turn supports the life that constantly regenerates it.

Mars, smaller and cooler than the Earth, is nevertheless the most likely planet other than Earth where life may have formed. Vast water channels show that it was once warmer and wetter; there may still be traces of former simple life forms, though whether life could thrive in its current cold, dry and thin atmosphere is doubtful. The ice caps are mainly frozen carbon dioxide, and whatever oxygen the planet once possessed is now locked up in the iron-bearing rock that covers its cratered surface and gives it its characteristic red hue. Mars is a dustbowl with occasional storms whirling the dust high into the air.

Jupiter masses almost three times as much as all the other planets combined; had it scooped up rather more matter during its formation, it might have evolved into a small companion star for the Sun. The planet is mostly gas, under intense pressure in the lower atmosphere above a core of fiercely compressed hydrogen and helium. The upper layers form strikingly-colored rotating belts, the outward sign of the intense storms created by Jupiter's rapid diurnal rotation. Close approaches by spacecraft have shown an orbiting ring system and discovered several previously unknown moons: Jupiter has at least 28 moons.

Saturn is structurally similar to Jupiter, rotating fast enough to produce an obvious bulge at its equator. It is composed of 89% hydrogen and 11% helium, and has wind velocities in the outer atmosphere of 1,600 feet per second. Ever since the invention of the telescope, however, Saturn's rings have been the feature that has attracted most observers. *Voyager* probes in 1980 and 1981 sent back detailed pictures that showed them to be composed of thousands of separate ringlets, each in turn made up of tiny icy particles.

Uranus was unknown to the ancients. Although it is faintly visible to the naked eye, it was not discovered until 1781. Its interior is largely water, with an atmosphere of hydrogen, helium and some methane, which gives the planet its blue-green color. Observations in 1977 suggested the presence of a faint ring system, amply confirmed when *Voyager 2* swung past the planet in 1986.

Neptune is always more than 2.5 billion miles from Earth, and despite its diameter of almost 30,000 miles, it can only be seen by telescope. Its 1846 discovery was the result of mathematical predictions by astronomers seeking to explain irregularities in the orbit of Uranus, but until *Voyager 2* closed with the planet in 1989, little was known of it. Like Uranus, it has a ring system; *Voyager*'s photographs revealed a total of eight moons.

Pluto is the most mysterious of the solar planets, if only because even the most powerful telescopes can scarcely resolve it from a point of light to a disk. It was discovered as recently as 1930, like Neptune as the result of perturbations in the orbits of the two then outermost planets. Its small size, as well as its eccentric and highly tilted orbit, has led to suggestions that it is a former satellite of Neptune, somehow liberated from its primary. In 1978 Pluto was found to have a moon of its own, Charon, apparently half the size of Pluto itself.

Mean distance from the Sun in million miles (not to scale)

Mercury	36.0
Venus	67.2
Earth	93.0
Mars	141.6
Jupiter	483.6
Saturn	886.6
Uranus	1,783.0
Neptune	2,793.9
Pluto	3,666.2

Diagram not drawn to scale

CARTOGRAPHY BY PHILIP'S. COPYRIGHT GEORGE PHILIP LTD

Time and Motion

The basic unit of time measurement is the day, that is, one rotation of the Earth on its axis. Our present calendar is based on the solar year of 365.24 days, the time taken by the Earth to orbit the Sun.

Calendars based on the movements of the Sun and Moon have been used since ancient times. The average length of the year, according to the Julian Calendar introduced by Julius Caesar, was about 11 minutes too long. The cumulative error was rectified in 1582 by the Gregorian Calendar, when Pope Gregory XIII decreed that the day following 4 October was 15 October, and in that century years did not count as leap years unless they were divisible by 400. England finally adopted the reformed calendar in 1752, when it was 11 days behind the European mainland.

The rotation of the Earth on its axis causes day and night. Because the Earth rotates through 360° every 24 hours, the world is divided into 24 time zones centered on lines of longitude at 15° longitude.

The tilt of the Earth's axis, also called the obliquity of the ecliptic, accounts for the seasons which are so familiar in the middle latitudes. But geological evidence shows that, over long periods of time, climates change and the advances and retreats of the ice during the Pleistocene Ice Age may have been caused by regular variations in the Earth's tilt, its orbit around the Sun, and changes in the season when it is closest to the Sun (perihelion).

Earth Data

Aphelion (maximum distance from Sun):
94,452,780 miles

Perihelion (minimum distance from Sun):
91,342,080 miles

Angle of tilt (obliquity of the ecliptic): 23° 27' 08"

Length of year – solar tropical (equinox to equinox): 365.24 days

Length of year: 365 days, 5 hours, 48 minutes, 46 seconds of mean solar time

Superficial area:
197,000,000 sq mi

Land surface:
57,500,000 sq mi (29.2%)

Water surface:
139,500,000 sq mi (70.8%)

Equatorial circumference:
24,903 mi

Polar circumference:
24,860 mi

Equatorial diameter:
7,926.7 mi

Polar diameter: 7,900.0 mi

Equatorial radius:
3,963.4 mi

Polar radius: 3,950.0 mi

Volume of the Earth:
260,000 x 10^6 cu mi

Mass of the Earth:
6.5 x 10^{21} tons

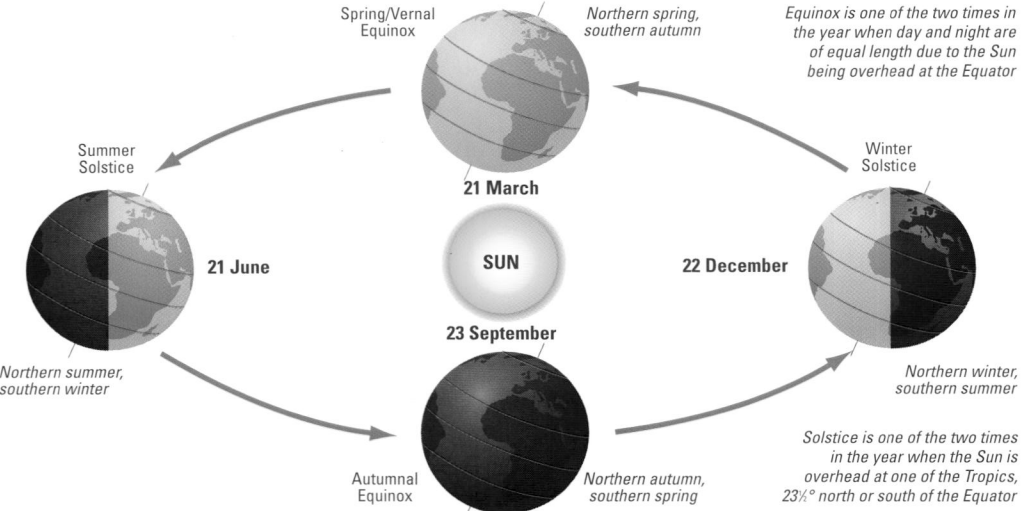

Spring/Vernal Equinox — Northern spring, southern autumn

Equinox is one of the two times in the year when day and night are of equal length due to the Sun being overhead at the Equator

21 March

Summer Solstice

Winter Solstice

21 June

SUN

22 December

23 September

Northern summer, southern winter

Northern winter, southern summer

Autumnal Equinox — Northern autumn, southern spring

Solstice is one of the two times in the year when the Sun is overhead at one of the Tropics, 23½° north or south of the Equator

The Seasons

Seasons occur because the Earth's axis is tilted at a constant angle of 23½°. When the northern hemisphere is tilted to a maximum extent toward the Sun, on 21 June, the Sun is overhead at the Tropic of Cancer (latitude 23½° North). This is midsummer, or the summer solstice, in the northern hemisphere.

On 22 or 23 September, the Sun is overhead at the Equator, and day and night are of equal length throughout the world. This is the autumn equinox in the northern hemisphere. On 21 or 22 December, the Sun is overhead at the Tropic of Capricorn (23½° South), the winter solstice in the northern hemisphere. The overhead Sun then tracks north until, on 21 March, it is overhead at the Equator. This is the spring (vernal) equinox in the northern hemisphere.

In the southern hemisphere, the seasons are the reverse of those in the north.

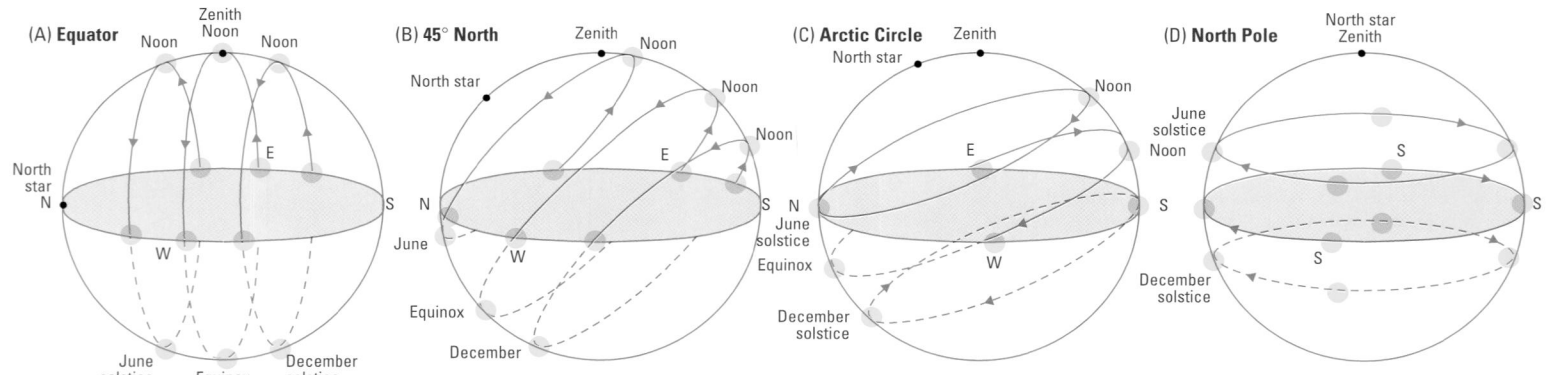

21 June

N

N. Pole: 6 months daylight

24 hours daylight — 10½ hours daylight

66½° — 23½°

12 hours daylight

13½ hours daylight

Sun's rays

23½° — 23½°

12 hours daylight

0°

SHORT NIGHT — LONG DAY — LONG NIGHT — SHORT DAY

Antarctic Circle: 24 hours darkness
S. Pole: 6 months darkness

22 December

N. Pole: 6 months darkness Arctic Circle: 24 hours darkness

10½ hours daylight

66½°

SHORT DAY — LONG NIGHT — SHORT NIGHT

0°

23½°

10½ hours daylight — 24 hours daylight

Antarctic Circle: 24 hours daylight
S. Pole: 6 months daylight

S

Day and Night

The Sun appears to rise in the east, reach its highest point at noon, and then set in the west, to be followed by night. In reality, it is not the Sun that is moving but the Earth rotating from west to east. The moment when the Sun's upper limb first appears above the horizon is termed sunrise; the moment when the Sun's upper limb disappears below the horizon is sunset.

At the summer solstice in the northern hemisphere (21 June), the Arctic has total daylight and the Antarctic total darkness. The opposite occurs at the winter solstice (21 or 22 December). At the Equator, the length of day and night are almost equal all year.

The Sun's Path

The diagrams on the right illustrate the apparent path of the Sun at (A) the Equator, (B) in midlatitude (45°), (C) at the Arctic Circle (66½°), and (D) at the North Pole, where there are six months of continuous daylight and six months of continuous night.

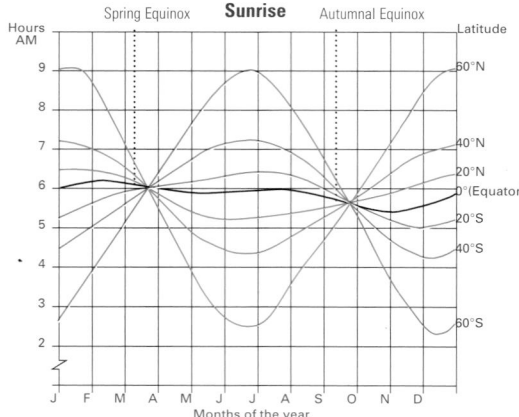

(A) Equator — Zenith Noon, Noon, Noon — North star N — E — S — W — June solstice, Equinox, December solstice

(B) 45° North — Zenith Noon, Noon, Noon — North star — E — S N — W — June, Equinox, December

(C) Arctic Circle — Zenith, North star, Noon — E — S N — W — June solstice, Equinox, December solstice

(D) North Pole — North star Zenith — June solstice Noon — S — S — December solstice — S

Sunrise and Sunset

The term equinox comes from two Latin words meaning "equal night." At the spring and autumn equinoxes, the Sun is vertically overhead at the Equator and all places on Earth have 12 hours of darkness and 12 of daylight. The graphs showing sunrise and sunset show that these occasions occur on 21 March and on 22 or 23 September. The graphs also show that, because the Sun remains high in the sky throughout the year, the length of the day and night at the Equator remain roughly the same throughout the year, with sunrise occurring around 6 AM and sunset at around 6 PM. The further north or south one travels, the greater the difference between the number of hours of daylight and darkness. For example, the graph, right, shows that at latitude 60°N, sunrise varies from just after 9 AM in midwinter (on 22 or 23 December) to about 2.30 AM in midsummer (around the summer solstice on 21 June). By contrast, the second graph, far right, shows that sunset at latitude 60°N occurs at about 2.45 PM in midwinter and 9.20 PM in midsummer.

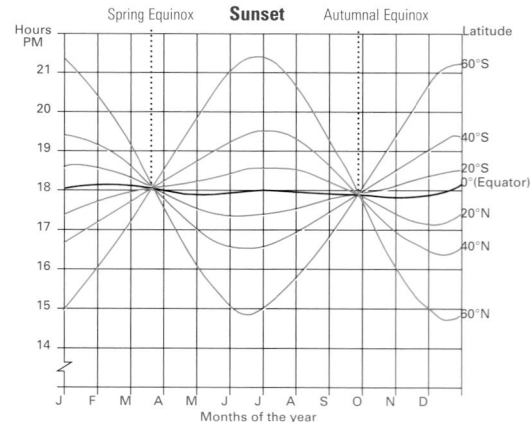

CARTOGRAPHY BY PHILIP'S. COPYRIGHT GEORGE PHILIP LTD

The Moon

The Moon rotates more slowly than the Earth, making one complete turn on its axis in just over 27 days. Since this corresponds to its period of revolution around the Earth, the Moon always presents the same hemisphere or face to us, and we never see "the dark side." The interval between one full Moon and the next (and between new Moons) is about 29½ days – a lunar month. The apparent changes in the shape of the Moon are caused by its changing position in relation to the Earth; like the planets, it produces no light of its own and shines only by reflecting the rays of the Sun.

Phases of the Moon

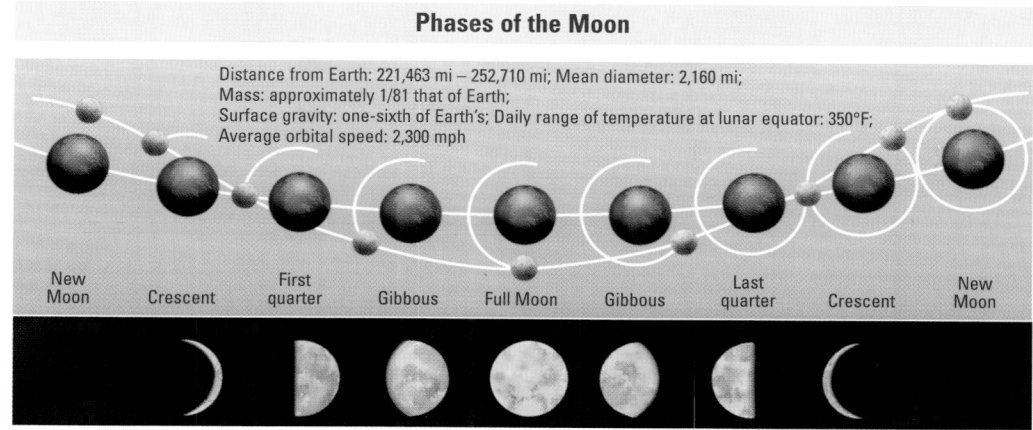

Distance from Earth: 221,463 mi – 252,710 mi; Mean diameter: 2,160 mi;
Mass: approximately 1/81 that of Earth;
Surface gravity: one-sixth of Earth's; Daily range of temperature at lunar equator: 350°F;
Average orbital speed: 2,300 mph

New Moon — Crescent — First quarter — Gibbous — Full Moon — Gibbous — Last quarter — Crescent — New Moon

Moon Data

Distance from Earth

The Moon orbits at a mean distance of 238,731 mi, at an average speed of 2,289 mph in relation to the Earth.

Size and mass

The average diameter of the Moon is 2,159.3 mi. It is 400 times smaller than the Sun but is about 400 times closer to the Earth, so we see them as the same size. The Moon has a mass of $7,975 \times 10^{19}$ tons, with a density 3.344 times that of water.

Visibility

Only 59% of the Moon's surface is directly visible from Earth. Reflected light takes 1.25 seconds to reach Earth – compared to 8 minutes 27.3 seconds for light to reach us from the Sun.

Temperature

With the Sun overhead, the temperature on the lunar equator can reach 243°F. At night it can sink to –261°F.

Eclipses

When the Moon passes between the Sun and the Earth it causes a partial eclipse of the Sun (1) if the Earth passes through the Moon's outer shadow (P), or a total eclipse (2) if the inner cone shadow crosses the Earth's surface. In a lunar eclipse, the Earth's shadow crosses the Moon and, again, provides either a partial or total eclipse.

Eclipses of the Sun and the Moon do not occur every month because of the 5° difference between the plane of the Moon's orbit and the plane in which the Earth moves. In the 1990s only 14 lunar eclipses were possible, for example, seven partial and seven total; each was visible only from certain, and variable, parts of the world. The same period witnessed 13 solar eclipses – six partial (or annular) and seven total.

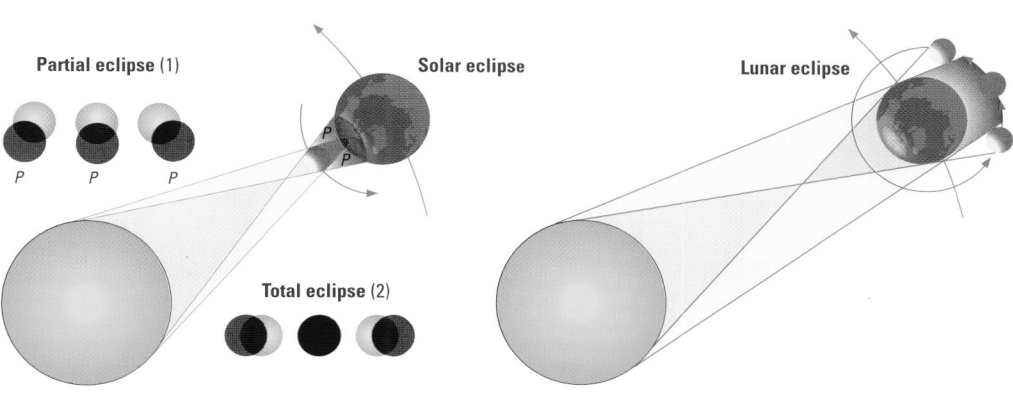

Partial eclipse (1) Solar eclipse Lunar eclipse

Total eclipse (2)

Tides

The daily rise and fall of the ocean's tides are the result of the gravitational pull of the Moon and that of the Sun, though the effect of the latter is only 46.6% as strong as that of the Moon. This effect is greatest on the hemisphere facing the Moon and causes a tidal "bulge." When the Sun, Earth and Moon are in line, tide-raising forces are at a maximum and Spring tides occur: high tide reaches the highest values, and low tide falls to low levels. When lunar and solar forces are least coincidental with the Sun and Moon at an angle (near the Moon's first and third quarters), Neap tides occur, which have a small tidal range.

Spring tide
New Moon
Last quarter
Neap tide
Spring tide
Full Moon
Gravitational pull by the Sun
Neap tide
First quarter

Time Zones

The Earth rotates through 360° in 24 hours, and so moves 15° every hour. The world is divided into 24 standard time zones, each centered on lines of longitude at 15° intervals. At the center of the first zone is the Prime meridian or Greenwich meridian. All places to the west of Greenwich are one hour behind for every 15° of longitude; places to the east are ahead by one hour for every 15°. When it is 12 noon at the Greenwich meridian, 180° east it is midnight of the same day – while 180° west the day is just beginning. To overcome this, the International Date Line was established, approximately following the 180° meridian. Thus, if you traveled eastward from Japan (140° East) to Samoa (170° West), you would pass from Sunday night into Sunday morning.

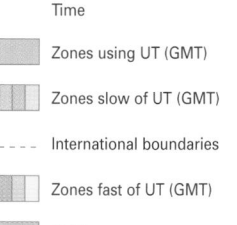

| 10 | Hours slow or fast of UT or Coordinated Universal Time |

Zones using UT (GMT)

Zones slow of UT (GMT)

International boundaries

Zones fast of UT (GMT)

Half-hour zones

Time zone boundaries

International Date Line

Actual Solar Time when time at Greenwich is 12:00 (noon)

Note: Certain of the above time zones are affected by the incidence of "Summer Time" in countries where it is adopted.

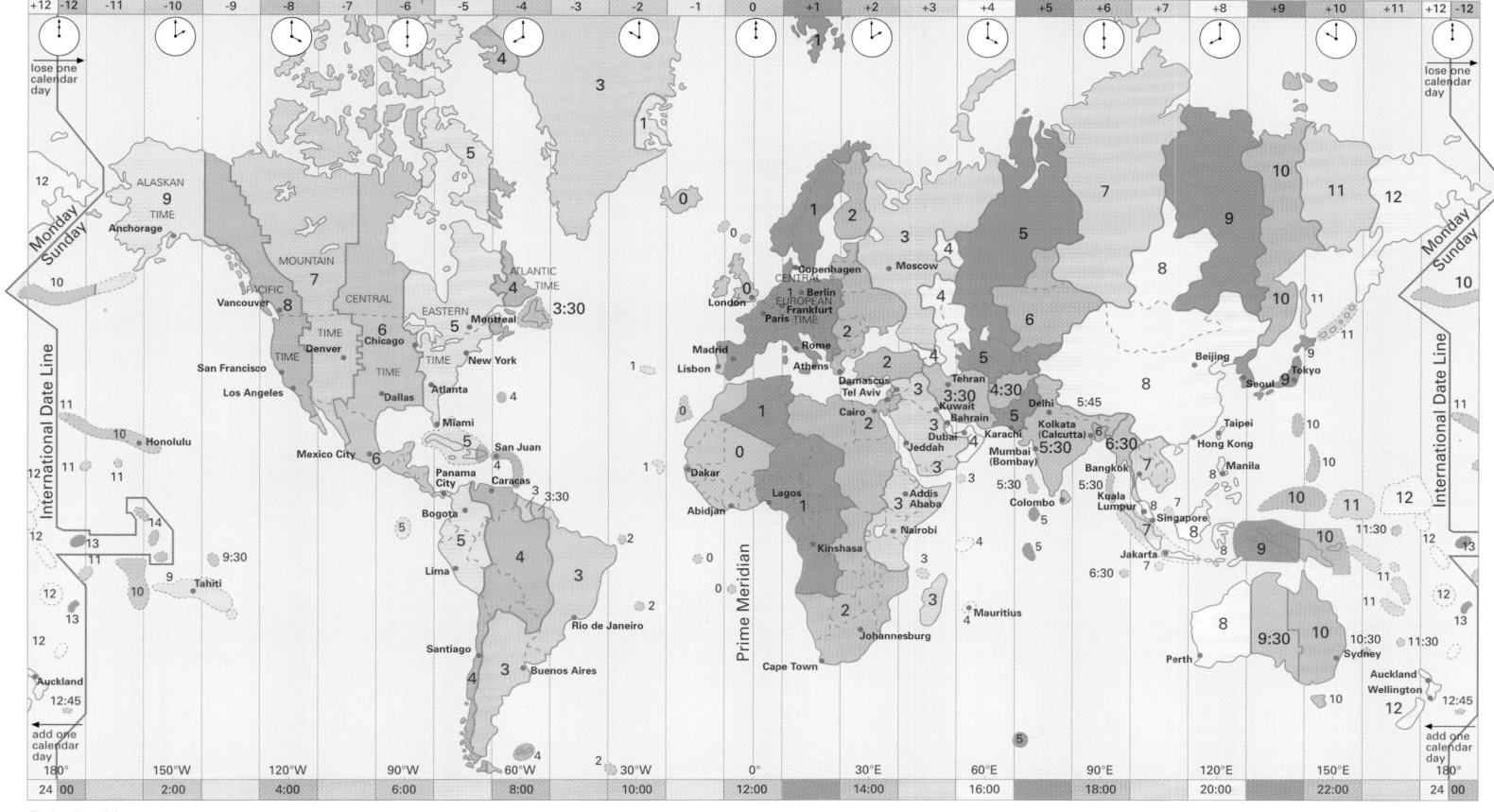

Projection: Mercator

CARTOGRAPHY BY PHILIP'S. COPYRIGHT GEORGE PHILIP LTD

Oceans

The last 40 years have been described as the "Space Age," but another exciting and perhaps even more important area of discovery, proceeding at the same time, has been the exploration of "inner space," namely the oceans which cover more than 70% of our planet. The study of the ocean floor and oceanic islands has revealed features that help to explain how continents move, and how the movements are related to earthquakes and volcanic activity.

Manned submersibles have established that life exists even in the deepest trenches, where the pressure reaches 1,000 atmospheres, the equivalent of the force of six and a half tons bearing down on every square inch. Further exploration in the pitch-black environment of the ocean ridges has revealed strange forms of marine life around scalding hot vents. The creatures include giant tubeworms, blind shrimps, and bacteria, some of which are genetically very different from any other known life forms. In 1996, an analysis of one microorganism revealed that at least half of its 1,700 or so genes were hitherto unknown. This environment, which is based on chemicals, not sunlight, may resemble the places where life on Earth first began.

Another vital area of contemporary research concerns the interactions between the oceans and the atmosphere, as exemplified in the El Niño–Southern Oscillation (ENSO), and the bearing that these have on climatic change.

Most geographers divide the world's ocean waters into four areas: the Pacific, Atlantic, Indian and Arctic oceans. The most active zone in the oceans is the sunlit upper layer, where the water is moved around by wind-blown currents. It is the home of most sea life and acts as a membrane through which the ocean breathes,

Seawater

The chemical composition of the sea, by percentage, excluding the elements of water itself

Chloride (Cl)	55.04%
Sodium (Na)	30.61%
Sulfate (SO₄)	7.69%
Magnesium (Mg)	3.69%
Calcium (Ca)	1.16%
Potassium (K)	1.10%
Bicarbonate (HCO₃)	0.41%
Bromide (Br)	0.19%
Boric Acid (H₃BO₃)	0.07%
Strontium (Sr)	0.04%
Fluoride (Fl)	0.003%
Lithium (Li)	trace
Rubidium (Rb)	trace
Phosphorus (P)	trace
Iodine (I)	trace
Barium (Ba)	trace
Arsenic (As)	trace
Cesium (Cs)	trace

Eleven constituents account for over 99% of the salt content of seawater, but seawater also contains virtually every other element. In natural conditions, its composition is broadly consistent across the world's seas and oceans; but in coastal areas especially, variations are sometimes substantial. The oceans are about 35 parts water to one part salt.

Life in the Oceans

An imaginary profile of the typical coastal and oceanic zones is shown, with a selection of the life forms that might occur in the water off the Pacific Coast of Central America. The animals illustrated are not drawn to scale as the range of sizes is too great. Most marine life is confined to the first 650 feet, the upper sunlit (photic) zone, where sunlight can still penetrate. Plant and animal plankton, the basis of life in the ocean, occur in great quantities in all zones.

In the pelagic environment (open sea), vertical gradients, including those of light, temperature and salinity, determine the distribution of organisms. From the tidal zone at the coastline, the continental shelf, geologically still part of the continental landmass, drops gently to about 650 feet – the sunlit zone. At the end of the shelf, the seabed falls away in the steeper angle of the continental slope. The subsequent descent to the deep ocean floor, known as the continental rise, is more gentle, with gradients between 1 in 100 and 1 in 700 until the abyssal plains and hills between 8,000 and 19,500 feet below the surface.

The deep sea floor contains seamounts, some of which are capped by coral reefs, ocean ridges, the longest mountain chains on Earth, and deep ocean trenches, especially in the Pacific Ocean where six trenches reach depths of more than 33,000 feet, including the Mariana Trench at 36,000 feet deep.

Each of these zones contains a distinctive community of species adapted to the different conditions of salinity, temperature and light intensity. Indeed, a few organisms have been found even in the abyssal darkness of the great ocean trenches.

absorbing great quantities of carbon dioxide and partly exchanging it for oxygen.

As the depth increases, so light fades and temperatures fall until just before 3,000 feet where there is a marked temperature change at the thermocline, the boundary between the warm surface zone and the cold deep zone. Below the thermocline, slow currents are caused by density differences between bodies of water with varying temperatures and salinity.

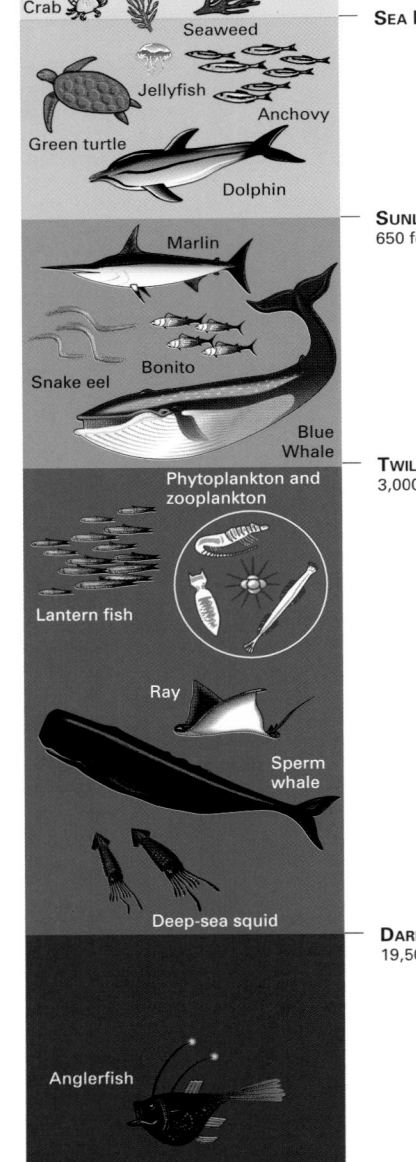

Crab — Seaweed — **SEA LEVEL**
Jellyfish
Green turtle — Anchovy
Dolphin — **SUNLIT ZONE** 650 feet

Marlin
Snake eel — Bonito — Blue Whale — **TWILIGHT ZONE** 3,000 feet

Phytoplankton and zooplankton
Lantern fish

Ray
Sperm whale

Deep-sea squid — **DARK ZONE** 19,500 feet

Anglerfish

Halosaur
Sea cucumber
Sponge

TRENCH ZONE 33,000 feet

Isopod

Atoll Building

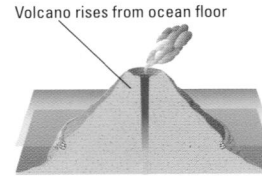

Volcano rises from ocean floor

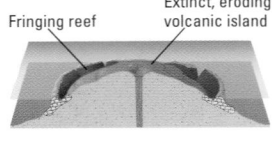

Fringing reef — Extinct, eroding volcanic island

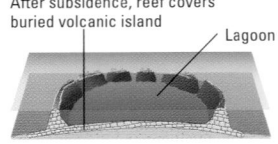

After subsidence, reef covers buried volcanic island — Lagoon

A coral atoll usually begins existence as a bare volcanic peak, thrusting above the surface of the ocean. A colony of coral – organisms with calcium carbonate skeletons – forms itself in the shallow water around the peak. The volcano is eroded and slowly sinks, leaving the coral forming a ring of hard limestone around its remnant. In time, the barrier reef of an atoll is all that remains.

The El Niño Phenomenon

The importance of the ocean–atmosphere interaction is nowhere more dramatically demonstrated than the El Niño phenomenon in the southern Pacific Ocean.

Under normal conditions, shown in the diagram, top right, surface water flows eastward from South America under the influence of trade winds while, near the coast, cold, nutrient-rich water (dark blue) rises to the surface and spreads westward. In the western Pacific, sea surface temperatures reach 82°F or more and warm air rises, creating a low pressure air system and causing heavy rains. The rising warm air spreads out and some of it descends over South America and the eastern Pacific creating a high pressure air system from which winds blow westward. This rotating system is called a Walker Circulation Cell.

An El Niño event, also called an El Niño–Southern Oscillation cycle, or ENSO cycle, is characterized by a reversal of currents whereby the eastward-moving South Equatorial Current extends much further eastward and the trade winds weaken. The upwelling of cold water off South America is greatly reduced and surface water temperatures rise, causing a drastic reduction in fish life. The heaviest rainfall is over the eastern Pacific, while Southeast Asia is much drier than usual. Warm air rises in the east and spreads out, descending in the western Pacific, which then becomes a high pressure area, as shown on the second diagram, below right.

During an intense El Niño, such as in 1982–83 when sea temperatures in the eastern Pacific rose by 11°F, the effects of the current and wind reversals affect the weather around the world. In Australia and Southeast Asia, the monsoon rainfall is reduced, while, in 1983–84, a severe drought occurred in the Sahel, south of the Sahara, and also in southern Africa. The southeast coast of the United States also suffered storms and heavy rainfall, and even Europe experienced changes in weather patterns, possibly as a result of consequent changes in the course of the jet stream.

Scientists have found evidence that the frequency of the El Niño event, which normally occurs every two to seven years, may have increased in recent years with warm conditions persisting in the eastern Pacific from 1990 until mid-1995, an unprecedented length of time during the 114 years for which data exist. Another intense El Niño occurred in 1997–98, with resultant freak weather conditions across the entire Pacific region. Scientists do not know the causes of the El Niño event, though some researchers are investigating possible connections between major volcanic eruptions in the tropical Pacific region, the ENSO cycle and atmospheric circulation.

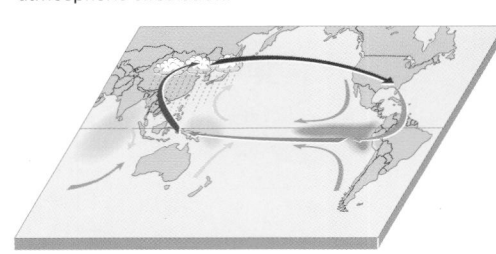

Normal year – Walker Circulation Cell

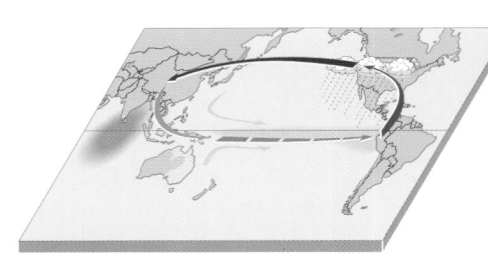

El Niño event

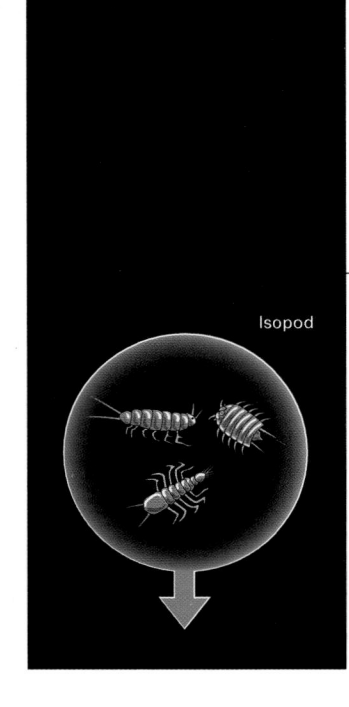

CARTOGRAPHY BY PHILIP'S. COPYRIGHT GEORGE PHILIP LTD

Ocean Currents

JANUARY CURRENTS AND TEMPERATURES
(Northern Hemisphere: winter)

ACTUAL SURFACE TEMPERATURE

°F
86
68
50
32
14
− 4
− 22
− 40

OCEAN CURRENTS

Cold	Warm	Speed (knots)
← - -	← - -	Less than 0.5
←	←	0.5 – 1.0
←	←	Over 1.0

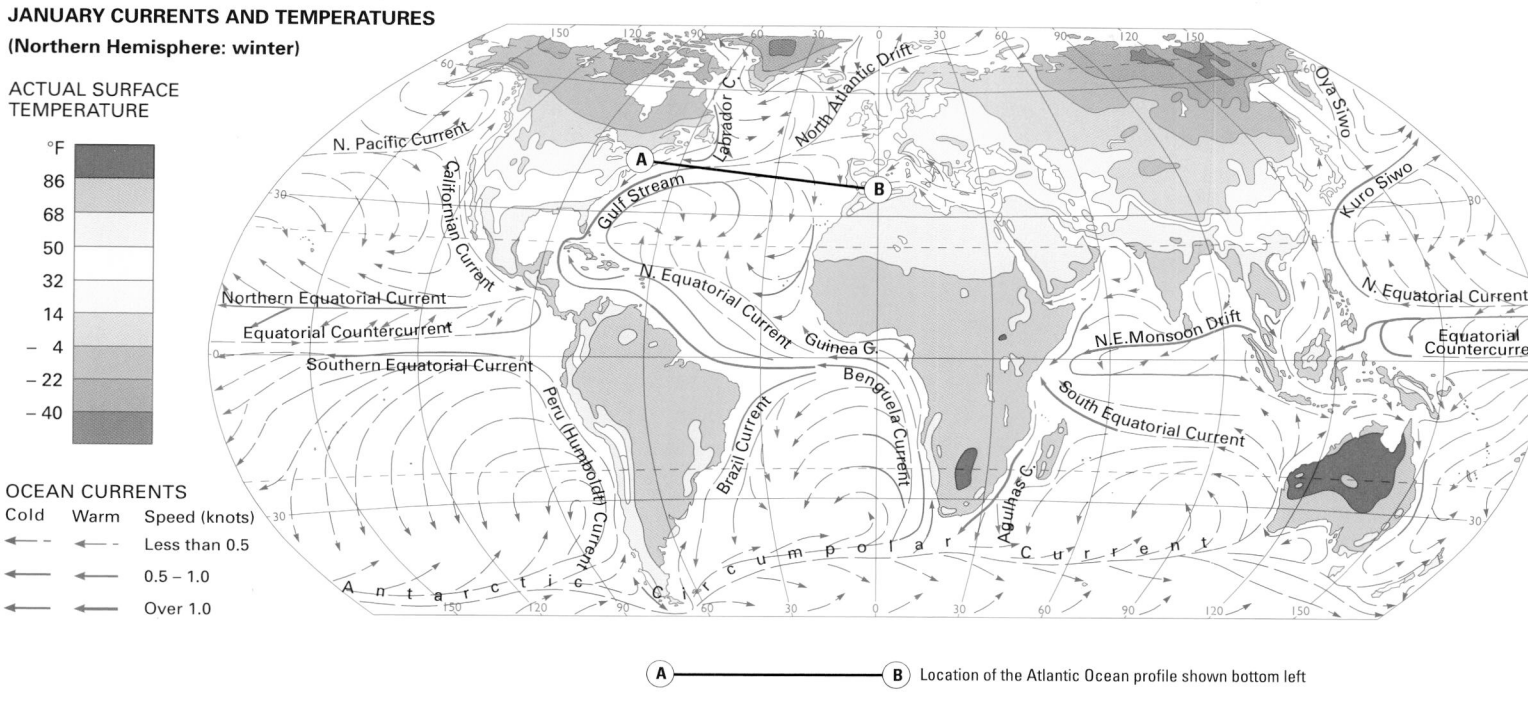

A ——————— B Location of the Atlantic Ocean profile shown bottom left

JULY CURRENTS AND TEMPERATURES
(Northern Hemisphere: summer)

ACTUAL SURFACE TEMPERATURE

°F
86
68
50
32
14

OCEAN CURRENTS

Cold	Warm	Speed (knots)
← - -	← - -	Less than 0.5
←	←	0.5 – 1.0
←	←	Over 1.0

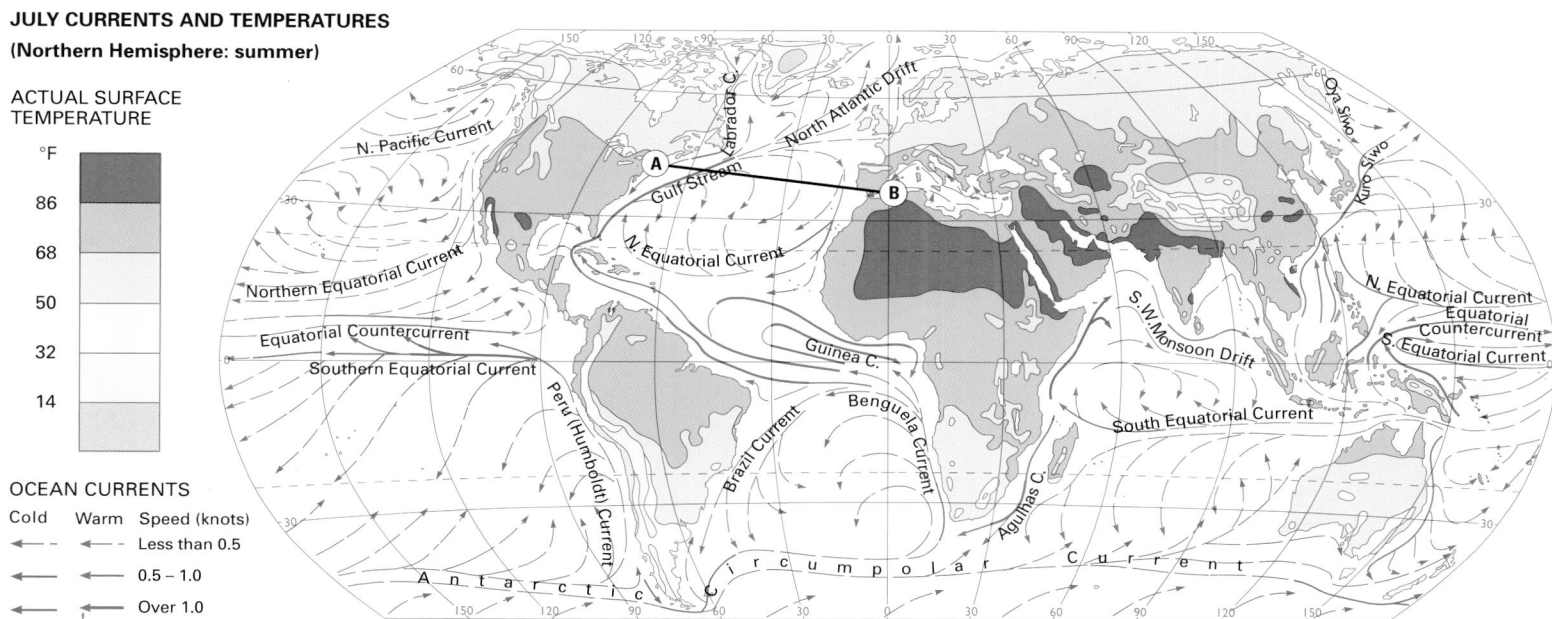

Moving immense quantities of energy as well as billions of tons of water every hour, the ocean currents are a vital part of the great heat engine that drives the Earth's climate. They themselves are produced by a twofold mechanism. At the surface, winds push huge masses of water before them; in the deep ocean, below an abrupt temperature gradient that separates the churning surface waters from the still depths, density variations cause slow vertical movements.

The pattern of circulation of the great surface currents is determined by the displacement known as the Coriolis effect. As the Earth turns beneath a moving object – whether it is a tennis ball or a vast mass of water – it appears to be deflected to one side. The deflection is most obvious near the Equator, where the Earth's surface is spinning eastward at 1,000 mph; currents moving poleward are curved clockwise in the northern hemisphere and counterclockwise in the southern.

The result is a system of spinning circles known as gyres. Warm currents move constantly from the Equator toward the poles, while cold water moves in the reverse direction. In this way, ocean currents act like a thermostat, helping to regulate temperatures around the world.

Depending on the annual movements of the prevailing wind belts, some currents on or near the Equator may reverse their direction in the course of the year, a variation on which Asia's monsoon rains depend and whose occasional failure has brought disaster to millions of people.

Topography of the Ocean Floor

Profile of the Atlantic Ocean

The deep ocean floor was once believed to be flat, but maps compiled from readings made by sonar equipment show that it is no more uniform than the surface of the continents. The profile, below, shows some of the features on the Atlantic Ocean floor between Massachusetts in North America and Gibraltar (for location of profile, see maps above). Around the continents are shallow continental shelves composed of rocks which are less dense than the underlying oceanic crust. The continents end at the top of the steep continental slope, which descends to the abyss via the continental rise, made up of sediments washed down from the continental shelves. The abyss contains large plains overlain by oozes but the plains are broken by volcanic seamounts and guyots (flat-topped seamounts), a few of which reach the surface as islands. The other main feature is the Mid-Atlantic Ridge, through which runs a rift valley where new crustal rock is being formed as the plates on either side move apart.

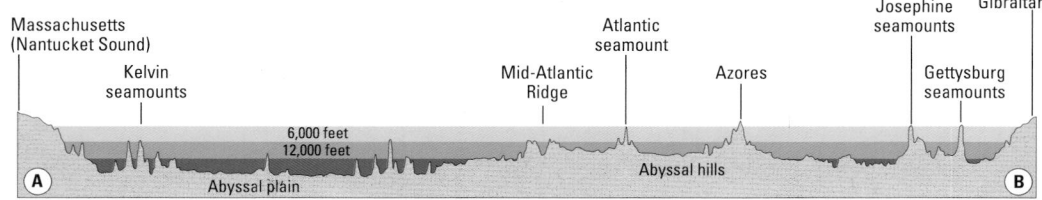

Topography of the ocean floor around Australia

In the image on the right, land areas are shown in gray, with shaded relief. The colors represent sea depth, with red representing the shallowest areas, through yellow and green to dark blue (the deepest). The data for the sea topography are from the Seasat radar satellite. The deep blue area in the upper left is the Java Trench which forms the boundary between the Indo-Australian plate and the Eurasian plate. In the top right, the New Guinea trench, which has a maximum depth of 29,865 feet, forms the border of the Indo-Australian and Pacific plates. Alongside the trenches are volcanic islands formed from magma, created as the edge of the Indo-Australian plate is subducted and melted.

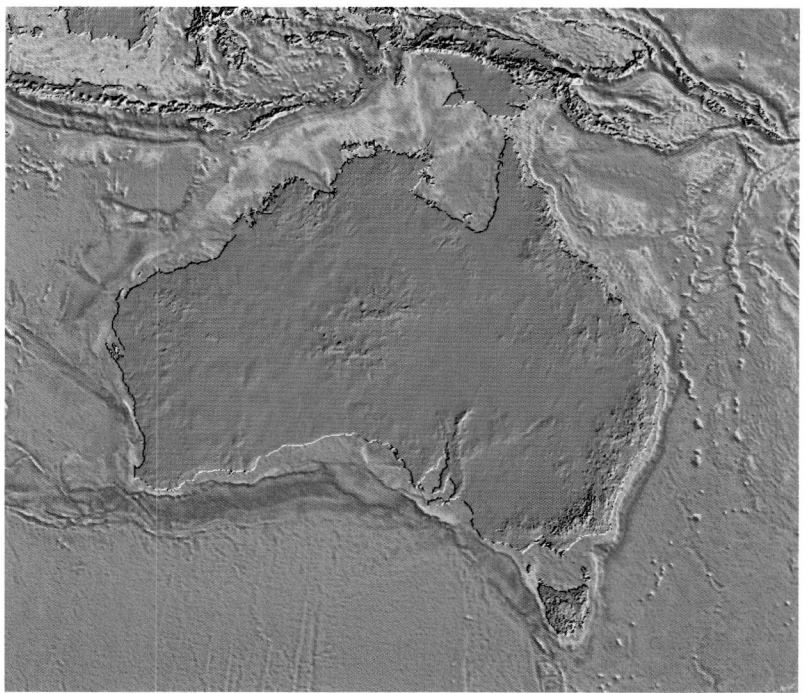

Geology of the Earth

Every year, earthquakes and volcanic eruptions cause much destruction throughout the world. Such phenomena were once thought to be unconnected but since the late 1960s, scientists have understood that these events are surface manifestations of the tremendous forces operating in the Earth's interior that are slowly but constantly changing the face of our planet.

The Earth is divided into three zones. The crust, a brittle, low-density zone, overlies the dense mantle. Separating the crust from the mantle is a distinct boundary called the Mohorovičić (or Moho) discontinuity. Enclosed by the mantle is the Earth's core, which consists mainly of iron and nickel.

Temperatures inside the Earth range from about 1,600°F in the upper mantle to perhaps 9,000°F in the core. Heat creates convection currents in a semimolten part of the mantle called the asthenosphere. Above the asthenosphere is the lithosphere, a solid layer about 40 miles thick, consisting of the crust and part of the mantle. The lithosphere is divided into rigid plates, moved around by the currents in the asthenosphere, a process named plate tectonics.

The Earth was formed around 4.6 billion years ago. Lighter elements floated toward the surface, where they formed crustal rocks. The oldest rocks so far discovered are nearly 4 billion years old, while the oldest fossils occur in rocks formed around 3.5 billion years ago. An explosion of life occurred at the start of the Cambrian period, 570 million years ago. The fossil record since the start of the Cambrian has enabled scientists to piece together the story of life on Earth.

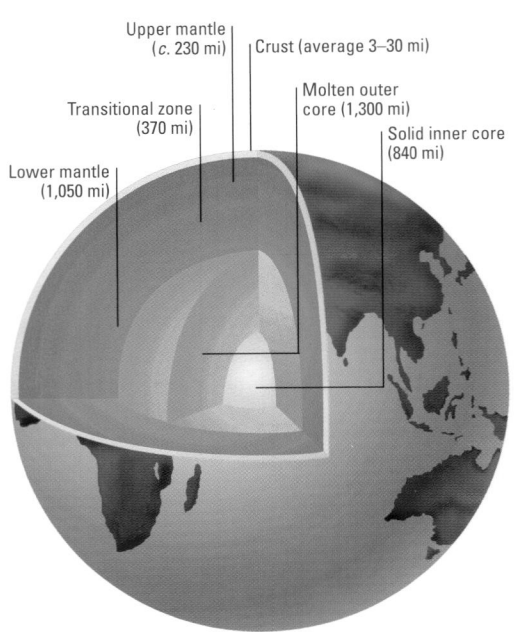

Upper mantle (c. 230 mi) | Crust (average 3–30 mi) | Transitional zone (370 mi) | Molten outer core (1,300 mi) | Solid inner core (840 mi) | Lower mantle (1,050 mi)

Plate Tectonics

In the early 20th century, the German scientist Alfred Wegener and others noticed similarities between the shapes of the continents. From a study of rocks and fossils in widely separated continents, they suggested that the continents had once been joined together and that somehow they had drifted apart. But no one knew of a mechanism that might cause continents to drift. However, in the 1950s and 1960s, evidence from studies of the ocean floor suggested that the low-density continents rest on huge slow-moving plates.

Seafloor spreading in the Indian Ocean and continental plate collision

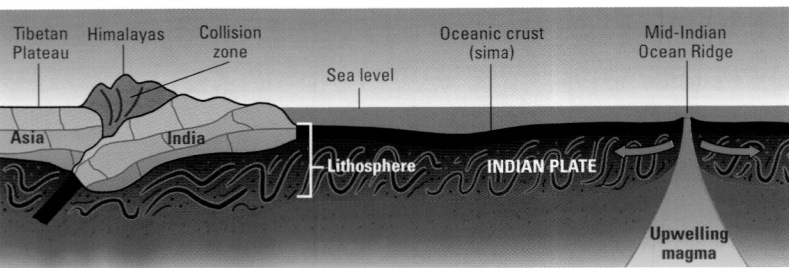

Tibetan Plateau | Himalayas | Collision zone | Oceanic crust (sima) | Mid-Indian Ocean Ridge | Sea level | Asia | India | Lithosphere | INDIAN PLATE | Upwelling magma

Seafloor spreading in the Atlantic Ocean and plate collision

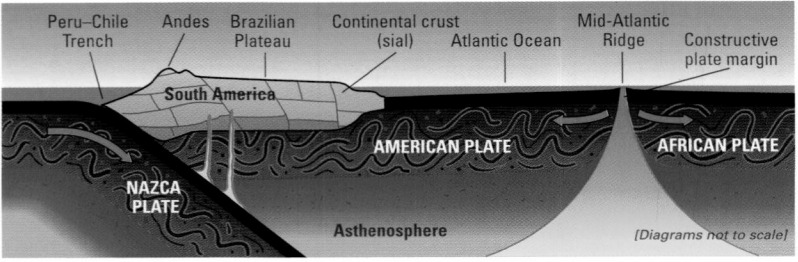

Peru–Chile Trench | Andes | Brazilian Plateau | Continental crust (sial) | Atlantic Ocean | Mid-Atlantic Ridge | Constructive plate margin | South America | AMERICAN PLATE | AFRICAN PLATE | NAZCA PLATE | Asthenosphere | [Diagrams not to scale]

The huge ridges that run through the oceans represent boundaries between plates. Here plates are diverging at rates of 1–2 inches a year. Molten magma from the mantle rises along a central rift valley to form new crustal rock. These ocean ridges, which are active zones where earthquakes and volcanic eruptions are common, are called constructive plate margins. Destructive plate margins, which occur when two plates converge, are marked by deep ocean trenches as one plate is forced under the other. The descending plate is melted to produce the magma that fuels volcanoes alongside the trenches. Movements of descending plates are often sudden and violent, triggering earthquakes in overlying continental areas. Where two continents collide, their margins are buckled up to form fold mountain ranges. A third type of plate margin, the transform fault, is not illustrated above. Along these plate margins, such as California's San Andreas fault, plates are moving parallel to each other.

The debate about plate tectonics is not over. Questions still arise as to why some active volcanoes lie far from plate margins, and why major earthquakes occur in midplate areas.

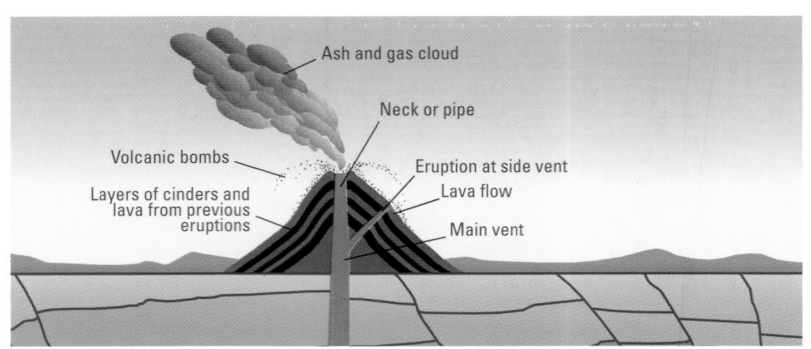

Ash and gas cloud | Neck or pipe | Volcanic bombs | Eruption at side vent | Layers of cinders and lava from previous eruptions | Lava flow | Main vent

Continental Drift

In 1915, Alfred Wegener produced a series of world maps proposing that, around 200 million years ago, the continents had been joined together in a super-continent which he called Pangaea. This land mass started to break up about 180 million years ago and the parts drifted to their present positions. The arrows on the present day world map shows that the continents are still on the move.

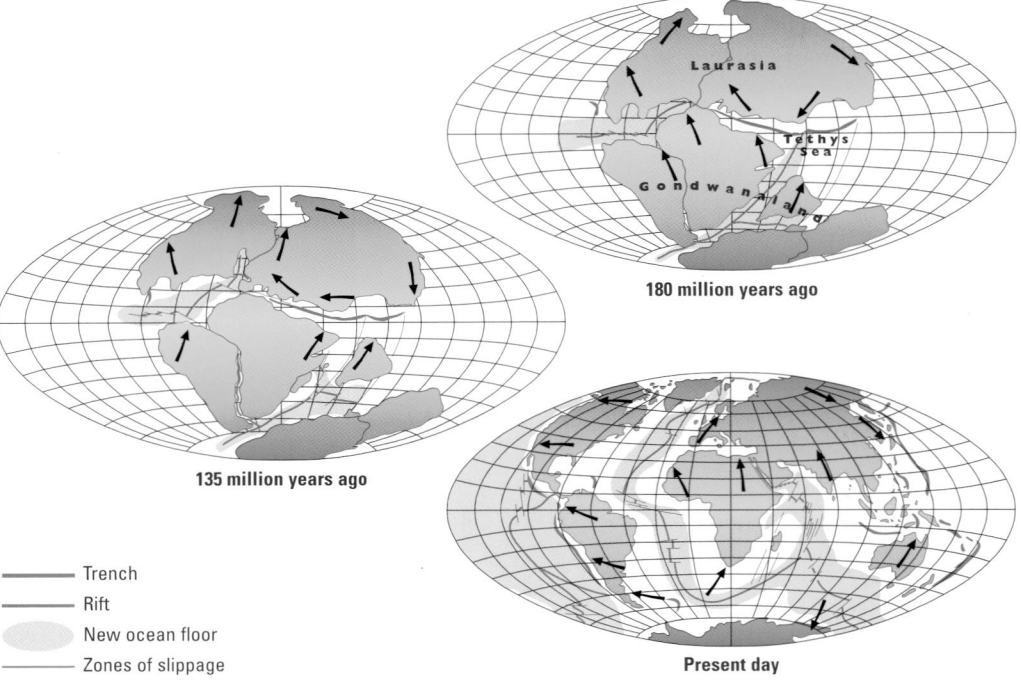

Laurasia | Tethys Sea | Gondwanaland | 180 million years ago | 135 million years ago | Present day

Trench
Rift
New ocean floor
Zones of slippage

Distribution of Volcanoes

Volcanoes occur when hot liquefied rock beneath the Earth's crust is pushed up by pressure to the surface as molten lava. There are some 550 known active volcanoes, around 20 of which are erupting at any one time.

▲ Land volcanoes active since 1700
↗ Direction of movement
〜 Boundaries of tectonic plates
• Submarine volcanoes
♦ Geysers

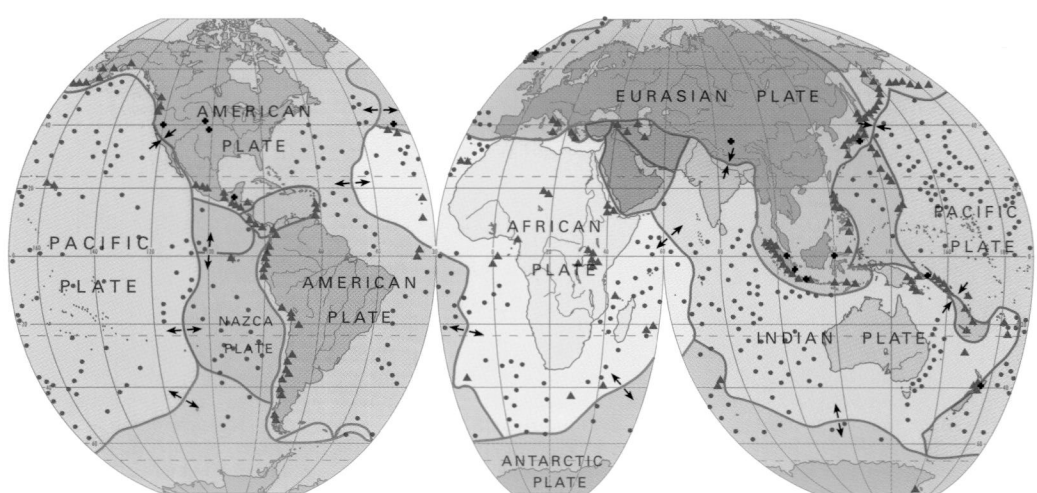

AMERICAN PLATE | PACIFIC PLATE | NAZCA PLATE | EURASIAN PLATE | AFRICAN PLATE | AMERICAN PLATE | PACIFIC PLATE | INDIAN PLATE | ANTARCTIC PLATE

CARTOGRAPHY BY PHILIP'S. COPYRIGHT GEORGE PHILIP LTD

Geological Time

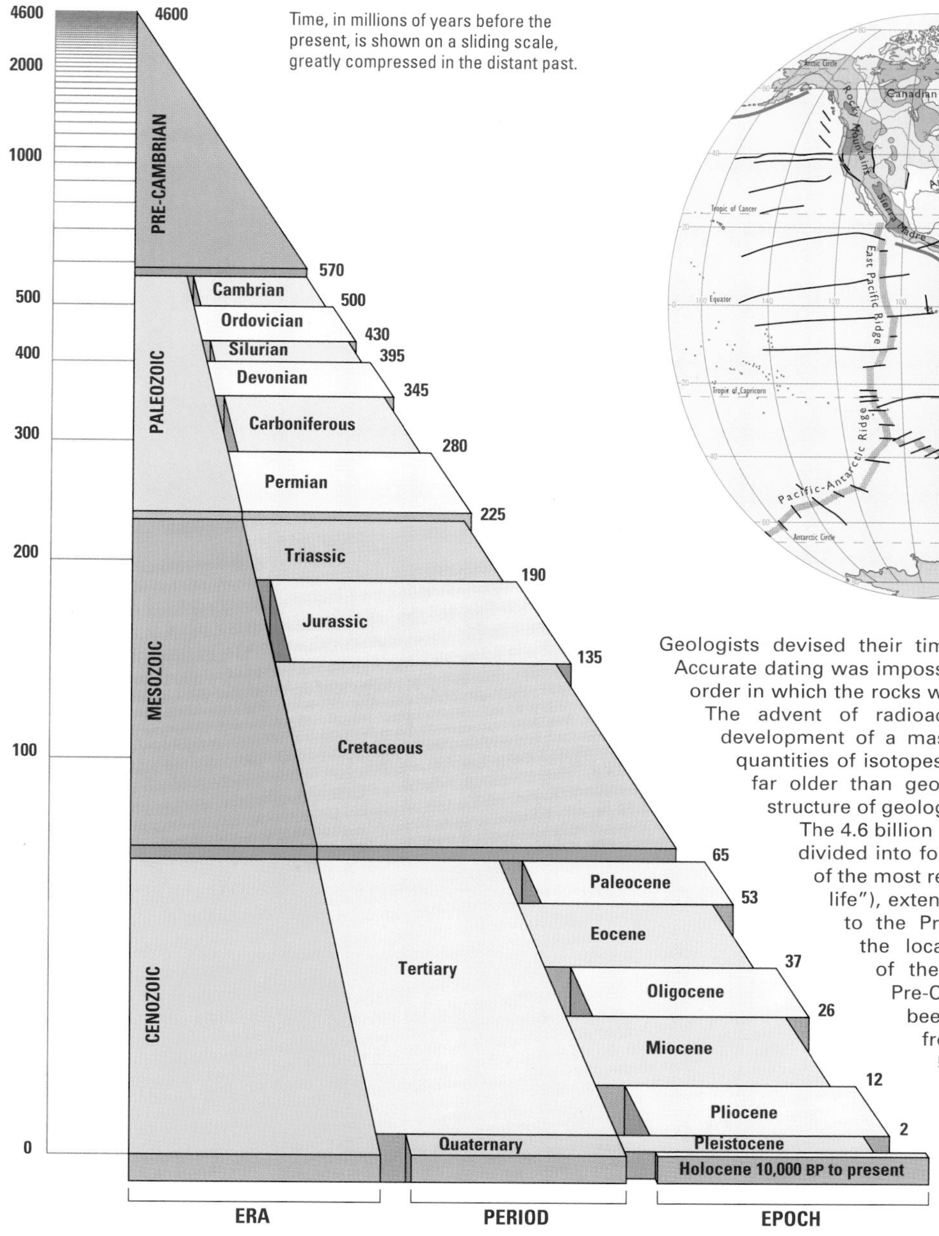

Time, in millions of years before the present, is shown on a sliding scale, greatly compressed in the distant past.

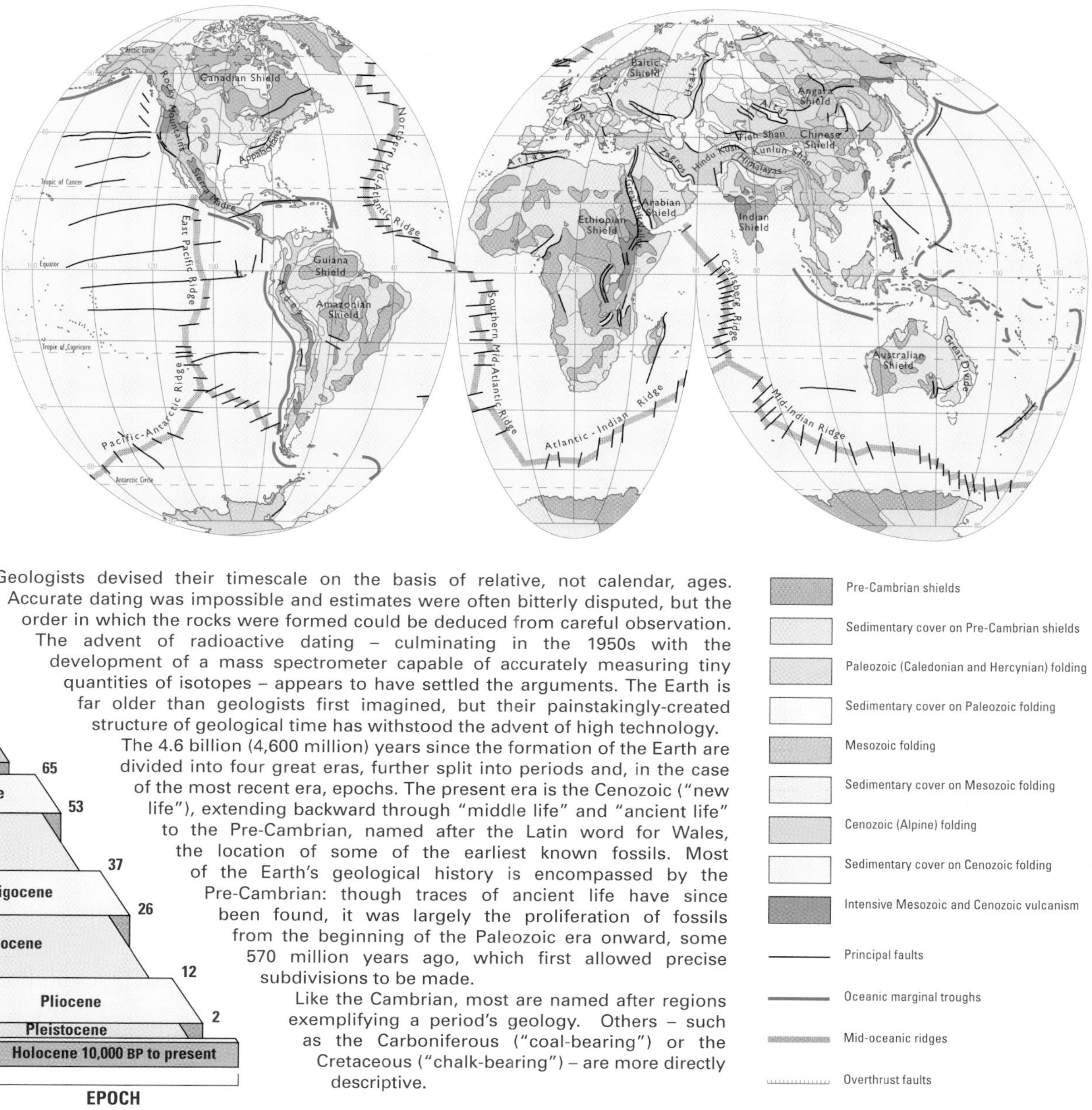

4600	4600
2000	
1000	PRE-CAMBRIAN
500	570 Cambrian
400	500 Ordovician / 430 Silurian / 395 Devonian
300	345 Carboniferous / 280 Permian
200	225 Triassic / 190 Jurassic
100	135 Cretaceous
0	65 Paleocene / 53 Eocene / 37 Oligocene / 26 Miocene / 12 Pliocene / 2 Pleistocene

PALEOZOIC
MESOZOIC
CENOZOIC

Tertiary
Quaternary
Holocene 10,000 BP to present

ERA — **PERIOD** — **EPOCH**

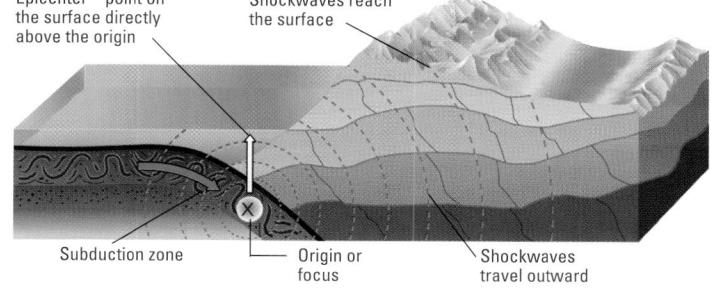

Geologists devised their timescale on the basis of relative, not calendar, ages. Accurate dating was impossible and estimates were often bitterly disputed, but the order in which the rocks were formed could be deduced from careful observation. The advent of radioactive dating – culminating in the 1950s with the development of a mass spectrometer capable of accurately measuring tiny quantities of isotopes – appears to have settled the arguments. The Earth is far older than geologists first imagined, but their painstakingly-created structure of geological time has withstood the advent of high technology.

The 4.6 billion (4,600 million) years since the formation of the Earth are divided into four great eras, further split into periods and, in the case of the most recent era, epochs. The present era is the Cenozoic ("new life"), extending backward through "middle life" and "ancient life" to the Pre-Cambrian, named after the Latin word for Wales, the location of some of the earliest known fossils. Most of the Earth's geological history is encompassed by the Pre-Cambrian: though traces of ancient life have since been found, it was largely the proliferation of fossils from the beginning of the Paleozoic era onward, some 570 million years ago, which first allowed precise subdivisions to be made.

Like the Cambrian, most are named after regions exemplifying a period's geology. Others – such as the Carboniferous ("coal-bearing") or the Cretaceous ("chalk-bearing") – are more directly descriptive.

Legend:
- Pre-Cambrian shields
- Sedimentary cover on Pre-Cambrian shields
- Paleozoic (Caledonian and Hercynian) folding
- Sedimentary cover on Paleozoic folding
- Mesozoic folding
- Sedimentary cover on Mesozoic folding
- Cenozoic (Alpine) folding
- Sedimentary cover on Cenozoic folding
- Intensive Mesozoic and Cenozoic vulcanism
- Principal faults
- Oceanic marginal troughs
- Mid-oceanic ridges
- Overthrust faults

Earthquakes

Earthquake magnitude is usually rated according to either the Richter or the Modified Mercalli scale, both devised by seismologists in the 1930s. The Richter scale measures absolute earthquake power with mathematical precision: each step upward represents a tenfold increase in the amplitude of the shockwave. Theoretically, there is no upper limit, but the largest earthquakes measured have been rated at between 8.8 and 8.9. The 12-point Mercalli scale, based on observed effects, is often more meaningful, ranging from I (earthquakes noticed only by seismographs) to XII (total destruction); intermediate points include V (people awakened at night; unstable objects overturned), VII (collapse of ordinary buildings; chimneys and monuments fall) and IX (conspicuous cracks in ground; serious damage to reservoirs).

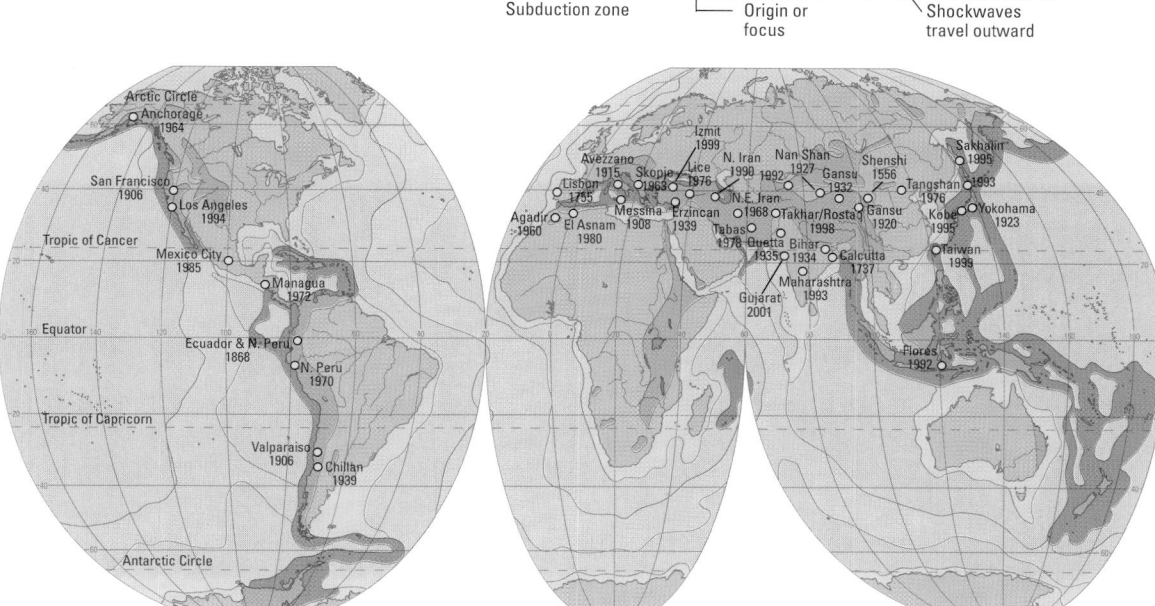

Epicenter – point on the surface directly above the origin
Shockwaves reach the surface
Subduction zone
Origin or focus
Shockwaves travel outward

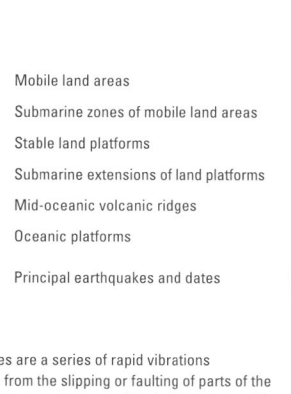

- Mobile land areas
- Submarine zones of mobile land areas
- Stable land platforms
- Submarine extensions of land platforms
- Mid-oceanic volcanic ridges
- Oceanic platforms

1976 ◯ Principal earthquakes and dates

Earthquakes are a series of rapid vibrations originating from the slipping or faulting of parts of the Earth's crust when stresses within build up to breaking point. They usually happen at depths varying from 5 to 20 miles. Severe earthquakes cause extensive damage when they take place in populated areas, destroying structures and severing communications. Most initial loss of life occurs due to secondary causes such as falling masonry, fires and flooding.

Notable Earthquakes Since 1900

Year	Location	Mag.	Deaths
1906	San Francisco, USA	8.3	503
1906	Valparaiso, Chile	8.6	22,000
1908	Messina, Italy	7.5	83,000
1915	Avezzano, Italy	7.5	30,000
1920	Gansu (Kansu), China	8.6	180,000
1923	Yokohama, Japan	8.3	143,000
1927	Nan Shan, China	8.3	200,000
1932	Gansu (Kansu), China	7.6	70,000
1933	Sanriku, Japan	8.9	2,990
1934	Bihar, India/Nepal	8.4	10,700
1935	Quetta, India*	7.5	60,000
1939	Chillan, Chile	8.3	28,000
1939	Erzincan, Turkey	7.9	30,000
1960	Agadir, Morocco	5.8	12,000
1962	Khorasan, Iran	7.1	12,230
1968	N.E. Iran	7.4	12,000
1970	N. Peru	7.7	66,794
1972	Managua, Nicaragua	6.2	5,000
1974	N. Pakistan	6.3	5,200
1976	Guatemala	7.5	22,778
1976	Tangshan, China	8.2	255,000
1978	Tabas, Iran	7.7	25,000
1980	El Asnam, Algeria	7.3	20,000
1980	S. Italy	7.2	4,800
1985	Mexico City, Mexico	8.1	4,200
1988	N.W. Armenia	6.8	55,000
1990	N. Iran	7.7	36,000
1992	Flores, Indonesia	6.8	1,895
1993	Maharashtra, India	6.4	30,000
1994	Los Angeles, USA	6.6	51
1995	Kobe, Japan	7.2	5,000
1995	Sakhalin Is., Russia	7.5	2,000
1996	Yunnan, China	7.0	240
1997	N.E. Iran	7.1	2,400
1998	Takhar, Afghanistan	6.1	4,200
1998	Rostaq, Afghanistan	7.0	5,000
1999	Izmit, Turkey	7.4	15,000
1999	Tapei, Taiwan	7.6	1,700
2001	Gujarat, India	7.7	18,600

The most devastating quake ever was at Shaanxi (Shenshi) province, central China, on 3 January 1556, when an estimated 830,000 people were killed.

* now Pakistan

CARTOGRAPHY BY PHILIP'S. COPYRIGHT GEORGE PHILIP LTD

Landforms

The theory of plate tectonics has offered new insights as to how the Earth works, elucidating mysteries concerning continental drift, volcanic eruptions and earthquakes. It has also contributed to our understanding of how plate collisions can squeeze up layers of sediments on seabeds into fold mountain ranges, such as the Himalayas.

Yet even as mountains rise, natural forces are wearing them away. In hot, dry climates, mechanical weathering, a result of rapid temperature changes, causes the outer layers of rocks to peel away, while, in cold mountain regions, boulders are prised apart when water freezes in cracks in rocks. Chemical weathering is responsible for hollowing out limestone caves and decomposing granites.

Climatic conditions have a great bearing on the principle agent of erosion in any particular area. Running water is most important in moist temperate regions. In cold regions, ice is the major agent of erosion, and in many mountain ranges, U-shaped valleys are evidence of the erosive power of valley glaciers. Ice sheets moulded much of the Earth's surface during the Ice Ages, the most recent of which, in the northern hemisphere, ended only 10,000 years ago. Polar climates also shape the scenery of the periglacial areas that border bodies of ice. Such areas are subject to constant freeze-thaw action, which creates such features as pingos (domed mounds).

Climatic change has also affected many of the landforms in hot deserts, which were shaped by running water at a time when the deserts enjoyed much wetter climates. However, the major agent of erosion in deserts today is wind-blown sand which erodes rock strata to form mushroom-shaped rocks and caves.

The surface of the Earth is under constant assault from tectonic processes and the agents of erosion. The products of erosion, fragments of rock such as sand, are deposited to form sedimentary rocks. Metamorphic rocks are created when igneous or sedimentary rocks are buried and metamorphosed by heat and pressure. Eventually the rocks are recycled to form magma, which rises upward to start the rock cycle all over again.

The Rock Cycle

James Hutton first proposed the rock cycle in the late 1700s after he observed the slow but steady effects of erosion.

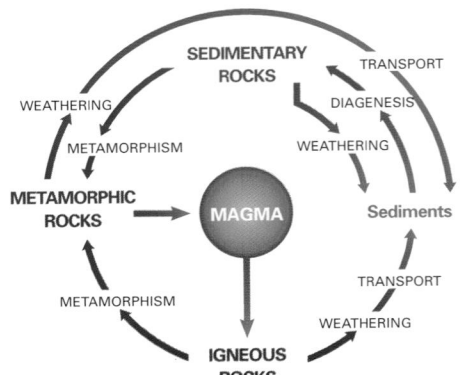

Rocks are divided into three types, according to the way in which they are formed:

Igneous rocks, including granite and basalt, are formed by the cooling of magma from within the Earth's crust.

Metamorphic rocks, such as slate, marble and quartzite, are formed below the Earth's surface by the compression or baking of existing rocks.

Sedimentary rocks, like sandstone and limestone, are formed on the surface of the Earth from the remains of living organisms and eroded fragments of older rocks.

Mountain Building

Mountains are formed when pressures on the Earth's crust caused by continental drift become so intense that the surface buckles or cracks. This happens where oceanic crust is subducted by continental crust or, more dramatically, where two tectonic plates collide: the Rockies, Andes, Alps, Urals and Himalayas resulted from such impacts. These are all known as fold mountains because they were formed by the compression of the rocks, forcing the surface to bend and fold like a crumpled rug. The Himalayas are formed from the folded former sediments of the Tethys Sea which was trapped in the collision zone between the Indian and Eurasian plates.

The other main mountain-building process occurs when the crust fractures to create faults, allowing rock to be forced upward in large blocks; or when the pressure of magma within the crust forces the surface to bulge into a dome, or erupts to form a volcano. Large mountain ranges may reveal a combination of those features; the Alps, for example, have been compressed so violently that the folds are fragmented by numerous faults and intrusions of molten igneous rock.

Over millions of years, even the greatest mountain ranges can be reduced by the agents of erosion (especially rivers) to a low rugged landscape known as a peneplain.

Types of faults: Faults occur where the crust is being stretched or compressed so violently that the rock strata break in a horizontal or vertical movement. They are classified by the direction in which the blocks of rock have moved. A normal fault results when a vertical movement causes the surface to break apart; compression causes a reverse fault. Horizontal movement causes shearing, known as a strike-slip fault. When the rock breaks in two places, the central block may be pushed up in a horst fault, or sink (creating a rift valley) in a graben fault.

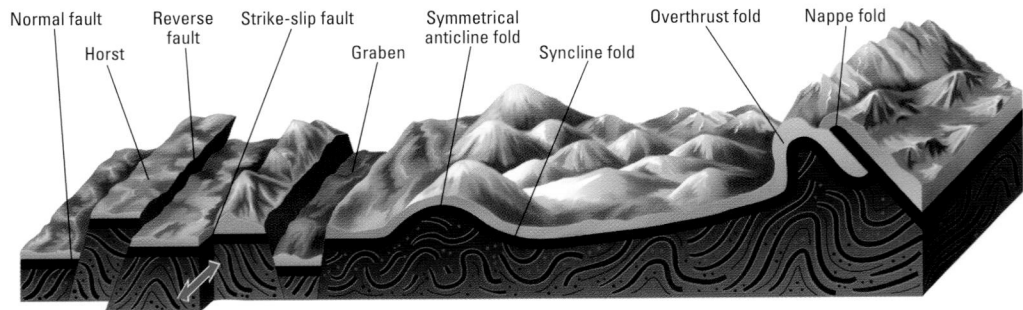

Types of fold: Folds occur when rock strata are squeezed and compressed. They are common, therefore, at destructive plate margins and where plates have collided, forcing the rocks to buckle into mountain ranges. Geographers give different names to the degrees of fold that result from continuing pressure on the rock. A simple fold may be symmetric, with even slopes on either side, but as the pressure builds up, one slope becomes steeper and the fold becomes asymmetric. Later, the ridge or "anticline" at the top of the fold may slide over the lower ground or "syncline" to form a recumbent fold. Eventually, the rock strata may break under the pressure to form an overthrust and finally a nappe fold.

Continental Glaciation

Annual Fluctuations for Selected Glaciers

Glacier name and location	Change in mass balance 1970–90
Wolverine, USA	+2,320
Storglaciaren, Sweden	−120
Djankuat, Russia	−1,890
Grasubreen, Norway	−2,530
Ürümqi, China	−3,828
Golubin, Kyrgyzstan	−7,105
Gries, Switzerland	−10,600
Careser, Italy	−11,610
Abramov, Tajikistan	−13,700
Sarennes, France	−15,020
Place, Canada	−15,175

The mass balance is defined as the difference between glacier accumulation and ablation (melting), and is expressed as water equivalent in millimeters. A minus indicates a reduction in the depth or length of a glacier. As can be seen from this geographically diverse selection, glaciers are retreating in many areas worldwide. The most dramatic and serious example of this phenomenon is the continuing distintegration of several large Antarctic ice shelves.

The extent to which glacial retreat is due to global warming, or to longer term climatic fluctuations, remains a matter for debate.

Many landforms in the northern hemisphere were shaped by ice sheets and meltwater during the Pleistocene Ice Age, which began about two million years ago. During the Ice Age, the ice sheets periodically advanced and retreated. The first map shows the ice cover at its greatest extent about 200,000 years BP (before the present), when it covered about 30% of the land surface, as compared with 10% today. About 18,000 years BP, the ice covered most of Canada and as far south as the Bristol Channel in England. Around the ice sheets, land areas experienced periglacial conditions.

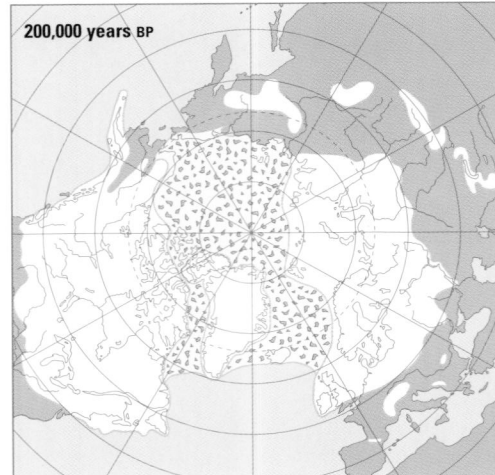

200,000 years BP

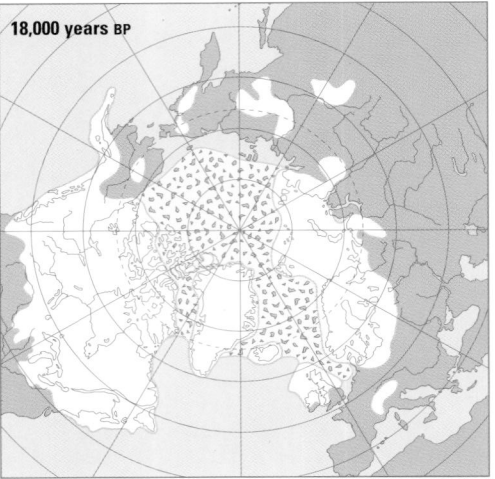

18,000 years BP

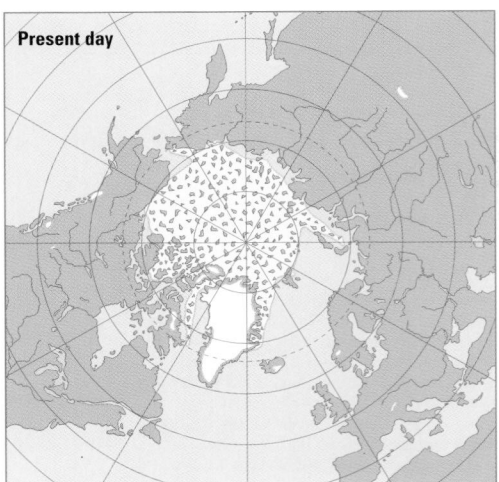

Present day

CARTOGRAPHY BY PHILIP'S. COPYRIGHT GEORGE PHILIP LTD

Natural Landforms

Natural landforms reflect the influence of plate tectonics through mountain-building and the generation of new rocks from the interior, together with the agents of erosion: running water, ice, winds and coastal waves. Over millions of years, mountains are gradually eroded, producing landforms that reflect the major forces that have been at work, as well as the underlying geology, the climatic conditions, which often vary over time, and the vegetation cover. The stylized diagram, below, shows some major natural landforms found in the midlatitudes.

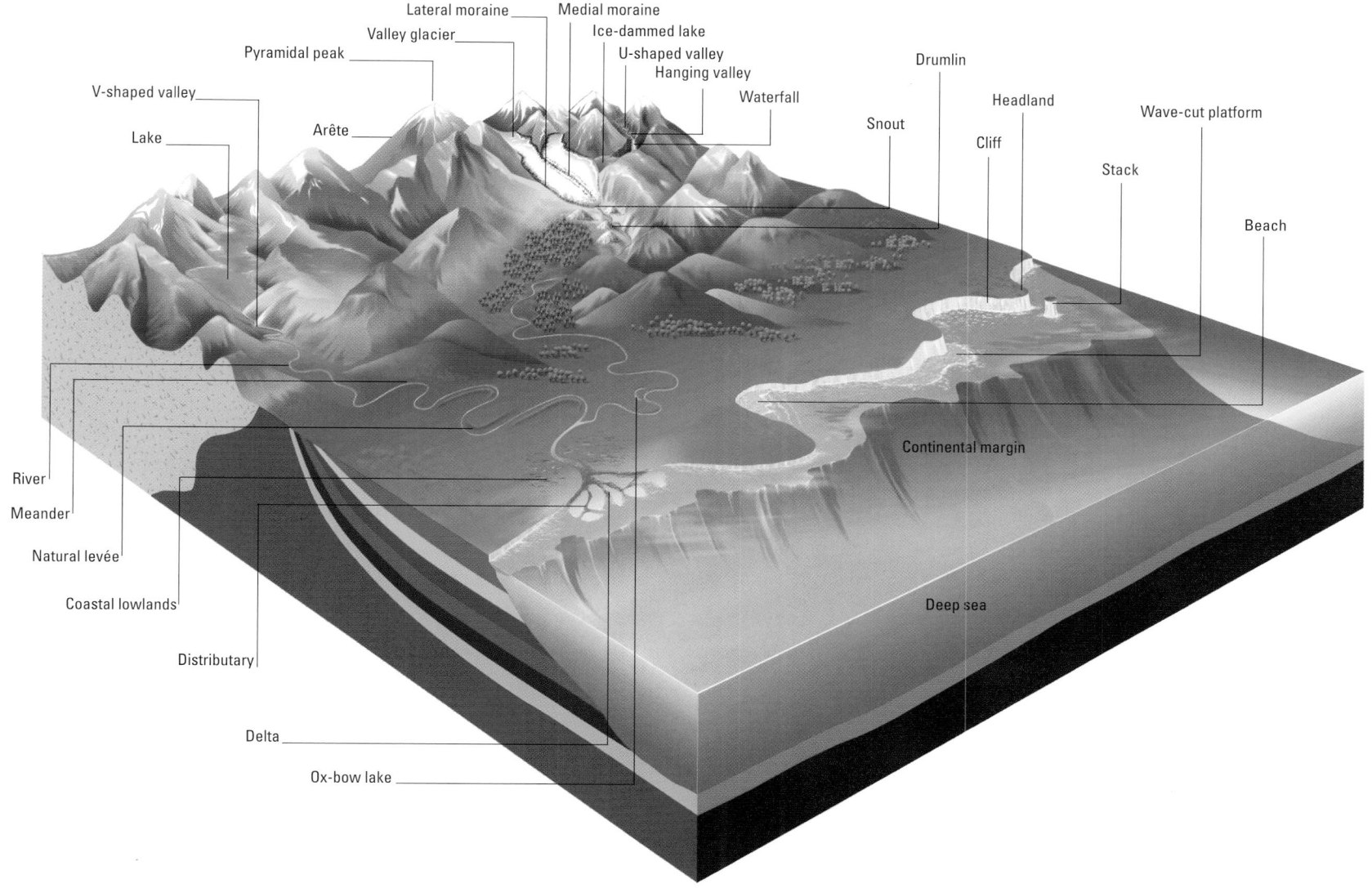

Lateral moraine — Medial moraine
Valley glacier — Ice-dammed lake
Pyramidal peak — U-shaped valley
Hanging valley
V-shaped valley — Waterfall — Drumlin
Headland — Wave-cut platform
Lake — Arête — Snout — Cliff — Stack
Beach
River
Meander
Natural levée — Continental margin
Coastal lowlands — Deep sea
Distributary
Delta
Ox-bow lake

Desert Landforms

Deserts are defined as places with an average annual precipitation of 10 inches per year, though places with a higher rainfall and a high evaporation rate may also qualify as deserts. The three types of desert landforms are known by their Arabic names, a reflection of the fact that the Sahara in North Africa is the world's largest desert. Sand desert, called erg, covers about one-fifth of the world's deserts. The rest is divided between hammada (areas of bare rock) and reg (broad plains covered by loose gravel or pebbles).

The shapes of dunes in sand deserts reflect the character of local winds. Where winds are constant in direction, the sand often piles up in crescent-shaped dunes, called barchans. Barchans are constantly on the move and their forward march, unless halted by vegetation, may overwhelm settlements at oases. Seif dunes, named after the Arabic word for sword, are long ridges of sand which lie parallel to the direction of the wind, but where winds are variable, the sand sheets are often featureless.

Wind-blown sand is an effective agent of erosion but because of the weight of sand grains, this type of erosion is confined to within 7 feet of the land surface, creating caves and mushroom-shaped rocks.

In assessing desert landforms, it is important to remember that other processes were at work in the past when the climate was very different from today. For example, cave paintings suggest that the Sahara had a much wetter climate after the end of the Ice Age and only began to dry up after about 5000 BC. However, human action, including overgrazing and the cutting down of trees for firewood, can turn a grassland region into desert – a process known as desertification.

Erg

Hammada

Reg

Surface Processes

Catastrophic changes to landforms are periodically caused by such phenomena as avalanches, landslides and volcanic eruptions, but most of the processes that shape the Earth's surface operate extremely slowly in human terms. One estimate, based on a study of landforms in the United States, suggests that, on average, just over 3 feet of land is removed from the entire surface of the country every 29,500 years. However, the terrain and the climate have a great effect on the erosion rate. For example, on cold plains, such as the Hudson Bay lowlands, the rate drops to around 3 feet for every 154,200 years, while in wet, tropical mountain areas, the rate may reach 3 feet for every 1,300 years.

Chemical weathering is at its greatest in warm, humid regions, while mechanical weathering, or the physical breakup of rocks, predominates in cold mountain or hot desert regions. The most familiar type of chemical weathering is caused by the reaction of rainwater containing dissolved carbon dioxide on limestone. This leads to the creation of labyrinthine cave networks dissolved by groundwater. Mechanical weathering includes frost action, while in hot deserts, rapid temperature changes cause the outer layers of rocks to expand and contract until they crack and peel away, a process called exfoliation.

The most important product of weathering is soil, which consists of rock fragments and humus, the decayed remains of plants and animals, together with living organisms, including vast numbers of micro-organisms. Soils vary in character according to the climate, ranging from the heavily leached, red laterite soils of wet tropical areas to the fertile, brown soils of dry grasslands. Soils are important because they support plants, which in turn anchor the soil and act as a protection against erosion. Soil erosion is greatest on sloping land because the steeper the slope, the greater the tendency for the soil to creep or flow downhill. The degree of movement of soil and rock downhill under the influence of gravity, called mass wasting, depends on a slope's stability. The stability may be disturbed by earthquakes or by heavy rain (water acts as a lubricant and increases the weight of the overlying material) which may trigger flows, slides or large falls of rock.

Running water is probably the world's leading agent of erosion and transportation. The energy of a river depends on several factors, including its velocity and volume, and its erosive power is at its peak when it is in full flood, sweeping soil, pebbles and even boulders along its course, cutting downward into the bedrock or widening its valley. Sea waves also exert tremendous erosive power during storms when they hurl pebbles and large rocks against the shore, undercutting cliffs and hollowing out caves. Headlands are often attacked on both sides, forming caves, then a natural arch and eventually an isolated stack.

Glacier ice forms in mountain hollows, called cirques, and spills out to form valley glaciers, which transport rocks shattered by frost action. As a glacier moves, rocks embedded in the base and sides scrape away bedrock, eroding steep-sided, flat-bottomed, U-shaped valleys. Evidence of past glaciation in mountain regions includes cirques, knife-edged ridges, or arêtes, and pyramidal peaks, or horns.

Geologists once considered that landforms evolved from "young," newly uplifted mountainous areas, through a "mature" hilly stage, to an "old age" stage when the land was reduced to an almost flat plain, or peneplain. This theory, called the "cycle of erosion," fell into disuse when it became evident that so many factors, including the effects of plate tectonics and climatic change, constantly interrupt the cycle, which takes no account of the highly complex interactions that shape the surface of our planet.

The Atmosphere

The atmosphere is a meteor shield, a radiation deflector, a thermal blanket and a source of chemical energy for the Earth's diverse life forms. Five-sixths of its mass is in the lowest layer, the troposphere which ranges in thickness from 11 to 6 miles between the Equator and the poles. Powered by the Sun, the air is always on the move, flowing generally from high- to low-pressure areas. The troposphere is the layer where virtually all weather phenomena, including clouds, precipitation and winds, occur. Above the troposphere is the stratosphere, which contains the important ozone layer and extends to about 30 miles above the Earth's surface. Beyond 60 miles, atmospheric density is lower than most laboratory vacuums.

Structure of the Atmosphere

HUBBLE SPACE TELESCOPE
370 miles

Pressure
10⁻³⁵ mb

350 mi

EXOSPHERE

10^{-22} mb

MIR SPACE STATION
200 miles — 200 mi

10^{-16} mb

SPACE SHUTTLE
170 miles

150 mi

THERMOSPHERE

10^{-10} mb

VOSTOCK MANNED CAPSULE
(first manned space flight, 1961)
110 miles — 100 mi

AURORAE

METEOR TRAILS 60 mi

MESOSPHERE

10^{-3} mb

OZONE LAYER 30 mi

STRATOSPHERE

CONCORDE
MOUNT EVEREST 6 mi
29,029 ft

TROPOSPHERE

10^3 mb

Circulation of the Air

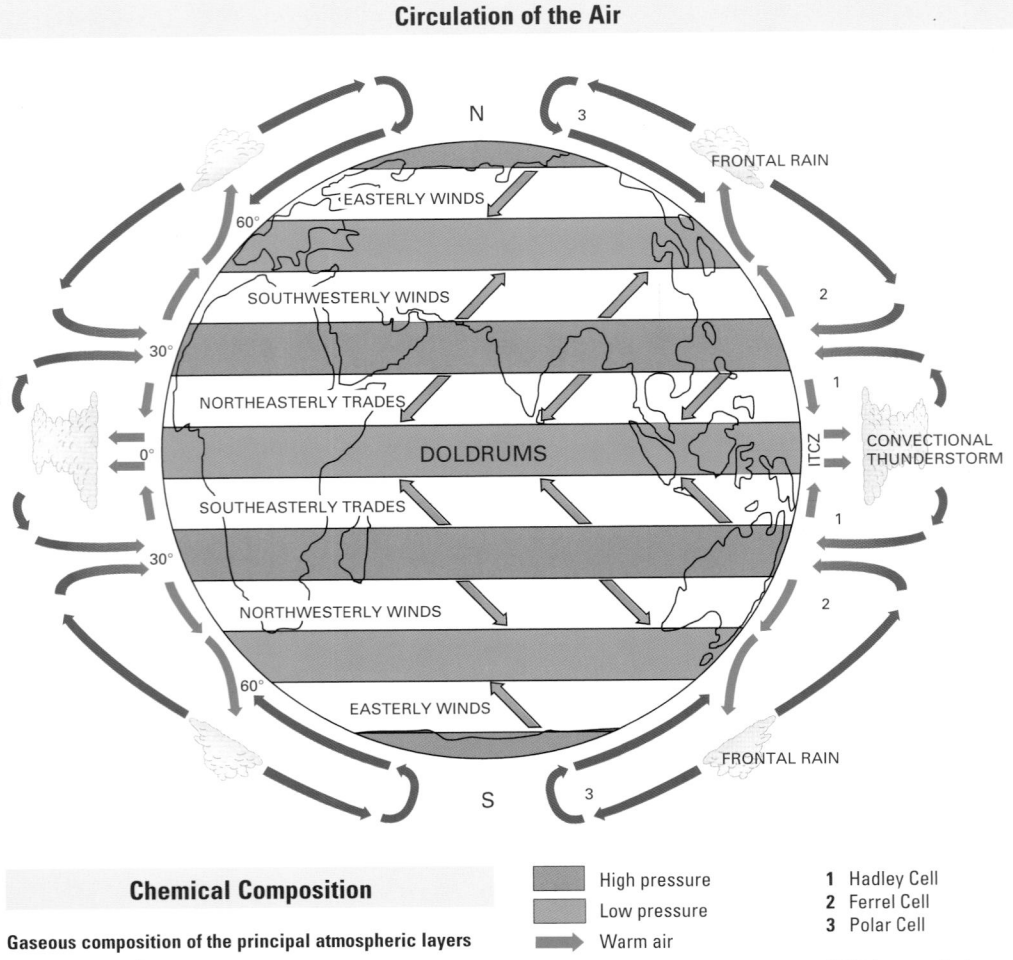

N
3
FRONTAL RAIN
60° EASTERLY WINDS
SOUTHWESTERLY WINDS
2
30°
NORTHEASTERLY TRADES
0° DOLDRUMS
ITCZ CONVECTIONAL THUNDERSTORM
1
SOUTHEASTERLY TRADES
30°
2
NORTHWESTERLY WINDS
60° EASTERLY WINDS
FRONTAL RAIN
S
3

Chemical Composition

Gaseous composition of the principal atmospheric layers

60–100% hydrogen | 25–50% helium
Exosphere
Helium vanishes with increasing altitude. Above 1,500 miles the exosphere is almost entirely composed of hydrogen.

70% nitrogen | 15% oxygen | 15% helium
Mesosphere
The high energy of mesospheric gas gives it a notional temperature of more than 3,600°F, although its density is negligible.

80% nitrogen | 18% oxygen | 1% argon | 1% ozone
Stratosphere
Stratospheric air contains enough ozone to make it poisonous, although it is in any case too rarified to breathe.

78% nitrogen | 21% oxygen | 1% argon
Troposphere
The narrowest of all the layers, this thin region contains about 85% of the atmosphere's total mass and almost all of its water vapor. It is also the realm of the Earth's weather.

Legend:
High pressure
Low pressure
Warm air
Cold air
Surface winds
Clouds

1 Hadley Cell
2 Ferrel Cell
3 Polar Cell

ITCZ Intertropical convergence zone

Frontal Systems

Depressions, or cyclones, form along the polar front where dense polar easterlies meet warm subtropical westerlies. Depressions occur when warm air flows into waves in the polar front, while cold air flows in behind it, creating rotating air systems that bring changeable weather. Along the warm front (the boundary on the ground between the warm and cold air), the warm air flows upward over the cold air, producing a sequence of clouds which help forecasters to predict a depression's advance. Along the cold front, the advancing cold air forces warm air to rise steeply. Towering cumulonimbus clouds form in the rising air. When the cold front overtakes the warm front, the warm air is pushed above ground level to form an occluded front. Cloud and rain persist along occlusions until temperatures equalize, the air mixes, and the depression dies out.

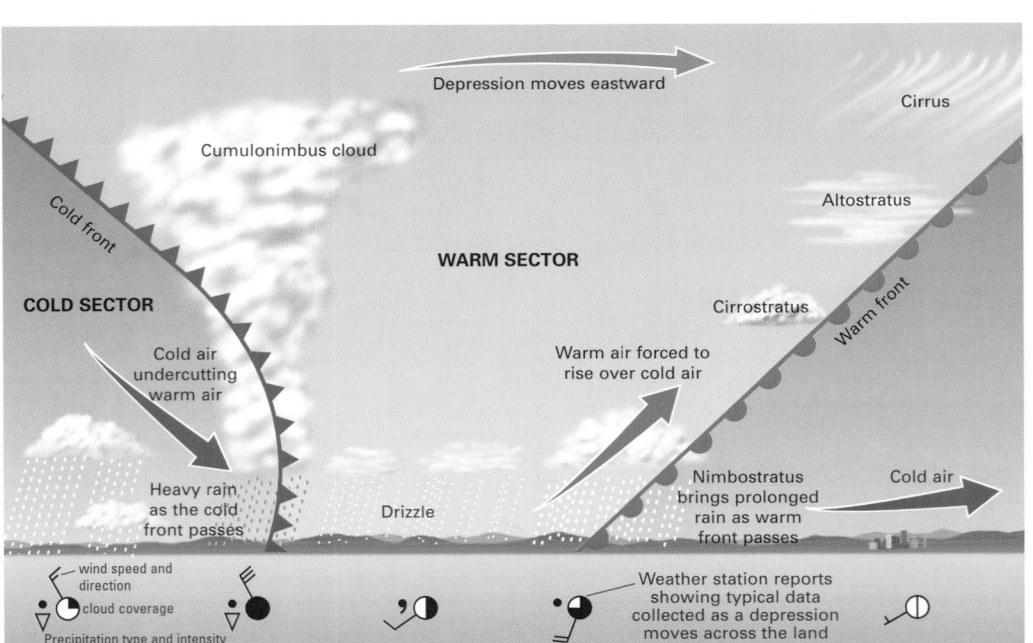

Depression moves eastward
Cirrus
Cumulonimbus cloud
Altostratus
Cold front
WARM SECTOR
Warm front
COLD SECTOR
Cirrostratus
Cold air undercutting warm air
Warm air forced to rise over cold air
Heavy rain as the cold front passes
Drizzle
Nimbostratus brings prolonged rain as warm front passes
Cold air

wind speed and direction
cloud coverage
Precipitation type and intensity
Weather station reports showing typical data collected as a depression moves across the land

CARTOGRAPHY BY PHILIP'S. COPYRIGHT GEORGE PHILIP LTD

Air Masses

Air masses are bodies of air whose characteristics are broadly the same over a large area. Around the Equator, where the Sun's heat creates relatively high surface temperatures, warm air rises to create a zone of low pressure called the doldrums. The air cools and finally spreads out toward the poles. Around latitudes 30° north and south, the air sinks back to the surface, becoming warmer as it descends and creating zones of high pressure called the horse latitudes.

The high- and low-pressure zones are both areas of comparative calm, but between them lie the prevailing trade wind belts. Air also flows north and south from the high-pressure horse latitudes and these air flows meet up with cold, dense air flowing from the poles along the polar front. This basic circulatory system is complicated by the Coriolis effect, brought about by the spinning Earth. Because of the Coriolis effect, the prevailing winds do not flow directly north–south but are deflected to the right in the northern hemisphere and to the left in the southern. Along the polar front, depressions form where the polar easterlies meet the westerlies.

The first classification of clouds was developed by a London chemist, Luke Howard, in 1803, and it was later modified by the World Meteorological Organization. The main types are divided into three groups according to their altitude, and into subgroups according to their shape, which vary from hairlike filaments (cirrus), heaps or piles (cumulus), and layers (stratus). Each cloud carries some kind of message, though not always a clear one, to weather forecasters.

Classification of Clouds

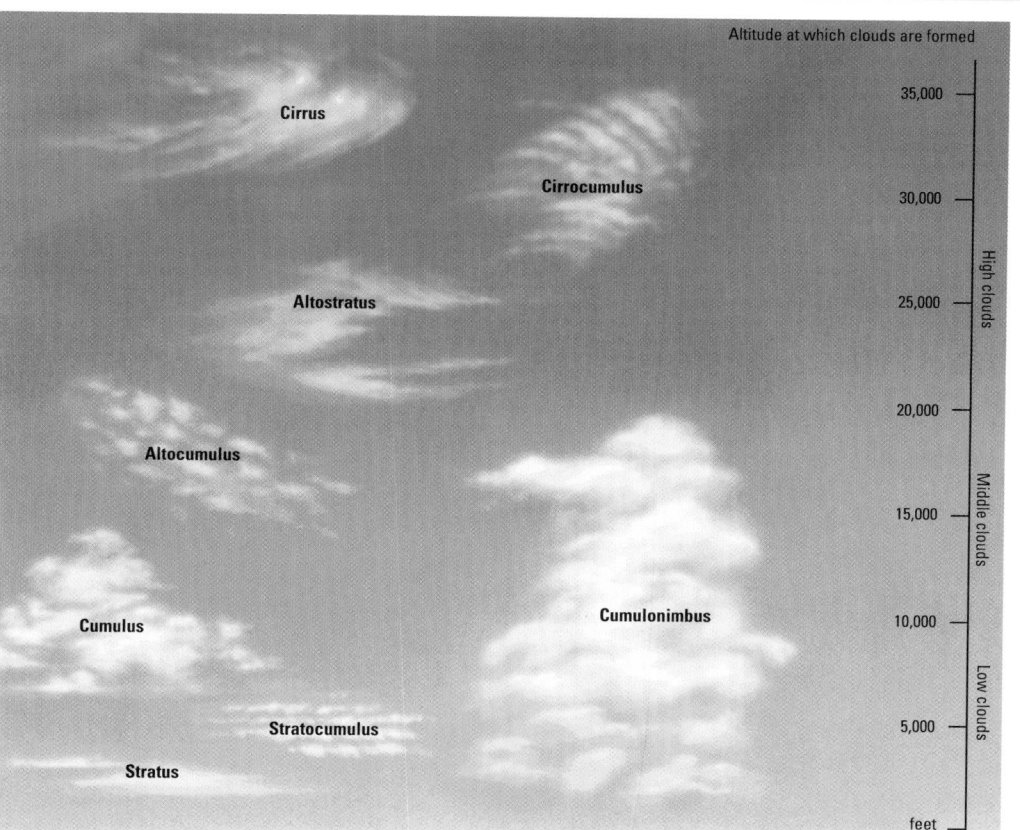

Clouds form when damp, usually rising, air is cooled. Thus they form when a wind rises to cross hills or mountains; when a mass of air rises over, or is pushed up by, another mass of denser air; or when local heating of the ground causes convection currents.

The types of clouds are classified according to altitude as high, middle or low. The high ones, composed of ice crystals, are cirrus, cirrostratus and cirrocumulus. The middle clouds are altostratus, a gray or bluish striated, fibrous or uniform sheet producing light drizzle, and altocumulus, a thicker and fluffier version of cirrocumulus.

Low clouds include nimbostratus, a dark grey layer that brings rain or snow; cumulus, a detached heap, dark at the base; stratus, which forms dull, overcast skies at low levels; and stratocumulus, which consists of fluffy grayish-white layers.

Cumulonimbus, associated with storms and rains, heavy and dense with a flat base and a high, fluffy outline, can be tall enough to occupy middle as well as low altitudes.

Pressure and Surface Winds

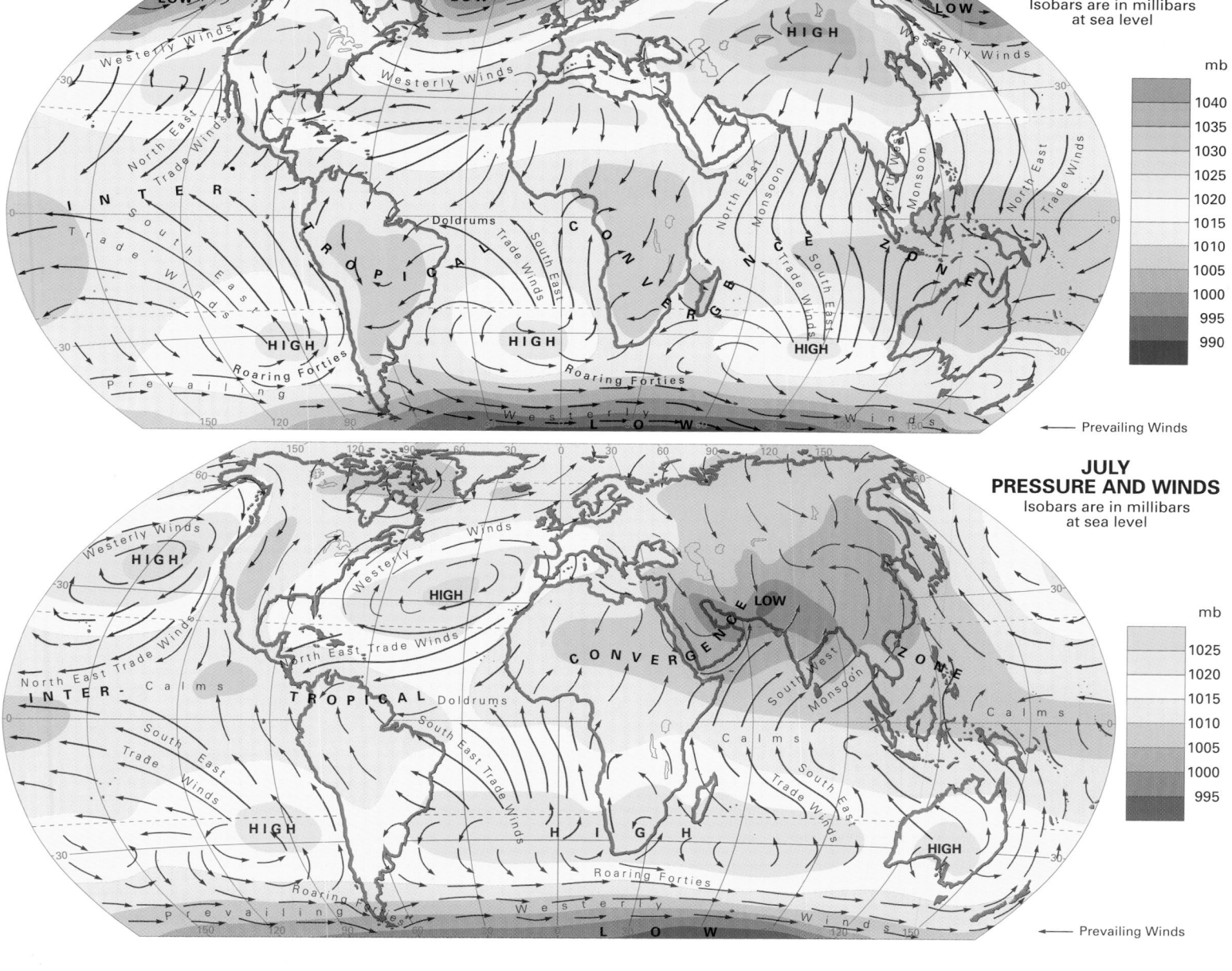

JANUARY PRESSURE AND WINDS
Isobars are in millibars at sea level

| mb |
| 1040 |
| 1035 |
| 1030 |
| 1025 |
| 1020 |
| 1015 |
| 1010 |
| 1005 |
| 1000 |
| 995 |
| 990 |

← Prevailing Winds

JULY PRESSURE AND WINDS
Isobars are in millibars at sea level

| mb |
| 1025 |
| 1020 |
| 1015 |
| 1010 |
| 1005 |
| 1000 |
| 995 |

← Prevailing Winds

Climate Records

Pressure and winds

Highest barometric pressure: Agata, Siberia, 1,083.8 mb at altitude 862 ft [262 m], December 31, 1968.

Lowest barometric pressure: Typhoon Tip, 300 miles [480 km] west of Guam, Pacific Ocean, 870 mb, October 12, 1979.

Highest recorded wind speed: Mt Washington, New Hampshire, USA, 231 mph [371 km/h], April 12, 1934. This is three times as strong as hurricane force on the Beaufort Scale.

Windiest place: Commonwealth Bay, George V Coast, Antarctica, where gales frequently reach over 200 mph [320 km/h].

Worst recorded storm: Bangladesh (then East Pakistan) cyclone*, November 13, 1970 – over 300,000 dead or missing. The 1991 cyclone, Bangladesh's and the world's second worst in terms of loss of life, killed an estimated 138,000 people.

Worst recorded tornado: Missouri/Illinois/Indiana, USA, March 18, 1925 – 792 deaths. The tornado was only 900 ft [275 m] wide.

Tropical cyclones are known as hurricanes in Central and North America, as typhoons in the Far East, and as willy-willies in northern Australia.

Climate

For more information:

9 Ocean currents
14 Circulation of the air
15 Classification of clouds
Pressure and winds
18 Hydrological cycle
19 Natural vegetation
21 Greenhouse effect
22 Global warming

Weather is the day-to-day or hour-to-hour condition of the air, while climate is weather in the long term, the seasonal pattern of hot and cold, wet and dry, averaged over a long period. Most classifications of climate are based on a system developed by a Russian meteorologist, Vladimir Köppen, in the early 19th century. Using a code based on letters and a classification centered on two main features, temperature and precipitation, he identified five main climatic types: tropical (A), dry (B), warm temperate (C), cold temperate (D), and polar (E). A highland mountain climate (H), was added later to account for the variety of altitudinal climatic zones on high mountains. Each of these main regions was then further subdivided.

Latitude is a major factor in determining climate, but other factors add to the complexity. They include the differential heating of land and sea, the distance from the sea, the effect of mountains on winds, and the influence of ocean currents. For example, New York City, Naples and the Gobi Desert share almost the same latitude, but their climates are very different.

Climates are not indefinitely stable. During the last Ice Age, the Earth underwent alternating cold periods, called glacials, separated by warm interglacials. The Milankovich theory suggests such cycles may be caused by variations in the Earth's path around the Sun, changing from almost circular to elliptical every 95,000 years, and variations in the Earth's tilt from 21.5° to 24.5° every 42,000 years. Another factor is that the Earth is now closest to the Sun in the middle of winter in the northern hemisphere and furthest away in summer. But 12,000 years ago, at the height of the last glacial period, the northern winter fell with the Sun at its most distant.

Studies of these cycles suggest that we are now in an interglacial with a new glacial period on the way. However, many scientists believe that global warming, largely a result of burning fossil fuels and deforestation, may be occurring much faster than the great, slow cycles of the Solar System.

Tropical rainy climates
All mean monthly temperatures above 64°F.
- Af Rain forest climate
- Am Monsoon climate
- Aw Savanna climate

Dry climates
Low rainfall combined with a wide range of temperatures
- BS Steppe climate
- BW Desert climate

Warm temperate rainy climates
The mean temperature is below 64°F but above 26°F and that of the warmest month is over 50°F.
- Cw Dry winter climate
- Cs Dry summer climate
- Cf Climate with no dry season

Cold temperate rainy climates
The mean temperature of the coldest month is below 37°F but that of the warmest month is still over 50°F.
- Dw Dry winter climate
- Df Climate with no dry season

Polar climates
The mean temperature of the warmest month is below 50°F, giving permanently frozen subsoil.
- ET Tundra climate

The mean temperature of the warmest month is below 32°F, giving permanent ice and snow.
- EF Polar climate

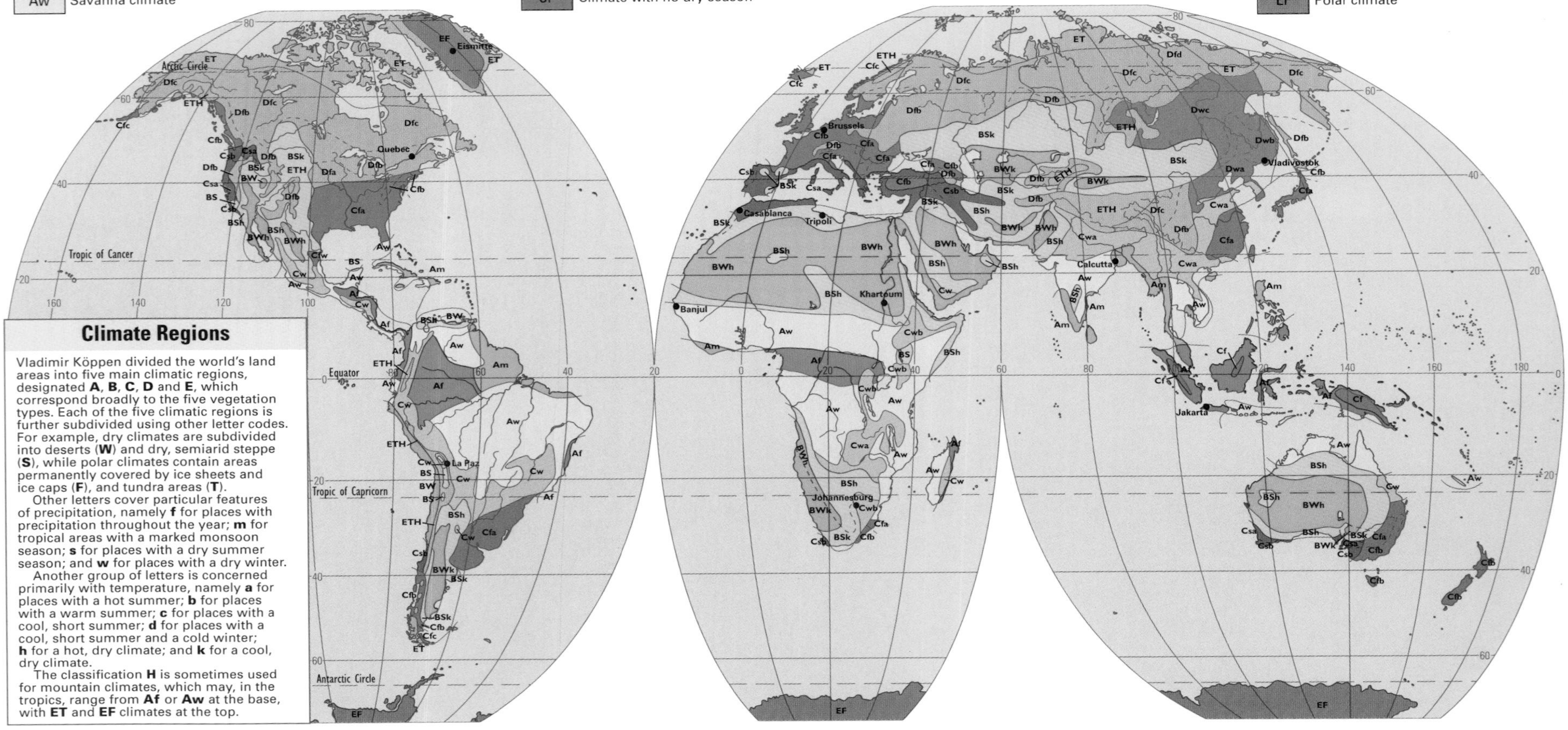

Climate Regions

Vladimir Köppen divided the world's land areas into five main climatic regions, designated **A**, **B**, **C**, **D** and **E**, which correspond broadly to the five vegetation types. Each of the five climatic regions is further subdivided using other letter codes. For example, dry climates are subdivided into deserts (**W**) and dry, semiarid steppe (**S**), while polar climates contain areas permanently covered by ice sheets and ice caps (**F**), and tundra areas (**T**).

Other letters cover particular features of precipitation, namely **f** for places with precipitation throughout the year; **m** for tropical areas with a marked monsoon season; **s** for places with a dry summer season; and **w** for places with a dry winter. Another group of letters is concerned primarily with temperature, namely **a** for places with a hot summer; **b** for places with a warm summer; **c** for places with a cool, short summer; **d** for places with a cool, short summer and a cold winter; **h** for a hot, dry climate; and **k** for a cool, dry climate.

The classification **H** is sometimes used for mountain climates, which may, in the tropics, range from **Af** or **Aw** at the base, with **ET** and **EF** climates at the top.

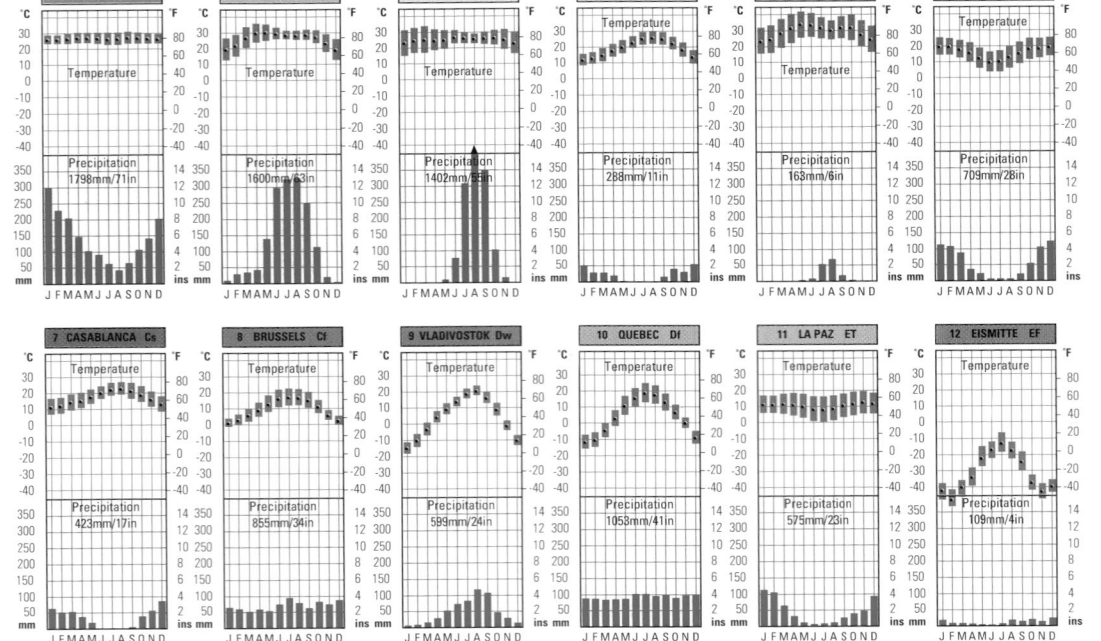

Climate and Weather Terms

Anticyclone: area of high pressure with light winds and generally quiet weather.
Absolute humidity: amount of water vapor contained in a given volume of air.
Cloud cover: amount of cloud in the sky; measured in oktas (from 1 – 8), with 0 clear, and 8 total cover.
Condensation: the conversion of water vapor, or moisture in the air, into liquid.
Cyclone: violent storm resulting from counterclockwise rotation of winds in the northern hemisphere and clockwise in the southern: called hurricane in N. America, typhoon in the Far East.
Depression: area of low pressure. The pressure gradient is toward the center.
Dew: water droplets condensed out of the air after the ground has cooled at night.
Dew point: temperature at which air becomes saturated (reaches a relative humidity of 100%) at a constant pressure.
Drizzle: precipitation where drops are less than 0.02 in [0.5 mm] in diameter.
Evaporation: conversion of water from liquid into vapor, or moisture in the air.
Front: the dividing line between two air masses.
Frost: dew that has frozen when the air temperature falls below freezing point.
Hail: frozen rain; small balls of ice, often falling during thunderstorms.
Hoar frost: formed on objects when the dew point is below freezing point.
Humidity: amount of moisture in the air.
Isobar: cartographic line connecting places of equal atmospheric pressure.
Isotherm: cartographic line connecting places of equal temperature.
Lightning: massive electrical discharge released in thunderstorm from cloud to cloud or cloud to ground, the result of the tip becoming positively charged and the bottom negatively charged.
Precipitation: measurable rain, snow, sleet or hail.
Prevailing wind: most common direction of wind at a given location.
Rain: precipitation of liquid particles with diameter larger than 0.02 in [0.5 mm].
Relative humidity: amount of water vapor contained in a given volume of air at a given temperature.
Snow: formed when water vapor condenses below freezing point.
Thunder: sound produced by the rapid expansion of air heated by lightning.
Tornado: severe funnel-shaped storm that twists as hot air spins vertically (waterspout at sea).
Whirlwind: rapidly rotating column of air, only a few feet across, made visible by dust.

CARTOGRAPHY BY PHILIP'S. COPYRIGHT GEORGE PHILIP LTD

Climate Change

Human factors, such as the emission of greenhouse gases through the burning of fossil fuels and deforestation, have contributed to global warming. The histogram, below, shows in blue the average global temperatures from 1860 (when sufficient observations became available for global averages to be calculated) to 1996. The red line is a 10-year running average. Overall, there is an upward trend, particularly so since the 1970s, when global warming became a matter of concern in scientific circles. The large year-to-year changes indicate the Earth's natural climatic variability and the influence of such factors as major volcanic eruptions.

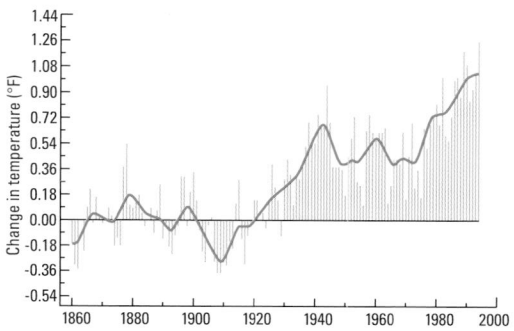

Data from the Hadley Centre for Climate Research and Prediction

Beaufort Wind Scale

Named after the 19th-century British naval officer who devised it, Admiral Beaufort, the Beaufort Scale assesses wind speed according to its effects. It was originally designed as an aid for sailors, but has since been adapted for use on the land. It is used internationally.

Scale	Wind speed km/h	mph	Effect
0	0–1	0–1	**Calm** Smoke rises vertically
1	1–5	1–3	**Light air** Wind direction shown only by smoke drift
2	6–11	4–7	**Light breeze** Wind felt on face; leaves rustle; vanes moved by wind
3	12–19	8–12	**Gentle breeze** Leaves and small twigs in constant motion; wind extends small flag
4	20–28	13–18	**Moderate** Raises dust and loose paper; small branches move
5	29–38	19–24	**Fresh** Small trees in leaf sway; crested wavelets on inland waters
6	39–49	25–31	**Strong** Large branches move; difficult to use umbrellas; overhead wires whistle
7	50–61	32–38	**Near gale** Whole trees in motion; difficult to walk against wind
8	62–74	39–46	**Gale** Twigs break from trees; walking very difficult
9	75–88	47–54	**Strong gale** Slight structural damage
10	89–102	55–63	**Storm** Trees uprooted; serious structural damage
11	103–117	64–72	**Violent storm** Widespread damage
12	118+	73+	**Hurricane**

The Monsoon

Monsoon is the term given to the seasonal reversal of wind direction, most noticeably in Southeast Asia. It results from a combination of factors: the extreme heating and cooling of large land masses in relation to the less marked changes in temperature of the adjacent seas; the northward movement of the Intertropical Convergence Zone (ITCZ); and the effect of the Himalayas on the circulation of the air.

In early March, which normally marks the end of the subcontinent's cool season and the start of the hot season, winds blow outward from the mainland. But as the overhead Sun and the ITCZ move northward, the land is intensely heated, and a low-pressure system develops. The southeast trade winds, which are drawn across the Equator, change direction and are sucked into the interior to become southwesterly winds, bringing heavy rain. By November, the overhead Sun and the ITCZ have again moved southward and the wind directions are again reversed. Cool winds blow from the Asian interior to the sea, losing any moisture on the Himalayas before descending to the coast.

Temperature

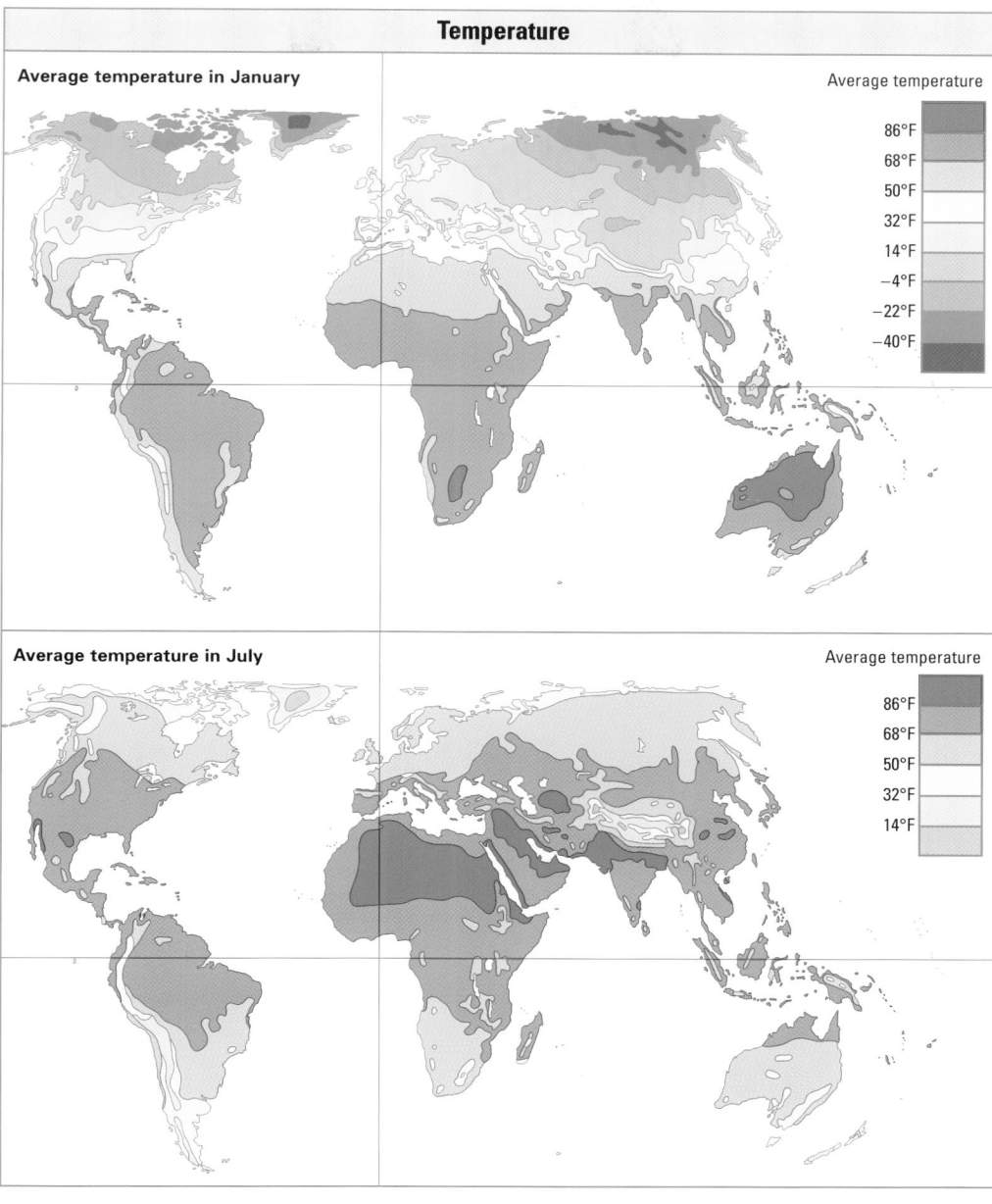

Average temperature in January

Average temperature

86°F
68°F
50°F
32°F
14°F
–4°F
–22°F
–40°F

Average temperature in July

Average temperature

86°F
68°F
50°F
32°F
14°F

Precipitation

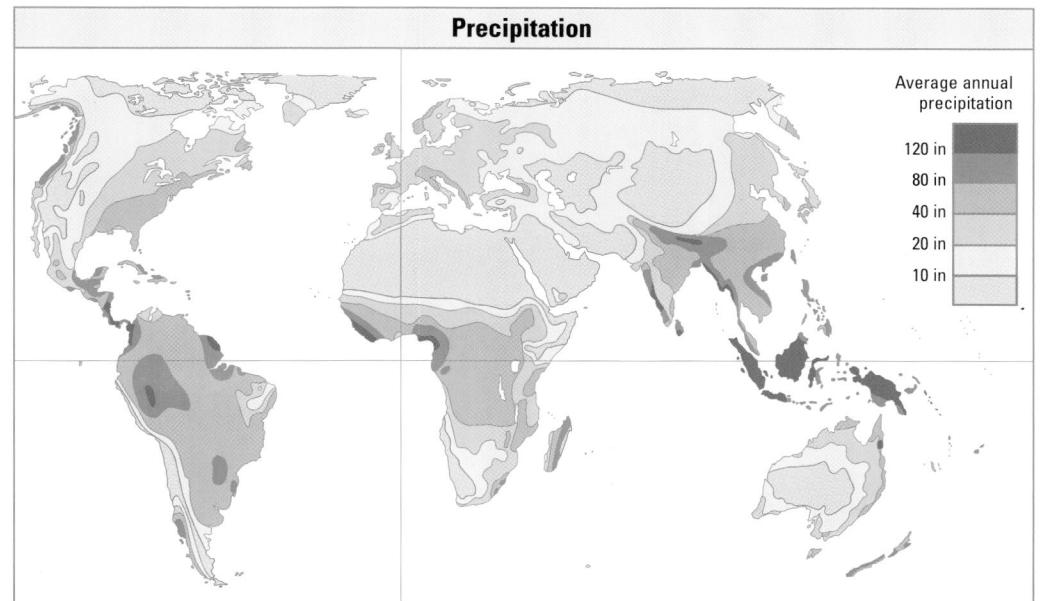

Average annual precipitation

120 in
80 in
40 in
20 in
10 in

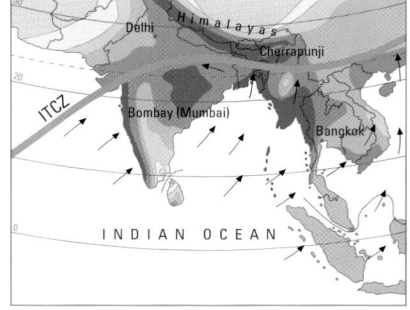

March – Start of the hot, dry season. The ITCZ is over the southern Indian Ocean.

July – The rainy season. The ITCZ has migrated northward; winds blow onshore.

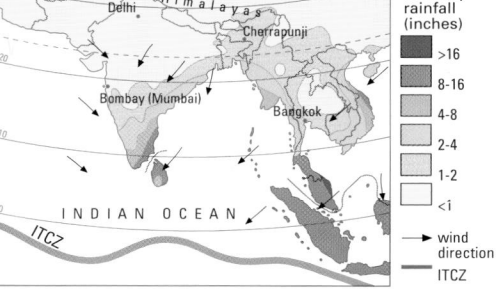

November – The ITCZ has returned south. The offshore winds are cool and dry.

Monthly rainfall (inches)

>16
8-16
4-8
2-4
1-2
<1

→ wind direction
ITCZ

Climate Records

Temperature

Highest recorded temperature: Al Aziziyah, Libya, 136.4°F [58°C], September 13, 1922.

Highest mean annual temperature: Dallol, Ethiopia, 94°F [34.4°C], 1960–66.

Longest heatwave: Marble Bar, W. Australia, 162 days over 100°F [38°C], October 23, 1923, to April 7, 1924.

Lowest recorded temperature (outside poles): Verkhoyansk, Siberia, –90°F [–68°C], February 6, 1933. Verkhoyansk also registered the greatest annual range of temperature: –94°F to 98°F [–70°C to 37°C].

Lowest mean annual temperature: Polus Nedostupnosti, Pole of Cold, Antarctica, –72°F [–57.8°C].

Precipitation

Driest place: Calama, N. Chile: no recorded rainfall in 400 years to 1971.

Wettest place (average): Tututendo, Colombia: mean annual rainfall 463.4 in [11,770 mm].

Wettest place (12 months): Cherrapunji, Meghalaya, N.E. India, 1,040 in [26,470 mm], August 1860 to August 1861. Cherrapunji also holds the record for rainfall in one month: 115 in [2,930 mm], July 1861. (See maps below.)

Wettest place (24 hours): Cilaos, Réunion, Indian Ocean, 73.6 in [1,870 mm], March 15–16, 1952.

Heaviest hailstones: Gopalganj, Bangladesh, up to 2.25 lb [1.02 kg], April 14, 1986 (killed 92 people).

Heaviest snowfall (continuous): Bessans, Savoie, France, 68 in [1,730 mm] in 19 hours, April 5–6, 1969.

Heaviest snowfall (season/year): Paradise Ranger Station, Mt Rainier, Washington, USA, 1,224.5 in [31,102 mm], February 19, 1971, to February 18, 1972.

CARTOGRAPHY BY PHILIP'S. COPYRIGHT GEORGE PHILIP LTD

17

Water and Vegetation

For more information:
12 Rivers and glaciers
14 Types of precipitation
20 Biodiversity

Without the hydrological cycle, whereby water is constantly recycled between the oceans, the atmosphere and the land, the continents would be barren. Precipitation enables plants to grow and soils to form, creating the world's natural vegetation regions and the ecosystems that support animal life. Running water also plays a

major role in shaping landforms. Yet in many parts of the world, people do not have safe water to drink and suffer from diseases caused by water-borne organisms or pollution. In addition, the limited water supplies have to be shared with agriculture and industry.

In 1996, UN experts argued that the

demand for water is increasing at about twice the rate of population growth. They predict that, by 2025, two-thirds of the world's population will face water shortages. This could lead to conflict and even boundary wars, especially because 300 major rivers cross national frontiers and access to their water is likely to be disputed.

The Hydrological Cycle

The world's water balance is regulated by the constant recycling of water between the oceans, atmosphere and land. The movement of water between these three reservoirs is known as the hydrological cycle. The oceans play a vital role in the hydrological cycle: 74% of the total precipitation falls over the oceans and 84% of the total evaporation comes from the oceans. Water vapor in the atmosphere circulates around the planet, transporting energy as well as the water itself. When the vapor cools, it falls as rain or snow. The whole cycle is driven by the Sun.

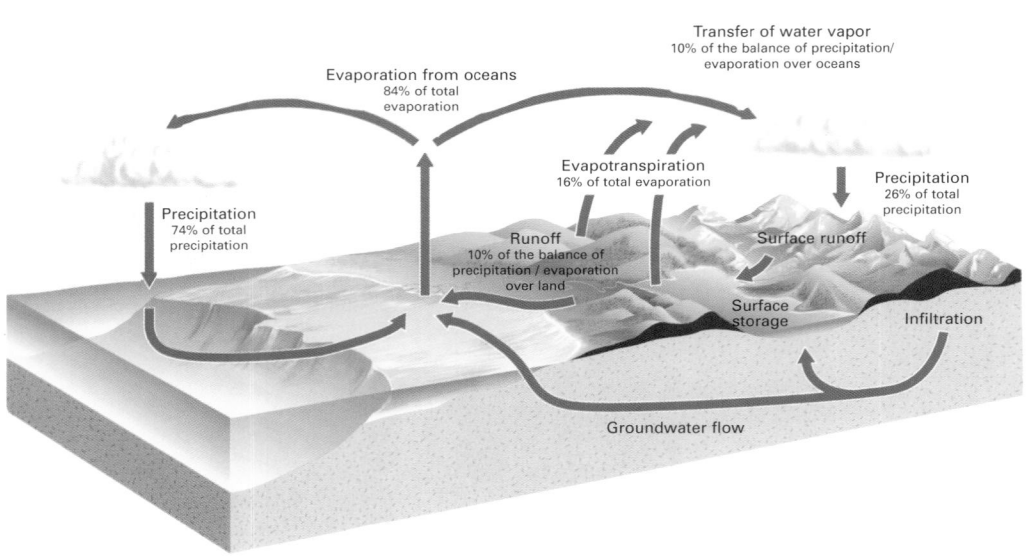

Water Distribution

The distribution of planetary water, by percentage. Oceans and ice caps together account for more than 99% of the total; the breakdown of the remainder is estimated.

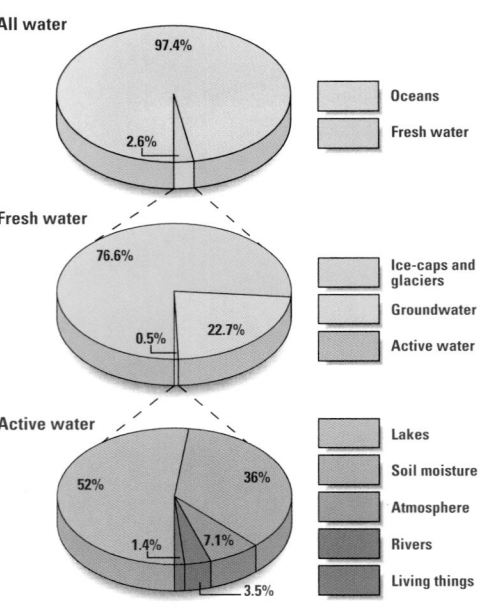

Almost all the world's water is 3 billion years old, and all of it cycles endlessly through the hydrosphere, though at different rates. Water vapor circulates over days, even hours; deep ocean water circulates over millennia; and ice-cap water remains solid for millions of years.

Water Utilization

The percentage breakdown of water usage by sector, selected countries (1996)

Domestic
Industrial
Agriculture

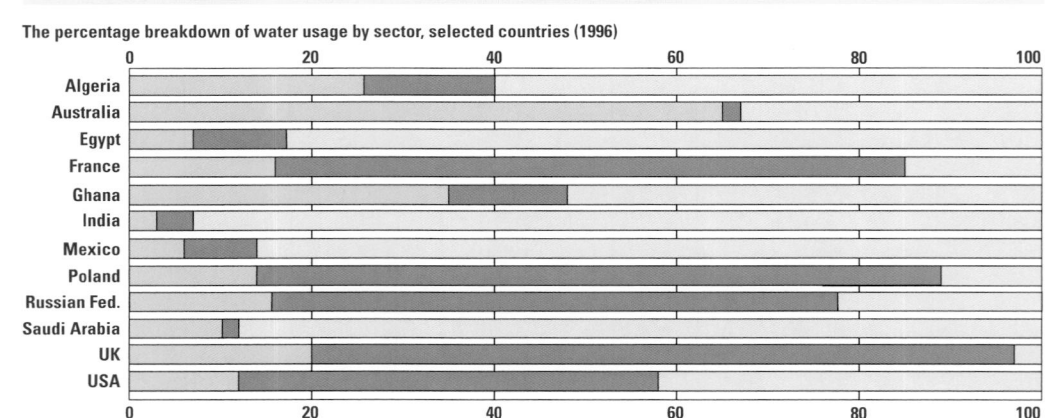

Water Runoff

Annual freshwater runoff by continent in cubic miles

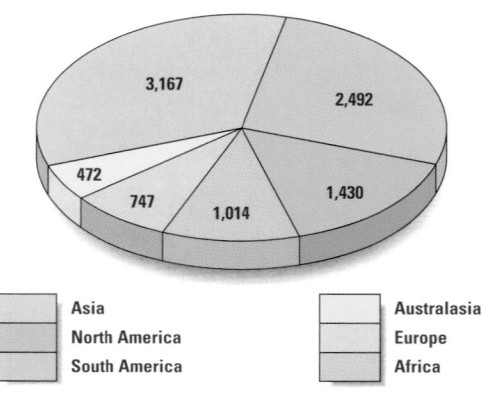

Asia — Australasia
North America — Europe
South America — Africa

Water Supply

Percentage of total population with access to safe drinking water (1995)

Over 90% with safe water
75 – 90% with safe water
60 – 75% with safe water
45 – 60% with safe water
30 – 45% with safe water
Under 30% with safe water

△ Under 80 liters average per capita daily water consumption
▲ Over 320 liters average per capita daily water consumption

Least well-provided countries

Country	%	Country	%
Paraguay	8%	Central Afr. Rep.	18%
Afghanistan	10%	Bhutan	21%
Cambodia	13%	Congo (D. Rep.)	25%

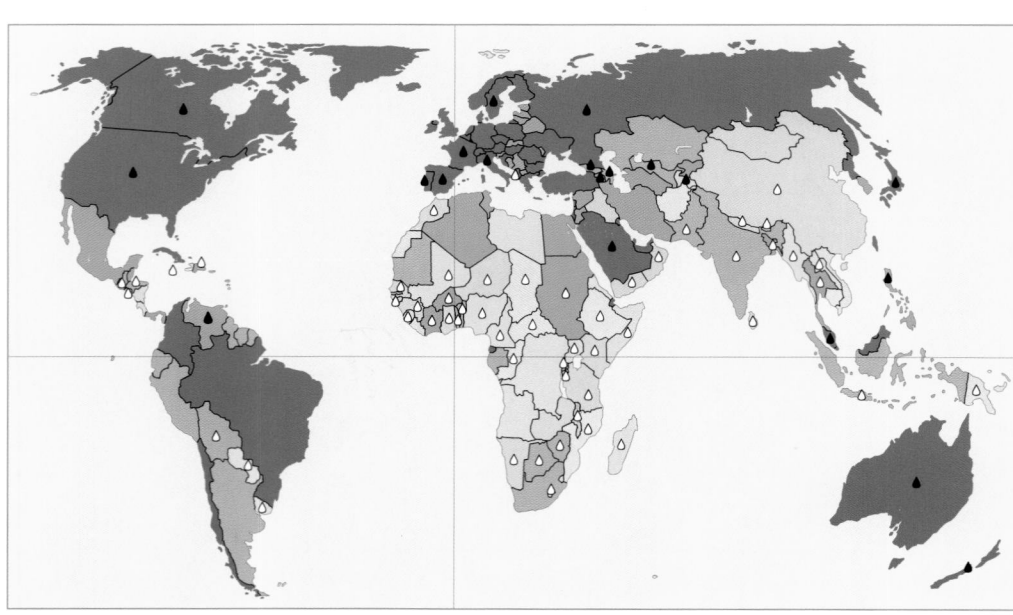
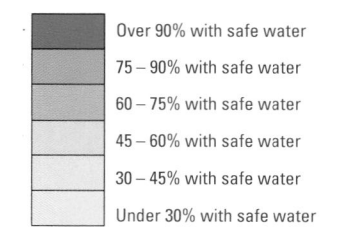

18

CARTOGRAPHY BY PHILIP'S. COPYRIGHT GEORGE PHILIP LTD

Watersheds

The world's major rivers; the rank of the world's 20 longest is shown in square brackets, led by the Nile and the Amazon.

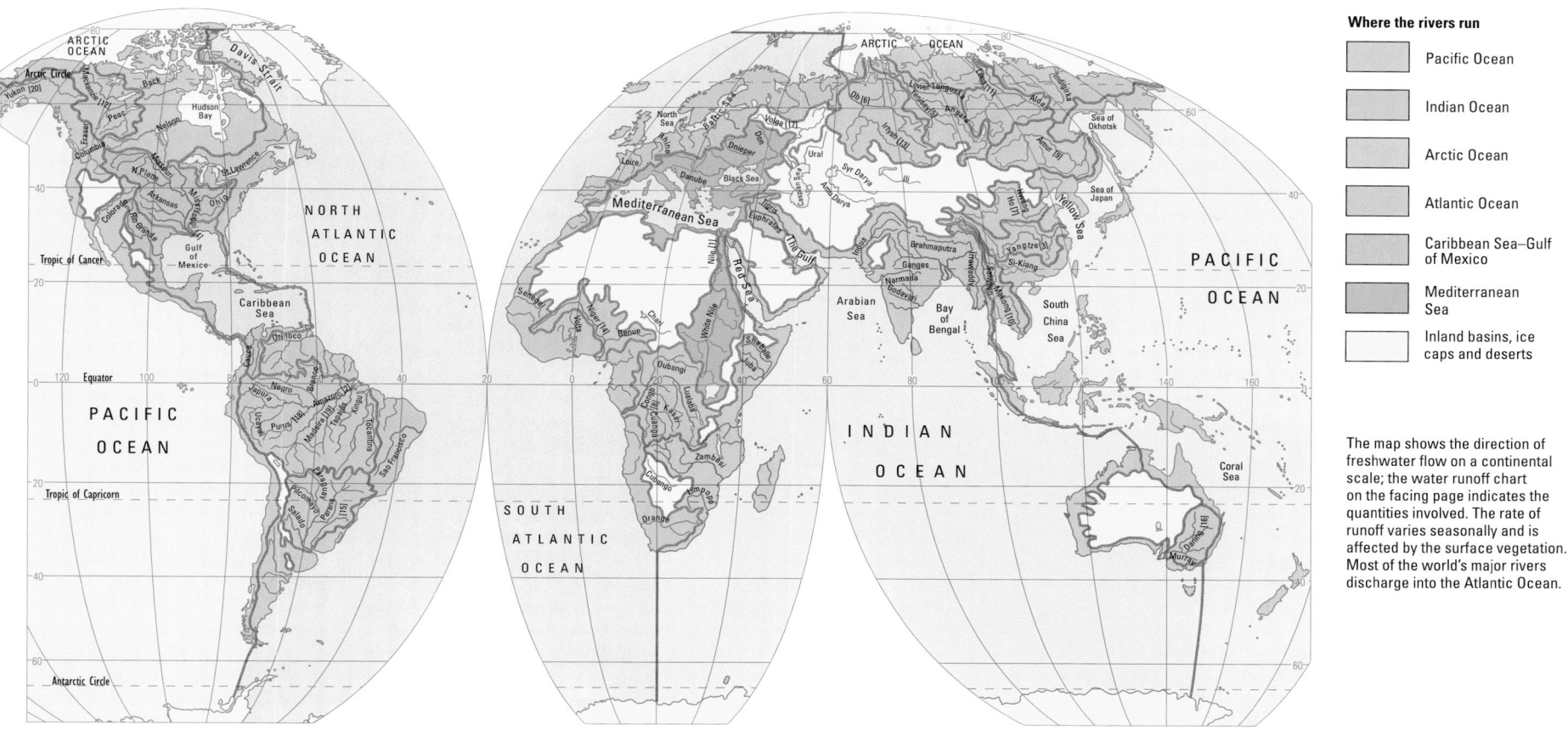

Where the rivers run

- Pacific Ocean
- Indian Ocean
- Arctic Ocean
- Atlantic Ocean
- Caribbean Sea–Gulf of Mexico
- Mediterranean Sea
- Inland basins, ice caps and deserts

The map shows the direction of freshwater flow on a continental scale; the water runoff chart on the facing page indicates the quantities involved. The rate of runoff varies seasonally and is affected by the surface vegetation. Most of the world's major rivers discharge into the Atlantic Ocean.

Annual Sediment Yield

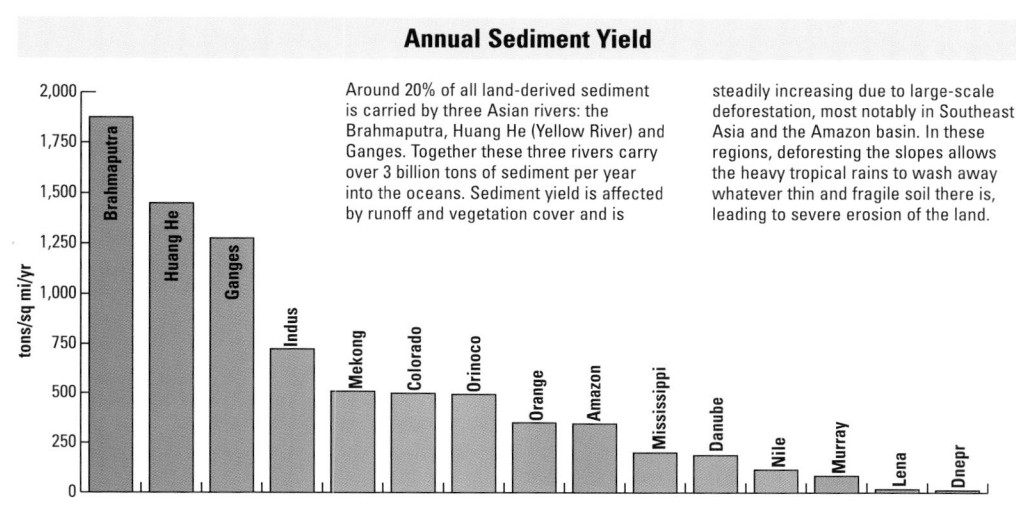

Around 20% of all land-derived sediment is carried by three Asian rivers: the Brahmaputra, Huang He (Yellow River) and Ganges. Together these three rivers carry over 3 billion tons of sediment per year into the oceans. Sediment yield is affected by runoff and vegetation cover and is steadily increasing due to large-scale deforestation, most notably in Southeast Asia and the Amazon basin. In these regions, deforesting the slopes allows the heavy tropical rains to wash away whatever thin and fragile soil there is, leading to severe erosion of the land.

Land Use by Continent

The proportion of productive land has reached its upper limit in Europe, and in Asia more than 80% of potential cropland is already under cultivation.

- Forest
- Permanent pasture and rough grazing
- Permanent crops and plantations
- Arable
- Non-productive

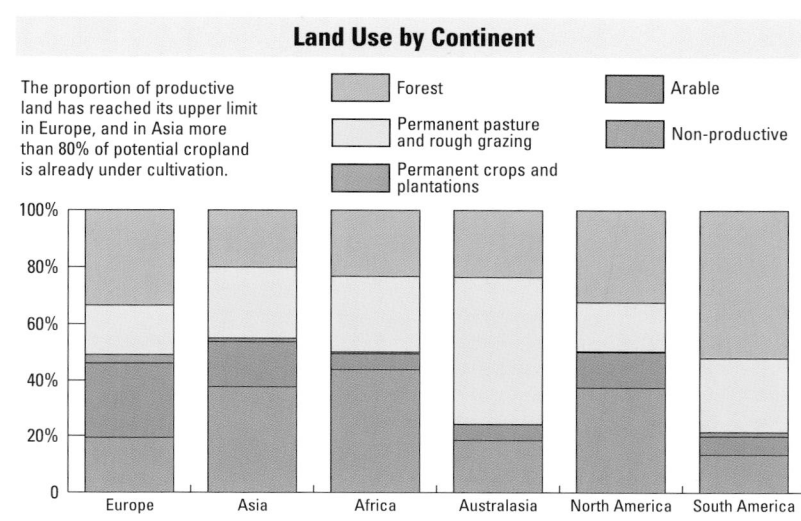

Natural Vegetation

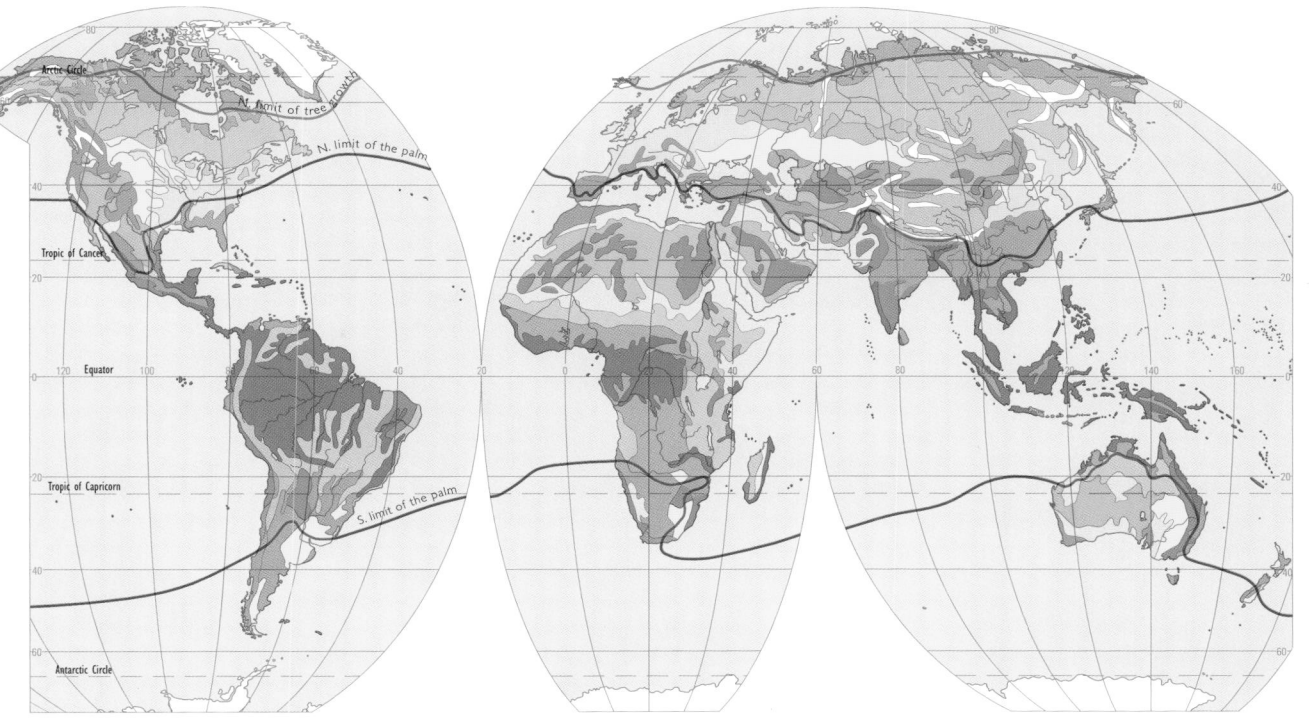

- Tropical rain forest
- Subtropical and temperate rain forest
- Monsoon woodland and open jungle
- Subtropical and temperate woodland, scrub and bush
- Tropical savanna, with low trees and bush
- Tropical savanna and grasslands
- Dry semidesert, with shrub and grass
- Desert shrub
- Desert
- Dry steppe and shrub
- Temperate grasslands, prairie and steppe
- Mediterranean hardwood forest and scrub
- Temperate deciduous forest and meadow
- Temperate deciduous and coniferous forest
- Northern coniferous forest (taiga)
- Mountainous forest, mainly coniferous
- High plateau steppe and tundra
- Arctic tundra
- Polar and mountainous ice desert

The map illustrates the natural "climax vegetation" of a region, as dictated by its climate and topography. In most cases, human agricultural activity has drastically altered the vegetation pattern. Western Europe, for example, lost most of its broadleaf forest many centuries ago, while elsewhere irrigation has turned some natural semidesert into productive land. The various vegetation regions support different kinds of animals and, in an undisturbed state, they are highly developed biological communities, or biomes.

The blue line on the map represents the northern limit of tree growth, and the red lines indicate the northern and southern limits of palm growth.

CARTOGRAPHY BY PHILIP'S. COPYRIGHT GEORGE PHILIP LTD

The Natural Environment

Recent discoveries of life forms in some of the world's most hostile environments, such as around the black smokers along the ocean ridges, prepared the way for the announcement by NASA scientists in 1996 that they had found microfossils in a Martian meteorite. But other scientists were sceptical, believing them to be natural mineral structures and not evidence of extraterrestrial life.

Until further evidence is available, the Earth remains the only planet where we know for sure that life exists. According to the fossil record, life on Earth appeared at least 3.5 billion years ago. Since then, it has evolved from its primitive beginnings to its modern biodiversity, including millions of plants, animals and micro-organisms. Living organisms have not only adapted to the environ-ment but they have also changed their environment to suit themselves. For example, the Earth's early atmosphere contained little oxygen but the emergence of multicelled, oxygen-producing algae, around 2 billion years ago, led to the creation of an oxygen-rich atmosphere. This enabled land animals to populate the ancient continents.

The amount of the greenhouse gas carbon dioxide in the atmosphere would steadily increase from its present 0.03% were it not for plants. Without them, the Earth's atmos-phere would, in a few million years, be similar to that of Venus, where surface temperatures reach 885°F. The Earth has evolved into a complex control system, sensing and reacting to changes and tending always to maintain the balance it has achieved.

Much discussion has centered on how that balance changes. Only recently, scientists were suggesting that we may be living in an interglacial stage of the Pleistocene Ice Age. From the 1980s, however, predictions of future climates have concentrated more on global warming, caused by pollution which has led to an increase in greenhouse gases in the atmosphere. Interference in the natural cycles that control the environment may have consequences that are hard to predict.

Furthermore, we are currently experien-cing a period of mass extinction of species, causing a rapid reduction in our planet's biodiversity. A report by the World Conser-vation Union in 1996 stated that, of the 4,327 known mammal species, 1,096 were at risk and 169 "critically endangered."

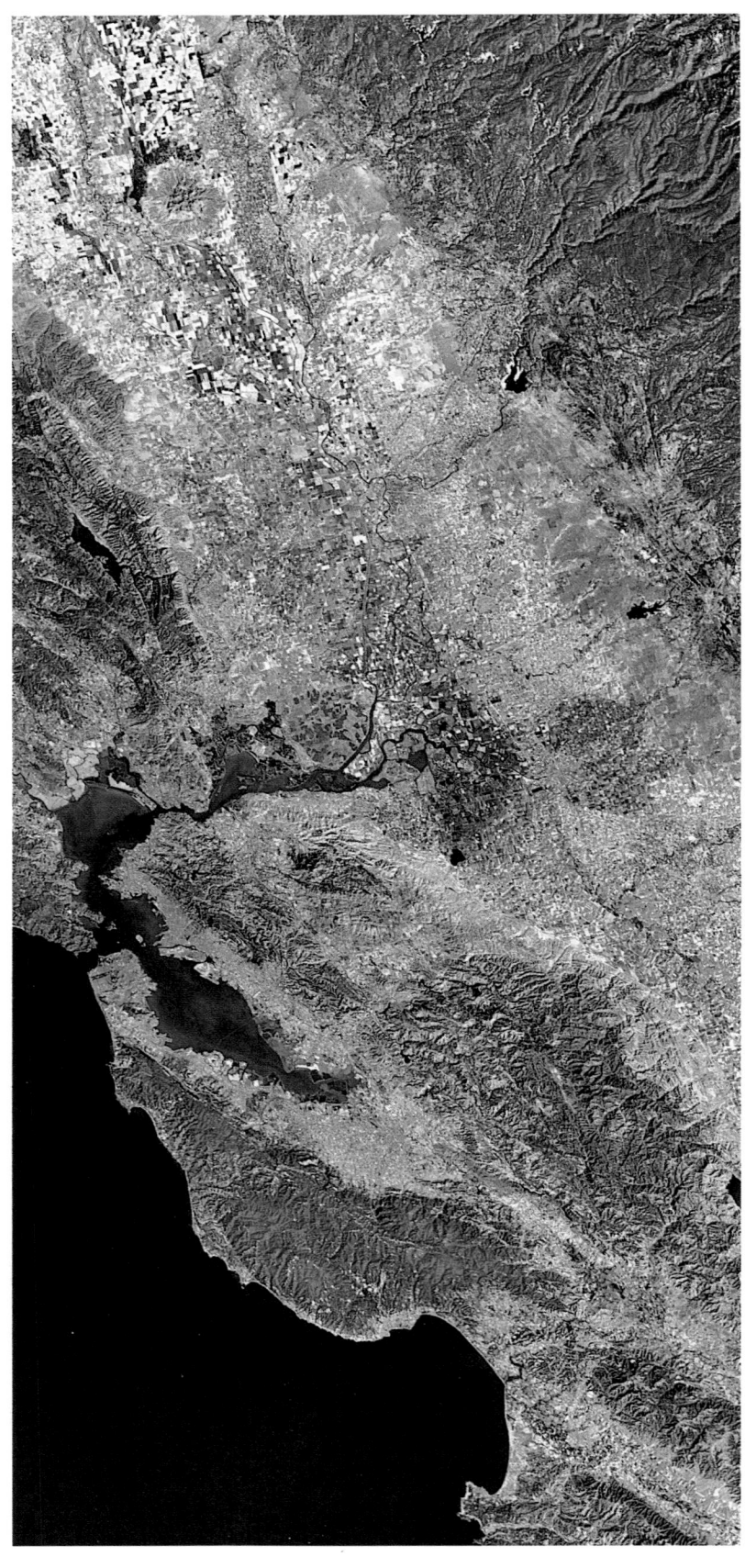

Biodiversity in California

The photograph, left, is a false color satellite image of central California in the southwestern United States. The large inlet of the Pacific Ocean is San Francisco Bay. San Francisco lies just below the entrance to the bay, with Oakland on the far side and San Jose to the southeast. California, nicknamed the Golden State, is the third largest state in the United States and the most populous.

Because of its varied terrain and climate, California has a wide range of diverse habitats within a relatively small area. East of the forested Coast Ranges (the gray and red areas just inland from the bay) lies the fertile Central Valley, which appears as a red and blue checkerboard. The Sierra Nevada is the red area in the top right corner. In the northwest and southwest of the state, not shown here, lie parts of the Basin and Range region, much of which is desert. It includes Death Valley, which contains the country's lowest point on land at 282 feet below sea level.

Forests cover about 40% of California and they include bristlecone pines, thought to be the oldest living things on Earth, together with coastal red-woods, the world's tallest trees. Wildlife is still abundant, though some species, such as the rare California condor, are on the endangered list.

The state has achieved much to protect its biodiversity. It contains eight of the 54 national parks in the United States. Two of them, Death Valley and Joshua Tree, were designated national parks as recently as 1994, as part of a conservation measure, including the protection of large areas of wilderness in the deserts.

California has vast resources and, were it a separate nation, it would rank among the world's ten most productive in terms of the total value of its goods and services. This means that, like the United States as a whole, it has resources, which many developing countries lack, to finance conservation measures. For example, the World Conservation Union reported in 1996 that 8% of mammals were threatened in the United States, as compared with 32% in the Philippines and 44% in Madagascar, two countries where habitat destruction has been on a large scale.

Endangered Species

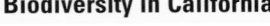
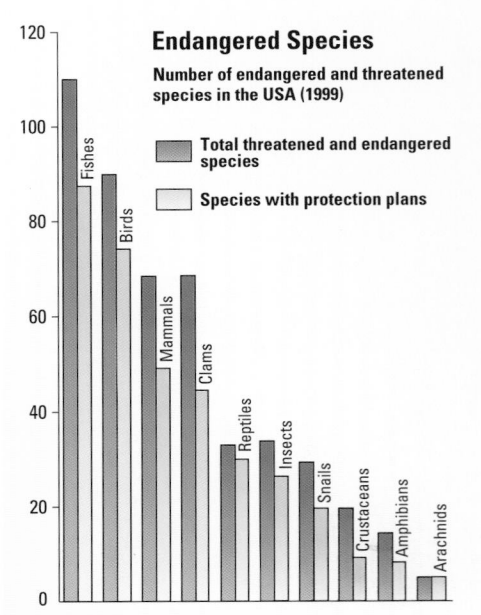

Number of endangered and threatened species in the USA (1999)

▮ Total threatened and endangered species

▯ Species with protection plans

Fishes, Birds, Mammals, Clams, Reptiles, Insects, Snails, Crustaceans, Amphibians, Arachnids

Threatened Mammals

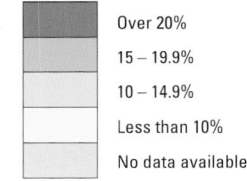

Percentage of mammal species classified as threatened (1996). Many scientists believe we are currently experiencing a period of mass extinction of species rivaling five other periods in the past half a billion years. Among the most threatened mammals are elephants, primates and rhinoceroses.

Over 20%
15 – 19.9%
10 – 14.9%
Less than 10%
No data available

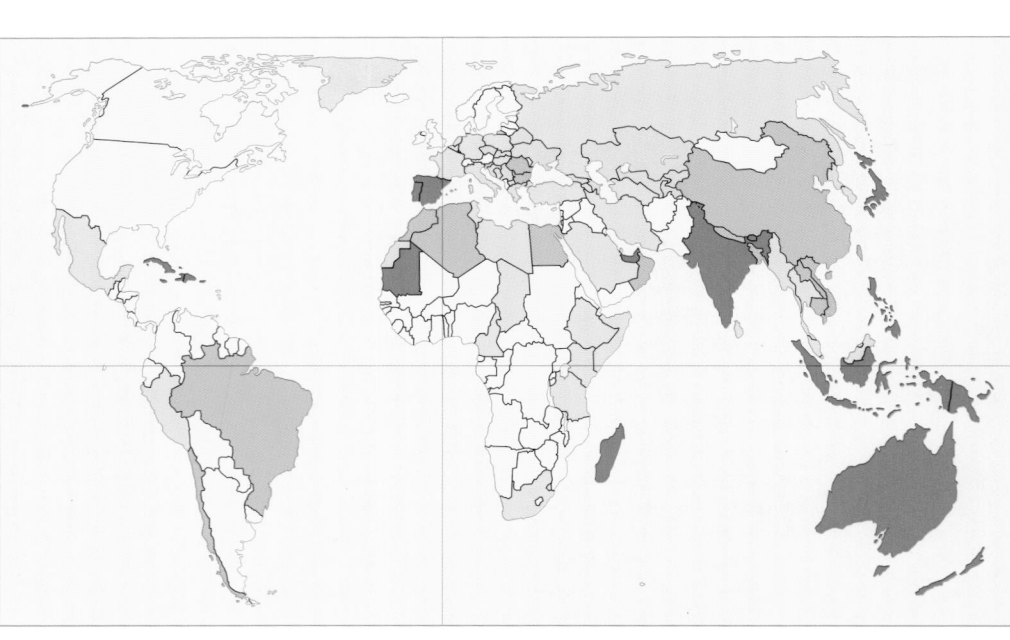

CARTOGRAPHY BY PHILIP'S. COPYRIGHT GEORGE PHILIP LTD

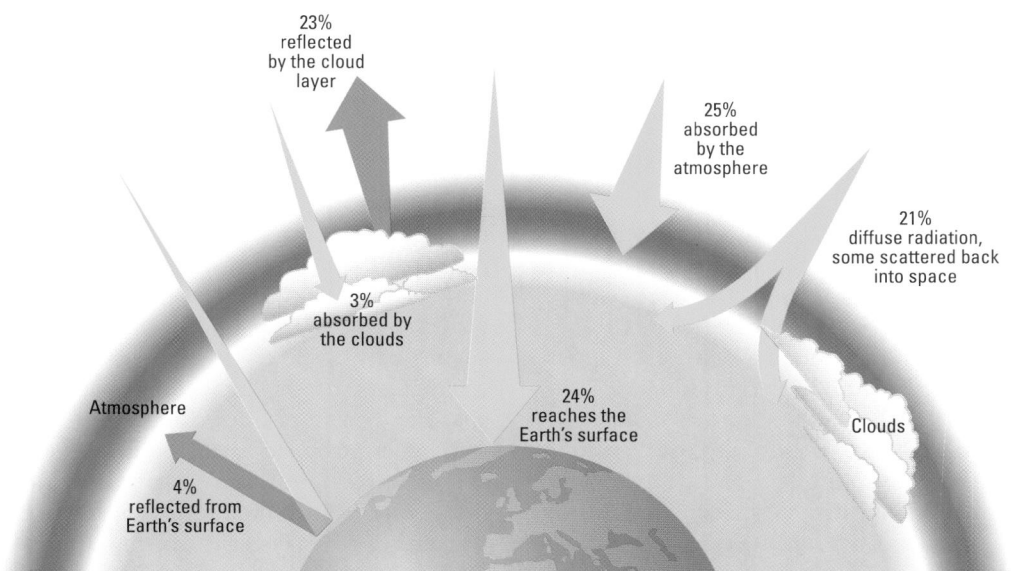

23% reflected by the cloud layer

25% absorbed by the atmosphere

21% diffuse radiation, some scattered back into space

3% absorbed by the clouds

Atmosphere

24% reaches the Earth's surface

Clouds

4% reflected from Earth's surface

The Earth's Energy Balance

Apart from a modest quantity of internal heat from its molten core, the Earth receives all of its energy from the Sun. If the planet is to remain at a constant temperature, it must reradiate exactly as much energy as it receives. Even a minute surplus would lead to a warmer Earth, a deficit to a cooler one. The temperature at which thermal equilibrium is reached depends on a multitude of interconnected factors. Two of the most important are the relative brightness of the Earth – its index of reflectivity, called the "albedo" – and the heat-trapping capacity of the atmosphere – the celebrated "greenhouse effect" (see below).

Because the Sun is very hot, most of its energy arrives in the form of relatively short-wave radiation: the shorter the waves, the more energy they carry. Some of the incoming energy is reflected straight back into space, exactly as it arrived; some is absorbed by the atmosphere on its way toward the surface; some is absorbed by the Earth itself. Absorbed energy heats the Earth and its atmosphere alike. But since its temperature is very much lower than that of the Sun, the outgoing energy is emitted at much longer infra-red wavelengths. Some of the outgoing radiation escapes directly into outer space; some of it is reabsorbed by the atmosphere. Atmospheric energy eventually finds its way back into space, too, after a complex series of interactions. These include the air movements we call the weather and, almost incidentally, the maintenance of life on Earth.

This diagram does not attempt to illustrate the actual mechanisms of heat exchange, but gives a reasonable account (in percentages) of what happens to 100 energy "units." Short-wave radiation is shown in yellow, long-wave in orange.

The Carbon Cycle

Most of the constituents of the atmosphere are kept in constant balance by complex cycles in which life plays an essential and indeed a dominant part. The control of carbon dioxide, which if left to its own devices would be the dominant atmospheric gas, is possibly the most important, although since all the Earth's biological and geophysical cycles interact and interlock, it is hard to separate them even in theory and quite impossible in practice.

The Earth has a huge supply of carbon, only a small quantity of which is in the form of carbon dioxide. Of that, around 98% is dissolved in the sea; the fraction circulating in the air amounts to only 340 parts per million of the atmosphere, where its capacity as a greenhouse gas is the key regulator of the planetary temperature. In turn, life regulates the regulator, keeping carbon dioxide concentrations below danger level.

If all life were to vanish from the Earth tomorrow, the atmosphere would begin the process of change immediately, although it might take several million years to achieve a new, inorganic stability. First, the oxygen content would begin to fall away; with no more assistance than a little solar radiation, a few electrical storms and its own high chemical potential, oxygen would steadily combine with atmospheric nitrogen and volcanic outgassing. In doing so, it would yield sufficient acid to react with carbonaceous rocks such as limestone, releasing carbon dioxide. Once carbon dioxide levels exceeded about 1%, its greenhouse power would increase disproportionately. Rising temperatures – well above the boiling point of water – would speed chemical reactions; in time, the Earth's atmosphere would consist of little more than carbon dioxide and superheated water vapor.

Living things, however, circulate carbon. They do so first by simply existing: after all, the carbon atom is the basic building block of living matter.

pool of CO_2 in atmosphere

combustion   photosynthesis

respiration   respiration   respiration

CO_2

CO_2

decay organisms

respiration

death

carbonification, gradual production of fossil fuels

death

decay organisms

peat

coal

oil and gas

During life, plants absorb carbon dioxide from the atmosphere and, along with various chemicals, as soluble salts from the soil, incorporating the carbon into their structure – leaves and trunks in the case of land plants, shells in the case of plankton and the tiny creatures that feed on it. The oxygen thereby freed is added to the atmosphere, at least for a time. The carbon is returned to circulation when the plants die or is passed up the food chain to the herbivores and then the carnivores that feed on them. As organisms at each of these trophic levels die, they decay, releasing the carbon which then combines once more with the oxygen released during life. However, a small proportion of carbon, about one part in 1,000, is removed almost permanently, buried beneath mud on land or at sea, sinking as dead matter to the ocean floor. In time, it is slowly compressed into sedimentary rocks such as limestone and chalk.

But in the evolution of the Earth, nothing is quite permanent. On an even longer timescale, the planet's crustal movements force new rock upward in mid-ocean ridges. Limestone deposits are moved, and sea levels change; ancient carboniferous rocks are exposed to weathering, and a little of their carbon is released to be fixed in turn by the current generation of plants.

The carbon cycle has continued quietly for an immensely long time, and without gross disturbance there is no reason why it would not continue almost indefinitely in the future. However, human beings have found a way to release fixed carbon at a rate far faster than existing global systems can recirculate it. The fossil fuels, coal, oil, gas and peat deposits, represent the work of millions of years of carbon accumulation; but it has taken only a few human generations of high-energy scavenging to endanger the entire complex regulatory cycle.

The Greenhouse Effect

Constituting less than 1% of the atmosphere, the natural greenhouse gases (water vapor, carbon dioxide, methane, nitrous oxide and ozone) have a hugely disproportionate effect on the Earth's climate and even its habitability. Like the glass panes in a greenhouse, the gases are transparent to most incoming short-wave radiation, which passes freely to heat the planet beneath. But when the warmed Earth retransmits that energy, in the form of longer-wave infra-red radiation, the gases function as an opaque shield preventing some of it from escaping, so that the planetary surface (like the interior of a greenhouse) stays relatively hot.

Over the last 150 years, there has been a gradual increase in the levels of greenhouse gases (with the exception of water vapor which remains a constant in the system). These increases are causing alarm – global warming associated with a runaway greenhouse effect could bring disaster – and what is more, predictions suggest that there could be a further rise of 2.5–8°F by the year 2100. A serious reduction in the greenhouse gases would be just as damaging; a total absence of CO_2, for example, would leave the planet with a temperature roughly 60°F colder than at present.

N.B. The thickness of the Earth's atmosphere is proportionately much thinner than the peel of an apple.

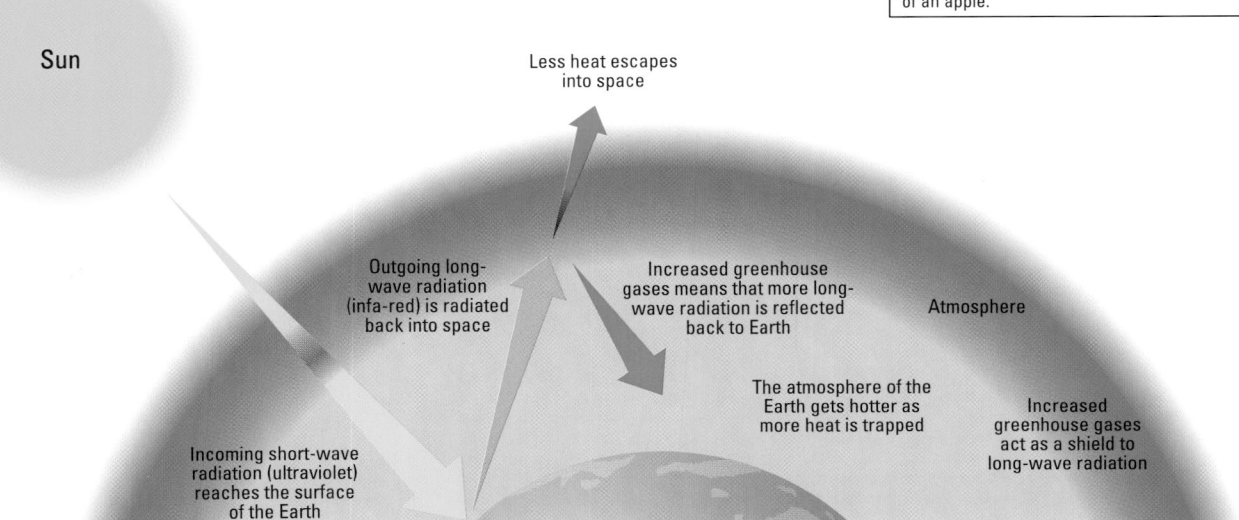

Sun

Less heat escapes into space

Outgoing long-wave radiation (infa-red) is radiated back into space

Increased greenhouse gases means that more long-wave radiation is reflected back to Earth

Atmosphere

The atmosphere of the Earth gets hotter as more heat is trapped

Increased greenhouse gases act as a shield to long-wave radiation

Incoming short-wave radiation (ultraviolet) reaches the surface of the Earth

CARTOGRAPHY BY PHILIP'S. COPYRIGHT GEORGE PHILIP LTD

People and the Environment

In 1996, the Intergovernmental Panel on Climate Change issued a report stating that "The balance of evidence suggests a discernible human influence on global climate through emissions of carbon dioxide and other greenhouse gases." The report acknowledged that average global temperatures have risen by about 0.9°F since the mid-19th century, but there were still reasons for caution, such as discrepancies between measurements of temperatures around the world. Furthermore, our knowledge about how climates change of their own accord is incomplete, as is our understanding of human interference, how this varies in different parts of the world and how it differs from natural climatic variability.

Human interference with nature is nothing new, at least since people turned from hunting and gathering to agriculture more than 10,000 years ago. At first, human actions seemed to have no ill effects because the systems that regulate the global environment were able to absorb damage. But from the late 18th century, the Industrial Revolution and the population explosion have caused pollution on a scale that threatens to overwhelm the Earth's ability to cope.

The 20th century witnessed many disasters, including the dumping of industrial wastes in rivers and seas, accidents at nuclear power stations, and the creation of acid rain through the release of sulphur dioxides and nitrous oxides by the burning of fossil fuels. The release of greenhouse gases are held to be the main reason for global warming, while CFCs (chlorofluoro-carbons) have damaged the ozone layer in the stratosphere, the planet's screen against ultraviolet radiation.

Global warming will lead to melting ice sheets and the flooding of fertile coastal plains. Computer models suggest that it might affect ocean currents so that north-western Europe, which owes its mild climate to the Gulf Stream, could expect bitterly cold winters. Some models have suggested that cloud cover could increase, reflecting more solar energy back into space and so start a new Ice Age.

In many tropical areas, deforestation is making productive land barren, while in the dry grasslands bordering deserts, the removal of plant cover is causing desertification. But human ingenuity can respond to this crisis in planet management.

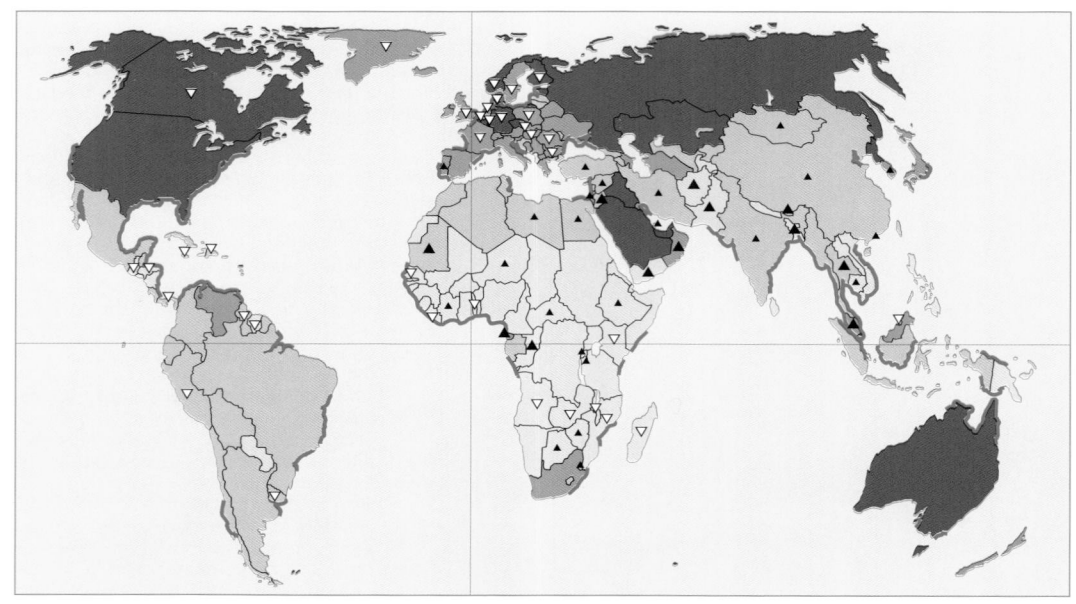

Global Warming

Carbon dioxide emissions in tons per person per year (1995)

- Over 10 tons of CO_2
- 5 – 10 tons of CO_2
- 1 – 5 tons of CO_2
- Under 1 ton of CO_2

Changes in CO_2 emissions 1980–90

- ▲ Over 100% increase
- ▲ 50–100% increase
- ▽ Reduction
- ▬ Coasts in danger of flooding from rising sea levels

Records of global mean surface temperatures from 1860 to the present show that 1995 was the warmest year and that nine of the ten warmest years have occurred since 1983. This evidence of global warming is attributed mainly to the Greenhouse Effect, caused by the emission of certain gases, notably carbon dioxide (CO_2), into the atmosphere since the start of the Industrial Revolution. At first, much of the CO_2 was absorbed by the oceans. However, the vast increase in fuel combustion since 1950 has led CO_2 content in the atmosphere to increase gradually from 280 parts per million to more than 350 parts per million. Despite international action to control the emissions of some greenhouse gases, CO_2 levels are still rising.

Greenhouse Power

Relative contributions to the Greenhouse Effect by the major heat-absorbing gases in the atmosphere

The chart combines greenhouse potency and volume. Carbon dioxide has a greenhouse potential of only 1, but its concentration of 350 parts per million makes it predominate. CFC 12, with 25,000 times the absorption capacity of CO_2, is present only as 0.00044 ppm.

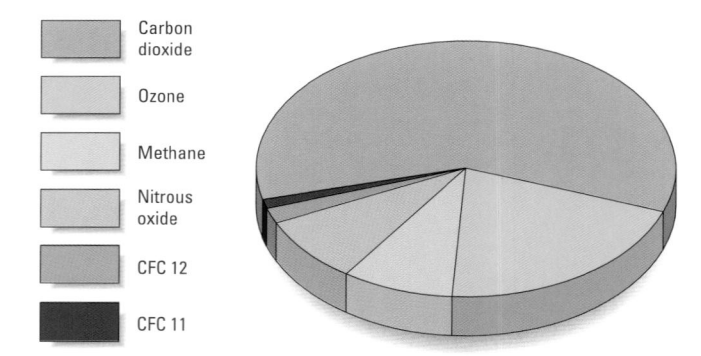

- Carbon dioxide
- Ozone
- Methane
- Nitrous oxide
- CFC 12
- CFC 11

Carbon Dioxide

Carbon dioxide released in millions of tons (latest available year)

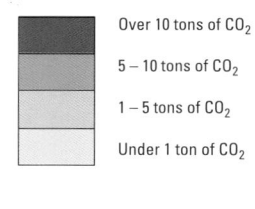

USA 4,932
Former USSR 3,581
China 2,543
Japan
Germany
India
UK
Iraq
Canada
Italy
France
Mexico

Temperature Rise

The rise in average temperatures caused by carbon dioxide and other greenhouse gases (1960–2020)

- assumes present trends continue
- assumes drastic emissions cuts in the 1990s

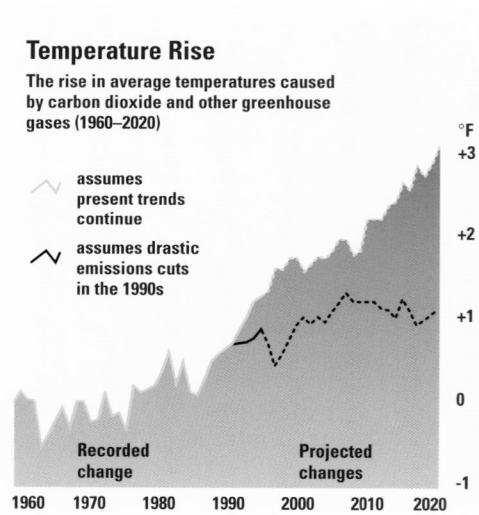

Recorded change | Projected changes

1960 1970 1980 1990 2000 2010 2020

The Thinning Ozone Layer

Total atmospheric ozone concentration in the southern and northern hemispheres (Dobson units, 1995)

In 1985, scientists working in Antarctica discovered a thinning of the ozone layer, commonly known as an "ozone hole." This caused immediate alarm because the ozone layer absorbs most of the Sun's dangerous ultraviolet radiation, which is believed to cause an increase in skin cancer, cataracts and damage to the immune system. Since 1985, ozone depletion has increased and, by 1996, the ozone hole over the South Pole was estimated to be as large as North America. The false color images, right, show the total atmospheric ozone concentration in the southern hemisphere (in October 1995) and the northern hemisphere (in March 1995) with the ozone hole clearly identifiable at the center. The data are from the Tiros Ozone Vertical Sounder, an instrument on the American TIROS weather satellite. The colors represent the ozone concentration in Dobson Units (DU). Normal healthy values are around 280 DU but the lowest value in the northern hemisphere reached 98 DU. Scientists agree that ozone depletion is caused by CFCs, a group of manufactured chemicals used in air conditioning systems and refrigerators. In a 1987 treaty most industrial nations agreed to phase out CFCs and a complete ban on most CFCs was agreed after the end of 1995. However, scientists believe that the chemicals will remain in the atmosphere for 50 to 100 years. As a result, ozone depletion will continue for many years.

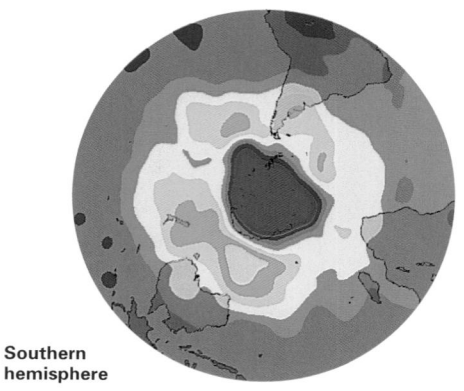

Southern hemisphere

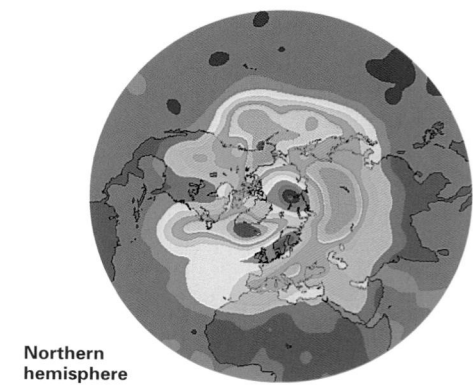

Northern hemisphere

CARTOGRAPHY BY PHILIP'S. COPYRIGHT GEORGE PHILIP LTD

World Pollution

Acid rain and sources of acidic emissions (latest available year)

Acid rain is caused by high levels of sulfur and nitrogen in the atmosphere. They combine with water vapor and oxygen to form acids (H_2SO_4 and HNO_3) which fall as precipitation.

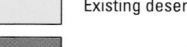 Regions where sulfur and nitrogen oxides are released in high concentrations, mainly from fossil fuel combustion

○ Major cities with high levels of air pollution (including nitrogen and sulfur emissions)

Areas of heavy acid deposition

pH numbers indicate acidity, decreasing from a neutral 7. Normal rain, slightly acid from dissolved carbon dioxide, never exceeds a pH of 5.6.

 pH less than 4.0 (most acidic)

 pH 4.0 to 4.5

 pH 4.5 to 5.0

 Areas where acid rain is a potential problem

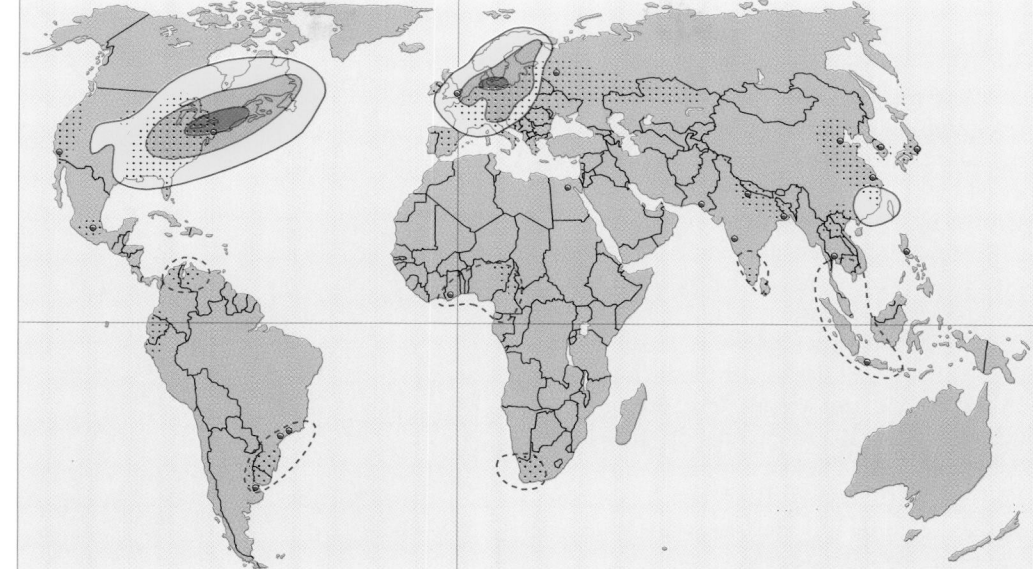

Desertification

 Existing deserts

Areas with a high risk of desertification

Areas with a moderate risk of desertification

Former areas of rain forest

Existing rain forest

Deforestation

Thousands of hectares of forest cleared annually, tropical countries surveyed 1981–85 and 1987–90. Loss as a percentage of remaining stocks is shown in figures on each column.

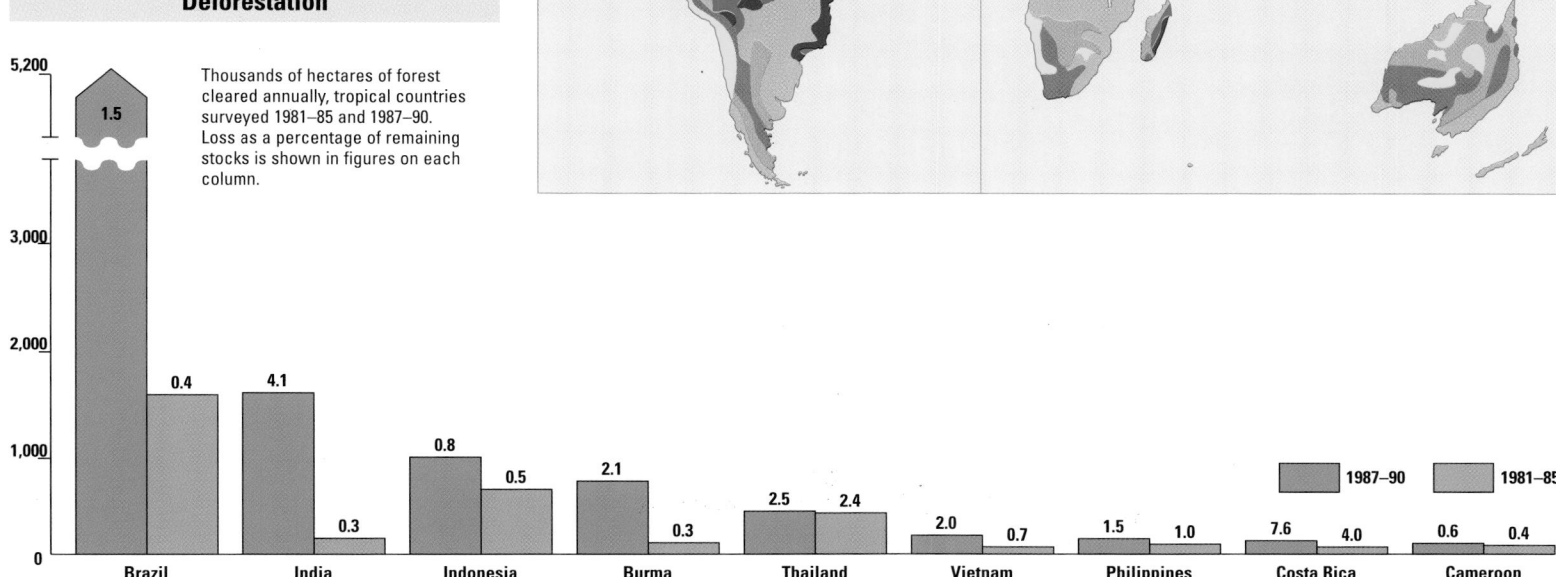

1987–90   1981–85

	Brazil	India	Indonesia	Burma	Thailand	Vietnam	Philippines	Costa Rica	Cameroon
1987–90	1.5	4.1	0.8	2.1	2.5	2.0	1.5	7.6	0.6
1981–85	0.4	0.3	0.5	0.3	2.4	0.7	1.0	4.0	0.4

Water Pollution

 Severely polluted sea areas and lakes

Polluted sea areas and lakes

Areas of frequent oil pollution by shipping

▶ Major oil tanker spills

▲ Major oil rig blow outs

▼ Offshore dumpsites for industrial and municipal waste

— Severely polluted rivers and estuaries

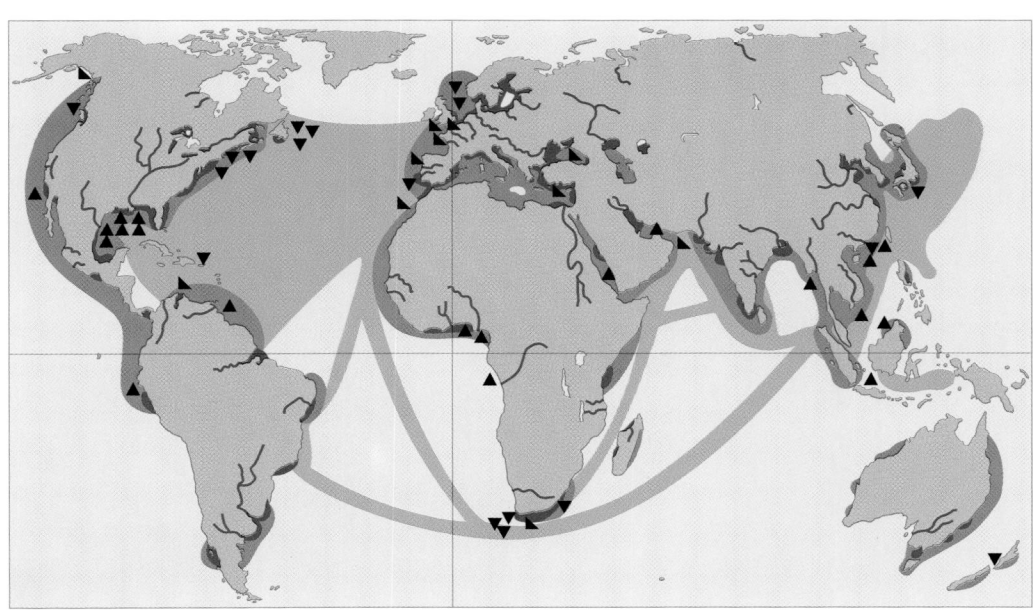

Antarctica

The vast Antarctic ice sheet, containing some 70% of the Earth's fresh water, plays a crucial role in the circulation of the atmosphere and oceans, and hence in determining the planetary climate. The frozen southern continent is also the last remaining wilderness – the largest area to remain free from human colonization.

Ever since Amundsen and Scott raced for the South Pole in 1911, various countries have pressed territorial claims over sections of Antarctica, spurred in recent years by its known and suspected mineral wealth: enough iron ore to supply the world at present levels for 200 years, large oil reserves and, probably, the biggest coal deposits on Earth.

However, the 1961 Antarctic Treaty set aside the area for peaceful uses only, guaranteeing freedom of scientific investigation, banning waste disposal and nuclear testing, and suspending the issue of territorial rights. By 1990, the original 12 signatories had grown to 25, with a further 15 nations granted observer status in subsequent deliberations. However, the Treaty itself was threatened by wrangles between different countries, government agencies and international pressure groups.

Finally, in July 1991, the belated agreement of the UK and the USA assured unanimity on a new accord to ban all mineral exploration for a further 50 years. The ban can only be rescinded if all the present signatories, plus a majority of any future adherents, agree. While the treaty has always lacked a formal mechanism for enforcement, it is firmly underwritten by public concern generated by the efforts of environmental pressure groups such as Greenpeace, which has been foremost in the campaign to have Antarctica declared a "World Park."

However, from the mid-1990s, the continent appeared to be under threat from global warming, which some scientists believe was the cause of the breakup of ice shelves along the Antarctic peninsula. Rising temperatures have also disturbed the breeding patterns of Adelie penguins.

Poisoned rivers, domestic sewage and oil spillage have combined in recent years to reduce the world's oceans to a sorry state of contamination, notably near the crowded coasts of industrialized nations. Shipping routes, too, are constantly affected by tanker discharges. Oil spills of all kinds, however, declined significantly during the 1980s, from a peak of 750,000 tons in 1979 to under 50,000 tons in 1990. The most notorious tanker spill of that period – when the *Exxon Valdez* (94,999 grt) ran aground in Prince William Sound, Alaska, in March 1989 – released only 267,000 barrels, a relatively small amount compared to the results of blow outs and war damage. Over 2,500,000 barrels were spilled during the Gulf War of 1991. The worst tanker accident in history occurred in July 1979, when the *Atlantic Empress* and the Aegean Captain collided off Trinidad, polluting the Caribbean with 1,890,000 barrels of crude oil.

Population

I n 8000 BC, following the development of agriculture, the world had an estimated population of 8 million and by AD 1000 it was about 300 million. The onset of the Industrial Revolution in the late 18th century led to a population explosion. The 1 billion mark was passed by 1850, it doubled by the 1920s and doubled again to 4 billion by 1975.

Most demographers agree that the world's population, which passed the 6 billion mark in October 1999, will reach 8.9 billion by 2050. It is not expected to level out until 2200, when it will peak at around 11 billion. After 2200, it is expected to level out or even decline a little. Rapid population growth is concentrated in the developing world; the populations of some developed countries, such as Belgium and Germany, are static or have even started to decline.

The developing world includes what the World Bank describes as low-income economies, with an average per capita GNP of US $380, and middle-income economies, with a per capita GNP of $2,520. Most developing countries are in Africa, Asia and Latin America. The developed world, made up of high-income, industrialized economies with an average per capita GNP of $23,420, contains Australasia, most of Europe and North America, and Japan in Asia.

In the poorer developing countries, a high proportion of the population is young, and they face high levels of expenditure on education and health until population growth rates start to decline. In developed countries, where the population pyramids are becoming increasingly top-heavy, expenditure on pensions and healthcare for the elderly is becoming a major social problem.

Largest Nations

The world's most populous nations, in millions (2000 est.)

1.	China	1,299
2.	India	1,041
3.	USA	266
4.	Indonesia	218
5.	Brazil	179
6.	Pakistan	162
7.	Russia	155
8.	Bangladesh	150
9.	Japan	128
10.	Mexico	107
11.	Nigeria	105
12.	Vietnam	82
13.	Philippines	77
14.	Germany	76
15.	Iran	68
16.	Turkey	66
17.	Egypt	64
18.	Thailand	63
19.	Ethiopia	61
20.	France	58
21.	UK	58
22.	Italy	57
23.	Ukraine	52
24.	Burma (Myanmar)	51

Crowded Nations

Population per square mile (1998), excluding nations of less than 1 million

1.	Monaco	32,894
2.	Macau	25,501
3.	Hong Kong	6,373
4.	Singapore	5,624
5.	Gibraltar	4,239
6.	Bermuda	1,199
7.	Malta	1,214
8.	Vatican City	1,090
9.	Maldives	909
10.	Bahrain	877
11.	Bangladesh	866
12.	Barbados	624
13.	Mauritius	559
14.	Nauru	529
15.	Armenia	487
16.	South Korea	466
17.	Puerto Rico	428
18.	Tuvalu	428
19.	San Marino	424
20.	Netherlands	384

Population Density

Inhabitants per square mile

	Over 500
	250 – 500
	125 – 250
	65 – 125
	15 – 65
	8 – 16
	3 – 8
	Under 3

Urban population

- ■ Over 10,000,000
- ● 5,000,000 – 10,000,000
- • 1,000,000 – 5,000,000

Places marked are conurbations, not city limits; San Francisco itself, for example, has an official population of less than a million.

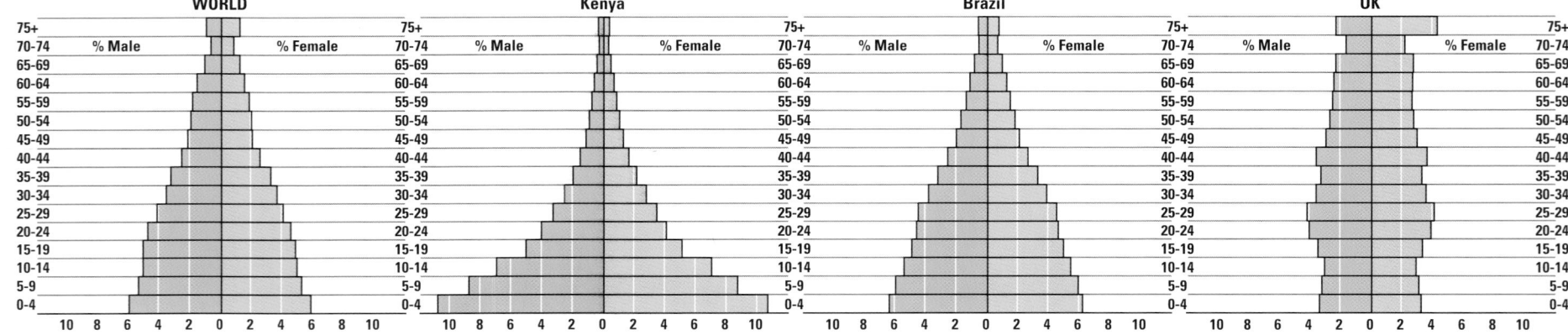

WORLD, Kenya, Brazil, UK population pyramids (% Male / % Female, age groups 0-4 through 75+)

Rates of Growth

The world population doubled between 1950 and 1990. Small rates of population growth led to dramatic increases over two or three generations. The table below translates annual percentage growth into the number of years required to double a population.

% change	Doubling time
0.5	139.0
1.0	69.7
1.5	46.6
2.0	35.0
2.5	28.1
3.0	23.4
3.5	20.1
4.0	17.7

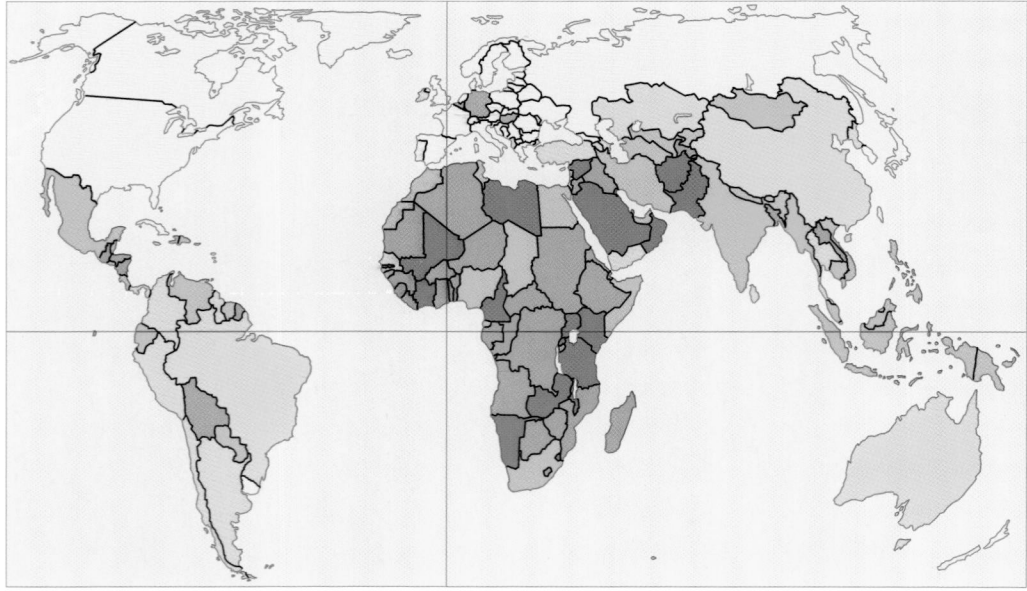

Population Change 1990–2000

The predicted population change for the years 1990–2000

	Over 40% population gain
	30 – 40% population gain
	20 – 30% population gain
	10 – 20% population gain
	0 – 10% population gain
	No change or population loss

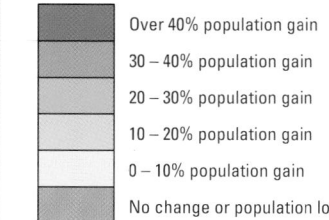

Top 5 countries		Bottom 5 countries	
Kuwait	+75.9%	Belgium	–0.1%
Namibia	+62.5%	Hungary	–0.2%
Afghanistan	+60.1%	Grenada	–2.4%
Mali	+55.5%	Germany	–3.2%
Tanzania	+54.6%	Tonga	–3.2%

CARTOGRAPHY BY PHILIP'S. COPYRIGHT GEORGE PHILIP LTD

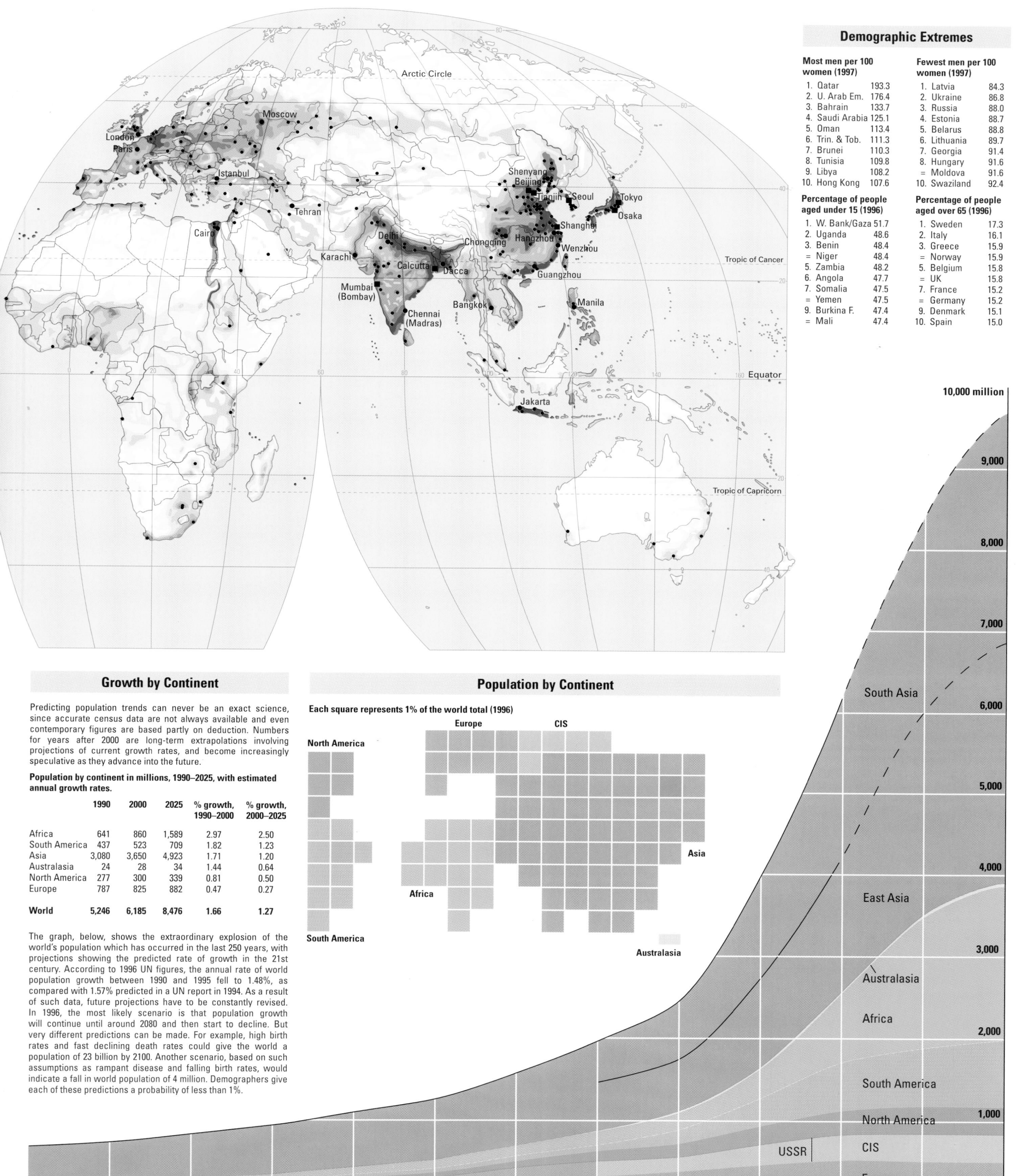

Arctic Circle

Moscow
London
Paris
Istanbul
Tehran
Cairo
Karachi
Delhi
Calcutta
Dacca
Mumbai (Bombay)
Chennai (Madras)
Bangkok
Shenyang
Beijing
Tianjin
Seoul
Tokyo
Osaka
Shanghai
Hangzhou
Chongqing
Wenzhou
Guangzhou
Manila
Jakarta

Tropic of Cancer

Equator

Tropic of Capricorn

Demographic Extremes

Most men per 100 women (1997)		Fewest men per 100 women (1997)	
1. Qatar	193.3	1. Latvia	84.3
2. U. Arab Em.	176.4	2. Ukraine	86.8
3. Bahrain	133.7	3. Russia	88.0
4. Saudi Arabia	125.1	4. Estonia	88.7
5. Oman	113.4	5. Belarus	88.8
6. Trin. & Tob.	111.3	6. Lithuania	89.7
7. Brunei	110.3	7. Georgia	91.4
8. Tunisia	109.8	8. Hungary	91.6
9. Libya	108.2	= Moldova	91.6
10. Hong Kong	107.6	10. Swaziland	92.4

Percentage of people aged under 15 (1996)		Percentage of people aged over 65 (1996)	
1. W. Bank/Gaza	51.7	1. Sweden	17.3
2. Uganda	48.6	2. Italy	16.1
3. Benin	48.4	3. Greece	15.9
= Niger	48.4	= Norway	15.9
5. Zambia	48.2	5. Belgium	15.8
6. Angola	47.7	= UK	15.8
7. Somalia	47.5	7. France	15.2
= Yemen	47.5	= Germany	15.2
9. Burkina F.	47.4	9. Denmark	15.1
= Mali	47.4	10. Spain	15.0

Growth by Continent

Predicting population trends can never be an exact science, since accurate census data are not always available and even contemporary figures are based partly on deduction. Numbers for years after 2000 are long-term extrapolations involving projections of current growth rates, and become increasingly speculative as they advance into the future.

Population by continent in millions, 1990–2025, with estimated annual growth rates.

	1990	2000	2025	% growth, 1990–2000	% growth, 2000–2025
Africa	641	860	1,589	2.97	2.50
South America	437	523	709	1.82	1.23
Asia	3,080	3,650	4,923	1.71	1.20
Australasia	24	28	34	1.44	0.64
North America	277	300	339	0.81	0.50
Europe	787	825	882	0.47	0.27
World	**5,246**	**6,185**	**8,476**	**1.66**	**1.27**

The graph, below, shows the extraordinary explosion of the world's population which has occurred in the last 250 years, with projections showing the predicted rate of growth in the 21st century. According to 1996 UN figures, the annual rate of world population growth between 1990 and 1995 fell to 1.48%, as compared with 1.57% predicted in a UN report in 1994. As a result of such data, future projections have to be constantly revised. In 1996, the most likely scenario is that population growth will continue until around 2080 and then start to decline. But very different predictions can be made. For example, high birth rates and fast declining death rates could give the world a population of 23 billion by 2100. Another scenario, based on such assumptions as rampant disease and falling birth rates, would indicate a fall in world population of 4 million. Demographers give each of these predictions a probability of less than 1%.

Population by Continent

Each square represents 1% of the world total (1996)

North America
Europe
CIS
Asia
Africa
South America
Australasia

10,000 million
9,000
8,000
7,000
6,000
5,000
4,000
3,000
2,000
1,000

South Asia
East Asia
Australasia
Africa
South America
North America
USSR
CIS
Europe

1750 1775 1800 1825 1850 1875 1900 1925 1950 1975 2000 2025 2050

CARTOGRAPHY BY PHILIP'S. COPYRIGHT GEORGE PHILIP LTD

Cities

For more information:
18 Water supply
24 Population density
48 The great ports

Following the development of agriculture more than 10,000 years ago, people began to live in farming villages. Around 5,500 years ago, the world's first cities appeared in the lower Tigris and Euphrates valleys in Mesopotamia. Cities were founded in Ancient Egypt around 5,000 years ago and in China around 3,600 years ago. By contrast with the villages, most people in the early cities were not engaged in farming. Instead, they worked in craft industries, in government services, in religion and in trade. The cities became centers of early civilizations and, through trade, their influence spread far and wide. However, they were dependent on the surrounding farming communities for their food and other materials.

In 1750, prior to the start of the Industrial Revolution, barely 3% of the world's population lived in urban areas. By 1850, London and Paris had more than a million people, and, by 1900, 14% of the world's population lived in cities. By 1950, the world had 83 cities with more than a million people, and

by 1996, there were 280. By 2015, experts predict that there will be more than 500. New York City was the only city with a population in excess of 10 million in 1950; by 2015 the experts predict 27 such cities worldwide, the majority located in the developing world.

By the end of the 20th century, more than half of the world's population was living in urban areas. Despite the rapid growth of cities in developing countries, urbanization is highest in industrialized countries. For example, 78% of the people in the United States live in urban areas, with the European Union not far behind with 77%. But in countries with low-income economies, which contained nearly 60% of the world's total population in 1996, only 28% lived in urban areas.

The rapid rate of urbanization has created problems, especially in cities which have not been able to provide enough jobs and services for the expanding population. Most new city dwellers are people from rural areas and because many of them are young there is a consequent acceleration in the rate of city

population growth. In developed countries, with highly mechanized agriculture, it is population pressure that drives many people into urban areas. In developing countries, the grinding poverty of rural life and the lack of services leads to migration to urban areas.

A typical city in a developing country contains millions of people living, often illegally, in shanty towns (or "informal settlements" in politically correct parlance), while thousands live on the streets. Yet many of these shanty towns are healthier than the industrial cities of 19th-century Europe and North America. Indeed, surveys have shown that the migrants to the cities in developing countries are less likely to face poverty than they are in rural areas, while benefiting from greater access to healthcare services and education.

Modern cities face many problems, including pollution, crime and unemployment. Yet, given competent central and local government, they are capable of generating the wealth they need to solve them, as well as making a major contribution to the economy.

The Urbanization of the Earth

City-building, 1850–2000; each white spot represents a city of at least 1 million inhabitants.

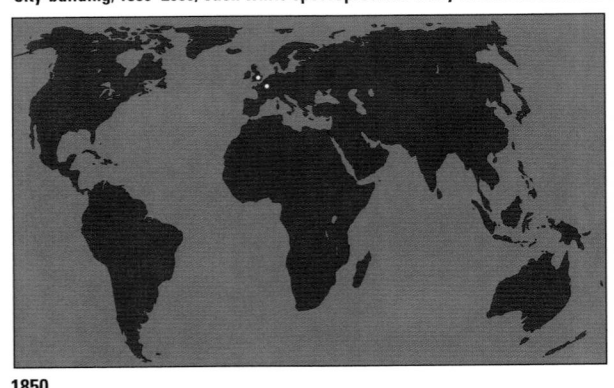

1850

1900

1925

1950

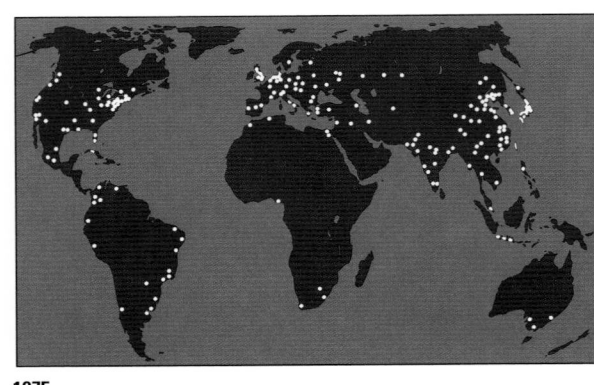

1975

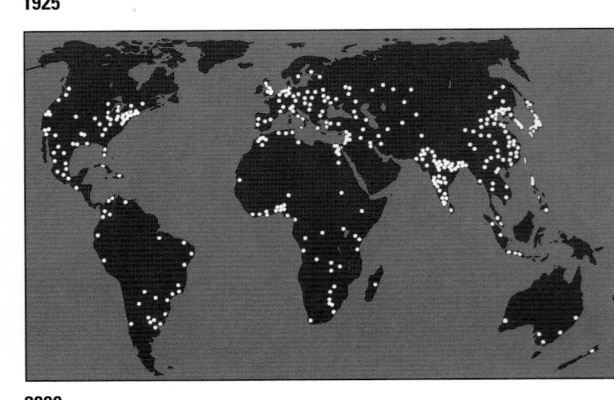

2000

Urban Population

Percentage of total population living in towns and cities (1997)

Most urbanized

Singapore	100%	Over 75%
Belgium	97%	50 – 75%
Israel	91%	25 – 50%
Uruguay	91%	10 – 25%
Netherlands	89%	Under 10%
[UK 89%]		

Least urbanized

Rwanda	6%
Bhutan	8%
Burundi	8%
Nepal	11%
Swaziland	12%

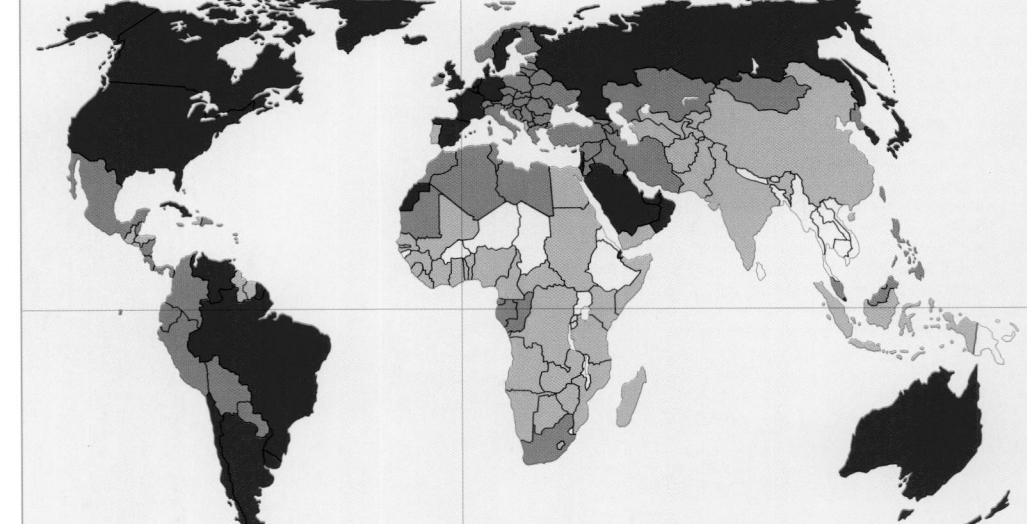

CARTOGRAPHY BY PHILIP'S, COPYRIGHT GEORGE PHILIP LTD

Expanding Cities

The growth of some of the world's largest cities in millions, 1950–2015.
Comparisons of city populations over time are problematic due to changes in the definition of the city limits.
These figures attempt to take such changes into consideration. The figure for London is the metropolitan region.

■ 1950   ■ 2015

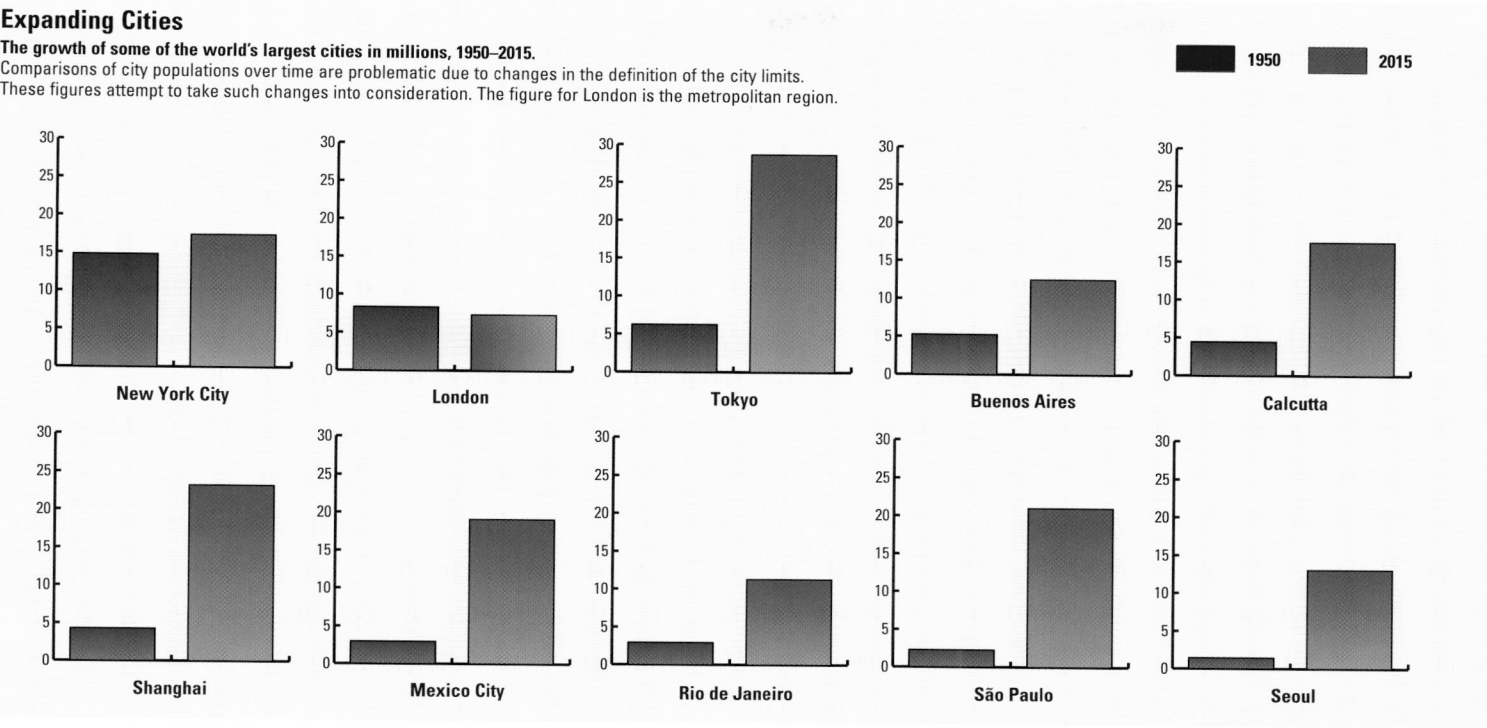

New York City · London · Tokyo · Buenos Aires · Calcutta
Shanghai · Mexico City · Rio de Janeiro · São Paulo · Seoul

The graphs show the projected growth of megacities between 1950 and 2015. New York City, the world's largest city in 1950, reached a peak in 1970, but it has experienced periods of negative growth. London's population also declined between 1970 and 1985, before resuming a modest rate of increase. In both cases, the divergence from world trends is explained in part by counting methods. Each lies at the center of a great agglomeration, and definitions of the "city limits" may vary over time. Also, in developing countries, many areas around the megacities which are counted as urban, are rural in character. The rates of city population growth in developing countries have also often been over-estimated. For example, it was once predicted that Calcutta would have a population of 40 million by the late 1990s. The reason why many estimates have proven incorrect is partly explained by a new trend, namely that rapid urban growth is now greatest, in some regions, in the smaller cities. For example, the main expansion in West Bengal is no longer in Calcutta, but in a rash of small cities across the state.

Cities in Danger

As the decade of the 1980s advanced, most industrial countries, alarmed by acid rain and urban smog, took significant steps to limit air pollution. Well into the 1990s, however, these controls proved expensive to install and difficult to enforce, and clean air remains a luxury most developed as well as developing cities must live without.

Those taking part in the United Nations' Global Environment Monitoring System (see right) frequently show dangerous levels of pollutants ranging from soot to sulfur dioxide and photo-chemical smog; air in the majority of cities without such sampling equipment is likely to be at least as bad. Traffic, a major source of air pollution worldwide, loses Thailand's work force 44 working days each year.

Urban Air Pollution

The world's most polluted cities: number of days each year when sulfur dioxide levels exceeded the WHO threshold of 150 micrograms per cubic meter (averaged over 4 to 15 years, 1970s – 1980s)

Sulfur dioxide is the main pollutant associated with industrial cities. According to the World Health Organization, more than seven days in a year above 150 µg per cubic meter bring a serious risk of respiratory disease: at least 600 million people live in urban areas where SO_2 concentrations regularly reach damaging levels.

Manila, Philippines
Calcutta, India
Milan, Italy
Zagreb, Croatia
Guangzhou, China
Madrid, Spain
Beijing, China
Xian, China
Seoul, South Korea
Tehran, Iran
Shenyang, China

120   90   60   30

Urban Housing Needs

Proportion of the population living in squatter settlements and the number of homeless per thousand, for selected cities (1993)

Urbanization in most developing countries has been proceeding so rapidly that local governments have been unable to provide the necessary services and housing. In some cities, many people find their homes in squatter settlements, frequently without power, water and sanitation. Yet these communities are often a dynamic part of the city's economy, while their inhabitants sometimes take all kinds of initiatives, including the setting up of their own local government and self-help associations. Some of the world's richest cities also have a homeless underclass, although calculating the numbers of people involved is problematic. Yet it is the case that homelessness and unemployment are currently affecting an increasing number of people in the developed world.

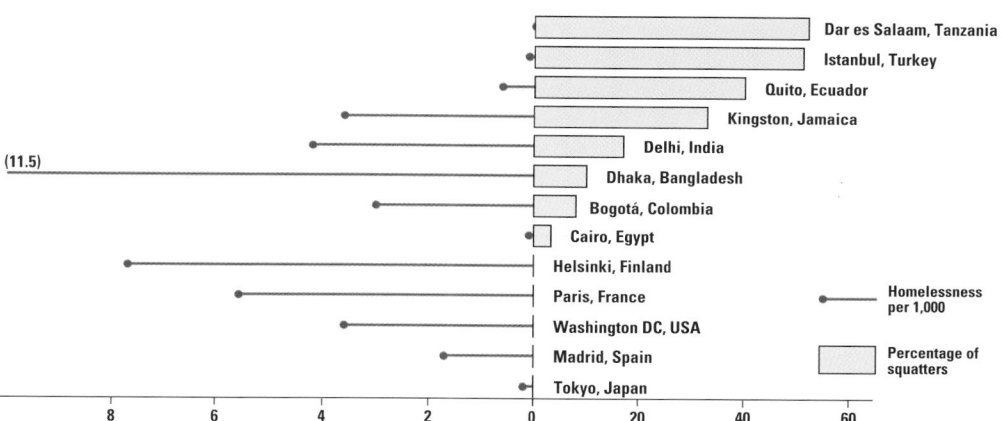

Dar es Salaam, Tanzania
Istanbul, Turkey
Quito, Ecuador
Kingston, Jamaica
Delhi, India
Dhaka, Bangladesh
Bogotá, Colombia
Cairo, Egypt
Helsinki, Finland
Paris, France
Washington DC, USA
Madrid, Spain
Tokyo, Japan

(11.5)

Homelessness per 1,000
Percentage of squatters

8   6   4   2   0   20   40   60

Largest Cities

Early in the 21st century for the first time in history, the majority of the world's population will live in cities. Below is a list of all the cities with more than 10 million inhabitants, based on estimates for the year 2015.

	City	
1.	Tokyo–Yokohama	28.7
2.	Bombay	27.4
3.	Lagos	24.1
4.	Shanghai	23.2
5.	Jakarta	21.5
6.	São Paulo	21.0
7.	Karachi	20.6
8.	Beijing	19.6
9.	Dhaka	19.2
10.	Mexico City	19.1
11.	Calcutta	17.6
12.	Delhi	17.5
13.	New York City	17.4
14.	Tianjin	17.1
15.	Manila	14.9
16.	Cairo	14.7
17.	Los Angeles	14.5
18.	Seoul	13.1
19.	Buenos Aires	12.5
20.	Istanbul	12.1
21.	Rio de Janeiro	11.3
22.	Lahore	10.9
23.	Hyderabad	10.6
24.	Bangkok	10.4
25.	Osaka	10.2
26.	Lima	10.1
27.	Tehran	10.0

City populations are based on urban agglomerations rather than legal city limits. In some cases where two adjacent cities have merged into one concentration, such as Tokyo–Yokohama, they have been regarded as a single unit.

Urban Advantages

Despite overcrowding and poor housing, living standards in the developing world's cities are almost invariably better than in the surrounding countryside. Resources – financial, material and administrative – are concentrated in the towns, which are usually also the centres of political activity and pressure. Governments – frequently unstable, and rarely established on a solid democratic base – are usually more responsive to urban discontent than rural misery.

In many countries, especially in Africa, food prices are kept artificially low, appeasing underemployed urban masses at the expense of agricultural development. The imbalance encourages further cityward migration, helping to account for the astonishing rate of post-1950 urbanization and putting great strain on the ability of many nations to provide even modest improvements for their people.

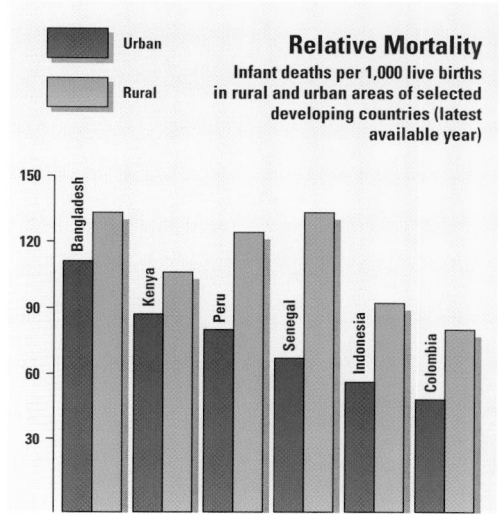

■ Urban ■ Rural
Relative Mortality
Infant deaths per 1,000 live births in rural and urban areas of selected developing countries (latest available year)

Bangladesh · Kenya · Peru · Senegal · Indonesia · Colombia

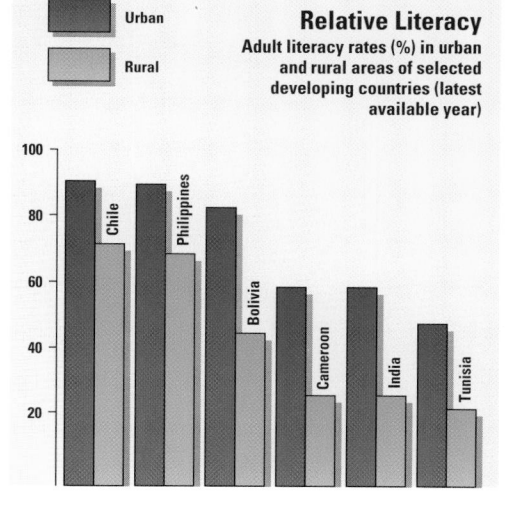

■ Urban ■ Rural
Relative Literacy
Adult literacy rates (%) in urban and rural areas of selected developing countries (latest available year)

Chile · Philippines · Bolivia · Cameroon · India · Tunisia

CARTOGRAPHY BY PHILIP'S. COPYRIGHT GEORGE PHILIP LTD

The Human Family

Racial, language and religious differences have led to appalling acts of inhumanity throughout history. Yet strictly speaking, all human beings belong to one species, *Homo sapiens*, which has no subspecies. The differences between the three racial types which most people identify – namely Caucasoid, Mongoloid and Negroid – reflect not so much evolutionary differences as long periods of separation.

Migration has recently mingled the various groups to an unprecedented extent, and most nations now have some degree of racial mixing. For example, the United States has often been called a melting pot, because of the large numbers of people from various geographical locations which make up the population. The country has no official language but, until recently, English was spoken by the vast majority of the people. But in recent years, some of the immigrants from Mexico, Cuba and other parts of Latin America have not learned English and speak only Spanish. This development disturbs those Americans who believe that the use of English binds the nation together, and several states have passed laws stating that English is their only official language.

Language is fundamental to human culture and any particular language is almost the definition of that particular culture. Because definitions of languages vary, estimates of the total number range from 3,000 to 6,000, although most are spoken by only a few people. The world's languages are grouped into families, the largest of which are the Indo-European and Sino-Tibetan. Chinese, a Sino-Tibetan language, is spoken by more people as a first language than any other. English, an Indo-European tongue, ranks second, but it is the leading international language, because so many people speak it as their second tongue.

Like language, religion encourages cohesion in single human groups and it satisfies a deep human need by assigning people a place in a divinely ordered world. Religion is a way in which a culture can express its individuality. For example, the rise of Islamic fundamentalism in the late 20th century was partly an expression of resentment that secular Western values are being imposed on Muslims.

World Migration

The greatest voluntary migration was the colonization of North America by 30–35 million European settlers during the 19th century. The greatest forced migration involved 9–11 million Africans taken as slaves to America between 1550 and 1860. The migrations shown on the map below are mostly international, as population movements within borders are not usually recorded. Many of the statistics are necessarily estimates as so many refugees and migrant workers enter countries illegally and unrecorded. Emigrants may have a variety of motives for leaving, thus making it difficult to distinguish between voluntary and involuntary migrations.

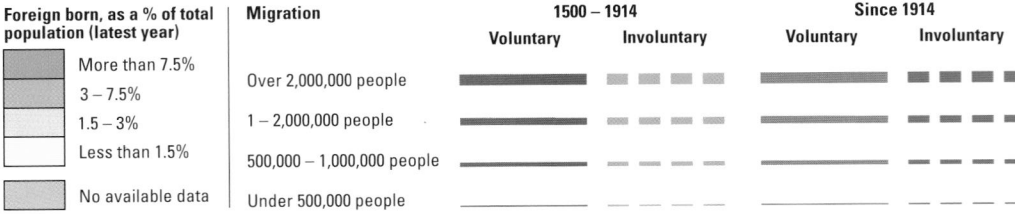

Foreign born, as a % of total population (latest year)
- More than 7.5%
- 3 – 7.5%
- 1.5 – 3%
- Less than 1.5%
- No available data

Migration	1500 – 1914		Since 1914	
	Voluntary	Involuntary	Voluntary	Involuntary
Over 2,000,000 people				
1 – 2,000,000 people				
500,000 – 1,000,000 people				
Under 500,000 people				

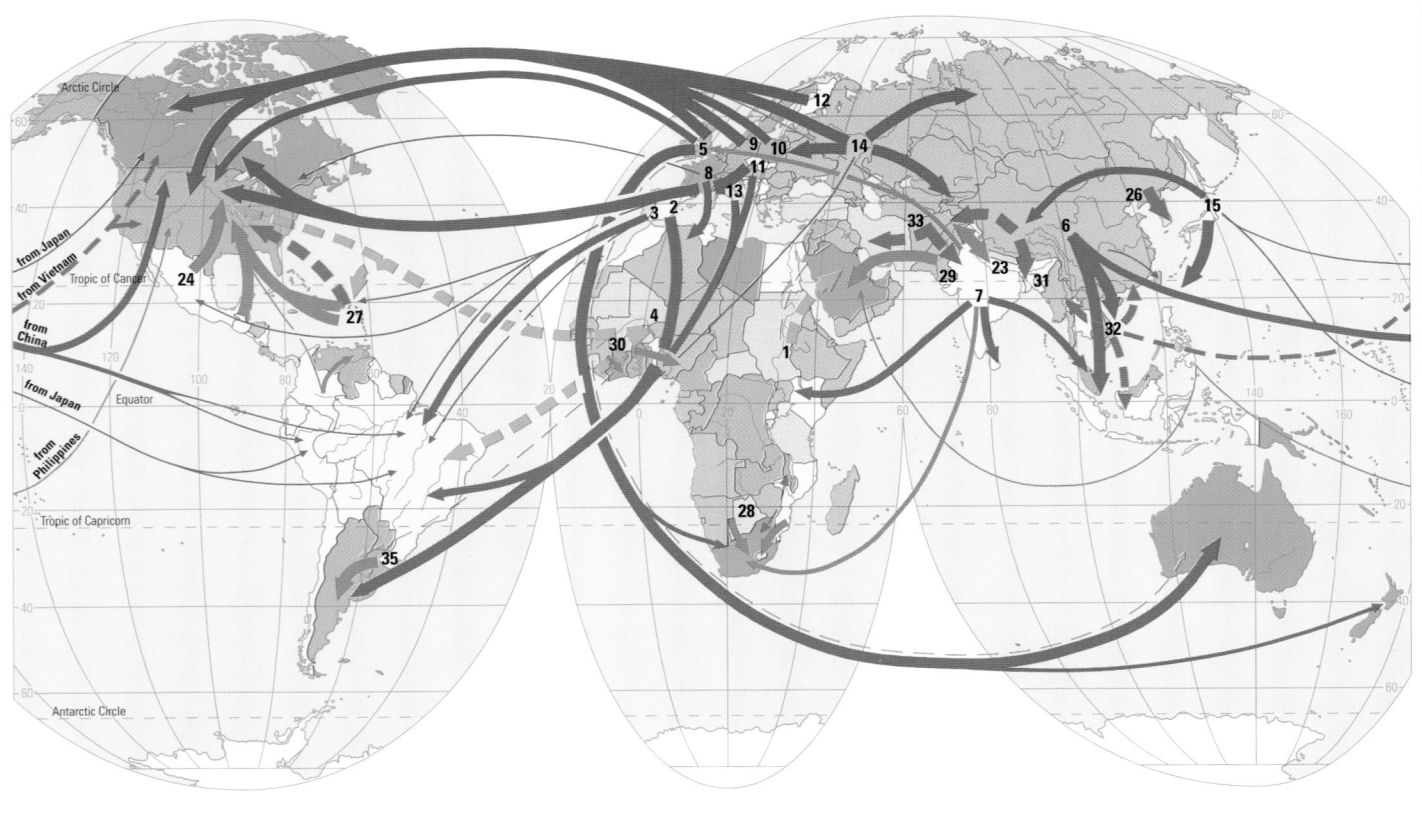

Europe Migrations since 1918

Middle East Migrations since 1945

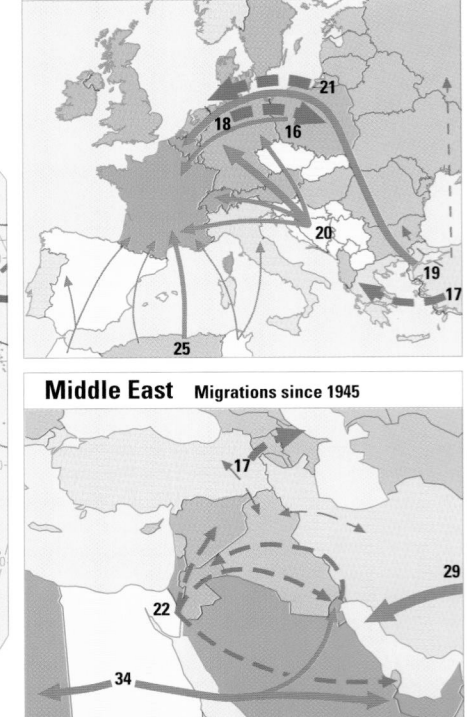

Building the USA

CARTOGRAPHY BY PHILIP'S. COPYRIGHT GEORGE PHILIP LTD

US Immigration 1820–1990

"Give me your tired, your poor / Your huddled masses yearning to breathe free...."

So starts Emma Lazarus's poem "The New Colossus," inscribed on the Statue of Liberty. For decades the USA was the magnet that attracted millions of immigrants, notably from Central and Eastern Europe, the flow peaking in the early years of the 20th century. By the mid-1990s the proportion of immigrants had increased again to pre-World War II rates. In 1993/4, net immigration accounted for 30% of US population growth. Of the 904,000 immigrants, 40% were from Asia and 31% from Central America and the Caribbean.

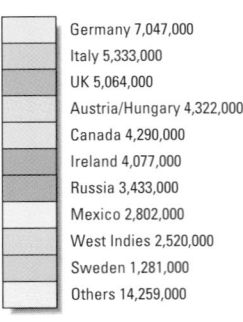

- Germany 7,047,000
- Italy 5,333,000
- UK 5,064,000
- Austria/Hungary 4,322,000
- Canada 4,290,000
- Ireland 4,077,000
- Russia 3,433,000
- Mexico 2,802,000
- West Indies 2,520,000
- Sweden 1,281,000
- Others 14,259,000

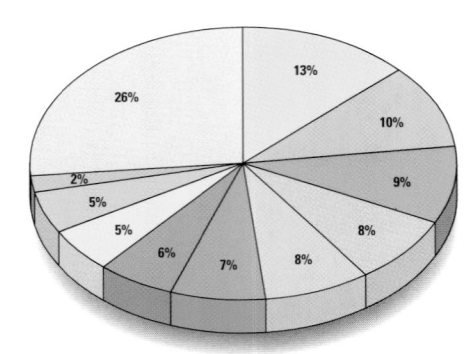

Major world migrations since 1500 (over 1,000,000 people)

1. North and East African slaves to Arabia (4.3m)..........1500–1900
2. Spanish to South and Central America (2.3m)...........1530–1914
3. Portuguese to Brazil (1.4m)...........................1530–1914
4. West African slaves to South America (4.6m)...........1550–1860
   to Caribbean (4m)...........1580–1860
   to North/Central America (1m)......1650–1820
5. British and Irish to North America (13.5m)..............1620–1914
   to Australasia and
   South Africa (3m)..................1790–1914
6. Chinese to South-east Asia (22m)....................1820–1914
   to North America (1m)...............1880–1914
7. Indian migrant workers (3m)...........................1850–1914
8. French to North Africa (1.5m)..........................1850–1914
9. Germans to North America (5m)........................1850–1914
10. Poles to North America (3.6m).........................1850–1914
11. Austro-Hungarians to North America (3.2m)...........1850–1914
    to Western Europe (3.4m)...........1850–1914
    to South America (1.8m)............1850–1914
12. Scandinavians to North America (2.7m)...............1850–1914
13. Italians to North America (5m)........................1860–1914
    to South America (3.7m)...........1860–1914
14. Russians to North America (2.2m)....................1880–1914
    to Western Europe (2.2m)..........1880–1914
    to Siberia (6m)....................1880–1914
    to Central Asia (4m)...............1880–1914
15. Japanese to Eastern Asia, Southeast Asia
    and America (8m)..........................1900–1914
16. Poles to Western Europe (1m)........................1920–1940
17. Greeks and Armenians from Turkey (1.6m)............1922–1923
18. European Jews to extermination camps (5m)..........1940–1944
19. Turks to Western Europe (1.9m) 1940–
20. Yugoslavs to Western Europe (2m)...................1940–
21. Germans to Western Europe (9.8m) 1945–1947
22. Palestinian refugees (2m)............................1947–
23. Indian and Pakistani refugees (15m)...................1947
24. Mexicans to North America (9m).....................1950–
25. North Africans to Western Europe (1.1m) 1950–
26. Korean refugees (5m)............................1950–1954
27. Latin Americans and West Indians to
    North America (4.7m)....................1960–
28. Migrant workers to South Africa (1.5m) 1960–
29. Indians and Pakistanis to The Gulf (2.4m)...........1970–
30. Migrant workers to Nigeria and Ivory Coast (3m)......1970–
31. Bangladeshi and Pakistani refugees (2m).............1972
32. Vietnamese and Cambodian refugees (1.5m).........1975–
33. Afghan refugees (6.1m)............................1979–
34. Egyptians to The Gulf and Libya (2.9m) 1980–
35. Migrant workers to Argentina (2m) 1980–
36. Mozambique refugees (1.7m) 1985–
37. Yugoslav/Balkan refugees (1.7m) 1992–
38. Rwanda/Burundi refugees (2.6m) 1994–

Predominant Languages

INDO-EUROPEAN FAMILY

1	Balto-Slavic group (incl. Russian, Ukrainian)
2	Germanic group (incl. English, German)
3	Celtic group
4	Greek
5	Albanian
6	Iranian group
7	Armenian
8	Romance group (incl. Spanish, Portuguese, French, Italian)
9	Indo-Aryan group (incl. Hindi, Bengali, Urdu, Punjabi, Marathi)
10	**CAUCASIAN FAMILY**

AFRO-ASIATIC FAMILY

11	Semitic group (incl. Arabic)
12	Kushitic group
13	Berber group
14	**KHOISAN FAMILY**
15	**NIGER-CONGO FAMILY**
16	**NILO-SAHARAN FAMILY**
17	**URALIC FAMILY**

ALTAIC FAMILY

18	Turkic group
19	Mongolian group
20	Tungus-Manchu group
21	Japanese and Korean

SINO-TIBETAN FAMILY

22	Sinitic (Chinese) languages
23	Tibetic-Burmic languages
24	**TAI FAMILY**

AUSTRO-ASIATIC FAMILY

25	Mon-Khmer group
26	Munda group
27	Vietnamese
28	**DRAVIDIAN FAMILY** (incl. Telugu, Tamil)
29	**AUSTRONESIAN FAMILY** (incl. Malay-Indonesian)
30	**OTHER LANGUAGES**

Official Languages

Language	Total population	World %
English	1,400m	27.0%
Chinese	1,070m	19.1%
Hindi	700m	13.5%
Spanish	280m	5.4%
Russian	270m	5.2%
French	220m	4.2%
Arabic	170m	3.3%
Portuguese	160m	3.0%
Malay	160m	3.0%
Bengali	150m	2.9%
Japanese	120m	2.3%

Languages form a kind of tree of development, splitting from a few ancient proto-tongues into branches that have grown apart and further divided with the passage of time. English and Hindi, for example, both belong to the great Indo-European family, although the relationship is only apparent after much analysis and comparison with non-Indo-European languages such as Chinese or Arabic; Hindi is part of the Indo-Aryan subgroup, whereas English is a member of Indo-European's Germanic branch; French, another Indo-European tongue, traces its descent through the Latin, or Romance, branch. A few languages – Basque is one example – have no apparent links with any other, living or dead. Most modern languages, of course, have acquired enormous quantities of vocabulary from each other.

Distribution of Living Languages

The figures refer to the number of languages currently in use in the regions shown.

- Europe 209
- Americas 949
- Asia 2,034
- Pacific 1,341
- Africa 1,995

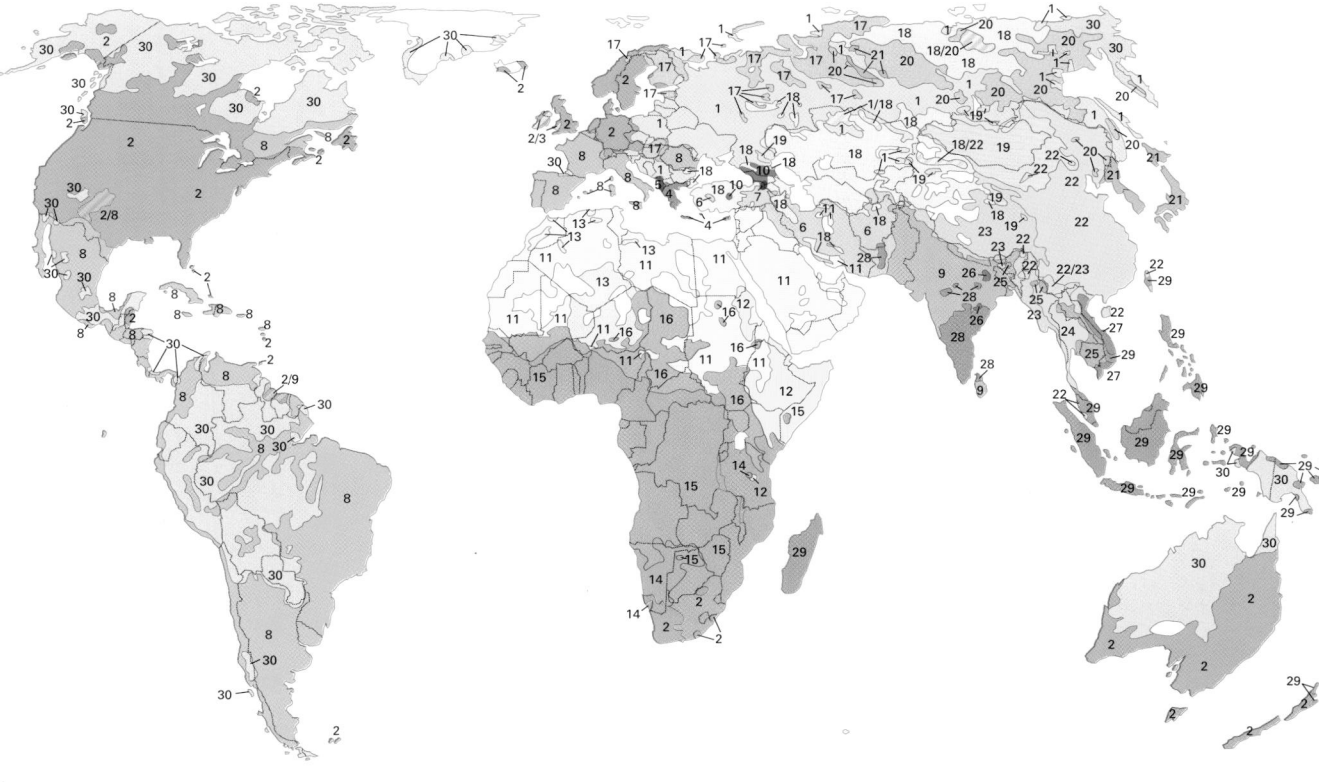

Predominant Religions

- ▲ Roman Catholicism
- Orthodox and other Eastern Churches
- • Protestantism
- Sunni Islam
- Shia Islam
- Buddhism
- Hinduism
- Confucianism
- ✶ Judaism
- Shintoism
- Tribal Religions

Religions are not as easily mapped as the physical contours of the land. Divisions are often blurred and frequently overlapping: most nations include people of many different faiths – or no faith at all. Some religions, like Islam and Christianity, have proselytes worldwide; others, like Hinduism and Confucianism, are restricted to a particular area, though modern migrations have taken some Indians and Chinese very far from their cultural origins. It is also difficult to show the degree to which religion controls daily life: Christian Western Europe, for example, is now far less dominated by its religion than are the Islamic nations of the Middle East. Similarly, figures for the major faiths' adherents make no distinction between nominal believers enrolled at birth and those for whom religion is a vital part of existence.

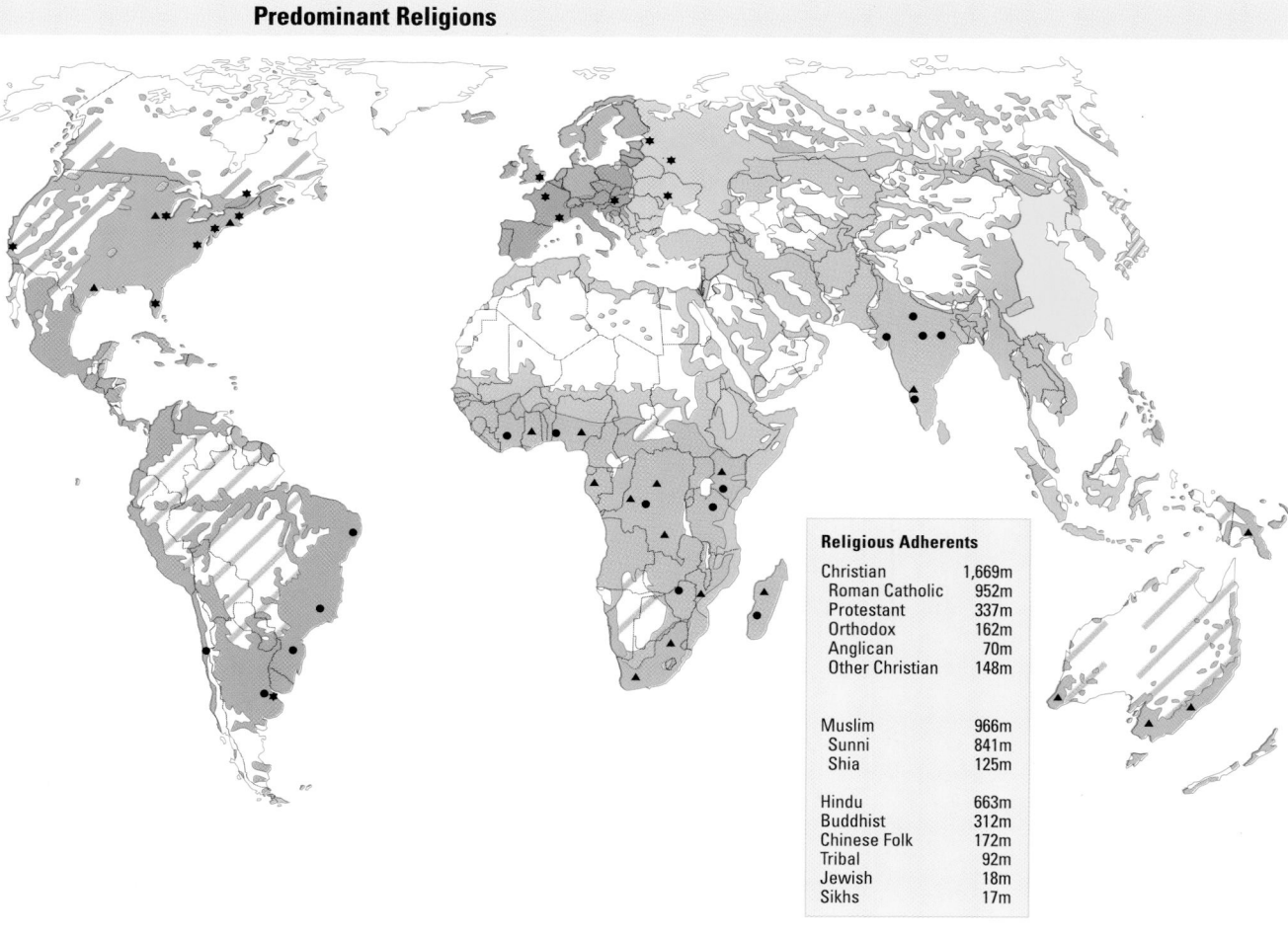

Religious Adherents

Christian	1,669m
Roman Catholic	952m
Protestant	337m
Orthodox	162m
Anglican	70m
Other Christian	148m
Muslim	966m
Sunni	841m
Shia	125m
Hindu	663m
Buddhist	312m
Chinese Folk	172m
Tribal	92m
Jewish	18m
Sikhs	17m

CARTOGRAPHY BY PHILIP'S. COPYRIGHT GEORGE PHILIP LTD

Conflict and Cooperation

For more information:
28 Migration
29 Religion

The 20th century witnessed two world wars, followed by a Cold War which several times threatened to erupt into a third world war, fought with nuclear weapons. The Cold War was marked by a great number of conflicts. Some were colonial wars, as the empires of the first half of the century fell apart, some were border wars, and some were civil wars. All the wars have caused great suffering among civilians, many of whom were forced to join the ranks of the world's refugees.

In the late 1980s, many people hoped that the end of the Cold War, following the collapse of Communist regimes in the former Soviet Union and Eastern Europe, would herald a new era of international stability. Instead, old ethnic and religious antagonisms surfaced in many areas, leading to civil war in such places as Chechenia, in Russia, and the former Yugoslavia. Nationalist rivalries, suppressed under Communist rule, replaced ideological factors as the major cause of conflict.

War is a very human activity, with no real equivalent in any other species. Yet humans also function well when they cooperate. Evolution has made this so. Hunter-gatherers in cooperative bands were far more effective than animals that prowled. Agriculture, urbanization and industrialization all depend on the ability of humans to cooperate.

The creation of the United Nations in 1945 held out hope that the world's nations, tired of war, would have the means to control humanity's aggressive instincts. Although the UN lacks the power to halt conflicts, it has often helped to achieve negotiation. Economic pressures have led to another kind of cooperation, the creation of common markets and economic unions, such as ASEAN in Southeast Asia, the European Union and NAFTA in North America.

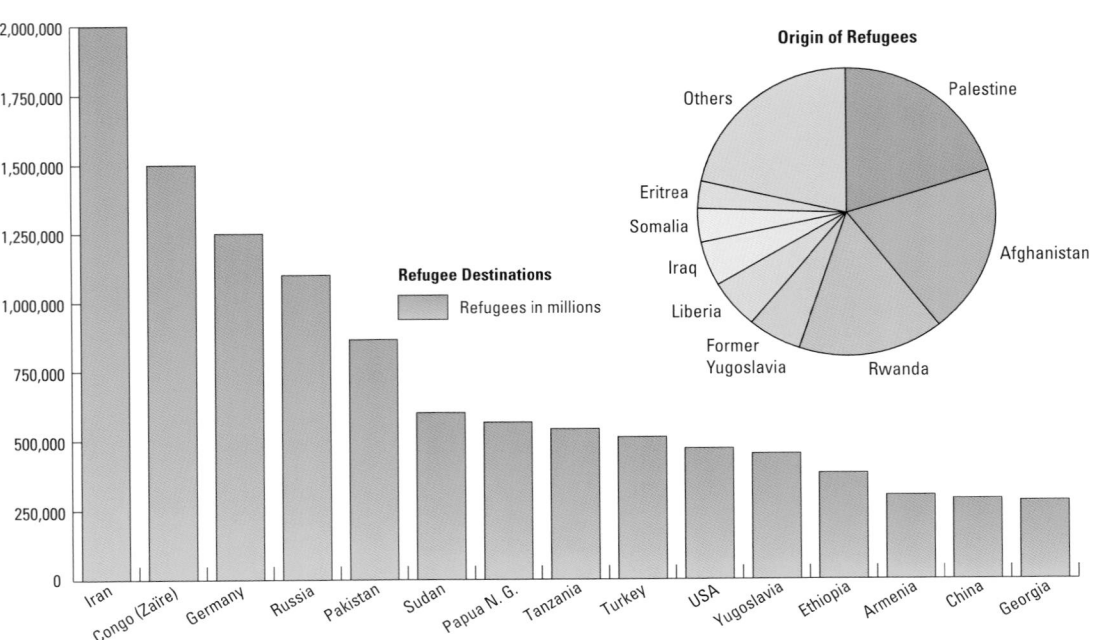

The World's Refugees

Refugees by host nation (bar chart, left) and by nation of origin (pie chart, left) (1995). The source is the United Nations High Commission for Refugees (UNHCR). The 3.2 million Palestinian refugees living in Jordan, Syria, Lebanon, Gaza and the West Bank fall under the mandate of United Nations Relief and Works Agency (UNRWA) and are not included on the bar chart.

The pie chart shows the origins of the world's refugees, while the bar chart below shows their destinations. According to the United Nations High Commission for Refugees (UNHCR) in 1995 there were 14.5 million refugees. However, the UNHCR definition of a refugee, "a person who has left or remains outside their own country because they have a well-founded fear of persecution, or because their safety is threatened by events seriously disturbing public order," does not include people who are in a refugee-like situation but who have not been formally recognized. In 1995, there were a further 3.5 million of these people worldwide and a further 4.5 million people who were internally displaced.

All but a few who cross international boundaries seek asylum in neighboring countries, which are often the least equipped to deal with them. Lacking any rights or power, they frequently become an unwelcome burden to their hosts. Usually, the best any refugee can hope for is rudimentary food and shelter in temporary camps. Many Palestinians have been forced to live in camps since 1948.

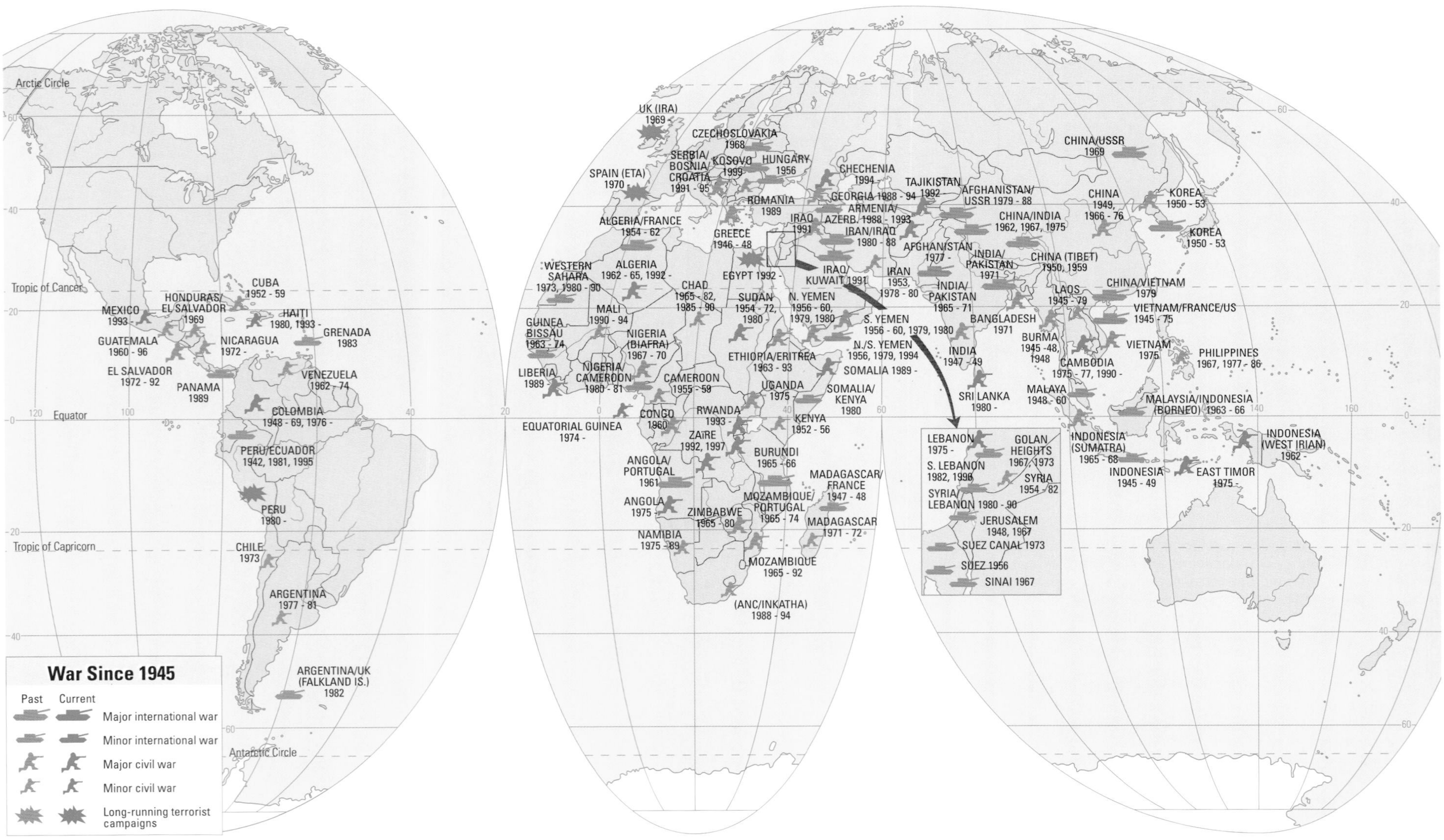

War Since 1945

Past	Current	
		Major international war
		Minor international war
		Major civil war
		Minor civil war
		Long-running terrorist campaigns

CARTOGRAPHY BY PHILIP'S. COPYRIGHT GEORGE PHILIP LTD

United Nations

The United Nations Organization was born as World War II drew to its conclusion. Six years of strife had strengthened the world's desire for peace, but an effective international organization was needed to help achieve it. That body would replace the League of Nations which, since its inception in 1920, had failed to curb the aggression of at least some of its member nations. At the United Nations Conference on International Organization held in San Francisco, the United Nations Charter was drawn up. Ratified by the Security Council and signed by the 51 original members, it came into effect on October 24, 1945.

The Charter set out the aims of the organization: to maintain peace and security, and develop friendly relations between nations; to achieve international cooperation in solving economic, social, cultural and humanitarian problems; to promote respect for human rights and fundamental freedoms; and to harmonize the activities of nations in order to achieve these common goals.

The United Nations has five principal organs :

The General Assembly
The forum at which member nations discuss moral and political issues affecting world development, peace and security meets annually in September, under a newly-elected President whose tenure lasts one year. Any member can bring business to the agenda, and each member nation has one vote.

The Security Council
A legislative and executive body, the Security Council is the primary instrument for establishing and maintaining international peace by attempting to settle disputes between nations. It has the power to dispatch UN forces, and member nations undertake to provide armed forces, assistance and facilities. The Security Council has ten temporary members elected by the General Assembly for two-year terms, and five permanent members – China, France, Russia, UK and USA.

The Economic and Social Council
By far the largest United Nations executive, the Council operates as a conduit between the General Assembly and the many United Nations agencies it instructs to implement Assembly decisions, and whose work it coordinates. The Council also commissions studies on economic conditions, collects data and makes recommendations to the Assembly.

The Secretariat
This is the staff of the United Nations, and its task is to administer the policies and programs of the UN and its organs, and assist and advise the Head of the Secretariat, the Secretary-General – a full-time, non-political appointment made by the General Assembly.

The Trusteeship Council
This no longer administers any of the original 11 trust territories as they are all now independent.

The International Court of Justice (the World Court)
The World Court is the judicial organ of the United Nations. It deals only with United Nations disputes and all members are subject to its jurisdiction. There are 15 judges, elected for nine-year terms by the General Assembly and the Security Council.

The social and humanitarian operations of the UN include:

United Nations Development Program (UNDP) Plans and funds projects to help developing countries make better use of their resources.

United Nations International Childrens' Fund (UNICEF) Created at the General Assembly's first session in 1945 to help children in the aftermath of World War II, it now provides basic health care and aid worldwide.

Food and Agriculture Organization (FAO) Aims to raise living standards and nutrition levels in rural areas by improving food production and distribution.

United Nations Educational, Scientific and Cultural Organization (UNESCO) Promotes international cooperation through broader and better education.

World Health Organization (WHO) Promotes and provides for better health care, public and environmental health and medical research.

United Nations agencies are involved in many aspects of international trade, safety and security:

International Maritime Organization (IMO) Promotes unity amongst merchant shipping, especially in regard to safety, marine pollution and standardization.

International Labor Organization (ILO) Seeks to improve labor conditions and promote productive employment to raise living standards.

World Meteorological Organization (WMO) Promotes cooperation in weather observation, reporting and forecasting.

World Trade Organization (WTO) On January 1, 1995, the WTO replaced GATT. It advocates a common code of conduct and its aim is the liberalization of world trade.

Disarmament Commission Considers and makes recommendations to the General Assembly on disarmament issues.

International Atomic Energy Agency (IAEA) Fosters development of peaceful uses for nuclear energy and establishes safety standards.

The World Bank comprises three United Nations agencies:

International Monetary Fund (IMF) Cultivates international monetary cooperation and expansion of trade.

International Bank for Reconstruction and Development (IBRD) Provides funds and technical assistance to developing countries.

International Finance Corporation (IFC) Encourages the growth of productive private enterprise in less developed countries.

Membership There are four independent states which are not members of the UN – Switzerland, Taiwan, Tuvalu and Vatican City. Official languages are Chinese, English, French, Russian, Spanish and Arabic.

Funding The UN budget for 1996–97 was US $2.6 billion. Contributions are assessed by the members' ability to pay, with the maximum 25% of the total, the minimum 0.01%.

Peacekeeping The UN has been involved in 43 peacekeeping operations worldwide since 1948. At the end of 1996 there were 16 areas of UN patrol and 25,649 "blue berets."

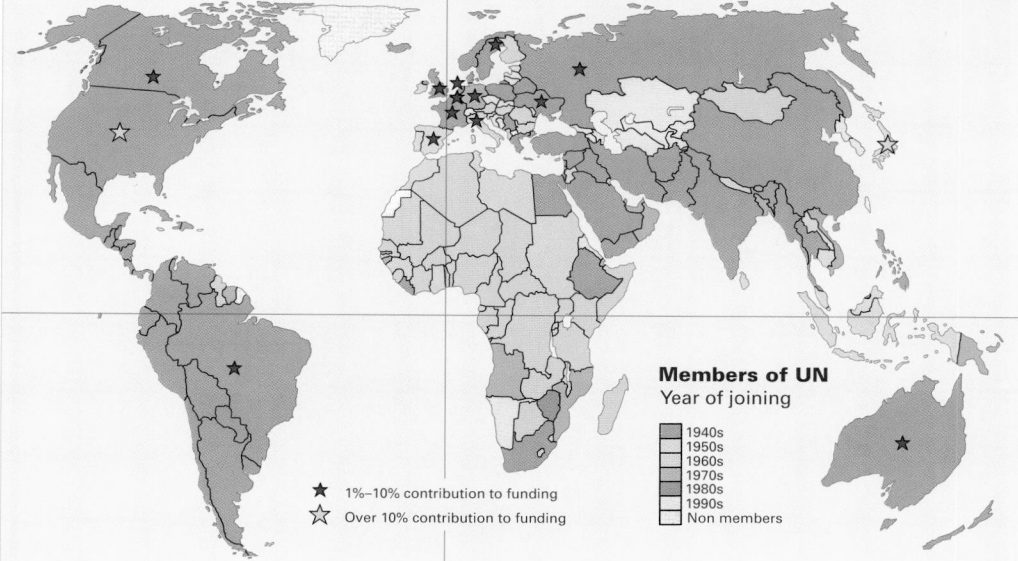

Members of UN
Year of joining

- 1940s
- 1950s
- 1960s
- 1970s
- 1980s
- 1990s
- Non members

★ 1%–10% contribution to funding
☆ Over 10% contribution to funding

Military Spending

Military expenditure as a % of GNP or GDP, ranked selection of countries (1994)

#	Country	%	#	Country	%
1.	Iraq	74.9%	14.	Jordan	7.5%
2.	North Korea	26.3%	15.	Laos	7.4%
3.	Angola	23.9%	16.	Pakistan	6.0%
4.	Oman	18.1%	17.	UAE	5.7%
5.	Syria	17.9%	18.	Seychelles	5.6%
6.	Sudan	17.1%	19.	Sierra Leone	4.9%
7.	Saudi Arabia	14.2%	20.	Taiwan	4.8%
8.	Yemen	14.1%	21.	Liberia	4.8%
9.	Russia	12.4%	22.	Singapore	4.5%
10.	Kuwait	11.1%	23.	Sri Lanka	4.5%
11.	Mozambique	8.7%	24.	USA	4.3%
12.	Israel	8.6%	25.	Malaysia	4.2%
13.	Rwanda	7.6%			

It is worth noting that the total amount of expenditure varies considerably depending on the size of the economy, so that although the percentages show the importance given to military spending within each country, they give no idea as to the total expenditure. In 1997, for example, the USA spent a total of US $271 billion, Russia US $70 billion, and the UK US $36 billion. In 1993, the USA also provided the most military assistance worldwide, providing US $3.4 billion, compared to a total of US $0.9 billion from Western Europe.

The period 1987–94 saw a decline in global military spending which generated what the United Nations Development Program term a "peace dividend" of US $935 billion. Unfortunately, there is no clear link between reduced military spending and enhanced expenditure on human development. Moreover, the poorest regions of the world (notably sub-Saharan Africa) failed to contain their military spending and, in some cases, it increased.

International Organizations

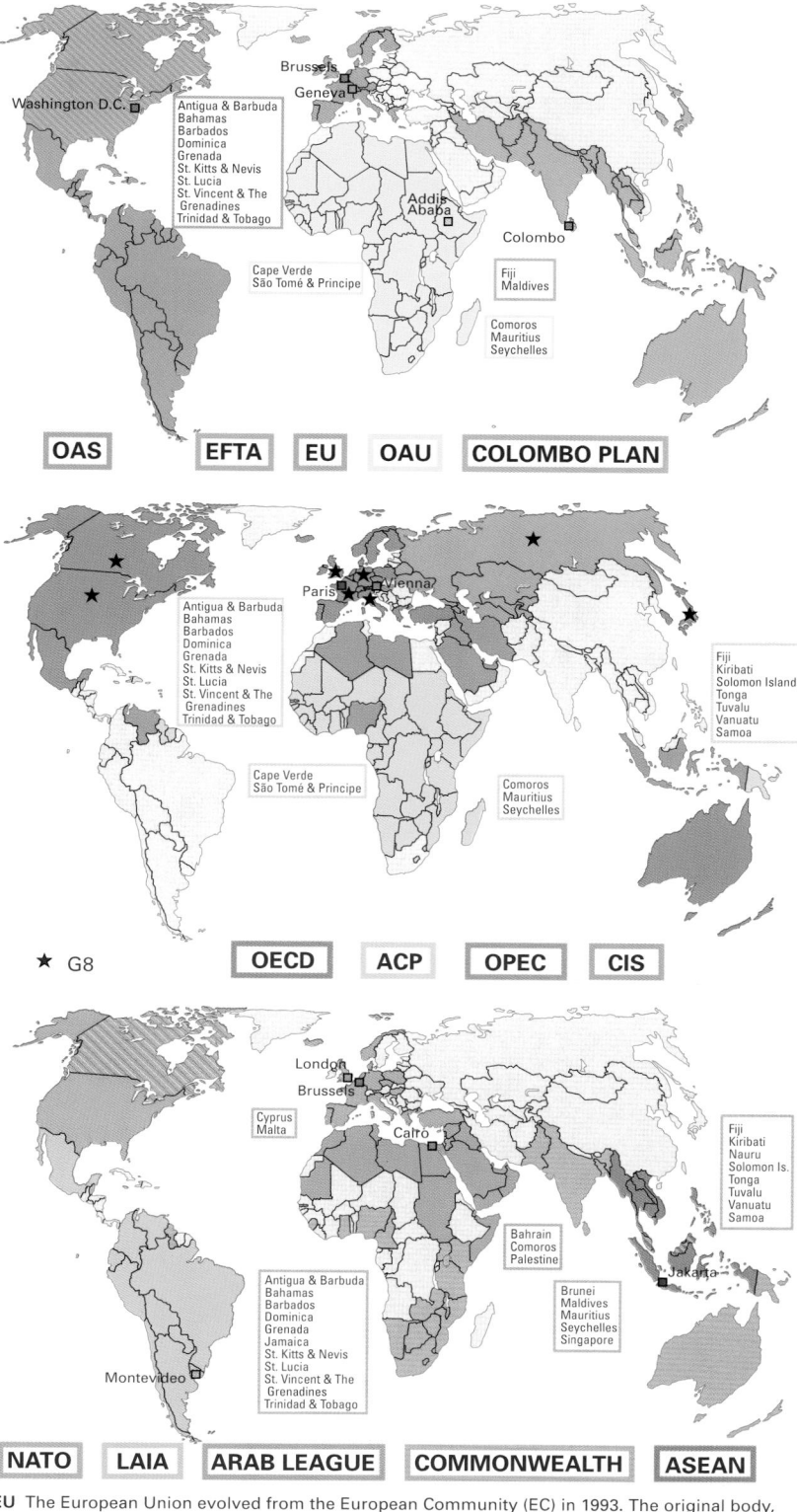

OAS   EFTA   EU   OAU   COLOMBO PLAN

★ G8

OECD   ACP   OPEC   CIS

NATO   LAIA   ARAB LEAGUE   COMMONWEALTH   ASEAN

EU The European Union evolved from the European Community (EC) in 1993. The original body, the European Coal and Steel Community (ECSC), was created in 1951 following the signing of the Treaty of Paris. The 15 members of the EU – Austria, Belgium, Denmark, Finland, France, Germany, Greece, Ireland, Italy, Luxembourg, Netherlands, Portugal, Spain, Sweden and the UK – aim to integrate economies, coordinate social developments and bring about political union. These members, of what is now the world's biggest market, share agricultural and industrial policies and tariffs on trade.

EFTA European Free Trade Association (formed in 1960). Portugal left the original "Seven" in 1989 to join what was then the EC, followed by Austria, Finland and Sweden in 1995. There are now only four members: Iceland, Liechtenstein, Norway, and Switzerland.

ACP African-Caribbean-Pacific (formed in 1963). Members enjoy economic ties with the EU.

NATO North Atlantic Treaty Organization (formed in 1949). It continues despite the winding up of the Warsaw Pact in 1991. The Czech Rep., Hungary and Poland were the latest to join in 1999.

OAS Organization of American States (formed in 1948). It aims to promote social and economic cooperation between countries in the developed North America and developing Latin America.

ASEAN Association of Southeast Asian Nations (formed in 1967). Cambodia joined in 1999.

OAU Organization of African Unity (1963). Its 53 members represent over 94% of Africa's population. Arabic, English, French, and Portuguese are recognized as working languages.

LAIA The Latin American Integration Association (formed in 1980) superceded the Latin American Free Trade Association formed in 1961. Its aim is to promote freer regional trade.

OECD Organization for Economic Cooperation and Development (formed in 1961). It comprises 29 major free-market economies. The "G8" is its "inner group" of leading industrial nations, comprising Canada, France, Germany, Italy, Japan, Russia, UK and the USA.

COMMONWEALTH The Commonwealth of Nations evolved from the British Empire; it comprises 16 nations recognizing the British monarch as head of state, 32 republics and 5 indigenous monarchies, giving a total of 53. Nigeria was suspended in 1995.

CIS The Commonwealth of Independent States (formed in 1991) comprises the countries of the former Soviet Union except for Estonia, Latvia and Lithuania.

OPEC Organization of Petroleum Exporting Countries (formed in 1960). It controls about three-quarters of the world's oil supply. Gabon formally withdrew from OPEC in August 1996.

ARAB LEAGUE (1945) Aims to promote economic, social, political and military cooperation.

COLOMBO PLAN (formed in 1951) Its 26 members aim to promote economic and social development in Asia and the Pacific.

Agriculture

Bad harvests in 1995 caused a drop in world grain reserves to a 20-year low. This revived the ongoing debate as to whether the population explosion will cause major food crises in the 21st century.

Experts estimate that 3.3 billion tons of cereals will be needed to feed the world's population in 25 years' time, as compared with 2 billion tons at present. To expand food production to this extent, some argue, will place great strain on the environment. One suggestion to alleviate the situation is that people in developed countries should eat less meat. This would release more grain, which is used as cattle fodder, to feed people.

Other experts argue that there should be no food crises. World grain production tripled between 1950 and 1990, largely as a result of the Green Revolution, during which genetically improved, high-yield varieties of maize, rice and wheat, the world's three leading staple crops, were developed. These new varieties have helped many developing countries to achieve food surpluses and prevent widespread starvation.

The only region of the world which seems likely to suffer food shortages in the 21st century is sub-Saharan Africa, where in the late 1990s the average daily calorie intake was 6% less than what was needed and where the population is expected to double in 20 years. Improved land management and a huge increase in global trade, especially in food distribution, is necessary if sub-Saharan Africans are not to go hungry.

The development of agriculture more than 10,000 years ago transformed human existence more than any other major advance. By supporting larger populations, it led to the growth of early civilizations and later it sustained people in the industrial cities which sprang up in the 19th century.

Today, agricultural production varies a great deal between the developed world, where it is highly mechanized and employs few people, such as 3% of the workforce in the United States, and the developing world, such as sub-Saharan Africa, where it employs 66% of the workforce. Many Africans are engaged in subsistence farming, providing the basic needs of their families but not contributing to the national economy. Much of Africa also suffers from economic mismanagement, as well as civil war and banditry.

Political problems have also affected food production in other parts of the world. The former USSR had much excellent farmland, but the failure of the collectives and state farms to maintain sufficiently high levels of production helped to bring about the collapse of Communism.

Farmers are under great pressure not only to maintain high levels of production but to increase them. However, the cultivation of marginal areas is one of the prime causes of soil erosion and desertification.

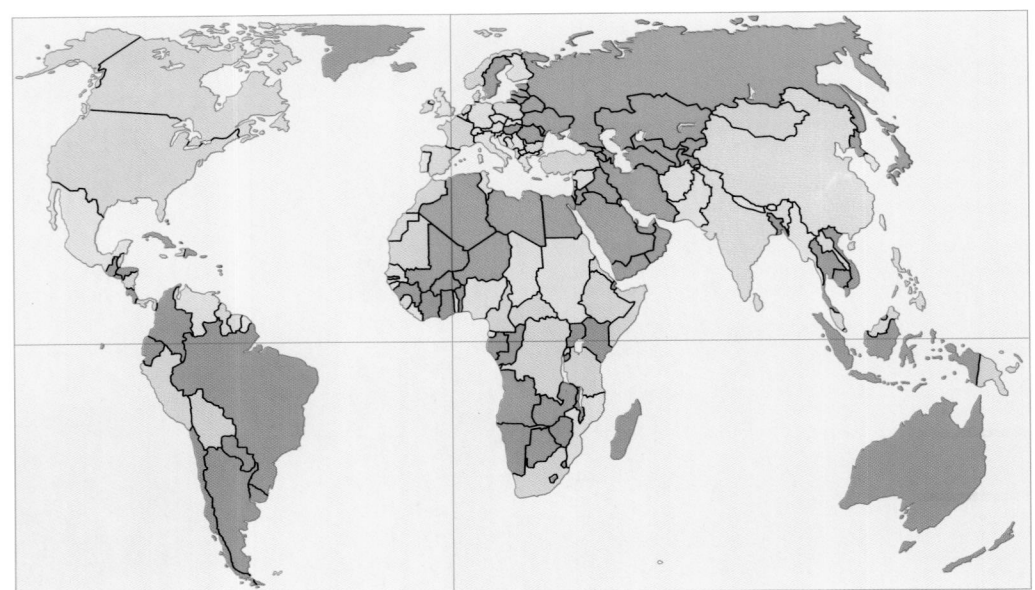

Self-sufficiency in Food

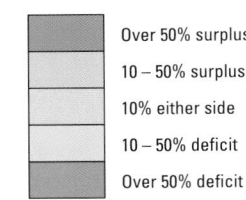

Balance of trade in food products as a percentage of total trade in food products – S.I.T.C. Classes 0, 1 and 4 (latest available year)

Over 50% surplus
10 – 50% surplus
10% either side
10 – 50% deficit
Over 50% deficit

Most self-sufficient		Least self-sufficient	
Argentina	95%	Algeria	−98%
Zimbabwe	87%	Djibouti	−97%
Honduras	81%	Yemen	−95%
Malawi	81%	Zambia	−95%
Costa Rica	79%	Japan	−91%
Iceland	78%	Gabon	−90%
Chile	75%	Kuwait	−90%
Uruguay	75%	Brunei	−89%
Ecuador	74%	Burkina Faso	−82%

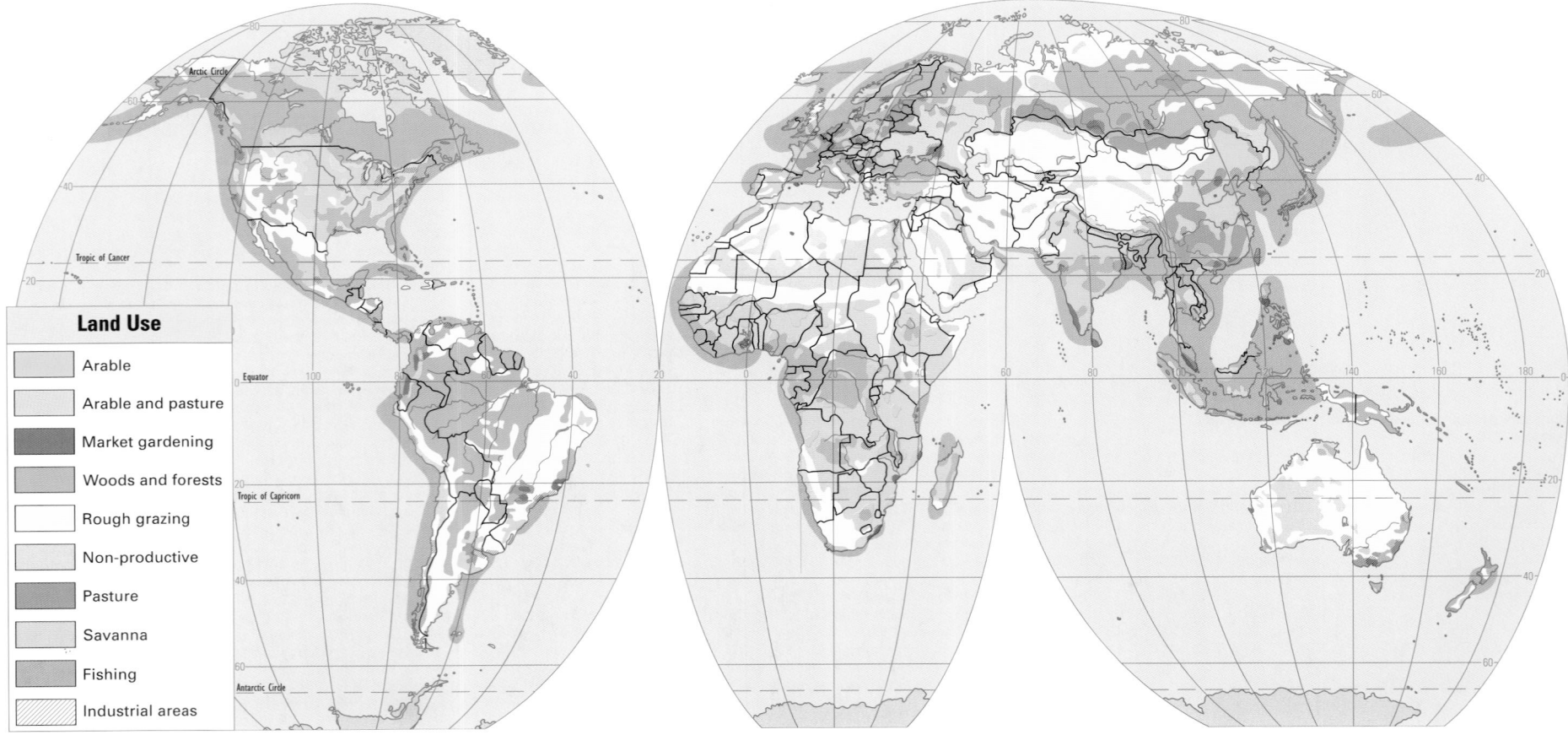

Land Use

Arable
Arable and pasture
Market gardening
Woods and forests
Rough grazing
Non-productive
Pasture
Savanna
Fishing
Industrial areas

CARTOGRAPHY BY PHILIP'S. COPYRIGHT GEORGE PHILIP LTD

Staple Crops

Wheat: Grown in a range of climates, with most varieties – including the highest-quality bread wheats – requiring temperate conditions. Mainly used in baking, it is also used for pasta and breakfast cereals.

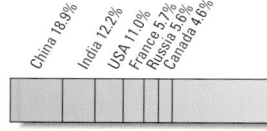

World total (1996): 584,874,000 tons

Maize: Originating in the New World and still an important human food in Africa and Latin America, in the developed world it is processed into breakfast cereals, oil, starches and adhesives. It is also used for animal feed.

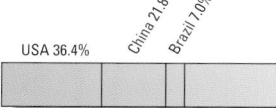

World total (1996): 576,821,000 tons

Oats: Most widely used to feed livestock, but eaten by humans as oatmeal or porridge. Oats have a beneficial effect on the cardiovascular system, and human consumption is likely to increase.

World total (1996): 28,794,000 tons

Millet: The name covers a number of small-grained cereals, members of the grass family with a short growing season. Used to produce flour, meal and animal feed, and fermented to make beer, especially in Africa.

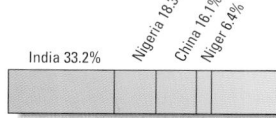

World total (1996): 29,563,000 tons

Sugars

Sugarcane: Confined to tropical regions, cane sugar accounts for the bulk of international trade in sugar. Most is produced as a foodstuff, but some countries, notably Brazil and South Africa, distill sugarcane to make motor fuels.

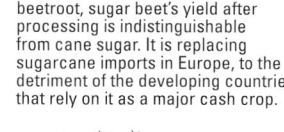

World total (1996): 1,192,555,000 tons

Cereals are grasses with starchy, edible seeds; every important civilization has depended on them as a source of food. The major cereal grains contain about 10% protein and 75% carbohydrate. Grain contributes more than any other group of foods to the energy and protein content of human diet. Starchy tuber crops or root crops are second in importance after cereals as staple foods; easily cultivated, they provide high yields for little effort.

Rice: Thrives on the high humidity and temperatures of the Far East, where it is the traditional staple food of half the human race. Usually grown standing in water, rice responds well to continuous cultivation, with three or four crops annually.

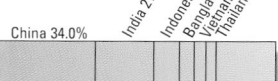

World total (1996): 562,259,000 tons

Potatoes: The most important of the edible tubers, potatoes grow in well-watered, temperate areas. Weight for weight less nutritious than grain, they are a human staple as well as an important animal feed.

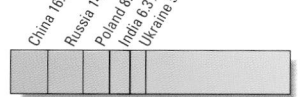

World total (1996): 294,834,000 tons

Soya: Beans from soya bushes are very high (30–40%) in protein. Most are processed into oil and proprietary protein foods. Consumption since 1950 has tripled, mainly due to the health-conscious developed world.

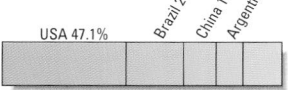

World total (1996): 130,302,000 tons

Cassava: A tropical shrub that needs high rainfall (over 125 inches annually) and a 10–30 month growing season to produce its large, edible tubers. Used as flour by humans, as cattle feed and in industrial starches.

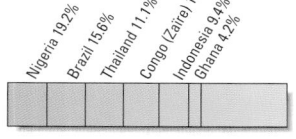

World total (1996): 162,942,000 tons

Sugar beet: Closely related to the beetroot, sugar beet's yield after processing is indistinguishable from cane sugar. It is replacing sugarcane imports in Europe, to the detriment of the developing countries that rely on it as a major cash crop.

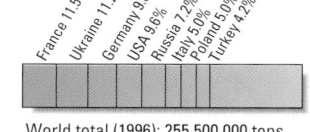

World total (1996): 255,500,000 tons

Food and Population

Comparison of food production and population by continent.

The left column indicates the % of world food production and the right shows population in proportion.

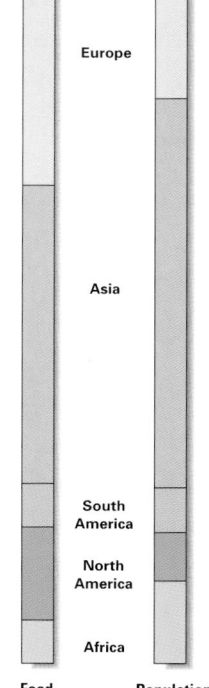

Agricultural Population

Percentage of the total population dependent on agriculture for their livelihood (1997)

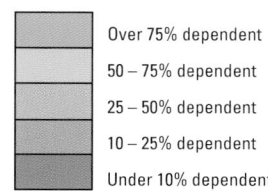
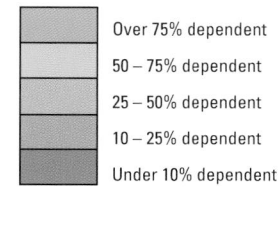

- Over 75% dependent
- 50 – 75% dependent
- 25 – 50% dependent
- 10 – 25% dependent
- Under 10% dependent

Top 5 countries (1997)		Bottom 5 countries (1997)	
Bhutan	94%	Singapore	0.2%
Nepal	93%	Kuwait	1.0%
Burkina Faso	92%	Brunei	1.0%
Rwanda	91%	Bahrain	1.3%
Burundi	91%	Qatar	1.7%

Animal Products

Traditionally, food animals subsisted on land unsuitable for cultivation, supporting agricultural production with their fertilizing dung. But free-ranging animals grow slowly and yield less meat than those more intensively reared; the demands of urban markets in the developed world have encouraged the growth of factory-like production methods. A large proportion of staple crops, especially cereals, are fed to animals, an inefficient way to produce protein but one likely to continue as long as people value meat and dairy products in their diet.

Cheese: Least perishable of all dairy products, cheese is milk fermented with selected bacterial strains to produce a foodstuff with a potentially immense range of flavors and textures. The vast majority of cheeses are made from cow's milk, although sheep and goat cheeses are highly prized.

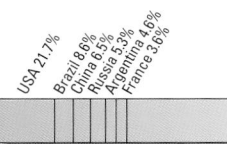

World total (1995): 14,754,000 tons

Beef and Veal: Most beef and veal is reared for home markets, and the top five producers are also the biggest consumers. The USA produces nearly a quarter of the world's beef and eats even more.

World total (1996): 53,965,000 tons

Milk: Many human groups, including most Asians, find raw milk indigestible after infancy, and it is often only the starting point for other dairy products such as butter, cheese and yoghurt. Most world production comes from cows, but sheep's milk and goats' milk are also important.

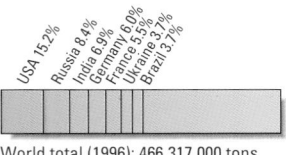

World total (1996): 466,317,000 tons

Butter: A traditional source of vitamin A as well as calories, butter has lost much popularity in the developed world for health reasons, although it remains a valuable food. Most butter from India, the world's largest producer, is clarified into ghee, which has religious as well as nutritional importance.

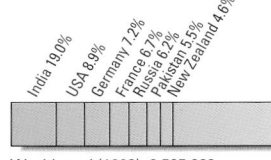

World total (1996): 6,565,000 tons

Pork: Although pork is forbidden to many millions, notably Muslims, on religious grounds, more is produced than any other meat in the world, mainly because it is the cheapest. It accounts for about 90% of China's meat output, although per capita meat consumption is relatively low.

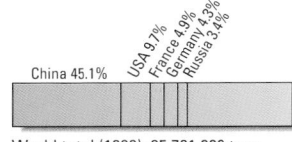

World total (1996): 85,761,000 tons

Crisis in Africa

Each year 40 million people, almost half of whom are children, die from starvation and related diseases. In 2000, 600 million people worldwide were estimated to be suffering from malnutrition. Africa suffers from more natural disasters than any other continent; pests such as locusts destroy crops, and tropical storms and flooding ruin harvests. Famines periodically affect parts of Africa causing widespread hardship, even though enough food is produced worldwide to feed everyone.

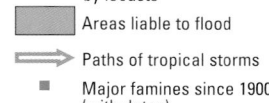

- Areas liable to invasions by locusts
- Areas liable to flood
- Paths of tropical storms
- Major famines since 1900 (with dates)

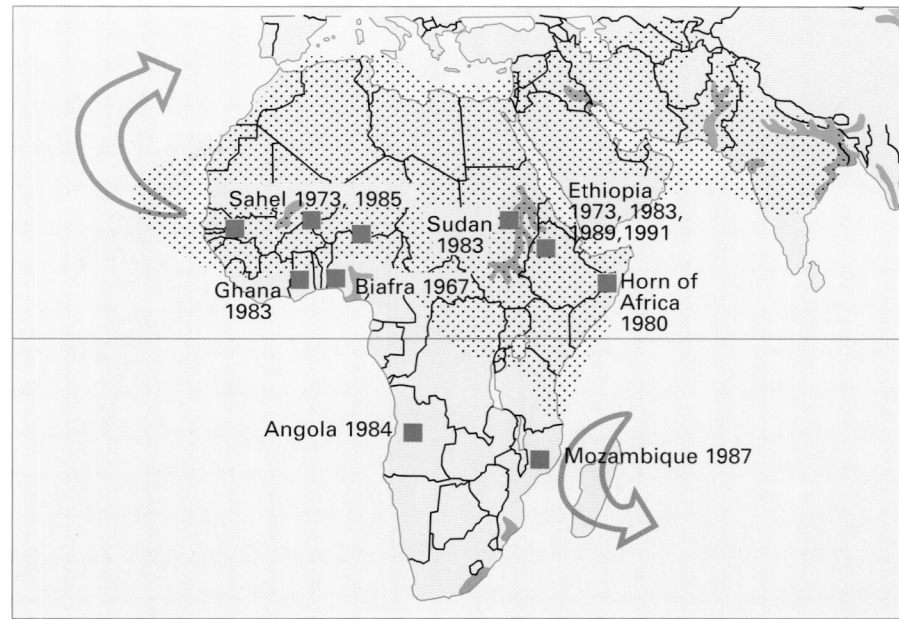

Energy

Every year, the world's energy consumption is about the equivalent of what would come from burning 8 billion tons of oil (8,000 MtOe) – a 20-fold increase since 1850. Two-fifths of this total actually comes from burning oil and most of the rest comes from coal and natural gas.

The oil crises in the 1970s precipitated concern over dependence on finite fossil fuels as the primary source of energy, and growing environmental awareness has added impetus to the search for alternative energy resources.

Fossil fuel combustion damages the environment through the release of gases and particulate matter but two other major sources of energy, hydroelectricity and nuclear power, are also controversial. For example, hydroelectricity production involves flooding large areas to create reservoirs, while nuclear power stations, which are costly to build, generate dangerous radioactive wastes, and can lead to disasters on an international scale.

Alternative energy resources may soon provide a much larger proportion of the world's energy consumption, especially in developing countries where millions of people currently have no access to electricity. Experts have predicted that solar and wind energy may have an important future in such countries as China and India, while other areas under development, such as tidal, wave and geothermal power, all have potential in appropriate areas. World Bank experts have calculated that solar power could, in theory, supply between five and ten times the present electricity supply of developing countries.

Conversions

For historical reasons, oil is still traded in barrels. The weight and volume equivalents shown below are all based on average density "Arabian light" crude oil, and should be considered approximate.

The energy equivalents given for a ton of oil are also somewhat imprecise: oil and coal of different qualities will have varying energy contents, a fact usually reflected in their price on world markets.

1 barrel:
0.15 tons
159 liters
35 Imperial gallons
42 US gallons

1 ton:
7.33 barrels
1185 liters
256 Imperial gallons
261 US gallons

1 ton oil:
1.5 tons hard coal
3.0 tons lignite
12,000 kWh

1 gallon (Imperial):
227,42 cubic inches
1.201 US gallons
4,546 liters

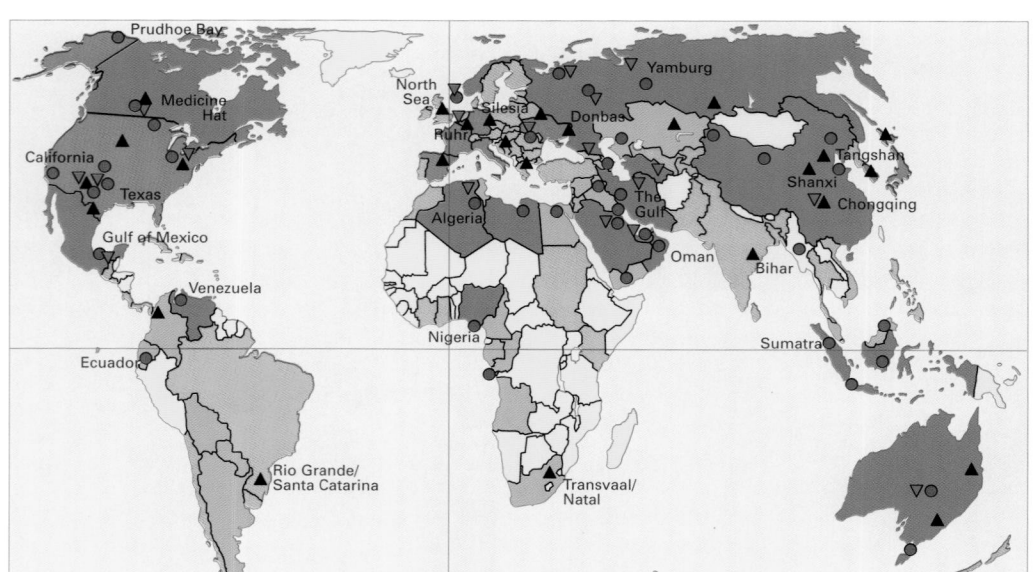

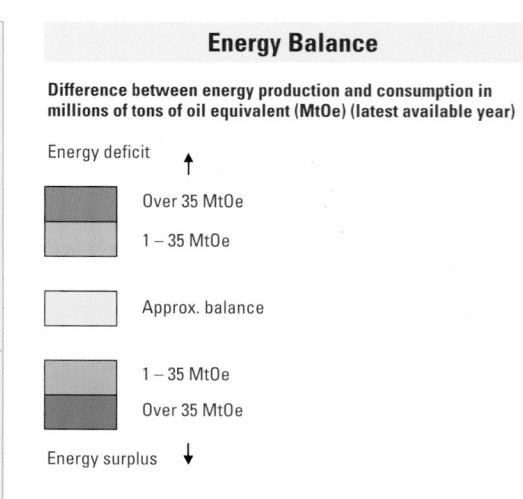

Energy Balance

Difference between energy production and consumption in millions of tons of oil equivalent (MtOe) (latest available year)

Energy deficit ↑

- Over 35 MtOe
- 1 – 35 MtOe
- Approx. balance
- 1 – 35 MtOe
- Over 35 MtOe

Energy surplus ↓

- ● Major oilfields
- ▽ Major gasfields
- ▲ Major coalfields

World Energy Consumption

Energy consumed by world regions, measured in million tons of oil equivalent in 1997. Total world consumption was 8,509 MtOe. Only energy from oil, gas, coal, nuclear and hydroelectric sources are included. Excluded are fuels such as wood, peat, animal waste, wind, solar and geothermal which, though important in some countries, are unreliably documented in terms of consumption statistics.

Oil   Gas   Coal   Nuclear   Hydro

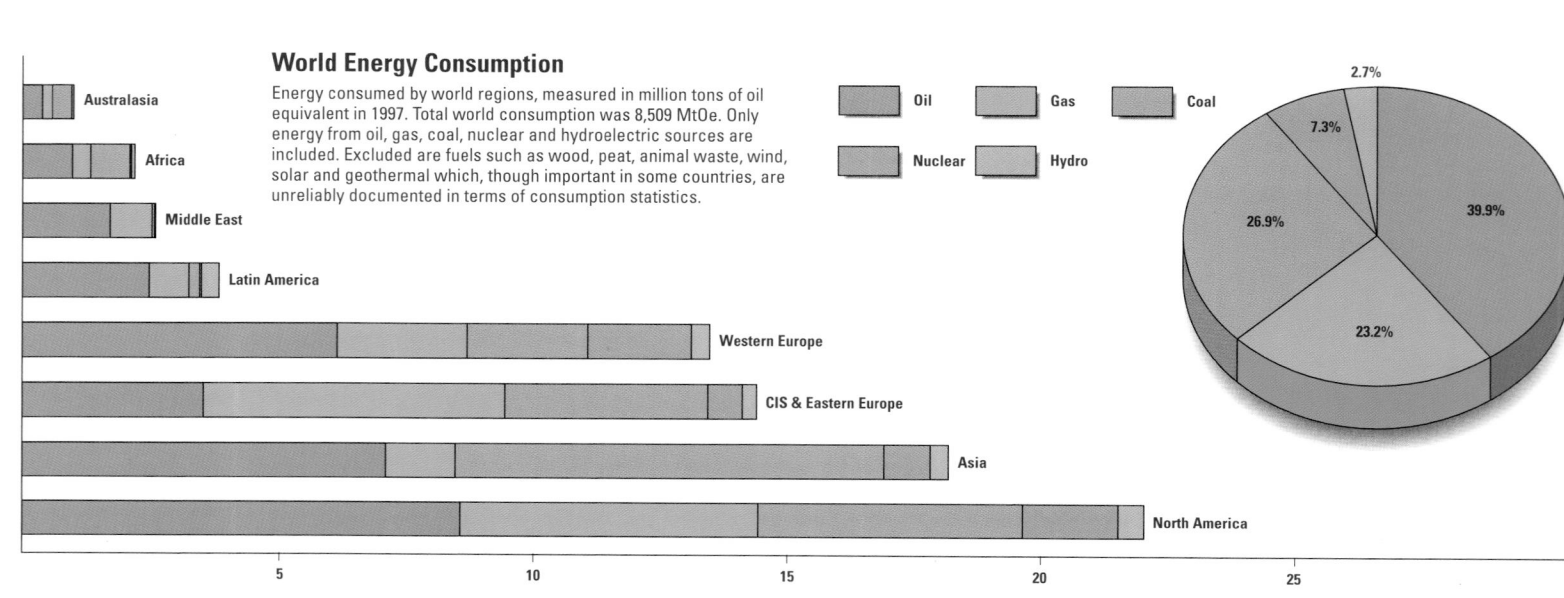

Energy Production

Primary energy production expressed in kilograms of coal equivalent per person (1994)

In developing countries traditional fuels are still very important. These so-called biomass fuels include wood, charcoal and dried dung. The pie chart highlights the importance of biomass in terms of energy consumption in Nigeria. Collecting fuelwood can be a time-consuming task, sometimes taking all day.

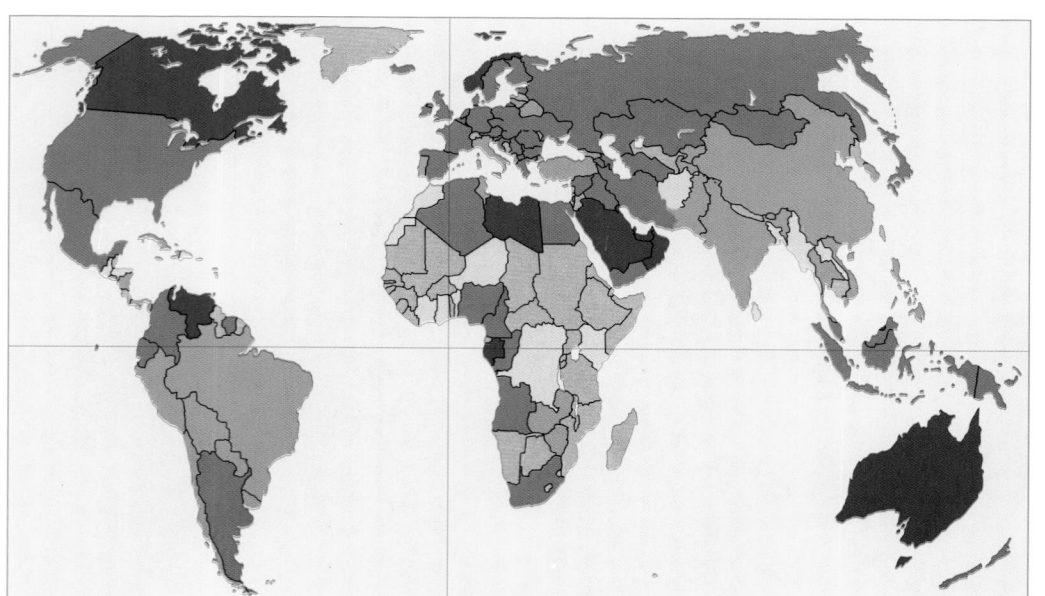

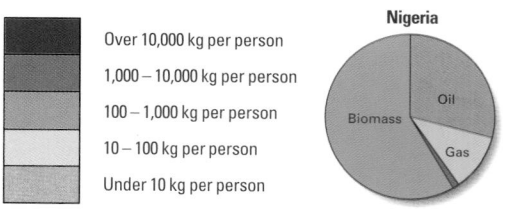

- Over 10,000 kg per person
- 1,000 – 10,000 kg per person
- 100 – 1,000 kg per person
- 10 – 100 kg per person
- Under 10 kg per person

CARTOGRAPHY BY PHILIP'S. COPYRIGHT GEORGE PHILIP LTD

Oil Movements

Major world movements of oil in millions of tons (1997)

Middle East to Asia (not Japan)	294.4
Middle East to Japan	218.1
Middle East to Western Europe	187.9
South and Central America to USA	132.1
North Africa to Western Europe	97.9
CIS to Western Europe	90.8
Middle East to USA	86.9
Canada to USA	72.7
West Africa to USA	68.3
Mexico to USA	68.0
West Africa to Western Europe	40.1
Western Europe to USA	32.9
Middle East to Africa	32.0
CIS to Central Europe	31.8
Middle East to South and Central America	27.8
Middle East to Central Europe	19.3

Total world imports ....1,978,900 billion tons

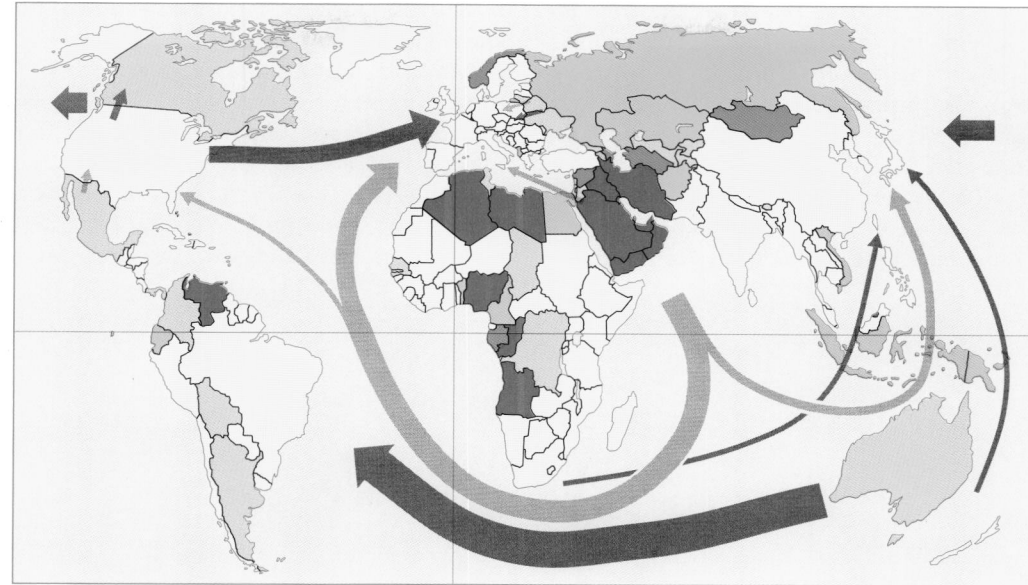

Fuel Exports

Fuels as a percentage of total value of exports (1996)

- Over 75%
- 50 – 75%
- 25 – 50%
- 10 – 25%
- Under 10%

➡ Major movements of coal
➡ Major movements of oil

In the 1970s, oil exports became a political issue when OPEC sought to increase the influence of developing countries in world affairs by raising oil prices and restricting production. But its power was short-lived, following a fall in demand for oil in the 1980s, due to an increase in energy efficiency and development of alternative resources.

Coal Reserves

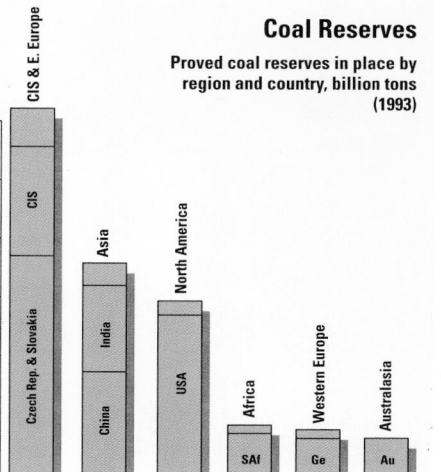

Proved coal reserves in place by region and country, billion tons (1993)

Gas Reserves

Proved recoverable natural gas reserves by region and country, billion tons (1993)

Oil Reserves

Crude oil reserves by region and country, billion tons (1993)

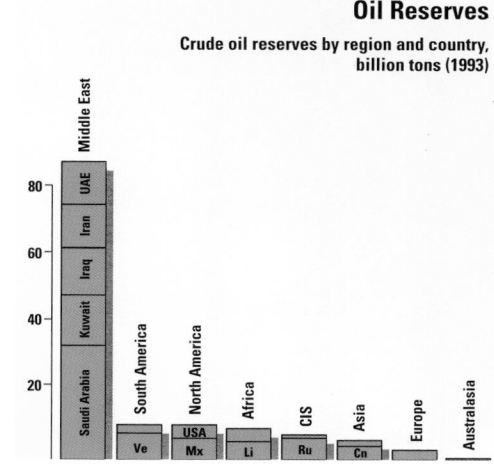

Al: Algeria
Au: Australia
Ca: Canada
Cn: China
Ge: Germany
Iq: Iraq
Ka: Kazakstan
Li: Libya
Ma: Malaysia
Mx: Mexico
Ni: Nigeria
No: Norway
Qa: Qatar
Ru: Russia
SA: Saudi Arabia
SAf: South Africa
Tm: Turkmenistan
Uk: Ukraine
Ve: Venezuela

Nuclear Power

Percentage of electricity generated by nuclear power stations, leading nations (1995)

1.	Lithuania	85%	11.	Spain	33%
2.	France	77%	12.	Finland	30%
3.	Belgium	56%	13.	Germany	29%
4.	Slovak Rep.	49%	14.	Japan	29%
5.	Sweden	48%	15.	UK	27%
6.	Bulgaria	41%	16.	Ukraine	27%
7.	Hungary	41%	17.	Czech Rep.	22%
8.	Switzerland	39%	18.	Canada	19%
9.	Slovenia	38%	19.	USA	18%
10.	South Korea	33%	20.	Russia	12%

Although the 1980s were a bad time for the nuclear power industry (major projects ran over budget and fears of long-term environmental damage were heavily reinforced by the 1986 disaster at Chernobyl), the industry picked up in the early 1990s. Whilst the number of reactors is still increasing, however, orders for new plants have shrunk. In 1997, the Swedish government began to decommission the country's 12 nuclear power plants; a bold environmental decision that could cost US $50 billion.

Renewable Energy

Average annual solar irradiance in kWh/ft², with selected major hydroelectric and geothermal power stations

- Over 24,000
- 21,000 – 24,000
- 18,000 – 21,000
- 15,000 – 18,000
- 12,000 – 15,000
- 9,000 – 12,000
- Under 9,000

▲ Hydroelectric plants
● Geothermal plants

Hydroelectricity

Percentage of electricity generated by hydroelectric power stations, leading nations (1995)

1.	Paraguay	99.9%	11.	Rwanda	97.6%
2.	Congo (Zaïre)	99.7%	12.	Malawi	97.6%
3.	Bhutan	99.6%	13.	Cameroon	96.9%
4.	Zambia	99.5%	14.	Nepal	96.7%
5.	Norway	99.4%	15.	Laos	95.3%
6.	Ghana	99.3%	16.	Albania	95.2%
7.	Congo	99.3%	17.	Iceland	94.0%
8.	Uganda	99.1%	18.	Brazil	92.2%
9.	Burundi	98.3%	19.	Honduras	87.6%
10.	Uruguay	98.0%	20.	Tanzania	87.1%

Countries heavily reliant on hydroelectricity are usually small and nonindustrial: a high proportion of hydroelectric power more often reflects a modest energy budget than vast hydroelectric resources. The USA, for instance, produces only 9% of power requirements from hydroelectricity; yet that 9% amounts to more than three times the hydropower generated by the whole of Africa.

Alternative Energy Resources

Solar: Each year the Sun bestows upon the Earth almost a million times as much energy as is locked up in all the planet's oil reserves, but only an insignificant fraction is trapped and used commercially. In a few installations around the world, mirrors focus the Sun's rays on to boilers, whose steam generates electricity by spinning turbines.

Wind: Caused by uneven heating of the Earth, winds are themselves a form of solar energy. Windmills have been used for centuries to turn wind power into mechanical work; recent models, often arranged in banks on wind-swept high ground, usually generate electricity. Figures for wind power worldwide are given in the table, right.

Tidal: The energy from tides is potentially enormous, although only a few installations have so far been built to exploit it. In theory at least, waves and currents could also provide almost unimaginable power, and the thermal differences in the ocean depths are another huge well of potential energy. But work on extracting it is still in the experimental stage.

Geothermal: The Earth's temperature rises by 1°F for every 50 feet descent, with much steeper temperature gradients in geologically active areas. El Salvador, for example, produces 39% of its electricity from geothermal power stations, whilst the USA, the world leader, produced 3,331 megawatts in 1993. Some of the oldest and most successful applications are in Iceland, where 86% of all households are heated by geothermal energy.

Biomass: The oldest of human fuels ranges from animal dung, still burned in cooking fires in much of North Africa and elsewhere, to sugarcane plantations feeding high-technology distilleries to produce ethanol for motor vehicle engines. In Brazil and South Africa, plant ethanol provides up to 25% of motor fuel. Throughout the developing world, most biomass energy comes from firewood: although accurate figures are impossible to obtain, it may yield as much as 10% of the world's total energy consumption.

Wind Power

World wind energy generating capacity, in megawatts

1980	10
1981	25
1982	90
1983	210
1984	600
1985	1,020
1986	1,270
1987	1,450
1988	1,580
1989	1,730
1990	1,930
1991	2,170
1992	2,510
1993	3,050
1994	3,710

Wind power is the fastest growing source of energy worldwide but still provides only 1% of the world's energy. Output grew by 33% in 1995.

CARTOGRAPHY BY PHILIP'S. COPYRIGHT GEORGE PHILIP LTD

Minerals

For more information:

The use of metals played a vital part in the evolving technologies of early peoples. Copper first came into use around 10,000 years ago, bronze about 5,000 years ago, and iron 3,300 years ago. In the early stages of the Industrial Revolution, the location of coal, iron ore and water power usually determined the location of new industries. But due to continuing improvements in transport, including oil pipelines, industries can now be located almost anywhere.

Minerals are distributed unevenly and some industrial countries, lacking their own mineral resources, import most of the raw materials they need. Some imports come from mineral-rich countries, such as Australia but others come from developing countries, especially in Africa and South America. Most of the developing countries export unprocessed ores, losing out on the much higher revenues gained from exporting metals.

Most minerals come from land deposits, because undersea deposits, with the exception of oil reserves under the continental shelves, have been regarded as inaccessible. But shortages of terrestrial minerals may one day encourage exploitation of the ocean floor.

Mineral Exports

Minerals and metals as a percentage of total exports (latest available year)

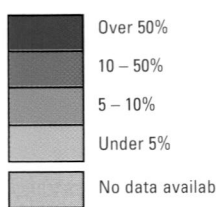

- Over 50%
- 10 – 50%
- 5 – 10%
- Under 5%
- No data available

Uranium

In its pure state, uranium is an immensely heavy, white metal; but although spent uranium is employed as projectiles in antimissile cannons, where its mass ensures a lethal punch, its main use is as a fuel in nuclear reactors, and in nuclear weaponry. Uranium is very scarce: the main source is the rare ore pitchblende, which itself contains only 0.2% uranium oxide. Only a minute fraction of that is the radioactive U^{235} isotope, though so-called breeder reactors can transmute the more common U^{238} into highly radioactive plutonium.

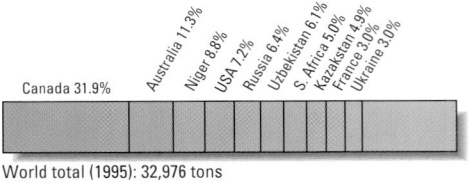

Canada 31.9% | Australia 11.3% | Niger 9.8% | USA 7.2% | Russia 6.4% | Uzbekistan 6.1% | S. Africa 5.0% | Kazakstan 5.0% | France 4.9% | Ukraine 3.0%

World total (1995): 32,976 tons

Metals

* Figures for aluminum are for refined metal; all other figures refer to ore production.

The world's leading producers of aluminum ore (bauxite) in 1995 were as follows:

1. Australia 41.9%
2. Papua New Guinea 14.3%
3. Jamaica 10.8%
4. Brazil 10.1%
5. Russia 6.7%
6. China 5.7%
7. India 5.0%
8. Surinam 2.8%
9. Venezuela 2.6%
10. Greece 1.9%

The figures shown above are in stark contrast to the figures showing aluminum production on the right. Australia, for example, produces 41.9% of the world's bauxite but only 5.9% of the aluminum metal. Papua New Guinea and Jamaica account for 25% of the bauxite mined but have no smelters and export virtually all of it to countries like the USA and Canada.

Diamond

Most of the world's diamond is found in kimberlite, or "blue ground," a basic peridotite rock; erosion may wash the diamond from its kimberlite matrix and deposit it with sand or gravel on river beds. Only a small proportion of the world's diamond, the most flawless, is cut into gemstones – "diamonds"; most is used in industry, where the material's remarkable hardness and abrasion resistance finds a use in cutting tools, drills and dies, as well as in styluses. Australia, not among the top 12 producers at the beginning of the 1980s, had by 1986 become world leader and by 1993 was the source of 40.6% of world production. The other main producers were Congo (then Zaïre) (16.3%), Botswana (14.6%), Russia (11.4%) and South Africa (9.7%). Between them, these five nations accounted for over 82% of the world total of 100,850,000 carats.

Aluminum: Produced mainly from its oxide, bauxite, which yields 25% of its weight in aluminum. The cost of refining and production is often too high for producer-countries to bear, so bauxite is largely exported. Lightweight and corrosion resistant, aluminum alloys are widely used in aircraft, vehicles, cans and packaging.

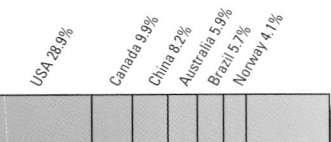

USA 26.9% | Canada 9.9% | China 8.2% | Australia 5.9% | Brazil 5.7% | Norway 4.1%

World total (1995): 22,706,000 tons *

Lead: A soft metal, obtained mainly from galena (lead sulfide), which occurs in veins associated with iron, zinc and silver sulfides. Its use in vehicle batteries accounts for the USA's prime consumer status; lead is also made into sheeting and piping. Its use as an additive to paints and petrol is decreasing.

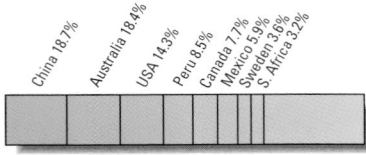

China 18.7% | Australia 18.4% | USA 14.3% | Peru 8.5% | Canada 7.7% | Mexico 5.9% | Sweden 3.6% | S. Africa 3.2%

World total (1995): 2,751,000 tons *

Tin: Soft, pliable and non-toxic, used to coat "tin" (tin-plated steel) cans, in the manufacture of foils and in alloys. The principal tin-bearing mineral is cassiterite (SnO_2), found in ore formed from molten rock. Producers and refiners were hit by a price collapse in 1991.

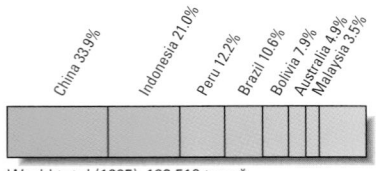

China 33.9% | Indonesia 21.0% | Peru 12.2% | Brazil 10.0% | Bolivia 7.9% | Australia 4.9% | Malaysia 3.5%

World total (1995): 182,518 tons *

Gold: Regarded for centuries as the most valuable metal in the world and used to make coins, gold is still recognized as the monetary standard. A soft metal, it is alloyed to make jewelry; the electronics industry values its corrosion resistance and conductivity.

S. Africa 27.7% | USA 16.9% | Australia 13.2% | Canada 7.9% | Indonesia 3.3% | Peru 2.9% | Ghana 2.9%

World total (1995): 1,889 tons *

Copper: Derived from low-yielding sulfide ores, copper is an important export for several developing countries. An excellent conductor of heat and electricity, it forms part of most electrical items, and is used in the manufacture of brass and bronze. Major importers include Japan and Germany.

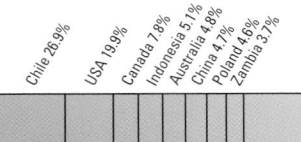

Chile 26.9% | USA 19.9% | Canada 7.8% | Indonesia 5.1% | Australia 4.8% | China 4.7% | Poland 4.6% | Zambia 3.7%

World total (1995): 9,311,000 tons *

Mercury: The only metal that is liquid at normal temperatures, most is derived from its sulfide, cinnabar, found only in small quantities in volcanic areas. Apart from its value in thermometers and other instruments, most mercury production is used in antifungal and antifouling preparations, and to make detonators.

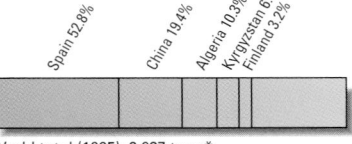

Spain 52.8% | China 18.4% | Algeria 10.3% | Kyrgystan 6.0% | Finland 3.2%

World total (1995): 2,837 tons *

Zinc: Often found in association with lead ores, zinc is highly resistant to corrosion, and about 40% of the refined metal is used to plate sheet steel, particularly vehicle bodies – a process known as galvanizing. Zinc is also used in dry batteries, paints and dyes.

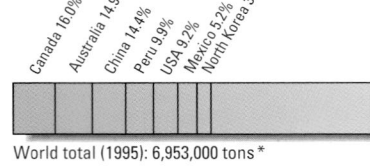

Canada 16.0% | Australia 14.9% | China 14.4% | Peru 9.9% | USA 8.2% | Mexico 5.2% | North Korea 3.1%

World total (1995): 6,953,000 tons *

Silver: Most silver comes from ores mined and processed for other metals (including lead and copper). Pure or alloyed with harder metals, it is used for jewelry and ornaments. Industrial use includes dentistry, electronics, photography and as a chemical catalyst.

USA 12.4% | Turkey 8.6% | Chile 7.8% | Poland 7.5% | Australia 6.9% | Bolivia 3.2%

World total (1995): 13,266 tons *

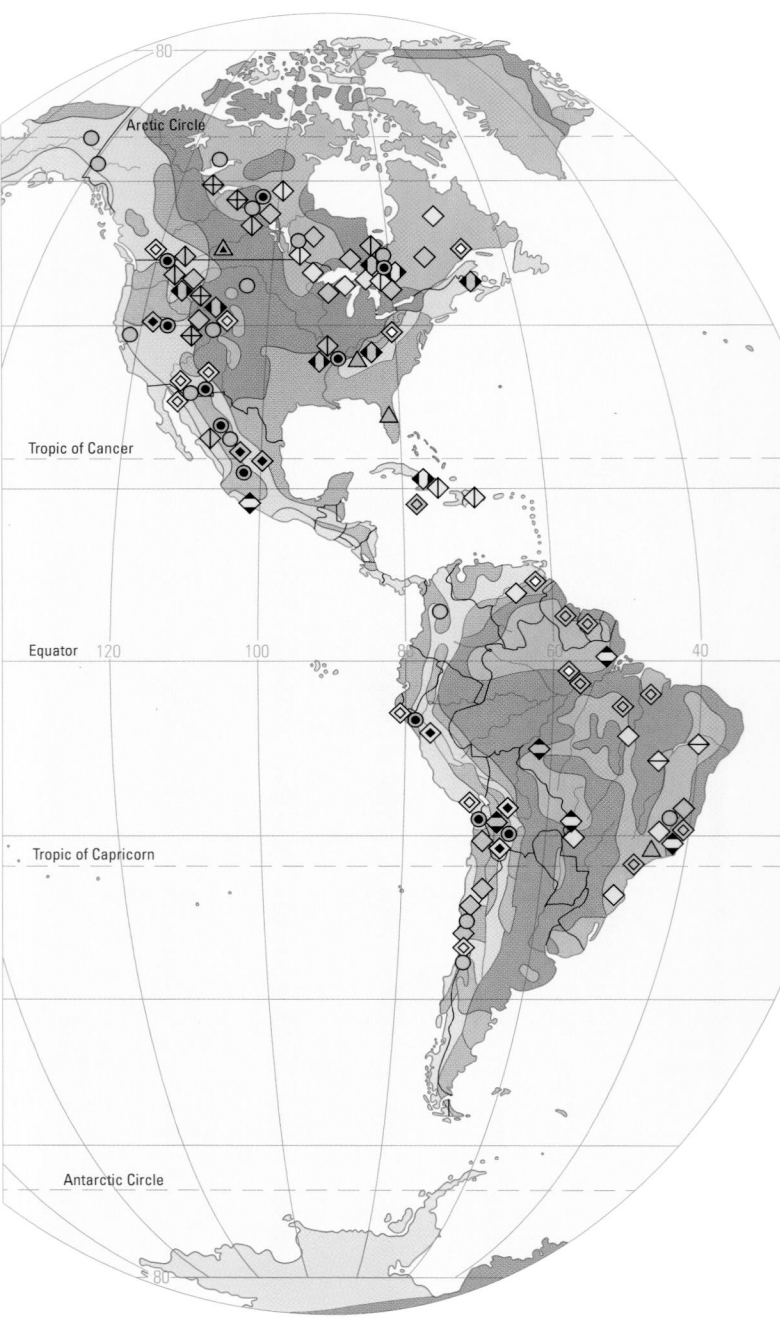

CARTOGRAPHY BY PHILIP'S. COPYRIGHT GEORGE PHILIP LTD

Strategic Minerals

Ever since the art of high-temperature smelting was discovered, some time in the second millennium BC, iron has been by far the most important metal known to man. The earliest iron plows transformed primitive agriculture and led to the first human population explosion, while iron weapons – or the lack of them – ensured the rise or fall of entire cultures.

Widely distributed around the world, iron ores usually contain 25–60% iron; blast furnaces process the raw product into pig iron, which is then alloyed with carbon and other minerals to produce steels of various qualities. From the time of the Industrial Revolution, steel has been almost literally the backbone of modern civilization, the prime structural material on which all else is built.

Iron smelting usually developed close to the sources of ore and, later, to the coalfields that fueled the furnaces. Today, most ore comes from a few richly-endowed locations where large-scale mining is possible. Iron and steel plants are generally built at coastal sites so that giant ore carriers, which account for a sizable proportion of the world's merchant fleet, can easily discharge their cargoes.

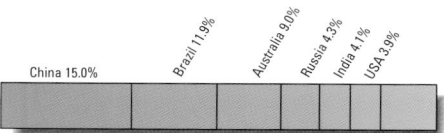

World total production of iron ore (1995): 1,020,000,000 tons

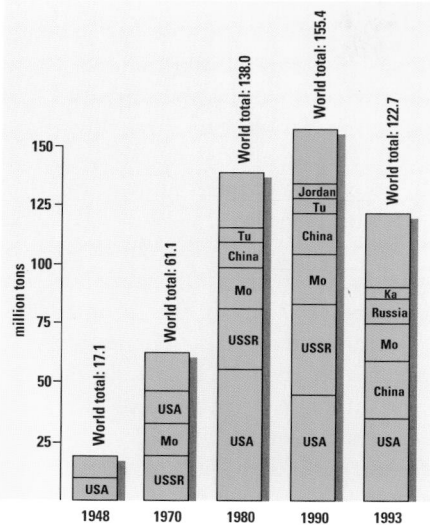

World production of phosphates in millions of tons (1993). Phosphate production is vital to the economies of several small countries. Nauru, for example, is heavily dependent on phosphate exports – the island has one of the world's richest deposits. In 1994, 613,000 tons were mined, employing 1,000 people. In Togo, earnings from phosphate exports have superseded all agricultural exports.

Percentage of total world phosphate production (1994)

1. USA	32.4%	7. Israel	3.1%
2. China	20.2%	8. Brazil	2.6%
3. Morocco	15.4%	9. South Africa	2.0%
4. Russia	6.2%	10. Togo	1.7%
5. Tunisia	4.4%	11. Kazakstan	1.6%
6. Jordan	3.3%	12. Senegal	1.4%

World production of pig iron and ferroalloys (1995). All countries with an annual output of more than 1 million tons are shown

Total world production: 690 million tons

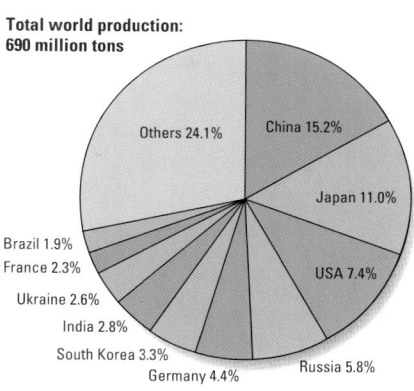

Manganese: In its pure state, manganese is a hard, brittle metal. Alloyed with chrome, iron and nickel, it produces abrasion-resistant steels; manganese-aluminum alloys are light but tough. Found in batteries and inks, manganese is also used in glass production. Manganese ores are frequently found in the same location as sedimentary iron ores. Pyrolusite (MnO_2) and psilomelane are the main economically-exploitable sources.

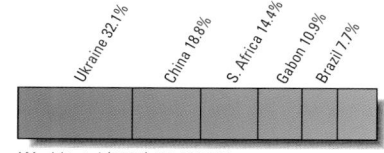

World total (1994): 22,180,000 tons

Chromium: Most of the world's chromium production is alloyed with iron and other metals to produce steels with various different properties. Combined with iron, nickel, cobalt and tungsten, chromium produces an exceptionally hard steel, resistant to heat; chrome steels are used for many household items where utility must be matched with appearance – cutlery, for example. Chromium is also used in production of refractory bricks, and its salts for tanning and dyeing leather and cloth.

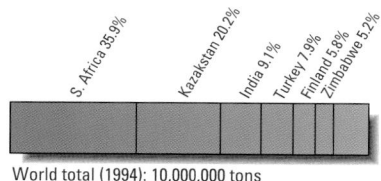

World total (1994): 10,000,000 tons

Nickel: Combined with chrome and iron, nickel produces stainless and high-strength steels; similar alloys go to make magnets and electrical heating elements. Nickel combined with copper is widely used to make coins; cupro-nickel alloy is very resistant to corrosion. Its ores yield only modest quantities of nickel – 0.5% to 3.0% – but also contain copper, iron and small amounts of precious metals. Japan, USA, UK, Germany and France are the principal importers.

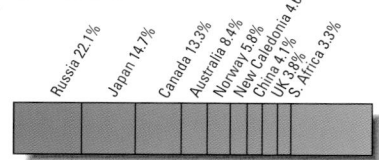

World total (1995): 920,000 tons

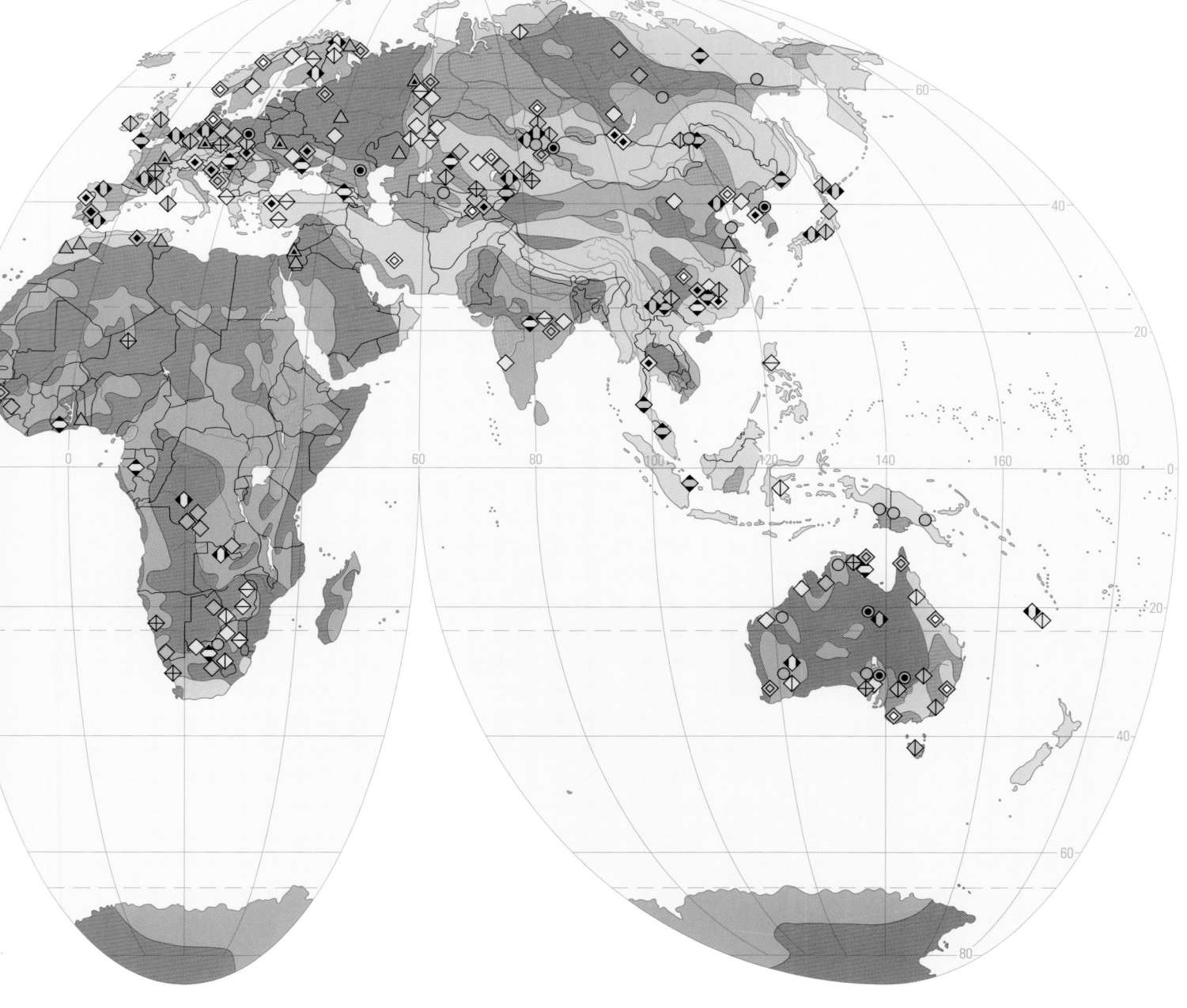

Distribution of Minerals

Structural Regions

- Pre-Cambrian shields
- Sedimentary cover on Pre-Cambrian shields
- Paleozoic (Caledonian and Hercynian) folding
- Sedimentary cover on Paleozoic folding
- Mesozoic folding
- Sedimentary cover on Mesozoic folding
- Cenozoic (Alpine) folding
- Sedimentary cover on Cenozoic folding
- Intensive Mesozoic and Cenozoic vulcanism

Distribution
Iron and ferro-alloys

- Chrome
- Cobalt
- Iron Ore
- Manganese
- Molybdenum
- Nickel Ore
- Tungsten

Non-ferrous metals

- Bauxite (Aluminum)
- Copper
- Lead
- Mercury
- Tin
- Zinc
- Uranium

Precious metals and stones

- Diamonds
- Gold
- Silver

Fertilizers

- Phosphates
- Potash

Manufacturing

The Industrial Revolution which began in Britain in the late 18th century, represented a major technological advance in the evolution of human society. It enabled a group of countries to become prosperous by replacing expensive human labor with increasingly sophisticated machinery. In economic terms, manufacturing is the transformation of raw materials, energy, labor and machines into finished goods, which have a higher value than the various elements used in production.

The economies of countries can be compared by reference to their per capita Gross National Products (or per capita GNPs), namely, the total value of goods and services produced in a country in a year, divided by the population.

The industrialized, or developed, countries accounted for 16% of the world's population in 1997 with an average per capita GNP of US $25,700. On the other hand, developing countries, with comparatively small industrial sectors and low-income economies, accounted for 35% of the world's population, with an average per capita GNP of just $350.

Kenya, with its low-income economy, had a per capita GNP in 1998 of $330. Agriculture employs 77% of the people, industry 8% and services 15%. The major industries are the processing of agricultural products and import substitution (the manufacture of such necessities as cement, footwear and textiles). Heavy industry plays a comparatively small part in the economy. By contrast, Germany, a major industrialized nation, had a per capita GNP in 1998 of $25,850. Agriculture employs only 1% of the population, with 32% in industry, and 67% in services. Germany's industrial sector differs greatly from Kenya's, with an emphasis on the manufacture of vehicles, machinery and chemicals.

Since the 1970s, some former developing countries in Asia have been transformed by rapid industrialization. These "economic tigers," including China, Malaysia, South Korea, Singapore, Taiwan, and Thailand, owe their success to low labor costs and substantial investment in education, together with advances in telecommunications, transport, and computers, which have made technology more readily transferable around the world than ever before. They have also benefited from economic freedom and trade liberalization.

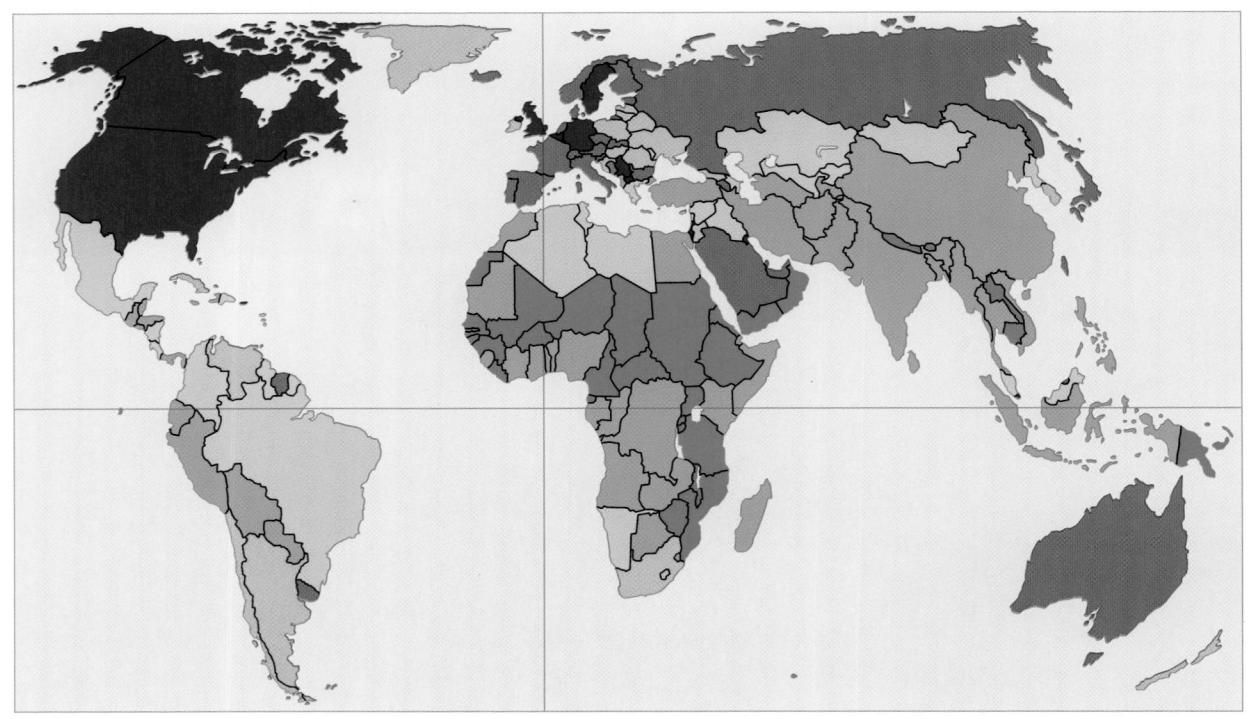

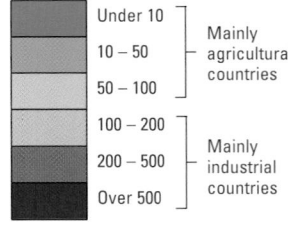

Employment

The number of workers employed in manufacturing for every 100 workers engaged in agriculture (latest available year)

Under 10	}	Mainly agricultural countries
10 – 50		
50 – 100		
100 – 200	}	Mainly industrial countries
200 – 500		
Over 500		

Selected countries (latest available year)

Singapore	8,860
UK	1,270
Belgium	820
Germany	800
Kuwait	767
Bahrain	660
USA	657
Israel	633

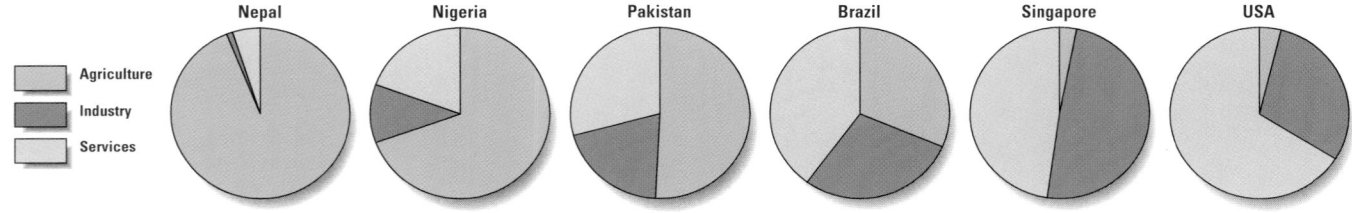

Nepal   Nigeria   Pakistan   Brazil   Singapore   USA

- Agriculture
- Industry
- Services

Division of Employment

Distribution of workers between agriculture, industry and services, selected countries (latest available year)

The six countries selected illustrate the usual stages of economic development, from dependence on agriculture through industrial growth to the expansion of the service sector.

The Work Force

Percentages of men and women between 15 and 64 in employment, selected countries (latest available year)

The figures include employees and the self-employed, who in developing countries are often subsistence farmers. People in full-time education are excluded. Because of the population age structure in developing countries, the employed population has to support a far larger number of non-workers than its industrial equivalent. For example, more than 52% of Kenya's people are under 15, an age group that makes up less than a tenth of the UK population.

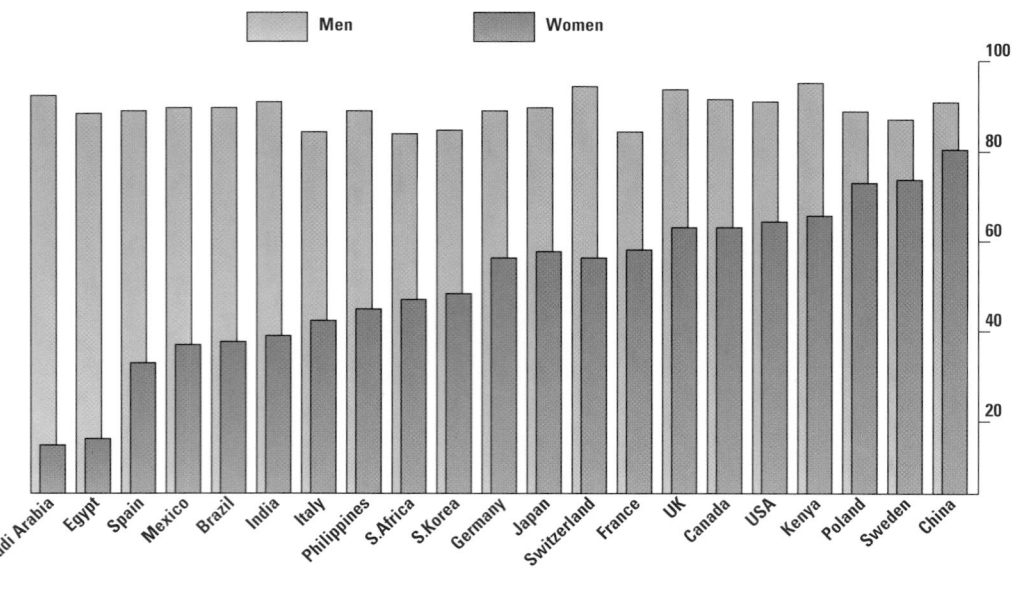

Men   Women

Saudi Arabia, Egypt, Spain, Mexico, Brazil, India, Italy, Philippines, S.Africa, S.Korea, Germany, Japan, Switzerland, France, UK, Canada, USA, Kenya, Poland, Sweden, China

Wealth Creation

The Gross National Product (GNP) of the world's largest economies, US $ million (1998)

1.	USA	7,922,651	21.	Austria	217,163
2.	Japan	4,089,910	22.	Turkey	200,505
3.	Germany	2,122,673	23.	Saudi Arabia	186,000
4.	Italy	1,666,178	24.	Denmark	176,374
5.	France	1,466,014	25.	Hong Kong	158,286
6.	UK	1,263,777	26.	Norway	152,082
7.	China	928,950	27.	Poland	150,798
8.	Botswana	758,043	28.	Indonesia	138,501
9.	Canada	612,332	29.	Thailand	134,433
10.	Spain	553,690	30.	Finland	124,293
11.	India	421,259	31.	Greece	122,880
12.	Netherlands	388,682	32.	South Africa	119,001
13.	Mexico	380,917	33.	Iran	109,645
14.	Australia	380,625	34.	Portugal	106,376
15.	South Korea	369,890	35.	Colombia	106,090
16.	Russia	337,914	36.	Israel	95,179
17.	Argentina	324,084	37.	Singapore	95,095
18.	Switzerland	284,808	38.	Venezuela	81,347
19.	Belgium	259,045	39.	Malaysia	79,848
20.	Sweden	226,861	40.	Egypt	79,208

CARTOGRAPHY BY PHILIP'S. COPYRIGHT GEORGE PHILIP LTD

Patterns of Production

Breakdown of industrial output by value, selected countries (latest available year)

	Food & agric. products	Textiles & clothing	Machinery & transport	Chemicals	Other
Algeria	26%	20%	11%	1%	41%
Argentina	24%	10%	16%	12%	37%
Australia	18%	7%	21%	8%	45%
Austria	17%	8%	25%	6%	43%
Belgium	19%	8%	23%	13%	36%
Brazil	15%	12%	24%	9%	40%
Burkina Faso	62%	18%	2%	1%	17%
Canada	15%	7%	25%	9%	44%
Denmark	22%	6%	23%	10%	39%
Egypt	20%	27%	13%	10%	31%
Finland	13%	6%	24%	7%	50%
France	18%	7%	33%	9%	33%
Germany	12%	5%	38%	10%	36%
Greece	20%	22%	14%	7%	38%
Hungary	6%	11%	37%	11%	35%
India	11%	16%	26%	15%	32%
Indonesia	23%	11%	10%	10%	47%
Iran	13%	22%	22%	7%	36%
Israel	13%	10%	28%	8%	42%
Ireland	28%	7%	20%	15%	28%
Italy	7%	13%	32%	10%	38%
Japan	10%	6%	38%	10%	37%
Kenya	35%	12%	14%	9%	29%
Malaysia	21%	5%	23%	14%	37%
Mexico	24%	12%	14%	12%	39%
Netherlands	19%	4%	28%	11%	38%
New Zealand	26%	10%	16%	6%	43%
Norway	21%	3%	26%	7%	44%
Pakistan	34%	21%	8%	12%	25%
Philippines	40%	7%	7%	10%	35%
Poland	15%	16%	30%	6%	33%
Portugal	17%	22%	16%	8%	38%
Singapore	6%	5%	46%	8%	36%
South Africa	14%	8%	17%	11%	49%
South Korea	15%	17%	24%	9%	35%
Spain	17%	9%	22%	9%	43%
Sweden	10%	2%	35%	8%	44%
Thailand	30%	17%	14%	6%	33%
Turkey	20%	14%	15%	8%	43%
UK	14%	6%	32%	11%	36%
USA	12%	5%	35%	10%	38%
Venezuela	23%	8%	9%	11%	49%

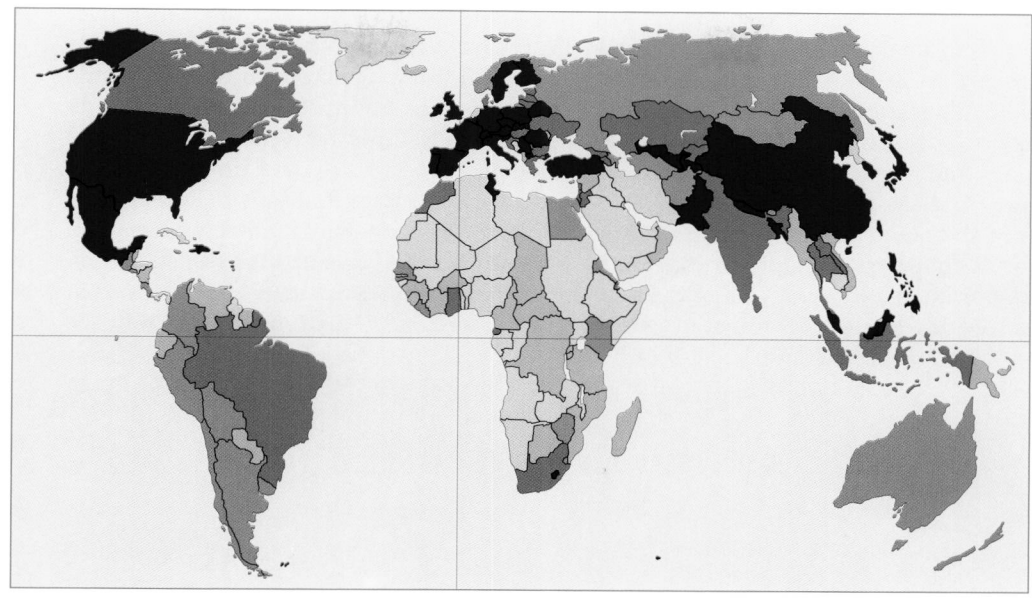

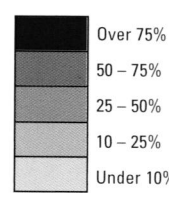

Industry and Trade

Manufactured goods (including machinery and transport) as a percentage of total exports (1996)

- Over 75%
- 50 – 75%
- 25 – 50%
- 10 – 25%
- Under 10%

The Far East and Southeast Asia (Japan 98%, Macau 96%, Taiwan 95%, Hong Kong [now part of China] 94%, South Korea 94%) are most dominant but many countries in Europe (e.g. Slovenia 93%) are also heavily dependent on manufactured goods.

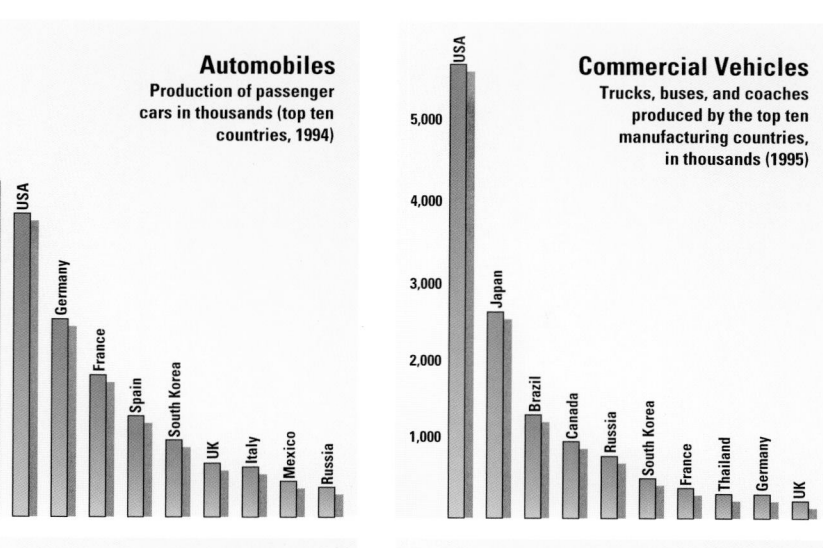

Automobiles
Production of passenger cars in thousands (top ten countries, 1994)

Commercial Vehicles
Trucks, buses, and coaches produced by the top ten manufacturing countries, in thousands (1995)

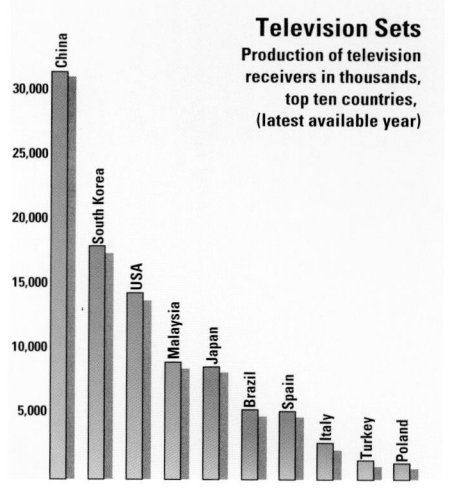

Television Sets
Production of television receivers in thousands, top ten countries, (latest available year)

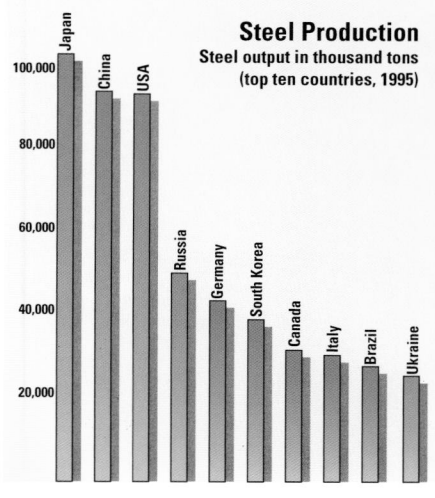

Steel Production
Steel output in thousand tons (top ten countries, 1995)

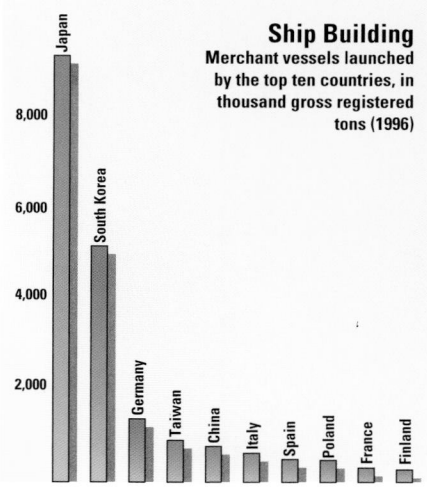

Ship Building
Merchant vessels launched by the top ten countries, in thousand gross registered tons (1996)

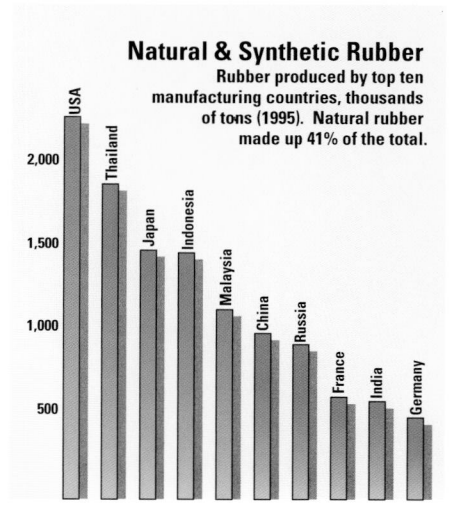

Natural & Synthetic Rubber
Rubber produced by top ten manufacturing countries, thousands of tons (1995). Natural rubber made up 41% of the total.

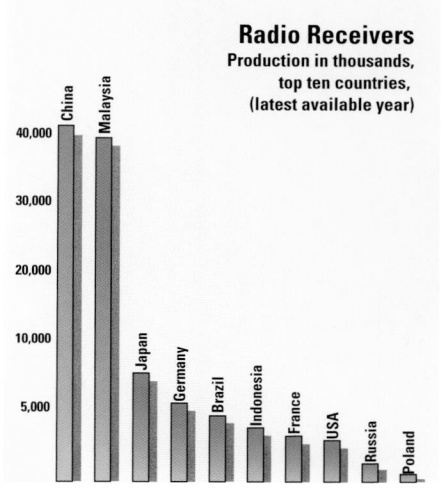

Radio Receivers
Production in thousands, top ten countries, (latest available year)

Industrial Output

Industrial output (mining, manufacturing, construction, energy, and water production), US $ billion (1995)

1.	Japan	1,941	21.	Sweden	73
2.	USA	1,808	22.	Saudi Arabia	67
3.	Germany	780	=	Thailand	67
4.	France	415	24.	Mexico	65
5.	UK	354	25.	Turkey	51
6.	Italy	337	26.	Denmark	50
7.	China	335	27.	Finland	46
8.	Brazil	255	=	Poland	46
9.	South Korea	196	29.	Norway	44
10.	Spain	187	30.	Malaysia	37
11.	Canada	174	=	Portugal	37
12.	Russia	131	32.	Ukraine	34
13.	Netherlands	107	33.	Greece	33
14.	Australia	98	34.	Singapore	30
15.	Switzerland	96	35.	Venezuela	29
16.	India	94	=	Israel	29
17.	Argentina	87	37.	Chile	24
18.	Belgium	83	=	Colombia	24
=	Indonesia	83	=	Hong Kong	24
20.	Austria	79	=	Philippines	24

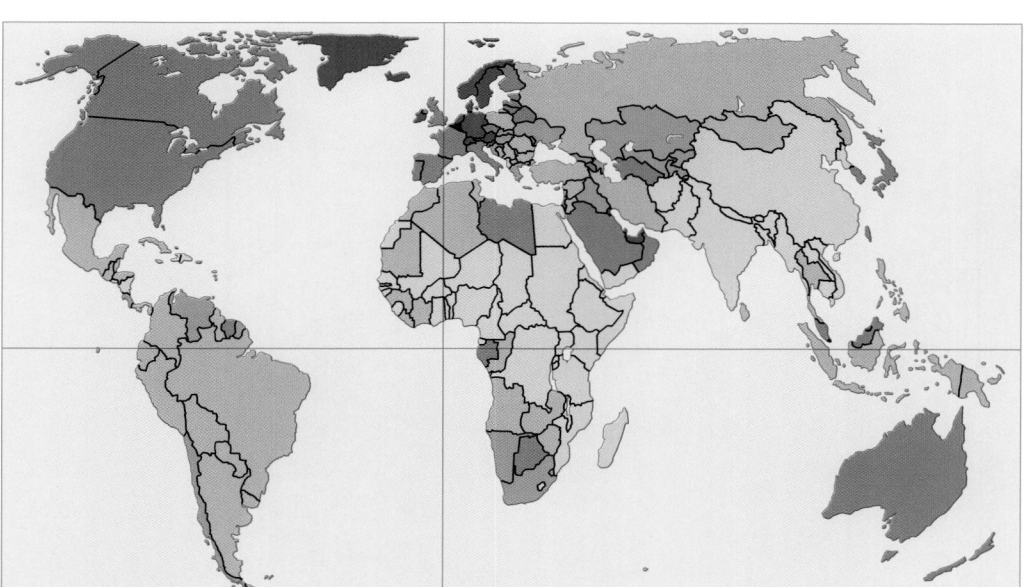

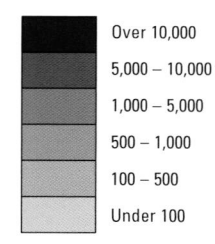

Exports Per Capita

Value of exports in US $, divided by total population (latest available year)

- Over 10,000
- 5,000 – 10,000
- 1,000 – 5,000
- 500 – 1,000
- 100 – 500
- Under 100

[UK 3,135] [USA 1,967]

Highest per capita exports (1993)
Singapore	25,787
Hong Kong	22,339
Benelux	12,295
Brunei	8,778
Netherlands	8,578
Switzerland	8,457

CARTOGRAPHY BY PHILIP'S. COPYRIGHT GEORGE PHILIP LTD

Trade

Trade played a vital role in the growth of early civilizations and it was later a spur to European exploration and colonization. The colonial powers grew rich by exporting cheap manufactures, such as clothing and footwear, while obtaining primary products from their colonies.

From the late 19th century to the early 1950s, as transport technology improved, primary products, especially oil in the later stages of this period, dominated world trade. However, since that time, manufactures have become the chief commodities in world trade, which is dominated by the industrialized countries. Nearly half of all world trade flows between the developed market economies of the European Union, the United States and Japan, although the Asian "tiger economies," notably Singapore, South Korea, Taiwan, Malaysia and Thailand, have increased their share in recent years. Recent predictions suggest that the next "tigers" might include Argentina and Chile in South America, Indonesia, the Philippines and Vietnam in Asia, and the Czech Republic and Poland in Europe.

There is little trade between developing countries, although some mineral- and oil-rich nations obtain a high proportion of their GNP from export sales. Growth in world trade is regarded as a sign of economic health, as is a favorable balance of trade (or trade surplus) in any country.

World Trade

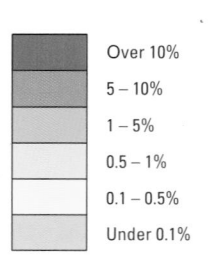

Percentage share of total world exports by value (1996)

- Over 10%
- 5 – 10%
- 1 – 5%
- 0.5 – 1%
- 0.1 – 0.5%
- Under 0.1%

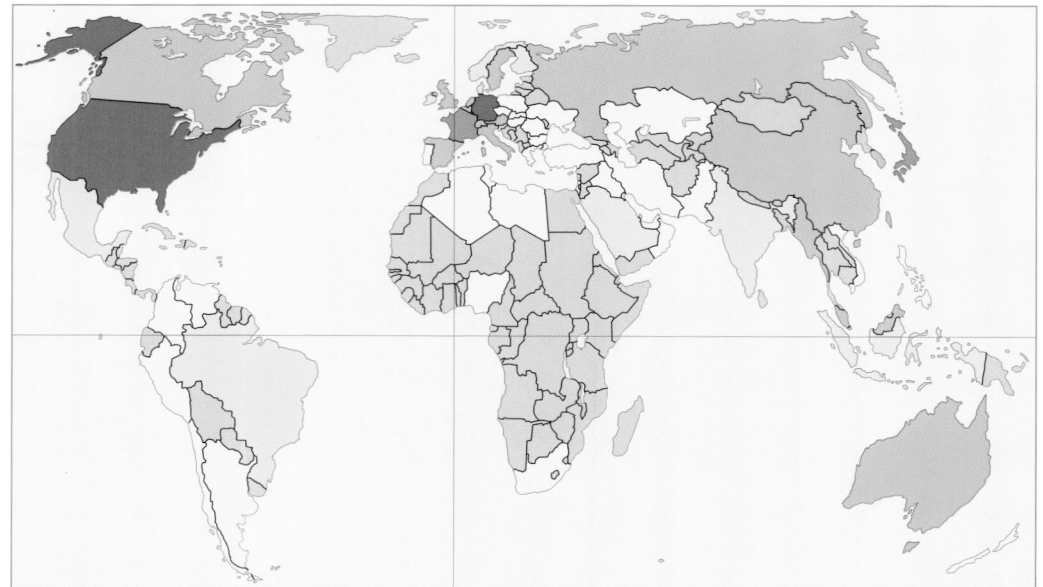

The Main Trading Nations

The imports and exports of the top ten trading nations as a percentage of world trade (1994). Each country's trade in manufactured goods is shown in dark blue. The graph shows that, in 1994, virtually all of Japan's imports and exports were manufactured goods.

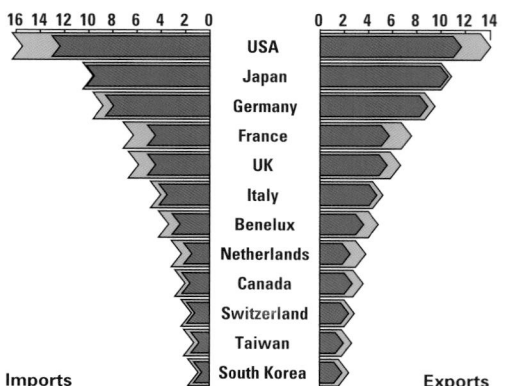

16 14 12 10 8 6 4 2 0   0 2 4 6 8 10 12 14

- USA
- Japan
- Germany
- France
- UK
- Italy
- Benelux
- Netherlands
- Canada
- Switzerland
- Taiwan
- South Korea

Imports   Exports

Dependence on Trade

Value of exports as a percentage of Gross Domestic Product (1997)

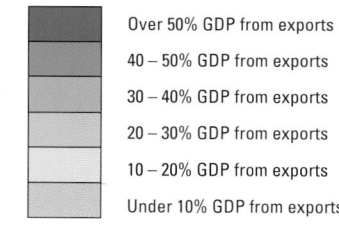

- Over 50% GDP from exports
- 40 – 50% GDP from exports
- 30 – 40% GDP from exports
- 20 – 30% GDP from exports
- 10 – 20% GDP from exports
- Under 10% GDP from exports

- ○ Most dependent on industrial exports (over 75% of total exports)
- ● Most dependent on fuel exports (over 75% of total exports)
- ○ Most dependent on metal and mineral exports (over 75% of total exports)

Major Exports

Leading manufactured items and their exporters, by percentage of world total in US $ (latest available year)

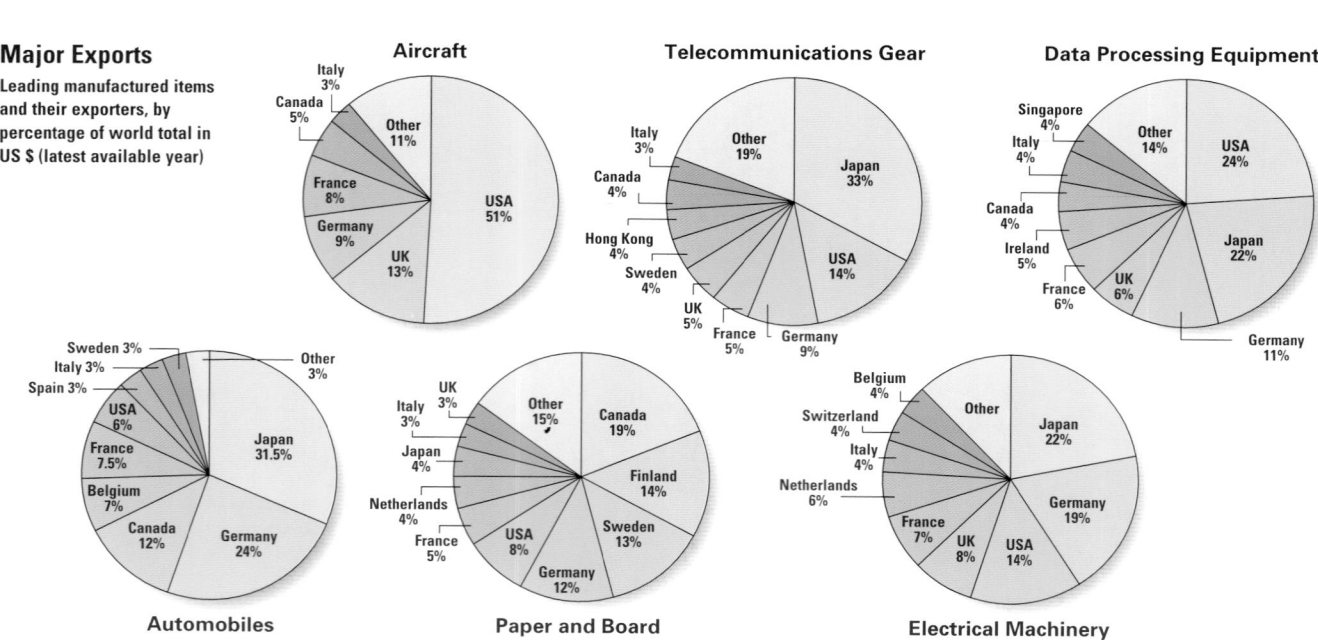

Aircraft
- USA 51%
- UK 13%
- Other 11%
- Germany 9%
- France 8%
- Canada 5%
- Italy 3%

Telecommunications Gear
- Japan 33%
- Other 19%
- USA 14%
- Germany 5%
- France 5%
- UK 5%
- Sweden 4%
- Hong Kong 4%
- Canada 4%
- Italy 3%

Data Processing Equipment
- USA 24%
- Japan 22%
- Other 14%
- Germany 11%
- France 6%
- UK 6%
- Ireland 5%
- Canada 4%
- Italy 4%
- Singapore 4%

Automobiles
- Japan 31.5%
- Germany 24%
- Canada 12%
- Belgium 7%
- France 7.5%
- USA 6%
- Spain 3%
- Italy 3%
- Sweden 3%
- Other 3%

Paper and Board
- Canada 19%
- Other 15%
- Finland 14%
- Sweden 13%
- Germany 12%
- USA 8%
- France 5%
- Japan 4%
- Netherlands 4%
- Italy 3%
- UK 3%

Electrical Machinery
- Japan 22%
- Germany 19%
- Other 14%
- USA 14%
- UK 8%
- France 7%
- Netherlands 6%
- Italy 4%
- Switzerland 4%
- Belgium 4%

Traded Products

Top ten manufactures traded, by value in billions of US $ (latest available year)

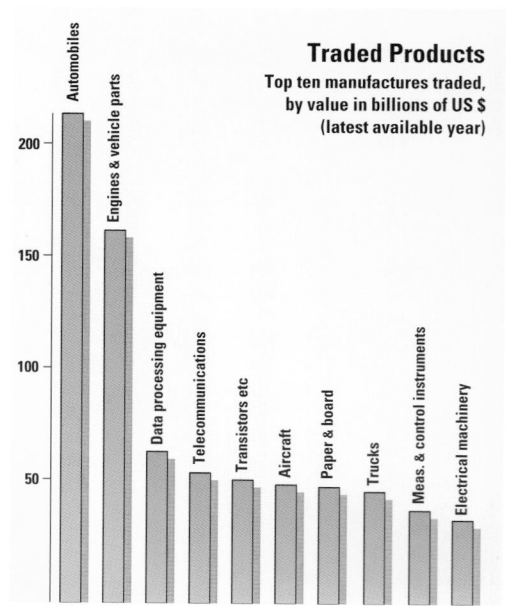

- Automobiles
- Engines & vehicle parts
- Data processing equipment
- Telecommunications
- Transistors etc
- Aircraft
- Paper & board
- Trucks
- Meas. & control instruments
- Electrical machinery

CARTOGRAPHY BY PHILIP'S, COPYRIGHT GEORGE PHILIP LTD

World Shipping

While ocean passenger traffic is nowadays relatively modest, sea transport still carries most of the world's trade. Oil and bulk carriers make up the majority of the world fleet, although the general cargo category is the fastest growing. Two innovations have revolutionized sea transport. The first is the development of the roll-on/roll-off (Ro-Ro) method where lorries or even trains loaded with freight are driven straight on to the ship, thus saving time. The second is containerization in which goods are packed into containers (the dimensions of which are fixed) at the factory, driven to the port and loaded on board by specialist machinery.

Almost 30% of world shipping sails under a "flag of convenience," whereby owners take advantage of low taxes by registering their vessels in a foreign country the ships will never see, notably Panama and Liberia.

Merchant Fleets

Merchant fleets in thousand gross tonnage (1996). A large number of vessels are registered in Liberia and Panama but they are not part of the national fleet.

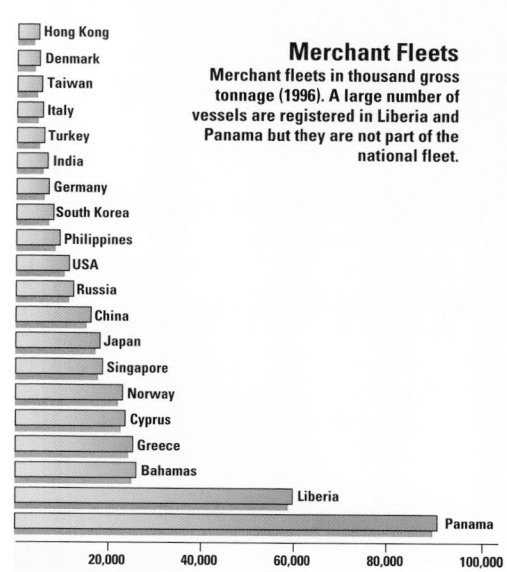

Hong Kong
Denmark
Taiwan
Italy
Turkey
India
Germany
South Korea
Philippines
USA
Russia
China
Japan
Singapore
Norway
Cyprus
Greece
Bahamas
Liberia
Panama

20,000   40,000   60,000   80,000   100,000

Trade in Primary Products

Primary products (excluding fuels, minerals and metals) as a percentage of total export value (latest available year)

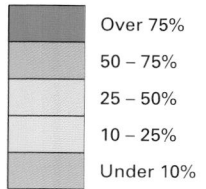

Over 75%
50 – 75%
25 – 50%
10 – 25%
Under 10%

Primary products are raw materials or partly processed products which form the basis for manufacturing. They are the necessary requirements of industries and include agricultural products, minerals and timber, as well as many semimanufactured goods such as cotton, which has been spun but not woven, wood pulp or flour. Many developed countries have few natural resources and rely on imports for the majority of their primary products. The countries of Southeast Asia export hardwoods to the rest of the world, whilst many South American countries are heavily dependent on coffee exports.

Balance of Trade

Value of exports in proportion to the value of imports (1995)

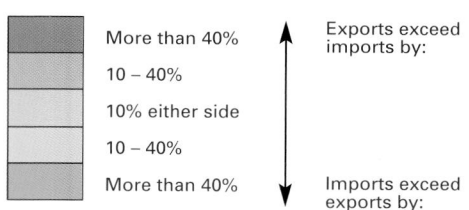

More than 40%   Exports exceed
10 – 40%   imports by:
10% either side
10 – 40%   Imports exceed
More than 40%   exports by:

The total world trade balance should amount to zero, since exports must equal imports on a global scale. In practice, at least $100 billion in exports go unrecorded, leaving the world with an apparent deficit and many countries in a better position than public accounting reveals. However, a favorable trade balance is not necessarily a sign of prosperity: many poorer countries must maintain a high surplus in order to service debts, and do so by restricting imports below the levels needed to sustain successful economies.

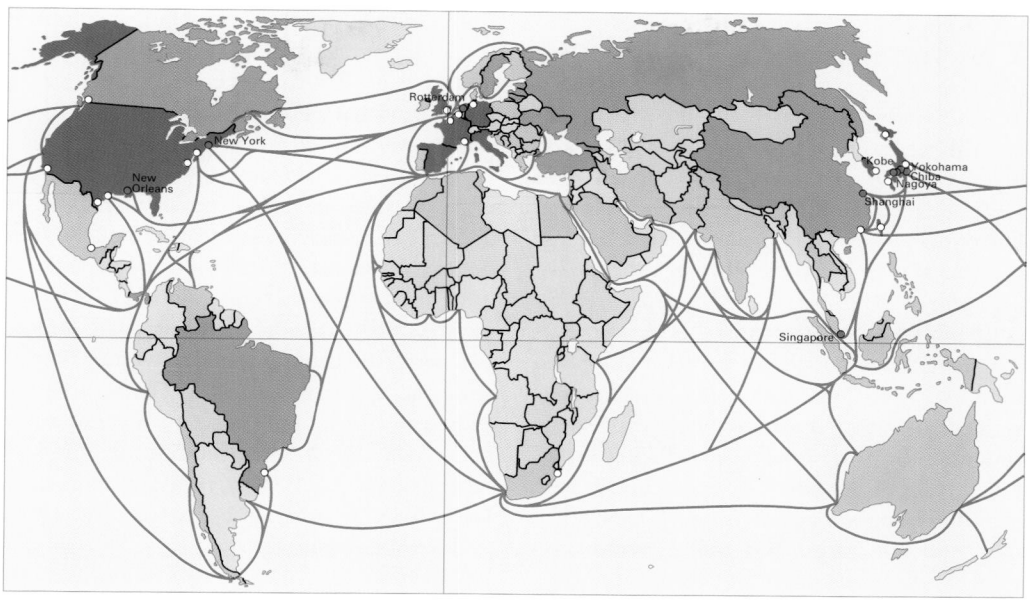

Types of Vessels

Oil tankers 38.4%
Ore & bulk carriers 29.9%
General cargo 16.1%
Others 9.7%
Ferries & passenger ships 0.5%
Liquid gas carriers 1.6%
Container ships 3.8%

The Great Ports

Total cargo traffic, thousand tons (1995)

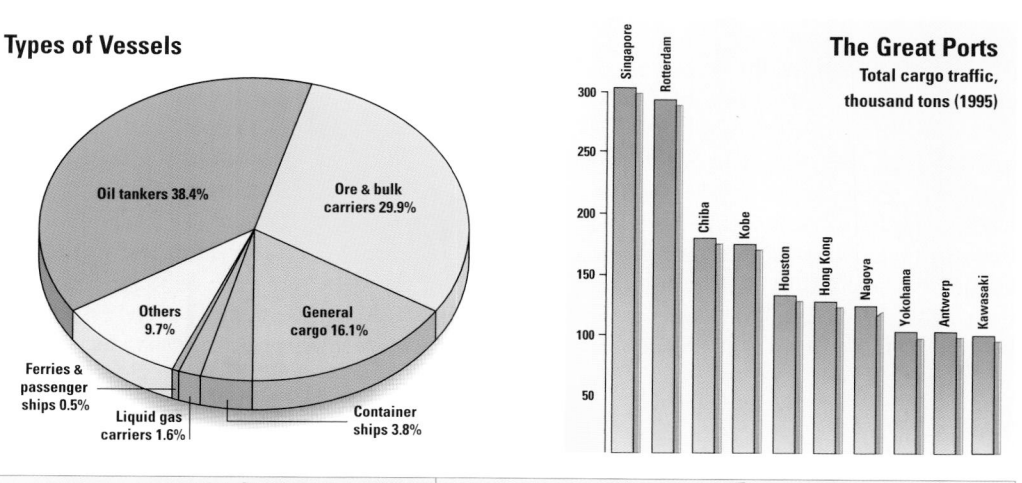

Singapore
Rotterdam
Chiba
Kobe
Houston
Hong Kong
Nagoya
Yokohama
Antwerp
Kawasaki

300
250
200
150
100
50

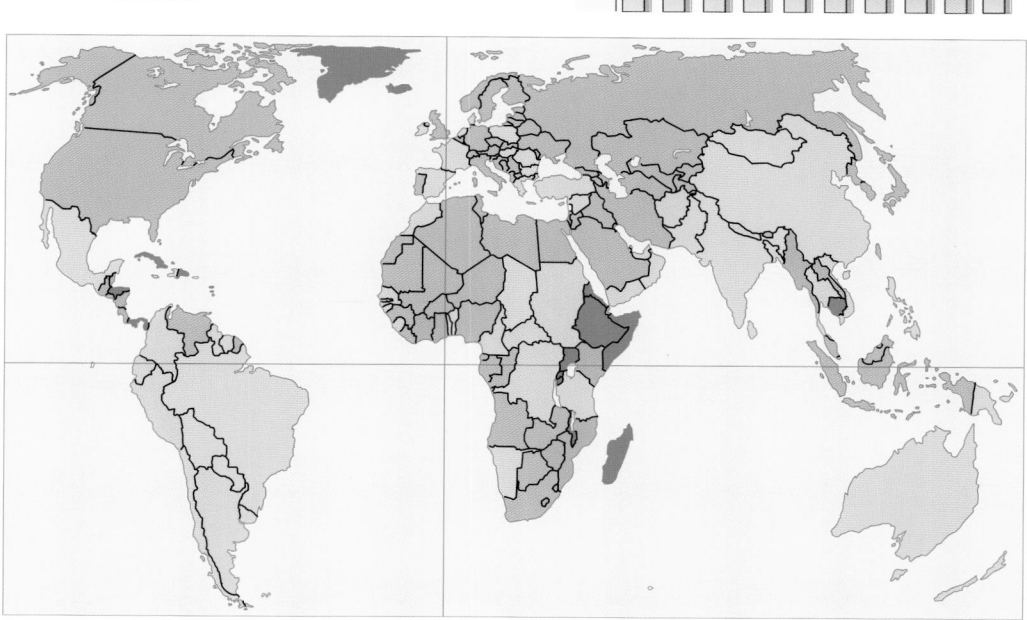

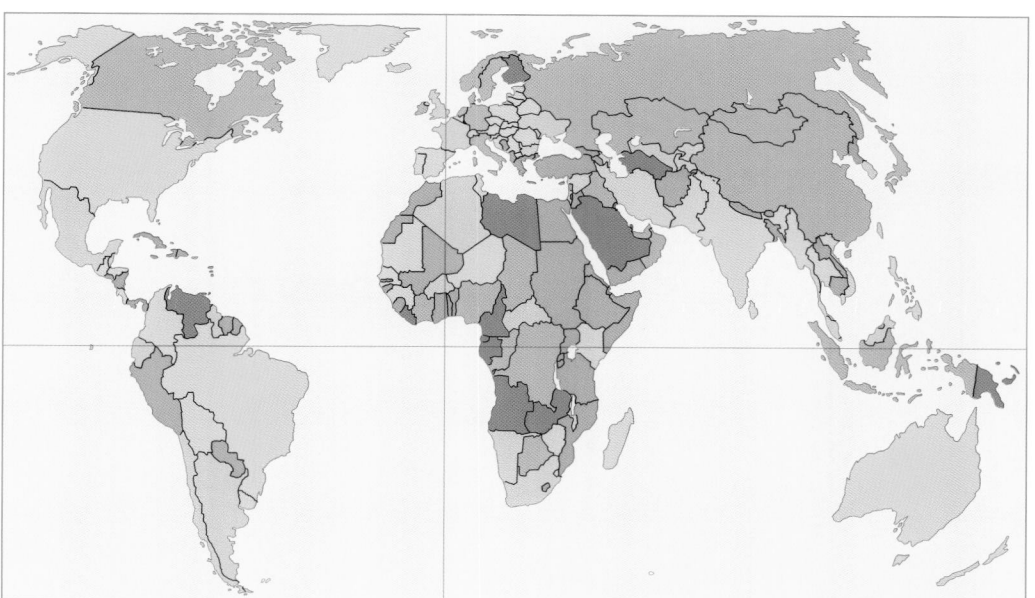

Freight

Freight unloaded in millions of tons (latest available year)

Over 100
50 – 100
10 – 50
5 – 10
Under 5
Landlocked countries

Major seaports

● Over 100 million tons per year
○ 50 – 100 million tons per year
— major shipping routes

Air Freight

Trends in air freight in million ton-km*, selected countries (1988–92)

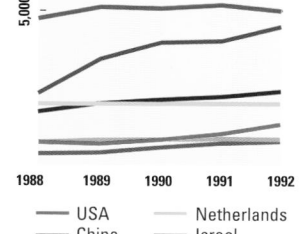

20,000
15,000
10,000
5,000

1988   1989   1990   1991   1992

— USA   — Netherlands
— China   — Israel
— Japan   — Malaysia
— UK

* Equivalent to million tons of air freight flown over 1 million km [650,000 miles] per year.

Air transport is important to countries of considerable size; where ground terrain is difficult; when crossing short stretches of sea; and where goods are of high value, light in weight or perishable. Recent deregulation of airlines (in the USA since 1978 and the EU in 1993) has led to increased competition and lower fares.

Health

Average life expectancies all over the world have never been higher. They range from an average of 77 years in high-income economies, to 67 years in middle-income economies and 63 in low-income economies. Even in poverty-stricken and strife-torn Burundi and Ethiopia, average life expectancies are around 50 years, as compared with less than 30 years for a citizen of Berlin in 1880.

In global terms, the radical improvements in health have much to do with improvements in agriculture and, hence, nutrition, as well as health education, an increase in sanitation and the quality of drinking water, together with advances in medicine. These radical changes have been responsible for falling death rates and rapid population growth, together with the expectation by most people that improvements in health will continue.

Health standards, life expectancies and causes of death vary considerably between the developed and developing world. The map on this page shows that in most of Africa, Asia and Latin America, the average daily calorie supply per person is so low as to cause malnutrition. (The daily requirement rated adequate by the World Health Organization is between 2,300 and 2,500 calories per person per day.) Malnutrition is a serious condition.

For example, among pregnant women it causes high rates of child mortality.

Deficiency diseases occur when people do not have a balanced diet. Protein deficiency causes stunting and kwashiorkor, which can be fatal, especially among young children, while vitamin deficiencies cause such illnesses as beri beri, pellagra, scurvy and rickets. Iron deficiency causes anemia, while a lack of iodine causes mental retardation. A UN report in the early 1990s reported that iodine deficiency affected 458 million women world-wide, as compared with 238 million men. Women's nutritional problems are especially acute in southern Asia. For example, the UN report stated that 88% of pregnant women in India were anemic, as compared with 15% in developed countries.

Infectious diseases in association, directly or indirectly, with deficient diets, continue to affect people in developing countries, especially the 48 countries in the low human development category, where, in 1990–95, only 32% of the people had access to sanitation and 68% to safe water supplies.

A World Health report in 1996 stated that infectious diseases cause 17 million deaths per year. Most of the victims are young and otherwise fit people in developing countries. The major killers in 1995 were respiratory infections, including pneumonia (which caused

4.4 million deaths), cholera, typhoid, dysentery (3.1 million together), tuberculosis (almost 3 million), malaria (2.1 million), hepatitis B (1.1 million), AIDS and measles (more than 1 million each). Many of these diseases are preventable and, according to the United Nations Children's Fund, an investment of US $25,000 million per year, about half the money spent annually on cigarettes in Europe alone, would save the lives of all the children who currently die from avoidable diseases.

Infectious diseases are much less important as causes of death in developed countries, where cancer and circulatory diseases, such as atherosclerosis and hypertension, which cause strokes and heart attacks, are the most common causes of fatality. Because these diseases tend to kill older people, they are relatively less important in developing countries where people have shorter lifespans.

Harmful habits are also generally practised more by the rich than the poor. For example, smoking is an important cause of death in developed countries, though, curiously, the Japanese, with an average life expectancy of 79 years in 1996, are among the highest tobacco consumers. Similarly, high alcohol consumption, although it has bad effects on health, does not seem to affect longevity. The leading consumers, the French, had a life expectancy of 78 in 1996.

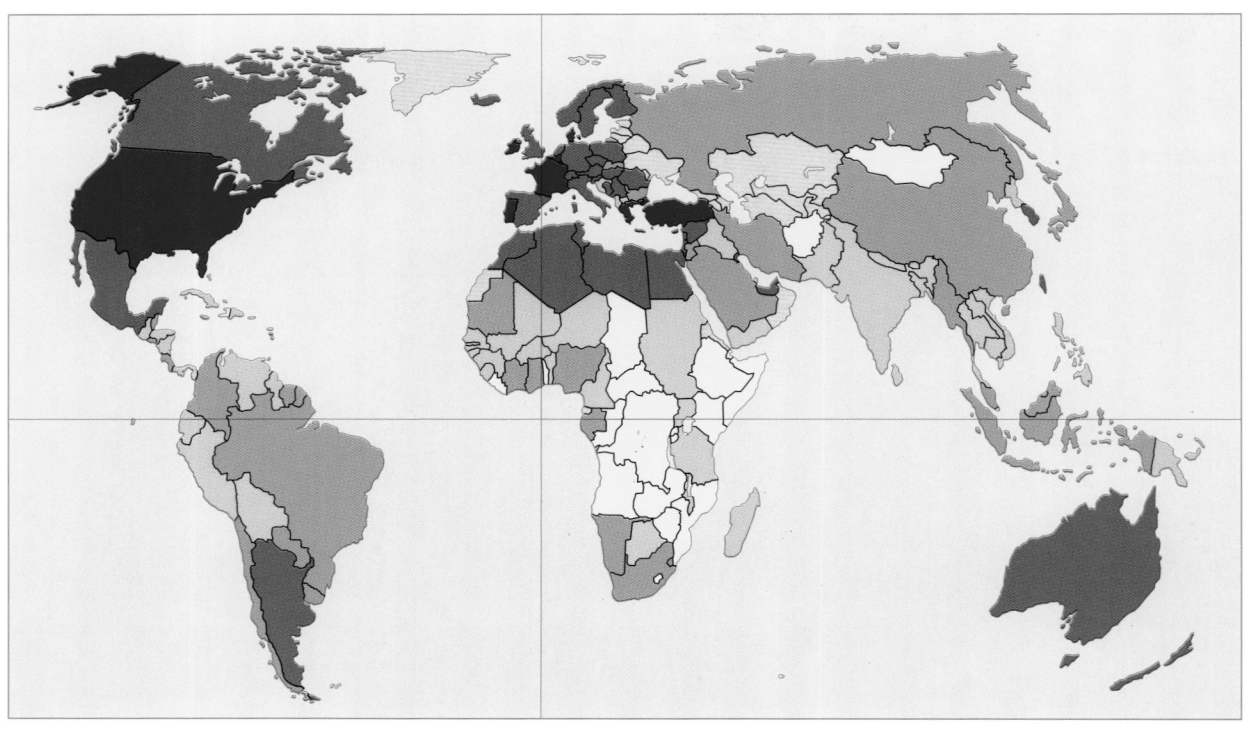

Food Consumption

Average daily food intake in calories per person (1995)

- Over 3,500 calories
- 3,000 – 3,500 calories
- 2,500 – 3,000 calories
- 2,000 – 2,500 calories
- Under 2,000 calories
- No available data

Top 5 countries

Cyprus .... 3,708 calories
Denmark .... 3,704 calories
Portugal .... 3,639 calories
Ireland .... 3,638 calories
USA .... 3,603 calories

Bottom 5 countries

Congo (D. Rep.) ...... 1,879 calories
Djibouti .... 1,831 calories
Togo .... 1,754 calories
Burundi .... 1,749 calories
Mozambique .... 1,678 calories

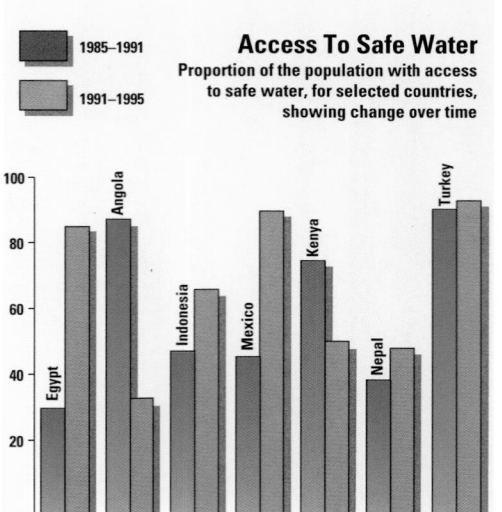

Access To Safe Water
Proportion of the population with access to safe water, for selected countries, showing change over time

- 1985–1991
- 1991–1995

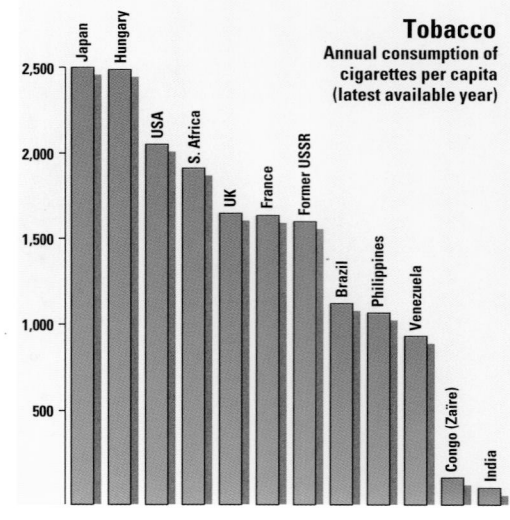

Tobacco
Annual consumption of cigarettes per capita (latest available year)

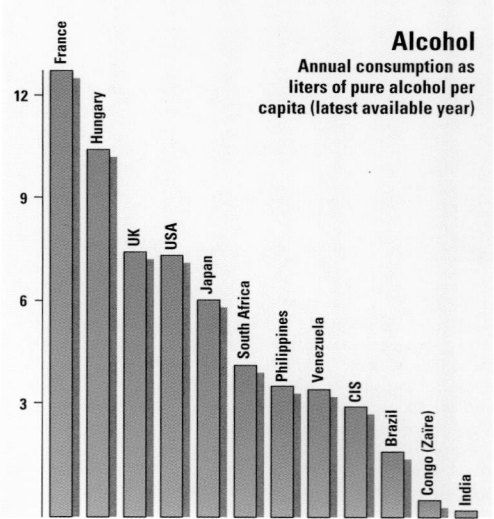

Alcohol
Annual consumption as liters of pure alcohol per capita (latest available year)

CARTOGRAPHY BY PHILIP'S, COPYRIGHT GEORGE PHILIP LTD

Life Expectancy

Years of life expectancy at birth, selected countries (1997)

The chart shows combined data for both sexes. On average, women live longer than men worldwide, even in developing countries with high maternal mortality rates. Overall, life expectancy is steadily rising, though the difference between rich and poor nations remains dramatic.

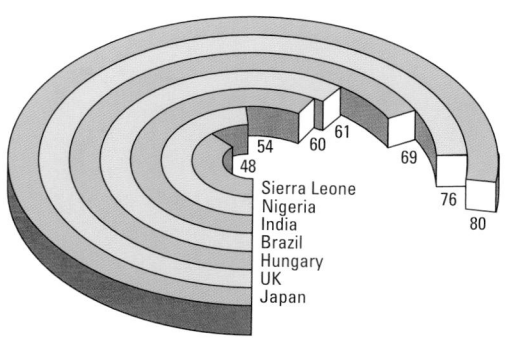

48 Sierra Leone
54 Nigeria
60 India
61 Brazil
69 Hungary
76 UK
80 Japan

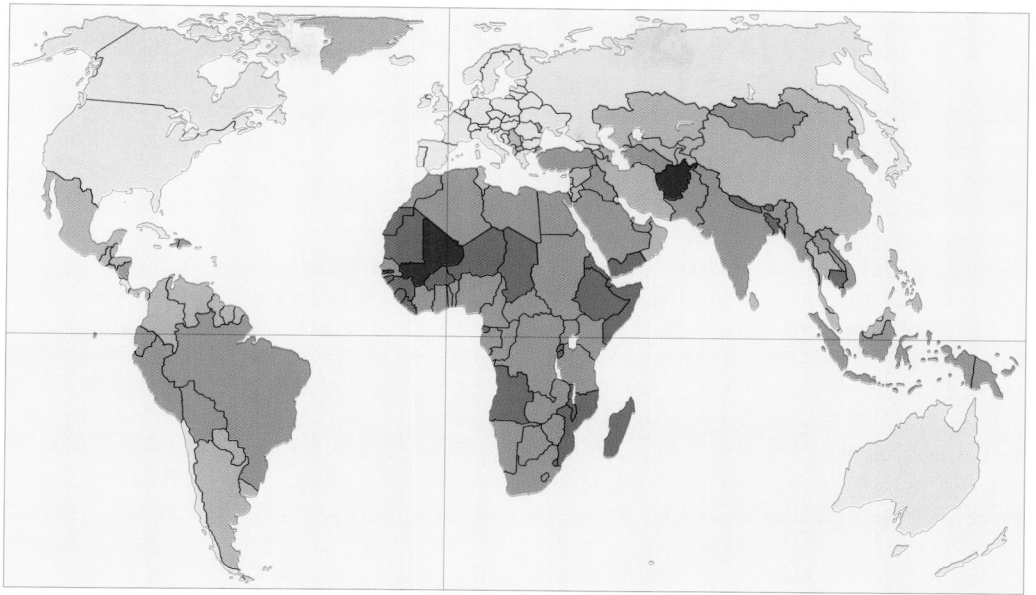

Child Mortality

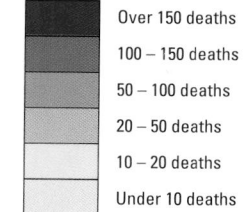

Number of babies who will die under the age of one, per 1,000 births (average 1990–95)

- Over 150 deaths
- 100 – 150 deaths
- 50 – 100 deaths
- 20 – 50 deaths
- 10 – 20 deaths
- Under 10 deaths

Highest child mortality
Afghanistan .... 162 deaths
Mali .... 159 deaths

Lowest child mortality
Iceland .... 5 deaths
Finland .... 5 deaths

[UK 8 deaths] [USA 8 deaths]

Expenditure on Health

Public expenditure on health as a percentage of GNP (1996)

Countries with the highest spending		Countries with the lowest spending	
USA	14.2	Sudan	0.3
Argentina	10.6	Cameroon	1.4
Germany	10.4	Ghana	1.4
Croatia	10.1	Nigeria	1.4
Switzerland	10.0	Indonesia	1.8
France	9.9	Sri Lanka	1.9
Canada	9.6	Eritrea	2.0
Czech Rep.	9.6	Bangladesh	2.4
Australia	8.9	Kenya	2.5

The allocation of limited funds for health care in developing countries is rarely evenly spread – the quality of treatment can vary enormously from place to place within the same country. Urban dwellers tend to have much better access to health provisions than those living in rural areas.

Medical Provision

Doctors per 100,000 population, selected countries (latest available year, 1996)

Although the ratio of people to doctors gives a good approximation of a country's health provision, it is not an absolute indicator. Raw numbers may mask inefficiency and other weaknesses: the high proportion of physicians in Hungary, for example, has not prevented infant mortality rates more than twice as high as in the United Kingdom.

The definition of a doctor also varies from nation to nation. As well as registered medical practitioners, it may include trained medical assistants – an especially important category in developing countries, where they provide many of the same services as fully qualified physicians, including simple operations.

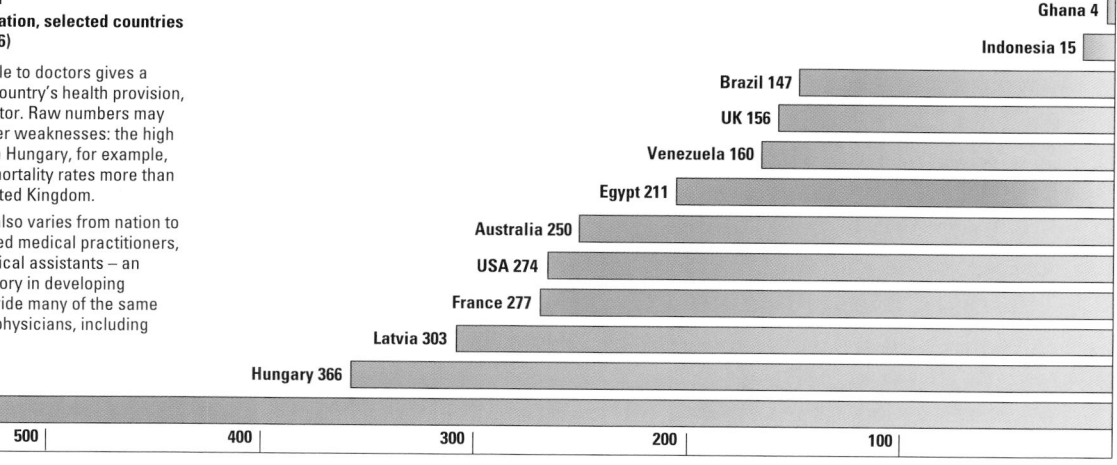

Ghana 4
Indonesia 15
Brazil 147
UK 156
Venezuela 160
Egypt 211
Australia 250
USA 274
France 277
Latvia 303
Hungary 366
Italy 518

500 400 300 200 100

The Aids Crisis

The Acquired Immune Deficiency Syndrome (AIDS) was first identified in 1981 when American doctors found otherwise healthy young men succumbing to rare infections. By 1984 the cause had been traced to the Human Immunodeficiency Virus (HIV) which can remain dormant for many years and perhaps indefinitely: only half of those known to carry the virus in 1981 had developed AIDS ten years later.

In Western countries in the mid-1990s, most AIDS deaths were among male homosexuals or needle-sharing drug-users. However, the disease is spreading fastest among heterosexual men and women, which is its usual vector in the developing world where most of its victims live.

The World Health Organization estimated that 1.3 million people died of AIDS in 1995 and that by the end of the same year 22 million people were HIV-positive. India has the largest number of HIV infections totaling more than 3 million, but two-thirds of all infections are in sub-Saharan Africa (where, unlike the rest of the world, more women are infected than men). It was estimated that 2 million African children would die of AIDS before the year 2000 and some 10 million would be orphaned.

Causes of Death

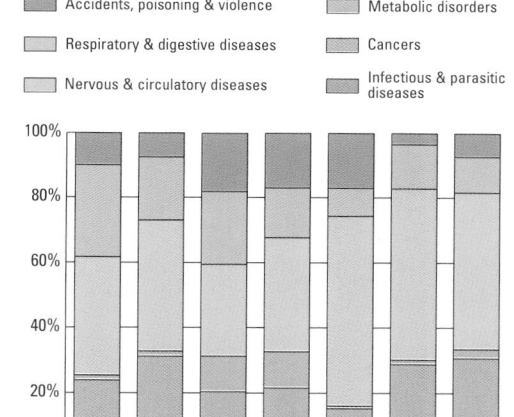

- Accidents, poisoning & violence
- Metabolic disorders
- Respiratory & digestive diseases
- Cancers
- Nervous & circulatory diseases
- Infectious & parasitic diseases

100%
80%
60%
40%
20%
0

China Japan Mexico Morocco Russia UK USA

Circulatory Disease in Europe

Diseases of the circulatory system per 100,000 people (latest available year 1992–95)

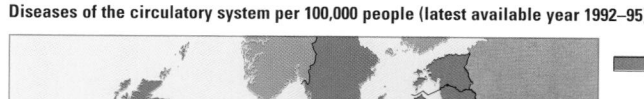
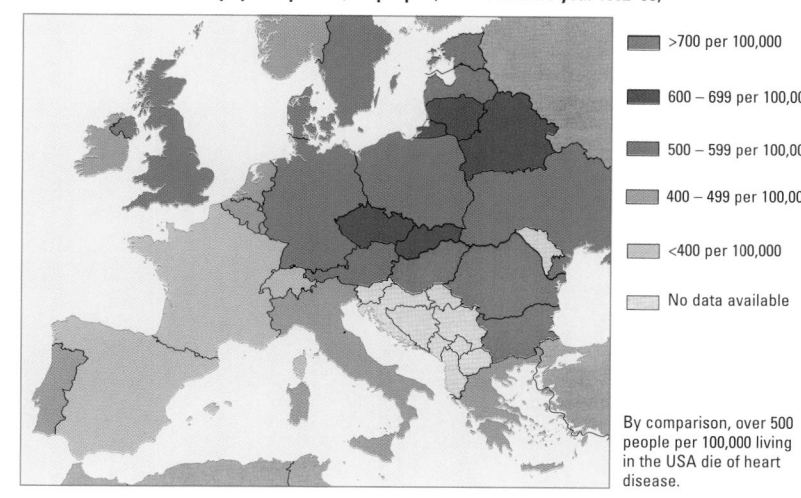

- >700 per 100,000
- 600 – 699 per 100,000
- 500 – 599 per 100,000
- 400 – 499 per 100,000
- <400 per 100,000
- No data available

By comparison, over 500 people per 100,000 living in the USA die of heart disease.

Aids

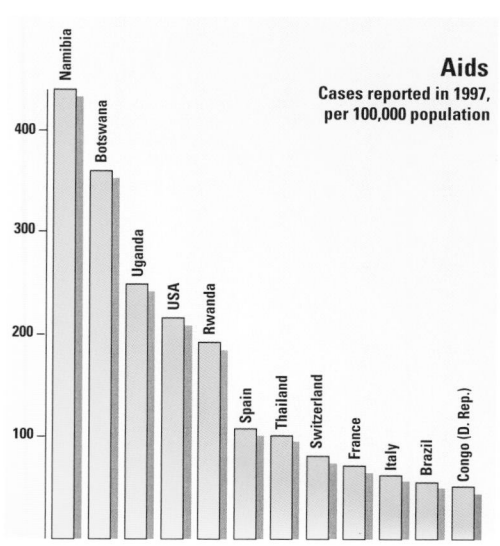

Cases reported in 1997, per 100,000 population

Namibia
Botswana
Uganda
USA
Rwanda
Spain
Thailand
Switzerland
France
Italy
Brazil
Congo (D. Rep.)

400
300
200
100

Sanitation

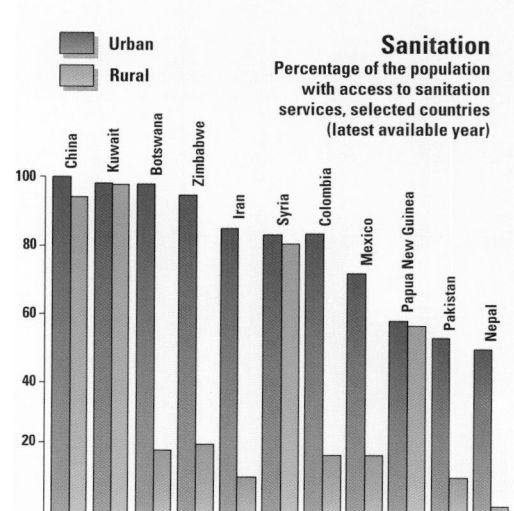

- Urban
- Rural

Percentage of the population with access to sanitation services, selected countries (latest available year)

China
Kuwait
Botswana
Zimbabwe
Iran
Syria
Colombia
Mexico
Papua New Guinea
Pakistan
Nepal

100
80
60
40
20

Malaria

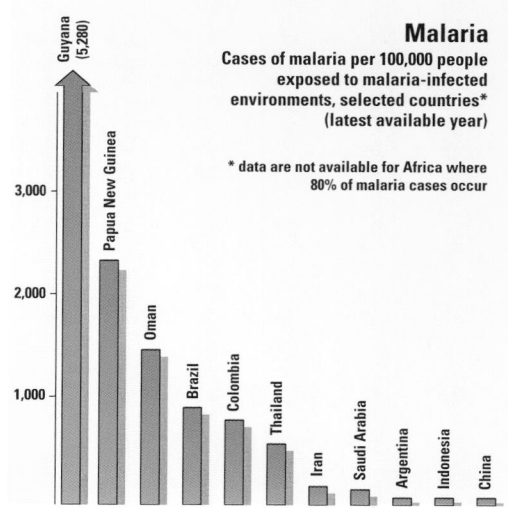

Cases of malaria per 100,000 people exposed to malaria-infected environments, selected countries* (latest available year)

* data are not available for Africa where 80% of malaria cases occur

Guyana (5,280)
Papua New Guinea
Oman
Brazil
Colombia
Thailand
Iran
Saudi Arabia
Argentina
Indonesia
China

3,000
2,000
1,000

Infectious and parasitic diseases, such as malaria, which claimed 2.1 million lives in 1995, remain a scourge in the developing countries. Respiratory infections and injury also claim more lives in developing countries, which lack the drugs and the medical personnel to deal with them. Developing countries lack the basic services taken for granted in developed nations. For example, in sub-Saharan Africa in 1990–95, only 31% of the population had access to sanitation and 45% to safe water, with the situation being worse in rural areas. By contrast, circulatory diseases and cancer are the main causes of death in the rich, industrialized countries. For example, in the UK in the mid-1990s, circulatory diseases, which cause heart attacks and strokes, accounted for nearly half the deaths, with cancer accounting for nearly a quarter.

Wealth

Perhaps the most glaring differences in the world today are those between the rich and the poor. The World Bank divides countries into three main groups based on average economic production expressed in terms of per capita GNP (Gross National Product). They are the low-income economies, including most African countries and much of Asia; the middle-income economies, including most of Latin America and most of the former USSR; and the high-income economies of Canada, the United States, Western Europe, Japan and Australia.

Per capita GNPs are a measure of the total goods and services produced by a country divided by the population, and then converted into US dollars at official exchange rates. They are useful indicators of a country's prosperity, though, like all statistics, they must be treated with care. For example, the prices for goods and services in China are far cheaper than they are in the United States. China's per capita GNP in 1998 was $750 (as compared with $29,340 in the USA) but the PPP (Purchasing-Power Parity) estimate of China's per capita GNP was considerably higher at $3,570. Another problem with per capita GNPs is that they are averages, which often conceal wide internal variations.

The pattern of poverty varies from region to region. In Latin America, much progress has been made through industrialization, though startling inequalities still exist between rich and poor. In Asia, the "tiger economies" have followed Japan's example in pursuing export-led industrial policies, while the success of China's Special Economic Zones, where foreign investment is encouraged, has led to a huge rise in China's per capita GNP, as shown on the map on page 45, bottom right.

Solutions to poverty in Africa are much harder to find because of its high population growth, civil wars, natural disasters and high inflation rates. Although Africa receives more aid than any other continent, aid is only a partial solution. Much aid has been wasted on overambitious projects, in the servicing of huge national debts, or lost by inexperienced or corrupt governments. One initiative in some African countries has been to improve the infrastructure and develop tourism, creating employment and providing much-needed foreign currency. But tourism alone cannot solve the problems of underdevelopment.

The International Monetary Fund and the World Bank argue that real economic progress in Africa will be achieved only when African countries create market-friendly economies that encourage trade through export-led manufacturing, while at the same time strictly controlling public spending on welfare, the civil service and other areas.

Continental Shares

Shares of population and of wealth (GNP) by continent

These generalized continental figures show the startling difference between rich and poor but mask the successes or failures of individual countries. Japan, for example, with less than 4% of Asia's population, produces almost 70% of the continent's output. Within countries, the difference between rich and poor can also be startling. In Brazil, for example, the richest 20% of the population own 60% of the wealth.

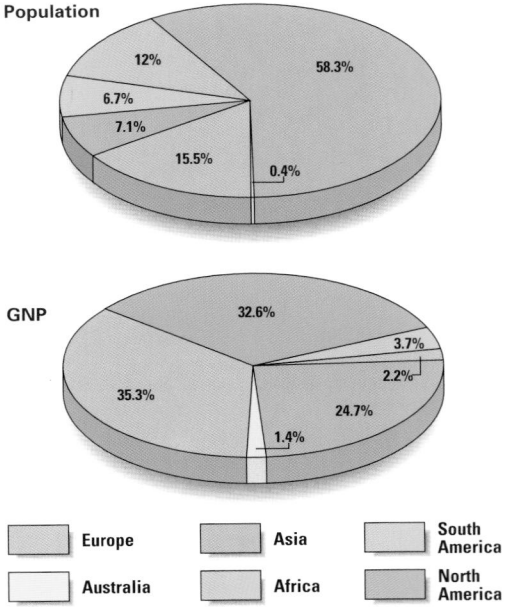

Population

GNP

Europe Asia South America
Australia Africa North America

Currencies

Currency units of the world's most powerful economies

1. USA: US dollar ($, US $)
   = 100 cents
2. Japan: Yen (Y, ¥)
   = 100 sen
3. Germany: Euro; Deutsche Mark (DM) = 100 Pfennig
4. France: Euro; French franc (Fr)
   = 100 centimes
5. Italy: Euro; Italian lira (L, £, Lit)
6. UK: Pound sterling (£)
   = 100 pence
7. Canada: Canadian dollar (C$, Can$) = 100 cents
8. China: Renminbi yuan (RMBY, $, Y) = 10 jiao = 100 fen
9. Brazil: Cruzeiro real (BRC)
   = 100 centavos
10. Spain: Euro; Peseta (Pta, Pa)
    = 100 céntimos
11. India: Indian rupee (Re, Rs)
    = 100 paisa
12. Australia: Australian dollar ($A) = 100 cents
13. Netherlands: Euro; Guilder, florin (Gld, f) = 100 centimes
14. Switzerland: Swiss franc (SFr, SwF) = 100 centimes
15. South Korea: Won (W)
    = 100 chon
16. Sweden: Swedish krona (SKr)
    = 100 ore
17. Mexico: Mexican peso (Mex$) = 100 centavos
18. Belgium: Euro; Belgian franc (BFr) = 100 centimes
19. Austria: Euro; Schilling (S, Sch) = 100 Groschen
20. Finland: Euro; Markka (FMk)
    = 100 penniä
21. Denmark: Danish krone (DKr)
    = 100 øre
22. Norway: Norwegian krone (NKr) = 100 øre
23. Saudi Arabia: Riyal (SAR, SRI$) = 100 halalah
24. Indonesia: Rupiah (Rp)
    = 100 sen
25. South Africa: Rand (R)
    = 100 cents

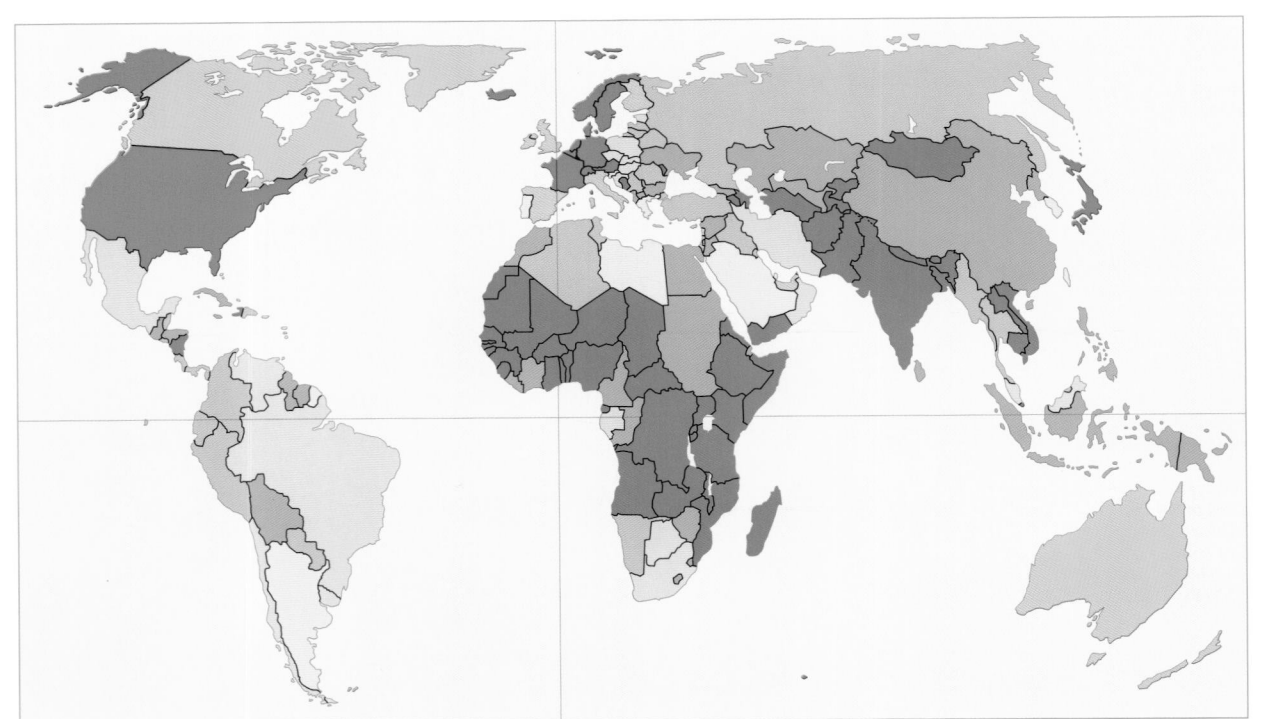

Levels of Income

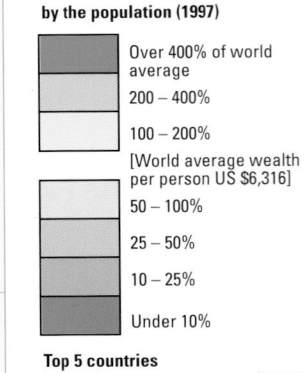

Gross National Product per capita: the value of total production divided by the population (1997)

Over 400% of world average
200 – 400%
100 – 200%
[World average wealth per person US $6,316]
50 – 100%
25 – 50%
10 – 25%
Under 10%

Top 5 countries

Luxembourg	$45,360
Switzerland	$44,220
Japan	$37,850
Norway	$36,090
Liechtenstein	$33,000

Bottom 5 countries

Mozambique	$90
Ethiopia	$110
Congo (Dem. Rep.)	$110
Burundi	$180
Sierra Leone	$200

Indicators

The gap between the world's rich and poor is now so great that it is difficult to illustrate on a single graph. Within each income group (as defined by the World Bank), however, comparisons have some meaning; the Chinese, perhaps because of propaganda value, have more TV sets than Indians, whereas Nigerians prefer to spend their money on radios. However, the wealth gap in many developing countries is wide, with a small, rich class and a large, impoverished majority, while many high-income countries contain an underclass of unemployed and homeless people.

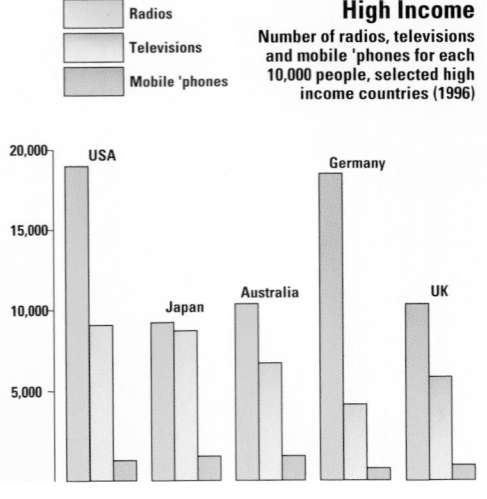

High Income
Number of radios, televisions and mobile 'phones for each 10,000 people, selected high income countries (1996)

Radios, Televisions, Mobile 'phones

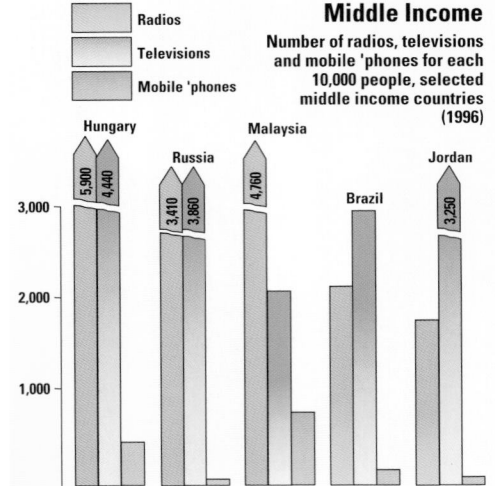

Middle Income
Number of radios, televisions and mobile 'phones for each 10,000 people, selected middle income countries (1996)

Radios, Televisions, Mobile 'phones

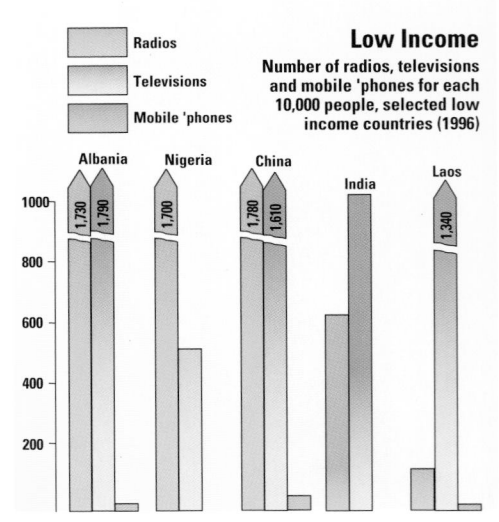

Low Income
Number of radios, televisions and mobile 'phones for each 10,000 people, selected low income countries (1996)

Radios, Televisions, Mobile 'phones

CARTOGRAPHY BY PHILIP'S. COPYRIGHT GEORGE PHILIP LTD

World Tourism

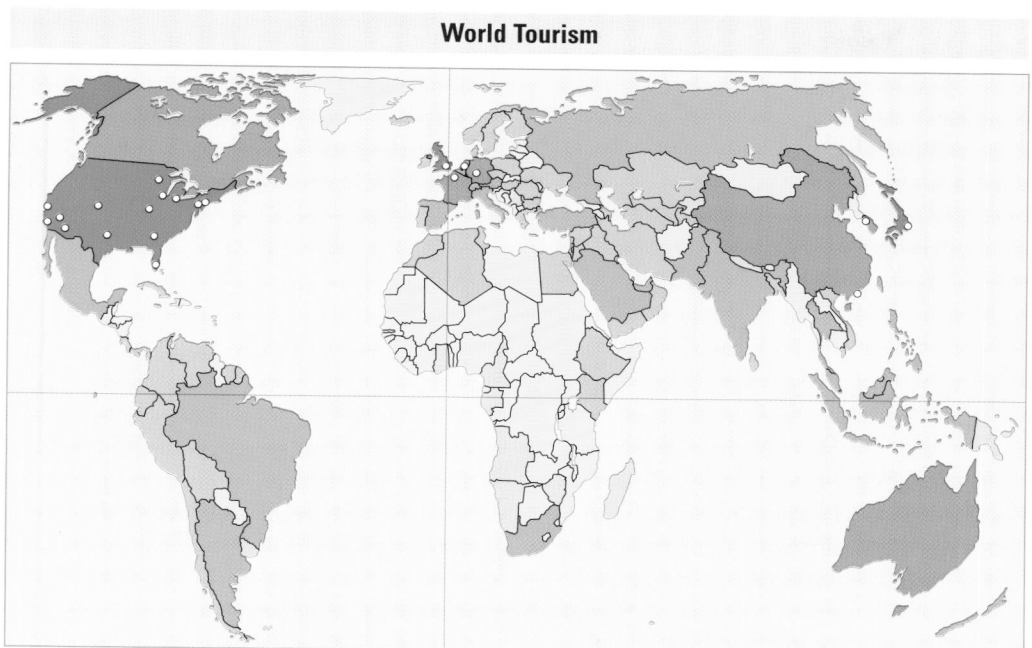

Passenger miles flown (the number of passengers multiplied by the distance flown by each passenger from the airport of origin) (1997)

- Over 60,000 million
- 30,000 – 60,000 million
- 6,000 – 30,000 million
- 600 – 6,000 million
- 300 – 600 million
- Under 300 million

○ Major airports (handling over 25 million passengers in 2000)

Leisure and tourism is the world's second largest industry in terms of revenue generated. Small economies in attractive areas are often completely dominated by tourism: in some Caribbean islands, tourist spending provides over 90% of the total income and is the biggest foreign exchange earner. In cash terms the USA is the world leader: its 1999 earnings exceeded US $74 billion, though that sum amounted to approximately 0.9% of its total GDP. Of the 48 million visitors to the USA, 34% came from Canada and 25% from Mexico. Germany spends the most on overseas tourism; this amounts to over US $50,000 million. The next biggest spenders are the USA, Japan and the UK.

The world's busiest airport in terms of total number of passengers is Atlanta (78.1 million passengers in 1999); the busiest international airport is London's Heathrow.

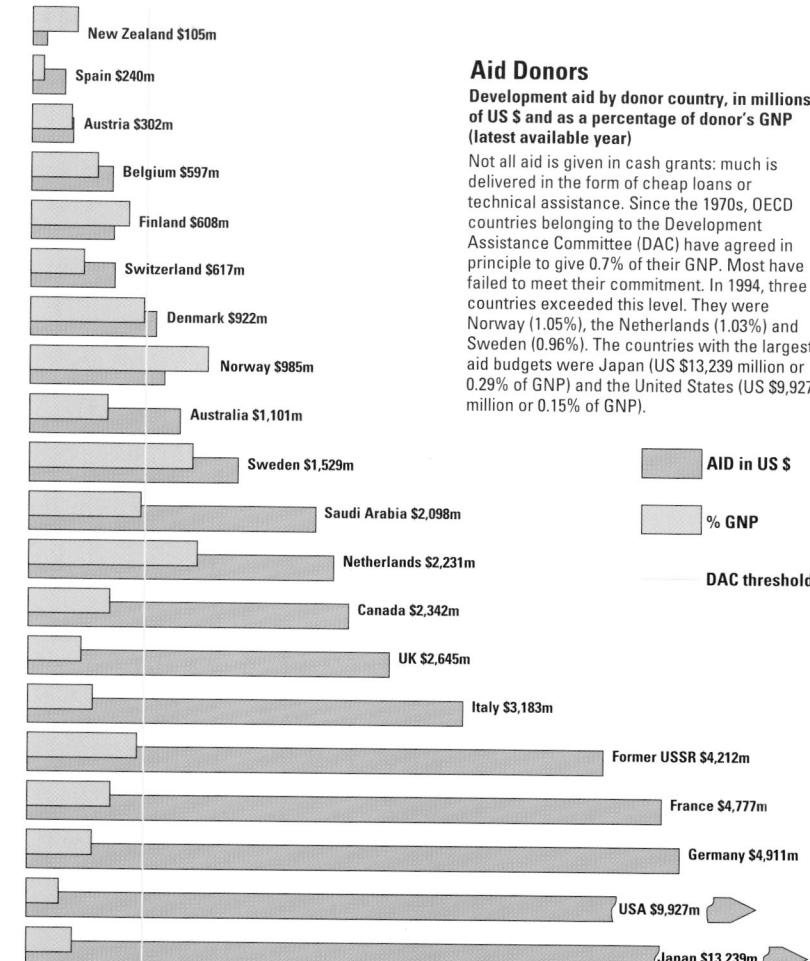

Aid Donors

Development aid by donor country, in millions of US $ and as a percentage of donor's GNP (latest available year)

Not all aid is given in cash grants: much is delivered in the form of cheap loans or technical assistance. Since the 1970s, OECD countries belonging to the Development Assistance Committee (DAC) have agreed in principle to give 0.7% of their GNP. Most have failed to meet their commitment. In 1994, three countries exceeded this level. They were Norway (1.05%), the Netherlands (1.03%) and Sweden (0.96%). The countries with the largest aid budgets were Japan (US $13,239 million or 0.29% of GNP) and the United States (US $9,927 million or 0.15% of GNP).

- AID in US $
- % GNP
- DAC threshold

New Zealand $105m
Spain $240m
Austria $302m
Belgium $597m
Finland $608m
Switzerland $617m
Denmark $922m
Norway $985m
Australia $1,101m
Sweden $1,529m
Saudi Arabia $2,098m
Netherlands $2,231m
Canada $2,342m
UK $2,645m
Italy $3,183m
Former USSR $4,212m
France $4,777m
Germany $4,911m
USA $9,927m
Japan $13,239m

0.5% 1% 1.5% 2% 2.5%

State Finance

Inflation rates, shown on the map, right, are an index of a country's financial stability and usually of its prosperity. Annual inflation rates above 20% are usually marked by slow or even negative growth of the GNP. Above 50%, it becomes hyperinflation and an economy is reeling. In the late 1980s and early 1990s, many high-income countries had to contend with annual inflation rates of 10% or more, while Japan, the growth leader, had an average inflation rate of 1.3% between 1985 and 1994.

The per capita GNP figures listed below are useful indicators of economic success or failure, but they do not account for living costs. Nor do they reveal the gaps between the rich and poor within countries.

Market-friendly policies, including low taxes and state spending, liberal trade policies and a welcome for foreign investors, are major factors in countries which have enjoyed rapid economic growth since 1980. For example, the setting up of Special Economic Zones in eastern China has led to a spectacular rise in the per capita GNP. Other successful countries include the "tiger economies" of South Korea, Thailand and Singapore, although an Asian market crash in 1997 temporarily halted the dramatic economic expansion in these countries.

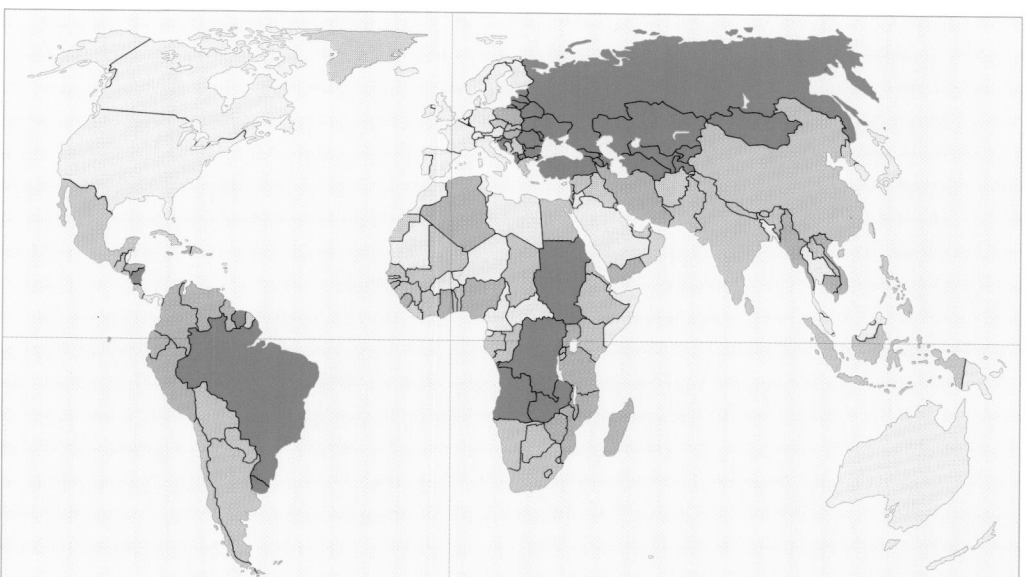

Inflation

Average annual rate of inflation (1990–96)

- Over 50%
- 20 – 50%
- 7.5 – 20%
- 1 – 7.5%
- Negative inflation
- No data available

Highest average inflation
Congo (Dem. R.) 2747%
Georgia 2279%
Angola 1103%

Lowest average inflation
Oman .... −3.0%
Bahrain .... −0.5%
Brunei .... −0.0%

The Wealth Gap

The world's richest and poorest countries, by Gross National Product per capita in US $ (1999 estimates)

1. Liechtenstein	50,000	1. Ethiopia	100
2. Luxembourg	44,640	2. Congo (D. Rep.)	110
3. Switzerland	38,350	3. Burundi	120
4. Bermuda	35,590	4. Sierra Leone	130
5. Norway	32,880	5. Guinea-Bissau	160
6. Japan	32,230	6. Niger	190
7. Denmark	32,030	7. Malawi	190
8. USA	30,600	8. Eritrea	200
9. Singapore	29,610	9. Chad	200
10. Iceland	29,280	10. Nepal	220
11. Austria	25,970	11. Angola	220
12. Germany	25,350	12. Mozambique	230
13. Sweden	25,040	13. Tanzania	240
14. Monaco	25,000	14. Burkina Faso	240
15. Belgium	24,510	15. Mali	240
16. Brunei	24,630	16. Rwanda	250
17. Netherlands	24,320	17. Madagascar	250
18. Finland	23,780	18. Cambodia	260
19. Hong Kong	23,520	19. São Tomé & Príncipe	270
20. France	23,480	20. Laos	280

GNP per capita is calculated by dividing a country's Gross National Product by its total population.

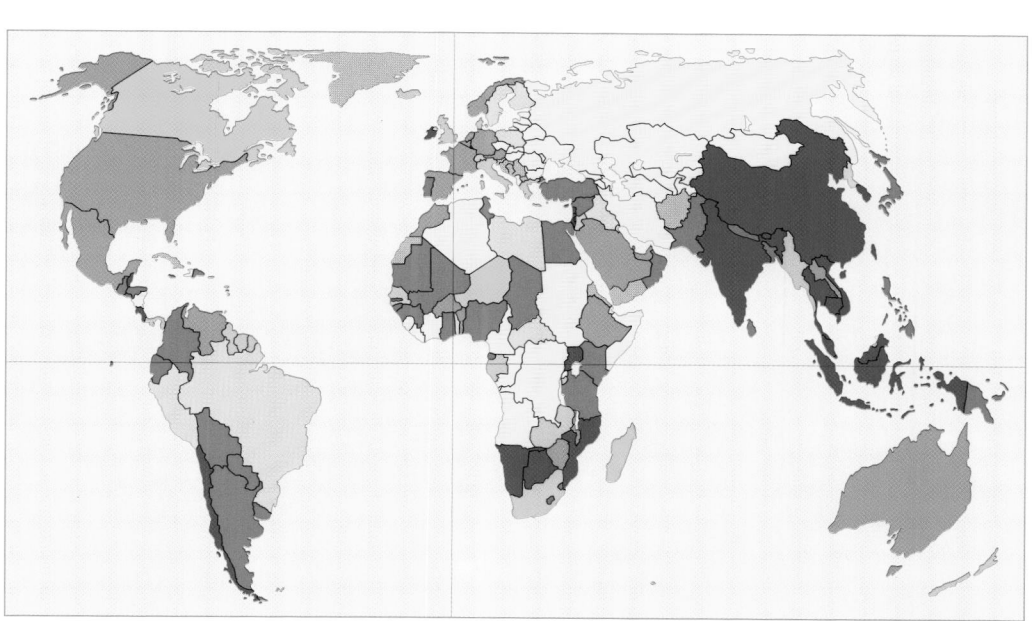

Growth in GNP

GNP per capita annual growth rate (1985–95)

- Over 5%
- 3 – 5%
- 2 – 3%
- 1 – 2%
- 0 – 1%
- Under 0%
- No data available

Countries with highest growth rates
Maldives 9.9%
Thailand 9.7%
China 9.3%
Botswana 9.0%
South Korea 8.5%

Standards of Living

Wealth is a basic factor in determining standards of living. Everywhere, the rich have more of everything, including higher average life expectancies, while the poor have to spend most of their income on basic human needs, such as food and clothing. Yet poverty and wealth are relative terms. Slum dwellers living on social security in an industrial society feel their poverty acutely, but they have far more resources than an average African living in a rural area.

In 1990 the United Nations Development Program published its first Human Development Index (HDI), an attempt to construct a comparative scale by which a simplified form of well-being might be measured. The HDI, expressed as a value between 0 and 0.999, combines figures for life expectancy and literacy with a wealth scale, based on Purchasing-Power Parity. The world's countries are divided into three groups, those with a high HDI (0.800 and above); those with a medium HDI (0.500 to 0.799); and those with a low HDI (below 0.500).

National scores for 1993 ranged from 0.951 for Canada to a low of 0.204 in Niger. In fact, of the 48 countries with a low HDI, 37 were from Africa, 10 from Asia, plus Haiti from the Caribbean.

Besides having low per capita GNPs, the average life expectancy in these countries was 56 years, while the adult literacy rate was 49%. By comparison, the average life expectancy at birth in countries in the high HDI group was 74 years, while the literacy rate was 97%.

Comparisons between countries with similar per capita GNPs reveal the effects of government actions. For example, the World Bank classifies both India and China as low-income economies, but India's HDI at 0.436 is much lower than that of China, at 0.609. This reflects not only China's economic progress in the 1980s and 1990s, but also differences in average life expectancies (61 years in India and 69 years in China), and adult literacy rates (51% in India and 80% in China).

Disparities in standards of living exist not only between countries but also between individuals, groups and regions within countries. For example, income distribution figures for 1995 show that, in the United States, the poorest 20% of households received less than 4% of the income.

Other contrasts exist in developing countries between rural communities, where incomes are low and basic services are often in short supply, and urban areas, where even those living in slums are generally better off than their rural neighbors. Other striking differences exist between men and women. For example, while adult literacy rates for men and women living in developed countries are more or less the same, large differences exist in many developing countries. In 1995, in countries in the lowest HDI category, only 37% of women were literate, as compared with 62% of men.

Female education is a factor in population control, especially as women's fertility rates appear to fall in direct proportion to the amount of secondary education they receive. This point was acknowledged in 1994 by the UN Population Fund, which defined four main objectives relating to women and population control. They were: the reduction of maternal, infant and child mortality; better education, especially for girls; universal access to reproductive health services; and gender equality.

Statistical analysis presents many problems of interpretation, especially when trying to define such intangible factors as a sense of well-being. For example, education helps create wealth; but are rich countries wealthy because their people are well-educated, or are they well-educated because they are rich?

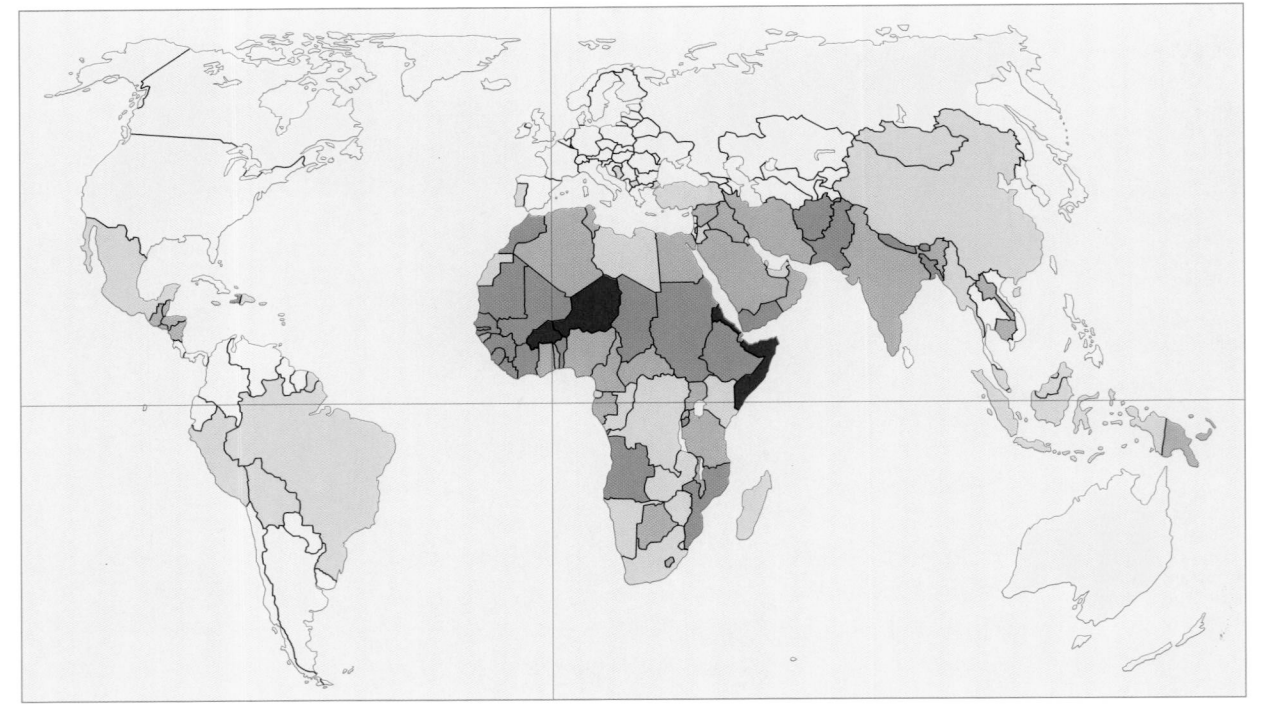

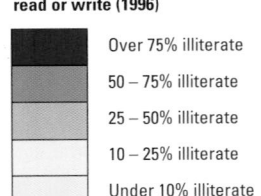

Illiteracy

% of the total population unable to read or write (1996)

- Over 75% illiterate
- 50 – 75% illiterate
- 25 – 50% illiterate
- 10 – 25% illiterate
- Under 10% illiterate

Educational expenditure per person (latest available year)

Top 5 countries

Sweden	$997
Qatar	$989
Canada	$983
Norway	$971
Switzerland	$796

Bottom 5 countries

Chad	$2
Bangladesh	$3
Ethiopia	$3
Nepal	$4
Somalia	$4

[UK $447]

Education

The developing countries made great efforts in the 1970s and 1980s to bring at least a basic education to their people. Primary school enrolments rose above 60% in all but the poorest nations. Figures often include teenagers or young adults, however, and there are still an estimated 300 million children worldwide who receive no schooling at all. A lack of resources has restricted the development of secondary and higher education. Most primary education is free in the poorer countries, but fees are often paid for secondary and higher education, thus heightening the differences between rich and poor.

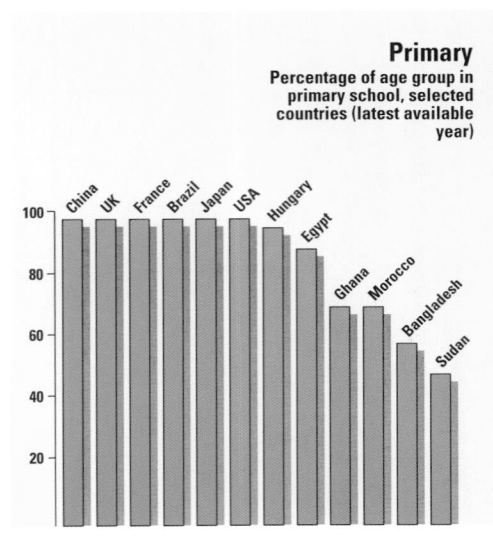

Primary
Percentage of age group in primary school, selected countries (latest available year)

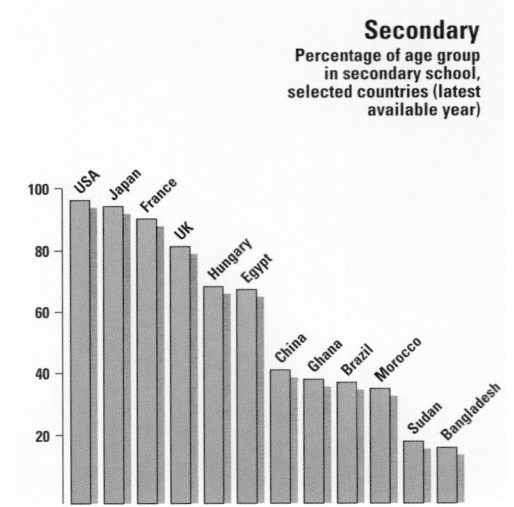

Secondary
Percentage of age group in secondary school, selected countries (latest available year)

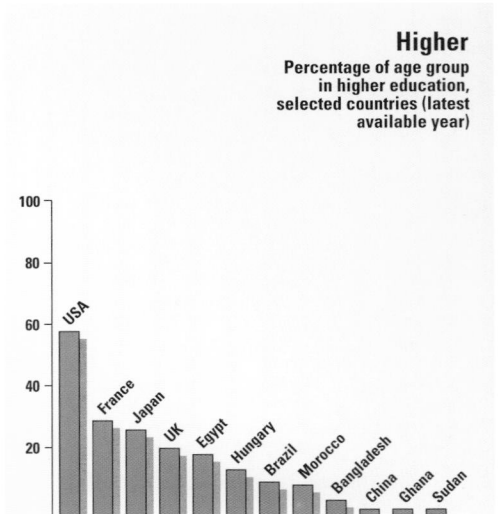

Higher
Percentage of age group in higher education, selected countries (latest available year)

CARTOGRAPHY BY PHILIP'S. COPYRIGHT GEORGE PHILIP LTD

Distribution of Spending

Percentage share of household spending (latest available year)

A high proportion of the average income of households in developing nations is spent on basic needs such as food and clothing. In most Western countries food and clothing account for less than 25% of expenditure.

Legend:
- Food
- Medicine & Education
- Clothing
- Transport
- Energy & Housing
- Other

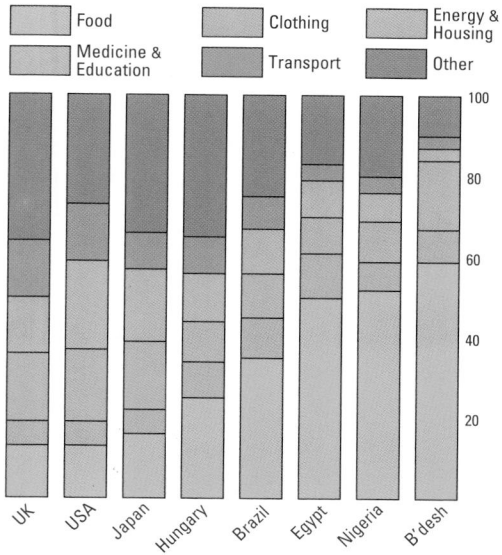

UK, USA, Japan, Hungary, Brazil, Egypt, Nigeria, B'desh

Distribution of Income

Percentage share of household income from poorest fifth to richest fifth, selected countries (latest available year)

The graph below shows that wealth is not distributed evenly throughout the population of the six countries. In every country worldwide the richest 20% of the population have a disproportionately high percentage of the income. This disparity between rich and poor is nowhere more pronounced than in Brazil, where the richest 20% of the population have over 60% of the income. The poorest 20%, on the other hand, have less than 5%.

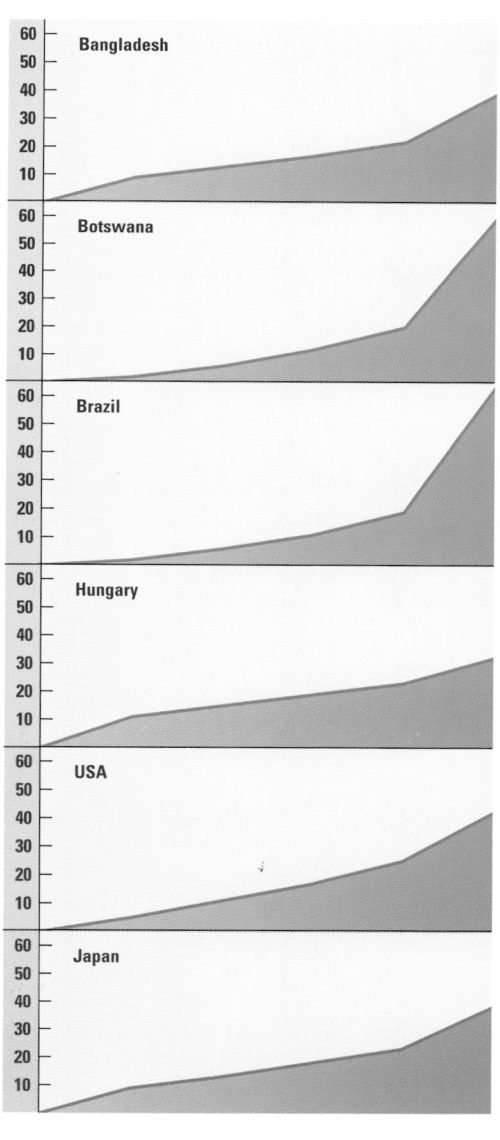

Bangladesh
Botswana
Brazil
Hungary
USA
Japan

Fertility and Education

Fertility rates compared with female education, selected countries (1992–95)

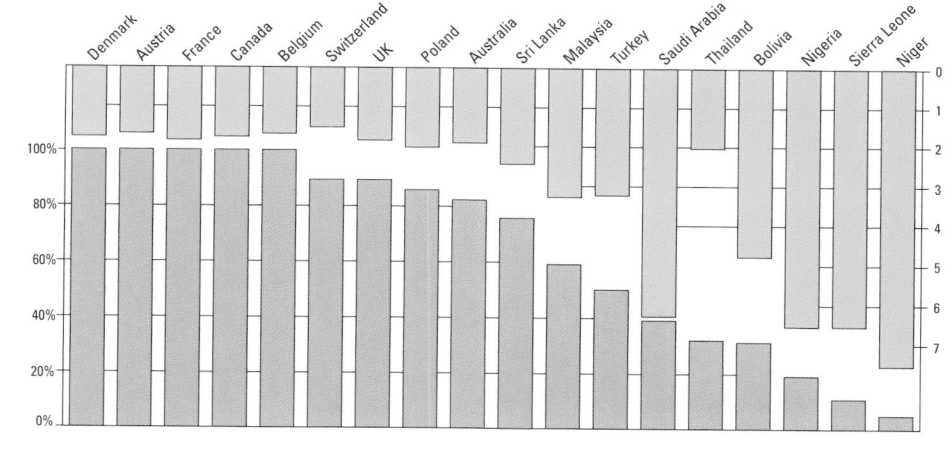

Denmark, Austria, France, Canada, Belgium, Switzerland, UK, Poland, Australia, Sri Lanka, Malaysia, Turkey, Saudi Arabia, Thailand, Bolivia, Nigeria, Sierra Leone, Niger

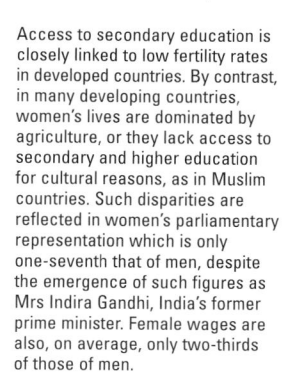

- Percentage of females aged 12–17 in secondary education
- Fertility rate: average number of children borne per woman

Access to secondary education is closely linked to low fertility rates in developed countries. By contrast, in many developing countries, women's lives are dominated by agriculture, or they lack access to secondary and higher education for cultural reasons, as in Muslim countries. Such disparities are reflected in women's parliamentary representation which is only one-seventh that of men, despite the emergence of such figures as Mrs Indira Gandhi, India's former prime minister. Female wages are also, on average, only two-thirds of those of men.

Women at Work

Women in paid employment as a percentage of the total work force (1996)

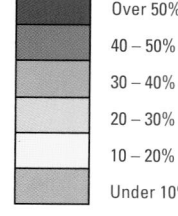

- Over 50%
- 40 – 50%
- 30 – 40%
- 20 – 30%
- 10 – 20%
- Under 10%

Most women in work

Cambodia	53%
Ghana	51%
Latvia	50%

Fewest women in work

Iraq	18%
Oman	15%
Saudi Arabia	14%

Car Ownership

Proportion of the world's vehicles, by region (1996)

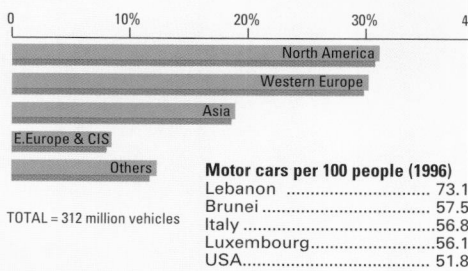

0   10%   20%   30%   40%

North America
Western Europe
Asia
E.Europe & CIS
Others

TOTAL = 312 million vehicles

Motor cars per 100 people (1996)

Lebanon	73.1
Brunei	57.5
Italy	56.8
Luxembourg	56.1
USA	51.8

Standards of Living in the USA by Race, Age and Region

A comparison of measures of income and education, by selected characteristics (1995)

Median income per household (US $), by age and region

15–24 years	20,979
25–34 years	34,701
35–44 years	43,465
45–54 years	48,058
55–64 years	38.077
65 years and over	19,096
Northeast	36,111
Midwest	35,839
South	30,942
West	35,979

Per capita income (US $), by race and Hispanic origin of householder

ALL RACES	17,227
White	18,304
Black	10,982
Asian & Pacific Is.	16,567
Hispanic (any race)	9,300

The poorest 20% of households received just 3.6% of the income, whereas the richest 20% received 48.2%.

Percentage of persons aged 25 and over who have completed High School, by race or origin

ALL RACES	1975	62.5
	1995	81.7
White	1975	64.5
	1995	83.0
Black	1975	42.5
	1995	73.8
Hispanic	1975	37.9
	1995	53.4

Regional Inequality in Italy

GERMANY, SWITZERLAND, AUSTRIA, HUNGARY, SLOVENIA, CROATIA, BOSNIA-HERZEGOVINA

Trento, Trieste, Venice, Aosta, Milan, Turin, Genoa, Bologna, Florence, Ancona, Perugia, L'Aquila, Rome, Campobasso, Naples, Bari, Potenza, Cagliari, Catanzaro, Palermo

MAP SCALE
0   100   200   300 km
0   100   200 miles

Gross Domestic Product (GDP) per capita in Italy, by region (1993)

- Over US $20,000
- $16,000 – $19,999
- $12,000 – $15,999
- $8,000 – $11,999
- Under $8,000

Average GDP per capita for Italy was $18,878. The per capita GDP, by comparison, for the UK was $17,920; for the USA $25,650; and for the EU $25,900.

The number of inhabitants per doctor, another social indicator, varies from less than 500 in the northwest of Italy to over 800 in the far south, with a national average of 607.

The southern part of Italy, known as the *Mezzogiorno* (or "Land of the midday sun"), has been described as the poorest part of the European Union. It is identifiable on the map, left, as all the regions with a GDP per capita of less than $12,000 (including the two islands of Sicily and Sardinia), plus Abruzzi whose capital is L'Aquila.

The *Mezzogiorno* region suffers from a lack of mineral and energy resources, industry, commerce, services and skilled labour. As a result, standards of living in the region are well below the rest of Italy and Europe. Employment is predominantly agricultural and small-scale.

The north of Italy accounts for 60% of the population but 80% of the GDP, whereas the *Mezzogiorno* accounts for 40% of the population and only 20% of the GDP. Manpower surpluses in the south led to emigration to other parts of Europe and the Americas. It has also led, especially in the last 50 years, to inter-regional migration from the islands and the southern mainland to the north. The main regions attracting migrants were the northwest – the prosperous Liguria–Piedmont–Lombardy triangle with its great industrial cities of Genoa, Milan and Turin – and the Venetia region in the northeast. As a result, the north has experienced much higher population growth rates than the rest of Italy.

In 1996 the Northern League, one of Italy's political parties, exploited the regional differences by declaring the north to be the independent "Republic of Padania." However, only a small minority of northerners supports secession.

CARTOGRAPHY BY PHILIP'S. COPYRIGHT GEORGE PHILIP LTD

— RHÔNE VALLEY, FRANCE —

From its source, the Rhône Glacier in Switzerland, the river
flows south past the Alps (right) to enter the Mediterranean
to the west of Marseille (at bottom right). Further west,
protected by sand bars, are the salt lagoons and marshes of
the Camargue, a UNESCO World Heritage site. On the
opposite bank, to the east, is a large lake, the Étang de Berre.
The pink area between the lake and the river is the arid,
boulder-strewn Plaine de Crau.

CITY MAPS

City Maps

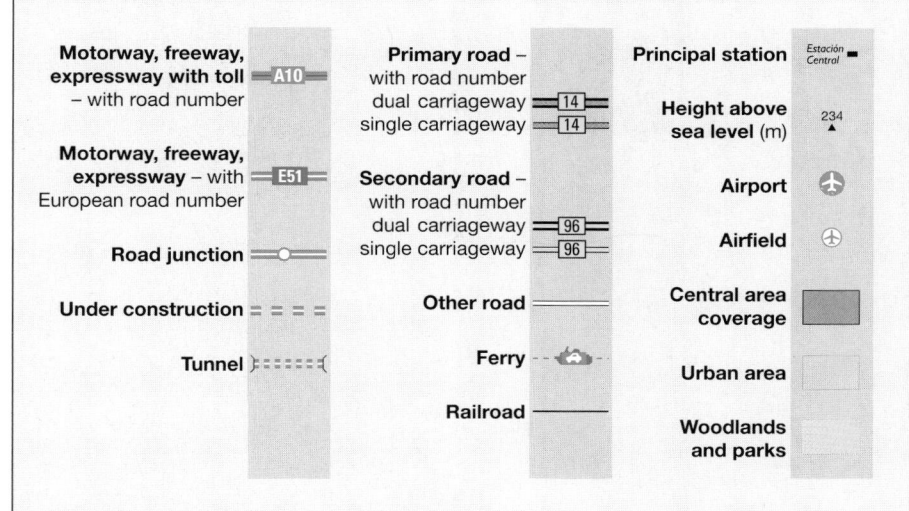

Central Area Maps

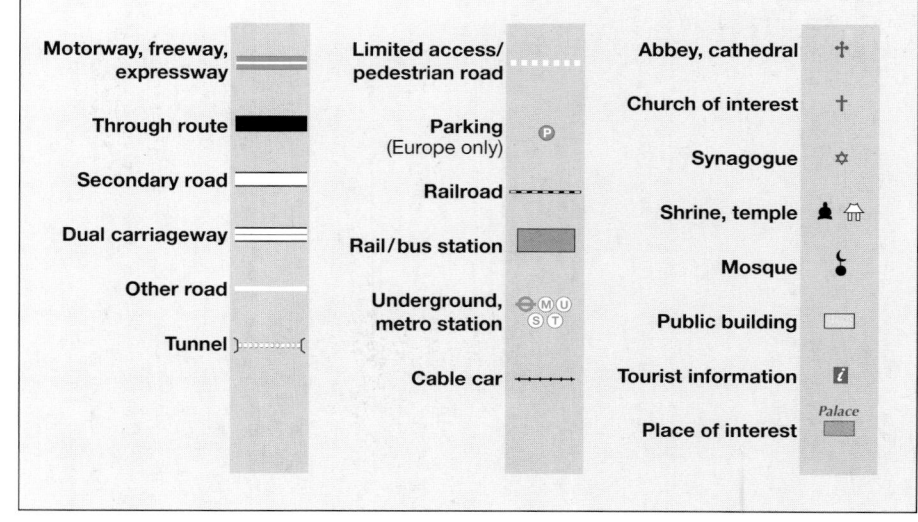

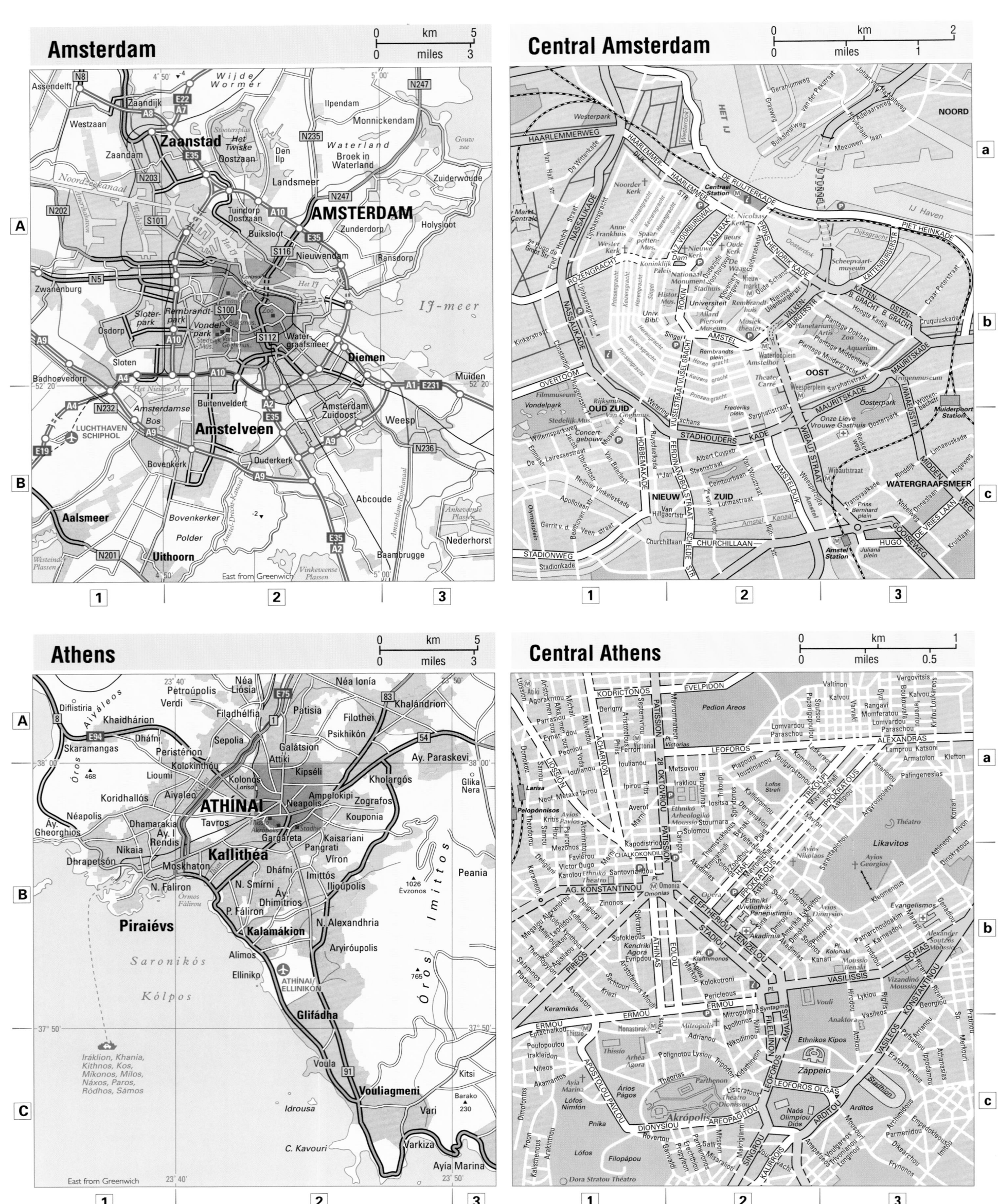

Amsterdam

km 5
miles 3

Assendelft
N8
Wijde Wormer
Zaandijk
E22
A8 A7
Ilpendam
Monnickendam
Westzaan
N235
Zaanstad
Het Twiske
N247
Den Ilp
Waterland
Broek in Waterland
Gouw zee
Zaandam
Oostzaan
Landsmeer
Zuiderwoude
Noordzeekanaal
N203
Tuindorp Oostzaan
A10
AMSTERDAM
Zunderdorp
Holysloot
N202
S101
Buiksloot
E35
N5
S116
Nieuwendam
Ransdorp
Zwanenburg
Centraal Stn
Het IJ
IJ-meer
Sloter park
Rembrandt park
Zoo
Water-graafsmeer
N232
Vondel park
S112
Diemen
Osdorp
A10
Stedelijk Mus.
S100
A1 E231
Muiden
Sloten
A10
52° 20'
Muiden
52° 20'
Badhoevedorp
A4
Het Nieuwe Meer
Buitenveldert
A2
Amsterdam Zuidoost
Weesp
A4
N232
Amsterdamse Bos
E35
A9
LUCHTHAVEN SCHIPHOL
A9
Ouderkerk
A9
N236
E19
Amstelveen
Bovenkerk
A9
Aalsmeer
Bovenkerker Polder
-2
Abcoude
Ankeveense Plassen
Westeinde Plassen
N201
Uithoorn
Vinkeveense Plassen
Nederhorst
4° 50'
East from Greenwich
5° 00'

A   B

1   2   3

Central Amsterdam

km 2
miles 1

NOORD
HAARLEMMERWEG
Westerpark
HET IJ
DE RUITERKADE
Centraal Station
IJ Haven
PIET HEINKADE
St. Nicolaas Kerk
Noorder Kerk
Scheepvaart-museum
Koninklijk Paleis
Dam
De Waag
OOST
Universiteit
Rembrandt-huis
Artis Zoo
Aquarium
OVERTOOM
Vondelpark
Filmmuseum
Rijksmuseum
Van Goghmus.
OUD ZUID
STADHOUDERS KADE
Weesperplein
Oosterpark
Tropenmuseum
Muiderpoort Station
Albert Cuypstr.
WIBAUT STRAAT
WATERGRAAFSMEER
NIEUW
ZUID
AMSTELDIJK
Amstel Kanaal
HUGO
STADIONWEG
CHURCHILLAAN
Amstel Station
Juliana plein
GOOISEWEG

a   b   c

1   2   3

Athens

km 5
miles 3

Diflistiria
8
Néa Liósia
Petroúpolis
Verdi
Néa Ionía
23° 50'
Khaidhárion
E94
Filadhélfia
E75
Patisia
Filothei
Khalándrion
Skaramangas
Dháfni
Peristérion
Sepolia
Psikhikón
83
Oros Aiyáleos
468
Lioumi
Galátsion
Attiki
Kipséli
Ay. Paraskevi
54
38° 00'
Koridhallós
Kolokinthou
Kolonos Larisa
Neapoli
Kholargós
Glika Nera
38° 00'
Néapolis
Aiyaleo
ATHÍNAI
Ampelokipi
Zografos
Ay. Gheorghios
Dhamarakia
Tavros
Akrópoli
Stádhion
Kouponia
Ay. I. Rendis
Gargaréta
Kaisariani
Píron
Nίkaia
Kallithéa
Pangrati
Dhrapetsón
Moskhaton
Dháfni
Imittós
Ilioúpolis
Peania
N. Faliron
N. Smírni
Oros Imittos
Piraiévs
Órmos Fálirou
Ay. Dhimitrios
1026 Évzonos
P. Fáliron
Kalamákion
N. Alexandhria
765
Saronikós
Alimos
Aryiróupolis
Elliniko
ATHÍNAI/ ELLINIKON
37° 50'
37° 50'
Iráklion, Khania, Kithnos, Kos, Míkonos, Milos, Náxos, Paros, Ródhos, Sámos
Glifádha
Kólpos
91
Voula
Idrousa
Kitsi
Vouliagmeni
Barako 230
Vari
East from Greenwich
23° 40'
Varkiza
23° 50'
Ayía Marina
C. Kavouri

A   B   C

1   2   3

Central Athens

km 1
miles 0.5

KODRICTONOS
EVELPIDON
Pedion Areos
Vergovitsis
ACHARNON
PATISSION
ALEXANDRAS
LEOFOROS ALEXANDRAS
Larisa
Pelopónnisos
28 OKTOVRIOU
Lofos Strefi
Likavitos
Ayios Georgios
AG. KONSTANTINOU
Omonia
Ethniki Vivliothiki
Panepistimio
IPPOKRATOUS
Théatro
Opera
STADIOU
ELEFTHERIOU VENIZELOU
Akadimia
Evangelismos
PIREOS
ATHINAS
Kendrikí Agora
EOLOU
VASILISSIS SOFIAS
Monastiraki
ERMOU
Pl. Klafthmonos
Mitrópolis
Syntagma
Voulí
VASILEOS KONSTANTINOU
Thissio
Arhéa Agora
Akrópolis
AMALIAS
ARDITTOU
Zappeio
LEOFOROS OLGAS
Lófos Nimfón
Dora Stratou Théatro
DIONYSIOU AREOPAGITOU
Naós Olimpíou Diós
SINGROU
KALLIROIS
Ardítos

a   b   c

1   2   3

COPYRIGHT GEORGE PHILIP LTD

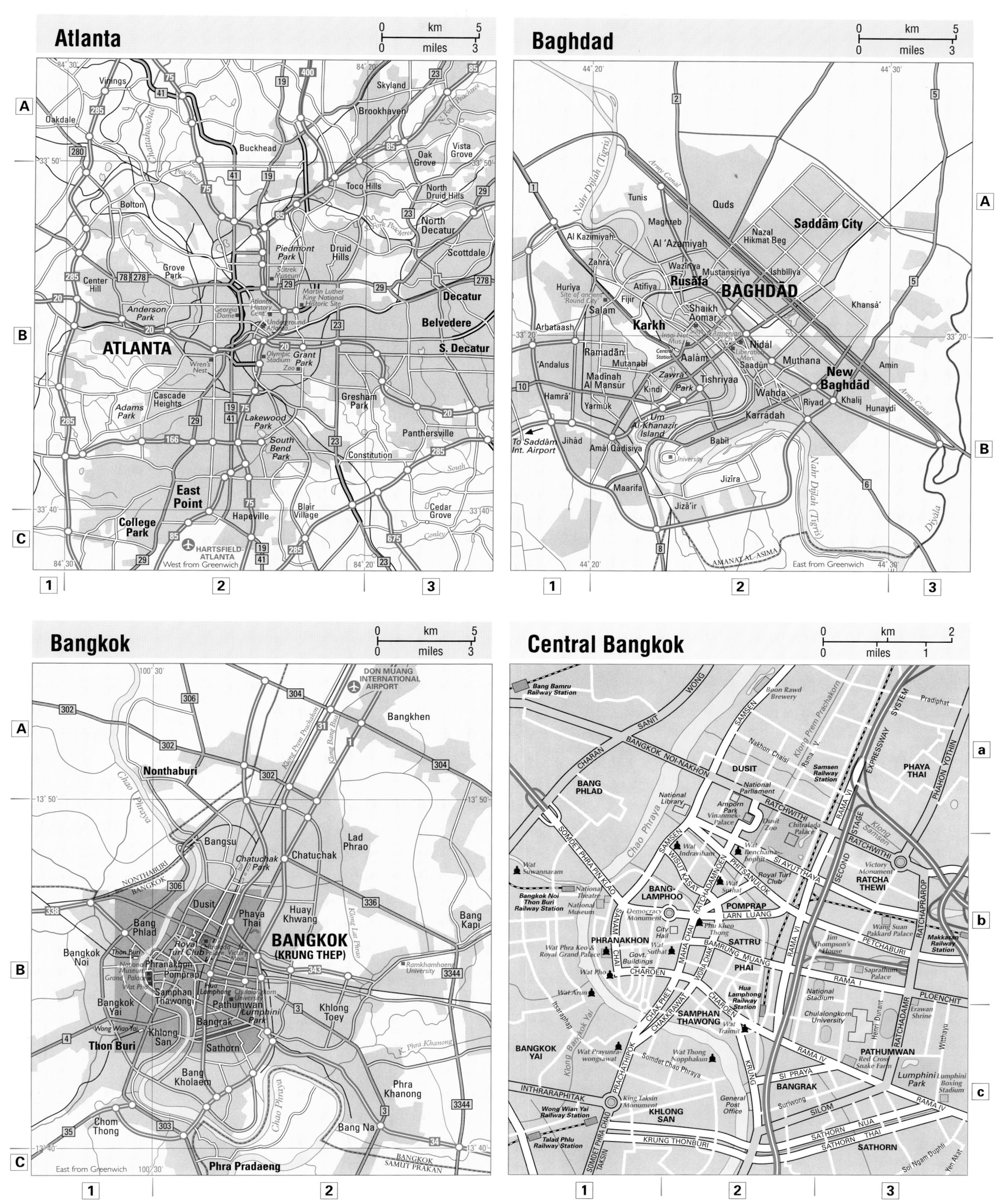

Atlanta

0 — km — 5
0 — miles — 3

84° 30' 84° 20'
75 41 19 400 85
Vinings Skyland 23
Oakdale 285 Brookhaven
A 33° 50' 280 Buckhead 85 33° 50'
41 19 Oak Grove Vista Grove
Peachtree 75 Toco Hills 85 North Druid Hills 29
Bolton 41 19 North Decatur 23
Piedmont Park 29 Scottdale 278
Grove Park 78 278 Scitrek Museum 29 Decatur
Center Hill Martin Luther King National Historic Site
285 20 Georgia Dome Druid Hills
B 33° 20' Anderson Park Underground Atlanta Belvedere
ATLANTA 20 Olympic Stadium 23 S. Decatur
Wren's Nest Grant Park Zoo 20
Cascade Heights Gresham Park
Adams Park 19 75 Lakewood Park 29 41 South Bend Park 23
166 285
285 29 Panthersville 20
East Point 75 Constitution 285
C 33° 40' College Park Hapeville Blair Village 675 Cedar Grove 33° 40'
85 Conley South
29 HARTSFIELD-ATLANTA 19 41 285 23
84° 30' West from Greenwich 84° 20'

1 2 3

Baghdad

0 — km — 5
0 — miles — 3

44° 20' 44° 30'
2 5
Nahr Dijlah (Tigris) Army Canal
Tunis Quds Saddām City
1 Maghteb Nazal Hikmat Beg
A Al Kazimiyah Al 'Azamiyah 5
Zahrā Waziriya Mustansiriya Ishbiliya
Huriya Atifiya Fijir Rusāfa BAGHDAD Khansā'
Site of ancient 'Round City' Salam Shaikh Aomar
Arbataash Karkh Central Station Armenian
B 33° 20' 'Andalus Ramadān Aalām Nidāl Muthana Amin 33° 20'
Mutanabi Saadūn New Baghdād
Madinah Al Mansūr Zawrā Park Tishriyaa Wahda
10 Hamrā' Kindi Riyad Khalij Amin
Yarmūk Babil Karrādah Hunaydi
To Saddām Int. Airport Jihād Amāl Qadisiya Um Al-Khanazir Island
University 6
Maarifa Jizīra Nahr Dijlah (Tigris) Diyala
Jizā'ir
8 AMANAT AL ASIMA East from Greenwich
44° 20' 44° 30'

1 2 3

Bangkok

0 — km — 5
0 — miles — 3

100° 30'
302 306 304 DON MUANG INTERNATIONAL AIRPORT
A 304 Bangkhen
302 Khlong Prem Prachakorn 31 Khlong Bang Bua 304
Nonthaburi 302
13° 50' Chao Phraya 13° 50'
Bangsu Bangsu Chatuchak Park Chatuchak Lad Phrao
NONTHABURI Klong Lat Phrao 336
BANGKOK 306 Dusit Phaya Thai Huay Khwang Bang Kapi
338 Royal Turf Club BANGKOK (KRUNG THEP) 343 Ramkhamhaeng University 3344
B Bang Phlad Thon Buri National Museum Grand Palace Phranakhon Khlong Toey 3
Bangkok Noi Pomprap Pathumwan Lumphini Park
Bangkok Yai Samphan Thawong Bangrak
4 Wong Wian Yai Khlong San Sathorn K. Phra Khanong
Thon Buri Bang Kholaem Phra Khanong
35 Chom Thong 303 Bang Na 3344
C 13° 40' East from Greenwich 100° 30' Phra Pradaeng BANGKOK SAMUT PRAKAN 34

1 2

Central Bangkok

0 — km — 2
0 — miles — 1

Bang Bamru Railway Station WONG Boon Rawd Brewery Pradiphat
CHARAN SANIT BANGKOK NOI-NAKHON SAMSEN EXPRESSWAY SYSTEM
a BANG PHLAD DUSIT Nakhon Chaisi Samsen Railway Station PHAYA THAI a
National Library RAMA VI PHAHON YOTHIN
National Parliament Amporn Park RATCHWITHI
Chao Phraya Vinmanmek-Palace Dusit Zoo
Wat Suwannaram SAMSEN Chitralada Palace RATCHWITHI
Wat Indraviham NUSIT KASAT Wat Benchama-bophit SI AYUTTHAYA Klong Samsen Victory Monument
Bangkok Noi Thon Buri Railway Station National Theatre RATCHADAMNEN PHITSANULOK Royal Turf Club RATCHA THEWI
National Museum BANG-LAMPHOO Wat Suthat SECOND STAGE
Democracy Monument POMPRAP LARN LUANG
b PHRANAKHON City Hall Phu Khao Thong SATTRU Wang Suan Pakkard Palace Makkasan Railway Station b
Wat Phra Keo & Royal Grand Palace MAHA CHAI Govt. Buildings BAMRUNG MUANG PHAI Jim Thompson's House PETCHABURI
Wat Pho CHAROEN RAMA VI RATCHAPRAROP
Wat Arun CHAK PHET Hua Lamphong Railway Station National Stadium Saprathum Palace RAMA I
CHAK KRAWAN CHAROEN Chulalongkorn University PLOENCHIT
BANGKOK YAI SAMPHAN THAWONG Wat Traimit Henri Dunant Erawan Shrine
Wat Prayunra-wongsawat Wat Thong Nopphakun KRUNG RAMA IV Red Cross Snake Farm RATCHADAMRI Withayu
INTHRAPHITAK Somdet Chao Phraya PATHUMWAN Lumphini Boxing Stadium
King Taksin Monument General Post Office BANGRAK Lumphini Park
Wong Wian Yai Railway Station PRACHATHIPOK SI PRAYA RAMA IV
c KHLONG SAN SILOM SATHORN c
Talad Phlu Railway Station KRUNG THONBURI Suriwong SATHORN NUA
SOMDET PHRA CHAO TAKSIN SATHORN THAI SATHORN
Soi Ngam Duphli Yen Akat

1 2 3

COPYRIGHT GEORGE PHILIP LTD

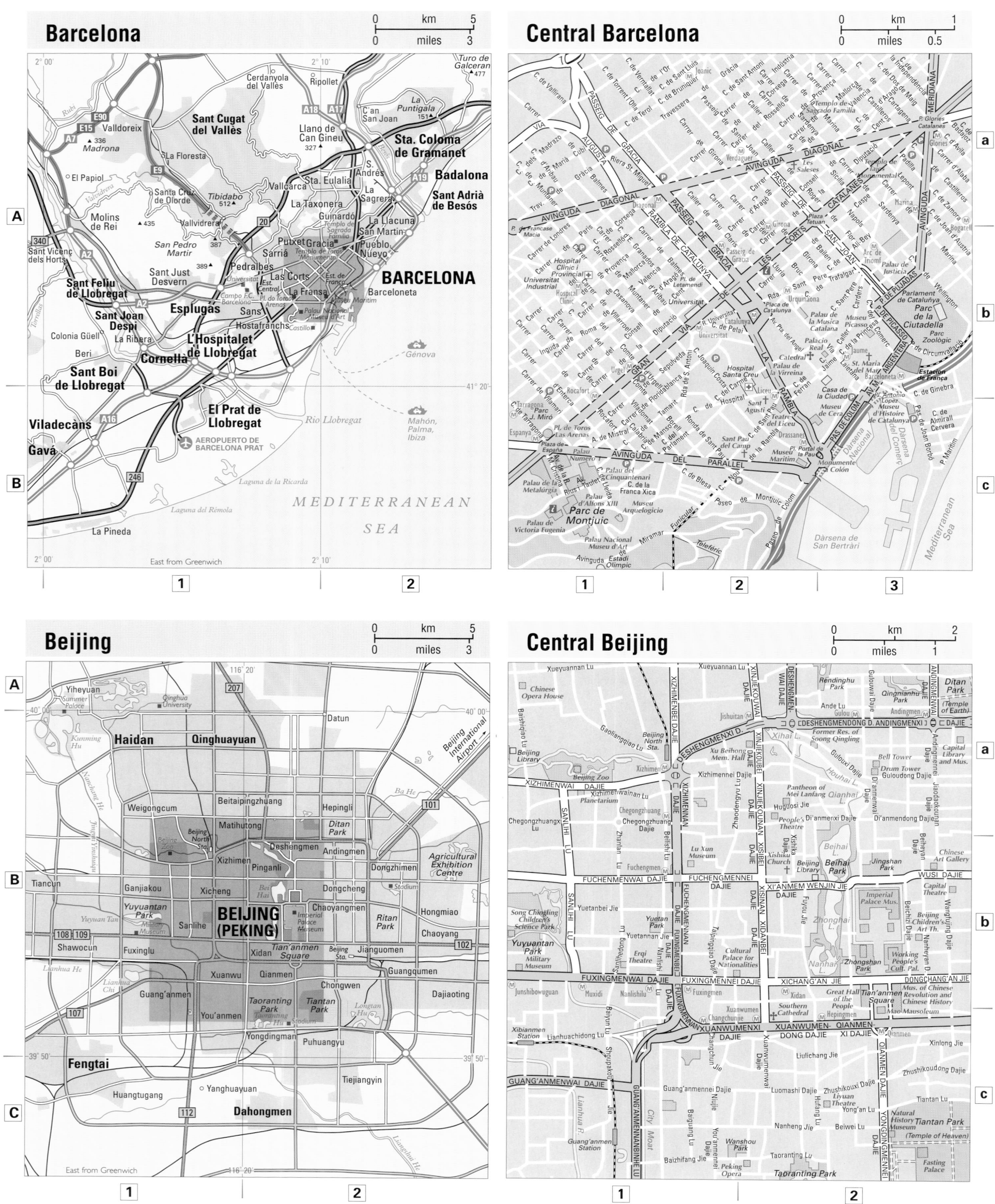

Barcelona

km 5 / miles 3

2° 00' | 2° 10'

Turo de Galceran 477

Cerdanyola del Vallès
Ripollet
E90
E15 Valldoreix
Sant Cugat del Vallès
C'an San Joan
La Puntigala 151▲
A18 A17
A7 ▲336 Madrona
Llano de Can Gineu 327
La Floresta
E9
Sta. Coloma de Gramanet
S. Andreu
Vallcarca
Sta. Eulàlia
A19 Badalona
El Papiol
Santa Cruz de Olorde
Tibidabo 512▲
La Taxonera
La Sagrera
Sant Adrià de Besós
A
Molins de Rei
San Pedro Martir 387
Vallvidrera
Gujnardó
Putxet
La Llacuna
Sant Martín
Pueblo Nuevo
20
Sàrriá
▲435
Templo de Toros Monumental
Sant Just Desvern
389▲
Pedralbes
Universitat Est. Central
La Fransa
BARCELONA
340
Sant Vicenç dels Horts
A2
Campo F.C. Barcelona
Las Corts
Pl. de Toros Arenas
Barceloneta
Moll Marítim
Sant Feliu de Llobregat
A2
Esplugas
Sans
Castillo
Palau Nacional Museu d'Art
Sant Joan Despi
Hostafranchs
Colonia Güell
La Ribera
Cornellà
L'Hospitalet de Llobregat
Beri
Génova
Sant Boi de Llobregat
41° 20'
Viladecans
A16
El Prat de Llobregat
Rio Llobregat
Mahón, Palma, Ibiza
B
246
Gavá
Laguna de la Ricarda
AEROPUERTO DE BARCELONA PRAT
Laguna del Rémola
MEDITERRANEAN SEA
La Pineda
2° 00'   East from Greenwich   2° 10'

1 | 2

Central Barcelona

km 1 / miles 0.5

C. de Vermella
C. de l'Or
C. de Sant Lluis
Joanic
Gracia
C. del Torrent d'Olla
C. de Bruniquer
de
C. de Sant Antoni
Industria
Carrer
C. de la Independencia
a
PASSEIG DE GRACIA
VIA AUGUSTA
DIAGONAL
AVINGUDA
PASSEIG DE GRACIA
CORTS
SANT JOAN
MERIDIANA
b
GRAN VIA
Plaça de Catalunya
Palau de la Música Catalana
Parc de la Ciutadella
Parc Zoològic
Universitat
Catedral
RAMBLA
St. María del Mar
Estació de França
c
AVINGUDA DEL PARAL·LEL
Palau Nacional Museu d'Art
Parc de Montjuic
Monumento Colón
Mediterranean Sea

1 | 2 | 3

Beijing

km 5 / miles 3

116° 20'
A
Yiheyuan Summer Palace
Qinghua University
207
Datun
40° 00'
Kunming Hu
Beijing International Airport
Haidan   **Qinghuayuan**
Ba He
Weigongcum
Beitaipingzhuang
Hepingli
101
Nanshan He
Matihutong
Beijing North Sta.
Ditan Park
B
Tiancun
Beijing Zoo
Deshengmen
Andingmen
Xizhimen
Pinganli
Dongzhimen
Agricultural Exhibition Centre
Yueyuan He
Ganjiakou
Xicheng
Bei Hai
Dongcheng
Stadium
Hongmiao
108 109
Yuyuantan Park
BEIJING (PEKING)
Chaoyangmen
Imperial Palace Museum
Ritan Park
Chaoyang
Shawocun
Sanlihe
Lianhua He
Fuxinglu
Xidan
Tian'anmen Square
Beijing Sta.
Jianguomen
Guangqumen
102
Lianhua Chi
Xuanwu
Qianmen
107
Guang'anmen
Chongwen
Dajiaoting
Taoranting Park
Tiantan Park
Longtan Hu
You'anmen
Taoranting Hu
Stadium
39° 50'
C
112
Yongdingmen
Puhuangyu
Fengtai
Huangtugang
Yanghuayuan
Tiejiangyin
Dahongmen
Longhua He
East from Greenwich
116° 20'

1 | 2

Central Beijing

km 2 / miles 1

Xueyuannan Lu
Xueyuannan Lu
XINJIEKOUWAI DAJIE
DESHENGMENWAI DAJIE
ANDINGMENWAI
Ditan Park
Chinese Opera House
Rendinghu Park
Qingnianhu Park
DAJIE
a
Baishiqiao Lu
Beijing North Sta.
Gulou
Andingmen
Capital Library and Mus.
Beijing Library
Jishuitan
XIZHIMENNEI DAJIE
Xihai
Former Res. of Soong Qingling
DONG D. ANDINGMENXI
Xu Beihong Mem. Hall
Houhai
Bell Tower
Drum Tower
XIZHIMENWAI DAJIE
Beijing Zoo
Xizhimennan Lu
Pantheon of Mei Lanfang
Di'anmen
Di'anmendong Dajie
Planetarium
Chegongzhuang Dajie
Huguosi Jie
SANLIHE LU
Lu Xun Museum
Xishiku Church
Beihai Park
Jingshan Park
Chinese Art Gallery
Chegongzhuang Lu
Fuchengmen
Beijing Library
FUCHENGMENNEI DAJIE
WUSI DAJIE
b
Song Chingling Children's Science Park
XISINAN XIDANBEI DAJIE
XI'ANMEN WENJIN JIE
Imperial Palace Mus.
Capital Theatre
Yuyuantan Park
Yuetanbei Jie
Zhonghai
Beijing Children's Art Th.
Yuetan Park
Cultural Palace for Nationalities
Working People's Cult. Pal.
Military Museum
Nanhai
Zhongshan Park
FUXINGMENWAI DAJIE
FUXINGMENNEI DAJIE
XICHANG'AN JIE
DONGCHANG'AN JIE
Muxidi
Fuxingmen
Xidan
Great Hall of the People
Tian'anmen Square
Mus. of Chinese Revolution and Chinese History
Mao Mausoleum
Southern Cathedral
Xuanwumen
XUANWUMEN QIANMEN
QIANMEN DAJIE
c
Xibianmen Station
Liulichang Jie
Zhushikou Liyuan Theatre
Tiantan Lu
City Moat
GUANG'ANMENWAI DAJIE
Guang'anmennei Dajie
Natural History Museum
Tiantan Park (Temple of Heaven)
Lianhua R.
GUANG'ANMENNEI LU
Peking Opera
Taoranting Park
YONGDINGMEN DAJIE
Fasting Palace

1 | 2

COPYRIGHT GEORGE PHILIP LTD

Berlin

0 km 5
0 miles 3

Wansdorf
Hennigsdorf
Lübars
Blankenfelde
Schwanebeck
Birkholzaue
Löhme
Werneuchen
Rudolfshöhe

E26
Hermsdorf
Schulzendorf
Waidmannslust
Bucholz
Neu Buch
Birkholz
E28
Seefeld

Alter Finkenkrug
Siedlung
Nieder Neuendorf
Heiligensee
Tegel
Rosenthal
Karow
Neu Lindenberg
Lindenberg
Blumberg
Krummensee

Waldheim
Falkensee
Schönwalde
Tegelort
Scharfenberg
Niederschönhausen
Blankenburg
BRANDENBURG BERLIN
Wegendorf
Neuhönow

Falkenhagen
Johannesstift
FLUGHAFEN BERLIN-TEGEL
Reinickendorf
Pankow
Heinersdorf
Malchow
Wartenberg
Ahrensfelde
Mehrow
Paulshof
Trappenfelde
Altlandsberg Nord

A
Finkenkrug
Seegefeld
Haselhorst
Volkspark Jungfernheide
Wedding
Weissensee
Hohenschönhausen
Eiche
Eiche Süd
Hönow
Seeberg
Friedrichslust
Altlandsberg
A

Döberitz
Spandau
Zitadelle
Siemensstadt
Spree
Tiergarten
Prenzlauerberg
Mitte
Falkenberg
Marzahn
Hellersdorf
Neuenhagen
Fredersdorf Nord

Dallgow
Staaken
Charlottenburg
Schlossgarten
Deutsche Oper
Friedrichshain
Lichtenburg
Wuhlgarten
Birkenstein
Bollensdorf

Seeburg
Olympia Stadion
Universität
BERLIN
Kreuzberg
Hauptbahnhof
Biesdorf
Kaulsdorf
Mahlsdorf
Dahlwitz-Hoppegarten

Gatow
Teufelsberg
Rathaus
Schöneberg
Neukölln
Treptow
Friedrichsfelde
Karlshorst
Münchehofe
Vogelsdorf

Grunewald
FLUGHAFEN BERLIN-TEMPELHOF
Heidemühle
Waldesruh
Kleinschönebeck
Schöneiche
Gratzwalde

Krampnitz
Gross Glienicke
Schmargendorf
Dahlem
Friedenau
Tempelhof
Oberschöneweide
Fichtenau
Schönblick
Woltersdorf

B
Neu Fahrland
Kladow
Schwanenwerder
Steglitz
Niederschöneweide
Köpenick
Grosse Müggelsee
Wilhelmshagen
Springeberg
B

Nedlitz
Pfaueninsel
Nikolassee
Zehlendorf
Britz
Johannisthal
Adlershof
Rahnsdorf
Erkner

Sacrow
Wannsee
Lichterfelde
Lankwitz
Mariendorf
Buckow
Rudow
Grünau
Wendenschloss
Müggelheim
Neu Buchhorst

Potsdam
Dreilinden
Kleinmachnow
Seehof
Osdorf
Marienfelde
Altglienicke
Bohnsdorf
FLUGHAFEN BERLIN-SCHÖNEFELD
Müggelberge
Karolinenhof
Gosen

Teltow
East from Greenwich

1 2 3 4 5

Central Berlin

0 km 1
0 miles 0.5

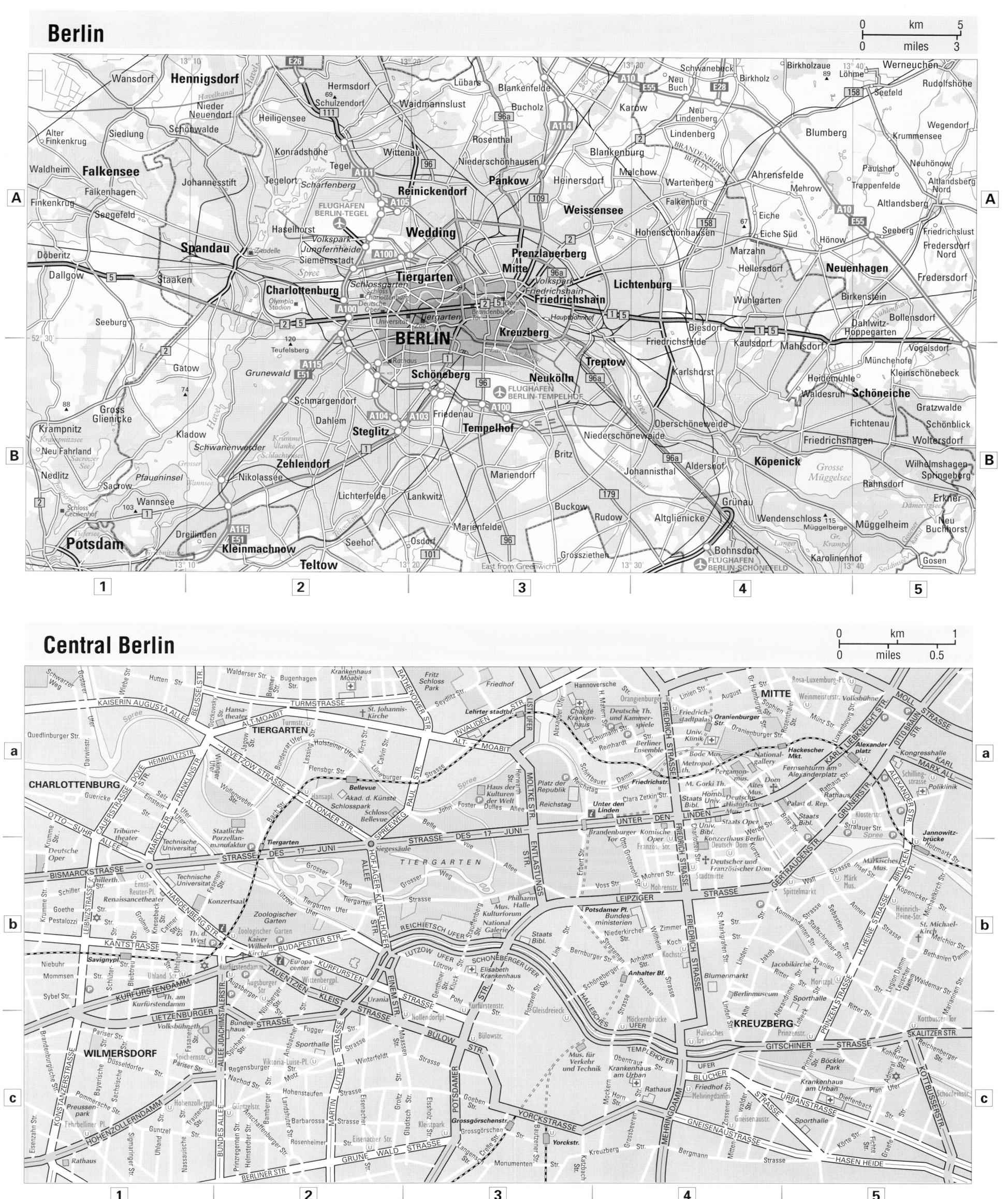

1 2 3 4 5

COPYRIGHT GEORGE PHILIP LTD

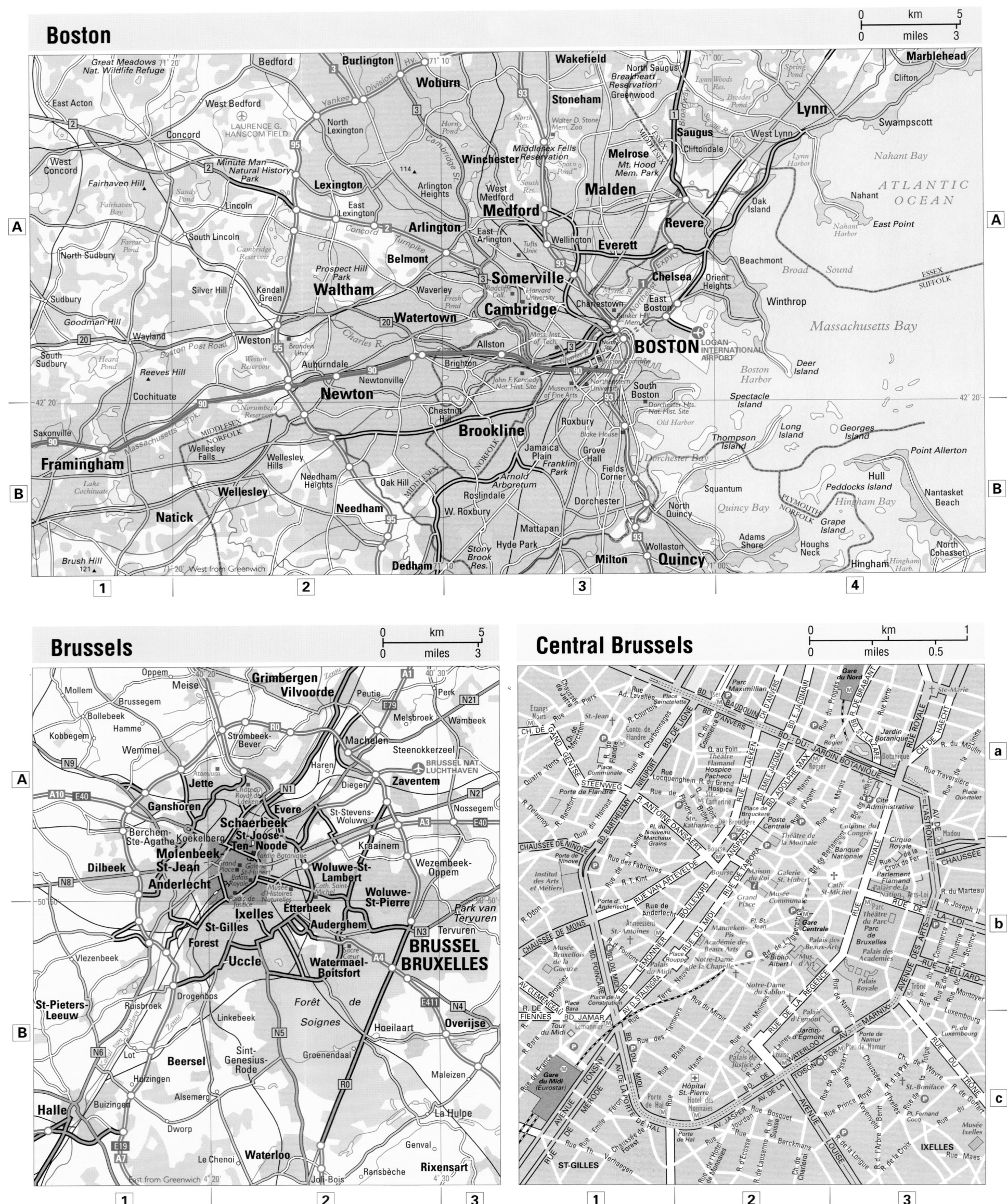

COPYRIGHT GEORGE PHILIP LTD

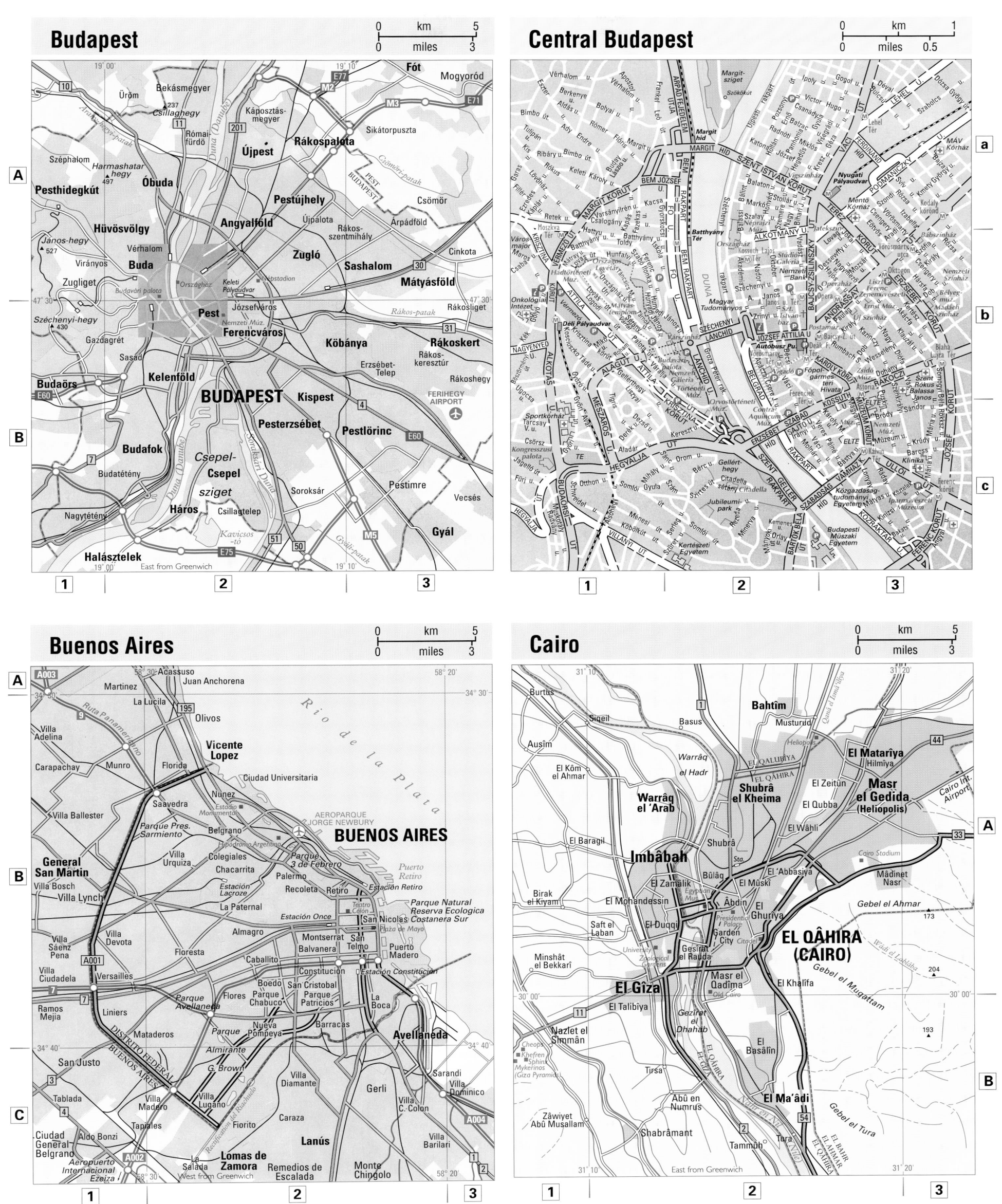

COPYRIGHT GEORGE PHILIP LTD

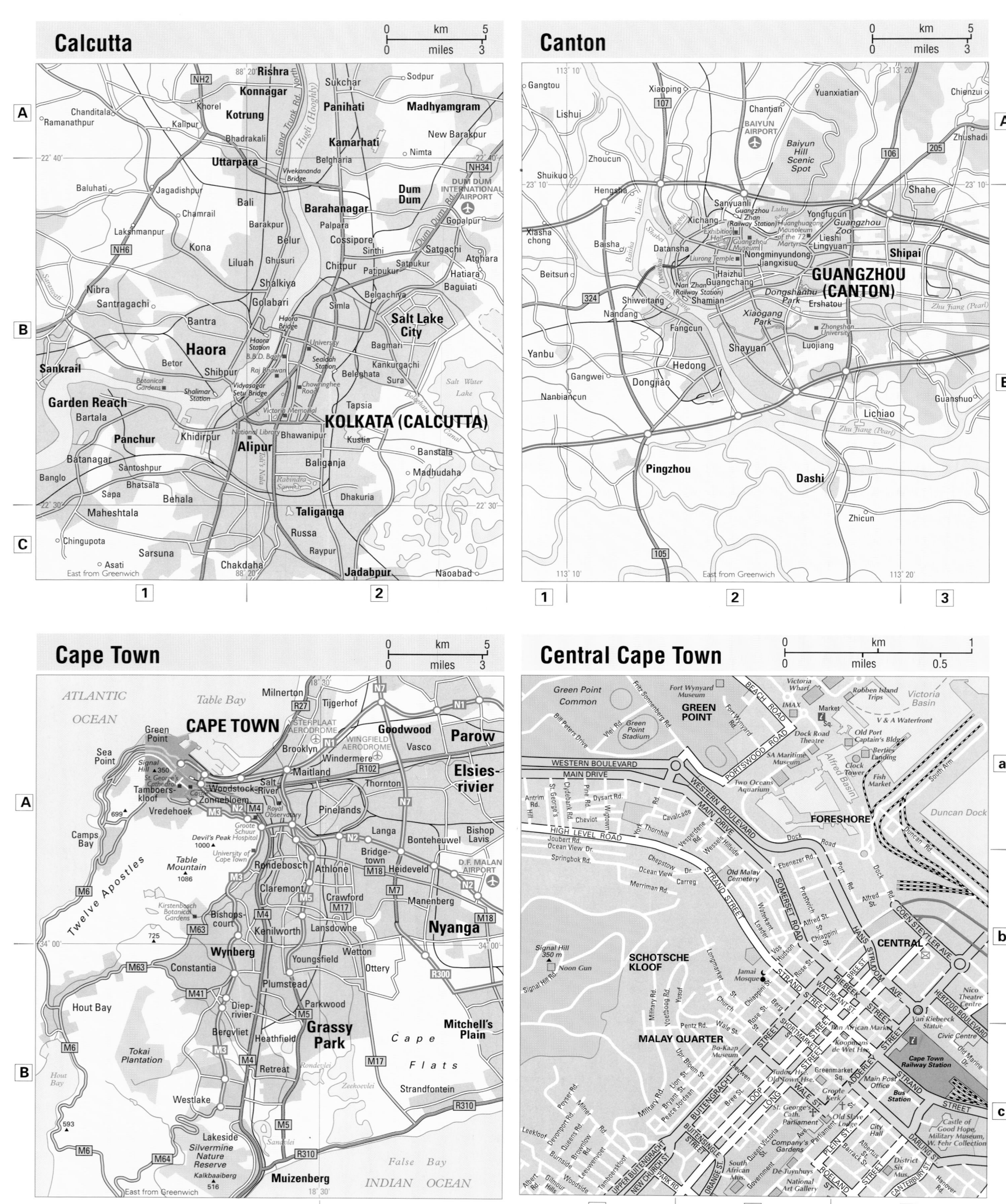

Calcutta

km 5 / miles 3

Rishra, Konnagar, Kotrung, Uttarpara, Kamarhati, Panihati, Madhyamgram, New Barakpur, Sukchar, Sodpur, Nimta, Dum Dum, Chanditala, Ramanathpur, Khorel, Kalipur, Kalpur, Bhadrakali, Belgharia, DUM DUM INTERNATIONAL AIRPORT, Baluhati, Jagadishpur, Chamrail, Bali, Barakpur, Palpara, Cossipore, Sinthi, Satgachi, Gopalpur, NH6, Lakshmanpur, Kona, Liluah, Ghusuri, Belur, Chitpur, Patipukur, Satpukur, Atghara, Hatiara, Baguiati, Nibra, Santragachi, Barahanagar, Shalkiya, Golabari, Simla, Belgachiya, Salt Lake City, Bantra, Haora Station, University, Sealdah Station, Bagmari, Kankurgachi, Sura, Sankrail, Betor, Shibpur, B.B.D. Bag, Raj Bhawan, Beleghata, Botanical Gardens, Shalimar Station, Vidyasagar Setu Bridge, Chowringhee Road, Tapsia, Salt Water Lake, Haora, Garden Reach, Bartala, National Library, Khidirpur, Alipur, Bhawanipur, Kustia, Banstala, Panchur, Victoria Memorial, KOLKATA (CALCUTTA), Batanagar, Santoshpur, Baliganja, Madhudaha, Banglo, Bhatsala, Sapa, Behala, Rabindra Sarovar, Dhakuria, Maheshtala, Chingupota, Sarsuna, Asati, Chakdaha, Taliganga, Russa, Raypur, Naoabad, Jadabpur

Canton

km 5 / miles 3

Gangtou, Xiaoping 107, Yuanxiatian, Chienzui, Lishui, Chantian, BAIYUN AIRPORT, Baiyun Hill Scenic Spot, Zhoucun, Zhushadi, Shuikuo, Hengsha, Sanyuanli, Guangzhou Zhan (Railway Station), Luhu, Yonfucun, Guangzhou Zoo, 106, 205, Shahe, Xiasha chong, Baisha, Xichang, Exhibition Hall, Wanghuaguodeng of the 72 Martyrs, Lieshi, Lingyuan, Shipai, Beitsun, Datansha, Guangzhou Museum, Liurong Temple, Nongminyundong, Jiangxisuo, Haizhu, Nan Zhan Guangchang, (Railway Station), Shamian, Dongshanhu Park, Ershatou, Zhu Jiang (Pearl), 324, Shiweitang, Nandang, Fangcun, Xiaogang Park, Zhongshan University, Yanbu, Shayuan, Luojiang, Guanshuo, Gangwei, Hedong, Zhu Jiang (Pearl), Lichiao, Nanbiancun, Dongjiao, Pingzhou, Dashi, Zhicun, 105

Cape Town

km 5 / miles 3

ATLANTIC OCEAN, Table Bay, Milnerton, Tijgerhof, N7, N1, CAPE TOWN, R27, Goodwood, Parow, Green Point, Brooklyn, WINGFIELD AERODROME, Vasco, Sea Point, Signal Hill 350, St. George's Cathedral, Woodstock, Maitland, Windermere, R102, Elsiesrivier, 699, Tamboerskloof, Zonnebloem, Salt River, Thornton, Camps Bay, Vredehoek, M3, Groote Schuur Hospital, Observatory, Pinelands, N7, Devil's Peak 1000, Langa, Bontehewel, Bishop Lavis, Table Mountain 1086, University of Cape Town, Rondebosch, Athlone, Bridgetown, Heideveld, D.F. MALAN AIRPORT, Kirstenbosch Botanical Gardens, Claremont, Crawford, M17, M7, N2, Twelve Apostles, M6, Bishopscourt, M5, Kenilworth, Lansdowne, Manenberg, M18, 725, M63, Wynberg, Wetton, Youngsfield, Nyanga, Constantia, M41, Plumstead, Ottery, R300, Hout Bay, Dieprivier, Parkwood, M5, Mitchell's Plain, Bergvliet, Heathfield, M3, M4, Grassy Park, Cape Flats, Tokai Plantation, M63, Retreat, M17, Ronderlei, 593, Westlake, Zeekoevlei, Strandfontein, M6, Lakeside, Silvermine Nature Reserve, M5, R310, Kalkbaaiberg 516, Muizenberg, False Bay, INDIAN OCEAN, Hout Bay, M64

Central Cape Town

km 1 / miles 0.5

Green Point Common, Fort Wynyard Museum, Victoria Wharf, Robben Island Trips, Victoria Basin, GREEN POINT, IMAX, V & A Waterfront, Green Point Stadium, Dock Road Theatre, Old Port Captain's Bldg, WESTERN BOULEVARD MAIN DRIVE, SA Maritime Museum, Berties Landing, Clock Tower, Fish Market, FORESHORE, Two Oceans Aquarium, South Arm, Duncan Dock, HIGH LEVEL ROAD, Alfred Basin, SCHOTSCHE KLOOF, Signal Hill 350 m, Noon Gun, CENTRAL, Nico Theatre Centre, Jamai Mosque, HERTZOG BOULEVARD, Van Riebeeck Statue, Civic Centre, MALAY QUARTER, Bo-Kaap Museum, Koopmans de Wet Hse, South African Museum, Old Slave Lodge, St. George's Cath., Parliament, Company's Gardens, Greenmarket Sq., Main Post Office, Bus Station, Cape Town Railway Station, City Hall, Castle of Good Hope, Military Museum, W. Fehr Collection, District Six Museum, South African National Art Gallery, De Tuynhuys, Government House

COPYRIGHT GEORGE PHILIP LTD

Chicago

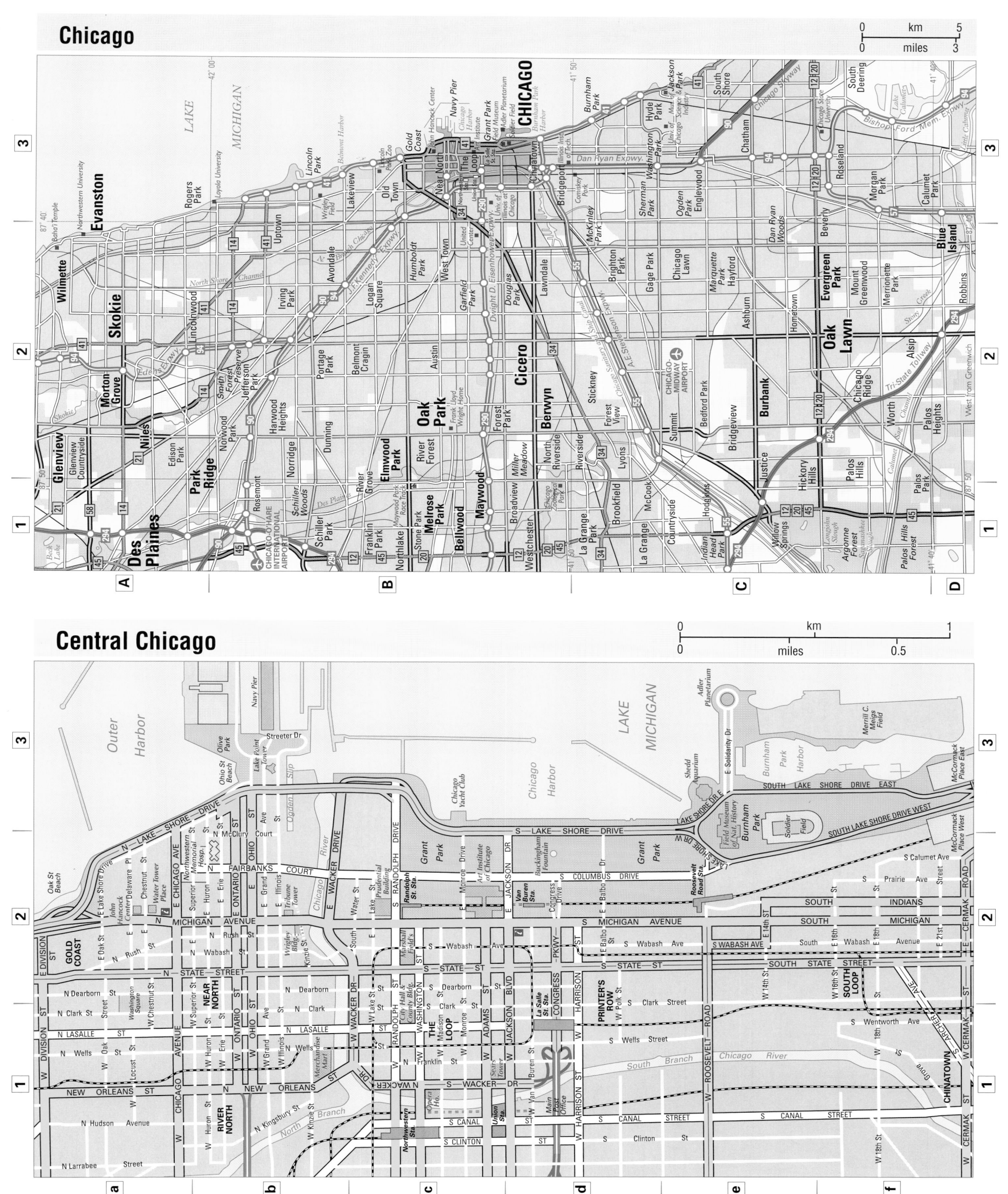

km 0 — 5
miles 0 — 3

LAKE MICHIGAN

Evanston
Wilmette
Skokie
Morton Grove
Niles
Glenview
Park Ridge
Des Plaines
Northwestern University
Baha'i Temple
Loyola University
Rogers Park
Lincolnwood
Edison Park
Norwood Park
Harwood Heights
Schiller Woods
Rosemont
CHICAGO O'HARE INTERNATIONAL AIRPORT
Schiller Park
Franklin Park
Northlake
Melrose Park
Bellwood
Maywood
Broadview
Westchester
La Grange Park
Brookfield
La Grange
Countryside
Indian Head Park
Willow Springs
Argonne Forest
Palos Hills Forest
Palos Park
Palos Heights
Worth
Hickory Hills
Justice
Hodgkins
McCook
Lyons
Riverside
North Riverside
Forest View
Summit
Bedford Park
Bridgeview
Burbank
Chicago Ridge
Oak Lawn
Evergreen Park
Mount Greenwood
Merrionette Park
Robbins
Blue Island
Beverly
Morgan Park
Calumet Park
Roseland
South Deering
Lake Calumet
Bishop Ford Mem. Expwy
Chicago Skyway
South Shore
Hyde Park
Chatham
Englewood
Sherman Park
Ogden Park
Gage Park
Marquette Park
Hayford
Ashburn
Hometown
Alsip
Tri-State Tollway
West from Greenwich
Dan Ryan Woods
Chicago Lawn
Brighton Park
McKinley Park
Comiskey Park
Bridgeport
Dan Ryan Expwy
A.E. Stevenson Expwy
Chicago Sanitary and Ship Canal
Stickney
Berwyn
Cicero
Oak Park
Forest Park
River Forest
Elmwood Park
River Grove
Stone Park
Maywood Park Race Track
Frank Lloyd Wright Home
Chicago Zoological Park
Dunning
Portage Park
Belmont Cragin
Austin
Lawndale
Garfield Park
Douglas Park
Humboldt Park
West Town
Univ. of Illinois at Chicago
United Center
The Loop
Near North
Gold Coast
Lincoln Park
Old Town
Lakeview
Wrigley Field
Uptown
Avondale
Logan Square
Irving Park
Jefferson Park
North Shore Channel
Skokie
Eden's Expwy
J.F. Kennedy Expwy
Dwight D. Eisenhower Expwy
Douglas Park
Illinois Inst. of Tech.
Chinatown
Grant Park
Art Institute
Field Museum
Adler Planetarium
Soldier Field
Burnham Park
Navy Pier
Chicago Harbor
Gold Coast
John Hancock Center
Lincoln Park Zoo
Belmont Harbor
Montrose Harbor
Burnham Harbor
Univ. of Chicago
Museum of Science & Industry
Jackson Park

Central Chicago

km 0 — 1
miles 0 — 0.5

LAKE MICHIGAN

Outer Harbor
Navy Pier
Olive Park
Ohio St Beach
Oak St Beach
Streeter Dr
Lake Point Tower
N McClurg Court
N Lake Shore Drive
John Hancock Center
Water Tower Place
Northwestern Memorial Hosp.
Fairbanks Court
Chicago River
Wrigley Bldg.
Tribune Tower
E Ontario
E Ohio
E Grand
E Illinois
E Erie
E Huron
E Superior
E Chicago Ave
E Delaware
E Chestnut
E Walton
E Oak
E Division
Gold Coast
Near North
N Dearborn
N Clark
N Wells
N LaSalle
N State
N Rush
N Wabash
N Michigan Avenue
N Kinzie St
Merchandise Mart
River North
N Hudson
N Larrabee
New Orleans St
N Canal
N Clinton
Union Sta.
Northwestern Sta.
Opera House
Sears Tower
Post Office
W Lake St
W Randolph
W Washington
W Madison
W Monroe
W Adams
W Jackson Blvd
W Van Buren
W Congress Pkwy
W Harrison
The Loop
City Hall County Bldg.
Marshall Field's
Prudential Building
Randolph St. Sta.
Van Buren St. Sta.
La Salle St. Sta.
Monroe Drive
Jackson Drive
Columbus Drive
Buckingham Fountain
Art Institute of Chicago
Grant Park
Randolph Drive
Lake Shore Drive
Balbo St
Congress
Printer's Row
W Polk St
W 9th St
Roosevelt Road Sta.
Roosevelt Road
South Loop
S Michigan Avenue
S Wabash Ave
S State St
S Canal Street
S Clinton
S Wells Street
S Clark Street
S Dearborn
W 14th St
W 16th St
W 18th St
S Indiana
S Prairie
S Calumet Ave
S Wabash
W Cermak
Chinatown
S Archer Ave
Wentworth Ave
S Roosevelt Road
South Branch Chicago River
Shedd Aquarium
Adler Planetarium
Field Museum of Nat. History
Soldier Field
Burnham Park
Burnham Park Harbor
McCormick Place East
McCormick Place West
South Lake Shore Drive East
South Lake Shore Drive West
Lake Shore Dr E
Merrill C. Meigs Field
Chicago Harbor
Chicago Yacht Club
E Solidarity Dr

COPYRIGHT GEORGE PHILIP LTD

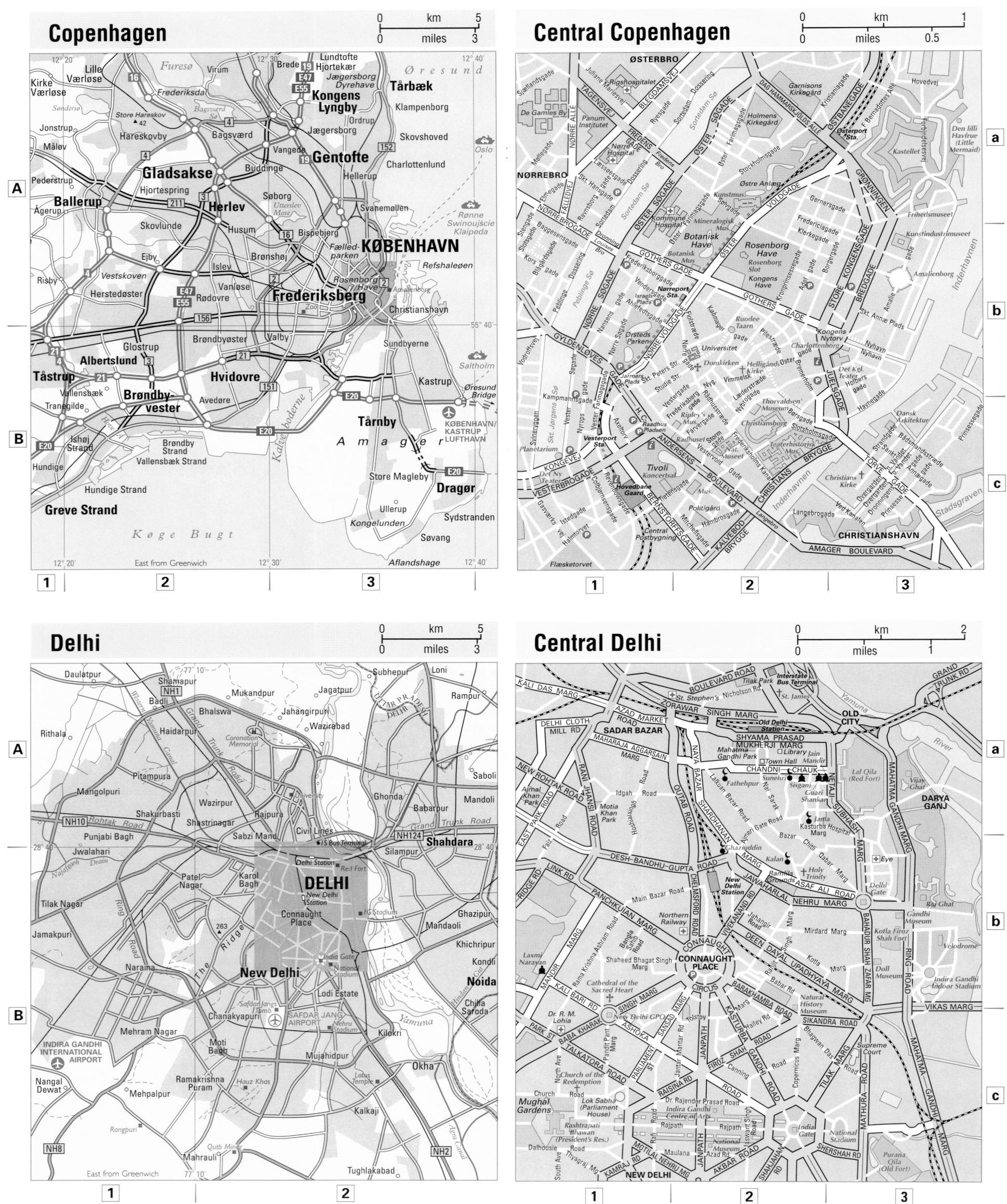

COPYRIGHT GEORGE PHILIP LTD

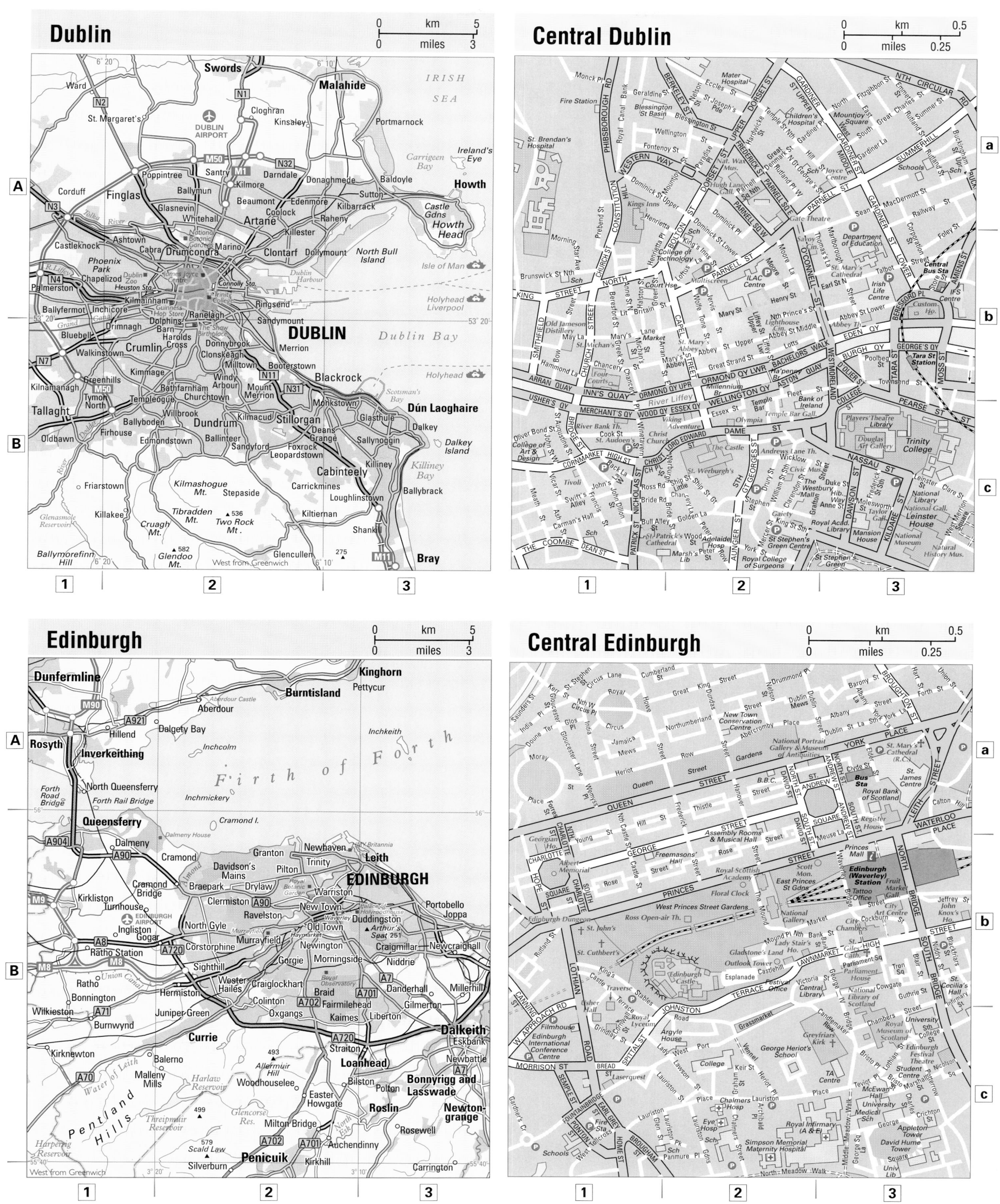

COPYRIGHT GEORGE PHILIP LTD

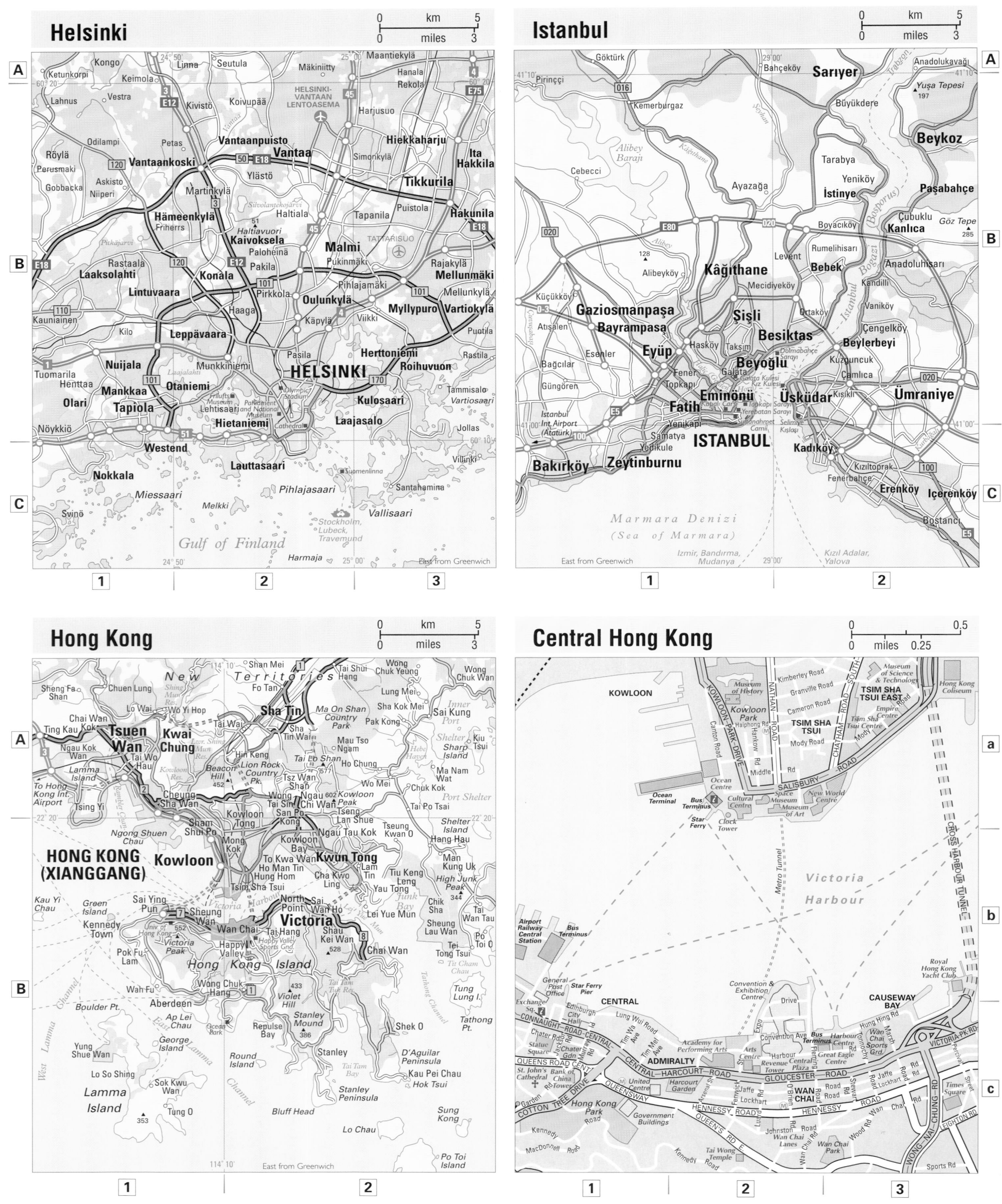

Helsinki

km 5
miles 3

Kongo Linna Seutula Mäkiniitty Maantiekylä
Ketunkorpi Keimola Hanala Rekola
Lahnus Kivistö Koivupää HELSINKI- Harjusuo
Vestra VANTAAN LENTOASEMA
Röylä Odilampi Petas Vantaanpuisto Hiekkaharju Ita Hakkila
Perusmaki Vantaankoski Vantaa Simonkylä Hakunila
Askisto Martinkylä Ylästö Tikkurila
Gobbacka Niiperi Hämeenkylä Haltiala Tapanila Puistola
Friherrs Kaivoksela Paloheinä Malmi Rajakylä Mellunmäki
Rastaala Konala Pakila Pukinmäki Mellunkylä
Laaksolahti Pirkkola Pihlajamäki Vartiokylä
Lintuvaara Haaga Oulunkylä Viikki Myllypuro
Kauniainen Kilo Käpylä Puotila
Leppävaara Munkkiniemi Pasila Herttoniemi Rastila
Nuijala HELSINKI Roihuvuon Tammisalo
Tuomarila Henttaa Otaniemi Kulosaari Vartiosaari
Mankkaa Tapiola Hietaniemi Laajasalo Jollas
Olari Westend Lauttasaari Villinki
Nöykkiö Nokkala Santahamina
Miessaari Melkki Pihlajasaari Vallisaari
Svinö Stockholm, Lubeck, Travemund
Gulf of Finland Harmaja East from Greenwich

Istanbul

km 5
miles 3

Göktürk Bahçeköy Sarıyer Anadolukavağı
Pirinçci Yuşa Tepesi 197
Kemerburgaz Büyükdere Beykoz
Cebecci Tarabya Yeniköy Paşabahçe
Ayazağa İstinye Çubuklu Göz Tepe 285
Boyacıköy Kanlıca
Küçükköy Levent Rumelihisarı Anadoluhisarı
Alibeyköy Kâğıthane Bebek Kandilli
Gaziosmanpaşa Mecidiyeköy Vaniköy
Bayrampaşa Şişli Ortaköy Çengelköy
Esenler Eyüp Beşiktaş Beylerbeyi
Bağcılar Haskoy Taksim Kuzguncuk
Güngören Fener Beyoğlu Çamlıca
Topkapı Galata Üsküdar Ümraniye
Yenikapı Eminönü Kısıklı
Istanbul Int. Airport (Atatürk) Fatih
Samatya ISTANBUL Kadıköy
Yedikule Kızıltoprak
Bakırköy Zeytinburnu Fenerbahçe Erenköy İçerenköy
Bostancı
Marmara Denizi (Sea of Marmara)
Izmir, Bandırma, Mudanya Kızıl Adalar, Yalova
East from Greenwich

Hong Kong

km 5
miles 3

Shan Mei Wong Chuk Yeung Wong Chuk Wan
Sheng Fa Shan *New Territories* Fo Tan Tai Shui Hang Lung Mei
Chuen Lung Wo Yi Hop Sha Tin Sha Kok Mei Sai Kung
Chai Wan Lo Wai Tai Wai Ma On Shan Country Park Pak Kong
Ting Kau Kok Tsuen Wan Kwai Chung Hin Keng Mau Tso Ngam Shelter
Ngau Kok Wan Tai Wo Hau Lion Rock Country Pk. Tai Lo Shan Ho Chung
Tsing Yi Cheung Sha Wan Tsz Wan Shan Ngau Chi Wan Ma Nam Wat
Sham Shui Po Kowloon Tong San Po Kong Tseng Lan Shue
HONG KONG (XIANGGANG) Kowloon Wong Tai Sin Kowloon Bay Ngau Tau Kok
Ngong Shuen Chau To Kwa Wan Kwun Tong
Green Island Sai Ying Pun Ho Man Tin Hung Hom Cha Kwo Ling Tiu Keng Leng
Kennedy Town Sheung Wan Tsim Sha Tsui North Point Yau Tong
Univ. of Hong Kong Wan Chai Victoria Sai Wan Ho Chik Sha
Pok Fu Lam *Victoria Peak* Happy Valley Shau Kei Wan Sheung Lau Wan
Wah Fu Happy Valley Sports Gnd Chai Wan Tei Tong Tsui
Hong Kong Island
Wong Chuk Hang Stanley Mound 386
Aberdeen Violet Hill 433 Shek O
Boulder Pt. Ap Lei Chau Repulse Bay Stanley
George Island *D'Aguilar Peninsula*
Yung Shue Wan Round Island Kau Pei Chau Hok Tsui
Lo So Shing Sok Kwu Wan *Stanley Peninsula* Sung Kong
Lamma Island Bluff Head Lo Chau Po Toi Island
Tung O 353
East from Greenwich

Central Hong Kong

0.5
miles 0.25

Museum of Science & Technology
KOWLOON Museum of History Kimberley Road Hong Kong Coliseum
Kowloon Park Granville Road TSIM SHA TSUI EAST
Haiphong Rd Cameron Road Empire Centre
Ocean Centre Canton Road Hankow Rd Middle TSIM SHA TSUI Mody Road
Ocean Terminal Cultural Centre Space Museum New World Centre
Bus Terminus Museum of Art SALISBURY
Star Ferry Clock Tower
Metro Tunnel *Victoria Harbour*
Airport Railway Central Station Bus Terminus
General Post Office Star Ferry Pier Royal Hong Kong Yacht Club
Exchange Edinburgh City Centre Convention & Exhibition Centre CAUSEWAY BAY
CONNAUGHT ROAD Tim Mei Ave Convention Ave Bus Terminus
Statue Square Chater Road CENTRAL Lung Wui Road Academy for Performing Arts Arts Centre Harbour Centre Great Eagle Centre
St. John's Cathedral CHATER ROAD CENTRAL ADMIRALTY HARCOURT ROAD Harbour Plaza Revenue Tower GLOUCESTER ROAD
Bank of China Tower QUEENSWAY Harcourt Garden WAN CHAI
Hong Kong Park United Centre Queensway HENNESSY ROAD Lockhart
COTTON TREE DRIVE Government Buildings QUEEN'S ROAD Johnston Road Wan Chai Lanes Wan Chai Park Times Square
Kennedy Road Tai Wong Temple WONG-NAI-CHUNG-RD LEIGHTON RD
MacDonnell Road Kennedy Road Sports Rd

COPYRIGHT GEORGE PHILIP LTD

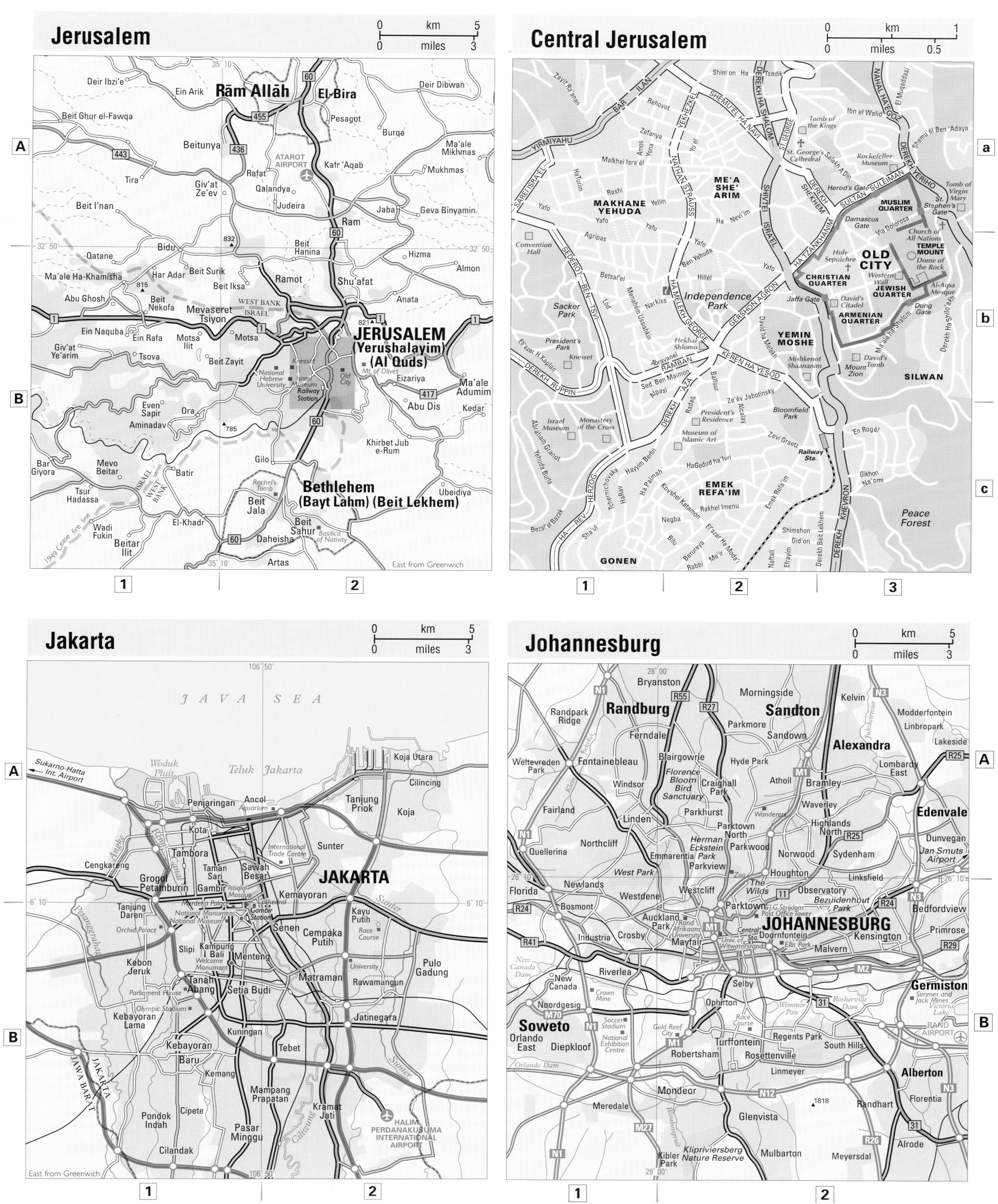

Jerusalem

0 — km — 5
0 — miles — 3

Deir Ibzi'e
Ein Arik
Rām Allāh   **El-Bira**
Deir Dibwan
Beit Ghur el-Fawqa
455
Pesagot
Burqa
Ma'ale Mikhmas
Beitunya
436
Ma'ale
Beit I'nan
443
Kafr 'Aqab
ATAROT AIRPORT
Mukhmas
Tira
Giv'at Ze'ev
Qalandya
Judeira
Jaba
Geva Binyamin
60
Qatane
Bidu
832
Beit Hanina
Ram
Ma'ale Ha-Khamisha
Har Adar
Beit Surik
Beit Iksa
Ramot
Shu'afat
Hizma
Almon
Abu Ghosh
815
Beit Nekofa
WEST BANK ISRAEL
Anata
Ein Naquba
Mevaseret Tsiyon
60
1
Ein Rafa
Motsa Ilit
1
Motsa
821
JERUSALEM (Yerushalayim) (Al Quds)
1
Giv'at Ye'arim
Tsova
Beit Zayit
National Hebrew University
Israel Museum Railway Station
Old City
Mt. of Olives
Eizariya
Ma'ale Adumim
Even Sapir
Ora
Aminadav
785
417
Abu Dis
Kedar
Bar Giyora
Mevo Beitar
Khirbet Jub e-Rum
Tsur Hadassa
ISRAEL WEST BANK
Batir
Gilo
Ubeidiya
Wadi Fukin
Beitar Ilit
El-Khadr
Beit Jala
Bethlehem (Bayt Lahm) (Beit Lekhem)
1949 Cease fire line
Rachel's Tomb
Beit Sahur
Basilica of Nativity
60
Daheisha
Artas
East from Greenwich

Central Jerusalem

0 — km — 1
0 — miles — 0.5

Zavit Ra'ana
BAR ILAN
Shim on Ha
Tsadik
NAHAL HAFEOZ
Ibn el Walid
YIRMIYAHU
Rehovot
SHEMU'EL HA NAVI
DEREKH HA SHALOM
ST GEORGE
Tomb of the Kings
St. George's Cathedral
Salāḥ A Din
Rockefeller Museum
Shemu'él Ben 'Adaya
Zefanya
Amōs
NATHAN STRAUSS
YEKHEZKEL
Yona
Herod's Gate
SULTAN SULEIMAN
Tomb of Virgin Mary
Rashi
Yellin
ME'A SHE' ARIM
SHIVTEI ISRAEL
SHEKHEM
MUSLIM QUARTER
St. Stephen's Gate
MAKHANE YEHUDA
Yafo
Ha Nevi'im
Damascus Gate
Via Dolorosa
Church of All Nations
Yafo
Agripas
Yafo
HA TZANKTANIM
DEREKH
Holy Sepulchre
OLD CITY
TEMPLE MOUNT
Convention Hall
Betsal'el
Ben Yehuda
Hillél
Yafo
CHRISTIAN QUARTER
Western Wall
Dome of the Rock
SEDEROT BEN-TSVI
HA MELEKH GEORGE
Narkiss
Menahem Usishkin
Independence Park
GERSHON AGRON
Jaffa Gate
David's Citadel
JEWISH QUARTER
Al-Aqsa Mosque
Sacker Park
Efrazat H.Kaplan
ARMENIAN QUARTER
Dung Gate
President's Park
Hekhal Shlomo
RAMBAN
KEREN HA YESOD
YEMIN MOSHE
Knesset
Abrazanel
Balfour
Ze'ev Jabotinsky
Mishkenot Sha'ananim
David's Tomb
Mount Zion
SILWAN
DEREKH RUPPIN
Sed. Ben Maimon
Alpasi
President's Residence
Bloomfield Park
Israel Museum
DEREKH AZA
Radaq
HERZOG
Monastery of the Cross
Museum of Islamic Art
Zevi Graetz
'En Rogél
Tchernichovsky
Hayyim Berlin
Museum of Islamic Art
HaGedud ha 'Ivri
Railway Sta.
Gikhon Na'omi
Abraham Granot
HaRav
HaGedud ha 'Ivri
Emek Refa'im
Yehuda Burla
Koyshel Katamon
Rakhel Imenu
DEREKH KHEVRON
Peace Forest
Bezal'el Bazak
Sha'ul
EMEK REFA'IM
Emek Refa'im
Negba
Shimshon
Gid'on
Berurya
Me'ir
Naftali
Efrayim
Rabbi
GONEN
Bilu
Er'azat Ha Moda'i
Beit Lakhem

Jakarta

0 — km — 5
0 — miles — 3

J A V A   S E A
106° 50'
Woduk Pluit
Teluk Jakarta
Koja Utara
A → Sukarno-Hatta Int. Airport
Penjaringan
Ancol
Aquarium
Cilincing
Tanjung Priok
Koja
Kota
Sunter
Cengkareng
Tambora
Taman Sari
Sawah Besar
International Trade Centre
Sunter
Grogol Petamburan
Gambir
Istiqlal Mosque
Kemayoran
Merdeka Palace
Cathedral
Tanjung Daren
National Monument
Gambir Station
Kayu Putih
JAKARTA
Orchid Palace
National Museum
Senen
Cempaka Putih
Slipi
Kampung I Bali
Welcome Monument
Menteng
Race Course
6° 10'
Kebon Jeruk
Tanah Abang
Setia Budi
University
Pulo Gadung
Parliament House
Rawamangun
Olympic Stadium
Matraman
Kebayoran Lama
Jatinegara
Kebayoran Baru
Kuningan
Tebet
JAWA BARAT
Kemang
Mampang Prapatan
Kramat Jati
Pondok Indah
Cipete
Pasar Minggu
Ciliwung
Cilandak
HALIM PERDANAKUSUMA INTERNATIONAL AIRPORT
106° 50'
East from Greenwich

Johannesburg

0 — km — 5
0 — miles — 3

28° 00'
Bryanston
N1
R55
Morningside
Kelvin
N3
Randpark Ridge
Randburg
R27
Sandton
Modderfontein
Linbropark
Ferndale
Parkmore
Sandown
Lakeside
Welteyreden Park
Fontainebleau
Blairgowrie
Hyde Park
Alexandra
R25
Fairland
Windsor
Florence Bloom Bird Sanctuary
Craighall Park
Atholl
Bramley
Lombardy East
A
Linden
Parkhurst
Wanderers
Highlands North
Edenvale
N1
Quellerina
Northcliff
Parktown North
Herman Eckstein Park
Parkwood
Norwood
Sydenham
Dunvegan
Jan Smuts Airport
West Park
Emmarentia Park
Parkview
Zoo
Houghton
Linksfield
26° 10'
Florida
Newlands
Westdene
Westcliff
The Wilds
11
Observatory
Bezuidenhout Park
R25
N3
Bosmont
Parktown
J.G.Strijdom Post Office Tower
R24
Bedfordview
New Canada Dam
Auckland Park
Rand Afrikaans University
JOHANNESBURG
Kensington
Primrose
R24
Industria
Crosby
Mayfair
Univ. of the Witwatersrand
Central Sta.
Doornfontein
Ellis Park
M1
Malvern
R29
New Canada
Riverlea
Selby
M2
R41
Germiston
Noordgesig
Crown Mine
Ophirton
Wemmer Pan
Rosherville Dam
Simmer and Jack Mines
Victoria Lake
Soweto
M70
Soccer Stadium
Gold Reef City
Turffontein
Race Course
RAND AIRPORT
B
Orlando East
N1
Diepkloof
National Exhibition Centre
M1
Robertsham
Rosettenville
South Hills
Orlando Dam
Linmeyer
Alberton
N3
Mondeor
M12
1818
Randhart
Florentia
Meredale
Glenvista
Kibler Park
Klipriviersberg Nature Reserve
M27
R26
Mulbarton
Meyersdal
Alrode
M1
28° 00'

COPYRIGHT GEORGE PHILIP LTD

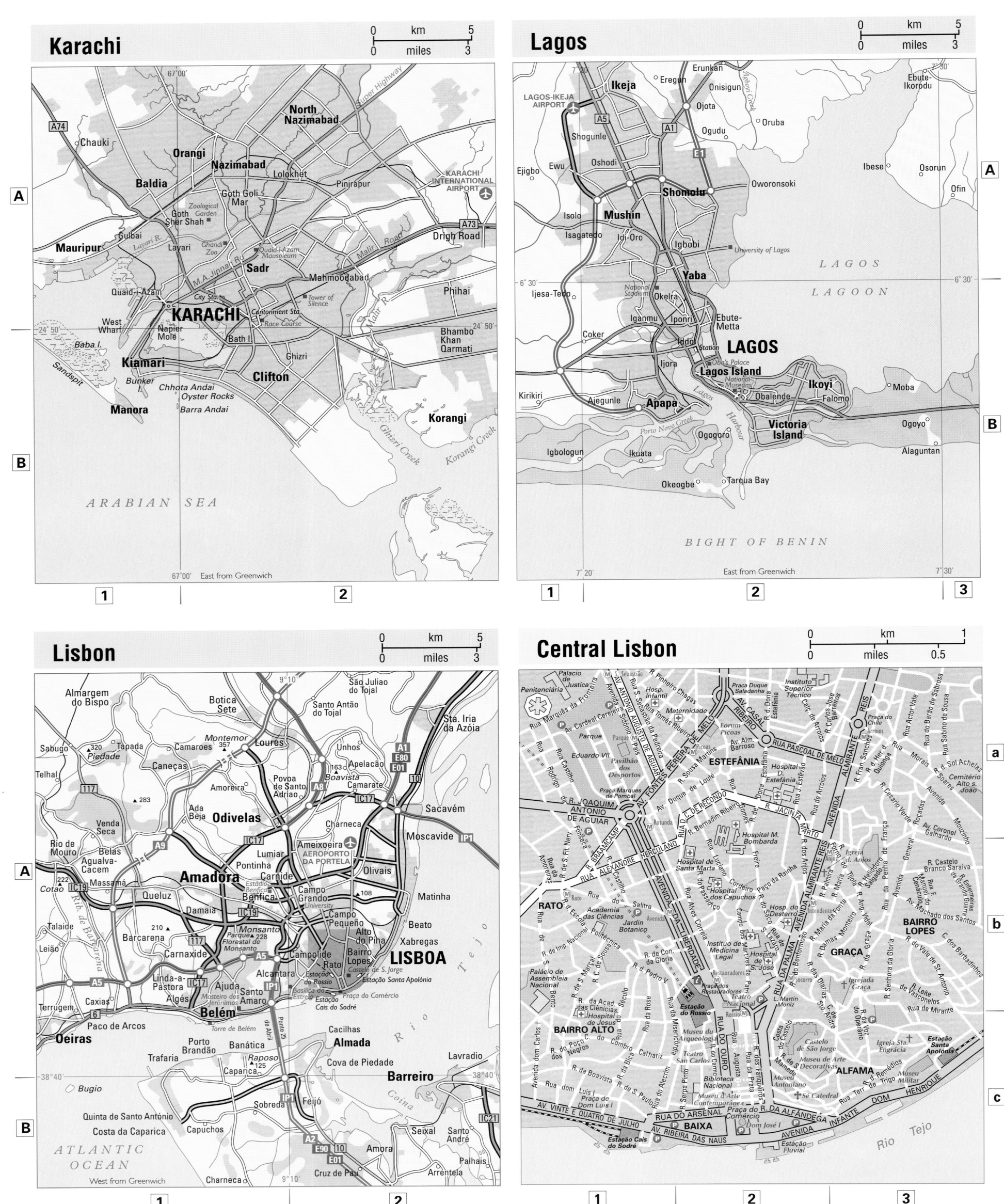

Karachi

0 — km — 5
0 — miles — 3

A74 · Chauki · 67°00'
North Nazimabad
Orangi
Nazimabad
Baldia
Lolokhet · Pinjirápur
Goth Goli Mar
Goth Sher Shah · Zoological Garden · Ghandi Zoo
A
Mauripur
Gulbai
Layari R. · Layari · Quaid-i-Azam Mausoleum · Malir Rd. · KARACHI INTERNATIONAL AIRPORT ✈
A73
M.A. Jinnah Rd.
Sadr
Drigh Road
Quaid-i-Azam
West Wharf · Napier Mole · City Sta. · Mahmoodabad · Malir R.
Baba I. · 24°50'
Cantonment Sta. · Tower of Silence · Phihai
Sandspit
Kiamari
Bath I. · Race Course · Ghizri
Bhambo Khan Qarmati
Bunker · Chhota Andai · Oyster Rocks
Clifton
24°50'
Manora
Barra Andai
B
Korangi
Ghizri Creek
Korangi Creek
ARABIAN SEA
67°00' · East from Greenwich

1 **2**

Lagos

0 — km — 5
0 — miles — 3

7°10' · Erunkan · 30'
Ikeja · Eregun · Onisigun · Ebute-Ikoródu
LAGOS-IKEJA AIRPORT ✈ · Shogunle · Ojota · Oruba
A5 · A1 · Ogudu
Ejigbo · Ewu · Oshodi · E1 · Ibese · Osorun
Isolo · Shomolu · Oworonsoki · **A** · Ofin
Mushin · Isagatedo · Idi-Oro · Igbobi
Ijesa-Tedo · University of Lagos · LAGOS LAGOON
Yaba · 6°30'
National Stadium · Okelra
Coker · Iganmu · Iponri · Ebute-Metta
Iddo · Station
Ijora · LAGOS
Kirikiri · Oba's Palace · National Museum · Lagos Island
Ajegunle · Ikoyi · Moba
Apapa · Obalénde · Falomo
Lagos Harbour · Victoria Island · Ogoyo
Igbologun · Porto Novo Creek · Ogogoro · Alaguntan · **B**
Ikuata
Okeogbe · Tarqua Bay
BIGHT OF BENIN
7°20' · East from Greenwich · 7°30'

1 **2** **3**

Lisbon

0 — km — 5
0 — miles — 3

9°10' · São Julião do Tojal
Almargem do Bispo · Botica Sete · Santo Antão do Tojal · Sta. Iria da Azóia
Sabugo · 320 · Tapada · Montemor 357 · Camaroes · Loures · Unhos · A1 · E80 · E01
Telhal · Piedade · Canecas · Apelação · 10
117 · 283 · Amoreira · Póvoa de Santo Adriao · 163 · Boavista · Camarate · IC17
Venda Seca · Ada Beja · Odivelas · Charneca · Sacavém
Rio de Mouro · Belas · A9 · IC17 · Lumiar · Ameixoeira · IC17 · Moscavide · IP1
222 · Agualva-Cacem · IC19 · Pontinha · AEROPORTO DA PORTELA · Olivais
A · Cotao · Massamá · Carnide · Campo Grande · Matinha
Amadora · 108
Queluz · Benfica · University · Campo Pequeno · Beato
Damaia · IC19 · Monsanto 228 · Alto do Pina · Xabregas
210 · Parque Florestal de Monsanto · Campolide · Bairro Lopes
Barcarena · Carnaxide · Castelo de S. Jorge · LISBOA
Leião · 117 · Alcântara · Estação do Rossio
Linda-a-Pastora · A5 · Ajuda · IP1 · Basílica da Estrela · Estação Santa Apolónia
Talaide · IC17 · Santo Amaro · Estação Cais do Sodré
Terrugem · 6 · Mosteiro dos Jerónimos · Praça do Comércio
Caxias · Belém · Torre de Belém · Cacilhas
Oeiras · Paco de Arcos · 125 · Almada
Porto Brandão · Raposo · Cova de Piedade · Lavradio
Trafaria · Banática · 38°40'
Caparica · 38°40' · Barreiro
Bugio · IP1 · Feijó · IC21
ATLANTIC OCEAN · Sobreda · Coina R.
Quinta de Santo António · Capuchos · Amora · Santo André
Costa da Caparica · **B** · Seixal
A2 · E90 · 10 · E01
West from Greenwich · Charneca · 9°10' · Cruz de Pau · Arrentela · Palhais

1 **2**

Central Lisbon

0 — km — 1
0 — miles — 0.5

Palácio da Penitenciária · R. Pinheiro Chagas · Praça Duque de Saldanha · Instituto Superior Técnico · **a**
Praça do Chile
Hosp. Infantil · Maternidade · Fórum Picoas
Eduardo VII · Pavilhão dos Desportos · ESTEFÂNIA · Hospital D. Estefânia
RATO · Parque Eduardo VII · Arroios
Académia das Ciências · Jardim Botânico · Hospital de Santa Marta · **b**
Palácio de Assembleia Nacional · Instituto de Medicina Legal · BAIRRO LOPES
BAIRRO ALTO · Museu do Arqueologia · GRAÇA · Igreja Graça
Teatro Nacional · Estação do Rossio · Castelo de São Jorge · Igreja Sta. Engrácia · Estação Santa Apolónia
Hospital de Jesus · Teatro S. Carlos · Museu de Arte Decorativas · **c**
Biblioteca Nacional · Museu Antoniano · ALFAMA
Museu de Arte Contemporânea · Sé Catedral
AV. VINTE E QUATRO DE JULHO · RUA DO ARSENAL · BAIXA · Praça do Comércio · Rio Tejo
Estação Cais do Sodré · AV. RIBEIRA DAS NAUS · Estação Fluvial

1 **2** **3**

COPYRIGHT GEORGE PHILIP LTD

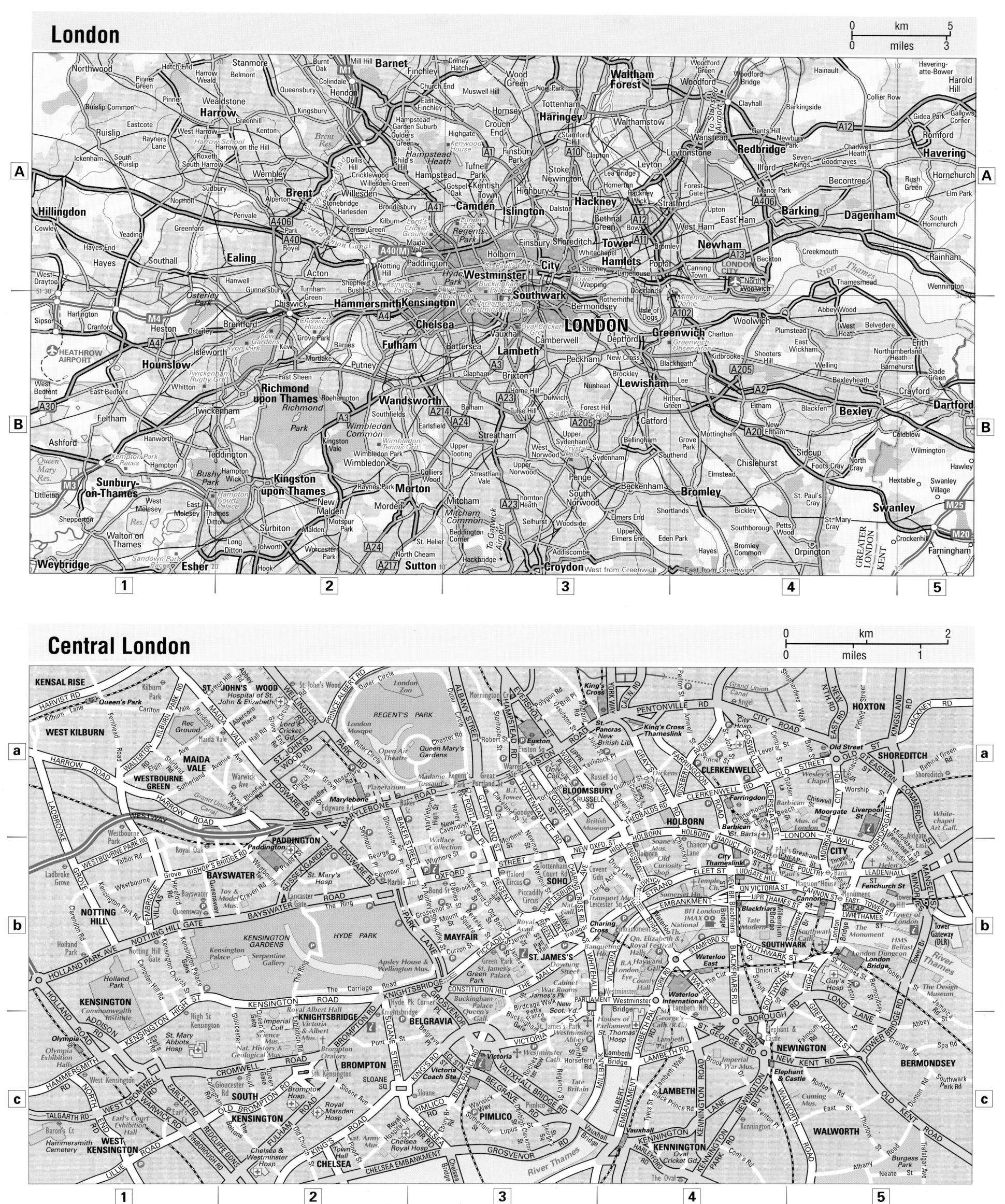

London

Central London

COPYRIGHT GEORGE PHILIP LTD

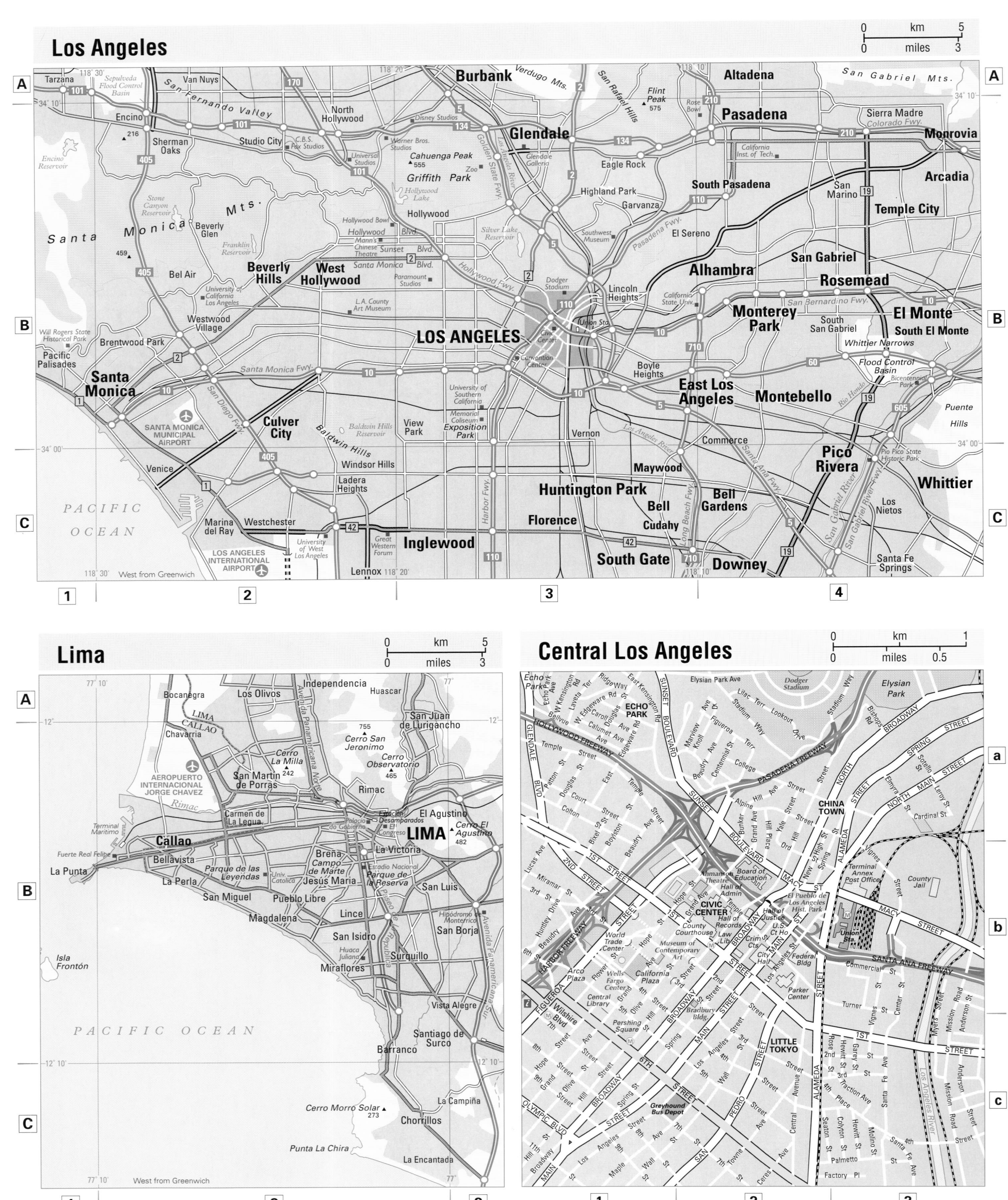

Los Angeles

0   km   5
0   miles   3

Tarzana
Van Nuys
Burbank
Verdugo Mts.
San Gabriel Mts.
Altadena
Sepulveda Flood Control Basin
Flint Peak 575
Rose Bowl
Pasadena
Sierra Madre
Colorado Fwy.
Encino
North Hollywood
Disney Studios
San Rafael Hills
California Inst. of Tech.
Monrovia
Sherman Oaks
Studio City
C.B.S. Studios
Warner Bros. Film Studios
Universal Studios
Glendale
Glendale Galleria
Eagle Rock
Arcadia
Encino Reservoir
Cahuenga Peak 555
Griffith Park
Hollywood Lake
Zoo
Highland Park
South Pasadena
Garvanza
San Marino
Temple City
Santa Monica Mts.
Beverly Glen
Hollywood Bowl
Mann's Chinese Theatre
Sunset Blvd.
Hollywood
Santa Monica Blvd.
Silver Lake Reservoir
Southwest Museum
El Sereno
San Gabriel
Bel Air
University of California Los Angeles
Beverly Hills
West Hollywood
Paramount Studios
Dodger Stadium
Lincoln Heights
California State Univ.
Alhambra
Rosemead
Westwood Village
L.A. County Art Museum
LOS ANGELES
Civic Center
Union Sta.
Monterey Park
South San Gabriel
El Monte
South El Monte
Will Rogers State Historical Park
Brentwood Park
Boyle Heights
Whittier Narrows
Flood Control Basin
Pacific Palisades
Santa Monica
Santa Monica Fwy.
University of Southern California
East Los Angeles
Montebello
Bicentennial Park
Puente Hills
PACIFIC OCEAN
Culver City
Baldwin Hills Reservoir
View Park
Memorial Coliseum Exposition Park
Vernon
Commerce
Pico Rivera
Pio Pico State Historic Park
Whittier
Venice
Windsor Hills
Maywood
Los Nietos
Marina del Ray
Ladera Heights
Westchester
Great Western Forum
Huntington Park
Bell
Bell Gardens
Cudahy
Florence
LOS ANGELES INTERNATIONAL AIRPORT
University of West Los Angeles
Inglewood
South Gate
Downey
Santa Fe Springs
Lennox

Lima

0   km   5
0   miles   3

Bocanegra
Los Olivos
Independencia
Huascar
LIMA CALLAO
Chavarria
Cerro San Jeronimo 755
San Juan de Lurigancho
Cerro La Milla
AEROPUERTO INTERNACIONAL JORGE CHAVEZ
San Martin de Porras
Cerro Observatorio 465
Rimac
Terminal Maritimo
Carmen de La Legua
Estación Desamparados
Palacio de Gobierno
El Agustino
Cerro El Agustino 482
Callao
Fuerte Real Felipe
La Victoria
La Punta
Bellavista
Breña
Campo de Marte
Estación del Congreso
La Perla
Parque de las Leyendas
Jesús Maria
Parque de la Reserva
San Luis
San Miguel
Univ. Catolica
Lince
Pueblo Libre
Huaca Juliana
San Isidro
Hipódromo de Monterrico
San Borja
Magdalena
Surquillo
Isla Frontón
Miraflores
PACIFIC OCEAN
Vista Alegre
Santiago de Surco
Barranco
La Campiña
Cerro Morro Solar 273
Chorrillos
Punta La Chira
La Encantada

West from Greenwich

Central Los Angeles

0   km   1
0   miles   0.5

Echo Park
Elysian Park Ave
Dodger Stadium
Elysian Park
ECHO PARK
SUNSET BOULEVARD
HOLLYWOOD FREEWAY
PASADENA FREEWAY
CHINA TOWN
GLENDALE BLVD
Temple Street
Terminal Annex Post Office
County Jail
SUNSET BOULEVARD
Alpine Street
ALAMEDA STREET
MACY ST
Board of Education
Hall of Admin
El Pueblo de Los Angeles Hist. Park
Union Sta.
HARBOR FREEWAY
CIVIC CENTER
County Courthouse
Ahmanson Theatre
Hall of Records
Hall of Justice
SANTA ANA FREEWAY
World Trade Center
Law Lib
City Hall
Federal Bldg
Commercial St
Arco Plaza
Museum of Contemporary Art
California Plaza
Parker Center
LITTLE TOKYO
Central Library
Wells Fargo Center
Bradbury Bldg
Wilshire Blvd
Pershing Square
BROADWAY
MAIN STREET
OLYMPIC BLVD
Greyhound Bus Depot
SAN PEDRO STREET
LOS ANGELES RIVER

COPYRIGHT GEORGE PHILIP LTD

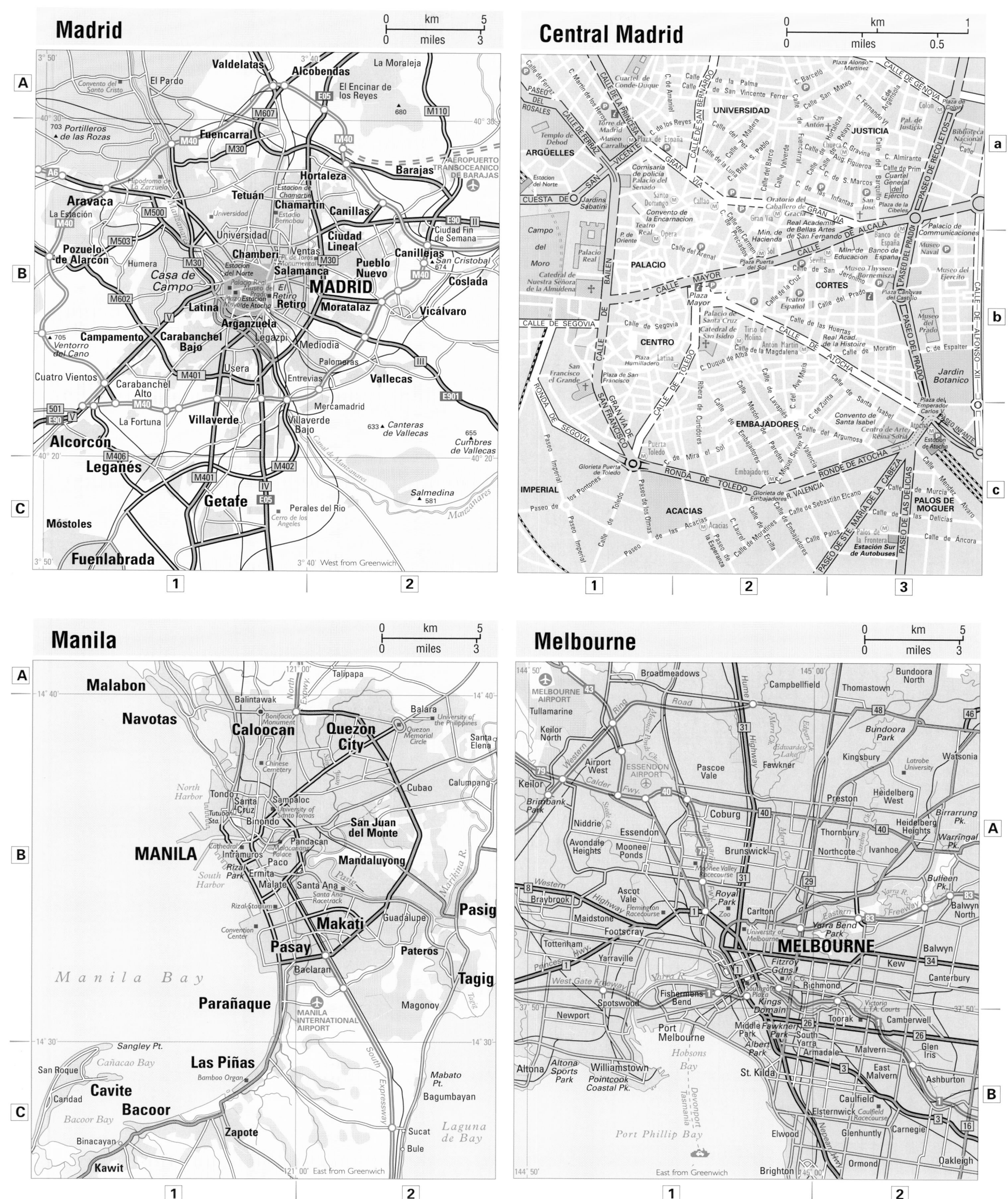

Madrid

km 0 — 5
miles 0 — 3

Central Madrid

km 0 — 1
miles 0 — 0.5

Manila

km 0 — 5
miles 0 — 3

Melbourne

km 0 — 5
miles 0 — 3

COPYRIGHT GEORGE PHILIP LTD

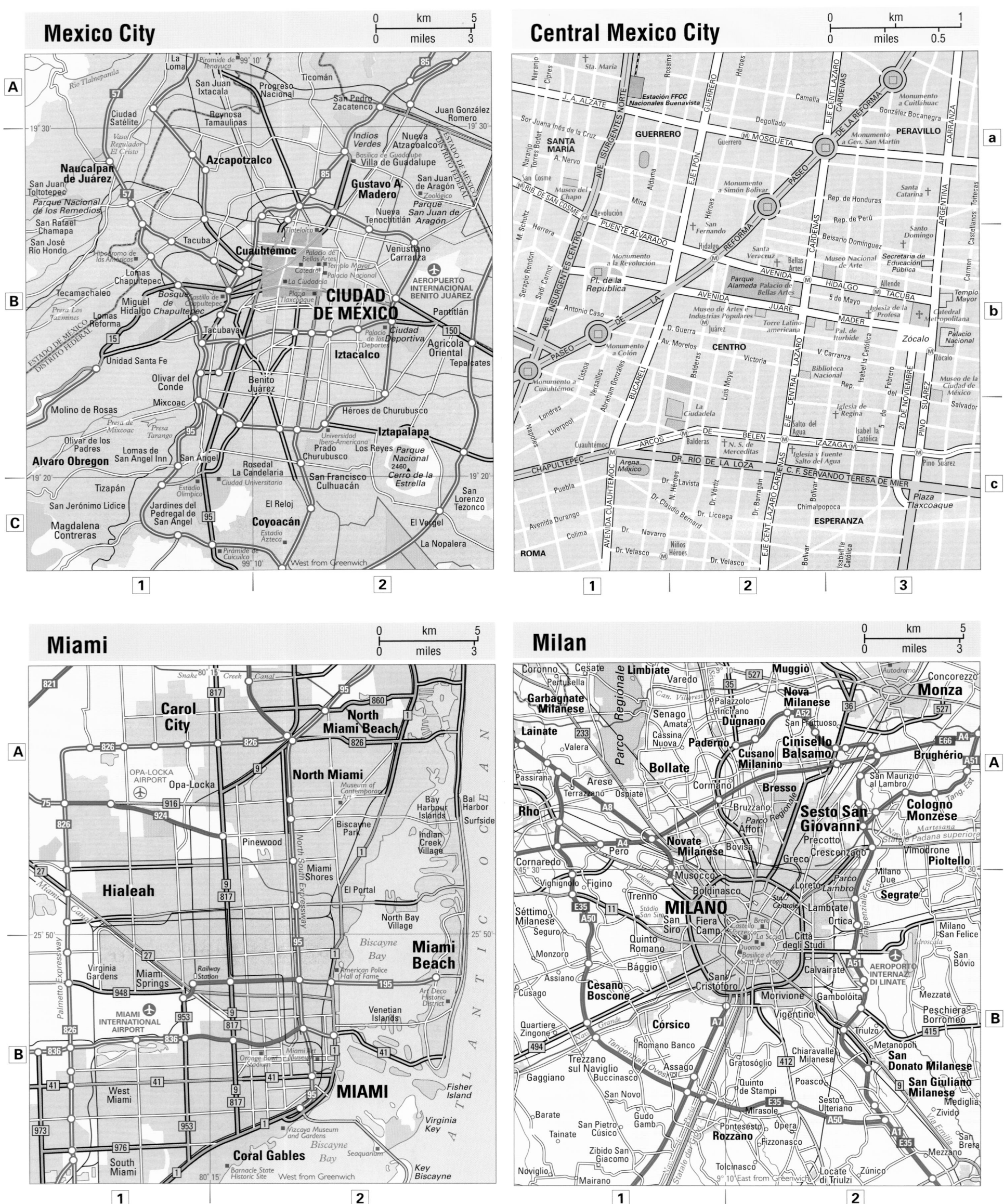

Mexico City

0 — km — 5
0 — miles — 3

Río Tlalnepantla
La Loma
Pirámide de Tenayuca
99° 10'
Ticomán
85
A
San Juan Ixtacala
Progreso Nacional
San Pedro Zacatenco
Juan González Romero
19° 30'
Ciudad Satélite
Reynosa Tamaulipas
19° 30'
57
Vaso Regulador El Cristo
Indios Verdes
Nueva Atzacoalco
Azcapotzalco
Basílica de Guadalupe
Villa de Guadalupe
85
Naucalpan de Juárez
Gustavo A. Madero
San Juan de Aragón
Zoológico
San Juan Toltotepec
Parque Nacional de los Remedios
Nueva Tenochtitlán
San Juan de Aragón
San Rafael Chamapa
Tlatelolco
Parque
57
Tacuba
Cuauhtémoc
Venustiano Carranza
San José Río Hondo
B
Hipódromo de las Américas
Palacio de Bellas Artes
Catedral
Templo Mayor
Palacio Nacional
AEROPUERTO INTERNACIONAL BENITO JUÁREZ
Tecamachaleo
Lomas Chapultepec
Bosque de Chapultepec
Castillo de Chapultepec
La Ciudadela
Plaza Tlaxcoaque
CIUDAD DE MÉXICO
Presa Los Tazmines
Miguel Hidalgo
Chapultepec
Paptitlán
Lomas Reforma
15
Tacubaya
Ciudad de los Deportes
150
Unidad Santa Fe
Iztacalco
Agrícola Oriental
Olivar del Conde
Benito Juárez
Tepalcates
Molino de Rosas
Mixcoac
Héroes de Churubusco
Presa de Mixcoac
Presa Tarango
95
Universidad Ibero-Americana
Iztapalapa
Olivar de los Padres
Prado Churubusco
Los Reyes
Álvaro Obregón
Lomas de San Angel Inn
San Angel
Parque Nacional 2460 Cerro de la Estrella
19° 20'
Tizapán
Rosedal La Candelaria
San Francisco Culhuacán
19° 20'
San Lorenzo Tezonco
San Jerónimo Lidice
Estadio Olímpico
Ciudad Universitaria
El Reloj
El Vergel
C
95
Jardines del Pedregal de San Angel
Coyoacán
Magdalena Contreras
Estadio Azteca
La Nopalera
Pirámide de Cuicuilco
99° 10'
West from Greenwich
1 **2**

Central Mexico City

0 — km — 1
0 — miles — 0.5

Naranjo
Sta. María
Cipres
Rossino
Héroes
+ Monumento a Cuitláhuac
a
J. A. ALZATE
Estación FFCC Nacionales Buenavista
GUERRERO
Camelia
González Bocanegra
Monumento a Gen. San Martín
PERAVILLO
Sor Juana Inés de la Cruz
A. Nervo
SANTA MARÍA
GUERRERO
Guerrero
Degollado
Monumento a Simón Bolívar
Rep. de Honduras
Santa Catarina
San Cosme
Museo del Chapo
Revolución
Héroes
+ San Fernando
Rep. de Perú
Santo Domingo
Herrera
PUENTE ALVARADO
Hidalgo
Santa Veracruz
Beisario Domínguez
Secretaría de Educación Pública
M. Schultz
Monumento a la Revolución
Pl. de la República
Reforma
Bellas Artes
Museo Nacional de Arte
Carmen
Allende
TACUBA
b
Antonio Caso
AVENIDA
Parque Alameda
Palacio de Bellas Artes
5 de Mayo
HIDALGO
Iglesia de la Profesa
Catedral Metropolitana
Templo Mayor
Monumento a Colón
D. Guerra
Juárez
JUARE
Pal. de Iturbide
Zócalo
Palacio Nacional
Monumento a Cuauhtémoc
Av. Morelos
Torre Latino-americana
CENTRO
V. Carranza
Zócalo
Londres
Listoni
Balderas
Victoria
Biblioteca Nacional
Museo de la Ciudad de México
La Ciudadela
Luis Moya
Isabel la Católica
Rep.
Salvador
Liverpool
Iglesia de Regina
Isabel la Católica
ARCOS
DE
BELEN
Balderas
Salto del Agua
c
CHAPULTEPEC
Arena México
N. S. de Mercedes
Iglesia y Fuente Salto del Agua
Pino Suárez
Puebla
DR. RÍO DE LA LOZA
D. Lavista
Dr. Barragán
Plaza Tlaxcoaque
Avenida Durango
D. Vértiz
Dr. Liceaga
Bolívar
Chimalpopoca
Colima
Dr. Navarro
Niños Héroes
ESPERANZA
ROMA
Dr. Velasco
Dr. Velasco
1 **2** **3**

Miami

0 — km — 5
0 — miles — 3

821
Snake 80° 15' Creek Canal
95
817
860
A
Carol City
826
North Miami Beach
826
826
1
OPA-LOCKA AIRPORT
9
North Miami
Bay Harbour Islands
Bal Harbor
75
916
Museum of Contemporary
Surfside
826
924
Biscayne Park
Indian Creek Village
1
Pinewood
Miami Shores
Hialeah
North South Expressway
El Portal
27
North Bay Village
25° 50'
95
25° 50'
Virginia Gardens
1
Miami Beach
27
Miami Springs
Railway Station
American Police Hall of Fame
948
MIAMI INTERNATIONAL AIRPORT
195
Art Deco Historic District
836
953
9
Miami Art Museum
826
836
817
41
Orange Bowl Stadium
Venetian Islands
B
41
1
27
9
West Miami
817
MIAMI
Fisher Island
973
953
Vizcaya Museum and Gardens
Virginia Key
976
Biscayne Bay
Seaquarium
South Miami
80° 15' West from Greenwich
Coral Gables
Barnacle State Historic Site
Key Biscayne
1 **2**

Milan

0 — km — 5
0 — miles — 3

Coronno
Cesate
Limbiate
Varedo
527
Muggiò
Concorezzo
A
Pertusella
Can. Villoresi
35
Garbagnate Milanese
Palazzolo
Nova Milanese
Autodromo
Monza
Senago
Amata
Trinciano
A52
Dugnano
San Fruttuoso
527
Lainate
233
Cassina Nuova
Paderno
Cinisello Balsamo
36
E66 A4
Valera
Cusano Milanino
A51
Brughério
Passirana
Ospiate
Cormano
Bollate
San Maurizio al Lambro
A4
Bresso
Rho
Arese
Bruzzano
Sesto San Giovanni
Cologno Monzese
Terrazzano
Affori
Precotto
A8
Parco Regionale
Vimodrone
Cornaredo
Novate Milanese
Bovisa
Crescenzago
45° 30'
Pero
Greco
Pioltello
45° 30'
Vighignolo
Figino
Musocco
Loreto
Milano Due
A4
Trenno
Boldinasco
Lambro
Segrate
E35
11
Stadio San Siro
Centrale
Séttimo Milanese
Lambrate
Milano San Felice
A50
MILANO
Seguro
San Siro
Fiera Camp.
Ortica
San Bóvio
Monzoro
Brera
La Scala
Castello
Città degli Studi
A51
Quinto Romano
Duomo
AEROPORTO INTERNAZ. DI LINATE
Bággio
Basilica di Sant'Ambrogio
Calvairate
Assiano
San Cristoforo
Mezzate
B
Cúsago
Morivione
Gambolóita
Peschiera Borromeo
Quartiere Zingone
Cesano Boscone
Vigentino
415
494
Triulzo
Romano Banco
A7
Trezzano sul Naviglio
Córsico
Chiaravalle Milanese
Metanopoli
San Donato Milanese
Gaggiano
Buccinasco
412
Gratosóglio
San Giuliano Milanese
Assago
Poasco
Quinto de Stampi
Barate
Medigia
San Novo
Sesto Ulteriano
Zivido
San Pietro Cúsico
Gudo Gamb.
A50
Opera
San Brera
Rozzano
Fizzonasco
A1
Zibido San Giacomo
Mirasole
Pontesesto
E35
Noviglio
Tolcinasco
9° 10' East from Greenwich
Locate di Triulzi
Zúnico
Mezzano
Mairano
1 **2**

COPYRIGHT GEORGE PHILIP LTD

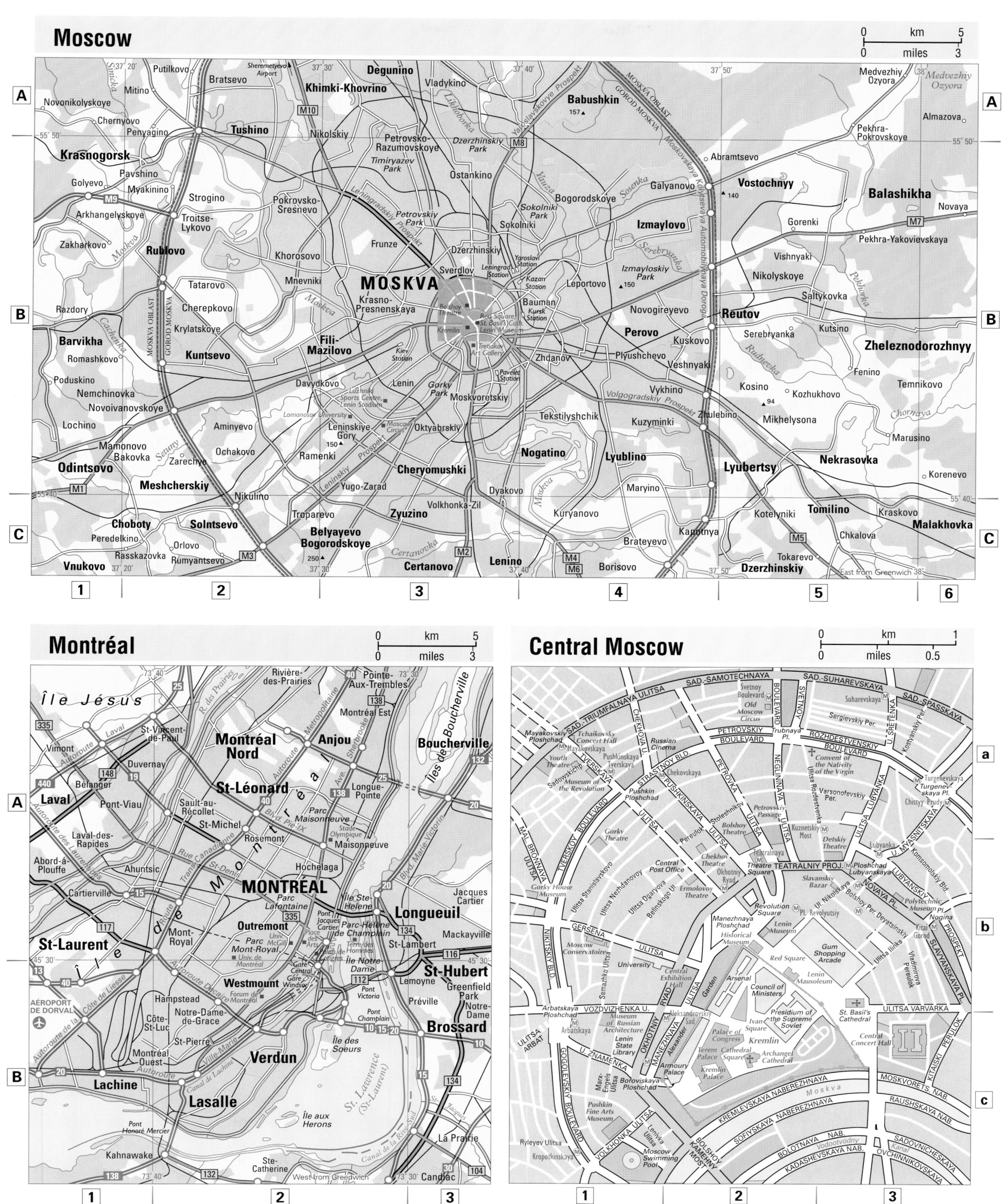

Moscow

km 0 5
miles 0 3

Medvezhiy Ozyora · Medvezhiy Ozyora
Novonikolyskoye · Mitino · Putilkovo · Sheremetyevo Airport · Bratsevo · Dégunino · Khimki-Khovrino · Vladykino · Babushkin · 157 · Pekhra-Pokrovskoye · Almazova
Chernyovo · Penyagino · M10 · Tushino · Nikolskiy · Petrovsko-Razumovskoye · M8 · Dzerzhinskiy Park · Ostankino · Abramtsevo · Vostochnyy · 140 · Balashikha · Novaya
Krasnogorsk · Pavshino · Myakinino · Strogino · Pokrovsko-Sresnevo · Timiryazev Park · Sokolniki Park · Bogorodskoye · Galyanovo · Izmaylovo · Gorenki · M7
Golyevo · M9 · Troitse-Lykovo · Frunze · Petrovskiy Park · Sokolniki · Izmayloskiy Park · Vishnyaki · Pekhra-Yakovievskaya
Arkhangelskoye · Zakharkovo · Rublovo · Tatarovo · Khorosovo · Mnevniki · MOSKVA · Krasno-Presnenskaya · Bolshoy Theatre · Leningrad Station · Yaroslavl Station · Kazan Station · Leportovo · 150 · Nikolyskoye · Saltykovka
Razdory · Cherepkovo · Krylatskoye · Sverdlov · Red Square · St Basil's Cath. · Lenin Museum · Bauman · Kursk Station · Novogireyevo · Reutov · Serebryanka · Kutsino · Zheleznodorozhnyy
Barvikha · Kremlin · Kiev Station · Tretiakov Art Gallery · Perovo · Kuskovo · Fenino · Temnikovo
Romashkovo · Kuntsevo · Fili-Mazilovo · Davydkovo · Lenin · Gorky Park · Moskvoretskiy · Zhdanov · Plyushchevo · Veshnyak · Vykhino · Kosino · Kozhukhovo · Mikhelysona · Marusino
Poduskino · Nemchinovka · Novoivanovskoye · Lomonosov University · Lenin Stadium · Luzhniki Sports Centre · Moscow Circus · Oktyabrskiy · Zhdanov · Tekstilyshchik · Kuzyminki · Zhulebino · 94 · Korenevo
Lochino · Aminyevo · Ochakovo · Leninskiye Gory · 150 · Ramenki · Cheryomushki · Nogatino · Lyublino · Nekrasovka
Mamonovo · Bakovka · Zarechye · Nikulino · Yugo-Zarad · Dyakovo · Maryino · Lyubertsy
Odintsovo · Meshcherskiy · M1 · Troparevo · Zyuzino · Volkhonka-Zil · Kuryanovo · Kotelniki · Tomilino · Kraskovo
Choboty · Solntsevo · Belyayevo Bogorodskoye · 250 · Kapotnya · Chkalova · Malakhovka
Peredelkino · Orlovo · Rumyantsevo · M3 · M2 · Certanovo · Lenino · M4 · Borisovo · Brateyevo · M5 · Tokarevo · Dzerzhinskiy
Vnukovo · Rasskazovka · M6 · Dzerzhinskiy · Tokarevo

East from Greenwich 38

1 2 3 4 5 6

A B C

Montréal

km 0 5
miles 0 3

Île Jésus · Rivière-des-Prairies · Pointe-Aux-Trembles · Boucherville
Vimont · Laval · St-Vincent-de-Paul · Montréal Nord · Anjou · Montréal Est
Duvernay · St-Léonard · Longue-Pointe · Boucherville
Laval · Bélanger · Pont-Viau · Sault-au-Récollet · Parc Maisonneuve
Abord-à-Plouffe · Ahuntsic · St-Michel · Rosemont · Stade Olympique · Maisonneuve
Laval-des-Rapides · Cartierville · Hochelaga
Cartierville · MONTRÉAL · Parc Lafontaine · Île Ste-Hélène · Jacques Cartier
St-Laurent · Outremont · Parc Mont-Royal · Parc Hélène Île Champlain · Longueuil · Mackayville
Mont-Royal · Univ. McGill · Place des Arts · St-Lambert
Univ. de Montréal · Gare Centrale · Lemoyne · St-Hubert
Westmount · Forum de Montréal · Pont Victoria · Préville · Greenfield Park · Notre-Dame
Hampstead · Côte-St-Luc · St-Pierre · Pont Champlain · Brossard
Notre-Dame-de-Grace · Montréal Ouest · Verdun · Île des Soeurs
Lachine · Lasalle · St. Lawrence (St-Laurent) · Île aux Herons
Kahnawake · Pont Honoré Mercier · Ste-Catherine · La Prairie · Candiac
West from Greenwich

AÉROPORT DE DORVAL

1 2 3

A B

Central Moscow

km 0 1
miles 0 0.5

SAD-SAMOTECHNAYA · SAD-SUHAREVSKAYA · SAD-SPASSKAYA
SAD-TRIUMFALNAYA ULITSA · Svetnoy Boulevard · Old Moscow Circus · Suharevskaya Ulitsa · Sergievskiy Per.
Mayakovskiy Ploshchad · Tchaikovsky Concert Hall · Russian Cinema · PETROVSKIY BOULEVARD · Trubnaya Pl. · ROZHDESTVENSKY · Kostyanskiy Per.
Youth Theatre · Pushkinskaya Iverskaya · Chekovskaya · Convent of the Nativity of the Virgin · Turgenevskaya Pl. · Chistyy Prudy
Museum of the Revolution · Pushkin Ploshchad · Petrovskiy Passage · Varsonofevskiy Per.
Gorky Theatre · Stoleshnikov Per. · Bolshoy Theatre · Kuznetskiy Most · Detskiy Theatre · Lubyanka
Gorky House Museum · Ulitsa Stanislavskoy · Chekhov Theatre · Teatralnaya · Theatre Square · TEATRALNIY PROJ. · Ploshchad Lubyanskaya · Komsomolskaya · Myasnitskaya
Central Post Office · Ermolovoy Theatre · Okhotny Ryad · Slavanskiy Bazar · Polytechnic Museum · Nagina
Moscow Conservatoire · Ulitsa Ogaryova · Revolution Square · Manezhnaya Ploshchad · Lenin Museum · Gum Shopping Arcade · Ilinka
University · Central Exhibition Hall · Historical Museum · Red Square · Lenin Mausoleum
Arbatskaya Ploshchad · Museum of Russian Architecture · Aleksandrovskiy Sad · Arsenal · Council of Ministers · St Basil's Cathedral · ULITSA VARVARKA · Central Concert Hall
Lenin State Library · Palace of Congress · Terem Cathedral Palace · Kremlin · Presidium of the Supreme Soviet
Arbatskaya Ploshchad · Armoury Palace · Kremlin Palace · Ivan Cathedral · Archangel Cathedral
Pushkin Fine Arts Museum · Borovitskaya Ploshchad · MOSKVORETS. NAB. · RAUSHSKAYA NAB.
Ryleyev Ulitsa · Kropotkinskaya · Moscow Swimming Pool · KREMLEVSKAYA NABEREZHNAYA · SOFIISKAYA NAB. · Vodootvodny Kanal · BOLOTNAYA NAB. · KADASHEVSKAYA NAB. · OVCHINNIKOVSKAYA

1 2 3

a b c

COPYRIGHT GEORGE PHILIP LTD

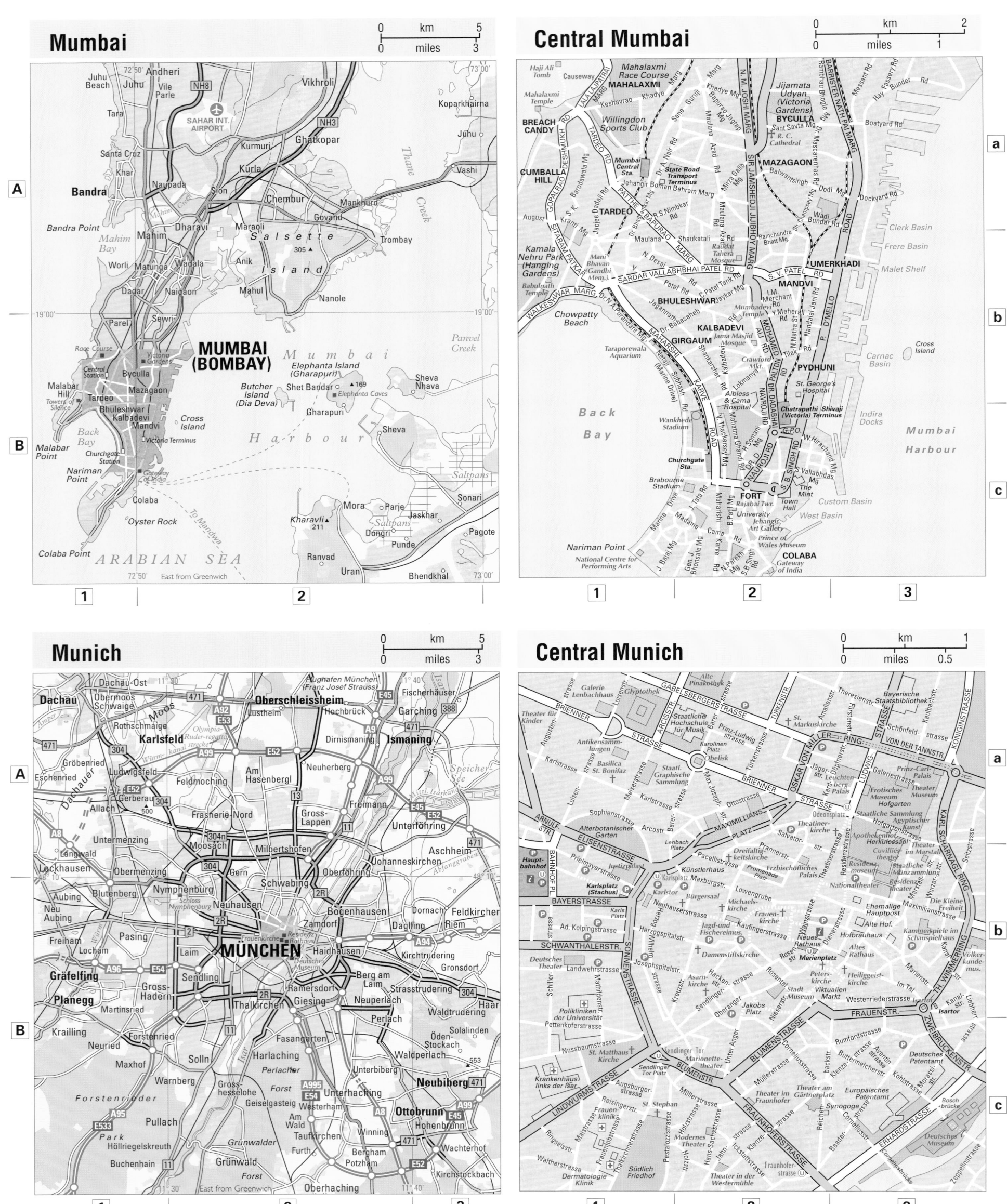

Mumbai

Central Mumbai

Munich

Central Munich

COPYRIGHT GEORGE PHILIP LTD

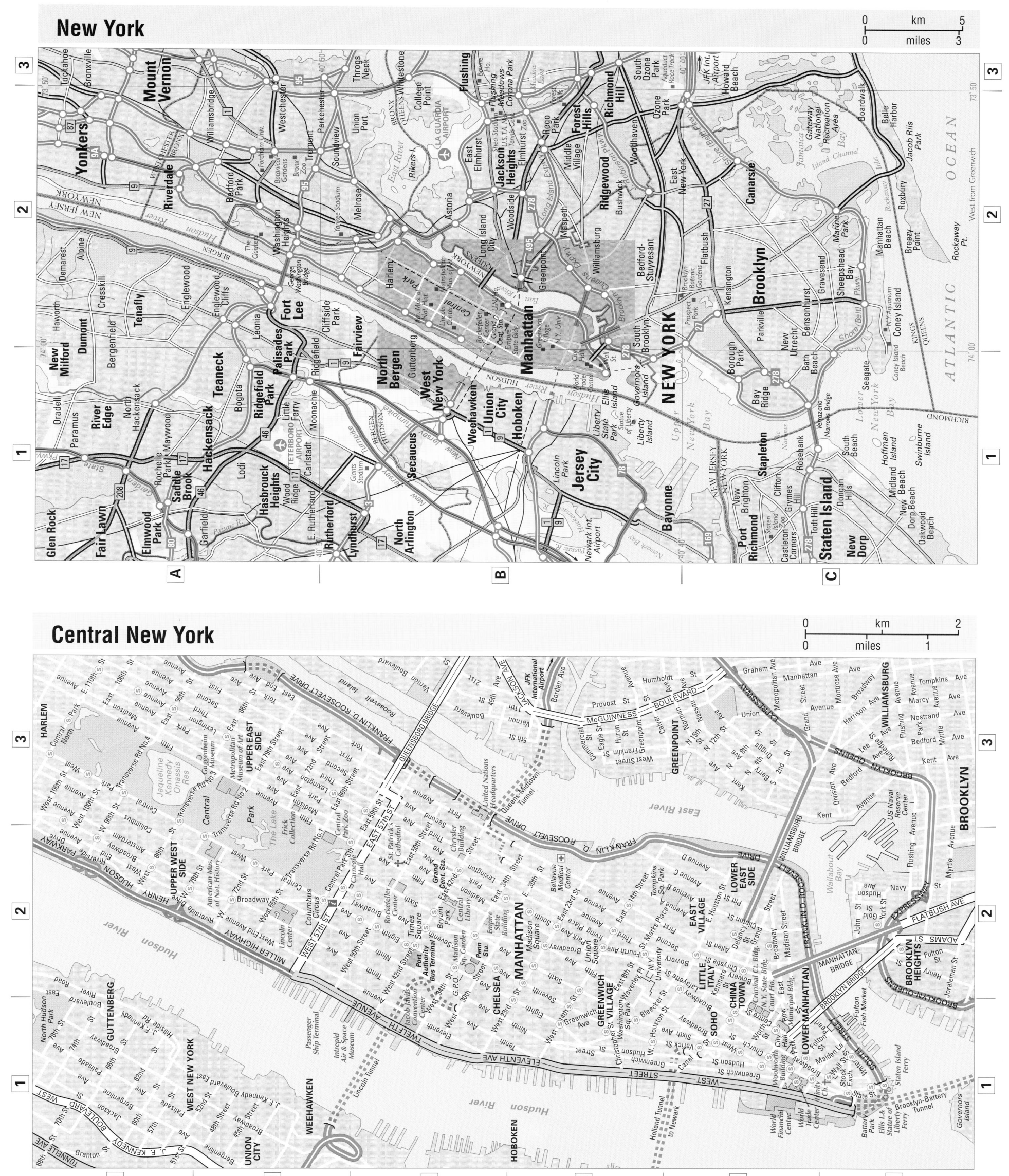

New York

0 — km — 5
0 — miles — 3

3
Tuckahoe · Bronxville · 87 · Mount Vernon · Williamsbridge · 95 · Westchester · Throgs Neck · Whitestone · Flushing · Flushing Mdws · Corona Park · Richmond Hill · South Ozone Park · JFK Int. Airport · Howard Beach · Boardwalk
Yonkers · 9A · 9 · Bronx · Fordham Univ · Parkchester · Soundview · Union Port · College Point · LA GUARDIA AIRPORT · East Elmhurst · Jackson Heights · Rego Park · Forest Hills · Ozone Park · Aqueduct Race Track · Belle Harbor · Jacob Riis Park

2
NEW JERSEY · NEW YORK · Riverdale · Bedford Park · Bronx Zoo · Botanic Gardens · Melrose · Yankee Stadium · Astoria · Woodside · Elmhurst · Elmhurst Zoo · Middle Village · Ridgewood · Bushwick · East New York · Canarsie · OCEAN · ATLANTIC · Rockaway Pt. · Breezy Point
Washington Heights · The Cloisters · George Washington Bridge · Long Island City · Williamsburg · Greenpoint · Bedford-Stuyvesant · Flatbush · Kensington · Brooklyn · Marine Park · Manhattan Beach

1
New Milford · Dumont · Demarest · Alpine · Cresskill · Tenafly · Englewood · Englewood Cliffs · Fort Lee · Leonia · Cliffside Park · Ridgefield · Fairview · North Bergen · Guttenberg · West New York · Weehawken · Union City · Hoboken · HUDSON · Manhattan · Central Park · Rockefeller Center · Empire State Bldg · City Hall · Wall St. · Governors Island · Ellis Island · Liberty Island · South Brooklyn · Borough Park · New Utrecht · Bath Beach · Bay Ridge · Verrazano Narrows Bridge · Coney Island · KINGS
Fair Lawn · Glen Rock · River Edge · Paramus · Oradell · Hackensack · Teaneck · Bogota · Palisades Park · Ridgefield Park · Little Ferry · Moonachie · TETERBORO AIRPORT · Carlstadt · Giants Stadium · Secaucus · New · NEW JERSEY · Lincoln Park · Jersey City · Liberty State Park · Statue of Liberty · Upper New York Bay · Stapleton · Rosebank · Grymes Hill · Clifton · South Beach · Midland Beach
Elmwood Park · Saddle Brook · Garfield · Lodi · Hasbrouck Heights · Wood Ridge · E. Rutherford · Rutherford · North Arlington · Lyndhurst · 17 · 280 · Newark Int. Airport · Newark Bay · Bayonne · 169 · Port Richmond · Castleton Corners · Dongan Hills · New Dorp · Oakwood Beach

A · B · C

Central New York

0 — km — 2
0 — miles — 1

3
HARLEM · Central Park North · E. 110th St · Jacqueline Kennedy Onassis Res. · UPPER EAST SIDE · Metropolitan Museum of Art · Guggenheim Museum · East 79th Street · Roosevelt Island · FRANKLIN D. ROOSEVELT DRIVE · QUEENSBORO BRIDGE · JFK International Airport · Vernon Boulevard · McGuinness Boulevard · GREENPOINT · BROOKLYN-QUEENS · WILLIAMSBURG · BROOKLYN

2
HUDSON RIVER · HENRY HUDSON PARKWAY · UPPER WEST SIDE · American Mus. of Nat. History · Lincoln Center · Columbus Circle · WEST 57TH ST · Carnegie Hall · Central Park South · EAST 57TH ST · Chrysler Building · United Nations Headquarters · Queens Midtown Tunnel · LOWER EAST SIDE · EAST VILLAGE · WILLIAMSBURG BRIDGE · Wallabout Bay · US Naval Reserve Center
MILLER HIGHWAY · WEST SIDE HIGHWAY · Times Square · Rockefeller Center · Bryant Park · N.Y. Public Library · Grand Central Sta. · Bellevue Medical Center · Empire State Building · Madison Square · Union Square · Tompkins Sq. Park · MANHATTAN · GREENWICH VILLAGE · LITTLE ITALY · CHINA TOWN · SOHO · MANHATTAN BRIDGE · BROOKLYN BRIDGE · BROOKLYN HEIGHTS

1
WEEHAWKEN · Lincoln Tunnel · Passenger Ship Terminal · Intrepid Air & Space Museum · Jacob Javits Convention Center · Port Authority Bus Terminal · Penn Sta. · Madison Sq. Garden · G.P.O. · TWELFTH AVENUE · ELEVENTH AVENUE · CHELSEA · WEST STREET · Holland Tunnel · HUDSON RIVER · LOWER MANHATTAN · Woolworth Building · World Financial Center · World Trade Center · Battery Park · Ellis Island · Statue of Liberty · Staten Island Ferry · Brooklyn-Battery Tunnel · Governors Island
WEST NEW YORK · GUTTENBERG · UNION CITY · HOBOKEN

a · b · c · d · e · f

COPYRIGHT GEORGE PHILIP LTD

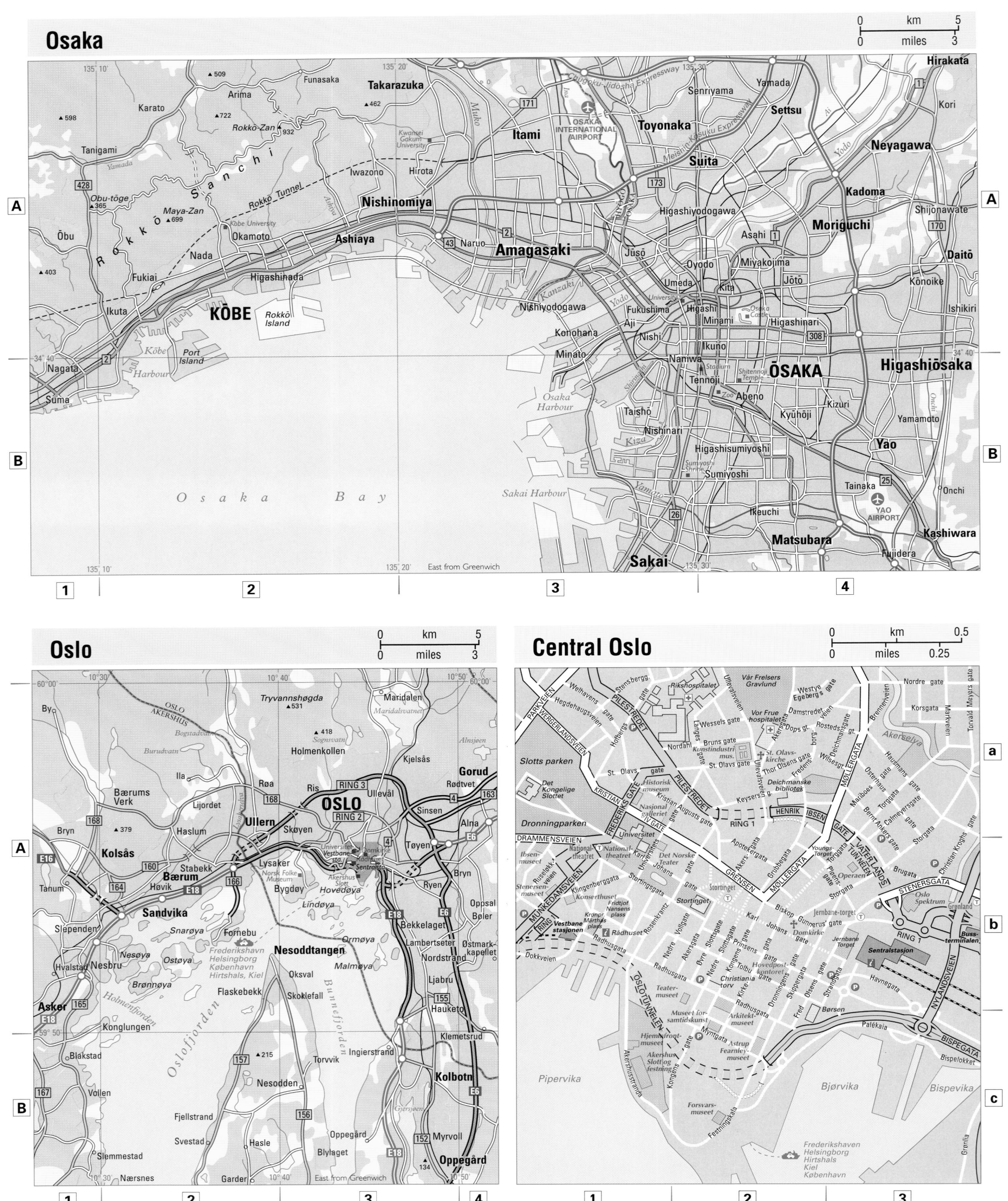

Osaka

km 5
miles 3

509
Arima
Karato
598
722
Rokkō-Zan
932
Takarazuka
Funasaka
462
Mukō
171
Ōgoku-Jidōshi Expressway
135°30′
Yamada
Senriyama
Hirakata
1
Kori
Tanigami
Yamada
428
Iwazono
Hirota
Itami
OSAKA
INTERNATIONAL
AIRPORT
Meishin-Kōsoku Expressway
Toyonaka
Settsu
Neyagawa
Obu-tōge
365
Rokkō Tunnel
173
Suita
Kadoma
A
Maya-Zan
699
Kōbe University
Nishinomiya
Higashiyodogawa
Asahi
1
Moriguchi
Shijonawate
170
A
Ōbu
Okamoto
43 Naruo
2
Jūsō
Ōyodo
Miyakojima
Daitō
403
Nada
Ashiaya
Amagasaki
Umeda
Jōtō
Fukiai
Higashihada
Nishiyodogawa
Fukushima
Higashi
Kōnoike
Ikuta
KŌBE
Rokkō
Island
Konohana
Aji
Nishi
Minami
Higashinari
308
Ishikiri
Nagata
2
Port
Island
Minato
Nanwa
Ikuno
34°40′
Higashiōsaka
Suma
Kōbe
Harbour
Tennōji
Abeno
ŌSAKA
Kizuri
Yamamoto
Osaka
Harbour
Taishō
Zoo
Shitennōji
Temple
Kyūhōji
Yao
Nishinari
Sakai Harbour
Kizu
Higashisumiyoshi
Tainaka
25
B
Sumiyoshi
Shrine
Onchi
B
Osaka Bay
Sumiyoshi
26
Ikeuchi
YAO
AIRPORT
Kashiwara
Matsubara
Sakai
135°30′
Fujidera
East from Greenwich

1   2   3   4

Oslo

km 5
miles 3

By
60°00′
10°30′
OSLO
AKERSHUS
Bogstadvan
10°40′
Tryvannshøgda
531
Maridalen
Maridalsvatnet
10°50′
60°00′
Burudvatn
418
Sognsvatn
Alnsjøen
Bærums
Verk
Ila
Røa
Ris
RING 3
Holmenkollen
Kjelsås
Gorud
Bryn
379
Lijordet
168
Ullevål
Rødtvet
163
A
168
Haslum
OSLO
RING 2
Sinsen
Alna
E6
A
160
Ullern
Skøyen
Tanum
164
Stabekk
166
Lysaker
Tøyen
Bryn
E18
Hovedøya
Ryen
Kolsås
Bærum
Høvik
Universitet
Vestbane
Domkirke
Rådhuset
Sentrortet
Norsk Folke
Museum
Akershus
Slott
Bygdøy
Oppsal
Bøler
E6
Sandvika
Snarøya
Fornebu
Lindøya
Bekkelaget
E18
Slependen
Nesøya
Ostøya
Frederikshavn
Helsingborg
København
Hirtshals, Kiel
Nesoddtangen
Lambertseter
Nordstrand
Østmark-
kapellet
Hvalstad Nesbru
Brønnøya
Oksval
Malmøya
Ljabru
Hauketo
Asker
165
Konglungen
Holmenfjorden
Flaskebekk
Skoklefall
155
E18
59°50′
Vollen
167
Blakstad
215
Nesodden
Torvvik
Ingierstrand
Klemetsrud
Kolbotn
E6
Slemmestad
Svestad
Hasle
157
Fjellstrand
156
Oppegård
Gjersjøen
Myrvoll
152
E18
Nærsnes
Garder
134
Oppegård
10°30′
10°40′
East from Greenwich
10°50′

1   2   3   4

Central Oslo

km 0.5
miles 0.25

Stensberg
Welhavens
gate
Rikshospitalet
Ullevålsvn
Vår Frelsers
Gravlund
Westye
Egeberg
gate
Nordre gate
Korsgata
Torvald Meyers gate
Marveien
PARKVEIEN
Hegdehaugsveien
WERGELANDSVEIEN
PILESTREDET
Vor Frue
hospitaletn
Damstredet
Rostedsgt.
Bremmerveien
Hausmans gate
a
Slotts parken
St. Olavs
gate
Langes
Nordahl
Bruns gate
Kunstindustri-
mus.
Akersgt
St. Olavs-
kirche
St. Olavs gate
Thor Olsens gate
Osterhaus gate
Torggata
Calmeyersgate
MØLLERGATA
Bernt Ankers gate
Storgata
Akerselva
Det Kongelige
Slottet
KRISTIAN IV GATE
FREDERIKS GATE
PILESTREDET
Keysersg.
Deichmanske
bibliotek
Youngs-
Torget
b
Dronningparken
Historisk
museum
Nasjonal
galleriet
HENRIK
IBSENS
GATE
Apotekergata
Grubbegata
VATERLANDS TUNNELEN
Brugata
Christian Krohgs gate
DRAMMENSVEIEN
Universitet
RING 1
Akersgt
Grensen
Karl
Youngs gate
Jernbanegt.
Stenersgata
Ibsen-
museet
National-
museet
National
theatret
Det Norske
Teater
Johans
Pipervn.
gate
Prof.
gate
Phars-
gate
Oslo
Spektrum
Stenersen-
museet
Klingenberggata
Stortings
gate
Karl
Johans
gate
Stortorget
Biskop
Gunnerus' gate
Domkirke
Grønland
b
MUNKEDAMSVEIEN
RING 1
Konserthuset
Fridtjof
Nansens
plass
Stortinget
Rosenkrantz
Prinsens
gate
Tollbu
gate
Jernbane
Torget
Sentralstasjon
RING 1
Buss-
terminalen
Dokkveien
Vestbane
stasjonen
Rådhuset
Øvre
Slottsgate
Nedre
Slottsgate
Kongens
gate
Skippergata
Strandgata
Havnegata
NYLANDSVEIEN
OSLO-TUNNELEN
Rådhusgata
Christiania
torv
Dronningens gate
Fred
Olsens gate
Børsen
BISPEGATA
Hovedpost-
kontoret
Teater-
museet
Museet for
samtidskunst
Arkitektur-
museet
Palékaia
Bispelokket
Hjemmefront-
museet
Myntgata
Astrup
Fearnley-
museet
Akershusstranda
Bjørvika
Bispevika
Pipervika
Akershus
Slott og
festning
Forsvars-
museet
Festningskaia
Frederikshaven
Helsingborg
Hirtshals
Kiel
København
Grenlia

1   2   3

a   b   c

COPYRIGHT GEORGE PHILIP LTD

Paris

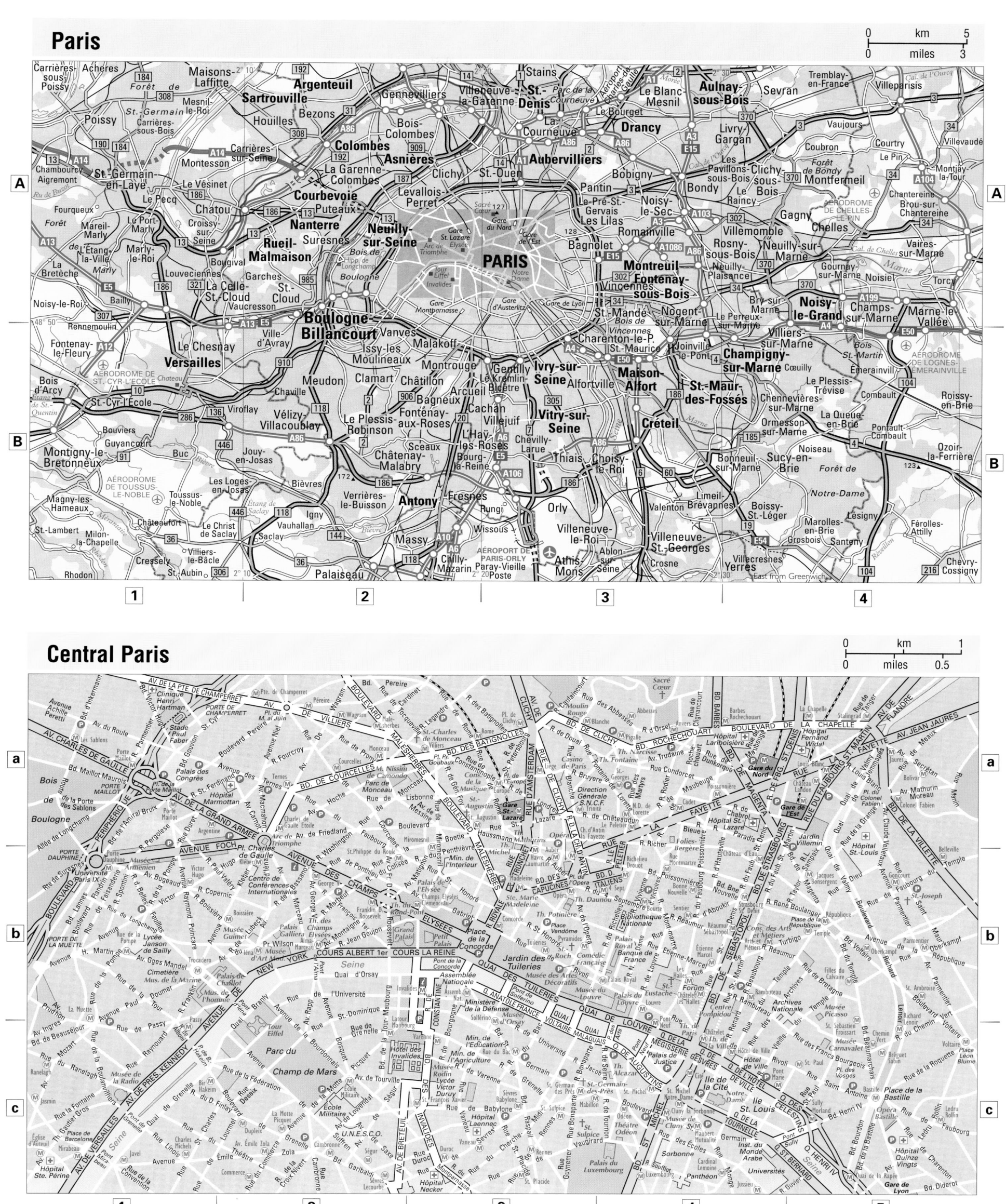

Central Paris

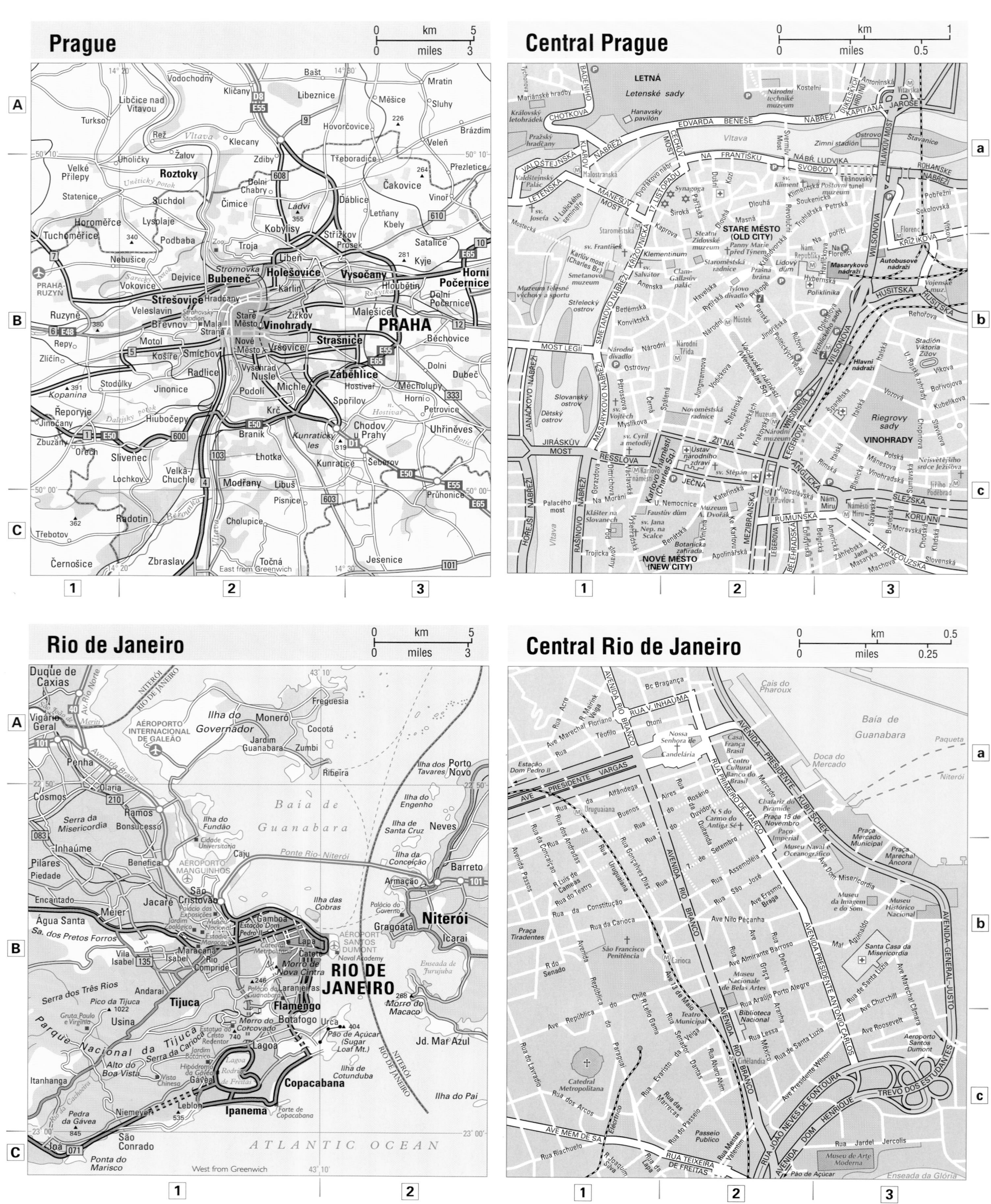

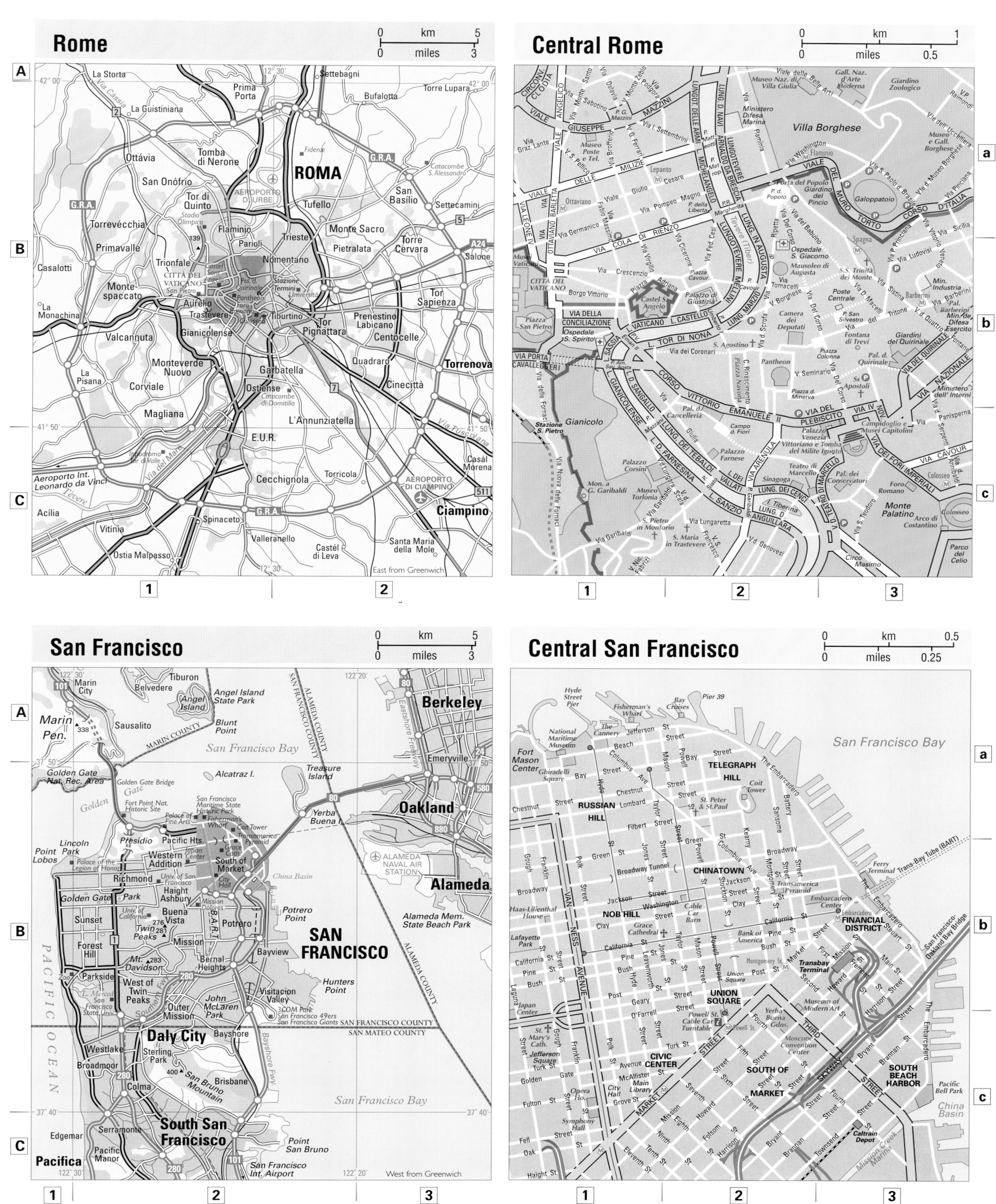

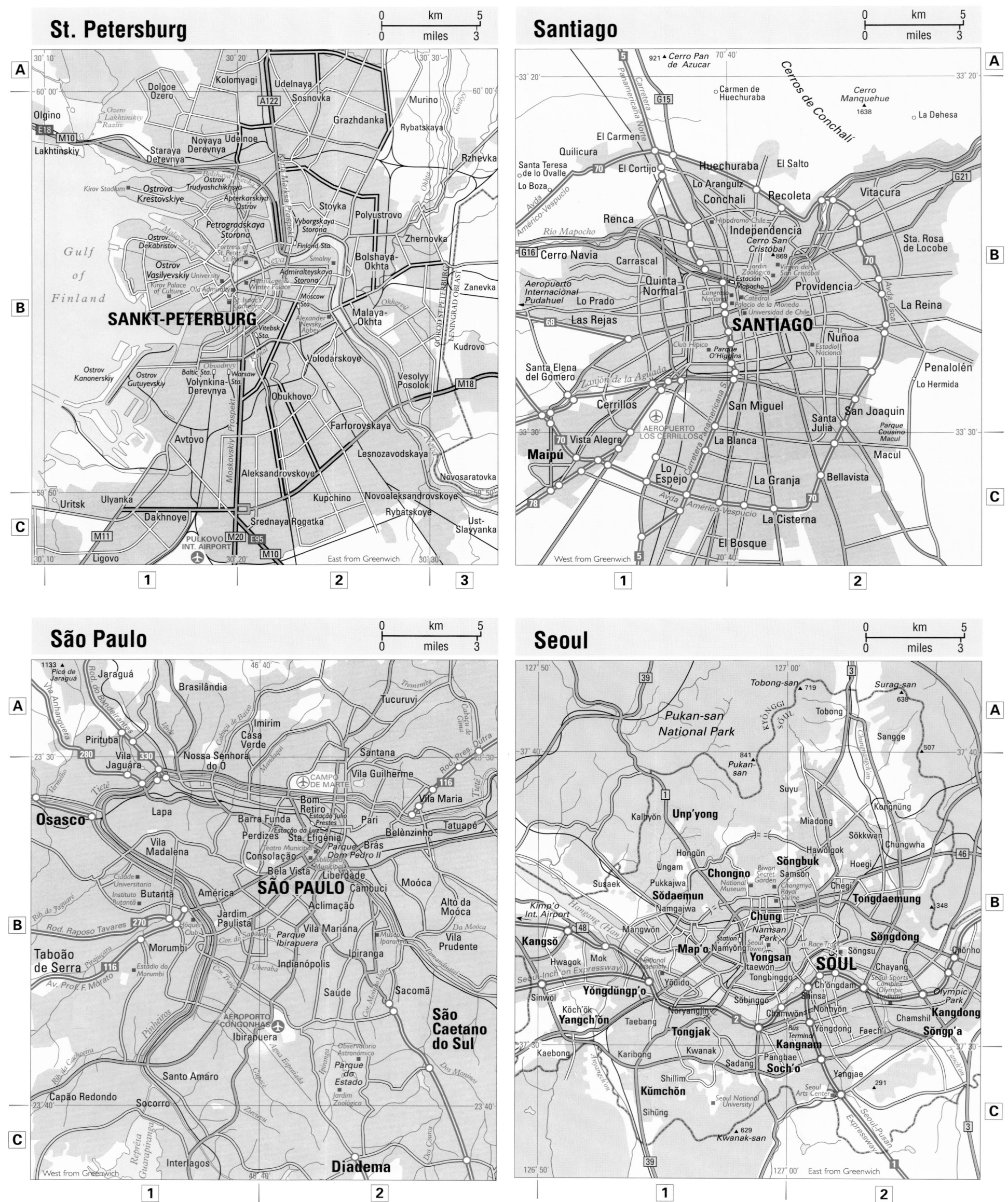

COPYRIGHT GEORGE PHILIP LTD

Shanghai

East from Greenwich 121°30'

Central Singapore

Singapore

East from Greenwich

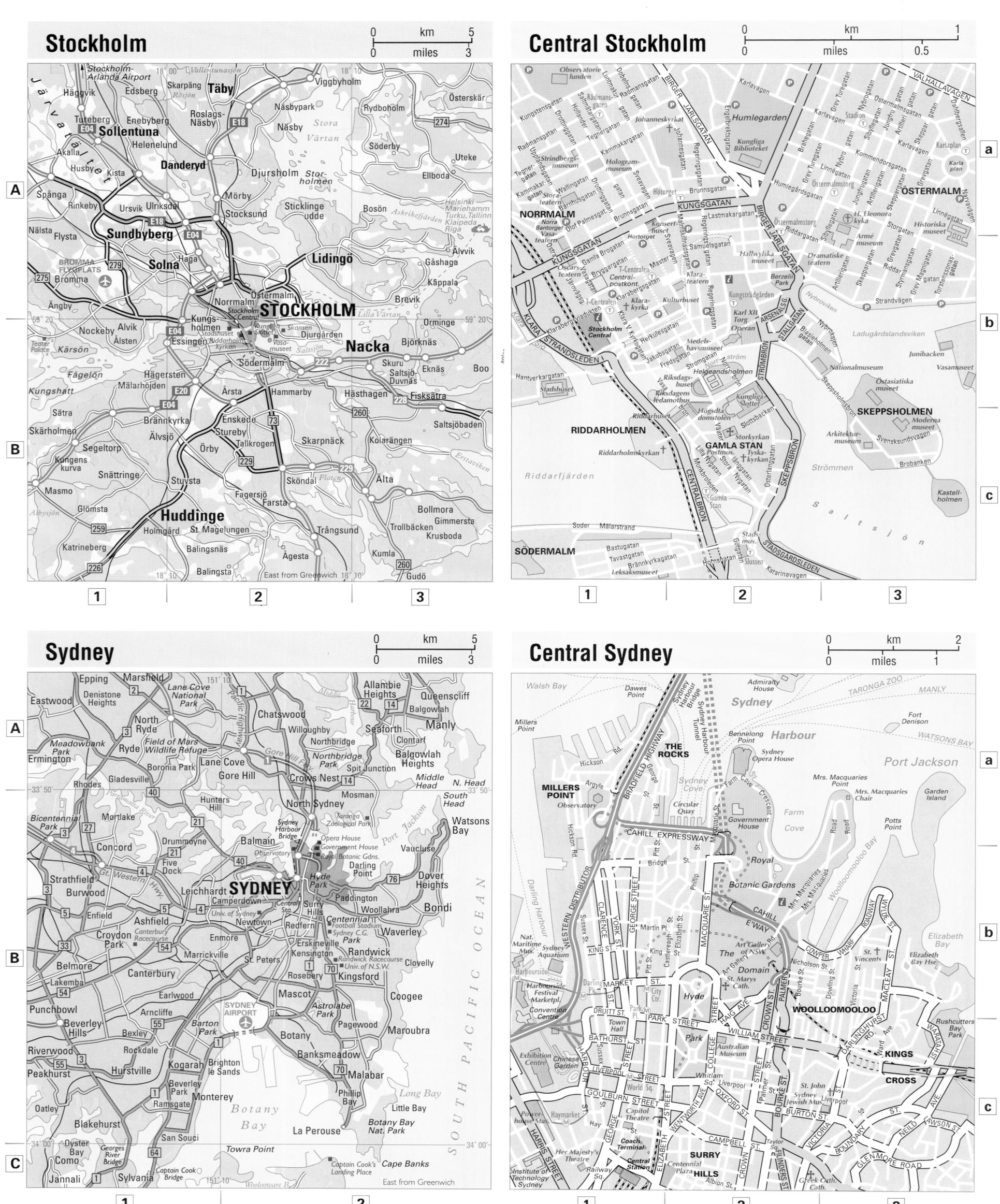

Stockholm

km 5
miles 3

Stockholm-Arlanda Airport
Häggvik
Tureberg
Sollentuna
Edsberg
Skarpäng
Täby
Viggbyholm
Österskär
Näsbypark
Roslags-
Näsby
Näsby
Rydboholm
274
Enebyberg
Helenelund
Danderyd
Djursholm
Stor-
holmen
Boson
Askrikefjärden
Helsinki
Mariehamn
Turku, Tallinn
Klaipeda
Riga
Akalla
Kista
Husby
Ursvik
Ulriksdal
Stocksund
Sticklinge
udde
Ellboda
Älvvik
Spånga
Rinkeby
Sundbyberg
Haga
Solna
Mörby
Gåshaga
Nälsta
Flysta
Lidingö
Käppala
BROMMA
FLYGPLATS
Bromma
Ängby
Nockeby
Alvik
Alsten
Kungs-
holmen
Östermalm
Norrmalm
STOCKHOLM
Brevik
Orminge
Teater
Palace
Kärsön
Essingen
Södermalm
Djurgården
Nacka
Björknäs
Fågelön
Hägersten
Mälarhöjden
Årsta
Hammarby
Skuru
Saltsjö-
Duvnäs
Eknäs
Boo
Kungshatt
Sätra
Skärholmen
Enskede
Stureby
Älvsjö
Örby
Tallkrogen
Skarpnäck
Hästhagen
Fisksätra
228
Kolarängen
Saltsjöbaden
Segeltorp
Kungens
kurva
Snättringe
Masmo
Glömsta
Stuvsta
229
229
Sköndal
Älta
Bollmora
Gimmersta
Krusboda
Huddinge
Holmgård
St. Magelungen
Fagersjö
Farsta
Trångsund
Trollbäcken
Katrineberg
Balingsnäs
Balingsta
Ågesta
Kumla
226
259
260
Gudö

Central Stockholm

km 1
miles 0.5

Observatorie
lunden
NORRMALM
ÖSTERMALM
RIDDARHOLMEN
GAMLA STAN
SKEPPSHOLMEN
SÖDERMALM
Riddarfjärden
Saltsjön
Strömmen

Sydney

km 5
miles 3

Epping
Marsfield
Eastwood
Denistone
Heights
North
Ryde
Lane Cove
National
Park
Chatswood
Allambie
Heights
Queenscliff
Balgowlah
Meadowbank
Park
Ermington
Ryde
Field of Mars
Wildlife Refuge
Willoughby
Northbridge
Seaforth
Manly
Clontarf
Boronia Park
Lane Cove
Northbridge
Park
Spit Junction
Balgowlah
Heights
Rhodes
Gladesville
Gore Hill
Crows Nest
Middle
Head
N. Head
Bicentennial
Park
Mortlake
Hunters
Hill
North Sydney
Mosman
South Head
Concord
Drummoyne
Sydney
Harbour
Bridge
Taronga
Zoological Park
Watsons
Bay
Strathfield
Burwood
Balmain
Opera House
Government House
Royal Botanic Gdns.
Observatory
Port Jackson
Ashfield
Leichhardt
SYDNEY
Camperdown
Hyde
Park
Darling
Point
Dover
Heights
Enfield
Croydon
Park
Univ. of Sydney
Newtown
Central
Sta.
Surry
Hills
Paddington
Woollahra
Bondi
Belmore
Canterbury
Racecourse
Enmore
Redfern
Centennial
Football Stadium
Centennial
Park
Waverley
Lakemba
Marrickville
St. Peters
Kensington
Univ. of N.S.W.
Randwick
Clovelly
Punchbowl
Earlwood
Roseberry
Randwick Racecourse
Kingsford
Coogee
Beverley
Hills
Arncliffe
Mascot
Astrolabe
Park
Pagewood
Maroubra
Riverwood
Bexley
SYDNEY
AIRPORT
Barton
Park
Botany
Banksmeadow
Peakhurst
Rockdale
Kogarah
Brighton
le Sands
Malabar
Oatley
Beverley
Park
Monterey
Phillip
Bay
Little Bay
Blakehurst
Ramsgate
Botany
Bay
La Perouse
Oyster
Bay
Como
Georges
River
Bridge
San Souci
Towra Point
Cape Banks
Jannali
Sylvania
Captain Cook
Bridge
Captain Cook's
Landing Place
Woolooware B.
SOUTH PACIFIC OCEAN

Central Sydney

km 2
miles 1

Walsh Bay
Dawes
Point
Admiralty
House
Sydney
TARONGA ZOO
MANLY
Millers
Point
Sydney
Harbour
Bridge
Sydney Harbour Tunnel
Bennelong
Point
Sydney Opera House
Fort
Denison
WATSONS BAY
THE
ROCKS
Harbour
Port Jackson
MILLERS
POINT
Observatory
Circular
Quay
Sydney
Cove
Farm
Cove
Mrs. Macquaries
Point
Mrs. Macquaries
Chair
Garden
Island
CAHILL EXPRESSWAY
Government
House
Potts
Point
Royal
Botanic Gardens
Woolloomooloo Bay
WOOLLOOMOOLOO
Elizabeth
Bay
KINGS
CROSS
SURRY
HILLS
Central
Station

East from Greenwich

COPYRIGHT GEORGE PHILIP LTD

Tokyo

Central Tokyo

COPYRIGHT GEORGE PHILIP LTD

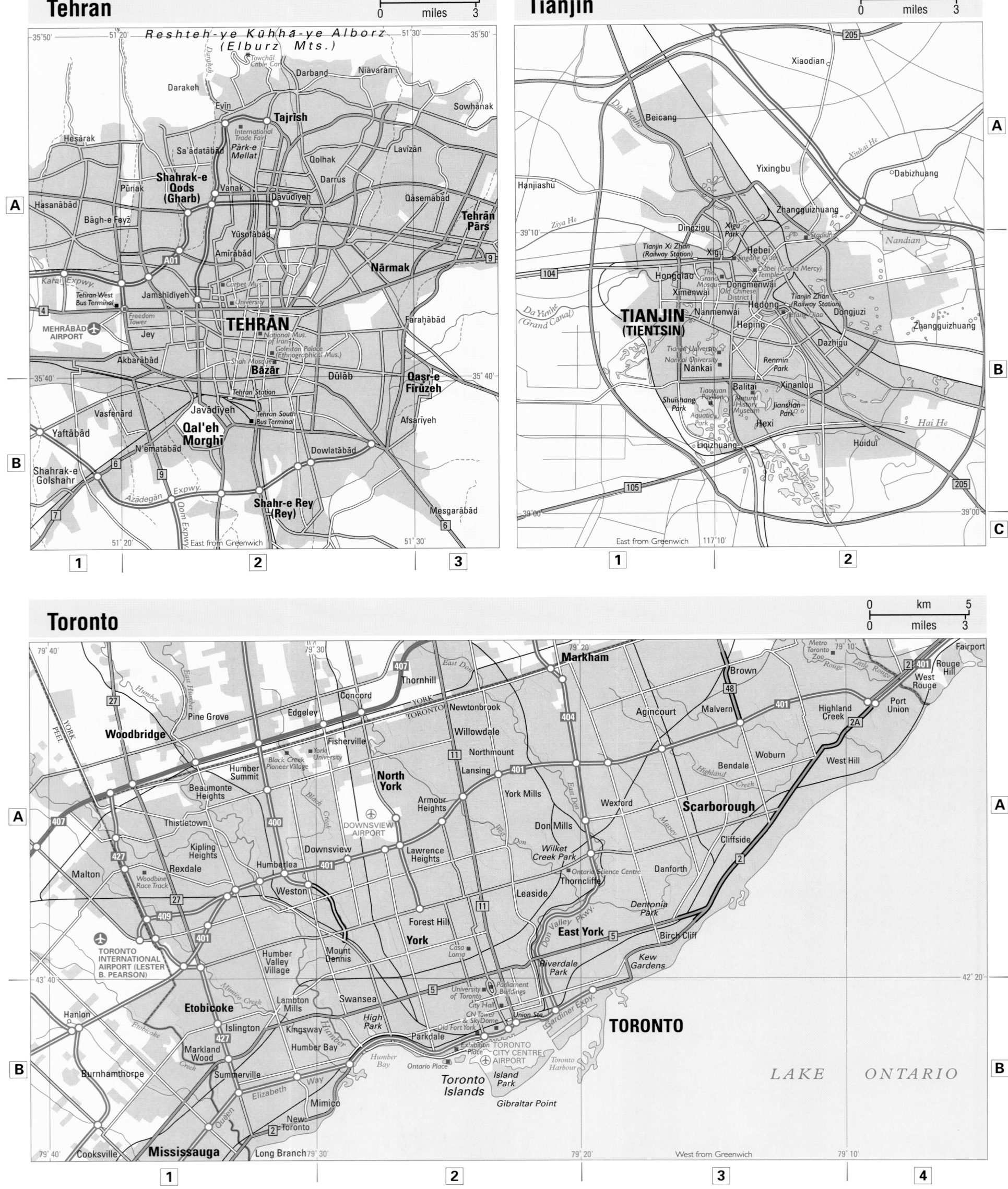

Tehran

0 — km — 5
0 — miles — 3

Reshteh-ye Kūhhā-ye Alborz
(Elburz Mts.)

35°50' 51°20' 51°30' 35°50'

Towchāl Cable Car
Darband
Niāvárán
Darakeh
Darband
Sowhānak
Evīn
Tajrīsh
International Trade Fair
Park-e Mellat
Qolhak
Lavīzān
Hesārak
Sa'ādatābād
Darrūs
Shahrak-e Qods (Gharb)
Pūnak
Vanak
Dāvūdiyeh
Qāsemābād
Tehrān Pārs
Hasanābād
Bāgh-e Feyż
Yūsofābād
Amīrābād
Nārmak
A01
Jamshīdiyeh
University
Farahābād
Tehran-West Bus Terminal
Freedom Tower
Corpet Mus.
4
MEHRĀBĀD AIRPORT
Jey
TEHRĀN
National Mus. of Iran
Golestan Palace (Ethnographical Mus.)
9
Akbarābād
Shah Mosque
Bāzār
Dūlāb
Qasr-e Fīrūzeh
35°40' 35°40'
Tehran Station
Vasfenārd
Javādiyeh
Tehran South Bus Terminal
Afsarīyeh
Yaftābād
N'ematābād
Qal'eh Morghī
Dowlatābād
Shahrak-e Golshahr
6
9
Shahr-e Rey (Rey)
Āzādegān Expwy.
Qom Expwy.
Mesgarābād
7
6
51°20' East from Greenwich 51°30'

1   2   3

Tianjin

0 — km — 5
0 — miles — 3

205
Xiaodian
A
Beicang
Da Yunhe
Dabizhuang
Yixingbu
Xinkai He
Nandian
Hanjiashū
Ziya He
Zhangguizhuang
39°10'
Dingzigu
Xigu Park
Da Yunhe (Grand Canal)
Tianjin Xi Zhan (Railway Station)
Xigu
Stadium
Jingde Qiao
104
Hebei
Hongqiao
Dàbēi (Grand Mercy) Temple
The Grand Mosque
Old Chinese District
Dongmenwai
Tianjin Zhan (Railway Station)
Ximenwai
Hedong
Dongjuzi
TIANJIN (TIENTSIN)
Nanmenwai
Jiefang Qiao
Zhangguizhuang
Tianjin University
Nankai University
Heping
Dazhigu
B
Nānkāi
Renmin Park
Xinanlou
Tiaoyuan Pavilion
Balitai
Natural History Museum
Shuishang Park
Aquatic Park
Jianshan Park
Hai He
Hexi
Huidui
Liqizhuang
39°00'
105
205
39°00'
East from Greenwich 117°10'
C

1   2

Toronto

0 — km — 5
0 — miles — 3

79°40' 79°30' 79°20' 79°10'
Fairport
Metro Toronto Zoo
Markham
407
Thornhill
Port Union
Brown
West Rouge
Rouge Hill
Pine Grove
Concord
Edgeley
Newtonbrook
York
48
Agincourt
Malvern
401
2A
Woodbridge
Fisherville
Willowdale
Highland Creek
27
York University
404
Northmount
Woburn
Humber Summit
Black Creek Pioneer Village
North York
11
Lansing
Woburn
Beaumonte Heights
Armour Heights
401
York Mills
Bendale
West Hill
Thistletown
400
Scarborough
A
DOWNSVIEW AIRPORT
Don Mills
Wexford
Kipling Heights
Downsview
Lawrence Heights
Cliffside
Rexdale
Humberlea
Wilket Creek Park
427
401
Ontario Science Centre
2
Malton
Weston
Thorncliffe
Danforth
Woodbine Race Track
27
11
Leaside
Dentonia Park
409
Forest Hill
5
East York
401
Birch Cliff
York
Kew Gardens
TORONTO INTERNATIONAL AIRPORT (LESTER B. PEARSON)
Humber Valley Village
Casa Loma
Don Valley Pkwy.
Riverdale Park
43°40' Mount Dennis 42°20'
Hanlon
Lambton Mills
Swansea
University of Toronto
Parliament Buildings
5
City Hall
Etobicoke
High Park
CN Tower & SkyDome
TORONTO
Islington
Kingsway
Old Fort York
Union Sta.
Markland Wood
Humber Bay
Parkdale
Exhibition Place
Gardiner Expwy.
427
Summerville
TORONTO CITY CENTRE AIRPORT
Burnhamthorpe
Ontario Place
Humber Bay
Toronto Harbour
LAKE ONTARIO
B
Elizabeth Way
Mimico
Toronto Islands
Island Park
New Toronto
2
Gibraltar Point
Cooksville Long Branch 79°30' **Mississauga** 79°20' West from Greenwich 79°10'

1   2   3   4

COPYRIGHT GEORGE PHILIP LTD

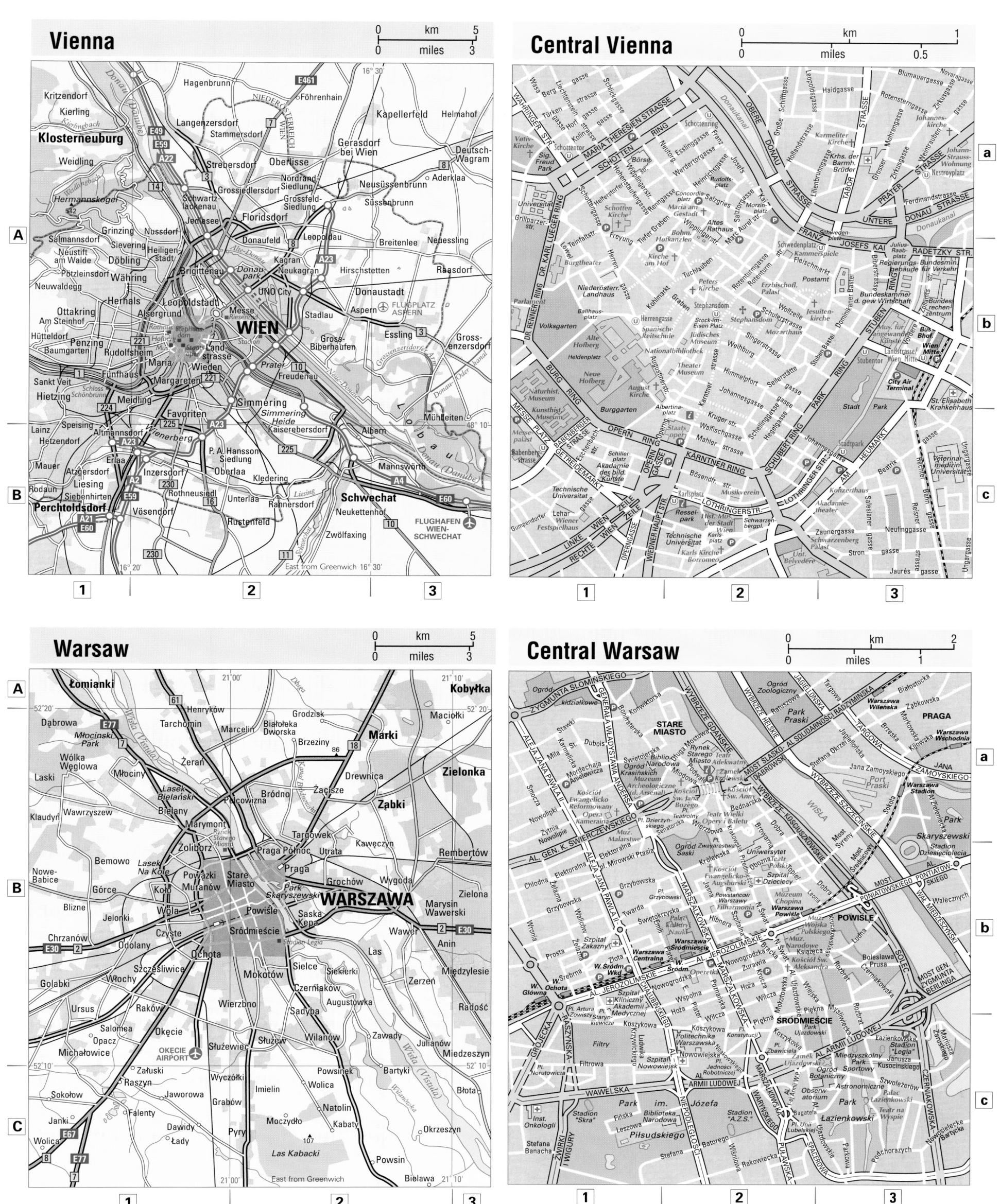

Vienna

| 0 | km | 5 |
| 0 | miles | 3 |

Central Vienna

| 0 | km | 1 |
| 0 | miles | 0.5 |

Warsaw

| 0 | km | 5 |
| 0 | miles | 3 |

Central Warsaw

| 0 | km | 2 |
| 0 | miles | 1 |

COPYRIGHT GEORGE PHILIP LTD

Washington

0 km 5
0 miles 3

77°20' 77°10' 77°00' 76°50'

A

Dranesville
Great Falls
Potomac
Cabin John Regional Park
Chevy Chase View
Silver Spring
Adelphi
Oak View
Greenbelt
39°00'
Great Falls Park
99
Woodmont
Bethesda
Chevy Chase
College Park
Lewisdale
Langley Park
Avenel
Berwyn Heights
Greenbelt Park
Lanham
Seabrook
Reston
MARYLAND
VIRGINIA
Cabin John
Glen Echo
Glen Mar Park
Somerset
Takoma Park
Brightwood
University Park
East Pines
New Carrollton
Belle View
Westgate
Brookmont
Langley
Rock Creek Park
Univ. of the Dist. of Col.
Chillum
Riverdale
Edmondston
Landover Hills
Glenarden
95/495
B
McLean
Washington Cath.
Nat. Zoological Park
American University
Hyattsville
Mt. Rainier
Kent Village
Bladensburg
Dulles Int. Airport
Dulles Airport Access Rd.
Wolf Trap Farm Park
Tysons Corner
Pimmit Hills
Franklin Park
Northern Va. Reg. Park
Marymount University
WASHINGTON
Georgetown
The White House
Union Station
Trinidad
National Arboretum
Kenilworth Aquatic Gardens
Cheverly
Fairmount Heights
Palmer Park
Hunters Valley
Vienna
Dunn Loring
Arlington
Rosslyn
Lincoln Memorial
U.S. Capitol
Library of Congress
Seat Pleasant
Vale
Oakton
Falls Church
Seven Corners
Hillwood
Arlington Nat. Cemetery
Pentagon
Jefferson Mem.
Mason Mem. Br.
East Potomac Park
Fort Dupont Park
Capitol Heights
Kettering
Lee Hwy.
East Arlington
Oakland
Millwood
Ritchie
50
Arlington Blvd.
Broyhill Park
50
Anacostia
Coral Hills
District Heights
66
FAIRFAX
Annalee Heights
Culmore
Baileys Crossroads
395
WASHINGTON NATIONAL AIRPORT
Forestville
Fairfax
495
Holmes Run Acres
Lake Barcroft
Parklawn
Suitland
38°50'
George Mason University
Little River Tpk.
Potomac River
Hillcrest Heights
Glassmanor
Silver Hill
Morningside
38°50'
29
Annandale
Kings Park
North Springfield
Alexandria
295
Forest Heights
Temple Hills
Camp Springs
ANDREWS AIR FORCE BASE
C
Fairfax Station
Kings Park West
West Springfield
Springfield
Franconia
Rose Hill
Huntington
Woodrow Wilson Memorial Bridge
Oxon Hill
South Lawn
Butts Corner
95
95/495
Groveton
Fort Foote Village
Oaklawn
West from Greenwich
77°20' 77°10' 77°00' 76°50'

1 2 3 4 5

Central Washington

0 km 1
0 miles 0.5

P ST.
Logan Circle
Scott Circle
16th St.
RHODE ISLAND AVE.
NEW JERSEY AVE.
N. CAPITOL ST.
a
CONNECTICUT AVE.
N ST.
N ST.
N ST.
M ST.
Thomas Circle
MASSACHUSETTS AVE.
13th St.
12th St.
11th St.
10th St.
9th St.
8th St.
7th St.
6th St.
M ST.
Mt. Vernon Sq.-UDC
NORTH WEST
NEW YORK AVE.
Farragut North
L ST.
VERMONT AVE.
L ST.
K ST.
K ST.
McPherson Square
Franklin Square
Mt. Vernon Square
Farragut West
I St.
H ST.
Lafayette Square
Convention Center
Metro Center
Gallery Place
Judiciary Sq.
Union Station
World Bank
G ST.
NEW YORK AVE.
National Place
Fords Theater
Nat. Mus. of American Art
b
18th St.
17th St.
F ST.
PENNSYLVANIA AVE.
The White House
15th St.
14th St.
13th St.
Federal Triangle
12th St.
Archives
MASSACHUSETTS AVE.
LOUISIANA AVE.
3rd ST.
Columbus Circle
Union Station Plaza
Dept. of the Interior
C ST.
The Ellipse
CONSTITUTION AVE.
Nat. Museum of Natural History
CONSTITUTION
Supreme Court
Reflecting Pool
Washington Monument
Nat. Museum of American History
Madison Dr.
National Gallery of Art
Grant Statue
U.S. Capitol
Library of Congress
D.C. War Memorial
The Mall
Jefferson Dr.
Smithsonian Institute
Hirshhorn Museum
Nat. Air & Space Museum
Botanic Gardens
INDEPENDENCE AVE.
INDEPENDENCE AVE.
INDEPENDENCE AVE.
US Holocaust Memorial Museum
Smithsonian
Federal Center SW
L'Enfant Plaza
c
Tidal Basin
Jefferson Memorial
Outlet Bridge
14th ST.
MAINE AVE.
7th ST.
SOUTHWEST FREEWAY
N. CAPITOL ST.
Capitol South
Francis Case Mem. Bridge
SOUTH WEST
G ST.
I ST.
Potomac R.
East Potomac Park
Washington Channel
Waterfront
M ST.
M ST.

1 2 3

Wellington

0 km 5
0 miles 3

175°50'
Rock Pt.
Elsdon
Porirua
Porirua East
58
Cook Strait
459 Colonial Knob
Linden
Haywards
A
Pipinui Pt.
Tawa
408
Manor Park
41°10'
Stokes Valley
Redwood
457 Belmont
Taita
Western Hutt Road
Glenside
Johnsonville
Normandale
Avalon
2
Hutt River
Lower Hutt
Naenae
445
Paparangi
Korokoro
Petone
Waterloo
Gracefield
Khandallah
Newlands
B
Ngaio
Ngauranga
Somes Island
Seaview
Wainuiomata
Otari Open Air Museum
Wadestown
Old St. Paul's Church
Port Nicholson
Lowry Bay
Botanic Gardens
Railway Station
WELLINGTON
Pt. Halswell
Days Bay
Karori
Maritime Museum
Ward I.
Eastbourne
Art Gallery and Mus.
Mount Victoria 196
Hataitai
706 McKerrow
Brooklyn
Zoo
Evans Bay
Miramar
Kilbirnie
Seatoun
570 Mount Grace
Island Bay
Lyall Bay
WELLINGTON INTERNATIONAL AIRPORT
248 Mount Cameron
41°20'
Owhiro Bay
Picton
Pencarrow Head
East from Greenwich
175°50'

1 2

COPYRIGHT GEORGE PHILIP LTD

INDEX TO CITY MAPS

The index contains the names of all the principal places and features shown on the City Maps. Each name is followed by an additional entry in italics giving the name of the City Map within which it is located.

The number in bold type which follows each name refers to the number of the City Map page where that feature or place will be found.

The letter and figure which are immediately after the page number give the grid square on the map within which the feature or place is situated. The letter represents the latitude and the figure the longitude. Upper case letters refer to the City Maps, lower case letters to the Central Area Maps. The full geographic reference is provided in the border of the City Maps.

The location given is the centre of the city, suburb or feature and is not necessarily the name. Rivers, canals and roads are indexed to their name. Rivers carry the symbol ➔ after their name.

An explanation of the alphabetical order rules and a list of the abbreviations used are to be found at the beginning of the World Map Index.

A

Aalām, *Baghdad* **3** B2
Aalsmeer, *Amsterdam* **2** B1
Abbey Wood, *London* **15** B4
Abcoude, *Amsterdam* **2** B2
Ābdīn, *Cairo* **7** A2
Abeno, *Osaka* **22** B4
Aberdeen, *Hong Kong* **12** B2
Aberdour, *Edinburgh* **11** A2
Aberdour Castle, *Edinburgh* **11** A2
Abfanggraben ➔, *Munich* **20** A3
Ablon-sur-Seine, *Paris* **23** B3
Abord-à-Plouffe, *Montreal* **19** A1
Abramtsevo, *Moscow* **19** B4
Abu Dis, *Jerusalem* **13** B2
Abū en Numrus, *Cairo* **7** B2
Abu Ghosh, *Jerusalem* **13** B1
Acacias, *Madrid* **17** c2
Acassuso, *Buenos Aires* **7** A1
Accotink Cr. ➔, *Washington* **32** B2
Achères, *Paris* **23** A1
Acilia, *Rome* **25** C1
Aclimação, *São Paulo* **26** B2
Acton, *London* **15** A2
Açúcar, Pão de,
Rio de Janeiro **24** B2
Ada Beja, *Lisbon* **14** A1
Adams Park, *Atlanta* **3** B2
Adams Shore, *Boston* **6** B4
Addiscombe, *London* **15** B3
Adelphi, *Washington* **32** A4
Aderklaa, *Vienna* **31** A3
Admiralteyskaya Storona,
St. Petersburg **26** B2
Áffori, *Milan* **18** A2
Aflandshage, *Copenhagen* **10** B3
Afsarīyeh, *Tehran* **30** B2
Agboyi Cr. ➔, *Lagos* **14** A2
Ågerup, *Copenhagen* **10** A1
Agesta, *Stockholm* **28** B2
Agincourt, *Toronto* **30** A3
Agora, Arhéa, *Athens* **2** c1
Agra Canal, *Delhi* **10** B2
Agricola Oriental,
Mexico City **18** B2
Agua Espraiada ➔,
São Paulo **26** B2
Agualva-Cacem, *Lisbon* **14** A1
Agustino, Cerro El, *Lima* **16** B2
Ahrensfelde, *Berlin* **5** A4
Ahuntsic, *Montreal* **19** A1
Ai ➔, *Osaka* **22** A4
Aigremont, *Paris* **23** A1
Air View Park, *Singapore* **27** A2
Airport West, *Melbourne* **17** A1
Aiyaleo, *Athens* **2** B2
Aiyáleos, Óros, *Athens* **2** B1
Ajegunle, *Lagos* **14** B2
Aji, *Osaka* **22** A3
Ajuda, *Lisbon* **14** A1
Akalla, *Stockholm* **28** A1
Akasaka, *Tokyo* **29** b3
Akbarābād, *Tehran* **30** A2
Akershus Slott, *Oslo* **22** A3
Akihabara, *Tokyo* **29** a5
Akrópolis, *Athens* **2** c2
Al 'Azamiyah, *Baghdad* **3** A2
Al Quds = Jerusalem,
Jerusalem **13** B2
Alaguntan, *Lagos* **14** B2
Alameda, *San Francisco* **25** B3
Alameda, Parque,
Mexico City **18** b2
Alameda Memorial State
Beach Park, *San Francisco* **25** B3
Albern, *Vienna* **31** A2
Albert Park, *Melbourne* **17** B1
Alberton, *Johannesburg* **13** B2
Albertslund, *Copenhagen* **10** A2
Albysjön, *Stockholm* **28** B1
Alcantara, *Lisbon* **14** A1
Alcatraz I., *San Francisco* **25** B2
Alcobendas, *Madrid* **17** A2
Alcorcón, *Madrid* **17** B1
Aldershof, *Berlin* **5** B4
Aldo Bonzi, *Buenos Aires* **7** C1
Aleksandrovskoye,
St. Petersburg **26** B2
Alexander Nevsky Abbey,
St. Petersburg **26** B2
Alexander Soutzos Moussío,
Athens **2** b3
Alexandra, *Johannesburg* **13** A2
Alexandra, *Singapore* **27** B2
Alexandria, *Washington* **32** C3
Alfama, *Lisbon* **14** c3
Alfortville, *Paris* **23** B3
Algés, *Lisbon* **14** A1
Alhambra, *Los Angeles* **16** B4
Alibey ➔, *Istanbul* **12** B1
Alibey Barajı, *Istanbul* **12** B1
Alibeyköy, *Istanbul* **12** B1
Alimos, *Athens* **2** B2
Alipur, *Calcutta* **8** B1
Allach, *Munich* **20** A1
Allambie Heights, *Sydney* **28** A2
Allard Pierson Museum,
Amsterdam **2** b2
Allermuir Hill, *Edinburgh* **11** B2
Allerton, Pt., *Boston* **6** B4
Allston, *Boston* **6** A3
Almada, *Lisbon* **14** A2
Almagro, *Buenos Aires* **7** B2
Almargem do Bispo, *Lisbon* **14** A1
Almazovo, *Moscow* **19** A6
Almirante G. Brown, Parque,
Buenos Aires **7** C2
Almon, *Jerusalem* **13** B2
Almond ➔, *Edinburgh* **11** B2
Alnabru, *Oslo* **22** A4
Alnsjøen, *Oslo* **22** A4
Alperton, *London* **15** A2
Alpine, *New York* **21** A2
Alrode, *Johannesburg* **13** B2
Alsemerg, *Brussels* **6** B1
Alsergrund, *Vienna* **31** A2
Alsip, *Chicago* **9** C2
Ålsten, *Stockholm* **28** B1
Ålta, *Stockholm* **28** B3
Altadena, *Los Angeles* **16** A4
Alte-Donau ➔, *Vienna* **31** A2
Alte Hofburg, *Vienna* **31** b1
Alter Finkenkrug, *Berlin* **5** A1
Altes Rathaus, *Munich* **20** b3
Altglienicke, *Berlin* **5** B4
Altlandsberg, *Berlin* **5** A5
Altlandsberg Nord, *Berlin* **5** A5
Altmannsdorf, *Vienna* **31** B1
Alto da Moóca, *São Paulo* **26** B2
Alto do Pina, *Lisbon* **14** A2
Altona, *Melbourne* **17** B1
Alvaro Obregon, *Mexico City* **18** B1
Alvik, *Stockholm* **28** B1
Älvsjo, *Stockholm* **28** B2
Älvvik, *Stockholm* **28** A3
Am Hasenbergl, *Munich* **20** A2
Am Steinhof, *Vienna* **31** A1
Am Wald, *Munich* **20** B2
Ama Keng, *Singapore* **27** A2
Amadora, *Lisbon* **14** A1
Amagasaki, *Osaka* **22** A3
Amager, *Copenhagen* **10** B3
Amāl Qādisiya, *Baghdad* **3** B2
Amalienborg, *Copenhagen* **10** b3
Amata, *Milan* **18** A1
Ameixoeira, *Lisbon* **14** A2
América, *São Paulo* **26** B1
Amin, *Baghdad* **3** B2
Aminadov, *Jerusalem* **13** B1
Aminyevo, *Moscow* **19** B2
Amīrābād, *Tehran* **30** A2
Amora, *Lisbon* **14** B2
Amoreira, *Lisbon* **14** A1
Ampelokipi, *Athens* **2** B2
Amper ➔, *Munich* **20** A1
Amstel, *Amsterdam* **2** b2
Amstel ➔, *Amsterdam* **2** c2
Amstel-Drecht-Kanaal,
Amsterdam **2** B2
Amstel Station, *Amsterdam* **2** c3
Amstelhof, *Amsterdam* **2** b2
Amstelveen, *Amsterdam* **2** B2
Amsterdam, *Amsterdam* **2** A2
Amsterdam-Rijnkanaal,
Amsterdam **2** B3
Amsterdam Zoo, *Amsterdam* **2** b3
Amsterdam Zuidoost,
Amsterdam **2** B2
Amsterdamse Bos,
Amsterdam **2** B1
Anacostia, *Washington* **32** B4
Anadoluhisarı, *Istanbul* **12** B2
Anadolukavağı, *Istanbul* **12** A2
Anata, *Jerusalem* **13** B2
Ancol, *Jakarta* **13** A1
'Andalus, *Baghdad* **3** B1
Andaraí, *Rio de Janeiro* **24** B1
Anderlecht, *Brussels* **6** A1
Anderson Park, *Atlanta* **3** B2
Andingmen, *Beijing* **4** B2
Andrews Air Force Base,
Washington **32** C4
Ang Mo Kio, *Singapore* **27** A3
Ängby, *Stockholm* **28** A1
Angel I., *San Francisco* **25** A2
Angel Island State Park,
San Francisco **25** A2
Angke, Kali ➔, *Jakarta* **13** A1
Angyalföld, *Budapest* **7** A2
Anik, *Mumbai* **20** A2
Anin, *Warsaw* **31** B2
Anjou, *Montreal* **19** A2
Annalee Heights,
Washington **32** B2
Annandale, *Washington* **32** C2
Anne Frankhuis, *Amsterdam* **2** a1
Antony, *Paris* **23** B2
Anyangch'on, *Seoul* **26** C1
Aoyama, *Tokyo* **29** b2
Ap Lei Chau, *Hong Kong* **12** B2
Apapa, *Lagos* **14** B2
Apelação, *Lisbon* **14** A2
Apterkarskiy Ostrov,
St. Petersburg **26** B2
Ar Kazimiyah, *Baghdad* **3** A2
Ara ➔, *Tokyo* **29** A4
Arakawa-Ku, *Tokyo* **29** A3
Arany-hegyi-patak ➔,
Budapest **7** A2
Aravaca, *Madrid* **17** B1
Arbataash, *Baghdad* **3** A1
Arc de Triomphe, *Paris* **23** a2
Arcadia, *Los Angeles* **16** B4
Arcueil, *Paris* **23** B2
Arco Plaza, *Los Angeles* **16** b1
Arese, *Milan* **18** A1
Arganzuela, *Madrid* **17** B1
Argenteuil, *Paris* **23** A2
Argonne Forest, *Chicago* **9** C1
Argüelles, *Madrid* **17** a1
Arima, *Osaka* **22** A2
Arima, *Tokyo* **29** B2
Áríos Págos, *Athens* **2** c1
Arkhangelskoye, *Moscow* **19** B1
Arlington, *Boston* **6** A2
Arlington, *Washington* **32** B3
Arlington Heights, *Boston* **6** A2
Arlington Nat. Cemetery,
Washington **32** B3
Armação, *Rio de Janeiro* **24** B2
Armadale, *Melbourne* **17** B2
Armenian Quarter,
Jerusalem **13** b3
Armour Heights, *Toronto* **30** A2
Arncliffe, *Sydney* **28** B1
Arnold Arboretum, *Boston* **6** B3
Árpádföld, *Budapest* **7** A3
Arrentela, *Lisbon* **14** B2
Årsta, *Stockholm* **28** B2
Art Institute, *Chicago* **9** c2
Artane, *Dublin* **11** A2
Artas, *Jerusalem* **13** B2
Arthur's Seat, *Edinburgh* **11** B3
Aryiroúpolis, *Athens* **2** B2
Asagaya, *Tokyo* **29** A2
Asahi, *Osaka* **22** A4
Asakusa, *Tokyo* **29** A3
Asakusabashi, *Tokyo* **29** a5
Asati, *Calcutta* **8** C1
Aschheim, *Munich* **20** A3
Ascot Vale, *Melbourne* **17** A1
Ashburn, *Chicago* **9** C2
Ashburton, *Melbourne* **17** B2
Ashfield, *Sydney* **28** B1
Ashford, *London* **15** B1
Ashiya, *Osaka* **22** A2
Ashiya ➔, *Osaka* **22** A2
Ashtown, *Dublin* **11** A2
Askisto, *Helsinki* **12** B1
Askrikefjärden, *Stockholm* **28** A3
Asnières, *Paris* **23** A2
Aspern, *Vienna* **31** A2
Aspern, Flugplatz, *Vienna* **31** A3
Assago, *Milan* **18** B1
Assemblée Nationale, *Paris* **23** b3
Assendelft, *Amsterdam* **2** A1
Assiano, *Milan* **18** B1
Astoria, *New York* **21** B2
Astrolabe Park, *Sydney* **28** B2
Atarot Airport, *Jerusalem* **13** A2
Atghara, *Calcutta* **8** B2
Athens = Athínai, *Athens* **2** B2
Athínai, *Athens* **2** B2
Athínai-Ellinikón Airport,
Athens **2** B2
Athis-Mons, *Paris* **23** B3
Athlone, *Cape Town* **8** A2
Atholl, *Johannesburg* **13** A2
Atīfiya, *Baghdad* **3** A2
Atişalen, *Istanbul* **12** B1
Atlanta, *Atlanta* **3** B2
Atlanta History Center,
Atlanta **3** B2
Atomium, *Brussels* **6** A2
Attiki, *Athens* **2** A2
Atzgersdorf, *Vienna* **31** B1
Aubervilliers, *Paris* **23** A3
Aubing, *Munich* **20** B1
Auburndale, *Boston* **6** A2
Auchendinny, *Edinburgh* **11** B2
Auckland Park,
Johannesburg **13** B2
Auderghem, *Brussels* **6** B2
Augusta, Mausoleo di, *Rome* **25** b2
Augustówka, *Warsaw* **31** B2
Aulnay-sous-Bois, *Paris* **23** A3
Aurelio, *Rome* **25** B1
Ausīm, *Cairo* **7** A1
Austerlitz, Gare d', *Paris* **23** A3
Austin, *Chicago* **9** B2
Avalon, *Wellington* **32** B2
Avedøre, *Copenhagen* **10** B2
Avellaneda, *Buenos Aires* **7** C2
Avenel, *Washington* **32** B4
Avondale, *Chicago* **9** B2
Avondale Heights,
Melbourne **17** A1
Avtovo, *St. Petersburg* **26** B1
Ayazağa, *Istanbul* **12** B1
Ayer Chawan, P., *Singapore* **27** B2
Ayer Merbau, P., *Singapore* **27** B2
Ayía Marina, *Athens* **2** C3
Ayía Paraskévi, *Athens* **2** A2
Áyios Dhimitrios, *Athens* **2** B2
Áyios Ioánnis Rendis, *Athens* **2** B1
Azabu, *Tokyo* **29** c3
Azcapotzalco, *Mexico City* **18** B1
Azteca, Estadia, *Mexico City* **18** C2
Azucar, Cerro Pan de,
Santiago **26** A1

B

Baambrugge, *Amsterdam* **2** B2
Baba I., *Karachi* **14** B1
Babarpur, *Delhi* **10** A2
Babushkin, *Moscow* **19** A4
Back B., *Mumbai* **20** B1
Baclaran, *Manila* **17** B2
Bacoor, *Manila* **17** C1
Bacoor B., *Manila* **17** C1
Badalona, *Barcelona* **4** A2
Badhoevedorp, *Amsterdam* **2** A1
Badli, *Delhi* **10** A1
Bærum, *Oslo* **22** A2
Bağcılar, *Istanbul* **12** B1
Bággio, *Milan* **18** B1
Bāgh-e-Feyz, *Tehran* **30** A1
Baghdād, *Baghdad* **3** A2
Bagmari, *Calcutta* **8** B2
Bagneux, *Paris* **23** B2
Bagnolet, *Paris* **23** A3
Bagsværd, *Copenhagen* **10** A2
Bagsværd Sø, *Copenhagen* **10** A2
Baguiati, *Calcutta* **8** B2
Bagumbayan, *Manila* **17** C2
Bahçeköy, *Istanbul* **12** A1
Bahtīm, *Cairo* **7** A2
Baileys Crossroads,
Washington **32** B3
Bailly, *Paris* **23** A1
Bairro Alto, *Lisbon* **14** c1
Bairro Lopes, *Lisbon* **14** b3
Baisha, *Canton* **8** B2
Baisha ➔, *Canton* **8** B2
Baixa, *Lisbon* **14** c2
Baiyun Airport, *Canton* **8** A2
Baiyun Hill Scenic Spot,
Canton **8** B2
Bakırköy, *Istanbul* **12** C1
Bakovka, *Moscow* **19** B2
Bal Harbor, *Miami* **18** A2
Balara, *Manila* **17** B2
Balashikha, *Moscow* **19** B5
Baldia, *Karachi* **14** A1
Baldoyle, *Dublin* **11** A3
Baldwin Hills, *Los Angeles* **16** B2
Baldwin Hills Res.,
Los Angeles **16** B2
Balgowlah, *Sydney* **28** A2
Balgowlah Heights, *Sydney* **28** A2
Balham, *London* **15** B3
Bali, *Calcutta* **8** B1
Baliganja, *Calcutta* **8** B2
Balingsnäs, *Stockholm* **28** B2
Balingsta, *Stockholm* **28** B2
Balintawak, *Manila* **17** B1
Balitai, *Tianjin* **30** B2
Ballerup, *Copenhagen* **10** A2
Ballinteer, *Dublin* **11** B2
Ballyboden, *Dublin* **11** B2
Ballybrack, *Dublin* **11** B3
Ballyfermot, *Dublin* **11** A1
Ballymorefinn Hill, *Dublin* **11** B1
Ballymun, *Dublin* **11** A2
Balmain, *Sydney* **28** B2
Baluhati, *Calcutta* **8** B1
Balvanera, *Buenos Aires* **7** B2
Balwyn, *Melbourne* **17** A2
Balwyn North, *Melbourne* **17** A2
Banática, *Lisbon* **14** A1
Banco do Brasil, Centro
Cultural, *Rio de Janeiro* **24** a2
Bandra, *Mumbai* **20** A1
Bandra Pt., *Mumbai* **20** A1
Bang Kapi, *Bangkok* **3** B2
Bang Kholaem, *Bangkok* **3** A2
Bang Na, *Bangkok* **3** B2
Bang Phlad, *Bangkok* **3** a1
Bangkhen, *Bangkok* **3** A2
Bangkok = Krung Thep,
Bangkok **3** B2
Bangkok Noi, *Bangkok* **3** B1
Bangkok Yai, *Bangkok* **3** B1
Banglamphoo, *Bangkok* **3** b1
Banglo, *Calcutta* **8** B1
Bangrak, *Bangkok* **3** B2
Bangsu, *Bangkok* **3** B2
Bank, *London* **15** b5
Bank of America,
San Francisco **25** b2
Bank of China Tower,
Hong Kong **12** c1
Banks, C., *Sydney* **28** C2
Banksmeadow, *Sydney* **28** B2
Banstala, *Calcutta* **8** B2
Bantra, *Calcutta* **8** B1
Baoshan, *Shanghai* **27** A1
Bar Giyora, *Jerusalem* **13** B1
Barahanagar, *Calcutta* **8** B2
Barajas, *Madrid* **17** B2
Barajas, Aeropuerto
Transoceanico de, *Madrid* **17** B2
Barakpur, *Calcutta* **8** A2
Barberini, Palazzo, *Rome* **25** b3
Barbican, *London* **15** a4
Barcarena, *Lisbon* **14** A1
Barcarena, Rib. de ➔,
Lisbon **14** A1
Barcelona, *Barcelona* **4** A2
Barcelona-Prat, Aeropuerta
de, *Barcelona* **4** B1
Barceloneta, *Barcelona* **4** A2
Barking, *London* **15** A4
Barkingside, *London* **15** A4
Barnes, *London* **15** B2
Barnet, *London* **15** A2
Barra Andai, *Karachi* **14** B2
Barra Funda, *São Paulo* **26** B2
Barracas, *Buenos Aires* **7** B2
Barranco, *Lima* **16** B2
Barreiro, *Lisbon* **14** B2
Barreto, *Rio de Janeiro* **24** B2
Bartala, *Calcutta* **8** B1
Barton Park, *Sydney* **28** B1
Bartyki, *Warsaw* **31** C2
Barvikha, *Moscow* **19** B1
Bastille, Place de la, *Paris* **23** c5
Basus, *Cairo* **7** A2
Batanagar, *Calcutta* **8** B1
Bath Beach, *New York* **21** C1
Bath I., *Karachi* **14** B2
Batir, *Jerusalem* **13** B1
Batok, Bukit, *Singapore* **27** A2
Battersea, *London* **15** B3
Battery Park, *New York* **21** f1
Bauman, *Moscow* **19** B4
Baumgarten, *Vienna* **31** A1
Bay Harbour Islands, *Miami* **18** A2
Bay Ridge, *New York* **21** C1
Bayonne, *New York* **21** B1
Bayshore, *San Francisco* **25** B3
Bayswater, *London* **15** b2
Bayt Lahm = Bethlehem,
Jerusalem **13** B2
Bayview, *San Francisco* **25** B2
Bāzār, *Tehran* **30** A2
Beachmont, *Boston* **6** A4
Beacon Hill, *Hong Kong* **12** A2
Beato, *Lisbon* **14** A2
Beaumont, *Dublin* **11** A2
Beaumonte Heights, *Toronto* **30** A1
Bebek, *Istanbul* **12** B2
Běchovice, *Prague* **24** B3
Beck L., *Chicago* **9** A1
Beckenham, *London* **15** B3
Beckton, *London* **15** A4
Becontree, *London* **15** A4
Beddington Corner, *London* **15** B3
Bedford, *Boston* **6** A2
Bedford Park, *Chicago* **9** C2
Bedford Park, *New York* **21** A2
Bedford Stuyvesant,
New York **21** B2
Bedford View, *Johannesburg* **13** B2
Bedok, *Singapore* **27** B3
Bedok, Res., *Singapore* **27** A3
Beersel, *Brussels* **6** B1
Behala, *Calcutta* **8** B1
Bei Hai, *Beijing* **4** B2
Beicai, *Shanghai* **27** B2
Beicang, *Tianjin* **30** A1
Beihai Park, *Beijing* **4** b2
Beijing, *Beijing* **4** B1
Beit Ghur el-Fawqa,
Jerusalem **13** A1
Beit Hanina, *Jerusalem* **13** B2
Beit Iksa, *Jerusalem* **13** B2
Beit I'nan, *Jerusalem* **13** A1
Beit Jala, *Jerusalem* **13** B2
Beit Lekhem = Bethlehem,
Jerusalem **13** B2
Beit Nekofa, *Jerusalem* **13** B1
Beit Sahur, *Jerusalem* **13** B2
Beit Surik, *Jerusalem* **13** B1
Beit Zayit, *Jerusalem* **13** B1
Beitaipingzhuan, *Beijing* **4** B1
Beitar Ilit, *Jerusalem* **13** B1
Beitsun, *Canton* **8** B2
Beitunya, *Jerusalem* **13** A2
Beixing Jing Park, *Shanghai* **27** B1
Békásmegyer, *Budapest* **7** A2
Bekkelaget, *Oslo* **22** A3
Bel Air, *Los Angeles* **16** B2
Bela Vista, *São Paulo* **26** B2
Bélanger, *Montreal* **19** A1
Belas, *Lisbon* **14** A1
Belas Artes, Museu
Nacionale de,
Rio de Janeiro **24** b2
Beleghata, *Calcutta* **8** B2
Belém, *Lisbon* **14** A1
Belém, Torre de, *Lisbon* **14** A1
Belenzinho, *São Paulo* **26** B2
Belgachia, *Calcutta* **8** B2
Belgharia, *Calcutta* **8** B2
Belgrano, *Buenos Aires* **7** B2
Belgravia, *London* **15** c3
Bell, *Los Angeles* **16** C3
Bell Gardens, *Los Angeles* **16** C4
Bell Tower, *Beijing* **4** a2
Bellavista, *Lima* **16** B2
Bellavista, *Santiago* **26** C2
Belle Harbor, *New York* **21** C2
Belle View, *Washington* **32** C3
Bellevue, Schloss, *Berlin* **5** a2
Bellingham, *London* **15** B3
Bellwood, *Chicago* **9** B1
Belmont, *Boston* **6** A2
Belmont, *London* **15** A2
Belmont, *Wellington* **32** B2
Belmont Harbor, *Chicago* **9** B3
Belmore, *Sydney* **28** B1
Belur, *Calcutta* **8** B2
Belvedere, *Atlanta* **3** B3
Belvedere, *London* **15** B4
Belvedere, *San Francisco* **25** A2
Belyayevo Bogorodskoye,
Moscow **19** C3
Bemowo, *Warsaw* **31** B1
Benaki, Moussío, *Athens* **2** b3
Bendale, *Toronto* **30** A3
Bendkhal, *Mumbai* **20** B2
Benefica, *Rio de Janeiro* **24** B1
Benfica, *Lisbon* **14** A1
Benito Juárez, *Mexico City* **18** B2
Benito Juárez, Aeropuerto
Int., *Mexico City* **18** B2
Bensonhurst, *New York* **21** C2
Berchem-Sainte-Agathe,
Brussels **6** A1
Berg am Laim, *Munich* **20** B2
Bergenfield, *New York* **21** A2
Bergham, *Munich* **20** B2
Bergvliet, *Cape Town* **8** B1
Beri, *Barcelona* **4** A1
Berkeley, *San Francisco* **25** A3
Berlin, *Berlin* **5** A3
Bermondsey, *London* **15** B3
Bernabeu, Estadio, *Madrid* **17** B1
Bernal Heights,
San Francisco **25** B2
Berwyn, *Chicago* **9** B2
Berwyn Heights, *Washington* **32** B4
Besiktas, *Istanbul* **12** B2
Besòs ➔, *Barcelona* **4** A2
Bethesda, *Washington* **32** B3
Bethlehem, *Jerusalem* **13** B2
Bethnal Green, *London* **15** A3
Betor, *Calcutta* **8** B1
Beurs, *Amsterdam* **2** b2
Beverley Hills, *Sydney* **28** B1
Beverley Park, *Sydney* **28** B1
Beverly, *Chicago* **9** C3
Beverly Glen, *Los Angeles* **16** B2
Beverly Hills, *Los Angeles* **16** B2
Bexley, *London* **15** B4
Bexley, *Sydney* **28** B1
Bexleyheath, *London* **15** B4
Beykoz, *Istanbul* **12** B2
Beylerbeyi, *Istanbul* **12** B2
Beyoğlu, *Istanbul* **12** B1
Bezons, *Paris* **23** A2
Bezuidenhout Park,
Johannesburg **13** B2
Bhadrakali, *Calcutta* **8** A2
Bhalswa, *Delhi* **10** A2
Bhambo Khan Qarmati,
Karachi **14** B2
Bhatsala, *Calcutta* **8** B1
Bhawanipur, *Calcutta* **8** B2
Bhuleshwar, *Mumbai* **20** b2
Białołeka Dworska, *Warsaw* **31** B2
Biblioteca Nacional,
Rio de Janeiro **24** c2
Bicentennial Park, *Sydney* **28** B1
Bickley, *London* **15** B4
Bidu, *Jerusalem* **13** B1
Bielany, *Warsaw* **31** B1
Bielawa, *Warsaw* **31** C2
Biesdorf, *Berlin* **5** A4
Bièvre ➔, *Paris* **23** B1
Bièvres, *Paris* **23** B2
Bilston, *Edinburgh* **11** B2
Binacayan, *Manila* **17** C1
Binondo, *Manila* **17** B1
Birak el Kiyam, *Cairo* **7** A1
Birch Cliff, *Toronto* **30** A3
Birkenstein, *Berlin* **5** A5
Birkholz, *Berlin* **5** A4
Birkholzaue, *Berlin* **5** A4
Birrarung Park, *Melbourne* **17** A2
Biscayne Bay, *Miami* **18** B2
Biscayne Park, *Miami* **18** A2
Bishop Lavis, *Cape Town* **8** A2
Bishopscourt, *Cape Town* **8** A1
Bispebjerg, *Copenhagen* **10** A3
Biwon Secret Garden, *Seoul* **26** B1
Björknäs, *Stockholm* **28** B3
Black Cr. ➔, *Toronto* **30** A2
Blackfen, *London* **15** B4
Blackheath, *London* **15** B4
Blackrock, *Dublin* **11** B2
Bladensburg, *Washington* **32** B4
Blair Village, *Atlanta* **3** C2
Blairgowrie, *Johannesburg* **13** A2
Blakehurst, *Sydney* **28** B1
Blakstad, *Oslo* **22** B1
Blankenburg, *Berlin* **5** A3
Blankenfelde, *Berlin* **5** A3
Blizne, *Warsaw* **31** B1
Bloomsbury, *London* **15** a3
Błota, *Warsaw* **31** C3
Blue Island, *Chicago* **9** C2
Bluebell, *Dublin* **11** B1
Bluff Hd., *Hong Kong* **12** B2
Blumberg, *Berlin* **5** A4
Blunt Pt., *San Francisco* **25** A2
Blutenberg, *Munich* **20** B1
Blylaget, *Oslo* **22** B3
Bo-Kaap Museum,
Cape Town **8** c2
Boa Vista, Alto do,
Rio de Janeiro **24** B1
Boardwalk, *New York* **21** C3
Boavista, *Lisbon* **14** A2
Bobigny, *Paris* **23** A3
Bocanegra, *Lima* **16** A2
Boedo, *Buenos Aires* **7** B2
Bogenhausen, *Munich* **20** B2
Bogorodskoye, *Moscow* **19** B4
Bogota, *New York* **21** A1
Bogstadvatnet, *Oslo* **22** A2
Bohnsdorf, *Berlin* **5** B4
Bois-Colombes, *Paris* **23** A2
Bois-d'Arcy, *Paris* **23** B1
Boissy-St.-Léger, *Paris* **23** B4
Boldinasco, *Milan* **18** B1
Bøler, *Oslo* **22** A4
Bollate, *Milan* **18** A1
Bollebeek, *Brussels* **6** A1
Bollensdorf, *Berlin* **5** A5
Bollmora, *Stockholm* **28** B3
Bolshaya-Okhta,
St. Petersburg **26** B2
Bolton, *Atlanta* **3** B2
Bom Retiro, *São Paulo* **26** B2
Bombay = Mumbai, *Mumbai* **20** B2
Bondi, *Sydney* **28** B2
Bondy, *Paris* **23** A3
Bondy, Forêt de, *Paris* **23** A4
Bonifacio Monument, *Manila* **17** B1
Bonneuil-sur-Marne, *Paris* **23** B4
Bonnington, *Edinburgh* **11** B1
Bonnyrig and Lasswade,
Edinburgh **11** B3
Bonsucesso, *Rio de Janeiro* **24** B1
Bonteheuwel, *Cape Town* **8** A2
Boo, *Stockholm* **28** A3
Booterstown, *Dublin* **11** B2
Borisovo, *Moscow* **19** C4
Borle, *Mumbai* **20** A2
Boronia Park, *Sydney* **28** A1
Borough Park, *New York* **21** C2
Bosmont, *Johannesburg* **13** B1
Bosön, *Stockholm* **28** A3
Bosporus = Istanbul Boğazi,
Istanbul **12** B2
Bostancı, *Istanbul* **12** C2
Boston Harbor, *Boston* **6** A4
Botafogo, *Rio de Janeiro* **24** B1
Botanisk Have, *Copenhagen* **10** b2
Botany, *Sydney* **28** B2
Botany B., *Sydney* **28** B2
Botany Bay Nat. Park,
Sydney **28** B2
Botič ➔, *Prague* **24** B3
Botica Sete, *Lisbon* **14** A1
Boucherville, *Montreal* **19** A3
Boucherville, Is. de, *Montreal* **19** A3
Bougival, *Paris* **23** A1
Boulder Pt., *Hong Kong* **12** B1
Boulogne, Bois de, *Paris* **23** A2
Boulogne-Billancourt, *Paris* **23** A2
Bourg-la-Reine, *Paris* **23** B2
Bouviers, *Paris* **23** B1
Bovenkerk, *Amsterdam* **2** B2
Bovenkerker Polder,
Amsterdam **2** B2
Bovisa, *Milan* **18** A2
Bow, *London* **15** A3
Bowery, *New York* **21** e2
Boyacıköy, *Istanbul* **12** B2
Boyle Heights, *Los Angeles* **16** B3
Bradbury Building,
Los Angeles **16** b2
Braepark, *Edinburgh* **11** B2
Braid, *Edinburgh* **11** B2
Bramley, *Johannesburg* **13** A2
Brandenburger Tor, *Berlin* **5** A3
Brani, P., *Singapore* **27** B3
Branik, *Prague* **24** B2
Brännkyrka, *Stockholm* **28** B2
Brás, *São Paulo* **26** B2
Brasilândia, *São Paulo* **26** A1
Brateyevo, *Moscow* **19** C4
Bratsevo, *Moscow* **19** A2
Bray, *Dublin* **11** B3
Braybrook, *Melbourne* **17** A1
Brázdim, *Prague* **24** A3
Breach Candy, *Mumbai* **20** a1
Breakheart Reservation,
Boston **6** A3
Brede, *Copenhagen* **10** A3
Breeds Pond, *Boston* **6** A4
Breezy Point, *New York* **21** C2
Breitenlee, *Vienna* **31** A3
Breña, *Lima* **16** B2
Brent, *London* **15** A2
Brent Res., *London* **15** A2
Brentford, *London* **15** B2
Brentwood Park,
Los Angeles **16** B2
Brera, *Milan* **18** B2
Bresso, *Milan* **18** A2
Brevik, *Stockholm* **28** A3
Břevnov, *Prague* **24** B2
Bridgeport, *Chicago* **9** B3
Bridgetown, *Cape Town* **8** A2
Bridgeview, *Chicago* **9** C2
Brighton, *Boston* **6** A3
Brighton, *Melbourne* **17** B1
Brighton le Sands, *Sydney* **28** B1
Brighton Park, *Chicago* **9** C2
Brightwood, *Washington* **32** B3
Brigittenau, *Vienna* **31** A2
Brimbank Park, *Melbourne* **17** A1
Brisbane, *San Francisco* **25** B2
British Museum, *London* **15** a3
Britz, *Berlin* **5** B3
Brixton, *London* **15** B3
Broad Sd., *Boston* **6** A4
Broadmeadows, *Melbourne* **17** A1
Broadmoor, *San Francisco* **25** B2
Broadview, *Chicago* **9** B1
Broadway, *New York* **21** e1
Brockley, *London* **15** B3
Bródno, *Warsaw* **31** B2
Bródnowski, Kanal, *Warsaw* **31** B2
Broek in Waterland,
Amsterdam **2** A2
Bromley, *London* **15** B4
Bromley Common, *London* **15** B4
Bromma, *Stockholm* **28** A1
Bromma flygplats, *Stockholm* **28** A1
Brompton, *London* **15** c2
Brøndby Strand, *Copenhagen* **10** B2
Brøndbyøster, *Copenhagen* **10** B2
Brøndbyvester, *Copenhagen* **10** B2
Brondesbury, *London* **15** A2
Brønnøya, *Oslo* **22** A2

34 Brønshøj

Brønshøj, *Copenhagen* 10 A2
Bronxville, *New York* 21 A3
Brookfield, *Chicago* 9 C1
Brookhaven, *Atlanta* 3 A2
Brookline, *Boston* 6 B3
Brooklyn, *Cape Town* 8 A1
Brooklyn, *New York* 21 C2
Brooklyn, *Wellington* 32 B1
Brooklyn Bridge, *New York* 21 f2
Brookmont, *Washington* 32 B3
Brossard, *Montreal* 19 B3
Brou-sur-Chantereine, *Paris* 23 A4
Brown, *Toronto* 30 A3
Broyhill Park, *Washington* 32 B2
Brughério, *Milan* 18 A2
Brunswick, *Melbourne* 17 A1
Brush Hill, *Boston* 6 B1
Brussegem, *Brussels* 6 A1
Brussel Nat. Luchthaven, *Brussels* 6 A2
Brussels = Bruxelles, *Brussels* 6 A2
Bruxelles, *Brussels* 6 A2
Bruzzano, *Milan* 18 A2
Bry-sur-Marne, *Paris* 23 A4
Bryanston, *Johannesburg* 13 A1
Bryn, *Oslo* 22 A1
Brzeziny, *Warsaw* 31 B2
Bubeneč, *Prague* 24 B2
Buc, *Paris* 23 B1
Buchenhain, *Munich* 20 B1
Buchholz, *Berlin* 5 A3
Buckhead, *Atlanta* 3 A2
Buckingham Palace, *London* 15 b3
Buckow, *Berlin* 5 B3
Buda, *Budapest* 7 A2
Budafok, *Budapest* 7 B2
Budaörs, *Budapest* 7 B1
Budapest, *Budapest* 7 B2
Budatétény, *Budapest* 7 B2
Budavaripalota, *Budapest* 7 b2
Buddinge, *Copenhagen* 10 A3
Budokan, *Tokyo* 29 a4
Buena Vista, *San Francisco* 25 B2
Buenos Aires, *Buenos Aires* 7 B2
Bufalotta, *Rome* 25 B2
Bugio, *Lisbon* 14 B1
Buiksloot, *Amsterdam* 2 A2
Buitenveldert, *Amsterdam* 2 B2
Buizingen, *Brussels* 6 B1
Bukit Panjang Nature Reserve, *Singapore* 27 A2
Bukit Timah Nature Reserve, *Singapore* 27 A2
Bukum, P., *Singapore* 27 B2
Bûlâq, *Cairo* 7 A2
Bule, *Manila* 17 C2
Bulim, *Singapore* 27 A2
Bullen Park, *Melbourne* 17 A2
Bundoora North, *Melbourne* 17 A2
Bundoora Park, *Melbourne* 17 A2
Bunker I., *Karachi* 14 B1
Bunkyo-Ku, *Tokyo* 29 A3
Bunnefjorden, *Oslo* 22 A3
Buona Vista Park, *Singapore* 27 B2
Burbank, *Chicago* 9 C2
Burbank, *Los Angeles* 16 A3
Burlington, *Boston* 6 A2
Burnham Park, *Chicago* 9 c2
Burnham Park Harbor, *Chicago* 9 B3
Burnhamthorpe, *Toronto* 30 B1
Burnt Oak, *London* 15 A2
Burntisland, *Edinburgh* 11 A2
Burnwynd, *Edinburgh* 11 B1
Burqa, *Jerusalem* 13 A2
Burtus, *Cairo* 7 A1
Burudvatn, *Oslo* 22 A2
Burwood, *Sydney* 28 B1
Bushwick, *New York* 21 B2
Bushy Park, *London* 15 B1
Butantã, *São Paulo* 26 B1
Butcher I., *Mumbai* 20 B2
Butts Corner, *Washington* 32 C2
Büyükdere, *Istanbul* 12 B2
Byculla, *Mumbai* 20 B2
Bygdøy, *Oslo* 22 A3

C

C.N. Tower, *Toronto* 30 B2
Cabaçu de Cima →, *São Paulo* 26 A2
Caballito, *Buenos Aires* 7 B2
Cabin John, *Washington* 32 B2
Cabin John Regional Park, *Washington* 32 A2
Cabinteely, *Dublin* 11 B3
Cabra, *Dublin* 11 A2
Cabuçú de Baixo →, *São Paulo* 26 A1
Cachan, *Paris* 23 B2
Cachenka →, *Moscow* 19 B1
Cachoeira, Rib. da →, *São Paulo* 26 B1
Cacilhas, *Lisbon* 14 A2
Cahuenga Pk., *Los Angeles* 16 B3
Cairo = El Qâhira, *Cairo* 7 A2
Caju, *Rio de Janeiro* 24 B1
Čakovice, *Prague* 24 B3
Calcutta = Kolkata, *Calcutta* 8 B2
California Inst. of Tech., *Los Angeles* 16 B4
California Plaza, *Los Angeles* 16 b1
California State Univ., *Los Angeles* 16 B3
Callao, *Lima* 16 B2
Caloocan, *Manila* 17 B1
Calumet Park, *Chicago* 9 C3
Calumet Sag Channel →, *Chicago* 9 C2
Calumpang, *Manila* 17 B2
Calvairate, *Milan* 18 B2
Camarate, *Lisbon* 14 A2
Camaroes, *Lisbon* 14 A1
Camberwell, *London* 15 B3
Camberwell, *Melbourne* 17 B2
Cambridge, *Boston* 6 A3
Cambridge Res., *Boston* 6 A2
Cambuci, *São Paulo* 26 B2
Camden, *London* 15 A3
Cameron, Mt., *Wellington* 32 B2
Çamlıca, *Istanbul* 12 B2
Camp Springs, *Washington* 32 C4
Campamento, *Madrid* 17 B1
Campbellfield, *Melbourne* 17 A1
Camperdown, *Sydney* 28 B2
Campidoglio, *Rome* 25 c3
Campo, Casa de, *Madrid* 17 B1
Campo F.C. Barcelona, *Barcelona* 4 A1
Campo Grando, *Lisbon* 14 A2
Campo Pequeño, *Lisbon* 14 A2
Campolide, *Lisbon* 14 A2
Camps Bay, *Cape Town* 8 A1
C'an San Joan, *Barcelona* 4 A2
Cañacao B., *Manila* 17 C1
Canarsie, *New York* 21 C2
Cancelleria, Palazzo dei, *Rome* 25 c2
Candiac, *Montreal* 19 B3
Caneças, *Lisbon* 14 A1
Canillas, *Madrid* 17 B2
Canillejas, *Madrid* 17 B2
Canning Town, *London* 15 A4
Canteras de Vallecas, *Madrid* 17 B2
Canterbury, *Melbourne* 17 A2
Canterbury, *Sydney* 28 B1
Canton = Guangzhou, *Canton* 8 B2
Caoheijing, *Shanghai* 27 B1
Capão Redondo, *São Paulo* 26 B1
Caparica, *Lisbon* 14 A2
Caparica, Costa da, *Lisbon* 14 B1
Cape Flats, *Cape Town* 8 B2
Cape Town, *Cape Town* 8 A1
Capitol Heights, *Washington* 32 B4
Capitol Hill, *Washington* 32 B4
Capitolini, Musei, *Rome* 25 c3
Captain Cook Bridge, *Sydney* 28 C1
Captain Cook Landing Place Park, *Sydney* 28 C2
Capuchos, *Lisbon* 14 B1
Carabanchel Alto, *Madrid* 17 B1
Carabanchel Bajo, *Madrid* 17 B1
Carapachay, *Buenos Aires* 7 B1
Caraza, *Buenos Aires* 7 C2
Caridad, *Manila* 17 C1
Carioca, Sa. da, *Rio de Janeiro* 24 B1
Carlstadt, *New York* 21 A1
Carlton, *Melbourne* 17 A1
Carmen de Huechuraba, *Santiago* 26 B1
Carmen de la Legua, *Lima* 16 B2
Carnaxide, *Lisbon* 14 A1
Carnegie, *Melbourne* 17 B2
Carnegie Hall, *New York* 21 c2
Carnide, *Lisbon* 14 A1
Carol City, *Miami* 18 A1
Carrascal, *Santiago* 26 B1
Carrickmines, *Dublin* 11 B3
Carrières-sous-Bois, *Paris* 23 A1
Carrières-sous-Poissy, *Paris* 23 A1
Carrières-sur-Seine, *Paris* 23 A2
Carrigeen Bay, *Dublin* 11 A3
Cartierville, *Montreal* 19 A1
Casa Verde, *São Paulo* 26 A1
Casal Morena, *Rome* 25 C2
Casalotti, *Rome* 25 B1
Cascade Heights, *Atlanta* 3 B2
Castél di Leva, *Rome* 25 C2
Castel Sant'Angelo, *Rome* 25 B1
Castle, *Dublin* 11 c2
Castle, *Edinburgh* 11 b2
Castle of Good Hope, *Cape Town* 8 c3
Castleknock, *Dublin* 11 A1
Castleton Corners, *New York* 21 C1
Catedral Metropolitana, *Mexico City* 18 b3
Catedral Metropolitana, *Rio de Janeiro* 24 c1
Catete, *Rio de Janeiro* 24 B1
Catford, *London* 15 B3
Caulfield, *Melbourne* 17 B2
Causeway Bay, *Hong Kong* 12 c3
Cavite, *Manila* 17 C1
Caxias, *Lisbon* 14 A1
Cebecci, *Istanbul* 12 B1
Cecchignola, *Rome* 25 C2
Cecilienhof, Schloss, *Berlin* 5 B1
Cedar Grove, *Atlanta* 3 C3
Cempaka Putih, *Jakarta* 13 B2
Çengelköy, *Istanbul* 12 B2
Cengkareng, *Jakarta* 13 A1
Centennial Park, *Sydney* 28 B2
Center Hill, *Atlanta* 3 B2
Centocelle, *Rome* 25 B2
Centraal Station, *Amsterdam* 2 a2
Central Park, *New York* 21 B2
Cerillos, *Santiago* 26 B1
Cerro de la Estrella, *Mexico City* 18 B2
Cerro de los Angeles, *Madrid* 17 C1
Cerro Navia, *Santiago* 26 B1
Certanovka →, *Moscow* 19 C3
Certanovo, *Moscow* 19 C3
Cesano Boscone, *Milan* 18 B1
Cesate, *Milan* 18 A1
Cha Kwo Ling, *Hong Kong* 12 B2
Chacarrita, *Buenos Aires* 7 B2
Chadwell Heath, *London* 15 A4
Chai Chee, *Singapore* 27 B3
Chai Wan, *Hong Kong* 12 B2
Chai Wan Kok, *Hong Kong* 12 A1
Chaillot, Palais de, *Paris* 23 b2
Chakdaha, *Calcutta* 8 C1
Chamartin, *Madrid* 17 B1
Chamberi, *Madrid* 17 B1
Chambourcy, *Paris* 23 A1
Champ de Mars, Parc du, *Paris* 23 c2
Champigny-sur-Marne, *Paris* 23 B4
Champlain, Pont, *Montreal* 19 B2
Champs Elysées, Avenue des, *Paris* 23 b2
Champs-sur-Marne, *Paris* 23 A4
Chamrail, *Calcutta* 8 B1
Chamshil, *Seoul* 26 B2
Chamwŏn, *Seoul* 26 B2
Chanakyapuri, *Delhi* 10 B2
Chanditala, *Calcutta* 8 A1
Changfeng Park, *Shanghai* 27 B1
Changi, *Singapore* 27 A3
Changi Int. Airport, *Singapore* 27 A3
Changning, *Shanghai* 27 B1
Chantereine, *Paris* 23 A4
Chantian, *Canton* 8 A2
Chao Phraya →, *Bangkok* 3 B2
Chaoyang, *Beijing* 4 B2
Chaoyangmen, *Beijing* 4 B2
Chapelizod, *Dublin* 11 A1
Chapultepec, Bosque de, *Mexico City* 18 B1
Chapultepec, Castillo de, *Mexico City* 18 B1
Charenton-le-Pont, *Paris* 23 B3
Charing Cross, *London* 15 b4
Charlerol, Kanal de →, *Brussels* 6 B1
Charles Bridge, *Prague* 24 b1
Charles Square, *Prague* 24 c1
Charlestown, *Boston* 6 A3
Charlottenburg, *Berlin* 5 A2
Charlottenburg, Schloss, *Berlin* 5 A2
Charlottenlund, *Copenhagen* 10 A3
Charlton, *London* 15 B4
Charneca, *Lisbon* 14 A2
Charneca, *Lisbon* 14 B1
Châteaufort, *Paris* 23 B1
Châtenay-Malabry, *Paris* 23 B2
Chatham, *Chicago* 9 C3
Châtillon, *Paris* 23 B2
Chatou, *Paris* 23 A1
Chatpur, *Calcutta* 8 B2
Chatswood, *Sydney* 28 A2
Chatuchak, *Bangkok* 3 B2
Chatuchak Park, *Bangkok* 3 B2
Chauki, *Karachi* 14 A1
Chavarria, *Lima* 16 B2
Chaville, *Paris* 23 B2
Chayang, *Seoul* 26 B2
Chegi, *Seoul* 26 B2
Chelles, *Paris* 23 A4
Chelles, Canal de, *Paris* 23 A4
Chels-le-Pin, Aérodrome, *Paris* 23 A4
Chelsea, *Boston* 6 A3
Chelsea, *London* 15 B2
Chelsea, *New York* 21 c1
Chembur, *Mumbai* 20 A2
Chennevières-sur-Marne, *Paris* 23 B4
Cheops, *Cairo* 7 B1
Cherepkovo, *Moscow* 19 B2
Chernyovo, *Moscow* 19 A1
Cheryomushki, *Moscow* 19 B3
Chestnut Hill, *Boston* 6 B2
Cheung Sha Wan, *Hong Kong* 12 A1
Cheverly, *Washington* 32 B4
Chevilly-Larue, *Paris* 23 B3
Chevry-Cossigny, *Paris* 23 B4
Chevy Chase, *Washington* 32 B3
Chevy Chase View, *Washington* 32 A3
Chia Keng, *Singapore* 27 A3
Chiaravalle Milanese, *Milan* 18 B2
Chicago, *Chicago* 9 B3
Chicago Harbor, *Chicago* 9 B3
Chicago Lawn, *Chicago* 9 C2
Chicago-Midway Airport, *Chicago* 9 C2
Chicago-O'Hare Int. Airport, *Chicago* 9 B1
Chicago Ridge, *Chicago* 9 C2
Chicago Sanitary and Ship Canal, *Chicago* 9 C2
Chienzui, *Canton* 8 A3
Chik Sha, *Hong Kong* 12 B2
Child's Hill, *London* 15 A2
Chilla Saroda, *Delhi* 10 B2
Chillum, *Washington* 32 B4
Chilly-Mazarin, *Paris* 23 B2
Chinatown, *Los Angeles* 16 a3
Chinatown, *New York* 21 e2
Chinatown, *San Francisco* 25 b2
Chinatown, *Singapore* 27 c2
Chingupota, *Calcutta* 8 C1
Chislehurst, *London* 15 B4
Chiswick, *London* 15 B2
Chiswick House, *London* 15 B2
Chitose, *Tokyo* 29 B2
Chitralada Palace, *Bangkok* 3 B2
Chiyoda-Ku, *Tokyo* 29 b4
Chkalova, *Moscow* 19 C5
Choa Chu Kang, *Singapore* 27 A2
Chobham, *Moscow* 19 C2
Chodov u Prahy, *Prague* 24 B3
Chōfu, *Tokyo* 29 B2
Choisy-le-Roi, *Paris* 23 B3
Cholupice, *Prague* 24 C2
Chom Thong, *Bangkok* 3 B1
Chong Pang, *Singapore* 27 A2
Ch'ŏngdam, *Seoul* 26 B2
Chongmyo Royal Shrine, *Seoul* 26 B1
Chongno, *Seoul* 26 B1
Chongwen, *Beijing* 4 B2
Chŏnho, *Seoul* 26 B2
Chopin, Muzeum, *Warsaw* 31 b2
Chornaya →, *Moscow* 19 B6
Chorrillos, *Lima* 16 C2
Chowpatty Beach, *Mumbai* 20 b1
Christian Quarter, *Jerusalem* 13 b3
Christiansborg, *Copenhagen* 10 c2
Christianshavn, *Copenhagen* 10 A3
Chrysler Building, *New York* 21 c2
Chrzanów, *Warsaw* 31 B1
Chuen Lung, *Hong Kong* 12 A1
Chuk Kok, *Hong Kong* 12 A2
Chulalongkom Univ., *Bangkok* 3 B2
Chung, *Seoul* 26 B1
Chunghwa, *Seoul* 26 B2
Chungnangch'on →, *Seoul* 26 B1
Chūō-Ku, *Tokyo* 29 b5
Church End, *London* 15 A2
Churchtown, *Dublin* 11 B2
Ciampino, *Rome* 25 C2
Ciampino, Aeroporto di, *Rome* 25 C2
Cicero, *Chicago* 9 B2
Cilandak, *Jakarta* 13 B1
Cilincing, *Jakarta* 13 A2
Ciliwung →, *Jakarta* 13 B2
Čimice, *Prague* 24 B2
Cinecittà, *Rome* 25 B2
Cinisello Bálsamo, *Milan* 18 A2
Cinkota, *Budapest* 7 A3
Cipete, *Jakarta* 13 B1
Citadella, *Budapest* 7 c2
Città degli Studi, *Milan* 18 B2
Città del Vaticano, *Rome* 25 B1
City, *London* 15 A3
City Hall, *New York* 21 e1
Ciudad Deportiva, *Mexico City* 18 B2
Ciudad Fin de Semana, *Madrid* 17 B2
Ciudad General Belgrano, *Buenos Aires* 7 C1
Ciudad Lineál, *Madrid* 17 B2
Ciudad Satélite, *Mexico City* 18 A1
Ciudad Universitaria, *Buenos Aires* 7 B2
Ciudad Universitaria, *Mexico City* 18 C1
Ciutadella, Parc de la, *Barcelona* 4 b3
Civic Center, *Los Angeles* 16 b2
Clamart, *Paris* 23 B2
Clapham, *London* 15 B3
Clapton, *London* 15 A3
Claremont, *Cape Town* 8 A1
Clayhall, *London* 15 A4
Clerkenwell, *London* 15 a4
Clermiston, *Edinburgh* 11 B2
Clichy, *Paris* 23 A2
Clichy-sous-Bois, *Paris* 23 A4
Cliffside, *Toronto* 30 A3
Cliffside Park, *New York* 21 B2
Clifton, *Boston* 6 A4
Clifton, *Karachi* 14 B2
Clifton, *New York* 21 C1
Cliftondale, *Boston* 6 A3
Cloghran, *Dublin* 11 A2
Clonskeagh, *Dublin* 11 B2
Clontarf, *Dublin* 11 A2
Clontarf, *Sydney* 28 A2
Clovelly, *Sydney* 28 B2
Cobras, I. das, *Rio de Janeiro* 24 B2
Coburg, *Melbourne* 17 A1
Cochituate, *Boston* 6 A1
Cochituate, L., *Boston* 6 B1
Cocotá, *Rio de Janeiro* 24 A1
Cœuilly, *Paris* 23 B4
Coina, *Lisbon* 14 B2
Coit Tower, *San Francisco* 25 a2
Coker, *Lagos* 14 B2
Colaba, *Mumbai* 20 B1
Colaba Pt., *Mumbai* 20 B1
Colegiales, *Buenos Aires* 7 B2
Colindale, *London* 15 A2
Colinton, *Edinburgh* 11 B2
College Park, *Atlanta* 3 C2
College Park, *Washington* 32 B4
College Point, *New York* 21 B2
Collégien, *Paris* 23 A4
Collier Row, *London* 15 A4
Colliers Wood, *London* 15 B2
Colma, *San Francisco* 25 B2
Colney Hatch, *London* 15 A3
Cologno Monzese, *Milan* 18 A2
Colombes, *Paris* 23 A2
Colón, Monumente, *Barcelona* 4 c3
Colon, Plaza de, *Madrid* 17 a3
Colonia Güell, *Barcelona* 4 A1
Colonial Knob, *Wellington* 32 A1
Colosseo, *Rome* 25 c3
Columbus Circus, *New York* 21 b2
Combault, *Paris* 23 B4
Comércio, Praça do, *Lisbon* 14 A2
Commerce, *Los Angeles* 16 B4
Como, *Sydney* 28 C1
Company's Gardens, *Cape Town* 8 c2
Conceição, I. da, *Rio de Janeiro* 24 B2
Concertgebouw, *Amsterdam* 2 c1
Conchali, *Santiago* 26 B2
Concord, *Boston* 6 A1
Concord, *Sydney* 28 B1
Concord, *Toronto* 30 A2
Concorde, Place de la, *Paris* 23 b3
Concorezzo, *Milan* 18 A2
Coney Island, *New York* 21 C2
Congonhas, Aéroporto, *São Paulo* 26 B2
Connaught Place, *Delhi* 10 B2
Conservatori, Palazzo dei, *Rome* 25 c3
Consolação, *São Paulo* 26 B2
Constantia, *Cape Town* 8 B1
Constitución, *Buenos Aires* 7 B2
Constitution, *Atlanta* 3 B2
Convention and Exhibition Centre, *Hong Kong* 12 b2
Coogee, *Sydney* 28 B2
Cook Str., *Wellington* 32 A1
Cooksville, *Toronto* 30 B1
Coolock, *Dublin* 11 A2
Copacabana, *Rio de Janeiro* 24 B1
Copenhagen = København, *Copenhagen* 10 A2
Coral Gables, *Miami* 18 B2
Coral Hills, *Washington* 32 B4
Corcovado, Morro do, *Rio de Janeiro* 24 B1
Corduff, *Dublin* 11 A1
Cormano, *Milan* 18 A2
Cornaredo, *Milan* 18 A1
Córsico, *Milan* 18 B1
Corsini, Palazzo, *Rome* 25 c1
Corviale, *Rome* 25 B1
Coslada, *Madrid* 17 B2
Cossigny, *Paris* 23 B4
Cossipore, *Calcutta* 8 B2
Costantino, Arco di, *Rome* 25 c3
Costorphine, *Edinburgh* 11 B2
Cotao, *Lisbon* 14 A1
Côte St.-Luc, *Montreal* 19 B2
Cotunduba, I. de, *Rio de Janeiro* 24 B2
Coubron, *Paris* 23 A4
Countryside, *Chicago* 9 C1
Courbevoie, *Paris* 23 A2
Courtry, *Paris* 23 A4
Covent Garden, *London* 15 b4
Cowgate, *Edinburgh* 11 b3
Cowley, *London* 15 A1
Coyoacán, *Mexico City* 18 B2
Cragin, *Chicago* 9 B2
Craighall Park, *Johannesburg* 13 A2
Craiglockhart, *Edinburgh* 11 B2
Craigmillar, *Edinburgh* 11 B3
Cramond, *Edinburgh* 11 B1
Cramond Bridge, *Edinburgh* 11 B1
Cramond I., *Edinburgh* 11 B1
Cranford, *London* 15 B1
Crawford, *Cape Town* 8 A2
Crayford, *London* 15 B5
Creekmouth, *London* 15 A4
Crescenzago, *Milan* 18 A2
Cressely, *Paris* 23 B1
Cresskill, *New York* 21 A2
Creteil, *Paris* 23 B3
Cricklewood, *London* 15 A2
Cristo Redentor, Estatua do, *Rio de Janeiro* 24 B1
Crockenhill, *London* 15 B4
Croissy-Beaubourg, *Paris* 23 B4
Croissy-sur-Seine, *Paris* 23 A1
Crosby, *Johannesburg* 13 B1
Crosne, *Paris* 23 B3
Cross I., *Mumbai* 20 B2
Crouch End, *London* 15 A3
Crown Mine, *Johannesburg* 13 B1
Crows Nest, *Sydney* 28 A2
Croydon, *London* 15 B3
Croydon Park, *Sydney* 28 B1
Cruagh Mt., *Dublin* 11 B2
Crumlin, *Dublin* 11 B2
Cruz de Pau, *Lisbon* 14 B2
Crystal Palace, *London* 15 B3
Csepel, *Budapest* 7 B2
Csepelsziget, *Budapest* 7 B2
Csillaghegy, *Budapest* 7 A2
Csillagtelep, *Budapest* 7 B2
Csömör, *Budapest* 7 A3
Csömöri-patak →, *Budapest* 7 A3
Cuatro Vientos, *Madrid* 17 B1
Cuauhtémoc, *Mexico City* 18 B2
Cubao, *Manila* 17 B2
Çubuklu, *Istanbul* 12 B2
Cudahy, *Los Angeles* 16 C3
Cuicuilco, Pirámido de, *Mexico City* 18 C1
Culver City, *Los Angeles* 16 B2
Cumballa Hill, *Mumbai* 20 a1
Cumbres de Vallecas, *Madrid* 17 B2
Cupecê, *São Paulo* 26 B1
Currie, *Edinburgh* 11 B2
Cusago, *Milan* 18 B1
Cusano Milanino, *Milan* 18 A2
Custom House, *Dublin* 11 b3
Çuvuşabaşi →, *Istanbul* 12 B1
Czerniaków, *Warsaw* 31 B2
Czyste, *Warsaw* 31 B1

D

D.F. Malan Airport, *Cape Town* 8 A2
Da Moóca →, *São Paulo* 26 B2
Da Yunhe →, *Tianjin* 30 A1
Dabizhuang, *Tianjin* 30 A2
Dablice, *Prague* 24 B2
Dąbrowa, *Warsaw* 31 B1
Dachang, *Shanghai* 27 B1
Dachang Airfield, *Shanghai* 27 B1
Dachau-Ost, *Munich* 20 A1
Dachauer Moos, *Munich* 20 A1
Dadar, *Mumbai* 20 A1
Dagenham, *London* 15 A4
Daglfing, *Munich* 20 B2
Daheisha, *Jerusalem* 13 B2
Dahlem, *Berlin* 5 B2
Dahlwitz-Hoppegarten, *Berlin* 5 A5
Dahongmen, *Beijing* 4 C2
Daitō, *Osaka* 22 A4
Dajiaoting, *Beijing* 4 B2
Dakhnoye, *St. Petersburg* 26 C1
Dalejsky potok →, *Prague* 24 B2
Dalgety Bay, *Edinburgh* 11 A1
Dalkeith, *Edinburgh* 11 B3
Dalkey, *Dublin* 11 B3
Dalkey Island, *Dublin* 11 B3
Dallgow, *Berlin* 5 A1
Dalmeny, *Edinburgh* 11 B1
Dalston, *London* 15 A3
Daly City, *San Francisco* 25 B2
Dam, *Amsterdam* 2 b2
Dam Rak, *Amsterdam* 2 a2
Damaia, *Lisbon* 14 A1
Dämeritzsee, *Berlin* 5 B5
Dan Ryan Woods, *Chicago* 9 C2
Danderhall, *Edinburgh* 11 B3
Danderyd, *Stockholm* 28 A2
Danforth, *Toronto* 30 A3
Darakeh, *Tehran* 30 A2
Darband, *Tehran* 30 A2
Darling Harbour, *Sydney* 28 b1
Darling Point, *Sydney* 28 B2
Darndale, *Dublin* 11 A2
Darrūs, *Tehran* 30 A2
Dartford, *London* 15 B5
Darya Ganj, *Delhi* 1 a3
Dashi, *Canton* 8 B2
Datansha, *Canton* 8 B2
Datun, *Beijing* 4 B2
Daulatpur, *Delhi* 10 A1
David's Citadel, *Jerusalem* 13 b3
David's Tomb, *Jerusalem* 13 b3
Davidson, Mt., *San Francisco* 25 B2
Davidson's Mains, *Edinburgh* 11 B2
Dāvūdiyeh, *Tehran* 30 A2
Davydkovo, *Moscow* 19 B2
Dawidy, *Warsaw* 31 C1
Days Bay, *Wellington* 32 B2
Dazhigu, *Tianjin* 30 B2
De Waag, *Amsterdam* 2 b2
Decatur, *Atlanta* 3 B3
Dedham, *Boston* 6 B2
Deer I., *Boston* 6 A4
Degunino, *Moscow* 19 A3
Deir Dibwan, *Jerusalem* 13 A2
Deir Ibzi'e, *Jerusalem* 13 A1
Dejvice, *Prague* 24 B2
Dekabristov, Ostrov, *St. Petersburg* 26 B1
Delhi, *Delhi* 10 B2
Delhi Gate, *Delhi* 1 b3
Demarest, *New York* 21 A2
Den Ilp, *Amsterdam* 2 A2
Denistone Heights, *Sydney* 28 A1
Dentonia Park, *Toronto* 30 A3
Deptford, *London* 15 B3
Deputati, Camera dei, *Rome* 25 b2
Des Plaines, *Chicago* 9 A1
Des Plaines →, *Chicago* 9 B1
Deshengmen, *Beijing* 4 B2
Deutsch-Wagram, *Vienna* 31 A3
Deutsche Oper, *Berlin* 5 A2
Deutscher Museum, *Munich* 20 B2
Devil's Peak, *Cape Town* 8 A1
Dhālni, *Athens* 2 B2
Dhakuria, *Calcutta* 8 B2
Dhamarakia, *Athens* 2 B1
Dharavi, *Mumbai* 20 A2
Dhrapersón, *Athens* 2 B1
Diadema, *São Paulo* 26 C2
Diegen, *Brussels* 6 A2
Diemen, *Amsterdam* 2 A2
Diepkloof, *Johannesburg* 13 B1
Dieprivier, *Cape Town* 8 B1
Difficult Run →, *Washington* 32 B2
Dilbeek, *Brussels* 6 A1
Dinzigu, *Tianjin* 30 A1
Dirnismaning, *Munich* 20 A2
District Heights, *Washington* 32 B4
Ditan Park, *Beijing* 4 a2
Diyāla →, *Baghdad* 3 B3
Djursholm, *Stockholm* 28 A2
Döberitz, *Berlin* 5 A1
Döbling, *Vienna* 31 A2
Docklands, *London* 15 A3
Dodder, R. →, *Dublin* 11 B1
Dodger Stadium, *Los Angeles* 16 B3
Dolgoe Ozero, *St. Petersburg* 26 A1
Doll Museum, *Delhi* 1 b3
Dollis Hill, *London* 15 A2
Dollymount, *Dublin* 11 A2
Dolni, *Prague* 24 B3
Dolni Chabry, *Prague* 24 B2
Dolni Počernice, *Prague* 24 B3
Dolphins Barn, *Dublin* 11 B2
Dom Pedro II, Parque, *São Paulo* 26 B2
Domain, The, *Sydney* 28 b2
Dome of the Rock, *Jerusalem* 13 b3
Don Mills, *Toronto* 30 A2
Don Muang Int. Airport, *Bangkok* 3 A2
Donaghmede, *Dublin* 11 A3
Donau-Oder Kanal, *Vienna* 31 A3
Donaufeld, *Vienna* 31 A2
Donaupark, *Vienna* 31 A2
Donaustadt, *Vienna* 31 A2
Dongan Hills, *New York* 21 C1
Dongcheng, *Beijing* 4 B2
Donggou, *Shanghai* 27 B2
Dongjiao, *Canton* 8 B2
Dongjuzi, *Tianjin* 30 B2
Dongmenwai, *Tianjin* 30 B2
Dongri, *Mumbai* 20 B2
Dongshanhu Park, *Canton* 8 B2
Dongzhimen, *Beijing* 4 B2
Donnybrook, *Dublin* 11 B2
Doornfontein, *Johannesburg* 13 B2
Dorchester, *Boston* 6 B3
Dorchester B., *Boston* 6 B3
Dornach, *Munich* 20 B3
Dorval, Aéroport de, *Montreal* 19 B1
Dos Couros →, *São Paulo* 26 C2
Dos Moninos →, *São Paulo* 26 C2
Douglas Park, *Chicago* 9 B2
Dover Heights, *Sydney* 28 B2
Dowlatābād, *Tehran* 30 B2
Downey, *Los Angeles* 16 C4
Downsview, *Toronto* 30 A1
Dragør, *Copenhagen* 10 B3
Drancy, *Paris* 23 A3
Dranesville, *Washington* 32 A1
Dreilinden, *Berlin* 5 B2
Drewnica, *Warsaw* 31 B2
Drigh Road, *Karachi* 14 A2
Drimnagh, *Dublin* 11 B2
Drogenbos, *Brussels* 6 B1
Druid Hills, *Atlanta* 3 B2
Drum Towwer, *Beijing* 4 a2
Drumcondra, *Dublin* 11 A2
Drummoyne, *Sydney* 28 B1
Drylaw, *Edinburgh* 11 B2
Dubeč, *Prague* 24 B3
Dublin, *Dublin* 11 A2
Dublin Airport, *Dublin* 11 A2
Dublin Bay, *Dublin* 11 B3
Dublin Harbour, *Dublin* 11 A2
Duddingston, *Edinburgh* 11 B3
Dugnano, *Milan* 18 A2
Dūlāb, *Tehran* 30 B2
Dulwich, *London* 15 B3
Dum Dum, *Calcutta* 8 B2
Dum Dum Int. Airport, *Calcutta* 8 B2
Dumont, *New York* 21 A2
Dūn Laoghaire, *Dublin* 11 B3
Duna →, *Budapest* 7 A2
Duncan Dock, *Cape Town* 8 a3
Dundrum, *Dublin* 11 B2
Dunearn, *Singapore* 27 B2
Dunfermline, *Edinburgh* 11 A1
Dunn Loring, *Washington* 32 B2
Dunning, *Chicago* 9 B2
Dunvegan, *Johannesburg* 13 A2
Duomo, *Milan* 18 B2
Duque de Caxias, *Rio de Janeiro* 24 A1
Dusit, *Bangkok* 3 B2
Dusit Zoo, *Bangkok* 3 a2
Duvernay, *Montreal* 19 A1
Dworp, *Brussels* 6 B1
Dyakovo, *Moscow* 19 B3
Dzerzhinskiy, *Moscow* 19 C5
Dzerzhinskiy, *Moscow* 19 B3
Dzerzhinskiy Park, *Moscow* 19 B3

E

Eagle Rock, *Los Angeles* 16 B3
Ealing, *London* 15 A2
Earl's Court, *London* 15 c1
Earlsfield, *London* 15 B2
Earlwood, *Sydney* 28 B1
East Acton, *Boston* 6 A1
East Arlington, *Boston* 6 A3
East Arlington, *Washington* 32 B3
East Bedfont, *London* 15 B1
East Boston, *Boston* 6 A3
East Don →, *Toronto* 30 A2
East Elmhurst, *New York* 21 B2
East Finchley, *London* 15 A2
East Ham, *London* 15 A4
East Humber →, *Toronto* 30 A1
East Lamma Channel, *Hong Kong* 12 B1
East Lexington, *Boston* 6 A2
East Los Angeles, *Los Angeles* 16 B3
East Molesey, *London* 15 B1
East New York, *New York* 21 B2
East Pines, *Washington* 32 B4
East Point, *Atlanta* 3 B2
East Potomac Park, *Washington* 32 B3
East Pt., *Boston* 6 A4
East River →, *New York* 21 B2
East Rutherford, *New York* 21 A1
East Sheen, *London* 15 B2
East Village, *New York* 21 e2
East Wickham, *London* 15 B4
East York, *Toronto* 30 A2
Eastbourne, *Wellington* 32 B2
Eastcote, *London* 15 A1
Easter Howgate, *Edinburgh* 11 B2
Eastwood, *Sydney* 28 A1
Ebara, *Tokyo* 29 B3
Ebisu, *Tokyo* 29 B3
Ebute-Ikorodu, *Lagos* 14 A2
Ebute-Metta, *Lagos* 14 B2
Echo Park, *Los Angeles* 16 a1
Eda, *Tokyo* 29 B2
Edendale, *Johannesburg* 13 A2
Edenmore, *Dublin* 11 A2
Edgars Cr. →, *Melbourne* 17 A1
Edgeley, *Toronto* 30 A1
Edgemar, *San Francisco* 25 C2
Edinburgh, *Edinburgh* 11 B2
Edison Park, *Chicago* 9 A2
Edmondston, *Washington* 32 B4
Edmondstown, *Dublin* 11 B2
Edo →, *Tokyo* 29 B4
Edogawa-Ku, *Tokyo* 29 A4
Edsberg, *Stockholm* 28 A1
Edwards L., *Melbourne* 17 A1
Eiche, *Berlin* 5 A4
Eiche Sud, *Berlin* 5 A4
Eiffel, Tour, *Paris* 23 A2
Ein Arik, *Jerusalem* 13 A1
Ein Naquba, *Jerusalem* 13 B1
Ein Rafa, *Jerusalem* 13 B1
Eizariya, *Jerusalem* 13 B2
Ejby, *Copenhagen* 10 A2
Ejigbo, *Lagos* 14 A1
Ekeberg, *Oslo* 22 A3
Eknäs, *Stockholm* 28 B3
El 'Abbasiya, *Cairo* 7 A2
El Agustino, *Lima* 16 B2
El Baragil, *Cairo* 7 A1
El Basâtîn, *Cairo* 7 B2
El-Bira, *Jerusalem* 13 A2
El Bosque, *Santiago* 26 C2
El Carmen, *Santiago* 26 B1
El Cortijo, *Santiago* 26 B1
El Duqqi, *Cairo* 7 A2
El Encinar de los Reyes, *Madrid* 17 A2
El Ghurîya, *Cairo* 7 A2
El Gîza, *Cairo* 7 A2
El-Khadr, *Jerusalem* 13 B1
El Khalîfa, *Cairo* 7 A2
El Kôm el Ahmar, *Cairo* 7 A2
El Ma'âdi, *Cairo* 7 B2
El Matarîya, *Cairo* 7 A2
El Mohandessin, *Cairo* 7 A2
El Monte, *Los Angeles* 16 B4
El Mûski, *Cairo* 7 A2
El Pardo, *Madrid* 17 A1
El Portal, *Miami* 18 A2
El Prat de Llobregat, *Barcelona* 4 B1
El Pueblo de L.A. Historic Park, *Los Angeles* 16 b2
El Qâhira, *Cairo* 7 A2
El Qubba, *Cairo* 7 A2
El Reloj, *Mexico City* 18 C2
El Retiro, *Madrid* 17 B1
El Salto, *Santiago* 26 B2
El Sereno, *Los Angeles* 16 B3
El Talibîya, *Cairo* 7 B2
El Vergel, *Mexico City* 18 C2
El Wâhli, *Cairo* 7 A2
El Zamâlik, *Cairo* 7 A2
El Zeitûn, *Cairo* 7 A2
Elephanta Caves, *Mumbai* 20 B2
Elephanta I., *Mumbai* 20 B2
Ellboda, *Stockholm* 28 A3
Ellinikón, *Athens* 2 B2
Ellis I., *New York* 21 B1
Elm Park, *London* 15 A5
Elmers End, *London* 15 B3
Elmhurst, *New York* 21 B2
Elmstead, *London* 15 B4
Elmwood Park, *Chicago* 9 B2
Elmwood Park, *New York* 21 A1
Elsdon, *Wellington* 32 A1
Elsiesrivier, *Cape Town* 8 A2
Elsternwick, *Melbourne* 17 B2
Eltham, *London* 15 B4
Elwood, *Melbourne* 17 B1
Élysée, *Paris* 23 A2
Elysian Park, *Los Angeles* 16 a3
Embajadores, *Madrid* 17 c2
Embarcadero Center, *San Francisco* 25 b3
Emek Refa'im, *Jerusalem* 13 c2
Émerainville, *Paris* 23 B4
Emeryville, *San Francisco* 25 A3
Eminönü, *Istanbul* 12 B1
Emmarentia, *Johannesburg* 13 A2
Empire State Building, *New York* 21 c2
Encantado, *Rio de Janeiro* 24 B1
Encino, *Los Angeles* 16 B2
Encino Res., *Los Angeles* 16 B1
Enebyberg, *Stockholm* 28 A1
Enfield, *Sydney* 28 B1
Engenho, I. do, *Rio de Janeiro* 24 B2
Englewood, *Chicago* 9 C3
Englewood, *New York* 21 A2
Englewood Cliffs, *New York* 21 A2
Enmore, *Sydney* 28 B2
Enskede, *Stockholm* 28 B2
Entrevias, *Madrid* 17 B1
Epping, *Sydney* 28 A1
Erawan Shrine, *Bangkok* 3 c3
Eregun, *Lagos* 14 A2
Erenköy, *Istanbul* 12 C2
Erith, *London* 15 B5
Erlaa, *Vienna* 31 B1
Ermington, *Sydney* 28 A1
Ermita, *Manila* 17 B1
Ershatou, *Canton* 8 B2
Erskineville, *Sydney* 28 B2
Erunkan, *Lagos* 14 A2
Erzsébet-Telep, *Budapest* 7 B3
Eschenried, *Munich* 20 A1
Esenler, *Istanbul* 12 B1
Esher, *London* 15 B1
Eskbank, *Edinburgh* 11 B3
Esperanza, *Mexico City* 18 c3
Esplanade Park, *Singapore* 27 c3
Esplugas, *Barcelona* 4 A1
Esposizione Univ. di Roma (E.U.R.), *Rome* 25 C1
Essendon, *Melbourne* 17 A1
Essendon Airport, *Melbourne* 17 A1
Essingen, *Stockholm* 28 B1
Essling, *Vienna* 31 A3
Est, Gare de l', *Paris* 23 a5
Estadio Maracanã, *Rio de Janeiro* 24 B1
Estado, Parque do, *São Paulo* 26 B2
Estefânia, *Lisbon* 14 a2
Estrela, Basilica da, *Lisbon* 14 A2
Ethnikó Arheologiko Mousslo, *Athens* 2 a2
Etobicoke, *Toronto* 30 B1
Etobicoke Cr. →, *Toronto* 30 B1
Etterbeek, *Brussels* 6 B2
Euston, *London* 15 a3
Evanston, *Chicago* 9 A2
Even Sapir, *Jerusalem* 13 B1
Evere, *Brussels* 6 A2
Everett, *Boston* 6 A3
Evergreen Park, *Chicago* 9 C2
Evīn, *Tehran* 30 A2
Évzonos, *Athens* 2 B2
Ewu, *Lagos* 14 A1
Exchange Square, *Hong Kong* 12 c1
Exposições, Palácio das, *Rio de Janeiro* 24 B1
Eyüp, *Istanbul* 12 B1

F

Fabour, Mt., *Singapore* 27 B2
Faechi, *Seoul* 26 B2
Fælledparken, *Copenhagen* 10 A3
Fågelön, *Stockholm* 28 B1
Fagersjö, *Stockholm* 28 B2
Fair Lawn, *New York* 21 A1
Fairfax, *Washington* 32 B2
Fairfax Station, *Washington* 32 C2
Fairhaven Bay, *Boston* 6 A1
Fairhaven Hill, *Boston* 6 A1
Fairland, *Johannesburg* 13 A1
Fairmilehead, *Edinburgh* 11 B2
Fairmount Heights, *Washington* 32 B4
Fairport, *Toronto* 30 A4
Fairview, *New York* 21 B2
Falenty, *Warsaw* 31 C1
Fálirou, Órmos, *Athens* 2 B2
Falkenberg, *Berlin* 5 A4
Falkenhagen, *Berlin* 5 A1
Falkensee, *Berlin* 5 A1
Falls Church, *Washington* 32 B2
Falomo, *Lagos* 14 B2
False Bay, *Cape Town* 8 B2
Fangcun, *Canton* 8 B2
Farahābād, *Tehran* 30 A2
Farforovskaya, *St. Petersburg* 26 B2
Farningham, *London* 15 B5
Farrar Pond, *Boston* 6 A1
Farsta, *Stockholm* 28 B2
Fasanerie-Nord, *Munich* 20 A2
Fasangarten, *Munich* 20 B2
Fasting Palace, *Beijing* 4 c2
Fatih, *Istanbul* 12 B1
Favoriten, *Vienna* 31 B2

Zyuzino 39

Tacubaya, *Mexico City* 18 B1
Taebang, *Seoul* 26 B1
Tagig, *Manila* 17 B2
Tagig →, *Manila* 17 B2
Tai Hang, *Hong Kong* 12 B2
Tai Lo Shan, *Hong Kong* 12 A2
Tai Po Tsai, *Hong Kong* 12 A2
Tai Seng, *Singapore* 27 A3
Tai Shui Hang, *Hong Kong* 12 A2
Tai Tam B., *Hong Kong* 12 B2
Tai Tam Tuk Res., *Hong Kong* 12 B2
Tai Wai, *Hong Kong* 12 A1
Tai Wan Tau, *Hong Kong* 12 B2
Tai Wo Hau, *Hong Kong* 12 A1
Tainaka, *Osaka* 22 B4
Taishō, *Osaka* 22 B3
Taita, *Wellington* 32 B2
Tajrīsh, *Tehran* 30 A2
Takaido, *Tokyo* 29 A2
Takaishi, *Tokyo* 29 B2
Takarazuka, *Osaka* 22 A2
Takasago, *Tokyo* 29 A4
Takatsu-Ku, *Tokyo* 29 B2
Takeshita, *Tokyo* 29 B2
Takinegawa, *Tokyo* 29 A3
Takoma Park, *Washington* 32 B3
Taksim, *Istanbul* 12 B1
Talaide, *Lisbon* 14 A1
Taliganga, *Calcutta* 8 B2
Talipapa, *Manila* 17 A2
Tallaght, *Dublin* 11 B1
Tallkrogen, *Stockholm* 28 B2
Tama, *Tokyo* 29 B1
Tama →, *Tokyo* 29 B2
Tama Kyūryō, *Tokyo* 29 B2
Tamaden, *Tokyo* 29 B2
Tamagawa-josui →, *Tokyo* 29 A1
Taman Sari, *Jakarta* 13 A1
Tamanduateí →, *São Paulo* 26 B2
Tamboerskloof, *Cape Town* 8 A1
Tambora, *Jakarta* 13 A1
Tammisalo, *Helsinki* 12 B3
Tammûh, *Cairo* 7 B2
Tampines, *Singapore* 27 A3
Tanah Abang, *Jakarta* 13 B1
Tanigami, *Osaka* 22 A2
Tanjung Duren, *Jakarta* 13 B1
Tanjung Priok, *Jakarta* 13 A2
Tanum, *Oslo* 22 A1
Taoranting Park, *Beijing* 4 c2
Tapada, *Lisbon* 14 A1
Tapanila, *Helsinki* 12 B3
Tapiales, *Buenos Aires* 7 C1
Tapiola, *Helsinki* 12 B1
Tapsia, *Calcutta* 8 B2
Tara, *Mumbai* 20 A1
Tarabya, *Istanbul* 12 B2
Tarango, Presa, *Mexico City* 18 B1
Tårbæk, *Copenhagen* 10 A3
Tarchomin, *Warsaw* 31 B1
Tardeo, *Mumbai* 20 B1
Targówek, *Warsaw* 31 B2
Tårnby, *Copenhagen* 10 B3
Tarqua Bay, *Lagos* 14 B2
Tåstrup, *Copenhagen* 10 B1
Tatarovo, *Moscow* 19 B2
Tathong Channel, *Hong Kong* 12 B2
Tathong Pt., *Hong Kong* 12 B2
Tatuapé, *São Paulo* 26 B2
Taufkirchen, *Munich* 20 B2
Tavares, I. dos, *Rio de Janeiro* 24 A2
Távros, *Athens* 2 B2
Tawa, *Wellington* 32 A1
Teaneck, *New York* 21 A1
Teatro Municipal, *Rio de Janeiro* 24 c2
Tebet, *Jakarta* 13 B2
Tecamachaleo, *Mexico City* 18 B1
Teddington, *London* 15 B1
Tegel, *Berlin* 5 A2
Tegel, Flughafen, *Berlin* 5 A2
Tegeler See, *Berlin* 5 A2
Tegelort, *Berlin* 5 A2
Tehrān, *Tehran* 30 A2
Tehrān Pārs, *Tehran* 30 A3
Tei Tong Tsui, *Hong Kong* 12 B2
Tejo, Rio →, *Lisbon* 14 A2
Tekstilyshchik, *Moscow* 19 B4
Telegraph hill, *San Francisco* 25 a2
Telhal, *Lisbon* 14 A1
Telok Blangah, *Singapore* 27 B2
Teltow, *Berlin* 5 B2
Teltow kanal, *Berlin* 5 B3
Temnikovo, *Moscow* 19 B6
Tempelhof, *Berlin* 5 B3
Tempelhof, Flughafen, *Berlin* 5 B3
Temple City, *Los Angeles* 16 B4
Temple Hills Park, *Washington* 32 C4
Temple Mount, *Jerusalem* 13 b3
Templeogue, *Dublin* 11 B2
Templo Mayor, *Mexico City* 18 b3
Tenafly, *New York* 21 A2
Tenayuca, Piramide de, *Mexico City* 18 A1
Tengah →, *Singapore* 27 A2
Tennoji, *Osaka* 22 B4
Tepalcates, *Mexico City* 18 B2
Terrazzano, *Milan* 18 A1
Terrugem, *Lisbon* 14 A1
Tervuren, *Brussels* 6 B3
Tervuren, Park van, *Brussels* 6 B3
Tetuán, *Madrid* 17 B1
Teufelsberg, *Berlin* 5 B2
Tévere →, *Rome* 25 B1
Thalkirchen, *Munich* 20 B2
Thames →, *London* 15 A4
Thames Ditton, *London* 15 B1
Thamesmead, *London* 15 A4
Thana Cr. →, *Mumbai* 20 A2
The Loop, *Chicago* 9 B3
The Ridge, *Delhi* 10 B2
The Wilds, *Johannesburg* 13 B2
Theater Carré, *Amsterdam* 2 b2
Théatro Dionissou, *Athens* 2 c2
Thiais, *Paris* 23 B3
Thissío, *Athens* 2 c1
Thistletown, *Toronto* 30 A1
Thomastown, *Melbourne* 17 A2
Thompson I., *Boston* 6 B4
Thon Buri, *Bangkok* 3 B1
Thornbury, *Melbourne* 17 A2
Thorncliffe, *Toronto* 30 A2
Thornhill, *Toronto* 30 A2
Thornton, *Cape Town* 8 A2
Thornton Heath, *London* 15 B3
Threipmuir Res., *Edinburgh* 11 B2
Throgs Neck, *New York* 21 B3
Thyssen Bornemisza, Museo, *Madrid* 17 b3
Tian'anmen Square, *Beijing* 4 B2
Tiancun, *Beijing* 4 B1
Tianjin, *Tianjin* 30 B1
Tiantan Park, *Beijing* 4 c2
Tibidabo, *Barcelona* 4 A1
Tibradden Mt., *Dublin* 11 B2
Tiburon, *San Francisco* 25 A2
Tiburtino, *Rome* 25 B2
Ticomán, *Mexico City* 18 A2
Tiefersee, *Berlin* 5 B1
Tiejiangyin, *Beijing* 4 C2
Tientsin = Tianjin, *Tianjin* 30 B1
Tiergarten, *Berlin* 5 A3
Tietê →, *São Paulo* 26 B2
Tigerhof, *Cape Town* 8 A2
Tigris = Nahr Dijlah →, *Baghdad* 3 B2
Tijuca, *Rio de Janeiro* 24 B1
Tijuca, Parque Nacional da, *Rio de Janeiro* 24 B1
Tijuca, Pico da, *Rio de Janeiro* 24 B1
Tikkurila, *Helsinki* 12 B3
Tilak Nagar, *Delhi* 10 B1
Tilanqiao, *Shanghai* 27 B1
Timah, Bukit, *Singapore* 27 A2
Times Square, *New York* 21 c2
Timiryazev Park, *Moscow* 19 B3
Ting Kau, *Hong Kong* 12 A1
Tira, *Jerusalem* 13 A1
Tirsa, *Cairo* 7 B2
Tishrīyaa, *Baghdad* 3 B2
Tiu Keng Leng, *Hong Kong* 12 B2
Tivoli, *Copenhagen* 10 a3
Tizapán, *Mexico City* 18 C1
Tlalnepantla →, *Mexico City* 18 A1
To Kwai Wan, *Hong Kong* 12 B2
Toa Payoh, *Singapore* 27 A3
Tobong, *Seoul* 26 B2
Tobong-san, *Seoul* 26 A2
Točná, *Prague* 24 C2
Toco Hills, *Atlanta* 3 B2
Todt Hill, *New York* 21 C1
Tōkagi, *Tokyo* 29 A4
Tokai Plantation, *Cape Town* 8 B1
Tōkaichiba, *Tokyo* 29 B2
Tokarevo, *Moscow* 19 C5
Tōkyō, *Tokyo* 29 B3
Tokyo B., *Tokyo* 29 B4
Tokyo-Haneda Int. Airport, *Tokyo* 29 B3
Tokyo Harbour, *Tokyo* 29 B3
Tolka R. →, *Dublin* 11 A1
Tolworth, *London* 15 B2
Tomb of Lu Xun, *Shanghai* 27 B1
Tomb of the Kings, *Jerusalem* 13 a2
Tomba di Nerone, *Rome* 25 B1
Tomilino, *Moscow* 19 C5
Tondo, *Manila* 17 B1
Tongbinggo, *Seoul* 26 B1
Tongjak, *Seoul* 26 B1
Tongmaemung, *Seoul* 26 B2
Tongqiao, *Shanghai* 27 A1
Toorak, *Melbourne* 17 B2
Topkapı, *Istanbul* 12 B1
Tor di Quinto, *Rome* 25 B1
Tor Pignattara, *Rome* 25 B2
Tor Sapienza, *Rome* 25 B2
Toranomon, *Tokyo* 29 c3
Torcy, *Paris* 23 A4
Toronto, *Toronto* 30 B3
Toronto, Univ. of, *Toronto* 30 B2
Toronto Harbour, *Toronto* 30 B2
Toronto I., *Toronto* 30 B2
Toronto Int. Airport, *Toronto* 30 A1
Toros Las Arenas, Pl. de, *Barcelona* 4 c1
Toros Monumental, Templo de, *Barcelona* 4 a3
Torre Latino-americana, *Mexico City* 18 b2
Torre Lupara, *Rome* 25 B2
Torre Nova, *Rome* 25 B2
Torrellas →, *Barcelona* 4 A1
Torrevécchia, *Rome* 25 B1
Toshima-Ku, *Tokyo* 29 A3
Toshimaen, *Tokyo* 29 A2
Tottenham, *London* 15 A3
Tottenham, *Melbourne* 17 A1
Tour Eiffel, *Paris* 23 c2
Toussus-le-Noble, *Paris* 23 B1
Toussus-le-Noble, Aérodrome de, *Paris* 23 B1
Tower Bridge, *London* 15 b5
Tower Hamlets, *London* 15 A3
Tower of London, *London* 15 A3
Towra Pt., *Sydney* 28 C2
Tøyen, *Oslo* 22 A3
Toyonaka, *Osaka* 22 A3
Trafalgar Square, *London* 15 b3
Trafaria, *Lisbon* 14 A1
Traição, Cor. →, *São Paulo* 26 B2
Tranegilde, *Copenhagen* 10 B2
Trångsund, *Stockholm* 28 B2
Transamerica Pyramid, *San Francisco* 25 b2
Transbay Terminal, *San Francisco* 25 b3
Trappenfelde, *Berlin* 5 A4
Trastévere, *Rome* 25 B1
Treasure I., *San Francisco* 25 B2
Třeboradice, *Prague* 24 B3
Třebotov, *Prague* 24 C1
Tremblay-en-France, *Paris* 23 A4
Tremembe →, *São Paulo* 26 A2
Tremont, *New York* 21 A2
Trenno, *Milan* 18 B1
Treptow, *Berlin* 5 B3
Trés Rios, Sa. dos, *Rio de Janeiro* 24 B1
Trevi, Fontana di, *Rome* 25 b3
Trezzano sul Navíglio, *Milan* 18 B1
Tribune Tower, *Chicago* 9 b2
Trieste, *Rome* 25 B2
Trinidad, *Washington* 32 B4
Trinity, *Edinburgh* 11 B2
Trinity College, *Dublin* 11 c3
Trionfale, *Rome* 25 B1
Triulzo, *Milan* 18 B2
Trocadero, *Paris* 23 b1
Troitse-Lykovo, *Moscow* 19 B2
Troja, *Prague* 24 B2
Trollbäcken, *Stockholm* 28 B3
Trombay, *Mumbai* 20 A2
Troparevo, *Moscow* 19 C2
Tropenmuseum, *Amsterdam* 2 b3
Trudyashchikhsya, Ostrov, *St. Petersburg* 26 B1
Tryvasshøgda, *Oslo* 22 A3
Tseng Lan Shue, *Hong Kong* 12 A2
Tsim Sha Tsui, *Hong Kong* 12 a2
Tsing Yi, *Hong Kong* 12 A1
Tsova, *Jerusalem* 13 B1
Tsuen Wan, *Hong Kong* 12 A1
Tsukiji, *Tokyo* 29 c5
Tsur Hadassa, *Jerusalem* 13 B1
Tsurumi →, *Tokyo* 29 B3
Tsz Wan Shan, *Hong Kong* 12 A2
Tuas, *Singapore* 27 B1
Tuchoměřice, *Prague* 24 B1
Tuckahoe, *New York* 21 A3
Tucuruvi, *São Paulo* 26 A2
Tufello, *Rome* 25 B2
Tufnell Park, *London* 15 A3
Tughlakabad, *Delhi* 10 B2
Tuileries, Jardin des, *Paris* 23 b3
Tuindorp Oostzaan, *Amsterdam* 2 A2
Tullamarine, *Melbourne* 17 A1
Tulse Hill, *London* 15 B3
Tung Lung I., *Hong Kong* 12 B2
Tung O, *Hong Kong* 12 B1
Tunis, *Baghdad* 3 A2
Tuomarila, *Helsinki* 12 B1
Tureberg, *Stockholm* 28 A1
Turffontein, *Johannesburg* 13 B2
Turkso, *Prague* 24 A1
Turnham Green, *London* 15 B2
Turnhouse, *Edinburgh* 11 B1
Tuscolana, Via, *Rome* 25 B2
Tushino, *Moscow* 19 A2
Twelve Apostles, *Cape Town* 8 A1
Twickenham, *London* 15 B1
Twickenham Rugby Ground, *London* 15 B1
Twin Peaks, *San Francisco* 25 B2
Two Rock Mt., *Dublin* 11 B2
Tymon North, *Dublin* 11 B1
Tysons Corner, *Washington* 32 B2

U

U.S. Capitol, *Washington* 32 b3
Ubeidiya, *Jerusalem* 13 B2
Uberaba →, *São Paulo* 26 B2
Ubin, P., *Singapore* 27 A3
Uccle, *Brussels* 6 B2
Udelnaya, *St. Petersburg* 26 A2
Udelnoe, *St. Petersburg* 26 B1
Udlding, *Munich* 20 A1
Ueno, *Tokyo* 29 A3
Üholičky, *Prague* 24 B1
Uhříněves, *Prague* 24 B3
Uithoorn, *Amsterdam* 2 B1
Újpalota, *Budapest* 7 A2
Újpest, *Budapest* 7 A2
Ukita, *Tokyo* 29 A4
Ullerup, *Copenhagen* 10 B3
Ullevål, *Oslo* 22 A3
Ulriksdal, *Stockholm* 28 A1
Ulyanka, *St. Petersburg* 26 B1
Um Al-Khanazir Island, *Baghdad* 3 B2
Umeda, *Osaka* 22 A3
Umerkhadi, *Mumbai* 20 b2
Ümraniye, *Istanbul* 12 B2
Underground Atlanta, *Atlanta* 3 B2
Unětický potok →, *Prague* 24 B2
Ŭngam, *Seoul* 26 B1
Unhos, *Lisbon* 14 A2
Unidad Santa Fe, *Mexico City* 18 B1
Union City, *New York* 21 B1
Union Port, *New York* 21 B2
Union Square, *New York* 21 d2
Union Square, *San Francisco* 25 b2
Union Station, *Washington* 32 b3
United Nations H.Q., *New York* 21 c3
Universidad, *Madrid* 17 B1
Universidad de Chile, *Santiago* 26 B2
University Park, *Washington* 32 B4
Unp'yong, *Seoul* 26 B1
Unter den Linden, *Berlin* 5 a4
Unterbiberg, *Munich* 20 B2
Unterföhring, *Munich* 20 A3
Unterhaching, *Munich* 20 B2
Unterlaa, *Vienna* 31 B2
Untermenzing, *Munich* 20 A1
Upper East Side, *New York* 21 b3
Upper Elmers End, *London* 15 B3
Upper New York B., *New York* 21 C1
Upper Norwood, *London* 15 B3
Upper Peirce Res., *Singapore* 27 A2
Upper Sydenham, *London* 15 B3
Upper Tooting, *London* 15 B3
Upper West Side, *New York* 21 a2
Upton, *London* 15 A4
Uptown, *Chicago* 9 B2
Uran, *Mumbai* 20 B2
Urayasu, *Tokyo* 29 B4
Urbe, Aeroporto d', *Rome* 25 B2
Urca, *Rio de Janeiro* 24 B2
Uritsk, *St. Petersburg* 26 C1
Üröm, *Budapest* 7 A2
Ursus, *Warsaw* 31 B1
Ursvik, *Stockholm* 28 A1
Usera, *Madrid* 17 B1
Ushigome, *Tokyo* 29 A3
Usina, *Rio de Janeiro* 24 B1
Üsküdar, *Istanbul* 12 B2
Ust-Slavyanka, *St. Petersburg* 26 C3
Uteke, *Stockholm* 28 A3
Utrata, *Warsaw* 31 B2
Uttarpara, *Calcutta* 8 B1
Utterslev Mose, *Copenhagen* 10 A2

V

Vadaul, *Mumbai* 20 A2
Vaires-sur-Marne, *Paris* 23 A4
Valby, *Copenhagen* 10 B2
Valcannuta, *Rome* 25 B1
Valdelatas, *Madrid* 17 A1
Vale, *Washington* 32 B1
Valenton, *Paris* 23 B3
Valera, *Milan* 18 A1
Vallcarca, *Barcelona* 4 A1
Valldoreix, *Barcelona* 4 A1
Vallecas, *Madrid* 17 B2
Vallensbæk, *Copenhagen* 10 B2
Vallensbæk Strand, *Copenhagen* 10 B2
Vallentunasjön, *Stockholm* 28 A2
Valleranello, *Rome* 25 C1
Vallisaari, *Helsinki* 12 C3
Vallvidrera, *Barcelona* 4 A1
Valvidrera →, *Barcelona* 4 A1
Van Goghmuseum, *Amsterdam* 2 c1
Vanak, *Tehran* 30 A2
Vangede, *Copenhagen* 10 A3
Vaniköy, *Istanbul* 12 B2
Vanløse, *Copenhagen* 10 A2
Vantaa, *Helsinki* 12 B2
Vantaa →, *Helsinki* 12 B2
Vantaankoski, *Helsinki* 12 B2
Vantaanpuisto, *Helsinki* 12 B2
Vanves, *Paris* 23 B2
Varedo, *Milan* 18 A1
Varkiza, *Athens* 2 C2
Varszínház, *Budapest* 7 b2
Vartiokylä, *Helsinki* 12 B3
Vartiosaari, *Helsinki* 12 B3
Vasamuseet, *Stockholm* 28 b3
Vasco, *Cape Town* 8 A2
Vasfanārd, *Tehran* 30 B2
Vashi, *Mumbai* 20 A2
Vasilyevskiy, Ostrov, *St. Petersburg* 26 B1
Vaso Regulador El Cristo, *Mexico City* 18 B1
Vaucluse, *Sydney* 28 B2
Vaucresson, *Paris* 23 A1
Vauhallan, *Paris* 23 B2
Vaujours, *Paris* 23 A4
Vauxhall, *London* 15 c4
Vecsés, *Budapest* 7 B3
Veleň, *Prague* 24 A3
Veleslavin, *Prague* 24 B2
Vélizy-Villacoublay, *Paris* 23 B2
Velka-Chuchle, *Prague* 24 B2
Velké Přilepy, *Prague* 24 B1
Venda Seca, *Lisbon* 14 A1
Venetian Islands, *Miami* 18 B2
Venezia, Palazzo, *Rome* 25 c2
Venice, *Los Angeles* 16 C2
Ventas, *Madrid* 17 B1
Ventorro del Cano, *Madrid* 17 B1
Venustiano Carranza, *Mexico City* 18 B2
Verde →, *São Paulo* 26 A1
Verdi, *Athens* 2 A2
Verdun, *Montreal* 19 B2
Vérhalom, *Budapest* 7 A2
Vermelho →, *São Paulo* 26 B1
Vernon, *Los Angeles* 16 B3
Verrières-le-Buisson, *Paris* 23 B2
Versailles, *Buenos Aires* 7 B1
Versailles, *Paris* 23 B1
Veshnyaki, *Moscow* 19 B4
Vesolyy Posolok, *St. Petersburg* 26 B2
Vestra, *Helsinki* 12 B1
Vestskoven, *Copenhagen* 10 A2
Vicálvaro, *Madrid* 17 B2
Vicente Lopez, *Buenos Aires* 7 B2
Victoria, *Hong Kong* 12 B2
Victoria, *London* 15 c3
Victoria, Mt., *Wellington* 32 B1
Victoria, Pont, *Montreal* 19 B2
Victoria and Albert Waterfront, *Cape Town* 8 a1
Victoria Gardens, *Mumbai* 20 B2
Victoria Harbour, *Hong Kong* 12 B1
Victoria Island, *Lagos* 14 B2
Victoria L., *Johannesburg* 13 B2
Victoria Lawn Tennis Courts, *Melbourne* 17 B2
Victoria Park, *Singapore* 27 B2
Victoria Peak, *Hong Kong* 12 B1
Victoria Wharf, *Cape Town* 8 a2
Vienna = Wien, *Vienna* 31 A2
Vienna, *Washington* 32 B2
View Park, *Los Angeles* 16 B3
Vigário Geral, *Rio de Janeiro* 24 A1
Vigentino, *Milan* 18 B2
Viggbyholm, *Stockholm* 28 A2
Vighignolo, *Milan* 18 B1
Viikki, *Helsinki* 12 B3
Vikhroli, *Mumbai* 20 A2
Vila Guilherme, *São Paulo* 26 B2
Vila Isabel, *Rio de Janeiro* 24 B1
Vila Jaguára, *São Paulo* 26 B1
Vila Madalena, *São Paulo* 26 B1
Vila Maria, *São Paulo* 26 B2
Vila Mariana, *São Paulo* 26 B2
Vila Prudente, *São Paulo* 26 B2
Viladecans, *Barcelona* 4 B1
Vile Parle, *Mumbai* 20 A2
Villa Adelina, *Buenos Aires* 7 B1
Villa Ballester, *Buenos Aires* 7 B1
Villa Barilari, *Buenos Aires* 7 C2
Villa Borghese, *Rome* 25 a3
Villa Bosch, *Buenos Aires* 7 B1
Villa C. Colon, *Buenos Aires* 7 C2
Villa Ciudadela, *Buenos Aires* 7 B1
Villa de Guadalupe, *Mexico City* 18 B2
Villa Devoto, *Buenos Aires* 7 B1
Villa Diamante, *Buenos Aires* 7 C2
Villa Dominico, *Buenos Aires* 7 C3
Villa Lugano, *Buenos Aires* 7 C2
Villa Lynch, *Buenos Aires* 7 B1
Villa Madero, *Buenos Aires* 7 C1
Villa Sáenz Pena, *Buenos Aires* 7 B1
Villa Urquiza, *Buenos Aires* 7 B2
Villaverde, *Madrid* 17 B1
Villaverde Bajo, *Madrid* 17 B1
Ville-d'Avray, *Paris* 23 B2
Villecresnes, *Paris* 23 B4
Villejuif, *Paris* 23 B3
Villemomble, *Paris* 23 A4
Villeneuve-la-Garenne, *Paris* 23 A2
Villeneuve-le-Roi, *Paris* 23 B3
Villeneuve-St.-Georges, *Paris* 23 B3
Villeparisis, *Paris* 23 A4
Villevaudé, *Paris* 23 A4
Villiers-le-Bâcle, *Paris* 23 B1
Villiers-sur-Marne, *Paris* 23 B4
Villinki, *Helsinki* 12 C3
Villoresi, Canale, *Milan* 18 A1
Vilvoorde, *Brussels* 6 A2
Vimodrone, *Milan* 18 A2
Vimont, *Montreal* 19 A1
Vinanmek Palace, *Bangkok* 3 a2
Vincennes, *Paris* 23 A3
Vincennes, Bois de, *Paris* 23 B3
Vinings, *Atlanta* 3 A2
Vinohrady, *Prague* 24 c3
Vinoř, *Prague* 24 B3
Violet Hill, *Hong Kong* 12 B2
Virányos, *Budapest* 7 A1
Virgen del San Cristóbal, *Santiago* 26 B2
Virginia Gardens, *Miami* 18 B1
Virginia Key, *Miami* 18 B2
Viroflay, *Paris* 23 B2
Víron, *Athens* 2 B2
Virum, *Copenhagen* 10 A2
Vishnyaki, *Moscow* 19 B5
Visitacion Valley, *San Francisco* 25 B2
Vista Alegre, *Lima* 16 B3
Vista Alegre, *Santiago* 26 C1
Vista Grove, *Atlanta* 3 A3
Vitacura, *Santiago* 26 B2
Vitinia, *Rome* 25 C1
Vitry-sur-Seine, *Paris* 23 B3
Vizandinó, Moussío, *Athens* 2 b3
Vladykino, *Moscow* 19 A3
Vlezenbeek, *Brussels* 6 B1
Vltava →, *Prague* 24 A2
Vnukovo, *Moscow* 19 C1
Vokovice, *Prague* 24 B2
Volgelsdorf, *Berlin* 5 B5
Volkhonka-Zil, *Moscow* 19 C3
Vollen, *Oslo* 22 B1
Volodarskoye, *St. Petersburg* 26 B2
Volynkina-Derevnya, *St. Petersburg* 26 B1
Vondelpark, *Amsterdam* 2 A2
Vösendorf, *Vienna* 31 B2
Vostochnyy, *Moscow* 19 B5
Voula, *Athens* 2 C2
Vouliagmeni, *Athens* 2 C2
Vredehoek, *Cape Town* 8 A1
Vršovice, *Prague* 24 B2
Vyborgskaya Storona, *St. Petersburg* 26 B2
Vykhino, *Moscow* 19 B4
Vyšehrad, *Prague* 24 B2

W

Wachterhof, *Munich* 20 B3
Wadala, *Mumbai* 20 A2
Wadestown, *Wellington* 32 B1
Wadi Fukin, *Jerusalem* 13 B1
Wah Fu, *Hong Kong* 12 B1
Wahda, *Baghdad* 3 B2
Währing, *Vienna* 31 A2
Waidmannslust, *Berlin* 5 A3
Wainuiomata, *Wellington* 32 B2
Wainuiomata R. →, *Wellington* 32 B2
Wakefield, *Boston* 6 A3
Waldesruh, *Berlin* 5 B4
Waldperlach, *Munich* 20 B3
Waldtrudering, *Munich* 20 B3
Walkinstown, *Dublin* 11 B1
Wall Street, *New York* 21 f1
Waltham, *Boston* 6 A2
Waltham Forest, *London* 15 A3
Walthamstow, *London* 15 A3
Walton on Thames, *London* 15 B1
Wambeek, *Brussels* 6 A3
Wan Chai, *Hong Kong* 12 B2
Wan Chai Lanes, *Hong Kong* 12 c2
Wandsworth, *London* 15 B2
Wankhede Stadium, *Mumbai* 20 c2
Wannsee, *Berlin* 5 B1
Wansdorf, *Berlin* 5 A1
Wanstead, *London* 15 A4
Wapping, *London* 15 A3
Ward, *Dublin* 11 A1
Ward I., *Wellington* 32 B2
Warnberg, *Munich* 20 B2
Warrâq el 'Arab, *Cairo* 7 A2
Warrâq el Hadr, *Cairo* 7 A2
Warringen Park, *Melbourne* 17 A2
Warriston, *Edinburgh* 11 B2
Warsaw = Warszawa, *Warsaw* 31 B2
Warszawa, *Warsaw* 31 B2
Wartenberg, *Berlin* 5 A4
Washington, *Washington* 32 B3
Washington Heights, *New York* 21 A2
Washington Monument, *Washington* 32 b1
Washington Nat. Airport, *Washington* 32 B3
Washington Park, *Chicago* 9 C3
Wat Arun, *Bangkok* 3 b1
Wat Pho, *Bangkok* 3 b1
Wat Phra Keo, *Bangkok* 3 b1
Wat Traimit, *Bangkok* 3 c2
Water of Leith, *Edinburgh* 11 B1
Water Tower Place, *Chicago* 9 a2
Watergraafsmeer, *Amsterdam* 2 A2
Waterland, *Amsterdam* 2 A2
Waterloo, *Brussels* 6 B2
Waterloo, *Wellington* 32 B2
Waterloo International, *London* 15 b4
Watermael-Boitsfort, *Brussels* 6 B2
Watertown, *Boston* 6 A2
Watsonia, *Melbourne* 17 A2
Waverley, *Boston* 6 A2
Waverley, *Johannesburg* 13 A2
Waverley, *Sydney* 28 B2
Waverley Station, *Edinburgh* 11 b3
Wawer, *Warsaw* 31 B2
Wawrzyszew, *Warsaw* 31 B1
Wayland, *Boston* 6 A1
Wazirabad, *Delhi* 10 A2
Wazīrīya, *Baghdad* 3 A2
Wazirpur, *Delhi* 10 A2
Wealdstone, *London* 15 A1
Wedding, *Berlin* 5 A3
Weehawken, *New York* 21 B1
Weesp, *Amsterdam* 2 B3
Weidling, *Vienna* 31 A1
Weidlingbach, *Vienna* 31 A1
Weigongcum, *Beijing* 4 B1
Weijin He →, *Tianjin* 30 B2
Weissensee, *Berlin* 5 A3
Wellesley, *Boston* 6 B2
Wellesley Falls, *Boston* 6 B2
Wellesley Hills, *Boston* 6 B2
Welling, *London* 15 B4
Wellington, *Boston* 6 A3
Wellington, *Wellington* 32 B1
Wells Fargo Center, *Los Angeles* 16 b1
Weltevreden Park, *Johannesburg* 13 A1
Wembley, *London* 15 A2
Wemmel, *Brussels* 6 A1
Wemmer Pan, *Johannesburg* 13 B2
Wenceslas Square, *Prague* 24 b2
Wendenschloss, *Berlin* 5 B4
Wenhuagong, *Tianjin* 30 B2
Wennington, *London* 15 A5
Werneuchen, *Berlin* 5 A5
West Bedford, *Boston* 6 A2
West Concord, *Boston* 6 A1
West Don →, *Toronto* 30 A2
West Drayton, *London* 15 A1
West Ham, *London* 15 A4
West Harrow, *London* 15 A1
West Heath, *London* 15 B4
West Hill, *Toronto* 30 A3
West Hollywood, *Los Angeles* 16 B2
West Kensington, *London* 15 c1
West Kilburn, *London* 15 a1
West Lamma Channel, *Hong Kong* 12 B1
West Lynn, *Boston* 6 A4
West Medford, *Boston* 6 A3
West Miami, *Miami* 18 B1
West Molesey, *London* 15 B1
West New York, *New York* 21 B1
West of Twin Peaks, *San Francisco* 25 B2
West Park, *Johannesburg* 13 A1
West Rouge, *Toronto* 30 A4
West Roxbury, *Boston* 6 B3
West Springfield, *Washington* 32 C2
West Town, *Chicago* 9 B2
West Wharf, *Karachi* 14 B1
Westbourne Green, *London* 15 a1
Westchester, *Chicago* 9 B1
Westchester, *Los Angeles* 16 C2
Westchester, *New York* 21 A2
Westcliff, *Johannesburg* 13 B2
Westdene, *Johannesburg* 13 B1
Westend, *Helsinki* 12 C1
Wester Hailes, *Edinburgh* 11 B2
Westerham, *Munich* 20 B2
Western Addition, *San Francisco* 25 B2
Western Wall, *Jerusalem* 13 b3
Westgate, *Washington* 32 B3
Westlake, *Cape Town* 8 B1
Westlake, *San Francisco* 25 B2
Westminster, *London* 15 A3
Westmount, *Montreal* 19 B2
Weston, *Boston* 6 A2
Weston, *Toronto* 30 A1
Weston Res., *Boston* 6 A2
Westwood Village, *Los Angeles* 16 B2
Westzaan, *Amsterdam* 2 A1
Wetton, *Cape Town* 8 B2
Wexford, *Toronto* 30 A3
Weybridge, *London* 15 B1
Wezembeek-Oppem, *Brussels* 6 A2
White House, The, *Washington* 32 b1
Whitechapel, *London* 15 A3
Whitehall, *Dublin* 11 A2
Whitehall, *London* 15 b3
Whittier, *Los Angeles* 16 C4
Whitton, *London* 15 B1
Wieden, *Vienna* 31 A2
Wien, *Vienna* 31 A2
Wien-Schwechat, Flughafen, *Vienna* 31 B3
Wienerberg, *Vienna* 31 B2
Wierzbno, *Warsaw* 31 B2
Wijde Wormer, *Amsterdam* 2 A2
Wilanów, *Warsaw* 31 B2
Wilanówka →, *Warsaw* 31 C2
Wilhelmshagen, *Berlin* 5 B5
Wilket Creek Park, *Toronto* 30 A2
Wilkieston, *Edinburgh* 11 B1
Willbrook, *Dublin* 11 B2
Willesden, *London* 15 A2
Willesden Green, *London* 15 A2
Williamsbridge, *New York* 21 A2
Williamsburg, *New York* 21 B2
Williamstown, *Melbourne* 17 B1
Willoughby, *Sydney* 28 A2
Willow Springs, *Chicago* 9 C1
Willowdale, *Toronto* 30 A2
Wilmersdorf, *Berlin* 5 c1
Wilmette, *Chicago* 9 A2
Wilmington, *London* 15 B5
Wilshire Boulevard, *Los Angeles* 16 c1
Wimbledon, *London* 15 B2
Wimbledon Common, *London* 15 B2
Wimbledon Park, *London* 15 B2
Wimbledon Tennis Ground, *London* 15 B2
Winchester, *Boston* 6 A3
Windermere, *Cape Town* 8 A2
Windsor, *Johannesburg* 13 A1
Windsor Hills, *Los Angeles* 16 C2
Windy Arbour, *Dublin* 11 B2
Winning, *Munich* 20 B2
Winthrop, *Boston* 6 A4
Wissous, *Paris* 23 B2
Wittenau, *Berlin* 5 A2
Witwatersrand, Univ. of, *Johannesburg* 13 B2
Włochy, *Warsaw* 31 B1
Wo Mei, *Hong Kong* 12 A2
Wo Yi Hop, *Hong Kong* 12 A1
Woburn, *Boston* 6 A3
Woburn, *Toronto* 30 A3
Woduk Pluit, *Jakarta* 13 A1
Wola, *Warsaw* 31 B1
Wolf Trap Farm Park, *Washington* 32 B2
Wolica, *Warsaw* 31 C2
Wolica, *Warsaw* 31 C1
Wólka Węglowa, *Warsaw* 31 B1
Wollaston, *Boston* 6 B3
Woltersdorf, *Berlin* 5 B5
Woluwe-Saint-Lambert, *Brussels* 6 A2
Woluwe-Saint-Pierre, *Brussels* 6 A2
Wong Chuk Hang, *Hong Kong* 12 B2
Wong Chuk Wan, *Hong Kong* 12 A2
Wong Chuk Yeung, *Hong Kong* 12 A2
Wong Tai Sin, *Hong Kong* 12 A2
Wood Green, *London* 15 A3
Wood Ridge, *New York* 21 A1
Woodbridge, *Toronto* 30 A1
Woodford, *London* 15 A4
Woodford Bridge, *London* 15 A4
Woodford Green, *London* 15 A4
Woodhaven, *New York* 21 B2
Woodhouselee, *Edinburgh* 11 B2
Woodlands New Town, *Singapore* 27 A2
Woodmont, *Washington* 32 B3
Woodside, *London* 15 B3
Woodside, *New York* 21 B2
Woodstock, *Cape Town* 8 A1
Woollahra, *Sydney* 28 B2
Woolloomooloo, *Sydney* 28 b2
Woolooware B., *Sydney* 28 C1
Woolwich, *London* 15 B4
Woolworth Building, *New York* 21 e1
World Trade Center, *New York* 21 B1
Worli, *Mumbai* 20 A1
Worth, *Chicago* 9 C2
Wren's Nest, *Atlanta* 3 B2
Wrigley Building, *Chicago* 9 b2
Wuhlgarten, *Berlin* 5 A4
Wujiaochang, *Shanghai* 27 B2
Würm →, *Munich* 20 B1
Würm-kanal, *Munich* 20 A1
Wusong, *Shanghai* 27 A1
Wyczółki, *Warsaw* 31 C1
Wygoda, *Warsaw* 31 B2
Wynberg, *Cape Town* 8 B1

X

Xabregas, *Lisbon* 14 A2
Xianggang = Hong Kong, *Hong Kong* 12 B1
Xiaodian, *Tianjin* 30 A2
Xiaogang Park, *Canton* 8 B2
Xiaoping, *Canton* 8 A2
Xiasha chong, *Canton* 8 B1
Xichang, *Canton* 8 B2
Xicheng, *Beijing* 4 B1
Xidan, *Beijing* 4 B2
Xigu Park, *Tianjin* 30 A2
Xigucun, *Tianjin* 30 A1
Ximenwai, *Tianjin* 30 B1
Xinanlou, *Tianjin* 30 B2
Xinkai He →, *Tianjin* 30 A2
Xizhimen, *Beijing* 4 B1
Xu Beihong Mem. Hall, *Beijing* 4 a1
Xuanwu, *Beijing* 4 B1
Xuhui, *Shanghai* 27 B1

Y

Yaba, *Lagos* 14 A2
Yaftābād, *Tehran* 30 B1
Yahara, *Tokyo* 29 A2
Yaho, *Tokyo* 29 A1
Yakire, *Tokyo* 29 A4
Yamada, *Osaka* 22 A4
Yamada, *Tokyo* 29 B2
Yamamoto, *Osaka* 22 B4
Yamato →, *Osaka* 22 B3
Yamuna →, *Delhi* 10 B2
Yan Kit, *Singapore* 27 A3
Yanbu, *Canton* 8 B1
Yangch'ŏn, *Seoul* 26 B1
Yanghuayuan, *Beijing* 4 C1
Yangjae, *Seoul* 26 C2
Yangjiazhuang, *Shanghai* 27 A1
Yangpu, *Shanghai* 27 B2
Yangpu Park, *Shanghai* 27 B2
Yao, *Osaka* 22 B4
Yao Airport, *Osaka* 22 B4
Yarmūk, *Baghdad* 3 B1
Yarra →, *Melbourne* 17 A1
Yarra Bend Park, *Melbourne* 17 A2
Yarraville, *Melbourne* 17 A1
Yau Tong, *Hong Kong* 12 B2
Yauza →, *Moscow* 19 A4
Yeading, *London* 15 A1
Yedikule, *Istanbul* 12 C1
Yemin Moshe, *Jerusalem* 13 b2
Yenikapı, *Istanbul* 12 B1
Yeniköy, *Istanbul* 12 B2
Yerba Buena Gardens, *San Francisco* 25 c2
Yerba Buena I., *San Francisco* 25 B2
Yerres, *Paris* 23 B4
Yerushalayim = Jerusalem, *Jerusalem* 13 B2
Yiheyuan, *Beijing* 4 A1
Yinhangzhen, *Shanghai* 27 A2
Yishun New Town, *Singapore* 27 A3
Yixingbu, *Tianjin* 30 A2
Ylästö, *Helsinki* 12 B2
Yodo →, *Osaka* 22 A4
Yongdingman, *Beijing* 4 B2
Yŏngdong, *Seoul* 26 B2
Yŏngdŭngp'o, *Seoul* 26 B1
Yongfucun, *Canton* 8 B2
Yongjing, *Shanghai* 27 B2
Yongsan, *Seoul* 26 B1
Yonkers, *New York* 21 A2
York, *Toronto* 30 A2
York Mills, *Toronto* 30 A2
Yotsuya, *Tokyo* 29 a2
You'anmen, *Beijing* 4 B1
Yŏŭido, *Seoul* 26 B1
Youndsfield, *Cape Town* 8 B1
Yuanxiatian, *Canton* 8 A2
Yugo-Zarad, *Moscow* 19 B3
Yung Shue Wan, *Hong Kong* 12 B1
Yūsofābād, *Tehran* 30 A2
Yuyuantan Park, *Beijing* 4 b2

Z

Zaandam, *Amsterdam* 2 A1
Zaandijk, *Amsterdam* 2 A1
Zaanstad, *Amsterdam* 2 A1
Záběhlice, *Prague* 24 B2
Ząbki, *Warsaw* 31 B2
Żacisze, *Warsaw* 31 B2
Zahrā, *Baghdad* 3 A1
Zakharkovo, *Moscow* 19 B1
Žalov, *Prague* 24 A2
Załuski, *Warsaw* 31 C1
Zamdorf, *Munich* 20 B2
Zamek Królewski, *Warsaw* 31 a2
Zamek Ujazdowski, *Warsaw* 31 c3
Zanevka, *St. Petersburg* 26 B3
Zapote, *Manila* 17 C1
Záppeio, *Athens* 2 c2
Zarechye, *Moscow* 19 B2
Zaventem, *Brussels* 6 A2
Zawady, *Warsaw* 31 B2
Zâwiyet Abû Musallam, *Cairo* 7 B1
Zawrā' Park, *Baghdad* 3 B2
Zbraslav, *Prague* 24 C2
Zbuzany, *Prague* 24 B1
Zdiby, *Prague* 24 B2
Zeekoevlei, *Cape Town* 8 B2
Zehlendorf, *Berlin* 5 B2
Zenne →, *Brussels* 6 B1
Żerań, *Warsaw* 31 B1
Zerzeń, *Warsaw* 31 B2
Zeytinburnu, *Istanbul* 12 C1
Zhabei, *Shanghai* 27 B1
Zhangguizhuang, *Tianjin* 30 B2
Zhdanov, *Moscow* 19 B4
Zheleznodorozhnyy, *Moscow* 19 B6
Zhenru, *Shanghai* 27 B1
Zhernovka, *St. Petersburg* 26 B2
Zhicun, *Canton* 8 B2
Zhongshan Park, *Beijing* 4 b2
Zhongshan Park, *Shanghai* 27 B1
Zhoucun, *Canton* 8 A2
Zhoujiadu, *Shanghai* 27 B1
Zhoujiazhen, *Shanghai* 27 B2
Zhu Jiang →, *Canton* 8 B3
Zhulebino, *Moscow* 19 B5
Zhushadi, *Canton* 8 A3
Zielona, *Warsaw* 31 B3
Zielonka, *Warsaw* 31 B2
Ziya He →, *Tianjin* 30 A1
Žižkov, *Prague* 24 B2
Zličin, *Prague* 24 B1
Zócalo, *Mexico City* 18 b3
Zografos, *Athens* 2 B2
Żoliborz, *Warsaw* 31 B1
Zonnenbloem, *Cape Town* 8 A1
Zoo, *Beijing* 4 a1
Zugliget, *Budapest* 7 B1
Zugló, *Budapest* 7 A2
Zuiderwoude, *Amsterdam* 2 A3
Zumbi, *Rio de Janeiro* 24 A1
Zunderdorp, *Amsterdam* 2 A2
Zuvuvu →, *São Paulo* 26 C1
Zwanenburg, *Amsterdam* 2 A1
Zwölfaxing, *Vienna* 31 B2
Zyuzino, *Moscow* 19 C3

– MT EVEREST, CHINA/NEPAL –

Part of the Himalaya range, Mt Everest - the highest
mountain in the world at 29,035 ft (8,850 m) - lies just
north of center in this image. The two arms of the Rongbuk
glacier flow away from the triangular shaded north wall, with
the Kangshung glacier due east. The international boundary
between China and Nepal bisects the peak, which was
first climbed on May 28, 1953.

WORLD MAPS

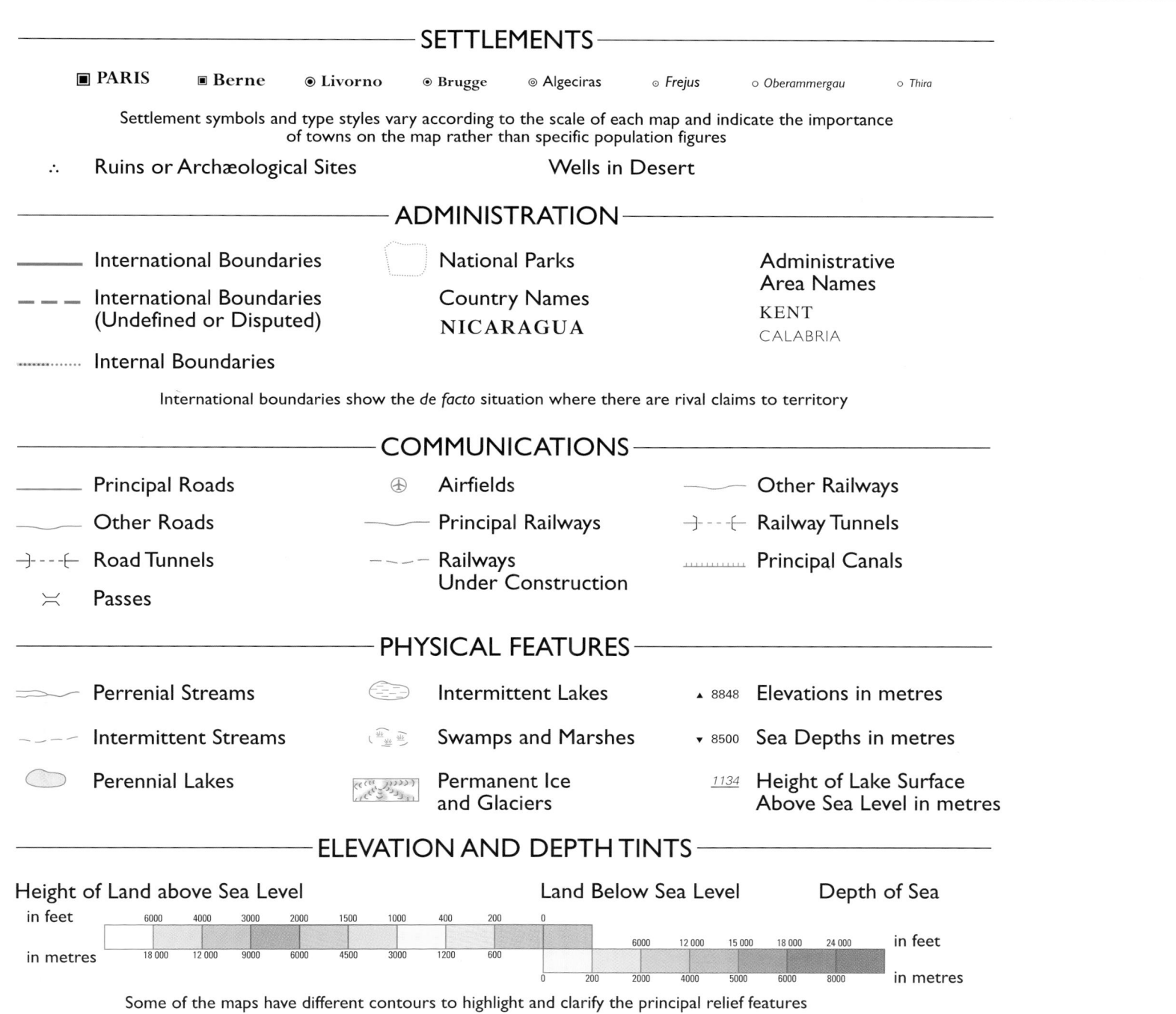

SETTLEMENTS

◼ PARIS ◼ Berne ◉ Livorno ◎ Brugge ⊚ Algeciras ○ Frejus ○ Oberammergau ○ Thira

Settlement symbols and type styles vary according to the scale of each map and indicate the importance
of towns on the map rather than specific population figures

∴ Ruins or Archæological Sites   Wells in Desert

ADMINISTRATION

——— International Boundaries

– – – International Boundaries
(Undefined or Disputed)

·········· Internal Boundaries

National Parks

Country Names
NICARAGUA

Administrative
Area Names
KENT
CALABRIA

International boundaries show the *de facto* situation where there are rival claims to territory

COMMUNICATIONS

——— Principal Roads

——— Other Roads

⊢--⊣ Road Tunnels

≍ Passes

⊕ Airfields

——— Principal Railways

–~– Railways
Under Construction

——— Other Railways

⊦--⊧ Railway Tunnels

········· Principal Canals

PHYSICAL FEATURES

⌇ Perrenial Streams

–·–· Intermittent Streams

⬭ Perennial Lakes

⬭ Intermittent Lakes

Swamps and Marshes

Permanent Ice
and Glaciers

▲ 8848 Elevations in metres

▾ 8500 Sea Depths in metres

1134 Height of Lake Surface
Above Sea Level in metres

ELEVATION AND DEPTH TINTS

Height of Land above Sea Level   Land Below Sea Level   Depth of Sea

in feet	6000	4000	3000	2000	1500	1000	400	200	0						in feet
										6000	12 000	15 000	18 000	24 000	
in metres	18 000	12 000	9000	6000	4500	3000	1200	600	0	200	2000	4000	5000	6000	8000	in metres

Some of the maps have different contours to highlight and clarify the principal relief features

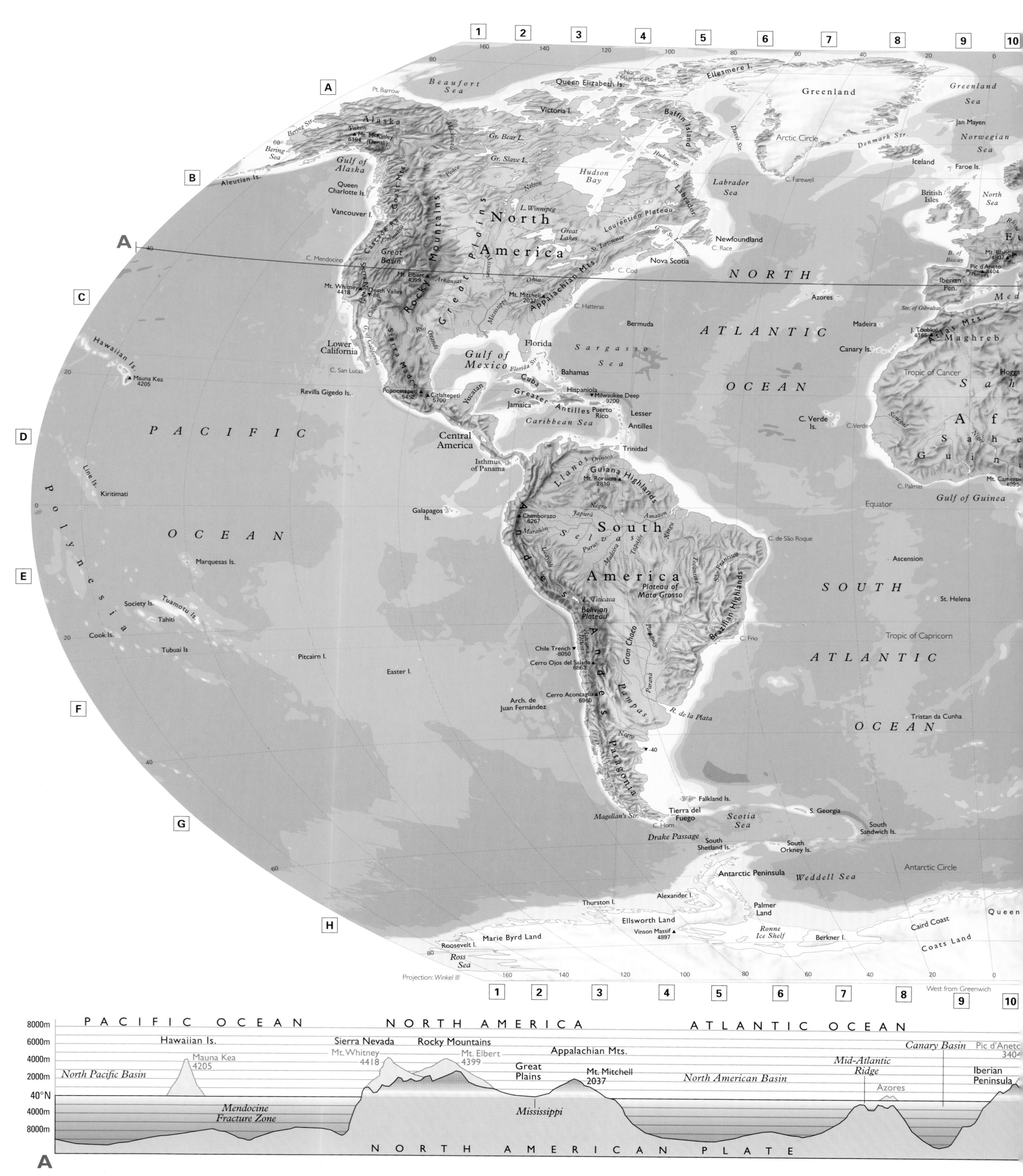

Projection: Winkel III

West from Greenwich

8000m
6000m
4000m
2000m
40°N
4000m
8000m

PACIFIC OCEAN   NORTH AMERICA   ATLANTIC OCEAN

Hawaiian Is.   Sierra Nevada   Rocky Mountains   Appalachian Mts.   Canary Basin   Pic d'Anet
Mauna Kea 4205   Mt. Whitney 4418   Mt. Elbert 4399   3404
North Pacific Basin   Great Plains   Mt. Mitchell 2037   North American Basin   Mid-Atlantic Ridge   Iberian Peninsula
Mendocine Fracture Zone   Mississippi   Azores

NORTH AMERICAN PLATE

A

ft m
18 000 6000
12 000 4000
6000 2000
600 200
0 0
600 4000
12 000
24 000 8000
ft m

1 12 13 14 15 16 17 18 19 20

A B C D E F G H

ARCTIC OCEAN
Barents Sea
Svalbard
N. Cape
Novaya Zemlya
Kara Sea
Severnaya Zemlya
Taimyr Pen.
Laptev Sea
New Siberian Is.
Wrangel I.
C. Dezhneva

Scandinavia
G. of Bothnia
White Sea
L. Onega
L. Ladoga
Baltic Sea
North European Plain
Central Russian Uplands
Europe
Carpathians
Danube
Adriatic Sea
Black Sea

Narodnaya 1894
Ural Mts.
Ob
Yenisey
West Siberian Plain
Siberian Plain
Irtysh
Angara
Lower Tunguska
Verhoyansk Ra.
Lena
Aldan
Cherski Ra.
Kolyma Ra.
Bering Sea
Kamchatka
Klyuchevskaya 4750
Aleutian Is.
-7822 Aleutian Trench

A S I A
Sayan Mts.
Altai
Baikal
Stanovoy Ra.
Amur
Sea of Okhotsk
Sakhalin
Kuril Is.
-10542 Kuril Trench
Hokkaido

Anatolia
Elbrus 5642
Caspian Sea
-28
Aral Sea
Syrdarya
Amudarya
L. Balkhash
Tian Shan
Tarim Basin
Gobi Desert
Manchuria
Hwang
Yellow Sea
Sea of Japan
Korea
Japan
Mt Fuji 3776
Shikoku
Kyushu
Ryukyu Is.
Japan Trench -10554

Mediterranean Sea
Mt Ararat 5165
Zagros
Elburz Mts. 5604
5496 4538
Hindu Kush
K2 8611
Karakoram
Pamirs
Kunlun Shan
Plateau of Tibet
Qilian Shan
China
East China Sea
Taiwan

Middle East
Dead Sea -411
Isthmus of Suez
The Gulf
Himalaya
Mt Everest 8850
Gongga Shan 7556
Yangtze
Si

Libyan Desert
Arabia
Red Sea
Rub' al Khali
-156
Arabian Sea
Ganges
Thar Desert
Indus
Deccan
W. Ghats
E. Ghats
India
Bay of Bengal
Andaman Is.
Isthmus of Kra
G. of Thailand
Indo-China
Hainan
Mekong
South China Sea
Luzon
Philippine Is.

Tibesti
Africa
L. Chad
Blue Nile
White Nile
Ethiopian Highlands
G. of Aden
Socotra
C. Guardafui
Somali Peninsula
Ceylon
C. Comorin
Nicobar Is.
Maldives
Malay Pen.
Sumatra
Sunda Is.
Borneo
Sulu Sea
Mindanao
Celebes Sea
Kinabalu 4101
Celebes
Moluccas
Banda Sea
Puncak Jaya 5029
New Guinea
Bismarck Arch.
New Britain
Solomon Is.

Rift Valley
Ruwenzori 5105
Mt Kenya 5199
Lake Victoria
Kilimanjaro 5895
L. Turkana
L. Tanganyika
L. Malawi
Zambezi
Congo Basin
Kasai
Comoros
Madagascar
Seychelles
Pic Boby 2658
Mauritius
Réunion
Rodriguez

INDIAN OCEAN
Java Sea
Java
-7450 Java Trench
Timor
Timor Sea
Arafura Sea
Torres Str.
C. York
PACIFIC OCEAN
Mariana Is.
Wake
Guam
Mariana Trench -11022
Caroline Is.
Belau
Micronesia
Melanesia
Nauru
Gilbert Is.
Phoenix Is.
Ellice Is.
Tokelau Is.
Samoa Is.
New Hebrides
Fiji Is.
Tonga Is.
-10822

Kalahari Desert
Namib Desert
Orange
Limpopo
Drakensberg
Cape of Good Hope
Mozambique Chan.

Cocos Is.
OCEAN
Amsterdam I.

Kimberley Plateau
Hamersley Ra.
Tanami Desert
MacDonnell Ra.
Coral Sea
New Caledonia
Great Barrier Reef
Cape York Pen.
Arnhem Land
Australia
Great Victoria Desert
L. Eyre -16
Nullarbor Plain
Great Australian Bight
C. Leeuwin
Murray
Darling
Great Dividing Ra.
Mt Kosciuszko 2237
Bass Str.
Tasmania
Tasman Sea
North I.
South I.
Aoraki Mt Cook 3753
New Zealand
Chatham Is.
Kermadec Is. -10047

Prince Edward Is.
Crozet Is.
Kerguelen
Heard I.
SOUTHERN OCEAN
Auckland Is.
Macquarie Is.

South Magnetic Pole
Amery Ice Shelf
Enderby Land
Queen Mary Coast
Wilkes Land
Victoria Land
Balleny Is.
Ross Sea
Mt Erebus 3743
Maud Land
Antarctica

East from Greenwich
11 12 13 14 15 16 17 18 19 20
20 40 60 80 100 120 140 160 180
80 60 40 20 0 20 40 60 80

Cross-section:
EUROPE ASIA PACIFIC OCEAN
Mt Blanc 4807
Tyrrhenian Sea
Apennines
Balkan Peninsula
Ægean Sea
Anatolia
Caucasus
Elbrus 5642
Caspian Sea
Pamirs
K2 8611
Tian Shan
Tarim Basin
Qilian Shan
Mt Everest 8850
Gongga Shan 7556
Yellow Sea
Korea
Sea of Japan
Honshū
Japan Trench
Emperor Seamount Chain
40°N
EURASIAN PLATE
B

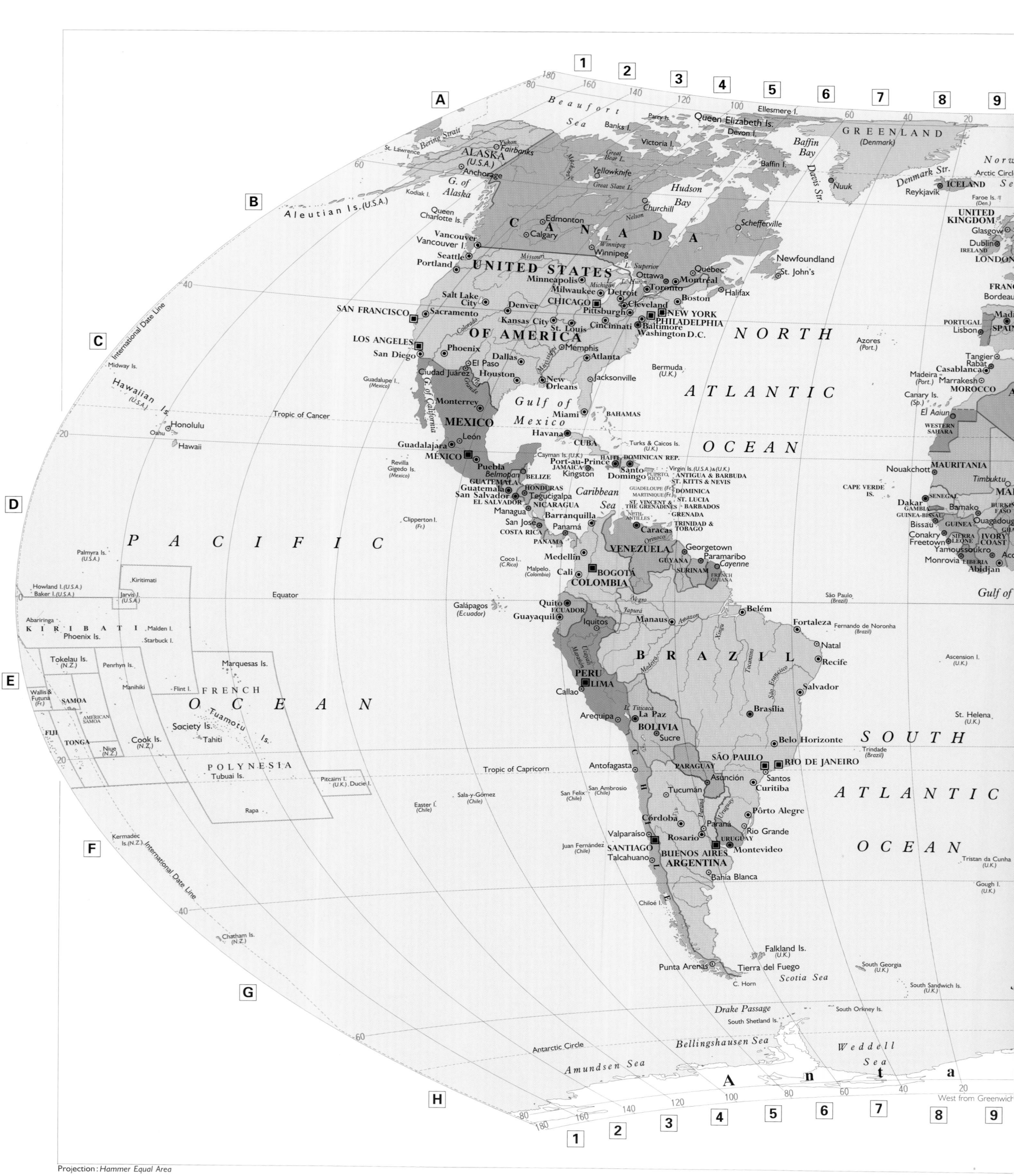

Projection: Hammer Equal Area

COPYRIGHT GEORGE PHILIP LTD.

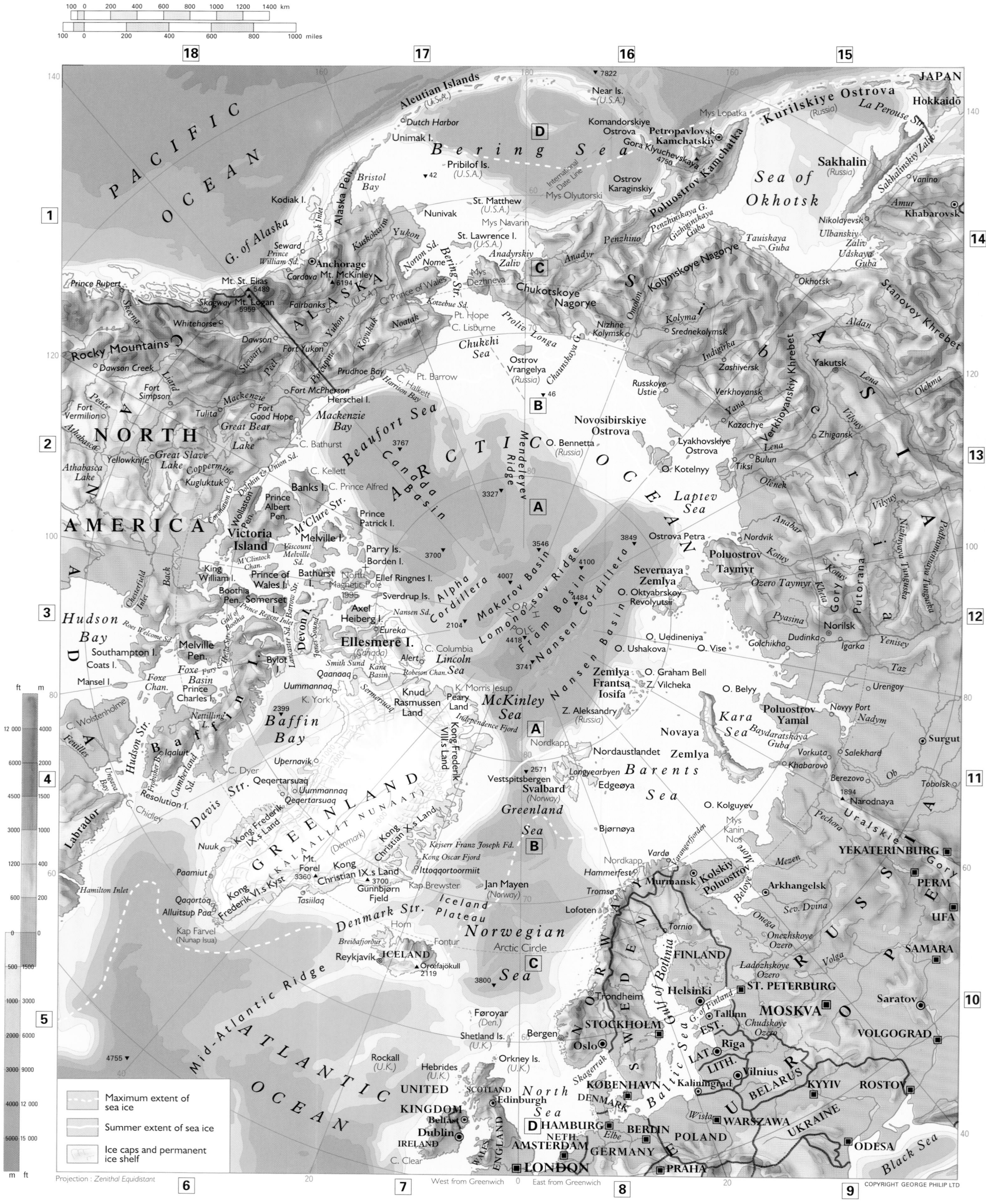

Projection : Zenithal Equidistant

West from Greenwich   East from Greenwich

COPYRIGHT GEORGE PHILIP LTD

Maximum extent of sea ice

Summer extent of sea ice

Ice caps and permanent ice shelf

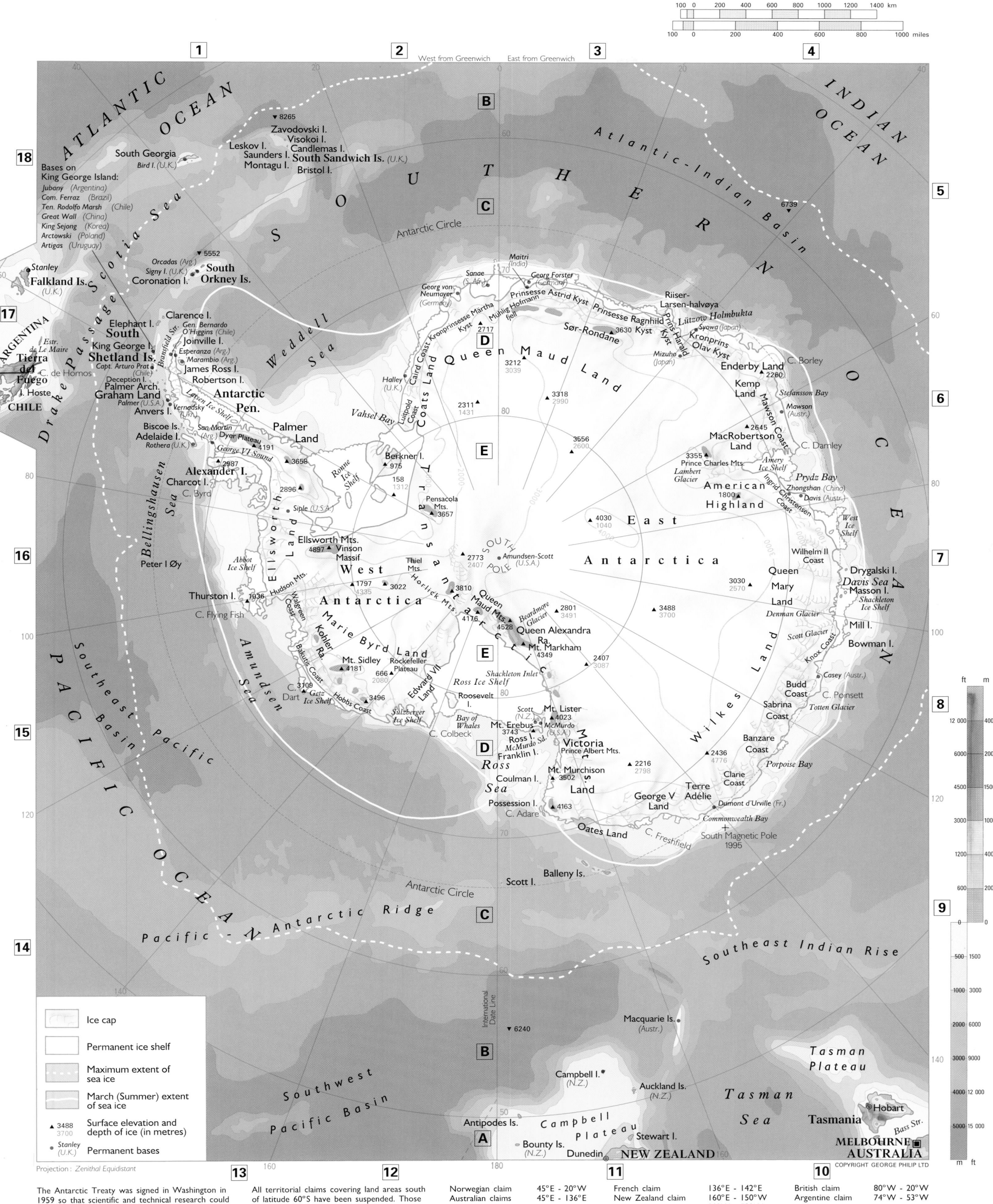

100 0 200 400 600 800 1000 1200 1400 km
100 0 200 400 600 800 1000 miles

1 **2** West from Greenwich East from Greenwich **3** **4**

ATLANTIC OCEAN

18

▲ 8265
Zavodovski I.
Visokoi I.
Leskov I. Candlemas I.
Saunders I. **South Sandwich Is.** (U.K.)
Montagu I. Bristol I.

B

INDIAN OCEAN

Bird I. (U.K.)
South Georgia

Bases on
King George Island:
Jubany (Argentina)
Com. Ferraz (Brazil)
Ten. Rodolfo Marsh (Chile)
Great Wall (China)
King Sejong (Korea)
Arctowski (Poland)
Artigas (Uruguay)

Atlantic-Indian Basin

5

C

Antarctic Circle

▲ 6739

17

Stanley
Falkland Is.
(U.K.)

▲ 5552
Orcadas (Arg.)
Signy I. (U.K.) **South**
Coronation I. **Orkney Is.**

Maitri
(India)
Sanae
(S. Afr.) Georg Forster
Georg von (Germany)
Neumayer
(Germany) Prinsesse Astrid Kyst
Prinsesse Martha Riiser-
Kronprinsesse Larsen-halvøya
Mühlig Hofmann Prinsesse Ragnhild Kyst Lützow Holmbukta
fjell Sør-Rondane Prins Harald Kyst Syowa (Japan)
Kronprins
Mizuho Olav Kyst
(Japan) **Enderby Land** C. Borley

Clarence I.
Gen. Bernardo
O'Higgins (Chile)
South Joinville I.
Shetland Is. Esperanza (Arg.)
Marambio (Arg.)
Capt. Arturo Prat James Ross I.
(Chile) Robertson I.
Deception I.

D

Queen Maud Land

▲ 3212
3039

▲ 3318
2990

Kemp
Land ▲ 2260

Stefansson Bay

Mawson
(Austr.)

6

ARGENTINA

Estr.
de le Maire
Tierra
del Fuego
J. Hoste C. de Hornos

CHILE

Elephant I.
King George I.
South

Palmer (U.S.A.)
Vernadsky
(U.K.)
Graham Land
Anvers I.

Halley
(U.K.)

Larsen Ice Shelf
Vahsel Bay

Caird Coast
Coats Land
Luitpold
Coast

▲ 2311
1431

▲ 3656
2600

MacRobertson
Land ▲ 2645

Prince Charles Mts.
Amery
Ice Shelf
Lambert
Glacier

C. Darnley

Drake Passage

Biscoe Is.
Adelaide I.
Rothera (U.K.)

San Martin
(Arg.) Dyer Plateau
Palmer
Land

Weddell
Sea

Berkner I.
▲ 975
158
1312

Ronne
Ice
Shelf

Pensacola
Mts.
▲ 3657

▲ 3355
1800

American

Highland

Prydz Bay
Zhongshan (China)
Davis (Austr.)
Ingrid Christensen Coast

80

Charcot I.
▲ 2987
C. Byrd

▲ 3658

Alexander I.

▲ 2896

Siple (U.S.A.)

▲ 2773
2407

▲ 3030
2570

Queen
Mary
Land

West Ice
Shelf

Wilhelm II
Coast

Drygalski I.

Davis Sea
Masson I.
Shackleton
Ice Shelf

7

16

Peter I Øy

Bellingshausen
Sea

Hudson Mts.

Ellsworth Land

Abbot
Ice Shelf

Ellsworth Mts.
4897 ▲ Vinson
Massif

South
Pole
Amundsen-Scott
(U.S.A.)

East

Antarctica

▲ 4030
1040

Denman Glacier
Scott Glacier
Knox Coast

Mill I.

Bowman I.

Thurston I.
▲ 1936

C. Flying Fish

Thiel
Mts.

Horlick Mts.

West
Antarctica

3022

▲ 3810

Queen
Maud Mts.

4176 ▲

Beardmore ▲ 2801
Glacier 3491

▲ 3488
3700

▲ 2407
3087

Casey (Austr.)
C. Poinsett
Totten Glacier

8

15

PACIFIC OCEAN

Walgreen
Coast
Bakutis Coast

Mt. Sidley
▲ 4181

Marie Byrd Land

1797
Rockefeller
666 Plateau
2080

4528 Queen Alexandra
Ra.
Mt. Markham
▲ 4349

Shackleton Inlet

Budd
Coast

Sabrina
Coast

Banzare
Coast
▲ 2436
4776

Southeast Pacific Basin

Kohler
Ra.

Dart
C. 3709

Getz
Ice Shelf Hobbs Coast

Edward VII
Land

Ross Ice Shelf

▲ 2216
2798

Clarie
Coast

Porpoise Bay

Amundsen
Sea

3496

Salzberger
Ice Shelf

Roosevelt
I.

80

Victoria

Terre
Adélie

9

14

Bay of
Whales

Scott
(N.Z.)
C. Colbeck

Mt. Erebus
Ross 3743
(U.S.A.)
Franklin I. McMurdo Sd.
McMurdo
(U.S.A.)

Mt. Lister
▲ 4023

Prince Albert Mts.

George V
Land

Dumont d'Urville (Fr.)

+
Commonwealth Bay
South Magnetic Pole
1995

Ross
Sea

Coulman I.
Possession I.
C. Adare

Mt. Murchison
▲ 3502

▲ 4163

Oates Land

C. Freshfield

Antarctic Circle

Scott I.

Balleny Is.

Southeast Indian Rise

C

Pacific-Antarctic Ridge

Macquarie Is.
(Austr.)

Tasman
Plateau

B

▼ 6240

Campbell I.•
(N.Z.) Auckland Is.
(N.Z.)

Tasman
Sea

Tasmania

•Hobart

Bass Str.

Southwest
Pacific Basin

Antipodes Is.

A Campbell
Plateau

Bounty Is.
(N.Z.) Stewart I.
Dunedin○ **NEW ZEALAND**

MELBOURNE
AUSTRALIA

COPYRIGHT GEORGE PHILIP LTD

ft m

12 000 4000

6000 2000

4500 1500

3000 1000

1200 400

600 200

0 0

500 1500
1000 3000
2000 6000
3000 9000
4000 12 000
5000 15 000

m ft

Ice cap

Permanent ice shelf

Maximum extent of
sea ice

March (Summer) extent
of sea ice

▲3488 Surface elevation and
3700 depth of ice (in metres)

• *Stanley*
(U.K.) Permanent bases

Projection : *Zenithal Equidistant*

13 160 **12** 180 **11** 160 **10**

The Antarctic Treaty was signed in Washington
in 1959 so that scientific and technical research could
continue unhampered by international politics.

All territorial claims covering land areas south
of latitude 60°S have been suspended. Those
claims were:

Norwegian claim 45°E - 20°W
Australian claims 45°E - 136°E
142°E - 160°E

French claim 136°E - 142°E
New Zealand claim 160°E - 150°W
Chilean claim 90°W - 53°W

British claim 80°W - 20°W
Argentine claim 74°W - 53°W

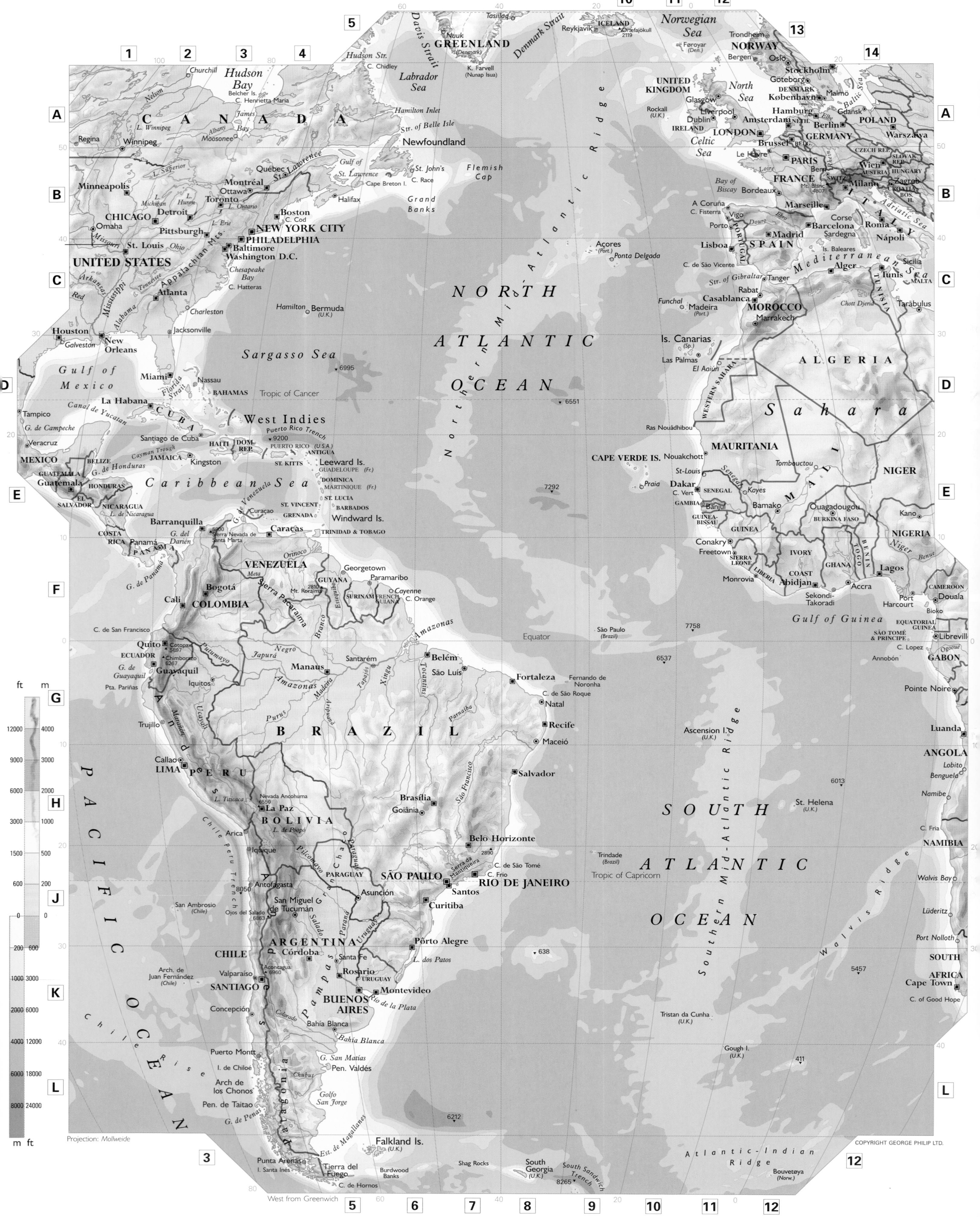

Grid references (top): 1 2 3 4 5 10 11 12 13 14

Grid references (sides): A B C D E F G H J K L

GREENLAND (Denmark)
Tasiilaq
Nuuk
K. Farvell (Nunap Isua)
C. Chidley
Hudson Str.
Davis Strait
Denmark Strait
Reykjavik
ICELAND
Öræfajökull 2119
Norwegian Sea
Føroyar (Den.)
Trondheim
NORWAY
Bergen
Oslo
Stockholm
Göteborg
Malmö
DENMARK
København
Gdańsk
POLAND
Warszawa

Churchill
Hudson Bay
Belcher Is.
James Bay
L. Henrietta Maria
Moosonee
Nelson
L. Winnipeg
CANADA
Regina
Winnipeg
Labrador Sea
Hamilton Inlet
Str. of Belle Isle
Newfoundland
Grand Banks
Flemish Cap
Northern Mid-Atlantic Ridge
UNITED KINGDOM
Rockall (U.K.)
Glasgow
Liverpool
Dublin
IRELAND
LONDON
Celtic Sea
North Sea
Amsterdam NETH.
Hamburg
Berlin
GERMANY
Brussel BELG.
CZECH REP.
SLOVAK REP.
HUNGARY
AUSTRIA
Wien
Mt. Blanc 4807
Zagreb
CROATIA
BOS. H.
Adriatic Sea

Minneapolis
CHICAGO
Detroit
L. Superior
L. Michigan
L. Huron
L. Erie
L. Ontario
Québec
Montréal
Ottawa
Toronto
St. Lawrence
Gulf of St. Lawrence
C. Breton I.
C. Race
St. John's
Halifax
Omaha
St. Louis
Missouri
Pittsburgh
BOSTON
C. Cod
NEW YORK CITY
PHILADELPHIA
Baltimore
Washington D.C.
UNITED STATES
Appalachian Mts.
Atlanta
Tennessee
Charleston
Chesapeake Bay
C. Hatteras
Bay of Biscay
Bordeaux
FRANCE
PARIS
Le Havre
Loire
A Coruña
C. Fisterra
Vigo
Porto
PORTUGAL
Doura
Lisboa
Madrid
SPAIN
Barcelona
Is. Baleares
Marseille
Corse
Sardegna
Roma
ITALY
Napoli
Milano
Bern

Houston
Galveston
New Orleans
Arkansas
Red
Mississippi
Alabama
Jacksonville
Bermuda (U.K.)
Hamilton
NORTH ATLANTIC OCEAN
6995
Açores (Port.)
Ponta Delgada
C. de São Vicente
Str. of Gibraltar
Tanger
Funchal
Madeira (Port.)
Casablanca
Rabat
MOROCCO
Marrakech
Alger
Tunis
TUNISIA
MALTA
Sicilia
Tarābulus
Mediterranean Sea

Gulf of Mexico
Miami
Florida Strait
Nassau
BAHAMAS
Tropic of Cancer
6551
Is. Canarias
Las Palmas
El Aaiún
WESTERN SAHARA
Sahara
ALGERIA

Tampico
G. de Campeche
Veracruz
MEXICO
Canal de Yucatán
La Habana
CUBA
Santiago de Cuba
West Indies
HAITI
DOM. REP.
PUERTO RICO (U.S.A.)
Puerto Rico Trench 9200
ANTIGUA
ST. KITTS
Leeward Is.
GUADELOUPE (Fr.)
DOMINICA
MARTINIQUE (Fr.)
ST. LUCIA
BARBADOS
ST. VINCENT
GRENADA
Windward Is.
7292
Ras Nouâdhibou
MAURITANIA
Nouadhibou
Nouakchott
CAPE VERDE IS.
St-Louis
Dakar
C. Vert
Praia
SENEGAL
GAMBIA
Banjul
GUINEA-BISSAU
MALI
Tombouctou
NIGER
Kayes
Bamako
Ouagadougou
BURKINA FASO
Kano
NIGERIA

BELIZE
GUATEMALA
G. de Honduras
JAMAICA
Kingston
Cayman Trough
HONDURAS
EL SALVADOR
NICARAGUA
L. de Nicaragua
COSTA RICA
Panamá
PANAMA
G. de Panamá
Caribbean Sea
Barranquilla
Sierra Nevada de Santa Marta
Curaçao
Venezuela
Caracas
TRINIDAD & TOBAGO
VENEZUELA
Orinoco
Georgetown
Paramaribo
GUYANA
SURINAM
FRENCH GUIANA
Cayenne
C. Orange
Mt. Roraima 2810
Sierra Pacaraima
CONAKRY
Freetown
SIERRA LEONE
GUINEA
LIBERIA
Monrovia
IVORY COAST
Abidjan
GHANA
Accra
Sekondi-Takoradi
TOGO
BENIN
Lagos
Port Harcourt
CAMEROON
Douala
Bioko
EQUATORIAL GUINEA
SÃO TOMÉ & PRÍNCIPE
C. Lopez
Libreville
GABON

Bogotá
Cali
COLOMBIA
C. de San Francisco
Quito
Cotopaxi 5897
ECUADOR
Chimborazo 6267
G. de Guayaquil
Guayaquil
Iquitos
Pta. Pariñas
Trujillo
Meta
Branco
Amazonas
Manaus
Santarém
Belém
São Luís
Fortaleza
Fernando de Noronha
C. de São Roque
Natal
7758
Annobón
Ogooué
6537
Equator
São Paulo (Brazil)
Gulf of Guinea

PACIFIC OCEAN
Negro
Japurá
Putumayo
Maranon
Ucayali
Purus
Madeira
Tapajós
Xingu
Tocantins
BRAZIL
Amazonas
Recife
Maceió
Ascension I. (U.K.)
Luanda
Pointe Noire
ANGOLA
Lobito
Benguela
Namibe
6013
St. Helena (U.K.)
Southern Mid-Atlantic Ridge

Callao
LIMA
PERU
L. Titicaca
Nevada Ancohuma 6550
La Paz
BOLIVIA
L. de Poopó
Arica
Iquique
Salvador
Brasília
Goiânia
São Francisco
Belo Horizonte
2890
C. de São Tomé
C. Frio
SOUTH ATLANTIC OCEAN
Trindade (Brazil)
Tropic of Capricorn
NAMIBIA
C. Fria
Walvis Bay
Walvis Ridge
Lüderitz

Antofagasta
8050
San Ambrosio (Chile)
Ojos del Salado 6863
San Miguel de Tucumán
PARAGUAY
Asunción
SÃO PAULO
Santos
Curitiba
Sierra da Mantiqueira
RIO DE JANEIRO
Port Nolloth
5457
SOUTH AFRICA
Cape Town
C. of Good Hope

Arch. de Juan Fernández (Chile)
Valparaíso
SANTIAGO
CHILE
Aconcagua 6960
Córdoba
ARGENTINA
Santa Fe
Rosario
URUGUAY
Montevideo
Pôrto Alegre
L. dos Patos
Río de la Plata
BUENOS AIRES
638
Tristan da Cunha (U.K.)
Chile Peru Trench

Concepción
Colorado
Pampas
Bahía Blanca
Bahía Blanca
Pen. Valdés
G. San Matías
Chubut
Golfo San Jorge
Puerto Montt
I. de Chiloé
Arch. de los Chonos
Pen. de Taitao
G. de Penas
6212
Gough I. (U.K.)
411

Punta Arenas
I. Santa Inés
Tierra del Fuego
C. de Hornos
Est. de Magallanes
Falkland Is. (U.K.)
Burdwood Banks
Shag Rocks
South Georgia (U.K.)
South Sandwich Trench 8265
Atlantic-Indian Ridge
Bouvetøya (Norw.)

Elevation scale
ft / m
12000 / 4000
9000 / 3000
6000 / 2000
3000 / 1000
1500 / 500
600 / 200
0
200 / 600
1000 / 3000
2000 / 6000
4000 / 12000
6000 / 18000
8000 / 24000
m ft

Projection: Mollweide

COPYRIGHT GEORGE PHILIP LTD.

West from Greenwich

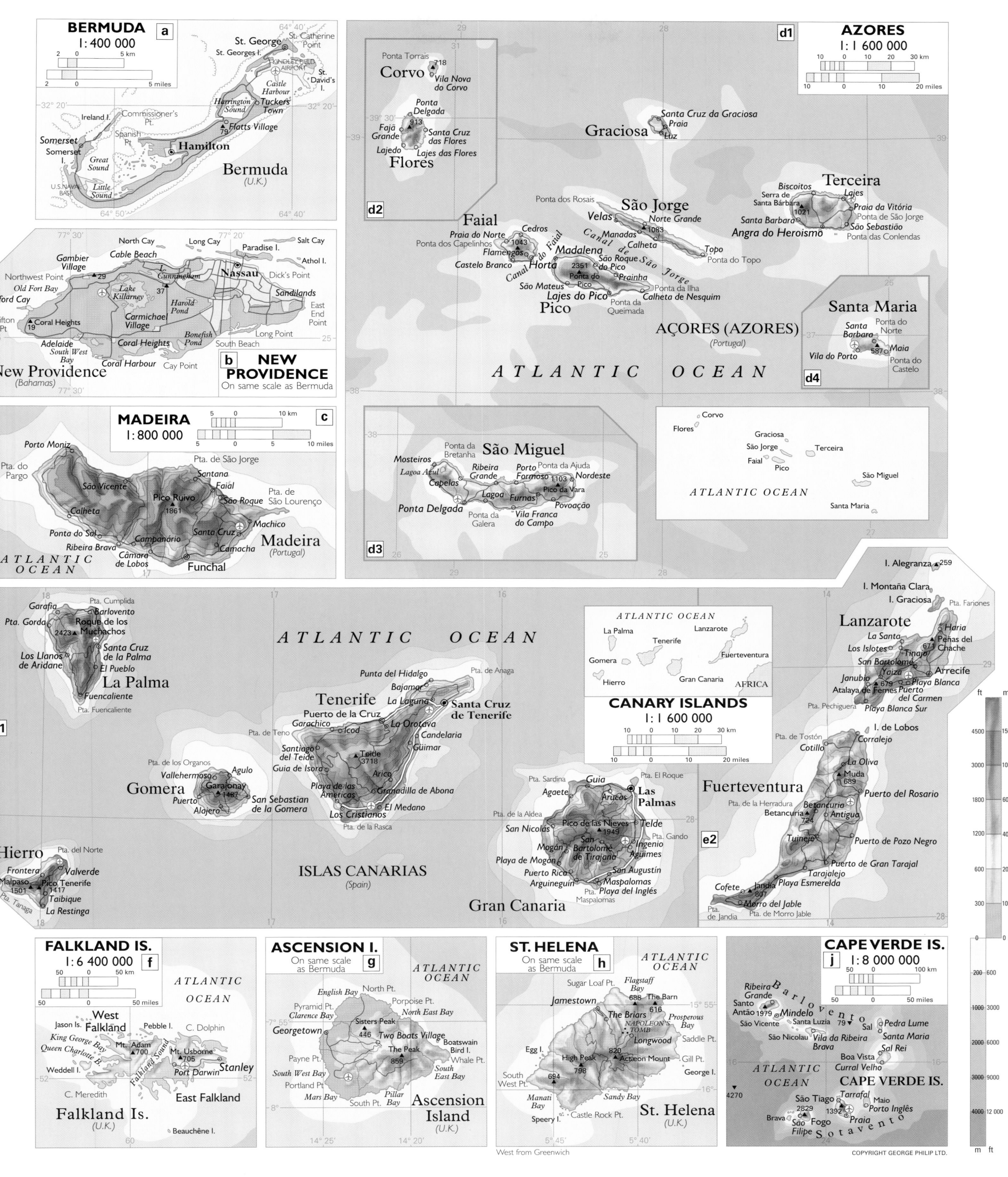

BERMUDA
1:400 000

St. George
St. Georges I.
St. Catherine Point
KINDLEY FIELD AIRPORT
St. David's I.
Castle Harbour
Harrington Sound
Tuckers Town
Flatts Village
Commissioner's Pt.
Ireland I.
Spanish Pt.
Somerset
Somerset I.
Great Sound
Hamilton
Little Sound
U.S. NAVAL BASE
Bermuda
(U.K.)

NEW PROVIDENCE
On same scale as Bermuda

North Cay
Long Cay
Paradise I.
Salt Cay
Gambier Village
Cable Beach
Athol I.
Northwest Point
Nassau
Dick's Point
Old Fort Bay
ford Cay
Cunningham
Lake Killarney
Clifton Pt.
Coral Heights
Harold Pond
Carmichael Village
Sandilands
East End Point
Adelaide
South West Bay
Coral Heights
Bonefish Pond
Long Point
Coral Harbour
Cay Point
South Beach
New Providence
(Bahamas)

MADEIRA
1:800 000

Porto Moniz
Pta. de São Jorge
Pta. do Pargo
São Vicente
Santana
Faial
São Roque
Pta. de São Lourenço
Calheta
Pico Ruivo 1861
Machico
Ponta do Sol
Campanário
Santa Cruz
Ribeira Brava
Câmara de Lobos
Camacha
Madeira
(Portugal)
Funchal
ATLANTIC OCEAN

AZORES
1:1 600 000

Corvo
Ponta Torrais 718
Vila Nova do Corvo
Ponta Delgada
Santa Cruz da Graciosa
Praia
Graciosa
Luz
Fajã Grande 913
Santa Cruz das Flores
Flores
Lajedo
Lajes das Flores
Ponta dos Rosais
São Jorge
Norte Grande 1083
Terceira
Biscoitos
Serra de Santa Bárbara 1021
Lajes
Velas
Manadas
Calheta
Praia da Vitória
Santa Barbara
Ponta de São Jorge
São Sebastião
Faial
Cedros
Ponta dos Capelinhos 1043
Flamengos
Madalena
Angra do Heroísmo
Ponta das Conlendas
Horta
Castelo Branco
São Roque do Pico
Topo
Ponta do Topo
2351
Prainha
São Mateus
Ponta do Pico
Lajes do Pico
Calheta de Nesquim
Pico
Ponta da Ilha
Ponta da Queimada
AÇORES (AZORES)
(Portugal)
ATLANTIC OCEAN
Santa Maria
Santa Barbara
Ponta do Norte
587
Maia
Vila do Porto
Ponta do Castelo

São Miguel
Mosteiros
Ponta da Bretanha
Ribeira Grande
Porto Formoso
Ponta da Ajuda
Nordeste
Lagoa Azul
Capelas
1103
Pico da Vara
Lagoa
Furnas
Ponta Delgada
Povoação
Ponta da Galera
Vila Franca do Campo

Corvo
Flores
Graciosa
São Jorge
Terceira
Faial
Pico
São Miguel
ATLANTIC OCEAN
Santa Maria

CANARY ISLANDS
1:1 600 000

ATLANTIC OCEAN
La Palma
Tenerife
Lanzarote
Gomera
Fuerteventura
Hierro
Gran Canaria
AFRICA

ATLANTIC OCEAN

Garafia
Pta. Cumplida
Barlovento
Pta. Gorda
Roque de los Muchachos 2423
Santa Cruz de la Palma
Los Llanos de Aridane
El Pueblo
La Palma
Fuencaliente
Pta. Fuencaliente

I. Alegranza 259
I. Montaña Clara
I. Graciosa
Pta. Fariones
Lanzarote
Haria
La Santa
Peñas del Chache 671
Los Islotes
Tinajo
San Bartolomé
Yaiza
Arrecife
Janubio 679
Atalaya de Femes
Playa Blanca
Puerto del Carmen
Pta. Pechiguera
Playa Blanca Sur

Punta del Hidalgo
Pta. de Anaga
Bajamar
Tenerife
La Laguna
Santa Cruz de Tenerife
Garachico
Puerto de la Cruz
Icod
La Orotava
Santiago del Teide
Teide 3718
Candelaria
Güimar
Pta. de Teno
Guia de Isora
Arico
Pta. de los Organos
Playa de las Américas
Granadilla de Abona
Vallehermoso
Agulo
El Medano
Gomera
Garajonay 1487
Pta. de la Rasca
Puerto
San Sebastian de la Gomera
Alajero

I. de Lobos
Corralejo
Cotillo
La Oliva
Pta. de Tostón
Muda 689
Fuerteventura
Puerto del Rosario
Pta. Sardina
Guia
Pta. El Roque
Agaete
Arucas
Las Palmas
Pta. de la Herradura
Betancuria
Betancuria 724
Antigua
San Nicolas
Pico de las Nieves 1949
Telde
Pta. Gando
Puerto de Pozo Negro
Mogán
San Bartolomé de Tirajana
Ingenio
Tuineje
Playa de Mogán
Agüimes
Tarajalejo
Puerto de Gran Tarajal
Puerto Rico
Maspalomas
Arguineguin
Playa del Inglés
Cofete
Jandia 807
Playa Esmerelda
Pta. de la Aldea
Maspalomas
Pta. de Jandia
Morro del Jable
Pta. de Morro Jable
Gran Canaria

Hierro
Frontera
Valverde
Malpaso
Pico Tenerife 1417
Taibique
Pta. Tanaga
La Restinga
Pta. del Norte
1501

ATLANTIC OCEAN

ISLAS CANARIAS
(Spain)

FALKLAND IS.
1:6 400 000

ATLANTIC OCEAN
West Falkland
Jason Is.
Pebble I.
C. Dolphin
King George Bay
Queen Charlotte B.
Mt. Adam 700
Mt. Usborne 705
Stanley
Weddell I.
Port Darwin
C. Meredith
East Falkland
Falkland Sound
Falkland Is.
(U.K.)
Beauchêne I.

ASCENSION I.
On same scale as Bermuda

ATLANTIC OCEAN
English Bay
North Pt.
Pyramid Pt.
Porpoise Pt.
Clarence Bay
North East Bay
Georgetown
Sisters Peak
Two Boats Village 446
Payne Pt.
The Peak 859
Boatswain Bird I.
South West Bay
South East Bay
Portland Pt.
Pillar Bay
Mars Bay
South Pt.
Ascension Island
(U.K.)

ST. HELENA
On same scale as Bermuda

ATLANTIC OCEAN
Sugar Loaf Pt.
Flagstaff Bay
Jamestown
The Barn 688
616
The Briars
Prosperous Bay
NAPOLEON'S TOMB
Longwood
Saddle Pt.
Egg I.
High Peak 820
Actaeon Mount
Gill Pt.
South West Pt.
798
694
George I.
Manati Bay
Sandy Bay
Speery I.
Castle Rock Pt.
St. Helena
(U.K.)

CAPE VERDE IS.
1:8 000 000

Ribeira Grande
Barlovento
Santo Antão 1979
Mindelo
São Vicente
Santa Luzia 79
Pedra Lume
Sal
Santa Maria
São Nicolau
Vila da Ribeira Brava
Sal Rei
Boa Vista
ATLANTIC OCEAN
Curral Velho
São Tiago 2829
Maio
Tarrafal
Porto Inglês
Brava
Sal 1392
Praia
São Filipe
Fogo
Sotavento
4270
CAPE VERDE IS.

West from Greenwich

COPYRIGHT GEORGE PHILIP LTD.

ft m
4500 1500
3000 1000
1800 600
1200 400
600 200
300 100
0 0
200 600
1000 3000
2000 6000
3000 9000
4000 12 000
m ft

100 0 100 200 300 400 500 km
100 0 50 100 150 200 250 300 350 miles

ARCTIC OCEAN

McKinley Sea

Nordaust-landet
Olgastredet
Nordkapp
Spitsbergen
Longyearbyen
Edgeøya
Barentsburg
Svalbard
(Norway)
Sørkapp
Storfjorden

GREENLAND SEA

Axel Heiberg I.
CANADA
Ellesmere Island
Lincoln Sea
Alert
Kap Morris Jesup
▲ 1920
Frederick E. Hyde Fjord
Nansen Land Peary Land
Robeson Chan.
Nyeboe Land
Wulff Land
J. P. Koch Fjord
Jørgen Brønlund Fjord
Heilprin Land
Independence Fjord
Station Nord
Nordostrundingen
Hall Land
Warming Land
Mylius Erichsen Land
Kronprins Christian Land
Ingolf Fjord
Mallemukfjeld

Kane Basin
Washington Land
Kronprins Frederik Land
Denmark Fjord
Hovgaard Ø
Nioghalvfjerdsfjorden
Norske Øer

Inglefield Land
Siorapaluk
Kap Kennedy Kanal
Knud Rasmussen Land
Lambert Land

Qaanaaq (Thule)
Qeqertarsuaq
▲ 2170
AVANNAARSUA) (NORDGRØNLAND)
Kong Frederik VIII.s Land
Franske Øer
Germania Land
Danmarkshavn

Jones Sd.
Devon Island
Kap Atholl
Uummannaq (Dundas)
Pituffik (Thule Air Base)
Kap York
Lauge Koch Kyst
Dove Bugt
Store Koldewey
Hochstetter Forland
Shannon

Melville Bugt
Steenstrup Gletscher
Dronning Margrethe II Land
Zackenberg
Wollaston Forland
Clavering Ø

Baffin Bay

Nuussuaq (Kraulshavn)
Nationalparken i Nord-og Østgrønland
Ole Rømer Land
Andrée Land
Kejserr Franz Joseph Fd.
Jan Mayen (Norway)

Clyde River
Upernavik
Kangersuatsiaq
Upernavik Kujalleq
▲ 2935
▲ 2940
Petermann Bjerg
Traill Ø
Mestersvig
Kong Oscar Fjord

Baffin I.
Nunavik
Illorsuit
Uummannaq
Maarmorilik
▲ 3220
KITAA (VESTGRØNLAND)
TUNU (ØSTGRØNLAND)
Stauning Alper
Renland
Jameson Land
Ittoqqortoormiut (Scoresbysund)

Qeqertarsuaq (Disko)
▲ 2092
Ikerasak
Saqqaq
Milne Land
Ittaajimmiut
Uunarteq
Kangerluk
Scoresby Sund
Kangikajik (Kap Brewster)

Qeqertarsuaq (Godhavn)
Disko Bugt
Ilulissat (Jakobshavn)
GREENLAND (KALAALLIT NUNAAT)
Kap Dalton
Aasiaat (Egedesminde)
Qasigiannguit (Christianshåb)
(Denmark)
IX.s Land

Kangaatsiaq
Ikamiut
Gunnbjørn Fjeld
▲ 3700
Blosseville Kyst
Arctic Circle

Nordre Strømfjord
Kong Frederik IX.s Land
Kangerdlugssuaq

Sisimiut (Holsteinsborg)
Kangerlussuaq (Søndre Strømfjord)
Hillea

Davis Strait
Søndre Strømfjord
Kangaamiut
Mt. Forel
▲ 3360
Kap Gustav Holm
Denmark Strait
Ísafjörður
Akureyri
Neskaupstaður
Eyjafjörður

Maniitsoq (Sukkertoppen)
Ikkatteq
Kuummiut
ICELAND
Vatnajökull
▲ 2119
Öræfajökull
Breidafjörður
Húnaflói

Nuuk (Godthåb)
Kapisillit
Isortoq
Kúlusuk
Tasiilaq (Ammassalik)
Dohrne Banke
Snæfellsnæs
Faxaflói
Reykjavík
Vestmannaeyjar
Heimaey
Surtsey

Dronning Ingrid Land
▲ 2850
Gyldenløve Fjord
Kap Møsting
Kap Moltke
Kap Skjold

Kangerluarsoruseq (Færingehavn)
Qeqertarsuatsiaat (Fiskenæsset)
Timmiarmiut
Mogens Heinesen Fjord
ATLANTIC OCEAN

Paamiut (Frederikshåb)
Narsalik
Kong Frederik VI.s Kyst

Kangilinnguit (Grønnedal)
Narsarsuaq
Arsuk
Narsaq
Ivittuut
Labrador Sea
Qaqortoq (Julianehåb)
Alluitsup Paa (Sydprøven)
Lindenow Fjord

Nanortalik
Nunap Isua (Kap Farvel)
Prins Christian Sund

ft m
3000 1000
1200 400
600 200
60 0
200 600
m ft

Projection: Conic
West from Greenwich
COPYRIGHT GEORGE PHILIP LTD.

Underlined towns give their name to the administrative area in which they stand.

10 0 10 20 30 40 50 60 70 80 100 km
10 0 10 20 30 40 50 60 miles

COPYRIGHT GEORGE PHILIP LTD.

Projection: Polyconic

West from Greenwich

NORWEGIAN SEA

ATLANTIC OCEAN

DENMARK STRAIT

ICELAND

Reykjavík

Vatnajökull

Arctic Circle

m 1000 400 200 100
ft 3000 1200 600 300

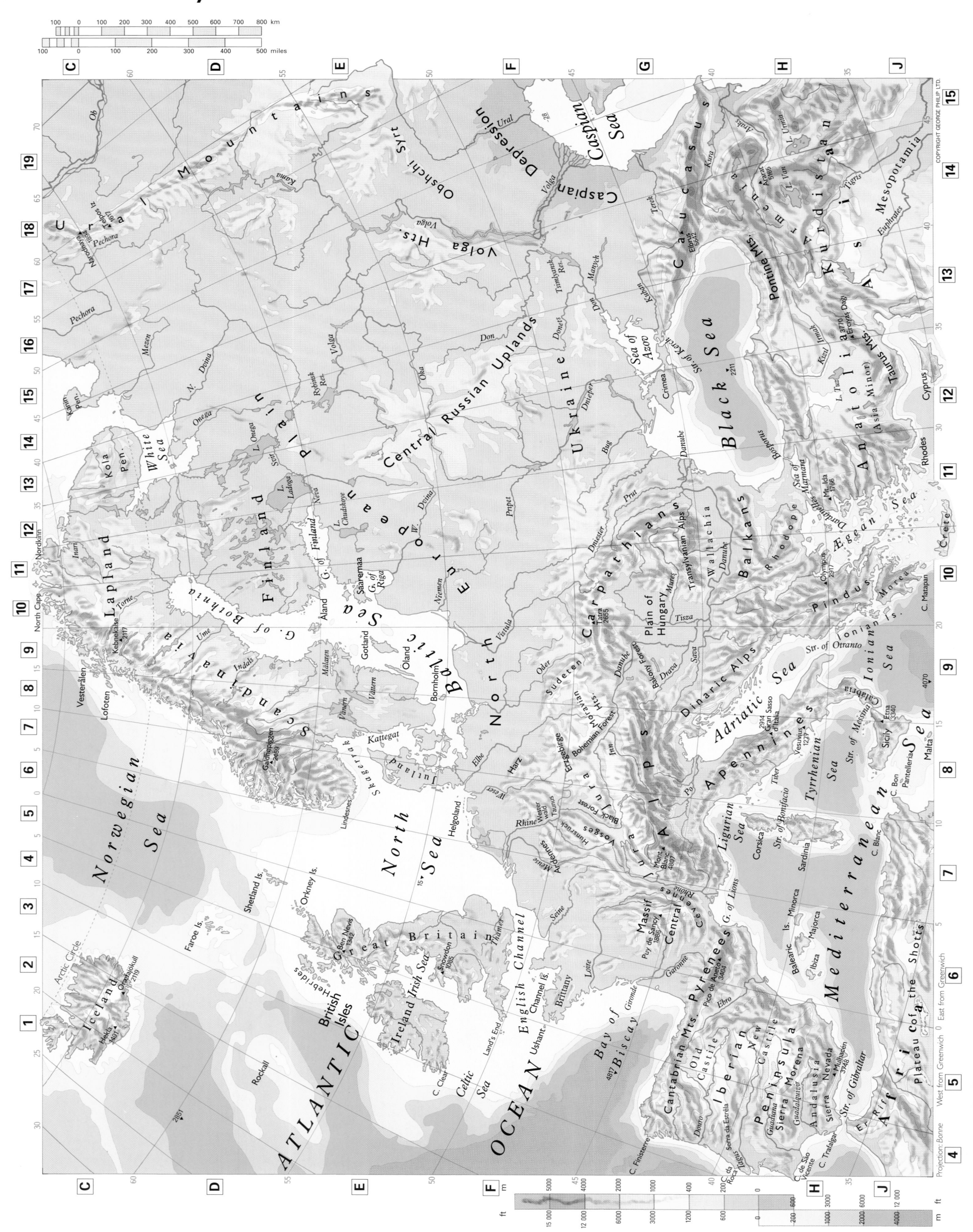

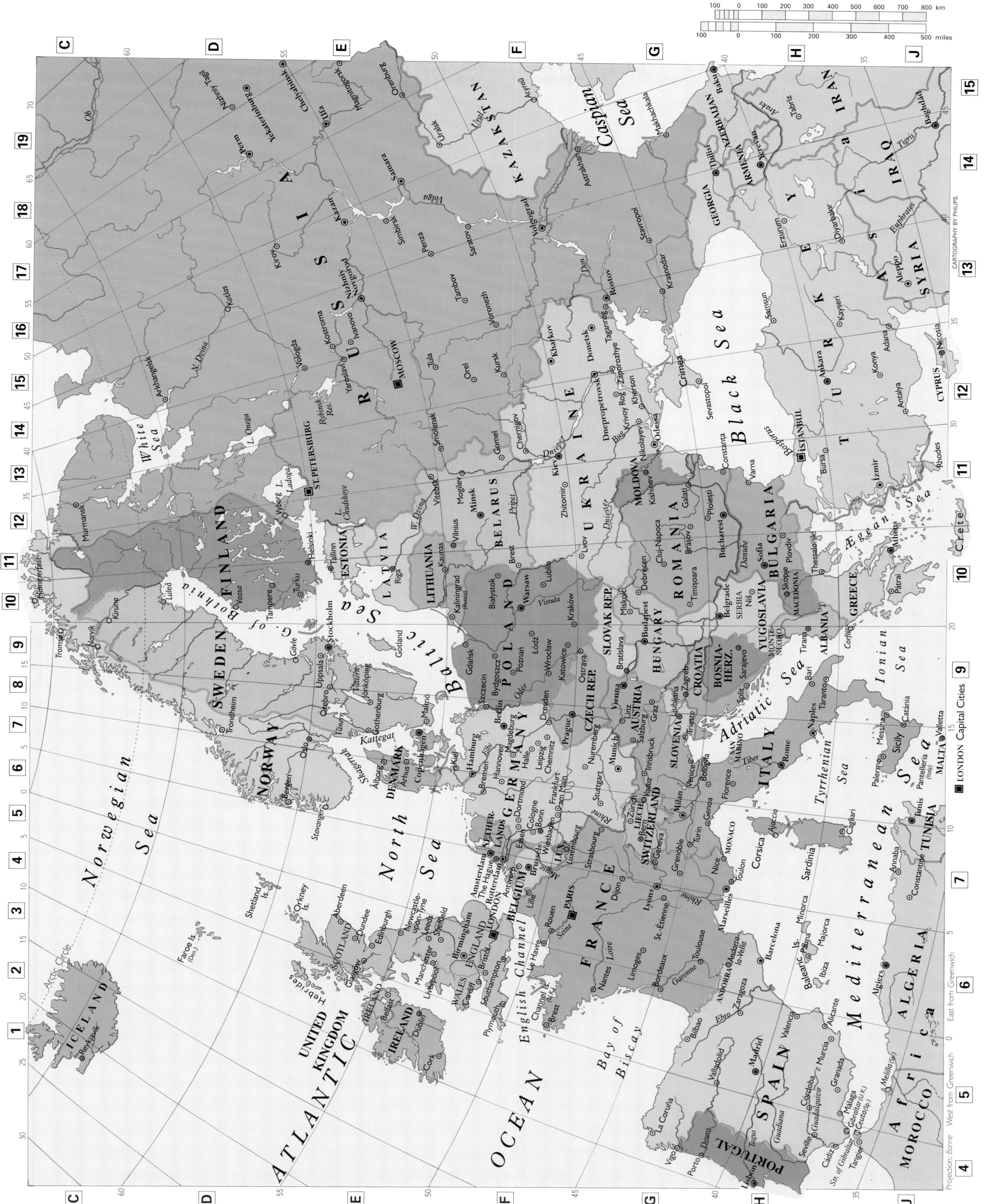

100   0   100   200   300   400   500   600   700   800 km
100   0   100   200   300   400   500 miles

CARTOGRAPHY BY PHILIP'S

Projection: Bonne

West from Greenwich   0   East from Greenwich

■ LONDON Capital Cities

SCANDINAVIA 1:4 000 000

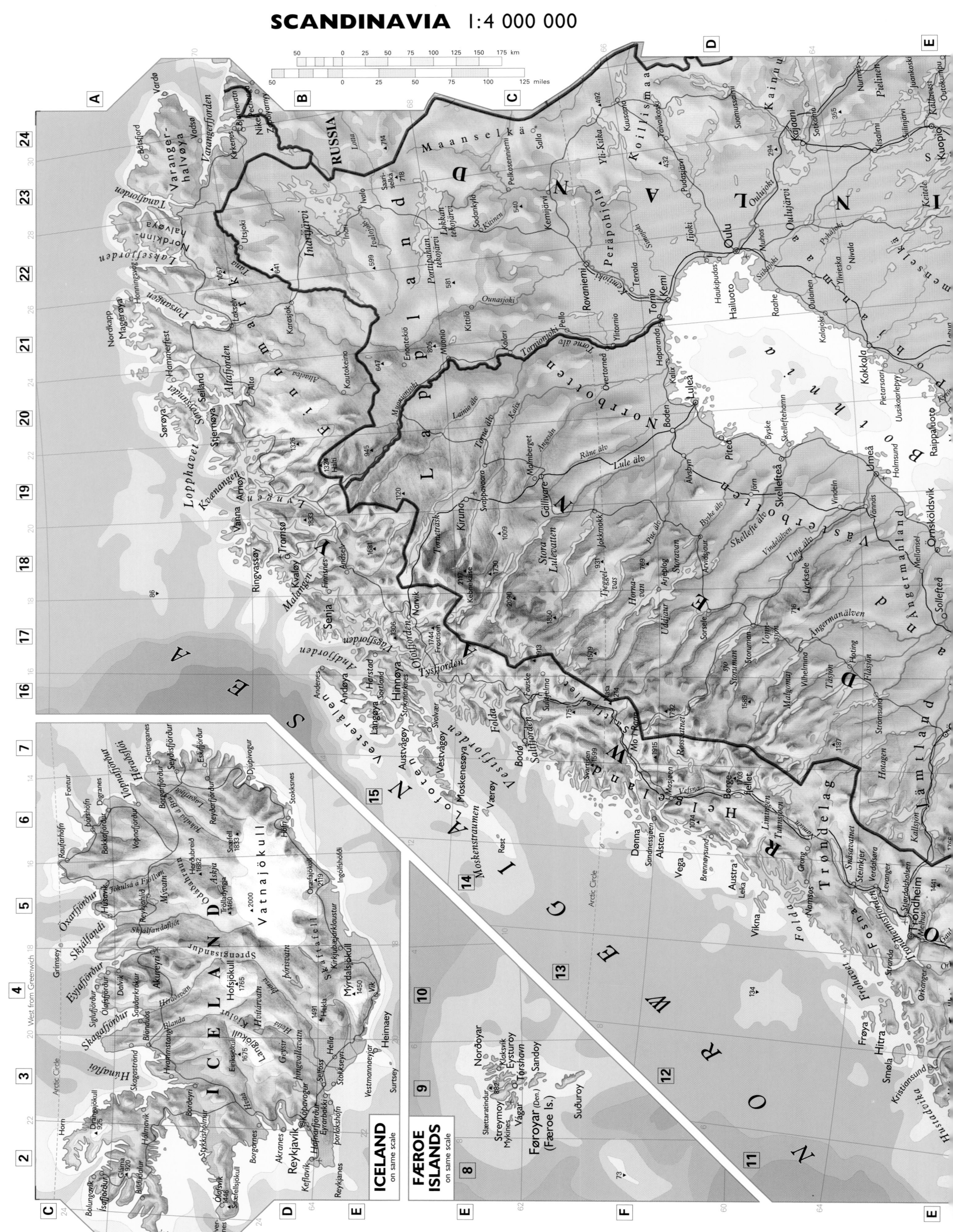

50   0   25 50 75 100 125 150 175 km

50   0   25   50   75   100 125 miles

RUSSIA

ICELAND
on same scale

FÆROE ISLANDS
on same scale

Føroyar (Den.)
(Færoe Is.)

15

COPYRIGHT GEORGE PHILIP LTD.

Projection: Conical with two standard parallels

East from Greenwich

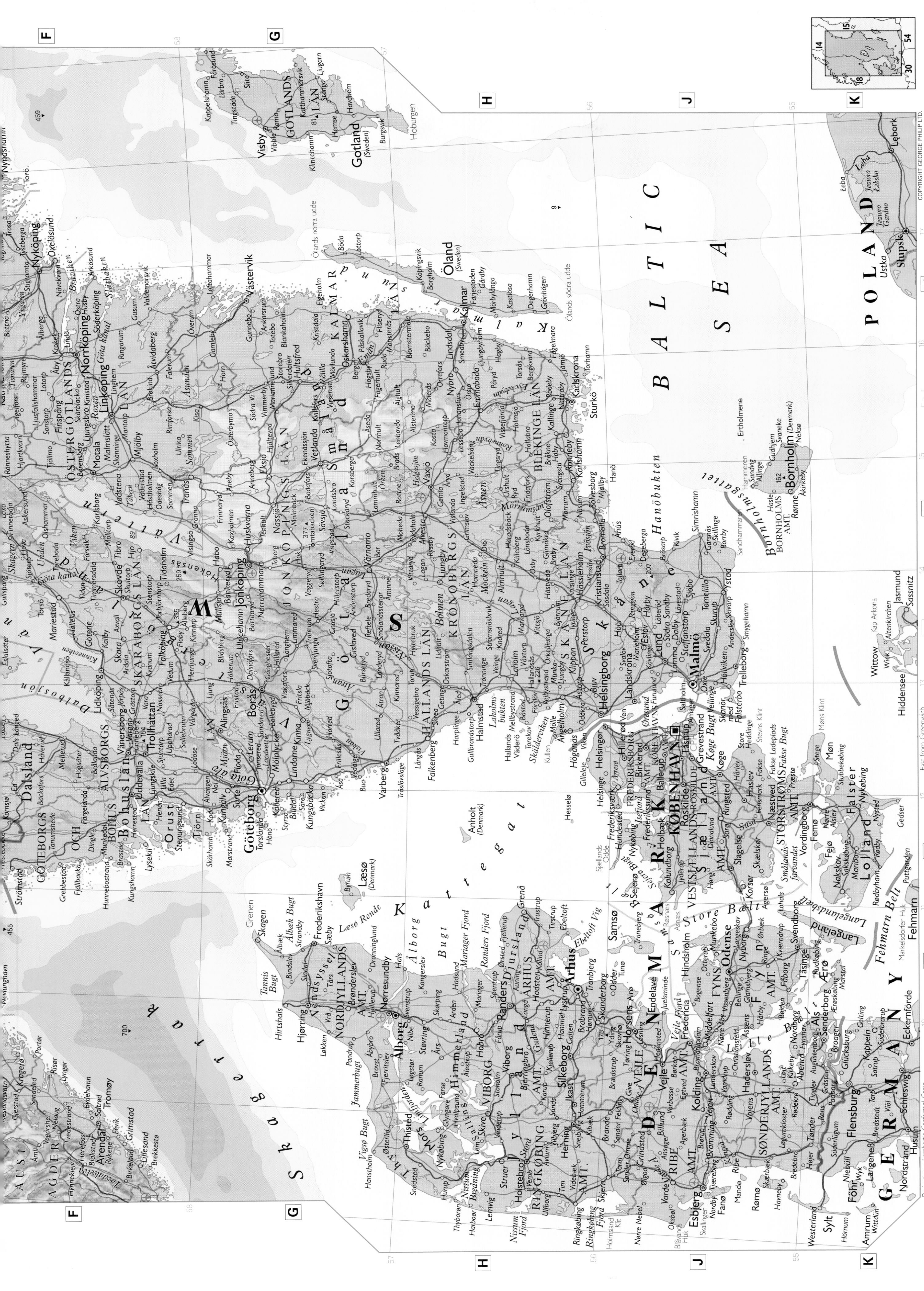

Map: Denmark and Southern Sweden

COPYRIGHT GEORGE PHILIP LTD.

Grid references: F G H J K

Sea / region labels:

BALTIC SEA

KATTEGAT

Skagerrak

Countries / regions:

POLAND

GERMANY

SWEDEN

DANMARK / DENMARK

AUST-AGDER

DALSLAND

BOHUSLÄN

VÄSTERGÖTLAND

GÖTEBORGS OCH BOHUS LÄN

ÄLVSBORGS LÄN

SKARABORGS LÄN

ÖSTERGÖTLANDS LÄN

JÖNKÖPINGS LÄN

KRONOBERGS LÄN

KALMAR LÄN

BLEKINGE LÄN

SKÅNE

HALLANDS LÄN

GOTLANDS LÄN

Gotland (Sweden)

Öland (Sweden)

Bornholm (Denmark)

BORNHOLMS AMT.

Major towns (Sweden):

Göteborg, Borås, Jönköping, Linköping, Norrköping, Nyköping, Oxelösund, Motala, Mariestad, Lidköping, Skövde, Falköping, Alingsås, Trollhättan, Vänersborg, Uddevalla, Kungälv, Varberg, Falkenberg, Halmstad, Helsingborg, Landskrona, Lund, Malmö, Trelleborg, Ystad, Kristianstad, Karlskrona, Karlshamn, Ronneby, Kalmar, Oskarshamn, Västervik, Växjö, Visby

Major towns (Denmark):

København, Roskilde, Køge, Helsingør, Hillerød, Frederikssund, Holbæk, Kalundborg, Slagelse, Korsør, Næstved, Vordingborg, Nykøbing, Odense, Svendborg, Nyborg, Assens, Faaborg, Middelfart, Ringe, Århus, Randers, Viborg, Silkeborg, Horsens, Vejle, Fredericia, Kolding, Haderslev, Aabenraa, Sønderborg, Tønder, Esbjerg, Varde, Ribe, Grindsted, Herning, Holstebro, Struer, Ringkøbing, Skjern, Ålborg, Frederikshavn, Hjørring, Skagen, Brønderslev, Nørresundby, Thisted, Nykøbing

Danish Amt (counties):

NORDJYLLANDS AMT., VIBORG AMT., ÅRHUS AMT., RINGKØBING AMT., VEJLE AMT., SØNDERJYLLANDS AMT., RIBE AMT., FYNS AMT., VESTSJÆLLANDS AMT., STORSTRØMS AMT., FREDERIKSBORG AMT., KØBENHAVNS AMT., ROSKILDE AMT.

Danish islands / regions:

Sjælland, Fyn, Lolland, Falster, Møn, Langeland, Ærø, Als, Samsø, Læsø (Denmark), Anholt (Denmark), Jylland, Vendsyssel, Himmerland, Djursland, Mors, Thy

German places:

Flensburg, Schleswig, Eckernförde, Husum, Sylt, Föhr, Amrum, Westerland, Niebüll, Kappeln, Nordstrand, Fehmarn, Puttgarden, Burg

Kiel Bay / Fehmarn Belt, Langelandsbælt, Store Bælt, Øresund, Lille Bælt

Straits and bays:

Ålborg Bugt, Mariager Fjord, Randers Fjord, Limfjorden, Jammerbugt, Tannis Bugt, Ålbæk Bugt, Kattegat, Store Bælt, Køge Bugt, Faxe Bugt, Hanöbukten

Lakes (Sweden):

Vättern, Vänern, Mälaren, Sommen, Bolmen, Åsnen, Roxen

Projection note:

Projection : Lambert's Conformal Conic

East from Greenwich

10 0 10 20 30 40 50 60 70 80 90 km
10 0 10 20 30 40 50 60 miles

NORWEGIAN SEA

Hitra
Trondheim
Smøla
Kristiansund
Bremsnes
Averøya
Molde
Nordmøre
MØRE OG
Troll-heimen
SØR-TRØNDELAG

Ålesund
Sunnmøre
Ørsta
Volda
ROMSDAL
Romsdal
Dovrefjell
Snøhetta 2286
Dombås

Stadlandet
Nordfjord
SOGN OG FJORDANE
Jostedalsbreen
Jotunheimen
Galdhøpiggen 2469
Rondane
HEDMARK
Femunden

Florø
Førde
Sognefjorden
OPPLAND
Gudbrandsdalen
Lillehammer
Gjøvik
Hamar
Mjøsa

Bergen
HORDALAND
Voss
Hardangervidda
Hardangerjøkulen
BUSKERUD
Hønefoss
Drammen
OSLO
AKERSHUS
Kongsvinger

Stord
Sunnhordland
TELEMARK
Gaustatoppen 1883
Kongsberg
VESTFOLD
Tønsberg
Sandefjord
Larvik
ØSTFOLD
Fredrikstad
Halden

Haugesund
Karmøy
RYFYLKE
ROGALAND
Setesdal
AUST-AGDER
Arendal
Kristiansand
Skagerrak

Stavanger
Sandnes
Jæren
VEST-AGDER
Flekkefjord
Egersund
Mandal
Lindesnes

SWEDEN
GÖTEBORGS OCH BOHUS LÄN
Uddevalla
Trollhättan
Vänersborg

Projection: Lambert's Conformal Conic
East from Greenwich
COPYRIGHT GEORGE PHILIP LTD.

ft / m
6000 2000
4500 1500
3000 1000
1500 500
600 200
0 0
50 150
100 300
200 600
500 1500
1000 3000
m ft

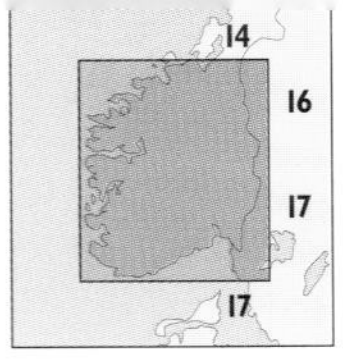

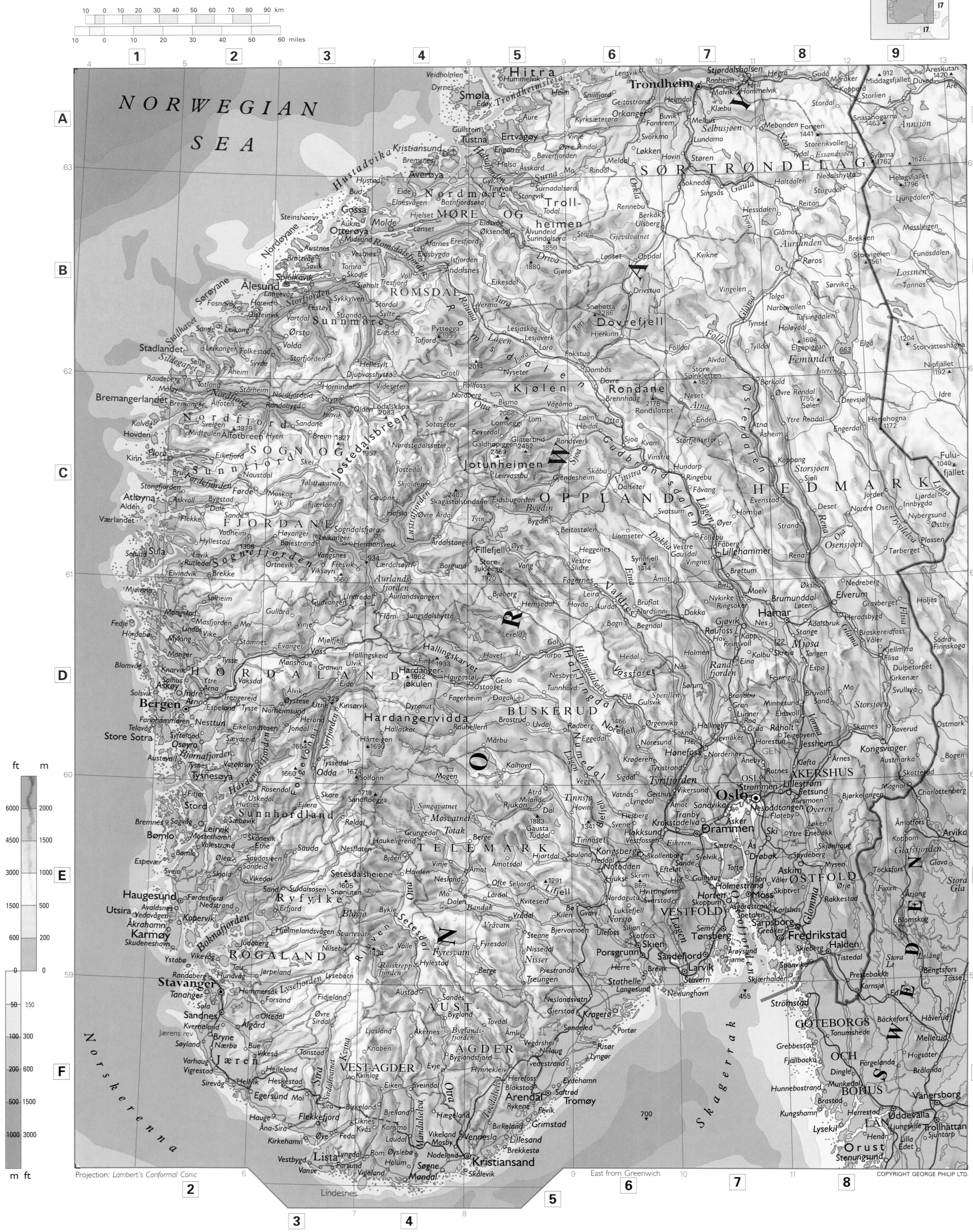

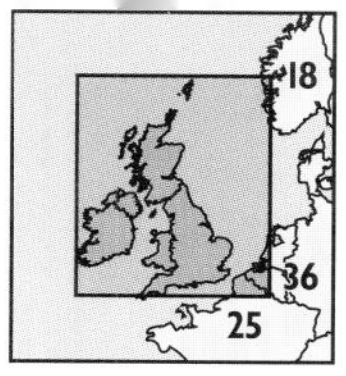

50 0 25 50 75 100 125 150 175 km
50 0 25 50 75 100 125 miles

ft m

NORWAY
Askøy
Bergen
Osøyro
Stord
Bømlo
Leirvik
Haugesund
Kopervik
Åkrahamn
Boknafjorden
Stavanger
Sandnes
Bryne
Nærbø

ATLANTIC OCEAN

Shetland Is.
Yell
Unst
Fetlar
Foula
Mainland
Lerwick
Fair Isle

Orkney Is.
Westray
Sanday
Stronsay
Mainland
Hoy
Kirkwall
South Ronaldsay

C. Wrath
Pentland Firth
Thurso
Wick

NORTH SEA

Outer Hebrides
Lewis
Stornoway
North Minch
St. Kilda
Harris
North Uist
Benbecula
South Uist
Inner Hebrides
Skye
Portree
Mallaig
Rhum
Eigg
Barra
Coll
Tiree
Tobermory
Mull
Oban
Colonsay
Jura
Islay

Helmsdale
Lairg
Golspie
Tain
Invergordon
Dingwall
L. Ness
Inverness
Nairn
Elgin
Buckie
Banff
Fraserburgh
Peterhead
Aviemore
Spey
Huntly
Inverurie
SCOTLAND
Grampian Mts.
Dee
Aberdeen
Ben Nevis
Fort William
Ballater
Stonehaven
Forfar
Montrose
Arbroath
Dundee
St. Andrews
Perth
L. Lomond
Stirling
Glenrothes
Kirkcaldy
Dunbar
Dunfermline
Glasgow **Edinburgh**
Greenock
Paisley
Clyde
Berwick-upon-Tweed
East Kilbride
Hamilton
Irvine
Kilmarnock
Galashiels
Jedburgh
Ayr
Southern Uplands
Cheviot Hills
Alnwick
Firth of Clyde
Campbeltown
Arran
Malin Hd.
North Channel
Girvan
Dumfries
Hawick
Buncrana
Aran I.
Letterkenny
Coleraine
Stranraer
Kirkcudbright
Annan
Carlisle
Hexham
Newcastle-upon-Tyne
South Shields
Gateshead
Sunderland
Durham
Hartlepool
Redcar
Middlesbrough
Stockton-on-Tees
Darlington
Scarborough
Bridlington

Londonderry
Ballymena
Larne
Antrim
Bangor
Lisburn
Belfast
Lough Neagh
Portadown
Lurgan
Armagh
Newry
NORTHERN IRELAND
Ulster
Lifford
Donegal
Omagh
Enniskillen
Lower L. Erne
Clones
Castleblaney
UNITED KINGDOM
Cumbrian Mts.
Whitehaven
Barrow-in-Furness
Lancaster
Workington
Pennines
Harrogate
York
Kingston upon Hull
Beverley
Leeds
Bradford
Keighley
Blackpool
Preston
Burnley
Halifax
Huddersfield
Barnsley
Scunthorpe
Grimsby
Blackburn
Bolton
Oldham
Doncaster
Rotherham
Manchester
Stockport
Sheffield
Lincoln
Louth
Skegness
Liverpool
Warrington
Chesterfield
Mansfield
Cromer
Crewe
Derby
Nottingham
Boston
The Wash
King's Lynn
Stoke-on-Trent
Stafford
Grantham
Norwich
Great Yarmouth
Shrewsbury
Telford
ENGLAND
Leicester
Corby
Peterborough
Lowestoft
Nuneaton
Welshpool
Coventry
Rugby
Northampton
Thetford
Bury St. Edmunds
Ipswich
BIRMINGHAM
Redditch
Royal Leamington Spa
Bedford
Cambridge
Worcester
Hereford
Milton Keynes
Felixstowe
Harwich
Colchester
Cheltenham
Gloucester
Cotswold Hills
Oxford
Hemel Hempstead
Luton
Harlow
Chelmsford
WALES
Brecon
Cwmbran
High Wycombe
Watford
Basildon
Southend-on-Sea
Newport
Swindon
Newbury
Reading
Slough
LONDON
Thames
Chatham
Margate
Cardiff
Bristol
Bath
Weston-super-Mare
Barry
Basingstoke
Guildford
Reigate
Maidstone
Canterbury
Dover
Folkestone
Bristol Channel
Exmoor
Taunton
Salisbury
Winchester
Crawley
Ashford
Barnstaple
Yeovil
Southampton
Fareham
Havant
Hastings
Eastbourne
Worthing
Brighton
Bude
Dartmoor
Exeter
Exmouth
Bournemouth
Poole
Weymouth
Newport
Isle of Wight
Portsmouth
Str. of Dover
C. Gris-Nez
Boulogne
Newquay
Truro
St. Austell
Torbay
Plymouth
Land's End
Penzance
Falmouth
Isles of Scilly

CELTIC SEA

IRELAND
Galway B.
Aran Is.
Galway
Ballinasloe
Roscommon
Longford
Athlone
Mullingar
Ballina
Castlebar
Westport
Lough Mask
Connemara
Lough Corrib
Lough Ree
Sligo
Leitrim
Cavan
Boyne
Dundalk
Drogheda
Dublin
Dun Laoghaire
Bray
Achill
L. Conn
Clew B.
Ceanannus Mor
Tullamore
Liffey
Anglesey
Holyhead
Bangor
Colwyn Bay
Ennis
Lough Derg
Birr
Port Laoise
Athy
Wicklow Mts.
Snowdon
Conwy
Chester
Cambrian Mts.
Kilrush
Nenagh
Thurles
Carlow
Kilkenny
Arklow
Wrexham
Pwllheli
Shannon
Listowel
Tipperary
Cardigan Bay
Aberystwyth
Tralee
Limerick
Clonmel
Carrick-on-Suir
Wexford
Rosslare
Fishguard
Carmarthen
Dingle
Mallow
Blackwater
Waterford
Dungarvan
Youghal
Haverfordwest
Milford Haven
Pembroke
Merthyr Tydfil
Neath
Llanelli
Swansea
Port Talbot
Rhondda
Killarney
Macgillycuddy's Reeks
Valencia
Cork
Cobh
Kinsale
Bantry
Bandon
C. Clear

IRISH SEA
Douglas
I. of Man
Mull of Galloway

St. George's Channel

ENGLAND ... **English Channel**

FRANCE
C. de la Hague
Pte. de Barfleur
Cherbourg
Le Havre
Bolbec
Rouen
Alderney
Guernsey
St. Peter Port
Sark
Channel Is. (U.K.)
St. Helier
Jersey
Cotentin
Valognes
Bayeux
Caen
Lisieux
Elbeuf
Seine
Trouville-sur-Mer
Fécamp
Le Tréport
Dieppe
Abbeville
St-Quentin
Cambrai
Valenciennes
Amiens
Pays de Caux
Picardie
Le Touquet-Paris-Plage
Calais
Dunkerque
St-Omer
Béthune
Bruay-la-Buissière
Lens
Lille
Tourcoing
Roubaix
Villeneuve-d'Ascq

NETHERLANDS
Texel
Den Helder
Alkmaar
Haarlem
's-Gravenhage (Den Haag)
Hoek van Holland
ROTTERDAM
Dordrecht
Vlissingen
Zeebrugge
Oostende
BELGIUM
BRUSSEL (Bruxelles)
Antwerpen
Brugge
Gent
Mechelen
Tournai

Projection: Conical with two standard parallels

West from Greenwich   East from Greenwich

CARTOGRAPHY BY PHILIP'S.

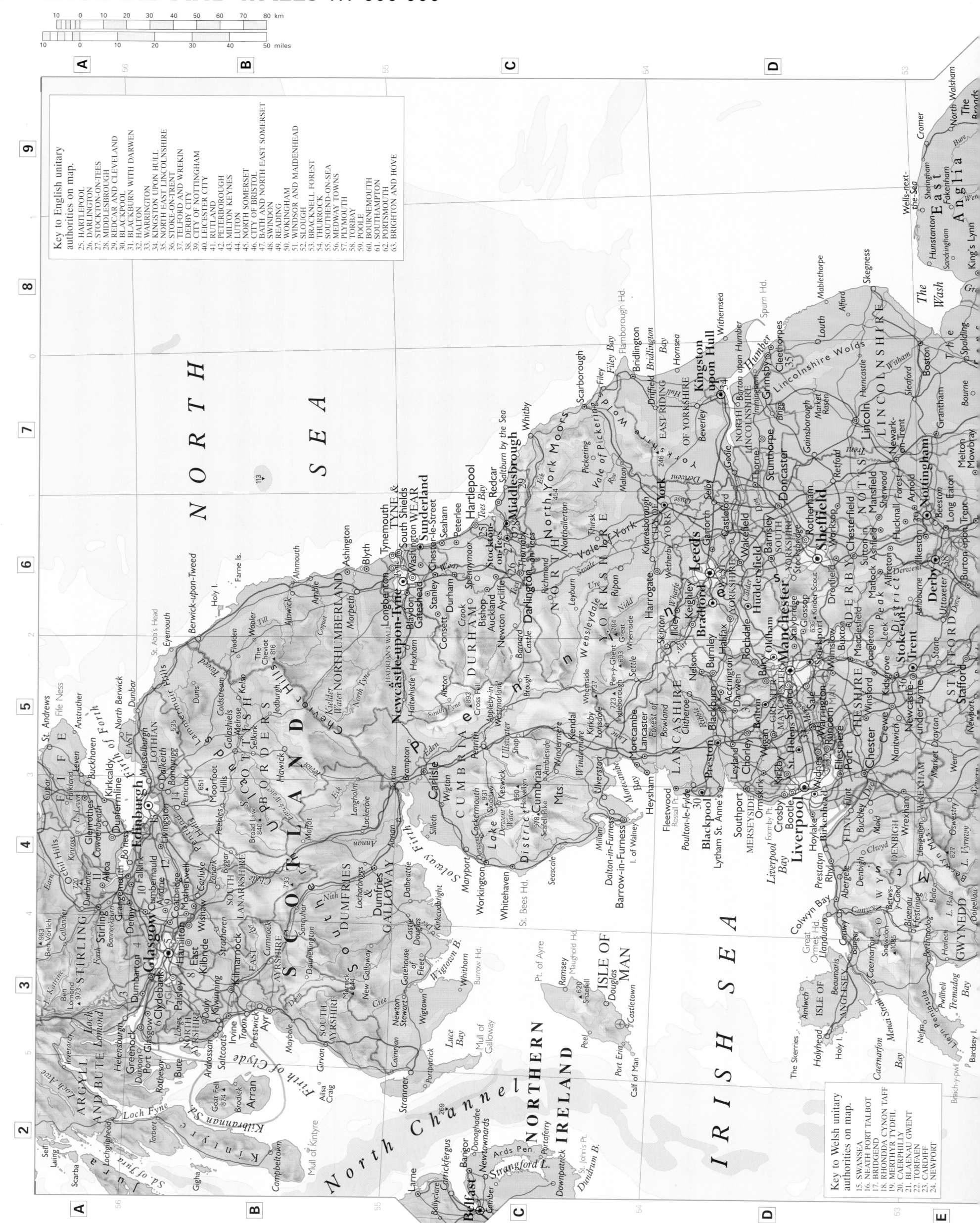

ENGLAND AND WALES 1:1 600 000

10 0 10 20 30 40 50 60 70 80 km
10   0   10   20   30   40   50 miles

Key to English unitary
authorities on map.

25. HARTLEPOOL
26. DARLINGTON
27. STOCKTON-ON-TEES
28. MIDDLESBROUGH
29. REDCAR AND CLEVELAND
30. BLACKPOOL
31. BLACKBURN WITH DARWEN
32. HALTON
33. WARRINGTON
34. KINGSTON UPON HULL
35. NORTH EAST LINCOLNSHIRE
36. STOKE-ON-TRENT
37. TELFORD AND WREKIN
38. DERBY CITY
39. CITY OF NOTTINGHAM
40. LEICESTER CITY
41. RUTLAND
42. PETERBOROUGH
43. MILTON KEYNES
44. LUTON
45. NORTH SOMERSET
46. CITY OF BRISTOL
47. BATH AND NORTH EAST SOMERSET
48. SWINDON
49. READING
50. WOKINGHAM
51. WINDSOR AND MAIDENHEAD
52. SLOUGH
53. BRACKNELL FOREST
54. THURROCK
55. SOUTHEND-ON-SEA
56. MEDWAY TOWNS
57. PLYMOUTH
58. TORBAY
59. POOLE
60. BOURNEMOUTH
61. SOUTHAMPTON
62. PORTSMOUTH
63. BRIGHTON AND HOVE

Key to Welsh unitary
authorities on map.

15. SWANSEA
16. NEATH PORT TALBOT
17. BRIDGEND
18. RHONDDA CYNON TAFF
19. MERTHYR TYDFIL
20. CAERPHILLY
21. BLAENAU GWENT
22. TORFAEN
23. CARDIFF
24. NEWPORT

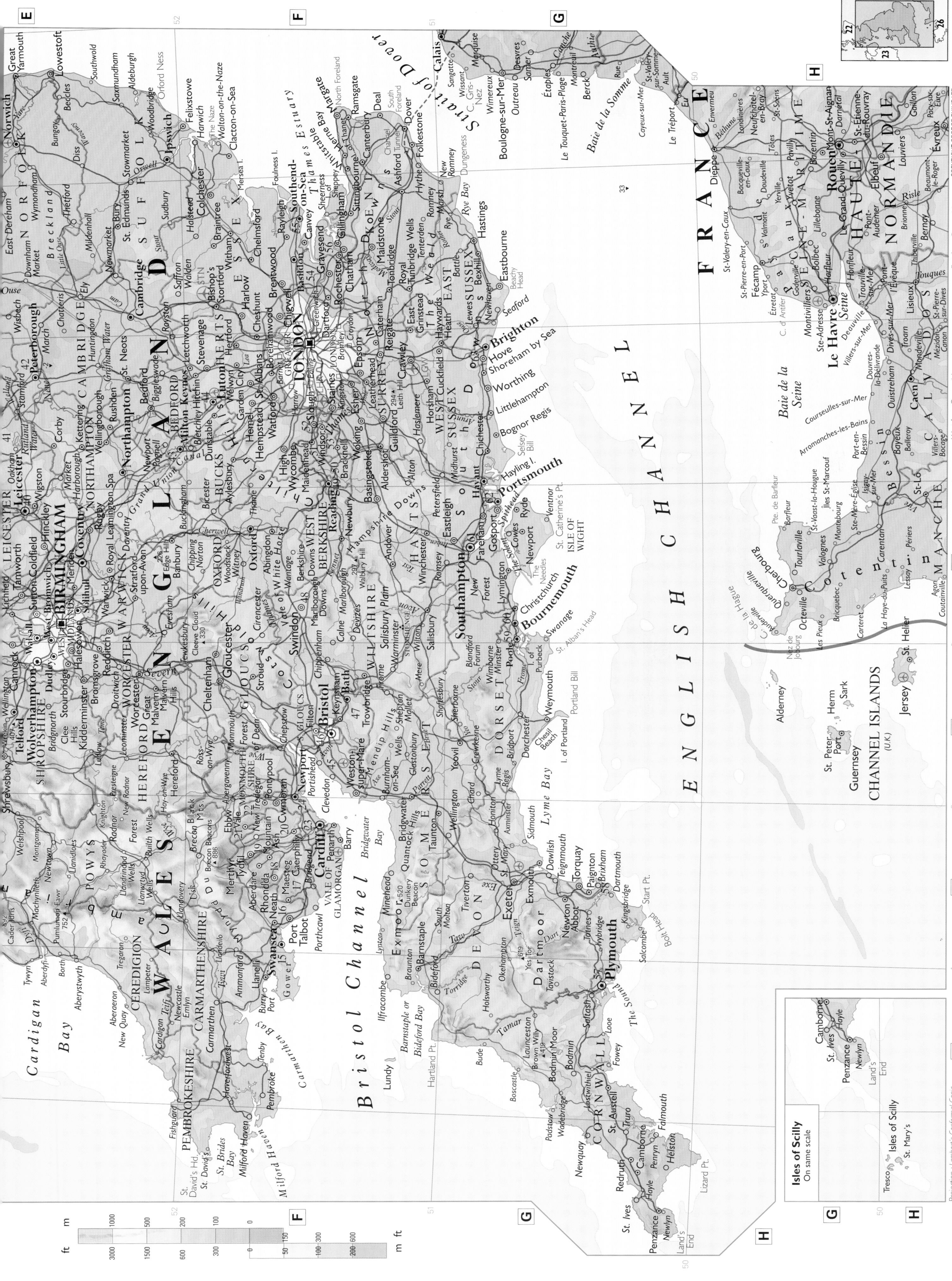

E **F** **G** **H**

Great Yarmouth · Lowestoft · Southwold · Norwich

Calais · Strait of Dover · Boulogne-sur-Mer · **FRANCE**

N O R F O L K · S U F F O L K · Ipswich · Felixstowe · Harwich · Clacton-on-Sea

Peterborough · Cambridge · C A M B R I D G E · E S S E X · Southend-on-Sea · Thames Estuary · Margate · Ramsgate · Dover · Folkestone

Dieppe · Le Havre · **Rouen** · HAUTE-NORMANDIE · Évreux

Leicester · Northampton · BEDFORD · HERTS · **LONDON** · GREATER LONDON · Dartford · Gravesend · Chatham · Maidstone · K E N T · Canterbury · Ashford

BIRMINGHAM · Coventry · WARWICK · OXFORD · BUCKS · Reading · BERKSHIRE · S U R R E Y · Guildford · W E S T S U S S E X · Worthing · **Brighton** · Hove · Eastbourne · Hastings

Baie de la Seine · Caen · CALVADOS · BASSE-NORMANDIE · MANCHE · Cherbourg

WALES · Cardiff · Swansea · CARMARTHENSHIRE · PEMBROKESHIRE · CEREDIGION · POWYS · Bristol Channel

Bristol · Bath · SOMERSET · WILTSHIRE · Salisbury · HANTS · Southampton · Portsmouth · ISLE OF WIGHT · Bournemouth · DORSET · Weymouth

E N G L I S H C H A N N E L

CHANNEL ISLANDS (U.K.) · Guernsey · Jersey · St. Helier · Alderney · Sark

D E V O N · Exeter · Plymouth · C O R N W A L L · Truro · Falmouth · Penzance · Land's End · Lizard Pt.

Cardigan Bay

Isles of Scilly · On same scale · St. Mary's · Tresco

Camborne · St. Ives · Penzance · Newlyn · Land's End

Projection: Lambert's Conformal Conic · COPYRIGHT GEORGE PHILIP LTD.

ft · m · 3000 · 1500 · 600 · 300 · 150 · 0 · 1000 · 500 · 200 · 100 · 50 · 0

10 0 10 20 30 40 50 60 70 80 km
10 0 10 20 30 40 50 miles

Key to Scottish unitary authorities on map
1. CITY OF ABERDEEN
2. DUNDEE CITY
3. WEST DUNBARTONSHIRE
4. EAST DUNBARTONSHIRE
5. CITY OF GLASGOW
6. INVERCLYDE
7. RENFREWSHIRE
8. EAST RENFREWSHIRE
9. NORTH LANARKSHIRE
10. FALKIRK
11. CLACKMANNANSHIRE
12. WEST LOTHIAN
13. CITY OF EDINBURGH
14. MIDLOTHIAN

ORKNEY IS.
On same scale

ORKNEY
North Ronaldsay
Papa Westray
Westray
Rousay
Eday
Sanday
Stronsay
Shapinsay
Brough Hd.
Mainland
Stromness
Kirkwall
St. Mary's
Burray
Hoy
Scapa Flow
South Ronaldsay
Burwick
Dunnet Hd.
Stroma
Duncansby Head
John o' Groats
Thurso
Sinclair's Bay
Pentland Firth

SHETLAND IS.
On same scale
Unst
Haroldswick
Esha Ness
St. Magnus Bay
Papa Stour
Yell
Fetlar
Whalsay
Voe
Bressay
Lerwick
Foula
Wollsa
Scalloway
West Burra
SHETLAND
Boddam
Sumburgh Hd.

ATLANTIC OCEAN

WESTERN ISLES
Butt of Lewis
Flannan Is.
Gallan Hd.
Stornoway
Broad Bay
Eye Peninsula
Lewis
Harris
Taransay
Clisham 799
North Uist
Lochmaddy
Benbecula
South Uist
Lochboisdale
Barra
Eriskay
Vatersay
Sandray
Barra Hd. 268

North Minch
C. Wrath
Durness
L. Eriboll
Strathy Pt.
Dounreay
Reay Forest
Ben Hope 927
Tongue
Naver
Halkirk
Thurso
Dunnet Hd. Stroma
Wick
Lybster
Sinclair's Bay
Noss Hd.
Ord of Caithness
Helmsdale
Brora
Golspie
Dornoch Firth
Tain
Tarbat Ness

Little Minch
Toe Hd.
Sound of Harris
Berneray
Pabbay
Balleshare
Grimsay
Ardivachar Pt.
Wiay
Ben Mhor 620

Sea of the Hebrides
Canna
Rhum (Rùm)
Eigg
Muck
Coll
Tiree
Pt. of Ardnamurchan

North West Highlands
L. Laxford
Eddrachillis B.
Pt. of Stoer
Enard B.
Rubha Coigeach
L. Assynt
Lochinver
Ben More Assynt 998
L. Shin
Lairg
Oykel
L. Broom
Ullapool
Greenstone Pt.
L. Ewe
Gruinard B.
L. Fannich
Garron
L. Maree 1053
L. Torridon
Ben Dearg 1081
Ben Wyvis 1045
Alness
Invergordon
Cromarty
Dingwall
Strathpeffer
Beauly
Fortrose
Nairn
Elgin
Lossiemouth
Portknockie
Portsoy
Buckie
Cullen
Banff
Macduff
Forres
Rothes
Keith
Aberchirder
Turriff
Huntly
Dufftown
MORAY
Grantown-on-Spey
Aviemore
Cairn Gorm 1245
Cairngorm Mts.
Kingussie
Newtonmore
Cairn Ban
Cairn Toul
Carn Eige 1182
Glen Affric
Glen Moriston
Fort Augustus
Loch Ness
Glen Garry
Monadhliath Mts.
Inverness
Beauly
Spey
Strath Spey
BUCHAN
Deveron
Ythan
Peterhead
Buchan Ness
Ellon
Oldmeldrum
Inverurie
Alford
Don
Dyce
Westhill
Aberdeen
Girdle Ness
Peterculter
Banchory
Stonehaven
Inverbervie
ABERDEENSHIRE
Tomintoul
Ballater
Aboyne
Braemar
Ben Macdhui 1309
Lochnagar
N. Esk
Brechin
Laurencekirk
Montrose
Arbroath
Carnoustie

Skye
Rubha Hunish
Uig
Sound of Raasay
Portree
Raasay
Scalpay
Rona
Stromeferry
Kyle of Lochalsh
L. Monar
Glen Affric
L. Carron
Cuillin Hills 992
Cuillin Sound
Loch Bracadale
S. of Sleat
Mallaig
Arisaig
L. Morar
L. Arkaig
L. Lochy
Glen Spean
Spean
Ben Nevis 1342
Fort William
L. Eil
L. Shiel
L. Sunart
Morvern
L. Etive
Glen Coe 1148
Rannoch Moor
L. Rannoch
Forest of Atholl
Blair Atholl
L. Ericht
Pitlochry
Ben Lawers 1214
Aberfeldy
L. Tay
Dunkeld
Blairgowrie
Alyth
Kirriemuir
Forfar
ANGUS
PERTH AND KINROSS
Strathmore
Sidlaw Hills

Hebrides
Tobermory
Mull
Ben More 966
Staffa
Ulva
Iona
Kerrera
Luing
Scarba
Colonsay
Oronsay
Jura
Islay
Bowmore
Port Ellen
Rhinns Pt.
Mull of Oa
Gigha

Passage of Tiree
Sound of Mull
Oban
Lorn
Firth of Lorn
Loch Awe
Inveraray
Loch Fyne
ARGYLL AND BUTE
Lochgilphead
Tarbert
Kintyre
Knapdale
Campbeltown
Mull of Kintyre
Ardnave Pt.
Rubh' a' Mhail

Ben Cruachan 1126
Ben More 1174
Ben Vorlich 983
L. Katrine
Ben Lomond 973
Loch Lomond
Callander
Crieff
STIRLING
Dunblane
Bridge of Allan
Ben Vorlich
Ochil Hills
Kinross
L. Leven
Falkland
Cupar
FIFE
St. Andrews
Fife Ness
Leven
Anstruther
Buckhaven
Glenrothes
Cowdenbeath
Kirkcaldy
Alloa
Bannockburn
Stirling
Grangemouth
Bo'ness
Dunfermline
Firth of Forth
North Berwick
EAST LOTHIAN
Dunbar
St. Abb's Head
Eyemouth

SCOTLAND
Dundee
New Scone
Perth
Tayport
Firth of Tay
Monifieth

NORTH SEA

Helensburgh
Dumbarton
Denny
Falkirk
Edinburgh
Musselburgh
Dalkeith
Bonnyrigg
Penicuik
Livingston
Greenock
Port Glasgow
Dunoon
Rothesay
Bute
Glasgow
Clydebank
Paisley
Cumbernauld
Airdrie
Coatbridge
Motherwell
Hamilton
Wishaw
Carluke
Lanark
East Kilbride
NORTH AYRSHIRE
Ardrossan
Saltcoats
Irvine
Kilwinning
Dalry
Kilmarnock
Troon
Prestwick
Ayr
EAST AYRSHIRE
Cumnock
Maybole
SOUTH AYRSHIRE
Girvan
Ailsa Craig
Goat Fell 874
Brodick
Arran
Firth of Clyde
Kilbrannan Sd.

SOUTH LANARKSHIRE
Strathaven
Biggar
Broad Law 840
Peebles
Moorfoot Hills
Pentland Hills
Melrose
Galashiels
Selkirk
SCOTTISH BORDERS
Hawick
Jedburgh
Kelso
Coldstream
Duns
Lammermuir Hills
Berwick-upon-Tweed
Holy I.
Farne Is.
The Cheviot 816
Cheviot Hills
Wooler
Flodden
Alnwick
Alnmouth
Amble
Coquet
NORTHUMBERLAND
Morpeth
Newcastle-upon-Tyne
Blaydon
Gateshead
Stanley
Consett
DURHAM
Crook
Bishop Auckland
Barnard Castle
Tees

Southern Uplands
Sanquhar
Moffat
Dumfries & Galloway
Lockerbie
Langholm
Lochmaben
Dumfries
Annan
Gretna
Carlisle
Brampton
Haltwhistle
Hexham
CUMBRIA
Penrith
Appleby-in-Westmorland
Alston
Cross Fell 893
Ullswater
Helvellyn 950
Keswick
Skiddaw
Derwent Water
Cockermouth
Workington
Maryport
Whitehaven
St. Bees Hd.
Silloth
Wigton
Kirkcudbright
Castle Douglas
Dalbeattie
Gatehouse of Fleet
Newton Stewart
New Galloway
Galloway
Merrick 844
Cairnryan
Stranraer
Portpatrick
Wigtown
Whithorn
Burrow Hd.
Wigtown B.
Luce Bay
Mull of Galloway
Solway Firth
Nith
Annan
Esk
Liddel Water
Tweed
Teviot
Ettrick Water
Ken

North Channel
NORTHERN IRELAND
Larne
Carrickfergus
Belfast L.
Bangor
Donaghadee
Newtownards
Belfast

Projection: Lambert's Conformal Conic
West from Greenwich
COPYRIGHT GEORGE PHILIP LTD.

ft m
3000 1000
1500 500
600 200
300 100
0 0
150 50
300 100
600 200
1500 500
3000 1000
m ft

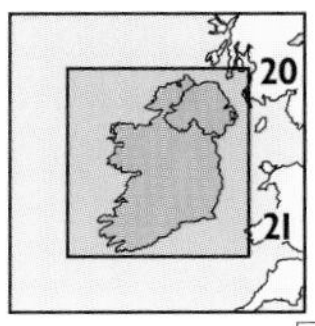

20
21

10 0 10 20 30 40 50 60 70 80 km
10 0 10 20 30 40 50 miles

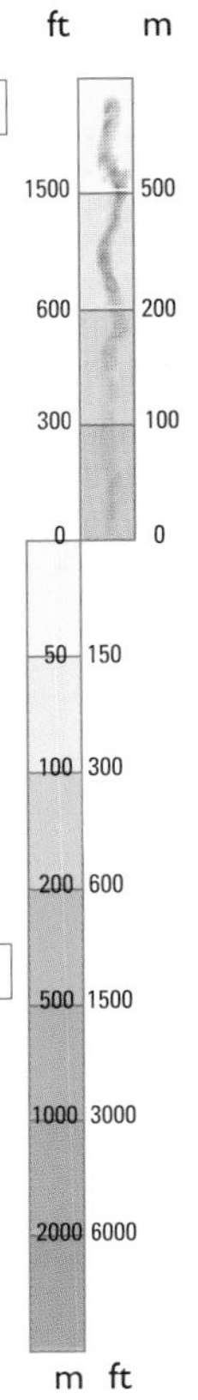

ATLANTIC OCEAN

NORTH CHANNEL

IRISH SEA

St. George's Channel

CELTIC SEA

Firth of Clyde
Kintyre
Campbeltown
Brodick
Arran
Mull of Oa
Mull of Kintyre
Ailsa Craig
Cairnryan
Stranraer
Portpatrick

Malin Hd.
Malin Pen.
Inishowen Pen.
Carndonagh
Moville
Buncrana
Lough Swilly
Fanad Hd.
Mulroy B.
Sheep Haven
Horn Hd.
Tory I.
Bloody Foreland
Inishfree B.
Gweedore
The Rosses
Errigal 752
683
Aran I.
Crohy Hd.
Gweebarra B.
Dawros Hd.
Laughros More B.
Rossan Pt.
Killybegs
St. John's Pt.
Donegal Bay
Ballyshannon
Bundoran

Giants Causeway
Rathlin I.
Portrush
Portstewart
Fair Hd.
Ballycastle
Garron Pt.
554
Trostan
Coleraine
Limavady
Ballymoney
Mts. of Antrim
LONDONDERRY
Londonderry
L. Foyle
Ballymena
Larne
Carrickfergus
269
Letterkenny
Rathmelton
Lifford
Strabane
Sawel Mt.
683
Sperrin Mts.
Magherafelt
Randalstown
Ballyclare
NORTHERN
Antrim
Belfast L.
Bangor
Donaghadee
Newtownards
DONEGAL
Derryveagh Mts.
Glenties
Lavagh More
676
Finn
Sion Mills
Newtownstewart
TYRONE
Omagh
Cookstown
Moneymore
Coalisland
Lough Neagh
Newtownabbey
Belfast
Lisburn
Comber
Strangford L.
Ards Pen.
Portaferry
Ballyquintin Pt.

U l s t e r
Donegal
Derg
Castlederg
Dromore
Irvinestown
Dungannon
Aughnacloy
Craigavon
Lurgan
Portadown
Lagan
Banbridge
Tandragee
DOWN
Ballynahinch
Downpatrick
St. John's Pt.

Enniskillen
FERMANAGH
Lower L. Erne
Erne
Upper L. Erne
Clones
Monaghan
MONAGHAN
Castleblaney
Cootehill
Annalee
Keady
Middletown
ARMAGH
Armagh
Newry
Slieve Gullion 577
Mourne Mts.
Slieve Donard 852
Newcastle
Dundrum B.
Warrenpoint
Greenore
Carlingford L.
Kilkeel

Broad Haven
Erris Hd.
Belmullet
Mullet Pen.
Inishkea North
Inishkea South
Blacksod Bay
Downpatrick Hd.
Killala B.
Killala
Ballina
Moy
Sligo Bay
Dromore West
544
S L I G O
Slieve Gamph
Sligo
Ballymote
Colloney
L. Arrow
L. Allen
Belturbet
LEITRIM
Leitrim
Carrick-on-Shannon
CAVAN
Cavan
Kingscourt
Carrickmacross
Clogher Hd.
Dunleer
LOUTH
Louth
Ardee
Dundalk
Dundalk Bay

Achill Hd.
Achill I.
Corraun Pen.
765
Croagh Patrick
819
Mweelrea
Clare I.
Clew Bay
Inishturk
Killary Harbour
Inishbofin
Inishshark
Slyne Hd.
Connemara
Clifden
Inishmore
Inishmaan
Inisheer
Aran Is.
Black Hd.
Galway Bay
Hags Hd.
Liscannor Bay
Mal Bay
Mutton I.
Loop Hd.

M A Y O
Newport
Westport
Castlebar
Knock
Claremorris
Ballinrobe
Ballyhaunis
Swinford
Charlestown
Ballaghaderreen
Boyle
Castlerea
806
L. Conn
Nephin
L. Mask
Lough Corrib
Oughterard
G A L W A Y
Galway
Tuam
Glennamaddy
ROSCOMMON
Roscommon
Castlerea
Longford
LONGFORD
Granard
L. Gowna
L. Sheelin
Oldcastle
Castlepollard
Ceannanus Mor (Kells)
Blackwater
An Uaimh (Navan)
Trim
MEATH
Boyne
Drogheda
Balbriggan
Rush
Lambay I.
Skerries

C o n n a c h t
IRELAND
Leinster
Lough Ree
Mullingar
WESTMEATH
Moate
Athlone
Ballinasloe
Athenry
Loughrea
368
Slieve Aughty
Portumna
Gort
Ennistimon
CLARE
Ennis
Tulla
Milltown Malbay
Lough Derg
Nenagh
Killaloe
Templemore
694
Keeper Hill
Thurles
TIPPERARY
Golden Vale
Tipperary
Cashel
Slievenamon 722
Caher
Clonmel
Carrick-on-Suir
Comeragh Mts. 792
Knockmealdown Mts. 795
Lismore
Dungarvan
Dungarvan Harbour

Royal Canal
Maynooth
Swords
Malahide
Howth Hd.
DUB
Dublin
Dun Laoghaire
Bray
Greystones
123
Edenderry
Allen
Bog of Allen
Clondalkin
KILDARE
Kildare
Naas
Droichead Nua
554
Blessington
Kippure
Poulaphouca Res.
WICKLOW
Wicklow
Wicklow Hd.
Lugnaquilla 926
Rathdrum
Arklow
Avoca

OFFALY
Tullamore
Daingean
Birr
Slieve Bloom
Arderin 529
Roscrea
Mountmellick
Portarlington
Port Laoise
LAOIS
Mountrath
Durrow
Athy
Carlow
Tullow
Muine Bheag
CARLOW
Mt. Leinster 796
Bunclody
Gorey
Shillelagh
Barrow
Mizen Hd.
Cahore Pt.

Kilkee
Kilrush
Shannon Airport
Sixmilebridge
Limerick
Foynes
LIMERICK
Rathkeale
Newcastle West
Listowel
Feale
Kilfinnane
920 Galtymore
Galty Mts.
Mitchelstown
Fermoy
Kilkenny
KILKENNY
Callan
Nore
Suir
Clonmel
WATERFORD
Waterford
Tramore
Tramore B.
Hook Hd.
Waterford Harbour
WEXFORD
New Ross
Wexford
Wexford Harbour
Rosslare
Greenore Pt.
Carnsore Pt.
Saltee Is.
Enniscorthy
Slaney

Kerry Hd.
Brandon B.
Tralee B.
Smerwick Harbour
953 Brandon Mt.
Dingle
Slieve Mish 853
Tralee
Maine
Newmarket
Kanturk
Buttevant
Mallow
Blackwater
Munster
Mouth of the Shannon

Great Blasket I.
Inishvickillane
Dunmore Hd.
Dingle Bay
Valencia I.
Puffin I.
Great Skellig
Killorglin
L. Leane
Killarney
KERRY
Carrauntoohill 1041
Macgillycuddy's Reeks
Caherciveen
Kenmare
Kenmare River
Boggeragh Mts. 646
Macroom
Blarney
CORK
Cork
Lee
Midleton
Youghal
Youghal B.
Cobh
Crosshaven
Passage West
Cork Harbour
Kinsale
Old Head of Kinsale
Bandon
Clonakilty
Clonakilty B.
Galley Hd.

Ballinskelligs B.
Scariff I.
Dursey I.
Crow Hd.
Castletown Bearhaven
Bear I.
Caha Mts. 686
Glengarriff
Bantry Bay
Bantry
Dunmanus B.
Mizen Hd.
Skull
Long I.
Sherkin I.
Clear I.
C. Clear
Skibbereen
Dunmanway

West from Greenwich

Projection : Lambert's Conformal Conic

COPYRIGHT GEORGE PHILIP LTD.

ft m
1500 500
600 200
300 100
0 0
50 150
100 300
200 600
500 1500
1000 3000
2000 6000
m ft

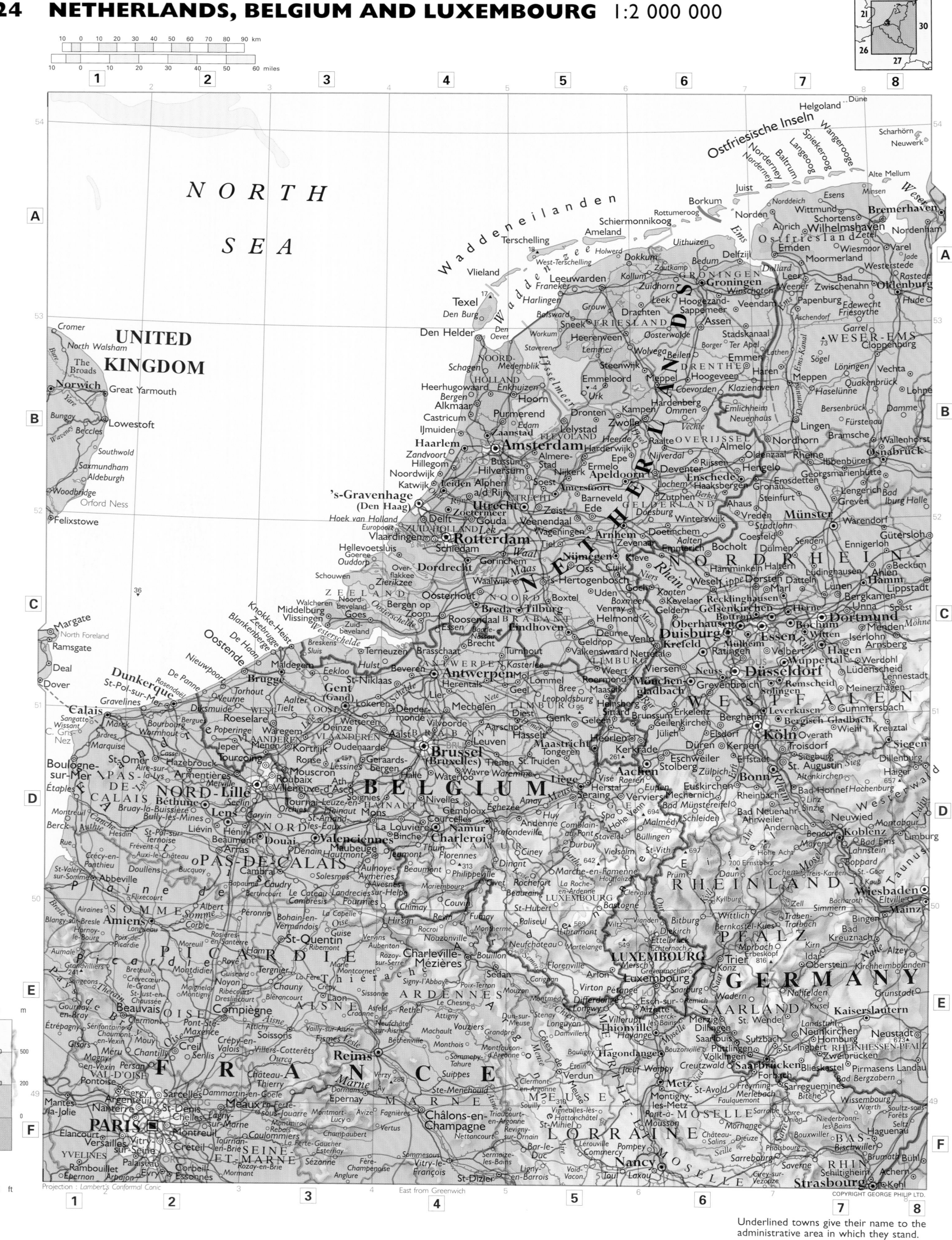

COPYRIGHT GEORGE PHILIP LTD.

Underlined towns give their name to the administrative area in which they stand.

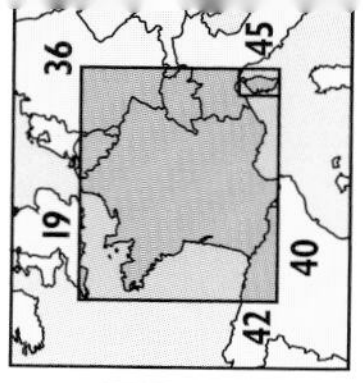

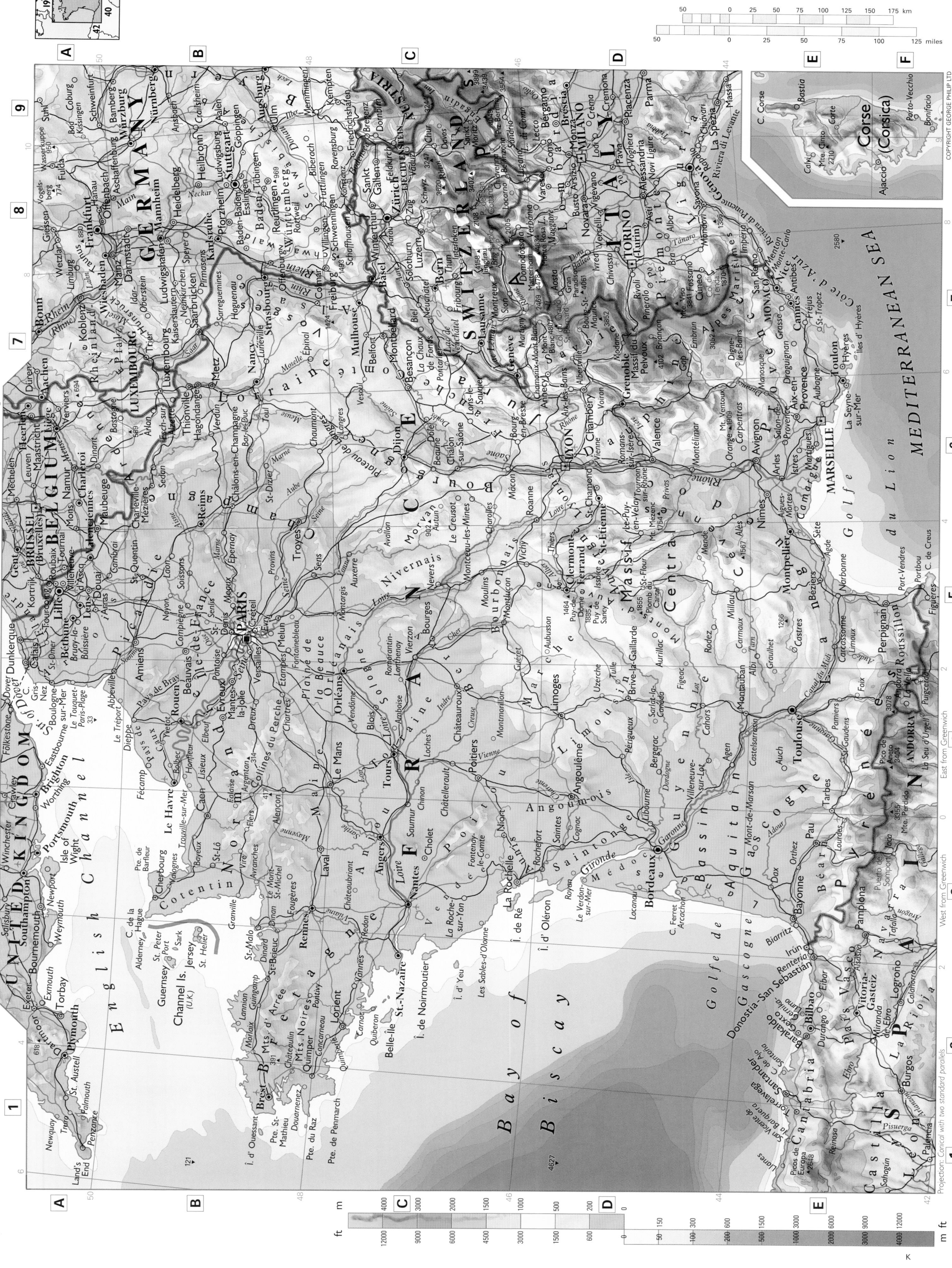

50   0   25   50   75   100   125   150   175 km

50   0   25   50   75   100   125 miles

COPYRIGHT GEORGE PHILIP LTD

Corse (Corsica)

MEDITERRANEAN SEA

UNITED KINGDOM

ENGLISH CHANNEL

BELGIUM

LUXEMBOURG

GERMANY

SWITZERLAND

ITALY

FRANCE

PARIS

MARSEILLE

LYON

Bay of Biscay

Golfe de Gascogne

ANDORRA

SPAIN

Golfe du Lion

Côte d'Azur

MONACO

Projection: Conical with two standard parallels

West from Greenwich

East from Greenwich

m ft

4000 3000 2000 1500 1000 500 200 0

ft 12000 9000 6000 4500 3000 1500 600 0

0 -50 -100 -150 -200 m

0 -150 -300 -600 -1000 -2000 -3000 -4000 ft

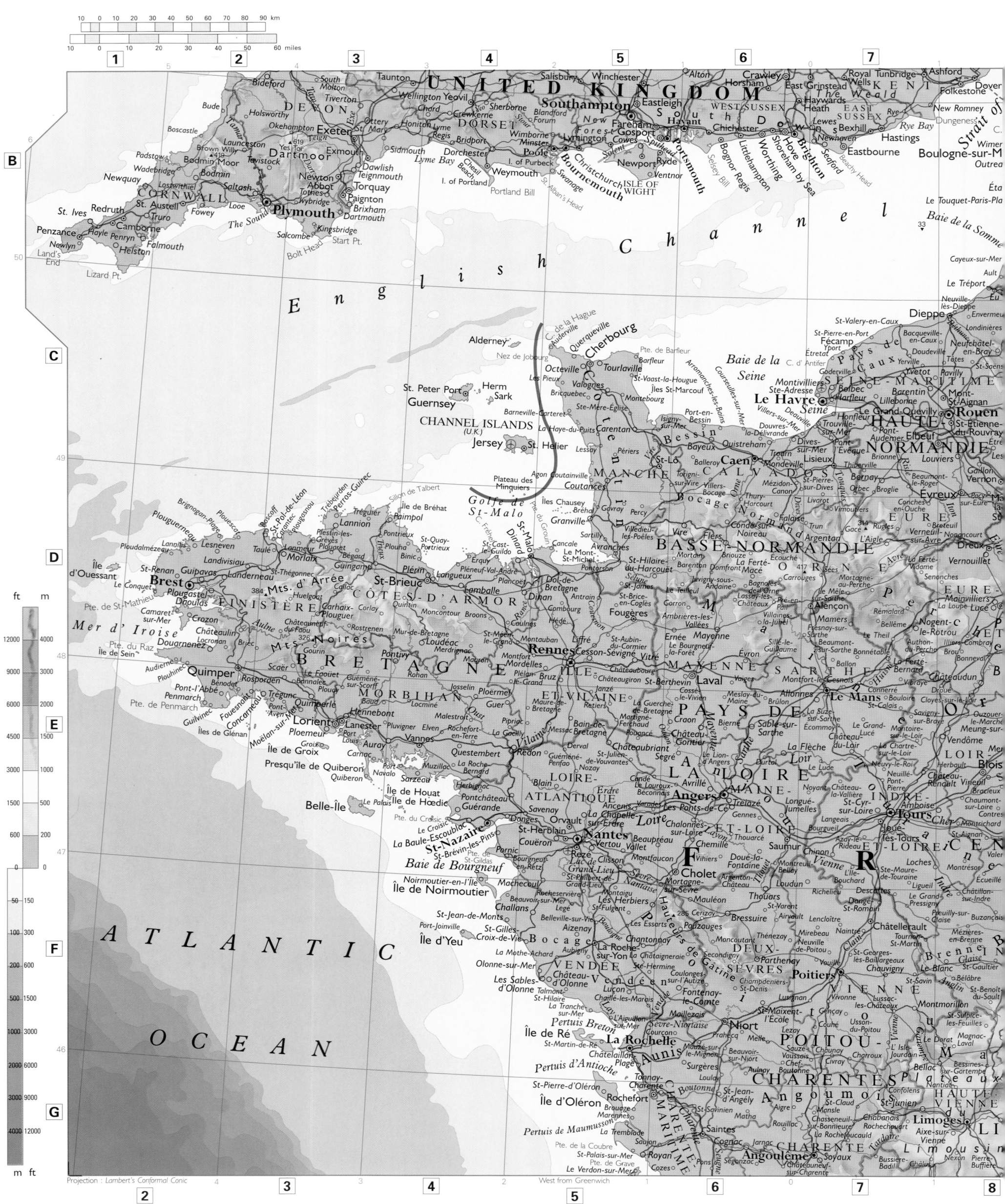

DÉPARTEMENTS IN THE PARIS AREA
1. Ville de Paris   3. Val-de-Marne
2. Seine-St-Denis   4. Hauts-de-Seine

Underlined towns give their name to the
administrative area in which they stand.

COPYRIGHT GEORGE PHILIP LTD.

East from Greenwich

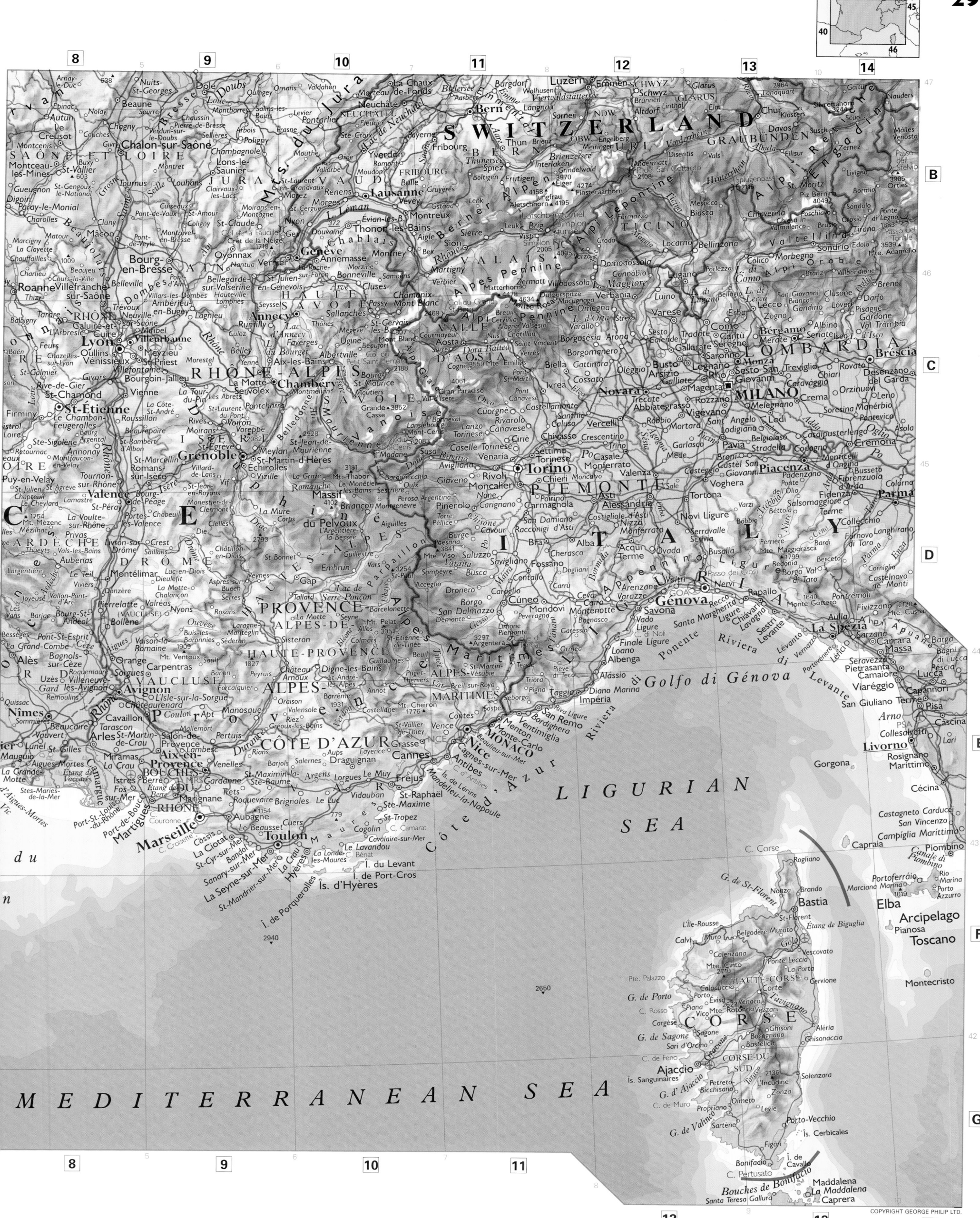

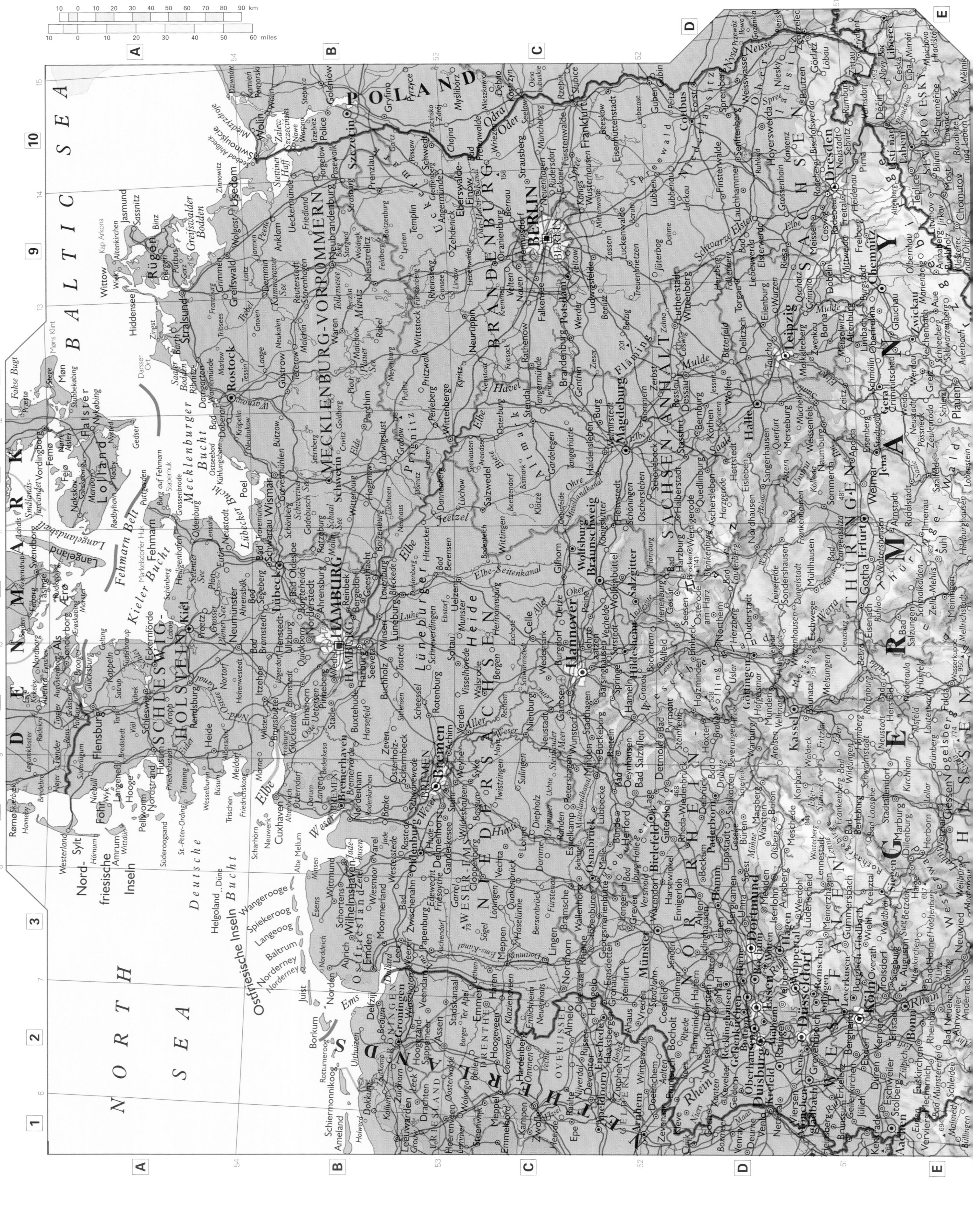
10 0 10 20 30 40 50 60 70 80 90 km
10 0 10 20 30 40 50 60 miles
NORTH SEA
BALTIC SEA
DENMARK
POLAND
NETHERLANDS
GERMANY
SCHLESWIG-HOLSTEIN
MECKLENBURG-VORPOMMERN
BRANDENBURG
NIEDERSACHSEN
SACHSEN-ANHALT
SACHSEN
THÜRINGEN
NORDRHEIN-WESTFALEN
HESSEN
BERLIN
HAMBURG
BREMEN
Hannover
Magdeburg
Leipzig
Dresden
Kiel
Lübeck
Rostock
Szczecin
Köln
Düsseldorf
Dortmund
Bielefeld
Kassel
Erfurt
Chemnitz
Lüneburger Heide
Ostfriesische Inseln
Nordfriesische Inseln
Deutsche Bucht
Mecklenburger Bucht
Fehmarn Belt
Kieler Bucht
Rügen

Underlined towns give their name to the administrative area in which they stand.

Projection: Lambert's Conformal Conic

COPYRIGHT GEORGE PHILIP LTD.

East from Greenwich

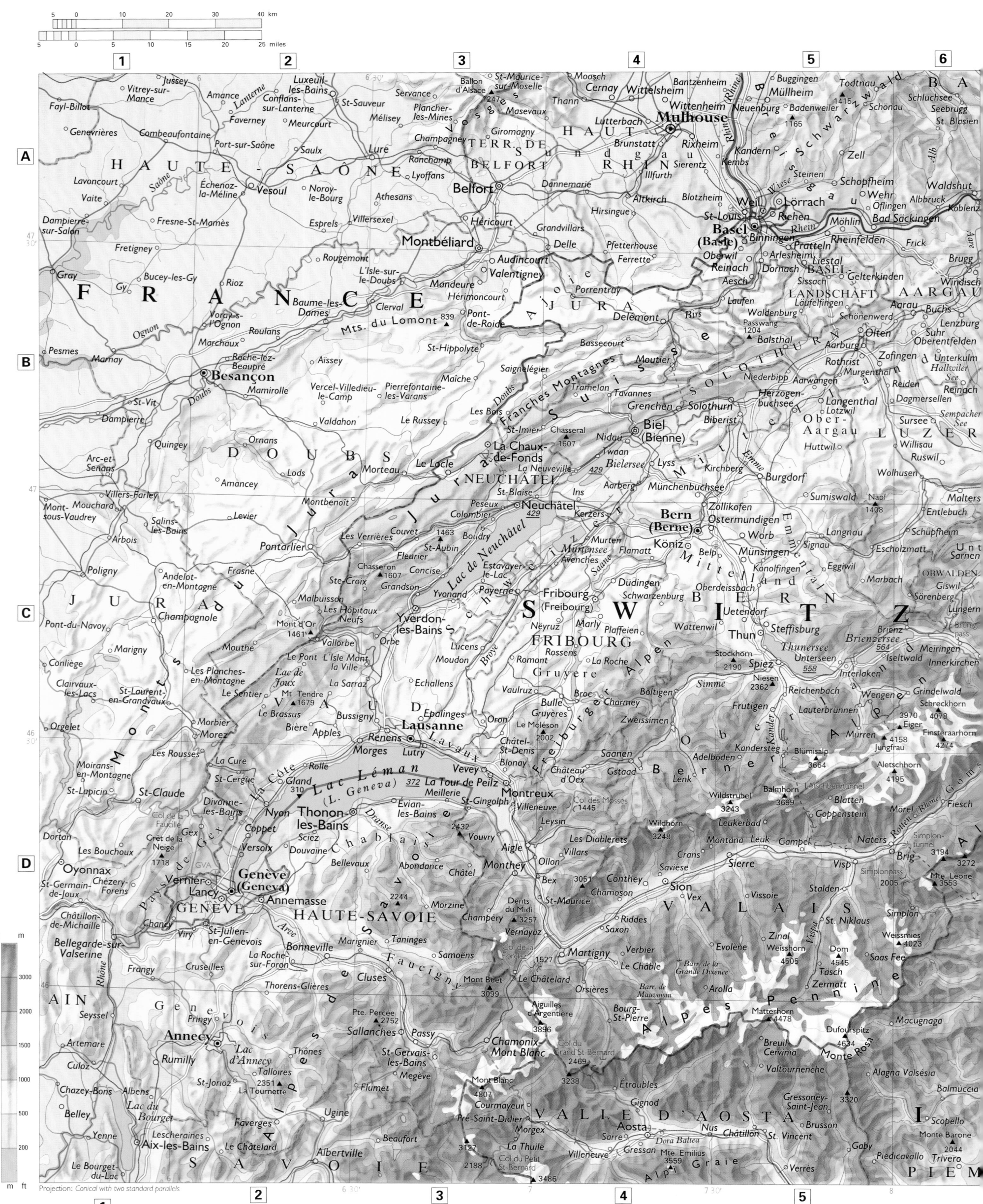

Underlined towns give their name to the
administrative area in which they stand.

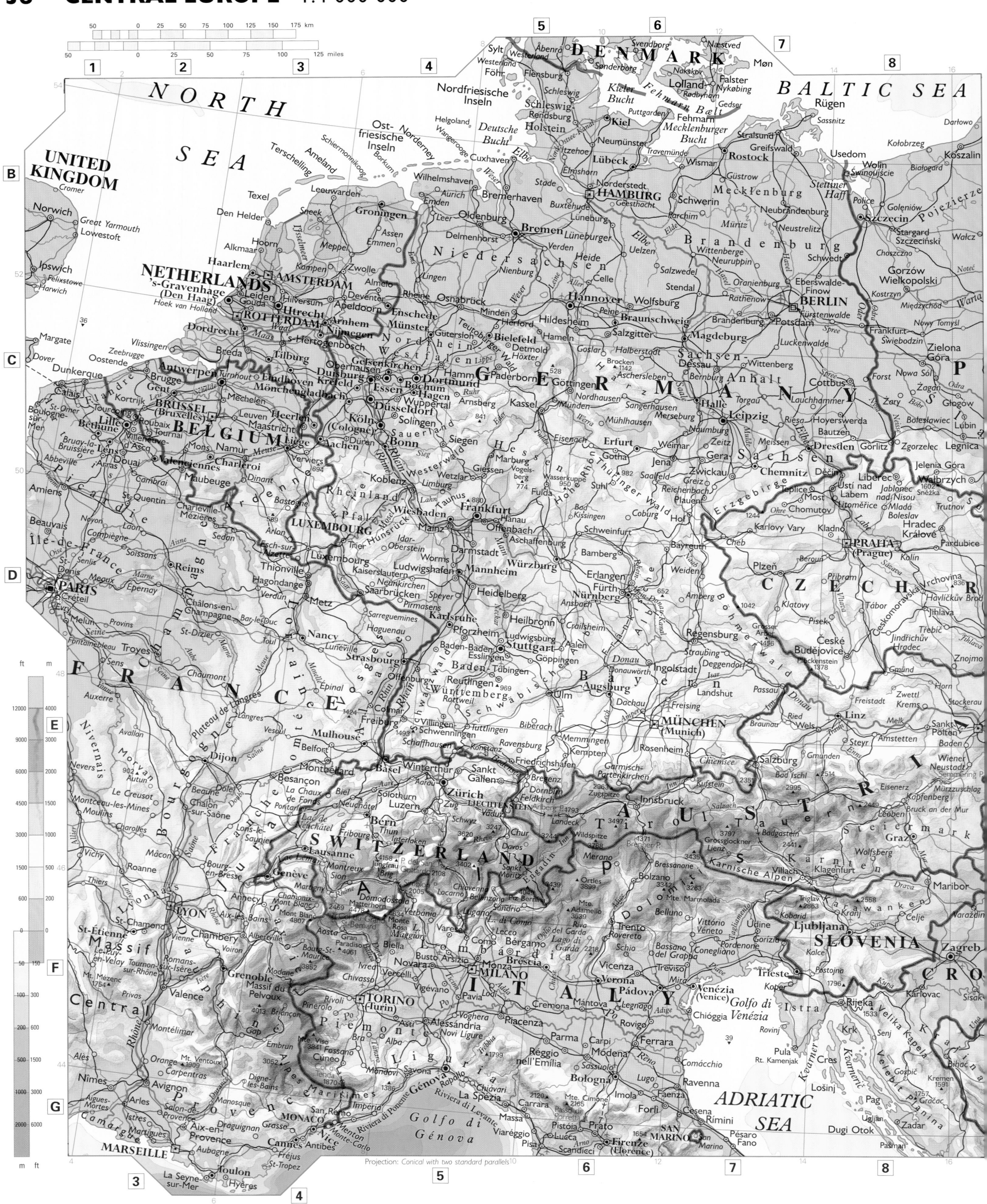

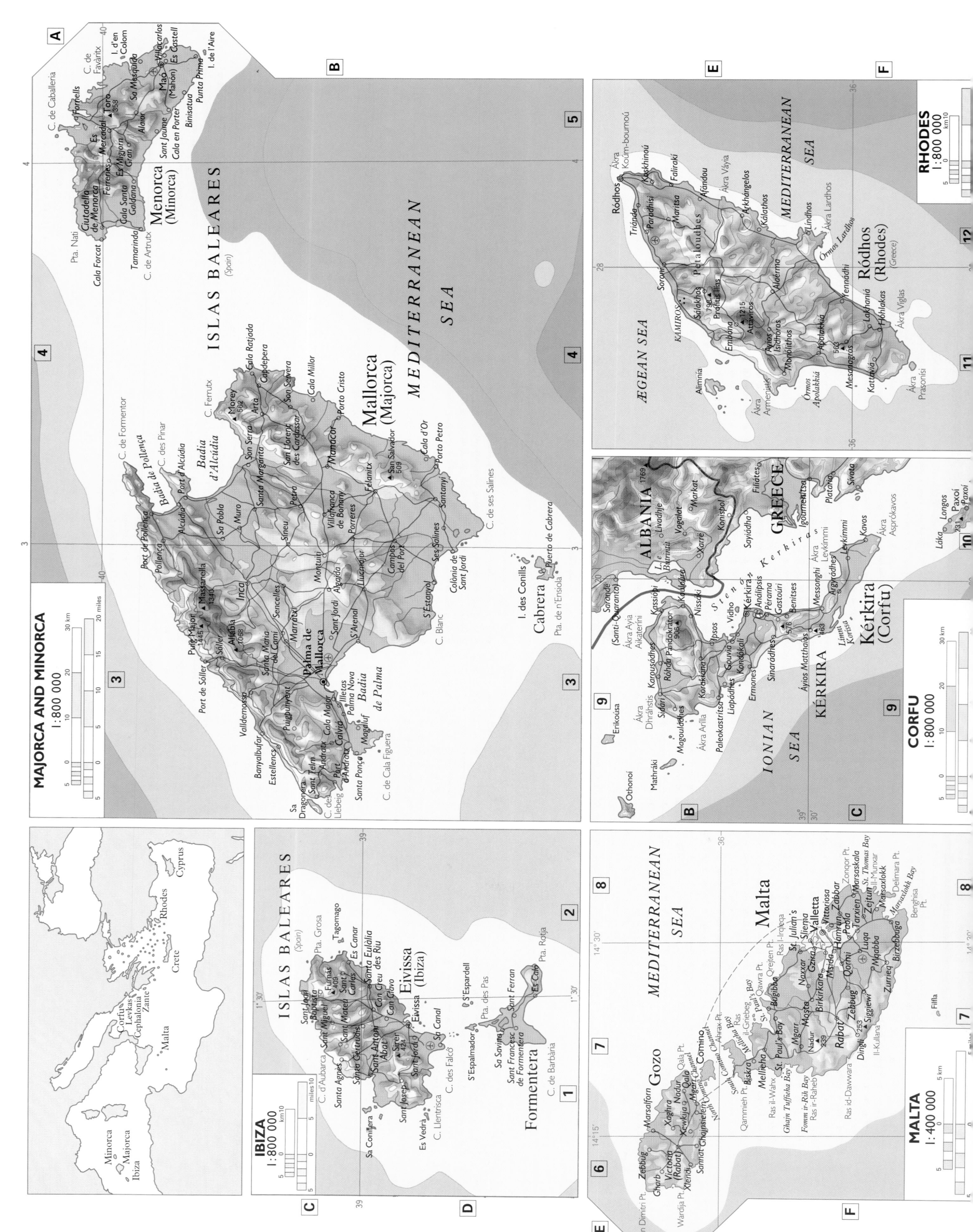

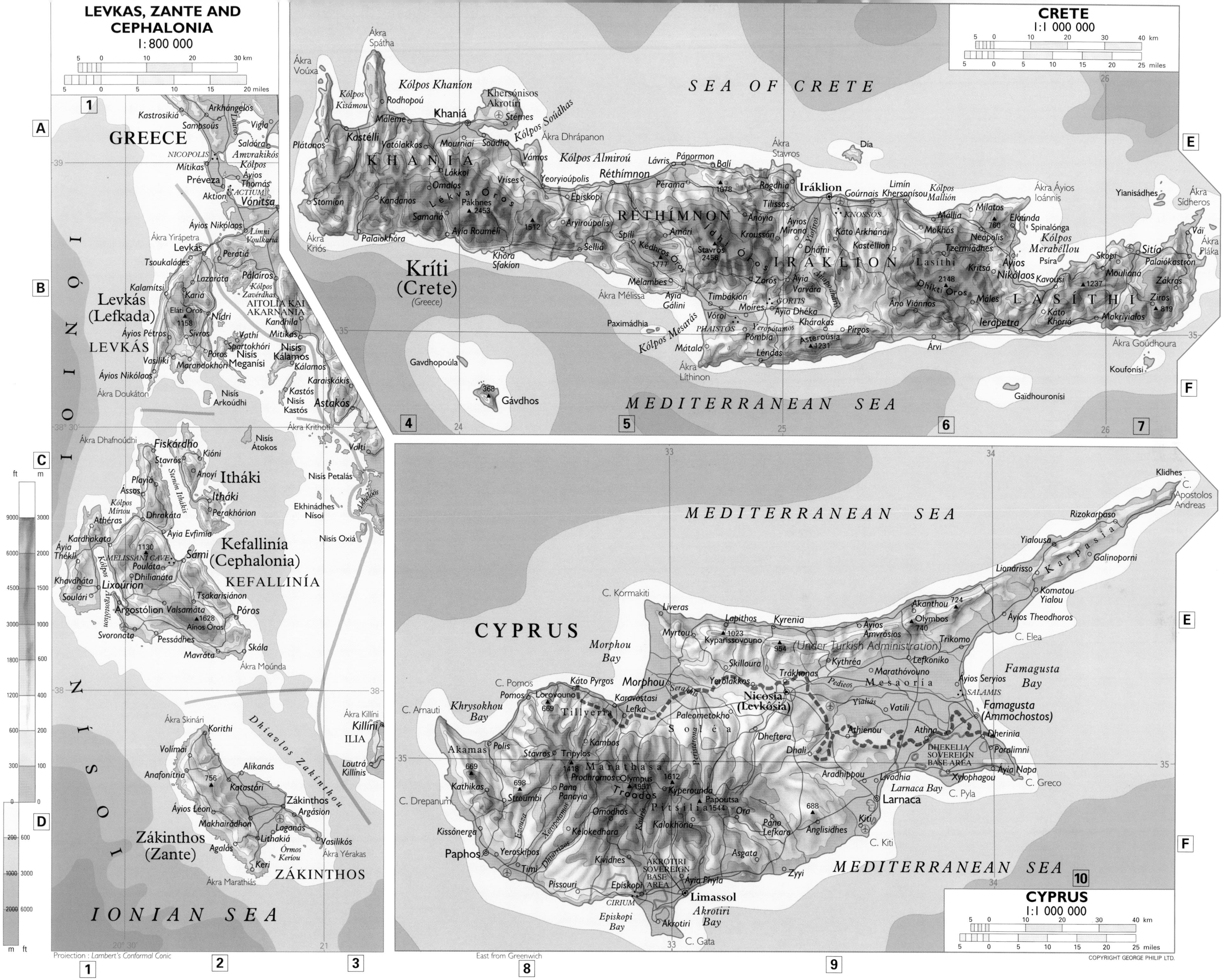

LEVKAS, ZANTE AND CEPHALONIA
1:800 000

CRETE
1:1 000 000

CYPRUS
1:1 000 000

GREECE

IONIAN SEA
NÍSOI IÓNIOI

Levkás (Lefkada)
LEVKÁS
AITOLÍA KAI AKARNANÍA
ACTIUM
Vónitsa
Préveza
NICOPOLIS

Ithaki
Anoyi Ithaki
Kefallinía (Cephalonia)
KEFALLINÍA
Sami
Póros
Skála

Zákinthos (Zante)
ZÁKINTHOS

SEA OF CRETE

KHANIÁ
Khaniá
Lévka Oros
Samariá
Khóra Sfakíon
Ákra Spátha
Ákra Voúxa

RÉTHIMNON
Réthimnon
Ídhi Oros
2456

IRÁKLION
Iráklion
Knosós
GORTYS
PHAISTOS

LASÍTHI
Áyios Nikólaos
Ierápetra
Sitía
Zákros

Kríti (Crete) (Greece)

MEDITERRANEAN SEA

Gávdhos

CYPRUS
MEDITERRANEAN SEA
Karpasía
Rizokárpaso
C. Apostolos Andreas

Kyrenia
Nicosia (Levkósia)
Famagusta (Ammochostos)
Famagusta Bay
Morphou Bay
Morphou
Tróodos
Olympus 1951
Limassol
Larnaca
Paphos
Akrotíri Bay
Episkopi Bay
SALAMIS
Under Turkish Administration
DHEKELIA SOVEREIGN BASE AREA
AKROTÍRI SOVEREIGN BASE AREA

East from Greenwich

Projection: Lambert's Conformal Conic

COPYRIGHT GEORGE PHILIP LTD.

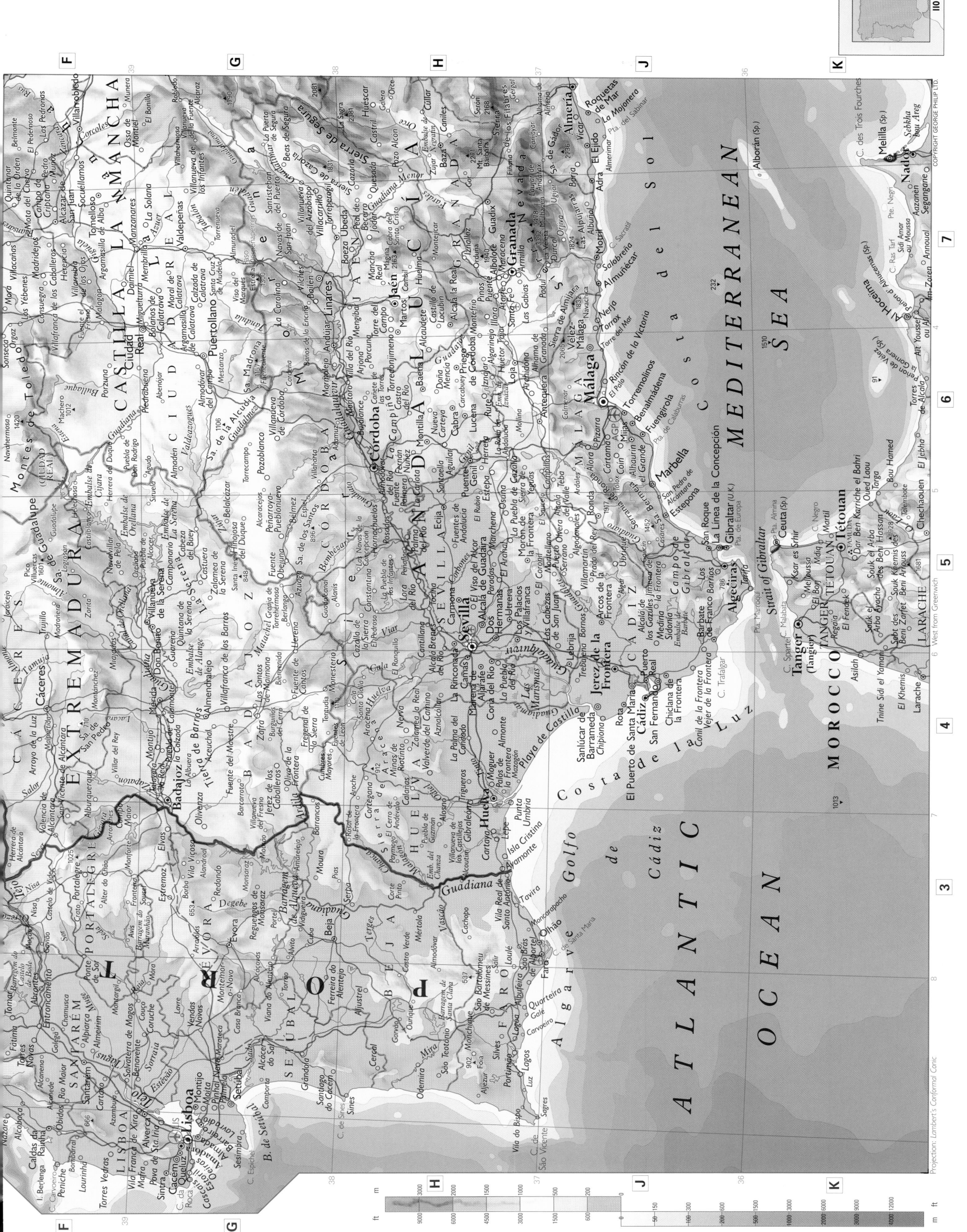

Underlined towns give their name to the
administrative area in which they stand.

Administrative divisions in Croatia:
1. Brodsko-Posavska   4. Medimurska   8. Virovitičko-Podravska
2. Koprivničko-Križevačka   6. Požeško-Slavonska   10. Zagrebačka
3. Krapinsko-Zagorska   7. Varaždinska

Inter-entity boundaries as agreed
at the 1995 Dayton Peace Agreement.

COPYRIGHT GEORGE PHILIP LTD.

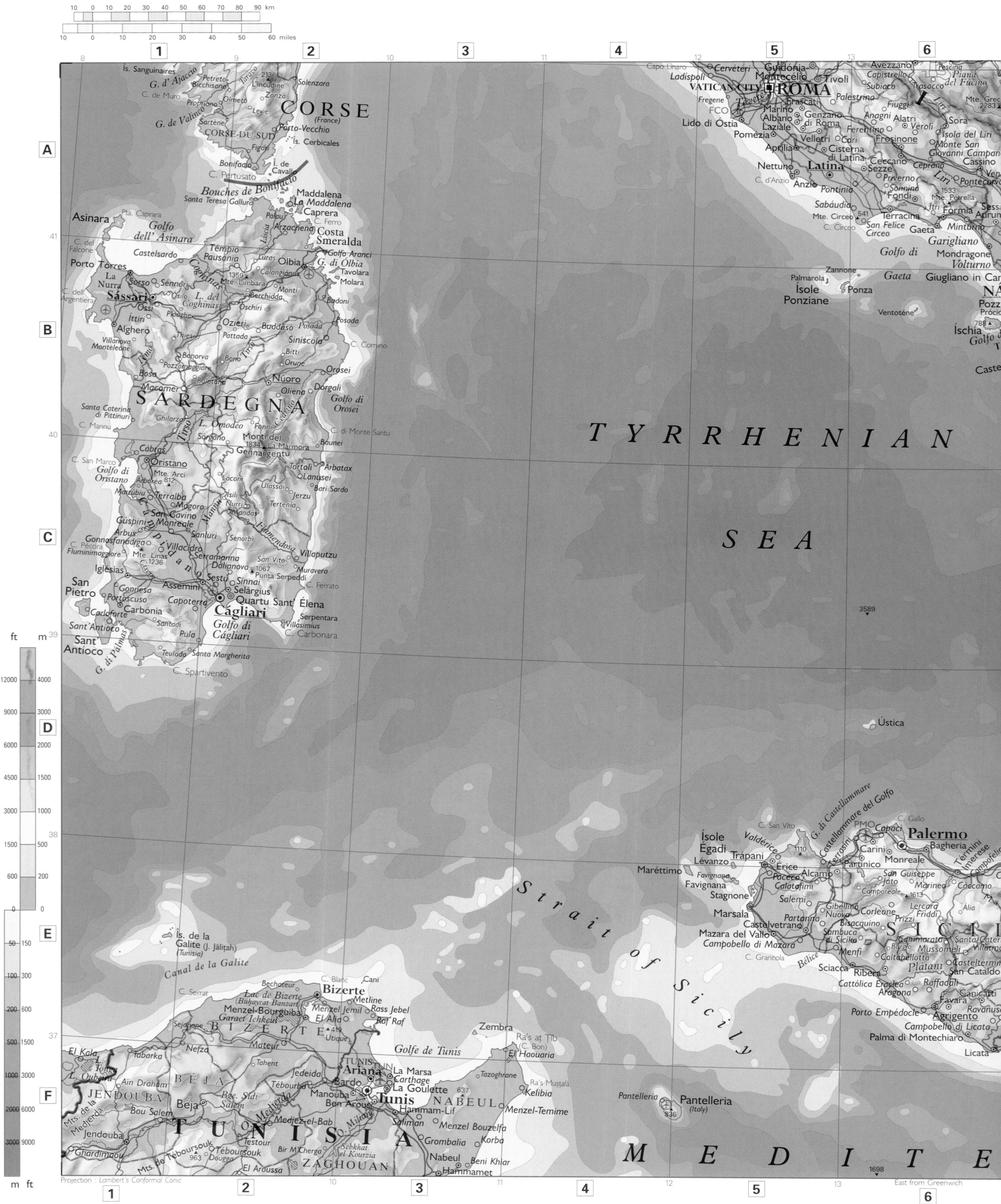

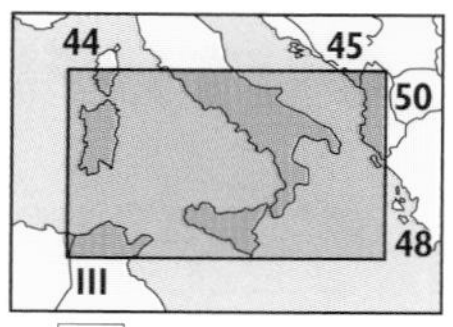

ADRIATIC SEA

IONIAN SEA

MEDITERRANEAN SEA

ALBANIA

GREECE

Strait of Otranto

Golfo di Táranto

Golfo di Manfredónia

Golfo di Salerno

Golfo di Squillace

Golfo di Sant' Eufémia

Golfo di Gioia

Golfo di Catánia

Golfo di Gela

Golfo di Noto

BASILICATA

CALÁBRIA

MOLISE

Ísole Eólie

Str. di Messina

Selected place names

Térmoli, Campomarino, L. di Lésina, Guglionesi, Montenero di Bisáccia, Sannicandro Gargánico, Vico del Gargano, Rodi Gargánico, Vieste, Agnone, Castel di Sangro, Castelmauro, Triveno, Larino, San Marco in Lámis, Mte. Calvo, Testa del Gargano, Apricena, San Severo, Campobasso, Ríccia, Lucera, Torremaggiore, San Paolo di Civitate, Monte Sant' Ángelo, Manfredónia, Fóggia, Isérnia, Campobasso, Bojano, Mte. Miletto, Piedmonte Matese, Guardia Sanframondi, Benevento, Caserta, Montesárchio, Ariano Irpino, Troía, Orta Nova, Orsara di Puglia, Candela, Cerignola, Canosa Andria, Barletta, Biscéglie, Molfetta, Giovinazzo, **Bari**, Mola di Bari, Polignano a Mare, Monópoli, Terlizzi, Corato, Bitonto, Ruvo di Púglia, Minervino Murge, Spinazzola, Gravina in Púglia, Altamura, Santéramo in Colle, Putignano, Noci, Acquaviva delle Fonti, Castellaneta, Mássafra, Grottáglie, Fasano, Cisternino, Ostuni, Céglie Messápico, San Vito dei Normanni, Mesagne, Francavilla Fontana, Latiano, **Brindisi**, Oria, Manduria, San Pietro Vernótico, Squinzano, **Lecce**, Copertino, Trepuzzi, Campi Salentina, Leverano, Nardo, Galatina, Martano, Otranto, Maglie, Poggiardo, Galátone, Gallipoli, Casarano, Taviano, Tricase, Ugento, Presicce, Gagliano del Capo, C. Santa Maria di Léuca, Sant' Andrea

Nápoli, Vesúvio, Torre del Greco, Torre Annunziata, Castellammare di Stabia, Sorrento, Amalfi, Cava de' Tirreni, **Salerno**, Battipáglia, Eboli, Campagna, Agrópoli, Capáccio, Castellabate, Punta Licosa, Ascea, Palinuro, C. Palinuro, Pisciotta, Camerota, Policastro, Sapri, Maratea, Práia a Mare, Scalea, Diamante, Belvedere Maríttimo, Cetraro, Fuscaldo, Páola, San Lúcido, Amantea, Nicastro, Gizzéria, Sambiase, Curinga, Pizzo, Vibo Valéntia, Tropea, C. Vaticano, Nicótera, Gioia Táuro, Rosarno, Palmi, Bagnara Cálabra, Scilla, Villa San Giovanni, **Messina**, **Réggio di Calábria**, Melito di Porto Salvo, Bova Marina, C. Spartivento

Potenza, Melfi, Rionero in Vúlture, Venosa, Lavello, Genzano di Lucánia, Palazzo San Gervasio, Irsina, Matera, **Matera**, Tricárico, Grassano, Ferrandina, Pisticci, Bernalda, Policoro, Nova Siri, Montalbano Iónico, San Mauro Forte, Tursi, Senise, Sant' Arcángelo, Lagonegro, Lauria, Moliterno, Castrovillari, Cassano allo Iónio, Trebisacce, Amendolara, Spezzano Albanese, Roggiano Gravina, San Marco Argentano, Rossano, Corigliano Cálabro, Crosia, Cariati, Bisignano, Acri, Longobucco, Rende, Montalto Uffugo, **Cosenza**, San Giovanni in Fiore, Cirò, Cirò Marina, Strongoli, Cótronei, Petilia Policastro, **Crotone**, Mesoraca, Sersale, Cutro, Isola di Capo Rizzuto, C. Rizzuto, Botricello, Tiriolo, **Catanzaro**, Borgia, Girifalco, Soverato, Chiaravalle Centrale, Guardavalle, Serra San Bruno, Polistena, Cittanova, Taurianova, Laureana di Borrello, Óppido Mamertina, Gioiosa Iónica, Roccella Iónica, Caulónia, Siderno, Locri, Ardore, Bovalino Marina, Montebello Iónico, Stromboli, Panarea, Salina, Filicudi, Alicudi, Lípari, Vulcano, Milazzo, Barcellona Pozzo di Gotto, Patti, Sant' Ágata Militello, Castroreale, Taormina, Giardini, Randazzo, Bronte, Adrano, Paternò, Biancavilla, Belpasso, Misterbianco, **Catánia**, Acireale, Giarre, Riposto, Máscali, Etna, Regalbuto, Leonforte, Nicosia, Enna, Piazza Armerina, **Caltanissetta**, Valguarnera Caropepe, Ramacca, Palagonia, Scordia, Lentini, Carlentini, Francofonte, Militello in Val di Catánia, Vizzini, Grammichele, Caltagirone, Butera, Gela, Vittoria, Cómiso, Ragusa, Módica, Scicli, Pozzallo, Íspica, Rosolini, Noto, Ávola, Siracusa, Canicattini Bagni, Floridia, Palazzolo Acreide, Chiaramonte Gulfi, Santa Croce Camerina, C. Scarámia, Pachino, C. Passero, C. Murro di Porco

Albania / Greece

Shëngjin, Lezhe, Rrëshen, MIRDITE, Rubik, Milot, Ullëz, Mamuras, Mat, Kruje, Laç, Fushë-Krujë, **Durrës**, **Tiranë**, Kavajë, Krrabe, Pequin, Elbasan, Cërrik, Lushnjë, Fier, Patos, Berat, Vlorë, Himare, Sarandë, Gjirokastër, Lukovë, Delvine, Finiq, Konispol, **KÉRKIRA**, **Kérkira (Corfu)**, Gastoúri, Igoumenítsa, Othonoi, Erikoúsa, Karousádhes, Paxoí

Underlined towns give their name to the
administrative area in which they stand.

COPYRIGHT GEORGE PHILIP LTD.

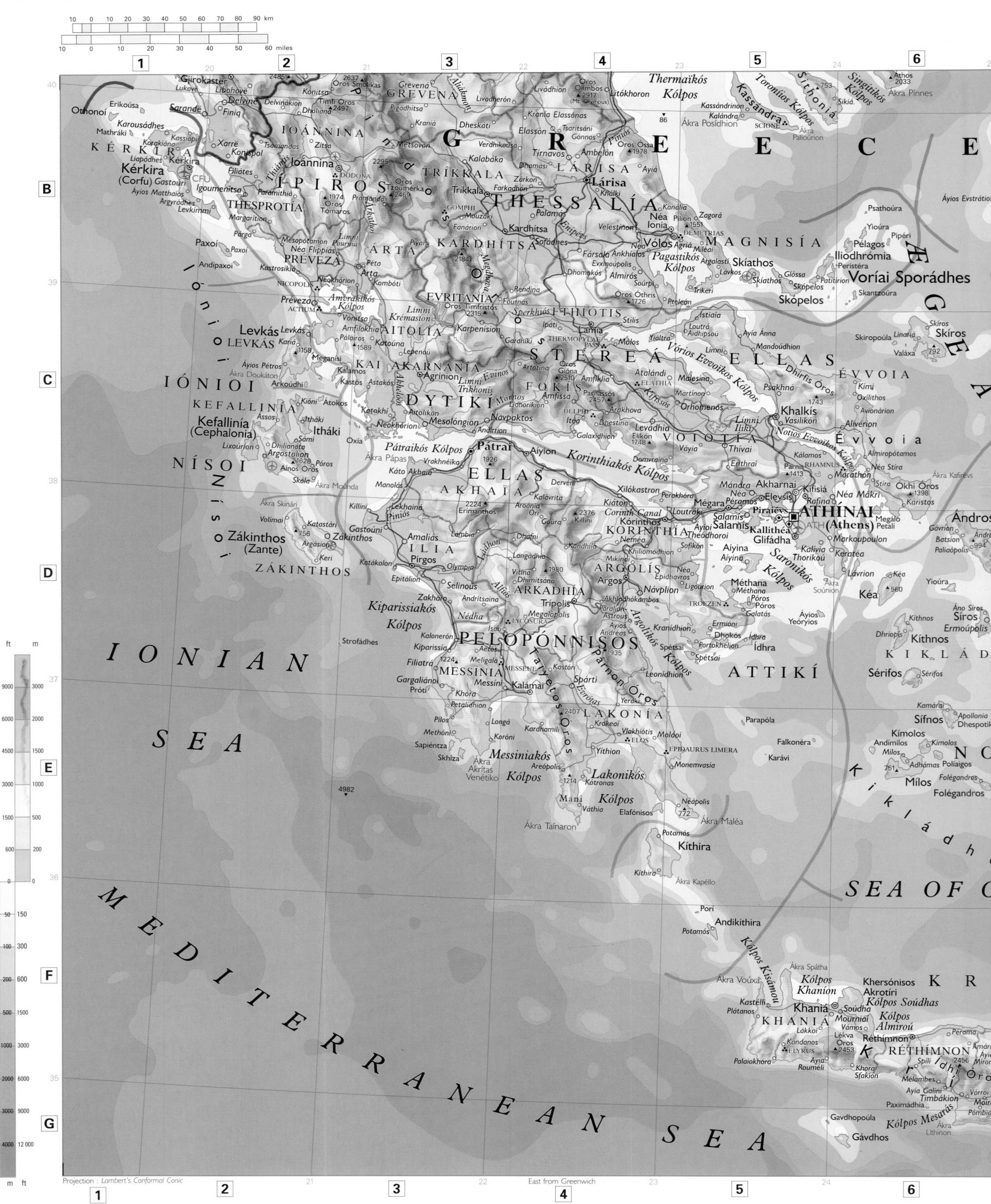

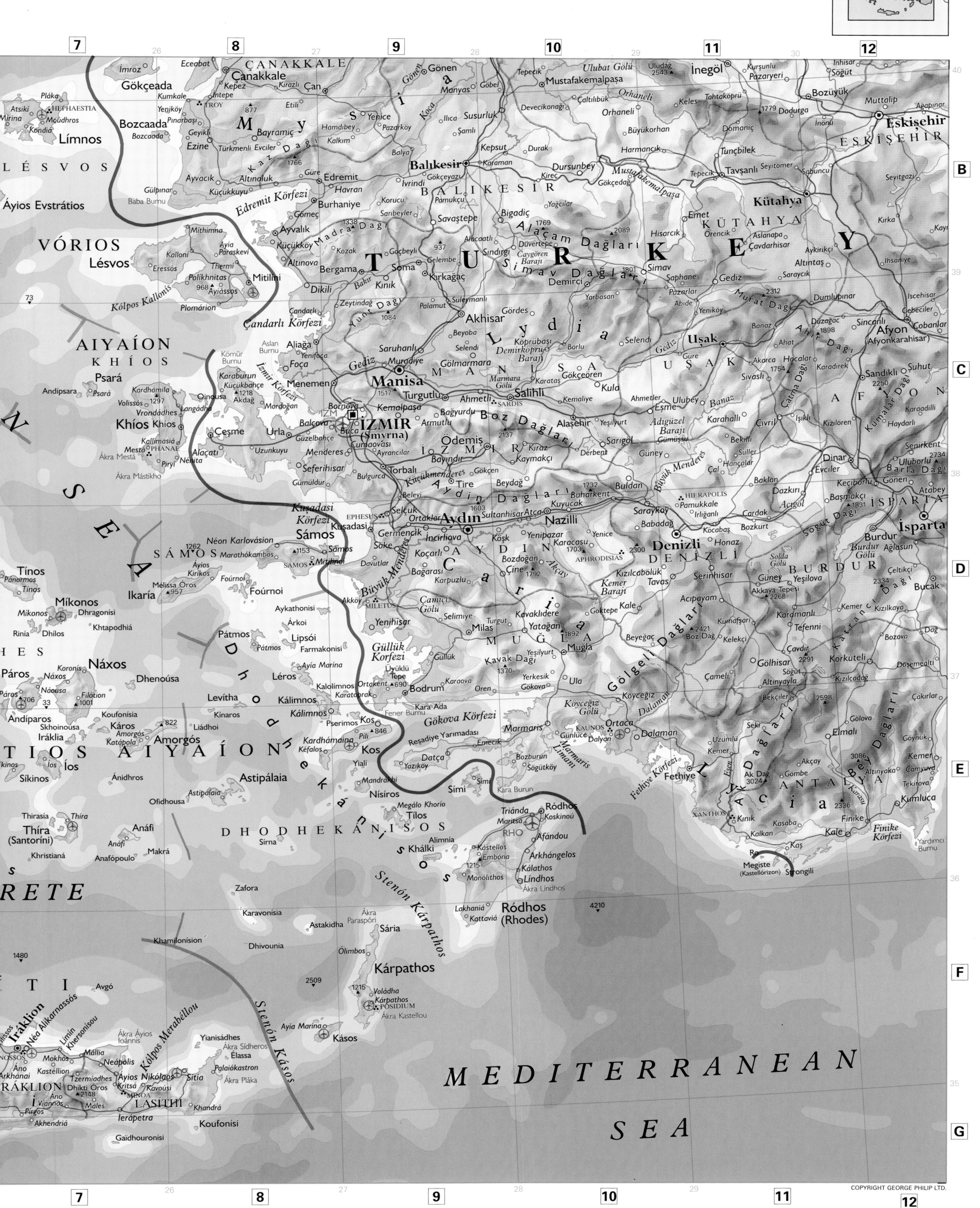

COPYRIGHT GEORGE PHILIP LTD.

Projection : Lambert's Conformal Conic

East from Greenwich

------- Inter-entity boundaries as agreed
at the 1995 Dayton Peace Agreement.

Underlined towns give their name to the administrative area in which they stand.

COPYRIGHT GEORGE PHILIP LTD.

Administrative divisions in Croatia:
1. Brodsko-Posavska   5. Osječko-Baranjska
2. Koprivničko-Križevačka 6. Požeško-Slavonska
4. Medimurska   8. Virovitičko-Podravska   9. Vukovarsko-Srijemska

Inter-entity boundaries as agreed
at the 1995 Dayton Peace Agreement.

Projection : Lambert's Conformal Conic   East from Greenwich

Underlined towns give their name to the
administrative area in which they stand.

COPYRIGHT GEORGE PHILIP LTD.

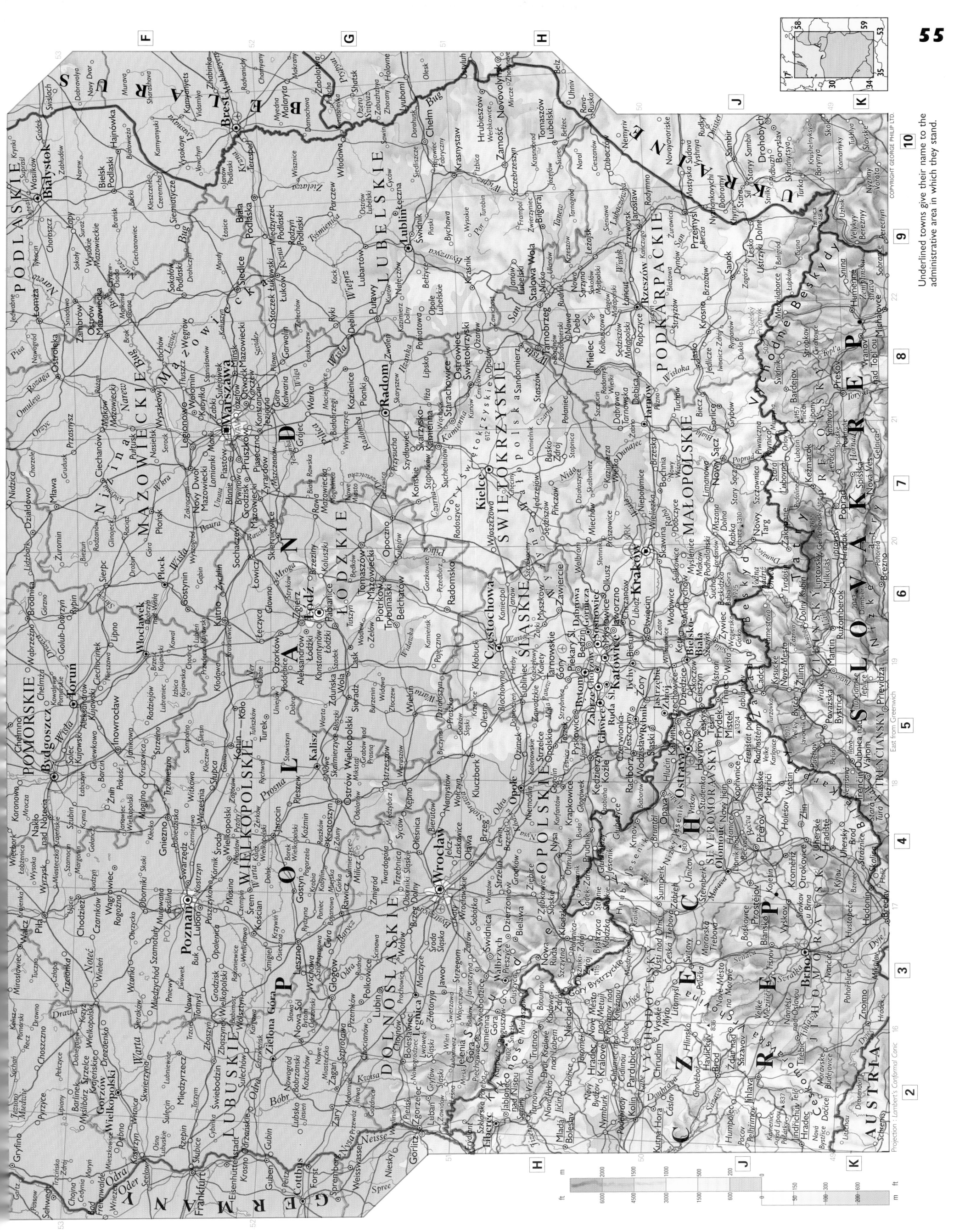

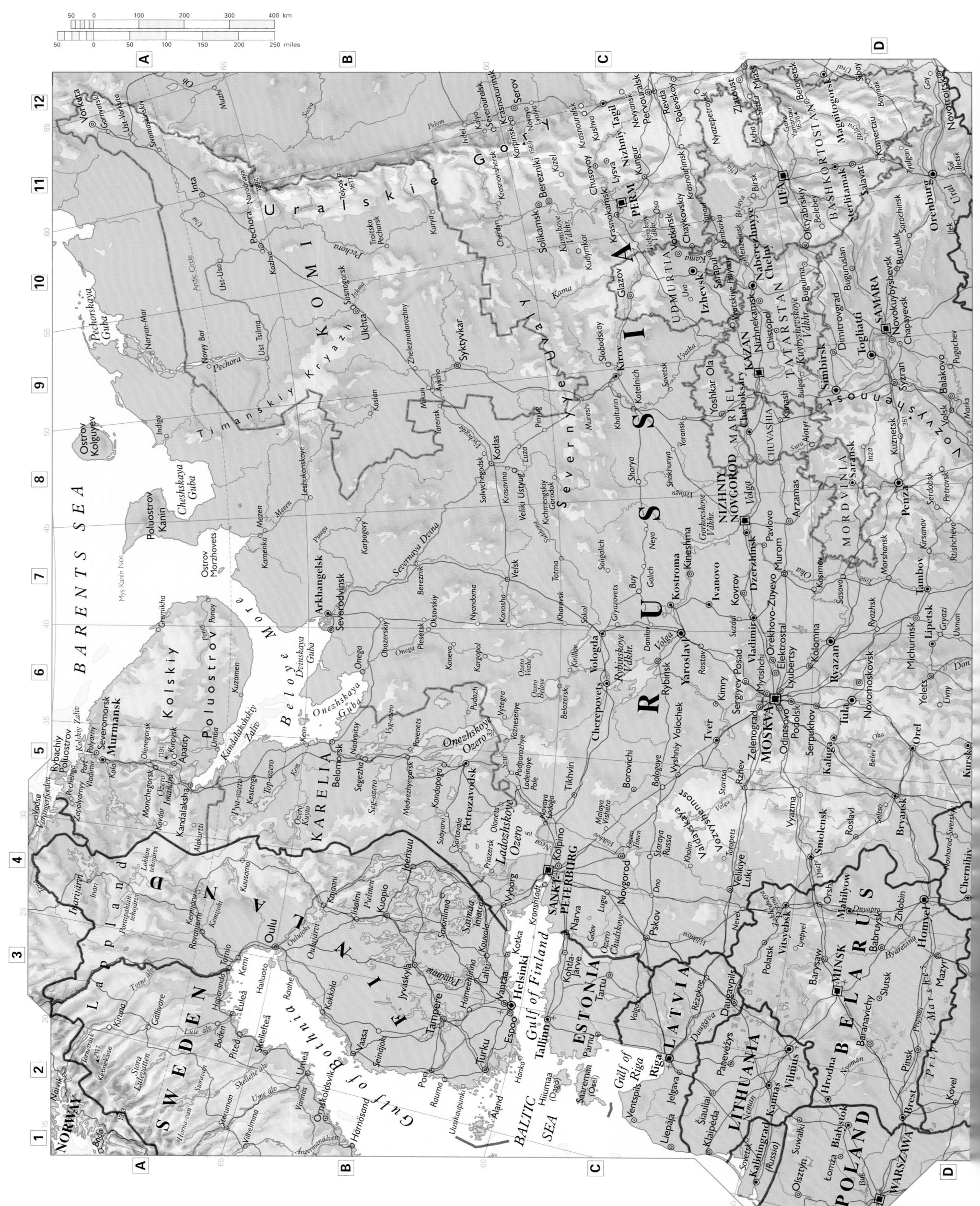

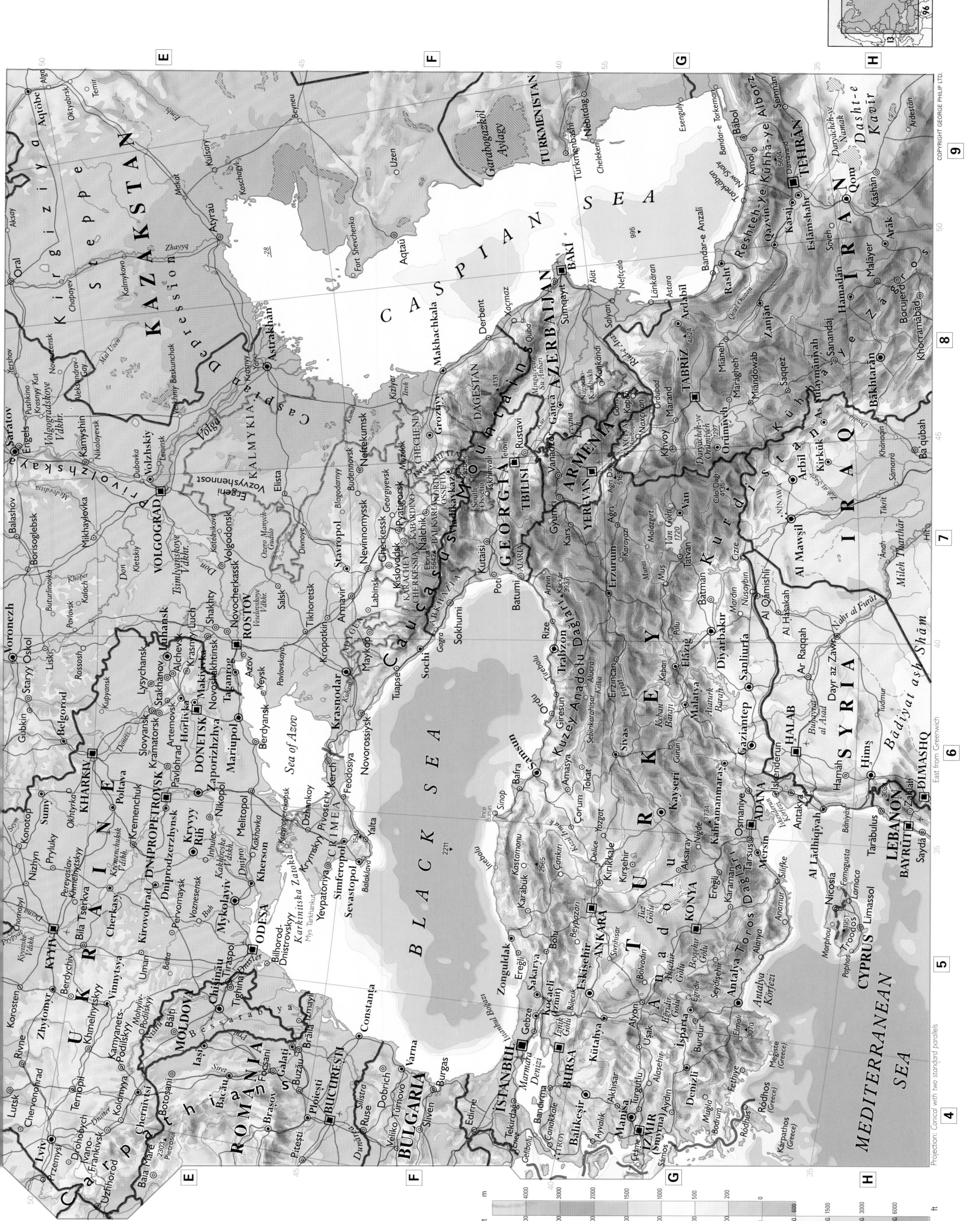

COPYRIGHT GEORGE PHILIP LTD.

Projection: Conical with two standard parallels

East from Greenwich

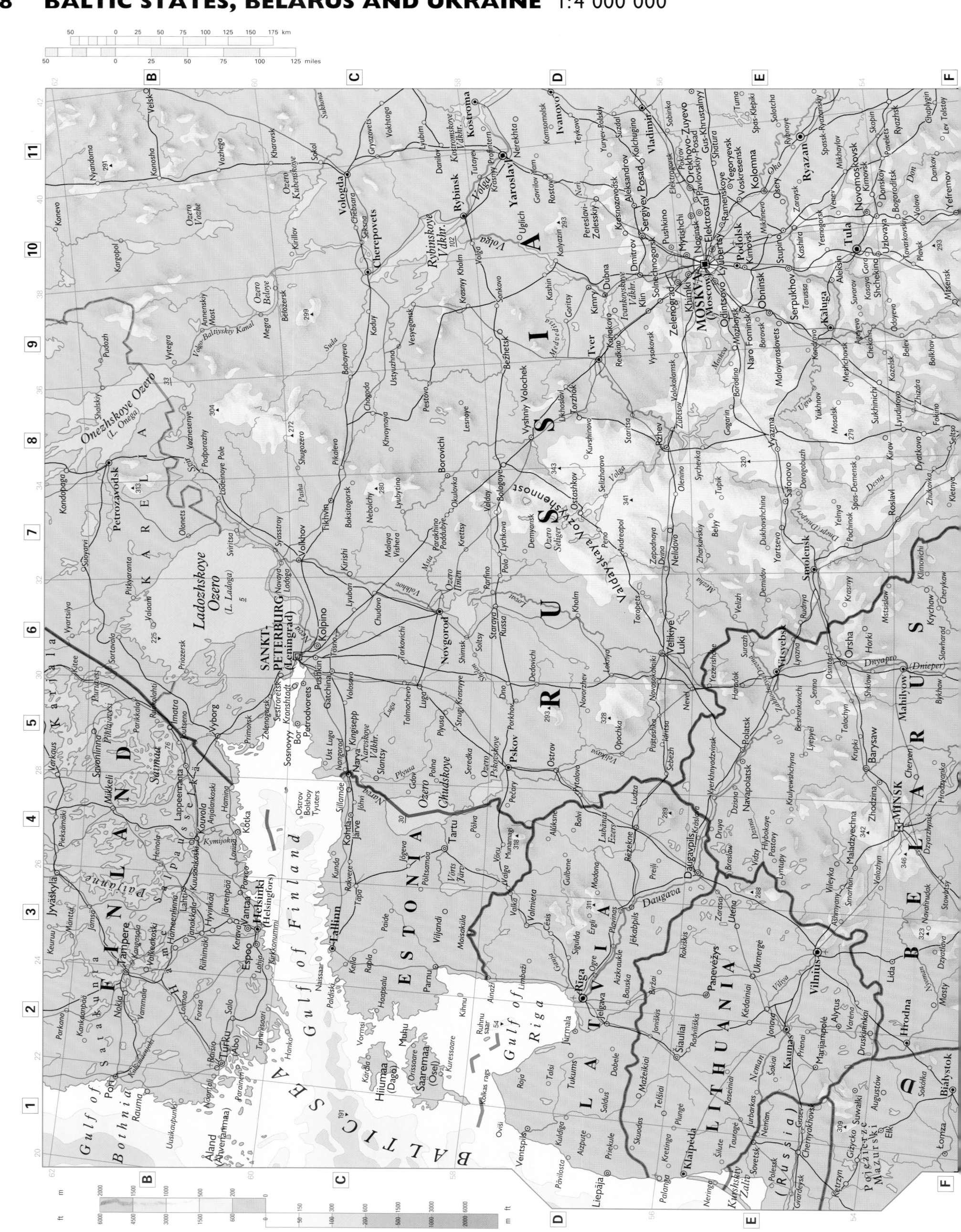

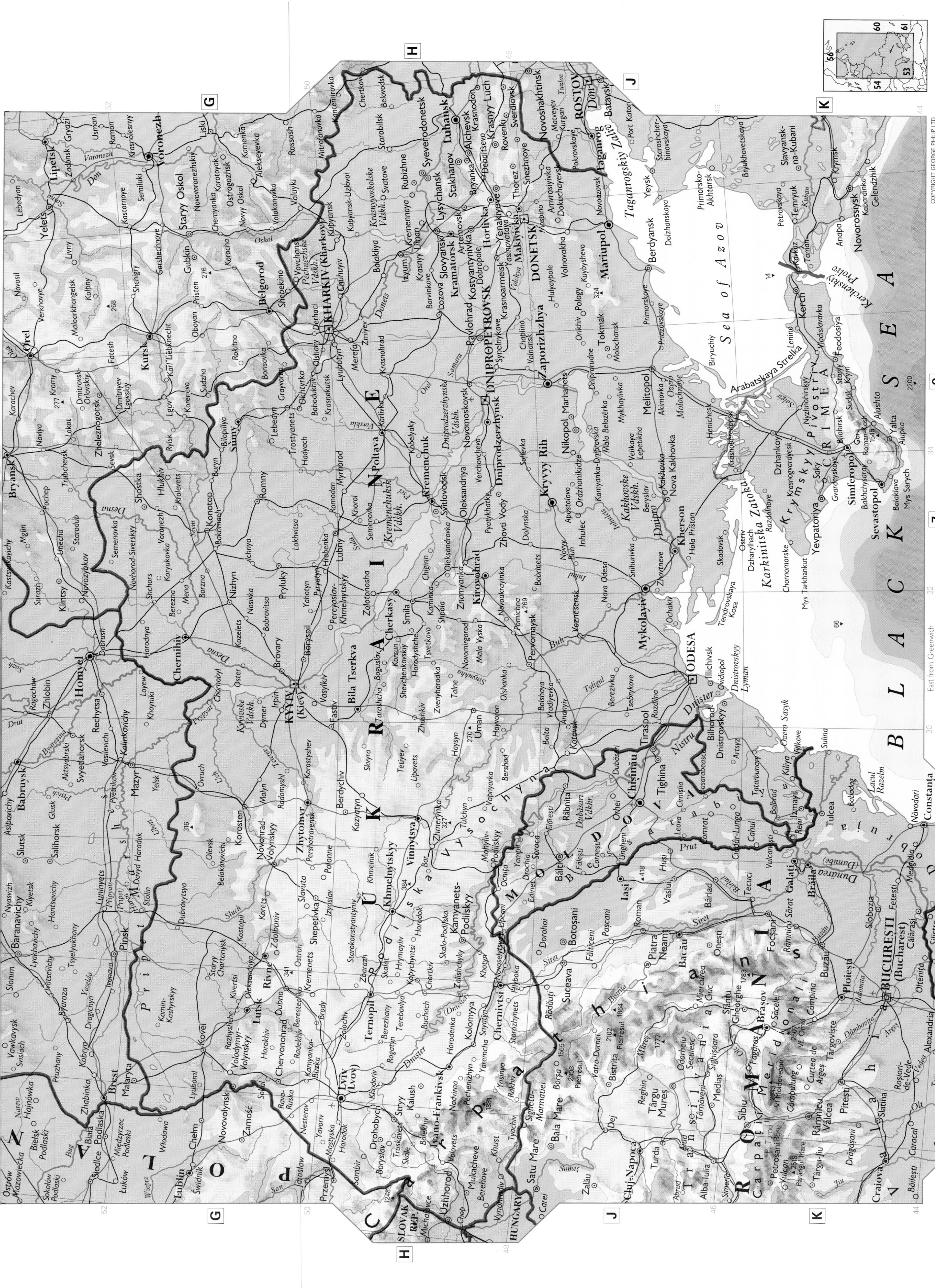

BLACK SEA

Sea of Azov

UKRAINE

ROMANIA

MOLDOVA

POLAND

SLOVAK REP.

HUNGARY

BULGARIA

CRIMEA

DONETSK

Taganrogskiy Zaliv

Kerchenskiy Proliv

KYIV (Kiev)

KHARKIV (Kharkov)

DNIPROPETROVSK

ROSTOV

ODESA

BUCUREŞTI (Bucharest)

Constanţa

Dunărea (Danube)

East from Greenwich

Projection: Conical with two standard parallels

COPYRIGHT GEORGE PHILIP LTD.

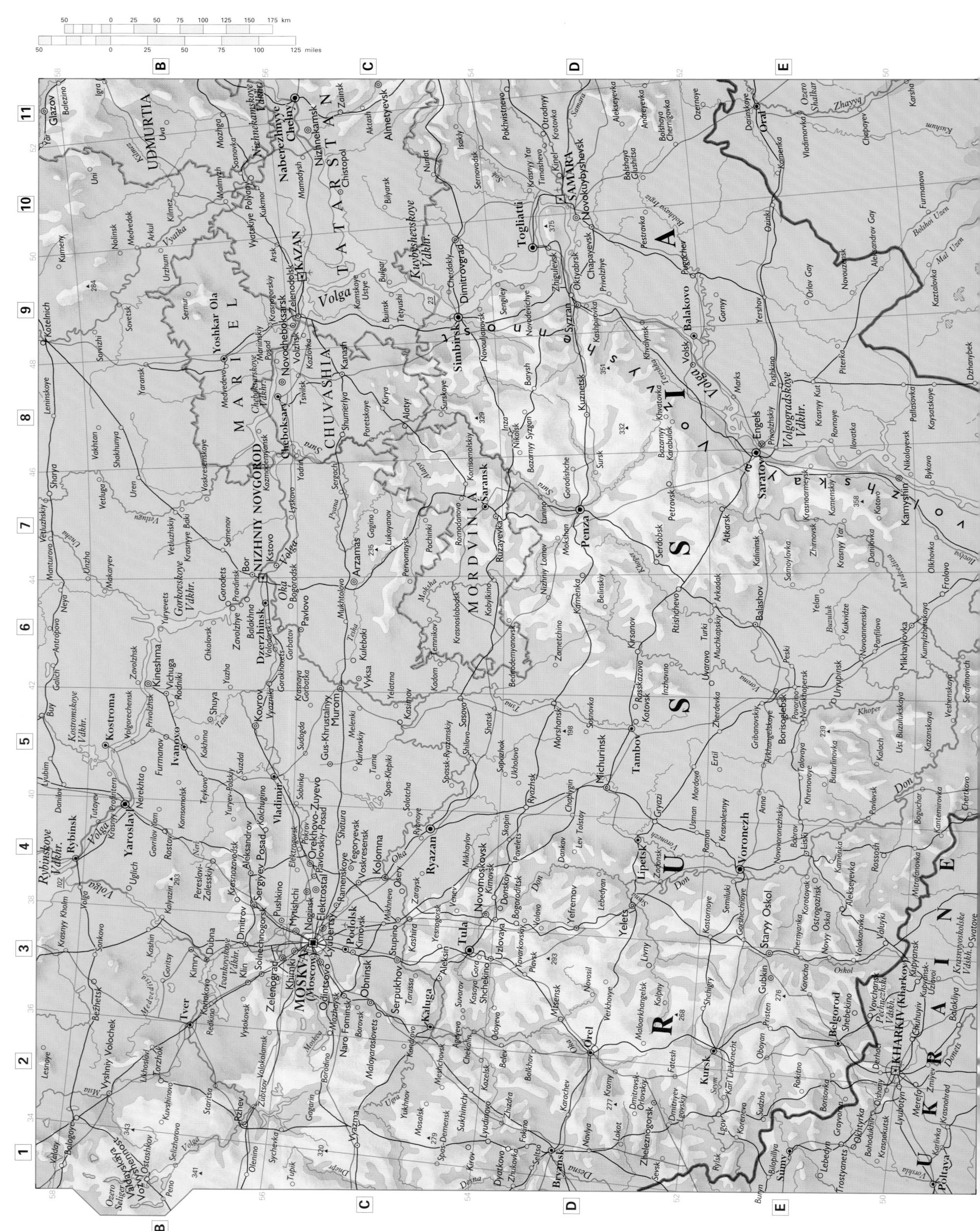

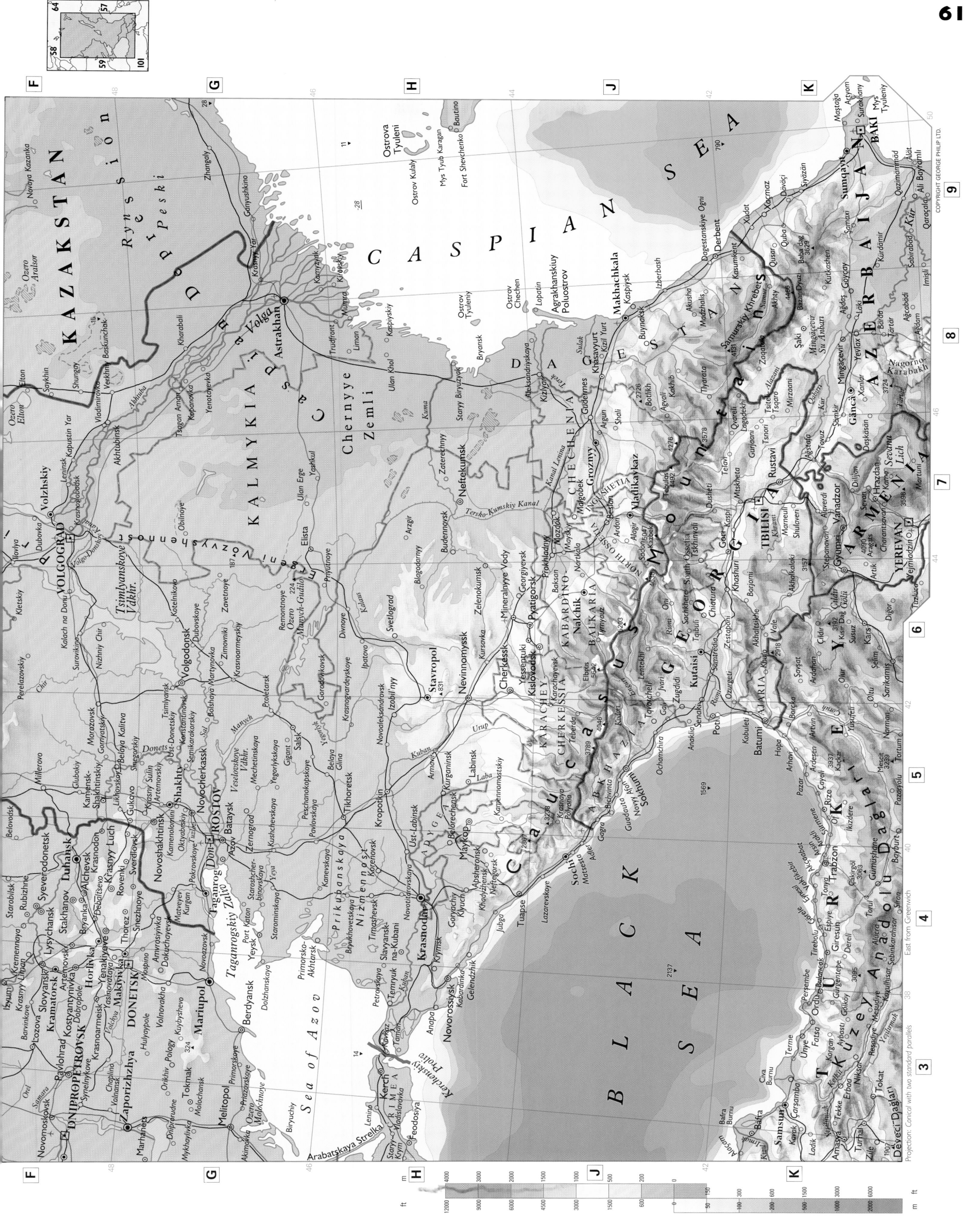

COPYRIGHT GEORGE PHILIP LTD.

Projection: Bonne

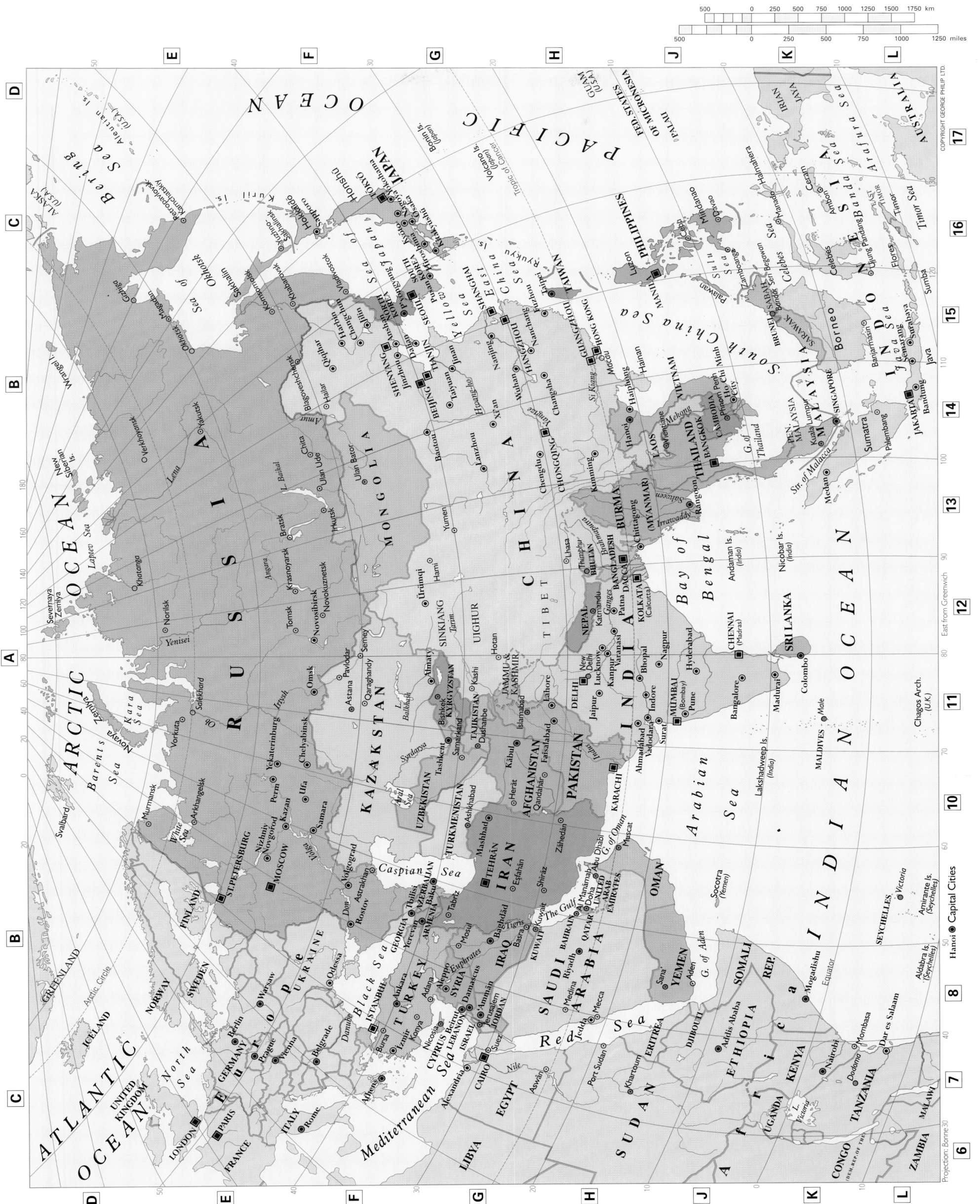

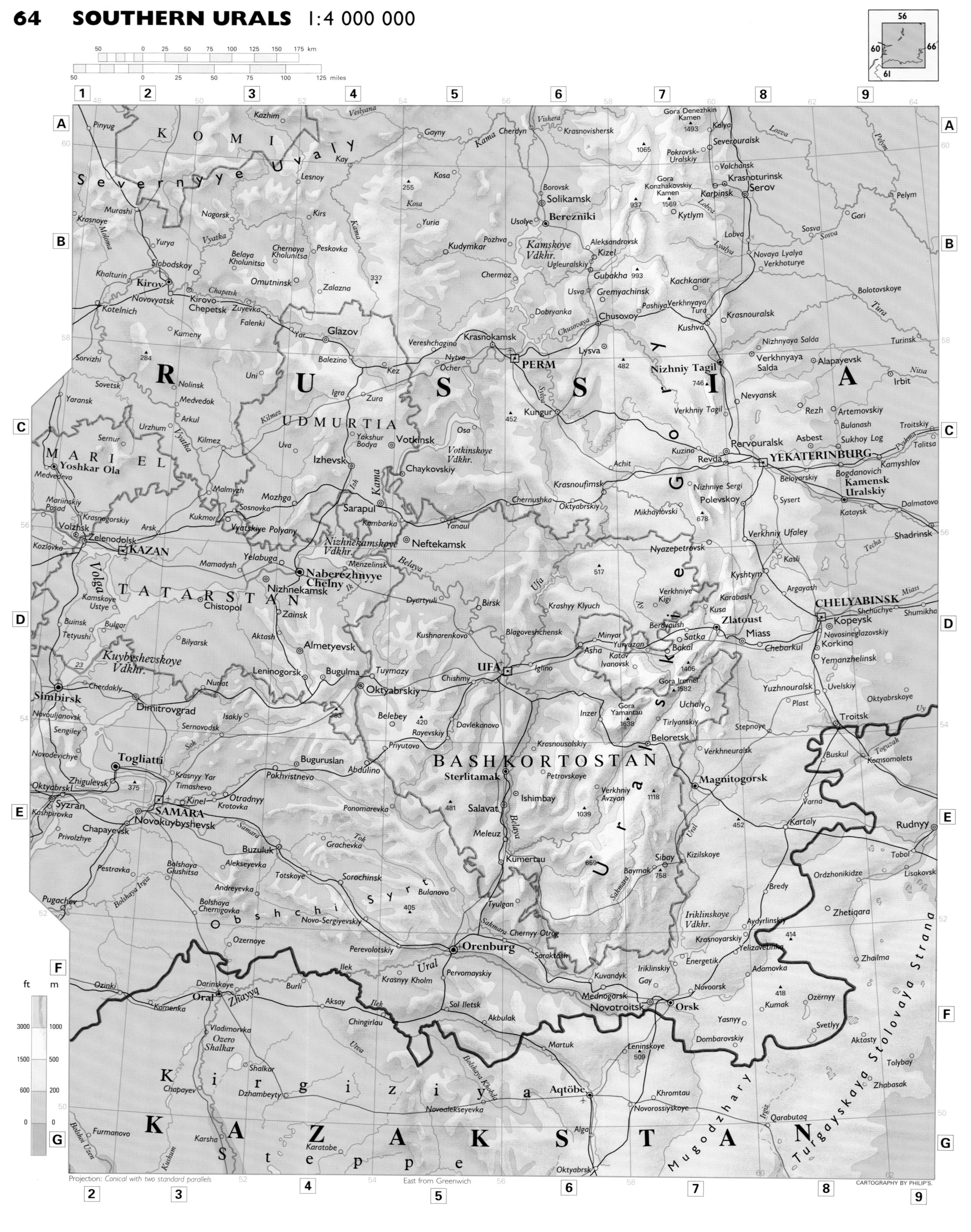

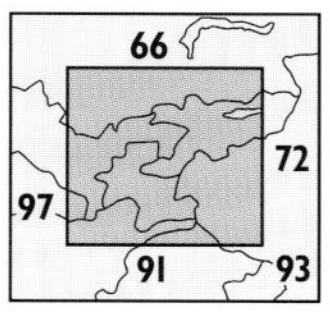

COPYRIGHT GEORGE PHILIP LTD.

East from Greenwich

Projection: Conical with two standard parallels

50 0 25 50 75 100 125 150 175 km
50 0 25 50 75 100 125 miles

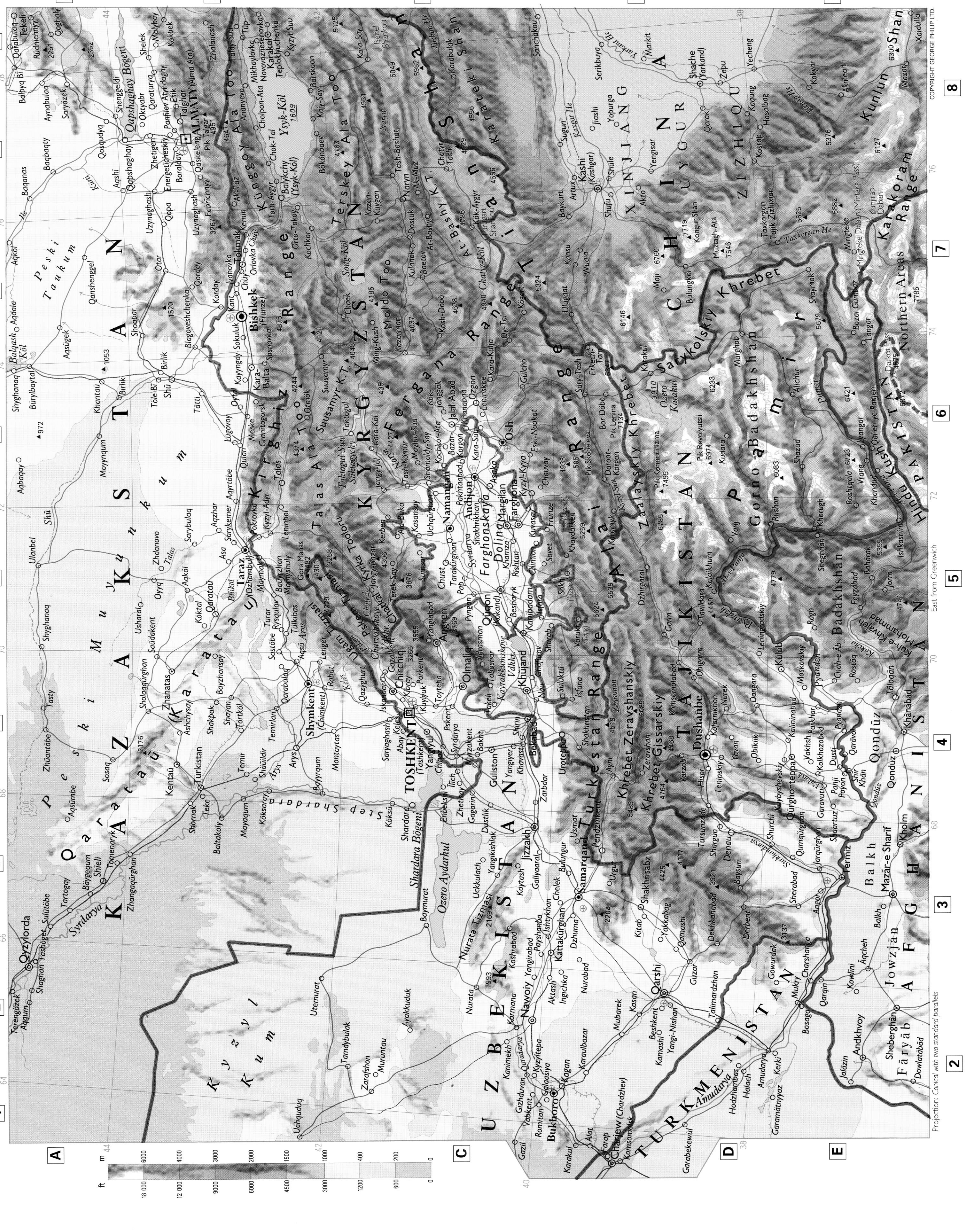

m ft
18 000 6000
12 000 4000 3000
9000 2000
6000 1500
4500 1000
3000 400
200 0

KAZAKSTAN

Peski Taukum
Peski Muyunkum
Betpak-Dala (Karatau)
Qaratau
Kyzyl Kum
Shardara Bögeni
Ozero Aydarkul
Step Shardara

Terengözek · Aqum · Toshkent · Shaghan · Oryzlorda · Qazaly

Balqash Köl · Shyghanaq · Aqqol

Tekeli · Qoghaly · Carabulaq · Rudnichnyy · Balpyq Bi · Aynabulaq · Saryőzek · Qapshaghay Bögeni · Shelek · Oqtyabr · Molodoy · Kökpek

ALMATY (Alma Ata) · Talghar · Esik · Qaskeleng · Energetichesky · Zhetigen

Bishkek (Frunze) · Kant · Sokuluk · Tokmak · Kemin

KYRGYZSTAN

Ysyk-Köl (Issyk-Köl) · Chok-Tal · Cholpon-Ata · Karakol · Teploklyuchenka

Kungöy Ala Too · Terskey Ala Too · Küngöy Ala Too

Kirghiz Range · Talas Ala Too · Suusamyr · Moldo Too

Fergana Range · Toktogul Suu · Song-Köl · Chatyr-Köl

Taraz (Dzhambul) · Shu · Lugovoy · Granitogorsk · Balta

Shymkent (Chimkent) · TOSHKENT (Tashkent) · Yangiyul · Chirchiq · Angren · Olmaliq · Bekabad · Khujand

Namangan · Andijon · Farghona (Fergana) · Margilan · Quqon (Kokand) · Osh · Jalal-Abad · Uzgen

UZBEKISTAN

Samarqand · Panjikent · Jizzakh · Guliston · Navoiy · Bukhoro · Qarshi

TAJIKISTAN

Dushanbe · Hisar · Qurghonteppa · Kůlob · Khorugh · Panji · Gorno-Badakhshan · Qondůz

Pamir · Sarykolskiy Khrebet · Zaalayskiy Khrebet · Turkestan Range · Khrebet Zeravshanskiy · Khrebet Gissarskiy · Alai Range · Badakhshan

Pik Lenina · Pik Kommunizma · Pik Revolyutsii

CHINA

XINJIANG UYGUR · ZIZHIQU

Kashi (Kashgar) · Shufu · Shule · Yengisar · Shache (Yarkand) · Yecheng · Kaxgar · Yopurga

Tian Shan · Karakax · Kunlun Shan · Karakoram Range

Kongur Shan 7719 · Muztagata 7546

AFGHANISTAN

Termiz · Mazar-e Sharif · Balkh · Kholm · Andkhvoy · Sheberghan · Fariab · Jowzjan · Hindu Kush · Northern Areas PAKISTAN

TURKMENISTAN

Charlew (Chardzhev) · Komsomol · Amudarya · Kerki · Kelif

Projection: Conical Orthomorphic with two standard parallels

COPYRIGHT GEORGE PHILIP LTD.

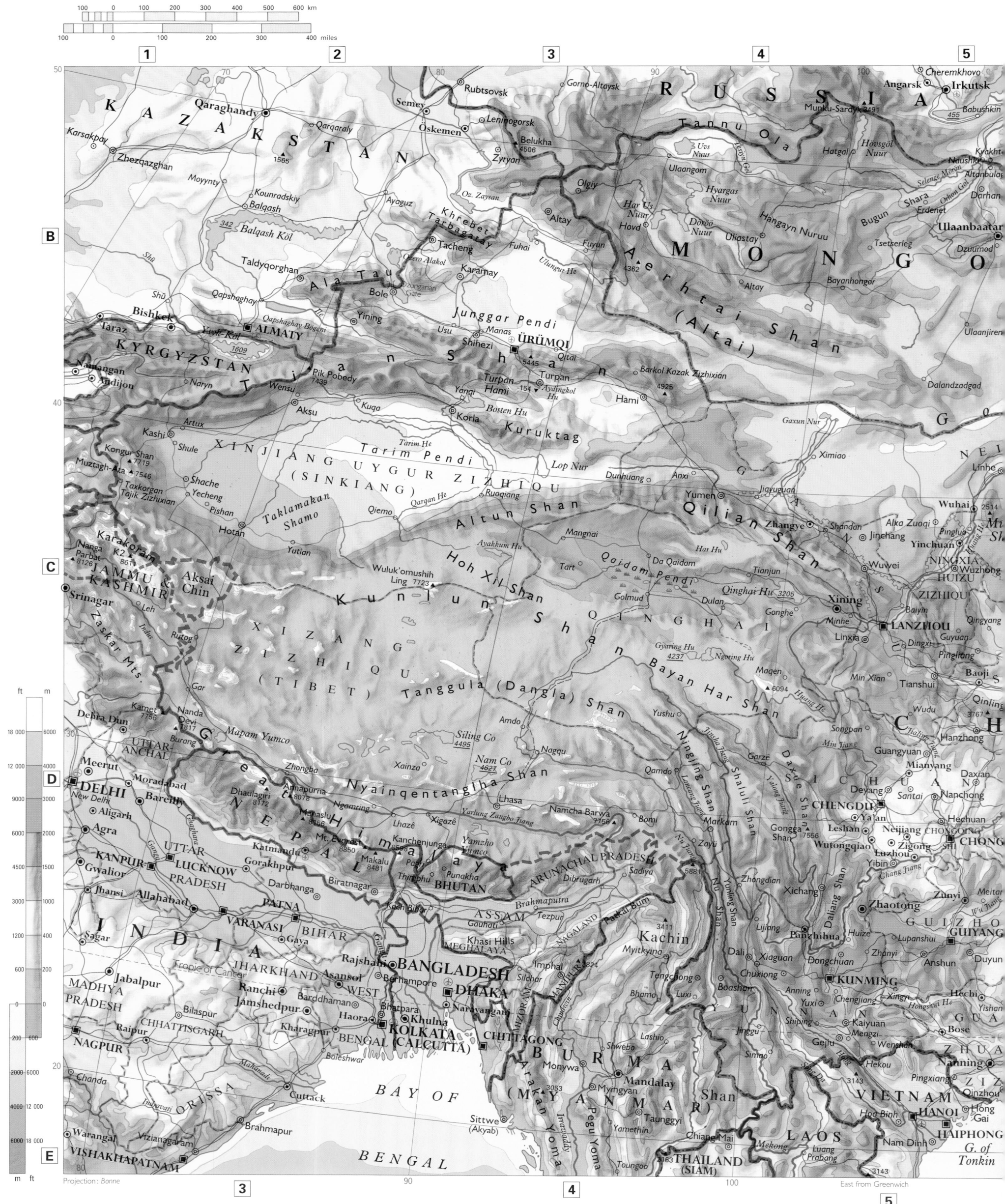

Projection: Bonne

East from Greenwich

JAPAN 1:4 000 000

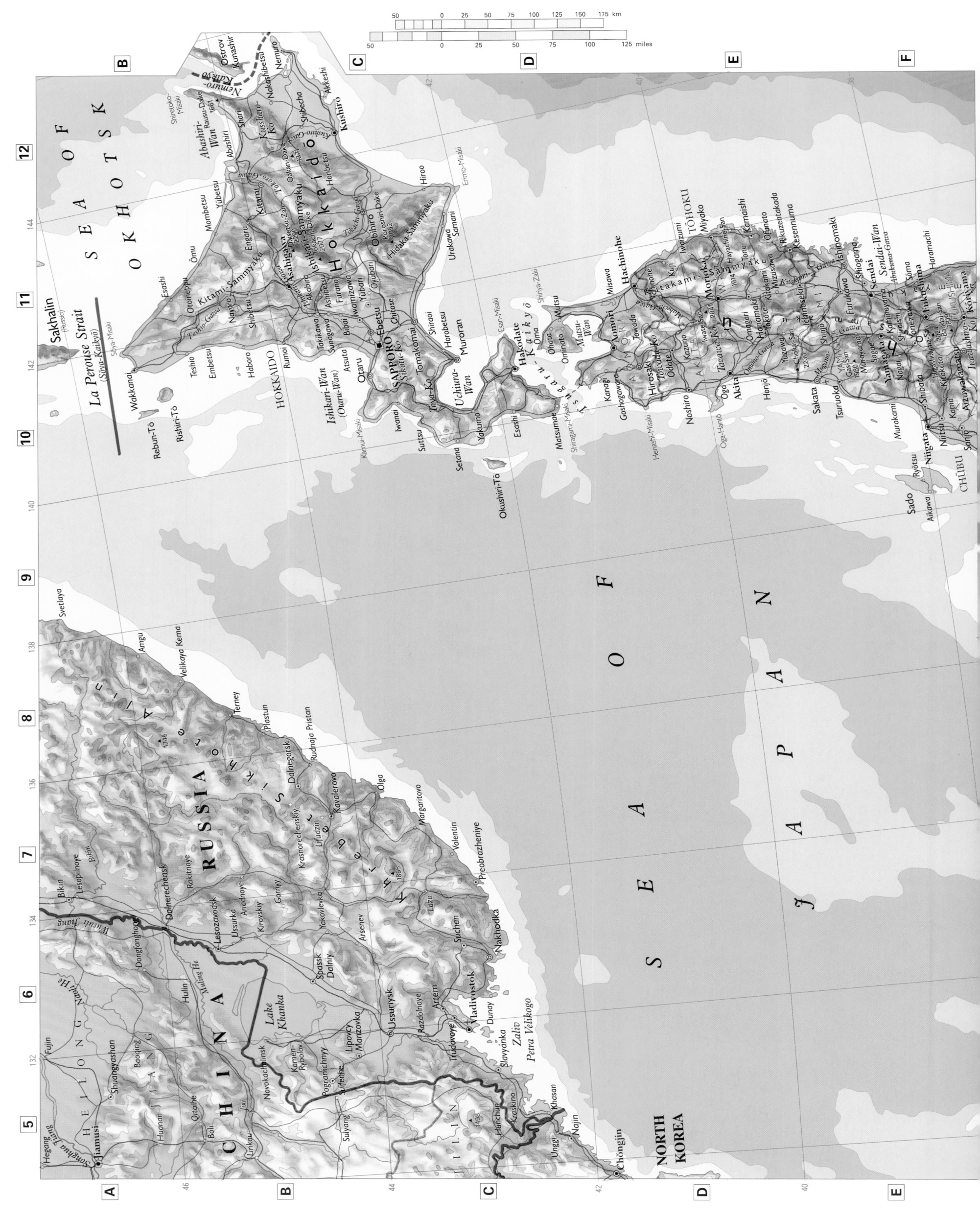

50 0 25 50 75 100 125 150 175 km

50 0 25 50 75 100 125 miles

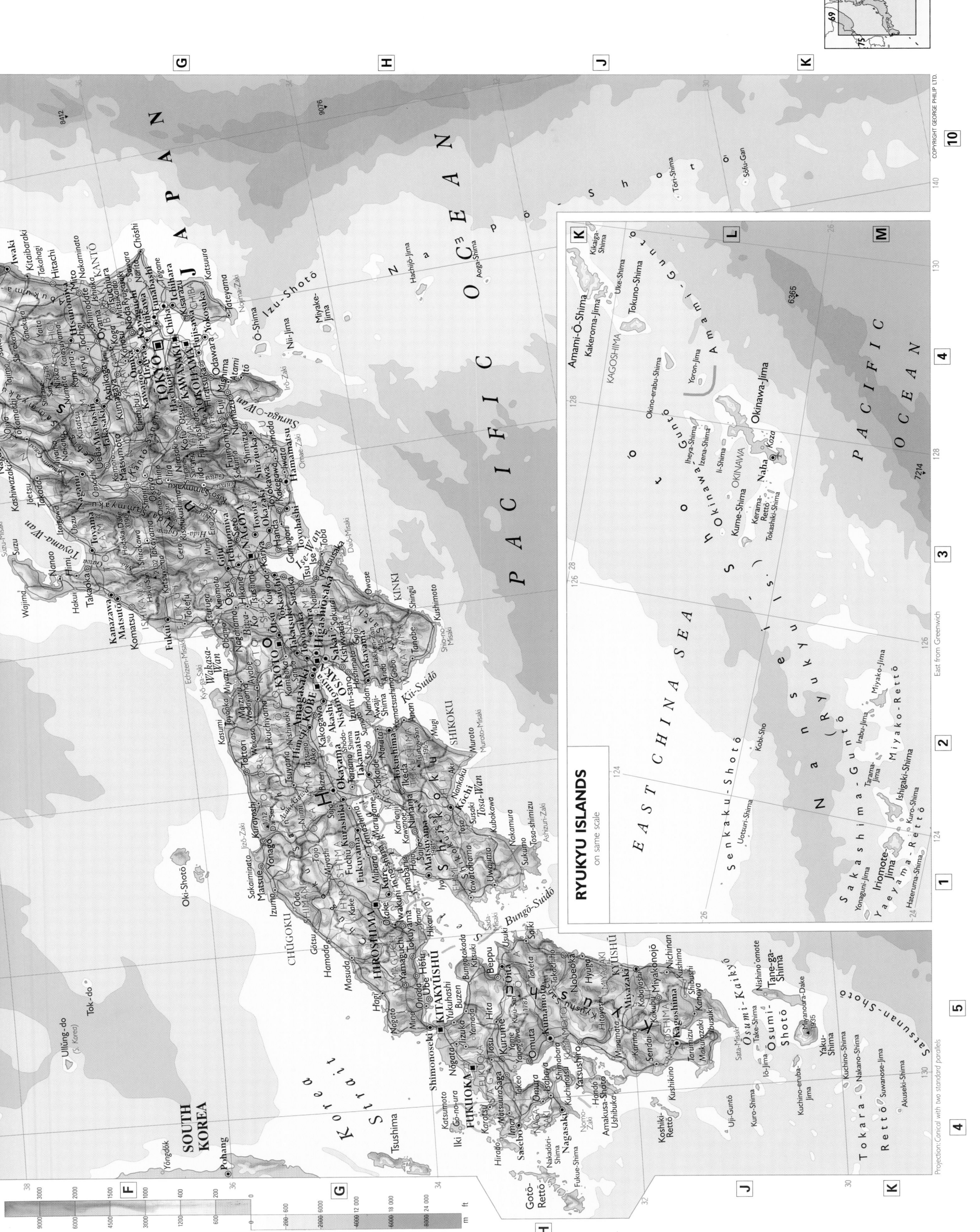

RYUKYU ISLANDS
on same scale

SOUTH KOREA

JAPAN

PACIFIC OCEAN

EAST CHINA SEA

PACIFIC OCEAN

COPYRIGHT GEORGE PHILIP LTD.

Projection: Conical with two standard parallels

East from Greenwich

10 0 10 20 30 40 50 60 70 80 90 km
10 0 10 20 30 40 50 60 miles

1 **2** **3** **4** **5** **6**

130 131 132 133 134 135

S E A   O F   J A P A N
(E A S T   S E A)

A

Yŏngdŏk

Chŏngha

Changgi-Ap

Daimanji-San
Dōgo ▲ 608
Oki-Shotō   Saigō

36

B

**SOUTH
KOREA**

Shimane-Hantō   Jizō-Zaki   Iwami   Kasumi
Matsue   Sakaiminato   Toyooka
Hirata Shinji-   Yonago   Kurayoshi   Tottori
Hi-no-Misaki   Ka   Yasugi   Dai-Sen   Wakasa   Hidaka
Taisha   Izumo   Daito   1729   Chizu   Suga-no-Sen
CHŪGOKU-DISTRICT   Kisuki   Dōgo-San   Katsuyama   Yamasaki   1510

35

Yunotsu   Sanbe-San   1269   Ochiai   Ikuno
Ōda   1126   Miyoshi   Shōbara   Tōjō   **OKAYAMA**   Yanahara   Sayō   **HYŌGO**
Gōtsu   **SHIMANE**   Niimi   Tsuyama   Nishiwaki
Hamada   **HIROSHIMA**   Fuchū   Ibara   Takahashi   Wake   Kasai
Bingo   Ochiai   Sōja   Bizen   Saidaiji   Ako   **Himeji**
Masuda   Kake   Yoshida   Higashi-   Fukuyama   **Okayama**   **Kurashiki**   Tatsuno   Aioi   Miki
Ōmi-Shima   Hagi   Aono-Yama   Kanmuri-Yama   Hiroshima   Onomichi   Kannabe   Konkō   Tamano   Shōdo-   Teshima-   **Kakogawa**   **Akashi**
34   Mi-Shima   908▲   1339   **HIROSHIMA**   Mihara   Kasaoka   Shotō   *Harima-*   Tsuna

C

Tsushima

Kara-Saki   Kamiagata
Kamitsushima
Mitsushima
Izuhara
Kō-Saki

Tsuno-Shima
Nagato   Atō
YAMAGUCHI
Hibiki-   Yamaguchi   Mine
Nada   Toyoura   Ogōri   San-yō
Higasi-Suidō   Ō-Shima   Nakama   Onoda Ube
Genkai-   Shimonoseki   Hōfu   Shin-Nan'yō   **Tokuyama**
Nada   **KITAKYŪSHŪ**   Kudamatsu   Yanai   Hikari

D

O-Shima
Iki
Gō-no-ura
Iki-Kaikyō
Ikitsuki-   Yobuko
Shima   Karatsu   Matsuura
Hirado   Imari   SAGA
Hirado-   Saza
Shima   Takeo   Taku
Sasebo   Arita   Saga
Ureshino
NAGASAKI   Ōmura-   1076   Tara
Ōmura   Wan

33

Hikari
Kanmuri-Yama
Hatsukaichi   Kure   Takehara   Omi-   Nada   Kawanoe
Ōtake   Iwakuni   Ondo   Shima   Kan'onji
FUKUOKA   Munakata   Suō-Nada   Naga-Shima   Yashiro-   Matsuyama   1981   Niihama
Fukuma   Iwai-Jima   Jima   Iyo   Ishizuchi-Yama
Dazaifu   Yamada   Nakatsu   Hime-Jima   **EHIME**   Sakawa
Chikushino   1200   Buzen   Futago-Yama   Heigun-Tō   Iyo-Mishima   Ikeda
Kasuga   Amagi   Usa   721   Kunisaki   Nagahama   Ōzu
Tosu   Hita   Kitsuki   *Iyo-Nada*   Uchiko   Tosa-Yamada
Kurume   Hiji   Beppu-Wan   Sada-Misaki-Hantō   Yawatahama   **KŌCHI**
Yanagawa   Kurogi   Yufu-Dake   Tsurusaki   Uwa   Tosa
Kashima   Yame   1584   **Beppu**   Saganoseki   Uwajima   Hiromi
Setaka   **ŌITA**   Ōita   Nankoku   Noichi
Chikugo   Oguni   Kujū-San   Usuki   Aki
Okawa   Aso   1787

E

Nagasaki   Isahaya
Unzen-Dake   Tamana
Nomo-Zaki   1360   Shimabara
Uto

32

F

31

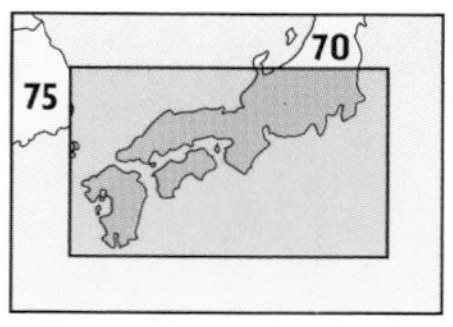

CHŪBU-DISTRICT

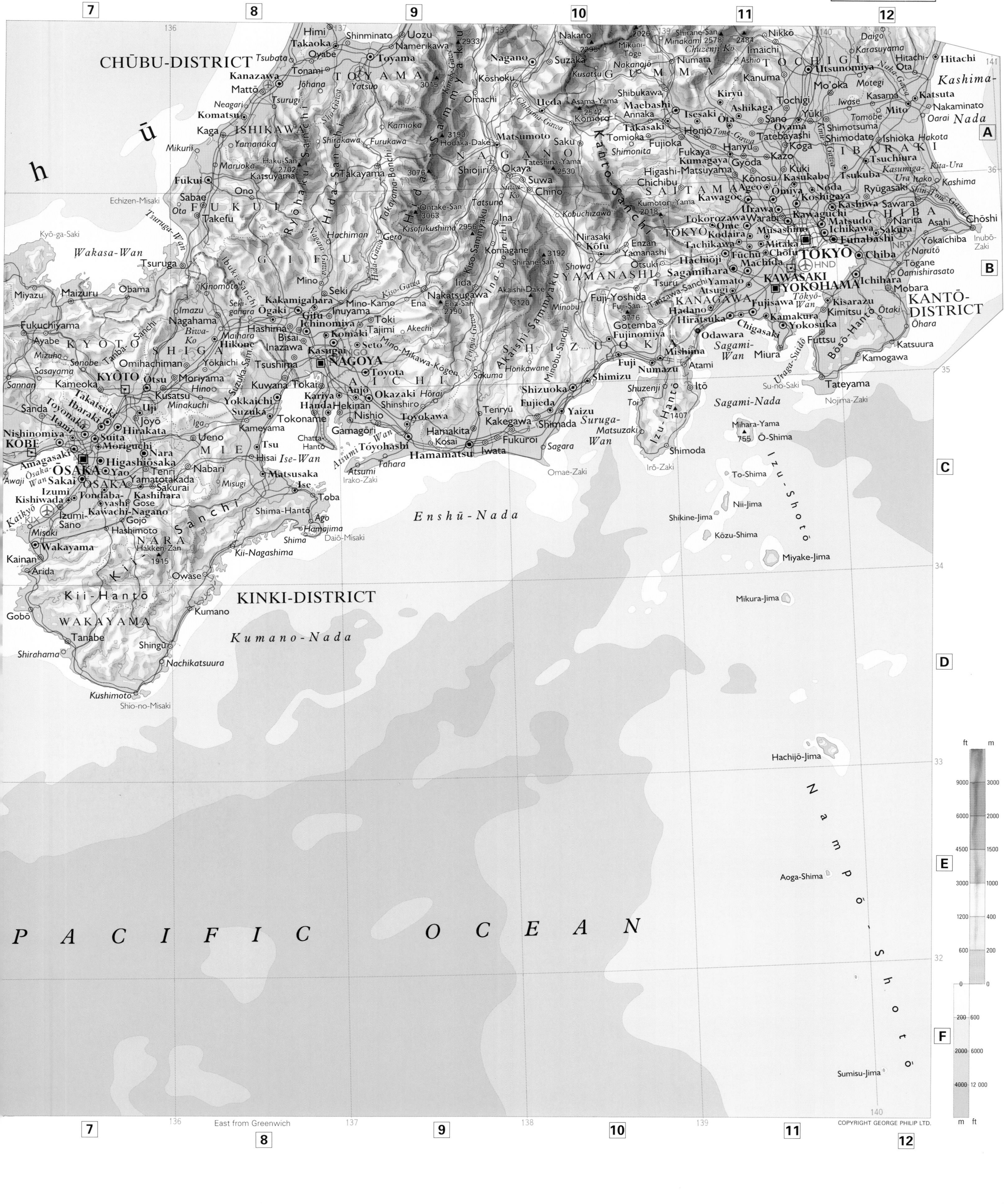

KANTŌ-DISTRICT

KINKI-DISTRICT

Kashima-Nada

Wakasa-Wan

Biwa-Ko

KYŌTO **ŌSAKA** **KOBE** **NAGOYA** **TOKYŌ** **YOKOHAMA** **KAWASAKI**

Ise-Wan *Atsumi-Wan* *Mikawa-Wan*

Kii-Hantō **WAKAYAMA** **NARA** **MIE**

Enshū-Nada

Kumano-Nada

Sagami-Nada *Sagami-Wan* *Suruga-Wan*

Izu-Shotō *Ō-Shima* *Nii-Jima* *Kōzu-Shima* *Miyake-Jima* *Mikura-Jima*

Hachijō-Jima *Aoga-Shima* *Sumisu-Jima*

Nampo Shoto

PACIFIC OCEAN

East from Greenwich

COPYRIGHT GEORGE PHILIP LTD.

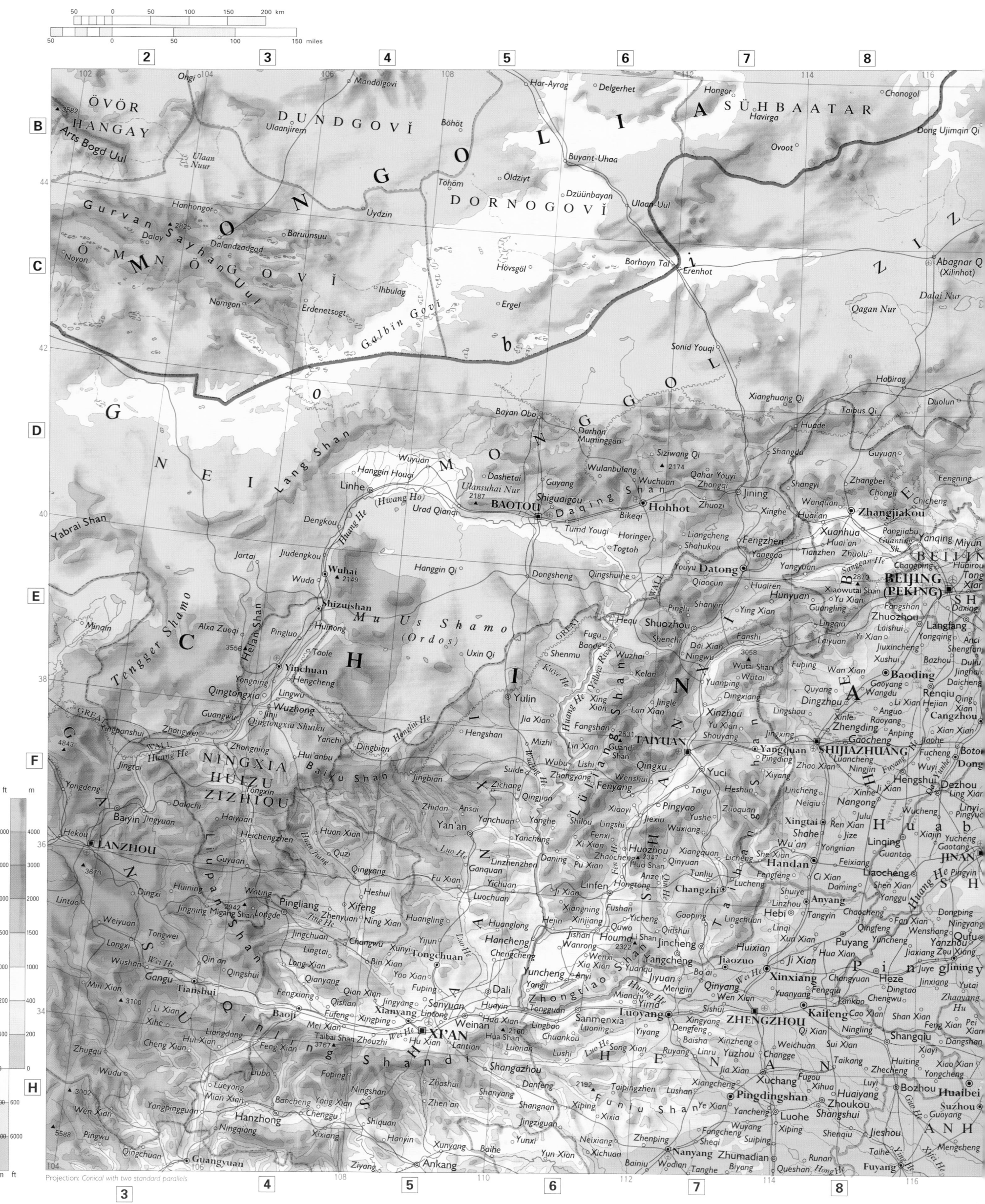

9   10   11   12   13   14   15   16

B

HEILONGJIANG

HARBIN   Bin Xian
Linkou   Jixi   Turiy Rog
Ozero
Khanka

Horqin Youyi Qianqi
(Ulanhot)
Zhenlai   Maoxing   Zhaoyuan   Shuangcheng   Acheng   Shangzhi   Yanshou
Baicheng   Da'an   Changchunling   Lalin   Yimianpo   Wuchang   Hengdaohezi   Maqiaohe   Pogranichnyy
Taonan   Anguang   Fuyu   Beitaolaizhao   Sanchahe   Yushu   Shanhetun   Mudanjiang   Xiachengzi
Tuquan   Qagan   Gorlos   Kaoshan   Dehui   Shulan   Hailin   Muling   Suiyang   Sufenhe   44
Hulingol   Hulin He   Nur Qian   Tongyu   Shenjingzi   Nong'an   Wulajie   Huangsongdian   Ning'an   Dongjingcheng   Dongning   Golenki
Jarud Qi   Zhanyu   Beizhengzhen   Fulongquan   Jiutai   Gangyao   Emu   Jingpo   Chunyang   Luozigou   Ussuriysk
Changling   Huaidezhen   JILIN   Jiaohe   Dunhua   Daxinggou   Wangqing   Shixian   Razdolnoye
Zhongai   CHANGCHUN   Fanjiatun   Huadian   Mingyuegue   Tumen   Hunchun   Artem   Tavrichanka
Maglin   Shuangyang   Panshi   Antu   Longjing   Yanji   Namyang   Vladivostok   C
Kailu   Tongliao   Shuangliao   Lishu   Gongzhuling   Yitong   Huadian   Baishan   Helong   Hoeamdong   Posyet
Xar Moron He   Jargalang   Siping   Liaoyuan   Dongfeng   Fusong   Changbai Shan   Hoeryong   Najin
Wutonghaolai   Bamiancheng   Huinan   Baihe   1677   Musan   Puryong   Pugodong   42
Hure Qi   Kaiyuan   Meihekou   Shanchengzhen   Liuhe   Linjiang   Paektu-san   Yuponadong   Nanam   CHONGJIN

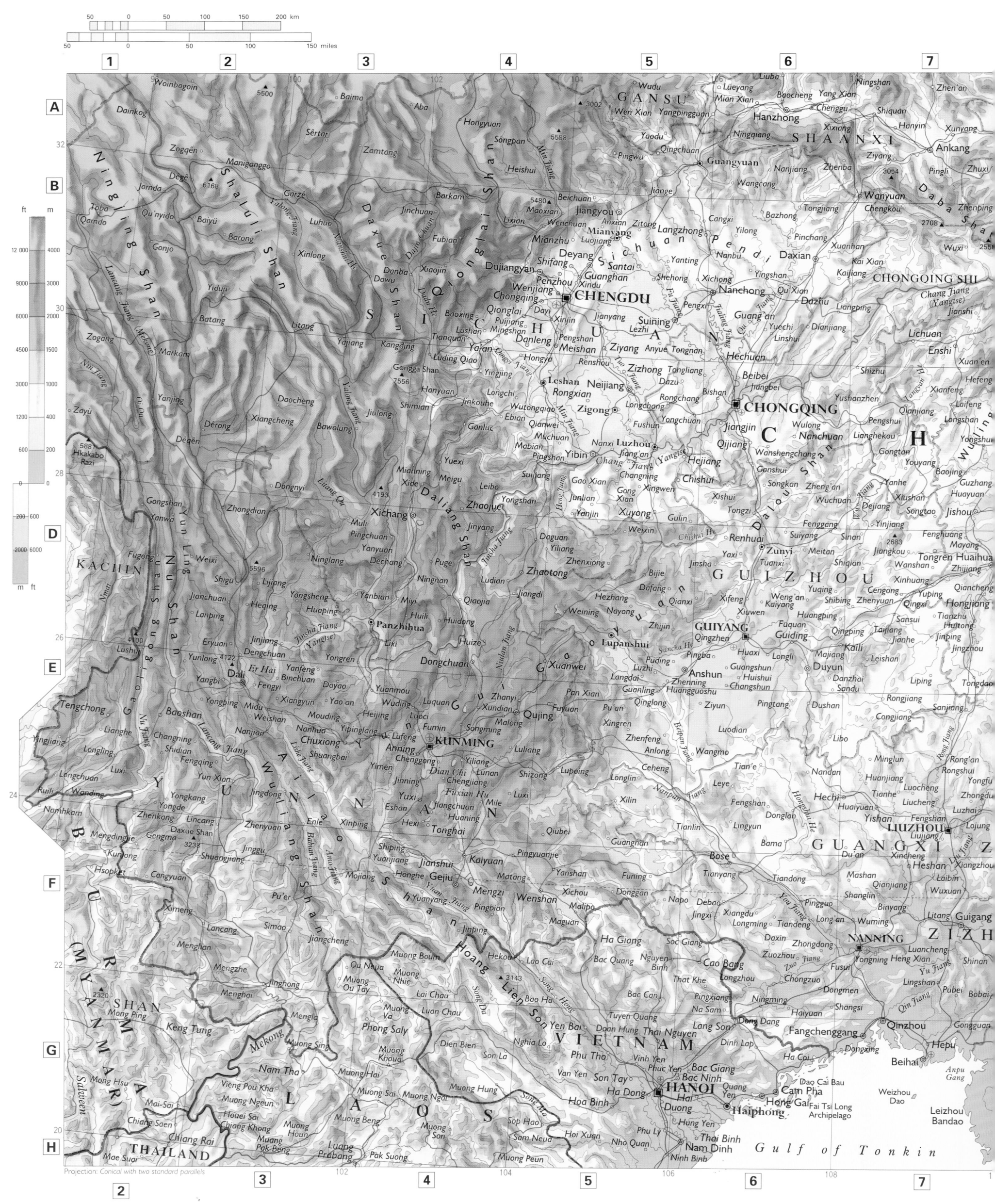

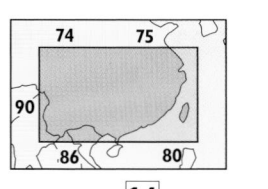

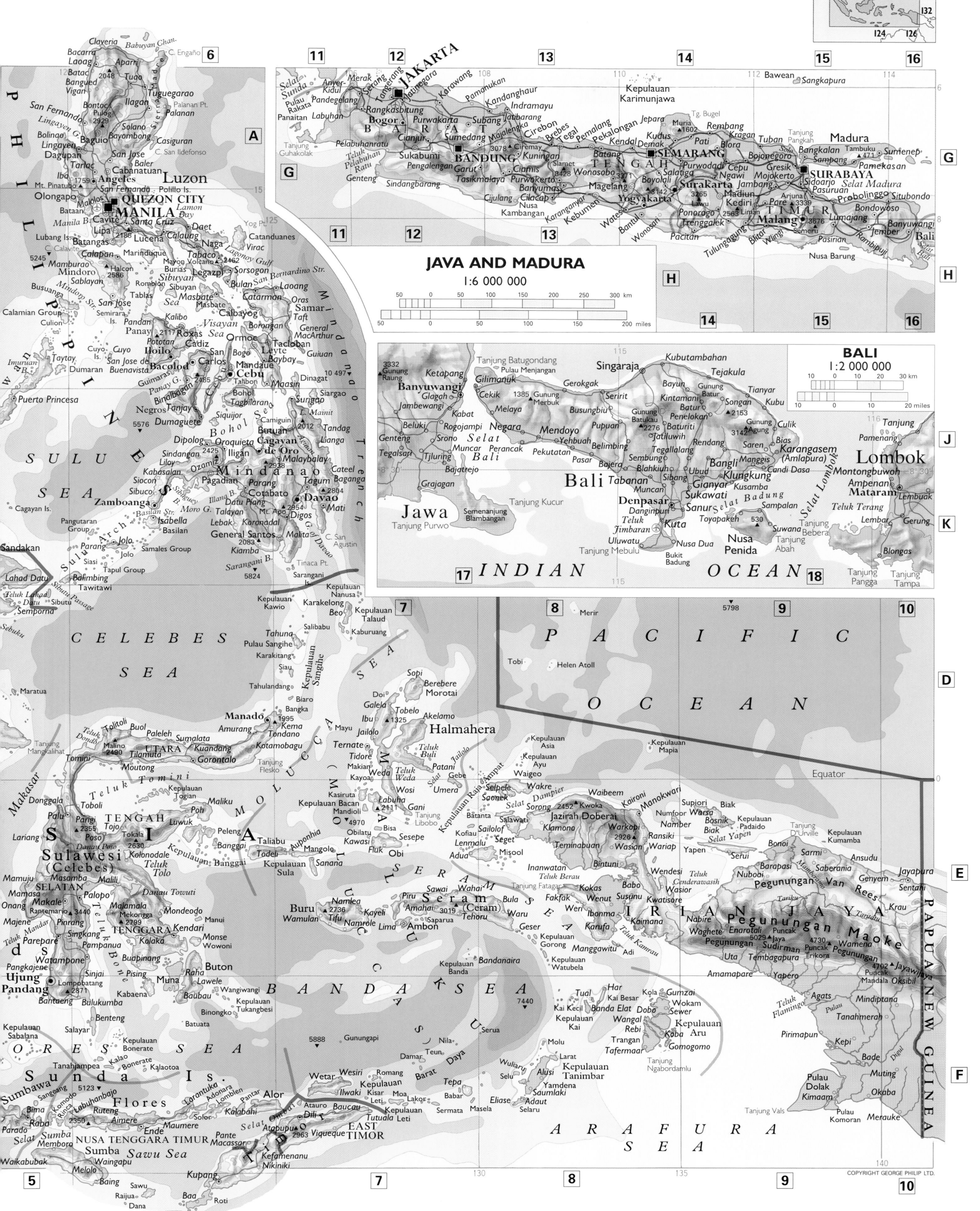

JAVA AND MADURA

1:6 000 000

50 0 50 100 150 200 250 300 km
50 0 50 100 150 200 miles

BALI

1:2 000 000

10 0 10 20 30 km
10 0 10 20 miles

COPYRIGHT GEORGE PHILIP LTD.

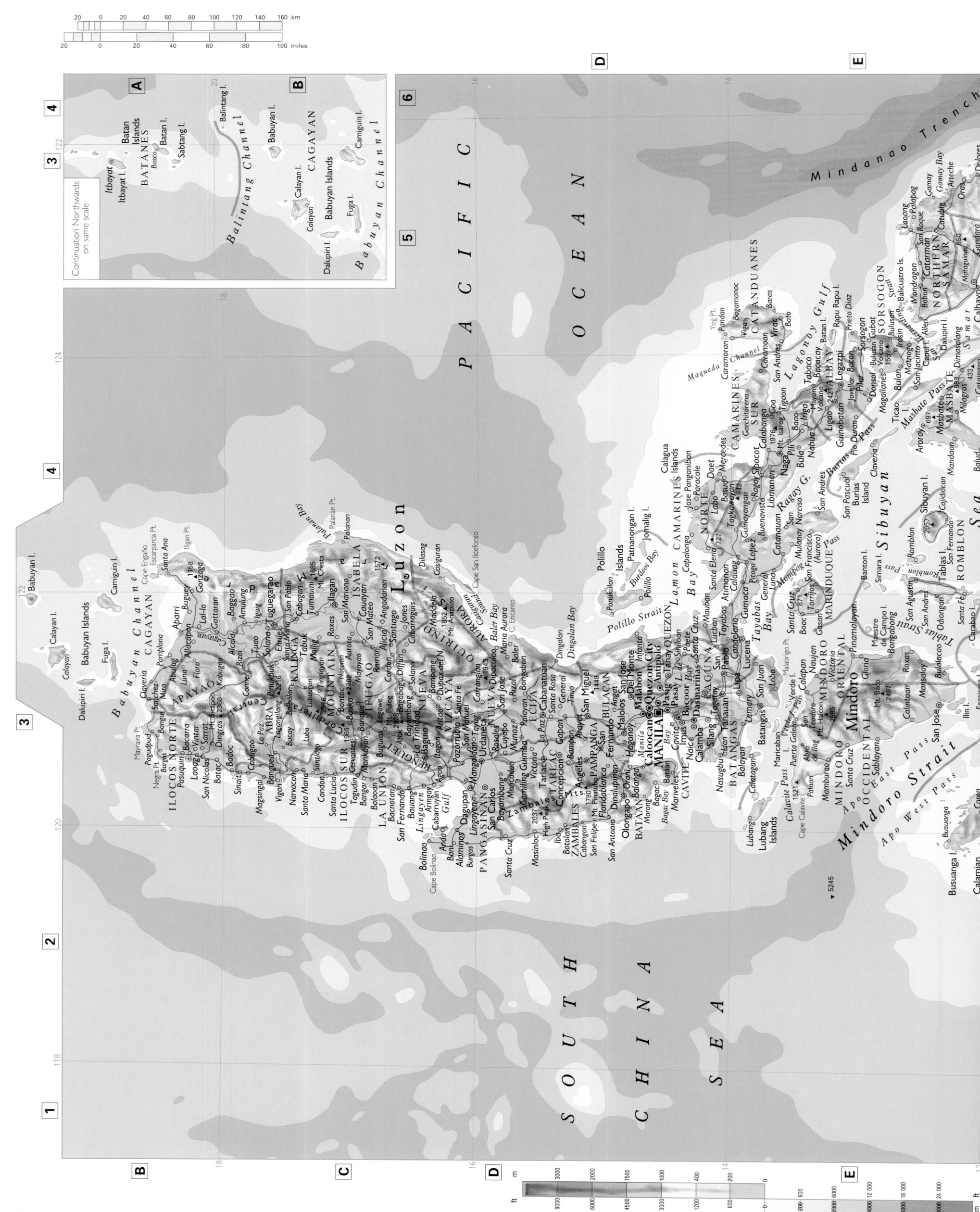

20 0 20 40 60 80 100 120 140 160 km
20 0 20 40 60 80 100 miles

A B 4 3 122 3

Continuation Northwards on same scale

Batan Islands
Itbayat I.
Itbayat I.
Batan
Bosco
Batan I.
BATANES
Sabtang I.
Balintang I.
Balintang Channel

CAGAYAN
Babuyan I.
Calayan I.
Calayan
Babuyan Islands
Fuga I.
Dalupiri I.
Camiguin I.
Babuyan Channel

D 16 E

6 5

P A C I F I C

O C E A N

Mindanao Trench

124

Luzon

ISABELA
AURORA
QUIRINO
NUEVA VIZCAYA
IFUGAO
MOUNTAIN
KALINGA
APAYAO
ABRA
BENGUET
NUEVA ECIJA
PANGASINAN
TARLAC
ZAMBALES
BULACAN
PAMPANGA
BATAAN
CAVITE
LAGUNA
BATANGAS
QUEZON
CAMARINES NORTE
CAMARINES SUR
ALBAY
SORSOGON

Polillo Islands
Polillo Strait
Polillo

MANILA
Caloocan
Quezon City

MINDORO ORIENTAL
MINDORO OCCIDENTAL
Mindoro

MARINDUQUE
ROMBLON
Sibuyan
MASBATE

Mindoro Strait

Lubang Islands

S O U T H

C H I N A

S E A

D 14 E

m 3000 2000 1500 1000 400 200 0 ft
ft 9000 6000 4500 3000 1200 600 0

0 200 2000 4000 6000 8000 m
0 600 6000 12 000 18 000 24 000 ft

B 18 C 16 D E

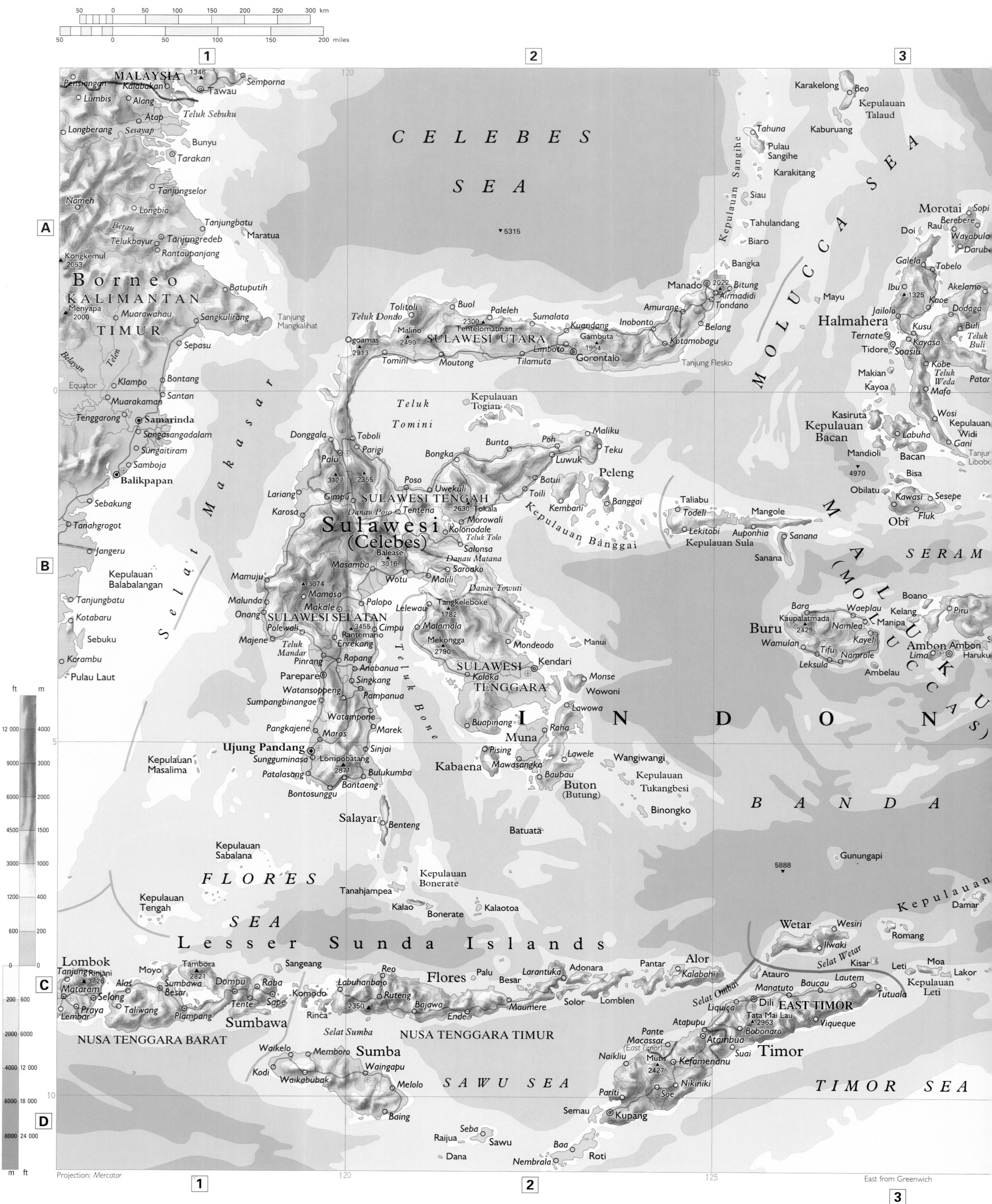

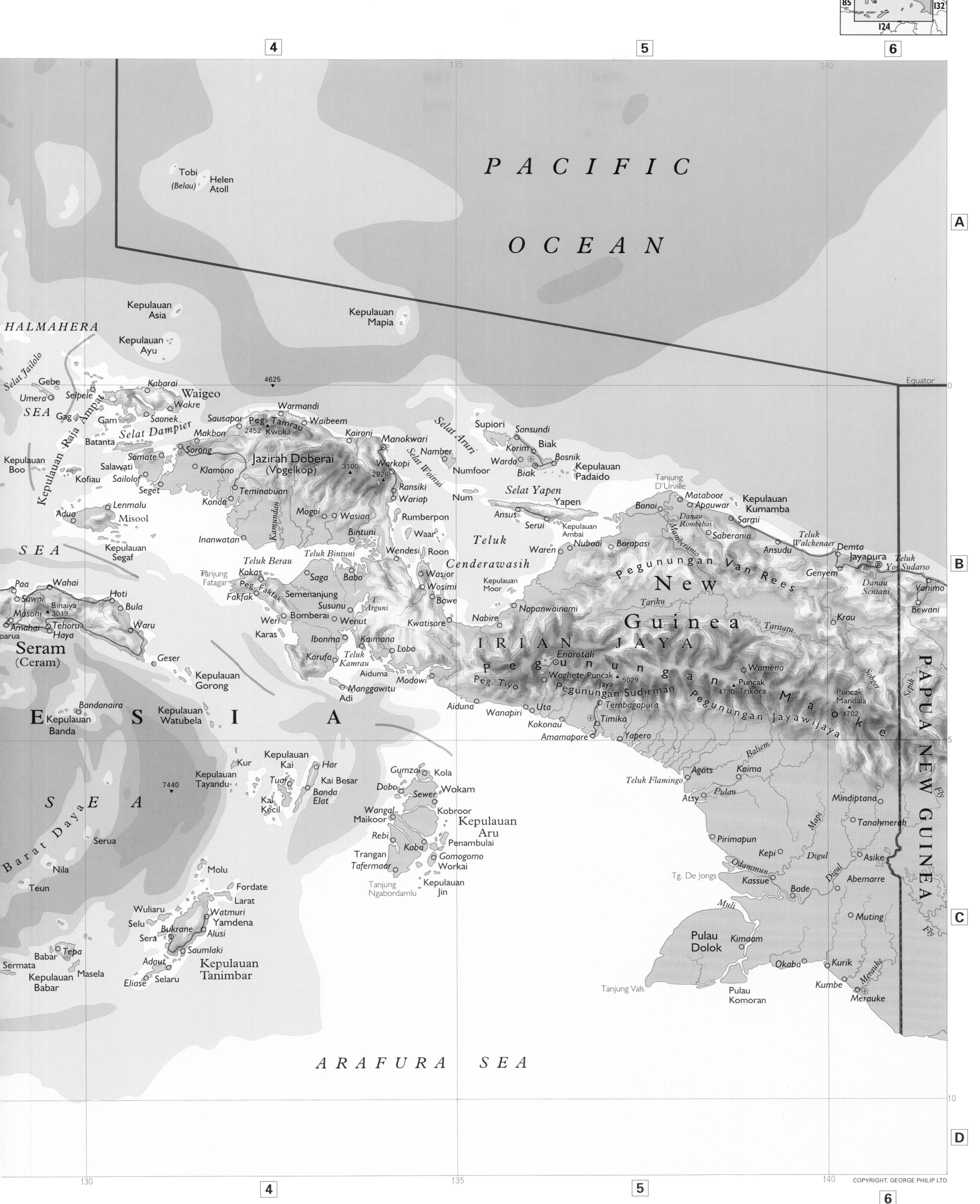

PACIFIC

OCEAN

HALMAHERA

Kepulauan Asia

Kepulauan Ayu

Kepulauan Mapia

Tobi
(*Belau*)
Helen Atoll

Selat Jailolo
Gebe
Umera
Selpele
SEA
Gag
Kabarai
Waigeo
Wakre
Warmandi
Waibeem

Kepulauan Boo
Batanta
Gam
Saonek
Salawati
Makbon
Sorong
Klamono
Samate
Kofiau
Sailolof
Seget
Konda
Selat Dampier

Kepulauan Raja Ampat

Peg. Tamrau
2452 Kwoka
Sausapor
Kaironi
Manokwari
4625
3100
Warkopi
2926

Jazirah Doberai
(Vogelkop)
Teminabuan
Mogoi
Wasian
Ransiki
Wariap
Rumberpon
Bintuni

Selat Amri
Supiori
Sansundi
Korim
Numfoor
Biak
Bosnik
Biak
Wardo

Namber

Selat Wornui
Num
Waar

Kepulauan Padaido

Selat Yapen
Ansus
Serui
Yapen
Kepulauan Ambai

Tanjung D'Urville
Mataboor
Apauwar
Danau Rombebai
Sargi
Saberania

Kepulauan Kumamba

Teluk Walckenaer
Ansudu
Demta
Genyem

Jayapura
Teluk Yos Sudarso
Vahimo
Danau Sentani
Bewani

Lenmalu
Adua
Misool
SEA
Kepulauan Segaf

Inanwatan
Teluk Berau
Kokas
Peg. Fakfak
Fakfak
Saga
Babo
Semenanjung
Susunu
Bomberai
Wenut
Weri
Karas
Ibonma
Karufa

Tanjung Fatagar
Kamundan

Teluk Bintuni
Wendesi
Roon
Wosimi
Bawe
T. Arguni
Teluk Kamrau
Kaimana
Lobo
Modowi
Adi

Manggawitu

Wasior
Teluk Cenderawasih
Waren
Nuboai
Kepulauan Moor
Napanwainami
Nabire

Barapasi

Pegunungan Van Rees

New
Guinea

Pegunungan Maoke

IRIAN   JAYA

Tariku

Krau

Taritatu

Puncak Mandala
4702

Paa
Sawai
Wahai
Masohi
Binaiya
3019
Tehoru
Haya
Amahai
Parua

Hoti
Bula
Waru

Geser
Kepulauan Gorong

Bandanaira
Kepulauan Banda
Kepulauan Watubela

Seram
(Ceram)

E   S   I   A

Kwatisore
Enarotali
Waghete Puncak
Jaya
Peg. Tiyo
Aiduna
Wanapiri
Uta
Kokonau
Amamapare
Timika
Tembagapura
Puncak
5029
Trikora
4730
Wamena

Pegunungan Sudirman
Pegunungan Jayawijaya

Yapero

Baliem
Agats
Kaima
Teluk Flamingo
Atsy
Pulau

Mindiptana
Tanahmerah

Kur
Kepulauan Kai
Har
Kai Besar
7440
Kepulauan Tayandu
Tual
Kai Kecil
Banda Elat

Gumzai
Dobo
Sewer
Wokam
Kola
Kobroor

Rebi
Koba
Maikoor
Wangal
Penambulai
Trangan
Tafermaar
Gomogomo
Workai

Kepulauan Aru

Pirimapun
Mapi
Kepi
Digul

Kassue
Bade
Odammun
Digul
Asike
Abemarre

Muting

Barat Daya

Nila
Serua
Teun

Molu
Fordate
Larat

SEA

Tanjung Ngabordamlu
Kepulauan Jin

Tg. De Jongs
Muli

Wuliaru
Selu
Sera
Babar
Tepa
Sermata
Kepulauan Masela
Babar

Watmuri
Yamdena
Alusi
Bukrane
Adaut
Saumlaki
Eliase
Selaru

Kepulauan Tanimbar

Tanjung Vals
Pulau Dolok

Kimaam
Okaba
Kurik
Kumbe

Pulau Komoran
Merauke

PAPUA NEW GUINEA

Fly

ARAFURA   SEA

COPYRIGHT. GEORGE PHILIP LTD

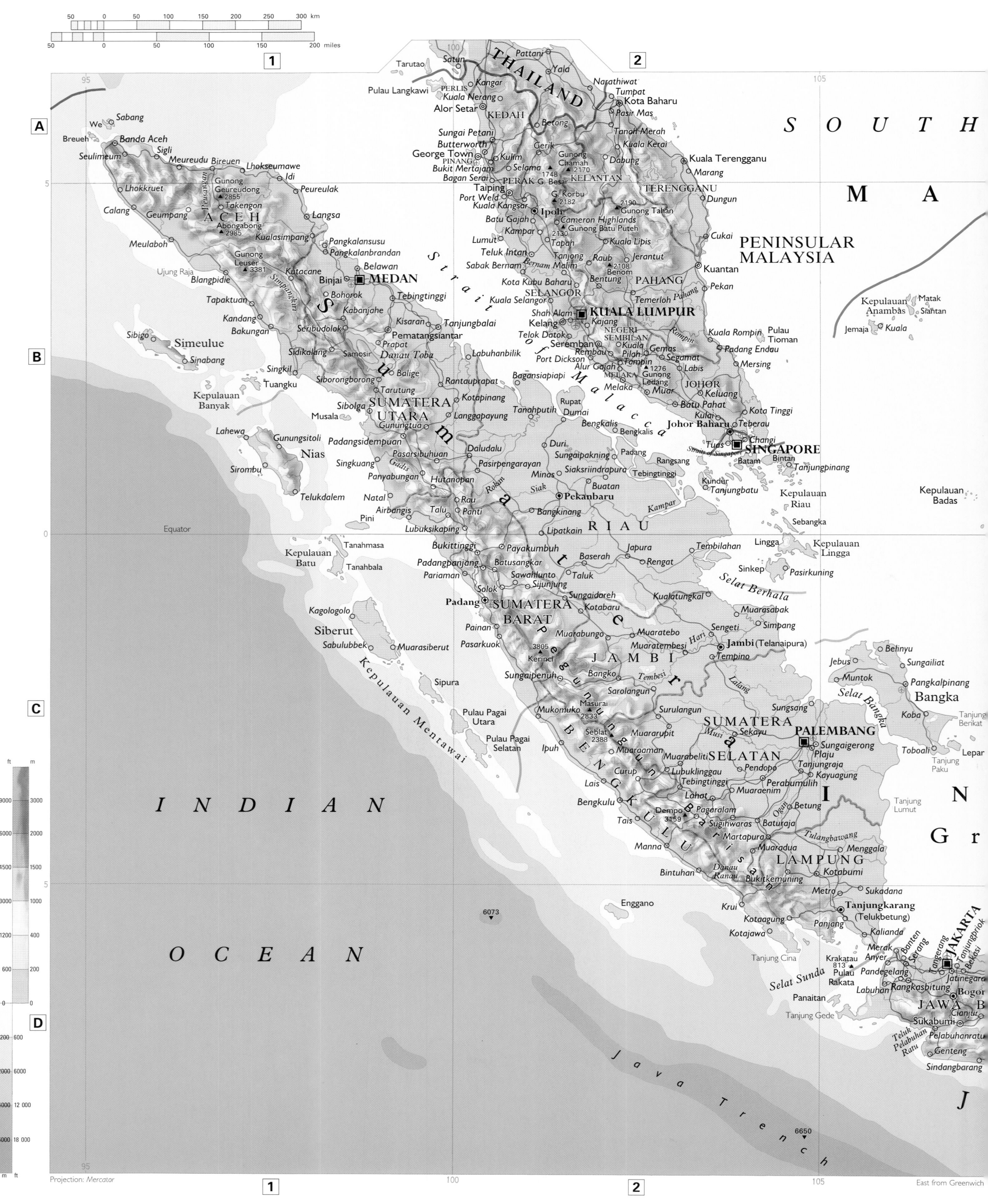

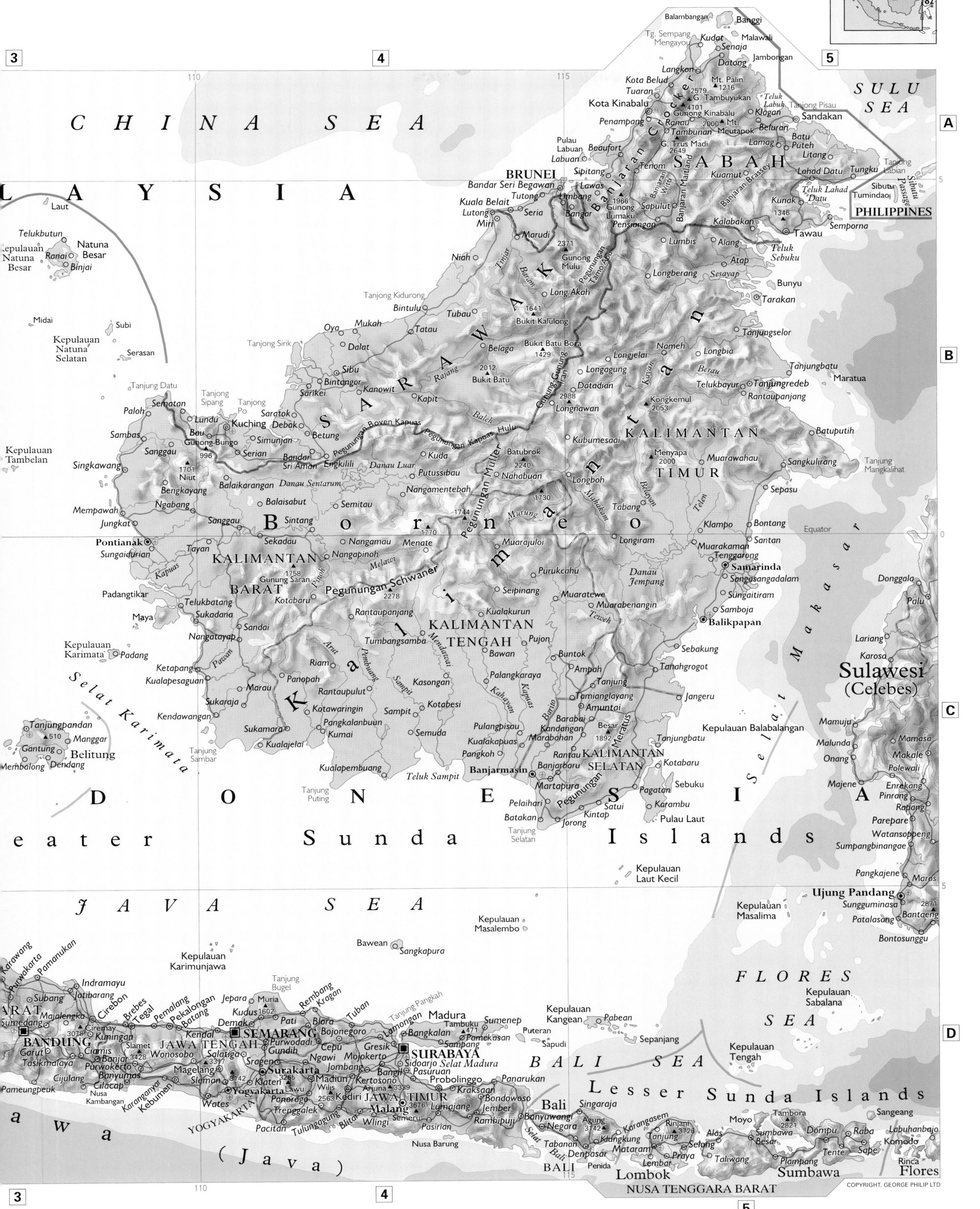

CHINA SEA

SULU SEA

MALAYSIA

Laut
Telukbutun
Kepulauan Natuna Besar
Natuna Besar
Ranai
Binjai
Midai
Subi
Kepulauan Natuna Selatan
Serasan
Tanjung Datu

BRUNEI
Bandar Seri Begawan
Kuala Belait
Tutong
Lutong
Seria
Miri
Marudi
Niah

Balambangan
Tg. Sempang Mengayou
Kudat
Malawali
Banggi
Langkon
Senaja
Datang
Jambongan
Kota Belud
Tuaran
Mt. Palin 1216
Tambuyukan
Kota Kinabalu
Penampang
Ranau
2000
Meutapok
Tambunan
SABAH
Sandakan
Tanjong Pisau
Teluk Labuk
Klagan
Beluran
Batu Puteh
Lamag
Litang
Lahad Datu
Tawau
Semporna
PHILIPPINES
Tungku
Tanjong Labian
Teluk Lahad Datu
Sibutu Passage
Tumindao

Pulau Labuan
Labuan
Beaufort
Sipitang
Lawas
Limbang
Bangar
Gunong Mulu
2371
Pegunungan Iran Apo
Long Akah
Tinjar
Baram
Gunong Ilumaku
Sapulut
Pensiangan
Lumis
Alang
Atap
Sesayap
Bunyu
Tarakan

Kepulauan Tambelan

Paloh
Sematan
Tanjong Sipang
Tanjong Po
Lundu
Bau
Gunong Bungo 996
Kuching
Debak
Sambas
Sanggau
1701
Niut
Singkawang
Simunjan
Bandar Sri Aman
Engkilili
Serian
Bengkayang
Ngabang
Balaikarangan
Mempawah
Jungkat

Tanjong Kidurong
Bintulu
Tubau
Oya
Mukah
Dalat
Tatau
Tanjong Sirik
Sibu
Bintangor
Sarikei
Kanowit
Kapit
Belaga
Bukit Batu Bora 1429
2012
Bukit Batu
Rajang
Kuda
Baleh
Pegunungan Kapuas Hulu
Datadian
2988
Longnawan
Nameh
Berau
Telukbayur
Longagung
Tanjungbatu
Maratua
Kubumesaai
Kongkemul 2053
Rantaupanjang
Batuputih

SARAWAK
KALIMANTAN
TIMUR
Tanjungselor
Longbia
Longjelai
Tanjungredeb

KALIMANTAN
BARAT
Pontianak
Sungaiduriaan
Tayan
Sekadau
Nangamau
Nangapinoh
Menate
Sintang
Semitau
Danau Sentarum
Balaisabut
Nangamentebah
Putussibau
Gunung Saran 1758
Pegunungan Schwaner 2278
Melawi
Kapuas
Batubrok 2240
Nahabuan
1730
Longboh
Kalimantan
1744
1770
Muarajuloi
Murung
Purukcahu
Menyapa 2000
Muarawahau
Sangkulirang
Tanjung Mangkalihat
Sepasu
Longiram
Muarakaman
Santan
Tenggarong
Equator
Samarinda
Songasangadalam
Sungaitiram
Samboja
Balikpapan
Danau Jempang
Muaratewe
Muarabenangin
Sebakung
Tanahgrogot
Lariang
Karosa
Donggala
Palu
Sulawesi
(Celebes)

Padangtikar
Telukbatang
Sukadana
Maya
Nangatayap
Sandai
Ketapang
Kualapesaguan
Marau
Riam
Panopah
Rantaupulut
Rantaupanjang
Tumbangsamba
Mendarai
KALIMANTAN
TENGAH
Bawan
Seipinang
Kualakurun
Pujon
Buntok
Ampah
Tanjung
Tamianglayang
Amuntai
Jangeru
Kepulauan Balabalangan
Mamuju
Malunda
Onang
Mamasa
Makale
Kepulauan Karimata
Padang
Sukaraja
Kendawangan
Sukamara
Kotawaringin
Kumai
Pangkalanbuun
Kasongan
Kotabesi
Sampit
Semuda
Pangkoh
Pulangpisau
Kualakapuas
Kahayan
Barabai
Kandangan
Marabahan
Besar 1892
Meratus
Tanjungbatu
Polewali
Majene
Enrekang
Pinrang
Rapang

Tanjungpandan
510
Manggar
Gantung
Belitung
Dendang
Membalong
Kualapembuang
Teluk Sampit
Tanjung Sambar
Tanjung Puting
Batakan
Banjarmasin
Martapura
Pelaihari
Banjarbaru
KALIMANTAN SELATAN
Pegunungan
Satui
Jorong
Kintap
Karambu
Pulau Laut
Kotabaru
Sebuku
Pagatan
Parepare
Watansoppeng
Sumpangbinangae
Pangkajene
Maros

Selat Karimata
Tanjung Selatan

DONESIA
Greater
Sunda
Islands

JAVA SEA
Kepulauan Masalembo
Bawean
Sangkapura
Kepulauan Masalima

Ujung Pandang
2871
Sungguminasa
Patalasang
Bantaeng
Bontosunggu

Kepulauan Karimunjawa
Tanjung Bugel
Jepara
Muria
Rembang
Krogan
Tuban
Tanjung Pangkah
Madura
Tambuku
471
Sumenep
Kepulauan Kangean
Pabean
Kepulauan Masalima

FLORES SEA
Kepulauan Sabalana
Kepulauan Tengah

Karawang
Purwakarta
Pamanukan
Indramayu
Subang
Jatibarang
Cirebon
Brebes
Tegal
Pemalang
Pekalongan
Batang
Kendal
SEMARANG
Demak
Kudus 1602
Pati
Blora
Bojonegoro
Cepu
Ngawi
Lamongan
Gresik
SURABAYA
Sidoarjo
Bangkalan
Sampang
Pamekasan
Sapudi
Sepanjang

BANDUNG
Garut
Tasikmalaya
Kuningan
Ciamis
Banjar
Slamet 3428
Wonosobo
Purwokerto
Banyumas
Cijulang
Cilacap
Nusa Kambangan
Majalengka
Ciremay 3078
Sumedang
JAWA TENGAH
Magelang
Salatiga
Purwodadi
Gundih
Sragen
3142
Sleman
Madiun
Willis 3265
Ponorogo
Kediri
Trenggalek
Tulungagung
Pacitan
YOGYAKARTA
Yogyakarta
Wates
Klaten
Surakarta
3337
Lawu 3265
Arjuna 3339
JAWA TIMUR
Malang 3676
Wlingi
Blitar
2563
Kertosono
Jombang
Mojokerto
Pasuruan
Probolinggo
Panarukan
Kraksaan
Bondowoso
Jember
Rambipuji
Lumajang
Semeru
Pasirian
Nusa Barung
Banyuwangi

Selat Madura
BALI SEA
Lesser Sunda Islands

JAVA
(Java)
Pameungpeuk
YOGYAKARTA
BALI
Bali
Singaraja
Negara
Agung 3142
Karangasem
Rinjani 3726
Klungkung
Denpasar
Penida
Lembar
Mataram
Praya
Taliwang
Lombok
NUSA TENGGARA BARAT
Selat Lombok
Tanjung
Selong
Alas
Sumbawa Besar
Moyo
Plampang
Tambora 2821
Dompu
Sumbawa
Tente
Raba
Sape
Komodo
Rinca
Flores
Sangeang
Labuhanbajo

Selat Makasar

COPYRIGHT. GEORGE PHILIP LTD

50 0 50 100 150 200 km
50 0 50 100 150 miles

Major features and regions shown on the map include:

GUANGXI ZHUANGZU ZIZHIQU, GUANGDONG, YUNNAN, HAINAN, G. of Tonkin, BURMA (MYANMAR), SHAN, KAYAH, KAREN, MON, PEGU, TENASSERIM, Dawna Range, Bilauk Taungdan, THAILAND, Chao Phraya, Cao Nguyen Khorat, Phnom Dangrek, LAOS, Annamite Chain, Annam, CAMBODIA, VIETNAM, Bac Phan, Trung Phan, Nam Phan, Mekong, Salween, Hong (Red), Lancang Jiang.

Selected settlements: Mandalay, RANGOON (YANGON), Moulmein, Chiang Mai, BANGKOK, Thon Buri, Phnom Penh region, Vientiane (Viangchan), HANOI, Haiphong, Da Nang, Hue, Qui Nhon, Nanning, Zhanjiang, Haikou, Beihai.

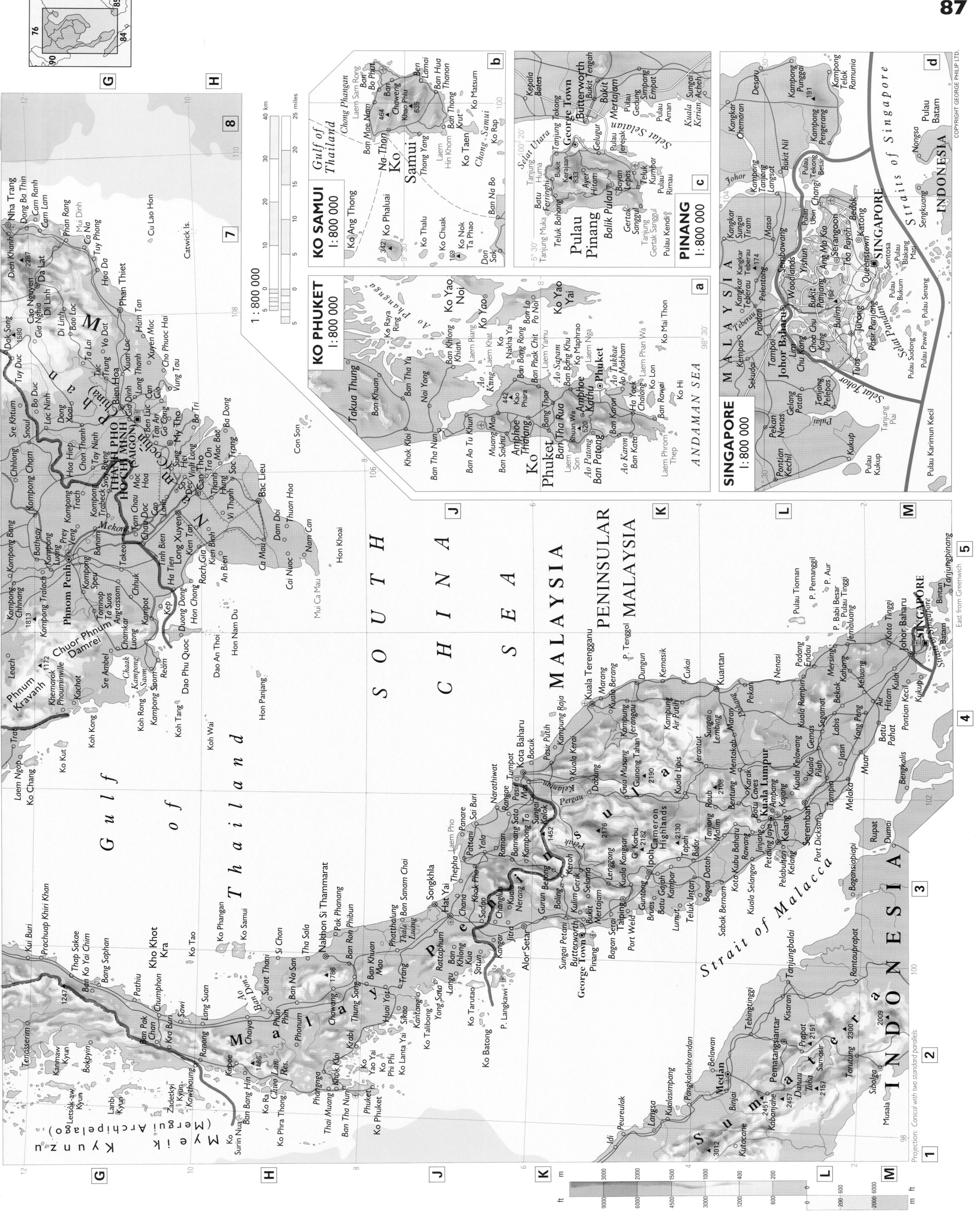

50 0 100 200 300 400 500 600 km
50 0 100 200 300 400 miles

B

C

D

E

ft m

18 000   6000
12 000   4000
9000   3000
6000   2000
3000   1000
1200   400
600   200
0   0
         200   600
         2000 6000
         4000 12000
m ft

Projection: Alber's Equal Area with two standard Parallels

TURKEY

Antalya Konya Kayseri Erzurum Gyumri Gäncä KAZAKSTAN Türkistan KAZA
Rodhos Toros Dağı Malatya Elâzığ YEREVAN ARMENIA AZERBAIJAN BAKI Nukus UZBEKISTAN
Mediterranean Adana Mersin Diyarbakır Muş Bitlis Van Gölü Orūmīyeh TABRĪZ Ardabīl Caspian Sea Urganch Amudarya
Sea CYPRUS Gaziantep Nusaybin Kurdistan Daryācheh-ye Rasht Garaboğazköl Aylagy Türkmenbashi Kara Charjew Samarqand
Nicosia HALAB (ALEPPO) Al Lādhiqīyah Al Mawṣil Orūmīyeh Zanjān Bābol Gorgan Kum TURKMENISTAN Qarshi
EL ISKANDARĪYA (ALEXANDRIA) Tarābulus Ḥamāh Nahr al Furāt Qazvin Reshteh-ye Kūhhā-ye Alborz Mary Ashgabat Kopet Dagh Bukhoro
LEBANON BAYRŪT (BEIRUT) SYRIA Ḥimṣ Al Qā'im Arbīl Kirkūk TEHRĀN Qolleh-ye Damāvand 5601 Emāmrūd Bayramaly Termiz
Damanhūr ISRAEL DIMASHQ (DAMASCUS) Al Jazīrah Zanjān Hamadān Qom Dasht-e Kavir Meymaneh Sheberghān Mazar-e Sharif
El Manṣūra Ḥaifa Tel Aviv-Yafo IRAQ Dayr az Zawr Ārāk Kāshān Gonābād HERĀT AFGHANISTAN Ghaznī
EL QĀHIRA (CAIRO) Jerusalem AMMĀN Bādiyat Ar Ramādī BAGHDĀD Kūhhā-ye Zagros ESFAHĀN 4548 Yazd Tabas Bīrjand Gereshk Farāh Qandahār
El Faiyūm JORDAN Baiyat ash Shām Karbalā Al Kūt Nahr Dijlah Dezfūl Kermānshāh Anār 4075 Dasht-e Lūt Dasht-e Mārgow Helmand
Es Sînâ' Ma'ān Ar'ar Al Ḥillah An Najaf Ahvāz Khorramshahr SHĪRĀZ Daryācheh-ye Seistān Helmand Nushki PAKISTAN Quetta
EGYPT Al 'Aqabah Tabuk Al Jawf An Nāṣirīyah Al Baṣrah Bandar-e Khomeynī Kāzerūn Sa'īdābād Zāhedān Mirjaveh Shikarpur
Qena Qeshm An Nafūd KUWAIT Shatt al 'Arab Būshehr Jahrom Bam Dasht-i Tahlāb Sibi Hyderabad
El Uqṣur Bûr Safâga Quseir Ḥā'il Al Kuwayt Al Qatif Kermān Bandar 'Abbās Jāsk Gābrik Nawabshah
Sharqīya Ras Banâs Yanbu' al Baḥr SAUDI Buraydah Ad Dammām BAHRAIN Al Manāmah Ra's al Khaymah Str. of Hormuz Central Makran Ra. Balūchistān Bela KARACHI
RED Rābigh ARABIA Ḥasā Al Mubarraz QATAR Ash Shāriqah Chāh Bahār Dasht Pasni Indus Delta
Al Madīnah AR RIYĀḌ Al Ḥufūf Ad Dawḥah Dubayy Ormara Gwādar G. of
SUDAN Halaib SEA JIDDAH (JEDDA) Makkah (Mecca) Aṭ Ṭā'if 2259 Layla UNITED ARAB EMIRATES Abū Ẓaby Al Ḥajar al Gharbī Masqat Suḥār Tropic of Cancer
Bûr Sûdân Suakin 'Asīr As Sulayyil Rub' al Khālī 3019 OMAN Maṣīrah Ras al Hadd
Haiya Jazā'ir Farasān Abhā Zufār Ra's al Madrakah Ras al Hadd
ERITREA Mitsiwa Dahlak Kebir Al Ḥudaydah Sana' Shibām Salālah J. Khurīyā Murīyā
Asmera Adwa 116 Ta'izz 3350 YEMEN Ḥaḍramawt Mirbāṭ Râs Fartak
Mekele Al Mukhā Shaqrā Al Mukallā Sayḥūt ARABIAN
Dese Aseb Al 'Adan (Aden) Madīnat ash Sha'b SEA
ETHIOPIA DJIBOUTI Djibouti Gulf of Aden Socotra (Yemen) Ras Asir (C. Guardafui)
Dire Dawa Berbera Bosaso Erigavo
Harer Hargeisa Burao Garoe Bender Beila
Ogaden SOMALI REP. Eil
Kebri Dehar
ETHIOPIA Giuba Obbia
Wabi Scebeli MUQDISHO (MOGADISHU) I N D I A

East from Greenwich

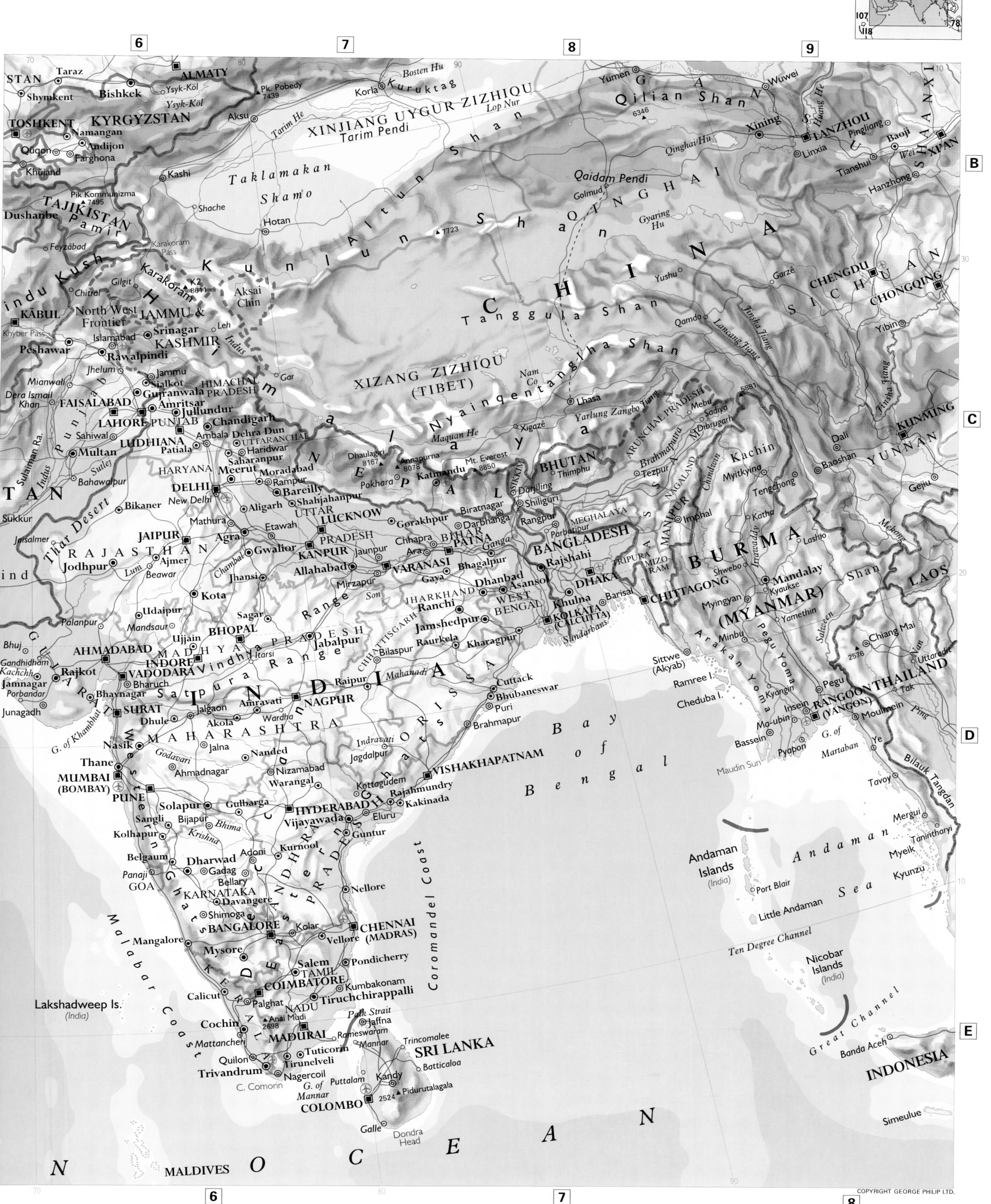

COPYRIGHT GEORGE PHILIP LTD.

1:4 800 000

50   0   50   100   150   200 km
50   0   50   100   150 miles

CHINA

XIZANG ZIZHIQU (TIBET)

NEPAL

BHUTAN

SIKKIM

ARUNACHAL PRADESH

Mishmi Hills

INDIA

ASSAM

NAGALAND

MANIPUR

MEGHALAYA

Khasi Hills

Garo Hills

RAJSHAHI

BANGLADESH

DHAKA

WEST BENGAL

KHULNA

KOLKATA

Haora

TRIPURA

MIZORAM

SYLHET

CHITTAGONG

CHIN HILLS

SAGAING

KACHIN

YUNNAN

CHINA

SHAN

BURMA (MYANMAR)

MANDALAY

MAGWE

ARAKAN

PEGU

KAYAH

THAILAND

Chiang Mai

RANGOON (YANGON)

MON

BAY OF BENGAL

INDIAN OCEAN

Mouths of the Ganges

The Sandheads

Sunderbans

Mouths of the Irrawaddy

G. of Martaban

Tropic of Cancer

ft   m
18 000 6000
12 000 4000
9000   3000
6000   2000
4500   1500
3000   1000
1200   400
600   200
0   0
200   600
2000   6000
m   ft

Projection: Conical with two standard parallels

East from Greenwich

COPYRIGHT GEORGE PHILIP LTD.

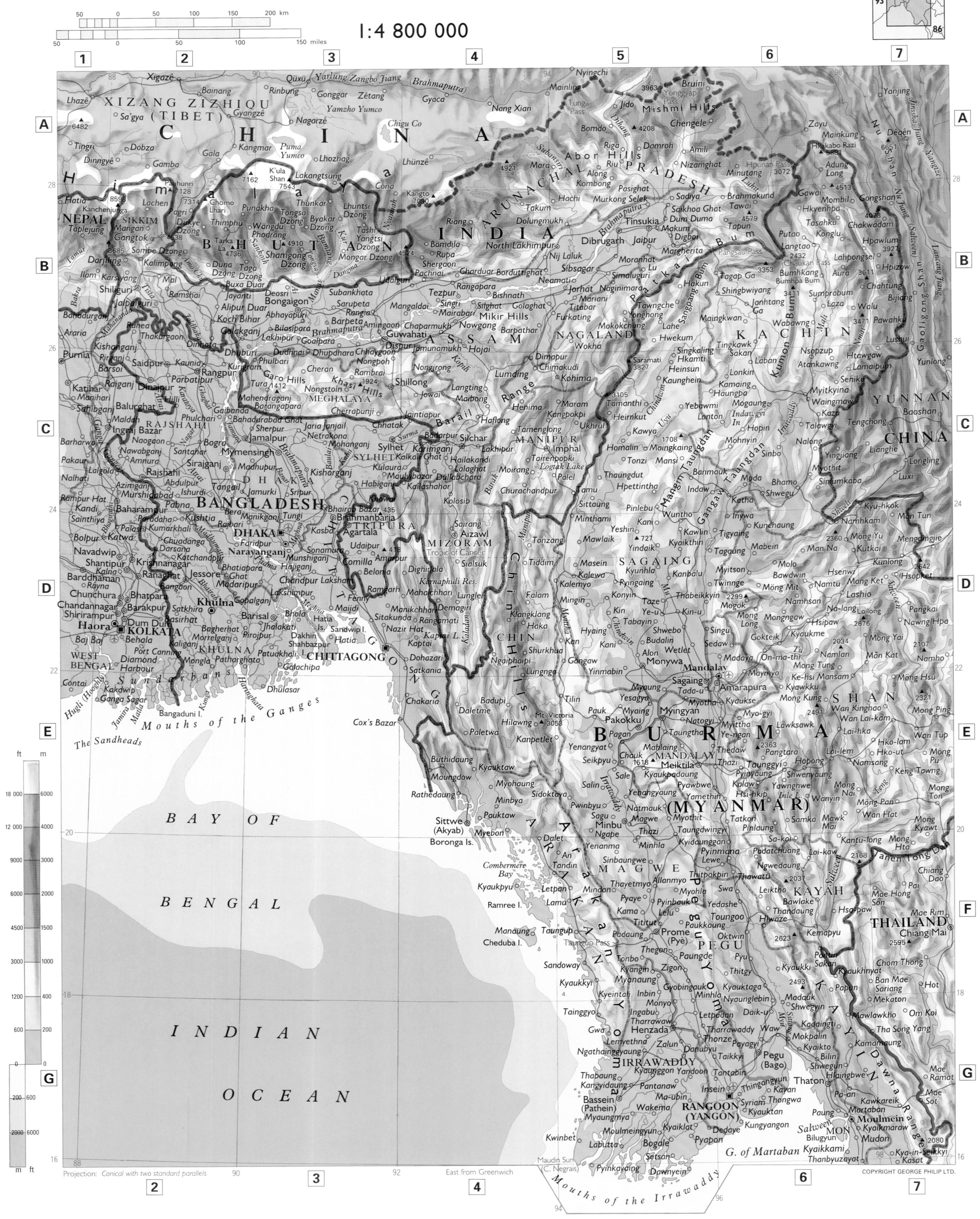

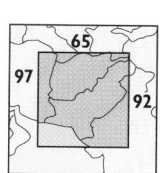

Projection: Conical with two standard parallels

COPYRIGHT GEORGE PHILIP LTD.

East from Greenwich

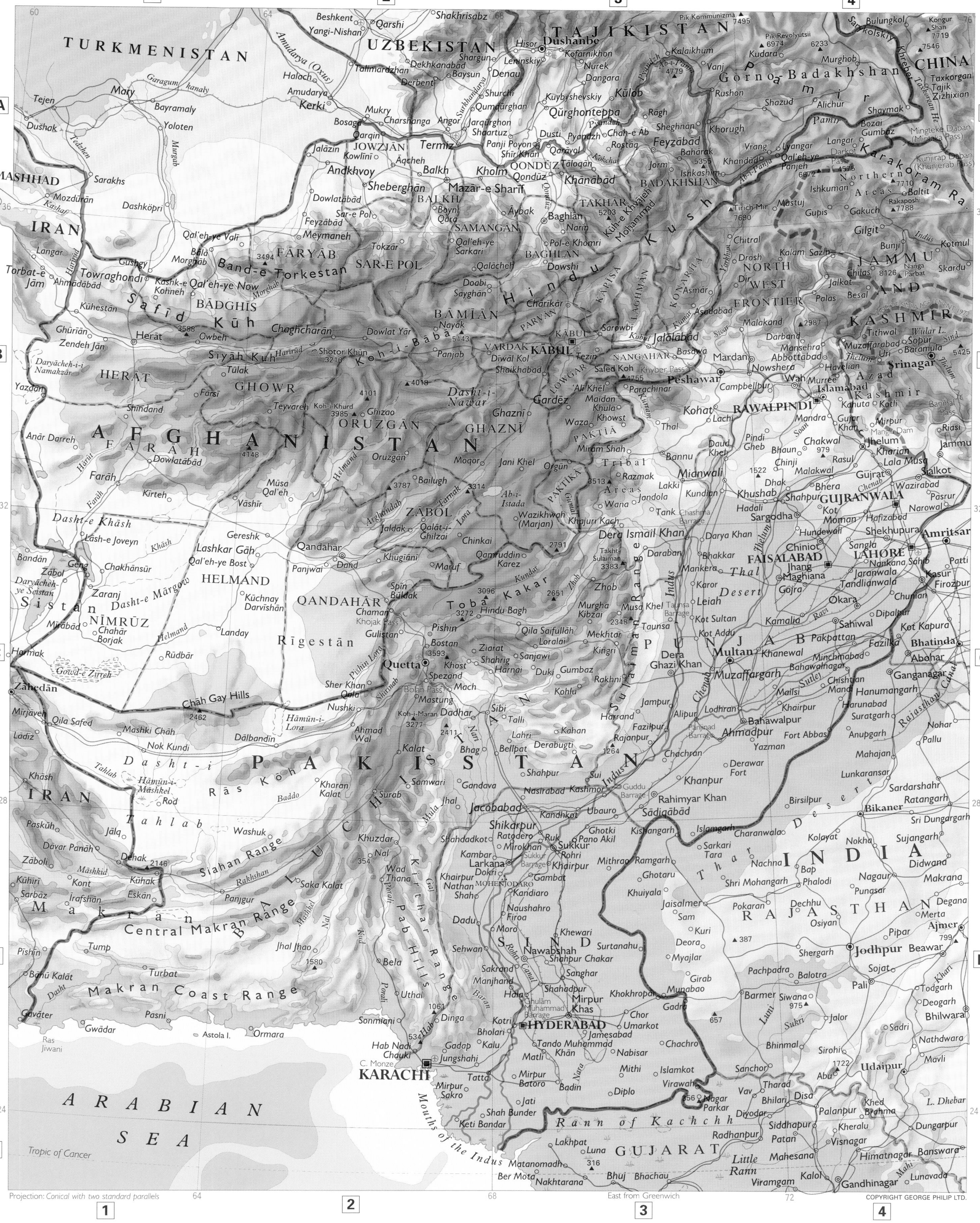

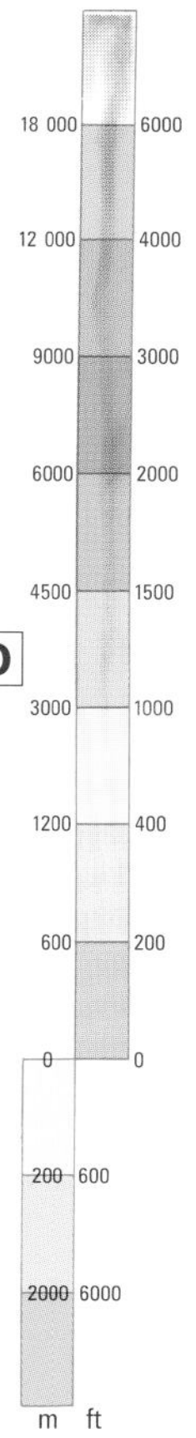

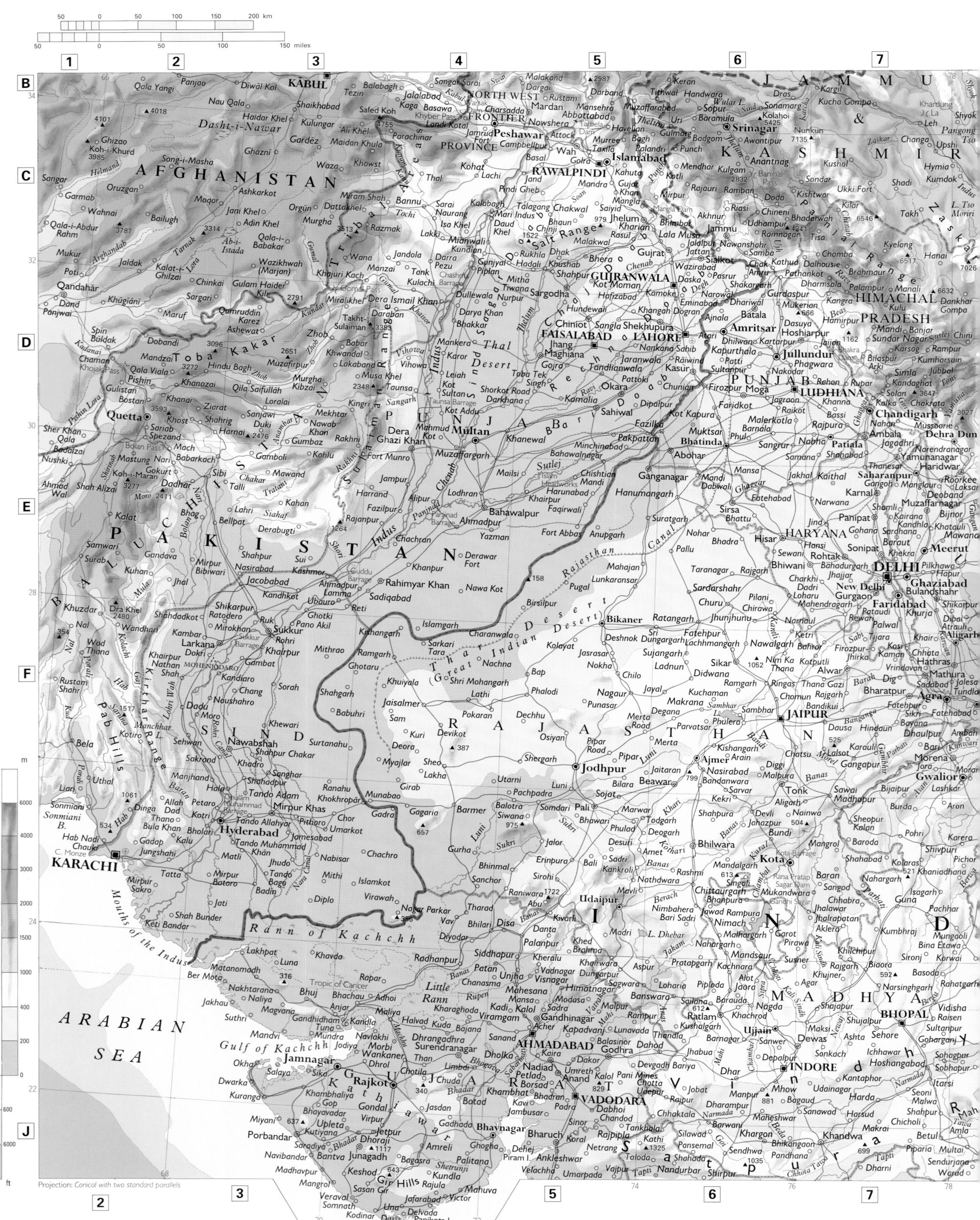

65
68
91
90
94

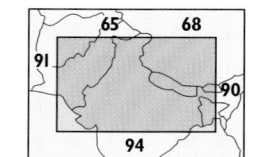

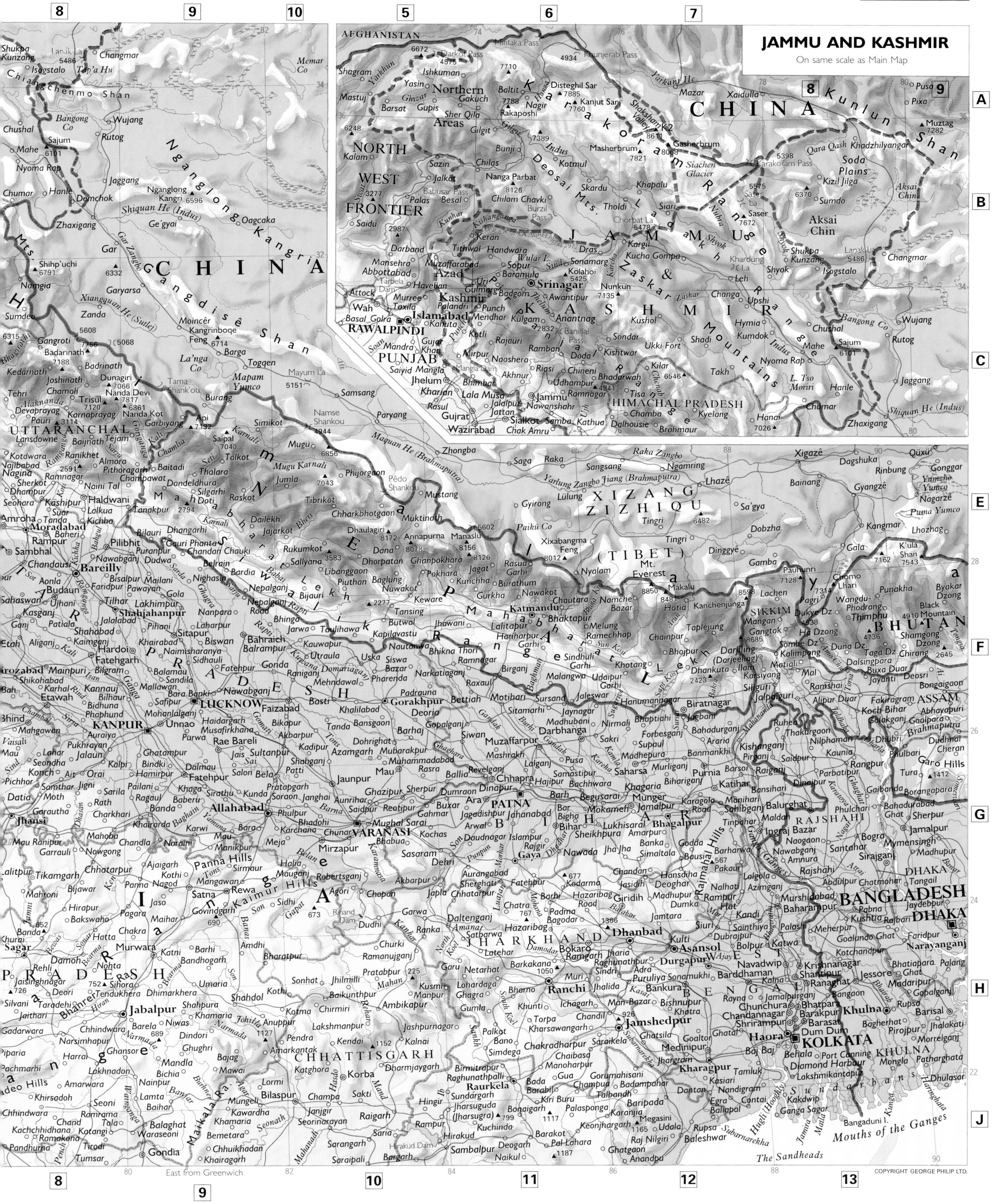

JAMMU AND KASHMIR
On same scale as Main Map
AFGHANISTAN
CHINA
Karakoram Range
Kunlun Shan
NORTH WEST FRONTIER
Northern Areas
Azad Kashmir
PUNJAB
JAMMU & KASHMIR
Zaskar Mountains
HIMACHAL PRADESH
Aksai Chin
Islamabad
RAWALPINDI
Srinagar
Jammu
K2 8611
Gasherbrum 8068
Nanga Parbat 8126
Deosai Mts.
Ladakh Range
CHINA
Nganglong Kangri
Gangdisê Shan
XIZANG ZIZHIQU (TIBET)
Mt. Everest 8850
NEPAL
Katmandu
Mahabharat Lekh
Siwalik Range
UTTARANCHAL
UTTAR PRADESH
LUCKNOW
KANPUR
Allahabad
VARANASI
BIHAR
PATNA
SIKKIM
Gangtok
BHUTAN
Thimphu
ASSAM
BANGLADESH
DHAKA
RAJSHAHI
KHULNA
JHARKHAND
Ranchi
WEST BENGAL
KOLKATA
CHHATTISGARH
MADHYA PRADESH
Jabalpur
Kaimur Hills
Mouths of the Ganges
The Sandheads
Sundarbans
East from Greenwich
COPYRIGHT GEORGE PHILIP LTD.
A
B
C
E
F
G
H
J
8
9
10
5
6
7
11
12
13

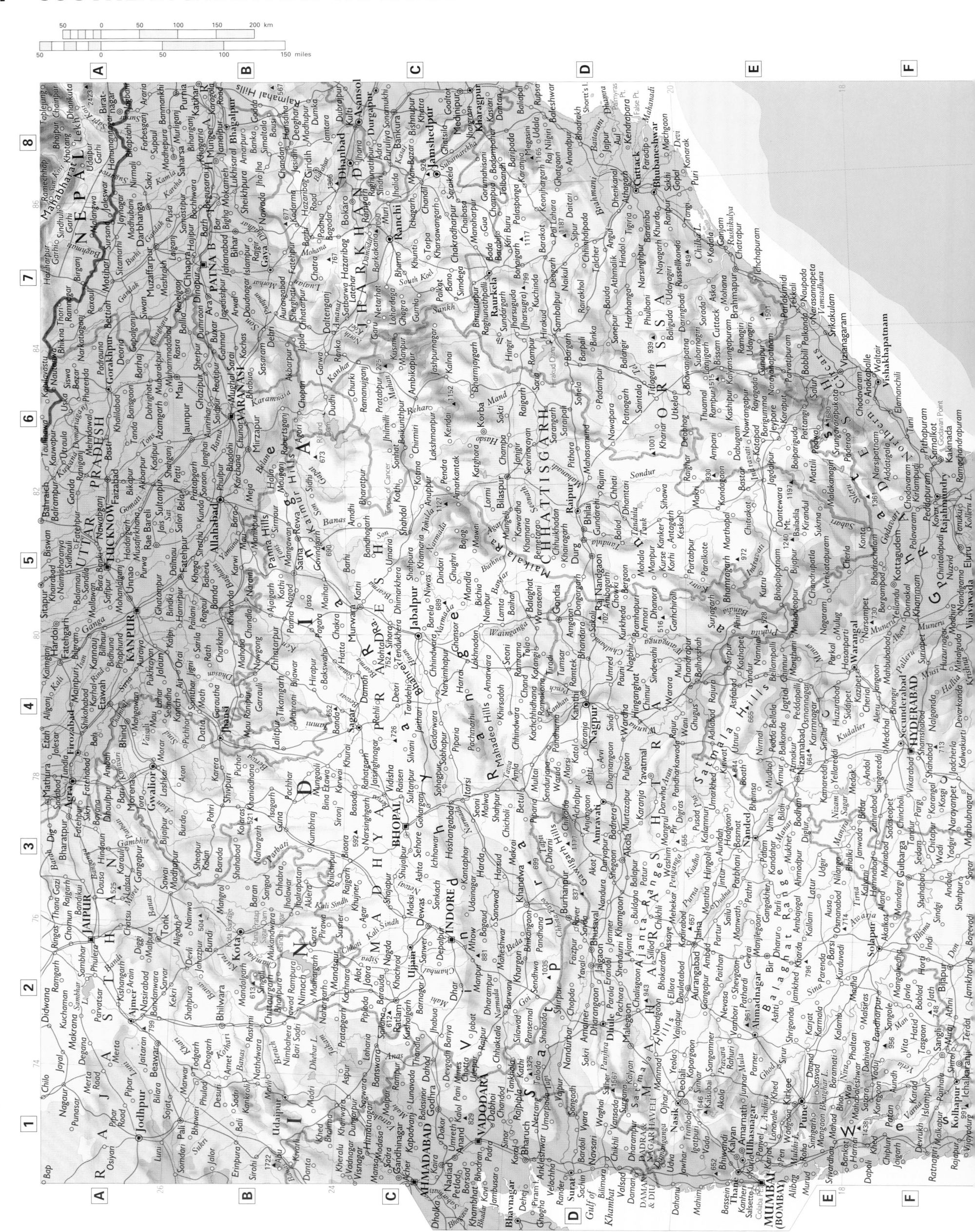

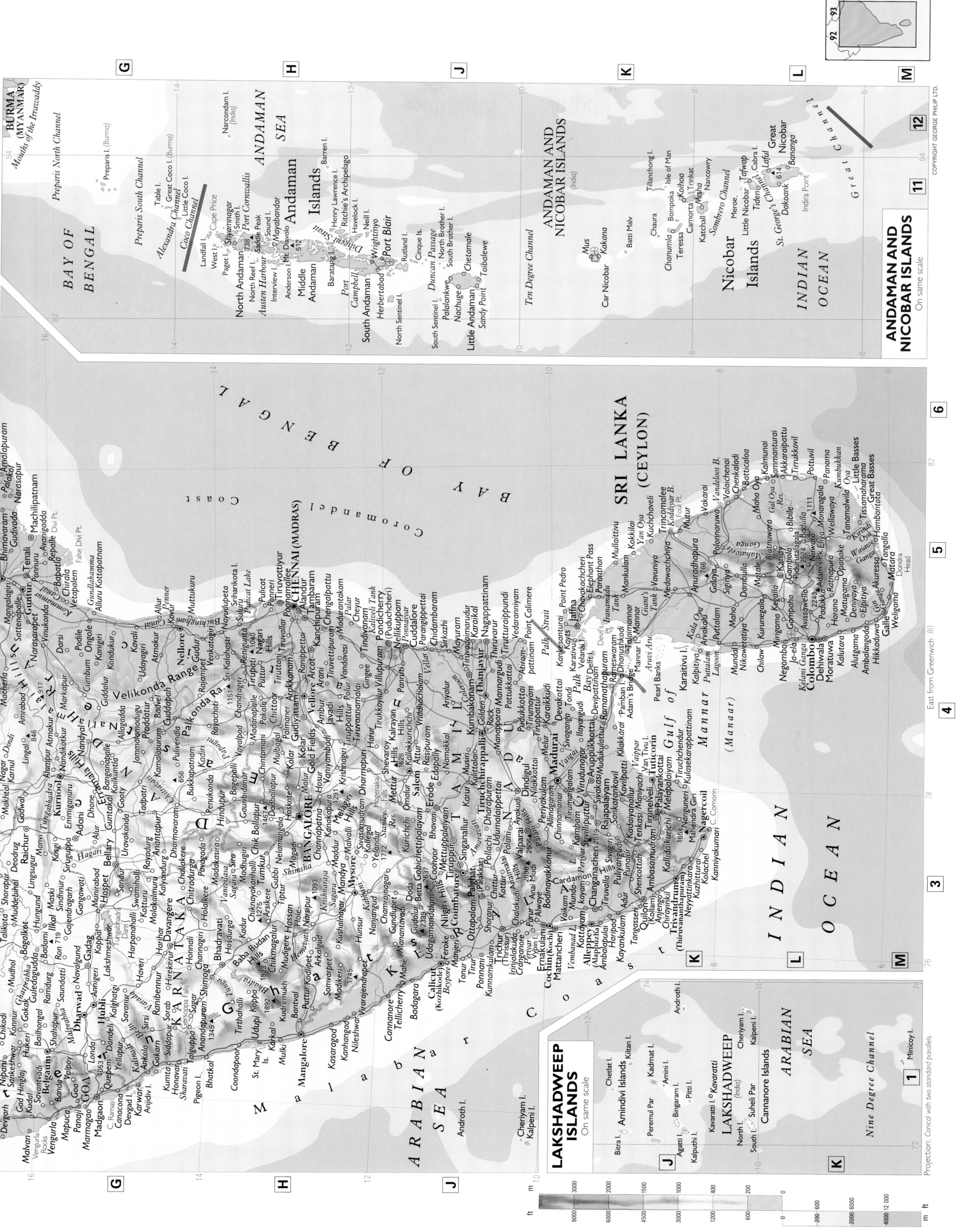

ANDAMAN AND NICOBAR ISLANDS
On same scale

LAKSHADWEEP ISLANDS
On same scale

Projection: Conical with two standard parallels

COPYRIGHT GEORGE PHILIP LTD.

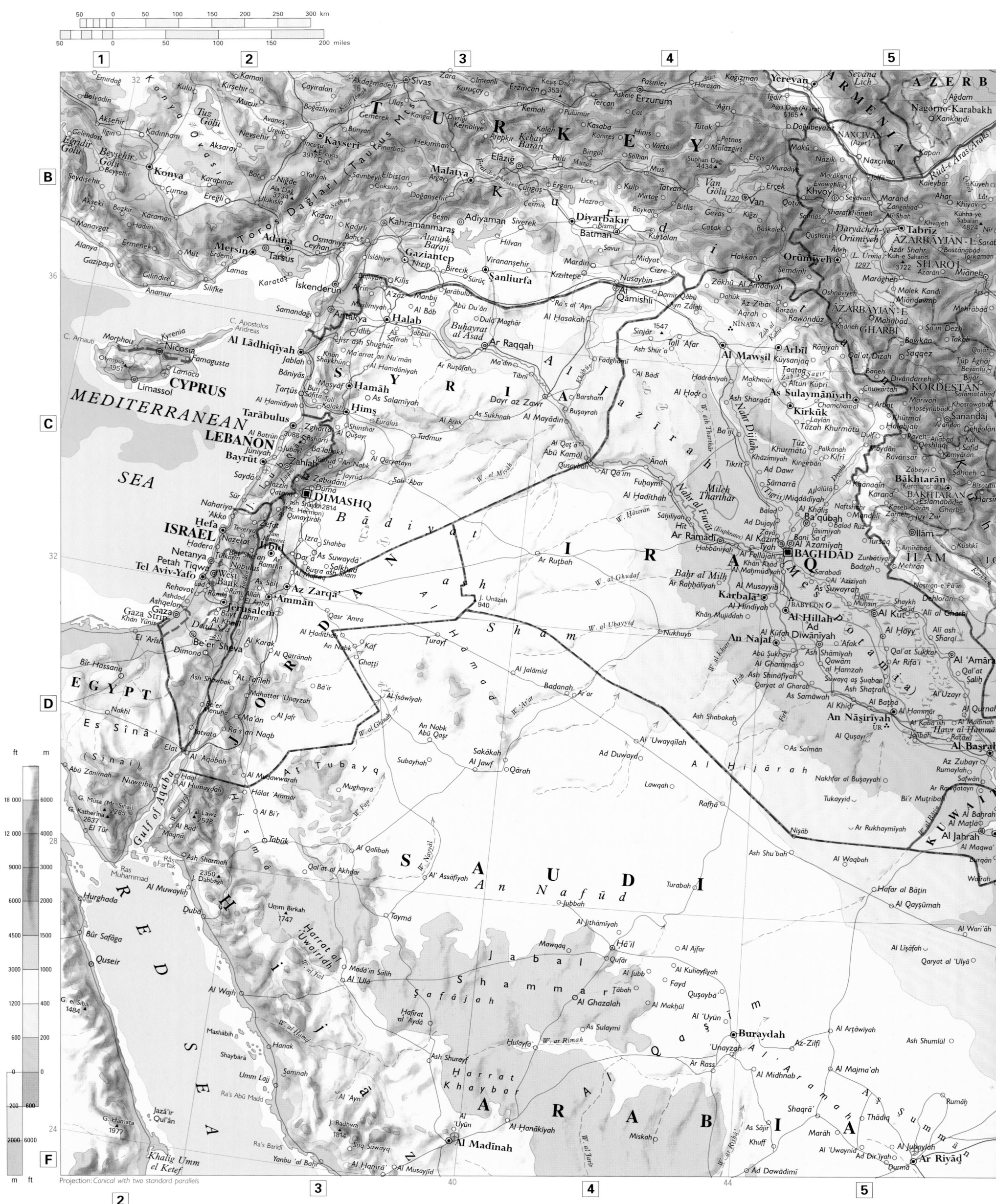

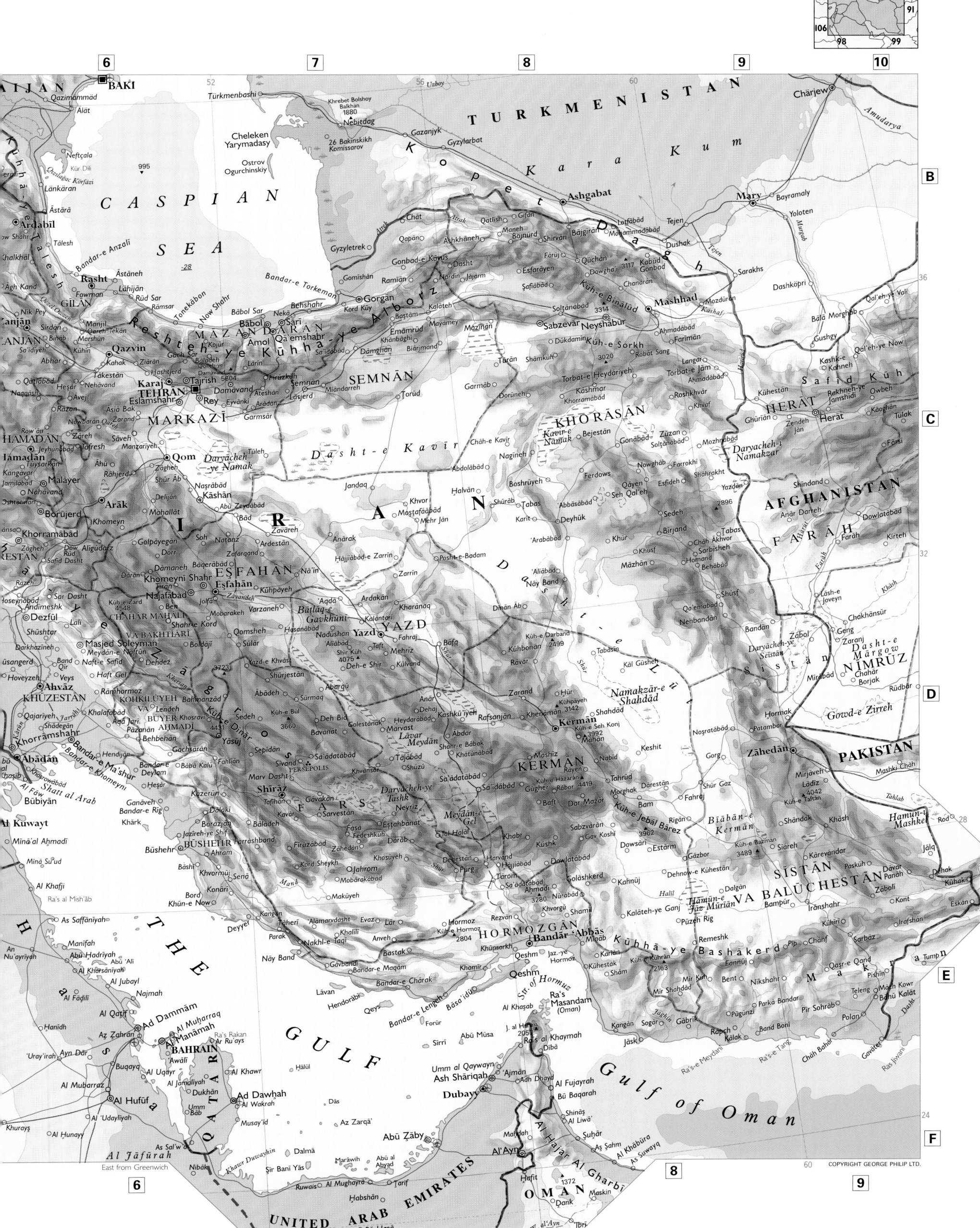

COPYRIGHT GEORGE PHILIP LTD.

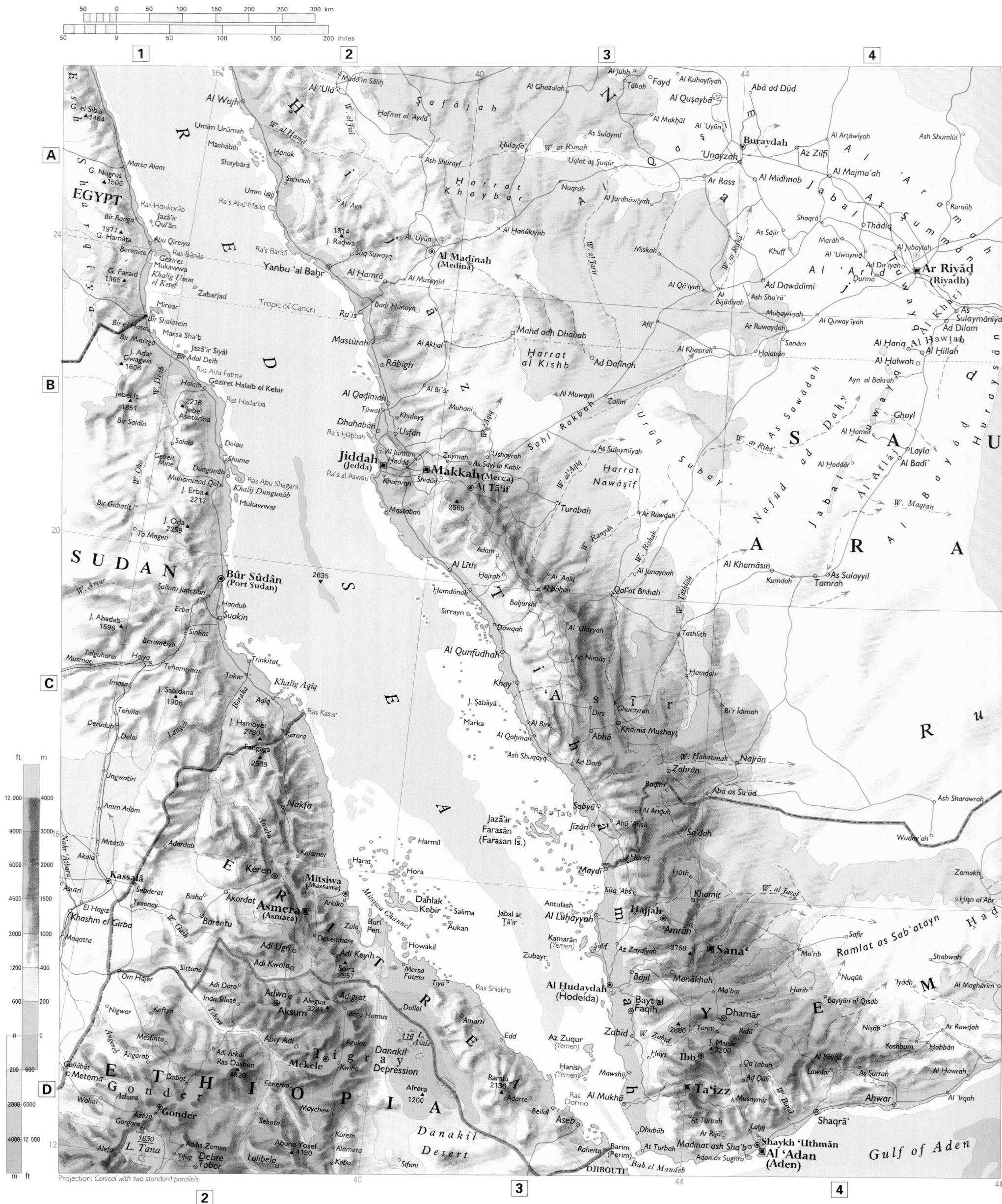

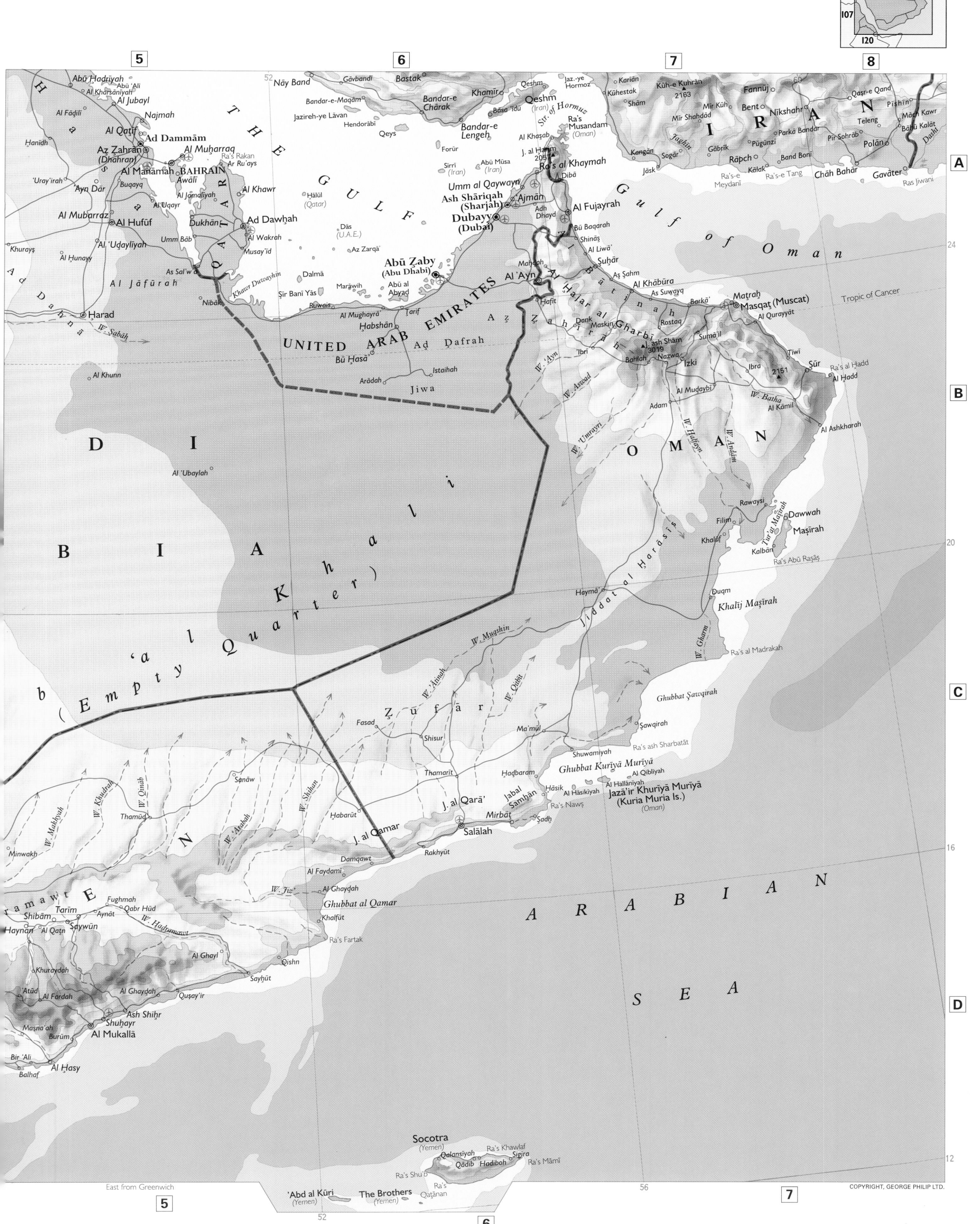

COPYRIGHT, GEORGE PHILIP LTD.

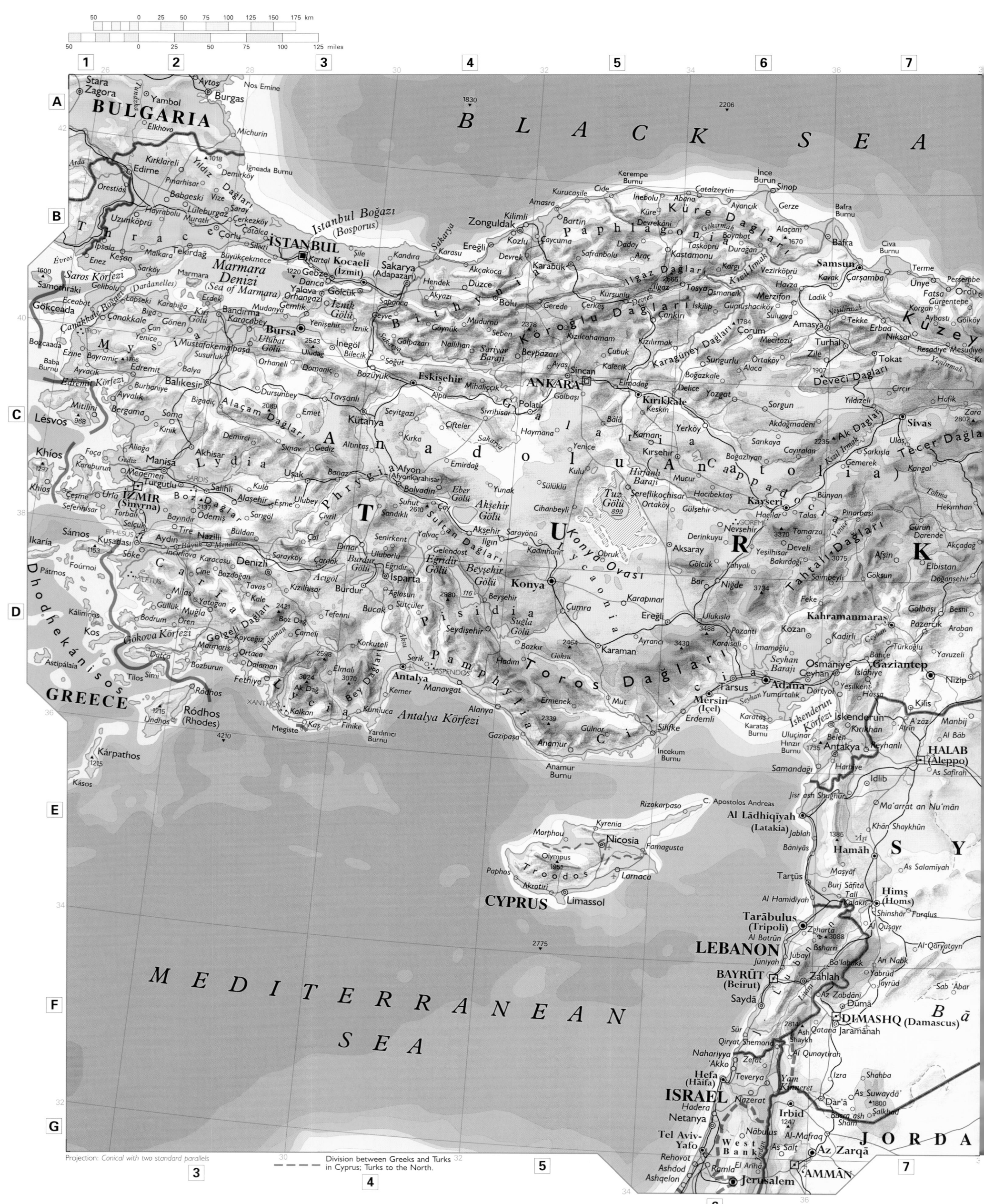

BULGARIA

BLACK SEA

İSTANBUL

ANKARA

İZMIR (Smyrna)

Bursa

Marmara Denizi (Sea of Marmara)

İstanbul Boğazı (Bosporus)

T U R K

A n a t o l i a

Toros Dağları

GREECE

CYPRUS

Nicosia

MEDITERRANEAN SEA

SYRIA

HALAB (Aleppo)

Hamāh

Hims (Homs)

Tarābulus (Tripoli)

LEBANON

BAYRŪT (Beirut)

DIMASHQ (Damascus)

ISRAEL

Hefa (Haifa)

Tel Aviv-Yafo

AMMĀN

Jerusalem

Az Zarqā

JORDAN

Projection: Conical with two standard parallels

Division between Greeks and Turks in Cyprus; Turks to the North.

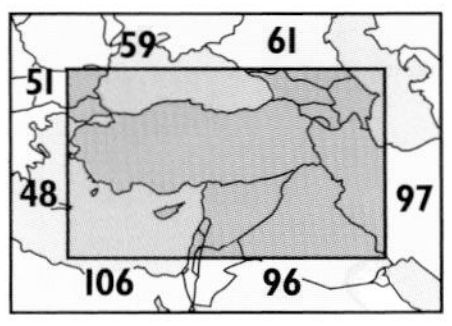

Caucasus Mountains

RUSSIA

GEORGIA

ARMENIA

AZERBAIJAN

CASPIAN SEA

TURKEY

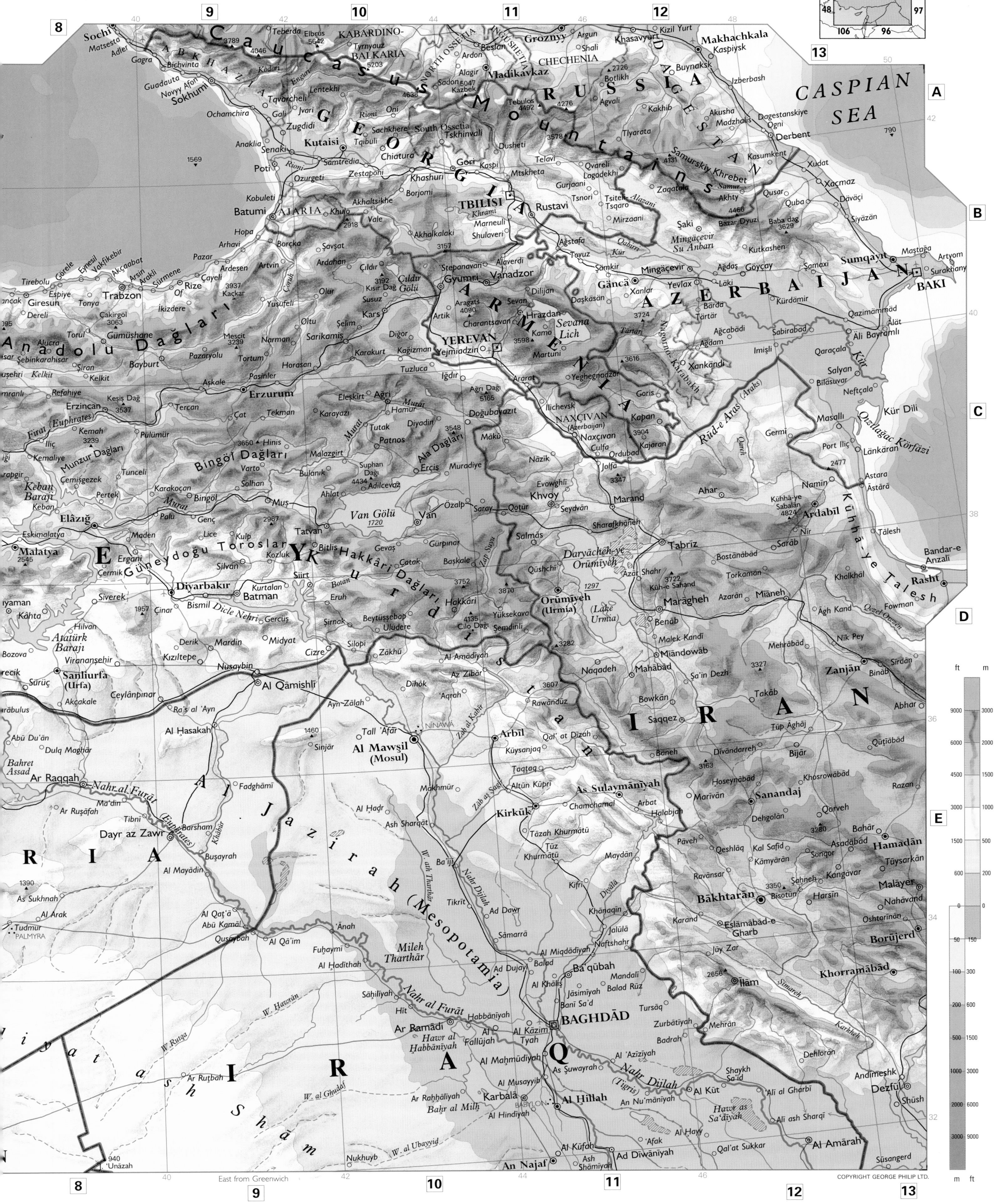

IRAQ

IRAN

SYRIA

Anadolu Dağları

Güneydoğu Toroslar

Mesopotamia

Al Jazirah (Mesopotamia)

Sochi · Matsesta · Adler · Gagra · Bichvinta · Guadauta · Novyy Afon · Sokhumi · Ochamchira · Gali · Zugdidi · Anaklia · Senaki · Poti · Kobuleti · Batumi · AJARIA · Hopa · Arhavi · Borçka · Pazar · Ardeşen · Çayeli · Rize · Of · Trabzon · Arsin · Akçaabat · Sürmene · İkizdere

Teberda · Elbrus 5642 · KABARDINO-BALKARIA · Tyrnyauz · 4046 · 5203 · Lentekhi · Kodori · Engari · Jvari · Oni · Rioni · Tqvarcheli · Sachkhere · Chiatura · Kutaisi · Samtredia · Zestaponi · Khashuri · Ozurgeti · Vale · Akhaltsikhe · Khulo · 2918 · Akhalkalaki · 3157

NORTH OSSETIA · INGUSHETIA · Grozny · Argun · Shali · Khasavyurt · Kizil Yurt · Makhachkala · Kaspiysk

Vladikavkaz · Beslan · Alagir · Ardon · Sadon · Kazbek · 4638 · Dusheti · Mtskheta · TBILISI · Khrami · Marneuli · Shulaveri · Rustavi · Mirzaani · Gori · Kaspi · Telavi · Gurjaani · Tsnori · Tsiteli-Tskaro

CHECHENIA · 2726 · Botlikh · DAGESTAN · Buynaksk · Izberbash · Tlyarata · 3578 · Kakhib · Agvali · Akusha · Madzhalis · Dagestanskiye Ogni · Derbent · 790 · Xudat · Xaçmaz · Qusar · Quba · Dəvəçi · Siyəzən

Samurskiy Khrebet · 4131 · Kasumkent · Akhty · Bazar Dyuzi · 4466 · Baba dağ 3629 · Şəki · Mingəçevir Su Anbarı · Kutkashen · Zaqatala · Qabırı · Ağdaş · Göyçay · Şamaxı · Sumqayıt · BAKI · Surakhany · Artyom · Maştağa

Eşnesil · Görele · Vakfıkebir · Tirebolu · Espiye · Giresun · Dereli · Gümüşhane · Çakırgöl 3063 · Tonya · Ikizdere · Aluçra · Şebinkarahisar · 3937 · Kaçkar · Yusufeli · Olur · Artvin · Ardahan · Çıldır · Kısır Dağ · Çıldır Gölü · Susuz · Kars · Sarıkamış · Selim · Digor · Karakurt · Kağızman · Tuzluca · İğdır · Ararat

Ardanuç · 3192 · Stepanavan · Alaverdi · Gyumri · Vanadzor · Dilijan · Sevan · Sevana Lich · Kamo · 3598 · Aragats 4090 · Artik · Hrazdan · YEREVAN · Yejmiadzin · Martuni · Yeghegnadzor

Şamkir · Ağstafa · Tovuz · Qazax · Gəncə · Xanlar · Yevlax · Mingəçevir · Daşkəsən · Göyçay · 3724 · Türtan · Tərtər · Ağdam · Xankəndi · Nagorno-Karabakh · 3616 · Goris · Qaraçala · Ağcabədi · Sabirabad · Salyan · Əli Bayramlı · İmişli · Kür · Kürdəmir · Bərdə · Qazımməmməd · Älät

Biləsuvar · Neftçala · Kür Dili · Masallı · Qızılağac Körfəzi · Port İliç · Lənkəran · 2477 · Namin · Astara · Ardabıl · Küh-ha-ye Talesh · Küh-ha-ye Sabalān 4824 · Nir · Sarāb · Tālesh · Germi · Qızıl Özen · Hashtpar · Fowman · Bandar-e Anzalī · Rasht

Erzincan · Refahiye · Keşiş Dağ 3537 · İliç · Kemah · 3239 · Pülümür · Tercan · Tekman · Çat · Erzurum · Aşkale · Pasinler · Horasan · Narman · Oltu · 3239 · Mescit

Eleşkirt · Ağrı · Murat · Hamur · Tutak · Karayazı · Patnos · Diyadin · Doğubayazıt · Ağrı Dağı 5165 · Māku · Nāzik · Qotūr · Khvoy · Marand · Ahar · Tabrīz · 3722 · Kūh-e Sahand · Bostānābād · Torkamān · Azārān · Mīāneh · Sarāb · Ardabīl

Kelkit · Bayburt · 3063 · Pazaryolu · Tortum · Sarıkamış · Karakurt · Horasan · NAXÇIVAN (Azerbaijan) · Naxçıvan · Culfa · Ordubad · 3904 · Kajaran · Kapan · Jolfa · Marand · 3347

Keban Barajı · Keban · Kemaliye · Kemah · Munzur Dağları · Çemişgezek · Pertek · Tunceli · Pülümür · Varto · Bingöl Dağları · Hınıs · 3650 · Malazgirt · Adilcevaz · Ahlat · Erciş · Muradiye · Van Gölü 1720 · Özalp · Saray · Seydvān · Salmās · Sharafkhāneh · Daryācheh-ye Orūmīyeh · Qūshchī · Āzar Shahr · Marāgheh

Elâzığ · Eskimalatya · Malatya 2545 · Ergani · Maden · Lice · Kulp · Muş · Solhan · Bingöl · Genç · Palu · 2967 · Tatvan · Bitlis · Gevaş · Gürpınar · Çatak · Başkale · 3752 · 3870 · Orūmīyeh (Urmia) · Lake Urmia · 1297 · Benāb · Malek Kandī · Miāndowāb · Bowkān · Saqqez

Çermik · Siverek · 1957 · Çınar · Diyarbakır · Bismil · Dicle Nehri · Batman · Kurtalan · Siirt · Gerçüş · Eruh · Şırnak · Botan · Beytüşşebap · Uludere · Hakkâri · Cilo Dağı 4135 · Şemdinli · Yüksekova · 3282 · Naqadeh · Mahābād · Sa'īn Dezh · 3327 · Takāb · Zanjān · Sırdān · Bināb · Abhar

Hilvan · Atatürk Barajı · Derik · Mardin · Midyat · Cizre · Silopi · Zākhū · Al Amādīyah · Az Zībār · 'Aqrah · Dīhōk · Rawāndūz · Qal'at Dīzah · Baneh · Dīvāndarreh · Bījār · Hoseynābād · Khosrowābād · Razan

Kâhta · Bozova · Viransehir · Kızıltepe · Nusaybin · Al Qāmishlī · Ra's al 'Ayn · Ayn Zālah · 1460 · Tall 'Afar · NĪNAWĀ · Al Mawsil (Mosul) · Makhmūr · Arbīl · Küysanjaq · Taqtaq · Altūn Küprī · As Sulaymānīyah · Halabjah · Marīvān · Sanandaj · Dehgolān · Qorveh · Bahār · 3280 · Asadābād · Hamadān

Şanlıurfa (Urfa) · Akçakale · Ceylânpınar · Al Hasakah · Sinjār · Ash Sharqāt · Tāzah Khurmātū · Kirkūk · Chamchamal · Arbat · Qeshlāq · Kāmyārān · Soṇqor · Kangāvar · Tūysarkān · Malāyer · Nahāvand

Sürüç · Harran · Bahret Assad · Ar Raqqah · Nahr al Furāt (Euphrates) · Ma'din · Ar Rusāfah · Fadghāmī · Al Hadr · Tūz Khurmātū · Qādir Karīm · Sahneh · Bīsotūn · 3350 · Bākhtarān · Eslāmābād-e Gharb · Harsin · Borūjerd

Dulq Maghār · Abū Du'ān · Tibnī · Barsham · Khābūr · Dayr az Zawr · Būsayrah · Al Mayādīn · As Sukhnah · W. ath Tharthār · Sāmarrā' · Maydān · Kifrī · Khānaqīn · Dīvānī · Jalūlā' · Karand · 3350 · Jūy Zar · Īlām · Mehrān · Khorramābād

1390 · Tudmur · PALMYRA · Al Arak · Al Qat'ā · Abū Kamāl · Al Qā'im · Fuhaymī · Al Hadīthah · Tikrīt · Ad Dawr · Mileh Tharthār · Nahr Dijlah · Ad Dujayl · Balad · Al Miqdādīyah · Balad Rūz · Mandalī · Naftshahr · 2656 · Dehlorān · Andīmeshk · Dezfūl · Shūsh

Ar Ruşāfah · Qusaybah · 'Ānah · SYRIA · Sāhilīyah · Hīt · Habbānīyah · Ar Ramādī · Al Fallūjah · BAGHDAD · Al Kāzimīyah · Al Mahmūdīyah · As Suwayrah · Zurbātīyah · Badrah · Shaykh Sa'd · Al Kūt · 'Alī al Gharbī · 'Alī ash Sharqī · Al Amārah

Ar Rutbah · W. Hawrān · W. Rutqa · W. al Ubayyid · W. al Ghudaf · Ar Rahhālīyah · Nukhayb · Hawr al Habbānīyah · Al Musayyib · BABYLON · Al Hillah · Al Hindīyah · An Najaf · Ash Shāmīyah · Ad Dīwānīyah · 'Afak · Al Kūfah · An Nu'mānīyah · Bahr al Milh · Hawr as Sa'dīyah · Al Hayy · Qal'at Sukkar · Süsangerd

Karbalā' · Al 'Azīzīyah · Bā'qūbah · Jāsimīyah · Banī Sa'd · Tursāq

940 · 'Unāzah · East from Greenwich

COPYRIGHT GEORGE PHILIP LTD.

ft m · 9000 3000 · 6000 2000 · 4500 1500 · 3000 1000 · 1500 500 · 600 200 · 0 0 · 50 150 · 100 300 · 200 600 · 500 1500 · 1000 3000 · 2000 6000 · 3000 9000 · m ft

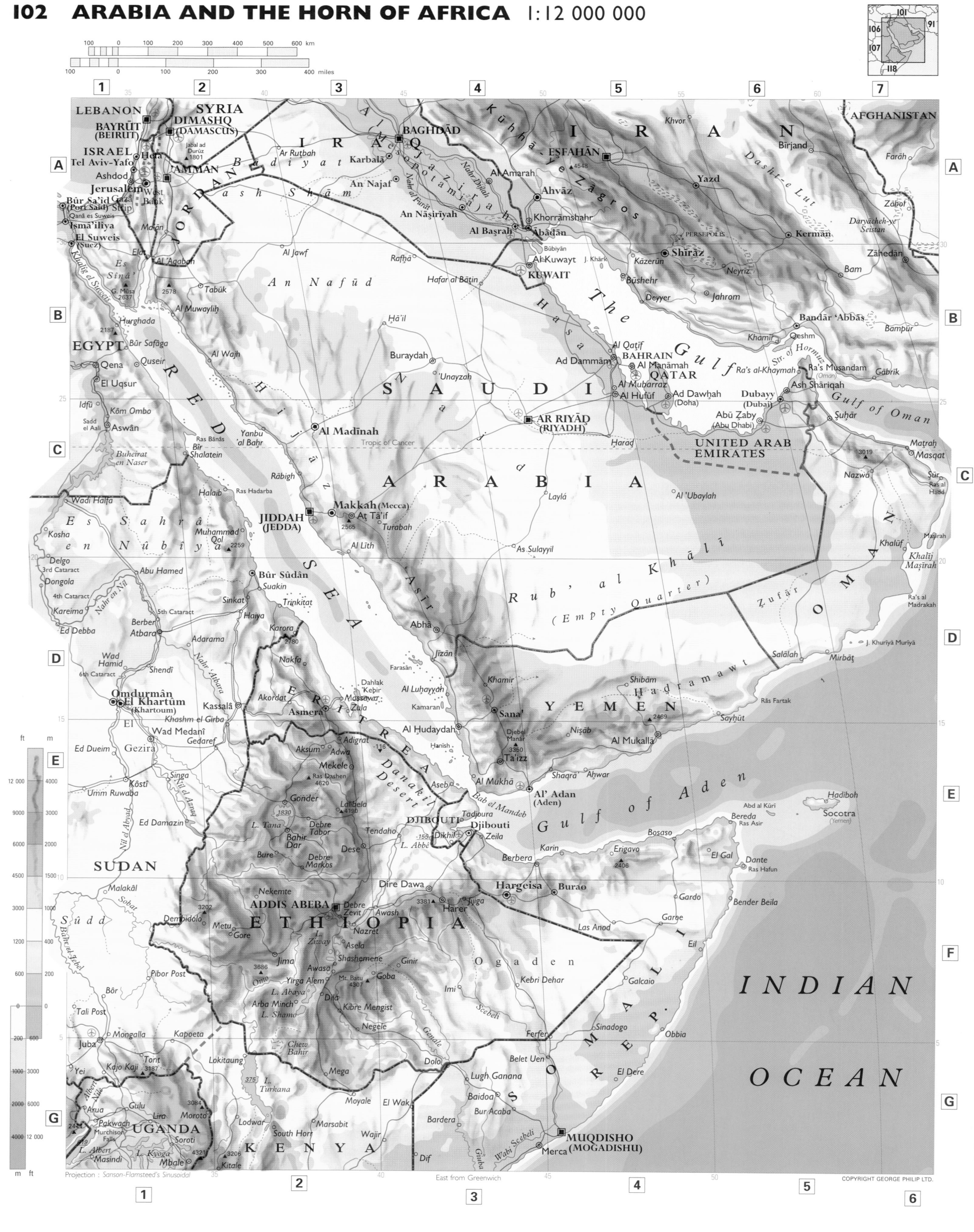

100 0 100 200 300 400 500 600 km
100 0 100 200 300 400 miles

LEBANON
BAYRŪT (BEIRUT)
SYRIA
DIMASHQ (DAMASCUS)
ISRAEL
Tel Aviv-Yafo
Ḥeifa
Ashdod
AMMĀN
Jabal ad Durūz 1801
JORDAN
IRAQ
BAGHDĀD
Karbalā'
Jerusalem
West Bank
Gaza Strip
Bûr Sa'id (Port Said)
Qanā es Suweis
Isma'iliya
El Suweis (Suez)
Ma'ān
Al 'Aqabah
Khalīg el Suweis
Es Sinā'
G. Mûsa 2637
2578
Tabûk
Al Muwayliḥ
2187
Hurghada
EGYPT
Bûr Safâga
Qena
Quseir
El Uqsur
Idfû
Kôm Ombo
Sadd el Aali
Aswân
Buheirat en Naser
Ar Ruṭbah
An Najaf
Nahr al Furāt
An Nāṣirīyah
Al Jawf
Rafḥā'
Hafar al Bāṭin
Hā'il
An Nafūd
Burayḍah
'Unayzah
Al Wajh
SAUDI
Ras Bânâs
Bîr Shalatein
Al Madīnah
Yanbu 'al Baḥr
Rābigh
Halaib
Ras Hadarba
Ḥijāz
Mecca Makkah
Aṭ Ṭā'if 2565
Muḥammad Qol 2259
Al Lith
ARABIA
Turabah
As Sulayyil
Laylá
AR RIYĀḌ (RIYADH)
Harad
Jabal ad Durūz
Al Basrah
Ahvāz
Khorramshahr
Ābādān
Būbiyān
J. Khārk
Al Kuwayt
KUWAIT
Al Amarah
ESFAHĀN
4548
Yazd
Kāzerūn
Shīrāz
PERSEPOLIS
Būshehr
Deyyer
Jahrom
Neyrīz
Kermān
Zāhedān
Bam
IRAN
Khvor
Bīrjand
Farāh
AFGHANISTAN
Zābol
Daryācheh-ye Seistan
Dasht-e Lut
The Gulf
Hasa
Ad Dammām
Al Qaṭīf
BAHRAIN
Al Manāmah
QATAR
Al Mubarraz
Al Hufūf
Ad Dawḥah (Doha)
Ra's al-Khaymah
Ash Shāriqah
Dubayy (Dubai)
Abū Ẓaby (Abu Dhabi)
UNITED ARAB EMIRATES
Al 'Ubaylah
Khamir
Qeshm
Bandār 'Abbās
Bampûr
Str. of Hormuz
Ra's Musandam (Oman)
Gābrīk
Maṭrah
Masqat
Nazwā 3019
Şūr
Ra's al Ḥadd
Khalūf
Maṣīrah
Rub' al Khālī (Empty Quarter)
OMAN
Zufār
Salālah
Mirbāṭ
Ra's al Madrakah
J. Khurīyā Murīyā
Khalīj Maṣīrah
'Asīr
Abha
Jīzān
Farasān
Abhā
Khamir
Shibām
Ḥadramawt
Rās Fartak
Sayḥūt
YEMEN
Sana'
Djebel Manār 3350
Nisāb
Al Mukallā
Ta'izz
Al Luḥayyah
Kamaran
Al Ḥudaydah
Dahlak Kebir
Massawa
Zula
Asmera
Adigrat
-116
Akordat
Nakfa 2780
Karora
Haiya
Trinkitat
Sinkat
Suakin
Bûr Sûdân
ERITREA
Danakil Desert
Adwa
Aksum
Mekele 4620
Ras Dashen 4620
Gonder 1830
Lalibela 4191
Debre Tabor
L. Tana
Bahir Dar
Bure
Dese
Debre Markos
Shaqrā'
Aḥwar
Al Mukhā
Bab el Mandeb
Al 'Adan (Aden)
Gulf of Aden
Abd al Kūrī
Hadiboh
Bereda
Ras Asir
Socotra (Yemen)
El Gal
Dante
Ras Hafun
Bosaso
Karin
Erigavo 2406
Berbera
Djibouti
Tadjoura
Zeila
Dikhil -155
DJIBOUTI
Aseb
L. Abbé
Tendaho
Dire Dawa
Hargeisa
Burao
Jijiga 3381
Harer
Gardo
Bender Beila
Garowe
SOMALI REP.
Ogaden
Las Anod
Kebri Dehar
Galcaio
Eil
Sinadogo
El Dere
Obbia
Ferfer
Gardo
Lugh Ganana
Belet Uen
Scebeli
Wabi Scebeli
Bur Acaba
Baidoa
Bardera
MUQDISHO (MOGADISHU)
Merca
Gituba
Genale
Dolo
INDIAN OCEAN
ADDIS ABEBA
Debre Zevit
Awash
Nazret
ETHIOPIA
Metu
Gore
Jima
3686
Awasa
Shashemene
Asela
Ginir
Goba
Mt. Batu 4307
Imi
Nekemte
Dembidolo
3202
Omo
Yirga Alem
Dila
Kibre Mengist
Negele
L. Abaya
Arba Minch
L. Shamo
Malakâl
Sobat
Sûdd
Bahr el Jebel
Bôr
Pibor Post
Tali Post
Juba
Mongalla
Kapoeta
Torit 3187
Yei
Chew Bahir
Mega
L. Turkana 375
Lokitaung
Lokichar
South Horn
Marsabit
Moyale
El Wak
Wajir
Dif
KENYA
Baidoa
Lodwar
Kitale
Mbale 4321
Soroti
Lira
Moroto 3084
Kdjo Kaji
UGANDA
2454
Pakwach
Arua
Gulu
Murchison Falls
L. Albert
L. Kyoga
Masindi
3206
Bû Sûdân
SUDAN
Omdurmân
El Khartûm (Khartoum)
Kassalâ
Khashm el Girba
Wad Medanî
Gedaref
El Gezira
Kôstî
Singa
Umm Ruwaba
Ed Dueim
Wad Hamid
Shendî
Berber
Atbara
Ed Debba
Kareima
Dongola
Delgo
Kosha
3rd Cataract
4th Cataract
5th Cataract
6th Cataract
Wadi Halfa
Abu Hamed
Nahr en Nil
Nahr 'Atbara
Es Sahrâ en Nûbîya
Nil el Abyad
Nil el Azraq
Ed Damazin
RED SEA
Badiyat ash Shâm
Al Jazira
Mesopotamia
Tropic of Cancer

East from Greenwich

Projection: Sanson-Flamsteed's Sinusoidal

COPYRIGHT GEORGE PHILIP LTD.

ft m
12 000 4000
9000 3000
6000 2000
4500 1500
3000 1000
1200 400
600 200
0 0
200 600
1000 3000
2000 6000
4000 12 000
m ft

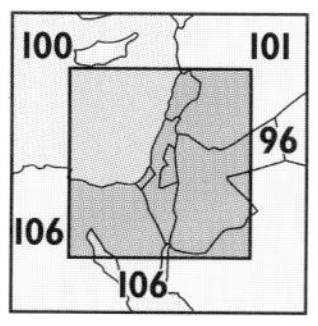

10 0 10 20 30 40 50 60 70 80 100 km
10 0 10 20 30 40 50 60 miles

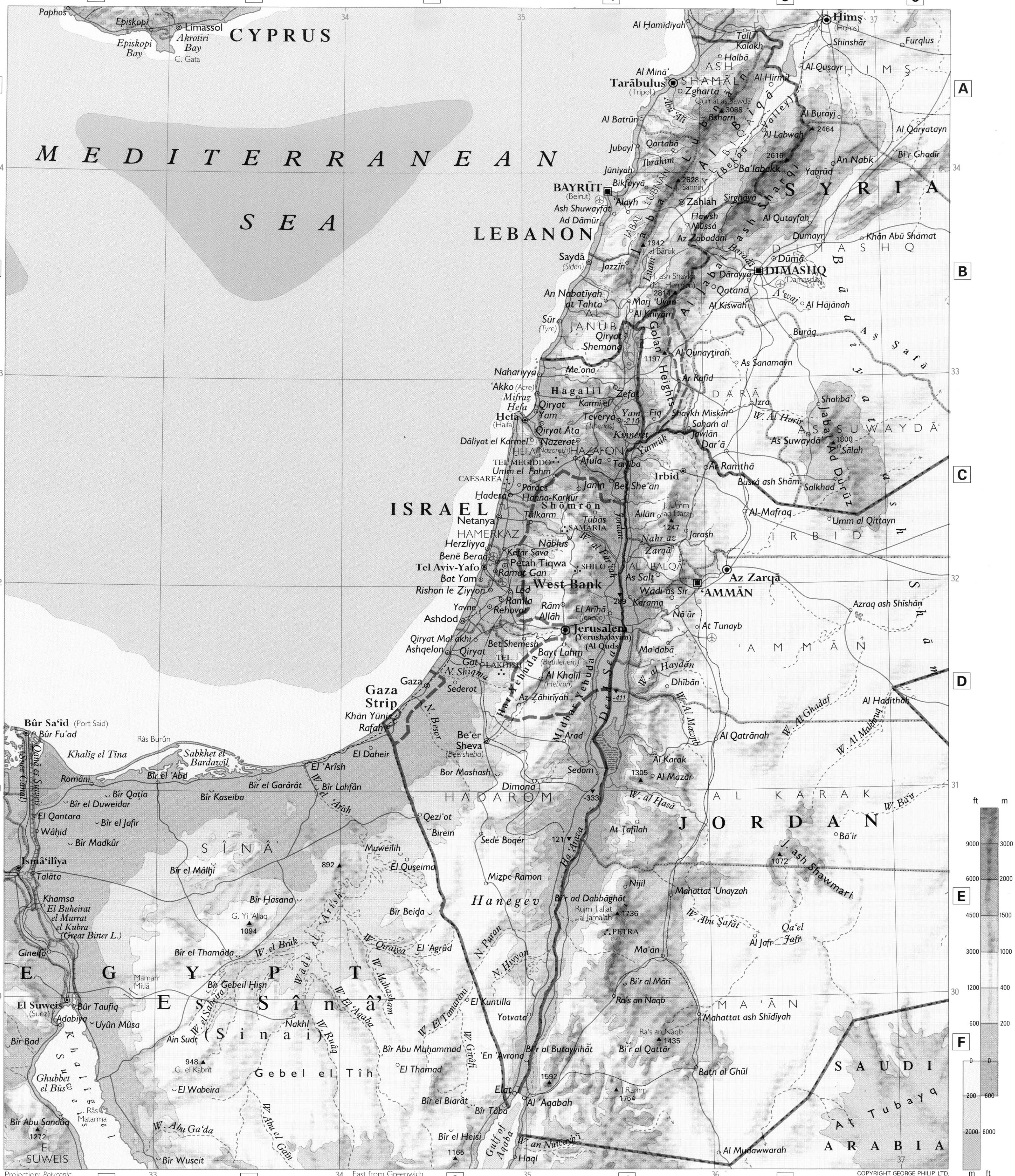

CYPRUS

Paphos
Episkopi
Akrotiri
Episkopi Bay
C. Gata
Limassol

M E D I T E R R A N E A N

S E A

Al Hamidiyah
Tall Kalakh
Halba
Al Hirmil
Al Qusayr
Shinshar
Furqlus
Ḥimṣ (Homs)

ASH SHAMĀL
Al Minā'
Ṭarābulus (Tripoli)
SHAMĀL
Zgharta
Qumat as Sawda
3088
Al Buray
2464
Al Qaryatayn

Al Batrūn
Bsharri
Al Labwah
Bi'r Ghadīr
Jubayl
Qartaba
2616
Ibrāhīm
Jūniyah
2628
Ba'labakk
Yabrūd
An Nabk

BAYRŪT (Beirut)
Sannin
2814
Zahlah
Sirghāyā
Dumayr
Khān Abū Shāmat
Ash Shuwayfat
Ad Dāmūr
'Alayh
Hawsh Mūssá
Al Qutayfah

LEBANON
Saydā (Sidon)
Az Zabadānī
DIMASHQ (Damascus)
Jazzīn
Dārayyā
Qatanā
An Nabaṭīyah at Tahta
Marj 'Uyūn
Al Ḥājānah
Sūr (Tyre)
Al Khiyām
Al Kiswah
AL JANŪB
Qiryat Shemona
1197
Al Qunayṭirah
As Sanamayn
Nahariyya
Me'ona
Ar Rafīd
Burāq

SYRIA
DIMASHQ
A'wai
J a b a l   a s h   S h a r q i
B ā d i y a   a s h   S h ā m

'Akko (Acre)
Hagalil
Zefat
DAR'Ā
Shahbā'
Mifraz Hefa
Qiryat Yam
Karmi'el
Yam
Fīq
Shaykh Miskin
Izra
Jabal ad Durūz
Hefa (Haifa)
Qiryat Ata
210
Saham al Jowlan
As Suwaydā'
1800
Dāliyat el Karmel
Nazerat (Nazareth)
Kinneret
Yarmūk
Dar'ā
AS SUWAYDĀ'
Ṭabariya
HEFA
HAZAFON
Afula
Al Harir

TEL MEGIDDO
Umm el Fahm
J. Umm ad Daraj
As Suwaydā'
Sālah
CAESAREA
Jenin
Bet She'an
Buṣrá ash Shām
Salkhad
Pardes
Hanna-Karkur
Ailūn
Al Mafraq
ISRAEL
Hadera
Ṭulkarm
Shōmrōn
Jordan
1247
Jarash
Umm al Qittayn

Netanya
Tūbās
SAMARIA
Nahr az Zarqā'
IRBID
HAMERKAZ
Nāblus
Herzliyya
Kefar Sava
AL BALQA
Benē Beraq
SHILO
As Salt
AMMĀN
Petah Tiqwa
Az Zarqā
Tel Aviv-Yafo
Ramat Gan
Wādī as Sīr
Bat Yam
West Bank
Azraq ash Shīshān
Rishon le Ziyyon
Lod
El Arīhā (Jericho)
Karama
Na'ūr
At Tunayb
Yavne
Ramla
Rām Allāh
289
Rehovot
'AMMĀN
Ashdod
Qiryat Mal'akhi
Bet Shemesh
Jerusalem (Yerushalayim) (Al Quds)
Ma'daba
Ashqelon
Qiryat Gat
Bayt Laḥm (Bethlehem)
TEL LAKHISH
Al Khalīl (Hebron)
W. al Ḥaydān
Gaza
Sederot
N. Shiqma
Az Ẓāhirīyah
Dhibān
Gaza Strip
Al Ḥadīthah
Khān Yūnis
Rafaḥ
N. Besor
Arad
Sedom
Al Karak
Bûr Sa'îd (Port Said)
Be'er Sheva (Beersheba)
1305
Al Mazār
Bûr Fu'ad
Rās Burûn
411
Khalîg el Tîna
Sabkhet el Bardawîl
El 'Arîsh
Bor Mashash
Al Qaṭrānah
Romāni
Bîr el 'Abd
Dimona
JORDAN
El Qantara
Bîr el Gararât
W. al Ḥasā
Bîr el Jafir
HADAROM
AL KARAK
El Qantara
W. 'Arîsh
Bîr el Duweidar
333
W. Bâr
Bîr Qaṭia
Bîr Kaseiba
At Ṭafīlah
El Qantara
Wâhid
Bîr Lahfân
J. ash Shawmari
Bîr Madkûr
S Î N Â '
1072
Ismâ'iliya
Qezi'ot
121
Birein
Nijil
Talâta
Sedé Boqér
Mahattat 'Unayzah
Khamsa
892
El Qusejma
Muweilih
W. Abu Safâi
El Buheirat el Murrat el Kubra (Great Bitter L.)
G. Yi 'Allâq
1094
Muweilih
Qa'el Jafr
Gineifo
Bîr Hasana
Mizpe Ramon
Al Jafr
Bîr el Thamâda
W. el Brûk
Bîr Beida
H a n e g e v
Bî'r ad Dabbâghât
1736
Ruim Tal'at al Jamâlah
El Suweis (Suez)
Bûr Taufiq
El 'Agrûd
N. Patan
W. Abu Safâi
Adabiya
Uyûn Mûsa
N. Hiyyon
Ma'ān
Bîr Bad'
Bîr Gebeil Hisn
El Kuntilla
Ra's an Naqb
MA'ĀN
948
El Thamad
Yotvata
Mahattat ash Shīdīyah
G. el Kabrît
'Ên 'Avrona
Bî'r al Mārī
1435
SAUDI
Ghubbet el Bûs
Gebel el Tîh
Bîr Abu Muḥammad
Bî'r al Butayyiḥât
Bî'r al Qaṭṭār
1272
Ghubbet el Bûs
E G Y P T
E S Î N Â' (Sinai)
1592
1754
Ramm
Baṭn al Ghûl
EL SUWEIS
Bîr el Biarât
Elat
ARABIA
Bîr Abu Sandûq
Bîr Wuseit
Bîr el Heisi
1165
Bîr Tâba
Āl 'Aqabah
At Tubayq
Ra's Matarma
W. Abu Ga'da
Gulf of Aqaba
Haql
Al Mudawwarah

Projection: Polyconic
East from Greenwich
COPYRIGHT GEORGE PHILIP LTD.

1974 Cease Fire Lines

See page VIII World: Regions in the News
for a map showing the areas under Palestinian control.

ft m
9000 3000
6000 2000
4500 1500
3000 1000
1200 400
600 200
0 0
200 600
2000 6000
m ft

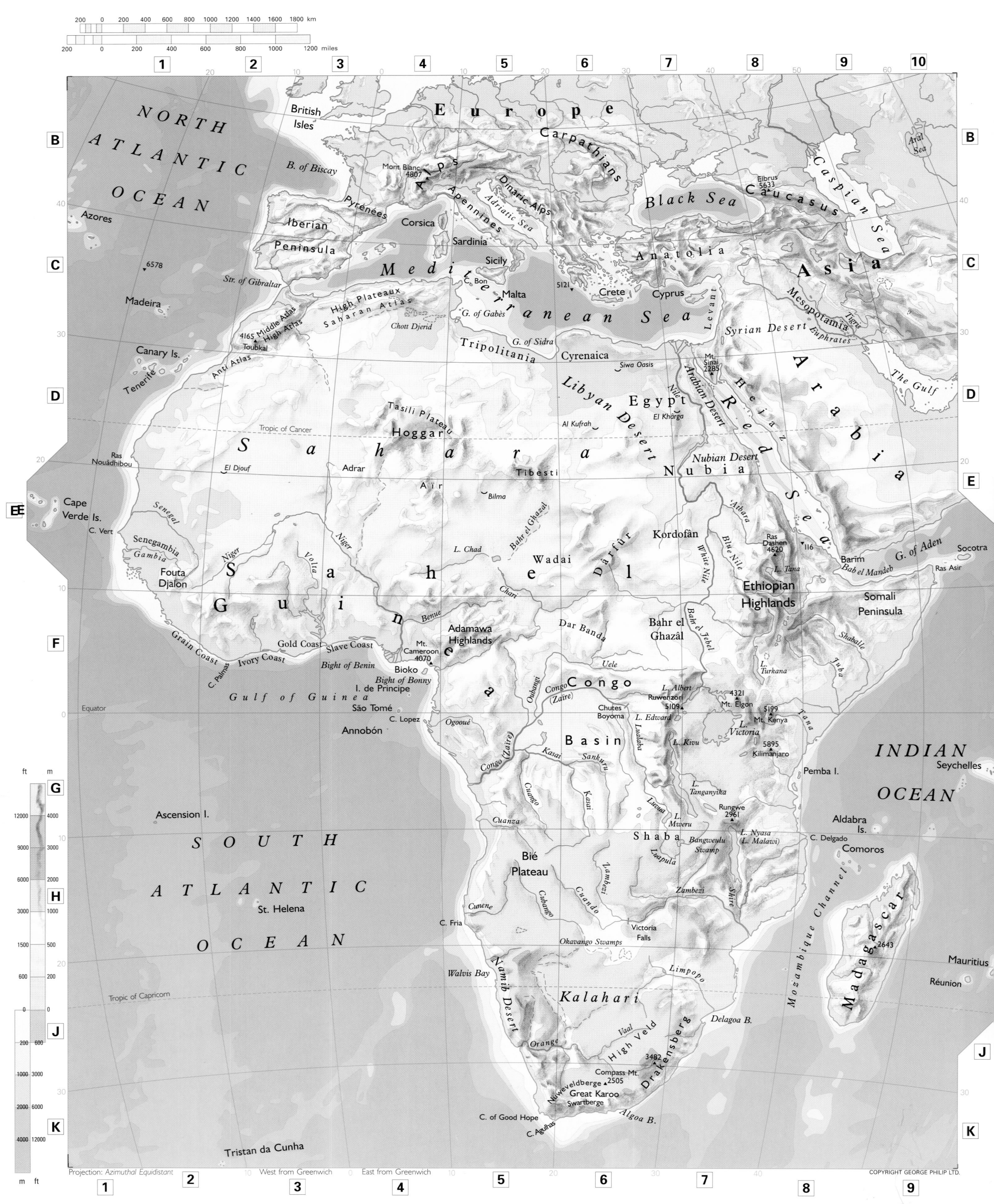

COPYRIGHT GEORGE PHILIP LTD.

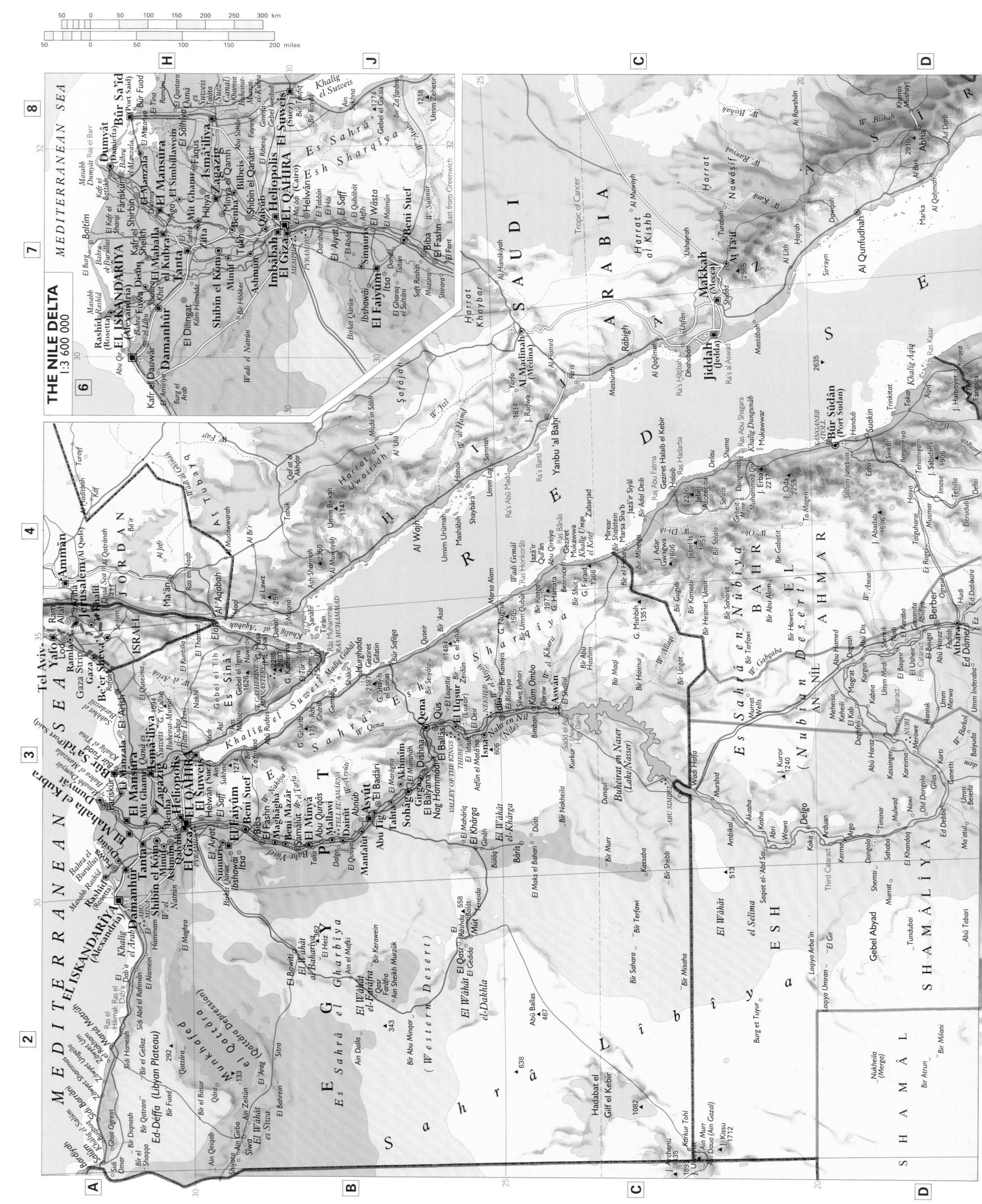

THE NILE DELTA
1:3 600 000

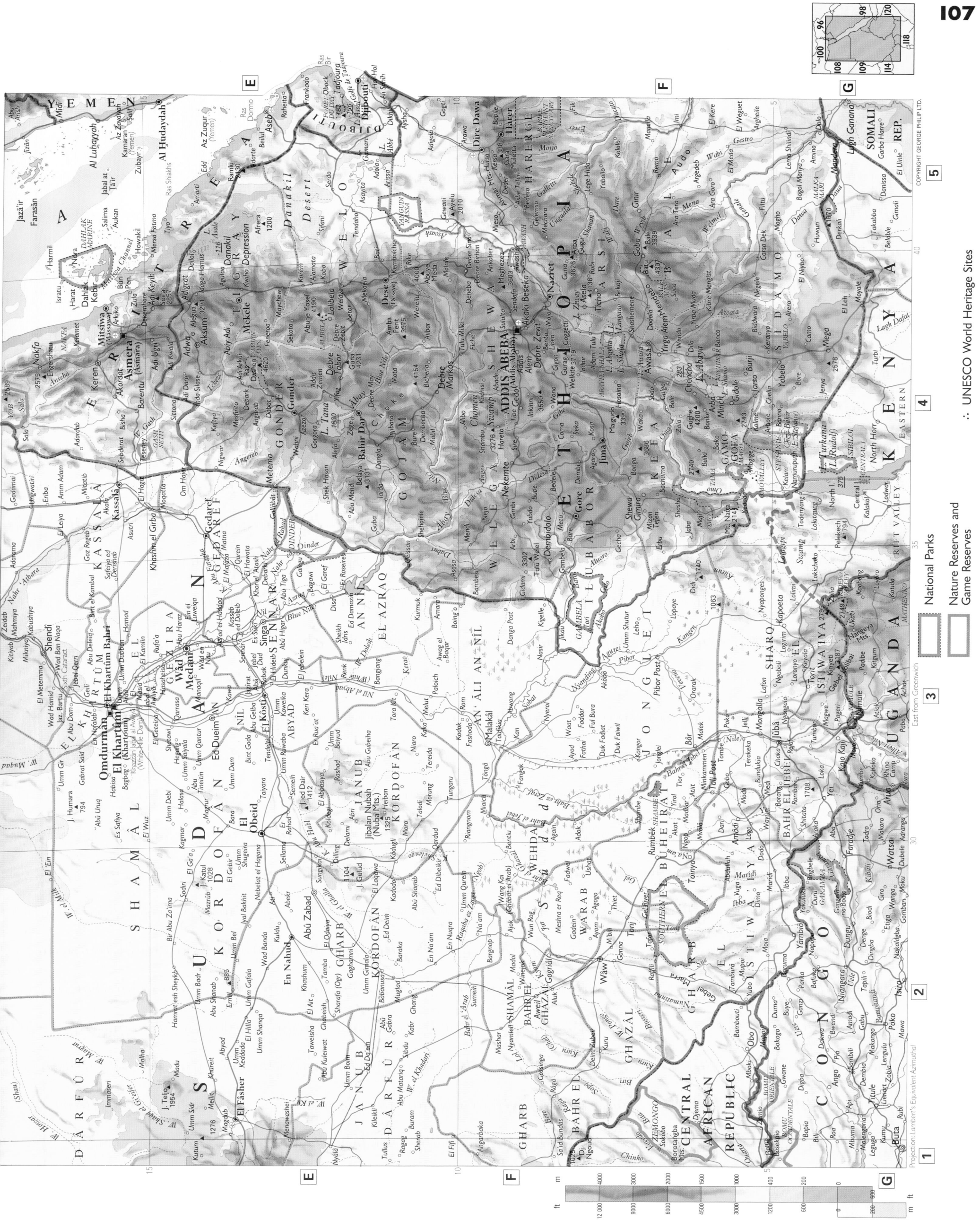

YEMEN

Al Luhayyah

Az Zuqur (Yemen)

Al Hudaydah

E R I T R E A

DJIBOUTI
Djibouti

Danakil Desert

Danakil Depression

WELLO

ETHIOPIA

HARERGE

Dire Dawa

Harer

SOMALI REP.

Asmera

GONDER

GOJAM

Bahir Dar

L. Tana

ADDIS ABEBA
(Addis Abeba)

ARSI

BALE

SIDAMO

S H E W A

WELEGA

KEFFA

GAMO-GOFA

GORE

ILUBABOR

KENYA

EASTERN

L. Turkana
(L. Rudolf)

El Fasher

DARFUR

KORDOFAN

S H A M A L

GHARB DARFUR

JANUB DARFUR

El Obeid

En Nahud

Khartoum
El Khartum

Omdurman

Wad Medani

GEZIRA

KASSALA

Kassala

Gedaref

GEDAREF

SENNAR

Singa

EL AZRAQ

AN NIL AL ANNIL

SHARQ

EL ISTIWAIYA

BAHR EL GHAZAL

BAHR EL JEBEL

JONGLEI

WARAB

WEHDA

SOUTHERN EL BUHEIRAT

EL BUHEIRAT

Wau

Malakal

Juba

UGANDA

CONGO

CENTRAL AFRICAN REPUBLIC

COPYRIGHT GEORGE PHILIP LTD.

East from Greenwich

∴ UNESCO World Heritage Sites

National Parks

Nature Reserves and Game Reserves

Projection Lambert's Equivalent Azimuthal

m ft
12 000
9000
6000
4500
3000
1500
1200
600
0
ft m
200-600

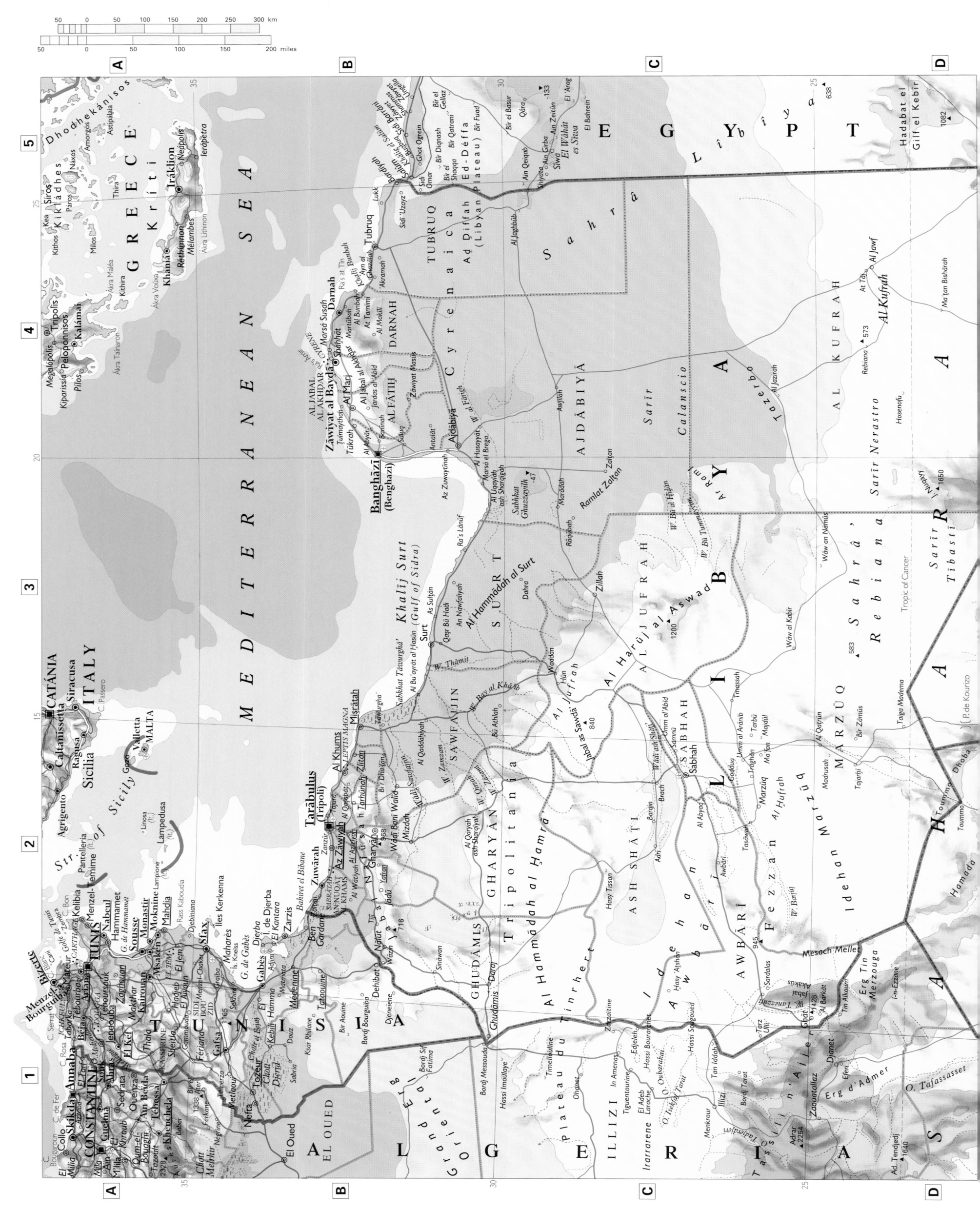

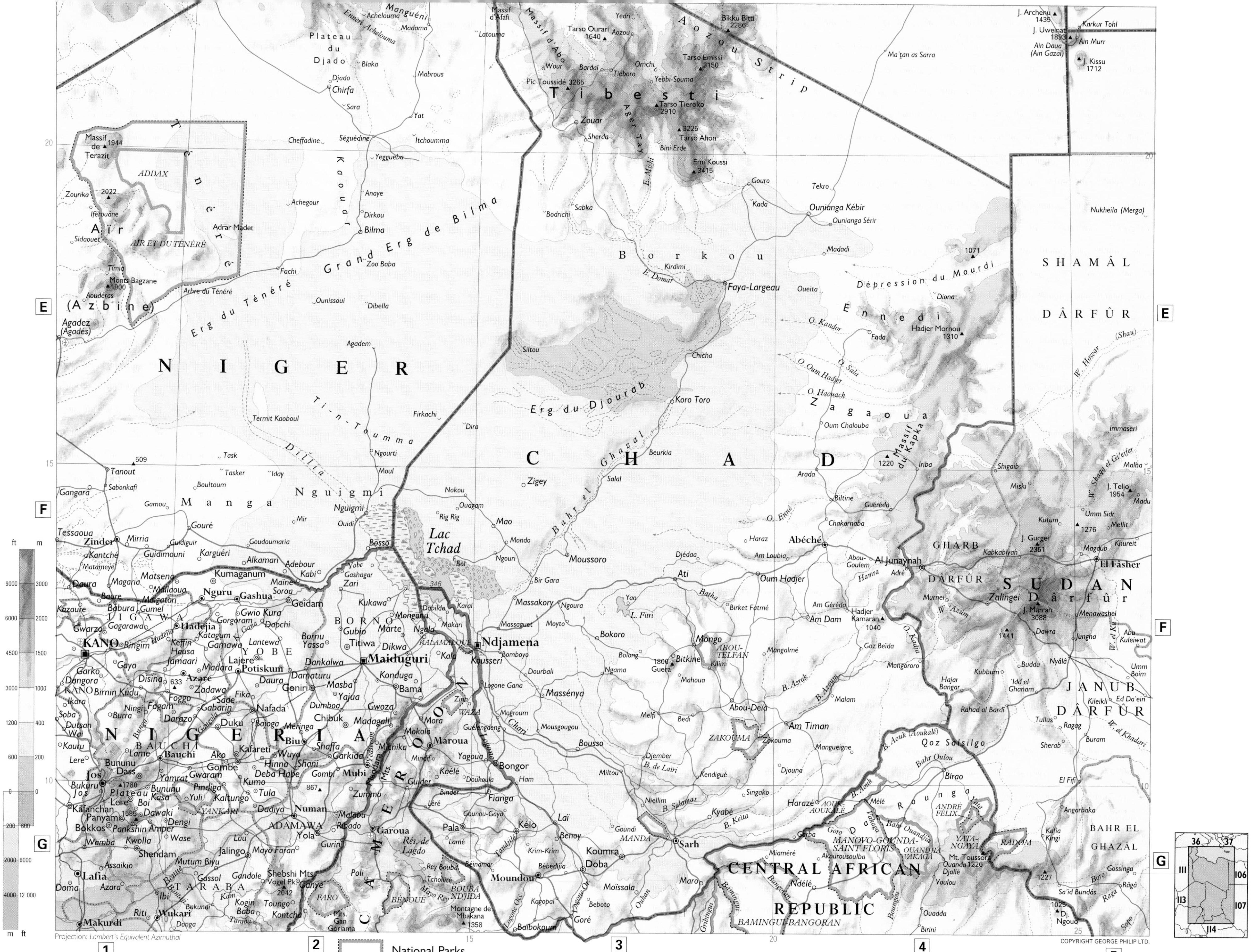

SHAMÂL DÂRFÛR

GHARB DÂRFÛR

SUDAN

JANUB DÂRFÛR

BAHR EL GHAZAL

CHAD

NIGER

NIGERIA

CAMEROUN

CENTRAL AFRICAN REPUBLIC

Tibesti

Aozou Strip

Ennedi

Borkou

Ergué du Djourab

Bahr el Ghazal

Erg du Ténéré

Grand Erg de Bilma

Kaouar

Plateau du Djado

Aïr (Azbine)

Manga

Nguigmi

Lac Tchad

Ndjamena

Maiduguri

Kano

Jos

Sarh

Abéché

Al Junaynah

El Fasher

Massif du Kapka

Dépression du Mourdi

Zaghaoua

Emi Koussi 3415
Pic Toussidé 3265
Tarso Emissi 3150
Bikkú Bitti 2286

Central African Republic

BAMINGUI-BANGORAN

MANOVO-GOUNDA-SAINT FLORIS

AOUK

ANDRÉ FÉLIX

ZAKOUMA

ABOU-TELFAN

BOUBA NDJIDA

BÉNOUÉ

FARO

WAZA

RÉS. DE DJA

ADDAX

AÏR ET DU TÉNÉRÉ

■ National Parks

□ Nature Reserves and Game Reserves

∴ UNESCO World Heritage Sites

Underlined towns give their name to the administrative area in which they stand.

COPYRIGHT GEORGE PHILIP LTD.

Projection: Lambert's Equivalent Azimuthal

m / ft scale bar

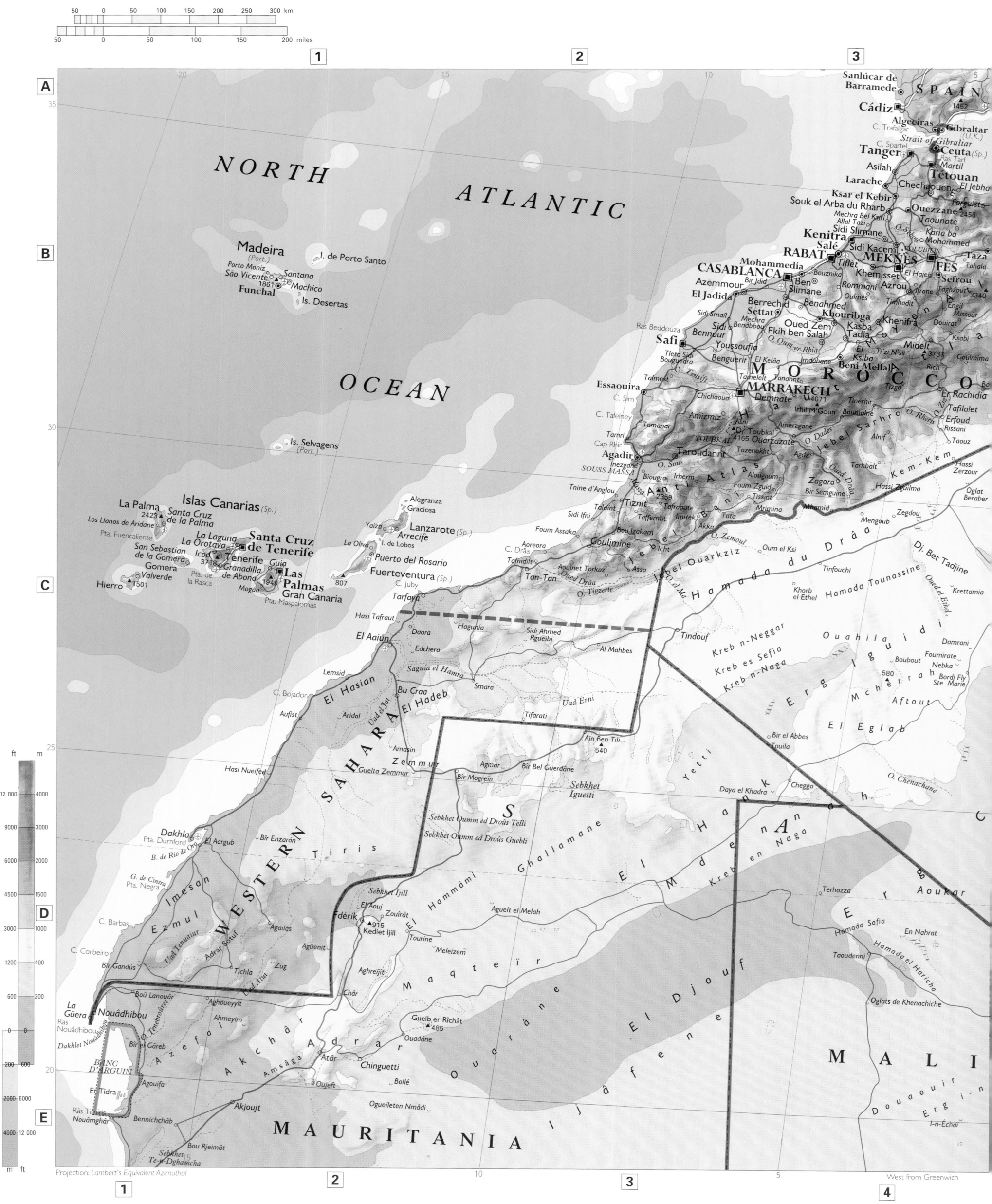

Projection: Lambert's Equivalent Azimuthal

West from Greenwich

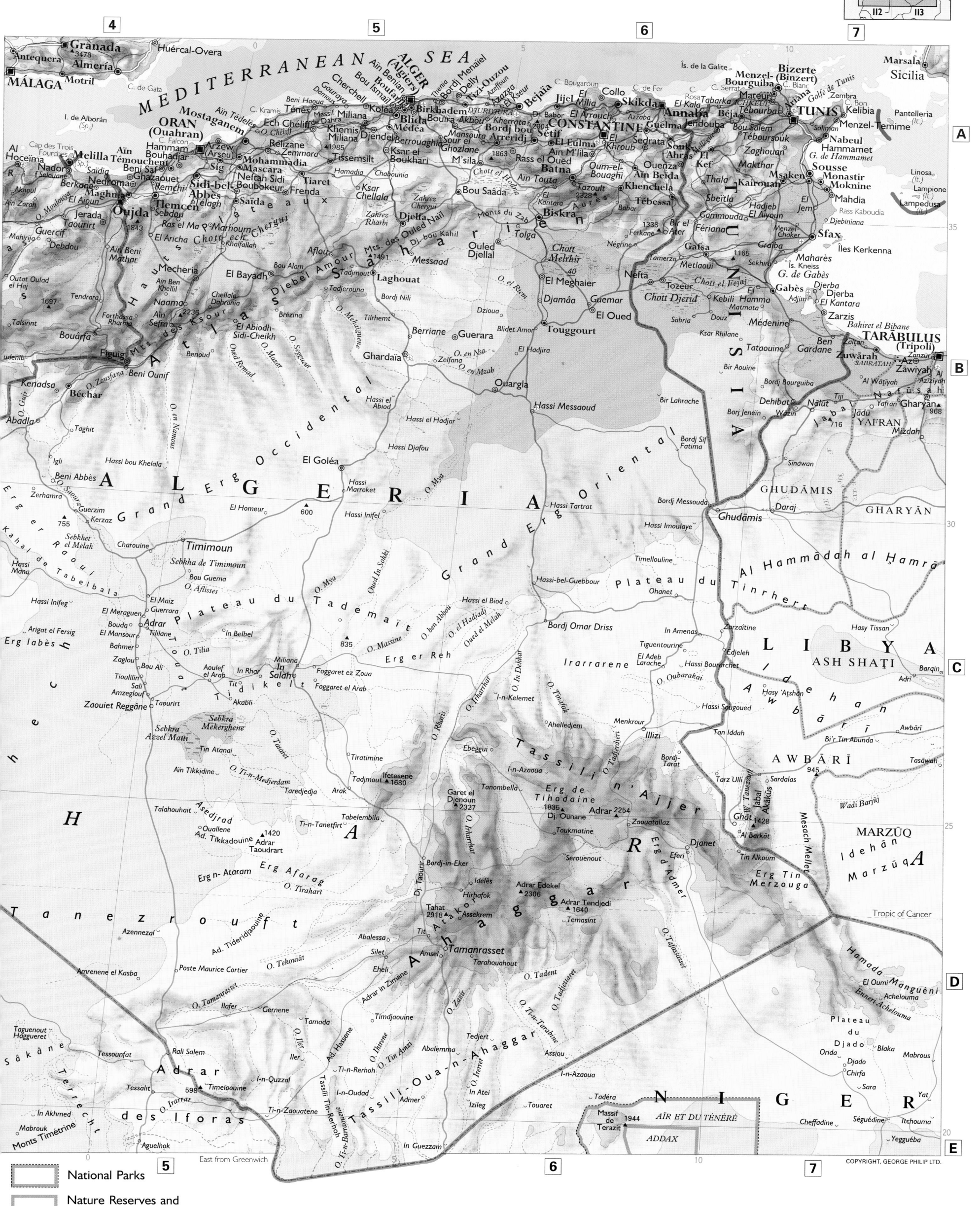

MEDITERRANEAN SEA

National Parks

Nature Reserves and Game Reserves

∴ **UNESCO World Heritage Sites**

COPYRIGHT, GEORGE PHILIP LTD.

East from Greenwich

50 0 50 100 150 200 250 300 km
50 0 50 100 150 200 miles

SAHA

Oujeft

Akjoujt

MAURITANIA

Tidjikja
420▲
Gâneb
Tîchît
Akreijît
Aratâne

Râs Tinirist

Benichchab

Nouâmghâr
BANC
D'ARGUIN
Et Tidra

Nouakchott

B

Bou Rjeimât

Sebkhet
Te-n-Dghâmcha

Mederdra

Boutilimit

Aleg Mâl

Moudjeria

Boûmdeïd

Togba

T a g â n t

A o u k â r

Tâmchekket

Tagourâret

Oualâta

Dayet en Naharat

In-Aleï

Araouane

Azaou

Guîr

Bou Djébéha

Rosso Dagana
Padi
Bogué
Kiffa
'Ayoûn el 'Atroûs
Néma
L. Faguibine
Tombouctou
(Timbuktu)
Koriodmé
Kabara
Diré

Richard
Toll
Thille-Boubacar
N'Dioum
Mbagne
Kaédi
Mbout
Masilf de l'Assaba
409▲
Kankossa
Kobenni
Timbedgha
Bassikounou
Ras el Mâ
Goundam
Sareyamou
Sébi
Niafounké
Akka
L. Débo

St. Louis
LANGUE
DE BARBARIE

Louga

DAKAR
Rufisque

SENEGAL

GAMBIA
Banjul

GUINEA-BISSAU
Arquipélago dos Bijagós
BISSAU

A T L A N T I C

O C E A N

G U L F

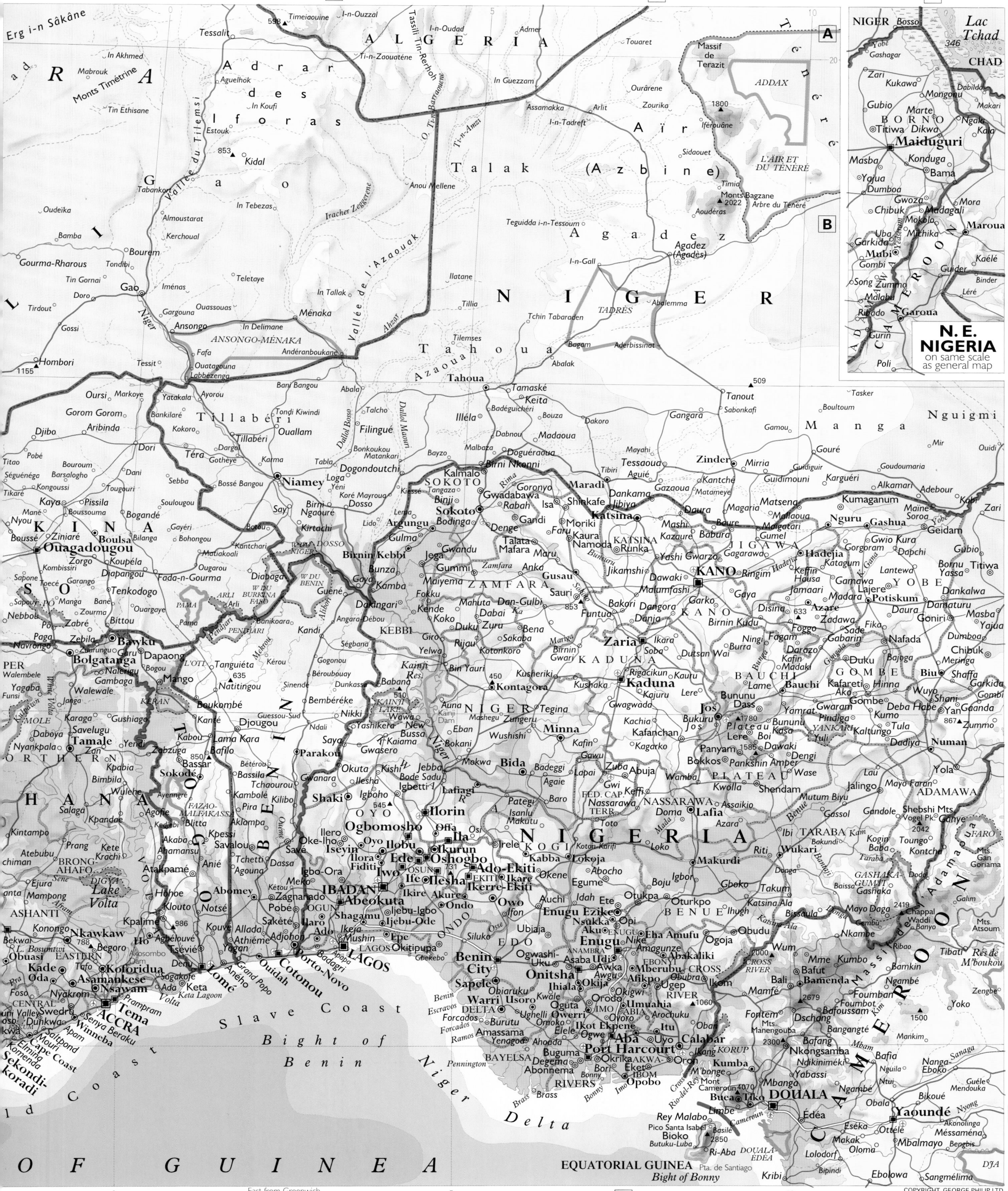

N. E. NIGERIA on same scale as general map

National Parks

Nature Reserves and Game Reserves

∴ UNESCO World Heritage Sites

COPYRIGHT, GEORGE PHILIP LTD.

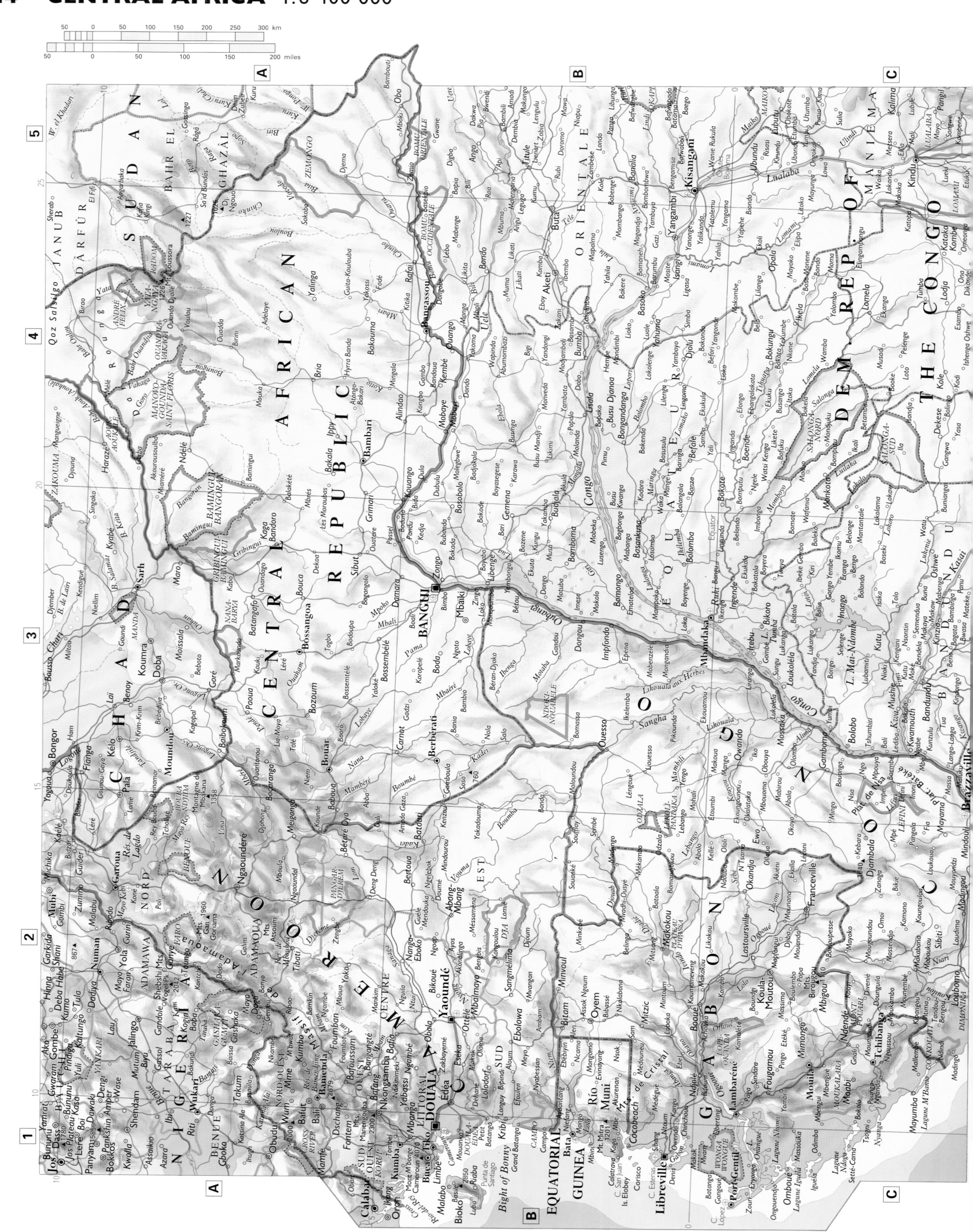

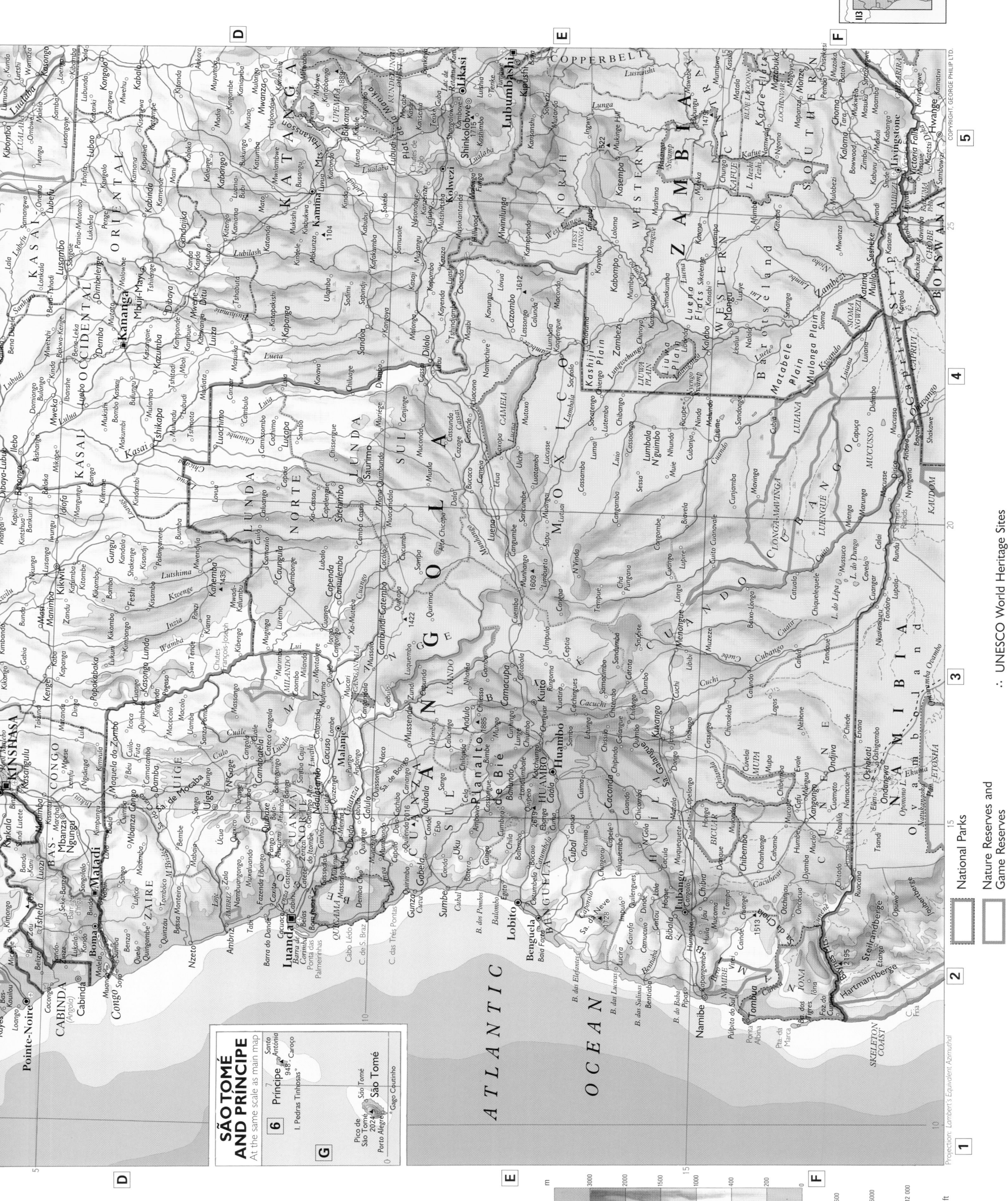

Map labels (selected)

115

COPYRIGHT, GEORGE PHILIP LTD.

SÃO TOMÉ AND PRÍNCIPE
At the same scale as main map

Príncipe
Santo António
948
Pico de São Tomé 2024
I. Pedras Tinhosas
São Tomé
Gago Coutinho
Porto Alegre

Projection: Lambert's Equivalent Azimuthal

Legend

National Parks

Nature Reserves and Game Reserves

:: UNESCO World Heritage Sites

Major regions / countries

KASAI ORIENTAL

KASAI OCCIDENTAL

KATANGA

LUNDA NORTE

LUNDA SUL

MOXICO

ZAMBIA

NAMIBIA

BOTSWANA

ANGOLA

CUANZA NORTE

CUANZA SUL

MALANJE

BENGUELA

HUAMBO

HUÍLA

CUNENE

CUANDO CUBANGO

BIÉ

ZAIRE

UÍGE

CABINDA

BAS-CONGO

KINSHASA

COPPERBELT

NORTH WESTERN

WESTERN

SOUTHERN

CENTRAL

CAPRIVI STRIP

Cities and towns (selected)

Pointe-Noire
Kinshasa
Cabinda
Boma
Matadi
Luanda
Lobito
Benguela
Namibe
Tombua
Huambo
Kuito
Lubango
Malanje
Saurimo
Kananga
Mbuji-Mayi
Kamina
Kolwezi
Likasi
Lubumbashi
Kipushi
Shinkolobwe
Kikwit
Livingstone
Mongu
Hwange

ATLANTIC OCEAN

SKELETON COAST

Scale bars

m
9000
6000
4500
3000
1200
600
200
ft

ft
30000
18000
12000
9000
6000
3000
600
m

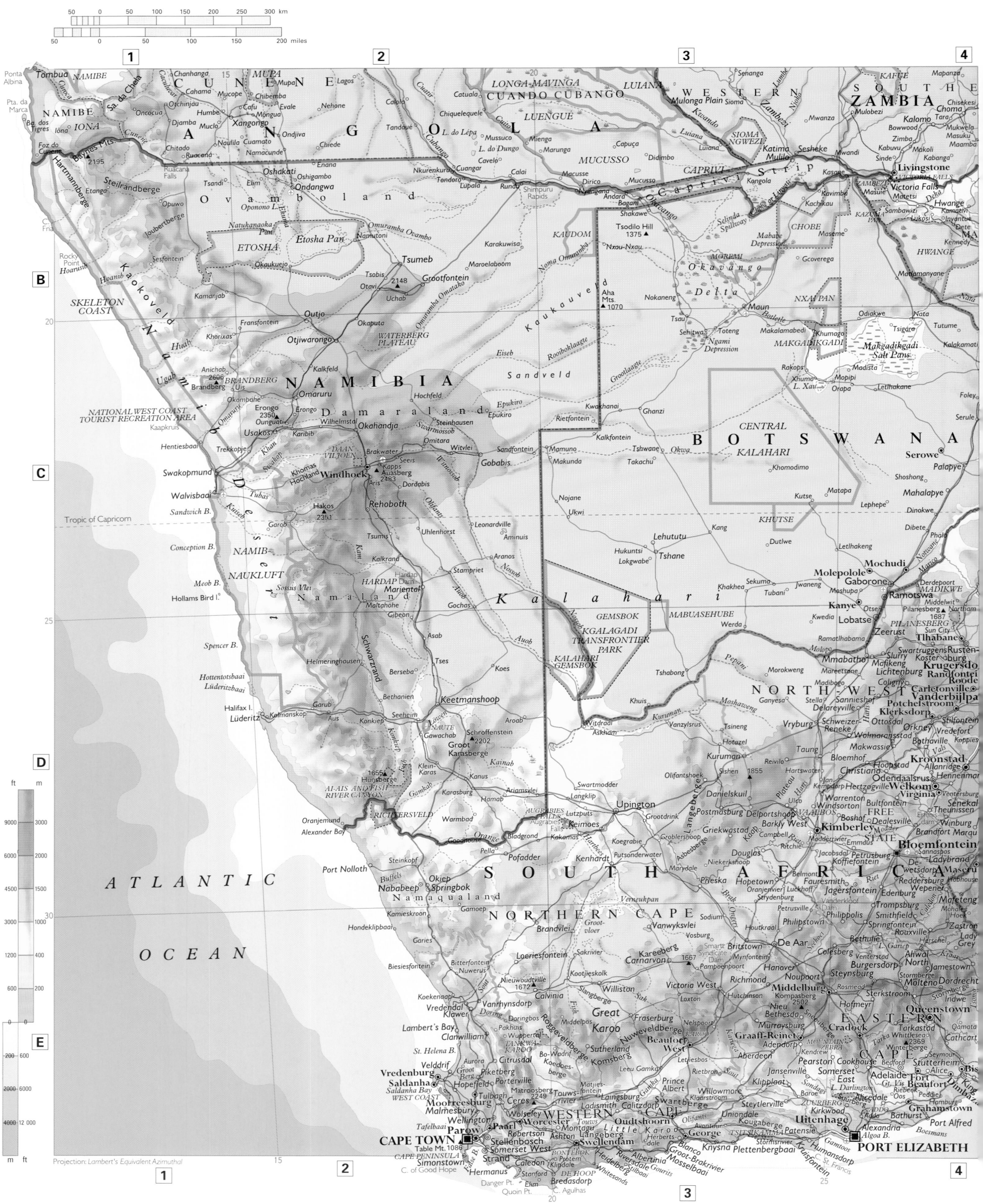

MOZAMBIQUE CHANNEL

INDIAN OCEAN

INDIAN OCEAN

MADAGASCAR

On same scale as General Map

COPYRIGHT GEORGE PHILIP LTD.

National Parks

Nature Reserves and
Game Reserves

⋄ UNESCO World Heritage Sites

East from Greenwich

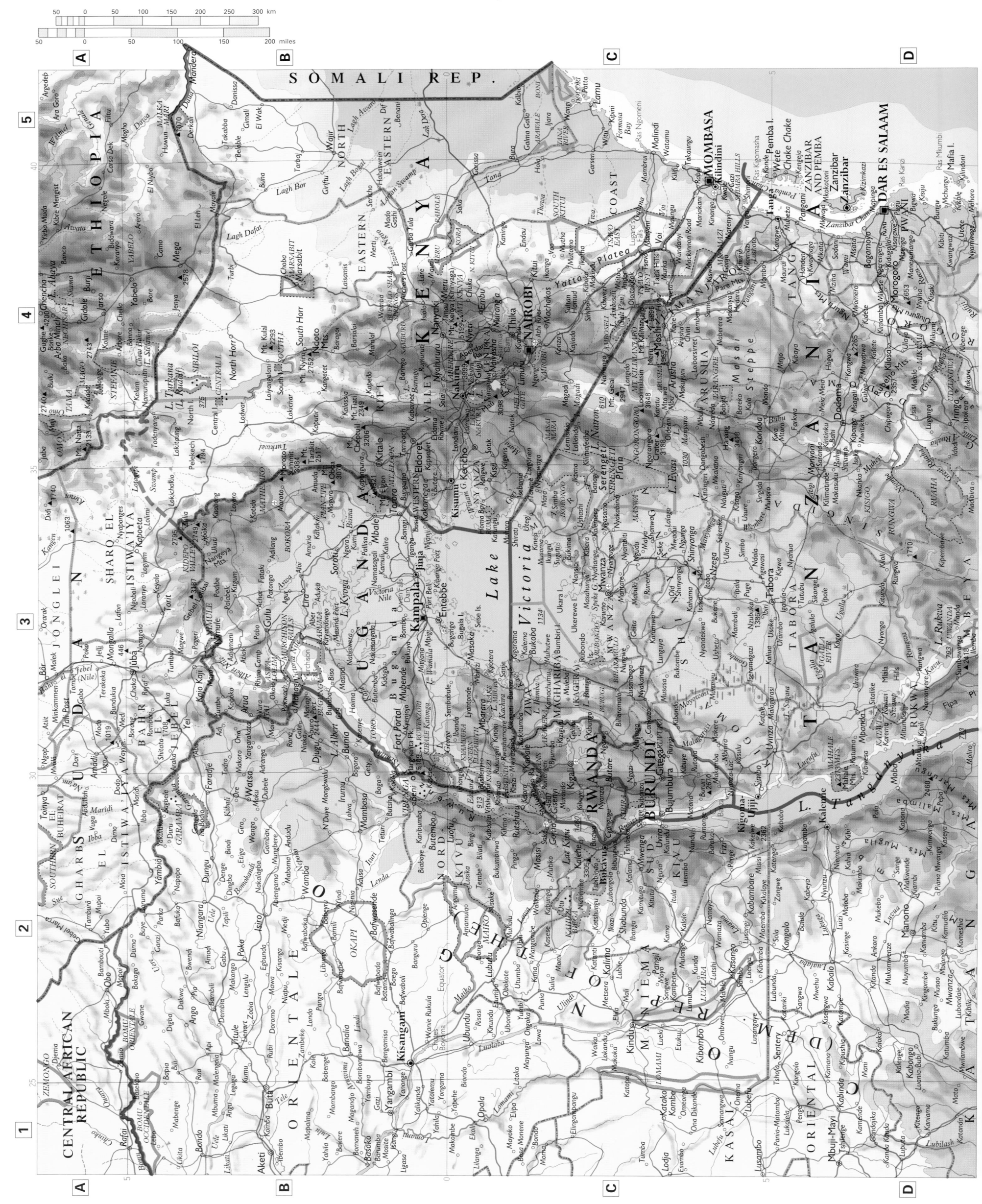

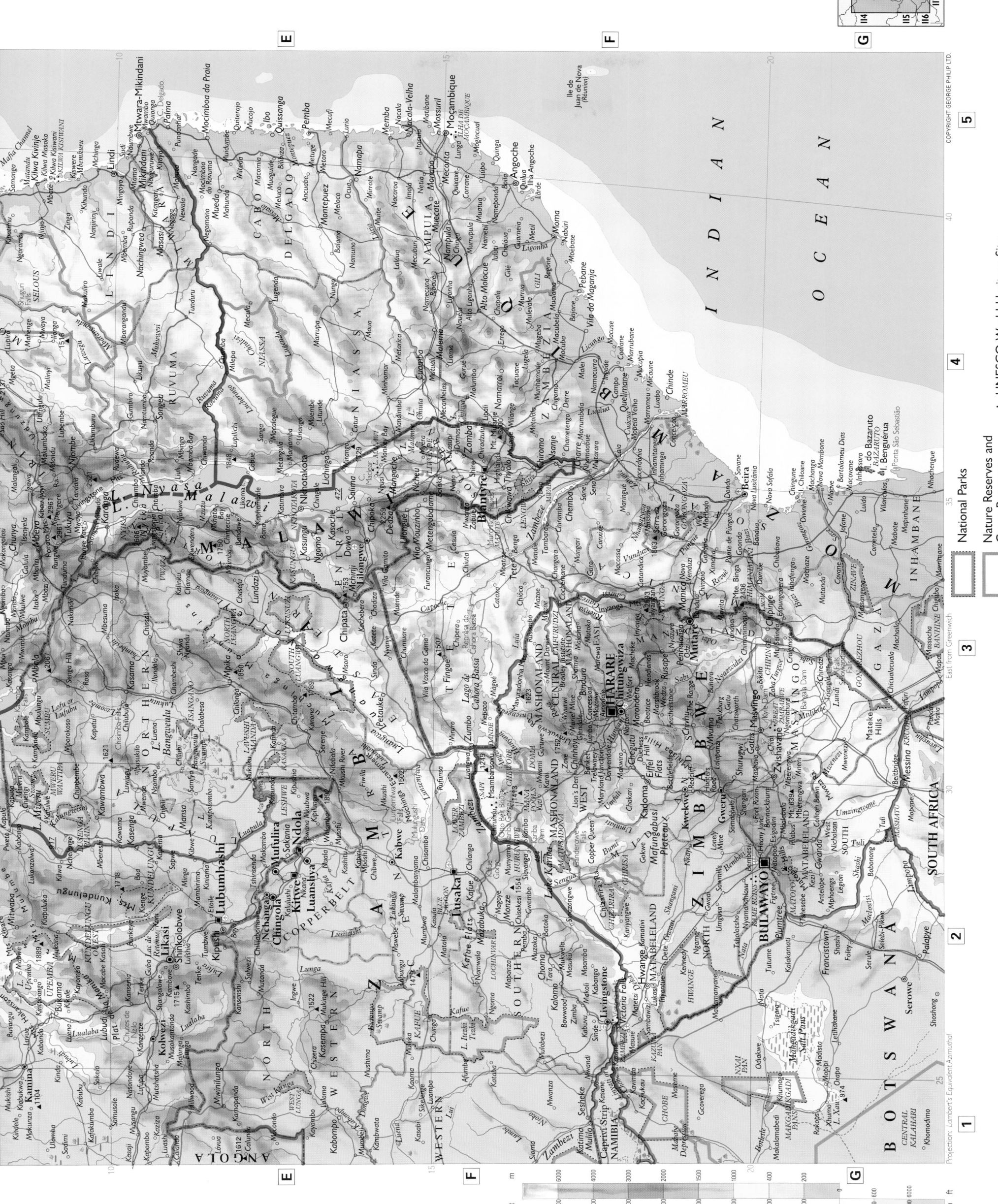

National Parks

Nature Reserves and
Game Reserves

∴ UNESCO World Heritage Sites

COPYRIGHT GEORGE PHILIP LTD.

Projection: Lambert's Equivalent Azimuthal

East from Greenwich

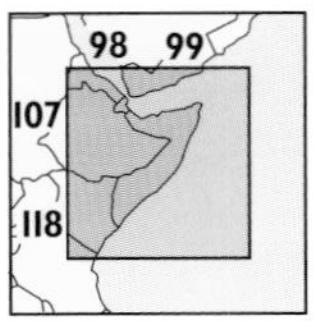

50 0 50 100 150 200 250 300 km
50 0 50 100 150 200 miles

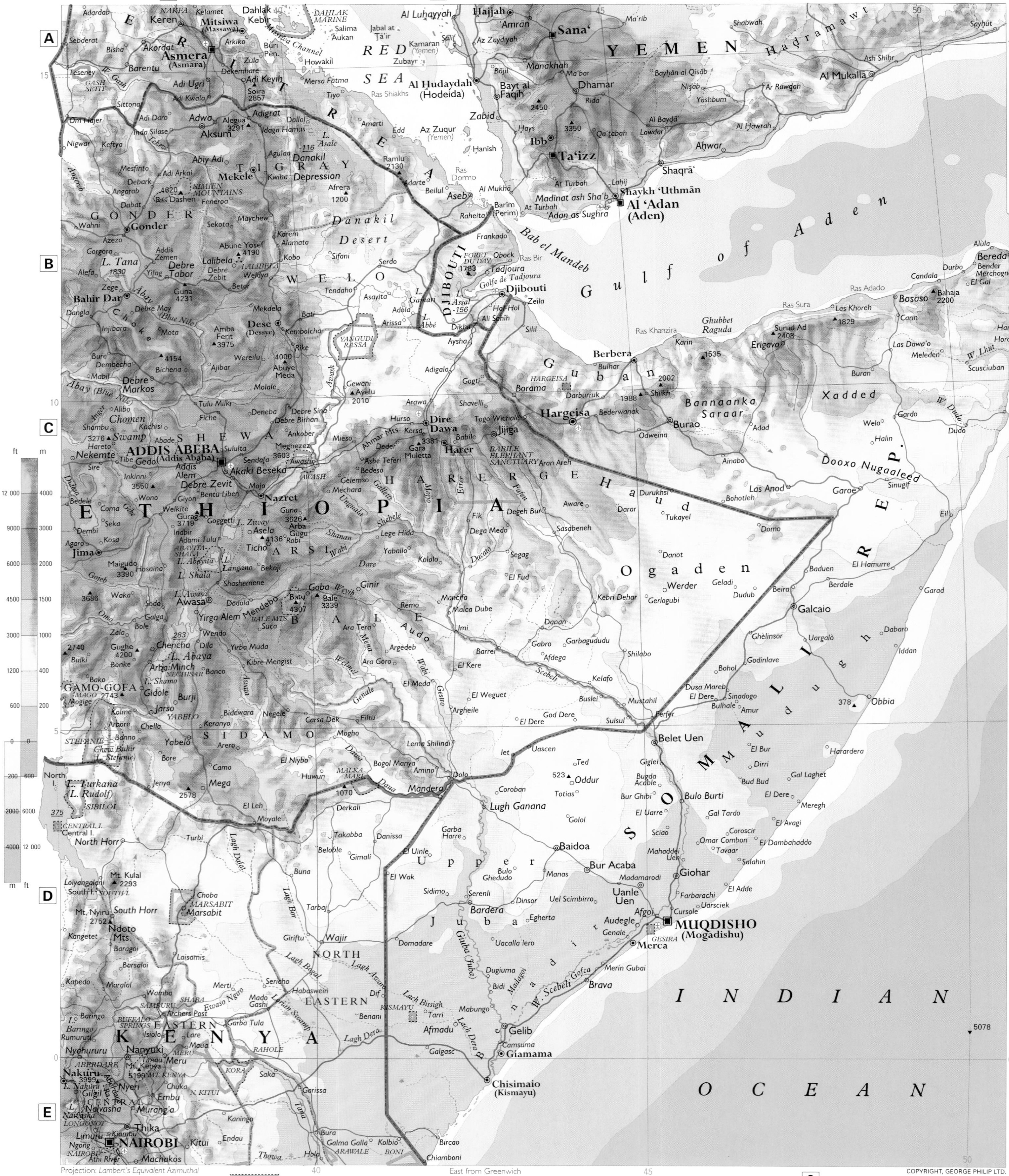

Projection: Lambert's Equivalent Azimuthal

COPYRIGHT, GEORGE PHILIP LTD.

East from Greenwich

Legend

National Parks

Nature Reserves and Game Reserves

∴ UNESCO World Heritage Sites

Major labels

R E D   S E A

Y E M E N

Gulf of Aden

E T H I O P I A

S O M A L I   R E P.

K E N Y A

DJIBOUTI

ERITREA

INDIAN OCEAN

ADDIS ABEBA (Addis Ababa)

MUQDISHO (Mogadishu)

NAIROBI

Sana'

Al 'Adan (Aden)

Djibouti

Ogaden

Danakil Desert

Danakil Depression

SIMIEN MOUNTAINS

Bab el Mandeb

L. Turkana (L. Rudolf)

L. Tana

Dooxo Nugaaleed

Bannaanka Saraar

Haud

Hadramawt

Blue Nile

Abay (Blue Nile)

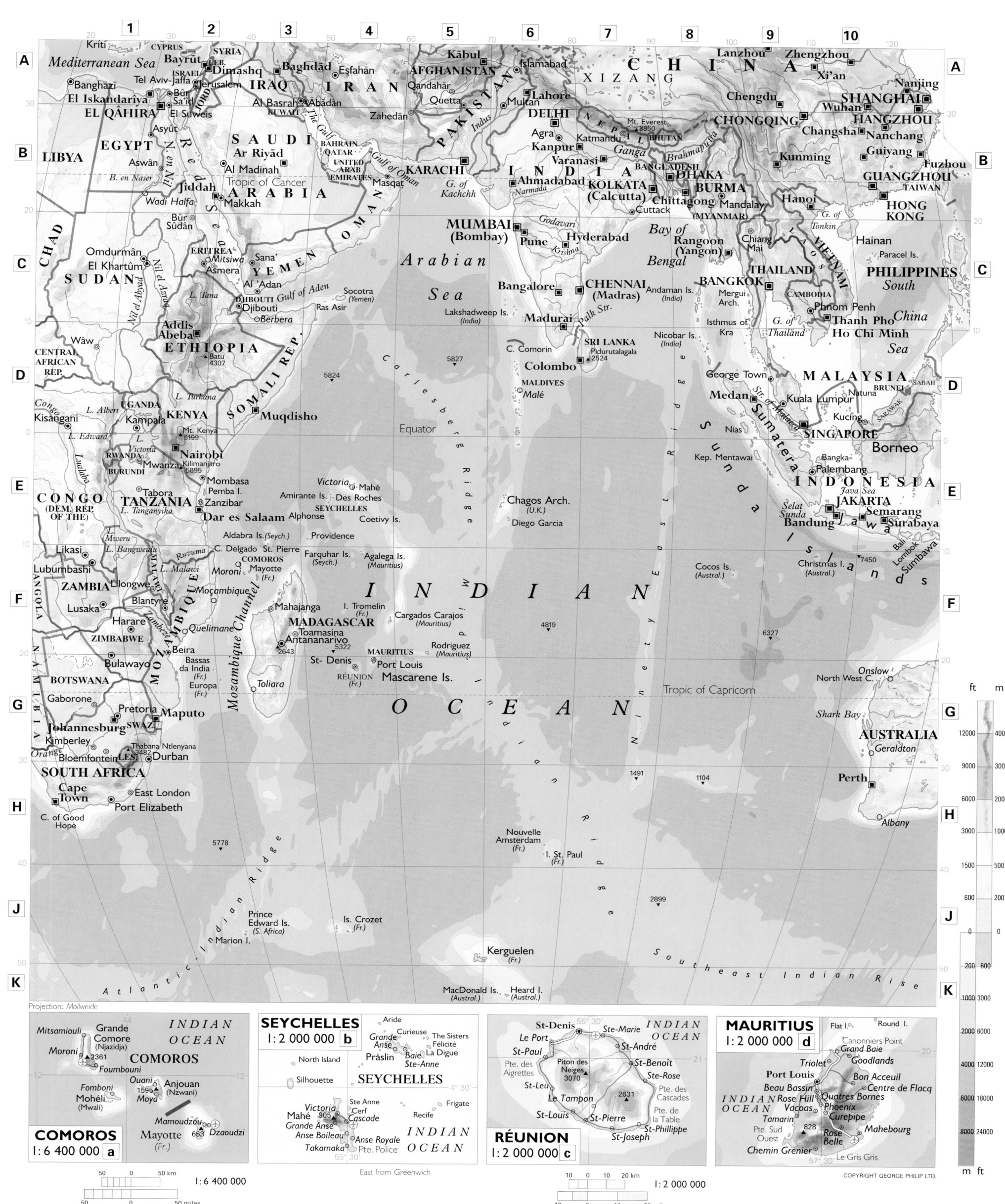

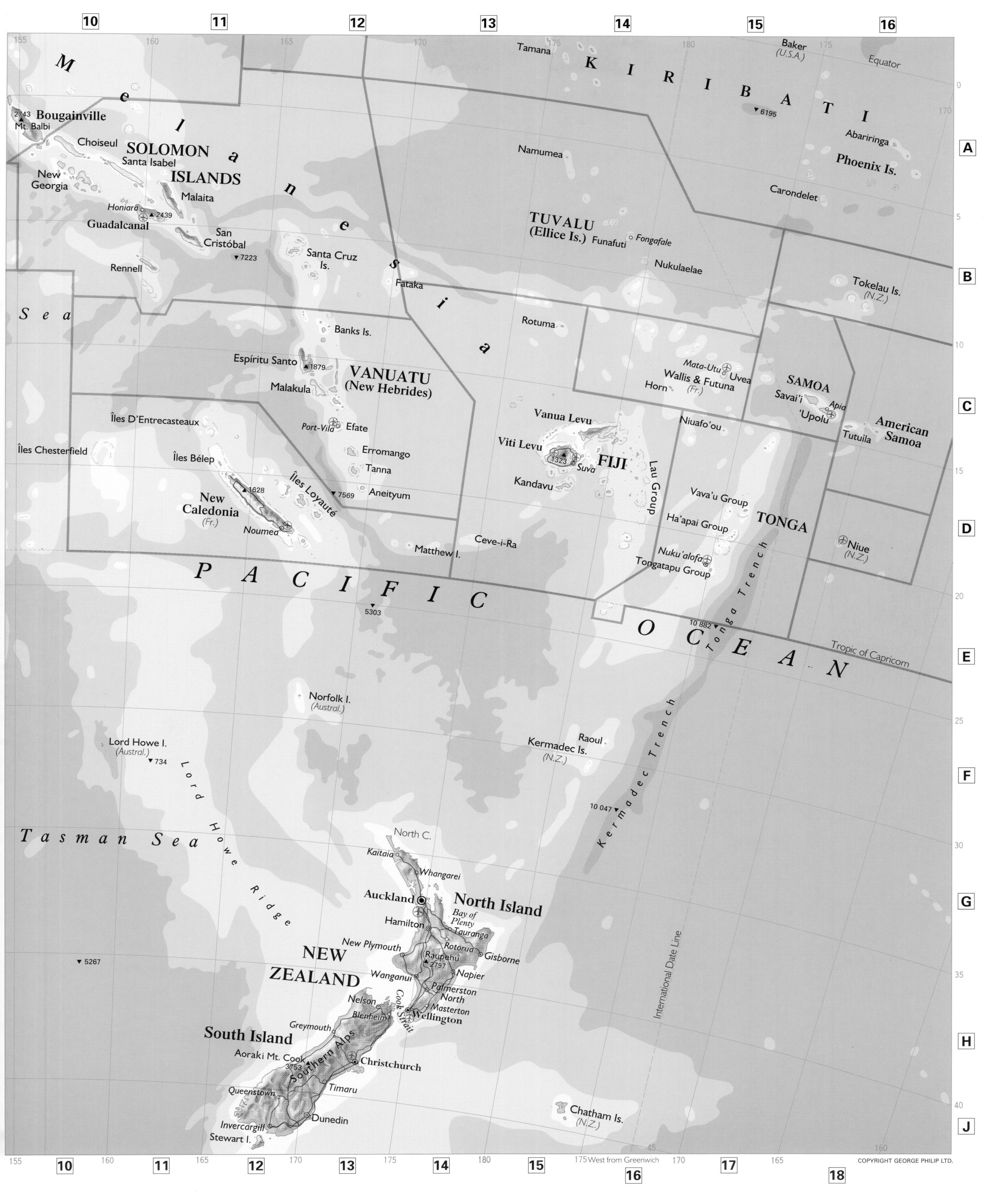

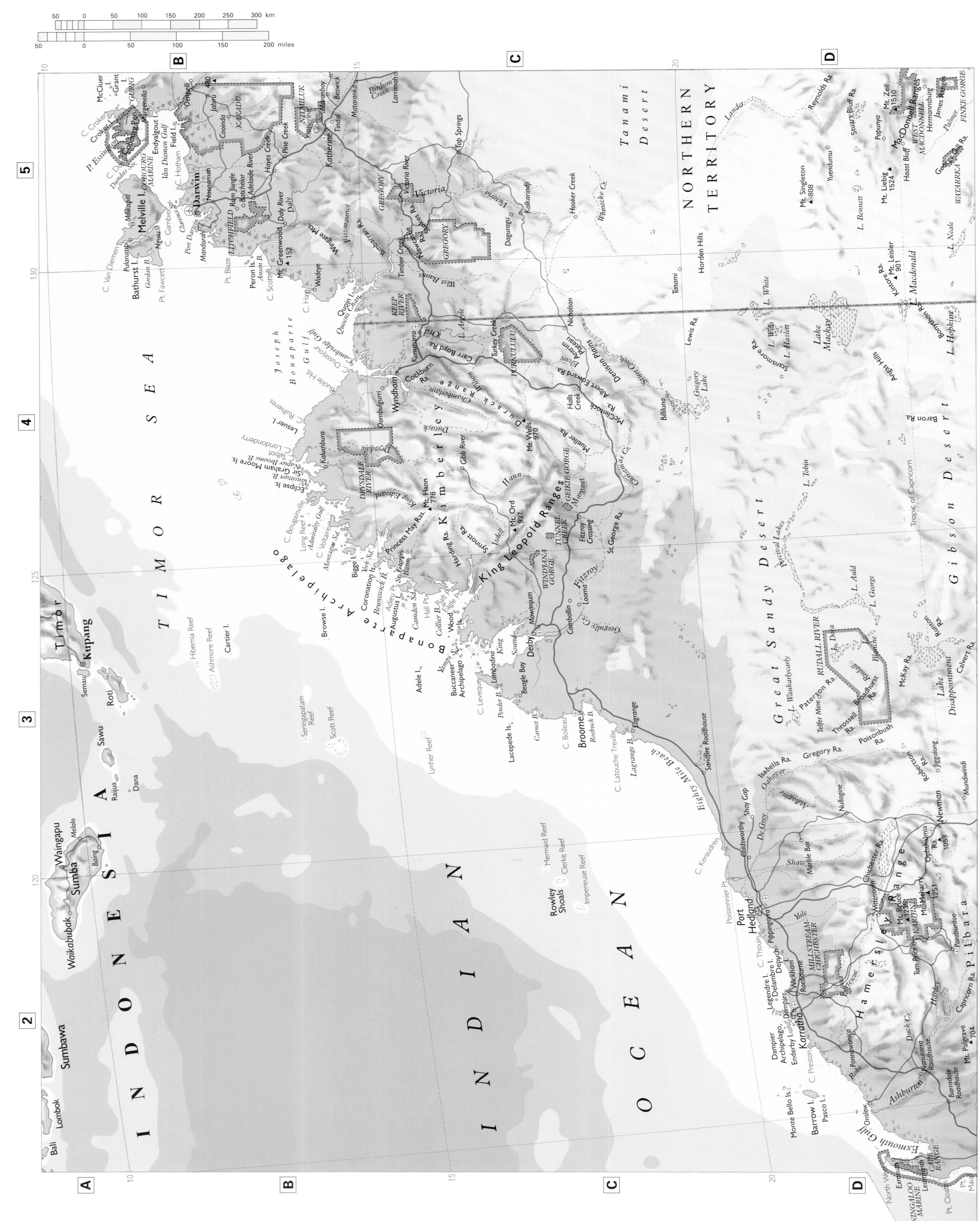

50 0 50 100 150 200 250 300 km
50 0 50 100 150 200 miles

A   B   C   D

INDONESIA

TIMOR SEA

INDIAN

OCEAN

NORTHERN TERRITORY

Tanami Desert

Gibson Desert

Great Sandy Desert

Kimberley

King Leopold Ranges

Bonaparte Archipelago

Joseph Bonaparte Gulf

Darwin

Melville I.
Bathurst I.

Timor

Sumba
Sumbawa
Lombok
Bali

Kupang
Waingapu
Waikabubak

Broome
Derby
Port Hedland
Karratha
Newman

Hamersley Range
Pilbara
Chichester Range

Exmouth Gulf

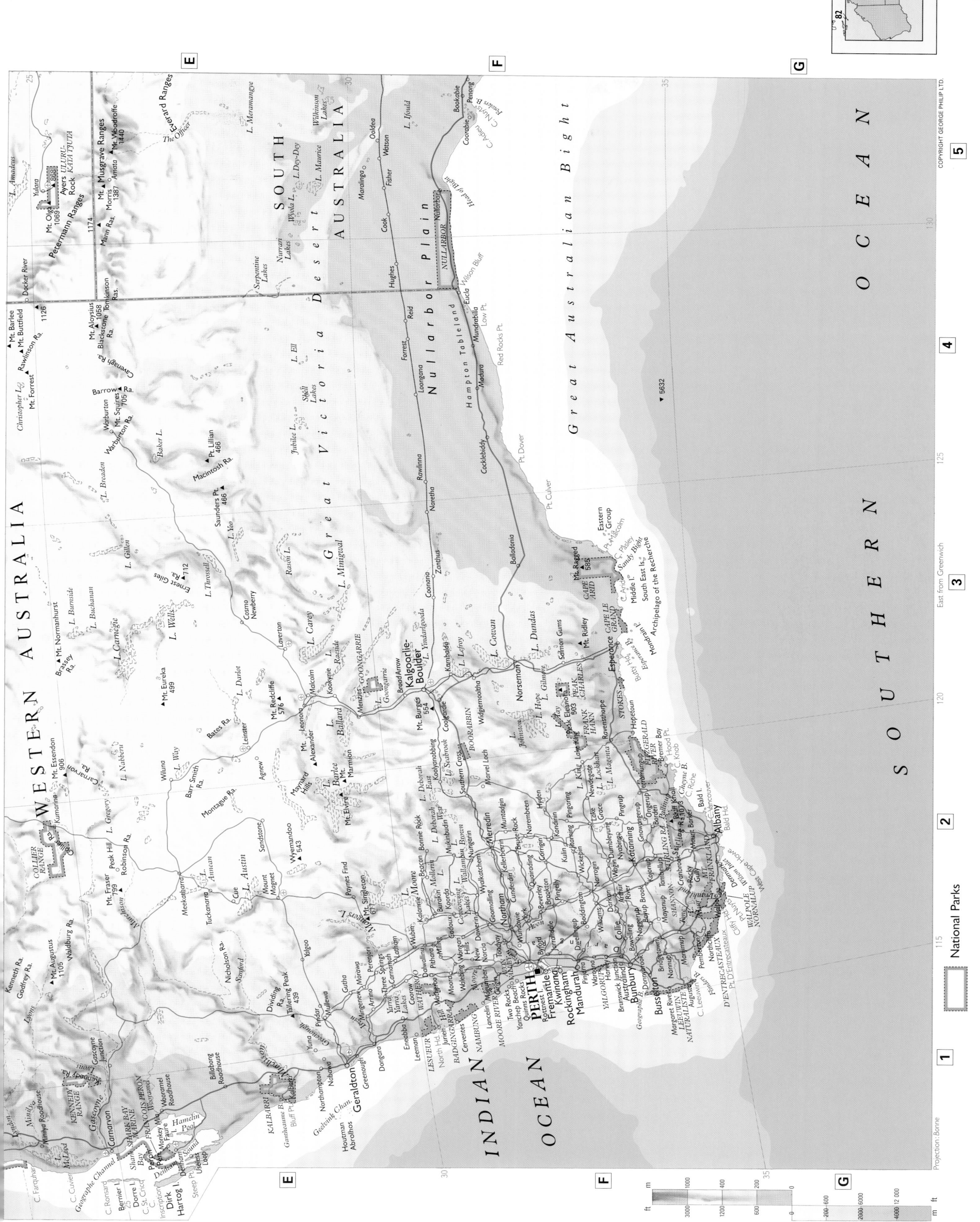

COPYRIGHT GEORGE PHILIP LTD.

WESTERN AUSTRALIA

SOUTH AUSTRALIA

INDIAN OCEAN

SOUTHERN OCEAN

Great Australian Bight

Great Victoria Desert

Nullarbor Plain

Hampton Tableland

National Parks

Projection Bonne

East from Greenwich

L. Amadeus
Everard Ranges
The Officer
Mt. Woodroffe 1440
Mt. Olga 1069
Ayers ULURU-Rock KATA TJUTA
Mt. Musgrave Ranges
Morris 1387 Amata
Mann Ras.
Wyola L.
L. Dey-Dey
L. Maurice
Serpentine Lakes
Wilkinson Lakes
L. Meramangye
Petermann Ranges
1174
Docker River
Christopher L.
Rawlinson Ra.
Mt. Forrest
1126
Mt. Buttfield 1058
Mt. Aloysius
Mt. Barlee
Blackstone Tomkinson Ras.
Cavenagh Ra.
Barrow Ra.
Warburton
Mt. Squires 705
Pt. Lillian 466
L. Ell
Shell Lakes
Jubilee L.
Baker L.
L. Breaden
Warburton Ra.
Macintosh Ra.
Saunders Pt. 466
L. Yeo
L. Gillen
L. Minigwal
Rason L.
Ernest Giles Ra.
L. Throssell
L. Wells
Cosmo Newberry
Laverton
L. Carey
Broad Arrow
Kalgoorlie-Boulder
Mt. Burges 554
Coolgardie
Kambalda
L. Lefroy
L. Cowan
L. Carnegie
L. Buchanan
L. Burnside
Mt. Normanhurst
Mt. Essendon 906
Carnarvon Ra.
Brassey Ra.
Kenneth Ra.
Godfrey Ra.
Lyons
Mt. Augustus 1105
Waldburg Ra.
Minnie
Minilya Roadhouse
Gascoyne
Goscoyne Junction
Mininya
Kumarina
Nicholson Ra.
Robinson Ra.
Peak Hill
Mt. Fraser Hill 799
Meekatharra
L. Nabberu
L. Way
Wiluna
Leinster
L. Carey
L. Darlot
Agnew
Leonora
Mt. Leonora
Menzies
Goongarrie
Bates Ra.
L. Mason
Montague Ra.
Cue
Tuckanarra
Sandstone
Wemandoo 543
Mt. Eureka 499
L. Austin
Barr Smith Ra.
Mt. Redcliffe 576
Mt. Alexander
L. Ballard
Maynard Hills
Mount Magnet
L. Annean
Yalgoo
Dividing Ra.
Tallering Peak 439
Paynes Find
Barlee Mt.
Mt. Elvira
L. Barlee
Mt. Marmion
L. Deborah East
L. Deborah West
Beacon Rock
Bonnie Rock
Mt. Singleton 671
Koorda
Mukinbudin
Kalannie
Burakin
Koolyanobbing
Southern Cross
Marvel Loch
Widgiemooltha
Norseman
Salmon Gums
Mt. Ridley
Nerren
Eneabba
Leeman
NAMBUNG
Cervantes
Lancelin
Jurien
North Hd.
Three Springs
Carnamah
Coorow
Moora
Dalwallinu
Wongan Hills
Wubin
Mullewa
Morawa
Perenjori
Arrino
Latham
Dongara
Greenough
GERALDTON
Northampton
Geraldton
KALBARRI
Galbraith Pt.
Billabong Roadhouse
Bluff Pt.
Houtman Abrolhos
Greenhead
HAMELIN POOL
Denham
Monkey Mia
Dirk Hartog I.
Hamelin Pool
FRANCOIS PERON
SHARK BAY MARINE
Useless Loop
Peron Pen.
Faure I.
Nanga
Overlander Roadhouse
Woomeral Roadhouse
Gladstone
Carnarvon
Babbage I.
C. Cuvier
C. Farquhar
Bernier I.
Dorre I.
C. Ronsard
C. St. Cruz
Inscription Pt.
Steep Pt.
L. McLeod
Yuna
Pindar
Gutha
Yalgoo
Maya
Goomalling
Dowerin
New Norcia
Bindoon
Gingin
Lancelin
Yanchep
Wanneroo
PERTH
Fremantle
Rottnest I.
Rockingham
Mandurah
Pinjarra
Dwellingup
Waroona
Harvey
YALGORUP
Brunswick Junction
Australind
Bunbury
Busselton
C. Naturaliste
Margaret River
Augusta
C. Leeuwin
LEEUWIN-NATURALISTE
D'ENTRECASTEAUX
Nornalup
Pemberton
Manjimup
Northcliffe
WALPOLE NORNALUP
C. Beaufort
SHANNON
Denmark
Walpole
Mt. Frankland
FRANK-LAND
MT. FRANKLAND
Pingrup
Ongerup
Jerramungup
Gnowangerup
Cranbrook
Mt. Barker
Kendenup
Rocky Gully
Tambellup
Broome Hill
Katanning
Nyabing
Pingaring
Lake Grace
Newdegate
Dumbleyung
Wagin
Woodanilling
Kukerin
Kukerin
Arthur River
Wickepin
Narrogin
Harrismith
Kulin
Pingelly
Cuballing
Williams
Darkan
Collie
Bowelling
Boyup Brook
Boddington
Wandering
Quairading
Corrigin
Kondinin
Beverley
Brookton
Pingelly
Kellerberrin
Bruce Rock
Narembeen
Hyden
Kondinin
York
Quairading
Beverley
Brookton
Toodyay
Northam
Meckering
Cunderdin
Kellerberrin
Merredin
Muntadgin
Tammin
Nungarin
Wyalkatchem
Trayning
Mukinbudin
Westonia
Bodallin
Moorine Rock
Marvel Loch
Bullfinch
Koolyanobbing
Bencubbin
Wundowie
Mundaring
Chidlows
Kalamunda
Armadale
Byford
Serpentine
Jarrahdale
Hopetoun
Ravensthorpe
Jerdacuttup
Bremer Bay
Borden
Boxwood Hill
STIRLING RANGE
Cheyne B.
Bluff Knoll
Bald Hd.
Bald I.
King George Sound
Albany
Cape Riche
Hood Pt.
Bremer Bay
Pt. Henry
Middle I.
Eastern Group
Archipelago of the Recherche
Cape Le Grand
CAPE LE GRAND
CAPE ARID
Mt. Arid 585
Mt. Ragged
Esperance
Israelite Bay
Pt. Malcolm
Pt. Paisley
South East Is.
Arid I.
Sandy Bight
Mondrain I.
Dundas Ra.
L. Dundas
Peak Charles 663
PEAK CHARLES
FRANK HANN
L. Hope
L. King
L. Gilmore
Grass Patch
Scaddan
Gibson
L. Johnston
Zanthus
Naretha
Loongana
Rawlinna
Cocklebiddy
Madura
Mundrabilla
Eucla
Wilson Bluff
NULLARBOR
Nullarbor
Forrest
Reid
Hughes
Cook
Fisher
Watson
Wynbring
Ooldea
Maralinga
Narrar Lakes
Bookabie
Coorabie
C. Adieu
Penong
C. Nuyts
Fowlers B.
Head of Bight
L. Ifould
Serpentine Lakes
5632
Low Pt.
Red Rocks Pt.
Pt. Culver
Pt. Dover
Point Malcolm

m ft
3000
2000-6000
1200-400
600-200
200-600
0
0
200
400
1000
4000 12 000

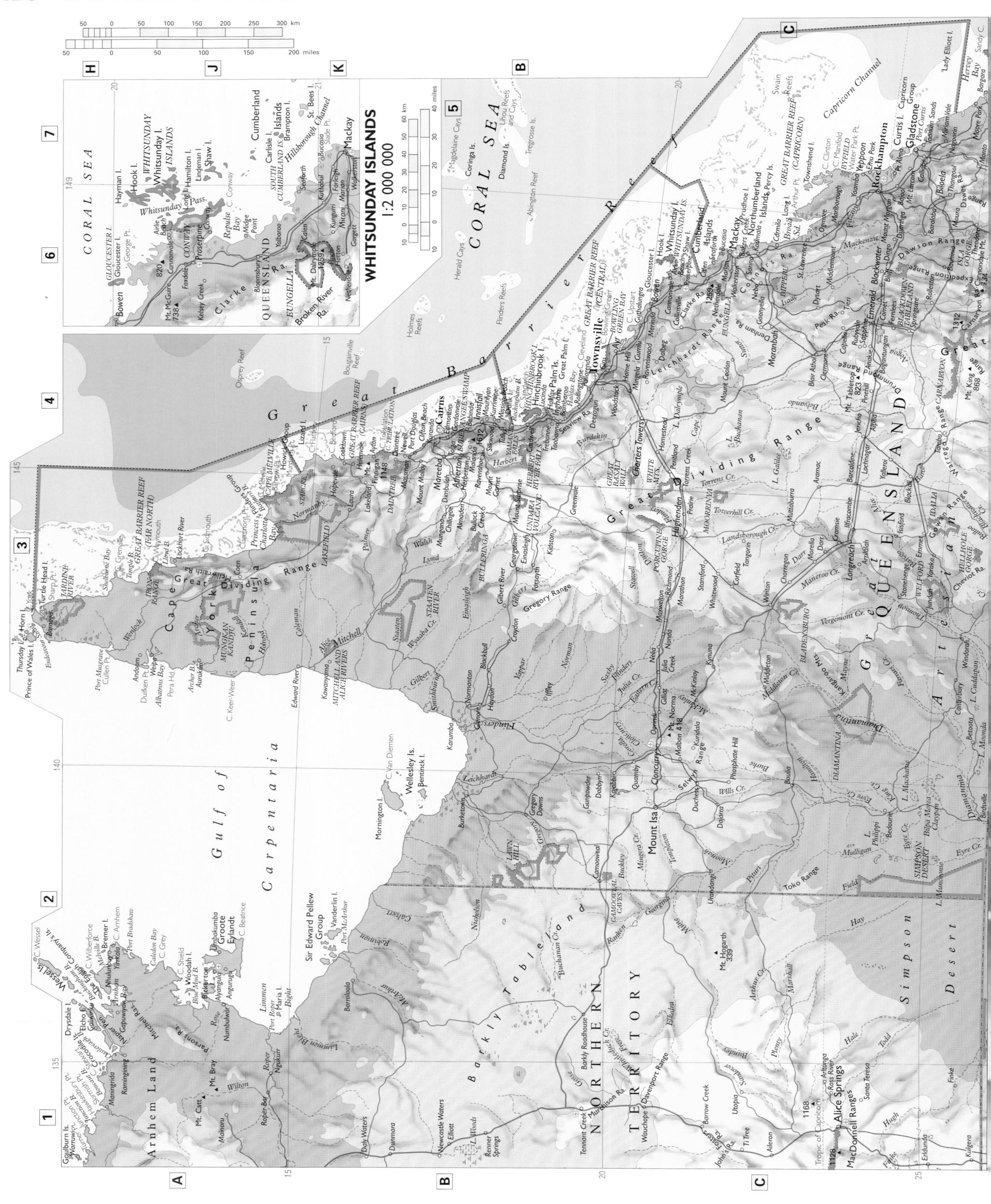

WHITSUNDAY ISLANDS
1:2 000 000

COPYRIGHT, GEORGE PHILIP LTD.

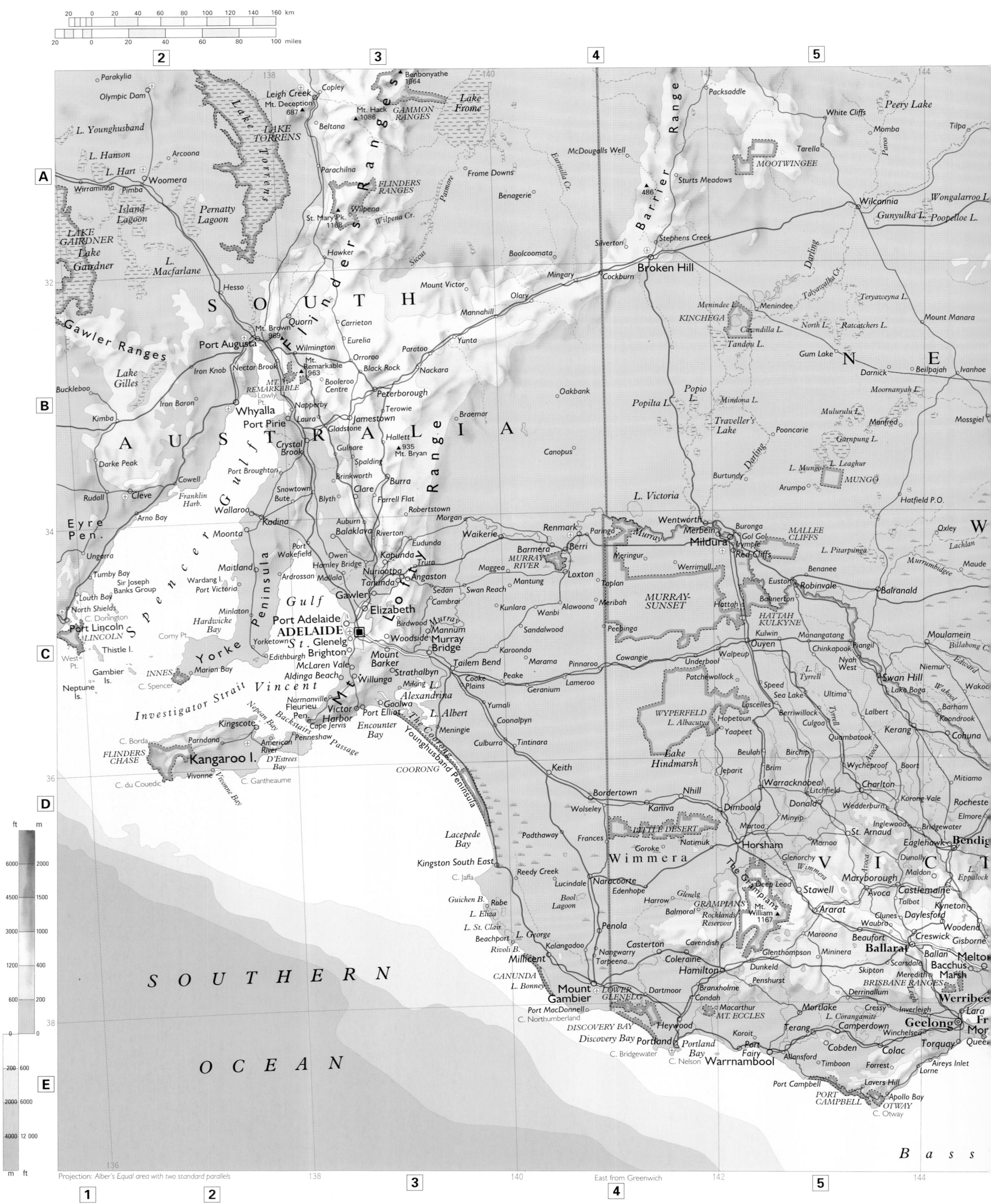

Projection: Alber's Equal area with two standard parallels

National Parks

131

10 0 20 40 60 80 100 120 140 km
10 0 20 40 60 80 100 miles

PACIFIC

OCEAN

C. Reinga
C. Maria van Diemen
North C.
Parengarenga Harbour
Houhora Heads
Ninety Mile Beach
Rangaunu B.
C. Karikari
Doubtless B.
Whangaroa Harb.
Awanui
Mangonui
Kaeo
Cavalli Is.
Ahipara B.
Kaitaia
Kerikeri
Kaikohe
B. of Islands
C. Brett
Russell
Paihia
Opua
Kawakawa
NORTHLAND
Herekino
Kohukohu
Okaihau
Moerewa
Whangaruru Harb.
Rawene
Kaikohe
Hikurangi
Poor Knights Is.
Hokianga Harbour
Omapere
▲776
Kamo
Onerahi
Whangarei
Donnelly's Crossing
Aranga
Wairoa
Whangarei Harb.
Bream Hd.
Hen & Chickens Is.
Dargaville
Kirikopuni
Bream B.
Waipu
Bream Tail
Te Kopuru
Waikiekie
Paparoa
Maungaturoto
Needles Pt.
Ruawai
Wellsford
Little Barrier I.
Port Fitzroy
Great Barrier I.
Matakana
C. Rodney
Kawau I.
Kaipara Harbour
Warkworth
Snells Beach
C. Barrier
Helensville
Hauraki G.
AUCKLAND
East Coast Bays
C. Colville
Cuvier I.
Port Charles
Takapuna
Birkenhead
Ostend
Coromandel
Mercury Is.
Waiheke I.
Whitianga
Mercury B.
AUCKLAND
Mount Wellington
Howick
Coromandel
Mount Roskill
Onehunga
Otahuhu
Coromandel Pen.
Papatoetoe
Papakura
Tairua
Manukau Harbour
835▲
Thames
Whangamata
Manukau
Pukekohe
Thames
Waiuku
Tuakau
Mercer
Turua
Waihi
Mayor I.
Waikato
Te Kauwhata
Paeroa
Waihi Beach
L. Waikare
Katikati
Tauranga Harb.
White I.
WAIKATO
Huntly
Waitoa
Te Aroha
Morrinsville
BAY OF PLENTY
C. Runaway
Hicks Bay
Ngaruawahia
Motiti I.
Te Araroa
Glen Afton
Mount Maunganui
Te Kaha
Glen Massey
Hamilton
Tauranga
Matamata
Bay of Plenty
East C.
Raglan Harbour
Raglan
Waharoa
Paengaroa
Matata
Edgecumbe
Whakatane
Hikurangi Ra.
1753▲
Cambridge
Karapiro
L. Rotorua
Te Puke
Ohiwa Harbour
Ruatoria
Aotea Harbour
Leamington
L. Rotoiti
Te Teko
Opotiki
Waipiro Bay
Te Awamutu
Tirau
Taneatua
Albatross Pt.
Arapuni
Putaruru
Mamaku
Kawerau
Tokomaru Bay
Kawhia Harbour
Kihikihi
Ngongotaha
Rotorua
L. Tarawera
UREWERA
Moutohora
Tirua Pt.
Otorohanga
Tokoroa
Mt. Tarawera
Galatea
GISBORNE
Te Kuiti
Kinleith
1111▲
Murupara
Huiarau Ra.
Puha
Tolaga Bay
Mokau
Aria
Mangakino
Atiamuri
Waiotapu
1392▲
Te Karaka
Mangaokino
Whakamaru
1165▲
Manuoha
Waikaretei
Ngatapa
Ormond
North Taranaki Bight
Ongarue
Mokai
Wairakei
Rangitaiki
Waikaremoana
Tuai
Gisborne
Ohura
Okahukura
L. Taupo
Taupo
369
Frasertown
Pututahi
Tuaheni Pt.
Waitara
Pukearuhe
Tahora
Taumarunui
Tokaanu
Turangi
1383▲
Mohaka
Wairoa
Poverty B.
New Plymouth
L. Rotoaira
Ahimanawa Mts.
Tarawera
Nuhaka
Waikokopu
Okato
Inglewood
Whangamomona
Mt. Ngauruhoe
Putorino
Table C.
TARANAKI
Huiroa
2291
Kaweka Ra.
Mahia Pen.
C. Egmont
Mt. Taranaki
Midhirst
TONGARIRO
Ruapehu
Portland I.
Rahotu
2518▲
Stratford
WHANGANUI
2796
Bay View
Opunake
Kaponga
Eltham
Rangataua
Kaimanawa Mts.
Taradale
Kapuni
Normanby
Ohakune
Ngaruroro
Napier
Manaia
Hawera
Piripiri
Raetihi
Clive
South Taranaki Bight
Patea
Waiouru
C. Kidnappers
Waverley
Maxwell
Waiotu
Hastings
Havelock North
Waitotara
Hunterville
Mangaweka▲1733
Opapa
Wanganui
Castlecliff
Mangaweka
Apiti
Otane
Turakina
Hawke Bay
Marton
Halcombe
Norsewood
Waipawa
Bulls
Feilding
Ruahine Ra.
Takapau
Waipukurau
MANAWATU-WANGANUI
Rangitikei
Bunnythorpe
Ormondville
Porangahau
Rongotea
Ashhurst
Dannevirke
Palmerston North
Woodville
Weber
Longburn
Manawatu
Pahiatua
Herbertville
Foxton
Shannon
Pukeroi Ra.
C. Turnagain
Levin
Eketahuna
Alfredton
Otaki
Mauriceville
Tinui
Kapiti I.
1571▲
Castlepoint
Paraparaumu
Mt. Mitre
Paekakariki
Masterton
Porirua
Carterton
Upper Hutt
Greytown
Lower Hutt
Featherston
WELLINGTON
Johnsonville
Petone
Martinborough
WELLINGTON
Eastbourne
Wainuiomata
L. Onoke
C. Palliser
Flat Pt.
Palliser B.

TASMAN

SEA

C. Farewell
Farewell Spit
Golden Bay
Collingwood
C. Stephens
Stephens I.
Kahurangi Pt.
Takaka
Separation Pt.
D'Urville I.
ABEL TASMAN
French Pass
Devil River Pk.
Tasman
Riwaka
Pelorus Sd.
Motueka
Forsyth I.
Kaiteriteri
Queen Charlotte
Kahurangi Mts.
1784▲
Tasman Bay
Karamea
Mt. Richmond
1756
Picton
KAHURANGI
Riwaka
Havelock
Arapawa
Brightwater
Nelson
Tuamarino
Cloudy B.
Wakefield
Stoke
Port Nicholson
NELSON
Richmond
Terawhiti
Belgrove
Aorangi Mts.
Tadmor
Renwick
983▲
Richmond Ra.
Blenheim
Mt. Owen
Glenhope
1875▲
Wairau
Seddon
Lyell
TASMAN
NELSON LAKES
Murchison
Mokihinui
Buller
L. Rotoiti
C. Campbell
Karamea
Ward
Atatare

ft m
9000 3000
6000 2000
3000 1000
1200 400
600 200
0 0
200 600
2000 6000
m ft

Projection: Conical with two standard parallels

East from Greenwich

COPYRIGHT. GEORGE PHILIP LTD

☐ National Parks

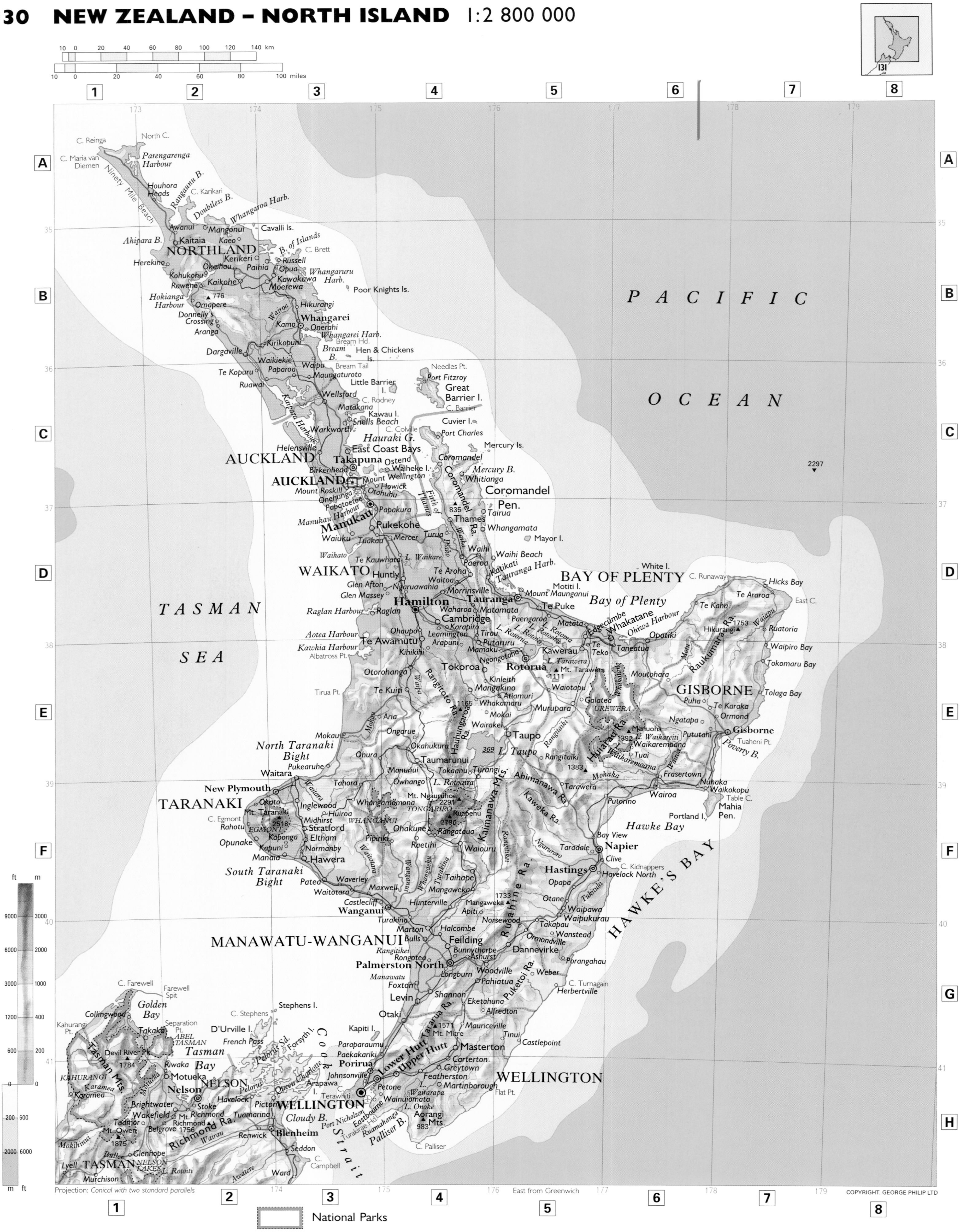

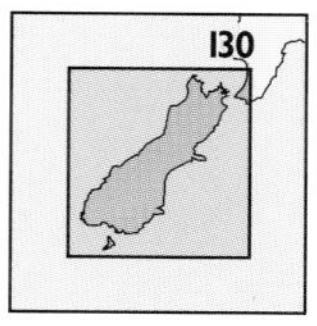

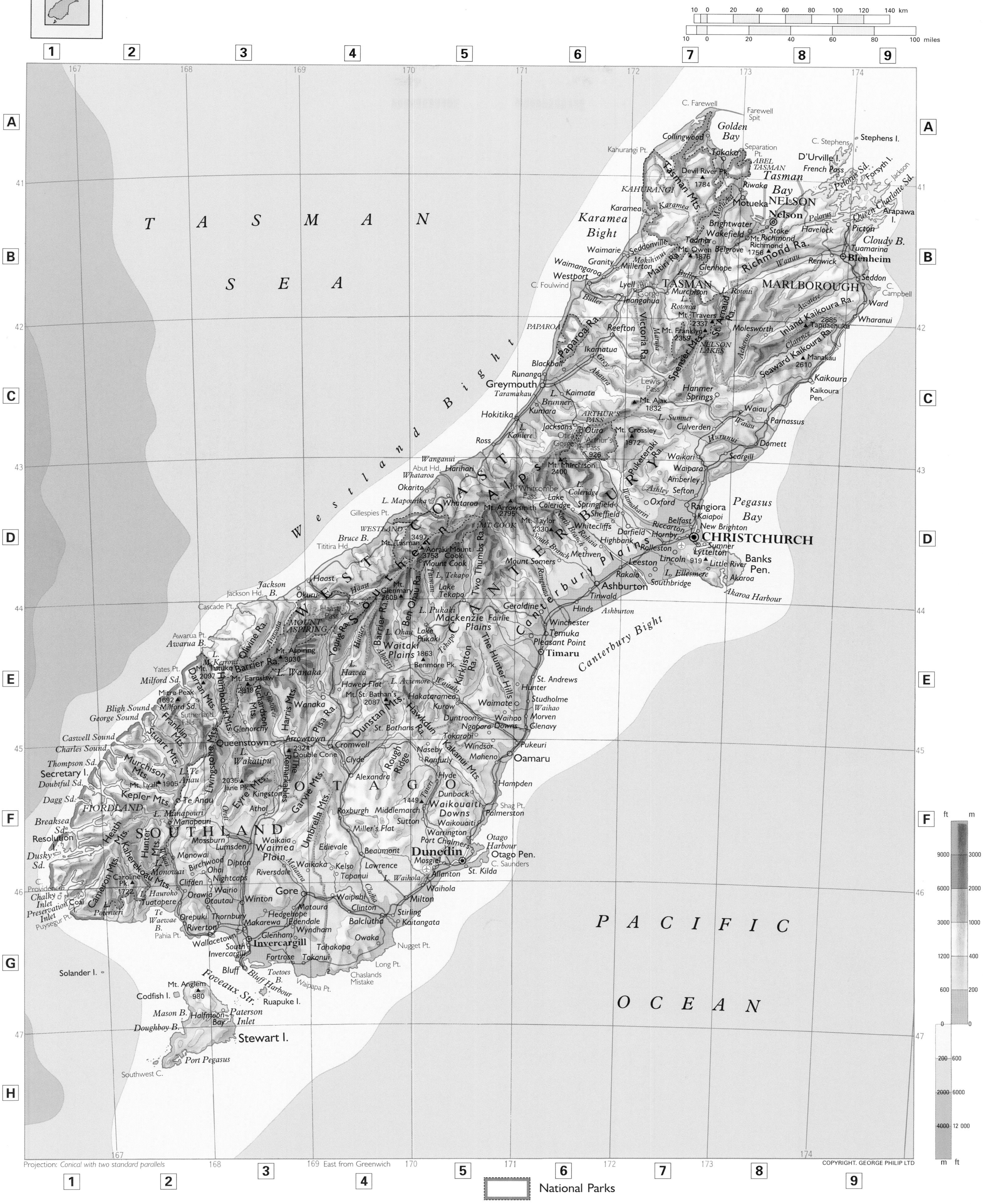

10 0 20 40 60 80 100 120 140 km
10 0 20 40 60 80 100 miles

TASMAN SEA

PACIFIC OCEAN

C. Farewell
Golden Bay
Collingwood
Farewell Spit
Takaka
Separation Pt.
C. Stephens
Stephens I.
D'Urville I.
French Pass
Kahurangi Pt.
ABEL TASMAN
Devil River Pk. 1784
Riwaka
Pelorus Sd.
Forsyth I.
Jackson
Queen Charlotte Sd.
Tasman Bay
KAHURANGI
Tasman Mts.
Motueka
NELSON
Arapawa I.
Karamea
Karamea
Brightwater
Stoke
Havelock
Picton
Karamea Bight
Nelson
Pelorus
Cloudy B.
Waimarie
Seddonville
Mokihinui
Wakefield
Mt. Owen 1876
Belgrove
Richmond
Tuamarina
Blenheim
Granity
Millerton
Matiri Ra.
Mt. Richmond 1756
Richmond Ra.
Renwick
Seddon
Westport
C. Foulwind
Lyell
Buller
Murchison
L. Rotoiti
Wairau
C. Campbell
MARLBOROUGH
Buller Gorge
Inangahua
Rotoroa
L. Rotoroa
St. Arnaud Ra.
Ward
PAPAROA
Reefton
Victoria Ra.
Mt. Franklyn 2353
Mt. Travers 2337
Acheron
2885
Tapuaenuku
Wharanui
Paparoa Ra.
Grey
Maruia
NELSON LAKES
Clarence
Inland Kaikoura Ra.
Blackball
Ikamatua
Molesworth
Manakau 2610
Runanga
Ahaura
Lewis Pass
Hanmer Springs
Seaward Kaikoura Ra.
Kaikoura
Greymouth
L. Kaimata
Hurunui
Taramakau
L. Brunner
ARTHUR'S PASS
Mt. Ajax 1832
Culverden
Waiau
Kaikoura Pen.
Hokitika
Kumara
Jacksons
Otira
Mt. Crossley 1972
Summer
Waiau
Parnassus
Ross
L. Kaniere
Arthur's Pass 926
Puketi...
Waikari
Scargill
Domett
Wanganui
Abut Hd.
Mt. Murchison 2400
Waipara
Whataroa
Harihari
Whitcombe Pass
L. Colendge
Oxford
Amberley
Okarito
Lake Coleridge
Springfield
Sefton
Ashley
Pegasus Bay
L. Mapourika
Whataroa
Mt. Arrowsmith 2795
Mt. Taylor 2330
Sheffield
Rangiora
Whitecliffs
Kaiapoi
Gillespies Pt.
Darfield
Riccarton
New Brighton
WESTLAND
Mt. Tasman 3497
Two Thumbs Ra.
South Branch
Highbank
Rolleston
Hornby
CHRISTCHURCH
Bruce B.
Aoraki Mount Cook 3753
Mount Cook
Mount Somers
Rakaia
Belfast
Lincoln 919
Lyttelton
Sumner
Tititira Hd.
Methven
Leeston
Little River
Banks Pen.
Akaroa
Haast
Mt. Glenmary 2608
Rangitata
Southbridge
L. Ellesmere
Jackson Hd.
Jackson B.
Okuru
Haast
Ben Ohau Ra.
L. Tekapo
Geraldine
Hinds
Ashburton
Tinwald
Akaroa Harbour
Cascade Pt.
L. Pukaki
Lake Tekapo
Mackenzie Plains
Fairlie Plains
Winchester
Temuka
OLIVINE Ra.
Mt. Aspiring 3030
Hunter
Waitaki Plains
Pleasant Point
Canterbury Bight
Awarua Pt.
Awarua B.
MOUNT ASPIRING
L. Ohau
Lake Pukaki
1863
Timaru
Yates Pt.
L. McKerrow
Mt. Tutoko 2097
Barrier Ra.
Mt. Earnslaw 2819
Young Ra.
Barrier Ra.
Alburn
Kirkliston Ra.
The Hunter Hills
Milford Sd.
Mitre Peak 1692
Milford Sd.
Harris Mts.
Richardson Mts.
L. Wanaka
Hawea
L. Avienore
Hakataramea
St. Andrews
Hunter
Bligh Sound
Sutherland Falls
Darran Mts.
Hawea Flat
Mt. St. Bathan's 2087
Kurow
Waimate
Studholme
George Sound
Franklin Mts.
Glenorchy
Wanaka
Duntroon
Waihao
Caswell Sound
Stuart Mts.
Eyre Mts.
Arrowtown
Dunstan Mts.
St. Bathans
Ngapara
Waihao Downs
Charles Sound
Queenstown
2324
Hawkdun Ra.
Tokarahi
Morven
Glenavy
Thompson Sd.
L. Te Anau
Double Cone
Cromwell
Kakanui Mts.
Maheno
Oamaru
Secretary I.
Murchison Mts.
The Remarkables
Clyde
Naseby
Windsor
Doubtful Sd.
Mt. Lyall 1905
2035
Jane Pk.
OTAGO
Garvie Mts.
Rough Ridge
Ranfurly
Pukeuri
Dagg Sd.
Kepler Mts.
Te Anau
Kingston
Alexandra
Hyde
Hampden
Breaksea Sd.
FIORDLAND
L. Manapouri
Athol
Umbrella Mts.
1449
Dunback
Shag Pt.
Palmerston
Resolution
Manapouri
Roxburgh
Middlemarch
Waikouaiti Downs
Dusky Sd.
Hauroko
SOUTHLAND
Mossburn
Lumsden
Waikaia
Miller's Flat
Sutton
Waikouaiti
C.
Murchison Mts.
Monowai
Birchwood
Dipton
Waimea Plain
Beaumont
Warrington
Otago Harbour
Providence
Cameron Mts.
Caroline Pk. 1722
Monowai
Ohai
Nightcaps
Waikaka
Edievale
Lawrence
Tapanui
Port Chalmers
Otago Pen.
Chalky Inlet
Coal
Kaherekoau Mts.
Riversdale
Kelso
L. Waihola
Dunedin
Mosgiel
C. Saunders
Preservation Inlet
Hunter Mts.
Orawia
Wairio
Winton
Gore
Waipahi
Milton
St. Kilda
Allanton
Puysegur Pt.
Takitimu Mts.
Orepuki
Otautau
Thornbury
Mataura
Clinton
Waihola
Te Waewae B.
Tuatapere
Makarewa
Hedgehope
Stirling
Pahia Pt.
Riverton
Glenham
Edendale
Balclutha
Kaitangata
Wallacetown
South Invercargill
Invercargill
Tahakopa
Owaka
Nugget Pt.
Bluff
Fortrose
Takanui
Long Pt.
Solander I.
Mt. Anglem
Bluff Harbour
Toetoes B.
Chaslands Mistake
Codfish I. 980
Ruapuke I.
Foveaux Str.
Waipapa Pt.
Mason B.
Halfmoon Bay
Paterson Inlet
Doughboy B.
Stewart I.
Port Pegasus
Southwest C.

WEST COAST
Southern ALPS
CANTERBURY
Canterbury Plains
Westland Bight

ft m
9000 3000
6000 2000
3000 1000
1200 400
600 200
0 0
200 600
2000 6000
4000 12000
m ft

Projection: Conical with two standard parallels

East from Greenwich

COPYRIGHT. GEORGE PHILIP LTD

National Parks

50 0 50 100 150 200 km
50 0 50 100 150 miles

83

126

A B C D E F G

COPYRIGHT GEORGE PHILIP LTD.

NORTH SOLOMONS

P A C I F I C   O C E A N

Lyra Reef

Nuguria Is.
Sable I.

NEW IRELAND

St. MATTHIAS Group
Mussau I.
Tabalo I.
Emirau I.
Eloaua I.

New Hanover
Tingwon
Ungat
Djaul
North C.
Kavieng

Nipuos
Taskul
Tench I.

Klinailau I.
Green Is.
Green I.
Feni Is. Babase I.
Ambitle I.

Buka I.
C. Hanpan
Hutjena
Mt. Balbi
2715
Sohano
Tinputz
Kunua
Torokina
Arawa Kieta
Panguna
Motupena Pt.
Buin
Boku

Treasury Is.
(Solomon Is.)

Shortland I.

Bougainville I.
Bougainville Trench 9140

Solomon Islands
Solomon Sea

Lihir Group
Lihir I.
Simberi I.
Tatau I. Tabar I.
Tanga Is.
Boang I.
Malendok I.

Schleinitz 1481
Konos
Lambu
Konogogo

Hans Meyer Ra.
Verron Ra.
Lambon
Metlik
C. St. George

St. George's Channel

Watom I.
Rabaul
Kerawat
Gazelle Peninsula
Kokopo
Mt. Sinewit 2438
Pondo
Ulamona
Lolobau I.
Wide Bay
Sampun
Pomio
Matong
Jacquinot Bay
Crater Pt.
Merai

NEW BRITAIN
EAST NEW BRITAIN
8320

Talasea
Willaumez Pen.
Garove I.
Kimbe Bay
Kimbe
Hoskins
Ewasse
Ubai

Nakanai Mts.

Bismarck Sea

Witu Is.
Unea I.
Garove I.
Ottilien Reef
Whirlwind Reef

Nakuru
2027
Whiteman Ra.

WEST NEW BRITAIN
WEST SOLOMON

Kandrian
C. Arukur C. Kablunga
Waku
Sag Sag
Aumo
Arawe
Gasmata

C. Gloucester
Sakar I.
Sialum
Umboi I.
Long I.
Crown I.
Tolokiwa I.
Sidssi
Dampier Strait
Vitiaz Strait

Finschhafen
C. Cretin
Tami Is.

Huon Peninsula
Wasu
Kabwum
Sio

MANUS
Admiralty Islands
Lorengau
Momote
Manus I.
Sori
Kali
South West Pt.
Rambutyo I.
Tong I.
Baluan I.

Hermit Is.
Ninigo Group

Circular Reef
Sherburne Reef
Bagabag I.
Karkar I.
Manam I.

MADANG
Madang
Saidor
Bibi
Matuka
Karkar I.
Bogia
Keram
Ramu

C. Girgir
C. Watam
Dumpu
Finisterre Ra.
Saruwaged Ra.
Mt. Bangeta 4121

Huon Gulf
Lae
Salamaua
Bulolo
Wau
Markham
Kaiapit
Erop

MOROBE
Morobe

Aua I.
Wyulu I.

WEST SEPIK
Wutung
Vanimo
Aitape
Sissano
Wewak
Muschu I.
Kairiru I.
Walis I.
Vokeo I.
Schouten Is.

EAST SEPIK
Angoram
Maprik
Drekikir
Ambunti
Pagwi
Yuat

Torricelli Mts.
Lumi
Nuku
Tabubil
Telefomin
Oksapmin

ENGA
Wabag
Laiagam
Wapenamanda

WESTERN HIGHLANDS
Mount Hagen
Banz
Minj
Tambul
Baiyer River
Kundiawa 4359

CHIMBU
Kerowagi
Gumine
Kundiawa

EASTERN HIGHLANDS
Goroka 4508
Mt. Michael 3647
Henganofi
Kainantu
Okapa
Kaugu
Aseki

Mt. Wilhelm 4508
Crater Mt. 3231

SOUTHERN HIGHLANDS
Mendi
Nipa
Kagua
Ialibu
Tari
Koroba
Lake Kopiago

New Guinea
Central Range

Mt. Capella 3993
Mt. Aiyang 3505
Victor Emanuel Ra.
West May May River
Pagei

PAPUA NEW GUINEA

Mt. Bosavi 2507
Muller Ra.
Kikori
Erave
Samberigi
Kutubu
Lake Kutubu
Porgera
Kandep

Kunga
Lake Murray
April River
Mamberamo
Nomad

WESTERN
Balimo
Lake Murray
Morehead
Wasua
Aramia
Guavi
Bamu
Fly
Awaba
Kiunga

Daru
Daru I.
Parama I.
Boze
Bristow I.
Wabuda I.
Umuda I.
Purutu I.
Kiwai I.
Aramia

Gulf of Papua

GULF
Kerema
Baimuru
Ihu
Malalaua
Kukipa
Kaintiba

Deception Bay
Blackwood
Vailala
Purari

Gulf of Papua

CENTRAL
Port Moresby
Hula
Hood Pt.
Kwikila
Abau
Kapa Kapa
Kalo
Keppel
Kupiano
Magarida
Abau

Kokoda
Kapagere
Sogeri
Kairuku
Yule I.
Bereina
Iokea
Lea Lea

OWEN STANLEY RANGE
Mt. Victoria 4035
Mt. Albert Edward 3989
Mt. St. Mary 3655
Tapini
Woitape
Menari
Itikinumu
Kokoda

VARIRATA
Mt. Suckling 3676
Mt. Simpson 2883

NORTHERN
Popondetta
Buna
Gona
Sanananda
Kokoda
Afore
Ioma
Kumusi
Sibium Mts.
Managalas
Sariri
Saiho
Tufi
C. Nelson

Kupiano
Amazon Bay
Mullins Hbr.

MILNE BAY
D'Entrecasteaux Islands
Goodenough I.
Bolubolu
Fergusson I.
Normanby I.
Esa'ala
Sewa Bay
Dobu
Salamo
Alotau
Samarai
East Cape
C. Frere
Ahioma

Trobriand Is.
Kiriwina I.
Kaileuna I.
Losuia
Kitava I.
Vakuta I.

Woodlark I.
Guasopa
Madau I.
Marshall Bennett Is.
Egum Atoll
Kulumadau

Louisiade Archipelago
Debaye Is.
Conflict Group
Nuakata I.
Dumoulin Is.
Basilaki I.
Rossel I.
Tagula
Misima I.
Tawa Tawa Mal Reef
The Calvados Chain
Sudest
Tagula I.

Pocklington Reef

C O R A L   S E A
Coral Sea
-- Tracks

Great Barrier Reef

AUSTRALIA

Cape York Peninsula
York
Shelburne Bay
C. Grenville
Temple Bay
Moa I.
Badu I.
Thursday I.
Wednesday I.
Prince of Wales I.
Horn I.
Turtle Head I.
C. York
Sharp Pt.
Torres Strait
Endeavour Strait
Cullen Pt.

Saibai
Boigu I.
Daru

INDONESIA

Sepik
Green River
Amanab

Projection: Lambert Conformal Conic

East from Greenwich

ft m (elevation scale)
18 000 6000
12 000 4000
6000 2000
3000 1000
1200 400
600 200
0 0

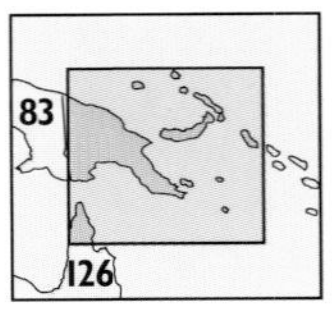

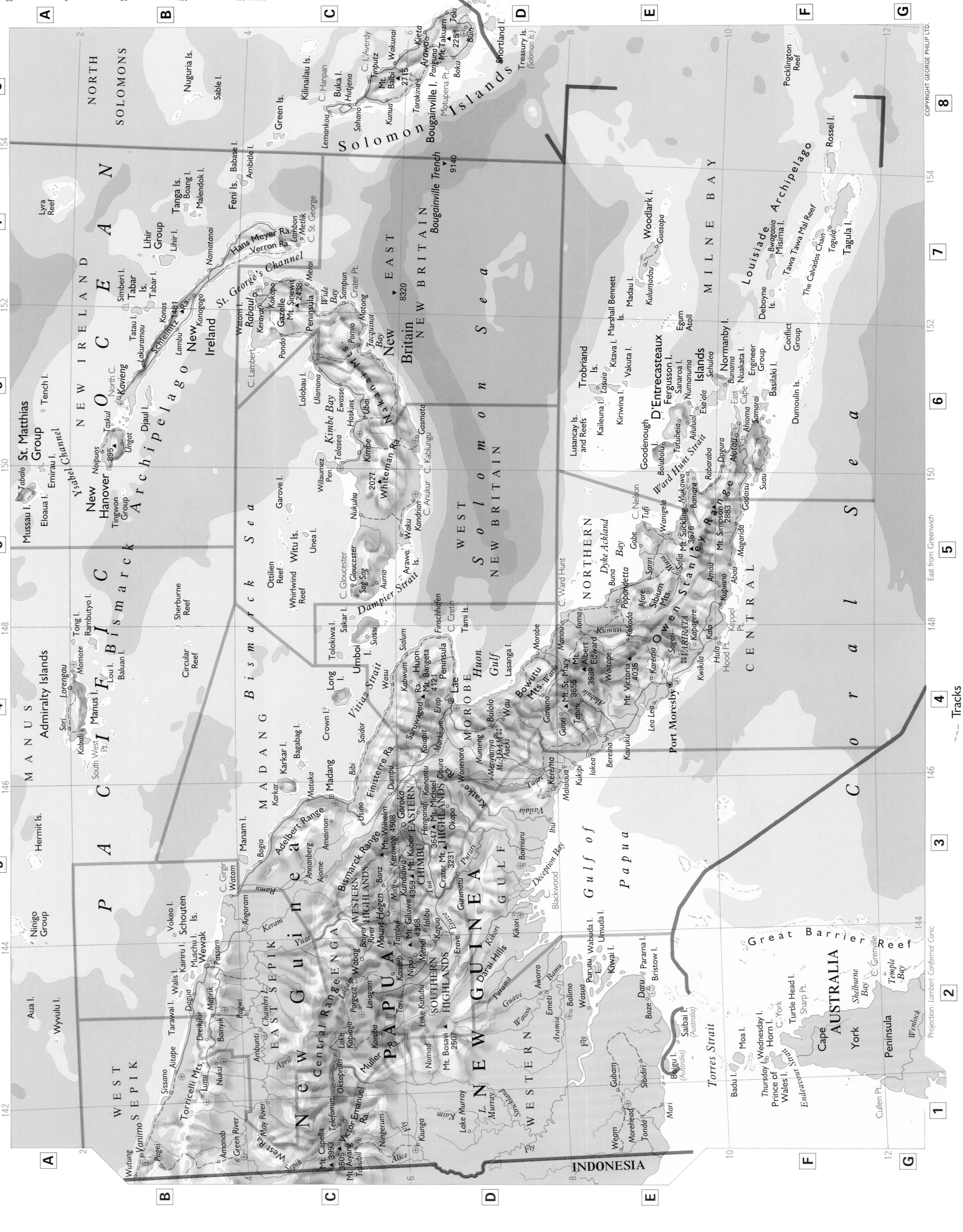

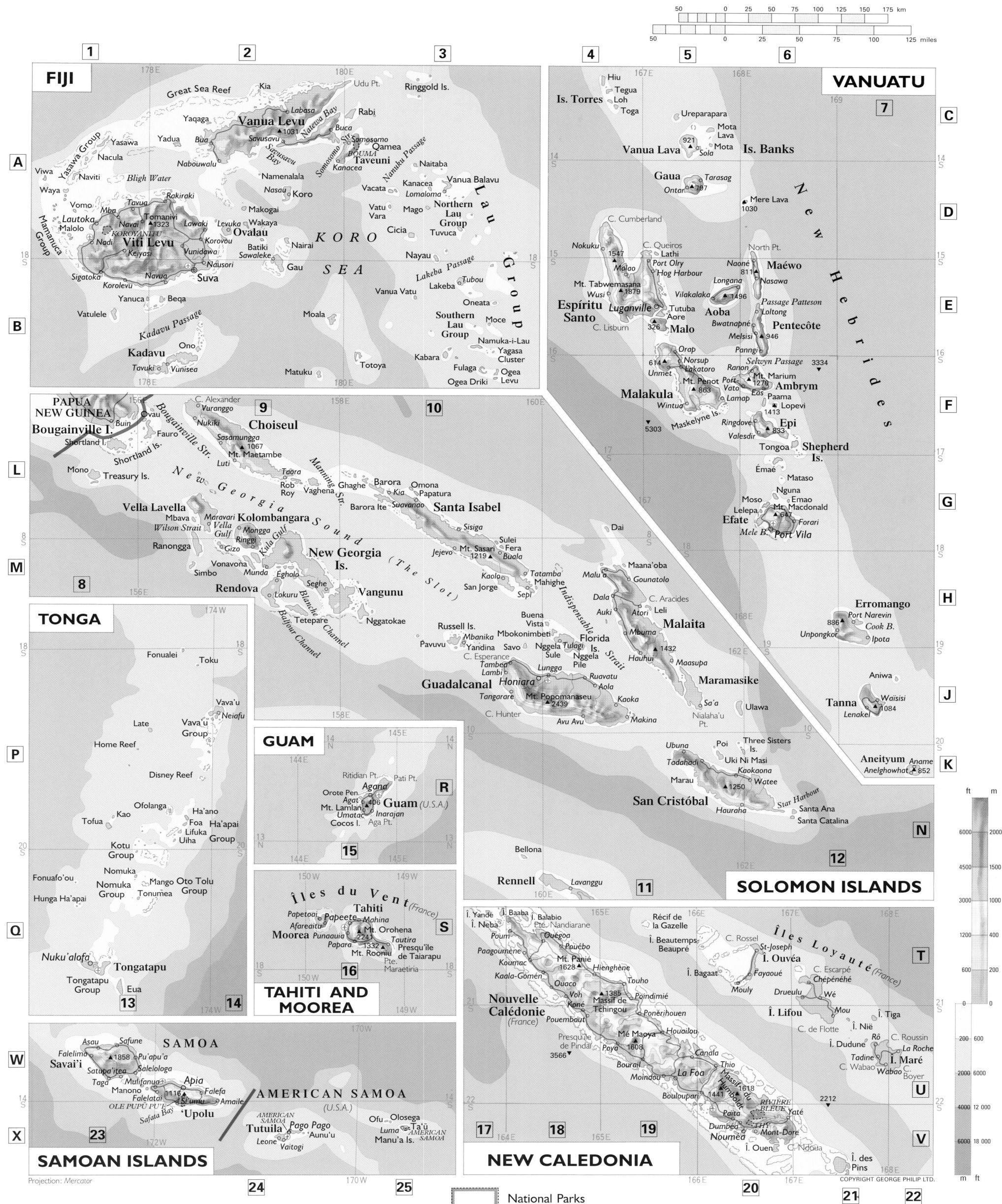

50   0   25 50 75 100 125 150 175 km

50   0   25   50   75   100 125 miles

1 **2** **3** **4** **5** **6**

FIJI **VANUATU** **7**

C

Great Sea Reef Kia Udu Pt.
Yaqaga Labasa Rabi Ringgold Is.
Yasawa Yadua Bua Savusavu ▲1031 Naidavu Bay Buca Somosomo Qamea Is. Torres Hiu Tegua Loh Toga Ureparapara Mota Lava Mota
Nacula Bua Sausavu Bay Somosomo BOUMA Taveuni Somosomo Vanua Lava ▲921 Is. Banks
Viwa Naviti Nabouwalu Namenalala Naitaba Gaua Tarasag Sola

A Vomo Tavua Rakiraki Makogai Wakaya Vatu Vanua Balavu D
Waya Mba Tavua Lawaki Levuka Ovalau Vara Kanacea Lomaloma C. Cumberland Mere Lava 1030
Mamanuca Group Lautoka Navai ▲1323 Ovalau Batiki Mago Northern Lau Group Nokuku ▲1547 C. Queiros North Pt. Naoné ▲1270 Maéwo
Malolo Nadi Viti Levu Korovou Sawaleke Nairai Cicia Tuvuca Malao Port Olry Longana 811 ▲ Nasawa
Keiyasi Vunidawa Nausori Gau Nayau Mt. Tabwemasana Hog Harbour Vilakalaka ▲1496 Aoba Passage Patteson

B Sigatoka Korolevu Navua Suva Lakeba Passage Tubou Espíritu Wusi ▲1879 Luganville Tutuba Loltong Pentecôte E
Vatulele Yanuca Beqa Kadavu Passage Vanua Vatu Lakeba Santo 326 Aore Bwatnapné Melsisi ▲946
Moala KORO SEA Oneata Moce C. Lisburn Malo Panngi
Kadavu Ono Southern Lau Group Fulaga Orap Norsup Ranon Selwyn Passage 3334
Tavuki Vunisea Matuku Totoya Kabara Namuka-i-Lau Yagasa Cluster 614 ▲ Lakatoro Mt. Marium Eas
Ogea Ogea Driki Levu Unmet Mt. Penot ▲863 Port Vato Ambrym F
Malakula 1413 Lamap Lopevi
Wintua Maskelyne Is. Ringdove ▲833 Epi
5303 Valesdir

PAPUA NEW GUINEA 156 C. Alexander **9** **10** Émaé Mataso G
Ovau Varanggo Nukiki Barora Omona Dai Tongoa Shepherd Is.
Bougainville I. Buin Choiseul Ghaghe Kia Papatura Nguna Moso Lelepa Emao
Shortland I. Fauro Sasamungga Santa Isabel Efate Mt. Macdonald ▲647 Forari
L Mono Shortland Is. Mt. Maetambe ▲1067 Taora Barora Ite Suavanao Sisiga Mele B. Port Vila
Treasury Is. Luti Ghatere Vaghena Rob Roy

New Georgia Sound Jejevo Sulei Fera Maana'oba H
M Vella Lavella Kolombangara Mt. Sasari 1219 ▲ Buala Gounatolo Erromango Port Narevin
Mbava Maravari Vella Gulf Mongga Kaolo Tatamba Dala C. Aracides 886 ▲ Cook B.
Wilson Strait Gizo Ringgi Kala Gulf San Jorge Mahighe Atori Leli Unpongkor Ipota
Ranongga Simbo New Georgia Is. Sepi Auki Mbuma Malaita

Vonavona Munda Egholo Buena Vista Malu a ▲1432 Aniwa
Rendova Lokuru Seghe Vangunu Mbokonimbeti Florida Maramasike Tanna Waisisi J
Tetepare Blanche Channel Nggatokae Russell Is. Mbanika Nggela Tulagi Is. Hauhau Lenakel ▲1084
Bafour Channel Pavuvu Yandina Savo Sule Nggela Pile Maasupa
C. Esperance Tambea Lambi Lungga Ruavatu Sa'a Ubuna Poi Three Sisters Is. Aneityum Aname
Guadalcanal Honiara Aola Ulawa Tadahadi Uki Ni Masi Anelghowhat ▲852 K

TONGA 174 W **8** Tangarare Mt. Popomanaseu ▲2439 Kaoka Kaokaona Watee
C. Hunter Avu Avu Makina Nialaha'u Pt. Marau ▲1250 N
Fonualei Toku San Cristóbal Hauraha Santa Ana Santa Catalina

P Vava'u Neiafu **GUAM** 145 E Rennell Lavanggu **11** **12** **SOLOMON ISLANDS**
Late Vava'u Group Ritidian Pt. Pati Pt. Bellona
Home Reef Agana **R**
Disney Reef Orote Pen. Agat ▲406 Guam (U.S.A.) **Îles Loyauté** (France)
Ofolanga Mt. Lamlam Inarajan Î. Yande Baaba Récif de la Gazelle
Tofua Kao Ha'ano Umatac Aga Pt. Î. Neba Balabio Nandiarane St-Joseph Î. Ouvéa T
Kotu Group Foa Lifuka Ha'apai Cocos I. **15** Poum Quégoa Î. Beautemps-Beaupré Fayaoué Mouly
Uiha Group Paagoumène Pouébo Î. Bagaat C. Escarpé Drueulu

Q Fonuafo'ou Nomuka Mango Oto Tolu **Îles du Vent** (France) Koumac Mt. Panié ▲1628 Hienghène Wé Chépénéhé
Nomuka Group Tonumea Group Papetoai Tahiti Kaala-Gómen Touho Î. Lifou
Hunga Ha'apai Afareaitu Papeete Mahina Ouaco Massif de Poindimié Mou Î. Tiga
Moorea Punaauia Mt. Orohena Voh Tchingou Î. Nié C. de Flotte
Papara ▲1332 ▲2241 Tautira Koné ▲1385 Î. Dudune Rô C. Roussin S
Mt. Roonui Presqu'île de Taiarapu Nouvelle Ponérihouen Tadine La Roche
Maraetiria Pte. Calédonie Mé Maoya Houailou C. Wabao Wabao Î. Maré
Nuku'alofa Eua **16** (France) ▲1608 Boyer
Tongatapu **TAHITI AND** Presqu'île de Pindaï Poya Canala U
Tongatapu Group Eua **MOOREA** 3566 ▼ Bourail La Foa Thio Massif du Rivière Bleue
13 **14** Moindou Humboldt ▲1618 Yaté V
SAMOA Bouloupari 1441 ▲ ▲2212
W Asau Safune Paita THY
Falelima ▲1858 Pu'apu'a Salelologa Dumbéa Mont-Dore
Savai'i Satupa'itea Taga Mulifanua Apia Falefa Nouméa
Falelatai Manono ▲1116 Afu'alu Amaile **AMERICAN SAMOA** (U.S.A.) **NEW CALEDONIA** Î. Ouen C. Ndoua Î. des Pins
OLE PUPŪ PU'E Falelatai 'Upolu Safata Bay AMERICAN SAMOA Ofu Olosega
23 Tutuila Pago Pago Luma Ta'ú
X Leone Vaitogi Manu'a Is. **17** **18** **19** **20** **21** **22** V

SAMOAN ISLANDS **NEW CALEDONIA**

Projection: Mercator **24** **25** COPYRIGHT GEORGE PHILIP LTD.

ft m
6000 2000
4500 1500
3000 1000
1200 400
600 200
0 0
200 600
2000 6000
4000 12 000
6000 18 000
m ft

National Parks

7   160   8   9   180   10
6
1   100   2   3   120   4   5   140

Bering Sea

Okhotsk

Sea of Okhotsk

Poluostrov Kamchatka

Komandorskiye Ostrova *(Russia)*
Near Is. *(U.S.A.)*
Andreanof Is. *(U.S.A.)*

B   MOSKVA   R   U   S   S   I   A
Yekaterinburg
Volga   Ob   Tomsk   *Lena*
Astana (Aqmola)   Novosibirsk   Irkutsk   Chita
Semey   *Oz. Baykal*   Blagoveshchensk   *Amur*   Khabarovsk   Sakhalin   Petropavlovsk-Kamchatskiy   *7822*
50

KAZAKSTAN
Aral Sea   *Balqash Köl*   MONGOLIA   Ulaanbaatar   Harbin   *La Perouse Str.*   Kurilskiye Ostrova *(Russia)*   *Kuril Trench*
C   Almaty   Ürümqi   *Altai*   Changchun   Vladivostok   Hakodate   *10,542*   *Aleutian*   *Aleutian Trench*
Toshkent   KYRGYZSTAN   SHENYANG   NORTH KOREA   Sapporo   *Sea of Japan*   *Emperor Seamount Chain*
TAJIKISTAN   BEIJING   TIANJIN   Dalian   SOUL   Sendai
40   AFGHANISTAN   CHINA   Taiyuan   *Huang He*   SOUTH KOREA   Nagoya   TOKYO   *Fuji-San 3776*   Yokohama
D   Kabul   Srinagar   Lanzhou   Xi'an   Qingdao   Kyōto   *Kitakyūshū*   Osaka JAPAN   *Japan Trench*   Midway Is. *(U.S.A.)*
PAKISTAN   *Kunlun Shan*   Nanjing   Shikoku   *10,554*   *Howaii*
Lahore   XIZANG   CHONGQING   Wuhan   *Yellow Sea*   Kyūshū   Lisianski I. *(U.S.A.)*
30   DELHI   *Himalaya*   Lhasa   Changsha   SHANGHAI   *South Honshu Ridge*   Ogasawara Gunto *(Japan)*   Minami-Tori-Shima *(Japan)*
Kanpur   Mt. Everest *8850*   HANGZHOU   *East China Sea*
E   *Ganga*   NEPAL   *Brahmaputra*   Kunming   Fuzhou   Taipei   Kazan-Rettō *(Japan)*
INDIA   BANGLADESH   KOLKATA (Calcutta)   DHAKA   GUANGZHOU   TAIWAN   Ryūkyū-rettō *(Japan)*   *Marcus*   *Necker Ridge*   Wake I. *(U.S.A.)*
BURMA   Mandalay   HONG KONG   Macau
20   Hyderabad   *Irrawaddy*   LAOS   Hanoi   *International Dateline*   P   A
F   *Bay of*   Rangoon   *Salween*   Hainan   C. Engano   NORTHERN MARIANAS *(U.S.A.)*   MARSHALL IS.
CHENNAI (Madras)   *Bengal*   THAILAND   *Mekong*   Luzon   Paracel Is.   Saipan   *Micro*
Andaman Is. *(India)*   BANGKOK   VIETNAM   MANILA   GUAM *(U.S.A.)* 11,022   Enewetak Atoll   Bikini Atoll
10   CAMBODIA   Phnom Penh   Mindoro   PHILIPPINES   *Mariana Trench*   *n e s i a*
Nicobar Is. *(India)*   Thanh Pho Ho Chi Minh   Palawan   Samar   Yap   Caroline Is.   Truk   Dalap-Uliga-Darrit
SRI LANKA   *G. of Thailand*   *South China Sea*   Mindanao   10,497   Koror   Pohnpei Palikir   Jaluit I.
G   Colombo   MALAYSIA   Sulu Sea   Mindanao Trench   PALAU   FEDERATED STATES OF MICRONESIA   Butaritari
0   Kuala Lumpur   PEN. MALAYSIA   4101   BRUNEI   SABAH   Celebes Sea   *Maluku*   *M e l a*   Tarawa   Gilbert Is.   Howland I. *(U.S.A.)*
SINGAPORE   *Sarawak*   Borneo   Sulawesi   Halmahera   Admiralty Is.   PAPUA NEW GUINEA   NAURU   Banaba   Baker I. *(U.S.A.)*
Sumatera   Palembang   Ujung Pandang   Buru   Seram   Puncak Jaya IRIAN JAYA 5029   Bismarck Arch.   New Ireland   *n e s i a*   KIR
H   *Java Sea*   JAKARTA   *Jawa*   Surabaya   *Flores Sea*   Banda Sea   New Guinea   Rabaul   Phoenix Is.   Abariringa Enderbury   O
Sunda Is   Bali   INDONESIA   Flores   7440   Lae   New Britain   SOLOMON IS.   Fongafale   Phoenix Is.   K   I   R
Selat Sunda   *Java Trench*   Sumbawa   Sumba   EAST TIMOR   Port Moresby   Honiara   TUVALU   Tokelau Is. *(N.Z.)*
10   *Mid-Indian Ridge*   Christmas I. *(Austral.)*   Timor   *Arafura Sea*   Torres Strait   Guadalcanal   Santa Cruz I. 9165
Cocos Is. *(Austral.)*   C. Arnhem   C. York   Louisiade Arch.   Rotuma   Is. Wallis & Futuna *(Fr.)*   SAMOA Apia
INDIAN   Darwin   *Gulf of Carpentaria*   Espíritu Santo   Vanua Levu
Nouvelle Amsterdam *(Fr.)*   Cairns   *Coral Sea*   VANUATU   Port Vila   Viti Levu   Suva   FIJI   Nuku'alofa
20   I. St. Paul *(Fr.)*   Broome   Townsville   Is. Chesterfield   NEW CALEDONIA *(Fr.)*   7570   Is. Loyauté   TONGA
OCEAN   North West C.   Mount Isa   AUSTRALIA   Rockhampton   Nouméa   10,822   *Tonga Trench*
Alice Springs   *L. Eyre*   Brisbane   Norfolk I. *(Austral.)*   Kermadec Is. *(N.Z.)*
30   Geraldton   Great Australian Bight   Lord Howe I. *(Austral.)*   *Kermadec Trench* 10,047
L   Perth   Sydney   Mt. Kosciuszko 2237   NEW ZEALAND
Albany   Adelaide   Canberra   *Tasman Sea*   Auckland   *Cook Strait*   Wellington
40   Melbourne   *Murray*   *Bass Str.*   Aoraki Mt. Cook 3753   Christchurch   Chatham Is. *(N.Z.)*
M   Is. Crozet *(Fr.)*   Tasmania   Hobart   Dunedin   Bounty Is. *(N.Z.)*
Kerguelen *(Fr.)*   Invercargill   Antipodes Is. *(N.Z.)*
50   Auckland Is. *(N.Z.)*
N   Heard I. *(Austral.)*   Macquarie Is. *(Austral.)*   Campbell I. *(N.Z.)*

ft   m
12 000   4000
9000   3000
6000   2000
3000   1000
1500   500
600   200
0   0
200   600
1000   3000
2000   6000
4000   12 000
6000   18 000
8000   24 000
m   ft

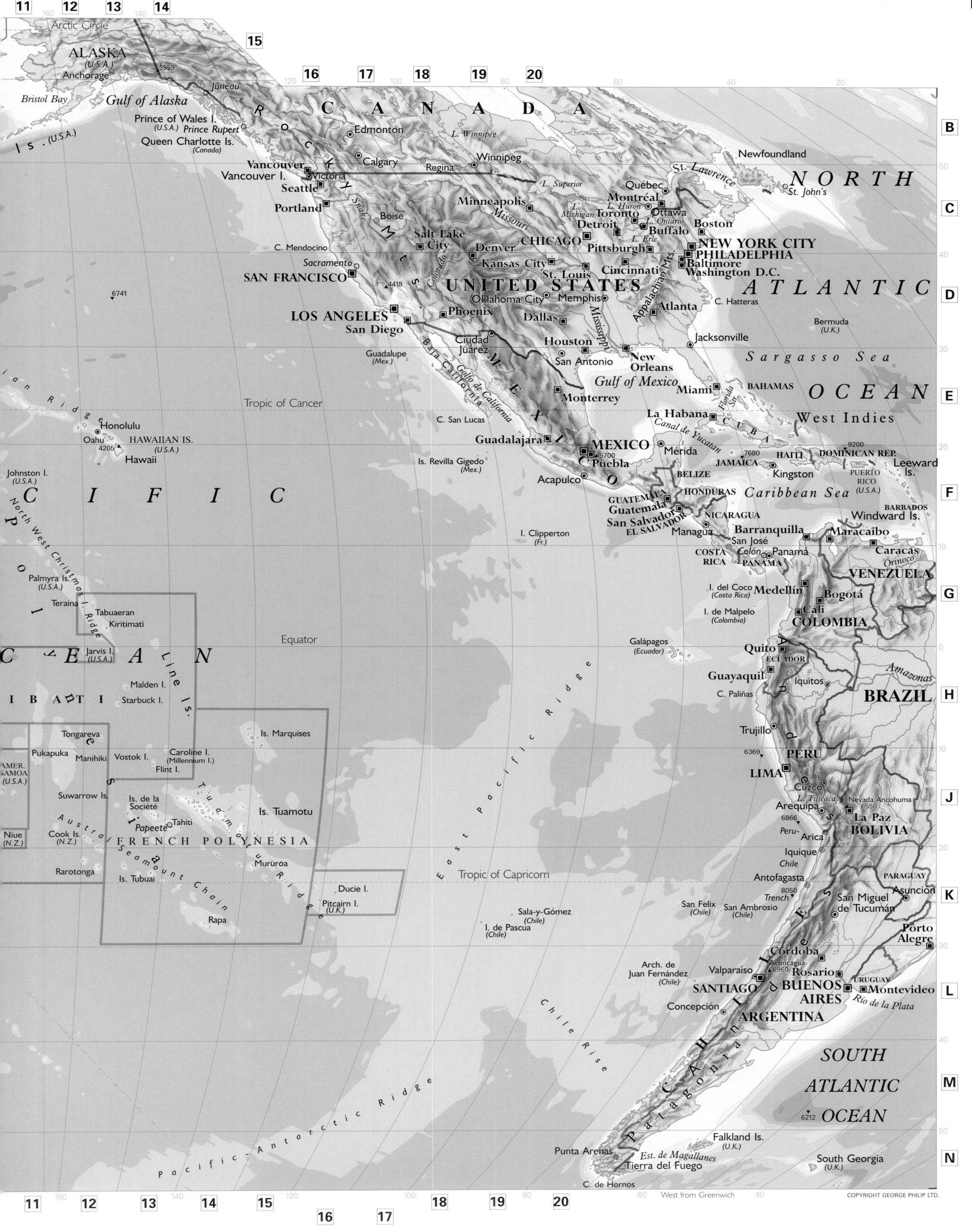

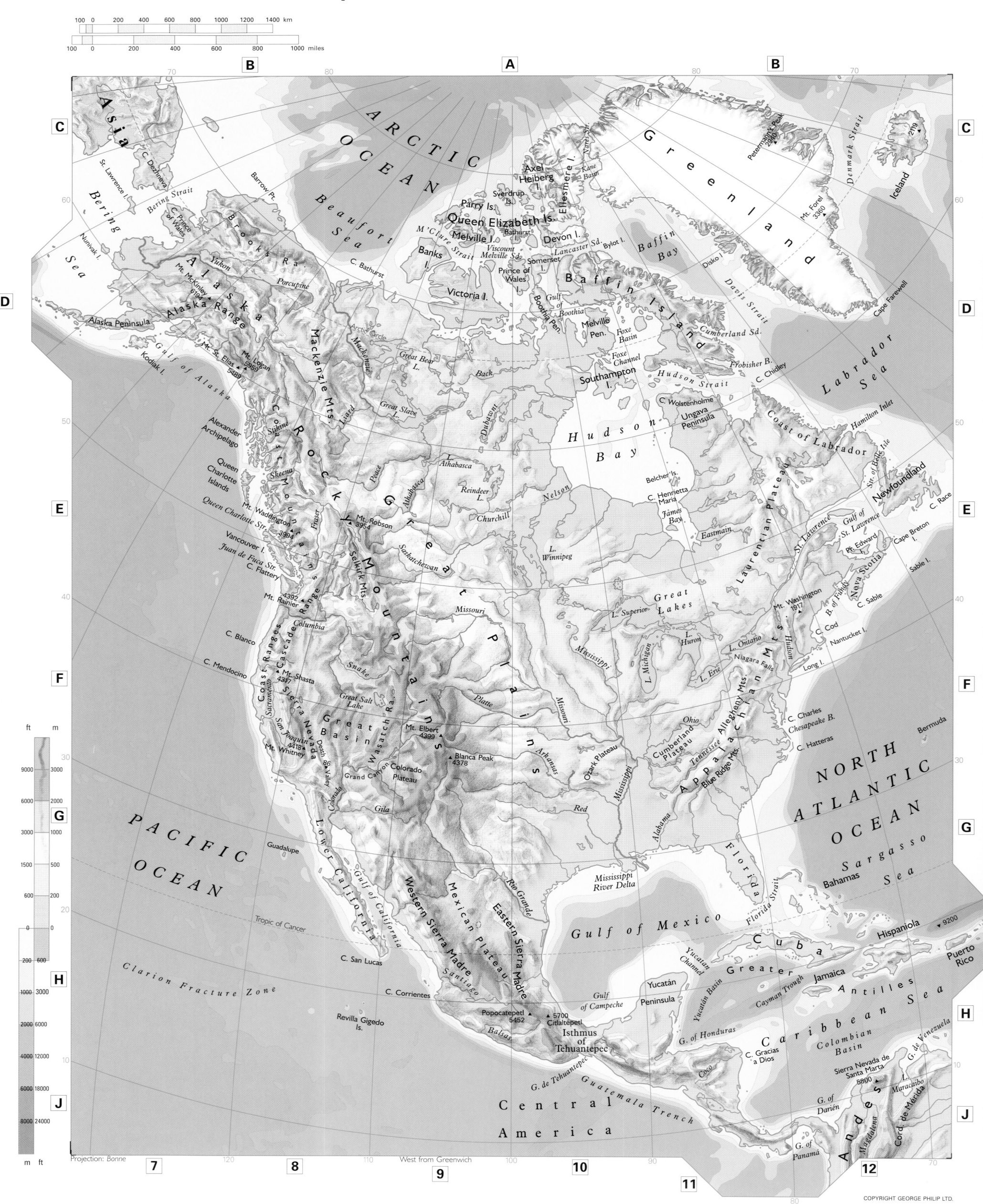

Projection: Bonne

West from Greenwich

COPYRIGHT GEORGE PHILIP LTD.

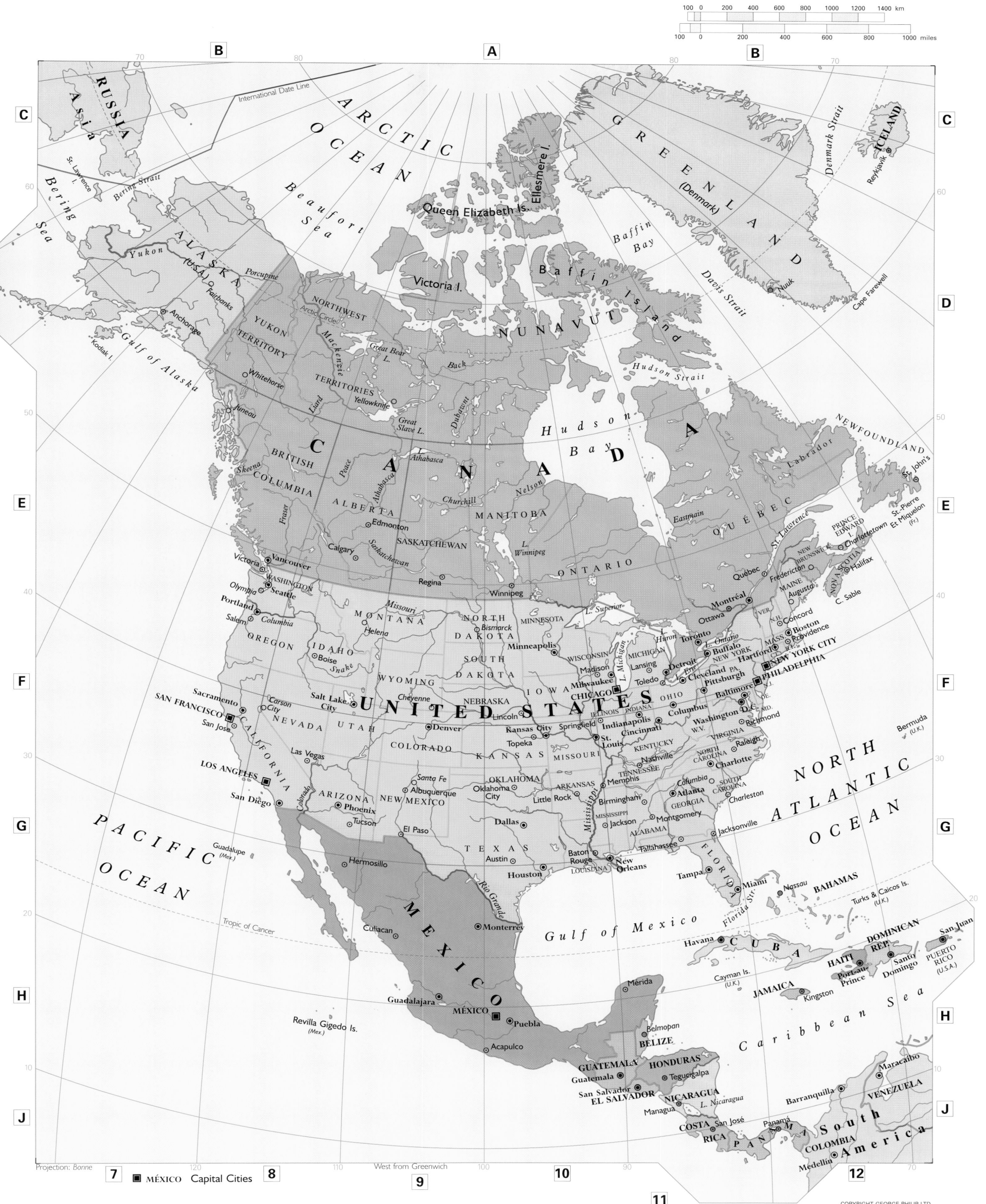

100 0 200 400 600 800 1000 1200 1400 km

100 0 200 400 600 800 1000 miles

7 ■ MÉXICO Capital Cities   **8**   West from Greenwich   **10**

Projection: *Bonne*

11

COPYRIGHT GEORGE PHILIP LTD.

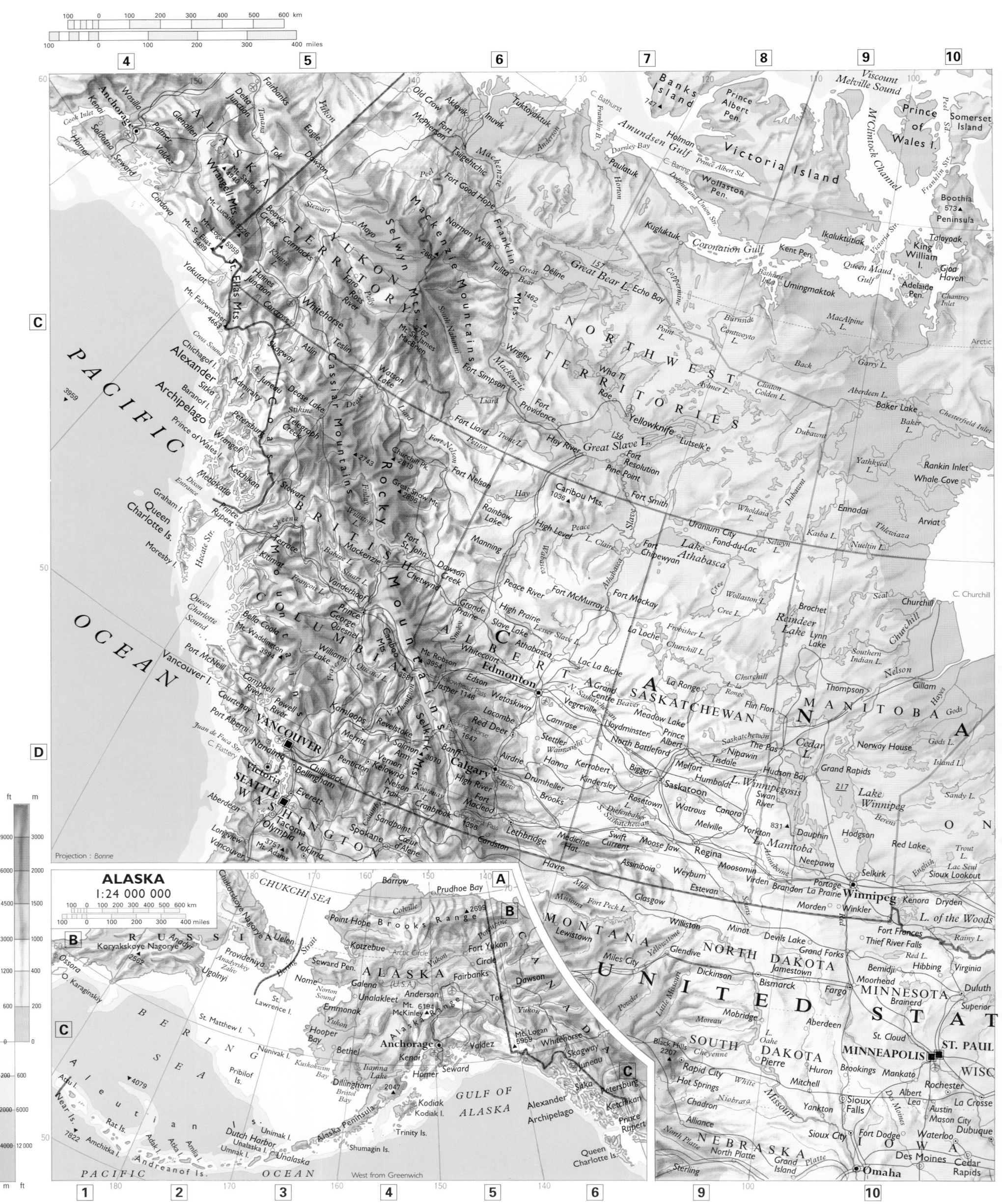

Projection : Bonne

ALASKA
1:24 000 000

West from Greenwich

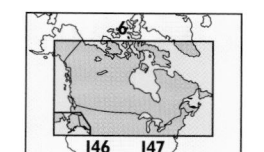

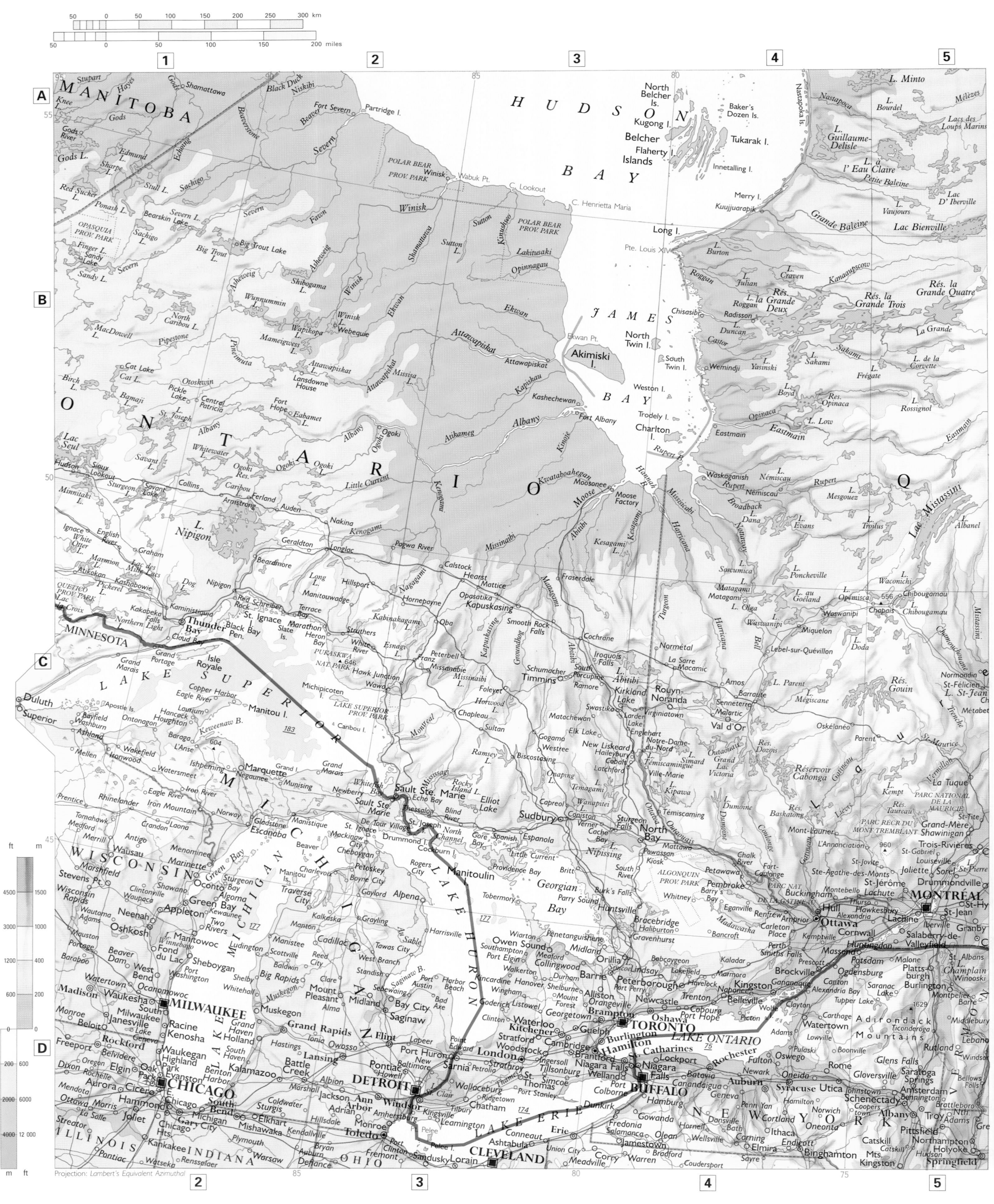

LABRADOR SEA

N E W F O U N D L A N D

Smallwood Reservoir

L a b r a d o r

Q U É B E C

Newfoundland

GULF OF ST. LAWRENCE

Î. d'Anticosti

Long Range Mts.

TERRA NOVA NAT. PARK

Corner Brook

GROS MORNE NAT. PARK

St. Lawrence

St. John's

ST-PIERRE ET MIQUELON (France)

Cabot Strait

CAPE BRETON HIGHLANDS NAT. PARK

PRINCE EDWARD ISLAND

Charlottetown

Cape Breton Island

Sydney

NEW BRUNSWICK

Fredericton

Moncton

NOVA SCOTIA

Halifax

Dartmouth

Saint John

Bay of Fundy

MAINE

Bangor

Augusta

Portland

KEJIMKUJIK NAT. PARK

Sable I. (Nova Scotia)

A T L A N T I C

O C E A N

NEW HAMPSHIRE

Manchester

Concord

BOSTON

Worcester

MASS.

UNITED STATES

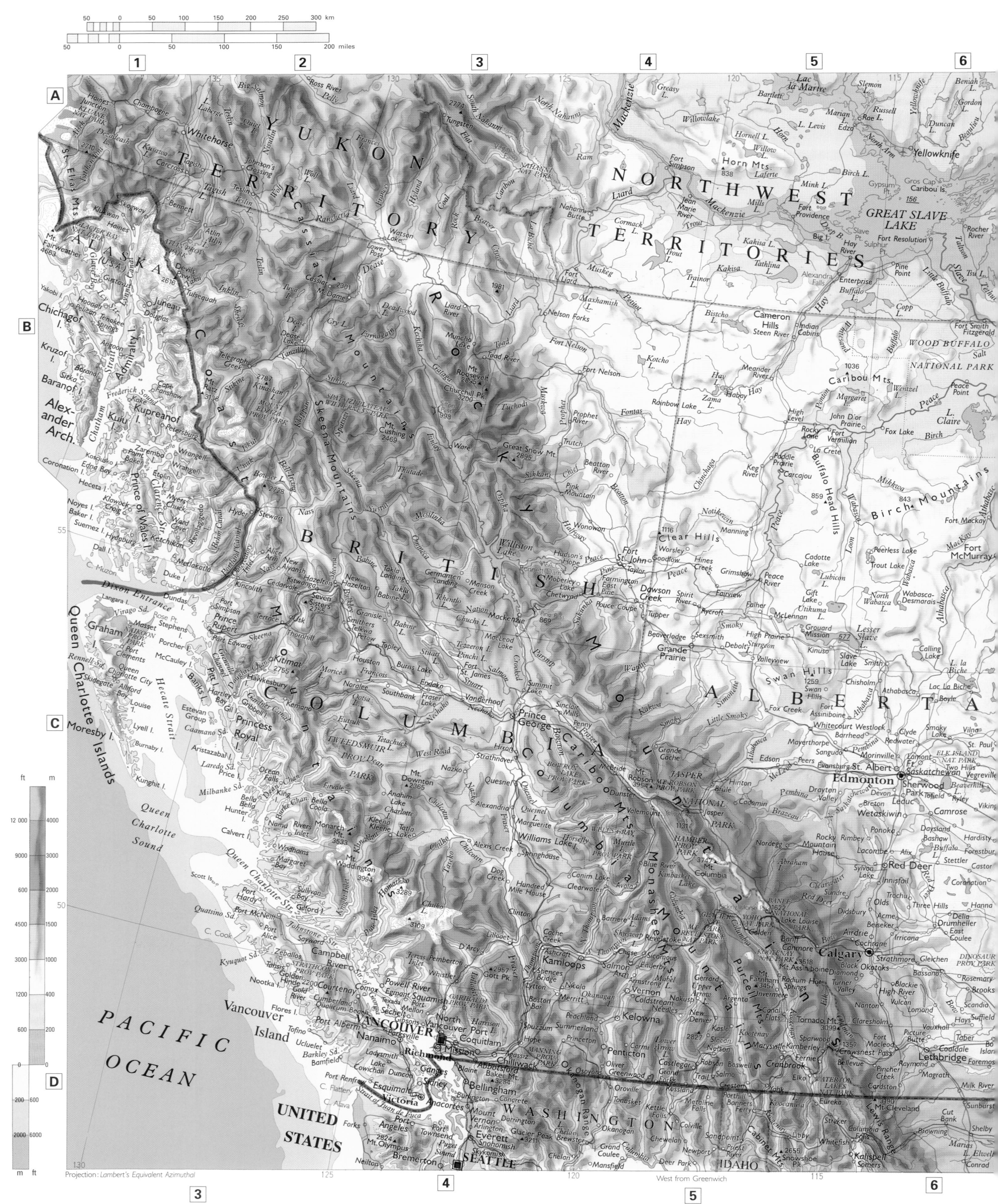

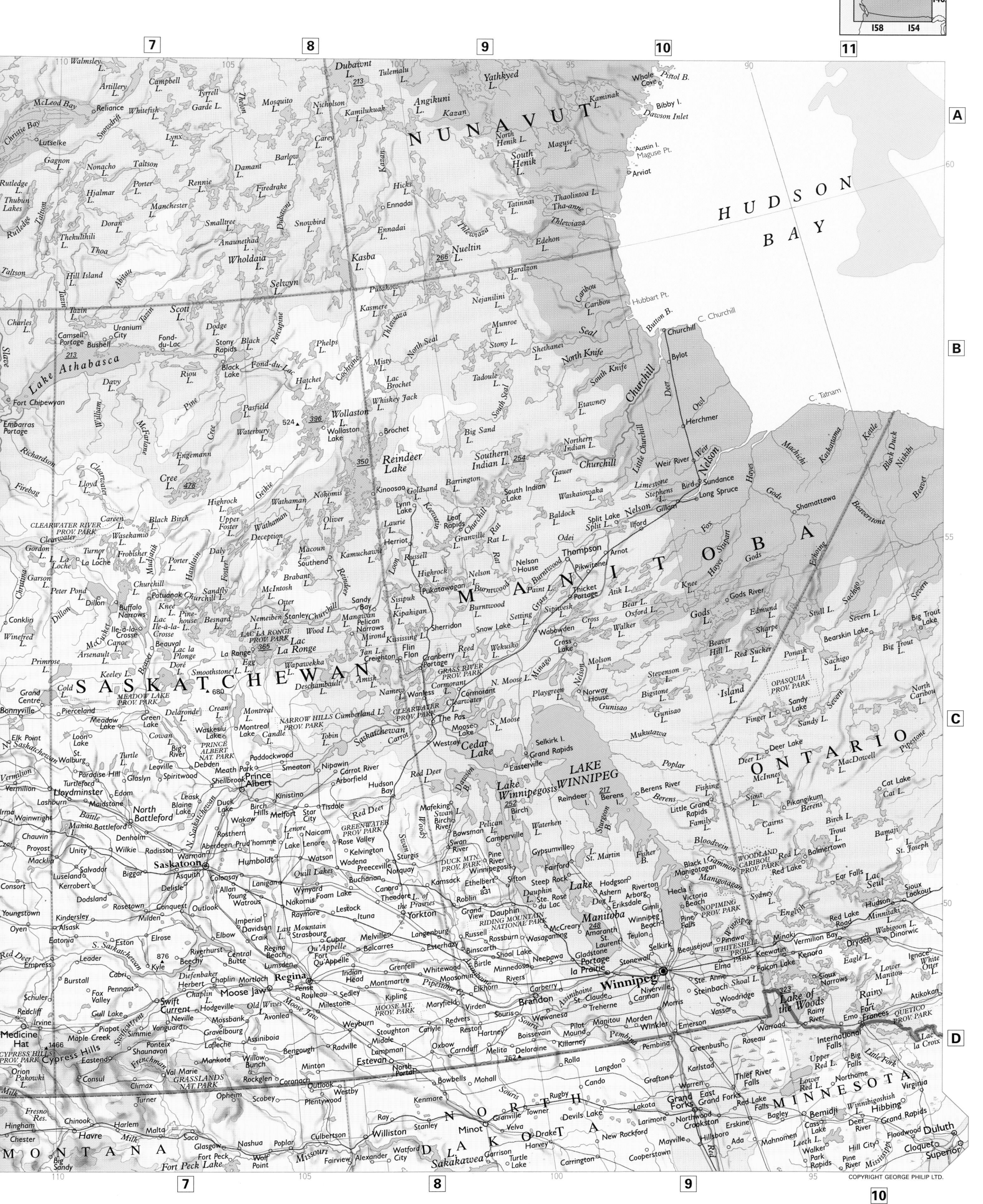

7   8   9   10   11

A

NUNAVUT

Dubawnt
Tulemalu
Yathkyed
Angikuni L.
Nicholson
Kamilukuak L.
Kazan
Carey
South Henik L.
Maguse
Whale Cove   Pistol B.
Austin I.   Maguse Pt.
Dawson Inlet
Arviat

Walmsley L.
Artillery L.
Campbell
Tyrrell L.
Garde L.
Thelon
Mosquito
McLeod Bay
Reliance   Whitefish
Snowdrift
Lynx   L.
Gagnon
Nonacho L.   Taltson
Rennie
Barlow L.
Firedrake L.
Hicks L.
North Henik L.
Kaminak L.
Tatinnai L.
Thaolintoa L.
Tha-anne

HUDSON BAY

B

Rutledge L.
Thubun Lakes
Hjalmar L.
Porter L.
Manchester
Damant L.
Rutledge   Taltson
Doran   L.
Smalltree L.
Dubawnt L.
Snowbird L.
Anaunethad L.
Ennadai
Ennadai L.
Thelwiaza
Nejanilini L.
Thlewiaza
Nueltin L.   266
Edehon L.
Thekulthili L.
Thoa
Wholdaia L.
Kasba L.
Baralzon L.
Caribou
Caribou
Hubbart Pt.
Taltson
Hill Island L.
Selwyn L.
Putahow
Seal
Button B.
C. Churchill

Charles L.
Tazin L.   Jasin
Scott L.
Dodge L.
Phelps L.
Kasmere L.
Munroe L.
Stony L.
Shethanei
North Knife L.
Churchill
Churchill
Bylot
Herchmer
C. Tatnam
Uranium City   Fond-du-Lac
Bushell
Camsell Portage   213
Stony Rapids   Black
Black L.
Fond-du-Lac
Hatchet L.
Cochrane
North Seal
Tadoule L.
South Seal
Etawney L.
Weir River
Weir
Nelson

Slave
Lake Athabasca
213
Fort Chipewyan
Embarras Portage
Richardson L.
William R.
Pine
Riou L.
Black Lake
Pasfield L.
524   396
Wollaston L.
Wollaston Lake
Whiskey Jack
Brochet
Lac Brochet
Misty L.
Big Sand L.
Southern Indian L.   254
Northern Indian L.
Churchill
Gauer L.
Waskaiowaka L.
Limestone
Stephens L.
Bird   Sundance
Long Spruce
Deer
Orel
Machichi
Kaskatama
Kettle
Black Duck
Niskbi
Beaver

Minerals / SASKATCHEWAN

Charles
Fort Chipewyan
Embarras Portage
Davy L.
Waterbury L.
Reindeer Lake
350
Kinoosao
Goldsand L.
Barrington L.
South Indian Lake
Gods L.
Gods River
Shamattawa
Beaverstone

Firebag
Lloyd L.
Clearwater
Cree L.   478
Highrock L.
Geikie
Wathaman L.
Nokomis L.
Oliver L.
Lynn Lake
Leaf Rapids
Laurie L.
Granville L.
Rat
Baldock L.
Split Lake   Nelson
Split L.
Ilford
Gillam
Fox
Hayes
Weir
Gods
Edmund L.
Sharpe L.
Still L.
Severn L.
Bearskin Lake
Big Trout Lake

CLEARWATER RIVER PROV PARK
Clearwater
Careen L.
Wasekamio L.
Black Birch L.
Upper Foster L.
Lower Foster L.
Deception L.
Macoun L.
Southend
Kamuchawie L.
Herriot
Loon
Russell L.
Highrock
Nelson
Nelson House
Burntwood
Paint L.
Thompson
Arnot
Pikwitonei
Odei
Knee L.
Oxford L.
Gods
Red Sucker L.
Ponask L.
Sachigo
Big Trout
Gordon L.
Wasekamio
Turnor L.
Porter L.
Daly L.
Brabant L.
Otter L.
Sisipuk L.
Kipahigan
Keewatin
Wabowden
Cross L.
Walker L.
Beaver Hill L.
Setting L.
Sipiwesk L.
Atik L.
Bear L.
Molson L.
Stull L.
Severn L.
McFarlane L.
Turnor
La Loche
Frobisher L.
Mudjatik
Foster
McIntosh L.
Brochet
Flin Flon
Cranberry Portage
Grass River PROV PARK
Snow Lake
Wekusko
Grass
Cross Lake
Norway House
Playgreen L.
Bigstone L.
Stevenson L.
Gunisao
Gunisao L.
Mukutawa
Finger L.
Sandy Lake
Sandy L.
North Caribou L.

Peter Pond L.
Dillon
Buffalo Narrows
Churchill L.
Knee L.
Pine-house L.
Sandy Bay
Manawan L.
Pelican Narrows
Mirond L.
Kississing L.
Reed L.
Creighton
Cormorant
N. Moose L.
Minago
Nelson
Island L.
OPASQUIA PROV. PARK
Deer
Deer L.
McInnes
MacDowell
Cat Lake
Cat L.

Conklin
Winefred L.
McCusker L.
Ile-à-la-Crosse
Lac Ile-à-la-Crosse
Besnard L.
Nemeiben L.
Stanley
Churchill
Wood L.
Jan L.
Wapawekka L.
Wanless
Cormorant L.
Cormorant
Clearwater L.
Moose Lake
S. Moose L.
Poplar
Berens River
Fishing
Stout L.
Pikangikum
Berens
Birch L.
Bamaji
St. Joseph

Cold L.
Primrose L.
Arsenault L.
Canoe L.
Beauval
Lac la Plonge
La Ronge
LAC LA RONGE PROV. PARK
365
Lac La Ronge
Egg L.
Smoothstone L.   680
Deschambault L.
Amisk L.
Namew L.
CLEARWATER L. PROV. PARK
GRASS RIVER PROV. PARK
The Pas
Cedar Lake
Easterville
Grand Rapids
LAKE WINNIPEG
Berens
Little Grand Rapids
Family
Cairns
Trout L.
Ear Falls

C

Grand Centre
Bonnyville
Pierceland
Meadow Lake
MEADOW LAKE PROV. PARK
Green Lake
Delaronde L.
Cree L.
Montreal L.
Montreal Lake
Candle L.
NARROW HILLS PROV. PARK
Cumberland L.
Cumberland House
Tobin L.
Saskatchewan
Carrot
Westray
Moose Lake
Selkirk I.
Grand Rapids
Lake Winnipegosis
252
Reindeer
217   Berens
Poplar
Deer L.
ONTARIO
MacDowell
Pipestone
Elk Point
N. Saskatchewan
St. Walburg
Loon Lake
Cowan
Big River
Waskesiu Lake
PRINCE ALBERT NAT. PARK
Paddockwood
Smeaton
Nipawin
Carrot River
Arborfield
Red Deer
Hudson Bay
Dawson
Swan L.
Lake Winnipegosis
Waterhen
St. Martin
Fisher
Berens River
Arborg
Fisher
Pine
Falls
Powell L.

Vermilion
Paradise Hill
Turtleford
Glaslyn
Spiritwood
Shellbrook
Prince Albert
Meath Park
Debden
Leask
Kinistino
Tisdale
Star City
Red Deer
Mafeking
Birch River
Pelican
Swan River
Camperville
Gypsumville
Fairford
Hodgson
Riverton
Hecla
Victoria Beach
Sydney
Pinewa
WHITESHELL PROV. PARK
Falcon Lake
Minaki
Kenora
Vermilion Bay
Dryden
Dinorwic

Lloydminster
Maidstone
Edam
Denholm
North Battleford
Battle
Blaine L.
Duck Lake
Birch Hills
Melfort
Lenore
Naicam
Watson
Kelvington
Rose Valley
Preeceville
Swan River
Winnipegosis
Dauphin
Ste. Rose du Lac
Dog L.
Eriksdale
Ashern
Arborg
Gimli
Winnipeg Beach
Pine Falls
Lac du Bonnet
Beausejour
Elma
Keewatin
Sioux Lookout
Minnitaki L.
Wabigoon L.
Wainwright
Irma
Lashburn
Mervin
Turtle L.
Leoville
Rosthern
Aberdeen
Prud'homme
Humboldt
Lanigan
Wadena
Buchanan
Canora
Roblin
Grand View
RIDING MOUNTAIN NATIONAL PARK
248
Amaranth
McCreary
Teulon
Selkirk
Stonewall
Pinawa
Steinbach
Shoal L.
Hudson
Red Lake Road
Minnitaki
Dryden
Eagle L.
Lower Manitou L.
White Otter L.

D

Chauvin
Provost
Macklin
Unity
Wilkie
Radisson
Warman
Saskatoon
Colonsay
Allan
Young
Watrous
Nokomis
Foam Lake
Theodore
Manitoba
Sheho
St. Martin
St. Laurent
Gladstone
Portage la Prairie
WINNIPEG
Niverville
Carman
Morris
Woodridge
Sprague
Sydney
Whitemouth
Rennie
Falcon Lake
Rainy
White
Ignace
Consort
Youngstown
Kindersley
Alsask
Oyen
Eatonia
Milden
Rosetown
Conquest
Outlook
Elrose
Kyle
Central Butte
Riverhurst
Davidson
Craik
Imperial
Last Mountain L.
Strasbourg
Raymore
Lestock
Ituna
Melville
Langenburg
Esterhazy
Russell
Rossburn
Binscarth
Shoal Lake
Neepawa
Minnedosa
Birtle
Beulah
Brandon
Carberry
Treherne
Elm Creek
St. Claude
Steinbach
Vassar
Warroad
International Falls
Fort Frances
QUETICO PROV. PARK
Lac la Croix
Atikokan

876
Eston
Kindersley
Milden
Elbow
Diefenbaker
Herbert
Chaplin
Mortlach
Moose Jaw
Regina
Pense
Rouleau
Milestone
Sedley
Qu'Appelle
Fort Qu'Appelle
Balcarres
Cupar
Regina Beach
Lumsden
Indian Head
Grenfell
Whitewood
Moosomin
Virden
Kipling
Montmartre
Pipestone
Elkhorn
Carberry
Souris
Glenboro
Wawanesa
Carman
Morden
Winkler
Altona
Emerson
Pembina
Warren
Roseau
Thief River Falls
Red Lake Falls
Crookston
Erskine
Cass L.
Bemidji
Hibbing
Virginia

Medicine Hat
CYPRESS HILLS PROV. PARK
1466
Cypress Hills
Maple Creek
Gull Lake
Swift Current
Chaplin
Old Wives L.
Moose Jaw
Avonlea
Weyburn
Stoughton
Carlyle
Redvers
Reston
Hartney
Souris
Pilot Mound
Manitou
Morden
Killarney
Boissevain
Deloraine
Melita
762
Killarney
Rolla
Langdon
Karlstad
Upper Red L.
Lower Red L.
Red L.
Bagley
Walker
Leech L.
Pine River
Grand Rapids
Hill City

Redcliff
Irvine
Piapot
Simmie
Neville
Vanguard
Gravelbourg
Assiniboia
Willow Bunch
Bengough
Radville
Lampman
Estevan
North Portal
Bowbells
Mohall
Rugby
Cando
Lakota
Devils Lake
Northwood
Grand Forks
Mayville
Hillsboro
Ada
Mahnomen
Park Rapids
Pine City
Floodwood
Cloquet

Schuler
Fox Valley
Pennant
Eastend
Shaunavon
Frenchman
Val Marie
Mankota
GRASSLANDS NAT PARK
Rockglen
Coronach
Minton
Outlook
Westby
Plentywood
Scobey
Kenmare
Stanley
Velva
Minot
Granville
Towner
Larimore
Grand Forks
East Grand Forks
Red
Warren
Greenbush
Fosston
Deer River
Grand Rapids

Orion
Pakowki L.
Consul
Turner
Opheim
Milk
Ray
Williston
Watford City
Garrison
Lake Sakakawea
Carrington
Cooperstown
Fargo
Bagley
Grand Rapids
Duluth
Superior

MONTANA
Big Sandy
Chinook
Havre
Chester
Harlem
Malta
Milk
Saco
Glasgow
Nashua
Poplar
Fort Peck Lake
Fort Peck
Wolf Point
Culbertson
Fairview
Alexander
NORTH DAKOTA
Minot
New Rockford
Jamestown
Harvey
MINNESOTA
Walker
Cass L.
Leech L.
Bemidji
Duluth
Mississippi
Cloquet
Superior

Fresno Res.
Hingham

7   8   9   10

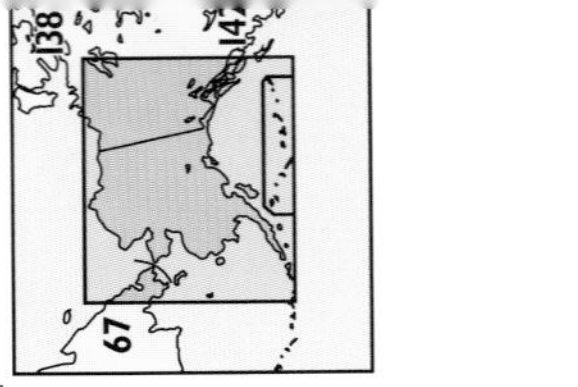

50 0 100 200 300 400 km
50 0 50 100 150 200 250 miles

Continuation Westwards on same scale

COPYRIGHT GEORGE PHILIP LTD.

CANADA

NORTH-WEST TERRITORIES

YUKON TERRITORY

BRITISH COLUMBIA

BEAUFORT SEA

ARCTIC OCEAN

CHUKCHI SEA

RUSSIA

Chukotskiy Poluostrov

BERING SEA

Gulf of Alaska

PACIFIC OCEAN

Aleutian Islands

Alexander Archipelago

Mackenzie Mts.
Franklin Mts.
Ogilvie Mts.
Selwyn Mountains
Pelly Mts.
Brooks Range
Endicott Mts.
Schwatka Mts.
De Long Mts.
Baird Mts.
Philip Smith Mts.
Romanzof Mts.
British Mts.
Richardson Mts.
White Mts.
Ray Mts.
Kuskokwim Mountains
ALASKA Range
Wrangell Mts.
Chugach Mts.
St. Elias Mts.
Kenai Mts.
Aleutian Range

Mt. McKinley 6194
Mt. Foraker 5304
Mt. Logan 5959
Mt. St. Elias 5489

Point Barrow
Barrow
Wainwright
Point Lay
Point Hope
Kotzebue
Nome
Bethel
Fairbanks
College
North Pole
Nenana
Anchorage
Palmer
Wasilla
Valdez
Cordova
Seward
Homer
Kenai
Soldotna
Kodiak
Dillingham
King Salmon
Juneau
Sitka
Ketchikan
Wrangell
Petersburg
Haines
Skagway
Whitehorse
Dawson
Inuvik
Fort McPherson
Old Crow
Eagle

Alaska Peninsula

Seward Peninsula

North Slope

Pribilof Is.
St. Paul I.
St. George I.
St. Lawrence I.
St. Matthew I.
Nunivak I.
Unimak I.
Unalaska
Dutch Harbor
Kodiak I.
Afognak I.
Shuyak I.
Montague I.

Near Is.
Attu I.
Agattu I.
Rat Islands
Kiska I.
Amchitka I.
Andreanof Islands
Adak I.
Atka I.
Tanaga I.
Islands of Four Mountains
Fox Islands
Umnak I.

Prince of Wales I.
Baranof I.
Chichagof I.
Admiralty I.
Kupreanof I.

Arctic Circle
Arctic Circle
International Date Line

West from Greenwich
East from Greenwich

Projection: Bipolar oblique conic conformal

ft m
9000 3000
6000 2000
4500 1500
3000 1000
1200 400
600 200
0 0
200 600
2000 6000
m ft

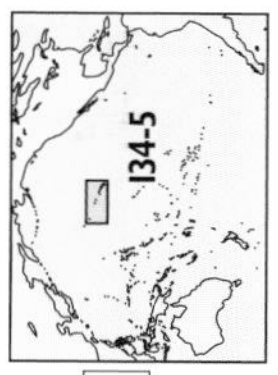

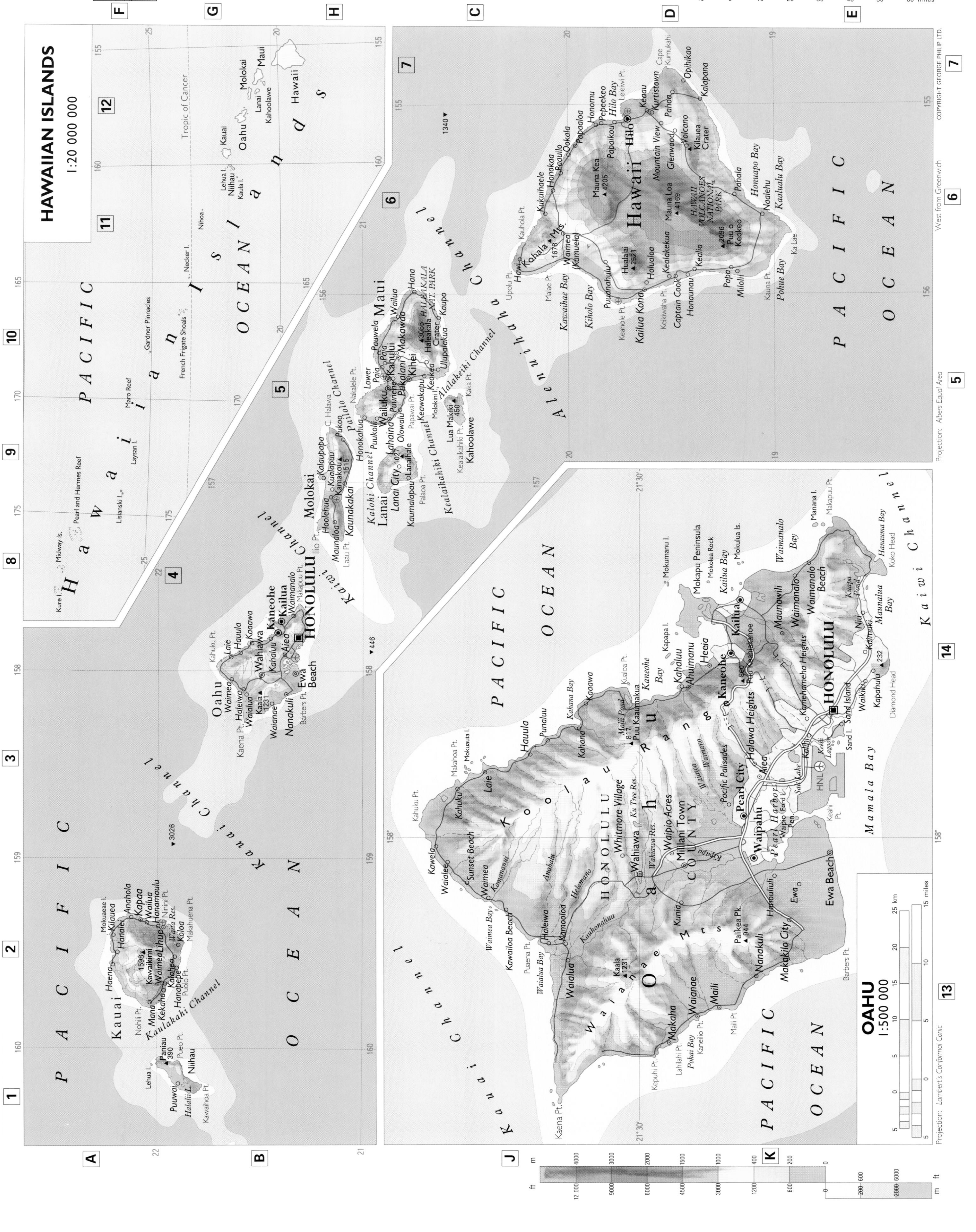

HAWAIIAN ISLANDS
1:20 000 000

10 0 10 20 30 40 50 60 70 80 90 km
10 0 10 20 30 40 50 60 miles

134–5

Main map labels

Tropic of Cancer

Kauai · Oahu · Molokai · Lanai · Maui · Kahoolawe · Hawaii

PACIFIC OCEAN

H a w a i i a n   I s l a n d s

Midway Is. · Kure I. · Pearl and Hermes Reef · Lisianski I. · Laysan I. · Maro Reef · Gardner Pinnacles · French Frigate Shoals · Necker I. · Nihoa · Lehua I. · Niihau · Kaula I.

Kauai
Haena · Kilauea · Mokuaeae · Anahola · Kapaa · Wailua · Hanamaulu · Lihue · Hanalei · Kekaha · Waimea · Kalaheo · Koloa · Kawaikini 1598 · Mana · Nohili Pt. · Iliiau Res. · Nonou Pt. · Makahuena Pt.

Niihau · Lehua I. · Puuwai 390 · Paniau · Halalii L. · Kawaihoa Pt. · Pueo Pt. · Kaulakahi Channel

Kauai Channel · ▼3026

Oahu
Kahuku Pt. · Laie · Waimea · Haleiwa · Kaaawa · Wahiawa · Kaneohe · Kailua · Kahaluu · Waimanalo · Aiea · HONOLULU · Kaala 1231 · Waianae · Nanakuli · Ewa Beach · Barbers Pt. · Kaena Pt. · ▼446

Kaiwi Channel

Molokai
Kalaupapa · Hoolehua · Hoolea · Kualapuu · Kamakou · Kaunakakai · Maunaloa · Ilio Pt. · Laau Pt. · Makapuu Pt.

Lanai
Lanai City · Kaumalapau · Palaoa Pt.

Maui
Honokohua · Lower Paia · Paia · Wailuku · Lahaina · Kahului · Puunene · Makawao · Kihei · Olowalu · Keokea · Ulupalakua · Kaupo · Makena · Hana · Wailua · Pauwela · HALEAKALA NAT. PARK · Haleakala Crater 3056 · Papawai Pt. · Molokini I. · Lua Makiki 450

Kahoolawe

Alalakeiki Channel · Kalohi Channel · Pailolo Channel · Kealaikahiki Channel · Kealaikahiki Pt. · Kaka Pt.

Alenuihaha Channel

Hawaii
Upolu Pt. · Hawi · Kohala Mts. · Kapaau · Honokaa · Kukuihaele · Waimea (Kamuela) 1677 · Honomu · Pepeekeo · Papaikou · Hilo · Kea'au · Keaau · Kurtistown · Mountain View · Glenwood · Volcano · Kilauea Crater · Pahoa · Kalapana · Opihikao · Cape Kumukahi · Mauna Kea ▲4205 · Mauna Loa ▲4169 · Hualalai ▲2521 · Kealakekua · Kealia · Puu o Keokeo ▲2096 · HAWAII VOLCANOES NATIONAL PARK · Kahola Pt. · Kawaihae Bay · Kailua Kona · Keauhou · Keahole Pt. · Kiholo Bay · Keokea · Captain Cook · Honaunau · Honuapo Bay · Papa · Milolii · Kaulualu Bay · Naalehu · Pahala · Ka Lae · Kauna Pt. · Pohue Bay · Malae Pt.

▼1340

PACIFIC OCEAN

West from Greenwich
Projection: Albers Equal Area
COPYRIGHT GEORGE PHILIP LTD.

OAHU inset
1:500 000

Kaena Pt. · Kawela · Waialee · Sunset Beach · Waimea · Kawailoa · Haleiwa · Kahuku · Laie · Hauula · Punaluu · Kahana · Kaaawa · Kualoa Pt. · Kaneohe Bay · Kahaluu · Heeia · Kaneohe · Mokapu Peninsula · Kailua Bay · Kailua · Mokulua Is. · Waimanalo · Waimanalo Beach · Makapuu Pt. · Manana I. · Mokolea Rock · Mokumanu I. · Kapapa I.

Waialua · Waialua Bay · Waimea Bay · Kamaloa · Anahulu · Wahiawa · Whitmore Village · Mililani Town · Waipio Acres · Wahiawa Res. · Ka Tree Res. · Waipahu · Waipio Pen. · Pearl City · Aiea · Pearl Harbor · Halawa Heights · Pacific Palisades · Puu Kaaumakua · Moli Paliali 817 · HONOLULU · Salt Lake · HNL · Sand Island · HONOLULU · Waikiki · Kaimuki · Kahala · Diamond Head · Niu 232 · Kuapa · Hanauma Bay · Koko Head · Kamehameha Heights · Puu Koaulelehoe

Waianae · Makaha · Maili · Nanakuli · Makakilo City · Honouliuli · Ewa · Ewa Beach · Barbers Pt. · Kaena Pt. · Kepuhi Pt. · Lahilahi Pt. · Makahoa Pt. · Kaneilio Pt. · Pokai Bay

Kaala 1231 · Palikea Pk. 944 · Waianae Range · Koolau Range · Kanehonua

Mamala Bay · Waimanalo Bay · Maunalua Bay

Kaiwi Channel · Kauai Channel

HONOLULU COUNTY

PACIFIC OCEAN

OAHU
1:500 000
5 0 5 10 15 20 25 km
5 0 5 10 15 miles

Projection: Lambert's Conformal Conic

Elevation scale
m · ft
4000 · 12000
3000 · 9000
2000 · 6000
1500 · 4500
1000 · 3000
600 · 1800
400 · 1200
200 · 600
0
200–600 · 2000
6000 · ft
m

A B C D E F G H J K
1 2 3 4 5 6 7
8 9 10 11 12 13 14

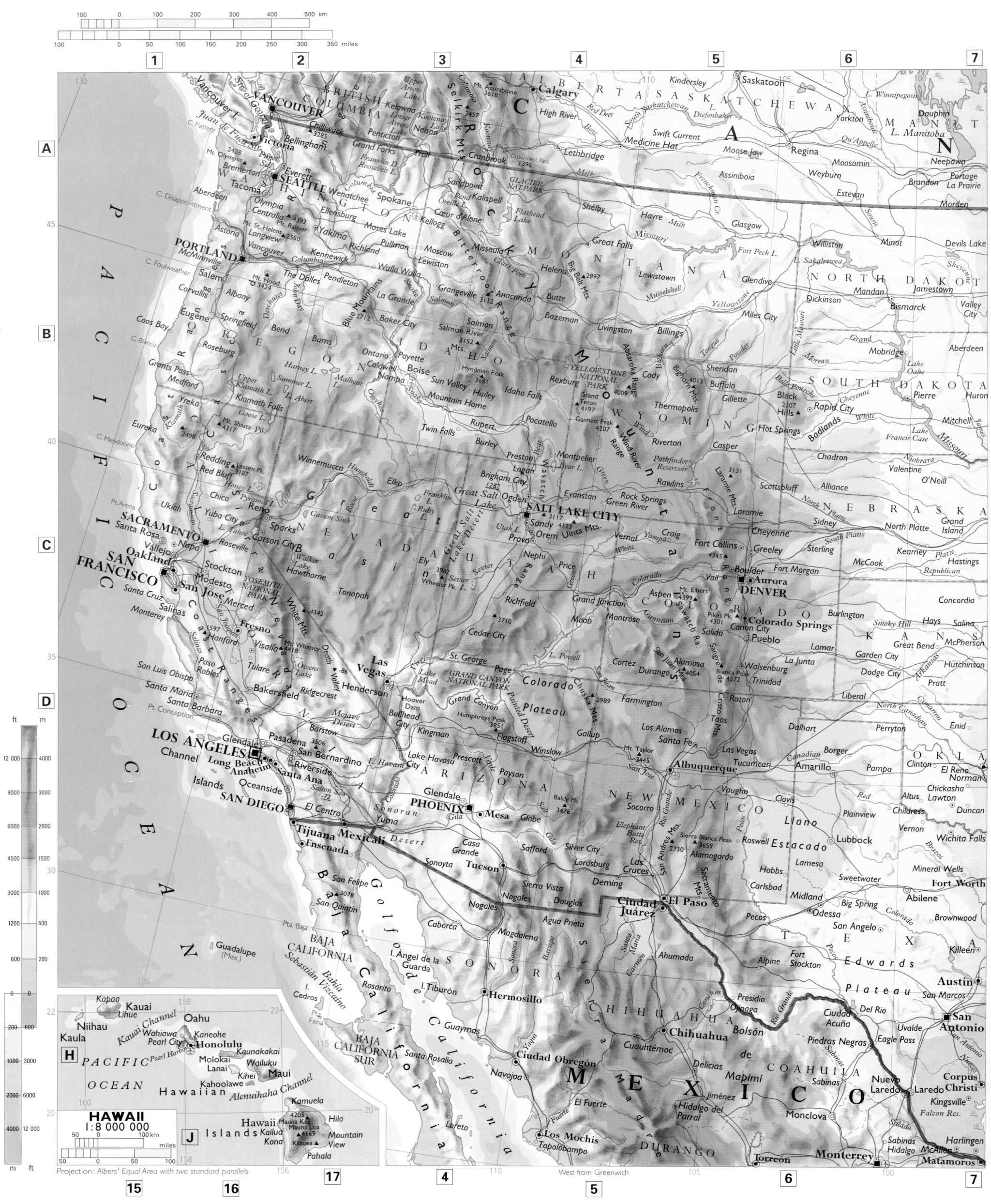

Projection: Albers' Equal Area with two standard parallels

COPYRIGHT GEORGE PHILIP LTD.

50   0   50   100   150   200 km
50   0   50   100   150 miles

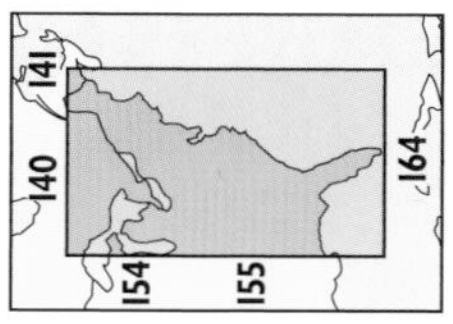

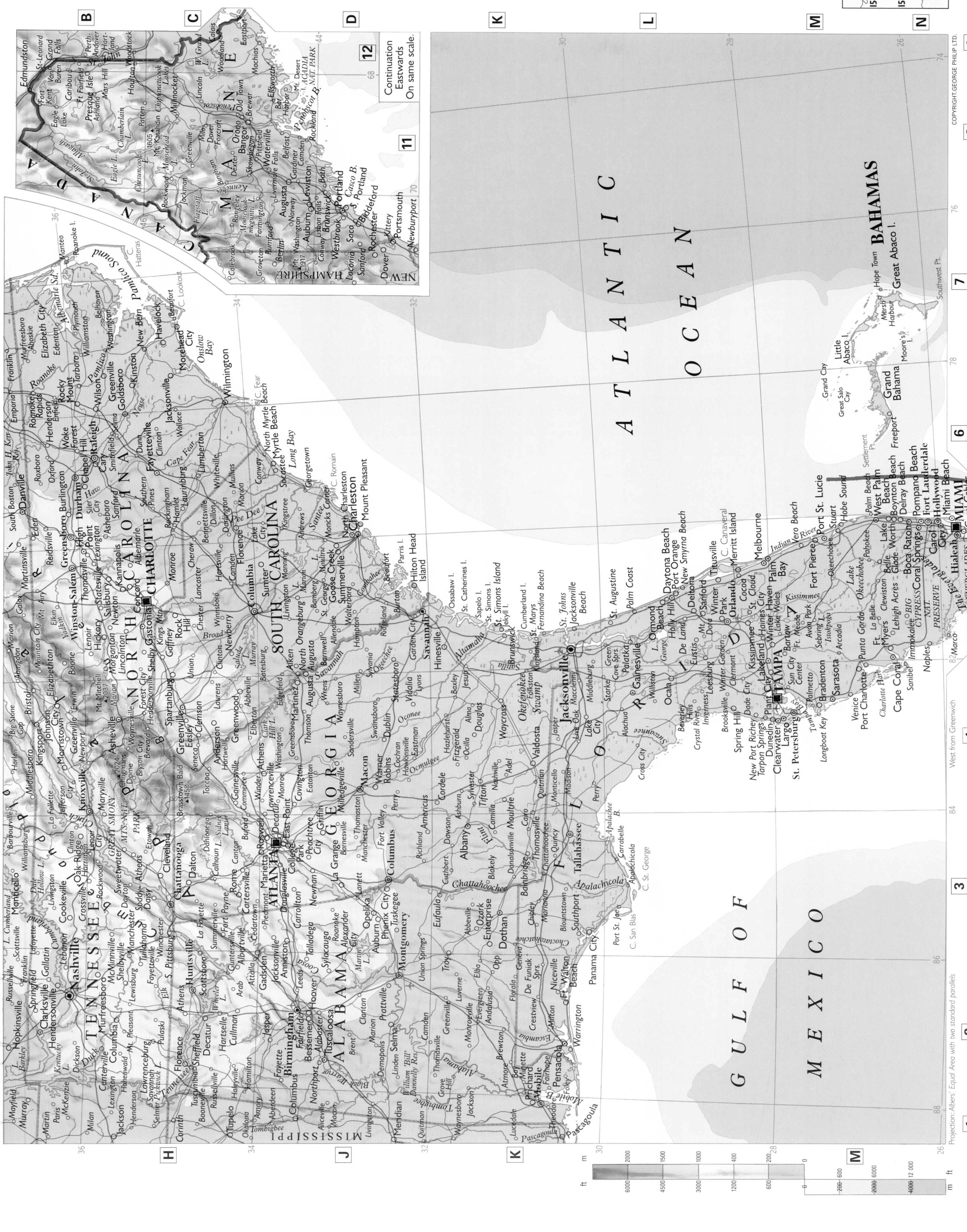

ATLANTIC OCEAN

GULF OF MEXICO

BAHAMAS

Great Abaco I.

Grand Bahama

FLORIDA

GEORGIA

ALABAMA

MISSISSIPPI

TENNESSEE

NORTH CAROLINA

SOUTH CAROLINA

MAINE

NEW HAMPSHIRE

CANADA

GREAT SMOKY MTS. NAT. PARK

EVERGLADES NAT. PARK

BIG CYPRESS NAT. PRESERVE

ACADIA NAT. PARK

ATLANTA

CHARLOTTE

TAMPA

MIAMI

Nashville

Jacksonville

Continuation Eastwards
On same scale.

Projection: Albers' Equal Area with two standard parallels

West from Greenwich

COPYRIGHT GEORGE PHILIP LTD.

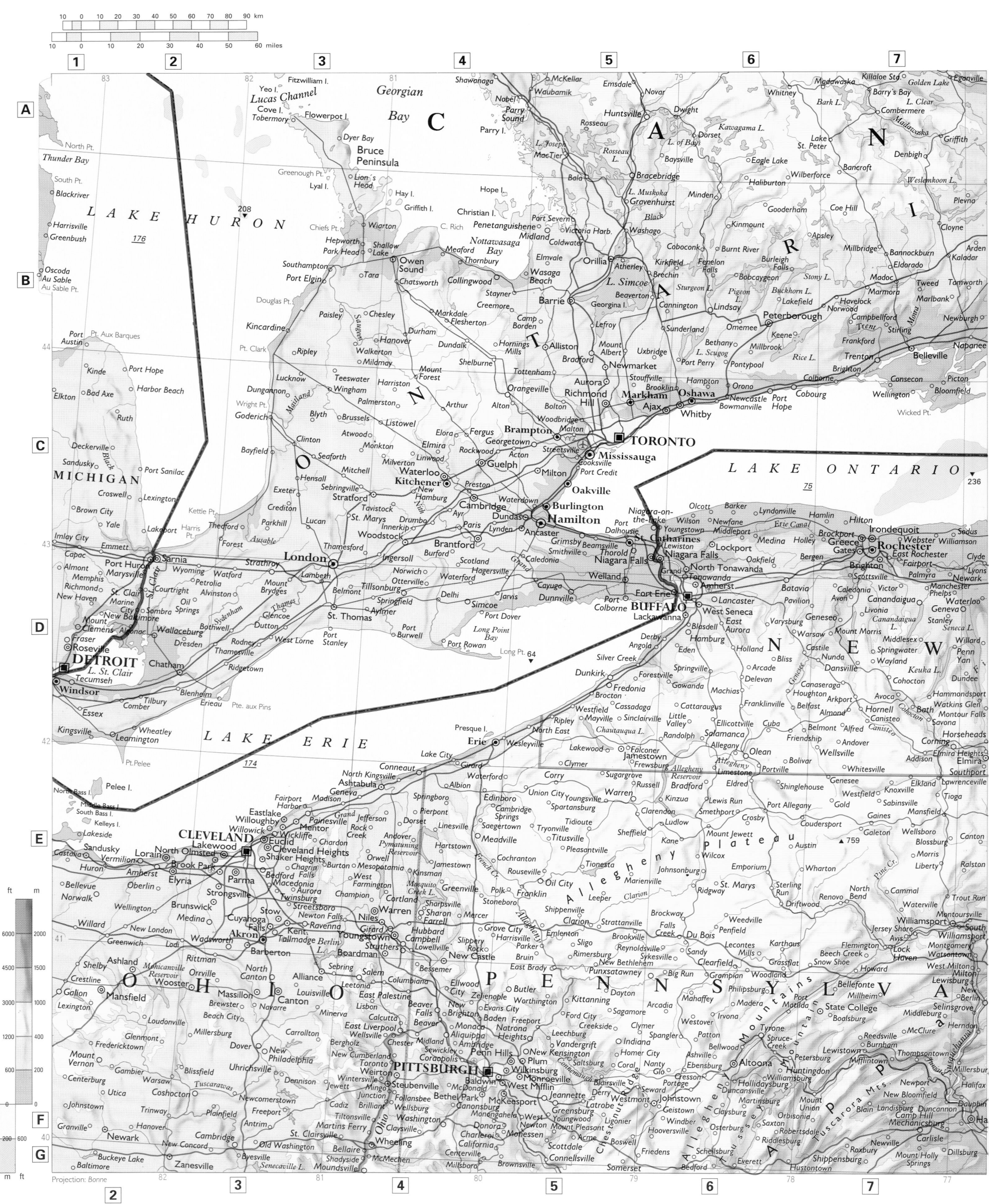

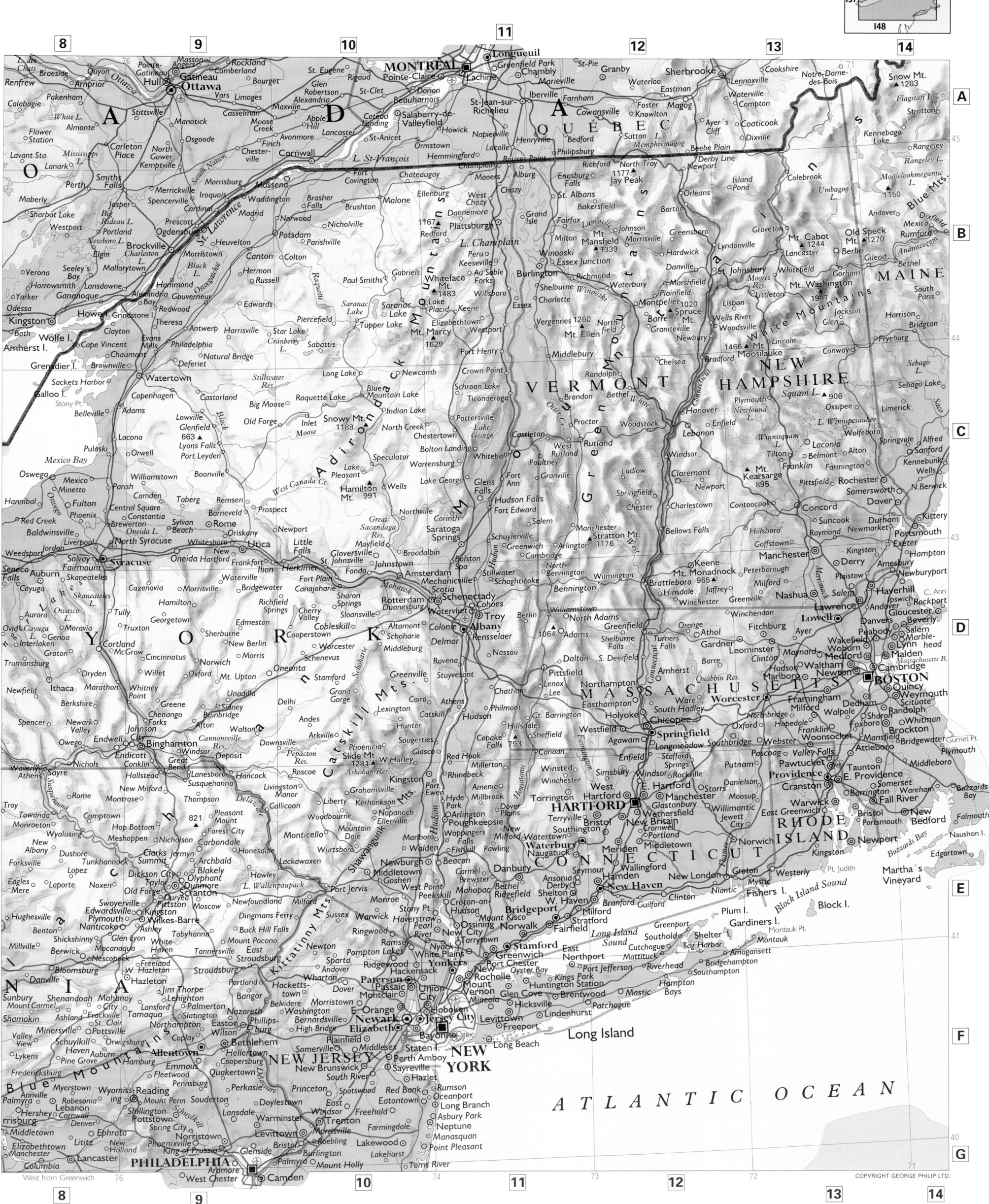

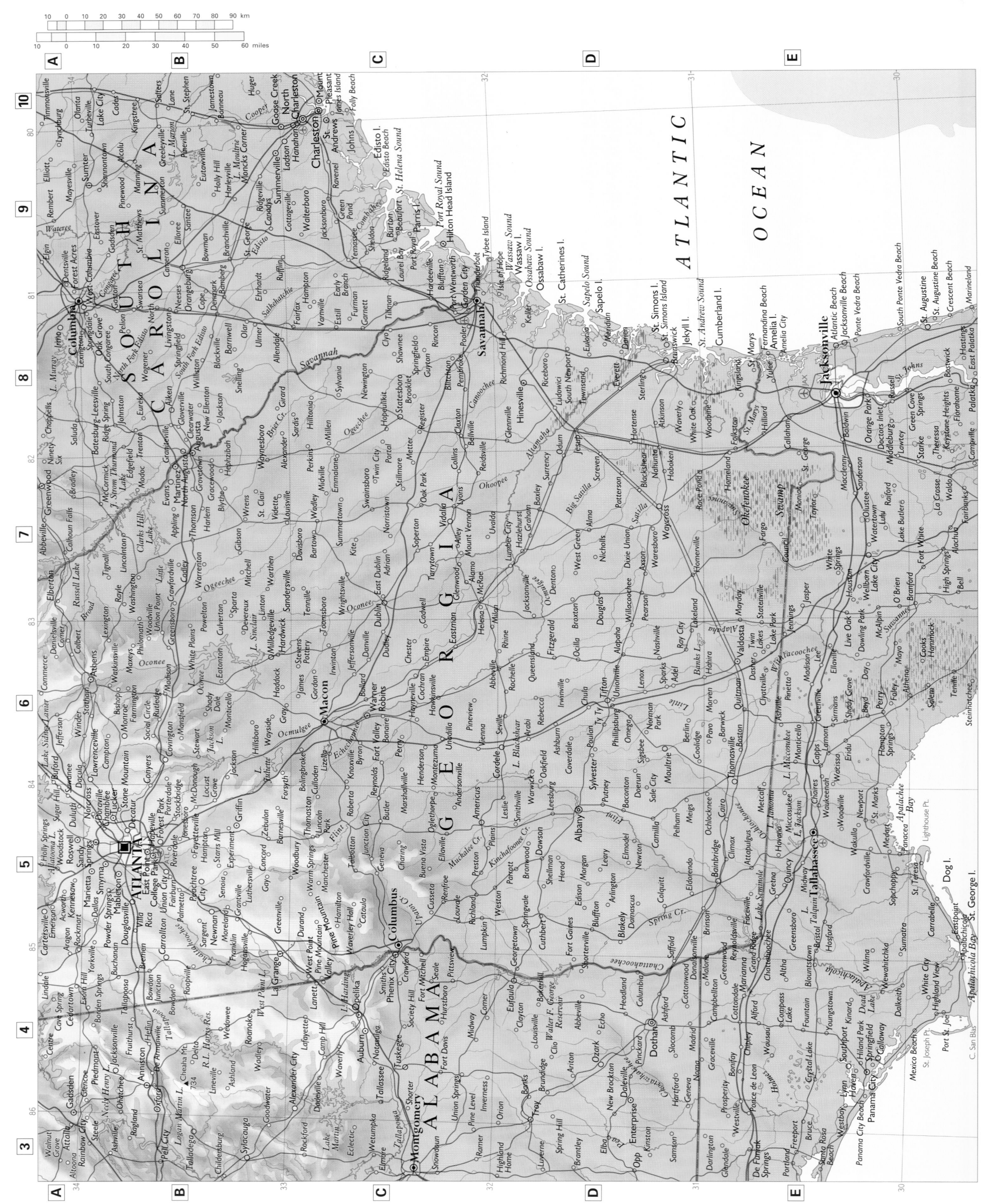

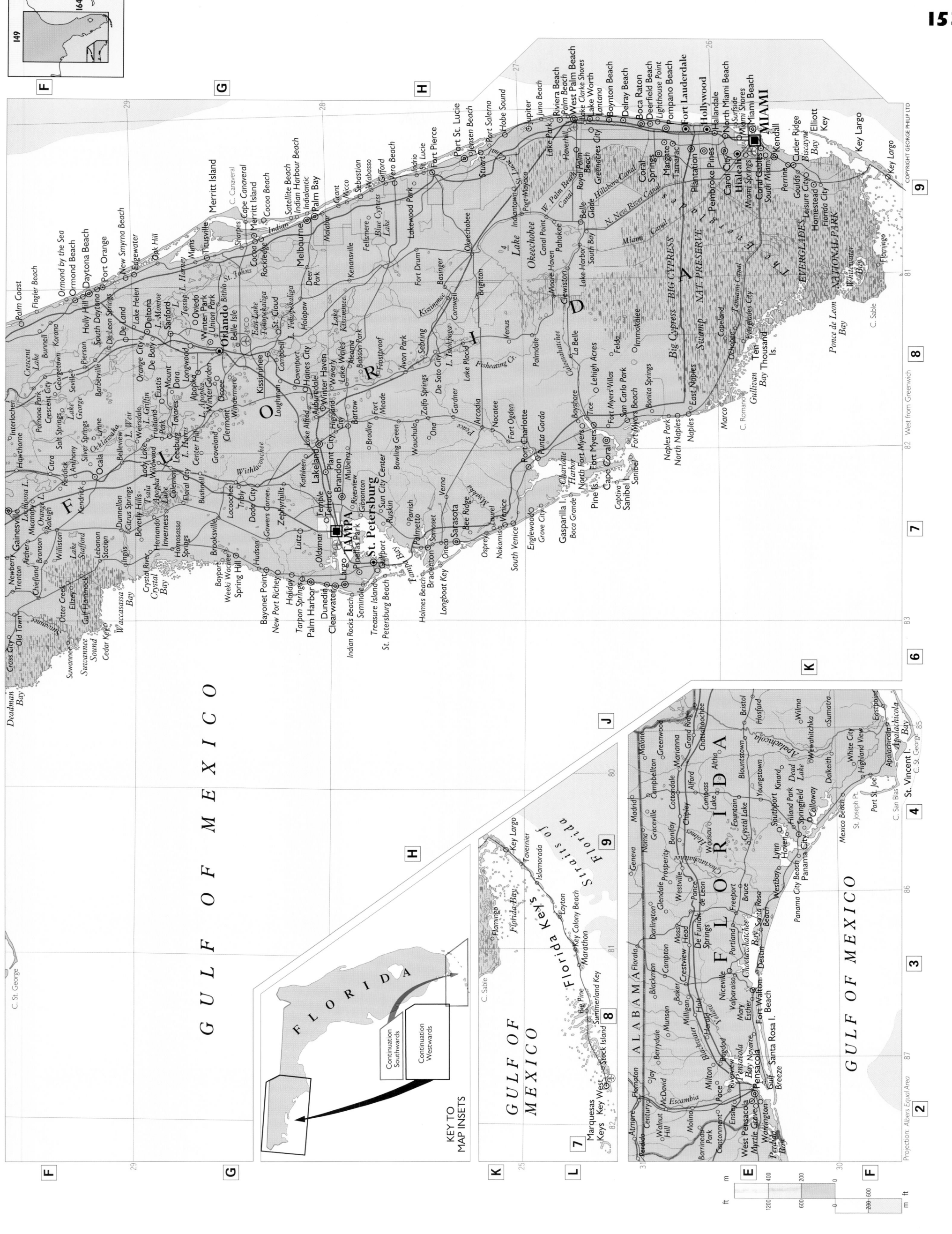

COPYRIGHT GEORGE PHILIP LTD

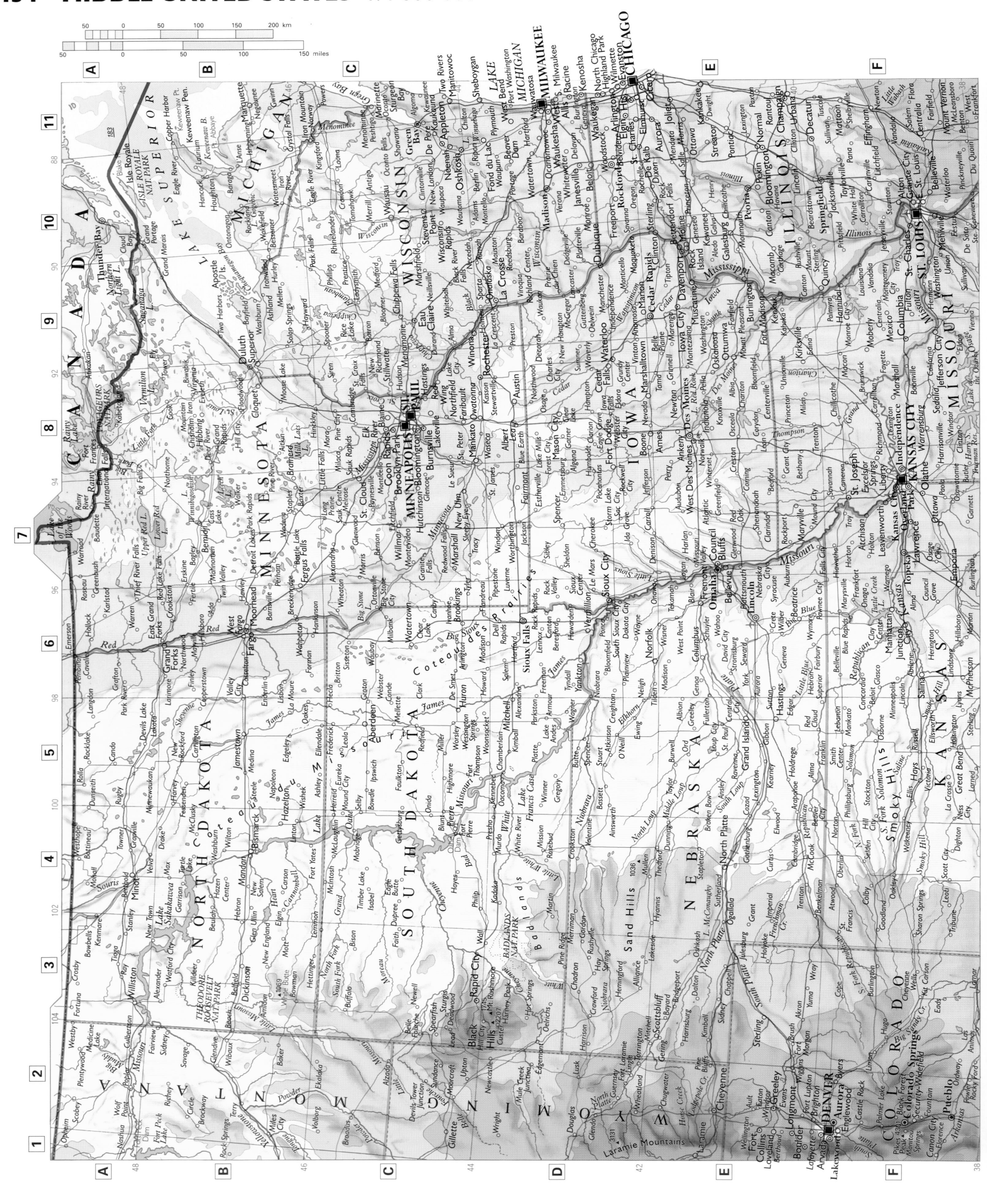

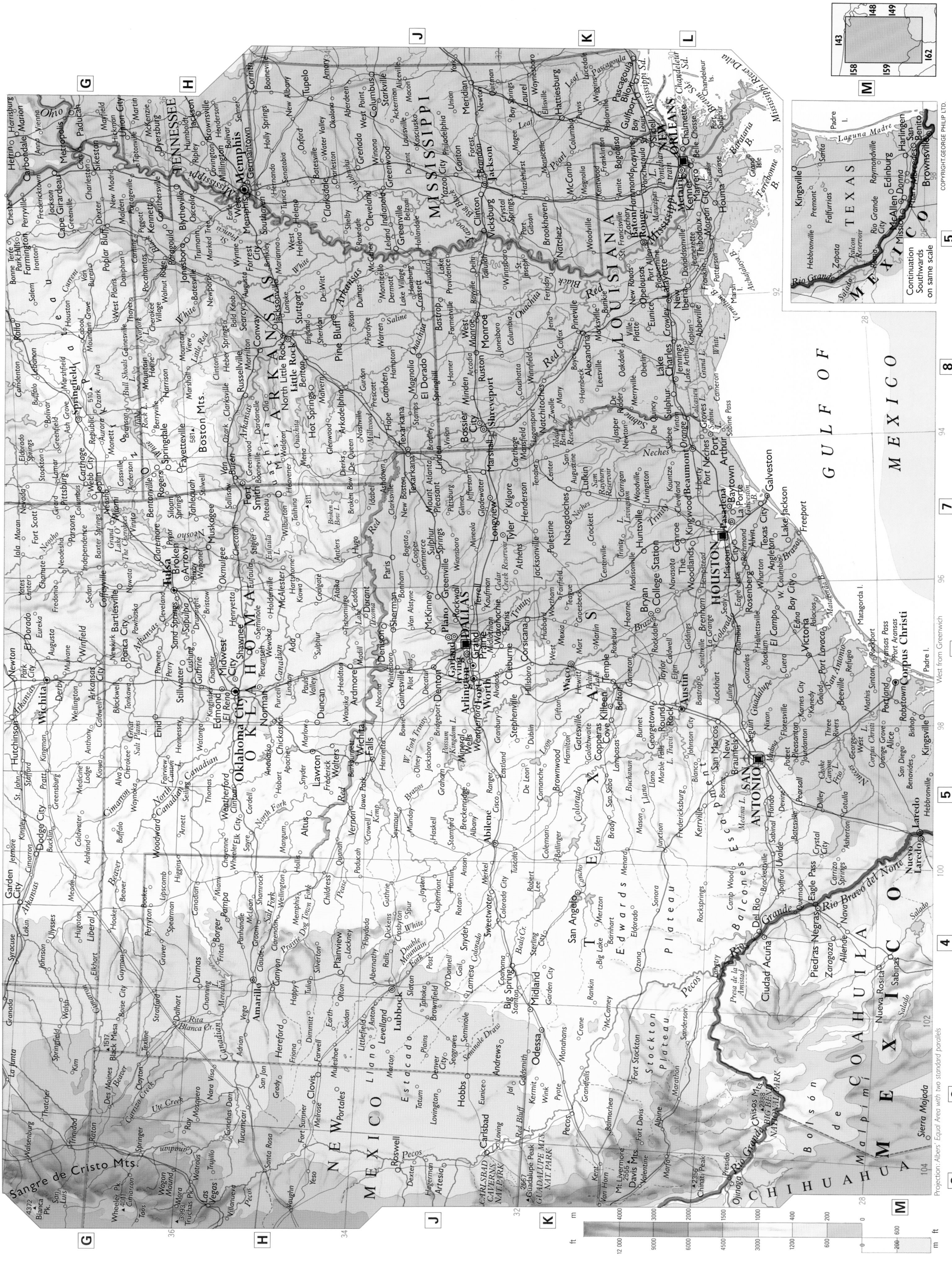

TENNESSEE

MISSISSIPPI

ARKANSAS

OKLAHOMA

LOUISIANA

TEXAS

NEW MEXICO

KANSAS

MEXICO

COAHUILA

CHIHUAHUA

GULF OF MEXICO

Memphis
Little Rock
Tulsa
Oklahoma City
Wichita
Dallas
Fort Worth
Arlington
Houston
San Antonio
Austin
Amarillo
Lubbock
Odessa
Midland
El Paso
Corpus Christi
Laredo
Nuevo Laredo
New Orleans
Baton Rouge
Shreveport
Jackson
Galveston
Beaumont
Port Arthur

Mississippi R.
Arkansas R.
Red R.
Rio Grande
Rio Bravo del Norte
Canadian R.
Pecos R.
Brazos R.
Colorado R.

Boston Mts.
Ouachita Mts.
Sangre de Cristo Mts.
Edwards Plateau
Llano Estacado
Stockton Plateau
Guadalupe Mts.
Davis Mts.
Chisos Mts.
Big Bend National Park
Carlsbad Caverns Nat. Park

Laguna Madre
Padre I.
Mississippi River Delta
Chandeleur Sd.

Gulf of Mexico

COPYRIGHT.GEORGE PHILIP LTD.

Continuation Southwards on same scale

Projection: Albers' Equal Area with two standard parallels

West from Greenwich

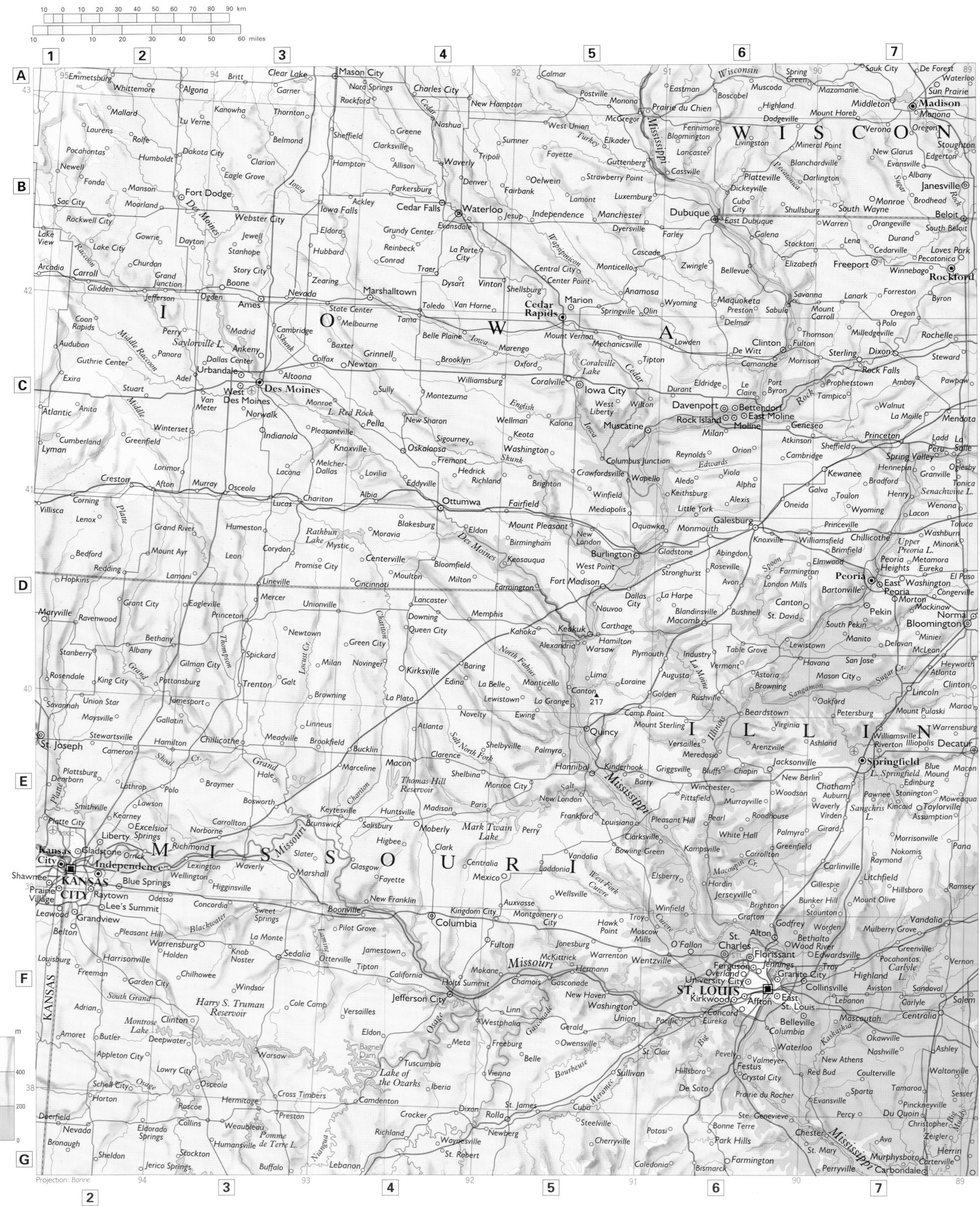

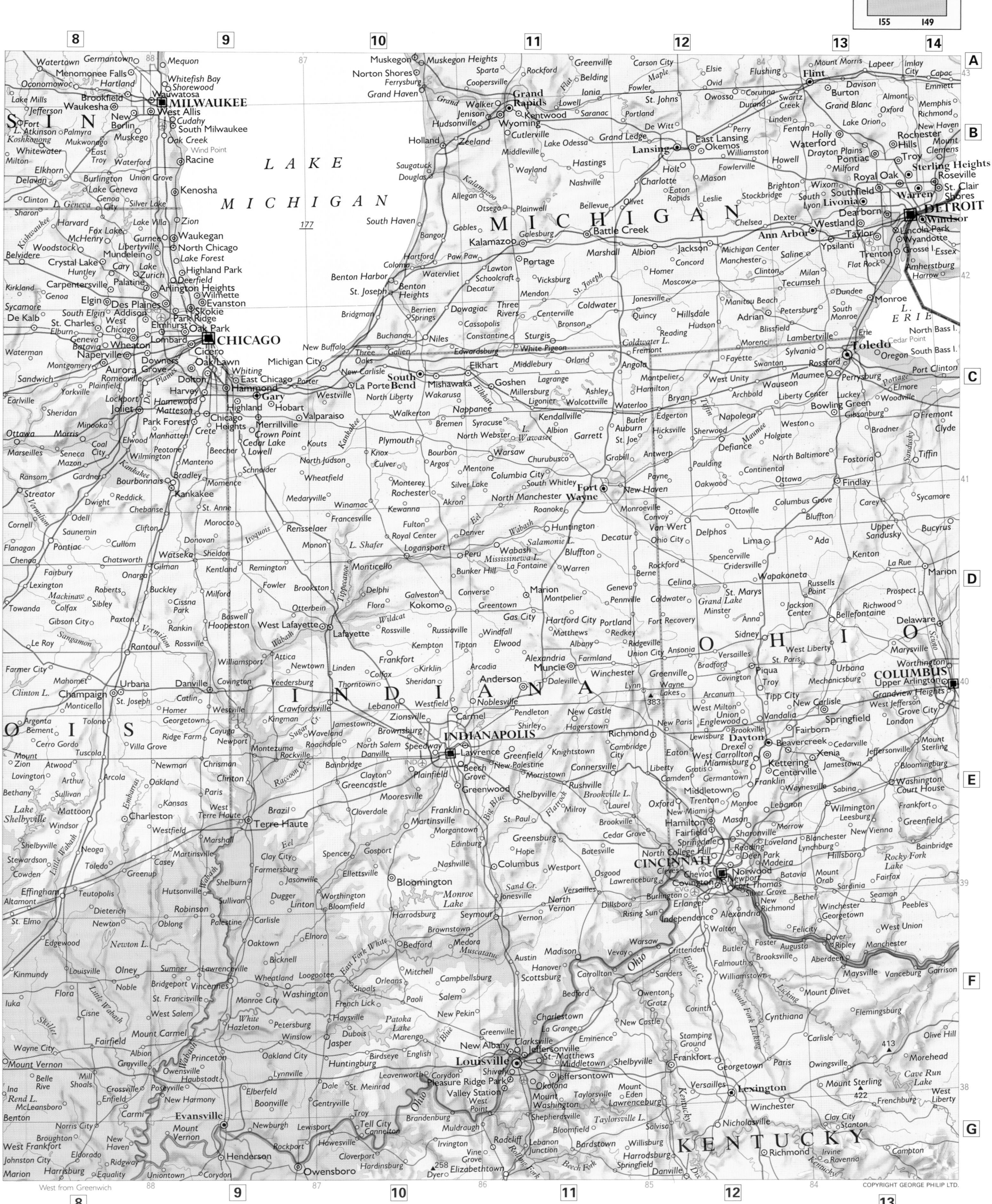

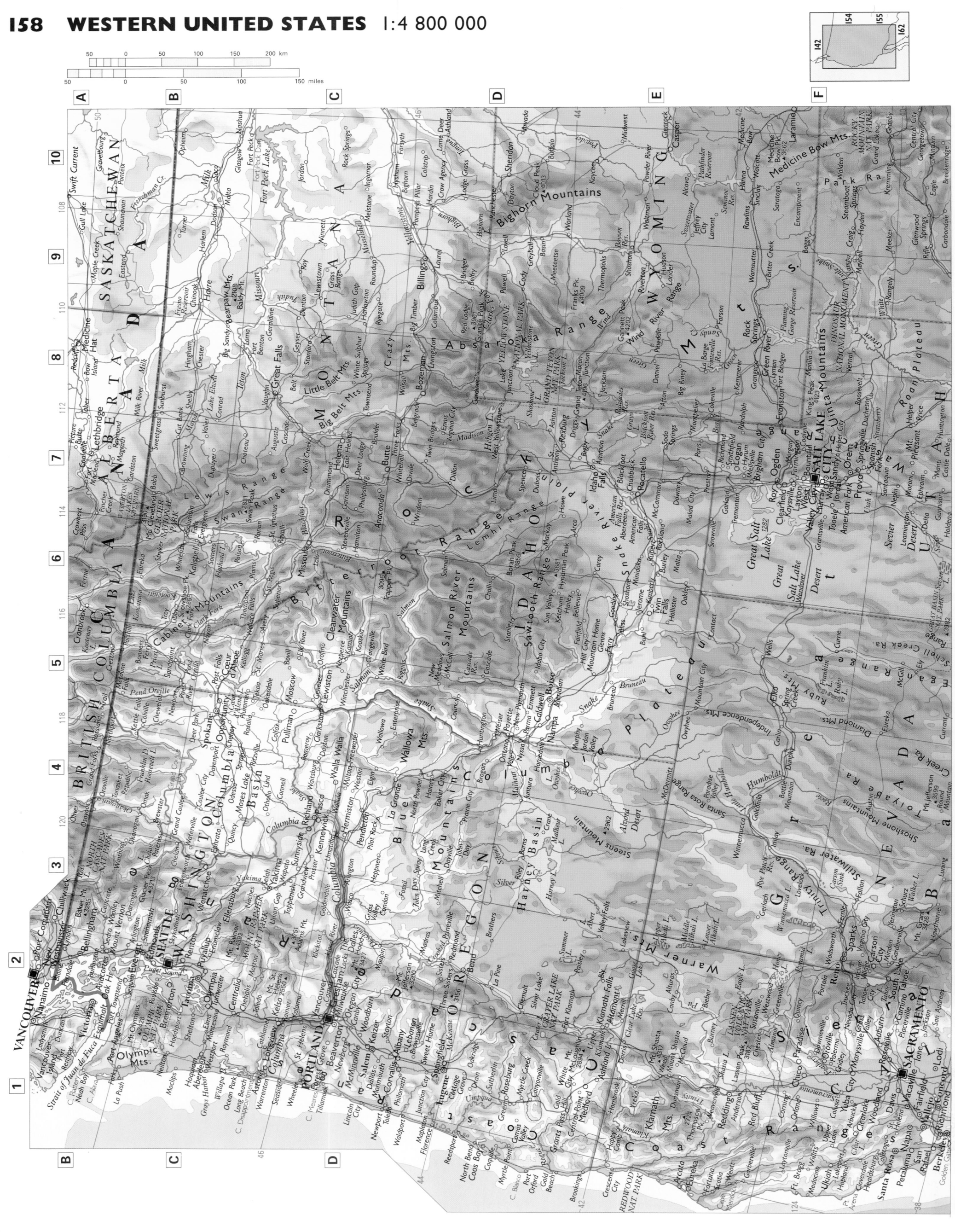

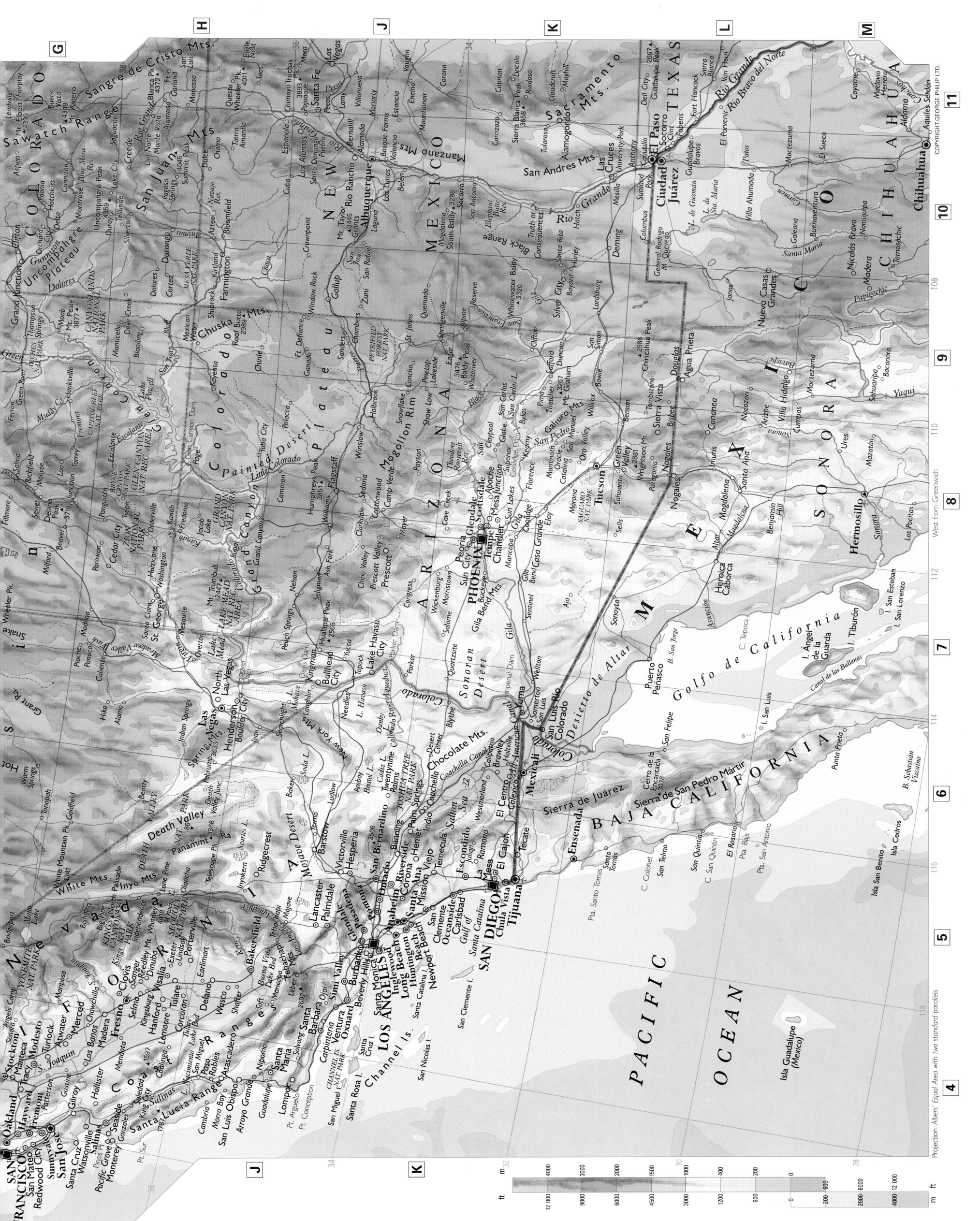

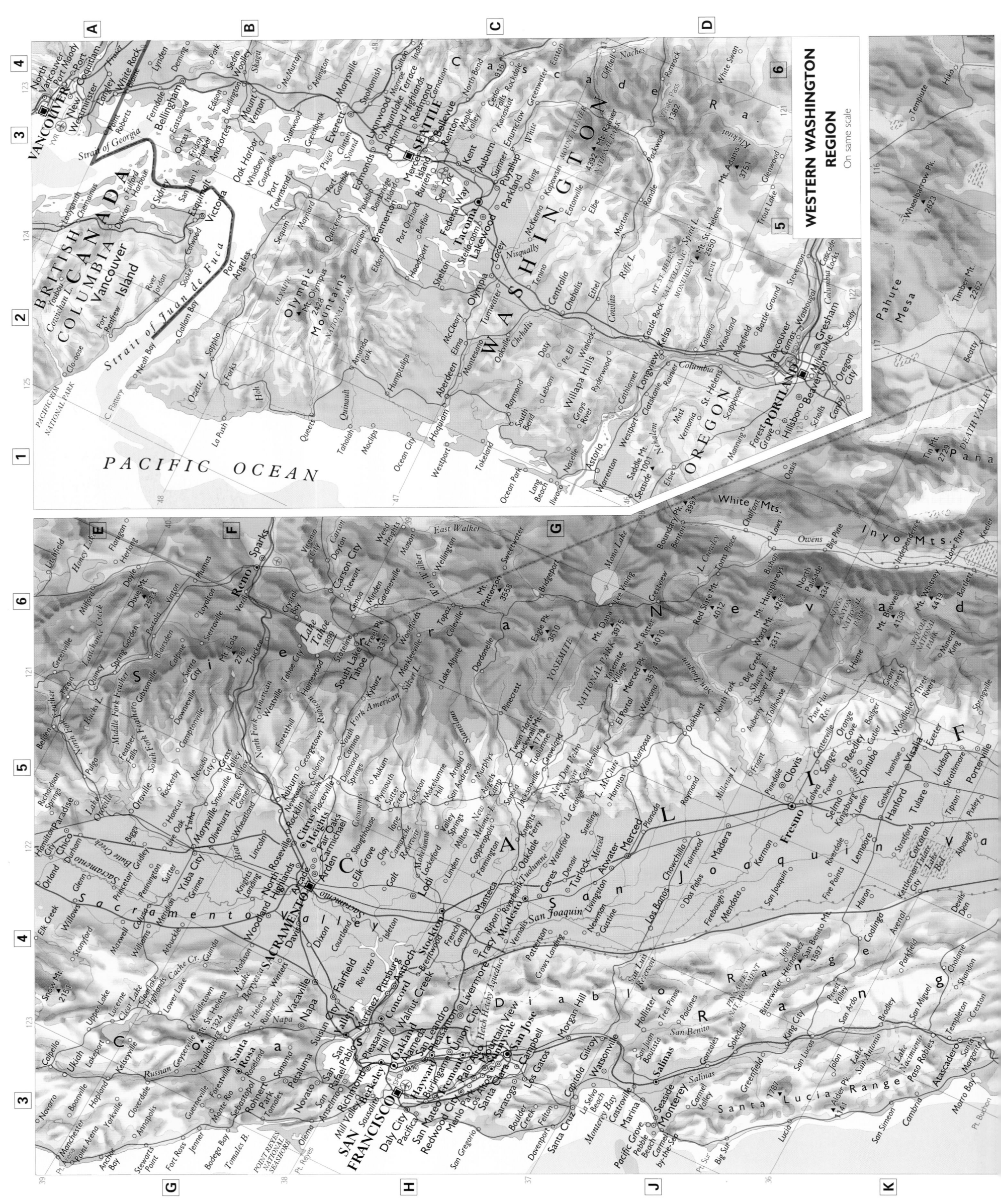

WESTERN WASHINGTON REGION
On same scale

PACIFIC OCEAN

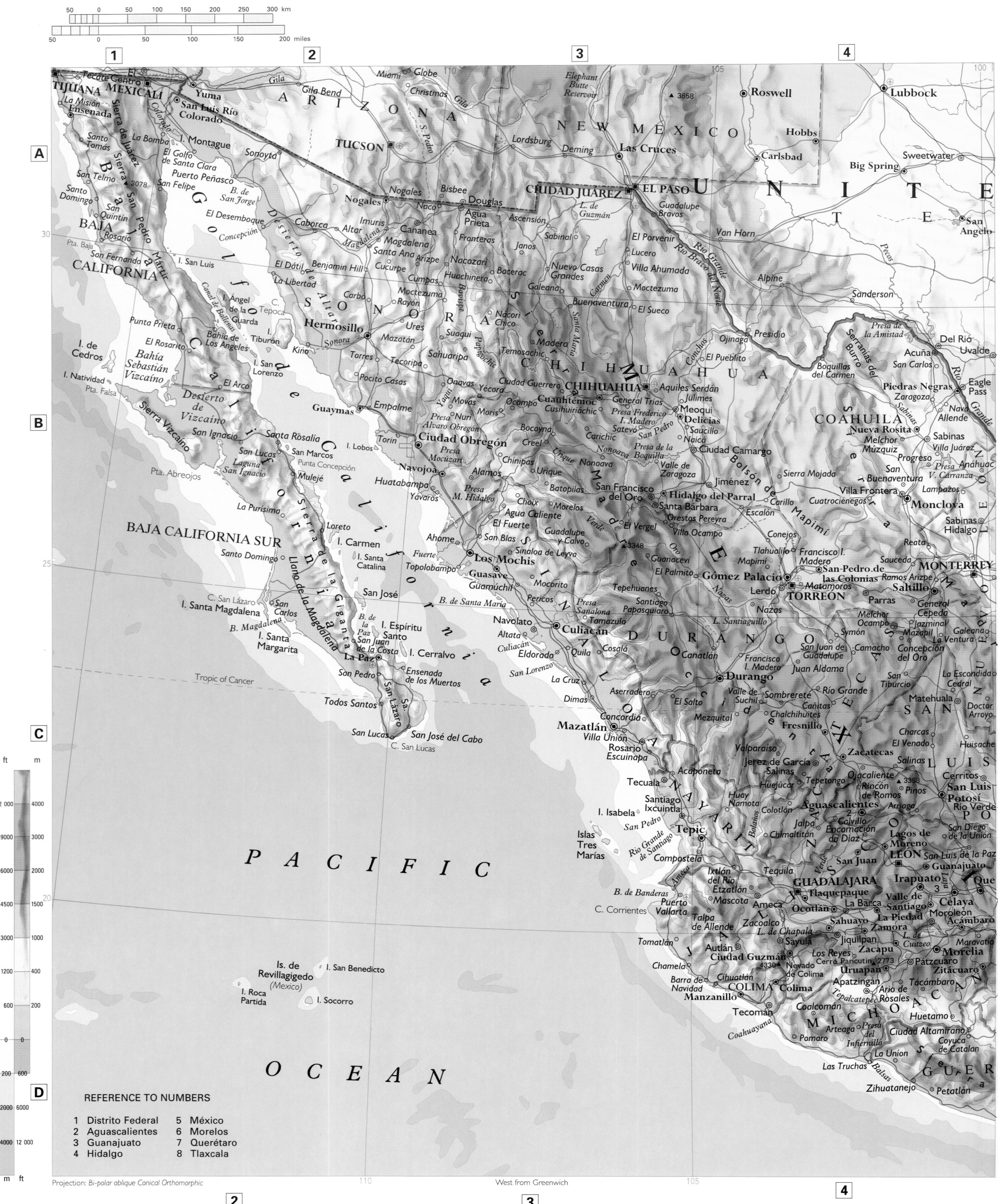

REFERENCE TO NUMBERS

1 Distrito Federal   5 México
2 Aguascalientes   6 Morelos
3 Guanajuato   7 Querétaro
4 Hidalgo   8 Tlaxcala

Projection: Bi-polar oblique Conical Orthomorphic   West from Greenwich

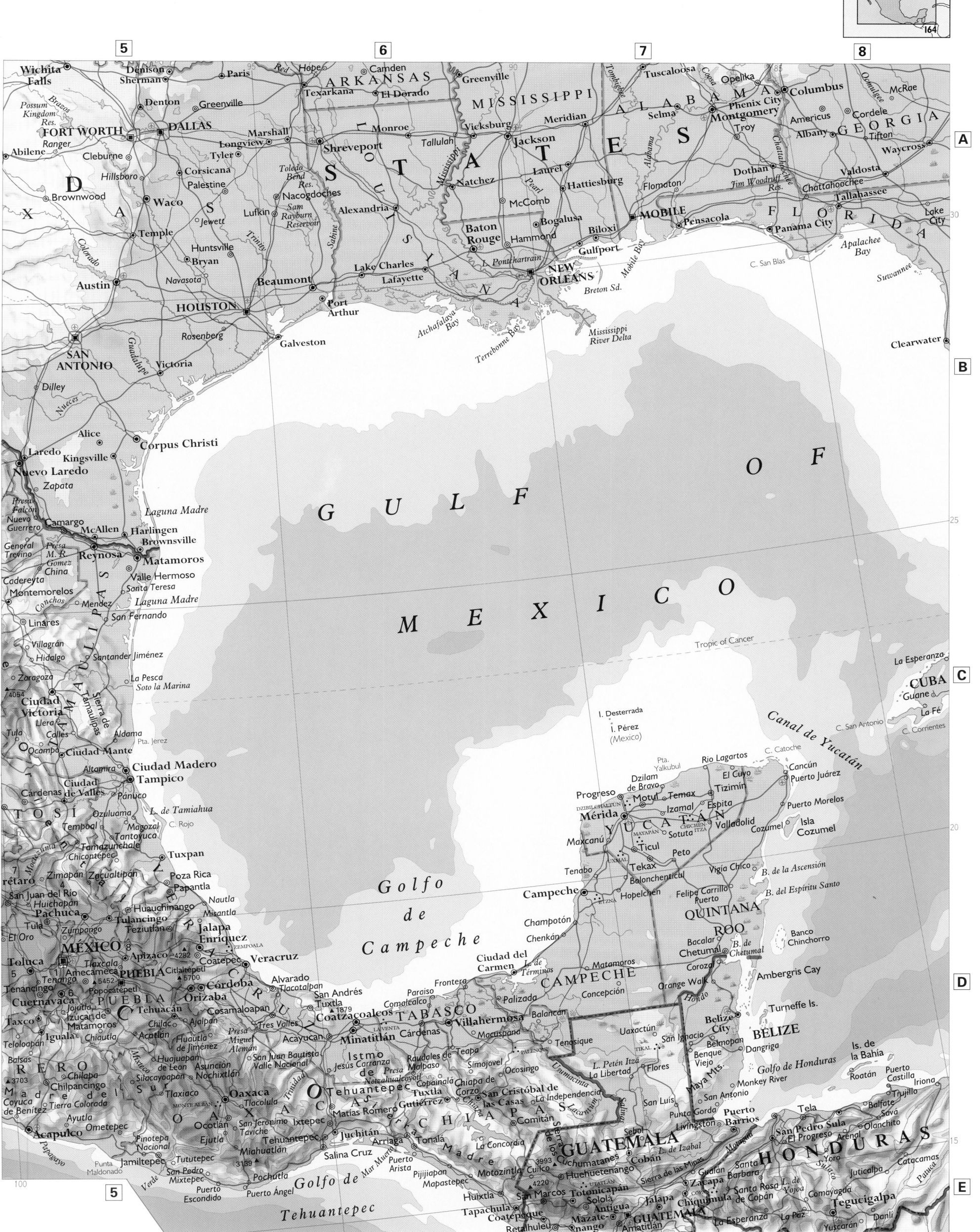

159 155 149
164

5 **6** **7** **8**

Wichita Falls
Denison
Sherman
Paris
Red
Hope
Camden
ARKANSAS
Greenville
Tuscaloosa
Opelika
Columbus
McRae
Oemulgee

Brownwood
Denton
Greenville
Texarkana
El Dorado
Monroe
Vicksburg
Meridian
Selma
Montgomery
Phenix City
Americus
Cordele
GEORGIA

FORT WORTH
DALLAS
Marshall
Longview
Shreveport
Jackson
Troy
Dothan
Albany
Tifton
Waycross

Ranger
Cleburne
Tyler
MISSISSIPPI
ALABAMA

Abilene
Hillsboro
Corsicana
Palestine
Natchez
Laurel
Flomaton
Chattahoochee
Valdosta

Waco
Nacogdoches
Alexandria
McComb
Hattiesburg
Pensacola
Panama City
Tallahassee
Lake City
FLORIDA

Temple
Lufkin
Baton Rouge
Bogalusa
MOBILE
Mobile Bay
C. San Blas
Apalachee Bay
Suwannee

Austin
Huntsville
Bryan
Beaumont
Lafayette
Lake Charles
Hammond
Gulfport
Biloxi

HOUSTON
Port Arthur
NEW ORLEANS
L. Pontchartrain
Breton Sd.
Clearwater

San Antonio
Rosenberg
Galveston
Atchafalaya Bay
Terrebonne Bay
Mississippi River Delta

GULF OF

Dilley
Victoria

Laredo
Alice
Corpus Christi

Kingsville

Nuevo Laredo
Zapata
Laguna Madre

Presa Falcón
Camargo
McAllen
Harlingen
Brownsville

Nueva Guerrero
Reynosa
Matamoros

General Treviño
Valle Hermoso
Santa Teresa

Cadereyta
Montemorelos
Laguna Madre

Linares
San Fernando

MEXICO

Villagrán
Hidalgo
Santander Jiménez

Zaragoza
La Pesca
Soto la Marina

Ciudad Victoria
Llera
Sierra de Tamaulipas
Pta. Jerez

Tula
Calles
Aldama

Ocampo
Ciudad Mante
Altamira
Ciudad Madero
Tampico

Cárdenas de Valles
Pánuco

Ozuluama
Tempoal
L. de Tamiahua
C. Rojo

Tamazunchale
Magozal
Tantoyuca

Chicontepec
Tuxpan

Zimapán
Zacualtipán
Poza Rica
Papantla

Querétaro
San Juan del Río
Huichapán
Nautla

Pachuca
Huauchinango
Misantla

Tula
El Oro
Zumpango
Tulancingo
Teziutlán

MÉXICO
Jalapa Enríquez
Coatepec
Veracruz

Toluca
Tlaxcala
Apizaco
ZEMPOALA

Tenancingo
Amecameca
PUEBLA
Citlaltépetl
Alvarado
San Andrés Tuxtla

Cuernavaca
Popocatépetl
Orizaba
Tlacotalpan
Paraíso
Comalcalco

Taxco
Izúcar de Matamoros
Córdoba
Cosamaloapan
Tres Valles
Frontera
Palizada

Iguala
Chiautla
Acayucan
Coatzacoalcos
Villahermosa
Balancán

Chilapa
Acatlán
Minatitlán
Cárdenas
Macuspana

Chilpancingo
Huajuapan de León
Asunción Nochixtlán
Jesús Carranza
Teapa
Tenosique

Tlaxiaco
Tres Valles
Ocosingo

Oaxaca
Tehuantepec
Tuxtla Gutiérrez
San Cristóbal de las Casas

Acapulco
Ometepec
Ocotlán
Ixtepec
Chiapa de Corzo
Comitán

Ejutla
San Jerónimo Taviche
Juchitán
Arriaga
Tonalá

Miahuatlán
Salina Cruz
La Concordia
Motozintla

Pochutla
Puerto Arista
GUATEMALA
Huehuetenango

Puerto Ángel
Pijijiapan
Mapastepec
Huixtla
Coban

Golfo de Tehuantepec
Tapachula
San Marcos
Totonicapán
Sololá

GUATEMALA

5 **6** **7** **8**

GULF OF MEXICO

I. Desterrada
I. Pérez (Mexico)

Tropic of Cancer

La Esperanza
CUBA
Guane
La Fé

Canal de Yucatán
C. San Antonio
C. Corrientes

C. Catoche
Río Lagartos
El Cuyo
Cancún
Puerto Juárez

Dzilam de Bravo
Temax
Tizimín

Progreso
Motul
Izamal
Espita
Puerto Morelos

Mérida
Valladolid
Cozumel
Isla Cozumel

YUCATÁN
MAYAPÁN
CHICHÉN ITZÁ
Sotuta

Maxcanú
Ticul
Peto

Tenabo
Tekax
UXMAL
Vigía Chico
B. de la Ascensión

Campeche
Bolonchenticul
Hopelchen
Felipe Carrillo Puerto
B. del Espíritu Santo

Champotón
Chenkán
QUINTANA ROO

Ciudad del Carmen
L. de Términos
Matamoros
Bacalar
Chetumal
Banco Chinchorro

Frontera
Concepción
Corozal
Orange Walk
Ambergris Cay

TABASCO
CAMPECHE
Hondo
Belize City
Turneffe Is.

Uaxactún
San Ignacio
BELIZE

TIKAL
Benque Viejo
Belmopan
Dangriga

L. Petén Itzá
La Libertad
Flores
Maya Mts.
Monkey River

San Luis
San Antonio
Golfo de Honduras
Is. de la Bahía

Punta Gorda
Puerto Barrios
Roatán
Trujillo

Livingston
Tela
San Pedro Sula
El Progreso
Arenal

Sebol
L. de Izabal
HONDURAS

Zacapa
Santa Bárbara
Yoro

Chiquimula
Santa Rosa de Copán
L. de Yojoa
Comayagua

Jalapa
Jutiapa
Tegucigalpa
Danlí

Golfo de Campeche

Golfo de Tehuantepec

COPYRIGHT GEORGE PHILIP LTD.

1:6 400 000

JAMAICA
1:2 400 000

CARIBBEAN SEA

Montego Bay, Falmouth, Runaway Bay, St. Ann's Bay, Galina Point, Port Maria, Annotto Bay, Moneague, Port Antonio, Lucea, Negril, Wakefield, Ocho Rios, Dry Harbour Mountains, Cambridge, The Cockpit Country, Mount Denham 985, Linstead, The Blue Mountains, Blue Mt. Pk., John Crow Mts., South Negril Pt., Maggotty, Don Figuero Mts., Santa Cruz Mts., Mandeville, Spanish Town, Portmore, KINGSTON, May Pen, Portland Bight, Morant Point, Savanna-la-Mar, Black River, Great Pedro Bluff, Alligator Pond, Portland Point, Morant Bay, Port Morant

JAMAICA

GULF OF MEXICO

I. Desterrada, I. Pérez (Mexico)

Progreso, Dzilam de Bravo, Rio Lagartos, C. Catoche, C. San Antonio, Punta Yalkubul, DZIBILCHALTÚN, Mérida, Motul, Temax, El Cuyo, Tizimin, Cancún, Maxcanú, Dzitya, Izamal, Espita, Puerto Juárez, Campeche, Calkini, Sotuta, MAYAPÁN, Ticul, CHICHÉN ITZÁ, Valladolid, El Díaz, Puerto Morelos, Tenabo, UXMAL, Tekax, Peto, Cozumel, Isla Cozumel, Champotón, Hopelchén, Bolonchenticul, Felipe Carrillo Puerto, Vigia Chico, Chenkán, San José Carpizo, B. de la Ascensión, Ciudad del Carmen, I. de Términos, MEXICO, Bacalar, B. del Espíritu Santo, Palizada, Pital, CAMPECHE, Matamoros, Concepción, Orange Walk, Banco Chinchorro, Balancán, Tenosique, Chetumal, Corozal, Ambergris Cay, PALENQUE, B. de Chetumal, Ocosingo, QUINTANA ROO, Pedro Antonio Santos, Hondo

Is. Santanilla (Swan Islands) (Honduras)

Cayman Islands (U.K.), Cayman Brac, Little Cayman, George Town, Grand Cayman, 7680, C. Cruz, Sierra Maestra, 2000, SANTIAGO DE CUBA

LA HABANA (Havana), Guanabacoa, Santa Cruz del Norte, Canal Nicholas, Marianao, Guanajay, Matanzas, Cárdenas, Sagua la Grande, Bahía Honda, Güines, Jovellanos, Colón, La Esperanza, San Antonio Batabanó, Jagüey Grande, Caibarién, Pinar del Río, Los Palacios, de los Baños, Santa Clara, Placetas, Morón, Cayo Romano, Guane, San Luis, CUBA, Cienfuegos, Trinidad, Júcaro, Sancti Spíritus, Tunas de Zaza, Florida, Camagüey, Nuevitas, C. Corrientes, La Fé, Nueva Gerona, I. de la Juventud, Arch. de los Canarreos, Arch. de Jardines de la Reina, Golfo de Guacanayabo, Santa Cruz del Sur, Manzanillo, Bayamo, Victoria de las Tunas, Palma Soriano, HOLGUÍN, Gibara, Puerto Padre, Puerto Manatí

U.S.A., L. Okeechobee, West Palm Beach, Fort Myers, Boca Raton, Fort Lauderdale, Naples, The Everglades, Hialeah, MIAMI, C. Romano, C. Sable, Dry Tortugas (U.S.A.), Key West, Florida Keys, Straits of Florida

Little Abaco I., West End, Grand Bahama, Hope Town, Freeport, Great Abaco I., Bimini Is., Berry Is., Northwest Providence Channel, Nicolls Town, Northeast Providence Channel, Eleuthera, Dunmore Town, Nassau, New Providence, Adelaide, Andros Island, Andros Town, Governor's Harbour, New Portsmouth (Rock Sound), BAH, Great Guana Cay, Great Exuma I., George Town, Exuma Sound, Jumentos Cays, Cay Sal Bank, Santaren Channel, Great Bahama Bank, Canal Viejo de Bahama, Duncan Town

Montego Bay, Falmouth, St. Ann's Bay, Lucea, Port Maria, Negril, Cambridge, Annotto Bay, Port Antonio, South Negril Pt., JAMAICA, Savanna-la-Mar, Black River, Mandeville, Spanish Town, May Pen, KINGSTON, Port Morant, Morant Cays (Jamaica), Pedro Cays (Jamaica)

GUATEMALA, Progreso, Flores, Petén, L. Petén Itzá, La Libertad, Sayaxché, San Luis, Belmopan, Belize City, Turneffe Is., BELIZE, Middlesex, Dangriga, Benque Viejo, Maya Mts., Monkey River, Punta Gorda, San Antonio, Livingston, Puerto Barrios, Puerto Cortés, Golfo de Honduras, Is. de la Bahía, Roatán, Puerto Castilla, Iriona, C. Camarón, Punta Patuca, Brus Laguna, Coban, L. de Izabal, Tela, La Ceiba, Balfate, Trujillo, Savá, Laguna Caratasca, Cuilco, Huehuetenango, Zacapa, Santa Barbara, San Pedro Sula, El Progreso, Olanchito, Sierra de las Minas, Chiquimula, Santa Rosa de Copán, L. de Yojoa, Yoro, Sulaco, Juticalpa, Catacamas, Mosquitia, C. Falso, Jalapa, HONDURAS, Comayagua, C. Gracias a Dios, Antigua, GUATEMALA, Amatitlán, La Esperanza, La Paz, Coco (Segovia), Puerto Cabezas, Escuintla, Santa Ana, TEGUCIGALPA, Danlí, Kisalaya, Puerto Lempira, Quezaltenango, Mazatenango, San José, Ahuachapán, Sonsonate, Cojutepeque, Zacatecoluca, Nacaome, Choluteca, Cayos Miskitos (Nicaragua), Pta. Gorda, Nueva San Salvador, SAN SALVADOR, San Miguel, La Unión, G. de Fonseca, Cord. Isabella, Estelí, Siuna, Bonanza, Tuma, EL SALVADOR, Usulután, Somoto, Jinotega, San Pedro del Norte, Tungla, Bajo Nuevo (Colombia)

Chinandega, Matagalpa, Muy Muy, Río Grande, Prinzapolca, Corinto, León, Boaco, Siquia, Santo Domingo, Rama, I. de Providencia (Colombia), La Paz Centro, L. de Managua, NICARAGUA, MANAGUA, Masaya, Juigalpa, Bluefields, Cayos Roncador (Colombia), Diriamba, Jinotepe, Granada, El Bluff, I. de San Andrés (Colombia), Rivas, Lago de Nicaragua, Cord. de Yolaina, B. de San Juan del Norte, Pta. Mico, Cayos de Albuquerque (Colombia), San Juan del Sur, I. de Ometepe, San Carlos, Punta de Perlas, Is. del Maíz (Nicaragua), B. de Salinas, La Cruz, Los Chiles, San Juan, San Juan del Norte, C. Santa Elena, G. de Papagayo, Liberia, Cord. de Guanacaste, COSTA, Cord. Central, Santa Cruz, Nicoya, Alajuela, Guápiles, Siquirres, Limón, I. de San Bernardo, Carmona, Pen. de Nicoya, Puntarenas, San José, Cartago, Pta. Mona, Esparta, RICA, Pta. Manzanillo, Nombre de Dios, Archipiélago de San Blas, CARTAGE, C. Blanco, G. de Nicoya, Bribri, Bocas del Toro, Portobelo, Golfo del Darién, Lorica, Pen. de Osa, Puerto Quepos, Chirripó, Buenos Aires, Cord. de Talamanca, 3837, L. de Chiriquí, Panama Canal, Colón, Cereté, Santiago, B. de Coronado, Puerto Cortés, San Vito, Volcán Barú 3374, Almirante, G. de los Mosquitos, La Chorrera, Balboa, PANAMÁ, Chimán, Montería, G. de Chiriquí, Puerto Armuelles, La Concepción, Remedios, David, Penonomé, Aguadulce, Río Hato, Las Perlas, San Miguel, del Rey, La Palma, Yaviza, I. de Coiba, I. de Cebaco, Chitré, Pocrí, Las Tablas, Tonosí, Garachiné, El Real, CÓR Monte, I. Jicarón, Pta. Mala, Punta Mariato, Pen. de Azuero, Serranía del Darién, G. de Urabá

GUADELOUPE
Pte. de la Grande Vigie, Port-Louis, Grande-Terre, Petit-Canal, Moule, La Désirade, Ste-Rose, Pointe-Noire, Pointe-à-Pitre, Ste-Anne, Pointe des Châteaux, Basse-Terre, Gosier, Îles de la Petite Terre, Bouillante, Capesterre-Belle-Eau, Soufrière 1467, St-Louis, Marie-Galante, Basse-Terre, Trois-Rivières, Grand-Bourg, Capesterre, Îles des Saintes, **GUADELOUPE** (Fr.), Pte. des Basses

MARTINIQUE
Cap St-Martin, Basse-Pointe, Le Prêcheur, Montagne Pelée 1397, Ste-Marie, St-Pierre, Presqu'île de la Caravelle, La Trinité, Schœlcher, Le Robert, Fort-de-France, Le Lamentin, Le François, Rivière-Salée, Le Vauclin, St-Joseph, Ducos, St-Esprit, Le Marin, **MARTINIQUE** (Fr.), Rivière-Pilote, Ste-Anne, Pte. d'Enfer

GUADELOUPE AND MARTINIQUE
1:1 600 000

PACIFIC OCEAN

Projection: Conical with two standard parallels

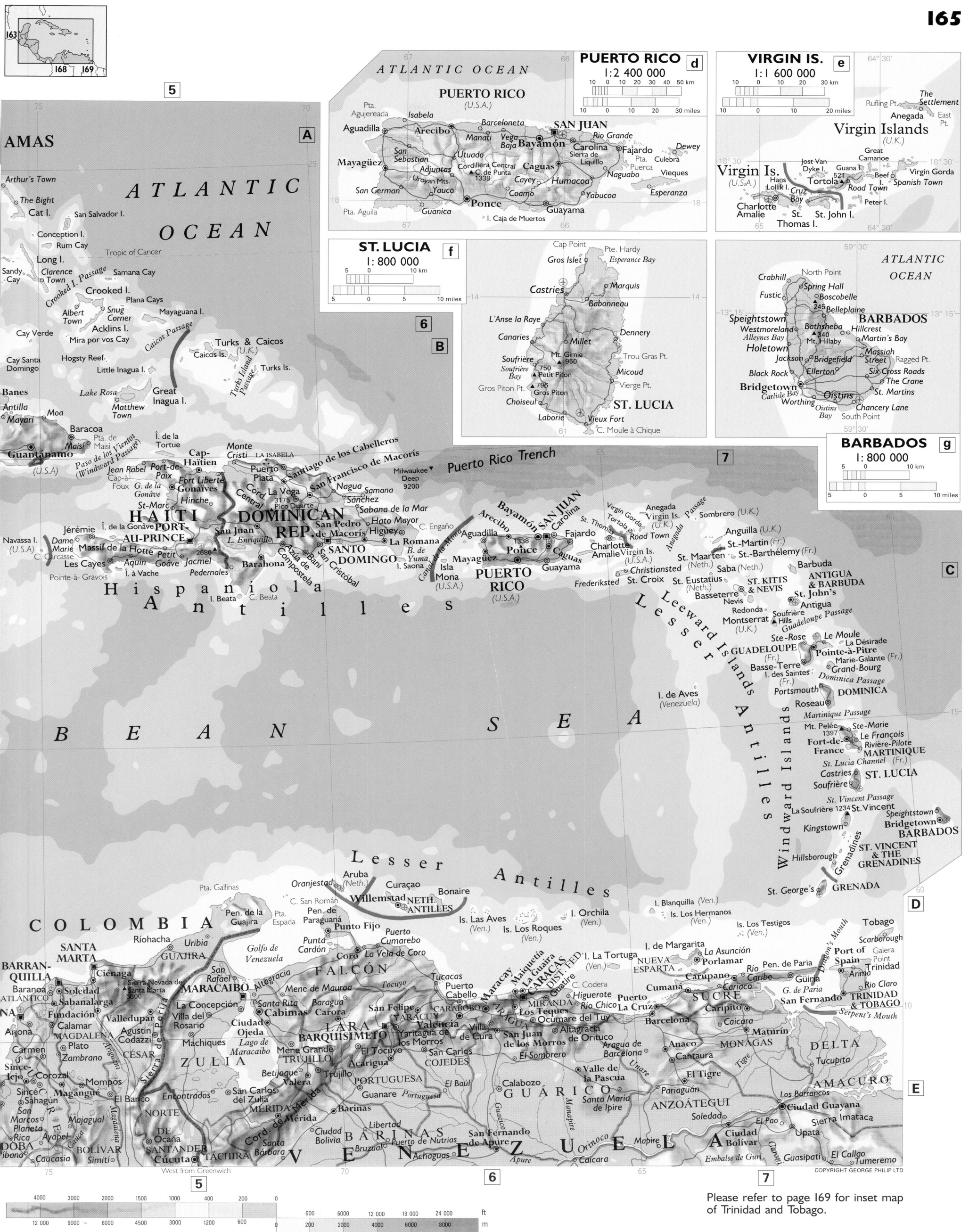

AMAS

ATLANTIC OCEAN

Arthur's Town
The Bight
Cat I.
San Salvador I.
Conception I.
Rum Cay
Long I.
Sandy
Cay *Clarence Town*
Samana Cay
Cay Verde
Plana Cays
Albert *Snug* Mayaguana I.
Town *Corner*
Acklins I.
Mira por vos Cay
Cay Santa Hogsty Reef
Domingo *Little Inagua I.*
Banes Lake Rosa
Antilla Matthew
Mayari Town *Great Inagua I.*
Moa
Baracoa
Guantánamo Pta. de
(U.S.A.) Maisí

Tropic of Cancer

ATLANTIC OCEAN

PUERTO RICO | d
1:2 400 000

PUERTO RICO
(U.S.A.)
Pta.
Agujereada
Isabela
Aguadilla Arecibo Barceloneta Vega Río Grande
Baja SAN JUAN
Mayagüez San Manatí Bayamón Carolina Fajardo
Sebastián Utuado Caguas Sierra de Pta.
Adjuntas Cordillera Central Liquillo Puerca Dewey
San German Uroyan Mts. ▲ C. de Punta Cayey Humacao Culebra
Yauco 1338 Coamo Naguabo
Pta. Aguila Ponce Yabucoa Vieques
Guánica Esperanza
Guayama
I. Caja de Muertos

VIRGIN IS. | e
1:1 600 000

Rufling Pt. The Settlement
Anegada East Pt.
Virgin Islands
(U.K.)
Virgin Is. Jost Van Great
(U.S.A.) Dyke I. Camanoe
Hans Guana I.
Lollik I. ▲521 Beef I.
Charlotte Cruz Tortola Virgin Gorda
Amalie Bay Road Town Spanish Town
St. St. John I. Peter I.
Thomas I.

ST. LUCIA | f
1:800 000

Cap Point
Gros Islet Pte. Hardy
Esperance Bay
Castries Marquis
Babonneau
L'Anse la Raye Millet Dennery
Canaries
Soufrière Mt. Gimie
Soufrière ▲950
Bay ▲750 Trou Gras Pt.
Petit Piton Micoud
Gros Piton Pt. ▲796 Vierge Pt.
Gros Piton
Choiseul
Laborie Vieux Fort
C. Moule à Chique
ST. LUCIA

Crabhill North Point **ATLANTIC
OCEAN**
Fustic Spring Hall
Boscobelle
▲245 Belleplaine
Speightstown **BARBADOS**
Westmoreland Bathsheba Hillcrest
Holetown Alleynes Bay ▲340 Martin's Bay
Mt. Hillaby
Jackson Massiah
Black Rock Bridgefield Street Ragged Pt.
Ellerton Six Cross Roads
Bridgetown Worthing The Crane
Carlisle Bay Oistins St. Martins
Worthing Chancery Lane
Bay South Point

BARBADOS | g
1:800 000

Cap-
Haïtien Santiago de los Cabelleros
Jean Rabel Port-de- Puerto Puerto Rico Trench
Paix Plata Milwaukee
G. de la La Vega San Francisco de Macorís Deep
Gonâve Cord. Nagua 9200
St-Marc Central Pico Duarte Samaná
Hinche ▲3175 Sánchez
Jérémie Î. de la Gonâve Sabana de la Mar
Navassa I. Dame HAITI DOMINICAN Hato Mayor
(U.S.A.) Marie PORT- REP. Higüey Bayamón San Juan
Massif de la Hotte AU-PRINCE San Juan San Pedro La Romana C. Engaño Arecibo Carolina
Les Cayes Petit ▲2680 de Macorís Fajardo
Aquin Goâve Jacmel Barahona SANTO Isla de B. de Aguadilla St. Thomas Road Town
Pointe-à- Gravois Pedernales DOMINGO Saona Yuma Isla Ponce Charlotte Anegada Sombrero (U.K.)
L. Enriquillo San Cristóbal Canal de la Mona Mona Mayagüez Caguas Amalie Virgin Is. Anguilla (U.K.)
Hispaniola PUERTO Guayama (U.S.A.) St.-Martin (Fr.)
Antilles RICO Christiansted St.-Barthélemy (Fr.)
(U.S.A.) Frederiksted St. Croix St. Eustatius Saba (Neth.) Barbuda
(Neth.) ST. KITTS ANTIGUA
Basseterre & NEVIS & BARBUDA
Nevis St. John's
Redonda Antigua
Montserrat Soufrière
(U.K.) ▲ Hills Guadeloupe Passage
Ste-Rose Le Moule
La Désirade
GUADELOUPE Pointe-à-Pitre
Basse-Terre Grand-Bourg Marie-Galante (Fr.)
I. des Saintes Dominica Passage
(Fr.)
Portsmouth DOMINICA
Roseau
Martinique Passage
Mt. Pelée Ste-Marie
▲1397 Le François
Fort-de- Rivière-Pilote
France MARTINIQUE
St. Lucia Channel (Fr.)
Castries ST. LUCIA
Soufrière
St. Vincent Passage
La Soufrière 1234 St. Vincent
Kingstown Speightstown
BARBADOS
Bridgetown
ST. VINCENT
Hillsborough & THE
GRENADINES
St. George's GRENADA

ARIBBEAN SEA (BEAN SEA)

Puerto Rico Trench

Lesser Antilles

Leeward Islands

Windward Islands

Oranjestad Aruba Curaçao
(Neth.)
Willemstad Bonaire
NETH.
ANTILLES Is. Las Aves
(Ven.) Is. Los Roques
(Ven.) I. Orchila
(Ven.)
I. Blanquilla (Ven.)
Is. Los Hermanos
(Ven.)
Is. Los Testigos
(Ven.)

COLOMBIA

Pta. Gallinas
Ríohacha PEN. de la I. de Margarita La Asunción Tobago
SANTA Uribia Guajira C. San Román GUAJIRA Porlamar Scarborough
MARTA PEN. de Punto Fijo NUEVA Port of
Baranoa Cienaga Paraguaná Golfo de Coro La Vela de Coro ESPARTA Spain Galera
BARRAN- Soledad GUAJIRA Venezuela Punta Tucacas Maiquetía Río Caribe Pen. de Paria Trinidad Point
QUILLA Sabanalarga Sierra Nevada de Cardón Puerto Coro CARACAS Cumaná Carúpano Arima
ATLÁNTICO San San Cabello DIST. FED. Güiria
Santa Marta Rafael Mene de Mauroa MARACAY MIRANDA Higuerote Río Claro
NA Fundación ▲5800 FALCÓN Maracay Los Teques Puerto SUCRE San Fernando TRINIDAD
Arjona Calamar MARACAIBO Altagracia Tocuyo CARABOBO ARAGUA La Cruz Caicara & TOBAGO
Carmen Magdalena Cabimas La Concepción San Felipe Valencia Barcelona Maturín Serpent's Mouth
Sincé Plato Zambrano Machiques Santa Rita Baragua YARACUY Villa Ocumare del Tuy Anaco
Sahagún CESAR Lago de Mene Grande El Tocuyo Yaritagua de los Morros Cantaura DELTA
San ZULIA Maracaibo BARQUISIMETO Valencia San Juan San Carlos MONAGAS AMACURO
Marcos Villa del LARA Villa de Acarigua de los Morros Anaco Tucupita
Corozal Rosario TRUJILLO de Cura El Sombrero
Since- Mompós Ciudad Agustín Betijoque PORTUGUESA San Carlos Valle de Ciudad Guayana
lejo Magangué Ojeda Codazzi Trujillo COJEDES la Pascua Soledad
San Caucasia Simití El Banco Valera MÉRIDA Calabozo Santa María El Pao Sierra Imataca
DOBA Mejagual Cúcuta NORTE Cord. de Mérida Barinas GUÁRICO de Ipire El Tigre Upata
ibano BOLÍVAR DE MÉRIDA Libertad ANZOÁTEGUI Ciudad
Ayapel SANTANDER Ciudad BARINAS San Fernando Bolívar
Caucasia TÁCHIRA Bolivia Puerto de Nutrias de Apure El Callao
Achaguas VENEZUELA Embalse de Guri Tumeremo
Arauca Apure Caicara Guasipati

COPYRIGHT GEORGE PHILIP LTD

Please refer to page 169 for inset map of Trinidad and Tobago.

West from Greenwich

4000 3000 2000 1500 1000 600 200 0
600 6000 12 000 18 000 24 000 ft
12 000 9000 6000 4500 3000 1200 600 0
200 2000 4000 6000 8000 m

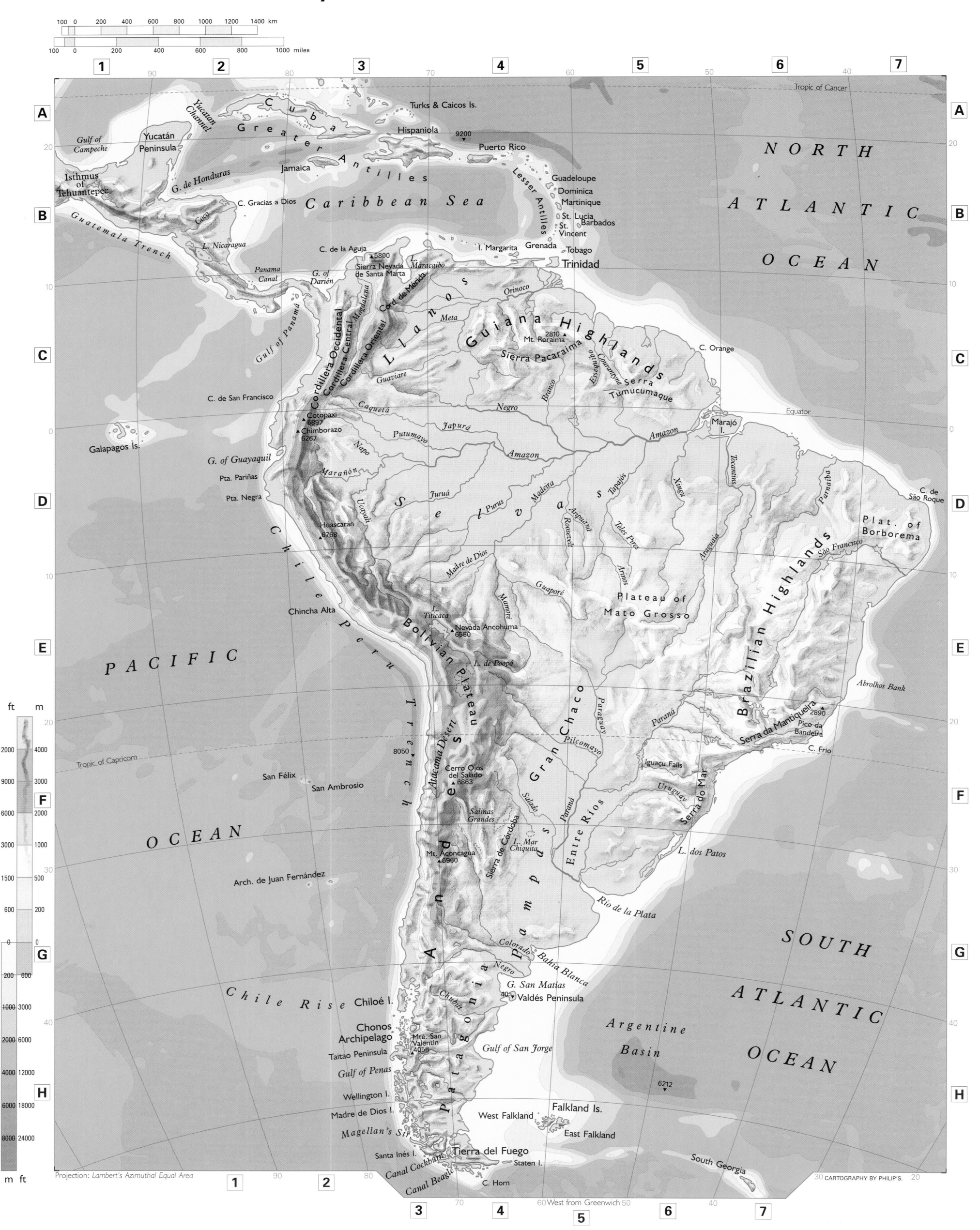

100 0   200 400 600 800 1000 1200 1400 km
100 0   200   400   600   800   1000 miles

ft   m
12000 4000
9000   3000
6000   2000
3000   1000
1500   500
600   200
0   0
200   600
1000   3000
2000   6000
4000   12000
6000   18000
8000   24000
m   ft

Projection: Lambert's Azimuthal Equal Area

Tropic of Cancer

Yucatán Channel
Gulf of Campeche
Yucatán Peninsula
Isthmus of Tehuantepec
Cuba
Greater Antilles
Turks & Caicos Is.
Hispaniola
9200
Puerto Rico
Jamaica
G. de Honduras
Coco
C. Gracias a Dios
L. Nicaragua
Caribbean Sea
Lesser Antilles
Guadeloupe
Dominica
Martinique
St. Lucia
St. Vincent
Barbados
Grenada
Tobago
Trinidad
I. Margarita

NORTH
ATLANTIC
OCEAN

Guatemala Trench
Panama Canal
Gulf of Panamá
C. de la Aguja
Sierra Nevada de Santa Marta 5800
Maracaibo
Cord. de Mérida
G. of Darién

Llanos
Orinoco
Meta
Guiana Highlands
Mt. Roraima 2810
Sierra Pacaraima
Cuyuni
Essequibo
Serra Tumucumaque
C. Orange

Cordillera Occidental
Cordillera Central
Cordillera Oriental
C. de San Francisco
Guaviare
Caquetá
Negro
Branco

Galapagos Is.
Cotopaxi 6897
Chimborazo 6267
Napo
Putumayo
Japurá
Amazon
Amazon
Marajó I.
Equator
C. de São Roque

G. of Guayaquil
Pta. Pariñas
Pta. Negra
Marañón
Ucayali
S e l v a s
Juruá
Purus
Madeira
Juruá
Tapajós
Teles Pires
Arinos
Xingu
Tocantins
Araguaia
Parnaíba
Plat. of Borborema

Huascarán 6768
Madre de Dios
Plateau of Mato Grosso
Guaporé
Mamoré
Aripuanã
Roosevelt
Jiparaná
São Francisco

Chincha Alta
L. Titicaca
Nevada Ancohuma 6560
L. de Poopó
Bolivian Plateau
Brazilian Highlands
Serra da Mantiqueira 2890
Pico da Bandeira

PACIFIC
OCEAN
Chile Peru Trench
A n d e s
Atacama Desert
8050
Cerro Ojos del Salado 6863
Tropic of Capricorn
San Félix
San Ambrosio

Abrolhos Bank

Gran Chaco
Pilcomayo
Paraguay
Paraná
Iguaçu Falls
Uruguay
Serra do Mar
C. Frio

Salinas Grandes
Salado
Entre Ríos
Paraná

Mt. Aconcagua 6960
Sierra de Córdoba
L. Mar Chiquita
Arch. de Juan Fernández

L. dos Patos

P a m p a s
Río de la Plata

Chile Rise
Chiloé I.
Colorado
Negro
Bahía Blanca
G. San Matías
Valdés Peninsula
40

SOUTH
ATLANTIC
OCEAN

Argentine Basin

Chonos Archipelago
Mte. San Valentín 4058
Taitao Peninsula
Gulf of Penas
Wellington I.
Madre de Dios I.
Chubut
P a t a g o n i a
Gulf of San Jorge
6212

Magellan's Str.
Santa Inés I.
Canal Cockburn
Tierra del Fuego
Canal Beagle
C. Horn
Staten I.
West Falkland
Falkland Is.
East Falkland
South Georgia

CARTOGRAPHY BY PHILIP'S.
West from Greenwich

100 0   200   400   600   800   1000 1200 1400 km
100   0   200   400   600   800   1000 miles

1   **2**   **3**   **4**   **5**   **6**   **7**

Tropic of Cancer

A

Havana   BAHAMAS
CUBA   Turks & Caicos Is.
                                        (U.K.)

NORTH

20

HAITI   DOMINICAN   Virgin Is.
JAMAICA   REP.   San Juan   (U.K.)
        Kingston   Port-au-   PUERTO   ANTIGUA &
MEXICO   Prince   RICO   BARBUDA
                              (U.S.A.)   GUADELOUPE
BELIZE   ST. KITTS   (Fr.)
GUATEMALA   & NEVIS
HONDURAS   Basse-Terre   DOMINICA
Guatemala   Tegucigalpa   Fort-de-France   MARTINIQUE
San Salvador   Castries   ST. LUCIA   (Fr.)
EL SALVADOR   NICARAGUA   ST. VINCENT   BARBADOS
Managua   Kingstown   St. George's   Bridgetown
COSTA   San José   GRENADA
RICA   Port of
PANAMA   Spain   TRINIDAD &
Panamá   TOBAGO

ATLANTIC

B

Caribbean Sea

OCEAN

Barranquilla   Aruba   Curaçao
C. de   Maracaibo   Caracas
Cartagena   la Aguja   Barquisimeto   Valencia
G. of
Darién   Cúcuta   Orinoco
Gulf of Panamá   San Cristóbal   Ciudad Guayana

10

Medellín   Bucaramanga   VENEZUELA
Magdalena   Georgetown
Bogotá   GUYANA   Paramaribo
Cali   SURINAM   Cayenne
COLOMBIA   RORAIMA   FRENCH   C. Orange
                        GUIANA

C

AMAPÁ

Galapagos Is.   Equator
(Ecuador)   Marajó
0   ECUADOR   Quito   Manaus   Amazon   I.   Belém
Guayaquil   Napo   Putumayo   Santarém   São Luís
G. of Guayaquil   Marañón   Japurá   PARÁ
        Iquitos   AMAZONAS   Amazon   Fortaleza
Chiclayo   Juruá   Purus   Madeira   Tapajós   Xingu   MARANHÃO   Teresina   C. de
Trujillo   ACRE   Pôrto Velho   São Roque
Chimbote   PERÚ   RONDÔNIA   Araguaia   PIAUÍ   Parnaíba   RIO G.   Natal
                                    PERNAMBUCO   DO NORTE
Callao   LIMA   BRAZIL   TOCANTINS   PARAÍBA
        Cuzco   Madre de Dios   Campina Grande   Recife
                        MATO GROSSO   BAHÍA   ALAGOAS   Maceió
L. Titicaca   Mamoré   GOIÁS   São Francisco   SERGIPE   Aracaju
        BOLIVIA   DIS. FED.   Brasília   Salvador
Arequipa   La Paz   Cochabamba   Cuiabá   Goiânia
        Sucre   Santa Cruz   MINAS GERAIS
Iquique   MATO GROSSO   Belo   ESPÍRITO
                DO SUL   Ribeirão   Horizonte   SANTO
                        Paraná   Prêto   Vitória
Tropic of Capricorn   PARAGUAY   SÃO PAULO   Juiz   Campos
                                de Fora
Antofagasta   Paraguay   PARANÁ   Campinas   R. DE J.   Niterói
San Félix   Salta   Pilcomayo   Asunción   SÃO   RIO DE
(Chile)   San Ambrosio   Resistencia   PAULO   Curitiba   JANEIRO
        (Chile)   San Miguel   SANTA CATARINA
                de Tucumán   Corrientes   Uruguay
                        RIO GRANDE   Pôrto Alegre
                Córdoba   DO SUL
Arch. de Juan Fernández   San Juan   Santa Fe   Pelotas
(Chile)   Viña del Mar   Mendoza   Paraná   Montevideo
        Valparaíso   Rosario   URUGUAY
        SANTIAGO   BUENOS AIRES
                La Plata   Río de la Plata
        Talca   Bahía   Mar del Plata
Concepción   Colorado   Blanca
Valdivia   Negro   Viedma
Puerto Montt   Chubut
        Comodoro Rivadavia
        Gulf of San Jorge
Gulf of Penas
        ARGENTINA
        Magellan's Str.
Punta Arenas   Tierra del Fuego
C. Horn

D

E

PACIFIC

F

OCEAN

G

H

Equator

SOUTH

ATLANTIC

OCEAN

West Falkland   FALKLAND IS.
        (U.K.)
        Stanley
        East Falkland

South Georgia
(U.K.)

Projection: Lambert's Azimuthal Equal Area   CARTOGRAPHY BY PHILIP'S.

1   **2**   **3**   **4**   **5**   **6**   **7**

LIMA Capital Cities   West from Greenwich

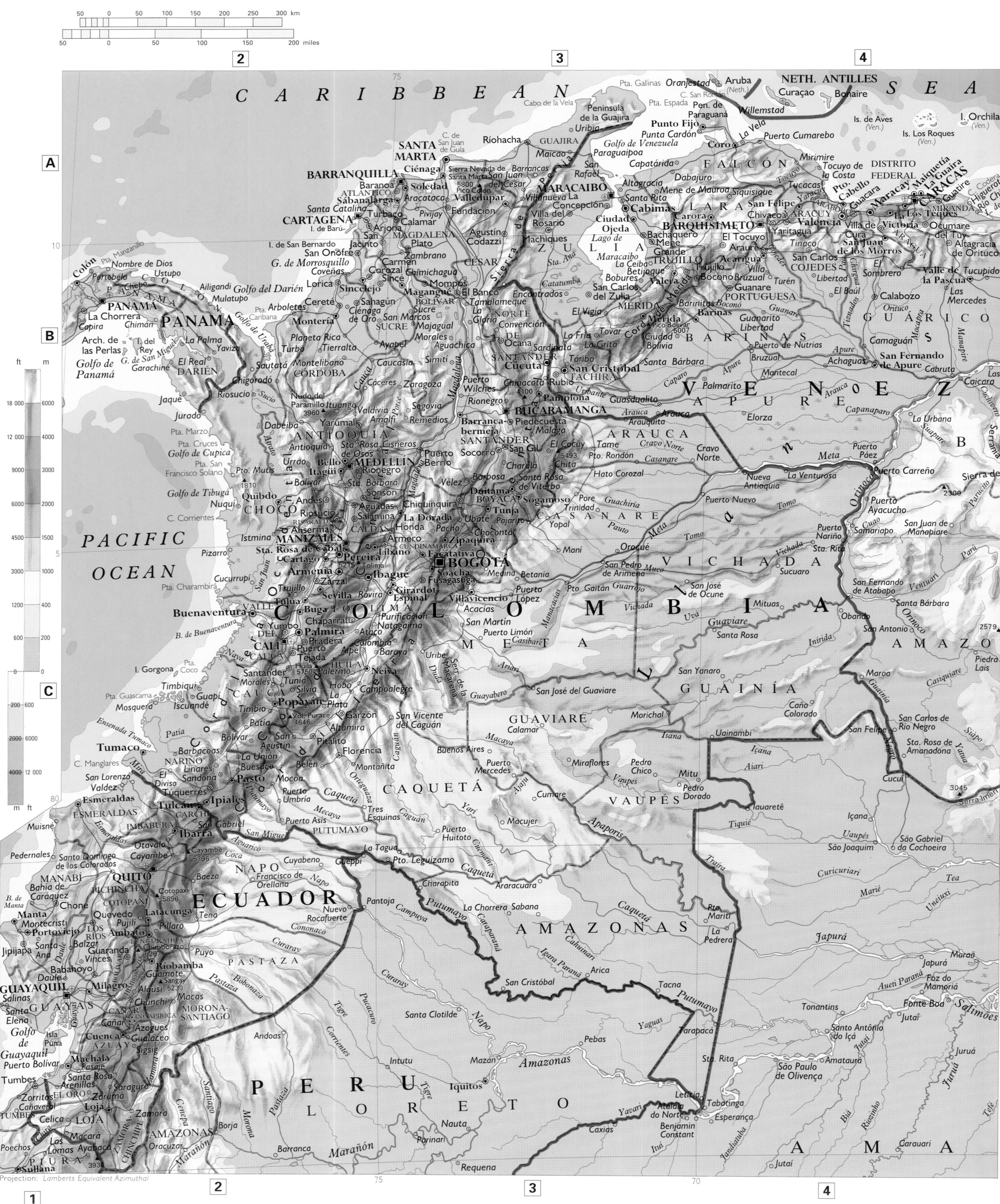

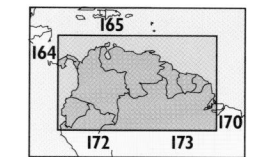

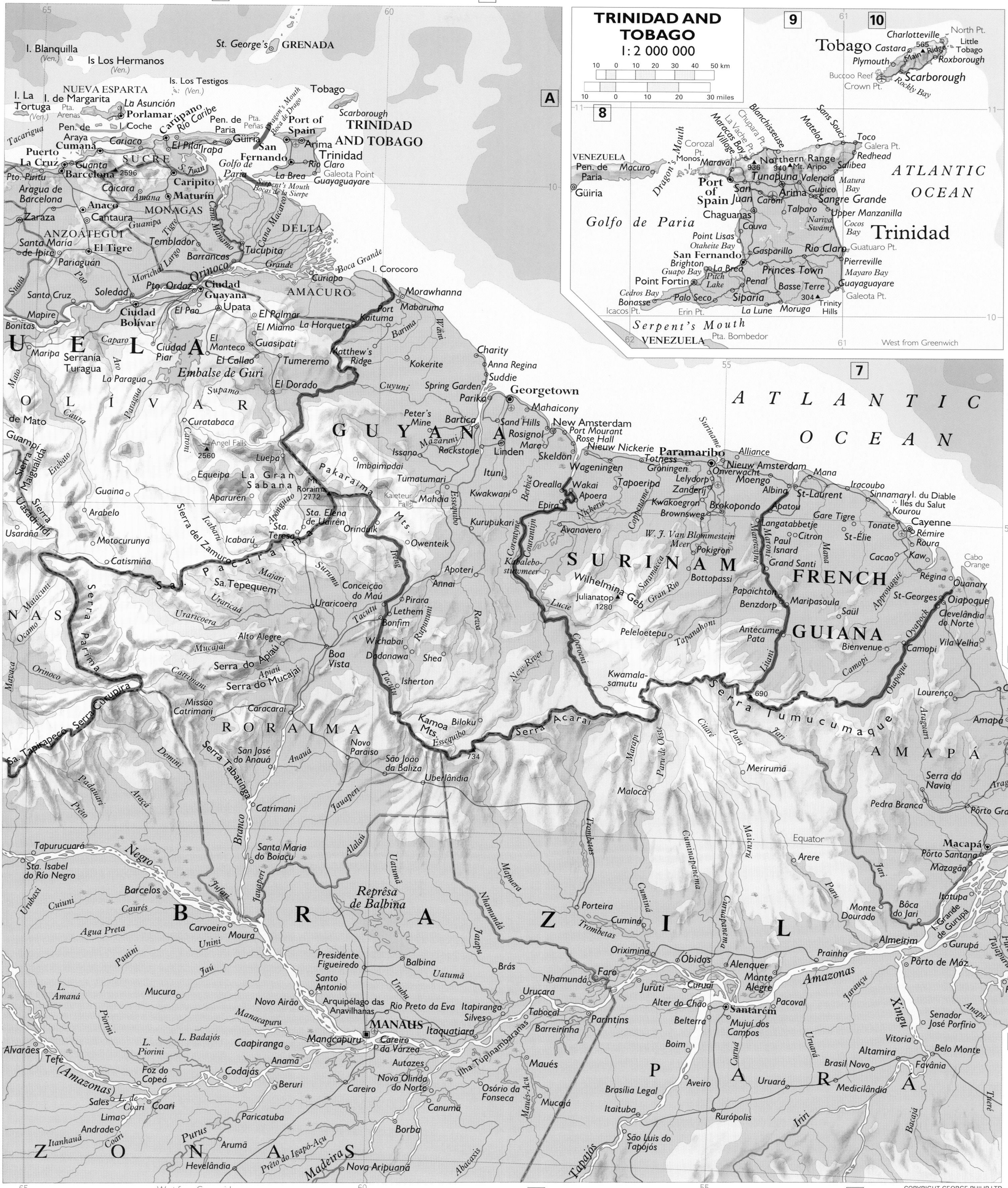

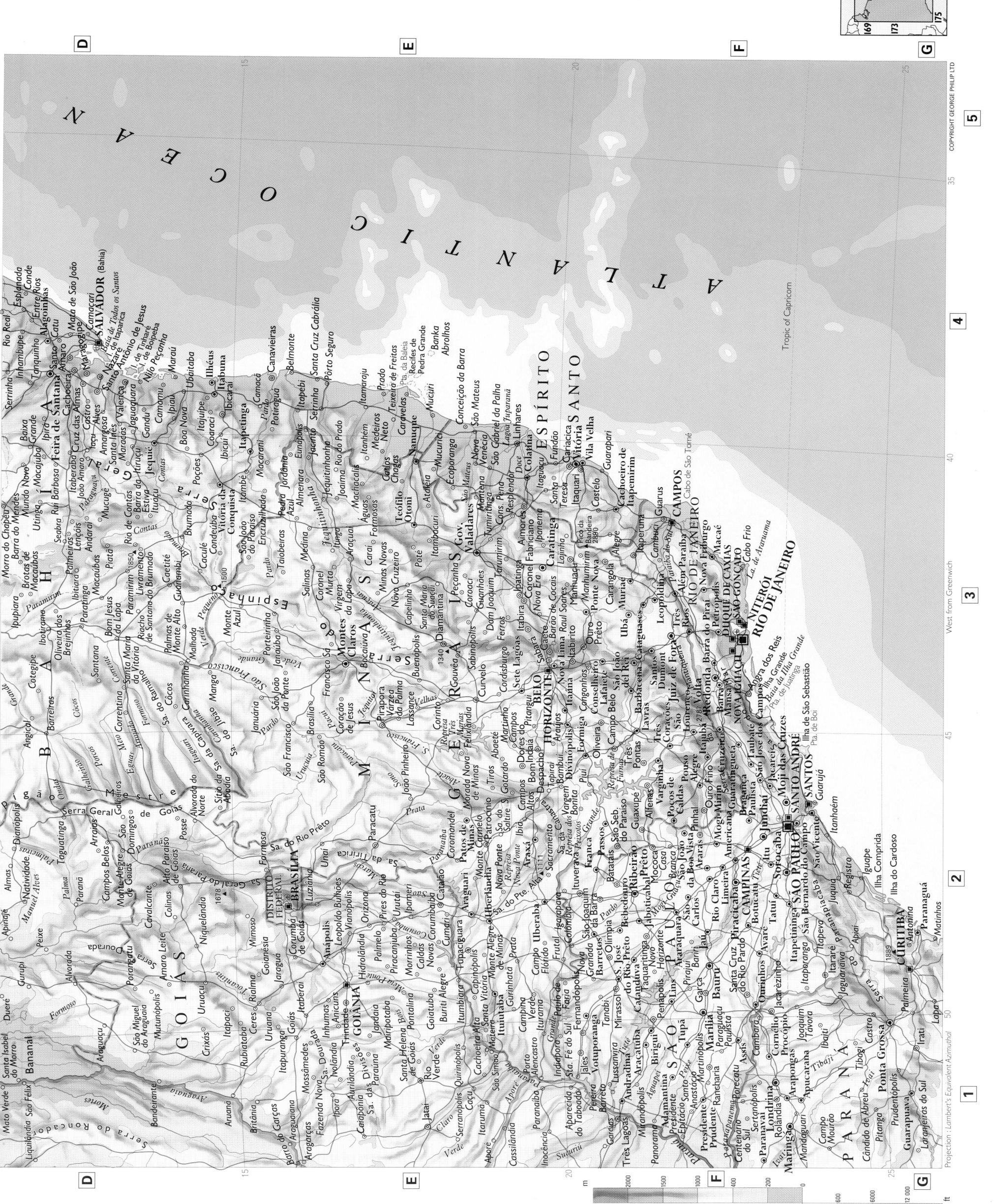

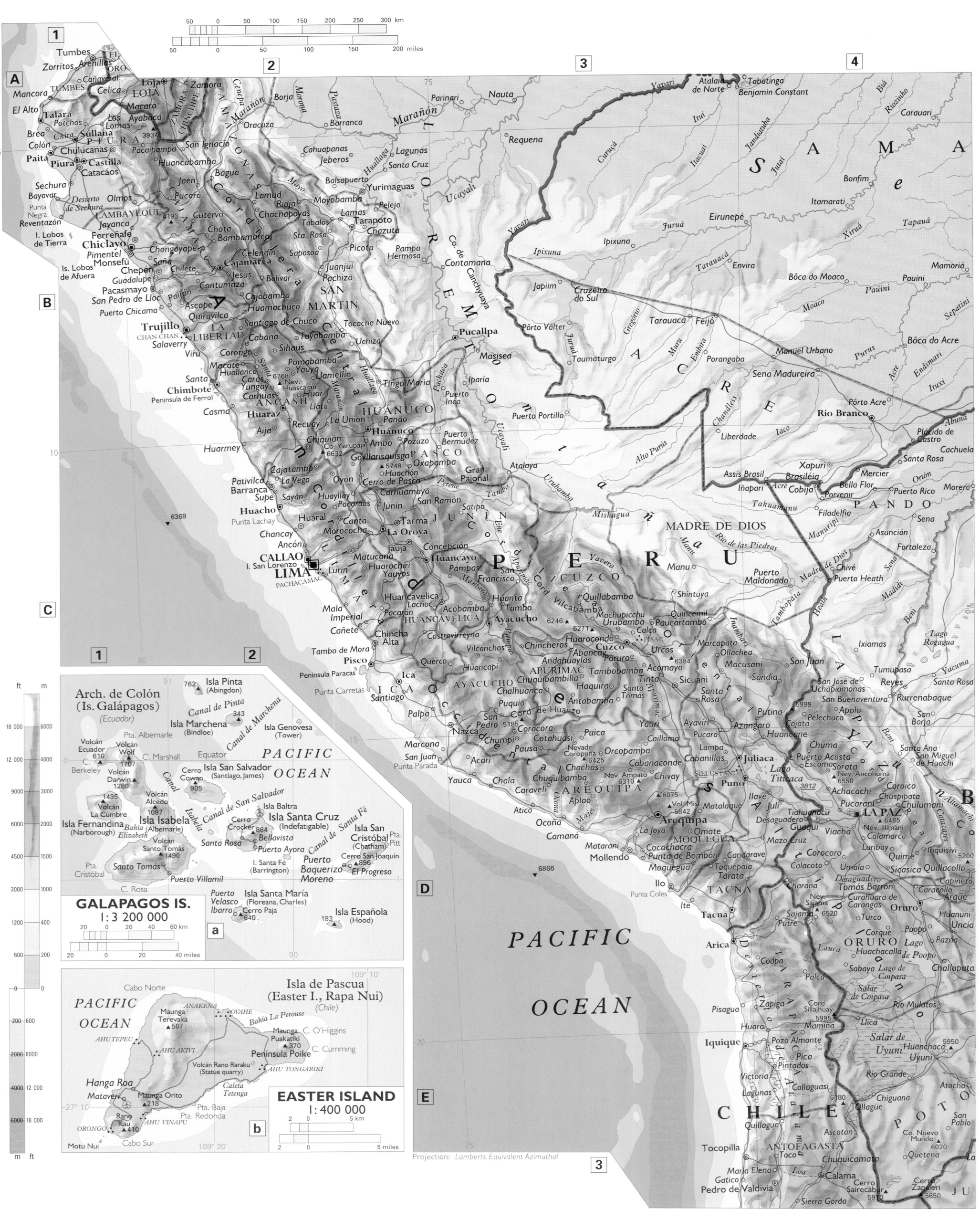

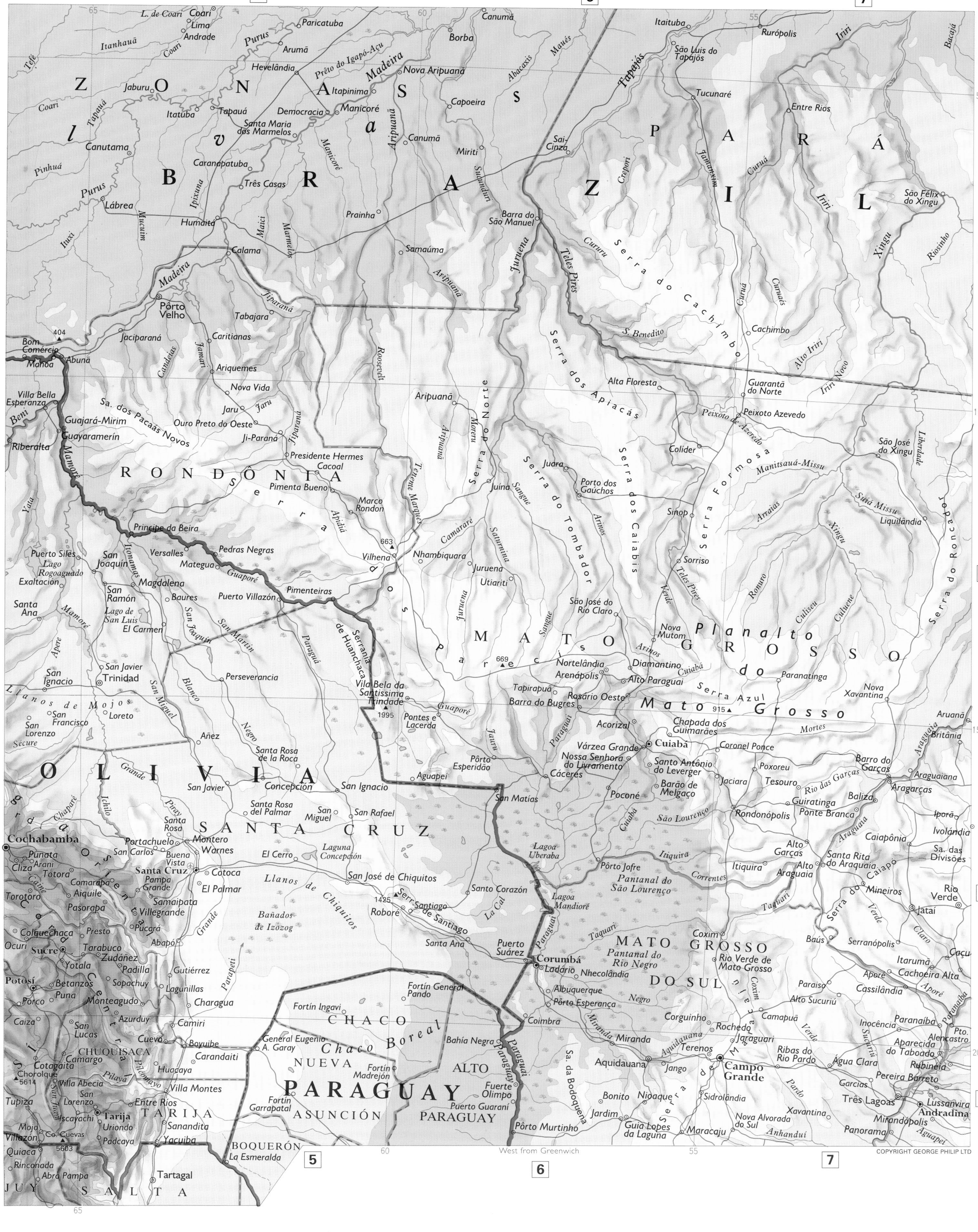

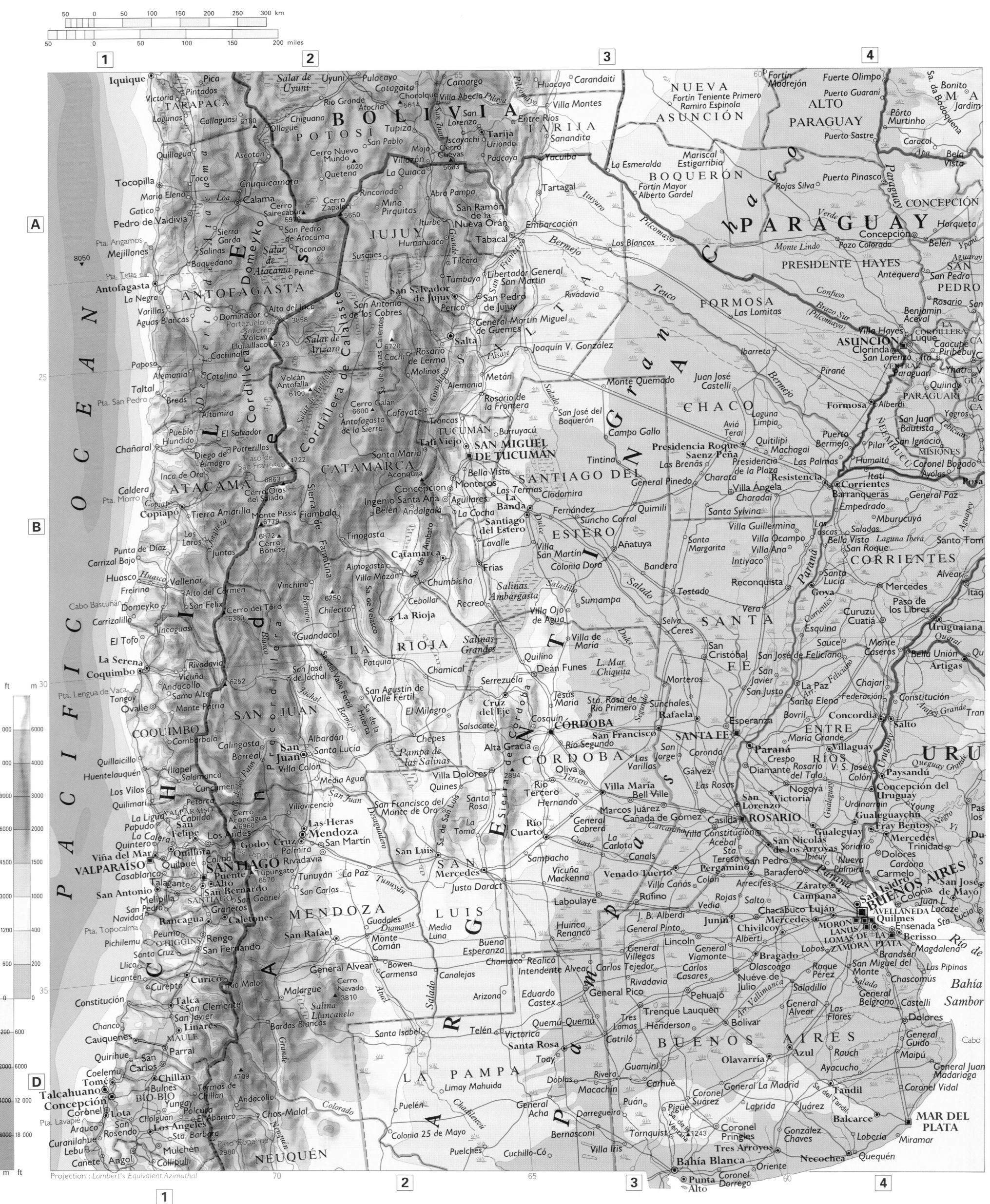

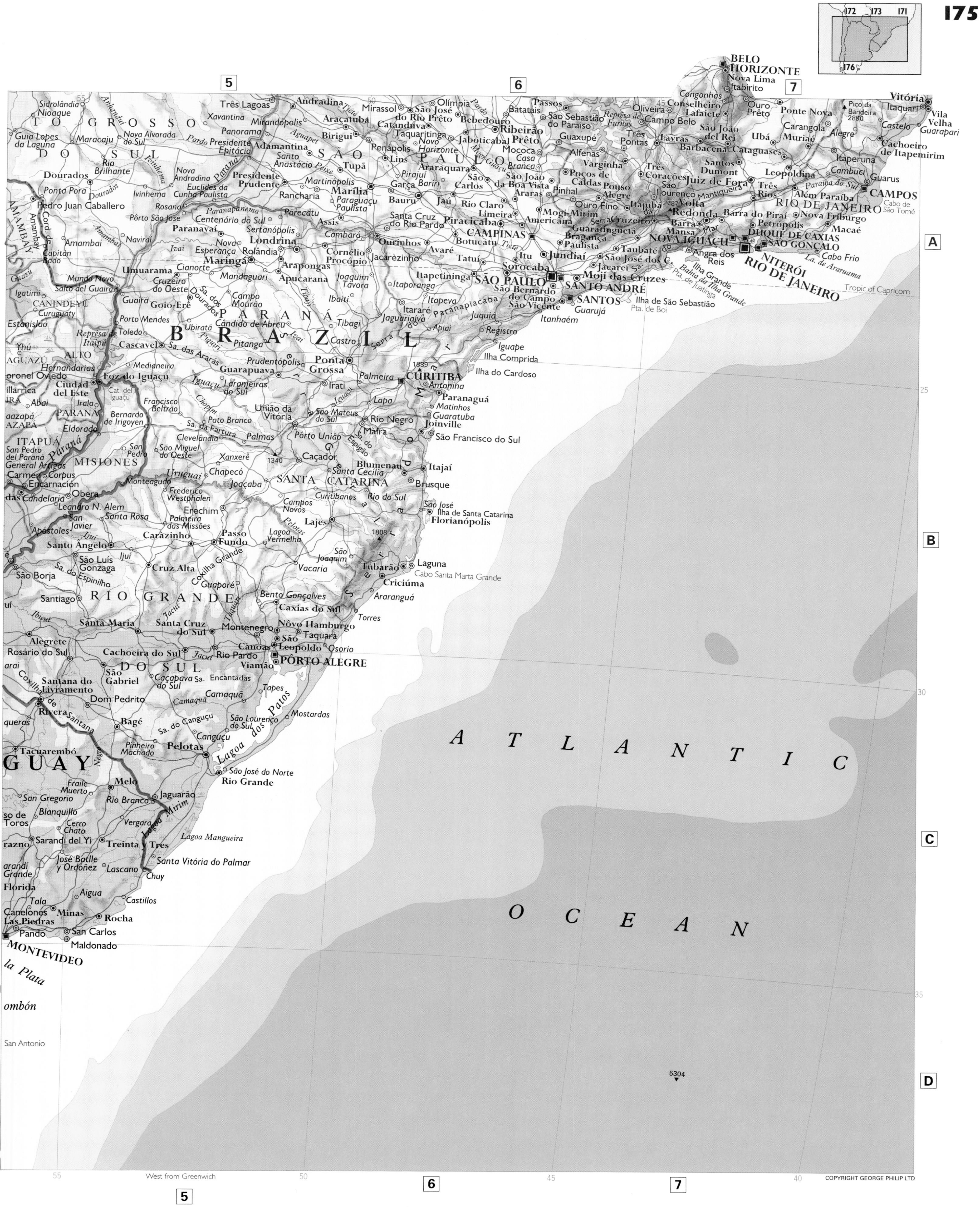

172 173 171
176
7

BELO HORIZONTE
Nova Lima
Itabirito
Congonhas
Conselheiro Lafaiete
Ouro Prêto
Ponte Nova
Vitória
Itaquari
Vila Velha
Guarapari

5

55
Sidrolândia
Nioaque
Três Lagoas
Andradina
Tietê
Mirassol
Olímpia
São José do Rio Prêto
Bebedouro
Passos
Batatais
Oliveira
Campo Belo
Carangola
Muriaé
Castelo
Cachoeiro de Itapemirim

TO GROSSO
Guia Lopes da Laguna
Maracaju
Nova Alvorada do Sul
Xavantina
Panorama
Araçatuba
Catanduva
São Sebastião do Paraíso
Ribeirão Prêto
Guaxupé
São Sebastião do Paraíso
Lafaiete
Lavras
São João del Rei
Ubá
Cataguases
Leopoldina
Campos

DO SUL
Dourados
Rio Brilhante
Presidente Epitácio
Adamantina
Birigui
Penápolis
Lins
Tupã
Jaboticabal
Novo
Mocóca
Casa Branca
Alfenas
Varginha
Pouso
Três Corações
Juiz de Fora
Santos
Barbacena
Leopoldina
Cabo de São Tomé

Douradina
Ponta Porã
Dourados
Santo Anastácio
da Cunha Paulista
Presidente Prudente
Martinópolis
Marília
Paraguaçu Paulista
Bauru
Garça
Bariri
Jaú
São Carlos
Araras
Pinhal
Poços de Caldas
Ouro Fino
Itajubá
Volta Redonda
Barra do Piraí
RIO DE JANEIRO
Macaé

Pedro Juan Caballero
Nova Andradina
Ivinhema
Rancharia
Rosana
Paranapanema
Assis
Cambará
Ourinhos
Santa Cruz do Rio Pardo
Piracicaba
Americana
CAMPINAS
Mogi-Mirim
Limeira
Rio Claro
Lorenço
Guaratinguetá
Bragança Paulista
Aparecida
Cruzeiro
Barra Mansa
Petrópolis
Nova Friburgo

AMAMBAY
Pôrto São José
Paranaví
Nova
Londrina
Rolândia
Cornélio Procópio
Jacarèzinho
Botucatu
Itu
Jundiaí
São José dos C.
Taubaté
Angra dos Reis
NOVA IGUAÇU
DUQUE DE CAXIAS
São Gonçalo
NITERÓI

Amambai
Naviraí
Ivaí
Maringá
Apucarana
Joaquim Távora
Avaré
Tatuí
Sorocaba
Moji das Cruzes
São José do C.
Ilha Grande
Baia da Ilha Grande
RIO DE JANEIRO

Capitán Bado
Mundo Novo
Salto del Guairá
Umuarama
Cianorte
Mandaguari
Ibaiti
Itapetininga
SÃO PAULO
Santo André
São Bernardo do Campo
São Vicente
SANTOS
Pta. de Juatinga
La. de Araruama
Cabo Frio

CANINDEYÚ
Igatimí
Guaíra
Goio-Erê
PARANÁ
Campo Mourão
Ibaiti
Itaporanga
Itapeva
Paranapiacaba
Juquiá
Guarujá
Ilha de São Sebastião
Pta. de Boi

Curuguaty
Estanislao
Porto Mendes
Ubiratã
Cândido de Abreu
Tibagi
Itararé
Apiaí
Registro
Itanhaém
Tropic of Capricorn

Yhú
ALTO
Cruzeiro do Oeste
Sa. dos Dourados
Castro
Iguape
Ilha Comprida

Coronel Oviedo
Hernandarias
Medianeira
Guarapuava
Prudentópolis
Ponta Grossa
Palmeira
CURITIBA
Antonina
Ilha do Cardoso

Villarica
Abai
Ciudad del Este
Irala
Cascavel
Laranjeiras do Sul
Irati
Lapa
Paranaguá
Matinhos
Guaratuba
25

IRA
PARANÁ
Cat. del Iguaçu
Francisco Beltrão
União da Vitória
São Mateus do Sul
Rio Negro
Mafra
Joinville
São Francisco do Sul

aazapá
AZAPÁ
Eldorado
Bernardo de Irigoyen
Pato Branco
Sa. da Fartura
Palmas
Pôrto União
Espigão
Caçador
1340
Xanxerê
Chapecó
Joaçaba
Canoinhas

ITAPUÁ
San Pedro del Paraná
General Artigas
San Pedro
Clevelândia
Palmas
Santa Cecília
Itajaí
Blumenau
Brusque

Carmen
Corpus
Encarnación
MISIONES
Uruguaí
Frederico Westphalen
Erechim
SANTA CATARINA
Curitibanos
Rio do Sul
São José de Santa Catarina

das Candelaria
Obera
Monteagudo
Palmeira das Missões
Campos Novos
Curitibanos
Florianópolis
Ilha de Santa Catarina

Apóstoles
Leandro N. Alem
Ijui
Uruguai
Lajes
1808

San Javier
Santa Rosa
Santo Ângelo
Ijuí
São Joaquim
Laguna
B

São Luís Gonzaga
Carazinho
Passo Fundo
Vacaria
Cabo Santa Marta Grande

São Borja
Sa. do Espinilho
Cruz Alta
Guaporé
Tubarão
Criciúma

Santiago
RIO GRANDE
Bento Gonçalves
Araranguá

ul
Santa Maria
Santa Cruz do Sul
Caxias do Sul
Torres

Alegrete
Rosário do Sul
DO SUL
Novo Hamburgo
Taquara

Santa Maria
Cachoeira do Sul
Montenegro
São Leopoldo
Canoas
Osório

arai
DO SUL
Rio Pardo
Viamão
PÔRTO ALEGRE

Santana do Livramento
São Gabriel
Caçapava do Sul
Encantadas
Tapes
30

Rivera
Santa
Dom Pedrito
Camaquã
Camaquã

queras
Bagé
Sa. do Canguçu
São Lourenço do Sul
Mostardas

Tacuarembó
Pinheiro Machado
Canguçu
Pelotas
Lagoa dos Patos

GUAY
Fraile Muerto
Melo
Rio Branco
Jaguarão
Rio Grande
São José do Norte

San Gregorio
Blanquillo
Cerro Chato
Mirim
ATLANTIC

so de Toros
Sarandi del Yi
Vergara
Lagoa Mangueira

razno
José Batlle y Ordóñez
Treinta y Tres
Santa Vitória do Palmar
Chuy

arandí
Florida
Lascano
Castillos
OCEAN

Grande
Tala
Aigua

Canelones
Minas
Rocha
Las Piedras
San Carlos

MONTEVIDEO
Pando
Maldonado

la Plata

ombón

San Antonio

5304

A T L A N T I C

O C E A N

5
West from Greenwich 50
6
45
7
40
COPYRIGHT GEORGE PHILIP LTD

174 175

50 0 50 100 150 200 250 300 km
50 0 50 100 150 200 miles

5

2 3 4

PACIFIC OCEAN

SOUTH ATLANTIC OCEAN

LA PAMPA

Colonia 25 de Mayo
Bernasconi
Puelches
Tornquist 1243
Coronel Pringles
Villa Iris
González Chaves
Juárez
Balcarce
Loberia
Quequén
Necochea
Oriente
Coronel Dorrego
Puelches
Cuchillo-Có
BUENOS AIRES
Bahía Blanca
Médanos
Punta Alta
B. Blanca
I. Trinidad
Mayor Buratovich

ARAUCO
Mulchén
Collipulli
Paso Copahue 2980
Cañete
Capitán Pastene
I. Mocha
Traiguén
Galvarino
Angol
Victoria
Longuimay
Las Lajas
Loncopué
Paso de los Indios
Anelo
Neuquén
Barda del Medio
Cipolletti
Fortín Uno
Allen
Gral. Roca
Chelforó
Temuco
Lautaro
Curacautín
Paso Pino Hachado 1824
Zabala
Cutral-Có
Río Colorado
Choele Choel
Puerto Saavedra
Nueva Imperial
Cunco
3124
Picún Leufú
Colorado
Lamarque
Carmen de Patagones
Toltén
Freire
Villarrica
Junín de los Andes
Limay
El Cuy
Negro
General Conesa
Stroeder
Viedma

ARAUCANIA
Pitrufquén
NEUQUÉN
Paso Mamuil Malal 1253 3778
RÍO NEGRO
Punta Rasa

Valdivia
Corral
Pta. Galera
Loncoche
Panguipulli
Las Coloradas
San Martín de los Andes
Piedra del Águila
La Esperanza
Sierra Colorada
Valcheta
Aguada Cecilio
San Antonio Oeste

La Unión
Osorno
Río Bueno
Lanco
L. Ranco
Lago Ranco
Puyehue
1314
Paso Flores
Los Menucos
Golfo San Matías

Bahía Mansa
Río Negro
Vol. Osorno 2660
L. Nahuel Huapí
Comallo
Maquinchao
Ingeniero Jacobacci
Meseta de Somuncurá
Salado
Sierra Grande
Cona Niyeu
Puerto Lobos
Pen. Valdés
Puerto Pirámides
Pta. Norte

LOS LAGOS
L. Llanquihue
Mte. Tronador 3554
San Carlos de Bariloche
El Cain
Verde
G. San José
Puerto Madryn

Puerto Varas
Puerto Montt
2185
El Bolsón
Norquinco
Quetrequile
1879
Puerto Pirámides -40
Punta Delgada

Los Muermos
G. de los Coronados
Pta. Huechucuicui
El Maitén
Gastre
Telsen
G. Nuevo
Puerto Madryn

Maullín
Ancud
G. de Ancud
Leleque
Gan Gan
Gaimán
Rawson
Trelew

Isla de Chiloé
Castro
820
Achao
CHUBUT
Gualjaina
Esquel
2470
L. Menéndez
Perdido
Las Plumas
Chubut

Chaitén
2440
Tecka
Pampa de Agnia
Cabo Raso

Puerto Quellón
C. Quilán
2300
Yelcho
El Corcovado
2075
Paso de Indios
Meseta de Montemayor
Camarones
B. Camarones
C. Dos Bahías

Boca del Guafo
I. Guafo
Islas Guaitecas
José de San Martín
Gran Laguna Salada
Chico

Archipiélago
I. Guamblin
Magdalena
Puerto Cisnes
L. General Vintter
Río Pico
1245
Camarones
B. Bustamante

de los
Chonos
C. Taitao
2020
L. Fontana
L. Musters
B. Bustamante

Peninsula de Taitao
Mte. San Valentín 4058
Alto Río Senguerr
Facundo
L. Colhué Huapi
Golfo San Jorge

Cerro Arenales 3437
Cochrane
Calhaique
Mayo
Río Mayo
Sarmiento
Holdich
Comodoro Rivadavia

Golfo de Penas
C. Tres Montes
Mte. San Lorenzo 3700
Balmaceda
L. Buenos Aires
Los Monos
Colonia Las Heras
Caleta Olivia

Archipiélago Guayaneco
I. Javier
Cerro Mellizo Sur 3050
Chile Chico
Perito Moreno
Los Antiguos
Pico Truncado

I. Campana
I. Patricio Lynch
2726
L. Gral. Carrera
Los Antiguos
1335
Mazarredo
C. Tres Puntas
C. Blanco

I. Esmeralda
Canal Baker
L. Pueyrredón
Bajo Caracoles
Fitz Roy
Jaramillo

I. Mornington
G. Ladrillero
Cerro Murallón 3600
Lago Posadas
Deseado
Puerto Deseado

G. Trinidad
Las Horquetas
2280
Mt. Inés 1120
Pta. Medanosa

I. Madre de Dios
I. Duque de York
SANTA CRUZ
Gobernador Gregores
Bahía Laura

C. Santiago
B. Salvación
Mte. Fitzroy 3375
Gran Altiplanicie Central
San Julián

I. Hanover
Lago San Martín
L. Cardiel
Tres Lagos
Comandante Luis Piedra Buena

I. Wellington
L. Viedma
Shehuen
Santa Cruz

Cerro Paine
Calafate
L. Argentina
Santa Cruz
Puerto Coig

FALKLAND ISLANDS (U.K.)
(ISLAS MALVINAS)
Jason Is.
Pebble I.
C. Dolphin
King George B.
Mt. Adam 700
Mt. Usborne 705
Queen Charlotte B.
Falkland Sound
Port Darwin
Stanley
Weddell I.
West Falkland
East Falkland
C. Meredith
Beauchêne I.

Esperanza
Río Turbio
El Turbio
Güer Aike
Río Gallegos
Gallegos
Morro Chico
Punta Delgada
Monte Dinero
C. Vírgenes

Puerto Natales
Almirante Montt
Seno Skyring
Strait of Magellan
Cerro Sombrero

C. Jorge
Estrecho Nelson
Pen. Muñoz
Gamero
Isla Grande de Tierra del Fuego
San Sebastián

Arch. Reina Adelaida
C. Deseado
C. Magallanes
Punta Arenas
Pen. de Brunswick
Porvenir
Río Grande

B. Otway
Santa Inés
I. Riesco
Seno de Otway
Ea. Cameron
TIERRA
DEL FUEGO

I. Desolación
Clarence I.
Capitán Aracena
Dawson I.
Whiteside
Ushuaia
L. Fagnano
C. San Diego
I. de los Estados (Staten I.)

Canal Cockburn
Pen. Brecknock
2469
Mte. Darwin
Canal Beagle
Picton
Nueva
Estr. de le Maire

I. Stewart
Gordon I.
Navarino
Lennox

I. Londonderry
B. Cook
I. Hoste
B. Nassau
Pen. Hardy
Islas Wollaston
Is. Hermite
Cabo de Hornos (Cape Horn)

Islas Diego Ramírez

Projection: Lambert's Equivalent Azimuthal

West from Greenwich

COPYRIGHT GEORGE PHILIP LTD

ft m
9000 3000
6000 2000
4500 1500
3000 1000
1200 400
600 200
0 0
200 600
2000 6000
4000 12000
m ft

INDEX TO
WORLD MAPS

How to use the index

The index contains the names of all the principal places and features shown on the World Maps. Each name is followed by an additional entry in italics giving the country or region within which it is located. The alphabetical order of names composed of two or more words is governed primarily by the first word and then by the second. This is an example of the rule:

Mīr Kūh, *Iran*	**97 E8**	26 22N 58 55 E
Mīr Shahdād, *Iran*	**97 E8**	26 15N 58 29 E
Mira, *Italy*	**45 C9**	45 26N 12 8 E
Mira por vos Cay, *Bahamas*	**165 B5**	22 9N 74 30W
Miraj, *India*	**94 F2**	16 50N 74 45 E

Physical features composed of a proper name (Erie) and a description (Lake) are positioned alphabetically by the proper name. The description is positioned after the proper name and is usually abbreviated:

Erie, L., *N. Amer.* **150 D4** 42 15N 81 0W

Where a description forms part of a settlement or administrative name however, it is always written in full and put in its true alphabetic position:

Mount Olive, *U.S.A.* **156 E7** 39 4N 89 44W

Names beginning with M' and Mc are indexed as if they were spelled Mac. Names beginning St. are alphabetised under Saint, but Sankt, Sint, Sant', Santa and San are all spelt in full and are alphabetised accordingly. If the same place name occurs two or more times in the index and all are in the same country, each is followed by the name of the administrative subdivision in which it is located.

The number in bold type which follows each name in the index refers to the number of the map page where that feature or place will be found. This is usually the largest scale at which the place or feature appears.

The letter and figure which are in bold type immediately after the page number give the grid square on the map page, within which the feature is situated. The letter represents the latitude and the figure the longitude. A lower case letter immediately after the page number refers to an inset map on that page.

In some cases the feature itself may fall within the specified square, while the name is outside. This is usually the case only with features which are larger than a grid square.

The geographical co-ordinates which follow the letter-figure references give the latitude and longitude of each place. The first co-ordinate indicates latitude – the distance north of the Equator. The second co-ordinate indicates longitude – the distance east or west of the Greenwich Meridian. Both latitude and longitude are measured in degrees and minutes (there are 60 minutes in a degree).

The latitude is followed by N(orth) or S(outh) and the longitude by E(ast) or W(est).

Rivers are indexed to their mouths or confluences, and carry the symbol ➔ after their names. A solid square ■ follows the name of a country, while an open square □ refers to a first order administrative area.

How to pronounce place names

English-speaking people usually have no difficulty in reading and pronouncing correctly English place names. However, foreign place name pronunciations may present many problems. Such problems can be minimised by following some simple rules. However, these rules cannot be applied to all situations, and there will be many exceptions.

1. In general, stress each syllable equally, unless your experience suggests otherwise.
2. Pronounce the letter 'a' as a broad 'a' as in 'arm'.
3. Pronounce the letter 'e' as a short 'e' as in 'elm'.
4. Pronounce the letter 'i' as a cross between a short 'i' and long 'e', as the two 'i's in 'California'.
5. Pronounce the letter 'o' as an intermediate 'o' as in 'soft'.
6. Pronounce the letter 'u' as an intermediate 'u' as in 'sure'.
7. Pronounce consonants hard, except in the Romance-language areas where 'g's are likely to be pronounced softly like 'j' in 'jam'; 'j' itself may be pronounced as 'y'; and 'x' may be pronounced as 'h'.
8. For names in mainland China, pronounce 'q' like the 'ch' in 'chin', 'x' like the 'sh' in 'she', 'zh' like the 'j' in 'jam', and 'z' as if it were spelled 'dz'. In general pronounce 'a' as in 'father', 'e' as in 'but', 'i' as in 'keep', 'o' as in 'or', and 'u' as in 'rule'.

Moreover, English has no diacritical marks (accent and pronunciation signs), although some languages do. The following is a brief and general guide to the pronunciation of those most frequently used in the principal Western European languages.

		Pronunciation as in
French	é	day and shows that the e is to be pronounced; e.g. Orléans.
	è	mare
	î	used over any vowel and does not affect pronunciation; shows contraction of the name, usually omission of 's' following a vowel.
	ç	's' before 'a', 'o' and 'u'.
	ë, ï, ü	over 'e', 'i' and 'u' when they are used with another vowel and shows that each is to be pronounced.
German	ä	fate
	ö	fur
	ü	no English equivalent; like French 'tu'
Italian	à, é	over vowels and indicates stress.
Portuguese	ã, õ	vowels pronounced nasally.
	ç	boss
	á	shows stress
	ô	shows that a vowel has an 'i' or 'u' sound combined with it.
Spanish	ñ	canyon
	ü	pronounced as w and separately from adjoining vowels.
	á	usually indicates that this is a stressed vowel.

Abbreviations

A.C.T. – Australian Capital Territory
A.R. – Autonomous Region
Afghan. – Afghanistan
Afr. – Africa
Ala. – Alabama
Alta. – Alberta
Amer. – America(n)
Arch. – Archipelago
Ariz. – Arizona
Ark. – Arkansas
Atl. Oc. – Atlantic Ocean
B. – Baie, Bahía, Bay, Bucht, Bugt
B.C. – British Columbia
Bangla. – Bangladesh
Barr. – Barrage
Bos.-H. – Bosnia-Herzegovina
C. – Cabo, Cap, Cape, Coast
C.A.R. – Central African Republic
C. Prov. – Cape Province
Calif. – California
Cat. – Catarata
Cent. – Central
Chan. – Channel
Colo. – Colorado
Conn. – Connecticut
Cord. – Cordillera
Cr. – Creek
Czech. – Czech Republic
D.C. – District of Columbia
Del. – Delaware
Dem. – Democratic
Dep. – Dependency
Des. – Desert
Dét. – Détroit
Dist. – District
Dj. – Djebel
Domin. – Dominica
Dom. Rep. – Dominican Republic

E. – East
E. Salv. – El Salvador
Eq. Guin. – Equatorial Guinea
Est. – Estrecho
Falk. Is. – Falkland Is.
Fd. – Fjord
Fla. – Florida
Fr. – French
G. – Golfe, Golfo, Gulf, Guba, Gebel
Ga. – Georgia
Gt. – Great, Greater
Guinea-Biss. – Guinea-Bissau
H.K. – Hong Kong
H.P. – Himachal Pradesh
Hants. – Hampshire
Harb. – Harbor, Harbour
Hd. – Head
Hts. – Heights
I.(s). – Île, Ilha, Insel, Isla, Island, Isle
Ill. – Illinois
Ind. – Indiana
Ind. Oc. – Indian Ocean
Ivory C. – Ivory Coast
J. – Jabal, Jebel
Jaz. – Jazīrah
Junc. – Junction
K. – Kap, Kapp
Kans. – Kansas
Kep. – Kepulauan
Ky. – Kentucky
L. – Lac, Lacul, Lago, Lagoa, Lake, Limni, Loch, Lough
La. – Louisiana
Ld. – Land
Liech. – Liechtenstein
Lux. – Luxembourg
Mad. P. – Madhya Pradesh
Madag. – Madagascar

Man. – Manitoba
Mass. – Massachusetts
Md. – Maryland
Me. – Maine
Medit. S. – Mediterranean Sea
Mich. – Michigan
Minn. – Minnesota
Miss. – Mississippi
Mo. – Missouri
Mont. – Montana
Mozam. – Mozambique
Mt.(s) – Mont, Montaña, Mountain
Mte. – Monte
Mti. – Monti
N. – Nord, Norte, North, Northern, Nouveau
N.B. – New Brunswick
N.C. – North Carolina
N. Cal. – New Caledonia
N. Dak. – North Dakota
N.H. – New Hampshire
N.I. – North Island
N.J. – New Jersey
N. Mex. – New Mexico
N.S. – Nova Scotia
N.S.W. – New South Wales
N.W.T. – North West Territory
N.Y. – New York
N.Z. – New Zealand
Nat. – National
Nebr. – Nebraska
Neths. – Netherlands
Nev. – Nevada
Nfld. – Newfoundland
Nic. – Nicaragua
O. – Oued, Ouadi
Occ. – Occidentale
Okla. – Oklahoma

Ont. – Ontario
Or. – Orientale
Oreg. – Oregon
Os. – Ostrov
Oz. – Ozero
P. – Pass, Passo, Pasul, Pulau
P.E.I. – Prince Edward Island
Pa. – Pennsylvania
Pac. Oc. – Pacific Ocean
Papua N.G. – Papua New Guinea
Pass. – Passage
Peg. – Pegunungan
Pen. – Peninsula, Péninsule
Phil. – Philippines
Pk. – Peak
Plat. – Plateau
Prov. – Province, Provincial
Pt. – Point
Pta. – Ponta, Punta
Pte. – Pointe
Qué. – Québec
Queens. – Queensland
R. – Rio, River
R.I. – Rhode Island
Ra. – Range
Raj. – Rajasthan
Recr. – Recreational, Récréatif
Reg. – Region
Rep. – Republic
Res. – Reserve, Reservoir
Rhld-Pfz. – Rheinland-Pfalz
S. – South, Southern, Sur
Si. Arabia – Saudi Arabia
S.C. – South Carolina
S. Dak. – South Dakota
S.I. – South Island
S. Leone – Sierra Leone
Sa. – Serra, Sierra

Sask. – Saskatchewan
Scot. – Scotland
Sd. – Sound
Sev. – Severnaya
Sib. – Siberia
Sprs. – Springs
St. – Saint
Sta. – Santa
Ste. – Sainte
Sto. – Santo
Str. – Strait, Stretto
Switz. – Switzerland
Tas. – Tasmania
Tenn. – Tennessee
Terr. – Territory, Territoire
Tex. – Texas
Tg. – Tanjung
Trin. & Tob. – Trinidad & Tobago
U.A.E. – United Arab Emirates
U.K. – United Kingdom
U.S.A. – United States of America
Ut. P. – Uttar Pradesh
Va. – Virginia
Vdkhr. – Vodokhranilishche
Vdskh. – Vodoskhovyshche
Vf. – Vírful
Vic. – Victoria
Vol. – Volcano
Vt. – Vermont
W. – Wadi, West
W. Va. – West Virginia
Wall. & F. Is. – Wallis and Futuna Is.
Wash. – Washington
Wis. – Wisconsin
Wlkp. – Wielkopolski
Wyo. – Wyoming
Yorks. – Yorkshire
Yug. – Yugoslavia

178 A Baña

A

A Baña, *Spain* **42 C2** 42 58N 8 46W
A Cañiza, *Spain* **42 C2** 42 13N 8 16W
A Coruña, *Spain* **42 B2** 43 20N 8 25W
A Estrada, *Spain* **42 C2** 42 43N 8 27W
A Fonsagrada, *Spain* **42 B3** 43 8N 7 4W
A Guarda, *Spain* **42 D2** 41 56N 8 52W
A Gudiña, *Spain* **42 C3** 42 4N 7 8W
A Rúa, *Spain* **42 C3** 42 24N 7 6W
Aachen, *Germany* **30 E2** 50 45N 6 6 E
Aadorf, *Switz.* **33 B7** 47 30N 8 55 E
Aalborg = Ålborg, *Denmark* **17 G3** 57 2N 9 54 E
Aalen, *Germany* **31 G6** 48 51N 10 6 E
A'Âli an Nîl □, *Sudan* **107 F3** 9 30N 33 0 E
Aalst, *Belgium* **24 D4** 50 56N 4 2 E
Aalten, *Neths.* **24 C6** 51 56N 6 35 E
Aalter, *Belgium* **24 C3** 51 5N 3 28 E
Äänekoski, *Finland* **15 E21** 62 36N 25 44 E
Aarau, *Switz.* **32 B6** 47 23N 8 4 E
Aarberg, *Switz.* **32 B4** 47 2N 7 16 E
Aarburg, *Switz.* **32 B5** 47 19N 7 54 E
Aare →, *Switz.* **32 A6** 47 33N 8 14 E
Aargau □, *Switz.* **32 B6** 47 26N 8 10 E
Aarhus = Århus, *Denmark* **17 H4** 56 8N 10 11 E
Aarschot, *Belgium* **24 D4** 50 59N 4 49 E
Aarwangen, *Switz.* **32 B5** 47 15N 7 46 E
Aasiaat, *Greenland* **10 D5** 68 43N 52 56W
Ab-i-Istada, *Afghan.* **91 B2** 32 29N 67 55 E
Ab-i-Panja = Pyandzh →, *Asia* **65 E4** 37 6N 68 20 E
Aba, *China* **76 A3** 32 59N 101 42 E
Aba, *Dem. Rep. of the Congo* **118 B3** 3 58N 30 17 E
Aba, *Nigeria* **113 D6** 5 10N 7 19 E
Abâ, Jazîrat, *Sudan* **107 E3** 13 30N 32 31 E
Abacaxis →, *Brazil* **169 D6** 3 54 S 58 47W
Abadab, J., *Sudan* **106 D4** 18 54N 35 56 E
Ābādān, *Iran* **97 D6** 30 22N 48 20 E
Abade, *Ethiopia* **107 F4** 9 22N 38 3 E
Ābādeh, *Iran* **97 D7** 31 8N 52 40 E
Abadin, *Spain* **42 B3** 43 21N 7 29W
Abadla, *Algeria* **111 B4** 31 2N 2 45W
Abaeté, *Brazil* **171 E2** 19 9 S 45 27W
Abaeté →, *Brazil* **171 E2** 18 2 S 45 12W
Abaetetuba, *Brazil* **170 B2** 1 40 S 48 50W
Abagnar Qi, *China* **74 C9** 43 52N 116 2 E
Abah, Tanjung, *Indonesia* **79 K18** 8 46 S 115 38 E
Abai, *Paraguay* **175 B4** 25 58 S 55 54W
Abak, *Nigeria* **113 E6** 4 58N 7 50 E
Abakaliki, *Nigeria* **113 D6** 6 22N 8 2 E
Abakan, *Russia* **67 D10** 53 40N 91 10 E
Abala, *Congo* **114 C3** 1 17 S 15 35 E
Abala, *Niger* **113 C5** 14 56N 3 22 E
Abalak, *Niger* **113 B6** 15 22N 6 21 E
Abalemma, *Algeria* **111 D6** 20 51N 5 59 E
Abalemma, *Niger* **113 B6** 16 12N 7 50 E
Abalessa, *Algeria* **111 D5** 22 58N 4 47 E
Abana, *Turkey* **100 B6** 41 59N 34 1 E
Abancay, *Peru* **172 C3** 13 35 S 72 55W
Abanga →, *Gabon* **114 C2** 0 20 S 10 30 E
Abano Terme, *Italy* **45 C8** 45 22N 11 46 E
Abapó, *Bolivia* **173 D5** 18 48 S 63 25W
Abarán, *Spain* **41 G3** 38 12N 1 23W
Abariringa, *Kiribati* **134 H10** 2 50 S 171 40W
Abarqū, *Iran* **97 D7** 31 10N 53 20 E
Abashiri, *Japan* **70 B12** 44 0N 144 15 E
Abashiri-Wan, *Japan* **70 C12** 44 0N 144 30 E
Abau, *Papua N. G.* **132 F5** 10 11 S 148 46 E
Abaújszántó, *Hungary* **52 B6** 48 16N 21 12 E
Abava →, *Latvia* **54 A8** 57 6N 21 54 E
Ābay = Nîl el Azraq →, *Sudan* **107 D3** 15 38N 32 31 E
Abay, *Kazakstan* **66 E8** 49 38N 72 53 E
Abaya, L., *Ethiopia* **107 F4** 6 30N 37 50 E
Abaya-Shala Lakes Nat. Park, *Ethiopia* **107 F4** 7 40N 38 37 E
Abaza, *Russia* **66 D9** 52 39N 90 6 E
Abba, *C.A.R.* **114 A3** 5 20N 15 11 E
Abbadia San Salvatore, *Italy* **45 F8** 42 53N 11 41 E
'Abbāsābād, *Iran* **97 C8** 33 34N 58 23 E
Abbay = Nîl el Azraq →, *Sudan* **107 D3** 15 38N 32 31 E
Abbaye, Pt., *U.S.A.* **148 B1** 46 58N 88 8W
Abbé, L., *Ethiopia* **107 E5** 11 8N 41 47 E
Abbeville, *France* **27 B8** 50 6N 1 49 E
Abbeville, *Ala., U.S.A.* **152 D4** 31 34N 85 15W
Abbeville, *Ga., U.S.A.* **152 D6** 31 59N 83 18W
Abbeville, *La., U.S.A.* **155 L8** 29 58N 92 8W
Abbeville, *S.C., U.S.A.* **152 A7** 34 11N 82 23W
Abbiategrasso, *Italy* **44 C5** 45 24N 8 54 E
Abbot Ice Shelf, *Antarctica* **7 D16** 73 0 S 92 0W
Abbottabad, *Pakistan* **92 B5** 34 10N 73 15 E
Abbou, O. ben →, *Algeria* **111 C5** 28 32N 5 14 E
Abd al Kūrī, *Yemen* **99 D6** 12 5N 52 20 E
Ābdar, *Iran* **97 D7** 30 16N 55 19 E
'Abdolābād, *Iran* **97 C8** 34 12N 56 30 E
Abdulino, *Russia* **64 E4** 53 42N 53 40 E
Abdulpur, *Bangla.* **90 C2** 24 15N 88 59 E
Abéché, *Chad* **109 F4** 13 50N 20 35 E
Abejar, *Spain* **40 D2** 41 48N 2 47W
Abekr, *Sudan* **107 E2** 12 45N 28 50 E
Abel Tasman Nat. Park, *N.Z.* **131 A8** 40 59 S 173 3 E
Abemarre, *Indonesia* **83 C6** 7 1 S 140 9 E
Abengourou, *Ivory C.* **112 D4** 6 42N 3 27W
Abenójar, *Spain* **43 G6** 38 53N 4 21W
Åbenrå, *Denmark* **17 J3** 55 3N 9 25 E
Abensberg, *Germany* **31 G7** 48 48N 11 51 E
Abeokuta, *Nigeria* **113 D5** 7 3N 3 19 E
Aber, *Uganda* **118 B3** 2 12N 32 25 E
Aberaeron, *U.K.* **21 E3** 52 15N 4 15W
Aberayron = Aberaeron, *U.K.* **21 E3** 52 15N 4 15W
Aberchirder, *U.K.* **22 D6** 57 34N 2 37W
Abercorn = Mbala, *Zambia* **119 D3** 8 46 S 31 24 E
Abercorn, *Australia* **127 D5** 25 12 S 151 5 E
Aberdare, *U.K.* **21 F4** 51 43N 3 27W
Aberdare Nat. Park, *Kenya* **118 C4** 0 22 S 36 44 E
Aberdare Ra., *Kenya* **118 C4** 0 15 S 36 50 E
Aberdeen, *Australia* **129 B9** 32 9 S 150 56 E
Aberdeen, *Canada* **143 C7** 52 20N 106 8W
Aberdeen, *China* **69 G11** 22 14N 114 9 E
Aberdeen, *S. Africa* **116 E3** 32 28 S 24 2 E
Aberdeen, *U.K.* **22 D6** 57 9N 2 5W
Aberdeen, *Ala., U.S.A.* **149 J1** 33 49N 88 33W
Aberdeen, *Idaho, U.S.A.* **158 E7** 42 57N 112 50W
Aberdeen, *Md., U.S.A.* **148 F7** 39 31N 76 10W
Aberdeen, *Ohio, U.S.A.* **157 F13** 38 39N 83 46W
Aberdeen, *S. Dak., U.S.A.* **154 C5** 45 28N 98 29W
Aberdeen, *Wash., U.S.A.* **160 D3** 46 59N 123 50W
Aberdeen, City of □, *U.K.* **22 D6** 57 10N 2 10W
Aberdeenshire □, *U.K.* **22 D6** 57 17N 2 36W
Aberdovey = Aberdyfi, *U.K.* **21 E3** 52 33N 4 3W
Aberdyfi, *U.K.* **21 E3** 52 33N 4 3W
Aberfeldy, *U.K.* **22 E5** 56 37N 3 51W
Abergavenny, *U.K.* **21 F4** 51 49N 3 1W
Abergele, *U.K.* **20 D4** 53 17N 3 35W
Abernathy, *U.S.A.* **155 J4** 33 50N 101 51W
Abert, L., *U.S.A.* **158 E3** 42 38N 120 14W
Aberystwyth, *U.K.* **21 E3** 52 25N 4 5W
Abhā, *Si. Arabia* **98 C3** 18 0N 42 34 E
Abhar, *Iran* **97 B6** 36 9N 49 13 E
Abhayapuri, *India* **90 B3** 26 24N 90 38 E
Abia □, *Nigeria* **113 D6** 5 30N 7 35 E
Abide, *Turkey* **49 C11** 38 55N 29 20 E
Abidiya, *Sudan* **106 D3** 18 18N 34 3 E
Abidjan, *Ivory C.* **112 D4** 5 26N 3 58W
Abilene, *Kans., U.S.A.* **154 F6** 38 55N 97 13W
Abilene, *Tex., U.S.A.* **155 J5** 32 28N 99 43W
Abingdon, *U.K.* **21 F6** 51 40N 1 17W
Abingdon, *Ill., U.S.A.* **156 D6** 40 48N 90 24W
Abingdon, *Va., U.S.A.* **149 G5** 36 43N 81 59W
Abington Reef, *Australia* **126 B4** 18 0 S 149 35 E
Abitau →, *Canada* **143 B7** 59 53N 109 3W
Abitibi →, *Canada* **140 B3** 51 3N 80 55W
Abitibi, L., *Canada* **140 C4** 48 40N 79 40W
Abiy Adi, *Ethiopia* **107 E4** 13 39N 39 3 E
Abkhaz Republic = Abkhazia □, *Georgia* **61 J5** 43 12N 41 5 E
Abkhazia □, *Georgia* **61 J5** 43 12N 41 5 E
Abminga, *Australia* **127 D1** 26 8 S 134 51 E
Abnûb, *Egypt* **106 B3** 27 18N 31 4 E
Åbo = Turku, *Finland* **15 F20** 60 30N 22 19 E
Abo, Massif d', *Chad* **109 D3** 21 41N 16 8 E
Abocho, *Nigeria* **113 D6** 7 35N 6 56 E
Abohar, *India* **92 D6** 30 10N 74 10 E
Aboisso, *Ivory C.* **112 D4** 5 30N 3 5W
Abolo, *Congo* **114 B2** 0 8N 14 16 E
Abomey, *Benin* **113 D5** 7 10N 2 5 E
Abong-Mbang, *Cameroon* **114 B2** 4 0N 13 8 E
Abongabong, *Indonesia* **84 B1** 4 15N 96 48 E
Abonnema, *Nigeria* **113 E6** 4 41N 6 49 E
Abony, *Hungary* **52 C5** 47 12N 20 3 E
Abor Hills, *India* **90 A5** 28 25N 94 46 E
Aborlan, *Phil.* **81 G2** 9 26N 118 33 E
Aboso, *Ghana* **112 D4** 5 23N 1 57W
Abou-Deïa, *Chad* **109 F3** 11 20N 19 20 E
Abou-Goulem, *Chad* **109 F4** 13 37N 21 38 E
Abou-Telfan, Réserve de Faune de l', *Chad* **109 F3** 12 2N 18 58 E
Aboyne, *U.K.* **22 D6** 57 4N 2 47W
Abra □, *Phil.* **80 C3** 17 35N 120 45 E
Abra de Ilog, *Phil.* **80 E3** 13 27N 120 44 E
Abra Pampa, *Argentina* **174 A2** 22 43 S 65 42W
Abraham L., *Canada* **142 C5** 52 15N 116 35W
Abrantes, *Portugal* **43 F2** 39 24N 8 7W
Abreojos, Pta., *Mexico* **162 B2** 26 50N 113 40W
Abri, *Esh Shamâliya, Sudan* **106 C3** 20 50N 30 27 E
Abri, *Janub Kordofân, Sudan* **107 E3** 11 40N 30 21 E
Abrolhos, Banka, *Brazil* **171 E4** 18 0 S 38 0W
Abrud, *Romania* **52 D8** 46 19N 23 5 E
Abruzzo □, *Italy* **45 F10** 42 15N 14 0 E
Absaroka Range, *U.S.A.* **158 D9** 44 45N 109 50W
Abtenau, *Austria* **34 D6** 47 33N 13 21 E
Abu, *India* **92 G5** 24 41N 72 50 E
Abū al Abyad, *U.A.E.* **97 E7** 24 11N 53 50 E
Abū al Khaṣīb, *Iraq* **97 D6** 30 25N 48 0 E
Abū 'Alī, *Si. Arabia* **97 E6** 27 20N 49 27 E
Abū 'Alī →, *Lebanon* **103 A4** 34 25N 35 50 E
Abu 'Arīsh, *Si. Arabia* **98 C3** 16 53N 42 48 E
Abu Ballas, *Egypt* **106 C2** 24 26N 27 36 E
Abu Deleiq, *Sudan* **107 D3** 15 57N 33 48 E
Abu Dhabi = Abū Ẓāby, *U.A.E.* **97 E7** 24 28N 54 22 E
Abu Dis, *Sudan* **106 D3** 19 12N 33 38 E
Abu Dom, *Sudan* **107 D3** 16 18N 32 25 E
Abū Du'ān, *Syria* **101 D8** 36 25N 38 15 E
Abu el Gairi, W. →, *Egypt* **103 F2** 29 35N 33 30 E
Abu Fatma, Ras, *Sudan* **106 C4** 22 25N 36 25 E
Abu Gabra, *Sudan* **107 E2** 11 2N 26 50 E
Abu Ga'da, W. →, *Egypt* **103 F1** 29 15N 32 53 E
Abu Gelba, *Sudan* **107 E3** 13 11N 31 52 E
Abu Gubeiha, *Sudan* **107 E3** 11 30N 31 15 E
Abu Habl, Khawr →, *Sudan* **107 E3** 12 37N 31 0 E
Abū Ḥadrīyah, *Si. Arabia* **97 E6** 27 20N 48 58 E
Abu Hamed, *Sudan* **106 D3** 19 32N 33 13 E
Abu Haraz, *An Nîl el Azraq, Sudan* **106 D3** 18 1N 33 58 E
Abu Haraz, *El Gezira, Sudan* **107 E3** 14 35N 33 30 E
Abu Haraz, *Esh Shamâliya, Sudan* **106 D3** 19 8N 32 18 E
Abu Higar, *Sudan* **107 E3** 12 50N 33 59 E
Abū Kamāl, *Syria* **101 E9** 34 30N 41 0 E
Abu Kuleiwat, *Sudan* **107 E2** 12 20N 26 0 E
Abū Madd, Ra's, *Si. Arabia* **96 E3** 24 50N 37 7 E
Abu Matariq, *Sudan* **107 E2** 10 59N 26 9 E
Abu Mendi, *Ethiopia* **107 E4** 11 45N 35 42 E
Abū Mūsā, *U.A.E.* **97 E7** 25 52N 55 3 E
Abū Qaṣr, *Si. Arabia* **96 D3** 30 21N 38 34 E
Abu Qir, *Egypt* **106 H7** 31 18N 30 0 E
Abu Qireiya, *Egypt* **106 C4** 24 5N 35 28 E
Abu Qurqâs, *Egypt* **106 B3** 28 1N 30 44 E
Abū Rasās, Ra's, *Oman* **99 B7** 20 10N 58 38 E
Abū Ṣafāt, W. →, *Jordan* **103 E5** 30 24N 36 7 E
Abu Shagara, Ras, *Sudan* **106 C4** 21 4N 37 19 E
Abu Shanab, *Sudan* **107 E2** 13 58N 27 49 E
Abu Simbel, *Egypt* **106 C3** 22 18N 31 40 E
Abū Şukhayr, *Iraq* **101 G11** 31 54N 44 30 E
Abu Sultân, *Egypt* **106 H8** 30 24N 32 21 E
Abu Tabari, *Sudan* **106 D2** 17 32N 28 32 E
Abu Tig, *Egypt* **106 B3** 27 4N 31 15 E
Abu Tiga, *Sudan* **107 E3** 12 47N 34 12 E
Abu Tineitin, *Sudan* **107 E3** 12 14N 31 1 E
Abu Uruq, *Sudan* **107 D3** 15 52N 30 25 E
Abu Zabad, *Sudan* **107 E2** 12 25N 29 10 E
Abū Ẓāby, *U.A.E.* **97 E7** 24 28N 54 22 E
Abū Zeydābād, *Iran* **97 C6** 33 54N 51 45 E
Abufari, *Brazil* **173 B5** 5 25 S 62 59W
Abuja, *Nigeria* **113 D6** 9 5N 7 32 E
Abukuma-Gawa →, *Japan* **70 E10** 38 6N 140 52 E
Abukuma-Sammyaku, *Japan* **70 F10** 37 30N 140 45 E
Abulug, *Phil.* **80 B3** 18 27N 121 27 E
Abumombazi, *Dem. Rep. of the Congo* **114 B4** 3 42N 22 10 E
Abunã, *Brazil* **173 B4** 9 40 S 65 20W
Abunã →, *Brazil* **173 B4** 9 41 S 65 20W
Abune Yosef, *Ethiopia* **107 E4** 12 5N 39 12 E
Aburatsu, *Japan* **72 F3** 31 34N 131 24 E
Aburo, *Dem. Rep. of the Congo* **118 B3** 2 4N 30 53 E
Abut Hd., *N.Z.* **131 D5** 43 7 S 170 15 E
Abuye Meda, *Ethiopia* **107 E4** 10 30N 39 49 E
Abuyog, *Phil.* **81 F5** 10 45N 125 0 E
Abwong, *Sudan* **107 F3** 9 2N 32 14 E
Åby, *Sweden* **17 F10** 58 40N 16 10 E
Aby, Lagune, *Ivory C.* **112 D4** 5 15N 3 14W
Abyad, *Sudan* **107 E2** 13 47N 26 24 E
Åbybro, *Denmark* **17 G3** 57 10N 9 44 E
Acacías, *Colombia* **168 C3** 3 59N 73 46W
Acadia Nat. Park, *U.S.A.* **149 C11** 44 20N 68 13W
Acajutla, *El Salv.* **164 D2** 13 36N 89 50W
Açailândia, *Brazil* **170 C2** 5 0 S 47 30W
Acámbaro, *Mexico* **162 D4** 20 0N 100 40W
Acanthus, *Greece* **50 F7** 40 27N 23 47 E
Acaponeta, *Mexico* **162 C3** 22 30N 105 20W
Acapulco, *Mexico* **163 D5** 16 51N 99 56W
Acará, *Brazil* **170 B2** 1 57 S 48 11W
Acarai, Serra, *Brazil* **169 C6** 1 50N 57 50W
Acaraú, *Brazil* **170 B3** 2 53 S 40 7W
Acari, *Brazil* **170 C4** 6 31 S 36 38W
Acari, *Peru* **172 D3** 15 25 S 74 36W
Acarigua, *Venezuela* **168 B4** 9 33N 69 12W
Acatlán, *Mexico* **163 D5** 18 10N 98 3W
Acayucan, *Mexico* **163 D6** 17 59N 94 58W
Accéglio, *Italy* **44 D4** 44 28N 6 59 E
Accomac, *U.S.A.* **148 G8** 37 43N 75 40W
Accous, *France* **28 E3** 43 0N 0 36W
Accra, *Ghana* **113 D4** 5 35N 0 6W
Accrington, *U.K.* **20 D5** 53 45N 2 22W
Acebal, *Argentina* **174 C3** 33 20 S 60 50W
Aceh □, *Indonesia* **84 B1** 4 15N 97 30 E
Acerra, *Italy* **47 B7** 40 57N 14 22 E
Aceuchal, *Spain* **43 G4** 38 39N 6 30W
Achacachi, *Bolivia* **172 D4** 16 3 S 68 43W
Achaguas, *Venezuela* **168 B4** 7 46N 68 14W
Achalpur, *India* **94 D3** 21 22N 77 32 E
Achao, *Chile* **176 B2** 42 28 S 73 30W
Achegour, *Niger* **109 E2** 19 10N 11 54 E
Achelouma, *Niger* **109 D2** 22 12N 12 50 E
Achelouma, E. →, *Niger* **109 D2** 21 55N 13 35 E
Acheng, *China* **75 B14** 45 30N 126 58 E
Achenkirch, *Austria* **34 D4** 47 32N 11 45 E
Achensee, *Austria* **34 D4** 47 26N 11 45 E
Acher, *India* **92 H5** 23 10N 72 32 E
Achern, *Germany* **31 G4** 48 37N 8 4 E
Acheron →, *N.Z.* **131 C8** 42 16 S 173 4 E
Achill Hd., *Ireland* **23 C1** 53 58N 10 15W
Achill I., *Ireland* **23 C1** 53 58N 10 1W
Achim, *Germany* **30 B5** 53 1N 9 3 E
Achinsk, *Russia* **67 D10** 56 20N 90 20 E
Achisay = Ashchysay, *Kazakstan* **65 B4** 43 35N 68 53 E
Achit, *Russia* **64 C6** 56 48N 57 54 E
Achouka, *Gabon* **114 C2** 0 52 S 9 45 E
Acıgöl, *Turkey* **49 D11** 37 50N 29 50 E
Acıpayam, *Turkey* **49 D11** 37 26N 29 22 E
Acireale, *Italy* **47 E8** 37 37N 15 10 E
Ackerman, *U.S.A.* **155 J10** 33 19N 89 11W
Ackley, *U.S.A.* **156 B3** 42 33N 93 3W
Acklins I., *Bahamas* **165 B5** 22 30N 74 0W
Acme, *Canada* **142 C6** 51 33N 113 30W
Acme, *U.S.A.* **150 F5** 40 8N 79 26W
Acobamba, *Peru* **172 C3** 12 52 S 74 35W
Acomayo, *Peru* **172 C3** 13 55 S 71 38W
Aconcagua, Cerro, *Argentina* **174 C2** 32 39 S 70 0W
Aconquija, Mt., *Argentina* **174 B2** 27 0 S 66 0W
Acopiara, *Brazil* **170 C4** 6 6 S 39 27W
Açores, Is. dos, *Atl. Oc.* **8 C9** 38 0N 27 0W
Acorizal, *Brazil* **173 D6** 15 12 S 56 22W
Acornhoek, *S. Africa* **117 C5** 24 37 S 31 2 E
Acquapendente, *Italy* **45 F8** 42 44N 11 52 E
Acquasanta Terme, *Italy* **45 F10** 42 46N 13 24 E
Acquasparta, *Italy* **45 F9** 42 41N 12 33 E
Acquaviva delle Fonti, *Italy* **47 B9** 40 54N 16 50 E
Ácqui Terme, *Italy* **44 D5** 44 41N 8 28 E
Acraman, L., *Australia* **127 E2** 32 2 S 135 23 E
Acre = 'Akko, *Israel* **103 C4** 32 55N 35 4 E
Acre □, *Brazil* **172 B3** 9 1 S 71 0W
Acre →, *Brazil* **172 B4** 8 45 S 67 22W
Acri, *Italy* **47 C9** 39 29N 16 23 E
Acs, *Hungary* **52 C3** 47 42N 18 2 E
Actæon Mt., *St. Helena* **9 h** 15 58 S 5 42W
Actium, *Greece* **39 B2** 38 57N 20 45 E
Acton, *Canada* **150 C4** 43 38N 80 3W
Açu, *Brazil* **170 C4** 5 34 S 36 54W
Acuña, *Mexico* **162 B4** 29 18N 100 55W
Acworth, *U.S.A.* **152 A5** 34 4N 84 41W
Ad Dafinah, *Si. Arabia* **98 B3** 23 18N 41 58 E
Ad Dafrah, *U.A.E.* **99 B6** 23 30N 54 30 E
Ad Dahnā, *Si. Arabia* **99 A5** 24 30N 48 10 E
Ad Dālī', *Yemen* **98 D4** 13 42N 44 44 E
Ad Dammām, *Si. Arabia* **97 E6** 26 20N 50 5 E
Ad Dāmūr, *Lebanon* **103 B4** 33 44N 35 27 E
Ad Darb, *Si. Arabia* **98 C3** 18 2N 43 7 E
Ad Dawādimī, *Si. Arabia* **96 E5** 24 35N 44 15 E
Ad Dawḩah, *Qatar* **97 E6** 25 15N 51 35 E
Ad Dawr, *Iraq* **101 E10** 34 27N 43 47 E
Ad Diffah, *Libya* **108 B4** 30 30N 24 30 E
Ad Dilam, *Si. Arabia* **98 B4** 23 55N 47 10 E
Ad Dir'īyah, *Si. Arabia* **96 E5** 24 44N 46 35 E
Ad Dīwānīyah, *Iraq* **101 F11** 32 0N 45 0 E
Ad Dujayl, *Iraq* **101 F11** 33 51N 44 14 E
Ad Duwayd, *Si. Arabia* **96 D4** 30 15N 42 17 E
Ada, *Ghana* **113 D5** 5 44N 0 40 E
Ada, *Serbia, Yug.* **52 E5** 45 49N 20 9 E
Ada, *Minn., U.S.A.* **154 B6** 47 18N 96 31W
Ada, *Ohio, U.S.A.* **157 D13** 40 46N 83 49W
Ada, *Okla., U.S.A.* **155 H6** 34 46N 96 41W
Adabiya, *Egypt* **103 F1** 29 53N 32 28 E
Adad, *Somali Rep.* **120 C3** 9 27N 46 49 E
Adair, C., *Canada* **139 A12** 71 31N 71 24W
Adaja →, *Spain* **42 D6** 41 32N 4 52W
Adak, *U.S.A.* **144 L3** 51 45N 176 45W
Adak I., *U.S.A.* **144 L3** 51 45N 176 45W
Ådalsbruk, *Norway* **18 D8** 60 43N 11 19 E
Adam, *Oman* **99 B7** 22 15N 57 28 E
Adam, Mt., *Falk. Is.* **9 f** 51 34 S 60 4W
Adamantina, *Brazil* **171 F1** 21 42 S 51 4W
Adamaoua, Massif de l', *Cameroon* **113 D7** 7 20N 12 20 E
Adamawa □, *Nigeria* **113 D7** 9 20N 12 30 E
Adamawa Highlands = Adamaoua, Massif de l', *Cameroon* **113 D7** 7 20N 12 20 E
Adamello, Mte., *Italy* **44 B7** 46 9N 10 30 E
Adami Tulu, *Ethiopia* **107 F4** 7 53N 38 41 E
Adaminaby, *Australia* **129 D8** 36 0 S 148 45 E
Adamovka, *Russia* **64 F7** 51 32N 59 56 E
Adams, *Mass., U.S.A.* **151 D11** 42 38N 73 7W
Adams, *N.Y., U.S.A.* **151 C8** 43 49N 76 1W
Adams, *Wis., U.S.A.* **154 D10** 43 57N 89 49W
Adam's Bridge, *Sri Lanka* **95 K4** 9 15N 79 40 E
Adams L., *Canada* **142 C5** 51 10N 119 40W
Adams Mt., *U.S.A.* **160 D5** 46 12N 121 30W
Adam's Peak, *Sri Lanka* **95 L5** 6 48N 80 30 E
Adamuz, *Spain* **43 G6** 38 2N 4 32W
Adana, *Turkey* **100 D6** 37 0N 35 16 E
Adanero, *Spain* **42 E6** 40 56N 4 36W
Adapazarı = Sakarya, *Turkey* **100 B4** 40 48N 30 25 E
Adar Gwagwa, J., *Sudan* **106 C4** 22 15N 35 20 E
Adarama, *Sudan* **107 D3** 17 10N 34 52 E
Adare, C., *Antarctica* **7 D11** 71 0 S 171 0 E
Adarte, *Eritrea* **107 E5** 13 18N 42 8 E
Adaut, *Indonesia* **83 C4** 8 8 S 131 7 E
Adavale, *Australia* **127 D3** 25 52 S 144 32 E
Adda →, *Italy* **44 C6** 45 8N 9 53 E
Addatigala, *India* **94 F6** 17 31N 82 3 E
Addax, Réserve Naturelle, *Niger* **109 E1** 19 17N 9 22 E
Addis Ababa = Addis Abeba, *Ethiopia* **107 F4** 9 2N 38 42 E
Addis Abeba, *Ethiopia* **107 F4** 9 2N 38 42 E
Addis Alem, *Ethiopia* **107 F4** 9 0N 38 17 E
Addis Zemen, *Ethiopia* **107 E4** 12 7N 37 47 E
Addison, *Ill., U.S.A.* **157 C8** 41 55N 88 0W
Addison, *N.Y., U.S.A.* **150 D7** 42 1N 77 14W
Addo, *S. Africa* **116 E4** 33 32 S 25 45 E
Addo Elephant Nat. Park, *S. Africa* **116 E4** 33 30 S 25 50 E
Adebour, *Niger* **113 C7** 13 17N 11 50 E
Ādeh, *Iran* **96 B5** 37 42N 45 11 E
Adel, *Ga., U.S.A.* **152 D6** 31 8N 83 25W
Adel, *Iowa, U.S.A.* **156 C2** 41 37N 94 1W
Adelaide, *Australia* **128 C3** 34 52 S 138 30 E
Adelaide, *Bahamas* **164 A4** 25 4N 77 31W
Adelaide, *S. Africa* **116 E4** 32 42 S 26 20 E
Adelaide I., *Antarctica* **7 C17** 67 15 S 68 30W
Adelaide Pen., *Canada* **138 B10** 68 15N 97 30W
Adelaide River, *Australia* **124 B5** 13 15 S 131 7 E
Adelanto, *U.S.A.* **161 L9** 34 35N 117 22W
Adelaye, *C.A.R.* **114 A4** 7 2N 22 49 E
Adelboden, *Switz.* **32 D5** 46 29N 7 33 E
Adele I., *Australia* **124 C3** 15 32 S 123 9 E
Adélie, Terre, *Antarctica* **7 C10** 68 0 S 140 0 E
Adélie Land = Adélie, Terre, *Antarctica* **7 C10** 68 0 S 140 0 E
Adelong, *Australia* **129 C8** 35 16 S 148 4 E
Ademuz, *Spain* **40 E3** 40 5N 1 13W
Aden = Al 'Adan, *Yemen* **98 D4** 12 45N 45 0 E
Aden, G. of, *Asia* **102 E4** 12 30N 47 30 E
Adendorp, *S. Africa* **116 E3** 32 15 S 24 30 E
Aderbissinat, *Niger* **113 B6** 15 34N 7 54 E
Adh Dhayd, *U.A.E.* **97 E7** 25 17N 55 53 E
Adhoi, *India* **92 H4** 23 26N 70 32 E
Adi, *Indonesia* **83 B4** 4 15 S 133 30 E
Adi Arkai, *Ethiopia* **107 E4** 13 35N 37 57 E
Adi Daro, *Ethiopia* **107 E4** 14 20N 38 14 E
Adi Keyih, *Eritrea* **107 E4** 14 51N 39 22 E
Adi Kwala, *Eritrea* **107 E4** 14 38N 38 48 E
Adi Ugri, *Eritrea* **107 E4** 14 58N 38 48 E
Adieu, C., *Australia* **125 F5** 32 0 S 132 10 E
Adieu Pt., *Australia* **124 C3** 15 14 S 124 35 E
Adigala, *Ethiopia* **107 E5** 10 24N 42 15 E
Adige →, *Italy* **45 C9** 45 9N 12 20 E
Adigrat, *Ethiopia* **107 E4** 14 20N 39 26 E
Adıgüzel Barajı, *Turkey* **49 C11** 38 13N 29 14 E
Adilabad, *India* **94 E4** 19 33N 78 20 E
Adilcevaz, *Turkey* **101 C10** 38 47N 42 43 E
Adirondack Mts., *U.S.A.* **151 C10** 44 0N 74 0W
Adıyaman, *Turkey* **101 D8** 37 45N 38 16 E
Adjim, *Tunisia* **108 B2** 33 47N 10 50 E
Adjohon, *Benin* **113 D5** 6 41N 2 32 E
Adjud, *Romania* **53 D12** 46 7N 27 10 E
Adjumani, *Uganda* **118 B3** 3 20N 31 50 E
Adjuntas, *Puerto Rico* **165 d** 18 10N 66 43W
Adlavik Is., *Canada* **141 B8** 55 0N 58 40W
Adler, *Russia* **61 J4** 43 28N 39 52 E
Adliswil, *Switz.* **33 B7** 47 19N 8 32 E
Admer, *Algeria* **111 D6** 20 21N 5 27 E
Admer, Erg d', *Algeria* **111 D6** 24 0N 9 5 E
Admiralty G., *Australia* **124 B4** 14 20 S 125 55 E
Admiralty I., *U.S.A.* **142 B2** 57 30N 134 30W
Admiralty Is., *Papua N. G.* **132 B4** 2 0 S 147 0 E
Ado, *Nigeria* **113 D5** 6 36N 2 56 E
Ado-Ekiti, *Nigeria* **113 D6** 7 38N 5 12 E
Adok, *Sudan* **107 F3** 8 10N 30 20 E
Adola, *Ethiopia* **107 E5** 11 14N 41 44 E
Adonara, *Indonesia* **82 C2** 8 15 S 123 5 E
Adoni, *India* **95 G3** 15 33N 77 18 E
Adony, *Hungary* **52 C3** 47 6N 18 52 E
Adour →, *France* **28 E2** 43 32N 1 32W
Adra, *India* **93 H12** 23 30N 86 42 E
Adra, *Spain* **43 J7** 36 43N 3 3W
Adrano, *Italy* **47 E7** 37 40N 14 50 E
Adrar, *Algeria* **111 C4** 27 51N 0 11 E
Adrar Madet, *Niger* **109 E2** 18 54N 10 35 E
Adrasman, *Tajikistan* **65 C4** 40 38N 69 58 E
Adré, *Chad* **109 F4** 13 40N 22 20 E
Adrī, *Libya* **108 C2** 27 32N 13 2 E
Ádria, *Italy* **45 C9** 45 3N 12 3 E
Adrian, *Ga., U.S.A.* **152 C7** 32 33N 82 35W
Adrian, *Mich., U.S.A.* **157 C12** 41 54N 84 2W
Adrian, *Mo., U.S.A.* **156 F2** 38 24N 94 21W
Adrian, *Tex., U.S.A.* **155 H3** 35 16N 102 40W
Adriatic Sea, *Medit. S.* **12 G9** 43 0N 16 0 E
Adua, *Indonesia* **83 B3** 1 45 S 129 50 E
Adula-Gruppe, *Switz.* **33 D8** 46 30N 9 3 E
Adung Long, *Burma* **90 A6** 28 7N 97 42 E
Adur, *India* **95 K3** 9 8N 76 40 E
Adwa, *Ethiopia* **107 E4** 14 15N 38 52 E
Adygea □, *Russia* **61 H5** 45 0N 40 0 E
Adzhar Republic = Ajaria □, *Georgia* **61 K6** 41 30N 42 0 E
Adzopé, *Ivory C.* **112 D4** 6 7N 3 49W
Ægean Sea, *Medit. S.* **49 C7** 38 30N 25 0 E
Aerhtai Shan, *Mongolia* **74 B4** 46 40N 92 45 E
Ærø, *Denmark* **17 K4** 54 52N 10 25 E
Ærøskøbing, *Denmark* **17 K4** 54 53N 10 24 E
Aesch, *Switz.* **32 B5** 47 28N 7 36 E
Aētós, *Greece* **48 D3** 37 15N 21 50 E
Afafi, Massif d', *Niger* **109 D3** 22 11N 15 10 E
'Afak, *Iraq* **101 F11** 32 4N 45 15 E
Afándou, *Greece* **38 E12** 36 18N 28 12 E
Afarag, Erg, *Algeria* **111 D5** 23 50N 2 47 E
Afareaitu, *Tahiti* **133 S16** 17 33 S 149 47W
Åfarnes, *Norway* **18 B4** 62 40N 7 32 E
Afdega, *Ethiopia* **120 C2** 6 4N 43 30 E
Affoltern, *Switz.* **33 B6** 47 17N 8 27 E
Affreville = Khemis Miliana, *Algeria* **111 A5** 36 11N 2 14 E
Affton, *U.S.A.* **156 F6** 38 33N 90 20W
Afghanistan ■, *Asia* **91 B2** 33 0N 65 0 E
Afgoi, *Somali Rep.* **120 D2** 2 7N 44 59 E
'Afīf, *Si. Arabia* **98 B3** 23 53N 42 56 E
Afikpo, *Nigeria* **113 D6** 5 53N 7 54 E
Aflisses, O. →, *Algeria* **111 C5** 28 40N 0 50 E
Aflou, *Algeria* **111 B5** 34 7N 2 3 E
Afmadu, *Somali Rep.* **120 D2** 0 31N 42 4 E
Afogados da Ingàzeira, *Brazil* **170 C4** 7 45 S 37 39W
Afognak I., *U.S.A.* **144 G9** 58 15N 152 30W
Afore, *Papua N. G.* **132 E5** 9 9 S 148 23 E
Afragóla, *Italy* **47 B7** 40 55N 14 18 E
Afram →, *Ghana* **113 D4** 7 0N 0 52W
Afrera, *Ethiopia* **107 E5** 13 16N 41 5 E
Africa **104 E6** 10 0N 20 0 E
'Afrīn, *Syria* **100 D7** 36 32N 36 50 E
Afşin, *Turkey* **100 C7** 38 14N 36 55 E
Afton, *Iowa, U.S.A.* **156 C2** 41 2N 94 12W
Afton, *N.Y., U.S.A.* **151 D9** 42 14N 75 32W
Afton, *Wyo., U.S.A.* **158 E8** 42 44N 110 56W
Aftout, *Algeria* **110 C4** 26 50N 3 45W
Afuá, *Brazil* **169 D7** 0 15 S 50 20W
'Afula, *Israel* **103 C4** 32 37N 35 17 E
Afumba, *Zambia* **115 F4** 15 38 S 24 56 E
Afyon, *Turkey* **49 C12** 38 45N 30 33 E
Afyon □, *Turkey* **49 C12** 38 25N 30 30 E
Afyonkarahisar = Afyon, *Turkey* **49 C12** 38 45N 30 33 E
Aga, *Egypt* **106 H7** 30 55N 31 10 E
Aga Pt., *Guam* **133 R15** 13 15N 144 43 E
Agadem, *Niger* **109 E2** 16 50N 13 11 E
Agadès = Agadez, *Niger* **113 B6** 16 58N 7 59 E
Agadez, *Niger* **113 B6** 16 58N 7 59 E
Agadir, *Morocco* **110 B3** 30 28N 9 55W
Agaete, *Canary Is.* **9 e1** 28 6N 15 43W
Agaie, *Nigeria* **113 D6** 9 1N 6 18 E
Agaiás, *Mauritania* **110 D2** 22 37N 14 22W
Again, *Sudan* **107 F2** 8 28N 29 55 E
Agalás, *Greece* **39 D2** 37 43N 20 47 E
Agalega Is., *Mauritius* **121 F4** 11 0 S 57 0 E
Agana, *Guam* **133 R15** 13 28N 144 45 E
Ağapınar, *Turkey* **49 B12** 39 48N 30 47 E
Agar, *India* **92 H7** 23 40N 76 2 E
Agar →, *India* **94 D6** 21 0N 82 57 E
Agaro, *Ethiopia* **107 F4** 7 50N 36 38 E
Agartala, *India* **90 D3** 23 50N 91 23 E
Ağaş, *Romania* **53 D11** 46 28N 26 15 E
Agassiz, *Canada* **142 D4** 49 14N 121 46W
Agat, *Guam* **133 R15** 13 25N 144 40 E
Agats, *Indonesia* **83 C5** 5 33 S 138 0 E
Agatti I., *India* **95 J1** 10 50N 72 12 E
Agattu I., *U.S.A.* **144 K1** 52 25N 173 35 E
Agawam, *U.S.A.* **151 D12** 42 5N 72 37W
Agbélouvé, *Togo* **113 D5** 6 35N 1 14 E
Agboville, *Ivory C.* **112 D4** 5 55N 4 15W
Ağcabädi, *Azerbaijan* **61 K8** 40 5N 47 27 E

Al Jawf 179

Ağdam, *Azerbaijan* **61 L8** 40 0N 46 58 E
Ağdaş, *Azerbaijan* **61 K8** 40 44N 47 22 E
Agde, *France* **28 E7** 43 19N 3 28 E
Agde, C. d', *France* **28 E7** 43 16N 3 28 E
Agdz, *Morocco* **110 B3** 30 47N 6 30W
Agdzhabedi = Ağcabädi, *Azerbaijan* **61 K8** 40 5N 47 27 E
Agen, *France* **28 D4** 44 12N 0 38 E
Ageo, *Japan* **73 B11** 35 58N 139 36 E
Ager Tay, *Chad* **109 E3** 20 0N 17 41 E
Agerbæk, *Denmark* **17 J2** 55 36N 8 48 E
Agersø, *Denmark* **17 J5** 55 13N 11 12 E
Ageyevo, *Russia* **58 E9** 54 10N 36 27 E
Āgh Kand, *Iran* **97 B6** 37 15N 48 4 E
Aghireşu, *Romania* **53 D8** 46 53N 23 15 E
Aghoueyyît, *Mauritania* **110 D1** 21 10N 15 6W
Aghreïjît, *Mauritania* **110 D2** 21 58N 12 11W
Aginskoye, *Russia* **67 D12** 51 6N 114 32 E
Ağlasun, *Turkey* **49 D12** 37 39N 30 31 E
Agly →, *France* **28 F7** 42 46N 3 3 E
Agmar, *Mauritania* **110 C2** 25 18N 10 50W
Agnew, *Australia* **125 E3** 28 1 S 120 31 E
Agnibilékrou, *Ivory C.* **112 D4** 7 10N 3 11W
Agnita, *Romania* **53 E9** 45 59N 24 40 E
Agno, *Switz.* **33 E7** 45 59N 8 53 E
Agnone, *Italy* **45 G11** 41 48N 14 22 E
Ago, *Japan* **73 C8** 34 20N 136 51 E
Agofie, *Ghana* **113 D5** 8 27N 0 15 E
Agogna →, *Italy* **44 C5** 45 4N 8 54 E
Agogo, *Sudan* **107 F2** 7 50N 28 45 E
Agön, *Sweden* **16 C11** 61 34N 17 23 E
Agon Coutainville, *France* **26 C5** 49 2N 1 34W
Agoo, *Phil.* **80 C3** 16 20N 120 22 E
Ágordo, *Italy* **45 B9** 46 18N 12 2 E
Agori, *India* **93 G10** 24 33N 82 57 E
Agouna, *Benin* **113 D5** 7 39N 1 47 E
Agout →, *France* **28 E5** 43 47N 1 41 E
Agra, *India* **92 F7** 27 17N 77 58 E
Agrakhanskiy Poluostrov, *Russia* **61 J8** 43 42N 47 36 E
Agramunt, *Spain* **40 D6** 41 48N 1 6 E
Agreda, *Spain* **40 D3** 41 51N 1 55W
Ağri, *Turkey* **101 C10** 39 44N 43 3 E
Agri →, *Italy* **47 B9** 40 13N 16 44 E
Ağri Daği, *Turkey* **101 C11** 39 50N 44 15 E
Ağri Karakose = Ağri, *Turkey* **101 C10** 39 44N 43 3 E
Agriá, *Greece* **48 B5** 39 20N 23 1 E
Agrigento, *Italy* **46 E6** 37 19N 13 34 E
Agrínion, *Greece* **48 C3** 38 37N 21 27 E
Agrópoli, *Italy* **47 B7** 40 21N 14 59 E
Ağstafa, *Azerbaijan* **61 K7** 41 7N 45 27 E
Água Branca, *Brazil* **170 C3** 5 50 S 42 40W
Agua Caliente, *Baja Calif., Mexico* **161 N10** 32 29N 116 59W
Agua Caliente, *Sinaloa, Mexico* **162 B3** 26 30N 108 20W
Agua Caliente Springs, *U.S.A.* **161 N10** 32 56N 116 19W
Água Clara, *Brazil* **173 E7** 20 25 S 52 45W
Agua Hechicero, *Mexico* **161 N10** 32 26N 116 14W
Agua Preta →, *Brazil* **169 D5** 1 41 S 63 48W
Agua Prieta, *Mexico* **162 A3** 31 20N 109 32W
Aguachica, *Colombia* **168 B3** 8 19N 73 38W
Aguada Cecilio, *Argentina* **176 B3** 40 51 S 65 51W
Aguadas, *Colombia* **168 B2** 5 40N 75 38W
Aguadilla, *Puerto Rico* **165 d** 18 26N 67 10W
Aguadulce, *Panama* **164 E3** 8 15N 80 32W
Aguanga, *U.S.A.* **161 M10** 33 27N 116 51W
Aguanish, *Canada* **141 B7** 50 14N 62 2W
Aguanus →, *Canada* **141 B7** 50 13N 62 5W
Aguapeí, *Brazil* **173 D6** 16 12 S 59 43W
Aguapeí →, *Brazil* **171 F1** 21 0 S 51 0W
Aguapey →, *Argentina* **174 B4** 29 7 S 56 36W
Aguaray Guazú →, *Paraguay* **174 A4** 24 47 S 57 19W
Aguarico →, *Ecuador* **168 D2** 0 59 S 75 11W
Aguas →, *Spain* **40 D4** 41 20N 0 30W
Aguas Blancas, *Chile* **174 A2** 24 15 S 69 55W
Aguas Calientes, Sierra de, *Argentina* **174 B2** 25 26 S 66 40W
Águas Formosas, *Brazil* **171 E3** 17 5 S 40 57W
Aguascalientes, *Mexico* **162 C4** 21 53N 102 12W
Aguascalientes □, *Mexico* **162 C4** 22 0N 102 20W
Agudo, *Spain* **43 G6** 38 59N 4 52W
Águeda, *Portugal* **42 E2** 40 34N 8 27W
Agueda →, *Spain* **42 D4** 41 2N 6 56W
Aguelhok, *Mali* **113 B5** 19 29N 0 52 E
Aguelt el Melah, *Mauritania* **110 D2** 23 3N 8 28W
Agüenit, *W. Sahara* **110 D2** 22 11N 13 8W
Aguié, *Niger* **113 C6** 13 31N 7 46 E
Aguila, Punta, *Puerto Rico* **165 d** 17 57N 67 13W
Aguilafuente, *Spain* **42 D6** 41 13N 4 7W
Aguilar, *Spain* **43 H6** 37 31N 4 40W
Aguilar de Campóo, *Spain* **42 C6** 42 47N 4 15W
Aguilares, *Argentina* **174 B2** 27 26 S 65 35W
Aguilas, *Spain* **41 H3** 37 23N 1 35W
Agüimes, *Canary Is.* **9 e1** 27 58N 15 27W
Aguja, C. de la, *Colombia* **168 A3** 11 18N 74 12W
Agujereada, Pta., *Puerto Rico* **165 d** 18 30N 67 8W
Agulaa, *Ethiopia* **107 E4** 13 40N 39 40 E
Agulhas, C., *S. Africa* **116 E3** 34 52 S 20 0 E
Agulo, *Canary Is.* **9 e1** 28 11N 17 12W
Agung, Gunung, *Indonesia* **85 D5** 8 20 S 115 28 E
Agur, *Uganda* **118 B3** 2 28N 32 55 E
Agusan →, *Phil.* **81 G5** 9 0N 125 30 E
Agusan del Norte □, *Phil.* **81 G5** 9 20N 125 10 E
Agusan del Sur □, *Phil.* **81 G5** 8 30N 125 30 E
Agustín Codazzi, *Colombia* **168 A3** 10 2N 73 14W
Agutaya I., *Phil.* **81 F3** 11 9N 120 58 E
Ağva, *Turkey* **51 E13** 41 8N 29 51 E
Agvali, *Russia* **61 J8** 42 36N 46 8 E
Aha Mts., *Botswana* **116 B3** 19 45 S 21 0 E
Ahaggar, *Algeria* **111 D6** 23 0N 6 30 E
Ahamansu, *Ghana* **113 D5** 7 38N 0 35 E
Ahar, *Iran* **101 C12** 38 35N 47 0 E
Ahat, *Turkey* **49 C11** 38 39N 29 47 E
Ahaura →, *N.Z.* **131 C6** 42 21 S 171 34 E
Ahaus, *Germany* **30 C2** 52 4N 7 0 E
Åheim, *Norway* **18 B2** 62 2N 5 13 E
Ahelledjem, *Algeria* **111 C6** 26 37N 6 58 E
Ahimanawa Ra., *N.Z.* **130 F5** 39 3 S 176 30 E
Ahioma, *Papua N. G.* **132 F6** 10 20 S 150 33 E
Ahipara B., *N.Z.* **130 B2** 35 5 S 173 5 E
Ahir Daği, *Turkey* **49 C12** 38 45N 30 10 E
Ahiri, *India* **94 E5** 19 30N 80 0 E
Ahlat, *Turkey* **101 C10** 38 45N 42 29 E
Ahlen, *Germany* **30 D3** 51 45N 7 53 E
Ahmad Wal, *Pakistan* **92 E1** 29 18N 65 58 E
Ahmadabad, *India* **92 H5** 23 0N 72 40 E
Aḩmadābād, *Khorāsān, Iran* **97 C9** 35 3N 60 50 E
Aḩmadābād, *Khorāsān, Iran* **97 C8** 35 49N 59 42 E
Aḩmadī, *Iran* **97 E8** 27 56N 56 42 E
Ahmadnagar, *India* **94 E2** 19 7N 74 46 E
Ahmadpur, *India* **94 E3** 18 40N 76 57 E
Ahmadpur, *Pakistan* **92 E4** 29 12N 71 10 E
Ahmadpur Lamma, *Pakistan* **92 E4** 28 19N 70 3 E
Ahmar, *Ethiopia* **107 F5** 9 20N 41 15 E
Ahmedabad = Ahmadabad, *India* **92 H5** 23 0N 72 40 E
Ahmednagar = Ahmadnagar, *India* **94 E2** 19 7N 74 46 E
Ahmetbey, *Turkey* **51 E11** 41 26N 27 34 E
Ahmetler, *Turkey* **49 C11** 38 28N 29 5 E
Ahmetli, *Turkey* **49 C9** 38 32N 27 57 E
Aḩmeyim, *Mauritania* **110 D2** 20 51N 14 25W
Ahoada, *Nigeria* **113 D6** 5 8N 6 36 E
Ahome, *Mexico* **162 B3** 25 55N 109 11W
Ahon, Tarso, *Chad* **110 D3** 20 23N 18 18 E
Ahoskie, *U.S.A.* **149 G7** 36 17N 76 59W
Ahr →, *Germany* **30 E3** 50 32N 7 16 E
Ahram, *Iran* **97 D6** 28 52N 51 16 E
Ahrax Pt., *Malta* **38 F7** 36 0N 14 22 E
Ahrensbök, *Germany* **30 A6** 54 2N 10 35 E
Ahrensburg, *Germany* **30 B6** 53 40N 10 13 E
Āhū, *Iran* **97 C6** 34 33N 50 2 E
Ahu Akivi, *Chile* **172 b** 27 7 S 109 24W
Ahu Tepeu, *Chile* **172 b** 27 6 S 109 25W
Ahu Tongariki, *Chile* **172 b** 27 8 S 109 17W
Ahu Vinapu, *Chile* **172 b** 27 10 S 109 25W
Ahuachapán, *El Salv.* **164 D2** 13 54N 89 52W
Ahun, *France* **27 F9** 46 4N 2 5 E
Ahuriri →, *N.Z.* **131 E5** 44 31 S 170 12 E
Åhus, *Sweden* **17 J8** 55 56N 14 18 E
Ahvāz, *Iran* **97 D6** 31 20N 48 40 E
Ahvenanmaa = Åland, *Finland* **15 F19** 60 15N 20 0 E
Aḩwar, *Yemen* **98 D4** 13 30N 46 40 E
Ahzar →, *Mali* **113 B5** 15 30N 3 20 E
Ai →, *India* **90 B3** 26 26N 90 44 E
Ai-Ais, *Namibia* **116 D2** 27 54 S 17 59 E
Ai-Ais and Fish River Canyon Nat. Park, *Namibia* **116 C2** 24 45 S 17 15 E
Aiari →, *Brazil* **168 C4** 1 22N 68 36W
Aichach, *Germany* **31 G7** 48 27N 11 8 E
Aichi □, *Japan* **73 C9** 35 0N 137 15 E
Aiduma, *Indonesia* **83 B4** 4 0 S 134 6 E
Aiduna, *Indonesia* **83 B5** 4 27 S 135 15 E
Aiea, *U.S.A.* **145 K14** 21 23N 157 56W
Aigle, *Switz.* **32 D3** 46 18N 6 58 E
Aignay-le-Duc, *France* **27 E11** 47 40N 4 43 E
Aigoual, Mt., *France* **28 D7** 44 8N 3 35 E
Aigre, *France* **28 C4** 45 54N 0 1 E
Aigrettes, Pte. des, *Réunion* **121 c** 21 3 S 55 13 E
Aigua, *Uruguay* **175 C5** 34 13 S 54 46W
Aigueperse, *France* **27 F10** 46 3N 3 13 E
Aigues →, *France* **29 D8** 44 7N 4 43 E
Aigues-Mortes, *France* **29 E8** 43 35N 4 12 E
Aigues-Mortes, G. d', *France* **29 E8** 43 31N 4 3 E
Aiguilles, *France* **29 D10** 44 47N 6 51 E
Aiguillon, *France* **28 D4** 44 18N 0 21 E
Aigurande, *France* **27 F8** 46 27N 1 49 E
Aihui, *China* **69 A7** 50 10N 127 30 E
Aija, *Peru* **172 B2** 9 50 S 77 45W
Aikawa, *Japan* **70 E9** 38 2N 138 15 E
Aiken, *U.S.A.* **152 B8** 33 34N 81 43W
Ailao Shan, *China* **76 F3** 24 0N 101 20 E
Aileron, *Australia* **126 C1** 22 39 S 133 20 E
Ailey, *U.S.A.* **152 C7** 32 11N 82 34W
Ailigandi, *Panama* **168 B2** 9 14N 78 1W
Aillant-sur-Tholon, *France* **27 E10** 47 52N 3 20 E
Aillik, *Canada* **141 A8** 55 11N 59 18W
Ailsa Craig, *U.K.* **22 F3** 55 15N 5 6W
Ailuluai, *Papua N. G.* **132 E6** 9 38 S 150 35 E
'Ailūn, *Jordan* **103 C4** 32 18N 35 47 E
Aim, *Russia* **67 D14** 59 0N 133 55 E
Aimere, *Indonesia* **79 F6** 8 45 S 121 3 E
Aimogasta, *Argentina* **174 B2** 28 33 S 66 50W
Aimorés, *Brazil* **171 E3** 19 30 S 41 4W
Ain □, *France* **27 F12** 46 5N 5 20 E
Ain →, *France* **29 C9** 45 45N 5 11 E
Aïn Beïda, *Algeria* **111 A6** 35 50N 7 29 E
Aïn Ben Khellil, *Algeria* **111 B4** 33 15N 0 49W
Aïn Ben Tili, *Mauritania* **110 C3** 25 59N 9 27W
Aïn Beni Mathar, *Morocco* **111 B4** 34 1N 2 0W
Aïn Benian, *Algeria* **111 A5** 36 48N 2 55 E
Ain Dalla, *Egypt* **106 B2** 27 20N 27 23 E
Ain el Mafki, *Egypt* **106 B2** 27 30N 28 15 E
Ain Girba, *Egypt* **106 B2** 29 20N 25 14 E
Aïn M'lila, *Algeria* **111 A6** 36 2N 6 35 E
Ain Murr, *Sudan* **106 C2** 21 50N 25 9 E
Ain Qeiqab, *Egypt* **106 B1** 29 42N 24 55 E
Aïn Sefra, *Algeria* **111 B4** 32 47N 0 37W
Ain Sheikh Murzûk, *Egypt* **106 B2** 26 47N 27 45 E
Ain Sudr, *Egypt* **103 F2** 29 50N 33 6 E
Ain Sukhna, *Egypt* **106 J8** 29 32N 32 20 E
Aïn Tédelès, *Algeria* **111 A5** 36 0N 0 21 E
Aïn Témouchent, *Algeria* **111 A4** 35 16N 1 8W
Aïn Tikkidine, *Algeria* **111 C5** 25 33N 1 24 E
Aïn Touta, *Algeria* **111 A6** 35 26N 5 54 E
Ain Zeitûn, *Egypt* **106 B2** 29 10N 25 48 E
Aïn Zorah, *Morocco* **111 B4** 34 37N 3 32W
Ainabo, *Somali Rep.* **120 C3** 9 0N 46 25 E
Ainaži, *Latvia* **15 H21** 57 50N 24 24 E
Aínos Óros, *Greece* **48 C2** 38 9N 20 40 E
Ainsworth, *U.S.A.* **154 D5** 42 33N 99 52W
Aioi, *Japan* **72 C6** 34 48N 134 28 E
Aiome, *Papua N. G.* **132 C3** 5 8 S 144 44 E
Aipe, *Colombia* **168 C2** 3 13N 75 15W
Aiquile, *Bolivia* **173 D4** 18 10 S 65 10W
Aïr, *Niger* **113 B6** 18 30N 8 0 E
Aïr et du Ténéré, Réserve Naturelle de L', *Niger* **109 E1** 18 12N 9 56 E
Air Force I., *Canada* **139 B12** 67 58N 74 5W
Air Hitam, *Malaysia* **87 M4** 1 55N 103 11 E
Aira, *Japan* **72 F2** 31 43N 130 43 E
Airaines, *France* **27 C8** 49 58N 1 55 E
Airão, *Brazil* **169 D5** 1 56 S 61 22W
Airdrie, *Canada* **142 C6** 51 18N 114 2W
Airdrie, *U.K.* **22 F5** 55 52N 3 57W
Aire →, *France* **27 C11** 49 18N 4 49 E
Aire →, *U.K.* **20 D7** 53 43N 0 55W
Aire, I. de l', *Spain* **38 B5** 39 48N 4 16 E
Aire-sur-la-Lys, *France* **27 B9** 50 37N 2 22 E
Aire-sur-l'Adour, *France* **28 E3** 43 42N 0 15W
Aireys Inlet, *Australia* **128 E6** 38 29 S 144 5 E
Airlie Beach, *Australia* **126 J6** 20 16 S 148 43 E
Airmadidi, *Indonesia* **82 A3** 1 25N 125 0 E
Airolo, *Switz.* **33 C7** 46 32N 8 37 E
Airvault, *France* **26 F6** 46 50N 0 8W
Aisch →, *Germany* **31 F6** 49 49N 10 58 E
Aisen □, *Chile* **176 C2** 46 30 S 73 0W
Aisne □, *France* **27 C10** 49 42N 3 40 E
Aisne →, *France* **27 C9** 49 26N 2 50 E
Ait, *India* **93 G8** 25 54N 79 14 E
Aitana, Sierra de, *Spain* **41 G4** 38 35N 0 24W
Aitape, *Papua N. G.* **132 B2** 3 11 S 142 22 E
Aitkin, *U.S.A.* **154 B8** 46 32N 93 42W
Aitolía Kai Akarnanía □, *Greece* **48 C3** 38 45N 21 18 E
Aitolikón, *Greece* **48 C3** 38 26N 21 21 E
Aiuaba, *Brazil* **170 C3** 6 38 S 40 7W
Aiud, *Romania* **53 D8** 46 19N 23 44 E
Aix-en-Provence, *France* **29 E9** 43 32N 5 27 E
Aix-la-Chapelle = Aachen, *Germany* **30 E2** 50 45N 6 6 E
Aix-les-Bains, *France* **29 C9** 45 41N 5 53 E
Aixe-sur-Vienne, *France* **28 C5** 45 47N 1 9 E
Aiyang, Mt., *Papua N. G.* **132 C1** 5 10 S 141 20 E
Aíyina, *Greece* **48 D5** 37 45N 23 26 E
Aiyínion, *Greece* **50 F6** 40 28N 22 28 E
Aíyion, *Greece* **48 C4** 38 15N 22 5 E
Aizawl, *India* **90 D4** 23 40N 92 44 E
Aizenay, *France* **26 F5** 46 44N 1 38W
Aizkraukle, *Latvia* **15 H21** 56 36N 25 11 E
Aizpute, *Latvia* **15 H19** 56 43N 21 40 E
Aizuwakamatsu, *Japan* **70 F9** 37 30N 139 56 E
Ajaccio, *France* **29 G12** 41 55N 8 40 E
Ajaccio, G. d', *France* **29 G12** 41 52N 8 40 E
Ajai Game Reserve, *Uganda* **118 B3** 2 52N 31 16 E
Ajaigarh, *India* **93 G9** 24 52N 80 16 E
Ajaju →, *Colombia* **168 C3** 0 59N 72 20W
Ajalpan, *Mexico* **163 D5** 18 22N 97 15W
Ajanta, *India* **94 D2** 20 30N 75 48 E
Ajanta Ra., *India* **94 D2** 20 28N 75 50 E
Ajari Rep. = Ajaria □, *Georgia* **61 K6** 41 30N 42 0 E
Ajaria □, *Georgia* **61 K6** 41 30N 42 0 E
Ajax, *Canada* **150 C5** 43 50N 79 1W
Ajax, Mt., *N.Z.* **131 C7** 42 35 S 172 5 E
Ajdābiyā, *Libya* **108 B4** 30 54N 20 4 E
Ajdovščina, *Slovenia* **45 C10** 45 54N 13 54 E
Ajibar, *Ethiopia* **107 E4** 10 35N 38 36 E
Ajka, *Hungary* **52 C2** 47 4N 17 31 E
'Ajmān, *U.A.E.* **97 E7** 25 25N 55 30 E
Ajmer, *India* **92 F6** 26 28N 74 37 E
Ajnala, *India* **92 D6** 31 50N 74 48 E
Ajo, *U.S.A.* **159 K7** 32 22N 112 52W
Ajo, C. de, *Spain* **42 B7** 43 31N 3 35W
Ajoie, *Switz.* **32 B4** 47 22N 7 0 E
Ajok, *Sudan* **107 F2** 9 15N 28 28 E
Ajuda, Pta. da, *Azores* **9 d3** 37 52N 25 19W
Ajuy, *Phil.* **81 F4** 11 10N 123 1 E
Ak Dağ, *Turkey* **49 E11** 36 30N 29 32 E
Ak Dağları, *Muğla, Turkey* **49 E10** 36 30N 29 30 E
Ak Dağları, *Sivas, Turkey* **100 C7** 39 32N 36 12 E
Ak-Muz, *Kyrgyzstan* **65 C8** 41 15N 76 10 E
Ak-Tüz, *Kyrgyzstan* **65 B8** 42 54N 76 7 E
Akaba, *Togo* **113 D5** 8 10N 1 2 E
Akabira, *Japan* **70 C11** 43 33N 142 5 E
Akabli, *Algeria* **111 C5** 26 49N 1 31 E
Akagera, Parc Nat. d', *Rwanda* **118 C3** 1 31 S 30 33 E
Akaishi-Dake, *Japan* **73 B10** 35 27N 138 9 E
Akaishi-Sammyaku, *Japan* **73 B10** 35 25N 138 10 E
Akaki Beseka, *Ethiopia* **107 F4** 8 55N 38 45 E
Akākūs, Jabal, *Libya* **111 C7** 25 20N 10 30 E
Akala, *Sudan* **107 D4** 15 39N 36 13 E
Akalkot, *India* **94 F3** 17 32N 76 13 E
Akamas, *Cyprus* **39 E8** 35 3N 32 18 E
Akanthou, *Cyprus* **39 E9** 35 22N 33 45 E
Akarca, *Turkey* **49 C11** 38 35N 29 35 E
Akaroa, *N.Z.* **131 D7** 43 49 S 172 59 E
Akaroa Harbour, *N.Z.* **131 D7** 43 50 S 172 55 E
Akasha, *Sudan* **106 C3** 21 10N 30 32 E
Akashi, *Japan* **72 C6** 34 45N 134 58 E
Akbarpur, *Bihar, India* **93 G10** 24 39N 83 58 E
Akbarpur, *Ut. P., India* **93 F10** 26 25N 82 32 E
Akbou, *Algeria* **111 A5** 36 31N 4 31 E
Akbulak, *Russia* **64 F5** 51 1N 55 37 E
Akçaabat, *Turkey* **101 B8** 41 1N 39 34 E
Akçadağ, *Turkey* **100 C7** 38 27N 37 43 E
Akçakale, *Turkey* **101 D8** 36 41N 38 56 E
Akçakoca, *Turkey* **100 B4** 41 5N 31 8 E
Akçaova, *Turkey* **51 E13** 41 2N 29 57 E
Akçay, *Turkey* **49 E11** 36 36N 29 45 E
Akçay →, *Turkey* **49 D10** 37 50N 28 15 E
Akchâr, *Mauritania* **110 D2** 20 20N 14 28W
Akdağ, *Turkey* **49 C8** 38 33N 26 30 E
Akdağmadeni, *Turkey* **100 C6** 39 39N 35 53 E
Akechi, *Japan* **73 B9** 35 18N 137 23 E
Akelamo, *Indonesia* **82 A3** 1 35N 129 40 E
Åkernes, *Norway* **18 F4** 58 45N 7 30 E
Åkers styckebruk, *Sweden* **16 E11** 59 15N 17 5 E
Åkersberga, *Sweden* **16 E12** 59 29N 18 18 E
Akershus □, *Norway* **18 D8** 60 0N 11 10 E
Akeru →, *India* **94 F5** 17 25N 80 5 E
Aketi, *Dem. Rep. of the Congo* **114 B4** 2 38N 23 47 E
Akhaïa □, *Greece* **48 C3** 38 5N 21 45 E
Akhalkalaki, *Georgia* **61 K6** 41 27N 43 25 E
Akhaltsikhe, *Georgia* **61 K6** 41 40N 43 0 E
Akharnaí, *Greece* **48 C5** 38 5N 23 44 E
Akhelóös →, *Greece* **48 C3** 38 19N 21 7 E
Akhendriá, *Greece* **49 G7** 34 59N 25 13 E
Akhiok, *U.S.A.* **144 H9** 56 57N 154 10W
Akhisar, *Turkey* **49 C9** 38 56N 27 48 E
Akhladhókambos, *Greece* **48 D4** 37 31N 22 35 E
Akhmîm, *Egypt* **106 B3** 26 31N 31 47 E
Akhnur, *India* **93 C6** 32 52N 74 45 E
Akhtopol, *Bulgaria* **51 D11** 42 6N 27 56 E
Akhtuba →, *Russia* **61 G8** 47 41N 46 55 E
Akhtubinsk, *Russia* **61 F8** 48 13N 46 7 E
Akhty, *Russia* **61 K8** 41 30N 47 45 E
Akhtyrka = Okhtyrka, *Ukraine* **59 G8** 50 25N 35 0 E
Aki, *Japan* **72 D5** 33 30N 133 54 E
Aki-Nada, *Japan* **72 C4** 34 5N 132 40 E
Akiachak, *U.S.A.* **144 F7** 60 55N 161 26W
Akiak, *U.S.A.* **144 F7** 60 55N 161 13W
Akiéni, *Gabon* **114 C2** 1 11 S 13 53 E
Akimiski I., *Canada* **140 B3** 52 50N 81 30W
Akimovka, *Ukraine* **59 J8** 46 44N 35 0 E
Åkirkeby, *Denmark* **17 J8** 55 4N 14 55 E
Akita, *Japan* **70 E10** 39 45N 140 7 E
Akita □, *Japan* **70 E10** 39 40N 140 30 E
Akjoujt, *Mauritania* **112 B2** 19 45N 14 15W
Akka, *Mali* **112 B4** 15 24N 4 11W
Akka, *Morocco* **110 C3** 29 22N 8 9W
Akkaraipattu, *Sri Lanka* **95 L5** 7 13N 81 51 E
Akkaya Tepesi, *Turkey* **49 D11** 37 25N 29 38 E
Akkeshi, *Japan* **70 C12** 43 2N 144 51 E
'Akko, *Israel* **103 C4** 32 55N 35 4 E
Akkol = Aqköl, *Kazakstan* **65 A7** 45 0N 75 39 E
Akkol = Aqköl, *Kazakstan* **65 B5** 43 36N 70 45 E
Akköy, *Turkey* **49 D9** 37 29N 27 15 E
Aklampa, *Benin* **113 D5** 8 15N 2 10 E
Aklan □, *Phil.* **81 F4** 11 50N 122 30 E
Aklavik, *Canada* **138 B6** 68 12N 135 0W
Aklera, *India* **92 G7** 24 26N 76 32 E
Akmené, *Lithuania* **54 B9** 56 15N 22 45 E
Akmenrags, *Latvia* **54 B8** 56 50N 21 4 E
Akmeqit, *China* **65 E8** 37 5N 76 55 E
Akmolinsk = Astana, *Kazakstan* **66 D8** 51 10N 71 30 E
Akmonte = Almonte, *Spain* **43 H4** 37 13N 6 38W
Aknoul, *Morocco* **111 B4** 34 40N 3 55W
Akō, *Japan* **72 C6** 34 45N 134 24 E
Ako, *Nigeria* **113 C7** 10 19N 10 48 E
Akôbô, *Sudan* **107 F3** 7 47N 33 1 E
Akobo →, *Ethiopia* **107 F3** 7 48N 33 3 E
Akola, *Maharashtra, India* **94 D3** 20 42N 77 2 E
Akola, *Maharashtra, India* **94 E2** 19 32N 74 3 E
Akolmiut, *U.S.A.* **144 F7** 60 55N 162 20W
Akonolinga, *Cameroon* **113 E7** 3 50N 12 18 E
Akor, *Mali* **112 C3** 14 59N 6 58W
Akordat, *Eritrea* **107 D4** 15 30N 37 40 E
Akosombo Dam, *Ghana* **113 D5** 6 20N 0 5 E
Akot, *India* **94 D3** 21 10N 77 10 E
Akot, *Sudan* **107 F3** 6 31N 30 9 E
Akoupé, *Ivory C.* **112 D4** 6 23N 3 54W
Akourousoulba, *C.A.R.* **114 A4** 8 58N 20 46 E
Akpatok I., *Canada* **139 B13** 60 25N 68 8W
Åkrahamn, *Norway* **15 G11** 59 15N 5 10 E
'Akramah, *Libya* **108 B4** 32 2N 23 41 E
Akranes, *Iceland* **11 C4** 64 19N 22 5W
Akreïjit, *Mauritania* **112 B3** 18 19N 9 11W
Akrítas Venétiko, Ákra, *Greece* **48 E3** 36 43N 21 54 E
Akron, *Colo., U.S.A.* **154 E3** 40 10N 103 13W
Akron, *Ind., U.S.A.* **157 C10** 41 2N 86 1W
Akron, *Ohio, U.S.A.* **150 E3** 41 5N 81 31W
Akrotiri, *Cyprus* **39 F8** 34 36N 32 57 E
Akrotiri, Ákra, *Greece* **51 F9** 40 26N 25 27 E
Akrotiri Bay, *Cyprus* **39 F9** 34 35N 33 10 E
Aksai Chin, *China* **93 B8** 35 15N 79 55 E
Aksaray, *Turkey* **100 C6** 38 25N 34 2 E
Aksay, *Kazakstan* **64 E5** 51 11N 53 0 E
Akşehir, *Turkey* **100 C4** 38 18N 31 30 E
Akşehir Gölü, *Turkey* **100 C4** 38 30N 31 25 E
Akstafa = Ağstafa, *Azerbaijan* **61 K7** 41 7N 45 27 E
Aksu, *China* **68 B3** 41 5N 80 10 E
Aksu →, *Turkey* **100 D4** 36 52N 30 57 E
Aksum, *Ethiopia* **107 E4** 14 5N 38 40 E
Aktash, *Russia* **60 C11** 55 2N 52 0 E
Aktash, *Uzbekistan* **65 D2** 39 55N 65 55 E
Aktasty, *Kazakstan* **64 F8** 50 42N 61 42 E
Aktion, *Greece* **39 B2** 38 57N 20 46 E
Akto, *China* **65 D7** 39 5N 75 59 E
Aktogay, *Kazakstan* **66 E8** 46 57N 79 40 E
Aktsyabrski, *Belarus* **59 F5** 52 38N 28 53 E
Aktyubinsk = Aqtöbe, *Kazakstan* **57 D10** 50 17N 57 10 E
Aktyuz = Ak-Tüz, *Kyrgyzstan* **65 B8** 42 54N 76 7 E
Aku, *Nigeria* **113 D6** 6 40N 7 18 E
Akula, *Dem. Rep. of the Congo* **114 B4** 2 22N 20 12 E
Akun I., *U.S.A.* **144 J6** 54 11N 165 32W
Akune, *Japan* **72 E2** 32 1N 130 12 E
Akure, *Nigeria* **113 D6** 7 15N 5 5 E
Akurenan, *Eq. Guin.* **114 B2** 1 2N 10 40 E
Akuressa, *Sri Lanka* **95 L5** 6 5N 80 29 E
Akureyri, *Iceland* **11 B8** 65 40N 18 6W
Akuseki-Shima, *Japan* **71 K4** 29 27N 129 37 E
Akusha, *Russia* **61 J8** 42 18N 47 30 E
Akutan, *U.S.A.* **144 J6** 54 8N 165 46W
Akutan I., *U.S.A.* **144 J6** 54 7N 165 55W
Akwa-Ibom □, *Nigeria* **113 E6** 4 30N 7 30 E
Akyab = Sittwe, *Burma* **90 E4** 20 18N 92 45 E
Akyazı, *Turkey* **100 B4** 40 40N 30 38 E
Ål, *Norway* **18 D5** 60 38N 8 33 E
Al Abyaḑ, *Libya* **108 C2** 26 49N 14 1 E
Al Abyār, *Libya* **108 B4** 32 9N 20 29 E
Al 'Adan, *Yemen* **98 D4** 12 45N 45 0 E
Al Aḩsā = Hasa □, *Si. Arabia* **97 E6** 25 50N 49 0 E
Al Ajfar, *Si. Arabia* **96 E4** 27 26N 43 0 E
Al Amādīyah, *Iraq* **101 D10** 37 5N 43 30 E
Al 'Amārah, *Iraq* **101 G12** 31 55N 47 15 E
Al 'Aqabah, *Jordan* **103 F4** 29 31N 35 0 E
Al 'Aqīq, *Si. Arabia* **98 B3** 20 39N 41 25 E
Al Arak, *Syria* **101 E8** 34 38N 38 35 E
Al 'Aramah, *Si. Arabia* **96 E5** 25 30N 46 0 E
Al 'Ariḑah, *Si. Arabia* **98 C3** 17 3N 43 5 E
Al Arṭāwīyah, *Si. Arabia* **96 E5** 26 31N 45 20 E
Al Ashkhara, *Oman* **99 B7** 21 50N 59 30 E
Al 'Āṣimah = 'Ammān □, *Jordan* **103 D5** 31 40N 36 30 E
Al 'Assāfīyah, *Si. Arabia* **96 D3** 28 17N 38 59 E
Al 'Ayn, *Oman* **97 E7** 24 15N 55 45 E
Al 'Ayn, *Si. Arabia* **96 E3** 25 4N 38 6 E
Al 'Aẓamīyah, *Iraq* **96 C5** 33 22N 44 22 E
Al 'Azīzīyah, *Iraq* **101 F11** 32 54N 45 4 E
Al 'Azīzīyah, *Libya* **108 B2** 32 30N 13 1 E
Al Bāb, *Syria* **100 D7** 36 23N 37 29 E
Al Bad', *Si. Arabia* **96 D2** 28 28N 35 1 E
Al Bādī, *Iraq* **96 C4** 35 56N 41 32 E
Al Badī', *Si. Arabia* **96 E5** 22 0N 46 35 E
Al Baḩrah, *Kuwait* **96 D5** 29 40N 47 52 E
Al Baḩral Mayyit = Dead Sea, *Asia* **103 D4** 31 30N 35 30 E
Al Balqā' □, *Jordan* **103 C4** 32 5N 35 45 E
Al Barkāt, *Libya* **108 D2** 24 56N 10 14 E
Al Bārūk, J., *Lebanon* **103 B4** 33 39N 35 40 E
Al Baṣrah, *Iraq* **96 D5** 30 30N 47 50 E
Al Baṭḩā, *Iraq* **96 D5** 31 6N 45 53 E
Al Batinah, *Oman* **99 A7** 24 10N 56 50 E
Al Batrūn, *Lebanon* **103 A4** 34 15N 35 40 E
Al Bayāḑ, *Si. Arabia* **98 B4** 22 0N 47 0 E
Al Bayḑā, *Libya* **108 B4** 32 50N 21 44 E
Al Bayḑā', *Yemen* **98 D4** 14 5N 45 42 E
Al Bi'ār, *Si. Arabia* **98 B2** 22 39N 39 40 E
Al Biqā, *Lebanon* **103 A5** 34 10N 36 10 E
Al Bi'r, *Si. Arabia* **96 D3** 28 51N 36 16 E
Al Birk, *Si. Arabia* **98 C3** 18 13N 41 33 E
Al Bu'ayrāt al Ḩasūn, *Libya* **108 B3** 31 24N 15 44 E
Al Bunbah, *Libya* **108 B4** 32 24N 23 8 E
Al Burayj, *Syria* **103 A5** 34 15N 36 46 E
Al Faḑilī, *Si. Arabia* **97 E6** 26 58N 49 10 E
Al Fallūjah, *Iraq* **101 F10** 33 20N 43 55 E
Al Fātiḩ □, *Libya* **108 B4** 32 0N 21 0 E
Al Fāw, *Iraq* **97 D6** 30 0N 48 30 E
Al Faydamī, *Yemen* **99 C6** 16 25N 52 26 E
Al Fujayrah, *U.A.E.* **97 E8** 25 7N 56 18 E
Al Ghadaf, W. →, *Jordan* **103 D5** 31 26N 36 43 E
Al Ghammās, *Iraq* **96 D5** 31 45N 44 37 E
Al Gharīb, *Libya* **108 B4** 32 35N 21 11 E
Al Ghayḑah, *Yemen* **99 C6** 16 13N 52 11 E
Al Ghayḑah, *Yemen* **99 D5** 14 55N 50 0 E
Al Ghayl, *Yemen* **99 D5** 15 30N 50 54 E
Al Ghazālah, *Si. Arabia* **96 E4** 26 48N 41 19 E
Al Ḩadd, *Oman* **99 B7** 22 32N 59 48 E
Al Ḩaddār, *Si. Arabia* **98 B4** 21 58N 45 57 E
Al Ḩadīthah, *Iraq* **101 E10** 34 0N 41 13 E
Al Ḩadīthah, *Si. Arabia* **103 D6** 31 28N 37 8 E
Al Ḩaḑr, *Iraq* **101 E10** 35 35N 42 44 E
Al Ḩājānah, *Syria* **103 B5** 33 20N 36 33 E
Al Ḩajar al Gharbī, *Oman* **97 E8** 24 10N 56 15 E
Al Ḩalfānīyah, *Oman* **99 C7** 18 30N 56 30 E
Al Ḩāmad, *Si. Arabia* **96 D3** 31 30N 39 30 E
Al Ḩamar, *Si. Arabia* **98 B4** 22 23N 46 12 E
Al Hamdānīyah, *Syria* **96 C3** 35 25N 36 50 E
Al Ḩamīdīyah, *Syria* **103 A4** 34 42N 35 57 E
Al Ḩammādah al Ḩamrā', *Libya* **108 C2** 29 30N 12 0 E
Al Ḩammār, *Iraq* **96 D5** 30 57N 46 51 E
Al Ḩamrā', *Si. Arabia* **96 E3** 24 2N 38 55 E
Al Ḩanākīyah, *Si. Arabia* **96 E4** 24 51N 40 31 E
Al Ḩarīq, *Si. Arabia* **98 B4** 23 29N 46 27 E
Al Ḩarīr, W. →, *Syria* **103 C4** 32 44N 35 59 E
Al Ḩarūj al Aswad, *Libya* **108 C3** 27 0N 17 10 E
Al Ḩasā, W. →, *Jordan* **103 D4** 31 4N 35 29 E
Al Ḩasakah, *Syria* **101 D9** 36 35N 40 45 E
Al Ḩāsikīyah, *Oman* **99 C6** 17 28N 55 36 E
Al Ḩasy, *Yemen* **99 D5** 14 3N 48 40 E
Al Ḩawrah, *Yemen* **98 D4** 13 50N 47 35 E
Al Ḩawṭah, *Si. Arabia* **98 B4** 23 30N 47 0 E
Al Ḩaydān, W. →, *Jordan* **103 D4** 31 29N 35 34 E
Al Ḩayy, *Iraq* **101 F12** 32 5N 46 5 E
Al Ḩijānah, *Asia* **96 D4** 30 0N 44 0 E
Al Ḩillah, *Iraq* **101 F11** 32 30N 44 25 E
Al Ḩillah, *Si. Arabia* **98 B4** 23 35N 46 50 E
Al Hindīyah, *Iraq* **101 F11** 32 30N 44 10 E
Al Hirmil, *Lebanon* **103 A5** 34 26N 36 24 E
Al Hoceïma, *Morocco* **110 A4** 35 8N 3 58W
Al Ḩudaydah, *Yemen* **98 D3** 14 50N 43 0 E
Al Ḩufrah, *Libya* **108 C3** 25 32N 14 1 E
Al Ḩufuf, *Si. Arabia* **97 E6** 25 25N 49 45 E
Al Ḩulwah, *Si. Arabia* **98 B4** 23 24N 46 48 E
Al Ḩumayḑah, *Si. Arabia* **96 D2** 29 14N 34 56 E
Al Ḩunayy, *Si. Arabia* **97 E6** 25 58N 48 45 E
Al Husayyāt, *Libya* **108 B4** 30 24N 20 37 E
Al 'Irqah, *Yemen* **98 D4** 13 39N 47 22 E
Al Īsāwīyah, *Si. Arabia* **96 D3** 30 43N 37 59 E
Al Ittihad = Madīnat ash Sha'b, *Yemen* **98 D4** 12 50N 45 0 E
Al Jabal al Akhḑar, *Libya* **108 B4** 32 30N 21 30 E
Al Jabal al Akhḑar □, *Libya* **108 B4** 32 30N 22 0 E
Al Jafr, *Jordan* **103 E5** 30 18N 36 14 E
Al Jāfūrah, *Si. Arabia* **97 E7** 25 0N 50 15 E
Al Jaghbūb, *Libya* **108 C4** 29 42N 24 38 E
Al Jahrah, *Kuwait* **96 D5** 29 25N 47 40 E
Al Jalāmīd, *Si. Arabia* **96 D3** 31 20N 40 6 E
Al Jamalīyah, *Qatar* **97 E6** 25 37N 51 5 E
Al Janūb □, *Lebanon* **103 B4** 33 20N 35 20 E
Al Jawf, *Libya* **108 D4** 24 10N 23 24 E

180 Al Jawf

Al Jawf, *Si. Arabia*	**96 D3**	29 55N	39 40 E
Al Jazirah, *Iraq*	**101 E10**	33 30N	44 0 E
Al Jazirah, *Libya*	**108 C4**	26 10N	21 20 E
Al Jithāmīyah, *Si. Arabia*	**96 E4**	27 41N	41 43 E
Al Jubayl, *Si. Arabia*	**97 E6**	27 0N	49 50 E
Al Jubaylah, *Si. Arabia*	**96 E5**	24 55N	46 25 E
Al Jubb, *Si. Arabia*	**96 E4**	27 11N	42 17 E
Al Jufrah, *Libya*	**108 C3**	29 10N	16 0 E
Al Jufrah □, *Libya*	**108 C3**	27 30N	17 30 E
Al Jumūm, *Si. Arabia*	**98 B2**	21 37N	39 42 E
Al Junaynah, *Sudan*	**109 F4**	13 27N	22 45 E
Al Kabā'ish, *Iraq*	**96 D5**	30 58N	47 0 E
Al Kāmil, *Oman*	**99 B7**	22 13N	59 12 E
Al Karak, *Jordan*	**103 D4**	31 11N	35 42 E
Al Karak □, *Jordan*	**103 E5**	31 0N	36 0 E
Al Kāzim Tyah, *Iraq*	**101 F11**	33 22N	44 12 E
Al Khābūra, *Oman*	**97 F8**	23 57N	57 5 E
Al Khafji, *Si. Arabia*	**97 E6**	28 24N	48 29 E
Al Khalīl, *West Bank*	**103 D4**	31 32N	35 6 E
Al Khāliş, *Iraq*	**101 F11**	33 49N	44 32 E
Al Khamāsīn, *Si. Arabia*	**98 B4**	20 29N	44 46 E
Al Kharj, *Si. Arabia*	**98 B4**	24 0N	47 0 E
Al Kharsānīyah, *Si. Arabia*	**97 E6**	27 13N	49 18 E
Al Khaşab, *Oman*	**97 E8**	26 14N	56 15 E
Al Khāşirah, *Si. Arabia*	**98 B3**	23 30N	43 47 E
Al Khawr, *Qatar*	**97 E6**	25 41N	51 30 E
Al Khiḑr, *Iraq*	**96 D5**	31 12N	45 33 E
Al Khiyām, *Lebanon*	**103 B4**	33 20N	35 36 E
Al Khums, *Libya*	**108 B2**	32 40N	14 17 E
Al Khums □, *Libya*	**108 B2**	31 20N	14 10 E
Al Kiswah, *Syria*	**103 B5**	33 23N	36 14 E
Al Kūfah, *Iraq*	**101 F11**	32 2N	44 24 E
Al Kufrah, *Libya*	**108 D4**	24 17N	23 15 E
Al Kuhayfīyah, *Si. Arabia*	**96 E4**	27 12N	43 3 E
Al Kūt, *Iraq*	**101 F11**	32 30N	46 0 E
Al Kuwayt, *Kuwait*	**96 D5**	29 30N	48 0 E
Al Labwah, *Lebanon*	**103 A5**	34 11N	36 20 E
Al Lādhiqīyah, *Syria*	**100 E6**	35 30N	35 45 E
Al Līth, *Si. Arabia*	**98 B3**	20 9N	40 15 E
Al Liwā', *Oman*	**97 E8**	24 31N	56 36 E
Al Luḩayyah, *Yemen*	**98 D3**	15 45N	42 40 E
Al Madīnah, *Iraq*	**96 D5**	30 57N	47 16 E
Al Madīnah, *Si. Arabia*	**96 E3**	24 35N	39 52 E
Al Mafraq, *Jordan*	**103 C5**	32 17N	36 14 E
Al Maghārīm, *Yemen*	**98 D4**	15 1N	47 49 E
Al Mahbes, *W. Sahara*	**110 C3**	27 10N	9 50W
Al Maḩmūdīyah, *Iraq*	**101 F11**	33 3N	44 21 E
Al Majma'ah, *Si. Arabia*	**96 E5**	25 57N	45 22 E
Al Makhruq, W. →, *Jordan*	**103 D6**	31 28N	37 0 E
Al Makḩūl, *Si. Arabia*	**96 E4**	26 37N	42 39 E
Al Makīlī, *Libya*	**108 B4**	32 10N	22 17 E
Al Manāmah, *Bahrain*	**97 E6**	26 10N	50 30 E
Al Maqwa', *Kuwait*	**96 D5**	29 10N	47 59 E
Al Marj, *Libya*	**108 B4**	32 25N	20 30 E
Al Maţlā, *Kuwait*	**96 D5**	29 24N	47 40 E
Al Mawjib, W. →, *Jordan*	**103 D4**	31 28N	35 36 E
Al Mawşil, *Iraq*	**101 D10**	36 15N	43 5 E
Al Mayādin, *Syria*	**101 E9**	35 1N	40 27 E
Al Mazār, *Jordan*	**103 D4**	31 4N	35 41 E
Al Midhnab, *Si. Arabia*	**96 E5**	25 50N	44 18 E
Al Minā', *Lebanon*	**103 A4**	34 24N	35 49 E
Al Miqdādīyah, *Iraq*	**101 E11**	34 0N	45 0 E
Al Mubarraz, *Si. Arabia*	**97 E6**	25 30N	49 40 E
Al Mudawwarah, *Jordan*	**103 F5**	29 19N	36 0 E
Al Muḑaybī, *Oman*	**99 B7**	22 34N	58 7 E
Al Mughayrā', *U.A.E.*	**97 E7**	24 5N	53 32 E
Al Muḩarraq, *Bahrain*	**97 E6**	26 15N	50 40 E
Al Mukallā, *Yemen*	**99 D5**	14 33N	49 2 E
Al Mukhā, *Yemen*	**98 D3**	13 18N	43 15 E
Al Musayjīd, *Si. Arabia*	**96 E3**	24 5N	39 5 E
Al Musayyib, *Iraq*	**101 F11**	32 49N	44 20 E
Al Muwayh, *Si. Arabia*	**106 C5**	22 41N	41 37 E
Al Muwayliḩ, *Si. Arabia*	**96 E2**	27 40N	35 30 E
Al Owuho = Otukpa, *Nigeria*	**113 D6**	7 9N	7 41 E
Al Qaddāḩīyah, *Libya*	**108 B3**	31 15N	15 9 E
Al Qaḑīmah, *Si. Arabia*	**98 B2**	22 20N	39 13 E
Al Qaḩmah, *Si. Arabia*	**98 C3**	18 0N	41 41 E
Al Qā'im, *Iraq*	**101 E9**	34 21N	41 7 E
Al Qalībah, *Si. Arabia*	**96 D3**	28 24N	37 42 E
Al Qāmishlī, *Syria*	**101 D9**	37 2N	41 14 E
Al Qaryah ash Sharqīyah, *Libya*	**108 B2**	30 28N	13 40 E
Al Qaryatayn, *Syria*	**103 A6**	34 12N	37 13 E
Al Qaşabát, *Libya*	**108 B2**	32 39N	14 1 E
Al Qaşīm, *Si. Arabia*	**96 E4**	26 0N	43 0 E
Al Qaţ'ā, *Syria*	**101 E9**	34 40N	40 48 E
Al Qaţīf, *Si. Arabia*	**97 E6**	26 35N	50 0 E
Al Qaţn, *Yemen*	**99 D5**	15 51N	48 26 E
Al Qatrānah, *Jordan*	**103 D5**	31 12N	36 6 E
Al Qaţrūn, *Libya*	**108 D3**	24 56N	15 3 E
Al Qayşūmah, *Si. Arabia*	**96 D5**	28 20N	46 7 E
Al Qiblīyah, *Oman*	**99 C7**	17 30N	56 20 E
Al Quds = Jerusalem, *Israel*	**103 D4**	31 47N	35 10 E
Al Qunayţirah, *Syria*	**103 C4**	32 55N	35 45 E
Al Qunfudhah, *Si. Arabia*	**98 C3**	19 3N	41 4 E
Al Qurḩ, *Yemen*	**99 C5**	16 44N	51 29 E
Al Qurnah, *Iraq*	**96 D5**	31 1N	47 25 E
Al Quşayr, *Iraq*	**96 D5**	30 39N	45 50 E
Al Quşayr, *Syria*	**103 A5**	34 31N	36 34 E
Al Qutayfah, *Syria*	**103 B5**	33 44N	36 36 E
Al Quway'īyah, *Si. Arabia*	**98 A4**	24 3N	45 15 E
Al 'Ubaylah, *Si. Arabia*	**99 B5**	21 59N	50 57 E
Al 'Uḑaylīyah, *Si. Arabia*	**97 E6**	25 8N	49 18 E
Al 'Ulā, *Si. Arabia*	**96 E3**	26 35N	38 0 E
Al 'Ulayyah, *Si. Arabia*	**98 C3**	19 39N	41 54 E
Al Uqaylah ash Sharqīgah, *Libya*	**108 B3**	30 12N	19 10 E
Al 'Uqayr, *Si. Arabia*	**97 E6**	25 40N	50 15 E
Al 'Uwaynid, *Si. Arabia*	**96 E5**	24 50N	46 0 E
Al 'Uwayqīlah, *Si. Arabia*	**96 D4**	30 30N	42 10 E
Al 'Uyūn, *Ḩijāz, Si. Arabia*	**96 E3**	24 33N	39 35 E
Al 'Uyūn, *Najd, Si. Arabia*	**96 E4**	26 30N	43 50 E
Al 'Uzayr, *Iraq*	**96 D5**	31 19N	47 25 E
Al Wajh, *Si. Arabia*	**96 E3**	26 10N	36 30 E
Al Wakrah, *Qatar*	**97 E6**	25 10N	51 40 E
Al Waqbah, *Si. Arabia*	**96 D5**	28 48N	45 33 E
Al Wari'āh, *Si. Arabia*	**96 E5**	27 51N	47 25 E
Al Wāţīyah, *Libya*	**108 B2**	32 28N	11 57 E
Ala, *Italy*	**44 C8**	45 45N	11 0 E
Ala-Buka, *Kyrgyzstan*	**65 C5**	41 23N	71 30 E
Ala Dağ, *Turkey*	**96 B2**	37 44N	35 9 E
Ala Dağları, *Turkey*	**101 C10**	39 15N	43 33 E
Ala Tau Shankou = Dzungarian Gates, *Asia*	**68 B3**	45 0N	82 0 E
Alabama □, *U.S.A.*	**149 J2**	33 0N	87 0W
Alabama →, *U.S.A.*	**149 K2**	31 8N	87 57W
Alabaster, *U.S.A.*	**149 J2**	33 15N	86 49W
Alabat I., *Phil.*	**80 D4**	14 7N	122 3 E
Alabel, *Phil.*	**81 H5**	6 4N	125 16 E
Alabule →, *Papua N. G.*	**132 E4**	8 31 S	146 56 E
Alaca, *Turkey*	**100 B6**	40 10N	34 51 E
Alacaatlı, *Turkey*	**49 B10**	39 15N	28 3 E
Alaçam, *Turkey*	**100 B6**	41 36N	35 36 E
Alaçam Dağları, *Turkey*	**49 B10**	39 18N	28 49 E
Alaçatı, *Turkey*	**49 C8**	38 15N	26 22 E
Alachua, *U.S.A.*	**152 F7**	29 47N	82 30W
Alaejos, *Spain*	**42 D5**	41 18N	5 13W
Alaérma, *Greece*	**38 E11**	36 9N	27 57 E
Alagir, *Russia*	**61 J7**	43 3N	44 14 E
Alagna Valsésia, *Italy*	**44 C4**	45 51N	7 56 E
Alagoa Grande, *Brazil*	**170 C4**	7 3 S	35 35W
Alagoas □, *Brazil*	**170 C4**	9 0 S	36 0W
Alagoinhas, *Brazil*	**171 D4**	12 7 S	38 20W
Alagón, *Spain*	**40 D3**	41 46N	1 12W
Alagón →, *Spain*	**42 F4**	39 44N	6 53W
Alai Range, *Asia*	**65 D5**	39 45N	72 0 E
Alaior, *Spain*	**38 B5**	39 57N	4 8 E
Alajero, *Canary Is.*	**9 e1**	28 3N	17 13W
Alajuela, *Costa Rica*	**164 D3**	10 2N	84 8W
Alakamisy, *Madag.*	**117 C8**	21 19 S	47 14 E
Alakanuk, *U.S.A.*	**144 E6**	62 41N	164 37W
Alaknanda →, *India*	**93 D8**	30 8N	78 36 E
Alakurtti, *Russia*	**56 A5**	67 0N	30 30 E
Alalakeiki Channel, *U.S.A.*	**145 C5**	20 30N	156 30W
Alalapura, *Surinam*	**169 C6**	2 20N	56 25W
Alalaú →, *Brazil*	**169 D5**	0 30 S	61 9W
Alamarvdasht, *Iran*	**97 E7**	27 37N	52 59 E
Alamata, *Ethiopia*	**107 E4**	12 25N	39 33 E
Alameda, *Calif., U.S.A.*	**160 H4**	37 46N	122 15W
Alameda, *N. Mex., U.S.A.*	**159 J10**	35 11N	106 37W
Alaminos, *Phil.*	**80 C2**	16 10N	119 59 E
Alamo, *Ga., U.S.A.*	**152 C7**	32 9N	82 47W
Alamo, *Nev., U.S.A.*	**161 J11**	37 22N	115 10W
Alamo Crossing, *U.S.A.*	**161 L13**	34 16N	113 33W
Alamogordo, *U.S.A.*	**159 K11**	32 54N	105 57W
Alamos, *Mexico*	**162 B3**	27 0N	109 0W
Alamosa, *U.S.A.*	**159 H11**	37 28N	105 52W
Alampur, *India*	**95 G4**	15 55N	78 6 E
Åland, *Finland*	**15 F19**	60 15N	20 0 E
Aland, *India*	**94 F3**	17 36N	76 35 E
Alandroal, *Portugal*	**43 G3**	38 41N	7 24W
Ålands hav, *Sweden*	**15 F18**	60 0N	19 30 E
Alandur, *India*	**95 H5**	13 0N	80 15 E
Alange, Presa de, *Spain*	**43 G4**	38 45N	6 18W
Alania = North Ossetia □, *Russia*	**61 J7**	43 30N	44 30 E
Alanís, *Spain*	**43 G5**	38 3N	5 43W
Alanya, *Turkey*	**100 D5**	36 38N	32 0 E
Alaotra, Farihin', *Madag.*	**117 B8**	17 30 S	48 30 E
Alapaha, *U.S.A.*	**152 D6**	31 23N	83 13W
Alapayevsk, *Russia*	**64 C8**	57 52N	61 42 E
Alappuzha = Alleppey, *India*	**95 K3**	9 30N	76 28 E
Alar del Rey, *Spain*	**42 C6**	42 38N	4 20W
Alaraz, *Spain*	**42 E5**	40 45N	5 17W
Alarcón, Embalse de, *Spain*	**40 F2**	39 36N	2 10W
Alarobia-Vohiposa, *Madag.*	**117 C8**	20 59 S	47 9 E
Alaşehir, *Turkey*	**49 C10**	38 23N	28 30 E
Alaska □, *U.S.A.*	**144 E9**	64 0N	154 0W
Alaska, G. of, *Pac. Oc.*	**144 G11**	58 0N	145 0W
Alaska Peninsula, *U.S.A.*	**144 J8**	56 0N	159 0W
Alaska Range, *U.S.A.*	**144 F10**	62 50N	151 0W
Alássio, *Italy*	**44 E5**	44 0N	8 10 E
Älät, *Azerbaijan*	**61 L9**	39 58N	49 25 E
Alat, *Uzbekistan*	**65 D1**	39 24N	63 47 E
Alatri, *Italy*	**45 G10**	41 43N	13 21 E
Alatyr, *Russia*	**60 C8**	54 55N	46 35 E
Alatyr →, *Russia*	**60 C8**	54 52N	46 36 E
Alausi, *Ecuador*	**168 D2**	2 0 S	78 50W
Álava □, *Spain*	**40 C2**	42 48N	2 28W
Alava, C., *U.S.A.*	**158 B1**	48 10N	124 44W
Alaverdi, *Armenia*	**61 K7**	41 15N	44 37 E
Alavus, *Finland*	**15 E20**	62 35N	23 36 E
Alawoona, *Australia*	**128 C4**	34 45 S	140 30 E
'Alayh, *Lebanon*	**103 B4**	33 46N	35 33 E
Alaykuu = Kögart, *Kyrgyzstan*	**65 C7**	40 15N	74 25 E
Alazani →, *Azerbaijan*	**61 K8**	41 5N	46 40 E
Alba, *Italy*	**44 D5**	44 42N	8 2 E
Alba □, *Romania*	**53 D8**	46 10N	23 30 E
Alba Adriática, *Italy*	**45 F10**	42 50N	13 56 E
Alba de Tormes, *Spain*	**42 E5**	40 50N	5 30W
Alba-Iulia, *Romania*	**53 D8**	46 8N	23 39 E
Albac, *Romania*	**52 D7**	46 28N	22 58 E
Albacete, *Spain*	**41 F3**	39 0N	1 50W
Albacete □, *Spain*	**41 G3**	38 50N	2 0W
Albacutya, L., *Australia*	**128 C4**	35 45 S	141 58 E
Ålbæk, *Denmark*	**17 G4**	57 36N	10 25 E
Ålbæk Bugt, *Denmark*	**17 G4**	57 35N	10 40 E
Albaida, *Spain*	**41 G4**	38 51N	0 31W
Albalate de las Nogueras, *Spain*	**40 E2**	40 22N	2 18W
Albalate del Arzobispo, *Spain*	**40 D4**	41 6N	0 31W
Alban, *France*	**28 E6**	43 53N	2 28 E
Albanel, L., *Canada*	**140 B5**	50 55N	73 12W
Albania ■, *Europe*	**50 E4**	41 0N	20 0 E
Albano Laziale, *Italy*	**45 G9**	41 44N	12 39 E
Albany, *Australia*	**125 G2**	35 1 S	117 58 E
Albany, *Ga., U.S.A.*	**152 D5**	31 35N	84 10W
Albany, *Ind., U.S.A.*	**157 D11**	40 18N	85 14W
Albany, *Mo., U.S.A.*	**156 D2**	40 15N	94 20W
Albany, *N.Y., U.S.A.*	**151 D11**	42 39N	73 45W
Albany, *Oreg., U.S.A.*	**158 D2**	44 38N	123 6W
Albany, *Tex., U.S.A.*	**155 J5**	32 44N	99 18W
Albany, *Wis., U.S.A.*	**156 B7**	42 43N	89 26W
Albany →, *Canada*	**140 B3**	52 17N	81 31W
Albardón, *Argentina*	**174 C2**	31 20 S	68 30W
Albarracín, *Spain*	**40 E3**	40 25N	1 26W
Albarracín, Sierra de, *Spain*	**40 E3**	40 30N	1 30W
Albatera, *Spain*	**41 G4**	38 11N	0 52W
Albatross B., *Australia*	**126 A3**	12 45 S	141 30 E
Albatross Pt., *N.Z.*	**130 E3**	38 7 S	174 44 E
Albay □, *Phil.*	**80 E4**	13 13N	123 33 E
Albegna →, *Italy*	**45 F8**	42 30N	11 11 E
Albemarle, *U.S.A.*	**149 H5**	35 21N	80 11W
Albemarle, Pta., *Ecuador*	**172 a**	0 11N	91 21W
Albemarle Sd., *U.S.A.*	**149 H7**	36 5N	76 0W
Albenga, *Italy*	**44 D5**	44 3N	8 13 E
Alberche →, *Spain*	**42 F6**	39 58N	4 46W
Alberdi, *Paraguay*	**174 B4**	26 14 S	58 20W
Alberes, Mts., *France*	**28 F6**	42 28N	2 56 E
Ålberga, *Sweden*	**17 F10**	58 44N	16 35 E
Albersdorf, *Germany*	**30 A5**	54 8N	9 17 E
Albert, *France*	**27 C9**	50 0N	2 38 E
Albert, L., *Africa*	**118 B3**	1 30N	31 0 E
Albert, L., *Australia*	**128 C3**	35 30 S	139 10 E
Albert Edward, Mt., *Papua N. G.*	**132 E4**	8 20 S	147 24 E
Albert Edward Ra., *Australia*	**124 C4**	18 17 S	127 57 E
Albert Lea, *U.S.A.*	**154 D8**	43 39N	93 22W
Albert Nile →, *Uganda*	**118 B3**	3 36N	32 2 E
Albert Town, *Bahamas*	**165 B5**	22 37N	74 33W
Alberta □, *Canada*	**142 C6**	54 40N	115 0W
Alberti, *Argentina*	**174 D3**	35 1 S	60 16W
Albertinia, *S. Africa*	**116 E3**	34 11 S	21 34 E
Albertirsa, *Hungary*	**52 C4**	47 14N	19 37 E
Alberton, *Canada*	**141 C7**	46 50N	64 0W
Albertville = Kalemie, *Dem. Rep. of the Congo*	**118 D2**	5 55 S	29 9 E
Albertville, *France*	**29 C10**	45 40N	6 22 E
Albertville, *U.S.A.*	**149 H2**	34 16N	86 13W
Albi, *France*	**28 E6**	43 56N	2 9 E
Albia, *U.S.A.*	**156 C4**	41 2N	92 48W
Albina, *Surinam*	**169 B7**	5 37N	54 15W
Albina, Ponta, *Angola*	**116 B1**	15 52 S	11 44 E
Albino, *Italy*	**44 C6**	45 46N	9 47 E
Albion, *Ill., U.S.A.*	**157 F8**	38 23N	88 4W
Albion, *Ind., U.S.A.*	**157 C11**	41 24N	85 25W
Albion, *Mich., U.S.A.*	**157 B12**	42 15N	84 45W
Albion, *Nebr., U.S.A.*	**154 E6**	41 42N	98 0W
Albion, *Pa., U.S.A.*	**150 E4**	41 53N	80 22W
Albocácer, *Spain*	**40 E5**	40 21N	0 1 E
Albolote, *Spain*	**43 H7**	37 14N	3 39W
Alborán, *Medit. S.*	**43 K7**	35 57N	3 0W
Alborea, *Spain*	**41 F3**	39 17N	1 24W
Ålborg, *Denmark*	**17 G3**	57 2N	9 54 E
Ålborg Bugt, *Denmark*	**17 H4**	56 50N	10 35 E
Alborz, Reshteh-ye Kūhhā-ye, *Iran*	**97 C7**	36 0N	52 0 E
Albosaggia, *Italy*	**33 D9**	46 8N	9 51 E
Albox, *Spain*	**41 H2**	37 23N	2 8W
Albuera, *Phil.*	**81 F5**	10 55N	124 42 E
Albufeira, *Portugal*	**43 H2**	37 5N	8 15W
Albula →, *Switz.*	**33 C8**	46 38N	9 28 E
Albuñol, *Spain*	**43 J7**	36 48N	3 11W
Albuquerque, *Brazil*	**173 D6**	19 23 S	57 26W
Albuquerque, *U.S.A.*	**159 J10**	35 5N	106 39W
Albuquerque, Cayos de, *Caribbean*	**164 D3**	12 10N	81 50W
Alburg, *U.S.A.*	**151 B11**	44 59N	73 18W
Alburno, Mte., *Italy*	**47 B8**	40 33N	15 17 E
Alburquerque, *Spain*	**43 F4**	39 15N	6 59W
Albury = Albury-Wodonga, *Australia*	**129 D7**	36 3 S	146 56 E
Albury-Wodonga, *Australia*	**129 D7**	36 3 S	146 56 E
Alcácer do Sal, *Portugal*	**43 G2**	38 22N	8 33W
Alcáçovas, *Portugal*	**43 G2**	38 23N	8 9W
Alcala, *Phil.*	**80 C3**	17 54N	121 39 E
Alcalá de Chivert, *Spain*	**40 E5**	40 19N	0 13 E
Alcalá de Guadaira, *Spain*	**43 H5**	37 20N	5 50W
Alcalá de Henares, *Spain*	**42 E7**	40 28N	3 22W
Alcalá de los Gazules, *Spain*	**43 J5**	36 29N	5 43W
Alcalá del Júcar, *Spain*	**41 F3**	39 12N	1 26W
Alcalá del Río, *Spain*	**43 H5**	37 31N	5 59W
Alcalá del Valle, *Spain*	**43 J5**	36 54N	5 10W
Alcalá la Real, *Spain*	**43 H7**	37 27N	3 57W
Álcamo, *Italy*	**46 E5**	37 59N	12 55 E
Alcanadre, *Spain*	**40 C2**	42 24N	2 7W
Alcanadre →, *Spain*	**40 D4**	41 43N	0 12W
Alcanar, *Spain*	**40 E5**	40 33N	0 28 E
Alcanede, *Portugal*	**43 F2**	39 25N	8 49W
Alcanena, *Portugal*	**43 F2**	39 27N	8 40W
Alcañices, *Spain*	**42 D4**	41 41N	6 21W
Alcaníz, *Spain*	**40 D4**	41 2N	0 8W
Alcântara, *Brazil*	**170 B3**	2 20 S	44 30W
Alcántara, *Spain*	**42 F4**	39 41N	6 57W
Alcántara, Embalse de, *Spain*	**42 F4**	39 44N	6 50W
Alcantarilla, *Spain*	**41 H3**	37 59N	1 12W
Alcaracejos, *Spain*	**43 G6**	38 24N	4 58W
Alcaraz, *Spain*	**41 G2**	38 40N	2 29W
Alcaraz, Sierra de, *Spain*	**41 G2**	38 40N	2 20W
Alcaudete, *Spain*	**43 H6**	37 35N	4 5W
Alcázar de San Juan, *Spain*	**43 F7**	39 24N	3 12W
Alcedo, Volcán, *Ecuador*	**172 a**	0 24 S	91 6W
Alchevsk, *Ukraine*	**59 H10**	48 30N	38 45 E
Alcira = Alzira, *Spain*	**41 F4**	39 9N	0 30W
Alcobaça, *Portugal*	**43 F2**	39 32N	8 58W
Alcobendas, *Spain*	**42 E7**	40 32N	3 38W
Alcolea del Pinar, *Spain*	**40 D2**	41 2N	2 28W
Alcoma, *U.S.A.*	**153 H8**	27 54N	81 29W
Alcora, *Spain*	**40 E4**	40 5N	0 14W
Alcorcón, *Spain*	**42 E7**	40 20N	3 50W
Alcoutim, *Portugal*	**43 H3**	37 25N	7 28W
Alcova, *U.S.A.*	**158 E10**	42 34N	106 43W
Alcoy, *Spain*	**41 G4**	38 43N	0 30W
Alcubierre, Sierra de, *Spain*	**40 D4**	41 45N	0 22W
Alcublas, *Spain*	**40 F4**	39 48N	0 43W
Alcúdia, *Spain*	**38 B4**	39 51N	3 7 E
Alcúdia, B. d', *Spain*	**38 B4**	39 47N	3 15 E
Alcudia, Sierra de la, *Spain*	**43 G6**	38 34N	4 30W
Aldabra Is., *Seychelles*	**105 G8**	9 22 S	46 28 E
Aldama, *Mexico*	**163 C5**	23 0N	98 4W
Aldan, *Russia*	**67 D13**	58 40N	125 30 E
Aldan →, *Russia*	**67 C13**	63 28N	129 35 E
Aldea, Pta. de la, *Canary Is.*	**9 e1**	28 0N	15 50W
Aldeburgh, *U.K.*	**21 E9**	52 10N	1 37 E
Alden, *Norway*	**18 C1**	61 19N	4 45 E
Alder Pk., *U.S.A.*	**160 K5**	35 53N	121 22W
Alderney, *U.K.*	**21 H5**	49 42N	2 11W
Aldershot, *U.K.*	**21 F7**	51 15N	0 44W
Aldinga Beach, *Australia*	**128 C3**	35 17 S	138 27 E
Åled, *Sweden*	**17 H6**	56 44N	12 57 E
Aledo, *U.S.A.*	**156 C6**	41 12N	90 45W
Alefa, *Ethiopia*	**107 E4**	11 55N	36 55 E
Aleg, *Mauritania*	**112 B2**	17 3N	13 55W
Alegranza, *Canary Is.*	**110 C2**	29 23N	13 32W
Alegranza, I., *Canary Is.*	**9 e2**	29 23N	13 32W
Alegre, *Brazil*	**171 F3**	20 50 S	41 30W
Alegrete, *Brazil*	**175 B4**	29 40 S	56 0W
Aleisk, *Russia*	**66 D9**	52 40N	83 0 E
Aleknagik, *U.S.A.*	**144 G8**	59 17N	158 36W
Aleksandriya = Oleksandriya, *Kirovohrad, Ukraine*	**59 H7**	48 42N	33 3 E
Aleksandriya = Oleksandriya, *Rivne, Ukraine*	**59 G4**	50 37N	26 19 E
Aleksandriyskaya, *Russia*	**61 J8**	43 58N	47 14 E
Aleksandrov, *Russia*	**58 D10**	56 23N	38 44 E
Aleksandrov Gay, *Russia*	**60 E9**	50 9N	48 34 E
Aleksandrovac, *Serbia, Yug.*	**50 C5**	43 28N	21 3 E
Aleksandrovac, *Serbia, Yug.*	**50 B5**	44 28N	21 13 E
Aleksandrovka = Oleksandrovka, *Ukraine*	**59 H7**	48 55N	32 20 E
Aleksandrovo, *Bulgaria*	**51 C8**	43 14N	24 51 E
Aleksandrovsk, *Russia*	**64 B6**	59 9N	57 33 E
Aleksandrovsk-Sakhalinskiy, *Russia*	**67 D15**	50 50N	142 20 E
Aleksandrów Kujawski, *Poland*	**55 F5**	52 53N	18 43 E
Aleksandrów Łódźki, *Poland*	**55 G6**	51 49N	19 17 E
Alekseyevka, *Samara, Russia*	**60 D10**	52 35N	51 17 E
Alekseyevka, *Voronezh, Russia*	**59 G10**	50 43N	38 40 E
Aleksin, *Russia*	**58 E9**	54 31N	37 9 E
Aleksinac, *Serbia, Yug.*	**50 C5**	43 31N	21 42 E
Além Paraíba, *Brazil*	**171 F3**	21 52 S	42 41W
Alemania, *Argentina*	**174 B2**	25 40 S	65 30W
Alemania, *Chile*	**174 B2**	25 10 S	69 55W
Alen, *Eq. Guin.*	**114 B2**	1 58N	11 19 E
Alençon, *France*	**26 D7**	48 27N	0 4 E
Alenuihaha Channel, *U.S.A.*	**145 C6**	20 30N	156 0W
Alépé, *Ivory C.*	**112 D4**	5 29N	3 40W
Aleppo = Ḩalab, *Syria*	**100 D7**	36 10N	37 15 E
Aléria, *France*	**29 F13**	42 5N	9 26 E
Aleru, *India*	**94 F4**	17 39N	79 3 E
Alès, *France*	**29 D8**	44 9N	4 5 E
Aleşd, *Romania*	**52 C7**	47 3N	22 22 E
Alessándria, *Italy*	**44 D5**	44 54N	8 37 E
Ålestrup, *Denmark*	**17 H3**	56 42N	9 29 E
Ålesund, *Norway*	**15 E12**	62 28N	6 12 E
Alet-les-Bains, *France*	**28 F6**	42 59N	2 14 E
Aletschhorn, *Switz.*	**32 D6**	46 28N	8 0 E
Aleutian Is., *Pac. Oc.*	**138 C2**	52 0N	175 0W
Aleutian Range, *U.S.A.*	**144 G9**	60 0N	154 0W
Aleutian Trench, *Pac. Oc.*	**134 C10**	48 0N	180 0 E
Alexander, *Ga., U.S.A.*	**152 B8**	33 1N	81 53W
Alexander, *N. Dak., U.S.A.*	**154 B3**	47 51N	103 39W
Alexander, C., *Solomon Is.*	**133 L9**	6 34 S	156 32 E
Alexander, Mt., *Australia*	**125 E3**	28 58 S	120 16 E
Alexander Arch., *U.S.A.*	**144 J14**	56 0N	136 0W
Alexander Bay, *S. Africa*	**116 D2**	28 40 S	16 30 E
Alexander City, *U.S.A.*	**152 C4**	32 56N	85 58W
Alexander I., *Antarctica*	**7 C17**	69 0 S	70 0W
Alexandra, *Australia*	**129 D6**	37 8 S	145 40 E
Alexandra, *N.Z.*	**131 F4**	45 14 S	169 25 E
Alexandra Channel, *Burma*	**95 G11**	14 7N	93 13 E
Alexandra Falls, *Canada*	**142 A5**	60 29N	116 18W
Alexandria = El Iskandarîya, *Egypt*	**106 H7**	31 13N	29 58 E
Alexandria, *B.C., Canada*	**142 C4**	52 35N	122 27W
Alexandria, *Ont., Canada*	**140 C5**	45 19N	74 38W
Alexandria, *Romania*	**53 G10**	43 57N	25 24 E
Alexandria, *S. Africa*	**116 E4**	33 38 S	26 28 E
Alexandria, *U.K.*	**22 F4**	55 59N	4 35W
Alexandria, *Ind., U.S.A.*	**157 D11**	40 16N	85 41W
Alexandria, *Ky., U.S.A.*	**157 F12**	38 58N	84 23W
Alexandria, *La., U.S.A.*	**155 K8**	31 18N	92 27W
Alexandria, *Minn., U.S.A.*	**154 C7**	45 53N	95 22W
Alexandria, *Mo., U.S.A.*	**156 D5**	40 27N	91 28W
Alexandria, *S. Dak., U.S.A.*	**154 D6**	43 39N	97 47W
Alexandria, *Va., U.S.A.*	**148 F7**	38 48N	77 3W
Alexandria Bay, *U.S.A.*	**151 B9**	44 20N	75 55W
Alexandrina, L., *Australia*	**128 C3**	35 25 S	139 10 E
Alexandroúpolis, *Greece*	**51 F9**	40 50N	25 54 E
Alexis, *U.S.A.*	**156 C6**	41 4N	90 33W
Alexis →, *Canada*	**141 B8**	52 33N	56 8W
Alexis Creek, *Canada*	**142 C4**	52 10N	123 20W
Alfabia, *Spain*	**38 B3**	39 44N	2 44 E
Alfambra, *Spain*	**40 E3**	40 33N	1 5W
Alfândega da Fé, *Portugal*	**42 D4**	41 20N	6 59W
Alfaro, *Spain*	**40 C3**	42 10N	1 50W
Alfatar, *Bulgaria*	**51 C11**	43 59N	27 13 E
Alfaz del Pi, *Spain*	**41 G4**	38 35N	0 5W
Alfeld, *Germany*	**30 D5**	51 59N	9 50 E
Alfenas, *Brazil*	**175 A6**	21 20 S	46 10W
Alfiós →, *Greece*	**48 D3**	37 40N	21 33 E
Alföld, *Hungary*	**52 D5**	46 30N	20 0 E
Alfonsine, *Italy*	**45 D9**	44 30N	12 3 E
Alfonso XIII = Quezon, *Phil.*	**81 G1**	9 15N	117 59 E
Alford, *Aberds., U.K.*	**22 D6**	57 14N	2 41W
Alford, *Lincs., U.K.*	**20 D8**	53 15N	0 10 E
Alford, *U.S.A.*	**152 E4**	30 42N	85 24W
Ålfotbreen, *Norway*	**18 C2**	61 45N	5 39 E
Ålfoten, *Norway*	**18 C2**	61 51N	5 41 E
Alfred, *Maine, U.S.A.*	**151 C14**	43 29N	70 43W
Alfred, *N.Y., U.S.A.*	**150 D7**	42 16N	77 48W
Alfredton, *N.Z.*	**130 G4**	40 41 S	175 54 E
Alfreton, *U.K.*	**20 D6**	53 6N	1 24W
Alfta, *Sweden*	**16 C10**	61 21N	16 4 E
Alga, *Kazakstan*	**57 E10**	49 53N	57 20 E
Algaida, *Spain*	**38 B3**	39 33N	2 53 E
Algar, *Spain*	**43 J5**	36 40N	5 39W
Ålgård, *Norway*	**15 G11**	58 46N	5 53 E
Algarinejo, *Spain*	**43 H6**	37 19N	4 9W
Algarve, *Portugal*	**43 J2**	36 58N	8 20W
Algeciras, *Spain*	**43 J5**	36 9N	5 28W
Algemesí, *Spain*	**41 F4**	39 11N	0 27W
Alger, *Algeria*	**111 A5**	36 42N	3 8 E
Algeria ■, *Africa*	**111 C5**	28 30N	2 0 E
Alghero, *Italy*	**46 B1**	40 33N	8 19 E
Älghult, *Sweden*	**17 G9**	57 0N	15 35 E
Algiers = Alger, *Algeria*	**111 A5**	36 42N	3 8 E
Algoa B., *S. Africa*	**116 E4**	33 50 S	25 45 E
Algodonales, *Spain*	**43 J5**	36 54N	5 24W
Algodor →, *Spain*	**42 F7**	39 55N	3 53W
Algoma, *U.S.A.*	**148 C2**	44 36N	87 26W
Algona, *U.S.A.*	**156 A2**	43 4N	94 14W
Algonac, *U.S.A.*	**150 D2**	42 37N	82 32W
Algonquin Prov. Park, *Canada*	**140 C4**	45 50N	78 30W
Alhama de Almería, *Spain*	**43 J8**	36 57N	2 34W
Alhama de Aragón, *Spain*	**40 D3**	41 18N	1 54W
Alhama de Granada, *Spain*	**43 H7**	37 0N	3 59W
Alhama de Murcia, *Spain*	**41 H3**	37 51N	1 25W
Alhambra, *U.S.A.*	**161 L8**	34 8N	118 6W
Alhaurín el Grande, *Spain*	**43 J6**	36 39N	4 41W
Alhucemas = Al Hoceïma, *Morocco*	**110 A4**	35 8N	3 58W
'Alī al Gharbī, *Iraq*	**101 F12**	32 30N	46 45 E
'Alī ash Sharqī, *Iraq*	**101 F12**	32 7N	46 44 E
Äli Bayramlı, *Azerbaijan*	**61 L9**	39 59N	48 52 E
'Alī Khēl, *Afghan.*	**91 B3**	33 57N	69 43 E
Ali Sahîh, *Djibouti*	**107 E5**	11 10N	42 44 E
Alī Shāh, *Iran*	**96 B5**	38 9N	45 50 E
Ália, *Italy*	**46 E6**	37 47N	13 43 E
'Alīābād, *Khorāsān, Iran*	**97 C8**	32 30N	57 30 E
'Alīābād, *Kordestān, Iran*	**96 C5**	35 4N	46 58 E
'Alīābād, *Yazd, Iran*	**97 D7**	31 41N	53 49 E
Aliaga, *Spain*	**40 E4**	40 40N	0 42W
Aliağa, *Turkey*	**49 C8**	38 47N	26 59 E
Aliákmon →, *Greece*	**50 F6**	40 30N	22 36 E
Alibag, *India*	**94 E1**	18 38N	72 56 E
Alibo, *Ethiopia*	**107 F4**	9 52N	37 5 E
Alibori →, *Benin*	**113 C5**	11 56N	3 17 E
Alibunar, *Serbia, Yug.*	**52 E5**	45 5N	20 57 E
Alicante, *Spain*	**41 G4**	38 23N	0 30W
Alicante □, *Spain*	**41 G4**	38 30N	0 37W
Alice, *S. Africa*	**116 E4**	32 48 S	26 55 E
Alice, *U.S.A.*	**155 M5**	27 45N	98 5W
Alice →, *Queens., Australia*	**126 C3**	24 2 S	144 50 E
Alice →, *Queens., Australia*	**126 B3**	15 35 S	142 20 E
Alice →, *Papua N. G.*	**132 D1**	6 10 S	141 8 E
Alice, Punta, *Italy*	**47 C10**	39 24N	17 9 E
Alice Arm, *Canada*	**142 B3**	55 29N	129 31W
Alice Springs, *Australia*	**126 C1**	23 40 S	133 50 E
Alicedale, *S. Africa*	**116 E4**	33 15 S	26 4 E
Aliceville, *U.S.A.*	**149 J1**	33 8N	88 9W
Alichur, *Tajikistan*	**65 E6**	37 45N	73 33 E
Alicia, *Bohol, Phil.*	**81 G5**	9 54N	124 26 E
Alicia, *Isabela, Phil.*	**80 C3**	16 46N	121 42 E
Alicudi, *Italy*	**47 D7**	38 33N	14 20 E
Aliganj, *India*	**93 F8**	27 30N	79 10 E
Aligarh, *Raj., India*	**92 G7**	25 55N	76 15 E
Aligarh, *Ut. P., India*	**92 F8**	27 55N	78 10 E
Alīgūdarz, *Iran*	**97 C6**	33 25N	49 45 E
Alijó, *Portugal*	**42 D3**	41 16N	7 27W
Alikanás, *Greece*	**39 D2**	37 51N	20 47 E
Alima →, *Congo*	**114 C3**	1 35 S	16 37 E
Alimnía, *Greece*	**38 E11**	36 16N	27 43 E
Alimodian, *Phil.*	**81 F4**	10 49N	122 26 E
Alindao, *C.A.R.*	**114 A4**	5 2N	21 13 E
Alingsås, *Sweden*	**17 G6**	57 56N	12 31 E
Alipur, *Pakistan*	**92 E4**	29 25N	70 55 E
Alipur Duar, *India*	**90 B2**	26 30N	89 35 E
Aliquippa, *U.S.A.*	**150 F4**	40 37N	80 15W
Alishan, *Taiwan*	**77 F13**	23 31N	120 48 E
Aliste →, *Spain*	**42 D5**	41 34N	5 58W
Alitus = Alytus, *Lithuania*	**15 J21**	54 24N	24 3 E
Alivérion, *Greece*	**48 C6**	38 24N	24 2 E
Aliwal North, *S. Africa*	**116 E4**	30 45 S	26 45 E
Alix, *Canada*	**142 C6**	52 24N	113 11W
Aljezur, *Portugal*	**43 H2**	37 18N	8 49W
Aljustrel, *Portugal*	**43 H2**	37 55N	8 10W
Alkamari, *Niger*	**113 C7**	13 27N	11 10 E
Alkmaar, *Neths.*	**24 B4**	52 37N	4 45 E
All American Canal, *U.S.A.*	**159 K6**	32 45N	115 15W
Allacapan, *Phil.*	**80 B3**	18 15N	121 35 E
Allada, *Benin*	**113 D5**	6 41N	2 9 E
Allagadda, *India*	**95 G4**	15 8N	78 30 E
Allagash →, *U.S.A.*	**149 B11**	47 5N	69 3W
Allah Dad, *Pakistan*	**92 G2**	25 38N	67 34 E
Allahabad, *India*	**93 G9**	25 25N	81 58 E
Allakaket, *U.S.A.*	**144 C9**	66 34N	152 39W
Allal Tazi, *Morocco*	**110 B3**	34 30N	6 20W
Allan, *Canada*	**143 C7**	51 53N	106 4W
Allanche, *France*	**28 C6**	45 14N	2 57 E
Allanmyo, *Burma*	**90 F5**	19 30N	95 17 E
Allanridge, *S. Africa*	**116 D4**	27 45 S	26 40 E
Allansford, *Australia*	**128 E5**	38 26 S	142 39 E
Allanton, *N.Z.*	**131 F5**	45 55 S	170 15 E
Allaqi, Wadi →, *Egypt*	**106 C3**	23 7N	32 47 E
Allariz, *Spain*	**42 C3**	42 11N	7 50W
Allassac, *France*	**28 C5**	45 15N	1 29 E
Allatoona L., *U.S.A.*	**152 A5**	34 10N	84 44W
Ålleberg, *Sweden*	**17 F7**	58 8N	13 36 E
Allegan, *U.S.A.*	**157 B11**	42 32N	85 51W

Amroha 181

Allegany, U.S.A. 150 D6 42 6N 78 30W
Allegheny →, U.S.A. 150 F5 40 27N 80 1W
Allegheny Mts., U.S.A. 148 G6 38 15N 80 10W
Allegheny Reservoir, U.S.A. 150 E6 41 50N 79 0W
Allègre, France 28 C7 45 12N 3 41 E
Allègre, P., Guadeloupe 164 b 16 22N 61 46W
Allen, Argentina 176 A3 38 58 S 67 50W
Allen, Phil. 80 E5 12 30N 124 17 E
Allen, Bog of, Ireland 23 C5 53 15N 7 0W
Allen, L., Ireland 23 B3 54 8N 8 4W
Allendale, U.S.A. 152 B8 33 1N 81 18W
Allende, Mexico 162 B4 28 20N 100 50W
Allensbach, Germany 33 A8 47 43N 9 4 E
Allentown, U.S.A. 151 F9 40 37N 75 29W
Allentsteig, Austria 34 C8 48 41N 15 20 E
Alleppey, India 95 K3 9 30N 76 28 E
Allepuz, Spain 40 E4 40 29N 0 44W
Aller →, Germany 30 C5 52 56N 9 12 E
Alleynes B., Barbados 165 g 13 13N 59 39W
Alliance, Surinam 169 B7 5 50N 54 50W
Alliance, Nebr., U.S.A. 154 D3 42 6N 102 52W
Alliance, Ohio, U.S.A. 150 F3 40 55N 81 6W
Allier □, France 27 F9 46 25N 2 40 E
Allier →, France 27 F10 46 57N 3 4 E
Alliford Bay, Canada 142 C2 53 12N 131 58W
Alligator Pond, Jamaica 164 a 17 52N 77 34W
Allinagaram, India 95 J3 10 2N 77 30 E
Allinge, Denmark 17 J8 55 17N 14 50 E
Allison, U.S.A. 156 B4 42 45N 92 48W
Alliston, Canada 140 D4 44 9N 79 52W
Alloa, U.K. 22 E5 56 7N 3 47W
Allones, France 26 D8 48 20N 1 40 E
Allora, Australia 127 D5 28 2 S 152 0 E
Allos, France 29 D10 44 15N 6 38 E
Alluitsup Paa, Greenland 10 E6 60 30N 45 35W
Allur, India 95 G5 14 40N 80 4 E
Alluru Kottapatnam, India 95 G5 15 24N 80 7 E
Alma, Canada 141 C5 48 35N 71 40W
Alma, Ga., U.S.A. 152 D7 31 33N 82 28W
Alma, Kans., U.S.A. 154 F6 39 1N 96 17W
Alma, Mich., U.S.A. 148 D3 43 23N 84 39W
Alma, Nebr., U.S.A. 154 E5 40 6N 99 22W
Alma Ata = Almaty, Kazakstan 66 E8 43 15N 76 57 E
Almacelles, Spain 40 D5 41 43N 0 27 E
Almada, Portugal 43 G1 38 40N 9 9W
Almaden, Australia 126 B3 17 22 S 144 40 E
Almadén, Spain 43 G6 38 49N 4 52W
Almalyk = Olmaliq, Uzbekistan 65 C4 40 50N 69 35 E
Almanor, L., U.S.A. 158 F3 40 14N 121 9W
Almansa, Spain 41 G3 38 51N 1 5W
Almanza, Spain 42 C5 42 39N 5 3W
Almanzor, Pico, Spain 42 E5 40 15N 5 18W
Almanzora →, Spain 41 H3 37 14N 1 46W
Almas, Brazil 171 D2 11 33 S 47 9W
Almaş, Munţii, Romania 52 F7 44 49N 22 12 E
Almassora, Spain 40 F4 39 57N 0 3W
Almaty, Kazakstan 66 E8 43 15N 76 57 E
Almazán, Spain 40 D2 41 30N 2 30W
Almeirim, Brazil 169 D7 1 30 S 52 34W
Almeirim, Portugal 43 F2 39 12N 8 37W
Almelo, Neths. 24 B6 52 22N 6 42 E
Almenar de Soria, Spain 40 D2 41 43N 2 12W
Almenara, Brazil 171 E3 16 11 S 40 42W
Almenara, Spain 40 F4 39 46N 0 14W
Almenara, Sierra de la, Spain 41 H3 37 34N 1 32W
Almendra, Embalse de, Spain 42 D4 41 10N 6 5W
Almendralejo, Spain 43 G4 38 41N 6 26W
Almere-Stad, Neths. 24 B5 52 20N 5 15 E
Almería, Spain 43 J8 36 52N 2 27W
Almería □, Spain 41 H2 37 20N 2 20W
Almería, G. de, Spain 41 J2 36 41N 2 28W
Almetyevsk, Russia 60 C11 54 53N 52 20 E
Älmhult, Sweden 17 H8 56 33N 14 8 E
Almirante, Panama 164 E3 9 10N 82 30W
Almirante Montt, G., Chile 176 D2 51 52 S 72 50W
Almirópótamos, Greece 48 C6 38 16N 24 11 E
Almirós, Greece 48 B4 39 11N 22 45 E
Almiroú, Kólpos, Greece 39 E5 35 23N 24 20 E
Almodôvar, Portugal 43 H2 37 31N 8 2W
Almodóvar del Campo, Spain 43 G6 38 43N 4 10W
Almodóvar del Río, Spain 43 H5 37 48N 5 1W
Almond, U.S.A. 150 D7 42 19N 77 44W
Almont, U.S.A. 150 D1 42 55N 83 3W
Almonte, Canada 151 A8 45 14N 76 12W
Almonte, Spain 43 H4 37 13N 6 38W
Almora, India 93 E8 29 38N 79 40 E
Almoradí, Spain 41 G4 38 7N 0 46W
Almorox, Spain 42 E6 40 14N 4 24W
Almoustarat, Mali 113 B5 17 35N 0 8 E
Älmsta, Sweden 16 E12 59 58N 18 50 E
Almudévar, Spain 40 C4 42 3N 0 35W
Almuñécar, Spain 43 J7 36 43N 3 41W
Almunge, Sweden 16 E12 59 53N 18 3 E
Almuradiel, Spain 43 G7 38 32N 3 28W
Alness, U.K. 22 D4 57 41N 4 16W
Alnif, Morocco 110 B3 31 10N 5 8W
Alnmouth, U.K. 20 B6 55 24N 1 37W
Alnwick, U.K. 20 B6 55 24N 1 42W
Aloi, Uganda 118 B3 2 16N 33 10 E
Alon, Burma 90 D5 22 12N 95 5 E
Along, India 90 A5 28 10N 94 46 E
Alor, Indonesia 82 C2 8 15 S 124 30 E
Alor Setar, Malaysia 87 J3 6 7N 100 22 E
Álora, Spain 43 J6 36 49N 4 46W
Alosno, Spain 43 H3 37 33N 7 7W
Alot, India 92 H6 23 56N 75 40 E
Alotau, Papua N. G. 132 F6 10 16 S 150 30 E
Alougoum, Morocco 110 B3 30 17N 6 56W
Aloum, Cameroon 114 B2 2 16N 10 34 E
Aloysius, Mt., Australia 125 E4 26 0 S 128 38 E
Alpaugh, U.S.A. 160 K7 35 53N 119 29W
Alpedrinha, Portugal 42 E3 40 6N 7 27W
Alpena, U.S.A. 148 C4 45 4N 83 27W
Alpercatas →, Brazil 170 C3 6 2 S 44 19W
Alpes-de-Haute-Provence □, France 29 D10 44 8N 6 10 E
Alpes-Maritimes □, France 29 E11 43 55N 7 10 E
Alpha, Australia 126 C4 23 39 S 146 37 E
Alpha, U.S.A. 156 C6 41 12N 90 23W
Alphen aan den Rijn, Neths. 24 B4 52 7N 4 40 E
Alphonse, Seychelles 121 E4 7 0 S 52 45 E
Alpiarça, Portugal 43 F2 39 15N 8 35W
Alpine, Ariz., U.S.A. 159 K9 33 51N 109 9W
Alpine, Calif., U.S.A. 161 N10 32 50N 116 46W
Alpine, Tex., U.S.A. 155 K3 30 22N 103 40W
Alpine Nat. Park, Australia 129 D7 37 15 S 146 45 E
Alpnach Dorf, Switz. 33 C6 46 57N 8 17 E
Alps, Europe 25 C8 46 30N 9 30 E
Alpu, Turkey 100 C4 39 46N 30 58 E
Alqueva, Barragem do, Portugal 43 G3 38 20N 7 25W
Alrø, Denmark 17 J4 55 52N 10 5 E
Als, Denmark 17 K3 54 59N 9 55 E
Alsace, France 27 D14 48 15N 7 25 E
Alsask, Canada 143 C7 51 21N 109 59W
Alsasua, Spain 40 C2 42 54N 2 10W
Alsek →, U.S.A. 142 B1 59 10N 138 12W
Alsfeld, Germany 30 E5 50 44N 9 16 E
Alsten, Norway 14 D15 65 58N 12 40 E
Alstermo, Sweden 17 H9 56 58N 15 38 E
Alston, U.K. 20 C5 54 49N 2 25W
Alta, Norway 14 B20 69 57N 23 10 E
Alta, Sierra, Spain 40 E3 40 31N 1 30W
Alta Floresta, Brazil 173 B6 9 57 S 55 58W
Alta Gracia, Argentina 174 C3 31 40 S 64 30W
Alta Sierra, U.S.A. 161 K8 35 42N 118 33W
Altaelva →, Norway 14 B20 69 54N 23 17 E
Altafjorden, Norway 14 A20 70 5N 23 5 E
Altagracia, Venezuela 168 A3 10 45N 71 30W
Altagracia de Orituco, Venezuela 168 B4 9 52N 66 23W
Altai = Aerhtai Shan, Mongolia 68 B4 46 40N 92 45 E
Altamachi →, Bolivia 172 D4 16 8 S 66 50W
Altamaha →, U.S.A. 152 D8 31 20N 81 20W
Altamira, Brazil 169 D7 3 12 S 52 10W
Altamira, Chile 174 B2 25 47 S 69 51W
Altamira, Colombia 168 C2 2 3N 75 47W
Altamira, Mexico 163 C5 22 24N 97 55W
Altamira, Cuevas de, Spain 42 B6 43 20N 4 5W
Altamont, Ill., U.S.A. 157 E8 39 4N 88 45W
Altamont, N.Y., U.S.A. 151 D10 42 43N 74 3W
Altamura, Italy 47 B9 40 49N 16 33 E
Altanbulag, Mongolia 68 A5 50 16N 106 30 E
Altar, Mexico 162 A2 30 40N 111 50W
Altar, Desierto de, Mexico 162 B2 30 10N 112 0W
Altata, Mexico 162 C3 24 30N 108 0W
Altavas, Phil. 81 F4 11 32N 122 29 E
Altavista, U.S.A. 148 G6 37 6N 79 17W
Altay, China 68 B3 47 48N 88 10 E
Altdorf, Switz. 33 C7 46 52N 8 36 E
Alte Mellum, Germany 30 B4 53 43N 8 10 E
Altea, Spain 41 G4 38 38N 0 2W
Altenberg, Germany 30 E9 50 45N 13 45 E
Altenbruch, Germany 30 B4 53 49N 8 46 E
Altenburg, Germany 30 E8 50 59N 12 25 E
Altenkirchen, Mecklenburg-Vorpommern, Germany 30 A9 54 38N 13 22 E
Altenkirchen, Rhld-Pfz., Germany 30 E3 50 41N 7 39 E
Altenmarkt, Austria 34 D7 47 43N 14 39 E
Alter do Chão, Brazil 169 D6 2 31 S 54 57W
Alter do Chão, Portugal 43 F3 39 12N 7 40W
Altha, U.S.A. 152 E4 30 34N 85 8W
Altınoluk, Turkey 49 B8 39 34N 26 45 E
Altınova, Turkey 49 B8 39 12N 26 47 E
Altıntaş, Turkey 49 B12 39 4N 30 7 E
Altınyaka, Turkey 49 E12 36 33N 30 20 E
Altınyayla, Turkey 49 D11 37 0N 29 33 E
Altiplano = Bolivian Plateau, S. Amer. 166 E4 20 0 S 67 30W
Altiplano, Bolivia 172 D4 17 0 S 68 0W
Altkirch, France 27 E14 47 37N 7 15 E
Altmark, Germany 30 C7 52 45N 11 30 E
Altmühl →, Germany 31 G7 48 54N 11 52 E
Altmunster, Austria 34 D6 47 54N 13 45 E
Alto Adige = Trentino-Alto Adige □, Italy 45 B8 46 30N 11 20 E
Alto Alegre, Brazil 169 C5 2 50N 61 20W
Alto Araguaia, Brazil 173 D7 17 15 S 53 20W
Alto Chicapa, Angola 115 E3 10 52 S 19 17 E
Alto Cuchumatanes = Cuchumatanes, Sierra de los, Guatemala 164 C1 15 35N 91 25W
Alto Cuito = Tempué, Angola 115 E3 13 27 S 18 49 E
Alto del Carmen, Chile 174 B1 28 46 S 70 30W
Alto del Inca, Chile 174 A2 24 10 S 68 10W
Alto Garças, Brazil 173 D7 16 56 S 53 32W
Alto Iriri →, Brazil 173 B7 8 50 S 53 25W
Alto Ligonha, Mozam. 119 F4 15 30 S 38 11 E
Alto Molocue, Mozam. 119 F4 15 50 S 37 35 E
Alto Paraguai, Brazil 173 C6 14 30 S 56 31W
Alto Paraguay □, Paraguay 174 A4 21 0 S 58 30W
Alto Paraiso de Goiás, Brazil 171 D2 14 7 S 47 31W
Alto Paraná □, Paraguay 175 B5 25 30 S 54 50W
Alto Parnaíba, Brazil 170 C2 9 6 S 45 57W
Alto Purús →, Peru 172 B3 9 12 S 70 28W
Alto Río Senguerr, Argentina 176 C2 45 2 S 70 50W
Alto Santo, Brazil 170 C4 5 31 S 38 15W
Alto Sucuriú, Brazil 173 D7 19 19 S 52 47W
Alto Turi, Brazil 170 B2 2 54 S 45 38W
Alton, Canada 150 C4 43 54N 80 5W
Alton, U.K. 21 F7 51 9N 0 59W
Alton, Ill., U.S.A. 156 F6 38 53N 90 11W
Alton, N.H., U.S.A. 151 C13 43 27N 71 13W
Altoona, Ala., U.S.A. 152 A3 34 2N 86 20W
Altoona, Iowa, U.S.A. 156 C3 41 39N 93 28W
Altoona, Pa., U.S.A. 150 F6 40 31N 78 24W
Altos, Brazil 170 C3 5 3 S 42 28W
Altötting, Germany 31 G8 48 12N 12 39 E
Altstätten, Switz. 33 B9 47 22N 9 33 E
Altūn Kūprī, Iraq 101 E11 35 45N 44 9 E
Altun Shan, China 68 C3 38 30N 88 0 E
Alturas, U.S.A. 158 F3 41 29N 120 32W
Altus, U.S.A. 155 H5 34 38N 99 20W
Alubijid, Phil. 81 G5 8 35N 124 29 E
Alucra, Turkey 101 B8 40 22N 38 47 E
Aluk, Sudan 107 F2 8 25N 27 30 E
Alūksne, Latvia 15 H22 57 24N 27 3 E
Alùla, Somali Rep. 120 B4 11 50N 50 45 E
Alunda, Sweden 16 D12 60 4N 18 5 E
Alunite, U.S.A. 161 K12 35 59N 114 55W
Aluoro →, Ethiopia 107 F3 8 26N 33 24 E
Alupka, Ukraine 59 K8 44 23N 34 2 E
Alur, India 95 E3 15 24N 77 15 E
Alur Gajah, Malaysia 84 B2 2 23N 102 13 E
Alushta, Ukraine 59 K8 44 40N 34 25 E
Alusi, Indonesia 83 C4 7 35 S 131 40 E
Alustante, Spain 40 E3 40 36N 1 40W
Alutgama, Sri Lanka 95 L4 6 26N 79 59 E
Alutnuwara, Sri Lanka 95 L5 7 19N 80 59 E
Alva, U.S.A. 155 G5 36 48N 98 40W
Alvaiázere, Portugal 42 F2 39 49N 8 23W
Älvängen, Sweden 17 G6 57 58N 12 8 E
Alvarado, Mexico 163 D5 18 40N 95 50W
Alvarado, U.S.A. 155 J6 32 24N 97 13W
Alvarães, Brazil 169 D5 3 12 S 64 50W
Alvaro Obregón, Presa, Mexico 162 B3 27 55N 109 52W
Alvdal, Norway 18 B7 62 6N 10 37 E
Älvdalen, Sweden 16 C8 61 13N 14 4 E
Alvear, Argentina 174 B4 29 5 S 56 30W
Alverca, Portugal 43 G1 38 56N 9 1W
Alvesta, Sweden 17 H8 56 54N 14 35 E
Ålvik, Norway 18 D3 60 26N 6 26 E
Alvin, U.S.A. 155 L7 29 26N 95 15W
Alvinston, Canada 150 D3 42 49N 81 52W
Alvito, Portugal 43 G3 38 15N 7 58W
Älvkarleby, Sweden 16 D11 60 34N 17 26 E
Alvorado, Brazil 171 D2 12 28 S 49 6W
Alvord Desert, U.S.A. 158 E4 42 30N 118 25W
Älvros, Sweden 16 B8 62 3N 14 38 E
Älvsbyn, Sweden 14 D19 65 40N 21 0 E
Ålvundeid, Norway 18 B5 62 46N 8 33 E
Alwar, India 92 F7 27 38N 76 34 E
Alwaye, India 95 J3 10 8N 76 24 E
Alxa Zuoqi, China 74 E3 38 50N 105 40 E
Alyangula, Australia 126 A2 13 55 S 136 30 E
Alyata = Älät, Azerbaijan 61 L9 39 58N 49 25 E
Alyth, U.K. 22 E5 56 38N 3 13W
Alytus, Lithuania 15 J21 54 24N 24 3 E
Alzada, U.S.A. 154 C2 45 2N 104 25W
Alzey, Germany 31 F4 49 45N 8 7 E
Alzira, Spain 41 F4 39 9N 0 30W
Am Dam, Chad 109 F4 12 40N 20 35 E
Am Géréda, Chad 109 F4 12 53N 21 14 E
Am Loubia, Chad 109 F4 13 39N 20 8 E
Am Timan, Chad 109 F4 11 0N 20 10 E
Amada Gaza, C.A.R. 114 B3 4 46N 15 9 E
Amadeus, L., Australia 124 D5 24 54 S 131 0 E
Amadi, Dem. Rep. of the Congo 118 B2 3 40N 26 40 E
Amâdi, Sudan 107 F3 5 29N 30 25 E
Amadjuak L., Canada 139 B12 65 0N 71 8W
Amadora, Portugal 43 G1 38 45N 9 13W
Amagansett, U.S.A. 151 F12 40 59N 72 9W
Amagasaki, Japan 73 C7 34 42N 135 20 E
Amager, Denmark 17 J6 55 37N 12 35 E
Amagi, Japan 72 D2 33 25N 130 39 E
Amagunze, Nigeria 113 D6 6 20N 7 40 E
Amahai, Indonesia 83 C3 3 20 S 128 55 E
Amaile, Samoa 133 W24 13 59 S 171 22W
Amaimon, Papua N. G. 132 C3 5 12 S 145 30 E
Amakusa-Nada, Japan 72 E2 32 35N 130 5 E
Amakusa-Shotō, Japan 72 E2 32 15N 130 10 E
Åmål, Sweden 16 E6 59 3N 12 42 E
Amalapuram, India 95 F5 16 35N 81 55 E
Amalfi, Colombia 168 B2 6 55N 75 4W
Amalfi, Italy 47 B7 40 38N 14 36 E
Amaliás, Greece 48 D3 37 47N 21 22 E
Amalner, India 94 D2 21 5N 75 5 E
Amamapare, Indonesia 83 B5 4 53 S 136 38 E
Amambaí, Brazil 175 A4 23 5 S 55 13W
Amambaí →, Brazil 175 A5 23 22 S 53 56W
Amambay □, Paraguay 175 A4 23 0 S 56 0W
Amambay, Cordillera de, S. Amer. 175 A4 23 0 S 55 45W
Amami-Guntō, Japan 71 L4 27 16N 129 21 E
Amami-Ō-Shima, Japan 71 L4 28 0N 129 0 E
Aman, Pulau, Malaysia 87 c 5 16N 100 24 E
Amana →, Venezuela 169 B5 9 45N 62 39W
Amaná, L., Brazil 169 D5 2 35 S 64 40W
Amanab, Papua N. G. 132 B1 3 40 S 141 14 E
Amanat →, India 93 G11 24 7N 84 4 E
Amanda Park, U.S.A. 160 C3 47 28N 123 55W
Amangeldy, Kazakstan 66 D7 50 10N 65 10 E
Amantea, Italy 47 C9 39 8N 16 4 E
Amapá, Brazil 169 C7 2 5N 50 50W
Amapá □, Brazil 169 C7 1 40N 52 0W
Amapari, Brazil 169 C7 0 37N 51 39W
Amara, Sudan 107 E3 10 25N 34 10 E
Amarante, Brazil 170 C3 6 14 S 42 50W
Amarante, Portugal 42 D2 41 16N 8 5W
Amarante do Maranhão, Brazil 170 C2 5 36 S 46 45W
Amaranth, Canada 143 C9 50 36N 98 43W
Amarapura, Burma 90 E6 21 54N 96 3 E
Amaravati →, India 95 J4 11 0N 78 15 E
Amareleja, Portugal 43 G3 38 12N 7 13W
Amargosa, Brazil 171 D4 13 2 S 39 36W
Amargosa →, U.S.A. 161 J10 36 14N 116 51W
Amargosa Range, U.S.A. 161 J10 36 20N 116 45W
Amári, Greece 39 E5 35 13N 24 40 E
Amarillo, U.S.A. 155 H4 35 13N 101 50W
Amarkantak, India 93 H9 22 40N 81 45 E
Amârna, Tell el', Sudan 106 B3 27 38N 30 52 E
Amarnath, India 94 E1 19 12N 73 22 E
Amaro, Mte., Italy 45 F11 42 5N 14 5 E
Amaro Leite, Brazil 171 D2 13 58 S 49 9W
Amarpur, Bihar, India 93 G12 25 5N 87 0 E
Amarpur, Tripura, India 90 D3 23 31N 91 39 E
Amarti, Eritrea 107 E5 14 17N 41 6 E
Amarwara, India 93 H8 22 18N 79 10 E
Amasin, W. Sahara 110 C2 25 45N 13 20W
Amasra, Turkey 100 B5 41 45N 32 23 E
Amassama, Nigeria 113 D6 5 1N 6 2 E
Amasya, Turkey 100 B6 40 40N 35 50 E
Amasya □, Turkey 57 F6 40 40N 35 50 E
Amata, Australia 125 E5 26 9 S 131 9 E
Amatauráa, Brazil 168 D4 3 29 S 68 6W
Amatignak I., U.S.A. 144 L3 51 16N 179 6W
Amatikulu, S. Africa 117 D5 29 3 S 31 33 E
Amatitlán, Guatemala 164 D1 14 29N 90 38W
Amatrice, Italy 45 F10 42 38N 13 17 E
Amau, Papua N. G. 132 F5 10 2 S 148 34 E
Amay, Belgium 24 D5 50 33N 5 19 E
Amazon = Amazonas →, S. Amer. 169 D7 0 5 S 50 0W
Amazonas □, Brazil 173 B5 5 0 S 65 0W
Amazonas □, Peru 172 B2 5 0 S 78 0W
Amazonas □, Venezuela 168 C4 3 30N 66 0W
Amazonas →, S. Amer. 169 D7 0 5 S 50 0W
Amba Ferit, Ethiopia 107 E4 10 55N 38 50 E
Ambad, India 94 E2 19 38N 75 50 E
Ambagarh Chowki, India 94 D5 20 47N 80 43 E
Ambah, India 92 F8 26 43N 78 13 E
Ambahakily, Madag. 117 C7 21 36 S 43 41 E
Ambahita, Madag. 117 C8 24 1 S 45 16 E
Ambajogal, India 94 E3 18 44N 76 23 E
Ambala, India 92 D7 30 23N 76 56 E
Ambalangoda, Sri Lanka 95 L5 6 15N 80 5 E
Ambalapulai, India 95 K3 9 25N 76 25 E
Ambalavao, Madag. 117 C8 21 50 S 46 56 E
Ambam, Cameroon 114 B2 2 20N 11 15 E
Ambanja, Madag. 117 A8 13 40 S 48 27 E
Ambararata, Madag. 117 B8 15 3 S 48 33 E
Ambarchik, Russia 67 C17 69 40N 162 20 E
Ambarijeby, Madag. 117 A8 14 56 S 47 41 E
Ambaro, Helodranon', Madag. 117 A8 13 23 S 48 38 E
Ambasamudram, India 95 K3 8 43N 77 25 E
Ambato, Ecuador 168 D2 1 5 S 78 42W
Ambato, Madag. 117 A8 13 24 S 48 29 E
Ambato, Sierra de, Argentina 174 B2 28 25 S 66 10W
Ambato Boeny, Madag. 117 B8 16 28 S 46 43 E
Ambatofinandrahana, Madag. 117 C8 20 33 S 46 48 E
Ambatolampy, Madag. 117 B8 19 20 S 47 35 E
Ambatomainty, Madag. 117 B8 17 41 S 45 40 E
Ambatomanoina, Madag. 117 B8 18 18 S 47 37 E
Ambatondrazaka, Madag. 117 B8 17 55 S 48 28 E
Ambatosoratra, Madag. 117 B8 17 37 S 48 31 E
Ambelau, Indonesia 82 B3 3 51 S 127 12 E
Ambelón, Greece 48 B4 39 45N 22 22 E
Ambenja, Madag. 117 B8 15 17 S 46 58 E
Amberg, Germany 31 F7 49 26N 11 52 E
Ambergris Cay, Belize 163 D7 18 0N 88 0W
Ambérieu-en-Bugey, France 29 C9 45 57N 5 20 E
Amberley, N.Z. 131 D7 43 9 S 172 44 E
Ambert, France 28 C7 45 33N 3 44 E
Ambidédi, Mali 112 C2 14 35N 11 47W
Ambikapur, India 93 H10 23 15N 83 15 E
Ambikol, Sudan 106 C3 21 20N 30 50 E
Ambilobé, Madag. 117 A8 13 10 S 49 3 E
Ambinanindrano, Madag. 117 C8 20 5 S 48 23 E
Ambinanitelo, Madag. 117 B8 15 21 S 49 35 E
Ambinda, Madag. 117 B8 16 25 S 45 52 E
Ambitle I., Papua N. G. 132 C7 4 5 S 153 37 E
Amble, U.K. 20 B6 55 20N 1 36W
Ambler, U.S.A. 144 C8 67 5N 157 52W
Ambleside, U.K. 20 C5 54 26N 2 58W
Ambo, Peru 172 C2 10 5 S 76 10W
Amboahangy, Madag. 117 C8 24 15 S 46 22 E
Ambodifototra, Madag. 117 B8 16 59 S 49 52 E
Ambodilazana, Madag. 117 B8 18 6 S 49 10 E
Ambodiriana, Madag. 117 B8 17 55 S 49 18 E
Ambohidratrimo, Madag. 117 B8 18 50 S 47 26 E
Ambohidray, Madag. 117 B8 18 36 S 48 18 E
Ambohimahamasina, Madag. 117 C8 21 56 S 47 11 E
Ambohimahasoa, Madag. 117 C8 21 7 S 47 13 E
Ambohimanga, Madag. 117 C8 20 52 S 47 36 E
Ambohimitombo, Madag. 117 C8 20 43 S 47 26 E
Ambohitra, Madag. 117 A8 12 30 S 49 10 E
Amboise, France 26 E8 47 24N 1 2 E
Amboiva, Angola 115 E2 11 33 S 14 43 E
Ambon, Indonesia 82 B3 3 43 S 128 12 E
Ambondro, Madag. 117 D8 25 13 S 45 44 E
Amboseli, L., Kenya 118 C4 2 40 S 37 10 E
Amboseli Nat. Park, Kenya 118 C4 2 37 S 37 13 E
Ambositra, Madag. 117 C8 20 31 S 47 25 E
Ambovombe, Madag. 117 D8 25 11 S 46 5 E
Amboy, Calif., U.S.A. 161 L11 34 33N 115 45W
Amboy, Ill., U.S.A. 156 C7 41 44N 89 20W
Amboyna Cay, S. China Sea 78 C4 7 50N 112 50 E
Ambridge, U.S.A. 150 F4 40 36N 80 14W
Ambriz, Angola 115 D2 7 48 S 13 8 E
Ambriz, Reserva de, Angola 115 D2 7 56 S 10 27 E
Ambrym, Vanuatu 133 F6 16 15 S 168 10 E
Ambunti, Papua N. G. 132 C2 4 13 S 142 52 E
Ambur, India 95 H4 12 48N 78 43 E
Amchitka I., U.S.A. 144 L2 51 32N 179 0 E
Amderma, Russia 66 C7 69 45N 61 30 E
Amdhi, India 93 H9 23 51N 81 27 E
Ameca, Mexico 162 C4 20 30N 104 0W
Ameca →, Mexico 162 C3 20 40N 105 15W
Amecameca, Mexico 163 D5 19 7N 98 46W
Ameland, Neths. 24 A5 53 27N 5 45 E
Amélia, Italy 45 F9 42 33N 12 25 E
Amelia City, U.S.A. 152 E8 30 35N 81 28W
Amelia I., U.S.A. 152 E8 30 40N 81 25W
Amendolara, Italy 47 C9 39 57N 16 35 E
Amenia, U.S.A. 151 E11 41 51N 73 33W
American Falls, U.S.A. 158 E7 42 47N 112 51W
American Falls Reservoir, U.S.A. 158 E7 42 47N 112 52W
American Fork, U.S.A. 158 F8 40 23N 111 48W
American Highland, Antarctica 7 D6 73 0 S 75 0 E
American River, Australia 128 C2 35 47 S 137 46 E
American Samoa ■, Pac. Oc. 133 X24 14 20 S 170 40W
American Samoa, Nat. Park of, Amer. Samoa 133 X24 14 15 S 170 28W
Americana, Brazil 175 A6 22 45 S 47 20W
Americus, U.S.A. 152 C5 32 4N 84 14W
Amersfoort, Neths. 24 B5 52 9N 5 23 E
Amersfoort, S. Africa 117 D4 26 59 S 29 53 E
Amery Ice Shelf, Antarctica 7 C6 69 30 S 72 0 E
Amerzgane, Morocco 110 B3 31 4N 7 14W
Ames, Spain 42 C2 42 54N 8 38W
Ames, U.S.A. 156 C3 42 2N 93 37W
Amesbury, U.S.A. 151 D14 42 51N 70 56W
Amet, India 92 G5 25 18N 73 56 E
Amfíklia, Greece 48 C4 38 38N 22 35 E
Amfilokhía, Greece 48 C3 38 52N 21 9 E
Amfípolis, Greece 50 F7 40 48N 23 52 E
Ámfissa, Greece 48 C4 38 32N 22 22 E
Amga, Russia 67 C14 60 50N 132 0 E
Amga →, Russia 67 C14 62 38N 134 32 E
Amgaon, India 94 D5 21 22N 80 22 E
Amgu, Russia 67 E14 45 45N 137 15 E
Amgun →, Russia 67 D14 52 56N 139 38 E
Amherst, Canada 141 C7 45 48N 64 8W
Amherst, Mass., U.S.A. 151 D12 42 23N 72 31W
Amherst, N.Y., U.S.A. 150 D6 42 59N 78 48W
Amherst, Ohio, U.S.A. 150 E2 41 24N 82 14W
Amherst I., Canada 151 B8 44 8N 76 43W
Amherstburg, Canada 140 D3 42 6N 83 6W
Amiata, Mte., Italy 45 F8 42 53N 11 37 E
Amidon, U.S.A. 154 B3 46 29N 103 19W
Amiens, France 27 C9 49 54N 2 16 E
Amili, India 90 A5 28 25N 95 52 E
Amindaion, Greece 50 F5 40 42N 21 42 E
Amindivi Is., India 95 J1 11 23N 72 23 E
Amingaon, India 90 B3 26 11N 91 40 E
Amini I., India 95 J1 11 6N 72 45 E
Äminne, Sweden 17 G7 57 7N 14 0 E
Amino, Ethiopia 107 G5 4 25N 41 52 E
Aminuis, Namibia 116 C2 23 43 S 19 21 E
Āmir, Ra's, Libya 108 B4 32 57N 21 43 E
Amīrābād, Iran 96 C5 33 20N 46 16 E
Amirante Is., Seychelles 62 K9 6 0 S 53 0 E
Amisk L., Canada 143 C8 54 35N 102 15W
Amistad, Presa de la, Mexico 162 B4 29 24N 101 0W
Amite, U.S.A. 155 K9 30 44N 90 30W
Amizmiz, Morocco 110 B3 31 12N 8 15W
Amla, India 92 J8 21 56N 78 7 E
Åmli, Norway 18 F5 58 45N 8 32 E
Amlia I., U.S.A. 144 K4 52 4N 173 30W
Amlwch, U.K. 20 D3 53 24N 4 20W
Amm Adam, Sudan 107 D4 16 20N 36 1 E
'Ammān, Jordan 103 D4 31 57N 35 52 E
'Ammān □, Jordan 103 D5 31 40N 36 30 E
Ammanford, U.K. 21 F4 51 48N 3 59W
Ammassalik = Tasiilaq, Greenland 10 D7 65 40N 37 20W
Ammerån →, Sweden 16 A10 63 9N 16 13 E
Ammersee, Germany 31 G7 48 0N 11 7 E
Ammochostos = Famagusta, Cyprus 39 E9 35 8N 33 55 E
Ammon, U.S.A. 158 E8 43 28N 111 58W
Amnat Charoen, Thailand 86 E5 15 51N 104 38 E
Amnura, Bangla. 93 G13 24 37N 88 25 E
Amo Jiang →, China 76 F3 23 0N 101 50 E
Āmol, Iran 97 B7 36 23N 52 20 E
Amoret, U.S.A. 156 F2 38 15N 94 35W
Amorgós, Greece 49 E7 36 50N 25 57 E
Amory, U.S.A. 149 J1 33 59N 88 29W
Amos, Canada 140 C4 48 35N 78 5W
Åmot, Buskerud, Norway 15 G13 59 57N 9 54 E
Åmot, Oppland, Norway 18 D7 61 0N 10 2 E
Åmot, Telemark, Norway 18 E5 59 34N 8 0 E
Åmotfors, Sweden 16 E6 59 47N 12 22 E
Åmotsdal, Norway 18 E5 59 37N 8 26 E
Amour, Djebel, Algeria 111 B5 33 42N 1 37 E
Amoy = Xiamen, China 77 E12 24 25N 118 4 E
Ampanavoana, Madag. 117 B9 15 41 S 50 22 E
Ampang, Malaysia 87 L3 3 8N 101 45 E
Ampangalana, Lakandranon', Madag. 117 C8 22 48 S 47 50 E
Ampani, India 94 E6 19 35N 82 38 E
Ampanihy, Madag. 117 C7 24 40 S 44 45 E
Amparafaravola, Madag. 117 B8 17 35 S 48 13 E
Ampasinambo, Madag. 117 C8 20 31 S 48 0 E
Ampasindava, Helodranon', Madag. 117 A8 13 40 S 48 15 E
Ampasindava, Saikanosy, Madag. 117 A8 13 42 S 47 55 E
Ampato, Nevado, Peru 172 D3 15 40 S 71 56W
Ampenan, Indonesia 85 D5 8 34 S 116 4 E
Amper, Nigeria 113 D6 9 25N 9 40 E
Amper →, Germany 31 G7 48 29N 11 55 E
Ampezzo, Italy 45 B9 46 25N 12 48 E
Amphoe Kathu, Thailand 87 a 7 55N 98 21 E
Amphoe Thalang, Thailand 87 a 8 1N 98 20 E
Ampitsikinana, Réunion 117 A8 12 57 S 49 49 E
Ampombiantambo, Madag. 117 A8 12 42 S 48 57 E
Amposta, Spain 40 E5 40 43N 0 34 E
Ampotaka, Madag. 117 D7 25 3 S 44 41 E
Ampoza, Madag. 117 C7 22 20 S 44 44 E
Amqui, Canada 141 C6 48 28N 67 27W
Amrabad, India 95 F4 16 23N 78 50 E
'Amrān, Yemen 98 D3 15 41N 43 55 E
Amravati, India 94 D3 20 55N 77 45 E
Amreli, India 92 J4 21 35N 71 17 E
Amrenene el Kasba, Algeria 111 D5 22 10N 0 30 E
Amriswil, Switz. 33 A8 47 33N 9 18 E
Amritsar, India 92 D6 31 35N 74 57 E
Amroha, India 93 E8 28 53N 78 30 E

182 Amrum

Amrum, *Germany* **30 A4** 54 38N 8 22 E
Amsâga, *Mauritania* **110 D2** 20 7N 14 10W
Amsel, *Algeria* **111 D6** 22 47N 5 29 E
Amsterdam, *Neths.* **24 B4** 52 23N 4 54 E
Amsterdam, *U.S.A.* **151 D10** 42 56N 74 11W
Amsterdam, I. = Nouvelle-
Amsterdam, I., *Ind. Oc.* **121 H6** 38 30 S 77 30 E
Amstetten, *Austria* **34 C7** 48 7N 14 51 E
Amudarya, *Turkmenistan* **65 E2** 37 53N 65 15 E
Amudarya →, *Uzbekistan* **66 E6** 43 58N 59 34 E
Amukta I., *U.S.A.* **144 K5** 52 30N 171 16W
Amukta Pass, *U.S.A.* **144 L5** 52 0N 172 0W
Amulung, *Phil.* **80 C3** 17 50N 121 43 E
Amundsen Gulf, *Canada* **138 A7** 71 0N 124 0W
Amundsen Sea, *Antarctica* **7 D15** 72 0 S 115 0W
Amungen, *Sweden* **16 C9** 61 10N 15 40 E
Amuntai, *Indonesia* **85 C5** 2 28 S 115 25 E
Amur, *Somali Rep.* **120 C3** 5 16N 46 30 E
Amur →, *Russia* **67 D15** 52 56N 141 10 E
Amur, W. →, *Sudan* **106 D3** 18 56N 33 34 E
Amurang, *Indonesia* **82 A2** 1 5N 124 40 E
Amurrio, *Spain* **40 B1** 43 3N 3 0W
Amursk, *Russia* **67 D14** 50 14N 136 54 E
Amusco, *Spain* **42 C6** 42 10N 4 28W
Amvrakikós Kólpos, *Greece* **48 C2** 39 0N 20 55 E
Amvrosiyivka, *Ukraine* **59 J10** 47 43N 38 30 E
Amyderya = Amudarya →,
Uzbekistan **66 E6** 43 58N 59 34 E
Amzeglouf, *Algeria* **111 C5** 26 50N 0 1 E
An, *Burma* **90 F5** 19 48N 94 0 E
An Bien, *Vietnam* **87 H5** 9 45N 105 0 E
An Hoa, *Vietnam* **86 E7** 15 40N 108 5 E
An Nabatīyah at Tahta, *Lebanon* **103 B4** 33 23N 35 27 E
An Nabk, *Si. Arabia* **96 D3** 31 20N 37 20 E
An Nabk, *Syria* **103 A5** 34 2N 36 44 E
An Nafūd, *Si. Arabia* **96 D4** 28 15N 41 0 E
An Najaf, *Iraq* **101 G11** 32 3N 44 15 E
An Nāṣirīyah, *Iraq* **96 D5** 31 0N 46 15 E
An Nawfaliyah, *Libya* **108 B3** 30 54N 17 58 E
An Nhon, *Vietnam* **86 F7** 13 55N 109 7 E
An Nîl □, *Sudan* **106 D3** 19 30N 33 0 E
An Nîl el Abyad □, *Sudan* **107 E3** 14 0N 32 15 E
An Nîl el Azraq □, *Sudan* **107 E3** 11 30N 34 30 E
An Nimāş, *Si. Arabia* **98 C3** 19 7N 42 8 E
An Nu'ayrīyah, *Si. Arabia* **97 E6** 27 30N 48 30 E
An Nu'mānīyah, *Iraq* **101 F11** 32 32N 45 25 E
An Nuwayb'ī, W. →, *Si. Arabia* **103 F3** 29 18N 34 57 E
An Thoi, Dao, *Vietnam* **87 H4** 9 58N 104 0 E
An Uaimh, *Ireland* **23 C5** 53 39N 6 41W
Åna-Sira, *Norway* **18 F3** 58 17N 6 25 E
Anabanua, *Indonesia* **82 B2** 3 57 S 120 4 E
Anabar →, *Russia* **67 B12** 73 8N 113 36 E
'Anabtā, *West Bank* **103 C4** 32 19N 35 7 E
Anaco, *Venezuela* **169 B5** 9 27N 64 28W
Anaconda, *U.S.A.* **158 C7** 46 8N 112 57W
Anacortes, *U.S.A.* **160 B4** 48 30N 122 37W
Anacuao, Mt., *Phil.* **80 C3** 16 16N 121 53 E
Anadarko, *U.S.A.* **155 H5** 35 4N 98 15W
Anadia, *Brazil* **170 C4** 9 42 S 36 18W
Anadia, *Portugal* **42 E2** 40 26N 8 27W
Anadolu, *Turkey* **100 C5** 39 0N 30 0 E
Anadyr, *Russia* **67 C18** 64 35N 177 20 E
Anadyr →, *Russia* **67 C18** 64 55N 176 5 E
Anadyrskiy Zaliv, *Russia* **67 C19** 64 0N 180 0 E
Anáfi, *Greece* **49 E7** 36 22N 25 48 E
Anafonítria, *Greece* **39 D2** 37 51N 20 39 E
Anafópoulo, *Greece* **49 E7** 36 17N 25 50 E
Anaga, Pta. de, *Canary Is.* **9 e1** 28 34N 16 9W
Anagni, *Italy* **45 G10** 41 44N 13 9 E
'Ānah, *Iraq* **101 E10** 34 25N 42 0 E
Anahalu →, *U.S.A.* **145 J13** 21 37N 158 6W
Anaheim, *U.S.A.* **161 M9** 33 50N 117 55W
Anahim Lake, *Canada* **142 C3** 52 28N 125 18W
Anahola, *U.S.A.* **145 A2** 22 9N 159 19W
Anáhuac, *Mexico* **162 B4** 27 14N 100 9W
Anai Mudi, *India* **95 J3** 10 12N 77 4 E
Anaimalai Hills, *India* **95 J3** 10 20N 76 40 E
Anajás, *Brazil* **170 B2** 0 59 S 49 57W
Anajatuba, *Brazil* **170 B3** 3 16 S 44 37W
Anakapalle, *India* **94 F6** 17 42N 83 6 E
Anakena, *Chile* **172 b** 27 5 S 109 20W
Anakie, *Australia* **126 C4** 23 32 S 147 45 E
Anaklia, *Georgia* **61 J5** 42 22N 41 35 E
Anaktuvuk Pass, *U.S.A.* **144 B10** 68 8N 151 45W
Analalava, *Madag.* **117 A8** 14 35 S 48 0 E
Analavoka, *Madag.* **117 C8** 22 23 S 46 30 E
Análipsis, *Greece* **38 B9** 39 36N 19 55 E
Anamã, *Brazil* **169 D5** 3 35 S 61 22W
Anambar →, *Pakistan* **92 D3** 30 15N 68 50 E
Anambas, Kepulauan, *Indonesia* **84 B3** 3 20N 106 30 E
Anambas Is. = Anambas,
Kepulauan, *Indonesia* **84 B3** 3 20N 106 30 E
Anambra □, *Nigeria* **113 D6** 6 20N 7 0 E
Aname, *Vanuatu* **133 K7** 20 8 S 169 47 E
Anamosa, *U.S.A.* **156 B5** 42 7N 91 17W
Anamur, *Turkey* **100 D5** 36 8N 32 58 E
Anamur Burnu, *Turkey* **100 D5** 36 2N 32 47 E
Anan, *Japan* **72 D6** 33 54N 134 40 E
Anand, *India* **92 H5** 22 32N 72 59 E
Anandapuram, *India* **95 G2** 14 5N 75 12 E
Anandpur, *India* **94 D8** 21 16N 86 13 E
Anánes, *Greece* **48 E6** 36 33N 24 9 E
Anantapur, *India* **95 G3** 14 39N 77 42 E
Anantnag, *India* **93 C6** 33 45N 75 10 E
Ananyevo, *Kyrgyzstan* **65 B8** 42 45N 77 40 E
Ananyiv, *Ukraine* **59 J5** 47 44N 29 58 E
Anapa, *Russia* **59 K9** 44 55N 37 25 E
Anapodháris →, *Greece* **39 F6** 34 59N 25 20 E
Anápolis, *Brazil* **171 E2** 16 15 S 48 50W
Anapu →, *Brazil* **169 D7** 1 53 S 50 53W
Anār, *Iran* **97 D7** 30 55N 55 13 E
Anār Darreh, *Afghan.* **91 B1** 32 46N 61 39 E
Anārak, *Iran* **97 C7** 33 25N 53 40 E
Anarisfjällen, *Sweden* **16 A7** 63 6N 13 10 E
Anas →, *India* **92 H5** 23 26N 74 0 E
Anatolia = Anadolu, *Turkey* **100 C5** 39 0N 30 0 E
Anatsogno, *Madag.* **117 C7** 23 33 S 43 46 E
Añatuya, *Argentina* **174 B3** 28 20 S 62 50W
Anauá →, *Brazil* **169 C5** 0 58N 61 21W
Anaunethad L., *Canada* **143 A8** 60 55N 104 25W
Anavilhanas, Arquipélago das,
Brazil **169 D5** 2 42 S 60 45W
Anaye, *Niger* **109 E2** 19 15N 12 50 E
Anbyŏn, *N. Korea* **75 E14** 39 1N 127 35 E
Ancares, Sierra de, *Spain* **42 C4** 42 51N 6 52W
Ancash □, *Peru* **172 B2** 9 30 S 77 45W
Ancaster, *Canada* **150 C5** 43 13N 79 59W
Ancenis, *France* **26 E5** 47 21N 1 10W
Ancho, Canal, *Chile* **176 D2** 50 0 S 74 20W
Anchor Bay, *U.S.A.* **160 G3** 38 48N 123 34W
Anchorage, *U.S.A.* **144 F10** 61 13N 149 54W
Anci, *China* **74 E9** 39 20N 116 40 E
Ancohuma, Nevada, *Bolivia* **172 D4** 16 0 S 68 50W
Ancón, *Peru* **172 C2** 11 50 S 77 10W
Ancona, *Italy* **45 E10** 43 38N 13 30 E
Ancud, *Chile* **176 B2** 42 0 S 73 50W
Ancud, G. de, *Chile* **176 B2** 42 0 S 73 0W
Ancy-le-Franc, *France* **27 E11** 47 46N 4 10 E
Anda, *China* **69 B7** 46 24N 125 19 E
Anda, *Phil.* **80 C2** 16 17N 119 57 E
Andacollo, *Argentina* **174 D1** 37 10 S 70 42W
Andacollo, *Chile* **174 C1** 30 14 S 71 6W
Andahuaylas, *Peru* **172 C3** 13 40 S 73 25W
Andaingo, *Madag.* **117 B8** 18 12 S 48 17 E
Andalgalá, *Argentina* **174 B2** 27 40 S 66 30W
Åndalsnes, *Norway* **15 E12** 62 35N 7 43 E
Andalucía □, *Spain* **43 H6** 37 35N 5 0W
Andalusia = Andalucía □, *Spain* **43 H6** 37 35N 5 0W
Andalusia, *U.S.A.* **149 K2** 31 18N 86 29W
Andaman & Nicobar Is. □, *India* **95 K11** 10 0N 93 0 E
Andaman Is., *Ind. Oc.* **95 H11** 12 30N 92 45 E
Andaman Sea, *Ind. Oc.* **78 B1** 13 0N 96 0 E
Andamooka Opal Fields, *Australia* **127 E2** 30 27 S 137 9 E
Andapa, *Madag.* **117 A8** 14 39 S 49 39 E
Andara, *Namibia* **116 B3** 18 2 S 21 9 E
Andaraí, *Brazil* **171 D3** 12 48 S 41 20W
Andeer, *Switz.* **33 C8** 46 36N 9 26 E
Andelfingen, *Switz.* **33 A7** 47 36N 8 41 E
Andelot-Blancheville, *France* **27 D12** 48 15N 5 18 E
Andenes, *Norway* **14 B17** 69 19N 16 18 E
Andenne, *Belgium* **24 D5** 50 28N 5 5 E
Andéranboukane, *Mali* **113 B5** 15 26N 3 2 E
Andermatt, *Switz.* **33 C7** 46 38N 8 35 E
Andernach, *Germany* **30 E3** 50 26N 7 24 E
Andernos-les-Bains, *France* **28 D2** 44 44N 1 6W
Anderslöv, *Sweden* **17 J7** 55 26N 13 19 E
Anderson, *Alaska, U.S.A.* **144 D10** 64 25N 149 15W
Anderson, *Calif., U.S.A.* **158 F2** 40 27N 122 18W
Anderson, *Ind., U.S.A.* **157 D11** 40 10N 85 41W
Anderson, *Mo., U.S.A.* **155 G7** 36 39N 94 27W
Anderson, *S.C., U.S.A.* **149 H4** 34 31N 82 39W
Anderson →, *Canada* **138 B7** 69 42N 129 0W
Anderson I., *India* **95 H11** 12 46N 92 43 E
Andersonville, *U.S.A.* **152 C5** 32 12N 84 9W
Anderstorp, *Sweden* **17 G7** 57 19N 13 39 E
Andes, *Colombia* **168 B2** 5 39N 75 54W
Andes, *U.S.A.* **151 D10** 42 12N 74 47W
Andes, Cord. de los, *S. Amer.* **172 C3** 20 0 S 68 0W
Andfjorden, *Norway* **14 B17** 69 10N 16 20 E
Andhra, L., *India* **94 E1** 18 54N 73 32 E
Andhra Pradesh □, *India* **95 F4** 18 0N 79 0 E
Andijon, *Uzbekistan* **66 E8** 41 10N 72 15 E
Andikíthira, *Greece* **48 F5** 35 52N 23 15 E
Andilamena, *Madag.* **117 B8** 17 1 S 48 35 E
Andīmeshk, *Iran* **97 C6** 32 27N 48 21 E
Andímilos, *Greece* **48 E6** 36 47N 24 12 E
Andíparos, *Greece* **49 D7** 37 0N 25 3 E
Andípaxoi, *Greece* **48 B2** 39 9N 20 13 E
Andípsara, *Greece* **49 C7** 38 30N 25 29 E
Andírrion, *Greece* **48 C3** 38 20N 21 46 E
Andizhan = Andijon, *Uzbekistan* **66 E8** 41 10N 72 15 E
Andkhvoy, *Afghan.* **65 E2** 36 52N 65 8 E
Andoain, *Spain* **40 B2** 43 13N 2 1W
Andoany, *Madag.* **117 A8** 13 25 S 48 16 E
Andoas, *Peru* **168 D2** 2 55 S 76 25W
Andohahela, Réserve Naturelle
Intégrale d', *Madag.* **117 C8** 24 4 S 46 44 E
Andol, *India* **94 F4** 17 51N 78 4 E
Andola, *India* **94 F3** 16 57N 76 50 E
Andong, *S. Korea* **75 F15** 36 40N 128 43 E
Andongwei, *China* **75 G10** 35 6N 119 20 E
Andoom, *Australia* **126 A3** 12 25 S 141 53 E
Andorra, *Spain* **40 E4** 40 59N 0 28W
Andorra ■, *Europe* **28 F5** 42 30N 1 30 E
Andorra La Vella, *Andorra* **28 F5** 42 31N 1 32 E
Andover, *U.K.* **21 F6** 51 12N 1 29W
Andover, *Maine, U.S.A.* **151 B14** 44 38N 70 45W
Andover, *Mass., U.S.A.* **151 D13** 42 40N 71 8W
Andover, *N.J., U.S.A.* **151 F10** 40 59N 74 45W
Andover, *N.Y., U.S.A.* **150 D7** 42 10N 77 48W
Andover, *Ohio, U.S.A.* **150 E4** 41 36N 80 34W
Andøya, *Norway* **14 B16** 69 10N 15 50 E
Andrade, *Brazil* **169 D5** 4 40 S 63 45W
Andradina, *Brazil* **171 F1** 20 54 S 51 23W
Andrahary, Mt., *Madag.* **117 A8** 13 37 S 49 17 E
Andramasina, *Madag.* **117 B8** 19 11 S 47 35 E
Andranopasy, *Madag.* **117 C7** 21 17 S 43 44 E
Andranovory, *Madag.* **117 C7** 23 8 S 44 10 E
Andratx, *Spain* **38 B3** 39 39N 2 25 E
André Félix, Parc Nat. d', *C.A.R.* **114 A4** 9 29N 23 18 E
Andreanof Is., *U.S.A.* **144 L4** 51 30N 176 0W
Andreapol, *Russia* **58 D7** 56 40N 32 17 E
Andrée Land, *Greenland* **10 C8** 73 40N 26 0W
Andrews, *S.C., U.S.A.* **149 J6** 33 27N 79 34W
Andrews, *Tex., U.S.A.* **155 J3** 32 19N 102 33W
Andreyevka, *Russia* **60 D10** 52 19N 51 55 E
Ándria, *Italy* **47 A9** 41 13N 16 17 E
Andriamena, *Madag.* **117 B8** 17 26 S 47 30 E
Andriandampy, *Madag.* **117 C8** 22 45 S 45 41 E
Andriba, *Madag.* **117 B8** 17 30 S 46 58 E
Andrijevica, *Montenegro, Yug.* **50 D3** 42 45N 19 48 E
Andringitra, Réserve Naturelle
Intégrale d', *Madag.* **117 C8** 22 13 S 46 5 E
Andrítsaina, *Greece* **48 D3** 37 29N 21 52 E
Androka, *Madag.* **117 C7** 24 58 S 44 2 E
Andropov = Rybinsk, *Russia* **58 C10** 58 5N 38 50 E
Ándros, *Greece* **48 D6** 37 50N 24 57 E
Andros I., *Bahamas* **164 B4** 24 30N 78 0W
Andros Town, *Bahamas* **164 B4** 24 43N 77 47W
Androscoggin →, *U.S.A.* **151 C14** 43 58N 70 0W
Androth I., *India* **95 J1** 10 50N 73 41 E
Andrychów, *Poland* **55 J6** 49 51N 19 18 E
Andselv, *Norway* **14 B18** 69 4N 18 34 E
Andújar, *Spain* **43 G6** 38 3N 4 5W
Andulo, *Angola* **115 E3** 11 25 S 16 45 E
Åneby, *Norway* **18 D7** 60 5N 10 51 E
Aneby, *Sweden* **17 G8** 57 48N 14 49 E
Anegada, B., *Argentina* **176 B4** 40 20 S 62 20W
Anegada I., *Br. Virgin Is.* **165 e** 18 45N 64 20W
Anegada Passage, *W. Indies* **165 C7** 18 15N 63 45W
Aného, *Togo* **113 D5** 6 12N 1 34 E
Aneityum, *Vanuatu* **133 K7** 20 12 S 169 45 E
Anelghowhat, *Vanuatu* **133 K7** 20 19 S 169 43 E
Añelo, *Argentina* **176 A3** 38 20 S 68 45W
Anenni-Noi, *Moldova* **53 D14** 46 53N 29 15 E
Aneto, Pico de, *Spain* **40 C5** 42 37N 0 40 E
Añez, *Bolivia* **173 D5** 15 40 S 63 10W
Anfu, *China* **77 D10** 27 21N 114 40 E
Ang Mo Kio, *Singapore* **87 d** 1 23N 103 50 E
Ang Thong, *Thailand* **86 E3** 14 35N 100 31 E
Ang Thong, Ko, *Thailand* **87 b** 9 37N 99 41 E
Angadanan, *Phil.* **80 C3** 16 45N 121 45 E
Angamos, Punta, *Chile* **174 A1** 23 1 S 70 32W
Angara →, *Russia* **67 D10** 58 5N 94 20 E
Angara-Débou, *Benin* **113 C5** 11 19N 3 3 E
Angarab, *Ethiopia* **107 E4** 13 11N 37 7 E
Angarbaka, *Sudan* **107 F1** 9 44N 24 44 E
Angarsk, *Russia* **67 D11** 52 30N 104 0 E
Angas Hills, *Australia* **124 D4** 23 0 S 127 50 E
Angaston, *Australia* **128 C3** 34 30 S 139 8 E
Angat, *Phil.* **80 D3** 14 56N 121 2 E
Ånge, *Sweden* **16 B9** 62 31N 15 35 E
Ángel, Salto = Angel Falls,
Venezuela **169 B5** 5 57N 62 30W
Ángel de la Guarda, I., *Mexico* **162 B2** 29 30N 113 30W
Angel Falls, *Venezuela* **169 B5** 5 57N 62 30W
Angeles, *Phil.* **80 D3** 15 9N 120 33 E
Ängelholm, *Sweden* **17 H6** 56 15N 12 58 E
Angels Camp, *U.S.A.* **160 G6** 38 4N 120 32W
Ängelsberg, *Sweden* **16 E10** 59 58N 16 0 E
Anger →, *Ethiopia* **107 F4** 9 37N 36 6 E
Angereb →, *Ethiopia* **107 E4** 13 45N 36 40 E
Ångermanälven →, *Sweden* **16 B11** 62 40N 18 0 E
Ångermanland, *Sweden* **14 E18** 63 36N 17 45 E
Angermünde, *Germany* **30 B9** 53 0N 14 0 E
Angers, *Canada* **151 A9** 45 31N 75 29W
Angers, *France* **26 E6** 47 30N 0 35W
Angerville, *France* **27 D9** 48 19N 2 0 E
Ängesån →, *Sweden* **14 C20** 66 16N 22 47 E
Angical, *Brazil* **171 D3** 12 0 S 44 42W
Angikuni L., *Canada* **143 A9** 62 0N 100 0W
Angkor, *Cambodia* **86 F4** 13 22N 103 50 E
Anglem, Mt., *N.Z.* **131 G2** 46 45 S 167 53 E
Anglès, *Spain* **40 D7** 41 57N 2 38 E
Anglesey, Isle of □, *U.K.* **20 D3** 53 16N 4 18W
Anglet, *France* **28 E2** 43 29N 1 31W
Angleton, *U.S.A.* **155 L7** 29 10N 95 26W
Anglin →, *France* **26 F7** 46 42N 0 52 E
Anglisidhes, *Cyprus* **39 F9** 34 51N 33 27 E
Anglure, *France* **27 D10** 48 35N 3 50 E
Angmagssalik = Tasiilaq,
Greenland **10 D7** 65 40N 37 20W
Ango, *Dem. Rep. of the Congo* **118 B2** 4 10N 26 5 E
Angoche, *Mozam.* **119 F4** 16 8 S 39 55 E
Angoche, I., *Mozam.* **119 F4** 16 20 S 39 50 E
Angol, *Chile* **174 D1** 37 56 S 72 45W
Angola, *Ind., U.S.A.* **157 C12** 41 38N 85 0W
Angola, *N.Y., U.S.A.* **150 D5** 42 38N 79 2W
Angola ■, *Africa* **115 E3** 12 0 S 18 0 E
Angoon, *U.S.A.* **144 H14** 57 30N 134 35W
Angor, *Uzbekistan* **65 E3** 37 27N 67 9 E
Angoram, *Papua N. G.* **132 C3** 4 4 S 144 4 E
Angoulême, *France* **28 C4** 45 39N 0 10 E
Angoumois, *France* **28 C4** 45 50N 0 25 E
Angra do Heroismo, *Azores* **9 d1** 38 39N 27 13W
Angra dos Reis, *Brazil* **175 A7** 23 0 S 44 10W
Angren, *Uzbekistan* **66 E8** 41 1N 70 12 E
Angtassom, *Cambodia* **87 G5** 11 1N 104 41 E
Angu, *Dem. Rep. of the Congo* **118 B1** 3 23N 24 30 E
Anguang, *China* **75 B12** 45 15N 123 45 E
Anguilla ■, *W. Indies* **165 C7** 18 14N 63 5W
Angul, *India* **94 D7** 20 51N 85 6 E
Anguo, *China* **74 E8** 38 28N 115 15 E
Angurugu, *Australia* **126 A2** 14 0 S 136 25 E
Angus □, *U.K.* **22 E6** 56 46N 2 56W
Angwa →, *Zimbabwe* **117 B5** 16 0 S 30 23 E
Anhanduí →, *Brazil* **175 A5** 21 46 S 52 9W
Anholt, *Denmark* **17 H5** 56 42N 11 33 E
Anhua, *China* **77 C8** 28 23N 111 12 E
Anhui □, *China* **77 B11** 32 0N 117 0 E
Anhwei = Anhui □, *China* **77 B11** 32 0N 117 0 E
Aniak, *U.S.A.* **144 F8** 61 35N 159 32W
Anichab, *Namibia* **116 C1** 21 0 S 14 46 E
Anicuns, *Brazil* **171 E2** 16 28 S 49 58W
Ánidhros, *Greece* **49 E7** 36 38N 25 43 E
Anié, *Togo* **113 D5** 7 42N 1 8 E
Anil, *Brazil* **170 B3** 2 32 S 44 14W
Animas →, *U.S.A.* **159 H9** 36 43N 108 13W
Anina, *Romania* **52 E6** 45 6N 21 51 E
Anini-y, *Phil.* **81 F3** 10 25N 121 55 E
Aninoasa, *Romania* **53 F9** 44 47N 24 10 E
Anita, *U.S.A.* **156 C2** 41 27N 94 46W
Anivorano, *Madag.* **117 B8** 18 44 S 48 58 E
Aniwa, *Vanuatu* **133 J7** 19 17 S 169 35 E
Anjalankoski, *Finland* **15 F22** 60 45N 26 51 E
Anjangaon, *India* **94 D3** 21 10N 77 20 E
Anjar, *India* **92 H4** 23 6N 70 10 E
Anjengo, *India* **95 K3** 8 40N 76 46 E
Anji, *China* **77 B12** 30 46N 119 40 E
Anjidiv I., *India* **95 G2** 14 40N 74 10 E
Anjō, *Japan* **73 C9** 34 57N 137 5 E
Anjou, *France* **26 E6** 47 20N 0 15W
Anjouan, *Comoros Is.* **121 a** 12 15 S 44 20 E
Anjozorobe, *Madag.* **117 B8** 18 22 S 47 52 E
Anju, *N. Korea* **75 E13** 39 36N 125 40 E
Anka, *Nigeria* **113 C6** 12 13N 5 58 E
Ankaboa, Tanjona, *Madag.* **117 C7** 21 58 S 43 20 E
Ankang, *China* **74 H5** 32 40N 109 1 E
Ankara, *Turkey* **100 C5** 39 57N 32 54 E
Ankarafantsika, Réserve Naturelle
Intégrale d', *Madag.* **117 B8** 16 8 S 47 5 E
Ankaramena, *Madag.* **117 C8** 21 57 S 46 39 E
Ankarsrum, *Sweden* **17 G10** 57 41N 16 20 E
Ankasakasa, *Madag.* **117 B7** 16 21 S 44 52 E
Ankavandra, *Madag.* **117 B8** 18 46 S 45 18 E
Ankazoabo, *Madag.* **117 C7** 22 18 S 44 31 E
Ankazobe, *Madag.* **117 B8** 18 20 S 47 10 E
Ankeny, *U.S.A.* **156 C3** 41 44N 93 36W
Ankilimalinika, *Madag.* **117 C7** 22 58 S 43 45 E
Ankilizato, *Madag.* **117 C8** 20 25 S 45 1 E
Ankisabe, *Madag.* **117 B8** 19 17 S 46 29 E
Anklam, *Germany* **30 B9** 53 51N 13 41 E
Ankleshwar, *India* **94 D1** 21 38N 73 3 E
Ankober, *Ethiopia* **107 F4** 9 35N 39 40 E
Ankola, *India* **95 G2** 14 40N 74 18 E
Ankoro, *Dem. Rep. of the Congo* **118 D2** 6 45 S 26 55 E
Ankororoka, *Madag.* **117 D8** 25 30 S 45 11 E
Anlong, *China* **76 E5** 25 2N 105 27 E
Anlu, *China* **77 B9** 31 15N 113 45 E
Anmyŏn-do, *S. Korea* **75 F14** 36 25N 126 25 E
Ånn, *Sweden* **16 A6** 63 16N 12 34 E
Ann, C., *U.S.A.* **151 D14** 42 38N 70 35W
Ann Arbor, *U.S.A.* **157 B13** 42 17N 83 45W
Anna, *Russia* **60 E5** 51 28N 40 23 E
Anna, *Ill., U.S.A.* **155 G10** 37 28N 89 15W
Anna, *Ohio, U.S.A.* **157 D12** 40 24N 84 11W
Anna Regina, *Guyana* **169 B6** 7 10N 58 30W
Annaba, *Algeria* **111 A6** 36 50N 7 46 E
Annaberg-Buchholz, *Germany* **30 E9** 50 34N 13 0 E
Annai, *Guyana* **169 C6** 3 57N 59 8W
Annaka, *Japan* **73 A10** 36 19N 138 54 E
Annalee →, *Ireland* **23 B4** 54 2N 7 24W
Annam, *Vietnam* **86 E7** 16 0N 108 0 E
Annamitique, Chaîne, *Asia* **86 D6** 17 0N 106 0 E
Annan, *U.K.* **22 G5** 54 59N 3 16W
Annan →, *U.K.* **22 G5** 54 58N 3 16W
Annanberg, *Papua N. G.* **132 C3** 4 52 S 144 42 E
Annapolis, *U.S.A.* **148 F7** 38 59N 76 30W
Annapolis Royal, *Canada* **141 D6** 44 44N 65 32W
Annapurna, *Nepal* **93 E10** 28 34N 83 50 E
Annean, L., *Australia* **125 E2** 26 54 S 118 14 E
Anneberg, *Sweden* **17 G8** 57 44N 14 49 E
Annecy, *France* **29 C10** 45 55N 6 8 E
Annecy, Lac d', *France* **29 C10** 45 52N 6 10 E
Annemasse, *France* **27 F13** 46 12N 6 16 E
Annenskiy Most, *Russia* **58 B9** 60 45N 37 10 E
Annette I., *U.S.A.* **144 J15** 55 9N 131 28W
Annigeri, *India* **95 G2** 15 26N 75 26 E
Anning, *China* **76 E4** 24 55N 102 26 E
Anniston, *U.S.A.* **152 B4** 33 39N 85 50W
Annobón, *Atl. Oc.* **105 G4** 1 25 S 5 36 E
Annonay, *France* **29 C8** 45 15N 4 40 E
Annot, *France* **29 E10** 43 58N 6 38 E
Annotto Bay, *Jamaica* **164 a** 18 17N 76 45W
Ånnsjön, *Sweden* **16 A6** 63 16N 12 34 E
Annville, *U.S.A.* **151 F8** 40 20N 76 31W
Annweiler, *Germany* **31 F3** 49 12N 7 57 E
Áno Arkhánai, *Greece* **49 F7** 35 16N 25 11 E
Áno Porróia, *Greece* **48 A4** 41 17N 23 2 E
Áno Síros, *Greece* **48 D6** 37 29N 24 56 E
Áno Viánnos, *Greece* **39 F6** 35 2N 25 21 E
Anorotsangana, *Madag.* **117 A8** 13 56 S 47 55 E
Anosibe, *Madag.* **117 B8** 19 26 S 48 13 E
Anou Mellene, *Mali* **113 B5** 17 29N 0 33 E
Anoumaba, *Ivory C.* **112 D4** 6 23N 4 38W
Anoyí, *Greece* **39 C2** 38 25N 20 40 E
Anóyia, *Greece* **39 E5** 35 16N 24 52 E
Anping, *Hebei, China* **74 E8** 38 15N 115 30 E
Anping, *Liaoning, China* **75 D12** 41 5N 123 30 E
Anpu Gang, *China* **76 G7** 21 25N 109 50 E
Anqing, *China* **77 B11** 30 30N 117 3 E
Anqiu, *China* **75 F10** 36 25N 119 10 E
Anren, *China* **77 D9** 26 43N 113 18 E
Ansager, *Denmark* **17 J2** 55 43N 8 45 E
Ansai, *China* **74 F5** 36 50N 109 20 E
Ansbach, *Germany* **31 F6** 49 28N 10 34 E
Anse Boileau, *Seychelles* **121 b** 4 43 S 55 29 E
Anse Royale, *Seychelles* **121 b** 4 44 S 55 31 E
Anseba →, *Eritrea* **107 D4** 16 0N 38 30 E
Anserma, *Colombia* **168 B2** 5 13N 75 48W
Ansfelden, *Austria* **34 C7** 48 12N 14 17 E
Anshan, *China* **75 D12** 41 5N 122 58 E
Anshun, *China* **76 D5** 26 18N 105 57 E
Ansião, *Portugal* **42 F2** 39 56N 8 27W
Ansley, *U.S.A.* **154 E5** 41 18N 99 23W
Ansó, *Spain* **40 C4** 42 51N 0 48W
Ansoain, *Spain* **40 C3** 42 50N 1 38W
Anson, *U.S.A.* **155 J5** 32 45N 99 54W
Anson B., *Australia* **124 B5** 13 20 S 130 6 E
Ansongo, *Mali* **113 B5** 15 25N 0 35 E
Ansongo-Ménaka, Réserve d',
Mali **113 B5** 15 0N 1 37 E
Ansonia, *Conn., U.S.A.* **151 E11** 41 21N 73 5W
Ansonia, *Ohio, U.S.A.* **157 D12** 40 13N 84 38W
Anstruther, *U.K.* **22 E6** 56 14N 2 41W
Ansudu, *Indonesia* **83 B5** 2 11 S 139 22 E
Ansus, *Indonesia* **83 B5** 1 44 S 135 49 E
Antabamba, *Peru* **172 C3** 14 40 S 73 0W
Antagarh, *India* **94 D5** 20 6N 81 9 E
Antakya, *Turkey* **100 D7** 36 14N 36 10 E
Antalaha, *Madag.* **117 A9** 14 57 S 50 20 E
Antalât, *Libya* **108 B4** 31 8N 20 42 E
Antalya, *Turkey* **100 D4** 36 52N 30 45 E
Antalya □, *Turkey* **49 E12** 36 30N 30 0 E
Antalya Körfezi, *Turkey* **100 D4** 36 15N 31 30 E
Antambohobe, *Madag.* **117 C8** 22 20 S 46 47 E
Antanambao-Manampotsy,
Madag. **117 B8** 19 29 S 48 34 E
Antanambe, *Madag.* **117 B8** 16 26 S 49 52 E
Antananarivo, *Madag.* **117 B8** 18 55 S 47 31 E
Antananarivo □, *Madag.* **117 B8** 19 0 S 47 0 E
Antanifotsy, *Madag.* **117 B8** 19 39 S 47 19 E
Antanimbaribe, *Madag.* **117 C7** 21 30 S 44 48 E
Antanimora, *Madag.* **117 C8** 24 49 S 45 40 E
Antarctic Pen., *Antarctica* **7 C18** 67 0 S 60 0W
Antarctica **7 E3** 90 0 S 0 0W
Antécume Pata, *Fr. Guiana* **169 C7** 3 17N 54 4W
Antelope, *Zimbabwe* **119 G2** 21 2 S 28 31 E
Antenor Navarro, *Brazil* **170 C4** 6 44 S 38 27W
Antequera, *Paraguay* **174 A4** 24 8 S 57 7W
Antequera, *Spain* **43 H6** 37 5N 4 33W
Antero, Mt., *U.S.A.* **159 G10** 38 41N 106 15W
Antevamena, *Madag.* **117 C7** 21 2 S 44 8 E
Anthemoús, *Greece* **50 F7** 40 31N 23 15 E
Anthony, *Fla., U.S.A.* **153 F7** 29 18N 82 7W
Anthony, *Kans., U.S.A.* **155 G5** 37 9N 98 2W
Anthony, *N. Mex., U.S.A.* **159 K10** 32 0N 106 36W
Anti Atlas, *Morocco* **110 C3** 30 0N 8 30W
Anti-Lebanon = Ash Sharqi, Al
Jabal, *Lebanon* **103 B5** 33 40N 36 10 E
Antibes, *France* **29 E11** 43 34N 7 6 E
Antibes, C. d', *France* **29 E11** 43 31N 7 7 E
Anticosti, Î. d', *Canada* **141 C7** 49 30N 63 0W
Antifer, C. d', *France* **26 C7** 49 41N 0 10 E
Antigo, *U.S.A.* **154 C10** 45 9N 89 9W
Antigonish, *Canada* **141 C7** 45 38N 61 58W
Antigua, *Canary Is.* **9 e2** 28 24N 14 1W
Antigua, *Guatemala* **164 D1** 14 34N 90 41W
Antigua, *W. Indies* **165 C7** 17 0N 61 50W
Antigua & Barbuda ■, *W. Indies* **165 C7** 17 20N 61 48W
Antilla, *Cuba* **164 B4** 20 40N 75 50W
Antilles = West Indies,
Cent. Amer. **165 D7** 15 0N 65 0W
Antioch, *U.S.A.* **160 G5** 38 1N 121 48W
Antioche, Pertuis d', *France* **28 B2** 46 6N 1 20W
Antioquia, *Colombia* **168 B2** 6 40N 75 55W
Antioquia □, *Colombia* **168 B2** 7 0N 75 30W
Antipodes Is., *Pac. Oc.* **134 M9** 49 45 S 178 40 E
Antipolo, *Phil.* **80 D3** 14 35N 121 10 E
Antique □, *Phil.* **81 F4** 11 10N 122 5 E
Antlers, *U.S.A.* **155 H7** 34 14N 95 37W
Antoetra, *Madag.* **117 C8** 20 46 S 47 20 E
Antofagasta, *Chile* **174 A1** 23 50 S 70 30W
Antofagasta □, *Chile* **174 A2** 24 0 S 69 0W
Antofagasta de la Sierra, *Argentina* **174 B2** 26 5 S 67 20W
Antofalla, *Argentina* **174 B2** 25 30 S 68 5W
Antofalla, Salar de, *Argentina* **174 B2** 25 40 S 67 45W
Anton, *U.S.A.* **155 J3** 33 49N 102 10W
Antongila, Helodrano, *Madag.* **117 B8** 15 30 S 49 50 E
Antonibé, *Madag.* **117 B8** 15 7 S 47 24 E
Antonibé, Presqu'île d', *Madag.* **117 A8** 14 55 S 47 20 E
Antonina, *Brazil* **175 B6** 25 26 S 48 42W
Antrain, *France* **26 D5** 48 28N 1 30W
Antrim, *U.K.* **23 B5** 54 43N 6 14W
Antrim, *U.S.A.* **150 F3** 40 7N 81 21W
Antrim □, *U.K.* **23 B5** 54 56N 6 25W
Antrim, Mts. of, *U.K.* **23 A5** 55 3N 6 14W
Antrim Plateau, *Australia* **124 C4** 18 8 S 128 20 E
Antrodoco, *Italy* **45 F10** 42 25N 13 5 E
Antropovo, *Russia* **60 A6** 58 24N 43 6 E
Antsakabary, *Madag.* **117 B8** 15 3 S 48 56 E
Antsalova, *Madag.* **117 B7** 18 40 S 44 37 E
Antsenavolo, *Madag.* **117 C8** 21 24 S 48 3 E
Antsiafabositra, *Madag.* **117 B8** 17 18 S 46 57 E
Antsirabe, *Antananarivo, Madag.* **117 B8** 19 55 S 47 2 E
Antsirabe, *Antsiranana, Madag.* **117 A8** 14 0 S 49 59 E
Antsirabe, *Mahajanga, Madag.* **117 B8** 15 57 S 48 58 E
Antsiranana, *Madag.* **117 A8** 12 25 S 49 20 E
Antsiranana □, *Madag.* **117 A8** 12 16 S 49 17 E
Antsohihy, *Madag.* **117 A8** 14 50 S 47 59 E
Antsohimbondrona Seranana,
Madag. **117 A8** 13 7 S 48 48 E
Antu, *China* **75 C15** 42 30N 128 20 E
Antufash, *Yemen* **98 D3** 15 42N 42 25 E
Antwerp = Antwerpen, *Belgium* **24 C4** 51 13N 4 25 E
Antwerp, *N.Y., U.S.A.* **151 B9** 44 12N 75 37W
Antwerp, *Ohio, U.S.A.* **157 C12** 41 11N 84 45W
Antwerpen, *Belgium* **24 C4** 51 13N 4 25 E
Antwerpen □, *Belgium* **24 C4** 51 15N 4 40 E
Anukur, C., *Papua N. G.* **132 D5** 6 18 S 149 37 E
Anupgarh, *India* **92 E5** 29 10N 73 10 E
Anuppur, *India* **93 H9** 23 6N 81 41 E
Anuradhapura, *Sri Lanka* **95 K5** 8 22N 80 28 E
Anveh, *Iran* **97 E7** 27 23N 54 11 E
Anvers = Antwerpen, *Belgium* **24 C4** 51 13N 4 25 E
Anvers I., *Antarctica* **7 C17** 64 30 S 63 40W
Anvik, *U.S.A.* **144 E7** 62 39N 160 13W
Anwen, *China* **77 C13** 29 4N 120 26 E
Anxi, *Fujian, China* **77 E12** 25 2N 118 12 E
Anxi, *Gansu, China* **68 B4** 40 30N 95 43 E
Anxian, *China* **76 B5** 31 40N 104 25 E
Anxiang, *China* **77 C9** 29 27N 112 11 E
Anxious B., *Australia* **127 E1** 33 24 S 134 45 E
Anyama, *Ivory C.* **112 D4** 5 30N 4 3W

Årkathos 183

Anyang, China 74 F8 36 5N 114 21 E
Anyer, Indonesia 84 D3 6 4 S 105 53 E
Anyer-Kidul, Indonesia 79 G11 6 4 S 105 53 E
Anyi, Jiangxi, China 77 C10 28 49N 115 25 E
Anyi, Shanxi, China 74 G6 35 2N 111 2 E
Anyuan, China 77 E10 25 9N 115 21 E
Anyue, China 76 B5 30 9N 105 50 E
Anza, U.S.A. 161 M10 33 35N 116 39W
Anze, China 74 F7 36 10N 112 12 E
Anzhero-Sudzhensk, Russia 66 D9 56 10N 86 0 E
Ánzio, Italy 46 A5 41 27N 12 37 E
Anzoátegui □, Venezuela 169 B5 9 0N 64 30W
Ao Makham, Thailand 87 a 7 50N 98 24 E
Aoba, Vanuatu 133 E5 15 25 S 167 50 E
Aoga-Shima, Japan 73 E11 32 28N 139 46 E
Aoiz, Spain 40 C3 42 46N 1 22W
Aola, Solomon Is. 133 M11 9 30 S 160 30 E
Aomen = Macau, China 77 F9 22 12N 113 33 E
Aomori, Japan 70 D10 40 45N 140 45 E
Aomori □, Japan 70 D10 40 45N 140 40 E
Aonla, India 93 E8 28 16N 79 11 E
Aono-Yama, Japan 72 C3 34 28N 131 48 E
Aoraki Mount Cook, N.Z. 131 D5 43 36 S 170 9 E
Aorangi Mts., N.Z. 130 H4 41 28 S 175 22 E
Aore, Vanuatu 133 E5 15 35 S 167 10 E
Aoreora, Morocco 110 C2 28 51N 10 53W
Aosta, Italy 44 C4 45 45N 7 20 E
Aotea Harbour, N.Z. 130 D3 38 0 S 174 50 E
Aoudéras, Niger 113 B6 17 45N 8 20 E
Aouinet Torkoz, Morocco 110 C3 28 31N 9 46W
Aouk, Bahr →, Africa 109 G3 8 51N 18 53 E
Aouk-Aoukalé, Réserve de Faune de l', C.A.R. 114 A4 9 52N 21 25 E
Aoukar, Mali 110 D4 23 50N 2 45W
Aoukâr, Mauritania 112 B3 17 40N 10 0W
Aoulef el Arab, Algeria 111 C5 26 55N 1 2 E
Aozou, Chad 109 D3 21 45N 17 28 E
Aozou Strip, Chad 109 D3 22 0N 19 0 E
Apa →, S. Amer. 174 A4 22 6 S 58 2W
Apache, U.S.A. 155 H5 34 54N 98 22W
Apache Junction, U.S.A. 159 K8 33 25N 111 33W
Apalachee B., U.S.A. 152 E5 30 0N 84 0W
Apalachicola, U.S.A. 152 F5 29 43N 84 59W
Apalachicola →, U.S.A. 152 F5 29 43N 84 58W
Apalachicola B., U.S.A. 152 F3 29 40N 85 0W
Apam, Ghana 113 D4 5 19N 0 42W
Apapa, Nigeria 113 D5 6 25N 3 25 E
Apaporis →, Colombia 168 D4 1 23 S 69 25W
Aparecida do Taboado, Brazil 171 F1 20 5 S 51 5W
Aparri, Phil. 80 B3 18 22N 121 38 E
Aparurén, Venezuela 169 B5 5 6N 62 8W
Apateu, Romania 52 D6 46 36N 21 47 E
Apatin, Serbia, Yug. 52 E4 45 40N 19 0 E
Apatity, Russia 56 A5 67 34N 33 22 E
Apatou, Fr. Guiana 169 B7 5 9N 54 20W
Apatzingán, Mexico 162 D4 19 0N 102 20W
Apauwar, Indonesia 83 B5 1 39 S 138 11 E
Apayao □, Phil. 80 B3 18 10N 121 10 E
Apeldoorn, Neths. 24 B5 52 13N 5 57 E
Apen, Germany 30 B3 53 13N 7 48 E
Apennines = Appennini, Italy 44 E7 44 0N 10 0 E
Apere →, Bolivia 173 C4 13 44 S 65 18W
Aphrodisias, Turkey 49 D10 37 42N 28 46 E
Apia, Samoa 133 W24 13 50 S 171 50W
Apiacás, Serra dos, Brazil 173 B6 9 50 S 57 0W
Apiai, Brazil 171 F2 24 31 S 48 50W
Apiaú →, Brazil 169 C5 2 39N 61 12W
Apiaú, Serra do, Brazil 169 C5 2 30N 62 0W
Apidiá →, Brazil 173 C5 11 39 S 61 11W
Apies →, S. Africa 117 D4 25 15 S 28 8 E
Apinajé, Brazil 171 D2 11 31 S 48 18W
Apiti, N.Z. 130 F4 39 58 S 175 54 E
Apizaco, Mexico 163 D5 19 26N 98 9W
Aplao, Peru 172 D3 16 0 S 72 40W
Apo, Mt., Phil. 81 H5 6 53N 125 14 E
Apo East Pass, Phil. 80 E3 12 40N 120 40 E
Apo West Pass, Phil. 80 E3 12 31N 120 22 E
Apodi, Brazil 170 C4 5 39 S 37 48W
Apoera, Surinam 169 B6 5 12N 57 10W
Apolakkiá, Greece 38 E11 36 5N 27 48 E
Apolakkiá, Órmos, Greece 38 E11 36 5N 27 45 E
Apolda, Germany 30 D7 51 2N 11 32 E
Apollo Bay, Australia 128 E5 38 45 S 143 40 E
Apollonia = Marsá Susah, Libya 108 B4 32 52N 21 59 E
Apollonia, Greece 48 E6 36 58N 24 43 E
Apolo, Bolivia 172 C4 14 30 S 68 30W
Apónguao →, Venezuela 169 C5 4 48N 61 36W
Apopka, U.S.A. 153 G8 28 40N 81 31W
Apopka L., U.S.A. 153 G8 28 38N 81 38W
Aporé, Brazil 173 D7 18 58 S 52 1W
Aporé →, Brazil 171 E1 19 27 S 50 57W
Aporema, Brazil 170 A1 1 14N 50 49W
Apostle Is., U.S.A. 154 B9 47 0N 90 40W
Apóstoles, Argentina 175 B4 28 0 S 56 0W
Apostolos Andreas, C., Cyprus 39 E10 35 42N 34 35 E
Apostolovo, Ukraine 59 J7 47 39N 33 39 E
Apoteri, Guyana 169 C6 4 2N 58 32W
Appalachian Mts., U.S.A. 148 G6 38 0N 80 0W
Äppelbo, Sweden 16 D8 60 29N 14 1 E
Appennini, Italy 44 E7 44 0N 10 0 E
Appennino Ligure, Italy 44 D6 44 30N 9 0 E
Appenzell, Switz. 33 B8 47 20N 9 25 E
Appenzell-Ausser Rhoden □, Switz. 33 B8 47 23N 9 23 E
Appenzell-Inner Rhoden □, Switz. 33 B8 47 20N 9 25 E
Appiano, Italy 45 B8 46 28N 11 15 E
Apple Hill, Canada 151 A10 45 13N 74 46W
Apple Valley, U.S.A. 161 L9 34 32N 117 14W
Appleby-in-Westmorland, U.K. 20 C5 54 35N 2 29W
Apples, Switz. 32 C2 46 33N 6 26 E
Appleton, U.S.A. 148 C1 44 16N 88 25W
Appleton City, U.S.A. 156 F2 38 11N 94 2W
Appling, U.S.A. 152 B7 33 33N 82 19W
Approuague, Fr. Guiana 169 C7 4 20N 52 0W
Aprica, Italy 33 D10 46 9N 10 6 E
Apricena, Italy 45 G12 41 47N 15 27 E
April →, Papua N. G. 132 C2 4 18 S 142 26 E
Aprília, Italy 46 A5 41 36N 12 39 E
Apsheronsk, Russia 61 H4 44 28N 39 42 E
Apsley, Canada 150 B6 44 45N 78 6W
Apt, France 29 E9 43 53N 5 24 E
Apuane, Alpi, Italy 44 D7 44 7N 10 14 E
Apuaú, Brazil 169 D5 2 25 S 60 53W
Apucarana, Brazil 175 A5 23 55 S 51 33W
Apulia = Púglia □, Italy 47 A9 41 15N 16 15 E
Apurauan, Phil. 81 G2 9 35N 118 20 E
Apure □, Venezuela 168 B4 7 10N 68 50W
Apure →, Venezuela 168 B4 7 37N 66 25W
Apurímac □, Peru 172 C3 14 0 S 73 0W
Apurimac →, Peru 172 C3 12 17 S 73 56W
Apuseni, Munţii, Romania 52 D7 46 30N 22 45 E
Āqā Jarī, Iran 97 D6 30 42N 49 50 E
Aqaba = Al 'Aqabah, Jordan 103 F4 29 31N 35 0 E
Aqaba, G. of, Red Sea 96 D2 28 15N 33 20 E
'Aqabah, Khalīj al = Aqaba, G. of, Red Sea 96 D2 28 15N 33 20 E
Aqbaqay, Kazakstan 65 A6 45 0N 72 47 E
Aqcheh, Afghan. 65 E3 36 56N 66 11 E
'Aqdā, Iran 97 C7 32 26N 53 37 E
Aqīq, Sudan 106 D4 18 14N 38 12 E
Aqīq, Khalīg, Sudan 106 D4 18 20N 38 10 E
'Aqīq, W. al →, Si. Arabia 98 B3 20 16N 41 40 E
Aqköl, Kazakstan 65 A7 45 0N 75 39 E
Aqköl, Kazakstan 65 B5 43 36N 70 45 E
Aqmola = Astana, Kazakstan 66 D8 51 10N 71 30 E
Aqqum, Kazakstan 65 A2 44 50N 65 8 E
'Aqrah, Iraq 101 D10 36 46N 43 45 E
Aqshī, Kazakstan 65 B8 43 59N 76 19 E
Aqsū, Kazakstan 65 B4 42 25N 69 50 E
Aqsügek, Kazakstan 65 A7 44 37N 74 30 E
Aqsümbe, Kazakstan 65 A3 44 26N 67 33 E
Aqtaū, Kazakstan 66 E6 43 39N 51 12 E
Aqtöbe, Kazakstan 57 D10 50 17N 57 10 E
Aquidauana, Brazil 173 E6 20 30 S 55 50W
Aquidauana →, Brazil 173 D6 19 44 S 56 50W
Aquiles Serdán, Mexico 162 B3 28 37N 105 54W
Aquin, Haiti 165 C5 18 16N 73 24W
Aquitain, Bassin, France 25 D3 44 0N 0 30W
Aquitaine □, France 28 D3 44 25N 0 30W
Aqviligjuaq = Pelly Bay, Canada 139 B11 68 38N 89 50W
Aqyrtöbe, Kazakstan 65 B6 42 59N 72 7 E
Aqzhar, Kazakstan 65 B5 43 8N 71 37 E
Ar Rachidiya = Er Rachidia, Morocco 110 B4 31 58N 4 20W
Ar Rafīd, Syria 103 C4 32 57N 35 52 E
Ar Raḩḩālīyah, Iraq 101 F10 32 44N 43 23 E
Ar Ramādī, Iraq 101 F10 33 25N 43 20 E
Ar Raml, Libya 108 C3 26 45N 19 40 E
Ar Ramthā, Jordan 103 C5 32 34N 36 0 E
Ar Raqqah, Syria 101 E8 35 59N 39 8 E
Ar Rass, Si. Arabia 96 E4 25 50N 43 40 E
Ar Rawḑah, Si. Arabia 98 B3 21 16N 42 50 E
Ar Rawḑah, Yemen 98 D4 14 28N 47 17 E
Ar Rawshān, Si. Arabia 106 C5 20 2N 42 36 E
Ar Rifā'ī, Iraq 96 D5 31 50N 46 10 E
Ar Rijā', Yemen 98 D4 13 1N 44 35 E
Ar Riyāḑ, Si. Arabia 96 E5 24 41N 46 42 E
Ar Ru'ays, Qatar 97 E6 26 8N 51 12 E
Ar Rukhaymīyah, Iraq 96 D5 29 22N 45 38 E
Ar Ruşāfah, Syria 101 E8 35 45N 38 49 E
Ar Ruţbah, Iraq 101 F9 33 0N 40 15 E
Ar Ruwaydah, Si. Arabia 98 B4 23 40N 44 40 E
Ara, India 93 G11 25 35N 84 32 E
Ara Goro, Ethiopia 107 F5 5 48N 41 18 E
Ara Tera, Ethiopia 107 F5 6 38N 40 57 E
Arab, U.S.A. 149 H2 34 19N 86 30W
'Arab, Bahr el →, Sudan 107 F2 9 0N 29 30 E
Arab, Khalîg el, Egypt 106 A2 30 55N 29 0 E
Arab, Shatt al →, Asia 97 D6 30 0N 48 31 E
'Araba, W. →, Egypt 106 J8 28 19N 33 31 E
'Arabābād, Iran 97 C8 33 2N 57 41 E
'Arabah, W. →, Yemen 105 C5 18 5N 51 26 E
Araban, Turkey 100 D7 37 28N 37 44 E
Arabatskaya Strelka, Ukraine 59 K8 45 40N 35 0 E
Arabba, Italy 45 B8 46 30N 11 52 E
Arabelo, Venezuela 169 C5 4 55N 64 13W
Arabi, U.S.A. 152 D6 31 50N 83 44W
Arabia, Asia 62 G8 25 0N 45 0 E
Arabian Desert = Es Sahrâ' Esh Sharqîya, Egypt 106 B3 27 30N 32 30 E
Arabian Gulf = Gulf, The, Asia 97 E6 27 0N 50 0 E
Arabian Sea, Ind. Oc. 62 H10 16 0N 65 0 E
Araç, Turkey 100 B5 41 15N 33 21 E
Aracaju, Brazil 170 D4 10 55 S 37 4W
Aracataca, Colombia 168 A3 10 38N 74 9W
Aracati, Brazil 170 B4 4 30 S 37 44W
Araçatuba, Brazil 175 A5 21 10 S 50 30W
Araceli, Phil. 81 F2 10 33N 119 59 E
Aracena, Spain 43 H4 37 53N 6 38W
Aracena, Sierra de, Spain 43 H4 37 50N 6 50W
Aracides, C., Solomon Is. 133 M11 8 21 S 161 0 E
Aračinovo, Macedonia 50 D5 42 1N 21 34 E
Araçuaí, Brazil 171 E3 16 52 S 42 4W
Araçuaí →, Brazil 171 E3 16 46 S 42 2W
'Arad, Israel 103 D4 31 15N 35 12 E
Arad, Romania 52 D6 46 10N 21 20 E
Arad □, Romania 52 D6 46 20N 22 0 E
Arada, Chad 109 F4 15 0N 20 20 E
Arādān, Iran 97 C7 35 21N 52 30 E
Aradhippou, Cyprus 39 F9 34 57N 33 36 E
Arafura Sea, E. Indies 83 C5 9 0 S 135 0 E
Aragarças, Brazil 173 D7 15 55 S 52 15W
Aragats, Armenia 61 K7 40 30N 44 15 E
Aragon, U.S.A. 152 A4 34 2N 85 3W
Aragón □, Spain 40 D4 41 25N 0 40W
Aragón →, Spain 40 C3 42 13N 1 44W
Aragona, Italy 46 E6 37 24N 13 27 E
Aragua □, Venezuela 168 B4 10 0N 67 10W
Aragua de Barcelona, Venezuela 169 B5 9 28N 64 49W
Araguacema, Brazil 170 C2 8 50 S 49 20W
Araguaçu, Brazil 171 D2 12 49 S 49 51W
Araguaia →, Brazil 170 C2 5 21 S 48 41W
Araguaiana, Brazil 173 D7 15 43 S 51 51W
Araguaína, Brazil 170 C2 7 12 S 48 12W
Araguari, Brazil 171 E2 18 38 S 48 11W
Araguari →, Brazil 169 C8 1 15N 49 55W
Araguatins, Brazil 170 C2 5 38 S 48 7W
Arain, India 92 F6 26 27N 75 2 E
Araioses, Brazil 170 B3 2 53 S 41 55W
Arak, Algeria 111 C5 25 20N 3 45 E
Arāk, Iran 97 C6 34 0N 49 40 E
Araka, Sudan 107 G3 4 20N 30 23 E
Arakan □, Burma 90 F5 19 0N 94 15 E
Arakan Yoma, Burma 90 F5 20 0N 94 40 E
Arákhova, Greece 48 C4 38 28N 22 35 E
Arakkonam, India 95 H4 13 7N 79 43 E
Arakli, Turkey 101 B8 41 6N 40 2 E
Araks = Aras, Rūd-e →, Asia 61 K9 40 5N 48 29 E
Aral, Kazakstan 66 E7 46 41N 61 45 E
Aral Sea, Asia 66 E7 44 30N 60 0 E
Aral Tengizi = Aral Sea, Asia 66 E7 44 30N 60 0 E
Aralsk = Aral, Kazakstan 66 E7 46 41N 61 45 E
Aralskoye More = Aral Sea, Asia 66 E7 44 30N 60 0 E
Aralsor, Ozero, Kazakstan 61 F9 49 5N 48 12 E
Aramac, Australia 126 C4 22 58 S 145 14 E
Aramia →, Papua N. G. 132 D2 7 55 S 143 22 E
Aran →, India 94 E4 19 55N 78 12 E
Aran Areh, Ethiopia 120 C2 9 2N 43 54 E
Aran I., Ireland 23 A3 55 0N 8 30W
Aran Is., Ireland 23 C2 53 6N 9 38W
Aranda de Duero, Spain 42 D7 41 39N 3 42W
Arandān, Iran 96 C5 35 23N 46 55 E
Aranđelovac, Serbia, Yug. 50 B4 44 18N 20 34 E
Aranga, N.Z. 130 B2 35 44 S 173 40 E
Arani, Bolivia 173 D4 17 34 S 65 46W
Arani, India 95 H4 12 43N 79 19 E
Aranjuez, Spain 42 E7 40 1N 3 40W
Aranos, Namibia 116 C2 24 9 S 19 7 E
Aransas Pass, U.S.A. 155 M6 27 55N 97 9W
Aranyaprathet, Thailand 86 F4 13 41N 102 30 E
Arao, Japan 72 E2 32 59N 130 25 E
Araouane, Mali 112 B4 18 55N 3 30W
Arapahoe, U.S.A. 154 E5 40 18N 99 54W
Arapari, Brazil 170 C2 5 34 S 49 15W
Arapawa I., N.Z. 131 B9 41 11 S 174 17 E
Arapey Grande →, Uruguay 174 C4 30 55 S 57 49W
Arapgir, Turkey 101 C8 39 5N 38 30 E
Arapiraca, Brazil 170 C4 9 45 S 36 39W
Arapongas, Brazil 175 A5 23 29 S 51 28W
Arapuni, N.Z. 130 E4 38 4 S 175 39 E
Ar'ar, Si. Arabia 96 D4 30 59N 41 2 E
Araracuara, Colombia 168 D3 0 24 S 72 17W
Araranguá, Brazil 175 B6 29 0 S 49 30W
Araraquara, Brazil 171 F2 21 50 S 48 0W
Araras, Brazil 171 F2 22 22 S 47 23W
Ararás, Serra das, Brazil 175 B5 25 0 S 53 10W
Ararat, Armenia 101 C11 39 48N 44 50 E
Ararat, Australia 128 D5 37 16 S 143 0 E
Ararat, Mt. = Ağrı Dağı, Turkey 101 C11 39 50N 44 15 E
Arari, Brazil 170 B3 3 28 S 44 47W
Araria, India 93 F12 26 9N 87 33 E
Araripe, Chapada do, Brazil 170 C3 7 20 S 40 0W
Araripina, Brazil 170 C3 7 33 S 40 34W
Araruama, L. de, Brazil 171 F3 22 53 S 42 12W
Araruna, Brazil 170 C4 6 52 S 35 44W
Aras, Rūd-e →, Asia 61 K9 40 5N 48 29 E
Aratāne, Mauritania 112 B3 18 24N 8 32W
Araticu, Brazil 170 B2 1 58 S 49 51W
Arauca, Colombia 168 B3 7 0N 70 40W
Arauca □, Colombia 168 B3 6 40N 71 0W
Arauca →, Venezuela 168 B4 7 24N 66 35W
Arauco, Chile 174 D1 37 16 S 73 25W
Araújos, Brazil 171 E2 19 56 S 45 14W
Arauquita, Colombia 168 B3 7 2N 71 25W
Araure, Venezuela 168 B4 9 34N 69 13W
Arawa, Ethiopia 107 F5 9 57N 41 58 E
Arawale Nat. Reserve, Kenya 118 C5 1 24 S 40 9 E
Arawata →, N.Z. 131 E3 44 0 S 168 40 E
Arawe Is., Papua N. G. 132 D5 6 6 S 149 0 E
Araxá, Brazil 171 E2 19 35 S 46 55W
Araya, Pen. de, Venezuela 169 A5 10 40N 64 0W
Arayat, Phil. 80 D3 15 10N 120 46 E
Arba Gugu, Ethiopia 107 F5 8 40N 40 15 E
Arba Minch, Ethiopia 107 F4 6 0N 37 30 E
Arbat, Iraq 101 E11 35 25N 45 35 E
Árbatax, Italy 46 C2 39 56N 9 42 E
Arbedo, Switz. 33 D8 46 12N 9 3 E
Arbi, Ethiopia 107 F4 9 4N 35 7 E
Arbīl, Iraq 101 D11 36 15N 44 5 E
Arboga, Sweden 16 E9 59 24N 15 52 E
Arbois, France 27 F12 46 55N 5 46 E
Arboletes, Colombia 168 B2 8 51N 76 26W
Arbon, Switz. 33 A8 47 31N 9 26 E
Arbore, Ethiopia 107 F4 5 3N 36 50 E
Arboréa, Italy 46 C1 39 46N 8 35 E
Arborfield, Canada 143 C8 53 6N 103 39W
Arborg, Canada 143 C9 50 54N 97 13W
Arbre du Ténéré, Niger 113 B7 17 50N 10 4 E
Arbroath, U.K. 22 E6 56 34N 2 35W
Arbuckle, U.S.A. 160 F4 39 1N 122 3W
Arbus, Italy 46 C1 39 30N 8 33 E
Arc →, France 29 C10 45 34N 6 12 E
Arc-lès-Gray, France 27 E12 47 28N 5 34 E
Arcachon, France 28 D2 44 40N 1 10W
Arcachon, Bassin d', France 28 D2 44 42N 1 10W
Arcade, Calif., U.S.A. 161 L8 34 2N 118 15W
Arcade, N.Y., U.S.A. 150 D6 42 32N 78 25W
Arcadia, Fla., U.S.A. 149 M5 27 13N 81 52W
Arcadia, Ind., U.S.A. 157 D10 40 11N 86 1W
Arcadia, Iowa, U.S.A. 156 B1 42 5N 95 3W
Arcadia, La., U.S.A. 155 J8 32 33N 92 55W
Arcadia, Pa., U.S.A. 150 F6 40 47N 78 51W
Arcanum, U.S.A. 157 E12 39 59N 84 33W
Arcata, U.S.A. 158 F1 40 52N 124 5W
Arcévia, Italy 45 E9 43 30N 12 56 E
Archangel = Arkhangelsk, Russia 56 B7 64 38N 40 36 E
Archar, Bulgaria 50 C6 43 50N 22 54 E
Archbald, U.S.A. 151 E9 41 30N 75 32W
Archbold, U.S.A. 157 C12 41 31N 84 18W
Archena, Spain 41 G3 38 9N 1 16W
Archenu, J., Chad 109 D4 22 15N 24 45 E
Archer, U.S.A. 153 F7 29 32N 82 32W
Archer →, Australia 126 A3 13 28 S 141 41 E
Archer B., Australia 126 A3 13 20 S 141 30 E
Archers Post, Kenya 118 B4 0 35N 37 35 E
Arches Nat. Park, U.S.A. 159 G9 38 45N 109 25W
Archidona, Spain 43 H6 37 6N 4 22W
Arci, Mte., Italy 46 C1 39 47N 8 45 E
Arcidosso, Italy 45 F8 42 52N 11 33 E
Arcila = Asilah, Morocco 110 A3 35 29N 6 0W
Arcis-sur-Aube, France 27 D11 48 32N 4 10 E
Arckaringa Cr. →, Australia 127 D2 28 10 S 135 22 E
Arco, Italy 44 C7 45 55N 10 53 E
Arco, U.S.A. 158 E7 43 38N 113 18W
Arcola, U.S.A. 157 E8 39 41N 88 19W
Arcoona, Australia 128 A2 31 2 S 137 1 E
Arcos = Arcos de Jalón, Spain 40 D2 41 12N 2 16W
Arcos de Jalón, Spain 40 D2 41 12N 2 16W
Arcos de la Frontera, Spain 43 J5 36 45N 5 49W
Arcos de Valdevez, Portugal 42 D2 41 55N 8 22W
Arcot, India 95 H4 12 53N 79 20 E
Arcoverde, Brazil 170 C4 8 25 S 37 4W
Arcozelo, Portugal 42 E3 40 32N 7 47W
Arctic Bay, Canada 139 A11 73 1N 85 7W
Arctic Ocean, Arctic 6 B18 78 0N 160 0W
Arctic Red River = Tsiigehtchic, Canada 138 B6 67 15N 134 0W
Arctic Village, U.S.A. 144 B11 68 8N 145 32W
Arda →, Bulgaria 51 E10 41 40N 26 30 E
Arda →, Italy 44 C7 45 2N 10 2 E
Ardabīl, Iran 97 B6 38 15N 48 18 E
Ardahan, Turkey 101 B10 41 7N 42 41 E
Ardakān = Sepīdān, Iran 97 D7 30 20N 52 5 E
Ardakān, Iran 97 C7 32 19N 53 59 E
Ardala, Sweden 17 F7 58 22N 13 19 E
Ardales, Spain 43 J6 36 53N 4 51W
Årdalstangen, Norway 18 C4 61 14N 7 43 E
Ardèche □, France 29 D8 44 42N 4 16 E
Ardèche →, France 29 D8 44 16N 4 39 E
Ardee, Ireland 23 C5 53 52N 6 33W
Arden, Canada 150 B8 44 43N 76 56W
Arden, Denmark 17 H3 56 46N 9 52 E
Arden, Calif., U.S.A. 160 G5 38 36N 121 33W
Arden, Nev., U.S.A. 161 J11 36 1N 115 14W
Ardenne, Belgium 36 D3 49 50N 5 5 E
Ardennes = Ardenne, Belgium 36 D3 49 50N 5 5 E
Ardennes □, France 27 C11 49 35N 4 40 E
Ardentes, France 27 F8 46 45N 1 50 E
Arderin, Ireland 23 C4 53 2N 7 39W
Ardeşen, Turkey 101 B9 41 12N 41 2 E
Ardestān, Iran 97 C7 33 20N 52 25 E
Ardez, Switz. 33 C10 46 47N 10 12 E
Árdhas →, Greece 51 E10 41 40N 26 30 E
Ardhéa, Greece 50 F6 40 58N 22 3 E
Ardila →, Portugal 43 G3 38 12N 7 28W
Ardino, Bulgaria 51 E9 41 34N 25 9 E
Ardivachar Pt., U.K. 22 D1 57 23N 7 26W
Ardlethan, Australia 129 C7 34 22 S 146 53 E
Ardmore, Okla., U.S.A. 155 H6 34 10N 97 8W
Ardmore, Pa., U.S.A. 151 G9 39 58N 75 18W
Ardnamurchan, Pt. of, U.K. 22 E2 56 43N 6 14W
Ardnave Pt., U.K. 22 F2 55 53N 6 20W
Ardon, Russia 61 J7 43 10N 44 18 E
Ardore, Italy 47 D9 38 11N 16 10 E
Ardres, France 27 B8 50 50N 1 59 E
Ardrossan, Australia 128 C2 34 26 S 137 53 E
Ardrossan, U.K. 22 F4 55 39N 4 49W
Ards Pen., U.K. 23 B6 54 33N 5 34W
Arduan, Sudan 106 D3 19 54N 30 20 E
Ardud, Romania 52 C7 47 37N 22 52 E
Åre, Sweden 16 A7 63 22N 13 15 E
Arecibo, Puerto Rico 165 d 18 29N 66 43W
Areia Branca, Brazil 170 B4 5 0 S 37 0W
Arena, Pt., U.S.A. 160 G3 38 57N 123 44W
Arenal, Honduras 164 C2 15 21N 86 50W
Arenales, Cerro, Chile 176 C2 47 5 S 73 40W
Arenápolis, Brazil 173 C6 14 26 S 56 49W
Arenas = Las Arenas, Spain 42 B6 43 17N 4 50W
Arenas, Pta., Venezuela 169 A5 10 31N 64 14W
Arenas de San Pedro, Spain 42 E5 40 12N 5 5W
Arendal, Norway 15 G13 58 28N 8 46 E
Arendsee, Germany 30 C7 52 52N 11 27 E
Arenillas, Ecuador 168 D1 3 33 S 80 10W
Arenys de Mar, Spain 40 D7 41 35N 2 33 E
Arenzano, Italy 44 D5 44 24N 8 41 E
Arenzville, U.S.A. 156 E6 39 53N 90 22W
Areópolis, Greece 48 E4 36 40N 22 22 E
Arequipa, Peru 172 D3 16 20 S 71 30W
Arequipa □, Peru 172 D3 16 0 S 72 50W
Arere, Brazil 169 D7 0 16 S 53 52W
Arero, Ethiopia 107 G4 4 41N 38 50 E
Arès, France 28 D2 44 47N 1 8W
Arévalo, Spain 42 D6 41 3N 4 43W
Arezzo, Italy 45 E8 43 25N 11 53 E
Arga, Turkey 96 B3 38 21N 37 59 E
Arga →, Spain 40 C3 42 18N 1 47W
Argalastí, Greece 48 B5 39 13N 23 13 E
Argamakmur, Indonesia 84 C2 3 35 S 102 0 E
Argamasilla de Alba, Spain 43 F7 39 8N 3 5W
Argamasilla de Calatrava, Spain 43 G6 38 44N 4 4W
Arganda, Spain 42 E7 40 19N 3 26W
Arganil, Portugal 42 E2 40 13N 8 3W
Argao, Phil. 81 G4 9 52N 123 36 E
Argásion 39 D2 37 45N 20 56 E
Argayash, Russia 64 D8 55 29N 60 52 E
Argedeb, Ethiopia 107 F5 6 11N 41 13 E
Argelès-Gazost, France 28 E3 43 0N 0 6W
Argelès-sur-Mer, France 28 F7 42 34N 3 1 E
Argens →, France 29 E10 43 24N 6 44 E
Argent-sur-Sauldre, France 27 E9 47 33N 2 25 E
Argenta, Canada 142 C5 50 11N 116 56W
Argenta, Italy 45 D8 44 37N 11 50 E
Argenta, U.S.A. 157 E8 39 59N 88 49W
Argentan, France 26 D6 48 45N 0 1W
Argentário, Mte., Italy 45 F8 42 24N 11 9 E
Argentat, France 28 C5 45 6N 1 56 E
Argentera, Italy 44 D4 44 12N 7 5 E
Argenteuil, France 27 D9 48 57N 2 14 E
Argentia, Canada 141 C9 47 18N 53 58W
Argentiera, C. dell', Italy 46 B1 40 44N 8 8 E
Argentière, Aiguilles d', Switz. 32 E4 45 58N 7 2 E
Argentina ■, S. Amer. 176 B3 35 0 S 66 0W
Argentina Is., Antarctica 7 C17 66 0 S 64 0W
Argentino, L., Argentina 176 D2 50 10 S 73 0W
Argenton-Château, France 26 F6 46 59N 0 27W
Argenton-sur-Creuse, France 27 F8 46 36N 1 30 E
Argeş □, Romania 53 F9 45 0N 24 45 E
Argeş →, Romania 53 F11 44 5N 26 38 E
Arghandab →, Afghan. 91 C2 31 30N 64 15 E
Argheile, Ethiopia 107 F5 5 19N 42 4 E
Argo, Sudan 106 D3 19 28N 30 30 E
Argolikós Kólpos, Greece 48 D4 37 20N 22 52 E
Argolís □, Greece 48 D4 37 38N 22 50 E
Argonne, France 27 C12 49 10N 5 0 E
Árgos, Greece 48 D4 37 40N 22 43 E
Argos, U.S.A. 157 C10 41 14N 86 15W
Árgos Orestikón, Greece 50 F5 40 27N 21 18 E
Argostólion, Greece 39 C2 38 11N 20 29 E
Argostólion, Kólpos, Greece 39 C1 38 10N 20 27 E
Arguedas, Spain 40 C3 42 11N 1 36W
Arguello, Pt., U.S.A. 161 L6 34 35N 120 39W
Arguineguín, Canary Is. 9 e1 27 46N 15 41W
Argun, Russia 61 J7 43 18N 45 52 E
Argun →, Russia 67 D13 53 20N 121 28 E
Argungu, Nigeria 113 C5 12 40N 4 31 E
Arguni, T., Indonesia 83 B4 3 6 S 133 42 E
Argus Pk., U.S.A. 161 K9 35 52N 117 26W
Argyle, L., Australia 124 C4 16 20 S 128 40 E
Argyll & Bute □, U.K. 22 E3 56 13N 5 28W
Arhavi, Turkey 101 B9 41 21N 41 18 E
Århus, Denmark 17 H4 56 8N 10 11 E
Århus Amtskommune □, Denmark 17 H4 56 15N 10 15 E
Aria, N.Z. 130 E4 38 33 S 175 0 E
Ariadnoye, Russia 70 B7 45 8N 134 25 E
Ariamsvlei, Namibia 116 D2 28 9 S 19 51 E
Ariana, Tunisia 108 A2 36 52N 10 12 E
Ariano Irpino, Italy 47 A8 41 9N 15 5 E
Ariari →, Colombia 168 C3 2 35N 72 47W
Aribinda, Burkina Faso 113 C4 14 17N 0 52W
Arica, Chile 172 D3 18 32 S 70 20W
Arica, Colombia 168 D3 2 0 S 71 50W
Arico, Canary Is. 9 e1 28 9N 16 29W
Arid, C., Australia 125 F3 34 1 S 123 10 E
Arida, Japan 73 C7 34 5N 135 8 E
Aridal, W. Sahara 110 C2 25 59N 13 54W
Aride, Seychelles 121 b 4 13 S 55 40 E
Ariège □, France 28 F5 42 56N 1 30 E
Ariège →, France 28 E5 43 30N 1 25 E
Arieş →, Romania 53 D8 46 24N 23 20 E
Arigat el Fersig, Algeria 111 C4 27 35N 2 7W
Arihā, Israel 106 A4 31 51N 35 27 E
Arilje, Serbia, Yug. 50 C4 43 44N 20 7 E
Arilla, Ákra, Greece 38 B9 39 43N 19 39 E
Arima, Trin. & Tob. 165 D7 10 38N 61 17W
Aringay, Phil. 80 C3 16 26N 120 21 E
Arinos →, Brazil 173 C6 10 25 S 58 20W
Ario de Rosales, Mexico 162 D4 19 12N 102 0W
Ariogala, Lithuania 54 C10 55 16N 23 28 E
Aripo, Mt., Trin. & Tob. 169 F9 10 45N 61 15W
Aripuanã, Brazil 173 B5 9 25 S 60 30W
Aripuanã →, Brazil 173 B5 5 7 S 60 25W
Ariquemes, Brazil 173 B5 9 55 S 63 6W
Arisaig, U.K. 22 E3 56 55N 5 51W
Arish, W. el →, Egypt 106 A3 31 9N 33 49 E
Arissa, Ethiopia 107 E5 11 10N 41 35 E
Aristazabal I., Canada 142 C3 52 40N 129 10W
Arita, Japan 72 D1 33 11N 129 54 E
Aritao, Phil. 80 C3 16 18N 121 2 E
Ariton, U.S.A. 152 D4 31 36N 85 43W
Arivonimamo, Madag. 117 B8 19 1 S 47 11 E
Ariyalur, India 95 J4 11 8N 79 8 E
Ariza, Spain 40 D2 41 19N 2 3W
Arizaro, Salar de, Argentina 174 A2 24 40 S 67 50W
Arizona, Argentina 174 D2 35 45 S 65 25W
Arizona □, U.S.A. 159 J8 34 0N 112 0W
Arizpe, Mexico 162 A2 30 20N 110 11W
Ärjäng, Sweden 16 E6 59 24N 12 8 E
Arjeplog, Sweden 14 D18 66 3N 18 2 E
Arjona, Colombia 168 A2 10 14N 75 22W
Arjona, Spain 43 H6 37 56N 4 4W
Arjuna, Indonesia 85 D4 7 49 S 112 34 E
Arka, Russia 67 C15 60 15N 142 0 E
Arkadak, Russia 60 E6 51 58N 43 30 E
Arkadelphia, U.S.A. 155 H8 34 7N 93 4W
Arkadhía □, Greece 48 D4 37 30N 22 20 E
Arkaig, L., U.K. 22 E3 56 59N 5 10W
Arkalgud, India 95 H3 12 46N 76 3 E
Arkalyk = Arqalyk, Kazakstan 66 D7 50 13N 66 50 E
Arkansas □, U.S.A. 155 H8 35 0N 92 30W
Arkansas →, U.S.A. 155 J9 33 47N 91 4W
Arkansas City, U.S.A. 155 G6 37 4N 97 2W
Arkaroola, Australia 127 E2 30 20 S 139 22 E
Årkathos →, Greece 48 B3 39 20N 21 4 E

Azuaga 185

Athena, *U.S.A.* **152 F6** 29 59N 83 30W
Athenry, *Ireland* **23 C3** 53 18N 8 44W
Athens = Athínai, *Greece* **48 D5** 37 58N 23 46 E
Athens, *Ala., U.S.A.* **149 H2** 34 48N 86 58W
Athens, *Ga., U.S.A.* **152 B6** 33 57N 83 23W
Athens, *N.Y., U.S.A.* **151 D11** 42 16N 73 49W
Athens, *Ohio, U.S.A.* **148 F4** 39 20N 82 6W
Athens, *Pa., U.S.A.* **151 E8** 41 57N 76 31W
Athens, *Tenn., U.S.A.* **149 H3** 35 27N 84 36W
Athens, *Tex., U.S.A.* **155 J7** 32 12N 95 51W
Athéras, *Greece* **39 C1** 38 19N 20 25 E
Atherley, *Canada* **150 B5** 44 37N 79 20W
Atherton, *Australia* **126 B4** 17 17 S 145 30 E
Athiéme, *Benin* **113 D5** 6 37N 1 40 E
Athienou, *Cyprus* **39 E9** 35 3N 33 32 E
Athínai, *Greece* **48 D5** 37 58N 23 46 E
Athlone, *Ireland* **23 C4** 53 25N 7 56W
Athmalik, *India* **94 D7** 20 43N 84 32 E
Athna, *Cyprus* **39 E9** 35 3N 33 47 E
Athni, *India* **94 F2** 16 44N 75 6 E
Athol, *N.Z.* **131 F3** 45 30 S 168 35 E
Athol, *U.S.A.* **151 D12** 42 36N 72 14W
Athol Is., *Bahamas* **9 b** 25 5N 77 16W
Atholl, Forest of, *U.K.* **22 E5** 56 51N 3 50W
Atholl, Kap, *Greenland* **10 B4** 76 25N 69 30W
Atholville, *Canada* **141 C6** 47 59N 66 43W
Áthos, *Greece* **51 F8** 40 9N 24 22 E
Athy, *Ireland* **23 C5** 53 0N 7 0W
Ati, *Chad* **109 F3** 13 13N 18 20 E
Ati, *Sudan* **107 E2** 13 5N 29 2 E
Atiak, *Uganda* **118 B3** 3 12N 32 2 E
Atiamuri, *N.Z.* **130 E5** 38 24 S 176 5 E
Atico, *Peru* **172 D3** 16 14 S 73 40W
Atienza, *Spain* **40 D2** 41 12N 2 52W
Atiit, *Sudan* **107 F3** 6 10N 30 35 E
Atik L., *Canada* **143 B9** 55 15N 96 0W
Atikameg →, *Canada* **140 B3** 52 30N 82 46W
Atikokan, *Canada* **140 C1** 48 45N 91 37W
Atikonak L., *Canada* **141 B7** 52 40N 64 32W
Atimonan, *Phil.* **80 D3** 14 0N 121 55 E
'Ātinah, W. →, *Oman* **99 C6** 18 23N 53 28 E
Atirampattinam, *India* **95 J4** 10 28N 79 20 E
Atka, *Russia* **67 C16** 60 50N 151 48 E
Atka, *U.S.A.* **144 K4** 52 12N 174 12W
Atka I., *U.S.A.* **144 K4** 52 7N 174 30W
Atkarsk, *Russia* **60 E7** 51 55N 45 2 E
Atkasuk = Meade River, *U.S.A.* **144 A8** 70 28N 157 24W
Atkinson, *Ga., U.S.A.* **152 D8** 31 13N 81 47W
Atkinson, *Ill., U.S.A.* **156 C6** 41 25N 90 1W
Atkinson, *Nebr., U.S.A.* **154 D5** 42 32N 98 59W
Atlanta, *Ga., U.S.A.* **152 B5** 33 45N 84 23W
Atlanta, *Ill., U.S.A.* **156 D7** 40 16N 89 14W
Atlanta, *Mo., U.S.A.* **156 E4** 39 54N 92 29W
Atlanta, *Tex., U.S.A.* **155 J7** 33 7N 94 10W
Atlantic, *U.S.A.* **156 C2** 41 24N 95 1W
Atlantic Beach, *U.S.A.* **152 E8** 30 20N 81 24W
Atlantic City, *U.S.A.* **148 F8** 39 21N 74 27W
Atlantic-Indian Ridge, *Atl. Oc.* **8 M11** 53 0 S 10 0 E
Atlantic Ocean **8 F8** 0 0 20 0W
Atlántico □, *Colombia* **168 A2** 10 45N 75 0W
Atlas Mts. = Haut Atlas, *Morocco* **110 B4** 32 30N 5 0W
Atlin, *Canada* **142 B2** 59 31N 133 41W
Atlin, L., *Canada* **142 B2** 59 26N 133 45W
Atlin Prov. Park, *Canada* **142 B2** 59 10N 134 30W
Atløyna, *Norway* **18 C1** 61 21N 4 58 E
Atmakur, *Andhra Pradesh, India* **94 E4** 18 45N 78 39 E
Atmakur, *Andhra Pradesh, India* **95 G4** 14 37N 79 40 E
Atmakur, *Andhra Pradesh, India* **95 G4** 15 53N 78 35 E
Atmore, *U.S.A.* **149 K2** 31 2N 87 29W
Atna, *Norway* **18 C7** 61 44N 10 49 E
Atna →, *Norway* **18 C7** 61 44N 10 49 E
Atō, *Japan* **72 C3** 34 25N 131 40 E
Atocha, *Bolivia* **172 E4** 20 56 S 66 14W
Atok, *Phil.* **80 C3** 16 35N 120 41 E
Atoka, *U.S.A.* **155 H6** 34 23N 96 8W
Átokos Nisís, *Greece* **39 C2** 38 28N 20 49 E
Atolia, *U.S.A.* **161 K9** 35 19N 117 37W
Atongo-Bakari, *C.A.R.* **114 A4** 5 49N 21 35 E
Atori, *Solomon Is.* **133 M11** 8 42 S 160 59 E
Atrå, *Norway* **18 E5** 59 59N 8 45 E
Atrai →, *Bangla.* **90 C2** 24 7N 89 22 E
Atrak = Atrek →, *Turkmenistan* **97 B8** 37 35N 53 58 E
Ätran, *Sweden* **17 G6** 57 7N 12 57 E
Ätran →, *Sweden* **17 H6** 56 53N 12 30 E
Atrato →, *Colombia* **168 B2** 8 17N 76 58W
Atrauli, *India* **92 E8** 28 2N 78 20 E
Atrek →, *Turkmenistan* **97 B8** 37 35N 53 58 E
Atri, *Italy* **45 F10** 42 35N 13 58 E
Atsikí, *Greece* **49 B7** 39 56N 25 13 E
Atsoum, Mts., *Cameroon* **113 D7** 6 41N 12 57 E
Atsugi, *Japan* **73 B11** 35 25N 139 21 E
Atsumi, *Japan* **73 C9** 34 35N 137 4 E
Atsumi-Wan, *Japan* **73 C9** 34 44N 137 13 E
Atsuta, *Japan* **70 C10** 43 24N 141 26 E
Atsy, *Indonesia* **83 C5** 5 48 S 138 20 E
Attalla, *U.S.A.* **152 A3** 34 1N 86 6W
Attapu, *Laos* **86 E6** 14 48N 106 50 E
Attapulgus, *U.S.A.* **152 E5** 30 45N 84 29W
Attáviros, *Greece* **38 E11** 36 12N 27 50 E
Attawapiskat, *Canada* **140 B3** 52 56N 82 24W
Attawapiskat →, *Canada* **140 B3** 52 57N 82 18W
Attawapiskat L., *Canada* **140 B2** 52 18N 87 54W
Attersee, *Austria* **34 D6** 47 55N 13 32 E
Attica, *Ind., U.S.A.* **157 D9** 40 18N 87 15W
Attica, *Ohio, U.S.A.* **150 E2** 41 4N 82 53W
Attichy, *France* **27 C10** 49 25N 3 3 E
Attigny, *France* **27 C11** 49 28N 4 35 E
Attika = Attikí □, *Greece* **48 D5** 37 10N 23 40 E
Attikamagen L., *Canada* **141 B6** 55 0N 66 30W
Attikí □, *Greece* **48 D5** 37 10N 23 40 E
Attleboro, *U.S.A.* **151 E13** 41 57N 71 17W
Attock, *Pakistan* **92 C5** 33 52N 72 20 E
Attopeu = Attapu, *Laos* **86 E6** 14 48N 106 50 E
Attu, *U.S.A.* **144 K1** 52 56N 173 15 E
Attu I., *U.S.A.* **144 K1** 52 55N 172 55 E
Attunga, *Australia* **129 A9** 30 55 S 150 50 E
Attur, *India* **95 J4** 11 35N 78 30 E
'Atūd, *Yemen* **99 D5** 14 53N 48 10 E
Atuel →, *Argentina* **174 D2** 36 17 S 66 50W
Åtvidaberg, *Sweden* **17 F10** 58 12N 16 0 E
Atwater, *U.S.A.* **160 H6** 37 21N 120 37W
Atwood, *Canada* **150 C3** 43 40N 81 1W
Atwood, *Ill., U.S.A.* **157 E8** 39 48N 88 28W
Atwood, *Kans., U.S.A.* **154 F4** 39 48N 101 3W
Atyraū, *Kazakstan* **57 E9** 47 5N 52 0 E
Au, *Austria* **33 B9** 47 19N 9 59 E
Au Sable, *U.S.A.* **150 B1** 44 25N 83 20W
Au Sable →, *U.S.A.* **148 C4** 44 25N 83 20W
Au Sable Forks, *U.S.A.* **151 B11** 44 27N 73 41W
Au Sable Pt., *U.S.A.* **150 B1** 44 20N 83 20W
Aubagne, *France* **29 E9** 43 17N 5 37 E
Aubarca, C. d', *Spain* **38 C1** 39 4N 1 22 E
Aube □, *France* **27 D11** 48 15N 4 10 E
Aube →, *France* **27 D10** 48 34N 3 43 E
Aubenas, *France* **29 D8** 44 37N 4 24 E
Aubenton, *France* **27 C11** 49 50N 4 12 E
Auberry, *U.S.A.* **160 H7** 37 7N 119 29W
Aubigny-sur-Nère, *France* **27 E9** 47 30N 2 24 E
Aubin, *France* **28 D6** 44 33N 2 15 E
Aubrac, Mts. d', *France* **28 D7** 44 40N 3 2 E
Auburn, *Australia* **128 C3** 34 1 S 138 42 E
Auburn, *Ala., U.S.A.* **152 C4** 32 36N 85 29W
Auburn, *Calif., U.S.A.* **160 G5** 38 54N 121 4W
Auburn, *Ill., U.S.A.* **156 E7** 39 36N 89 45W
Auburn, *Ind., U.S.A.* **157 C11** 41 22N 85 4W
Auburn, *Maine, U.S.A.* **149 C10** 44 6N 70 14W
Auburn, *N.Y., U.S.A.* **151 D8** 42 56N 76 34W
Auburn, *Nebr., U.S.A.* **154 E7** 40 23N 95 51W
Auburn, *Pa., U.S.A.* **151 F8** 40 36N 76 6W
Auburn, *Wash., U.S.A.* **160 C4** 47 18N 122 14W
Auburn Ra., *Australia* **127 D5** 25 15 S 150 30 E
Auburndale, *U.S.A.* **149 L5** 28 4N 81 48W
Aubusson, *France* **28 C6** 45 57N 2 11 E
Auce, *Latvia* **54 B9** 56 28N 22 53 E
Auch, *France* **28 E4** 43 39N 0 36 E
Auchi, *Nigeria* **113 D6** 7 6N 6 13 E
Auckland, *N.Z.* **130 C3** 36 52 S 174 46 E
Auckland □, *N.Z.* **130 E6** 36 50 S 175 0 E
Auckland Is., *Pac. Oc.* **134 N8** 50 40 S 166 5 E
Aude □, *France* **28 E6** 43 8N 2 28 E
Aude →, *France* **28 E7** 43 13N 3 14 E
Audegle, *Somali Rep.* **120 D2** 1 59N 44 50 E
Auden, *Canada* **140 B2** 50 14N 87 53W
Auderville, *France* **26 C5** 49 43N 1 57W
Audierne, *France* **26 D2** 48 1N 4 34W
Audincourt, *France* **27 E13** 47 30N 6 50 E
Audo, *Ethiopia* **107 F5** 6 20N 41 50 E
Audubon, *U.S.A.* **156 C2** 41 43N 94 56W
Aue, *Germany* **30 E8** 50 35N 12 41 E
Auerbach, *Germany* **30 E8** 50 30N 12 24 E
Aueti Paraná →, *Brazil* **168 D4** 1 51 S 65 37W
Aufist, *W. Sahara* **110 C2** 25 44N 14 39W
Augathella, *Australia* **127 D4** 25 48 S 146 35 E
Aughnacloy, *U.K.* **23 B5** 54 25N 6 59W
Augrabies Falls, *S. Africa* **116 D3** 28 35 S 20 20 E
Augrabies Falls Nat. Park,
S. Africa **116 D3** 28 40 S 20 22 E
Augsburg, *Germany* **31 G6** 48 25N 10 52 E
Augusta, *Australia* **125 F2** 34 19 S 115 9 E
Augusta, *Italy* **47 E8** 37 13N 15 13 E
Augusta, *Ark., U.S.A.* **155 H9** 35 17N 91 22W
Augusta, *Ga., U.S.A.* **152 B8** 33 28N 81 58W
Augusta, *Ill., U.S.A.* **156 D6** 40 14N 90 57W
Augusta, *Kans., U.S.A.* **155 G6** 37 41N 96 59W
Augusta, *Ky., U.S.A.* **157 F12** 38 47N 84 0W
Augusta, *Maine, U.S.A.* **139 D13** 44 19N 69 47W
Augusta, *Mont., U.S.A.* **158 C7** 47 30N 112 24W
Augustenborg, *Denmark* **17 K3** 54 57N 9 53 E
Augustine I., *U.S.A.* **144 G9** 59 22N 153 26W
Augustów, *Poland* **54 E9** 53 51N 23 0 E
Augustus, Mt., *Australia* **125 D2** 24 20 S 116 50 E
Augustus I., *Australia* **124 C3** 15 20 S 124 30 E
Aukan, *Eritrea* **107 D5** 15 29N 40 50 E
Auki, *Solomon Is.* **133 M11** 8 45 S 160 42 E
Aukra, *Norway* **18 B3** 62 47N 6 55 E
Aukum, *U.S.A.* **160 G6** 38 34N 120 43W
Aul, *India* **94 D8** 20 41N 86 39 E
Auld, L., *Australia* **124 D3** 22 25 S 123 50 E
Aulla, *Italy* **44 D6** 44 12N 9 58 E
Aulnay, *France* **28 B3** 46 2N 0 22W
Aulne →, *France* **26 D2** 48 17N 4 16W
Aulnoye-Aymeries, *France* **27 B10** 50 12N 3 50 E
Ault, *France* **26 B8** 50 8N 1 26 E
Ault, *U.S.A.* **154 E2** 40 35N 104 44W
Aulus-les-Bains, *France* **28 F5** 42 49N 1 19 E
Aumale, *France* **27 C8** 49 46N 1 46 E
Aumo, *Papua N. G.* **132 C5** 5 44 S 148 30 E
Aumont-Aubrac, *France* **28 D7** 44 43N 3 17 E
Auna, *Nigeria* **113 C5** 10 9N 4 42 E
Aundah, *India* **94 E3** 19 32N 77 3 E
Aundh, *India* **94 F2** 17 33N 74 23 E
Auning, *Denmark* **17 H4** 56 26N 10 22 E
Aunis, *France* **28 B3** 46 5N 0 50W
'Aunu'u, *Amer. Samoa* **133 X24** 14 20 S 170 31W
Auponhia, *Indonesia* **82 B3** 1 58 S 125 27 E
Aups, *France* **29 E10** 43 37N 6 15 E
Aur, Pulau, *Malaysia* **87 L5** 2 35N 104 10 E
Aura, *Burma* **90 B6** 26 59N 97 57 E
Auraiya, *India* **93 F8** 26 28N 79 33 E
Aurangabad, *Bihar, India* **93 G11** 24 45N 84 18 E
Aurangabad, *Maharashtra, India* **94 E2** 19 50N 75 23 E
Auray, *France* **26 E4** 47 40N 2 59W
Aurdal, *Norway* **18 D6** 60 55N 9 26 E
Aure, *Norway* **18 A5** 63 16N 8 33 E
Aurès, *Algeria* **111 A6** 35 8N 6 30 E
Aurich, *Germany* **30 B3** 53 28N 7 28 E
Aurilândia, *Brazil* **171 E1** 16 44 S 50 28W
Aurillac, *France* **28 D6** 44 55N 2 26 E
Aurlandsfjorden, *Norway* **18 C4** 61 3N 7 1 E
Aurlandsvangen, *Norway* **18 D4** 60 55N 7 12 E
Auronzo di Cadore, *Italy* **45 B9** 46 33N 12 26 E
Aurora = Maéwo, *Vanuatu* **133 E6** 15 10 S 168 10 E
Aurora = San Francisco, *Phil.* **80 E4** 13 21N 122 31 E
Aurora, *Canada* **150 C5** 44 0N 79 28W
Aurora, *Isabela, Phil.* **80 C3** 16 59N 121 38 E
Aurora, *Zamboanga del S., Phil.* **81 H4** 7 57N 123 36 E
Aurora, *S. Africa* **116 E2** 32 40 S 18 29 E
Aurora, *Colo., U.S.A.* **154 F2** 39 44N 104 52W
Aurora, *Ill., U.S.A.* **157 C8** 41 45N 88 19W
Aurora, *Mo., U.S.A.* **155 G8** 36 58N 93 43W
Aurora, *N.Y., U.S.A.* **151 D8** 42 45N 76 42W
Aurora, *Nebr., U.S.A.* **154 E6** 40 52N 98 0W
Aurora, *Ohio, U.S.A.* **150 E3** 41 21N 81 20W
Aurora □, *Phil.* **80 D3** 15 30N 121 30 E
Aursmoen, *Norway* **18 E8** 59 55N 11 26 E
Aursunden, *Norway* **18 B8** 62 40N 11 40 E
Aurukun, *Australia* **126 A3** 13 20 S 141 45 E
Aus, *Namibia* **116 D2** 26 35 S 16 12 E
Ausa, *India* **94 E3** 18 15N 76 30 E
Ausable →, *Canada* **150 C3** 43 19N 81 46W
Auschwitz = Oświęcim, *Poland* **55 H6** 50 2N 19 11 E
Aust-Agder □, *Norway* **18 F4** 58 45N 8 0 E
Austad, *Norway* **18 F4** 58 58N 7 37 E
Austen Harbour, *India* **95 H11** 12 55N 92 45 E
Austerlitz = Slavkov u Brna,
Czech Rep. **35 B9** 49 10N 16 52 E
Austevoll, *Norway* **18 D2** 60 5N 5 13 E
Austin, *Ind., U.S.A.* **157 F11** 38 45N 85 49W
Austin, *Minn., U.S.A.* **154 D8** 43 40N 92 58W
Austin, *Nev., U.S.A.* **158 G5** 39 30N 117 4W
Austin, *Pa., U.S.A.* **150 E6** 41 38N 78 6W
Austin, *Tex., U.S.A.* **155 K6** 30 17N 97 45W
Austin, L., *Australia* **125 E2** 27 40 S 118 0 E
Austin I., *Canada* **143 A10** 61 10N 94 0W
Austmarka, *Norway* **18 D9** 60 6N 12 21 E
Austnes, *Norway* **18 B3** 62 38N 6 16 E
Austra, *Norway* **14 D14** 65 8N 11 55 E
Austral Is. = Tubuai Is., *Pac. Oc.* **135 K13** 25 0 S 150 0W
Austral Seamount Chain, *Pac. Oc.* **135 K13** 24 0 S 150 0W
Australia ■, *Oceania* **134 K5** 23 0 S 135 0 E
Australian Capital Territory □,
Australia **129 C8** 35 30 S 149 0 E
Australind, *Australia* **125 F2** 33 17 S 115 42 E
Austria ■, *Europe* **34 E7** 47 0N 14 0 E
Austur-Skaftafellssýsla □, *Iceland* **11 C10** 64 15N 16 0W
Austvågøy, *Norway* **14 B16** 68 20N 14 40 E
Autazes, *Brazil* **169 D6** 3 35 S 59 8W
Auterive, *France* **28 E5** 43 21N 1 29 E
Authie →, *France* **27 B8** 50 22N 1 38 E
Authon-du-Perche, *France* **26 D7** 48 12N 0 54 E
Autlán, *Mexico* **162 D4** 19 40N 104 30W
Autun, *France* **27 F11** 46 58N 4 17 E
Auvergne, *France* **28 C7** 45 20N 3 15 E
Auvergne, Mts. d', *France* **28 C6** 45 20N 2 55 E
Auvézère →, *France* **28 C4** 45 12N 0 50 E
Auxerre, *France* **27 E10** 47 48N 3 32 E
Auxi-le-Château, *France* **27 B9** 50 15N 2 8 E
Auxonne, *France* **27 E12** 47 10N 5 20 E
Auxvasse, *U.S.A.* **156 E5** 39 1N 91 54W
Auzances, *France* **27 F9** 46 2N 2 30 E
Ava, *Ill., U.S.A.* **156 G7** 37 53N 89 30W
Ava, *Mo., U.S.A.* **155 G8** 36 57N 92 40W
Avaldsnes, *Norway* **18 E2** 59 21N 5 20 E
Avallon, *France* **27 E10** 47 30N 3 53 E
Avalon, *U.S.A.* **161 M8** 33 21N 118 20W
Avalon Pen., *Canada* **141 C9** 47 30N 53 20W
Avanavero, *Surinam* **169 C6** 4 51N 57 22W
Avanigadda, *India* **95 G5** 16 0N 80 56 E
Avannaarsua □, *Greenland* **10 B5** 80 0N 55 0W
Avanos, *Turkey* **96 B2** 38 43N 34 51 E
Avaré, *Brazil* **175 A6** 23 4 S 48 58W
Ávas, *Greece* **51 F9** 40 57N 25 56 E
Avawatz Mts., *U.S.A.* **161 K10** 35 40N 116 30W
Avdan Dağı, *Turkey* **51 F13** 40 23N 29 46 E
Aveiro, *Brazil* **169 D6** 3 10 S 55 5W
Aveiro, *Portugal* **42 E2** 40 37N 8 38W
Aveiro □, *Portugal* **42 E2** 40 40N 8 35W
Āvej, *Iran* **97 C6** 35 40N 49 15 E
Avellaneda, *Argentina* **174 C4** 34 50 S 58 10W
Avellino, *Italy* **47 B7** 40 54N 14 47 E
Avenal, *U.S.A.* **160 K6** 36 0N 120 8W
Avenches, *Switz.* **32 C4** 46 53N 7 2 E
Averøya, *Norway* **18 A4** 63 0N 7 35 E
Aversa, *Italy* **47 B7** 40 58N 14 12 E
Avery, *U.S.A.* **158 C6** 47 15N 115 49W
Aves, Is. las, *Venezuela* **165 D6** 12 0N 67 30W
Avesnes-sur-Helpe, *France* **27 B10** 50 8N 3 55 E
Avesta, *Sweden* **16 D10** 60 9N 16 10 E
Aveyron □, *France* **28 D6** 44 22N 2 45 E
Aveyron →, *France* **28 D5** 44 5N 1 16 E
Avezzano, *Italy* **45 F10** 42 2N 13 25 E
Avgó, *Greece* **49 F7** 35 33N 25 37 E
Aviá Terai, *Argentina* **174 B3** 26 45 S 60 50W
Aviano, *Italy* **45 B9** 46 4N 12 36 E
Aviemore, *U.K.* **22 D5** 57 12N 3 50W
Aviemore, L., *N.Z.* **131 E5** 44 37 S 170 18 E
Avigliana, *Italy* **44 C4** 45 5N 7 23 E
Avigliano, *Italy* **47 B8** 40 44N 15 43 E
Avignon, *France* **29 E8** 43 57N 4 50 E
Ávila, *Spain* **42 E6** 40 39N 4 43W
Ávila □, *Spain* **42 E6** 40 30N 5 0W
Ávila, Sierra de, *Spain* **42 E5** 40 40N 5 15W
Avila Beach, *U.S.A.* **161 K6** 35 11N 120 44W
Avilés, *Spain* **42 B5** 43 35N 5 57W
Avintes, *Portugal* **42 D2** 41 7N 8 33W
Avionárion, *Greece* **48 C6** 38 31N 24 8 E
Avis, *Portugal* **43 F3** 39 4N 7 53W
Avis, *U.S.A.* **150 E7** 41 11N 77 19W
Avísio →, *Italy* **44 B8** 46 7N 11 5 E
Avissawella, *Sri Lanka* **95 L5** 6 56N 80 11 E
Aviston, *U.S.A.* **156 F7** 38 36N 89 36W
Aviz = Avis, *Portugal* **43 F3** 39 4N 7 53W
Avize, *France* **27 D11** 48 59N 4 1 E
Avlum, *Denmark* **17 H2** 56 16N 8 47 E
Avoca, *Australia* **128 D5** 37 5 S 143 26 E
Avoca, *U.S.A.* **150 D7** 42 25N 77 25W
Avoca →, *Australia* **128 C5** 35 40 S 143 43 E
Avoca →, *Ireland* **23 D5** 52 48N 6 10W
Avola, *Canada* **142 C5** 51 45N 119 19W
Avola, *Italy* **47 F8** 36 56N 15 7 E
Avon, *Ill., U.S.A.* **156 D6** 40 40N 90 26W
Avon, *N.Y., U.S.A.* **150 D7** 42 55N 77 45W
Avon, *S. Dak., U.S.A.* **154 D5** 43 0N 98 4W
Avon →, *Australia* **125 F2** 31 40 S 116 7 E
Avon →, *Bristol, U.K.* **21 F5** 51 29N 2 41W
Avon →, *Dorset, U.K.* **21 G6** 50 44N 1 46W
Avon →, *Warks., U.K.* **21 E5** 52 0N 2 8W
Avon Park, *U.S.A.* **153 H8** 27 36N 81 31W
Avondale, *Zimbabwe* **119 F3** 17 43 S 30 58 E
Avonlea, *Canada* **143 D8** 50 0N 105 0W
Avonmore, *Canada* **151 A10** 45 10N 74 58W
Avramov, *Bulgaria* **51 D10** 42 45N 26 38 E
Avranches, *France* **26 D5** 48 40N 1 20W
Avre →, *France* **26 D8** 48 47N 1 22 E
Avrig, *Romania* **53 E9** 45 43N 24 21 E
Avrillé, *France* **26 E6** 47 30N 0 35W
Avtovac, *Bos.-H.* **50 C2** 43 9N 18 35 E
Avu Avu, *Solomon Is.* **133 M11** 9 50 S 160 22 E
Awag el Baqar, *Sudan* **107 E3** 10 10N 33 10 E
A'waj →, *Syria* **103 B5** 33 23N 36 20 E
Awaji, *Japan* **73 C7** 34 32N 135 1 E
Awaji-Shima, *Japan* **72 C6** 34 30N 134 50 E
'Awālī, *Bahrain* **97 E6** 26 0N 50 30 E
Awantipur, *India* **93 C6** 33 55N 75 3 E
Awanui, *N.Z.* **130 B2** 35 4 S 173 17 E
Awarja →, *India* **94 F3** 17 5N 76 15 E
Awarua B., *N.Z.* **131 E3** 44 28 S 168 4 E
Awarua Pt., *N.Z.* **131 E3** 44 15 S 168 5 E
Awasa, *Ethiopia* **107 F4** 7 2N 38 28 E
Awasa, L., *Ethiopia* **107 F4** 7 0N 38 30 E
Awash, *Ethiopia* **107 F5** 9 1N 40 10 E
Awash →, *Ethiopia* **107 E5** 11 45N 41 5 E
Awash Nat. Park and Reserve,
Ethiopia **107 F5** 9 8N 40 0 E
Awaso, *Ghana* **112 D4** 6 15N 2 22W
Awatere →, *N.Z.* **131 B9** 41 37 S 174 10 E
Awbārī, *Libya* **108 C2** 26 46N 12 57 E
Awbārī □, *Libya* **108 C2** 26 35N 12 46 E
Awbārī, Idehan, *Libya* **108 C2** 27 10N 11 30 E
Awe, L., *U.K.* **22 E3** 56 17N 5 16W
Aweil, *Sudan* **107 F2** 8 42N 27 20 E
Awgu, *Nigeria* **113 D6** 6 4N 7 24 E
Awjilah, *Libya* **108 C4** 29 8N 21 7 E
Awka, *Nigeria* **113 D6** 6 12N 7 5 E
Aworro, *Papua N. G.* **132 D2** 7 43 S 143 11 E
Ax-les-Thermes, *France* **28 F5** 42 44N 1 50 E
Axat, *France* **28 F6** 42 48N 2 13 E
Axe →, *U.K.* **21 F5** 50 42N 3 4W
Axel Heiberg I., *Canada* **6 B3** 80 0N 90 0W
Axim, *Ghana* **112 E4** 4 51N 2 15W
Aximim, *Brazil* **169 D6** 4 2 S 59 22W
Axintele, *Romania* **53 F11** 44 37N 26 47 E
Axioma, *Brazil* **173 B5** 6 45 S 64 31W
Axiós →, *Greece* **50 F6** 40 57N 22 35 E
Axminster, *U.K.* **21 G4** 50 46N 3 0W
Axson, *U.S.A.* **152 D7** 31 17N 82 44W
Axvall, *Sweden* **17 F7** 58 23N 13 34 E
Ay, *France* **27 C11** 49 3N 4 1 E
Ay →, *Russia* **64 C6** 56 8N 57 40 E
Ayaantang, *Eq. Guin.* **114 B2** 1 58N 10 24 E
Ayabaca, *Peru* **172 A2** 4 40 S 79 53W
Ayabe, *Japan* **73 B7** 35 20N 135 20 E
Ayacucho, *Argentina* **174 D4** 37 5 S 58 20W
Ayacucho, *Peru* **172 C3** 13 0 S 74 0W
Ayacucho □, *Peru* **172 C3** 14 0 S 74 0W
Ayaguz, *Kazakstan* **66 E9** 48 10N 80 10 E
Ayakkuduk, *Uzbekistan* **65 C2** 41 12N 65 12 E
Ayakudi, *India* **95 J3** 10 28N 77 56 E
Ayakum Hu, *China* **88 D5** 37 30N 89 20 E
Ayala, *Phil.* **81 H3** 6 57N 121 57 E
Ayamé, *Ivory C.* **112 D4** 5 35N 3 9W
Ayamonte, *Spain* **43 H3** 37 12N 7 24W
Ayan, *Russia* **67 D14** 56 30N 138 16 E
Ayancık, *Turkey* **100 B6** 41 57N 34 18 E
Ayapel, *Colombia* **168 B2** 8 19N 75 9W
Ayas, *Turkey* **100 B5** 40 2N 32 21 E
Ayaviri, *Peru* **172 C3** 14 50 S 70 35W
Āybak, *Afghan.* **91 A3** 36 15N 68 5 E
Aybastı, *Turkey* **100 B7** 40 41N 37 23 E
Aydarkul Ozero, *Uzbekistan* **65 C3** 40 50N 67 10 E
Aydın, *Turkey* **100 D2** 37 51N 27 51 E
Aydin □, *Turkey* **49 D9** 37 50N 28 0 E
Aydin Dağları, *Turkey* **49 D10** 38 0N 28 0 E
Aydyrlinskiy, *Russia* **64 E7** 52 3N 59 50 E
Ayelu, *Ethiopia* **107 E5** 10 5N 40 42 E
Ayenngré, *Togo* **113 D5** 8 40N 1 1 E
Ayer, *U.S.A.* **151 D13** 42 34N 71 35W
Ayer Hitam, *Malaysia* **87 c** 5 24N 100 16 E
Ayerbe, *Spain* **40 C4** 42 17N 0 41W
Ayer's Cliff, *Canada* **151 A12** 45 10N 72 3W
Ayers Rock, *Australia* **125 E5** 25 23 S 131 5 E
Ayiá, *Greece* **48 B4** 39 43N 22 45 E
Ayia Aikateríni, Ákra, *Greece* **38 B9** 39 50N 19 50 E
Ayía Ánna, *Greece* **48 C5** 38 52N 23 24 E
Ayía Dhéka, *Greece* **39 E5** 35 3N 24 58 E
Ayía Gálini, *Greece* **39 E5** 35 6N 24 41 E
Ayía Marína, Kásos, *Greece* **49 F8** 35 27N 26 53 E
Ayía Marína, Léros, *Greece* **49 D8** 37 11N 26 48 E
Ayia Napa, *Cyprus* **39 F10** 34 59N 34 0 E
Ayía Paraskeví, *Greece* **49 B8** 39 14N 26 21 E
Áyia Phyla, *Cyprus* **39 F9** 34 43N 33 1 E
Ayía Rouméli, *Greece* **39 E4** 35 14N 23 58 E
Ayía Varvára, *Greece* **39 E6** 35 8N 25 1 E
Ayiássos, *Greece* **49 B8** 39 5N 26 23 E
Áyioi Theódhoroi, *Greece* **48 D5** 37 55N 23 9 E
Áyion Óros □, *Greece* **51 F8** 40 25N 24 6 E
Áyios Amvrósios, *Cyprus* **39 E9** 35 20N 33 35 E
Áyios Andréas, *Greece* **48 D4** 37 21N 22 45 E
Áyios Evstrátios, *Greece* **48 B6** 39 34N 24 58 E
Áyios Ioánnis, Ákra, *Greece* **39 E6** 35 20N 25 40 E
Áyios Isidhoros, *Greece* **38 E11** 36 9N 27 51 E
Áyios Kiríkos, *Greece* **49 D8** 37 34N 26 17 E
Áyios Léon, *Greece* **39 D2** 37 47N 20 43 E
Áyios Matthaíos, *Greece* **38 C9** 39 30N 19 47 E
Áyios Míronos, *Greece* **39 E6** 35 15N 25 1 E
Áyios Nikólaos,
Aitolía kai Akarnanía, Greece **39 B2** 38 52N 20 48 E
Áyios Nikólaos, *Kríti, Greece* **39 E6** 35 11N 25 41 E
Áyios Nikólaos, *Levkás, Greece* **39 B2** 38 36N 20 34 E
Áyios Pétros, *Greece* **39 B2** 38 40N 20 36 E
Áyios Seryios, *Cyprus* **39 E9** 35 12N 33 53 E
Áyios Theódhoros, *Cyprus* **39 E10** 35 22N 34 1 E
Áyios Thomás, *Greece* **39 B3** 38 58N 20 47 E
Áyios Yeóryios, *Greece* **48 D5** 37 28N 23 57 E
Aykathonisi, *Greece* **49 D8** 37 28N 27 0 E
Aykino, *Russia* **56 B8** 62 15N 49 56 E
Aykirikçi, *Turkey* **49 B12** 39 8N 30 9 E
Aylesbury, *U.K.* **21 F7** 51 49N 0 49W
Aylmer, *Canada* **150 D4** 42 46N 80 59W
Aylmer, L., *Canada* **138 B8** 64 0N 110 8W
'Ayn, Wādī al, *Oman* **97 F7** 22 15N 55 28 E
'Ayn al Ghazālah, *Libya* **108 B4** 32 10N 23 20 E
Ayn Dār, *Si. Arabia* **97 E7** 25 55N 49 10 E
Ayn Zālah, *Iraq* **101 D10** 36 45N 42 35 E
Ayna, *Spain* **41 G2** 38 34N 2 3W
Aynabulaq, *Kazakstan* **65 A8** 44 36N 77 56 E
Aynāt, *Yemen* **99 C5** 16 4N 49 9 E
Ayni, *Tajikistan* **65 D4** 39 23N 68 32 E
Ayod, *Sudan* **107 F3** 8 7N 31 26 E
Ayolas, *Paraguay* **174 B4** 27 10 S 56 59W
Ayom, *Sudan* **107 F2** 7 49N 28 23 E
Ayon, Ostrov, *Russia* **67 C17** 69 50N 169 0 E
Ayora, *Spain* **41 F3** 39 3N 1 3W
Ayorou, *Niger* **113 C5** 14 53N 1 0 E
Ayos, *Cameroon* **114 B2** 3 53N 12 31 E
'Ayoûn el 'Atroûs, *Mauritania* **112 B3** 16 38N 9 37W
Ayr, *Australia* **126 B4** 19 35 S 147 25 E
Ayr, *Canada* **150 C4** 43 17N 80 27W
Ayr, *U.K.* **22 F4** 55 28N 4 38W
Ayr →, *U.K.* **22 F4** 55 28N 4 38W
Ayrancı, *Turkey* **100 D5** 37 21N 33 41 E
Ayrancılar, *Turkey* **49 C9** 38 15N 27 18 E
Ayre, Pt. of, *U.K.* **20 C3** 54 25N 4 21W
Aysha, *Ethiopia* **107 E5** 10 50N 42 23 E
Ayton, *Australia* **126 B4** 15 56 S 145 22 E
Aytos, *Bulgaria* **51 D11** 42 42N 27 16 E
Aytoska Planina, *Bulgaria* **51 D11** 42 45N 27 30 E
Ayu, Kepulauan, *Indonesia* **83 A4** 0 35N 131 5 E
Ayutla, *Guatemala* **164 D1** 14 40N 92 10W
Ayutla, *Mexico* **163 D5** 16 58N 99 17W
Ayvacık, *Turkey* **100 C2** 39 36N 26 24 E
Ayvalık, *Turkey* **49 B8** 39 20N 26 46 E
Az Zabadānī, *Syria* **103 B5** 33 43N 36 5 E
Az Zahirāh, *Asia* **99 B7** 23 40N 56 10 E
Az Zāhirīyah, *West Bank* **103 D3** 31 25N 34 58 E
Az Zahrān, *Si. Arabia* **97 E6** 26 10N 50 7 E
Az Zarqā, *Jordan* **103 C5** 32 5N 36 4 E
Az Zarqā', *U.A.E.* **97 E7** 24 53N 53 4 E
Az Zāwiyah, *Libya* **108 B2** 32 52N 12 56 E
Az Zaydīyah, *Yemen* **98 D3** 15 20N 43 1 E
Az Zībār, *Iraq* **101 D11** 36 52N 44 4 E
Az Zilfī, *Si. Arabia* **96 E5** 26 12N 44 52 E
Az Zubayr, *Iraq* **96 D5** 30 26N 47 40 E
Az Zuqur, *Yemen* **98 D3** 14 0N 42 45 E
Az Zuwaytīnah, *Libya* **108 B4** 30 58N 20 7 E
Azad Kashmir □, *Pakistan* **93 C5** 33 50N 73 50 E
Azambuja, *Portugal* **43 F2** 39 4N 8 51W
Azamgarh, *India* **93 F10** 26 5N 83 13 E
Azangaro, *Peru* **172 C3** 14 55 S 70 13W
Azaoua, *Niger* **113 B5** 15 50N 4 0 E
Azaouad, *Mali* **112 B4** 19 0N 3 0W
Azaouak, Vallée de l', *Mali* **113 B5** 15 50N 3 20 E
Āzār Shahr, *Iran* **101 D11** 37 45N 45 59 E
Azara, *Nigeria* **113 D6** 8 22N 9 12 E
Azarān, *Iran* **101 D12** 37 25N 47 16 E
Azärbayjan = Azerbaijan ■, *Asia* **61 K9** 40 20N 48 0 E
Āzarbāyjān-e Gharbī □, *Iran* **96 B5** 37 0N 44 30 E
Āzarbāyjān-e Sharqī □, *Iran* **96 B5** 37 20N 47 0 E
Azare, *Nigeria* **113 C7** 11 55N 10 10 E
Azay-le-Rideau, *France* **26 E7** 47 16N 0 30 E
A'zāz, *Syria* **100 D7** 36 36N 37 4 E
Azazga, *Algeria* **111 A5** 36 48N 4 22 E
Azbine = Aïr, *Niger* **113 B6** 18 30N 8 0 E
Azefal, *Mauritania* **110 D2** 21 0N 14 45W
Azeffoun, *Algeria* **111 A5** 36 51N 4 26 E
Azemmour, *Morocco* **110 B3** 33 20N 9 20W
Azennezal, *Algeria* **111 D5** 22 58N 0 43 E
Azerbaijan ■, *Asia* **61 K9** 40 20N 48 0 E
Azerbaijchan = Azerbaijan ■, *Asia* **61 K9** 40 20N 48 0 E
Azezo, *Ethiopia* **107 E4** 12 28N 37 15 E
Azimganj, *India* **93 G13** 24 14N 88 16 E
Aznalcóllar, *Spain* **43 H4** 37 32N 6 17W
Azogues, *Ecuador* **168 D2** 2 35 S 78 0W
Azores = Açores, Is. dos, *Atl. Oc.* **8 C9** 38 0N 27 0W
Azoum, B. →, *Chad* **109 F4** 10 53N 20 15 E
Azov, *Russia* **61 G4** 47 3N 39 25 E
Azov, Sea of, *Europe* **59 J9** 46 0N 36 30 E
Azovskoye More = Azov, Sea of,
Europe **59 J9** 46 0N 36 30 E
Azpeitia, *Spain* **40 B2** 43 12N 2 19W
Azrak, B. →, *Chad* **109 F4** 10 52N 20 15 E
Azraq ash Shīshān, *Jordan* **103 D5** 31 50N 36 49 E
Azrou, *Morocco* **110 B3** 33 28N 5 19W
Aztec, *U.S.A.* **159 H10** 36 49N 107 59W
Azúa de Compostela, *Dom. Rep.* **165 C5** 18 25N 70 44W
Azuaga, *Spain* **43 G5** 38 16N 5 39W

186 Azuara

Azuara, Spain 40 D4 41 15N 0 53W
Azuay □, Ecuador 168 D2 2 55 S 79 0W
Azuer →, Spain 43 F7 39 8N 3 36W
Azuero, Pen. de, Panama 164 E3 7 30N 80 30W
Azuga, Romania 53 E10 45 27N 25 33 E
Azul, Argentina 174 D4 36 42 S 59 43W
Azul, Lagoa, Azores 9 d3 37 52N 25 47W
Azul, Serra, Brazil 173 C7 14 50 S 54 50W
Azurduy, Bolivia 173 D5 19 59 S 64 29W
Azusa, U.S.A. 161 L9 34 8N 117 52W
Azzaba, Algeria 111 A6 36 48N 7 6 E
Azzano Décimo, Italy 45 C9 45 52N 12 56 E
Azzel Mati, Sebkra, Algeria 111 C5 26 10N 0 43 E

B

Ba Don, Vietnam 86 D6 17 45N 106 26 E
Ba Dong, Vietnam 87 H6 9 40N 106 33 E
Ba Ngoi = Cam Lam, Vietnam 87 G7 11 54N 109 10 E
Ba Tri, Vietnam 87 G6 10 2N 106 36 E
Ba Xian = Bazhou, China 74 E9 39 8N 116 22 E
Baa, Indonesia 82 D2 10 50 S 123 0 E
Baaba, Î., N. Cal. 133 T18 20 3 S 163 59 E
Baamonde, Spain 42 B3 43 7N 7 44W
Baao, Phil. 80 E4 13 27N 123 22 E
Baar, Switz. 33 B7 47 12N 8 32 E
Baardeere = Bardera, Somali Rep. 120 D2 2 20N 42 27 E
Baarle-Nassau, Belgium 24 C4 51 27N 4 56 E
Bab el Mandeb, Red Sea 98 D3 12 35N 43 25 E
Baba, Bulgaria 50 D7 42 44N 23 59 E
Baba, B. do, Angola 115 E2 14 50 S 12 14 E
Bābā, Koh-i-, Afghan. 91 B2 34 30N 67 0 E
Baba Budan Hills, India 95 H2 13 30N 75 44 E
Baba Burnu, Turkey 49 B8 39 29N 26 2 E
Baba dag, Azerbaijan 61 K9 41 0N 48 19 E
Bābā Kalū, Iran 97 D6 30 7N 50 49 E
Babaçulândia, Brazil 170 C2 7 13 S 47 46W
Babadag, Romania 53 F13 44 53N 28 44 E
Babadağ, Turkey 49 D10 37 49N 28 52 E
Babadayhan, Turkmenistan 66 F7 37 42N 60 23 E
Babaeski, Turkey 51 E11 41 26N 27 6 E
Babahoyo, Ecuador 168 D2 1 40 S 79 30W
Babai = Sarju →, India 93 F9 27 21N 81 23 E
Babak, Phil. 81 H5 7 8N 125 41 E
Babana, Nigeria 113 C5 10 31N 3 46 E
Babanusa, Sudan 107 E2 11 20N 27 48 E
Babar, Algeria 111 A6 35 10N 7 6 E
Babar, Indonesia 83 C3 8 0 S 129 30 E
Babar, Pakistan 92 D3 31 7N 69 32 E
Babar, Kepulauan, Indonesia 83 C4 8 0 S 131 30 E
Babarkach, Pakistan 92 E3 29 45N 68 0 E
Babase I., Papua N. G. 132 B7 4 0 S 153 42 E
Babayevo, Russia 58 C8 59 24N 35 55 E
Babb, U.S.A. 158 B7 48 51N 113 27W
Babenhausen, Germany 31 F4 49 57N 8 57 E
Băbeni, Romania 53 F9 44 59N 24 11 E
Baberu, India 93 G9 25 33N 80 43 E
Babi Besar, Pulau, Malaysia 87 L4 2 25N 103 59 E
Babia Gora, Europe 55 J6 49 38N 19 38 E
Babian Jiang →, China 76 F3 22 55N 101 47 E
Babile, Ethiopia 107 F5 9 16N 42 11 E
Babile Elephant Sanctuary, Ethiopia 120 C2 8 45N 42 20 E
Babimost, Poland 55 F2 52 10N 15 49 E
Babinda, Australia 126 B4 17 20 S 145 56 E
Babine, Canada 142 B3 55 22N 126 37W
Babine →, Canada 142 B3 55 45N 127 44W
Babine L., Canada 142 C3 54 48N 126 0W
Babo, Indonesia 83 B4 2 30 S 133 30 E
Babócsa, Hungary 52 D2 46 2N 17 21 E
Bābol, Iran 97 B7 36 40N 52 50 E
Bābol Sar, Iran 97 B7 36 45N 52 45 E
Babor, Dj., Algeria 111 A6 36 31N 5 25 E
Baborów, Poland 55 H5 50 7N 18 1 E
Baboua, C.A.R. 114 A2 5 49N 14 58 E
Babruysk, Belarus 59 F5 53 10N 29 15 E
Babson Park, U.S.A. 153 H8 27 49N 81 32W
Babuhri, India 92 F3 26 49N 69 43 E
Babuna, Macedonia 50 E5 41 30N 21 40 E
Babura, Nigeria 113 C6 12 51N 8 59 E
Babusar Pass, Pakistan 93 B5 35 12N 73 59 E
Babušnica, Serbia, Yug. 50 C6 43 7N 22 27 E
Babuyan, Phil. 81 F2 10 0N 118 54 E
Babuyan Chan., Phil. 80 B3 18 40N 121 30 E
Babuyan I., Phil. 80 B3 19 32N 121 57 E
Babuyan Is., Phil. 80 B3 19 10N 121 40 E
Babylon, Iraq 101 F11 32 34N 44 22 E
Bač, Serbia, Yug. 52 E4 45 29N 19 17 E
Bâc →, Moldova 53 D14 46 55N 29 26 E
Bac Can, Vietnam 76 F5 22 8N 105 49 E
Bac Giang, Vietnam 76 G6 21 16N 106 11 E
Bac Lieu, Vietnam 87 H5 9 17N 105 43 E
Bac Ninh, Vietnam 76 G6 21 13N 106 4 E
Bac Phan, Vietnam 86 B5 22 0N 105 0 E
Bac Quang, Vietnam 76 F5 22 30N 104 48 E
Bacabal, Brazil 170 B3 4 15 S 44 45W
Bacacay, Phil. 80 E4 13 18N 123 47 E
Bacajá →, Brazil 169 D7 3 25 S 51 50W
Bacalar, Mexico 163 D7 18 50N 87 27W
Bacan, Indonesia 82 B3 0 50 S 127 30 E
Bacan, Kepulauan, Indonesia 82 B3 0 35 S 127 30 E
Bacarra, Phil. 80 B3 18 15N 120 37 E
Bacău, Romania 53 D11 46 35N 26 55 E
Bacău □, Romania 53 D11 46 30N 26 45 E
Baccarat, France 27 D13 48 28N 6 42 E
Bacchus Marsh, Australia 128 D6 37 43 S 144 27 E
Bacerac, Mexico 162 A3 30 18N 108 50W
Băceşti, Romania 53 D12 46 50N 27 11 E
Bach, Austria 33 B10 47 16N 10 25 E
Bach Long Vi, Dao, Vietnam 86 B6 20 10N 107 40 E
Bachaquero, Venezuela 168 B3 9 56N 71 8W
Bacharach, Germany 31 E3 50 3N 7 44 E
Bachelina, Russia 66 D7 57 45N 67 20 E
Bachhwara, India 93 G11 25 35N 85 54 E
Bachuma, Ethiopia 107 F4 6 48N 35 53 E
Bačina, Serbia, Yug. 50 C5 43 42N 21 23 E
Back →, Canada 138 B9 65 10N 104 0W
Bačka Palanka, Serbia, Yug. 52 E4 45 17N 19 27 E
Bačka Topola, Serbia, Yug. 52 E4 45 49N 19 39 E
Bäckebo, Sweden 17 H10 56 53N 16 4 E
Bäckefors, Sweden 17 F6 58 48N 12 9 E
Bäckhammar, Sweden 16 E8 59 10N 14 11 E
Bački Petrovac, Serbia, Yug. 52 E4 45 29N 19 32 E
Backnang, Germany 31 G5 48 56N 9 26 E
Backstairs Passage, Australia 128 C3 35 40 S 138 5 E
Baco, Mt., Phil. 80 E3 12 49N 121 10 E
Bacolod, Phil. 81 F4 10 40N 122 57 E
Bacon, Phil. 80 E5 13 3N 124 3 E
Baconton, U.S.A. 152 D5 31 23N 84 10W
Bacoor, Phil. 80 D3 14 28N 120 56 E
Bacqueville-en-Caux, France 26 C8 49 47N 1 0 E
Bács-Kiskun □, Hungary 52 D4 46 43N 19 30 E
Bácsalmás, Hungary 52 D4 46 8N 19 17 E
Bacuag = Placer, Phil. 81 G5 9 36N 125 38 E
Bacuk, Malaysia 87 J4 6 4N 102 25 E
Bād, Iran 97 C7 33 41N 52 1 E
Bad →, U.S.A. 154 C4 44 21N 100 22W
Bad Aussee, Austria 34 D6 47 43N 13 45 E
Bad Axe, U.S.A. 150 C2 43 48N 83 0W
Bad Bergzabern, Germany 31 F3 49 6N 7 59 E
Bad Berleburg, Germany 30 D4 51 2N 8 26 E
Bad Bevensen, Germany 30 B6 53 5N 10 35 E
Bad Bramstedt, Germany 30 B5 53 55N 9 53 E
Bad Brückenau, Germany 31 E5 50 18N 9 47 E
Bad Doberan, Germany 30 A7 54 6N 11 53 E
Bad Driburg, Germany 30 D5 51 43N 9 1 E
Bad Ems, Germany 31 E3 50 20N 7 43 E
Bad Frankenhausen, Germany 30 D7 51 21N 11 5 E
Bad Freienwalde, Germany 30 C10 52 46N 14 1 E
Bad Goisern, Austria 34 D6 47 38N 13 38 E
Bad Harzburg, Germany 30 D6 51 52N 10 34 E
Bad Hersfeld, Germany 30 E5 50 52N 9 42 E
Bad Hofgastein, Austria 34 D6 47 17N 13 6 E
Bad Homburg, Germany 31 E4 50 13N 8 38 E
Bad Honnef, Germany 30 E3 50 38N 7 13 E
Bad Iburg, Germany 30 C4 52 10N 8 3 E
Bad Ischl, Austria 34 D6 47 44N 13 38 E
Bad Kissingen, Germany 31 E6 50 11N 10 4 E
Bad Königshofen, Germany 31 E6 50 17N 10 28 E
Bad Kreuznach, Germany 31 F3 49 50N 7 51 E
Bad Krozingen, Germany 31 H3 47 54N 7 42 E
Bad Laasphe, Germany 30 E4 50 56N 8 25 E
Bad Lands, U.S.A. 154 D3 43 40N 102 10W
Bad Langensalza, Germany 30 D6 51 5N 10 38 E
Bad Lauterberg, Germany 30 D6 51 38N 10 28 E
Bad Leonfelden, Austria 34 C7 48 31N 14 18 E
Bad Liebenwerda, Germany 30 D9 51 31N 13 24 E
Bad Mergentheim, Germany 31 F5 49 28N 9 42 E
Bad Münstereifel, Germany 30 E2 50 33N 6 46 E
Bad Nauheim, Germany 31 E4 50 21N 8 43 E
Bad Neuenahr-Ahrweiler, Germany 30 E3 50 32N 7 5 E
Bad Neustadt, Germany 31 E6 50 18N 10 13 E
Bad Oeynhausen, Germany 30 C4 52 12N 8 46 E
Bad Oldesloe, Germany 30 B6 53 48N 10 22 E
Bad Orb, Germany 31 E5 50 12N 9 22 E
Bad Pyrmont, Germany 30 D5 51 59N 9 16 E
Bad Ragaz, Switz. 33 C9 47 0N 9 30 E
Bad Reichenhall, Germany 31 H8 47 43N 12 54 E
Bad Säckingen, Germany 31 H3 47 33N 7 56 E
Bad Salzuflen, Germany 30 C4 52 5N 8 45 E
Bad Salzungen, Germany 30 E6 50 48N 10 14 E
Bad Schwartau, Germany 30 B6 53 55N 10 41 E
Bad Segeberg, Germany 30 B6 53 56N 10 17 E
Bad St. Leonhard, Austria 34 E7 46 58N 14 47 E
Bad Tölz, Germany 31 H7 47 45N 11 34 E
Bad Urach, Germany 31 G5 48 29N 9 23 E
Bad Vöslau, Austria 35 D9 47 58N 16 12 E
Bad Waldsee, Germany 31 H5 47 55N 9 45 E
Bad Wildungen, Germany 30 D5 51 6N 9 7 E
Bad Wimpfen, Germany 31 F5 49 13N 9 11 E
Bad Windsheim, Germany 31 F6 49 36N 10 25 E
Bad Zwischenahn, Germany 30 B4 53 12N 8 1 E
Bada Barabil, India 93 H11 22 7N 85 24 E
Badagara, India 95 J2 11 35N 75 40 E
Badagri, Nigeria 113 D5 6 25N 2 55 E
Badajós, L., Brazil 169 D5 3 15 S 62 50W
Badajoz, Spain 43 G4 38 50N 6 59W
Badajoz □, Spain 43 G4 38 40N 6 30W
Badakhshān □, Afghan. 65 E5 36 30N 71 0 E
Badalona, Spain 40 D7 41 26N 2 15 E
Badalzai, Afghan. 92 E1 29 50N 65 35 E
Badami, India 95 G2 15 55N 75 41 E
Badampahar, India 94 C8 22 10N 86 10 E
Badanah, Si. Arabia 96 D4 30 58N 41 30 E
Badarinath, India 93 D8 30 45N 79 30 E
Badarpur, India 90 C4 24 54N 92 36 E
Badas, Kepulauan, Indonesia 84 B3 0 45N 107 5 E
Baddo →, Pakistan 91 D2 28 0N 64 20 E
Bade, Indonesia 83 C5 7 10 S 139 35 E
Badeggi, Nigeria 113 D6 9 1N 6 8 E
Badéguichéri, Niger 113 C6 14 30N 5 22 E
Baden, Austria 35 C9 48 1N 16 13 E
Baden, Switz. 33 B6 47 28N 8 18 E
Baden, U.S.A. 150 F4 40 38N 80 14W
Baden-Baden, Germany 31 G4 48 44N 8 13 E
Baden-Württemberg □, Germany 31 G4 48 20N 8 40 E
Badgastein, Austria 34 D6 47 7N 13 9 E
Badger, Canada 141 C8 49 0N 56 4W
Badger, U.S.A. 160 J7 36 38N 119 1W
Bādghīs □, Afghan. 91 B1 35 0N 63 0 E
Badgingarra Nat. Park, Australia 125 F2 30 23 S 115 22 E
Badgom, India 93 B6 34 1N 74 45 E
Badia Polésine, Italy 45 C8 45 5N 11 29 E
Badian, Phil. 81 G4 9 55N 123 24 E
Badiar, Parc Nat. du, Guinea 112 C2 13 37N 13 11W
Badin, Pakistan 91 D3 24 38N 68 54 E
Badinka, Réserve du, Mali 112 C3 13 31N 9 28W
Badjokola, Dem. Rep. of the Congo 114 B4 3 54N 20 17 E
Badlands Nat. Park, U.S.A. 154 D3 43 38N 102 56W
Badnera, India 94 D3 20 48N 77 44 E
Badoc, Phil. 80 C3 17 56N 120 28 E
Badogo, Mali 112 C3 11 2N 8 13W
Badoumbé, Mali 112 C2 13 42N 10 15W
Badr Ḩunayn, Si. Arabia 98 B2 23 44N 38 46 E
Badrah, Iraq 101 F11 33 6N 45 58 E
Badrinath, India 93 D8 30 44N 79 29 E
Badu I., Papua N. G. 132 F2 10 5 S 142 10 E
Baduen, Somali Rep. 120 C3 7 15N 47 40 E
Badulla, Sri Lanka 95 L5 7 1N 81 7 E
Badung, Selat, Indonesia 79 K18 8 40 S 115 22 E
Badupi, Burma 90 E4 21 36N 93 27 E
Badvel, India 95 G4 14 45N 79 3 E
Baena, Spain 43 H6 37 37N 4 20W
Baerami, N.S.W., Australia 129 B9 32 24 S 150 29 E
Baerami, N.S.W., Australia 129 B9 32 27 S 150 27 E
Baetov, Kyrgyzstan 65 C7 41 13N 74 54 E
Baeza, Ecuador 168 D2 0 25 S 77 53W
Baeza, Spain 43 H7 37 57N 3 25W
Bafang, Cameroon 113 D7 5 9N 10 11 E
Bafatá, Guinea-Biss. 112 C2 12 8N 14 40W
Baffin B., Canada 139 A13 72 0N 64 0W
Baffin I., Canada 139 B12 68 0N 75 0W
Bafia, Cameroon 113 E7 4 40N 11 10 E
Bafilo, Togo 113 D5 9 22N 1 22 E
Bafing →, Mali 112 C2 13 49N 10 50W
Bafing, Parc Nat. du, Mali 112 C2 12 50N 10 28W
Bafliyūn, Syria 96 B3 36 37N 36 59 E
Bafoulabé, Mali 112 C2 13 50N 10 55W
Bafoussam, Cameroon 113 D7 5 28N 10 25 E
Bāfq, Iran 97 D7 31 40N 55 25 E
Bafra, Turkey 100 B6 41 34N 35 54 E
Bafra Burnu, Turkey 100 B7 41 45N 36 2 E
Bāft, Iran 97 D8 29 15N 56 38 E
Bafut, Cameroon 113 D7 6 6N 10 2 E
Bafwasende, Dem. Rep. of the Congo 118 B2 1 3N 27 5 E
Bagaat, Î., N. Cal. 133 K4 20 40 S 166 15 E
Bagabag, Phil. 80 C3 16 30N 121 15 E
Bagabag I., Papua N. G. 132 C4 4 48 S 146 14 E
Bagac, Phil. 80 D3 14 36N 120 23 E
Bagac Bay, Phil. 80 D3 14 36N 120 20 E
Bagalkot, India 95 F2 16 10N 75 40 E
Bagam, Niger 113 B6 15 43N 6 35 E
Bagamanoc, Phil. 80 E5 13 57N 124 17 E
Bagamoyo, Tanzania 118 D4 6 28 S 38 55 E
Bagan Datoh, Malaysia 87 L3 3 59N 100 47 E
Bagan Serai, Malaysia 87 K3 5 1N 100 32 E
Baganga, Phil. 81 H6 7 34N 126 33 E
Bagani, Namibia 116 B3 18 7 S 21 41 E
Bagansiapiapi, Indonesia 84 B2 2 12N 100 50 E
Bagasra, India 92 J4 21 30N 71 0 E
Bagata, Dem. Rep. of the Congo 114 C3 3 44 S 17 57 E
Bagaud, India 92 H6 22 19N 75 53 E
Bagawi, Sudan 107 E3 12 20N 34 18 E
Bagbag, Sudan 107 D3 15 23N 31 30 E
Bagdad, Calif., U.S.A. 161 L11 34 35N 115 53W
Bagdad, Fla., U.S.A. 153 E2 30 36N 87 2W
Bagdarin, Russia 67 D12 54 26N 113 36 E
Bagé, Brazil 175 C5 31 20 S 54 15W
Bagenalstown = Muine Bheag, Ireland 23 D5 52 42N 6 58W
Bagepalli, India 95 H3 13 47N 77 47 E
Bagevadi, India 94 F2 16 35N 75 58 E
Baggao, Phil. 80 C3 17 56N 121 46 E
Baggs, U.S.A. 158 F10 41 2N 107 39W
Bagh, Pakistan 93 C5 33 59N 73 45 E
Baghain →, India 93 G9 25 32N 81 1 E
Baghdād, Iraq 101 F11 33 20N 44 30 E
Bagherhat, Bangla. 90 D2 22 40N 89 47 E
Bagheria, Italy 46 D6 38 5N 13 30 E
Baghlān, Afghan. 91 A3 32 12N 68 46 E
Baghlān □, Afghan. 91 B3 36 0N 68 30 E
Bagley, U.S.A. 154 B7 47 32N 95 24W
Bagn, Norway 18 D6 60 49N 9 34 E
Bagnara Cálabra, Italy 47 D8 38 17N 15 48 E
Bagnasco, Italy 44 D5 44 18N 8 2 E
Bagnell Dam, U.S.A. 156 F4 38 14N 92 36W
Bagnères-de-Bigorre, France 28 E4 43 5N 0 9 E
Bagnères-de-Luchon, France 28 F4 42 47N 0 38 E
Bagni di Lucca, Italy 44 D7 44 1N 10 35 E
Bagno di Romagna, Italy 45 E8 43 50N 11 57 E
Bagnoles-de-l'Orne, France 26 D6 48 32N 0 25W
Bagnols-sur-Cèze, France 29 D8 44 10N 4 36 E
Bagnorégio, Italy 45 F9 42 37N 12 5 E
Bago = Pegu, Burma 90 G6 17 20N 96 29 E
Bago, Phil. 81 F4 10 32N 122 50 E
Bagodar, India 93 G11 24 5N 85 52 E
Bagrationovsk, Russia 15 J19 54 23N 20 39 E
Bagrdan, Serbia, Yug. 50 B5 44 5N 21 11 E
Bagua, Peru 172 B2 5 35 S 78 22W
Baguio, Phil. 80 C3 16 26N 120 34 E
Bağyurdu, Turkey 49 C9 38 25N 27 41 E
Bagzane, Monts, Niger 113 B6 17 43N 8 45 E
Bah, India 93 F8 26 53N 78 36 E
Bahabón de Esgueva, Spain 42 D7 41 52N 3 43W
Bahadurabad Ghat, Bangla. 90 C2 25 11N 89 44 E
Bahadurganj, India 93 F12 26 16N 87 49 E
Bahadurgarh, India 92 E7 28 40N 76 57 E
Bahama, Canal Viejo de, W. Indies 164 B4 22 10N 77 30W
Bahamas ■, N. Amer. 165 B5 24 0N 75 0W
Bahār, Iran 101 E13 34 54N 48 26 E
Baharak, Afghan. 65 E5 37 0N 70 53 E
Baharampur, India 93 G13 24 2N 88 27 E
Baharîya, El Wâhât al, Egypt 106 B2 28 0N 28 50 E
Bahawalnagar, Pakistan 91 C4 30 0N 73 15 E
Bahawalpur, Pakistan 91 C3 29 24N 71 40 E
Bahçe, Turkey 100 D7 37 13N 36 34 E
Bahçecik, Turkey 51 F13 40 41N 29 44 E
Baheli, Phil. 81 F2 10 0N 118 47 E
Baheri, India 93 E8 28 45N 79 34 E
Bahgul →, India 93 F8 27 45N 79 36 E
Bahi, Tanzania 118 D4 5 58 S 35 21 E
Bahi Swamp, Tanzania 118 D4 6 10 S 35 0 E
Bahía = Salvador, Brazil 171 D4 13 0 S 38 30W
Bahía □, Brazil 171 D3 12 0 S 42 0W
Bahía, Is. de la, Honduras 164 C2 16 45N 86 15W
Bahía Blanca, Argentina 174 D3 38 35 S 62 13W
Bahía de Caráquez, Ecuador 168 D1 0 40 S 80 27W
Bahía Honda, Cuba 164 B3 22 54N 83 10W
Bahía Laura, Argentina 176 C3 48 10 S 66 30W
Bahía Mansa, Chile 176 B2 40 33 S 73 46W
Bahía Negra, Paraguay 173 E6 20 5 S 58 5W
Bahir Dar, Ethiopia 107 E4 11 37N 37 10 E
Bahlah, Oman 99 B7 22 58N 57 18 E
Bahmanzād, Iran 97 D6 31 15N 51 47 E
Bahmer, Algeria 111 C4 27 32N 0 10W
Bahr el Ahmar □, Sudan 106 D4 20 0N 35 0 E
Bahr el Ghazâl □, Sudan 107 F2 7 0N 28 0 E
Bahr el Jabal □, Sudan 107 G3 4 0N 31 0 E
Bahraich, India 93 F9 27 38N 81 37 E
Bahrain ■, Asia 97 E6 26 0N 50 35 E
Bahror, India 92 F7 27 51N 76 20 E
Bāhū Kalāt, Iran 97 E9 25 43N 61 25 E
Bai, Mali 112 C4 13 35N 3 28W
Bai Bung, Mui = Ca Mau, Mui, Vietnam 87 H5 8 38N 104 44 E
Bai Duc, Vietnam 86 C5 18 3N 105 49 E
Bai Thuong, Vietnam 86 C5 19 54N 105 23 E
Baia de Aramă, Romania 52 E7 45 0N 22 50 E
Baía dos Tigres, Angola 115 F2 16 40 S 11 47 E
Baia Farta, Angola 115 E2 12 40 S 13 11 E
Baia Mare, Romania 53 C8 47 40N 23 35 E
Baia-Sprie, Romania 53 C8 47 41N 23 43 E
Baião, Brazil 170 B2 2 40 S 49 40W
Baïbokoum, Chad 109 G3 7 46N 15 43 E
Baicheng, China 75 B12 45 38N 122 42 E
Băicoi, Romania 53 E10 45 3N 25 52 E
Baidoa, Somali Rep. 120 D2 3 8N 43 30 E
Baie Comeau, Canada 141 C6 49 12N 68 10W
Baie-St-Paul, Canada 141 C5 47 28N 70 32W
Baie Ste-Anne, Seychelles 121 b 4 18 S 55 45 E
Baie Trinité, Canada 141 C6 49 25N 67 20W
Baie Verte, Canada 141 C8 49 55N 56 12W
Baignes-Ste-Radegonde, France 28 C3 45 23N 0 25W
Baigneux-les-Juifs, France 27 E11 47 31N 4 39 E
Baihar, India 93 H9 22 6N 80 33 E
Baihe, China 74 H6 32 50N 110 5 E
Ba'ījī, Iraq 101 E10 35 0N 43 30 E
Baijnath, India 93 E8 29 55N 79 37 E
Baikal, L. = Baykal, Oz., Russia 67 D11 53 0N 108 0 E
Baikunthpur, India 93 H10 23 15N 82 33 E
Bailadila, Mt., India 94 E5 18 43N 81 15 E
Baile Atha Cliath = Dublin, Ireland 23 C5 53 21N 6 15W
Băile Govora, Romania 53 E9 45 5N 24 11 E
Băile Herculane, Romania 52 F7 44 53N 22 26 E
Băile Olăneşti, Romania 53 E9 45 12N 24 14 E
Băile Tuşnad, Romania 53 D10 46 9N 25 51 E
Bailén, Spain 43 G7 38 8N 3 48W
Băileşti, Romania 53 F8 44 1N 23 20 E
Bailhongal, India 95 G2 15 55N 74 53 E
Bailique, Ilha, Brazil 170 A2 1 2N 49 58W
Bailugh, Afghan. 91 B2 32 40N 66 47 E
Bailundo, Angola 115 E3 12 10 S 15 50 E
Baima, China 76 A3 33 0N 100 26 E
Baimuru, Papua N. G. 132 D3 7 35 S 144 51 E
Bain-de-Bretagne, France 26 E5 47 50N 1 40W
Bainbridge, Ga., U.S.A. 152 E5 30 55N 84 35W
Bainbridge, Ind., U.S.A. 157 E10 39 46N 86 49W
Bainbridge, N.Y., U.S.A. 151 D9 42 18N 75 29W
Bainbridge, Ohio, U.S.A. 157 E13 39 14N 83 16W
Baing, Indonesia 82 D2 10 14 S 120 34 E
Bainiu, China 74 H7 32 50N 112 15 E
Bainyik, Papua N. G. 132 B2 3 40 S 143 4 E
Baiona, Spain 42 C2 42 6N 8 52W
Bā'ir, Jordan 103 E5 30 45N 36 55 E
Baird Mts., U.S.A. 144 C8 67 0N 160 0W
Bairin Youqi, China 75 C10 43 30N 118 35 E
Bairin Zuoqi, China 75 C10 43 58N 119 15 E
Bairnsdale, Australia 129 D7 37 48 S 147 36 E
Bais, Phil. 81 G4 9 35N 123 7 E
Baisha, China 74 G7 34 20N 112 32 E
Baissa, Nigeria 113 D7 7 14N 10 38 E
Baitadi, Nepal 93 E9 29 35N 80 25 E
Baitarani →, India 94 D8 20 45N 86 48 E
Baixa Grande, Brazil 171 D3 11 57 S 40 11W
Baixo-Longa, Angola 115 F3 15 41 S 18 45 E
Baiyer River, Papua N. G. 132 C3 5 32 S 144 9 E
Baiyin, China 74 F3 36 45N 104 14 E
Baiyü, China 76 B2 31 16N 98 50 E
Baiyu Shan, China 74 F4 37 15N 107 30 E
Baiyuda, Sudan 106 D3 17 35N 32 7 E
Baj Baj, India 93 H13 22 30N 88 5 E
Baja, Hungary 52 D3 46 12N 18 59 E
Baja, Pta., Chile 172 b 27 10 S 109 22W
Baja, Pta., Mexico 162 B1 29 50N 116 0W
Baja California, Mexico 162 A1 31 10N 115 12W
Baja California □, Mexico 162 B2 30 0N 115 0W
Baja California Sur □, Mexico 162 B2 25 50N 111 50W
Bajag, India 93 H9 22 40N 81 21 E
Bajamar, Canary Is. 9 e1 28 33N 16 20W
Bajana, India 92 H4 23 7N 71 49 E
Bajatrejo, Indonesia 79 J17 8 29 S 114 19 E
Bajawa, Indonesia 82 C2 8 47 S 120 59 E
Bajera, Indonesia 79 J18 8 31 S 115 2 E
Bājgīrān, Iran 97 B8 37 36N 58 24 E
Bājil, Yemen 98 D3 15 4N 43 17 E
Bajimba, Mt., Australia 127 D5 29 17 S 152 6 E
Bajina Bašta, Serbia, Yug. 50 C3 43 58N 19 35 E
Bajmok, Serbia, Yug. 52 E4 45 57N 19 24 E
Bajo Caracoles, Argentina 176 C2 47 27 S 70 56W
Bajo Nuevo, Caribbean 164 C4 15 40N 78 50W
Bajoga, Nigeria 113 C7 10 57N 11 20 E
Bajool, Australia 126 C5 23 40 S 150 35 E
Bak, Hungary 52 D1 46 43N 16 51 E
Bakal, Russia 64 D7 54 56N 58 48 E
Bakala, C.A.R. 114 A4 6 15N 20 20 E
Bakanas = Baqanas, Kazakstan 65 A8 44 50N 76 15 E
Bakar, Croatia 45 C11 45 18N 14 32 E
Bakel, Senegal 112 C2 14 56N 12 20W
Baker, Calif., U.S.A. 161 K10 35 16N 116 4W
Baker, Fla., U.S.A. 153 E3 30 48N 86 41W
Baker, Mont., U.S.A. 154 B2 46 22N 104 17W
Baker, Canal, Chile 176 C2 47 45 S 74 45W
Baker, L., Canada 138 B10 64 0N 96 0W
Baker City, U.S.A. 158 D5 44 47N 117 50W
Baker I., Pac. Oc. 134 G10 0 10N 176 35W
Baker I., U.S.A. 142 B2 55 20N 133 40W
Baker L., Australia 125 E4 26 54 S 126 5 E
Baker Lake, Canada 138 B10 64 20N 96 3W
Baker Mt., U.S.A. 158 B3 48 50N 121 49W
Bakere, Dem. Rep. of the Congo 114 B4 1 36N 23 50 E
Bakerhill, U.S.A. 152 D4 31 47N 85 18W
Bakers Creek, Australia 126 C4 21 13 S 149 7 E
Baker's Dozen Is., Canada 140 A4 56 45N 78 45W
Bakersfield, Calif., U.S.A. 161 K8 35 23N 119 1W
Bakersfield, Vt., U.S.A. 151 B12 44 45N 72 48W
Bakhchysaray, Ukraine 59 K7 44 40N 33 45 E
Bakhmach, Ukraine 59 G7 51 10N 32 45 E
Bakht, Uzbekistan 65 C4 40 43N 68 42 E
Bākhtarān, Iran 101 E12 34 23N 47 0 E
Bākhtarān □, Iran 96 C5 34 0N 46 30 E
Bakı, Azerbaijan 61 K9 40 29N 49 56 E
Bakır →, Turkey 49 C9 38 55N 27 0 E
Bakırdaği, Turkey 100 C6 38 13N 35 46 E
Bakkafjörður, Iceland 11 A12 66 2N 14 48W
Bakkaflói, Iceland 11 A12 66 10N 14 45W
Baklan, Turkey 49 C11 38 0N 29 36 E
Bako, Ethiopia 107 F4 5 51N 36 23 E
Bako, Ivory C. 112 D3 9 8N 7 40W
Bakony, Hungary 52 C2 47 10N 17 30 E
Bakony Forest = Bakony, Hungary 52 C2 47 10N 17 30 E
Bakori, Nigeria 113 C6 11 34N 7 25 E
Bakouma, C.A.R. 114 A4 5 40N 22 56 E
Bakpakty = Baqbaqty, Kazakstan 65 A8 44 35N 76 40 E
Baksan, Russia 61 J6 43 42N 43 32 E
Bakswaho, India 93 G8 24 15N 79 18 E
Baku = Bakı, Azerbaijan 61 K9 40 29N 49 56 E
Bakundi, Nigeria 113 D7 8 2N 10 45 E
Bakutis Coast, Antarctica 7 D15 74 0 S 120 0W
Bakwa-Kenge, Dem. Rep. of the Congo 115 C4 4 51 S 22 4 E
Baky = Bakı, Azerbaijan 61 K9 40 29N 49 56 E
Bala, Canada 150 A5 45 1N 79 37W
Bala, Senegal 112 C2 14 1N 13 8W
Bâlâ, Turkey 100 C5 39 32N 33 6 E
Bala, U.K. 20 E4 52 54N 3 36W
Bala, L., U.K. 20 E4 52 53N 3 37W
Bālā Morghāb, Afghan. 91 B1 35 35N 63 20 E
Balabac, Phil. 81 H1 7 59N 117 4 E
Balabac I., Phil. 81 G1 8 0N 117 0 E
Balabac Str., E. Indies 78 C5 7 53N 117 5 E
Balabagh, Afghan. 92 B4 34 25N 70 12 E
Ba'labakk, Lebanon 103 B5 34 0N 36 10 E
Balabalangan, Kepulauan, Indonesia 85 C5 2 20 S 117 30 E
Balabio, Î., N. Cal. 133 T18 20 7 S 164 11 E
Bălăciţa, Romania 53 F8 44 23N 23 8 E
Balad, Iraq 101 F11 34 1N 44 9 E
Balad Rūz, Iraq 101 F11 33 42N 45 5 E
Bālādeh, Fārs, Iran 97 D6 29 17N 51 56 E
Bālādeh, Māzandaran, Iran 97 B6 36 12N 51 48 E
Balaghat, India 94 D5 21 49N 80 12 E
Balaghat Ra., India 94 E3 18 50N 76 30 E
Balaguer, Spain 40 D5 41 50N 0 50 E
Balaka, Dem. Rep. of the Congo 115 C3 4 52 S 19 57 E
Balakété, C.A.R. 114 A3 6 56N 19 54 E
Balakhna, Russia 60 B6 56 25N 43 32 E
Balaklava, Australia 128 C3 34 7 S 138 22 E
Balaklava, Ukraine 59 K7 44 30N 33 30 E
Balakliya, Ukraine 59 H9 49 28N 36 55 E
Balakovo, Russia 60 D8 52 4N 47 55 E
Balamau, India 93 F9 27 10N 80 21 E
Balamban, Phil. 81 F4 10 30N 123 43 E
Balambangan, Malaysia 85 A5 7 17N 116 55 E
Bălan, Romania 53 D10 46 39N 25 49 E
Balancán, Mexico 163 D6 17 48N 91 32W
Balanga, Phil. 80 D3 14 41N 120 32 E
Balangala, Dem. Rep. of the Congo 114 B3 0 30N 19 56 E
Balangiga, Phil. 81 F5 11 7N 125 23 E
Balangir, India 94 D6 20 43N 83 35 E
Balaoan, Phil. 80 C3 16 49N 120 24 E
Balapur, India 94 D3 20 40N 76 45 E
Balashov, Russia 60 E6 51 30N 43 10 E
Balasinor, India 92 H5 22 57N 73 23 E
Balasore = Baleshwar, India 94 D8 21 35N 87 3 E
Balassagyarmat, Hungary 52 B4 48 4N 19 15 E
Balât, Egypt 106 B2 25 36N 29 19 E
Balaton, Hungary 52 D2 46 50N 17 40 E
Balatonboglár, Hungary 52 D2 46 46N 17 40 E
Balatonfüred, Hungary 52 D2 46 58N 17 54 E
Balatonszentgyörgy, Hungary 52 D2 46 41N 17 19 E
Balayan, Phil. 80 E3 13 57N 120 44 E
Balazote, Spain 41 G2 38 54N 2 9W
Balbalan, Phil. 80 C3 17 27N 121 12 E
Balbi, Mt., Papua N. G. 132 C8 5 55 S 154 58 E
Balbieriškis, Lithuania 54 D10 54 32N 23 52 E
Balbigny, France 29 C8 45 49N 4 11 E
Balbina, Brazil 169 D6 1 58 S 59 29W
Balbina, Reprêsa de, Brazil 169 D6 2 0 S 59 30W

Barail Range 187

Balboa, Panama 164 E4 8 57N 79 34W
Balbriggan, Ireland 23 C5 53 37N 6 11W
Balcarce, Argentina 174 D4 38 0 S 58 10W
Balcarres, Canada 143 C8 50 50N 103 35W
Bălceşti, Romania 53 F8 44 37N 23 57 E
Balchik, Bulgaria 51 C12 43 28N 28 11 E
Balclutha, N.Z. 131 G4 46 15 S 169 45 E
Balcones Escarpment, U.S.A. 155 L5 29 30N 99 15W
Balçova, Turkey 49 C9 38 22N 27 4 E
Bald Hd., Australia 125 G2 35 6 S 118 1 E
Bald I., Australia 125 F2 34 57 S 118 27 E
Bald Knob, U.S.A. 155 H9 35 19N 91 34W
Baldock L., Canada 143 B9 56 33N 97 57W
Baldwin, Fla., U.S.A. 152 E8 30 18N 81 59W
Baldwin, Mich., U.S.A. 148 D3 43 54N 85 51W
Baldwin, Pa., U.S.A. 150 F5 40 23N 79 59W
Baldwinsville, U.S.A. 151 C8 43 10N 76 20W
Baldy Mt., U.S.A. 158 B9 48 9N 109 39W
Baldy Peak, U.S.A. 159 K9 33 54N 109 34W
Bale, Croatia 45 C10 45 4N 13 46 E
Bale, Ethiopia 107 F5 6 57N 40 8 E
Bale □, Ethiopia 107 F5 6 20N 41 30 E
Bale Mountains Nat. Park, Ethiopia 107 F4 6 59N 39 52 E
Baleares, Is., Spain 38 B4 39 30N 3 0 E
Balearic Is. = Baleares, Is., Spain 38 B4 39 30N 3 0 E
Balease, Indonesia 82 B2 2 24 S 120 33 E
Baleia, Pta. da, Brazil 171 E4 17 40 S 39 7W
Baleine = Whale →, Canada 141 A6 58 15N 67 40W
Băleni, Romania 53 E12 45 48N 27 51 E
Baler, Phil. 80 D3 15 46N 121 34 E
Baler Bay, Phil. 80 D3 15 50N 121 35 E
Balerna, Switz. 33 E8 45 52N 9 0 E
Baleshare, U.K. 22 D1 57 31N 7 22W
Baleshwar, India 94 D8 21 35N 87 3 E
Balestrand, Norway 18 C3 61 11N 6 31 E
Balezino, Russia 60 B11 58 2N 53 6 E
Balfate, Honduras 164 C2 15 48N 86 25W
Balfour Channel, Solomon Is. 133 M9 8 43 S 157 27 E
Balharshah, India 94 E4 19 50N 79 23 E
Bali, Cameroon 113 D7 5 54N 10 0 E
Bali, Dem. Rep. of the Congo 114 C3 2 50 S 16 12 E
Balí, Greece 39 E5 35 25N 24 47 E
Bali, India 92 G5 25 11N 73 17 E
Bali, Indonesia 85 D4 8 20 S 115 0 E
Bali □, Indonesia 85 D4 8 20 S 115 0 E
Bali, Selat, Indonesia 85 D4 8 18 S 114 25 E
Bali Sea, Indonesia 85 D5 8 0 S 115 0 E
Balia, S. Leone 112 D2 9 22N 11 1W
Baliapal, India 93 J12 21 40N 87 17 E
Balicuatro Is., Phil. 80 E5 12 39N 124 24 E
Baliem →, Indonesia 83 C5 5 44 S 138 8 E
Baligród, Poland 55 J9 49 20N 22 17 E
Baliguda, India 94 D6 20 12N 83 55 E
Balik Pulau, Malaysia 87 c 5 21N 100 14 E
Balikeşir, Turkey 49 B9 39 39N 27 53 E
Balikeşir □, Turkey 49 B9 39 45N 28 0 E
Balıkılıçeşme, Turkey 51 F11 40 18N 27 5 E
Balikpapan, Indonesia 85 C5 1 10 S 116 55 E
Balimbing, Phil. 81 J2 5 5N 119 58 E
Balimo, Papua N. G. 132 E2 8 6 S 142 57 E
Baling, Malaysia 87 K3 5 41N 100 55 E
Balingasag, Phil. 81 G5 8 45N 124 47 E
Balingen, Germany 31 G4 48 16N 8 51 E
Balinţ, Romania 52 E6 45 48N 21 54 E
Balintang Channel, Phil. 80 B3 19 49N 121 40 E
Balintang I., Phil. 80 B4 19 58N 122 9 E
Baliza, Brazil 173 D7 16 0 S 52 20W
Baljurshī, Si. Arabia 98 C3 19 51N 41 33 E
Balkan Mts. = Stara Planina, Bulgaria 50 C7 43 15N 23 0 E
Balkh, Afghan. 65 E3 36 44N 66 47 E
Balkh □, Afghan. 65 E3 36 50N 67 0 E
Balkhash = Balqash, Kazakstan 66 E8 46 50N 74 50 E
Balkhash, Ozero = Balqash Köl, Kazakstan 66 E8 46 0N 74 50 E
Balkonda, India 94 E4 18 52N 78 21 E
Ballachulish, U.K. 22 E3 56 41N 5 8W
Balladonia, Australia 125 F3 32 27 S 123 51 E
Ballaghaderreen, Ireland 23 C3 53 55N 8 34W
Ballan, Australia 128 D6 37 35 S 144 13 E
Ballarat, Australia 128 D5 37 33 S 143 50 E
Ballard, L., Australia 125 E3 29 20 S 120 40 E
Ballater, U.K. 22 D5 57 3N 3 3W
Ballé, Mali 112 B3 15 18N 8 33W
Ballenas, Canal de, Mexico 162 B2 29 10N 113 45W
Balleny Is., Antarctica 7 C11 66 30 S 163 0 E
Balleroy, France 26 C6 49 11N 0 50W
Ballerup, Denmark 17 J6 55 44N 12 21 E
Ballı, Turkey 51 F11 40 50N 27 3 E
Ballia, India 93 G11 25 46N 84 12 E
Ballina, Australia 127 D5 28 50 S 153 31 E
Ballina, Ireland 23 B2 54 7N 9 9W
Ballinasloe, Ireland 23 C3 53 20N 8 13W
Ballinger, U.S.A. 155 K5 31 45N 99 57W
Ballinrobe, Ireland 23 C2 53 38N 9 13W
Ballinskelligs B., Ireland 23 E1 51 48N 10 13W
Ballon, France 26 D7 48 10N 0 14 E
Ballsh, Albania 50 F3 40 36N 19 44 E
Ballston Spa, U.S.A. 151 D11 43 0N 73 51W
Ballycastle, U.K. 23 A5 55 12N 6 15W
Ballyclare, U.K. 23 B5 54 46N 6 0W
Ballyhaunis, Ireland 23 C3 53 46N 8 46W
Ballymena, U.K. 23 B5 54 52N 6 17W
Ballymoney, U.K. 23 A5 55 5N 6 31W
Ballymote, Ireland 23 B3 54 5N 8 31W
Ballynahinch, U.K. 23 B6 54 24N 5 54W
Ballyquintin Pt., U.K. 23 B6 54 20N 5 30W
Ballyshannon, Ireland 23 B3 54 30N 8 11W
Balmaceda, Chile 176 C2 46 0 S 71 50W
Balmaseda, Spain 40 B1 43 11N 3 12W
Balmazújváros, Hungary 52 C6 47 37N 21 21 E
Balmertown, Canada 143 C10 51 4N 93 41W
Balmhorn, Switz. 32 D5 46 26N 7 42 E
Balmoral, Australia 128 D4 37 15 S 141 48 E
Balmorhea, U.S.A. 155 K3 30 59N 103 45W
Balochistan = Baluchistan □, Pakistan 91 D2 27 30N 65 0 E
Balod, India 94 D5 20 44N 81 13 E
Balombo, Angola 115 E2 12 21 S 14 46 E
Balombo →, Angola 115 E2 11 57 S 13 46 E
Balonne →, Australia 127 D4 28 47 S 147 56 E
Balotra, India 92 G5 25 50N 72 14 E
Balpyq Bī, Kazakstan 65 A9 44 52N 78 12 E
Balqash, Kazakstan 66 E8 46 50N 74 50 E
Balqash Köl, Kazakstan 66 E8 46 0N 74 50 E
Balrampur, India 93 F10 27 30N 82 20 E
Balranald, Australia 128 C5 34 38 S 143 33 E
Balş, Romania 53 F9 44 22N 24 5 E
Balsapuerto, Peru 172 B2 5 48 S 76 33W
Balsas, Mexico 163 D5 18 0N 99 40W
Balsas →, Maranhão, Brazil 170 C3 7 15 S 44 35W
Balsas →, Tocantins, Brazil 170 C2 9 58 S 47 52W
Balsas →, Mexico 162 D4 17 55N 102 10W
Bålsta, Sweden 16 E11 59 35N 17 30 E
Balsthal, Switz. 32 B5 47 19N 7 41 E
Balston Spa, U.S.A. 151 D11 43 0N 73 52W
Balta, Romania 52 F7 44 54N 22 38 E
Balta, Ukraine 59 J5 48 2N 29 45 E
Baltanás, Spain 42 D6 41 56N 4 15W
Bălţi, Moldova 53 C12 47 48N 27 58 E
Baltic Sea, Europe 15 H18 57 0N 19 0 E
Baltîm, Egypt 106 H7 31 35N 31 10 E
Baltimore, Ireland 23 E2 51 29N 9 22W
Baltimore, Md., U.S.A. 148 F7 39 17N 76 37W
Baltimore, Ohio, U.S.A. 150 G2 39 51N 82 36W
Baltit, Pakistan 93 A6 36 15N 74 40 E
Baltiysk, Russia 15 J18 54 41N 19 58 E
Baltra, I., Ecuador 172 a 0 26 S 90 16W
Baltrum, Germany 30 B3 53 43N 7 24 E
Baluan I., Papua N. G. 132 B4 2 33 S 147 17 E
Baluchistan □, Pakistan 91 D2 27 30N 65 0 E
Balud, Phil. 80 E4 12 2N 123 12 E
Balurghat, India 90 C2 25 15N 88 44 E
Balvi, Latvia 15 H22 57 8N 27 15 E
Balya, Turkey 49 B9 39 44N 27 35 E
Balykchy, Kyrgyzstan 65 B8 42 26N 76 12 E
Balzar, Ecuador 168 D2 2 2 S 79 54W
Bam, Iran 97 D8 29 7N 58 14 E
Bama, China 76 E6 24 8N 107 12 E
Bama, Nigeria 113 C7 11 33N 13 41 E
Bamaga, Australia 126 A3 10 50 S 142 25 E
Bamaji L., Canada 140 B1 51 9N 91 25W
Bamako, Mali 112 C3 12 34N 7 55W
Bamba, Dem. Rep. of the Congo 115 D3 5 45 S 18 23 E
Bamba, Mali 113 B4 17 5N 1 24W
Bambamarca, Peru 172 B2 6 36 S 78 32W
Bambang, Phil. 80 C3 16 23N 121 6 E
Bambannan I., Phil. 81 J3 5 37N 120 17 E
Bambara Maoundé, Mali 112 B4 13 26N 4 3W
Bambari, C.A.R. 114 A4 5 40N 20 35 E
Bambaroo, Australia 126 B4 18 50 S 146 10 E
Bambaya, Guinea 112 D2 10 55N 13 38W
Bamberg, Germany 31 F6 49 54N 10 54 E
Bamberg, U.S.A. 152 B8 33 18N 81 2W
Bambesi, Ethiopia 107 F3 9 45N 34 40 E
Bambey, Senegal 112 C1 14 42N 16 28W
Bambili, Dem. Rep. of the Congo 118 B2 3 40N 26 0 E
Bambinga, Dem. Rep. of the Congo 114 C3 3 43 S 18 53 E
Bambio, C.A.R. 114 B3 3 55N 16 57 E
Bamboi, Ghana 112 D4 8 13N 2 1W
Bambouti, C.A.R. 114 A5 5 24N 27 12 E
Bambuí, Brazil 171 F2 20 1 S 45 58W
Bamenda, Cameroon 113 D7 5 57N 10 11 E
Bamfield, Canada 142 D3 48 45N 125 10W
Bāmīān □, Afghan. 91 B2 35 0N 67 0 E
Bamiancheng, China 75 C13 43 15N 124 2 E
Bamingui, C.A.R. 114 A4 7 34N 20 11 E
Bamingui →, C.A.R. 114 A3 8 33N 19 5 E
Bamingui-Bangoran, Parc Nat. du, C.A.R. 114 A3 8 30N 19 46 E
Bamkin, Cameroon 113 D7 6 3N 11 27 E
Bampan, Phil. 80 D3 15 40N 120 20 E
Bampūr, Iran 97 E9 27 15N 60 21 E
Bamu →, Papua N. G. 132 E2 8 1 S 143 33 E
Ban, Burkina Faso 112 C4 14 5N 2 27W
Ban Ao Tu Khun, Thailand 87 a 8 9N 98 20 E
Ban Ban, Laos 86 C4 19 31N 103 30 E
Ban Bang Hin, Thailand 87 H2 9 32N 98 35 E
Ban Bang Khu, Thailand 87 a 7 57N 98 23 E
Ban Bang Rong, Thailand 87 a 8 3N 98 25 E
Ban Bo Phut, Thailand 87 b 9 33N 100 2 E
Ban Chaweng, Thailand 87 b 9 32N 100 3 E
Ban Chiang Klang, Thailand 86 C3 19 25N 100 55 E
Ban Chik, Laos 86 D4 17 15N 102 22 E
Ban Choho, Thailand 86 E4 15 2N 102 9 E
Ban Dan Lan Hoi, Thailand 86 D2 17 0N 99 35 E
Ban Don = Surat Thani, Thailand 87 H2 9 6N 99 20 E
Ban Don, Vietnam 86 F6 12 53N 107 48 E
Ban Don, Ao →, Thailand 87 H2 9 20N 99 25 E
Ban Dong, Thailand 86 C3 19 30N 100 59 E
Ban Hong, Thailand 86 C2 18 18N 98 50 E
Ban Hua Thanon, Thailand 87 b 9 26N 100 1 E
Ban Kaeng, Thailand 86 D3 17 29N 100 7 E
Ban Kantang, Thailand 87 J2 7 25N 99 31 E
Ban Karon, Thailand 87 a 7 51N 98 18 E
Ban Kata, Thailand 87 a 7 50N 98 18 E
Ban Keun, Laos 86 C4 18 22N 102 35 E
Ban Khai, Thailand 86 F3 12 46N 101 18 E
Ban Kheun, Laos 86 B3 20 13N 101 7 E
Ban Khlong Khian, Thailand 87 a 8 10N 98 26 E
Ban Khlong Kua, Thailand 87 J3 6 57N 100 8 E
Ban Khuan, Thailand 87 a 8 20N 98 25 E
Ban Khuan Mao, Thailand 87 J2 7 50N 99 37 E
Ban Ko Yai Chim, Thailand 87 G2 11 17N 99 26 E
Ban Kok, Thailand 86 D4 16 40N 103 40 E
Ban Laem, Thailand 86 F2 13 13N 99 59 E
Ban Lamai, Thailand 87 b 9 28N 100 3 E
Ban Lao Ngam, Laos 86 E6 15 28N 106 10 E
Ban Le Kathe, Thailand 86 E2 15 49N 98 53 E
Ban Lo Po Noi, Thailand 87 a 8 1N 98 34 E
Ban Mae Chedi, Thailand 86 C2 19 11N 99 31 E
Ban Mae Laeng, Thailand 86 B2 20 1N 99 17 E
Ban Mae Nam, Thailand 87 b 9 34N 100 0 E
Ban Mae Sariang, Thailand 86 C1 18 10N 97 56 E
Ban Mê Thuôt = Buon Ma Thuot, Vietnam 86 F7 12 40N 108 3 E
Ban Mi, Thailand 86 E3 15 3N 100 32 E
Ban Muong Mo, Laos 86 C4 19 4N 103 58 E
Ban Na Bo, Thailand 87 b 9 19N 99 41 E
Ban Na Mo, Laos 86 D5 17 7N 105 40 E
Ban Na San, Thailand 87 H2 8 53N 99 52 E
Ban Na Tong, Laos 86 B3 20 56N 101 47 E
Ban Nam Bac, Laos 86 B4 20 38N 102 20 E
Ban Nam Ma, Laos 86 A3 22 2N 101 37 E
Ban Ngang, Laos 86 E6 15 59N 106 11 E
Ban Nong Bok, Laos 86 D5 17 5N 104 48 E
Ban Nong Boua, Laos 86 E6 15 40N 106 33 E
Ban Nong Pling, Thailand 86 E3 15 40N 100 10 E
Ban Pak Chan, Thailand 87 G2 10 32N 98 51 E
Ban Patong, Thailand 87 a 7 54N 98 18 E
Ban Phai, Thailand 86 D4 16 4N 102 44 E
Ban Phak Chit, Thailand 87 a 8 0N 98 24 E
Ban Pong, Thailand 86 F2 13 50N 99 55 E
Ban Rawai, Thailand 87 a 7 47N 98 20 E
Ban Ron Phibun, Thailand 87 H2 8 9N 99 51 E
Ban Sakhu, Thailand 87 a 8 4N 98 18 E
Ban Sanam Chai, Thailand 87 J3 7 33N 100 25 E
Ban Sangkha, Thailand 86 E4 14 37N 103 52 E
Ban Tak, Thailand 86 D2 17 2N 99 4 E
Ban Tako, Thailand 86 E4 14 5N 102 40 E
Ban Tha Dua, Thailand 86 D2 17 59N 98 39 E
Ban Tha Li, Thailand 86 D3 17 37N 101 25 E
Ban Tha Nun, Thailand 87 a 8 12N 98 18 E
Ban Tha Rua, Thailand 87 a 7 59N 98 22 E
Ban Tha Yu, Thailand 87 a 8 17N 98 22 E
Ban Thahine, Laos 86 E5 14 12N 105 33 E
Ban Thong Krut, Thailand 87 b 9 25N 99 57 E
Ban Xien Kok, Laos 86 B3 20 54N 100 39 E
Ban Yen Nhan, Vietnam 86 B6 20 57N 106 2 E
Banā, W. →, Yemen 98 D4 13 3N 45 24 E
Banaba, Kiribati 134 H8 0 45 S 169 50 E
Banalia, Dem. Rep. of the Congo 118 B2 1 32N 25 5 E
Banam, Cambodia 87 G5 11 20N 105 17 E
Banamba, Mali 112 C3 13 29N 7 22W
Banana Is., S. Leone 112 D2 8 7N 13 15W
Bananal, I. do, Brazil 171 D1 11 30 S 50 30W
Bananga, India 95 L11 6 57N 93 54 E
Banaras = Varanasi, India 93 G10 25 22N 83 0 E
Banas →, Gujarat, India 92 H4 23 45N 71 25 E
Banas →, Mad. P., India 93 G9 24 15N 81 30 E
Bânâs, Ras, Egypt 106 C4 23 57N 35 59 E
Banaue, Phil. 80 C3 16 55N 121 4 E
Banaz, Turkey 49 C11 38 46N 29 46 E
Banaz →, Turkey 49 C11 38 12N 29 14 E
Banbridge, U.K. 23 B5 54 22N 6 16W
Banbury, U.K. 21 E6 52 4N 1 20W
Banc d'Arguin, Parc Nat. du, Mauritania 110 D1 20 10N 16 20W
Banchory, U.K. 22 D6 57 3N 2 29W
Banco, Ethiopia 107 F4 6 12N 38 13 E
Bancroft, Canada 140 C4 45 3N 77 51W
Band, Romania 53 D9 46 30N 24 25 E
Band Bonī, Iran 97 E8 25 30N 59 33 E
Band-e Torkestan, Afghan. 91 B2 35 30N 64 0 E
Band Qīr, Iran 97 D6 31 39N 48 53 E
Banda, Cameroon 114 B2 3 58N 14 32 E
Banda, Mad. P., India 93 G8 24 3N 78 57 E
Banda, Maharashtra, India 95 G1 15 49N 73 52 E
Banda, Ut. P., India 93 G9 25 30N 80 26 E
Banda, Kepulauan, Indonesia 83 B3 4 37 S 129 50 E
Banda Aceh, Indonesia 84 A1 5 35N 95 20 E
Banda Banda, Mt., Australia 129 A10 31 10 S 152 28 E
Banda Elat, Indonesia 83 C4 5 40 S 133 5 E
Banda Is. = Banda, Kepulauan, Indonesia 83 B3 4 37 S 129 50 E
Banda Kani, Dem. Rep. of the Congo 115 C2 4 48 S 13 52 E
Banda Sea, Indonesia 82 C3 6 0 S 130 0 E
Bandai-San, Japan 70 F10 37 36N 140 4 E
Bandak, Norway 18 E5 59 23N 8 29 E
Bandama →, Ivory C. 112 D3 6 32N 4 30W
Bandama Blanc →, Ivory C. 112 D3 6 55N 5 30W
Bandama Rouge →, Ivory C. 112 D4 6 55N 5 30W
Bandān, Iran 97 D9 31 23N 60 44 E
Bandanaira, Indonesia 83 B3 4 32 S 129 54 E
Bandanwara, India 92 F6 26 9N 74 38 E
Bandar = Machilipatnam, India 95 F5 16 12N 81 8 E
Bandar 'Abbās, Iran 97 E8 27 15N 56 15 E
Bandar-e Anzalī, Iran 97 B6 37 30N 49 30 E
Bandar-e Bushehr = Būshehr, Iran 97 D6 28 55N 50 55 E
Bandar-e Chārak, Iran 97 E7 26 45N 54 20 E
Bandar-e Deylam, Iran 97 D6 30 5N 50 10 E
Bandar-e Khomeynı, Iran 97 D6 30 30N 49 5 E
Bandar-e Lengeh, Iran 97 E7 26 35N 54 58 E
Bandar-e Maqām, Iran 97 E7 26 56N 53 29 E
Bandar-e Ma'shur, Iran 97 D6 30 35N 49 10 E
Bandar-e Rīg, Iran 97 D6 29 29N 50 38 E
Bandar-e Torkeman, Iran 97 B7 37 0N 54 10 E
Bandar Maharani = Muar, Malaysia 87 L4 2 3N 102 34 E
Bandar Penggaram = Batu Pahat, Malaysia 87 M4 1 50N 102 56 E
Bandar Seri Begawan, Brunei 85 B4 4 52N 115 0 E
Bandar Sri Aman, Malaysia 85 B4 1 15N 111 32 E
Bandawe, Malawi 119 E3 11 58 S 34 5 E
Bande, Spain 42 C3 42 3N 7 58W
Bandeira, Pico da, Brazil 171 F3 20 26 S 41 47W
Bandeirante, Brazil 171 D1 13 41 S 50 48W
Bandera, Argentina 174 B3 28 55 S 62 20W
Banderas, B. de, Mexico 162 C3 20 40N 105 30W
Bandhogarh, India 93 H9 23 40N 81 2 E
Bandi →, India 92 G6 26 12N 75 47 E
Bandia →, India 94 E5 19 2N 80 28 E
Bandiagara, Mali 112 C4 14 12N 3 29W
Bandikui, India 92 F7 27 3N 76 34 E
Bandırma, Turkey 51 F11 40 20N 28 0 E
Bandol, France 29 E9 43 8N 5 46 E
Bandon, Ireland 23 E3 51 44N 8 44W
Bandon →, Ireland 23 E3 51 43N 8 37W
Bandoua, C.A.R. 114 B4 4 39N 21 42 E
Bandula, Mozam. 119 F3 19 0 S 33 7 E
Bandundu, Dem. Rep. of the Congo 114 C3 3 15 S 17 22 E
Bandundu □, Dem. Rep. of the Congo 114 C3 3 30 S 17 30 E
Bandung, Indonesia 85 D3 6 54 S 107 36 E
Bané, Burkina Faso 113 C4 11 42N 0 15W
Băneasa, Romania 53 E12 45 56N 27 55 E
Bāneh, Iran 101 E11 35 59N 45 53 E
Bañeres, Spain 41 G4 38 44N 0 38W
Banes, Cuba 165 B4 21 0N 75 42W
Banff, Canada 142 C5 51 10N 115 34W
Banff, U.K. 22 D6 57 40N 2 33W
Banff Nat. Park, Canada 142 C5 51 30N 116 15W
Banfora, Burkina Faso 112 C4 10 40N 4 40W
Bang Fai →, Laos 86 D5 16 57N 104 45 E
Bang Hieng →, Laos 86 D5 16 10N 105 10 E
Bang Krathum, Thailand 86 D3 16 34N 100 18 E
Bang Lamung, Thailand 86 F3 13 3N 100 56 E
Bang Mun Nak, Thailand 86 D3 16 2N 100 23 E
Bang Pa In, Thailand 86 E3 14 14N 100 35 E
Bang Rakam, Thailand 86 D3 16 45N 100 7 E
Bang Saphan, Thailand 87 G2 11 14N 99 28 E
Bang Thao, Thailand 87 a 7 59N 98 18 E
Banga, Angola 115 D3 8 43 S 15 13 E
Banga, Dem. Rep. of the Congo 115 D4 5 25 S 20 28 E
Banga, Aklan, Phil. 81 F4 11 38N 122 20 E
Banga, S. Cotabato, Phil. 81 H5 6 21N 124 47 E
Bangaduni I., India 90 E2 21 34N 88 52 E
Bangala Dam, Zimbabwe 119 G3 21 7 S 31 25 E
Bangalore, India 95 H3 12 59N 77 40 E
Banganapalle, India 95 G4 15 19N 78 14 E
Banganga →, India 92 F6 27 6N 77 25 E
Bangangté, Cameroon 113 D7 5 8N 10 32 E
Bangaon, India 93 H13 23 0N 88 47 E
Bangar, Phil. 80 C3 16 54N 120 25 E
Bangassou, C.A.R. 114 B4 4 55N 23 7 E
Bangeta, Mt., Papua N. G. 132 D4 6 21 S 147 3 E
Banggai, Indonesia 82 B2 1 34 S 123 30 E
Banggai, Kepulauan, Indonesia 82 B2 1 40 S 123 30 E
Banggai Arch. = Banggai, Kepulauan, Indonesia 82 B2 1 40 S 123 30 E
Banggi, Malaysia 85 A5 7 17N 117 12 E
Banghāzī, Libya 108 B4 32 11N 20 3 E
Banghāzī □, Libya 108 B4 32 7N 20 4 E
Bangil, Indonesia 85 D4 7 36 S 112 50 E
Bangjang, Sudan 107 E3 11 23N 32 41 E
Bangka, Sulawesi, Indonesia 82 A3 1 50N 125 5 E
Bangka, Sumatera, Indonesia 84 C3 2 0 S 105 50 E
Bangka, Selat, Indonesia 84 C3 2 30 S 105 30 E
Bangkalan, Indonesia 85 D4 7 2 S 112 46 E
Bangkinang, Indonesia 84 B2 0 18N 101 5 E
Bangko, Indonesia 84 C2 2 5 S 102 9 E
Bangkok, Thailand 86 F3 13 45N 100 35 E
Bangladesh ■, Asia 90 C3 24 0N 90 0 E
Bangli, Indonesia 79 J18 8 27 S 115 21 E
Bangolo, Ivory C. 112 D3 7 1N 7 29W
Bangong Co, India 93 B8 35 50N 79 20 E
Bangor, Down, U.K. 23 B6 54 40N 5 40W
Bangor, Gwynedd, U.K. 20 D3 53 14N 4 8W
Bangor, Maine, U.S.A. 139 D13 44 48N 68 46W
Bangor, Mich., U.S.A. 157 B10 42 18N 86 7W
Bangor, Pa., U.S.A. 151 F9 40 52N 75 13W
Bangoran →, C.A.R. 114 A3 8 42N 19 6 E
Bangu, Dem. Rep. of the Congo 115 D4 0 3 S 19 12 E
Bangued, Phil. 80 C3 17 40N 120 37 E
Bangui, C.A.R. 114 B3 4 23N 18 35 E
Bangui, Phil. 80 B3 18 32N 120 46 E
Banguru, Dem. Rep. of the Congo 118 B2 0 30N 27 10 E
Bangweulu, L., Zambia 119 E3 11 0 S 30 0 E
Bangweulu Swamp, Zambia 119 E3 11 20 S 30 15 E
Banhine, Parque Nacional de, Mozam. 117 C5 22 49 S 32 55 E
Bani, Dom. Rep. 165 C5 18 16N 70 22W
Bani, Phil. 80 C2 16 11N 119 52 E
Bani →, Mali 112 C4 14 30N 4 12W
Bani, Jebel, Morocco 110 C3 29 16N 8 0W
Bani Bangou, Niger 113 B5 15 3N 2 42 E
Banī Sa'd, Iraq 101 F11 33 34N 44 32 E
Bania, C.A.R. 114 B3 4 1N 16 7 E
Bania, Ivory C. 112 D4 9 4N 3 6W
Baniara, Papua N. G. 132 E5 9 44 S 149 54 E
Banihal Pass, India 93 C6 33 30N 75 12 E
Banikoara, Benin 113 C5 11 18N 2 26 E
Banīnah, Libya 108 B4 32 0N 20 12 E
Bāniyās, Syria 100 E6 35 10N 36 0 E
Banja Luka, Bos.-H. 52 F2 44 49N 17 11 E
Banjar, India 92 D7 31 38N 77 21 E
Banjar, Indonesia 85 D3 7 24 S 108 30 E
Banjar →, India 93 H9 22 36N 80 22 E
Banjarmasin, Indonesia 85 C4 3 20 S 114 35 E
Banjarnegara, Indonesia 85 D3 7 24 S 109 42 E
Banjul, Gambia 112 C1 13 28N 16 40W
Banka, India 93 G12 24 53N 86 55 E
Bankas, Mali 112 C4 14 4N 3 31W
Bankeryd, Sweden 17 G8 57 53N 14 6 E
Banket, Zimbabwe 119 F3 17 27 S 30 19 E
Bankilaré, Niger 113 C5 14 35N 0 44 E
Bankot, India 94 F1 17 58N 73 2 E
Banks, U.S.A. 152 D4 31 49N 85 51W
Banks I. = Moa, I., Papua N. G. 132 F2 10 10 S 142 15 E
Banks I., B.C., Canada 142 C3 53 20N 130 0W
Banks I., N.W.T., Canada 138 A7 73 15N 121 30W
Banks Is., Vanuatu 133 C5 13 50 S 167 30 E
Banks L., U.S.A. 152 D6 31 2N 83 6W
Banks Pen., N.Z. 131 D8 43 45 S 173 15 E
Banks Str., Australia 127 G4 40 40 S 148 10 E
Bankumuna, Dem. Rep. of the Congo 115 C3 4 28 S 19 57 E
Bankura, India 93 H12 23 11N 87 18 E
Bankya, Bulgaria 50 D7 42 43N 23 8 E
Banmankhi, India 93 G12 25 53N 87 11 E
Banmauk, Burma 90 C5 24 24N 95 51 E
Bann →, Arm., U.K. 23 B5 54 30N 6 31W
Bann →, L'derry., U.K. 23 A5 55 8N 6 41W
Bannaanka Saraar, Somali Rep. 120 C3 9 25N 46 17 E
Bannalec, France 26 E3 47 57N 3 42W
Bannang Sata, Thailand 87 J3 6 16N 101 16 E
Bannerton, Australia 128 C5 34 42 S 142 47 E
Banning, U.S.A. 161 M10 33 56N 116 53W
Banningville = Bandundu, Dem. Rep. of the Congo 114 C3 3 15 S 17 22 E
Banno, Ethiopia 107 G4 4 51N 37 24 E
Bannockburn, Canada 150 B7 44 39N 77 33W
Bannockburn, U.K. 22 E5 56 5N 3 55W
Bannockburn, Zimbabwe 119 G2 20 17 S 29 48 E
Bannu, Pakistan 91 B3 33 0N 70 18 E
Bano, India 93 H11 22 40N 84 55 E
Bañolas = Banyoles, Spain 40 C7 42 16N 2 44 E
Banon, France 29 D9 44 2N 5 38 E
Baños de la Encina, Spain 43 G7 38 10N 3 46W
Baños de Molgas, Spain 42 C3 42 15N 7 40W
Bánovce nad Bebravou, Slovak Rep. 35 C11 48 44N 18 16 E
Banovići, Bos.-H. 52 F3 44 25N 18 32 E
Bansalan, Phil. 81 H5 6 55N 125 13 E
Bansgaon, India 93 F10 26 33N 83 21 E
Banská Bystrica, Slovak Rep. 35 C12 48 46N 19 14 E
Banská Štiavnica, Slovak Rep. 35 C11 48 25N 18 55 E
Bansko, Bulgaria 50 E7 41 52N 23 28 E
Banskobystrický □, Slovak Rep. 35 C12 48 20N 19 0 E
Banswara, India 92 H6 23 32N 74 24 E
Bantaeng, Indonesia 82 C1 5 32 S 119 56 E
Bantaji, Nigeria 113 D7 8 6N 10 5 E
Bantayan, Phil. 81 F4 11 10N 123 43 E
Bantayan I., Phil. 81 F4 11 13N 123 44 E
Banten, Indonesia 84 D3 6 5 S 106 8 E
Banton I., Phil. 80 E4 12 56N 122 4 E
Bantry, Ireland 23 E2 51 41N 9 27W
Bantry B., Ireland 23 E2 51 37N 9 44W
Bantul, Indonesia 85 D4 7 55 S 110 19 E
Bantva, India 92 J4 21 29N 70 12 E
Bantval, India 95 H2 12 55N 75 0 E
Banya, Bulgaria 51 D8 42 33N 24 50 E
Banyak, Kepulauan, Indonesia 84 B1 2 10N 97 10 E
Banyalbufar, Spain 38 B3 39 42N 2 31 E
Banyo, Cameroon 113 D7 6 52N 11 45 E
Banyoles, Spain 40 C7 42 16N 2 44 E
Banyuls-sur-Mer, France 28 F7 42 28N 3 8 E
Banyumas, Indonesia 85 D3 7 32 S 109 18 E
Banyuwangi, Indonesia 85 D4 8 13 S 114 21 E
Banz, Papua N. G. 132 C3 5 47 S 144 37 E
Banza, Dem. Rep. of the Congo 114 B4 0 28N 20 10 E
Banzare Coast, Antarctica 7 C9 68 0 S 125 0 E
Bao Ha, Vietnam 76 F5 22 11N 104 21 E
Bao Lac, Vietnam 86 A5 22 57N 105 40 E
Bao Loc, Vietnam 87 G6 11 32N 107 48 E
Bao'an = Shenzhen, China 77 F10 22 33N 114 5 E
Baocheng, China 74 H4 33 12N 106 56 E
Baode, China 74 E6 39 1N 111 5 E
Baodi, China 75 E9 39 38N 117 20 E
Baoding, China 74 E8 38 50N 115 28 E
Baoji, China 74 G4 34 20N 107 5 E
Baojing, China 76 C7 28 45N 109 41 E
Baokang, China 77 B8 31 54N 111 12 E
Baoro, C.A.R. 114 A3 5 40N 15 58 E
Baoshan, Shanghai, China 77 B13 31 27N 121 26 E
Baoshan, Yunnan, China 76 E2 25 10N 99 5 E
Baotou, China 74 D6 40 32N 110 2 E
Baoxing, China 76 B4 30 24N 102 50 E
Baoying, China 75 H10 33 17N 119 20 E
Bap, India 92 F5 27 23N 72 18 E
Bapatla, India 95 G5 15 55N 80 30 E
Bapaume, France 27 B9 50 7N 2 50 E
Baqanas, Kazakstan 65 A8 44 50N 76 15 E
Baqbaqty, Kazakstan 65 A8 44 35N 76 40 E
Bāqerābād, Iran 97 C6 33 2N 51 58 E
Ba'qūbah, Iraq 101 F11 33 45N 44 50 E
Baquedano, Chile 174 A2 23 20 S 69 52W
Bar, Montenegro, Yug. 50 D3 42 8N 19 6 E
Bar, Ukraine 59 H4 49 4N 27 40 E
Bar Bigha, India 93 G11 25 21N 85 47 E
Bar Harbor, U.S.A. 149 C11 44 23N 68 13W
Bar-le-Duc, France 27 D12 48 47N 5 10 E
Bar-sur-Aube, France 27 D11 48 14N 4 40 E
Bar-sur-Seine, France 27 D11 48 7N 4 20 E
Bara, India 93 G9 25 16N 81 43 E
Bara, Indonesia 82 B3 3 8 S 126 11 E
Bâra, Romania 53 C12 47 2N 27 3 E
Bara Banki, India 93 F9 26 55N 81 12 E
Barabai, Indonesia 85 C5 2 32 S 115 34 E
Baraboo, U.S.A. 154 D10 43 28N 89 45W
Baracoa, Cuba 165 B5 20 20N 74 30W
Baradā →, Syria 103 B5 33 33N 36 34 E
Baradero, Argentina 174 C4 33 52 S 59 29W
Baradine, Australia 129 A8 30 56 S 149 4 E
Baraga, U.S.A. 154 B10 46 47N 88 30W
Bărăganul, Romania 53 F12 44 29N 27 31 E
Barah →, India 92 F6 27 42N 77 5 E
Barahona, Dom. Rep. 165 C5 18 13N 71 7W
Barahona, Spain 40 D2 41 17N 2 39W
Barail Range, India 90 C4 25 15N 93 20 E

188 Barak

Barak →, *India* **90 C4** 24 52N 92 30 E
Baraka, *Sudan* **107 E2** 10 59N 27 59 E
Baraka →, *Sudan* **106 D4** 18 13N 37 35 E
Barakaldo, *Spain* **40 B2** 43 18N 2 59W
Barakar →, *India* **93 G12** 24 7N 86 14 E
Barakot, *India* **93 J11** 21 33N 84 59 E
Barakpur, *India* **93 H13** 22 44N 88 30 E
Baralaba, *Australia* **126 C4** 24 13 S 149 50 E
Baralla, *Spain* **42 C3** 42 53N 7 15W
Baralzon L., *Canada* **143 B9** 60 0N 98 3W
Baram →, *Malaysia* **85 B4** 4 35N 113 58 E
Baramati, *India* **94 E2** 18 11N 74 33 E
Baramba, *India* **94 D7** 20 25N 85 23 E
Barameiya, *Sudan* **106 D4** 18 32N 36 38 E
Baramula, *India* **93 B6** 34 15N 74 20 E
Baran, *India* **92 G7** 25 9N 76 40 E
Baran →, *Pakistan* **92 G3** 25 13N 68 17 E
Barañain, *Spain* **40 C3** 42 48N 1 40W
Baranavichy, *Belarus* **59 F4** 53 10N 26 0 E
Barani, *Burkina Faso* **112 C4** 13 9N 3 51W
Baranoa, *Colombia* **168 A3** 10 48N 74 55W
Baranof, *U.S.A.* **142 B2** 57 5N 134 50W
Baranof I., *U.S.A.* **144 H14** 57 0N 135 0W
Baranów Sandomierski, *Poland* **55 H8** 50 29N 21 30 E
Baranya □, *Hungary* **52 E3** 46 0N 18 15 E
Barão de Cocais, *Brazil* **171 E3** 19 56 S 43 28W
Barão de Grajaú, *Brazil* **170 C3** 6 45 S 43 1W
Barão de Melgaço, *Mato Grosso, Brazil* **173 D6** 16 14 S 55 52W
Barão de Melgaço, *Rondônia, Brazil* **173 C5** 11 50 S 60 45W
Baraolt, *Romania* **53 D10** 46 5N 25 34 E
Barapasi, *Indonesia* **83 B5** 2 15 S 137 5 E
Barapina = Panguna, *Papua N. G.* **132 D8** 6 21 S 155 25 E
Baras, *Phil.* **80 E5** 13 40N 124 22 E
Barasat, *India* **93 H13** 22 46N 88 31 E
Barat Daya, Kepulauan, *Indonesia* **82 C3** 7 30 S 128 0 E
Baratang I., *India* **95 H11** 12 13N 92 45 E
Barataria B., *U.S.A.* **155 L10** 29 20N 89 55W
Barauda, *India* **92 H6** 23 33N 75 15 E
Baraut, *India* **92 E7** 29 13N 77 7 E
Baraya, *Colombia* **168 C2** 3 10N 75 4W
Barbacan = Roxas, *Phil.* **81 F2** 10 20N 119 21 E
Barbacena, *Brazil* **171 F3** 21 15 S 43 56W
Barbacoas, *Colombia* **168 C2** 1 45N 78 0W
Barbados ■, *W. Indies* **165 g** 13 10N 59 30W
Barbalha, *Brazil* **170 C4** 7 19 S 39 17W
Barban, *Croatia* **45 C11** 45 5N 14 2 E
Barbària, C. de, *Spain* **38 D1** 38 39N 1 24 E
Barbaros, *Turkey* **51 F11** 40 54N 27 27 E
Barbas, C., *W. Sahara* **110 D1** 22 20N 16 42W
Barbastro, *Spain* **40 C5** 42 2N 0 5 E
Barbate = Barbate de Franco, *Spain* **43 J5** 36 13N 5 56W
Barbate de Franco, *Spain* **43 J5** 36 13N 5 56W
Barbaza, *Phil.* **81 F4** 11 12N 122 2 E
Barberino di Mugello, *Italy* **45 E8** 44 0N 11 15 E
Barbers Pt., *U.S.A.* **145 K13** 21 18N 158 7W
Barberton, *S. Africa* **117 D5** 25 42 S 31 2 E
Barberton, *U.S.A.* **150 E3** 41 0N 81 39W
Barberville, *U.S.A.* **153 F8** 29 11N 81 26W
Barbezieux-St-Hilaire, *France* **28 C3** 45 28N 0 9W
Barbonneau, *St. Lucia* **165 f** 13 59N 60 58W
Barbosa, *Colombia* **168 B3** 5 57N 73 37W
Barbourville, *U.S.A.* **149 G4** 36 52N 83 53W
Barbuda, *W. Indies* **165 C7** 17 30N 61 40W
Bârca, *Romania* **53 G8** 43 59N 23 36 E
Barcaldine, *Australia* **126 C4** 23 43 S 145 6 E
Barcarena, *Brazil* **170 B2** 1 30 S 48 40W
Barcarrota, *Spain* **43 G4** 38 31N 6 51W
Barcellona Pozzo di Gotto, *Italy* **47 D8** 38 9N 15 13 E
Barcelona, *Spain* **40 D7** 41 21N 2 10 E
Barcelona, *Venezuela* **169 A5** 10 10N 64 40W
Barcelona □, *Spain* **40 D7** 41 30N 2 0 E
Barceloneta, *Puerto Rico* **165 d** 18 27N 66 32W
Barcelonette, *France* **29 D10** 44 23N 6 40 E
Barcelos, *Brazil* **169 D5** 1 0 S 63 0W
Barcin, *Poland* **55 F4** 52 52N 17 55 E
Barclayville, *Liberia* **112 E3** 4 48N 8 10W
Barcoo →, *Australia* **126 D3** 25 30 S 142 50 E
Barcs, *Hungary* **52 E2** 45 58N 17 28 E
Barczewo, *Poland* **54 E7** 53 50N 20 42 E
Bärdä, *Azerbaijan* **61 K8** 40 25N 47 10 E
Barda del Medio, *Argentina* **176 A3** 38 45 S 68 11W
Bardaï, *Chad* **109 D3** 21 25N 17 0 E
Bardas Blancas, *Argentina* **174 D2** 35 49 S 69 45W
Bardawîl, Sabkhet el, *Egypt* **103 D2** 31 10N 33 15 E
Barddhaman, *India* **93 H12** 23 14N 87 39 E
Bardejov, *Slovak Rep.* **35 B14** 49 18N 21 15 E
Bardera, *Somali Rep.* **120 D2** 2 20N 42 27 E
Barð, *Iceland* **11 A7** 66 3N 19 8W
Bárðarbunga, *Iceland* **11 C9** 64 38N 17 32W
Barðastrandarsýsla □, *Iceland* **11 B3** 65 40N 23 0W
Bardi, *Italy* **44 D6** 44 38N 9 44 E
Bardīyah, *Libya* **108 B5** 31 45N 25 5 E
Bardoli, *India* **94 D1** 21 12N 73 5 E
Bardolino, *Italy* **44 C7** 45 33N 10 43 E
Bardonécchia, *Italy* **44 C3** 45 5N 6 42 E
Bardsey I., *U.K.* **20 E3** 52 45N 4 47W
Bardstown, *U.S.A.* **157 G11** 37 49N 85 28W
Bareilly, *India* **93 E8** 28 22N 79 27 E
Barela, *India* **93 H9** 23 6N 80 3 E
Barellan, *Australia* **129 C7** 34 16 S 146 24 E
Barentin, *France* **26 C7** 49 33N 0 58 E
Barenton, *France* **26 D6** 48 38N 0 50W
Barents Sea, *Arctic* **6 B9** 73 0N 39 0 E
Barentu, *Eritrea* **107 D4** 15 2N 37 35 E
Barfleur, *France* **26 C5** 49 40N 1 17W
Barfleur, Pte. de, *France* **26 C5** 49 42N 1 16W
Barga, *Italy* **44 D7** 44 4N 10 29 E
Bargal, *Somali Rep.* **120 B4** 11 25N 51 0 E
Bargara, *Australia* **126 C5** 24 50 S 152 25 E
Bargarh, *India* **94 D6** 21 20N 83 37 E
Bargas, *Spain* **42 F6** 39 56N 4 3W
Bârgăului Bistriţa, *Romania* **53 C9** 47 13N 24 46 E
Barge, *Italy* **44 D4** 44 43N 7 20 E
Bargnop, *Sudan* **107 F2** 9 32N 28 25 E
Bargo, *Australia* **129 C9** 34 18 S 150 35 E
Bargteheide, *Germany* **30 B6** 53 44N 10 14 E
Barguzin, *Russia* **67 D11** 53 37N 109 37 E
Barh, *India* **93 G11** 25 29N 85 46 E
Barhaj, *India* **93 F10** 26 18N 83 44 E
Barham, *Australia* **128 C6** 35 36 S 144 8 E
Barharwa, *India* **93 G12** 24 52N 87 47 E
Barhi, *India* **93 G11** 24 15N 85 25 E
Bari, *Dem. Rep. of the Congo* **114 B3** 3 20N 19 25 E
Bari, *India* **92 F7** 26 39N 77 39 E
Bari, *Italy* **47 A9** 41 8N 16 51 E
Bari Doab, *Pakistan* **92 D5** 30 20N 73 0 E
Bari Sadri, *India* **92 G6** 24 28N 74 30 E
Bari Sardo, *Italy* **46 C2** 39 50N 9 38 E
Barīdī, Ra's, *Si. Arabia* **96 E3** 24 17N 37 31 E
Barīm, *Yemen* **98 D3** 12 39N 43 25 E
Barima →, *Guyana* **169 B5** 8 33N 60 25W
Barinas, *Venezuela* **168 B3** 8 36N 70 15W
Barinas □, *Venezuela* **168 B4** 8 10N 69 50W
Baring, *U.S.A.* **156 D4** 40 15N 92 12W
Baring, C., *Canada* **138 B8** 70 0N 117 30W
Baringa, *Dem. Rep. of the Congo* **114 B4** 0 45N 20 52 E
Baringo, *Kenya* **118 B4** 0 47N 36 16 E
Baringo, L., *Kenya* **118 B4** 0 47N 36 16 E
Barinitas, *Venezuela* **168 B3** 8 45N 70 25W
Baripada, *India* **94 D8** 21 57N 86 45 E
Bariri, *Brazil* **171 F2** 22 4 S 48 44W
Bârîs, *Egypt* **106 C3** 24 42N 30 31 E
Barisal, *Bangla.* **90 D3** 22 45N 90 20 E
Barisan, Bukit, *Indonesia* **78 E2** 3 30 S 102 15 E
Barito →, *Indonesia* **85 C4** 4 0 S 114 50 E
Barjac, *France* **29 D8** 44 20N 4 22 E
Barjols, *France* **29 E10** 43 34N 6 2 E
Barjūj, Wadi →, *Libya* **108 C2** 25 26N 12 12 E
Bark L., *Canada* **150 A7** 45 27N 77 51W
Barka = Baraka →, *Sudan* **106 D4** 18 13N 37 35 E
Barkakana, *India* **93 H11** 23 37N 85 29 E
Barkald, *Norway* **18 C7** 61 59N 10 53 E
Barkam, *China* **76 B4** 31 51N 102 28 E
Barker, *U.S.A.* **150 C6** 43 20N 78 33W
Barkley, L., *U.S.A.* **149 G2** 37 1N 88 14W
Barkley Sound, *Canada* **142 D3** 48 50N 125 10W
Barkly East, *S. Africa* **116 E4** 30 58 S 27 33 E
Barkly Roadhouse, *Australia* **126 B2** 19 52 S 135 50 E
Barkly Tableland, *Australia* **126 B2** 17 50 S 136 40 E
Barkly West, *S. Africa* **116 D3** 28 5 S 24 31 E
Barkol, Wadi →, *Sudan* **106 D3** 17 40N 32 0 E
Barkol Kazak Zizhixian, *China* **68 B4** 43 37N 93 2 E
Barla Dağı, *Turkey* **49 C12** 38 5N 30 40 E
Bârlad, *Romania* **53 D12** 46 15N 27 38 E
Bârlad →, *Romania* **53 E12** 45 38N 27 32 E
Barlee, L., *Australia* **125 E2** 29 15 S 119 30 E
Barlee, Mt., *Australia* **125 D4** 24 38 S 128 13 E
Barletta, *Italy* **47 A9** 41 19N 16 17 E
Barlinek, *Poland* **55 F2** 53 0N 15 15 E
Barlovento, *Canary Is.* **9 e1** 28 48N 17 48W
Barlovento, *C. Verde Is.* **9 j** 17 0N 25 0W
Barlow L., *Canada* **143 A8** 62 0N 103 0W
Barmedman, *Australia* **129 C7** 34 9 S 147 21 E
Barmer, *India* **92 G4** 25 45N 71 20 E
Barmera, *Australia* **128 C4** 34 15 S 140 28 E
Barmouth, *U.K.* **20 E3** 52 44N 4 4W
Barmstedt, *Germany* **30 B5** 53 47N 9 46 E
Barn, The, *St. Helena* **9 h** 15 55 S 5 40W
Barna →, *India* **93 G10** 25 21N 83 3 E
Barnagar, *India* **92 H6** 23 7N 75 19 E
Barnala, *India* **92 D6** 30 23N 75 33 E
Barnard →, *Australia* **129 A9** 31 34 S 151 25 E
Barnard Castle, *U.K.* **20 C6** 54 33N 1 55W
Barnato, *Australia* **129 A6** 31 38 S 145 0 E
Barnaul, *Russia* **66 D9** 53 20N 83 40 E
Barnes, *Australia* **128 D6** 36 2 S 144 49 E
Barnesville, *U.S.A.* **152 B5** 33 3N 84 9W
Barnet □, *U.K.* **21 F7** 51 38N 0 9W
Barneveld, *Neths.* **24 B5** 52 7N 5 36 E
Barneveld, *U.S.A.* **151 C9** 43 16N 75 14W
Barneville-Cartevert, *France* **26 C5** 49 23N 1 46W
Barnhart, *U.S.A.* **155 K4** 31 8N 101 10W
Barnsley, *U.K.* **20 D6** 53 34N 1 27W
Barnstaple, *U.K.* **21 F3** 51 5N 4 4W
Barnstaple Bay = Bideford Bay, *U.K.* **21 F3** 51 5N 4 20W
Barnsville, *U.S.A.* **154 B6** 46 43N 96 28W
Barnwell, *U.S.A.* **152 B8** 33 15N 81 23W
Baro, *Nigeria* **113 D6** 8 35N 6 18 E
Baro →, *Ethiopia* **107 F3** 8 26N 33 13 E
Barobo, *Phil.* **81 G6** 8 33N 126 7 E
Baroda = Vadodara, *India* **92 H5** 22 20N 73 10 E
Baroda, *India* **92 G7** 25 29N 76 35 E
Baroe, *S. Africa* **116 E3** 33 13 S 24 33 E
Baron Ra., *Australia* **124 D4** 23 30 S 127 45 E
Barong, *China* **76 B2** 31 3N 99 20 E
Barora, *Solomon Is.* **133 L10** 7 30 S 158 20 E
Barora Ite, *Solomon Is.* **133 L10** 7 36 S 158 24 E
Barotseland, *Zambia* **115 F4** 15 0 S 24 0 E
Barouéli, *Mali* **112 C3** 13 4N 6 50W
Barpali, *India* **94 D6** 21 11N 83 35 E
Barpathar, *India* **90 B4** 26 17N 93 53 E
Barpeta, *India* **90 B3** 26 20N 91 10 E
Barqin, *Libya* **108 C2** 27 33N 13 34 E
Barques, Pt. Aux, *U.S.A.* **150 B2** 44 4N 82 58W
Barquísimeto, *Venezuela* **168 A4** 10 4N 69 19W
Barr, Ras el, *Egypt* **106 H7** 31 32N 31 50 E
Barr Smith Range, *Australia* **125 E3** 27 4 S 120 20 E
Barra, *Brazil* **170 D3** 11 5 S 43 10W
Barra, *U.K.* **22 E1** 57 0N 7 29W
Barra, Sd. of, *U.K.* **22 D1** 57 4N 7 25W
Barra da Estiva, *Brazil* **171 D3** 13 38 S 41 19W
Barra de Navidad, *Mexico* **162 D4** 19 12N 104 41W
Barra do Bugres, *Brazil* **173 C6** 15 0 S 57 11W
Barra do Corda, *Brazil* **170 C2** 5 30 S 45 10W
Barra do Dande, *Angola* **115 D2** 8 28 S 13 22 E
Barra do Mendes, *Brazil* **171 D3** 11 43 S 42 4W
Barra do Piraí, *Brazil* **171 F3** 22 30 S 43 50W
Barra Falsa, Pta. da, *Mozam.* **117 C6** 22 58 S 35 37 E
Barra Hd., *U.K.* **22 E1** 56 47N 7 40W
Barra Mansa, *Brazil* **171 F3** 22 35 S 44 12W
Barraba, *Australia* **129 A9** 30 21 S 150 35 E
Barracão do Barreto, *Brazil* **173 B6** 8 48 S 58 24W
Barrackpur = Barakpur, *India* **93 H13** 22 44N 88 30 E
Barradale Roadhouse, *Australia* **124 D1** 22 42 S 114 58 E
Barrafranca, *Italy* **47 E7** 37 22N 14 12 E
Barraigh = Barra, *U.K.* **22 E1** 57 0N 7 29W
Barranca, *Lima, Peru* **172 C2** 10 45 S 77 50W
Barranca, *Loreto, Peru* **168 D2** 4 50 S 76 50W
Barrancabermeja, *Colombia* **168 B3** 7 0N 73 50W
Barrancas, *Colombia* **168 A3** 10 57N 72 50W
Barrancas, *Venezuela* **169 B5** 8 55N 62 5W
Barrancos, *Portugal* **43 G4** 38 10N 6 58W
Barranqueras, *Argentina* **174 B4** 27 30 S 59 0W
Barranquilla, *Colombia* **168 A3** 11 0N 74 50W
Barras, *Brazil* **170 B3** 4 15 S 42 18W
Barras, *Colombia* **168 D3** 1 45 S 73 13W
Barraute, *Canada* **140 C4** 48 26N 77 38W
Barre, *Mass., U.S.A.* **151 D12** 42 25N 72 6W
Barre, *Vt., U.S.A.* **151 B12** 44 12N 72 30W
Barreal, *Argentina* **174 C2** 31 33 S 69 28W
Barrei, *Ethiopia* **120 C2** 6 10N 42 49 E
Barreiras, *Brazil* **171 D3** 12 8 S 45 0W
Barreirinha, *Brazil* **169 D6** 2 47 S 57 3W
Barreirinhas, *Brazil* **170 B3** 2 30 S 42 50W
Barreiro, *Portugal* **43 G1** 38 40N 9 6W
Barreiros, *Brazil* **170 C4** 8 49 S 35 12W
Barrême, *France* **29 E10** 43 57N 6 23 E
Barren, Nosy, *Madag.* **117 B7** 18 25 S 43 40 E
Barren I., *India* **95 H11** 12 16N 93 51 E
Barren Is., *U.S.A.* **144 G9** 58 55N 152 15W
Barretos, *Brazil* **171 F2** 20 30 S 48 35W
Barrhead, *Canada* **142 C6** 54 10N 114 24W
Barrie, *Canada* **140 D4** 44 24N 79 40W
Barrier, C., *N.Z.* **130 C4** 36 25 S 175 32 E
Barrier Ra., *Australia* **128 A4** 31 0 S 141 30 E
Barrier Ra., *Otago, N.Z.* **131 E4** 44 15 S 169 32 E
Barrier Ra., *W. Coast, N.Z.* **131 E3** 44 30 S 168 30 E
Barrière, *Canada* **142 C4** 51 12N 120 7W
Barrineau Park, *U.S.A.* **153 E2** 30 42N 87 26W
Barrington, *U.S.A.* **151 E13** 41 44N 71 18W
Barrington L., *Canada* **143 B8** 56 55N 100 15W
Barrington Tops, *Australia* **129 B9** 32 6 S 151 28 E
Barrington Tops Nat. Park, *Australia* **129 B9** 32 4 S 151 25 E
Barringun, *Australia* **127 D4** 29 1 S 145 41 E
Barro do Garças, *Brazil* **173 D7** 15 54 S 52 16W
Barron, *U.S.A.* **154 C9** 45 24N 91 51W
Barrow, *U.S.A.* **144 A8** 71 18N 156 47W
Barrow →, *Ireland* **23 D5** 52 25N 6 58W
Barrow Creek, *Australia* **126 C1** 21 30 S 133 55 E
Barrow I., *Australia* **124 D2** 20 45 S 115 20 E
Barrow-in-Furness, *U.K.* **20 C4** 54 7N 3 14W
Barrow Pt., *Australia* **126 A3** 14 20 S 144 40 E
Barrow Pt., *U.S.A.* **144 A8** 71 10N 156 20W
Barrow Ra., *Australia* **125 E4** 26 0 S 127 40 E
Barrow Str., *Canada* **6 B3** 74 20N 95 0W
Barruecopardo, *Spain* **42 D4** 41 4N 6 40W
Barruelo de Santullán, *Spain* **42 C6** 42 54N 4 17W
Barry, *U.K.* **21 F4** 51 24N 3 16W
Barry, *U.S.A.* **156 E5** 39 42N 91 2W
Barry's Bay, *Canada* **140 C4** 45 29N 77 41W
Barsalogho, *Burkina Faso* **113 C4** 13 25N 1 3W
Barsat, *Pakistan* **93 A5** 36 10N 72 45 E
Barsham, *Syria* **101 E9** 35 21N 40 33 E
Barsi, *India* **94 E2** 18 10N 75 50 E
Barsinghausen, *Germany* **30 C5** 52 18N 9 28 E
Barskoon, *Kyrgyzstan* **65 B8** 42 10N 77 37 E
Barstow, *U.S.A.* **161 L9** 34 54N 117 1W
Barth, *Germany* **30 A8** 54 22N 12 42 E
Barthélemy, Col, *Vietnam* **86 C5** 19 26N 104 6 E
Bartica, *Guyana* **169 B6** 6 25N 58 40W
Bartin, *Turkey* **100 B5** 41 38N 32 21 E
Bartlesville, *U.S.A.* **155 G7** 36 45N 95 59W
Bartlett, *U.S.A.* **160 J8** 36 29N 118 2W
Bartlett, L., *Canada* **142 A5** 63 5N 118 20W
Bartolomeu Dias, *Mozam.* **119 G4** 21 10 S 35 8 E
Barton, *Phil.* **81 F2** 10 24N 119 8 E
Barton, *U.S.A.* **151 B12** 44 45N 72 11W
Barton upon Humber, *U.K.* **20 D7** 53 41N 0 25W
Bartonville, *U.S.A.* **156 D7** 40 39N 89 39W
Bartoszyce, *Poland* **54 D7** 54 15N 20 55 E
Bartow, *Fla., U.S.A.* **149 M5** 27 54N 81 50W
Bartow, *Ga., U.S.A.* **152 C7** 32 53N 82 29W
Barú, I. de, *Colombia* **168 A2** 10 15N 75 35W
Barú, Volcan, *Panama* **164 E3** 8 55N 82 35W
Barumba, *Dem. Rep. of the Congo* **118 B1** 1 3N 23 37 E
Barumbu, *Dem. Rep. of the Congo* **114 B4** 1 14N 23 31 E
Baruth, *Germany* **30 C9** 52 4N 13 30 E
Baruunsuu, *Mongolia* **74 C3** 43 43N 105 35 E
Barvinkove, *Ukraine* **59 H9** 48 57N 37 0 E
Barwani, *India* **92 H6** 22 2N 74 57 E
Barwice, *Poland* **54 E3** 53 44N 16 21 E
Barwick, *U.S.A.* **152 E6** 30 54N 83 44W
Barycz →, *Poland* **55 G3** 51 42N 16 15 E
Barysaw, *Belarus* **58 E5** 54 17N 28 28 E
Barysh, *Russia* **60 D8** 53 39N 47 8 E
Barzān, *Iraq* **96 B5** 36 55N 44 3 E
Bârzava, *Romania* **52 D6** 46 7N 21 59 E
Bas-Congo □, *Dem. Rep. of the Congo* **115 D2** 5 0 S 15 0 E
Bas-Kouilou, *Congo* **115 C2** 4 28 S 11 42 E
Bas-Rhin □, *France* **27 D14** 48 40N 7 30 E
Bašaid, *Serbia, Yug.* **52 E5** 45 38N 20 25 E
Bāsa'idū, *Iran* **97 E7** 26 35N 55 20 E
Basal, *Pakistan* **92 C5** 33 33N 72 13 E
Basankusa, *Dem. Rep. of the Congo* **114 B3** 1 5N 19 50 E
Basarabeasca, *Moldova* **53 D13** 46 21N 28 58 E
Basarabi, *Romania* **53 F13** 44 10N 28 26 E
Basarabia = Bessarabiya, *Moldova* **59 J5** 47 0N 28 10 E
Basauri, *Spain* **40 B2** 43 13N 2 53W
Basawa, *Afghan.* **91 B3** 34 15N 70 50 E
Basco, *Phil.* **80 A3** 20 27N 121 58 E
Bascuñán, C., *Chile* **174 B1** 28 52 S 71 35W
Basekpio, *Dem. Rep. of the Congo* **114 B4** 4 43N 24 36 E
Basel, *Switz.* **32 A5** 47 35N 7 35 E
Basel-Landschaft □, *Switz.* **32 B5** 47 26N 7 45 E
Basel-Stadt □, *Switz.* **32 A5** 47 35N 7 35 E
Basento →, *Italy* **47 B9** 40 20N 16 49 E
Basey, *Phil.* **81 F5** 11 17N 125 4 E
Bashākerd, Kūhhā-ye, *Iran* **97 E8** 26 42N 58 35 E
Bashaw, *Canada* **142 C6** 52 35N 112 58W
Bāshī, *Iran* **97 D6** 28 41N 51 4 E
Bashkir Republic = Bashkortostan □, *Russia* **64 E6** 54 0N 57 0 E
Bashkortostan □, *Russia* **64 E6** 54 0N 57 0 E
Basibasy, *Madag.* **117 C7** 22 10 S 43 40 E
Basilaki I., *Papua N. G.* **132 F6** 10 35 S 151 0 E
Basilan □, *Phil.* **81 H4** 6 33N 122 4 E
Basilan I., *Phil.* **81 H4** 6 35N 122 0 E
Basilan Str., *Phil.* **81 H4** 6 50N 122 0 E
Basildon, *U.K.* **21 F8** 51 34N 0 28 E
Basile, *Eq. Guin.* **113 E6** 3 42N 8 48 E
Basilicata □, *Italy* **47 B9** 40 30N 16 30 E
Basim = Washim, *India* **94 D3** 20 3N 77 0 E
Basin, *U.S.A.* **158 D9** 44 23N 108 2W
Basinger, *U.S.A.* **153 H8** 27 23N 81 2W
Basingstoke, *U.K.* **21 F6** 51 15N 1 5W
Basirhat, *Bangla.* **90 D2** 22 40N 88 54 E
Baška, *Croatia* **45 D11** 44 58N 14 45 E
Başkale, *Turkey* **101 C10** 38 2N 43 59 E
Baskatong, Rés., *Canada* **140 C4** 46 46N 75 50W
Basle = Basel, *Switz.* **32 A5** 47 35N 7 35 E
Başmakçı, *Turkey* **49 D12** 37 54N 30 1 E
Basmat, *India* **94 E3** 19 15N 77 12 E
Basoda, *India* **92 H7** 23 52N 77 54 E
Basodino, *Switz.* **33 D6** 46 25N 8 28 E
Basoko, *Dem. Rep. of the Congo* **118 B1** 1 16N 23 40 E
Basongo, *Dem. Rep. of the Congo* **115 C4** 4 15 S 20 20 E
Basque, Pays, *France* **28 E2** 43 15N 1 20W
Basque Provinces = País Vasco □, *Spain* **40 C2** 42 50N 2 45W
Basra = Al Başrah, *Iraq* **96 D5** 30 30N 47 50 E
Bass Str., *Australia* **127 F4** 39 15 S 146 30 E
Bassano, *Canada* **142 C6** 50 48N 112 20W
Bassano del Grappa, *Italy* **45 C8** 45 46N 11 44 E
Bassar, *Togo* **113 D5** 9 19N 0 57 E
Bassas da India, *Ind. Oc.* **121 G2** 22 0 S 39 0 E
Basse-Normandie □, *France* **26 D6** 48 45N 0 30W
Basse-Pointe, *Martinique* **164 c** 14 52N 61 8W
Basse Santa-Su, *Gambia* **112 C2** 13 13N 14 15W
Basse-Terre, *Guadeloupe* **164 b** 16 0N 61 44W
Basse Terre, *Trin. & Tob.* **169 F9** 10 7N 61 19W
Bassecourt, *Switz.* **32 B4** 47 20N 7 15 E
Bassein, *Burma* **90 G5** 16 45N 94 30 E
Bassein, *India* **94 E1** 19 26N 72 48 E
Basses, Pte. des, *Guadeloupe* **164 b** 15 52N 61 17W
Basseterre, *St. Kitts & Nevis* **165 C7** 17 17N 62 43W
Bassett, *U.S.A.* **154 D5** 42 35N 99 32W
Bassi, *India* **92 D7** 30 44N 76 21 E
Bassigny, *France* **27 E12** 48 0N 5 30 E
Bassikounou, *Mauritania* **112 B3** 15 55N 6 1W
Bassila, *Benin* **113 D5** 9 1N 1 46 E
Bassum, *Germany* **30 C4** 52 50N 8 40 E
Båstad, *Sweden* **17 H6** 56 25N 12 51 E
Bastak, *Iran* **97 E7** 27 15N 54 25 E
Baştām, *Iran* **97 B7** 36 29N 55 4 E
Bastar, *India* **94 E5** 19 15N 81 40 E
Bastelica, *France* **29 F13** 42 1N 9 3 E
Basti, *India* **93 F10** 26 52N 82 55 E
Bastia, *France* **29 F13** 42 40N 9 30 E
Bastogne, *Belgium* **24 D5** 50 1N 5 43 E
Bastrop, *La., U.S.A.* **155 J9** 32 47N 91 55W
Bastrop, *Tex., U.S.A.* **155 K6** 30 7N 97 19W
Basud, *Phil.* **80 D4** 14 4N 122 58 E
Bat Yam, *Israel* **103 C3** 32 2N 34 44 E
Bata, *Eq. Guin.* **114 B1** 1 57N 9 50 E
Bata, *Romania* **52 D7** 46 1N 22 4 E
Bataan □, *Phil.* **80 D3** 14 40N 120 25 E
Batabanó, *Cuba* **164 B3** 22 40N 82 20W
Batabanó, G. de, *Cuba* **164 B3** 22 30N 82 30W
Batac, *Phil.* **80 B3** 18 3N 120 34 E
Batagai, *Russia* **67 C14** 67 38N 134 38 E
Batajnica, *Serbia, Yug.* **50 B4** 44 54N 20 17 E
Batak, *Bulgaria* **51 E8** 41 57N 24 12 E
Batala, *India* **92 D6** 31 48N 75 12 E
Batalha, *Portugal* **42 F2** 39 40N 8 50W
Batam, *Indonesia* **84 B2** 1 5N 104 3 E
Batama, *Dem. Rep. of the Congo* **118 B2** 0 58N 26 33 E
Batamay, *Russia* **67 C13** 63 30N 129 15 E
Batan I., *Albay, Phil.* **80 E4** 13 15N 124 0 E
Batan I., *Batanes, Phil.* **80 A3** 20 26N 121 58 E
Batanes □, *Phil.* **80 A3** 20 40N 121 55 E
Batanes Is., *Phil.* **80 A3** 20 30N 122 0 E
Batang, *China* **76 B2** 30 1N 99 0 E
Batang, *Indonesia* **85 D3** 6 55 S 109 45 E
Batanga, *Gabon* **114 C1** 0 21 S 9 18 E
Batangafo, *C.A.R.* **114 A3** 7 25N 18 20 E
Batangas, *Phil.* **80 E3** 13 35N 121 10 E
Batangas □, *Phil.* **80 E3** 13 40N 121 5 E
Batanghari, *Indonesia* **84 C2** 1 36 S 103 37 E
Batanta, *Indonesia* **83 B4** 0 55 S 130 40 E
Bataraza, *Phil.* **81 G1** 8 40N 117 37 E
Batas I., *Phil.* **81 F2** 11 10N 119 36 E
Batatais, *Brazil* **175 A6** 20 54 S 47 37W
Batavia, *Ill., U.S.A.* **157 C8** 41 51N 88 19W
Batavia, *N.Y., U.S.A.* **150 D6** 43 0N 78 11W
Batavia, *Ohio, U.S.A.* **157 E12** 39 5N 84 11W
Bataysk, *Russia* **59 J10** 47 3N 39 45 E
Batchelor, *Australia* **124 B5** 13 4 S 131 1 E
Batdambang, *Cambodia* **86 F4** 13 7N 103 12 E
Batéké, Plateau, *Congo* **114 C3** 3 30 S 15 45 E
Batemans B., *Australia* **129 C9** 35 40 S 150 12 E
Batemans Bay, *Australia* **129 C9** 35 44 S 150 11 E
Bates Ra., *Australia* **125 E3** 27 27 S 121 5 E
Batesburg-Leesville, *U.S.A.* **152 B8** 33 54N 81 33W
Batesville, *Ark., U.S.A.* **155 H9** 35 46N 91 39W
Batesville, *Ind., U.S.A.* **157 E11** 39 18N 85 13W
Batesville, *Miss., U.S.A.* **155 H10** 34 19N 89 57W
Batesville, *Tex., U.S.A.* **155 L5** 28 58N 99 37W
Bath, *Canada* **151 B8** 44 11N 76 47W
Bath, *U.K.* **21 F5** 51 23N 2 22W
Bath, *Maine, U.S.A.* **149 D11** 43 55N 69 49W
Bath, *N.Y., U.S.A.* **150 D7** 42 20N 77 19W
Bath, *S.C., U.S.A.* **152 B8** 33 31N 81 51W
Bath & North East Somerset □, *U.K.* **21 F5** 51 21N 2 27W
Batha →, *Chad* **109 F3** 12 47N 17 34 E
Batheay, *Cambodia* **87 G5** 11 59N 104 57 E
Bathsheba, *Barbados* **165 g** 13 13N 59 31W
Bathurst = Banjul, *Gambia* **112 C1** 13 28N 16 40W
Bathurst, *Australia* **129 B8** 33 25 S 149 31 E
Bathurst, *Canada* **141 C6** 47 37N 65 43W
Bathurst, *S. Africa* **116 E4** 33 30 S 26 50 E
Bathurst, C., *Canada* **138 A7** 70 34N 128 0W
Bathurst B., *Australia* **126 A3** 14 16 S 144 25 E
Bathurst Harb., *Australia* **127 G4** 43 15 S 146 10 E
Bathurst I., *Australia* **124 B5** 11 30 S 130 10 E
Bathurst I., *Canada* **6 B2** 76 0N 100 30W
Bathurst Inlet, *Canada* **138 B9** 66 50N 108 1W
Bati, *Ethiopia* **107 E5** 11 10N 40 0 E
Batie, *Burkina Faso* **112 D4** 9 53N 2 53W
Batiki, *Fiji* **133 A2** 17 48 S 179 10 E
Batlow, *Australia* **129 C8** 35 31 S 148 9 E
Batman, *Turkey* **101 D9** 37 55N 41 5 E
Baţn al Ghūl, *Jordan* **103 F4** 29 36N 35 56 E
Batna, *Algeria* **111 A6** 35 34N 6 15 E
Batnfjordsøra, *Norway* **18 B4** 62 53N 7 42 E
Bato, *Catanduanes, Phil.* **80 E5** 13 36N 124 18 E
Bato, *Leyte, Phil.* **81 F5** 10 13N 124 48 E
Bato Bato, *Phil.* **81 J2** 5 6N 119 49 E
Batoala, *Gabon* **114 B2** 0 48N 13 27 E
Batobato = San Isidro, *Phil.* **81 H6** 6 50N 126 5 E
Batočina, *Serbia, Yug.* **50 B5** 44 7N 21 5 E
Batoka, *Zambia* **119 F2** 16 45 S 27 15 E
Baton Rouge, *U.S.A.* **155 K9** 30 27N 91 11W
Batong, Ko, *Thailand* **87 J2** 6 32N 99 12 E
Bátonyterenye, *Hungary* **52 C4** 47 59N 19 50 E
Batopilas, *Mexico* **162 B3** 27 0N 107 45W
Batouri, *Cameroon* **114 B2** 4 30N 14 25 E
Båtsfjord, *Norway* **14 A23** 70 38N 29 39 E
Battambang = Batdambang, *Cambodia* **86 F4** 13 7N 103 12 E
Batti Malv, *India* **95 K11** 8 50N 92 51 E
Batticaloa, *Sri Lanka* **95 L5** 7 43N 81 45 E
Battipáglia, *Italy* **47 B7** 40 37N 14 58 E
Battle, *U.K.* **21 G8** 50 55N 0 30 E
Battle →, *Canada* **143 C7** 52 43N 108 15W
Battle Creek, *U.S.A.* **157 B11** 42 19N 85 11W
Battle Ground, *U.S.A.* **160 E4** 45 47N 122 32W
Battle Harbour, *Canada* **141 B8** 52 16N 55 35W
Battle Lake, *U.S.A.* **154 B7** 46 17N 95 43W
Battle Mountain, *U.S.A.* **158 F5** 40 38N 116 56W
Battlefields, *Zimbabwe* **119 F2** 18 37 S 29 47 E
Battleford, *Canada* **143 C7** 52 45N 108 15W
Battonya, *Hungary* **52 D6** 46 16N 21 3 E
Batu, *Ethiopia* **107 F4** 6 55N 39 45 E
Batu, Bukit, *Malaysia* **85 B4** 2 16N 113 43 E
Batu, Kepulauan, *Indonesia* **84 C1** 0 30 S 98 25 E
Batu Bora, Bukit, *Malaysia* **85 B4** 2 43N 114 43 E
Batu Caves, *Malaysia* **87 L3** 3 15N 101 40 E
Batu Ferringhi, *Malaysia* **87 c** 5 28N 100 15 E
Batu Gajah, *Malaysia* **87 K3** 4 28N 101 3 E
Batu Is. = Batu, Kepulauan, *Indonesia* **84 C1** 0 30 S 98 25 E
Batu Pahat, *Malaysia* **87 M4** 1 50N 102 56 E
Batu Puteh, Gunong, *Malaysia* **84 B2** 4 15N 101 31 E
Batuata, *Indonesia* **82 C2** 6 12 S 122 42 E
Batugondang, Tanjung, *Indonesia* **79 J17** 8 6 S 114 29 E
Batui, *Indonesia* **82 B2** 1 17 S 122 33 E
Batukau, Gunung, *Indonesia* **79 J18** 8 20 S 115 5 E
Batulaki, *Phil.* **81 J5** 5 34N 125 19 E
Batumi, *Georgia* **61 K5** 41 39N 41 44 E
Batur, *Indonesia* **79 J18** 8 15 S 115 20 E
Batur, Gunung, *Indonesia* **79 J18** 8 14 S 115 23 E
Baturaja, *Indonesia* **84 C2** 4 11 S 104 15 E
Baturité, *Brazil* **170 B4** 4 28 S 38 45W
Baturiti, *Indonesia* **79 J18** 8 19 S 115 11 E
Batusangkar, *Indonesia* **84 C2** 0 27 S 100 35 E
Bau, *Malaysia* **85 B4** 1 25N 110 9 E
Bauang, *Phil.* **80 C3** 16 31N 120 20 E
Baubau, *Indonesia* **82 C2** 5 25 S 122 38 E
Baucau, *E. Timor* **82 C3** 8 27 S 126 27 E
Bauchi, *Nigeria* **113 C6** 10 22N 9 48 E
Bauchi □, *Nigeria* **113 C7** 10 30N 10 0 E
Baud, *France* **26 E3** 47 52N 3 1W
Bauda, *India* **94 D7** 20 50N 84 25 E
Baudette, *U.S.A.* **154 A7** 48 43N 94 36W
Bauen, *Switz.* **33 C7** 46 56N 8 35 E
Bauer, C., *Australia* **127 E1** 32 44 S 134 4 E
Bauhinia, *Australia* **126 C4** 24 35 S 149 18 E
Baukau = Baucau, *E. Timor* **82 C3** 8 27 S 126 27 E
Bauko, *Phil.* **80 C3** 17 0N 120 52 E
Baulai →, *Bangla.* **90 C3** 24 22N 91 1 E
Bauld, C., *Canada* **139 C14** 51 38N 55 26W
Bauma, *Switz.* **33 B7** 47 23N 8 53 E
Baume-les-Dames, *France* **27 E13** 47 22N 6 22 E
Baunatal, *Germany* **30 D5** 51 14N 9 24 E
Baunei, *Italy* **46 B2** 40 2N 9 40 E
Baure, *Nigeria* **113 C6** 12 52N 8 50 E

Belvidere 189

Baures, Bolivia 173 C5 13 35 S 63 35W
Bauru, Brazil 175 A6 22 10 S 49 0W
Baús, Brazil 173 D7 18 22 S 52 47W
Bausi, India 93 G12 24 48N 87 1 E
Bauska, Latvia 15 H21 56 24N 24 15 E
Bautino, Kazakstan 61 H10 44 35N 50 14 E
Bautzen, Germany 30 D10 51 10N 14 26 E
Bauya, S. Leone 112 D2 8 12N 12 38W
Baŭyrzhan Momyshuly, Kazakstan 65 B5 42 36N 70 47 E
Bavānāt, Iran 97 D7 30 28N 53 27 E
Bavanište, Serbia, Yug. 52 F5 44 49N 20 55 E
Bavaria = Bayern □, Germany 31 G7 48 50N 12 0 E
Båven, Sweden 16 E10 59 0N 16 56 E
Bavispe →, Mexico 162 B3 29 30N 109 11W
Baw Baw Nat. Park, Australia 129 D7 37 50 S 146 17 E
Bawdwin, Burma 90 D6 23 5N 97 20 E
Bawe, Indonesia 83 B4 2 59 S 134 43 E
Bawean, Indonesia 85 D4 5 46 S 112 35 E
Bawku, Ghana 113 C4 11 3N 0 19W
Bawlake, Burma 90 F6 19 11N 97 21 E
Bawolung, China 76 C3 28 50N 101 16 E
Baxley, U.S.A. 152 D7 31 47N 82 21W
Baxoi, China 76 B1 30 1N 96 50 E
Baxter, Iowa, U.S.A. 156 C3 41 49N 93 9W
Baxter, Minn., U.S.A. 154 B7 46 21N 94 17W
Baxter Springs, U.S.A. 155 G7 37 2N 94 44W
Bay, L. de, Phil. 80 D3 14 20N 121 11 E
Bay al Khā'ib, Wādī →, Libya 108 B3 30 55N 15 29 E
Bay City, Mich., U.S.A. 148 D4 43 36N 83 54W
Bay City, Tex., U.S.A. 155 L7 28 59N 95 58W
Bay Minette, U.S.A. 149 K2 30 53N 87 46W
Bay of Plenty □, N.Z. 130 D5 38 0 S 177 0 E
Bay Roberts, Canada 141 C9 47 36N 53 16W
Bay St. Louis, U.S.A. 155 K10 30 19N 89 20W
Bay Springs, U.S.A. 155 K10 31 59N 89 17W
Bay View, N.Z. 130 F5 39 25 S 176 50 E
Baya, Dem. Rep. of the Congo 119 E2 11 53 S 27 25 E
Bayambang, Phil. 80 D3 15 49N 120 27 E
Bayamo, Cuba 164 B4 20 20N 76 40W
Bayamón, Puerto Rico 165 d 18 24N 66 10W
Bayan Har Shan, China 68 C4 34 0N 98 0 E
Bayan Hot = Alxa Zuoqi, China 74 E3 38 50N 105 40 E
Bayan Lepas, Malaysia 87 c 5 17N 100 16 E
Bayan Obo, China 74 D5 41 52N 109 59 E
Bayan-Ovoo = Erdenetsogt, Mongolia 74 C4 42 55N 106 5 E
Bayana, India 92 F7 26 55N 77 18 E
Bayanaūyl, Kazakstan 66 D8 50 45N 75 45 E
Bayandalay, Mongolia 74 C2 43 30N 103 29 E
Bayanhongor, Mongolia 68 B5 46 8N 102 43 E
Bayard, N. Mex., U.S.A. 159 K9 32 46N 108 8W
Bayard, Nebr., U.S.A. 154 E3 41 45N 103 20W
Bayawan, Phil. 81 G4 9 46N 122 45 E
Baybay, Phil. 81 F5 10 40N 124 55 E
Bayburt, Turkey 101 B9 40 15N 40 20 E
Baydhabo = Baidoa, Somali Rep. 120 D2 3 8N 43 30 E
Bayelsa □, Nigeria 113 E6 4 30N 6 0 E
Bayerische Alpen, Germany 31 H7 47 35N 11 30 E
Bayerischer Wald, Germany 31 G8 48 56N 12 50 E
Bayern □, Germany 31 G7 48 50N 12 0 E
Bayeux, France 26 C6 49 17N 0 42W
Bayfield, Canada 150 C3 43 34N 81 42W
Bayfield, U.S.A. 154 B9 46 49N 90 49W
Bäygequm, Kazakstan 65 A3 44 19N 66 27 E
Bayḩān al Qiṣāb, Yemen 98 D4 15 48N 45 44 E
Bayındır, Turkey 49 C9 38 13N 27 39 E
Baykal, Oz., Russia 67 D11 53 0N 108 0 E
Baykan, Turkey 96 B4 38 7N 41 44 E
Baykonur = Bayqongyr, Kazakstan 66 E7 47 48N 65 50 E
Baykurt, China 65 D7 39 56N 75 33 E
Baymak, Russia 64 E7 52 36N 58 19 E
Baymurat, Uzbekistan 65 C3 41 8N 66 25 E
Baynes Mts., Namibia 116 B1 17 15 S 13 0 E
Bayombong, Phil. 80 C3 16 30N 121 10 E
Bayon, France 27 D13 48 30N 6 20 E
Bayona = Baiona, Spain 42 C2 42 6N 8 52W
Bayonne, France 28 E2 43 30N 1 28W
Bayonne, U.S.A. 151 F10 40 40N 74 7W
Bayovar, Peru 172 B1 5 50 S 81 0W
Bayport, U.S.A. 153 G7 28 32N 82 39W
Bayqongyr, Kazakstan 66 E7 47 48N 65 50 E
Bayram-Ali = Bayramaly, Turkmenistan 66 F7 37 37N 62 10 E
Bayramaly, Turkmenistan 66 F7 37 37N 62 10 E
Bayramiç, Turkey 49 B8 39 48N 26 36 E
Bayreuth, Germany 31 F7 49 56N 11 35 E
Bayrischzell, Germany 31 H8 47 41N 12 0 E
Bayrūt, Lebanon 103 B4 33 53N 35 31 E
Bays, L. of, Canada 150 A5 45 15N 79 4W
Bayshore, U.S.A. 153 J8 26 43N 81 50W
Baysun, Uzbekistan 65 D3 38 12N 67 12 E
Baysville, Canada 150 A5 45 9N 79 7W
Bayt al Faqīh, Yemen 98 D3 14 31N 43 19 E
Bayt Lahm, West Bank 103 D4 31 43N 35 12 E
Baytown, U.S.A. 155 L7 29 43N 94 59W
Bayugan, Phil. 81 G5 8 43N 125 42 E
Bayun, Indonesia 79 J18 8 11 S 115 16 E
Bayyrqum, Kazakstan 65 B4 42 7N 68 3 E
Bayzhansay, Kazakstan 65 B4 43 14N 69 54 E
Bayzo, Niger 113 C5 13 52N 4 35 E
Baza, Spain 43 H8 37 30N 2 47W
Bazar Dyuzi, Russia 61 K8 41 12N 47 50 E
Bazar-Korgon, Kyrgyzstan 65 C6 41 0N 72 43 E
Bazardüzü = Bazar Dyuzi, Russia 61 K8 41 12N 47 50 E
Bazarny Karabulak, Russia 60 D8 52 20N 46 29 E
Bazarnyy Syzgan, Russia 60 D8 53 45N 46 40 E
Bazaruto, I. do, Mozam. 117 C6 21 40 S 35 28 E
Bazaruto, Parque Nacional de, Mozam. 117 C6 21 42 S 35 26 E
Bazas, France 28 D3 44 27N 0 13W
Bazhong, China 76 B6 31 52N 106 46 E
Bazhou, China 74 E9 39 8N 116 22 E
Bazmān, Kūh-e, Iran 97 D9 28 4N 60 1 E
Beach, U.S.A. 154 B3 46 58N 104 0W
Beach City, U.S.A. 150 F3 40 39N 81 35W
Beachport, Australia 128 D4 37 29 S 140 0 E
Beachy Hd., U.K. 21 G8 50 44N 0 15 E
Beacon, Australia 125 F2 30 26 S 117 52 E
Beacon, U.S.A. 151 E11 41 30N 73 58W
Beaconsfield, Australia 127 G4 41 11 S 146 48 E
Beagle, Canal, S. Amer. 176 E3 55 0 S 68 30W
Beagle Bay, Australia 124 C3 16 58 S 122 40 E
Bealanana, Madag. 117 A8 14 33 S 48 44 E
Beals Cr. →, U.S.A. 155 J4 32 10N 100 51W
Beamsville, Canada 150 C5 43 12N 79 28W
Bear →, Calif., U.S.A. 160 G5 38 56N 121 36W
Bear →, Utah, U.S.A. 146 B4 41 30N 112 8W
Béar, C., France 28 F7 42 31N 3 8 E
Bear I., Ireland 23 E2 51 38N 9 50W
Bear L., Canada 143 B9 55 8N 96 0W
Bear L., U.S.A. 158 F8 41 59N 111 21W
Beardmore, Canada 140 C2 49 36N 87 57W
Beardmore Glacier, Antarctica 7 E11 84 30 S 170 0 E
Beardstown, U.S.A. 156 E6 40 1N 90 26W
Bearma →, India 93 G8 24 20N 79 51 E
Béarn, France 28 E3 43 20N 0 30W
Bearpaw Mts., U.S.A. 158 B9 48 12N 109 30W
Bearskin Lake, Canada 140 B1 53 58N 91 2W
Beas →, India 92 D6 31 10N 74 59 E
Beas de Segura, Spain 43 G8 38 15N 2 53W
Beasain, Spain 40 B2 43 3N 2 11W
Beata, C., Dom. Rep. 165 C5 17 40N 71 30W
Beata, I., Dom. Rep. 165 C5 17 34N 71 31W
Beatrice, U.S.A. 154 E6 40 16N 96 45W
Beatrice, Zimbabwe 119 F3 18 15 S 30 55 E
Beatrice, C., Australia 126 A2 14 20 S 136 55 E
Beatton →, Canada 142 B4 56 15N 120 45W
Beatton River, Canada 142 B4 57 26N 121 20W
Beatty, U.S.A. 160 J10 36 54N 116 46W
Beau Bassin, Mauritius 121 d 20 13 S 57 27 E
Beaucaire, France 29 E8 43 48N 4 39 E
Beauce, Plaine de la, France 27 D8 48 10N 1 45 E
Beauceville, Canada 141 C5 46 13N 70 46W
Beauchêne, I., Falk. Is. 9 f 52 55 S 59 15W
Beaudesert, Australia 127 D5 27 59 S 153 0 E
Beaufort, Australia 128 D5 37 25 S 143 25 E
Beaufort, France 29 C10 45 44N 6 34 E
Beaufort, Malaysia 85 A5 5 30N 115 40 E
Beaufort, N.C., U.S.A. 149 H7 34 43N 76 40W
Beaufort, S.C., U.S.A. 152 C9 32 26N 80 40W
Beaufort Sea, Arctic 6 B1 72 0N 140 0W
Beaufort West, S. Africa 116 E3 32 18 S 22 36 E
Beaugency, France 27 E8 47 47N 1 38 E
Beauharnois, Canada 151 A11 45 20N 73 52W
Beaujeu, France 27 F11 46 10N 4 35 E
Beaujolais, France 27 F11 46 0N 4 22 E
Beaulieu →, Canada 142 A6 62 3N 113 11W
Beaulieu-sur-Dordogne, France 28 D5 44 58N 1 50 E
Beaulieu-sur-Mer, France 29 E11 43 42N 7 20 E
Beauly, U.K. 22 D4 57 30N 4 28W
Beauly →, U.K. 22 D4 57 29N 4 27W
Beaumaris, U.K. 20 D3 53 16N 4 6W
Beaumont, Belgium 24 D4 50 15N 4 14 E
Beaumont, France 28 D4 44 45N 0 46 E
Beaumont, N.Z. 131 F4 45 50 S 169 33 E
Beaumont, U.S.A. 155 K7 30 5N 94 6W
Beaumont-de-Lomagne, France 28 E5 43 53N 1 0 E
Beaumont-le-Roger, France 26 C7 49 4N 0 47 E
Beaumont-sur-Sarthe, France 26 D7 48 13N 0 8 E
Beaune, France 27 E11 47 2N 4 50 E
Beaune-la-Rolande, France 27 D9 48 4N 2 25 E
Beaupré, Canada 141 C5 47 3N 70 54W
Beaupréau, France 26 E6 47 12N 1 0W
Beauraing, Belgium 24 D4 50 7N 4 57 E
Beaurepaire, France 29 C9 45 22N 5 1 E
Beauséjour, Canada 143 C9 50 5N 96 35W
Beautemps-Beaupré, Î., N. Cal. 133 K4 20 24 S 166 9 E
Beauvais, France 27 C9 49 25N 2 8 E
Beauval, Canada 143 B7 55 9N 107 37W
Beauvoir-sur-Mer, France 26 F4 46 55N 2 2W
Beauvoir-sur-Niort, France 28 B3 46 12N 0 30W
Beaver, Alaska, U.S.A. 144 C11 66 22N 147 24W
Beaver, Okla., U.S.A. 155 G4 36 49N 100 31W
Beaver, Pa., U.S.A. 150 F4 40 42N 80 19W
Beaver, Utah, U.S.A. 159 G7 38 17N 112 38W
Beaver →, B.C., Canada 142 B4 59 52N 124 20W
Beaver →, Ont., Canada 140 A2 55 55N 87 48W
Beaver →, Sask., Canada 143 B7 55 26N 107 45W
Beaver →, U.S.A. 155 G5 36 35N 99 30W
Beaver City, U.S.A. 154 E5 40 8N 99 50W
Beaver Creek, Canada 138 B5 63 0N 141 0W
Beaver Dam, U.S.A. 154 D10 43 28N 88 50W
Beaver Falls, U.S.A. 150 F4 40 46N 80 20W
Beaver Hill L., Canada 143 C10 54 5N 94 50W
Beaver I., U.S.A. 148 C3 45 40N 85 33W
Beavercreek, U.S.A. 157 E12 39 43N 84 11W
Beaverhill L., Canada 142 C6 53 27N 112 32W
Beaverlodge, Canada 142 B5 55 11N 119 29W
Beaverstone →, Canada 140 B2 54 59N 89 25W
Beaverton, Canada 150 B5 44 26N 79 9W
Beaverton, U.S.A. 160 E4 45 29N 122 48W
Beawar, India 92 F6 26 3N 74 18 E
Bebedouro, Brazil 175 A6 21 0 S 48 25W
Bebera, Tanjung, Indonesia 79 K18 8 44 S 115 51 E
Beboa, Madag. 117 B7 17 22 S 44 33 E
Beboto, Chad 109 G3 8 16N 16 56 E
Bebra, Germany 30 E5 50 58N 9 48 E
Beccles, U.K. 21 E9 52 27N 1 35 E
Bečej, Serbia, Yug. 52 E5 45 36N 20 3 E
Beceni, Romania 53 E11 45 23N 26 48 E
Becerreá, Spain 42 C3 42 51N 7 10W
Béchar, Algeria 111 B4 31 38N 2 18W
Becharof L., U.S.A. 144 H8 57 56N 156 23W
Bechyně, Czech Rep. 34 B7 49 17N 14 29 E
Beckley, U.S.A. 148 G5 37 47N 81 11W
Beckum, Germany 30 D4 51 45N 8 3 E
Beclean, Romania 53 C9 47 11N 24 11 E
Bečov nad Teplou, Czech Rep. 34 A5 50 5N 12 49 E
Bečva →, Czech Rep. 35 B10 49 31N 17 20 E
Bédar, Spain 41 H3 37 11N 1 59W
Bédarieux, France 28 E7 43 37N 3 10 E
Beddouza, Ras, Morocco 110 B3 32 33N 9 9W
Bedele, Ethiopia 107 F4 8 31N 36 23 E
Bederkesa, Germany 30 B4 53 37N 8 50 E
Bederwanak, Somali Rep. 120 C2 9 34N 44 23 E
Bedeso, Ethiopia 107 F5 9 58N 40 52 E
Bedford, Canada 151 A12 45 7N 72 59W
Bedford, S. Africa 116 E4 32 40 S 26 10 E
Bedford, U.K. 21 E7 52 8N 0 28W
Bedford, Ind., U.S.A. 157 F10 38 52N 86 29W
Bedford, Iowa, U.S.A. 156 D2 40 40N 94 44W
Bedford, Ky., U.S.A. 157 F11 38 36N 85 19W
Bedford, Ohio, U.S.A. 150 E3 41 23N 81 32W
Bedford, Pa., U.S.A. 150 F6 40 1N 78 30W
Bedford, Va., U.S.A. 148 G6 37 20N 79 31W
Bedford, C., Australia 126 B4 15 14 S 145 21 E
Bedfordshire □, U.K. 21 E7 52 4N 0 28W
Bedi, Chad 109 F3 11 6N 18 33 E
Będków, Poland 55 G6 51 36N 19 44 E
Bednja →, Croatia 45 B13 46 20N 16 52 E
Bednodemyanovsk, Russia 60 D6 53 55N 43 15 E
Bedok, Singapore 87 d 1 19N 103 56 E
Bedónia, Italy 44 D6 44 30N 9 38 E
Bedourie, Australia 126 C2 24 30 S 139 30 E
Bedretto, Switz. 33 C7 46 31N 8 31 E
Bedti →, India 95 G2 14 50N 74 44 E
Bedum, Neths. 24 A6 53 18N 6 36 E
Będzin, Poland 55 H6 50 19N 19 7 E
Bee Ridge, U.S.A. 153 H7 27 17N 82 29W
Beebe Plain, Canada 151 A12 45 1N 72 9W
Beech Creek, U.S.A. 150 E7 41 5N 77 36W
Beech Fork →, U.S.A. 157 G11 37 46N 85 41W
Beech Grove, U.S.A. 157 E10 39 44N 86 3W
Beecher, U.S.A. 157 C9 41 21N 87 38W
Beechworth, Australia 129 D7 36 22 S 146 43 E
Beef I., Br. Virgin Is. 165 e 18 26N 64 30W
Beelitz, Germany 30 C8 52 14N 12 58 E
Beenleigh, Australia 127 D5 27 43 S 153 10 E
Be'er Menuḥa, Israel 96 D2 30 19N 35 8 E
Be'er Sheva, Israel 103 D3 31 15N 34 48 E
Beersheba = Be'er Sheva, Israel 103 D3 31 15N 34 48 E
Beeskow, Germany 30 C10 52 10N 14 15 E
Beestekraal, S. Africa 117 D4 25 23 S 27 38 E
Beeston, U.K. 20 E6 52 56N 1 14W
Beetzendorf, Germany 30 C7 52 42N 11 6 E
Beeville, U.S.A. 155 L6 28 24N 97 45W
Befale, Dem. Rep. of the Congo 114 B4 0 25N 20 45 E
Befandriana, Mahajanga, Madag. 117 B8 15 16 S 48 32 E
Befandriana, Toliara, Madag. 117 C7 21 55 S 44 0 E
Befasy, Madag. 117 C7 20 33 S 44 22 E
Befori, Dem. Rep. of the Congo 114 B4 0 8N 22 22 E
Befotaka, Antsiranana, Madag. 117 A8 13 15 S 48 16 E
Befotaka, Fianarantsoa, Madag. 117 C8 23 49 S 47 0 E
Bega, Australia 129 D8 36 41 S 149 51 E
Bega, Canalul, Romania 52 E5 45 37N 20 46 E
Bégard, France 26 D3 48 38N 3 18W
Beğendik, Turkey 51 F10 40 55N 26 34 E
Begndal, Norway 18 D6 60 49N 9 46 E
Begoro, Ghana 113 D4 6 23N 0 23W
Begusarai, India 93 G12 25 24N 86 9 E
Behābād, Iran 97 C8 32 24N 59 47 E
Behala, India 93 H13 22 30N 88 20 E
Behara, Madag. 117 C8 24 55 S 46 20 E
Behbehān, Iran 97 D6 30 30N 50 15 E
Behm Canal, U.S.A. 142 B2 55 10N 131 0W
Behshahr, Iran 97 B7 36 45N 53 35 E
Bei Jiang →, China 77 F9 23 2N 112 58 E
Bei'an, China 69 B7 48 10N 126 20 E
Beibei, China 76 C6 29 47N 106 22 E
Beichuan, China 76 B5 31 55N 104 39 E
Beihai, China 76 G7 21 28N 109 6 E
Beijing, China 74 E9 39 55N 116 20 E
Beijing □, China 74 E9 39 55N 116 20 E
Beilen, Neths. 24 B6 52 52N 6 27 E
Beiliu, China 77 F8 22 41N 110 21 E
Beilngries, Germany 31 F7 49 2N 11 28 E
Beilpajah, Australia 128 B5 32 54 S 143 52 E
Beilul, Eritrea 107 E5 13 2N 42 20 E
Béinamar, Chad 109 G3 8 40N 15 23 E
Beinn na Faoghla = Benbecula, U.K. 22 D1 57 26N 7 21W
Beipan Jiang, China 76 E5 25 7N 106 1 E
Beipiao, China 75 D11 41 52N 120 32 E
Beira, Mozam. 119 F3 19 50 S 34 52 E
Beira, Somali Rep. 120 C3 6 57N 47 19 E
Beirut = Bayrūt, Lebanon 103 B4 33 53N 35 31 E
Beiseker, Canada 142 C6 51 23N 113 32W
Beitaolaizhao, China 75 B13 44 58N 125 58 E
Beitbridge, Zimbabwe 119 G3 22 12 S 30 0 E
Beiuş, Romania 52 D7 46 40N 22 21 E
Beizhen = Binzhou, China 75 F10 37 20N 118 2 E
Beizhen, China 75 D11 41 38N 121 54 E
Beizhengzhen, China 75 B12 44 31N 123 30 E
Beja, Portugal 43 G3 38 2N 7 53W
Béja, Tunisia 108 A1 36 43N 9 12 E
Beja □, Portugal 43 H3 37 55N 7 55W
Bejaïa, Algeria 111 A6 36 42N 5 2 E
Béjar, Spain 42 E5 40 23N 5 46W
Bejestān, Iran 97 C8 34 30N 58 5 E
Bekabad, Uzbekistan 65 C4 40 13N 69 14 E
Bekasi, Indonesia 84 D3 6 14 S 106 59 E
Bekçiler, Turkey 49 E11 36 56N 29 44 E
Békés, Hungary 52 D6 46 47N 21 9 E
Békés □, Hungary 52 D6 46 45N 21 0 E
Békéscsaba, Hungary 52 D6 46 40N 21 5 E
Bekilli, Turkey 49 C11 38 17N 29 27 E
Bekily, Madag. 117 C8 24 13 S 45 19 E
Bekisopa, Madag. 117 C8 21 40 S 45 54 E
Bekitro, Madag. 117 C8 24 33 S 45 18 E
Bekodoka, Madag. 117 B8 16 58 S 45 7 E
Bekoji, Ethiopia 107 F4 7 40N 39 17 E
Bekok, Malaysia 87 L4 2 20N 103 7 E
Bekopaka, Madag. 117 B7 19 9 S 44 48 E
Bekuli, Indonesia 79 J17 8 22 S 114 13 E
Bekwai, Ghana 113 D4 6 30N 1 34W
Bela, India 93 G10 25 50N 82 0 E
Bela, Pakistan 91 D2 26 12N 66 20 E
Bela Crkva, Serbia, Yug. 52 F6 44 55N 21 27 E
Bela Palanka, Serbia, Yug. 50 C6 43 13N 22 17 E
Bela Vista, Brazil 174 A4 22 12 S 56 20W
Bela Vista, Mozam. 117 D5 26 10 S 32 44 E
Bélâbre, France 28 B5 46 34N 1 8 E
Belaga, Malaysia 85 B4 2 42N 113 47 E
Belalcázar, Spain 43 G5 38 35N 5 10W
Belan →, India 93 G9 24 2N 81 45 E
Belang, Indonesia 82 A2 0 57N 124 47 E
Belanovica, Serbia, Yug. 50 B4 44 15N 20 23 E
Belarus ■, Europe 58 F4 53 30N 27 0 E
Belas, Angola 115 D2 8 55 S 13 9 E
Belau = Palau ■, Pac. Oc. 62 J17 7 30N 134 30 E
Belavenona, Madag. 117 C8 24 50 S 47 4 E
Belawan, Indonesia 84 B1 3 33N 98 32 E
Belaya, Ethiopia 107 E4 11 25N 36 8 E
Belaya →, Russia 64 D6 54 40N 56 0 E
Belaya Glina, Russia 61 G5 46 5N 40 48 E
Belaya Kalitva, Russia 61 F5 48 13N 40 50 E
Belaya Kholunitsa, Russia 64 B3 58 51N 50 53 E
Belaya Tserkov = Bila Tserkva, Ukraine 59 H6 49 45N 30 10 E
Belayan →, Indonesia 85 C5 0 14 S 116 36 E
Belceşti, Romania 53 C12 47 19N 27 7 E
Bełchatów, Poland 55 G6 51 21N 19 22 E
Belcher Is., Canada 140 A3 56 15N 78 45W
Belchite, Spain 40 D4 41 18N 0 43W
Belden, U.S.A. 160 E5 40 2N 121 17W
Belding, U.S.A. 157 A11 43 6N 85 14W
Belebey, Russia 64 D5 54 7N 54 7 E
Beled Weyne = Belet Uen, Somali Rep. 120 D3 4 30N 45 5 E
Belém, Brazil 170 B2 1 20 S 48 30W
Belém de São Francisco, Brazil 170 C4 8 46 S 38 58W
Belén, Argentina 174 B2 27 40 S 67 5W
Belén, Colombia 168 C2 1 26N 75 56W
Belén, Paraguay 174 A4 23 30 S 57 6W
Belen, U.S.A. 159 J10 34 40N 106 46W
Belene, Bulgaria 51 C9 43 39N 25 10 E
Beleni, Turkey 100 D7 36 31N 36 10 E
Bélep, Is., N. Cal. 123 D11 19 45 S 163 40 E
Bélesta, France 28 F5 42 55N 1 56 E
Belet Uen, Somali Rep. 120 D3 4 30N 45 5 E
Belev, Russia 58 F9 53 50N 36 5 E
Belevi, Turkey 49 C9 38 0N 27 28 E
Belfair, U.S.A. 160 C4 47 27N 122 50W
Belfast, N.Z. 131 D7 43 27 S 172 39 E
Belfast, S. Africa 117 D5 25 42 S 30 2 E
Belfast, U.K. 23 B6 54 37N 5 56W
Belfast, Maine, U.S.A. 149 C11 44 26N 69 1W
Belfast, N.Y., U.S.A. 150 D6 42 21N 78 7W
Belfast L., U.K. 23 B6 54 40N 5 50W
Belfield, U.S.A. 154 B3 46 53N 103 12W
Belfort, France 27 E13 47 38N 6 50 E
Belfort, Territoire de □, France 27 E13 47 40N 6 55 E
Belfry, U.S.A. 158 D9 45 9N 109 1W
Belgaum, India 95 G2 15 55N 74 35 E
Belgioioso, Italy 44 C6 45 10N 9 19 E
Belgium ■, Europe 24 D4 50 30N 5 0 E
Belgodère, France 29 F13 42 35N 9 1 E
Belgorod, Russia 59 G9 50 35N 36 35 E
Belgorod-Dnestrovskiy = Bilhorod-Dnistrovskyy, Ukraine 59 J6 46 11N 30 23 E
Belgrade = Beograd, Serbia, Yug. 50 B4 44 50N 20 37 E
Belgrade, U.S.A. 158 D8 45 47N 111 11W
Belgrove, N.Z. 131 B7 41 27 S 172 59 E
Belhaven, U.S.A. 149 H7 35 33N 76 37W
Beli Drim →, Europe 50 D4 42 6N 20 25 E
Beli Manastir, Croatia 52 E3 45 45N 18 36 E
Beli Timok →, Serbia, Yug. 50 C6 43 53N 22 14 E
Bélice →, Italy 46 E5 37 35N 12 55 E
Belimbing, Indonesia 79 J18 8 24 S 115 2 E
Belinga, Gabon 114 B2 1 10N 13 2 E
Belinskiy, Russia 60 D6 53 0N 43 25 E
Belinyu, Indonesia 84 C3 1 35 S 105 50 E
Beliton Is. = Belitung, Indonesia 85 C3 3 10 S 107 50 E
Belitung, Indonesia 85 C3 3 10 S 107 50 E
Beliu, Romania 52 D6 46 30N 22 0 E
Belize, Angola 115 C2 4 39 S 12 46 E
Belize ■, Cent. Amer. 163 D7 17 0N 88 30W
Belize City, Belize 163 D7 17 25N 88 0W
Beljakovci, Macedonia 50 D5 42 6N 21 59 E
Beljanica, Serbia, Yug. 50 B5 44 8N 21 43 E
Belkovskiy, Ostrov, Russia 67 B14 75 32N 135 44 E
Bell, U.S.A. 152 F7 29 45N 82 52W
Bell →, Canada 140 C4 49 48N 77 38W
Bell I., Canada 141 B8 50 46N 55 35W
Bell-Irving →, Canada 142 B3 56 12N 129 5W
Bell Peninsula, Canada 139 B11 63 50N 82 0W
Bell Ville, Argentina 174 C3 32 40 S 62 40W
Bella, Italy 47 B8 40 45N 15 32 E
Bella Bella, Canada 142 C3 52 10N 128 10W
Bella Coola, Canada 142 C3 52 25N 126 40W
Bella Flor, Bolivia 172 C4 11 9 S 67 49W
Bella Unión, Uruguay 174 C4 30 15 S 57 40W
Bella Vista, Corrientes, Argentina 174 B4 28 33 S 59 0W
Bella Vista, Tucuman, Argentina 174 B2 27 10 S 65 25W
Bellac, France 28 B5 46 7N 1 3 E
Bellágio, Italy 44 C6 45 59N 9 15 E
Bellaire, U.S.A. 150 F4 40 1N 80 45W
Bellária, Italy 45 D9 44 9N 12 28 E
Bellary, India 95 G3 15 10N 76 56 E
Bellata, Australia 127 D4 29 53 S 149 46 E
Bellavista, Ecuador 172 a 0 41 S 90 18W
Belle, U.S.A. 156 F5 38 17N 91 43W
Belle-Chasse, U.S.A. 155 L10 29 51N 89 59W
Belle Fourche, U.S.A. 154 C3 44 40N 103 51W
Belle Fourche →, U.S.A. 154 C3 44 26N 102 18W
Belle Glade, U.S.A. 149 M5 26 41N 80 40W
Belle-Île, France 26 E3 47 20N 3 10W
Belle Isle, Canada 141 B8 51 57N 55 25W
Belle Isle, U.S.A. 153 G8 28 27N 81 21W
Belle Isle, Str. of, Canada 141 B8 51 30N 56 30W
Belle Plaine, U.S.A. 156 C4 41 54N 92 17W
Belle Rive, U.S.A. 157 F8 38 14N 88 45W
Belle Yella, Liberia 112 D3 7 24N 10 0W
Belledonne, France 29 C10 45 20N 6 10 E
Bellefontaine, U.S.A. 157 D13 40 22N 83 46W
Bellefonte, U.S.A. 150 F7 40 55N 77 47W
Bellegarde, France 27 E9 47 59N 2 26 E
Bellegarde-en-Marche, France 28 C6 45 59N 2 18 E
Bellegarde-sur-Valserine, France 27 F12 46 4N 5 50 E
Bellême, France 26 D7 48 22N 0 34 E
Belleoram, Canada 141 C8 47 31N 55 25W
Belleplaine, Barbados 165 g 13 15N 59 34W
Belleview, U.S.A. 153 F7 29 4N 82 3W
Belleville, Canada 150 B7 44 10N 77 23W
Belleville, France 27 F11 46 7N 4 45 E
Belleville, Ill., U.S.A. 156 F7 38 31N 89 59W
Belleville, Kans., U.S.A. 154 F6 39 50N 97 38W
Belleville, N.Y., U.S.A. 151 C8 43 46N 76 10W
Belleville-sur-Vie, France 26 F5 46 46N 1 25W
Bellevue, Canada 142 D6 49 35N 114 22W
Bellevue, Idaho, U.S.A. 158 E6 43 28N 114 16W
Bellevue, Iowa, U.S.A. 156 B6 42 16N 90 26W
Bellevue, Mich., U.S.A. 157 B11 42 27N 85 1W
Bellevue, Nebr., U.S.A. 154 E7 41 8N 95 53W
Bellevue, Ohio, U.S.A. 150 E2 41 17N 82 51W
Bellevue, Wash., U.S.A. 160 C4 47 37N 122 12W
Belley, France 29 C9 45 46N 5 41 E
Bellin = Kangirsuk, Canada 139 B13 60 0N 70 0W
Bellinge, Denmark 17 J4 55 20N 10 20 E
Bellingen, Australia 129 A10 30 25 S 152 50 E
Bellingham, U.S.A. 138 D7 48 46N 122 29W
Bellingshausen Sea, Antarctica 7 C17 66 0 S 80 0W
Bellinzona, Switz. 33 D8 46 11N 9 1 E
Bello, Colombia 168 B2 6 20N 75 33W
Bellona, Solomon Is. 133 N10 11 17 S 159 47 E
Bellows Falls, U.S.A. 151 C12 43 8N 72 27W
Bellpat, Pakistan 92 E3 29 0N 68 5 E
Bellpuig d'Urgell, Spain 40 D6 41 37N 1 1 E
Belluno, Italy 45 B9 46 9N 12 13 E
Bellville, U.S.A. 152 C8 32 9N 81 59W
Bellwood, U.S.A. 150 F6 40 36N 78 20W
Bélmez, Spain 43 G5 38 17N 5 17W
Belmond, U.S.A. 156 B3 42 51N 93 37W
Belmont, Australia 129 B9 33 4 S 151 42 E
Belmont, Canada 150 D3 42 53N 81 5W
Belmont, S. Africa 116 D3 29 28 S 24 22 E
Belmont, U.S.A. 150 D6 42 14N 78 2W
Belmonte, Brazil 171 E4 16 0 S 39 0W
Belmonte, Portugal 42 E3 40 21N 7 20W
Belmonte, Spain 41 F2 39 34N 2 43W
Belmopan, Belize 163 D7 17 18N 88 30W
Belmullet, Ireland 23 B2 54 14N 9 58W
Belo, Dem. Rep. of the Congo 114 C4 0 32 S 23 13 E
Belo Horizonte, Brazil 171 E3 19 55 S 43 56W
Belo Jardim, Brazil 170 C4 8 20 S 36 26W
Belo Monte, Brazil 169 D7 3 5 S 51 46W
Belo-sur-Mer, Madag. 117 C7 20 42 S 44 0 E
Belo-Tsiribihina, Madag. 117 B7 19 40 S 44 30 E
Belogorsk = Bilohirsk, Ukraine 59 K8 45 3N 34 35 E
Belogorsk, Russia 67 D13 51 0N 128 20 E
Belogradchik, Bulgaria 50 C6 43 53N 22 42 E
Belogradets, Bulgaria 51 C11 43 22N 27 18 E
Beloha, Madag. 117 D8 25 10 S 45 3 E
Beloit, Kans., U.S.A. 154 F5 39 28N 98 6W
Beloit, Wis., U.S.A. 156 B7 42 31N 89 2W
Belokorovichi, Ukraine 59 G5 51 7N 28 2 E
Belomorsk, Russia 56 B5 64 35N 34 54 E
Belondo, Dem. Rep. of the Congo 114 C3 0 15 S 19 31 E
Belonge, Dem. Rep. of the Congo 114 C3 2 7 S 19 33 E
Belonia, India 90 D3 23 15N 91 30 E
Belopolye = Bilopillya, Ukraine 59 G8 51 14N 34 20 E
Belorechensk, Russia 61 H4 44 46N 39 52 E
Beloretsk, Russia 64 E7 53 58N 58 24 E
Belorussia = Belarus ■, Europe 58 F4 53 30N 27 0 E
Beloslav, Bulgaria 51 C11 43 11N 27 42 E
Belovo, Bulgaria 51 D8 42 13N 24 1 E
Belovo, Russia 66 D9 54 30N 86 0 E
Belovodsk, Ukraine 59 H10 49 13N 39 36 E
Beloyarskiy, Russia 64 C8 56 45N 61 24 E
Beloye, Ozero, Russia 58 B9 60 10N 37 35 E
Beloye More, Russia 56 A6 66 30N 38 0 E
Belozem, Bulgaria 51 D9 42 12N 25 2 E
Belozersk, Russia 58 B9 60 1N 37 45 E
Belp, Switz. 32 C5 46 53N 7 30 E
Belpasso, Italy 47 E7 37 35N 14 58 E
Belpre, U.S.A. 148 F5 39 17N 81 34W
Belrain, India 93 E9 28 23N 80 55 E
Belt, U.S.A. 158 C8 47 23N 110 55W
Beltana, Australia 128 A3 30 48 S 138 25 E
Belterra, Brazil 169 D7 2 45 S 55 0W
Beltinci, Slovenia 45 B13 46 37N 16 20 E
Belton, Mo., U.S.A. 156 F2 38 49N 94 32W
Belton, Tex., U.S.A. 155 K6 31 3N 97 28W
Belton L., U.S.A. 155 K6 31 8N 97 32W
Beltsy = Bălţi, Moldova 53 C12 47 48N 27 58 E
Belturbet, Ireland 23 B4 54 6N 7 26W
Belukha, Russia 66 E9 49 50N 86 50 E
Beluran, Malaysia 78 C5 5 48N 117 35 E
Beluša, Slovak Rep. 35 B11 49 5N 18 17 E
Belušić, Serbia, Yug. 50 C5 43 50N 21 10 E
Belvedere Marittimo, Italy 47 C8 39 37N 15 52 E
Belvès, France 28 D5 44 46N 1 0 E
Belvidere, Ill., U.S.A. 154 D10 42 15N 88 50W
Belvidere, N.J., U.S.A. 151 F9 40 50N 75 5W

190 Belvis de la Jara

Belvis de la Jara, *Spain* **42 F6** 39 45N 4 57W
Belyando →, *Australia* **126 C4** 21 38 S 146 50 E
Belyy, *Russia* **58 E7** 55 49N 33 3 E
Belyy, Ostrov, *Russia* **66 B8** 73 30N 71 0 E
Belyy Yar, *Russia* **66 D9** 58 26N 84 39 E
Belyye Vody = Aqsū, *Kazakstan* **65 B4** 42 25N 69 50 E
Bełżec, *Poland* **55 H10** 50 23N 23 26 E
Belzig, *Germany* **30 C8** 52 8N 12 35 E
Belzoni, *U.S.A.* **155 J9** 33 11N 90 29W
Bełżyce, *Poland* **55 G9** 51 11N 22 17 E
Bemaraha, Lembalemban' i, *Madag.* **117 B7** 18 40 S 44 45 E
Bemarivo, *Madag.* **117 C7** 21 45 S 44 45 E
Bemarivo →, *Antsiranana, Madag.* **117 A9** 14 9 S 50 9 E
Bemarivo →, *Mahajanga, Madag.* **117 B8** 15 27 S 47 40 E
Bemavo, *Madag.* **117 C8** 21 33 S 45 25 E
Bembe, *Angola* **115 D2** 7 3 S 14 25 E
Bembéréke, *Benin* **113 C5** 10 11N 2 43 E
Bembesi, *Zimbabwe* **119 G2** 20 0 S 28 58 E
Bembesi →, *Zimbabwe* **119 F2** 18 57 S 27 47 E
Bembézar →, *Spain* **43 H5** 37 45N 5 13W
Bembibre, *Spain* **42 C4** 42 37N 6 25W
Bemboka Nat. Park, *Australia* **129 D8** 36 35 S 149 41 E
Bement, *U.S.A.* **157 E8** 39 55N 88 34W
Bemetara, *India* **93 J9** 21 42N 81 32 E
Bemidji, *U.S.A.* **154 B7** 47 28N 94 53W
Bemolanga, *Madag.* **117 B8** 17 44 S 45 6 E
Ben, *Iran* **97 C6** 32 32N 50 45 E
Ben Boyd Nat. Park, *Australia* **129 D8** 37 0 S 149 55 E
Ben Cruachan, *U.K.* **22 E3** 56 26N 5 8W
Ben Dearg, *U.K.* **22 D4** 57 47N 4 56W
Ben Gardane, *Tunisia* **108 B2** 33 11N 11 11 E
Ben Hope, *U.K.* **22 C4** 58 25N 4 36W
Ben Lawers, *U.K.* **22 E4** 56 32N 4 14W
Ben Lomond, *N.S.W., Australia* **127 E5** 30 1 S 151 43 E
Ben Lomond, *Tas., Australia* **127 G4** 41 38 S 147 42 E
Ben Lomond, *U.K.* **22 E4** 56 11N 4 38W
Ben Lomond Nat. Park, *Australia* **127 G4** 41 33 S 147 39 E
Ben Luc, *Vietnam* **87 G6** 10 39N 106 29 E
Ben Macdhui, *U.K.* **22 D5** 57 4N 3 40W
Ben Mhor, *U.K.* **22 D1** 57 15N 7 18W
Ben More, *Arg. & Bute, U.K.* **22 E2** 56 26N 6 1W
Ben More, *Stirl., U.K.* **22 E4** 56 23N 4 32W
Ben More Assynt, *U.K.* **22 C4** 58 8N 4 52W
Ben Nevis, *U.K.* **22 E3** 56 48N 5 1W
Ben Ohau Ra., *N.Z.* **131 E5** 44 1 S 170 4 E
Ben Quang, *Vietnam* **86 D6** 17 3N 106 55 E
Ben Slimane, *Morocco* **110 B3** 33 38N 7 7W
Ben Vorlich, *U.K.* **22 E4** 56 21N 4 14W
Ben Wyvis, *U.K.* **22 D4** 57 40N 4 35W
Bena, *Nigeria* **113 C6** 11 20N 5 50 E
Bena-Dibele, *Dem. Rep. of the Congo* **115 C4** 4 4 S 22 50 E
Bena-Leka, *Dem. Rep. of the Congo* **115 D4** 5 8 S 22 10 E
Bena-Tshadi, *Dem. Rep. of the Congo* **115 C4** 4 40 S 22 49 E
Benāb, *Iran* **101 D12** 37 20N 46 4 E
Benadir, *Somali Rep.* **120 D2** 1 30N 44 30 E
Benagerie, *Australia* **128 A4** 31 25 S 140 22 E
Benahmed, *Morocco* **110 B3** 33 4N 7 9W
Benalla, *Australia* **129 D7** 36 30 S 146 0 E
Benalmádena, *Spain* **43 J6** 36 36N 4 34W
Benambra, Mt., *Australia* **129 D7** 36 31 S 147 34 E
Benanee, *Australia* **128 C5** 34 31 S 142 52 E
Benares = Varanasi, *India* **93 G10** 25 22N 83 0 E
Bénat, C., *France* **29 E10** 43 5N 6 22 E
Benavente, *Portugal* **43 G2** 38 59N 8 49W
Benavente, *Spain* **42 C5** 42 2N 5 43W
Benavides, *U.S.A.* **155 M5** 27 36N 98 25W
Benavides de Órbigo, *Spain* **42 C5** 42 30N 5 54W
Benbecula, *U.K.* **22 D1** 57 26N 7 21W
Benbonyathe, *Australia* **128 A3** 30 25 S 139 11 E
Bend, *U.S.A.* **158 D3** 44 4N 121 19W
Bendela, *Dem. Rep. of the Congo* **114 C3** 3 18 S 17 36 E
Bendemeer, *Australia* **129 A9** 30 53 S 151 8 E
Bender Beila, *Somali Rep.* **120 C4** 9 30N 50 48 E
Bender Merchagno, *Somali Rep.* **120 B4** 11 41N 50 34 E
Bendery = Tighina, *Moldova* **53 D14** 46 50N 29 30 E
Bendigo, *Australia* **128 D6** 36 40 S 144 15 E
Bendorf, *Germany* **30 E3** 50 25N 7 35 E
Benē Beraq, *Israel* **103 C3** 32 6N 34 51 E
Beneditinos, *Brazil* **170 C3** 5 27 S 42 22W
Benedito Leite, *Brazil* **170 C3** 7 13 S 44 34W
Bénéna, *Mali* **112 C4** 13 9N 4 17W
Benenitra, *Madag.* **117 C8** 23 27 S 45 5 E
Benešov, *Czech Rep.* **34 B7** 49 46N 14 41 E
Benevento, *Italy* **47 A7** 41 8N 14 45 E
Benfeld, *France* **27 D14** 48 22N 7 34 E
Benga, *Mozam.* **119 F3** 16 11 S 33 40 E
Bengal, Bay of, *Ind. Oc.* **62 H12** 15 0N 90 0 E
Bengbis, *Cameroon* **113 E7** 3 27N 12 36 E
Bengbu, *China* **75 H9** 32 58N 117 20 E
Benghazi = Banghāzī, *Libya* **108 B4** 32 11N 20 3 E
Benghisa Point, *Malta* **38 F8** 35 49N 14 33 E
Bengkalis, *Indonesia* **84 B2** 1 30N 102 10 E
Bengkulu, *Indonesia* **84 C2** 3 50 S 102 12 E
Bengkulu □, *Indonesia* **84 C2** 3 48 S 102 16 E
Bengo, *Dem. Rep. of the Congo* **114 C3** 2 11 S 19 5 E
Bengo □, *Angola* **115 D2** 9 0 S 13 10 E
Bengough, *Canada* **143 D7** 49 25N 105 10W
Bengtsfors, *Sweden* **16 E6** 59 2N 12 14 E
Benguela, *Angola* **115 E2** 12 37 S 13 25 E
Benguela □, *Angola* **115 E2** 13 0 S 13 30 E
Benguerir, *Morocco* **110 B3** 32 16N 7 56W
Benguérua, I., *Mozam.* **117 C6** 21 58 S 35 28 E
Benguet □, *Phil.* **80 C3** 16 30N 120 40 E
Benha, *Egypt* **106 H7** 30 26N 31 8 E
Beni, *Dem. Rep. of the Congo* **118 B2** 0 30N 29 27 E
Beni □, *Bolivia* **173 C4** 14 0 S 65 0W
Beni →, *Bolivia* **173 C4** 10 23 S 65 24W
Beni Abbès, *Algeria* **111 B4** 30 5N 2 5W
Beni Haoua, *Algeria* **111 A5** 36 30N 1 30 E
Beni Mazâr, *Egypt* **106 B3** 28 32N 30 44 E
Beni Mellal, *Morocco* **110 B3** 32 21N 6 21W
Beni Ounif, *Algeria* **111 B4** 32 0N 1 10W
Beni Saf, *Algeria* **111 A4** 35 17N 1 15W
Beni Suef, *Egypt* **106 J7** 29 5N 31 6 E
Beniah L., *Canada* **142 A6** 63 23N 112 17W
Benicarló, *Spain* **40 E5** 40 23N 0 23 E
Benicássim, *Spain* **40 E5** 40 3N 0 4 E
Benicia, *U.S.A.* **160 G4** 38 3N 122 9W
Benidorm, *Spain* **41 G4** 38 33N 0 9W
Benin ■, *Africa* **113 D5** 10 0N 2 0 E
Benin →, *Nigeria* **113 D6** 5 45N 5 4 E
Benin, Bight of, *W. Afr.* **113 E5** 5 0N 3 0 E
Benin City, *Nigeria* **113 D6** 6 20N 5 31 E
Benisa, *Spain* **41 G5** 38 43N 0 3 E
Benitses, *Greece* **38 B9** 39 32N 19 55 E
Benjamin Aceval, *Paraguay* **174 A4** 24 58 S 57 34W
Benjamin Constant, *Brazil* **168 D3** 4 40 S 70 15W
Benjamin Hill, *Mexico* **162 A2** 30 10N 111 10W
Benkelman, *U.S.A.* **154 E4** 40 3N 101 32W
Benkovac, *Croatia* **45 D12** 44 2N 15 37 E
Benmore Pk., *N.Z.* **131 E5** 44 25 S 170 8 E
Bennett, *Canada* **142 B2** 59 56N 134 53W
Bennett, L., *Australia* **124 D5** 22 50 S 131 2 E
Bennetta, Ostrov, *Russia* **67 B15** 76 21N 148 56 E
Bennettsville, *U.S.A.* **149 H6** 34 37N 79 41W
Bennichchāb, *Mauritania* **112 B1** 19 32N 15 12W
Bennington, *N.H., U.S.A.* **151 D11** 43 0N 71 55W
Bennington, *Vt., U.S.A.* **151 D11** 42 53N 73 12W
Beno, *Dem. Rep. of the Congo* **114 C3** 3 41 S 17 49 E
Bénodet, *France* **26 E2** 47 53N 4 7W
Benoni, *S. Africa* **117 D4** 26 11 S 28 18 E
Benoud, *Algeria* **111 B5** 32 20N 0 16 E
Bénoué, Parc Nat. de la, *Cameroon* **114 A2** 8 30N 13 55 E
Benoy, *Chad* **109 G3** 8 59N 16 19 E
Benque Viejo, *Belize* **163 D7** 17 5N 89 8W
Bensheim, *Germany* **31 F4** 49 40N 8 38 E
Benson, *Ariz., U.S.A.* **159 L8** 31 58N 110 18W
Benson, *Minn., U.S.A.* **154 C7** 45 19N 95 36W
Bent, *Iran* **97 E8** 26 20N 59 31 E
Benteng, *Indonesia* **82 C2** 6 10 S 120 30 E
Bentiaba, *Angola* **115 E2** 14 15 S 12 21 E
Bentinck I., *Australia* **126 B2** 17 3 S 139 35 E
Bentiu, *Sudan* **107 F2** 9 10N 29 55 E
Bento Gonçalves, *Brazil* **175 B5** 29 10 S 51 31W
Benton, *Ark., U.S.A.* **155 H8** 34 34N 92 35W
Benton, *Calif., U.S.A.* **160 H8** 37 48N 118 32W
Benton, *Ill., U.S.A.* **156 G8** 38 0N 88 55W
Benton, *Pa., U.S.A.* **151 E8** 41 12N 76 23W
Benton Harbor, *U.S.A.* **157 B10** 42 6N 86 27W
Benton Heights, *U.S.A.* **157 B10** 42 7N 86 24W
Bentonville, *U.S.A.* **155 G7** 36 22N 94 13W
Bentu Liben, *Ethiopia* **107 F4** 8 32N 38 21 E
Bentung, *Malaysia* **87 L3** 3 31N 101 55 E
Benue □, *Nigeria* **113 D6** 7 20N 8 45 E
Benue →, *Nigeria* **113 D6** 7 48N 6 46 E
Benxi, *China* **75 D12** 41 20N 123 48 E
Benza, *Dem. Rep. of the Congo* **115 D2** 4 49 S 13 17 E
Benzdorp, *Surinam* **169 C7** 3 44N 54 5W
Beo, *Indonesia* **82 A3** 4 25N 126 50 E
Beograd, *Serbia, Yug.* **50 B4** 44 50N 20 37 E
Beoumi, *Ivory C.* **112 D3** 7 45N 5 23W
Bepan Jiang →, *China* **76 E6** 24 55N 106 5 E
Beppu, *Japan* **72 D3** 33 15N 131 30 E
Beppu-Wan, *Japan* **72 D3** 33 18N 131 34 E
Beqa, *Fiji* **133 B2** 18 23 S 178 8 E
Beqaa Valley = Al Biqā, *Lebanon* **103 A5** 34 10N 36 10 E
Ber Mota, *India* **92 H3** 23 27N 68 34 E
Bera, *Bangla.* **90 C2** 24 5N 89 37 E
Berach →, *India* **92 G6** 25 15N 75 2 E
Beraketa, *Madag.* **117 C7** 23 7 S 44 25 E
Béran-Djoko, *Congo* **114 B3** 3 15N 17 0 E
Berane, *Montenegro, Yug.* **50 D3** 42 51N 19 52 E
Berat, *Albania* **50 F3** 40 43N 19 59 E
Berau →, *Indonesia* **85 B5** 2 10N 117 42 E
Berau, Teluk, *Indonesia* **83 B4** 2 30 S 132 30 E
Beravina, *Madag.* **117 B8** 18 10 S 45 14 E
Berber, *Sudan* **106 D3** 18 0N 34 0 E
Berbera, *Somali Rep.* **120 B3** 10 30N 45 2 E
Berbérati, *C.A.R.* **114 B3** 4 15N 15 40 E
Berbice →, *Guyana* **169 B6** 6 20N 57 32W
Berceto, *Italy* **44 D6** 44 31N 9 51 E
Berchidda, *Italy* **46 B2** 40 47N 9 10 E
Berchtesgaden, *Germany* **31 H8** 47 38N 13 0 E
Berck, *France* **27 B8** 50 25N 1 36 E
Berdale, *Somali Rep.* **120 C3** 7 4N 47 51 E
Berdichev = Berdychiv, *Ukraine* **59 H5** 49 57N 28 30 E
Berdsk, *Russia* **66 D9** 54 47N 83 2 E
Berdyansk, *Ukraine* **59 J9** 46 45N 36 50 E
Berdyaush, *Russia* **64 D7** 55 9N 59 9 E
Berdychiv, *Ukraine* **59 H5** 49 57N 28 30 E
Berea, *U.S.A.* **148 G3** 37 34N 84 17W
Berebere, *Indonesia* **82 A3** 2 25N 128 45 E
Bereda, *Somali Rep.* **120 B4** 11 45N 51 0 E
Berehove, *Ukraine* **59 H2** 48 15N 22 35 E
Bereina, *Papua N. G.* **132 E4** 8 39 S 146 30 E
Berekum, *Ghana* **112 D4** 7 29N 2 34W
Berenice, *Egypt* **106 C4** 24 2N 35 25 E
Berens →, *Canada* **143 C9** 52 25N 97 2W
Berens I., *Canada* **143 C9** 52 18N 97 18W
Berens River, *Canada* **143 C9** 52 25N 97 0W
Beresford, *U.S.A.* **154 D6** 43 5N 96 47W
Berestechko, *Ukraine* **59 G3** 50 22N 25 5 E
Bereşti, *Romania* **53 D12** 46 6N 27 50 E
Beretău →, *Romania* **52 C6** 47 10N 21 50 E
Berettyó →, *Hungary* **52 D6** 46 59N 21 7 E
Berettyóújfalu, *Hungary* **52 C6** 47 13N 21 33 E
Berevo, *Mahajanga, Madag.* **117 B7** 17 14 S 44 17 E
Berevo, *Toliara, Madag.* **117 B7** 19 44 S 44 58 E
Bereza = Byaroza, *Belarus* **59 F3** 52 31N 24 51 E
Berezhany, *Ukraine* **59 H3** 49 26N 24 58 E
Berezina = Byarezina →, *Belarus* **59 F6** 52 33N 30 14 E
Berezivka, *Ukraine* **59 J6** 47 14N 30 55 E
Berezna, *Ukraine* **59 G6** 51 35N 31 46 E
Bereznik, *Russia* **56 B7** 62 51N 42 40 E
Berezniki, *Russia* **64 B6** 59 24N 56 46 E
Berezovo, *Russia* **66 C7** 64 0N 65 0 E
Berga, *Spain* **40 C6** 42 6N 1 48 E
Berga, *Sweden* **17 G10** 57 14N 16 3 E
Bergama, *Turkey* **49 B9** 39 8N 27 11 E
Bérgamo, *Italy* **44 C6** 45 41N 9 43 E
Bergaon, *India* **94 D5** 20 41N 80 27 E
Bergara, *Spain* **40 B2** 43 9N 2 28W
Bergby, *Sweden* **16 D11** 60 57N 17 2 E
Bergedorf, *Germany* **30 B6** 53 28N 10 6 E
Bergeforsen, *Sweden* **16 B11** 62 32N 17 23 E
Bergen, *Mecklenburg-Vorpommern, Germany* **30 A9** 54 25N 13 25 E
Bergen, *Niedersachsen, Germany* **30 C5** 52 49N 9 57 E
Bergen, *Neths.* **24 B4** 52 40N 4 43 E
Bergen, *Norway* **15 F11** 60 20N 5 20 E
Bergen, *U.S.A.* **150 C7** 43 5N 77 57W
Bergen op Zoom, *Neths.* **24 C4** 51 28N 4 18 E
Bergerac, *France* **28 D4** 44 51N 0 30 E
Bergheim, *Germany* **30 E2** 50 57N 6 38 E
Bergholz, *U.S.A.* **150 F4** 40 31N 80 53W
Bergisch Gladbach, *Germany* **24 D7** 50 59N 7 8 E
Bergkamen, *Germany* **30 D3** 51 37N 7 38 E
Bergkvara, *Sweden* **17 H10** 56 23N 16 5 E
Bergshamra, *Sweden* **16 E12** 59 38N 18 37 E
Bergsjö, *Sweden* **16 C11** 61 59N 17 3 E
Bergues, *France* **27 B9** 50 58N 2 24 E
Bergviken, *Sweden* **16 C10** 61 15N 16 40 E
Bergville, *S. Africa* **117 D4** 28 52 S 29 18 E
Berhala, Selat, *Indonesia* **84 C2** 1 0 S 104 15 E
Berhampore = Baharampur, *India* **93 G13** 24 2N 88 27 E
Berhampur = Brahmapur, *India* **94 E7** 19 15N 84 54 E
Berheci →, *Romania* **53 E12** 45 58N 27 28 E
Bering Glacier, *U.S.A.* **144 F12** 60 20N 143 30W
Bering Sea, *Pac. Oc.* **138 C1** 58 0N 171 0 E
Bering Strait, *Pac. Oc.* **144 D5** 65 30N 169 0W
Beringen, *Switz.* **33 A7** 47 38N 8 34 E
Beringovskiy, *Russia* **67 C18** 63 3N 179 19 E
Berisso, *Argentina* **174 C4** 34 56 S 57 50W
Berja, *Spain* **43 J8** 36 50N 2 56W
Berkåk, *Norway* **18 B6** 62 50N 10 0 E
Berkane, *Morocco* **111 B4** 34 52N 2 20W
Berkeley, *U.S.A.* **160 H4** 37 52N 122 16W
Berkeley, C., *Ecuador* **172 a** 0 1N 91 35W
Berkner I., *Antarctica* **7 D18** 79 30 S 50 0W
Berkovitsa, *Bulgaria* **50 C7** 43 16N 23 8 E
Berkshire, *U.S.A.* **151 D8** 42 19N 76 11W
Berkshire Downs, *U.K.* **21 F6** 51 33N 1 29W
Berlanga, *Spain* **43 G5** 38 17N 5 50W
Berlenga, I., *Portugal* **43 F1** 39 25N 9 30W
Berlin, *Germany* **30 C9** 52 30N 13 25 E
Berlin, *Ga., U.S.A.* **152 D6** 31 4N 83 37W
Berlin, *Md., U.S.A.* **148 F8** 38 20N 75 13W
Berlin, *N.H., U.S.A.* **151 B13** 44 28N 71 11W
Berlin, *N.Y., U.S.A.* **151 D11** 42 42N 73 23W
Berlin, *Wis., U.S.A.* **148 D1** 43 58N 88 57W
Berlin □, *Germany* **30 C9** 52 30N 13 20 E
Berlin L., *U.S.A.* **150 E4** 41 3N 81 0W
Bermagui, *Australia* **129 D9** 36 25 S 150 4 E
Bermeja, Sierra, *Spain* **43 J5** 36 30N 5 11W
Bermejo →, *Formosa, Argentina* **174 B4** 26 51 S 58 23W
Bermejo →, *San Juan, Argentina* **174 C2** 32 30 S 67 30W
Bermen, L., *Canada* **141 B6** 53 35N 68 55W
Bermeo, *Spain* **40 B2** 43 25N 2 47W
Bermillo de Sayago, *Spain* **42 D4** 41 22N 6 8W
Bermuda ■, *Atl. Oc.* **9 a** 32 45N 65 0W
Bern, *Switz.* **32 C4** 46 57N 7 28 E
Bern □, *Switz.* **32 C5** 46 45N 7 40 E
Bernalda, *Italy* **47 B9** 40 24N 16 41 E
Bernalillo, *U.S.A.* **159 J10** 35 18N 106 33W
Bernam →, *Malaysia* **84 B2** 3 45N 101 5 E
Bernardo de Irigoyen, *Argentina* **175 B5** 26 15 S 53 40W
Bernardo O'Higgins □, *Chile* **174 C1** 34 15 S 70 45W
Bernardsville, *U.S.A.* **151 F10** 40 43N 74 34W
Bernasconi, *Argentina* **174 D3** 37 55 S 63 44W
Bernau, *Bayern, Germany* **31 H8** 47 47N 12 22 E
Bernau, *Brandenburg, Germany* **30 C9** 52 40N 13 35 E
Bernay, *France* **26 C7** 49 5N 0 35 E
Bernburg, *Germany* **30 D7** 51 47N 11 44 E
Berndorf, *Austria* **34 D9** 47 59N 16 1 E
Berne = Bern, *Switz.* **32 C4** 46 57N 7 28 E
Berne = Bern □, *Switz.* **32 C5** 46 45N 7 40 E
Berne, *U.S.A.* **157 D12** 40 39N 84 57W
Berner Alpen, *Switz.* **32 D5** 46 27N 7 35 E
Berneray, *U.K.* **22 D1** 57 43N 7 11W
Bernese Oberland = Oberland, *Switz.* **32 C5** 46 35N 7 38 E
Bernier I., *Australia* **125 D1** 24 50 S 113 12 E
Bernina, Passo del, *Switz.* **33 D10** 46 25N 10 2 E
Bernina, Piz, *Switz.* **33 D9** 46 20N 9 54 E
Bernkastel-Kues, *Germany* **31 F3** 49 55N 7 3 E
Bero →, *Angola* **115 F2** 15 10 S 12 9 E
Beroroha, *Madag.* **117 C8** 21 40 S 45 10 E
Béroubouay, *Benin* **113 C5** 10 34N 2 46 E
Beroun, *Czech Rep.* **34 B7** 49 57N 14 5 E
Berounka →, *Czech Rep.* **34 B7** 50 0N 14 22 E
Berovo, *Macedonia* **50 E6** 41 38N 22 51 E
Berrahal, *Algeria* **111 A6** 36 54N 7 33 E
Berre, Étang de, *France* **29 E9** 43 27N 5 5 E
Berre-l'Étang, *France* **29 E9** 43 27N 5 10 E
Berrechid, *Morocco* **110 B3** 33 18N 7 36W
Berri, *Australia* **128 C4** 34 14 S 140 35 E
Berriane, *Algeria* **111 B5** 32 50N 3 46 E
Berridale, *Australia* **129 D8** 36 22 S 148 48 E
Berrien Springs, *U.S.A.* **157 C10** 41 57N 86 20W
Berrigan, *Australia* **129 C6** 35 38 S 145 49 E
Berriwillock, *Australia* **128 C5** 35 36 S 142 59 E
Berrouaghia, *Algeria* **111 A5** 36 10N 2 53 E
Berry, *Australia* **129 C9** 34 46 S 150 43 E
Berry, *France* **27 F8** 46 50N 2 0 E
Berry Is., *Bahamas* **164 A4** 25 40N 77 50W
Berrydale, *U.S.A.* **153 E2** 30 53N 87 3W
Berryessa L., *U.S.A.* **160 G4** 38 31N 122 6W
Berryville, *U.S.A.* **155 G8** 36 22N 93 34W
Berseba, *Namibia* **116 D2** 26 0 S 17 46 E
Bersenbrück, *Germany* **30 C3** 52 34N 7 56 E
Bershad, *Ukraine* **59 H5** 48 22N 29 31 E
Berthold, *U.S.A.* **154 A4** 48 19N 101 44W
Berthoud, *U.S.A.* **154 E2** 40 19N 105 5W
Bertincourt, *France* **27 B9** 50 5N 2 58 E
Bertolínia, *Brazil* **170 C3** 7 38 S 43 57W
Bertoua, *Cameroon* **114 B2** 4 30N 13 45 E
Bertraghboy B., *Ireland* **23 C2** 53 22N 9 54W
Berufjörður, *Iceland* **11 C12** 64 48N 14 29W
Berunes, *Iceland* **11 C12** 64 42N 14 16W
Beruri, *Brazil* **169 D5** 3 54 S 61 22W
Berwick, *U.S.A.* **151 E8** 41 3N 76 14W
Berwick-upon-Tweed, *U.K.* **20 B6** 55 46N 2 0W
Berwyn Mts., *U.K.* **20 E4** 52 54N 3 26W
Beryslav, *Ukraine* **59 J7** 46 50N 33 30 E
Berzasca, *Romania* **52 F6** 44 39N 21 58 E
Berzence, *Hungary* **52 D2** 46 12N 17 11 E
Besal, *Pakistan* **93 B5** 35 4N 73 56 E
Besalampy, *Madag.* **117 B7** 16 43 S 44 29 E
Besançon, *France* **27 E13** 47 15N 6 2 E
Besar, *Indonesia* **85 C5** 2 40 S 116 0 E
Besar, Gunong, *Malaysia* **84 A2** 5 10N 101 18 E
Besharyk, *Uzbekistan* **65 C5** 40 26N 70 36 E
Beshenkovichi, *Belarus* **58 E5** 55 2N 29 29 E
Beshkent, *Uzbekistan* **65 D2** 38 49N 65 39 E
Beška, *Serbia, Yug.* **52 E5** 45 8N 20 6 E
Beslan, *Russia* **61 J7** 43 15N 44 28 E
Besna Kobila, *Serbia, Yug.* **50 D6** 42 31N 22 10 E
Besnard L., *Canada* **143 B7** 55 25N 106 0W
Besni, *Turkey* **100 D7** 37 41N 37 52 E
Besor, N. →, *Egypt* **103 D3** 31 28N 34 22 E
Bessa Monteiro, *Angola* **115 D2** 7 7 S 13 44 E
Bessarabiya, *Moldova* **59 J5** 47 0N 28 10 E
Bessarabka = Basarabeasca, *Moldova* **53 D13** 46 21N 28 58 E
Bessèges, *France* **29 D8** 44 18N 4 8 E
Bessemer, *Ala., U.S.A.* **149 J2** 33 24N 86 58W
Bessemer, *Mich., U.S.A.* **154 B9** 46 29N 90 3W
Bessemer, *Pa., U.S.A.* **150 F4** 40 59N 80 30W
Bessin, *France* **26 C6** 49 18N 1 0W
Bessines-sur-Gartempe, *France* **28 B5** 46 6N 1 22 E
Beswick, *Australia* **124 B5** 14 34 S 132 53 E
Bet She'an, *Israel* **103 C4** 32 30N 35 30 E
Bet Shemesh, *Israel* **103 D4** 31 44N 35 0 E
Bet Tadjine, Djebel, *Algeria* **110 C4** 29 0N 3 30W
Betafo, *Madag.* **117 B8** 19 50 S 46 51 E
Betamba, *Dem. Rep. of the Congo* **114 C4** 2 17 S 21 24 E
Betancuria, *Canary Is.* **9 e2** 28 25N 14 3W
Betancuria, Mt., *Canary Is.* **9 e2** 28 25N 14 6W
Betania, *Colombia* **168 C3** 4 22N 72 54W
Betanzos, *Bolivia* **173 D4** 19 34 S 65 27W
Betanzos, *Spain* **42 B2** 43 15N 8 12W
Bétaré Oya, *Cameroon* **114 A2** 5 40N 14 5 E
Betatao, *Madag.* **117 B8** 18 11 S 47 52 E
Bétera, *Spain* **41 F4** 39 35N 0 28W
Bétérou, *Benin* **113 D5** 9 12N 2 16 E
Bethal, *S. Africa* **117 D4** 26 27 S 29 28 E
Bethalto, *U.S.A.* **156 F6** 38 55N 90 2W
Bethanien, *Namibia* **116 D2** 26 31 S 17 8 E
Bethany, *Canada* **150 B6** 44 11N 78 34W
Bethany, *Ill., U.S.A.* **157 E8** 39 39N 88 45W
Bethany, *Mo., U.S.A.* **156 D2** 40 16N 94 2W
Bethel, *Alaska, U.S.A.* **144 F7** 60 48N 161 45W
Bethel, *Conn., U.S.A.* **151 E11** 41 22N 73 25W
Bethel, *Maine, U.S.A.* **151 B14** 44 25N 70 47W
Bethel, *Ohio, U.S.A.* **157 F12** 38 58N 84 5W
Bethel, *Vt., U.S.A.* **151 C12** 43 50N 72 38W
Bethel Park, *U.S.A.* **150 F4** 40 20N 80 1W
Béthenville, *France* **27 C11** 49 18N 4 23 E
Bethlehem = Bayt Lahm, *West Bank* **103 D4** 31 43N 35 12 E
Bethlehem, *S. Africa* **117 D4** 28 14 S 28 18 E
Bethlehem, *U.S.A.* **151 F9** 40 37N 75 23W
Bethulie, *S. Africa* **116 E4** 30 30 S 25 59 E
Béthune, *France* **27 B9** 50 30N 2 38 E
Béthune →, *France* **26 C8** 49 53N 1 4 E
Bethungra, *Australia* **129 C7** 34 45 S 147 51 E
Betijoque, *Venezuela* **168 B3** 9 23N 70 44W
Betioky, *Madag.* **117 C7** 23 48 S 44 20 E
Betong, *Thailand* **87 K3** 5 45N 101 5 E
Betoota, *Australia* **126 D3** 25 45 S 140 42 E
Betor, *Ethiopia* **107 E4** 11 37N 39 2 E
Bétou, *Congo* **114 B3** 3 2N 18 32 E
Betroka, *Madag.* **117 C8** 23 16 S 46 0 E
Betsiamites, *Canada* **141 C6** 48 56N 68 40W
Betsiamites →, *Canada* **141 C6** 48 56N 68 38W
Betsiboka →, *Madag.* **117 B8** 16 3 S 46 36 E
Bettendorf, *U.S.A.* **156 C6** 41 32N 90 30W
Bettiah, *India* **93 F11** 26 48N 84 33 E
Bettna, *Sweden* **17 F10** 58 55N 16 38 E
Béttola, *Italy* **44 D6** 44 47N 9 36 E
Betul, *India* **94 D3** 21 58N 77 59 E
Betung, *Malaysia* **85 B4** 1 24N 111 31 E
Betws-y-Coed, *U.K.* **20 D4** 53 5N 3 48W
Betxi, *Spain* **40 F4** 39 56N 0 12W
Betzdorf, *Germany* **30 E3** 50 46N 7 52 E
Béu, *Angola* **115 D3** 6 15 S 15 32 E
Beuil, *France* **29 D10** 44 6N 6 59 E
Beulah, *Australia* **128 C5** 35 58 S 142 29 E
Beulah, *Mich., U.S.A.* **148 C2** 44 38N 86 6W
Beulah, *N. Dak., U.S.A.* **154 B4** 47 16N 101 47W
Beurkia, *Chad* **109 E3** 15 20N 17 56 E
Beuvron →, *France* **26 E8** 47 29N 1 15 E
Beveren, *Belgium* **24 C4** 51 12N 4 16 E
Beverley, *Australia* **125 F2** 32 9 S 116 56 E
Beverley, *U.K.* **20 D7** 53 51N 0 26W
Beverley Hills, *U.S.A.* **149 L4** 28 56N 82 28W
Beverly, *U.S.A.* **151 D14** 42 33N 70 53W
Beverly Hills, *U.S.A.* **161 L8** 34 4N 118 25W
Beverungen, *Germany* **30 D5** 51 39N 9 22 E
Bevoalavo, *Madag.* **117 D7** 25 13 S 45 26 E
Bewani, *Papua N. G.* **83 B6** 3 2 S 141 10 E
Bewas →, *India* **93 H8** 23 59N 79 21 E
Bex, *Switz.* **32 D4** 46 15N 7 1 E
Bexhill, *U.K.* **21 G8** 50 51N 0 29 E
Bey Dağları, *Turkey* **49 E12** 36 38N 30 29 E
Beyānlū, *Iran* **96 C5** 36 0N 47 51 E
Beyazköy, *Turkey* **51 E11** 41 21N 27 42 E
Beyçayırı, *Turkey* **51 F10** 40 15N 26 55 E
Beydağ, *Turkey* **49 C10** 38 5N 28 13 E
Beyeğaç, *Turkey* **49 D10** 37 14N 28 53 E
Beyin, *Ghana* **112 D4** 5 1N 2 41W
Beykoz, *Turkey* **51 E13** 41 8N 29 7 E
Beyla, *Guinea* **112 D3** 8 30N 8 38W
Beynat, *France* **28 C5** 45 8N 1 44 E
Beyneu, *Kazakstan* **57 E10** 45 18N 55 9 E
Beyoba, *Turkey* **49 C9** 38 48N 27 47 E
Beyoğlu, *Turkey* **51 E12** 41 2N 29 0 E
Beypazarı, *Turkey* **100 B4** 40 10N 31 56 E
Beypore →, *India* **95 J2** 11 10N 75 47 E
Beyşehir, *Turkey* **100 D4** 37 41N 31 43 E
Beyşehir Gölü, *Turkey* **100 D4** 37 41N 31 33 E
Beytüşşebap, *Turkey* **101 D10** 37 35N 43 10 E
Bezau, *Austria* **33 B9** 47 23N 9 54 E
Bezdan, *Serbia, Yug.* **52 E3** 45 50N 18 57 E
Bezhetsk, *Russia* **58 D9** 57 47N 36 39 E
Béziers, *France* **28 E7** 43 20N 3 12 E
Bezwada = Vijayawada, *India* **94 F5** 16 31N 80 39 E
Bhabua, *India* **93 G10** 25 3N 83 37 E
Bhadar →, *Gujarat, India* **92 H5** 22 17N 72 20 E
Bhadar →, *Gujarat, India* **92 J3** 21 27N 69 47 E
Bhadarwah, *India* **93 C6** 32 58N 75 46 E
Bhadohi, *India* **93 G10** 25 25N 82 34 E
Bhadra, *India* **92 E6** 29 8N 75 14 E
Bhadra →, *India* **95 H2** 14 0N 75 20 E
Bhadrachalam, *India* **94 F5** 17 40N 80 53 E
Bhadrakh, *India* **94 D8** 21 10N 86 30 E
Bhadran, *India* **92 H5** 22 19N 72 6 E
Bhadravati, *India* **95 H2** 13 49N 75 40 E
Bhag, *Pakistan* **92 E2** 29 2N 67 49 E
Bhagalpur, *India* **93 G12** 25 10N 87 0 E
Bhagirathi →, *Uttaranchal, India* **93 D8** 30 8N 78 35 E
Bhagirathi →, *W. Bengal, India* **93 H13** 23 25N 88 23 E
Bhainsa, *India* **94 E3** 19 10N 77 58 E
Bhairab →, *Bangla.* **90 D2** 22 51N 89 34 E
Bhairab Bazar, *Bangla.* **90 C3** 24 4N 90 58 E
Bhakkar, *Pakistan* **91 C3** 31 40N 71 5 E
Bhakra Dam, *India* **92 D7** 31 30N 76 45 E
Bhaktapur, *Nepal* **93 F11** 27 38N 85 24 E
Bhalki, *India* **94 E3** 18 2N 77 13 E
Bhamo, *Burma* **90 C6** 24 15N 97 15 E
Bhamragarh, *India* **94 E5** 19 30N 80 40 E
Bhandara, *India* **94 D4** 21 5N 79 42 E
Bhanpura, *India* **92 G6** 24 31N 75 44 E
Bhanrer Ra., *India* **93 H8** 23 40N 79 45 E
Bhaptiahi, *India* **93 F12** 26 19N 86 44 E
Bharat = India ■, *Asia* **89 C6** 20 0N 78 0 E
Bharatpur, *Chhattisgarh, India* **93 H9** 23 44N 81 46 E
Bharatpur, *Raj., India* **92 F7** 27 15N 77 30 E
Bharno, *India* **93 H11** 23 14N 84 53 E
Bharuch, *India* **94 D1** 21 47N 73 0 E
Bhatghar L., *India* **94 E1** 18 10N 73 48 E
Bhatiapara Ghat, *Bangla.* **90 D2** 23 13N 89 42 E
Bhatinda, *India* **92 D6** 30 15N 74 57 E
Bhatkal, *India* **95 H2** 13 58N 74 35 E
Bhatpara, *India* **93 H13** 22 50N 88 25 E
Bhattu, *India* **92 E6** 29 36N 75 19 E
Bhaun, *Pakistan* **92 C5** 32 55N 72 40 E
Bhaunagar = Bhavnagar, *India* **94 D1** 21 45N 72 10 E
Bhavani, *India* **95 J3** 11 27N 77 43 E
Bhavnagar, *India* **94 D1** 21 45N 72 10 E
Bhawanipatna, *India* **94 E5** 19 55N 80 10 E
Bhawari, *India* **92 G5** 25 42N 73 4 E
Bhayavadar, *India* **92 J4** 21 51N 70 15 E
Bhera, *Pakistan* **92 C5** 32 29N 72 57 E
Bhikangaon, *India* **92 J6** 21 52N 75 57 E
Bhilai, *India* **94 D5** 21 13N 81 26 E
Bhilsa = Vidisha, *India* **92 H7** 23 28N 77 53 E
Bhilwara, *India* **92 G6** 25 25N 74 38 E
Bhima →, *India* **94 F3** 16 25N 77 17 E
Bhimavaram, *India* **95 F5** 16 30N 81 30 E
Bhimbar, *Pakistan* **93 C6** 32 59N 74 3 E
Bhind, *India* **93 F8** 26 30N 78 46 E
Bhinga, *India* **93 F9** 27 43N 81 56 E
Bhinmal, *India* **92 G5** 25 0N 72 15 E
Bhiwandi, *India* **94 E1** 19 20N 73 0 E
Bhiwani, *India* **92 E7** 28 50N 76 9 E
Bhogava →, *India* **92 H5** 22 26N 72 20 E
Bhokardan, *India* **94 D2** 20 16N 75 46 E
Bhola, *Bangla.* **90 D3** 22 45N 90 35 E
Bholari, *Pakistan* **92 G3** 25 19N 68 13 E
Bhongir, *India* **94 F4** 17 30N 78 56 E
Bhopal, *India* **92 H7** 23 20N 77 30 E
Bhopalpatnam, *India* **94 E5** 18 52N 80 23 E
Bhor, *India* **94 E1** 18 12N 73 53 E
Bhubaneshwar, *India* **94 D7** 20 15N 85 50 E
Bhuj, *India* **92 H3** 23 15N 69 49 E
Bhusaval, *India* **94 D2** 21 3N 75 46 E
Bhutan ■, *Asia* **90 B3** 27 25N 90 30 E
Biá →, *Brazil* **168 D4** 3 28 S 67 23W
Biafra, B. of = Bonny, Bight of, *Africa* **113 E6** 3 30N 9 20 E
Biak, *Indonesia* **83 B5** 1 10 S 136 6 E
Biała, *Poland* **55 H4** 50 24N 17 40 E
Biała →, *Poland* **55 H7** 50 3N 20 55 E
Biała Piska, *Poland* **54 E9** 53 37N 22 5 E
Biała Podlaska, *Poland* **55 F10** 52 4N 23 6 E
Biała Rawska, *Poland* **55 G7** 51 48N 20 29 E
Białobrzegi, *Poland* **55 G7** 51 39N 20 57 E
Białogard, *Poland* **54 D2** 54 2N 15 58 E

Białowieża, Poland 55 F10 52 41N 23 49 E
Biały Bór, Poland 54 E3 53 53N 16 51 E
Białystok, Poland 55 E10 53 10N 23 10 E
Bian →, Indonesia 83 C5 8 6 S 139 58 E
Biancavilla, Italy 47 E7 37 38N 14 52 E
Bianco, Italy 47 D9 38 5N 16 9 E
Biankouma, Ivory C. 112 D3 7 50N 7 40W
Biaora, India 92 H7 23 56N 76 56 E
Bīārjmand, Iran 97 B7 36 6N 55 53 E
Biaro, Indonesia 82 A3 2 5N 125 26 E
Biarritz, France 28 E2 43 29N 1 33W
Bias, Indonesia 79 J18 8 24 S 115 36 E
Biasca, Switz. 33 D7 46 22N 8 58 E
Biavela, Angola 115 E3 14 43 S 19 47 E
Biba, Egypt 106 J7 28 55N 31 0 E
Bibai, Japan 70 C10 43 19N 141 52 E
Bibala, Angola 115 E2 14 44 S 13 24 E
Bibane, Bahiret el, Tunisia 108 B2 33 16N 11 13 E
Bibassé, Gabon 114 B2 1 27N 11 37 E
Bibbiena, Italy 45 E8 43 42N 11 49 E
Bibby I., Canada 143 A10 61 55N 93 0W
Bibel →, Spain 42 C3 42 24N 7 13W
Biberach, Germany 31 G5 48 5N 9 47 E
Biberist, Switz. 32 B5 47 11N 7 34 E
Bibi, Papua N. G. 132 C4 5 30 S 146 2 E
Bibiani, Ghana 112 D4 6 30N 2 8W
Bibile, Sri Lanka 95 L5 7 10N 81 25 E
Bibungwa, Dem. Rep. of the Congo 118 C2 2 40 S 28 15 E
Bic, Canada 141 C6 48 20N 68 41W
Bicaj, Albania 50 E4 41 58N 20 25 E
Bicaz, Romania 53 D11 46 53N 26 5 E
Bicazu Ardelean, Romania 53 D10 46 51N 25 56 E
Bìccari, Italy 47 A8 41 23N 15 12 E
Bicester, U.K. 21 F6 51 54N 1 9W
Bichena, Ethiopia 107 E4 10 28N 38 10 E
Bicheno, Australia 127 G4 41 52 S 148 18 E
Bichia, India 93 H9 22 27N 80 42 E
Bichvinta, Georgia 61 J5 43 9N 40 21 E
Bickerton I., Australia 126 A2 13 45 S 136 10 E
Bicknell, U.S.A. 157 F9 38 47N 87 19W
Bicske, Hungary 52 C3 47 29N 18 38 E
Bicuar, Parque Nacional do,
Angola 115 F2 15 14 S 14 45 E
Bida, Dem. Rep. of the Congo 114 B3 4 55N 19 56 E
Bida, Nigeria 113 D6 9 3N 5 58 E
Bidar, India 94 F3 17 55N 77 35 E
Biddeford, U.S.A. 149 D10 43 30N 70 28W
Biddwara, Ethiopia 107 F4 5 11N 38 34 E
Bideford, U.K. 21 F3 51 1N 4 13W
Bideford Bay, U.K. 21 F3 51 5N 4 20W
Bidhuna, India 93 F8 26 49N 79 31 E
Bidon 5 = Poste Maurice Cortier,
Algeria 111 D5 22 14N 1 2 E
Bidor, Malaysia 87 K3 4 6N 101 15 E
Bidzar, Cameroon 114 A2 9 54N 14 7 E
Bie, Sweden 16 E10 59 5N 16 12 E
Bié □, Angola 115 E3 12 30 S 17 0 E
Bié, Planalto de, Angola 115 E3 12 0 S 16 0 E
Bieber, U.S.A. 158 F3 41 7N 121 8W
Biebrza →, Poland 55 E9 53 13N 22 25 E
Biecz, Poland 55 J8 49 44N 21 15 E
Biel, Switz. 32 B4 47 8N 7 14 E
Bielawa, Poland 55 H3 50 43N 16 37 E
Bielefeld, Germany 30 C4 52 1N 8 33 E
Bielersee, Switz. 32 B4 47 6N 7 5 E
Biella, Italy 44 C5 45 34N 8 3 E
Bielsk Podlaski, Poland 55 F10 52 47N 23 12 E
Bielsko-Biała, Poland 55 J6 49 50N 19 2 E
Bien Hoa, Vietnam 87 G6 10 57N 106 49 E
Bienne = Biel, Switz. 32 B4 47 8N 7 14 E
Bienno, Italy 33 E10 45 56N 10 18 E
Bienvenida, Spain 43 G4 38 18N 6 12W
Bienvenue, Fr. Guiana 171 C7 3 0N 52 30W
Bienville, L., Canada 140 A5 55 5N 72 40W
Bière, Switz. 32 C2 46 33N 6 20 E
Bierné, France 26 E6 47 48N 0 33W
Bierun, Poland 55 H6 50 6N 19 6 E
Bierutów, Poland 55 G4 51 7N 17 32 E
Biescas, Spain 40 C4 42 37N 0 20W
Biese →, Germany 30 C7 52 53N 11 46 E
Biesiesfontein, S. Africa 116 E2 30 57 S 17 58 E
Bietigheim-Bissingen, Germany 31 G5 48 58N 9 8 E
Bieżuń, Poland 55 F6 52 58N 19 55 E
Biferno →, Italy 45 G12 41 59N 15 2 E
Bifoum, Gabon 114 C2 0 20 S 10 23 E
Big →, Canada 141 B8 54 50N 58 55W
Big →, U.S.A. 156 F6 38 28N 90 37W
Big B., Canada 141 A7 55 43N 60 35W
Big Bear City, U.S.A. 161 L10 34 16N 116 51W
Big Bear Lake, U.S.A. 161 L10 34 15N 116 56W
Big Belt Mts., U.S.A. 158 C8 46 30N 111 25W
Big Bend, Swaziland 117 D5 26 50 S 31 58 E
Big Bend Nat. Park, U.S.A. 155 L3 29 20N 103 5W
Big Black →, U.S.A. 155 K9 32 3N 91 4W
Big Blue →, Ind., U.S.A. 157 E11 39 12N 85 56W
Big Blue →, Kans., U.S.A. 156 F6 39 35N 96 34W
Big Creek, U.S.A. 160 H7 37 11N 119 14W
Big Cypress Nat. Preserve, U.S.A. 149 M5 26 0N 81 10W
Big Cypress Swamp, U.S.A. 153 J8 26 15N 81 30W
Big Delta, U.S.A. 144 D11 64 10N 145 51W
Big Falls, U.S.A. 154 A8 48 12N 93 48W
Big Fork →, U.S.A. 154 A8 48 31N 93 43W
Big Horn Mts. = Bighorn Mts.,
U.S.A. 158 D10 44 30N 107 30W
Big I., Canada 142 A5 61 7N 116 45W
Big Lake, U.S.A. 155 K4 31 12N 101 28W
Big Moose, U.S.A. 151 C10 43 49N 74 58W
Big Muddy →, U.S.A. 156 G8 38 0N 89 0W
Big Muddy Cr. →, U.S.A. 154 A2 48 8N 104 36W
Big Pine, Calif., U.S.A. 160 H8 37 10N 118 17W
Big Pine, Fla., U.S.A. 153 L8 24 40N 81 21W
Big Piney, U.S.A. 158 E8 42 32N 110 7W
Big Rapids, U.S.A. 148 D3 43 42N 85 29W
Big Rideau L., Canada 151 B8 44 40N 76 15W
Big River, Canada 143 C7 53 50N 107 0W
Big Run, U.S.A. 150 F6 40 57N 78 55W
Big Sable Pt., U.S.A. 148 C2 44 3N 86 1W
Big Salmon →, Canada 142 A2 61 52N 134 55W
Big Sand L., Canada 143 B9 57 45N 99 45W
Big Sandy, U.S.A. 158 B8 48 11N 110 7W
Big Sandy →, U.S.A. 148 F4 38 25N 82 36W
Big Sandy Cr. →, U.S.A. 154 F3 38 7N 102 29W
Big Satilla →, U.S.A. 152 D7 31 27N 82 3W
Big Sioux →, U.S.A. 154 D6 42 29N 96 27W
Big Spring, U.S.A. 155 J4 32 15N 101 28W
Big Stone City, U.S.A. 154 C6 45 18N 96 28W
Big Stone Gap, U.S.A. 149 G4 36 52N 82 47W
Big Stone L., U.S.A. 154 C6 45 30N 96 35W
Big Sur, U.S.A. 160 J5 36 15N 121 48W
Big Timber, U.S.A. 158 D9 45 50N 109 57W
Big Trout L., Canada 140 B2 53 40N 90 0W
Big Trout Lake, Canada 140 B2 53 45N 90 0W
Biğa, Turkey 51 F11 40 13N 27 14 E
Biga →, Turkey 51 F11 40 20N 27 14 E
Bigadiç, Turkey 49 B10 39 22N 28 7 E
Biganos, France 28 D3 44 39N 0 59W
Biggar, Canada 143 C7 52 4N 108 0W
Biggar, U.K. 22 F5 55 38N 3 32W
Bigge I., Australia 124 B4 14 35 S 125 10 E
Biggenden, Australia 127 D5 25 31 S 152 4 E
Biggleswade, U.K. 21 E7 52 5N 0 14W
Biggs, U.S.A. 160 F5 39 25N 121 43W
Bighorn, U.S.A. 158 C10 46 10N 107 27W
Bighorn →, U.S.A. 158 C10 46 10N 107 28W
Bighorn L., U.S.A. 158 D9 44 55N 108 15W
Bighorn Mts., U.S.A. 158 D10 44 30N 107 30W
Bigi, Dem. Rep. of the Congo 114 B4 3 2N 22 25 E
Bignasco, Switz. 33 D7 46 21N 8 37 E
Bignona, Senegal 112 C1 12 52N 16 14W
Bigorre, France 28 E4 43 10N 0 5 E
Bigstone L., Canada 143 C9 53 42N 95 44W
Biguglia, Étang de, France 29 F13 42 36N 9 29 E
Bigwa, Tanzania 118 D4 7 10 S 39 10 E
Bihać, Bos.-H. 45 D12 44 49N 15 57 E
Bihar, India 93 G11 25 5N 85 40 E
Bihar □, India 93 G12 25 0N 86 0 E
Biharamulo, Tanzania 118 C3 2 25 S 31 25 E
Biharamulo Game Reserve,
Tanzania 118 C3 2 24 S 31 26 E
Bihariganj, India 93 G12 25 44N 86 59 E
Biharkeresztes, Hungary 52 C6 47 8N 21 44 E
Bihor □, Romania 52 D7 47 0N 22 10 E
Bihor, Munţii, Romania 52 D7 46 29N 22 47 E
Bijagós, Arquipélago dos,
Guinea-Biss. 112 C1 11 15N 16 10W
Bijaipur, India 92 F7 26 2N 77 20 E
Bijapur, Chhattisgarh, India 94 E5 18 50N 80 50 E
Bijapur, Karnataka, India 94 F2 16 50N 75 55 E
Bījār, Iran 101 E12 35 52N 47 35 E
Bijawar, India 93 G8 24 38N 79 30 E
Bijeljina, Bos.-H. 52 F4 44 46N 19 14 E
Bijelo Polje, Montenegro, Yug. 50 C3 43 1N 19 45 E
Bijie, China 76 D5 27 20N 105 16 E
Bijnor, India 92 E8 29 27N 78 11 E
Bikaner, India 92 E5 28 2N 73 18 E
Bikapur, India 93 F10 26 30N 82 7 E
Bikeqi, China 74 D6 40 43N 111 20 E
Bikfayyā, Lebanon 103 B4 33 55N 35 41 E
Bikié, Congo 114 C2 3 7 S 13 52 E
Bikin, Russia 67 E14 46 50N 134 20 E
Bikin →, Russia 70 A7 46 51N 134 2 E
Bikini Atoll, Marshall Is. 134 F8 12 0N 167 30 E
Bikita, Zimbabwe 117 C5 20 6 S 31 41 E
Bīkkū Bīttī, Libya 109 D3 22 0N 19 12 E
Bikoro, Dem. Rep. of the Congo 114 C3 0 48 S 18 15 E
Bikoué, Cameroon 113 E7 3 55N 11 50 E
Bila Tserkva, Ukraine 59 H6 49 45N 30 10 E
Bilanga, Burkina Faso 113 C4 12 40N 0 1W
Bilara, India 92 F5 26 14N 73 53 E
Bilasipara, India 90 B3 26 13N 90 14 E
Bilaspur, Chhattisgarh, India 93 H10 22 2N 82 15 E
Bilaspur, Punjab, India 92 D7 31 19N 76 50 E
Biläsuvar, Azerbaijan 101 C13 39 27N 48 32 E
Bilauk Taungdan, Thailand 86 F2 13 0N 99 0 E
Bilbao, Spain 40 B2 43 16N 2 56W
Bilbeis, Egypt 106 H7 30 25N 31 34 E
Bilbo = Bilbao, Spain 40 B2 43 16N 2 56W
Bilbor, Romania 53 C10 47 6N 25 30 E
Bilciureşti, Romania 53 F10 44 44N 25 48 E
Bíldudalur, Iceland 11 B3 65 41N 23 36W
Bílé Karpaty, Europe 35 B11 49 5N 18 0 E
Bileća, Bos.-H. 50 D2 42 53N 18 27 E
Bilecik, Turkey 100 B4 40 5N 30 5 E
Biłgoraj, Poland 55 H9 50 33N 22 42 E
Bilgram, India 93 F9 27 11N 80 2 E
Bilhaur, India 93 F9 26 51N 80 5 E
Bilhorod-Dnistrovskyy, Ukraine 59 J6 46 11N 30 23 E
Bili →, Dem. Rep. of the Congo 114 B4 4 9N 22 29 E
Bilibino, Russia 67 C17 68 3N 166 20 E
Bilibiza, Mozam. 119 E5 12 30 S 40 20 E
Bilikŏl, Kazakstan 65 B5 43 5N 70 45 E
Bilimora, India 94 D1 20 45N 72 57 E
Bilin, Burma 90 G6 17 14N 97 15 E
Biliran □, Phil. 81 F5 11 35N 124 28 E
Bilisht, Albania 50 F5 40 37N 21 2 E
Billabalong Roadhouse, Australia 125 E2 27 25 S 115 49 E
Billabong Cr. →, Australia 128 C6 35 5 S 144 2 E
Billdal, Sweden 17 G5 57 35N 11 57 E
Billiluna, Australia 124 C4 19 37 S 127 41 E
Billings, U.S.A. 158 D9 45 47N 108 30W
Billiton Is. = Belitung, Indonesia 85 C3 3 10 S 107 50 E
Billsta, Sweden 16 A12 63 20N 18 28 E
Billund, Denmark 17 J3 55 44N 9 6 E
Bilma, Niger 109 E2 18 50N 13 30 E
Bilo Gora, Croatia 52 E2 45 53N 17 15 E
Biloela, Australia 126 C5 24 24 S 150 31 E
Bilohirsk, Ukraine 59 K8 45 3N 34 35 E
Biloku, Guyana 169 C6 1 50N 58 25W
Biloli, India 94 E3 18 46N 77 44 E
Bilopillya, Ukraine 59 G8 51 14N 34 20 E
Biloxi, U.S.A. 155 K10 30 24N 88 53W
Bilpa Morea Claypan, Australia 126 D3 25 0 S 140 0 E
Biltine, Chad 109 F4 14 40N 20 50 E
Bilugyun, Burma 90 G6 16 24N 97 32 E
Bilyarsk, Russia 60 C10 54 58N 50 22 E
Bima, Indonesia 85 D5 8 22 S 118 49 E
Bimban, Egypt 106 C3 24 24N 32 54 E
Bimbe, Angola 115 E3 11 50 S 15 50 E
Bimberi Pk., Australia 129 C8 35 44 S 148 51 E
Bimbila, Ghana 113 D5 8 54N 0 5 E
Bimbo, C.A.R. 114 B3 4 15N 18 33 E
Bimini Is., Bahamas 164 A4 25 42N 79 25W
Bin Xian, Heilongjiang, China 75 B14 45 42N 127 32 E
Bin Xian, Shaanxi, China 74 G5 35 2N 108 4 E
Bin Yauri, Nigeria 113 C5 10 46N 4 45 E
Bina-Etawah, India 92 G8 24 13N 78 14 E
Bināb, Iran 97 B6 36 35N 48 41 E
Binaiya, Indonesia 83 B3 3 11 S 129 26 E
Binalbagan, Phil. 81 F4 10 12N 122 50 E
Binalong, Australia 129 C8 34 40 S 148 39 E
Bīnālūd, Kūh-e, Iran 97 B8 36 30N 58 30 E
Binatang = Bintangor, Malaysia 85 B4 2 10N 111 40 E
Binche, Belgium 24 D4 50 26N 4 10 E
Binchuan, China 76 E3 25 42N 100 38 E
Binda, Dem. Rep. of the Congo 115 D2 5 52 S 13 14 E
Binder, Chad 113 D7 9 56N 14 27 E
Bindki, India 93 F9 26 2N 80 36 E
Bindoy, Phil. 81 G4 9 48N 123 5 E
Bindslev, Denmark 17 G4 57 33N 10 11 E
Bindura, Zimbabwe 119 F3 17 18 S 31 18 E
Binefar, Spain 40 D5 41 51N 0 18 E
Bingara, Australia 127 D5 29 52 S 150 36 E
Bingaram I., India 94 H1 10 56N 72 17 E
Bingen, Germany 31 F3 49 57N 7 55 E
Bingerville, Ivory C. 112 D4 5 18N 3 49W
Bingham, U.S.A. 149 C11 45 3N 69 53W
Binghamton, U.S.A. 151 D9 42 6N 75 55W
Bingo-Ochiai, Japan 72 C4 34 59N 133 8 E
Bingöl, Turkey 101 C9 38 53N 40 29 E
Bingöl Dağları, Turkey 101 C9 39 16N 41 9 E
Bingsjö, Sweden 16 C9 61 1N 15 39 E
Binh Dinh = An Nhon, Vietnam 86 F7 13 55N 109 7 E
Binh Khe, Vietnam 86 F7 13 57N 108 51 E
Binh Son, Vietnam 86 E7 15 20N 108 40 E
Binhai, China 75 G10 34 2N 119 49 E
Binic, France 26 D4 48 46N 2 50W
Binisatua, Spain 38 B5 39 50N 4 11 E
Binjai, Indonesia 84 B1 3 20N 98 30 E
Binji, Nigeria 113 C5 13 10N 4 55 E
Binka, India 94 D6 21 2N 83 48 E
Binnaway, Australia 129 A8 31 28 S 149 24 E
Binningen, Switz. 32 A5 47 32N 7 34 E
Binongko, Indonesia 82 C2 5 57 S 124 2 E
Binscarth, Canada 143 C8 50 37N 101 17W
Bint Goda, Sudan 107 E3 13 17N 31 33 E
Bintan, Indonesia 84 B2 1 0N 104 0 E
Bintangor, Malaysia 85 B4 2 10N 111 40 E
Bintulu, Malaysia 78 D4 3 10N 113 0 E
Bintuni, Indonesia 83 B4 2 7 S 133 32 E
Bintuni, Teluk, Indonesia 83 B4 2 20 S 133 30 E
Binyang, China 76 F7 23 12N 108 47 E
Binz, Germany 30 A9 54 24N 13 35 E
Binza, Dem. Rep. of the Congo 115 C3 4 21 S 15 14 E
Binzert = Bizerte, Tunisia 108 A1 37 15N 9 50 E
Binzhou, China 75 F10 37 20N 118 2 E
Bío Bío □, Chile 174 D1 37 35 S 72 0W
Biograd na Moru, Croatia 45 E12 43 56N 15 29 E
Bioko, Eq. Guin. 113 E6 3 30N 8 40 E
Biokovo, Croatia 45 E14 43 23N 17 0 E
Biougra, Morocco 110 B3 30 15N 9 14W
Bipindi, Cameroon 113 E7 3 6N 10 30 E
Bir, India 94 E2 19 4N 75 46 E
Bir, Ras, Djibouti 107 E5 12 0N 43 20 E
Bîr Abu Hashim, Egypt 106 C3 23 42N 34 6 E
Bîr Abu Minqar, Egypt 106 B2 26 33N 27 33 E
Bîr Abu Muḥammad, Egypt 103 F3 29 44N 34 14 E
Bi'r ad Dabbāghāt, Jordan 103 E4 30 26N 35 32 E
Bîr Adal Deib, Sudan 106 C4 22 35N 36 10 E
Bi'r al Butayyihāt, Jordan 103 F4 29 47N 35 20 E
Bi'r al Mārī, Jordan 103 E4 30 4N 35 33 E
Bi'r al Qaţţār, Jordan 103 F4 29 47N 35 32 E
Bir 'Ali, Yemen 99 D5 14 1N 48 20 E
Bir Aouine, Tunisia 108 B1 32 25N 9 18 E
Bîr 'Asal, Egypt 106 B3 25 55N 34 20 E
Bir Atrun, Sudan 106 D2 18 15N 26 40 E
Bîr Beiḍa, Egypt 103 E3 30 25N 34 29 E
Bîr Bel Guerdâne, Mauritania 110 C2 25 24N 10 31W
Bi'r Dhu'fān, Libya 108 B2 31 59N 14 32 E
Bîr Diqnash, Egypt 106 A2 31 3N 25 23 E
Bir el Abbes, Algeria 110 C3 26 7N 6 9W
Bîr el 'Abd, Egypt 103 D2 31 2N 33 0 E
Bir el Ater, Algeria 111 B6 34 46N 8 3 E
Bîr el Basur, Egypt 106 B2 29 51N 25 49 E
Bîr el Biarât, Egypt 103 F3 29 30N 34 43 E
Bîr el Duweidar, Egypt 103 E1 30 56N 32 32 E
Bîr el Garârât, Egypt 103 D2 31 3N 33 34 E
Bîr el Gâreb, Mauritania 110 D1 20 33N 16 12W
Bîr el Gellaz, Egypt 106 A2 30 50N 26 40 E
Bîr el Heisi, Egypt 103 F3 29 22N 34 36 E
Bîr el Jafir, Egypt 103 E1 30 50N 32 41 E
Bîr el Mâlḥi, Egypt 103 E2 30 38N 33 19 E
Bîr el Shaqqa, Egypt 106 A2 30 54N 25 1 E
Bîr el Thamâda, Egypt 103 E2 30 12N 33 27 E
Bîr Enzarán, W. Sahara 110 D2 23 53N 14 32W
Bîr Fuad, Egypt 106 A2 30 35N 26 28 E
Bîr Gandús, W. Sahara 110 D1 21 36N 16 30W
Bir Gara, Chad 109 F3 13 11N 15 58 E
Bîr Gebeil Ḥişn, Egypt 103 E2 30 2N 33 18 E
Bi'r Ghadīr, Syria 103 A6 34 6N 37 3 E
Bîr Haimur, Egypt 106 C3 22 45N 33 40 E
Bîr Ḥasana, Egypt 103 E2 30 29N 33 46 E
Bîr Hööker, Egypt 106 H7 30 22N 30 21 E
Bi'r Idimah, Si. Arabia 98 C4 18 31N 44 12 E
Bir Jdid, Morocco 110 B3 33 26N 8 0W
Bîr Kanayis, Egypt 106 C3 24 59N 33 15 E
Bîr Kaseiba, Egypt 103 E2 31 0N 33 17 E
Bîr Kerawein, Egypt 106 B2 27 10N 28 25 E
Bîr Lahfân, Egypt 103 E2 31 0N 33 51 E
Bir Lahrache, Algeria 111 B6 32 1N 8 12 E
Bîr Madkûr, Egypt 103 E1 30 44N 32 33 E
Bîr Maql, Egypt 106 C3 23 7N 33 40 E
Bîr Mîneiga, Sudan 106 C4 22 47N 35 12 E
Bîr Misaha, Egypt 106 C2 22 13N 27 59 E
Bir Mogreïn, Mauritania 110 C2 25 10N 11 25W
Bîr Murr, Egypt 106 C3 23 28N 30 10 E
Bi'r Muţribah, Kuwait 96 D5 29 54N 47 17 E
Bîr Nakheila, Egypt 106 C3 24 1N 30 50 E
Bîr Qaţia, Egypt 103 E1 30 58N 32 45 E
Bîr Qatrani, Egypt 106 A2 30 55N 26 10 E
Bîr Ranga, Egypt 106 C4 24 25N 35 15 E
Bîr Sahara, Egypt 106 C2 22 54N 28 40 E
Bîr Seiyâla, Egypt 106 B3 26 10N 33 50 E
Bir Semguine, Morocco 110 B3 30 1N 5 39W
Bîr Shalatein, Egypt 106 C4 23 5N 35 25 E
Bîr Shebb, Egypt 106 C2 22 25N 29 40 E
Bîr Shût, Egypt 106 C4 23 50N 35 15 E
Bîr Terfawi, Egypt 106 C2 22 57N 28 55 E
Bi'r Tin Abunda, Libya 111 C7 26 28N 12 27 E
Bîr Umm Qubûr, Egypt 106 C3 24 35N 34 2 E
Bîr Ungât, Egypt 106 C3 22 8N 33 48 E
Bîr Za'farâna, Egypt 106 J8 29 10N 32 40 E
Bi'r Zāmūs, Libya 108 D3 24 16N 15 6 E
Bîr Zeidûn, Egypt 106 B3 25 45N 33 40 E
Bira, Indonesia 83 B4 2 3 S 132 2 E
Biramféro, Guinea 112 C3 11 40N 9 10W
Birao, C.A.R. 114 A4 10 20N 22 47 E
Biratnagar, Nepal 93 F12 26 27N 87 17 E
Birawa, Dem. Rep. of the Congo 118 C2 2 20 S 28 48 E
Birch →, Canada 142 B6 58 28N 112 17W
Birch Hills, Canada 143 C7 52 59N 105 25W
Birch I., Canada 143 C9 52 26N 99 54W
Birch L., N.W.T., Canada 142 A5 62 4N 116 33W
Birch L., Ont., Canada 140 B1 51 23N 92 18W
Birch Mts., Canada 142 B6 57 30N 113 10W
Birch River, Canada 143 C8 52 24N 101 6W
Birchip, Australia 128 C5 35 56 S 142 55 E
Birchiş, Romania 52 E7 45 58N 22 9 E
Birchwood, N.Z. 131 F2 45 55 S 167 53 E
Bird, Canada 143 B10 56 30N 94 13W
Bird I. = Las Aves, Is., W. Indies 165 C7 15 45N 63 55W
Birdseye, U.S.A. 157 F10 38 19N 86 42W
Birdsville, Australia 126 D2 25 51 S 139 20 E
Birdum Cr. →, Australia 124 C5 15 14 S 133 0 E
Birdwood, Australia 128 C3 34 51 S 138 58 E
Birecik, Turkey 101 D8 37 2N 38 0 E
Birein, Israel 103 E3 30 50N 34 28 E
Bireuen, Indonesia 84 A1 5 14N 96 39 E
Biri, Norway 18 D7 60 58N 10 35 E
Biri →, Sudan 107 F2 7 56N 26 33 E
Birifo, Gambia 112 C2 13 30N 14 0W
Birigui, Brazil 175 A5 21 18 S 50 16W
Birini, C.A.R. 114 B4 7 51N 22 24 E
Birjand, Iran 97 C8 32 53N 59 13 E
Birkeland, Norway 18 F4 58 24N 7 12 E
Birkenfeld, Germany 31 F3 49 38N 7 9 E
Birkenhead, N.Z. 130 C3 36 49 S 174 46 E
Birkenhead, U.K. 20 D4 53 23N 3 2W
Birkerød, Denmark 17 J6 55 50N 12 25 E
Birket Fatmé, Chad 109 F3 12 55N 19 7 E
Birket Qârûn, Egypt 106 J7 29 30N 30 40 E
Birkfeld, Austria 34 D8 47 21N 15 45 E
Birkhadem, Algeria 111 A5 36 43N 3 3 E
Birkirkara, Malta 38 F7 35 54N 14 28 E
Bîrlad = Bârlad, Romania 53 D12 46 15N 27 38 E
Birlik, Kazakstan 65 B6 43 40N 73 49 E
Birlik, Kazakstan 65 A6 44 5N 73 31 E
Birmingham, U.K. 21 E6 52 29N 1 52W
Birmingham, Ala., U.S.A. 149 J2 33 31N 86 48W
Birmingham, Iowa, U.S.A. 156 D5 40 53N 91 57W
Birmitrapur, India 94 C7 22 24N 84 46 E
Birni Ngaouré, Niger 113 C5 13 5N 2 51 E
Birni Nkonni, Niger 113 C6 13 55N 5 15 E
Birnin Gwari, Nigeria 113 C6 11 0N 6 45 E
Birnin Kebbi, Nigeria 113 C5 12 32N 4 12 E
Birnin Kudu, Nigeria 113 C6 11 30N 9 29 E
Birobidzhan, Russia 67 E14 48 50N 132 50 E
Birougou, Mts., Gabon 114 C2 1 51 S 12 20 E
Birr, Ireland 23 C4 53 6N 7 54W
Birrie →, Australia 127 D4 29 43 S 146 37 E
Birs →, Switz. 32 B5 47 24N 7 32 E
Birsilpur, India 92 E5 28 11N 72 15 E
Birsk, Russia 64 D5 55 25N 55 30 E
Birštonas, Lithuania 54 D11 54 37N 24 2 E
Birtle, Canada 143 C8 50 30N 101 5W
Biryuchiy, Ukraine 59 J8 46 10N 35 0 E
Biržai, Lithuania 55 H21 56 11N 24 45 E
Birzebbugga, Malta 38 F8 35 50N 14 32 E
Bisa, Indonesia 82 B3 1 15 S 127 28 E
Bisáccia, Italy 47 A8 41 1N 15 22 E
Bisacquino, Italy 46 E6 37 42N 13 15 E
Bisai, Japan 73 B8 35 16N 136 44 E
Bisalpur, India 93 E8 28 14N 79 48 E
Bisbee, U.S.A. 159 L9 31 27N 109 55W
Biscarrosse, France 28 D2 44 22N 1 20W
Biscarrosse et de Parentis, Étang
de, France 28 D2 44 21N 1 10W
Biscay, B. of, Atl. Oc. 8 B11 45 0N 2 0W
Biscayne B., U.S.A. 149 N5 25 40N 80 12W
Bisceglie, Italy 47 A9 41 14N 16 30 E
Bischheim, France 27 D14 48 37N 7 46 E
Bischofshofen, Austria 34 D6 47 26N 13 14 E
Bischofswerda, Germany 30 D10 51 7N 14 10 E
Bischofszell, Switz. 33 B8 47 29N 9 15 E
Bischwiller, France 27 D14 48 46N 7 50 E
Biscoe Bay, Antarctica 7 D13 77 0 S 152 0W
Biscoe Is., Antarctica 7 C17 66 0 S 67 0W
Biscoitos, Azores 9 d1 38 47N 27 15W
Biscostasing, Canada 140 C3 47 18N 82 9W
Biševo, Croatia 45 F13 42 57N 16 3 E
Bisha, Eritrea 107 D4 15 30N 37 31 E
Bishah, W. →, Si. Arabia 98 B3 21 24N 43 26 E
Bishan, China 76 C6 29 33N 106 12 E
Bishanga, Dem. Rep. of the Congo 115 C4 4 31 S 21 2 E
Bishkek, Kyrgyzstan 66 E8 42 54N 74 46 E
Bishnath, India 90 B4 26 40N 93 10 E
Bishnupur, India 93 H12 23 8N 87 20 E
Bisho, S. Africa 117 E4 32 50 S 27 23 E
Bishop, Calif., U.S.A. 160 H8 37 22N 118 24W
Bishop, Ga., U.S.A. 152 B6 33 49N 83 26W
Bishop, Tex., U.S.A. 155 M6 27 35N 97 48W
Bishop Auckland, U.K. 20 C6 54 39N 1 40W
Bishop's Falls, Canada 141 C8 49 2N 55 30W
Bishop's Stortford, U.K. 21 F8 51 52N 0 10 E
Bisignano, Italy 47 C9 39 31N 16 17 E
Bisina, L., Uganda 118 B3 1 38N 33 56 E
Biskra, Algeria 111 B6 34 50N 5 44 E
Biskra, Malta 38 F7 35 58N 14 21 E
Biskupiec, Poland 54 E7 53 53N 20 58 E
Bismarck, Mo., U.S.A. 156 G6 37 46N 90 38W
Bismarck, N. Dak., U.S.A. 154 B4 46 48N 100 47W
Bismarck Arch., Papua N. G. 132 B5 2 30 S 150 0 E
Bismarck Ra., Papua N. G. 132 C3 5 35 S 145 0 E
Bismarck Sea, Papua N. G. 132 C4 4 10 S 146 50 E
Bismark, Germany 30 C7 52 40N 11 33 E
Bismil, Turkey 101 D9 37 51N 40 40 E
Bismo, Norway 18 C5 61 54N 8 15 E
Biso, Uganda 118 B3 1 44N 31 26 E
Bison, U.S.A. 154 C3 45 31N 102 28W
Bīsotūn, Iran 101 E12 34 23N 47 26 E
Bispgården, Sweden 16 A10 63 2N 16 40 E
Bissagos = Bijagós, Arquipélago
dos, Guinea-Biss. 112 C1 11 15N 16 10W
Bissam Cuttack, India 94 E6 19 31N 83 31 E
Bissau, Guinea-Biss. 112 C1 11 45N 15 45W
Bissaula, Nigeria 113 D7 7 0N 10 27 E
Bissikrima, Guinea 112 C2 10 50N 10 58W
Bissorã, Guinea-Biss. 112 C1 12 16N 15 35W
Bistcho L., Canada 142 B5 59 45N 118 50W
Bistreţ, Romania 53 G8 43 54N 23 23 E
Bistrica = Ilirska-Bistrica, Slovenia 45 C11 45 34N 14 14 E
Bistriţa, Romania 53 C9 47 9N 24 35 E
Bistriţa →, Romania 53 D11 46 30N 26 57 E
Bistriţa Năsăud □, Romania 53 C9 47 15N 24 30 E
Bistriţei, Munţii, Romania 53 C10 47 15N 25 40 E
Biswan, India 93 F9 27 29N 81 2 E
Bisztynek, Poland 54 D7 54 8N 20 53 E
Bita →, C.A.R. 114 A4 6 26N 24 43 E
Bitam, Gabon 114 B2 2 5N 11 25 E
Bitburg, Germany 31 F2 49 58N 6 31 E
Bitche, France 27 C14 49 2N 7 25 E
Bithlo, U.S.A. 153 G8 28 33N 81 6W
Bithynia, Turkey 100 B4 40 40N 31 0 E
Bitkine, Chad 109 F3 11 59N 18 13 E
Bitlis, Turkey 101 C10 38 20N 42 3 E
Bitola, Macedonia 50 E5 41 1N 21 20 E
Bitolj = Bitola, Macedonia 50 E5 41 1N 21 20 E
Bitonto, Italy 47 A9 41 6N 16 41 E
Bitra I., India 95 J1 11 33N 72 9 E
Bitter Creek, U.S.A. 158 F9 41 33N 108 33W
Bitter L. = Buheirat-Murrat-el-
Kubra, Egypt 106 H8 30 18N 32 26 E
Bitterfeld, Germany 30 D8 51 37N 12 20 E
Bitterfontein, S. Africa 116 E2 31 1 S 18 32 E
Bitterroot →, U.S.A. 158 C6 46 52N 114 7W
Bitterroot Range, U.S.A. 158 D6 46 0N 114 20W
Bitterwater, U.S.A. 160 J6 36 23N 121 0W
Bitti, Italy 46 B2 40 29N 9 23 E
Bittou, Burkina Faso 113 C4 11 17N 0 18W
Bitung, Indonesia 82 A3 1 27N 125 11 E
Biu, Nigeria 113 C7 10 40N 12 3 E
Bivolari, Romania 53 C12 47 31N 27 27 E
Bivolu, Vf., Romania 53 C10 47 16N 25 58 E
Biwa-Ko, Japan 73 B8 35 15N 136 10 E
Biwabik, U.S.A. 154 B8 47 32N 92 21W
Bixad, Romania 53 C8 47 56N 23 28 E
Bixby, U.S.A. 155 H7 35 57N 95 53W
Biyang, China 74 H7 32 38N 113 21 E
Biysk, Russia 66 D9 52 40N 85 0 E
Bizana, S. Africa 117 E4 30 50 S 29 52 E
Bizen, Japan 72 C6 34 43N 134 8 E
Bizerte, Tunisia 108 A1 37 15N 9 50 E
Bjåen, Norway 18 E4 59 37N 7 26 E
Bjargtangar, Iceland 11 B2 65 30N 24 30W
Bjarkalundur, Iceland 11 B4 65 33N 22 9W
Bjärnum, Sweden 17 H7 56 17N 13 43 E
Bjästa, Sweden 16 A12 63 12N 18 29 E
Bjelasica, Montenegro, Yug. 50 D3 42 50N 19 40 E
Bjelašnica, Bos.-H. 52 G3 43 43N 18 9 E
Bjelland, Norway 18 F4 58 23N 7 32 E
Bjelovar, Croatia 45 C13 45 56N 16 49 E
Bjerringbro, Denmark 17 H3 56 23N 9 39 E
Bjervamoen, Norway 18 E6 59 17N 9 5 E
Bjøberg, Norway 18 D5 60 56N 8 13 E
Björbo, Sweden 16 D8 60 27N 14 44 E
Bjørkelangen, Norway 18 E8 59 53N 11 34 E
Björklinge, Sweden 16 D11 60 2N 17 33 E
Bjørnafjorden, Norway 18 D2 60 7N 5 28 E
Björneborg, Sweden 16 E8 59 14N 14 16 E
Bjørnevatn, Norway 14 B23 69 40N 30 0 E
Bjørnøya, Arctic 6 B8 74 30N 19 0 E
Bjursås, Sweden 16 D9 60 45N 15 25 E
Bjuv, Sweden 17 H6 56 5N 12 55 E
Bla, Mali 112 C3 12 56N 5 47W

192 Blace

Blace, Serbia, Yug. 50 C5 43 18N 21 17 E
Blachownia, Poland 55 H5 50 49N 18 56 E
Black = Da →, Vietnam 76 G5 21 15N 105 20 E
Black →, Canada 150 B5 44 42N 79 19W
Black →, Alaska, U.S.A. 144 C11 66 42N 144 42W
Black →, Ariz., U.S.A. 159 K8 33 44N 110 13W
Black →, Ark., U.S.A. 155 H9 35 38N 91 20W
Black →, Mich., U.S.A. 150 D2 42 59N 82 27W
Black →, N.Y., U.S.A. 151 C8 43 59N 76 4W
Black →, Wis., U.S.A. 154 D9 43 57N 91 22W
Black Bay Pen., Canada 140 C2 48 38N 88 21W
Black Birch L., Canada 143 B7 56 53N 107 45W
Black Diamond, Canada 142 C6 50 45N 114 14W
Black Duck →, Canada 140 A2 56 51N 89 2W
Black Forest = Schwarzwald, Germany 31 G4 48 30N 8 20 E
Black Forest, U.S.A. 154 F2 39 0N 104 43W
Black Hd., Ireland 23 C2 53 9N 9 16W
Black Hills, U.S.A. 154 D3 44 0N 103 45W
Black I., Canada 143 C9 51 12N 96 30W
Black L., Canada 143 B7 59 12N 105 15W
Black L., Mich., U.S.A. 148 C3 45 28N 84 16W
Black L., N.Y., U.S.A. 151 B9 44 31N 75 36W
Black Lake, Canada 143 B7 59 11N 105 20W
Black Mesa, U.S.A. 155 G3 36 58N 102 58W
Black Mountain, Australia 129 A9 30 18 S 151 39 E
Black Mt. = Mynydd Du, U.K. 21 F4 51 52N 3 50W
Black Mts., U.K. 21 F4 51 55N 3 7W
Black Range, U.S.A. 159 K10 33 15N 107 50W
Black River, Jamaica 164 a 18 0N 77 50W
Black River Falls, U.S.A. 154 C9 44 18N 90 51W
Black Rock, Australia 128 B3 32 50 S 138 44 E
Black Rock, Barbados 165 g 13 7N 59 37W
Black Sea, Eurasia 57 F6 43 30N 35 0 E
Black Tickle, Canada 141 B8 53 28N 55 45W
Black Volta →, Africa 112 D4 8 41N 1 33W
Black Warrior →, U.S.A. 149 J2 32 32N 87 51W
Blackall, Australia 126 C4 24 25 S 145 45 E
Blackball, N.Z. 131 C6 42 22 S 171 26 E
Blackbull, Australia 126 B3 17 55 S 141 45 E
Blackburn, U.K. 20 D5 53 45N 2 29W
Blackburn, Mt., U.S.A. 144 F12 61 44N 143 26W
Blackburn with Darwen □, U.K. 20 D5 53 45N 2 29W
Blackdown Tableland Nat. Park, Australia 126 C4 23 52 S 149 8 E
Blackfoot, U.S.A. 158 E7 43 11N 112 21W
Blackfoot →, U.S.A. 158 C7 46 52N 113 53W
Blackfoot River Reservoir, U.S.A. 158 E8 43 0N 111 43W
Blackman, U.S.A. 153 E3 30 56N 86 38W
Blackpool, U.K. 20 D4 53 49N 3 3W
Blackpool □, U.K. 20 D4 53 49N 3 3W
Blackriver, U.S.A. 150 B1 44 46N 83 17W
Blacks Harbour, Canada 141 C6 45 3N 66 49W
Blacksburg, U.S.A. 148 G5 37 14N 80 25W
Blackshear, U.S.A. 152 D7 31 18N 82 14W
Blackshear, L., U.S.A. 152 D6 31 51N 83 56W
Blacksod B., Ireland 23 B1 54 6N 10 0W
Blackstone, U.S.A. 148 G7 37 4N 78 0W
Blackstone Ra., Australia 125 E4 26 0 S 128 30 E
Blackville, U.S.A. 152 B8 33 22N 81 16W
Blackwater, Australia 126 C4 23 35 S 148 53 E
Blackwater →, Cork, Ireland 19 E3 52 5N 9 3W
Blackwater →, Meath, Ireland 23 C4 53 39N 6 41W
Blackwater →, Waterford, Ireland 23 D4 52 4N 7 52W
Blackwater →, U.K. 23 B5 54 31N 6 35W
Blackwater →, Fla., U.S.A. 153 E2 30 36N 87 2W
Blackwater →, Mo., U.S.A. 156 F4 38 59N 92 59W
Blackwell, U.S.A. 155 G6 36 48N 97 17W
Blackwells Corner, U.S.A. 161 K7 35 37N 119 47W
Blackwood, C., Papua N. G. 132 D3 7 49 S 144 31 E
Bladensburg Nat. Park, Australia 126 C3 22 30 S 142 59 E
Blaenau Ffestiniog, U.K. 20 E4 53 0N 3 56W
Blaenau Gwent □, U.K. 21 F4 51 48N 3 12W
Bláfell, Iceland 11 C7 64 30N 19 51W
Bláfjall, Iceland 11 B10 65 26N 16 50W
Blagaj, Bos.-H. 50 C1 43 16N 17 55 E
Blagnac, France 28 E5 43 37N 1 23 E
Blagodarnoye = Blagodarnyy, Russia 61 H6 45 7N 43 37 E
Blagodarnyy, Russia 61 H6 45 7N 43 37 E
Blagoevgrad, Bulgaria 50 D7 42 2N 23 5 E
Blagoveshchenka, Kazakstan 65 B7 43 18N 74 12 E
Blagoveshchensk, Amur, Russia 67 D13 50 20N 127 30 E
Blagoveshchensk, Bashkortostan, Russia 64 D5 55 1N 55 59 E
Blahkiuh, Indonesia 79 J18 8 31 S 115 12 E
Blain, France 26 E5 47 29N 1 45W
Blain, U.S.A. 150 F7 40 20N 77 31W
Blaine, Minn., U.S.A. 154 C8 45 10N 93 13W
Blaine, Wash., U.S.A. 160 B4 48 59N 122 45W
Blaine Lake, Canada 143 C7 52 51N 106 52W
Blair, U.S.A. 154 E6 41 33N 96 8W
Blair Athol, Australia 126 C4 22 42 S 147 31 E
Blair Atholl, U.K. 22 E5 56 46N 3 50W
Blairgowrie, U.K. 22 E5 56 35N 3 21W
Blairsden, U.S.A. 160 F6 39 47N 120 37W
Blairsville, U.S.A. 150 F5 40 26N 79 16W
Blaj, Romania 53 D8 46 10N 23 57 E
Blaka, Niger 109 D2 21 21N 12 47 E
Blakang Mati, Pulau, Singapore 87 d 1 15N 103 50 E
Blake Pt., U.S.A. 154 A10 48 11N 88 25W
Blakely, Ga., U.S.A. 152 D5 31 23N 84 56W
Blakely, Pa., U.S.A. 151 E9 41 28N 75 37W
Blakesburg, U.S.A. 156 D4 40 58N 92 38W
Blakstad, Norway 18 F5 58 30N 8 39 E
Blâmont, France 27 D13 48 35N 6 50 E
Blanc, C., Spain 38 B3 39 21N 2 51 E
Blanc, C., Tunisia 108 A1 37 15N 9 56 E
Blanc, Mont, Alps 29 C10 45 48N 6 50 E
Blanc-Sablon, Canada 141 B8 51 24N 57 12W
Blanca, B., Argentina 176 A4 39 10 S 61 30W
Blanca Peak, U.S.A. 159 H11 37 35N 105 29W
Blanchardville, U.S.A. 156 B7 42 49N 89 52W
Blanche, C., Australia 127 E1 33 1 S 134 9 E
Blanche, L., S. Austral., Australia 127 D2 29 15 S 139 40 E
Blanche, L., W. Austral., Australia 124 D3 22 25 S 123 17 E
Blanche Channel, Solomon Is. 133 M9 8 30 S 157 30 E
Blanchester, U.S.A. 157 E13 39 17N 83 59W
Blanchisseuse, Trin. & Tob. 169 F9 10 48N 61 18W
Blanco, S. Africa 116 E3 33 55 S 22 23 E
Blanco, U.S.A. 155 K5 30 6N 98 25W
Blanco →, Argentina 174 C2 30 20 S 68 42W
Blanco →, Bolivia 173 C5 12 30 S 64 18W
Blanco, C., Costa Rica 164 E2 9 34N 85 8W
Blanco, C., U.S.A. 158 E1 42 51N 124 34W
Blanda →, Iceland 11 B6 65 37N 20 9W
Blandford Forum, U.K. 21 G5 50 51N 2 9W
Blanding, U.S.A. 159 H9 37 37N 109 29W
Blandinsville, U.S.A. 156 D6 40 33N 90 52W
Blanes, Spain 40 D7 41 40N 2 48 E
Blangy-sur-Bresle, France 27 C8 49 55N 1 37 E
Blanice →, Czech Rep. 34 B7 49 10N 14 5 E
Blankaholm, Sweden 17 G10 57 36N 16 31 E
Blankenberge, Belgium 24 C3 51 20N 3 9 E
Blankenburg, Germany 30 D6 51 47N 10 57 E
Blanquefort, France 28 D3 44 55N 0 38W
Blanquilla, I., Venezuela 165 D7 11 51N 64 37W
Blanquillo, Uruguay 175 C4 32 53 S 55 37W
Blansko, Czech Rep. 35 B9 49 22N 16 40 E
Blantyre, Malawi 119 F4 15 45 S 35 0 E
Blarney, Ireland 23 E3 51 56N 8 33W
Blasdell, U.S.A. 150 D6 42 48N 78 50W
Blåsjø, Norway 18 E3 59 20N 6 50 E
Błaszki, Poland 55 G5 51 38N 18 30 E
Blatná, Czech Rep. 34 B6 49 25N 13 52 E
Blato, Croatia 45 F13 42 56N 16 48 E
Blatten, Switz. 32 D5 46 20N 7 50 E
Blaubeuren, Germany 31 G5 48 24N 9 46 E
Blaustein, Germany 31 G5 48 25N 9 53 E
Blåvands Huk, Denmark 17 J2 55 33N 8 4 E
Blaydon, U.K. 20 C6 54 58N 1 42W
Blaye, France 28 C3 45 8N 0 40W
Blaye-les-Mines, France 28 D6 44 1N 2 8 E
Blayney, Australia 129 B8 33 32 S 149 14 E
Blaze, Pt., Australia 124 B5 12 56 S 130 11 E
Błażowa, Poland 55 J9 49 53N 22 7 E
Bleckede, Germany 30 B6 53 17N 10 43 E
Bled, Slovenia 45 B11 46 27N 14 7 E
Blefjell, Norway 18 E6 59 48N 9 10 E
Bleiburg, Austria 34 E7 46 35N 14 49 E
Blejeşti, Romania 53 F10 44 19N 25 27 E
Blekinge, Sweden 15 H16 56 25N 15 20 E
Blekinge län □, Sweden 17 H9 56 20N 15 20 E
Blenheim, Canada 150 D3 42 20N 82 0W
Blenheim, N.Z. 131 B8 41 38 S 173 57 E
Bléone →, France 29 D10 44 5N 6 0 E
Blérancourt, France 27 C10 49 31N 3 9 E
Bletchley, U.K. 21 F7 51 59N 0 44W
Blida, Algeria 111 A5 36 30N 2 49 E
Blidet Amor, Algeria 111 B6 32 59N 5 58 E
Blidö, Sweden 16 E12 59 37N 18 53 E
Blidsberg, Sweden 17 G7 57 56N 13 30 E
Blieskastel, Germany 31 F3 49 14N 7 12 E
Bligh Sound, N.Z. 131 E2 44 47 S 167 32 E
Bligh Water, Fiji 133 A2 17 0 S 178 0 E
Blind River, Canada 140 C3 46 10N 82 58W
Blinisht, Albania 50 E3 41 52N 19 59 E
Blinnenhorn, Switz. 33 D6 46 26N 8 19 E
Bliss, Idaho, U.S.A. 158 E6 42 56N 114 57W
Bliss, N.Y., U.S.A. 150 D6 42 34N 78 15W
Blissfield, Mich., U.S.A. 157 C13 41 50N 83 52W
Blissfield, Ohio, U.S.A. 150 F3 40 24N 81 58W
Blitar, Indonesia 85 D4 8 5 S 112 11 E
Blitchton, U.S.A. 152 C8 32 12N 81 26W
Blitta, Togo 113 D5 8 23N 1 6 E
Block I., U.S.A. 151 E13 41 11N 71 35W
Block Island Sd., U.S.A. 151 E13 41 15N 71 40W
Bloemfontein, S. Africa 116 D4 29 6 S 26 7 E
Bloemhof, S. Africa 116 D4 27 38 S 25 32 E
Blois, France 26 E8 47 35N 1 20 E
Blomskog, Sweden 16 E6 59 16N 12 2 E
Blomstermåla, Sweden 17 H10 56 59N 16 21 E
Blomvåg, Norway 18 D1 60 32N 4 50 E
Blonay, Switz. 32 D3 46 28N 6 54 E
Blönduós, Iceland 11 B6 65 40N 20 12W
Blongas, Indonesia 79 K19 8 53 S 116 2 E
Błonie, Poland 55 F7 52 12N 20 37 E
Bloodvein →, Canada 143 C9 51 47N 96 43W
Bloody Foreland, Ireland 23 A3 55 10N 8 17W
Bloomer, U.S.A. 154 C9 45 6N 91 29W
Bloomfield, Canada 150 C7 43 59N 77 14W
Bloomfield, Ind., U.S.A. 157 E10 39 1N 86 57W
Bloomfield, Iowa, U.S.A. 156 D4 40 45N 92 25W
Bloomfield, Ky., U.S.A. 157 G11 37 55N 85 19W
Bloomfield, N. Mex., U.S.A. 159 H10 36 43N 107 59W
Bloomfield, Nebr., U.S.A. 154 D6 42 36N 97 39W
Bloomingburg, U.S.A. 157 E13 39 36N 83 24W
Bloomingdale, U.S.A. 152 C8 32 8N 81 18W
Bloomington, Ill., U.S.A. 156 D8 40 28N 89 0W
Bloomington, Ind., U.S.A. 157 E10 39 10N 86 32W
Bloomington, Minn., U.S.A. 154 C8 44 50N 93 17W
Bloomington, Wis., U.S.A. 156 B6 42 53N 90 55W
Bloomsburg, U.S.A. 151 F8 41 0N 76 27W
Bloomsbury, Australia 126 J6 20 48 S 148 38 E
Blora, Indonesia 85 D4 6 57 S 111 25 E
Blossburg, U.S.A. 150 E7 41 41N 77 4W
Blosseville Kyst, Greenland 10 D8 68 50N 26 30W
Blotzheim, France 32 A4 47 36N 7 29 E
Blouberg, S. Africa 117 C4 23 8 S 28 59 E
Blountstown, U.S.A. 152 E4 30 27N 85 3W
Bludenz, Austria 34 D2 47 10N 9 50 E
Blue →, U.S.A. 157 F10 38 11N 86 19W
Blue Cypress L., U.S.A. 153 H9 27 44N 80 45W
Blue Earth, U.S.A. 154 D8 43 38N 94 6W
Blue Lagoon Nat. Park, Zambia 119 F2 15 28 S 27 26 E
Blue Mesa Reservoir, U.S.A. 159 G10 38 28N 107 20W
Blue Mound, U.S.A. 156 E7 39 42N 89 7W
Blue Mountain Lake, U.S.A. 151 C10 43 52N 74 30W
Blue Mountain Pk., Jamaica 164 a 18 3N 76 36W
Blue Mountains, The, Jamaica 164 a 18 3N 76 36W
Blue Mountains Nat. Park, Australia 129 C9 34 2 S 150 15 E
Blue Mts., Australia 129 B9 33 40 S 150 15 E
Blue Mts., Maine, U.S.A. 151 B14 44 50N 70 35W
Blue Mts., Oreg., U.S.A. 158 D4 45 15N 119 0W
Blue Mts., Pa., U.S.A. 151 F8 40 30N 76 30W
Blue Mud B., Australia 126 A2 13 30 S 136 0 E
Blue Nile = Nîl el Azraq →, Sudan 107 D3 15 38N 32 31 E
Blue Rapids, U.S.A. 154 F6 39 41N 96 39W
Blue Ridge Mts., U.S.A. 149 G5 36 30N 80 15W
Blue River, Canada 142 C5 52 6N 119 18W
Blue Springs, U.S.A. 156 E2 39 1N 94 17W
Bluefield, U.S.A. 148 G5 37 15N 81 17W
Bluefields, Nic. 164 D3 12 20N 83 50W
Bluff, Australia 126 C4 23 35 S 149 4 E
Bluff, N.Z. 131 G3 46 37 S 168 20 E
Bluff, U.S.A. 159 H9 37 17N 109 33W
Bluff Harbour, N.Z. 131 G3 46 36 S 168 21 E
Bluff Knoll, Australia 125 F2 34 24 S 118 15 E
Bluff Pt., Australia 125 E1 27 50 S 114 5 E
Bluffs, U.S.A. 156 E6 39 45N 90 32W
Bluffton, Ga., U.S.A. 152 D5 31 31N 84 52W
Bluffton, Ind., U.S.A. 157 D11 40 44N 85 11W
Bluffton, Ohio, U.S.A. 157 D13 40 54N 83 54W
Bluffton, S.C., U.S.A. 152 C9 32 14N 80 52W
Blumenau, Brazil 175 B6 27 0 S 49 0W
Blümisalphorn, Switz. 32 D5 46 28N 7 47 E
Blunt, U.S.A. 154 C5 44 31N 99 59W
Bly, U.S.A. 158 E3 42 24N 121 3W
Blyde River Canyon Nature Reserve, S. Africa 117 C5 24 37 S 31 2 E
Blyth, Australia 128 B3 33 49 S 138 28 E
Blyth, Canada 150 C3 43 44N 81 26W
Blyth, U.K. 20 B6 55 8N 1 31W
Blythe, Calif., U.S.A. 161 M12 33 37N 114 36W
Blythe, Ga., U.S.A. 152 B7 33 17N 82 12W
Blytheville, U.S.A. 155 H10 35 56N 89 55W
Bø, Norway 18 E6 59 25N 9 3 E
Bo, S. Leone 112 D2 7 55N 11 50W
Bo Duc, Vietnam 87 G6 11 58N 106 50 E
Bo Hai, China 75 E10 39 0N 119 0 E
Bō-no-Misaki, Japan 72 F2 31 15N 130 13 E
Bo Xian = Bozhou, China 74 H8 33 55N 115 41 E
Boa Esperança, Brazil 169 C5 3 21N 61 23W
Boa Esperança, Represa, Brazil 170 C3 6 50 S 43 50W
Boa Nova, Brazil 171 D3 14 22 S 40 10W
Boa Viagem, Brazil 170 C4 5 7 S 39 44W
Boa Vista, Brazil 169 C5 2 48N 60 30W
Boa Vista, C. Verde Is. 9 j 16 0N 22 49W
Boac, Phil. 80 E3 13 27N 121 50 E
Boaco, Nic. 164 D2 12 29N 85 35W
Bo'ai, China 74 G7 35 10N 113 3 E
Boal, Spain 42 B4 43 25N 6 49W
Boali, C.A.R. 114 B3 4 48N 18 7 E
Boalsburg, U.S.A. 150 F7 40 46N 77 47W
Boane, Mozam. 117 D5 26 6 S 32 19 E
Boang I., Papua N. G. 132 B7 3 23 S 153 18 E
Boano, Indonesia 82 B3 3 0 S 127 56 E
Boardman, U.S.A. 150 E4 41 2N 80 40W
Boath, India 94 E4 19 20N 78 20 E
Boatswain Bird I., Ascension I. 9 g 7 56 S 14 18W
Bobadah, Australia 129 B7 32 19 S 146 41 E
Bobai, China 76 F7 22 17N 109 59 E
Bobbili, India 94 E6 18 35N 83 30 E
Bòbbio, Italy 44 D6 44 46N 9 23 E
Bobcaygeon, Canada 140 D4 44 33N 78 33W
Boblad, India 94 F2 17 13N 75 26 E
Böblingen, Germany 31 G5 48 40N 9 1 E
Bobo-Dioulasso, Burkina Faso 112 C4 11 8N 4 13W
Bobolice, Poland 54 E3 53 58N 16 37 E
Bobon, Phil. 80 E5 12 32N 124 34 E
Bobonaro, E. Timor 82 C3 9 2 S 125 22 E
Bobonaza →, Ecuador 168 D2 2 36 S 76 38W
Boboshevo, Bulgaria 50 D7 42 9N 23 0 E
Bobov Dol, Bulgaria 50 D6 42 20N 23 0 E
Bóbr →, Poland 55 F2 52 4N 15 4 E
Bobraomby, Tanjon' i, Madag. 117 A8 12 40 S 49 10 E
Bobrinets, Ukraine 59 H7 48 4N 32 5 E
Bobrov, Russia 60 E5 51 5N 40 2 E
Bobrovitsa, Ukraine 59 G6 50 45N 31 23 E
Bobruysk = Babruysk, Belarus 59 F5 53 10N 29 15 E
Bobures, Venezuela 168 B3 9 15N 71 11W
Boca de Drago, Venezuela 169 F9 11 0N 61 50W
Bôca do Acre, Brazil 172 B4 8 50 S 67 27W
Bôca do Jari, Brazil 169 D7 1 7 S 51 58W
Bôca do Moaco, Brazil 172 B4 7 41 S 68 17W
Boca Grande, U.S.A. 153 J7 26 45N 82 16W
Boca Grande, Venezuela 169 B5 8 40N 60 40W
Boca Raton, U.S.A. 149 M5 26 21N 80 5W
Bocaiúva, Brazil 171 E3 17 7 S 43 49W
Bocanda, Ivory C. 112 D4 7 5N 4 31W
Bocaranga, C.A.R. 114 A3 7 0N 15 35 E
Bocas del Toro, Panama 164 E3 9 15N 82 20W
Boceguillas, Spain 42 D7 41 20N 3 39W
Bochnia, Poland 55 J7 49 58N 20 27 E
Bocholt, Germany 30 D2 51 50N 6 36 E
Bochum, Germany 30 D3 51 28N 7 13 E
Bockenem, Germany 30 C6 52 1N 10 8 E
Boćki, Poland 55 F10 52 39N 23 3 E
Bocognano, France 29 F13 42 5N 9 4 E
Bocoio, Angola 115 E2 12 28 S 14 10 E
Boconó, Venezuela 168 B3 9 15N 70 16W
Boconó →, Venezuela 168 B4 8 43N 69 34W
Bocoyna, Mexico 162 B3 27 52N 107 35W
Bocşa, Romania 52 E6 45 21N 21 47 E
Boda, C.A.R. 114 B3 4 19N 17 26 E
Boda, Dalarnas, Sweden 16 C9 61 1N 15 13 E
Böda, Kalmar, Sweden 17 G11 57 15N 17 3 E
Boda, Västernorrland, Sweden 16 B10 62 52N 16 39 E
Bodafors, Sweden 17 G8 57 48N 14 23 E
Bodaybo, Russia 67 D12 57 50N 114 0 E
Boddam, U.K. 22 B7 59 56N 1 17W
Boddington, Australia 125 F2 32 50 S 116 30 E
Bode Sadu, Nigeria 113 D5 9 0N 4 47 E
Bodega Bay, U.S.A. 160 G3 38 20N 123 3W
Boden, Sweden 14 D19 65 50N 21 42 E
Bodensee, Europe 33 A8 47 35N 9 25 E
Bodenteich, Germany 30 C6 52 50N 10 42 E
Bodhan, India 94 E3 18 40N 77 44 E
Bodinayakkanur, India 95 J3 10 2N 77 10 E
Bodinga, Nigeria 113 C6 12 58N 5 10 E
Bodio, Switz. 33 D7 46 23N 8 55 E
Bodmin, U.K. 21 G3 50 28N 4 43W
Bodmin Moor, U.K. 21 G3 50 33N 4 36W
Bodø, Norway 14 C16 67 17N 14 24 E
Bodoquena, Serra da, Brazil 173 E6 21 0 S 56 50W
Bodoupa, C.A.R. 114 A3 5 43N 17 36 E
Bodrichi, Chad 109 E3 19 11N 15 54 E
Bodrog →, Hungary 52 B6 48 11N 21 22 E
Bodrum, Turkey 49 D9 37 3N 27 30 E
Boduna, Dem. Rep. of the Congo 114 A3 5 5N 19 44 E
Bódva →, Hungary 52 B5 48 19N 20 45 E
Boembé, Congo 114 C3 2 54 S 15 39 E
Boën, France 29 C8 45 44N 4 1 E
Boende, Dem. Rep. of the Congo 114 C4 0 24 S 21 12 E
Boerne, U.S.A. 155 L5 29 47N 98 44W
Boesmans →, S. Africa 116 E4 33 42 S 26 39 E
Boffa, Guinea 112 C2 10 16N 14 3W
Bofuku, Dem. Rep. of the Congo 114 C4 0 57 S 20 53 E
Bogale, Burma 90 G5 16 17N 95 24 E
Bogalusa, U.S.A. 155 K10 30 47N 89 52W
Bogan →, N.S.W., Australia 127 D4 29 59 S 146 17 E
Bogan →, N.S.W., Australia 129 A7 30 20 S 146 55 E
Bogan Gate, Australia 129 B7 33 7 S 147 49 E
Bogandé, Burkina Faso 113 C4 13 2N 0 8W
Bogangolo, C.A.R. 114 A3 5 34N 18 15 E
Bogantungan, Australia 126 C4 23 41 S 147 17 E
Bogata, U.S.A. 155 J7 33 28N 95 13W
Bogatić, Serbia, Yug. 50 B3 44 51N 19 30 E
Boğazkale, Turkey 100 B6 40 2N 34 37 E
Boğazlıyan, Turkey 100 C6 39 11N 35 14 E
Bogbonga, Dem. Rep. of the Congo 114 B3 1 36N 19 24 E
Bogdanovich, Russia 64 C9 56 47N 62 1 E
Bogen, Sweden 16 D6 60 4N 12 33 E
Bogense, Denmark 17 J4 55 34N 10 5 E
Bogetići, Montenegro, Yug. 50 D2 42 41N 18 58 E
Boggabilla, Australia 127 D5 28 36 S 150 24 E
Boggabri, Australia 129 A9 30 45 S 150 5 E
Boggeragh Mts., Ireland 23 D3 52 2N 8 55W
Bogia, Papua N. G. 132 C3 4 9 S 145 0 E
Boglan = Solhan, Turkey 101 C9 38 57N 41 3 E
Bognor Regis, U.K. 21 G7 50 47N 0 40W
Bogo, Phil. 81 F4 11 3N 124 0 E
Bogodukhov = Bohodukhiv, Ukraine 59 G8 50 9N 35 33 E
Bogol Manya, Ethiopia 107 G5 4 34N 41 29 E
Bogong, Mt., Australia 129 D7 36 47 S 147 17 E
Bogor, Indonesia 84 D3 6 36 S 106 48 E
Bogoroditsk, Russia 58 F10 53 47N 38 8 E
Bogorodsk, Russia 60 B6 56 4N 43 30 E
Bogoso, Ghana 112 D4 5 38N 2 3W
Bogotá, Colombia 168 C3 4 34N 74 0W
Bogotol, Russia 66 D9 56 15N 89 50 E
Bogou, Togo 113 C5 10 40N 0 12 E
Bogra, Bangla. 90 C2 24 51N 89 22 E
Boguchany, Russia 67 D10 58 40N 97 30 E
Boguchar, Russia 60 F5 49 55N 40 32 E
Bogué, Mauritania 112 B2 16 45N 14 10W
Boguslav, Ukraine 59 H6 49 33N 30 56 E
Boguszów-Gorce, Poland 55 H3 50 45N 16 12 E
Bohain-en-Vermandois, France 27 C10 49 59N 3 28 E
Bohemian Forest = Böhmerwald, Germany 31 F9 49 8N 13 14 E
Bohena Cr. →, Australia 129 A8 30 17 S 149 42 E
Bohinjska Bistrica, Slovenia 45 B11 46 17N 14 1 E
Böhmerwald, Germany 31 F9 49 8N 13 14 E
Bohmte, Germany 30 C4 52 22N 8 19 E
Bohodukhiv, Ukraine 59 G8 50 9N 35 33 E
Bohol, Somali Rep. 120 C3 5 45N 46 9 E
Bohol □, Phil. 81 G5 9 50N 124 10 E
Bohol Sea, Phil. 81 G5 9 0N 124 0 E
Bohol Str., Phil. 81 G4 9 45N 123 40 E
Bohongou, Burkina Faso 113 C5 12 30N 0 40 E
Böhönye, Hungary 52 D2 46 25N 17 28 E
Bohotleh, Somali Rep. 120 C3 8 20N 46 25 E
Bohuslän, Sweden 17 F5 58 25N 12 0 E
Boi, Nigeria 113 D6 9 35N 9 27 E
Boi, Pta. de, Brazil 175 A6 23 55 S 45 15W
Boiaçu, Brazil 169 D5 0 27 S 61 46W
Boigu I., Australia 132 E2 9 15 S 142 14 E
Boileau, C., Australia 124 C3 17 40 S 122 7 E
Boim, Brazil 169 D6 2 49 S 55 10W
Boing'o, Sudan 107 F3 9 58N 33 44 E
Boipariguda, India 94 E6 18 46N 82 26 E
Boipeba, I. de, Brazil 171 D4 13 39 S 38 55W
Boiro, Spain 42 C2 42 39N 8 54W
Bois →, Brazil 171 E1 18 35 S 50 2W
Boise, U.S.A. 158 E5 43 37N 116 13W
Boise City, U.S.A. 155 G3 36 44N 102 31W
Boissevain, Canada 143 D8 49 15N 100 5W
Bóite →, Italy 45 B9 46 5N 12 5 E
Boitzenburg, Germany 30 B9 53 16N 13 35 E
Boizenburg, Germany 30 B6 53 23N 10 43 E
Bojador, C., W. Sahara 110 C2 26 0N 14 30W
Bojana →, Albania 50 E3 41 52N 19 22 E
Bojano, Italy 47 A7 41 29N 14 29 E
Bojanowo, Poland 55 G3 51 43N 16 42 E
Bøjden, Denmark 17 J4 55 6N 10 7 E
Bojnūrd, Iran 97 B8 37 30N 57 20 E
Bojonegoro, Indonesia 85 D4 7 11 S 111 54 E
Boju, Nigeria 113 D6 7 22N 7 55 E
Boka, Serbia, Yug. 52 E5 45 22N 20 52 E
Boka Kotorska, Montenegro, Yug. 50 D2 42 23N 18 32 E
Bokada, Dem. Rep. of the Congo 114 B3 4 8N 19 23 E
Bokala, Dem. Rep. of the Congo 114 C3 3 8 S 17 4 E
Bokala, Ivory C. 112 D4 8 31N 4 33W
Bokani, Nigeria 113 D6 9 28N 5 10 E
Bokaro, India 93 H11 23 46N 85 55 E
Bokatola, Dem. Rep. of the Congo 114 C3 0 38 S 18 46 E
Boké, Guinea 112 C2 10 56N 14 17W
Bokela, Dem. Rep. of the Congo 114 C4 1 10 S 21 59 E
Bokenda, Dem. Rep. of the Congo 114 B4 1 16N 21 22 E
Bokhara →, Australia 127 D4 29 55 S 146 42 E
Bokkos, Nigeria 113 D6 9 17N 9 1 E
Boknafjorden, Norway 15 G11 59 14N 5 40 E
Bokode, Dem. Rep. of the Congo 114 B3 3 55N 19 30 E
Bokolo, Gabon 114 C2 2 40 S 10 10 E
Bökönbaev, Kyrgyzstan 65 B8 42 10N 76 55 E
Bokondo, Dem. Rep. of the Congo 114 B4 0 15N 22 32 E
Bokora Game Reserve, Uganda 118 B3 2 12N 31 32 E
Bokoro, Chad 109 F3 12 25N 17 14 E
Bokota, Dem. Rep. of the Congo 114 C4 0 56 S 22 24 E
Bokote, Dem. Rep. of the Congo 114 C4 0 12 S 21 8 E
Bokpyin, Burma 87 G2 11 18N 98 42 E
Boksitogorsk, Russia 58 C7 59 22N 33 50 E
Boku, Papua N. G. 132 D8 6 34 S 155 21 E
Bokungu, Dem. Rep. of the Congo 114 C4 0 35 S 22 50 E
Bol, Chad 109 F2 13 30N 14 40 E
Bol, Croatia 45 E13 43 18N 16 38 E
Bolama, Guinea-Biss. 112 C1 11 30N 15 30W
Bolan →, Pakistan 92 E2 28 38N 67 42 E
Bolan Pass, Pakistan 91 C2 29 50N 67 20 E
Bolaños →, Mexico 162 C4 21 14N 104 8W
Bolaños de Calatrava, Spain 43 G7 38 54N 3 40W
Bolayır, Turkey 51 F10 40 31N 26 45 E
Bolbec, France 26 C7 49 30N 0 30 E
Boldājī, Iran 97 D6 31 56N 51 3 E
Boldeşti-Scăeni, Romania 53 E11 45 3N 26 2 E
Bole, China 68 B3 45 11N 81 37 E
Bole, Ethiopia 107 F4 6 36N 37 20 E
Bole, Ghana 112 D4 9 3N 2 23W
Bolekhiv, Ukraine 59 H2 49 0N 23 57 E
Boleko, Dem. Rep. of the Congo 114 C3 1 35 S 19 50 E
Bolesławiec, Poland 55 G2 51 17N 15 37 E
Bolgatanga, Ghana 113 C4 10 44N 0 53W
Bolgrad = Bolhrad, Ukraine 59 K5 45 40N 28 32 E
Bolhrad, Ukraine 59 K5 45 40N 28 32 E
Bolia, Dem. Rep. of the Congo 114 C3 1 36 S 18 22 E
Bolinao, Phil. 80 C2 16 23N 119 54 E
Bolinao, C., Phil. 80 C2 16 23N 119 55 E
Bolingbroke, U.S.A. 152 C6 32 57N 83 48W
Bolingo, Dem. Rep. of the Congo 114 C4 3 31 S 21 43 E
Bolintin-Vale, Romania 53 F10 44 27N 25 46 E
Bolívar, Argentina 174 D3 36 15 S 60 53W
Bolívar, Antioquía, Colombia 168 B2 5 50N 76 1W
Bolívar, Cauca, Colombia 168 C2 2 0N 77 0W
Bolívar, Peru 172 B2 7 18 S 77 48W
Bolivar, Mo., U.S.A. 155 G8 37 37N 93 25W
Bolivar, N.Y., U.S.A. 150 D6 42 4N 78 10W
Bolivar, Tenn., U.S.A. 155 H10 35 12N 89 0W
Bolívar □, Colombia 168 B3 9 0N 74 40W
Bolívar □, Ecuador 168 D2 1 15 S 79 5W
Bolívar □, Venezuela 169 B5 6 20N 63 30W
Bolivia ■, S. Amer. 173 D5 17 6 S 64 0W
Bolivian Plateau, S. Amer. 166 E4 20 0 S 67 30W
Boljevac, Serbia, Yug. 50 C5 43 51N 21 58 E
Bolkhov, Russia 58 F9 53 25N 36 0 E
Bolków, Poland 55 H3 50 55N 16 6 E
Bollé, Mauritania 110 D2 20 8N 11 40W
Bollebygd, Sweden 17 G6 57 40N 12 35 E
Bollène, France 29 D8 44 18N 4 45 E
Bollnäs, Sweden 16 C10 61 21N 16 24 E
Bollon, Australia 127 D4 28 2 S 147 29 E
Bollstabruk, Sweden 16 B11 62 59N 17 40 E
Bolmen, Sweden 17 H7 56 55N 13 40 E
Bolobo, Dem. Rep. of the Congo 114 C3 2 6 S 16 20 E
Bologna, Italy 45 D8 44 29N 11 20 E
Bologoye, Russia 58 D8 57 55N 34 5 E
Bolomba, Dem. Rep. of the Congo 114 B3 0 35N 19 0 E
Bolombo →, Dem. Rep. of the Congo 114 B4 1 32N 21 14 E
Bolonchenticul, Mexico 163 D7 20 0N 89 49W
Bolondo, Dem. Rep. of the Congo 114 C3 2 12 S 18 42 E
Bolong, Chad 109 F3 12 3N 17 45 E
Bolong, Phil. 81 H4 7 6N 122 14 E
Bolongongo, Angola 115 D3 8 28 S 15 16 E
Bolótana, Italy 46 B1 40 20N 8 52 E
Bolotovskoye, Russia 64 B9 58 31N 62 28 E
Boloven, Cao Nguyen, Laos 86 E6 15 10N 106 30 E
Bolpur, India 93 H12 23 40N 87 45 E
Bolsena, Italy 45 F8 42 39N 11 59 E
Bolsena, L. di, Italy 45 F8 42 36N 11 56 E
Bolshaya Chernigovka, Russia 60 D10 52 6N 50 52 E
Bolshaya Glushitsa, Russia 60 D10 52 28N 50 30 E
Bolshaya Khobda →, Kazakstan 64 F5 50 56N 54 34 E
Bolshaya Martynovka, Russia 61 G5 47 19N 41 37 E
Bolshaya Vradiyevka, Ukraine 59 J6 47 50N 30 40 E
Bolshevik, Ostrov, Russia 67 B11 78 30N 102 0 E
Bolshoi Kavkas = Caucasus Mountains, Eurasia 61 J7 42 50N 44 0 E
Bolshoy Anyuy →, Russia 67 C17 68 30N 160 49 E
Bolshoy Begichev, Ostrov, Russia 67 B12 74 20N 112 30 E
Bolshoy Lyakhovskiy, Ostrov, Russia 67 B15 73 35N 142 0 E
Bolshoy Tokmak = Tokmak, Ukraine 59 J8 47 16N 35 42 E
Bolshoy Tyuters, Ostrov, Russia 15 G22 59 51N 27 13 E
Bólstaðarhlíð, Iceland 11 B7 65 31N 19 49W
Bolsward, Neths. 24 A5 53 3N 5 32 E
Bolt Head, U.K. 21 G4 50 12N 3 48W
Boltaña, Spain 40 C5 42 28N 0 4 E
Boltigen, Switz. 32 C4 46 38N 7 24 E
Bolton, Canada 150 C5 43 54N 79 45W
Bolton, U.K. 20 D5 53 35N 2 26W
Bolton Landing, U.S.A. 151 C11 43 32N 73 35W

Boxmeer 193

Bolu, Turkey 100 B4 40 45N 31 35 E
Bolubolu, Papua N. G. 132 E6 9 21 S 150 20 E
Bolungavík, Iceland 11 A3 66 9N 23 15W
Boluo, China 77 F10 23 3N 114 21 E
Bolvadin, Turkey 100 C4 38 45N 31 4 E
Bolzano, Italy 45 B8 46 31N 11 22 E
Bom Comércio, Brazil 173 B4 9 45 S 65 54W
Bom Conselho, Brazil 170 C4 9 10 S 36 41W
Bom Despacho, Brazil 171 E2 19 43 S 45 15W
Bom Jesus, Angola 115 D2 9 11 S 13 34 E
Bom Jesus, Brazil 170 C3 9 4 S 44 22W
Bom Jesus da Gurguéia, Serra, Brazil 170 C3 9 0 S 43 0W
Bom Jesus da Lapa, Brazil 171 D3 13 15 S 43 25W
Boma, Dem. Rep. of the Congo 115 D2 5 50 S 13 4 E
Bomaderry, Australia 129 C9 34 52 S 150 37 E
Bomandjokou, Congo 114 B2 0 34N 14 23 E
Bomaneh, Dem. Rep. of the Congo 114 B4 1 18N 23 47 E
Bomassa, Congo 114 B3 2 12N 16 12 E
Bomate, Dem. Rep. of the Congo 114 C3 2 14N 25 15 E
Bombala, Australia 129 D8 36 56 S 149 15 E
Bombarral, Portugal 43 F1 39 15N 9 9W
Bombay = Mumbai, India 94 E1 18 55N 72 50 E
Bombedor, Pta., Venezuela 169 G9 9 53N 61 37W
Bomberai, Semenanjung, Indonesia 83 B4 3 0 S 133 0 E
Bombo Kasani, Dem. Rep. of the Congo 115 D4 5 51 S 21 54 E
Bomboma, Dem. Rep. of the Congo 114 B3 2 25N 18 55 E
Bombombwa, Dem. Rep. of the Congo 118 B2 1 40N 25 40 E
Bomboyo, Chad 109 F3 12 1N 15 28 E
Bomdila, India 90 B4 27 18N 92 22 E
Bomdo, India 90 A5 28 44N 94 54 E
Bomi Hills, Liberia 112 D2 7 1N 10 38W
Bomili, Dem. Rep. of the Congo 118 B2 1 45N 27 5 E
Bømlo, Norway 15 G11 59 37N 5 13 E
Bomokandi →, Dem. Rep. of the Congo 118 B2 3 39N 26 8 E
Bomongo, Dem. Rep. of the Congo 114 B3 1 27N 18 21 E
Bompoka, India 95 K11 8 15N 93 13 E
Bomputu, Dem. Rep. of the Congo 114 C4 0 23 S 20 6 E
Bomu →, C.A.R. 114 B4 4 40N 22 30 E
Bomu Occidentale, Réserve de Faune de la, Dem. Rep. of the Congo 114 B4 4 48N 24 17 E
Bomu Orientale, Réserve de Faune de la, Dem. Rep. of the Congo 114 B2 5 0N 25 50 E
Bon, C., Tunisia 108 A2 37 1N 11 2 E
Bon Acceuil, Mauritius 121 d 20 10 S 57 39 E
Bon Sar Pa, Vietnam 86 F6 12 24N 107 35 E
Bonaduz, Switz. 33 C8 46 49N 9 25 E
Bonaigarh, India 93 J11 21 50N 84 57 E
Bonaire, Neth. Ant. 165 D6 12 10N 68 15W
Bonaire, U.S.A. 152 C6 32 33N 83 36W
Bonang, Australia 129 D8 37 11 S 148 41 E
Bonanza, Nic. 164 D3 13 54N 84 35W
Bonaparte Arch., Australia 124 B3 14 0 S 124 30 E
Boñar, Spain 42 C5 42 52N 5 19W
Bonasse, Trin. & Tob. 169 F9 10 5N 61 54W
Bonaventure, Canada 141 C6 48 5N 65 32W
Bonavista, Canada 141 C9 48 40N 53 5W
Bonavista, C., Canada 141 C9 48 42N 53 5W
Bonavista B., Canada 141 C9 48 45N 53 25W
Bondeno, Italy 45 D8 44 53N 11 25 E
Bondo, Équateur, Dem. Rep. of the Congo 114 C4 1 22 S 23 54 E
Bondo, Orientale, Dem. Rep. of the Congo 118 B1 3 55N 23 53 E
Bondoukou, Ivory C. 112 D4 8 2N 2 47W
Bondowoso, Indonesia 85 D4 7 55 S 113 49 E
Bone, Teluk, Indonesia 82 B2 4 10 S 120 50 E
Bonefish Pond, Bahamas 9 b 25 59N 77 23W
Bonerate, Indonesia 82 C2 7 25 S 121 5 E
Bonerate, Kepulauan, Indonesia 82 C2 6 30 S 121 10 E
Bo'ness, U.K. 22 E5 56 1N 3 37W
Bonete, Cerro, Argentina 174 B2 27 55 S 68 40W
Bonfim, Brazil 169 C6 3 33N 59 25W
Bong Son = Hoai Nhon, Vietnam 86 E7 14 28N 109 1 E
Bonga, Ethiopia 107 F4 7 15N 36 14 E
Bongabon, Phil. 80 D3 15 38N 121 8 E
Bongabong, Phil. 80 E3 12 45N 121 29 E
Bongaigon, India 90 B3 26 28N 90 34 E
Bongandanga, Dem. Rep. of the Congo 114 B4 1 24N 21 3 E
Bongao, Phil. 81 J2 5 2N 119 46 E
Bongka, Indonesia 82 B2 0 58 S 121 27 E
Bongo, Dem. Rep. of the Congo 114 C3 1 47 S 17 41 E
Bongo, Sa. de, Angola 115 E3 10 3 S 15 15 E
Bongor, Chad 109 F3 10 35N 15 20 E
Bongouanou, Ivory C. 112 D4 6 42N 4 15W
Bonham, U.S.A. 155 J6 33 35N 96 11W
Boni, Mali 112 B4 15 3N 2 10W
Boni Nat. Reserve, Kenya 118 C5 1 35 S 41 18 E
Bonifacio, France 29 G13 41 24N 9 10 E
Bonifacio, Bouches de, Medit. S. 46 A2 41 12N 9 15 E
Bonifay, U.S.A. 152 E4 30 47N 85 41W
Bonin Is. = Ogasawara Gunto, Pac. Oc. 62 G18 27 0N 142 0 E
Bonita Springs, U.S.A. 153 J8 26 21N 81 47W
Bonito, Brazil 173 21 8 S 56 28W
Bonke, Ethiopia 107 F4 6 5N 37 16 E
Bonkoukou, Niger 113 C5 14 0N 3 15 E
Bonn, Germany 30 E3 50 46N 7 6 E
Bonnat, France 27 F8 46 20N 1 54 E
Bonne Terre, U.S.A. 155 G9 37 55N 90 33W
Bonneau, U.S.A. 152 B10 33 16N 79 58W
Bonners Ferry, U.S.A. 158 B5 48 42N 116 19W
Bonnétable, France 26 D7 48 11N 0 25 E
Bonneval, Eure-et-Loir, France 26 D8 48 11N 1 24 E
Bonneval, Savoie, France 29 C11 45 22N 7 3 E
Bonneville, France 27 F13 46 4N 6 24 E
Bonney, L., Australia 128 D4 37 50 S 140 20 E
Bonnie Doon, Australia 129 D6 37 2 S 145 53 E
Bonnie Rock, Australia 125 F2 30 29 S 118 22 E
Bonny, Nigeria 113 E6 4 25N 7 13 E
Bonny →, Nigeria 113 E6 4 20N 7 10 E
Bonny, Bight of, Africa 113 E6 3 30N 9 20 E
Bonny Hills, Australia 129 A10 31 36 S 152 51 E
Bonny-sur-Loire, France 27 E9 47 33N 2 50 E
Bonnyrigg, U.K. 22 F5 55 53N 3 6W
Bonnyville, Canada 143 C6 54 20N 110 45W
Bono, Italy 46 B2 40 25N 9 2 E
Bonoi, Indonesia 83 B5 1 45 S 137 41 E
Bonorva, Italy 46 B1 40 25N 8 46 E
Bonsall, U.S.A. 161 M9 33 16N 117 14W
Bontang, Indonesia 85 B5 0 10N 117 30 E
Bontebok Nat. Park, S. Africa 116 E3 34 5 S 20 28 E
Bonthe, S. Leone 112 D2 7 30N 12 33W
Bontoc, Phil. 80 C3 17 7N 120 58 E
Bontosunggu, Indonesia 82 C1 5 41 S 119 42 E
Bonyeri, Ghana 112 D4 5 1N 2 46W
Bonyhád, Hungary 52 D3 46 18N 18 32 E
Bonython Ra., Australia 124 D4 23 40 S 128 45 E
Boo, Kepulauan, Indonesia 83 B3 1 12 S 129 24 E
Bookabie, Australia 125 F5 31 50 S 132 41 E
Booke, Dem. Rep. of the Congo 114 C4 2 34 S 22 3 E
Booker, U.S.A. 155 G4 36 27N 100 32W
Bool Lagoon, Australia 128 D4 37 7 S 140 40 E
Boola, Guinea 112 D3 8 22N 8 41 E
Boolcoomata, Australia 128 A4 31 57 S 140 33 E
Booleroo Centre, Australia 128 B3 32 53 S 138 21 E
Booligal, Australia 129 B6 33 58 S 144 53 E
Boonah, Australia 127 D5 27 58 S 152 41 E
Boone, Iowa, U.S.A. 156 B3 42 4N 93 53W
Boone, N.C., U.S.A. 149 G5 36 13N 81 41W
Booneville, Ark., U.S.A. 155 H8 35 8N 93 55W
Booneville, Miss., U.S.A. 149 H1 34 39N 88 34W
Boonville, Calif., U.S.A. 160 F3 39 1N 123 22W
Boonville, Ind., U.S.A. 157 F9 38 3N 87 16W
Boonville, Mo., U.S.A. 156 F4 38 58N 92 44W
Boonville, N.Y., U.S.A. 151 C9 43 29N 75 20W
Boorabbin Nat. Park, Australia 125 F3 31 30 S 129 57 E
Boorindal, Australia 127 E4 30 22 S 146 11 E
Boorowa, Australia 129 C8 34 28 S 148 44 E
Boort, Australia 128 D5 36 7 S 143 46 E
Boosaaso = Bosaso, Somali Rep. 120 E3 11 12N 49 18 E
Boothia, Gulf of, Canada 139 A11 71 0N 90 0W
Boothia Pen., Canada 138 A10 71 0N 94 0W
Bootle, U.K. 20 D4 53 28N 3 1W
Booué, Gabon 114 C2 0 5 S 11 55 E
Bopako, Dem. Rep. of the Congo 114 B4 1 53N 21 13 E
Boppard, Germany 31 E3 50 13N 7 35 E
Boquerón □, Paraguay 173 E5 23 0 S 60 0W
Boquete, Panama 164 E3 8 46N 82 27W
Boquilla, Presa de la, Mexico 162 B3 27 40N 105 30W
Boquillas del Carmen, Mexico 162 B4 29 17N 102 53W
Bor, Czech Rep. 34 B5 49 41N 12 45 E
Bor, Russia 60 B7 56 28N 43 59 E
Bor, Serbia, Yug. 50 B6 44 5N 22 7 E
Bôr, Sudan 107 F3 6 10N 31 40 E
Bor, Sweden 17 G8 57 9N 14 10 E
Bor, Turkey 100 D6 37 54N 34 32 E
Bor Döbö, Kyrgyzstan 65 D6 39 31N 73 16 E
Bor Mashash, Israel 103 D3 31 7N 34 50 E
Borah Peak, U.S.A. 158 D7 44 8N 113 47W
Boralday, Kazakstan 65 B8 43 20N 76 51 E
Borama, Somali Rep. 120 C2 9 55N 43 7 E
Borang, Sudan 107 G3 4 50N 30 59 E
Borangapara, India 90 C3 25 14N 90 14 E
Borås, Sweden 17 G6 57 43N 12 56 E
Borāzjān, Iran 97 D6 29 22N 51 10 E
Borba, Brazil 169 D6 4 12 S 59 34W
Borba, Portugal 43 G3 38 50N 7 26W
Borbon, Phil. 81 F5 10 50N 124 2 E
Borborema, Planalto da, Brazil 170 C4 7 0 S 37 0W
Borcea, Romania 53 F12 44 20N 27 45 E
Borçka, Turkey 101 B9 41 25N 41 41 E
Bord Khūn-e Now, Iran 97 D6 28 3N 51 28 E
Borda, C., Australia 128 C2 35 45 S 136 34 E
Bordeaux, France 28 D3 44 50N 0 36W
Borden, Australia 125 F2 34 3 S 118 12 E
Borden, Canada 141 C7 46 18N 63 47W
Borden I., Canada 6 B2 78 30N 111 30W
Borden Pen., Canada 139 A11 73 0N 83 0W
Borden Springs, U.S.A. 152 B4 33 56N 85 28W
Border Ranges Nat. Park, Australia 127 D5 28 24 S 152 56 E
Borders = Scottish Borders □, U.K. 22 F6 55 35N 2 50W
Bordertown, Australia 128 D4 36 19 S 140 45 E
Borðeyri, Iceland 11 B5 65 12N 21 6W
Bordighera, Italy 44 E4 43 46N 7 39 E
Bordj bou Arreridj, Algeria 111 A5 36 4N 4 45 E
Bordj Bourguiba, Tunisia 108 B2 32 12N 10 2 E
Bordj Fly Ste. Marie, Algeria 110 C4 27 19N 2 32W
Bordj-in-Eker, Algeria 111 D6 24 9N 5 3 E
Bordj Menaïel, Algeria 111 A5 36 46N 3 43 E
Bordj Messouda, Algeria 111 B6 30 12N 9 25 E
Bordj Nili, Algeria 111 B5 33 28N 3 2 E
Bordj Omar Driss, Algeria 111 C6 28 10N 6 40 E
Bordj Sif Fatima, Algeria 111 B6 31 6N 8 41 E
Bordj Tarat, Algeria 111 C6 25 55N 9 3 E
Borduttighat, India 90 B4 26 57N 93 58 E
Bore, Ethiopia 107 G4 4 39N 37 39 E
Borehamwood, U.K. 21 F7 51 40N 0 15W
Borek Wielkopolski, Poland 55 G4 51 54N 17 11 E
Borensberg, Sweden 17 F9 58 34N 15 17 E
Borgå = Porvoo, Finland 15 F21 60 24N 25 40 E
Borgampad, India 94 F5 17 39N 80 52 E
Borgarfjarðarsýsla □, Iceland 11 C5 64 32N 21 55W
Borgarfjörður, Borgarfjarðarsýsla, Iceland 11 C4 64 30N 22 0W
Borgarfjörður, Norður-Múlasýsla, Iceland 14 D7 65 31N 13 49W
Borgarnes, Iceland 11 C5 64 32N 21 55W
Børgefjellet, Norway 14 D15 65 20N 13 45 E
Borger, Neths. 24 B6 52 54N 6 44 E
Borger, U.S.A. 155 H4 35 39N 101 24W
Borgholm, Sweden 17 H10 56 52N 16 39 E
Bòrghia, Italy 47 D9 38 49N 16 30 E
Borgo San Dalmazzo, Italy 44 D4 44 20N 7 30 E
Borgo San Lorenzo, Italy 45 E8 43 57N 11 23 E
Borgo Val di Taro, Italy 44 D6 44 29N 9 46 E
Borgo Valsugana, Italy 45 B8 46 3N 11 27 E
Borgomanero, Italy 44 C5 45 42N 8 28 E
Borgorose, Italy 45 F10 42 11N 13 13 E
Borgosésia, Italy 44 C5 45 43N 8 16 E
Borgund, Norway 18 C4 61 3N 7 48 E
Borhoyn Tal, Mongolia 74 C6 43 50N 111 58 E
Bori, Nigeria 113 E6 4 42N 7 21 E
Borigumma, India 94 E6 19 3N 82 33 E
Borikhane, Laos 86 C4 18 33N 103 43 E
Borisoglebsk, Russia 60 E6 51 27N 42 5 E
Borisov = Barysaw, Belarus 58 E5 54 17N 28 28 E
Borisovka, Russia 59 G9 50 36N 36 1 E
Borja, Peru 168 D2 4 20 S 77 40W
Borja, Spain 40 D3 41 48N 1 34W
Borjas Blancas = Les Borges Blanques, Spain 40 D5 41 31N 0 52 E
Borjomi, Georgia 61 K6 41 48N 43 28 E
Børkop, Denmark 17 J3 55 39N 9 39 E
Borkou, Chad 109 E3 18 15N 18 50 E
Borkum, Germany 30 B2 53 34N 6 40 E
Borlänge, Sweden 16 D9 60 29N 15 26 E
Borley, C., Antarctica 7 C5 66 15 S 52 30 E
Borlu, Turkey 49 C10 38 44N 28 27 E
Bormida →, Italy 44 D5 44 23N 8 13 E
Bórmio, Italy 44 B7 46 28N 10 22 E
Borna, Germany 30 D8 51 7N 12 29 E
Borne Sulinowo, Poland 54 E3 53 32N 16 36 E
Borneo, E. Indies 85 B4 1 0N 115 0 E
Bornholm, Denmark 17 J8 55 10N 15 0 E
Bornholms Amtskommune □, Denmark 17 J8 55 5N 15 0 E
Bornholmsgattet, Europe 17 J8 55 15N 14 20 E
Borno, Italy 33 E10 45 56N 10 12 E
Borno □, Nigeria 113 C7 11 30N 13 0 E
Bornos, Spain 43 J5 36 48N 5 42W
Bornova, Turkey 49 C9 38 27N 27 14 E
Bornu Yassa, Nigeria 113 C7 12 14N 12 25 E
Boro →, Sudan 107 F2 8 52N 26 11 E
Borobudur, Indonesia 85 D4 7 36 S 110 13 E
Borodino, Russia 58 E8 55 31N 35 40 E
Borogontsy, Russia 67 C14 62 42N 131 8 E
Boromo, Burkina Faso 112 C4 11 45N 2 58W
Boron, U.S.A. 161 L9 35 0N 117 39W
Borongan Is., Burma 90 F4 19 58N 93 6 E
Borongan, Phil. 81 F5 11 37N 125 26 E
Borotangba Mts., C.A.R. 107 F2 6 30N 25 0 E
Borotou, Ivory C. 112 D3 8 46N 7 30W
Borovan, Bulgaria 50 C7 43 27N 23 45 E
Borovichi, Russia 58 C7 58 25N 33 55 E
Borovsk, Berezniki, Russia 64 B6 59 43N 56 40 E
Borovsk, Moskva, Russia 58 E9 55 12N 36 24 E
Borrby, Sweden 17 J8 55 27N 14 10 E
Borrego Springs, U.S.A. 161 M10 33 15N 116 23W
Borriol, Spain 40 E4 40 4N 0 4W
Borroloola, Australia 126 B2 16 4 S 136 17 E
Borşa, Cluj, Romania 53 D8 46 56N 23 40 E
Borşa, Maramureş, Romania 53 C9 47 41N 24 50 E
Borsad, India 92 H5 22 25N 72 54 E
Borsec, Romania 53 D10 46 57N 25 34 E
Borsod-Abaúj-Zemplén □, Hungary 52 B6 48 20N 21 0 E
Bort-les-Orgues, France 28 C6 45 24N 2 29 E
Borth, U.K. 21 E3 52 29N 4 2W
Börtnan, Sweden 16 B7 62 45N 13 50 E
Borūjerd, Iran 97 C6 33 55N 48 50 E
Boryslav, Ukraine 59 H2 49 18N 23 28 E
Boryspil, Ukraine 59 G6 50 21N 30 59 E
Borzhomi = Borjomi, Georgia 61 K6 41 48N 43 28 E
Borzna, Ukraine 59 G7 51 18N 32 26 E
Borzya, Russia 67 D12 50 24N 116 31 E
Bosa, Italy 46 B1 40 18N 8 30 E
Bosa Monene, Dem. Rep. of the Congo 114 C4 1 16 S 23 40 E
Bosaga, Turkmenistan 65 E2 37 33N 65 41 E
Bosambi, Dem. Rep. of the Congo 114 B4 2 24N 22 39 E
Bosanska Dubica, Bos.-H. 45 C13 45 10N 16 50 E
Bosanska Gradiška, Bos.-H. 52 E2 45 10N 17 15 E
Bosanska Kostajnica, Bos.-H. 45 C13 45 11N 16 33 E
Bosanska Krupa, Bos.-H. 45 D13 44 53N 16 10 E
Bosanski Brod, Bos.-H. 52 E2 45 10N 18 0 E
Bosanski Novi, Bos.-H. 45 C13 45 2N 16 22 E
Bosanski Petrovac, Bos.-H. 45 D13 44 35N 16 21 E
Bosanski Šamac, Bos.-H. 52 E3 45 3N 18 29 E
Bosansko Grahovo, Bos.-H. 45 D13 44 12N 16 26 E
Bosaso, Somali Rep. 120 B3 11 12N 49 18 E
Bosavi, Mt., Papua N. G. 132 D2 6 30 S 142 49 E
Boscastle, U.K. 21 G3 50 41N 4 42W
Boscobel, U.S.A. 156 A6 43 8N 90 42W
Boscobelle, Barbados 165 g 13 16N 59 34W
Bose, China 76 F6 23 53N 106 35 E
Boseki, Dem. Rep. of the Congo 114 C3 2 34 S 19 38 E
Boshan, China 75 F9 36 28N 117 49 E
Boshof, S. Africa 116 D4 28 31 S 25 13 E
Boshrūyeh, Iran 97 C8 33 50N 57 30 E
Bosilegrad, Serbia, Yug. 50 D6 42 30N 22 27 E
Boskovice, Czech Rep. 35 B9 49 29N 16 40 E
Bosna →, Bos.-H. 52 E3 45 4N 18 29 E
Bosna i Hercegovina = Bosnia-Herzegovina ■, Europe 52 G2 44 0N 18 0 E
Bosnia-Herzegovina ■, Europe 52 G2 44 0N 18 0 E
Bosnik, Indonesia 83 B5 1 5 S 136 10 E
Bōsō-Hantō, Japan 73 B12 35 20N 140 20 E
Bosobolo, Dem. Rep. of the Congo 114 B3 4 15N 19 50 E
Bosporus = İstanbul Boğazı, Turkey 51 E13 41 10N 29 10 E
Bosque Farms, U.S.A. 159 J10 34 53N 106 40W
Bossangoa, C.A.R. 114 A3 6 35N 17 30 E
Bossé Bangou, Niger 113 C5 13 20N 1 18 E
Bossembélé, C.A.R. 114 A3 5 25N 17 40 E
Bossemtélé, C.A.R. 114 A3 5 41N 16 38 E
Bossier City, U.S.A. 155 J8 32 31N 93 44W
Bosso, Niger 113 C7 13 43N 13 19 E
Bosso, Dallol →, Niger 113 C5 12 25N 2 50 E
Bostan, Pakistan 92 D2 30 26N 67 2 E
Bostānābād, Iran 101 D12 37 50N 46 50 E
Bosten Hu, China 68 B3 41 55N 87 40 E
Boston, Phil. 81 H6 7 52N 126 22 E
Boston, U.K. 20 E7 52 59N 0 2W
Boston, Ga., U.S.A. 152 E6 30 47N 83 47W
Boston, Mass., U.S.A. 151 D13 42 22N 71 4W
Boston Bar, Canada 142 D4 49 52N 121 30W
Boston Mts., U.S.A. 155 H8 35 42N 93 15W
Bostwick, U.S.A. 152 F8 29 46N 81 38W
Bosumtwi, L., Ghana 113 D4 6 30N 1 25W
Bosusulu, Dem. Rep. of the Congo 114 B4 0 50N 20 45 E
Bosut →, Croatia 52 E3 45 20N 18 45 E
Boswell, Canada 142 D5 49 28N 116 45W
Boswell, Ind., U.S.A. 157 D9 40 31N 87 23W
Boswell, Pa., U.S.A. 150 F5 40 10N 79 2W
Bosworth, U.S.A. 156 E4 39 28N 93 20W
Botad, India 92 H4 22 15N 71 40 E
Botan →, Turkey 101 D10 37 57N 42 2 E
Botene, Laos 86 D3 17 35N 101 12 E
Botera, Angola 115 E2 11 37 S 14 16 E
Botev, Bulgaria 51 D8 42 44N 24 52 E
Botevgrad, Bulgaria 50 D7 42 55N 23 47 E
Bothaville, S. Africa 116 D4 27 23 S 26 34 E
Bothnia, G. of, Europe 14 E19 63 0N 20 15 E
Bothwell, Australia 127 G4 42 20 S 147 1 E
Bothwell, Canada 150 D3 42 38N 81 52W
Boticas, Portugal 42 D3 41 41N 7 40W
Botletle →, Botswana 116 C3 20 10 S 23 15 E
Botlikh, Russia 61 J8 42 39N 46 11 E
Botna →, Moldova 53 D14 46 45N 29 34 E
Botola, Dem. Rep. of the Congo 114 C3 1 17 S 18 13 E
Botolan, Phil. 80 D3 15 17N 120 1 E
Botoroaga, Romania 53 F10 44 8N 25 32 E
Botoşani, Romania 53 C11 47 42N 26 41 E
Botoşani □, Romania 53 C11 47 50N 26 50 E
Botou, Burkina Faso 113 C5 12 42N 1 59 E
Botricello, Italy 47 D9 38 56N 16 51 E
Botro, Ivory C. 112 D3 7 51N 5 19W
Botswana ■, Africa 116 C3 22 0 S 24 0 E
Bottineau, U.S.A. 154 A4 48 50N 100 27W
Bottnaryd, Sweden 17 G7 57 47N 13 50 E
Bottopassi, Surinam 169 C6 4 14N 55 27W
Bottrop, Germany 24 C6 51 31N 6 58 E
Botucatu, Brazil 175 A6 22 55 S 48 30W
Botwood, Canada 141 C8 49 6N 55 23W
Bou Alam, Algeria 111 B5 33 50N 1 26 E
Bou Ali, Algeria 111 C4 27 11N 0 4W
Bou Djébéha, Mali 112 B4 18 25N 2 45W
Bou Guema, Algeria 111 C5 28 49N 0 19 E
Bou Ismaïl, Algeria 111 A5 36 38N 2 42 E
Bou Izakarn, Morocco 110 C3 29 12N 9 46W
Boû Lanouâr, Mauritania 110 D1 21 12N 16 34W
Boû Rjeïmât, Mauritania 112 B1 19 4N 15 3W
Bou Saâda, Algeria 111 A5 35 11N 4 9 E
Bou Salem, Tunisia 108 A1 36 45N 9 2 E
Bouaflé, Ivory C. 112 D3 7 1N 5 47W
Bouaké, Ivory C. 112 D3 7 40N 5 2W
Bouanga, Congo 114 C3 2 7 S 16 8 E
Bouar, C.A.R. 114 A3 6 0N 15 40 E
Bouârfa, Morocco 111 B4 32 32N 1 58W
Bouba Ndjida, Parc Nat. de, Cameroon 114 A2 8 50N 14 45 E
Bouboui, Algeria 110 C4 27 26N 4 30W
Bouca, C.A.R. 114 A3 6 45N 18 25 E
Boucaut B., Australia 126 A1 12 0 S 134 25 E
Bouches-du-Rhône □, France 29 E9 43 37N 5 2 E
Boucle de Baoule, Parc Nat. de la, Mali 112 C3 13 53N 9 0W
Bouda, Algeria 111 C4 27 50N 0 27W
Boudenib, Morocco 110 B4 31 59N 3 31W
Boudry, Switz. 32 C3 46 57N 6 50 E
Boufarik, Algeria 111 A5 36 34N 2 58 E
Bougainville, C., Australia 124 B4 13 57 S 126 4 E
Bougainville I., Papua N. G. 133 L8 6 0 S 155 0 E
Bougainville Reef, Australia 126 B4 15 30 S 147 5 E
Bougainville Str., Solomon Is. 133 L9 6 40 S 156 10 E
Bougaroun, C., Algeria 111 A6 37 6N 6 30 E
Bougie = Bejaïa, Algeria 111 A6 36 42N 5 2 E
Bougouni, Mali 112 C3 11 30N 7 20W
Bouillon, Belgium 24 E5 49 44N 5 3 E
Bouïra, Algeria 111 A5 36 20N 3 59 E
Boukombé, Benin 113 C5 10 13N 1 9 E
Boulal, Mali 112 B3 15 8N 8 21W
Boulazac, France 28 C4 45 10N 0 47 E
Boulder, Colo., U.S.A. 154 E2 40 1N 105 17W
Boulder, Mont., U.S.A. 158 C7 46 14N 112 7W
Boulder City, U.S.A. 161 K12 35 59N 114 50W
Boulder Creek, U.S.A. 160 H4 37 7N 122 7W
Boulder Dam = Hoover Dam, U.S.A. 161 K12 36 1N 114 44W
Boulembo, Gabon 114 C2 1 26 S 12 0 E
Bouli, Mauritania 112 B2 15 17N 12 18W
Boulia, Australia 126 C2 22 52 S 139 51 E
Bouligny, France 27 C12 49 17N 5 45 E
Boulogne →, France 26 E5 47 12N 1 47W
Boulogne-sur-Gesse, France 28 E4 43 18N 0 38 E
Boulogne-sur-Mer, France 27 B8 50 42N 1 36 E
Bouloire, France 26 E7 47 59N 0 45 E
Boulou →, C.A.R. 114 A4 6 45N 24 16 E
Boulouli, Mali 112 B3 15 30N 9 25W
Bouloupari, N. Cal. 133 U20 21 52 S 166 4 E
Bouloupesse, Congo 114 C2 1 58 S 12 40 E
Boulsa, Burkina Faso 113 C4 12 39N 0 34W
Boultoum, Niger 113 C7 14 45N 10 25 E
Bouma Nat. Heritage Park, Fiji 133 A2 16 50 S 179 52 E
Boumalne, Morocco 110 B3 31 25N 6 0W
Boumba →, Cameroon 114 B2 2 2N 15 12 E
Boumbé →, C.A.R. 114 B3 4 4N 15 23 E
Boûmdeïd, Mauritania 112 B2 17 25N 9 50W
Boun Neua, Laos 86 B3 21 38N 101 54 E
Boun Tai, Laos 86 B3 21 23N 101 58 E
Bouna, Ivory C. 112 D4 9 10N 3 0W
Boundary, U.S.A. 144 D12 64 4N 141 6W
Boundary Peak, U.S.A. 160 H8 37 51N 118 21W
Boundgi, Gabon 114 C2 1 0 S 11 51 E
Boundiali, Ivory C. 112 D3 9 30N 6 20W
Boungou →, C.A.R. 114 A4 8 21N 23 48 E
Bountiful, U.S.A. 158 F8 40 53N 111 53W
Bounty Is., Pac. Oc. 134 M9 48 0 S 178 30 E
Boura, Mali 112 C4 12 25N 4 33W
Bourail, N. Cal. 133 U19 21 34 S 165 30 E
Bourbeuse →, U.S.A. 156 F6 38 24N 90 53W
Bourbon, U.S.A. 157 C10 41 18N 86 7W
Bourbon-Lancy, France 27 F10 46 37N 3 45 E
Bourbon-l'Archambault, France 27 F10 46 36N 3 4 E
Bourbonnais, France 27 F10 46 28N 3 0 E
Bourbonnais, U.S.A. 157 C9 41 9N 87 52W
Bourbonne-les-Bains, France 27 E12 47 54N 5 45 E
Bourbourg, France 27 B9 50 56N 2 12 E
Bourdel L., Canada 140 A5 56 43N 74 10W
Bourem, Mali 113 B4 17 0N 0 24W
Bourg, France 28 C3 45 3N 0 34W
Bourg-Argental, France 29 C8 45 18N 4 32 E
Bourg-de-Péage, France 29 C9 45 2N 5 3 E
Bourg-en-Bresse, France 27 F12 46 13N 5 12 E
Bourg-Lastic, France 28 C6 45 39N 2 35 E
Bourg-Madame, France 28 F5 42 26N 1 55 E
Bourg-St-Andéol, France 29 D8 44 23N 4 39 E
Bourg-St-Maurice, France 29 C10 45 35N 6 46 E
Bourg-St. Pierre, Switz. 32 E4 45 57N 7 12 E
Bourganeuf, France 28 C5 45 57N 1 45 E
Bourges, France 27 E9 47 9N 2 25 E
Bourget, Canada 151 A9 45 26N 75 9W
Bourget, Lac du, France 29 C9 45 44N 5 52 E
Bourgneuf, B. de, France 26 E4 47 3N 2 10W
Bourgneuf-en-Retz, France 26 E5 47 2N 1 58W
Bourgogne, France 27 F11 47 0N 4 50 E
Bourgoin-Jallieu, France 29 C9 45 36N 5 17 E
Bourgueil, France 26 E7 47 17N 0 10 E
Bourke, Australia 127 E4 30 8 S 145 55 E
Bourne, U.K. 20 E7 52 47N 0 22W
Bournemouth, U.K. 21 G6 50 43N 1 52W
Bournemouth □, U.K. 21 G6 50 43N 1 52W
Bouroum, Burkina Faso 113 C4 13 37N 0 39W
Bouse, U.S.A. 161 M13 33 56N 114 0W
Boussac, France 27 F9 46 22N 2 13 E
Boussé, Burkina Faso 113 C4 12 39N 1 53W
Bousso, Chad 109 F3 10 34N 16 52 E
Boussouma, Burkina Faso 113 C4 12 52N 1 13W
Boutilimit, Mauritania 112 B2 17 45N 14 40W
Boutonne →, France 28 C3 45 54N 0 50W
Bouvet I. = Bouvetøya, Antarctica 8 M12 54 26 S 3 24 E
Bouvetøya, Antarctica 8 M12 54 26 S 3 24 E
Bouxwiller, France 27 D14 48 49N 7 27 E
Bouza, Niger 113 C6 14 29N 6 2 E
Bouznika, Morocco 110 B3 33 46N 7 6W
Bouzonville, France 27 C13 49 17N 6 32 E
Bova Marina, Italy 47 E8 37 56N 15 55 E
Bovalino Marina, Italy 47 D9 38 10N 16 10 E
Bovec, Slovenia 45 B10 46 20N 13 33 E
Boven Kapuas, Pegunungan, Malaysia 85 B4 1 25N 113 15 E
Bøverdal, Norway 18 C5 61 44N 8 20 E
Bøverfjorden, Norway 18 A5 63 1N 8 12 E
Bovill, U.S.A. 158 C5 46 51N 116 24W
Bovino, Italy 47 A8 41 15N 15 20 E
Bovril, Argentina 174 C4 31 21 S 59 26W
Bow →, Canada 142 C6 49 57N 111 41W
Bow Island, Canada 142 D6 49 50N 111 23W
Bowbells, U.S.A. 154 A3 48 48N 102 15W
Bowdle, U.S.A. 154 C5 45 27N 99 39W
Bowdon, U.S.A. 152 B4 33 32N 85 15W
Bowdon Junction, U.S.A. 152 B4 33 40N 85 9W
Bowelling, Australia 125 F2 33 25 S 116 30 E
Bowen, Argentina 174 D2 35 0 S 67 31W
Bowen, Australia 126 J6 20 0 S 148 16 E
Bowen Mts., Australia 129 D7 37 0 S 147 50 E
Bowie, Ariz., U.S.A. 159 K9 32 19N 109 29W
Bowie, Tex., U.S.A. 155 J6 33 34N 97 51W
Bowkān, Iran 101 D12 36 31N 46 12 E
Bowland, Forest of, U.K. 20 D5 54 0N 2 30W
Bowling Green, Fla., U.S.A. 153 H8 27 38N 81 50W
Bowling Green, Ky., U.S.A. 148 G2 36 59N 86 27W
Bowling Green, Mo., U.S.A. 156 E5 39 21N 91 12W
Bowling Green, Ohio, U.S.A. 157 C13 41 23N 83 39W
Bowling Green, C., Australia 126 B4 19 19 S 147 25 E
Bowling Green Bay Nat. Park, Australia 126 B4 19 26 S 146 57 E
Bowman, N. Dak., U.S.A. 154 B3 46 11N 103 24W
Bowman, S.C., U.S.A. 152 B9 33 21N 80 41W
Bowman I., Antarctica 7 C8 65 0 S 104 0 E
Bowmanville, Canada 150 C6 43 55N 78 41W
Bowmore, U.K. 22 F2 55 45N 6 17W
Bowral, Australia 129 C9 34 26 S 150 27 E
Bowraville, Australia 127 E5 30 37 S 152 52 E
Bowron →, Canada 142 C4 54 3N 121 50W
Bowron Lake Prov. Park, Canada 142 C4 53 10N 121 5W
Bowser L., Canada 142 B3 56 30N 129 30W
Bowsman, Canada 143 C8 52 14N 101 12W
Bowutu Mts., Papua N. G. 132 D4 7 45 S 147 10 E
Bowwood, Zambia 119 F2 17 5 S 26 20 E
Box Cr. →, Australia 127 E3 34 10 S 143 50 E
Boxholm, Sweden 17 F9 58 12N 15 3 E
Boxmeer, Neths. 24 C5 51 38N 5 56 E

194 Boxtel

Boxtel, *Neths.* **24 C5** 51 36N 5 20 E
Boyabat, *Turkey* **100 B6** 41 28N 34 47 E
Boyabo, *Dem. Rep. of the Congo* . **114 B3** 3 43N 18 46 E
Boyaca □, *Colombia* **168 B3** 5 30N 73 20W
Boyalıca, *Turkey* **51 F13** 40 29N 29 33 E
Boyang, *China* **77 C11** 29 0N 116 38 E
Boyasegese, *Dem. Rep. of the Congo* **114 B4** 3 29N 20 33 E
Boyce, *U.S.A.* **155 K8** 31 23N 92 40W
Boyd, *U.S.A.* **152 E6** 30 11N 83 37W
Boyd L., *Canada* **140 B4** 52 46N 76 42W
Boyenge, *Dem. Rep. of the Congo* **114 B3** 0 14N 18 55 E
Boyer, C., *N. Cal.* **133 U22** 21 37 S 168 6 E
Boyera, *Dem. Rep. of the Congo* . **114 C3** 0 40 S 19 23 E
Boyle, *Canada* **142 C6** 54 35N 112 49W
Boyle, *Ireland* **23 C3** 53 59N 8 18W
Boyne →, *Ireland* **23 C5** 53 43N 6 15W
Boyne City, *U.S.A.* **148 C3** 45 13N 85 1W
Boyni Qara, *Afghan.* **91 A2** 36 20N 67 0 E
Boynitsa, *Bulgaria* **50 C6** 43 58N 22 32 E
Boynton Beach, *U.S.A.* **149 M5** 26 32N 80 4W
Boyolali, *Indonesia* **85 D4** 7 32 S 110 35 E
Boyoma, Chutes, *Dem. Rep. of the Congo* **118 B2** 0 35N 25 23 E
Boysen Reservoir, *U.S.A.* **158 E9** 43 25N 108 11W
Boyup Brook, *Australia* **125 F2** 33 50 S 116 23 E
Boz Burun, *Turkey* **51 F12** 40 32N 28 46 E
Boz Dağ, *Turkey* **49 D11** 37 18N 29 11 E
Boz Dağları, *Turkey* **49 C10** 38 20N 28 0 E
Bozai Gumbaz, *Afghan.* **65 E7** 37 8N 74 0 E
Bozburun, *Turkey* **49 E10** 36 43N 28 4 E
Bozcaada, *Turkey* **100 C2** 39 49N 26 3 E
Bozdoğan, *Turkey* **49 D10** 37 40N 28 17 E
Boze, *Papua N. G.* **132 E2** 9 3 S 143 3 E
Bozeman, *U.S.A.* **158 D8** 45 41N 111 2W
Bozen = Bolzano, *Italy* **45 B8** 46 31N 11 22 E
Bozene, *Dem. Rep. of the Congo* . **114 B3** 2 56N 19 12 E
Boževac, *Serbia, Yug.* **50 B5** 44 32N 21 24 E
Bozhou, *China* **74 H8** 33 55N 115 41 E
Bozkır, *Turkey* **100 D5** 37 11N 32 14 E
Bozkurt, *Turkey* **49 D11** 37 50N 29 37 E
Bozouls, *France* **28 D6** 44 28N 2 43 E
Bozoum, *C.A.R.* **114 A3** 6 25N 16 35 E
Bozova, *Antalya, Turkey* **49 D12** 37 13N 30 18 E
Bozova, *Sanliurfa, Turkey* **101 D8** 37 21N 38 32 E
Bozovici, *Romania* **52 F7** 44 56N 22 0 E
Bozüyük, *Turkey* **49 B12** 39 54N 30 3 E
Bra, *Italy* **44 D4** 44 42N 7 51 E
Braås, *Sweden* **17 G9** 57 4N 15 3 E
Brabant □, *Belgium* **24 D4** 50 46N 4 30 E
Brabant L., *Canada* **143 B8** 55 58N 103 43W
Brabrand, *Denmark* **17 H4** 56 9N 10 7 E
Brač, *Croatia* **45 E13** 43 20N 16 40 E
Bracadale, L., *U.K.* **22 D2** 57 20N 6 30W
Bracciano, *Italy* **45 F9** 42 6N 12 10 E
Bracciano, L. di, *Italy* **45 F9** 42 7N 12 14 E
Bracebridge, *Canada* **140 C4** 45 2N 79 19W
Brach, *Libya* **108 C2** 27 31N 14 20 E
Bracieux, *France* **26 E8** 47 30N 1 30 E
Bräcke, *Sweden* **16 B9** 62 45N 15 26 E
Brackettville, *U.S.A.* **155 L4** 29 19N 100 25W
Bracki Kanal, *Croatia* **45 E13** 43 24N 16 40 E
Bracknell, *U.K.* **21 F7** 51 25N 0 43W
Bracknell Forest □, *U.K.* **21 F7** 51 25N 0 44W
Brad, *Romania* **52 D7** 46 10N 22 50 E
Brádano →, *Italy* **47 B9** 40 23N 16 51 E
Bradenton, *U.S.A.* **149 M4** 27 30N 82 34W
Bradford, *Canada* **150 B5** 44 7N 79 34W
Bradford, *U.K.* **20 D6** 53 47N 1 45W
Bradford, *Ill., U.S.A.* **156 C7** 41 11N 89 39W
Bradford, *Ohio, U.S.A.* **157 D12** 40 8N 84 27W
Bradford, *Pa., U.S.A.* **150 E6** 41 58N 78 38W
Bradford, *Vt., U.S.A.* **151 C12** 43 59N 72 9W
Bradley, *Ark., U.S.A.* **155 J8** 33 6N 93 39W
Bradley, *Calif., U.S.A.* **160 K6** 35 52N 120 48W
Bradley, *Fla., U.S.A.* **153 H8** 27 48N 81 59W
Bradley, *Ill., U.S.A.* **157 C9** 41 9N 87 52W
Bradley Institute, *Zimbabwe* **119 F3** 17 7 S 31 25 E
Bradner, *U.S.A.* **157 C13** 41 20N 83 26W
Brady, *U.S.A.* **155 K5** 31 9N 99 20W
Brædstrup, *Denmark* **17 J3** 55 58N 9 37 E
Braemar, *Australia* **128 B3** 33 12 S 139 35 E
Braeside, *Canada* **151 A8** 45 28N 76 24W
Braga, *Portugal* **42 D2** 41 35N 8 25W
Braga □, *Portugal* **42 D2** 41 30N 8 30W
Bragadiru, *Romania* **53 G10** 43 46N 25 31 E
Bragado, *Argentina* **174 D3** 35 2 S 60 27W
Bragança, *Brazil* **170 B2** 1 0 S 47 2W
Bragança, *Portugal* **42 D4** 41 48N 6 50W
Bragança □, *Portugal* **42 D4** 41 30N 6 45W
Bragança Paulista, *Brazil* **175 A6** 22 55 S 46 32W
Brahmakund, *India* **90 B6** 27 52N 96 22 E
Brahmanbaria, *Bangla.* **90 D3** 23 58N 91 15 E
Brahmani →, *India* **94 D8** 20 39N 86 46 E
Brahmapur, *India* **94 E7** 19 15N 84 54 E
Brahmaputra →, *Asia* **90 D2** 23 58N 89 50 E
Brahmaputra →, *India* **90 B5** 27 48N 95 30 E
Braich-y-pwll, *U.K.* **20 E3** 52 47N 4 46W
Braidwood, *Australia* **129 C8** 35 27 S 149 49 E
Brăila, *Romania* **53 E12** 45 19N 27 59 E
Brăila □, *Romania* **53 E12** 45 5N 27 30 E
Brainerd, *U.S.A.* **154 B7** 46 22N 94 12W
Braintree, *U.K.* **21 F8** 51 53N 0 34 E
Braintree, *U.S.A.* **151 D14** 42 13N 71 0W
Brak →, *S. Africa* **116 D3** 29 35 S 22 55 E
Brake, *Germany* **30 B4** 53 20N 8 28 E
Brakel, *Germany* **30 D5** 51 42N 9 11 E
Bräkne-Hoby, *Sweden* **17 H9** 56 14N 15 6 E
Brakwater, *Namibia* **116 C2** 22 28 S 17 3 E
Brålanda, *Sweden* **17 F6** 58 34N 12 21 E
Bramberg, *Germany* **31 E6** 50 6N 10 40 E
Bramdrupdam, *Denmark* **17 J3** 55 31N 9 28 E
Bramhapuri, *India* **94 D4** 20 36N 79 52 E
Bramming, *Denmark* **17 J2** 55 28N 8 42 E
Brämön, *Sweden* **16 B11** 62 14N 17 40 E
Brampton, *Canada* **140 D4** 43 45N 79 45W
Brampton, *U.K.* **20 C5** 54 57N 2 44W
Bramsche, *Germany* **30 C3** 52 24N 7 59 E
Bramton I., *Australia* **126 J7** 20 50 S 149 17 E
Branchville, *U.S.A.* **151 C11** 43 41N 73 4W
Branco →, *Brazil* **169 D5** 1 20 S 61 50W
Branco, C., *Brazil* **170 C5** 7 9 S 34 47W
Brandberg, *Namibia* **116 B2** 21 10 S 14 33 E
Brandberg Nature Reserve, *Namibia* **116 C1** 21 10 S 14 30 E
Brandbu, *Norway* **18 D7** 60 26N 10 28 E
Brande, *Denmark* **17 J3** 55 57N 9 8 E
Brandenburg = Neubrandenburg, *Germany* **30 B9** 53 33N 13 15 E
Brandenburg, *Germany* **30 C8** 52 25N 12 33 E
Brandenburg, *U.S.A.* **157 G10** 38 0N 86 10W
Brandenburg □, *Germany* **30 C9** 52 50N 13 0 E
Brandfort, *S. Africa* **116 D4** 28 40 S 26 30 E
Brando, *France* **29 F13** 42 47N 9 27 E
Brandon, *Canada* **143 D9** 49 50N 99 57W
Brandon, *Fla., U.S.A.* **153 H7** 27 56N 82 17W
Brandon, *Vt., U.S.A.* **151 C11** 43 48N 73 4W
Brandon B., *Ireland* **23 D1** 52 17N 10 8W
Brandon Mt., *Ireland* **23 D1** 52 15N 10 15W
Brandsen, *Argentina* **174 D4** 35 10 S 58 15W
Brandvlei, *S. Africa* **116 E3** 30 25 S 20 30 E
Brandýs nad Labem, *Czech Rep.* . **34 A7** 50 10N 14 40 E
Brănești, *Romania* **53 F11** 44 27N 26 20 E
Branford, *Conn., U.S.A.* **151 E12** 41 17N 72 49W
Branford, *Fla., U.S.A.* **152 F7** 29 58N 82 56W
Braniewo, *Poland* **54 D6** 54 25N 19 50 E
Bransfield Str., *Antarctica* **7 C18** 63 0 S 59 0W
Brańsk, *Poland* **55 F9** 52 45N 22 50 E
Branson, *U.S.A.* **155 G8** 36 39N 93 13W
Brantford, *Canada* **140 D3** 43 10N 80 15W
Brantley, *U.S.A.* **152 D3** 31 35N 86 16W
Brantôme, *France* **28 C4** 45 22N 0 39 E
Branxholme, *Australia* **128 D4** 37 52 S 141 49 E
Branxton, *Australia* **129 B9** 32 38 S 151 21 E
Branzi, *Italy* **44 B6** 46 1N 9 46 E
Brás, *Brazil* **169 D6** 2 5 S 58 10W
Bras d'Or L., *Canada* **141 C7** 45 50N 60 50W
Brasher Falls, *U.S.A.* **151 B10** 44 49N 74 47W
Brasil, Planalto, *Brazil* **166 E6** 18 0 S 46 30W
Brasil Novo, *Brazil* **169 D7** 3 19 S 52 38W
Brasiléia, *Brazil* **172 C4** 11 0 S 68 45W
Brasília, *Distrito Federal, Brazil* . **171 E2** 15 47 S 47 55W
Brasília, *Minas Gerais, Brazil* **171 E3** 16 12 S 44 26W
Brasília Legal, *Brazil* **169 D6** 3 49 S 55 36W
Braskereidfoss, *Norway* **18 D8** 60 44N 11 46 E
Braslaw, *Belarus* **15 J22** 55 38N 27 0 E
Braslovče, *Slovenia* **45 B12** 46 21N 15 3 E
Brașov, *Romania* **53 E10** 45 38N 25 35 E
Brașov □, *Romania* **53 E10** 45 45N 25 15 E
Brass, *Nigeria* **113 E6** 4 35N 6 14 E
Brass →, *Nigeria* **113 E6** 4 15N 6 13 E
Brassac-les-Mines, *France* **28 C7** 45 24N 3 20 E
Brasschaat, *Belgium* **24 C4** 51 19N 4 27 E
Brassey, Banjaran, *Malaysia* **85 B5** 5 0N 117 15 E
Brassey Ra., *Australia* **125 E3** 25 8 S 122 15 E
Brasstown Bald, *U.S.A.* **149 H4** 34 53N 83 49W
Brastad, *Sweden* **17 F5** 58 23N 11 30 E
Brastavățu, *Romania* **53 G9** 43 55N 24 24 E
Bratan = Morozov, *Bulgaria* **51 D9** 42 30N 25 10 E
Brateș, *Romania* **53 E11** 45 50N 26 4 E
Bratislava, *Slovak Rep.* **35 C10** 48 10N 17 7 E
Bratislavský □, *Slovak Rep.* **35 C10** 48 15N 17 20 E
Bratsigovo, *Bulgaria* **51 D8** 42 1N 24 22 E
Bratsk, *Russia* **67 D11** 56 10N 101 30 E
Brattleboro, *U.S.A.* **151 D12** 42 51N 72 34W
Brattvåg, *Norway* **18 B3** 62 37N 6 25 E
Bratunac, *Bos.-H.* **52 F4** 44 13N 19 21 E
Braunau, *Austria* **34 C6** 48 15N 13 3 E
Braunschweig, *Germany* **30 C6** 52 15N 10 31 E
Braunton, *U.K.* **21 F3** 51 7N 4 10W
Brava, *C. Verde Is.* **9 j** 15 0N 24 40W
Brava, *Somali Rep.* **120 D2** 1 20N 44 8 E
Bravicea, *Moldova* **53 C13** 47 22N 28 27 E
Bråviken, *Sweden* **17 F10** 58 38N 16 32 E
Bravo del Norte, Rio = Grande, Rio →, *U.S.A.* **155 N6** 25 58N 97 9W
Brawley, *U.S.A.* **161 N11** 32 59N 115 31W
Bray, *Ireland* **23 C5** 53 13N 6 7W
Bray, Mt., *Australia* **126 A1** 14 0 S 134 30 E
Bray, Pays de, *France* **25 B4** 49 46N 1 26 E
Bray-sur-Seine, *France* **27 D10** 48 25N 3 14 E
Braymer, *U.S.A.* **156 E3** 39 35N 93 48W
Brazeau →, *Canada* **142 C5** 52 55N 115 14W
Brazil, *U.S.A.* **157 E9** 39 32N 87 8W
Brazil ■, *S. Amer.* **171 D2** 12 0 S 50 0W
Brazilian Highlands = Brasil, Planalto, *Brazil* **166 E6** 18 0 S 46 30W
Brazo Sur →, *S. Amer.* **174 B4** 25 21 S 57 42W
Brazos →, *U.S.A.* **155 L7** 28 53N 95 23W
Brazzaville, *Congo* **115 C3** 4 9 S 15 12 E
Brčko, *Bos.-H.* **52 F3** 44 54N 18 46 E
Brda →, *Poland* **55 E5** 53 8N 18 8 E
Brdy, *Czech Rep.* **34 B6** 49 43N 13 55 E
Brea, *Peru* **172 A1** 4 40 S 81 7W
Breaden, L., *Australia* **125 E4** 25 51 S 125 28 E
Breaksea Sd., *N.Z.* **131 F1** 45 35 S 166 35 E
Bream B., *N.Z.* **130 B3** 35 56 S 174 28 E
Bream Hd., *N.Z.* **130 B3** 35 51 S 174 36 E
Bream Tail, *N.Z.* **130 C3** 36 3 S 174 36 E
Breas, *Chile* **174 B1** 25 29 S 70 24W
Breaza, *Romania* **53 E10** 45 11N 25 40 E
Brebes, *Indonesia* **85 D3** 6 52 S 109 3 E
Brechin, *Canada* **150 B5** 44 32N 79 10W
Brechin, *U.K.* **22 E6** 56 44N 2 39W
Brecht, *Belgium* **24 C4** 51 21N 4 38 E
Breckenridge, *Colo., U.S.A.* **158 G10** 39 29N 106 3W
Breckenridge, *Minn., U.S.A.* **154 B6** 46 16N 96 35W
Breckenridge, *Tex., U.S.A.* **155 J5** 32 45N 98 54W
Breckland, *U.K.* **21 E8** 52 30N 0 40 E
Brecknock, Pen., *Chile* **176 D2** 54 35 S 71 30W
Břeclav, *Czech Rep.* **35 C9** 48 46N 16 53 E
Brecon, *U.K.* **21 F4** 51 57N 3 23W
Brecon Beacons, *U.K.* **21 F4** 51 53N 3 26W
Breda, *Neths.* **24 C4** 51 35N 4 45 E
Bredaryd, *Sweden* **17 G7** 57 10N 13 45 E
Bredasdorp, *S. Africa* **116 E3** 34 33 S 20 2 E
Bredbo, *Australia* **129 C8** 35 58 S 149 10 E
Bredebro, *Denmark* **17 J2** 55 4N 8 50 E
Bredstedt, *Germany* **30 A4** 54 37N 8 55 E
Bredy, *Russia* **64 E8** 52 26N 60 21 E
Bree, *Belgium* **24 C5** 51 8N 5 35 E
Bregalnica →, *Macedonia* **50 E6** 41 43N 22 9 E
Bregenz, *Austria* **34 D2** 47 30N 9 45 E
Bregenzer Wald, *Austria* **33 B9** 47 20N 10 0 E
Bregovo, *Bulgaria* **50 B6** 44 9N 22 39 E
Bréhal, *France* **26 D5** 48 53N 1 30W
Bréhat, Î. de, *France* **26 D4** 48 51N 3 0W
Breiðafjörður, *Iceland* **11 B3** 65 15N 23 15W
Breiðdalsvík, *Iceland* **11 C13** 64 44N 14 0W
Breil-sur-Roya, *France* **29 E11** 43 56N 7 31 E
Breim, *Norway* **18 C3** 61 44N 6 25 E
Breisach, *Germany* **31 G3** 48 1N 7 36 E
Brejinho de Nazaré, *Brazil* **170 D2** 11 1 S 48 34W
Brejo, *Brazil* **170 B3** 3 41 S 42 47W
Brekke, *Norway* **18 C2** 61 1N 5 26 E
Brekken, *Norway* **18 B8** 62 40N 11 51 E
Brekkestø, *Norway* **18 F5** 58 11N 8 22 E
Bremanger, *Norway* **18 C1** 61 51N 4 58 E
Bremangerlandet, *Norway* **18 C1** 61 51N 5 0 E
Bremen, *Germany* **30 B4** 53 4N 8 47 E
Bremen, *Ga., U.S.A.* **153 B4** 33 43N 85 9W
Bremen, *Ind., U.S.A.* **157 C10** 41 27N 86 9W
Bremen □, *Germany* **30 B4** 53 4N 8 50 E
Bremer Bay, *Australia* **125 F2** 34 21 S 119 20 E
Bremer I., *Australia* **126 A2** 12 5 S 136 45 E
Bremerhaven, *Germany* **30 B4** 53 33N 8 36 E
Bremerton, *U.S.A.* **160 C4** 47 34N 122 38W
Bremervörde, *Germany* **30 B5** 53 29N 9 8 E
Bremgarten, *Switz.* **33 B6** 47 22N 8 20 E
Bremnes, *Norway* **18 E2** 59 47N 5 8 E
Bremsnes, *Norway* **18 A4** 63 6N 7 40 E
Brenes, *Spain* **43 H5** 37 32N 5 54W
Brenham, *U.S.A.* **155 K6** 30 10N 96 24W
Brenne, *France* **28 B5** 46 44N 1 14 E
Brennerpass, *Austria* **34 D4** 47 2N 11 30 E
Brennhaug, *Norway* **18 C6** 61 54N 9 21 E
Breno, *Italy* **44 C7** 45 57N 10 18 E
Brent, *U.S.A.* **149 J2** 32 56N 87 10W
Brenta →, *Italy* **45 C9** 45 11N 12 18 E
Brentwood, *U.K.* **21 F8** 51 37N 0 19 E
Brentwood, *Calif., U.S.A.* **160 H5** 37 56N 121 42W
Brentwood, *N.Y., U.S.A.* **151 F11** 40 47N 73 15W
Bréscia, *Italy* **44 C7** 45 33N 10 15 E
Breskens, *Neths.* **24 C3** 51 23N 3 33 E
Breslau = Wrocław, *Poland* **55 G4** 51 5N 17 5 E
Bresle →, *France* **26 B8** 50 4N 1 22 E
Bressanone, *Italy* **45 B8** 46 43N 11 39 E
Bressay, *U.K.* **22 A7** 60 9N 1 6W
Bresse, *France* **27 F12** 46 50N 5 10 E
Bressuire, *France* **26 F6** 46 51N 0 30W
Brest, *Belarus* **59 F2** 52 10N 23 40 E
Brest, *France* **26 D2** 48 24N 4 31W
Brest-Litovsk = Brest, *Belarus* **59 F2** 52 10N 23 40 E
Bretagne, *France* **26 D3** 48 10N 3 0W
Bretanha, Pta. da, *Azores* **9 d3** 37 54N 25 47W
Bretçu, *Romania* **53 D11** 46 7N 26 18 E
Bretenoux, *France* **28 D5** 44 54N 1 51 E
Breteuil, *Eure, France* **26 D7** 48 50N 0 57 E
Breteuil, *Oise, France* **27 C9** 49 38N 2 18 E
Breton, *Canada* **142 C6** 53 7N 114 28W
Breton, Pertuis, *France* **28 B2** 46 17N 1 25W
Breton Sd., *U.S.A.* **155 L10** 29 35N 89 15W
Brett, C., *N.Z.* **130 B3** 35 10 S 174 20 E
Bretten, *Germany* **31 F4** 49 2N 8 42 E
Breuil-Cervínia, *Italy* **44 C4** 45 56N 7 38 E
Brevard, *U.S.A.* **149 H4** 35 14N 82 44W
Breves, *Brazil* **170 B1** 1 40 S 50 29W
Brevig Mission, *U.S.A.* **144 D6** 65 20N 166 29W
Brevik, *Norway* **18 E6** 59 4N 9 42 E
Brewarrina, *Australia* **127 E4** 30 0 S 146 51 E
Brewer, *U.S.A.* **149 C11** 44 48N 68 46W
Brewer, Mt., *U.S.A.* **160 J8** 36 44N 118 28W
Brewerville, *Liberia* **112 D2** 6 26N 10 47W
Brewster, *N.Y., U.S.A.* **151 E11** 41 23N 73 37W
Brewster, *Ohio, U.S.A.* **150 F3** 40 43N 81 36W
Brewster, *Wash., U.S.A.* **158 B4** 48 6N 119 47W
Brewster, Kap = Kangikajik, *Greenland* **10 C8** 70 7N 22 0W
Brewton, *U.S.A.* **149 K2** 31 7N 87 4W
Breyten, *S. Africa* **117 D5** 26 16 S 30 0 E
Breza, *Bos.-H.* **52 F3** 44 2N 18 16 E
Brezhnev = Naberezhnyye Chelny, *Russia* **60 C11** 55 42N 52 19 E
Brežice, *Slovenia* **45 C12** 45 54N 15 35 E
Brézina, *Algeria* **111 B5** 33 4N 1 14 E
Březnice, *Czech Rep.* **34 B6** 49 32N 13 57 E
Breznik, *Bulgaria* **50 D6** 42 44N 22 55 E
Brezno, *Slovak Rep.* **35 C12** 48 50N 19 40 E
Brezoi, *Romania* **53 E9** 45 21N 24 15 E
Brezovica, *Kosovo, Yug.* **50 D5** 42 15N 21 3 E
Brezovo, *Bulgaria* **51 D9** 42 21N 25 5 E
Bria, *C.A.R.* **114 A4** 6 30N 21 58 E
Briançon, *France* **29 D10** 44 54N 6 39 E
Briare, *France* **27 E9** 47 38N 2 45 E
Briático, *Italy* **47 D9** 38 43N 16 2 E
Bribie I., *Australia* **127 D5** 27 0 S 153 10 E
Bribri, *Costa Rica* **164 E3** 9 38N 82 50W
Briceni, *Moldova* **53 B12** 48 22N 27 6 E
Bricquebec, *France* **26 C5** 49 28N 1 38W
Bridgefield, *Barbados* **165 g** 13 9N 59 36W
Bridgehampton, *U.S.A.* **151 F12** 40 56N 72 19W
Bridgend, *U.K.* **21 F4** 51 30N 3 34W
Bridgend □, *U.K.* **21 F4** 51 36N 3 36W
Bridgeport, *Calif., U.S.A.* **160 G7** 38 15N 119 14W
Bridgeport, *Conn., U.S.A.* **151 E11** 41 11N 73 12W
Bridgeport, *Ill., U.S.A.* **157 F9** 38 43N 87 46W
Bridgeport, *Nebr., U.S.A.* **154 E3** 41 40N 103 6W
Bridgeport, *Tex., U.S.A.* **155 J6** 33 13N 97 45W
Bridger, *U.S.A.* **158 D9** 45 18N 108 55W
Bridgeton, *U.S.A.* **148 F8** 39 26N 75 14W
Bridgetown, *Australia* **125 F2** 33 58 S 116 7 E
Bridgetown, *Barbados* **165 g** 13 5N 59 30W
Bridgetown, *Canada* **141 D6** 44 55N 65 18W
Bridgewater, *Australia* **128 D5** 36 36 S 143 59 E
Bridgewater, *Canada* **141 D7** 44 25N 64 31W
Bridgewater, *Mass., U.S.A.* **151 E14** 41 59N 70 58W
Bridgewater, *N.Y., U.S.A.* **151 D9** 42 53N 75 15W
Bridgewater, C., *Australia* **128 E4** 38 23 S 141 23 E
Bridgewater-Gagebrook, *Australia* **127 G4** 42 44 S 147 14 E
Bridgman, *U.S.A.* **157 C10** 41 57N 86 33W
Bridgnorth, *U.K.* **21 E5** 52 32N 2 25W
Bridgton, *U.S.A.* **151 B14** 44 3N 70 42W
Bridgwater, *U.K.* **21 F5** 51 8N 2 59W
Bridgwater B., *U.K.* **21 F5** 51 15N 3 15W
Bridlington, *U.K.* **20 C7** 54 5N 0 12W
Bridlington B., *U.K.* **20 C7** 54 4N 0 10W
Bridport, *Australia* **127 G4** 40 59 S 147 23 E
Bridport, *U.K.* **21 G5** 50 44N 2 45W
Briec, *France* **26 D2** 48 6N 4 0W
Brienne-le-Château, *France* **27 D11** 48 24N 4 30 E
Brienon-sur-Armançon, *France* **27 E10** 47 59N 3 38 E
Brienz, *Switz.* **32 C6** 46 46N 8 2 E
Brienzersee, *Switz.* **32 C5** 46 44N 7 53 E
Brier Cr. →, *U.S.A.* **152 C8** 32 44N 81 26W
Brig, *Switz.* **32 D5** 46 18N 7 59 E
Brigg, *U.K.* **20 D7** 53 34N 0 28W
Brigham City, *U.S.A.* **158 F7** 41 31N 112 1W
Bright, *Australia* **129 D7** 36 42 S 146 56 E
Brighton, *Australia* **128 C3** 35 5 S 138 30 E
Brighton, *Canada* **150 B7** 44 2N 77 44W
Brighton, *Trin. & Tob.* **169 F9** 10 13N 61 39W
Brighton, *U.K.* **21 G7** 50 49N 0 7W
Brighton, *Colo., U.S.A.* **154 F2** 39 59N 104 49W
Brighton, *Fla., U.S.A.* **153 H8** 27 14N 81 6W
Brighton, *Ill., U.S.A.* **156 E6** 39 2N 90 8W
Brighton, *Iowa, U.S.A.* **156 C5** 41 10N 91 49W
Brighton, *Mich., U.S.A.* **157 B13** 42 32N 83 47W
Brighton, *N.Y., U.S.A.* **150 C7** 43 8N 77 34W
Brightwater, *N.Z.* **131 B8** 41 22 S 173 9 E
Brignogan-Plage, *France* **26 D2** 48 40N 4 20W
Brignoles, *France* **29 E10** 43 25N 6 5 E
Brihuega, *Spain* **40 E2** 40 45N 2 52W
Brikama, *Gambia* **112 C1** 13 15N 16 45W
Brilliant, *U.S.A.* **150 F4** 40 15N 80 39W
Brilon, *Germany* **30 D4** 51 23N 8 35 E
Brim, *Australia* **128 D5** 36 3 S 142 27 E
Brimfield, *U.S.A.* **156 D7** 40 50N 89 53W
Bríndisi, *Italy* **47 B10** 40 39N 17 55 E
Brinje, *Croatia* **45 D12** 44 59N 15 9 E
Brinkley, *U.S.A.* **155 H9** 34 53N 91 12W
Brinkworth, *Australia* **128 B3** 33 42 S 138 26 E
Brinnon, *U.S.A.* **160 C4** 47 41N 122 54W
Brinson, *U.S.A.* **152 E5** 30 59N 84 44W
Brion, I., *Canada* **141 C7** 47 46N 61 26W
Brionne, *France* **26 C7** 49 11N 0 43 E
Brionski, *Croatia* **45 D10** 44 55N 13 45 E
Brioude, *France* **28 C7** 45 18N 3 24 E
Briouze, *France* **26 D6** 48 42N 0 23W
Brisbane, *Australia* **127 D5** 27 25 S 153 2 E
Brisbane →, *Australia* **127 D5** 27 24 S 153 9 E
Brisbane Ranges Nat. Park, *Australia* **128 D6** 37 47 S 144 16 E
Brisighella, *Italy* **45 D8** 44 13N 11 46 E
Brissago, *Switz.* **33 D7** 46 7N 8 43 E
Bristol, *U.K.* **21 F5** 51 26N 2 35W
Bristol, *Conn., U.S.A.* **151 E12** 41 40N 72 57W
Bristol, *Fla., U.S.A.* **152 E5** 30 26N 84 59W
Bristol, *Pa., U.S.A.* **151 F10** 40 6N 74 51W
Bristol, *R.I., U.S.A.* **151 E13** 41 40N 71 16W
Bristol, *Tenn., U.S.A.* **149 G4** 36 36N 82 11W
Bristol, City of □, *U.K.* **21 F5** 51 27N 2 36W
Bristol B., *U.S.A.* **144 H8** 58 0N 160 0W
Bristol Channel, *U.K.* **21 F3** 51 18N 4 30W
Bristol I., *Antarctica* **7 B1** 58 45 S 28 0W
Bristol L., *U.S.A.* **159 J5** 34 23N 116 50W
Bristow, *U.S.A.* **155 H6** 35 50N 96 23W
Bristow I., *Papua N. G.* **132 E2** 9 8 S 143 14 E
Britain = Great Britain, *Europe* **19 D5** 54 0N 2 15W
Britânia, *Brazil* **173 D7** 15 14 S 51 9W
British Columbia □, *Canada* **142 C3** 55 0N 125 15W
British Indian Ocean Terr. = Chagos Arch., *Ind. Oc.* **62 K11** 6 0 S 72 0 E
British Isles, *Europe* **19 D5** 54 0N 4 0W
Brits, *S. Africa* **117 D4** 25 37 S 27 48 E
Britstown, *S. Africa* **116 E3** 30 37 S 23 30 E
Britt, *Canada* **140 C3** 45 46N 80 34W
Britt, *U.S.A.* **156 A3** 43 6N 93 48W
Brittany = Bretagne, *France* **26 D3** 48 10N 3 0W
Britton, *U.S.A.* **154 C6** 45 48N 97 45W
Brive-la-Gaillarde, *France* **28 C5** 45 10N 1 32 E
Briviesca, *Spain* **42 C7** 42 32N 3 19W
Brixen = Bressanone, *Italy* **45 B8** 46 43N 11 39 E
Brixham, *U.K.* **21 G4** 50 23N 3 31W
Brlik = Birlik, *Kazakstan* **65 B6** 43 40N 73 49 E
Brlik = Birlik, *Kazakstan* **65 A6** 44 5N 73 31 E
Brnaze, *Croatia* **45 E13** 43 41N 16 40 E
Brno, *Czech Rep.* **35 B9** 49 10N 16 35 E
Broach = Bharuch, *India* **94 D1** 21 47N 73 0 E
Broad →, *Ga., U.S.A.* **152 B7** 33 59N 82 39W
Broad →, *S.C., U.S.A.* **149 J5** 34 1N 81 4W
Broad Arrow, *Australia* **125 F3** 30 23 S 121 15 E
Broad B., *U.K.* **22 C2** 58 14N 6 18W
Broad Haven, *Ireland* **23 B2** 54 20N 9 55W
Broad Law, *U.K.* **22 F5** 55 30N 3 21W
Broad Sd., *Australia* **126 C4** 22 0 S 149 45 E
Broadalbin, *U.S.A.* **151 C10** 43 4N 74 12W
Broadback →, *Canada* **140 B4** 51 21N 78 52W
Broadford, *Australia* **129 D6** 37 14 S 145 4 E
Broadhurst Ra., *Australia* **124 D3** 22 30 S 122 30 E
Broads, The, *U.K.* **20 E9** 52 45N 1 30 E
Broadus, *U.S.A.* **154 C2** 45 27N 105 25W
Broager, *Denmark* **17 K3** 54 53N 9 40 E
Broby, *Sweden* **17 H8** 56 15N 14 4 E
Broc, *Switz.* **32 C4** 46 37N 7 6 E
Brocēni, *Latvia* **54 B9** 56 42N 22 32 E
Brochet, *Canada* **143 B8** 57 53N 101 40W
Brochet, L., *Canada* **143 B8** 58 36N 101 35W
Brocken, *Germany* **30 D6** 51 47N 10 37 E
Brocklehurst, *Australia* **129 B8** 32 9 S 148 38 E
Brockport, *U.S.A.* **150 C7** 43 13N 77 56W
Brockton, *U.S.A.* **151 D13** 42 5N 71 1W
Brockville, *Canada* **140 D4** 44 35N 75 41W
Brockway, *Mont., U.S.A.* **154 B2** 47 18N 105 45W
Brockway, *Pa., U.S.A.* **150 E6** 41 15N 78 47W
Brocton, *U.S.A.* **150 D5** 42 23N 79 26W
Brod, *Macedonia* **50 E5** 41 32N 21 17 E
Brodarevo, *Serbia, Yug.* **50 C3** 43 14N 19 44 E
Brodeur Pen., *Canada* **139 A11** 72 30N 88 10W
Brodhead, *U.S.A.* **156 B7** 42 37N 89 22W
Brodhead, Mt., *U.S.A.* **150 E7** 41 39N 77 47W
Brodick, *U.K.* **22 F3** 55 35N 5 9W
Brodnica, *Poland* **55 E6** 53 15N 19 25 E
Brody, *Ukraine* **59 G3** 50 5N 25 10 E
Brogan, *U.S.A.* **158 D5** 44 15N 117 31W
Broglie, *France* **26 C7** 49 2N 0 30 E
Brok, *Poland* **55 F8** 52 43N 21 52 E
Broken Arrow, *U.S.A.* **155 G7** 36 3N 95 48W
Broken Bow, *Nebr., U.S.A.* **154 E5** 41 24N 99 38W
Broken Bow, *Okla., U.S.A.* **155 H7** 34 2N 94 44W
Broken Bow Lake, *U.S.A.* **155 H7** 34 9N 94 40W
Broken Hill = Kabwe, *Zambia* **119 E2** 14 30 S 28 29 E
Broken Hill, *Australia* **128 A4** 31 58 S 141 29 E
Broken River Ra., *Australia* **126 K6** 21 0 S 148 22 E
Brokind, *Sweden* **17 F9** 58 13N 15 42 E
Brokopondo, *Surinam* **169 B7** 5 3N 54 59W
Bromley □, *U.K.* **21 F8** 51 24N 0 2 E
Bromölla, *Sweden* **17 H8** 56 5N 14 28 E
Bromsgrove, *U.K.* **21 E5** 52 21N 2 2W
Bronaugh, *U.S.A.* **156 G2** 37 41N 94 28W
Brønderslev, *Denmark* **17 G3** 57 16N 9 57 E
Brong-Ahafo □, *Ghana* **112 D4** 7 50N 2 0W
Broni, *Italy* **44 C6** 45 4N 9 16 E
Bronkhorstspruit, *S. Africa* **117 D4** 25 46 S 28 45 E
Brønnøysund, *Norway* **14 D15** 65 28N 12 14 E
Bronson, *Fla., U.S.A.* **153 F7** 29 27N 82 39W
Bronson, *Mich., U.S.A.* **157 C11** 41 52N 85 12W
Bronte, *Italy* **47 E7** 37 47N 14 50 E
Bronwood, *U.S.A.* **152 D5** 31 50N 84 22W
Brook Park, *U.S.A.* **150 E4** 41 24N 81 51W
Brooke's Point, *Phil.* **81 G1** 8 47N 117 50 E
Brookfield, *Mo., U.S.A.* **156 E3** 39 47N 93 4W
Brookfield, *Wis., U.S.A.* **157 A8** 43 4N 88 9W
Brookhaven, *U.S.A.* **155 K9** 31 35N 90 26W
Brookings, *Oreg., U.S.A.* **158 E1** 42 3N 124 17W
Brookings, *S. Dak., U.S.A.* **154 C6** 44 19N 96 48W
Brooklet, *U.S.A.* **152 C8** 32 23N 81 40W
Brooklin, *Canada* **150 C6** 43 55N 78 55W
Brooklyn, *U.S.A.* **156 C4** 41 44N 92 27W
Brooklyn Park, *U.S.A.* **154 C8** 45 6N 93 23W
Brooks, *Canada* **142 C6** 50 35N 111 55W
Brooks Range, *U.S.A.* **144 C10** 68 0N 152 0W
Brookston, *U.S.A.* **157 D10** 40 36N 86 52W
Brooksville, *Fla., U.S.A.* **149 L4** 28 33N 82 23W
Brooksville, *Ky., U.S.A.* **157 F12** 38 41N 84 4W
Brookton, *Australia* **125 F2** 32 22 S 117 0 E
Brookville, *Ind., U.S.A.* **157 E12** 39 25N 85 1W
Brookville, *Ohio, U.S.A.* **157 E12** 39 50N 84 27W
Brookville, *Pa., U.S.A.* **150 E5** 41 10N 79 5W
Brookville L., *U.S.A.* **157 E11** 39 28N 85 0W
Broom, L., *U.K.* **22 D3** 57 55N 5 15W
Broome, *Australia* **124 C3** 18 0 S 122 15 E
Broons, *France* **26 D4** 48 20N 2 16W
Brora, *U.K.* **22 C5** 58 0N 3 52W
Brora →, *U.K.* **22 C5** 58 0N 3 51W
Brørup, *Denmark* **17 J2** 55 29N 9 1 E
Brösarp, *Sweden* **17 J8** 55 43N 14 6 E
Brosna →, *Ireland* **23 C4** 53 14N 7 58W
Broșteni, *Mehedinți, Romania* **52 F7** 44 45N 22 59 E
Broșteni, *Suceava, Romania* **53 C10** 47 14N 25 43 E
Brostrud, *Norway* **18 D5** 60 18N 8 34 E
Brotas de Macaúbas, *Brazil* **171 D3** 12 0 S 42 38W
Brothers, *U.S.A.* **158 E3** 43 49N 120 36W
Brøttum, *Norway* **18 C7** 61 2N 10 34 E
Brou, *France* **26 D8** 48 13N 1 11 E
Brouage, *France* **28 C2** 45 52N 1 4W
Brough, *U.K.* **20 C5** 54 32N 2 18W
Brough Hd., *U.K.* **22 B5** 59 8N 3 20W
Broughton, *U.S.A.* **157 G8** 37 56N 88 27W
Broughton Island = Qikiqtarjuaq, *Canada* **139 B13** 67 33N 63 0W
Broumov, *Czech Rep.* **35 A9** 50 35N 16 20 E
Brovary, *Ukraine* **59 G6** 50 34N 30 48 E
Brovst, *Denmark* **17 G3** 57 6N 9 31 E
Brown, L., *Australia* **125 F2** 31 5 S 118 15 E
Brown, Mt., *Australia* **128 B3** 32 30 S 138 0 E
Brown, Pt., *Australia* **127 E1** 32 32 S 133 50 E
Brown City, *U.S.A.* **150 C2** 43 13N 82 59W
Brown Willy, *U.K.* **21 G3** 50 35N 4 37W
Brownfield, *U.S.A.* **155 J3** 33 11N 102 17W
Browning, *Ill., U.S.A.* **156 D6** 40 8N 90 22W
Browning, *Mo., U.S.A.* **156 D3** 40 3N 93 12W
Browning, *Mont., U.S.A.* **158 B7** 48 34N 113 1W
Brownsburg, *U.S.A.* **157 E10** 39 51N 86 24W
Brownstown, *U.S.A.* **157 F10** 38 53N 86 3W

196 Burnt River

Burnt River, *Canada* **150 B6** 44 41N 78 42W
Burntwood →, *Canada* **143 B9** 56 8N 96 34W
Burntwood L., *Canada* **143 B8** 55 22N 100 26W
Buronga, *Australia* **128 C5** 34 18 S 142 20 E
Burqān, *Kuwait* **96 D5** 29 0N 47 57 E
Burra, *Australia* **128 B3** 33 40 S 138 55 E
Burra, *Nigeria* **113 C6** 11 0N 8 56 E
Burragorang, L., *Australia* **129 B9** 33 52 S 150 37 E
Burray, *U.K.* **22 C6** 58 51N 2 54W
Burrel, *Albania* **50 E4** 41 36N 20 1 E
Burren Junction, *Australia* **127 E4** 30 7 S 148 59 E
Burrendong, L., *Australia* **129 B8** 32 45 S 149 10 E
Burriana, *Spain* **40 F4** 39 50N 0 4W
Burrinjuck Res., *Australia* **129 C8** 35 0 S 148 36 E
Burro, Serranías del, *Mexico* **162 B4** 29 0N 102 0W
Burrow Hd., *U.K.* **22 G4** 54 41N 4 24W
Burrowa Pine Mountain Nat. Park, *Australia* **129 D7** 36 6 S 147 45 E
Burrum Coast Nat. Park, *Australia* **127 D5** 25 13 S 152 36 E
Burruyacú, *Argentina* **174 B3** 26 30 S 64 40W
Burry Port, *U.K.* **21 F3** 51 41N 4 15W
Bursa, *Turkey* **51 F13** 40 15N 29 5 E
Burseryd, *Sweden* **17 G7** 57 12N 13 17 E
Burstall, *Canada* **143 C7** 50 39N 109 54W
Burton, *Mich., U.S.A.* **157 B13** 43 0N 83 40W
Burton, *Ohio, U.S.A.* **150 E3** 41 28N 81 8W
Burton, *S.C., U.S.A.* **149 J5** 32 25N 80 45W
Burton, L., *Canada* **140 B4** 54 45N 78 20W
Burton upon Trent, *U.K.* **20 E6** 52 48N 1 38W
Burtundy, *Australia* **128 B5** 33 45 S 142 15 E
Buru, *Indonesia* **82 B3** 3 30 S 126 30 E
Buruanga, *Phil.* **81 F3** 11 51N 121 53 E
Burugi Game Reserve, *Tanzania* **118 C3** 2 20 S 31 6 E
Burullus, Bahra el, *Egypt* **106 H7** 31 25N 31 0 E
Burūm, *Yemen* **99 D5** 14 22N 48 59 E
Burûn, Râs, *Egypt* **103 D2** 31 14N 33 7 E
Burunday = Boralday, *Kazakstan* **65 B8** 43 20N 76 51 E
Burundi ■, *Africa* **118 C3** 3 15 S 30 0 E
Bururi, *Burundi* **118 C2** 3 57 S 29 37 E
Burutu, *Nigeria* **113 D6** 5 20N 5 29 E
Burwell, *U.S.A.* **154 E5** 41 47N 99 8W
Burwick, *U.K.* **22 C5** 58 45N 2 58W
Bury, *U.K.* **20 D5** 53 35N 2 17W
Bury St. Edmunds, *U.K.* **21 E8** 52 15N 0 43 E
Buryatia □, *Russia* **67 D11** 53 0N 110 0 E
Būrylbaytal, *Kazakstan* **65 A7** 45 5N 74 1 E
Buryn, *Ukraine* **59 G7** 51 13N 33 50 E
Burzenin, *Poland* **55 G5** 51 28N 18 47 E
Busa, Mt., *Phil.* **81 H5** 6 8N 124 39 E
Busalla, *Italy* **44 D5** 44 34N 8 57 E
Busan = Pusan, *S. Korea* **75 G15** 35 5N 129 0 E
Busanga, *Dem. Rep. of the Congo* **114 C4** 0 53 S 22 7 E
Busango Swamp, *Zambia* **119 E2** 14 15 S 25 45 E
Buşayrah, *Syria* **101 E9** 35 9N 40 26 E
Busca, *Italy* **44 D4** 44 31N 7 29 E
Bushat, *Albania* **50 E3** 41 58N 19 34 E
Būshehr, *Iran* **97 D6** 28 55N 50 55 E
Būshehr □, *Iran* **97 D6** 28 20N 51 45 E
Bushell, *Canada* **143 B7** 59 31N 108 45W
Bushenyi, *Uganda* **118 C3** 0 35 S 30 10 E
Bushimaie →, *Dem. Rep. of the Congo* **115 D4** 6 2 S 23 45 E
Bushire = Būshehr, *Iran* **97 D6** 28 55N 50 55 E
Bushnell, *Fla., U.S.A.* **153 G7** 28 40N 82 7W
Bushnell, *Ill., U.S.A.* **156 D6** 40 33N 90 31W
Busie, *Ghana* **112 C4** 10 29N 2 22W
Businga, *Dem. Rep. of the Congo* **114 B4** 3 16N 20 59 E
Buskerud □, *Norway* **18 D5** 60 20N 9 0 E
Busko-Zdrój, *Poland* **55 H7** 50 28N 20 42 E
Buskul, *Kazakstan* **64 E8** 53 45N 61 12 E
Buslei, *Ethiopia* **120 C2** 5 28N 44 25 E
Busovača, *Bos.-H.* **52 F2** 44 6N 17 53 E
Buşra ash Shām, *Syria* **103 C5** 32 30N 36 25 E
Busselton, *Australia* **125 F2** 33 42 S 115 15 E
Busseri →, *Sudan* **107 F2** 7 41N 28 3 E
Busseto, *Italy* **44 D7** 44 59N 10 2 E
Bussière-Badil, *France* **28 C4** 45 39N 0 36 E
Bussigny, *Switz.* **32 C3** 46 33N 6 33 E
Bussolengo, *Italy* **44 C7** 45 28N 10 51 E
Bussum, *Neths.* **24 B5** 52 16N 5 10 E
Bustamante, B., *Argentina* **176 C3** 45 5 S 66 18W
Buşteni, *Romania* **53 E10** 45 24N 25 32 E
Busto, C., *Spain* **42 B4** 43 34N 6 28W
Busto Arsízio, *Italy* **44 C5** 45 37N 8 51 E
Busu Djanoa, *Dem. Rep. of the Congo* **114 B4** 1 43N 21 23 E
Busu Kwanga, *Dem. Rep. of the Congo* **114 B4** 1 48N 20 21 E
Busu Mandji, *Dem. Rep. of the Congo* **114 B4** 2 52N 21 14 E
Busuanga, *Phil.* **80 E2** 12 14N 119 52 E
Busuanga I., *Phil.* **80 E2** 12 10N 120 0 E
Büsum, *Germany* **30 A4** 54 7N 8 51 E
Busungbiu, *Indonesia* **79 J17** 8 16 S 114 58 E
Buta, *Dem. Rep. of the Congo* **118 B1** 2 50N 24 53 E
Butare, *Rwanda* **118 C2** 2 31 S 29 52 E
Butaritari, *Kiribati* **134 G9** 3 30N 174 0 E
Bute, *Australia* **128 B3** 33 51 S 138 2 E
Bute, *U.K.* **22 F3** 55 48N 5 2W
Bute Inlet, *Canada* **142 C4** 50 40N 124 53W
Butemba, *Uganda* **118 B3** 1 9N 31 37 E
Butembo, *Dem. Rep. of the Congo* **118 B2** 0 9N 29 18 E
Buteni, *Romania* **52 D7** 46 19N 22 7 E
Butera, *Italy* **47 E7** 37 11N 14 11 E
Butha Qi, *China* **69 B7** 48 0N 122 32 E
Buthidaung, *Burma* **90 E4** 20 52N 92 32 E
Butiaba, *Uganda* **118 B3** 1 50N 31 20 E
Butler, *Ga., U.S.A.* **152 C5** 32 33N 84 14W
Butler, *Ind., U.S.A.* **157 C12** 41 26N 84 52W
Butler, *Ky., U.S.A.* **157 F12** 38 47N 84 22W
Butler, *Mo., U.S.A.* **156 F2** 38 16N 94 20W
Butler, *Pa., U.S.A.* **150 F5** 40 52N 79 54W
Buton, *Indonesia* **82 C2** 5 0 S 122 45 E
Butrintit, L. e, *Albania* **38 B10** 39 43N 20 5 E
Bütschwil, *Switz.* **33 B8** 47 23N 9 5 E
Butte, *Mont., U.S.A.* **158 C7** 46 0N 112 32W
Butte, *Nebr., U.S.A.* **154 D5** 42 58N 98 51W
Butte Creek →, *U.S.A.* **160 F5** 39 12N 121 56W
Butterworth = Gcuwa, *S. Africa* **117 E4** 32 20 S 28 11 E
Butterworth, *Malaysia* **87 c** 5 24N 100 23 E
Buttevant, *Ireland* **23 D3** 52 14N 8 40W
Buttfield, Mt., *Australia* **125 D4** 24 45 S 128 9 E
Button B., *Canada* **143 B10** 58 45N 94 23W
Buttonwillow, *U.S.A.* **161 K7** 35 24N 119 28W
Butty Hd., *Australia* **125 F3** 33 54 S 121 39 E
Butuan, *Phil.* **81 G5** 8 57N 125 33 E
Butuku-Luba, *Eq. Guin.* **113 E6** 3 29N 8 33 E
Butung = Buton, *Indonesia* **82 C2** 5 0 S 122 45 E
Buturlinovka, *Russia* **60 E5** 50 50N 40 35 E
Butzbach, *Germany* **31 E4** 50 25N 8 40 E
Bützow, *Germany* **30 B7** 53 50N 11 58 E
Buulobarde = Bulo Burti, *Somali Rep.* **120 D3** 3 50N 45 33 E
Buur Hakaba = Bur Acaba, *Somali Rep.* **120 D2** 3 12N 44 20 E
Buvik, *Norway* **18 A7** 63 18N 10 11 E
Buxa Duar, *India* **93 F13** 27 45N 89 35 E
Buxar, *India* **93 G10** 25 34N 83 58 E
Buxtehude, *Germany* **30 B5** 53 28N 9 39 E
Buxton, *Guyana* **169 B6** 6 48N 58 2W
Buxton, *U.K.* **20 D6** 53 16N 1 54W
Buxy, *France* **27 F11** 46 44N 4 40 E
Buy, *Russia* **60 A5** 58 28N 41 28 E
Buynaksk, *Russia* **61 J8** 42 48N 47 7 E
Buyo, *Ivory C.* **112 D3** 6 21N 7 5W
Buyo, L. de, *Ivory C.* **112 D3** 6 16N 7 10W
Büyük Menderes →, *Turkey* **49 D9** 37 28N 27 11 E
Büyükçekmece, *Turkey* **51 E12** 41 2N 28 35 E
Büyükkarıştiran, *Turkey* **51 E11** 41 18N 27 33 E
Büyükkemikli Burnu, *Turkey* **51 F10** 40 18N 26 14 E
Büyükorhan, *Turkey* **49 B10** 39 46N 28 56 E
Büyükyoncalı, *Turkey* **51 E11** 41 20N 27 55 E
Buzançais, *France* **26 F8** 46 54N 1 25 E
Buzău, *Romania* **53 E11** 45 10N 26 50 E
Buzău □, *Romania* **53 E11** 45 20N 26 30 E
Buzău →, *Romania* **53 E12** 45 26N 27 44 E
Buzău, Pasul, *Romania* **53 E11** 45 35N 26 12 E
Buzen, *Japan* **72 D3** 33 35N 131 5 E
Buzet, *Croatia* **45 C10** 45 24N 13 58 E
Buzi →, *Mozam.* **119 F3** 19 50 S 34 43 E
Buziaş, *Romania* **52 E6** 45 38N 21 36 E
Buzuluk, *Russia* **64 E4** 52 48N 52 12 E
Buzuluk →, *Russia* **60 E6** 50 15N 42 7 E
Buzzards B., *U.S.A.* **151 E14** 41 45N 70 37W
Buzzards Bay, *U.S.A.* **151 E14** 41 44N 70 37W
Bwagaoia, *Papua N. G.* **132 F7** 10 40 S 152 52 E
Bwana Mkubwe, *Dem. Rep. of the Congo* **119 E2** 13 8 S 28 38 E
Bwasa, *Dem. Rep. of the Congo* **114 C3** 3 55 S 18 24 E
Bwatnapné, *Vanuatu* **133 E6** 15 41 S 168 9 E
Bwindi Impenetrable Forest Nat. Park, *Uganda* **118 C2** 1 2 S 29 42 E
Byala, *Ruse, Bulgaria* **51 C9** 43 28N 25 44 E
Byala, *Varna, Bulgaria* **51 D11** 42 53N 27 55 E
Byala Slatina, *Bulgaria* **50 C7** 43 26N 23 58 E
Byarezina →, *Belarus* **59 F6** 52 33N 30 14 E
Byaroza, *Belarus* **59 F3** 52 31N 24 51 E
Bychawa, *Poland* **55 G9** 51 1N 22 36 E
Byczyna, *Poland* **55 G5** 51 7N 18 12 E
Bydgoszcz, *Poland* **55 E5** 53 10N 18 0 E
Byelarus = Belarus ■, *Europe* **58 F4** 53 30N 27 0 E
Byelorussia = Belarus ■, *Europe* **58 F4** 53 30N 27 0 E
Byers, *U.S.A.* **154 F2** 39 43N 104 14W
Byesville, *U.S.A.* **150 G3** 39 58N 81 32W
Byfield Nat. Park, *Australia* **126 C5** 22 52 S 150 45 E
Byford, *Australia* **125 F2** 32 15 S 116 0 E
Bygdin, *Norway* **18 C5** 61 21N 8 32 E
Bygland, *Norway* **18 F4** 58 50N 7 48 E
Byglandsfjorden, *Norway* **18 F4** 58 44N 7 50 E
Bygstad, *Norway* **18 C2** 61 23N 5 40 E
Bykhaw, *Belarus* **58 F6** 53 31N 30 14 E
Bykhov = Bykhaw, *Belarus* **58 F6** 53 31N 30 14 E
Bykle, *Norway* **18 E4** 59 20N 7 22 E
Bykovo, *Russia* **60 F7** 49 50N 45 25 E
Bylas, *U.S.A.* **159 K8** 33 8N 110 7W
Bylot, *Canada* **143 B10** 58 25N 94 8W
Bylot I., *Canada* **139 A12** 73 13N 78 34W
Byrd, C., *Antarctica* **7 C17** 69 38 S 76 7W
Byrock, *Australia* **129 A7** 30 40 S 146 27 E
Byron, *Ga., U.S.A.* **152 C6** 32 39N 83 46W
Byron, *Ill., U.S.A.* **156 B7** 42 8N 89 15W
Byron Bay, *Australia* **127 D5** 28 43 S 153 37 E
Byrranga, Gory, *Russia* **67 B11** 75 0N 100 0 E
Byrranga Mts. = Byrranga, Gory, *Russia* **67 B11** 75 0N 100 0 E
Byrum, *Denmark* **17 G5** 57 16N 11 0 E
Byske, *Sweden* **14 D19** 64 57N 21 11 E
Byske älv →, *Sweden* **14 D19** 64 57N 21 13 E
Bystrovka = Kemin, *Kyrgyzstan* **65 B7** 42 47N 75 42 E
Bystrzyca →, *Dolnośląskie, Poland* **55 G3** 51 12N 16 55 E
Bystrzyca →, *Lubelskie, Poland* **55 G9** 51 21N 22 46 E
Bystrzyca Kłodzka, *Poland* **55 H3** 50 19N 16 39 E
Bytča, *Slovak Rep.* **35 B11** 49 13N 18 34 E
Bytom, *Poland* **55 H5** 50 25N 18 54 E
Bytom Odrzański, *Poland* **55 G2** 51 44N 15 48 E
Bytów, *Poland* **54 D4** 54 10N 17 30 E
Byumba, *Rwanda* **118 C3** 1 35 S 30 4 E
Bzenec, *Czech Rep.* **35 C10** 48 58N 17 18 E
Bzura →, *Poland* **55 F7** 52 25N 20 15 E

C

Ca →, *Vietnam* **86 C5** 18 45N 105 45 E
Ca Mau, *Vietnam* **87 H5** 9 7N 105 8 E
Ca Mau, Mui, *Vietnam* **87 H5** 8 38N 104 44 E
Ca Na, *Vietnam* **87 G7** 11 20N 108 54 E
Caacupé, *Paraguay* **174 B4** 25 23 S 57 5W
Caála, *Angola* **115 E3** 12 46 S 15 30 E
Caamano Sd., *Canada* **142 C3** 52 55N 129 25W
Caapiranga, *Brazil* **169 D5** 3 18 S 61 13W
Caazapá, *Paraguay* **174 B4** 26 8 S 56 19W
Caazapá □, *Paraguay* **175 B4** 26 10 S 56 0W
Cabadbaran, *Phil.* **81 G5** 9 10N 125 38 E
Cabagan, *Phil.* **80 C3** 17 26N 121 46 E
Cabalian = San Juan, *Phil.* **81 F5** 10 16N 125 10 E
Caballeria, C. de, *Spain* **38 A5** 40 5N 4 5 E
Cabana, *Peru* **172 B2** 8 25 S 78 5W
Cabana, *Spain* **42 B2** 43 13N 8 54W
Cabanaconde, *Peru* **172 D3** 15 38 S 71 58W
Cabañaquinta, *Spain* **42 B5** 43 10N 5 38W
Cabanatuan, *Phil.* **80 D3** 15 30N 120 58 E
Cabanes, *Spain* **40 E5** 40 9N 0 2 E
Cabangon, *Phil.* **80 D3** 15 10N 120 3 E
Cabanillas, *Peru* **172 D3** 15 36 S 70 28W
Cabano, *Canada* **141 C6** 47 40N 68 56W
Čabar, *Croatia* **45 C11** 45 36N 14 39 E
Cabarroguis, *Phil.* **80 C3** 16 50N 121 30 E
Cabarruyan I., *Phil.* **80 C2** 16 18N 119 59 E
Cabazon, *U.S.A.* **161 M10** 33 55N 116 47W
Cabedelo, *Brazil* **170 C5** 7 0 S 34 50W
Cabeza del Buey, *Spain* **43 G5** 38 44N 5 13W
Cabezón de la Sal, *Spain* **42 B6** 43 18N 4 14W
Cabildo, *Chile* **174 C1** 32 30 S 71 5W
Cabimas, *Venezuela* **168 A3** 10 23N 71 25W
Cabinda, *Angola* **115 D2** 5 33 S 12 11 E
Cabinda □, *Angola* **115 D2** 5 0 S 12 30 E
Cabinet Mts., *U.S.A.* **158 C6** 48 0N 115 30W
Cabiri, *Angola* **115 D2** 8 52 S 13 39 E
Cable Beach, *Bahamas* **9 b** 25 4N 77 24W
Cabo Blanco, *Argentina* **176 C3** 47 15 S 65 47W
Cabo Frio, *Brazil* **171 F3** 22 51 S 42 3W
Cabo Pantoja, *Peru* **168 D2** 1 0 S 75 10W
Cabo Raso, *Argentina* **176 B3** 44 20 S 65 15W
Cabonga, Réservoir, *Canada* **140 C4** 47 20N 76 40W
Cabool, *U.S.A.* **155 G8** 37 7N 92 6W
Caboolture, *Australia* **127 D5** 27 5 S 152 58 E
Cabora Bassa Dam = Cahora Bassa, Reprêsa de, *Mozam.* **119 F3** 15 20 S 32 50 E
Caborca, *Mexico* **162 A2** 30 40N 112 10W
Cabot, Mt., *U.S.A.* **151 B13** 44 30N 71 25W
Cabot Hd., *Canada* **150 A3** 45 14N 81 17W
Cabot Str., *Canada* **141 C8** 47 15N 59 40W
Cabra, *Spain* **43 H6** 37 30N 4 28W
Cabra del Santo Cristo, *Spain* **43 H7** 37 42N 3 16W
Cabra I., *India* **95 L11** 7 18N 93 50 E
Cábras, *Italy* **46 C1** 39 56N 8 32 E
Cabrera, *Spain* **38 B3** 39 8N 2 57 E
Cabrera, Sierra, *Spain* **42 C4** 42 12N 6 40W
Cabri, *Canada* **143 C7** 50 35N 108 25W
Cabriel →, *Spain* **41 F3** 39 14N 1 3W
Cabruta, *Venezuela* **168 B4** 7 50N 66 10W
Cabucgayan, *Phil.* **81 F5** 11 29N 124 34 E
Cabugao, *Phil.* **80 C3** 17 48N 120 27 E
Cabulauan Is., *Phil.* **81 F3** 11 25N 120 8 E
Cabulo, *Angola* **115 E3** 10 18 S 16 22 E
Caburan = Jose Abad Santos, *Phil.* **81 J5** 5 55N 125 39 E
Cabuta, *Angola* **115 D2** 9 48 S 14 58 E
Cabuyaro, *Colombia* **168 C3** 4 18N 72 49W
Cacabelos, *Spain* **42 C4** 42 36N 6 44W
Caçador, *Brazil* **175 B5** 26 47 S 51 0W
Čačak, *Serbia, Yug.* **50 C4** 43 54N 20 20 E
Cacao, *Fr. Guiana* **169 C7** 4 33N 52 26W
Caçapava do Sul, *Brazil* **175 C5** 30 30 S 53 30W
Cáccamo, *Italy* **46 E6** 37 56N 13 40 E
Cacém, *Portugal* **43 G1** 38 46N 9 18W
Cáceres, *Brazil* **173 D6** 16 5 S 57 40W
Cáceres, *Colombia* **168 B2** 7 35N 75 20W
Cáceres, *Spain* **43 F4** 39 26N 6 23W
Cáceres □, *Spain* **42 F5** 39 45N 6 0W
Cache Bay, *Canada* **140 C4** 46 22N 80 0W
Cache Cr. →, *U.S.A.* **160 G5** 38 42N 121 42W
Cache Creek, *Canada* **142 C4** 50 48N 121 19W
Cacheu, *Guinea-Biss.* **112 C1** 12 14N 16 8W
Cachi, *Argentina* **174 B2** 25 5 S 66 10W
Cachimbo, *Brazil* **173 B7** 8 57 S 54 54W
Cachimbo, Serra do, *Brazil* **173 B6** 9 30 S 55 30W
Cachimo, *Angola* **115 D4** 8 21 S 21 24 E
Cachinal de la Sierra, *Chile* **174 A2** 24 58 S 69 32W
Cachingues, *Angola* **115 E3** 13 5 S 16 43 E
Cachoeira, *Brazil* **171 D4** 12 30 S 39 0W
Cachoeira Alta, *Brazil* **171 E1** 18 48 S 50 58W
Cachoeira do Sul, *Brazil* **175 C5** 30 3 S 52 53W
Cachoeiro de Itapemirim, *Brazil* **171 F3** 20 51 S 41 7W
Cachoeiro do Arari, *Brazil* **170 B2** 1 1 S 48 58W
Cachopo, *Portugal* **43 H3** 37 20N 7 49W
Cachuela Esperanza, *Bolivia* **173 C4** 10 32 S 65 38W
Cacine, *Guinea-Biss.* **112 C1** 11 8N 14 57W
Cacoal, *Brazil* **173 C5** 11 30 S 61 25W
Cacólo, *Angola* **115 E3** 10 9 S 19 21 E
Caconda, *Angola* **115 E3** 13 48 S 15 8 E
Cacongo, *Angola* **115 D2** 5 11 S 12 5 E
Caçu, *Brazil* **171 E1** 18 37 S 51 4W
Cacuaco, *Angola* **115 D2** 8 47 S 13 21 E
Cacuchi →, *Angola* **115 E3** 14 26 S 16 46 E
Cacula, *Angola* **115 E2** 14 29 S 14 10 E
Caculé, *Brazil* **171 D3** 14 30 S 42 13W
Caculuvar →, *Angola* **115 F2** 16 47 S 14 56 E
Cacuso, *Angola* **115 D3** 9 25 S 15 45 E
Čadca, *Slovak Rep.* **35 B11** 49 26N 18 45 E
Caddo, *U.S.A.* **155 H6** 34 7N 96 16W
Cadenazzo, *Switz.* **33 D7** 46 9N 8 57 E
Cader Idris, *U.K.* **21 E4** 52 42N 3 53W
Cadereyta, *Mexico* **162 B5** 25 36N 100 0W
Cades, *U.S.A.* **152 B10** 33 47N 79 47W
Cadí, Sierra del, *Spain* **40 C6** 42 17N 1 42 E
Cadibarrawirracanna, L., *Australia* **127 D2** 28 52 S 135 27 E
Cadillac, *France* **28 D3** 44 38N 0 20W
Cadillac, *U.S.A.* **148 C3** 44 15N 85 24W
Cadiz, *Phil.* **81 F4** 10 57N 123 15 E
Cádiz, *Spain* **43 J4** 36 30N 6 20W
Cadiz, *Calif., U.S.A.* **161 L11** 34 30N 115 28W
Cadiz, *Ohio, U.S.A.* **150 F4** 40 22N 81 0W
Cádiz □, *Spain* **43 J5** 36 36N 5 45W
Cádiz, G. de, *Spain* **43 J3** 36 40N 7 0W
Cadiz L., *U.S.A.* **159 J6** 34 18N 115 24W
Cadley, *U.S.A.* **152 B7** 33 32N 82 40W
Cadney Park, *Australia* **127 D1** 27 55 S 134 3 E
Cadomin, *Canada* **142 C5** 53 2N 117 20W
Cadotte Lake, *Canada* **142 B5** 56 26N 116 23W
Cadours, *France* **28 E5** 43 44N 1 2 E
Cadoux, *Australia* **125 F2** 30 46 S 117 7 E
Cadwell, *U.S.A.* **152 C6** 32 20N 83 3W
Caen, *France* **26 C6** 49 10N 0 22W
Caernarfon, *U.K.* **20 D3** 53 8N 4 16W
Caernarfon B., *U.K.* **20 D3** 53 4N 4 40W
Caernarvon = Caernarfon, *U.K.* **20 D3** 53 8N 4 16W
Caerphilly, *U.K.* **21 F4** 51 35N 3 13W
Caerphilly □, *U.K.* **21 F4** 51 37N 3 12W
Caesarea, *Israel* **103 C3** 32 30N 34 53 E
Caeté, *Brazil* **171 E3** 19 55 S 43 40W
Caetité, *Brazil* **171 D3** 13 50 S 42 32W
Cafayate, *Argentina* **174 B2** 26 2 S 66 0W
Cafu, *Angola* **116 B2** 16 30 S 15 8 E
Cagayan □, *Phil.* **80 C3** 18 0N 121 50 E
Cagayan →, *Phil.* **80 B3** 18 25N 121 42 E
Cagayan de Oro, *Phil.* **81 G5** 8 30N 124 40 E
Cagayan Is., *Phil.* **81 G3** 9 40N 121 16 E
Cagayan Sulu I., *Phil.* **81 H2** 7 1N 118 30 E
Cagli, *Italy* **45 E9** 43 33N 12 39 E
Cágliari, *Italy* **46 C2** 39 13N 9 7 E
Cágliari, G. di, *Italy* **46 C2** 39 8N 9 11 E
Cagnano Varano, *Italy* **45 G12** 41 49N 15 47 E
Cagnes-sur-Mer, *France* **29 E11** 43 40N 7 9 E
Caguán →, *Colombia* **168 D3** 0 8 S 74 18W
Caguas, *Puerto Rico* **165 d** 18 14N 66 2W
Caha Mts., *Ireland* **23 E2** 51 45N 9 40W
Cahama, *Angola* **116 B1** 16 17 S 14 19 E
Caher, *Ireland* **23 D4** 52 22N 7 56W
Caherciveen, *Ireland* **23 E1** 51 56N 10 14W
Cahora Bassa, L. de, *Mozam.* **119 F3** 15 35 S 32 0 E
Cahora Bassa, Reprêsa de, *Mozam.* **119 F3** 15 20 S 32 50 E
Cahore Pt., *Ireland* **23 D5** 52 33N 6 12W
Cahors, *France* **28 D5** 44 27N 1 27 E
Cahuapanas, *Peru* **172 B2** 5 15 S 77 0W
Cahuinari →, *Colombia* **168 D3** 1 21 S 70 44W
Cahul, *Moldova* **53 E13** 45 50N 28 15 E
Caì Bau, Dao, *Vietnam* **76 G6** 21 10N 107 27 E
Cai Nuoc, *Vietnam* **87 H5** 8 56N 105 1 E
Caia, *Mozam.* **119 F4** 17 51 S 35 24 E
Caiabis, Serra dos, *Brazil* **173 C6** 11 30 S 56 30W
Caianda, *Angola* **119 E1** 11 2 S 23 31 E
Caiapó, Serra do, *Brazil* **173 D7** 17 0 S 52 0W
Caiapônia, *Brazil* **173 D7** 16 57 S 51 49W
Caibarién, *Cuba* **164 B4** 22 30N 79 30W
Caibiran, *Phil.* **81 F5** 11 34N 124 35 E
Caicara, *Bolívar, Venezuela* **168 B4** 7 38N 66 10W
Caicara, *Monagas, Venezuela* **169 B5** 9 52N 63 38W
Caicó, *Brazil* **170 C4** 6 20 S 37 0W
Caicos Is., *Turks & Caicos* **165 B5** 21 40N 71 40W
Caicos Passage, *W. Indies* **165 B5** 22 45N 72 45W
Caidian, *China* **77 B10** 30 35N 114 2 E
Cailloma, *Peru* **172 D3** 15 9 S 71 45W
Căinari, *Moldova* **53 D14** 46 41N 29 3 E
Cainde, *Angola* **115 F2** 15 29 S 13 24 E
Caine →, *Bolivia* **173 D4** 18 23 S 65 21W
Caird Coast, *Antarctica* **7 D1** 75 0 S 25 0W
Cairn Gorm, *U.K.* **22 D5** 57 7N 3 39W
Cairngorm Mts., *U.K.* **22 D5** 57 6N 3 42W
Cairnryan, *U.K.* **22 G3** 54 59N 5 1W
Cairns, *Australia* **126 B4** 16 57 S 145 45 E
Cairns L., *Canada* **143 C10** 51 42N 94 30W
Cairo = El Qâhira, *Egypt* **106 H7** 30 1N 31 14 E
Cairo, *Ga., U.S.A.* **152 E5** 30 52N 84 13W
Cairo, *Ill., U.S.A.* **155 G10** 37 0N 89 11W
Cairo, *N.Y., U.S.A.* **151 D11** 42 18N 74 0W
Cairo Montenotte, *Italy* **44 D5** 44 23N 8 16 E
Cairofa, *Angola* **115 E2** 14 3 S 12 54 E
Caithness, Ord of, *U.K.* **22 C5** 58 8N 3 36W
Caitou, *Angola* **115 E2** 14 28 S 13 7 E
Caiundo, *Angola* **115 F3** 15 50 S 17 28 E
Caiza, *Bolivia* **173 E4** 20 2 S 65 40W
Caja de Muertos, I., *Puerto Rico* **165 d** 17 54N 66 32W
Cajabamba, *Peru* **172 B2** 7 38 S 78 4W
Cajamarca, *Peru* **172 B2** 7 5 S 78 28W
Cajamarca □, *Peru* **172 B2** 6 15 S 78 50W
Cajapió, *Brazil* **170 B3** 2 58 S 44 48W
Cajarc, *France* **28 D5** 44 29N 1 50 E
Cajatambo, *Peru* **172 C2** 10 30 S 77 2W
Cajàzeiras, *Brazil* **170 C4** 6 52 S 38 30W
Čajetina, *Serbia, Yug.* **50 C3** 43 47N 19 42 E
Cajidiocan, *Phil.* **80 E4** 12 22N 122 41 E
Çakirgol, *Turkey* **101 B8** 40 33N 39 40 E
Çakırlar, *Turkey* **49 E12** 36 52N 30 33 E
Čakovec, *Croatia* **45 B13** 46 23N 16 26 E
Çal, *Turkey* **49 C11** 38 4N 29 23 E
Cala, *Spain* **43 H4** 37 59N 6 21W
Cala →, *Spain* **43 H4** 37 38N 6 5W
Cala Cadolar, Punta de = Rotja, Pta., *Spain* **38 D2** 38 38N 1 35 E
Cala d'Or, *Spain* **38 B4** 39 23N 3 14 E
Cala en Porter, *Spain* **38 B5** 39 52N 4 8 E
Cala Figuera, C. de, *Spain* **38 B3** 39 27N 2 31 E
Cala Forcat, *Spain* **38 B4** 40 0N 3 47 E
Cala Major, *Spain* **38 B3** 39 33N 2 37 E
Cala Mezquida = Sa Mesquida, *Spain* **38 B5** 39 55N 4 16 E
Cala Millor, *Spain* **38 B4** 39 35N 3 22 E
Cala Ratjada, *Spain* **38 B4** 39 43N 3 27 E
Cala Santa Galdana, *Spain* **38 B4** 39 56N 3 58 E
Calabanga, *Phil.* **80 E4** 13 42N 123 17 E
Calabar, *Nigeria* **113 E6** 4 57N 8 20 E
Calabogie, *Canada* **151 A8** 45 18N 76 43W
Calabozo, *Venezuela* **168 B4** 9 0N 67 28W
Calábria □, *Italy* **47 C9** 39 0N 16 30 E
Calaburras, Pta. de, *Spain* **43 J6** 36 30N 4 38W
Calaceite, *Spain* **40 D5** 41 1N 0 11 E
Calacoto, *Bolivia* **172 D4** 17 16 S 68 38W
Calacuccia, *France* **29 F13** 42 21N 9 1 E
Calafat, *Romania* **52 G7** 43 58N 22 59 E
Calafate, *Argentina* **176 D2** 50 19 S 72 15W
Calafell, *Spain* **40 D6** 41 11N 1 34 E
Calagua Is., *Phil.* **80 D4** 14 30N 122 55 E
Calahorra, *Spain* **40 C3** 42 18N 1 59W
Calai, *Angola* **115 F3** 17 47 S 19 41 E
Calais, *France* **27 B8** 50 57N 1 56 E
Calais, *U.S.A.* **149 C12** 45 11N 67 17W
Calalaste, Cord. de, *Argentina* **174 B2** 25 0 S 67 0W
Calama, *Brazil* **173 B5** 8 0 S 62 50W
Calama, *Chile* **174 A2** 22 30 S 68 55W
Calamar, *Bolívar, Colombia* **168 A3** 10 15N 74 55W
Calamar, *Vaupés, Colombia* **168 C3** 1 58N 72 32W
Calamarca, *Bolivia* **172 D4** 16 55 S 68 9W
Calamba, *Cavite, Phil.* **80 D3** 14 13N 121 10 E
Calamba, *Mis. Occ., Phil.* **81 G4** 8 35N 123 39 E
Calamian Group, *Phil.* **81 F2** 11 50N 119 55 E
Calamocha, *Spain* **40 E3** 40 50N 1 17W
Calamonte, *Spain* **43 G4** 38 53N 6 23W
Călan, *Romania* **52 E7** 45 44N 22 59 E
Calañas, *Spain* **43 H4** 37 40N 6 53W
Calanda, *Spain* **40 E4** 40 56N 0 15W
Calandagan I., *Phil.* **81 F3** 10 39N 120 15 E
Calandula, *Angola* **115 D3** 9 6 S 15 57 E
Calang, *Indonesia* **84 B1** 4 37N 95 37 E
Calangiánus, *Italy* **46 B2** 40 56N 9 11 E
Calanscio, Sarīr, *Libya* **108 C4** 27 0N 21 30 E
Calapan, *Phil.* **80 E3** 13 25N 121 7 E
Călărasi, *Moldova* **53 C13** 47 16N 28 19 E
Călăraşi, *Romania* **53 F12** 44 12N 27 20 E
Călăraşi □, *Romania* **53 F12** 44 10N 27 0 E
Calasparra, *Spain* **41 G3** 38 14N 1 41W
Calatafimi, *Italy* **46 E5** 37 55N 12 52 E
Calatagan, *Phil.* **80 E3** 13 50N 120 38 E
Calatayud, *Spain* **40 D3** 41 20N 1 40W
Călăţele, *Romania* **52 D8** 46 46N 23 1 E
Calato = Kálathos, *Greece* **38 E12** 36 9N 28 8 E
Calatrava, *Eq. Guin.* **114 B1** 1 6N 9 25 E
Calauag, *Phil.* **80 E4** 13 55N 122 15 E
Calavà, C., *Italy* **47 D7** 38 11N 14 55 E
Calavite, C., *Phil.* **80 E3** 13 26N 120 20 E
Calavite Pass, *Phil.* **80 E3** 13 36N 120 25 E
Calayan, *Phil.* **80 B3** 19 16N 121 28 E
Calayan I., *Phil.* **80 B3** 19 20N 121 27 E
Calbayog, *Phil.* **80 E5** 12 4N 124 38 E
Calbiga, *Phil.* **81 F5** 11 38N 125 0 E
Calca, *Peru* **172 C3** 13 22 S 72 0W
Calcasieu L., *U.S.A.* **155 L8** 29 55N 93 18W
Calcutta = Kolkata, *India* **93 H13** 22 36N 88 24 E
Calcutta, *U.S.A.* **150 F4** 40 40N 80 34W
Caldaro, *Italy* **45 B8** 46 25N 11 14 E
Caldas □, *Colombia* **168 B2** 5 15N 75 30W
Caldas da Rainha, *Portugal* **43 F1** 39 24N 9 8W
Caldas de Reis, *Spain* **42 C2** 42 36N 8 39W
Caldas Novas, *Brazil* **171 E2** 17 45 S 48 38W
Calder →, *U.K.* **20 D6** 53 44N 1 22W
Caldera, *Chile* **174 B1** 27 5 S 70 55W
Caldwell, *Idaho, U.S.A.* **158 E5** 43 40N 116 41W
Caldwell, *Kans., U.S.A.* **155 G6** 37 2N 97 37W
Caldwell, *Tex., U.S.A.* **155 K6** 30 32N 96 42W
Caledon, *S. Africa* **116 E2** 34 14 S 19 26 E
Caledon →, *S. Africa* **116 E4** 30 31 S 26 5 E
Caledon B., *Australia* **126 A2** 12 45 S 137 0 E
Caledonia, *Canada* **150 C5** 43 7N 79 58W
Caledonia, *Mo., U.S.A.* **156 G6** 37 45N 90 46W
Caledonia, *N.Y., U.S.A.* **150 D7** 42 58N 77 51W
Calella, *Spain* **40 D7** 41 37N 2 40 E
Calemba, *Angola* **116 B2** 16 0 S 15 44 E
Calen, *Australia* **126 J6** 20 56 S 148 48 E
Calenzana, *France* **29 F12** 42 31N 8 51 E
Caleta Olivia, *Argentina* **176 C3** 46 25 S 67 25W
Caletones, *Chile* **174 C1** 34 6 S 70 27W
Calexico, *U.S.A.* **161 N11** 32 40N 115 30W
Calf of Man, *U.K.* **20 C3** 54 3N 4 48W
Calgary, *Canada* **142 C6** 51 0N 114 10W
Calheta, *Azores* **9 d1** 38 36N 28 1W
Calheta, *Madeira* **9 c** 32 44N 17 11W
Calheta de Nesquim, *Azores* **9 d1** 38 24N 28 5W
Calhoun, *U.S.A.* **149 H3** 34 30N 84 57W
Calhoun Falls, *U.S.A.* **152 A7** 34 6N 82 36W
Cali, *Colombia* **168 C2** 3 25N 76 35W
Calicut, *India* **95 J2** 11 15N 75 43 E
Caliente, *U.S.A.* **159 H6** 37 37N 114 31W
California, *Mo., U.S.A.* **156 F4** 38 38N 92 34W
California, *Pa., U.S.A.* **150 F5** 40 4N 79 54W
California □, *U.S.A.* **160 H7** 37 30N 119 30W
California, Baja, *Mexico* **162 A1** 32 10N 115 12W
California, Baja, T.N. = Baja California □, *Mexico* **162 B2** 30 0N 115 0W
California, Baja, T.S. = Baja California Sur □, *Mexico* **162 B2** 25 50N 111 50W
California, G. de, *Mexico* **162 B2** 27 0N 111 0W
California City, *U.S.A.* **161 K9** 35 10N 117 55W
California Hot Springs, *U.S.A.* **161 K8** 35 51N 118 41W
Călimăneşti, *Romania* **53 E9** 45 14N 24 20 E
Călimani, Munţii, *Romania* **53 C10** 47 12N 25 0 E
Calingasta, *Argentina* **174 C2** 31 15 S 69 30W
Calinog, *Phil.* **81 F4** 11 7N 122 32 E
Calintaan, *Phil.* **80 E3** 12 35N 120 57 E
Calipatria, *U.S.A.* **161 M11** 33 8N 115 31W
Calistoga, *U.S.A.* **160 G4** 38 35N 122 35W
Calitri, *Italy* **47 B8** 40 54N 15 26 E

Capivara, Serra da 197

Calitzdorp, *S. Africa* **116 E3** 33 33 S 21 42 E
Callabonna, L., *Australia* **127 D3** 29 40 S 140 5 E
Callac, *France* **26 D3** 48 25N 3 27W
Callahan, *U.S.A.* **152 E8** 30 34N 81 50W
Callan, *Ireland* **23 D4** 52 32N 7 24W
Callander, *U.K.* **22 E4** 56 15N 4 13W
Callao, *Peru* **172 C2** 12 0 S 77 0W
Callaway, *U.S.A.* **152 E4** 30 8N 85 36W
Calles, *Mexico* **163 C5** 23 2N 98 42W
Callicoon, *U.S.A.* **151 E9** 41 46N 75 3W
Calling Lake, *Canada* **142 B6** 55 15N 113 12W
Calliope, *Australia* **126 C5** 24 0 S 151 16 E
Callosa de Ensarriá, *Spain* **41 G4** 38 40N 0 8W
Callosa de Segura, *Spain* **41 G4** 38 7N 0 53W
Calmar, *U.S.A.* **156 A5** 43 11N 91 52W
Calne, *U.K.* **21 F6** 51 26N 2 0W
Calola, *Angola* **116 B2** 16 25 S 17 48 E
Calolbon = San Andres, *Phil.* **80 E5** 13 36N 124 6 E
Calonge, *Spain* **40 D8** 41 52N 3 5 E
Caloocan, *Phil.* **80 D3** 14 39N 120 58 E
Caloosahatchee →, *U.S.A.* **153 J7** 26 31N 82 1W
Calore →, *Italy* **47 A7** 41 11N 14 28 E
Caloundra, *Australia* **127 D5** 26 45 S 153 10 E
Calpe, *Spain* **41 G5** 38 39N 0 3 E
Calpella, *U.S.A.* **160 F3** 39 14N 123 12W
Calpine, *U.S.A.* **160 F6** 39 40N 120 27W
Calstock, *Canada* **140 C3** 49 47N 84 9W
Caltabellotta, *Italy* **46 E6** 37 34N 13 13 E
Caltagirone, *Italy* **47 E7** 37 14N 14 31 E
Caltanissetta, *Italy* **47 E7** 37 29N 14 4 E
Çaltılıbük, *Turkey* **51 G12** 39 57N 28 36 E
Caluango, *Angola* **115 D3** 8 20 S 19 39 E
Calubian, *Phil.* **81 F5** 11 27N 124 26 E
Calucinga, *Angola* **115 E3** 11 18 S 16 12 E
Caluire-et-Cuire, *France* **27 G11** 45 48N 4 52 E
Calulo, *Angola* **115 E2** 10 1 S 14 56 E
Calunda, *Angola* **115 E4** 12 7 S 23 36 E
Caluquembe, *Angola* **115 E2** 13 47 S 14 44 E
Caluso, *Italy* **44 C4** 45 18N 7 53 E
Caluya I., *Phil.* **81 F3** 11 55N 121 34 E
Calvados □, *France* **26 C6** 49 5N 0 15W
Calvert →, *Australia* **126 B2** 16 17 S 137 44 E
Calvert I., *Canada* **142 C3** 51 30N 128 0W
Calvert Ra., *Australia* **124 D3** 24 0 S 122 30 E
Calvi, *France* **29 F12** 42 34N 8 45 E
Calviá, *Spain* **38 B3** 39 34N 2 31 E
Calvillo, *Mexico* **162 C4** 21 51N 102 43W
Calvinia, *S. Africa* **116 E2** 31 28 S 19 45 E
Calvo = Calvo, Mte., *Italy* **45 G12** 41 44N 15 46 E
Calvo, Mte., *Italy* **45 G12** 41 44N 15 46 E
Calwa, *U.S.A.* **160 J7** 36 42N 119 46W
Calzada Almuradiel = Almuradiel, *Spain* **43 G7** 38 32N 3 28W
Calzada de Calatrava, *Spain* **43 G7** 38 42N 3 46W
Cam →, *U.K.* **21 E8** 52 21N 0 16 E
Cam Lam, *Vietnam* **87 G7** 11 54N 109 10 E
Cam Pha, *Vietnam* **76 G6** 21 7N 107 18 E
Cam Ranh, *Vietnam* **87 G7** 11 54N 109 12 E
Cam Xuyen, *Vietnam* **86 C6** 18 15N 106 0 E
Camabatela, *Angola* **115 D3** 8 20 S 15 26 E
Camacã, *Brazil* **171 E4** 15 24 S 39 30W
Camaçari, *Brazil* **171 D4** 12 41 S 38 18W
Camacha, *Madeira* **9 c** 32 41N 16 49W
Camacho, *Mexico* **162 C4** 24 25N 102 18W
Camacupa, *Angola* **115 E3** 11 58 S 17 22 E
Camaguán, *Venezuela* **168 B4** 8 6N 67 36W
Camagüey, *Cuba* **164 B4** 21 20N 78 0W
Camaiore, *Italy* **44 E7** 43 56N 10 18 E
Camamu, *Brazil* **171 D4** 13 57 S 39 7W
Camaná, *Peru* **172 D3** 16 30 S 72 50W
Camanche, *U.S.A.* **156 C6** 41 47N 90 15W
Camanche Reservoir, *U.S.A.* **160 G6** 38 14N 121 1W
Camapuã, *Brazil* **173 D7** 19 30 S 54 5W
Camaquã, *Brazil* **175 C5** 30 51 S 51 49W
Camaquã →, *Brazil* **175 C5** 31 17 S 51 47W
Câmara de Lobos, *Madeira* **9 c** 32 39N 16 59W
Camararé →, *Brazil* **173 C6** 12 15 S 58 55W
Camarat, C., *France* **29 E10** 43 12N 6 41 E
Camarès, *France* **28 E6** 43 49N 2 53 E
Camaret-sur-Mer, *France* **26 D2** 48 16N 4 37W
Camargo, *Bolivia* **173 E4** 20 38 S 65 15W
Camargo, *Mexico* **163 B5** 26 19N 98 50W
Camargue, *France* **29 E8** 43 34N 4 34 E
Camarillo, *U.S.A.* **161 L7** 34 13N 119 2W
Camariñas, *Spain* **42 B1** 43 8N 9 12W
Camarines Norte □, *Phil.* **80 D4** 14 10N 122 45 E
Camarines Sur □, *Phil.* **80 E4** 13 40N 123 20 E
Camarón, C., *Honduras* **164 C2** 16 0N 85 5W
Camarones, *Argentina* **176 B3** 44 50 S 65 40W
Camarones, B., *Argentina* **176 B3** 44 45 S 65 35W
Camas, *Spain* **43 H4** 37 24N 6 2W
Camas, *U.S.A.* **160 E4** 45 35N 122 24W
Camas Valley, *U.S.A.* **158 E2** 43 2N 123 40W
Camatambo, *Angola* **115 D3** 6 31 S 15 21 E
Camaxilo, *Angola* **115 D3** 8 21 S 18 56 E
Camba Cassai, *Angola* **115 D3** 9 47 S 19 9 E
Camballin, *Australia* **124 C3** 17 59 S 124 12 E
Cambamba, *Angola* **115 D2** 8 53 S 14 44 E
Cambará, *Brazil* **175 A5** 23 2 S 50 5W
Cambay = Khambhat, *India* **92 H5** 22 23N 72 33 E
Cambay, G. of = Khambhat, G. of, *India* **89 C6** 20 45N 72 30 E
Cambil, *Spain* **43 H7** 37 40N 3 33W
Cambo, *Angola* **115 D3** 10 55 S 20 6 E
Cambo-les-Bains, *France* **28 E2** 43 22N 1 23W
Cambodia ■, *Asia* **86 F5** 12 15N 105 0 E
Camborne, *U.K.* **21 G2** 50 12N 5 19W
Cambrai, *Australia* **128 C3** 34 40 S 139 16 E
Cambrai, *France* **27 B10** 50 11N 3 14 E
Cambre, *Spain* **42 B2** 43 17N 8 20W
Cambria, *U.S.A.* **160 K5** 35 34N 121 5W
Cambrian Mts., *U.K.* **21 E4** 52 3N 3 57W
Cambridge, *Canada* **140 D3** 43 23N 80 15W
Cambridge, *Jamaica* **164 a** 18 18N 77 54W
Cambridge, *N.Z.* **130 D4** 37 54 S 175 29 E
Cambridge, *U.K.* **21 E8** 52 12N 0 8 E
Cambridge, *Ill., U.S.A.* **156 C6** 41 18N 90 12W
Cambridge, *Iowa, U.S.A.* **156 C3** 41 54N 93 32W
Cambridge, *Mass., U.S.A.* **151 D13** 42 22N 71 6W
Cambridge, *Minn., U.S.A.* **154 C8** 45 34N 93 13W
Cambridge, *N.Y., U.S.A.* **151 C11** 43 2N 73 22W
Cambridge, *Nebr., U.S.A.* **154 E4** 40 17N 100 10W
Cambridge, *Ohio, U.S.A.* **150 F3** 40 2N 81 35W
Cambridge Bay = Ikaluktutiak, *Canada* **138 B9** 69 10N 105 0W
Cambridge City, *U.S.A.* **157 E11** 39 49N 85 10W
Cambridge G., *Australia* **124 B4** 14 55 S 128 15 E
Cambridge Springs, *U.S.A.* **150 E4** 41 48N 80 4W
Cambridgeshire □, *U.K.* **21 E7** 52 25N 0 7W
Cambrils, *Spain* **40 D6** 41 8N 1 3 E
Cambuci, *Brazil* **171 F3** 21 35 S 41 55W
Cambulo, *Angola* **115 D4** 7 49 S 21 15 E
Cambundi-Catembo, *Angola* **115 E3** 10 10 S 17 35 E
Camden, *Australia* **129 C9** 34 1 S 150 43 E
Camden, *Ala., U.S.A.* **149 K2** 31 59N 87 17W
Camden, *Ark., U.S.A.* **155 J8** 33 35N 92 50W
Camden, *Maine, U.S.A.* **149 C11** 44 13N 69 4W
Camden, *N.J., U.S.A.* **151 G9** 39 56N 75 7W
Camden, *N.Y., U.S.A.* **151 C9** 43 20N 75 45W
Camden, *Ohio, U.S.A.* **157 E12** 39 38N 84 39W
Camden, *S.C., U.S.A.* **149 H5** 34 16N 80 36W
Camden Bay, *U.S.A.* **144 A11** 70 10N 145 15W
Camden Sd., *Australia* **124 C3** 15 27 S 124 25 E
Camdenton, *U.S.A.* **155 F8** 38 1N 92 45W
Cameia, Parque Nacional da, *Angola* **115 E4** 12 5 S 21 40 E
Çameli, *Turkey* **49 D11** 37 5N 29 24 E
Camenca, *Moldova* **53 B13** 48 3N 28 42 E
Camerino, *Italy* **45 E10** 43 8N 13 4 E
Cameron, *Ariz., U.S.A.* **159 J8** 35 53N 111 25W
Cameron, *La., U.S.A.* **155 L8** 29 48N 93 20W
Cameron, *Mo., U.S.A.* **156 E2** 39 44N 94 14W
Cameron, *S.C., U.S.A.* **152 B9** 33 34N 80 43W
Cameron, *Tex., U.S.A.* **155 K6** 30 51N 96 59W
Cameron Highlands, *Malaysia* **87 K3** 4 27N 101 22 E
Cameron Hills, *Canada* **142 B5** 59 48N 118 0W
Cameron Mts., *N.Z.* **131 G1** 46 1 S 167 0 E
Cameroon ■, *Africa* **114 A2** 6 0N 12 30 E
Camerota, *Italy* **47 B8** 40 2N 15 22 E
Cameroun →, *Cameroon* **113 E6** 4 0N 9 35 E
Cameroun, Mt., *Cameroon* **113 E6** 4 13N 9 10 E
Cametá, *Brazil* **170 B2** 2 12 S 49 30W
Çamiçi Gölü, *Turkey* **49 D9** 37 29N 27 28 E
Camiguin □, *Phil.* **81 G5** 9 11N 124 42 E
Camiguin I., *Phil.* **80 B3** 18 56N 121 55 E
Camiling, *Phil.* **80 D3** 15 42N 120 24 E
Camilla, *U.S.A.* **152 D5** 31 14N 84 12W
Caminha, *Portugal* **42 D2** 41 50N 8 50W
Camino, *U.S.A.* **160 G6** 38 44N 120 41W
Camira Creek, *Australia* **127 D5** 29 15 S 152 58 E
Camiranga, *Brazil* **170 B2** 1 48 S 46 17W
Camiri, *Bolivia* **173 E5** 20 3 S 63 31W
Camissombo, *Angola* **115 D4** 8 7 S 20 38 E
Cammal, *U.S.A.* **150 E7** 41 24N 77 28W
Cammarata, *Italy* **46 E6** 37 38N 13 38 E
Camocim, *Brazil* **170 B3** 2 55 S 40 50W
Camooweal, *Australia* **126 B2** 19 56 S 138 7 E
Camooweal Caves Nat. Park, *Australia* **126 C2** 20 1 S 138 11 E
Camopi, *Fr. Guiana* **169 C7** 3 12N 52 17W
Camopi →, *Fr. Guiana* **169 C7** 3 10N 52 20W
Camorta, *India* **95 K11** 8 8N 93 30 E
Camotes Is., *Phil.* **81 F5** 10 40N 124 24 E
Camotes Sea, *Phil.* **81 F5** 10 30N 124 15 E
Camp Borden, *Canada* **150 B5** 44 18N 79 56W
Camp Hill, *Ala., U.S.A.* **152 C4** 32 48N 85 39W
Camp Hill, *Pa., U.S.A.* **150 F8** 40 14N 76 55W
Camp Nelson, *U.S.A.* **161 J8** 36 8N 118 39W
Camp Pendleton, *U.S.A.* **161 M9** 33 16N 117 23W
Camp Point, *U.S.A.* **156 D5** 40 3N 91 4W
Camp Verde, *U.S.A.* **159 J8** 34 34N 111 51W
Camp Wood, *U.S.A.* **155 L5** 29 40N 100 1W
Campagna, *Italy* **47 B8** 40 40N 15 6 E
Campana, *Argentina* **174 C4** 34 10 S 58 55W
Campana, I., *Chile* **176 C1** 48 20 S 75 20W
Campanário, *Madeira* **9 c** 32 39N 17 2W
Campanario, *Spain* **43 G5** 38 52N 5 36W
Campánia □, *Italy* **47 B7** 41 0N 14 30 E
Campbell, *S. Africa* **116 D3** 28 48 S 23 44 E
Campbell, *Calif., U.S.A.* **160 H5** 37 17N 121 57W
Campbell, *Ohio, U.S.A.* **150 E4** 41 5N 80 37W
Campbell, C., *N.Z.* **131 B9** 41 47 S 174 18 E
Campbell I., *Pac. Oc.* **134 N8** 52 30 S 169 0 E
Campbell L., *Canada* **143 A7** 63 14N 106 55W
Campbell River, *Canada* **142 C3** 50 5N 125 20W
Campbell Town, *Australia* **127 G4** 41 52 S 147 30 E
Campbellford, *Canada* **150 B7** 44 18N 77 48W
Campbellpur, *Pakistan* **92 C5** 33 46N 72 26 E
Campbellsburg, *U.S.A.* **157 F10** 38 39N 86 16W
Campbellsville, *U.S.A.* **148 G3** 37 21N 85 20W
Campbellton, *Canada* **141 C6** 47 57N 66 43W
Campbellton, *U.S.A.* **152 E4** 30 57N 85 24W
Campbelltown, *Australia* **129 C9** 34 4 S 150 49 E
Campbeltown, *U.K.* **22 F3** 55 26N 5 36W
Campeche, *Mexico* **163 D6** 19 50N 90 32W
Campeche □, *Mexico* **163 D6** 19 50N 90 32W
Campeche, Golfo de, *Mexico* **163 D6** 19 30N 93 0W
Campello, *Spain* **41 G4** 38 26N 0 24W
Câmpeni, *Romania* **52 D8** 46 22N 23 3 E
Camperdown, *Australia* **128 E5** 38 14 S 143 9 E
Camperville, *Canada* **143 C8** 51 59N 100 9W
Campi Salentina, *Italy* **47 B11** 40 24N 18 1 E
Câmpia Turzii, *Romania* **53 D8** 46 34N 23 53 E
Campidano, *Italy* **46 C1** 39 30N 8 47 E
Campíglia Maríttima, *Italy* **44 E7** 43 4N 10 37 E
Campillo de Altobuey, *Spain* **41 F3** 39 36N 1 49W
Campillos, *Spain* **43 H6** 37 4N 4 51W
Câmpina, *Romania* **53 E10** 45 10N 25 45 E
Campina Grande, *Brazil* **170 C4** 7 20 S 35 47W
Campina Verde, *Brazil* **171 E2** 19 31 S 49 28W
Campinas, *Brazil* **175 A6** 22 50 S 47 0W
Campli, *Italy* **45 F10** 42 43N 13 41 E
Campo = Ntem →, *Cameroon* **114 B2** 2 21N 9 49 E
Campo, *Cameroon* **114 B1** 2 22N 9 50 E
Campo, *Spain* **40 C5** 42 25N 0 24 E
Campo, Réserve de, *Cameroon* **114 B2** 2 23N 10 5 E
Campo Belo, *Brazil* **171 F2** 20 52 S 45 16W
Campo de Criptana, *Spain* **43 F7** 39 24N 3 7W
Campo de Diauarum, *Brazil* **173 C7** 11 12 S 53 14W
Campo de Gibraltar, *Spain* **43 J5** 36 15N 5 25W
Campo Flórido, *Brazil* **171 E2** 19 47 S 48 35W
Campo Formoso, *Brazil* **170 D3** 10 30 S 40 20W
Campo Grande, *Brazil* **173 E7** 20 25 S 54 40W
Campo Maíor, *Brazil* **170 B3** 4 50 S 42 12W
Campo Maior, *Portugal* **43 F3** 39 2N 7 7W
Campo Mourão, *Brazil* **175 A5** 24 3 S 52 22W
Campo Tencia, *Switz.* **33 D7** 46 26N 8 43 E
Campo Túres, *Italy* **45 B8** 46 53N 11 55 E
Campoalegre, *Colombia* **168 C2** 2 41N 75 20W
Campobasso, *Italy* **47 A7** 41 34N 14 39 E
Campobello di Licata, *Italy* **46 E6** 37 15N 13 55 E
Campobello di Mazara, *Italy* **46 E5** 37 38N 12 45 E
Campofelice di Roccella, *Italy* **46 E6** 37 59N 13 53 E
Campomarino, *Italy* **45 G12** 41 57N 15 2 E
Camporeale, *Italy* **46 E6** 37 54N 13 6 E
Camporrobles, *Spain* **40 F3** 39 39N 1 24W
Campos, *Brazil* **171 F3** 21 50 S 41 20W
Campos Altos, *Brazil* **171 E2** 19 47 S 46 10W
Campos Belos, *Brazil* **171 D2** 13 10 S 47 3W
Campos del Port, *Spain* **38 B4** 39 26N 3 1 E
Campos Novos, *Brazil* **175 B5** 27 21 S 51 50W
Campos Sales, *Brazil* **170 C3** 7 4 S 40 23W
Camprodón, *Spain* **40 C7** 42 19N 2 23 E
Campton, *Fla., U.S.A.* **153 E3** 30 53N 86 31W
Campton, *Ga., U.S.A.* **152 B6** 33 52N 83 43W
Campton, *Ky., U.S.A.* **157 G13** 37 44N 83 33W
Camptonville, *U.S.A.* **160 F5** 39 27N 121 3W
Camptown, *U.S.A.* **151 E8** 41 44N 76 14W
Câmpulung, *Argeş, Romania* **53 E10** 45 17N 25 3 E
Câmpulung, *Suceava, Romania* **53 C10** 47 32N 25 30 E
Câmpuri, *Romania* **53 D11** 46 0N 26 50 E
Campuya →, *Peru* **168 D3** 1 40 S 73 30W
Campville, *U.S.A.* **152 F7** 29 40N 82 7W
Camrose, *Canada* **142 C6** 53 0N 112 50W
Camsell Portage, *Canada* **143 B7** 59 37N 109 15W
Camucuio, *Angola* **115 E2** 14 7 S 13 15 E
Çamyuva, *Turkey* **49 E12** 36 30N 30 30 E
Çan, *Turkey* **51 F11** 40 2N 27 3 E
Can Clavo, *Spain* **38 D1** 38 57N 1 27 E
Can Creu, *Spain* **38 D1** 38 58N 1 28 E
Can Gio, *Vietnam* **87 G6** 10 25N 106 58 E
Can Tho, *Vietnam* **87 G5** 10 2N 105 46 E
Canaan, *U.S.A.* **151 D11** 42 2N 73 20W
Canacona, *India* **95 G2** 15 1N 74 4 E
Canada ■, *N. Amer.* **138 C10** 60 0N 100 0W
Cañada de Gómez, *Argentina* **174 C3** 32 40 S 61 30W
Canadian, *U.S.A.* **155 H4** 35 55N 100 23W
Canadian →, *U.S.A.* **155 H7** 35 28N 95 3W
Canadys, *U.S.A.* **152 B9** 33 3N 80 37W
Canajoharie, *U.S.A.* **151 D10** 42 54N 74 35W
Çanakkale, *Turkey* **51 F10** 40 8N 26 24 E
Çanakkale □, *Turkey* **51 F10** 40 10N 26 25 E
Çanakkale Boğazı, *Turkey* **51 F10** 40 17N 26 32 E
Canal Flats, *Canada* **142 C5** 50 10N 115 48W
Canal Point, *U.S.A.* **153 J9** 26 52N 80 38W
Canala, *N. Cal.* **133 U19** 21 32 S 165 57 E
Canalejas, *Argentina* **174 D2** 35 15 S 66 34W
Canals, *Argentina* **174 C3** 33 35 S 62 53W
Canals, *Spain* **41 G4** 38 58N 0 35W
Canandaigua, *U.S.A.* **150 D7** 42 54N 77 17W
Canandaigua L., *U.S.A.* **150 D7** 42 47N 77 19W
Cananea, *Mexico* **162 A2** 31 0N 110 20W
Cañar, *Ecuador* **168 D2** 2 33 S 78 56W
Cañar □, *Ecuador* **168 D2** 2 30 S 79 0W
Canarias, Is., *Atl. Oc.* **9 e1** 28 30N 16 0W
Canaries, *St. Lucia* **165 f** 13 55N 61 4W
Canarreos, Arch. de los, *Cuba* **164 B3** 21 35N 81 40W
Canary Is. = Canarias, Is., *Atl. Oc.* **9 e1** 28 30N 16 0W
Canaseraga, *U.S.A.* **150 D7** 42 27N 77 45W
Canastra, Serra da, *Brazil* **171 F2** 20 0 S 46 20W
Canatlán, *Mexico* **162 C4** 24 31N 104 47W
Cañaveral, *Peru* **168 D1** 3 56 S 80 39W
Canaveral, C., *U.S.A.* **149 L5** 28 27N 80 32W
Cañaveruelas, *Spain* **40 E2** 40 24N 2 38W
Canavieiras, *Brazil* **171 E4** 15 39 S 39 0W
Canbelego, *Australia* **129 A7** 31 32 S 146 18 E
Canberra, *Australia* **129 C8** 35 15 S 149 8 E
Canby, *Calif., U.S.A.* **158 F3** 41 27N 120 52W
Canby, *Minn., U.S.A.* **154 C6** 44 43N 96 16W
Canby, *Oreg., U.S.A.* **160 E4** 45 16N 122 42W
Cancale, *France* **26 D5** 48 40N 1 50W
Canche →, *France* **27 B8** 50 31N 1 39 E
Canchyuaya, Cordillera de, *Peru* **172 B3** 7 30 S 74 0W
Cancún, *Mexico* **163 C7** 21 8N 86 44W
Candala, *Somali Rep.* **120 B3** 11 30N 49 58 E
Candanchu, *Spain* **40 C4** 42 47N 0 32W
Candarave, *Peru* **172 D3** 17 15 S 70 13W
Çandarlı, *Turkey* **49 C8** 38 56N 26 56 E
Çandarlı Körfezi, *Turkey* **49 C8** 38 52N 26 55 E
Candas, *Spain* **42 B5** 43 35N 5 45W
Candé, *France* **26 E5** 47 34N 1 2W
Candeias →, *Brazil* **173 B5** 8 39 S 63 31W
Candela, *Italy* **47 A8** 41 8N 15 31 E
Candelaria, *Argentina* **175 B4** 27 29 S 55 44W
Candelaria, *Canary Is.* **9 e1** 28 22N 16 22W
Candelaria, *Phil.* **80 E3** 13 56N 121 25 E
Candeleda, *Spain* **42 E5** 40 10N 5 14W
Candelo, *Australia* **129 D8** 36 47 S 149 43 E
Candi Dasa, *Indonesia* **79 J18** 8 30 S 115 34 E
Candia = Iráklion, *Greece* **39 E6** 35 20N 25 12 E
Candia, Sea of = Crete, Sea of, *Greece* **49 E7** 36 0N 25 0 E
Cândido de Abreu, *Brazil* **171 F1** 24 35 S 51 20W
Cândido Mendes, *Brazil* **170 B2** 1 27 S 45 43W
Candle, *U.S.A.* **144 D7** 65 55N 161 56W
Candle L., *Canada* **143 C7** 53 50N 105 18W
Candlemas I., *Antarctica* **7 B1** 57 3 S 26 40W
Cando, *U.S.A.* **154 A5** 48 32N 99 12W
Candon, *Phil.* **80 C3** 17 12N 120 27 E
Canea = Khaniá, *Greece* **39 E5** 35 30N 24 4 E
Canela, *Brazil* **170 D2** 10 15 S 48 25W
Canelli, *Italy* **44 D5** 44 43N 8 17 E
Canelones, *Uruguay* **175 C4** 34 32 S 56 17W
Canet-Plage, *France* **28 F7** 42 41N 3 2 E
Cañete, *Chile* **174 D1** 37 50 S 73 30W
Cañete, *Peru* **172 C2** 13 8 S 76 30W
Cañete, *Spain* **40 E3** 40 3N 1 54W
Cañete de las Torres, *Spain* **43 H6** 37 53N 4 19W
Cangamba, *Angola* **115 E3** 13 40 S 19 54 E
Cangandala, *Angola* **115 D3** 9 45 S 16 33 E
Cangandala, Parque Nacional da, *Angola* **115 D3** 9 53 S 16 42 E
Cangas, *Spain* **42 C2** 42 16N 8 47W
Cangas de Narcea, *Spain* **42 B4** 43 10N 6 32W
Cangas de Onís, *Spain* **42 B5** 43 21N 5 8W
Cangnan, *China* **77 D13** 27 30N 120 23 E
Cangoa, *Angola* **115 E3** 13 8 S 18 30 E
Cangola, *Angola* **115 D3** 7 58 S 15 53 E
Cangolo, *Angola* **115 E2** 15 0 S 13 52 E
Cangombe, *Angola* **115 E3** 14 24 S 19 59 E
Cangongo, *Angola* **115 D3** 9 24 S 17 30 E
Canguaretama, *Brazil* **170 C4** 6 20 S 35 5W
Canguçu, *Brazil* **175 C5** 31 22 S 52 43W
Canguçu, Serra do, *Brazil* **175 C5** 31 20 S 52 40W
Cangumbe, *Angola* **115 E3** 11 58 S 19 12 E
Cangwu, *China* **77 F8** 23 25N 111 17 E
Cangxi, *China* **76 B5** 31 47N 105 59 E
Cangyuan, *China* **76 F2** 23 12N 99 14 E
Cangzhou, *China* **74 E9** 38 19N 116 52 E
Canhoca, *Angola* **115 D2** 9 15 S 14 41 E
Cani, I., *Tunisia* **108 A2** 37 21N 10 5 E
Caniapiscau →, *Canada* **141 A6** 56 40N 69 30W
Caniapiscau, Rés. de, *Canada* **141 B6** 54 10N 69 55W
Canicattì, *Italy* **46 E6** 37 21N 13 51 E
Canicattini Bagni, *Italy* **47 E8** 37 2N 15 4 E
Canigao Channel, *Phil.* **81 F5** 10 15N 124 42 E
Caniles, *Spain* **43 H8** 37 26N 2 43W
Canim Lake, *Canada* **142 C4** 51 47N 120 54W
Canindé, *Brazil* **170 B4** 4 22 S 39 19W
Canindé →, *Brazil* **170 C3** 6 15 S 42 52W
Canindeyu □, *Paraguay* **175 A5** 24 10 S 55 0W
Canino, *Italy* **45 F8** 42 28N 11 45 E
Canisteo, *U.S.A.* **150 D7** 42 16N 77 36W
Canisteo →, *U.S.A.* **150 D7** 42 7N 77 8W
Cañitas, *Mexico* **162 C4** 23 36N 102 43W
Cañizal, *Spain* **42 D5** 41 12N 5 22W
Canjáyar, *Spain* **43 H8** 37 1N 2 44W
Canjinge, *Angola* **115 E4** 10 12 S 21 17 E
Çankırı, *Turkey* **100 B5** 40 40N 33 37 E
Cankuzo, *Burundi* **118 C3** 3 10 S 30 31 E
Canlaon, *Phil.* **81 F4** 10 22N 123 12 E
Canlaon Volcano, *Phil.* **81 F4** 10 24N 123 8 E
Canmore, *Canada* **142 C5** 51 7N 115 18W
Cann River, *Australia* **129 D8** 37 35 S 149 7 E
Canna, *U.K.* **22 D2** 57 3N 6 33W
Cannanore, *India* **95 J2** 11 53N 75 27 E
Cannanore Is., *India* **95 J1** 10 30N 72 30 E
Cannelton, *U.S.A.* **157 G10** 37 55N 86 45W
Cannes, *France* **29 E11** 43 32N 7 1 E
Canning Town = Port Canning, *India* **93 H13** 22 23N 88 40 E
Cannington, *Canada* **150 B5** 44 20N 79 2W
Cannóbio, *Italy* **44 B5** 46 4N 8 42 E
Cannock, *U.K.* **21 E5** 52 41N 2 1W
Cannon Ball →, *U.S.A.* **154 B4** 46 20N 100 38W
Cannondale Mt., *Australia* **126 D4** 25 13 S 148 57 E
Cannonsville Reservoir, *U.S.A.* **151 D9** 42 4N 75 22W
Cannonvale, *Australia* **126 J6** 20 17 S 148 43 E
Caño Colorado, *Colombia* **168 C4** 2 18N 68 22W
Canoas, *Brazil* **175 B5** 29 56 S 51 11W
Canoe L., *Canada* **143 B7** 55 10N 108 15W
Canon City, *U.S.A.* **154 F2** 38 27N 105 14W
Canonniers Pt., *Mauritius* **121 d** 20 2 S 57 32 E
Canoochee →, *U.S.A.* **152 D8** 31 59N 81 19W
Canopus, *Australia* **128 B4** 33 29 S 140 42 E
Canora, *Canada* **143 C8** 51 40N 102 30W
Canosa di Púglia, *Italy* **47 A9** 41 13N 16 4 E
Canowindra, *Australia* **129 B8** 33 35 S 148 38 E
Canso, *Canada* **141 C7** 45 20N 61 0W
Canta, *Peru* **172 C2** 11 29 S 76 37W
Cantabria □, *Spain* **42 B7** 43 10N 4 0W
Cantabria, Sierra de, *Spain* **40 C2** 42 40N 2 30W
Cantabrian Mts. = Cantábrica, Cordillera, *Spain* **42 C5** 43 0N 5 10W
Cantábrica, Cordillera, *Spain* **42 C5** 43 0N 5 10W
Cantal □, *France* **28 C6** 45 5N 2 45 E
Cantal, Plomb du, *France* **28 C6** 45 3N 2 45 E
Cantanhede, *Portugal* **42 E2** 40 20N 8 36W
Cantaura, *Venezuela* **169 B5** 9 19N 64 21W
Cantavieja, *Spain* **40 E4** 40 31N 0 25W
Čantavir, *Serbia, Yug.* **52 E4** 45 55N 19 46 E
Cantemir, *Moldova* **53 D13** 46 17N 28 14 E
Canterbury, *Australia* **126 D3** 25 23 S 141 53 E
Canterbury, *U.K.* **21 F9** 51 16N 1 6 E
Canterbury □, *N.Z.* **131 D6** 43 45 S 171 19 E
Canterbury Bight, *N.Z.* **131 E6** 44 16 S 171 55 E
Canterbury Plains, *N.Z.* **131 D6** 43 55 S 171 22 E
Cantil, *U.S.A.* **161 K9** 35 18N 117 58W
Cantilan, *Phil.* **81 G5** 9 20N 125 58 E
Cantillana, *Spain* **43 H5** 37 36N 5 50W
Canto do Buriti, *Brazil* **170 C3** 8 7 S 42 58W
Canton = Guangzhou, *China* **77 F9** 23 5N 113 10 E
Canton, *Ga., U.S.A.* **149 H3** 34 14N 84 29W
Canton, *Ill., U.S.A.* **156 D6** 40 33N 90 2W
Canton, *Miss., U.S.A.* **155 J9** 32 37N 90 2W
Canton, *Mo., U.S.A.* **156 D5** 40 8N 91 32W
Canton, *N.Y., U.S.A.* **151 B9** 44 36N 75 10W
Canton, *Ohio, U.S.A.* **150 F3** 40 48N 81 23W
Canton, *Pa., U.S.A.* **150 E8** 41 39N 76 51W
Canton, *S. Dak., U.S.A.* **154 D6** 43 18N 96 35W
Canton L., *U.S.A.* **155 G5** 36 6N 98 35W
Cantonment, *U.S.A.* **153 E2** 30 37N 87 20W
Cantù, *Italy* **44 C6** 45 44N 9 8 E
Cantwell, *U.S.A.* **144 E10** 63 24N 148 57W
Canudos, *Brazil* **173 B6** 7 13 S 58 5W
Canumã, *Amazonas, Brazil* **169 D6** 4 2 S 59 4W
Canumã, *Amazonas, Brazil* **173 B5** 6 8 S 60 10W
Canumã →, *Brazil* **173 A6** 3 55 S 59 10W
Canunda Nat. Park, *Australia* **128 D4** 37 42 S 140 16 E
Canutama, *Brazil* **173 B5** 6 30 S 64 20W
Canutillo, *U.S.A.* **159 L10** 31 55N 106 36W
Canvey, *U.K.* **21 F8** 51 31N 0 37 E
Canyon, *U.S.A.* **155 H4** 34 59N 101 55W
Canyonlands Nat. Park, *U.S.A.* **159 G9** 38 15N 110 0W
Canyonville, *U.S.A.* **158 E2** 42 56N 123 17W
Canzar, *Angola* **115 D4** 7 35 S 21 34 E
Cao Bang, *Vietnam* **76 F6** 22 40N 106 15 E
Cao He →, *China* **75 D13** 40 10N 124 32 E
Cao Lanh, *Vietnam* **87 G5** 10 27N 105 38 E
Cao Xian, *China* **74 G8** 34 50N 115 35 E
Caombo, *Angola* **115 D3** 8 42 S 16 33 E
Càorle, *Italy* **45 C9** 45 36N 12 53 E
Cap-aux-Meules, *Canada* **141 C7** 47 23N 61 52W
Cap-Chat, *Canada* **141 C6** 49 6N 66 40W
Cap-de-la-Madeleine, *Canada* **140 C5** 46 22N 72 31W
Cap-Haïtien, *Haiti* **165 C5** 19 40N 72 20W
Cap I., *Phil.* **81 J3** 5 57N 120 6 E
Cap Pt., *St. Lucia* **165 f** 14 7N 60 57W
Capac, *U.S.A.* **150 C2** 43 1N 82 56W
Capáccio, *Italy* **47 B8** 40 25N 15 5 E
Capaci, *Italy* **46 D6** 38 10N 13 14 E
Capaia, *Angola* **115 D4** 8 27 S 20 13 E
Capalonga, *Phil.* **80 D4** 14 20N 122 30 E
Capanaparo →, *Venezuela* **168 B4** 7 1N 67 7W
Capanema, *Brazil* **170 B2** 1 12 S 47 11W
Capangombe, *Angola* **115 F2** 15 6 S 13 8 E
Capánnori, *Italy* **44 E7** 43 50N 10 34 E
Caparo →, *Barinas, Venezuela* **168 B3** 7 46N 70 23W
Caparo →, *Bolívar, Venezuela* **169 B5** 7 30N 64 0W
Capatárida, *Venezuela* **168 A3** 11 11N 70 37W
Capayas, *Phil.* **81 F2** 10 28N 119 39 E
Capbreton, *France* **28 E2** 43 39N 1 26W
Capdenac, *France* **28 D6** 44 34N 2 5 E
Capdepera, *Spain* **38 B4** 39 42N 3 26 E
Cape →, *Australia* **126 C4** 20 59 S 146 51 E
Cape Arid Nat. Park, *Australia* **125 F3** 33 58 S 123 13 E
Cape Barren I., *Australia* **127 G4** 40 25 S 148 15 E
Cape Breton Highlands Nat. Park, *Canada* **141 C7** 46 50N 60 40W
Cape Breton I., *Canada* **141 C7** 46 0N 60 30W
Cape Canaveral, *U.S.A.* **153 G9** 28 24N 80 36W
Cape Charles, *U.S.A.* **148 G8** 37 16N 76 1W
Cape Coast, *Ghana* **113 D4** 5 5N 1 15W
Cape Coral, *U.S.A.* **149 M5** 26 33N 81 57W
Cape Dorset, *Canada* **139 B12** 64 14N 76 32W
Cape Fear →, *U.S.A.* **149 H6** 33 53N 78 1W
Cape Girardeau, *U.S.A.* **155 G10** 37 19N 89 32W
Cape Jervis, *Australia* **128 C3** 35 40 S 138 5 E
Cape Lee Nat. Park, *Australia* **125 F3** 33 54 S 122 26 E
Cape Lisburne = Wevok, *U.S.A.* **144 B6** 68 53N 166 13W
Cape May, *U.S.A.* **148 F8** 38 56N 74 56W
Cape May Point, *U.S.A.* **148 F8** 38 56N 74 58W
Cape Melville Nat. Park, *Australia* **126 A3** 14 26 S 144 28 E
Cape Mount Nat. Park, *Liberia* **112 D2** 6 44N 11 24W
Cape Peninsula Nat. Park, *S. Africa* **116 E2** 34 20 S 18 28 E
Cape Pole, *U.S.A.* **144 J14** 55 58N 133 48W
Cape Range Nat. Park, *Australia* **124 D1** 22 3 S 111 0 E
Cape Tormentine, *Canada* **141 C7** 46 8N 63 47W
Cape Town, *S. Africa* **116 E2** 33 55 S 18 22 E
Cape Tribulation Nat. Park, *Australia* **126 B4** 16 5 S 145 25 E
Cape Verde Is. ■, *Atl. Oc.* **8 E9** 16 0N 24 0W
Cape Vincent, *U.S.A.* **151 B8** 44 8N 76 20W
Cape Yakataga, *U.S.A.* **144 F12** 60 4N 142 26W
Cape York Peninsula, *Australia* **126 A3** 12 0 S 142 30 E
Capela, *Brazil* **170 D4** 10 30 S 37 0W
Capela de Campo, *Brazil* **170 B3** 4 40 S 41 55W
Capelas, *Azores* **9 d3** 37 50N 25 41W
Capele, *Angola* **115 E2** 13 39 S 14 53 E
Capelengue, *Angola* **115 D3** 8 53 S 19 42 E
Capelinha, *Brazil* **171 E3** 17 42 S 42 31W
Capelinhos, Pta. dos, *Azores* **9 d1** 38 36N 28 50W
Capella, *Australia* **126 C4** 23 2 S 148 1 E
Capella, Mt., *Papua N. G.* **132 C1** 5 4 S 141 8 E
Capelongo, *Angola* **115 E3** 14 54 S 15 8 E
Capenda Camulemba, *Angola* **115 D3** 9 24 S 18 27 E
Capendu, *France* **28 E6** 43 11N 2 31 E
Capertree, *Australia* **129 B8** 33 6 S 149 58 E
Capestang, *France* **28 E7** 43 20N 3 2 E
Capesterre, *Guadeloupe* **164 b** 15 53N 61 14W
Capesterre-Belle-Eau, *Guadeloupe* **164 b** 16 4N 61 36W
Capim, *Brazil* **170 B2** 1 41 S 47 47W
Capim →, *Brazil* **170 B2** 1 40 S 47 47W
Capinópolis, *Brazil* **171 E2** 18 41 S 49 35W
Capinota, *Bolivia* **172 D4** 17 43 S 66 14W
Capira, *Panama* **168 B2** 8 45N 79 53W
Capistrello, *Italy* **45 G10** 41 57N 13 23 E
Capitan, *U.S.A.* **159 K11** 33 35N 105 35W
Capitán Aracena, I., *Chile* **176 D2** 54 10 S 71 20W
Capitán Pastene, *Chile* **176 A2** 38 13 S 73 1W
Capitol Reef Nat. Park, *U.S.A.* **159 G8** 38 15N 111 10W
Capitola, *U.S.A.* **160 J5** 36 59N 121 57W
Capivara, Serra da, *Brazil* **171 D3** 14 35 S 45 0W

198 Capiz

Capiz □, *Phil.* **81 F4** 11 35N 122 30 E
Capizzi, *Italy* **47 E7** 37 51N 14 29 E
Capoche →, *Mozam.* **119 F3** 15 35 S 33 0 E
Capoeira, *Brazil* **173 B6** 5 37 S 59 33W
Capolo, *Angola* **115 E2** 10 22 S 14 7 E
Caporolo →, *Angola* **115 E2** 12 56 S 12 58 E
Capoterra, *Italy* **46 C1** 39 11N 8 58 E
Cappadocia, *Turkey* **100 C6** 39 0N 35 0 E
Capraia, *Italy* **44 E6** 43 2N 9 50 E
Caprara, Pta., *Italy* **46 A1** 41 7N 8 19 E
Caprarola, *Italy* **45 F9** 42 19N 12 14 E
Capreol, *Canada* **140 C3** 46 43N 80 56W
Caprera, *Italy* **46 A2** 41 12N 9 28 E
Capri, *Italy* **47 B7** 40 33N 14 14 E
Capricorn Group, *Australia* **126 C5** 23 30 S 151 55 E
Capricorn Ra., *Australia* **124 D2** 23 20 S 116 50 E
Caprino Veronese, *Italy* **44 C7** 45 36N 10 47 E
Caprivi Game Park, *Namibia* **116 B3** 17 55 S 22 37 E
Caprivi Strip, *Namibia* **116 B3** 18 0 S 23 0 E
Captain Cook, *U.S.A.* **145 D6** 19 30N 155 55W
Captain's Flat, *Australia* **129 C8** 35 35 S 149 27 E
Captieux, *France* **28 D3** 44 18N 0 16W
Captiva, *U.S.A.* **153 J7** 26 31N 82 11W
Capuça, *Angola* **115 F4** 17 22 S 21 18 E
Capul I., *Phil.* **80 E5** 12 26N 124 10 E
Capunda, *Angola* **115 E3** 10 41 S 17 23 E
Caquetá □, *Colombia* **168 C3** 1 0N 74 0W
Caquetá →, *Colombia* **168 D4** 1 15 S 69 15W
Car Nicobar, *India* **95 K11** 9 10N 92 47 E
Carabao I., *Phil.* **80 E3** 12 4N 121 56 E
Carabobo □, *Venezuela* **168 A4** 10 10N 68 5W
Caracal, *Romania* **53 F9** 44 8N 24 22 E
Caracaraí, *Brazil* **169 C5** 1 50N 61 8W
Caracas, *Venezuela* **168 A4** 10 30N 66 55W
Caracol, *Mato Grosso do Sul, Brazil* **174 A4** 22 18 S 57 1W
Caracol, *Piauí, Brazil* **170 C3** 9 15 S 43 22W
Caracollo, *Bolivia* **172 D4** 17 39 S 67 10W
Caraga, *Phil.* **81 H6** 7 20N 126 34 E
Caragabal, *Australia* **129 B7** 33 49 S 147 45 E
Caráglio, *Italy* **44 D4** 44 25N 7 26 E
Carahue, *Chile* **176 A2** 38 43 S 73 12W
Caraí, *Brazil* **171 E3** 17 12 S 41 42W
Carajás, *Brazil* **170 C1** 2 57 S 51 22W
Carajás, Serra dos, *Brazil* **170 C1** 6 0 S 51 30W
Caramoan, *Phil.* **80 E4** 13 46N 123 52 E
Caramoran, *Phil.* **80 D5** 14 0N 124 8 E
Caranapatuba, *Brazil* **173 B5** 6 38 S 62 34W
Carandaiti, *Bolivia* **173 E5** 20 45 S 63 4W
Carangola, *Brazil* **171 F3** 20 44 S 42 5W
Caransebeş, *Romania* **52 E7** 45 28N 22 18 E
Carantec, *France* **26 D3** 48 40N 3 55W
Caraparaná →, *Colombia* **168 D3** 1 45 S 73 13W
Caraquet, *Canada* **141 C6** 47 48N 64 57W
Caras, *Peru* **172 B2** 9 3 S 77 47W
Caraş Severin □, *Romania* **52 E7** 45 10N 22 10 E
Caraşova, *Romania* **52 E6** 45 11N 21 51 E
Caratasca, L., *Honduras* **164 C3** 15 20N 83 40W
Caratinga, *Brazil* **171 E3** 19 50 S 42 10W
Carauari, *Brazil* **168 D4** 4 52 S 66 54W
Caraúbas, *Brazil* **170 C4** 5 43 S 37 33W
Caravaca = Caravaca de la Cruz, *Spain* **41 G3** 38 8N 1 52W
Caravaca de la Cruz, *Spain* **41 G3** 38 8N 1 52W
Caravággio, *Italy* **44 C6** 45 30N 9 38 E
Caravela, *Guinea-Biss.* **112 C1** 11 30N 16 30W
Caravelas, *Brazil* **171 E4** 17 45 S 39 15W
Caraveli, *Peru* **172 D3** 15 45 S 73 25W
Caravelle, Presqu'île de la, *Martinique* **164 c** 14 46N 60 48W
Caràzinho, *Brazil* **175 B5** 28 16 S 52 46W
Carballino = O Carballiño, *Spain* **42 C2** 42 26N 8 5W
Carballo, *Spain* **42 B2** 43 13N 8 41W
Carberry, *Canada* **143 D9** 49 50N 99 25W
Carbó, *Mexico* **162 B2** 29 42N 110 58W
Carbonara, C., *Italy* **46 C2** 39 6N 9 31 E
Carbondale, *Colo., U.S.A.* **158 G10** 39 24N 107 13W
Carbondale, *Ill., U.S.A.* **155 G10** 37 44N 89 13W
Carbondale, *Pa., U.S.A.* **151 E9** 41 35N 75 30W
Carbonear, *Canada* **141 C9** 47 42N 53 13W
Carboneras, *Spain* **41 J3** 36 59N 1 53W
Carboneras de Guadazaón, *Spain* **40 F3** 39 54N 1 50W
Carbónia, *Italy* **46 C1** 39 10N 8 30 E
Carcabuey, *Spain* **43 H6** 37 27N 4 17W
Carcagente = Carcaixent, *Spain* **41 F4** 39 8N 0 28W
Carcaixent, *Spain* **41 F4** 39 8N 0 28W
Carcajou, *Canada* **142 B5** 57 47N 117 6W
Carcar, *Phil.* **81 F4** 10 6N 123 38 E
Carcarana →, *Argentina* **174 C3** 32 27 S 60 48W
Carcasse, C., *Haiti* **165 C5** 18 30N 74 28W
Carcassonne, *France* **28 E6** 43 13N 2 20 E
Carchi □, *Ecuador* **168 C2** 0 45N 78 0W
Carcoar, *Australia* **129 B8** 33 36 S 149 8 E
Carcross, *Canada* **142 A2** 60 13N 134 45W
Çardak, *Çanakkale, Turkey* **51 F10** 40 22N 26 43 E
Çardak, *Denizli, Turkey* **49 D11** 37 49N 29 39 E
Cardamon Hills, *India* **95 K3** 9 30N 77 15 E
Cardeña, *Spain* **43 G6** 38 16N 4 20W
Cárdenas, *Cuba* **164 B3** 23 0N 81 30W
Cárdenas, *San Luis Potosí, Mexico* **163 C5** 22 0N 99 41W
Cárdenas, *Tabasco, Mexico* **163 D6** 17 59N 93 21W
Cardenete, *Spain* **40 F3** 39 46N 1 41W
Cardiel, L., *Argentina* **176 C2** 48 55 S 71 10W
Cardiff, *U.K.* **21 F4** 51 29N 3 10W
Cardiff □, *U.K.* **21 F4** 51 31N 3 12W
Cardiff-by-the-Sea, *U.S.A.* **161 M9** 33 1N 117 17W
Cardigan, *U.K.* **21 E3** 52 5N 4 40W
Cardigan B., *U.K.* **21 E3** 52 30N 4 30W
Cardinal, *Canada* **151 B9** 44 47N 75 23W
Cardón, Punta, *Venezuela* **168 A3** 11 37N 70 14W
Cardona, *Spain* **40 D6** 41 56N 1 40 E
Cardona, *Uruguay* **174 C4** 33 53 S 57 18W
Cardoner →, *Spain* **40 D6** 41 41N 1 51 E
Cardoso, Ilha do, *Brazil* **175 B5** 25 8 S 47 58W
Cardston, *Canada* **142 D6** 49 15N 113 20W
Cardwell, *Australia* **126 B4** 18 14 S 146 2 E
Careen L., *Canada* **143 B7** 57 0N 108 11W
Carei, *Romania* **52 C7** 47 40N 22 29 E
Careiro, *Brazil* **169 D6** 3 12 S 59 45W
Careme = Ciremay, *Indonesia* **85 D3** 6 55 S 108 27 E
Carentan, *France* **26 C5** 49 19N 1 15W
Carey, *Idaho, U.S.A.* **158 E7** 43 19N 113 57W
Carey, *Ohio, U.S.A.* **157 D13** 40 57N 83 23W
Carey, L., *Australia* **125 E3** 29 0 S 122 15 E
Carey L., *Canada* **143 A8** 62 12N 102 55W
Careysburg, *Liberia* **112 D2** 6 34N 10 30W
Cargados Garajos, *Ind. Oc.* **121 F4** 17 0 S 59 0 E
Cargèse, *France* **29 F12** 42 7N 8 35 E
Carhaix-Plouguer, *France* **26 D3** 48 18N 3 36W
Carhuamayo, *Peru* **172 C2** 10 51 S 76 4W
Carhuas, *Peru* **172 B2** 9 15 S 77 39W
Carhué, *Argentina* **174 D3** 37 10 S 62 50W
Caria, *Turkey* **49 D10** 37 20N 28 10 E
Cariacica, *Brazil* **171 F3** 20 16 S 40 25W
Cariaco, *Venezuela* **169 A5** 10 29N 63 33W
Cariango, *Angola* **115 E3** 10 37 S 15 20 E
Cariati, *Italy* **47 C9** 39 30N 16 57 E
Caribbean Sea, *W. Indies* **165 D5** 15 0N 75 0W
Cariboo Mts., *Canada* **142 C4** 53 0N 121 0W
Caribou, *U.S.A.* **149 B12** 46 52N 68 1W
Caribou →, *Man., Canada* **143 B10** 59 20N 94 44W
Caribou →, *N.W.T., Canada* **142 A3** 61 27N 125 45W
Caribou I., *Canada* **140 C2** 47 22N 85 49W
Caribou Is., *Canada* **142 A6** 61 55N 113 15W
Caribou L., *Man., Canada* **143 B9** 59 21N 96 10W
Caribou L., *Ont., Canada* **140 B2** 50 25N 89 5W
Caribou Mts., *Canada* **142 B5** 59 12N 115 40W
Carichic, *Mexico* **162 B3** 27 56N 107 3W
Carigara, *Phil.* **81 F5** 11 18N 124 41 E
Carignan, *France* **27 C12** 49 38N 5 10 E
Carignano, *Italy* **44 D4** 44 55N 7 40 E
Carillo, *Mexico* **162 B4** 26 50N 103 55W
Carin, *Somali Rep.* **120 B3** 10 59N 49 13 E
Carinda, *Australia* **129 A7** 30 28 S 147 41 E
Cariñena, *Spain* **40 D3** 41 20N 1 13W
Carinhanha, *Brazil* **171 D3** 14 15 S 44 46W
Carinhanha →, *Brazil* **171 D3** 14 20 S 43 47W
Carini, *Italy* **46 D6** 38 8N 13 11 E
Cariño, *Spain* **42 B3** 43 45N 7 52W
Carínola, *Italy* **46 A6** 41 11N 13 58 E
Carinthia = Kärnten □, *Austria* **34 E6** 46 52N 13 30 E
Caripito, *Venezuela* **169 A5** 10 8N 63 6W
Cariré, *Brazil* **170 B3** 3 57 S 40 27W
Caritianas, *Brazil* **173 B5** 9 20 S 63 6W
Carlbrod = Dimitrovgrad, *Serbia, Yug.* **50 C6** 43 2N 22 48 E
Carles, *Phil.* **81 F4** 11 34N 123 8 E
Carlesberg Ridge, *Ind. Oc.* **121 D5** 1 0N 66 0 E
Carlet, *Spain* **41 F4** 39 14N 0 31W
Carleton, Mt., *Canada* **141 C6** 47 23N 66 53W
Carleton Place, *Canada* **140 C4** 45 8N 76 9W
Carletonville, *S. Africa* **116 D4** 26 23 S 27 22 E
Cârlibaba, *Romania* **53 C10** 47 35N 25 8 E
Carlin, *U.S.A.* **158 F5** 40 43N 116 7W
Carlingford L., *U.K.* **23 B5** 54 3N 6 9W
Carlinville, *U.S.A.* **156 E7** 39 17N 89 53W
Carlisle, *U.K.* **20 C5** 54 54N 2 56W
Carlisle, *Ind., U.S.A.* **157 F9** 38 58N 87 24W
Carlisle, *Ky., U.S.A.* **157 F12** 38 19N 84 1W
Carlisle, *Pa., U.S.A.* **150 F7** 40 12N 77 12W
Carlisle B., *Barbados* **165 g** 13 5N 59 37W
Carlisle I., *Australia* **126 J7** 20 49 S 149 18 E
Carlit, Pic, *France* **28 F5** 42 35N 1 55 E
Carloforte, *Italy* **46 C1** 39 8N 8 18 E
Carlos Casares, *Argentina* **174 D3** 35 32 S 61 20W
Carlos Chagas, *Brazil* **171 E3** 17 43 S 40 45W
Carlos Tejedor, *Argentina* **174 D3** 35 25 S 62 25W
Carlow, *Ireland* **23 D5** 52 50N 6 56W
Carlow □, *Ireland* **23 D5** 52 43N 6 50W
Carlsbad, *Calif., U.S.A.* **161 M9** 33 10N 117 21W
Carlsbad, *N. Mex., U.S.A.* **155 J2** 32 25N 104 14W
Carlsbad Caverns Nat. Park, *U.S.A.* **155 J2** 32 10N 104 35W
Carluke, *U.K.* **22 F5** 55 45N 3 50W
Carlyle, *Canada* **143 D8** 49 40N 102 20W
Carlyle, *U.S.A.* **156 F7** 38 37N 89 22W
Carlyle L., *U.S.A.* **156 F7** 38 37N 89 21W
Carmacks, *Canada* **138 B6** 62 5N 136 16W
Carmagnola, *Italy* **44 D4** 44 51N 7 43 E
Carman, *Canada* **143 D9** 49 30N 98 0W
Carmarthen, *U.K.* **21 F3** 51 52N 4 19W
Carmarthen B., *U.K.* **21 F3** 51 40N 4 30W
Carmarthenshire □, *U.K.* **21 F3** 51 55N 4 13W
Carmaux, *France* **28 D6** 44 3N 2 10 E
Carmel, *Ind., U.S.A.* **157 E10** 39 59N 86 8W
Carmel, *N.Y., U.S.A.* **151 E11** 41 26N 73 41W
Carmel-by-the-Sea, *U.S.A.* **160 J5** 36 33N 121 55W
Carmel Valley, *U.S.A.* **160 J5** 36 29N 121 43W
Carmelo, *Uruguay* **174 C4** 34 0 S 58 20W
Carmen, *Bolivia* **172 C4** 11 40 S 67 51W
Carmen, *Colombia* **168 B2** 9 43N 75 8W
Carmen, *Paraguay* **175 B4** 27 13 S 56 12W
Carmen, *Bohol, Phil.* **81 G5** 9 50N 124 12 E
Carmen, *Cebu, Phil.* **81 F5** 10 35N 124 1 E
Carmen, *Cotabato, Phil.* **81 H5** 7 13N 124 45 E
Carmen, *Venezuela* **168 C4** 1 16N 66 52W
Carmen →, *Mexico* **162 A3** 30 42N 106 29W
Carmen, I., *Mexico* **162 B2** 26 0N 111 20W
Carmen de Patagones, *Argentina* **176 B4** 40 50 S 63 0W
Cármenes, *Spain* **42 C5** 42 58N 5 34W
Carmensa, *Argentina* **174 D2** 35 15 S 67 40W
Carmi, *Canada* **142 D5** 49 36N 119 8W
Carmi, *U.S.A.* **157 F8** 38 5N 88 10W
Carmichael, *U.S.A.* **160 G5** 38 38N 121 19W
Carmichael Village, *Bahamas* **9 b** 25 0N 77 26W
Carmila, *Australia* **126 C4** 21 55 S 149 24 E
Carmona, *Costa Rica* **164 E2** 10 0N 85 15W
Carmona, *Spain* **43 H5** 37 28N 5 42W
Carn Ban, *U.K.* **22 D4** 57 7N 4 15W
Carn Eige, *U.K.* **22 D3** 57 17N 5 8W
Carnac, *France* **25 C2** 47 35N 3 6W
Carnamah, *Australia* **125 E2** 29 41 S 115 53 E
Carnarvon, *Australia* **125 D1** 24 51 S 113 42 E
Carnarvon, *S. Africa* **116 E3** 30 56 S 22 8 E
Carnarvon Nat. Park, *Australia* **126 C4** 24 54 S 148 2 E
Carnarvon Ra., *Queens., Australia* **126 D4** 25 15 S 148 30 E
Carnarvon Ra., *W. Austral., Australia* **125 E3** 25 20 S 120 45 E
Carnatic, *India* **95 K3** 9 40N 77 50 E
Carnation, *U.S.A.* **160 C5** 47 39N 121 55W
Carndonagh, *Ireland* **23 A4** 55 16N 7 15W
Carnduff, *Canada* **143 D8** 49 10N 101 50W
Carnegie, *U.S.A.* **150 F4** 40 24N 80 5W
Carnegie, L., *Australia* **125 E3** 26 5 S 122 30 E
Carnic Alps = Karnische Alpen, *Europe* **34 E6** 46 36N 13 0 E
Carniche Alpi = Karnische Alpen, *Europe* **34 E6** 46 36N 13 0 E
Carnot, *C.A.R.* **114 B3** 4 59N 15 56 E
Carnot, C., *Australia* **127 E2** 34 57 S 135 38 E
Carnot B., *Australia* **124 C3** 17 20 S 122 15 E
Carnoustie, *U.K.* **22 E6** 56 30N 2 42W
Carnsore Pt., *Ireland* **23 D5** 52 10N 6 22W
Caro, *U.S.A.* **148 D4** 43 29N 83 24W
Caroço, *São Tomé & Principe* **115 G6** 1 32N 7 27 E
Carol City, *U.S.A.* **149 N5** 25 56N 80 16W
Carolina, *Brazil* **170 C2** 7 10 S 47 30W
Carolina, *Puerto Rico* **165 d** 18 23N 65 58W
Carolina, *S. Africa* **117 D5** 26 5 S 30 6 E
Caroline I., *Kiribati* **135 H12** 9 58 S 150 13W
Caroline Is., *Micronesia* **62 J17** 8 0N 150 0 E
Caroline Pk., *N.Z.* **131 F2** 45 57 S 167 15 E
Carondelet, *Kiribati* **123 B16** 5 33 S 173 50 E
Caroni, *Trin. & Tob.* **169 F9** 10 34N 61 23W
Caroní →, *Venezuela* **169 B5** 8 21N 62 43W
Caronie = Nébrodi, Monti, *Italy* **47 E7** 37 54N 14 35 E
Caroona, *Australia* **129 A9** 31 24 S 150 26 E
Carora, *Venezuela* **168 A3** 10 11N 70 5W
Carpathians, *Europe* **37 D11** 49 30N 21 0 E
Carpaţii Meridionali, *Romania* **53 E9** 45 30N 25 0 E
Carpentaria, G. of, *Australia* **126 A2** 14 0 S 139 0 E
Carpentersville, *U.S.A.* **157 B8** 42 6N 88 17W
Carpentras, *France* **29 D9** 44 3N 5 2 E
Carpi, *Italy* **44 D7** 44 47N 10 53 E
Carpina, *Brazil* **170 C4** 7 51 S 35 15W
Cărpineni, *Moldova* **53 D13** 46 46N 28 22 E
Carpinteria, *U.S.A.* **161 L7** 34 24N 119 31W
Carpio, *Spain* **42 D5** 41 13N 5 7W
Carr Boyd Ra., *Australia* **124 C4** 16 15 S 128 35 E
Carrabelle, *U.S.A.* **152 F5** 29 51N 84 40W
Carral, *Spain* **42 B2** 43 13N 8 21W
Carranglan, *Phil.* **80 D3** 15 58N 121 4 E
Carranza, Presa V., *Mexico* **162 B4** 27 20N 100 50W
Carrara, *Italy* **44 D7** 44 5N 10 6 E
Carrascal, *Phil.* **81 G5** 9 22N 125 56 E
Carrascosa del Campo, *Spain* **40 E2** 40 2N 2 45W
Carrauntoohill, *Ireland* **23 D2** 52 0N 9 45W
Carretas, Punta, *Peru* **172 C2** 14 12 S 76 17W
Carrick-on-Shannon, *Ireland* **23 C3** 53 57N 8 5W
Carrick-on-Suir, *Ireland* **23 D4** 52 21N 7 24W
Carrickfergus, *U.K.* **23 B6** 54 43N 5 49W
Carrickmacross, *Ireland* **23 C5** 53 59N 6 43W
Carrieton, *Australia* **128 B3** 32 25 S 138 31 E
Carrington, *U.S.A.* **154 B5** 47 27N 99 8W
Carrión →, *Spain* **42 D6** 41 53N 4 32W
Carrión de los Condes, *Spain* **42 C6** 42 20N 4 37W
Carrizal Bajo, *Chile* **174 B1** 28 5 S 71 20W
Carrizalillo, *Chile* **174 B1** 29 5 S 71 30W
Carrizo Cr. →, *U.S.A.* **155 G3** 36 55N 103 55W
Carrizo Springs, *U.S.A.* **155 L5** 28 31N 99 52W
Carrizozo, *U.S.A.* **159 K11** 33 38N 105 53W
Carroll, *U.S.A.* **156 B2** 42 4N 94 52W
Carrollton, *Ga., U.S.A.* **152 B4** 33 35N 85 5W
Carrollton, *Ill., U.S.A.* **156 E6** 39 18N 90 24W
Carrollton, *Ky., U.S.A.* **157 F11** 38 41N 85 11W
Carrollton, *Mo., U.S.A.* **156 E3** 39 22N 93 30W
Carrollton, *Ohio, U.S.A.* **150 F3** 40 34N 81 5W
Carron →, *U.K.* **22 D4** 57 53N 4 22W
Carron, L., *U.K.* **22 D3** 57 22N 5 35W
Carrot →, *Canada* **143 C8** 53 50N 101 17W
Carrot River, *Canada* **143 C8** 53 17N 103 35W
Carrouges, *France* **26 D6** 48 34N 0 10W
Carrù, *Italy* **44 D4** 44 29N 7 52 E
Carruthers, *Canada* **143 C7** 52 52N 109 16W
Carsa Dek, *Ethiopia* **107 F4** 5 13N 39 50 E
Çarşamba, *Turkey* **100 B7** 41 11N 36 44 E
Carsóli, *Italy* **45 F10** 42 6N 13 5 E
Carson, *Calif., U.S.A.* **161 M8** 33 48N 118 17W
Carson, *N. Dak., U.S.A.* **154 B4** 46 25N 101 34W
Carson →, *U.S.A.* **160 F8** 39 45N 118 40W
Carson City, *Mich., U.S.A.* **157 A12** 43 11N 84 51W
Carson City, *Nev., U.S.A.* **160 F7** 39 10N 119 46W
Carson Sink, *U.S.A.* **158 G4** 39 50N 118 25W
Cartagena, *Colombia* **168 A2** 10 25N 75 33W
Cartagena, *Spain* **41 H4** 37 38N 0 59W
Cartago, *Colombia* **168 C2** 4 45N 75 55W
Cartago, *Costa Rica* **164 E3** 9 50N 83 55W
Cártama, *Spain* **43 J6** 36 43N 4 39W
Cartaxo, *Portugal* **43 F2** 39 10N 8 47W
Cartaya, *Spain* **43 H3** 37 16N 7 9W
Cartersville, *U.S.A.* **152 A5** 34 10N 84 48W
Carterton, *N.Z.* **130 H4** 41 2 S 175 31 E
Carterville, *U.S.A.* **156 G7** 37 46N 89 5W
Carthage, *Tunisia* **46 F3** 36 50N 10 21 E
Carthage, *Ill., U.S.A.* **156 D5** 40 25N 91 8W
Carthage, *Mo., U.S.A.* **155 G7** 37 11N 94 19W
Carthage, *N.Y., U.S.A.* **148 D8** 43 59N 75 37W
Carthage, *Tex., U.S.A.* **155 J7** 32 9N 94 20W
Cartier I., *Australia* **124 B3** 12 31 S 123 29 E
Cartwright, *Canada* **141 B8** 53 41N 56 58W
Caruaru, *Brazil* **170 C4** 8 15 S 35 55W
Carúpano, *Venezuela* **169 A5** 10 39N 63 15W
Caruray, *Phil.* **81 F2** 10 20N 119 0 E
Carutapera, *Brazil* **170 B2** 1 13 S 46 1W
Caruthersville, *U.S.A.* **155 G10** 36 11N 89 39W
Carvalho, *Brazil* **169 D7** 2 16 S 51 29W
Carvin, *France* **27 B9** 50 30N 2 57 E
Carvoeiro, *Brazil* **169 D5** 1 30 S 61 59W
Carvoeiro, C., *Portugal* **43 F1** 39 21N 9 24W
Cary, *Ill., U.S.A.* **157 B8** 42 13N 88 14W
Cary, *N.C., U.S.A.* **149 H6** 35 47N 78 46W
Casa Branca, *Brazil* **171 F2** 21 46 S 47 4W
Casa Branca, *Portugal* **43 G2** 38 29N 8 12W
Casa Grande, *U.S.A.* **159 K8** 32 53N 111 45W
Casablanca, *Chile* **174 C1** 33 20 S 71 25W
Casablanca, *Morocco* **110 B3** 33 36N 7 36W
Casacalenda, *Italy* **45 G11** 41 44N 14 51 E
Casalbordino, *Italy* **45 F11** 42 9N 14 35 E
Casale Monferrato, *Italy* **44 C5** 45 8N 8 27 E
Casalmaggiore, *Italy* **44 D7** 44 59N 10 26 E
Casalpusterlengo, *Italy* **44 C6** 45 11N 9 39 E
Casamance →, *Senegal* **112 C1** 12 33N 16 46W
Casanare □, *Colombia* **168 B3** 5 30N 72 0W
Casanare →, *Colombia* **168 B4** 6 2N 69 51W
Casarano, *Italy* **47 B11** 40 0N 18 10 E
Casares, *Spain* **43 J5** 36 27N 5 16W
Casas Ibáñez, *Spain* **41 F3** 39 17N 1 30W
Casasimarro, *Spain* **41 F2** 39 22N 2 3W
Casatejada, *Spain* **42 F5** 39 54N 5 40W
Casavieja, *Spain* **42 E6** 40 17N 4 46W
Cascade, *Seychelles* **121 b** 4 39 S 55 29 E
Cascade, *Idaho, U.S.A.* **158 D5** 44 31N 116 2W
Cascade, *Iowa, U.S.A.* **156 B6** 42 18N 91 0W
Cascade, *Mont., U.S.A.* **158 C8** 47 16N 111 42W
Cascade Locks, *U.S.A.* **160 E5** 45 40N 121 54W
Cascade Pt., *N.Z.* **131 E3** 44 1 S 168 20 E
Cascade Ra., *U.S.A.* **160 D5** 47 0N 121 30W
Cascade Reservoir, *U.S.A.* **158 D5** 44 32N 116 3W
Cascades, Pte. des, *Réunion* **121 c** 21 9 S 55 51 E
Cascais, *Portugal* **43 G1** 38 41N 9 25W
Cascavel, *Ceará, Brazil* **170 B4** 4 7 S 38 14W
Cascavel, *Paraná, Brazil* **175 A5** 24 57 S 53 28W
Càscina, *Italy* **44 E7** 43 41N 10 33 E
Casco B., *U.S.A.* **149 D10** 43 45N 70 0W
Caselle Torinese, *Italy* **44 C4** 45 10N 7 39 E
Caserta, *Italy* **47 A7** 41 4N 14 20 E
Casey, *U.S.A.* **157 E9** 39 18N 87 59W
Caseyr, Raas = Asir, Ras, *Somali Rep.* **120 B4** 11 55N 51 10 E
Cashel, *Ireland* **23 D4** 52 30N 7 53W
Casibare →, *Colombia* **168 C3** 3 48N 72 18W
Casiguran, *Phil.* **80 C4** 16 22N 122 7 E
Casiguran Sound, *Phil.* **80 C3** 16 6N 121 58 E
Casilda, *Argentina* **174 C3** 33 10 S 61 10W
Casimcea, *Romania* **53 F13** 44 45N 28 23 E
Casino, *Australia* **127 D5** 28 52 S 153 3 E
Casiquiare →, *Venezuela* **168 C4** 2 1N 67 7W
Casitas, *Peru* **172 A1** 3 54 S 80 39W
Čáslav, *Czech Rep.* **34 B8** 49 54N 15 22 E
Casma, *Peru* **172 B2** 9 30 S 78 20W
Casmalia, *U.S.A.* **161 L6** 34 50N 120 32W
Cásola Valsénio, *Italy* **45 D8** 44 12N 11 40 E
Cásoli, *Italy* **45 F11** 42 7N 14 18 E
Caspe, *Spain* **40 D4** 41 14N 0 1W
Casper, *U.S.A.* **158 E10** 42 51N 106 19W
Caspian Depression, *Eurasia* **61 G9** 47 0N 48 0 E
Caspian Sea, *Eurasia* **57 F9** 43 0N 50 0 E
Cass Lake, *U.S.A.* **154 B7** 47 23N 94 37W
Cassà de la Selva, *Spain* **40 D7** 41 53N 2 52 E
Cassadaga, *U.S.A.* **150 D5** 42 20N 79 19W
Cassai, *Angola* **115 E4** 10 33 S 21 59 E
Cassai →, *Angola* **115 E4** 11 0 S 16 57 E
Cassamba, *Angola* **115 E4** 13 6 S 20 18 E
Cassano allo Iónio, *Italy* **47 C9** 39 47N 16 20 E
Casse, Grande, *France* **29 C10** 45 24N 6 49 E
Cassel, *France* **27 B9** 50 48N 2 30 E
Casselman, *Canada* **151 A9** 45 19N 75 5W
Casselton, *U.S.A.* **154 B6** 46 54N 97 13W
Cassiar, *Canada* **142 B3** 59 16N 129 40W
Cassiar Mts., *Canada* **142 B2** 59 30N 130 30W
Cassilândia, *Brazil* **173 D7** 19 9 S 51 45W
Cassilis, *Australia* **129 B8** 32 3 S 149 58 E
Cassinga, *Angola* **115 F3** 15 5 S 16 4 E
Cassino, *Italy* **46 A6** 41 30N 13 49 E
Cassis, *France* **29 E9** 43 14N 5 32 E
Cassoalala, *Angola* **115 D2** 9 30 S 14 22 E
Cassoango, *Angola* **115 E4** 13 42 S 20 56 E
Cassongue, *Angola* **115 E3** 11 53 S 15 2 E
Cassopolis, *U.S.A.* **157 C10** 41 55N 86 1W
Cassunda, *Angola* **115 E4** 10 57 S 21 3 E
Cassville, *Mo., U.S.A.* **155 G8** 36 41N 93 52W
Cassville, *Wis., U.S.A.* **156 B6** 42 43N 90 59W
Castagneto Carducci, *Italy* **44 E7** 43 9N 10 36 E
Castaic, *U.S.A.* **161 L8** 34 30N 118 38W
Castalia, *U.S.A.* **150 E2** 41 24N 82 49W
Castanhal, *Brazil* **170 B2** 1 18 S 47 55W
Castara, *Trin. & Tob.* **169 E10** 11 17N 60 42W
Castasegna, *Switz.* **33 D9** 46 20N 9 31 E
Castéggio, *Italy* **44 C6** 45 0N 9 7 E
Castejón de Monegros, *Spain* **40 D4** 41 37N 0 15W
Castèl di Sangro, *Italy* **45 G11** 41 47N 14 6 E
Castèl San Giovanni, *Italy* **44 C6** 45 4N 9 26 E
Castèl San Pietro Terme, *Italy* **45 D8** 44 24N 11 35 E
Castelbuono, *Italy* **47 E7** 37 56N 14 5 E
Castelfidardo, *Italy* **45 E10** 43 28N 13 33 E
Castelfiorentino, *Italy* **44 E7** 43 36N 10 58 E
Castelfranco Emília, *Italy* **44 D8** 44 37N 11 3 E
Castelfranco Véneto, *Italy* **45 C8** 45 40N 11 55 E
Casteljaloux, *France* **28 D4** 44 19N 0 6 E
Castellabate, *Italy* **47 B7** 40 17N 14 57 E
Castellammare, G. di, *Italy* **46 D5** 38 8N 12 54 E
Castellammare del Golfo, *Italy* **46 D5** 38 1N 12 53 E
Castellammare di Stábia, *Italy* **47 B7** 40 42N 14 29 E
Castellamonte, *Italy* **44 C4** 45 23N 7 42 E
Castellane, *France* **29 E10** 43 50N 6 31 E
Castellaneta, *Italy* **47 B9** 40 38N 16 56 E
Castelli, *Argentina* **174 D4** 36 7 S 57 47W
Castelló de la Plana, *Spain* **40 F4** 39 58N 0 3W
Castellón de la Plana □, *Spain* **40 E4** 40 15N 0 5W
Castellote, *Spain* **40 E4** 40 48N 0 15W
Castelmáuro, *Italy* **45 G11** 41 50N 14 43 E
Castelnau-de-Médoc, *France* **28 C3** 45 2N 0 48W
Castelnau-Magnoac, *France* **28 E4** 43 17N 0 31 E
Castelnaudary, *France* **28 E5** 43 20N 1 58 E
Castelnovo ne' Monti, *Italy* **44 D7** 44 26N 10 24 E
Castelnuovo di Val di Cécina, *Italy* **44 E7** 43 12N 10 59 E
Castelo, *Brazil* **171 F3** 20 33 S 41 14W
Castelo, Pta. do, *Azores* **9 d4** 36 56N 25 1W
Castelo Branco, *Azores* **9 d1** 38 31N 28 44W
Castelo Branco, *Portugal* **42 F3** 39 50N 7 31W
Castelo Branco □, *Portugal* **42 F3** 39 52N 7 45W
Castelo de Paiva, *Portugal* **42 D2** 41 2N 8 16W
Castelo de Vide, *Portugal* **43 F3** 39 25N 7 27W
Castelo do Piauí, *Brazil* **170 C3** 5 20 S 41 33W
Castelsardo, *Italy* **46 B1** 40 55N 8 43 E
Castelsarrasin, *France* **28 D5** 44 2N 1 7 E
Casteltérmini, *Italy* **46 E6** 37 32N 13 39 E
Castelvetrano, *Italy* **46 E5** 37 41N 12 47 E
Castendo, *Angola* **115 D2** 8 39 S 14 10 E
Casterton, *Australia* **128 D4** 37 30 S 141 30 E
Castets, *France* **28 E2** 43 52N 1 6W
Castiglion Fiorentino, *Italy* **45 E8** 43 20N 11 55 E
Castiglione del Lago, *Italy* **45 E9** 43 7N 12 3 E
Castiglione della Pescáia, *Italy* **44 F7** 42 46N 10 53 E
Castiglione delle Stiviere, *Italy* **44 C7** 45 23N 10 29 E
Castilblanco, *Spain* **43 F5** 39 17N 5 5W
Castile, *U.S.A.* **150 D6** 42 38N 78 3W
Castilla, *Peru* **172 B1** 5 12 S 80 38W
Castilla, Playa de, *Spain* **43 J4** 37 0N 6 33W
Castilla-La Mancha □, *Spain* **12 H5** 39 30N 3 30W
Castilla y Leon □, *Spain* **42 D6** 42 0N 5 0W
Castillo de Locubín, *Spain* **43 H7** 37 32N 3 56W
Castillon-en-Couserans, *France* **28 F5** 42 56N 1 1 E
Castillonès, *France* **28 D4** 44 39N 0 37 E
Castillos, *Uruguay* **175 C5** 34 12 S 53 52W
Castle Dale, *U.S.A.* **158 G8** 39 13N 111 1W
Castle Douglas, *U.K.* **22 G5** 54 56N 3 56W
Castle Harbour, *Bermuda* **9 a** 32 21N 64 40W
Castle Rock, *Colo., U.S.A.* **154 F2** 39 22N 104 51W
Castle Rock, *Wash., U.S.A.* **160 D4** 46 17N 122 54W
Castle Rock Pt., *St. Helena* **9 h** 16 1 S 5 45W
Castlebar, *Ireland* **23 C2** 53 52N 9 18W
Castleblaney, *Ireland* **23 B5** 54 7N 6 44W
Castlecliff, *N.Z.* **130 F3** 39 57 S 174 59 E
Castlederg, *U.K.* **23 B4** 54 42N 7 35W
Castleford, *U.K.* **20 D6** 53 43N 1 21W
Castlegar, *Canada* **142 D5** 49 20N 117 40W
Castlemaine, *Australia* **128 D6** 37 2 S 144 12 E
Castlepoint, *N.Z.* **130 G5** 40 54 S 176 15 E
Castlepollard, *Ireland* **23 C4** 53 41N 7 19W
Castlerea, *Ireland* **23 C3** 53 46N 8 29W
Castlereagh →, *N.S.W., Australia* **129 A7** 30 12 S 147 32 E
Castlereagh →, *N.S.W., Australia* **129 A7** 30 12 S 147 32 E
Castlereagh B., *Australia* **126 A2** 12 10 S 135 10 E
Castleton, *U.S.A.* **151 C11** 43 37N 73 11W
Castletown, *U.K.* **20 C3** 54 5N 4 38W
Castletown Bearhaven, *Ireland* **23 E2** 51 39N 9 55W
Castor, *Canada* **142 C6** 52 15N 111 50W
Castor →, *Canada* **140 B4** 53 24N 78 58W
Castorland, *U.S.A.* **151 C9** 43 53N 75 31W
Castres, *France* **28 E6** 43 37N 2 13 E
Castricum, *Neths.* **24 B4** 52 33N 4 40 E
Castries, *St. Lucia* **165 f** 14 2N 60 58W
Castril, *Spain* **43 H8** 37 48N 2 46W
Castro, *Brazil* **175 A6** 24 45 S 50 0W
Castro, *Chile* **176 B2** 42 30 S 73 50W
Castro Alves, *Brazil* **171 D4** 12 46 S 39 33W
Castro del Río, *Spain* **43 H6** 37 41N 4 29W
Castro-Urdiales, *Spain* **42 B7** 43 23N 3 11W
Castro Verde, *Portugal* **43 H2** 37 41N 8 4W
Castrojeriz, *Spain* **42 C6** 42 17N 4 9W
Castropol, *Spain* **42 B4** 43 32N 7 0W
Castroreale, *Italy* **47 D8** 38 6N 15 12 E
Castrovillari, *Italy* **47 C9** 39 49N 16 12 E
Castroville, *U.S.A.* **160 J5** 36 46N 121 45W
Castrovirreyna, *Peru* **172 C2** 13 20 S 75 18W
Castuera, *Spain* **43 G5** 38 43N 5 37W
Caswell Sound, *N.Z.* **131 E2** 44 59 S 167 8 E
Çat, *Turkey* **101 C9** 39 40N 41 3 E
Cat Ba, Dao, *Vietnam* **86 B6** 20 50N 107 0 E
Cat I., *Bahamas* **165 B4** 24 30N 75 30W
Cat L., *Canada* **140 B1** 51 40N 91 50W
Cat Lake, *Canada* **140 B1** 51 40N 91 50W
Čata, *Slovak Rep.* **35 D11** 47 58N 18 38 E
Catabola, *Angola* **115 E3** 12 9 S 17 16 E
Catacamas, *Honduras* **164 D2** 14 54N 85 56W
Catacáos, *Peru* **172 B1** 5 20 S 80 45W
Cataguases, *Brazil* **171 F3** 21 23 S 42 39W
Catagupan, *Phil.* **81 G1** 8 1N 116 58 E
Cataingan, *Phil.* **80 E4** 12 0N 124 0 E
Çatak, *Turkey* **101 C10** 38 1N 43 8 E
Catalão, *Brazil* **171 E2** 18 10 S 47 57W
Çatalca, *Turkey* **51 E12** 41 8N 28 27 E
Catalina, *Canada* **141 C9** 48 31N 53 4W
Catalina, *Chile* **174 B2** 25 13 S 69 43W
Catalina, *U.S.A.* **159 K8** 32 30N 110 50W
Catalonia = Cataluña □, *Spain* **40 D6** 41 40N 1 15 E
Cataluña □, *Spain* **40 D6** 41 40N 1 15 E
Çatalzeytin, *Turkey* **100 B6** 41 57N 34 12 E
Catamarca, *Argentina* **174 B2** 28 30 S 65 50W
Catamarca □, *Argentina* **174 B2** 27 0 S 65 50W
Catanauan, *Phil.* **80 E4** 13 36N 122 19 E
Catanduanes □, *Phil.* **80 E5** 13 50N 124 20 E
Catanduva, *Brazil* **175 A6** 21 5 S 48 58W

200 Changde

Changde, *China* **77 C8** 29 4N 111 35 E
Changdo-ri, *N. Korea* **75 E14** 38 30N 127 40 E
Changfeng, *China* **77 A11** 32 28N 117 10 E
Changhai = Shanghai, *China* **77 B13** 31 15N 121 26 E
Changhua, *China* **77 B12** 30 12N 119 12 E
Changhua, *Taiwan* **77 E13** 24 2N 120 30 E
Changhŭng, *S. Korea* **75 G14** 34 41N 126 52 E
Changhŭngni, *N. Korea* **75 D15** 40 24N 128 19 E
Changi, *Malaysia* **84 B2** 1 23N 103 59 E
Changi, *Singapore* **87 d** 1 23N 103 59 E
Changjiang, *China* **86 C7** 19 20N 108 55 E
Changjiang Shuiku, *China* **69 G10** 22 29N 113 27 E
Changjin, *N. Korea* **75 D14** 40 23N 127 15 E
Changjin-chŏsuji, *N. Korea* **75 D14** 40 30N 127 15 E
Changle, *China* **77 E12** 25 59N 119 27 E
Changli, *China* **75 E10** 39 40N 119 13 E
Changling, *China* **75 B12** 44 20N 123 58 E
Changlun, *Malaysia* **87 J3** 6 25N 100 26 E
Changning, *Hunan, China* **77 D9** 26 28N 112 22 E
Changning, *Sichuan, China* **76 C5** 28 40N 104 56 E
Changning, *Yunnan, China* **76 E2** 24 45N 99 30 E
Changping, *China* **74 D9** 40 14N 116 12 E
Changsha, *China* **77 C9** 28 12N 113 0 E
Changshan, *China* **77 C12** 28 55N 118 27 E
Changshu, *China* **77 B13** 31 38N 120 43 E
Changshun, *China* **76 D6** 26 3N 106 25 E
Changtai, *China* **77 E11** 24 35N 117 42 E
Changting, *China* **77 E11** 25 50N 116 22 E
Changwu, *China* **74 G4** 35 10N 107 45 E
Changxing, *China* **77 B12** 31 0N 119 55 E
Changyang, *China* **77 B8** 30 30N 111 10 E
Changyi, *China* **75 F10** 36 40N 119 30 E
Changyŏn, *N. Korea* **75 E13** 38 15N 125 6 E
Changyuan, *China* **74 G8** 35 15N 114 42 E
Changzhi, *China* **74 F7** 36 10N 113 6 E
Changzhou, *China* **77 B12** 31 47N 119 58 E
Chanhanga, *Angola* **116 B1** 16 0 S 14 8 E
Chanlar = Xanlar, *Azerbaijan* **61 K8** 40 37N 46 12 E
Channagiri, *India* **95 G2** 14 2N 75 56 E
Channapatna, *India* **95 H3** 12 40N 77 15 E
Channel Is., *U.K.* **21 H5** 49 19N 2 24W
Channel Is., *U.S.A.* **161 M7** 33 40N 119 15W
Channel Islands Nat. Park, *U.S.A.* **161 M8** 33 30N 119 0W
Channel-Port aux Basques, *Canada* **141 C8** 47 30N 59 9W
Channel Tunnel, *Europe* **21 F9** 51 0N 1 30 E
Channing, *U.S.A.* **155 H3** 35 41N 102 20W
Chantada, *Spain* **42 C3** 42 36N 7 46W
Chanthaburi, *Thailand* **86 F4** 12 38N 102 12 E
Chantilly, *France* **27 C9** 49 12N 2 29 E
Chantonnay, *France* **26 F5** 46 40N 1 3W
Chantrey Inlet, *Canada* **138 B10** 67 48N 96 20W
Chanumla, *India* **95 K11** 8 19N 93 5 E
Chanute, *U.S.A.* **155 G7** 37 41N 95 27W
Chanza →, *Spain* **43 H3** 37 32N 7 30W
Chao Hu, *China* **77 B11** 31 30N 117 30 E
Chao Phraya →, *Thailand* **86 F3** 13 32N 100 36 E
Chao Phraya Lowlands, *Thailand* **86 E3** 15 30N 100 0 E
Chaocheng, *China* **74 F8** 36 4N 115 37 E
Chaohu, *China* **77 B11** 31 38N 117 50 E
Chaoyang, *Guangdong, China* **77 F11** 23 17N 116 30 E
Chaoyang, *Liaoning, China* **75 D11** 41 35N 120 22 E
Chaozhou, *China* **77 F11** 23 42N 116 32 E
Chapada dos Guimarães, *Brazil* **173 D6** 15 26 S 55 45W
Chapais, *Canada* **140 C5** 49 47N 74 51W
Chapala, *Mozam.* **119 F4** 15 50 S 37 35 E
Chapala, L. de, *Mexico* **162 C4** 20 10N 103 20W
Chaparé →, *Bolivia* **173 D5** 15 58 S 64 42W
Chaparmukh, *India* **90 B4** 26 12N 92 31 E
Chaparral, *Colombia* **168 C2** 3 43N 75 28W
Chapayev, *Kazakstan* **60 E10** 50 25N 51 10 E
Chapayevsk, *Russia* **60 D9** 53 0N 49 40 E
Chapecó, *Brazil* **175 B5** 27 14 S 52 41W
Chapel Hill, *U.S.A.* **149 H6** 35 55N 79 4W
Chapetsk →, *Russia* **64 B3** 58 36N 50 4 E
Chapin, *U.S.A.* **156 E6** 39 46N 90 24W
Chapleau, *Canada* **140 C3** 47 50N 83 24W
Chaplin, *Canada* **143 C7** 50 28N 106 40W
Chaplin L., *Canada* **143 C7** 50 22N 106 36W
Chaplino, *Ukraine* **59 H9** 48 8N 36 15 E
Chaplygin, *Russia* **58 F11** 53 15N 40 0 E
Chappell, *U.S.A.* **154 E3** 41 6N 102 28W
Chappells, *U.S.A.* **152 A8** 34 11N 81 52W
Chapra = Chhapra, *India* **93 G11** 25 48N 84 44 E
Châr, *Mauritania* **110 D2** 21 32N 12 45W
Chara, *Russia* **67 D12** 56 54N 118 20 E
Charadai, *Argentina* **174 B4** 27 35 S 59 55W
Charagua, *Bolivia* **173 D5** 19 45 S 63 10W
Charalá, *Colombia* **168 B3** 6 17N 73 10W
Charambirá, Punta, *Colombia* **168 C2** 4 16N 77 32W
Charaña, *Bolivia* **172 D4** 17 30 S 69 25W
Charantsavan, *Armenia* **61 K7** 40 35N 44 41 E
Charanwala, *India* **92 F5** 27 51N 72 10 E
Charapita, *Colombia* **168 D3** 0 37 S 74 21W
Charata, *Argentina* **174 B3** 27 13 S 61 14W
Charcas, *Mexico* **162 C4** 23 10N 101 20W
Chard, *U.K.* **21 G5** 50 52N 2 58W
Chardon, *U.S.A.* **150 E3** 41 35N 81 12W
Charduar, *India* **90 B4** 26 51N 92 46 E
Chardzhou = Chärjew, *Turkmenistan* **66 F7** 39 6N 63 34 E
Charente □, *France* **28 C4** 45 50N 0 16 E
Charente →, *France* **28 C2** 45 57N 1 5W
Charente-Maritime □, *France* **28 C3** 45 45N 0 45W
Charenton-du-Cher, *France* **27 F9** 46 44N 2 39 E
Chari →, *Chad* **109 F2** 12 58N 14 31 E
Chārīkār, *Afghan.* **91 B3** 35 0N 69 10 E
Charing, *U.S.A.* **152 C5** 32 28N 84 22W
Chariton, *U.S.A.* **156 C3** 41 1N 93 19W
Chariton →, *U.S.A.* **156 E4** 39 19N 92 58W
Charity, *Guyana* **169 B6** 7 24N 58 36W
Chärjew, *Turkmenistan* **66 F7** 39 6N 63 34 E
Charkhari, *India* **93 G8** 25 24N 79 45 E
Charkhi Dadri, *India* **92 E7** 28 37N 76 17 E
Charleroi, *Belgium* **24 D4** 50 24N 4 27 E
Charleroi, *U.S.A.* **150 F5** 40 9N 79 57W
Charles, C., *U.S.A.* **148 G8** 37 7N 75 58W
Charles City, *U.S.A.* **156 A4** 43 4N 92 41W
Charles L., *Canada* **143 B6** 59 50N 110 33W
Charles Sound, *N.Z.* **131 F2** 45 2 S 167 4 E
Charles Town, *U.S.A.* **148 F7** 39 17N 77 52W
Charleston, *Ill., U.S.A.* **157 E8** 39 30N 88 10W
Charleston, *Miss., U.S.A.* **155 H9** 34 1N 90 4W
Charleston, *Mo., U.S.A.* **155 G10** 36 55N 89 21W
Charleston, *S.C., U.S.A.* **152 C10** 32 46N 79 56W
Charleston, *W. Va., U.S.A.* **148 F5** 38 21N 81 38W
Charleston L., *Canada* **151 B9** 44 32N 76 0W
Charleston Peak, *U.S.A.* **161 J11** 36 16N 115 42W
Charlestown, *Ireland* **23 C3** 53 58N 8 48W
Charlestown, *S. Africa* **117 D4** 27 26 S 29 53 E
Charlestown, *Ind., U.S.A.* **157 F11** 38 27N 85 40W
Charlestown, *N.H., U.S.A.* **151 C12** 43 14N 72 25W
Charleville = Rath Luirc, *Ireland* **23 D3** 52 21N 8 40W
Charleville, *Australia* **127 D4** 26 24 S 146 15 E
Charleville-Mézières, *France* **27 C11** 49 44N 4 40 E
Charlevoix, *U.S.A.* **148 C3** 45 19N 85 16W
Charlieu, *France* **27 F11** 46 10N 4 10 E
Charlotte, *Mich., U.S.A.* **157 B12** 42 34N 84 50W
Charlotte, *N.C., U.S.A.* **149 H5** 35 13N 80 51W
Charlotte, *Vt., U.S.A.* **151 B11** 44 19N 73 14W
Charlotte Amalie, *U.S. Virgin Is.* **165 e** 18 21N 64 56W
Charlotte Harbor, *U.S.A.* **149 M4** 26 50N 82 10W
Charlotte L., *Canada* **142 C3** 52 12N 125 19W
Charlottenberg, *Sweden* **16 E6** 59 54N 12 17 E
Charlottesville, *U.S.A.* **148 F6** 38 2N 78 30W
Charlottetown, *Nfld., Canada* **141 B8** 52 46N 56 7W
Charlottetown, *P.E.I., Canada* **141 C7** 46 14N 63 8W
Charlotteville, *Trin. & Tob.* **169 E10** 11 20N 60 33W
Charlton, *Australia* **128 D5** 36 16 S 143 24 E
Charlton, *U.S.A.* **154 E8** 40 59N 93 20W
Charlton I., *Canada* **140 B4** 52 0N 79 20W
Charmes, *France* **27 D13** 48 22N 6 17 E
Charmey, *Switz.* **32 C4** 46 37N 7 10 E
Charny, *Canada* **141 C5** 46 43N 71 15W
Charolles, *France* **27 F11** 46 27N 4 16 E
Chârost, *France* **27 F9** 47 0N 2 7 E
Charouine, *Algeria* **111 C4** 29 0N 0 15W
Charre, *Mozam.* **119 F4** 17 13 S 35 10 E
Charroux, *France* **28 B4** 46 9N 0 25 E
Charsadda, *Pakistan* **92 B4** 34 7N 71 45 E
Charshanga, *Turkmenistan* **65 E3** 37 30N 66 1 E
Charters Towers, *Australia* **126 C4** 20 5 S 146 13 E
Chartres, *France* **26 D8** 48 29N 1 30 E
Charvakskoye Vdkhr., *Uzbekistan* **65 C5** 41 35N 70 0 E
Chascomús, *Argentina* **174 D4** 35 30 S 58 0W
Chasefu, *Zambia* **119 E3** 11 55 S 33 8 E
Chashma Barrage, *Pakistan* **91 B3** 32 27N 71 20 E
Chaslands Mistake, *N.Z.* **131 G4** 46 38 S 169 22 E
Chasseneuil-sur-Bonnieure, *France* **28 C4** 45 52N 0 29 E
Chasseron, *Switz.* **32 C3** 46 52N 6 32 E
Chāt, *Iran* **97 B7** 37 59N 55 16 E
Chatal Balkan = Udvoy Balkan, *Bulgaria* **51 D10** 42 50N 26 50 E
Chatanika, *U.S.A.* **144 D11** 65 7N 147 28W
Château-Arnoux, *France* **29 D10** 44 6N 6 0 E
Château-Chinon, *France* **27 E10** 47 4N 3 56 E
Château d'Oex, *Switz.* **32 D4** 46 28N 7 8 E
Château-d'Olonne, *France* **28 B2** 46 30N 1 44W
Château-du-Loir, *France* **26 E7** 47 40N 0 25 E
Château-Gontier, *France* **26 E6** 47 50N 0 48W
Château-la-Vallière, *France* **26 E7** 47 30N 0 20 E
Château-Landon, *France* **27 D9** 48 8N 2 40 E
Château-Renault, *France* **26 E7** 47 36N 0 56 E
Château-Salins, *France* **27 D13** 48 50N 6 30 E
Château-Thierry, *France* **27 C10** 49 3N 3 20 E
Châteaubourg, *France* **26 D5** 48 7N 1 25W
Châteaubriant, *France* **26 E5** 47 43N 1 23W
Châteaudun, *France* **26 D8** 48 3N 1 20 E
Chateaugay, *U.S.A.* **151 B10** 44 56N 74 5W
Châteaugiron, *France* **26 D5** 48 3N 1 30W
Châteauguay, L., *Canada* **141 A5** 56 26N 70 3W
Châteaulin, *France* **26 D2** 48 11N 4 8W
Châteaumeillant, *France* **27 F9** 46 35N 2 12 E
Châteauneuf-du-Faou, *France* **26 D3** 48 11N 3 50W
Châteauneuf-sur-Charente, *France* **28 C3** 45 36N 0 3W
Châteauneuf-sur-Cher, *France* **27 F9** 46 52N 2 18 E
Châteauneuf-sur-Loire, *France* **27 E9** 47 52N 2 13 E
Châteaurenard, *Bouches-du-Rhône, France* **29 E8** 43 53N 4 51 E
Châteaurenard, *Loiret, France* **27 E9** 47 56N 2 55 E
Châteauroux, *France* **27 F8** 46 50N 1 40 E
Châteauvillain, *France* **27 D11** 48 2N 4 55 E
Châteaux, Pte. des, *Guadeloupe* **164 b** 16 15N 61 10W
Châtel-St.-Denis, *Switz.* **32 C3** 46 32N 6 54 E
Châtelaillon-Plage, *France* **28 B2** 46 5N 1 5W
Châtelguyon, *France* **28 C7** 45 55N 3 4 E
Châtellerault, *France* **26 F7** 46 50N 0 30 E
Châtelus-Malvaleix, *France* **27 F9** 46 18N 2 1 E
Chatham = Miramichi, *Canada* **141 C6** 47 2N 65 28W
Chatham, *Canada* **140 D3** 42 24N 82 11W
Chatham, *U.K.* **21 F8** 51 22N 0 32 E
Chatham, *Ill., U.S.A.* **156 E7** 39 40N 89 42W
Chatham, *N.Y., U.S.A.* **151 D11** 42 21N 73 36W
Chatham, I., *Chile* **176 D2** 50 40 S 74 25W
Chatham Is., *Pac. Oc.* **134 M10** 44 0 S 176 40W
Châtillon, *Italy* **44 C4** 45 45N 7 37 E
Châtillon-Coligny, *France* **27 E9** 47 50N 2 51 E
Châtillon-en-Diois, *France* **29 D9** 44 41N 5 29 E
Châtillon-sur-Indre, *France* **26 F8** 46 59N 1 10 E
Châtillon-sur-Loire, *France* **27 E9** 47 35N 2 44 E
Châtillon-sur-Seine, *France* **27 E11** 47 50N 4 33 E
Chatkal →, *Uzbekistan* **65 C5** 41 38N 70 1 E
Chatkal Kyrka Tooloru, *Kyrgyzstan* **65 C5** 41 30N 70 45 E
Chatmohar, *Bangla.* **93 G13** 24 15N 89 15 E
Chatra, *India* **93 G11** 24 12N 84 56 E
Chatrapur, *India* **94 E7** 19 22N 85 2 E
Chats, L. des, *Canada* **151 A8** 45 30N 76 20W
Chatsu, *India* **92 F6** 26 36N 75 57 E
Chatsworth, *Canada* **150 B4** 44 27N 80 54W
Chatsworth, *U.S.A.* **157 D8** 40 45N 88 18W
Chatsworth, *Zimbabwe* **119 F3** 19 38 S 31 13 E
Chatta-Hantō, *Japan* **73 C8** 34 45N 136 55 E
Chattahoochee, *U.S.A.* **152 E5** 30 42N 84 51W
Chattahoochee →, *U.S.A.* **152 E5** 30 54N 84 57W
Chattanooga, *U.S.A.* **149 H3** 35 3N 85 19W
Chatteris, *U.K.* **21 E8** 52 28N 0 2 E
Chaturat, *Thailand* **86 E3** 15 40N 101 51 E
Chatyr-Köl, *Kyrgyzstan* **65 C7** 40 40N 75 18 E
Chatyr-Tash, *Kyrgyzstan* **65 C8** 40 55N 76 25 E
Chau Doc, *Vietnam* **87 G5** 10 42N 105 7 E
Chaudes-Aigues, *France* **28 D7** 44 51N 3 1 E
Chauffailles, *France* **27 F11** 46 13N 4 20 E
Chauk, *Burma* **90 E5** 20 53N 94 49 E
Chaukan Pass, *Burma* **90 B6** 27 8N 97 10 E
Chaumont, *France* **27 D12** 48 7N 5 8 E
Chaumont, *U.S.A.* **151 B8** 44 4N 76 8W
Chaumont-en-Vexin, *France* **27 C8** 49 16N 1 53 E
Chaumont-sur-Loire, *France* **26 E8** 47 29N 1 11 E
Chaunay, *France* **28 B4** 46 13N 0 9 E
Chauny, *France* **27 C10** 49 37N 3 12 E
Chaura, *India* **95 K11** 8 27N 93 2 E
Chausey, Îs., *France* **26 D5** 48 52N 1 49W
Chaussin, *France* **27 F12** 46 59N 5 22 E
Chautauqua L., *U.S.A.* **150 D5** 42 10N 79 24W
Chauvay, *Kyrgyzstan* **65 C6** 40 8N 72 8 E
Chauvigny, *France* **26 F7** 46 34N 0 39 E
Chauvin, *Canada* **143 C6** 52 45N 110 10W
Chavakachcheri, *Sri Lanka* **95 K5** 9 39N 80 9 E
Chavanges, *France* **27 D11** 48 30N 4 35 E
Chavantina, *Brazil* **173 C7** 14 40 S 52 21W
Chaves, *Brazil* **170 B2** 0 15 S 49 55W
Chaves, *Portugal* **42 D3** 41 45N 7 32W
Chavuma, *Zambia* **115 E4** 13 4 S 22 40 E
Chawang, *Thailand* **87 H2** 8 25N 99 30 E
Chayan = Shayan, *Kazakstan* **65 B4** 43 5N 69 25 E
Chaykovskiy, *Russia* **64 C5** 56 47N 54 9 E
Chazelles-sur-Lyon, *France* **29 C8** 45 39N 4 22 E
Chazuta, *Peru* **172 B2** 6 30 S 76 0W
Chazy, *U.S.A.* **151 B11** 44 53N 73 26W
Cheaha Mt., *U.S.A.* **152 B4** 33 29N 85 49W
Cheb, *Czech Rep.* **34 A5** 50 9N 12 28 E
Chebanse, *U.S.A.* **157 D9** 41 0N 87 54W
Chebarkul, *Russia* **64 D8** 55 0N 60 25 E
Cheboksarskoye Vdkhr., *Russia* **60 B8** 56 13N 46 58 E
Cheboksary, *Russia* **60 B8** 56 8N 47 12 E
Cheboygan, *U.S.A.* **148 C3** 45 39N 84 29W
Chebsara, *Russia* **58 C10** 59 10N 38 59 E
Chech, Erg, *Africa* **110 D4** 25 0N 2 15W
Chechaouen, *Morocco* **110 A3** 35 9N 5 15W
Chechen, Ostrov, *Russia* **61 H8** 43 59N 47 40 E
Chechenia □, *Russia* **61 J7** 43 30N 45 29 E
Checheno-Ingush Republic = Chechenia □, *Russia* **61 J7** 43 30N 45 29 E
Chechnya = Chechenia □, *Russia* **61 J7** 43 30N 45 29 E
Chech'ŏn, *S. Korea* **75 F15** 37 8N 128 12 E
Chęciny, *Poland* **55 H7** 50 46N 20 28 E
Checotah, *U.S.A.* **155 H7** 35 28N 95 31W
Chedabucto B., *Canada* **141 C7** 45 25N 61 8W
Cheduba I., *Burma* **90 F4** 18 45N 93 40 E
Cheepie, *Australia* **127 D4** 26 33 S 145 1 E
Chef-Boutonne, *France* **28 B3** 46 7N 0 4W
Cheffadine, *Niger* **109 D2** 19 57N 12 11 E
Chefornak, *U.S.A.* **144 F6** 60 13N 164 12W
Chegdomyn, *Russia* **67 D14** 51 7N 133 1 E
Chegga, *Mauritania* **110 C3** 25 27N 5 40W
Chegutu, *Zimbabwe* **119 F3** 18 10 S 30 14 E
Chehalis, *U.S.A.* **160 D4** 46 40N 122 58W
Chehalis →, *U.S.A.* **160 D3** 46 57N 123 50W
Cheiron, Mt., *France* **29 E10** 43 49N 6 58 E
Cheju do, *S. Korea* **75 H14** 33 29N 126 34 E
Chekalin, *Russia* **58 E9** 54 10N 36 10 E
Chekiang = Zhejiang □, *China* **77 C13** 29 0N 120 0 E
Chel = Kuru, Bahr el →, *Sudan* **107 F2** 8 10N 26 50 E
Chela, Sa. da, *Angola* **116 B1** 16 20 S 13 20 E
Chelan, *U.S.A.* **158 C4** 47 51N 120 1W
Chelan, L., *U.S.A.* **158 B3** 48 11N 120 30W
Chelek, *Uzbekistan* **65 D3** 39 55N 66 51 E
Cheleken, *Turkmenistan* **57 G9** 39 34N 53 16 E
Cheleken Yarymadasy, *Turkmenistan* **97 B7** 39 30N 53 15 E
Chelforó, *Argentina* **176 A3** 39 0 S 66 33W
Chéliff, O. →, *Algeria* **111 A5** 36 0N 0 8 E
Chelkar = Shalqar, *Kazakstan* **66 E6** 47 48N 59 39 E
Chelkar Tengiz, Solonchak, *Kazakstan* **66 E7** 48 5N 63 7 E
Chella, *Ethiopia* **107 F4** 5 0N 37 26 E
Chellala Dahrania, *Algeria* **111 B5** 33 2N 0 1 E
Chelles, *France* **27 D9** 48 52N 2 33 E
Chełm, *Poland* **55 G10** 51 8N 23 30 E
Chełmno, *Poland* **55 E5** 53 20N 18 30 E
Chelmsford, *U.K.* **21 F8** 51 44N 0 29 E
Chełmża, *Poland* **55 E5** 53 10N 18 39 E
Chelsea, *Australia* **129 E6** 38 5 S 145 8 E
Chelsea, *Mich., U.S.A.* **157 B12** 42 19N 84 1W
Chelsea, *Vt., U.S.A.* **151 C12** 43 59N 72 27W
Cheltenham, *U.K.* **21 F5** 51 54N 2 4W
Chelva, *Spain* **40 F4** 39 45N 1 0W
Chelyabinsk, *Russia* **64 D8** 55 10N 61 24 E
Chelyuskin, C., *Russia* **62 B14** 77 30N 103 0 E
Chemainus, *Canada* **160 B3** 48 55N 123 42W
Chembar = Belinskiy, *Russia* **60 D6** 53 0N 43 25 E
Chemillé, *France* **26 E6** 47 14N 0 45W
Chemin Grenier, *Mauritius* **121 d** 20 29 S 57 28 E
Chemnitz, *Germany* **30 E8** 50 51N 12 54 E
Chemult, *U.S.A.* **158 E3** 43 14N 121 47W
Chen, Gora, *Russia* **67 C15** 65 16N 141 50 E
Chenab →, *Pakistan* **91 C3** 30 23N 71 2 E
Chenachane, O. →, *Algeria* **110 C4** 25 20N 3 20W
Chenango Forks, *U.S.A.* **151 D9** 42 15N 75 51W
Chencha, *Ethiopia* **107 F4** 6 15N 37 32 E
Chenchiang = Zhenjiang, *China* **77 A12** 32 11N 119 26 E
Cheney, *U.S.A.* **158 C5** 47 30N 117 35W
Cheng Xian, *China* **74 H3** 33 43N 105 42 E
Chengalpattu, *India* **95 H4** 12 42N 79 58 E
Chengbu, *China* **77 D8** 26 18N 110 16 E
Chengcheng, *China* **74 G5** 35 8N 109 56 E
Chengchou = Zhengzhou, *China* **74 G7** 34 45N 113 34 E
Chengde, *China* **75 D9** 40 59N 117 58 E
Chengdong Hu, *China* **77 A11** 32 15N 116 20 E
Chengdu, *China* **76 B5** 30 38N 104 2 E
Chengele, *India* **90 A6** 28 47N 96 16 E
Chenggong, *China* **76 E4** 24 52N 102 56 E
Chenggu, *China* **74 H4** 33 10N 107 21 E
Chenghai, *China* **77 F11** 23 30N 116 42 E
Chengjiang, *China* **76 E4** 24 39N 103 0 E
Chengkou, *China* **76 B7** 31 54N 108 31 E
Ch'engmai, *China* **86 C7** 19 50N 109 58 E
Ch'engtu = Chengdu, *China* **76 B5** 30 38N 104 2 E
Chengwu, *China* **74 G8** 34 58N 115 50 E
Chengxi Hu, *China* **77 A11** 32 15N 116 10 E
Chengyang, *China* **75 F11** 36 18N 120 21 E
Chenjiagang, *China* **75 G10** 34 23N 119 47 E
Chenkaladi, *Sri Lanka* **95 L5** 7 47N 81 35 E
Chenkán, *Mexico* **163 D6** 19 8N 90 58W
Chennai, *India* **95 H5** 13 8N 80 19 E
Chenoa, *U.S.A.* **157 D8** 40 45N 88 43W
Chenôve, *France* **27 E12** 47 16N 5 1 E
Chenxi, *China* **77 C8** 28 2N 110 12 E
Chenzhou, *China* **77 E9** 25 47N 113 1 E
Cheo Reo, *Vietnam* **78 B3** 13 25N 108 28 E
Cheom Ksan, *Cambodia* **86 E5** 14 13N 104 56 E
Chepelare, *Bulgaria* **51 E8** 41 44N 24 40 E
Chepén, *Peru* **172 B2** 7 15 S 79 23W
Chépénéhé, *Vanuatu* **133 K5** 20 47 S 167 9 E
Chepes, *Argentina* **174 C2** 31 20 S 66 35W
Chepo, *Panama* **164 E4** 9 10N 79 6W
Chepstow, *U.K.* **21 F5** 51 38N 2 41W
Cheptsa → = Chapetsk →, *Russia* **64 B3** 58 36N 50 4 E
Cheptulil, Mt., *Kenya* **118 B4** 1 25N 35 35 E
Chequamegon B., *U.S.A.* **154 B9** 46 40N 90 30W
Cher □, *France* **27 E9** 47 10N 2 30 E
Cher →, *France* **26 E7** 47 21N 0 29 E
Chéradi, *Italy* **47 B10** 40 27N 17 10 E
Cheran, *India* **90 C3** 25 45N 90 44 E
Cherasco, *Italy* **44 D4** 44 39N 7 51 E
Cheraw, *U.S.A.* **149 H6** 34 42N 79 53W
Cherbourg, *France* **26 C5** 49 39N 1 40W
Cherchell, *Algeria* **111 A5** 36 35N 2 12 E
Cherdakly, *Russia* **60 C9** 54 25N 48 50 E
Cherdyn, *Russia* **64 A6** 60 24N 56 29 E
Cheremkhovo, *Russia* **67 D11** 53 8N 103 1 E
Cherepanovo, *Russia* **66 D9** 54 15N 83 30 E
Cherepovets, *Russia* **58 C9** 59 5N 37 55 E
Chergui, Chott ech, *Algeria* **111 B5** 34 21N 0 25 E
Chergui, Zahrez, *Algeria* **111 B5** 35 11N 3 31 E
Cherial, *India* **94 F4** 17 55N 78 59 E
Cherikov = Cherykaw, *Belarus* **58 F6** 53 32N 31 20 E
Cheriyam I., *India* **95 J1** 10 9N 73 40 E
Cherkasy, *Ukraine* **59 H7** 49 27N 32 4 E
Cherkessk, *Russia* **61 H6** 44 15N 42 5 E
Cherla, *India* **94 E5** 18 5N 80 49 E
Cherlak, *Russia* **66 D8** 54 15N 74 55 E
Chermoz, *Russia* **64 B6** 58 46N 56 10 E
Chernak = Shornak, *Kazakstan* **65 B4** 43 24N 68 2 E
Chernaya, *Russia* **67 B9** 70 30N 89 10 E
Chernaya Kholunitsa, *Russia* **64 B3** 58 57N 51 39 E
Cherni, *Bulgaria* **50 D7** 42 35N 23 18 E
Chernigov = Chernihiv, *Ukraine* **59 G6** 51 28N 31 20 E
Chernihiv, *Ukraine* **59 G6** 51 28N 31 20 E
Chernivtsi, *Ukraine* **59 H3** 48 15N 25 52 E
Chernobyl = Chornobyl, *Ukraine* **59 G6** 51 20N 30 15 E
Chernogorsk, *Russia* **67 D10** 53 49N 91 18 E
Chernomorskoye = Chornomorske, *Ukraine* **59 K7** 45 31N 32 40 E
Chernovtsy = Chernivtsi, *Ukraine* **59 H3** 48 15N 25 52 E
Chernushka, *Russia* **64 C6** 56 29N 56 3 E
Chernyakhovsk, *Russia* **15 J19** 54 36N 21 48 E
Chernyanka, *Russia* **59 G9** 50 56N 37 49 E
Chernysheyskiy, *Russia* **67 C12** 63 0N 112 30 E
Chernyy Otrog, *Russia* **64 F6** 51 53N 56 0 E
Chernyye Zemli, *Russia* **61 H8** 46 10N 46 0 E
Cherokee, *Iowa, U.S.A.* **154 D7** 42 45N 95 33W
Cherokee, *Okla., U.S.A.* **155 G5** 36 45N 98 21W
Cherokee Village, *U.S.A.* **155 G9** 36 17N 91 30W
Cherokees, Grand Lake O' The, *U.S.A.* **155 G7** 36 28N 95 2W
Cherquenco, *Chile* **176 A2** 38 35 S 72 0W
Cherrapunji, *India* **90 C3** 25 17N 91 47 E
Cherry Valley, *Calif., U.S.A.* **161 M10** 33 59N 116 57W
Cherry Valley, *N.Y., U.S.A.* **151 D10** 42 48N 74 45W
Cherryville, *U.S.A.* **156 G5** 37 51N 91 16W
Cherskiy, *Russia* **67 C17** 68 45N 161 18 E
Cherskogo Khrebet, *Russia* **67 C15** 65 0N 143 0 E
Chertkovo, *Russia* **59 H11** 49 25N 40 19 E
Cherven, *Belarus* **58 F5** 53 45N 28 28 E
Cherven-Bryag, *Bulgaria* **51 C8** 43 17N 24 7 E
Chervonohrad, *Ukraine* **59 G3** 50 25N 24 10 E
Cherwell →, *U.K.* **21 F6** 51 44N 1 14W
Cherykaw, *Belarus* **58 F6** 53 32N 31 20 E
Chesapeake, *U.S.A.* **148 G7** 36 50N 76 17W
Chesapeake B., *U.S.A.* **148 G7** 38 0N 76 10W
Cheshire □, *U.K.* **20 D5** 53 14N 2 30W
Cheshskaya Guba, *Russia* **56 A8** 67 20N 47 0 E
Cheshunt, *U.K.* **21 F7** 51 43N 0 1W
Chesil Beach, *U.K.* **21 G5** 50 37N 2 33W
Chesley, *Canada* **150 B3** 44 17N 81 5W
Cheste, *Spain* **41 F4** 39 30N 0 41W
Chester, *U.K.* **20 D5** 53 12N 2 53W
Chester, *Calif., U.S.A.* **158 F3** 40 19N 121 14W
Chester, *Ga., U.S.A.* **152 C6** 32 24N 83 9W
Chester, *Ill., U.S.A.* **155 G10** 37 55N 89 49W
Chester, *Mont., U.S.A.* **158 B8** 48 31N 110 58W
Chester, *Pa., U.S.A.* **148 F8** 39 51N 75 22W
Chester, *S.C., U.S.A.* **149 H5** 34 43N 81 12W
Chester, *Vt., U.S.A.* **151 C12** 43 16N 72 36W
Chester, *W. Va., U.S.A.* **150 F4** 40 37N 80 34W
Chester-le-Street, *U.K.* **20 C6** 54 51N 1 34W
Chesterfield, *U.K.* **20 D6** 53 15N 1 25W
Chesterfield, Is., *N. Cal.* **134 J7** 19 52 S 158 15 E
Chesterfield Inlet, *Canada* **138 B10** 63 30N 90 45W
Chesterton Ra., *Australia* **127 D4** 25 30 S 147 27 E
Chesterton Range Nat. Park, *Australia* **127 D4** 26 16 S 147 22 E
Chestertown, *U.S.A.* **151 C11** 43 40N 73 48W
Chesterville, *Canada* **151 A9** 45 6N 75 14W
Chestnut Ridge, *U.S.A.* **150 F5** 40 20N 79 10W
Chesuncook L., *U.S.A.* **149 C11** 46 0N 69 21W
Chetamale, *India* **95 J11** 10 43N 92 33 E
Chéticamp, *Canada* **141 C7** 46 37N 60 59W
Chetlat I., *India* **95 J1** 11 42N 72 42 E
Chetrosu, *Moldova* **53 B12** 48 5N 27 54 E
Chetumal, *Mexico* **163 D7** 18 30N 88 20W
Chetumal, B. de, *Mexico* **163 D7** 18 40N 88 10W
Chetwynd, *Canada* **142 B4** 55 45N 121 36W
Chevak, *U.S.A.* **144 F6** 61 32N 165 35W
Chevanceaux, *France* **28 C3** 45 18N 0 14W
Cheviot, *U.S.A.* **157 E12** 39 10N 84 37W
Cheviot, The, *U.K.* **20 B5** 55 29N 2 9W
Cheviot Hills, *U.K.* **20 B5** 55 20N 2 30W
Cheviot Ra., *Australia* **126 D3** 25 20 S 143 45 E
Chew Bahir, *Ethiopia* **107 G4** 4 40N 36 50 E
Chewelah, *U.S.A.* **158 B5** 48 17N 117 43W
Chewore Safari Area, *Zimbabwe* **119 F2** 16 0 S 29 52 E
Cheyenne, *Okla., U.S.A.* **155 H5** 35 37N 99 40W
Cheyenne, *Wyo., U.S.A.* **154 E2** 41 8N 104 49W
Cheyenne →, *U.S.A.* **154 C4** 44 41N 101 18W
Cheyenne Wells, *U.S.A.* **154 F3** 38 49N 102 21W
Cheyne B., *Australia* **125 F2** 34 35 S 118 50 E
Cheyur, *India* **95 H5** 12 21N 80 0 E
Chhabra, *India* **92 G7** 24 40N 76 54 E
Chhaktala, *India* **92 H6** 22 6N 74 11 E
Chhapra, *India* **93 G11** 25 48N 84 44 E
Chhata, *India* **92 F7** 27 42N 77 30 E
Chhatak, *Bangla.* **90 C3** 25 5N 91 37 E
Chhatarpur, *Jharkhand, India* **93 G11** 24 23N 84 11 E
Chhatarpur, *Mad. P., India* **93 G8** 24 55N 79 35 E
Chhati, *India* **94 D5** 20 47N 81 40 E
Chhattisgarh □, *India* **93 J10** 22 0N 82 0 E
Chhaygaon, *India* **90 B3** 26 3N 91 24 E
Chhep, *Cambodia* **86 F5** 13 45N 105 24 E
Chhindwara, *Mad. P., India* **93 H8** 23 3N 79 29 E
Chhindwara, *Mad. P., India* **93 H8** 22 2N 78 59 E
Chhinhdipada, *India* **94 D7** 21 6N 84 52 E
Chhlong, *Cambodia* **87 F5** 12 15N 105 58 E
Chhota Tawa →, *India* **92 H7** 22 14N 76 36 E
Chhoti Kali Sindh →, *India* **92 G6** 24 2N 75 31 E
Chhuikhadan, *India* **93 J9** 21 32N 80 59 E
Chhuk, *Cambodia* **87 G5** 10 46N 104 28 E
Chi →, *Thailand* **86 E5** 15 11N 104 43 E
Chiai, *Taiwan* **77 F13** 23 29N 120 25 E
Chiali, *Taiwan* **77 F13** 23 10N 120 11 E
Chiamussu = Jiamusi, *China* **69 B8** 46 40N 130 26 E
Chianciano Terme, *Italy* **45 E8** 43 2N 11 49 E
Chiang Dao, *Thailand* **86 C2** 19 22N 98 58 E
Chiang Kham, *Thailand* **86 C3** 19 32N 100 18 E
Chiang Khan, *Thailand* **86 D3** 17 52N 101 36 E
Chiang Khong, *Thailand* **76 G3** 20 17N 100 24 E
Chiang Mai, *Thailand* **86 C2** 18 47N 98 59 E
Chiang Rai, *Thailand* **76 H2** 19 52N 99 50 E
Chiang Saen, *Thailand* **76 G3** 20 16N 100 5 E
Chiange, *Angola* **115 F2** 15 35 S 13 40 E
Chiapa →, *Mexico* **163 D6** 16 42N 93 0W
Chiapa de Corzo, *Mexico* **163 D6** 16 42N 93 0W
Chiapas □, *Mexico* **163 D6** 17 0N 92 45W
Chiaramonte Gulfi, *Italy* **47 E7** 37 2N 14 42 E
Chiaravalle, *Italy* **45 E10** 43 36N 13 19 E
Chiaravalle Centrale, *Italy* **47 D9** 38 41N 16 25 E
Chiari, *Italy* **44 C6** 45 32N 9 56 E
Chiasso, *Switz.* **33 E8** 45 50N 9 2 E
Chiatura, *Georgia* **61 J6** 42 15N 43 17 E
Chiautla, *Mexico* **163 D5** 18 18N 98 34W
Chiávari, *Italy* **44 D6** 44 19N 9 19 E
Chiavenna, *Italy* **44 B6** 46 19N 9 24 E
Chiba, *Japan* **73 B12** 35 30N 140 7 E
Chiba □, *Japan* **73 B12** 35 30N 140 20 E
Chibabava, *Mozam.* **117 C5** 20 17 S 33 35 E
Chibango, *Angola* **115 E4** 13 38 S 21 56 E
Chibemba, *Cunene, Angola* **115 F2** 15 48 S 14 8 E
Chibemba, *Huila, Angola* **116 B2** 16 20 S 15 20 E
Chibi, *Zimbabwe* **117 C5** 20 18 S 30 25 E
Chibia, *Angola* **115 F2** 15 10 S 13 42 E
Chibougamau, *Canada* **140 C5** 49 56N 74 24W
Chibougamau, L., *Canada* **140 C5** 49 50N 74 20W
Chibuk, *Nigeria* **113 C7** 10 52N 12 50 E
Chibuto, *Mozam.* **117 C5** 24 40 S 33 33 E
Chic-Chocs, Mts., *Canada* **141 C6** 48 55N 66 0W
Chicacole = Srikakulam, *India* **94 E6** 18 14N 83 58 E
Chicago, *U.S.A.* **157 C9** 41 53N 87 38W
Chicago Heights, *U.S.A.* **157 C9** 41 30N 87 38W
Chicapa →, *Dem. Rep. of the Congo* **115 D4** 6 25 S 20 48 E
Chicha, *Chad* **109 E3** 16 57N 18 34 E
Chichagof I., *U.S.A.* **144 H14** 57 30N 135 30W
Chichaoua, *Morocco* **110 B3** 31 32N 8 44W
Chichén-Itzá, *Mexico* **163 C7** 20 40N 88 36W
Chicheng, *China* **74 D8** 40 55N 115 55 E
Chichester, *U.K.* **21 G7** 50 50N 0 47W
Chichester Ra., *Australia* **124 D2** 22 12 S 119 15 E
Chichibu, *Japan* **73 A11** 35 59N 139 10 E
Ch'ich'ihaerh = Qiqihar, *China* **67 E13** 47 26N 124 0 E
Chicholi, *India* **92 H8** 22 1N 77 40 E
Chickasha, *U.S.A.* **155 H6** 35 3N 97 58W
Chicken, *U.S.A.* **144 D12** 64 5N 141 56W

Cincinnatus 201

Chiclana de la Frontera, *Spain* **43 J4** 36 26N 6 9W
Chiclayo, *Peru* **172 B2** 6 42 S 79 50W
Chico, *U.S.A.* **160 F5** 39 44N 121 50W
Chico →, *Chubut, Argentina* **176 B3** 44 0 S 67 0W
Chico →, *Santa Cruz, Argentina* **176 C3** 50 0 S 68 30W
Chicomba, *Angola* **115 E2** 14 10 S 14 52 E
Chicomo, *Mozam.* **117 C5** 24 31 S 34 6 E
Chicontepec, *Mexico* **163 C5** 20 58N 98 10W
Chicopee, *U.S.A.* **151 D12** 42 9N 72 37W
Chicoutimi, *Canada* **141 C5** 48 28N 71 5W
Chicualacuala, *Mozam.* **117 C5** 22 6 S 31 42 E
Chicuma, *Angola* **115 E2** 13 26 S 14 50 E
Chidambaram, *India* **95 J4** 11 20N 79 45 E
Chidenguele, *Mozam.* **117 C5** 24 55 S 34 11 E
Chidley, C., *Canada* **139 B13** 60 23N 64 26W
Chiducuane, *Mozam.* **117 C5** 24 35 S 34 25 E
Chiede, *Angola* **116 B2** 17 15 S 16 22 E
Chiefland, *U.S.A.* **153 F7** 29 29N 82 52W
Chiefs Pt., *Canada* **150 B3** 44 41N 81 18W
Chiem Hoa, *Vietnam* **86 A5** 22 12N 105 17 E
Chiemsee, *Germany* **31 H8** 47 53N 12 28 E
Chiengi, *Zambia* **119 D2** 8 45 S 29 10 E
Chiengmai = Chiang Mai, *Thailand* **86 C2** 18 47N 98 59 E
Chiengo, *Angola* **115 E4** 13 20 S 21 55 E
Chienti →, *Italy* **45 E10** 43 18N 13 45 E
Chieri, *Italy* **44 C4** 45 1N 7 49 E
Chiers →, *France* **27 C11** 49 39N 4 59 E
Chiesa in Valmalenco, *Italy* **44 B6** 46 16N 9 51 E
Chiese →, *Italy* **44 C7** 45 8N 10 25 E
Chieti, *Italy* **45 F11** 42 21N 14 10 E
Chifeng, *China* **75 C10** 42 18N 118 58 E
Chigasaki, *Japan* **73 B11** 35 19N 139 24 E
Chigirin, *Ukraine* **59 H7** 49 4N 32 38 E
Chignecto B., *Canada* **141 C7** 45 30N 64 40W
Chignik, *U.S.A.* **144 H8** 56 18N 158 24W
Chigorodó, *Colombia* **168 B2** 7 41N 76 42W
Chiguana, *Bolivia* **174 A2** 21 0 S 67 58W
Chigwell, *U.K.* **21 F8** 51 37N 0 5 E
Chiha-ri, *N. Korea* **75 E14** 38 40N 126 30 E
Chihli, G. of = Bo Hai, *China* **75 E10** 39 0N 119 0 E
Chihuahua, *Mexico* **162 B3** 28 40N 106 3W
Chihuahua □, *Mexico* **162 B3** 28 40N 106 3W
Chiili = Shīeli, *Kazakstan* **66 E7** 44 20N 66 15 E
Chik Bollapur, *India* **95 H3** 13 25N 77 45 E
Chikalda, *India* **94 D3** 21 24N 77 19 E
Chikhli, *Ahmadabad, India* **94 D1** 20 45N 73 4 E
Chikhli, *Maharashtra, India* **94 D3** 20 20N 76 18 E
Chikmagalur, *India* **95 H2** 13 15N 75 45 E
Chiknayakanhalli, *India* **95 H3** 13 26N 76 37 E
Chikodi, *India* **95 F2** 16 26N 74 38 E
Chikugo, *Japan* **72 D2** 33 14N 130 28 E
Chikuma-Gawa →, *Japan* **73 A10** 36 59N 138 35 E
Chikushino, *Japan* **72 D2** 33 30N 130 30 E
Chikwawa, *Malawi* **119 F3** 16 2 S 34 50 E
Chila, *Angola* **115 E2** 12 3 S 14 29 E
Chilac, *Mexico* **163 D5** 18 20N 97 24W
Chilam Chavki, *Pakistan* **93 B6** 35 5N 75 5 E
Chilanga, *Zambia* **119 F2** 15 33 S 28 16 E
Chilapa, *Mexico* **163 D5** 17 40N 99 11W
Chilas, *Pakistan* **93 B6** 35 25N 74 5 E
Chilaw, *Sri Lanka* **95 L4** 7 30N 79 50 E
Chilcotin →, *Canada* **142 C4** 51 44N 122 23W
Childers, *Australia* **127 D5** 25 15 S 152 17 E
Childersburg, *U.S.A.* **152 B3** 33 16N 86 21W
Childress, *U.S.A.* **155 H4** 34 25N 100 13W
Chile ■, *S. Amer.* **176 B2** 35 0 S 72 0W
Chile Chico, *Chile* **176 C2** 46 33 S 71 44W
Chile Rise, *Pac. Oc.* **135 L18** 38 0 S 92 0W
Chilecito, *Argentina* **174 B2** 29 10 S 67 30W
Chilesso, *Angola* **115 E3** 11 35 S 16 34 E
Chilete, *Peru* **172 B2** 7 10 S 78 50W
Chilhowee, *U.S.A.* **156 F3** 38 36N 93 51W
Chilia, Braţul →, *Romania* **53 E14** 45 14N 29 42 E
Chilik = Shelek, *Kazakstan* **65 B9** 43 33N 78 17 E
Chililabombwe, *Zambia* **119 E2** 12 18 S 27 43 E
Chilin = Jilin, *China* **75 C14** 43 44N 126 30 E
Chilka L., *India* **94 E7** 19 40N 85 25 E
Chilko →, *Canada* **142 C4** 52 0N 123 40W
Chilko L., *Canada* **142 C4** 51 20N 124 10W
Chillagoe, *Australia* **126 B3** 17 7 S 144 33 E
Chillán, *Chile* **174 D1** 36 40 S 72 10W
Chillicothe, *Ill., U.S.A.* **156 D7** 40 55N 89 29W
Chillicothe, *Mo., U.S.A.* **156 E3** 39 48N 93 33W
Chillicothe, *Ohio, U.S.A.* **148 F4** 39 20N 82 59W
Chilliwack, *Canada* **142 D4** 49 10N 121 54W
Chilo, *India* **92 F5** 27 25N 73 32 E
Chiloane, I., *Mozam.* **117 C5** 20 40 S 34 55 E
Chiloé, I. de, *Chile* **176 B2** 42 30 S 73 50W
Chilonda, *Angola* **115 E3** 11 19 S 16 12 E
Chilongo, *Angola* **115 E3** 13 55 S 16 35 E
Chilpancingo, *Mexico* **163 D5** 17 30N 99 30W
Chiltern, *Australia* **129 D7** 36 10 S 146 36 E
Chiltern Hills, *U.K.* **21 F7** 51 40N 0 53W
Chilton, *U.S.A.* **148 C1** 44 2N 88 10W
Chiluage, *Angola* **115 D4** 9 30 S 21 50 E
Chilubi, *Zambia* **119 E2** 11 5 S 29 58 E
Chilubula, *Zambia* **119 E3** 10 14 S 30 51 E
Chilumba, *Malawi* **119 E3** 10 28 S 34 12 E
Chilung, *Taiwan* **77 E13** 25 3N 121 45 E
Chilwa, L., *Malawi* **119 F4** 15 15 S 35 40 E
Chimakela, *Angola* **115 F3** 15 24 S 16 58 E
Chimakudi, *India* **90 C4** 25 47N 93 48 E
Chimaltitán, *Mexico* **162 C4** 21 46N 103 50W
Chimán, *Panama* **164 E4** 8 45N 78 40W
Chimanimani, *Zimbabwe* **117 B5** 19 48 S 32 52 E
Chimanimani Nat. Park, *Zimbabwe* **119 F3** 19 48 S 33 0 E
Chimay, *Belgium* **24 D4** 50 3N 4 20 E
Chimayo, *U.S.A.* **159 H11** 36 0N 105 56W
Chimbay, *Uzbekistan* **66 E6** 42 57N 59 47 E
Chimborazo, *Ecuador* **168 D2** 1 29 S 78 55W
Chimborazo □, *Ecuador* **168 D2** 1 0 S 78 40W
Chimbote, *Peru* **172 B2** 9 0 S 78 35W
Chimbu □, *Papua N. G.* **132 D3** 6 15 S 144 50 E
Chimichagua, *Colombia* **168 B3** 9 15N 73 49W
Chimion, *Uzbekistan* **65 C5** 40 15N 71 32 E
Chimkent = Shymkent, *Kazakstan* **66 E7** 42 18N 69 36 E
Chimoio, *Mozam.* **119 F3** 19 4 S 33 30 E
Chimpembe, *Zambia* **119 D2** 9 31 S 29 33 E
Chimur, *India* **94 D4** 20 30N 79 23 E
Chin □, *Burma* **90 D4** 22 0N 93 0 E
Chin Hills, *Burma* **90 D4** 22 30N 93 30 E
Chin Ling Shan = Qinling Shandi, *China* **74 H5** 33 50N 108 10 E
China, *Mexico* **163 B5** 25 40N 99 20W
China ■, *Asia* **69 C6** 30 0N 110 0 E
China Lake, *U.S.A.* **161 K9** 35 44N 117 37W
Chinacota, *Colombia* **168 B3** 7 37N 72 36W
Chinan = Jinan, *China* **74 F9** 36 38N 117 1 E
Chinandega, *Nic.* **164 D2** 12 35N 87 12W
Chinati Peak, *U.S.A.* **155 L2** 29 57N 104 29W
Chinaz, *Uzbekistan* **65 C4** 40 56N 68 46 E
Chincha Alta, *Peru* **172 C2** 13 25 S 76 7W
Chinchaga →, *Canada* **142 B5** 58 53N 118 20W
Chincheros, *Peru* **172 C3** 13 30 S 73 44W
Chinchilla, *Australia* **127 D5** 26 45 S 150 38 E
Chinchilla de Monte Aragón, *Spain* **41 G3** 38 53N 1 40W
Chincholi, *India* **94 E3** 17 28N 77 26 E
Chinchorro, Banco, *Mexico* **163 D7** 18 35N 87 20W
Chinchou = Jinzhou, *China* **75 D11** 41 5N 121 3 E
Chinchoua, *Gabon* **114 B1** 0 1N 9 48 E
Chincoteague, *U.S.A.* **148 G8** 37 56N 75 23W
Chinde, *Mozam.* **119 F4** 18 35 S 36 30 E
Chindo, *S. Korea* **75 G14** 34 28N 126 15 E
Chindwin →, *Burma* **90 E5** 21 26N 95 15 E
Chineni, *India* **93 C6** 33 2N 75 15 E
Chinga, *Mozam.* **119 F4** 15 13 S 38 35 E
Chingirlau, *Kazakstan* **64 F5** 51 7N 54 7 E
Chingola, *Zambia* **119 E2** 12 31 S 27 53 E
Chingole, *Malawi* **119 E3** 13 4 S 34 17 E
Chingoroi, *Angola* **115 E2** 13 37 S 14 1 E
Ch'ingtao = Qingdao, *China* **75 F11** 36 5N 120 20 E
Chinguar, *Angola* **115 E3** 12 25 S 16 45 E
Chinguetti, *Mauritania* **110 D2** 20 25N 12 24W
Chingune, *Mozam.* **117 C5** 20 33 S 34 58 E
Chinhae, *S. Korea* **75 G15** 35 9N 128 47 E
Chinhanguanine, *Mozam.* **117 D5** 25 21 S 32 30 E
Chinhoyi, *Zimbabwe* **119 F3** 17 20 S 30 8 E
Chini, *India* **92 D8** 31 32N 78 15 E
Chiniot, *Pakistan* **91 C4** 31 45N 73 0 E
Chínipas, *Mexico* **162 B3** 27 22N 108 32W
Chinji, *Pakistan* **92 C5** 32 42N 72 22 E
Chinju, *S. Korea* **75 G15** 35 12N 128 2 E
Chinkai, *Afghan.* **91 C2** 31 57N 67 26 E
Chinkapook, *Australia* **128 C5** 35 11 S 142 57 E
Chinko →, *C.A.R.* **114 B4** 4 50N 23 53 E
Chinle, *U.S.A.* **159 H9** 36 9N 109 33W
Chinmen, *Taiwan* **77 E13** 24 26N 118 19 E
Chinmen Tao, *Taiwan* **77 E12** 24 27N 118 23 E
Chinnamanur, *India* **95 K3** 9 50N 77 24 E
Chinnampo = Namp'o, *N. Korea* **75 E13** 38 52N 125 10 E
Chinnur, *India* **94 E4** 18 57N 79 49 E
Chino, *Japan* **73 B10** 35 59N 138 9 E
Chino, *U.S.A.* **161 L9** 34 1N 117 41W
Chino Valley, *U.S.A.* **159 J7** 34 45N 112 27W
Chinon, *France* **26 E7** 47 10N 0 15 E
Chinook, *U.S.A.* **158 B9** 48 35N 109 14W
Chinoya, *Zambia* **115 E4** 13 55 S 23 16 E
Chinsali, *Zambia* **119 E3** 10 30 S 32 2 E
Chintalapudi, *India* **94 F5** 17 4N 80 59 E
Chintamani, *India* **95 H4** 13 26N 78 3 E
Chióggia, *Italy* **45 C9** 45 13N 12 17 E
Chíos = Khíos, *Greece* **49 C8** 38 27N 26 9 E
Chipata, *Zambia* **119 E3** 13 38 S 32 28 E
Chiperceni, *Moldova* **53 C13** 47 31N 28 50 E
Chipindo, *Angola* **115 E3** 13 49 S 15 48 E
Chipinge, *Zimbabwe* **119 G3** 20 13 S 32 28 E
Chipinge Safari Area, *Zimbabwe* **119 G3** 20 14 S 33 0 E
Chipiona, *Spain* **43 J4** 36 44N 6 26W
Chipley, *U.S.A.* **152 E4** 30 47N 85 32W
Chiplun, *India* **94 F1** 17 31N 73 34 E
Chipman, *Canada* **141 C6** 46 6N 65 53W
Chipoka, *Malawi* **119 E3** 13 57 S 34 28 E
Chippenham, *U.K.* **21 F5** 51 27N 2 6W
Chippewa →, *U.S.A.* **154 C8** 44 25N 92 5W
Chippewa Falls, *U.S.A.* **154 C9** 44 56N 91 24W
Chipping Norton, *U.K.* **21 F6** 51 56N 1 32W
Chiprovtsi, *Bulgaria* **50 C6** 43 24N 22 52 E
Chiputneticook Lakes, *U.S.A.* **149 C11** 45 35N 67 35W
Chiquelequele, *Angola* **115 F3** 16 44 S 19 5 E
Chiquián, *Peru* **172 C2** 10 10 S 77 0W
Chiquimula, *Guatemala* **164 D2** 14 51N 89 37W
Chiquinquira, *Colombia* **168 B3** 5 37N 73 50W
Chiquitos, Llanos de, *Bolivia* **173 D5** 18 0 S 61 30W
Chir →, *Russia* **61 F6** 48 30N 43 0 E
Chira →, *Peru* **168 D1** 4 54 S 81 8W
Chirala, *India* **95 G5** 15 50N 80 26 E
Chiramba, *Mozam.* **119 F3** 16 55 S 34 39 E
Chirawa, *India* **92 E6** 28 14N 75 42 E
Chirayinkil, *India* **95 K3** 8 41N 76 49 E
Chirchiq, *Uzbekistan* **66 E7** 41 29N 69 35 E
Chiredzi, *Zimbabwe* **117 C5** 21 0 S 31 38 E
Chirfa, *Niger* **109 D2** 20 55N 12 22 E
Chirgua →, *Venezuela* **168 B4** 8 54N 67 58W
Chiricahua Peak, *U.S.A.* **159 L9** 31 51N 109 18W
Chiriquí, G. de, *Panama* **164 E3** 8 0N 82 10W
Chiriquí, L. de, *Panama* **164 E3** 9 10N 82 0W
Chirisa Safari Area, *Zimbabwe* **119 F2** 17 53 S 28 15 E
Chirivira Falls, *Zimbabwe* **119 G3** 21 10 S 32 12 E
Chirnogi, *Romania* **53 F11** 44 7N 26 32 E
Chirpan, *Bulgaria* **51 D9** 42 10N 25 19 E
Chirripó Grande, Cerro, *Costa Rica* **164 E3** 9 29N 83 29W
Chirundu, *Zimbabwe* **117 B4** 16 3 S 28 50 E
Chisamba, *Zambia* **119 E2** 14 55 S 28 20 E
Chisasibi, *Canada* **140 B4** 53 50N 79 0W
Ch'ishan, *Taiwan* **77 F13** 22 44N 120 31 E
Chishmy, *Russia* **64 D5** 54 35N 55 23 E
Chisholm, *Canada* **142 C6** 54 55N 114 10W
Chisholm, *U.S.A.* **154 B8** 47 29N 92 53W
Chishtian Mandi, *Pakistan* **92 E5** 29 50N 72 55 E
Chishui, *China* **76 C5** 28 30N 105 42 E
Chishui He →, *China* **76 C5** 28 49N 105 50 E
Chisimaio, *Somali Rep.* **120 E2** 0 22 S 42 32 E
Chisimba Falls, *Zambia* **119 E3** 10 12 S 30 56 E
Chişinău, *Moldova* **53 C13** 47 2N 28 50 E
Chişineu Criş, *Romania* **52 D6** 46 32N 21 37 E
Chisone →, *Italy* **44 D4** 44 49N 7 25 E
Chisos Mts., *U.S.A.* **155 L3** 29 5N 103 15W
Chissengue, *Angola* **115 D4** 9 13 S 20 34 E
Chissilo, *Angola* **115 E3** 13 48 S 16 31 E
Chistochina, *U.S.A.* **144 E11** 62 34N 144 40W
Chistopol, *Russia* **60 C10** 55 25N 50 38 E
Chita, *Colombia* **168 B3** 6 11N 72 28W
Chita, *Russia* **67 D12** 52 0N 113 35 E
Chitado, *Angola* **115 F2** 17 10 S 14 8 E
Chitanda →, *Angola* **115 F3** 16 1 S 15 12 E
Chitapur, *India* **94 F3** 17 10N 77 5 E
Chitembo, *Angola* **115 E3** 13 30 S 16 50 E
Chitina, *U.S.A.* **144 F11** 61 31N 144 26W
Chitipa, *Malawi* **119 D3** 9 41 S 33 19 E
Chitose, *Japan* **70 C10** 42 49N 141 39 E
Chitradurga, *India* **95 G3** 14 14N 76 24 E
Chitrakot, *India* **94 E5** 19 10N 81 40 E
Chitral, *Pakistan* **91 B3** 35 50N 71 56 E
Chitravati →, *India* **95 G4** 14 45N 78 15 E
Chitré, *Panama* **164 E3** 7 59N 80 27W
Chittagong, *Bangla.* **90 D3** 22 19N 91 48 E
Chittagong □, *Bangla.* **90 C3** 24 5N 91 0 E
Chittaurgarh, *India* **92 G6** 24 52N 74 38 E
Chittoor, *India* **95 H4** 13 15N 79 5 E
Chittur, *India* **95 J3** 10 40N 76 45 E
Chitungwiza, *Zimbabwe* **119 F3** 18 0 S 31 6 E
Chiumbe →, *Dem. Rep. of the Congo* **115 D4** 6 59 S 21 12 E
Chiumbo, *Angola* **115 E3** 12 29 S 16 8 E
Chiume, *Angola* **115 F4** 15 3 S 21 14 E
Chiuro, *Italy* **33 D9** 46 10N 9 59 E
Chiusi, *Italy* **45 E8** 43 1N 11 57 E
Chiva, *Spain* **41 F4** 39 27N 0 41W
Chivacoa, *Venezuela* **168 A4** 10 10N 68 54W
Chivasso, *Italy* **44 C4** 45 11N 7 53 E
Chivay, *Peru* **172 D3** 15 40 S 71 35W
Chivé, *Bolivia* **172 C4** 12 23 S 68 35W
Chivhu, *Zimbabwe* **119 F3** 19 2 S 30 52 E
Chivilcoy, *Argentina* **174 C4** 34 55 S 60 0W
Chiwanda, *Tanzania* **119 E3** 11 23 S 34 55 E
Chixi, *China* **77 G9** 22 0N 112 58 E
Chizarira, *Zimbabwe* **119 F2** 17 36 S 27 45 E
Chizarira Nat. Park, *Zimbabwe* **119 F2** 17 44 S 27 52 E
Chizela, *Zambia* **115 E4** 13 8 S 25 0 E
Chizera, *Zambia* **119 E2** 13 10 S 25 0 E
Chizu, *Japan* **72 B6** 35 16N 134 14 E
Chkalov = Orenburg, *Russia* **64 F5** 51 45N 55 6 E
Chkolovsk, *Russia* **60 B6** 56 50N 43 10 E
Chloride, *U.S.A.* **161 K12** 35 25N 114 12W
Chlumec nad Cidlinou, *Czech Rep.* **34 A8** 50 9N 15 29 E
Chmielnik, *Poland* **55 H7** 50 37N 20 43 E
Cho Bo, *Vietnam* **76 G5** 20 46N 105 10 E
Cho-do, *N. Korea* **75 E13** 38 30N 124 40 E
Cho Phuoc Hai, *Vietnam* **87 G6** 10 26N 107 18 E
Choa Chu Kang, *Singapore* **87 d** 1 22N 103 41 E
Choba, *Kenya* **118 B4** 2 30N 38 5 E
Chobe Nat. Park, *Botswana* **116 B4** 18 37 S 24 23 E
Choch'iwŏn, *S. Korea* **75 F14** 36 37N 127 18 E
Chocianów, *Poland* **55 G2** 51 27N 15 55 E
Chociwel, *Poland* **54 E2** 53 29N 15 21 E
Chocó □, *Colombia* **168 B2** 6 0N 77 0W
Chocolate Mts., *U.S.A.* **161 M11** 33 15N 115 15W
Chocontá, *Colombia* **168 B3** 5 9N 73 41W
Choctawhatchee →, *U.S.A.* **152 E3** 30 25N 86 8W
Chodavaram, *Andhra Pradesh, India* **94 F6** 17 50N 82 57 E
Chodavaram, *Andhra Pradesh, India* **94 F5** 17 27N 81 46 E
Chodecz, *Poland* **55 F6** 52 24N 19 2 E
Chodov, *Czech Rep.* **34 A5** 50 15N 12 45 E
Chodziez, *Poland* **55 F3** 52 58N 16 58 E
Choele Choel, *Argentina* **176 A3** 39 11 S 65 40W
Chōfu, *Japan* **73 B11** 35 39N 139 33 E
Choiseul, *St. Lucia* **165 f** 13 47N 61 3W
Choiseul, *Solomon Is.* **133 L9** 7 0 S 156 40 E
Choix, *Mexico* **162 B3** 26 40N 108 23W
Chojna, *Poland* **55 F1** 52 58N 14 25 E
Chojnice, *Poland* **54 E4** 53 42N 17 32 E
Chojnów, *Poland* **55 G2** 51 18N 15 58 E
Chok-Tal, *Kyrgyzstan* **65 B8** 42 35N 76 45 E
Chōkai-San, *Japan* **70 E10** 39 6N 140 3 E
Choke, *Ethiopia* **107 E4** 11 18N 37 15 E
Choke Canyon L., *U.S.A.* **155 L5** 28 30N 98 20W
Chokurdakh, *Russia* **67 B15** 70 38N 147 55 E
Cholame, *U.S.A.* **160 K6** 35 44N 120 18W
Cholet, *France* **26 E6** 47 4N 0 52W
Cholguan, *Chile* **174 D1** 37 10 S 72 3W
Cholpon-Ata, *Kyrgyzstan* **65 B8** 42 40N 77 6 E
Choluteca, *Honduras* **164 D2** 13 20N 87 14W
Choluteca →, *Honduras* **164 D2** 13 0N 87 20W
Chom Bung, *Thailand* **86 F2** 13 37N 99 36 E
Chom Thong, *Thailand* **86 C2** 18 25N 98 41 E
Choma, *Zambia* **119 F2** 16 48 S 26 59 E
Chomen Swamp, *Ethiopia* **107 F4** 9 20N 37 10 E
Chomun, *India* **92 F6** 27 15N 75 40 E
Chomutov, *Czech Rep.* **34 A6** 50 28N 13 23 E
Chon Buri, *Thailand* **86 F3** 13 21N 101 1 E
Chon Thanh, *Vietnam* **87 G6** 11 24N 106 36 E
Ch'onan, *S. Korea* **75 F14** 36 48N 127 9 E
Chone, *Ecuador* **168 D2** 0 40 S 80 0W
Chong Kai, *Cambodia* **86 F4** 13 57N 103 35 E
Chong Mek, *Thailand* **86 E5** 15 10N 105 27 E
Chong Phangan, *Thailand* **87 b** 9 39N 100 0 E
Chong Samui, *Thailand* **87 b** 9 21N 99 50 E
Chongde, *China* **77 B13** 30 32N 120 26 E
Chŏngdo, *S. Korea* **75 G15** 35 38N 128 42 E
Chŏngha, *S. Korea* **75 F15** 36 12N 129 21 E
Chŏngjin, *N. Korea* **75 D15** 41 47N 129 50 E
Chŏngjiu, *S. Korea* **75 F14** 36 39N 127 27 E
Chŏngju, *N. Korea* **75 E13** 39 40N 125 5 E
Chongli, *China* **74 D8** 40 58N 115 15 E
Chongming, *China* **77 B13** 31 38N 121 23 E
Chongming Dao, *China* **77 B13** 31 40N 121 30 E
Chongoyape, *Peru* **172 B2** 6 35 S 79 25W
Chongqing, *Chongqing, China* **76 C6** 29 35N 106 25 E
Chongqing, *Sichuan, China* **76 B4** 30 38N 103 40 E
Chongqing Shi □, *China* **76 C6** 30 0N 108 0 E
Chongren, *China* **77 D11** 27 46N 116 3 E
Chonguene, *Mozam.* **117 C5** 25 3 S 33 49 E
Chŏngŭp, *S. Korea* **75 G14** 35 35N 126 50 E
Chongyi, *China* **77 E10** 25 45N 114 29 E
Chongzuo, *China* **76 F6** 22 23N 107 20 E
Chŏnju, *S. Korea* **75 G14** 35 50N 127 4 E
Chonos, Arch. de los, *Chile* **176 C2** 45 0 S 75 0W
Chop, *Ukraine* **59 H2** 48 26N 22 12 E
Chopda, *India* **94 D2** 21 20N 75 15 E
Chopim →, *Brazil* **175 B5** 25 35 S 53 5W
Chor, *Pakistan* **92 G3** 25 31N 69 46 E
Chorbat La, *India* **93 B7** 34 42N 76 37 E
Chorley, *U.K.* **20 D5** 53 39N 2 38W
Chornobyl, *Ukraine* **59 G6** 51 20N 30 15 E
Chornomorske, *Ukraine* **59 K7** 45 31N 32 40 E
Chorolque, Cerro, *Bolivia* **174 A2** 20 59 S 66 5W
Choroszcz, *Poland* **55 E9** 53 10N 22 59 E
Chorregon, *Australia* **126 C3** 22 40 S 143 32 E
Chortkiv, *Ukraine* **59 H3** 49 2N 25 46 E
Ch'ŏrwon, *S. Korea* **75 E14** 38 15N 127 10 E
Chorzele, *Poland* **55 E7** 53 15N 20 55 E
Chorzów, *Poland* **55 H5** 50 18N 18 57 E
Chos-Malal, *Argentina* **174 D1** 37 20 S 70 15W
Ch'osan, *N. Korea* **75 D13** 40 50N 125 47 E
Chōshi, *Japan* **73 B12** 35 45N 140 51 E
Choszczno, *Poland* **55 E2** 53 7N 15 25 E
Chota, *Peru* **172 B2** 6 33 S 78 39W
Choteau, *U.S.A.* **158 C7** 47 49N 112 11W
Chotěboř, *Czech Rep.* **34 B8** 49 43N 15 40 E
Chotila, *India* **92 H4** 22 23N 71 15 E
Chotta Udepur, *India* **92 H6** 22 19N 74 1 E
Chowchilla, *U.S.A.* **160 H6** 37 7N 120 16W
Choybalsan, *Mongolia* **69 B6** 48 4N 114 30 E
Chrisman, *U.S.A.* **156 E9** 39 48N 87 41W
Christchurch, *N.Z.* **131 D7** 43 33 S 172 47 E
Christchurch, *U.K.* **21 G6** 50 44N 1 47W
Christian I., *Canada* **150 B4** 44 50N 80 12W
Christian Sd., *U.S.A.* **144 J14** 55 56N 134 40W
Christiana, *S. Africa* **116 D4** 27 52 S 25 8 E
Christiansfeld, *Denmark* **17 J3** 55 21N 9 29 E
Christianshåb = Qasigiannguit, *Greenland* **10 D5** 68 50N 51 18W
Christiansted, *U.S. Virgin Is.* **165 C7** 17 45N 64 42W
Christie B., *Canada* **143 A6** 62 32N 111 10W
Christina →, *Canada* **143 B6** 56 40N 111 3W
Christmas Cr. →, *Australia* **124 C4** 18 29 S 125 23 E
Christmas I. = Kiritimati, *Kiribati* **135 G12** 1 58N 157 27W
Christmas I., *Ind. Oc.* **121 F9** 10 30 S 105 40 E
Christopher, *U.S.A.* **156 G7** 37 59N 89 3W
Christopher L., *Australia* **125 D4** 24 49 S 127 42 E
Chrudim, *Czech Rep.* **34 B8** 49 58N 15 43 E
Chrzanów, *Poland* **55 H6** 50 10N 19 21 E
Chtimba, *Malawi* **119 E3** 10 35 S 34 13 E
Chu = Shū, *Kazakstan* **66 E8** 43 36N 73 42 E
Chu →, *Vietnam* **86 C5** 19 53N 105 45 E
Chu Lai, *Vietnam* **86 E7** 15 28N 108 45 E
Chuadanga, *Bangla.* **90 D2** 23 38N 88 51 E
Chuak, Ko, *Thailand* **87 b** 9 28N 99 41 E
Ch'uanchou = Quanzhou, *China* **77 E12** 24 55N 118 34 E
Chuankou, *China* **74 G6** 34 20N 110 59 E
Chuathbaluk, *U.S.A.* **144 F8** 61 35N 159 15W
Chubbuck, *U.S.A.* **158 E7** 42 55N 112 28W
Chūbu □, *Japan* **73 A9** 36 45N 137 30 E
Chubut □, *Argentina* **176 B3** 43 30 S 69 0W
Chubut →, *Argentina* **176 B3** 43 20 S 65 5W
Chuchi L., *Canada* **142 B4** 55 12N 124 30W
Chuda, *India* **92 H4** 22 29N 71 41 E
Chudovo, *Russia* **58 C6** 59 10N 31 41 E
Chudskoye, Ozero, *Russia* **15 G22** 58 13N 27 30 E
Chugach Mts., *U.S.A.* **144 F11** 60 45N 147 0W
Chugach Nat. Forest, *U.S.A.* **144 G9** 58 15N 152 45W
Chugiak, *U.S.A.* **144 F10** 61 24N 149 29W
Chuginadak I., *U.S.A.* **144 K5** 52 50N 169 45W
Chūgoku □, *Japan* **72 C5** 35 0N 133 0 E
Chūgoku-Sanchi, *Japan* **72 C5** 35 0N 133 0 E
Chuguyev = Chuhuyiv, *Ukraine* **59 H9** 49 55N 36 45 E
Chugwater, *U.S.A.* **154 E2** 41 46N 104 50W
Chuhuyiv, *Ukraine* **59 H9** 49 55N 36 45 E
Chukchi Sea, *Russia* **67 C19** 68 0N 175 0W
Chukotskoye Nagorye, *Russia* **67 C18** 68 0N 175 0 E
Chula, *U.S.A.* **152 D6** 31 33N 83 32W
Chula Vista, *U.S.A.* **161 N9** 32 39N 117 5W
Chulakkurgan = Sholaqqūrghan, *Kazakstan* **65 B4** 43 46N 69 9 E
Chulband →, *India* **94 D4** 20 40N 79 54 E
Chulucanas, *Peru* **172 B1** 5 8 S 80 10W
Chulumani, *Bolivia* **172 D4** 16 24 S 67 31W
Chulym →, *Russia* **66 D9** 57 43N 83 51 E
Chum Phae, *Thailand* **86 D4** 16 40N 102 6 E
Chum Saeng, *Thailand* **86 E3** 15 55N 100 15 E
Chuma, *Bolivia* **172 D4** 15 24 S 68 56W
Chumar, *India* **93 C8** 32 40N 78 35 E
Chumbicha, *Argentina* **174 B2** 29 0 S 66 10W
Chumerna, *Bulgaria* **51 D9** 42 45N 25 55 E
Chumikan, *Russia* **67 D14** 54 40N 135 10 E
Chumphon, *Thailand* **87 G2** 10 35N 99 14 E
Chumpi, *Peru* **172 D3** 15 4 S 73 46W
Chumuare, *Mozam.* **119 E3** 14 31 S 31 50 E
Chumunjin, *S. Korea* **75 F15** 37 55N 128 54 E
Chuna →, *Russia* **67 D10** 57 47N 94 37 E
Chun'an, *China* **77 C12** 29 35N 119 3 E
Ch'unch'ŏn, *S. Korea* **75 F14** 37 58N 127 44 E
Chunchura, *India* **93 H13** 22 53N 88 27 E
Chunga, *Zambia* **119 F2** 15 0 S 26 2 E
Chunggang-ŭp, *N. Korea* **75 D14** 41 48N 126 48 E
Chunghwa, *N. Korea* **75 E13** 38 52N 125 47 E
Ch'ungju, *S. Korea* **75 F14** 36 58N 127 58 E
Chungking = Chongqing, *China* **76 C6** 29 35N 106 25 E
Chungli, *Taiwan* **77 E13** 24 57N 121 13 E
Ch'ungmu, *S. Korea* **75 G15** 34 50N 128 20 E
Chungt'iaoshan = Zhongtiao Shan, *China* **74 G6** 35 0N 111 10 E
Chungyang Shanmo, *Taiwan* **77 F13** 23 10N 121 0 E
Chunian, *Pakistan* **92 D6** 30 57N 74 0 E
Chunya, *Tanzania* **119 D3** 8 30 S 33 27 E
Chunyang, *China* **75 C15** 43 38N 129 23 E
Chupara Pt., *Trin. & Tob.* **169 F9** 10 49N 61 22W
Chuquibamba, *Peru* **172 D3** 15 47 S 72 44W
Chuquibambilla, *Peru* **172 C3** 14 7 S 72 41W
Chuquicamata, *Chile* **174 A2** 22 15 S 69 0W
Chuquisaca □, *Bolivia* **173 E5** 20 30 S 63 30W
Chur, *Switz.* **33 C9** 46 52N 9 32 E
Churachandpur, *India* **90 C4** 24 20N 93 40 E
Churchill, *Australia* **129 E7** 38 19 S 146 25 E
Churchill, *Canada* **143 B10** 58 47N 94 11W
Churchill →, *Man., Canada* **143 B10** 58 47N 94 12W
Churchill →, *Nfld., Canada* **141 B7** 53 19N 60 10W
Churchill, C., *Canada* **143 B10** 58 46N 93 12W
Churchill Falls, *Canada* **141 B7** 53 36N 64 19W
Churchill L., *Canada* **143 B7** 55 55N 108 20W
Churchill Pk., *Canada* **142 B3** 58 10N 125 10W
Churdan, *U.S.A.* **156 B2** 42 9N 94 29W
Churfisten, *Switz.* **33 B8** 47 8N 9 17 E
Churki, *India* **93 H10** 23 50N 83 12 E
Churu, *India* **92 E6** 28 20N 74 50 E
Churubusco, *U.S.A.* **157 C11** 41 14N 85 19W
Churún Merú = Angel Falls, *Venezuela* **169 B5** 5 57N 62 30W
Churwalden, *Switz.* **33 C9** 46 47N 9 33 E
Chushal, *India* **93 C8** 33 40N 78 40 E
Chuska Mts., *U.S.A.* **159 H9** 36 15N 108 50W
Chusovaya →, *Russia* **64 B6** 58 12N 56 54 E
Chusovoy, *Russia* **64 B6** 58 22N 57 50 E
Chuspipata, *Bolivia* **172 D4** 16 18 S 67 48W
Chust, *Uzbekistan* **65 C5** 41 0N 71 13 E
Chute-aux-Outardes, *Canada* **141 C6** 49 7N 68 24W
Chuuronjang, *N. Korea* **75 D15** 41 35N 129 40 E
Chuvash Republic = Chuvashia □, *Russia* **60 C8** 55 30N 47 0 E
Chuvashia □, *Russia* **60 C8** 55 30N 47 0 E
Chuwārtah, *Iraq* **96 C5** 35 43N 45 34 E
Chuxiong, *China* **76 E3** 25 2N 101 28 E
Chüy = Shū →, *Kazakstan* **65 A3** 45 0N 67 44 E
Chüy, *Kyrgyzstan* **65 B7** 42 55N 75 15 E
Chuy, *Uruguay* **175 C5** 33 41 S 53 27W
Chuzenji-Ko, *Japan* **73 A11** 36 44N 139 27 E
Chuzhou, *China* **77 A12** 32 19N 118 20 E
Ci Xian, *China* **74 F8** 36 20N 114 25 E
Ciacova, *Romania* **52 E6** 45 35N 21 10 E
Ciadâr-Lunga, *Moldova* **53 D13** 46 3N 28 51 E
Ciamis, *Indonesia* **85 D3** 7 20 S 108 21 E
Cianjur, *Indonesia* **84 D3** 6 49 S 107 8 E
Cianorte, *Brazil* **175 A5** 23 37 S 52 37W
Cibola, *U.S.A.* **161 M12** 33 17N 114 42W
Cicero, *U.S.A.* **157 C9** 41 51N 87 45W
Cícero Dantas, *Brazil* **170 D4** 10 36 S 38 23W
Cicia, *Fiji* **133 A3** 17 45 S 179 18W
Cidacos →, *Spain* **40 C3** 42 21N 1 38W
Cide, *Turkey* **100 B5** 41 53N 33 1 E
Ciechanów, *Poland* **55 F7** 52 52N 20 38 E
Ciechanowiec, *Poland* **55 F9** 52 40N 22 31 E
Ciechocinek, *Poland* **55 F5** 52 53N 18 45 E
Ciego de Avila, *Cuba* **164 B4** 21 50N 78 50W
Ciénaga, *Colombia* **168 A3** 11 1N 74 15W
Ciénaga de Oro, *Colombia* **168 B2** 8 53N 75 37W
Cienfuegos, *Cuba* **164 B3** 22 10N 80 30W
Cierp, *France* **28 F4** 42 55N 0 40 E
Cíes, Is., *Spain* **42 C2** 42 12N 8 55W
Cieszanów, *Poland* **55 H10** 50 14N 23 8 E
Cieszyn, *Poland* **55 J5** 49 45N 18 35 E
Cieza, *Spain* **41 G3** 38 17N 1 23W
Çifteler, *Turkey* **100 C4** 39 22N 31 2 E
Cifuentes, *Spain* **40 E2** 40 47N 2 37W
Cihanbeyli, *Turkey* **100 C5** 38 40N 32 55 E
Cihuatlán, *Mexico* **162 D4** 19 14N 104 35W
Cijara, Embalse de, *Spain* **43 F6** 39 18N 4 52W
Cijulang, *Indonesia* **79 G13** 7 42 S 108 27 E
Cilacap, *Indonesia* **85 D3** 7 43 S 109 0 E
Çıldır, *Turkey* **101 B10** 41 7N 43 8 E
Çıldır Gölü, *Turkey* **101 B10** 41 5N 43 15 E
Cili, *China* **77 C8** 29 30N 111 8 E
Cilibia, *Romania* **53 E12** 45 4N 27 4 E
Cilicia, *Turkey* **100 D5** 36 30N 33 40 E
Cill Chainnigh = Kilkenny, *Ireland* **23 D4** 52 39N 7 15W
Cilo Dağı, *Turkey* **101 D10** 37 28N 43 55 E
Cima, *U.S.A.* **161 K11** 35 14N 115 30W
Cimarron, *Kans., U.S.A.* **155 G4** 37 48N 100 21W
Cimarron, *N. Mex., U.S.A.* **155 G2** 36 31N 104 55W
Cimarron →, *U.S.A.* **155 G6** 36 10N 96 17W
Cimişlia, *Moldova* **53 D13** 46 34N 28 44 E
Cimone, Mte., *Italy* **44 D7** 44 12N 10 42 E
Cimpu, *Indonesia* **82 B2** 3 25 S 120 22 E
Çinar, *Turkey* **101 D9** 37 46N 40 19 E
Çınarcık, *Turkey* **51 F13** 40 38N 29 5 E
Cinca →, *Spain* **40 D5** 41 26N 0 21 E
Cincar, *Bos.-H.* **52 G2** 43 55N 17 5 E
Cincinnati, *Iowa, U.S.A.* **156 D4** 40 38N 92 56W
Cincinnati, *Ohio, U.S.A.* **157 E12** 39 6N 84 31W
Cincinnatus, *U.S.A.* **151 D9** 42 33N 75 54W

Correntina 203

Colmenar Viejo, Spain 42 E7 40 39N 3 47W
Colo →, Australia 129 B9 33 25 S 150 52 E
Cologne = Köln, Germany 30 E2 50 56N 6 57 E
Colom, I. d'en, Spain 38 B5 39 58N 4 16 E
Coloma, Calif., U.S.A. 160 G6 38 48N 120 53W
Coloma, Mich., U.S.A. 157 B10 42 11N 86 19W
Colomb-Béchar = Béchar, Algeria 111 B4 31 38N 2 18W
Colombey-les-Belles, France 27 D12 48 32N 5 54 E
Colombey-les-Deux-Églises, France 27 D11 48 13N 4 50 E
Colômbia, Brazil 171 F2 20 10 S 48 40W
Colombia ■, S. Amer. 168 C3 3 45N 73 0W
Colombian Basin, S. Amer. 136 H12 14 0N 76 0W
Colombier, Switz. 32 C3 46 58N 6 53 E
Colombo, Sri Lanka 95 L4 6 56N 79 58 E
Colomiers, France 28 E5 43 36N 1 21 E
Colón, Buenos Aires, Argentina 174 C3 33 53 S 61 7W
Colón, Entre Ríos, Argentina 174 C4 32 12 S 58 10W
Colón, Cuba 164 B3 22 42N 80 54W
Colón, Panama 164 E4 9 20N 79 54W
Colón, Peru 172 A1 5 0 S 81 0W
Colón, Arch. de, Ecuador 172 a 0 0 91 0W
Colonia 25 de Mayo, Argentina 176 A3 37 48 S 67 41W
Colònia de Sant Jordi, Spain 38 B3 39 19N 2 59 E
Colonia del Sacramento, Uruguay 174 C4 34 25 S 57 50W
Colonia Dora, Argentina 174 B3 28 34 S 62 59W
Colonia Las Heras, Argentina 176 C3 46 33 S 68 57W
Colonial Beach, U.S.A. 148 F7 38 15N 76 58W
Colonie, U.S.A. 151 D11 42 43N 73 50W
Colonna, C., Italy 47 C10 39 2N 17 12 E
Colonsay, Canada 143 C7 51 59N 105 52W
Colonsay, U.K. 22 E2 56 5N 6 12W
Colorado □, U.S.A. 159 G10 39 30N 105 30W
Colorado →, Argentina 176 A4 39 50 S 62 8W
Colorado →, N. Amer. 159 L6 31 45N 114 40W
Colorado →, U.S.A. 155 L7 28 36N 95 59W
Colorado City, U.S.A. 155 J4 32 24N 100 52W
Colorado Plateau, U.S.A. 159 H8 37 0N 111 0W
Colorado River Aqueduct, U.S.A. 161 L12 34 17N 114 10W
Colorado Springs, U.S.A. 154 F2 38 50N 104 49W
Colorno, Italy 44 D7 44 56N 10 23 E
Colotlán, Mexico 162 C4 22 6N 103 16W
Colquechaca, Bolivia 173 D4 18 40 S 66 1W
Colquitt, U.S.A. 152 D5 31 10N 84 44W
Colstrip, U.S.A. 158 D10 45 53N 106 38W
Colton, U.S.A. 151 B10 44 33N 74 56W
Columbia, Ala., U.S.A. 152 D4 31 18N 85 7W
Columbia, Ill., U.S.A. 156 F6 38 27N 90 12W
Columbia, Ky., U.S.A. 148 G3 37 6N 85 18W
Columbia, La., U.S.A. 155 J8 32 6N 92 5W
Columbia, Miss., U.S.A. 155 K10 31 15N 89 50W
Columbia, Mo., U.S.A. 156 F4 38 57N 92 20W
Columbia, Pa., U.S.A. 151 F8 40 2N 76 30W
Columbia, S.C., U.S.A. 152 A8 34 0N 81 2W
Columbia, Tenn., U.S.A. 149 H2 35 37N 87 2W
Columbia →, N. Amer. 160 D2 46 15N 124 5W
Columbia, C., Canada 6 A4 83 0N 70 0W
Columbia, District of □, U.S.A. 148 F7 38 55N 77 0W
Columbia, Mt., Canada 142 C5 52 8N 117 20W
Columbia Basin, U.S.A. 158 C4 46 45N 119 5W
Columbia City, U.S.A. 157 C11 41 10N 85 29W
Columbia Falls, U.S.A. 158 B6 48 23N 114 11W
Columbia Mts., Canada 142 C5 52 0N 119 0W
Columbia Plateau, U.S.A. 158 D5 44 0N 117 30W
Columbiana, U.S.A. 150 F4 40 53N 80 42W
Columbretes, Is., Spain 40 F5 39 50N 0 50 E
Columbus, Ga., U.S.A. 152 C5 32 28N 84 59W
Columbus, Ind., U.S.A. 157 E11 39 13N 85 55W
Columbus, Kans., U.S.A. 155 G7 37 10N 94 50W
Columbus, Miss., U.S.A. 149 J1 33 30N 88 25W
Columbus, Mont., U.S.A. 158 D9 45 38N 109 15W
Columbus, N. Mex., U.S.A. 159 L10 31 50N 107 38W
Columbus, Nebr., U.S.A. 154 E6 41 26N 97 22W
Columbus, Ohio, U.S.A. 157 E13 39 58N 83 0W
Columbus, Tex., U.S.A. 155 L6 29 42N 96 33W
Columbus Grove, U.S.A. 157 D12 40 55N 84 4W
Columbus Junction, U.S.A. 156 C5 41 17N 91 22W
Colunga, Spain 42 B5 43 29N 5 16W
Colusa, U.S.A. 160 F4 39 13N 122 1W
Colville, U.S.A. 158 B5 48 33N 117 54W
Colville →, U.S.A. 144 A10 70 25N 150 30W
Colville, C., N.Z. 130 C4 36 29 S 175 21 E
Colwood, Canada 160 B3 48 26N 123 29W
Colwyn Bay, U.K. 20 D4 53 18N 3 44W
Coma, Ethiopia 107 F4 8 29N 36 53 E
Comácchio, Italy 45 D9 44 42N 12 11 E
Comalcalco, Mexico 163 D6 18 16N 93 13W
Comallo, Argentina 176 B2 41 0 S 70 5W
Comana, Romania 53 F11 44 10N 26 10 E
Comanche, U.S.A. 155 K5 31 54N 98 36W
Comandante Luis Piedrabuena, Argentina 176 C3 49 59 S 68 54W
Comănești, Romania 53 D11 46 25N 26 26 E
Comarapa, Bolivia 173 D5 17 54 S 64 29W
Comarnic, Romania 53 E10 45 15N 25 38 E
Comayagua, Honduras 164 D2 14 25N 87 37W
Combahee →, U.S.A. 149 J5 32 30N 80 31W
Combarbalá, Chile 174 C1 31 11 S 71 2W
Combeaufontaine, France 27 E12 47 38N 5 54 E
Comber, Canada 150 D2 42 14N 82 33W
Comber, U.K. 23 B6 54 33N 5 45W
Combermere, Canada 150 A7 45 22N 77 37W
Combermere Bay, Burma 90 F4 19 37N 93 34 E
Comblain-au-Pont, Belgium 24 D5 50 29N 5 35 E
Combourg, France 26 D5 48 25N 1 46W
Comboyne, Australia 129 A10 31 34 S 152 27 E
Combrailles, France 27 F9 46 8N 2 8 E
Combronde, France 28 C7 45 58N 3 5 E
Comer, Ala., U.S.A. 152 C4 32 2N 85 23W
Comer, Ga., U.S.A. 152 A6 34 4N 83 8W
Comeragh Mts., Ireland 23 D4 52 18N 7 34W
Comet, Australia 126 C4 23 36 S 148 38 E
Comilla, Bangla. 90 D3 23 28N 91 10 E
Comino, Malta 38 E7 36 1N 14 20 E
Comino, C., Italy 46 B2 40 32N 9 49 E
Cómiso, Italy 47 F7 36 56N 14 36 E
Comitán, Mexico 163 D6 16 18N 92 9W
Commentry, France 27 F9 46 20N 2 46 E
Commerce, Ga., U.S.A. 149 H4 34 12N 83 28W
Commerce, Tex., U.S.A. 155 J7 33 15N 95 54W
Commercy, France 27 D12 48 43N 5 34 E
Commissioner's Pt., Bermuda 9 a 32 19N 64 49W
Committee B., Canada 139 B11 68 30N 86 30W
Commonwealth B., Antarctica 7 C10 67 0 S 144 0 E
Commoron Cr. →, Australia 127 D5 28 22 S 150 8 E
Communism Pk. = Kommunizma, Pik, Tajikistan 66 F8 39 0N 72 2 E
Como, Italy 44 C6 45 47N 9 5 E
Como, Lago di, Italy 44 B6 46 0N 9 11 E
Comodoro Rivadavia, Argentina 176 C3 45 50 S 67 40W
Comoé, Parc Nat. de la, Ivory C. 112 D4 9 0N 3 35W
Comorâște, Romania 52 E6 45 10N 21 35 E
Comorin, C., India 95 K3 8 3N 77 40 E
Comoro Is. = Comoros ■, Ind. Oc. 105 H8 12 10 S 44 15 E
Comoros ■, Ind. Oc. 105 H8 12 10 S 44 15 E
Comox, Canada 142 D4 49 42N 124 55W
Compass Lake, U.S.A. 152 E4 30 36N 85 24W
Compiègne, France 27 C9 49 24N 2 50 E
Comporta, Portugal 43 G2 38 22N 8 46W
Compostela, Mexico 162 C4 21 15N 104 53W
Compostela, Phil. 81 H6 7 40N 126 2 E
Comprida, I., Brazil 175 A6 24 50 S 47 42W
Compton, Canada 151 A13 45 14N 71 49W
Compton, U.S.A. 161 M8 33 54N 118 13W
Comrat, Moldova 53 D13 46 18N 28 40 E
Con Cuong, Vietnam 86 C5 19 2N 104 54 E
Con Son, Vietnam 87 H6 8 41N 106 37 E
Cona Niyeu, Argentina 176 B3 41 58 S 67 0W
Conakry, Guinea 112 D2 9 29N 13 49W
Conara, Australia 127 G4 41 50 S 147 26 E
Conargo, Australia 129 C6 35 16 S 145 10 E
Concarneau, France 26 E3 47 52N 3 56W
Conceição, Brazil 170 C4 7 33 S 38 31W
Conceição, Mozam. 119 F4 18 47 S 36 7 E
Conceição da Barra, Brazil 171 E4 18 35 S 39 45W
Conceição do Araguaia, Brazil 170 C2 8 0 S 49 2W
Conceição do Canindé, Brazil 170 C3 7 54 S 41 34W
Conceição do Maú, Brazil 169 C6 3 35N 59 53W
Concepción, Argentina 174 B2 27 20 S 65 35W
Concepción, Bolivia 173 D5 16 15 S 62 8W
Concepción, Chile 174 D1 36 50 S 73 0W
Concepción, Mexico 163 D6 18 15N 90 5W
Concepción, Paraguay 174 A4 23 22 S 57 26W
Concepción, Peru 172 C2 11 54 S 75 19W
Concepcion, Phil. 80 D3 15 27N 120 47 E
Concepción □, Chile 174 D1 37 0 S 72 30W
Concepción →, Mexico 162 A2 30 32N 113 2W
Concepción, Est. de, Chile 176 D2 50 30 S 74 55W
Concepción, L., Bolivia 173 D5 17 20 S 61 20W
Concepción, Punta, Mexico 162 B2 26 55N 111 59W
Concepción del Oro, Mexico 162 C4 24 40N 101 30W
Concepción del Uruguay, Argentina 174 C4 32 35 S 58 20W
Conception, Pt., U.S.A. 161 L6 34 27N 120 28W
Conception B., Canada 141 C9 47 45N 53 0W
Conception B., Namibia 116 C1 23 55 S 14 22 E
Conception I., Bahamas 165 B4 23 52N 75 9W
Concession, Zimbabwe 119 F3 17 27 S 30 56 E
Conchas Dam, U.S.A. 155 H2 35 22N 104 11W
Conches-en-Ouche, France 26 D7 48 58N 0 56 E
Concho, U.S.A. 159 J9 34 28N 109 36W
Concho →, U.S.A. 155 K5 31 34N 99 43W
Conchos →, Chihuahua, Mexico 162 B4 29 32N 105 0W
Conchos →, Tamaulipas, Mexico 163 B5 25 9N 98 35W
Concise, Switz. 32 C3 46 51N 6 43 E
Concord, Calif., U.S.A. 160 H4 37 59N 122 2W
Concord, Ga., U.S.A. 152 B5 33 5N 84 27W
Concord, Mich., U.S.A. 157 B12 42 11N 84 38W
Concord, Mo., U.S.A. 156 F6 38 32N 90 23W
Concord, N.C., U.S.A. 149 H5 35 25N 80 35W
Concord, N.H., U.S.A. 151 C13 43 12N 71 32W
Concordia, Argentina 174 C4 31 20 S 58 2W
Concórdia, Brazil 168 D4 4 36 S 66 36W
Concordia, Mexico 162 C3 23 18N 106 2W
Concordia, Kans., U.S.A. 154 F6 39 34N 97 40W
Concordia, Mo., U.S.A. 156 F3 38 59N 93 34W
Concrete, U.S.A. 158 B3 48 32N 121 45W
Conda, Angola 115 E2 11 9 S 14 20 E
Condah, Australia 128 D4 37 57 S 141 44 E
Condamine, Australia 127 D5 26 56 S 150 9 E
Condat, France 28 C6 45 21N 2 46 E
Condé, Angola 115 E2 10 50 S 14 37 E
Conde, Brazil 171 D4 11 49 S 37 37W
Conde, U.S.A. 154 C5 45 9N 98 6W
Condé-sur-Noireau, France 26 D6 48 51N 0 33W
Condeúba, Brazil 171 D3 14 52 S 42 0W
Condobolin, Australia 129 B7 33 4 S 147 6 E
Condom, France 28 E4 43 57N 0 22 E
Condon, U.S.A. 158 D3 45 14N 120 11W
Conegliano, Italy 45 C9 45 53N 12 18 E
Conejera, I. = Conills, I. des, Spain 38 B3 39 11N 2 58 E
Conejos, Mexico 162 B4 26 14N 103 53W
Conflict Group, Papua N. G. 132 F6 10 47 S 151 45 E
Confolens, France 28 B4 46 2N 0 40 E
Confuso →, Paraguay 174 B4 25 9 S 57 34W
Congaree →, U.S.A. 152 B9 33 44N 80 38W
Congaz, Moldova 53 D13 46 7N 28 36 E
Congerville, U.S.A. 156 D7 40 38N 89 11W
Conghua, China 77 F9 23 36N 113 31 E
Congjiang, China 76 E7 25 43N 108 52 E
Congleton, U.K. 20 D5 53 10N 2 13W
Congo, Brazil 170 C4 7 48 S 36 40W
Congo (Kinshasa) = Congo, Dem. Rep. of the ■, Africa 115 C4 3 0 S 23 0 E
Congo ■, Africa 114 C3 1 0 S 16 0 E
Congo →, Africa 115 D2 6 4 S 12 24 E
Congo, Dem. Rep. of the ■, Africa 115 C4 3 0 S 23 0 E
Congo Basin, Africa 104 G6 0 10 S 24 30 E
Congonhas, Brazil 171 F3 20 30 S 43 52W
Congress, U.S.A. 159 J7 34 9N 112 51W
Conil = Conil de la Frontera, Spain 43 J4 36 17N 6 10W
Conil de la Frontera, Spain 43 J4 36 17N 6 10W
Conills, I. des, Spain 38 B3 39 11N 2 58 E
Coniston, Canada 140 C3 46 29N 80 51W
Conjeeveram = Kanchipuram, India 95 H4 12 52N 79 45 E
Conklin, Canada 143 B6 55 38N 111 5W
Conklin, U.S.A. 151 D9 42 2N 75 49W
Conkouati, Réserve de Faune de, Congo 114 C2 3 50 S 11 28 E
Conlendas, Pta. das, Azores 9 d1 38 38N 27 14W
Conn, L., Ireland 23 B2 54 3N 9 15W
Connacht □, Ireland 23 C2 53 43N 9 12W
Conneaut, U.S.A. 150 E4 41 57N 80 34W
Connecticut □, U.S.A. 151 E12 41 30N 72 45W
Connecticut →, U.S.A. 151 E12 41 16N 72 20W
Connell, U.S.A. 158 C4 46 40N 118 52W
Connellsville, U.S.A. 150 F5 40 1N 79 35W
Connemara, Ireland 23 C2 53 29N 9 45W
Connemaugh →, U.S.A. 150 F5 40 28N 79 19W
Conner, Phil. 80 C3 17 48N 121 19 E
Connerré, France 26 D7 48 3N 0 30 E
Connersville, U.S.A. 157 E11 39 39N 85 8W
Connors Ra., Australia 126 C4 21 40 S 149 10 E
Conoble, Australia 129 B6 32 55 S 144 33 E
Cononaco →, Ecuador 168 D2 1 32 S 75 35W
Conques, France 28 D6 44 36N 2 23 E
Conquest, Canada 143 C7 51 32N 107 14W
Conrad, Iowa, U.S.A. 156 B4 42 14N 92 52W
Conrad, Mont., U.S.A. 158 B8 48 10N 111 57W
Conran, C., Australia 129 D8 37 49 S 148 44 E
Conroe, U.S.A. 155 K7 30 19N 95 27W
Consecon, Canada 150 C7 44 0N 77 31W
Conselheiro Lafaiete, Brazil 171 F3 20 40 S 43 48W
Conselheiro Pena, Brazil 171 E3 19 10 S 41 30W
Conselve, Italy 45 C8 45 14N 11 52 E
Consett, U.K. 20 C6 54 51N 1 50W
Consort, Canada 143 C6 52 1N 110 46W
Constance = Konstanz, Germany 31 H5 47 40N 9 10 E
Constance, L. = Bodensee, Europe 33 A8 47 35N 9 25 E
Constanța, Romania 53 F13 44 14N 28 38 E
Constanța □, Romania 53 F13 44 15N 28 15 E
Constantia, U.S.A. 151 C8 43 15N 76 1W
Constantina, Spain 43 H5 37 51N 5 40W
Constantine, Algeria 111 A6 36 25N 6 42 E
Constantine, U.S.A. 157 C11 41 50N 85 40W
Constantine, C., U.S.A. 144 G8 58 24N 158 54W
Constitución, Chile 174 D1 35 20 S 72 30W
Constitución, Uruguay 174 C4 31 0 S 57 50W
Consuegra, Spain 43 F7 39 28N 3 36W
Consul, Canada 143 D7 49 20N 109 30W
Contact, U.S.A. 158 F6 41 46N 114 45W
Contai, India 93 J12 21 54N 87 46 E
Contamana, Peru 172 B3 7 19 S 74 55W
Contarina, Italy 45 C9 45 1N 12 13 E
Contas →, Brazil 171 D4 14 17 S 39 1W
Contes, France 29 E11 43 49N 7 19 E
Conthey, Switz. 32 D4 46 14N 7 18 E
Continental, U.S.A. 157 C12 41 6N 84 16W
Contoocook, U.S.A. 151 C13 43 13N 71 45W
Contra Costa, Mozam. 117 D5 25 9 S 33 30 E
Contres, France 26 E8 47 24N 1 26 E
Contrexéville, France 27 D12 48 10N 5 53 E
Controller B., U.S.A. 144 F11 60 7N 144 15W
Contumaza, Peru 172 B2 7 23 S 78 57W
Contwoyto L., Canada 138 B8 65 42N 110 50W
Convención, Colombia 168 B3 8 28N 73 21W
Conversano, Italy 47 B10 40 58N 17 7 E
Converse, U.S.A. 157 D11 40 35N 85 52W
Convoy, U.S.A. 157 D12 40 55N 84 43W
Conway = Conwy, U.K. 20 D4 53 17N 3 50W
Conway = Conwy →, U.K. 20 D4 53 17N 3 50W
Conway, Australia 126 J6 20 24 S 148 41 E
Conway, Ark., U.S.A. 155 H8 35 5N 92 26W
Conway, N.H., U.S.A. 151 C13 43 59N 71 7W
Conway, S.C., U.S.A. 149 J6 33 51N 79 3W
Conway, C., Australia 126 J6 20 34 S 148 46 E
Conway, L., Australia 127 D2 28 17 S 135 35 E
Conwy, U.K. 20 D4 53 17N 3 50W
Conwy □, U.K. 20 D4 53 10N 3 44W
Conwy →, U.K. 20 D4 53 17N 3 50W
Conyers, U.S.A. 152 B5 33 40N 84 1W
Coober Pedy, Australia 127 D1 29 1 S 134 43 E
Cooch Behar = Koch Bihar, India 90 B2 26 22N 89 29 E
Cooinda, Australia 124 B5 13 15 S 130 5 E
Cook, Australia 125 F5 30 37 S 130 25 E
Cook, U.S.A. 154 B8 47 49N 92 39W
Cook, B., Chile 176 E2 55 10 S 70 0W
Cook, C., Canada 142 C3 50 8N 127 55W
Cook, Mt. = Aoraki Mount Cook, N.Z. 131 D5 43 36 S 170 9 E
Cook B., Vanuatu 133 H7 18 46 S 169 15 E
Cook Inlet, U.S.A. 144 G10 60 0N 152 0W
Cook Is., Pac. Oc. 135 J12 17 0 S 160 0W
Cook Strait, N.Z. 130 H3 41 15 S 174 29 E
Cooke Plains, Australia 128 C3 35 23 S 139 34 E
Cookeville, U.S.A. 149 G3 36 10N 85 30W
Cookhouse, S. Africa 116 E4 32 44 S 25 47 E
Cooks Hammock, U.S.A. 152 F6 29 56N 83 17W
Cookshire, Canada 151 A13 45 25N 71 38W
Cookstown, U.K. 23 B5 54 39N 6 45W
Cooksville, Canada 150 C5 43 36N 79 35W
Cooktown, Australia 126 B4 15 30 S 145 16 E
Coolabah, Australia 129 A7 31 1 S 146 43 E
Cooladdi, Australia 127 D4 26 37 S 145 23 E
Coolah, Australia 129 A8 31 48 S 149 41 E
Coolamon, Australia 129 C7 34 46 S 147 8 E
Coolgardie, Australia 125 F3 30 55 S 121 8 E
Coolidge, Ariz., U.S.A. 159 K8 32 59N 111 31W
Coolidge, Ga., U.S.A. 152 E6 31 1N 83 52W
Coolidge Dam, U.S.A. 159 K8 33 0N 110 20W
Cooloola Nationl Park, Australia 127 D5 26 13 S 153 2 E
Cooma, Australia 129 D8 36 12 S 149 8 E
Coon Rapids, Iowa, U.S.A. 156 C2 41 53N 94 41W
Coon Rapids, Minn., U.S.A. 154 C8 45 9N 93 19W
Coonabarabran, Australia 129 A8 31 14 S 149 18 E
Coonalpyn, Australia 128 C3 35 43 S 139 52 E
Coonamble, Australia 129 A8 30 56 S 148 27 E
Coonana, Australia 125 F3 31 0 S 123 0 E
Coondapoor, India 95 H2 13 42N 74 40 E
Cooninie, L., Australia 127 D2 26 4 S 139 59 E
Coonoor, India 95 J3 11 21N 76 45 E
Cooper, U.S.A. 155 J7 33 23N 95 42W
Cooper →, U.S.A. 152 C10 32 50N 79 56W
Cooper Cr. →, N. Terr., Australia 122 C5 12 7 S 132 41 E
Cooper Cr. →, S. Austral., Australia 127 D2 28 29 S 137 46 E
Cooperstown, N. Dak., U.S.A. 154 B5 47 27N 98 8W
Cooperstown, N.Y., U.S.A. 151 D10 42 42N 74 56W
Coopersville, U.S.A. 157 A11 43 4N 85 57W
Coopracambra Nat. Park, Australia 129 D8 37 20 S 149 20 E
Coorabie, Australia 125 F5 31 54 S 132 18 E
Coorong, The, Australia 128 C3 35 50 S 139 20 E
Coorong Nat. Park, Australia 128 D3 36 0 S 139 29 E
Coorow, Australia 125 E2 29 53 S 116 2 E
Cooroy, Australia 127 D5 26 22 S 152 54 E
Coos Bay, U.S.A. 158 E1 43 22N 124 13W
Coosa →, U.S.A. 149 J2 32 30N 86 16W
Cootamundra, Australia 129 C8 34 36 S 148 1 E
Cootehill, Ireland 23 B4 54 4N 7 5W
Copahue Paso, Argentina 174 D1 37 49 S 71 8W
Copainalá, Mexico 163 D6 17 8N 93 11W
Copake Falls, U.S.A. 151 D11 42 7N 73 31W
Copalnic Mănăștur, Romania 53 C8 47 30N 23 41 E
Copán, Honduras 164 D2 14 50N 89 9W
Copatana, Brazil 168 D4 2 48 S 67 4W
Cope, Colo., U.S.A. 154 F3 39 40N 102 51W
Cope, S.C., U.S.A. 152 B8 33 23N 81 0W
Cope, C., Spain 41 H3 37 26N 1 28W
Copeland, U.S.A. 153 K8 25 57N 81 22W
Copenhagen = København, Denmark 17 J6 55 41N 12 34 E
Copenhagen, U.S.A. 151 C9 43 54N 75 41W
Copertino, Italy 47 B11 40 16N 18 3 E
Copiapó, Chile 174 B1 27 30 S 70 20W
Copiapó →, Chile 174 B1 27 19 S 70 56W
Coplay, U.S.A. 151 F9 40 44N 75 29W
Copley, Australia 128 A3 30 36 S 138 26 E
Copp L., Canada 142 A6 60 14N 114 40W
Copparo, Italy 45 D8 44 54N 11 49 E
Coppename →, Surinam 169 B6 5 48N 55 55W
Copper →, U.S.A. 144 F11 60 18N 145 3W
Copper Center, U.S.A. 144 F11 61 58N 145 18W
Copper Harbor, U.S.A. 148 B2 47 28N 87 53W
Copper Queen, Zimbabwe 119 F2 17 29 S 29 18 E
Copperas Cove, U.S.A. 155 K6 31 8N 97 54W
Copperbelt □, Zambia 119 E2 13 15 S 27 30 E
Coppermine = Kugluktuk, Canada 138 B8 67 50N 115 5W
Coppermine →, Canada 138 B8 67 49N 116 4W
Copperopolis, U.S.A. 160 H6 37 58N 120 38W
Coppet, Switz. 32 D2 46 19N 6 12 E
Copșa Mică, Romania 53 D9 46 6N 24 15 E
Coquet →, U.K. 20 B6 55 20N 1 32W
Coquille, U.S.A. 158 E1 43 11N 124 11W
Coquimbo, Chile 174 C1 30 0 S 71 20W
Coquimbo □, Chile 174 C1 31 0 S 71 0W
Corabia, Romania 53 G9 43 48N 24 30 E
Coração de Jesus, Brazil 171 E3 16 43 S 44 22W
Coracora, Peru 172 D3 15 5 S 73 45W
Coraki, Australia 127 D5 28 59 S 153 17 E
Coral, U.S.A. 150 F5 40 29N 79 10W
Coral Bay, Phil. 81 G1 8 25N 117 20 E
Coral Gables, U.S.A. 149 N5 25 45N 80 16W
Coral Harbour = Salliq, Canada 139 B11 64 8N 83 10W
Coral Harbour, Bahamas 9 b 24 58N 77 28W
Coral Heights, Bahamas 9 b 25 3N 77 25W
Coral Hts., Bahamas 9 b 25 1N 77 33W
Coral Sea, Pac. Oc. 132 F3 15 0 S 150 0 E
Coral Springs, U.S.A. 149 M5 26 16N 80 13W
Coralville, U.S.A. 156 C5 41 40N 91 35W
Coralville L., U.S.A. 156 C5 41 50N 91 40W
Corangamite, L., Australia 128 E5 38 5 S 143 30 E
Corantijn →, Surinam 169 B6 5 50N 57 8W
Coraopolis, U.S.A. 150 F4 40 31N 80 10W
Corato, Italy 47 A9 41 9N 16 25 E
Corbeil-Essonnes, France 27 D9 48 36N 2 26 E
Corbeiro, C., W. Sahara 110 D1 21 50N 17 0W
Corbie, France 27 C9 49 54N 2 30 E
Corbières, France 28 F6 42 55N 2 35 E
Corbigny, France 27 E10 47 16N 3 40 E
Corbin, U.S.A. 148 G3 36 57N 84 6W
Corbones →, Spain 43 H5 37 36N 5 39W
Corbu, Romania 53 F13 44 25N 28 39 E
Corby, U.K. 21 E7 52 30N 0 41W
Corcaigh = Cork, Ireland 23 E3 51 54N 8 29W
Corcoran, U.S.A. 160 J7 36 6N 119 33W
Cordele, U.S.A. 152 D6 31 58N 83 47W
Cordell, U.S.A. 155 H5 35 17N 98 59W
Cordenòns, Italy 45 C9 45 59N 12 42 E
Cordes, France 28 D5 44 5N 1 57 E
Cordisburgo, Brazil 171 E3 19 7 S 44 21W
Córdoba, Argentina 174 C3 31 20 S 64 10W
Córdoba, Mexico 163 D5 18 50N 97 0W
Córdoba, Spain 43 H6 37 50N 4 50W
Córdoba □, Argentina 174 C3 31 22 S 64 15W
Córdoba □, Colombia 168 B2 8 20N 75 40W
Córdoba □, Spain 43 G6 38 5N 5 0W
Córdoba, Sierra de, Argentina 174 C3 31 10 S 64 25W
Cordon, Phil. 80 C3 16 42N 121 32 E
Cordova, U.S.A. 144 F11 60 33N 145 45W
Corella, Spain 40 C3 42 7N 1 48W
Corella →, Australia 126 B3 19 34 S 140 47 E
Coremas, Brazil 170 C4 7 1 S 37 58W
Corentyne →, Guyana 169 B6 5 50N 57 8W
Corfield, Australia 126 C3 21 40 S 143 21 E
Corfu = Kérkira, Greece 38 B9 39 38N 19 50 E
Corgo = O Corgo, Spain 42 C3 42 56N 7 25W
Corguinho, Brazil 173 D7 19 53 S 54 52W
Cori, Italy 46 A5 41 39N 12 55 E
Coria, Spain 42 F4 39 58N 6 33W
Coria del Río, Spain 43 H4 37 16N 6 3W
Coricudgy, Australia 129 B9 32 51 S 150 24 E
Corigliano Cálabro, Italy 47 C9 39 36N 16 31 E
Corimba, Barra de, Angola 115 D2 8 52 S 13 9 E
Coringa Is., Australia 126 B4 16 58 S 149 58 E
Corinth = Kórinthos, Greece 48 D4 37 56N 22 55 E
Corinth, Ky., U.S.A. 157 F12 38 30N 84 34W
Corinth, Miss., U.S.A. 149 H1 34 56N 88 31W
Corinth, N.Y., U.S.A. 151 C11 43 15N 73 49W
Corinth, G. of = Korinthiakós Kólpos, Greece 48 C4 38 16N 22 30 E
Corinth Canal, Greece 48 D4 37 58N 23 0 E
Corinto, Brazil 171 E3 18 20 S 44 30W
Corinto, Nic. 164 D2 12 30N 87 10W
Corisco, Eq. Guin. 114 B1 0 55N 9 18 E
Cork, Ireland 23 E3 51 54N 8 29W
Cork □, Ireland 23 E3 51 57N 8 40W
Cork Harbour, Ireland 23 E3 51 47N 8 16W
Corlay, France 26 D3 48 20N 3 5W
Corleone, Italy 46 E6 37 49N 13 18 E
Corleto Perticara, Italy 47 B9 40 23N 16 2 E
Çorlu, Turkey 51 E11 41 11N 27 49 E
Cormack L., Canada 142 A4 60 56N 121 37W
Cormòns, Italy 45 C10 45 58N 13 28 E
Cormorant, Canada 143 C8 54 14N 100 35W
Cormorant L., Canada 143 C8 54 15N 100 50W
Corn Is. = Maiz, Is. del, Nic. 164 D3 12 15N 83 4W
Cornélio Procópio, Brazil 175 A5 23 7 S 50 40W
Cornell, U.S.A. 157 D8 41 0N 88 44W
Corner Brook, Canada 141 C8 48 57N 57 58W
Corner Inlet, Australia 129 E7 38 45 S 146 20 E
Cornești, Moldova 53 C13 47 21N 28 1 E
Corníglio, Italy 44 D7 44 29N 10 5 E
Corning, Ark., U.S.A. 155 G9 36 25N 90 35W
Corning, Calif., U.S.A. 158 G2 39 56N 122 11W
Corning, Iowa, U.S.A. 156 D2 40 59N 94 44W
Corning, N.Y., U.S.A. 150 D7 42 9N 77 3W
Corno Grande, Italy 45 F10 42 28N 13 34 E
Cornwall, Canada 140 C5 45 2N 74 44W
Cornwall, U.S.A. 151 F8 40 17N 76 25W
Cornwall □, U.K. 21 G3 50 26N 4 40W
Cornwell, U.S.A. 153 H8 27 23N 81 6W
Corny Pt., Australia 128 C2 34 55 S 137 0 E
Coro, Venezuela 168 A4 11 25N 69 41W
Coroaci, Brazil 171 E3 18 35 S 42 17W
Coroatá, Brazil 170 B3 4 8 S 44 0W
Coroban, Somali Rep. 120 D2 3 58N 42 44 E
Corocoro, Bolivia 172 D4 17 15 S 68 28W
Corocoro, I., Venezuela 169 B5 8 30N 60 10W
Coroico, Bolivia 172 D4 16 0 S 67 50W
Coromandel, Brazil 171 E2 18 28 S 47 13W
Coromandel, N.Z. 130 C4 36 45 S 175 31 E
Coromandel Coast, India 95 H5 12 30N 81 0 E
Coromandel Pen., N.Z. 130 C4 37 0 S 175 45 E
Coromandel Ra., N.Z. 130 C4 37 0 S 175 40 E
Coron, Phil. 80 E3 12 1N 120 12 E
Coron Bay, Phil. 81 F3 11 54N 120 8 E
Coron I., Phil. 81 F3 11 55N 120 14 E
Corona, Calif., U.S.A. 161 M9 33 53N 117 34W
Corona, N. Mex., U.S.A. 159 J11 34 15N 105 36W
Coronach, Canada 143 D7 49 7N 105 31W
Coronado, U.S.A. 161 N9 32 41N 117 11W
Coronado, B. de, Costa Rica 164 E3 9 0N 83 40W
Coronados, G. de los, Chile 176 B2 41 40 S 74 0W
Coronados, Is. los, U.S.A. 161 N9 32 25N 117 15W
Coronation, Canada 142 C6 52 5N 111 27W
Coronation Gulf, Canada 138 B8 68 25N 110 0W
Coronation I., Antarctica 7 C18 60 45 S 46 0W
Coronation Is., Australia 124 B3 14 57 S 124 55 E
Coronda, Argentina 174 C3 31 58 S 60 56W
Coronel, Chile 174 D1 37 0 S 73 10W
Coronel Bogado, Paraguay 174 B4 27 11 S 56 18W
Coronel Dorrego, Argentina 174 D3 38 40 S 61 10W
Coronel Fabriciano, Brazil 171 E3 19 31 S 42 38W
Coronel Murta, Brazil 171 E3 16 37 S 42 11W
Coronel Oviedo, Paraguay 174 B4 25 24 S 56 30W
Coronel Ponce, Brazil 173 D6 15 34 S 55 1W
Coronel Pringles, Argentina 174 D3 38 0 S 61 30W
Coronel Suárez, Argentina 174 D3 37 30 S 61 52W
Coronel Vidal, Argentina 174 D4 37 28 S 57 45W
Corongo, Peru 172 B2 8 30 S 77 53W
Coropuna, Nevado, Peru 172 D3 15 30 S 72 41W
Çorovodë, Albania 50 F4 40 31N 20 14 E
Corowa, Australia 129 C7 35 58 S 146 21 E
Corozal, Belize 163 D7 18 23N 88 23W
Corozal, Colombia 168 B2 9 19N 75 18W
Corozal Pt., Trin. & Tob. 169 F9 10 44N 61 40W
Corps, France 29 D9 44 50N 5 56 E
Corpus, Argentina 175 B4 27 10 S 55 30W
Corpus Christi, U.S.A. 155 M6 27 47N 97 24W
Corpus Christi, L., U.S.A. 155 L6 28 2N 97 52W
Corque, Bolivia 172 D4 18 20 S 67 41W
Corral, Chile 176 A2 39 52 S 73 26W
Corral de Almaguer, Spain 42 F7 39 45N 3 10W
Corralejo, Canary Is. 9 e2 28 43N 13 53W
Corraun Pen., Ireland 23 C2 53 54N 9 54W
Corréggio, Italy 44 D7 44 46N 10 47 E
Corrente, Brazil 170 D2 10 27 S 45 10W
Corrente →, Brazil 171 D3 13 8 S 43 28W
Correntes →, Brazil 173 D6 17 38 S 55 8W
Correntes, C. das, Mozam. 117 C6 24 6 S 35 34 E
Correntina, Brazil 171 D3 13 20 S 44 39W

204 Corrèze

Corrèze □, *France* **28 C5** 45 20N 1 45 E
Corrèze →, *France* **28 C5** 45 10N 1 28 E
Corrib, L., *Ireland* **23 C2** 53 27N 9 16W
Corridónia, *Italy* **45 E10** 43 15N 13 30 E
Corrientes, *Argentina* **174 B4** 27 30 S 58 45W
Corrientes □, *Argentina* **174 B4** 28 0 S 57 0W
Corrientes →, *Argentina* **174 C4** 30 42 S 59 38W
Corrientes →, *Peru* **168 D3** 3 43 S 74 35W
Corrientes, C., *Colombia* **168 B2** 5 30N 77 34W
Corrientes, C., *Cuba* **164 B3** 21 43N 84 30W
Corrientes, C., *Mexico* **162 C3** 20 25N 105 42W
Corrigan, *U.S.A.* **155 K7** 31 0N 94 52W
Corrigin, *Australia* **125 F2** 32 20 S 117 53 E
Corry, *U.S.A.* **150 E5** 41 55N 79 39W
Corryong, *Australia* **129 D7** 36 12 S 147 53 E
Corse, *France* **29 G13** 42 0N 9 0 E
Corse, C., *France* **29 E13** 43 1N 9 25 E
Corse-du-Sud □, *France* **29 G13** 41 45N 9 0 E
Corsica = Corse, *France* **29 G13** 42 0N 9 0 E
Corsicana, *U.S.A.* **155 J6** 32 6N 96 28W
Corte, *France* **29 F13** 42 19N 9 11 E
Corte Pinto, *Portugal* **43 H3** 37 42N 7 29W
Cortegana, *Spain* **43 H4** 37 52N 6 49W
Cortes, *Phil.* **81 G6** 9 17N 126 11 E
Cortez, *U.S.A.* **159 H9** 37 21N 108 35W
Cortina d'Ampezzo, *Italy* **45 B9** 46 32N 12 8 E
Cortland, *N.Y., U.S.A.* **151 D8** 42 36N 76 11W
Cortland, *Ohio, U.S.A.* **150 E4** 41 20N 80 44W
Cortona, *Italy* **45 E8** 43 16N 11 59 E
Corubal →, *Guinea-Biss.* **112 C2** 11 57N 15 5W
Coruche, *Portugal* **43 G2** 38 57N 8 30W
Çoruh →, *Turkey* **61 K5** 41 38N 41 38 E
Çorum, *Turkey* **100 B6** 40 30N 34 57 E
Corumbá, *Brazil* **173 D6** 19 0 S 57 30W
Corumbá →, *Brazil* **171 E2** 18 19 S 48 55W
Corumbá de Goiás, *Brazil* **171 E2** 16 0 S 48 50W
Corumbaíba, *Brazil* **171 E2** 18 9 S 48 34W
Corund, *Romania* **53 D10** 46 30N 25 13 E
Corunna = A Coruña, *Spain* **42 B2** 43 20N 8 25W
Corunna, *U.S.A.* **157 B12** 42 59N 84 7W
Corvallis, *U.S.A.* **158 D2** 44 34N 123 16W
Corvette, L. de la, *Canada* **140 B5** 53 25N 74 3W
Corvo, *Azores* **9 d2** 39 42N 31 6W
Corydon, *Ind., U.S.A.* **157 F10** 38 13N 86 7W
Corydon, *Iowa, U.S.A.* **156 D3** 40 46N 93 19W
Corydon, *Ky., U.S.A.* **157 G9** 37 44N 87 43W
Cosalá, *Mexico* **162 C3** 24 28N 106 40W
Cosamaloapan, *Mexico* **163 D5** 18 23N 95 50W
Cosenza, *Italy* **47 C9** 39 18N 16 15 E
Coşereni, *Romania* **53 F11** 44 38N 26 35 E
Coshocton, *U.S.A.* **150 F3** 40 16N 81 51W
Cosmo Newberry, *Australia* **125 E3** 28 0 S 122 54 E
Cosne-Cours-sur-Loire, *France* **27 E9** 47 24N 2 54 E
Coso Junction, *U.S.A.* **161 J9** 36 3N 117 57W
Coso Pk., *U.S.A.* **161 J9** 36 13N 117 44W
Cospeito, *Spain* **42 B3** 43 12N 7 34W
Cosquín, *Argentina* **174 C3** 31 15 S 64 30W
Cossato, *Italy* **44 C5** 45 34N 8 10 E
Cossé-le-Vivien, *France* **26 E6** 47 57N 0 54W
Cosson →, *France* **26 E8** 47 30N 1 15 E
Costa Blanca, *Spain* **41 G4** 38 25N 0 10W
Costa Brava, *Spain* **40 D8** 41 30N 3 0 E
Costa del Sol, *Spain* **43 J6** 36 30N 4 30W
Costa Dorada, *Spain* **40 D6** 41 12N 1 15 E
Costa Mesa, *U.S.A.* **161 M9** 33 38N 117 55W
Costa Rica ■, *Cent. Amer.* **164 E3** 10 0N 84 0W
Costa Smeralda, *Italy* **46 A2** 41 5N 9 35 E
Costeşti, *Romania* **53 F9** 44 40N 24 53 E
Costigliole d'Asti, *Italy* **44 D5** 44 47N 8 11 E
Cosumnes →, *U.S.A.* **160 G5** 38 16N 121 26W
Coswig, *Sachsen, Germany* **30 D9** 51 7N 13 34 E
Coswig, *Sachsen-Anhalt, Germany* **30 D8** 51 53N 12 27 E
Cotabato, *Phil.* **81 H5** 7 14N 124 15 E
Cotabato □, *Phil.* **81 H5** 7 10N 125 0 E
Cotacajes →, *Bolivia* **172 D4** 16 0 S 67 1W
Cotagaita, *Bolivia* **174 A2** 20 45 S 65 40W
Cotahuasi, *Peru* **172 D3** 15 12 S 72 50W
Côte d'Azur, *France* **29 E11** 43 25N 7 10 E
Côte-d'Ivoire = Ivory Coast ■, *Africa* **112 D4** 7 30N 5 0W
Côte d'Or, *France* **27 E11** 47 30N 4 50 E
Côte-d'Or □, *France* **27 E11** 47 10N 4 50 E
Coteau des Prairies, *U.S.A.* **154 C6** 45 20N 97 50W
Coteau du Missouri, *U.S.A.* **154 B4** 47 0N 100 0W
Coteau Landing, *Canada* **151 A10** 45 15N 74 13W
Cotegipe, *Brazil* **171 D3** 12 2 S 44 15W
Cotentin, *France* **26 C5** 49 15N 1 30W
Côtes-d'Armor □, *France* **26 D4** 48 25N 2 40W
Côtes de Meuse, *France* **27 C12** 49 15N 5 22 E
Côtes-du-Nord = Côtes-d'Armor □, *France* **26 D4** 48 25N 2 40W
Cotiella, *Spain* **40 C5** 42 31N 0 19 E
Cotillo, *Canary Is.* **9 e2** 28 41N 14 1W
Cotiujeni, *Moldova* **53 C13** 47 51N 28 33 E
Cotoca, *Bolivia* **173 D5** 17 49 S 63 3W
Cotonou, *Benin* **113 D5** 6 20N 2 25 E
Cotopaxi, *Ecuador* **168 D2** 0 40 S 78 30W
Cotopaxi □, *Ecuador* **168 D2** 0 5 S 78 55W
Cotronei, *Italy* **47 C9** 39 9N 16 47 E
Cotswold Hills, *U.K.* **21 F5** 51 42N 2 10W
Cottage Grove, *U.S.A.* **158 E2** 43 48N 123 3W
Cottageville, *U.S.A.* **152 C9** 32 56N 80 29W
Cottbus, *Germany* **30 D10** 51 45N 14 20 E
Cottondale, *U.S.A.* **152 E4** 30 48N 85 23W
Cottonwood, *Ala., U.S.A.* **152 D4** 31 3N 85 18W
Cottonwood, *Ariz., U.S.A.* **159 J7** 34 45N 112 1W
Cotulla, *U.S.A.* **155 L5** 28 26N 99 14W
Coubre, Pte. de la, *France* **28 C2** 45 42N 1 15W
Couches, *France* **27 F11** 46 53N 4 30 E
Couço, *Portugal* **43 G2** 38 59N 8 17W
Coudersport, *U.S.A.* **150 E6** 41 46N 78 1W
Couedic, C. du, *Australia* **128 D2** 36 5 S 136 40 E
Couëron, *France* **26 E5** 47 13N 1 44W
Couesnon →, *France* **26 D5** 48 38N 1 32W
Couhé, *France* **28 B4** 46 17N 0 11 E
Coulanges-sur-Yonne, *France* **27 E10** 47 31N 3 33 E
Coulee City, *U.S.A.* **158 C4** 47 37N 119 17W
Coulman I., *Antarctica* **7 D11** 73 35 S 170 0 E
Coulommiers, *France* **27 D10** 48 50N 3 3 E
Coulon →, *France* **29 E9** 43 51N 5 6 E
Coulonge →, *Canada* **140 C4** 45 52N 76 46W
Coulonges-sur-l'Autize, *France* **28 B3** 46 29N 0 36W
Coulounieix-Chamiers, *France* **28 C4** 45 11N 0 42 E
Coulterville, *Calif., U.S.A.* **160 H6** 37 43N 120 12W
Coulterville, *Ill., U.S.A.* **156 F7** 38 11N 89 36W
Council, *Ga., U.S.A.* **152 E7** 30 37N 82 31W
Council, *Idaho, U.S.A.* **158 D5** 44 44N 116 26W
Council Bluffs, *U.S.A.* **154 E7** 41 16N 95 52W
Council Grove, *U.S.A.* **154 F6** 38 40N 96 29W
Coupeville, *U.S.A.* **160 B4** 48 13N 122 41W
Courantyne →, *S. Amer.* **169 B6** 5 55N 57 5W
Courcelles, *Belgium* **24 D4** 50 28N 4 22 E
Courçon, *France* **28 B3** 46 15N 0 50W
Courmayeur, *Italy* **44 C3** 45 47N 6 58 E
Couronne, C., *France* **29 E9** 43 19N 5 3 E
Cours-la-Ville, *France* **27 F11** 46 7N 4 19 E
Coursan, *France* **28 E7** 43 14N 3 4 E
Courseulles-sur-Mer, *France* **26 C6** 49 20N 0 29W
Courtenay, *Canada* **142 D4** 49 45N 125 0W
Courtenay, *France* **27 D10** 48 2N 3 3 E
Courtland, *U.S.A.* **160 G5** 38 20N 121 34W
Courtrai = Kortrijk, *Belgium* **24 D3** 50 50N 3 17 E
Courtright, *Canada* **150 D2** 42 49N 82 28W
Coushatta, *U.S.A.* **155 J8** 32 1N 93 21W
Coutances, *France* **26 C5** 49 3N 1 28W
Coutras, *France* **28 C3** 45 3N 0 8W
Coutts Crossing, *Australia* **127 D5** 29 49 S 152 55 E
Couva, *Trin. & Tob.* **169 F9** 10 24N 61 30W
Couvet, *Switz.* **32 C3** 46 57N 6 38 E
Couvin, *Belgium* **24 D4** 50 3N 4 29 E
Covarrubias, *Spain* **42 C7** 42 4N 3 31W
Covasna, *Romania* **53 E11** 45 50N 26 10 E
Covasna □, *Romania* **53 E10** 45 50N 26 0 E
Cove I., *Canada* **150 A3** 45 17N 81 44W
Coveñas, *Colombia* **168 B2** 9 24N 75 44W
Coventry, *U.K.* **21 E6** 52 25N 1 28W
Coverdale, *U.S.A.* **152 D6** 31 38N 83 58W
Covilhã, *Portugal* **42 E3** 40 17N 7 31W
Covington, *Ga., U.S.A.* **152 B6** 33 36N 83 51W
Covington, *Ind., U.S.A.* **157 D9** 40 9N 87 24W
Covington, *Ky., U.S.A.* **157 E12** 39 5N 84 31W
Covington, *Ohio, U.S.A.* **157 D12** 40 7N 84 21W
Covington, *Okla., U.S.A.* **155 G6** 36 18N 97 35W
Covington, *Tenn., U.S.A.* **155 H10** 35 34N 89 39W
Covington, *Va., U.S.A.* **150 G4** 37 47N 79 59W
Cowal, L., *Australia* **129 B7** 33 40 S 147 25 E
Cowan, Cerro, *Ecuador* **172 a** 0 12 S 90 48W
Cowan, L., *Australia* **125 F3** 31 45 S 121 45 E
Cowan L., *Canada* **143 C7** 54 0N 107 15W
Cowangie, *Australia* **128 C4** 35 12 S 141 26 E
Cowansville, *Canada* **140 C5** 45 14N 72 46W
Coward Springs, *Australia* **127 D2** 29 24 S 136 49 E
Cowcowing Lakes, *Australia* **125 F2** 30 55 S 117 20 E
Cowden, *U.S.A.* **157 E8** 39 15N 88 52W
Cowdenbeath, *U.K.* **22 E5** 56 7N 3 21W
Cowell, *Australia* **128 B2** 33 39 S 136 56 E
Cowes, *Australia* **129 E6** 38 28 S 145 14 E
Cowes, *U.K.* **21 G6** 50 45N 1 18W
Cowichan L., *Canada* **160 B2** 48 53N 124 17W
Cowlitz →, *U.S.A.* **160 D4** 46 6N 122 55W
Cowra, *Australia* **129 B8** 33 49 S 148 42 E
Cox, *Spain* **41 G4** 38 8N 0 53W
Coxilha Grande, *Brazil* **175 B5** 28 18 S 51 30W
Coxim, *Brazil* **173 D7** 18 30 S 54 55W
Coxim →, *Brazil* **173 D7** 18 34 S 54 46W
Cox's Bazar, *Bangla.* **90 E3** 21 26N 91 59 E
Coyote Wells, *U.S.A.* **161 N11** 32 44N 115 58W
Coyuca de Benítez, *Mexico* **163 D4** 17 1N 100 8W
Coyuca de Catalan, *Mexico* **163 D4** 18 18N 100 41W
Cozad, *U.S.A.* **154 E5** 40 52N 99 59W
Cozes, *France* **28 C3** 45 34N 0 49W
Cozumel, *Mexico* **163 C7** 20 31N 86 55W
Cozumel, Isla, *Mexico* **163 C7** 20 30N 86 40W
Crabhill, *Barbados* **165 g** 13 19N 59 38W
Cracow = Kraków, *Poland* **55 H6** 50 4N 19 57 E
Cracow, *Australia* **127 D5** 25 17 S 150 17 E
Cradle Mt.-Lake St. Clair Nat. Park, *Australia* **127 G4** 41 49 S 147 56 E
Cradock, *Australia* **127 E2** 32 6 S 138 31 E
Cradock, *S. Africa* **116 E4** 32 8 S 25 36 E
Craig, *Alaska, U.S.A.* **144 J14** 55 29N 133 9W
Craig, *Colo., U.S.A.* **158 F10** 40 31N 107 33W
Craigavon, *U.K.* **23 B5** 54 27N 6 23W
Craigieburn, *Australia* **129 D6** 37 36 S 144 56 E
Craigmore, *Zimbabwe* **119 G3** 20 28 S 32 50 E
Craik, *Canada* **143 C7** 51 3N 105 49W
Crailsheim, *Germany* **31 F6** 49 8N 10 5 E
Craiova, *Romania* **53 F8** 44 21N 23 48 E
Cramsie, *Australia* **126 C3** 23 20 S 144 15 E
Cranberry L., *U.S.A.* **151 B10** 44 11N 74 50W
Cranberry Portage, *Canada* **143 C8** 54 35N 101 23W
Cranbrook, *Australia* **125 F2** 34 18 S 117 33 E
Cranbrook, *Canada* **142 D5** 49 30N 115 46W
Crandon, *U.S.A.* **154 C10** 45 34N 88 54W
Crane, *Oreg., U.S.A.* **158 E4** 43 25N 118 35W
Crane, *Tex., U.S.A.* **155 K3** 31 24N 102 21W
Cranganore, *India* **95 J3** 10 13N 76 13 E
Cranston, *U.S.A.* **151 E13** 41 47N 71 26W
Craon, *France* **26 E6** 47 50N 0 58W
Craonne, *France* **27 C10** 49 27N 3 46 E
Craponne-sur-Arzon, *France* **28 C7** 45 19N 3 51 E
Crasna, *Romania* **53 D12** 46 32N 27 51 E
Crasna →, *Romania* **52 C7** 47 44N 22 35 E
Crasnei, Munţii, *Romania* **53 C8** 47 0N 23 20 E
Crater L., *U.S.A.* **158 E2** 42 56N 122 6W
Crater Lake Nat. Park, *U.S.A.* **158 E2** 42 55N 122 10W
Crater Mt., *Papua N. G.* **132 D3** 6 37 S 145 7 E
Crater Pt., *Papua N. G.* **132 C7** 5 25 S 152 9 E
Crateús, *Brazil* **170 C3** 5 10 S 40 39W
Crati →, *Italy* **47 C9** 39 43N 16 31 E
Crato, *Brazil* **170 C4** 7 10 S 39 25W
Crato, *Portugal* **43 F3** 39 16N 7 39W
Craven, L., *Canada* **140 B4** 54 20N 76 56W
Cravo Norte, *Colombia* **168 B3** 6 18N 70 12W
Cravo Norte →, *Colombia* **168 B3** 6 18N 70 12W
Crawford, *Ala., U.S.A.* **152 C4** 32 27N 85 11W
Crawford, *Nebr., U.S.A.* **154 D3** 42 41N 103 25W
Crawfordsville, *Ind., U.S.A.* **157 D10** 40 2N 86 54W
Crawfordsville, *Iowa, U.S.A.* **156 C5** 41 12N 91 32W
Crawfordville, *Fla., U.S.A.* **152 E5** 30 11N 84 23W
Crawfordville, *Ga., U.S.A.* **152 B7** 33 33N 82 54W
Crawley, *U.K.* **21 F7** 51 7N 0 11W
Crazy Mts., *U.S.A.* **158 C8** 46 12N 110 20W
Crean L., *Canada* **143 C7** 54 5N 106 9W
Crécy-en-Ponthieu, *France* **27 B8** 50 15N 1 53 E
Crediton, *Canada* **150 C3** 43 17N 81 33W
Cree →, *Canada* **143 B7** 58 57N 105 47W
Cree →, *U.K.* **22 G4** 54 55N 4 25W
Cree L., *Canada* **143 B7** 57 30N 106 30W
Creede, *U.S.A.* **159 H10** 37 51N 106 56W
Creekside, *U.S.A.* **150 F5** 40 40N 79 11W
Creel, *Mexico* **162 B3** 27 45N 107 38W
Creemore, *Canada* **150 B4** 44 19N 80 6W
Creighton, *Canada* **143 C8** 54 45N 101 54W
Creighton, *U.S.A.* **154 D6** 42 28N 97 54W
Creil, *France* **27 C9** 49 15N 2 29 E
Crema, *Italy* **44 C6** 45 22N 9 41 E
Cremona, *Italy* **44 C7** 45 7N 10 2 E
Crepaja, *Serbia, Yug.* **52 E5** 45 1N 20 38 E
Crepori →, *Brazil* **173 B6** 5 42 S 57 8W
Crépy, *France* **27 C10** 49 35N 3 32 E
Crépy-en-Valois, *France* **27 C9** 49 14N 2 54 E
Cres, *Croatia* **45 D11** 44 58N 14 25 E
Crescent Beach, *U.S.A.* **152 F8** 29 46N 81 15W
Crescent City, *Calif., U.S.A.* **158 F1** 41 45N 124 12W
Crescent City, *Fla., U.S.A.* **153 F8** 29 26N 81 31W
Crescent Hd., *Australia* **129 A10** 31 11 S 152 59 E
Crescent L., *U.S.A.* **153 F8** 29 28N 81 30W
Crescentino, *Italy* **44 C5** 45 11N 8 6 E
Crespo, *Argentina* **174 C3** 32 2 S 60 19W
Cresson, *U.S.A.* **150 F6** 40 28N 78 36W
Cressy, *Australia* **128 E5** 38 2 S 143 40 E
Crest, *France* **29 D9** 44 44N 5 2 E
Cresta, Mt., *Phil.* **80 C4** 17 17N 122 6 E
Crestline, *Calif., U.S.A.* **161 L9** 34 14N 117 18W
Crestline, *Ohio, U.S.A.* **150 F2** 40 47N 82 44W
Creston, *Canada* **142 D5** 49 10N 116 31W
Creston, *Calif., U.S.A.* **160 K6** 35 32N 120 33W
Creston, *Iowa, U.S.A.* **156 C2** 41 4N 94 22W
Crestview, *Calif., U.S.A.* **160 H8** 37 46N 118 58W
Crestview, *Fla., U.S.A.* **149 K2** 30 46N 86 34W
Creswick, *Australia* **128 D5** 37 25 S 143 58 E
Crêt de la Neige, *France* **27 F12** 46 16N 5 58 E
Crete = Kríti, *Greece* **39 E6** 35 15N 25 0 E
Crete, *Ill., U.S.A.* **157 C9** 41 27N 87 38W
Crete, *Nebr., U.S.A.* **154 E6** 40 38N 96 58W
Crete, Sea of, *Greece* **49 E7** 36 0N 25 0 E
Créteil, *France* **27 D9** 48 47N 2 28 E
Cretin, C., *Papua N. G.* **132 D4** 6 40 S 147 53 E
Creus, C. de, *Spain* **40 C8** 42 20N 3 19 E
Creuse □, *France* **27 F9** 46 10N 2 0 E
Creuse →, *France* **28 B4** 47 0N 0 34 E
Creutzwald, *France* **27 C13** 49 12N 6 42 E
Creuzburg, *Germany* **30 D6** 51 3N 10 14 E
Crèvecœur-le-Grand, *France* **27 C9** 49 37N 2 5 E
Crevillente, *Spain* **41 G4** 38 12N 0 48W
Crewe, *U.K.* **20 D5** 53 6N 2 26W
Crewkerne, *U.K.* **21 G5** 50 53N 2 48W
Criciúma, *Brazil* **175 B6** 28 40 S 49 23W
Cricova, *Moldova* **53 C13** 47 8N 28 52 E
Cridersville, *U.S.A.* **157 D12** 40 39N 84 9W
Crieff, *U.K.* **22 E5** 56 22N 3 50W
Crikvenica, *Croatia* **45 C11** 45 11N 14 40 E
Crimea □, *Ukraine* **59 K8** 45 30N 33 10 E
Crimean Pen. = Krymskyy Pivostriv, *Ukraine* **59 K8** 45 0N 34 0 E
Crimmitschau, *Germany* **30 E8** 50 48N 12 24 E
Cristal, Mts. de, *Gabon* **114 B2** 0 30N 10 30 E
Cristalândia, *Brazil* **170 D2** 10 36 S 49 11W
Cristino Castro, *Brazil* **170 C3** 8 49 S 44 13W
Cristóbal, Pta., *Ecuador* **172 a** 0 54 S 91 31W
Cristuru Secuiesc, *Romania* **53 D10** 46 17N 25 2 E
Crişul Alb →, *Romania* **52 D6** 46 42N 21 17 E
Crişul Negru →, *Romania* **52 D6** 46 42N 21 16 E
Crişul Repede →, *Romania* **52 D5** 46 55N 20 59 E
Crittenden, *U.S.A.* **157 F12** 38 47N 84 36W
Criuleni, *Moldova* **53 C14** 47 13N 29 10 E
Crivitz, *Germany* **30 B7** 53 34N 11 39 E
Crixás, *Brazil* **171 D2** 14 27 S 49 58W
Crna →, *Macedonia* **50 E5** 41 33N 21 59 E
Crna Gora = Montenegro □, *Yugoslavia* **50 D3** 42 40N 19 20 E
Crna Gora, *Macedonia* **50 D5** 42 10N 21 30 E
Crna Reka = Crna →, *Macedonia* **50 E5** 41 33N 21 59 E
Crna Trava, *Serbia, Yug.* **50 D6** 42 49N 22 19 E
Crni Drim →, *Macedonia* **50 E4** 41 17N 20 40 E
Crni Timok →, *Serbia, Yug.* **50 C6** 43 53N 22 15 E
Crnoljeva Planina, *Kosovo, Yug.* **50 D5** 42 20N 21 0 E
Črnomelj, *Slovenia* **45 C12** 45 33N 15 10 E
Croagh Patrick, *Ireland* **23 C2** 53 46N 9 40W
Croajingolong Nat. Park, *Australia* **129 D8** 37 45 S 149 26 E
Croatia ■, *Europe* **45 C13** 45 20N 16 0 E
Crocker, *U.S.A.* **156 G4** 37 57N 92 16W
Crocker, Banjaran, *Malaysia* **85 A5** 5 40N 116 30 E
Crocker, Cerro, *Ecuador* **172 a** 0 36 S 90 21W
Crockett, *U.S.A.* **155 K7** 31 19N 95 27W
Crocodile = Krokodil →, *Mozam.* **117 D5** 25 14 S 32 18 E
Crocodile Is., *Australia* **126 A1** 12 3 S 134 58 E
Crocq, *France* **28 C6** 45 52N 2 21 E
Crodo, *Italy* **44 B5** 46 13N 8 19 E
Crohy Hd., *Ireland* **23 B3** 54 55N 8 26W
Croisette, C., *France* **29 E9** 43 14N 5 22 E
Croisic, Pte. du, *France* **26 E4** 47 19N 2 31W
Croix, L. La, *Canada* **140 C1** 48 20N 92 15W
Croker, C., *Australia* **124 B5** 10 58 S 132 35 E
Croker, C., *Canada* **150 B4** 44 58N 80 59W
Croker I., *Australia* **124 B5** 11 12 S 132 32 E
Cromarty, *U.K.* **22 D4** 57 40N 4 2W
Cromer, *U.K.* **20 E9** 52 56N 1 17 E
Cromwell, *N.Z.* **131 F4** 45 3 S 169 14 E
Cromwell, *U.S.A.* **151 E12** 41 36N 72 39W
Cronat, *France* **27 F10** 46 43N 3 40 E
Crook, *U.K.* **20 C6** 54 43N 1 45W
Crooked →, *Canada* **142 C4** 54 50N 122 54W
Crooked →, *U.S.A.* **158 D3** 44 32N 121 16W
Crooked Creek, *U.S.A.* **144 F8** 61 52N 158 7W
Crooked I., *Bahamas* **165 B5** 22 50N 74 10W
Crooked Island Passage, *Bahamas* **165 B5** 23 0N 74 30W
Crookston, *Minn., U.S.A.* **154 B6** 47 47N 96 37W
Crookston, *Nebr., U.S.A.* **154 D4** 42 56N 100 45W
Crookwell, *Australia* **129 C8** 34 28 S 149 24 E
Crosby, *U.K.* **20 D4** 53 30N 3 3W
Crosby, *N. Dak., U.S.A.* **154 A3** 48 55N 103 18W
Crosby, *Pa., U.S.A.* **150 E6** 41 45N 78 23W
Crosbyton, *U.S.A.* **155 J4** 33 40N 101 14W
Crosía, *Italy* **47 C9** 39 35N 16 45 E
Cross →, *Nigeria* **113 E6** 4 42N 8 21 E
Cross City, *U.S.A.* **153 F6** 29 38N 83 7W
Cross Fell, *U.K.* **20 C5** 54 43N 2 28W
Cross L., *Canada* **143 C9** 54 45N 97 30W
Cross Lake, *Canada* **143 C9** 54 37N 97 47W
Cross River □, *Nigeria* **113 D6** 6 0N 8 0 E
Cross River Nat. Park, *Nigeria* **113 D6** 5 50N 9 50 E
Cross Sound, *U.S.A.* **144 H14** 58 0N 135 0W
Cross Timbers, *U.S.A.* **156 F3** 38 1N 93 14W
Crossett, *U.S.A.* **155 J9** 33 8N 91 58W
Crosshaven, *Ireland* **23 E3** 51 47N 8 17W
Crossley, Mt., *N.Z.* **131 C7** 42 50 S 172 5 E
Crossville, *Ill., U.S.A.* **157 F8** 38 10N 88 4W
Crossville, *Tenn., U.S.A.* **149 G3** 35 57N 85 2W
Croswell, *U.S.A.* **150 C2** 43 16N 82 37W
Croton-on-Hudson, *U.S.A.* **151 E11** 41 12N 73 55W
Crotone, *Italy* **47 C10** 39 5N 17 8 E
Crow →, *Canada* **142 B4** 59 41N 124 20W
Crow Agency, *U.S.A.* **158 D10** 45 36N 107 28W
Crow Hd., *Ireland* **23 E1** 51 35N 10 9W
Crowdy Bay Nat. Park, *Australia* **129 A10** 31 45 S 152 45 E
Crowell, *U.S.A.* **155 J5** 33 59N 99 43W
Crowl Cr. →, *Australia* **129 B6** 32 0 S 145 30 E
Crowley, *U.S.A.* **155 K8** 30 13N 92 22W
Crowley, L., *U.S.A.* **160 H8** 37 35N 118 42W
Crown I., *Papua N. G.* **132 C4** 5 7 S 146 58 E
Crown Point, *Ind., U.S.A.* **157 C9** 41 25N 87 22W
Crown Point, *N.Y., U.S.A.* **151 C11** 43 57N 73 26W
Crown Pt., *Trin. & Tob.* **169 E10** 11 18N 60 51W
Crownpoint, *U.S.A.* **159 J9** 35 41N 108 9W
Crows Landing, *U.S.A.* **160 H5** 37 23N 121 6W
Crows Nest, *Australia* **127 D5** 27 16 S 152 4 E
Crowsnest Pass, *Canada* **142 D6** 49 40N 114 40W
Croydon, *Australia* **126 B3** 18 13 S 142 14 E
Croydon □, *U.K.* **21 F7** 51 22N 0 5W
Crozet, Is., *Ind. Oc.* **121 J4** 46 27 S 52 0 E
Crozon, *France* **26 D2** 48 15N 4 30W
Cruces, Punta, *Colombia* **168 B2** 6 39N 77 32W
Cruz, C., *Cuba* **164 C4** 19 50N 77 50W
Cruz Alta, *Brazil* **175 B5** 28 45 S 53 40W
Cruz Bay, *U.S. Virgin Is.* **165 e** 18 20N 64 48W
Cruz das Almas, *Brazil* **171 D4** 12 0 S 39 6W
Cruz de Incio, *Spain* **42 C3** 42 39N 7 21W
Cruz de Malta, *Brazil* **170 C3** 8 15 S 40 20W
Cruz del Eje, *Argentina* **174 C3** 30 45 S 64 50W
Cruzeiro, *Brazil* **171 F2** 22 33 S 45 0W
Cruzeiro do Oeste, *Brazil* **175 A5** 23 46 S 53 4W
Cruzeiro do Sul, *Brazil* **172 B3** 7 35 S 72 35W
Cry L., *Canada* **142 B3** 58 45N 129 0W
Crystal B., *U.S.A.* **153 G7** 28 50N 82 45W
Crystal Bay, *U.S.A.* **160 F7** 39 15N 120 0W
Crystal Brook, *Australia* **128 B3** 33 21 S 138 12 E
Crystal City, *Mo., U.S.A.* **156 F6** 38 13N 90 23W
Crystal City, *Tex., U.S.A.* **155 L5** 28 41N 99 50W
Crystal Falls, *U.S.A.* **148 B1** 46 5N 88 20W
Crystal Lake, *Fla., U.S.A.* **152 E4** 30 26N 85 42W
Crystal Lake, *Ill., U.S.A.* **157 B8** 42 14N 88 19W
Crystal River, *U.S.A.* **149 L4** 28 54N 82 35W
Crystal Springs, *U.S.A.* **155 K9** 31 59N 90 21W
Csenger, *Hungary* **52 C7** 47 50N 22 41 E
Csongrád, *Hungary* **52 D5** 46 43N 20 12 E
Csongrád □, *Hungary* **52 D5** 46 32N 20 15 E
Csorna, *Hungary* **52 C2** 47 38N 17 18 E
Csurgo, *Hungary* **52 D2** 46 16N 17 9 E
Cu Lao Hon, *Vietnam* **87 G7** 10 54N 108 18 E
Cua Rao, *Vietnam* **86 C5** 19 16N 104 27 E
Cuácua →, *Mozam.* **119 F4** 17 54 S 37 0 E
Cuále, *Angola* **115 D3** 8 22 S 16 10 E
Cuále →, *Angola* **115 D3** 8 29 S 15 1 E
Cuamato, *Angola* **116 B2** 17 2 S 15 7 E
Cuamba, *Mozam.* **119 E4** 14 45 S 36 22 E
Cuando, *Angola* **115 E3** 14 34 S 19 1 E
Cuando →, *Angola* **115 F4** 17 30 S 23 15 E
Cuando Cubango □, *Angola* **116 B3** 16 25 S 20 0 E
Cuangar, *Angola* **116 B2** 17 36 S 18 39 E
Cuango = Kwango →, *Dem. Rep. of the Congo* **114 C3** 3 14 S 17 22 E
Cuango, *Lunda Norte, Angola* **115 D3** 9 8 S 18 3 E
Cuango, *Moxico, Angola* **115 E3** 6 20 S 16 42 E
Cuango, *Uíge, Angola* **115 D3** 6 15 S 16 42 E
Cuanza →, *Angola* **115 D2** 9 21 S 13 9 E
Cuanza Norte □, *Angola* **115 D2** 8 50 S 14 30 E
Cuanza Sul □, *Angola* **115 E2** 10 50 S 14 50 E
Cuao →, *Venezuela* **168 C4** 4 55N 67 40W
Cuarto →, *Argentina* **174 C3** 33 25 S 63 2W
Cuatir →, *Angola* **115 F3** 17 1 S 18 9 E
Cuatrociénegas, *Mexico* **162 B4** 26 59N 102 5W
Cuauhtémoc, *Mexico* **162 B3** 28 25N 106 52W
Cuba, *Portugal* **43 G3** 38 10N 7 54W
Cuba, *Mo., U.S.A.* **156 F5** 38 4N 91 24W
Cuba, *N. Mex., U.S.A.* **159 J10** 36 1N 107 4W
Cuba, *N.Y., U.S.A.* **150 D6** 42 13N 78 17W
Cuba ■, *W. Indies* **164 B4** 22 0N 79 0W
Cuba City, *U.S.A.* **156 B6** 42 36N 90 26W
Cubal, *Angola* **115 E2** 12 26 S 14 3 E
Cubal →, *Angola* **115 E2** 12 13 S 13 39 E
Cubango →, *Africa* **116 B3** 18 50 S 22 25 E
Cubanja, *Angola* **115 E4** 14 49 S 21 20 E
Cubia, *Angola* **115 F4** 15 58 S 21 42 E
Çubuk, *Turkey* **100 B5** 40 14N 33 3 E
Cuchi, *Angola* **115 E3** 14 37 S 16 58 E
Cuchi →, *Angola* **115 F3** 15 13 S 17 20 E
Cuchillo-Có, *Argentina* **176 A4** 38 20 S 64 37W
Cuchivero →, *Venezuela* **168 B4** 7 40N 65 57W
Cuchumatanes, Sierra de los, *Guatemala* **164 C1** 15 35N 91 25W
Cuckfield, *U.K.* **21 F7** 51 1N 0 8W
Cucuí, *Brazil* **168 C4** 1 12N 66 50W
Cucumbi, *Angola* **115 E3** 10 17 S 19 5 E
Cucurpe, *Mexico* **162 A2** 30 20N 110 43W
Cucurrupí, *Colombia* **168 C2** 4 23N 76 56W
Cúcuta, *Colombia* **168 B3** 7 54N 72 31W
Cudahy, *U.S.A.* **157 B9** 42 58N 87 52W
Cudalbi, *Romania* **53 E12** 45 46N 27 41 E
Cuddalore, *India* **95 J4** 11 46N 79 45 E
Cuddapah, *India* **95 G4** 14 30N 78 47 E
Cuddapan, L., *Australia* **126 D3** 25 45 S 141 26 E
Cudgewa, *Australia* **129 D7** 36 10 S 147 42 E
Cudillero, *Spain* **42 B4** 43 33N 6 9W
Cue, *Australia* **125 E2** 27 25 S 117 54 E
Cuebe →, *Angola* **115 F3** 15 46 S 17 32 E
Cuéllar, *Spain* **42 D6** 41 23N 4 21W
Cuemba, *Angola* **115 E3** 11 50 S 17 42 E
Cuenca, *Ecuador* **168 D2** 2 50 S 79 9W
Cuenca, *Spain* **40 E2** 40 5N 2 10W
Cuenca □, *Spain* **40 F3** 40 0N 2 0W
Cuenca, Serranía de, *Spain* **40 F3** 39 55N 1 50W
Cuerdo del Pozo, Embalse de la, *Spain* **40 D2** 41 51N 2 44W
Cuernavaca, *Mexico* **163 D5** 18 55N 99 15W
Cuero, *U.S.A.* **155 L6** 29 6N 97 17W
Cuers, *France* **29 E10** 43 14N 6 5 E
Cuevas, Cerro, *Bolivia* **173 E4** 22 0 S 65 12W
Cuevas del Almanzora, *Spain* **41 H3** 37 18N 1 58W
Cuevo, *Bolivia* **173 E5** 20 15 S 63 30W
Cugir, *Romania* **53 E8** 45 48N 23 25 E
Cugnaux, *France* **28 E5** 43 32N 1 20 E
Cuhai-Bakony →, *Hungary* **52 C2** 47 35N 17 54 E
Cuiabá, *Brazil* **173 D6** 15 30 S 56 0W
Cuiabá →, *Brazil* **173 D6** 17 5 S 56 36W
Cuihangcun, *China* **69 G10** 22 27N 113 32 E
Cuijk, *Neths.* **24 C5** 51 44N 5 50 E
Cuilco, *Guatemala* **164 C1** 15 24N 91 58W
Cuillin Hills, *U.K.* **22 D2** 57 13N 6 15W
Cuillin Sd., *U.K.* **22 D2** 57 4N 6 20W
Cuilo, *Angola* **115 D3** 8 12 S 19 28 E
Cuilo-Futa, *Angola* **115 D3** 6 28 S 15 51 E
Cuima, *Angola* **115 E3** 13 25 S 15 45 E
Cuimba, *Angola* **115 D2** 6 10 S 14 41 E
Cuiseaux, *France* **27 F12** 46 30N 5 22 E
Cuité, *Brazil* **170 C4** 6 29 S 36 9W
Cuito →, *Angola* **116 B3** 18 1 S 20 48 E
Cuito Cuanavale, *Angola* **115 F3** 15 10 S 19 10 E
Cuitzeo, L. de, *Mexico* **162 D4** 19 55N 101 5W
Cuiuni →, *Brazil* **169 D5** 0 45 S 63 7W
Cuivre →, *U.S.A.* **156 F6** 38 55N 90 44W
Cuivre, West Fork →, *U.S.A.* **156 E6** 39 2N 90 58W
Cujmir, *Romania* **52 F7** 44 13N 22 57 E
Cukai, *Malaysia* **87 K4** 4 13N 103 25 E
Culasi, *Phil.* **81 F4** 11 26N 122 3 E
Culbertson, *U.S.A.* **154 A2** 48 9N 104 31W
Culburra, *N.S.W., Australia* **129 C9** 34 56 S 150 46 E
Culburra, *S. Austral., Australia* **128 C3** 35 50 S 139 58 E
Culcairn, *Australia* **129 C7** 35 41 S 147 3 E
Culebra, Isla de, *Puerto Rico* **165 d** 18 19N 65 18W
Culebra, Sierra de la, *Spain* **42 D4** 41 55N 6 20W
Culfa, *Azerbaijan* **101 C11** 38 57N 45 38 E
Culgoa, *Australia* **128 C5** 35 44 S 143 6 E
Culgoa →, *Australia* **127 D4** 29 56 S 146 20 E
Culgoa Flood Plain Nat. Park, *Australia* **127 D4** 28 58 S 147 5 E
Culiacán, *Mexico* **162 C3** 24 50N 107 23W
Culiacán →, *Mexico* **162 C3** 24 30N 107 42W
Culik, *Indonesia* **79 J18** 8 21 S 115 37 E
Culion, *Phil.* **81 F3** 11 54N 119 58 E
Culion I., *Phil.* **81 F2** 11 50N 120 0 E
Culiseu →, *Brazil* **173 C7** 12 14 S 53 17W
Cúllar, *Spain* **43 H8** 37 35N 2 34W
Cullarin Ra., *Australia* **129 C8** 34 30 S 149 30 E
Cullen, *U.K.* **22 D6** 57 42N 2 49W
Cullen Bullen, *Australia* **129 B9** 33 18 S 150 2 E
Cullen Pt., *Australia* **126 A3** 11 57 S 141 54 E
Cullera, *Spain* **41 F4** 39 9N 0 17W
Cullman, *U.S.A.* **149 H2** 34 11N 86 51W
Culloden, *U.S.A.* **152 C5** 32 52N 84 6W
Cullom, *U.S.A.* **157 D8** 40 53N 88 16W
Culo →, *Angola* **115 D3** 6 13 S 15 14 E
Culoz, *France* **29 C9** 45 47N 5 46 E
Culpeper, *U.S.A.* **148 F7** 38 30N 78 0W
Culuene →, *Brazil* **173 C7** 12 56 S 52 51W
Culver, *U.S.A.* **157 C10** 41 13N 86 25W
Culver, Pt., *Australia* **125 F3** 32 54 S 124 43 E
Culverden, *N.Z.* **131 C7** 42 47 S 172 49 E
Culverton, *U.S.A.* **152 B7** 33 19N 82 54W
Cuma, *Angola* **115 E3** 12 52 S 15 5 E
Cumaná, *Venezuela* **169 A5** 10 30N 64 5W
Cumaovası, *Turkey* **49 C9** 38 15N 27 9 E
Cumare, *Colombia* **168 C3** 0 49N 72 32W

Daraj 205

Cumari, *Brazil* **171 E2** 18 16 S 48 11W
Cumberland, *B.C., Canada* **142 D4** 49 40N 125 0W
Cumberland, *Ont., Canada* **151 A9** 45 29N 75 24W
Cumberland, *Iowa, U.S.A.* **156 C2** 41 16N 94 52W
Cumberland, *Md., U.S.A.* **148 F6** 39 39N 78 46W
Cumberland →, *U.S.A.* **149 G2** 36 15N 87 0W
Cumberland, C., *Vanuatu* **133 D4** 14 39 S 166 37 E
Cumberland, L., *U.S.A.* **149 G3** 36 57N 84 55W
Cumberland I., *U.S.A.* **152 E8** 30 50N 81 25W
Cumberland Is., *Australia* **126 J7** 20 35 S 149 10 E
Cumberland L., *Canada* **143 C8** 54 3N 102 18W
Cumberland Pen., *Canada* **139 B13** 67 0N 64 0W
Cumberland Plateau, *U.S.A.* **149 H3** 36 0N 85 0W
Cumberland Sd., *Canada* **139 B13** 65 30N 66 0W
Cumbernauld, *U.K.* **22 F5** 55 57N 3 58W
Cumbira, *Angola* **115 E3** 12 11 S 15 8 E
Cumborah, *Australia* **127 D4** 29 40 S 147 45 E
Cumbres Mayores, *Spain* **43 G4** 38 4N 6 39W
Cumbria □, *U.K.* **20 C5** 54 42N 2 52W
Cumbrian Mts., *U.K.* **20 C5** 54 30N 3 0W
Cumbum, *India* **95 G4** 15 40N 79 10 E
Cuminá, *Brazil* **169 D6** 1 57 S 56 2W
Cuminá →, *Brazil* **169 D6** 1 30 S 56 0W
Cuminapanema →, *Brazil* **169 D7** 1 9 S 54 54W
Cumming, C., *Chile* **172 b** 27 6 S 109 14W
Cummings Mt., *U.S.A.* **161 K8** 35 2N 118 34W
Cummins, *Australia* **127 E2** 34 16 S 135 43 E
Cumnock, *Australia* **129 B8** 32 59 S 148 46 E
Cumnock, *U.K.* **22 F4** 55 28N 4 17W
Cumpas, *Mexico* **162 B3** 30 0N 109 48W
Cumplida, Pta., *Canary Is.* **9 e1** 28 50N 17 48W
Çumra, *Turkey* **100 D5** 37 34N 32 45 E
Cuncumén, *Chile* **174 C1** 31 53 S 70 38W
Cunderdin, *Australia* **125 F2** 31 37 S 117 12 E
Cundinamarca □, *Colombia* **168 C3** 5 0N 74 0W
Cunene □, *Angola* **115 F3** 16 30 S 15 0 E
Cunene →, *Angola* **116 B1** 17 20 S 11 50 E
Cúneo, *Italy* **44 D4** 44 23N 7 32 E
Çüngüş, *Turkey* **96 B3** 38 13N 39 17 E
Cunhinga, *Angola* **115 E3** 12 11 S 16 47 E
Cunillera, I. = Sa Conillera, *Spain* **38 D1** 38 59N 1 13 E
Cunjamba, *Angola* **115 F4** 15 27 S 20 10 E
Cunlhat, *France* **28 C7** 45 38N 3 32 E
Cunnamulla, *Australia* **127 D4** 28 2 S 145 38 E
Cunningham, *Bahamas* **9 b** 25 5N 77 26W
Cuorgnè, *Italy* **44 C4** 45 23N 7 39 E
Cupar, *Canada* **143 C8** 50 57N 104 10W
Cupar, *U.K.* **22 E5** 56 19N 3 1W
Cupcini, *Moldova* **53 B12** 48 6N 27 23 E
Cupica, G. de, *Colombia* **168 B2** 6 25N 77 30W
Čuprija, *Serbia, Yug.* **50 C5** 43 57N 21 26 E
Curaçá, *Brazil* **170 C4** 8 59 S 39 54W
Curaçao, *Neth. Ant.* **165 D6** 12 10N 69 0W
Curacautín, *Chile* **176 A2** 38 26 S 71 53W
Curahuara de Carangas, *Bolivia* **172 D4** 17 52 S 68 26W
Curanilahue, *Chile* **174 D1** 37 29 S 73 28W
Curaray →, *Peru* **168 D3** 2 20 S 74 5W
Curatabaca, *Venezuela* **169 B5** 6 19N 62 51W
Cure →, *France* **27 E10** 47 40N 3 41 E
Curepipe, *Mauritius* **121 d** 20 19 S 57 31 E
Curepto, *Chile* **174 D1** 35 8 S 72 1W
Curiapo, *Venezuela* **169 B5** 8 33N 61 5W
Curicó, *Chile* **174 C1** 34 55 S 71 20W
Curicuriari →, *Brazil* **168 D4** 0 14 S 66 48W
Curieuse, *Seychelles* **121 b** 4 15 S 55 44 E
Curimatá, *Brazil* **170 D3** 10 2 S 44 17W
Curinga, *Italy* **47 D9** 38 49N 16 19 E
Curiplaya, *Colombia* **168 C3** 0 16N 74 52W
Curitiba, *Brazil* **175 B6** 25 20 S 49 10W
Curitibanos, *Brazil* **175 B5** 27 18 S 50 36W
Curlewis, *Australia* **129 A9** 31 7 S 150 16 E
Curoca →, *Angola* **115 F2** 15 43 S 11 55 E
Currabubula, *Australia* **129 A9** 31 16 S 150 44 E
Currais Novos, *Brazil* **170 C4** 6 13 S 36 30W
Curral Velho, *C. Verde Is.* **9 j** 16 8N 22 48W
Curralinho, *Brazil* **170 B2** 1 45 S 49 46W
Currant, *U.S.A.* **158 G6** 38 51N 115 32W
Curraweena, *Australia* **129 A6** 30 47 S 145 54 E
Currawinya Nat. Park, *Australia* **127 D3** 28 55 S 144 27 E
Current →, *U.S.A.* **155 G9** 36 15N 90 55W
Currie, *Australia* **127 F3** 39 56 S 143 53 E
Currie, *U.S.A.* **158 F6** 40 16N 114 45W
Cursole, *Somali Rep.* **120 D3** 2 14N 45 25 E
Curtea de Argeş, *Romania* **53 E9** 45 12N 24 42 E
Curtici, *Romania* **52 D6** 46 21N 21 18 E
Curtis, *U.S.A.* **154 E4** 40 38N 100 31W
Curtis Group, *Australia* **127 F4** 39 30 S 146 37 E
Curtis I., *Australia* **126 C5** 23 35 S 151 10 E
Curuá →, *Pará, Brazil* **169 D7** 2 24 S 54 5W
Curuá →, *Pará, Brazil* **173 B7** 5 23 S 54 22W
Curuá, I., *Brazil* **170 A1** 0 48N 50 10W
Curuaés →, *Brazil* **173 B7** 7 30 S 54 45W
Curuaí, *Brazil* **169 D6** 2 17 S 55 29W
Curuápanema →, *Brazil* **169 D6** 2 25 S 55 2W
Curuçá, *Brazil* **170 B2** 0 43 S 47 50W
Curuçá →, *Brazil* **172 B3** 4 27 S 71 23W
Curuguaty, *Paraguay* **175 A4** 24 31 S 55 42W
Curup, *Indonesia* **84 C2** 4 26 S 102 13 E
Curupira, Serra, *S. Amer.* **169 C5** 1 25N 64 30W
Cururu →, *Brazil* **173 B6** 7 12 S 58 3W
Cururupu, *Brazil* **170 B3** 1 50 S 44 50W
Curuzú Cuatiá, *Argentina* **174 B4** 29 50 S 58 5W
Curvelo, *Brazil* **171 E3** 18 45 S 44 27W
Cushing, *U.S.A.* **155 H6** 35 59N 96 46W
Cushing, Mt., *Canada* **142 B3** 57 35N 126 57W
Cusihuiriáchic, *Mexico* **162 B3** 28 10N 106 50W
Cusna, Mte., *Italy* **44 D7** 44 17N 10 23 E
Cusset, *France* **27 F10** 46 8N 3 28 E
Cusseta, *U.S.A.* **152 C5** 32 18N 84 47W
Cusso, Sa. do, *Angola* **115 D2** 6 30 S 14 58 E
Custer, *U.S.A.* **154 D3** 43 46N 103 36W
Cut Bank, *U.S.A.* **158 B7** 48 38N 112 20W
Cutchogue, *U.S.A.* **151 E12** 41 1N 72 30W
Cutervo, *Peru* **172 B2** 6 25 S 78 55W
Cuthbert, *U.S.A.* **152 D5** 31 46N 84 48W
Cutler, *U.S.A.* **160 J7** 36 31N 119 17W
Cutler Ridge, *U.S.A.* **153 K9** 25 35N 80 20W
Cutlerville, *U.S.A.* **157 B11** 42 50N 85 40W
Cutral-Có, *Argentina* **176 A3** 38 58 S 69 15W
Cutro, *Italy* **47 C9** 39 2N 16 59 E
Cuttaburra →, *Australia* **127 D3** 29 43 S 144 22 E
Cuttack, *India* **94 D7** 20 25N 85 57 E
Cuva →, *Angola* **115 E2** 11 42 S 14 52 E
Cuvelai, *Angola* **115 F3** 15 44 S 15 50 E
Cuvier, C., *Australia* **125 D1** 23 14 S 113 22 E
Cuvier I., *N.Z.* **130 C4** 36 27 S 175 50 E
Cuxhaven, *Germany* **30 B4** 53 51N 8 41 E
Cuyabeno, *Ecuador* **168 D2** 0 16 S 75 53W
Cuyahoga Falls, *U.S.A.* **150 E3** 41 8N 81 29W
Cuyapo, *Phil.* **80 D3** 15 46N 120 40 E
Cuyo, *Phil.* **81 F3** 10 50N 121 5 E
Cuyo East Pass, *Phil.* **81 F3** 11 0N 121 28 E
Cuyo I., *Phil.* **81 F3** 10 51N 121 2 E
Cuyo Islands, *Phil.* **81 F3** 11 4N 120 57 E
Cuyo West Pass, *Phil.* **81 F3** 11 0N 120 30 E
Cuyuni →, *Guyana* **169 B6** 6 23N 58 41W
Cuzco, *Bolivia* **172 E4** 20 0 S 66 50W
Cuzco, *Peru* **172 C3** 13 32 S 72 0W
Cuzco □, *Peru* **172 C3** 13 31 S 71 59W
Čvrsnica, *Bos.-H.* **52 G2** 43 36N 17 35 E
Cwmbran, *U.K.* **21 F4** 51 39N 3 2W
Cyangugu, *Rwanda* **118 C2** 2 29 S 28 54 E
Cybinka, *Poland* **55 F1** 52 12N 14 46 E
Cyclades = Kikládhes, *Greece* **48 E6** 37 0N 24 30 E
Cygnet, *Australia* **127 G4** 43 8 S 147 1 E
Cynthiana, *U.S.A.* **157 F12** 38 23N 84 18W
Cypress Hills, *Canada* **143 D7** 49 40N 109 30W
Cypress Hills Prov. Park, *Canada* **143 D7** 49 40N 109 30W
Cyprus ■, *Asia* **39 F9** 35 0N 33 0 E
Cyrenaica, *Libya* **108 B4** 27 0N 23 0 E
Cyrene = Shaḥḥāt, *Libya* **108 B4** 32 48N 21 54 E
Cyrene, *Libya* **108 B4** 32 53N 21 52 E
Czaplinek, *Poland* **54 E3** 53 34N 16 14 E
Czar, *Canada* **143 C6** 52 27N 110 50W
Czarna →, *Łódzkie, Poland* **55 G6** 51 18N 19 55 E
Czarna →, *Świętokrzyskie, Poland* **55 H8** 50 28N 21 21 E
Czarna Białostocka, *Poland* **55 E10** 53 18N 23 17 E
Czarna Woda, *Poland* **54 E5** 53 51N 18 6 E
Czarne, *Poland* **54 E3** 53 42N 16 58 E
Czarnków, *Poland* **55 F3** 52 55N 16 38 E
Czech Rep. ■, *Europe* **34 B8** 50 0N 15 0 E
Czechowice-Dziedzice, *Poland* **55 J5** 49 54N 18 59 E
Czempiń, *Poland* **55 F3** 52 9N 16 43 E
Czeremcha, *Poland* **55 F10** 52 31N 23 21 E
Czerniejewo, *Poland* **55 F4** 52 26N 17 30 E
Czersk, *Poland* **54 E4** 53 46N 17 58 E
Czerwieńsk, *Poland* **55 F2** 52 1N 15 23 E
Czerwionka-Leszczyny, *Poland* **55 H5** 50 7N 18 37 E
Częstochowa, *Poland* **55 H6** 50 49N 19 7 E
Człopa, *Poland* **55 E3** 53 6N 16 6 E
Człuchów, *Poland* **54 E4** 53 41N 17 22 E
Czyżew-Osada, *Poland* **55 F9** 52 48N 22 19 E

D

Da →, *Vietnam* **76 G5** 21 15N 105 20 E
Da Hinggan Ling, *China* **69 B7** 48 0N 121 0 E
Da Lat, *Vietnam* **87 G7** 11 56N 108 25 E
Da Nang, *Vietnam* **86 D7** 16 4N 108 13 E
Da Qaidam, *China* **68 C4** 37 50N 95 15 E
Da Yunhe →, *China* **75 G11** 34 25N 120 5 E
Da'an, *China* **75 B13** 45 30N 124 7 E
Daan Viljoen Game Park, *Namibia* **116 C2** 22 2 S 16 45 E
Daanbantayan, *Phil.* **81 F5** 11 17N 124 2 E
Dab'a, Ras el, *Egypt* **106 H6** 31 3N 28 31 E
Daba Shan, *China* **76 B7** 32 0N 109 0 E
Dabai, *Nigeria* **113 C6** 11 25N 5 15 E
Dabajuro, *Venezuela* **168 A3** 11 2N 70 40W
Dabakala, *Ivory C.* **112 D4** 8 15N 4 20W
Dabaro, *Somali Rep.* **120 C3** 6 21N 48 43 E
Dabas, *Hungary* **52 C4** 47 11N 19 19 E
Dabat, *Ethiopia* **107 E4** 12 58N 37 41 E
Dabbagh, Jabal, *Si. Arabia* **96 E2** 27 52N 35 45 E
Dabeiba, *Colombia* **168 B2** 7 1N 76 16W
Dabhoi, *India* **92 H5** 22 10N 73 20 E
Dąbie, *Poland* **55 F5** 52 5N 18 50 E
Dabie Shan, *China* **77 B10** 31 20N 115 20 E
Dabilda, *Cameroon* **113 C7** 12 45N 14 35 E
Dabilda, *Cent. Amer.* **109 F2** 12 14N 14 34 E
Dabnou, *Niger* **113 C6** 14 10N 5 22 E
Dabo = Pasirkuning, *Indonesia* **84 C2** 0 30 S 104 33 E
Dabola, *Guinea* **112 C2** 10 50N 11 5W
Dabou, *Ivory C.* **112 D4** 5 20N 4 23W
Daboya, *Ghana* **113 D4** 9 30N 1 20W
Dąbrowa Białostocka, *Poland* **54 E10** 53 40N 23 21 E
Dąbrowa Górnicza, *Poland* **55 H6** 50 15N 19 10 E
Dąbrowa Tarnowska, *Poland* **55 H7** 50 10N 20 59 E
Dabu, *China* **77 E11** 24 22N 116 41 E
Dabugam, *India* **94 E6** 19 27N 82 26 E
Dabung, *Malaysia* **87 K4** 5 23N 102 1 E
Dabus →, *Ethiopia* **107 E4** 10 48N 35 10 E
Dacato →, *Ethiopia* **107 F5** 7 25N 42 40 E
Dacca = Dhaka, *Bangla.* **90 D3** 23 43N 90 26 E
Dacca = Dhaka □, *Bangla.* **90 C3** 24 25N 90 25 E
Dachau, *Germany* **31 G7** 48 15N 11 26 E
Dachstein, Hoher, *Austria* **34 D6** 47 28N 13 35 E
Dačice, *Czech Rep.* **34 B8** 49 5N 15 26 E
Dacula, *U.S.A.* **152 B6** 33 59N 83 54W
Dadanawa, *Guyana* **169 C6** 2 50N 59 30W
Daday, *Turkey* **100 B5** 41 28N 33 27 E
Dade City, *U.S.A.* **149 L4** 28 22N 82 11W
Dadès, Oued →, *Morocco* **110 B3** 30 58N 6 44W
Dadeville, *U.S.A.* **152 C4** 32 50N 85 46W
Dadhar, *Pakistan* **92 E2** 29 28N 67 39 E
Dadiya, *Nigeria* **113 D7** 9 35N 11 24 E
Dadra & Nagar Haveli □, *India* **94 D1** 20 5N 73 0 E
Dadri = Charkhi Dadri, *India* **92 E7** 28 37N 76 17 E
Dadu, *Pakistan* **91 D2** 26 45N 67 45 E
Dadu He →, *China* **76 C4** 29 31N 103 46 E
Daet, *Phil.* **80 D4** 14 2N 122 55 E
Dafang, *China* **76 D5** 27 9N 105 39 E
Dağ, *Turkey* **49 D12** 37 12N 30 31 E
Dagali, *Norway* **18 D5** 60 25N 8 28 E
Dagana, *Senegal* **112 B1** 16 30N 15 35W
Dagash, *Sudan* **106 D3** 19 19N 33 25 E
Dagestan □, *Russia* **61 J8** 42 30N 47 0 E
Dagestanskiye Ogni, *Russia* **61 J9** 42 6N 48 12 E
Dagg Sd., *N.Z.* **131 F1** 45 23 S 166 45 E
Daggett, *U.S.A.* **161 L10** 34 52N 116 52W
Daghestan Republic = Dagestan □, *Russia* **61 J8** 42 30N 47 0 E
Daghfeli, *Sudan* **106 D3** 19 18N 32 40 E
Dağlıq Qarabağ = Nagorno-Karabakh, *Azerbaijan* **101 C12** 39 55N 46 45 E
Dagmersellen, *Switz.* **32 B5** 47 13N 7 59 E
Dagö = Hiiumaa, *Estonia* **15 G20** 58 50N 22 45 E
Dagu, *China* **75 E9** 38 59N 117 40 E
Dagua, *Papua N. G.* **132 B2** 3 27 S 143 20 E
Daguan, *China* **76 D4** 27 43N 103 56 E
Dagupan, *Phil.* **80 C3** 16 3N 120 20 E
Daguragu, *Australia* **124 C5** 17 33 S 130 30 E
Dahab, *Egypt* **106 B3** 28 31N 34 31 E
Dahanu, *India* **94 E1** 19 58N 72 44 E
Dahivadi, *India* **94 F2** 17 43N 74 33 E
Dahlak Kebir, *Eritrea* **107 D5** 15 50N 40 10 E
Dahlak Marine Nat. Park, *Eritrea* **107 D5** 15 35N 40 1 E
Dahlenburg, *Germany* **30 B6** 53 11N 10 44 E
Dahlonega, *U.S.A.* **149 H4** 34 32N 83 59W
Dahme, *Germany* **30 D9** 51 52N 13 25 E
Dahod, *India* **92 H6** 22 50N 74 15 E
Dahomey = Benin ■, *Africa* **113 D5** 10 0N 2 0 E
Dahong Shan, *China* **77 B9** 31 25N 113 0 E
Dahra, *Libya* **108 C3** 29 30N 17 50 E
Dahra, *Senegal* **112 B1** 15 22N 15 30W
Dahra, Massif de, *Algeria* **111 A5** 36 7N 1 21 E
Dahshûr, *Egypt* **106 J7** 29 45N 31 14 E
Dahūk, *Iraq* **101 D10** 36 50N 43 1 E
Daḥy, Nafūd ad, *Si. Arabia* **98 B4** 22 0N 45 25 E
Dai, *Solomon Is.* **133 L11** 7 54 S 160 40 E
Dai Hao, *Vietnam* **86 C6** 18 1N 106 25 E
Dai-Sen, *Japan* **72 B5** 35 22N 133 32 E
Dai Shan, *China* **77 B14** 30 25N 122 10 E
Dai Xian, *China* **74 E7** 39 4N 112 58 E
Daicheng, *China* **74 E9** 38 42N 116 38 E
Daigo, *Japan* **73 A12** 36 46N 140 21 E
Daik-u, *Burma* **90 G6** 17 47N 96 40 E
Daimanji-San, *Japan* **72 A5** 36 14N 133 20 E
Daimiel, *Spain* **43 F7** 39 5N 3 35W
Daingean, *Ireland* **23 C4** 53 18N 7 17W
Dainkog, *China* **76 A1** 32 30N 97 58 E
Daintree, *Australia* **126 B4** 16 20 S 145 20 E
Daintree Nat. Park, *Australia* **126 B4** 16 8 S 145 2 E
Daiō-Misaki, *Japan* **73 C8** 34 15N 136 45 E
Dair, J. ed, *Sudan* **107 E3** 12 27N 30 42 E
Dairût, *Egypt* **106 B3** 27 34N 30 43 E
Daisetsu-Zan, *Japan* **70 C11** 43 30N 142 57 E
Daitari, *India* **94 D7** 21 10N 85 46 E
Daito, *Japan* **72 B4** 35 19N 132 58 E
Dajarra, *Australia* **126 C2** 21 42 S 139 30 E
Dajin Chuan →, *China* **76 B3** 31 16N 101 59 E
Dak Dam, *Cambodia* **86 F6** 12 20N 107 21 E
Dak Nhe, *Vietnam* **86 E6** 15 28N 107 48 E
Dak Pek, *Vietnam* **86 E6** 15 4N 107 44 E
Dak Song, *Vietnam* **87 F6** 12 19N 107 35 E
Dak Sui, *Vietnam* **86 E6** 14 55N 107 43 E
Dakar, *Senegal* **112 C1** 14 34N 17 29W
Dakhin, *Bangla.* **90 D3** 22 30N 90 45 E
Dakhla, *W. Sahara* **110 D1** 23 50N 15 53W
Dakhla, El Wâhât el-, *Egypt* **106 B2** 25 30N 28 50 E
Dakingari, *Nigeria* **113 C5** 11 37N 4 1 E
Dakoank, *India* **95 L11** 7 2N 93 43 E
Dakor, *India* **92 H5** 22 45N 73 11 E
Dakoro, *Niger* **113 C6** 14 31N 6 46 E
Dakota City, *Iowa, U.S.A.* **156 B2** 42 43N 94 12W
Dakota City, *Nebr., U.S.A.* **154 D6** 42 25N 96 25W
Đakovica, *Kosovo, Yug.* **50 D4** 42 22N 20 26 E
Đakovo, *Croatia* **52 E3** 45 19N 18 24 E
Dal, *Norway* **18 E5** 59 53N 8 40 E
Dala, *Lunda Sul, Angola* **115 E4** 11 3 S 20 17 E
Dala, *Uíge, Angola* **115 D3** 8 5 S 15 49 E
Dala, *Solomon Is.* **133 M11** 8 30 S 160 41 E
Dala-Cachibo, *Angola* **115 E2** 10 30 S 14 41 E
Dalaas, *Austria* **33 B10** 47 7N 10 0 E
Dalaba, *Guinea* **112 C2** 10 47N 12 12W
Dalachi, *China* **74 F3** 36 48N 105 0 E
Dalaguete, *Phil.* **81 G4** 9 46N 123 32 E
Dalai Nur, *China* **74 C9** 43 20N 116 45 E
Dālakī, *Iran* **97 D6** 29 26N 51 17 E
Dalälven →, *Sweden* **16 D10** 60 12N 16 43 E
Dalaman, *Turkey* **49 E10** 36 48N 28 47 E
Dalaman →, *Turkey* **49 E10** 36 41N 28 43 E
Dalandzadgad, *Mongolia* **74 C3** 43 27N 104 30 E
Dalanganem Is., *Phil.* **81 F3** 10 40N 120 17 E
Dalap-Uliga-Darrit, *Marshall Is.* **134 G9** 7 7N 171 24 E
Dalarna, *Sweden* **16 D8** 61 0N 14 0 E
Dalarnas län □, *Sweden* **16 C8** 61 0N 14 15 E
Dalasýsla □, *Iceland* **11 B4** 65 15N 22 0W
Dalat, *Malaysia* **85 B4** 2 44N 111 56 E
Dālbandīn, *Pakistan* **91 C2** 29 0N 64 23 E
Dalbeattie, *U.K.* **22 G5** 54 56N 3 50W
Dalbeg, *Australia* **126 C4** 20 16 S 147 18 E
Dalbosjön, *Sweden* **17 F6** 58 40N 12 45 E
Dalby, *Australia* **127 D5** 27 10 S 151 17 E
Dalby, *Sweden* **17 J7** 55 40N 13 22 E
Dale, *Norway* **18 C2** 61 22N 5 23 E
Dale, *U.S.A.* **157 F10** 38 10N 86 59W
Dale City, *U.S.A.* **148 F7** 38 38N 77 18W
Dale Hollow L., *U.S.A.* **149 G3** 36 32N 85 27W
Dalen, *Norway* **18 E4** 59 26N 8 0 E
Dalet, *Burma* **90 F4** 19 59N 93 51 E
Daletme, *Burma* **90 E4** 21 36N 92 46 E
Daleville, *Ala., U.S.A.* **152 D4** 31 19N 85 43W
Daleville, *Ind., U.S.A.* **157 D11** 40 7N 85 33W
Dalga, *Egypt* **106 B3** 27 39N 30 41 E
Dalgān, *Iran* **97 E8** 27 31N 59 19 E
Dalhart, *U.S.A.* **155 G3** 36 4N 102 31W
Dalhousie, *Canada* **141 C6** 48 5N 66 26W
Dalhousie, *India* **92 C6** 32 38N 75 58 E
Dali, *Shaanxi, China* **74 G5** 34 48N 109 58 E
Dali, *Yunnan, China* **76 E3** 25 40N 100 10 E
Dalian, *China* **75 E11** 38 50N 121 40 E
Daliang Shan, *China* **76 D4** 28 0N 102 45 E
Daling He →, *China* **75 D11** 40 55N 121 40 E
Dāliyat el Karmel, *Israel* **103 C4** 32 43N 35 2 E
Dalj, *Croatia* **52 E3** 45 29N 18 59 E
Dalkeith, *U.K.* **22 F5** 55 54N 3 4W
Dalkeith, *U.S.A.* **152 E4** 30 0N 85 9W
Dallas, *Ga., U.S.A.* **152 B5** 33 55N 84 51W
Dallas, *Oreg., U.S.A.* **158 D2** 44 55N 123 19W
Dallas, *Tex., U.S.A.* **155 J6** 32 47N 96 49W
Dallas Center, *U.S.A.* **156 C3** 41 41N 93 58W
Dallas City, *U.S.A.* **156 D5** 40 38N 91 10W
Dallol, *Ethiopia* **107 E5** 14 14N 40 17 E
Dalmā, *U.A.E.* **97 E7** 24 30N 52 20 E
Dalmacija, *Croatia* **45 E13** 43 20N 17 0 E
Dalmas, L., *Canada* **141 B5** 53 30N 71 50W
Dalmatia = Dalmacija, *Croatia* **45 E13** 43 20N 17 0 E
Dalmatovo, *Russia* **64 C9** 56 16N 62 56 E
Dalmau, *India* **93 F9** 26 4N 81 2 E
Dalmellington, *U.K.* **22 F4** 55 19N 4 23W
Dalmeny, *Australia* **129 D9** 36 10 S 150 8 E
Dalnegorsk, *Russia* **67 E14** 44 32N 135 33 E
Dalnerechensk, *Russia* **67 E14** 45 50N 133 40 E
Daloa, *Ivory C.* **112 D3** 7 0N 6 30W
Dalou Shan, *China* **76 C6** 28 15N 107 0 E
Dalry, *U.K.* **22 F4** 55 42N 4 43W
Dalrymple, L., *Australia* **126 C4** 20 40 S 147 0 E
Dalrymple, Mt., *Australia* **126 K6** 21 1 S 148 39 E
Dals Långed, *Sweden* **17 F6** 58 56N 12 18 E
Dalseter, *Norway* **18 C6** 61 28N 9 26 E
Dalsjöfors, *Sweden* **17 G7** 57 46N 13 5 E
Dalsland, *Sweden* **17 F6** 58 50N 12 15 E
Dalsmynni, *Iceland* **11 C5** 64 48N 21 29W
Daltenganj, *India* **93 H11** 24 0N 84 4 E
Dalton, *Ga., U.S.A.* **149 H3** 34 46N 84 58W
Dalton, *Mass., U.S.A.* **151 D11** 42 28N 73 11W
Dalton, *Nebr., U.S.A.* **154 E3** 41 25N 102 58W
Dalton, Kap, *Greenland* **10 D8** 69 25N 24 3W
Dalton-in-Furness, *U.K.* **20 C4** 54 10N 3 11W
Dalupiri I., *Cagayan, Phil.* **80 B3** 19 5N 121 12 E
Dalupiri I., *N. Samar, Phil.* **80 E5** 12 25N 124 16 E
Dalvík, *Iceland* **11 B8** 65 58N 18 32W
Dalwallinu, *Australia* **125 F2** 30 17 S 116 40 E
Daly →, *Australia* **124 B5** 13 35 S 130 19 E
Daly City, *U.S.A.* **160 H4** 37 42N 122 28W
Daly L., *Canada* **143 B7** 56 32N 105 39W
Daly River, *Australia* **124 B5** 13 46 S 130 42 E
Daly Waters, *Australia* **126 B1** 16 15 S 133 24 E
Dalyan, *Turkey* **49 E10** 36 50N 28 39 E
Dam Doi, *Vietnam* **87 H5** 8 50N 105 12 E
Dam Ha, *Vietnam* **86 B6** 21 21N 107 36 E
Daman, *India* **94 D1** 20 25N 72 57 E
Daman & Diu □, *India* **94 D1** 20 25N 72 58 E
Dāmaneh, *Iran* **97 C6** 33 1N 50 29 E
Damanganga →, *India* **94 D1** 20 25N 72 56 E
Damanhûr, *Egypt* **106 H7** 31 0N 30 30 E
Damant L., *Canada* **143 A7** 61 45N 105 5W
Damanzhuang, *China* **74 E9** 38 5N 116 35 E
Damar, *Indonesia* **82 C3** 7 7 S 128 40 E
Damara, *C.A.R.* **114 B3** 4 58N 18 42 E
Damaraland, *Namibia* **116 C2** 20 0 S 15 0 E
Damascus = Dimashq, *Syria* **103 B5** 33 30N 36 18 E
Damascus, *U.S.A.* **152 D5** 31 18N 84 43W
Damaturu, *Nigeria* **113 C7** 11 45N 11 55 E
Damāvand, *Iran* **97 C7** 35 47N 52 0 E
Damāvand, Qolleh-ye, *Iran* **97 C7** 35 56N 52 10 E
Damba, *Angola* **115 D3** 6 44 S 15 20 E
Dâmboviţa □, *Romania* **53 F10** 45 0N 25 30 E
Dâmboviţa →, *Romania* **53 F11** 44 12N 26 26 E
Dâmbovnic →, *Romania* **53 F10** 44 28N 25 18 E
Dambulla, *Sri Lanka* **95 L5** 7 51N 80 39 E
Dame Marie, *Haiti* **165 C5** 18 36N 74 26W
Dāmghān, *Iran* **97 B7** 36 10N 54 17 E
Dămienesti, *Romania* **53 D11** 46 44N 26 59 E
Damietta = Dumyât, *Egypt* **106 H7** 31 24N 31 48 E
Daming, *China* **74 F8** 36 15N 115 6 E
Damīr Qābū, *Syria* **96 B4** 36 58N 41 51 E
Dammai I., *Phil.* **81 J3** 5 47N 120 25 E
Dammam = Ad Dammām, *Si. Arabia* **97 E6** 26 20N 50 5 E
Dammarie-les-Lys, *France* **27 D9** 48 31N 2 39 E
Dammartin-en-Goële, *France* **27 C9** 49 3N 2 41 E
Dammastock, *Switz.* **33 C6** 46 38N 8 24 E
Damme, *Germany* **30 C4** 52 32N 8 11 E
Damodar →, *India* **93 H12** 23 17N 87 35 E
Damoh, *India* **93 H8** 23 50N 79 28 E
Damous, *Algeria* **111 A5** 36 31N 1 42 E
Dampier, *Australia* **124 D2** 20 41 S 116 42 E
Dampier, Selat, *Indonesia* **83 B4** 0 40 S 131 0 E
Dampier Arch., *Australia* **124 D2** 20 38 S 116 32 E
Dampier Str., *Papua N. G.* **132 C5** 5 50 S 148 0 E
Dampierre-sur Salon, *France* **32 A1** 47 33N 5 41 E
Damqawt, *Yemen* **99 C6** 16 34N 52 50 E
Damrani, *Algeria* **110 C4** 27 45N 2 56W
Damrei, Chuor Phnum, *Cambodia* **87 G4** 11 30N 103 0 E
Damroh, *India* **90 A5** 28 26N 95 14 E
Damüls, *Austria* **33 B9** 47 17N 9 53 E
Damvillers, *France* **27 C12** 49 20N 5 21 E
Dan-Gulbi, *Nigeria* **113 C6** 11 40N 6 15 E
Dan Xian, *China* **86 C7** 19 31N 109 33 E
Dana, *Indonesia* **82 D2** 11 0 S 122 52 E
Dana, L., *Canada* **140 B4** 50 53N 77 20W
Dana, Mt., *U.S.A.* **160 H7** 37 54N 119 12W
Danakil Desert, *Ethiopia* **107 E5** 12 45N 41 0 E
Danané, *Ivory C.* **112 D3** 7 16N 8 9W
Danao, *Phil.* **81 F5** 10 31N 124 1 E
Danau Poso, *Indonesia* **79 E6** 1 52 S 120 35 E
Danba, *China* **76 B3** 30 54N 101 48 E
Danbury, *U.S.A.* **151 E11** 41 24N 73 28W
Danby L., *U.S.A.* **159 J6** 34 13N 115 5W
Dand, *Afghan.* **91 C2** 31 28N 65 32 E
Dande →, *Angola* **115 D2** 6 15 S 15 34 E
Dande Safari Area, *Zimbabwe* **119 F3** 15 56 S 30 16 E
Dandeldhura, *Nepal* **93 E9** 29 20N 80 35 E
Dandeli, *India* **95 G2** 15 5N 74 30 E
Dandenong, *Australia* **129 E6** 38 0 S 145 15 E
Dandîl, *Egypt* **106 J7** 29 10N 31 2 E
Dandong, *China* **75 D13** 40 10N 124 20 E
Danfeng, *China* **74 H6** 33 45N 110 25 E
Dangan Liedao, *China* **77 F10** 22 2N 114 8 E
Dangara, *Tajikistan* **65 D4** 38 6N 69 22 E
Dange, *Angola* **115 D3** 7 56 S 15 3 E
Dangé-St-Romain, *France* **28 B4** 46 56N 0 36 E
Dângeni, *Romania* **53 C11** 47 51N 26 58 E
Danger Is. = Pukapuka, *Cook Is.* **135 J11** 10 53 S 165 49W
Danger Pt., *S. Africa* **116 E2** 34 40 S 19 17 E
Danginpuri, *Indonesia* **79 K18** 8 40 S 115 13 E
Dangla, *Ethiopia* **107 E4** 11 18N 36 56 E
Dangla Shan = Tanggula Shan, *China* **68 C4** 32 40N 92 10 E
Dangora, *Nigeria* **113 C6** 11 30N 8 7 E
Dangouadougou, *Burkina Faso* **112 D4** 10 9N 4 56W
Dangrek, Phnom, *Thailand* **86 E5** 14 15N 105 0 E
Dangriga, *Belize* **163 D7** 17 0N 88 13W
Dangshan, *China* **74 G9** 34 27N 116 22 E
Dangtu, *China* **77 B12** 31 32N 118 25 E
Dangyang, *China* **77 B8** 30 52N 111 44 E
Dani, *Burkina Faso* **113 C4** 13 43N 0 10W
Daniel, *U.S.A.* **158 E8** 42 52N 110 4W
Daniel's Harbour, *Canada* **141 B8** 50 13N 57 35W
Danielskuil, *S. Africa* **116 D3** 28 11 S 23 33 E
Danielson, *U.S.A.* **151 E13** 41 48N 71 53W
Danielsville, *U.S.A.* **152 A6** 34 8N 83 13W
Danilov, *Russia* **58 C11** 58 16N 40 13 E
Danilovgrad, *Montenegro, Yug.* **50 D3** 42 38N 19 4 E
Danilovka, *Russia* **60 E7** 50 25N 44 12 E
Daning, *China* **74 F6** 36 28N 110 45 E
Danissa, *Kenya* **118 B5** 3 15N 40 58 E
Danja, *Nigeria* **113 C6** 11 21N 7 30 E
Danje-la-Menha, *Angola* **115 D2** 9 32 S 14 39 E
Danjiangkou, *China* **77 A8** 32 31N 111 30 E
Danjiangkou Shuiku, *China* **77 A8** 32 37N 111 30 E
Ḍank, *Oman* **97 F8** 23 33N 56 16 E
Dạnkalwa, *Nigeria* **113 C7** 11 52N 12 12 E
Dankama, *Nigeria* **113 C6** 13 20N 7 44 E
Dankov, *Russia* **58 F10** 53 20N 39 5 E
Danleng, *China* **76 B4** 30 1N 103 31 E
Danlí, *Honduras* **164 D2** 14 4N 86 35W
Danmark Fjord, *Greenland* **10 A8** 81 30N 22 0W
Danmarkshavn, *Greenland* **10 B9** 76 45N 18 50W
Dannemora, *U.S.A.* **151 B11** 44 43N 73 44W
Dannenberg, *Germany* **30 B7** 53 6N 11 5 E
Dannevirke, *N.Z.* **130 G5** 40 12 S 176 8 E
Dannhauser, *S. Africa* **117 D5** 28 0 S 30 3 E
Danot, *Ethiopia* **120 C3** 7 33N 45 17 E
Dansville, *U.S.A.* **150 D7** 42 34N 77 42W
Danta, *India* **92 G5** 24 11N 72 46 E
Dantan, *India* **93 J12** 21 57N 87 20 E
Dantewara, *India* **94 E5** 18 54N 81 21 E
Danube = Dunărea →, *Europe* **53 E14** 45 20N 29 40 E
Danubyu, *Burma* **90 G5** 17 15N 95 35 E
Danvers, *U.S.A.* **151 D14** 42 34N 70 56W
Danville, *Ga., U.S.A.* **152 C6** 32 37N 83 15W
Danville, *Ill., U.S.A.* **157 D9** 40 8N 87 37W
Danville, *Ind., U.S.A.* **157 E10** 39 46N 86 32W
Danville, *Ky., U.S.A.* **157 G12** 37 39N 84 46W
Danville, *Pa., U.S.A.* **151 F8** 40 58N 76 37W
Danville, *Va., U.S.A.* **149 G6** 36 36N 79 23W
Danville, *Vt., U.S.A.* **151 B12** 44 25N 72 9W
Danyang, *China* **77 B12** 32 0N 119 31 E
Danzhai, *China* **76 D6** 26 11N 107 48 E
Danzig = Gdańsk, *Poland* **54 D5** 54 22N 18 40 E
Dao = Tobias Fornier, *Phil.* **81 F3** 10 30N 121 57 E
Dao, *Phil.* **81 F4** 11 24N 122 41 E
Dão →, *Portugal* **42 E2** 40 20N 8 11W
Dao Xian, *China* **77 E8** 25 36N 111 31 E
Daocheng, *China* **76 C3** 29 0N 100 10 E
Daora, *W. Sahara* **110 C2** 27 5N 12 59W
Daoud = Aïn Beïda, *Algeria* **111 A6** 35 50N 7 29 E
Daoukro, *Ivory C.* **112 D4** 7 10N 3 58W
Dapa, *Phil.* **81 G6** 9 46N 126 3 E
Dapaong, *Togo* **113 C5** 10 55N 0 16 E
Dapchi, *Nigeria* **113 C7** 12 32N 11 31 E
Dapiak, Mt., *Phil.* **81 G4** 8 15N 123 28 E
Dapitan, *Phil.* **81 G4** 8 39N 123 25 E
Dapoli, *India* **94 F1** 17 46N 73 11 E
Daqing Shan, *China* **74 D6** 40 40N 111 0 E
Daqu Shan, *China* **77 B14** 30 25N 122 20 E
Dar Banda, *Africa* **104 F6** 8 0N 23 0 E
Dar el Beida = Casablanca, *Morocco* **110 B3** 33 36N 7 36W
Dar es Salaam, *Tanzania* **118 D4** 6 50 S 39 12 E
Dar Mazār, *Iran* **97 D8** 29 14N 57 20 E
Dar Rounga, *C.A.R.* **114 A4** 0 45N 22 20 E
Dar'ā, *Syria* **103 C5** 32 36N 36 7 E
Dar'ā □, *Syria* **103 C5** 32 55N 36 10 E
Dārāb, *Iran* **97 D7** 28 50N 54 30 E
Daraban, *Pakistan* **92 D4** 31 44N 70 20 E
Darabani, *Romania* **53 B11** 48 10N 26 39 E
Darai Hills, *Papua N. G.* **132 D2** 7 8 S 143 33 E
Daraina, *Madag.* **117 A8** 13 12 S 49 40 E
Daraj, *Libya* **108 B2** 30 10N 10 28 E

Djambala 207

Denpasar, Indonesia 85 D5 8 39 S 115 13 E
Denton, Ga., U.S.A. 152 D7 31 44N 82 42W
Denton, Mont., U.S.A. 158 C9 47 19N 109 57W
Denton, Tex., U.S.A. 155 J6 33 13N 97 8W
D'Entrecasteaux, Pt., Australia 125 F2 34 50 S 115 57 E
D'Entrecasteaux Is., Papua N. G. 132 E6 9 0 S 151 0 E
D'Entrecasteaux Nat. Park, Australia 125 F2 34 20 S 115 33 E
Dents du Midi, Switz. 32 D3 46 10N 6 56 E
Dentsville, U.S.A. 152 A9 34 4N 80 58W
Denu, Ghana 113 D5 6 4N 1 8 E
Denver, Colo., U.S.A. 154 F2 39 44N 104 59W
Denver, Ind., U.S.A. 157 D10 40 52N 86 5W
Denver, Iowa, U.S.A. 156 B4 42 40N 92 20W
Denver, Pa., U.S.A. 151 F8 40 14N 76 8W
Denver City, U.S.A. 155 J3 32 58N 102 50W
Deoband, India 92 E7 29 42N 77 43 E
Deobhog, India 94 E6 19 53N 82 44 E
Deodrug, India 95 F3 16 26N 76 55 E
Deogarh, Orissa, India 94 D7 21 32N 84 45 E
Deogarh, Raj., India 92 G5 25 32N 73 54 E
Deoghar, India 93 G12 24 30N 86 42 E
Deolali, India 94 E1 19 58N 73 50 E
Deoli = Devli, India 92 G6 25 50N 75 20 E
Déols, France 27 F8 46 50N 1 43 E
Deora, India 92 F4 26 22N 70 55 E
Deori, India 93 H8 23 24N 79 1 E
Deoria, India 93 F10 26 31N 83 48 E
Deosai Mts., Pakistan 93 B6 35 40N 75 0 E
Deosri, India 90 B3 26 46N 90 29 E
Depalpur, India 92 H6 22 51N 75 33 E
Deping, China 75 F9 37 25N 116 58 E
Deposit, U.S.A. 151 D9 42 4N 75 25W
Depuch I., Australia 124 D2 20 37 S 117 44 E
Deputatskiy, Russia 67 C14 69 18N 139 54 E
Dêqên, China 76 C2 28 34N 98 51 E
Deqing, China 77 F8 23 8N 111 42 E
Dera Ghazi Khan, Pakistan 91 C3 30 5N 70 43 E
Dera Ismail Khan, Pakistan 91 C3 31 50N 70 50 E
Derabugti, Pakistan 92 E3 29 2N 69 9 E
Derawar Fort, Pakistan 92 E4 28 46N 71 20 E
Derbent, Russia 61 J9 42 5N 48 15 E
Derbent, Turkey 49 C10 38 11N 28 33 E
Derbent, Uzbekistan 65 D3 38 13N 67 1 E
Derby, Australia 124 C3 17 18 S 123 38 E
Derby, U.K. 20 E6 52 56N 1 28W
Derby, Conn., U.S.A. 151 E11 41 19N 73 5W
Derby, Kans., U.S.A. 155 G6 37 33N 97 16W
Derby, N.Y., U.S.A. 150 D6 42 41N 78 58W
Derby City □, U.K. 20 E6 52 56N 1 28W
Derby Line, U.S.A. 151 B12 45 0N 72 6W
Derbyshire □, U.K. 20 D6 53 11N 1 38W
Derecske, Hungary 52 C6 47 20N 21 33 E
Dereköy, Turkey 51 E11 41 55N 27 21 E
Dereli, Turkey 101 B8 40 44N 38 26 E
Derg →, U.K. 23 B4 54 44N 7 26W
Derg, L., Ireland 23 D3 53 0N 8 20W
Dergachi = Derhaci, Ukraine 59 G9 50 9N 36 11 E
Derhaci, Ukraine 59 G9 50 9N 36 11 E
Derik, Turkey 101 D9 37 21N 40 18 E
Derinkuyu, Turkey 100 C6 38 22N 34 45 E
Dermantsi, Bulgaria 51 C8 43 8N 24 17 E
Dermott, U.S.A. 155 J9 33 32N 91 26W
Dêrong, China 76 C2 28 44N 99 9 E
Derrinallum, Australia 128 D5 37 57 S 143 15 E
Derry = Londonderry, U.K. 23 B4 55 0N 7 20W
Derry = Londonderry □, U.K. 23 B4 55 0N 7 20W
Derry, N.H., U.S.A. 151 D13 42 53N 71 19W
Derry, Pa., U.S.A. 150 F5 40 20N 79 18W
Derryveagh Mts., Ireland 23 B3 54 56N 8 11W
Derudub, Sudan 106 D4 17 31N 36 7 E
Derval, France 26 E5 47 40N 1 41W
Dervéni, Greece 48 C4 38 8N 22 25 E
Derventa, Bos.-H. 52 F2 44 59N 17 55 E
Derwent →, Cumb., U.K. 20 C4 54 39N 3 33W
Derwent →, Derby, U.K. 20 E6 52 57N 1 28W
Derwent →, N. Yorks., U.K. 20 D7 53 45N 0 58W
Derwent Water, U.K. 20 C4 54 35N 3 9W
Des Moines, Iowa, U.S.A. 156 C3 41 35N 93 37W
Des Moines, N. Mex., U.S.A. 155 G3 36 46N 103 50W
Des Moines →, U.S.A. 156 D5 40 23N 91 25W
Des Plaines, U.S.A. 157 B9 42 3N 87 52W
Des Plaines →, U.S.A. 157 C8 41 23N 88 15W
Desa, Romania 52 G8 43 52N 23 2 E
Desaguadero, Peru 172 D4 16 34 S 69 3W
Desaguadero →, Argentina 174 C2 34 30 S 66 46W
Desaguadero →, Bolivia 172 D4 16 35 S 69 5W
Desar, Malaysia 87 d 1 31N 104 17 E
Descanso, Pta., Mexico 161 N9 32 21N 117 3W
Descartes, France 28 B4 46 59N 0 42 E
Deschaillons, Canada 141 C5 46 32N 72 7W
Deschambault L., Canada 143 C8 54 50N 103 30W
Deschutes →, U.S.A. 158 D3 45 38N 120 55W
Dese, Ethiopia 107 E4 11 5N 39 40 E
Deseado, C., Chile 176 D2 52 45 S 74 42W
Desenzano del Garda, Italy 44 C7 45 28N 10 32 E
Desert Center, U.S.A. 161 M11 33 43N 115 24W
Desert Hot Springs, U.S.A. 161 M10 33 58N 116 30W
Desertas, Ilhas, Madeira 110 B1 32 30N 16 30W
Deset, Norway 18 C8 61 20N 11 26 E
Deshnok, India 92 F5 27 48N 73 21 E
Desna →, Ukraine 59 G6 50 33N 30 32 E
Desnătui →, Romania 53 G8 43 53N 23 35 E
Desolación, I., Chile 176 D2 53 0 S 74 0W
Despeñaperros, Paso, Spain 43 G7 38 24N 3 30W
Despotovac, Serbia, Yug. 50 B5 44 6N 21 30 E
Dessau, Germany 30 D8 51 51N 12 14 E
Dessye = Dese, Ethiopia 107 E4 11 5N 39 40 E
Destin, U.S.A. 153 E3 30 24N 86 30W
D'Estrees B., Australia 128 C2 35 55 S 137 45 E
Desuri, India 92 G5 25 18N 73 35 E
Desvres, France 27 B8 50 40N 1 48 E
Det Udom, Thailand 86 E5 14 54N 105 5 E
Deta, Romania 52 E6 45 24N 21 13 E
Dete, Zimbabwe 116 B4 18 38 S 26 50 E
Đetinja →, Serbia, Yug. 50 C4 43 51N 20 5 E
Detmold, Germany 30 D4 51 56N 8 52 E
Detour, Pt., U.S.A. 148 C2 45 40N 86 40W
Detroit, U.S.A. 150 D1 42 20N 83 3W
Detroit Lakes, U.S.A. 154 B7 46 49N 95 51W
Detva, Slovak Rep. 35 C12 48 34N 19 25 E
Deurne, Neths. 24 C5 51 27N 5 49 E
Deutsche Bucht, Germany 30 A4 54 15N 8 0 E
Deutschlandsberg, Austria 34 E8 46 49N 15 14 E
Deux-Sèvres □, France 26 F6 46 35N 0 20W
Deva, Romania 52 E7 45 53N 22 55 E
Deva Nat. Park, Australia 129 C8 35 55 S 149 48 E
Devakottai, India 95 K4 9 55N 78 45 E
Devaprayag, India 93 D8 30 13N 78 35 E
Devarkonda, India 94 F4 16 42N 78 56 E
Dévaványa, Hungary 52 C5 47 2N 20 59 E
Deveci Dağları, Turkey 100 B7 40 10N 36 15 E
Devecikonağı, Turkey 51 G12 39 55N 28 34 E
Devecser, Hungary 52 C2 47 6N 17 26 E
Develi, Turkey 100 C6 38 23N 35 29 E
Deventer, Neths. 24 B6 52 15N 6 10 E
Devereux, U.S.A. 152 B6 33 13N 83 5W
Deveron →, U.K. 22 D6 57 41N 2 32W
Devesel, Romania 52 F7 44 28N 22 41 E
Devgad I., India 95 G2 14 48N 74 5 E
Devgadh Bariya, India 92 H5 22 40N 73 55 E
Devgarh, India 95 F1 16 23N 73 23 E
Devi →, India 94 E8 19 59N 86 24 E
Devikot, India 92 F4 26 42N 71 12 E
Devil River Pk., N.Z. 131 A7 40 56 S 172 37 E
Devils Den, U.S.A. 160 K7 35 46N 119 58W
Devils Lake, U.S.A. 154 A5 48 7N 98 52W
Devils Paw, Canada 142 B2 58 47N 134 0W
Devil's Pt., Sri Lanka 95 K5 9 26N 80 6 E
Devils Tower Junction, U.S.A. 154 C2 44 31N 104 57W
Devin, Bulgaria 51 E8 41 44N 24 24 E
Devine, U.S.A. 155 L5 29 8N 98 54W
Devipattinam, India 95 K4 9 29N 78 54 E
Devizes, U.K. 21 F6 51 22N 1 58W
Devli, India 92 G6 25 50N 75 20 E
Devnya, Bulgaria 51 C11 43 13N 27 33 E
Devoll →, Albania 50 F4 40 57N 20 15 E
Devon, Canada 142 C6 53 24N 113 44W
Devon □, U.K. 21 G4 50 50N 3 40W
Devon I., Canada 6 B3 75 10N 85 0W
Devonport, Australia 127 G4 41 10 S 146 22 E
Devrek, Turkey 100 B4 41 13N 31 57 E
Devrekâni, Turkey 100 B5 41 36N 33 50 E
Devrez →, Turkey 100 B6 41 6N 34 25 E
Devrukh, India 94 F1 17 3N 73 37 E
Dewas, India 92 H7 22 59N 76 3 E
Dewetsdorp, S. Africa 116 D4 29 33 S 26 39 E
Dewey, Puerto Rico 165 d 18 18N 65 18W
Dexing, China 77 C11 28 46N 117 30 E
Dexter, Maine, U.S.A. 149 C11 45 1N 69 18W
Dexter, Mich., U.S.A. 157 B13 42 20N 83 53W
Dexter, Mo., U.S.A. 155 G10 36 48N 89 57W
Dexter, N. Mex., U.S.A. 155 J2 33 12N 104 22W
Dey-Dey, L., Australia 125 E5 29 12 S 131 4 E
Deyang, China 76 B5 31 3N 104 27 E
Deyhūk, Iran 97 C8 33 15N 57 30 E
Deyyer, Iran 97 E6 27 55N 51 55 E
Dezadeash L., Canada 142 A1 60 28N 136 58W
Dezfūl, Iran 97 C6 32 20N 48 30 E
Dezhneva, Mys, Russia 67 C19 66 5N 169 40W
Dezhou, China 74 F9 37 26N 116 18 E
Dhadhar →, India 93 G11 24 56N 85 24 E
Dháfni, Kríti, Greece 39 E6 35 13N 25 3 E
Dháfni, Pelóponnisos, Greece 48 D4 37 48N 22 1 E
Dhafnoúdhi, Ákra, Greece 39 C2 38 28N 20 32 E
Dhahabān, Si. Arabia 98 B2 21 58N 39 3 E
Dhahiriya = Az Ẓāhirīyah, West Bank 103 D3 31 25N 34 58 E
Dhahran = Az Ẓahrān, Si. Arabia 97 E6 26 10N 50 7 E
Dhak, Pakistan 92 C5 32 25N 72 33 E
Dhaka, Bangla. 90 D3 23 43N 90 26 E
Dhaka □, Bangla. 90 C3 24 25N 90 25 E
Dhali, Cyprus 39 E9 35 1N 33 25 E
Dhamangaon, India 94 D4 20 48N 78 9 E
Dhamār, Yemen 98 D4 14 30N 44 20 E
Dhamási, Greece 48 B4 39 43N 22 11 E
Dhampur, India 93 E8 29 19N 78 33 E
Dhamra →, India 94 D8 20 47N 86 58 E
Dhamtari, India 94 D5 20 42N 81 35 E
Dhanbad, India 93 H12 23 50N 86 30 E
Dhankuta, Nepal 93 F12 26 55N 87 40 E
Dhanora, India 94 D5 20 20N 80 22 E
Dhanushkodi, India 95 K4 9 11N 79 24 E
Dhar, India 92 H6 22 35N 75 26 E
Dharampur, Gujarat, India 94 D1 20 32N 73 17 E
Dharampur, Mad. P., India 92 H6 22 13N 75 18 E
Dharamsala = Dharmsala, India 92 C7 32 16N 76 23 E
Dharangaon, India 94 D2 21 1N 75 16 E
Dharapuram, India 95 J3 10 45N 77 34 E
Dhariwal, India 92 D6 31 57N 75 19 E
Dharla →, Bangla. 93 G13 25 46N 89 42 E
Dharmapuri, India 95 H4 12 10N 78 10 E
Dharmavaram, India 95 G3 14 29N 77 44 E
Dharmjaygarh, India 93 H10 22 28N 83 13 E
Dharmsala, India 92 C7 32 16N 76 23 E
Dharni, India 92 J7 21 33N 76 53 E
Dharug Nat. Park, Australia 129 B9 33 20 S 151 2 E
Dharur, India 94 E3 18 3N 76 8 E
Dharwad, India 95 G2 15 30N 75 4 E
Dhasan →, India 93 G8 25 48N 79 24 E
Dhaulagiri, Nepal 93 E10 28 39N 83 28 E
Dhebar, L., India 92 G6 24 10N 74 0 E
Dheftera, Cyprus 39 E9 35 5N 33 16 E
Dhenkanal, India 94 D7 20 45N 85 35 E
Dhenoúsa, Greece 49 D7 37 8N 25 48 E
Dherinia, Cyprus 39 E9 35 3N 33 57 E
Dheskáti, Greece 50 G5 39 55N 21 49 E
Dhespotikó, Greece 48 E6 36 57N 24 58 E
Dhestina, Greece 48 C4 38 25N 22 31 E
Dhiarrizos →, Cyprus 39 F8 34 41N 32 34 E
Dhíavlos Zakínthou, Greece 39 D2 37 50N 21 0 E
Dhībān, Jordan 103 D4 31 30N 35 46 E
Dhidhimótikhon, Greece 51 E10 41 22N 26 29 E
Dhíkti Óros, Greece 39 E6 35 8N 25 30 E
Dhilianáta, Greece 39 C2 38 13N 20 31 E
Dhílos, Greece 49 D7 37 23N 25 15 E
Dhilwan, India 92 D6 31 31N 75 21 E
Dhimarkhera, India 93 H9 23 28N 80 22 E
Dhimitsána, Greece 48 D4 37 36N 22 3 E
Dhírfis Óros, Greece 48 C5 38 40N 23 54 E
Dhodhekánisos, Greece 49 E8 36 35N 27 0 E
Dhodhekánisos □, Greece 49 E8 36 35N 27 0 E
Dhokós, Greece 48 D5 37 20N 23 20 E
Dholiana, Greece 50 G4 39 54N 20 32 E
Dholka, India 92 H5 22 44N 72 29 E
Dhomokós, Greece 48 B4 39 10N 22 18 E
Dhone, India 95 E3 15 25N 77 53 E
Dhoraji, India 92 J4 21 45N 70 37 E
Dhoxáton, Greece 51 E8 41 9N 24 16 E
Dhragonísi, Greece 49 D7 37 27N 25 29 E
Dhráhstis, Ákra, Greece 38 B9 39 48N 19 40 E
Dhrakáta, Greece 39 C2 38 20N 20 33 E
Dhrangadhra, India 92 H4 22 59N 71 31 E
Dhrápanon, Ákra, Greece 39 E5 35 28N 24 14 E
Dhriopís, Greece 48 D6 37 25N 24 26 E
Dhrol, India 92 H4 22 33N 70 25 E
Dhubāb, Yemen 98 D3 12 56N 43 25 E
Dhuburi, India 90 B2 26 2N 89 59 E
Dhulasar, Bangla. 90 E3 21 52N 90 14 E
Dhule, India 94 D2 20 58N 74 50 E
Dhupdhara, India 90 B3 26 10N 91 4 E
Dhuusa Marreeb = Dusa Mareb, Somali Rep. 120 C3 5 30N 46 15 E
Di-ib, W. →, Sudan 106 C4 22 38N 36 6 E
Di Linh, Vietnam 87 G7 11 35N 108 4 E
Di Linh, Cao Nguyen, Vietnam 87 G7 11 30N 108 0 E
Día, Greece 39 E6 35 28N 25 14 E
Diabakania, Guinea 112 C2 10 38N 10 58W
Diable, Île du, Fr. Guiana 169 B7 5 15N 52 34W
Diablo, Mt., U.S.A. 160 H5 37 53N 121 56W
Diablo Range, U.S.A. 160 J5 37 20N 121 25W
Diafarabé, Mali 112 C4 14 9N 4 57W
Diala, Mali 112 C3 14 10N 9 58W
Dialakoro, Mali 112 C3 12 18N 7 54W
Dialakoto, Senegal 112 C2 13 21N 13 19W
Diallassagou, Mali 112 C4 13 47N 3 41W
Diamante, Argentina 174 C3 32 5 S 60 40W
Diamante, Italy 47 C8 39 41N 15 49 E
Diamante →, Argentina 174 C2 34 30 S 66 46W
Diamantina, Brazil 171 E3 18 17 S 43 40W
Diamantina →, Australia 127 D2 26 45 S 139 10 E
Diamantina Nat. Park, Australia 126 C3 23 33 S 141 23 E
Diamantino, Brazil 173 C6 14 30 S 56 30W
Diamond Bar, U.S.A. 161 L9 34 1N 117 48W
Diamond Harbour, India 93 H13 22 11N 88 14 E
Diamond Head, U.S.A. 145 K14 21 16N 157 49W
Diamond Is., Australia 126 B5 17 25 S 151 5 E
Diamond Mts., U.S.A. 158 G6 39 50N 115 30W
Diamond Springs, U.S.A. 160 G6 38 42N 120 49W
Dian Chi, China 76 E4 24 50N 102 43 E
Dianalund, Denmark 17 J5 55 32N 11 30 E
Dianbai, China 77 G8 21 33N 111 0 E
Diancheng, China 77 G8 21 30N 111 4 E
Dianjiang, China 76 B6 30 24N 107 20 E
Diano Marina, Italy 44 E5 43 54N 8 5 E
Dianópolis, Brazil 171 D2 11 38 S 46 50W
Dianra, Ivory C. 112 D3 8 45N 6 14W
Diapaga, Burkina Faso 113 C5 12 5N 1 46 E
Diapangou, Burkina Faso 113 C5 12 5N 0 10 E
Diariguila, Guinea 112 C2 10 35N 10 2W
Diavolo, Mt., India 95 H11 12 40N 92 56 E
Dibā, Oman 97 E8 25 45N 56 16 E
Dibai, India 92 E8 28 13N 78 15 E
Dibaya, Dem. Rep. of the Congo 115 D4 6 30 S 22 57 E
Dibaya-Lubue, Dem. Rep. of the Congo 115 C3 4 12 S 19 54 E
Dibella, Niger 109 E2 17 32N 13 6 E
Dibete, Botswana 116 C4 23 45 S 26 32 E
Dibrugarh, India 90 B5 27 29N 94 55 E
Dickens, U.S.A. 155 J4 33 37N 100 50W
Dickeyville, U.S.A. 156 B6 42 38N 90 36W
Dickinson, U.S.A. 154 B3 46 53N 102 47W
Dick's Pt., Bahamas 9 b 25 4N 77 18W
Dickson = Dikson, Russia 66 B9 73 40N 80 5 E
Dickson, U.S.A. 149 G2 36 5N 87 23W
Dickson City, U.S.A. 151 E9 41 29N 75 40W
Dicle Nehri →, Turkey 101 D9 37 44N 41 10 E
Dicomano, Italy 45 E8 43 53N 11 31 E
Didesa, W. →, Ethiopia 107 E4 10 2N 35 32 E
Didi, Sudan 107 F3 6 18N 34 29 E
Didiéni, Mali 112 C3 13 53N 8 6W
Didimbo, Angola 115 F4 17 30 S 21 45 E
Didsbury, Canada 142 C6 51 35N 114 10W
Didwana, India 92 F6 27 23N 74 36 E
Die, France 29 D9 44 47N 5 22 E
Diébougou, Burkina Faso 112 C4 11 0N 3 15W
Diecke, Guinea 112 D3 7 27N 8 54W
Diefenbaker, L., Canada 143 C7 51 0N 106 55W
Diego de Almagro, Chile 174 B1 26 22 S 70 3W
Diego Garcia, Ind. Oc. 121 E6 7 50 S 72 50 E
Diego Ramírez, Islas, Chile 176 E3 56 30 S 68 44W
Diekirch, Lux. 24 E6 49 52N 6 10 E
Diéma, Mali 112 C3 14 32N 9 12W
Diembéring, Senegal 112 C1 12 29N 16 47W
Dien Ban, Vietnam 86 E7 15 53N 108 16 E
Dien Bien, Vietnam 76 G4 21 20N 103 0 E
Dien Khanh, Vietnam 87 F7 12 15N 109 6 E
Diepholz, Germany 30 C4 52 37N 8 22 E
Diepoldsau, Switz. 33 B9 47 23N 9 40 E
Dieppe, France 26 C8 49 54N 1 4 E
Dierks, U.S.A. 155 H8 34 7N 94 1W
Diessenhofen, Switz. 33 A7 47 42N 8 46 E
Diest, Belgium 24 D5 50 58N 5 4 E
Dieterich, U.S.A. 157 E8 39 4N 88 23W
Dietikon, Switz. 33 B6 47 24N 8 24 E
Dieulefit, France 29 D9 44 32N 5 4 E
Dieuze, France 27 D13 48 49N 6 43 E
Dif, Somali Rep. 102 G3 0 59N 0 56 E
Differdange, Lux. 24 E5 49 31N 5 54 E
Diffun, Phil. 80 C3 16 36N 121 33 E
Dig, India 92 F7 27 28N 77 20 E
Digba, Dem. Rep. of the Congo 118 B2 4 25N 25 48 E
Digboi, India 90 B5 27 23N 95 38 E
Digby, Canada 141 D6 44 38N 65 50W
Diggi, India 92 F6 26 22N 75 26 E
Dighinala, Bangla. 90 D4 23 15N 92 5 E
Dighton, U.S.A. 154 F4 38 29N 100 28W
Diglur, India 94 E3 18 34N 77 33 E
Digna, Mali 112 C3 14 48N 8 10W
Digne-les-Bains, France 29 D10 44 5N 6 12 E
Digoin, France 27 F11 46 29N 4 1 E
Digor, Turkey 101 B10 40 22N 43 25 E
Digos, Phil. 81 H5 6 45N 125 20 E
Digranes, Iceland 11 A12 66 4N 14 44W
Digras, India 94 D3 20 6N 77 45 E
Digul →, Indonesia 83 C5 7 7 S 138 42 E
Digya Nat. Park, Ghana 113 D5 7 15N 0 5 E
Dihang = Brahmaputra →, India 90 B5 27 48N 95 30 E
Dijlah, Nahr →, Asia 96 D5 31 0N 47 25 E
Dijon, France 27 E12 47 20N 5 3 E
Dikhil, Djibouti 107 E5 11 8N 42 20 E
Dikili, Turkey 49 B8 39 4N 26 53 E
Dikirnis, Egypt 106 H7 31 6N 31 35 E
Dikkil = Dikhil, Djibouti 107 E5 11 8N 42 20 E
Dikodougou, Ivory C. 112 D3 9 4N 5 45W
Diksmuide, Belgium 24 C2 51 2N 2 52 E
Dikson, Russia 66 B9 73 40N 80 5 E
Dikwa, Nigeria 113 C7 12 4N 13 30 E
Dila, Ethiopia 107 F4 6 21N 38 22 E
Dilasag, Phil. 80 C4 16 25N 122 11 E
Dili, E. Timor 82 C3 8 39 S 125 34 E
Diligent Strait, India 95 H11 12 11N 92 57 E
Dilijan, Armenia 61 K7 40 46N 44 57 E
Dilizhan = Dilijan, Armenia 61 K7 40 46N 44 57 E
Dilj, Croatia 52 E3 45 29N 18 1 E
Dillenburg, Germany 30 E4 50 43N 8 17 E
Dilley, U.S.A. 155 L5 28 40N 99 10W
Dillia →, Niger 109 F2 14 9N 12 50 E
Dilling, Sudan 107 E2 12 3N 29 35 E
Dillingen, Bayern, Germany 31 G6 48 36N 10 30 E
Dillingen, Saarland, Germany 31 F2 49 20N 6 43 E
Dillingham, U.S.A. 144 G8 59 3N 158 28W
Dillon, Canada 143 B7 55 56N 108 35W
Dillon, Mont., U.S.A. 158 D7 45 13N 112 38W
Dillon, S.C., U.S.A. 149 H6 34 25N 79 22W
Dillon →, Canada 143 B7 55 56N 108 56W
Dillsboro, U.S.A. 157 E11 39 1N 85 4W
Dillsburg, U.S.A. 150 F7 40 7N 77 2W
Dilly, Mali 112 C3 15 1N 7 40W
Dilolo, Dem. Rep. of the Congo 115 E4 10 28 S 22 18 E
Dimapur, India 90 C4 25 54N 93 45 E
Dimas, Mexico 162 C3 23 43N 106 47W
Dimasalang, Phil. 80 E4 12 12N 123 51 E
Dimashq, Syria 103 B5 33 30N 36 18 E
Dimashq □, Syria 103 B5 33 30N 36 30 E
Dimbaza, S. Africa 117 E4 32 50 S 27 14 E
Dimbelenge, Dem. Rep. of the Congo 115 D4 5 33 S 23 7 E
Dimbokro, Ivory C. 112 D4 6 45N 4 46W
Dimboola, Australia 128 D5 36 28 S 142 7 E
Dîmbovița = Dâmbovița →, Romania 53 F11 44 12N 26 26 E
Dimbulah, Australia 126 B4 17 8 S 145 4 E
Dimitrovgrad, Bulgaria 51 D9 42 5N 25 35 E
Dimitrovgrad, Russia 60 C9 54 14N 49 39 E
Dimitrovgrad, Serbia, Yug. 50 C6 43 2N 22 48 E
Dimitrovo = Pernik, Bulgaria 50 D7 42 35N 23 2 E
Dimmitt, U.S.A. 155 H3 34 33N 102 19W
Dimo, Sudan 107 F2 5 19N 29 10 E
Dimona, Israel 103 D4 31 2N 35 1 E
Dimonika, Réserve de la Biosphere de, Congo 114 C2 4 13 S 12 21 E
Dimovo, Bulgaria 50 C6 43 43N 22 50 E
Dinagat, Phil. 81 F5 10 10N 125 40 E
Dinaig, Phil. 81 H5 7 11N 124 10 E
Dinajpur, Bangla. 90 C2 25 33N 88 43 E
Dinalupihan, Phil. 80 D3 14 52N 120 28 E
Dinan, France 26 D4 48 28N 2 2W
Dīnān Āb, Iran 97 C8 32 4N 56 49 E
Dinant, Belgium 24 D4 50 16N 4 55 E
Dinapur, India 93 G11 25 38N 85 5 E
Dinar, Turkey 49 C12 38 5N 30 10 E
Dīnār, Kūh-e, Iran 97 D6 30 42N 51 46 E
Dinara Planina, Croatia 45 D13 44 0N 16 30 E
Dinard, France 26 D4 48 38N 2 6W
Dinaric Alps = Dinara Planina, Croatia 45 D13 44 0N 16 30 E
Dinas, Phil. 81 H4 7 38N 123 20 E
Dindanko, Mali 112 C3 14 8N 9 30W
Dinde, Angola 115 E2 14 17 S 13 42 E
Dinder, Nahr ed →, Sudan 107 E3 14 6N 33 40 E
Dinder Nat. Park, Sudan 107 E4 12 30N 35 10 E
Dindi →, India 95 F4 16 24N 78 15 E
Dindigul, India 95 J4 10 25N 78 0 E
Dindori, India 93 H9 22 57N 81 5 E
Ding Xian = Dingzhou, China 74 E8 38 30N 114 59 E
Dinga, Dem. Rep. of the Congo 115 D3 5 17 S 16 42 E
Dinga, Pakistan 92 G2 25 26N 67 10 E
Dingalan, Phil. 80 D3 15 18N 121 25 E
Dingalan Bay, Phil. 80 D3 15 18N 121 25 E
Dingbian, China 74 F4 37 35N 107 32 E
Dingelstädt, Germany 30 D6 51 18N 10 19 E
Dingle, Ireland 23 D1 52 9N 10 17W
Dingle, Sweden 17 F5 58 32N 11 35 E
Dingle B., Ireland 23 D1 52 3N 10 20W
Dingli, Malta 38 F7 35 52N 14 23 E
Dingmans Ferry, U.S.A. 151 E10 41 13N 74 55W
Dingnan, China 77 E10 24 45N 115 0 E
Dingo, Australia 126 C4 23 38 S 149 19 E
Dingolfing, Germany 31 G8 48 37N 12 30 E
Dingras, Phil. 80 B3 18 6N 120 42 E
Dingtao, China 74 G8 35 5N 115 35 E
Dinguira, Mali 112 C2 14 11N 11 16W
Dinguiraye, Guinea 112 C2 11 18N 10 49W
Dingwall, U.K. 22 D4 57 36N 4 26W
Dingxi, China 74 G3 35 30N 104 33 E
Dingxiang, China 74 E7 38 30N 112 58 E
Dingyuan, China 77 A11 32 32N 117 41 E
Dingzhou, China 74 E8 38 30N 114 59 E
Dinh, Mui, Vietnam 87 G7 11 22N 109 1 E
Dinh Lap, Vietnam 76 G6 21 33N 107 6 E
Dinhata, India 90 B2 26 8N 89 27 E
Dinokwe, Botswana 116 C4 23 29 S 26 37 E
Dinorwic, Canada 143 D10 49 41N 92 30W
Dinosaur Nat. Monument, U.S.A. 158 F9 40 30N 108 45W
Dinosaur Prov. Park, Canada 142 C6 50 47N 111 30W
Dinsor, Somali Rep. 120 D2 2 24N 42 59 E
Dinuba, U.S.A. 160 J7 36 32N 119 23W
Diö, Sweden 17 H8 56 37N 14 15 E
Dioïla, Mali 112 C3 12 23N 6 50W
Dioka, Mali 112 C2 14 57N 10 4W
Diomede, U.S.A. 144 D5 65 47N 169 0W
Diona, Chad 109 E4 17 51N 22 36 E
Diongoï, Mali 112 C3 14 38N 8 34W
Diósgyör, Hungary 52 B5 48 7N 20 43 E
Diosig, Romania 52 C7 47 18N 22 2 E
Diougani, Mali 112 C4 14 19N 2 44W
Diouloulou, Senegal 112 C1 13 5N 16 38W
Dioura, Mali 112 C3 14 59N 5 12W
Diourbel, Senegal 112 C1 14 39N 16 12W
Dipaculao, Phil. 80 D3 15 51N 121 32 E
Dipalpur, Pakistan 92 D5 30 40N 73 39 E
Diplo, Pakistan 92 G3 24 35N 69 35 E
Dipolog, Phil. 81 G4 8 36N 123 20 E
Dipperu Nat. Park, Australia 126 C4 21 56 S 148 42 E
Dipton, N.Z. 131 F3 45 54 S 168 22 E
Dir, Pakistan 91 B3 35 8N 71 59 E
Diré, Mali 112 B4 16 20N 3 25W
Dire Dawa, Ethiopia 107 F5 9 35N 41 45 E
Diriamba, Nic. 164 D2 11 51N 86 19W
Dirico, Angola 115 F4 17 50 S 20 42 E
Dirk Hartog I., Australia 125 E1 25 50 S 113 5 E
Dirkou, Niger 109 E2 19 1N 12 53 E
Dirranbandi, Australia 127 D4 28 33 S 148 17 E
Dirs, Si. Arabia 98 C3 18 32N 42 5 E
Disa, India 92 G5 24 18N 72 10 E
Disa, Sudan 107 E3 12 5N 34 15 E
Disappointment, C., U.S.A. 158 C2 46 18N 124 5W
Disappointment, L., Australia 124 D3 23 20 S 122 40 E
Disaster B., Australia 129 D8 37 15 S 149 58 E
Discovery B., Australia 128 E4 38 10 S 140 40 E
Discovery B., China 69 G11 22 18N 114 1 E
Discovery Bay Nat. Park, Australia 128 E4 38 9 S 141 16 E
Disentis Muster, Switz. 33 C7 46 42N 8 50 E
Dishna, Egypt 106 B3 26 9N 32 32 E
Disina, Nigeria 113 C6 11 35N 9 50 E
Disko = Qeqertarsuaq, Greenland 10 D5 69 45N 53 30W
Disko Bugt, Greenland 10 D5 69 10N 52 0W
Disna = Dzisna →, Belarus 58 E5 55 34N 28 12 E
Disney Reef, Tonga 133 P13 19 17 S 174 7W
Dispur, India 90 B3 26 3N 91 52 E
Diss, U.K. 21 E9 52 23N 1 7 E
Disteghil Sar, Pakistan 93 A6 36 20N 75 12 E
Distrito Federal □, Brazil 171 E2 15 45 S 47 45W
Distrito Federal □, Mexico 163 D5 19 15N 99 10W
Distrito Federal □, Venezuela 168 A4 10 30N 66 55W
Disûq, Egypt 106 H7 31 8N 30 35 E
Diu, India 92 J4 20 45N 70 58 E
Diuata Mts., Phil. 81 G5 9 0N 125 50 E
Dīvāndarreh, Iran 101 E12 35 55N 47 2 E
Divenié, Congo 114 C2 2 43 S 12 1 E
Dives →, France 26 C6 49 18N 0 7W
Dives-sur-Mer, France 26 C6 49 18N 0 8W
Divi Pt., India 95 G5 15 59N 81 9 E
Divichi = Däväçi, Azerbaijan 61 K9 41 15N 48 57 E
Divide, U.S.A. 158 D7 45 45N 112 45W
Dividing Ra., Australia 125 E2 27 45 S 116 0 E
Divinópolis, Brazil 171 F3 20 10 S 44 54W
Divisões, Serra dos, Brazil 171 E1 17 0 S 51 0W
Divjake, Albania 50 F3 41 0N 19 32 E
Divnoye, Russia 61 H6 45 55N 43 21 E
Divo, Ivory C. 112 D3 5 48N 5 15W
Divriği, Turkey 101 C8 39 22N 38 7 E
Dīwāl Kol, Afghan. 91 B2 34 23N 67 52 E
Dix →, U.S.A. 157 G12 37 49N 84 43W
Dixie Mt., U.S.A. 160 F6 39 55N 120 16W
Dixie Union, U.S.A. 152 D7 31 20N 82 28W
Dixon, Calif., U.S.A. 160 G5 38 27N 121 49W
Dixon, Ill., U.S.A. 156 C7 41 50N 89 29W
Dixon, Mo., U.S.A. 156 G4 37 59N 92 6W
Dixon Entrance, U.S.A. 138 C6 54 30N 132 0W
Dixville, Canada 151 A13 45 4N 71 46W
Diyadin, Turkey 101 C10 39 33N 43 40 E
Diyālā →, Iraq 101 F11 33 14N 44 31 E
Diyarbakır, Turkey 101 D9 37 55N 40 18 E
Diyodar, India 92 G4 24 8N 71 50 E
Dja, Réserve du, Cameroon 114 B2 3 10N 12 58 E
Djadié →, Gabon 114 B2 0 46N 12 58 E
Djado, Niger 109 D2 21 4N 12 14 E
Djado, Plateau du, Niger 109 D2 21 29N 12 21 E
Djakarta = Jakarta, Indonesia 84 D3 6 9 S 106 49 E
Djamâa, Algeria 111 B6 33 32N 5 59 E
Djamba, Angola 116 B1 16 45 S 13 58 E
Djambala, Congo 114 C2 2 32 S 14 30 E

208 Djanet

Djanet, *Algeria* **111 D6** 24 35N 9 32 E
Djaul I., *Papua N. G.* **132 B6** 2 58 S 150 57 E
Djawa = Jawa, *Indonesia* **85 D4** 7 0 S 110 0 E
Djebiniana, *Tunisia* **108 A2** 35 1N 11 0 E
Djédaa, *Chad* **109 F3** 13 31N 18 34 E
Djelfa, *Algeria* **111 B5** 34 40N 3 15 E
Djema, *C.A.R.* **118 A2** 6 3N 25 15 E
Djember, *Chad* **109 F3** 10 25N 17 50 E
Djembo, *Dem. Rep. of the Congo* **115 D4** 9 54 S 22 18 E
Djendel, *Algeria* **111 A5** 36 15N 2 25 E
Djeneïene, *Tunisia* **108 B2** 31 45N 10 9 E
Djenné, *Mali* **112 C4** 14 0N 4 30W
Djenoun, Garet el, *Algeria* **111 C6** 25 4N 5 31 E
Djerba, *Tunisia* **108 B2** 33 52N 10 51 E
Djerba, I. de, *Tunisia* **108 B2** 33 50N 10 48 E
Djeréme →, *Cameroon* **114 A2** 5 20N 13 24 E
Djerid, Chott, *Tunisia* **108 B1** 33 42N 8 30 E
Djiba, *Gabon* **114 C2** 1 20 S 13 9 E
Djibo, *Burkina Faso* **113 C4** 14 9N 1 35W
Djibouti, *Djibouti* **107 E5** 11 30N 43 5 E
Djibouti ■, *Africa* **107 E5** 12 0N 43 0 E
Djohong, *Cameroon* **114 A2** 6 47N 14 20 E
Djolu, *Dem. Rep. of the Congo* **114 B4** 0 35N 22 5 E
Djouab →, *Gabon* **114 B2** 1 13N 13 12 E
Djougou, *Benin* **113 D5** 9 40N 1 45 E
Djoum, *Cameroon* **114 B2** 2 41N 12 35 E
Djouna, *Chad* **109 F4** 10 27N 20 4 E
Djourab, Erg du, *Chad* **109 E3** 16 40N 18 50 E
Djugu, *Dem. Rep. of the Congo* **118 B3** 1 55N 30 35 E
Djúpavík, *Iceland* **11 B5** 65 57N 21 34W
Djúpivogur, *Iceland* **11 C12** 64 39N 14 17W
Djupvasshytta, *Norway* **18 B4** 62 2N 7 16 E
Djurås, *Sweden* **16 D9** 60 34N 15 8 E
Djurdjura, Parc Nat. du, *Algeria* **111 A5** 35 20N 4 15 E
Djursland, *Denmark* **17 H4** 56 27N 10 45 E
Dmitriya Lapteva, Proliv, *Russia* **67 B15** 73 0N 140 0 E
Dmitriyev Lgovskiy, *Russia* **59 F8** 52 10N 35 0 E
Dmitrov, *Russia* **58 D9** 56 25N 37 32 E
Dmitrovsk-Orlovskiy, *Russia* **59 F8** 52 29N 35 10 E
Dnepr → = Dnipro →, *Ukraine* **59 J7** 46 30N 32 18 E
Dneprodzerzhinsk = Dniprodzerzhynsk, *Ukraine* **59 H8** 48 32N 34 37 E
Dneprodzerzhinskoye Vdkhr. = Dniprodzerzhynske Vdskh., *Ukraine* **59 H8** 48 49N 34 8 E
Dnepropetrovsk = Dnipropetrovsk, *Ukraine* **59 H8** 48 30N 35 0 E
Dneprorudnoye = Dniprorudne, *Ukraine* **59 J8** 47 21N 34 58 E
Dnestr → = Dnister →, *Europe* **59 J6** 46 18N 30 17 E
Dnestrovski = Belgorod, *Russia* **59 G9** 50 35N 36 35 E
Dnieper = Dnipro →, *Ukraine* **59 J7** 46 30N 32 18 E
Dniester = Dnister →, *Europe* **59 J6** 46 18N 30 17 E
Dnipro →, *Ukraine* **59 J7** 46 30N 32 18 E
Dniprodzerzhynsk, *Ukraine* **59 H8** 48 32N 34 37 E
Dniprodzerzhynske Vdskh., *Ukraine* **59 H8** 48 49N 34 8 E
Dnipropetrovsk, *Ukraine* **59 H8** 48 30N 35 0 E
Dniprorudne, *Ukraine* **59 J8** 47 21N 34 58 E
Dnister →, *Europe* **59 J6** 46 18N 30 17 E
Dnistrovskyy Lyman, *Ukraine* **59 J6** 46 15N 30 17 E
Dno, *Russia* **58 D5** 57 50N 29 58 E
Dnyapro = Dnipro →, *Ukraine* **59 J7** 46 30N 32 18 E
Doabi, *Afghan.* **91 A3** 36 1N 69 32 E
Doaktown, *Canada* **141 C6** 46 33N 66 8W
Doan Hung, *Vietnam* **76 G5** 21 30N 105 10 E
Doany, *Madag.* **117 A8** 14 21 S 49 30 E
Doba, *Chad* **109 G3** 8 40N 16 50 E
Dobandi, *Pakistan* **92 D2** 31 13N 66 50 E
Dobbiaco, *Italy* **45 B9** 46 44N 12 14 E
Dobbyn, *Australia* **126 B3** 19 44 S 140 2 E
Dobczyce, *Poland* **55 J7** 49 52N 20 5 E
Dobele, *Latvia* **15 H20** 56 37N 23 16 E
Dobele □, *Latvia* **54 B10** 56 35N 23 5 E
Döbeln, *Germany* **30 D9** 51 6N 13 7 E
Doberai, Jazirah, *Indonesia* **83 B4** 1 25 S 133 0 E
Dobiegniew, *Poland* **55 F2** 52 59N 15 45 E
Doblas, *Argentina* **174 D3** 37 5 S 64 0W
Dobo, *Dem. Rep. of the Congo* **114 B4** 2 20N 22 11 E
Dobo, *Indonesia* **83 C4** 5 45 S 134 15 E
Doboj, *Bos.-H.* **52 F3** 44 46N 18 4 E
Dobra, *Wielkopolskie, Poland* **55 G5** 51 55N 18 37 E
Dobra, *Zachodnio-Pomorskie, Poland* **54 E2** 53 34N 15 20 E
Dobra, *Dîmbovita, Romania* **53 F10** 44 52N 25 40 E
Dobra, *Hunedoara, Romania* **52 E7** 45 54N 22 36 E
Dobre Miasto, *Poland* **54 E7** 53 58N 20 26 E
Dobreşti, *Romania* **52 D7** 46 51N 22 18 E
Dobrich, *Bulgaria* **51 C11** 43 37N 27 49 E
Dobrinishta, *Bulgaria* **50 E7** 41 49N 23 34 E
Dobříš, *Czech Rep.* **34 B7** 49 46N 14 10 E
Dobrodzień, *Poland* **55 H5** 50 45N 18 25 E
Dobropole, *Ukraine* **59 H9** 48 25N 37 2 E
Dobruja, *Europe* **53 F13** 44 30N 28 15 E
Dobrush, *Belarus* **59 F6** 52 25N 31 22 E
Dobryanka, *Russia* **64 B6** 58 27N 56 25 E
Dobrzany, *Poland* **54 E2** 53 22N 15 25 E
Dobrzyń nad Wisłą, *Poland* **55 F6** 52 39N 19 22 E
Doc, Mui, *Vietnam* **86 D6** 17 58N 106 30 E
Doc Can I., *Phil.* **81 J2** 5 55N 119 56 E
Doce →, *Brazil* **171 E4** 19 37 S 39 49W
Docker River, *Australia* **125 D4** 24 52 S 129 5 E
Docksta, *Sweden* **16 A12** 63 3N 18 18 E
Doctor Arroyo, *Mexico* **162 C4** 23 40N 100 11W
Doctors Inlet, *U.S.A.* **152 E8** 30 6N 81 47W
Doda, *India* **93 C6** 33 10N 75 34 E
Doda, L., *Canada* **140 C4** 49 25N 75 13W
Doda Betta, *India* **95 J3** 11 24N 76 44 E
Dodaga, *Indonesia* **82 A3** 1 9N 128 11 E
Dodballapur, *India* **95 H3** 13 18N 77 32 E
Dodecanese = Dhodhekánisos, *Greece* **49 E8** 36 35N 27 0 E
Dodge City, *U.S.A.* **155 G5** 37 45N 100 1W
Dodge L., *Canada* **143 B7** 59 50N 105 36W
Dodgeville, *U.S.A.* **156 B6** 42 58N 90 8W
Dodo, *Cameroon* **113 D7** 7 30N 12 3 E
Dodo, *Sudan* **107 F2** 5 10N 29 57 E
Dodola, *Ethiopia* **107 F4** 6 59N 39 11 E
Dodoma, *Tanzania* **118 D4** 6 8 S 35 45 E
Dodoma □, *Tanzania* **118 D4** 6 0 S 36 0 E
Dodona, *Greece* **48 B2** 39 40N 20 46 E
Dodori Nat. Reserve, *Kenya* **118 C5** 1 55 S 41 7 E
Dodsland, *Canada* **143 C7** 51 50N 108 45W
Dodson, *U.S.A.* **158 B9** 48 24N 108 15W
Dodurga, *Turkey* **49 B11** 39 49N 29 57 E
Doerun, *U.S.A.* **152 D6** 31 19N 83 55W
Doesburg, *Neths.* **24 B6** 52 1N 6 9 E
Doetinchem, *Neths.* **24 C6** 51 59N 6 18 E
Dog Creek, *Canada* **142 C4** 51 35N 122 14W
Dog I., *U.S.A.* **152 F5** 29 48N 84 36W
Dog L., *Man., Canada* **143 C9** 51 2N 98 31W
Dog L., *Ont., Canada* **140 C2** 48 48N 89 30W
Doğanşehir, *Turkey* **100 C7** 38 5N 37 53 E
Dogliani, *Italy* **44 D4** 44 32N 7 56 E
Dōgo, *Japan* **72 A5** 36 15N 133 16 E
Dōgo-San, *Japan* **72 B5** 35 2N 133 13 E
Dogondoutchi, *Niger* **113 C5** 13 38N 4 2 E
Dogran, *Pakistan* **92 D5** 31 48N 73 35 E
Doğubayazıt, *Turkey* **101 C11** 39 31N 44 5 E
Doguéraoua, *Niger* **113 C6** 14 0N 5 31 E
Dogura, *Papua N. G.* **132 F6** 10 6 S 150 5 E
Doha = Ad Dawḩah, *Qatar* **97 E6** 25 15N 51 35 E
Dohazari, *Bangla.* **90 D4** 22 10N 92 5 E
Dohinog = Manukan, *Phil.* **81 G4** 8 32N 123 12 E
Dohrighat, *India* **93 F10** 26 16N 83 31 E
Dohrn Banke, *Greenland* **10 D8** 65 55N 25 50W
Doi, *Indonesia* **82 A3** 2 14N 127 49 E
Doi Luang, *Thailand* **86 C3** 18 30N 101 0 E
Doi Saket, *Thailand* **86 C2** 18 52N 99 9 E
Dois Irmãos, Sa., *Brazil* **170 C3** 9 0 S 42 30W
Dojransko Jezero, *Macedonia* **50 E6** 41 13N 22 44 E
Dokka, *Norway* **18 D7** 60 49N 10 7 E
Dokka →, *Norway* **18 D7** 60 49N 10 7 E
Dokkum, *Neths.* **24 A5** 53 20N 5 59 E
Dokri, *Pakistan* **92 F3** 27 25N 68 7 E
Dokuchayevsk, *Ukraine* **59 J9** 47 44N 37 40 E
Dol-de-Bretagne, *France* **26 D5** 48 34N 1 47W
Dolac, *Kosovo, Yug.* **50 D4** 42 36N 20 36 E
Dolak, Pulau, *Indonesia* **83 C5** 8 0 S 138 30 E
Dolbeau, *Canada* **141 C5** 48 53N 72 18W
Dole, *France* **27 E12** 47 7N 5 31 E
Doleib, Wadi →, *Sudan* **107 E3** 12 10N 33 15 E
Dolenji Logatec, *Slovenia* **45 C11** 45 56N 14 15 E
Dolgellau, *U.K.* **20 E4** 52 45N 3 53W
Dolgelley = Dolgellau, *U.K.* **20 E4** 52 45N 3 53W
Dolhasca, *Romania* **53 C11** 47 26N 26 36 E
Dolianova, *Italy* **46 C2** 39 22N 9 10 E
Dolinskaya = Dolynska, *Ukraine* **59 H7** 48 6N 32 46 E
Dolj □, *Romania* **53 F8** 44 10N 23 30 E
Dollard, *Neths.* **24 A7** 53 20N 7 10 E
Dolna Banya, *Bulgaria* **50 D7** 42 18N 23 44 E
Dolni Chiflik, *Bulgaria* **51 D11** 42 59N 27 43 E
Dolni Dŭbnik, *Bulgaria* **51 C8** 43 24N 24 26 E
Dolnośląskie □, *Poland* **55 G3** 51 10N 16 30 E
Dolný Kubín, *Slovak Rep.* **35 B12** 49 12N 19 18 E
Dolo, *Ethiopia* **107 G5** 4 11N 42 3 E
Dolo, *Italy* **45 C9** 45 25N 12 5 E
Dolomites = Dolomiti, *Italy* **45 B8** 46 23N 11 51 E
Dolomiti, *Italy* **45 B8** 46 23N 11 51 E
Dolores, *Argentina* **174 D4** 36 20 S 57 40W
Dolores, *Phil.* **80 E5** 12 2N 125 29 E
Dolores, *Uruguay* **174 C4** 33 34 S 58 15W
Dolores, *U.S.A.* **159 H9** 37 28N 108 30W
Dolores →, *U.S.A.* **159 G9** 38 49N 109 17W
Dolovo, *Serbia, Yug.* **52 F5** 44 55N 20 52 E
Dolphin, C., *Falk. Is.* **9 f** 51 10 S 59 0W
Dolphin and Union Str., *Canada* **138 B8** 69 5N 114 45W
Dolsk, *Poland* **55 G4** 51 59N 17 3 E
Dolton, *U.S.A.* **157 C9** 41 38N 87 36W
Dolungmukh, *India* **90 B5** 27 30N 94 18 E
Dolynska, *Ukraine* **59 H7** 48 6N 32 46 E
Dolzhanskaya, *Russia* **59 J9** 46 37N 37 48 E
Dom, *Switz.* **32 D5** 46 6N 7 50 E
Dom Joaquim, *Brazil* **171 E3** 18 57 S 43 16W
Dom Pedrito, *Brazil* **175 C5** 31 0 S 54 40W
Dom Pedro, *Brazil* **170 B3** 4 59 S 44 27W
Doma, *Nigeria* **113 D6** 8 25N 8 18 E
Doma Safari Area, *Zimbabwe* **119 F3** 16 28 S 30 12 E
Domaniç, *Turkey* **49 B11** 39 48N 29 36 E
Domar, E. →, *Chad* **109 E3** 18 11N 18 4 E
Domariaganj →, *India* **93 F10** 26 17N 83 44 E
Domasi, *Malawi* **119 F4** 15 15 S 35 22 E
Domat Ems, *Switz.* **33 C8** 46 50N 9 27 E
Domažlice, *Czech Rep.* **34 B5** 49 28N 12 58 E
Dombarovskiy, *Russia* **64 F7** 50 46N 59 32 E
Dombås, *Norway* **15 E13** 62 4N 9 8 E
Dombasle-sur-Meurthe, *France* **27 D13** 48 38N 6 21 E
Dombes, *France* **29 C9** 45 58N 5 0 E
Dombóvár, *Hungary* **52 D3** 46 21N 18 9 E
Dombrád, *Hungary* **52 B6** 48 13N 21 54 E
Domel I. = Letsôk-aw Kyun, *Burma* **87 G2** 11 30N 98 25 E
Domérat, *France* **27 F9** 46 21N 2 32 E
Domett, *N.Z.* **131 C8** 42 53 S 173 12 E
Domeyko, *Chile* **174 B1** 29 0 S 71 0W
Domeyko, Cordillera, *Chile* **174 A2** 24 30 S 69 0W
Domfront, *France* **26 D6** 48 37N 0 40W
Dominador, *Chile* **174 A2** 24 21 S 69 20W
Dominica ■, *W. Indies* **165 C7** 15 20N 61 20W
Dominica Passage, *W. Indies* **165 C7** 15 10N 61 20W
Dominican Rep. ■, *W. Indies* **165 C5** 19 0N 70 30W
Domiongo, *Dem. Rep. of the Congo* **115 C4** 4 37 S 21 15 E
Dömitz, *Germany* **30 B7** 53 8N 11 15 E
Domme, *France* **28 D5** 44 48N 1 12 E
Domneşti, *Romania* **53 E9** 45 12N 24 50 E
Domo, *Ethiopia* **120 C3** 7 50N 47 10 E
Domodóssola, *Italy* **44 B5** 46 7N 8 17 E
Dompaire, *France* **27 D13** 48 14N 6 14 E
Dompierre-sur-Besbre, *France* **27 F10** 46 31N 3 41 E
Dompim, *Ghana* **112 D4** 5 10N 2 5W
Dompu, *Indonesia* **85 D5** 8 32 S 118 28 E
Domrémy-la-Pucelle, *France* **27 D12** 48 26N 5 40 E
Domville, Mt., *Australia* **127 D5** 28 1 S 151 15 E
Domvraína, *Greece* **48 C4** 38 15N 22 59 E
Domžale, *Slovenia* **45 B11** 46 9N 14 35 E
Don →, *India* **95 F3** 16 20N 76 15 E
Don →, *Russia* **59 J10** 47 4N 39 18 E
Don →, *Aberds., U.K.* **22 D6** 57 11N 2 5W
Don →, *S. Yorks., U.K.* **20 D7** 53 41N 0 52W
Don, C., *Australia* **124 B5** 11 18 S 131 46 E
Don Benito, *Spain* **43 G5** 38 53N 5 51W
Don Figuero Mts., *Jamaica* **164 a** 18 5N 77 36W
Don Sak, *Thailand* **87 b** 9 18N 99 41 E
Dona Ana = Nhamaabué, *Mozam.* **119 F4** 17 25 S 35 5 E
Doña Mencía, *Spain* **43 H6** 37 33N 4 21W
Donaghadee, *U.K.* **23 B6** 54 39N 5 33W
Donald, *Australia* **128 D5** 36 23 S 143 0 E
Donaldsonville, *U.S.A.* **155 K9** 30 6N 90 59W
Donalsonville, *U.S.A.* **152 D5** 31 3N 84 53W
Donau = Dunărea →, *Europe* **53 E14** 45 20N 29 40 E
Donau →, *Austria* **24 D3** 48 10N 17 0 E
Donaueschingen, *Germany* **31 H4** 47 56N 8 29 E
Donauwörth, *Germany* **31 G6** 48 43N 10 47 E
Doncaster, *U.K.* **20 D6** 53 32N 1 6W
Dondo, *Angola* **115 D2** 9 45 S 14 25 E
Dondo, *Dem. Rep. of the Congo* **114 B4** 4 11N 21 39 E
Dondo, *Mozam.* **119 F3** 19 33 S 34 46 E
Dondo, Teluk, *Indonesia* **82 A2** 0 50N 120 30 E
Dondra Head, *Sri Lanka* **95 M5** 5 55N 80 40 E
Donduşeni, *Moldova* **53 B12** 48 14N 27 36 E
Donegal, *Ireland* **23 B3** 54 39N 8 5W
Donegal □, *Ireland* **23 B4** 54 53N 8 0W
Donegal B., *Ireland* **23 B3** 54 31N 8 49W
Donets →, *Russia* **61 G5** 47 33N 40 55 E
Donetsk, *Ukraine* **59 J9** 48 0N 37 45 E
Dong Ba Thin, *Vietnam* **87 F7** 12 8N 109 13 E
Dong Dang, *Vietnam* **76 G6** 21 54N 106 42 E
Dong Giam, *Vietnam* **86 C5** 19 25N 105 31 E
Dong Ha, *Vietnam* **86 D6** 16 55N 107 8 E
Dong Hene, *Laos* **86 D5** 16 40N 105 18 E
Dong Hoi, *Vietnam* **86 D6** 17 29N 106 36 E
Dong Jiang →, *China* **77 F10** 23 6N 114 0 E
Dong Khe, *Vietnam* **86 A6** 22 26N 106 27 E
Dong Ujimqin Qi, *China* **74 B9** 45 32N 116 55 E
Dong Van, *Vietnam* **86 A5** 23 16N 105 22 E
Dong Xoai, *Vietnam* **87 G6** 11 32N 106 55 E
Donga, *Nigeria* **113 D7** 7 45N 10 2 E
Donga →, *Nigeria* **113 D7** 8 20N 9 58 E
Dong'an, *China* **77 D8** 26 23N 111 12 E
Dongara, *Australia* **125 E1** 29 14 S 114 57 E
Dongargarh, *India* **94 D5** 21 10N 80 40 E
Dongbei, *China* **75 D13** 45 0N 125 0 E
Dongchuan, *China* **76 D4** 26 8N 103 1 E
Donges, *France* **26 E4** 47 18N 2 4W
Dongfang, *China* **86 C7** 18 50N 108 33 E
Dongfeng, *China* **75 C13** 42 40N 125 34 E
Donggala, *Indonesia* **82 B1** 0 30 S 119 40 E
Donggan, *China* **76 F5** 23 22N 105 9 E
Donggou, *China* **75 E13** 39 52N 124 10 E
Dongguan, *China* **77 F9** 22 58N 113 44 E
Dongguang, *China* **74 F9** 37 50N 116 30 E
Donghai Dao, *China* **77 G8** 21 0N 110 15 E
Dongjingcheng, *China* **75 B15** 44 5N 129 10 E
Dongkou, *China* **77 D8** 27 6N 110 35 E
Donglan, *China* **76 E6** 24 30N 107 21 E
Dongliu, *China* **77 B11** 30 13N 116 55 E
Dongmen, *China* **76 F6** 22 20N 107 48 E
Dongning, *China* **75 B16** 44 2N 131 5 E
Dongnyi, *China* **76 C3** 28 3N 100 15 E
Dongo, *Angola* **115 E3** 14 36 S 15 48 E
Dongo, *Dem. Rep. of the Congo* **114 A3** 5 50 S 19 45 E
Dongobe, *Dem. Rep. of the Congo* **114 B4** 4 35N 23 13 E
Dongola, *Sudan* **106 D3** 19 9N 30 22 E
Dongou, *Congo* **114 B3** 2 0N 18 5 E
Dongping, *China* **74 G9** 35 55N 116 20 E
Dongsha Dao, *China* **77 G11** 20 45N 116 43 E
Dongshan, *China* **77 F11** 23 43N 117 30 E
Dongsheng, *China* **74 E6** 39 50N 110 0 E
Dongtai, *China* **75 H11** 32 51N 120 21 E
Dongting Hu, *China* **77 C9** 29 18N 112 45 E
Dongtou, *China* **77 D13** 27 51N 121 10 E
Dongwe →, *Zambia* **115 E4** 13 59 S 23 53 E
Dongxiang, *China* **77 C11** 28 11N 116 34 E
Dongxing, *China* **76 G7** 21 34N 108 0 E
Dongyang, *China* **77 C13** 29 13N 120 15 E
Dongzhi, *China* **77 B11** 30 9N 117 0 E
Donington, C., *Australia* **128 C2** 34 45 S 136 0 E
Doniphan, *U.S.A.* **155 G9** 36 37N 90 50W
Donja Stubica, *Croatia* **45 C12** 45 59N 15 59 E
Donji Dušnik, *Serbia, Yug.* **50 C6** 43 12N 22 5 E
Donji Miholjac, *Croatia* **52 E3** 45 45N 18 10 E
Donji Milanovac, *Serbia, Yug.* **50 B6** 44 28N 22 6 E
Donji Vakuf, *Bos.-H.* **52 F2** 44 8N 17 24 E
Dønna, *Norway* **14 C15** 66 6N 12 30 E
Donna, *U.S.A.* **155 M5** 26 9N 98 4W
Donnaconna, *Canada* **141 C5** 46 41N 71 41W
Donnelly's Crossing, *N.Z.* **130 B2** 35 42 S 173 38 E
Donnybrook, *Australia* **125 F2** 33 34 S 115 48 E
Donnybrook, *S. Africa* **117 D4** 29 59 S 29 48 E
Donora, *U.S.A.* **150 F5** 40 11N 79 52W
Donostia = Donostia-San Sebastián, *Spain* **40 B3** 43 17N 1 58W
Donostia-San Sebastián, *Spain* **40 B3** 43 17N 1 58W
Donovan, *U.S.A.* **157 D9** 40 53N 87 37W
Donque, *Angola* **115 F2** 15 28 S 14 6 E
Donskoy, *Russia* **58 F10** 53 55N 38 15 E
Donsol, *Phil.* **80 E4** 12 54N 123 36 E
Donzère, *France* **29 D8** 44 28N 4 43 E
Donzy, *France* **27 E10** 47 20N 3 6 E
Dookie, *Australia* **129 D6** 36 20 S 145 41 E
Doon →, *U.K.* **22 F4** 55 27N 4 39W
Dora, L., *Australia* **124 D3** 22 0 S 123 0 E
Dora Báltea →, *Italy* **44 C5** 45 11N 8 3 E
Dora Ripária →, *Italy* **44 C4** 45 5N 7 44 E
Doran L., *Canada* **143 A7** 61 13N 108 6W
Doraville, *U.S.A.* **152 B5** 33 54N 84 17W
Dorchester, *U.K.* **21 G5** 50 42N 2 27W
Dorchester, C., *Canada* **139 B12** 65 27N 77 27W
Dordabis, *Namibia* **116 C2** 22 52 S 17 38 E
Dordogne □, *France* **28 C4** 45 5N 0 40 E
Dordogne →, *France* **28 C3** 45 2N 0 36W
Dordrecht, *Neths.* **24 C4** 51 48N 4 39 E
Dordrecht, *S. Africa* **116 E4** 31 20 S 27 3 E
Dore →, *France* **28 C7** 45 50N 3 35 E
Dore, Mts., *France* **28 C6** 45 32N 2 50 E
Doré L., *Canada* **143 C7** 54 46N 107 17W
Doré Lake, *Canada* **143 C7** 54 38N 107 36W
Dores do Indaiá, *Brazil* **171 E2** 19 27 S 45 36W
Dorfen, *Germany* **31 G8** 48 15N 12 8 E
Dorgali, *Italy* **46 B2** 40 17N 9 35 E
Dori, *Burkina Faso* **113 C4** 14 3N 0 2W
Doring →, *S. Africa* **116 E2** 31 54 S 18 39 E
Doringbos, *S. Africa* **116 E2** 31 59 S 19 16 E
Dorion, *Canada* **151 A10** 45 23N 74 3W
Dormaa-Ahenkro, *Ghana* **112 D4** 7 15N 2 52W
Dormans, *France* **27 C10** 49 4N 3 38 E
Dormo, Ras, *Eritrea* **107 E5** 13 14N 42 35 E
Dornach, *Switz.* **32 B5** 47 29N 7 37 E
Dornakal, *India* **94 F5** 17 27N 80 10 E
Dornbirn, *Austria* **34 D2** 47 25N 9 45 E
Dornes, *France* **27 F10** 46 48N 3 18 E
Dorneşti, *Romania* **53 C11** 47 52N 26 1 E
Dornie, *U.K.* **22 D3** 57 17N 5 31W
Dornoch, *U.K.* **22 D4** 57 53N 4 2W
Dornoch Firth, *U.K.* **22 D4** 57 51N 4 4W
Dornogovĭ □, *Mongolia* **74 C6** 44 0N 110 0 E
Doro, *Mali* **113 B4** 16 9N 0 51W
Dorog, *Hungary* **52 C3** 47 42N 18 45 E
Dorogobuzh, *Russia* **58 E7** 54 50N 33 18 E
Dorohoi, *Romania* **53 C11** 47 56N 26 23 E
Döröö Nuur, *Mongolia* **68 B4** 48 0N 93 0 E
Dorr, *Iran* **97 C6** 33 17N 50 38 E
Dorre I., *Australia* **125 E1** 25 13 S 113 12 E
Dorrigo, *Australia* **129 A10** 30 20 S 152 44 E
Dorrigo Nat. Park, *Australia* **129 A10** 30 22 S 152 47 E
Dorris, *U.S.A.* **158 F3** 41 58N 121 55W
Dorset, *Canada* **150 A6** 45 14N 78 54W
Dorset, *U.S.A.* **150 E4** 41 40N 80 40W
Dorset □, *U.K.* **21 G5** 50 45N 2 26W
Dorsten, *Germany* **30 D2** 51 40N 6 58 E
Dortmund, *Germany* **30 D3** 51 30N 7 28 E
Dortmund-Ems-Kanal →, *Germany* **30 D3** 51 50N 7 26 E
Dörtyol, *Turkey* **100 D7** 36 50N 36 13 E
Dorum, *Germany* **30 B4** 53 41N 8 34 E
Doruma, *Dem. Rep. of the Congo* **118 B2** 4 42N 27 33 E
Dorūneh, *Iran* **97 C8** 35 10N 57 18 E
Dos Bahías, C., *Argentina* **176 B3** 44 58 S 65 32W
Dos Hermanas, *Spain* **43 H5** 37 16N 5 55W
Dos Palos, *U.S.A.* **160 J6** 36 59N 120 37W
Döşemealtı, *Turkey* **49 D12** 37 4N 30 36 E
Dosso, *Niger* **113 C5** 13 0N 3 13 E
Dosso, Réserve Partielle de, *Niger* **113 C5** 12 36N 2 36 E
Dostuk, *Kyrgyzstan* **65 C7** 41 20N 75 30 E
Dot Lake, *U.S.A.* **144 E11** 63 40N 144 4W
Dothan, *U.S.A.* **152 D4** 31 13N 85 24W
Döttingen, *Switz.* **32 A6** 47 34N 8 15 E
Doty, *U.S.A.* **160 D3** 46 38N 123 17W
Douai, *France* **27 B10** 50 21N 3 4 E
Douako, *Guinea* **112 D2** 9 45N 10 8W
Douala, *Cameroon* **113 E6** 4 0N 9 45 E
Douala-Édéa, Réserve de, *Cameroon* **114 B1** 3 20N 9 41 E
Douaouir, *Mali* **110 D4** 20 45N 3 0W
Douarnenez, *France* **26 D2** 48 6N 4 21W
Doubabougou, *Mali* **112 C3** 14 13N 7 59W
Double Cone, *N.Z.* **131 F3** 45 4 S 168 49 E
Double Island Pt., *Australia* **127 D5** 25 56 S 153 11 E
Double Mountain Fork →, *U.S.A.* **155 J4** 33 16N 100 0W
Doubrava →, *Czech Rep.* **34 A8** 50 2N 15 20 E
Doubs □, *France* **27 E13** 47 10N 6 20 E
Doubs →, *France* **27 F12** 46 53N 5 1 E
Doubtful Sd., *N.Z.* **131 F1** 45 20 S 166 49 E
Doubtless B., *N.Z.* **130 A2** 34 55 S 173 26 E
Doudeville, *France* **26 C7** 49 43N 0 47 E
Doué-la-Fontaine, *France* **26 E6** 47 11N 0 16W
Douentza, *Mali* **112 C4** 14 58N 2 48W
Douentza, Réserve de, *Mali* **112 B4** 15 40N 2 25W
Dougga, *Tunisia* **108 A1** 36 30N 8 55 E
Doughboy B., *N.Z.* **131 H2** 47 2 S 167 40 E
Douglas, *S. Africa* **116 D3** 29 4 S 23 46 E
Douglas, *U.K.* **20 C3** 54 10N 4 28W
Douglas, *Alaska, U.S.A.* **144 G14** 58 17N 134 24W
Douglas, *Ariz., U.S.A.* **159 L9** 31 21N 109 33W
Douglas, *Ga., U.S.A.* **152 D7** 31 31N 82 51W
Douglas, *Mich., U.S.A.* **157 B10** 42 39N 86 14W
Douglas, *Wyo., U.S.A.* **154 D2** 42 45N 105 24W
Douglas Apsley Nat. Park, *Australia* **127 G4** 41 45 S 148 11 E
Douglas C., *U.S.A.* **144 G9** 58 51N 153 15W
Douglas Chan., *Canada* **142 C3** 53 40N 129 20W
Douglas Pt., *Canada* **150 B3** 44 19N 81 37W
Douglasville, *U.S.A.* **152 B5** 33 45N 84 45W
Douirat, *Morocco* **110 B4** 33 2N 4 11W
Doukáton, Ákra, *Greece* **39 B2** 38 34N 20 33 E
Doukoula, *Cameroon* **114 A2** 10 0N 15 0 E
Doukoula, *Cent. Amer.* **109 F2** 10 10N 15 0 E
Doulevant-le-Château, *France* **27 D11** 48 23N 4 55 E
Doullens, *France* **27 B9** 50 10N 2 20 E
Doumé, *Cameroon* **114 B2** 4 15N 13 25 E
Doumen, *China* **77 F9** 22 10N 113 18 E
Douna, *Mali* **112 C3** 13 13N 6 0W
Dounguila, *Congo* **114 C2** 2 53 S 11 58 E
Dounreay, *U.K.* **22 C5** 58 35N 3 44W
Dourada, Serra, *Brazil* **171 D2** 13 10 S 48 45W
Dourados, *Brazil* **175 A5** 22 9 S 54 50W
Dourados →, *Brazil* **175 A5** 21 58 S 54 18W
Dourados, Serra dos, *Brazil* **175 A5** 23 30 S 53 30W
Dourbali, *Chad* **109 F3** 11 49N 15 52 E
Dourdan, *France* **27 D9** 48 30N 2 1 E
Douro →, *Europe* **42 D2** 41 8N 8 40W
Douvaine, *France* **27 F13** 46 19N 6 16 E
Douvres-la-Délivrande, *France* **26 C6** 49 17N 0 23W
Douz, *Tunisia* **108 B1** 33 25N 9 0 E
Douze →, *France* **28 E3** 43 54N 0 30W
Dove →, *U.K.* **20 E6** 52 51N 1 36W
Dove Creek, *U.S.A.* **159 H9** 37 46N 108 54W
Dover, *Australia* **127 G4** 43 18 S 147 2 E
Dover, *U.K.* **21 F9** 51 7N 1 19 E
Dover, *Del., U.S.A.* **148 F8** 39 10N 75 32W
Dover, *Ky., U.S.A.* **157 F13** 38 43N 83 52W
Dover, *N.H., U.S.A.* **151 C14** 43 12N 70 56W
Dover, *N.J., U.S.A.* **151 F10** 40 53N 74 34W
Dover, *Ohio, U.S.A.* **150 F3** 40 32N 81 29W
Dover, Pt., *Australia* **125 F4** 32 32 S 125 32 E
Dover, Str. of, *Europe* **21 G9** 51 0N 1 30 E
Dover-Foxcroft, *U.S.A.* **149 C11** 45 11N 69 13W
Dover Plains, *U.S.A.* **151 E11** 41 43N 73 35W
Dovey = Dyfi →, *U.K.* **21 E3** 52 32N 4 3W
Dovre, *Norway* **18 C6** 61 58N 9 15 E
Dovrefjell, *Norway* **15 E13** 62 15N 9 33 E
Dow Rūd, *Iran* **97 C6** 33 28N 49 4 E
Dowa, *Malawi* **119 E3** 13 38 S 33 58 E
Dowagiac, *U.S.A.* **157 C10** 41 59N 86 6W
Dowerin, *Australia* **125 F2** 31 12 S 117 2 E
Dowgha'i, *Iran* **97 B8** 36 54N 58 32 E
Dowlat Yār, *Afghan.* **91 B2** 34 30N 65 45 E
Dowlatābād, *Farāh, Afghan.* **91 B1** 32 47N 62 40 E
Dowlatābād, *Fāryāb, Afghan.* **65 E2** 36 26N 64 55 E
Dowlatābād, *Iran* **97 D8** 28 20N 56 40 E
Dowling Park, *U.S.A.* **152 E6** 30 15N 83 15W
Down □, *U.K.* **23 B5** 54 23N 6 2W
Downers Grove, *U.S.A.* **157 C8** 41 48N 88 1W
Downey, *Calif., U.S.A.* **161 M8** 33 56N 118 7W
Downey, *Idaho, U.S.A.* **158 E7** 42 26N 112 7W
Downham Market, *U.K.* **21 E8** 52 37N 0 23 E
Downieville, *U.S.A.* **160 F6** 39 34N 120 50W
Downing, *U.S.A.* **156 D4** 40 29N 92 22W
Downpatrick, *U.K.* **23 B6** 54 20N 5 43W
Downpatrick Hd., *Ireland* **23 B2** 54 20N 9 21W
Downsville, *U.S.A.* **151 D10** 42 5N 74 50W
Downton, Mt., *Canada* **142 C4** 52 42N 124 52W
Dowsārī, *Iran* **97 D8** 28 25N 57 59 E
Dowshī, *Afghan.* **91 B3** 35 35N 68 43 E
Doyle, *U.S.A.* **160 E6** 40 2N 120 6W
Doylestown, *U.S.A.* **151 F9** 40 21N 75 10W
Dōzen, *Japan* **72 A5** 36 5N 133 5 E
Dozois, Rés., *Canada* **140 C4** 47 30N 77 5W
Dra Khel, *Pakistan* **92 F2** 27 58N 66 45 E
Drâa, C., *Morocco* **110 C2** 28 47N 11 0W
Drâa, Hamada du, *Algeria* **110 C3** 28 0N 7 0W
Drâa, Oued →, *Morocco* **110 C2** 28 40N 11 10W
Drac →, *France* **29 C9** 45 12N 5 42 E
Dračevo, *Macedonia* **50 E5** 41 56N 21 31 E
Drachten, *Neths.* **24 A6** 53 7N 6 5 E
Drăgăneşti, *Moldova* **53 C13** 47 43N 28 15 E
Drăgăneşti-Olt, *Romania* **53 F9** 44 9N 24 32 E
Drăgăneşti-Vlaşca, *Romania* **53 F10** 44 5N 25 33 E
Dragaš, *Kosovo, Yug.* **50 D4** 42 5N 20 41 E
Drăgăşani, *Romania* **53 F9** 44 39N 24 17 E
Dragichyn, *Belarus* **59 F3** 52 15N 25 8 E
Dragocvet, *Serbia, Yug.* **50 C5** 43 58N 21 15 E
Dragovishtitsa, *Bulgaria* **50 D6** 42 22N 22 39 E
Draguignan, *France* **29 E10** 43 32N 6 27 E
Drain, *U.S.A.* **158 E2** 43 40N 123 19W
Drake, *U.S.A.* **154 B4** 47 55N 100 23W
Drake Passage, *S. Ocean* **7 B17** 58 0 S 68 0W
Drakensberg, *S. Africa* **117 D4** 31 0 S 28 0 E
Dráma, *Greece* **51 E8** 41 9N 24 10 E
Dráma □, *Greece* **51 E8** 41 20N 24 0 E
Drammen, *Norway* **15 G14** 59 42N 10 12 E
Drangajökull, *Iceland* **11 A4** 66 9N 22 15W
Drangedal, *Norway* **18 E6** 59 6N 9 3 E
Drangsnes, *Iceland* **11 B5** 65 41N 21 27W
Dranov, Ostrov, *Romania* **53 F14** 44 55N 29 30 E
Dras, *India* **93 B6** 34 25N 75 48 E
Drau = Drava →, *Croatia* **52 E3** 45 33N 18 55 E
Drava →, *Croatia* **52 E3** 45 33N 18 55 E
Dravograd, *Slovenia* **45 B12** 46 36N 15 5 E
Drawa →, *Poland* **55 F2** 52 52N 15 59 E
Drawno, *Poland* **55 E2** 53 13N 15 46 E
Drawsko Pomorskie, *Poland* **54 E2** 53 35N 15 50 E
Drayton Plains, *U.S.A.* **157 B13** 42 42N 83 23W
Drayton Valley, *Canada* **142 C6** 53 12N 114 58W
Dreieich, *Germany* **31 E4** 50 1N 8 41 E
Dreikikir, *Papua N. G.* **132 B2** 3 35 S 142 46 E
Dren, *Kosovo, Yug.* **50 C4** 43 8N 20 46 E
Drenthe □, *Neths.* **24 B6** 52 52N 6 40 E
Drepanum, C., *Cyprus* **39 F8** 34 54N 32 19 E
Dresden, *Canada* **150 D2** 42 35N 82 11W
Dresden, *Germany* **30 D9** 51 3N 13 44 E
Dreux, *France* **26 D8** 48 44N 1 23 E
Drevsjø, *Norway* **18 C9** 61 53N 12 1 E
Drexel, *U.S.A.* **157 E12** 39 45N 84 18W
Drezdenko, *Poland* **55 F2** 52 50N 15 49 E
Driffield, *U.K.* **20 C7** 54 0N 0 26W
Driftwood, *U.S.A.* **150 E6** 41 20N 78 8W
Driggs, *U.S.A.* **158 E8** 43 44N 111 6W
Drin →, *Albania* **50 D3** 42 1N 19 38 E
Drin i Zi →, *Albania* **50 E4** 41 37N 20 28 E
Drina →, *Bos.-H.* **50 B3** 44 53N 19 21 E
Drincea →, *Romania* **52 F7** 44 20N 22 55 E
Drinjača →, *Bos.-H.* **52 F4** 44 15N 19 8 E

East Retford 209

Drissa = Vyerkhnyadzvinsk, Belarus 58 E4 55 45N 27 58 E
Driva →, Norway 18 B6 62 41N 9 31 E
Drivstua, Norway 18 B6 62 26N 9 47 E
Drniš, Croatia 45 E13 43 51N 16 10 E
Drøbak, Norway 15 G14 59 39N 10 39 E
Drobeta-Turnu Severin, Romania 52 F7 44 39N 22 41 E
Drobin, Poland 55 F6 52 42N 19 58 E
Drochia, Moldova 53 B12 48 2N 27 48 E
Drogheda, Ireland 23 C5 53 43N 6 22W
Drogichin = Dragichyn, Belarus 59 F3 52 15N 25 8 E
Drogobych = Drohobych, Ukraine 59 H2 49 20N 23 30 E
Drohiczyn, Poland 55 F9 52 24N 22 39 E
Drohobych, Ukraine 59 H2 49 20N 23 30 E
Droichead Atha = Drogheda, Ireland 23 C5 53 43N 6 22W
Droichead Nua, Ireland 23 C5 53 11N 6 48W
Droitwich, U.K. 21 E5 52 16N 2 8W
Drôme □, France 29 D9 44 38N 5 15 E
Drôme →, France 29 D8 44 46N 4 46 E
Dromedary, C., Australia 129 D9 36 17 S 150 10 E
Dromore, U.K. 23 B4 54 31N 7 28W
Dromore West, Ireland 23 B3 54 15N 8 52W
Dronero, Italy 44 D4 44 28N 7 22 E
Dronfield, U.K. 20 D6 53 19N 1 27W
Dronne →, France 28 C3 45 2N 0 9W
Dronning Ingrid Land, Greenland 10 D5 66 25N 52 5W
Dronninglund, Denmark 17 G4 57 10N 10 19 E
Dronten, Neths. 24 B5 52 32N 5 43 E
Dropt →, France 28 D3 44 35N 0 6W
Drosendorf, Austria 34 C8 48 52N 15 37 E
Drosh, Pakistan 91 B3 35 33N 71 48 E
Droué, France 26 D8 48 3N 1 6 E
Drouin, Australia 129 E6 38 10 S 145 53 E
Drueulu, N. Cal. 133 K5 20 56 S 167 5 E
Drumbo, Canada 150 C4 43 16N 80 35W
Drumheller, Canada 142 C6 51 25N 112 40W
Drummond, U.S.A. 158 C7 46 40N 113 9W
Drummond I., U.S.A. 148 C4 46 1N 83 39W
Drummond Pt., Australia 127 E2 34 9 S 135 16 E
Drummond Ra., Australia 126 C4 23 45 S 147 10 E
Drummondville, Canada 140 C5 45 55N 72 25W
Drumright, U.S.A. 155 H6 35 59N 96 36W
Druskininkai, Lithuania 15 J20 54 3N 23 58 E
Drut →, Belarus 59 F6 53 8N 30 5 E
Druya, Belarus 58 E4 55 45N 27 28 E
Druzhba, Bulgaria 51 C12 43 15N 28 1 E
Druzhina, Russia 67 C15 68 14N 145 18 E
Drvar, Bos.-H. 45 D13 44 21N 16 23 E
Drvenik, Croatia 45 E13 43 27N 16 3 E
Drwęca →, Poland 55 E5 53 0N 18 42 E
Dry Harbour Mts., Jamaica 164 a 18 19N 77 24W
Dry Tortugas, U.S.A. 164 B3 24 38N 82 55W
Dryanovo, Bulgaria 51 D9 42 59N 25 28 E
Dryden, Canada 143 D10 49 47N 92 50W
Dryden, U.S.A. 151 D8 42 30N 76 18W
Drygalski I., Antarctica 7 C7 66 0 S 92 0 E
Drysdale →, Australia 124 B4 13 59 S 126 51 E
Drysdale I., Australia 126 A2 11 41 S 136 0 E
Drysdale River Nat. Park, Australia 124 B4 14 56 S 127 2 E
Drzewica, Poland 55 G7 51 27N 20 29 E
Drzewiczka →, Poland 55 G7 51 36N 20 36 E
Dschang, Cameroon 113 D7 5 32N 10 3 E
Du Bois, U.S.A. 150 E6 41 8N 78 46W
Du Gué →, Canada 140 A5 57 21N 70 45W
Du He, China 77 A8 32 48N 110 40 E
Du Quoin, U.S.A. 156 G7 38 1N 89 14W
Du'an, China 76 F7 23 59N 108 3 E
Duanesburg, U.S.A. 151 D10 42 45N 74 11W
Duaringa, Australia 126 C4 23 42 S 149 42 E
Duarte, Pico, Dom. Rep. 165 D5 19 2N 70 59W
Dubā, Si. Arabia 96 E2 27 10N 35 40 E
Dubai = Dubayy, U.A.E. 97 E7 25 18N 55 20 E
Dubăsari, Moldova 53 C14 47 15N 29 10 E
Dubăsari Vdkhr., Moldova 53 C13 47 30N 29 0 E
Dubawnt →, Canada 143 A8 64 33N 100 6W
Dubawnt, L., Canada 143 A8 63 4N 101 42W
Dubayy, U.A.E. 97 E7 25 18N 55 20 E
Dubbo, Australia 129 B8 32 11 S 148 35 E
Dubele, Dem. Rep. of the Congo 118 B2 2 56N 29 35 E
Dübendorf, Switz. 33 B7 47 24N 8 37 E
Dubica, Croatia 45 C13 45 11N 16 48 E
Dublin, Ireland 23 C5 53 21N 6 15W
Dublin, Ga., U.S.A. 152 C7 32 32N 82 54W
Dublin, Tex., U.S.A. 155 J5 32 5N 98 21W
Dublin □, Ireland 23 C5 53 24N 6 20W
Dubna, Russia 58 D9 56 44N 37 10 E
Dubnica nad Váhom, Slovak Rep. 35 C11 48 58N 18 11 E
Dubno, Ukraine 59 G3 50 25N 25 45 E
Dubois, Idaho, U.S.A. 158 D7 44 10N 112 14W
Dubois, Ind., U.S.A. 157 F10 38 27N 86 48W
Dubossary = Dubăsari, Moldova 53 C14 47 15N 29 10 E
Dubossary Vdkhr. = Dubăsari Vdkhr., Moldova 53 C13 47 30N 29 0 E
Dubovka, Russia 61 F7 49 5N 44 50 E
Dubovskoye, Russia 61 G6 47 28N 42 46 E
Dubrajpur, India 93 H12 23 48N 87 25 E
Dubréka, Guinea 112 D2 9 46N 13 31W
Dubrovitsa = Dubrovytsya, Ukraine 59 G4 51 31N 26 35 E
Dubrovnik, Croatia 50 D2 42 39N 18 6 E
Dubrovytsya, Ukraine 59 G4 51 31N 26 35 E
Dubulu, Dem. Rep. of the Congo 114 B4 4 18N 20 16 E
Dubuque, U.S.A. 156 B6 42 30N 90 41W
Dubysa →, Lithuania 54 C10 55 5N 23 26 E
Duchang, China 77 C11 29 18N 116 12 E
Duchesne, U.S.A. 158 F8 40 10N 110 24W
Duchess, Australia 126 C2 21 20 S 139 50 E
Ducie I., Pac. Oc. 135 K15 24 40 S 124 48W
Duck →, U.S.A. 149 G2 36 2N 87 52W
Duck Cr. →, Australia 124 D2 22 37 S 116 53 E
Duck Lake, Canada 143 C7 52 50N 106 16W
Duck Mountain Prov. Park, Canada 143 C8 51 45N 101 0W
Duckwall, Mt., U.S.A. 160 H6 37 58N 120 7W
Duda →, Colombia 168 C3 2 34N 74 3W
Duderstadt, Germany 30 D6 51 31N 10 15 E
Dudhnai, India 90 C3 25 59N 90 47 E
Düdingen, Switz. 32 C4 46 52N 7 12 E
Dudinka, Russia 67 C9 69 30N 86 13 E
Dudley, U.K. 21 E5 52 31N 2 5W
Dudley, U.S.A. 152 C6 32 32N 83 5W
Dudna →, India 94 E3 19 17N 76 54 E
Dudo, Somali Rep. 120 C4 9 20N 50 12 E
Dudub, Ethiopia 120 C3 6 55N 46 43 E
Dudune, Î., N. Cal. 133 U21 21 21 S 167 46 E
Dudwa, India 93 E9 28 30N 80 41 E
Duékoué, Ivory C. 112 D3 6 40N 7 15W
Duenas, Phil. 81 F4 11 4N 122 37 E
Dueñas, Spain 42 D6 41 52N 4 33W
Dueré, Brazil 171 D2 11 20 S 49 17W
Duero = Douro →, Europe 42 D2 41 8N 8 40W
Dufftown, U.K. 22 D5 57 27N 3 8W
Dufourspitz, Switz. 32 E5 45 56N 7 52 E
Dugger, U.S.A. 157 E9 39 4N 87 18W
Dugi Otok, Croatia 45 D11 44 0N 15 3 E
Duguma, Somali Rep. 120 D2 1 15N 42 34 E
Dugo Selo, Croatia 45 C13 45 51N 16 18 E
Duifken Pt., Australia 126 A3 12 33 S 141 38 E
Duisburg, Germany 30 D2 51 26N 6 45 E
Duitama, Colombia 168 B3 5 50N 73 2W
Duiwelskloof, S. Africa 117 C5 23 42 S 30 10 E
Dujiangyan, China 76 B4 31 2N 103 38 E
Duk Fadiat, Sudan 107 F3 7 45N 31 25 E
Duk Faiwil, Sudan 107 F3 7 30N 31 29 E
Dukat, Albania 50 F3 40 16N 19 32 E
Dūkdamīn, Iran 97 C8 35 59N 57 43 E
Dukelský Průsmyk, Slovak Rep. 35 B14 49 25N 21 42 E
Dukhān, Qatar 97 E6 25 25N 50 50 E
Dukhovshchina, Russia 58 E7 55 15N 32 27 E
Duki, Pakistan 91 C3 30 14N 68 25 E
Dukla, Poland 55 J8 49 30N 21 35 E
Duku, Bauchi, Nigeria 113 C7 10 43N 10 43 E
Duku, Sokoto, Nigeria 113 C5 11 11N 4 55 E
Dula, Dem. Rep. of the Congo 114 B4 4 40N 20 21 E
Dulag, Phil. 81 F5 10 57N 125 2 E
Dulce, U.S.A. 159 H10 36 56N 107 0W
Dulce →, Argentina 174 C3 30 32 S 62 33W
Dulce, G., Costa Rica 164 E3 8 40N 83 20W
Dulf, Iraq 96 C5 35 7N 45 51 E
Dŭlgopol, Bulgaria 51 C11 43 3N 27 22 E
Dulit, Banjaran, Malaysia 78 D4 3 15N 114 30 E
Duliu, China 74 E9 39 2N 116 55 E
Dullabchara, India 90 C4 24 30N 92 26 E
Dullewala, Pakistan 92 D4 31 50N 71 25 E
Dullstroom, S. Africa 117 D5 25 27 S 30 7 E
Dülmen, Germany 30 D3 51 49N 7 17 E
Dulovo, Bulgaria 51 C11 43 48N 27 9 E
Dulpetorpet, Norway 18 D9 60 34N 12 19 E
Dulq Maghār, Syria 101 D8 36 22N 38 39 E
Duluth, Ga., U.S.A. 152 A5 34 0N 84 9W
Duluth, Minn., U.S.A. 154 B8 46 47N 92 6W
Dum Dum, India 93 H13 22 39N 88 33 E
Dum Duma, India 90 B5 27 40N 95 40 E
Dūmā, Syria 103 B5 33 34N 36 24 E
Dumaguete, Phil. 81 G4 9 17N 123 15 E
Dumai, Indonesia 84 B2 1 35N 101 28 E
Dumalinao, Phil. 81 H4 7 49N 123 23 E
Dumanguilas Bay, Phil. 81 H4 7 34N 123 4 E
Dumanjug, Phil. 81 F4 10 4N 123 26 E
Dumaran, Phil. 81 F2 10 33N 119 50 E
Dumaran I., Phil. 81 F2 10 33N 119 51 E
Dumarao, Phil. 81 F4 11 16N 122 41 E
Dumas, Ark., U.S.A. 155 J9 33 53N 91 29W
Dumas, Tex., U.S.A. 155 H4 35 52N 101 58W
Dumayr, Syria 103 B5 33 39N 36 42 E
Dumbarton, U.K. 22 F4 55 57N 4 33W
Dumbéa, N. Cal. 133 V20 22 10 S 166 27 E
Ďumbier, Slovak Rep. 35 C12 48 56N 19 38 E
Dumbleyung, Australia 125 F2 33 17 S 117 42 E
Dumbo, Angola 115 E3 14 6 S 17 24 E
Dumboa, Nigeria 113 C7 11 15N 12 55 E
Dumbrăveni, Romania 53 D9 46 14N 24 34 E
Dumfries, U.K. 22 F5 55 4N 3 37W
Dumfries & Galloway □, U.K. 22 F5 55 9N 3 58W
Dumingag, Phil. 81 G4 8 20N 123 20 E
Dumitreşti, Romania 53 E11 45 33N 26 55 E
Dumka, India 93 G12 24 12N 87 15 E
Dumlupınar, Turkey 49 C12 38 53N 30 0 E
Dümmer, Germany 30 C4 52 31N 8 20 E
Dumoine →, Canada 140 C4 46 13N 77 51W
Dumoine, L., Canada 140 C4 46 55N 77 55W
Dumoulin Is., Papua N. G. 132 F6 10 54 S 150 46 E
Dumpu, Papua N. G. 132 C3 5 53 S 145 44 E
Dumraon, India 93 G11 25 33N 84 8 E
Dumyât, Egypt 106 H7 31 24N 31 48 E
Dumyât, Masabb, Egypt 106 H7 31 28N 31 51 E
Dún Dealgan = Dundalk, Ireland 23 B5 54 1N 6 24W
Dun Laoghaire, Ireland 23 C5 53 17N 6 8W
Dun-le-Palestel, France 27 F8 46 18N 1 39 E
Dun-sur-Auron, France 27 F9 46 53N 2 33 E
Dun-sur-Meuse, France 27 C12 49 23N 5 11 E
Duna = Dunărea →, Europe 53 E14 45 20N 29 40 E
Duna →, Hungary 52 E3 45 51N 18 48 E
Duna-völgyi-főcsatorna, Hungary 52 D4 46 40N 19 14 E
Dunaföldvár, Hungary 52 D3 46 50N 18 57 E
Dunagiri, India 93 D8 30 31N 79 52 E
Dunaj = Dunărea →, Europe 53 E14 45 20N 29 40 E
Dunaj →, Slovak Rep. 35 D11 47 50N 18 50 E
Dunajec →, Poland 55 H7 50 15N 20 44 E
Dunajská Streda, Slovak Rep. 35 C10 48 0N 17 37 E
Dunakeszi, Hungary 52 C4 47 37N 19 8 E
Dunapataj, Hungary 52 D4 46 39N 19 4 E
Dunărea →, Europe 53 E14 45 20N 29 40 E
Dunaszekcső, Hungary 52 D3 46 6N 18 45 E
Dunaújváros, Hungary 52 D3 46 58N 18 57 E
Dunav = Dunărea →, Europe 53 E14 45 20N 29 40 E
Dunavaţu de Jos, Romania 53 F14 44 59N 29 13 E
Dunavtsi, Bulgaria 50 C6 43 57N 22 53 E
Dunay, Russia 70 C6 42 52N 132 22 E
Dunback, N.Z. 131 F5 45 23 S 170 36 E
Dunbar, U.K. 22 E6 56 0N 2 31W
Dunblane, U.K. 22 E5 56 11N 3 58W
Duncan, Canada 142 D4 48 45N 123 40W
Duncan, Ariz., U.S.A. 159 K9 32 43N 109 6W
Duncan, Okla., U.S.A. 155 H6 34 30N 97 57W
Duncan, L., Canada 140 B4 53 29N 77 58W
Duncan L., Canada 142 A6 62 51N 113 58W
Duncan Passage, India 95 J11 11 0N 92 0 E
Duncan Town, Bahamas 164 B4 22 15N 75 45W
Duncannon, U.S.A. 150 F7 40 23N 77 2W
Duncansby Head, U.K. 22 C5 58 38N 3 1W
Duncansville, U.S.A. 150 F6 40 25N 78 26W
Dundaga, Latvia 54 A9 57 31N 22 21 E
Dundalk, Canada 150 B4 44 10N 80 24W
Dundalk, Ireland 23 B5 54 1N 6 24W
Dundalk, U.S.A. 148 F7 39 16N 76 32W
Dundalk Bay, Ireland 23 C5 53 55N 6 15W
Dundas = Uummannaq, Greenland 10 B4 77 0N 69 0W
Dundas, Canada 150 C5 43 17N 79 59W
Dundas, L., Australia 125 F3 32 35 S 121 50 E
Dundas I., Canada 142 C2 54 30N 130 50W
Dundas Str., Australia 124 B5 11 15 S 131 35 E
Dundee, S. Africa 117 D5 28 11 S 30 15 E
Dundee, U.K. 22 E6 56 28N 2 59W
Dundee, Mich., U.S.A. 157 C13 41 57N 83 40W
Dundee, N.Y., U.S.A. 150 D8 42 32N 76 59W
Dundee City □, U.K. 22 E6 56 30N 2 58W
Dundgovĭ □, Mongolia 74 B4 45 10N 106 0 E
Dundrum, U.K. 23 B6 54 16N 5 52W
Dundrum B., U.K. 23 B6 54 13N 5 47W
Dunedin, N.Z. 131 F5 45 50 S 170 33 E
Dunedin, U.S.A. 149 L4 28 1N 82 47W
Dunedoo, Australia 129 A8 32 0 S 149 25 E
Dunfermline, U.K. 22 E5 56 5N 3 27W
Dungannon, Canada 150 C3 43 51N 81 36W
Dungannon, U.K. 23 B5 54 31N 6 46W
Dungarpur, India 92 H5 23 52N 73 45 E
Dungarvan, Ireland 23 D4 52 5N 7 37W
Dungarvan Harbour, Ireland 23 D4 52 4N 7 35W
Dungeness, U.K. 21 G8 50 54N 0 59 E
Dungo, L. do, Angola 116 B2 17 15 S 19 0 E
Dungog, Australia 129 B9 32 22 S 151 46 E
Dungu, Dem. Rep. of the Congo 118 B2 3 40N 28 32 E
Dungun, Malaysia 87 K4 4 45N 103 25 E
Dungunâb, Sudan 106 C4 21 10N 37 9 E
Dungunâb, Khalîg, Sudan 106 C4 21 5N 37 12 E
Dunhua, China 75 C15 43 20N 128 14 E
Dunhuang, China 68 B4 40 8N 94 36 E
Dunk I., Australia 126 B4 17 59 S 146 29 E
Dunkassa, Benin 113 C5 10 21N 3 10 E
Dunkeld, Queens., Australia 127 E4 33 25 S 149 29 E
Dunkeld, Vic., Australia 128 D5 37 40 S 142 22 E
Dunkeld, U.K. 22 E5 56 34N 3 35W
Dunkerque, France 27 A9 51 2N 2 20 E
Dunkery Beacon, U.K. 21 F4 51 9N 3 36W
Dunkirk = Dunkerque, France 27 A9 51 2N 2 20 E
Dunkirk, U.S.A. 150 D5 42 29N 79 20W
Dunkuj, Sudan 107 E3 12 50N 32 49 E
Dunkwa, Central, Ghana 112 D4 6 0N 1 47W
Dunkwa, Central, Ghana 113 D4 5 30N 1 0W
Dúnleary = Dun Laoghaire, Ireland 23 C5 53 17N 6 8W
Dunleer, Ireland 23 C5 53 50N 6 24W
Dunmanus B., Ireland 23 E2 51 31N 9 50W
Dunmanway, Ireland 23 E2 51 43N 9 6W
Dunmara, Australia 126 B1 16 42 S 133 25 E
Dunmore, U.S.A. 151 E9 41 25N 75 38W
Dunmore Hd., Ireland 23 D1 52 10N 10 35W
Dunmore Town, Bahamas 164 A4 25 30N 76 39W
Dunn, U.S.A. 149 H6 35 19N 78 37W
Dunnellon, U.S.A. 149 L4 29 3N 82 28W
Dunnet Hd., U.K. 22 C5 58 40N 3 21W
Dunning, U.S.A. 154 E4 41 50N 100 6W
Dunnville, Canada 150 D5 42 54N 79 36W
Dunolly, Australia 128 D5 36 51 S 143 44 E
Dunoon, U.K. 22 F4 55 57N 4 56W
Dunphy, U.S.A. 158 F5 40 42N 116 31W
Dunqul, Egypt 106 C3 23 26N 31 37 E
Duns, U.K. 22 F6 55 47N 2 20W
Dunseith, U.S.A. 154 A4 48 50N 100 3W
Dunsmuir, U.S.A. 158 F2 41 13N 122 16W
Dunstable, U.K. 21 F7 51 53N 0 32W
Dunstan Mts., N.Z. 131 E4 44 53 S 169 35 E
Dunster, Canada 142 C5 53 8N 119 50W
Duntroon, N.Z. 131 E5 44 51 S 170 40 E
Dunvegan L., Canada 143 A7 60 8N 107 10W
Duolun, China 74 C9 42 12N 116 28 E
Duong Dong, Vietnam 87 G4 10 13N 103 58 E
Dupax, Phil. 80 C3 16 17N 121 5 E
Dupree, U.S.A. 154 C4 45 4N 101 35W
Dupuyer, U.S.A. 158 B7 48 13N 112 30W
Duqm, Oman 99 C7 19 39N 57 42 E
Duque de Caxias, Brazil 171 F3 22 45 S 43 19W
Duque de York, I., Chile 176 D1 50 37 S 75 25W
Durack →, Australia 124 C4 15 33 S 127 52 E
Durack Ra., Australia 124 C4 16 50 S 127 40 E
Durağan, Turkey 100 B6 41 25N 35 3 E
Durak, Turkey 49 B10 39 42N 28 17 E
Đurakovac, Kosovo, Yug. 50 D4 42 43N 20 29 E
Durance →, France 29 E8 43 55N 4 45 E
Durand, Ga., U.S.A. 152 C5 32 54N 84 51W
Durand, Ill., U.S.A. 156 B7 42 26N 89 20W
Durand, Mich., U.S.A. 157 B13 42 55N 83 59W
Durand, Wis., U.S.A. 154 C9 44 38N 91 58W
Durango, Mexico 162 C4 24 3N 104 39W
Durango, U.S.A. 159 H10 37 16N 107 53W
Durango □, Mexico 162 C4 25 0N 105 0W
Durankulak, Bulgaria 51 C12 43 41N 28 32 E
Durant, Iowa, U.S.A. 156 C6 41 36N 90 54W
Durant, Miss., U.S.A. 155 J10 33 4N 89 51W
Durant, Okla., U.S.A. 155 J6 33 59N 96 25W
Duratón →, Spain 42 D6 41 37N 4 7W
Durazno, Uruguay 174 C4 33 25 S 56 31W
Durazzo = Durrës, Albania 50 E3 41 19N 19 28 E
Durban, France 28 F6 42 59N 2 49 E
Durban, S. Africa 117 D5 29 49 S 31 1 E
Durbo, Somali Rep. 120 B4 11 37N 50 20 E
Durbuy, Belgium 24 D5 50 21N 5 28 E
Dúrcal, Spain 43 J7 36 59N 3 34W
Đurđevac, Croatia 52 D2 46 2N 17 3 E
Düren, Germany 30 E2 50 48N 6 29 E
Durg, India 94 D5 21 15N 81 22 E
Durgapur, India 93 H12 23 30N 87 20 E
Durham, Canada 140 D3 44 10N 80 49W
Durham, U.K. 20 C6 54 47N 1 34W
Durham, Calif., U.S.A. 160 F5 39 39N 121 48W
Durham, N.C., U.S.A. 149 H6 35 59N 78 54W
Durham, N.H., U.S.A. 151 C14 43 8N 70 56W
Durham □, U.K. 20 C6 54 42N 1 45W
Durleşti, Moldova 53 C13 47 1N 28 46 E
Ḑurmā, Si. Arabia 96 E5 24 37N 46 8 E
Durmitor, Montenegro, Yug. 50 C2 43 10N 19 0 E
Durness, U.K. 22 C4 58 34N 4 45W
Durnford, Pta., W. Sahara 110 D1 23 37N 16 0W
Durrës, Albania 50 E3 41 19N 19 28 E
Durrow, Ireland 23 D4 52 51N 7 24W
Dursey I., Ireland 23 E1 51 36N 10 12W
Dursunbey, Turkey 49 B10 39 35N 28 37 E
Durtal, France 26 E6 47 40N 0 18W
Duru, Dem. Rep. of the Congo 118 B2 4 14N 28 50 E
Duru Gölü, Turkey 51 E12 41 20N 28 35 E
Durusu, Turkey 51 E12 41 17N 28 41 E
Durūz, Jabal ad, Jordan 103 C5 32 35N 36 40 E
D'Urville, Tanjung, Indonesia 83 B5 1 28 S 137 54 E
D'Urville I., N.Z. 131 A8 40 50 S 173 55 E
Duryea, U.S.A. 151 E9 41 20N 75 45W
Dusa Mareb, Somali Rep. 120 C3 5 30N 46 15 E
Dûsh, Egypt 106 C3 24 35N 30 41 E
Dushak, Turkmenistan 66 F7 37 13N 60 1 E
Dushan, China 76 E6 25 48N 107 30 E
Dushanbe, Tajikistan 66 F7 38 33N 68 48 E
Dusheti, Georgia 61 J7 42 10N 44 42 E
Dushore, U.S.A. 151 E8 41 31N 76 24W
Dusky Sd., N.Z. 131 F1 45 47 S 166 30 E
Dussejour, C., Australia 124 B4 14 45 S 128 13 E
Düsseldorf, Germany 30 D2 51 14N 6 47 E
Dusti, Tajikistan 65 E4 37 20N 68 40 E
Dustlik, Uzbekistan 65 C4 40 31N 68 2 E
Duszniki-Zdrój, Poland 55 H3 50 24N 16 24 E
Dutch Harbor, U.S.A. 144 K6 53 53N 166 32W
Dutlwe, Botswana 116 C3 23 58 S 23 46 E
Dutsan Wai, Nigeria 113 C6 10 50N 8 10 E
Dutton, Canada 150 D3 42 39N 81 30W
Dutton →, Australia 126 C3 20 44 S 143 10 E
Duved, Sweden 16 A6 63 24N 12 55 E
Düvertepe, Turkey 49 B10 39 14N 28 27 E
Duwayhin, Khawr, U.A.E. 97 E6 24 20N 51 25 E
Duyun, China 76 D6 26 18N 107 29 E
Düzağac, Turkey 49 C12 38 48N 30 10 E
Düzce, Turkey 100 B4 40 50N 31 10 E
Duzdab = Zāhedān, Iran 97 D9 29 30N 60 50 E
Dve Mogili, Bulgaria 51 C9 43 35N 25 55 E
Dvina, Severnaya →, Russia 56 B7 64 32N 40 30 E
Dvinsk = Daugavpils, Latvia 15 J22 55 53N 26 32 E
Dvinskaya Guba, Russia 56 B6 65 0N 39 0 E
Dvor, Croatia 45 C13 45 4N 16 22 E
Dvůr Králové nad Labem, Czech Rep. 34 A8 50 27N 15 50 E
Dwarka, India 92 H3 22 18N 69 8 E
Dwellingup, Australia 125 F2 32 43 S 116 4 E
Dwight, Canada 150 A5 45 20N 79 1W
Dwight, U.S.A. 157 C8 41 5N 88 26W
Dyatkovo, Russia 58 F8 53 40N 34 27 E
Dyatlovo = Dzyatlava, Belarus 58 F3 53 28N 25 28 E
Dyce, U.K. 22 D6 57 13N 2 12W
Dyer, U.S.A. 157 G10 37 24N 86 13W
Dyer, C., Canada 139 B13 66 40N 61 0W
Dyer Bay, Canada 150 A3 45 10N 81 20W
Dyer Plateau, Antarctica 7 D17 70 45 S 65 30W
Dyersburg, U.S.A. 155 G10 36 3N 89 23W
Dyersville, U.S.A. 156 B5 42 29N 91 8W
Dyfi →, U.K. 21 E3 52 32N 4 3W
Dyje →, Czech Rep. 35 C9 48 37N 16 56 E
Dyke Ackland B., Papua N. G. 132 E5 9 0 S 148 45 E
Dymer, Ukraine 59 G6 50 47N 30 18 E
Dynów, Poland 55 J9 49 50N 22 11 E
Dyranut, Norway 18 D4 60 22N 7 31 E
Dyrhólaey, Iceland 11 D7 63 24N 19 8W
Dyrnes, Norway 18 A4 63 25N 7 52 E
Dysart, Australia 126 C4 22 32 S 148 23 E
Dysart, U.S.A. 156 B4 42 10N 92 18W
Dyurtyuli, Russia 64 D5 55 9N 54 40 E
Dzamin Üüd = Borhoyn Tal, Mongolia 74 C6 43 50N 111 58 E
Dzaoudzi, Mayotte 121 a 12 47 S 45 16 E
Dzerzhinsk, Russia 60 B6 56 14N 43 30 E
Dzhalal-Abad = Jalal-Abad, Kyrgyzstan 65 C6 40 56N 73 0 E
Dzhalinda, Russia 67 D13 53 26N 124 0 E
Dzhambeyty, Kazakstan 64 F4 50 16N 52 35 E
Dzhambul = Taraz, Kazakstan 66 E8 42 54N 71 22 E
Dzhankoy, Ukraine 59 K8 45 40N 34 20 E
Dzhanybek, Kazakstan 60 F8 49 25N 46 50 E
Dzharkurgan = Jarqŭrghon, Uzbekistan 65 E3 37 31N 67 25 E
Dzharylhach, Ostriv, Ukraine 59 J7 46 2N 32 55 E
Dzhezkazgan = Zhezqazghan, Kazakstan 66 E7 47 44N 67 40 E
Dzhirgatal, Tajikistan 65 D5 39 13N 71 12 E
Dzhizak = Jizzakh, Uzbekistan 66 E7 40 6N 67 50 E
Dzhugdzur, Khrebet, Russia 67 D14 57 30N 138 0 E
Dzhuma, Uzbekistan 65 D3 39 42N 66 40 E
Dzhungarskiye Vorota = Dzungarian Gates, Asia 68 B3 45 0N 82 0 E
Dzhvari = Jvari, Georgia 61 J6 42 42N 42 4 E
Działdowo, Poland 55 E7 53 15N 20 15 E
Działoszyce, Poland 55 H7 50 22N 20 20 E
Działoszyn, Poland 55 G5 51 6N 18 50 E
Dzibilchaltun, Mexico 163 C7 21 5N 89 36W
Dzierzgoń, Poland 54 E6 53 58N 19 20 E
Dzierżoniów, Poland 55 H3 50 45N 16 39 E
Dzilam de Bravo, Mexico 163 C7 21 24N 88 53W
Dzioua, Algeria 111 B6 33 14N 5 14 E
Dzisna, Belarus 58 E5 55 34N 28 12 E
Dzisna →, Belarus 58 E5 55 34N 28 12 E
Dziwnów, Poland 54 D1 54 2N 14 45 E
Dzungaria = Junggar Pendi, China 68 B3 44 30N 86 0 E
Dzungarian Gates, Asia 68 B3 45 0N 82 0 E
Dzuumod, Mongolia 68 B5 47 45N 106 58 E
Dzyarzhynsk, Belarus 58 F4 53 40N 27 1 E
Dzyatlava, Belarus 58 F3 53 28N 25 28 E

E

Eabamet L., Canada 140 B2 51 30N 87 46W
Eads, U.S.A. 154 F3 38 29N 102 47W
Eagar, U.S.A. 159 J9 34 6N 109 17W
Eagle, Alaska, U.S.A. 144 D12 64 47N 141 12W
Eagle, Colo., U.S.A. 158 G10 39 39N 106 50W
Eagle →, Canada 141 B8 53 36N 57 26W
Eagle Butte, U.S.A. 154 C4 45 0N 101 10W
Eagle Cr. →, U.S.A. 157 F11 38 36N 85 4W
Eagle Grove, U.S.A. 156 B3 42 40N 93 54W
Eagle L., Canada 143 D10 49 42N 93 13W
Eagle L., Calif., U.S.A. 158 F3 40 39N 120 45W
Eagle L., Maine, U.S.A. 149 B11 46 20N 69 22W
Eagle Lake, Canada 150 A6 45 8N 78 29W
Eagle Lake, Maine, U.S.A. 149 B11 47 3N 68 36W
Eagle Lake, Tex., U.S.A. 155 L6 29 35N 96 20W
Eagle Mountain, U.S.A. 161 M11 33 49N 115 27W
Eagle Nest, U.S.A. 159 H11 36 33N 105 16W
Eagle Pass, U.S.A. 155 L4 28 43N 100 30W
Eagle Pk., U.S.A. 160 G7 38 10N 119 25W
Eagle Pt., Australia 124 C3 16 11 S 124 23 E
Eagle River, Mich., U.S.A. 148 B1 47 24N 88 18W
Eagle River, Wis., U.S.A. 154 C10 45 55N 89 15W
Eaglehawk, N.S.W., Australia 127 F3 36 44 S 144 15 E
Eaglehawk, Vic., Australia 128 D6 36 44 S 144 15 E
Eagles Mere, U.S.A. 151 E8 41 25N 76 33W
Eagleville, U.S.A. 156 D3 40 28N 93 59W
Ealing □, U.K. 21 F7 51 30N 0 20W
Ear Falls, Canada 143 C10 50 38N 93 13W
Earle, U.S.A. 155 H9 35 16N 90 28W
Earlimart, U.S.A. 161 K7 35 53N 119 16W
Earlville, U.S.A. 157 C8 41 35N 88 55W
Early Branch, U.S.A. 152 C9 32 45N 80 55W
Earn →, U.K. 22 E5 56 21N 3 18W
Earn, L., U.K. 22 E4 56 23N 4 13W
Earnslaw, Mt., N.Z. 131 E3 44 32 S 168 27 E
Earth, U.S.A. 155 H3 34 14N 102 24W
Eas, Vanuatu 133 F6 16 20 S 168 15 E
Easley, U.S.A. 149 H4 34 50N 82 36W
East Anglia, U.K. 20 E9 52 30N 1 0 E
East Angus, Canada 141 C5 45 30N 71 40W
East Aurora, U.S.A. 150 D6 42 46N 78 37W
East Ayrshire □, U.K. 22 F4 55 26N 4 11W
East Beskids = Vychodné Beskydy, Europe 35 B15 49 20N 22 0 E
East Brady, U.S.A. 150 F5 40 59N 79 36W
East C., N.Z. 130 D7 37 42 S 178 35 E
East C., Papua N. G. 132 F6 10 13 S 150 53 E
East Chicago, U.S.A. 157 C9 41 38N 87 27W
East China Sea, Asia 69 D7 30 0N 126 0 E
East Coast Bays, N.Z. 130 C3 36 45 S 174 46 E
East Coulee, Canada 142 C6 51 23N 112 27W
East Dereham, U.K. 21 E8 52 41N 0 57 E
East Dublin, U.S.A. 152 C7 32 32N 82 52W
East Dubuque, U.S.A. 156 B6 42 30N 90 39W
East Dunbartonshire □, U.K. 22 F4 55 57N 4 13W
East End Pt., Bahamas 9 b 25 3N 77 16W
East Falkland, Falk. Is. 9 f 51 30 S 58 30W
East Grand Forks, U.S.A. 154 B6 47 56N 97 1W
East Greenwich, U.S.A. 151 E13 41 40N 71 27W
East Grinstead, U.K. 21 F8 51 7N 0 0W
East Hartford, U.S.A. 151 E12 41 46N 72 39W
East Helena, U.S.A. 158 C8 46 35N 111 56W
East Indies, Asia 62 K15 0 0 120 0 E
East Kilbride, U.K. 22 F4 55 47N 4 11W
East Lamma Channel, China 69 G11 22 14N 114 9 E
East Lansing, U.S.A. 157 B12 42 44N 84 29W
East Liverpool, U.S.A. 150 F4 40 37N 80 35W
East London, S. Africa 117 E4 33 0 S 27 55 E
East Lothian □, U.K. 22 F6 55 58N 2 44W
East Main = Eastmain, Canada 140 B4 52 10N 78 30W
East Moline, U.S.A. 156 C6 41 32N 90 26W
East Naples, U.S.A. 153 J8 26 8N 81 46W
East New Britain □, Papua N. G. 132 D7 6 30 S 152 30 E
East Northport, U.S.A. 151 F11 40 53N 73 20W
East Orange, U.S.A. 151 F10 40 46N 74 13W
East Pacific Ridge, Pac. Oc. 135 J17 15 0 S 110 0W
East Palatka, U.S.A. 152 F8 29 39N 81 36W
East Palestine, U.S.A. 150 F4 40 50N 80 33W
East Peoria, U.S.A. 156 D7 40 40N 89 34W
East Pine, Canada 142 B4 55 48N 120 12W
East Point, U.S.A. 152 B5 33 41N 84 27W
East Providence, U.S.A. 151 E13 41 49N 71 23W
East Pt., Br. Virgin Is. 165 e 18 40N 64 18W
East Pt., Canada 141 C7 46 27N 61 58W
East Renfrewshire □, U.K. 22 F4 55 46N 4 21W
East Retford = Retford, U.K. 20 D7 53 19N 0 56W

210 East Riding of Yorkshire

East Riding of Yorkshire □, U.K. 20 D7 53 55N 0 30W
East Rochester, U.S.A. 150 C7 43 7N 77 29W
East St. Louis, U.S.A. 156 F6 38 37N 90 9W
East Schelde = Oosterschelde →, Neths. 24 C4 51 33N 4 0 E
East Sea = Japan, Sea of, Asia 70 E7 40 0N 135 0 E
East Sepik □, Papua N. G. 132 C2 4 0 S 143 45 E
East Siberian Sea, Russia 67 B17 73 0N 160 0 E
East Stroudsburg, U.S.A. 151 E9 41 1N 75 11W
East Sussex □, U.K. 21 G8 50 56N 0 19 E
East Tawas, U.S.A. 148 C4 44 17N 83 29W
East Timor ■, Asia 82 C3 8 50 S 126 0 E
East Tohopekaliga, Lake, U.S.A. 153 G8 28 18N 81 15W
East Toorale, Australia 127 E4 30 27 S 145 28 E
East Troy, U.S.A. 157 B8 42 47N 88 24W
East Walker →, U.S.A. 160 G7 38 52N 119 10W
East Windsor, U.S.A. 151 F10 40 17N 74 34W
Eastbourne, N.Z. 130 H3 41 19 S 174 55 E
Eastbourne, U.K. 21 G8 50 46N 0 18 E
Eastend, Canada 143 D7 49 32N 108 50W
Easter I. = Pascua, I. de, Chile 172 b 27 7 S 109 23W
Eastern □, Ghana 113 D4 6 30N 0 30W
Eastern □, Kenya 118 C4 0 0 38 30 E
Eastern Cape □, S. Africa 116 E4 32 0 S 26 0 E
Eastern Cr. →, Australia 126 C3 20 40 S 141 35 E
Eastern Ghats, India 95 H4 14 0N 78 50 E
Eastern Group = Lau Group, Fiji 133 A3 17 0 S 178 30W
Eastern Group, Australia 125 F3 33 30 S 124 30 E
Eastern Highlands □, Papua N. G. 132 D3 6 30 S 145 35 E
Eastern Province □, S. Leone 112 D2 8 15N 11 0W
Eastern Samar □, Phil. 81 F5 11 40N 125 40 E
Eastern Transvaal = Mpumalanga □, S. Africa 117 B5 26 0 S 30 0 E
Easterville, Canada 143 C9 53 8N 99 49W
Easthampton, U.S.A. 151 D12 42 16N 72 40W
Eastlake, U.S.A. 150 E3 41 40N 81 26W
Eastland, U.S.A. 155 J5 32 24N 98 49W
Eastleigh, U.K. 21 G6 50 58N 1 21W
Eastmain, Canada 140 B4 52 10N 78 30W
Eastmain →, Canada 140 B4 52 27N 78 26W
Eastman, Canada 151 A12 45 18N 72 19W
Eastman, Ga., U.S.A. 152 C6 32 12N 83 11W
Eastman, Wis., U.S.A. 156 A5 43 10N 91 1W
Easton, Md., U.S.A. 148 F7 38 47N 76 5W
Easton, Pa., U.S.A. 151 F9 40 41N 75 13W
Easton, Wash., U.S.A. 160 C5 47 14N 121 11W
Eastover, U.S.A. 152 B9 33 52N 80 41W
Eastpoint, U.S.A. 152 F5 29 44N 84 53W
Eastpointe, U.S.A. 150 D2 42 27N 82 56W
Eastport, U.S.A. 149 C12 44 56N 67 0W
Eastsound, U.S.A. 160 B4 48 42N 122 55W
Eaton, Colo., U.S.A. 154 E2 40 32N 104 42W
Eaton, Ohio, U.S.A. 157 E12 39 45N 84 38W
Eaton Rapids, U.S.A. 157 B12 42 31N 84 39W
Eatonia, Canada 143 C7 51 13N 109 25W
Eatonton, U.S.A. 152 B6 33 20N 83 23W
Eatontown, U.S.A. 151 F10 40 19N 74 4W
Eatonville, U.S.A. 160 D4 46 52N 122 16W
Eau Claire, Fr. Guiana 169 C7 3 30N 53 40W
Eau Claire, U.S.A. 154 C9 44 49N 91 30W
Eau Claire, L. à l', Canada 140 A5 56 10N 74 25W
Eauze, France 28 E4 43 53N 0 7 E
Eban, Nigeria 113 D5 9 40N 4 50 E
Ebanga, Angola 115 E2 12 45 S 14 45 E
Ebangalakata, Dem. Rep. of the Congo 114 C4 0 29 S 21 29 E
Ebbw Vale, U.K. 21 F4 51 46N 3 12W
Ebebiyín, Eq. Guin. 114 B2 2 9N 11 20 E
Ebeggui, Algeria 111 C6 26 2N 6 0 E
Ebel, Gabon 114 B2 0 7N 11 5 E
Ebeltoft, Denmark 17 H4 56 12N 10 41 E
Ebeltoft Vig, Denmark 17 H4 56 10N 10 35 E
Ebensburg, U.S.A. 150 F6 40 29N 78 44W
Ebensee, Austria 34 D6 47 48N 13 46 E
Eber Gölü, Turkey 100 C4 38 38N 31 11 E
Eberbach, Germany 31 F4 49 28N 8 59 E
Eberswalde-Finow, Germany 30 C9 52 50N 13 49 E
Ebetsu, Japan 70 C10 43 7N 141 34 E
Ebian, China 76 C4 29 11N 103 13 E
Ebikon, Switz. 33 B6 47 5N 8 21 E
Ebingen, Germany 31 G5 48 13N 9 1 E
Ebino, Japan 72 E2 32 2N 130 48 E
Ebnat-Kappel, Switz. 33 B8 47 16N 9 7 E
Ebo, Angola 115 E2 11 40 S 14 40 E
Ebola →, Dem. Rep. of the Congo 114 B4 3 20N 20 57 E
Éboli, Italy 47 B8 40 39N 15 2 E
Ebolowa, Cameroon 113 E7 2 55N 11 10 E
Ebonyi □, Nigeria 113 D6 6 20N 8 0 E
Eboy, Dem. Rep. of the Congo 114 B4 2 50N 23 11 E
Ebrach, Germany 31 F6 49 51N 10 29 E
Ébrié, Lagune, Ivory C. 112 D4 5 12N 4 26W
Ebro →, Spain 40 E5 40 43N 0 54 E
Ebro, Embalse del, Spain 42 C7 43 0N 3 58W
Ebstorf, Germany 30 B6 53 2N 10 24 E
Eceabat, Turkey 51 F10 40 11N 26 21 E
Ech Chéliff, Algeria 111 A5 36 10N 1 20 E
Echallens, Switz. 32 C3 46 38N 6 38 E
Echeconnee →, U.S.A. 152 C6 32 39N 83 36W
Echigo-Sammyaku, Japan 71 F9 36 50N 139 50 E
Échirolles, France 29 C9 45 8N 5 44 E
Echizen-Misaki, Japan 73 B7 35 59N 135 57 E
Echmiadzin = Yejmiadzin, Armenia 61 K7 40 12N 44 19 E
Echo, U.S.A. 152 D4 31 29N 85 28W
Echo Bay, N.W.T., Canada 138 B8 66 5N 117 55W
Echo Bay, Ont., Canada 140 C3 46 29N 84 4W
Echoing →, Canada 140 B1 55 51N 92 5W
Echternach, Lux. 24 E6 49 49N 6 25 E
Echuca, Australia 129 D6 36 10 S 144 45 E
Ecija, Spain 43 H5 37 30N 5 10W
Eckental, Germany 31 F7 49 35N 11 12 E
Eckernförde, Germany 30 A5 54 28N 9 50 E
Eclectic, U.S.A. 152 C3 32 38N 86 2W
Eclipse Is., Australia 124 B4 13 54 S 126 19 E
Eclipse Sd., Canada 139 A11 72 38N 79 0W
Écommoy, France 26 E7 47 50N 0 17 E
Ecoporanga, Brazil 171 E3 18 23 S 40 50W
Écouché, France 26 D6 48 42N 0 10W
Ecuador ■, S. Amer. 168 D2 2 0 S 78 0W
Ecuador, Volcán, Ecuador 172 a 1 1 S 91 32W
Écueillé, France 26 E8 47 5N 1 21 E
Ed, Sweden 17 F5 58 55N 11 55 E
Ed Dabbura, Sudan 106 D3 17 40N 34 15 E
Ed Da'ein, Sudan 107 E2 11 26N 26 9 E
Ed Dâmer, Sudan 106 D3 17 27N 34 0 E
Ed Debba, Sudan 106 D3 18 0N 30 51 E
Ed-Déffa, Egypt 106 A2 30 40N 26 30 E
Ed Deim, Sudan 107 E2 10 10N 28 20 E
Ed Dueim, Sudan 107 E3 14 0N 32 10 E
Edam, Canada 143 C7 53 11N 108 46W
Edam, Neths. 24 B5 52 31N 5 3 E
Edane, Sweden 16 E6 59 38N 12 49 E
Edapally, India 95 J4 11 19N 78 3 E
Eday, U.K. 22 B6 59 11N 2 47W
Edchera, W. Sahara 110 C2 27 2N 13 4W
Edd, Eritrea 107 E5 14 0N 41 38 E
Eddrachillis B., U.K. 22 C3 58 17N 5 14W
Eddystone Pt., Australia 127 G4 40 59 S 148 20 E
Eddyville, U.S.A. 156 C4 41 9N 92 38W
Ede, Neths. 24 B5 52 4N 5 40 E
Ede, Nigeria 113 D5 7 45N 4 29 E
Édéa, Cameroon 113 E7 3 51N 10 9 E
Edebäck, Sweden 16 D7 60 4N 13 32 E
Edehon L., Canada 143 A9 60 25N 97 15W
Edekel, Adrar, Algeria 111 D6 23 56N 6 47 E
Edelény, Hungary 52 B5 48 18N 20 44 E
Eden, Australia 129 D8 37 3 S 149 55 E
Eden, N.C., U.S.A. 149 G6 36 29N 79 53W
Eden, N.Y., U.S.A. 150 D6 42 39N 78 55W
Eden, Tex., U.S.A. 155 K5 31 13N 99 51W
Eden →, U.K. 20 C4 54 57N 3 1W
Edenburg, S. Africa 116 D4 29 43 S 25 58 E
Edendale, N.Z. 131 G3 46 19 S 168 48 E
Edendale, S. Africa 117 D5 29 39 S 30 18 E
Edenderry, Ireland 23 C4 53 21N 7 4W
Edenhope, Australia 128 D4 37 4 S 141 19 E
Edenton, U.S.A. 149 G7 36 4N 76 39W
Edenville, S. Africa 117 D4 27 37 S 27 34 E
Eder →, Germany 30 D5 51 12N 9 28 E
Eder-Stausee, Germany 30 D4 51 10N 8 57 E
Edewecht, Germany 30 B3 53 8N 7 58 E
Edgar, U.S.A. 154 E6 40 22N 97 58W
Edgartown, U.S.A. 151 E14 41 23N 70 31W
Edge Hill, U.K. 21 E6 52 8N 1 26W
Edgecumbe, N.Z. 130 D5 37 59 S 176 47 E
Edgefield, U.S.A. 152 B8 33 47N 81 56W
Edgeley, U.S.A. 154 B5 46 22N 98 43W
Edgemont, U.S.A. 154 D3 43 18N 103 50W
Edgeøya, Svalbard 6 B9 77 45N 22 30 E
Edgerton, Ohio, U.S.A. 157 C12 41 27N 84 45W
Edgerton, Wis., U.S.A. 156 B7 42 50N 89 4W
Edgewater, U.S.A. 153 G9 28 59N 80 54W
Edgewood, U.S.A. 157 F8 38 55N 88 40W
Édhessa, Greece 50 F6 40 48N 22 5 E
Edievale, N.Z. 131 F4 45 49 S 169 22 E
Edina, Liberia 112 D2 6 0N 10 10W
Edina, U.S.A. 156 D4 40 10N 92 11W
Edinboro, U.S.A. 150 E4 41 52N 80 8W
Edinburg, Ill., U.S.A. 156 E7 39 39N 89 23W
Edinburg, Ind., U.S.A. 157 E11 39 21N 85 58W
Edinburg, Tex., U.S.A. 155 M5 26 18N 98 10W
Edinburgh, U.K. 22 F5 55 57N 3 13W
Edinburgh, City of □, U.K. 22 F5 55 57N 3 17W
Edineţ, Moldova 53 B12 48 9N 27 18 E
Edirne, Turkey 51 E10 41 40N 26 34 E
Edirne □, Turkey 51 E10 41 12N 26 30 E
Edison, Ga., U.S.A. 152 D5 31 34N 84 44W
Edison, Wash., U.S.A. 160 B4 48 33N 122 27W
Edisto →, U.S.A. 152 C9 32 29N 80 21W
Edisto Beach, U.S.A. 152 C9 32 29N 80 20W
Edisto I., U.S.A. 152 C9 32 35N 80 20W
Edithburgh, Australia 128 C2 35 5 S 137 43 E
Edjeleh, Algeria 111 C6 28 38N 9 50 E
Edmeston, U.S.A. 151 D9 42 42N 75 15W
Edmond, U.S.A. 155 H6 35 39N 97 29W
Edmonds, U.S.A. 160 C4 47 49N 122 23W
Edmonton, Australia 126 B4 17 2 S 145 46 E
Edmonton, Canada 142 C6 53 30N 113 30W
Edmund L., Canada 140 B1 54 45N 93 17W
Edmundston, Canada 141 C6 47 23N 68 20W
Edna, U.S.A. 155 L6 28 59N 96 39W
Edo □, Nigeria 113 D6 6 30N 6 0 E
Edolo, Italy 44 B7 46 10N 10 21 E
Edøy, Norway 18 A5 63 18N 8 10 E
Edremit, Turkey 49 B9 39 34N 27 0 E
Edremit Körfezi, Turkey 49 B8 39 30N 26 45 E
Edsbro, Sweden 16 E12 59 54N 18 29 E
Edsbyn, Sweden 16 C9 61 23N 15 49 E
Edson, Canada 142 C5 53 35N 116 28W
Eduardo Castex, Argentina 174 D3 35 50 S 64 18W
Edward →, Australia 128 C5 35 5 S 143 30 E
Edward, L., Africa 118 C2 0 25 S 29 40 E
Edward River, Australia 126 A3 14 59 S 141 26 E
Edward VII Land, Antarctica 7 E13 80 0 S 150 0W
Edwards, Calif., U.S.A. 161 L9 34 55N 117 51W
Edwards, N.Y., U.S.A. 151 B9 44 20N 75 15W
Edwards →, U.S.A. 156 C6 41 9N 90 59W
Edwards Air Force Base, U.S.A. 161 L9 34 50N 117 40W
Edwards Plateau, U.S.A. 155 K4 30 45N 101 20W
Edwardsburg, U.S.A. 157 C10 41 48N 86 6W
Edwardsville, Ill., U.S.A. 156 F7 38 49N 89 58W
Edwardsville, Pa., U.S.A. 151 E9 41 15N 75 56W
Edzo, Canada 142 A5 62 49N 116 4W
Eek, U.S.A. 144 F7 60 14N 162 2W
Eeklo, Belgium 24 C3 51 11N 3 33 E
Eel →, Ind., U.S.A. 157 E10 39 7N 86 57W
Eel →, Ind., U.S.A. 157 D10 40 45N 86 22W
Efate, Vanuatu 133 G6 17 40 S 168 25 E
Efate, I., Vanuatu 133 G6 17 40 S 168 25 E
Eferding, Austria 34 C7 48 18N 14 1 E
Eferi, Algeria 111 D6 24 30N 9 28 E
Effingham, U.S.A. 157 E8 39 7N 88 33W
Effretikon, Switz. 33 B7 47 25N 8 42 E
Eforie, Romania 53 F13 44 1N 28 37 E
Efoulen, Cameroon 114 B2 2 46N 10 43 E
Efteløt, Norway 18 E6 59 33N 9 49 E
Ega →, Spain 46 E5 37 55N 12 16 E
Égadi, Ìsole, Italy 46 E5 37 55N 12 16 E
Egan Range, U.S.A. 158 G6 39 35N 114 55W
Eganville, Canada 140 C4 45 32N 77 5W
Egedesminde = Aasiaat, Greenland 10 D5 68 43N 52 56W
Egegik, U.S.A. 144 G8 58 13N 157 22W
Eger = Cheb, Czech Rep. 34 A5 50 9N 12 28 E
Eger, Hungary 52 C5 47 53N 20 27 E
Eger →, Hungary 52 C5 47 38N 20 50 E
Egersund, Norway 15 G12 58 26N 6 1 E
Egg, Austria 33 B9 47 26N 9 54 E
Egg, Switz. 33 B7 47 18N 8 41 E
Egg I., St. Helena 9 h 15 58 S 5 47W
Egg L., Canada 143 B7 55 5N 105 30W
Eggedal, Norway 18 D6 60 14N 9 22 E
Eggenburg, Austria 34 C8 48 38N 15 50 E
Eggenfelden, Germany 31 G8 48 23N 12 46 E
Eggiwil, Switz. 32 C5 46 52N 7 47 E
Egherta, Somali Rep. 120 D2 2 4N 43 11 E
Éghezée, Belgium 24 D4 50 35N 4 55 E
Egholo, Solomon Is. 133 M9 8 25 S 157 25 E
Egilsstaðir, Iceland 11 B12 65 16N 14 25W
Egito, Angola 115 E2 12 4 S 13 58 E
Égletons, France 28 C6 45 24N 2 3 E
Eglisau, Switz. 33 A7 47 35N 8 31 E
Egmont, Canada 142 D4 49 45N 123 56W
Egmont, C., N.Z. 130 F2 39 16 S 173 45 E
Egmont, Mt. = Taranaki, Mt., N.Z. 130 F3 39 17 S 174 5 E
Egmont Nat. Park, N.Z. 130 F3 39 17 S 174 4 E
Egra, India 93 J12 21 54N 87 32 E
Eğridir, Turkey 100 D4 37 52N 30 51 E
Eğridir Gölü, Turkey 100 D4 37 53N 30 50 E
Egtved, Denmark 17 J3 55 38N 9 18 E
Éguas →, Brazil 171 D3 13 26 S 44 14W
Egum Atoll, Papua N. G. 132 E7 9 25 S 152 0 E
Egume, Nigeria 113 D6 7 30N 7 14 E
Éguzon-Chantôme, France 27 F8 46 27N 1 33 E
Egvekinot, Russia 67 C19 66 19N 179 50W
Egyek, Hungary 52 C5 47 39N 20 52 E
Egypt ■, Africa 106 B3 28 0N 31 0 E
Eha Amufu, Nigeria 113 D6 6 30N 7 46 E
Eheli, Algeria 111 D5 22 26N 4 40 E
Ehime □, Japan 72 D4 33 30N 132 40 E
Ehingen, Germany 31 G5 48 16N 9 43 E
Ehrenberg, U.S.A. 161 M12 33 36N 114 31W
Ehrhardt, U.S.A. 152 B8 33 6N 81 1W
Ehrwald, Austria 34 D3 47 24N 10 56 E
Eibar, Spain 40 B2 43 11N 2 28W
Eichstätt, Germany 31 G7 48 54N 11 11 E
Eide, Hordaland, Norway 18 D3 60 31N 6 44 E
Eide, Møre og Romsdal, Norway 18 B4 62 55N 7 27 E
Eider →, Germany 30 A4 54 19N 8 57 E
Eidsbugarden, Norway 18 C5 61 23N 8 16 E
Eidsbygda, Norway 18 B4 62 36N 7 30 E
Eidsdal, Norway 18 B4 62 16N 7 10 E
Eidsvåg, Norway 18 B5 62 46N 8 2 E
Eidsvold, Australia 127 D5 25 25 S 151 12 E
Eidsvoll, Norway 15 F14 60 19N 11 14 E
Eifel, Germany 31 E2 50 15N 6 50 E
Eiffel Flats, Zimbabwe 119 F3 18 20 S 30 0 E
Eiger, Switz. 32 C6 46 34N 8 1 E
Eigg, U.K. 22 E2 56 54N 6 10W
Eighty Mile Beach, Australia 124 C3 19 30 S 120 40 E
Eikefjord, Norway 18 C2 61 35N 5 27 E
Eikelandsosen, Norway 18 D2 60 15N 5 43 E
Eiken, Norway 18 F4 58 29N 7 14 E
Eikeren, Norway 18 E6 59 38N 9 58 E
Eikesdal, Norway 18 B5 62 28N 8 12 E
Eil, Somali Rep. 120 C3 8 0N 49 50 E
Eil, L., U.K. 22 E3 56 51N 5 16W
Eildon, Australia 129 D6 37 14 S 145 55 E
Eildon, L., Australia 129 D7 37 10 S 146 0 E
Eilenburg, Germany 30 D8 51 27N 12 36 E
Ein el Luweiqa, Sudan 107 E3 14 5N 33 50 E
Eina, Norway 18 D7 60 38N 10 35 E
Einarsstaðir, Iceland 11 B9 65 44N 17 24W
Einasleigh, Australia 126 B3 18 32 S 144 5 E
Einasleigh →, Australia 126 B3 17 30 S 142 17 E
Einbeck, Germany 30 D5 51 49N 9 53 E
Eindhoven, Neths. 24 C5 51 26N 5 28 E
Einsiedeln, Switz. 33 B7 47 7N 8 46 E
Eire = Ireland ■, Europe 23 C4 53 50N 7 52W
Eiríksjökull, Iceland 11 C6 64 46N 20 24W
Eiríksstaðir, Iceland 11 B11 65 7N 15 25W
Eirunepé, Brazil 172 B4 6 35 S 69 53W
Eiseb →, Namibia 116 C2 20 33 S 20 59 E
Eisenach, Germany 30 E6 50 58N 10 19 E
Eisenberg, Germany 30 E7 50 58N 11 54 E
Eisenerz, Austria 34 D7 47 32N 14 54 E
Eisenhüttenstadt, Germany 30 C10 52 9N 14 38 E
Eisenkappel, Austria 34 E7 46 29N 14 36 E
Eisenstadt, Austria 35 D9 47 51N 16 31 E
Eisfeld, Germany 31 E6 50 25N 10 54 E
Eisleben, Germany 30 D7 51 32N 11 32 E
Eislingen, Germany 31 G5 48 41N 9 42 E
Eivindvik, Norway 18 D2 60 59N 5 5 E
Eivissa, Spain 38 D1 38 54N 1 26 E
Eixe, Serra do, Spain 42 C4 42 24N 6 54W
Ejea de los Caballeros, Spain 40 C3 42 7N 1 9W
Ejeda, Madag. 117 C7 24 20 S 44 31 E
Ejura, Ghana 113 D4 7 23N 1 15W
Ejutla, Mexico 163 D5 16 34N 96 44W
Ekalaka, U.S.A. 154 C2 45 53N 104 33W
Ekalla, Gabon 114 C2 1 27 S 14 0 E
Ekanga, Dem. Rep. of the Congo 114 C4 2 23 S 23 14 E
Ekenässjön, Sweden 17 G9 57 28N 15 1 E
Ekerö, Sweden 16 E11 59 16N 17 45 E
Eket, Nigeria 113 E6 4 38N 7 56 E
Eketahuna, N.Z. 130 G4 40 38 S 175 43 E
Ekhinádhes Nísoi, Greece 39 C3 38 25N 21 2 E
Ekhínos, Greece 51 E9 41 16N 25 1 E
Ekibastuz, Kazakstan 66 D8 51 50N 75 10 E
Ekiti □, Nigeria 113 D6 7 25N 5 20 E
Ekoli, Dem. Rep. of the Congo 118 C1 0 23 S 24 13 E
Ekoln, Sweden 16 E11 59 45N 17 37 E
Ekouamou, Congo 114 B3 0 8N 16 31 E
Ekoungounou, Congo 114 C3 1 10 S 15 52 E
Ekshärad, Sweden 16 D7 60 10N 13 30 E
Eksjö, Sweden 17 G8 57 40N 14 58 E
Ekukola, Dem. Rep. of the Congo 114 C3 0 31 S 18 56 E
Ekuku, Dem. Rep. of the Congo 114 C4 0 41 S 21 42 E
Ekukula, Dem. Rep. of the Congo 114 B4 0 15N 21 30 E
Ekuma →, Namibia 116 B2 18 40 S 16 2 E
Ekuta, Dem. Rep. of the Congo 114 B3 3 0N 18 50 E
Ekwan →, Canada 140 B3 53 12N 82 15W
Ekwan Pt., Canada 140 B3 53 16N 82 7W
Ekwok, U.S.A. 144 G8 59 22N 157 30W
El Aaiún, W. Sahara 110 C2 27 9N 13 12W
El Aargub, Mauritania 110 D1 23 37N 15 52W
El Abanico, Chile 174 D1 37 20 S 71 31W
El Abbasiya, Sudan 107 E3 12 10N 31 18 E
El Abiodh-Sidi-Cheikh, Algeria 111 B5 32 53N 0 31 E
El Adde, Somali Rep. 120 D3 2 35N 46 9 E
El 'Agrûd, Egypt 103 E3 30 14N 34 24 E
El Aïoun, Morocco 111 B4 34 33N 2 30W
El Ait, Sudan 107 E2 12 22N 27 27 E
El 'Aiyat, Egypt 106 J7 29 36N 31 15 E
El Alamein, Egypt 106 A2 30 48N 28 58 E
El Alto, Peru 172 A1 4 15 S 81 14W
El Aouj, Mauritania 110 D2 22 53N 12 49W
El 'Aqaba, W. →, Egypt 103 E2 30 7N 33 54 E
El 'Arag, Egypt 106 B2 28 40N 26 20 E
El Arahal, Spain 43 H5 37 15N 5 33W
El Aricha, Algeria 111 B4 34 13N 1 10W
El Arīḩā, West Bank 103 D4 31 52N 35 27 E
El 'Arîsh, Egypt 103 D2 31 8N 33 50 E
El 'Arîsh, W. →, Egypt 103 D2 31 8N 33 47 E
El Arrouch, Algeria 111 A6 36 37N 6 53 E
El Asnam = Ech Chéliff, Algeria 111 A5 36 10N 1 20 E
El Astillero, Spain 42 B7 43 24N 3 49W
El Badâri, Egypt 106 B3 27 4N 31 25 E
El Bahrein, Egypt 106 B2 28 30N 26 25 E
El Ballâs, Egypt 106 B3 26 2N 32 43 E
El Balyana, Egypt 106 B3 26 10N 32 3 E
El Banco, Colombia 168 B3 9 0N 73 58W
El Baqeir, Sudan 106 D3 18 40N 33 40 E
El Barco de Ávila, Spain 42 E5 40 21N 5 31W
El Barco de Valdeorras = O Barco, Spain 42 C4 42 23N 6 58W
El Bauga, Sudan 106 D3 18 18N 33 52 E
El Baúl, Venezuela 168 B4 8 57N 68 17W
El Bawiti, Egypt 106 B2 28 25N 28 45 E
El Bayadh, Algeria 111 B5 33 40N 1 1 E
El Bierzo, Spain 42 C4 42 45N 6 30W
El Bluff, Nic. 164 D3 11 59N 83 40W
El Bolsón, Argentina 176 B2 41 55 S 71 30W
El Bonillo, Spain 41 G2 38 57N 2 35W
El Brûk, W. →, Egypt 103 E2 30 15N 33 50 E
El Buheirat □, Sudan 107 F3 7 0N 30 0 E
El Bur, Somali Rep. 120 D3 4 40N 46 37 E
El Burgo de Osma, Spain 40 D1 41 35N 3 4W
El Caín, Argentina 176 B3 41 38 S 68 19W
El Cajon, U.S.A. 161 N10 32 48N 116 58W
El Callao, Venezuela 169 B5 7 18N 61 50W
El Campo, U.S.A. 155 L6 29 12N 96 16W
El Carmen, Bolivia 173 C5 13 40 S 63 55W
El Centro, U.S.A. 161 N11 32 48N 115 34W
El Cerro, Bolivia 173 D5 17 30 S 61 40W
El Cerro de Andévalo, Spain 43 H4 37 45N 6 57W
El Cocuy, Colombia 168 B3 6 25N 72 27W
El Compadre, Mexico 161 N10 32 20N 116 14W
El Corcovado, Argentina 176 B2 43 25 S 71 35W
El Coronil, Spain 43 H5 37 5N 5 38W
El Cuy, Argentina 176 A3 39 55 S 68 25W
El Cuyo, Mexico 163 C7 21 30N 87 40W
El Dab'a, Egypt 106 H6 31 0N 28 27 E
El Daheir, Egypt 103 D3 31 13N 34 10 E
El Dambahaddo, Somali Rep. 120 D3 3 17N 46 40 E
El Dátil, Mexico 162 B2 30 7N 112 15W
El Deir, Egypt 106 B3 25 25N 32 20 E
El Dere, Ethiopia 120 C2 5 6N 43 50 E
El Dere, Somali Rep. 120 D3 3 50N 47 8 E
El Dere, Somali Rep. 120 C3 5 22N 46 11 E
El Descanso, Mexico 161 N10 32 12N 116 58W
El Desemboque, Mexico 162 A2 30 30N 112 57W
El Dilingat, Egypt 106 H7 30 50N 30 31 E
El Diviso, Colombia 168 C2 1 22N 78 14W
El Djouf, Mauritania 104 D3 20 0N 9 0W
El Dorado, Ark., U.S.A. 155 J8 33 12N 92 40W
El Dorado, Kans., U.S.A. 155 G6 37 49N 96 52W
El Dorado, Venezuela 169 B5 6 55N 61 37W
El Eglab, Algeria 110 C4 26 20N 4 30W
El 'Ein, Sudan 107 D2 16 35N 29 22 E
El Ejido, Spain 43 J8 36 47N 2 49W
El Escorial, Spain 42 E6 40 35N 4 7W
El Espinar, Spain 42 D6 41 43N 4 15W
El Eulma, Algeria 111 A6 36 9N 5 42 E
El Faiyûm, Egypt 106 J7 29 19N 30 50 E
El Fâsher, Sudan 107 E2 13 33N 25 26 E
El Fashn, Egypt 106 J7 28 50N 30 54 E
El Ferrol = Ferrol, Spain 42 B2 43 29N 8 15W
El Fifi, Sudan 107 E2 10 4N 25 0 E
El Fud, Ethiopia 120 C2 7 15N 42 52 E
El Fuerte, Mexico 162 B3 26 30N 108 40W
El Ga'a, Sudan 107 E2 14 16N 29 59 E
El Gal, Somali Rep. 120 B4 10 58N 50 20 E
El Garef, Sudan 107 E3 12 3N 34 19 E
El Gebir, Sudan 107 E2 13 40N 29 40 E
El Gedida, Egypt 106 B2 25 40N 28 30 E
El Geneina = Al Junaynah, Sudan 109 F4 13 27N 22 45 E
El Geteina, Sudan 107 E3 14 50N 32 27 E
El Gezira □, Sudan 107 E3 15 0N 33 0 E
El Gir, Sudan 106 D2 19 50N 28 18 E
El Gîza, Egypt 106 J7 30 0N 31 10 E
El Goléa, Algeria 111 B5 30 30N 2 50 E
El Grau, Spain 41 G4 39 0N 0 7W
El Hadeb, W. Sahara 110 C2 25 51N 13 0W
El Hadjira, Algeria 111 B6 32 36N 5 30 E
El Hagiz, Sudan 107 D4 15 15N 35 50 E
El Hâi, Egypt 106 J7 29 39N 31 18 E
El Hajeb, Morocco 110 B3 33 43N 5 13W
El Hamma, Tunisia 108 B1 33 54N 9 48 E
El Hammam, Egypt 106 A2 30 52N 29 25 E
El Hammâmi, Mauritania 110 D2 23 3N 11 30W
El Hamurre, Somali Rep. 120 C3 7 13N 48 54 E
El Hank, Mauritania 110 D3 24 30N 7 0W
El Hasian, W. Sahara 110 C2 26 20N 14 0W
El Hawata, Sudan 107 E3 13 25N 34 42 E
El Heiz, Egypt 106 B2 27 50N 28 40 E
El Hideib, Sudan 107 E3 13 0N 32 50 E
El Hilla, Sudan 107 E2 13 24N 27 2 E
El Homeur, Algeria 111 C5 29 43N 1 45 E
El 'Idisât, Egypt 106 B3 25 30N 32 35 E
El Iskandarîya, Egypt 106 H7 31 13N 29 58 E
El Jadida, Morocco 110 B3 33 11N 8 17W
El Jardal, Honduras 164 D2 14 54N 88 50W
El Jebelein, Sudan 107 E3 12 40N 32 55 E
El Jebha, Morocco 110 A4 35 11N 4 43W
El Jem, Tunisia 108 A2 35 18N 10 42 E
El Kab, Sudan 106 D3 19 27N 32 46 E
El Kabrît, G., Egypt 103 F2 29 42N 33 16 E
El Kafr el Sharqi, Egypt 106 H7 31 16N 31 10 E
El Kala, Algeria 111 A6 36 50N 8 30 E
El Kamlin, Sudan 107 D3 15 3N 33 11 E
El Kantara, Algeria 111 A6 35 14N 5 45 E
El Kantara, Tunisia 108 B2 33 45N 10 58 E
El Karaba, Sudan 106 D3 18 32N 33 41 E
El Kef, Tunisia 108 A1 36 12N 8 47 E
El Kelâa, Morocco 110 B3 32 4N 7 27W
El Kere, Ethiopia 107 F5 5 50N 42 5 E
El Khandaq, Sudan 106 D3 18 30N 30 30 E
El Khârga, Egypt 106 B3 25 30N 30 33 E
El Khartûm, Sudan 107 D3 15 31N 32 35 E
El Khartûm □, Sudan 107 D3 16 0N 33 0 E
El Khartûm Bahrî, Sudan 107 D3 15 40N 32 31 E
El Khroub, Algeria 111 A6 36 10N 6 55 E
El Kseur, Algeria 111 A5 36 46N 4 49 E
El Ksiba, Morocco 110 B3 32 45N 6 1W
El Kuntilla, Egypt 103 E3 30 1N 34 45 E
El Laqâwa, Sudan 107 E2 11 25N 29 1 E
El Laqeita, Egypt 106 B3 25 50N 33 15 E
El Leh, Ethiopia 107 G4 3 46N 39 13 E
El Leiya, Sudan 107 D4 16 15N 35 28 E
El Maestrazgo, Spain 40 E4 40 30N 0 25W
El Mafâza, Sudan 107 E3 13 38N 34 30 E
El Maghra, Egypt 106 A2 30 15N 28 55 E
El Mahalla el Kubra, Egypt 106 H7 31 0N 31 0 E
El Mahârîq, Egypt 106 B3 25 35N 30 35 E
El Maîmûn, Egypt 106 J7 29 14N 31 12 E
El Maitén, Argentina 176 B2 42 3 S 71 10W
El Maiz, Algeria 111 C4 28 19N 0 9W
El Maks el Bahari, Egypt 106 C3 24 30N 30 40 E
El Manshâh, Egypt 106 B3 26 26N 31 50 E
El Mansour, Algeria 111 C4 27 47N 0 14W
El Mansûra, Egypt 106 H7 31 0N 31 19 E
El Manteco, Venezuela 169 B5 7 38N 62 45W
El Manzala, Egypt 106 H7 31 10N 31 50 E
El Marâgha, Egypt 106 B3 26 35N 31 10 E
El Masid, Sudan 107 D3 15 15N 33 0 E
El Masnou, Spain 40 D7 41 28N 2 20 E
El Matariya, Egypt 106 H8 31 15N 32 0 E
El Meda, Ethiopia 107 F5 5 39N 41 47 E
El Medano, Canary Is. 9 e1 28 3N 16 32W
El Meghaier, Algeria 111 B6 33 55N 5 58 E
El Meraguen, Algeria 111 C4 28 0N 0 7W
El Metemma, Sudan 107 D3 16 50N 33 10 E
El Miamo, Venezuela 169 B5 7 39N 61 46W
El Milagro, Argentina 174 C2 30 59 S 65 59W
El Milia, Algeria 111 A6 36 51N 6 13 E
El Minyâ, Egypt 106 B3 28 7N 30 33 E
El Monte, U.S.A. 161 L8 34 4N 118 1W
El Montseny, Spain 40 D7 41 55N 2 25 E
El Mreyye, Mauritania 110 D3 18 0N 6 0W
El Nido, Phil. 81 F2 11 10N 119 25 E
El Niybo, Ethiopia 107 G4 4 40N 39 55 E
El Obeid, Sudan 107 E3 13 8N 30 10 E
El Odaiya, Sudan 107 E2 12 8N 28 12 E
El Oro, Mexico 163 D4 19 48N 100 8W
El Oro □, Ecuador 168 D2 3 30 S 79 50W
El Oued, Algeria 111 B6 33 20N 6 58 E
El Oumi, Niger 111 D7 20 11N 0 15 E
El Palmar, Bolivia 173 D5 17 50 S 63 9W
El Palmar, Venezuela 169 B5 7 58N 61 53W
El Palmito, Presa, Mexico 162 B3 25 40N 105 30W
El Paso, Ill., U.S.A. 156 D7 40 44N 89 1W
El Paso, Tex., U.S.A. 159 L10 31 45N 106 29W
El Paso Robles, U.S.A. 160 K6 35 38N 120 41W
El Pedernoso, Spain 41 F2 39 29N 2 45W
El Pedroso, Spain 43 H5 37 51N 5 45W
El Pilar, Venezuela 169 A5 10 32N 63 9W
El Pobo de Dueñas, Spain 40 E3 40 46N 1 39W
El Portal, U.S.A. 160 H7 37 41N 119 47W
El Porvenir, Mexico 162 A3 31 15N 105 51W
El Prat de Llobregat, Spain 40 D7 41 18N 2 3 E
El Progreso, Ecuador 172 a 0 54 S 89 33W
El Progreso, Honduras 164 C2 15 26N 87 51W
El Pueblito, Mexico 162 B3 29 3N 105 4W

Erdao Jiang 211

El Pueblo, *Canary Is.* **9 e1** 28 36N 17 47W
El Puente del Arzobispo, *Spain* **42 F5** 39 48N 5 10W
El Puerto de Santa María, *Spain* **43 J4** 36 36N 6 13W
El Qâhira, *Egypt* **106 H7** 30 1N 31 14 E
El Qantara, *Egypt* **103 E1** 30 51N 32 20 E
El Qasr, *Egypt* **106 B2** 25 44N 28 42 E
El Qubâbât, *Egypt* **106 J7** 29 28N 31 16 E
El Quseima, *Egypt* **103 E3** 30 40N 34 15 E
El Quseîya, *Egypt* **106 B3** 27 29N 30 44 E
El Râshda, *Egypt* **106 B2** 25 36N 28 57 E
El Reno, *U.S.A.* **155 H6** 35 32N 97 57W
El Ridisiya, *Egypt* **106 C3** 24 56N 32 51 E
El Rio, *U.S.A.* **161 L7** 34 14N 119 10W
El Ronquillo, *Spain* **43 H4** 37 44N 6 10W
El Roque, Pta., *Canary Is.* **9 e1** 28 10N 15 25W
El Rosarito, *Mexico* **162 B2** 28 38N 114 4W
El Rubio, *Spain* **43 H5** 37 22N 5 0W
El Saff, *Egypt* **106 J7** 29 34N 31 16 E
El Saheira, W. →, *Egypt* **103 E2** 30 5N 33 25 E
El Salto, *Mexico* **162 C3** 23 47N 105 22W
El Salvador ■, *Cent. Amer.* **164 D2** 13 50N 89 0W
El Sauce, *Nic.* **164 D2** 13 0N 86 40W
El Saucejo, *Spain* **43 H5** 37 4N 5 6W
El Shallal, *Egypt* **106 C3** 24 0N 32 53 E
El Simbillawein, *Egypt* **106 H7** 30 48N 31 13 E
El Sombrero, *Venezuela* **168 B4** 9 23N 67 3W
El Sueco, *Mexico* **162 B3** 29 54N 106 24W
El Suweis, *Egypt* **106 J8** 29 58N 32 31 E
El Tabbîn, *Egypt* **106 J7** 29 47N 31 18 E
El Tamarâni, W. →, *Egypt* **103 E3** 30 7N 34 43 E
El Thamad, *Egypt* **103 F3** 29 40N 34 28 E
El Tigre, *Venezuela* **169 B5** 8 44N 64 15W
El Tîh, Gebal, *Egypt* **103 F2** 29 40N 33 50 E
El Tîna, *Egypt* **106 H8** 31 3N 32 22 E
El Tîna, Khalîg, *Egypt* **103 D1** 31 10N 32 40 E
El Tocuyo, *Venezuela* **168 B4** 9 47N 69 48W
El Tofo, *Chile* **174 B1** 29 22 S 71 18W
El Tránsito, *Chile* **174 B1** 28 52 S 70 17W
El Tûr, *Egypt* **96 D2** 28 14N 33 36 E
El Turbio, *Argentina* **176 D2** 51 45 S 72 5W
El Uinle, *Somali Rep.* **120 D3** 1 4N 41 42 E
El Uqsur, *Egypt* **106 B3** 25 41N 32 38 E
El Venado, *Mexico* **162 C4** 22 56N 101 10W
El Vendrell, *Spain* **40 D6** 41 10N 1 30 E
El Vergel, *Mexico* **162 B3** 26 28N 106 22W
El Vigía, *Venezuela* **168 B3** 8 38N 71 39W
El Viso del Alcor, *Spain* **43 H5** 37 23N 5 43W
El Wabeira, *Egypt* **103 F2** 29 34N 33 6 E
El Wak, *Kenya* **118 B5** 2 49N 40 56 E
El Wak, *Somali Rep.* **120 D2** 2 44N 41 1 E
El Waqf, *Egypt* **106 B3** 25 45N 32 15 E
El Weguet, *Ethiopia* **107 F5** 5 28N 42 17 E
El Wuz, *Sudan* **107 D3** 15 5N 30 7 E
Elafónisos, *Greece* **48 E4** 36 29N 22 56 E
Elamanchili, *India* **94 F6** 17 33N 82 50 E
Élancourt, *France* **27 D8** 48 47N 1 58 E
Elands, *Australia* **129 A10** 31 37 S 152 20 E
Élassa, *Greece* **49 F8** 35 18N 26 21 E
Elassón, *Greece* **48 B4** 39 53N 22 12 E
Elat, *Israel* **103 F3** 29 30N 34 56 E
Eláthia, *Greece* **48 C4** 38 37N 22 46 E
Eláti Óros, *Greece* **39 B2** 38 43N 20 39 E
Elâzığ, *Turkey* **101 C8** 38 37N 39 14 E
Elba, *Italy* **44 F7** 42 46N 10 17 E
Elba, *U.S.A.* **152 D3** 31 25N 86 4W
Elbasan, *Albania* **50 E4** 41 9N 20 9 E
Elbe, *U.S.A.* **160 D4** 46 45N 122 10W
Elbe →, *Europe* **26 B4** 53 50N 9 0 E
Elbe-Seitenkanal, *Germany* **30 C6** 52 45N 10 32 E
Elberfeld, *U.S.A.* **157 F9** 38 10N 87 27W
Elbert, Mt., *U.S.A.* **159 G10** 39 7N 106 27W
Elberton, *U.S.A.* **152 A7** 34 7N 82 52W
Elbeuf, *France* **26 C8** 49 17N 1 2 E
Elbidtan, *Turkey* **96 B3** 38 13N 37 12 E
Elbing = Elbląg, *Poland* **54 D6** 54 10N 19 25 E
Elbistan, *Turkey* **100 C7** 38 13N 37 15 E
Elbląg, *Poland* **54 D6** 54 10N 19 25 E
Elbow, *Canada* **143 C7** 51 7N 106 35W
Elbow, Pta., *W. Sahara* **110 D1** 24 5N 15 35W
Elbrus, *Asia* **61 J6** 43 21N 42 30 E
Elburn, *U.S.A.* **157 C8** 41 54N 88 28W
Elburz Mts. = Alborz, Reshteh-ye Kūhhā-ye, *Iran* **97 C7** 36 0N 52 0 E
Elche, *Spain* **41 G4** 38 15N 0 42W
Elche de la Sierra, *Spain* **41 G2** 38 27N 2 3W
Elcho I., *Australia* **126 A2** 11 55 S 135 45 E
Elda, *Spain* **41 G4** 38 29N 0 47W
Elde →, *Germany* **30 B7** 53 7N 11 15 E
Eldon, *Iowa, U.S.A.* **156 D4** 40 55N 92 13W
Eldon, *Mo., U.S.A.* **156 F4** 38 21N 92 35W
Eldon, *Wash., U.S.A.* **160 C3** 47 33N 123 3W
Eldora, *U.S.A.* **156 B3** 42 22N 93 5W
Eldorado, *Argentina* **175 B5** 26 28 S 54 43W
Eldorado, *Canada* **150 B7** 44 35N 77 31W
Eldorado, *Mexico* **162 C3** 24 20N 107 22W
Eldorado, *Ill., U.S.A.* **157 G8** 37 49N 88 26W
Eldorado, *Tex., U.S.A.* **155 K4** 30 52N 100 36W
Eldorado Springs, *U.S.A.* **155 G8** 37 52N 94 1W
Eldorendo, *U.S.A.* **152 D5** 31 3N 84 39W
Eldoret, *Kenya* **118 B4** 0 30N 35 17 E
Eldred, *U.S.A.* **150 E6** 41 58N 78 23W
Eldridge, *U.S.A.* **156 C6** 41 39N 90 35W
Elea, C., *Cyprus* **39 E10** 35 19N 34 4 E
Eleanora, Pk., *Australia* **125 F3** 32 57 S 121 9 E
Elefantes →, *Mozam.* **117 C5** 24 10 S 32 40 E
Elefantes, B. das, *Angola* **115 E2** 13 13 S 12 44 E
Elefantes, G., *Chile* **176 C2** 46 28 S 73 49W
Elefantes do Maputo, Reserva de, *Mozam.* **117 D5** 26 23 S 32 48 E
Elektrogorsk, *Russia* **58 E10** 55 56N 38 50 E
Elektrostal, *Russia* **58 E10** 55 41N 38 32 E
Elele, *Nigeria* **113 D6** 5 5N 6 50 E
Elena, *Bulgaria* **51 D9** 42 55N 25 53 E
Elephant Butte Reservoir, *U.S.A.* **159 K10** 33 9N 107 11W
Elephant I., *Antarctica* **7 C18** 61 0 S 55 0W
Elephant Pass, *Sri Lanka* **95 K5** 9 35N 80 25 E
Elesbão Veloso, *Brazil* **170 C3** 6 13 S 42 8W
Eleshnitsa, *Bulgaria* **50 E7** 41 52N 23 36 E
Eleşkirt, *Turkey* **101 C10** 39 50N 42 50 E
Eleuthera, *Bahamas* **164 B4** 25 0N 76 20W
Elevsís, *Greece* **48 C5** 38 4N 23 26 E
Elevtheroúpolis, *Greece* **51 F8** 40 52N 24 20 E
Elfin Cove, *U.S.A.* **144 G13** 58 12N 136 22W
Elgå, *Norway* **18 B8** 62 10N 11 56 E
Elgepiggen, *Norway* **18 B8** 62 10N 11 21 E
Elgg, *Switz.* **33 B7** 47 29N 8 52 E
Elgin, *Canada* **151 B8** 44 36N 76 13W
Elgin, *U.K.* **22 D5** 57 39N 3 19W
Elgin, *Ill., U.S.A.* **157 B8** 42 2N 88 17W
Elgin, *N. Dak., U.S.A.* **154 B4** 46 24N 101 51W
Elgin, *Oreg., U.S.A.* **158 D5** 45 34N 117 55W
Elgin, *S.C., U.S.A.* **152 A9** 34 10N 80 48W
Elgin, *Tex., U.S.A.* **155 K6** 30 21N 97 22W
Elgoibar, *Spain* **40 B2** 43 13N 2 24W
Elgon, Mt., *Africa* **118 B3** 1 10N 34 30 E
Eliase, *Indonesia* **83 C4** 8 21 S 130 48 E
Elikón, *Greece* **48 C4** 38 18N 22 45 E
Elim, *Namibia* **116 B2** 17 48 S 15 31 E
Elim, *S. Africa* **116 E2** 34 35 S 19 45 E
Elim, *U.S.A.* **144 D7** 64 37N 162 15W
Elin Pelin, *Bulgaria* **50 D7** 42 40N 23 36 E
Elingampangu, *Dem. Rep. of the Congo* **114 C4** 2 0 S 24 4 E
Elipa, *Dem. Rep. of the Congo* **114 C4** 1 3 S 24 20 E
Eliseu Martins, *Brazil* **170 C3** 8 13 S 43 42W
Elista, *Russia* **61 G7** 46 16N 44 14 E
Eliza, L., *Australia* **128 D3** 37 15 S 139 50 E
Elizabeth, *Australia* **128 C3** 34 42 S 138 41 E
Elizabeth, *Ill., U.S.A.* **156 B6** 42 19N 90 13W
Elizabeth, *N.J., U.S.A.* **151 F10** 40 39N 74 13W
Elizabeth, *N.J., U.S.A.* **151 F10** 40 40N 74 13W
Elizabeth, B., *Ecuador* **172 a** 0 36 S 91 12W
Elizabeth City, *U.S.A.* **149 G7** 36 18N 76 14W
Elizabethton, *U.S.A.* **149 G4** 36 21N 82 13W
Elizabethtown, *Ky., U.S.A.* **157 G11** 37 42N 85 52W
Elizabethtown, *N.Y., U.S.A.* **151 B11** 44 13N 73 36W
Elizabethtown, *Pa., U.S.A.* **151 F8** 40 9N 76 36W
Elizondo, *Spain* **40 B3** 43 12N 1 30W
Ełk, *Poland* **54 E9** 53 50N 22 21 E
Elk →, *Canada* **142 C5** 49 11N 115 14W
Ełk →, *Poland* **54 E9** 53 41N 22 28 E
Elk →, *U.S.A.* **149 H2** 34 46N 87 16W
Elk City, *U.S.A.* **155 H5** 35 25N 99 25W
Elk Creek, *U.S.A.* **160 F4** 39 36N 122 32W
Elk Grove, *U.S.A.* **160 G5** 38 25N 121 22W
Elk Island Nat. Park, *Canada* **142 C6** 53 35N 112 59W
Elk Lake, *Canada* **140 C3** 47 40N 80 25W
Elk Point, *Canada* **143 C6** 53 54N 110 55W
Elk River, *Idaho, U.S.A.* **158 C5** 46 47N 116 11W
Elk River, *Minn., U.S.A.* **154 C8** 45 18N 93 35W
Elkader, *U.S.A.* **156 B5** 42 51N 91 24W
Elkedra →, *Australia* **126 C2** 21 8 S 136 22 E
Elkhart, *Ind., U.S.A.* **157 C11** 41 41N 85 58W
Elkhart, *Kans., U.S.A.* **155 G4** 37 0N 101 54W
Elkhart →, *U.S.A.* **157 C11** 41 41N 85 58W
Elkhorn, *Canada* **143 D8** 49 59N 101 14W
Elkhorn, *U.S.A.* **157 B8** 42 40N 88 33W
Elkhorn →, *U.S.A.* **154 E6** 41 8N 96 19W
Elkhovo, *Bulgaria* **51 D10** 42 10N 26 35 E
Elkin, *U.S.A.* **149 G5** 36 15N 80 51W
Elkins, *U.S.A.* **148 F6** 38 55N 79 51W
Elkland, *U.S.A.* **150 E7** 41 59N 77 19W
Elko, *Canada* **142 D5** 49 20N 115 10W
Elko, *U.S.A.* **158 F6** 40 50N 115 46W
Elkton, *U.S.A.* **150 C1** 43 49N 83 11W
Ell, L., *Australia* **125 E4** 29 13 S 127 46 E
Ellaville, *U.S.A.* **152 C5** 32 14N 84 19W
Ellef Ringnes I., *Canada* **6 B2** 78 30N 102 2W
Ellen, Mt., *U.S.A.* **151 B12** 44 9N 72 56W
Ellenburg, *U.S.A.* **151 B11** 44 54N 73 48W
Ellendale, *U.S.A.* **154 B5** 46 0N 98 32W
Ellensburg, *U.S.A.* **158 C3** 46 59N 120 34W
Ellenville, *U.S.A.* **151 E10** 41 43N 74 24W
Ellerton, *Barbados* **165 g** 13 7N 59 33W
Ellery, Mt., *Australia* **129 D8** 37 28 S 148 47 E
Ellesmere, L., *N.Z.* **131 H7** 43 47 S 172 28 E
Ellesmere I., *Canada* **6 B4** 79 30N 80 0W
Ellesmere Port, *U.K.* **20 D5** 53 17N 2 54W
Ellettsville, *U.S.A.* **157 E10** 39 14N 86 38W
Ellice Is. = Tuvalu ■, *Pac. Oc.* **134 H9** 8 0 S 178 0 E
Ellicottville, *U.S.A.* **150 D6** 42 17N 78 40W
Elliot, *Australia* **126 B1** 17 33 S 133 32 E
Elliot, *S. Africa* **117 E4** 31 22 S 27 48 E
Elliot Lake, *Canada* **140 C3** 46 25N 82 35W
Elliotdale = Xhora, *S. Africa* **117 E4** 31 55 S 28 38 E
Elliott, *U.S.A.* **152 A9** 34 6N 80 10W
Elliott Key, *U.S.A.* **153 K9** 25 27N 80 12W
Ellis, *U.S.A.* **154 F5** 38 56N 99 34W
Elliston, *Australia* **127 E1** 33 39 S 134 53 E
Ellisville, *U.S.A.* **155 K10** 31 36N 89 12W
Ellon, *U.K.* **22 D6** 57 22N 2 4W
Ellora, *India* **94 D2** 20 1N 75 10 E
Ellore = Eluru, *India* **94 F5** 16 48N 81 8 E
Elloree, *U.S.A.* **152 B9** 33 32N 80 34W
Ellsworth, *Kans., U.S.A.* **154 F5** 38 44N 98 14W
Ellsworth, *Maine, U.S.A.* **149 C11** 44 33N 68 25W
Ellsworth Land, *Antarctica* **7 D16** 76 0 S 89 0W
Ellsworth Mts., *Antarctica* **7 D16** 78 30 S 85 0W
Ellwangen, *Germany* **31 G6** 48 57N 10 8 E
Ellwood City, *U.S.A.* **150 F4** 40 52N 80 17W
Ellzey, *U.S.A.* **153 F7** 29 19N 82 48W
Elm, *Switz.* **33 C8** 46 54N 9 10 E
Elma, *Canada* **143 D9** 49 52N 95 55W
Elma, *U.S.A.* **160 D3** 47 0N 123 25W
Elmadağ, *Turkey* **100 C5** 39 55N 33 14 E
Elmalı, *Turkey* **49 E11** 36 44N 29 56 E
Elmhurst, *U.S.A.* **157 C9** 41 53N 87 56W
Elmina, *Ghana* **113 D4** 5 5N 1 21W
Elmira, *Canada* **150 C4** 43 36N 80 33W
Elmira, *U.S.A.* **150 D8** 42 6N 76 48W
Elmira Heights, *U.S.A.* **150 D8** 42 8N 76 50W
Elmodel, *U.S.A.* **152 D5** 31 21N 84 29W
Elmore, *Australia* **128 D6** 36 30 S 144 37 E
Elmore, *Ala., U.S.A.* **152 C3** 32 32N 86 19W
Elmore, *Calif., U.S.A.* **161 M11** 33 7N 115 49W
Elmore, *Minn., U.S.A.* **157 C13** 41 29N 83 18W
Elmshorn, *Germany* **30 B5** 53 43N 9 40 E
Elmvale, *Canada* **150 B5** 44 35N 79 52W
Elmwood, *U.S.A.* **156 D7** 40 47N 89 58W
Elne, *France* **28 F6** 42 36N 2 58 E
Elnesvågen, *Norway* **18 B4** 62 52N 7 10 E
Elnora, *U.S.A.* **157 F9** 38 53N 87 5W
Eloaua I., *Papua N. G.* **132 A5** 1 38 S 149 40 E
Elobey, Is., *Eq. Guin.* **114 B1** 1 1N 9 29 E
Elongo, *Dem. Rep. of the Congo* **114 C4** 0 19 S 21 39 E
Elora, *Canada* **150 C4** 43 41N 80 26W
Elorza, *Venezuela* **168 B4** 7 3N 69 31W
Elos, *Greece* **48 E4** 36 46N 22 43 E
Eloúnda, *Greece* **39 E6** 35 16N 25 42 E
Eloy, *U.S.A.* **159 K8** 32 45N 111 33W
Éloyes, *France* **27 D13** 48 6N 6 36 E
Elpitiya, *Sri Lanka* **95 L5** 6 17N 80 10 E
Elrose, *Canada* **143 C7** 51 12N 108 0W
Elsberry, *U.S.A.* **156 E6** 39 10N 90 47W
Elsdorf, *Germany* **30 E2** 50 55N 6 34 E
Elsie, *Mich., U.S.A.* **157 A12** 43 5N 84 23W
Elsie, *Oreg., U.S.A.* **160 E3** 45 52N 123 36W
Elsinore = Helsingør, *Denmark* **17 H6** 56 2N 12 35 E
Elster →, *Germany* **30 D7** 51 25N 11 57 E
Elsterwerda, *Germany* **30 D9** 51 27N 13 31 E
Eltham, *N.Z.* **130 F3** 39 26 S 174 19 E
Elton, *Russia* **61 F8** 49 5N 46 52 E
Elton, Ozero, *Russia* **61 F8** 49 5N 46 42 E
Eltville, *Germany* **31 E4** 50 2N 8 7 E
Eluru, *India* **94 F5** 16 48N 81 8 E
Elvas, *Portugal* **43 G3** 38 50N 7 10W
Elven, *France* **26 E4** 47 44N 2 36W
Elverum, *Norway* **15 F14** 60 53N 11 34 E
Elvire →, *Australia* **124 C4** 17 51 S 128 11 E
Elvire, Mt., *Australia* **125 E2** 29 22 S 119 36 E
Elvo →, *Italy* **44 C5** 45 23N 8 21 E
Elwell, L., *U.S.A.* **158 B8** 48 22N 111 17W
Elwood, *Ill., U.S.A.* **157 C8** 41 24N 88 7W
Elwood, *Ind., U.S.A.* **157 D11** 40 17N 85 50W
Elwood, *Nebr., U.S.A.* **154 E5** 40 36N 99 52W
Elx = Elche, *Spain* **41 G4** 38 15N 0 42W
Ely, *U.K.* **21 E8** 52 24N 0 16 E
Ely, *Minn., U.S.A.* **154 B9** 47 55N 91 51W
Ely, *Nev., U.S.A.* **158 G6** 39 15N 114 54W
Elyria, *U.S.A.* **150 E2** 41 22N 82 7W
Elyrus, *Greece* **48 F5** 35 15N 23 45 E
Elz →, *Germany* **31 G3** 48 18N 7 44 E
Emådalen, *Sweden* **16 C8** 61 20N 14 44 E
Émaé, *Vanuatu* **133 G6** 17 4 S 168 24 E
Emāmrūd, *Iran* **97 B7** 36 30N 55 0 E
Emån →, *Sweden* **17 G10** 57 8N 16 30 E
Emao, *Vanuatu* **133 G6** 17 29 S 168 30 E
Emateloa, *Dem. Rep. of the Congo* **114 B3** 1 16N 18 42 E
Emba, *Kazakstan* **66 E6** 48 50N 58 8 E
Emba →, *Kazakstan* **57 E9** 46 55N 53 28 E
Embarcación, *Argentina* **174 A3** 23 10 S 64 0W
Embarras →, *U.S.A.* **157 F9** 38 39N 87 37W
Embarras Portage, *Canada* **143 B6** 58 27N 111 28W
Embetsu, *Japan* **70 B10** 44 44N 141 47 E
Embi = Emba, *Kazakstan* **66 E6** 48 50N 58 8 E
Embi = Emba →, *Kazakstan* **57 E9** 46 55N 53 28 E
Embira →, *Brazil* **172 B3** 7 19 S 70 15W
Embóna, *Greece* **38 E11** 36 13N 27 51 E
Embrach, *Switz.* **33 B7** 47 30N 8 36 E
Embrun, *France* **29 D10** 44 34N 6 30 E
Embu, *Kenya* **118 C4** 0 32 S 37 38 E
Emden, *Germany* **30 B3** 53 21N 7 12 E
Emecik, *Turkey* **49 E9** 36 46N 27 49 E
Emerald, *Queens., Australia* **126 C4** 23 32 S 148 10 E
Emerald, *Vic., Australia* **122 E8** 37 56 S 145 29 E
Emerson, *Canada* **143 D9** 49 0N 97 10W
Emerson, *U.S.A.* **152 A5** 34 8N 84 45W
Emet, *Turkey* **49 B11** 39 20N 29 15 E
Emeti, *Papua N. G.* **132 D2** 7 53 S 143 15 E
Emi Koussi, *Chad* **109 E3** 19 45N 18 55 E
Emília-Romagna □, *Italy* **44 D8** 44 45N 11 0 E
Emilius, Mte., *Italy* **44 C4** 45 45N 7 20 E
Eminabad, *Pakistan* **92 C6** 32 2N 74 8 E
Emine, Nos, *Bulgaria* **51 D11** 42 40N 27 56 E
Eminence, *U.S.A.* **157 F11** 38 22N 85 11W
Emirau I., *Papua N. G.* **132 A6** 1 40 S 150 0 E
Emirdağ, *Turkey* **100 C4** 39 2N 31 8 E
Emissi, Tarso, *Chad* **109 D3** 21 27N 18 36 E
Emlenton, *U.S.A.* **150 E5** 41 11N 79 43W
Emlichheim, *Germany* **30 C2** 52 37N 6 51 E
Emmaboda, *Sweden* **17 H9** 56 37N 15 32 E
Emmalane, *U.S.A.* **152 C7** 32 46N 82 0W
Emmaus, *S. Africa* **116 D4** 29 2 S 25 15 E
Emmaus, *U.S.A.* **151 F9** 40 32N 75 30W
Emme →, *Switz.* **32 B5** 47 14N 7 32 E
Emmeloord, *Neths.* **24 B5** 52 44N 5 46 E
Emmen, *Neths.* **24 B6** 52 48N 6 57 E
Emmen, *Switz.* **31 H4** 47 5N 8 18 E
Emmenbrücke, *Switz.* **33 B6** 47 4N 8 16 E
Emmendingen, *Germany* **31 G3** 48 6N 7 51 E
Emmental, *Switz.* **32 C4** 46 55N 7 40 E
Emmerich, *Germany* **30 D2** 51 50N 6 14 E
Emmet, *Australia* **126 C3** 24 45 S 144 30 E
Emmetsburg, *U.S.A.* **156 A2** 43 7N 94 41W
Emmett, *Idaho, U.S.A.* **158 E5** 43 52N 116 30W
Emmett, *Mich., U.S.A.* **150 D2** 42 59N 82 46W
Emmiganuru, *India* **95 E3** 15 44N 77 29 E
Emmonak, *U.S.A.* **144 E6** 62 46N 164 30W
Emo, *Canada* **143 D10** 48 38N 93 50W
Emőd, *Hungary* **52 C5** 47 57N 20 47 E
Emona, *Bulgaria* **51 D11** 42 43N 27 53 E
Empalme, *Mexico* **162 B2** 28 1N 110 49W
Empangeni, *S. Africa* **117 D5** 28 50 S 31 52 E
Empedrado, *Argentina* **174 B4** 28 0 S 58 46W
Emperor Seamount Chain, *Pac. Oc.* **134 D9** 40 0N 170 0 E
Empire, *U.S.A.* **152 C6** 32 21N 83 18W
Empoli, *Italy* **44 E7** 43 43N 10 57 E
Emporia, *Kans., U.S.A.* **154 F6** 38 25N 96 11W
Emporia, *Va., U.S.A.* **149 G7** 36 42N 77 32W
Emporium, *U.S.A.* **150 E6** 41 31N 78 14W
Empress, *Canada* **143 C7** 50 57N 110 0W
Empty Quarter = Rub' al Khālī, *Si. Arabia* **99 C5** 19 0N 48 0 E
Ems →, *Germany* **30 B3** 53 20N 7 12 E
Emsdale, *Canada* **150 A5** 45 32N 79 19W
Emsdetten, *Germany* **30 C3** 52 10N 7 32 E
Emu, *China* **75 C15** 43 40N 128 6 E
Emu Park, *Australia* **126 C5** 23 13 S 150 50 E
'En 'Avrona, *Israel* **103 F4** 29 43N 35 0 E
En Nahrat, *Mali* **110 D4** 22 55N 3 36W
En Nahud, *Sudan* **107 E2** 12 45N 28 25 E
En Nofalab, *Sudan* **107 D3** 15 52N 32 32 E
Ena, *Japan* **73 B9** 35 25N 137 25 E
Ena-San, *Japan* **73 B9** 35 26N 137 36 E
Enambú, *Colombia* **168 C3** 1 1N 70 17W
Enana, *Namibia* **116 B2** 17 30 S 16 23 E
Enånger, *Sweden* **16 C11** 61 30N 17 9 E
Enard B., *U.K.* **22 C3** 58 5N 5 20W
Enare = Inarijärvi, *Finland* **14 B22** 69 0N 28 0 E
Enarotali, *Indonesia* **83 B5** 3 55 S 136 21 E
Enbekshi, *Kazakstan* **65 C4** 41 22N 68 3 E
Encampment, *U.S.A.* **158 F10** 41 12N 106 47W
Encantadas, Serra, *Brazil* **175 C5** 30 40 S 53 0W
Encarnación, *Paraguay* **175 B4** 27 15 S 55 50W
Encarnación de Diaz, *Mexico* **162 C4** 21 30N 102 13W
Enchi, *Ghana* **112 D4** 5 53N 2 48W
Encinitas, *U.S.A.* **161 M9** 33 3N 117 17W
Encino, *U.S.A.* **159 J11** 34 39N 105 28W
Encontrados, *Venezuela* **168 B3** 9 3N 72 14W
Encounter B., *Australia* **128 C3** 35 45 S 138 45 E
Encruzilhada, *Brazil* **171 E3** 15 31 S 40 54W
Encs, *Hungary* **52 B6** 48 20N 21 8 E
Endako, *Canada* **142 C3** 54 6N 125 2W
Ende, *Indonesia* **82 C2** 8 45 S 121 40 E
Endeavour Str., *Australia* **126 A3** 10 45 S 142 0 E
Endelave, *Denmark* **17 J4** 55 46N 10 18 E
Enden, *Norway* **18 C7** 61 47N 10 15 E
Enderbury I., *Kiribati* **134 H10** 3 8 S 171 5W
Enderby, *Canada* **142 C5** 50 35N 119 10W
Enderby I., *Australia* **124 D2** 20 35 S 116 30 E
Enderby Land, *Antarctica* **7 C5** 66 0 S 53 0 E
Enderlin, *U.S.A.* **154 B6** 46 38N 97 36W
Endicott, *U.S.A.* **151 D8** 42 6N 76 4W
Endicott Mts., *U.S.A.* **144 C10** 68 0N 152 0W
Endimari →, *Brazil* **172 B4** 8 46 S 66 7W
Endwell, *U.S.A.* **151 D8** 42 6N 76 2W
Endyalgout I., *Australia* **124 B5** 11 40 S 132 35 E
Ene →, *Peru* **172 C3** 11 10 S 74 18W
Eneabba, *Australia* **125 E2** 29 49 S 115 16 E
Energetīcheskīy, *Kazakstan* **65 B8** 43 25N 77 1 E
Energetik, *Russia* **64 F7** 51 45N 58 45 E
Enewetak Atoll, *Marshall Is.* **134 F8** 11 30N 162 15 E
Enez, *Turkey* **51 F10** 40 45N 26 5 E
Enfer, Pte. d', *Martinique* **164 c** 14 22N 60 54W
Enfield, *Canada* **141 D7** 44 56N 63 32W
Enfield, *Conn., U.S.A.* **151 E12** 41 58N 72 36W
Enfield, *Ill., U.S.A.* **157 F8** 38 6N 88 20W
Enfield, *N.H., U.S.A.* **151 C12** 43 39N 72 9W
Enga □, *Papua N. G.* **132 C2** 5 30 S 143 30 E
Engadin, *Switz.* **31 J6** 46 45N 10 10 E
Engan, *Norway* **18 A5** 63 8N 8 31 E
Engaño, C., *Dom. Rep.* **165 C6** 18 30N 68 20W
Engaño, C., *Phil.* **80 B4** 18 35N 122 23 E
Engaru, *Japan* **70 B11** 44 3N 143 31 E
Engcobo, *S. Africa* **117 E4** 31 37 S 28 0 E
Engelberg, *Switz.* **33 C6** 46 48N 8 26 E
Engels, *Russia* **60 E8** 51 28N 46 6 E
Engemann L., *Canada* **143 B7** 58 0N 106 55W
Engerdal, *Norway* **18 C8** 61 45N 11 58 E
Engershatu, *Eritrea* **107 D4** 16 7N 38 34 E
Enggano, *Indonesia* **82 C1** 5 20 S 102 40 E
Engil, *Morocco* **110 B4** 33 12N 4 32W
Engineer Group, *Papua N. G.* **132 F6** 10 35 S 151 20 E
Engkilili, *Malaysia* **85 B4** 1 3N 111 42 E
England, *U.S.A.* **155 H9** 34 33N 91 58W
England □, *U.K.* **20 D7** 53 0N 2 0W
Englee, *Canada* **141 B8** 50 45N 56 5W
Englehart, *Canada* **140 C4** 47 49N 79 52W
Englewood, *Colo., U.S.A.* **154 F2** 39 39N 104 59W
Englewood, *Fla., U.S.A.* **153 J7** 26 58N 82 21W
Englewood, *Ohio, U.S.A.* **157 E12** 39 53N 84 18W
English, *U.S.A.* **157 F10** 38 20N 86 28W
English →, *Canada* **143 C10** 50 35N 93 30W
English →, *U.S.A.* **156 C5** 41 29N 91 32W
English B., *Ascension I.* **9 g** 7 54 S 14 23W
English Bazar = Ingraj Bazar, *India* **93 G13** 24 58N 88 10 E
English Channel, *Europe* **21 G6** 50 0N 2 0W
English River, *Canada* **140 C1** 49 14N 91 0W
Engures ezers, *Latvia* **54 A10** 57 16N 23 6 E
Enguri →, *Georgia* **61 J5** 42 27N 41 38 E
Enid, *U.S.A.* **155 G6** 36 24N 97 53W
Enipévs →, *Greece* **48 B4** 39 22N 22 17 E
Enkhuizen, *Neths.* **24 B5** 52 42N 5 17 E
Enköping, *Sweden* **16 E11** 59 37N 17 4 E
Enle, *China* **76 F3** 24 0N 101 9 E
Enna, *Italy* **47 E7** 37 34N 14 16 E
Ennadai, *Canada* **143 A8** 61 8N 100 53W
Ennadai L., *Canada* **143 A8** 61 0N 101 0W
Enné, O. →, *Chad* **109 F4** 14 24N 18 45 E
Ennedi, *Chad* **109 E4** 17 15N 22 0 E
Enneri Achelouma →, *Niger* **111 D7** 21 55N 13 35 E
Enngonia, *Australia* **127 D4** 29 21 S 145 50 E
Ennigerloh, *Germany* **30 D4** 51 50N 8 2 E
Ennis, *Ireland* **23 D3** 52 51N 8 59W
Ennis, *Mont., U.S.A.* **158 D8** 45 21N 111 44W
Ennis, *Tex., U.S.A.* **155 J6** 32 20N 96 38W
Enniscorthy, *Ireland* **23 D5** 52 30N 6 34W
Enniskillen, *U.K.* **23 B4** 54 21N 7 39W
Ennistimon, *Ireland* **23 D2** 52 57N 9 17W
Enns, *Austria* **34 C7** 48 12N 14 28 E
Enns →, *Austria* **34 C7** 48 14N 14 32 E
Enontekiö, *Finland* **14 B20** 68 23N 23 37 E
Enosburg Falls, *U.S.A.* **151 B12** 44 55N 72 48W
Enping, *China* **77 F9** 22 16N 112 21 E
Enrekang, *Indonesia* **82 B1** 3 34 S 119 47 E
Enrile, *Phil.* **80 C3** 17 34N 121 42 E
Enriquillo, L., *Dom. Rep.* **165 C5** 18 20N 72 5W
Enschede, *Neths.* **24 B6** 52 13N 6 53 E
Ensenada, *Argentina* **174 C4** 34 55 S 57 55W
Ensenada, *Mexico* **162 A1** 31 50N 116 50W
Ensenada de los Muertos, *Mexico* **162 C2** 23 59N 109 50W
Enshi, *China* **76 B7** 30 18N 109 29 E
Enshū-Nada, *Japan* **73 C9** 34 27N 137 38 E
Ensiola, Pta. de n', *Spain* **38 B3** 39 7N 2 55 E
Ensisheim, *France* **27 E14** 47 50N 7 20 E
Ensley, *U.S.A.* **153 E2** 30 31N 87 16W
Entebbe, *Uganda* **118 B3** 0 4N 32 28 E
Enterprise, *Canada* **142 A5** 60 47N 115 45W
Enterprise, *Ala., U.S.A.* **152 D4** 31 19N 85 51W
Enterprise, *Oreg., U.S.A.* **158 D5** 45 25N 117 17W
Entlebuch, *Switz.* **32 C6** 46 59N 8 4 E
Entraygues-sur-Truyère, *France* **28 D6** 44 38N 2 35 E
Entre Ríos, *Bolivia* **174 A3** 21 30 S 64 25W
Entre Rios, *Bahia, Brazil* **171 D4** 11 56 S 38 5W
Entre Rios, *Pará, Brazil* **173 B7** 5 24 S 54 21W
Entre Ríos □, *Argentina* **174 C4** 30 30 S 58 30W
Entrepeñas, Embalse de, *Spain* **40 E2** 40 34N 2 42W
Entroncamento, *Portugal* **43 F2** 39 28N 8 28W
Enugu, *Nigeria* **113 D6** 6 30N 7 30 E
Enugu □, *Nigeria* **113 D6** 6 30N 7 45 E
Enugu Ezike, *Nigeria* **113 D6** 7 0N 7 29 E
Enumclaw, *U.S.A.* **160 C5** 47 12N 121 59W
Envermeu, *France* **26 C8** 49 53N 1 15 E
Envigado, *Colombia* **168 B2** 6 10N 75 35W
Enviken, *Sweden* **16 D9** 60 49N 15 46 E
Envira, *Brazil* **172 B3** 7 18 S 70 13W
Enying, *Hungary* **52 D3** 46 56N 18 15 E
Enyonga, *Gabon* **114 C1** 0 59 S 9 22 E
Enza →, *Italy* **44 D7** 44 54N 10 31 E
Enzan, *Japan* **73 B10** 35 42N 138 44 E
Eólie, Ís., *Italy* **47 D7** 38 30N 14 57 E
Epalinges, *Switz.* **32 C3** 46 33N 6 40 E
Epanomí, *Greece* **50 F6** 40 25N 22 59 E
Epe, *Neths.* **24 B5** 52 21N 5 59 E
Epe, *Nigeria* **113 D5** 6 36N 3 59 E
Epéna, *Congo* **114 B3** 1 22N 17 29 E
Épernay, *France* **27 C10** 49 3N 3 56 E
Épernon, *France* **27 D8** 48 35N 1 40 E
Ephesus, *Turkey* **49 D9** 37 55N 27 22 E
Ephraim, *U.S.A.* **158 G8** 39 22N 111 35W
Ephrata, *Pa., U.S.A.* **151 F8** 40 11N 76 11W
Ephrata, *Wash., U.S.A.* **158 C4** 47 19N 119 33W
Epi, *Vanuatu* **133 F6** 16 43 S 168 15 E
Epidaurus Limera, *Greece* **48 E5** 36 46N 23 0 E
Épila, *Spain* **40 D3** 41 36N 1 17W
Épinac, *France* **27 F11** 46 59N 4 31 E
Épinal, *France* **27 D13** 48 10N 6 27 E
Epira, *Guyana* **169 B6** 5 5N 57 20W
Episkopi, *Cyprus* **39 F8** 34 40N 32 54 E
Episkopí, *Greece* **39 E5** 35 20N 24 20 E
Episkopi Bay, *Cyprus* **39 F8** 34 35N 32 50 E
Epitálion, *Greece* **48 D3** 37 37N 21 30 E
Eppalock, L., *Australia* **128 D6** 36 52 S 144 34 E
Eppan = Appiano, *Italy* **45 B8** 46 28N 11 15 E
Eppingen, *Germany* **31 F4** 49 8N 8 53 E
Epsom, *U.K.* **21 F7** 51 19N 0 16W
Epukiro, *Namibia* **116 C2** 21 40 S 19 9 E
Equality, *U.S.A.* **157 G8** 37 44N 88 20W
Équateur □, *Dem. Rep. of the Congo* **114 B4** 2 0N 21 0 E
Equatorial Guinea ■, *Africa* **114 B1** 2 0N 8 0 E
Equeipa, *Venezuela* **169 B5** 5 22N 62 43W
Er Hai, *China* **76 E3** 25 48N 100 11 E
Er Rachidia, *Morocco* **110 B4** 31 58N 4 20W
Er Rahad, *Sudan* **107 E3** 12 45N 30 32 E
Er Rif, *Morocco* **111 A4** 35 1N 4 1W
Er Rogel, *Sudan* **106 D4** 18 10N 35 25 E
Er Roseires, *Sudan* **107 E3** 11 55N 34 30 E
Er Rua'at, *Sudan* **107 E3** 12 21N 32 17 E
Eraclea, *Italy* **45 C9** 45 35N 12 40 E
Eran, *Phil.* **81 G1** 9 4N 117 42 E
Erandol, *India* **94 D2** 20 56N 75 20 E
Eranga, *Dem. Rep. of the Congo* **114 C3** 1 52 S 18 56 E
Erap, *Papua N. G.* **132 D4** 6 37 S 146 51 E
Erave, *Papua N. G.* **132 D2** 6 39 S 144 0 E
Erave →, *Papua N. G.* **132 D3** 6 54 S 144 47 E
Erāwadī Myit = Irrawaddy →, *Burma* **90 G5** 15 50N 95 6 E
Erāwadī Myitwanya = Irrawaddy, Mouths of the, *Burma* **90 H5** 15 30N 95 0 E
Erba, *Italy* **44 C6** 45 48N 9 15 E
Erba, *Sudan* **106 D4** 19 5N 36 51 E
Erba, J., *Sudan* **106 C4** 20 48N 36 47 E
Erbaa, *Turkey* **100 B7** 40 42N 36 36 E
Erbeskopf, *Germany* **31 F3** 49 44N 7 2 E
Erbil = Arbīl, *Iraq* **101 D11** 36 15N 44 5 E
Erbu, *Ethiopia* **107 E3** 6 44N 34 53 E
Erçek, *Turkey* **96 B4** 38 39N 43 36 E
Erçis, *Turkey* **101 C10** 39 2N 43 21 E
Ercıyaş Dağı, *Turkey* **57 G6** 38 30N 35 30 E
Érd, *Hungary* **52 C3** 47 22N 18 56 E
Erdao Jiang →, *China* **75 C14** 43 0N 127 0 E

212 Erdek

Erdek, Turkey 51 F11 40 23N 27 47 E
Erdemli, Turkey 100 D6 36 36N 34 19 E
Erdene = Ulaan-Uul, Mongolia 74 B6 44 13N 111 10 E
Erdenetsogt, Mongolia 74 C4 42 55N 106 5 E
Erding, Germany 31 G7 48 18N 11 54 E
Erdre →, France 26 E5 47 13N 1 32W
Erebato →, Venezuela 169 B5 5 54N 64 16W
Erebus, Mt., Antarctica 7 D11 77 35 S 167 0 E
Erechim, Brazil 175 B5 27 35 S 52 15W
Ereğli, Konya, Turkey 100 D6 37 31N 34 4 E
Ereğli, Zonguldak, Turkey 100 B4 41 15N 31 24 E
Erei, Monti, Italy 47 E7 37 20N 14 20 E
Erenhot, China 74 C7 43 48N 112 2 E
Eresfjord, Norway 18 B5 62 40N 8 8 E
Eresma →, Spain 42 D6 41 26N 4 45W
Eressós, Greece 49 B7 39 11N 25 57 E
Erfenisdam, S. Africa 116 D4 28 30 S 26 50 E
Erfjord, Norway 18 E3 59 20N 6 14 E
Erfoud, Morocco 110 B4 31 30N 4 15W
Erfstadt, Germany 30 E2 50 50N 6 50 E
Erft →, Germany 30 D2 51 11N 6 44 E
Erfurt, Germany 30 E7 50 58N 11 2 E
Ergani, Turkey 101 C8 38 17N 39 49 E
Ergel, Mongolia 74 C5 43 8N 109 5 E
Ergene →, Turkey 51 E10 41 1N 26 22 E
Ergeni Vozvyshennost, Russia 61 G7 47 0N 44 0 E
Ērgli, Latvia 15 H21 56 54N 25 38 E
Erhlin, Taiwan 77 F13 23 54N 120 22 E
Eria →, Spain 42 C5 42 3N 5 44W
Eriba, Sudan 107 D4 16 40N 36 10 E
Eriboll, L., U.K. 22 C4 58 30N 4 42W
Érice, Italy 46 D5 38 2N 12 35 E
Eridu, U.S.A. 152 E6 30 18N 83 45W
Erie, Mich., U.S.A. 157 C13 41 47N 83 31W
Erie, Pa., U.S.A. 150 D4 42 8N 80 5W
Erie, L., N. Amer. 150 D4 42 15N 81 0W
Erie Canal, U.S.A. 150 C7 43 5N 78 43W
Erieau, Canada 150 D3 42 16N 81 57W
Erigavo, Somali Rep. 120 B3 10 35N 47 20 E
Erikoúsa, Greece 38 B9 39 53N 19 34 E
Eriksdale, Canada 143 C9 50 52N 98 7W
Erímanthos, Greece 48 D3 37 57N 21 50 E
Erimo-misaki, Japan 70 D11 41 50N 143 15 E
Erin Pt., Trin. & Tob. 169 F9 10 13N 61 40W
Erinpura, India 92 G5 25 9N 73 3 E
Eriskay, U.K. 22 D1 57 4N 7 18W
Eriswil, Switz. 32 B5 47 5N 7 46 E
Erithraí, Greece 48 C5 38 13N 23 20 E
Eritrea ■, Africa 107 E4 14 0N 38 30 E
Erjas →, Portugal 42 F3 39 40N 7 1W
Erkech-Tam, Kyrgyzstan 65 D6 39 41N 73 55 E
Erkelenz, Germany 30 D2 51 4N 6 19 E
Erkner, Germany 30 C9 52 25N 13 44 E
Erlangen, Germany 31 F6 49 36N 11 0 E
Erlanger, U.S.A. 157 E12 39 1N 84 36W
Erldunda, Australia 126 D1 25 14 S 133 12 E
Ermelo, Neths. 24 B5 52 18N 5 35 E
Ermelo, S. Africa 117 D4 26 31 S 29 59 E
Ermenek, Turkey 100 D5 36 38N 33 0 E
Ermil, Sudan 107 E2 13 35N 27 40 E
Ermióni, Greece 48 D5 37 23N 23 15 E
Ermones, Greece 38 B9 39 37N 19 46 E
Ermoúpolis = Síros, Greece 48 D6 37 28N 24 57 E
Erne →, Ireland 23 B3 54 30N 8 16W
Erne, Lower L., U.K. 23 B4 54 28N 7 47W
Erne, Upper L., U.K. 23 B4 54 14N 7 32W
Ernée, France 26 D6 48 18N 0 56W
Ernest Giles Ra., Australia 125 E3 27 0 S 123 45 E
Ernstberg, Germany 31 E2 50 13N 6 47 E
Erode, India 95 J3 11 24N 77 45 E
Eromanga, Australia 127 D3 26 40 S 143 11 E
Erongo, Namibia 116 C2 21 39 S 15 58 E
Erquy, France 26 D4 48 38N 2 29W
Err, Piz d', Switz. 33 C9 46 34N 9 43 E
Erramala Hills, India 95 G4 15 30N 78 15 E
Errer →, Ethiopia 107 F5 7 32N 42 35 E
Errigal, Ireland 23 A3 55 2N 8 6W
Errinundra Nat. Park, Australia 129 D8 37 20 S 148 47 E
Erris Hd., Ireland 23 B1 54 19N 10 0W
Erromango, Vanuatu 133 H7 18 45 S 169 5 E
Erseké, Albania 50 F4 40 22N 20 40 E
Erskine, U.S.A. 154 B7 47 40N 96 0W
Erstein, France 27 D14 48 25N 7 38 E
Erstfeld, Switz. 33 C7 46 50N 8 38 E
Ertholmene, Denmark 17 J9 55 19N 15 11 E
Ertil, Russia 60 E5 51 55N 40 50 E
Ertis = Irtysh →, Russia 66 C7 61 4N 68 52 E
Ertvågøy, Norway 18 A5 63 13N 8 26 E
Eruh, Turkey 101 D10 37 46N 42 13 E
Eruwa, Nigeria 113 D5 7 33N 3 26 E
Ervy-le-Châtel, France 27 D10 48 2N 3 55 E
Erwin, U.S.A. 149 G4 36 9N 82 25W
Eryuan, China 76 D2 26 7N 99 57 E
Erzgebirge, Germany 30 E8 50 27N 12 55 E
Erzin, Russia 67 D10 50 15N 95 10 E
Erzincan, Turkey 101 C8 39 46N 39 30 E
Erzurum, Turkey 101 C9 39 57N 41 15 E
Es Caló, Spain 38 D2 38 40N 1 30 E
Es Canar, Spain 38 C2 39 2N 1 36 E
Es Mercadal, Spain 38 B5 39 59N 4 5 E
Es Migjorn Gran, Spain 38 B5 39 57N 4 3 E
Es Safiya, Sudan 107 D3 15 31N 30 7 E
Es Sahrâ' Esh Sharqîya, Egypt 106 B3 27 30N 32 30 E
Es Sînâ', Egypt 103 F3 29 0N 34 0 E
Es Sûkî, Sudan 107 E3 13 20N 33 58 E
Es Vedrà, Spain 38 D1 38 52N 1 12 E
Esa'ala, Papua N. G. 132 E6 9 45 S 150 49 E
Esambo, Dem. Rep. of the Congo 118 C1 3 48 S 23 30 E
Esan-Misaki, Japan 70 D10 41 40N 141 10 E
Esashi, Hokkaidō, Japan 70 B11 44 56N 142 35 E
Esashi, Hokkaidō, Japan 70 D10 41 52N 140 7 E
Esbjerg, Denmark 17 J2 55 29N 8 29 E
Escada, Brazil 170 C4 8 22 S 35 8W
Escalante, U.S.A. 159 H8 37 47N 111 36W
Escalante →, U.S.A. 159 H8 37 24N 110 57W
Escalente, Phil. 81 F4 10 50N 123 33 E
Escalón, Mexico 162 B4 26 46N 104 20W
Escambia →, U.S.A. 149 K2 30 32N 87 11W
Escanaba, U.S.A. 148 C2 45 45N 87 4W
Escarparda Pt., Phil. 80 B4 18 31N 122 13 E
Escarpé, C., Vanuatu 133 K5 20 41 S 167 13 E
Esch-sur-Alzette, Lux. 24 E6 49 32N 6 0 E
Eschede, Germany 30 C6 52 44N 10 14 E
Escholzmatt, Switz. 32 C5 46 55N 7 56 E
Eschwege, Germany 30 D6 51 11N 10 2 E
Eschweiler, Germany 30 E2 50 49N 6 15 E
Escoma, Bolivia 172 D4 15 40 S 69 8W
Escondido, U.S.A. 161 M9 33 7N 117 5W
Escravos →, Nigeria 113 D6 5 35N 5 10 E
Escuinapa, Mexico 162 C3 22 50N 105 50W
Escuintla, Guatemala 164 D1 14 20N 90 48W
Eséka, Cameroon 113 E7 3 41N 10 44 E
Eşen →, Turkey 49 E11 36 27N 29 16 E
Esenguly, Turkmenistan 66 F6 37 37N 53 59 E
Esens, Germany 30 B3 53 38N 7 36 E
Esenyurt, Turkey 51 E12 41 3N 28 48 E
Esera →, Spain 40 C5 42 6N 0 15 E
Eşfahān, Iran 97 C6 32 39N 51 43 E
Eşfahān □, Iran 97 C6 32 50N 51 50 E
Esfarāyen, Iran 97 B8 37 4N 57 30 E
Esfideh, Iran 97 C8 33 39N 59 46 E
Esgueva →, Spain 42 D6 41 40N 4 43W
Esh Sham = Dimashq, Syria 103 B5 33 30N 36 18 E
Esh Shamâlîya □, Sudan 106 D2 19 0N 29 0 E
Esha Ness, U.K. 22 A7 60 29N 1 38W
Eshan, China 76 E4 24 11N 102 24 E
Esher, U.K. 21 F7 51 21N 0 20W
Eshkāshem = Ishkashim, Tajikistan 65 E5 36 44N 71 37 E
Eshowe, S. Africa 117 D5 28 50 S 31 30 E
Esiama, Ghana 112 E4 4 56N 2 25W
Esigodini, Zimbabwe 117 C4 20 18 S 28 56 E
Esik, Kazakstan 65 B8 43 21N 77 27 E
Esil = Ishim →, Russia 66 D8 57 45N 71 10 E
Esino →, Italy 45 E10 43 39N 13 22 E
Esira, Madag. 117 C8 24 20 S 46 42 E
Esk →, Cumb., U.K. 22 G5 54 58N 3 2W
Esk →, N. Yorks., U.K. 20 C7 54 30N 0 37W
Eskān, Iran 91 D1 26 48N 63 9 E
Esker, Canada 141 B6 53 53N 66 25W
Eski-Nookat, Kyrgyzstan 65 C6 40 16N 72 36 E
Eskifjörður, Iceland 11 B13 65 3N 13 55W
Eskilsäter, Sweden 17 F7 58 57N 13 10 E
Eskilstuna, Sweden 16 E10 59 22N 16 32 E
Eskimalatya, Turkey 101 C8 38 24N 38 22 E
Eskimo Pt., Canada 138 B10 61 10N 94 15W
Eskişehir, Turkey 49 B12 39 50N 30 30 E
Eskişehir □, Turkey 49 B12 39 40N 31 0 E
Esla →, Spain 42 D4 41 29N 6 3W
Eslāmābād-e Gharb, Iran 101 E12 34 10N 46 30 E
Eslāmshahr, Iran 97 C6 35 40N 51 10 E
Eslöv, Sweden 17 J7 55 50N 13 20 E
Eşme, Turkey 49 C10 38 23N 28 58 E
Esmeralda, I., Chile 176 C1 48 55 S 75 25W
Esmeraldas, Ecuador 168 C2 1 0N 79 40W
Esmeraldas □, Ecuador 168 C2 0 40N 79 30W
Esmeraldas →, Ecuador 168 C2 0 58N 79 38W
Esnagi L., Canada 140 C3 48 36N 84 33W
Esom Hill, U.S.A. 152 B4 33 57N 85 23W
Espa, Norway 18 D8 60 34N 11 16 E
Espada, Pta., Colombia 168 A3 12 5N 71 7W
Espalion, France 28 D6 44 32N 2 47 E
Espanola, Canada 140 C3 46 15N 81 46W
Espanola, U.S.A. 159 H10 35 59N 106 5W
Española, I., Ecuador 172 a 1 23 S 89 39W
Esparreguera, Spain 40 D6 41 33N 1 52 E
Esparta, Costa Rica 164 E3 9 59N 84 40W
Espeland, Norway 18 D2 60 23N 5 28 E
Espelkamp, Germany 30 C4 52 24N 8 36 E
Espenberg, C., U.S.A. 144 C7 66 33N 163 36W
Esperança, Amazonas, Brazil 168 D4 4 24 S 69 52W
Esperança, Paraíba, Brazil 170 C4 7 1 S 35 51W
Esperance, Australia 125 F3 33 45 S 121 55 E
Esperance, C., Solomon Is. 133 M10 9 15 S 159 43 E
Esperance B., Australia 125 F3 33 48 S 121 55 E
Esperance B., St. Lucia 165 f 14 4N 60 55W
Esperantinópolis, Brazil 170 B3 4 53 S 44 53W
Esperanza, Santa Cruz, Argentina 176 D2 51 1 S 70 49W
Esperanza, Santa Fe, Argentina 174 C3 31 29 S 61 3W
Esperanza, Agusan del S., Phil. 81 G5 8 43N 125 36 E
Esperanza, Masbate, Phil. 81 F5 11 45N 124 3 E
Esperanza, Puerto Rico 165 d 18 6N 65 28W
Espéraza, France 28 F6 42 56N 2 14 E
Espevær, Norway 18 E2 59 35N 5 7 E
Espichel, C., Portugal 43 G1 38 22N 9 16W
Espiel, Spain 43 G5 38 11N 5 1W
Espigão, Serra do, Brazil 175 B5 26 35 S 50 30W
Espinal, Colombia 168 C3 4 9N 74 53W
Espinar, Peru 172 C3 14 51 S 71 24W
Espinazo, Sierra del = Espinhaço, Serra do, Brazil 171 E3 17 30 S 43 30W
Espinhaço, Serra do, Brazil 171 E3 17 30 S 43 30W
Espinho, Portugal 42 D2 41 1N 8 38W
Espinilho, Serra do, Brazil 175 B5 28 30 S 55 0W
Espinosa de los Monteros, Spain 42 B7 43 5N 3 34W
Espírito Santo □, Brazil 171 F3 20 0 S 40 45W
Espíritu Santo, Vanuatu 133 E4 15 15 S 166 50 E
Espíritu Santo, B. del, Mexico 163 D7 19 15N 87 0W
Espíritu Santo, I., Mexico 162 C2 24 30N 110 23W
Espita, Mexico 163 C7 21 1N 88 19W
Espiye, Turkey 101 B8 40 56N 38 43 E
Esplanada, Brazil 171 D4 11 47 S 37 57W
Espluga de Francolí, Spain 40 D6 41 24N 1 7 E
Espoo, Finland 15 F21 60 12N 24 40 E
Esprels, France 32 A2 47 32N 6 22 E
Espuña, Sierra de, Spain 41 H3 37 51N 1 35W
Espungabera, Mozam. 117 C5 20 29 S 32 45 E
Esquel, Argentina 176 B2 42 55 S 71 20W
Esquimalt, Canada 142 D4 48 26N 123 25W
Esquina, Argentina 174 C4 30 0 S 59 30W
Essandsjøen, Norway 18 A8 63 0N 12 0 E
Essaouira, Morocco 110 B3 31 32N 9 42W
Essebie, Dem. Rep. of the Congo 118 B3 2 58N 30 40 E
Essen, Belgium 24 C4 51 28N 4 28 E
Essen, Germany 30 D3 51 28N 7 2 E
Essendon, Mt., Australia 125 E3 25 0 S 120 29 E
Essequibo →, Guyana 169 B6 6 50N 58 30W
Essex, Canada 150 D2 42 10N 82 49W
Essex, Calif., U.S.A. 161 L11 34 44N 115 15W
Essex, N.Y., U.S.A. 151 B11 44 19N 73 21W
Essex □, U.K. 21 F8 51 54N 0 27 E
Essex Junction, U.S.A. 151 B11 44 29N 73 7W
Esslingen, Germany 31 G5 48 44N 9 18 E
Essonne □, France 27 D9 48 30N 2 20 E
Estaca de Bares, C. de, Spain 42 B3 43 46N 7 42W
Estadilla, Spain 40 C5 42 4N 0 16 E
Estados, I. de Los, Argentina 176 D4 54 40 S 64 30W
Estagel, France 28 F6 42 47N 2 40 E
Eşţahbānāt, Iran 97 D7 29 8N 54 4 E
Estância, Brazil 170 D4 11 16 S 37 26W
Estancia, U.S.A. 159 J10 34 46N 106 4W
Estancia Cameron, Chile 176 D3 53 38 S 69 39W
Estārm, Iran 97 D8 28 21N 58 21 E
Estarreja, Portugal 42 E2 40 45N 8 35W
Estats, Pic d', Spain 40 C6 42 40N 1 24 E
Estavayer-le-Lac, Switz. 32 C3 46 51N 6 51 E
Estcourt, S. Africa 117 D4 29 0 S 29 53 E
Este, Italy 45 C8 45 14N 11 39 E
Estelí, Nic. 164 D2 13 9N 86 22W
Estella, Spain 40 C2 42 40N 2 0W
Estellencs, Spain 38 B3 39 39N 2 29 E
Estena →, Spain 43 F6 39 23N 4 44W
Estepa, Spain 43 H6 37 17N 4 52W
Estepona, Spain 43 J5 36 24N 5 7W
Esterhazy, Canada 143 C8 50 37N 102 5W
Esterias, C., Gabon 114 B1 0 40N 9 20 E
Esternay, France 27 D10 48 44N 3 33 E
Esterri d'Aneu, Spain 40 C6 42 38N 1 5 E
Estevan, Canada 143 D8 49 10N 102 59W
Estevan Group, Canada 142 C3 53 3N 129 38W
Estherville, U.S.A. 154 D7 43 24N 94 50W
Estill, U.S.A. 152 C8 32 45N 81 15W
Estissac, France 27 D10 48 16N 3 48 E
Eston, Canada 143 C7 51 8N 108 40W
Estonia ■, Europe 15 G21 58 30N 25 30 E
Estoril, Portugal 43 G1 38 42N 9 23W
Estouk, Mali 113 B5 18 14N 1 2 E
Estrela, Serra da, Portugal 42 E3 40 10N 7 45W
Estrella, Spain 43 G7 38 25N 3 35W
Estremoz, Portugal 43 G3 38 51N 7 39W
Estrondo, Serra do, Brazil 170 C2 7 20 S 48 0W
Esztergom, Hungary 53 D8 47 47N 18 44 E
Et Tîdra, Mauritania 112 B1 19 45N 16 20W
Etah, India 93 F8 27 35N 78 40 E
Étain, France 27 C12 49 13N 5 38 E
Étampes, France 27 D9 48 26N 2 10 E
Etanga, Namibia 116 B1 17 55 S 13 0 E
Étaples, France 27 B8 50 30N 1 39 E
Etawah, India 93 F8 26 48N 79 6 E
Etawney L., Canada 143 B9 57 50N 96 50W
Ete, Nigeria 113 D6 7 2N 7 28 E
Etéké, Gabon 114 C2 1 29 S 11 35 E
Ethel, U.S.A. 160 D4 46 32N 122 46W
Ethel, Oued el →, Algeria 110 C4 28 31N 3 37W
Ethelbert, Canada 143 C8 51 32N 100 25W
Ethiopia ■, Africa 102 F3 8 0N 40 0 E
Ethiopian Highlands, Ethiopia 62 J7 10 0N 37 0 E
Etili, Turkey 51 G10 39 59N 26 54 E
Etive, L., U.K. 22 E3 56 29N 5 10W
Etna, Italy 47 E7 37 50N 14 55 E
Etna →, Norway 18 C6 60 49N 10 7 E
Etne, Norway 18 E2 59 40N 5 58 E
Etoile, Dem. Rep. of the Congo 119 E2 11 33 S 27 30 E
Etolin Strait, U.S.A. 144 F6 60 20N 165 15W
Etosha Nat. Park, Namibia 116 B2 19 0 S 16 0 E
Etosha Pan, Namibia 116 B2 18 40 S 16 30 E
Etoumbi, Congo 114 C2 0 1 S 14 57 E
Etowah, U.S.A. 149 H3 35 20N 84 32W
Étréchy, France 27 D9 48 30N 2 12 E
Étrépagny, France 27 C8 49 18N 1 36 E
Étretat, France 26 C7 49 42N 0 12 E
Etropole, Bulgaria 51 D8 42 50N 24 0 E
Ettelbruck, Lux. 24 E6 49 51N 6 5 E
Ettlingen, Germany 31 G4 48 56N 8 25 E
Ettrick Water →, U.K. 22 F6 55 31N 2 55W
Etuku, Dem. Rep. of the Congo 118 C2 3 42 S 25 45 E
Etulia, Moldova 53 E13 45 32N 28 27 E
Etzatlán, Mexico 162 C4 20 48N 104 5W
Etzná, Mexico 163 D6 19 35N 90 15W
Eu, France 26 B8 50 3N 1 26 E
Eua, Tonga 133 Q13 21 22 S 174 56W
Eubenangee Swamp Nat. Park, Australia 126 B4 16 25 S 146 1 E
Euboea = Évvoia, Greece 48 C6 38 30N 24 0 E
Euchareena, Australia 129 B8 32 57 S 149 6 E
Eucla, Australia 125 F4 31 41 S 128 52 E
Euclid, U.S.A. 150 E3 41 34N 81 32W
Euclides da Cunha, Brazil 170 D4 10 31 S 39 1W
Eucumbene, L., Australia 129 D8 36 2 S 148 40 E
Eudora, U.S.A. 155 J9 33 7N 91 16W
Eudunda, Australia 128 C3 34 12 S 139 7 E
Eufaula, Ala., U.S.A. 152 D4 31 54N 85 9W
Eufaula, Okla., U.S.A. 155 H7 35 17N 95 35W
Eufaula L., U.S.A. 155 H7 35 18N 95 21W
Eugene, U.S.A. 158 E2 44 5N 123 4W
Eugowra, Australia 129 B8 33 22 S 148 24 E
Eulo, Australia 127 D4 28 10 S 145 3 E
Eulonia, U.S.A. 152 D8 31 32N 81 26W
Eumungerie, Australia 129 A8 31 56 S 148 36 E
Eungella Nat. Park, Australia 126 C4 20 57 S 148 40 E
Eunice, La., U.S.A. 155 K8 30 30N 92 25W
Eunice, N. Mex., U.S.A. 155 J3 32 26N 103 10W
Eupen, Belgium 24 D6 50 37N 6 3 E
Euphrates = Furāt, Nahr al →, Asia 96 D5 31 0N 47 25 E
Eure □, France 26 C8 49 10N 1 0 E
Eure →, France 26 C8 49 18N 1 12 E
Eure-et-Loir □, France 26 D8 48 22N 1 30 E
Eureka, Canada 6 B3 80 0N 85 56W
Eureka, Calif., U.S.A. 158 F1 40 47N 124 9W
Eureka, Ill., U.S.A. 156 D7 40 43N 89 16W
Eureka, Kans., U.S.A. 155 G6 37 49N 96 17W
Eureka, Mo., U.S.A. 156 F6 38 30N 90 38W
Eureka, Mont., U.S.A. 158 B6 48 53N 115 3W
Eureka, Nev., U.S.A. 158 G5 39 31N 115 58W
Eureka, S.C., U.S.A. 152 B8 33 42N 81 46W
Eureka, S. Dak., U.S.A. 154 C5 45 46N 99 38W
Eureka, Mt., Australia 125 E3 26 35 S 121 35 E
Eurelia, Australia 128 B3 32 33 S 138 35 E
Eurinilla Cr. →, Australia 128 A4 30 53 S 140 11 E
Euroa, Australia 129 D6 36 44 S 145 35 E
Europa, Île, Ind. Oc. 121 G2 22 20 S 40 22 E
Europa, Picos de, Spain 42 B6 43 10N 4 49W
Europa, Pta. de, Gib. 43 J5 36 3N 5 21W
Europe 12 E10 50 0N 20 0 E
Europoort, Neths. 24 C4 51 57N 4 10 E
Euskirchen, Germany 30 E2 50 39N 6 48 E
Eustis, U.S.A. 149 L5 28 51N 81 41W
Euston, Australia 128 C5 34 30 S 142 46 E
Eutawville, U.S.A. 152 B9 33 24N 80 21W
Eutin, Germany 30 A6 54 8N 10 36 E
Eutsuk L., Canada 142 C3 53 20N 126 45W
Eva, Brazil 169 D6 3 9 S 59 56W
Evale, Angola 116 B2 16 33 S 15 44 E
Evanger, Norway 18 D3 60 39N 6 7 E
Evans, U.S.A. 154 E2 40 23N 104 41W
Evans, L., Canada 140 B4 50 50N 77 0W
Evans City, U.S.A. 150 F4 40 46N 80 4W
Evans Head, Australia 127 D5 29 7 S 153 27 E
Evans Mills, U.S.A. 151 B9 44 6N 75 48W
Evansburg, Canada 142 C5 53 36N 114 59W
Evansdale, U.S.A. 156 B4 42 30N 92 17W
Evanston, Ill., U.S.A. 157 B9 42 3N 87 41W
Evanston, Wyo., U.S.A. 158 F8 41 16N 110 58W
Evansville, Ill., U.S.A. 156 F7 38 5N 89 56W
Evansville, Ind., U.S.A. 157 G9 37 58N 87 35W
Evansville, Wis., U.S.A. 156 B7 42 47N 89 18W
Évaux-les-Bains, France 27 F9 46 12N 2 29 E
Evaz, Iran 97 E7 27 46N 53 59 E
Eveciler, Afyon, Turkey 49 C11 38 4N 29 54 E
Eveciler, Çanakkale, Turkey 49 B8 39 47N 26 44 E
Eveleth, U.S.A. 154 B8 47 28N 92 32W
Evensk, Russia 67 C16 62 12N 159 30 E
Evenstad, Norway 18 C8 61 25N 11 7 E
Everard, L., Australia 127 E2 31 30 S 135 0 E
Everard Ranges, Australia 125 E5 27 5 S 132 28 E
Everest, Mt., Nepal 93 E12 28 5N 86 58 E
Everett, Ga., U.S.A. 152 D8 31 24N 81 38W
Everett, Pa., U.S.A. 150 F6 40 1N 78 23W
Everett, Wash., U.S.A. 160 C4 47 59N 122 12W
Everglades, The, U.S.A. 149 N5 25 50N 81 0W
Everglades City, U.S.A. 149 N5 25 52N 81 23W
Everglades Nat. Park, U.S.A. 149 N5 25 30N 81 0W
Evergreen, Ala., U.S.A. 149 K2 31 26N 86 57W
Evergreen, Mont., U.S.A. 158 B6 48 9N 114 13W
Everöd, Sweden 17 J8 55 53N 14 5 E
Everton, Australia 129 D7 36 25 S 146 33 E
Evertsberg, Sweden 16 C7 61 8N 13 58 E
Evesham, U.K. 21 E6 52 6N 1 56W
Evfimía, Ayía, Greece 39 C2 38 18N 20 36 E
Évian-les-Bains, France 27 F13 46 24N 6 35 E
Evinayong, Eq. Guin. 114 B2 1 26N 10 35 E
Évinos →, Greece 48 C3 38 27N 21 40 E
Évisa, France 29 F12 42 15N 8 48 E
Evje, Norway 15 G12 58 36N 7 51 E
Evolène, Switz. 32 D4 46 7N 7 30 E
Évora, Portugal 43 G3 38 33N 7 57W
Évora □, Portugal 43 G3 38 33N 7 50W
Evowghlī, Iran 101 C11 38 43N 45 13 E
Évreux, France 26 C8 49 3N 1 8 E
Evritanía □, Greece 48 B3 39 5N 21 30 E
Évron, France 26 D6 48 10N 0 24W
Évros □, Greece 51 E10 41 10N 26 0 E
Évros →, Greece 100 B2 41 40N 26 34 E
Evrótas →, Greece 48 E4 36 50N 22 40 E
Évry, France 27 D9 48 38N 2 27 E
Évvoia, Greece 48 C6 38 30N 24 0 E
Évvoia □, Greece 48 C5 38 40N 23 40 E
Evxinoúpolis, Greece 48 B4 39 12N 22 42 E
Ewa, U.S.A. 145 K13 21 20N 158 3W
Ewa Beach, U.S.A. 145 K13 21 19N 158 1W
Ewasse, Papua N. G. 132 C6 5 19 S 151 1 E
Ewe, L., U.K. 22 D3 57 49N 5 38W
Ewing, Mo., U.S.A. 156 E5 40 6N 91 43W
Ewing, Nebr., U.S.A. 154 D5 42 16N 98 21W
Ewo, Congo 114 C2 0 48 S 14 45 E
Exaltación, Bolivia 173 C4 13 10 S 65 20W
Excelsior Springs, U.S.A. 156 E2 39 20N 94 13W
Excideuil, France 28 C5 45 20N 1 4 E
Exe →, U.K. 21 G4 50 41N 3 29W
Exeter, Canada 150 C3 43 21N 81 29W
Exeter, U.K. 21 G4 50 43N 3 31W
Exeter, Calif., U.S.A. 160 J7 36 18N 119 9W
Exeter, N.H., U.S.A. 151 D14 42 59N 70 57W
Exira, U.S.A. 156 C2 41 35N 94 52W
Exmoor, U.K. 21 F4 51 12N 3 45W
Exmouth, Australia 124 D1 21 54 S 114 10 E
Exmouth, U.K. 21 G4 50 37N 3 25W
Exmouth G., Australia 124 D1 22 15 S 114 15 E
Expedition Nat. Park, Australia 127 D4 25 41 S 149 7 E
Expedition Ra., Australia 126 C4 24 30 S 149 12 E
Experiment, U.S.A. 152 B5 33 17N 84 17W
Extremadura □, Spain 43 F4 39 30N 6 5W
Exuma Sound, Bahamas 164 B4 24 30N 76 20W
Eyak, U.S.A. 144 F11 60 32N 145 36W
Eyasi, L., Tanzania 118 C4 3 30 S 35 0 E
Eydehamn, Norway 18 F5 58 30N 8 53 E
Eye Pen., U.K. 22 C2 58 13N 6 10W
Eyemouth, U.K. 22 F6 55 52N 2 5W
Eygurande, France 27 G9 45 40N 2 26 E
Eyjafjallajökull, Iceland 11 D7 63 38N 19 36W
Eyjafjarðarsýsla □, Iceland 11 B8 65 30N 18 30W
Eyjafjörður, Iceland 11 A8 66 15N 18 30W
Eymet, France 28 D4 44 40N 0 25 E
Eymoutiers, France 28 C5 45 40N 1 45 E
Eynesil, Turkey 101 B8 41 4N 39 9 E
Eyrarbakki, Iceland 11 D5 63 52N 21 9W
Eyre (North), L., Australia 127 D2 28 30 S 137 20 E
Eyre (South), L., Australia 127 D2 29 18 S 137 25 E
Eyre, L., Australia 122 F6 29 30 S 137 26 E
Eyre Mts., N.Z. 131 F3 45 25 S 168 25 E
Eyre Pen., Australia 127 E2 33 30 S 136 17 E
Eysturoy, Færoe Is. 14 E9 62 13N 6 54W
Eyvānkī, Iran 97 C6 35 24N 51 56 E
Ez Zeidab, Sudan 106 D3 17 25N 33 55 E
Ezcaray, Spain 40 C1 42 19N 3 0W
Ežerėlis, Lithuania 54 D10 54 53N 23 37 E
Ezhou, China 77 B10 30 23N 114 50 E
Ezine, Turkey 49 B8 39 48N 26 20 E
Ezmul, Mauritania 110 D1 22 15N 15 40W
Ezouza →, Cyprus 39 F8 34 44N 32 27 E

F

F.Y.R.O.M. = Macedonia ■, Europe 50 E5 41 53N 21 40 E
Fabala, Guinea 112 D3 9 44N 9 5W
Fabens, U.S.A. 159 L10 31 30N 106 10W
Fåberg, Norway 18 C7 61 10N 10 25 E
Fabero, Spain 42 C4 42 46N 6 37W
Fåborg, Denmark 17 J4 55 6N 10 15 E
Fabriano, Italy 45 E9 43 20N 12 54 E
Fabrīchnyy, Kazakstan 65 B8 43 9N 76 24 E
Făcăeni, Romania 53 F12 44 32N 27 53 E
Facatativá, Colombia 168 C3 4 49N 74 22W
Faceville, U.S.A. 152 E5 30 45N 84 38W
Fachi, Niger 109 E2 18 6N 11 34 E
Facundo, Argentina 176 C3 45 18 S 69 58W
Fada, Chad 109 E4 17 13N 21 34 E
Fada-n-Gourma, Burkina Faso 113 C5 12 10N 0 30 E
Fadd, Hungary 52 D3 46 28N 18 49 E
Faddeyevskiy, Ostrov, Russia 67 B15 76 0N 144 0 E
Faddor, Sudan 107 F3 8 7N 32 17 E
Fadghāmī, Syria 101 E9 35 53N 40 52 E
Fadlab, Sudan 106 D3 17 42N 34 2 E
Faenza, Italy 45 D8 44 17N 11 53 E
Færingehavn = Kangerluarsoruseq, Greenland 10 E5 63 45N 51 27W
Færoe Is. = Føroyar, Atl. Oc. 14 F9 62 0N 7 0W
Fafa, Mali 113 B5 15 22N 0 48 E
Fafe, Portugal 42 D2 41 27N 8 11W
Fagam, Nigeria 113 C7 11 1N 10 1 E
Făgăras, Romania 53 E9 45 48N 24 58 E
Făgăras, Munţii, Romania 53 E9 45 40N 24 40 E
Fågelmara, Sweden 17 H9 56 16N 15 58 E
Fagerheim, Norway 18 D4 60 26N 7 46 E
Fagerhult, Sweden 17 G9 57 8N 15 40 E
Fagernes, Norway 18 D6 60 59N 9 14 E
Fagersta, Sweden 16 D9 60 1N 15 46 E
Făget, Romania 52 E7 45 52N 22 10 E
Făget, Munţii, Romania 53 C8 47 40N 23 10 E
Fagnano, L., Argentina 176 D3 54 30 S 68 0W
Fagnières, France 27 D11 48 58N 4 20 E
Faguibine, L., Mali 112 B4 16 45N 4 0W
Fahlīān, Iran 97 D6 30 11N 51 28 E
Fahraj, Kermān, Iran 97 D8 29 0N 59 0 E
Fahraj, Yazd, Iran 97 D7 31 46N 54 36 E
Fai Tsi Long Archipelago, Vietnam 76 G6 21 0N 107 30 E
Faial, Azores 9 d1 38 34N 28 42W
Faial, Madeira 9 c 32 47N 16 53W
Faial, Canal do, Azores 9 d1 38 33N 28 35W
Faido, Switz. 33 D7 46 29N 8 48 E
Fair Haven, U.S.A. 148 D9 43 36N 73 16W
Fair Hd., U.K. 23 A5 55 14N 6 9W
Fair Isle, U.K. 19 B6 59 32N 1 40W
Fair Oaks, U.S.A. 160 G5 38 39N 121 16W
Fairbank, U.S.A. 156 B4 42 38N 92 3W
Fairbanks, Alaska, U.S.A. 144 D11 64 51N 147 43W
Fairbanks, Fla., U.S.A. 152 F7 29 44N 82 16W
Fairborn, U.S.A. 157 E12 39 49N 84 2W
Fairburn, U.S.A. 152 B5 33 34N 84 35W
Fairbury, Ill., U.S.A. 157 D8 40 45N 88 31W
Fairbury, Nebr., U.S.A. 154 E6 40 8N 97 11W
Fairfax, Ohio, U.S.A. 157 E12 39 5N 83 37W
Fairfax, S.C., U.S.A. 152 C8 32 59N 81 15W
Fairfax, Vt., U.S.A. 151 B11 44 40N 73 1W
Fairfield, Australia 129 B9 33 53 S 150 57 E
Fairfield, Ala., U.S.A. 149 J2 33 29N 86 55W
Fairfield, Calif., U.S.A. 160 G4 38 15N 122 3W
Fairfield, Conn., U.S.A. 151 E11 41 9N 73 16W
Fairfield, Idaho, U.S.A. 158 E6 43 21N 114 44W
Fairfield, Ill., U.S.A. 157 F8 38 23N 88 22W
Fairfield, Iowa, U.S.A. 156 D5 40 56N 91 57W
Fairfield, Ohio, U.S.A. 157 E12 39 21N 84 34W
Fairfield, Tex., U.S.A. 155 K7 31 44N 96 10W
Fairford, Canada 143 C9 51 37N 98 38W
Fairhope, U.S.A. 149 K2 30 31N 87 54W
Fairlie, N.Z. 131 E5 44 5 S 170 49 E
Fairmead, U.S.A. 160 H6 37 5N 120 10W
Fairmont, Minn., U.S.A. 154 D7 43 39N 94 28W
Fairmont, W. Va., U.S.A. 148 F5 39 29N 80 9W
Fairmont, Calif., U.S.A. 161 L8 34 45N 118 26W
Fairmount, N.Y., U.S.A. 151 C8 43 5N 76 12W

Finley 213

Fairplay, *U.S.A.* 159 G11 39 15N 106 2W
Fairport, *U.S.A.* 150 C7 43 6N 77 27W
Fairport Harbor, *U.S.A.* 150 E3 41 45N 81 17W
Fairview, *Canada* 142 B5 56 5N 118 25W
Fairview, *Mont., U.S.A.* 154 B2 47 51N 104 3W
Fairview, *Okla., U.S.A.* 155 G5 36 16N 98 29W
Fairweather, Mt., *U.S.A.* 142 B1 58 55N 137 32W
Faisalabad, *Pakistan* 91 C4 31 30N 73 5 E
Faith, *U.S.A.* 154 C3 45 2N 102 2W
Faizabad, *India* 93 F10 26 45N 82 10 E
Faizpur, *India* 94 D2 21 14N 75 49 E
Fajã Grande, *Azores* 9 d2 39 27N 31 16W
Fajardo, *Puerto Rico* 165 d 18 20N 65 39W
Fajr, W. →, *Si. Arabia* 96 D3 29 10N 38 10 E
Fakenham, *U.K.* 20 E8 52 51N 0 51 E
Fåker, *Sweden* 16 A8 63 0N 14 34 E
Fakfak, *Indonesia* 83 B4 2 55 S 132 18 E
Fakfak, Peg., *Indonesia* 83 B4 2 50 S 132 20 E
Fakiya, *Bulgaria* 51 D11 42 10N 27 6 E
Fakobli, *Ivory C.* 112 D3 7 23N 7 23W
Fakse, *Denmark* 17 J6 55 15N 12 8 E
Fakse Bugt, *Denmark* 17 J6 55 11N 12 15 E
Fakse Ladeplads, *Denmark* 17 J6 55 11N 12 9 E
Faku, *China* 75 C12 42 32N 123 21 E
Falaba, *S. Leone* 112 D2 9 54N 11 22W
Falaise, *France* 26 D6 48 54N 0 12W
Falaise, Mui, *Vietnam* 86 C5 19 6N 105 45 E
Falakrón Óros, *Greece* 50 E7 41 15N 23 58 E
Falam, *Burma* 90 D4 23 0N 93 45 E
Falces, *Spain* 40 C3 42 24N 1 48W
Fălciu, *Romania* 53 D13 46 17N 28 7 E
Falcó, C. des, *Spain* 38 D1 38 50N 1 23 E
Falcón □, *Venezuela* 168 A4 11 0N 69 50W
Falcon, C., *Algeria* 111 A4 35 50N 0 50W
Falcón, Presa, *Mexico* 163 B5 26 35N 99 10W
Falcon Lake, *Canada* 143 D9 49 42N 95 15W
Falcon Reservoir, *U.S.A.* 155 M5 26 34N 99 10W
Falconara Marittima, *Italy* 45 E10 43 37N 13 24 E
Falcone, C. del, *Italy* 46 B1 40 58N 8 12 E
Falconer, *U.S.A.* 150 D5 42 7N 79 13W
Faléa, *Mali* 112 C2 12 16N 11 17W
Falefa, *Samoa* 133 W24 13 54 S 171 31W
Falelatai, *Samoa* 133 W24 13 55 S 171 59W
Falelima, *Samoa* 133 W23 13 32 S 172 41W
Falémé →, *Senegal* 112 C2 14 46N 12 14W
Falenki, *Russia* 64 B3 58 22N 51 35 E
Falerum, *Sweden* 17 F10 58 8N 16 13 E
Faleshty = Fălești, *Moldova* 53 C12 47 32N 27 44 E
Fălești, *Moldova* 53 C12 47 32N 27 44 E
Falfurrias, *U.S.A.* 155 M5 27 14N 98 9W
Falher, *Canada* 142 B5 55 44N 117 15W
Falirakí, *Greece* 38 E12 36 22N 28 12 E
Falkenberg, *Germany* 30 D9 51 35N 13 14 E
Falkenberg, *Sweden* 17 H6 56 54N 12 30 E
Falkensee, *Germany* 30 C9 52 34N 13 4 E
Falkirk, *U.K.* 22 F5 56 0N 3 47W
Falkirk □, *U.K.* 22 F5 55 58N 3 49W
Falkland, *U.K.* 22 E5 56 16N 3 12W
Falkland, East, I., *Falk. Is.* 176 D5 51 40 S 58 30W
Falkland, West, I., *Falk. Is.* 176 D4 51 40 S 60 0W
Falkland Is. □, *Atl. Oc.* 9 f 51 30 S 59 0W
Falkland Sd., *Falk. Is.* 9 f 52 0 S 60 0W
Falkonéra, *Greece* 48 E5 36 50N 23 52 E
Falköping, *Sweden* 17 F7 58 12N 13 33 E
Fall River, *U.S.A.* 151 E13 41 43N 71 10W
Fällanden, *Switz.* 33 B7 47 22N 8 38 E
Fallbrook, *U.S.A.* 161 M9 33 23N 117 15W
Fallon, *U.S.A.* 158 G4 39 28N 118 47W
Falls City, *U.S.A.* 154 E7 40 3N 95 36W
Falls Creek, *U.S.A.* 150 E6 41 9N 78 48W
Falmouth, *Jamaica* 164 a 18 30N 77 40W
Falmouth, *U.K.* 21 G2 50 9N 5 5W
Falmouth, *Ky., U.S.A.* 157 F12 38 41N 84 20W
Falmouth, *Mass., U.S.A.* 151 E14 41 33N 70 37W
Falsa, Pta., *Mexico* 162 B1 27 51N 115 3W
False B., *S. Africa* 116 E2 34 15 S 18 40 E
False Divi Pt., *India* 95 G5 15 43N 80 50 E
False Pass, *U.S.A.* 144 J7 54 51N 163 25W
False Pt., *India* 94 D8 20 18N 86 48 E
Falso, C., *Honduras* 164 C3 15 12N 83 21W
Falster, *Denmark* 17 K5 54 45N 11 55 E
Falsterbo, *Sweden* 15 J15 55 23N 12 50 E
Fălticeni, *Romania* 53 C11 47 21N 26 20 E
Falun, *Sweden* 16 D9 60 37N 15 37 E
Famagusta, *Cyprus* 39 E9 35 8N 33 55 E
Famagusta Bay, *Cyprus* 39 E10 35 15N 34 0 E
Famatina, Sierra de, *Argentina* 174 B2 27 30 S 68 0W
Family L., *Canada* 143 C9 51 54N 95 27W
Famoso, *U.S.A.* 161 K7 35 37N 119 12W
Fan Xian, *China* 74 G8 35 55N 115 38 E
Fana, *Mali* 112 C3 13 0N 6 56W
Fanad Hd., *Ireland* 23 A4 55 17N 7 38W
Fanahammaren, *Norway* 18 D2 60 16N 5 20 E
Fanárion, *Greece* 48 B3 39 24N 21 47 E
Fandriana, *Madag.* 117 C8 20 14 S 47 21 E
Fang, *Thailand* 76 H2 19 55N 99 13 E
Fang Xian, *China* 77 A8 32 3N 110 40 E
Fangaga, *Sudan* 106 D4 17 40N 37 50 E
Fangak, *Sudan* 107 F3 9 4N 30 53 E
Fangchang, *China* 77 B12 31 5N 118 4 E
Fangcheng, *China* 74 H7 33 18N 112 59 E
Fangchenggang, *China* 76 G7 21 42N 108 21 E
Fangliao, *Taiwan* 77 F13 22 22N 120 38 E
Fangshan, *China* 74 E6 38 3N 111 25 E
Fangzi, *China* 75 F10 36 33N 119 10 E
Fani i Madh →, *Albania* 50 E4 41 56N 20 16 E
Fanjakana, *Madag.* 117 C8 21 10 S 46 53 E
Fanjiatun, *China* 75 C13 43 40N 125 15 E
Fanling, *China* 69 F11 22 30N 114 8 E
Fannich, L., *U.K.* 22 D4 57 38N 4 59W
Fannrem, *Norway* 18 A6 63 16N 9 50 E
Fannūj, *Iran* 97 E8 26 35N 59 38 E
Fanø, *Denmark* 17 J2 55 25N 8 25 E
Fano, *Italy* 45 E10 43 50N 13 1 E
Fanshi, *China* 74 E7 39 12N 113 20 E
Fao = Al Fāw, *Iraq* 97 D6 30 0N 48 30 E
Faqirwali, *Pakistan* 92 E5 29 27N 73 0 E
Fâqûs, *Egypt* 106 H7 30 44N 31 47 E
Fara in Sabina, *Italy* 45 F9 42 12N 12 43 E
Faradje, *Dem. Rep. of the Congo* 118 B2 3 50N 29 45 E
Farafangana, *Madag.* 117 C8 22 49 S 47 50 E
Farâfra, El Wâhât el-, *Egypt* 106 B2 27 15N 28 20 E
Farāh, *Afghan.* 91 B1 32 20N 62 7 E
Farāh □, *Afghan.* 91 B1 32 25N 62 10 E
Farahalana, *Madag.* 117 A9 14 26 S 50 10 E
Faraid, Gebel, *Egypt* 106 C4 23 33N 35 19 E
Farako, *Ivory C.* 112 D4 10 45N 6 50W
Faramana, *Burkina Faso* 112 C4 11 56N 4 45W
Faranah, *Guinea* 112 C2 10 3N 10 45W
Farap, *Turkmenistan* 65 D1 39 9N 63 36 E
Farasān, Jazā'ir, *Si. Arabia* 98 C3 16 45N 41 55 E
Farasan Is. = Farasān, Jazā'ir, *Si. Arabia* 98 C3 16 45N 41 55 E
Faratsiho, *Madag.* 117 B8 19 24 S 46 57 E
Farbarachi, *Somali Rep.* 120 D3 2 30N 45 30 E
Fardes →, *Spain* 43 H7 37 35N 3 0W
Fareham, *U.K.* 21 G6 50 51N 1 11W
Farewell, *U.S.A.* 144 E9 62 31N 153 54W
Farewell, C., *N.Z.* 131 A7 40 29 S 172 43 E
Farewell C. = Nunap Isua, *Greenland* 10 F6 59 48N 43 55W
Farewell Spit, *N.Z.* 131 A8 40 35 S 173 0 E
Färgelanda, *Sweden* 17 F5 58 34N 12 0 E
Farghona, *Uzbekistan* 66 E8 40 23N 71 19 E
Farghonskaya Dolina, *Uzbekistan* 65 C5 40 50N 71 30 E
Fargo, *Ga., U.S.A.* 152 E7 30 41N 82 34W
Fargo, *N. Dak., U.S.A.* 154 B6 46 53N 96 48W
Fār'iah, W. al →, *West Bank* 103 C4 32 12N 35 27 E
Faribault, *U.S.A.* 154 C8 44 18N 93 16W
Faridabad, *India* 92 E6 28 26N 77 19 E
Faridkot, *India* 92 D6 30 44N 74 45 E
Faridpur, *Bangla.* 90 D2 23 15N 89 55 E
Faridpur, *India* 93 E8 28 13N 79 33 E
Fārigh, W. al →, *Libya* 108 B3 30 28N 20 44 E
Färila, *Sweden* 16 C9 61 48N 15 50 E
Farim, *Guinea-Biss.* 112 C1 12 27N 15 9W
Farīmān, *Iran* 97 C8 35 40N 59 49 E
Farina, *Australia* 127 E2 30 3 S 138 15 E
Farinha →, *Brazil* 170 C2 6 51 S 47 30W
Fariones, Pta., *Canary Is.* 9 e2 29 13N 13 28W
Fâriskûr, *Egypt* 106 H7 31 20N 31 43 E
Färjestaden, *Sweden* 17 H10 56 39N 16 27 E
Farkadhón, *Greece* 48 B4 39 36N 22 4 E
Farkhor = Parkhar, *Tajikistan* 65 E4 37 30N 69 34 E
Farleigh, *Australia* 126 K7 21 4 S 149 8 E
Farley, *U.S.A.* 156 B6 42 27N 91 0W
Farmakonisi, *Greece* 49 D9 37 17N 27 5 E
Farmer City, *U.S.A.* 157 D8 40 15N 88 39W
Farmersburg, *U.S.A.* 157 E9 39 15N 87 23W
Farmerville, *U.S.A.* 155 J8 32 47N 92 24W
Farmingdale, *U.S.A.* 151 F10 40 12N 74 10W
Farmington, *Canada* 142 B4 55 54N 120 30W
Farmington, *Calif., U.S.A.* 160 H6 37 55N 120 59W
Farmington, *Ga., U.S.A.* 152 B6 33 47N 83 26W
Farmington, *Ill., U.S.A.* 156 D7 40 42N 90 0W
Farmington, *Iowa, U.S.A.* 156 D5 40 38N 91 44W
Farmington, *Maine, U.S.A.* 149 C10 44 40N 70 9W
Farmington, *Mo., U.S.A.* 155 G9 37 47N 90 25W
Farmington, *N.H., U.S.A.* 151 C13 43 24N 71 4W
Farmington, *N. Mex., U.S.A.* 159 H9 36 44N 108 12W
Farmington, *Utah, U.S.A.* 158 F8 41 0N 111 12W
Farmington →, *U.S.A.* 151 E12 41 51N 72 38W
Farmland, *U.S.A.* 157 D11 40 15N 85 5W
Farmville, *U.S.A.* 148 G6 37 18N 78 24W
Färnäs, *Sweden* 16 D8 61 0N 14 39 E
Farne Is., *U.K.* 20 B6 55 38N 1 37W
Farnham, *Canada* 151 A12 45 17N 72 59W
Farnham, Mt., *Canada* 142 C5 50 29N 116 30W
Faro, *Brazil* 169 D6 2 10 S 56 39W
Faro, *Canada* 138 B6 62 11N 133 22W
Faro, *Portugal* 43 H3 37 2N 7 55W
Fårö, *Sweden* 15 H18 57 55N 19 5 E
Faro □, *Portugal* 43 H2 37 12N 8 10W
Faro, Réserve de, *Cameroon* 114 A2 8 15N 12 37 E
Fårösund, *Sweden* 17 G13 57 52N 19 2 E
Farquhar, C., *Australia* 125 D1 23 50 S 113 36 E
Farquhar Is., *Seychelles* 121 F4 11 0 S 52 0 E
Farrars Cr. →, *Australia* 126 D3 25 35 S 140 43 E
Farrāshband, *Iran* 97 D7 28 57N 52 5 E
Farrell, *U.S.A.* 150 E4 41 13N 80 30W
Farrell Flat, *Australia* 128 B3 33 48 S 138 48 E
Farrokhī, *Iran* 97 C8 33 50N 59 31 E
Farruch, C. = Ferrutx, C., *Spain* 38 B4 39 47N 3 21 E
Fārs □, *Iran* 97 D7 29 30N 55 0 E
Fársala, *Greece* 48 B4 39 17N 22 23 E
Fārsī, *Afghan.* 91 B1 33 47N 63 15 E
Farsø, *Denmark* 17 H3 56 46N 9 19 E
Farson, *U.S.A.* 158 E9 42 6N 109 27W
Farsund, *Norway* 15 G12 58 5N 6 55 E
Fartak, Râs, *Si. Arabia* 96 D2 28 5N 34 34 E
Fartak, Ra's, *Yemen* 99 D6 15 38N 52 15 E
Fârțănești, *Romania* 53 E12 45 49N 27 59 E
Fartura, Serra da, *Brazil* 175 B5 26 21 S 52 52W
Faru, *Nigeria* 113 C6 12 48N 6 12 E
Fārūj, *Iran* 97 B8 37 14N 58 14 E
Fårup, *Denmark* 17 H3 56 33N 9 51 E
Farvel, Kap = Nunap Isua, *Greenland* 10 F6 59 48N 43 55W
Farwell, *U.S.A.* 155 H3 34 23N 103 2W
Faryāb □, *Afghan.* 65 E2 36 0N 65 0 E
Fasā, *Iran* 97 D7 29 0N 53 39 E
Fasano, *Italy* 47 B10 40 50N 17 22 E
Fashoda, *Sudan* 107 F3 9 50N 32 2 E
Fassa, *Mali* 112 C3 13 26N 8 15 E
Fastiv, *Ukraine* 59 G5 50 7N 29 57 E
Fastov = Fastiv, *Ukraine* 59 G5 50 7N 29 57 E
Fatagar, Tanjung, *Indonesia* 83 B4 2 46 S 131 57 E
Fataka, *Solomon Is.* 123 C12 11 55 S 170 12 E
Fatehabad, *Haryana, India* 92 E6 29 31N 75 27 E
Fatehabad, *Ut. P., India* 92 F8 27 1N 78 19 E
Fatehgarh, *India* 93 F8 27 25N 79 35 E
Fatehpur, *Bihar, India* 93 G11 24 38N 85 14 E
Fatehpur, *Raj., India* 92 F6 28 0N 74 40 E
Fatehpur, *Ut. P., India* 93 G9 25 56N 81 13 E
Fatehpur, *Ut. P., India* 93 F9 27 10N 81 13 E
Fatehpur Sikri, *India* 92 F6 27 6N 77 40 E
Fatesh, *Russia* 59 F8 52 8N 35 57 E
Fathai, *Sudan* 107 F3 8 5N 31 48 E
Fatick, *Senegal* 112 C1 14 19N 16 27W
Fatima, *Canada* 141 C7 47 24N 61 53W
Fátima, *Portugal* 43 F2 39 37N 8 39W
Fatoya, *Guinea* 112 C3 11 37N 9 10W
Fatsa, *Turkey* 100 B7 41 2N 37 31 E
Faucille, Col de la, *France* 27 F13 46 22N 6 2 E
Faulkton, *U.S.A.* 154 C5 45 2N 99 8W
Faulquemont, *France* 27 C13 49 3N 6 36 E
Faure I., *Australia* 125 E1 25 52 S 113 50 E
Făurei, *Romania* 53 E12 45 6N 27 19 E
Fauresmith, *S. Africa* 116 D4 29 44 S 25 17 E
Fauro, *Solomon Is.* 133 L9 6 55 S 156 7 E
Fauske, *Norway* 14 C16 67 17N 15 25 E
Fåvang, *Norway* 18 C7 61 27N 10 11 E
Favânia, *Brazil* 169 D7 3 7 S 51 48W
Favara, *Italy* 46 E6 37 19N 13 39 E
Favàritx, C. de, *Spain* 38 B5 40 0N 4 15 E
Faverges, *France* 29 C10 45 45N 6 17 E
Favignana, *Italy* 46 E5 37 56N 12 20 E
Favignana, I., *Italy* 46 E5 37 56N 12 19 E
Fawcett, Pt., *Australia* 124 B5 11 46 S 130 2 E
Fawn →, *Canada* 140 A2 55 20N 87 35W
Fawnskin, *U.S.A.* 161 L10 34 16N 116 56W
Faxaflói, *Iceland* 11 C3 64 29N 23 0W
Faxälven →, *Sweden* 16 A10 63 13N 17 13 E
Faya-Largeau, *Chad* 109 E3 17 58N 19 6 E
Fayaoué, *Vanuatu* 133 K4 20 38 S 166 33 E
Fayd, *Si. Arabia* 96 E4 27 1N 42 52 E
Fayence, *France* 29 E10 43 38N 6 42 E
Fayette, *Ala., U.S.A.* 149 J2 33 41N 87 50W
Fayette, *Iowa, U.S.A.* 156 B5 42 51N 91 48W
Fayette, *Mo., U.S.A.* 156 E4 39 9N 92 41W
Fayette, *Ohio, U.S.A.* 157 C12 41 40N 84 20W
Fayetteville, *Ark., U.S.A.* 155 G7 36 4N 94 10W
Fayetteville, *Ga., U.S.A.* 152 B5 33 27N 84 27W
Fayetteville, *N.C., U.S.A.* 149 H6 35 3N 78 53W
Fayetteville, *Tenn., U.S.A.* 149 H2 35 9N 86 34W
Fayied, *Egypt* 106 H8 30 18N 32 16 E
Fayón, *Spain* 40 D5 41 15N 0 20 E
Fazao-Malfakassa, Parc Nat. de, *Togo* 113 D5 8 45N 0 50 E
Fazenda Libongo, *Angola* 115 D2 8 24 S 13 24 E
Fazenda Nova, *Brazil* 171 E1 16 11 S 50 48W
Fazilka, *India* 92 D6 30 27N 74 2 E
Fazilpur, *Pakistan* 92 E4 29 18N 70 29 E
Fdérik, *Mauritania* 110 D2 22 40N 12 45W
Feale →, *Ireland* 23 D2 52 27N 9 37W
Fear, C., *U.S.A.* 149 J7 33 50N 77 58W
Feather →, *U.S.A.* 158 G3 38 47N 121 36W
Feather Falls, *U.S.A.* 160 F5 39 36N 121 16W
Featherston, *N.Z.* 130 H4 41 6 S 175 20 E
Featherstone, *Zimbabwe* 119 F3 18 42 S 30 55 E
Fécamp, *France* 26 C7 49 45N 0 22 E
Feda, *Norway* 18 F3 58 17N 6 50 E
Fedala = Mohammedia, *Morocco* 110 B3 33 44N 7 21W
Federación, *Argentina* 174 C4 31 0 S 57 55W
Federal Capital Terr. □, *Nigeria* 113 D6 9 0N 7 10 E
Federal Way, *U.S.A.* 160 C4 47 18N 122 19W
Fedeshkūh, *Iran* 97 D7 28 49N 53 50 E
Fedje, *Norway* 18 D1 60 47N 4 43 E
Fehérgyarmat, *Hungary* 52 C7 47 58N 22 30 E
Fehmarn, *Germany* 30 A7 54 27N 11 7 E
Fehmarn Bælt, *Europe* 17 K5 54 35N 11 20 E
Fehmarn Belt = Fehmarn Bælt, *Europe* 17 K5 54 35N 11 20 E
Fei Xian, *China* 75 G9 35 18N 117 59 E
Feijó, *Brazil* 172 B3 8 9 S 70 21W
Feilding, *N.Z.* 130 G4 40 13 S 175 35 E
Feira de Santana, *Brazil* 171 D4 12 15 S 38 57W
Feiring, *Norway* 18 D8 60 30N 11 10 E
Feixi, *China* 77 B11 31 43N 117 59 E
Feixiang, *China* 74 F8 36 30N 114 45 E
Fejaj, Chott el, *Tunisia* 108 B1 33 52N 9 14 E
Fejér □, *Hungary* 52 C3 47 9N 18 30 E
Fejø, *Denmark* 17 K5 54 55N 11 30 E
Feke, *Turkey* 100 D6 37 48N 35 56 E
Fekete →, *Hungary* 52 E3 45 47N 18 15 E
Felanitx, *Spain* 38 B4 39 28N 3 9 E
Felda, *U.S.A.* 153 J8 26 34N 81 26W
Feldbach, *Austria* 34 E8 46 57N 15 52 E
Feldberg, *Baden-W., Germany* 31 H3 47 52N 8 0 E
Feldberg, *Mecklenburg-Vorpommern, Germany* 30 B9 53 20N 13 25 E
Feldkirch, *Austria* 34 D2 47 15N 9 37 E
Feldkirchen, *Austria* 34 E7 46 44N 14 6 E
Felicité, *Seychelles* 121 b 4 19 S 55 52 E
Felicity, *U.S.A.* 157 F12 38 51N 84 6W
Felipe Carrillo Puerto, *Mexico* 163 D7 19 38N 88 3W
Felixburg, *Zimbabwe* 117 B5 19 29 S 30 51 E
Felixlândia, *Brazil* 171 E3 18 47 S 44 55W
Felixstowe, *U.K.* 21 F9 51 58N 1 23 E
Felletin, *France* 28 C6 45 53N 2 11 E
Fellingsbro, *Sweden* 16 E9 59 26N 15 37 E
Fellsmere, *U.S.A.* 153 H9 27 46N 80 36W
Felton, *U.S.A.* 160 H4 37 3N 122 4W
Feltre, *Italy* 45 B8 46 1N 11 54 E
Femer Bælt = Fehmarn Bælt, *Europe* 17 K5 54 35N 11 20 E
Femø, *Denmark* 17 K5 54 58N 11 35 E
Femunden, *Norway* 15 E14 62 10N 11 53 E
Fen He →, *China* 74 G6 35 36N 110 42 E
Fene, *Spain* 42 B2 43 27N 8 9W
Fenelon Falls, *Canada* 150 B6 44 32N 78 45W
Fener Burnu, *Turkey* 49 E9 36 58N 27 18 E
Feneroa, *Ethiopia* 107 E4 13 5N 39 3 E
Feng Xian, *Jiangsu, China* 74 G9 34 43N 116 35 E
Feng Xian, *Shaanxi, China* 74 H4 33 54N 106 40 E
Fengári, *Greece* 51 F9 40 25N 25 32 E
Fengcheng, *Jiangxi, China* 77 C10 28 12N 115 48 E
Fengcheng, *Liaoning, China* 75 D13 40 28N 124 5 E
Fengfeng, *China* 74 F8 36 28N 114 8 E
Fenggang, *China* 76 D6 27 57N 107 47 E
Fenghua, *China* 77 C13 29 40N 121 25 E
Fenghuang, *China* 76 D7 27 57N 109 29 E
Fengkai, *China* 77 F8 23 24N 111 30 E
Fengkang, *Taiwan* 77 F13 22 12N 120 41 E
Fengle, *China* 77 B9 31 29N 112 29 E
Fenglin, *Taiwan* 77 F13 23 45N 121 26 E
Fengning, *China* 74 D9 41 10N 116 33 E
Fengqing, *China* 76 E2 24 38N 99 55 E
Fengqiu, *China* 74 G8 35 2N 114 25 E
Fengrun, *China* 75 E10 39 48N 118 8 E
Fengshan, *Guangxi Zhuangzu, China* 76 E7 24 39N 109 15 E
Fengshan, *Guangxi Zhuangzu, China* 76 E6 24 31N 107 3 E
Fengshan, *Taiwan* 77 F13 22 38N 120 21 E
Fengshun, *China* 77 F11 23 46N 116 10 E
Fengtai, *Anhui, China* 77 A11 32 50N 116 40 E
Fengtai, *Beijing, China* 74 E9 39 50N 116 18 E
Fengxian, *China* 77 B13 30 55N 121 26 E
Fengxiang, *China* 74 G4 34 29N 107 25 E
Fengxin, *China* 77 C10 28 41N 115 18 E
Fengyang, *China* 75 H9 32 51N 117 29 E
Fengyi, *China* 76 E3 25 37N 100 20 E
Fengyüan, *Taiwan* 77 E13 24 15N 120 35 E
Fengzhen, *China* 74 D7 40 25N 113 2 E
Feni Is., *Papua N. G.* 132 C7 4 0 S 153 40 E
Fennimore, *U.S.A.* 156 B6 42 59N 90 39W
Fenny, *Bangla.* 90 D3 22 55N 91 32 E
Feno, C. de, *France* 29 G12 41 58N 8 33 E
Fenoarivo, *Fianarantsoa, Madag.* 117 C8 21 43 S 46 24 E
Fenoarivo, *Fianarantsoa, Madag.* 117 C8 20 52 S 46 53 E
Fenoarivo Afovoany, *Madag.* 117 B8 18 26 S 46 34 E
Fenoarivo Atsinanana, *Madag.* 117 B8 17 22 S 49 25 E
Fens, The, *U.K.* 20 E7 52 38N 0 2W
Fensmark, *Denmark* 17 J5 55 17N 11 48 E
Fenton, *U.S.A.* 157 B13 42 48N 83 42W
Fenxi, *China* 74 F6 36 40N 111 31 E
Fenyang, *China* 74 F6 37 18N 111 48 E
Fenyi, *China* 77 D10 27 45N 114 47 E
Feodosiya, *Ukraine* 59 K8 45 2N 35 16 E
Fer, C. de, *Algeria* 111 A6 37 3N 7 10 E
Fera, *Solomon Is.* 133 M10 8 6 S 159 37 E
Ferdows, *Iran* 97 C8 33 58N 58 2 E
Fère-Champenoise, *France* 27 D10 48 45N 3 59 E
Fère-en-Tardenois, *France* 27 C10 49 10N 3 30 E
Ferentino, *Italy* 45 G10 41 42N 13 15 E
Ferfer, *Somali Rep.* 120 C3 5 4N 45 9 E
Fergana = Farghona, *Uzbekistan* 66 E8 40 23N 71 19 E
Fergana Range, *Asia* 65 C6 41 0N 73 50 E
Ferganskaya Dolina = Farghonskaya Dolina, *Uzbekistan* 65 C5 40 50N 71 30 E
Fergus, *Canada* 150 C4 43 43N 80 24W
Fergus Falls, *U.S.A.* 154 B6 46 17N 96 4W
Ferguson, *U.S.A.* 156 F6 38 45N 90 18W
Fergusson I., *Papua N. G.* 132 E6 9 30 S 150 45 E
Fériana, *Tunisia* 108 B1 34 59N 8 33 E
Feričanci, *Croatia* 52 E2 45 32N 18 0 E
Ferkane, *Algeria* 111 B6 34 37N 7 26 E
Ferkéssédougou, *Ivory C.* 112 D3 9 35N 5 6W
Ferlach, *Austria* 34 E7 46 32N 14 18 E
Ferland, *Canada* 140 B2 50 19N 88 27W
Ferlo, Vallée du, *Senegal* 112 B2 15 15N 14 15W
Ferlo-Nord, Réserve de Faune du, *Senegal* 112 B2 15 43N 14 0W
Ferlo-Sud, Réserve de Faune du, *Senegal* 112 B2 15 43N 14 0W
Fermanagh □, *U.K.* 23 B4 54 21N 7 40W
Fermo, *Italy* 45 E10 43 9N 13 43 E
Fermont, *Canada* 141 B6 52 47N 67 5W
Fermoselle, *Spain* 42 D4 41 19N 6 27W
Fermoy, *Ireland* 23 D3 52 9N 8 16W
Fernán Nuñéz, *Spain* 43 H6 37 40N 4 44W
Fernández, *Argentina* 174 B3 27 55 S 63 50W
Fernandina, I., *Ecuador* 172 a 0 25 S 91 30W
Fernandina Beach, *U.S.A.* 152 E8 30 40N 81 27W
Fernando de Noronha, *Brazil* 170 B5 4 0 S 33 10W
Fernando Póo = Bioko, *Eq. Guin.* 113 E6 3 30N 8 40 E
Fernandópolis, *Brazil* 171 F1 20 16 S 50 14W
Ferndale, *U.S.A.* 160 B4 48 51N 122 36W
Fernie, *Canada* 142 D5 49 30N 115 5W
Fernlees, *Australia* 126 C4 23 51 S 148 7 E
Fernley, *U.S.A.* 158 G4 39 36N 119 15W
Feroke, *India* 95 J2 11 9N 75 46 E
Ferozepore = Firozpur, *India* 92 D6 30 55N 74 40 E
Férrai, *Greece* 51 F10 40 53N 26 10 E
Ferrandina, *Italy* 47 B9 40 29N 16 27 E
Ferrara, *Italy* 45 D8 44 50N 11 35 E
Ferrato, C., *Italy* 46 C2 39 18N 9 38 E
Ferreira do Alentejo, *Portugal* 43 G2 38 4N 8 6W
Ferreira Gomes, *Brazil* 170 A1 0 48N 51 8W
Ferreñafe, *Peru* 172 B2 6 42 S 79 50W
Ferrerías, *Spain* 38 B5 39 59N 4 1 E
Ferret, C., *France* 28 D2 44 38N 1 15W
Ferrette, *France* 27 E14 47 30N 7 20 E
Ferriday, *U.S.A.* 155 K9 31 38N 91 33W
Ferriere, *Italy* 44 D6 44 40N 9 30 E
Ferrières, *France* 27 D9 48 5N 2 48 E
Ferro, Capo, *Italy* 46 A2 41 9N 9 31 E
Ferrol, *Spain* 42 B2 43 29N 8 15W
Ferrol, Pen. de, *Peru* 172 B2 9 10S 78 35W
Ferron, *U.S.A.* 159 G8 39 5N 111 8W
Ferros, *Brazil* 171 E3 19 14 S 43 2W
Ferrutx, C., *Spain* 38 B4 39 47N 3 21 E
Ferryland, *Canada* 141 C9 47 2N 52 53W
Ferrysburg, *U.S.A.* 157 A10 43 5N 86 13W
Fertile, *U.S.A.* 154 B6 47 32N 96 17W
Fertőszentmiklós, *Hungary* 52 C1 47 35N 16 53 E
Fès, *Morocco* 110 B4 34 0N 5 0W
Feshi, *Dem. Rep. of the Congo* 115 D3 6 8 S 18 10 E
Fessenden, *U.S.A.* 154 B5 47 39N 99 38W
Festøy, *Norway* 18 B3 62 22N 6 19 E
Festus, *U.S.A.* 156 F6 38 13N 90 24W
Feté Bowé, *Senegal* 112 C2 14 56N 13 30W
Fetești, *Romania* 53 F12 44 22N 27 51 E
Fethiye, *Turkey* 49 E11 36 36N 29 6 E
Fethiye Körfezi, *Turkey* 49 E10 36 40N 28 50 E
Fetlar, *U.K.* 22 A8 60 36N 0 52W
Fetsund, *Norway* 18 E8 59 56N 11 10 E
Feuchten, *Austria* 33 B11 47 2N 10 44 E
Feuerthalen, *Switz.* 33 A7 47 37N 8 38 E
Feuilles →, *Canada* 139 C12 58 47N 70 4W
Feurs, *France* 29 C8 45 45N 4 13 E
Fevik, *Norway* 18 F5 58 22N 8 39 E
Feyẕābād, *Badākhshān, Afghan.* 65 E5 37 7N 70 33 E
Feyẕābād, *Fāryāb, Afghan.* 91 A2 36 17N 64 52 E
Fez = Fès, *Morocco* 110 B4 34 0N 5 0W
Fezzan, *Libya* 108 C2 27 0N 13 0 E
Fia, *Congo* 114 C2 3 25 S 14 49 E
Fiambalá, *Argentina* 174 B2 27 45 S 67 37W
Fianarantsoa, *Madag.* 117 C8 21 26 S 47 5 E
Fianarantsoa □, *Madag.* 117 B8 19 30 S 47 0 E
Fianga, *Cameroon* 109 G3 9 55N 15 9 E
Fiche, *Ethiopia* 107 F4 9 50N 38 46 E
Fichtelgebirge, *Germany* 31 E7 50 2N 11 55 E
Ficksburg, *S. Africa* 117 D4 28 51 S 27 53 E
Fidenza, *Italy* 44 D7 44 52N 10 3 E
Fiditi, *Nigeria* 113 D5 7 45N 3 53 E
Fidjeland, *Norway* 18 F3 58 57N 6 56 E
Field →, *Australia* 126 C2 23 48 S 138 0 E
Field I., *Australia* 124 B5 12 5 S 132 23 E
Fieni, *Romania* 53 E10 45 8N 25 25 E
Fier, *Albania* 50 F3 40 43N 19 33 E
Fierzë, *Albania* 50 D4 42 15N 20 1 E
Fiesch, *Switz.* 32 D6 46 25N 8 12 E
Fife □, *U.K.* 22 E5 56 16N 3 1W
Fife Ness, *U.K.* 22 E6 56 17N 2 35W
Fifth Cataract, *Sudan* 106 D3 18 22N 33 50 E
Figari, *France* 29 G13 41 29N 9 7 E
Figeac, *France* 28 D6 44 37N 2 2 E
Figeholm, *Sweden* 17 G10 57 22N 16 33 E
Figline Valdarno, *Italy* 45 E8 43 37N 11 28 E
Figtree, *Zimbabwe* 119 G2 20 22 S 28 20 E
Figueira Castelo Rodrigo, *Portugal* 42 E4 40 57N 6 58W
Figueira da Foz, *Portugal* 42 E2 40 7N 8 54W
Figueiró dos Vinhos, *Portugal* 42 F2 39 55N 8 16W
Figueres, *Spain* 40 C7 42 18N 2 58 E
Figuig, *Morocco* 111 B4 32 5N 1 11W
Fihaonana, *Madag.* 117 B8 18 36 S 47 12 E
Fiherenana, *Madag.* 117 B8 18 29 S 48 24 E
Fiherenana →, *Madag.* 117 C7 23 19 S 43 37 E
Fiji ■, *Pac. Oc.* 133 A2 17 20 S 179 0 E
Fik, *Ethiopia* 107 F5 8 10N 42 19 E
Fika, *Nigeria* 113 C7 11 15N 11 13 E
Filabres, Sierra de los, *Spain* 43 H8 37 13N 2 20W
Filabusi, *Zimbabwe* 117 C4 20 34 S 29 20 E
Filadelfia, *Bolivia* 172 C4 11 20 S 68 46W
Filadélfia, *Brazil* 170 C2 7 21 S 47 30W
Filadélfia, *Italy* 47 D9 38 47N 16 17 E
Fil'akovo, *Slovak Rep.* 35 C12 48 17N 19 50 E
Filey, *U.K.* 20 C7 54 12N 0 18W
Filey B., *U.K.* 20 C7 54 12N 0 15W
Filfla, *Malta* 38 F7 35 47N 14 24 E
Filiași, *Romania* 53 F8 44 32N 23 31 E
Filiátes, *Greece* 38 B10 39 38N 20 16 E
Filiatrá, *Greece* 48 D3 37 9N 21 35 E
Filicudi, *Italy* 47 D7 38 35N 14 33 E
Filim, *Oman* 99 B7 20 37N 58 12 E
Filingué, *Niger* 113 C5 14 21N 3 22 E
Filiourí →, *Greece* 51 E9 41 15N 25 40 E
Filipstad, *Sweden* 16 E8 59 43N 14 9 E
Filisur, *Switz.* 33 C9 46 41N 9 40 E
Fillefjell, *Norway* 18 C5 61 8N 8 10 E
Fillmore, *Calif., U.S.A.* 161 L8 34 24N 118 55W
Fillmore, *Utah, U.S.A.* 159 G7 38 58N 112 20W
Filótion, *Greece* 49 D7 37 3N 25 30 E
Filottrano, *Italy* 45 E10 43 26N 13 21 E
Filtu, *Ethiopia* 107 F5 5 8N 40 35 E
Fimi →, *Dem. Rep. of the Congo* 114 C3 3 1S 16 58 E
Fina, Réserve de, *Mali* 112 C3 13 15N 8 46W
Finale Emília, *Italy* 45 D8 44 50N 11 18 E
Finale Lígure, *Italy* 44 D5 44 10N 8 20 E
Fiñana, *Spain* 43 H8 37 10N 2 50W
Finch, *Canada* 151 A9 45 11N 75 7W
Finch Hatton, *Australia* 126 K6 20 25 S 148 39 E
Findhorn →, *U.K.* 22 D5 57 38N 3 38W
Findlay, *U.S.A.* 157 C13 41 2N 83 39W
Finger L., *Canada* 140 B1 53 33N 93 30W
Finger Lakes, *U.S.A.* 151 D8 42 40N 76 30W
Fíngoè, *Mozam.* 119 E3 14 55 S 31 50 E
Finike, *Turkey* 49 E12 36 21N 30 10 E
Finike Körfezi, *Turkey* 49 E12 36 17N 30 16 E
Finiq, *Albania* 50 G4 39 54N 20 3 E
Finistère □, *France* 26 D3 48 20N 4 0W
Finisterre = Fisterra, *Spain* 42 C1 42 54N 9 16W
Finisterre, C. = Fisterra, C., *Spain* 42 C1 42 50N 9 19W
Finisterre Ra., *Papua N. G.* 132 D4 6 0 S 146 30 E
Finke, *Australia* 126 D1 25 34 S 134 35 E
Finke Gorge Nat. Park, *Australia* 124 D5 24 8 S 132 49 E
Finland ■, *Europe* 14 E22 63 0N 27 0 E
Finland, G. of, *Europe* 15 G21 60 0N 26 0 E
Finlay →, *Canada* 142 B3 57 0N 125 10W
Finley, *Australia* 129 C6 35 38 S 145 35 E

Gal Tardo 215

Fox Valley, *Canada* **143 C7** 50 30N 109 25W
Foxboro, *U.S.A.* **151 D13** 42 4N 71 16W
Foxdale, *Australia* **126 J6** 20 22 S 148 35 E
Foxe Basin, *Canada* **139 B12** 66 0N 77 0W
Foxe Chan., *Canada* **139 B11** 65 0N 80 0W
Foxe Pen., *Canada* **139 B12** 65 0N 76 0W
Foxen, *Sweden* **16 E5** 59 25N 11 55 E
Foxton, *N.Z.* **130 G4** 40 29 S 175 18 E
Foyle, Lough, *U.K.* **23 A4** 55 7N 7 4W
Foynes, *Ireland* **23 D2** 52 37N 9 7W
Foz, *Spain* **42 B3** 43 33N 7 20W
Foz do Copeá, *Brazil* **169 D5** 3 52 S 63 19W
Foz do Cunene, *Angola* **116 B1** 17 15 S 11 48 E
Foz do Gregório, *Brazil* **172 B3** 6 47 S 70 44W
Foz do Iguaçu, *Brazil* **175 B5** 25 30 S 54 30W
Foz do Mamoriá, *Brazil* **168 D4** 2 27 S 66 32W
Foz do Riosinho, *Brazil* **172 B3** 7 11 S 71 50W
Frackville, *U.S.A.* **151 F8** 40 47N 76 14W
Fraga, *Spain* **40 D5** 41 32N 0 21 E
Fraile Muerto, *Uruguay* **175 C5** 32 31 S 54 32W
Framingham, *U.S.A.* **151 D13** 42 17N 71 25W
Framnes, *Iceland* **11 A6** 66 1N 20 26W
Frampol, *Poland* **55 H9** 50 41N 22 40 E
Franca, *Brazil* **171 F2** 20 33 S 47 30W
Francavilla al Mare, *Italy* **45 F11** 42 25N 14 17 E
Francavilla Fontana, *Italy* **47 B10** 40 32N 17 35 E
France ■, *Europe* **25 C5** 47 0N 3 0 E
Frances, *Australia* **128 D4** 36 41 S 140 55 E
Frances →, *Canada* **142 A3** 60 16N 129 10W
Frances L., *Canada* **142 A3** 61 23N 129 30W
Francesville, *U.S.A.* **157 D10** 40 59N 86 53W
Franceville, *Gabon* **114 C2** 1 40 S 13 32 E
Franche-Comté, *France* **27 F12** 46 50N 5 55 E
Franches Montagnes, *Switz.* **32 B4** 47 10N 7 0 E
Francis Case, L., *U.S.A.* **154 D5** 43 4N 98 34W
Francisco Beltrão, *Brazil* **175 B5** 26 5 S 53 4W
Francisco de Orellana, *Ecuador* **168 D2** 0 28 S 76 58W
Francisco I. Madero, *Coahuila, Mexico* **162 B4** 25 48N 103 18W
Francisco I. Madero, *Durango, Mexico* **162 C4** 24 32N 104 22W
Francisco Sá, *Brazil* **171 E3** 16 28 S 43 30W
Francistown, *Botswana* **117 C4** 21 7 S 27 33 E
Francofonte, *Italy* **47 E7** 37 14N 14 53 E
François, *Canada* **141 C8** 47 35N 56 45W
François-Joseph, Chutes, *Dem. Rep. of the Congo* **115 D3** 7 37 S 17 17 E
François L., *Canada* **142 C3** 54 0N 125 30W
Francois Peron Nat. Park, *Australia* **125 E1** 25 42 S 113 33 E
Franeker, *Neths.* **24 A5** 53 12N 5 33 E
Frank Hann Nationa Park, *Australia* **125 F3** 32 52 S 120 19 E
Frankado, *Djibouti* **107 E5** 12 30N 43 12 E
Frankenberg, *Germany* **30 D4** 51 3N 8 48 E
Frankenwald, *Germany* **31 E7** 50 20N 11 30 E
Frankford, *Canada* **150 B7** 44 12N 77 36W
Frankford, *U.S.A.* **156 E5** 39 29N 91 19W
Frankfort, *S. Africa* **117 D4** 27 17 S 28 30 E
Frankfort, *Ind., U.S.A.* **157 D10** 40 17N 86 31W
Frankfort, *Kans., U.S.A.* **154 F6** 39 42N 96 25W
Frankfort, *Ky., U.S.A.* **157 F12** 38 12N 84 52W
Frankfort, *N.Y., U.S.A.* **151 C9** 43 2N 75 4W
Frankfort, *Ohio, U.S.A.* **157 E13** 39 24N 83 11W
Frankfurt, *Brandenburg, Germany* **30 C10** 52 20N 14 32 E
Frankfurt, *Hessen, Germany* **31 E4** 50 7N 8 41 E
Fränkische Alb, *Germany* **31 F7** 49 10N 11 23 E
Fränkische Rezat →, *Germany* **31 F7** 49 11N 11 1 E
Fränkische Saale →, *Germany* **31 E5** 50 3N 9 42 E
Fränkische Schweiz, *Germany* **31 F7** 49 50N 11 16 E
Frankland →, *Australia* **125 G2** 35 0 S 116 48 E
Franklin, *Ga., U.S.A.* **153 E7** 33 17N 85 6W
Franklin, *Ind., U.S.A.* **157 E10** 39 29N 86 3W
Franklin, *Ky., U.S.A.* **149 G2** 36 43N 86 35W
Franklin, *La., U.S.A.* **155 L9** 29 48N 91 30W
Franklin, *Mass., U.S.A.* **151 D13** 42 5N 71 24W
Franklin, *N.H., U.S.A.* **151 C13** 43 27N 71 39W
Franklin, *Nebr., U.S.A.* **154 E5** 40 6N 98 57W
Franklin, *Ohio, U.S.A.* **157 E12** 39 34N 84 18W
Franklin, *Pa., U.S.A.* **150 E5** 41 24N 79 50W
Franklin, *Va., U.S.A.* **149 G7** 36 41N 76 56W
Franklin, *W. Va., U.S.A.* **148 F6** 38 39N 79 20W
Franklin, Pt., *U.S.A.* **144 A8** 70 55N 158 48W
Franklin B., *Canada* **138 B7** 69 45N 126 0W
Franklin D. Roosevelt L., *U.S.A.* **158 B4** 48 18N 118 9W
Franklin-Gordon Wild Rivers Nat. Park, *Australia* **127 G4** 42 19 S 145 51 E
Franklin Harb., *Australia* **128 B2** 33 43 S 136 55 E
Franklin I., *Antarctica* **7 D11** 76 10 S 168 30 E
Franklin L., *U.S.A.* **158 F6** 40 25N 115 22W
Franklin Mts., *Canada* **138 B7** 65 0N 125 0W
Franklin Mts., *N.Z.* **131 E2** 44 55 S 167 45 E
Franklin Str., *Canada* **138 A10** 72 0N 96 0W
Franklinton, *U.S.A.* **155 K9** 30 51N 90 9W
Franklinville, *U.S.A.* **150 D6** 42 20N 78 27W
Franklyn Mt., *N.Z.* **131 C7** 42 4 S 172 42 E
Franks Pk., *U.S.A.* **158 E9** 43 58N 109 18W
Frankston, *Australia* **129 E6** 38 8 S 145 8 E
Frånö, *Sweden* **16 B11** 62 55N 17 50 E
Fransfontein, *Namibia* **116 C2** 20 12 S 15 1 E
Fränsta, *Sweden* **16 B10** 62 30N 16 11 E
Frantsa Iosifa, Zemlya, *Russia* **66 A6** 82 0N 55 0 E
Franz, *Canada* **140 C3** 48 25N 84 30W
Franz Josef Land = Frantsa Iosifa, Zemlya, *Russia* **66 A6** 82 0N 55 0 E
Franzburg, *Germany* **30 A8** 54 11N 12 51 E
Frascati, *Italy* **45 G9** 41 48N 12 41 E
Fraser, *U.S.A.* **150 D2** 42 32N 82 57W
Fraser →, *B.C., Canada* **142 D4** 49 7N 123 11W
Fraser →, *Nfld., Canada* **141 A7** 56 39N 62 10W
Fraser, Mt., *Australia* **125 E2** 25 35 S 118 20 E
Fraser I., *Australia* **127 D5** 25 15 S 153 10 E
Fraser Lake, *Canada* **142 C4** 54 0N 124 50W
Fraser Nat. Park, *Australia* **129 D6** 37 9 S 145 51 E
Fraserburg, *S. Africa* **116 E3** 31 55 S 21 30 E
Fraserburgh, *U.K.* **22 D6** 57 42N 2 1W
Fraserdale, *Canada* **140 C3** 49 55N 81 37W
Frasertown, *N.Z.* **130 E6** 38 58 S 177 28 E
Frashër, *Albania* **50 F4** 40 23N 20 30 E
Frasne, *France* **27 F13** 46 50N 6 10 E
Frătești, *Romania* **53 G10** 43 58N 25 58 E
Frauenfeld, *Switz.* **33 A7** 47 34N 8 54 E
Fray Bentos, *Uruguay* **174 C4** 33 10 S 58 15W
Frechilla, *Spain* **42 C6** 42 8N 4 50W
Fredericia, *Denmark* **17 J3** 55 34N 9 45 E
Frederick, *Md., U.S.A.* **148 F7** 39 25N 77 25W
Frederick, *Okla., U.S.A.* **155 H5** 34 23N 99 1W
Frederick, *S. Dak., U.S.A.* **154 C5** 45 50N 98 31W
Frederick E. Hyde Fjord, *Greenland* **10 A8** 83 25N 29 0W
Fredericksburg, *Pa., U.S.A.* **151 F8** 40 27N 76 26W
Fredericksburg, *Tex., U.S.A.* **155 K5** 30 16N 98 52W
Fredericksburg, *Va., U.S.A.* **148 F7** 38 18N 77 28W
Fredericktown, *Mo., U.S.A.* **155 G9** 37 34N 90 18W
Fredericktown, *Ohio, U.S.A.* **150 F2** 40 29N 82 33W
Frederico I. Madero, Presa, *Mexico* **162 B3** 28 7N 105 40W
Frederico Westphalen, *Brazil* **175 B5** 27 22 S 53 24W
Fredericton, *Canada* **141 C6** 45 57N 66 40W
Fredericton Junction, *Canada* **141 C6** 45 41N 66 40W
Frederiksborg Amtskommune □, *Denmark* **17 J6** 55 50N 12 10 E
Frederikshåb = Paamiut, *Greenland* **10 E6** 62 0N 49 43W
Frederikshavn, *Denmark* **17 G4** 57 28N 10 31 E
Frederikssund, *Denmark* **17 J6** 55 50N 12 3 E
Frederiksted, *U.S. Virgin Is.* **165 C7** 17 43N 64 53W
Frederiksværk, *Denmark* **17 J6** 55 58N 12 4 E
Fredonia, *Ariz., U.S.A.* **159 H7** 36 57N 112 32W
Fredonia, *Kans., U.S.A.* **155 G7** 37 32N 95 49W
Fredonia, *N.Y., U.S.A.* **150 D5** 42 26N 79 20W
Fredriksberg, *Sweden* **16 D8** 60 8N 14 23 E
Fredrikstad, *Norway* **15 G14** 59 13N 10 57 E
Free State □, *S. Africa* **116 D4** 28 30 S 27 0 E
Freeburg, *U.S.A.* **156 F5** 38 19N 91 56W
Freehold, *U.S.A.* **151 F10** 40 16N 74 17W
Freel Peak, *U.S.A.* **160 G7** 38 52N 119 54W
Freeland, *U.S.A.* **151 E9** 41 1N 75 54W
Freels, C., *Canada* **141 C9** 49 15N 53 30W
Freeman, *Calif., U.S.A.* **161 K9** 35 35N 117 53W
Freeman, *Mo., U.S.A.* **156 F2** 38 37N 94 30W
Freeman, *S. Dak., U.S.A.* **154 D6** 43 21N 97 26W
Freeport, *Bahamas* **164 A4** 26 30N 78 47W
Freeport, *Fla., U.S.A.* **152 E3** 30 30N 86 8W
Freeport, *Ill., U.S.A.* **156 B7** 42 17N 89 36W
Freeport, *N.Y., U.S.A.* **151 F11** 40 39N 73 35W
Freeport, *Ohio, U.S.A.* **150 F3** 40 12N 81 15W
Freeport, *Pa., U.S.A.* **150 F5** 40 41N 79 41W
Freeport, *Tex., U.S.A.* **155 L7** 28 57N 95 21W
Freetown, *S. Leone* **112 D2** 8 30N 13 17W
Frégate, L., *Canada* **140 B5** 53 15N 74 45W
Fregenal de la Sierra, *Spain* **43 G4** 38 10N 6 39W
Fregene, *Italy* **45 G9** 41 51N 12 12 E
Fréhel, C., *France* **26 D4** 48 40N 2 20W
Freiberg, *Germany* **30 E9** 50 55N 13 20 E
Freibourg = Fribourg, *Switz.* **32 C4** 46 49N 7 9 E
Freiburg, *Baden-W., Germany* **31 H3** 47 59N 7 51 E
Freiburg, *Niedersachsen, Germany* **30 B5** 53 49N 9 16 E
Freiburger Alpen, *Switz.* **32 C4** 46 37N 7 10 E
Freilassing, *Germany* **31 H8** 47 50N 12 58 E
Freire, *Chile* **176 A2** 38 54 S 72 38W
Freirina, *Chile* **174 B1** 28 30 S 71 10W
Freising, *Germany* **31 G7** 48 24N 11 45 E
Freistadt, *Austria* **34 C7** 48 30N 14 30 E
Freital, *Germany* **30 D9** 51 1N 13 39 E
Fréjus, *France* **29 E10** 43 25N 6 44 E
Fremantle, *Australia* **125 F2** 32 7 S 115 47 E
Fremont, *Calif., U.S.A.* **160 H4** 37 32N 121 57W
Fremont, *Ind., U.S.A.* **157 C12** 41 44N 84 56W
Fremont, *Iowa, U.S.A.* **156 C4** 41 13N 92 26W
Fremont, *Mich., U.S.A.* **148 D3** 43 28N 85 57W
Fremont, *Nebr., U.S.A.* **154 E6** 41 26N 96 30W
Fremont, *Ohio, U.S.A.* **157 C13** 41 21N 83 7W
Fremont →, *U.S.A.* **159 G8** 38 24N 110 42W
French Camp, *U.S.A.* **160 H5** 37 53N 121 16W
French Creek →, *U.S.A.* **150 E5** 41 24N 79 50W
French Frigate Shoals, *U.S.A.* **145 G10** 23 45N 166 10W
French Guiana ■, *S. Amer.* **169 C7** 4 0N 53 0W
French I., *Australia* **129 E6** 38 20 S 145 22 E
French Lick, *U.S.A.* **157 F10** 38 33N 86 37W
French Pass, *N.Z.* **131 A8** 40 55 S 173 55 E
French Polynesia ■, *Pac. Oc.* **135 K13** 20 0 S 145 0W
Frenchburg, *U.S.A.* **157 G13** 37 57N 83 38W
Frenchman Cr. →, *N. Amer.* **158 B10** 48 31N 107 10W
Frenchman Cr. →, *U.S.A.* **154 E4** 40 14N 100 50W
Frenda, *Algeria* **111 A5** 35 2N 1 1 E
Frenštát pod Radhoštěm, *Czech Rep.* **35 B11** 49 33N 18 13 E
Fresco, *Ivory C.* **112 D3** 5 3N 5 31W
Fresco →, *Brazil* **173 B7** 7 15 S 51 30W
Freshfield, C., *Antarctica* **7 C10** 68 25 S 151 10 E
Fresnay-sur-Sarthe, *France* **26 D7** 48 17N 0 1 E
Fresnillo, *Mexico* **162 C4** 23 10N 103 0W
Fresno, *U.S.A.* **160 J7** 36 44N 119 47W
Fresno Alhandiga, *Spain* **42 E5** 40 42N 5 37W
Fresno Reservoir, *U.S.A.* **158 B9** 48 36N 109 57W
Fresvik, *Norway* **18 C3** 61 4N 6 55 E
Freudenstadt, *Germany* **31 G4** 48 27N 8 24 E
Frévent, *France* **27 B9** 50 15N 2 17 E
Frew →, *Australia* **126 C2** 20 0 S 135 38 E
Frewsburg, *U.S.A.* **150 D5** 42 3N 79 10W
Freycinet Nat. Park, *Australia* **127 G4** 42 11 S 148 19 E
Freycinet Pen., *Australia* **127 G4** 42 10 S 148 25 E
Freyming-Merlebach, *France* **27 C13** 49 8N 6 48 E
Freyung, *Germany* **31 G9** 48 48N 13 31 E
Fria, *Guinea* **112 C2** 10 27N 13 38W
Fria, C., *Namibia* **116 B1** 18 0 S 12 0 E
Friant, *U.S.A.* **160 J7** 36 59N 119 43W
Frías, *Argentina* **174 B2** 28 40 S 65 5W
Fribourg, *Switz.* **32 C4** 46 49N 7 9 E
Fribourg □, *Switz.* **32 C4** 46 40N 7 0 E
Frick, *Switz.* **32 A6** 47 31N 8 1 E
Fridafors, *Sweden* **17 H8** 56 25N 14 39 E
Friday Harbor, *U.S.A.* **160 B3** 48 32N 123 1W
Friedberg, *Bayern, Germany* **31 G6** 48 21N 10 59 E
Friedberg, *Hessen, Germany* **31 E4** 50 19N 8 45 E
Friedens, *U.S.A.* **150 F6** 40 3N 78 59W
Friedland, *Germany* **30 B9** 53 40N 13 33 E
Friedrichshafen, *Germany* **31 H5** 47 39N 9 30 E
Friedrichskoog, *Germany* **30 A4** 54 1N 8 53 E
Friedrichstadt, *Germany* **30 A5** 54 23N 9 6 E
Friendly Is. = Tonga ■, *Pac. Oc.* **133 P13** 19 50 S 174 30W
Friendship, *U.S.A.* **150 D6** 42 12N 78 8W
Friesach, *Austria* **34 E7** 46 57N 14 24 E
Friesack, *Germany* **30 C8** 52 44N 12 34 E
Friesland □, *Neths.* **24 A5** 53 5N 5 50 E
Friesoythe, *Germany* **30 B3** 53 1N 7 51 E
Frigate, *Seychelles* **121 b** 4 35 S 55 56 E
Friggesund, *Sweden* **16 C10** 61 54N 16 33 E
Frillesås, *Sweden* **17 G6** 57 20N 12 12 E
Frinnaryd, *Sweden* **17 G8** 57 55N 14 50 E
Frio →, *U.S.A.* **155 L5** 28 26N 98 11W
Frio, C., *Brazil* **166 F6** 22 50 S 41 50W
Friol, *Spain* **42 B3** 43 2N 7 47W
Friona, *U.S.A.* **155 H3** 34 38N 102 43W
Fristad, *Sweden* **17 G6** 57 50N 13 0 E
Fritch, *U.S.A.* **155 H4** 35 38N 101 36W
Fritsla, *Sweden* **17 G6** 57 33N 12 47 E
Fritzlar, *Germany* **30 D5** 51 7N 9 16 E
Friuli-Venézia Giulia □, *Italy* **45 B9** 46 0N 13 0 E
Frobisher B., *Canada* **139 B13** 62 30N 66 0W
Frobisher Bay = Iqaluit, *Canada* **139 B13** 63 44N 68 31W
Frobisher L., *Canada* **143 B7** 56 20N 108 15W
Frohavet, *Norway* **14 E13** 64 0N 9 30 E
Frohnleiten, *Austria* **34 D8** 47 16N 15 19 E
Frolovo, *Russia* **60 F6** 49 45N 43 40 E
Frombork, *Poland* **54 D6** 54 21N 19 41 E
Frome, *U.K.* **21 F5** 51 14N 2 19W
Frome →, *U.K.* **21 G5** 50 41N 2 6W
Frome, L., *Australia* **128 A3** 30 45 S 139 45 E
Frome Downs, *Australia* **128 A3** 31 13 S 139 45 E
Frómista, *Spain* **42 C6** 42 16N 4 25W
Front Range, *U.S.A.* **146 C5** 40 25N 105 45W
Front Royal, *U.S.A.* **148 F6** 38 55N 78 12W
Fronteira, *Portugal* **43 F3** 39 3N 7 39W
Fronteiras, *Brazil* **170 C3** 7 5 S 40 37W
Frontera, *Canary Is.* **9 e1** 27 47N 17 59W
Frontera, *Mexico* **163 D6** 18 30N 92 40W
Fronteras, *Mexico* **162 A3** 30 56N 109 31W
Frontignan, *France* **28 E7** 43 27N 3 45 E
Frosinone, *Italy* **46 A6** 41 38N 13 19 E
Frostburg, *U.S.A.* **148 F6** 39 39N 78 56W
Frostisen, *Norway* **14 B17** 68 14N 17 10 E
Frostproof, *U.S.A.* **153 H8** 27 45N 81 32W
Frouard, *France* **27 D13** 48 47N 6 8 E
Frövi, *Sweden* **16 E9** 59 28N 15 24 E
Frøya, *Norway* **14 E13** 63 43N 8 40 E
Fruithurst, *U.S.A.* **152 B4** 33 44N 85 26W
Fruitland Park, *U.S.A.* **153 G8** 28 51N 81 54W
Frumoasa, *Romania* **53 D10** 46 28N 25 48 E
Frunze = Bishkek, *Kyrgyzstan* **66 E8** 42 54N 74 46 E
Frunze, *Kyrgyzstan* **65 C5** 40 7N 71 44 E
Fruška Gora, *Serbia, Yug.* **52 E4** 45 7N 19 30 E
Frutal, *Brazil* **171 F2** 20 0 S 49 0W
Frutigen, *Switz.* **32 C5** 46 35N 7 38 E
Frýdek-Místek, *Czech Rep.* **35 B11** 49 40N 18 20 E
Frýdlant, *Czech Rep.* **34 A8** 50 56N 15 9 E
Fryeburg, *U.S.A.* **151 B14** 44 1N 70 59W
Fryvaldov = Jeseník, *Czech Rep.* **35 A10** 50 14N 17 8 E
Fthiótis □, *Greece* **48 C4** 38 50N 22 25 E
Fu Jiang →, *China* **76 C6** 30 0N 106 16 E
Fu Xian = Wafangdian, *China* **75 E11** 39 38N 121 58 E
Fu Xian, *China* **74 G5** 36 0N 109 20 E
Fu'an, *China* **77 D12** 27 11N 119 36 E
Fubian, *China* **76 B4** 31 17N 102 22 E
Fucécchio, *Italy* **44 E7** 43 44N 10 48 E
Fucheng, *China* **74 F9** 37 50N 116 10 E
Fuchou = Fuzhou, *China* **77 D12** 26 5N 119 16 E
Fuchū, *Hiroshima, Japan* **72 C5** 34 34N 133 14 E
Fūchū, *Tōkyō, Japan* **73 B11** 35 40N 139 29 E
Fuchuan, *China* **77 E8** 24 50N 111 5 E
Fuchun Jiang →, *China* **77 B13** 30 5N 120 5 E
Fúcino, Piana del, *Italy* **45 F10** 42 1N 13 31 E
Fuding, *China* **77 D13** 27 20N 120 12 E
Fuencaliente, *Canary Is.* **9 e1** 28 28N 17 50W
Fuencaliente, *Spain* **43 G6** 38 25N 4 18W
Fuencaliente, Pta., *Canary Is.* **9 e1** 28 27N 17 51W
Fuengirola, *Spain* **43 J6** 36 32N 4 41W
Fuenlabrada, *Spain* **42 E7** 40 17N 3 48W
Fuensalida, *Spain* **42 E6** 40 3N 4 12W
Fuente-Álamo, *Spain* **41 G3** 38 44N 1 24W
Fuente-Álamo de Murcia, *Spain* **41 H3** 37 42N 1 6W
Fuente de Cantos, *Spain* **43 G4** 38 15N 6 18W
Fuente del Maestre, *Spain* **43 G4** 38 31N 6 28W
Fuente el Fresno, *Spain* **43 F7** 39 14N 3 46W
Fuente Obejuna, *Spain* **43 G5** 38 15N 5 25W
Fuente Palmera, *Spain* **43 H5** 37 42N 5 6W
Fuentes de Andalucía, *Spain* **43 H5** 37 28N 5 20W
Fuentes de Ebro, *Spain* **40 D4** 41 31N 0 38W
Fuentes de León, *Spain* **43 G4** 38 5N 6 32W
Fuentes de Oñoro, *Spain* **42 E4** 40 33N 6 52W
Fuentesaúco, *Spain* **42 D5** 41 15N 5 30W
Fuerte →, *Mexico* **162 B3** 25 50N 109 25W
Fuerte Olimpo, *Paraguay* **174 A4** 21 0 S 57 51W
Fuerteventura, *Canary Is.* **9 e2** 28 30N 14 0W
Fufeng, *China* **74 G5** 34 22N 108 0 E
Fuga I., *Phil.* **80 B3** 18 52N 121 20 E
Fughmah, *Yemen* **99 C5** 16 9N 49 26 E
Fugong, *China* **76 D2** 27 5N 98 47 E
Fugou, *China* **74 G8** 34 3N 114 25 E
Fugu, *China* **74 E6** 39 2N 111 3 E
Fuhai, *China* **68 B3** 47 2N 87 25 E
Fuḩaymī, *Iraq* **101 E10** 34 16N 42 10 E
Fuji, *Japan* **73 B10** 35 9N 138 39 E
Fuji-San, *Japan* **73 B10** 35 22N 138 44 E
Fuji-Yoshida, *Japan* **73 B10** 35 30N 138 46 E
Fujian □, *China* **77 E12** 26 0N 118 0 E
Fujieda, *Japan* **73 C10** 34 52N 138 16 E
Fujinomiya, *Japan* **73 B10** 35 10N 138 40 E
Fujioka, *Japan* **73 A11** 36 15N 139 5 E
Fujisawa, *Japan* **73 B11** 35 22N 139 29 E
Fujiyama, Mt. = Fuji-San, *Japan* **73 B10** 35 22N 138 44 E
Fukaya, *Japan* **73 A11** 36 12N 139 12 E
Fukiage, *Japan* **72 F2** 31 27N 130 17 E
Fukien = Fujian □, *China* **77 E12** 26 0N 118 0 E
Fukuchiyama, *Japan* **73 B7** 35 19N 135 9 E
Fukue-Shima, *Japan* **71 H4** 32 40N 128 45 E
Fukui, *Japan* **73 A8** 36 5N 136 10 E
Fukui □, *Japan* **73 B8** 36 0N 136 12 E
Fukuma, *Japan* **72 D2** 33 46N 130 28 E
Fukuoka, *Japan* **72 D2** 33 39N 130 21 E
Fukuoka □, *Japan* **72 D3** 33 30N 131 0 E
Fukuroi, *Japan* **73 C9** 34 45N 137 55 E
Fukushima, *Japan* **70 F10** 37 44N 140 28 E
Fukushima □, *Japan* **70 F10** 37 30N 140 15 E
Fukuyama, *Japan* **72 C5** 34 35N 133 20 E
Fulacunda, *Guinea-Biss.* **112 C1** 11 44N 15 3W
Fulaga, *Fiji* **133 B3** 19 8 S 178 33W
Fulda, *Germany* **30 E5** 50 32N 9 40 E
Fulda →, *Germany* **30 D5** 51 25N 9 39 E
Fulford Harbour, *Canada* **160 B3** 48 47N 123 27W
Fuliang, *China* **77 C11** 29 23N 117 14 E
Fullerton, *Calif., U.S.A.* **161 M9** 33 53N 117 56W
Fullerton, *Nebr., U.S.A.* **154 E6** 41 22N 97 58W
Fulongquan, *China* **75 B13** 44 20N 124 42 E
Fülöpszállás, *Hungary* **52 D4** 46 49N 19 15 E
Fulton, *Ill., U.S.A.* **156 C6** 41 52N 90 11W
Fulton, *Ind., U.S.A.* **157 D10** 40 57N 86 16W
Fulton, *Mo., U.S.A.* **156 F5** 38 52N 91 57W
Fulton, *N.Y., U.S.A.* **151 C8** 43 19N 76 25W
Fuluälven →, *Sweden* **16 C7** 61 18N 13 4 E
Fulufjället, *Sweden* **16 C6** 61 32N 12 41 E
Fumay, *France* **27 C11** 49 58N 4 40 E
Fumel, *France* **28 D4** 44 30N 0 58 E
Fumin, *China* **76 E4** 25 10N 102 20 E
Funabashi, *Japan* **73 B12** 35 45N 140 0 E
Funafuti = Fongafale, *Tuvalu* **134 H9** 8 31 S 179 13 E
Funäsdalen, *Sweden* **16 B6** 62 33N 12 32 E
Funchal, *Madeira* **9 c** 32 38N 16 54W
Fundación, *Colombia* **168 A3** 10 31N 74 11W
Fundão, *Brazil* **171 E3** 19 55 S 40 24W
Fundão, *Portugal* **42 E3** 40 8N 7 30W
Fundu Moldovei, *Romania* **53 C10** 47 32N 25 24 E
Fundulea, *Romania* **53 F11** 44 28N 26 31 E
Fundy, B. of, *Canada* **141 D6** 45 0N 66 0W
Funhalouro, *Mozam.* **117 C5** 23 3 S 34 25 E
Funing, *Hebei, China* **75 E10** 39 53N 119 12 E
Funing, *Jiangsu, China* **75 H10** 33 45N 119 50 E
Funing, *Yunnan, China* **76 F5** 23 35N 105 45 E
Funiu Shan, *China* **74 H7** 33 30N 112 20 E
Funsi, *Ghana* **112 C4** 10 21N 1 54W
Funtua, *Nigeria* **113 C6** 11 30N 7 18 E
Fuping, *Hebei, China* **74 E8** 38 48N 114 12 E
Fuping, *Shaanxi, China* **74 G5** 34 42N 109 10 E
Fuqing, *China* **77 E12** 25 41N 119 21 E
Fuquan, *China* **76 D6** 26 40N 107 27 E
Furano, *Japan* **70 C11** 43 21N 142 23 E
Furāt, Nahr al →, *Asia* **96 D5** 31 0N 47 25 E
Fürg, *Iran* **97 D7** 28 18N 55 13 E
Furkapass, *Switz.* **33 C7** 46 34N 8 35 E
Furkating, *India* **93 F19** 26 28N 93 59 E
Furman, *U.S.A.* **152 C8** 32 41N 81 11W
Furmanov, *Russia* **60 B5** 57 10N 41 9 E
Furmanovo, *Kazakstan* **60 F9** 49 42N 49 25 E
Furnas, *Azores* **9 d3** 37 46N 25 19W
Furnás, *Spain* **38 C2** 39 3N 1 32 E
Furnas, Reprêsa de, *Brazil* **171 F2** 20 50 S 45 30W
Furneaux Group, *Australia* **127 G4** 40 10 S 147 50 E
Furqlus, *Syria* **103 A6** 34 36N 37 8 E
Fürstenau, *Germany* **30 C3** 52 31N 7 40 E
Fürstenberg, *Germany* **30 B9** 53 10N 13 8 E
Fürstenfeld, *Austria* **34 D9** 47 3N 16 3 E
Fürstenfeldbruck, *Germany* **31 G7** 48 11N 11 15 E
Fürstenwalde, *Germany* **30 C10** 52 22N 14 3 E
Fürth, *Germany* **31 F6** 49 28N 10 59 E
Furth im Wald, *Germany* **31 F8** 49 18N 12 50 E
Furtwangen, *Germany* **31 G4** 48 2N 8 12 E
Furudal, *Sweden* **16 C9** 61 10N 15 11 E
Furukawa, *Gifu, Japan* **73 A9** 36 14N 137 11 E
Furukawa, *Miyagi, Japan* **70 E10** 38 34N 140 58 E
Furulund, *Sweden* **17 J7** 55 46N 13 6 E
Fury and Hecla Str., *Canada* **139 B11** 69 56N 84 0W
Fusagasuga, *Colombia* **168 C3** 4 21N 74 22W
Fuscaldo, *Italy* **47 C9** 39 25N 16 2 E
Fushan, *Shandong, China* **75 F11** 37 30N 121 15 E
Fushan, *Shanxi, China* **74 G6** 35 58N 111 51 E
Fushë Arrëz, *Albania* **50 D4** 42 4N 20 2 E
Fushë Krujë, *Albania* **50 E3** 41 29N 19 43 E
Fushun, *Liaoning, China* **75 D12** 41 50N 123 56 E
Fushun, *Sichuan, China* **76 C5** 29 13N 104 52 E
Fusio, *Switz.* **33 D7** 46 27N 8 40 E
Fusong, *China* **75 C14** 42 20N 127 15 E
Füssen, *Germany* **31 H6** 47 34N 10 42 E
Fustic, *Barbados* **165 g** 13 16N 59 38W
Fusui, *China* **76 F6** 22 40N 107 56 E
Futago-Yama, *Japan* **72 D3** 33 35N 131 36 E
Futian, *China* **69 F11** 22 32N 114 4 E
Futog, *Yugoslavia* **52 E4** 45 15N 19 42 E
Futrono, *Chile* **176 B2** 40 8 S 72 24W
Futtsu, *Japan* **73 B10** 35 13N 139 49 E
Futuna, *Wall. & F. Is.* **134 J9** 14 25 S 178 20W
Fuwa, *Egypt* **106 H7** 31 12N 30 33 E
Fuxian Hu, *China* **76 E4** 24 30N 102 53 E
Fuxin, *China* **75 C11** 42 5N 121 48 E
Fuyang, *Anhui, China* **74 H8** 33 0N 115 48 E
Fuyang, *Zhejiang, China* **77 B12** 30 5N 119 57 E
Fuyang He →, *China* **74 E9** 38 12N 117 0 E
Fuying Dao, *China* **77 D13** 26 34N 120 9 E
Fuyong, *China* **69 F10** 22 40N 113 49 E
Fuyu, *China* **75 B13** 45 12N 124 43 E
Fuyuan, *China* **76 E5** 25 40N 104 16 E
Füzesgyarmat, *Hungary* **52 C6** 47 6N 21 14 E
Fuzhou, *China* **77 D12** 26 5N 119 16 E
Fylde, *U.K.* **20 D5** 53 50N 2 58W
Fyn, *Denmark* **17 J4** 55 20N 10 30 E
Fyne, L., *U.K.* **22 F3** 55 59N 5 23W
Fyns Amtskommune □, *Denmark* **17 J4** 55 15N 10 30 E
Fynshav, *Denmark* **17 K3** 54 59N 9 59 E
Fyresdal, *Norway* **18 E5** 59 11N 8 5 E
Fyresvatn, *Norway* **18 E5** 59 6N 8 10 E

G

Ga, *Ghana* **112 D4** 9 47N 2 30W
Gaanda, *Nigeria* **113 C7** 10 10N 12 27 E
Gabarin, *Nigeria* **113 C7** 11 8N 10 27 E
Gabas →, *France* **28 E3** 43 46N 0 42W
Gabela, *Angola* **115 E2** 11 0 S 14 24 E
Gabès, *Tunisia* **108 B2** 33 53N 10 2 E
Gabès, G. de, *Tunisia* **108 B2** 34 0N 10 30 E
Gabgaba, W. →, *Egypt* **106 C3** 22 10N 33 5 E
Gabia, *Dem. Rep. of the Congo* **115 C3** 4 37 S 17 14 E
Gąbin, *Poland* **55 F6** 52 23N 19 41 E
Gabon ■, *Africa* **114 C2** 0 10 S 10 0 E
Gabon →, *Gabon* **114 B1** 0 25N 9 20 E
Gaborone, *Botswana* **116 C4** 24 45 S 25 57 E
Gabriels, *U.S.A.* **151 B10** 44 26N 74 12W
Gābrīk, *Iran* **97 E8** 25 44N 58 28 E
Gabro, *Ethiopia* **120 C2** 6 18N 43 16 E
Gabrovo, *Bulgaria* **51 D9** 42 52N 25 19 E
Gacé, *France* **26 D7** 48 49N 0 20 E
Gāch Sār, *Iran* **97 B6** 36 7N 51 19 E
Gachsārān, *Iran* **97 D6** 30 15N 50 45 E
Gacko, *Bos.-H.* **50 C2** 43 10N 18 33 E
Gad Hinglaj, *India* **95 F2** 16 14N 74 21 E
Gadag, *India* **95 G2** 15 30N 75 45 E
Gadaisu, *Papua N. G.* **132 F5** 10 22 S 149 46 E
Gadamai, *Sudan* **107 D4** 17 11N 36 10 E
Gadap, *Pakistan* **92 G2** 25 5N 67 28 E
Gadarwara, *India* **93 H8** 22 50N 78 50 E
Gadebusch, *Germany* **30 B7** 53 42N 11 7 E
Gadein, *Sudan* **107 F2** 8 10N 28 45 E
Gadhada, *India* **92 J4** 22 0N 71 35 E
Gadmen, *Switz.* **33 C6** 46 45N 8 16 E
Gádor, Sierra de, *Spain* **43 J8** 36 57N 2 45W
Gadra, *Pakistan* **92 G4** 25 40N 70 38 E
Gadsden, *Ala., U.S.A.* **152 A3** 34 1N 86 1W
Gadsden, *S.C., U.S.A.* **152 B9** 33 51N 80 46W
Gadwal, *India* **95 F3** 16 10N 77 50 E
Gadyach = Hadyach, *Ukraine* **59 G8** 50 21N 34 0 E
Gadzi, *C.A.R.* **114 B3** 4 47N 16 42 E
Găești, *Romania* **53 F10** 44 48N 25 19 E
Gaeta, *Italy* **46 A6** 41 12N 13 35 E
Gaeta, G. di, *Italy* **46 A6** 41 6N 13 30 E
Gaffney, *U.S.A.* **149 H5** 35 5N 81 39W
Gafsa, *Tunisia* **108 B1** 34 24N 8 43 E
Gag, *Indonesia* **83 B3** 0 27 S 129 52 E
Gagarawa, *Nigeria* **113 C6** 12 25N 9 32 E
Gagaria, *India* **92 G4** 25 43N 70 46 E
Gagarin, *Russia* **58 E8** 55 38N 35 0 E
Gagarin, *Uzbekistan* **65 C4** 40 39N 68 10 E
Gaggenau, *Germany* **31 G4** 48 48N 8 18 E
Gaghamni, *Sudan* **107 E2** 11 41N 28 19 E
Gagino, *Russia* **60 C7** 55 15N 45 1 E
Gagliano del Capo, *Italy* **47 C11** 39 50N 18 22 E
Gagnef, *Sweden* **16 D9** 60 36N 15 5 E
Gagnoa, *Ivory C.* **112 D3** 6 56N 5 16W
Gagnon, *Canada* **141 B6** 51 50N 68 5W
Gagnon, L., *Canada* **143 A6** 62 3N 110 27W
Gago Coutinho, *São Tomé & Principe* **115 G6** 0 1 S 6 32 E
Gagra, *Georgia* **61 J5** 43 20N 40 10 E
Gahini, *Rwanda* **118 C3** 1 50 S 30 30 E
Gahmar, *India* **93 G10** 25 27N 83 49 E
Gai Xian = Gaizhou, *China* **75 D12** 40 22N 122 20 E
Gaibanda, *Bangla.* **90 C2** 25 20N 89 36 E
Gaïdhouronísi, *Greece* **39 F6** 34 53N 25 41 E
Gail, *U.S.A.* **155 J4** 32 46N 101 27W
Gail →, *Austria* **34 E6** 46 36N 13 53 E
Gaillac, *France* **28 E5** 43 54N 1 54 E
Gaillimh = Galway, *Ireland* **23 C2** 53 17N 9 3W
Gaillon, *France* **26 C8** 49 10N 1 20 E
Gaimán, *Argentina* **176 B3** 43 10 S 65 25W
Gaines, *U.S.A.* **150 E7** 41 46N 77 35W
Gainesville, *Fla., U.S.A.* **153 F7** 29 40N 82 20W
Gainesville, *Ga., U.S.A.* **149 H4** 34 18N 83 50W
Gainesville, *Mo., U.S.A.* **155 G8** 36 36N 92 26W
Gainesville, *Tex., U.S.A.* **155 J6** 33 38N 97 8W
Gainsborough, *U.K.* **20 D7** 53 24N 0 46W
Gairdner, L., *Australia* **128 A2** 31 30 S 136 0 E
Gairloch, L., *U.K.* **22 D3** 57 43N 5 45W
Gais, *Switz.* **33 B8** 47 22N 9 27 E
Gaizhou, *China* **75 D12** 40 22N 122 20 E
Gaj, *Croatia* **52 E2** 45 28N 17 3 E
Gaj →, *Pakistan* **92 F2** 26 26N 67 21 E
Gajendragarh, *India* **95 G2** 15 44N 75 59 E
Gakona, *U.S.A.* **144 E11** 62 18N 145 18W
Gakuch, *Pakistan* **93 A5** 36 7N 73 45 E
Gal Laghet, *Somali Rep.* **120 D3** 4 9N 47 10 E
Gal Oya Res., *Sri Lanka* **95 L5** 7 5N 81 30 E
Gal Tardo, *Somali Rep.* **120 D3** 3 34N 45 58 E

216 Galaasiya

Galaasiya, *Uzbekistan* **65 D2** 39 51N 64 26 E
Galachipa, *Bangla.* **90 D3** 22 8N 90 26 E
Galala, Gebel el, *Egypt* **106 J8** 29 21N 32 22 E
Galán, Cerro, *Argentina* **174 B2** 25 55 S 66 52W
Galana →, *Kenya* **118 C5** 3 9 S 40 8 E
Galangue, *Angola* **115 E3** 13 42 S 16 9 E
Galangue, Serra, *Angola* **115 E3** 14 18 S 15 52 E
Galanta, *Slovak Rep.* **35 C10** 48 11N 17 45 E
Galapagar, *Spain* **42 E7** 40 36N 3 58W
Galápagos = Colón, Arch. de, *Ecuador* **172 a** 0 0 91 0W
Galashiels, *U.K.* **22 F6** 55 37N 2 49W
Galatás, *Greece* **48 D5** 37 30N 23 26 E
Galatea, *N.Z.* **130 E5** 38 24 S 176 45 E
Galaţi, *Romania* **53 E13** 45 27N 28 2 E
Galaţi □, *Romania* **53 E12** 45 45N 27 30 E
Galatia, *Turkey* **100 C5** 39 30N 33 0 E
Galatina, *Italy* **47 B11** 40 10N 18 10 E
Galátone, *Italy* **47 B11** 40 9N 18 4 E
Galax, *U.S.A.* **149 G5** 36 40N 80 56W
Galaxídhion, *Greece* **48 C4** 38 22N 22 23 E
Galcaio, *Somali Rep.* **120 C3** 6 30N 47 30 E
Galdhøpiggen, *Norway* **15 F12** 61 38N 8 18 E
Galeana, *Chihuahua, Mexico* **162 A3** 30 7N 107 38W
Galeana, *Nuevo León, Mexico* **162 A3** 24 50N 100 4W
Galegu, *Sudan* **107 E4** 12 36N 35 2 E
Galela, *Indonesia* **82 A3** 1 50N 127 49 E
Galena, *Alaska, U.S.A.* **144 D8** 64 44N 156 56W
Galena, *Ill., U.S.A.* **156 B6** 42 25N 90 26W
Galeota Pt., *Trin. & Tob.* **169 F10** 10 8N 60 59W
Galera, *Spain* **41 H2** 37 45N 2 33W
Galera, Pta., *Chile* **176 A2** 39 59 S 73 43W
Galera, Pta. da, *Azores* **9 d3** 37 42N 25 30W
Galera Pt., *Trin. & Tob.* **165 D7** 10 49N 60 54W
Galesburg, *Ill., U.S.A.* **156 D6** 40 57N 90 22W
Galesburg, *Mich., U.S.A.* **157 B11** 42 17N 85 26W
Galeton, *U.S.A.* **150 E7** 41 44N 77 39W
Galga, *Ethiopia* **107 F4** 6 39N 37 47 E
Galgasc, *Somali Rep.* **120 D2** 0 11N 41 38 E
Galheirão →, *Brazil* **171 D2** 12 23 S 45 5W
Galheiros, *Brazil* **171 D2** 13 18 S 46 25W
Gali, *Georgia* **61 J5** 42 37N 41 46 E
Galicea Mare, *Romania* **53 F8** 44 4N 23 19 E
Galich, *Russia* **60 A6** 58 22N 42 24 E
Galiche, *Bulgaria* **50 C7** 43 34N 23 53 E
Galicia □, *Spain* **42 C3** 42 43N 7 45W
Galien, *U.S.A.* **157 C10** 41 48N 86 30W
Galilee = Hagalil, *Israel* **103 C4** 32 53N 35 18 E
Galilee, L., *Australia* **126 C4** 22 20 S 145 50 E
Galilee, Sea of = Yam Kinneret, *Israel* **103 C4** 32 45N 35 35 E
Galim, *Cameroon* **113 D7** 7 6N 12 25 E
Galina Pt., *Jamaica* **164 a** 18 24N 76 58W
Galinoporni, *Cyprus* **39 E10** 35 31N 34 18 E
Galion, *U.S.A.* **150 F2** 40 44N 82 47W
Galite, Is. de la, *Tunisia* **111 A6** 37 30N 8 59 E
Galiuro Mts., *U.S.A.* **159 K8** 32 30N 110 20W
Galiwinku, *Australia* **126 A2** 12 2 S 135 34 E
Gallabat, *Sudan* **107 E4** 12 58N 36 11 E
Gallan Hd., *U.K.* **22 C1** 58 15N 7 2W
Gallarate, *Italy* **44 C5** 45 40N 8 48 E
Gallatin, *Mo., U.S.A.* **156 E3** 39 55N 93 58W
Gallatin, *Tenn., U.S.A.* **149 G2** 36 24N 86 27W
Galle, *Sri Lanka* **95 L5** 6 5N 80 10 E
Gállego →, *Spain* **40 D4** 41 39N 0 51W
Gallegos →, *Argentina* **176 D3** 51 35 S 69 0W
Galletti →, *Ethiopia* **107 F5** 8 46N 41 10 E
Galley Hd., *Ireland* **23 E3** 51 32N 8 55W
Galliate, *Italy* **44 C5** 45 29N 8 42 E
Gallinas, Pta., *Colombia* **168 A3** 12 28N 71 40W
Gallipoli = Gelibolu, *Turkey* **51 F10** 40 28N 26 43 E
Gallípoli, *Italy* **47 B10** 40 3N 17 58 E
Gallipolis, *U.S.A.* **148 F4** 38 49N 82 12W
Gällivare, *Sweden* **14 C19** 67 9N 20 40 E
Gallneukirchen, *Austria* **34 C7** 48 21N 14 25 E
Gällö, *Sweden* **16 B9** 62 55N 15 13 E
Gallo, C., *Italy* **46 D6** 38 13N 13 19 E
Gallocanta, L. de, *Spain* **40 E3** 40 58N 1 30W
Galloo I., *U.S.A.* **151 C8** 43 55N 76 25W
Galloway, *U.K.* **22 F4** 55 1N 4 29W
Galloway, Mull of, *U.K.* **22 G4** 54 39N 4 52W
Gallup, *U.S.A.* **159 J9** 35 32N 108 45W
Gallur, *Spain* **40 D3** 41 52N 1 19W
Gallyaaral, *Uzbekistan* **65 C3** 40 2N 67 35 E
Galong, *Australia* **129 C8** 34 37 S 148 34 E
Galoya, *Sri Lanka* **95 K5** 8 10N 80 55 E
Galt, *Calif., U.S.A.* **160 G5** 38 15N 121 18W
Galt, *Mo., U.S.A.* **156 D3** 40 8N 93 23W
Galtee Mts., *Ireland* **23 D3** 52 22N 8 10W
Galten, *Denmark* **17 H3** 56 9N 9 54 E
Galtür, *Austria* **34 E3** 46 58N 10 11 E
Galty Mts., *Ireland* **23 D3** 52 22N 8 10W
Galtymore, *Ireland* **23 D3** 52 21N 8 11W
Galva, *U.S.A.* **156 C6** 41 10N 90 3W
Galvarino, *Chile* **176 A2** 38 24 S 72 47W
Galve de Sorbe, *Spain* **40 D1** 41 13N 3 10W
Galveston, *Ind., U.S.A.* **157 D10** 40 35N 86 11W
Galveston, *Tex., U.S.A.* **155 L7** 29 18N 94 48W
Galveston B., *U.S.A.* **155 L7** 29 36N 94 50W
Gálvez, *Argentina* **174 C3** 32 0 S 61 14W
Galway, *Ireland* **23 C2** 53 17N 9 3W
Galway □, *Ireland* **23 C2** 53 22N 9 1W
Galway B., *Ireland* **23 C2** 53 13N 9 10W
Gam, *Indonesia* **83 B4** 0 27 S 130 36 E
Gam →, *Vietnam* **86 B5** 21 55N 105 12 E
Gamagōri, *Japan* **73 C9** 34 50N 137 14 E
Gamari, L., *Ethiopia* **107 E5** 11 32N 41 40 E
Gamawa, *Nigeria* **113 C7** 12 10N 10 31 E
Gamay, *Phil.* **80 E5** 12 23N 125 18 E
Gamay Bay, *Phil.* **80 E5** 12 21N 125 21 E
Gamba, *Angola* **115 E3** 11 42 S 17 14 E
Gambaga, *Ghana* **113 C4** 10 30N 0 28W
Gambat, *Pakistan* **92 F3** 27 17N 68 26 E
Gambela, *Ethiopia* **107 F3** 8 14N 34 38 E
Gambela Nat. Park, *Ethiopia* **107 F3** 8 0N 34 0 E
Gambell, *U.S.A.* **144 E5** 63 47N 171 45W
Gambhir →, *India* **92 F6** 26 58N 77 27 E
Gambia ■, *W. Afr.* **112 C1** 13 25N 16 0W
Gambia →, *W. Afr.* **112 C1** 13 28N 16 34W
Gambier, *U.S.A.* **150 F2** 40 22N 82 23W
Gambier, C., *Australia* **124 B5** 11 56 S 130 57 E
Gambier Is., *Australia* **128 C2** 35 3 S 136 30 E
Gambier Village, *Bahamas* **9 b** 25 4N 77 30W
Gambo, *C.A.R.* **114 B4** 4 39N 22 16 E
Gambo, *Canada* **141 C9** 48 47N 54 13W
Gamboli, *Pakistan* **92 E3** 29 53N 68 24 E
Gamboma, *Congo* **114 C3** 1 55 S 15 52 E
Gamboula, *C.A.R.* **114 B3** 4 8N 15 9 E
Gambuta, *Indonesia* **82 A2** 0 30N 123 20 E
Gamka →, *S. Africa* **116 E3** 33 18 S 21 39 E
Gamkab →, *Namibia* **116 D2** 28 4 S 17 54 E
Gamla Uppsala, *Sweden* **16 E11** 59 54N 17 40 E
Gamlakarleby = Kokkola, *Finland* **14 E20** 63 50N 23 8 E
Gamleby, *Sweden* **17 G10** 57 54N 16 24 E
Gammon →, *Canada* **143 C9** 51 24N 95 44W
Gammouda, *Tunisia* **108 A1** 35 3N 9 39 E
Gamo-Gofa □, *Ethiopia* **107 F4** 5 40N 36 40 E
Gamoda-Saki, *Japan* **72 D6** 33 50N 134 45 E
Gamou, *Niger* **113 C6** 14 20N 9 55 E
Gampaha, *Sri Lanka* **95 L4** 7 5N 79 59 E
Gampel, *Switz.* **32 D5** 46 19N 7 44 E
Gampola, *Sri Lanka* **95 L5** 7 10N 80 34 E
Gams, *Switz.* **33 B8** 47 12N 9 26 E
Gamtoos →, *S. Africa* **116 E4** 33 58 S 25 1 E
Gan, *France* **28 E3** 43 12N 0 27W
Gan Gan, *Argentina* **176 B3** 42 30 S 68 10W
Gan Goriama, Mts., *Cameroon* **113 D7** 7 44N 12 45 E
Gan Jiang →, *China* **77 C11** 29 15N 116 0 E
Ganado, *U.S.A.* **159 J9** 35 43N 109 33W
Gananita, *Sudan* **106 D3** 18 22N 33 50 E
Gananoque, *Canada* **140 D4** 44 20N 76 10W
Ganassi, *Phil.* **81 H5** 7 49N 124 6 E
Ganāveh, *Iran* **97 D6** 29 35N 50 35 E
Gäncä, *Azerbaijan* **61 K8** 40 45N 46 20 E
Gancheng, *China* **86 C7** 18 51N 108 37 E
Gand = Gent, *Belgium* **24 C3** 51 2N 3 42 E
Ganda, *Angola* **115 E2** 13 3 S 14 35 E
Gandajika, *Dem. Rep. of the Congo* **115 D4** 6 46 S 23 58 E
Gandak →, *India* **93 G11** 25 39N 85 13 E
Gandara, *Phil.* **80 E5** 12 1N 124 49 E
Gandava, *Pakistan* **91 C2** 28 32N 67 32 E
Gander, *Canada* **141 C9** 48 58N 54 35W
Gander L., *Canada* **141 C9** 48 58N 54 35W
Ganderkesee, *Germany* **30 B4** 53 2N 8 32 E
Ganderowe Falls, *Zimbabwe* **119 F2** 17 20 S 29 10 E
Gandesa, *Spain* **40 D5** 41 3N 0 26 E
Gandhi Sagar, *India* **92 G6** 24 40N 75 40 E
Gandhinagar, *India* **92 H5** 23 15N 72 45 E
Gandi, *Nigeria* **113 C6** 12 55N 5 49 E
Gandía, *Spain* **41 G4** 38 58N 0 9W
Gandino, *Italy* **44 C6** 45 49N 9 54 E
Gando, Pta., *Canary Is.* **9 e1** 27 55N 15 22W
Gandole, *Nigeria* **113 D7** 8 28N 11 35 E
Gandou, *Congo* **114 B3** 2 25N 17 25 E
Gandu, *Brazil* **171 D4** 13 45 S 39 30W
Gâneb, *Mauritania* **112 B2** 18 29N 10 8W
Ganedidalem = Gani, *Indonesia* **82 B3** 0 48 S 128 14 E
Ganetti, *Sudan* **106 D3** 18 0N 31 10 E
Ganga →, *India* **93 H14** 23 20N 90 30 E
Ganga Sagar, *India* **93 J13** 21 38N 88 5 E
Gangafani, *Mali* **112 C4** 14 20N 2 20W
Gangakher, *India* **94 E3** 18 57N 76 45 E
Gangan →, *India* **93 E8** 28 38N 78 58 E
Ganganagar, *India* **92 E5** 29 56N 73 56 E
Gangapur, *Maharashtra, India* **94 E2** 19 41N 75 1 E
Gangapur, *Raj., India* **92 F7** 26 32N 76 49 E
Gangara, *Niger* **113 C6** 14 35N 8 29 E
Gangaw, *Burma* **90 D5** 22 5N 94 5 E
Gangaw Taungdan, *Burma* **90 C6** 24 55N 96 35 E
Gangawati, *India* **95 G3** 15 30N 76 36 E
Ganges = Ganga →, *India* **93 H14** 23 20N 90 30 E
Ganges, *Canada* **142 D4** 48 51N 123 31W
Ganges, *France* **28 E7** 43 56N 3 42 E
Ganges, Mouths of the, *India* **90 E3** 21 30N 90 0 E
Gånghester, *Sweden* **17 G7** 57 42N 13 1 E
Gangi, *Italy* **47 E7** 37 48N 14 12 E
Gângiova, *Romania* **53 G8** 43 54N 23 50 E
Gangoh, *India* **92 E7** 29 46N 77 18 E
Gangroti, *India* **93 D8** 30 50N 79 10 E
Gangtok, *India* **90 B2** 27 20N 88 37 E
Gangu, *China* **74 G3** 34 40N 105 15 E
Gangwa, *Dem. Rep. of the Congo* **114 C4** 3 30 S 20 54 E
Gangyao, *China* **75 B14** 44 12N 126 37 E
Gani, *Indonesia* **82 B3** 0 48 S 128 14 E
Ganj, *India* **93 F8** 27 45N 78 57 E
Ganjam, *India* **94 E7** 19 23N 85 4 E
Ganluc, *China* **76 C4** 28 58N 102 59 E
Ganmain, *Australia* **129 C7** 34 47 S 147 1 E
Gannat, *France* **27 F10** 46 7N 3 11 E
Gannett Peak, *U.S.A.* **158 E9** 43 11N 109 39W
Ganquan, *China* **74 F5** 36 20N 109 20 E
Gänserdorf, *Austria* **35 C9** 48 20N 16 43 E
Ganshui, *China* **76 C6** 28 40N 106 40 E
Gansu □, *China* **74 G3** 36 0N 104 0 E
Ganta, *Liberia* **112 D3** 7 15N 8 59W
Gantheaume, C., *Australia* **128 D2** 36 4 S 137 32 E
Gantheaume B., *Australia* **125 E1** 27 40 S 114 10 E
Gantsevichi = Hantsavichy, *Belarus* **59 F4** 52 49N 26 30 E
Ganye, *Nigeria* **113 D7** 8 25N 12 4 E
Ganyem = Genyem, *Indonesia* **83 B6** 2 46 S 140 12 E
Ganyu, *China* **75 G10** 34 50N 119 8 E
Ganyushkino, *Kazakstan* **61 G9** 46 35N 49 20 E
Ganzhou, *China* **77 E10** 25 51N 114 56 E
Gao, *Mali* **113 B4** 16 15N 0 5W
Gao Xian, *China* **76 C5** 28 21N 104 32 E
Gao'an, *China* **77 C10** 28 26N 115 17 E
Gaochun, *China* **77 B12** 31 20N 118 49 E
Gaohe, *China* **77 F9** 22 46N 112 57 E
Gaohebu, *China* **77 B11** 30 43N 116 49 E
Gaokeng, *China* **77 D9** 27 40N 113 58 E
Gaolan Dao, *China* **77 G9** 21 55N 113 10 E
Gaoligong Shan, *China* **76 E2** 24 45N 98 45 E
Gaomi, *China* **75 F10** 36 20N 119 42 E
Gaoming, *China* **77 F9** 36 9N 113 1 E
Gaoping, *China* **74 G7** 35 45N 112 55 E
Gaotang, *China* **74 F9** 36 50N 116 15 E
Gaoua, *Burkina Faso* **112 C4** 10 20N 3 8W
Gaoual, *Guinea* **112 C2** 11 45N 13 25W
Gaoxiong = Kaohsiung, *Taiwan* **77 F13** 22 35N 120 16 E
Gaoyang, *China* **74 E8** 38 40N 115 45 E
Gaoyao, *China* **77 F9** 23 3N 112 27 E
Gaoyou, *China* **77 A12** 32 47N 119 26 E
Gaoyou Hu, *China* **75 H10** 32 45N 119 20 E
Gaoyuan, *China* **75 F9** 37 8N 117 58 E
Gaozhou, *China* **77 G8** 21 58N 110 50 E
Gap, *France* **29 D10** 44 33N 6 5 E
Gapan, *Phil.* **80 D3** 15 19N 120 57 E
Gapat →, *India* **93 G10** 24 30N 82 28 E
Gapuwiyak, *Australia* **126 A2** 12 25 S 135 43 E
Gar, *China* **68 C2** 32 10N 79 58 E
Garabekewül, *Turkmenistan* **65 D2** 38 30N 64 8 E
Garabogazköl Aylagy, *Turkmenistan* **57 F9** 41 0N 53 30 E
Garachico, *Canary Is.* **9 e1** 28 22N 16 46W
Garachiné, *Panama* **164 E4** 8 0N 78 12W
Garad, *Somali Rep.* **120 C3** 6 57N 49 24 E
Garafía, *Canary Is.* **9 e1** 28 48N 17 57W
Garah, *Australia* **127 D4** 29 5 S 149 38 E
Garaina, *Papua N. G.* **132 D4** 7 53 S 147 8 E
Garajonay, *Canary Is.* **9 e1** 28 7N 17 14W
Garamätnyyaz, *Turkmenistan* **65 E2** 37 45N 64 34 E
Garamba, Parc Nat. de la, *Dem. Rep. of the Congo* **118 B2** 4 10N 29 40 E
Garango, *Burkina Faso* **113 C4** 11 48N 0 34W
Garanhuns, *Brazil* **170 C4** 8 50 S 36 30W
Garautha, *India* **93 G8** 25 34N 79 18 E
Garavuti, *Tajikistan* **65 E4** 37 34N 68 26 E
Garawe, *Liberia* **112 E3** 4 35N 8 0W
Garba Harre, *Somali Rep.* **120 D2** 3 19N 42 13 E
Garba Tula, *Kenya* **118 B4** 0 30N 38 32 E
Garbagududu, *Ethiopia* **120 C2** 6 12N 43 50 E
Garbahaarrey = Garba Harre, *Somali Rep.* **120 D2** 3 19N 42 13 E
Garberville, *U.S.A.* **158 F2** 40 6N 123 48W
Garbiyang, *India* **93 D9** 30 8N 80 54 E
Garbsen, *Germany* **30 C5** 52 26N 9 36 E
Garça, *Brazil* **171 F2** 22 14 S 49 37W
Garças →, *Mato Grosso, Brazil* **173 D7** 15 54 S 52 16W
Garças →, *Pernambuco, Brazil* **170 C4** 8 43 S 39 41W
Garchitorena, *Phil.* **80 E4** 13 53N 123 40 E
Garcia Hernandez, *Phil.* **81 G5** 9 37N 124 18 E
Garcias, *Brazil* **173 E7** 20 34 S 52 13W
Gard □, *France* **29 D8** 44 2N 4 10 E
Gard →, *France* **29 E8** 43 51N 4 37 E
Garda, L. di, *Italy* **44 C7** 45 40N 10 41 E
Gardanne, *France* **29 E9** 43 27N 5 27 E
Gårdby, *Sweden* **17 H10** 56 36N 16 38 E
Garde L., *Canada* **143 A7** 62 50N 106 13W
Gardelegen, *Germany* **30 C7** 52 32N 11 24 E
Garden City, *Ga., U.S.A.* **152 C8** 32 6N 81 9W
Garden City, *Kans., U.S.A.* **155 G4** 37 58N 100 53W
Garden City, *Mo., U.S.A.* **156 F2** 38 34N 94 12W
Garden City, *Tex., U.S.A.* **155 K4** 31 52N 101 29W
Garden Grove, *U.S.A.* **161 M9** 33 47N 117 55W
Gardēz, *Afghan.* **91 B3** 33 37N 69 9 E
Gardhíki, *Greece* **48 C3** 38 50N 21 55 E
Garðsur, *Iceland* **11 A10** 66 4N 16 46W
Gardiner, *Maine, U.S.A.* **149 C11** 44 14N 69 47W
Gardiner, *Mont., U.S.A.* **158 D8** 45 2N 110 22W
Gardiners I., *U.S.A.* **151 E12** 41 6N 72 6W
Gardner, *Fla., U.S.A.* **153 H8** 27 21N 81 48W
Gardner, *Ill., U.S.A.* **157 C8** 41 12N 88 17W
Gardner, *Mass., U.S.A.* **151 D13** 42 34N 71 59W
Gardner Canal, *Canada* **142 C3** 53 27N 128 8W
Gardner Pinnacles, *U.S.A.* **145 G10** 25 0N 167 55W
Gardnerville, *U.S.A.* **160 G7** 38 56N 119 45W
Gardno, Jezioro, *Poland* **54 D4** 54 40N 17 7 E
Gardo, *Somali Rep.* **120 C3** 9 30N 49 6 E
Gardone Val Trómpia, *Italy* **44 C7** 45 41N 10 11 E
Gárdony, *Hungary* **52 C3** 47 12N 18 39 E
Gare Tigre, *Fr. Guiana* **169 C7** 4 58N 53 9W
Gareloi I., *U.S.A.* **144 L3** 51 48N 178 48W
Garešnica, *Croatia* **45 C13** 45 36N 16 56 E
Garéssio, *Italy* **44 D5** 44 12N 8 2 E
Garey, *U.S.A.* **161 L6** 34 53N 120 19W
Garfield, *U.S.A.* **158 C5** 47 1N 117 9W
Garforth, *U.K.* **20 D6** 53 47N 1 24W
Gargaliánoi, *Greece* **48 D3** 37 4N 21 38 E
Gargan, Mt., *France* **28 C5** 45 37N 1 39 E
Gargett, *Australia* **126 K6** 21 9 S 148 46 E
Gargouna, *Mali* **113 B5** 15 56N 0 13 E
Gargždai, *Lithuania* **55 C8** 55 43N 21 24 E
Garhchiroli, *India* **94 D5** 20 10N 80 0 E
Gari, *Russia* **64 B9** 59 26N 62 21 E
Garibaldi Prov. Park, *Canada* **142 D4** 49 50N 122 40W
Gariep, L., *S. Africa* **116 E4** 30 40 S 25 40 E
Garies, *S. Africa* **116 E2** 30 32 S 17 59 E
Garigliano →, *Italy* **46 A6** 41 13N 13 45 E
Garissa, *Kenya* **118 C4** 0 25 S 39 40 E
Garkida, *Nigeria* **113 C7** 10 27N 12 36 E
Garko, *Nigeria* **113 C6** 11 45N 8 35 E
Garland, *Tex., U.S.A.* **155 J6** 32 55N 96 38W
Garland, *Utah, U.S.A.* **158 F7** 41 47N 112 10W
Garlasco, *Italy* **44 C5** 45 12N 8 55 E
Garliava, *Lithuania* **54 D10** 54 49N 23 52 E
Garlin, *France* **28 E3** 43 33N 0 16W
Garm, *Tajikistan* **66 F8** 39 0N 70 20 E
Garmāb, *Iran* **97 C8** 35 25N 56 45 E
Garmisch-Partenkirchen, *Germany* **31 H7** 47 30N 11 6 E
Garmo, Qullai = Kommunizma, Pik, *Tajikistan* **66 F8** 39 0N 72 2 E
Garmsār, *Iran* **97 C7** 35 20N 52 25 E
Garner, *U.S.A.* **156 A3** 43 6N 93 36W
Garnett, *U.S.A.* **154 F7** 38 17N 95 14W
Garnpung L., *Australia* **128 B5** 33 25 S 143 10 E
Garo Hills, *India* **90 C3** 25 30N 90 30 E
Garoe, *Somali Rep.* **120 C3** 8 25N 48 33 E
Garonne →, *France* **28 C3** 45 2N 0 36W
Garonne, Canal Latéral à la, *France* **28 D4** 44 15N 0 18 E
Garoowe = Garoe, *Somali Rep.* **120 C3** 8 25N 48 33 E
Garot, *India* **92 G6** 24 19N 75 41 E
Garoua, *Cameroon* **113 D7** 9 19N 13 21 E
Garove I., *Papua N. G.* **132 C5** 4 42 S 149 30 E
Garpenberg, *Sweden* **16 D10** 60 19N 16 12 E
Garphyttan, *Sweden* **16 E8** 59 18N 14 56 E
Garrauli, *India* **93 G8** 25 5N 79 22 E
Garrel, *Germany* **30 C4** 52 57N 8 1 E
Garrett, *U.S.A.* **157 C11** 41 21N 85 8W
Garrigue = Garrigues, *France* **28 E7** 43 40N 3 55 E
Garrigues, *France* **28 E7** 43 40N 3 55 E
Garrison, *Ky., U.S.A.* **157 F13** 38 36N 83 10W
Garrison, *Mont., U.S.A.* **158 C7** 46 31N 112 49W
Garrison, *N. Dak., U.S.A.* **154 B4** 47 40N 101 25W
Garrison Res. = Sakakawea, L., *U.S.A.* **154 B4** 47 30N 101 25W
Garron Pt., *U.K.* **23 A6** 55 3N 5 59W
Garrovillas, *Spain* **43 F4** 39 40N 6 33W
Garrucha, *Spain* **41 H3** 37 11N 1 49W
Garry →, *U.K.* **22 E5** 56 44N 3 47W
Garry, L., *Canada* **138 B9** 65 58N 100 18W
Garsen, *Kenya* **118 C5** 2 20 S 40 5 E
Gärsnäs, *Sweden* **17 J8** 55 32N 14 10 E
Garson L., *Canada* **143 B6** 56 19N 110 2W
Gartempe →, *France* **28 B4** 46 47N 0 49 E
Gartz, *Germany* **30 B10** 53 13N 14 22 E
Garu, *Ghana* **113 C4** 10 55N 0 11W
Garu, *India* **93 H11** 23 40N 84 14 E
Garub, *Namibia* **116 D2** 26 37 S 16 0 E
Garut, *Indonesia* **85 D3** 7 14 S 107 53 E
Garvão, *Portugal* **43 H2** 37 42N 8 21W
Garvie Mts., *N.Z.* **131 F3** 45 30 S 168 50 E
Garwa = Garoua, *Cameroon* **113 D7** 9 19N 13 21 E
Garwa, *India* **93 G10** 24 11N 83 47 E
Garwolin, *Poland* **55 G8** 51 55N 21 38 E
Gary, *U.S.A.* **157 C9** 41 36N 87 20W
Garz, *Germany* **30 A9** 54 19N 13 20 E
Garzê, *China* **76 B3** 31 38N 100 1 E
Garzón, *Colombia* **168 C2** 2 10N 75 40W
Gas City, *U.S.A.* **157 D11** 40 29N 85 37W
Gas-San, *Japan* **70 E10** 38 32N 140 1 E
Gasan, *Phil.* **80 E3** 13 19N 121 51 E
Gasan Kuli = Esenguly, *Turkmenistan* **66 F6** 37 37N 53 59 E
Gaschurn, *Austria* **33 C10** 46 59N 10 2 E
Gascogne, *France* **28 E4** 43 45N 0 20 E
Gascogne, G. de, *Europe* **28 E2** 44 0N 2 0W
Gasconade, *U.S.A.* **156 F5** 38 40N 91 34W
Gasconade →, *U.S.A.* **156 F5** 38 41N 91 33W
Gascony = Gascogne, *France* **28 E4** 43 45N 0 20 E
Gascoyne →, *Australia* **125 D1** 24 52 S 113 37 E
Gascoyne Junction, *Australia* **125 E2** 25 2 S 115 17 E
Gascueña, *Spain* **40 E2** 40 18N 2 31W
Gash, Wadi →, *Ethiopia* **107 D4** 16 48N 35 51 E
Gash-Setit Wildlife Reserve, *Eritrea* **107 D4** 15 12N 36 58 E
Gashagar, *Nigeria* **113 C7** 13 22N 12 47 E
Gashaka, *Nigeria* **113 D7** 7 20N 11 29 E
Gashaka-Gumti Nat. Park, *Nigeria* **113 D7** 7 23N 11 34 E
Gasherbrum, *Pakistan* **93 B7** 35 40N 76 40 E
Gashua, *Nigeria* **113 C7** 12 54N 11 0 E
Gasmata, *Papua N. G.* **132 D6** 6 17 S 150 20 E
Gasparilla I., *U.S.A.* **153 J7** 26 46N 82 16W
Gasparillo, *Trin. & Tob.* **169 F9** 10 18N 61 26W
Gaspé, *Canada* **141 C7** 48 52N 64 30W
Gaspé, C. de, *Canada* **141 C7** 48 48N 64 7W
Gaspé, Pén. de, *Canada* **141 C6** 48 45N 65 40W
Gaspésie, Parc de Conservation de la, *Canada* **141 C6** 48 55N 65 50W
Gassan, *Burkina Faso* **112 C4** 12 49N 3 12W
Gassol, *Nigeria* **113 D7** 8 34N 10 25 E
Gasteiz = Vitoria-Gasteiz, *Spain* **40 C2** 42 50N 2 41W
Gaston, *U.S.A.* **152 B8** 33 49N 81 5W
Gastonia, *U.S.A.* **149 H5** 35 16N 81 11W
Gastoúni, *Greece* **48 D3** 37 51N 21 15 E
Gastoúri, *Greece* **38 B9** 39 34N 19 54 E
Gastre, *Argentina* **176 B3** 42 20 S 69 15W
Gästrikland, *Sweden* **16 D10** 60 45N 16 40 E
Gata, C., *Cyprus* **39 F9** 34 34N 33 2 E
Gata, C. de, *Spain* **41 J2** 36 41N 2 13W
Gata, Sierra de, *Spain* **42 E4** 40 20N 6 45W
Gataga →, *Canada* **142 B3** 58 35N 126 59W
Gătaia, *Romania* **52 E6** 45 26N 21 30 E
Gatchina, *Russia* **58 C6** 59 35N 30 9 E
Gatehouse of Fleet, *U.K.* **22 G4** 54 53N 4 12W
Gates, *U.S.A.* **150 C7** 43 9N 77 42W
Gateshead, *U.K.* **20 C6** 54 57N 1 35W
Gatesville, *U.S.A.* **155 K6** 31 26N 97 45W
Gaths, *Zimbabwe* **119 G3** 20 2 S 30 32 E
Gatico, *Chile* **174 A1** 22 29 S 70 20W
Gâtinais, *France* **27 D9** 48 5N 2 40 E
Gâtine, Hauteurs de, *France* **28 B3** 46 35N 0 45W
Gatineau, *Canada* **151 A9** 45 29N 75 38W
Gatineau →, *Canada* **140 C4** 45 27N 75 42W
Gatineau, Parc Nat. de la, *Canada* **140 C4** 45 40N 76 0W
Gattaran, *Phil.* **80 B3** 18 4N 121 38 E
Gattinara, *Italy* **44 C5** 45 37N 8 22 E
Gatton, *Australia* **127 D5** 27 32 S 152 17 E
Gatun, L., *Panama* **164 E4** 9 7N 79 56W
Gatyana, *S. Africa* **117 E4** 32 16 S 28 31 E
Gau, *Fiji* **133 B2** 18 2 S 179 18 E
Gaua, *Vanuatu* **133 D5** 14 15 S 167 30 E
Gaucín, *Spain* **43 J5** 36 31N 5 19W
Gauer L., *Canada* **143 B9** 57 0N 97 50W
Gauhati = Guwahati, *India* **90 B3** 26 10N 91 45 E
Gauja →, *Latvia* **15 H21** 57 10N 24 16 E
Gaula →, *Norway* **14 E14** 63 21N 10 14 E
Gaupne, *Norway* **18 C4** 61 25N 7 18 E
Gaurdak = Gowurdak, *Turkmenistan* **65 E3** 37 50N 66 4 E
Gauri Phanta, *India* **93 E9** 28 41N 80 36 E
Gauribidanur, *India* **95 H3** 13 37N 77 32 E
Gausta, *Norway* **15 G13** 59 48N 8 40 E
Gauteng □, *S. Africa* **117 D4** 26 0 S 28 0 E
Gāv Koshī, *Iran* **97 D8** 28 38N 57 12 E
Gāvakān, *Iran* **97 D7** 29 37N 53 10 E
Gavallai Nat. Park, *Liberia* **112 D3** 5 8N 7 20W
Gavarnie, *France* **28 F3** 42 44N 0 1W
Gavāter, *Iran* **97 E9** 25 10N 61 31 E
Gāvbandī, *Iran* **97 E7** 27 12N 53 4 E
Gavdhopoúla, *Greece* **39 F5** 34 56N 24 0 E
Gávdhos, *Greece* **39 F5** 34 50N 24 5 E
Gavi, *Italy* **44 D5** 44 41N 8 49 E
Gavião, *Portugal* **43 F3** 39 28N 7 56W
Gaviota, *U.S.A.* **161 L6** 34 29N 120 13W
Gāvkhūnī, Bātlāq-e, *Iran* **97 C7** 32 6N 52 52 E
Gävle, *Sweden* **16 D11** 60 40N 17 9 E
Gävleborgs län □, *Sweden* **16 C10** 61 30N 16 15 E
Gävlebukten, *Sweden* **16 D11** 60 40N 17 20 E
Gavorrano, *Italy* **44 F7** 42 55N 10 54 E
Gavray, *France* **26 D5** 48 55N 1 20W
Gavrilov Yam, *Russia* **58 D10** 57 18N 39 49 E
Gávrion, *Greece* **48 D6** 37 54N 24 44 E
Gawachab, *Namibia* **116 D2** 27 4 S 17 55 E
Gawai, *Burma* **90 B6** 27 56N 97 30 E
Gawilgarh Hills, *India* **94 D3** 21 15N 76 45 E
Gawler, *Australia* **128 C3** 34 30 S 138 42 E
Gawler Ranges, *Australia* **128 B2** 32 30 S 136 0 E
Gawu, *Nigeria* **113 D6** 9 14N 6 52 E
Gaxun Nur, *China* **68 B5** 42 22N 100 30 E
Gay, *Russia* **64 F7** 51 27N 58 27 E
Gay, *U.S.A.* **152 B5** 33 6N 84 35W
Gaya, *India* **93 G11** 24 47N 85 4 E
Gaya, *Niger* **113 C5** 11 52N 3 28 E
Gaya, *Nigeria* **113 C6** 11 57N 9 0 E
Gayéri, *Burkina Faso* **113 C5** 12 39N 0 29 E
Gaylord, *U.S.A.* **148 C3** 45 2N 84 41W
Gayndah, *Australia* **127 D5** 25 35 S 151 32 E
Gayny, *Russia* **64 A5** 60 18N 54 19 E
Gaysin = Haysyn, *Ukraine* **59 H5** 48 57N 29 25 E
Gayvoron = Hayvoron, *Ukraine* **59 H5** 48 22N 29 52 E
Gaza, *Gaza Strip* **103 D3** 31 30N 34 28 E
Gaza □, *Mozam.* **117 C5** 23 10 S 32 45 E
Gaza Strip □, *Asia* **103 D3** 31 29N 34 25 E
Gazalkent, *Uzbekistan* **65 C4** 41 33N 69 46 E
Gazanjyk, *Turkmenistan* **97 B7** 39 16N 55 32 E
Gazaoua, *Niger* **113 C6** 13 32N 7 55 E
Gāzbor, *Iran* **97 D8** 28 5N 58 51 E
Gazelle, Récif de la, *N. Cal.* **133 T19** 20 10 S 165 30 E
Gazelle Pen., *Papua N. G.* **132 C6** 4 40 S 152 0 E
Gazi, *Dem. Rep. of the Congo* **118 B1** 1 3N 24 30 E
Gaziantep, *Turkey* **100 D7** 37 6N 37 23 E
Gazipaşa, *Turkey* **100 D5** 36 16N 32 18 E
Gbarnga, *Liberia* **112 D3** 7 19N 9 13W
Gbekebo, *Nigeria* **113 D5** 6 20N 4 56 E
Gboko, *Nigeria* **113 D6** 7 17N 9 4 E
Gbongan, *Nigeria* **113 D5** 7 28N 4 20 E
Gcoverega, *Botswana* **116 B3** 19 8 S 24 18 E
Gcuwa, *S. Africa* **117 E4** 32 20 S 28 11 E
Gdańsk, *Poland* **54 D5** 54 22N 18 40 E
Gdańska, Zatoka, *Poland* **54 D6** 54 30N 19 20 E
Gdov, *Russia* **15 G22** 58 48N 27 55 E
Gdynia, *Poland* **54 D5** 54 35N 18 33 E
Geba →, *Guinea-Biss.* **112 C1** 11 46N 15 36W
Gebe, *Indonesia* **83 A3** 0 5N 129 25 E
Gebeciler, *Turkey* **49 C12** 38 46N 30 46 E
Gebeit Mine, *Sudan* **106 C4** 21 3N 36 29 E
Gebel Abyad, *Sudan* **106 D2** 19 0N 28 0 E
Gebel Iweibid, *Egypt* **106 H8** 30 8N 32 13 E
Gebze, *Turkey* **51 F13** 40 47N 29 25 E
Gecha, *Ethiopia* **107 F4** 7 30N 35 18 E
Gedaref, *Sudan* **107 E4** 14 2N 35 28 E
Gedaref □, *Sudan* **107 E4** 14 0N 35 0 E
Gede, Tanjung, *Indonesia* **84 D3** 6 46 S 105 12 E
Gediz, *Turkey* **49 B11** 39 1N 29 24 E
Gediz →, *Turkey* **49 C8** 38 35N 26 48 E
Gedo, *Ethiopia* **107 F4** 9 2N 37 25 E
Gèdre, *France* **28 F4** 42 47N 0 2 E
Gedser, *Denmark* **17 K5** 54 35N 11 55 E
Gedung, Pulau, *Malaysia* **87 c** 5 17N 100 23 E
Geegully Cr. →, *Australia* **124 C3** 18 32 S 123 41 E
Geel, *Belgium* **24 C4** 51 10N 4 59 E
Geelong, *Australia* **128 E6** 38 10 S 144 22 E
Geelvink B. = Cenderwasih, Teluk, *Indonesia* **79 E9** 3 0 S 135 20 E
Geelvink Chan., *Australia* **125 E1** 28 30 S 114 0 E
Geesthacht, *Germany* **30 B6** 53 26N 10 22 E
Geidam, *Nigeria* **113 C7** 12 57N 11 57 E
Geikie →, *Canada* **143 B8** 57 45N 103 52W
Geikie Gorge Nat. Park, *Australia* **124 C4** 18 3 S 125 41 E
Geilenkirchen, *Germany* **30 E2** 50 57N 6 8 E
Geili, *Sudan* **107 D3** 16 1N 32 37 E
Geilo, *Norway* **18 D5** 60 32N 8 14 E
Geisingen, *Germany* **31 H4** 47 54N 8 38 E
Geislingen, *Germany* **31 G5** 48 37N 9 50 E
Geistown, *U.S.A.* **150 F6** 40 18N 78 52W
Geita, *Tanzania* **118 C3** 2 48 S 32 12 E
Geitastrand, *Norway* **18 A6** 63 22N 9 56 E
Geithus, *Norway* **18 E6** 59 57N 9 59 E
Gejiu, *China* **76 F4** 23 20N 103 10 E
Gel →, *Sudan* **107 F2** 7 5N 29 10 E
Gel, Meydān-e, *Iran* **97 D7** 29 4N 54 50 E
Gel River, *Sudan* **107 F2** 7 5N 29 10 E

218 Glasgow

Glasgow, *Ky., U.S.A.* **148 G3** 37 0N 85 55W
Glasgow, *Mo., U.S.A.* **156 E4** 39 14N 92 51W
Glasgow, *Mont., U.S.A.* **158 B10** 48 12N 106 38W
Glasgow, City of □, *U.K.* **22 F4** 55 51N 4 12W
Glaslyn, *Canada* **143 C7** 53 22N 108 21W
Glastonbury, *U.K.* **21 F5** 51 9N 2 43W
Glastonbury, *U.S.A.* **151 E12** 41 43N 72 37W
Glatt →, *Switz.* **33 B7** 47 28N 8 32 E
Glattfelden, *Switz.* **33 A7** 47 33N 8 30 E
Glauchau, *Germany* **30 E8** 50 49N 12 31 E
Glava, *Sweden* **16 E6** 59 33N 12 35 E
Glavice, *Croatia* **45 E13** 43 43N 16 41 E
Glazov, *Russia* **60 A11** 58 9N 52 40 E
Gleichen, *Canada* **142 C6** 50 52N 113 3W
Gleisdorf, *Austria* **34 D8** 47 6N 15 44 E
Gleiwitz = Gliwice, *Poland* **55 H5** 50 22N 18 41 E
Glen, *U.S.A.* **151 B13** 44 7N 71 11W
Glen Affric, *U.K.* **22 D3** 57 17N 5 1W
Glen Afton, *N.Z.* **130 D4** 37 37 S 175 4 E
Glen Canyon, *U.S.A.* **159 H8** 37 30N 110 40W
Glen Canyon Dam, *U.S.A.* **159 H8** 36 57N 111 29W
Glen Canyon Nat. Recr. Area, *U.S.A.* **159 H8** 37 15N 111 0W
Glen Coe, *U.K.* **22 E3** 56 40N 5 0W
Glen Cove, *U.S.A.* **151 F11** 40 52N 73 38W
Glen Garry, *U.K.* **22 D3** 57 3N 5 7W
Glen Innes, *Australia* **127 D5** 29 44 S 151 44 E
Glen Lyon, *U.S.A.* **151 E8** 41 10N 76 5W
Glen Massey, *N.Z.* **130 D4** 37 38 S 175 2 E
Glen Mor, *U.K.* **22 D4** 57 9N 4 37W
Glen Moriston, *U.K.* **22 D4** 57 11N 4 52W
Glen Robertson, *Canada* **151 A10** 45 22N 74 30W
Glen Spean, *U.K.* **22 E4** 56 53N 4 40W
Glen Ullin, *U.S.A.* **154 B4** 46 49N 101 50W
Glénan, Îs. de, *France* **26 E3** 47 42N 4 0W
Glenavy, *N.Z.* **131 E6** 44 54 S 171 7 E
Glenburn, *Australia* **129 D6** 37 27 S 145 26 E
Glencoe, *Canada* **150 D3** 42 45N 81 43W
Glencoe, *S. Africa* **117 D5** 28 11 S 30 11 E
Glencoe, *Ala., U.S.A.* **152 B4** 33 57N 85 56W
Glencoe, *Minn., U.S.A.* **154 C7** 44 46N 94 9W
Glendale, *Ariz., U.S.A.* **159 K7** 33 32N 112 11W
Glendale, *Calif., U.S.A.* **161 L8** 34 9N 118 15W
Glendale, *Fla., U.S.A.* **152 E3** 30 52N 86 7W
Glendale, *Zimbabwe* **119 F3** 17 22 S 31 5 E
Glendive, *U.S.A.* **154 B2** 47 7N 104 43W
Glendo, *U.S.A.* **154 D2** 42 30N 105 2W
Glenelg, *Australia* **128 C3** 34 58 S 138 31 E
Glenelg →, *Australia* **128 E4** 38 4 S 140 59 E
Glenfield, *U.S.A.* **151 C9** 43 43N 75 24W
Glengarriff, *Ireland* **23 E2** 51 45N 9 34W
Glenham, *N.Z.* **131 G3** 46 26 S 168 52 E
Glenhope, *N.Z.* **131 B7** 41 40 S 172 39 E
Glenmary, Mt., *N.Z.* **131 D4** 43 55 S 169 55 E
Glenmont, *U.S.A.* **150 F2** 40 31N 82 6W
Glenmorgan, *Australia* **127 D4** 27 14 S 149 42 E
Glenn, *U.S.A.* **160 F4** 39 31N 122 1W
Glennallen, *U.S.A.* **144 E11** 62 7N 145 33W
Glennamaddy, *Ireland* **23 C3** 53 37N 8 33W
Glenns Ferry, *U.S.A.* **158 E6** 42 57N 115 18W
Glennville, *U.S.A.* **152 D8** 31 56N 81 56W
Glenorchy, *Australia* **128 D5** 36 55 S 142 41 E
Glenorchy, *N.Z.* **131 E3** 44 51 S 168 24 E
Glenore, *Australia* **126 B3** 17 50 S 141 12 E
Glenreagh, *Australia* **127 E5** 30 2 S 153 1 E
Glenrock, *U.S.A.* **158 E11** 42 52N 105 52W
Glenrothes, *U.K.* **22 E5** 56 12N 3 10W
Glenrowan, *Australia* **129 D7** 36 29 S 146 13 E
Glens Falls, *U.S.A.* **151 C11** 43 19N 73 39W
Glenside, *U.S.A.* **151 F9** 40 6N 75 9W
Glenthompson, *Australia* **128 D5** 37 38 S 142 38 E
Glenties, *Ireland* **23 B3** 54 49N 8 16W
Glenville, *U.S.A.* **148 F5** 38 56N 80 50W
Glenwood, *Canada* **141 C9** 49 0N 54 58W
Glenwood, *Ark., U.S.A.* **155 H8** 34 20N 93 33W
Glenwood, *Ga., U.S.A.* **152 C7** 32 11N 82 40W
Glenwood, *Hawaii, U.S.A.* **145 D6** 19 29N 155 9W
Glenwood, *Iowa, U.S.A.* **154 E7** 41 3N 95 45W
Glenwood, *Minn., U.S.A.* **154 C7** 45 39N 95 23W
Glenwood, *Wash., U.S.A.* **160 D5** 46 1N 121 17W
Glenwood Springs, *U.S.A.* **158 G10** 39 33N 107 19W
Gletsch, *Switz.* **33 C6** 46 34N 8 22 E
Glettinganes, *Iceland* **11 B13** 65 30N 13 37W
Glidden, *U.S.A.* **156 B2** 42 4N 94 44W
Glifádha, *Greece* **48 D5** 37 52N 23 45 E
Glimåkra, *Sweden* **17 H8** 56 19N 14 7 E
Glina, *Croatia* **45 C13** 45 20N 16 6 E
Glinojeck, *Poland* **55 F7** 52 49N 20 21 E
Glittertind, *Norway* **18 C5** 61 40N 8 32 E
Gliwice, *Poland* **55 H5** 50 22N 18 41 E
Globe, *U.S.A.* **159 K8** 33 24N 110 47W
Glodeanu Siliştea, *Romania* **53 F11** 44 50N 26 48 E
Glodeni, *Moldova* **53 C12** 47 45N 27 31 E
Glödnitz, *Austria* **34 E7** 46 53N 14 7 E
Gloggnitz, *Austria* **34 D8** 47 41N 15 56 E
Głogów, *Poland* **55 G3** 51 37N 16 5 E
Głogówek, *Poland* **55 H4** 50 21N 17 53 E
Glomma →, *Norway* **15 G14** 59 12N 10 57 E
Gloria, *Phil.* **80 E3** 12 59N 121 30 E
Glorieuses, Is., *Ind. Oc.* **117 A8** 11 30 S 47 20 E
Glóssa, *Greece* **48 B5** 39 10N 23 45 E
Glossop, *U.K.* **20 D6** 53 27N 1 56W
Gloucester, *Australia* **129 B9** 32 0 S 151 59 E
Gloucester, *Papua N. G.* **132 C5** 5 31 S 148 31 E
Gloucester, *U.K.* **21 F5** 51 53N 2 15W
Gloucester, *U.S.A.* **151 D14** 42 37N 70 40W
Gloucester, C., *Papua N. G.* **132 C5** 5 26 S 148 21 E
Gloucester I., *Australia* **126 J6** 20 0 S 148 30 E
Gloucester Island Nat. Park, *Australia* **126 J6** 20 2 S 148 30 E
Gloucester Point, *U.S.A.* **148 G7** 37 15N 76 29W
Gloucestershire □, *U.K.* **21 F5** 51 46N 2 15W
Gloversville, *U.S.A.* **151 C10** 43 3N 74 21W
Glovertown, *Canada* **141 C9** 48 40N 54 3W
Gloverville, *U.S.A.* **152 B8** 33 32N 81 48W
Głowno, *Poland* **55 G6** 51 59N 19 42 E
Głubczyce, *Poland* **55 H4** 50 13N 17 52 E
Glubokiy, *Russia* **61 F5** 48 35N 40 25 E
Glubokoye = Hlybokaye, *Belarus* **58 E4** 55 10N 27 45 E
Głuchołazy, *Poland* **55 H4** 50 19N 17 24 E
Glücksburg, *Germany* **30 A5** 54 50N 9 33 E
Glückstadt, *Germany* **30 B5** 53 45N 9 25 E
Glukhov = Hlukhiv, *Ukraine* **59 G7** 51 40N 33 58 E
Glusk, *Belarus* **59 F5** 52 53N 28 41 E
Głuszyca, *Poland* **55 H3** 50 41N 16 23 E
Glyngøre, *Denmark* **17 H2** 56 46N 8 52 E
Gmünd, *Kärnten, Austria* **34 E6** 46 54N 13 31 E
Gmünd, *Niederösterreich, Austria* **34 C8** 48 45N 15 0 E
Gmunden, *Austria* **34 D6** 47 55N 13 48 E
Gnali, *Gabon* **114 C2** 2 34 S 11 18 E
Gnarp, *Sweden* **16 B11** 62 3N 17 16 E
Gnesta, *Sweden* **16 E11** 59 3N 17 17 E
Gniew, *Poland* **54 E5** 53 50N 18 50 E
Gniewkowo, *Poland* **55 F5** 52 54N 18 25 E
Gniezno, *Poland* **55 F4** 52 30N 17 35 E
Gnjilane, *Kosovo, Yug.* **50 D5** 42 28N 21 29 E
Gnoien, *Germany* **30 B8** 53 58N 12 41 E
Gnosjö, *Sweden* **17 G7** 57 22N 13 43 E
Gnowangerup, *Australia* **125 F2** 33 58 S 117 59 E
Go Cong, *Vietnam* **87 G6** 10 22N 106 40 E
Gō-Gawa →, *Japan* **72 B4** 35 2N 132 13 E
Gō-no-ura, *Japan* **72 D1** 33 44N 129 40 E
Goa, *India* **95 G1** 15 33N 73 59 E
Goa, *Phil.* **80 E4** 13 42N 123 29 E
Goa □, *India* **95 G1** 15 33N 73 59 E
Goalen Hd., *Australia* **129 D9** 36 33 S 150 4 E
Goalpara, *India* **90 B3** 26 10N 90 40 E
Goaltor, *India* **93 H12** 22 43N 87 10 E
Goalundo Ghat, *Bangla.* **93 H13** 23 50N 89 47 E
Goaso, *Ghana* **112 D4** 6 48N 2 30W
Goat Fell, *U.K.* **22 F3** 55 38N 5 11W
Goba, *Ethiopia* **107 F4** 7 1N 39 59 E
Goba, *Mozam.* **117 D5** 26 15 S 32 13 E
Gobabis, *Namibia* **116 C2** 22 30 S 19 0 E
Gobe, *Papua N. G.* **132 E5** 9 4 S 149 0 E
Göbel, *Turkey* **51 F12** 40 0N 28 9 E
Gobernador Gregores, *Argentina* **176 C2** 48 46 S 70 15W
Gobi, *Asia* **74 C6** 44 0N 110 0 E
Gobichettipalayam, *India* **95 J3** 11 31N 77 21 E
Gobles, *U.S.A.* **157 B11** 42 22N 85 53W
Gobō, *Japan* **73 D7** 33 53N 135 10 E
Gobo, *Sudan* **107 F3** 5 40N 31 10 E
Göçbeyli, *Turkey* **49 B9** 39 13N 27 25 E
Goch, *Germany* **30 D2** 51 41N 6 9 E
Gochas, *Namibia* **116 C2** 24 59 S 18 55 E
Godavari →, *India* **94 F6** 16 25N 82 18 E
Godavari Pt., *India* **94 F6** 17 0N 82 20 E
Godbout, *Canada* **141 C6** 49 20N 67 38W
Godda, *India* **93 G12** 24 50N 87 13 E
Goddua, *Libya* **108 C2** 26 26N 14 19 E
Godech, *Bulgaria* **50 C7** 43 1N 23 4 E
Goderich, *Canada* **140 D3** 43 45N 81 41W
Goderville, *France* **26 C7** 49 38N 0 22 E
Godfrey, *U.S.A.* **156 F6** 38 58N 90 11W
Godfrey Ra., *Australia* **125 D2** 24 0 S 117 0 E
Goðafoss, *Iceland* **11 B9** 65 41N 17 33W
Godhavn = Qeqertarsuaq, *Greenland* **10 D5** 69 15N 53 38W
Goðdalir, *Iceland* **11 B7** 65 20N 19 6W
Godhra, *India* **92 H5** 22 49N 73 40 E
Godinlave, *Somali Rep.* **120 C3** 5 54N 46 38 E
Gödöllő, *Hungary* **52 C4** 47 38N 19 25 E
Godoy Cruz, *Argentina* **174 C2** 32 56 S 68 52W
Gods →, *Canada* **140 A1** 56 22N 92 51W
Gods L., *Canada* **140 B1** 54 40N 94 15W
Gods River, *Canada* **143 C10** 54 50N 94 5W
Godthåb = Nuuk, *Greenland* **10 E5** 64 10N 51 35W
Godwin Austen = K2, *Pakistan* **93 B7** 35 58N 76 32 E
Goeie Hoop, Kaap die = Good Hope, C. of, *S. Africa* **116 E2** 34 24 S 18 30 E
Goéland, L. au, *Canada* **140 C4** 49 50N 76 48W
Goeree, *Neths.* **24 C3** 51 50N 4 0 E
Goes, *Neths.* **24 C3** 51 30N 3 55 E
Goffstown, *U.S.A.* **151 C13** 43 1N 71 36W
Gogama, *Canada* **140 C3** 47 35N 81 43W
Gogebic, L., *U.S.A.* **154 B10** 46 30N 89 35W
Goggetti, *Ethiopia* **107 F4** 8 11N 38 35 E
Goglin, *Poland* **55 H5** 50 30N 18 0 E
Gogonou, *Benin* **113 C5** 10 50N 2 50 E
Gogra = Ghaghara →, *India* **93 G11** 25 45N 84 40 E
Gogriâl, *Sudan* **107 F2** 8 30N 28 8 E
Gogti, *Ethiopia* **107 E5** 10 7N 42 51 E
Gohana, *India* **92 E7** 29 8N 76 42 E
Goharganj, *India* **92 H7** 23 1N 77 41 E
Goi →, *India* **92 H6** 22 4N 74 46 E
Goiana, *Brazil* **170 C5** 7 33 S 34 59W
Goianésia, *Brazil* **171 E2** 15 18 S 49 7W
Goiânia, *Brazil* **171 E2** 16 43 S 49 20W
Goiás, *Brazil* **171 E1** 15 55 S 50 10W
Goiás □, *Brazil* **170 D2** 12 10 S 48 0W
Goiatuba, *Brazil* **171 E2** 18 1 S 49 23W
Goio-Erê, *Brazil* **175 A5** 24 12 S 53 1W
Góis, *Portugal* **42 E2** 40 10N 8 6W
Gojam □, *Ethiopia* **107 E4** 10 55N 36 30 E
Gojeb, Wabi →, *Ethiopia* **107 F4** 7 12N 36 40 E
Gojō, *Japan* **73 C7** 34 21N 135 42 E
Gojra, *Pakistan* **92 D5** 31 10N 72 40 E
Gokak, *India* **95 F2** 16 11N 74 52 E
Gokarn, *India* **95 G2** 14 33N 74 17 E
Gökçeada, *Turkey* **51 F9** 40 10N 25 50 E
Gökçedağ, *Turkey* **49 B10** 39 33N 28 52 E
Gökçen, *Turkey* **49 C9** 38 7N 27 53 E
Gökçeören, *Turkey* **49 C10** 38 37N 28 35 E
Gökçeyazı, *Turkey* **49 B9** 39 40N 27 40 E
Gökırmak →, *Turkey* **100 B6** 41 25N 35 8 E
Gökova, *Turkey* **49 D10** 37 1N 28 17 E
Gökova Körfezi, *Turkey* **49 E9** 36 55N 27 50 E
Göksu →, *Turkey* **100 D6** 36 19N 34 5 E
Göksun, *Turkey* **100 C7** 38 2N 36 30 E
Gokteik, *Burma* **90 D6** 22 26N 97 0 E
Göktepe, *Turkey* **49 D10** 37 25N 28 34 E
Gokurt, *Pakistan* **92 E2** 29 40N 67 26 E
Gokwe, *Zimbabwe* **117 B4** 18 7 S 28 58 E
Gol, *Norway* **18 D5** 60 42N 8 55 E
Gol Gol, *Australia* **128 C5** 34 12 S 142 14 E
Gola, *India* **93 E9** 28 3N 80 32 E
Golaghat, *India* **90 B5** 26 30N 94 0 E
Golakganj, *India* **90 B2** 26 8N 89 52 E
Golan Heights = Hagolan, *Syria* **103 C4** 33 0N 35 45 E
Gołańcz, *Poland* **55 F4** 52 57N 17 18 E
Golāshkerd, *Iran* **97 E8** 27 59N 57 16 E
Golaya Pristen = Hola Pristan, *Ukraine* **59 J7** 46 29N 32 32 E
Gölbaşı, *Adiyaman, Turkey* **100 D7** 37 43N 37 25 E
Gölbaşı, *Ankara, Turkey* **100 C5** 39 47N 32 49 E
Golchikha, *Russia* **6 B12** 71 45N 83 30 E
Golconda, *U.S.A.* **158 F5** 40 58N 117 30W
Gölcük, *Kocaeli, Turkey* **51 F13** 40 42N 29 48 E
Gölcük, *Niğde, Turkey* **100 C6** 38 14N 34 47 E
Gold, *U.S.A.* **150 E7** 41 52N 77 50W
Gold Beach, *U.S.A.* **158 E1** 42 25N 124 25W
Gold Coast, *Australia* **122 F9** 28 0 S 153 25 E
Gold Coast, *W. Afr.* **113 E4** 4 0N 1 40W
Gold Creek, *U.S.A.* **144 E10** 62 46N 149 41W
Gold Hill, *U.S.A.* **158 E2** 42 26N 123 3W
Gold River, *Canada* **142 D3** 49 46N 126 3W
Goldach, *Switz.* **33 B8** 47 28N 9 28 E
Goldap, *Poland* **54 D9** 54 19N 22 18 E
Goldau, *Switz.* **33 B7** 47 3N 8 33 E
Goldberg, *Germany* **30 B8** 53 35N 12 4 E
Golden, *Canada* **142 C5** 51 20N 116 59W
Golden, *U.S.A.* **154 F2** 39 42N 105 15W
Golden B., *N.Z.* **131 A7** 40 40 S 172 50 E
Golden Gate, *U.S.A.* **158 H2** 37 54N 122 30W
Golden Gate Highlands Nat. Park, *S. Africa* **117 D4** 28 40 S 28 40 E
Golden Hinde, *Canada* **142 D3** 49 40N 125 44W
Golden Lake, *Canada* **150 A7** 45 34N 77 21W
Golden Rock, *India* **95 J4** 10 45N 78 48 E
Golden Vale, *Ireland* **23 D3** 52 33N 8 17W
Goldendale, *U.S.A.* **158 D3** 45 49N 120 50W
Goldfield, *U.S.A.* **159 H5** 37 42N 117 14W
Goldsand L., *Canada* **143 B8** 57 2N 101 8W
Goldsboro, *U.S.A.* **149 H7** 35 23N 77 59W
Goldsmith, *U.S.A.* **155 K3** 31 59N 102 37W
Goldsworthy, *Australia* **124 D2** 20 21 S 119 30 E
Goldthwaite, *U.S.A.* **155 K5** 31 27N 98 34W
Golegã, *Portugal* **43 F2** 39 24N 8 29W
Goleniów, *Poland* **54 E1** 53 35N 14 50 E
Golestānak, *Iran* **99 D7** 30 36N 54 14 E
Goleta, *U.S.A.* **161 L7** 34 27N 119 50W
Golfito, *Costa Rica* **164 E3** 8 41N 83 5W
Golfo Aranci, *Italy* **46 B2** 40 59N 9 38 E
Gölgeli Dağları, *Turkey* **49 D10** 37 10N 28 55 E
Gölhisar, *Turkey* **49 D11** 37 8N 29 31 E
Goliad, *U.S.A.* **155 L6** 28 40N 97 23W
Golija, *Montenegro, Yug.* **50 C2** 43 5N 18 45 E
Golija, *Serbia, Yug.* **50 C4** 43 22N 20 15 E
Golina, *Poland* **55 F5** 52 15N 18 4 E
Gölköy, *Turkey* **100 B7** 40 41N 37 37 E
Göllersdorf, *Austria* **34 C9** 48 29N 16 7 E
Gölmarmara, *Turkey* **49 C9** 38 42N 27 55 E
Golo →, *France* **29 F13** 42 31N 9 32 E
Golol, *Somali Rep.* **120 D2** 3 38N 43 49 E
Gölova, *Turkey* **49 E12** 36 48N 30 5 E
Golovin, *U.S.A.* **144 D7** 64 33N 163 2W
Golpāyegān, *Iran* **97 C6** 33 27N 50 18 E
Gölpazarı, *Turkey* **100 B4** 40 16N 30 18 E
Golra, *Pakistan* **92 C5** 33 37N 72 56 E
Golspie, *U.K.* **22 D5** 57 58N 3 59W
Golub-Dobrzyń, *Poland* **55 E6** 53 7N 19 2 E
Golubac, *Serbia, Yug.* **50 B5** 44 38N 21 38 E
Golungo Alto, *Angola* **115 D2** 9 8 S 14 46 E
Golyam Perelik, *Bulgaria* **51 E8** 41 36N 24 33 E
Golyama Kamchiya →, *Bulgaria* **51 C11** 43 10N 27 55 E
Goma, *Dem. Rep. of the Congo* **118 C2** 1 37 S 29 10 E
Gomal Pass, *Pakistan* **92 D3** 31 56N 69 20 E
Gomati →, *India* **93 G10** 25 32N 83 11 E
Gombari, *Dem. Rep. of the Congo* **118 B2** 2 45N 29 3 E
Gombe, *Dem. Rep. of the Congo* **114 C3** 0 45 S 17 36 E
Gombe, *Nigeria* **113 C7** 10 19N 11 2 E
Gombe, *Turkey* **49 E11** 36 33N 29 38 E
Gombe □, *Nigeria* **113 C7** 10 0N 11 0 E
Gombe →, *Tanzania* **118 C3** 4 38 S 31 40 E
Gombi, *Nigeria* **113 C7** 10 12N 12 30 E
Gomel = Homyel, *Belarus* **59 F6** 52 28N 31 0 E
Gomera, *Canary Is.* **9 e1** 28 7N 17 14W
Gómez Palacio, *Mexico* **162 B4** 25 40N 104 0W
Gomīshān, *Iran* **97 B7** 37 4N 54 6 E
Gommern, *Germany* **30 C7** 52 4N 11 50 E
Gomogomo, *Indonesia* **83 C4** 6 39 S 134 43 E
Gomotartsi, *Bulgaria* **50 B6** 44 6N 22 57 E
Gompa = Ganta, *Liberia* **112 D3** 7 15N 8 59W
Gomphi, *Greece* **48 B3** 39 26N 21 36 E
Goms, *Switz.* **32 D6** 46 27N 8 15 E
Gonābād, *Iran* **97 C8** 34 15N 58 45 E
Gonaïves, *Haiti* **165 C5** 19 20N 72 42W
Gonarezhou Nat. Park, *Zimbabwe* **119 G3** 21 32 S 31 55 E
Gonâve, G. de la, *Haiti* **165 C5** 19 29N 72 42W
Gonâve, I. de la, *Haiti* **165 C5** 18 45N 73 0W
Gonbad-e Kāvūs, *Iran* **97 B7** 37 20N 55 25 E
Gönc, *Hungary* **52 B6** 48 28N 21 14 E
Gonda, *India* **93 F9** 27 9N 81 58 E
Gondal, *India* **92 J4** 21 58N 70 52 E
Gonder, *Ethiopia* **107 E4** 12 39N 37 30 E
Gonder □, *Ethiopia* **107 E4** 12 55N 37 30 E
Gondia, *India* **94 D5** 21 23N 80 10 E
Gondola, *Mozam.* **119 F3** 19 10 S 33 37 E
Gondomar, *Portugal* **42 D2** 41 10N 8 35W
Gondrecourt-le-Château, *France* **27 D12** 48 31N 5 30 E
Gönen, *Balıkesir, Turkey* **51 F11** 40 6N 27 39 E
Gönen, *Isparta, Turkey* **49 D12** 37 57N 30 31 E
Gönen →, *Turkey* **51 F11** 40 6N 27 39 E
Gong Xian, *China* **76 C5** 28 23N 104 47 E
Gong'an, *China* **77 B9** 30 7N 112 12 E
Gongbei, *China* **69 G10** 22 12N 113 32 E
Gongcheng, *China* **77 E8** 24 50N 110 49 E
Gongga Shan, *China* **76 C3** 29 40N 101 55 E
Gongguan, *China* **76 G7** 21 48N 109 36 E
Gonghe, *China* **68 C5** 36 18N 100 32 E
Gongming, *China* **69 F10** 22 47N 113 53 E
Gongo Yembe, *Dem. Rep. of the Congo* **114 C3** 1 58 S 18 40 E
Gongola →, *Nigeria* **113 D7** 9 30N 12 4 E
Gongolgon, *Australia* **127 E4** 30 21 S 146 54 E
Gongoué, *Gabon* **114 C1** 0 31 S 9 13 E
Gongshan, *China* **76 D2** 27 43N 98 29 E
Gongtan, *China* **76 C7** 28 55N 108 20 E
Gongzhuling, *China* **75 C13** 43 30N 124 40 E
Goniadz, *Poland* **54 E9** 53 30N 22 44 E
Goniri, *Nigeria* **113 C7** 11 30N 12 15 E
Gonjo, *China* **76 B2** 30 52N 98 17 E
Gonnesa, *Italy* **46 C1** 39 16N 8 28 E
Gónnos, *Greece* **48 B4** 39 52N 22 29 E
Gonnosfanàdiga, *Italy* **46 C1** 39 29N 8 39 E
Gonzaga, *Phil.* **80 B4** 18 16N 122 0 E
Gonzales, *Calif., U.S.A.* **160 J5** 36 30N 121 26W
Gonzales, *Tex., U.S.A.* **155 L6** 29 30N 97 27W
González Chaves, *Argentina* **174 D3** 38 2 S 60 5W
Goobang Nat. Park, *Australia* **129 B8** 33 0 S 148 32 E
Good Hope, C. of, *S. Africa* **116 E2** 34 24 S 18 30 E
Goodenough I., *Papua N. G.* **132 E6** 9 20 S 150 15 E
Gooderham, *Canada* **150 B6** 44 54N 78 21W
Goodhouse, *S. Africa* **116 D2** 28 57 S 18 13 E
Gooding, *U.S.A.* **158 E6** 42 56N 114 43W
Goodland, *U.S.A.* **154 F4** 39 21N 101 43W
Goodlands, *Mauritius* **121 d** 20 2 S 57 39 E
Goodlow, *Canada* **142 B4** 56 20N 120 8W
Goodnews Bay, *U.S.A.* **144 G7** 59 7N 161 35W
Goodooga, *Australia* **127 D4** 29 3 S 147 28 E
Goodsprings, *U.S.A.* **161 K11** 35 49N 115 27W
Goodwater, *U.S.A.* **152 B3** 33 4N 86 3W
Goole, *U.K.* **20 D7** 53 42N 0 53W
Goolgowi, *Australia* **129 B6** 33 58 S 145 41 E
Goolwa, *Australia* **128 C3** 35 30 S 138 47 E
Goomalling, *Australia* **125 F2** 31 15 S 116 49 E
Goomeri, *Australia* **127 D5** 26 12 S 152 6 E
Goonda, *Mozam.* **119 F3** 19 48 S 33 57 E
Goondiwindi, *Australia* **127 D5** 28 30 S 150 21 E
Goongarrie, L., *Australia* **125 F3** 30 3 S 121 9 E
Goongarrie Nat. Park, *Australia* **125 F3** 30 7 S 121 30 E
Goonyella, *Australia* **126 C4** 21 47 S 147 58 E
Goose →, *Canada* **141 B7** 53 20N 60 35W
Goose Creek, *U.S.A.* **152 C9** 32 59N 80 2W
Goose L., *U.S.A.* **158 F3** 41 56N 120 26W
Gooty, *India* **95 G3** 15 7N 77 41 E
Gopalganj, *Bangla.* **90 D2** 23 1N 89 50 E
Gopalganj, *India* **93 F11** 26 28N 84 30 E
Goppenstein, *Switz.* **32 D5** 46 23N 7 46 E
Göppingen, *Germany* **31 G5** 48 42N 9 39 E
Gor, *Spain* **43 H8** 37 23N 2 58W
Góra, *Dolnośląskie, Poland* **55 G3** 51 40N 16 31 E
Góra, *Mazowieckie, Poland* **55 F7** 52 39N 20 6 E
Góra Kalwaria, *Poland* **55 G8** 51 59N 21 14 E
Gorakhpur, *India* **93 F10** 26 47N 83 23 E
Goražde, *Bos.-H.* **52 G3** 43 38N 18 58 E
Gorbatov, *Russia* **60 B6** 56 12N 43 2 E
Gorbea, Peña, *Spain* **40 B4** 43 1N 2 50W
Gorda, *U.S.A.* **160 K5** 35 53N 121 26W
Gorda, Pta., *Canary Is.* **9 e1** 28 45N 18 0W
Gorda, Pta., *Nic.* **164 D3** 14 20N 83 10W
Gordan B., *Australia* **124 B5** 11 35 S 130 10 E
Gördes, *Turkey* **49 C10** 38 54N 28 17 E
Gordon, *Ga., U.S.A.* **152 C6** 32 54N 83 20W
Gordon, *Nebr., U.S.A.* **154 D3** 42 48N 102 12W
Gordon →, *Australia* **127 G4** 42 27 S 145 30 E
Gordon, L., *Chile* **176 D3** 54 55 S 69 30W
Gordon L., *Alta., Canada* **143 B6** 56 30N 110 25W
Gordon L., *N.W.T., Canada* **142 A6** 63 5N 113 11W
Gordonvale, *Australia* **126 B4** 17 5 S 145 50 E
Goré, *Chad* **109 G3** 7 59N 16 31 E
Gore, *Ethiopia* **107 F4** 8 12N 35 32 E
Gore, *N.Z.* **131 G3** 46 5 S 168 58 E
Gore Bay, *Canada* **140 C3** 45 57N 82 28W
Görele, *Turkey* **101 B8** 41 2N 39 0 E
Goreme, *Turkey* **100 C6** 38 35N 34 52 E
Gorey, *Ireland* **23 D5** 52 41N 6 18W
Gorg, *Iran* **97 D8** 29 29N 59 43 E
Gorgān, *Iran* **97 B7** 36 50N 54 29 E
Gorgona, *Italy* **44 E6** 43 26N 9 54 E
Gorgora, *Ethiopia* **107 E4** 12 15N 37 17 E
Gorgoram, *Nigeria* **113 C7** 12 40N 10 45 E
Gorham, *U.S.A.* **151 B13** 44 23N 71 10W
Gori, *Georgia* **61 J7** 42 0N 44 7 E
Goriganga →, *India* **93 E9** 29 45N 80 23 E
Gorinchem, *Neths.* **24 C4** 51 50N 4 59 E
Gorinhatã, *Brazil* **171 E2** 19 15 S 49 45W
Goris, *Armenia* **101 C12** 39 31N 46 22 E
Goritsy, *Russia* **58 D9** 57 4N 36 43 E
Gorízia, *Italy* **45 C10** 45 56N 13 37 E
Gorj □, *Romania* **53 E8** 45 5N 23 25 E
Gorki = Horki, *Belarus* **58 E6** 54 17N 30 59 E
Gorki = Nizhniy Novgorod, *Russia* **60 B7** 56 20N 44 0 E
Gorkiy = Nizhniy Novgorod, *Russia* **60 B7** 56 20N 44 0 E
Gorkovskoye Vdkhr., *Russia* **60 B6** 57 2N 43 4 E
Gorlice, *Poland* **55 J8** 49 35N 21 11 E
Görlitz, *Germany* **30 D10** 51 9N 14 58 E
Gorlovka = Horlivka, *Ukraine* **59 H10** 48 19N 38 5 E
Gorman, *U.S.A.* **161 L8** 34 47N 118 51W
Gorna Dzhumayo = Blagoevgrad, *Bulgaria* **50 D7** 42 2N 23 5 E
Gorna Oryakhovitsa, *Bulgaria* **51 C9** 43 7N 25 40 E
Gornja Radgona, *Slovenia* **45 B13** 46 40N 16 2 E
Gornja Tuzla, *Bos.-H.* **52 F3** 44 35N 18 46 E
Gornji Grad, *Slovenia* **45 B11** 46 20N 14 52 E
Gornji Milanovac, *Serbia, Yug.* **50 B4** 44 3N 20 29 E
Gornji Vakuf, *Bos.-H.* **52 G2** 43 57N 17 34 E
Gorno Ablanovo, *Bulgaria* **51 C9** 43 37N 25 43 E
Gorno-Altay □, *Russia* **66 D9** 51 0N 86 0 E
Gorno-Altaysk, *Russia* **66 D9** 51 50N 86 5 E
Gorno-Badakhshan □, *Tajikistan* **65 D6** 38 30N 73 0 E
Gornyatski, *Russia* **56 A11** 67 32N 64 3 E
Gornyatskiy, *Russia* **61 F5** 48 18N 40 56 E
Gornyy, *Saratov, Russia* **60 E9** 51 50N 48 30 E
Gornyy, *Sib., Russia* **70 B6** 44 57N 133 59 E
Goro →, *C.A.R.* **114 A4** 9 14N 21 16 E
Gorodenka = Horodenka, *Ukraine* **59 H3** 48 41N 25 29 E
Gorodets, *Russia* **60 B6** 56 38N 43 28 E
Gorodishche = Horodyshche, *Ukraine* **59 H6** 49 17N 31 27 E
Gorodishche, *Russia* **60 D7** 53 13N 45 40 E
Gorodnya = Horodnya, *Ukraine* **59 G6** 51 55N 31 33 E
Gorodok = Haradok, *Belarus* **58 E6** 55 30N 30 3 E
Gorodok = Horodok, *Ukraine* **59 H2** 49 46N 23 32 E
Gorodovikovsk, *Russia* **61 G5** 46 8N 41 58 E
Goroka, *Papua N. G.* **132 D3** 6 7 S 145 25 E
Goroke, *Australia* **128 D4** 36 43 S 141 29 E
Gorokhov = Horokhiv, *Ukraine* **59 G3** 50 30N 24 45 E
Gorokhovets, *Russia* **60 B6** 56 13N 42 39 E
Gorom Gorom, *Burkina Faso* **113 C4** 14 26N 0 14W
Goromonzi, *Zimbabwe* **119 F3** 17 52 S 31 22 E
Gorong, Kepulauan, *Indonesia* **83 B4** 3 59 S 131 25 E
Gorongosa, Parque Nacional de, *Mozam.* **117 B5** 18 50 S 34 29 E
Gorongose →, *Mozam.* **117 C5** 20 30 S 34 40 E
Gorongoza, *Mozam.* **119 F3** 18 44 S 34 2 E
Gorongoza, Sa. da, *Mozam.* **119 F3** 18 27 S 34 2 E
Gorontalo, *Indonesia* **82 A2** 0 35N 123 5 E
Goronyo, *Nigeria* **113 C6** 13 29N 5 39 E
Górowo Iławeckie, *Poland* **54 D7** 54 17N 20 30 E
Gorron, *France* **26 D6** 48 25N 0 50W
Gorshechnoye, *Russia* **59 G10** 51 31N 38 2 E
Gort, *Ireland* **23 C3** 53 3N 8 49W
Gortis, *Greece* **39 E5** 35 4N 24 58 E
Gorumahisani, *India* **94 C8** 22 20N 86 24 E
Góry Bystrzyckie, *Poland* **55 H3** 50 16N 16 33 E
Goryachiy Klyuch, *Russia* **61 H4** 44 38N 39 8 E
Gorzkowice, *Poland* **55 G6** 51 13N 19 36 E
Górzno, *Poland* **55 E6** 53 12N 19 38 E
Gorzów Śląski, *Poland* **55 G5** 51 3N 18 22 E
Gorzów Wielkopolski, *Poland* **55 F2** 52 43N 15 15 E
Göschenen, *Switz.* **33 C7** 46 40N 8 36 E
Gose, *Japan* **73 C7** 34 27N 135 44 E
Gosford, *Australia* **129 B9** 33 23 S 151 18 E
Goshen, *Calif., U.S.A.* **160 J7** 36 21N 119 25W
Goshen, *Ind., U.S.A.* **157 C11** 41 35N 85 50W
Goshen, *N.Y., U.S.A.* **151 E10** 41 24N 74 20W
Goshogawara, *Japan* **70 D10** 40 48N 140 27 E
Gosier, *Guadeloupe* **164 b** 16 12N 61 30W
Goslar, *Germany* **30 D6** 51 54N 10 25 E
Gospič, *Croatia* **45 D12** 44 35N 15 23 E
Gosport, *U.K.* **21 G6** 50 48N 1 9W
Gosport, *U.S.A.* **157 E10** 39 21N 86 40W
Gossa, *Norway* **18 B3** 62 52N 6 50 E
Gossas, *Senegal* **112 C1** 14 28N 16 0W
Gossau, *Switz.* **33 B8** 47 25N 9 15 E
Gosse →, *Australia* **126 B1** 19 32 S 134 37 E
Gossi, *Mali* **113 B4** 15 48N 1 20W
Gossinga, *Sudan* **107 F2** 8 36N 25 59 E
Gostivar, *Macedonia* **50 E4** 41 48N 20 57 E
Gostyń, *Poland* **55 G4** 51 50N 17 3 E
Gostynin, *Poland* **55 F6** 52 26N 19 29 E
Göta älv →, *Sweden* **17 G5** 57 42N 11 54 E
Göta kanal, *Sweden* **17 F9** 58 30N 15 58 E
Götaland, *Sweden* **17 G8** 57 30N 14 30 E
Göteborg, *Sweden* **17 G5** 57 43N 11 59 E
Gotemba, *Japan* **73 B10** 35 18N 138 56 E
Götene, *Sweden* **17 F7** 58 32N 13 30 E
Goteşti, *Moldova* **53 D13** 46 9N 28 10 E
Gotha, *Germany* **30 E6** 50 56N 10 42 E
Gothenburg = Göteborg, *Sweden* **17 G5** 57 43N 11 59 E
Gothenburg, *U.S.A.* **154 E4** 40 56N 100 10W
Gothèye, *Niger* **113 C5** 13 52N 1 34 E
Gotland, *Sweden* **17 G12** 57 30N 18 33 E
Gotlands län □, *Sweden* **17 G12** 57 15N 18 30 E
Gotō-Rettō, *Japan* **71 H4** 32 55N 129 5 E
Gotse Delchev, *Bulgaria* **50 E7** 41 36N 23 46 E
Gotska Sandön, *Sweden* **15 G18** 58 24N 19 15 E
Gōtsu, *Japan* **72 C4** 35 0N 132 14 E
Gott Pk., *Canada* **142 C4** 50 18N 122 16W
Göttero, Monte, *Italy* **44 D6** 44 22N 9 42 E
Göttingen, *Germany* **30 D5** 51 31N 9 55 E
Gottwald = Zmiyev, *Ukraine* **59 H9** 49 39N 36 27 E
Gottwaldov = Zlín, *Czech Rep.* **35 B10** 49 14N 17 40 E
Götzis, *Austria* **33 B9** 47 20N 9 38 E
Goubangzi, *China* **75 D11** 41 20N 121 52 E
Gouda, *Neths.* **24 B4** 52 1N 4 42 E
Goúdhoura, Ákra, *Greece* **39 F7** 34 59N 26 6 E
Goudiry, *Senegal* **112 C2** 14 15N 12 45W
Goudoumaria, *Niger* **113 C7** 13 40N 11 10 E
Gouéké, *Guinea* **112 D3** 8 2N 8 43W
Gough I., *Atl. Oc.* **8 L11** 40 10 S 9 45W
Gouin, Rés., *Canada* **140 C5** 48 35N 74 40W
Gouitafla, *Ivory C.* **112 D3** 7 30N 5 53W
Goulburn, *Australia* **129 C8** 34 44 S 149 44 E
Goulburn Is., *Australia* **126 A1** 11 40 S 133 20 E
Goulburn River Nat. Park, *Australia* **129 B9** 32 19 S 150 10 E
Goulds, *U.S.A.* **153 K9** 25 33N 80 23W
Goulia, *Ivory C.* **112 C3** 10 1N 7 11W
Goulimine, *Morocco* **110 C3** 28 56N 10 0W
Goulmima, *Morocco* **110 B4** 31 41N 4 57W
Goumbou, *Mali* **112 B3** 15 2N 7 25W

Grimma 219

Gouménissa, Greece 50 F6 40 56N 22 37 E
Gounatolo, Solomon Is. 133 M11 8 25 S 160 52 E
Goundam, Mali 112 B4 16 27N 3 40W
Goundi, Chad 109 G3 9 22N 17 21 E
Gounou-Gaya, Chad 109 G3 9 38N 15 31 E
Goúra, Greece 48 D4 37 56N 22 20 E
Gouraya, Algeria 111 A5 36 31N 1 56 E
Gourbassi, Mali 112 C2 13 24N 11 38W
Gourdon, France 28 D5 44 44N 1 23 E
Gouré, Niger 113 C7 14 0N 10 10 E
Gouri, Chad 109 E3 18 50N 16 49 E
Gourin, France 26 D3 48 8N 3 37W
Gourits →, S. Africa 116 E3 34 21 S 21 52 E
Gourma-Rharous, Mali 113 B4 16 55N 1 50W
Goúrnais, Greece 39 E6 35 19N 25 16 E
Gournay-en-Bray, France 27 C8 49 29N 1 44 E
Gouro, Chad 109 E3 19 36N 19 36 E
Gourock Ra., Australia 129 D8 36 0 S 149 25 E
Goursi, Burkina Faso 112 C4 12 42N 2 37W
Gouvêa, Brazil 171 E3 18 27 S 43 44W
Gouverneur, U.S.A. 151 B9 44 20N 75 28W
Gouviá, Greece 38 B9 39 39N 19 50 E
Gouzon, France 27 F9 46 12N 2 14 E
Governador Valadares, Brazil 171 E3 18 15 S 41 57W
Governor Generoso, Phil. 81 H6 6 39N 126 5 E
Governor's Harbour, Bahamas 164 A4 25 10N 76 14W
Govindgarh, India 93 G9 24 23N 81 18 E
Gowan Ra., Australia 126 D4 25 0 S 145 0 E
Gowanda, U.S.A. 150 D6 42 28N 78 56W
Gower, U.K. 21 F3 51 35N 4 10W
Gowna, L., Ireland 23 C4 53 51N 7 34W
Gowrie, U.S.A. 156 B2 42 17N 94 17W
Gowurdak, Turkmenistan 65 E3 37 50N 66 4 E
Goya, Argentina 174 B4 29 10 S 59 10W
Göyçay, Azerbaijan 61 K8 40 42N 47 43 E
Goyder Lagoon, Australia 127 D2 27 3 S 138 58 E
Goyllarisquisga, Peru 172 C2 10 31 S 76 24W
Göynük, Antalya, Turkey 49 E12 36 41N 30 33 E
Göynük, Bolu, Turkey 100 B4 40 24N 30 48 E
Goz Beïda, Chad 109 F4 12 10N 21 20 E
Goz Regeb, Sudan 107 D4 16 3N 35 33 E
Gozdnica, Poland 55 G2 51 28N 15 4 E
Gozo, Malta 38 E7 36 3N 14 15 E
Graaff-Reinet, S. Africa 116 E3 32 13 S 24 32 E
Grabill, U.S.A. 157 C12 41 13N 84 57W
Grabo, Ivory C. 112 D3 4 57N 7 30W
Grabow, Germany 30 B7 53 17N 11 34 E
Grabów nad Prosną, Poland 55 G5 51 31N 18 7 E
Grabs, Switz. 33 B8 47 11N 9 27 E
Gračac, Croatia 45 D12 44 18N 15 57 E
Gračanica, Bos.-H. 52 F3 44 43N 18 18 E
Graçay, France 27 E8 47 10N 1 50 E
Graceville, U.S.A. 152 E4 30 58N 85 31W
Gracewood, U.S.A. 152 B7 33 22N 82 2W
Grachevka, Russia 64 E4 52 55N 52 52 E
Gracias a Dios, C., Honduras 164 D3 15 0N 83 10W
Graciosa, Azores 9 d1 39 4N 28 0W
Graciosa, I., Canary Is. 9 e2 29 15N 13 32W
Grad Sofiya □, Bulgaria 50 D7 42 35N 23 20 E
Gradac, Montenegro, Yug. 50 C3 43 23N 19 9 E
Gradačac, Bos.-H. 52 F3 44 52N 18 26 E
Gradaús, Brazil 170 C1 7 43 S 51 11W
Gradaús, Serra dos, Brazil 170 C1 8 0 S 50 45W
Gradeśka Planina, Macedonia 50 E6 41 30N 22 15 E
Gradets, Bulgaria 51 D10 42 46N 26 30 E
Gradišče, Slovenia 45 B12 46 37N 15 50 E
Grădiştea de Munte, Romania 53 E8 45 37N 23 13 E
Grado, Italy 45 C10 45 40N 13 23 E
Grado, Spain 42 B4 43 23N 6 4W
Grady, U.S.A. 155 H3 34 49N 103 19W
Graeca, Lacul, Romania 53 F11 44 5N 26 10 E
Grafarnes, Iceland 11 C3 64 55N 23 16W
Grafenau, Germany 31 G9 48 51N 13 22 E
Gräfenberg, Germany 31 F7 49 39N 11 14 E
Grafham Water, U.K. 21 E7 52 19N 0 18W
Grafton, Australia 127 D5 29 38 S 152 58 E
Grafton, Ill., U.S.A. 156 F6 38 58N 90 26W
Grafton, N. Dak., U.S.A. 154 A6 48 25N 97 25W
Grafton, W. Va., U.S.A. 148 F5 39 21N 80 2W
Graham, Canada 140 C1 49 20N 90 30W
Graham, Ga., U.S.A. 152 D7 31 50N 82 30W
Graham, Tex., U.S.A. 155 J5 33 6N 98 35W
Graham, Mt., U.S.A. 159 K9 32 42N 109 52W
Graham Bell, Ostrov = Greem-Bell, Ostrov, Russia 66 A7 81 0N 62 0 E
Graham I., Canada 142 C2 53 40N 132 30W
Graham Land, Antarctica 7 C17 65 0 S 64 0W
Grahamstown, S. Africa 116 E4 33 19 S 26 31 E
Grahamsville, U.S.A. 151 E10 41 51N 74 33W
Grahovo, Montenegro, Yug. 50 D2 42 40N 18 40 E
Graïba, Tunisia 108 B2 34 30N 10 13 E
Graie, Alpi, Europe 29 C11 45 30N 7 10 E
Grain Coast, W. Afr. 112 E3 4 20N 10 0W
Grajagan, Indonesia 79 K17 8 35 S 114 13 E
Grajagan, Teluk, Indonesia 79 K17 8 40 S 114 18 E
Grajaú, Brazil 170 C2 5 50 S 46 4W
Grajaú →, Brazil 170 B3 3 41 S 44 48W
Grajewo, Poland 54 E9 53 39N 22 30 E
Gramada, Bulgaria 50 C6 43 49N 22 39 E
Gramat, France 28 D5 44 48N 1 43 E
Grammichele, Italy 47 E7 37 13N 14 38 E
Grámmos, Óros, Greece 50 F4 40 18N 20 47 E
Grampian, U.S.A. 150 F6 40 58N 78 37W
Grampian Highlands = Grampian Mts., U.K. 22 E5 56 50N 4 0W
Grampian Mts., U.K. 22 E5 56 50N 4 0W
Grampians, The, Australia 128 D5 37 0 S 142 20 E
Grampians Nat. Park, Australia 128 D5 37 15 S 142 28 E
Gramsh, Albania 50 F4 40 52N 20 12 E
Gran, Norway 18 D7 60 23N 10 31 E
Gran →, Surinam 169 C6 4 1N 55 30W
Gran Altiplanicie Central, Argentina 176 C3 49 0 S 69 30W
Gran Canaria, Canary Is. 9 e1 27 55N 15 35W
Gran Chaco, S. Amer. 174 B3 25 0 S 61 0W
Gran Laguna Salada, Argentina 176 B3 44 24 S 67 23W
Gran Pajonal, Peru 172 C3 10 45 S 74 30W
Gran Paradiso, Italy 44 C4 45 33N 7 17 E
Gran Sasso d'Itália, Italy 45 F10 42 27N 13 42 E
Granada, Nic. 164 D2 11 58N 86 0W
Granada, Spain 43 H7 37 10N 3 35W
Granada, U.S.A. 155 F3 38 4N 102 19W
Granada □, Spain 43 H7 37 18N 3 0W
Granadilla de Abona, Canary Is. 9 e1 28 7N 16 33W
Granard, Ireland 23 C4 53 47N 7 30W
Granbury, U.S.A. 155 J6 32 27N 97 47W
Granby, Canada 140 C5 45 25N 72 45W
Granby, U.S.A. 158 F11 40 5N 105 56W
Grand →, Canada 150 D5 42 51N 79 34W
Grand →, Mich., U.S.A. 157 A10 43 4N 86 15W
Grand →, Mo., U.S.A. 156 E3 39 23N 93 7W
Grand →, S. Dak., U.S.A. 154 C4 45 40N 100 45W
Grand Anse, Seychelles 121 b 4 18 S 55 45 E
Grand Bahama, Bahamas 164 A4 26 40N 78 30W
Grand Baie, Mauritius 121 d 20 0 S 57 35 E
Grand Bank, Canada 141 C8 47 6N 55 48W
Grand Banks, Atl. Oc. 8 B6 45 0N 52 0W
Grand Bassam, Ivory C. 112 D4 5 10N 3 49W
Grand Batanga, Cameroon 114 B1 2 50N 9 55 E
Grand Béréby, Ivory C. 112 E3 4 38N 6 55W
Grand Blanc, U.S.A. 157 B13 42 56N 83 38W
Grand-Bourg, Guadeloupe 164 b 15 53N 61 19W
Grand Canal = Yun Ho →, China 75 E9 39 10N 117 10 E
Grand Canyon, U.S.A. 159 H7 36 3N 112 9W
Grand Canyon Nat. Park, U.S.A. 159 H7 36 15N 112 30W
Grand Cayman, Cayman Is. 164 C3 19 20N 81 20W
Grand Centre, Canada 143 C6 54 25N 110 13W
Grand Cess, Liberia 112 E3 4 40N 8 12W
Grand Coulee, U.S.A. 158 C4 47 57N 119 0W
Grand Coulee Dam, U.S.A. 158 C4 47 57N 118 59W
Grand Erg de Bilma, Niger 109 E2 18 30N 14 0 E
Grand Falls, Canada 141 C6 47 3N 67 44W
Grand Falls-Windsor, Canada 141 C8 48 56N 55 40W
Grand Forks, Canada 142 D5 49 0N 118 30W
Grand Forks, U.S.A. 154 B6 47 55N 97 3W
Grand Gorge, U.S.A. 151 D10 42 21N 74 29W
Grand Haven, U.S.A. 157 A10 43 4N 86 13W
Grand I., Mich., U.S.A. 148 B2 46 31N 86 40W
Grand I., N.Y., U.S.A. 150 D6 43 0N 78 58W
Grand Island, U.S.A. 154 E5 40 55N 98 21W
Grand Isle, La., U.S.A. 155 L9 29 14N 90 0W
Grand Isle, Vt., U.S.A. 151 B11 44 43N 73 18W
Grand Junction, Colo., U.S.A. 159 G9 39 4N 108 33W
Grand Junction, Iowa, U.S.A. 156 B2 42 2N 94 14W
Grand L., N.B., Canada 141 C6 45 57N 66 7W
Grand L., Nfld., Canada 141 C8 49 0N 57 30W
Grand L., Nfld., Canada 141 B7 53 40N 60 30W
Grand L., La., U.S.A. 155 L8 29 55N 92 47W
Grand L., Ohio, U.S.A. 157 D12 40 32N 84 25W
Grand Lahou, Ivory C. 112 D3 5 10N 5 5W
Grand Lake, U.S.A. 158 F11 40 15N 105 49W
Grand Ledge, U.S.A. 157 B12 42 45N 84 45W
Grand-Lieu, L. de, France 26 E5 47 6N 1 40W
Grand Manan I., Canada 141 D6 44 45N 66 52W
Grand Marais, Canada 154 B9 47 45N 90 25W
Grand Marais, U.S.A. 148 B3 46 40N 85 59W
Grand-Mère, Canada 140 C5 46 36N 72 40W
Grand Popo, Benin 113 D5 6 15N 1 57 E
Grand Portage, U.S.A. 154 B10 47 58N 89 41W
Grand Prairie, U.S.A. 155 J6 32 47N 97 0W
Grand Rapids, Canada 143 C9 53 12N 99 19W
Grand Rapids, Mich., U.S.A. 157 B10 42 58N 85 40W
Grand Rapids, Minn., U.S.A. 154 B8 47 14N 93 31W
Grand Ridge, U.S.A. 152 E4 30 43N 85 1W
Grand River, U.S.A. 156 D3 40 49N 93 58W
Grand St-Bernard, Col du, Europe 32 E4 45 50N 7 10 E
Grand Santi, Fr. Guiana 169 C7 4 20N 54 24W
Grand Teton, U.S.A. 158 E8 43 54N 111 50W
Grand Teton Nat. Park, U.S.A. 158 D8 43 50N 110 50W
Grand Union Canal, U.K. 21 E7 52 7N 0 53W
Grand View, Canada 143 C8 51 10N 100 42W
Grand-Vigie, Pte. de la, Guadeloupe 164 b 16 32N 61 27W
Grandas de Salime, Spain 42 B4 43 13N 6 53W
Grande →, Jujuy, Argentina 174 A2 24 20 S 65 2W
Grande →, Mendoza, Argentina 174 D2 36 52 S 69 45W
Grande →, Bolivia 173 D5 15 51 S 64 39W
Grande →, Bahia, Brazil 170 D3 11 30 S 44 30W
Grande →, Minas Gerais, Brazil 171 F1 20 6 S 51 4W
Grande →, Venezuela 169 B5 8 36N 61 39W
Grande, B., Argentina 176 D3 50 30 S 68 20W
Grande, I., Brazil 171 F3 23 9 S 44 14W
Grande, Rio →, U.S.A. 155 N6 25 58N 97 9W
Grande, Serra, Piauí, Brazil 170 C2 8 0 S 45 10W
Grande, Serra, Tocantins, Brazil 170 D2 11 15 S 46 30W
Grande Anse, Seychelles 121 b 4 40 S 55 26 E
Grande Baleine, R. de la →, Canada 140 A4 55 16N 77 47W
Grande Cache, Canada 142 C5 53 53N 119 8W
Grande Comore, Comoros Is. 121 a 11 35 S 43 20 E
Grande Dixence, Barr. de la, Switz. 32 D4 46 5N 7 23 E
Grande-Entrée, Canada 141 C7 47 30N 61 40W
Grande Prairie, Canada 142 B5 55 10N 118 50W
Grande-Rivière, Canada 141 C7 48 26N 64 30W
Grande-Terre, I., Guadeloupe 164 b 16 20N 61 25W
Grande-Vallée, Canada 141 C6 49 14N 65 8W
Grandfalls, U.S.A. 155 K3 31 20N 102 51W
Grândola, Portugal 43 G2 38 12N 8 35W
Grandpré, France 27 C11 49 20N 4 50 E
Grandson, Switz. 32 C3 46 49N 6 39 E
Grandview, Mo., U.S.A. 156 F2 38 53N 94 32W
Grandview, Wash., U.S.A. 158 C4 46 15N 119 54W
Grandview Heights, U.S.A. 157 E13 39 58N 83 2W
Grandvilliers, France 27 C8 49 40N 1 57 E
Graneros, Chile 174 C1 34 5 S 70 45W
Grangemouth, U.K. 22 E5 56 1N 3 42W
Granger, U.S.A. 158 F9 41 35N 109 58W
Grängesberg, Sweden 16 D9 60 6N 15 1 E
Grangeville, U.S.A. 158 D5 45 56N 116 7W
Granisle, Canada 142 C3 54 53N 126 13W
Granite City, U.S.A. 156 F6 38 42N 90 9W
Granite Falls, U.S.A. 154 C7 44 49N 95 33W
Granite L., Canada 141 C8 48 8N 57 5W
Granite Mt., U.S.A. 161 M10 33 5N 116 28W
Granite Pk., U.S.A. 158 D9 45 10N 109 48W
Graniteville, S.C., U.S.A. 152 B8 33 34N 81 49W
Graniteville, Vt., U.S.A. 151 B12 44 8N 72 29W
Granītogorsk, Kazakstan 65 B6 42 44N 73 28 E
Granitola, C., Italy 46 E5 37 34N 12 39 E
Granity, N.Z. 131 B6 41 39 S 171 51 E
Granja, Brazil 170 B3 3 7 S 40 50W
Granja de Moreruela, Spain 42 D5 41 48N 5 44W
Granja de Torrehermosa, Spain 43 G5 38 19N 5 35W
Gränna, Sweden 17 F8 58 1N 14 28 E
Granollers, Spain 40 D7 41 39N 2 18 E
Gransee, Germany 30 B9 53 1N 13 8 E
Grant, Fla., U.S.A. 153 H9 27 56N 80 32W
Grant, Nebr., U.S.A. 154 E4 40 53N 101 42W
Grant, Mt., U.S.A. 158 G4 38 34N 118 48W
Grant City, U.S.A. 156 D2 40 29N 94 25W
Grant I., Australia 124 B5 11 10 S 132 52 E
Grant Range, U.S.A. 159 G6 38 30N 115 25W
Grantham, U.K. 20 E7 52 55N 0 38W
Grantown-on-Spey, U.K. 22 D5 57 20N 3 36W
Grants, U.S.A. 159 J10 35 9N 107 52W
Grants Pass, U.S.A. 158 E2 42 26N 123 19W
Grantsville, U.S.A. 158 F7 40 36N 112 28W
Grantville, U.S.A. 152 B5 33 14N 84 50W
Granville, France 26 D5 48 50N 1 35W
Granville, Ill., U.S.A. 156 C7 41 16N 89 14W
Granville, N. Dak., U.S.A. 154 A4 48 16N 100 47W
Granville, N.Y., U.S.A. 151 C11 43 24N 73 16W
Granville, Ohio, U.S.A. 150 F2 40 4N 82 31W
Granville L., Canada 143 B8 56 18N 100 30W
Granvin, Norway 18 D3 60 33N 6 45 E
Graskop, S. Africa 117 C5 24 56 S 30 49 E
Gräsö, Sweden 16 D12 60 28N 18 35 E
Grass →, Canada 143 B9 56 3N 96 33W
Grass Range, U.S.A. 158 C9 47 0N 109 0W
Grass River Prov. Park, Canada 143 C8 54 40N 100 50W
Grass Valley, Calif., U.S.A. 160 F6 39 13N 121 4W
Grass Valley, Oreg., U.S.A. 158 D3 45 22N 120 47W
Grassano, Italy 47 B9 40 38N 16 17 E
Grasse, France 29 E10 43 38N 6 56 E
Grassflat, U.S.A. 150 F6 41 0N 78 6W
Grasslands Nat. Park, Canada 143 D7 49 11N 107 38W
Grassy, Australia 127 G3 40 3 S 144 5 E
Gråsten, Denmark 17 K3 54 55N 9 35 E
Grästorp, Sweden 17 F6 58 20N 12 40 E
Gratis, U.S.A. 157 E12 39 38N 84 32W
Gratkorn, Austria 34 D8 47 8N 15 21 E
Gratz, U.S.A. 157 F12 38 28N 84 57W
Graubünden □, Switz. 33 C9 46 45N 9 30 E
Graulhet, France 28 E5 43 45N 1 59 E
Graus, Spain 40 C5 42 11N 0 20 E
Gravatá, Brazil 170 C4 8 10 S 35 29W
Gravberget, Norway 18 D9 60 53N 12 14 E
Grave, Pte. de, France 28 C2 45 34N 1 4W
Gravelbourg, Canada 143 D7 49 50N 106 35W
Gravelines, France 27 A9 51 1N 2 10 E
's-Gravenhage, Neths. 24 B4 52 7N 4 17 E
Gravenhurst, Canada 140 D4 44 52N 79 20W
Gravesend, Australia 127 D5 29 35 S 150 20 E
Gravesend, U.K. 21 F8 51 26N 0 22 E
Gravina in Púglia, Italy 47 B9 40 49N 16 25 E
Gravois, Pointe-à-, Haiti 165 C5 18 15N 73 56W
Gravone →, France 29 G12 41 58N 8 45 E
Gray, France 27 E12 47 22N 5 35 E
Gray, U.S.A. 152 B6 33 1N 83 32W
Grayling, Alaska, U.S.A. 144 E7 62 57N 160 3W
Grayling, Mich., U.S.A. 148 C3 44 40N 84 43W
Grays Harbor, U.S.A. 158 C1 46 59N 124 1W
Grays L., U.S.A. 158 E8 43 4N 111 26W
Grays River, U.S.A. 160 D3 46 21N 123 37W
Grayville, U.S.A. 157 F9 38 16N 88 0W
Grayvoron, Russia 59 G8 50 29N 35 41 E
Graz, Austria 34 D8 47 4N 15 27 E
Grdelica, Serbia, Yug. 50 D6 42 55N 22 3 E
Greåker, Norway 18 E8 59 16N 11 12 E
Greasy L., Canada 142 A4 62 55N 122 12W
Great Abaco I., Bahamas 164 A4 26 25N 77 10W
Great Artesian Basin, Australia 126 C3 23 0 S 144 0 E
Great Australian Bight, Australia 125 F5 33 30 S 130 0 E
Great Bahama Bank, Bahamas 164 B4 23 15N 78 0W
Great Barrier I., N.Z. 130 C4 36 11 S 175 25 E
Great Barrier Reef, Australia 126 B4 18 0 S 146 50 E
Great Barrier Reef Commonwealth Marine Park, Australia 126 B4 20 0 S 150 0 E
Great Barrington, U.S.A. 151 D11 42 12N 73 22W
Great Basalt Wall Nat. Park, Australia 126 B4 19 52 S 145 43 E
Great Basin, U.S.A. 158 G5 40 0N 117 0W
Great Basin Nat. Park, U.S.A. 158 G6 38 55N 114 14W
Great Basses, Sri Lanka 95 L5 6 11N 81 29 E
Great Bear →, Canada 138 B7 65 0N 124 0W
Great Bear L., Canada 138 B7 65 30N 120 0W
Great Belt = Store Bælt, Denmark 17 J4 55 20N 11 0 E
Great Bend, Kans., U.S.A. 154 F5 38 22N 98 46W
Great Bend, Pa., U.S.A. 151 E9 41 58N 75 45W
Great Blasket I., Ireland 23 D1 52 6N 10 32W
Great Britain, Europe 19 D5 54 0N 2 15W
Great Camanoe, Br. Virgin Is. 165 e 18 30N 64 35W
Great Channel, Asia 95 L11 6 0N 94 0 E
Great Coco I., Burma 95 G11 14 7N 93 22 E
Great Codroy, Canada 141 C8 47 51N 59 16W
Great Dividing Ra., Australia 126 C4 23 0 S 146 0 E
Great Driffield = Driffield, U.K. 20 C7 54 0N 0 26W
Great Exuma I., Bahamas 164 B4 23 30N 75 50W
Great Falls, U.S.A. 158 C8 47 30N 111 17W
Great Fish = Groot Vis →, S. Africa 116 E4 33 28 S 27 5 E
Great Guana Cay, Bahamas 164 B4 24 0N 76 20W
Great Inagua I., Bahamas 165 B5 21 0N 73 20W
Great Indian Desert = Thar Desert, India 92 F5 28 0N 72 0 E
Great Karoo, S. Africa 116 E3 31 55 S 21 0 E
Great Lake, Australia 127 G4 41 50 S 146 40 E
Great Lakes, N. Amer. 136 E11 46 0N 84 0W
Great Malvern, U.K. 21 E5 52 7N 2 18W
Great Miami →, U.S.A. 148 F3 39 20N 84 40W
Great Nicobar, India 95 L11 7 0N 93 50 E
Great Ormes Head, U.K. 20 D4 53 20N 3 52W
Great Ouse →, U.K. 20 E8 52 48N 0 21 E
Great Palm I., Australia 126 B4 18 45 S 146 40 E
Great Pedro Bluff, Jamaica 164 a 17 51N 77 44W
Great Plains, N. Amer. 136 E9 47 0N 105 0W
Great Ruaha →, Tanzania 118 D4 7 56 S 37 52 E
Great Sacandaga Res., U.S.A. 151 C10 43 6N 74 16W
Great Saint Bernard Pass = Grand St-Bernard, Col du, Europe 32 E4 45 50N 7 10 E
Great Salt L., U.S.A. 158 F7 41 15N 112 40W
Great Salt Lake Desert, U.S.A. 158 F7 40 50N 113 30W
Great Salt Plains L., U.S.A. 155 G5 36 45N 98 8W
Great Sandy Desert, Australia 124 D3 21 0 S 124 0 E
Great Sandy Nat. Park, Australia 127 D5 26 13 S 153 2 E
Great Sangi = Sangihe, Pulau, Indonesia 82 A3 3 35N 125 30 E
Great Scarcies →, S. Leone 112 D2 9 0N 13 0W
Great Sd., Bermuda 9 a 32 17N 64 51W
Great Sea Reef, Fiji 133 A2 16 15 S 179 0 E
Great Sitkin I., U.S.A. 144 K3 52 3N 176 6W
Great Skellig, Ireland 23 E1 51 47N 10 33W
Great Slave L., Canada 142 A5 61 23N 115 38W
Great Smoky Mts. Nat. Park, U.S.A. 149 H4 35 40N 83 40W
Great Snow Mt., Canada 142 B4 57 26N 124 0W
Great Stour = Stour →, U.K. 21 F9 51 18N 1 22 E
Great Victoria Desert, Australia 125 E4 29 30 S 126 30 E
Great Wall, China 74 E5 38 30N 109 30 E
Great Whernside, U.K. 20 C6 54 10N 1 58W
Great Yarmouth, U.K. 21 E9 52 37N 1 44 E
Great Zimbabwe, Zimbabwe 119 G3 20 16 S 30 54 E
Greater Antilles, W. Indies 165 C5 17 40N 74 0W
Greater London □, U.K. 21 F7 51 31N 0 6W
Greater Manchester □, U.K. 20 D5 53 30N 2 15W
Greater St. Lucia Wetlands Park, S. Africa 117 D5 28 6 S 32 27 E
Greater Sunda Is., Indonesia 78 F4 7 0 S 112 0 E
Grebbestad, Sweden 17 F5 58 42N 11 15 E
Grebenka = Hrebenka, Ukraine 59 G7 50 9N 32 22 E
Greco, C., Cyprus 39 F10 34 57N 34 5 E
Greco, Mte., Italy 45 G10 41 48N 13 58 E
Gredos, Sierra de, Spain 42 E6 40 20N 5 0W
Greece, U.S.A. 150 C7 43 13N 77 41W
Greece ■, Europe 48 B3 40 0N 23 0 E
Greeley, Colo., U.S.A. 154 E2 40 25N 104 42W
Greeley, Nebr., U.S.A. 154 E5 41 33N 98 32W
Greeleyville, U.S.A. 152 B10 33 40N 79 59W
Greem-Bell, Ostrov, Russia 66 A7 81 0N 62 0 E
Green, U.S.A. 158 E2 43 9N 123 22W
Green →, Ky., U.S.A. 148 G2 37 54N 87 30W
Green →, Utah, U.S.A. 159 G9 38 11N 109 53W
Green B., U.S.A. 148 C2 45 0N 87 30W
Green Bay, U.S.A. 148 C2 44 31N 88 0W
Green C., Australia 129 D9 37 13 S 150 1 E
Green City, U.S.A. 156 D4 40 16N 92 57W
Green Cove Springs, U.S.A. 152 F8 29 59N 81 42W
Green Is., Papua N. G. 132 C8 4 35 S 154 10 E
Green Island Bay, Phil. 81 F2 10 12N 119 22 E
Green Lake, Canada 143 C7 54 17N 107 47W
Green Mts., U.S.A. 151 C12 43 45N 72 45W
Green Pond, U.S.A. 152 C9 32 44N 80 37W
Green River, Papua N. G. 132 B1 3 54 S 141 11 E
Green River, Utah, U.S.A. 159 G8 38 59N 110 10W
Green River, Wyo., U.S.A. 158 F9 41 32N 109 28W
Green Valley, U.S.A. 159 L8 31 52N 110 56W
Greenacres City, U.S.A. 153 J9 26 38N 80 7W
Greenbank, U.S.A. 160 B4 48 6N 122 34W
Greenbush, Mich., U.S.A. 150 B1 44 35N 83 19W
Greenbush, Minn., U.S.A. 154 A6 48 42N 96 11W
Greencastle, U.S.A. 157 E10 39 38N 86 52W
Greene, Iowa, U.S.A. 156 B4 42 54N 92 48W
Greene, N.Y., U.S.A. 151 D9 42 20N 75 46W
Greenfield, Calif., U.S.A. 160 J5 36 19N 121 15W
Greenfield, Calif., U.S.A. 161 K8 35 15N 119 0W
Greenfield, Ill., U.S.A. 156 E6 39 21N 90 12W
Greenfield, Ind., U.S.A. 157 E11 39 47N 85 46W
Greenfield, Iowa, U.S.A. 156 C2 41 18N 94 28W
Greenfield, Mass., U.S.A. 151 D12 42 35N 72 36W
Greenfield, Mo., U.S.A. 155 G8 37 25N 93 51W
Greenfield, Ohio, U.S.A. 157 E13 39 21N 83 23W
Greenfield Park, Canada 151 A11 45 29N 73 29W
Greenland ■, N. Amer. 10 D6 66 0N 45 0W
Greenland Sea, Arctic 10 B10 73 0N 10 0W
Greenock, U.K. 22 F4 55 57N 4 46W
Greenore, Ireland 23 B5 54 2N 6 8W
Greenore Pt., Ireland 23 D5 52 14N 6 19W
Greenough, Australia 125 E1 28 58 S 114 43 E
Greenough →, Australia 125 E1 28 51 S 114 38 E
Greenough Pt., Canada 150 B3 44 58N 81 26W
Greenport, U.S.A. 151 E12 41 6N 72 22W
Greensboro, Fla., U.S.A. 152 E5 30 34N 84 45W
Greensboro, Ga., U.S.A. 152 B6 33 35N 83 11W
Greensboro, N.C., U.S.A. 149 G6 36 4N 79 48W
Greensboro, Vt., U.S.A. 151 B12 44 36N 72 18W
Greensburg, Ind., U.S.A. 157 E11 39 20N 85 29W
Greensburg, Kans., U.S.A. 155 G5 37 36N 99 18W
Greensburg, Pa., U.S.A. 150 F5 40 18N 79 33W
Greenstone Pt., U.K. 22 D3 57 55N 5 37W
Greentown, U.S.A. 157 D11 40 29N 85 58W
Greenup, U.S.A. 157 E8 39 15N 88 10W
Greenvale, Australia 126 B4 18 59 S 145 7 E
Greenville, Liberia 112 D3 5 1N 9 6W
Greenville, Ala., U.S.A. 149 K2 31 50N 86 38W
Greenville, Calif., U.S.A. 160 E6 40 8N 120 57W
Greenville, Fla., U.S.A. 152 E6 30 28N 83 38W
Greenville, Ga., U.S.A. 152 B5 33 2N 84 43W
Greenville, Ill., U.S.A. 156 F7 38 53N 89 25W
Greenville, Ind., U.S.A. 157 F11 38 22N 85 59W
Greenville, Maine, U.S.A. 149 C11 45 28N 69 35W
Greenville, Mich., U.S.A. 157 A11 43 11N 85 15W
Greenville, Miss., U.S.A. 155 J9 33 24N 91 4W
Greenville, Mo., U.S.A. 155 G9 37 8N 90 27W
Greenville, N.C., U.S.A. 149 H7 35 37N 77 23W
Greenville, N.H., U.S.A. 151 D13 42 46N 71 49W
Greenville, N.Y., U.S.A. 151 D10 42 25N 74 1W
Greenville, Ohio, U.S.A. 157 D12 40 6N 84 38W
Greenville, Pa., U.S.A. 150 E4 41 24N 80 23W
Greenville, S.C., U.S.A. 149 H4 34 51N 82 24W
Greenville, Tenn., U.S.A. 149 G4 36 13N 82 51W
Greenville, Tex., U.S.A. 155 J6 33 8N 96 7W
Greenwater Lake Prov. Park, Canada 143 C8 52 32N 103 30W
Greenwich, Conn., U.S.A. 151 E11 41 2N 73 38W
Greenwich, N.Y., U.S.A. 151 C11 43 5N 73 30W
Greenwich, Ohio, U.S.A. 150 E2 41 2N 82 31W
Greenwich □, U.K. 21 F8 51 29N 0 1 E
Greenwood, Canada 142 D5 49 10N 118 40W
Greenwood, Ark., U.S.A. 155 H7 35 13N 94 16W
Greenwood, Fla., U.S.A. 152 E4 30 52N 85 10W
Greenwood, Ind., U.S.A. 157 E10 39 37N 86 7W
Greenwood, Miss., U.S.A. 155 J9 33 31N 90 11W
Greenwood, S.C., U.S.A. 149 H4 34 12N 82 10W
Greenwood, Mt., Australia 124 B5 13 48 S 130 4 E
Gregbe, Ivory C. 112 D3 6 48N 6 43W
Gregório →, Brazil 172 B3 6 50 S 70 46W
Gregory, U.S.A. 154 D5 43 14N 99 20W
Gregory →, Australia 126 B2 17 53 S 139 17 E
Gregory, L., S. Austral., Australia 127 D2 28 55 S 139 0 E
Gregory, L., W. Austral., Australia 125 E2 25 38 S 119 58 E
Gregory Downs, Australia 126 B2 18 35 S 138 45 E
Gregory L., Australia 124 D4 20 0 S 127 40 E
Gregory Nat. Park, Australia 124 C5 15 38 S 131 15 E
Gregory Ra., Queens., Australia 126 B3 19 30 S 143 40 E
Gregory Ra., W. Austral., Australia 124 D3 21 20 S 121 12 E
Greiffenberg, Germany 30 B9 53 5N 13 57 E
Greifswald, Germany 30 A9 54 5N 13 23 E
Greifswalder Bodden, Germany 30 A9 54 12N 13 35 E
Grein, Austria 34 C7 48 14N 14 51 E
Greiz, Germany 30 E8 50 39N 12 10 E
Gremikha, Russia 56 A6 67 59N 39 47 E
Gremyachinsk, Russia 64 B6 58 34N 57 51 E
Grenå, Denmark 17 H4 56 25N 10 53 E
Grenada, U.S.A. 155 J10 33 47N 89 49W
Grenada ■, W. Indies 165 D7 12 10N 61 40W
Grenade, France 28 E5 43 47N 1 17 E
Grenadier I., U.S.A. 151 B8 44 3N 76 22W
Grenadines, St. Vincent 165 D7 12 40N 61 20W
Grenchen, Switz. 32 B4 47 12N 7 24 E
Grenen, Denmark 17 G4 57 44N 10 40 E
Grenfell, Australia 129 B8 33 52 S 148 8 E
Grenfell, Canada 143 C8 50 30N 102 56W
Grenivík, Iceland 11 B8 65 57N 18 11W
Grenjaðarstaður, Iceland 11 B9 65 49N 17 21W
Grenoble, France 29 C9 45 12N 5 42 E
Grenville, C., Australia 126 A3 12 0 S 143 13 E
Grenville Chan., Canada 142 C3 53 40N 129 46W
Gréoux-les-Bains, France 29 E9 43 45N 5 52 E
Gresham, U.S.A. 160 E4 45 30N 122 26W
Gresik, Indonesia 85 D4 7 13 S 112 38 E
Gressan, Italy 32 E4 45 43N 7 17 E
Gretna, U.K. 22 F5 55 0N 3 3W
Gretna, U.S.A. 152 E5 30 37N 84 40W
Greven, Germany 30 C3 52 6N 7 37 E
Grevená, Greece 50 F5 40 4N 21 25 E
Grevená □, Greece 50 F5 40 2N 21 25 E
Grevenbroich, Germany 30 D2 51 5N 6 35 E
Grevenmacher, Lux. 24 E6 49 41N 6 26 E
Grevesmühlen, Germany 30 B7 53 52N 11 12 E
Grevestrand, Denmark 17 J6 55 36N 12 19 E
Grey →, Canada 141 C8 47 34N 57 6W
Grey →, N.Z. 131 C6 42 27 S 171 12 E
Grey, C., Australia 126 A2 13 0 S 136 35 E
Grey Ra., Australia 127 D3 27 0 S 143 30 E
Greybull, U.S.A. 158 D9 44 30N 108 3W
Greymouth, N.Z. 131 C6 42 29 S 171 13 E
Greystones, Ireland 23 C5 53 9N 6 5W
Greytown, N.Z. 130 H4 41 5 S 175 29 E
Greytown, S. Africa 117 D5 29 1 S 30 36 E
Gribanovskiy, Russia 60 E5 51 28N 41 50 E
Gribbell I., Canada 142 C3 53 23N 129 0W
Gribës, Mal i, Albania 50 F3 40 17N 19 45 E
Gribingui →, C.A.R. 114 A3 8 33N 19 5 E
Gribingui-Bamingui, Réserve de Faune du, C.A.R. 114 A3 7 45N 19 17 E
Gridley, U.S.A. 160 F5 39 22N 121 42W
Griebeg, Ras il-, Malta 38 F7 35 58N 14 23 E
Griekwastad, S. Africa 116 D3 28 49 S 23 15 E
Griesheim, Germany 31 F4 49 51N 8 33 E
Grieskirchen, Austria 34 C6 48 16N 13 48 E
Griffin, U.S.A. 152 B5 33 15N 84 16W
Griffin, L., U.S.A. 153 G8 28 52N 81 51W
Griffith, Australia 129 C7 34 18 S 146 2 E
Griffith, Canada 150 A7 45 15N 77 10W
Griffith I., Canada 150 B4 44 50N 80 55W
Griggsville, U.S.A. 156 E6 39 43N 90 43W
Grignols, France 28 D3 44 23N 0 2W
Grigoriopol, Moldova 53 C14 47 9N 29 18 E
Grimari, C.A.R. 114 A4 5 43N 20 6 E
Grimaylov = Hrymayliv, Ukraine 59 H4 49 20N 26 5 E
Grimes, U.S.A. 160 F5 39 4N 121 54W
Grimma, Germany 30 D8 51 14N 12 43 E

220 Grimmen

Grimmen, Germany 30 A9 54 7N 13 3 E
Grimsay, U.K. 22 D1 57 29N 7 14W
Grimsby, Canada 150 C5 43 12N 79 34W
Grimsby, U.K. 20 D7 53 34N 0 5W
Grimselpass, Switz. 33 C6 46 34N 8 23 E
Grímsey, Iceland 11 A9 66 33N 17 58W
Grimshaw, Canada 142 B5 56 10N 117 40W
Grimslöv, Sweden 17 H8 56 44N 14 34 E
Grímsstaðir, Iceland 11 B10 65 39N 16 7W
Grimstad, Norway 15 G13 58 20N 8 35 E
Grímsvötn, Iceland 11 C9 64 26N 17 22W
Grindavík, Iceland 11 D4 63 50N 22 26W
Grindelwald, Switz. 32 C6 46 38N 8 2 E
Grindsted, Denmark 17 J2 55 46N 8 55 E
Grindstone I., Canada 151 B8 44 43N 76 14W
Grindu, Romania 53 F11 44 44N 26 50 E
Grinnell, U.S.A. 156 C4 41 45N 92 43W
Grintavec, Slovenia 45 B11 46 22N 14 32 E
Gris-Nez, C., France 27 B8 50 52N 1 35 E
Grisolles, France 28 E5 43 49N 1 19 E
Grisons = Graubünden □, Switz. 33 C9 46 45N 9 30 E
Grisslehamn, Sweden 16 D12 60 5N 18 49 E
Grmeč Planina, Bos.-H. 45 D13 44 43N 16 16 E
Groais I., Canada 141 B8 50 55N 55 35W
Grobiņa, Latvia 54 B8 56 33N 21 10 E
Groblersdal, S. Africa 117 D4 25 15 S 29 25 E
Grobming, Austria 34 D6 47 27N 13 54 E
Grocka, Serbia, Yug. 50 B4 44 40N 20 42 E
Gródek, Poland 55 E10 53 6N 23 40 E
Grodków, Poland 55 H4 50 43N 17 21 E
Grodno = Hrodna, Belarus 58 F2 53 42N 23 52 E
Grodzisk Mazowiecki, Poland 55 F7 52 7N 20 37 E
Grodzisk Wielkopolski, Poland 55 F3 52 15N 16 22 E
Grodzyanka = Hrodzyanka, Belarus 58 F5 53 31N 28 42 E
Groesbeck, U.S.A. 155 K6 30 48N 96 31W
Groix, France 26 E3 47 38N 3 29W
Groix, Î. de, France 26 E3 47 38N 3 28W
Grójec, Poland 55 G7 51 50N 20 58 E
Gronau, Niedersachsen, Germany 30 C5 52 5N 9 47 E
Gronau, Nordrhein-Westfalen, Germany 30 C3 52 12N 7 2 E
Grong, Norway 14 D15 64 25N 12 8 E
Grönhögen, Sweden 17 H10 56 16N 16 24 E
Groningen, Neths. 24 A6 53 15N 6 35 E
Groningen, Surinam 169 B6 5 48N 55 28W
Groningen □, Neths. 24 A6 53 16N 6 40 E
Grønnedal = Kangilinnguit, Greenland 10 E6 61 20N 47 57W
Groom, U.S.A. 155 H4 35 12N 101 6W
Groot →, S. Africa 116 E3 33 45 S 24 36 E
Groot Berg →, S. Africa 116 E2 32 47 S 18 8 E
Groot-Brakrivier, S. Africa 116 E3 34 2 S 22 18 E
Groot Karasberge, Namibia 116 D2 27 20 S 18 40 E
Groot-Kei →, S. Africa 117 E4 32 41 S 28 22 E
Groot Vis →, S. Africa 116 E4 33 28 S 27 5 E
Grootdrink, S. Africa 116 D3 28 33 S 21 42 E
Groote Eylandt, Australia 126 A2 14 0 S 136 40 E
Grootfontein, Namibia 116 B2 19 31 S 18 6 E
Grootlaagte →, Africa 116 C3 20 55 S 21 27 E
Grootvloer →, S. Africa 116 E3 30 0 S 20 40 E
Gros C., Canada 142 A6 61 59N 113 32W
Gros Islet, St. Lucia 165 f 14 5N 60 58W
Gros Morne Nat. Park, Canada 141 C8 49 40N 57 50W
Gros Piton, St. Lucia 165 f 13 49N 61 5W
Gros Piton Pt., St. Lucia 165 f 13 49N 61 5W
Grósio, Italy 44 B7 46 18N 10 16 E
Grosne →, France 27 F11 46 42N 4 56 E
Grosotto, Italy 33 D10 46 17N 10 15 E
Grossa, Pta., Spain 38 C2 39 6N 1 36 E
Grosse I., U.S.A. 157 B13 42 8N 83 9W
Grossenbrode, Germany 30 A7 54 21N 11 4 E
Grossenhain, Germany 30 D9 51 17N 13 32 E
Grosser Arber, Germany 31 F9 49 6N 13 8 E
Grosser Plöner See, Germany 30 A6 54 10N 10 22 E
Grosseto, Italy 45 F8 42 46N 11 8 E
Grossgerungs, Austria 34 C7 48 34N 14 57 E
Grossglockner, Austria 34 D5 47 5N 12 40 E
Groswater B., Canada 141 B8 54 20N 57 40W
Grotli, Norway 18 B4 62 2N 7 42 E
Groton, Conn., U.S.A. 151 E12 41 21N 72 5W
Groton, N.Y., U.S.A. 151 D8 42 36N 76 22W
Groton, S. Dak., U.S.A. 154 C5 45 27N 98 6W
Grottáglie, Italy 47 B10 40 32N 17 26 E
Grottaminarda, Italy 47 A8 41 4N 15 2 E
Grottammare, Italy 45 F10 42 59N 13 52 E
Grouard Mission, Canada 142 B5 55 33N 116 9W
Grouin, Pte. du, France 26 D5 48 43N 1 51W
Groundhog →, Canada 140 C3 48 45N 82 58W
Grouw, Neths. 24 A5 53 5N 5 51 E
Grove City, Ohio, U.S.A. 157 E13 39 53N 83 6W
Grove City, Pa., U.S.A. 150 E4 41 10N 80 5W
Grove Hill, U.S.A. 149 K2 31 42N 87 47W
Groveland, Calif., U.S.A. 160 H6 37 50N 120 14W
Groveland, Fla., U.S.A. 153 G8 28 34N 81 51W
Grover City, U.S.A. 161 K6 35 7N 120 37W
Groves, U.S.A. 155 L8 29 57N 93 54W
Groveton, U.S.A. 151 B13 44 36N 71 31W
Grovetown, U.S.A. 152 B7 33 27N 82 12W
Grožnjan, Croatia 45 C10 45 22N 13 43 E
Groznyy, Russia 61 J7 43 20N 45 45 E
Grua, Norway 18 D7 60 16N 10 40 E
Grubišno Polje, Croatia 52 E2 45 44N 17 12 E
Grudovo, Bulgaria 51 D11 42 21N 27 10 E
Grudusk, Poland 55 E7 53 3N 20 38 E
Grudziądz, Poland 54 E5 53 30N 18 47 E
Gruinard B., U.K. 22 D3 57 56N 5 35W
Gruissan, France 28 E7 43 8N 3 7 E
Grumo Áppula, Italy 47 A9 41 1N 16 42 E
Grums, Sweden 16 E7 59 22N 13 5 E
Grünberg, Germany 30 E4 50 35N 8 58 E
Grund, Iceland 11 B8 65 31N 18 9W
Gründau, Germany 31 E5 50 10N 9 9 E
Grundy Center, U.S.A. 156 B4 42 22N 92 47W
Grungedal, Norway 18 E4 59 44N 7 43 E
Grünstadt, Germany 31 F4 49 34N 8 9 E
Gruvberget, Sweden 16 C10 61 6N 16 10 E
Gruver, U.S.A. 155 G4 36 16N 101 24W
Gruyères, Switz. 32 C4 46 35N 7 4 E
Gruža, Serbia, Yug. 50 C4 43 54N 20 46 E
Gryazi, Russia 59 F10 52 30N 39 58 E
Gryazovets, Russia 58 C11 58 50N 40 10 E
Grybów, Poland 55 J7 49 36N 20 55 E
Grycksbo, Sweden 16 D9 60 40N 15 29 E
Gryfice, Poland 54 E2 53 55N 15 13 E
Gryfino, Poland 55 E1 53 16N 14 29 E
Gryfów Śląski, Poland 55 G2 51 2N 15 24 E
Grythyttan, Sweden 16 E8 59 41N 14 32 E
Gstaad, Switz. 32 D4 46 28N 7 18 E
Gua Musang, Malaysia 87 K3 4 53N 101 58 E
Guacanayabo, G. de, Cuba 164 B4 20 40N 77 20W
Guacara, Venezuela 168 A4 10 14N 67 53W
Guachípas →, Argentina 174 B2 25 40 S 65 30W
Guachiría →, Colombia 168 B3 5 27N 70 36W
Guadajoz →, Spain 43 H6 37 50N 4 51W
Guadalajara, Mexico 162 C4 20 40N 103 20W
Guadalajara, Spain 40 E1 40 37N 3 12W
Guadalajara □, Spain 40 E2 40 47N 2 30W
Guadalcanal, Solomon Is. 133 M11 9 32 S 160 12 E
Guadalcanal, Spain 43 G5 38 5N 5 52W
Guadalén →, Spain 43 G7 38 5N 3 32W
Guadales, Argentina 174 C2 34 30 S 67 55W
Guadalete →, Spain 43 J4 36 35N 6 13W
Guadalimar →, Spain 43 G7 38 5N 3 28W
Guadalmena →, Spain 43 G8 38 19N 2 56W
Guadalmez →, Spain 43 G5 38 46N 5 4W
Guadalope →, Spain 40 D4 41 15N 0 3W
Guadalquivir →, Spain 43 J4 36 47N 6 22W
Guadalupe = Guadeloupe ■, W. Indies 164 b 16 20N 61 40W
Guadalupe, Brazil 170 C3 6 44 S 43 47W
Guadalupe, Mexico 161 N10 32 4N 116 32W
Guadalupe, Spain 43 F5 39 27N 5 17W
Guadalupe, U.S.A. 161 L6 34 59N 120 33W
Guadalupe →, Mexico 161 N10 32 6N 116 51W
Guadalupe →, U.S.A. 155 L6 28 27N 96 47W
Guadalupe, Sierra de, Spain 43 F5 39 28N 5 30W
Guadalupe Bravos, Mexico 162 A3 31 20N 106 10W
Guadalupe I., Pac. Oc. 136 G8 29 0N 118 50W
Guadalupe Mts. Nat. Park, U.S.A. 155 K2 32 0N 104 30W
Guadalupe Peak, U.S.A. 155 K2 31 50N 104 52W
Guadalupe y Calvo, Mexico 162 B3 26 6N 106 58W
Guadarrama, Sierra de, Spain 42 E7 41 0N 4 0W
Guadauta, Georgia 61 J5 43 7N 40 32 E
Guadeloupe ■, W. Indies 164 b 16 20N 61 40W
Guadeloupe Passage, W. Indies 165 C7 16 50N 62 15W
Guadelupe, Peru 172 B2 7 15 S 79 29W
Guadiamar →, Spain 43 J4 36 55N 6 24W
Guadiana →, Portugal 43 H3 37 14N 7 22W
Guadiana Menor →, Spain 43 H7 37 56N 3 15W
Guadiaro →, Spain 43 J5 36 17N 5 17W
Guadiato →, Spain 43 H5 37 48N 5 5W
Guadiela →, Spain 40 E2 40 22N 2 49W
Guadix, Spain 43 H7 37 18N 3 11W
Guafo, Boca del, Chile 176 B2 43 35 S 74 0W
Guafo, I., Chile 176 B2 43 35 S 74 50W
Guaico, Trin. & Tob. 169 F9 10 35N 61 9W
Guainía □, Colombia 168 C4 2 30N 69 0W
Guainía →, Colombia 168 C4 2 1N 67 7W
Guaíra, Brazil 175 A5 24 5 S 54 10W
Guaíra □, Paraguay 174 B4 25 45 S 56 30W
Guaitecas, Is., Chile 176 B2 44 0 S 74 30W
Guajará-Mirim, Brazil 173 C4 10 50 S 65 20W
Guajira □, Colombia 168 A3 11 30N 72 30W
Guajira, Pen. de la, Colombia 168 A3 12 0N 72 0W
Gualaceo, Ecuador 168 D2 2 54 S 78 47W
Gualán, Guatemala 164 C2 15 8N 89 22W
Gualdo Tadino, Italy 45 E9 43 14N 12 47 E
Gualeguay, Argentina 174 C4 33 10 S 59 14W
Gualeguaychú, Argentina 174 C4 33 3 S 59 31W
Gualequay →, Argentina 174 C4 33 19 S 59 39W
Gualicho, Salina, Argentina 176 B3 40 25 S 65 20W
Gualjaina, Argentina 176 B2 42 45 S 70 30W
Guam ■, Pac. Oc. 133 R15 13 27N 144 45 E
Guamá, Brazil 170 B2 1 37 S 47 29W
Guamá →, Brazil 170 B2 1 29 S 48 30W
Guamblin, I., Chile 176 B1 44 50 S 75 0W
Guaminí, Argentina 174 D3 37 1 S 62 28W
Guamote, Ecuador 168 D2 1 56 S 78 43W
Guampí, Sierra de, Venezuela 169 B4 6 0N 65 35W
Guamúchil, Mexico 162 B3 25 25N 108 3W
Guana I., Br. Virgin Is. 165 e 18 30N 64 30W
Guanabacoa, Cuba 164 B3 23 8N 82 18W
Guanacaste, Cordillera del, Costa Rica 164 D2 10 40N 85 4W
Guanaceví, Mexico 162 B3 25 40N 106 0W
Guanahani = San Salvador I., Bahamas 165 B5 24 0N 74 40W
Guanajay, Cuba 164 B3 22 56N 82 42W
Guanajuato, Mexico 162 C4 21 0N 101 20W
Guanajuato □, Mexico 162 C4 20 40N 101 20W
Guanambi, Brazil 171 D3 14 13 S 42 47W
Guanare, Venezuela 168 B4 8 42N 69 12W
Guanare →, Venezuela 168 B4 8 13N 67 46W
Guandacol, Argentina 174 B2 29 30 S 68 40W
Guane, Cuba 164 B3 22 10N 84 7W
Guang'an, China 76 B6 30 28N 106 35 E
Guangchang, China 77 D11 26 50N 116 21 E
Guangde, China 77 B12 30 54N 119 25 E
Guangdong □, China 77 F9 23 0N 113 0 E
Guangfeng, China 77 C12 28 20N 118 15 E
Guanghan, China 76 B5 30 58N 104 17 E
Guangling, China 74 E8 39 47N 114 22 E
Guangnan, China 76 E5 24 5N 105 4 E
Guangning, China 77 F9 23 40N 112 22 E
Guangrao, China 75 F10 37 5N 118 25 E
Guangshui, China 77 B9 31 37N 114 0 E
Guangshun, China 76 D6 26 8N 106 21 E
Guangwu, China 74 F3 37 48N 105 57 E
Guangxi Zhuangzu Zizhiqu □, China 76 F7 24 0N 109 0 E
Guangyuan, China 76 A5 32 26N 105 51 E
Guangze, China 77 D11 27 30N 117 12 E
Guangzhou, China 77 F9 23 5N 113 10 E
Guanhães, Brazil 171 E3 18 47 S 42 57W
Guanica, Puerto Rico 165 d 17 59N 66 55W
Guanipa →, Venezuela 169 B5 9 56N 62 26W
Guanling, China 76 E5 25 56N 105 35 E
Guannan, China 75 G10 34 8N 119 21 E
Guanta, Venezuela 169 A5 10 14N 64 36W
Guantánamo, Cuba 165 B4 20 10N 75 14W
Guantao, China 74 F8 36 42N 115 25 E
Guanyang, China 77 E8 25 30N 111 8 E
Guanyun, China 75 G10 34 20N 119 18 E
Guapí, Colombia 168 C2 2 36N 77 54W
Guápiles, Costa Rica 164 D3 10 10N 83 46W
Guapo B., Trin. & Tob. 169 F9 10 12N 61 41W
Guaporé, Brazil 175 B5 28 51 S 51 54W
Guaporé →, Brazil 173 C4 11 55 S 65 4W
Guaqui, Bolivia 172 D4 16 41 S 68 54W
Guara, Sierra de, Spain 40 C4 42 19N 0 15W
Guarabira, Brazil 170 C4 6 51 S 35 29W
Guaranda, Ecuador 168 D2 1 36 S 79 0W
Guarapari, Brazil 171 F3 20 40 S 40 30W
Guarapuava, Brazil 171 G1 25 20 S 51 30W
Guaratinguetá, Brazil 175 A6 22 49 S 45 9W
Guaratuba, Brazil 175 B6 25 53 S 48 38W
Guarda, Portugal 42 E3 40 32N 7 20W
Guarda □, Portugal 42 E3 40 40N 7 20W
Guardafui, C. = Asir, Ras, Somali Rep. 120 B4 11 55N 51 10 E
Guardamar del Segura, Spain 41 G4 38 5N 0 39W
Guardavalle, Italy 47 D9 38 30N 16 30 E
Guárdia Sanframondi, Italy 47 A7 41 15N 14 36 E
Guardiagrele, Italy 45 F11 42 11N 14 13 E
Guardo, Spain 42 C6 42 47N 4 50W
Guareña, Spain 43 G4 38 51N 6 6W
Guareña →, Spain 42 D5 41 29N 5 23W
Guari, Papua N. G. 132 E4 8 3 S 146 52 E
Guárico □, Venezuela 168 B4 8 40N 66 35W
Guarrojo →, Colombia 168 C3 4 6N 70 42W
Guarujá, Brazil 175 A6 24 2 S 46 25W
Guarus, Brazil 171 F3 21 44 S 41 20W
Guasave, Mexico 162 B3 25 34N 108 27W
Guascama, Pta., Colombia 168 C2 2 32N 78 24W
Guasdualito, Venezuela 168 B3 7 15N 70 44W
Guasipati, Venezuela 169 B5 7 28N 61 54W
Guasopa, Papua N. G. 132 E7 9 12 S 152 56 E
Guastalla, Italy 44 D7 44 55N 10 39 E
Guatemala, Guatemala 164 D1 14 40N 90 22W
Guatemala ■, Cent. Amer. 164 C1 15 40N 90 30W
Guatire, Venezuela 168 A4 10 28N 66 32W
Guatuaro Pt., Trin. & Tob. 169 F10 10 19N 60 59W
Guavi →, Papua N. G. 132 D2 7 48 S 143 16 E
Guaviare □, Colombia 168 C3 2 0N 72 30W
Guaviare →, Colombia 168 C4 4 3N 67 44W
Guaxupé, Brazil 175 A6 21 10 S 47 5W
Guayabero →, Colombia 168 C3 2 36N 72 47W
Guayaguayare, Trin. & Tob. 169 F9 10 12N 61 3W
Guayama, Puerto Rico 165 d 17 59N 66 7W
Guayaneco, Arch., Chile 176 C1 47 45 S 75 10W
Guayaquil, Ecuador 168 D2 2 15 S 79 52W
Guayaquil, G. de, Ecuador 168 D1 3 10 S 81 0W
Guayaramerín, Bolivia 173 C4 10 48 S 65 23W
Guayas →, Ecuador 168 D2 2 36 S 79 52W
Guaymas, Mexico 162 B2 27 59N 110 54W
Guba, Dem. Rep. of the Congo 119 E2 10 38 S 26 27 E
Guba, Ethiopia 107 E4 11 17N 35 20 E
Gubakha, Russia 64 B6 58 52N 57 36 E
Gûbâl, Madîq, Egypt 106 B3 27 30N 34 0 E
Gubam, Papua N. G. 132 E1 8 39 S 141 53 E
Guban, Somali Rep. 120 B1 10 30N 44 0 E
Gubat, Phil. 80 E5 12 55N 124 7 E
Gubbi, India 95 H3 13 19N 76 56 E
Gúbbio, Italy 45 E9 43 21N 12 35 E
Guben, Germany 30 D10 51 57N 14 42 E
Gubin, Poland 55 G1 51 57N 14 43 E
Gubio, Nigeria 113 C7 12 30N 12 42 E
Gubkin, Russia 59 G9 51 17N 37 32 E
Guča, Serbia, Yug. 50 C4 43 46N 20 15 E
Gucheng, China 77 A8 32 20N 111 30 E
Gudå, Norway 18 A8 63 27N 11 36 E
Gudalur, India 95 J3 11 30N 76 29 E
Gudata = Guadauta, Georgia 61 J5 43 7N 40 32 E
Gudbrandsdalen, Norway 15 F14 61 33N 10 10 E
Gudenå →, Denmark 17 H4 56 29N 10 13 E
Gudermes, Russia 61 J8 43 24N 46 5 E
Gudhjem, Denmark 17 J8 55 12N 14 58 E
Gudivada, India 95 F5 16 30N 81 3 E
Gudiyattam, India 95 H4 12 57N 78 55 E
Gudur, India 95 G4 14 12N 79 55 E
Gudvangen, Norway 18 D3 60 52N 6 49 E
Guebwiller, France 27 E14 47 55N 7 12 E
Guecho = Getxo, Spain 40 B2 43 21N 2 59W
Guékédou, Guinea 112 D2 8 40N 10 5W
Guelb er Rîchât, Mauritania 110 D2 21 7N 11 24W
Guéle Mendouka, Cameroon 113 E7 4 23N 12 55 E
Guélengdeng, Chad 109 F3 10 55N 15 31 E
Guelma, Algeria 111 A6 36 25N 7 29 E
Guelmine = Goulimine, Morocco 110 C3 28 56N 10 0W
Guelph, Canada 140 D3 43 35N 80 20W
Guelta Zemmur, W. Sahara 110 C2 25 8N 12 22W
Guemar, Algeria 111 B6 33 30N 6 49 E
Guéméné-Penfao, France 26 E5 47 38N 1 50W
Guéméné-sur-Scorff, France 26 D3 48 4N 3 13W
Guéné, Benin 113 C5 11 44N 3 16 E
Güeppí, Peru 168 D2 0 7 S 75 15W
Guer, France 26 E4 47 54N 2 8W
Güer Aike, Argentina 176 D3 51 39 S 69 35W
Guera, Chad 109 F3 11 55N 18 12 E
Guérande, France 26 E4 47 20N 2 26W
Guerara, Algeria 111 B5 32 51N 4 22 E
Guercif, Morocco 111 B4 34 14N 3 21W
Guéréda, Chad 109 F4 14 31N 22 5 E
Guéret, France 27 F8 46 11N 1 51 E
Guérigny, France 27 E10 47 6N 3 10 E
Guerneville, U.S.A. 160 G4 38 30N 123 0W
Guernica = Gernika-Lumo, Spain 40 B2 43 19N 2 40W
Guernsey, U.K. 21 H5 49 26N 2 35W
Guernsey, U.S.A. 154 D2 42 19N 104 45W
Guerrara, Algeria 111 C4 28 5N 0 8W
Guerrero □, Mexico 163 D5 17 30N 100 0W
Guerzim, Algeria 111 C4 29 39N 1 40W
Guessou-Sud, Benin 113 C5 10 3N 2 38 E
Gueugnon, France 27 F11 46 36N 4 4 E
Guéyo, Ivory C. 112 D3 5 25N 6 5W
Gufuðalur, Iceland 11 B4 65 34N 22 25W
Gughe, Ethiopia 107 F4 6 12N 37 30 E
Gūgher, Iran 97 D8 29 28N 56 27 E
Guglionesi, Italy 45 G11 41 55N 14 55 E
Guhakolak, Tanjung, Indonesia 79 G11 6 50 S 105 14 E
Gui Jiang →, China 77 F8 23 30N 111 15 E
Guia, Canary Is. 9 e1 28 8N 15 38W
Guia de Isora, Canary Is. 9 e1 28 12N 16 46W
Guia Lopes da Laguna, Brazil 175 A4 21 26 S 56 7W
Guiana, S. Amer. 166 C4 5 10N 60 40W
Guiana, Venezuela 169 B5 5 9N 63 36W
Guibéroua, Ivory C. 112 D3 6 14N 6 10W
Guichen B., Australia 128 D3 37 10 S 139 45 E
Guichi, China 77 B11 30 39N 117 27 E
Guider, Cameroon 113 D7 9 56N 13 57 E
Guidiguir, Niger 113 C6 13 40N 9 50 E
Guidimouni, Niger 113 C6 13 42N 9 31 E
Guiding, China 76 D6 26 34N 107 11 E
Guidong, China 77 D9 26 7N 113 57 E
Guidónia-Montecélio, Italy 45 F9 42 1N 12 45 E
Guiers, L. de, Senegal 112 B1 16 10N 15 50W
Guigang, China 76 F7 23 8N 109 35 E
Guiglo, Ivory C. 112 D3 6 45N 7 30W
Guihulñgan, Phil. 81 F4 10 7N 123 16 E
Guijá, Mozam. 117 C5 24 27 S 33 0 E
Guijuelo, Spain 42 E5 40 33N 5 40W
Guildford, U.K. 21 F7 51 14N 0 34W
Guilford, U.S.A. 151 E12 41 17N 72 41W
Guilin, China 77 E8 25 18N 110 15 E
Guillaume-Delisle L., Canada 140 A4 56 15N 76 17W
Guillaumes, France 29 D10 44 5N 6 52 E
Guillestre, France 29 D10 44 39N 6 40 E
Guilvinec, France 26 E2 47 48N 4 17W
Güimar, Canary Is. 9 e1 28 18N 16 24W
Guimarães, Brazil 170 B3 2 9 S 44 42W
Guimarães, Portugal 42 D2 41 28N 8 24W
Guimaras □, Phil. 81 F4 10 35N 122 37 E
Guimba, Phil. 80 D3 15 40N 120 46 E
Guinayangan, Phil. 80 E4 13 54N 122 27 E
Guinda, U.S.A. 160 G4 38 50N 122 12W
Guindulman, Phil. 81 G5 9 46N 124 29 E
Guinea, Africa 104 F4 8 0N 8 0 E
Guinea ■, W. Afr. 112 C2 10 20N 11 30W
Guinea, Gulf of, Atl. Oc. 113 E5 3 0N 2 30 E
Guinea-Bissau ■, Africa 112 C2 12 0N 15 0W
Güines, Cuba 164 B3 22 50N 82 0W
Guingamp, France 26 D3 48 34N 3 10W
Guinguinéo, Senegal 112 C1 14 20N 15 57W
Guinobatan, Phil. 80 E4 13 11N 123 36 E
Guipavas, France 26 D2 48 26N 4 29W
Guiping, China 77 F8 23 21N 110 2 E
Guipúzcoa □, Spain 40 B2 43 12N 2 15W
Guir, Mali 112 B4 18 52N 2 52W
Guir, O. →, Algeria 111 B4 31 29N 2 17W
Guiratinga, Brazil 173 D7 16 21 S 53 45W
Guirel, Mauritania 112 B3 15 30N 7 3W
Güiria, Venezuela 169 F8 10 32N 62 18W
Guiscard, France 27 C10 49 40N 3 1 E
Guise, France 27 C10 49 52N 3 35 E
Guita-Koulouba, C.A.R. 114 A4 5 58N 23 21 E
Guitiriz, Spain 42 B3 43 11N 7 50W
Guitri, Ivory C. 112 D3 5 30N 5 14W
Guiuan, Phil. 81 F5 11 5N 125 55 E
Guixi, China 77 C11 28 16N 117 15 E
Guiyang, Guizhou, China 76 D6 26 32N 106 40 E
Guiyang, Hunan, China 77 E9 25 46N 112 42 E
Guizhou □, China 76 D6 27 0N 107 0 E
Gujan-Mestras, France 28 D2 44 38N 1 4W
Gujar Khan, Pakistan 92 C5 33 16N 73 19 E
Gujarat □, India 92 H4 23 20N 71 0 E
Gujiang, China 77 D10 27 11N 114 47 E
Gujranwala, Pakistan 91 B4 32 10N 74 12 E
Gujrat, Pakistan 91 B4 32 40N 74 2 E
Gukovo, Russia 61 F5 48 1N 39 58 E
Gulargambone, Australia 129 A8 31 20 S 148 30 E
Gulbarga, India 94 F3 17 20N 76 50 E
Gulbene, Latvia 15 H22 57 8N 26 52 E
Gülchö, Kyrgyzstan 65 C6 40 19N 73 26 E
Guledagudda, India 95 F2 16 3N 75 48 E
Gulf □, Papua N. G. 132 D3 8 0 S 145 0 E
Gulf, The, Asia 97 E6 27 0N 50 0 E
Gulf Breeze, U.S.A. 153 E2 30 22N 87 9W
Gulf Hammock, U.S.A. 153 F7 29 15N 82 43W
Gulfport, Fla., U.S.A. 153 H7 27 44N 82 43W
Gulfport, Miss., U.S.A. 155 K10 30 22N 89 6W
Gulgong, Australia 129 B8 32 20 S 149 49 E
Gulin, China 76 C5 28 1N 105 50 E
Gulistan, Pakistan 92 D2 30 30N 66 35 E
Guliston, Uzbekistan 65 C4 40 29N 68 46 E
Gulkana, U.S.A. 144 E11 62 16N 145 23W
Gull Lake, Canada 143 C7 50 10N 108 29W
Gullbrå, Norway 18 D3 60 50N 6 17 E
Gullbrandstorp, Sweden 17 H6 56 42N 12 43 E
Gullbringusýsla □, Iceland 11 D4 64 0N 22 0W
Gullfoss, Iceland 11 C6 64 20N 20 8W
Gullhaug, Norway 18 E7 59 30N 10 15 E
Gullivan B., U.S.A. 153 K8 25 45N 81 40W
Gullspång, Sweden 17 F8 58 59N 14 6 E
Gullstein, Norway 18 A5 63 13N 8 9 E
Güllük, Turkey 49 D9 37 14N 27 35 E
Güllük Korfezi, Turkey 49 D9 37 12N 27 30 E
Gulma, Nigeria 113 C5 12 40N 4 23 E
Gulmarg, India 93 B6 34 3N 74 25 E
Gülnar, Turkey 100 D5 36 19N 33 24 E
Gulnare, Australia 128 B3 33 27 S 138 27 E
Gülpınar, Turkey 49 B8 39 32N 26 7 E
Gülşehir, Turkey 100 C6 38 44N 34 37 E
Gulshad, Kazakstan 66 E8 46 45N 74 25 E
Gulsvik, Norway 18 D6 60 24N 9 38 E
Gulu, Uganda 118 B3 2 48N 32 17 E
Gŭlŭbovo, Bulgaria 51 D9 42 8N 25 55 E
Gulud, J., Sudan 107 E2 11 41N 29 31 E
Gulwe, Tanzania 118 D4 6 30 S 36 25 E
Gulyaypole = Hulyaypole, Ukraine 59 J9 47 45N 36 21 E
Gum Lake, Australia 128 B5 32 42 S 143 9 E
Gumaca, Phil. 80 E4 13 55N 122 6 E
Gumal →, Pakistan 92 D4 31 40N 71 50 E
Gumbaz, Pakistan 92 D3 30 2N 69 0 E
Gumel, Nigeria 113 C6 12 39N 9 22 E
Gumiel de Hizán, Spain 42 D7 41 46N 3 41W
Gumla, India 93 H11 23 3N 84 33 E
Gumlu, Australia 126 B4 19 53 S 147 41 E
Gumma □, Japan 73 A10 36 30N 138 20 E
Gummersbach, Germany 30 D3 51 1N 7 34 E
Gummi, Nigeria 113 C6 12 4N 5 9 E
Gümüldür, Turkey 49 C9 38 6N 27 0 E
Gümüşçay, Turkey 51 F11 40 16N 27 17 E
Gümüşhaciköy, Turkey 100 B6 40 50N 35 18 E
Gümüşhane, Turkey 101 B8 40 30N 39 30 E
Gümüşsu, Turkey 49 C11 38 14N 29 1 E
Gumzai, Indonesia 83 C4 5 28 S 134 42 E
Guna, Ethiopia 107 F4 8 18N 39 52 E
Guna, India 92 G7 24 40N 77 19 E
Gundagai, Australia 129 C8 35 3 S 148 6 E
Gundarehi, India 94 D5 20 57N 81 17 E
Gundelfingen, Germany 31 G6 48 34N 10 22 E
Gundih, Indonesia 85 D4 7 10 S 110 56 E
Gundlakamma →, India 95 G5 15 30N 80 15 E
Gundlupet, India 95 J3 11 48N 76 41 E
Gunebang, Australia 129 B7 33 1 S 146 38 E
Güney, Burdur, Turkey 49 D11 37 29N 29 34 E
Güney, Denizli, Turkey 49 C11 38 10N 29 4 E
Güneydoğu Toroslar, Turkey 101 C9 38 20N 40 30 E
Gungal, Australia 129 B9 32 17 S 150 32 E
Gungo, Angola 115 E2 10 58 S 15 30 E
Gungu, Dem. Rep. of the Congo 115 D3 5 43 S 19 20 E
Gunisao →, Canada 143 C9 53 56N 97 53W
Gunisao L., Canada 143 C9 53 33N 96 15W
Gunjyal, Pakistan 92 C4 32 20N 71 55 E
Günlüce, Turkey 49 E10 36 50N 28 20 E
Gunnarskog, Sweden 16 E6 59 49N 12 34 E
Gunnbjørn Fjeld, Greenland 10 D8 68 55N 29 47W
Gunnebo, Sweden 17 G10 57 44N 16 32 E
Gunnedah, Australia 129 A9 30 59 S 150 15 E
Gunnewin, Australia 127 D4 25 59 S 148 33 E
Gunningbar Cr. →, Australia 129 A7 31 14 S 147 6 E
Gunnison, Colo., U.S.A. 159 G10 38 33N 106 56W
Gunnison, Utah, U.S.A. 158 G8 39 9N 111 49W
Gunnison →, U.S.A. 159 G9 39 4N 108 35W
Gunpowder, Australia 126 B2 19 42 S 139 22 E
Guntakal, India 95 G3 15 11N 77 27 E
Guntersville, U.S.A. 149 H2 34 21N 86 18W
Guntong, Malaysia 87 K3 4 36N 101 3 E
Guntur, India 95 F5 16 23N 80 30 E
Gunungapi, Indonesia 82 C3 6 45 S 126 30 E
Gunungsitoli, Indonesia 84 B1 1 15N 97 30 E
Gunupur, India 94 E6 19 5N 83 50 E
Günz →, Germany 31 G6 48 27N 10 16 E
Gunza, Angola 115 E2 10 50 S 13 50 E
Günzburg, Germany 31 G6 48 26N 10 17 E
Gunzenhausen, Germany 31 F6 49 7N 10 44 E
Guo He →, China 75 H9 32 59N 117 10 E
Guoyang, China 74 H9 33 32N 116 12 E
Gupis, Pakistan 93 A5 36 15N 73 20 E
Gura Humorului, Romania 53 C10 47 35N 25 53 E
Gura-Teghii, Romania 53 E11 45 30N 26 25 E
Gurag, Ethiopia 107 F4 8 20N 38 20 E
Gurahonţ, Romania 52 D7 46 16N 22 21 E
Gurdaspur, India 92 C6 32 5N 75 31 E
Gurdon, U.S.A. 155 J8 33 55N 93 9W
Güre, Balıkesir, Turkey 49 B8 39 36N 26 54 E
Güre, Uşak, Turkey 49 C11 38 39N 29 10 E
Gurgaon, India 92 E7 28 27N 77 1 E
Gürgentepe, Turkey 100 B7 40 51N 37 50 E
Gurghiu, Munţii, Romania 53 D10 46 41N 25 15 E
Gurgueia →, Brazil 170 C3 6 50 S 43 24W
Gurha, India 92 G4 25 12N 71 39 E
Guri, Embalse de, Venezuela 169 B5 7 50N 62 52W
Gurig Nat. Park, Australia 124 B5 11 36 S 132 7 E
Gurimatu, Papua N. G. 132 D3 6 45 S 144 45 E
Gurin, Nigeria 113 D7 9 5N 12 54 E
Gurinhatã, Brazil 171 E2 19 14 S 49 48W
Gurjaani, Georgia 61 K7 41 43N 45 52 E
Gurk →, Austria 34 E7 46 35N 14 31 E
Gurkha, Nepal 93 E11 28 5N 84 40 E
Gurley, Australia 127 D4 29 45 S 149 48 E
Gurnee, U.S.A. 157 B9 42 22N 87 55W
Gurnet Point, U.S.A. 151 D14 42 1N 70 34W
Guro, Mozam. 119 F3 17 26 S 32 30 E
Gürpınar, İst., Turkey 51 F12 40 59N 28 37 E
Gürpınar, Van, Turkey 101 C10 38 18N 43 25 E
Gürsu, Turkey 51 F13 40 13N 29 11 E
Gurué, Mozam. 119 F4 15 25 S 36 58 E
Gurun, Malaysia 87 K3 5 49N 100 27 E
Gürün, Turkey 100 C7 38 43N 37 15 E
Gurupá, Brazil 169 D7 1 25 S 51 35W
Gurupá, I. Grande de, Brazil 169 D7 1 25 S 51 45W
Gurupi, Brazil 171 D2 11 43 S 49 4W

222 Hanover

Hanover, *Ind., U.S.A.* **157 F11** 38 43N 85 28W
Hanover, *N.H., U.S.A.* **151 C12** 43 42N 72 17W
Hanover, *Ohio, U.S.A.* **150 F2** 40 4N 82 16W
Hanover, *Pa., U.S.A.* **148 F7** 39 48N 76 59W
Hanover, I., *Chile* **176 D2** 51 0S 74 50W
Hanpan, C., *Papua N. G.* **132 C8** 5 0S 154 35 E
Hans Lollik I., *U.S. Virgin Is.* **165 e** 18 24N 64 53W
Hans Meyer Ra., *Papua N. G.* **132 C7** 4 20S 152 55 E
Hansdiha, *India* **93 G12** 24 36N 87 5 E
Hanshou, *China* **77 C8** 28 56N 111 50 E
Hansi, *India* **92 E6** 29 10N 75 57 E
Hanson, L., *Australia* **128 A2** 31 0S 136 15 E
Hanstholm, *Denmark* **17 G2** 57 7N 8 36 E
Hantsavichy, *Belarus* **59 F4** 52 49N 26 30 E
Hanumangarh, *India* **92 E6** 29 35N 74 19 E
Hanyin, *China* **76 A7** 32 54N 108 28 E
Hanyū, *Japan* **73 A11** 36 10N 139 32 E
Hanyuan, *China* **76 C4** 29 21N 102 40 E
Hanzhong, *China* **74 H4** 33 10N 107 1 E
Hanzhuang, *China* **75 G9** 34 33N 117 23 E
Haora, *India* **93 H13** 22 37N 88 20 E
Haouach, O. →, *Chad* **109 E4** 16 45N 19 35 E
Haoxue, *China* **77 B9** 30 3N 112 24 E
Haparanda, *Sweden* **14 D21** 65 52N 24 8 E
Hapeville, *U.S.A.* **152 B5** 33 40N 84 25W
Happy, *U.S.A.* **155 H4** 34 45N 101 52W
Happy Camp, *U.S.A.* **158 F2** 41 48N 123 23W
Happy Valley-Goose Bay, *Canada* **141 B7** 53 15N 60 20W
Hapsu, *N. Korea* **75 D15** 41 13N 128 51 E
Hapur, *India* **92 E7** 28 45N 77 45 E
Ḥaql, *Si. Arabia* **103 F3** 29 10N 34 58 E
Haquira, *Peru* **172 C3** 14 14S 72 12W
Har, *Indonesia* **83 C4** 5 16S 133 14 E
Har-Ayrag, *Mongolia* **74 B5** 45 47N 109 16 E
Har Hu, *China* **68 C4** 38 20N 97 38 E
Har Us Nuur, *Mongolia* **68 B4** 48 0N 92 0 E
Har Yehuda, *Israel* **103 D3** 31 35N 34 57 E
Ḥaraḍ, *Si. Arabia* **99 A5** 24 22N 49 0 E
Ḥaraḍ, *Yemen* **98 C3** 16 26N 43 5 E
Haradok, *Belarus* **58 E6** 55 30N 30 3 E
Häradsbäck, *Sweden* **17 H8** 56 32N 14 26 E
Haranomachi, *Japan* **70 F10** 37 38N 140 58 E
Harardera, *Somali Rep.* **120 D3** 4 33N 47 38 E
Harare, *Zimbabwe* **119 F3** 17 43S 31 2 E
Ḥarāsīs, Jiddat al, *Oman* **99 C7** 19 30N 56 0 E
Harat, *Eritrea* **107 D4** 16 5N 39 26 E
Haraz, *Chad* **109 F3** 14 20N 19 12 E
Harazé, *Chad* **109 G4** 9 57N 20 48 E
Harbhanga, *India* **94 D7** 20 38N 84 36 E
Harbin, *China* **75 B14** 45 48N 126 40 E
Harbiye, *Turkey* **100 D7** 36 10N 36 8 E
Harbo, *Sweden* **16 D11** 60 7N 17 12 E
Harboør, *Denmark* **17 H2** 56 38N 8 10 E
Harbor Beach, *U.S.A.* **150 C2** 43 51N 82 39W
Harbour Breton, *Canada* **141 C8** 47 29N 55 50W
Harbour Deep, *Canada* **141 B8** 50 25N 56 32W
Harburg, *Germany* **30 B5** 53 27N 9 58 E
Hårby, *Denmark* **17 J4** 55 13N 10 7 E
Harda, *India* **92 H7** 22 27N 77 5 E
Hardangerfjorden, *Norway* **15 F12** 60 5N 6 0 E
Hardangerjøkulen, *Norway* **18 D4** 60 30N 7 27 E
Hardangervidda, *Norway* **15 F12** 60 7N 7 20 E
Hardap Dam, *Namibia* **116 C2** 24 32S 17 50 E
Hardap Recreational Resort, *Namibia* **116 C2** 24 29S 17 45 E
Hardeeville, *U.S.A.* **152 C8** 32 17N 81 5W
Harden, *Australia* **129 C8** 34 32S 148 24 E
Hardenberg, *Neths.* **24 B6** 52 34N 6 37 E
Harderwijk, *Neths.* **24 B5** 52 21N 5 38 E
Hardey →, *Australia* **124 D2** 22 45S 116 8 E
Hardin, *Ill., U.S.A.* **156 E6** 39 10N 90 37W
Hardin, *Mont., U.S.A.* **158 D10** 45 44N 107 37W
Harding, *S. Africa* **117 E4** 30 35S 29 55 E
Harding, L., *U.S.A.* **152 C4** 32 40N 85 5W
Harding Ra., *Australia* **124 C3** 16 17S 124 55 E
Hardinsburg, *U.S.A.* **157 G10** 37 47N 86 28W
Hardisty, *Canada* **142 C6** 52 40N 111 18W
Hardoi, *India* **93 F9** 27 26N 80 6 E
Hardwar = Haridwar, *India* **92 E8** 29 58N 78 9 E
Hardwick, *Ga., U.S.A.* **152 B6** 33 4N 83 14W
Hardwick, *Vt., U.S.A.* **151 B12** 44 30N 72 22W
Hardwicke B., *Australia* **128 C2** 34 55S 137 20 E
Hardy, Pen., *Chile* **176 E3** 55 30S 68 20W
Hardy, Pte., *St. Lucia* **165 f** 14 6N 60 56W
Hare B., *Canada* **141 B8** 51 15N 55 45W
Hareid, *Norway* **15 E12** 62 22N 6 1 E
Haren, *Germany* **30 C3** 52 47N 7 13 E
Harer, *Ethiopia* **107 F5** 9 20N 42 8 E
Harerge □, *Ethiopia* **107 F5** 7 12N 42 0 E
Harestua, *Norway* **18 D7** 60 11N 10 44 E
Hareto, *Ethiopia* **107 F4** 9 23N 37 6 E
Harfleur, *France* **26 C7** 49 30N 0 10 E
Hargeisa, *Somali Rep.* **120 C2** 9 30N 44 2 E
Hargeisa Game Park, *Somali Rep.* **120 B2** 10 2N 44 2 E
Harghita □, *Romania* **53 D10** 46 30N 25 30 E
Harghita, Munţii, *Romania* **53 D10** 46 25N 25 35 E
Hargshamn, *Sweden* **16 D12** 60 12N 18 30 E
Hari →, *Indonesia* **84 C2** 1 16S 104 5 E
Haría, *Canary Is.* **9 e2** 29 8N 13 32W
Ḥarīb, *Yemen* **98 D4** 14 56N 45 30 E
Haricha, Hamada el, *Mali* **110 D4** 22 40N 3 15W
Haridwar, *India* **92 E8** 29 58N 78 9 E
Harihar, *India* **95 G2** 14 32N 75 44 E
Harihari, *N.Z.* **131 D5** 43 9S 170 33 E
Harim, Jabal al, *Oman* **97 E8** 25 58N 56 14 E
Harima-Nada, *Japan* **72 C6** 34 30N 134 35 E
Haringhata →, *Bangla.* **90 E2** 22 0N 89 58 E
Haripad, *India* **95 K3** 9 14N 76 28 E
Harīrūd →, *Asia* **91 A1** 37 24N 60 38 E
Härjedalen, *Sweden* **16 B7** 62 22N 13 5 E
Harlan, *Iowa, U.S.A.* **154 E7** 41 39N 95 19W
Harlan, *Ky., U.S.A.* **149 G4** 36 51N 83 19W
Hărlău, *Romania* **53 C11** 47 23N 26 55 E
Harlech, *U.K.* **20 E3** 52 52N 4 6W
Harlem, *Ga., U.S.A.* **152 B7** 33 25N 82 19W
Harlem, *Mont., U.S.A.* **158 B9** 48 32N 108 47W
Hårlev, *Denmark* **17 J6** 55 21N 12 14 E
Harleyville, *U.S.A.* **152 B9** 33 13N 80 27W
Harlingen, *Neths.* **24 A5** 53 11N 5 25 E
Harlingen, *U.S.A.* **155 M6** 26 12N 97 42W
Harlow, *U.K.* **21 F8** 51 46N 0 8 E
Harlowton, *U.S.A.* **158 C9** 46 26N 109 50W
Harmancık, *Turkey* **49 B11** 39 41N 29 9 E
Harmånger, *Sweden* **16 C11** 61 55N 17 20 E
Harmil, *Eritrea* **107 D5** 16 30N 40 10 E
Harnai, *India* **94 F1** 17 48N 73 6 E
Harnai, *Pakistan* **92 D2** 30 6N 67 56 E
Harney, L., *U.S.A.* **153 G8** 28 45N 81 3W
Harney Basin, *U.S.A.* **158 E4** 43 30N 119 0W
Harney L., *U.S.A.* **158 E4** 43 14N 119 8W
Harney Peak, *U.S.A.* **154 D3** 43 52N 103 32W
Härnön, *Sweden* **16 B12** 62 36N 18 0 E
Härnösand, *Sweden* **16 B11** 62 38N 17 55 E
Haro, *Spain* **40 C2** 42 35N 2 55W
Harold, *U.S.A.* **153 E3** 30 40N 86 53W
Harold Pond, *Bahamas* **9 b** 25 2N 77 22W
Haroldswick, *U.K.* **22 A8** 60 48N 0 50W
Harp L., *Canada* **141 A7** 55 5N 61 50W
Harpanahalli, *India* **95 G3** 14 47N 76 2 E
Harper, *Liberia* **112 E3** 4 25N 7 43W
Harper, Mt., *U.S.A.* **144 D12** 64 14N 143 51W
Harplinge, *Sweden* **17 H6** 56 45N 12 45 E
Harr, *Mauritania* **112 B2** 15 20N 12 28W
Harrai, *India* **93 H8** 22 37N 79 13 E
Harrand, *Pakistan* **92 E4** 29 28N 70 3 E
Ḥarrat Khaybar, *Si. Arabia* **106 B5** 25 30N 39 45 E
Ḥarrat Nawāşīf, *Si. Arabia* **106 C5** 21 20N 42 10 E
Harricana →, *Canada* **140 B4** 50 56N 79 32W
Harriman, *U.S.A.* **149 H3** 35 56N 84 33W
Harrington, *Australia* **129 A10** 31 52S 152 42 E
Harrington Harbour, *Canada* **141 B8** 50 31N 59 30W
Harrington Sd., *Bermuda* **9 a** 32 20N 64 44W
Harris, *U.K.* **22 D2** 57 50N 6 55W
Harris, L., *U.S.A.* **153 G8** 28 47N 81 49W
Harris, Sd. of, *U.K.* **22 D1** 57 44N 7 6W
Harris L., *Australia* **127 E2** 31 10S 135 10 E
Harris Mts., *N.Z.* **131 E3** 44 49S 168 49 E
Harris Pt., *Canada* **150 C2** 43 6N 82 9W
Harrisburg, *Ill., U.S.A.* **155 G10** 37 44N 88 32W
Harrisburg, *Nebr., U.S.A.* **154 E3** 41 33N 103 44W
Harrisburg, *Pa., U.S.A.* **150 F8** 40 16N 76 53W
Harrismith, *S. Africa* **117 D4** 28 15S 29 8 E
Harrison, *Ark., U.S.A.* **155 G8** 36 14N 93 7W
Harrison, *Maine, U.S.A.* **151 B14** 44 7N 70 39W
Harrison, *Nebr., U.S.A.* **154 D3** 42 41N 103 53W
Harrison, C., *Canada* **141 B8** 54 55N 57 55W
Harrison Bay, *U.S.A.* **144 A10** 70 40N 151 0W
Harrison L., *Canada* **142 D4** 49 33N 121 50W
Harrisonburg, *U.S.A.* **148 F6** 38 27N 78 52W
Harrisonville, *U.S.A.* **156 F2** 38 39N 94 21W
Harriston, *Canada* **150 C4** 43 57N 80 53W
Harrisville, *Mich., U.S.A.* **150 B1** 44 39N 83 17W
Harrisville, *N.Y., U.S.A.* **151 B9** 44 9N 75 19W
Harrisville, *Pa., U.S.A.* **150 E5** 41 8N 80 0W
Harrodsburg, *Ind., U.S.A.* **157 E10** 39 1N 86 33W
Harrodsburg, *Ky., U.S.A.* **157 G12** 37 46N 84 51W
Harrogate, *U.K.* **20 C6** 54 0N 1 33W
Harrow, *Australia* **128 D4** 37 9S 141 35 E
Harrow, *Canada* **157 B14** 42 2N 82 55W
Harrow □, *U.K.* **21 F7** 51 35N 0 21W
Harrowsmith, *Canada* **151 B8** 44 24N 76 40W
Harry S. Truman Reservoir, *U.S.A.* **156 F3** 38 16N 93 24W
Harsefeld, *Germany* **30 B5** 53 27N 9 30 E
Harsewinkel, *Germany* **30 D4** 51 56N 8 14 E
Harsīn, *Iran* **101 E12** 34 18N 47 33 E
Hârşova, *Romania* **53 F12** 44 40N 27 59 E
Harstad, *Norway* **14 B17** 68 48N 16 30 E
Harsud, *India* **92 H7** 22 6N 76 44 E
Hart, *U.S.A.* **148 D2** 43 42N 86 22W
Hart, L., *Australia* **128 A2** 31 10S 136 25 E
Hartbees →, *S. Africa* **116 D3** 28 45S 20 32 E
Hartberg, *Austria* **34 D8** 47 17N 15 58 E
Hårteigen, *Norway* **18 D4** 60 11N 7 3 E
Hartford, *Ala., U.S.A.* **152 D4** 31 6N 85 42W
Hartford, *Conn., U.S.A.* **151 E12** 41 46N 72 41W
Hartford, *Ky., U.S.A.* **148 G2** 37 27N 86 55W
Hartford, *Mich., U.S.A.* **157 B10** 42 13N 86 10W
Hartford, *S. Dak., U.S.A.* **154 D6** 43 38N 96 57W
Hartford, *Wis., U.S.A.* **154 D10** 43 19N 88 22W
Hartford City, *U.S.A.* **157 D11** 40 27N 85 22W
Hartland, *Canada* **141 C6** 46 20N 67 32W
Hartland, *U.S.A.* **157 A8** 43 6N 88 21W
Hartland Pt., *U.K.* **21 F3** 51 1N 4 32W
Hartlepool, *U.K.* **20 C6** 54 42N 1 13W
Hartlepool □, *U.K.* **20 C6** 54 42N 1 17W
Hartley Bay, *Canada* **142 C3** 53 25N 129 15W
Hartmannberge, *Namibia* **116 B1** 17 0S 13 0 E
Hartney, *Canada* **143 D8** 49 30N 100 35W
Hârtop, *Moldova* **53 D13** 46 39N 28 40 E
Harts →, *S. Africa* **116 D3** 28 24S 24 17 E
Hartselle, *U.S.A.* **149 H2** 34 27N 86 56W
Hartshorne, *U.S.A.* **155 H7** 34 51N 95 34W
Hartstown, *U.S.A.* **150 E4** 41 33N 80 23W
Hartsville, *U.S.A.* **149 H5** 34 23N 80 4W
Hartswater, *S. Africa* **116 D3** 27 34S 24 43 E
Hartwell, *U.S.A.* **149 H4** 34 21N 82 56W
Haruku, *Indonesia* **82 B3** 3 34S 128 29 E
Harunabad, *Pakistan* **92 E5** 29 35N 73 8 E
Harur, *India* **95 H4** 12 3N 78 29 E
Harūt →, *Afghan.* **91 C1** 31 29N 61 24 E
Harvand, *Iran* **97 D7** 28 25N 55 43 E
Harvard, *U.S.A.* **157 B8** 42 25N 88 37W
Harvey, *Australia* **125 F2** 33 5S 115 54 E
Harvey, *Ill., U.S.A.* **157 C9** 41 36N 87 50W
Harvey, *N. Dak., U.S.A.* **154 B5** 47 47N 99 56W
Harwich, *U.K.* **21 F9** 51 56N 1 17 E
Haryana □, *India* **92 E7** 29 0N 76 10 E
Haryn →, *Belarus* **59 F4** 52 7N 27 17 E
Harz, *Germany* **30 D6** 51 38N 10 44 E
Harzgerode, *Germany* **30 D7** 51 38N 11 8 E
Hasa □, *Si. Arabia* **97 E6** 25 50N 49 0 E
Hasaheisa, *Sudan* **107 E3** 14 44N 33 20 E
Hasalbag, *China* **65 E8** 37 52N 76 42 E
Ḥasanābād, *Iran* **97 C7** 32 8N 52 44 E
Hasanparti, *India* **94 E4** 18 4N 79 32 E
Hasdo →, *India* **93 J10** 21 44N 82 44 E
Häselgehr, *Austria* **33 B10** 47 19N 10 30 E
Haselünne, *Germany* **30 C3** 52 40N 7 29 E
Hashima, *Japan* **73 B8** 35 20N 136 40 E
Hashimoto, *Japan* **73 C7** 34 19N 135 37 E
Hashtjerd, *Iran* **97 C6** 35 52N 50 40 E
Hasi Nueifed, *W. Sahara* **110 D2** 24 54N 14 49W
Hasi Tafraut, *W. Sahara* **110 C2** 27 24N 13 15W
Ḥāsik, *Oman* **99 C6** 17 22N 55 17 E
Haskell, *U.S.A.* **155 J5** 33 10N 99 44W
Hasköy, *Turkey* **51 E10** 41 38N 26 52 E
Haslach, *Germany* **31 G4** 48 16N 8 5 E
Hasle, *Denmark* **17 J8** 55 11N 14 44 E
Haslemere, *U.K.* **21 F7** 51 5N 0 43W
Haslev, *Denmark* **17 J5** 55 18N 11 57 E
Hasparren, *France* **28 E2** 43 24N 1 18W
Hassa, *Turkey* **100 D7** 36 48N 36 29 E
Hassan, *India* **95 H3** 13 0N 76 5 E
Hassela, *Sweden* **16 B10** 62 7N 16 42 E
Hasselt, *Belgium* **24 D5** 50 56N 5 21 E
Hassene, Adrar, *Algeria* **111 D5** 21 0N 4 0 E
Hassfurt, *Germany* **31 E6** 50 2N 10 30 E
Hassi bou Khelala, *Algeria* **111 B4** 30 17N 0 18W
Hassi Bourarchet, *Algeria* **111 C6** 27 26N 9 19 E
Hassi Djafou, *Algeria* **111 B5** 30 55N 3 35 E
Hassi el Abiod, *Algeria* **111 B5** 31 47N 3 37 E
Hassi el Biod, *Algeria* **111 C6** 28 30N 6 0 E
Hassi el Hadjar, *Algeria* **111 B5** 31 28N 4 45 E
Hassi Imoulaye, *Algeria* **111 C6** 29 54N 9 10 E
Hassi Inifeg, *Algeria* **111 C4** 28 15N 1 30W
Hassi Inifel, *Algeria* **111 C5** 29 50N 3 41 E
Hassi Mana, *Algeria* **111 C4** 28 48N 2 37W
Hassi Messaoud, *Algeria* **111 B6** 31 51N 6 1 E
Hassi Sougoued, *Algeria* **111 C6** 26 50N 9 28 E
Hassi Tartrat, *Algeria* **111 B6** 30 5N 6 28 E
Hassi Zerzour, *Morocco* **110 B4** 30 51N 3 56W
Hassi Zguilma, *Algeria* **111 B4** 30 12N 2 19W
Hässleholm, *Sweden* **17 H7** 56 10N 13 46 E
Hassloch, *Germany* **31 F4** 49 22N 8 16 E
Hästholmen, *Sweden* **17 F8** 58 17N 14 38 E
Hastings, *Australia* **129 E6** 38 18S 145 12 E
Hastings, *N.Z.* **130 F5** 39 39S 176 52 E
Hastings, *U.K.* **21 G8** 50 51N 0 35 E
Hastings, *Fla., U.S.A.* **152 F8** 29 43N 81 31W
Hastings, *Mich., U.S.A.* **157 B11** 42 39N 85 17W
Hastings, *Minn., U.S.A.* **154 C8** 44 44N 92 51W
Hastings, *Nebr., U.S.A.* **154 E5** 40 35N 98 23W
Hastings Ra., *Australia* **129 A10** 31 15S 152 14 E
Hästveda, *Sweden* **17 H7** 56 17N 13 55 E
Ḥasy 'Aṭshān, *Libya* **108 C2** 27 20N 10 25 E
Hasy Tissan, *Libya* **111 C7** 28 14N 12 26 E
Hat Yai, *Thailand* **87 J3** 7 1N 100 27 E
Hatanbulag = Ergel, *Mongolia* **74 C5** 43 8N 109 5 E
Hatay = Antalya, *Turkey* **100 D4** 36 52N 30 45 E
Hatch, *U.S.A.* **159 K10** 32 40N 107 9W
Hatchet L., *Canada* **143 B8** 58 36N 103 40W
Haţeg, *Romania* **52 E7** 45 36N 22 55 E
Hateruma-Shima, *Japan* **71 M1** 24 3N 123 47 E
Hatfield P.O., *Australia* **128 B5** 33 54S 143 49 E
Hatgal, *Mongolia* **68 A5** 50 26N 100 9 E
Hathras, *India* **92 F8** 27 36N 78 6 E
Hatia, *Bangla.* **90 D3** 22 30N 91 5 E
Hatia Is., *Bangla.* **90 D3** 22 30N 91 0 E
Ḥāţibah, Ra's, *Si. Arabia* **106 C4** 21 55N 38 57 E
Hatid, *India* **94 F2** 17 17N 75 3 E
Hato Corozal, *Colombia* **164 C3** 6 11N 71 45W
Hato Mayor, *Dom. Rep.* **165 C6** 18 46N 69 15W
Hatsukaichi, *Japan* **72 C4** 34 22N 132 22 E
Hatta, *India* **93 G8** 24 7N 79 36 E
Hattah, *Australia* **128 C5** 34 48S 142 17 E
Hattah Kulkyne Nat. Park, *Australia* **128 C5** 35 40S 142 22 E
Hatteras, C., *U.S.A.* **149 H8** 35 14N 75 32W
Hattiesburg, *U.S.A.* **155 K10** 31 20N 89 17W
Hatvan, *Hungary* **52 C4** 47 40N 19 45 E
Hau Bon = Cheo Reo, *Vietnam* **78 B3** 13 25N 108 28 E
Hau Duc, *Vietnam* **86 E7** 15 20N 108 13 E
Haubstadt, *U.S.A.* **157 F9** 38 12N 87 34W
Haud, *Ethiopia* **120 C2** 8 0N 45 0 E
Hauganes, *Iceland* **11 B8** 65 55N 18 18W
Haugastøl, *Norway* **18 D4** 60 30N 7 50 E
Hauge, *Norway* **18 F3** 58 20N 6 15 E
Haugesund, *Norway* **15 G11** 59 23N 5 13 E
Hauhui, *Solomon Is.* **133 M11** 9 10S 160 59 E
Hauhungaroa Ra., *N.Z.* **130 E4** 38 42S 175 40 E
Haukeligrend, *Norway* **18 E4** 59 44N 7 33 E
Haukipudas, *Finland* **14 D21** 65 12N 25 20 E
Haultain →, *Canada* **143 B7** 55 51N 106 46W
Haungpa, *Burma* **90 C6** 25 29N 96 7 E
Hauraha, *Solomon Is.* **133 N11** 10 46S 161 59 E
Hauraki G., *N.Z.* **130 C4** 36 35S 175 5 E
Hauroko L., *N.Z.* **131 F2** 45 59S 167 21 E
Hausruck, *Austria* **34 C6** 48 6N 13 30 E
Hausstock, *Switz.* **33 C8** 46 53N 9 3 E
Haut Atlas, *Morocco* **110 B4** 32 30N 5 0W
Haut Niger, Parc Nat. du, *Guinea* **112 C2** 10 20N 10 20W
Haut-Rhin □, *France* **27 E14** 48 0N 7 15 E
Haut-Zaïre = Orientale □, *Dem. Rep. of the Congo* **118 B2** 2 20N 26 0 E
Haute-Corse □, *France* **29 F13** 42 30N 9 30 E
Haute-Garonne □, *France* **28 E5** 43 30N 1 30 E
Haute-Loire □, *France* **28 C7** 45 5N 3 50 E
Haute-Marne □, *France* **27 D12** 48 10N 5 20 E
Haute-Normandie □, *France* **26 C7** 49 20N 1 0 E
Haute-Saône □, *France* **27 E13** 47 45N 6 10 E
Haute-Savoie □, *France* **29 C10** 46 0N 6 20 E
Haute-Vienne □, *France* **28 C5** 45 50N 1 10 E
Hautes-Alpes □, *France* **29 D10** 44 42N 6 20 E
Hautes Fagnes = Hohe Venn, *Belgium* **24 D6** 50 30N 6 5 E
Hautes-Pyrénées □, *France* **28 F4** 43 0N 0 10 E
Hauteville-Lompnès, *France* **29 C9** 45 58N 5 36 E
Hautmont, *France* **27 B10** 50 15N 3 55 E
Hauts-de-Seine □, *France* **27 D9** 48 52N 2 15 E
Hauts Plateaux, *Algeria* **111 B5** 35 0N 1 0 E
Hauula, *U.S.A.* **145 J14** 21 37N 157 55W
Hauzenberg, *Germany* **31 G9** 48 40N 13 37 E
Havana = La Habana, *Cuba* **164 B3** 23 8N 82 22W
Havana, *Fla., U.S.A.* **153 E5** 30 37N 84 25W
Havana, *Ill., U.S.A.* **156 D6** 40 18N 90 4W
Havant, *U.K.* **21 G7** 50 51N 0 58W
Havârna, *Romania* **53 B11** 48 4N 26 43 E
Havasu, L., *U.S.A.* **161 L12** 34 18N 114 28W
Havdhem, *Sweden* **17 G12** 57 10N 18 20 E
Havel →, *Germany* **30 C8** 52 50N 12 3 E
Havelian, *Pakistan* **92 B5** 34 2N 73 10 E
Havelock, *Canada* **140 D4** 44 26N 77 53W
Havelock, *N.Z.* **131 B8** 41 17S 173 48 E
Havelock, *U.S.A.* **149 H7** 34 53N 76 54W
Havelock I., *India* **95 J11** 11 58N 93 0 E
Havelock North, *N.Z.* **130 F5** 39 40S 176 53 E
Haverfordwest, *U.K.* **21 F3** 51 48N 4 58W
Haverhill, *Fla., U.S.A.* **153 J9** 26 42N 80 7W
Haverhill, *Mass., U.S.A.* **151 D13** 42 47N 71 5W
Haveri, *India* **95 G2** 14 53N 75 24 E
Haverstraw, *U.S.A.* **151 E11** 41 12N 73 58W
Håverud, *Sweden* **17 F6** 58 50N 12 28 E
Havirga, *Mongolia* **74 B7** 45 41N 113 5 E
Havířov, *Czech Rep.* **35 B11** 49 46N 18 20 E
Havlíčkův Brod, *Czech Rep.* **34 B8** 49 36N 15 33 E
Havneby, *Denmark* **17 J2** 55 5N 8 34 E
Havran, *Turkey* **49 B9** 39 33N 27 6 E
Havre, *U.S.A.* **158 B9** 48 33N 109 41W
Havre-Aubert, *Canada* **141 C7** 47 12N 61 56W
Havre-St.-Pierre, *Canada* **141 B7** 50 18N 63 33W
Havsa, *Turkey* **51 E10** 41 31N 26 48 E
Havza, *Turkey* **100 B6** 41 0N 35 35 E
Haw →, *U.S.A.* **149 H6** 35 36N 79 3W
Hawaii, *U.S.A.* **145 D6** 19 30N 155 30W
Hawaii □, *U.S.A.* **145 D5** 19 30N 156 30W
Hawaii I., *Pac. Oc.* **146 J17** 20 0N 155 0W
Hawaii Volcanoes Nat. Park, *U.S.A.* **145 D6** 19 23N 155 17W
Hawaiian Is., *Pac. Oc.* **135 E12** 20 30N 156 0W
Hawaiian Ridge, *Pac. Oc.* **135 E11** 24 0N 165 0W
Hawarden, *U.S.A.* **154 D6** 43 0N 96 29W
Hawea, L., *N.Z.* **131 E4** 44 28S 169 19 E
Hawea Flat, *N.Z.* **131 E4** 44 40S 169 19 E
Hawera, *N.Z.* **130 F3** 39 35S 174 19 E
Hawesville, *U.S.A.* **157 G10** 37 54N 86 45W
Hawi, *U.S.A.* **145 C6** 20 14N 155 50W
Hawick, *U.K.* **22 F6** 55 26N 2 47W
Hawk Junction, *Canada* **140 C3** 48 5N 84 38W
Hawk Point, *U.S.A.* **156 F5** 38 58N 91 8W
Hawkdun Ra., *N.Z.* **131 E5** 44 53S 170 5 E
Hawke B., *N.Z.* **130 F6** 39 25S 177 20 E
Hawker, *Australia* **128 A3** 31 59S 138 22 E
Hawke's Bay □, *N.Z.* **130 F5** 39 45S 176 35 E
Hawkesbury, *Canada* **140 C5** 45 37N 74 37W
Hawkesbury I., *Canada* **142 C3** 53 37N 129 3W
Hawkesbury Pt., *Australia* **126 A1** 11 55S 134 5 E
Hawkinsville, *U.S.A.* **152 C6** 32 17N 83 28W
Hawks Nest, *Australia* **129 B10** 32 41S 152 11 E
Hawley, *Minn., U.S.A.* **154 B6** 46 53N 96 19W
Hawley, *Pa., U.S.A.* **151 E9** 41 28N 75 11W
Ḥawrān, W. →, *Iraq* **101 F10** 33 58N 42 34 E
Hawsh Müssá, *Lebanon* **103 B4** 33 45N 35 55 E
Hawthorne, *Fla., U.S.A.* **153 F7** 29 36N 82 5W
Hawthorne, *Nev., U.S.A.* **158 G4** 38 32N 118 38W
Hay, *Australia* **129 C6** 34 30S 144 51 E
Hay →, *Australia* **126 C2** 24 50S 138 0 E
Hay →, *Canada* **142 A5** 60 50N 116 26W
Hay, C., *Australia* **124 B4** 14 5S 129 29 E
Hay I., *Canada* **150 B4** 44 53N 80 58W
Hay L., *Canada* **142 B5** 58 50N 118 50W
Hay-on-Wye, *U.K.* **21 E4** 52 5N 3 8W
Hay River, *Canada* **142 A5** 60 51N 115 44W
Hay Springs, *U.S.A.* **154 D3** 42 41N 102 41W
Haya = Tehoru, *Indonesia* **83 B3** 3 23S 129 30 E
Hayachine-San, *Japan* **70 E10** 39 34N 141 29 E
Hayange, *France* **27 C13** 49 20N 6 2 E
Hayato, *Japan* **72 F2** 31 40N 130 43 E
Haydarlı, *Turkey* **49 C12** 38 16N 30 23 E
Hayden, *U.S.A.* **158 F10** 40 30N 107 16W
Haydon, *Australia* **126 B3** 18 0S 141 30 E
Hayes, *U.S.A.* **154 C4** 44 23N 101 1W
Hayes →, *Canada* **140 A1** 57 3N 92 12W
Hayes, Mt., *U.S.A.* **144 E11** 63 37N 146 43W
Hayes Creek, *Australia* **124 B5** 13 43S 131 22 E
Hayle, *U.K.* **21 G2** 50 11N 5 26W
Hayling I., *U.K.* **21 G7** 50 48N 0 59W
Haymana, *Turkey* **100 C5** 39 26N 32 31 E
Haymen I., *Australia* **126 J6** 20 3S 148 52 E
Haynan, *Yemen* **99 D5** 15 50N 48 18 E
Hayneville, *U.S.A.* **152 C6** 32 23N 83 37W
Hayrabolu, *Turkey* **51 E11** 41 12N 27 5 E
Hays, *Canada* **142 C6** 50 6N 111 48W
Hays, *U.S.A.* **154 F5** 38 53N 99 20W
Ḥays, *Yemen* **98 D3** 13 56N 43 29 E
Haysville, *U.S.A.* **157 F10** 38 28N 86 55W
Haysyn, *Ukraine* **59 H5** 48 57N 29 25 E
Hayvoron, *Ukraine* **59 H5** 48 22N 29 52 E
Hayward, *Calif., U.S.A.* **160 H4** 37 40N 122 5W
Hayward, *Wis., U.S.A.* **154 B9** 46 1N 91 29W
Haywards Heath, *U.K.* **21 G7** 51 0N 0 5W
Hazafon □, *Israel* **103 C4** 32 40N 35 20 E
Hazārān, Kūh-e, *Iran* **97 D8** 29 35N 57 20 E
Hazard, *U.S.A.* **148 G4** 37 15N 83 12W
Hazaribag, *India* **93 H11** 23 58N 85 26 E
Hazaribag Road, *India* **93 G11** 24 12N 85 57 E
Hazebrouck, *France* **27 B9** 50 42N 2 31 E
Hazelton, *Canada* **142 B3** 55 20N 127 42W
Hazelton, *U.S.A.* **154 B4** 46 29N 100 17W
Hazen, *U.S.A.* **154 B4** 47 18N 101 38W
Hazlehurst, *Ga., U.S.A.* **152 D7** 31 52N 82 36W
Hazlehurst, *Miss., U.S.A.* **155 K9** 31 52N 90 24W
Hazlet, *U.S.A.* **151 F10** 40 25N 74 12W
Hazleton, *Ind., U.S.A.* **157 F9** 38 29N 87 33W
Hazleton, *Pa., U.S.A.* **151 F9** 40 57N 75 59W
Hazlett, L., *Australia* **124 D4** 21 30S 128 48 E
Hazro, *Turkey* **96 B4** 38 15N 40 47 E
He Xian, *Anhui, China* **77 B12** 31 45N 118 20 E
He Xian, *Guangxi Zhuangzu, China* **77 E8** 24 27N 111 30 E
Head of Bight, *Australia* **125 F5** 31 30S 131 25 E
Headland, *U.S.A.* **152 D4** 31 21N 85 21W
Headlands, *Zimbabwe* **119 F3** 18 15S 32 2 E
Healdsburg, *U.S.A.* **160 G4** 38 37N 122 52W
Healdton, *U.S.A.* **155 H6** 34 14N 97 29W
Healesville, *Australia* **129 D6** 37 35S 145 30 E
Healy, *U.S.A.* **144 E10** 63 52N 148 58W
Heany Junction, *Zimbabwe* **117 C4** 20 6S 28 54 E
Heard I., *Ind. Oc.* **121 K6** 53 0S 74 0 E
Hearne, *U.S.A.* **155 K6** 30 53N 96 36W
Hearst, *Canada* **140 C3** 49 40N 83 41W
Heart →, *U.S.A.* **154 B4** 46 46N 100 50W
Heart's Content, *Canada* **141 C9** 47 54N 53 27W
Heath →, *Bolivia* **172 C4** 12 31S 68 38W
Heath Mts., *N.Z.* **131 F2** 45 39S 167 9 E
Heath Pt., *Canada* **141 C7** 49 8N 61 40W
Heathcote, *Australia* **129 D6** 36 56S 144 45 E
Heavener, *U.S.A.* **155 H7** 34 53N 94 36W
Hebbronville, *U.S.A.* **155 M5** 27 18N 98 41W
Hebei □, *China* **74 E9** 39 0N 116 0 E
Hebel, *Australia* **127 D4** 28 58S 147 47 E
Heber, *U.S.A.* **161 N11** 32 44N 115 32W
Heber City, *U.S.A.* **158 F8** 40 31N 111 25W
Heber Springs, *U.S.A.* **155 H9** 35 30N 92 2W
Hebert, *Canada* **143 C7** 50 30N 107 10W
Hebgen L., *U.S.A.* **158 D8** 44 52N 111 20W
Hebi, *China* **74 G8** 35 57N 114 7 E
Hebrides, *U.K.* **12 D4** 57 30N 7 0W
Hebrides, Sea of the, *U.K.* **22 D2** 57 5N 7 0W
Hebron = Al Khalīl, *West Bank* **103 D4** 31 32N 35 6 E
Hebron, *Canada* **139 C13** 58 5N 62 30W
Hebron, *N. Dak., U.S.A.* **154 B3** 46 54N 102 3W
Hebron, *Nebr., U.S.A.* **154 E6** 40 10N 97 35W
Heby, *Sweden* **16 E10** 59 56N 16 53 E
Hecate Str., *Canada* **142 C2** 53 10N 130 30W
Heceta I., *U.S.A.* **142 B2** 55 46N 133 40W
Hechi, *China* **76 E7** 24 40N 108 2 E
Hechingen, *Germany* **31 G4** 48 21N 8 57 E
Hechuan, *China* **76 B6** 30 2N 106 12 E
Hecla, *U.S.A.* **154 C5** 45 53N 98 9W
Hecla I., *Canada* **143 C9** 51 10N 96 43W
Hedal, *Norway* **18 D6** 60 37N 9 41 E
Heddal, *Norway* **18 E6** 59 36N 9 9 E
Hédé, *France* **26 D5** 48 18N 1 49W
Hede, *Sweden* **16 B7** 62 23N 13 30 E
Hedemora, *Sweden* **16 D9** 60 18N 15 58 E
Hedensted, *Denmark* **17 J3** 55 46N 9 42 E
Hedesunda, *Sweden* **16 D10** 60 24N 17 0 E
Hedgehope, *N.Z.* **131 G3** 46 12S 168 34 E
Hedmark □, *Norway* **18 C8** 61 17N 11 40 E
Hedrick, *U.S.A.* **156 C4** 41 11N 92 19W
Heerde, *Neths.* **24 B6** 52 24N 6 2 E
Heerenveen, *Neths.* **24 B5** 52 57N 5 55 E
Heerhugowaard, *Neths.* **24 B4** 52 40N 4 51 E
Heerlen, *Neths.* **24 D5** 50 55N 5 58 E
Ḥefa, *Israel* **103 C4** 32 46N 35 0 E
Ḥefa □, *Israel* **103 C4** 32 40N 35 0 E
Hefei, *China* **77 B11** 31 52N 117 18 E
Hefeng, *China* **77 C8** 29 55N 109 52 E
Heflin, *U.S.A.* **152 B4** 33 39N 85 35W
Hegalig, *Sudan* **107 E3** 14 36N 31 54 E
Hegang, *China* **69 B8** 47 20N 130 19 E
Heggenes, *Norway* **18 C6** 61 9N 9 4 E
Hegra, *Norway* **18 A8** 63 27N 11 8 E
Hei Ling Chau, *China* **69 G11** 22 15N 114 2 E
Heiban, *Sudan* **107 E3** 11 13N 30 31 E
Heichengzhen, *China* **74 F4** 36 24N 106 3 E
Heidal, *Norway* **18 C6** 61 45N 9 19 E
Heide, *Germany* **30 A5** 54 11N 9 6 E
Heidelberg, *Germany* **31 F4** 49 24N 8 42 E
Heidelberg, *S. Africa* **116 E3** 34 6S 20 59 E
Heidenau, *Germany* **30 E9** 50 57N 13 52 E
Heidenheim, *Germany* **31 G6** 48 41N 10 9 E
Heigun-Tō, *Japan* **72 D4** 33 47N 132 14 E
Heijing, *China* **76 E3** 25 22N 101 44 E
Heilbad Heiligenstadt, *Germany* **30 D6** 51 22N 10 8 E
Heilbron, *S. Africa* **117 D4** 27 16S 27 59 E
Heilbronn, *Germany* **31 F5** 49 9N 9 13 E
Heiligenblut, *Austria* **34 D5** 47 2N 12 51 E
Heiligenhafen, *Germany* **30 A6** 54 22N 10 59 E
Heilongjiang □, *China* **69 B7** 48 0N 126 0 E
Heilprin Land, *Greenland* **10 A7** 82 5N 33 0W
Heilunkiang = Heilongjiang □, *China* **69 B7** 48 0N 126 0 E
Heim, *Norway* **18 A6** 63 26N 9 5 E
Heimaey, *Iceland* **11 D6** 63 26N 20 17W
Heimdal, *Norway* **18 A7** 63 21N 10 22 E
Heinola, *Finland* **15 F22** 61 13N 26 2 E
Heinsberg, *Germany* **30 D2** 51 3N 6 5 E
Heinsun, *Burma* **90 C5** 25 52N 95 35 E
Heinze Kyun, *Burma* **86 E1** 14 25N 97 45 E
Heirnkut, *Burma* **90 C5** 25 14N 94 44 E
Heishan, *China* **75 D12** 41 40N 122 5 E
Heishui, *Liaoning, China* **75 C10** 42 8N 119 30 E
Heishui, *Sichuan, China* **76 A4** 32 4N 103 2 E

Hejaz = Ḥijāz □, Si. Arabia 96 E3 24 0N 40 0 E
Hejian, China 74 E9 38 25N 116 5 E
Hejiang, China 76 C5 28 43N 105 46 E
Hejin, China 74 G6 35 35N 110 42 E
Hekımhan, Turkey 100 C7 38 50N 37 55 E
Hekinan, Japan 73 C9 34 52N 137 0 E
Hekla, Iceland 11 D7 63 56N 19 35W
Hekou, Guangdong, China 77 F9 23 13N 112 45 E
Hekou, Yunnan, China 76 F4 22 30N 103 59 E
Hel, Poland 54 D5 54 37N 18 47 E
Helagsfjället, Sweden 16 B6 62 54N 12 25 E
Helan Shan, China 74 E3 38 30N 105 55 E
Helechosa, Spain 43 F6 39 22N 4 53W
Helemano →, U.S.A. 145 J13 21 35N 158 7W
Helen Atoll, Pac. Oc. 83 A4 2 40N 132 0 E
Helena, Ark., U.S.A. 155 H9 34 32N 90 36W
Helena, Ga., U.S.A. 152 C7 32 5N 82 55W
Helena, Mont., U.S.A. 158 C7 46 36N 112 2W
Helendale, U.S.A. 161 L9 34 44N 117 19W
Helensburgh, Australia 129 C9 34 11 S 151 1 E
Helensburgh, U.K. 22 E4 56 1N 4 43W
Helensville, N.Z. 130 C3 36 41 S 174 29 E
Helenvale, Australia 126 B4 15 43 S 145 14 E
Helgasjön, Sweden 17 H8 56 55N 14 50 E
Helgeland, Norway 14 C15 66 7N 13 29 E
Helgoland, Germany 30 A3 54 10N 7 53 E
Heligoland = Helgoland, Germany 30 A3 54 10N 7 53 E
Heligoland B. = Deutsche Bucht, Germany 30 A4 54 15N 8 0 E
Heliopolis, Egypt 106 H7 30 6N 31 17 E
Hell, Norway 18 A7 63 26N 10 54 E
Hella, Iceland 11 D6 63 50N 20 24W
Helleland, Norway 18 F3 58 33N 6 7 E
Hellertown, U.S.A. 151 F9 40 35N 75 21W
Hellespont = Çanakkale Boğazı, Turkey 51 F10 40 17N 26 32 E
Hellesylt, Norway 18 B3 62 6N 6 51 E
Hellevoetsluis, Neths. 24 C4 51 50N 4 8 E
Hellhole Gorge Nat. Park, Australia 126 D3 25 31 S 144 12 E
Hellín, Spain 41 G3 38 31N 1 40W
Hellissandur, Iceland 11 C3 64 55N 23 54W
Hell's Gate Nat. Park, Kenya 118 C4 0 54 S 36 19 E
Hellvik, Norway 18 F2 58 29N 5 52 E
Helmand □, Afghan. 91 C2 31 20N 64 0 E
Helmand →, Afghan. 91 C1 31 12N 61 34 E
Helme →, Germany 30 D7 51 20N 11 21 E
Helmeringhausen, Namibia 116 D2 25 54 S 16 57 E
Helmond, Neths. 24 C5 51 29N 5 41 E
Helmsdale, U.K. 22 C5 58 7N 3 39W
Helmsdale →, U.K. 22 C5 58 7N 3 40W
Helmstedt, Germany 30 C7 52 12N 11 0 E
Helong, China 75 C15 42 40N 129 0 E
Helper, U.S.A. 158 G8 39 41N 110 51W
Helsingborg, Sweden 17 H6 56 3N 12 42 E
Helsinge, Denmark 17 H6 56 2N 12 12 E
Helsingfors = Helsinki, Finland 15 F21 60 15N 25 3 E
Helsingør, Denmark 17 H6 56 2N 12 35 E
Helsinki, Finland 15 F21 60 15N 25 3 E
Helska, Mierzeja, Poland 54 D5 54 45N 18 40 E
Helston, U.K. 21 G2 50 6N 5 17W
Helvellyn, U.K. 20 C4 54 32N 3 1W
Helwân, Egypt 106 J7 29 50N 31 20 E
Hemavati →, India 95 H3 12 30N 76 20 E
Hemel Hempstead, U.K. 21 F7 51 44N 0 28W
Hemet, U.S.A. 161 M10 33 45N 116 58W
Hemingford, U.S.A. 154 D3 42 19N 103 4W
Hemmingford, Canada 151 A11 45 3N 73 35W
Hempe, Dem. Rep. of the Congo 114 B4 1 54N 22 42 E
Hempstead, U.S.A. 155 K6 30 6N 96 5W
Hemse, Sweden 17 G12 57 15N 18 22 E
Hemsedal, Norway 18 D5 60 53N 8 30 E
Hemsön, Sweden 16 B12 62 42N 18 5 E
Hen, Norway 18 D7 60 13N 10 14 E
Hen and Chickens Is., N.Z. 130 B3 35 58 S 174 45 E
Henån, Sweden 17 F5 58 14N 11 40 E
Henan □, China 74 H8 34 0N 114 0 E
Henares →, Spain 42 E7 40 24N 3 30W
Henashi-Misaki, Japan 70 D9 40 37N 139 51 E
Hendaye, France 28 E2 43 23N 1 47W
Hendek, Turkey 100 B4 40 48N 30 44 E
Henderson, Argentina 174 D3 36 18 S 61 43W
Henderson, Ga., U.S.A. 152 C6 32 21N 83 47W
Henderson, Ky., U.S.A. 157 G9 37 50N 87 35W
Henderson, N.C., U.S.A. 149 G6 36 20N 78 25W
Henderson, Nev., U.S.A. 161 J12 36 2N 114 59W
Henderson, Tenn., U.S.A. 149 H1 35 26N 88 38W
Henderson, Tex., U.S.A. 155 J7 32 9N 94 48W
Hendersonville, N.C., U.S.A. 149 H4 35 19N 82 28W
Hendersonville, Tenn., U.S.A. 149 G2 36 18N 86 37W
Hendījān, Iran 97 D6 30 14N 49 43 E
Hendorābī, Iran 97 E7 26 40N 53 37 E
Heng Jiang, China 76 C5 28 40N 104 25 E
Heng Xian, China 76 F7 22 40N 109 17 E
Henganofi, Papua N. G. 132 D3 6 15 S 145 38 E
Hengcheng, China 74 E4 38 18N 106 28 E
Hëngchun, Taiwan 77 F13 22 0N 120 44 E
Hengdaohezi, China 75 B15 44 52N 129 0 E
Hengelo, Neths. 24 B6 52 16N 6 48 E
Hengfeng, China 77 C10 28 12N 115 48 E
Henggang, China 69 F11 22 39N 114 12 E
Hengmen, China 69 F10 22 33N 113 35 E
Hengqin Dao, China 69 G10 22 7N 113 34 E
Hengshan, Hunan, China 77 D9 27 16N 112 45 E
Hengshan, Shaanxi, China 74 F5 37 58N 109 5 E
Hengshui, China 74 F8 37 41N 115 40 E
Hengyang, China 77 D9 26 59N 112 22 E
Henichesk, Ukraine 59 J8 46 12N 34 50 E
Henima, India 90 C4 25 22N 93 36 E
Hénin-Beaumont, France 27 B9 50 25N 2 58 E
Henlopen, C., U.S.A. 148 F8 38 48N 75 6W
Hennan, Sweden 16 B9 62 2N 15 54 E
Hennebont, France 26 E3 47 49N 3 19W
Hennenman, S. Africa 116 D4 27 59 S 27 1 E
Hennepin, U.S.A. 156 C7 41 15N 89 21W
Hennessey, U.S.A. 155 G6 36 6N 97 54W
Hennigsdorf, Germany 30 C9 52 38N 13 12 E
Henrietta, U.S.A. 155 J5 33 49N 98 12W
Henrietta, Ostrov = Genriyetty, Ostrov, Russia 67 B16 77 6N 156 30 E
Henrietta Maria, C., Canada 140 A3 55 9N 82 20W
Henry, U.S.A. 156 C7 41 7N 89 22W
Henry Lawrence I., India 95 H11 12 9N 93 5 E
Henryetta, U.S.A. 155 H7 35 27N 95 59W
Henryville, Canada 151 A11 45 8N 73 11W
Hensall, Canada 150 C3 43 26N 81 30W
Henstedt-Ulzburg, Germany 30 B6 53 47N 10 0 E
Hentiesbaai, Namibia 116 C1 22 8 S 14 18 E
Hentiyn Nuruu, Mongolia 69 B5 48 30N 108 30 E
Henty, Australia 129 C7 35 30 S 147 0 E
Henzada, Burma 90 G5 17 38N 95 26 E
Hephaestia, Greece 49 B7 39 55N 25 14 E
Hephzibah, U.S.A. 152 B7 33 19N 82 6W
Heping, China 77 E10 24 29N 115 0 E
Heppner, U.S.A. 158 D4 45 21N 119 33W
Hepu, China 76 G7 21 40N 109 12 E
Hepworth, Canada 150 B3 44 37N 81 9W
Heqing, China 76 D3 26 37N 100 11 E
Hequ, China 74 E6 39 20N 111 15 E
Héraðsflói, Iceland 11 B12 65 42N 14 12W
Héraðsvötn →, Iceland 11 B7 65 45N 19 25W
Heradsbygd, Norway 18 D8 60 49N 11 39 E
Herald Cays, Australia 126 B4 16 58 S 149 9 E
Herand, Norway 18 D3 60 20N 6 22 E
Herāt, Afghan. 91 B1 34 20N 62 7 E
Herāt □, Afghan. 91 B1 35 0N 62 0 E
Hérault □, France 28 E7 43 34N 3 15 E
Hérault →, France 28 E7 43 17N 3 26 E
Herbault, France 26 E8 47 36N 1 8 E
Herbert →, Australia 126 B4 18 31 S 146 17 E
Herbert I., U.S.A. 144 K5 52 45N 170 7W
Herbert River Falls Nat. Park, Australia 126 B4 18 15 S 145 32 E
Herbertabad, India 95 J11 11 43N 92 37 E
Herberton, Australia 126 B4 17 20 S 145 25 E
Herbertsdale, S. Africa 116 E3 34 1 S 21 46 E
Herbertville, N.Z. 130 G5 40 30 S 176 33 E
Herbignac, France 26 E4 47 27N 2 18W
Herborn, Germany 30 E4 50 40N 8 18 E
Herby, Poland 55 H5 50 45N 18 50 E
Herceg-Novi, Montenegro, Yug. 50 D2 42 30N 18 33 E
Herchmer, Canada 143 B10 57 22N 94 10W
Herðubreið, Iceland 11 B10 65 11N 16 21W
Hereford, U.K. 21 E5 52 4N 2 43W
Hereford, U.S.A. 155 H3 34 49N 102 24W
Herefordshire □, U.K. 21 E5 52 8N 2 40W
Herefoss, Norway 18 F5 58 32N 8 23 E
Herehoga, Sweden 18 C9 61 44N 12 8 E
Hereke, Turkey 51 F13 40 47N 29 38 E
Herekino, N.Z. 130 B2 35 18 S 173 11 E
Herencia, Spain 43 F7 39 21N 3 22W
Herentals, Belgium 24 C4 51 12N 4 51 E
Herford, Germany 30 C4 52 7N 8 39 E
Héricourt, France 27 E13 47 32N 6 45 E
Herington, U.S.A. 154 F6 38 40N 96 57W
Herisau, Switz. 33 B8 47 22N 9 17 E
Hérisson, France 27 F9 46 32N 2 42 E
Herkimer, U.S.A. 151 D10 43 0N 74 59W
Herlong, U.S.A. 160 E6 40 8N 120 8W
Herm, U.K. 21 H5 49 30N 2 28W
Hermann, U.S.A. 156 F5 38 42N 91 27W
Hermannsburg, Australia 124 D5 23 57 S 132 45 E
Hermannsburg, Germany 30 C6 52 50N 10 5 E
Hermansverk, Norway 18 C4 61 11N 6 52 E
Hermanus, S. Africa 116 E2 34 27 S 19 12 E
Herment, France 28 C6 45 45N 2 24 E
Hermidale, Australia 129 A7 31 30 S 146 42 E
Hermiston, U.S.A. 158 D4 45 51N 119 17W
Hermit Is., Papua N. G. 132 A3 1 32 S 145 5 E
Hermitage, U.S.A. 156 G3 37 56N 93 19W
Hermite, I., Chile 176 E3 55 50 S 68 0W
Hermon, U.S.A. 151 B9 44 28N 75 14W
Hermon, Mt. = Shaykh, J. ash, Lebanon 103 B4 33 25N 35 50 E
Hermosillo, Baja Calif., Mexico 137 F8 32 27N 114 56W
Hermosillo, Sonora, Mexico 162 B2 29 10N 111 0W
Hernád →, Hungary 52 C6 47 56N 21 8 E
Hernandarias, Paraguay 175 B5 25 20 S 54 40W
Hernandez, U.S.A. 160 J6 36 24N 120 46W
Hernando, Argentina 174 C3 32 28 S 63 40W
Hernando, Fla., U.S.A. 153 G7 28 54N 82 23W
Hernando, Miss., U.S.A. 155 H10 34 50N 90 0W
Hernani, Spain 40 B3 43 16N 1 58W
Herndon, U.S.A. 150 F8 40 43N 76 51W
Herne, Germany 24 C7 51 32N 7 14 E
Herne Bay, U.K. 21 F9 51 21N 1 8 E
Herning, Denmark 17 H2 56 8N 8 58 E
Herod, U.S.A. 152 D5 31 42N 84 26W
Heroica = Caborca, Mexico 162 A2 30 40N 112 10W
Heroica Nogales = Nogales, Mexico 162 A2 31 20N 110 56W
Heron Bay, Canada 140 C2 48 40N 86 25W
Herradura, Pta. de la, Canary Is. 9 e2 28 26N 14 8W
Herre, Norway 18 E6 59 6N 9 34 E
Herreid, U.S.A. 154 C4 45 50N 100 4W
Herrenberg, Germany 31 G4 48 35N 8 52 E
Herrera, Spain 43 H6 37 26N 4 55W
Herrera de Alcántara, Spain 43 F3 39 39N 7 25W
Herrera de Pisuerga, Spain 42 C6 42 35N 4 20W
Herrera del Duque, Spain 43 F5 39 10N 5 3W
Herrestad, Sweden 17 F5 58 21N 11 50 E
Herrin, U.S.A. 155 G10 37 48N 89 2W
Herriot, Canada 143 B8 56 22N 101 16W
Herrljunga, Sweden 17 F7 58 5N 13 1 E
Hersbruck, Germany 31 F7 49 30N 11 26 E
Hershey, U.S.A. 151 F8 40 17N 76 39W
Herstal, Belgium 24 D5 50 40N 5 38 E
Hertford, U.K. 21 F7 51 48N 0 4W
Hertfordshire □, U.K. 21 F7 51 51N 0 5W
's-Hertogenbosch, Neths. 24 C5 51 42N 5 17 E
Hertzogville, S. Africa 116 D4 28 9 S 25 30 E
Hervás, Spain 42 E5 40 16N 5 52W
Hervey B., Australia 126 C5 25 0 S 152 52 E
Herzberg, Brandenburg, Germany 30 D9 51 41N 13 14 E
Herzberg, Niedersachsen, Germany 30 D6 51 38N 10 20 E
Herzliyya, Israel 103 C3 32 10N 34 50 E
Herzogenbuchsee, Switz. 32 B5 47 11N 7 42 E
Herzogenburg, Austria 34 C8 48 17N 15 41 E
Ḥeṣār, Fārs, Iran 97 D6 29 52N 50 16 E
Ḥeṣār, Markazī, Iran 97 C6 35 50N 49 12 E
Hesdin, France 27 B9 50 21N 2 2 E
Heshan, China 76 F7 23 50N 108 53 E
Heshui, China 74 G5 35 48N 108 0 E
Heshun, China 74 F7 37 22N 113 32 E
Heskestad, Norway 18 F3 58 28N 6 22 E
Hesperia, U.S.A. 161 L9 34 25N 117 18W
Hessdalen, Norway 18 B8 62 48N 11 10 E
Hesse = Hessen □, Germany 30 E4 50 30N 9 0 E
Hessen □, Germany 30 E4 50 30N 9 0 E
Hesso, Australia 128 B2 32 8 S 137 27 E
Hesteyri, Iceland 11 A4 66 20N 22 53W
Hestra, Sweden 17 G7 57 26N 13 35 E
Hetch Hetchy Aqueduct, U.S.A. 160 H5 37 29N 122 19W
Hettinger, U.S.A. 154 C3 46 0N 102 42W
Hettstedt, Germany 30 D7 51 39N 11 31 E
Heuvelton, U.S.A. 151 B9 44 37N 75 25W
Heveländia, Brazil 169 E5 5 12 S 61 50W
Heves, Hungary 52 C5 47 36N 20 17 E
Heves □, Hungary 52 C5 47 50N 20 0 E
Hewitt, U.S.A. 155 K6 31 27N 97 11W
Hexham, U.K. 20 C5 54 58N 2 4W
Hexi, Yunnan, China 76 E4 24 9N 102 38 E
Hexi, Zhejiang, China 77 D12 27 58N 119 38 E
Hexigten Qi, China 75 C9 43 18N 117 30 E
Ḥeydarābād, Iran 97 D7 30 33N 55 38 E
Heyfield, Australia 129 D7 37 59 S 146 47 E
Heysham, U.K. 20 C5 54 3N 2 53W
Heyuan, China 77 F10 23 39N 114 40 E
Heywood, Australia 128 E4 38 8 S 141 37 E
Heyworth, U.S.A. 156 D8 40 19N 88 59W
Heze, China 74 G8 35 14N 115 20 E
Hezhang, China 76 D5 27 8N 104 41 E
Hi, Ko, Thailand 87 a 7 44N 98 22 E
Hi-no-Misaki, Japan 72 B4 35 26N 132 38 E
Hi Vista, U.S.A. 161 L9 34 45N 117 46W
Hialeah, U.S.A. 149 N5 25 50N 80 17W
Hiawatha, U.S.A. 154 F7 39 51N 95 32W
Hibbing, U.S.A. 154 B8 47 25N 92 56W
Hibbs B., Australia 127 G4 42 35 S 145 15 E
Hibernia Reef, Australia 124 B3 12 0 S 123 23 E
Hibiki-Nada, Japan 72 D2 34 0N 130 0 E
Hickman, U.S.A. 155 G10 36 34N 89 11W
Hickory, U.S.A. 149 H5 35 44N 81 21W
Hicks, Pt., Australia 129 D8 37 49 S 149 17 E
Hicks Bay, N.Z. 130 D7 37 34 S 178 21 E
Hicks L., Canada 143 A9 61 25N 100 0W
Hicksville, N.Y., U.S.A. 151 F11 40 46N 73 32W
Hicksville, Ohio, U.S.A. 157 C12 41 18N 84 46W
Hida, Romania 53 C8 47 10N 23 19 E
Hida-Gawa →, Japan 73 B9 35 26N 137 3 E
Hida-Sammyaku, Japan 73 A9 36 30N 137 40 E
Hida-Sanchi, Japan 73 A9 36 10N 137 0 E
Hidaka, Japan 72 B6 35 30N 134 44 E
Hidaka-Sammyaku, Japan 70 C11 42 35N 142 45 E
Hidalgo, Mexico 163 C5 24 15N 99 26W
Hidalgo □, Mexico 163 C5 20 30N 99 10W
Hidalgo, Presa M., Mexico 162 B3 26 30N 108 35W
Hidalgo del Parral, Mexico 162 B3 26 58N 105 40W
Hiddensee, Germany 30 A9 54 32N 13 6 E
Hidrolândia, Brazil 171 E2 17 0 S 49 15W
Hieflau, Austria 34 D7 47 36N 14 46 E
Hiendelaencina, Spain 40 D2 41 5N 3 0W
Hienghène, N. Cal. 133 T18 20 41 S 164 56 E
Hierro, Canary Is. 9 e1 27 44N 18 0W
Higashi-Hiroshima, Japan 72 C4 34 25N 132 45 E
Higashi-Matsuyama, Japan 73 A11 36 2N 139 25 E
Higashiajima-San, Japan 70 F10 37 40N 140 10 E
Higashiōsaka, Japan 73 C7 34 40N 135 37 E
Higasi-Suidō, Japan 72 D1 34 0N 129 30 E
Higbee, U.S.A. 156 E4 39 19N 92 31W
Higgins, U.S.A. 155 G4 36 7N 100 2W
Higgins Corner, U.S.A. 160 F5 39 2N 121 5W
Higginsville, U.S.A. 156 E3 39 4N 93 43W
High Atlas = Haut Atlas, Morocco 110 B4 32 30N 5 0W
High Bridge, U.S.A. 151 F10 40 40N 74 54W
High Island Res., China 69 G11 22 22N 114 21 E
High Level, Canada 142 B5 58 31N 117 8W
High Peak, Phil. 80 D3 15 29N 120 7 E
High Pk., St. Helena 9 h 15 58 S 5 44W
High Point, U.S.A. 149 H6 35 57N 80 0W
High Prairie, Canada 142 B5 55 30N 116 30W
High River, Canada 142 C6 50 30N 113 50W
High Springs, U.S.A. 153 F7 29 50N 82 36W
High Tatra = Tatry, Slovak Rep. 35 B13 49 20N 20 0 E
High Veld, Africa 104 J6 27 0 S 27 0 E
High Wycombe, U.K. 21 F7 51 37N 0 45W
Highbank, N.Z. 131 D6 43 37 S 171 45 E
Highland, Ill., U.S.A. 156 F7 38 44N 89 41W
Highland, Ind., U.S.A. 157 C9 41 33N 87 28W
Highland, Wis., U.S.A. 156 A6 43 5N 90 22W
Highland □, U.K. 22 D4 57 17N 4 21W
Highland City, U.S.A. 153 H8 27 58N 81 53W
Highland Home, U.S.A. 152 D3 31 57N 86 19W
Highland Mills = Experiment, U.S.A. 152 B5 33 17N 84 17W
Highland Park, U.S.A. 157 B9 42 11N 87 48W
Highland View, U.S.A. 152 F4 29 50N 85 19W
Highmore, U.S.A. 154 C5 44 31N 99 27W
Highrock L., Man., Canada 143 B8 55 45N 100 30W
Highrock L., Sask., Canada 143 B7 57 5N 105 32W
Higüey, Dom. Rep. 165 C6 18 37N 68 42W
Hihya, Egypt 106 H7 30 40N 31 36 E
Hiiumaa, Estonia 15 G20 58 50N 22 45 E
Híjar, Spain 40 D4 41 10N 0 27W
Ḥijāz □, Si. Arabia 96 E3 24 0N 40 0 E
Hiji, Japan 72 D3 33 22N 131 32 E
Hijo = Tagum, Phil. 81 H5 7 33N 125 53 E
Hikari, Japan 72 D3 33 58N 131 58 E
Hiketa, Japan 72 C6 34 13N 134 24 E
Hikkaduwa, Sri Lanka 95 L5 6 8N 80 6 E
Hikmak, Ras el, Egypt 106 A2 31 15N 27 51 E
Hiko, U.S.A. 160 H11 37 32N 115 14W
Hikone, Japan 73 B8 35 15N 136 10 E
Hikurangi, Gisborne, N.Z. 130 E5 37 55 S 178 4 E
Hikurangi, Northland, N.Z. 130 B3 35 36 S 174 17 E
Hiland Park, U.S.A. 152 E4 30 12N 85 33W
Hilawng, Burma 90 E4 21 23N 93 48 E
Hildburghausen, Germany 30 E6 50 25N 10 42 E
Hildesheim, Germany 30 C5 52 9N 9 56 E
Hilðarendi, Iceland 11 D7 63 44N 19 57W
Hill →, Australia 125 F2 30 23 S 115 3 E
Hill City, Idaho, U.S.A. 158 E6 43 18N 115 3W
Hill City, Kans., U.S.A. 154 F5 39 22N 99 51W
Hill City, S. Dak., U.S.A. 154 D3 43 56N 103 35W
Hill Island L., Canada 143 A7 60 30N 109 50W
Hillaby, Mt., Barbados 165 g 13 12N 59 35W
Hillared, Sweden 17 G7 57 37N 13 10 E
Hillcrest, Barbados 165 g 13 13N 59 32W
Hillcrest Center, U.S.A. 161 K8 35 23N 118 57W
Hillegom, Neths. 24 B4 52 18N 4 35 E
Hillerød, Denmark 17 J6 55 56N 12 19 E
Hillerstorp, Sweden 17 G7 57 20N 13 52 E
Hilli, Bangla. 90 C2 25 17N 89 1 E
Hilliard, U.S.A. 152 E8 30 41N 81 55W
Hillsboro, Ga., U.S.A. 152 B6 33 11N 83 38W
Hillsboro, Ill., U.S.A. 156 E7 39 9N 89 29W
Hillsboro, Kans., U.S.A. 154 F6 38 21N 97 12W
Hillsboro, Mo., U.S.A. 156 F6 38 14N 90 34W
Hillsboro, N. Dak., U.S.A. 154 B6 47 26N 97 3W
Hillsboro, N.H., U.S.A. 151 C13 43 7N 71 54W
Hillsboro, Ohio, U.S.A. 157 E13 39 12N 83 37W
Hillsboro, Oreg., U.S.A. 160 E4 45 31N 122 59W
Hillsboro, Tex., U.S.A. 155 J6 32 1N 97 8W
Hillsboro Canal, U.S.A. 153 J9 26 30N 80 15W
Hillsborough, Grenada 165 D7 12 28N 61 28W
Hillsborough Channel, Australia 126 J7 20 56 S 149 15 E
Hillsdale, Mich., U.S.A. 157 C12 41 56N 84 38W
Hillsdale, N.Y., U.S.A. 151 D11 42 11N 73 30W
Hillsport, Canada 140 C2 49 27N 85 34W
Hillston, Australia 129 B6 33 30 S 145 31 E
Hilltonia, U.S.A. 152 C8 32 53N 81 40W
Hilo, U.S.A. 145 D6 19 44N 155 5W
Hilo B., U.S.A. 145 D6 19 45N 155 5W
Hilton, U.S.A. 150 C7 43 17N 77 48W
Hilton Head Island, U.S.A. 152 C9 32 13N 80 45W
Hilvan, Turkey 101 D8 37 34N 38 58 E
Hilversum, Neths. 24 B5 52 14N 5 10 E
Hilzingen, Germany 33 A7 47 46N 8 47 E
Himachal Pradesh □, India 92 D7 31 30N 77 0 E
Himalaya, Asia 93 E11 29 0N 84 0 E
Himamaylan, Phil. 81 F4 10 6N 122 52 E
Himarë, Albania 50 F3 40 8N 19 43 E
Hime-Jima, Japan 72 D3 33 43N 131 40 E
Himeji, Japan 72 B6 34 50N 134 40 E
Himi, Japan 73 A8 36 50N 136 55 E
Himmerland, Denmark 17 H3 56 45N 9 30 E
Ḥimṣ, Syria 103 A5 34 40N 36 45 E
Ḥimṣ □, Syria 103 A6 34 30N 37 0 E
Hinatuan, Phil. 81 G6 8 23N 126 20 E
Hinatuan Passage, Phil. 81 G5 9 45N 125 47 E
Hinche, Haiti 165 C5 19 9N 72 1W
Hinchinbrook I., Australia 126 B4 18 20 S 146 15 E
Hinchinbrook Island Nat. Park, Australia 126 B4 18 14 S 146 6 E
Hinckley, U.K. 21 E6 52 33N 1 22W
Hinckley, U.S.A. 154 B8 46 1N 92 56W
Hindaun, India 92 F7 26 44N 77 5 E
Hindmarsh, L., Australia 128 D4 36 5 S 141 55 E
Hindol, India 94 D7 20 40N 85 10 E
Hinds, N.Z. 131 D6 43 59 S 171 36 E
Hindsholm, Denmark 17 J4 55 30N 10 40 E
Hinglaj Bagh, Pakistan 91 C2 30 56N 67 50 E
Hindu Kush, Asia 65 E5 36 0N 71 0 E
Hindupur, India 95 H3 13 49N 77 32 E
Hines Creek, Canada 142 B5 56 20N 118 40W
Hinesville, U.S.A. 152 D8 31 51N 81 36W
Hinganghat, India 94 D4 20 30N 78 52 E
Hingham, U.S.A. 158 B8 48 33N 110 25W
Hingir, India 93 J10 21 57N 83 41 E
Hingoli, India 94 E3 19 41N 77 15 E
Hinigaran, Phil. 81 F4 10 16N 122 50 E
Hinis, Turkey 101 C9 39 22N 41 43 E
Hinna = Imi, Ethiopia 107 F5 6 28N 42 10 E
Hinna, Nigeria 113 C7 10 25N 11 35 E
Hinnerup, Denmark 17 H4 56 16N 10 4 E
Hinnøya, Norway 14 B16 68 35N 15 50 E
Hino, Japan 73 C8 35 0N 136 15 E
Hinoba-an, Phil. 81 G4 9 35N 122 28 E
Hinojosa del Duque, Spain 43 G5 38 30N 5 9W
Hinokage, Japan 72 E3 32 39N 131 24 E
Hinsdale, U.S.A. 151 D12 42 47N 72 29W
Hinterrhein →, Switz. 33 C8 46 40N 9 25 E
Hinton, Canada 142 C5 53 26N 117 34W
Hinton, U.S.A. 148 G5 37 40N 80 54W
Hinuangan, Phil. 81 F5 10 25N 125 12 E
Hinwil, Switz. 33 B7 47 18N 8 51 E
Hınzır Burnu, Turkey 100 D6 36 19N 35 46 E
Hirado, Japan 72 D1 33 22N 129 33 E
Hirado-Shima, Japan 72 D1 33 20N 129 30 E
Hirakata, Japan 73 C7 34 48N 135 40 E
Hirakud, India 94 D6 21 32N 83 51 E
Hirakud Dam, India 94 D6 21 32N 83 45 E
Hiran →, India 93 H8 23 6N 79 21 E
Hirapur, India 93 G8 24 22N 79 13 E
Hirata, Japan 72 B4 35 24N 132 49 E
Hiratsuka, Japan 73 B11 35 19N 139 21 E
Hirekerur, India 95 G2 14 28N 75 23 E
Hirfanlı Barajı, Turkey 100 C5 39 18N 33 31 E
Hirhafok, Algeria 111 D6 23 49N 5 45 E
Hiromi, Japan 72 D4 33 13N 132 36 E
Hiroo, Japan 70 C11 42 17N 143 19 E
Hirosaki, Japan 70 D10 40 34N 140 28 E
Hiroshima, Japan 72 C4 34 24N 132 30 E
Hiroshima □, Japan 72 C4 34 50N 133 0 E
Hiroshima-Wan, Japan 72 C4 34 5N 132 20 E
Hirson, France 27 C11 49 55N 4 4 E
Hirtshals, Denmark 17 G3 57 36N 9 57 E
Hisai, Japan 73 C8 34 40N 136 28 E
Hisar, India 92 E6 29 12N 75 45 E
Hisarcık, Turkey 49 B11 39 15N 29 14 E
Hisaria, Bulgaria 51 D8 42 30N 24 44 E
Hisb →, Iraq 96 D5 31 45N 44 17 E
Ḥismá, Si. Arabia 96 D3 28 30N 36 0 E
Ḥiṣn al 'Abr, Yemen 98 C4 16 8N 47 14 E
Hisor, Tajikistan 65 D4 38 31N 68 33 E
Hispaniola, W. Indies 165 C5 19 0N 71 0W
Hīt, Iraq 101 F10 33 38N 42 49 E
Hita, Japan 72 D2 33 20N 130 58 E
Hitachi, Japan 73 A12 36 36N 140 39 E
Hitachi-Ōta, Japan 73 A12 36 30N 140 30 E
Hitchin, U.K. 21 F7 51 58N 0 16W
Hitoyoshi, Japan 72 E2 32 13N 130 45 E
Hitra, Norway 14 E13 63 30N 8 45 E
Hittisau, Austria 33 B9 47 28N 9 58 E
Hitzacker, Germany 30 B7 53 9N 11 2 E
Hiu, Vanuatu 133 C4 13 10 S 166 35 E
Hiuchi-Nada, Japan 72 C5 34 5N 133 20 E
Hixon, Canada 142 C4 53 25N 122 35W
Ḥiyyon, N. →, Israel 103 E4 30 25N 35 10 E
Hjalmar L., Canada 143 A7 61 33N 109 25W
Hjälmaren, Sweden 16 E9 59 18N 15 40 E
Hjältevad, Sweden 17 G9 57 38N 15 20 E
Hjartdal, Norway 18 E5 59 37N 8 41 E
Hjelmelandsvågen, Norway 18 E3 59 14N 6 10 E
Hjelset, Norway 18 B4 62 48N 7 30 E
Hjerkinn, Norway 18 B6 62 13N 9 33 E
Hjo, Sweden 17 F8 58 22N 14 17 E
Hjørring, Denmark 17 G3 57 29N 9 59 E
Hjortkvarn, Sweden 17 F9 58 54N 15 26 E
Hjukse, Norway 18 E6 59 31N 9 19 E
Hkakabo Razi, Burma 90 B6 28 17N 97 46 E
Hko-lam, Burma 90 E7 21 7N 98 5 E
Hko-ut, Burma 90 E7 20 58N 98 2 E
Hkyenhpa, Burma 90 B7 27 43N 97 25 E
Hlaingbwe, Burma 90 G6 17 8N 97 50 E
Hlinsko, Czech Rep. 34 B8 49 45N 15 54 E
Hlobane, S. Africa 117 D5 27 42 S 31 0 E
Hlohovec, Slovak Rep. 35 C10 48 26N 17 49 E
Hlučín, Czech Rep. 35 B11 49 54N 18 11 E
Hluhluwe, S. Africa 117 D5 28 1 S 32 15 E
Hluhluwe Game Reserve, S. Africa 117 C5 22 10 S 32 5 E
Hlukhiv, Ukraine 59 G7 51 40N 33 58 E
Hlwaze, Burma 90 F6 18 54N 96 37 E
Hlyboka, Ukraine 59 H3 48 5N 25 56 E
Hlybokaye, Belarus 58 E4 55 10N 27 45 E
Hnappadalssýsla □, Iceland 11 C4 64 50N 22 30W
Hnífsdalur, Iceland 11 A3 66 7N 23 8W
Hnúšt'a, Slovak Rep. 35 C12 48 35N 19 58 E
Ho, Ghana 113 D5 6 37N 0 27 E
Ho Chi Minh City = Thanh Pho Ho Chi Minh, Vietnam 87 G6 10 58N 106 40 E
Ho Thuong, Vietnam 86 C5 19 32N 105 48 E
Hoa Binh, Vietnam 76 G5 20 50N 105 20 E
Hoa Da, Vietnam 87 G7 11 16N 108 40 E
Hoa Hiep, Vietnam 87 G5 11 34N 105 51 E
Hoai Nhon, Vietnam 86 E7 14 28N 109 1 E
Hoang Lien Son, Vietnam 76 F4 22 0N 104 0 E
Hoanib →, Namibia 116 B2 19 27 S 12 46 E
Hoare B., Canada 139 B13 65 17N 62 30W
Hoarusib →, Namibia 116 B2 19 3 S 12 36 E
Hobart, Australia 127 G4 42 50 S 147 21 E
Hobart, Ind., U.S.A. 157 C9 41 32N 87 15W
Hobart, Okla., U.S.A. 155 H5 35 1N 99 6W
Hobbs, U.S.A. 155 J3 32 42N 103 8W
Hobbs Coast, Antarctica 7 D14 74 50 S 131 0W
Hobe Sound, U.S.A. 153 H9 27 4N 80 8W
Hobo, Colombia 168 C2 2 35N 75 30W
Hoboken, Ga., U.S.A. 152 D7 31 11N 82 8W
Hoboken, N.J., U.S.A. 151 F10 40 45N 74 4W
Hobro, Denmark 17 H3 56 39N 9 46 E
Hoburgen, Sweden 17 H12 56 55N 18 7 E
Hocalar, Turkey 49 C11 38 36N 30 0 E
Hochdorf, Switz. 33 B6 47 10N 8 17 E
Hochfeld, Namibia 116 C2 21 28 S 17 58 E
Hochschwab, Austria 34 D8 47 35N 15 0 E
Höchstadt, Germany 31 F6 49 42N 10 47 E
Hockenheim, Germany 31 F4 49 19N 8 32 E
Hodaka-Dake, Japan 73 A9 36 17N 137 39 E
Hodeida = Al Ḥudaydah, Yemen 98 D3 14 50N 43 0 E
Hodgeville, Canada 143 C7 50 7N 106 58W
Hodgson, Canada 143 C9 51 13N 97 36W
Hódmezővásárhely, Hungary 52 D5 46 28N 20 22 E
Hodna, Chott el, Algeria 111 A6 35 26N 4 43 E
Hodna, Monts du, Algeria 111 A5 35 52N 4 42 E
Hodonín, Czech Rep. 35 C10 48 50N 17 10 E
Hodzhambas, Turkmenistan 65 D2 38 7N 65 0 E
Hoeamdong, N. Korea 75 C16 42 30N 130 16 E
Hœdic, Î. de, France 26 E4 47 20N 2 53W
Hoek van Holland, Neths. 24 C4 52 0N 4 7 E
Hoengsŏng, S. Korea 75 F14 37 29N 127 59 E
Hoeryong, N. Korea 75 C15 42 30N 129 45 E
Hoeyang, N. Korea 75 E14 38 43N 127 36 E
Hof, Germany 31 E7 50 19N 11 55 E
Hof, Norður-Múlasýsla, Iceland 11 B11 65 39N 15 0W

Hof, *Suður-Múlasýsla, Iceland* ... **11 C12** 64 33N 14 40W
Hof, *Norway* ... **18 E7** 59 32N 10 5 E
Hoffell, *Iceland* ... **11 C11** 64 23N 15 20W
Hofgeismar, *Germany* ... **30 D5** 51 29N 9 23 E
Hofheim, *Germany* ... **31 E4** 50 5N 8 26 E
Hofmeyr, *S. Africa* ... **116 E4** 31 39 S 25 50 E
Höfn, *Iceland* ... **11 C11** 64 15N 15 13W
Hofors, *Sweden* ... **16 D10** 60 31N 16 15 E
Hofsjökull, *Iceland* ... **11 C8** 64 49N 18 48W
Hofsós, *Iceland* ... **11 B7** 65 53N 19 26W
Hōfu, *Japan* ... **72 C3** 34 3N 131 34 E
Hog Harbour, *Vanuatu* ... **133 E5** 15 8 S 167 6 E
Hogan Group, *Australia* ... **127 F4** 39 13 S 147 1 E
Höganäs, *Sweden* ... **17 H6** 56 12N 12 33 E
Hogansville, *U.S.A.* ... **152 B5** 33 10N 84 55W
Hogarth, Mt., *Australia* ... **126 C2** 21 48 S 136 58 E
Hogenakai Falls, *India* ... **95 H3** 12 6N 77 50 E
Hoggar = Ahaggar, *Algeria* ... **111 D6** 23 0N 6 30 E
Högsäter, *Sweden* ... **17 F6** 58 38N 12 5 E
Högsby, *Sweden* ... **17 G10** 57 10N 16 1 E
Högsjö, *Sweden* ... **16 E9** 59 4N 15 44 E
Hogsty Reef, *Bahamas* ... **165 B5** 21 41N 73 48W
Hoh →, *U.S.A.* ... **160 C2** 47 45N 124 29W
Hohe Acht, *Germany* ... **31 E3** 50 22N 7 0 E
Hohe Tauern, *Austria* ... **34 D5** 47 11N 12 40 E
Hohe Venn, *Belgium* ... **24 D6** 50 30N 6 5 E
Hohenau, *Austria* ... **35 C9** 48 36N 16 55 E
Hohenems, *Austria* ... **34 D2** 47 22N 9 42 E
Hohenloher Ebene, *Germany* ... **31 F5** 49 14N 9 36 E
Hohenwald, *U.S.A.* ... **149 H2** 35 33N 87 33W
Hohenwestedt, *Germany* ... **30 A5** 54 5N 9 40 E
Hoher Freschen, *Austria* ... **33 B9** 47 18N 9 46 E
Hoher Rhön = Rhön, *Germany* ... **30 E5** 50 24N 9 58 E
Hohhot, *China* ... **74 D6** 40 52N 111 40 E
Hóhlakas, *Greece* ... **38 F11** 35 57N 27 53 E
Hohoe, *Ghana* ... **113 D5** 7 8N 0 32 E
Hoi An, *Vietnam* ... **86 E7** 15 30N 108 19 E
Hoi Xuan, *Vietnam* ... **76 G5** 20 25N 105 9 E
Hoisington, *U.S.A.* ... **154 F5** 38 31N 98 47W
Hojai, *India* ... **90 B4** 26 2N 92 54 E
Højer, *Denmark* ... **17 K2** 54 58N 8 42 E
Hōjō, *Japan* ... **72 D4** 33 58N 132 46 E
Hok, *Sweden* ... **17 G8** 57 31N 14 16 E
Hökensås, *Sweden* ... **17 G8** 58 0N 14 5 E
Hökerum, *Sweden* ... **17 G7** 57 51N 13 16 E
Hokianga Harbour, *N.Z.* ... **130 B2** 35 31 S 173 22 E
Hokitika, *N.Z.* ... **131 C5** 42 42 S 171 0 E
Hokkaidō □, *Japan* ... **70 C11** 43 30N 143 0 E
Hokksund, *Norway* ... **18 E6** 59 48N 9 54 E
Hokuriko Tunnel, *Japan* ... **73 B8** 35 40N 136 6 E
Hol-Hol, *Djibouti* ... **107 E5** 11 20N 42 50 E
Hola Pristan, *Ukraine* ... **59 J7** 46 29N 32 32 E
Holalkere, *India* ... **95 G3** 14 2N 76 11 E
Hólar, *Iceland* ... **11 B7** 65 44N 19 8W
Holbæk, *Denmark* ... **17 J5** 55 43N 11 43 E
Holbrook, *Australia* ... **129 C7** 35 42 S 147 18 E
Holbrook, *U.S.A.* ... **159 J8** 34 54N 110 10W
Holden, *Mo., U.S.A.* ... **156 F3** 38 43N 94 0W
Holden, *Utah, U.S.A.* ... **158 G7** 39 6N 112 16W
Holdenville, *U.S.A.* ... **155 H6** 35 5N 96 24W
Holdich, *Argentina* ... **176 C3** 45 57 S 68 13W
Holdrege, *U.S.A.* ... **154 E5** 40 26N 99 23W
Hole-Narsipur, *India* ... **95 H3** 12 48N 76 16 E
Holešov, *Czech Rep.* ... **35 B10** 49 20N 17 35 E
Holetown, *Barbados* ... **165 g** 13 11N 59 38W
Holgate, *U.S.A.* ... **157 C12** 41 15N 84 8W
Holguín, *Cuba* ... **164 B4** 20 50N 76 20W
Holíč, *Slovak Rep.* ... **35 C10** 48 49N 17 10 E
Holice, *Czech Rep.* ... **34 A8** 50 5N 16 0 E
Holiday, *U.S.A.* ... **153 G7** 28 13N 82 43W
Höljes, *Sweden* ... **16 D6** 60 50N 12 35 E
Hollabrunn, *Austria* ... **34 C9** 48 34N 16 5 E
Hollams Bird I., *Namibia* ... **116 C1** 24 40 S 14 30 E
Holland, *Mich., U.S.A.* ... **157 B10** 42 47N 86 7W
Holland, *N.Y., U.S.A.* ... **156 D6** 42 38N 78 32W
Hollandale, *U.S.A.* ... **155 J9** 33 10N 90 51W
Hollandia = Jayapura, *Indonesia* ... **83 B6** 2 28 S 140 38 E
Holley, *U.S.A.* ... **150 C6** 43 14N 78 2W
Hollfeld, *Germany* ... **31 F7** 49 56N 11 18 E
Hollidaysburg, *U.S.A.* ... **150 F6** 40 26N 78 24W
Hollis, *U.S.A.* ... **155 H5** 34 41N 99 55W
Hollister, *Calif., U.S.A.* ... **160 J5** 36 51N 121 24W
Hollister, *Idaho, U.S.A.* ... **158 E6** 42 21N 114 35W
Höllviken = Höllviksnäs, *Sweden* ... **17 J6** 55 26N 12 58 E
Höllviksnäs, *Sweden* ... **17 J6** 55 26N 12 58 E
Holly, *U.S.A.* ... **157 B13** 42 48N 83 38W
Holly Hill, *Fla., U.S.A.* ... **149 L5** 29 16N 81 3W
Holly Hill, *S.C., U.S.A.* ... **152 B9** 33 19N 80 25W
Holly Springs, *Ga., U.S.A.* ... **152 A5** 34 10N 84 30W
Holly Springs, *Miss., U.S.A.* ... **155 H10** 34 46N 89 27W
Hollywood, *U.S.A.* ... **149 N5** 26 1N 80 9W
Holman, *Canada* ... **138 A8** 70 44N 117 44W
Hólmavík, *Iceland* ... **14 D3** 65 42N 21 40W
Holmen, *Norway* ... **18 D7** 60 40N 10 22 E
Holmen, *U.S.A.* ... **154 D9** 43 58N 91 15W
Holmes →, *U.S.A.* ... **152 E4** 30 30N 85 50W
Holmes Beach, *U.S.A.* ... **153 H7** 27 31N 82 43W
Holmes Reefs, *Australia* ... **126 B4** 16 27 S 148 0 E
Holmestrand, *Norway* ... **18 E7** 59 31N 10 14 E
Holmsjö, *Sweden* ... **17 H9** 56 25N 15 32 E
Holmsjön, *Västernorrland, Sweden* ... **16 B10** 62 41N 16 33 E
Holmsjön, *Västernorrland, Sweden* ... **16 B9** 62 26N 15 20 E
Holmsland Klit, *Denmark* ... **17 J2** 56 0N 8 5 E
Holmsund, *Sweden* ... **14 E19** 63 41N 20 20 E
Holod, *Romania* ... **52 D7** 46 49N 22 8 E
Holopaw, *U.S.A.* ... **153 G8** 28 8N 81 5W
Holøydal, *Norway* ... **18 B8** 62 12N 11 27 E
Holroyd →, *Australia* ... **126 A3** 14 10 S 141 36 E
Holstebro, *Denmark* ... **17 H2** 56 22N 8 37 E
Holsteinsborg = Sisimiut, *Greenland* ... **10 D5** 66 40N 53 30W
Holsworthy, *U.K.* ... **21 G3** 50 48N 4 22W
Holt, *Iceland* ... **11 D7** 63 33N 19 48W
Holt, *Fla., U.S.A.* ... **153 E3** 30 43N 86 45W
Holt, *Mich., U.S.A.* ... **157 B12** 42 39N 84 31W
Holton, *Canada* ... **141 B8** 54 31N 57 12W
Holton, *U.S.A.* ... **154 F7** 39 28N 95 44W
Holts Summit, *U.S.A.* ... **156 F4** 38 38N 92 7W
Holtville, *U.S.A.* ... **161 N11** 32 49N 115 23W
Holualoa, *U.S.A.* ... **145 D6** 19 37N 155 57W
Holum, *Norway* ... **18 F4** 58 6N 7 32 E
Holwerd, *Neths.* ... **24 A5** 53 22N 5 54 E
Holy Cross, *U.S.A.* ... **144 E8** 62 12N 159 46W
Holy I., *Angl., U.K.* ... **20 D3** 53 17N 4 37W
Holy I., *Northumb., U.K.* ... **20 B6** 55 40N 1 47W
Holyhead, *U.K.* ... **20 D3** 53 18N 4 38W
Holyoke, *Colo., U.S.A.* ... **154 E3** 40 35N 102 18W
Holyoke, *Mass., U.S.A.* ... **151 D12** 42 12N 72 37W
Holyrood, *Canada* ... **141 C9** 47 27N 53 8W
Holzkirchen, *Germany* ... **31 H7** 47 52N 11 42 E
Holzminden, *Germany* ... **30 D5** 51 50N 9 28 E
Homa Bay, *Kenya* ... **118 C3** 0 36 S 34 30 E
Homalin, *Burma* ... **90 C5** 24 55N 95 0 E
Homand, *Iran* ... **97 C8** 32 28N 59 37 E
Homathko →, *Canada* ... **142 C4** 51 0N 124 56W
Homberg, *Germany* ... **30 D5** 51 2N 9 25 E
Hombori, *Mali* ... **113 B4** 15 20N 1 38W
Homburg, *Germany* ... **31 F3** 49 28N 7 18 E
Home B., *Canada* ... **139 B13** 68 40N 67 10W
Home Hill, *Australia* ... **126 B4** 19 43 S 147 25 E
Home Reef, *Tonga* ... **133 P13** 18 59 S 174 47W
Homedale, *U.S.A.* ... **158 E5** 43 37N 116 56W
Homeland, *U.S.A.* ... **152 E7** 30 51N 82 1W
Homer, *Alaska, U.S.A.* ... **144 G10** 59 39N 151 33W
Homer, *Ill., U.S.A.* ... **157 D9** 40 4N 87 57W
Homer, *La., U.S.A.* ... **155 J8** 32 48N 93 4W
Homer, *Mich., U.S.A.* ... **157 B12** 42 9N 84 49W
Homer City, *U.S.A.* ... **150 F5** 40 32N 79 10W
Homerville, *U.S.A.* ... **152 D7** 31 2N 82 45W
Homestead, *Australia* ... **126 C4** 20 20 S 145 40 E
Homestead, *U.S.A.* ... **149 N5** 25 28N 80 29W
Homewood, *Calif., U.S.A.* ... **160 F6** 39 4N 120 8W
Homewood, *Ill., U.S.A.* ... **157 C9** 41 34N 87 40W
Hommelvik, *Norway* ... **18 A7** 63 25N 10 48 E
Hommersåk, *Norway* ... **18 F2** 58 56N 5 50 E
Homnabad, *India* ... **94 F3** 17 45N 77 11 E
Homoine, *Mozam.* ... **117 C6** 23 55 S 35 8 E
Homoljske Planina, *Serbia, Yug.* ... **50 B5** 44 10N 21 45 E
Homonhon I., *Phil.* ... **81 F5** 10 44N 125 43 E
Homorod, *Romania* ... **53 D10** 46 5N 25 15 E
Homosassa Springs, *U.S.A.* ... **153 G7** 28 48N 82 35W
Homs = Ḥimṣ, *Syria* ... **103 A5** 34 40N 36 45 E
Homyel, *Belarus* ... **59 F6** 52 28N 31 0 E
Hon Chong, *Vietnam* ... **87 G5** 10 25N 104 30 E
Hon Me, *Vietnam* ... **86 C5** 19 23N 105 56 E
Honan = Henan □, *China* ... **74 H8** 34 0N 114 0 E
Honaunau, *U.S.A.* ... **145 D6** 19 26N 155 55W
Honavar, *India* ... **95 G2** 14 17N 74 27 E
Honaz, *Turkey* ... **49 D11** 37 46N 29 18 E
Honbetsu, *Japan* ... **70 C11** 43 7N 143 37 E
Honcut, *U.S.A.* ... **160 F5** 39 20N 121 32W
Honda, *Colombia* ... **168 B3** 5 12N 74 45W
Honda Bay, *Phil.* ... **81 G2** 9 53N 118 49 E
Hondarribia, *Spain* ... **40 B3** 43 22N 1 47W
Hondeklipbaai, *S. Africa* ... **116 E2** 30 19 S 17 17 E
Hondo, *Japan* ... **72 E2** 32 27N 130 12 E
Hondo, *U.S.A.* ... **155 L5** 29 21N 99 9W
Hondo →, *Belize* ... **163 D7** 18 25N 88 21W
Honduras ■, *Cent. Amer.* ... **164 D2** 14 40N 86 30W
Honduras, G. de, *Caribbean* ... **164 C2** 16 50N 87 0W
Hønefoss, *Norway* ... **15 F14** 60 10N 10 18 E
Honesdale, *U.S.A.* ... **151 E9** 41 34N 75 16W
Honey L., *U.S.A.* ... **160 E6** 40 15N 120 19W
Honfleur, *France* ... **26 C7** 49 25N 0 13 E
Høng, *Denmark* ... **17 J5** 55 31N 11 18 E
Hong →, *Vietnam* ... **76 F5** 22 0N 104 0 E
Hong Gai, *Vietnam* ... **76 G6** 20 57N 107 5 E
Hong He →, *China* ... **74 H8** 32 25N 115 35 E
Hong Hu, *China* ... **77 C9** 29 54N 113 24 E
Hong Kong □, *China* ... **77 F10** 22 11N 114 14 E
Hong Kong I., *China* ... **69 G11** 22 16N 114 12 E
Honga, *Angola* ... **115 F3** 15 9 S 15 12 E
Hong'an, *China* ... **77 B10** 31 20N 114 40 E
Hongch'ŏn, *S. Korea* ... **75 F14** 37 44N 127 53 E
Honghai Wan, *China* ... **77 F10** 22 40N 115 0 E
Honghe, *China* ... **76 F4** 23 25N 102 25 E
Honghu, *China* ... **77 C9** 29 50N 113 30 E
Hongjiang, *China* ... **76 D7** 27 7N 109 59 E
Hongliu He →, *China* ... **74 F5** 38 0N 109 50 E
Hongor, *Mongolia* ... **74 B7** 45 45N 112 50 E
Hongsa, *Laos* ... **86 C3** 19 43N 101 20 E
Hongshui He →, *China* ... **76 F7** 23 48N 109 30 E
Hongsŏng, *S. Korea* ... **75 F14** 36 37N 126 38 E
Hongtong, *China* ... **74 F6** 36 16N 111 40 E
Honguedo, Détroit d', *Canada* ... **141 C7** 49 15N 64 0W
Hongwon, *N. Korea* ... **75 E14** 40 0N 127 56 E
Hongya, *China* ... **76 C4** 29 57N 103 22 E
Hongyuan, *China* ... **76 A4** 32 51N 102 40 E
Hongze Hu, *China* ... **75 H10** 33 15N 118 35 E
Honiara, *Solomon Is.* ... **133 M10** 9 27 S 159 57 E
Honiton, *U.K.* ... **21 G4** 50 47N 3 11W
Honjō, *Akita, Japan* ... **70 E10** 39 23N 140 3 E
Honjō, *Gumma, Japan* ... **73 A11** 36 14N 139 11 E
Honkawane, *Japan* ... **73 B10** 35 5N 138 5 E
Honkorâb, Ras, *Egypt* ... **106 C4** 24 35N 35 10 E
Honnali, *India* ... **95 G2** 14 15N 75 40 E
Honningsvåg, *Norway* ... **14 A21** 70 59N 25 59 E
Hönö, *Sweden* ... **17 G5** 57 41N 11 39 E
Honokaa, *U.S.A.* ... **145 C6** 20 5N 155 28W
Honokahua, *U.S.A.* ... **145 C5** 21 0N 156 40W
Honolulu, *U.S.A.* ... **145 K14** 21 19N 157 52W
Honomu, *U.S.A.* ... **145 D6** 19 52N 155 7W
Honouliuli, *U.S.A.* ... **145 K13** 21 22N 158 2W
Honshū, *Japan* ... **73 A8** 36 0N 138 0 E
Hontoria del Pinar, *Spain* ... **40 D1** 41 50N 3 10W
Hoopapo B., *U.S.A.* ... **145 D6** 19 5N 155 33W
Hood, Mt., *U.S.A.* ... **158 D3** 45 23N 121 42W
Hood, Pt., *Australia* ... **125 F2** 34 23 S 119 34 E
Hood Pt., *Papua N. G.* ... **132 F4** 10 4 S 147 45 E
Hood River, *U.S.A.* ... **158 D3** 45 43N 121 31W
Hoodsport, *U.S.A.* ... **160 C3** 47 24N 123 9W
Hooge, *Germany* ... **30 A4** 54 34N 8 33 E
Hoogeveen, *Neths.* ... **24 B6** 52 44N 6 28 E
Hoogezand-Sappemeer, *Neths.* ... **24 A6** 53 9N 6 45 E
Hooghly = Hugli →, *India* ... **93 J13** 21 56N 88 4 E
Hooghly-Chinsura = Chunchura, *India* ... **93 H13** 22 53N 88 27 E
Hook Hd., *Ireland* ... **23 D5** 52 7N 6 56W
Hook I., *Australia* ... **126 J6** 20 4 S 149 0 E
Hook of Holland = Hoek van Holland, *Neths.* ... **24 C4** 52 0N 4 7 E
Hooker, *U.S.A.* ... **155 G4** 36 52N 101 13W
Hooker Creek, *Australia* ... **124 C5** 18 23 S 130 38 E
Hoolehua, *U.S.A.* ... **145 B4** 21 10N 157 5W
Hoonah, *U.S.A.* ... **142 B1** 58 7N 135 27W
Hooper Bay, *U.S.A.* ... **144 F6** 61 32N 166 6W
Hoopeston, *U.S.A.* ... **157 D9** 40 28N 87 40W
Hoopstad, *S. Africa* ... **116 D4** 27 50 S 25 55 E
Höör, *Sweden* ... **17 J7** 55 56N 13 33 E
Hoorn, *Neths.* ... **24 B5** 52 38N 5 4 E
Hoover, *U.S.A.* ... **152 B3** 33 20N 86 11W
Hoover Dam, *U.S.A.* ... **161 K12** 36 1N 114 44W
Hooversville, *U.S.A.* ... **150 F6** 40 9N 78 55W
Hop Bottom, *U.S.A.* ... **151 E9** 41 42N 75 46W
Hopa, *Turkey* ... **101 B9** 41 28N 41 30 E
Hope, *Canada* ... **142 D4** 49 25N 121 25W
Hope, *Ariz., U.S.A.* ... **161 M13** 33 43N 113 42W
Hope, *Ark., U.S.A.* ... **155 J8** 33 40N 93 36W
Hope, *Ind., U.S.A.* ... **157 E11** 39 18N 85 46W
Hope, L., *S. Austral., Australia* ... **127 D2** 28 24 S 139 18 E
Hope, L., *W. Austral., Australia* ... **125 F3** 32 35 S 120 15 E
Hope I., *Canada* ... **150 B4** 44 55N 80 11W
Hope Town, *Bahamas* ... **164 A4** 26 35N 76 57W
Hopedale, *Canada* ... **141 A7** 55 28N 60 13W
Hopedale, *U.S.A.* ... **151 D13** 42 8N 71 33W
Hopefield, *S. Africa* ... **116 E2** 33 3 S 18 22 E
Hopei = Hebei □, *China* ... **74 E9** 39 0N 116 0 E
Hopelchén, *Mexico* ... **163 D7** 19 46N 89 50W
Hopetoun, *Vic., Australia* ... **128 C5** 35 42 S 142 22 E
Hopetoun, *W. Austral., Australia* ... **125 F3** 33 57 S 120 7 E
Hopetown, *S. Africa* ... **116 D3** 29 34 S 24 3 E
Hopevale, *Australia* ... **126 B4** 15 16 S 145 20 E
Hopewell, *U.S.A.* ... **148 G7** 37 18N 77 17W
Hopfgarten, *Austria* ... **34 D5** 47 27N 12 10 E
Hopin, *Burma* ... **90 C6** 24 58N 96 30 E
Hopkins, *U.S.A.* ... **156 D2** 40 33N 94 49W
Hopkins, L., *Australia* ... **124 D4** 24 15 S 128 35 E
Hopkinsville, *U.S.A.* ... **149 G2** 36 52N 87 29W
Hopland, *U.S.A.* ... **160 G3** 38 58N 123 7W
Hopong, *Burma* ... **90 E6** 20 47N 97 11 E
Hoque, *Angola* ... **115 E2** 14 40 S 13 55 E
Hoquiam, *U.S.A.* ... **160 D3** 46 59N 123 53W
Hōrai, *Japan* ... **73 C9** 34 58N 137 32 E
Horana, *Sri Lanka* ... **95 L5** 6 43N 80 4 E
Horasan, *Turkey* ... **101 B10** 40 3N 42 11 E
Horažďovice, *Czech Rep.* ... **34 B6** 49 19N 13 42 E
Horb, *Germany* ... **31 G4** 48 26N 8 47 E
Hörby, *Sweden* ... **17 J7** 55 51N 13 40 E
Horcajo de Santiago, *Spain* ... **40 F1** 39 50N 3 1W
Hordabø, *Norway* ... **18 D1** 60 42N 4 54 E
Hordaland □, *Norway* ... **18 D3** 60 25N 6 15 E
Horden Hills, *Australia* ... **124 D5** 20 15 S 130 0 E
Hordio, *Somali Rep.* ... **120 B4** 10 33N 51 6 E
Horezu, *Romania* ... **53 E8** 45 6N 24 0 E
Horgen, *Switz.* ... **33 B7** 47 15N 8 35 E
Horgoš, *Serbia, Yug.* ... **52 D4** 46 10N 20 0 E
Hořice, *Czech Rep.* ... **34 A8** 50 21N 15 39 E
Horinger, *China* ... **74 D6** 40 28N 111 48 E
Horki, *Belarus* ... **58 E6** 54 17N 30 59 E
Horlick Mts., *Antarctica* ... **7 E15** 84 0 S 102 0W
Horlivka, *Ukraine* ... **59 H10** 48 19N 38 5 E
Hormak, *Iran* ... **97 D9** 29 58N 60 51 E
Hormoz, *Iran* ... **97 E7** 27 35N 55 0 E
Hormoz, Jaz.-ye, *Iran* ... **97 E8** 27 8N 56 28 E
Hormozgān □, *Iran* ... **97 E8** 27 30N 56 0 E
Hormuz, Kūh-e, *Iran* ... **97 E7** 27 27N 55 10 E
Hormuz, Str. of, *The Gulf* ... **97 E8** 26 30N 56 30 E
Horn, *Austria* ... **34 C8** 48 39N 15 40 E
Horn, *Iceland* ... **14 C2** 66 28N 22 28W
Horn, *Sweden* ... **17 G9** 57 54N 15 51 E
Horn →, *Canada* ... **142 A5** 61 30N 118 1W
Horn, Cape = Hornos, C. de, *Chile* ... **176 E3** 55 50 S 67 30W
Horn, Is., *Wall. & F. Is.* ... **123 C15** 14 16 S 178 6W
Horn Head, *Ireland* ... **23 A3** 55 14N 8 0W
Horn I., *Australia* ... **126 A3** 10 37 S 142 17 E
Horn Mts., *Canada* ... **142 A5** 62 15N 119 15W
Hornachuelos, *Spain* ... **43 H5** 37 50N 5 14W
Hornavan, *Sweden* ... **14 C17** 66 15N 17 30 E
Hornbeck, *U.S.A.* ... **155 K8** 31 20N 93 24W
Hornbjarg, *Iceland* ... **11 A4** 66 28N 22 25W
Hornbrook, *U.S.A.* ... **158 F2** 41 55N 122 33W
Hornburg, *Germany* ... **30 C6** 52 2N 10 37 E
Hornby, *N.Z.* ... **131 D7** 43 33 S 172 33 E
Horncastle, *U.K.* ... **20 D7** 53 13N 0 7W
Horndal, *Sweden* ... **16 D10** 60 18N 16 23 E
Hornell, *U.S.A.* ... **150 D7** 42 20N 77 40W
Hornell L., *Canada* ... **142 A5** 62 20N 119 25W
Hornepayne, *Canada* ... **140 C3** 49 14N 84 48W
Horní Planá, *Czech Rep.* ... **34 C7** 48 46N 14 2 E
Hornindal, *Norway* ... **18 C3** 61 58N 6 30 E
Hornings Mills, *Canada* ... **150 B4** 44 9N 80 12W
Hornitos, *U.S.A.* ... **160 H6** 37 30N 120 14W
Hornos, C. de, *Chile* ... **176 E3** 55 50 S 67 30W
Hornos Is., *Papua N. G.* ... **132 B4** 2 12 S 147 45 E
Hornoy-le-Bourg, *France* ... **27 C8** 49 50N 1 54 E
Hornsby, *Australia* ... **129 B9** 33 42 S 151 2 E
Hornsea, *U.K.* ... **20 D7** 53 55N 0 11W
Hornsjø, *Norway* ... **18 C7** 61 19N 10 38 E
Hornslandet, *Sweden* ... **16 C11** 61 35N 17 37 E
Hörnum, *Germany* ... **30 A4** 54 45N 8 17 E
Horobetsu, *Japan* ... **70 C10** 42 24N 141 6 E
Horodenka, *Ukraine* ... **59 H3** 48 41N 25 29 E
Horodnya, *Ukraine* ... **59 G6** 51 55N 31 33 E
Horodok, *Khmelnytskyy, Ukraine* ... **59 H4** 49 10N 26 34 E
Horodok, *Lviv, Ukraine* ... **59 H2** 49 46N 23 32 E
Horodyshche, *Ukraine* ... **59 H6** 49 17N 31 27 E
Horokhiv, *Ukraine* ... **59 G3** 50 30N 24 45 E
Horovice, *Czech Rep.* ... **34 B6** 49 48N 13 53 E
Horqin Youyi Qianqi, *China* ... **75 A12** 46 5N 122 3 E
Horqueta, *Paraguay* ... **174 A4** 23 15 S 56 55W
Horred, *Sweden* ... **17 G6** 57 22N 12 28 E
Horse Creek, *U.S.A.* ... **154 E3** 41 57N 105 10W
Horse Is., *Canada* ... **141 B8** 50 15N 55 50W
Horsefly L., *Canada* ... **142 C4** 52 25N 121 0W
Horseheads, *U.S.A.* ... **150 D8** 42 10N 76 49W
Horsens, *Denmark* ... **17 J3** 55 52N 9 51 E
Horsham, *Australia* ... **128 D5** 36 44 S 142 13 E
Horsham, *U.K.* ... **21 F7** 51 4N 0 20W
Horšovský Týn, *Czech Rep.* ... **34 B5** 49 31N 12 58 E
Horta, *Azores* ... **9 d1** 38 32N 28 38W
Horten, *Norway* ... **15 G14** 59 25N 10 32 E
Hortense, *U.S.A.* ... **152 D8** 31 20N 81 57W
Horti, *India* ... **94 F2** 17 7N 75 47 E
Hortobágy →, *Hungary* ... **52 C6** 47 30N 21 6 E
Horton, *Kans., U.S.A.* ... **154 F7** 39 40N 95 32W
Horton, *Mo., U.S.A.* ... **156 G2** 37 58N 94 22W
Horton →, *Canada* ... **138 B7** 69 56N 126 52W
Horw, *Switz.* ... **33 B6** 47 1N 8 19 E
Horwood L., *Canada* ... **140 C3** 48 5N 82 20W
Hosaina, *Ethiopia* ... **107 F4** 7 30N 37 47 E
Hosdurga, *India* ... **95 H3** 13 49N 76 17 E
Hose, Gunung-Gunung, *Malaysia* ... **78 D4** 2 5N 114 6 E
Hosenofu, *Libya* ... **108 D4** 23 41N 21 4 E
Ḩoseynābād, *Khuzestān, Iran* ... **97 C6** 32 45N 48 20 E
Ḩoseynābād, *Kordestān, Iran* ... **101 E12** 35 33N 47 8 E
Hosford, *U.S.A.* ... **152 E5** 30 23N 84 48W
Hoshangabad, *India* ... **92 H7** 22 45N 77 45 E
Hoshiarpur, *India* ... **92 D6** 31 30N 75 58 E
Hoskins, *Papua N. G.* ... **132 C6** 5 29 S 150 27 E
Hoskote, *India* ... **95 H3** 13 4N 77 48 E
Hospental, *Switz.* ... **33 C7** 46 37N 8 34 E
Hospet, *India* ... **95 G3** 15 15N 76 20 E
Hoste, I., *Chile* ... **176 E3** 55 0 S 69 0W
Hostens, *France* ... **28 D3** 44 30N 0 40W
Hosur, *India* ... **95 H3** 12 43N 77 49 E
Hot, *Thailand* ... **86 C2** 18 8N 98 29 E
Hot Creek Range, *U.S.A.* ... **158 G6** 38 40N 116 20W
Hot Springs, *Ark., U.S.A.* ... **155 H8** 34 31N 93 3W
Hot Springs, *S. Dak., U.S.A.* ... **154 D3** 43 26N 103 29W
Hotagen, *Sweden* ... **14 E16** 63 50N 14 30 E
Hotan, *China* ... **68 C2** 37 25N 79 55 E
Hotazel, *S. Africa* ... **116 D3** 27 17 S 22 58 E
Hotchkiss, *U.S.A.* ... **159 G10** 38 48N 107 43W
Hotham, C., *Australia* ... **124 B5** 12 2 S 131 18 E
Hoti, *Indonesia* ... **83 B4** 3 0 S 130 22 E
Hoting, *Sweden* ... **14 D17** 64 8N 16 15 E
Hotolisht, *Albania* ... **50 E4** 41 10N 20 25 E
Hotte, Massif de la, *Haiti* ... **165 C5** 18 30N 73 45W
Hottentotsbaai, *Namibia* ... **116 D1** 26 8 S 14 59 E
Hou Hai, *China* ... **69 F10** 22 32N 113 56 E
Houailou, *N. Cal.* ... **133 U19** 21 17 S 165 38 E
Houat, Î. de, *France* ... **26 E4** 47 24N 2 58W
Houdan, *France* ... **27 D8** 48 48N 1 35 E
Houei Sai, *Laos* ... **76 G3** 20 18N 100 26 E
Houeillès, *France* ... **28 D4** 44 12N 0 2 E
Houffalize, *Belgium* ... **24 D5** 50 8N 5 48 E
Houghton, *Mich., U.S.A.* ... **154 B10** 47 7N 88 34W
Houghton, *N.Y., U.S.A.* ... **150 D6** 42 25N 78 10W
Houghton L., *U.S.A.* ... **148 C3** 44 21N 84 44W
Houhora Heads, *N.Z.* ... **130 A2** 34 49 S 173 9 E
Houlton, *U.S.A.* ... **149 B12** 46 8N 67 51W
Houma, *U.S.A.* ... **155 L9** 29 36N 90 43W
Houndé, *Burkina Faso* ... **112 C4** 11 34N 3 31W
Hourtin, *France* ... **28 C2** 45 11N 1 4W
Hourtin-Carcans, Étang d', *France* ... **28 C2** 45 10N 1 6W
Housatonic →, *U.S.A.* ... **151 E11** 41 10N 73 7W
Houston, *Canada* ... **142 C3** 54 25N 126 39W
Houston, *Fla., U.S.A.* ... **152 E7** 30 15N 82 54W
Houston, *Mo., U.S.A.* ... **155 G9** 37 22N 91 58W
Houston, *Tex., U.S.A.* ... **155 L7** 29 46N 95 22W
Hout →, *S. Africa* ... **117 C4** 23 4 S 29 36 E
Houtkraal, *S. Africa* ... **116 E3** 30 23 S 24 5 E
Houtman Abrolhos, *Australia* ... **125 E1** 28 43 S 113 48 E
Hov, *Norway* ... **18 D7** 60 42N 10 20 E
Hovd, *Mongolia* ... **68 B4** 48 2N 91 37 E
Hovda, *Norway* ... **18 D6** 60 53N 9 11 E
Hovden, *Aust-Agder, Norway* ... **18 E4** 59 33N 7 22 E
Hovden, *Sogn og Fjordane, Norway* ... **18 C1** 61 41N 4 52 E
Hove, *U.K.* ... **21 G7** 50 50N 0 10W
Hovet, *Norway* ... **18 D5** 60 38N 8 8 E
Hoveyzeh, *Iran* ... **97 D6** 31 27N 48 4 E
Hovgaard Ø, *Greenland* ... **10 B9** 79 55N 18 50W
Hovin, *Norway* ... **18 E6** 59 51N 9 0 E
Hovmantorp, *Sweden* ... **17 H9** 56 47N 15 7 E
Hövsgöl, *Mongolia* ... **74 C5** 43 37N 109 39 E
Hövsgöl Nuur, *Mongolia* ... **68 A5** 51 0N 100 30 E
Hovsta, *Sweden* ... **16 E9** 59 22N 15 15 E
Howakil, *Eritrea* ... **107 D5** 15 10N 40 16 E
Howar, Wadi →, *Sudan* ... **107 D2** 17 30N 27 8 E
Howard, *Australia* ... **127 D5** 25 16 S 152 32 E
Howard, *Pa., U.S.A.* ... **150 F7** 41 1N 77 40W
Howard, *S. Dak., U.S.A.* ... **154 C6** 44 1N 97 32W
Howe, *U.S.A.* ... **158 E7** 43 48N 113 0W
Howe, C., *Australia* ... **129 D9** 37 30 S 150 0 E
Howe I., *Canada* ... **151 B8** 44 16N 76 17W
Howell, *U.S.A.* ... **157 B13** 42 36N 83 56W
Howick, *Canada* ... **151 A11** 45 11N 73 51W
Howick, *N.Z.* ... **130 C3** 36 54 S 174 56 E
Howick, *S. Africa* ... **117 D5** 29 28 S 30 14 E
Howick Group, *Australia* ... **126 A4** 14 20 S 145 30 E
Howitt, L., *Australia* ... **127 D2** 27 40 S 138 40 E
Howland I., *Pac. Oc.* ... **134 G10** 0 48N 176 38W
Howlong, *Australia* ... **129 C7** 35 59 S 146 38 E
Howrah = Haora, *India* ... **93 H13** 22 37N 88 20 E
Howth Hd., *Ireland* ... **23 C5** 53 22N 6 3W
Höxter, *Germany* ... **30 D5** 51 46N 9 22 E
Hoy, *U.K.* ... **22 C5** 58 50N 3 15W
Hoya, *Germany* ... **30 C5** 52 49N 9 8 E
Høyanger, *Norway* ... **15 F12** 61 13N 6 4 E
Hoyerswerda, *Germany* ... **30 D10** 51 26N 14 14 E
Hoylake, *U.K.* ... **20 D4** 53 24N 3 10W
Hōyo-Kaikyō, *Japan* ... **72 D3** 33 20N 131 58 E
Hoyos, *Spain* ... **42 E4** 40 9N 6 45W
Hpa-an = Pa-an, *Burma* ... **90 G6** 16 51N 97 40 E
Hpawlum, *Burma* ... **90 B7** 27 12N 98 12 E
Hpettintha, *Burma* ... **90 C5** 24 14N 95 23 E
Hpizow, *Burma* ... **90 B7** 26 57N 98 24 E
Hpunan Pass, *India* ... **90 A6** 28 9N 97 20 E
Hradec Králové, *Czech Rep.* ... **34 A8** 50 15N 15 50 E
Hrádek, *Czech Rep.* ... **35 C9** 48 46N 16 16 E
Hrafnseyri, *Iceland* ... **11 B3** 65 46N 23 28W
Hranice, *Czech Rep.* ... **35 B10** 49 34N 17 45 E
Hrazdan, *Armenia* ... **61 K7** 40 30N 44 46 E
Hrebenka, *Ukraine* ... **59 G7** 50 9N 32 22 E
Hrífunes, *Iceland* ... **11 D8** 63 38N 18 30W
Hrísey, *Iceland* ... **11 B8** 66 0N 18 23W
Hrodna, *Belarus* ... **58 F2** 53 42N 23 52 E
Hrodzyanka, *Belarus* ... **58 F5** 53 31N 28 42 E
Hron →, *Slovak Rep.* ... **35 D11** 47 49N 18 45 E
Hrubieszów, *Poland* ... **55 H10** 50 49N 23 51 E
Hrubý Jeseník, *Czech Rep.* ... **35 A10** 50 5N 17 10 E
Hrvatska = Croatia ■, *Europe* ... **45 C13** 45 20N 16 0 E
Hrymayliv, *Ukraine* ... **59 H4** 49 20N 26 5 E
Hsa-paw, *Burma* ... **90 F6** 19 1N 97 30 E
Hsenwi, *Burma* ... **90 D6** 23 22N 97 55 E
Hsi-hkip, *Burma* ... **90 E6** 20 25N 96 42 E
Hsiamen = Xiamen, *China* ... **77 E12** 24 25N 118 4 E
Hsian = Xi'an, *China* ... **74 G5** 34 15N 109 0 E
Hsinchu, *Taiwan* ... **77 E13** 24 48N 120 58 E
Hsinhailien = Lianyungang, *China* ... **75 G10** 34 40N 119 11 E
Hsinying, *Taiwan* ... **77 F13** 23 18N 120 19 E
Hsipaw, *Burma* ... **90 D6** 22 37N 97 18 E
Hsopket, *Burma* ... **76 F2** 23 11N 98 26 E
Hsüchou = Xuzhou, *China* ... **75 G9** 34 18N 117 10 E
Htawgaw, *Burma* ... **90 C7** 25 57N 98 23 E
Hu Xian, *China* ... **74 G5** 34 8N 108 42 E
Hua Hin, *Thailand* ... **86 F2** 12 34N 99 58 E
Hua Xian, *Henan, China* ... **74 G8** 35 30N 114 30 E
Hua Xian, *Shaanxi, China* ... **74 G5** 34 30N 109 48 E
Hua'an, *China* ... **77 E11** 25 1N 117 32 E
Huab →, *Namibia* ... **116 B2** 20 52 S 13 25 E
Huacaya, *Bolivia* ... **173 E5** 20 45 S 63 43W
Huachacalla, *Bolivia* ... **172 D4** 18 45 S 68 17W
Huacheng, *China* ... **77 E10** 24 4N 115 37 E
Huachinera, *Mexico* ... **162 A3** 30 9N 108 55W
Huacho, *Peru* ... **172 C2** 11 10 S 77 35W
Huachón, *Peru* ... **172 C2** 10 35 S 76 0W
Huade, *China* ... **74 D7** 41 55N 113 59 E
Huadian, *China* ... **75 C14** 43 0N 126 40 E
Huadu, *China* ... **77 F9** 23 22N 113 12 E
Huai He →, *China* ... **77 A12** 33 0N 118 30 E
Huai Yot, *Thailand* ... **87 J2** 7 45N 99 37 E
Huai'an, *Hebei, China* ... **74 D8** 40 30N 114 20 E
Huai'an, *Jiangsu, China* ... **75 H10** 33 30N 119 10 E
Huaibei, *China* ... **74 G9** 34 0N 116 48 E
Huaibin, *China* ... **77 A10** 32 32N 115 27 E
Huaide = Gongzhuling, *China* ... **75 C13** 43 30N 124 40 E
Huaidezhen, *China* ... **75 C13** 43 48N 124 50 E
Huaihua, *China* ... **76 D7** 27 32N 109 57 E
Huaiji, *China* ... **77 F9** 23 55N 112 12 E
Huainan, *China* ... **77 A11** 32 38N 116 58 E
Huaining, *China* ... **77 B11** 30 24N 116 40 E
Huairen, *China* ... **74 E7** 39 48N 113 20 E
Huairou, *China* ... **74 D9** 40 20N 116 35 E
Huaiyang, *China* ... **74 H8** 33 40N 114 52 E
Huaiyin, *China* ... **75 H10** 33 30N 119 2 E
Huaiyuan, *Anhui, China* ... **75 H9** 32 55N 117 10 E
Huaiyuan, *Guangxi Zhuangzu, China* ... **76 E7** 24 31N 108 22 E
Huajianzi, *China* ... **75 D13** 41 23N 125 20 E
Huajuapan de Leon, *Mexico* ... **163 D5** 17 50N 97 48W
Hualalai, *U.S.A.* ... **145 D6** 19 42N 155 52W
Hualapai Peak, *U.S.A.* ... **159 J7** 35 5N 113 54W
Hualien, *Taiwan* ... **77 E13** 24 0N 121 30 E
Huallaga →, *Peru* ... **172 B2** 5 15 S 75 30W
Huallanca, *Peru* ... **172 B2** 8 50 S 77 56W
Huamachuco, *Peru* ... **172 B2** 7 50 S 78 5W
Huambo, *Angola* ... **115 E3** 12 42 S 15 54 E
Huambo □, *Angola* ... **115 E3** 13 0 S 16 0 E
Huan Jiang →, *China* ... **74 G5** 34 28N 109 0 E
Huan Xian, *China* ... **74 F4** 36 33N 107 7 E
Huancabamba, *Peru* ... **172 B2** 5 10 S 79 15W
Huancane, *Peru* ... **172 D4** 15 10 S 69 44W
Huancapi, *Peru* ... **172 C3** 13 40 S 74 0W
Huancavelica, *Peru* ... **172 C2** 12 50 S 75 5W
Huancavelica □, *Peru* ... **172 C3** 13 0 S 75 0W
Huancayo, *Peru* ... **172 C2** 12 5 S 75 12W
Huanchaca, *Bolivia* ... **172 E4** 20 15 S 66 40W
Huanchaca, Serranía de, *Bolivia* ... **173 C5** 14 30 S 60 39W
Huang Hai = Yellow Sea, *China* ... **75 G12** 35 0N 123 0 E
Huang He →, *China* ... **75 F10** 37 55N 118 50 E
Huang Xian, *China* ... **75 F11** 37 38N 120 30 E
Huangchuan, *China* ... **77 A10** 32 15N 115 10 E
Huanggang, *China* ... **77 B10** 30 29N 114 52 E
Huangguoshu, *China* ... **76 E5** 26 0N 105 40 E
Huangling, *China* ... **74 G5** 35 34N 109 15 E
Huanglong, *China* ... **74 G5** 35 30N 109 59 E
Huanglongtan, *China* ... **77 A8** 32 40N 110 33 E
Huangmei, *China* ... **77 B10** 30 5N 115 56 E
Huangpi, *China* ... **77 B10** 30 50N 114 22 E
Huangping, *China* ... **76 D6** 26 52N 107 54 E
Huangshan, *China* ... **77 C12** 29 42N 118 25 E
Huangshi, *China* ... **77 B10** 30 10N 115 3 E

Ijebu-Ode 225

Huangsongdian, *China* **75 C14** 43 45N 127 25 E
Huangyan, *China* **77 C13** 28 38N 121 19 E
Huangyangsi, *China* **77 D8** 26 33N 111 39 E
Huaning, *China* **76 E4** 24 17N 102 56 E
Huanjiang, *China* **76 E7** 24 50N 108 18 E
Huanta, *Peru* **172 C3** 12 55 S 74 20W
Huantai, *China* **75 F9** 36 58N 117 56 E
Huánuco, *Peru* **172 B2** 9 55 S 76 15W
Huánuco □, *Peru* **172 B2** 9 55 S 76 14W
Huanuni, *Bolivia* **172 D4** 18 16 S 66 51W
Huanzo, Cordillera de, *Peru* **172 C3** 14 35 S 73 20W
Huaping, *China* **76 D3** 26 46N 101 25 E
Huara, *Chile* **172 D4** 19 59 S 69 47W
Huaral, *Peru* **172 C2** 11 32 S 77 13W
Huaraz, *Peru* **172 B2** 9 30 S 77 32W
Huari, *Peru* **172 B2** 9 14 S 77 14W
Huarmey, *Peru* **172 C2** 10 5 S 78 5W
Huarochiri, *Peru* **172 C2** 12 9 S 76 15W
Huarocondo, *Peru* **172 C3** 13 26 S 72 14W
Huarong, *China* **77 C9** 29 29N 112 30 E
Huascarán, *Peru* **172 B2** 9 8 S 77 36W
Huascarán, Nevado, *Peru* **172 B2** 9 7 S 77 37W
Huasco, *Chile* **174 B1** 28 30 S 71 15W
Huasco →, *Chile* **174 B1** 28 27 S 71 13W
Huasna, *U.S.A.* **161 K6** 35 6N 120 24W
Huatabampo, *Mexico* **162 B3** 26 50N 109 50W
Huauchinango, *Mexico* **163 C5** 20 11N 98 3W
Huautla de Jiménez, *Mexico* **163 D5** 18 8N 96 51W
Huaxi, *China* **76 D6** 26 25N 106 40 E
Huay Namota, *Mexico* **162 C4** 21 56N 104 30W
Huayin, *China* **74 G6** 34 35N 110 5 E
Huayllay, *Peru* **172 C2** 11 3 S 76 21W
Huayuan, *China* **76 C7** 28 37N 109 29 E
Huayun, *China* **76 B6** 30 14N 106 40 E
Huazhou, *China* **77 G8** 21 33N 110 33 E
Hubbard, *Iowa, U.S.A.* **156 B3** 42 18N 93 18W
Hubbard, *Ohio, U.S.A.* **150 E4** 41 9N 80 34W
Hubbard, *Tex., U.S.A.* **155 K6** 31 51N 96 48W
Hubbart Pt., *Canada* **143 B10** 59 21N 94 41W
Hubei □, *China* **77 B9** 31 0N 112 0 E
Hubli, *India* **95 G2** 15 22N 75 15 E
Huch'ang, *N. Korea* **75 D14** 41 25N 127 2 E
Hucknall, *U.K.* **20 D6** 53 3N 1 13W
Huddersfield, *U.K.* **20 D6** 53 39N 1 47W
Hude, *Germany* **30 B4** 53 7N 8 26 E
Hudi, *Sudan* **106 D3** 17 43N 34 18 E
Hudiksvall, *Sweden* **16 C11** 61 43N 17 10 E
Hudson, *Canada* **140 B1** 50 6N 92 9W
Hudson, *Fla., U.S.A.* **153 G7** 28 22N 82 42W
Hudson, *Mass., U.S.A.* **151 D13** 42 23N 71 34W
Hudson, *Mich., U.S.A.* **157 C12** 41 51N 84 21W
Hudson, *N.Y., U.S.A.* **151 D11** 42 15N 73 46W
Hudson, *Wis., U.S.A.* **154 C8** 44 58N 92 45W
Hudson, *Wyo., U.S.A.* **158 E9** 42 54N 108 35W
Hudson →, *U.S.A.* **151 F10** 40 42N 74 2W
Hudson Bay, *Nunavut, Canada* **139 C11** 60 0N 86 0W
Hudson Bay, *Sask., Canada* **143 C8** 52 51N 102 23W
Hudson Falls, *U.S.A.* **151 C11** 43 18N 73 35W
Hudson Mts., *Antarctica* **7 D16** 74 32 S 99 20W
Hudson Str., *Canada* **139 B13** 62 0N 70 0W
Hudson's Hope, *Canada* **142 B4** 56 0N 121 54W
Hudsonville, *U.S.A.* **157 B11** 42 52N 85 52W
Hue, *Vietnam* **86 D6** 16 30N 107 35 E
Huebra →, *Spain* **42 D4** 41 2N 6 48W
Huechucuicui, Pta., *Chile* **176 B2** 41 48 S 74 2W
Huedin, *Romania* **52 D8** 46 52N 23 2 E
Huehuetenango, *Guatemala* **164 C1** 15 20N 91 28W
Huejúcar, *Mexico* **162 C4** 22 21N 103 13W
Huélamo, *Spain* **40 E3** 40 17N 1 48W
Huelgoat, *France* **26 D3** 48 22N 3 46W
Huelma, *Spain* **43 H7** 37 39N 3 28W
Huelva, *Spain* **43 H4** 37 18N 6 57W
Huelva □, *Spain* **43 H4** 37 40N 7 0W
Huelva →, *Spain* **43 H5** 37 27N 6 0W
Huentelauquén, *Chile* **174 C1** 31 38 S 71 33W
Huércal-Overa, *Spain* **41 H3** 37 23N 1 57W
Huerta, Sa. de la, *Argentina* **174 C2** 31 10 S 67 30W
Huertas, C. de las, *Spain* **41 G4** 38 21N 0 24W
Huerva →, *Spain* **40 D4** 41 39N 0 52W
Huesca, *Spain* **40 C4** 42 8N 0 25W
Huesca □, *Spain* **40 C5** 42 20N 0 1 E
Huéscar, *Spain* **41 H2** 37 44N 2 35W
Huetamo, *Mexico* **162 D4** 18 36N 100 54W
Huete, *Spain* **40 E2** 40 10N 2 43W
Huger, *U.S.A.* **152 B10** 33 6N 79 48W
Hugh →, *Australia* **126 D1** 25 1 S 134 1 E
Hughenden, *Australia* **126 C3** 20 52 S 144 10 E
Hughes, *Australia* **125 F4** 30 42 S 129 31 E
Hughes, *U.S.A.* **144 C9** 66 3N 154 15W
Hughesville, *U.S.A.* **151 E8** 41 14N 76 44W
Hugli →, *India* **93 J13** 21 56N 88 4 E
Hugo, *Colo., U.S.A.* **154 F3** 39 8N 103 28W
Hugo, *Okla., U.S.A.* **155 H7** 34 1N 95 31W
Hugoton, *U.S.A.* **155 G4** 37 11N 101 21W
Hui Xian = Huixian, *China* **74 G7** 35 27N 113 12 E
Hui Xian, *China* **74 H4** 33 50N 106 4 E
Hui'an, *China* **77 E12** 25 1N 118 43 E
Hui'anbu, *China* **74 F4** 37 28N 106 38 E
Huiarau Ra., *N.Z.* **130 E5** 38 45 S 176 55 E
Huichang, *China* **77 E10** 25 32N 115 45 E
Huichapán, *Mexico* **163 C5** 20 24N 99 40W
Huidong, *Guangdong, China* **77 F10** 22 58N 114 43 E
Huidong, *Sichuan, China* **76 D4** 26 34N 102 35 E
Huifa He →, *China* **75 C14** 43 0N 127 50 E
Huíla, *Angola* **115 F2** 15 4 S 13 32 E
Huíla □, *Angola* **115 E2** 14 0 S 15 0 E
Huila □, *Colombia* **168 C2** 2 30N 75 45W
Huila, Nevado del, *Colombia* **168 C2** 3 0N 76 0W
Huilai, *China* **77 F11** 23 0N 116 18 E
Huili, *China* **76 D4** 26 35N 102 17 E
Huimin, *China* **75 F9** 37 27N 117 28 E
Huinan, *China* **75 C14** 42 40N 126 2 E
Huinca Renancó, *Argentina* **174 C3** 34 51 S 64 22W
Huining, *China* **74 G3** 35 38N 105 0 E
Huinong, *China* **74 E4** 39 5N 106 35 E
Huiroa, *N.Z.* **130 F3** 39 15 S 174 30 E
Huisache, *Mexico* **162 C4** 22 55N 100 25W
Huishui, *China* **76 D6** 26 7N 106 38 E
Huisne →, *France* **26 E7** 47 59N 0 11 E
Huiting, *China* **74 G9** 34 5N 116 5 E
Huitong, *China* **76 D7** 26 51N 109 45 E
Huixian, *China* **74 G7** 35 27N 113 12 E
Huixtla, *Mexico* **163 D6** 15 9N 92 28W
Huize, *China* **76 D4** 26 24N 103 15 E
Huizhou, *China* **77 F10** 23 0N 114 23 E
Hukeri, *India* **95 F2** 16 14N 74 36 E
Hukou, *China* **77 C11** 29 45N 116 21 E
Hŭksan-chedo, *S. Korea* **75 G13** 34 40N 125 30 E
Hukuntsi, *Botswana* **116 C3** 23 58 S 21 45 E
Hula, *Papua N. G.* **132 F4** 10 5 S 147 43 E
Ḩulayfā', *Si. Arabia* **96 E4** 25 58N 40 45 E
Huld = Ulaanjirem, *Mongolia* **74 B3** 45 5N 105 30 E
Hulin He →, *China* **75 B12** 45 0N 122 10 E
Hull = Kingston upon Hull, *U.K.* **20 D7** 53 45N 0 21W
Hull, *Canada* **140 C4** 45 25N 75 44W
Hull →, *U.K.* **20 D7** 53 44N 0 20W
Hulst, *Neths.* **24 C4** 51 17N 4 2 E
Hultsfred, *Sweden* **17 G9** 57 30N 15 52 E
Hulun Nur, *China* **69 B6** 49 0N 117 30 E
Hulyaypole, *Ukraine* **59 J9** 47 45N 36 21 E
Huma, Tanjung, *Malaysia* **87 c** 5 29N 100 16 E
Humacao, *Puerto Rico* **165 d** 18 9N 65 50W
Humahuaca, *Argentina* **174 A2** 23 10 S 65 25W
Humaitá, *Brazil* **173 B5** 7 35 S 63 1W
Humaitá, *Paraguay* **174 B4** 27 2 S 58 31W
Humansdorp, *S. Africa* **116 E3** 34 2 S 24 46 E
Humansville, *U.S.A.* **156 G3** 37 48N 93 35W
Humara, J., *Sudan* **107 D3** 16 16N 30 59 E
Humbe, *Angola* **116 B1** 16 40 S 14 55 E
Humber →, *U.K.* **20 D7** 53 42N 0 27W
Humboldt, *Canada* **143 C7** 52 15N 105 9W
Humboldt, *Iowa, U.S.A.* **156 B2** 42 44N 94 13W
Humboldt, *Tenn., U.S.A.* **155 H10** 35 50N 88 55W
Humboldt →, *U.S.A.* **158 F4** 39 59N 118 36W
Humboldt, Massif du, *N. Cal.* **133 U20** 21 53 S 166 25 E
Humboldt Gletscher, *Greenland* **10 B4** 79 30N 62 0W
Humboldt Mts., *N.Z.* **131 E3** 44 30 S 168 15 E
Hume, *U.S.A.* **160 J8** 36 48N 118 54W
Hume, L., *Australia* **129 D7** 36 0 S 147 5 E
Humen, *China* **69 F10** 22 50N 113 40 E
Humenné, *Slovak Rep.* **35 C14** 48 55N 21 50 E
Humeston, *U.S.A.* **156 D3** 40 52N 93 30W
Hummelsta, *Sweden* **16 E10** 59 34N 16 58 E
Hummelvik, *Norway* **18 A5** 63 29N 8 19 E
Humpata, *Angola* **115 F2** 15 2 S 13 24 E
Humphreys, Mt., *U.S.A.* **160 H8** 37 17N 118 40W
Humphreys Peak, *U.S.A.* **159 J8** 35 21N 111 41W
Humpolec, *Czech Rep.* **34 B8** 49 31N 15 20 E
Humptulips, *U.S.A.* **160 C3** 47 14N 123 57W
Humula, *Australia* **129 C7** 35 30 S 147 46 E
Hūn, *Libya* **108 C3** 29 2N 16 0 E
Hun Jiang →, *China* **75 D13** 40 50N 125 38 E
Húnaflói, *Iceland* **11 B6** 65 50N 20 50W
Hunan □, *China* **77 D9** 27 30N 112 0 E
Húnavatnssýsla □, *Iceland* **11 B6** 65 30N 20 25W
Hunchun, *China* **75 C16** 42 52N 130 28 E
Hundested, *Denmark* **17 J5** 55 58N 11 52 E
Hundewali, *Pakistan* **92 D5** 31 55N 72 38 E
Hundorp, *Norway* **18 C7** 61 33N 9 59 E
Hundred Mile House, *Canada* **142 C4** 51 38N 121 18W
Hundvåg, *Norway* **18 E2** 59 0N 5 43 E
Hunedoara, *Romania* **52 E7** 45 40N 22 50 E
Hunedoara □, *Romania* **52 E7** 45 50N 22 54 E
Hünfeld, *Germany* **30 E5** 50 39N 9 46 E
Hung Yen, *Vietnam* **76 G6** 20 39N 106 4 E
Hunga Ha'apai, *Tonga* **133 Q13** 20 41 S 175 7W
Hungary ■, *Europe* **35 D12** 47 20N 19 20 E
Hungary, Plain of, *Europe* **12 F10** 47 0N 20 0 E
Hungerford, *Australia* **127 D3** 28 58 S 144 24 E
Hŭngnam, *N. Korea* **75 E14** 39 49N 127 45 E
Hungt'ou Hsü, *Taiwan* **77 G13** 22 0N 121 30 E
Hungund, *India* **95 F3** 16 4N 76 3 E
Huni Valley, *Ghana* **112 D4** 5 33N 1 56W
Hunneberg, *Sweden* **17 F6** 58 18N 12 30 E
Hunnebostrand, *Sweden* **17 F5** 58 27N 11 18 E
Hunsberge, *Namibia* **116 D2** 27 45 S 17 12 E
Hunsrück, *Germany* **31 F3** 49 56N 7 27 E
Hunstanton, *U.K.* **20 E8** 52 56N 0 29 E
Hunsur, *India* **95 H3** 12 16N 76 16 E
Hunte →, *Germany* **30 B4** 53 14N 8 28 E
Hunter, *N.Z.* **131 E6** 44 36 S 171 2 E
Hunter, *U.S.A.* **151 D10** 42 13N 74 13W
Hunter →, *Australia* **129 B9** 32 52 S 151 46 E
Hunter →, *N.Z.* **131 E4** 44 21 S 169 27 E
Hunter, C., *Solomon Is.* **133 M10** 9 48 S 159 50 E
Hunter I., *Australia* **127 G3** 40 30 S 144 45 E
Hunter I., *Canada* **142 C3** 51 55N 128 0W
Hunter Mts., *N.Z.* **131 F2** 45 43 S 167 25 E
Hunter Ra., *Australia* **129 B9** 32 45 S 150 15 E
Hunters Road, *Zimbabwe* **119 F2** 19 9 S 29 49 E
Hunterville, *N.Z.* **130 F4** 39 56 S 175 35 E
Huntingburg, *U.S.A.* **157 F10** 38 18N 86 57W
Huntingdon, *Canada* **140 C5** 45 6N 74 10W
Huntingdon, *U.K.* **21 E7** 52 20N 0 11W
Huntingdon, *U.S.A.* **150 F6** 40 30N 78 1W
Huntington, *Ind., U.S.A.* **157 D11** 40 53N 85 30W
Huntington, *Oreg., U.S.A.* **158 D5** 44 21N 117 16W
Huntington, *Utah, U.S.A.* **158 G8** 39 20N 110 58W
Huntington, *W. Va., U.S.A.* **148 F4** 38 25N 82 27W
Huntington Beach, *U.S.A.* **161 M9** 33 40N 118 5W
Huntington Station, *U.S.A.* **151 F11** 40 52N 73 26W
Huntley, *U.S.A.* **157 B8** 42 10N 88 26W
Huntly, *N.Z.* **130 D4** 37 34 S 175 11 E
Huntly, *U.K.* **22 D6** 57 27N 2 47W
Huntsville, *Canada* **140 C4** 45 20N 79 14W
Huntsville, *Ala., U.S.A.* **149 H2** 34 44N 86 35W
Huntsville, *Mo., U.S.A.* **156 E4** 39 26N 92 33W
Huntsville, *Tex., U.S.A.* **155 K7** 30 43N 95 33W
Hunyani →, *Zimbabwe* **119 F3** 15 57 S 30 39 E
Hunyuan, *China* **74 E7** 39 42N 113 42 E
Hunza →, *India* **93 B6** 35 54N 74 20 E
Huo Xian = Huozhou, *China* **74 F6** 36 36N 111 42 E
Huon G., *Papua N. G.* **132 D4** 7 0 S 147 30 E
Huon Pen., *Papua N. G.* **132 D4** 6 20 S 147 30 E
Huong Hoa, *Vietnam* **86 D6** 16 37N 106 45 E
Huong Khe, *Vietnam* **86 C5** 18 13N 105 41 E
Huonville, *Australia* **127 G4** 43 0 S 147 5 E
Huoqiu, *China* **77 A11** 32 20N 116 12 E
Huoshan, *Anhui, China* **77 A12** 32 28N 118 30 E
Huoshan, *Anhui, China* **77 B11** 31 25N 116 20 E
Huoshao Dao = Lü-Tao, *Taiwan* **77 F13** 22 40N 121 30 E
Huozhou, *China* **74 F6** 36 36N 111 42 E
Hupeh = Hubei □, *China* **77 B9** 31 0N 112 0 E
Ḩūr, *Iran* **97 D8** 30 50N 57 7 E
Hurbanovo, *Slovak Rep.* **35 D11** 47 51N 18 11 E
Hurd, C., *Canada* **150 A3** 45 13N 81 44W
Hure Qi, *China* **75 C11** 42 45N 121 45 E
Hurezani, *Romania* **53 F8** 44 49N 23 40 E
Hurghada, *Egypt* **106 B3** 27 15N 33 50 E
Hurley, *N. Mex., U.S.A.* **159 K9** 32 42N 108 8W
Hurley, *Wis., U.S.A.* **154 B9** 46 27N 90 11W
Huron, *Calif., U.S.A.* **160 J6** 36 12N 120 6W
Huron, *Ohio, U.S.A.* **150 E2** 41 24N 82 33W
Huron, *S. Dak., U.S.A.* **154 C5** 44 22N 98 13W
Huron, L., *U.S.A.* **150 B2** 44 30N 82 40W
Hurricane, *U.S.A.* **159 H7** 37 11N 113 17W
Hurso, *Ethiopia* **107 F5** 9 35N 41 33 E
Hurstboro, *U.S.A.* **153 J3** 32 15N 85 25W
Hurungwe Safari Area, *Zimbabwe* **119 F2** 16 7 S 29 5 E
Hurunui →, *N.Z.* **131 C8** 42 54 S 173 18 E
Hurup, *Denmark* **17 H2** 56 46N 8 25 E
Húsafell, *Iceland* **11 C6** 64 42N 20 53W
Húsavík, *Iceland* **11 A9** 66 3N 17 21W
Huşi, *Romania* **53 D13** 46 41N 28 7 E
Huskisson, *Australia* **129 C9** 35 2 S 150 41 E
Huskvarna, *Sweden* **17 G8** 57 47N 14 15 E
Huslia, *U.S.A.* **144 D8** 65 41N 156 24W
Husnes, *Norway* **18 E2** 59 52N 5 45 E
Hustad, *Norway* **18 B4** 62 57N 7 6 E
Hustadvika, *Norway* **14 E12** 63 0N 7 0 E
Hustontown, *U.S.A.* **150 F6** 40 3N 78 2W
Hustopeče, *Czech Rep.* **35 C9** 48 57N 16 43 E
Husum, *Germany* **30 A5** 54 28N 9 4 E
Husum, *Sweden* **16 A13** 63 21N 19 12 E
Hutchinson, *Kans., U.S.A.* **155 F6** 38 5N 97 56W
Hutchinson, *Minn., U.S.A.* **154 C7** 44 54N 94 22W
Ḩūth, *Yemen* **98 C3** 16 14N 43 58 E
Hutjena, *Papua N. G.* **132 C8** 5 23 S 154 42 E
Hutsonville, *U.S.A.* **157 E9** 39 7N 87 40W
Hutte Sauvage, L. de la, *Canada* **141 A7** 56 15N 64 45W
Hüttenberg, *Austria* **34 E7** 46 56N 14 33 E
Hutton, Mt., *Australia* **127 D4** 25 51 S 148 20 E
Huttwil, *Switz.* **32 B5** 47 7N 7 50 E
Huwun, *Ethiopia* **107 G5** 4 23N 40 6 E
Huy, *Belgium* **24 D5** 50 31N 5 15 E
Huzhou, *China* **77 B13** 30 51N 120 8 E
Huzurabad, *India* **94 E4** 18 12N 79 25 E
Huzurnagar, *India* **94 F4** 16 54N 79 53 E
Hvalpsund, *Denmark* **17 H3** 56 42N 9 11 E
Hvammsfjörður, *Iceland* **11 B4** 65 4N 22 5W
Hvammstangi, *Iceland* **11 B6** 65 24N 20 57W
Hvammur, *Mýrasýsla, Iceland* **11 C5** 64 50N 21 21W
Hvammur, *Skagafjarðarsýsla, Iceland* **11 B7** 65 53N 19 51W
Hvannadalshnúkur, *Iceland* **11 C10** 64 1N 16 41W
Hvanneyri, *Iceland* **11 C5** 64 34N 21 36W
Hvar, *Croatia* **45 E13** 43 11N 16 28 E
Hvarski Kanal, *Croatia* **45 E13** 43 15N 16 35 E
Hveragerði, *Iceland* **11 C5** 64 0N 21 12W
Hvítá →, *Iceland* **11 C5** 64 30N 21 58W
Hvítárvatn, *Iceland* **11 C7** 64 37N 19 50W
Hvittingfoss, *Norway* **18 E7** 59 29N 10 0 E
Hvolsvöllur, *Iceland* **11 D6** 63 45N 20 14W
Hwachŏn-chŏsuji, *S. Korea* **75 E14** 38 5N 127 50 E
Hwang Ho = Huang He →, *China* **75 F10** 37 55N 118 50 E
Hwange, *Zimbabwe* **119 F2** 18 18 S 26 30 E
Hwange Nat. Park, *Zimbabwe* **116 B4** 19 0 S 26 30 E
Hwekum, *Burma* **90 B5** 26 7N 95 22 E
Hyaing, *Burma* **90 D5** 22 39N 94 44 E
Hyannis, *Mass., U.S.A.* **148 E10** 41 39N 70 17W
Hyannis, *Nebr., U.S.A.* **154 E4** 42 0N 101 46W
Hyargas Nuur, *Mongolia* **68 B4** 49 0N 93 0 E
Hybo, *Sweden* **16 C10** 61 49N 16 15 E
Hydaburg, *U.S.A.* **142 B2** 55 15N 132 50W
Hyde, *N.Z.* **131 F5** 45 18 S 170 16 E
Hyde Park, *Guyana* **169 B6** 6 30N 58 16W
Hyde Park, *U.S.A.* **151 E11** 41 47N 73 56W
Hyden, *Australia* **125 F2** 32 24 S 118 53 E
Hyder, *U.S.A.* **142 B2** 55 55N 130 5W
Hyderabad, *India* **94 F4** 17 22N 78 29 E
Hyderabad, *Pakistan* **91 D3** 25 23N 68 24 E
Hyen, *Norway* **18 C2** 61 44N 5 56 E
Hyères, *France* **29 E10** 43 8N 6 9 E
Hyères, Îs. d', *France* **29 F10** 43 0N 6 20 E
Hyesan, *N. Korea* **75 D15** 41 20N 128 10 E
Hyland →, *Canada* **142 B3** 59 52N 128 12W
Hylestad, *Norway* **18 E4** 59 6N 7 29 E
Hyllestad, *Norway* **18 C2** 61 10N 5 17 E
Hyltebruk, *Sweden* **17 H7** 56 59N 13 15 E
Hymia, *India* **93 C8** 33 40N 78 2 E
Hyndman Peak, *U.S.A.* **158 E6** 43 45N 114 8W
Hynnekleiv, *Norway* **18 F5** 58 36N 8 25 E
Hyōgo □, *Japan* **72 B6** 35 15N 134 50 E
Hyrra Banda, *C.A.R.* **114 A4** 5 58N 22 1 E
Hyrum, *U.S.A.* **158 F8** 41 38N 111 51W
Hysham, *U.S.A.* **158 C10** 46 18N 107 14W
Hythe, *U.K.* **21 F9** 51 4N 1 5 E
Hyūga, *Japan* **72 E3** 32 25N 131 35 E
Hyvinge = Hyvinkää, *Finland* **15 F21** 60 38N 24 50 E
Hyvinkää, *Finland* **15 F21** 60 38N 24 50 E

I

I-n-Azaoua, *Illizi, Algeria* **111 C6** 25 42N 6 54 E
I-n-Azaoua, *Tamanrasset, Algeria* **111 D6** 20 46N 7 32 E
I-n-Échaï, *Mali* **110 D4** 20 10N 2 5W
I-n-Gall, *Niger* **113 B6** 16 51N 7 1 E
I-n-Kelemet, *Algeria* **111 C6** 26 57N 5 47 E
I-n-Oudad, *Algeria* **111 D5** 20 17N 4 38 E
I-n-Ouzzal, *Algeria* **113 A5** 20 40N 2 35 E
I-n-Quzzal, *Algeria* **111 D5** 20 41N 2 34 E
I-n-Tadreft, *Niger* **113 B6** 19 5N 6 38 E
Iabès, Erg, *Algeria* **111 C4** 27 30N 2 2W
Iablanița, *Romania* **52 F7** 44 57N 22 19 E
Iaco →, *Brazil* **172 B4** 9 3 S 68 34W
Iacobeni, *Romania* **53 C10** 47 25N 25 20 E
Iaçu, *Brazil* **171 D3** 12 45 S 40 13W
Iakora, *Madag.* **117 C8** 23 6 S 46 40 E
Ialibu, *Papua N. G.* **132 D2** 6 17 S 143 59 E
Ialomița □, *Romania* **53 F12** 44 30N 27 30 E
Ialomița →, *Romania* **53 F12** 44 42N 27 51 E
Ialoveni, *Moldova* **53 D13** 46 56N 28 47 E
Ialpug →, *Moldova* **53 E13** 45 41N 28 35 E
Iamonia L., *U.S.A.* **152 E5** 30 38N 84 14W
Ianca, *Romania* **53 E12** 45 6N 27 29 E
Iara, *Romania* **53 D8** 46 31N 23 35 E
Iarda, *Ethiopia* **107 E4** 11 9N 35 53 E
Iargara, *Moldova* **53 D13** 46 24N 28 23 E
Iași, *Romania* **53 C12** 47 10N 27 40 E
Iași □, *Romania* **53 C12** 47 20N 27 0 E
Íasmos, *Greece* **51 E9** 41 8N 25 11 E
Iauaretê, *Colombia* **168 C4** 0 36N 69 12W
Ib →, *India* **93 J10** 21 34N 83 48 E
Iba, *Phil.* **80 D2** 15 22N 120 0 E
Ibadan, *Nigeria* **113 D5** 7 22N 3 58 E
Ibagué, *Colombia* **168 C2** 4 20N 75 20W
Ibaiti, *Brazil* **171 F1** 23 50 S 50 10W
Ibajay, *Phil.* **81 F4** 11 49N 122 10 E
Iballë, *Albania* **50 D4** 42 12N 20 2 E
Ibănești, *Botoșani, Romania* **53 B11** 48 4N 26 22 E
Ibănești, *Mureș, Romania* **53 D9** 46 45N 24 57 E
Ibanshe, *Dem. Rep. of the Congo* **115 C4** 4 58 S 21 30 E
Ibar →, *Serbia, Yug.* **50 C4** 43 43N 20 45 E
Ibara, *Japan* **72 C5** 34 36N 133 28 E
Ibaraki, *Japan* **73 C7** 34 49N 135 34 E
Ibaraki □, *Japan* **73 A12** 36 10N 140 10 E
Ibarra, *Ecuador* **168 C2** 0 21N 78 7W
Ibb, *Yemen* **98 D4** 14 2N 44 10 E
Ibba, *Sudan* **107 G2** 4 49N 29 2 E
Ibba, Bahr el →, *Sudan* **107 F2** 5 30N 28 55 E
Ibbenbüren, *Germany* **30 C3** 52 16N 7 43 E
Ibeke Gembo, *Dem. Rep. of the Congo* **114 C3** 1 24 S 18 51 E
Ibembo, *Dem. Rep. of the Congo* **118 B1** 2 35N 23 35 E
Ibenga →, *Congo* **114 B3** 2 19N 18 9 E
Ibera, L., *Argentina* **174 B4** 28 30 S 57 9W
Iberia, *U.S.A.* **156 F4** 38 5N 92 18W
Iberian Peninsula, *Europe* **12 H5** 40 0N 5 0W
Iberville, *Canada* **140 C5** 45 19N 73 17W
Iberville, Lac d', *Canada* **140 A5** 55 55N 73 15W
Ibi, *Nigeria* **113 D6** 8 15N 9 44 E
Ibi, *Spain* **41 G4** 38 38N 0 34W
Ibiá, *Brazil* **171 E2** 19 30 S 46 30W
Ibiapaba, Sa. da, *Brazil* **170 B3** 4 0 S 41 30W
Ibicaraí, *Brazil* **171 D4** 14 51 S 39 36W
Ibicuí, *Brazil* **171 D4** 14 51 S 39 59W
Ibicuí →, *Brazil* **175 B4** 29 25 S 56 47W
Ibicuy, *Argentina* **174 C4** 33 55 S 59 10W
Ibipetuba, *Brazil* **170 D3** 11 0 S 44 32W
Ibitiara, *Brazil* **171 D3** 12 39 S 42 13W
Ibiza = Eivissa, *Spain* **38 D1** 38 54N 1 26 E
Íblei, Monti, *Italy* **47 E7** 37 15N 14 45 E
Ibo, *Mozam.* **119 E5** 12 22 S 40 40 E
Ibonma, *Indonesia* **83 B4** 3 29 S 133 31 E
Ibotirama, *Brazil* **171 D3** 12 13 S 43 12W
Ibrāhīm →, *Lebanon* **103 A4** 34 4N 35 38 E
'Ibrī, *Oman* **97 F8** 23 14N 56 30 E
İbriktepe, *Turkey* **51 E10** 41 0N 26 30 E
Ibshawâi, *Egypt* **106 J7** 29 21N 30 40 E
Ibu, *Indonesia* **82 A3** 1 35N 127 33 E
Ibuki-Sanchi, *Japan* **73 B8** 35 25N 136 18 E
Ibusuki, *Japan* **72 F2** 31 12N 130 40 E
Ica, *Peru* **172 C2** 14 0 S 75 48W
Ica □, *Peru* **172 C2** 14 20 S 75 30W
Iça →, *Brazil* **172 A4** 2 55 S 67 58W
Icabarú, *Venezuela* **169 C5** 4 20N 61 45W
Icabarú →, *Venezuela* **169 C5** 4 45N 62 15W
Icacos Pt., *Trin. & Tob.* **169 F9** 10 3N 61 57W
Içana, *Brazil* **168 C4** 0 21N 67 19W
Içana →, *Brazil* **168 C4** 0 26N 67 19W
Icatu, *Brazil* **170 B3** 2 46 S 44 4W
İçel = Mersin, *Turkey* **100 D6** 36 51N 34 36 E
Iceland ■, *Europe* **11 C8** 64 45N 19 0W
Ichalkaranji, *India* **94 F2** 16 40N 74 33 E
Ich'ang = Yichang, *China* **77 B8** 30 40N 111 20 E
Ichchapuram, *India* **94 E7** 19 10N 84 40 E
Ichhawar, *India* **92 H7** 23 1N 77 1 E
Ichihara, *Japan* **73 B12** 35 28N 140 5 E
Ichikawa, *Japan* **73 B11** 35 44N 139 55 E
Ichilo →, *Bolivia* **173 D5** 15 57 S 64 50W
Ichinohe, *Japan* **70 D10** 40 13N 141 17 E
Ichinomiya, *Gifu, Japan* **73 B8** 35 18N 136 48 E
Ichinomiya, *Kumamoto, Japan* **72 E3** 32 58N 131 5 E
Ichinoseki, *Japan* **70 E10** 38 55N 141 8 E
Ichkeul Nat. Park, *Tunisia* **108 A1** 37 5N 9 37 E
Ichnya, *Ukraine* **59 G7** 50 52N 32 24 E
Icht, *Morocco* **110 C3** 29 6N 8 54W
Icó, *Brazil* **170 C4** 6 24 S 38 51W
Icoca, *Angola* **115 D3** 6 12 S 16 20 E
Icod, *Canary Is.* **9 e1** 28 22N 16 43W
Icoraci, *Brazil* **170 B2** 1 18 S 48 28W
Icy C., *U.S.A.* **144 A7** 70 20N 161 52W
Ida Grove, *U.S.A.* **154 D7** 42 21N 95 28W
Idabel, *U.S.A.* **155 J7** 33 54N 94 50W
Idaga Hamus, *Ethiopia* **107 E4** 14 13N 39 48 E
Idah, *Nigeria* **113 D6** 7 5N 6 40 E
Idaho □, *U.S.A.* **158 D7** 45 0N 115 0W
Idaho City, *U.S.A.* **158 E6** 43 50N 115 50W
Idaho Falls, *U.S.A.* **158 E7** 43 30N 112 2W
Idalia Nat. Park, *Australia* **126 C3** 24 49 S 144 36 E
Idanha-a-Nova, *Portugal* **42 F3** 39 50N 7 15W
Idar-Oberstein, *Germany* **31 F3** 49 43N 7 16 E
Iday, *Niger* **109 F2** 14 54N 11 33 E
'Idd el Ghanam, *Sudan* **109 F4** 11 30N 24 19 E
Iddan, *Somali Rep.* **120 C3** 6 10N 48 55 E
Idelès, *Algeria* **111 D6** 23 50N 5 53 E
Idfû, *Egypt* **106 C3** 24 55N 32 49 E
Ídhi Óros, *Greece* **39 E5** 35 15N 24 45 E
Ídhra, *Greece* **48 D5** 37 20N 23 28 E
Idi, *Indonesia* **84 A1** 5 2N 97 37 E
Idiofa, *Dem. Rep. of the Congo* **115 C3** 4 55 S 19 42 E
Idkerberget, *Sweden* **16 D9** 60 22N 15 15 E
Idku, Bahra el, *Egypt* **106 H7** 31 18N 30 18 E
Idlib, *Syria* **100 E7** 35 55N 36 36 E
Idre, *Sweden* **16 C6** 61 52N 12 42 E
Idria, *U.S.A.* **160 J6** 36 25N 120 41W
Idrija, *Slovenia* **45 C11** 46 0N 14 5 E
Idritsa, *Russia* **58 D5** 56 17N 28 53 E
Idro, *Italy* **33 E10** 45 44N 10 29 E
Idutywa, *S. Africa* **117 E4** 32 8 S 28 18 E
Ieper, *Belgium* **24 D2** 50 51N 2 53 E
Ierápetra, *Greece* **39 F6** 35 1N 25 44 E
Ierissós, *Greece* **50 F7** 40 22N 23 52 E
Ierissóu Kólpos, *Greece* **50 F7** 40 27N 23 57 E
Iernut, *Romania* **53 D9** 46 27N 24 15 E
Ieshima-Shotō, *Japan* **72 C6** 34 40N 134 32 E
Iesi, *Italy* **45 E10** 43 31N 13 14 E
Iésolo, *Italy* **45 C9** 45 32N 12 38 E
Ifach, Peñón de, *Spain* **41 G5** 38 38N 0 5 E
'Ifâl, W. al →, *Si. Arabia* **96 D2** 28 7N 35 3 E
Ifanadiana, *Madag.* **117 C8** 21 19 S 47 39 E
Ife, *Nigeria* **113 D5** 7 30N 4 31 E
Iférouâne, *Niger* **113 B6** 19 5N 8 24 E
Ifetesene, *Algeria* **111 C5** 25 30N 4 33 E
Iffley, *Australia* **126 B3** 18 53 S 141 12 E
Ifon, *Nigeria* **113 D6** 6 58N 5 40 E
Iforas, Adrar des, *Africa* **111 D5** 19 40N 1 40 E
Ifould, L., *Australia* **125 F5** 30 52 S 132 6 E
Ifrane, *Morocco* **110 B3** 33 33N 5 7W
Ifugao □, *Phil.* **80 C3** 16 40N 121 10 E
Iga, *Japan* **73 C8** 34 45N 136 10 E
Iganga, *Uganda* **118 B3** 0 37N 33 28 E
Igara Paraná →, *Colombia* **168 D3** 2 9 S 71 47W
Igarapava, *Brazil* **171 F2** 20 3 S 47 47W
Igarapé Açu, *Brazil* **170 B2** 1 4 S 47 33W
Igarapé-Mirim, *Brazil* **170 B2** 1 59 S 48 58W
Igarka, *Russia* **66 C9** 67 30N 86 33 E
Igatimi, *Paraguay* **175 A4** 24 5 S 55 40W
Igatpuri, *India* **94 E1** 19 40N 73 35 E
Igbetti, *Nigeria* **113 D5** 8 44N 4 8 E
Igbo-Ora, *Nigeria* **113 D5** 7 29N 3 15 E
Igboho, *Nigeria* **113 D5** 8 53N 3 50 E
Igbor, *Nigeria* **113 D6** 7 27N 8 34 E
Iğdır, *Turkey* **101 C11** 39 55N 44 2 E
Igelfors, *Sweden* **17 F9** 58 52N 15 41 E
Iggesund, *Sweden* **16 C11** 61 39N 17 10 E
Ighil Izane = Relizane, *Algeria* **111 A5** 35 44N 0 31 E
Igiugig, *U.S.A.* **144 G9** 59 20N 155 55W
Iglésias, *Italy* **46 C1** 39 19N 8 32 E
Igli, *Algeria* **111 B4** 30 25N 2 19W
Iglino, *Russia* **64 D6** 54 50N 56 26 E
Igloolik, *Canada* **139 B11** 69 20N 81 49W
Igluligaarjuk, *Canada* **139 B10** 63 21N 90 42W
Iglulik = Igloolik, *Canada* **139 B11** 69 20N 81 49W
'Igma, Gebel el, *Egypt* **106 B3** 28 55N 34 0 E
Ignace, *Canada* **140 C1** 49 30N 91 40W
İğneada, *Turkey* **51 E11** 41 52N 27 59 E
İğneada Burnu, *Turkey* **51 E12** 41 53N 28 2 E
Igoumenítsa, *Greece* **38 B10** 39 32N 20 18 E
Igra, *Russia* **60 B11** 57 33N 53 7 E
Iguaçu →, *Brazil* **175 B5** 25 36 S 54 36W
Iguaçu, Cat. del, *Brazil* **175 B5** 25 41 S 54 26W
Iguaçu Falls = Iguaçu, Cat. del, *Brazil* **175 B5** 25 41 S 54 26W
Iguala, *Mexico* **163 D5** 18 20N 99 40W
Igualada, *Spain* **40 D6** 41 37N 1 37 E
Iguape, *Brazil* **171 F2** 24 43 S 47 33W
Iguassu = Iguaçu →, *Brazil* **175 B5** 25 36 S 54 36W
Iguatu, *Brazil* **170 C4** 6 20 S 39 18W
Iguéla, *Gabon* **114 C1** 2 0 S 9 16 E
Iguéla, Lagune, *Gabon* **114 C2** 1 45 S 9 16 E
Iguetti, Sebkhet, *Mauritania* **110 C3** 25 5N 9 50W
Iguig, *Phil.* **80 C3** 17 45N 121 44 E
Iharana, *Madag.* **117 A9** 13 25 S 50 0 E
Ihbulag, *Mongolia* **74 C4** 43 11N 107 10 E
Iheya-Shima, *Japan* **71 L3** 27 4N 127 58 E
Ihiala, *Nigeria* **113 D6** 5 51N 6 55 E
Ihirene →, *Algeria* **111 D5** 20 28N 4 37 E
Ihosy, *Madag.* **117 C8** 22 24 S 46 8 E
Ihotry, Farihy, *Madag.* **117 C7** 21 56 S 43 41 E
Ihu, *Papua N. G.* **132 D3** 7 55 S 145 24 E
Ihugh, *Nigeria* **113 D6** 7 2N 9 0 E
Ii, *Finland* **14 D21** 65 19N 25 22 E
Ii-Shima, *Japan* **71 L3** 26 43N 127 47 E
Iida, *Japan* **73 B9** 35 35N 137 50 E
Iijoki →, *Finland* **14 D21** 65 20N 25 20 E
Iisalmi, *Finland* **14 E22** 63 32N 27 10 E
Iiyama, *Japan* **71 F9** 36 51N 138 22 E
Iizuka, *Japan* **72 D2** 33 38N 130 42 E
Ijâfene, *Mauritania* **110 D3** 20 40N 8 0W
Ijebu-Igbo, *Nigeria* **113 D5** 6 56N 4 1 E
Ijebu-Ode, *Nigeria* **113 D5** 6 47N 3 58 E

226 Ijill, Sebkhet

Ijill, Sebkhet, *Mauritania* **110 D2** 22 47N 12 53W
IJmuiden, *Neths.* **24 B4** 52 28N 4 35 E
IJssel →, *Neths.* **24 B5** 52 35N 5 50 E
IJsselmeer, *Neths.* **24 B5** 52 45N 5 20 E
Ijuí, *Brazil* **175 B5** 28 23 S 53 55W
Ijuí →, *Brazil* **175 B4** 27 58 S 55 20W
Ijūin, *Japan* **72 F2** 31 37N 130 24 E
Ik →, *Russia* **64 D4** 55 41N 53 29 E
Ikalamavony, *Madag.* **117 C8** 21 9 S 46 35 E
Ikale, *Nigeria* **113 D6** 7 40N 5 37 E
Ikali, *Dem. Rep. of the Congo* **114 C4** 2 2 S 21 4 E
Ikaluktutiak, *Canada* **138 B9** 69 10N 105 0W
Ikamatua, *N.Z.* **131 C6** 42 16 S 171 41 E
Ikang, *Nigeria* **113 E6** 4 49N 8 30 E
Ikara, *Nigeria* **113 C6** 11 12N 8 15 E
Ikare, *Nigeria* **113 D6** 7 32N 5 40 E
Ikaría, *Greece* **49 D8** 37 35N 26 10 E
Ikast, *Denmark* **17 H3** 56 8N 9 10 E
Ikeda, *Japan* **72 C5** 34 1N 133 48 E
Ikeja, *Nigeria* **113 D5** 6 36N 3 23 E
Ikela, *Dem. Rep. of the Congo* **114 C4** 1 6 S 23 6 E
Ikélemba, *Congo* **114 B3** 1 12N 16 38 E
Ikélemba →, *Dem. Rep. of the Congo* **114 B3** 0 7N 18 17 E
Ikengo, *Dem. Rep. of the Congo* **114 C3** 0 8 S 18 8 E
Ikerre-Ekiti, *Nigeria* **113 D6** 7 25N 5 19 E
Ikhtiman, *Bulgaria* **50 D7** 42 27N 23 48 E
Iki, *Japan* **72 D1** 33 45N 129 42 E
Iki-Kaikyō, *Japan* **72 D1** 33 40N 129 45 E
Ikimba L., *Tanzania* **118 C3** 1 30 S 31 20 E
Ikire, *Nigeria* **113 D5** 7 23N 4 15 E
Ikitsuki-Shima, *Japan* **72 D1** 33 23N 129 26 E
Ikizdere, *Turkey* **101 B9** 40 46N 40 32 E
Iko, *Congo* **114 C3** 0 35 S 16 0 E
Ikom, *Nigeria* **113 D6** 6 0N 8 42 E
Ikomu, *Dem. Rep. of the Congo* **114 C3** 1 53 S 19 40 E
Ikongo, *Madag.* **117 C8** 21 52 S 47 27 E
Ikopa →, *Madag.* **117 B8** 16 45 S 46 40 E
Ikorongo Game Reserve, *Tanzania* **118 C3** 1 50 S 34 53 E
Ikot Ekpene, *Nigeria* **113 D6** 5 12N 7 40 E
Ikungu, *Tanzania* **118 C3** 1 33 S 33 42 E
Ikuno, *Japan* **72 B6** 35 10N 134 48 E
Ikurun, *Nigeria* **113 D5** 7 54N 4 40 E
Il-Kullana, *Malta* **38 F7** 35 50N 14 24 E
Il-Munxar, *Malta* **38 F8** 35 51N 14 34 E
Ila, *Dem. Rep. of the Congo* **114 C4** 2 53 S 21 7 E
Ila, *Nigeria* **113 D5** 8 0N 4 39 E
Ilafer, *Algeria* **111 D5** 21 40N 1 58 E
Ilagan, *Phil.* **80 C3** 17 7N 121 53 E
Ilaka, *Madag.* **117 B8** 19 33 S 48 52 E
Īlām, *Iran* **101 F12** 33 36N 46 36 E
Ilam, *Nepal* **93 F12** 26 58N 87 58 E
Īlām □, *Iran* **96 C5** 33 0N 47 0 E
Ilan, *Taiwan* **77 E13** 24 45N 121 44 E
Ilanskiy, *Russia* **67 D10** 56 14N 96 3 E
Ilanz, *Switz.* **33 C8** 46 46N 9 12 E
Ilaro, *Nigeria* **113 D5** 6 53N 3 3 E
Ilatane, *Niger* **113 B5** 16 30N 4 45 E
Ilave, *Peru* **172 D4** 16 5 S 69 40W
Iława, *Poland* **54 E6** 53 36N 19 34 E
Ilayangudi, *India* **95 K4** 9 34N 78 37 E
Ile →, *Kazakstan* **66 E8** 45 53N 77 10 E
Ile-à-la-Crosse, *Canada* **143 B7** 55 27N 107 53W
Ile-à-la-Crosse, Lac, *Canada* **143 B7** 55 40N 107 45W
Île-de-France □, *France* **27 D9** 49 0N 2 20 E
Ileanda, *Romania* **53 C8** 47 20N 23 38 E
Ilebo, *Dem. Rep. of the Congo* **115 C4** 4 17 S 20 55 E
Ilek, *Russia* **64 F4** 51 32N 53 21 E
Ilek →, *Russia* **64 F4** 51 30N 53 22 E
Iler, *Algeria* **111 D5** 20 57N 3 21 E
Iler, O. →, *Algeria* **111 D5** 20 59N 3 14 E
Ilero, *Nigeria* **113 D5** 8 0N 3 20 E
Ilesha, *Kwara, Nigeria* **113 D5** 8 57N 3 28 E
Ilesha, *Oyo, Nigeria* **113 D5** 7 37N 4 40 E
Ilford, *Canada* **143 B9** 56 4N 95 35W
Ilfracombe, *Australia* **126 C3** 23 30 S 144 30 E
Ilfracombe, *U.K.* **21 F3** 51 12N 4 8W
Ilgaz, *Turkey* **100 B5** 40 55N 33 37 E
Ilgaz Dağları, *Turkey* **100 B5** 41 10N 33 50 E
Ilgın, *Turkey* **100 C4** 38 16N 31 55 E
Ilha, Pta. da, *Azores* **9 d1** 38 25N 28 3W
Ilha de Moçambique, *Mozam.* **119 F5** 15 4 S 40 52 E
Ilha Grande, *Brazil* **169 D4** 0 27 S 65 2W
Ilha Grande, B. da, *Brazil* **171 F3** 23 9 S 44 30W
Ílhavo, *Portugal* **42 E2** 40 33N 8 43W
Ilhéus, *Brazil* **171 D4** 14 49 S 39 2W
Ili = Ile →, *Kazakstan* **66 E8** 45 53N 77 10 E
Ilia, *Romania* **52 E7** 45 57N 22 40 E
Ilia □, *Greece* **48 D3** 37 45N 21 35 E
Iliamna, *U.S.A.* **144 G9** 59 45N 154 55W
Iliamna L., *U.S.A.* **144 G9** 59 30N 155 0W
Ilian, Mt., *Phil.* **81 F2** 10 26N 119 33 E
Iliç, *Turkey* **101 C8** 39 27N 38 33 E
Ilıca, *Turkey* **49 B9** 39 52N 27 46 E
Ilich, *Kazakstan* **65 C4** 40 50N 68 27 E
Ilichevsk, *Azerbaijan* **101 C11** 39 22N 45 5 E
Iligan, *Phil.* **81 G5** 8 12N 124 13 E
Iligan Bay, *Phil.* **81 G5** 8 25N 124 5 E
Iligan Pt., *Phil.* **80 B4** 18 25N 122 25 E
Ilíki, L., *Greece* **48 C5** 38 24N 23 15 E
Ilin I., *Phil.* **80 E3** 12 14N 121 5 E
Ilio Pt., *U.S.A.* **145 B4** 21 13N 157 16W
Iliodhrómia, *Greece* **48 B5** 39 12N 23 50 E
Ilion, *U.S.A.* **151 D9** 43 1N 75 2W
Ilirska-Bistrica, *Slovenia* **45 C11** 45 34N 14 14 E
Ilkal, *India* **95 G3** 15 57N 76 8 E
Ilkeston, *U.K.* **20 E6** 52 58N 1 19W
Ilkley, *U.K.* **20 D6** 53 56N 1 48W
Illampu = Ancohuma, Nevada, *Bolivia* **172 D4** 16 0 S 68 50W
Illana B., *Phil.* **81 H4** 7 35N 123 45 E
Illapel, *Chile* **174 C1** 32 0 S 71 10W
Ille-et-Vilaine □, *France* **26 D5** 48 10N 1 30W
Ille-sur-Têt, *France* **28 F6** 42 40N 2 38 E
Illéla, *Niger* **113 C6** 14 32N 5 20 E
Iller →, *Germany* **31 G5** 48 23N 9 58 E
Illertissen, *Germany* **31 G6** 48 12N 10 7 E
Illescas, *Spain* **42 E7** 40 8N 3 51W
Illetas, *Spain* **38 B3** 39 32N 2 35 E
Illichivsk, *Ukraine* **59 J6** 46 20N 30 35 E
Illiers-Combray, *France* **26 D8** 48 18N 1 15 E
Illimani, Nevado, *Bolivia* **172 D4** 16 30 S 67 50W
Illinois □, *U.S.A.* **156 D7** 40 15N 89 30W
Illinois →, *U.S.A.* **156 F6** 38 58N 90 28W
Illiopolis, *U.S.A.* **156 E7** 39 51N 89 15W
Illium = Troy, *Turkey* **49 B8** 39 57N 26 12 E
Illizi, *Algeria* **111 C6** 26 31N 8 32 E
Illkirch-Graffenstaden, *France* **27 D14** 48 34N 7 42 E
Íllora, *Spain* **43 H7** 37 17N 3 53W
Ilulissat, *Greenland* **10 D5** 69 12N 51 10W
Ilm →, *Germany* **30 D7** 51 6N 11 40 E
Ilmajoki, *Finland* **15 E20** 62 44N 22 34 E
Ilmen, Ozero, *Russia* **58 C6** 58 15N 31 10 E
Ilmenau, *Germany* **30 E6** 50 41N 10 54 E
Ilo, *Peru* **172 D3** 17 40 S 71 20W
Ilobu, *Nigeria* **113 D5** 7 45N 4 25 E
Ilocos Norte □, *Phil.* **80 B3** 18 10N 120 45 E
Ilocos Sur □, *Phil.* **80 C3** 17 20N 120 35 E
Iloilo, *Phil.* **81 F4** 10 45N 122 33 E
Iloilo □, *Phil.* **81 F4** 11 0N 122 40 E
Ilora, *Nigeria* **113 D5** 7 45N 3 50 E
Ilorin, *Nigeria* **113 D5** 8 30N 4 35 E
Ilovatka, *Russia* **60 E7** 50 30N 45 50 E
Ilovlya, *Russia* **61 F7** 49 15N 44 2 E
Ilovlya →, *Russia* **61 F7** 49 14N 44 0 E
Iłowa, *Poland* **55 G2** 51 30N 15 10 E
Ilubabor □, *Ethiopia* **107 F4** 7 25N 35 0 E
Ilva Mică, *Romania* **53 C9** 47 17N 24 40 E
Ilwaco, *U.S.A.* **160 D2** 46 19N 124 3W
Ilwaki, *Indonesia* **82 C3** 7 55 S 126 30 E
Ilyichevsk = Illichivsk, *Ukraine* **59 J6** 46 20N 30 35 E
Iłża, *Poland* **55 G8** 51 10N 21 15 E
Iłzanka →, *Poland* **55 G8** 51 14N 21 48 E
Imabari, *Japan* **72 C5** 34 4N 133 0 E
Imaichi, *Japan* **73 A11** 36 43N 139 46 E
Imaloto →, *Madag.* **117 C8** 23 27 S 45 13 E
İmamoğlu, *Turkey* **100 D6** 37 15N 35 38 E
Imandra, Ozero, *Russia* **56 A5** 67 30N 33 0 E
Imanombo, *Madag.* **117 C8** 24 26 S 45 49 E
Imari, *Japan* **72 D1** 33 15N 129 52 E
Imasa, *Sudan* **106 D4** 18 0N 36 12 E
Imathía □, *Greece* **50 F6** 40 30N 22 15 E
Imatra, *Finland* **58 B5** 61 12N 28 48 E
Imazu, *Japan* **73 B8** 35 24N 136 2 E
Imbabura □, *Ecuador* **168 C2** 0 30N 78 45W
Imbaimadai, *Guyana* **169 B5** 5 44N 60 17W
Imbil, *Australia* **127 D5** 26 22 S 152 32 E
Imbonga, *Dem. Rep. of the Congo* **114 C3** 0 43 S 19 44 E
Imdahane, *Morocco* **110 B3** 32 8N 7 0W
Iménas, *Mali* **113 B5** 16 20N 0 40 E
imeni 26 Bakinskikh Komissarov = Neftçala, *Azerbaijan* **97 B6** 39 19N 49 12 E
imeni 26 Bakinskikh Komissarov, *Turkmenistan* **97 B7** 39 22N 54 10 E
Imeri, Serra, *Brazil* **168 C4** 0 50N 65 25W
Imerimandroso, *Madag.* **117 B8** 17 26 S 48 35 E
Imesan, *Mauritania* **110 D1** 22 54N 15 30W
Imese, *Dem. Rep. of the Congo* **114 B3** 2 6N 18 9 E
Imi, *Ethiopia* **107 F5** 6 28N 42 10 E
Imishly = Imişli, *Azerbaijan* **61 L9** 39 55N 48 4 E
Imişli, *Azerbaijan* **61 L9** 39 55N 48 4 E
Imitek, *Morocco* **110 C3** 29 43N 8 10W
Imlay, *U.S.A.* **158 F4** 40 40N 118 9W
Imlay City, *U.S.A.* **150 D1** 43 2N 83 5W
Immaseri, *Sudan* **107 D2** 15 40N 25 31 E
Immenstadt, *Germany* **31 H6** 47 33N 10 13 E
Immingham, *U.K.* **20 D7** 53 37N 0 13W
Immokalee, *U.S.A.* **149 M5** 26 25N 81 25W
Imo □, *Nigeria* **113 D6** 5 30N 7 10 E
Imo →, *Nigeria* **113 E6** 4 36N 7 35 E
Ímola, *Italy* **45 D8** 44 20N 11 42 E
Imotski, *Croatia* **45 E14** 43 27N 17 12 E
Impé, *Congo* **114 C3** 2 45 S 15 16 E
Imperatriz, *Amazonas, Brazil* **172 B4** 5 18 S 67 11W
Imperatriz, *Maranhão, Brazil* **170 C2** 5 30 S 47 29W
Impéria, *Italy* **44 E5** 43 53N 8 3 E
Imperial, *Canada* **143 C7** 51 21N 105 28W
Imperial, *Peru* **172 C2** 13 4 S 76 21W
Imperial, *Calif., U.S.A.* **161 N11** 32 51N 115 34W
Imperial, *Nebr., U.S.A.* **154 E4** 40 31N 101 39W
Imperial Beach, *U.S.A.* **161 N9** 32 35N 117 8W
Imperial Dam, *U.S.A.* **161 N12** 32 55N 114 25W
Imperial Reservoir, *U.S.A.* **161 N12** 32 53N 114 28W
Imperial Valley, *U.S.A.* **161 N11** 33 0N 115 30W
Imperieuse Reef, *Australia* **124 C2** 17 36 S 118 50 E
Impfondo, *Congo* **114 B3** 1 40N 18 0 E
Imphal, *India* **90 C4** 24 48N 93 56 E
Imphy, *France* **27 F10** 46 55N 3 16 E
Impulo, *Angola* **115 E2** 13 51 S 13 39 E
İmranlı, *Turkey* **101 C8** 39 54N 38 7 E
İmroz = Gökçeada, *Turkey* **51 F9** 40 10N 25 50 E
İmroz, *Turkey* **51 F9** 40 10N 25 55 E
Imst, *Austria* **34 D3** 47 15N 10 44 E
Imuris, *Mexico* **162 A2** 30 47N 110 52W
Imuruan B., *Phil.* **81 F2** 10 40N 119 10 E
Imus, *Phil.* **80 D3** 14 26N 120 56 E
In Akhmed, *Mali* **113 B4** 19 49N 0 56W
In Aleï, *Mali* **112 B4** 17 42N 2 30W
In Amenas, *Algeria* **111 C6** 28 5N 9 33 E
In Atei, *Algeria* **111 D6** 20 33N 6 4 E
In Belbel, *Algeria* **111 C5** 27 55N 1 12 E
In Dekkar, O. →, *Algeria* **111 C6** 27 12N 6 16 E
In Delimane, *Mali* **113 B5** 15 52N 1 31 E
In Guezzam, *Algeria* **111 E6** 19 37N 5 52 E
In Koufi, *Mali* **113 B5** 19 11N 1 25 E
In Rhar, *Algeria* **111 C5** 27 10N 1 59 E
In Salah, *Algeria* **111 C5** 27 10N 2 32 E
In Tallak, *Mali* **113 B5** 16 19N 3 15 E
In Tebezas, *Mali* **113 B5** 17 49N 1 53 E
Ina, *Japan* **73 B9** 35 50N 137 55 E
Ina, *U.S.A.* **157 F8** 38 9N 88 54W
Ina-Bonchi, *Japan* **73 B9** 35 45N 137 58 E
Inabanga, *Phil.* **81 F5** 10 2N 124 4 E
Inagauan, *Phil.* **81 G2** 9 33N 118 39 E
Inajá, *Brazil* **170 C4** 8 54 S 37 49W
Inambari →, *Peru* **172 C4** 12 41 S 69 44W
Inangahua, *N.Z.* **131 B6** 41 52 S 171 59 E
Inanwatan, *Indonesia* **83 B4** 2 8 S 132 10 E
Iñapari, *Peru* **172 C4** 11 0 S 69 40W
Inarajan, *Guam* **133 R15** 13 16N 144 45 E
Inari, *Finland* **14 B22** 68 54N 27 5 E
Inarijärvi, *Finland* **14 B22** 69 0N 28 0 E
Inawashiro-Ko, *Japan* **70 F10** 37 29N 140 6 E
Inazawa, *Japan* **73 B8** 35 15N 136 47 E
Inbin, *Burma* **90 F5** 18 6N 95 16 E
Inca, *Spain* **38 B3** 39 43N 2 54 E
Inca de Oro, *Chile* **174 B2** 26 45 S 69 54W
Incaguasi, *Chile* **174 B1** 29 12 S 71 5W
Ince Burun, *Turkey* **100 A6** 42 7N 34 56 E
Incekum Burnu, *Turkey* **100 D5** 36 13N 33 57 E
Incesu, *Turkey* **96 B2** 38 38N 35 11 E
Inch'ŏn, *S. Korea* **75 F14** 37 27N 126 40 E
Incio = Cruz de Incio, *Spain* **42 C3** 42 39N 7 21W
Incirliova, *Turkey* **49 D9** 37 50N 27 41 E
Incline Village, *U.S.A.* **158 G4** 39 10N 119 58W
Incomáti →, *Mozam.* **117 D5** 25 46 S 32 43 E
Inda Silase, *Ethiopia* **107 E4** 14 10N 38 15 E
Indal, *Sweden* **16 B11** 62 35N 17 5 E
Indalsälven →, *Sweden* **16 B11** 62 36N 17 30 E
Indaw, *Burma* **90 C6** 24 15N 96 5 E
Indawgyi, L., *Burma* **90 C6** 25 8N 96 20 E
Indbir, *Ethiopia* **107 F4** 8 7N 37 52 E
Independence, *Calif., U.S.A.* **160 J8** 36 48N 118 12W
Independence, *Iowa, U.S.A.* **156 B5** 42 28N 91 54W
Independence, *Kans., U.S.A.* **155 G7** 37 14N 95 42W
Independence, *Ky., U.S.A.* **157 F12** 38 57N 84 33W
Independence, *Mo., U.S.A.* **156 E2** 39 6N 94 25W
Independence Fjord, *Greenland* **10 A8** 82 10N 29 0W
Independence Mts., *U.S.A.* **158 F5** 41 20N 116 0W
Independência, *Brazil* **170 C3** 5 23 S 40 19W
Independenţa, *Romania* **53 E12** 45 25N 27 42 E
Index, *U.S.A.* **160 C5** 47 50N 121 33W
Indi, *India* **94 F2** 17 10N 75 58 E
India ■, *Asia* **89 C6** 20 0N 78 0 E
Indialantic, *U.S.A.* **153 G9** 28 6N 80 34W
Indian →, *Fla., U.S.A.* **149 M5** 27 59N 80 34W
Indian →, *Fla., U.S.A.* **153 H9** 27 10N 80 10W
Indian Cabins, *Canada* **142 B5** 59 52N 117 40W
Indian Harbour, *Canada* **141 B8** 54 27N 57 13W
Indian Harbour Beach, *U.S.A.* **153 G9** 28 10N 80 35W
Indian Head, *Canada* **143 C8** 50 30N 103 41W
Indian Lake, *U.S.A.* **151 C10** 43 47N 74 16W
Indian Ocean **62 K11** 5 0 S 75 0 E
Indian Rocks Beach, *U.S.A.* **153 H7** 27 53N 82 51W
Indian Springs, *U.S.A.* **161 J11** 36 35N 115 40W
Indiana, *U.S.A.* **150 F5** 40 37N 79 9W
Indiana □, *U.S.A.* **157 E11** 40 0N 86 0W
Indianapolis, *U.S.A.* **157 E10** 39 46N 86 9W
Indianola, *Iowa, U.S.A.* **156 C3** 41 22N 93 34W
Indianola, *Miss., U.S.A.* **155 J9** 33 27N 90 39W
Indiantown, *U.S.A.* **153 H9** 27 1N 80 28W
Indiapora, *Brazil* **171 E1** 19 57 S 50 17W
Indiga, *Russia* **56 A8** 67 38N 49 9 E
Indigirka →, *Russia* **67 B15** 70 48N 148 54 E
Indija, *Serbia, Yug.* **52 E5** 45 6N 20 7 E
Indio, *U.S.A.* **161 M10** 33 43N 116 13W
Indira Pt., *India* **95 L11** 6 44N 93 49 E
Indispensable Strait, *Solomon Is.* **133 M11** 9 0 S 160 30 E
Indo-China, *Asia* **62 H14** 15 0N 102 0 E
Indonesia ■, *Asia* **85 C4** 5 0 S 115 0 E
Indore, *India* **92 H6** 22 42N 75 53 E
Indramayu, *Indonesia* **85 D3** 6 20 S 108 19 E
Indravati →, *India* **94 E5** 19 20N 80 20 E
Indre □, *France* **27 F8** 46 50N 1 39 E
Indre →, *France* **26 E7** 47 16N 0 11 E
Indre Arna, *Norway* **18 D2** 60 26N 5 30 E
Indre-et-Loire □, *France* **26 E7** 47 20N 0 40 E
Indrio, *U.S.A.* **153 H9** 27 31N 80 21W
Indulkana, *Australia* **127 D1** 26 58 S 133 5 E
Indungo, *Angola* **115 E3** 14 48 S 16 17 E
Indus →, *Pakistan* **91 D2** 24 20N 67 47 E
Indus, Mouths of the, *Pakistan* **91 E3** 24 0N 68 0 E
Industry, *U.S.A.* **156 D6** 40 20N 90 36W
İnebolu, *Turkey* **100 B5** 41 55N 33 40 E
İnecik, *Turkey* **51 F11** 40 56N 27 16 E
İnegöl, *Turkey* **51 F13** 40 5N 29 31 E
Inés, Mt., *Argentina* **176 C3** 48 30 S 69 40W
Ineu, *Romania* **52 D6** 46 26N 21 51 E
Inezgane, *Morocco* **110 B3** 30 25N 9 29W
Infanta, *Phil.* **80 D3** 14 45N 121 39 E
Infantes = Villanueva de los Infantes, *Spain* **43 G7** 38 43N 3 1W
Infiernillo, Presa del, *Mexico* **162 D4** 18 9N 102 0W
Infiesto, *Spain* **42 B5** 43 21N 5 21W
Inga, Barrage d', *Dem. Rep. of the Congo* **115 D2** 5 39 S 13 39 E
Ingabu, *Burma* **90 G5** 17 37N 95 20 E
Inganda, *Dem. Rep. of the Congo* **114 C4** 0 5 S 20 57 E
Ingapirca, *Ecuador* **168 D2** 2 38 S 78 56W
Ingelstad, *Sweden* **17 H8** 56 45N 14 56 E
Ingende, *Dem. Rep. of the Congo* **114 C3** 0 12 S 18 57 E
Ingeniero Jacobacci, *Argentina* **176 B3** 41 20 S 69 36W
Ingenio, *Canary Is.* **9 e1** 27 55N 15 26W
Ingenio Santa Ana, *Argentina* **174 B2** 27 25 S 65 40W
Ingersoll, *Canada* **140 D3** 43 4N 80 55W
Ingham, *Australia* **126 B4** 18 43 S 146 10 E
Ingichka, *Uzbekistan* **65 D2** 39 47N 65 58 E
Ingleborough, *U.K.* **20 C5** 54 10N 2 22W
Inglefield Land, *Greenland* **10 B4** 78 30N 70 0W
Inglewood, *Queens., Australia* **127 D5** 28 25 S 151 2 E
Inglewood, *Vic., Australia* **128 D5** 36 29 S 143 53 E
Inglewood, *N.Z.* **130 F3** 39 9 S 174 14 E
Inglewood, *U.S.A.* **161 M8** 33 58N 118 21W
Inglis, *U.S.A.* **153 F7** 29 2N 82 40W
Ingolf Fjord, *Greenland* **10 A9** 80 35N 17 30W
Ingólfshöfði, *Iceland* **14 E5** 63 48N 16 39W
Ingolstadt, *Germany* **31 G7** 48 46N 11 26 E
Ingomar, *U.S.A.* **158 C10** 46 35N 107 23W
Ingonish, *Canada* **141 C7** 46 42N 60 18W
Ingore, *Guinea-Biss.* **112 C1** 12 24N 15 48W
Ingraj Bazar, *India* **93 G13** 24 58N 88 10 E
Ingrid Christensen Coast, *Antarctica* **7 C6** 69 30 S 76 0 E
Ingul → = Inhul →, *Ukraine* **59 J7** 46 50N 32 0 E
Ingulec = Inhulec, *Ukraine* **59 J7** 47 42N 33 14 E
Ingulets → = Inhulets →, *Ukraine* **59 J7** 46 46N 32 47 E
Inguri → = Enguri →, *Georgia* **61 J5** 42 27N 41 38 E
Ingushetia □, *Russia* **61 J7** 43 20N 44 50 E
Ingwavuma, *S. Africa* **117 D5** 27 9 S 31 59 E
Inhaca, *Mozam.* **117 D5** 26 1 S 32 57 E
Inhafenga, *Mozam.* **117 C5** 20 36 S 33 53 E
Inhambane, *Mozam.* **117 C6** 23 54 S 35 30 E
Inhambane □, *Mozam.* **117 C5** 22 30 S 34 20 E
Inhambupe, *Brazil* **171 D4** 11 47 S 38 21W
Inhaminga, *Mozam.* **119 F4** 18 26 S 35 0 E
Inharrime, *Mozam.* **117 C6** 24 30 S 35 0 E
Inharrime →, *Mozam.* **117 C6** 24 30 S 35 0 E
Inhisar, *Turkey* **49 A12** 40 3N 30 23 E
Inhul →, *Ukraine* **59 J7** 46 50N 32 0 E
Inhulec, *Ukraine* **59 J7** 47 42N 33 14 E
Inhulets →, *Ukraine* **59 J7** 46 46N 32 47 E
Inhuma, *Brazil* **170 C3** 6 40 S 41 42W
Inhumas, *Brazil* **171 E2** 16 22 S 49 30W
Iniesta, *Spain* **41 F3** 39 27N 1 45W
Ining = Yining, *China* **66 E9** 43 58N 81 10 E
Inini □, *Fr. Guiana* **169 C7** 4 0N 53 0W
Inírida →, *Colombia* **168 C4** 3 55N 67 52W
Inishbofin, *Ireland* **23 C1** 53 37N 10 13W
Inisheer, *Ireland* **23 C2** 53 3N 9 32W
Inishfree B., *Ireland* **23 A3** 55 4N 8 23W
Inishkea North, *Ireland* **23 B1** 54 9N 10 11W
Inishkea South, *Ireland* **23 B1** 54 7N 10 12W
Inishmaan, *Ireland* **23 C2** 53 5N 9 35W
Inishmore, *Ireland* **23 C2** 53 8N 9 45W
Inishowen Pen., *Ireland* **23 A4** 55 14N 7 15W
Inishshark, *Ireland* **23 C1** 53 37N 10 16W
Inishturk, *Ireland* **23 C1** 53 42N 10 7W
Inishvickillane, *Ireland* **23 D1** 52 3N 10 37W
Injibara, *Ethiopia* **107 E4** 10 59N 37 0 E
Injune, *Australia* **127 D4** 25 53 S 148 32 E
Inkisi →, *Dem. Rep. of the Congo* **115 D3** 4 46 S 14 52 E
Inklin →, *Canada* **142 B2** 58 50N 133 10W
Inland Kaikoura Ra., *N.Z.* **131 B8** 41 59 S 173 41 E
Inland Sea = Setonaikai, *Japan* **72 C5** 34 20N 133 30 E
Inle L., *Burma* **90 E6** 20 30N 96 58 E
Inlet, *U.S.A.* **151 C10** 43 45N 74 48W
Inn →, *Austria* **34 C6** 48 35N 13 28 E
Innamincka, *Australia* **127 D3** 27 44 S 140 46 E
Innbygda, *Norway* **18 C9** 61 19N 12 17 E
Inner Hebrides, *U.K.* **22 E2** 57 0N 6 30W
Inner Mongolia = Nei Monggol Zizhiqu □, *China* **74 D7** 42 0N 112 0 E
Inner Sound, *U.K.* **22 D3** 57 30N 5 55W
Innerkip, *Canada* **150 C4** 43 13N 80 42W
Innerkirchen, *Switz.* **32 C6** 46 43N 8 14 E
Innes Nat. Park, *Australia* **128 C2** 35 52 S 136 53 E
Innetalling I., *Canada* **140 A4** 56 0N 79 0W
Innisfail, *Australia* **126 B4** 17 33 S 146 5 E
Innisfail, *Canada* **142 C6** 52 0N 113 57W
In'noshima, *Japan* **72 C5** 34 19N 133 10 E
Innsbruck, *Austria* **34 D4** 47 16N 11 23 E
Innviertel, *Austria* **34 C6** 48 15N 13 15 E
Innvik, *Norway* **18 C3** 61 51N 6 37 E
Inny →, *Ireland* **23 C4** 53 30N 7 50W
Ino, *Japan* **72 D5** 33 33N 133 26 E
Inobonto, *Indonesia* **82 A2** 0 52N 123 57 E
Inocência, *Brazil* **171 E1** 19 47 S 51 48W
Inongo, *Dem. Rep. of the Congo* **114 C3** 1 55 S 18 30 E
Inoni, *Congo* **114 C3** 3 4 S 15 39 E
İnönü, *Turkey* **49 B12** 39 48N 30 9 E
Inoucdjouac = Inukjuak, *Canada* **139 C12** 58 25N 78 15W
Inowrocław, *Poland* **55 F5** 52 50N 18 12 E
Inpundong, *N. Korea* **75 D14** 41 25N 126 34 E
Inquisivi, *Bolivia* **172 D4** 16 50 S 67 10W
Ins, *Switz.* **32 B4** 47 1N 7 7 E
Inscription, C., *Australia* **125 E1** 25 29 S 112 59 E
Insein, *Burma* **90 G6** 16 50N 96 5 E
Insjön, *Sweden* **16 D9** 60 41N 15 6 E
Ińsko, *Poland* **54 E2** 53 25N 15 32 E
Însurăţei, *Romania* **53 F12** 44 50N 27 40 E
Inta, *Russia* **56 A11** 66 5N 60 8 E
Intendente Alvear, *Argentina* **174 D3** 35 12 S 63 32W
Intepe, *Turkey* **49 A8** 40 1N 26 20 E
Interlachen, *U.S.A.* **153 F8** 29 37N 81 53W
Interlaken, *Switz.* **32 C5** 46 41N 7 50 E
Interlaken, *U.S.A.* **151 D8** 42 37N 76 44W
International Falls, *U.S.A.* **154 A8** 48 36N 93 25W
Interview I., *India* **95 H11** 12 55N 92 43 E
Intiyaco, *Argentina* **174 B3** 28 43 S 60 5W
Întorsura Buzăului, *Romania* **53 E11** 45 41N 26 2 E
Intragna, *Switz.* **33 D7** 46 11N 8 42 E
Intutu, *Peru* **168 D3** 3 32 S 74 48W
Inubō-Zaki, *Japan* **73 B12** 35 42N 140 52 E
Inukjuak, *Canada* **139 C12** 58 25N 78 15W
Inútil, B., *Chile* **176 D2** 53 30 S 70 15W
Inuvik, *Canada* **138 B6** 68 16N 133 40W
Inuyama, *Japan* **73 B8** 35 23N 136 56 E
Inveraray, *U.K.* **22 E3** 56 14N 5 5W
Inverbervie, *U.K.* **22 E6** 56 51N 2 17W
Invercargill, *N.Z.* **131 G3** 46 24 S 168 24 E
Inverclyde □, *U.K.* **22 F4** 55 55N 4 49W
Inverell, *Australia* **127 D5** 29 45 S 151 8 E
Invergordon, *U.K.* **22 D4** 57 41N 4 10W
Inverleigh, *Australia* **128 E6** 38 6 S 144 3 E
Inverloch, *Australia* **127 F4** 38 38 S 145 45 E
Invermere, *Canada* **142 C5** 50 30N 116 2W
Inverness, *Canada* **141 C7** 46 15N 61 19W
Inverness, *U.K.* **22 D4** 57 29N 4 13W
Inverness, *Ala., U.S.A.* **152 C4** 32 1N 85 45W
Inverness, *Fla., U.S.A.* **149 L4** 28 50N 82 20W
Inverurie, *U.K.* **22 D6** 57 17N 2 23W
Investigator Group, *Australia* **127 E1** 34 45 S 134 20 E
Investigator Str., *Australia* **128 C2** 35 30 S 137 0 E
Inya, *Russia* **66 D9** 50 28N 86 37 E
Inyanga, *Zimbabwe* **119 F3** 18 12 S 32 40 E
Inyangani, *Zimbabwe* **119 F3** 18 5 S 32 50 E
Inyantue, *Zimbabwe* **116 B4** 18 33 S 26 39 E
Inyo Mts., *U.S.A.* **160 J9** 36 40N 118 0W
Inyokern, *U.S.A.* **161 K9** 35 39N 117 49W
Inywa, *Burma* **90 D6** 23 56N 96 17 E
Inza, *Russia* **60 D8** 53 55N 46 25 E
Inzer, *Russia* **64 D6** 54 14N 57 34 E
Inzhavino, *Russia* **60 D6** 52 22N 42 30 E
Inzia →, *Dem. Rep. of the Congo* **115 C3** 4 35 S 17 57 E
Iō-Jima, *Japan* **71 J5** 30 48N 130 18 E
Ioánnina, *Greece* **48 B2** 39 42N 20 47 E
Ioánnina □, *Greece* **48 B2** 39 39N 20 57 E
Iokea, *Papua N. G.* **132 E4** 8 25 S 146 16 E
Iola, *U.S.A.* **155 G7** 37 55N 95 24W
Ioma, *Papua N. G.* **132 E4** 8 19 S 147 52 E
Ion Corvin, *Romania* **53 F12** 44 7N 27 50 E
Iôna, *Angola* **115 F2** 16 54 S 12 34 E
Iona, *U.K.* **22 E2** 56 20N 6 25W
Iona, Parque Nacional do, *Angola* **115 F2** 16 47 S 12 20 E
Ione, *U.S.A.* **160 G6** 38 21N 120 56W
Iongo, *Angola* **115 D3** 9 11 S 17 45 E
Ionia, *U.S.A.* **157 B11** 42 59N 85 4W
Ionian Is. = Iónioi Nísoi, *Greece* **39 B1** 38 40N 20 0 E
Ionian Sea, *Medit. S.* **12 H9** 37 30N 17 30 E
Iónioi Nísoi, *Greece* **39 B1** 38 40N 20 0 E
Iónioi Nísoi □, *Greece* **39 B2** 38 40N 20 8 E
Íos, *Greece* **49 E7** 36 41N 25 20 E
Iowa □, *U.S.A.* **156 C3** 42 18N 93 30W
Iowa →, *U.S.A.* **156 C5** 41 10N 91 1W
Iowa City, *U.S.A.* **156 C5** 41 40N 91 32W
Iowa Falls, *U.S.A.* **156 B3** 42 31N 93 16W
Iowa Park, *U.S.A.* **155 J5** 33 57N 98 40W
Ipala, *Tanzania* **118 C3** 4 30 S 32 52 E
Ipameri, *Brazil* **171 E2** 17 44 S 48 9W
Ipanema, *Brazil* **171 E3** 19 47 S 41 44W
Iparía, *Peru* **172 B3** 9 17 S 74 29W
Ipáti, *Greece* **48 C4** 38 52N 22 14 E
Ipatinga, *Brazil* **171 E3** 19 32 S 42 30W
Ipatovo, *Russia* **61 H6** 45 45N 42 50 E
Ipel' →, *Europe* **35 D11** 47 48N 18 53 E
Ipiales, *Colombia* **168 C2** 0 50N 77 37W
Ipiaú, *Brazil* **171 D4** 14 8 S 39 44W
Ipil, *Phil.* **81 H4** 7 47N 122 35 E
Ipin = Yibin, *China* **76 C5** 28 45N 104 32 E
Ipirá, *Brazil* **171 D4** 12 10 S 39 44W
Ipiranga, *Brazil* **168 D4** 3 13 S 65 57W
Ípiros □, *Greece* **48 B2** 39 30N 20 30 E
Ipixuna, *Brazil* **172 B3** 7 0 S 71 40W
Ipixuna →, *Amazonas, Brazil* **172 B3** 7 11 S 71 51W
Ipixuna →, *Amazonas, Brazil* **173 B5** 5 45 S 63 2W
Ipoh, *Malaysia* **87 K3** 4 35N 101 5 E
Iporá, *Brazil* **173 D7** 16 28 S 51 7W
Ipota, *Vanuatu* **133 H7** 18 52 S 169 20 E
Ippy, *C.A.R.* **114 A4** 6 5N 21 7 E
Ipsala, *Turkey* **51 F10** 40 55N 26 23 E
Ipsárion, Óros, *Greece* **51 F8** 40 40N 24 40 E
Ipsos, *Greece* **38 B9** 39 43N 19 48 E
Ipswich, *Australia* **127 D5** 27 35 S 152 40 E
Ipswich, *U.K.* **21 E9** 52 4N 1 10 E
Ipswich, *Mass., U.S.A.* **151 D14** 42 41N 70 50W
Ipswich, *S. Dak., U.S.A.* **154 C5** 45 27N 99 2W
Ipu, *Brazil* **170 B3** 4 23 S 40 44W
Ipueiras, *Brazil* **170 B3** 4 33 S 40 43W
Ipupiara, *Brazil* **171 D3** 11 49 S 42 37W
Iqaluit, *Canada* **139 B13** 63 44N 68 31W
Iquique, *Chile* **172 E3** 20 19 S 70 5W
Iquitos, *Peru* **168 D3** 3 45 S 73 10W
Irabu-Jima, *Japan* **71 M2** 24 50N 125 10 E
Iracoubo, *Fr. Guiana* **169 B7** 5 30N 53 10W
Īrafshān, *Iran* **97 E9** 26 42N 61 56 E
Irahuan, *Phil.* **81 G2** 9 48N 118 41 E
Iráklia, *Kikládhes, Greece* **49 E7** 36 50N 25 28 E
Iráklia, *Sérrai, Greece* **50 E7** 41 10N 23 16 E
Iráklion, *Greece* **39 E6** 35 20N 25 12 E
Iráklion □, *Greece* **39 E6** 35 10N 25 10 E
Irako-Zaki, *Japan* **73 C9** 34 35N 137 1 E
Irala, *Paraguay* **175 B5** 25 55 S 54 35W
Iran ■, *Asia* **97 C7** 33 0N 53 0 E
Iran, Gunung-Gunung, *Malaysia* **85 B4** 2 20N 114 50 E
Iran, Plateau of, *Asia* **62 F9** 32 0N 55 0 E
Iran Ra. = Iran, Gunung-Gunung, *Malaysia* **85 B4** 2 20N 114 50 E
Iranamadu Tank, *Sri Lanka* **95 K5** 9 23N 80 29 E
Īrānshahr, *Iran* **97 E9** 27 15N 60 40 E
Irapa, *Venezuela* **169 A5** 10 34N 62 35W
Irapuato, *Mexico* **162 C4** 20 40N 101 30W
Iraq ■, *Asia* **101 F10** 33 0N 44 0 E
Irarrar, O. →, *Mali* **111 E5** 20 0N 1 30 E
Irarrarene, *Algeria* **111 C6** 27 37N 7 30 E
Irati, *Brazil* **175 B5** 25 25 S 50 38W
Irbes saurums, *Latvia* **54 A9** 57 45N 22 5 E
Irbid, *Jordan* **103 C4** 32 35N 35 48 E
Irbid □, *Jordan* **103 C5** 32 15N 36 35 E
Irbit, *Russia* **64 C9** 57 41N 63 3 E
Irebu, *Dem. Rep. of the Congo* **114 C3** 0 40 S 17 46 E
Irecê, *Brazil* **170 D3** 11 18 S 41 52W
Iregua →, *Spain* **40 C7** 42 27N 2 24 E
Ireland ■, *Europe* **23 C4** 53 50N 7 52W
Ireland I., *Bermuda* **9 a** 32 19N 64 50W

Jaguaribe 227

Irele, *Nigeria* **113 D6** 7 40N 5 40 E
Iremel, Gora, *Russia* **64 D7** 54 33N 58 50 E
Ireng →, *Brazil* **169 C6** 3 33N 59 51W
Irerrer, O. →, *Algeria* **111 E6** 19 25N 5 47 E
Irgiz, Bolshaya →, *Russia* **60 D9** 52 10N 49 10 E
Irharhar, O. →, *Algeria* **111 C6** 28 3N 6 15 E
Irherm, *Morocco* **110 B3** 30 7N 8 18W
Irhil M'Goun, *Morocco* **110 B3** 31 30N 6 28W
Irhyangdong, *N. Korea* **75 D15** 41 15N 129 30 E
Iri, *S. Korea* **75 G14** 35 59N 127 0 E
Irian Jaya □, *Indonesia* **83 B5** 4 0 S 137 0 E
Iriba, *Chad* **109 E4** 15 7N 22 15 E
Irié, *Guinea* **112 D3** 8 15N 9 10W
Iriga, *Phil.* **80 E4** 13 25N 123 25 E
Iriklinskiy, *Russia* **64 F7** 51 39N 58 38 E
Iriklinskoye Vdkhr., *Russia* **64 F7** 52 0N 59 0 E
Iringa, *Tanzania* **118 D4** 7 48 S 35 43 E
Iringa □, *Tanzania* **118 D4** 7 48 S 35 43 E
Irinjalakuda, *India* **95 J3** 10 21N 76 14 E
Iriomote-Jima, *Japan* **71 M1** 24 19N 123 48 E
Iriona, *Honduras* **164 C2** 15 57N 85 11W
Iriri →, *Brazil* **169 D7** 3 52 S 52 37W
Iriri Novo →, *Brazil* **173 B7** 8 46 S 53 22W
Irish Republic ■, *Europe* **23 C3** 53 0N 8 0W
Irish Sea, *U.K.* **20 D3** 53 38N 4 48W
Irkeshtam = Erkech-Tam, *Kyrgyzstan* **65 D6** 39 41N 73 55 E
Irkutsk, *Russia* **67 D11** 52 18N 104 20 E
Irlığanlı, *Turkey* **49 D11** 37 53N 29 12 E
Irma, *Canada* **143 C6** 52 55N 111 14W
Irō-Zaki, *Japan* **73 C10** 34 36N 138 51 E
Iroise, Mer d', *France* **26 D2** 48 15N 4 45W
Iron Baron, *Australia* **128 B2** 32 58 S 137 11 E
Iron Gate = Portile de Fier, *Europe* **52 F7** 44 44N 22 30 E
Iron Knob, *Australia* **128 B2** 32 46 S 137 8 E
Iron Mountain, *U.S.A.* **148 C1** 45 49N 88 4W
Iron Range Nat. Park, *Australia* **126 A3** 12 34 S 143 18 E
Iron River, *U.S.A.* **154 B10** 46 6N 88 39W
Irondequoit, *U.S.A.* **150 C7** 43 13N 77 35W
Ironton, *Mo., U.S.A.* **155 G9** 37 36N 90 38W
Ironton, *Ohio, U.S.A.* **148 F4** 38 32N 82 41W
Ironwood, *U.S.A.* **154 B9** 46 27N 90 9W
Iroquois, *Canada* **151 B9** 44 51N 75 19W
Iroquois →, *U.S.A.* **157 C9** 41 5N 87 49W
Iroquois Falls, *Canada* **140 C3** 48 46N 80 41W
Irosin, *Phil.* **80 E5** 12 42N 124 2 E
Irpin, *Ukraine* **59 G6** 50 30N 30 15 E
Irqieqa, Ras I-, *Malta* **38 F7** 35 56N 14 29 E
Irrara Cr. →, *Australia* **127 D4** 29 35 S 145 31 E
Irrawaddy □, *Burma* **90 G5** 17 0N 95 0 E
Irrawaddy →, *Burma* **90 G5** 15 50N 95 6 E
Irrawaddy, Mouths of the, *Burma* **90 H5** 15 30N 95 0 E
Irricana, *Canada* **142 C6** 51 19N 113 37W
Irsina, *Italy* **47 B9** 40 45N 16 14 E
Irtysh →, *Russia* **66 C7** 61 4N 68 52 E
Irumu, *Dem. Rep. of the Congo* **118 B2** 1 32N 29 53 E
Irún, *Spain* **40 B3** 43 20N 1 52W
Irunea = Pamplona, *Spain* **40 C3** 42 48N 1 38W
Irurzun, *Spain* **40 C3** 42 55N 1 50W
Irvine, *U.K.* **22 F4** 55 37N 4 41W
Irvine, *Calif., U.S.A.* **161 M9** 33 41N 117 46W
Irvine, *Ky., U.S.A.* **157 G13** 37 42N 83 58W
Irvinestown, *U.K.* **23 B4** 54 28N 7 39W
Irving, *U.S.A.* **155 J6** 32 49N 96 56W
Irvington, *U.S.A.* **157 G10** 37 53N 86 17W
Irvona, *U.S.A.* **150 F6** 40 46N 78 33W
Irwin →, *Australia* **125 E1** 29 15 S 114 54 E
Irwinton, *U.S.A.* **152 C6** 32 49N 83 10W
Irwinville, *U.S.A.* **152 D6** 31 39N 83 23W
Irymple, *Australia* **128 C5** 34 14 S 142 8 E
Is, Jebel, *Sudan* **106 C4** 21 52N 35 28 E
Is-sur-Tille, *France* **27 E12** 47 30N 5 8 E
Isa, *Nigeria* **113 C6** 13 14N 6 24 E
Isa Khel, *Pakistan* **92 C4** 32 41N 71 17 E
Isaac →, *Australia* **126 C4** 22 55 S 149 20 E
Isabel, *U.S.A.* **154 C4** 45 24N 101 26W
Isabela, *Basilan, Phil.* **81 H3** 6 40N 121 59 E
Isabela, *Negros, Phil.* **81 F4** 10 12N 122 59 E
Isabela, *Puerto Rico* **165 d** 18 30N 67 2W
Isabela □, *Phil.* **80 C4** 17 0N 122 0 E
Isabela, Canal, *Ecuador* **172 a** 0 20 S 90 55W
Isabela, I., *Ecuador* **172 a** 0 30 S 91 4W
Isabela, I., *Mexico* **162 C3** 21 51N 105 55W
Isabelia, Cord., *Nic.* **164 D2** 13 30N 85 25W
Isabella Ra., *Australia* **124 D3** 21 0 S 121 4 E
Isaccea, *Romania* **53 E13** 45 16N 28 28 E
Ísafjarðardjúp, *Iceland* **11 A3** 66 10N 23 0W
Ísafjarðarsýsla □, *Iceland* **11 B3** 66 0N 23 0W
Ísafjörður, *Iceland* **11 A3** 66 5N 23 9W
Isagarh, *India* **92 G7** 24 48N 77 51 E
Isahaya, *Japan* **72 E2** 32 52N 130 2 E
Isaka, *Dem. Rep. of the Congo* **114 C3** 2 33 S 18 54 E
Isaka, *Tanzania* **118 C3** 3 56 S 32 59 E
Isakly, *Russia* **60 C10** 54 8N 51 32 E
Işalniţa, *Romania* **53 F8** 44 24N 23 44 E
Isalo, Parc Nat. de l', *Madag.* **117 C8** 22 23 S 45 16 E
Isan →, *India* **93 F9** 26 51N 80 7 E
Isana = Içana →, *Brazil* **168 C4** 0 26N 67 19W
Isandja, *Dem. Rep. of the Congo* **114 C4** 2 59 S 21 59 E
Isangano Nat. Park, *Zambia* **119 E3** 11 8 S 30 35 E
Isangi, *Dem. Rep. of the Congo* **114 B4** 0 52N 24 10 E
Isanlu Makutu, *Nigeria* **113 D6** 8 20N 5 50 E
Isar →, *Germany* **31 G8** 48 48N 12 57 E
Isarco →, *Italy* **45 B8** 46 27N 11 18 E
Ísari, *Greece* **48 D3** 37 22N 22 0 E
Isarog, Mt., *Phil.* **80 E4** 13 39N 123 23 E
Íscar, *Spain* **42 D6** 41 22N 4 32W
Iscayachi, *Bolivia* **173 E4** 21 31 S 65 3W
Iscehisar, *Turkey* **49 C12** 38 51N 30 45 E
Ischgl, *Austria* **33 B10** 47 1N 10 17 E
Íschia, *Italy* **46 B6** 40 44N 13 57 E
Iscuandé, *Colombia* **168 C2** 2 28N 77 59W
Isdell →, *Australia* **124 C3** 16 27 S 124 51 E
Ise, *Japan* **73 C8** 34 25N 136 45 E
Ise-Wan, *Japan* **73 C8** 34 43N 136 43 E
Isefjord, *Denmark* **17 J5** 55 53N 11 50 E
Isel →, *Austria* **34 E5** 46 50N 12 47 E
Iseltwald, *Switz.* **32 C5** 46 43N 7 58 E
Isenthal, *Switz.* **33 C7** 46 55N 8 34 E
Iseo, *Italy* **44 C7** 45 39N 10 3 E
Iseo, L. d', *Italy* **44 C7** 45 43N 10 4 E
Iseramagazi, *Tanzania* **118 C3** 4 37 S 32 10 E
Isère □, *France* **29 C9** 45 15N 5 40 E
Isère →, *France* **29 D8** 44 59N 4 51 E
Iserlohn, *Germany* **30 D3** 51 22N 7 41 E
Isérnia, *Italy* **47 A7** 41 36N 14 14 E
Isesaki, *Japan* **73 A11** 36 19N 139 12 E
Iseyin, *Nigeria* **113 D5** 8 0N 3 36 E
Isfahan = Eşfahān, *Iran* **97 C6** 32 39N 51 43 E
Isfana, *Kyrgyzstan* **65 D4** 39 50N 69 31 E
Isfara, *Tajikistan* **65 C5** 40 7N 70 38 E
Isfjorden, *Norway* **18 B4** 62 35N 7 49 E
Ishëm, *Albania* **50 E3** 41 33N 19 34 E
Ishenga Oshwe, *Dem. Rep. of the Congo* **114 C4** 3 57 S 22 33 E
Isherton, *Guyana* **169 C6** 2 20N 59 25W
Ishigaki-Shima, *Japan* **71 M2** 24 20N 124 10 E
Ishikari-Gawa →, *Japan* **70 C10** 43 15N 141 23 E
Ishikari-Sammyaku, *Japan* **70 C11** 43 30N 143 0 E
Ishikari-Wan, *Japan* **70 C10** 43 25N 141 1 E
Ishikawa □, *Japan* **73 A8** 36 30N 136 30 E
Ishim, *Russia* **66 D7** 56 10N 69 30 E
Ishim →, *Russia* **66 D8** 57 45N 71 10 E
Ishimbay, *Russia* **64 E6** 53 28N 56 2 E
Ishinomaki, *Japan* **70 E10** 38 32N 141 20 E
Ishioka, *Japan* **73 A12** 36 11N 140 16 E
Ishizuchi-Yama, *Japan* **72 D5** 33 45N 133 6 E
Ishkashim, *Tajikistan* **65 E5** 36 44N 71 37 E
Ishkuman, *Pakistan* **93 A5** 36 30N 73 50 E
Ishpeming, *U.S.A.* **148 B2** 46 29N 87 40W
Ishtykhan, *Uzbekistan* **65 D3** 39 58N 66 29 E
Ishurdi, *Bangla.* **90 C2** 24 9N 89 3 E
Isigny-sur-Mer, *France* **26 C5** 49 19N 1 6W
Isıklar Dağı, *Turkey* **51 F11** 40 45N 27 15 E
Işıklı, *Turkey* **49 C11** 38 19N 29 51 E
Isil Kul, *Russia* **66 D8** 54 55N 71 16 E
Ísili, *Italy* **46 C2** 39 44N 9 6 E
Isiolo, *Kenya* **118 B4** 0 24N 37 33 E
Isiro, *Dem. Rep. of the Congo* **118 B2** 2 53N 27 40 E
Isisford, *Australia* **126 C3** 24 15 S 144 21 E
Iskandar, *Uzbekistan* **65 C4** 41 36N 69 41 E
İskenderun, *Turkey* **100 D7** 36 32N 36 10 E
İskenderun Körfezi, *Turkey* **100 D6** 36 40N 35 50 E
Iski-Naukat = Eski-Nookat, *Kyrgyzstan* **65 C6** 40 16N 72 36 E
İskilip, *Turkey* **100 B6** 40 45N 34 29 E
Iskŭr →, *Bulgaria* **51 C8** 43 45N 24 25 E
Iskŭr, Yazovir, *Bulgaria* **50 D7** 42 23N 23 30 E
Iskut →, *Canada* **142 B2** 56 45N 131 49W
Isla →, *U.K.* **22 E5** 56 32N 3 20W
Isla Cristina, *Spain* **43 H3** 37 13N 7 17W
Isla Gorge Nat. Park, *Australia* **126 D4** 25 10 S 149 57 E
Isla Vista, *U.S.A.* **161 L7** 34 25N 119 53W
İslâhiye, *Turkey* **100 D7** 37 0N 36 35 E
Islam Headworks, *Pakistan* **92 E5** 29 49N 72 33 E
Islamabad, *Pakistan* **91 B4** 33 40N 73 10 E
Islamgarh, *Pakistan* **92 F4** 27 51N 70 48 E
Islamkot, *Pakistan* **92 G4** 24 42N 70 13 E
Islamorada, *U.S.A.* **153 L9** 24 56N 80 37W
Islampur, *Bihar, India* **93 G11** 25 9N 85 12 E
Islampur, *Maharashtra, India* **94 F2** 17 2N 74 20 E
Island Bay, *Phil.* **81 G2** 9 6N 118 10 E
Island L., *Canada* **143 C10** 53 47N 94 25W
Island Lagoon, *Australia* **128 A2** 31 30 S 136 40 E
Island Pond, *U.S.A.* **151 B13** 44 49N 71 53W
Islands, B. of, *Canada* **141 C8** 49 11N 58 15W
Islands, B. of, *N.Z.* **130 B3** 35 15 S 174 6 E
Islay, *U.K.* **22 F2** 55 46N 6 10W
Isle →, *France* **28 D3** 44 55N 0 15W
Isle aux Morts, *Canada* **141 C8** 47 35N 59 0W
Isle of Hope, *U.S.A.* **152 D8** 31 58N 81 5W
Isle of Wight □, *U.K.* **21 G6** 50 41N 1 17W
Isle Royale Nat. Park, *U.S.A.* **154 B10** 48 0N 88 55W
Isleton, *U.S.A.* **160 G5** 38 10N 121 37W
Ismail = Izmayil, *Ukraine* **59 K5** 45 22N 28 46 E
Ismâ'ilîya, *Egypt* **106 H8** 30 37N 32 18 E
Ismaning, *Germany* **31 G7** 48 13N 11 40 E
Isna, *Egypt* **106 B3** 25 17N 32 30 E
Isoanala, *Madag.* **117 C8** 23 50 S 45 44 E
Isogstalo, *India* **93 B8** 34 15N 78 46 E
Ísola del Liri, *Italy* **45 G10** 41 41N 13 34 E
Ísola della Scala, *Italy* **44 C7** 45 16N 11 0 E
Ísola di Capo Rizzuto, *Italy* **47 D10** 38 58N 17 6 E
İsparta, *Turkey* **49 D12** 37 47N 30 30 E
Isperikh, *Bulgaria* **51 C10** 43 43N 26 50 E
Íspica, *Italy* **47 F7** 36 47N 14 55 E
Israel ■, *Asia* **103 D3** 32 0N 34 50 E
Isratu, *Eritrea* **107 D4** 16 20N 39 51 E
Issano, *Guyana* **169 B6** 5 49N 59 26W
Issia, *Ivory C.* **112 D3** 6 33N 6 33W
Issoire, *France* **28 C7** 45 32N 3 15 E
Issoudun, *France* **27 F8** 46 57N 1 59 E
Issyk-Kul = Balykchy, *Kyrgyzstan* **65 B8** 42 26N 76 12 E
Issyk-Kul, Ozero = Ysyk-Köl, *Kyrgyzstan* **66 E8** 42 25N 77 15 E
Ist, *Croatia* **45 D11** 44 17N 14 47 E
Istaihah, *U.A.E.* **99 B6** 23 19N 54 4 E
Istállós-kő, *Hungary* **52 B5** 48 4N 20 26 E
İstanbul, *Turkey* **51 E12** 41 0N 29 0 E
İstanbul □, *Turkey* **51 E12** 41 0N 29 0 E
İstanbul Boğazı, *Turkey* **51 E13** 41 10N 29 10 E
Isteren, *Norway* **18 B8** 61 58N 11 47 E
Istiaía, *Greece* **48 C5** 38 57N 23 9 E
Istmina, *Colombia* **168 B2** 5 10N 76 39W
Isto, Mt., *U.S.A.* **144 B12** 69 12N 143 48W
Istok, *Kosovo, Yug.* **50 D4** 42 45N 20 24 E
Istokpoga, L., *U.S.A.* **149 M5** 27 23N 81 17W
Istra, *Croatia* **45 C10** 45 10N 14 0 E
Istres, *France* **29 E8** 43 31N 4 59 E
Istria = Istra, *Croatia* **45 C10** 45 10N 14 0 E
Isugod, *Phil.* **81 G2** 9 19N 118 5 E
Isulan, *Phil.* **81 H5** 6 30N 124 29 E
Itá, *Paraguay* **174 B4** 25 29 S 57 21W
Itabaiana, *Paraíba, Brazil* **170 C4** 7 18 S 35 19W
Itabaiana, *Sergipe, Brazil* **170 D4** 10 41 S 37 37W
Itabaianinha, *Brazil* **170 D4** 11 16 S 37 47W
Itaberaba, *Brazil* **171 D3** 12 32 S 40 18W
Itaberaí, *Brazil* **171 E2** 16 2 S 49 48W
Itabira, *Brazil* **171 E3** 19 37 S 43 13W
Itabirito, *Brazil* **171 F3** 20 15 S 43 48W
Itaboca, *Brazil* **169 D5** 4 50 S 62 40W
Itabuna, *Brazil* **171 D4** 14 48 S 39 16W
Itacajá, *Brazil* **170 C2** 8 19 S 47 46W
Itacaunas →, *Brazil* **170 C2** 5 21 S 49 8W
Itacoatiara, *Brazil* **169 D6** 3 8 S 58 25W
Itacuaí →, *Brazil* **172 A3** 4 20 S 70 12W
Itaguaçu, *Brazil* **171 E3** 19 48 S 40 51W
Itaguari →, *Brazil* **171 D3** 14 11 S 44 40W
Itaguatins, *Brazil* **170 C2** 5 47 S 47 29W
Itaim →, *Brazil* **170 C3** 7 2 S 42 2W
Itainópolis, *Brazil* **170 C3** 7 24 S 41 31W
Itaipú, Represa de, *Brazil* **175 B5** 25 30 S 54 30W
Itaituba, *Brazil* **169 D6** 4 10 S 55 50W
Itajaí, *Brazil* **175 B6** 27 50 S 48 39W
Itajubá, *Brazil* **171 F2** 22 24 S 45 30W
Itajuípe, *Brazil* **171 D4** 14 41 S 39 22W
Itaka, *Tanzania* **119 D3** 8 50 S 32 49 E
Itako, *Japan* **73 B12** 35 56N 140 33 E
Itala Nature Reserve, *S. Africa* **117 D5** 27 30 S 31 7 E
Italy ■, *Europe* **13 G8** 42 0N 13 0 E
Itamaraju, *Brazil* **171 E4** 17 4 S 39 32W
Itamarati, *Brazil* **172 B4** 6 24 S 68 15W
Itamataré, *Brazil* **170 B2** 2 16 S 46 24W
Itambacuri, *Brazil* **171 E3** 18 1 S 41 42W
Itambé, *Brazil* **171 E3** 15 15 S 40 37W
Itami, *Japan* **73 C7** 34 46N 135 25 E
Itampolo, *Madag.* **117 C7** 24 41 S 43 57 E
Itandrano, *Madag.* **117 C8** 21 47 S 45 17 E
Itanhaém, *Brazil* **171 F2** 24 11 S 46 47W
Itanhauã →, *Brazil* **169 D5** 4 45 S 63 48W
Itanhém, *Brazil* **171 E3** 17 9 S 40 20W
Itano, *Japan* **72 C6** 34 7N 134 28 E
Itapaci, *Brazil* **171 D2** 14 57 S 49 34W
Itapagé, *Brazil* **170 B4** 3 41 S 39 34W
Itaparica, I. de, *Brazil* **171 D4** 12 54 S 38 42W
Itapebi, *Brazil* **171 E4** 15 56 S 39 32W
Itapecuru-Mirim, *Brazil* **170 B3** 3 24 S 44 20W
Itaperuna, *Brazil* **171 F3** 21 10 S 41 54W
Itapetinga, *Brazil* **171 E3** 15 15 S 40 15W
Itapetininga, *Brazil* **175 A6** 23 36 S 48 7W
Itapeva, *Brazil* **175 A6** 23 59 S 48 59W
Itapicuru →, *Bahia, Brazil* **170 D4** 11 47 S 37 32W
Itapicuru →, *Maranhão, Brazil* **170 B3** 2 52 S 44 12W
Itapinima, *Brazil* **173 B5** 5 25 S 60 44W
Itapipoca, *Brazil* **170 B4** 3 30 S 39 35W
Itapiranga, *Brazil* **169 D6** 2 45 S 58 1W
Itapiúna, *Brazil* **170 B4** 4 33 S 38 57W
Itaporanga, *Paraíba, Brazil* **170 C4** 7 18 S 38 0W
Itaporanga, *São Paulo, Brazil* **171 F2** 23 42 S 49 29W
Itapuá □, *Paraguay* **175 B4** 26 40 S 55 40W
Itapuranga, *Brazil* **171 E2** 15 40 S 49 59W
Itaquari, *Brazil* **171 F3** 20 20 S 40 25W
Itaquatiara, *Brazil* **169 D6** 2 58 S 58 30W
Itaquí, *Brazil* **174 B4** 29 8 S 56 30W
Itararé, *Brazil* **175 A6** 24 6 S 49 23W
Itarsi, *India* **92 H7** 22 36N 77 51 E
Itarumã, *Brazil* **171 E1** 18 42 S 51 25W
Itatí, *Argentina* **174 B4** 27 16 S 58 15W
Itatira, *Brazil* **170 B4** 4 30 S 39 37W
Itatuba, *Brazil* **173 B5** 5 46 S 63 20W
Itatupa, *Brazil* **169 D7** 0 37 S 51 12W
Itaueira, *Brazil* **170 C3** 7 36 S 43 2W
Itaueira →, *Brazil* **170 C3** 6 41 S 42 55W
Itaúna, *Brazil* **171 F3** 20 4 S 44 34W
Itbayat, *Phil.* **80 A3** 20 47N 121 51 E
Itbayat I., *Phil.* **80 A3** 20 45N 121 50 E
Itchen →, *U.K.* **21 G6** 50 55N 1 22W
Itchouma, *Niger* **111 D7** 20 14N 13 32 E
Itchoumma, *Niger* **109 D2** 20 14N 13 32 E
Ite, *Peru* **172 D3** 17 55 S 70 57W
Itéa, *Greece* **48 C4** 38 25N 22 25 E
Itezhi Tezhi, L., *Zambia* **119 F2** 15 30 S 25 30 E
Ithaca = Itháki, *Greece* **39 C2** 38 25N 20 40 E
Ithaca, *U.S.A.* **151 D8** 42 27N 76 30W
Itháki, *Greece* **39 C2** 38 25N 20 40 E
Itinga, *Brazil* **171 E3** 16 36 S 41 47W
Itiquira, *Brazil* **173 D7** 17 12 S 54 7W
Itiquira →, *Brazil* **173 D6** 17 18 S 56 44W
Itiruçu, *Brazil* **171 D3** 13 31 S 40 9W
Itiúba, *Brazil* **170 D4** 10 43 S 39 51W
Itkilik →, *U.S.A.* **144 A10** 70 9N 150 56W
Itō, *Japan* **73 C11** 34 58N 139 5 E
Itogon, *Phil.* **80 C3** 16 22N 120 41 E
Itoigawa, *Japan* **71 F8** 37 2N 137 51 E
Itoko, *Dem. Rep. of the Congo* **114 C4** 1 0 S 21 48 E
Iton →, *France* **26 C8** 49 9N 1 12 E
Itonamas →, *Bolivia* **173 C5** 12 28 S 64 24W
Itri, *Italy* **46 A6** 41 17N 13 32 E
Itsa, *Egypt* **106 J7** 29 15N 30 47 E
Itsuki, *Japan* **72 E2** 32 24N 130 50 E
Íttiri, *Italy* **46 B1** 40 36N 8 34 E
Ittoqqortoormiit, *Greenland* **10 C8** 70 20N 23 0W
Itu, *Brazil* **175 A6** 23 17 S 47 15W
Itu, *Nigeria* **113 D6** 5 10N 7 58 E
Itu Aba I., *S. China Sea* **78 B4** 10 23N 114 21 E
Ituaçu, *Brazil* **171 D3** 13 50 S 41 18W
Ituango, *Colombia* **168 B2** 7 4N 75 45W
Ituí →, *Brazil* **168 D3** 4 38 S 70 19W
Ituiutaba, *Brazil* **171 E2** 19 0 S 49 25W
Itumbiara, *Brazil* **171 E2** 18 20 S 49 10W
Ituna, *Canada* **143 C8** 51 10N 103 24W
Itunge Port, *Tanzania* **119 D3** 9 40 S 33 55 E
Iturí, *Guyana* **169 B6** 5 28N 58 15W
Itupiranga, *Brazil* **170 C2** 5 9 S 49 20W
Iturama, *Brazil* **171 E1** 19 44 S 50 11W
Iturbe, *Argentina* **174 A2** 23 0 S 65 25W
Ituri →, *Dem. Rep. of the Congo* **118 B2** 1 40N 27 1 E
Iturup, Ostrov, *Russia* **67 E15** 45 0N 148 0 E
Ituverava, *Brazil* **171 F2** 20 20 S 47 47W
Ituxi →, *Brazil* **173 B5** 7 18 S 64 51W
Ituyuro →, *Argentina* **174 A3** 22 40 S 63 50W
Itzehoe, *Germany* **30 B5** 53 55N 9 31 E
Iuka, *U.S.A.* **157 F8** 38 37N 88 47W
Ivahona, *Madag.* **117 C8** 23 27 S 46 10 E
Ivaí →, *Brazil* **175 A5** 23 18 S 53 42W
Ivalo, *Finland* **14 B22** 68 38N 27 35 E
Ivalojoki →, *Finland* **14 B22** 68 40N 27 40 E
Ivanava, *Belarus* **59 F3** 52 7N 25 29 E
Ivančice, *Czech Rep.* **35 B9** 49 6N 16 23 E
Ivăneşti, *Romania* **53 D12** 46 39N 27 27 E
Ivangorod, *Russia* **58 C5** 59 27N 28 13 E
Ivanhoe, *N.S.W., Australia* **128 B6** 32 56 S 144 20 E
Ivanhoe, *Vic., Australia* **129 D6** 37 46 S 145 2 E
Ivanhoe, *Calif., U.S.A.* **160 J7** 36 23N 119 13W
Ivanhoe, *Minn., U.S.A.* **154 C6** 44 28N 96 15W
Ivanić Grad, *Croatia* **45 C13** 45 41N 16 25 E
Ivanjica, *Serbia, Yug.* **50 C4** 43 35N 20 12 E
Ivanjska, *Bos.-H.* **52 F2** 44 55N 17 4 E
Ivankoyskoye Vdkhr., *Russia* **58 D9** 56 37N 36 32 E
Ivano-Frankivsk, *Ukraine* **59 H3** 48 40N 24 40 E
Ivano-Frankovsk = Ivano-Frankivsk, *Ukraine* **59 H3** 48 40N 24 40 E
Ivanof Bay, *U.S.A.* **144 J8** 55 54N 159 29W
Ivanovka, *Kyrgyzstan* **65 B7** 42 53N 75 6 E
Ivanovo = Ivanava, *Belarus* **59 F3** 52 7N 25 29 E
Ivanovo, *Russia* **58 D11** 57 5N 41 0 E
Ivanšćica, *Croatia* **45 B13** 46 12N 16 13 E
Ivato, *Madag.* **117 C8** 20 37 S 47 10 E
Ivatsevichy, *Belarus* **59 F3** 52 43N 25 21 E
Ivaylovgrad, *Bulgaria* **51 E10** 41 32N 26 8 E
Ivdel, *Russia* **56 B11** 60 42N 60 24 E
Ivindo →, *Gabon* **114 C2** 0 9 S 12 9 E
Ivinheima →, *Brazil* **175 A5** 23 14 S 53 42W
Ivinhema, *Brazil* **175 A5** 22 10 S 53 37W
Ivittuut, *Greenland* **141 B10** 61 14N 48 12W
Ivohibe, *Madag.* **117 C8** 22 31 S 46 57 E
Ivolândia, *Brazil* **171 E1** 16 34 S 50 51W
Ivory Coast, *W. Afr.* **112 E4** 4 20N 5 0W
Ivory Coast ■, *Africa* **112 D4** 7 30N 5 0W
Ivösjön, *Sweden* **17 H8** 56 8N 14 25 E
Ivrea, *Italy* **44 C4** 45 28N 7 52 E
Ivrindi, *Turkey* **49 B9** 39 34N 27 30 E
Ivujivik, *Canada* **139 B12** 62 24N 77 55W
Ivybridge, *U.K.* **21 G4** 50 23N 3 56W
Iwai-Jima, *Japan* **72 D3** 33 47N 131 58 E
Iwaizumi, *Japan* **70 E10** 39 50N 141 45 E
Iwaki, *Japan* **71 F10** 37 3N 140 55 E
Iwakuni, *Japan* **72 C4** 34 15N 132 8 E
Iwami, *Japan* **72 B6** 35 32N 134 15 E
Iwamizawa, *Japan* **70 C10** 43 12N 141 46 E
Iwanai, *Japan* **70 C10** 42 58N 140 30 E
Iwase, *Japan* **73 A12** 36 21N 140 6 E
Iwata, *Japan* **73 C9** 34 42N 137 51 E
Iwate □, *Japan* **70 E10** 39 30N 141 30 E
Iwate-San, *Japan* **70 E10** 39 51N 141 0 E
Iwo, *Nigeria* **113 D5** 7 39N 4 9 E
Iwonicz-Zdrój, *Poland* **55 J8** 49 37N 21 47 E
Iwungu, *Dem. Rep. of the Congo* **115 D3** 5 16 S 19 17 E
Ixiamas, *Bolivia* **172 C4** 13 50 S 68 5W
Ixopo, *S. Africa* **117 E5** 30 11 S 30 5 E
Ixtepec, *Mexico* **163 D5** 16 32N 95 10W
Ixtlán del Río, *Mexico* **162 C4** 21 5N 104 21W
'Iyādh, *Yemen* **98 D4** 14 59N 46 51 E
Iyal Bakhit, *Sudan* **107 E2** 13 20N 28 39 E
Iyo, *Japan* **72 D4** 33 45N 132 45 E
Iyo-Mishima, *Japan* **72 D5** 33 58N 133 30 E
Iyo-Nada, *Japan* **72 D4** 33 40N 132 20 E
Izabal, L. de, *Guatemala* **164 C2** 15 30N 89 10W
Izamal, *Mexico* **163 C7** 20 56N 89 1W
Izberbash, *Russia* **61 J8** 42 35N 47 52 E
Izbica, *Poland* **55 H10** 50 53N 23 10 E
Izbica Kujawska, *Poland* **55 F5** 52 25N 18 40 E
Izbiceni, *Romania* **53 G9** 43 45N 24 40 E
Izena-Shima, *Japan* **71 L3** 26 56N 127 56 E
Izgrev, *Bulgaria* **51 C10** 43 36N 26 58 E
Izh →, *Russia* **64 C4** 56 9N 53 0 E
Izhevsk, *Russia* **64 C4** 56 51N 53 14 E
Izhma →, *Russia* **56 A9** 65 19N 52 54 E
Izileg, *Algeria* **111 D6** 20 20N 6 4 E
Izkī, *Oman* **99 B7** 22 56N 57 46 E
Izmayil, *Ukraine* **59 K5** 45 22N 28 46 E
İzmir, *Turkey* **49 C9** 38 25N 27 8 E
İzmir □, *Turkey* **49 C9** 38 15N 27 40 E
İzmir Körfezi, *Turkey* **49 C8** 38 30N 26 50 E
İzmit = Kocaeli, *Turkey* **51 F13** 40 45N 29 50 E
Iznájar, *Spain* **43 H6** 37 15N 4 19W
Iznalloz, *Spain* **43 H7** 37 24N 3 30W
İznik, *Turkey* **100 B3** 40 23N 29 46 E
İznik Gölü, *Turkey* **51 F13** 40 27N 29 30 E
Izobil'nyy, *Russia* **61 H5** 45 25N 41 44 E
Izola, *Slovenia* **45 C10** 45 32N 13 39 E
Izozog, Bañados de, *Bolivia* **173 D5** 18 48 S 62 10W
Izra, *Syria* **103 C5** 32 51N 36 15 E
Iztochni Rodopi, *Bulgaria* **51 E9** 41 45N 25 30 E
Izu-Hantō, *Japan* **73 C11** 34 45N 139 0 E
Izu-Shotō, *Japan* **71 G10** 34 30N 140 0 E
Izúcar de Matamoros, *Mexico* **163 D5** 18 36N 98 28W
Izuhara, *Japan* **72 C1** 34 12N 129 17 E
Izumi, *Kagoshima, Japan* **72 E2** 32 5N 130 22 E
Izumi, *Ōsaka, Japan* **73 C7** 34 28N 135 24 E
Izumi-Sano, *Japan* **73 C7** 34 23N 135 18 E
Izumo, *Japan* **72 B4** 35 20N 132 46 E
Izyaslav, *Ukraine* **59 G4** 50 5N 26 50 E
Izyum, *Ukraine* **59 H9** 49 12N 37 19 E

J

J.F. Rodrigues, *Brazil* **170 B1** 2 55 S 50 20W
J.P. Koch Fjord, *Greenland* **10 A6** 82 45N 44 0W
Ja-ela, *Sri Lanka* **95 L4** 7 5N 79 53 E
Jaba, *Ethiopia* **107 F4** 6 20N 35 7 E
Jabal at Ṭā'ir, *Red Sea* **107 D5** 15 35N 41 52 E
Jabalón →, *Spain* **43 G6** 38 53N 4 5W
Jabalpur, *India* **93 H8** 23 9N 79 58 E
Jabbūl, *Syria* **96 B3** 36 4N 37 30 E
Jabiru, *Australia* **124 B5** 12 40 S 132 53 E
Jablah, *Syria* **100 E6** 35 20N 36 0 E
Jablanac, *Croatia* **45 D11** 44 42N 14 56 E
Jablanica, *Bos.-H.* **52 G2** 43 40N 17 45 E
Jablonec nad Nisou, *Czech Rep.* **34 A8** 50 43N 15 10 E
Jablonica, *Slovak Rep.* **35 C10** 48 37N 17 26 E
Jabłonowo Pomorskie, *Poland* **54 E6** 53 23N 19 10 E
Jablunkov, *Czech Rep.* **35 B11** 49 35N 18 46 E
Jaboatão, *Brazil* **170 C4** 8 7 S 35 1W
Jabonga, *Phil.* **81 G5** 9 20N 125 32 E
Jaboticabal, *Brazil* **175 A6** 21 15 S 48 17W
Jabukovac, *Serbia, Yug.* **50 B6** 44 22N 22 21 E
Jaburu, *Brazil* **173 B5** 5 30 S 64 0W
Jaca, *Spain* **40 C4** 42 35N 0 33W
Jacaré →, *Brazil* **170 D3** 10 3 S 42 13W
Jacareí, *Brazil* **175 A6** 23 20 S 46 0W
Jacarèzinho, *Brazil* **175 A6** 23 5 S 49 58W
Jaciara, *Brazil* **173 D7** 15 59 S 54 57W
Jacinto, *Brazil* **171 E3** 16 10 S 40 17W
Jaciparaná, *Brazil* **173 B5** 9 15 S 64 23W
Jackman, *U.S.A.* **149 C10** 45 35N 70 17W
Jacksboro, *U.S.A.* **155 J5** 33 14N 98 15W
Jackson, *Barbados* **165 g** 13 7N 59 36W
Jackson, *Ala., U.S.A.* **149 K2** 31 31N 87 53W
Jackson, *Calif., U.S.A.* **160 G6** 38 21N 120 46W
Jackson, *Ga., U.S.A.* **152 B6** 33 20N 83 57W
Jackson, *Ky., U.S.A.* **148 G4** 37 33N 83 23W
Jackson, *Mich., U.S.A.* **157 B12** 42 15N 84 24W
Jackson, *Minn., U.S.A.* **154 D7** 43 37N 95 1W
Jackson, *Miss., U.S.A.* **155 J9** 32 18N 90 12W
Jackson, *Mo., U.S.A.* **155 G10** 37 23N 89 40W
Jackson, *N.H., U.S.A.* **151 B13** 44 10N 71 11W
Jackson, *Ohio, U.S.A.* **148 F4** 39 3N 82 39W
Jackson, *S.C., U.S.A.* **152 B8** 33 20N 81 47W
Jackson, *Tenn., U.S.A.* **149 H1** 35 37N 88 49W
Jackson, *Wyo., U.S.A.* **158 E8** 43 29N 110 46W
Jackson, C., *N.Z.* **131 A9** 40 59 S 174 20 E
Jackson B., *N.Z.* **131 D3** 43 58 S 168 42 E
Jackson Center, *U.S.A.* **157 D12** 40 27N 84 4W
Jackson Hd., *N.Z.* **131 D3** 43 58 S 168 37 E
Jackson L., *Fla., U.S.A.* **152 E5** 30 30N 84 17W
Jackson L., *Ga., U.S.A.* **152 B6** 33 19N 83 50W
Jackson L., *Wyo., U.S.A.* **158 E8** 43 52N 110 36W
Jacksons, *N.Z.* **131 C6** 42 46 S 171 32 E
Jackson's Arm, *Canada* **141 C8** 49 52N 56 47W
Jacksonville, *Ala., U.S.A.* **152 B4** 33 49N 85 46W
Jacksonville, *Ark., U.S.A.* **155 H8** 34 52N 92 7W
Jacksonville, *Calif., U.S.A.* **160 H6** 37 52N 120 24W
Jacksonville, *Fla., U.S.A.* **152 E8** 30 20N 81 39W
Jacksonville, *Ga., U.S.A.* **152 D7** 31 49N 82 59W
Jacksonville, *Ill., U.S.A.* **156 E6** 39 44N 90 14W
Jacksonville, *N.C., U.S.A.* **149 H7** 34 45N 77 26W
Jacksonville, *Tex., U.S.A.* **155 K7** 31 58N 95 17W
Jacksonville Beach, *U.S.A.* **152 E8** 30 17N 81 24W
Jacmel, *Haiti* **165 C5** 18 14N 72 32W
Jacob Lake, *U.S.A.* **159 H7** 36 43N 112 13W
Jacobabad, *Pakistan* **91 C3** 28 20N 68 29 E
Jacobina, *Brazil* **170 D3** 11 11 S 40 30W
Jacques Cartier, Dét. de, *Canada* **141 C7** 50 0N 63 30W
Jacques Cartier, Mt., *Canada* **141 C6** 48 57N 66 0W
Jacques Cartier, Parc Prov., *Canada* **141 C5** 47 15N 71 33W
Jacqueville, *Ivory C.* **112 D4** 5 12N 4 25W
Jacuí →, *Brazil* **175 C5** 30 2 S 51 15W
Jacumba, *U.S.A.* **161 N10** 32 37N 116 11W
Jacundá →, *Brazil* **170 B1** 1 57 S 50 26W
Jadcherla, *India* **94 F4** 16 46N 78 9 E
Jade, *Germany* **30 B4** 53 20N 8 14 E
Jadebusen, *Germany* **30 B4** 53 29N 8 12 E
Jadotville = Likasi, *Dem. Rep. of the Congo* **119 E2** 10 55 S 26 48 E
Jadovnik, *Serbia, Yug.* **50 C3** 43 20N 19 45 E
Jadraque, *Spain* **40 E2** 40 55N 2 55W
Jādū, *Libya* **108 B2** 32 0N 12 0 E
Jaén, *Peru* **172 B2** 5 25 S 78 40W
Jaén, *Spain* **43 H7** 37 44N 3 43W
Jaén □, *Spain* **43 H7** 37 50N 3 30W
Jæren, *Norway* **18 F2** 58 45N 5 47 E
Jærens rev, *Norway* **18 F2** 58 45N 5 45 E
Jafarabad, *India* **92 J4** 20 52N 71 22 E
Jafène, *Africa* **110 D3** 20 35N 5 30W
Jaffa = Tel Aviv-Yafo, *Israel* **103 C3** 32 4N 34 48 E
Jaffa, C., *Australia* **128 D3** 36 58 S 139 40 E
Jaffna, *Sri Lanka* **95 K5** 9 45N 80 2 E
Jaffrey, *U.S.A.* **151 D12** 42 49N 72 2W
Jagadhri, *India* **92 D7** 30 10N 77 20 E
Jagadishpur, *India* **93 G11** 25 30N 84 21 E
Jagdalpur, *India* **94 E6** 19 3N 82 0 E
Jagersfontein, *S. Africa* **116 D4** 29 44 S 25 27 E
Jaghīn →, *Iran* **97 E8** 27 17N 57 13 E
Jagna, *Phil.* **81 G5** 9 39N 124 22 E
Jagodina, *Serbia, Yug.* **50 B5** 44 5N 21 15 E
Jagst →, *Germany* **31 F5** 49 14N 9 10 E
Jagtial, *India* **94 E4** 18 50N 79 0 E
Jaguaquara, *Brazil* **171 D4** 13 32 S 39 58W
Jaguariaíva, *Brazil* **175 A6** 24 10 S 49 50W
Jaguaribe, *Brazil* **170 C4** 5 53 S 38 37W

228 Jaguaribe

Jaguaribe →, *Brazil* **170 B4** 4 25 S 37 45W
Jaguaruana, *Brazil* **170 B4** 4 50 S 37 47W
Jagüey Grande, *Cuba* **164 B3** 22 35N 81 7W
Jagungal, Mt., *Australia* **129 D8** 36 8 S 148 22 E
Jahanabad, *India* **93 G11** 25 13N 84 59 E
Jahazpur, *India* **92 G6** 25 37N 75 17 E
Jahrom, *Iran* **97 D7** 28 30N 53 31 E
Jaicós, *Brazil* **170 C3** 7 21 S 41 8W
Jaigarh, *India* **94 F1** 17 17N 73 13 E
Jaijon, *India* **92 D7** 31 21N 76 9 E
Jailolo, *Indonesia* **82 A3** 1 5N 127 30 E
Jailolo, Selat, *Indonesia* **83 A3** 0 5N 129 5 E
Jaintiapur, *Bangla.* **90 C4** 25 8N 92 7 E
Jaipur, *Assam, India* **90 B5** 27 16N 95 24 E
Jaipur, *Raj., India* **92 F6** 27 0N 75 50 E
Jais, *India* **93 F9** 26 15N 81 32 E
Jaisalmer, *India* **92 F4** 26 55N 70 54 E
Jaisinghnagar, *India* **93 H8** 23 38N 78 34 E
Jaitaran, *India* **92 F5** 26 12N 73 56 E
Jaithari, *India* **93 H8** 23 14N 78 37 E
Jājarm, *Iran* **97 B8** 36 58N 56 27 E
Jajce, *Bos.-H.* **52 F2** 44 19N 17 17 E
Jajpur, *India* **94 D8** 20 53N 86 22 E
Jakam →, *India* **92 H6** 23 54N 74 13 E
Jakarta, *Indonesia* **84 D3** 6 9 S 106 49 E
Jakhal, *India* **92 E6** 29 48N 75 50 E
Jakhau, *India* **92 H3** 23 13N 68 43 E
Jakobshavn = Illulissat, *Greenland* **10 D5** 69 12N 51 10W
Jakobstad = Pietarsaari, *Finland* **14 E20** 63 40N 22 43 E
Jakupica, *Macedonia* **50 E5** 41 45N 21 22 E
Jal, *U.S.A.* **155 J3** 32 7N 103 12W
Jalal-Abad, *Kyrgyzstan* **65 C6** 40 56N 73 0 E
Jalālābād, *Afghan.* **91 B3** 34 30N 70 29 E
Jalalabad, *India* **93 F8** 27 41N 79 42 E
Jalalpur Jattan, *Pakistan* **92 C6** 32 38N 74 11 E
Jalama, *U.S.A.* **161 L6** 34 29N 120 29W
Jalapa, *Guatemala* **164 D2** 14 39N 89 59W
Jalapa Enríquez, *Mexico* **163 D5** 19 32N 96 55W
Jalasjärvi, *Finland* **15 E20** 62 29N 22 47 E
Jalaun, *India* **93 F8** 26 8N 79 25 E
Jalāzin, *Afghan.* **65 E2** 37 2N 64 49 E
Jaldak, *Afghan.* **91 C2** 31 58N 66 43 E
Jaldhaka →, *Bangla.* **90 B2** 26 16N 89 16 E
Jales, *Brazil* **171 F1** 20 10 S 50 33W
Jalesar, *India* **92 F8** 27 29N 78 19 E
Jaleswar, *Nepal* **93 F11** 26 38N 85 48 E
Jalgaon, *India* **94 D2** 21 0N 75 42 E
Jalībah, *Iraq* **96 D5** 30 35N 46 32 E
Jalingo, *Nigeria* **113 D7** 8 55N 11 25 E
Jalisco □, *Mexico* **162 D4** 20 0N 104 0W
Jalkot, *Pakistan* **93 B5** 35 14N 73 24 E
Jallas →, *Spain* **42 C1** 42 54N 9 8W
Jalna, *India* **94 E2** 19 48N 75 38 E
Jalón →, *Spain* **40 D3** 41 47N 1 4W
Jalor, *India* **92 G5** 25 21N 72 37 E
Jalpa, *Mexico* **162 C4** 21 38N 102 58W
Jalpaiguri, *India* **90 B2** 26 32N 88 46 E
Jālq, *Iran* **91 D1** 27 35N 62 46 E
Jaluit I., *Marshall Is.* **134 G8** 6 0N 169 30 E
Jalūlā, *Iraq* **101 E11** 34 16N 45 10 E
Jamaane = Giamama, *Somali Rep.* **120 D2** 0 4N 42 44 E
Jamaari, *Nigeria* **113 C6** 11 44N 9 53 E
Jamaica ■, *W. Indies* **164 a** 18 10N 77 30W
Jamalpur, *Bangla.* **90 C2** 24 52N 89 56 E
Jamalpur, *India* **93 G12** 25 18N 86 28 E
Jamalpurganj, *India* **93 H13** 23 2N 87 59 E
Jamanxim →, *Brazil* **173 A6** 4 43 S 56 18W
Jamari, *Brazil* **173 B5** 8 45 S 63 27W
Jamari →, *Brazil* **173 B5** 8 27 S 63 30W
Jamba, *Angola* **115 E3** 14 40 S 16 2 E
Jambewangi, *Indonesia* **79 J17** 8 17 S 114 7 E
Jambi, *Indonesia* **84 C2** 1 38 S 103 30 E
Jambi □, *Indonesia* **84 C2** 1 30 S 102 30 E
Jambusar, *India* **92 H5** 22 3N 72 51 E
James, *U.S.A.* **152 C6** 32 58N 83 29W
James →, *S. Dak., U.S.A.* **154 D6** 42 52N 97 18W
James →, *Va., U.S.A.* **148 G7** 36 56N 76 27W
James B., *Canada* **140 B3** 54 0N 80 0W
James Island, *U.S.A.* **152 C10** 32 45N 79 55W
James Ranges, *Australia* **124 D5** 24 10 S 132 30 E
James Ross I., *Antarctica* **7 C18** 63 58 S 57 50W
Jamesabad, *Pakistan* **92 G3** 25 17N 69 15 E
Jameson Land, *Greenland* **10 C8** 71 0N 23 30W
Jamesport, *U.S.A.* **156 E3** 39 58N 93 48W
Jamestown, *Australia* **128 B3** 33 10 S 138 32 E
Jamestown, *St. Helena* **9 h** 15 55 S 5 43W
Jamestown, *S. Africa* **116 E4** 31 6 S 26 45 E
Jamestown, *Ind., U.S.A.* **157 E10** 39 56N 86 38W
Jamestown, *Mo., U.S.A.* **156 F4** 38 48N 92 30W
Jamestown, *N. Dak., U.S.A.* **154 B5** 46 54N 98 42W
Jamestown, *N.Y., U.S.A.* **150 D5** 42 6N 79 14W
Jamestown, *Ohio, U.S.A.* **157 E13** 39 39N 83 33W
Jamestown, *Pa., U.S.A.* **150 E4** 41 29N 80 27W
Jamestown, *S.C., U.S.A.* **152 B10** 33 17N 79 42W
Jamīlābād, *Iran* **97 C6** 34 24N 48 28 E
Jamiltepec, *Mexico* **163 D5** 16 17N 97 49W
Jamira →, *India* **93 J13** 21 35N 88 28 E
Jämjö, *Sweden* **17 H9** 56 12N 15 49 E
Jamkhandi, *India* **94 F2** 16 30N 75 15 E
Jamkhed, *India* **94 E2** 18 43N 75 19 E
Jammalamadugu, *India* **95 G4** 14 51N 78 25 E
Jammerbugt, *Denmark* **17 G3** 57 15N 9 20 E
Jammu, *India* **92 C6** 32 43N 74 54 E
Jammu & Kashmir □, *India* **93 B7** 34 25N 77 0 E
Jamnagar, *India* **92 H4** 22 30N 70 6 E
Jamner, *India* **94 D2** 20 45N 75 52 E
Jamni →, *India* **93 G8** 25 13N 78 35 E
Jampur, *Pakistan* **91 C3** 29 39N 70 40 E
Jamrud, *Pakistan* **92 C4** 33 59N 71 24 E
Jämsä, *Finland* **15 F21** 61 53N 25 10 E
Jamshedpur, *India* **93 H12** 22 44N 86 12 E
Jamtara, *India* **93 H12** 23 59N 86 49 E
Jämtland, *Sweden* **14 E15** 63 31N 14 0 E
Jämtlands län □, *Sweden* **16 B7** 62 40N 13 50 E
Jamuna →, *Bangla.* **90 D2** 23 51N 89 45 E
Jamunamukh, *India* **90 B4** 26 6N 92 44 E
Jamurki, *Bangla.* **90 C2** 24 9N 90 2 E
Jan L., *Canada* **143 C8** 54 56N 102 55W
Jan Mayen, *Arctic* **6 B7** 71 0N 9 0W
Janakkala, *Finland* **15 F21** 60 54N 24 36 E
Janaúba, *Brazil* **171 E3** 15 48 S 43 19W
Janaucu, I., *Brazil* **170 A1** 0 30N 50 10W
Jand, *Pakistan* **92 C5** 33 30N 72 6 E
Jandaia, *Brazil* **171 E1** 17 6 S 50 7W
Jandaq, *Iran* **97 C7** 34 3N 54 22 E
Jandia, *Canary Is.* **9 e2** 28 6N 14 21W
Jandia, Pta. de, *Canary Is.* **9 e2** 28 3N 14 31W
Jandiatuba →, *Brazil* **168 D4** 3 28 S 68 42W
Jandola, *Pakistan* **92 C4** 32 20N 70 9 E
Jandowae, *Australia* **127 D5** 26 45 S 151 7 E
Jándula →, *Spain* **43 G6** 38 3N 4 6W
Jane Pk., *N.Z.* **131 F3** 45 15 S 168 20 E
Janesville, *U.S.A.* **156 B7** 42 41N 89 1W
Janga, *Ghana* **113 C4** 10 5N 1 0W
Jangamo, *Mozam.* **117 C6** 24 6 S 35 21 E
Janghai, *India* **93 G10** 25 33N 82 19 E
Jango, *Brazil* **173 E6** 20 27 S 55 29W
Jangoon, *India* **94 F4** 17 44N 79 5 E
Jangy-Bazar, *Kyrgyzstan* **65 C5** 41 40N 70 53 E
Jangy-Jol, *Kyrgyzstan* **65 C6** 41 36N 72 9 E
Janhtang Ga, *Burma* **90 B6** 26 32N 96 38 E
Jani Khel, *Afghan.* **91 B3** 32 46N 68 24 E
Janikowo, *Poland* **55 F5** 52 45N 18 7 E
Janīn, *West Bank* **103 C4** 32 28N 35 18 E
Janinà = Ioánnina □, *Greece* **48 B2** 39 39N 20 57 E
Janiuay, *Phil.* **81 F4** 10 58N 122 30 E
Janja, *Bos.-H.* **52 F4** 44 40N 19 14 E
Janjevo, *Kosovo, Yug.* **50 D5** 42 35N 21 19 E
Janjgir, *India* **93 J10** 22 1N 82 34 E
Janjina, *Croatia* **45 F14** 42 58N 17 25 E
Janjina, *Madag.* **117 C8** 20 30 S 45 50 E
Janos, *Mexico* **162 A3** 30 45N 108 10W
Jánoshalma, *Hungary* **52 D4** 46 18N 19 21 E
Jánosháza, *Hungary* **52 C2** 47 8N 17 12 E
Jánossomorja, *Hungary* **52 C2** 47 47N 17 11 E
Janów, *Poland* **55 H6** 50 44N 19 27 E
Janów Lubelski, *Poland* **55 H9** 50 48N 22 23 E
Janów Podlaski, *Poland* **55 F10** 52 11N 23 11 E
Janowiec Wielkopolski, *Poland* **55 F4** 52 45N 17 30 E
Januária, *Brazil* **171 E3** 15 25 S 44 25W
Janub Dârfûr □, *Sudan* **107 E2** 11 0N 25 0 E
Janub Kordofân □, *Sudan* **107 E3** 12 0N 30 0 E
Janubio, *Canary Is.* **9 e2** 28 56N 13 50W
Janville, *France* **27 D8** 48 10N 1 50 E
Janwada, *India* **94 E3** 18 0N 77 29 E
Janzé, *France* **26 E5** 47 55N 1 28W
Jaora, *India* **92 H6** 23 40N 75 10 E
Japan ■, *Asia* **71 G8** 36 0N 136 0 E
Japan, Sea of, *Asia* **70 E7** 40 0N 135 0 E
Japan Trench, *Pac. Oc.* **62 F18** 32 0N 142 0 E
Japen = Yapen, *Indonesia* **83 B5** 1 50 S 136 0 E
Japiim, *Brazil* **172 B3** 7 37 S 72 54W
Japla, *India* **93 G11** 24 33N 84 1 E
Japurá, *Brazil* **168 D4** 1 48 S 66 34W
Japurá →, *Brazil* **168 D4** 3 8 S 65 46W
Jaquarão, *Brazil* **175 C5** 32 34 S 53 23W
Jaqué, *Panama* **164 E4** 7 27N 78 8W
Jarābulus, *Syria* **101 D8** 36 49N 38 1 E
Jaraguá, *Brazil* **171 E2** 15 45 S 49 20W
Jaraguari, *Brazil* **173 E7** 20 9 S 54 35W
Jaraicejo, *Spain* **43 F5** 39 40N 5 49W
Jaraíz de la Vera, *Spain* **42 E5** 40 4N 5 45W
Jarama →, *Spain* **42 E7** 40 24N 3 32W
Jaramānah, *Syria* **100 F7** 33 29N 36 21 E
Jaramillo, *Argentina* **176 C3** 47 10 S 67 7W
Jarandilla, *Spain* **42 E5** 40 8N 5 39W
Jaranwala, *Pakistan* **91 C4** 31 15N 73 26 E
Jarash, *Jordan* **103 C4** 32 17N 35 54 E
Jarauçu →, *Brazil* **169 D7** 1 48 S 52 22W
Järbo, *Sweden* **16 D10** 60 43N 16 36 E
Jardas al 'Abīd, *Libya* **108 B4** 32 18N 20 59 E
Jardim, *Brazil* **174 A4** 21 28 S 56 2W
Jardín →, *Spain* **41 G2** 38 50N 2 10W
Jardine River Nat. Park, *Australia* **126 A3** 11 9 S 142 21 E
Jardines de la Reina, Arch. de los, *Cuba* **164 B4** 20 50N 78 50W
Jargalang, *China* **75 C12** 43 5N 122 55 E
Jargalant = Hovd, *Mongolia* **68 B4** 48 2N 91 37 E
Jari →, *Brazil* **169 D7** 1 9 S 51 54W
Jaria Janjail, *Bangla.* **90 C3** 25 0N 90 40 E
Jarīr, W. al →, *Si. Arabia* **96 E4** 25 38N 42 30 E
Järlåsa, *Sweden* **16 E11** 59 53N 17 12 E
Jarmen, *Germany* **30 B9** 53 54N 13 20 E
Järna, *Dalarnas, Sweden* **16 D8** 60 33N 14 26 E
Järna, *Stockholm, Sweden* **16 E11** 59 6N 17 34 E
Jarnac, *France* **28 C3** 45 40N 0 11W
Jarny, *France* **27 C12** 49 9N 5 53 E
Jaro, *Phil.* **81 F5** 11 11N 124 47 E
Jarocin, *Poland* **55 G4** 51 59N 17 29 E
Jaroměř, *Czech Rep.* **34 A8** 50 22N 15 52 E
Jarosław, *Poland* **55 H9** 50 2N 22 42 E
Järpås, *Sweden* **17 F6** 58 23N 12 57 E
Järpen, *Sweden* **16 A7** 63 21N 13 26 E
Jarqūrghon, *Uzbekistan* **65 E3** 37 31N 67 25 E
Jarrahdale, *Australia* **125 F2** 32 24 S 116 5 E
Jarrahi →, *Iran* **97 D6** 30 49N 48 48 E
Jarres, Plaine des, *Laos* **86 C4** 19 27N 103 10 E
Jarso, *Ethiopia* **107 F4** 5 15N 37 30 E
Jartai, *China* **74 E3** 39 45N 105 48 E
Jaru, *Brazil* **173 C5** 10 26 S 62 27W
Jaru →, *Brazil* **173 C5** 10 5 S 61 59W
Jarud Qi, *China* **75 B11** 44 28N 120 50 E
Järvenpää, *Finland* **15 F21** 60 29N 25 5 E
Jarvis, *Canada* **150 D4** 42 53N 80 6W
Jarvis I., *Pac. Oc.* **135 H12** 0 15 S 160 5W
Jarvorník, *Czech Rep.* **35 A10** 50 23N 17 2 E
Järvsö, *Sweden* **16 C10** 61 43N 16 10 E
Jarwa, *India* **93 F10** 27 38N 82 30 E
Jaša Tomić, *Serbia, Yug.* **52 E5** 45 26N 20 50 E
Jasaan, *Phil.* **81 G5** 8 39N 124 45 E
Jasdan, *India* **92 H4** 22 2N 71 12 E
Jashpurnagar, *India* **93 H11** 22 54N 84 9 E
Jasidih, *India* **93 G12** 24 31N 86 39 E
Jasień, *Poland* **55 G2** 51 46N 15 0 E
Jāsimīyah, *Iraq* **101 F11** 33 45N 44 41 E
Jasin, *Malaysia* **87 L4** 2 20N 102 26 E
Jāsk, *Iran* **97 E8** 25 38N 57 45 E
Jasło, *Poland* **55 J8** 49 45N 21 30 E
Jasmund, *Germany* **30 A9** 54 32N 13 35 E
Jaso, *India* **93 G9** 24 30N 80 29 E
Jason Is., *Falk. Is.* **9 f** 51 0 S 61 0W
Jasonville, *U.S.A.* **157 E9** 39 10N 87 12W
Jasper, *Alta., Canada* **142 C5** 52 55N 118 5W
Jasper, *Ont., Canada* **151 B9** 44 52N 75 57W
Jasper, *Ala., U.S.A.* **149 J2** 33 50N 87 17W
Jasper, *Fla., U.S.A.* **152 E7** 30 31N 82 57W
Jasper, *Ind., U.S.A.* **157 F10** 38 24N 86 56W
Jasper, *Tex., U.S.A.* **155 K8** 30 56N 94 1W
Jasper Nat. Park, *Canada* **142 C5** 52 50N 118 8W
Jasrasar, *India* **92 F5** 27 43N 73 49 E
Jastarnia, *Poland* **54 D5** 54 42N 18 40 E
Jastrebarsko, *Croatia* **45 C12** 45 41N 15 39 E
Jastrowie, *Poland* **54 E3** 53 26N 16 49 E
Jastrzębie Zdrój, *Poland* **55 J5** 49 57N 18 35 E
Jász-Nagykun-Szolnok □, *Hungary* **52 C5** 47 15N 20 30 E
Jászapáti, *Hungary* **52 C5** 47 32N 20 10 E
Jászárokszállás, *Hungary* **52 C4** 47 39N 19 58 E
Jászberény, *Hungary* **52 C4** 47 30N 19 55 E
Jászkisér, *Hungary* **52 C5** 47 27N 20 20 E
Jászladány, *Hungary* **52 C5** 47 23N 20 10 E
Jataí, *Brazil* **171 E1** 17 58 S 51 48W
Jatapu →, *Brazil* **169 D6** 2 13 S 58 17W
Jath, *India* **94 F2** 17 3N 75 13 E
Jati, *Pakistan* **92 G3** 24 20N 68 19 E
Jatibarang, *Indonesia* **85 D3** 6 28 S 108 18 E
Jatiluwih, *Indonesia* **79 J18** 8 23 S 115 8 E
Jatinegara, *Indonesia* **84 D3** 6 13 S 106 52 E
Játiva = Xàtiva, *Spain* **41 G4** 38 59N 0 32W
Jättendal, *Sweden* **16 C11** 61 58N 17 15 E
Jaú, *Angola* **115 F2** 15 12 S 13 31 E
Jaú, *Brazil* **175 A6** 22 10 S 48 30W
Jaú →, *Brazil* **169 D5** 1 54 S 61 26W
Jauaperí →, *Brazil* **169 D5** 1 26 S 61 35W
Jauja, *Peru* **172 C2** 11 45 S 75 15W
Jaunpur, *India* **93 G10** 25 46N 82 44 E
Jauru →, *Brazil* **173 D6** 16 22 S 57 46W
Java = Jawa, *Indonesia* **85 D4** 7 0 S 110 0 E
Java Barat □, *Indonesia* **79 G12** 7 0 S 107 0 E
Java Sea, *Indonesia* **85 C3** 4 35 S 107 15 E
Java Tengah □, *Indonesia* **79 G14** 7 0 S 110 0 E
Java Timur □, *Indonesia* **79 G15** 8 0 S 113 0 E
Java Trench, *Ind. Oc.* **84 D2** 9 0 S 105 0 E
Javadi Hills, *India* **95 H4** 12 40N 78 40 E
Javalambre, Sa. de, *Spain* **40 E4** 40 6N 1 0W
Jávea, *Spain* **41 G5** 38 48N 0 10 E
Javhlant = Ulyasutay, *Mongolia* **68 B4** 47 56N 97 28 E
Javier, I., *Chile* **176 C2** 47 5 S 74 25W
Javla, *India* **94 F2** 17 18N 75 9 E
Jawa, *Indonesia* **85 D4** 7 0 S 110 0 E
Jawad, *India* **92 G6** 24 36N 74 51 E
Jawf, W. al →, *Yemen* **98 D4** 15 50N 45 30 E
Jawhar, *India* **94 E1** 19 55N 73 14 E
Jawor, *Poland* **55 G3** 51 4N 16 11 E
Jaworzno, *Poland* **55 H6** 50 13N 19 11 E
Jaworzyna Śląska, *Poland* **55 H3** 50 55N 16 28 E
Jay, *U.S.A.* **153 E2** 30 57N 87 9W
Jay Peak, *U.S.A.* **151 B12** 44 55N 72 32W
Jaya, Puncak, *Indonesia* **83 B5** 3 57 S 137 17 E
Jayanca, *Peru* **172 B2** 6 24 S 79 50W
Jayanti, *India* **90 B2** 26 45N 89 40 E
Jayapura, *Indonesia* **83 B6** 2 28 S 140 38 E
Jayawijaya, Pegunungan, *Indonesia* **83 B5** 5 0 S 139 0 E
Jayrūd, *Syria* **100 F7** 33 49N 36 44 E
Jayton, *U.S.A.* **155 J4** 33 15N 100 34W
Jāz Mūrīān, Hāmūn-e, *Iran* **97 E8** 27 20N 58 55 E
Jazīreh-ye Shīf, *Iran* **97 D6** 29 4N 50 54 E
Jazminal, *Mexico* **162 C4** 24 56N 101 25W
Jazzīn, *Lebanon* **103 B4** 33 31N 35 35 E
Jean, *U.S.A.* **161 K11** 35 47N 115 20W
Jean Marie River, *Canada* **142 A4** 61 32N 120 38W
Jean Rabel, *Haiti* **165 C5** 19 50N 73 5W
Jeanerette, *U.S.A.* **155 L9** 29 55N 91 40W
Jeanette, Ostrov = Zhannetty, Ostrov, *Russia* **67 B16** 76 43N 158 0 E
Jeannette, *U.S.A.* **150 F5** 40 20N 79 36W
Jebāl Bārez, Kūh-e, *Iran* **97 D8** 28 30N 58 20 E
Jebba, *Nigeria* **113 D5** 9 9N 4 48 E
Jebel, Bahr el →, *Sudan* **107 F3** 9 30N 30 25 E
Jebel Dud, *Sudan* **107 E3** 13 25N 33 9 E
Jebel Qerri, *Sudan* **107 D3** 16 16N 32 50 E
Jeberos, *Peru* **172 B2** 5 15 S 76 10W
Jedburgh, *U.K.* **22 F6** 55 29N 2 33W
Jedda = Jiddah, *Si. Arabia* **98 B2** 21 29N 39 10 E
Jeddore L., *Canada* **141 C8** 48 3N 55 55W
Jedlicze, *Poland* **55 J8** 49 43N 21 40 E
Jędrzejów, *Poland* **55 H7** 50 35N 20 15 E
Jedwabne, *Poland* **55 E9** 53 17N 22 18 E
Jeetzel →, *Germany* **30 B7** 53 9N 11 3 E
Jefferson, *Ga., U.S.A.* **152 A6** 34 7N 83 35W
Jefferson, *Iowa, U.S.A.* **156 B2** 42 1N 94 23W
Jefferson, *Ohio, U.S.A.* **150 E4** 41 44N 80 46W
Jefferson, *Tex., U.S.A.* **155 J7** 32 46N 94 21W
Jefferson, *Wis., U.S.A.* **157 B8** 43 0N 88 48W
Jefferson, Mt., *Nev., U.S.A.* **158 G5** 38 51N 117 0W
Jefferson, Mt., *Oreg., U.S.A.* **158 D3** 44 41N 121 48W
Jefferson City, *Mo., U.S.A.* **156 F4** 38 34N 92 10W
Jefferson City, *Tenn., U.S.A.* **149 G4** 36 7N 83 30W
Jeffersontown, *U.S.A.* **157 F11** 38 12N 85 35W
Jeffersonville, *Ga., U.S.A.* **152 C6** 32 41N 83 20W
Jeffersonville, *Ind., U.S.A.* **157 F11** 38 17N 85 44W
Jeffersonville, *Ohio, U.S.A.* **157 E13** 39 39N 83 34W
Jeffrey City, *U.S.A.* **158 E10** 42 30N 107 49W
Jega, *Nigeria* **113 C5** 12 15N 4 23 E
Jejevo, *Solomon Is.* **133 M10** 8 6 S 159 8 E
Jēkabpils, *Latvia* **15 H21** 56 29N 25 57 E
Jekyll I., *U.S.A.* **152 D8** 31 4N 81 25W
Jelcz-Laskowice, *Poland* **55 G4** 51 2N 17 19 E
Jelenia Góra, *Poland* **55 H2** 50 50N 15 45 E
Jelgava, *Latvia* **15 H20** 56 41N 23 49 E
Jelgava □, *Latvia* **54 B10** 56 35N 23 45 E
Jelica, *Serbia, Yug.* **50 C4** 43 50N 20 17 E
Jelli, *Sudan* **107 F3** 5 25N 31 45 E
Jelšava, *Slovak Rep.* **35 C13** 48 37N 20 15 E
Jemaja, *Indonesia* **87 L5** 3 5N 105 45 E
Jemaluang, *Malaysia* **87 L4** 2 16N 103 52 E
Jember, *Indonesia* **85 D4** 8 11 S 113 41 E
Jembongan, *Malaysia* **78 C5** 6 45N 117 20 E
Jena, *Germany* **30 E7** 50 54N 11 35 E
Jena, *U.S.A.* **155 K8** 31 41N 92 8W
Jenbach, *Austria* **34 D4** 47 24N 11 47 E
Jendouba, *Tunisia* **108 A1** 36 29N 8 47 E
Jenison, *U.S.A.* **157 B11** 42 54N 85 47W
Jenkins, *U.S.A.* **148 G4** 37 10N 82 38W
Jenner, *U.S.A.* **160 G3** 38 27N 123 7W
Jennings, *Fla., U.S.A.* **152 E6** 30 36N 83 6W
Jennings, *La., U.S.A.* **155 K8** 30 13N 92 40W
Jennings, *Mo., U.S.A.* **156 F6** 38 43N 90 16W
Jensen Beach, *U.S.A.* **153 H9** 27 15N 80 14W
Jepara, *Indonesia* **85 D3** 7 40 S 109 14 E
Jeparit, *Australia* **128 D5** 36 8 S 142 1 E
Jequié, *Brazil* **171 D3** 13 51 S 40 5W
Jequitaí →, *Brazil* **171 E3** 17 4 S 44 50W
Jequitinhonha, *Brazil* **171 E3** 16 30 S 41 0W
Jequitinhonha →, *Brazil* **171 E4** 15 51 S 38 53W
Jerada, *Morocco* **111 B4** 34 17N 2 10W
Jerantut, *Malaysia* **87 L4** 3 56N 102 22 E
Jerejak, Pulau, *Malaysia* **87 c** 5 19N 100 19 E
Jérémie, *Haiti* **165 C5** 18 40N 74 10W
Jeremoabo, *Brazil* **170 D4** 10 4 S 38 21W
Jerez, Punta, *Mexico* **163 C5** 22 58N 97 40W
Jerez de García Salinas, *Mexico* **162 C4** 22 39N 103 0W
Jerez de la Frontera, *Spain* **43 J4** 36 41N 6 7W
Jerez de los Caballeros, *Spain* **43 G4** 38 20N 6 45W
Jericho = El Arīḥā, *West Bank* **103 D4** 31 52N 35 27 E
Jericho, *Australia* **126 C4** 23 38 S 146 6 E
Jerichow, *Germany* **30 C8** 52 30N 12 1 E
Jericho Springs, *U.S.A.* **156 G2** 37 37N 94 1W
Jerid, Chott el = Djerid, Chott, *Tunisia* **108 B1** 33 42N 8 30 E
Jerilderie, *Australia* **129 C6** 35 20 S 145 41 E
Jermyn, *U.S.A.* **151 E9** 41 31N 75 31W
Jerome, *U.S.A.* **158 E6** 42 44N 114 31W
Jerramungup, *Australia* **125 F2** 33 55 S 118 55 E
Jersey, *U.K.* **21 H5** 49 11N 2 7W
Jersey City, *U.S.A.* **151 F10** 40 44N 74 4W
Jersey Shore, *U.S.A.* **150 E7** 41 12N 77 15W
Jerseyville, *U.S.A.* **156 E6** 39 7N 90 20W
Jerumenha, *Brazil* **170 C3** 7 5 S 43 30W
Jerusalem, *Israel* **103 D4** 31 47N 35 10 E
Jervis B., *Australia* **129 C9** 35 8 S 150 46 E
Jervis Inlet, *Canada* **142 C4** 50 0N 123 57W
Jerzu, *Italy* **46 C2** 39 47N 9 31 E
Jesenice, *Slovenia* **45 B11** 46 28N 14 3 E
Jeseník, *Czech Rep.* **35 A10** 50 14N 17 8 E
Jesenké, *Slovak Rep.* **35 C13** 48 20N 20 10 E
Jesi = Iesi, *Italy* **45 E10** 43 31N 13 14 E
Jesselton = Kota Kinabalu, *Malaysia* **85 A5** 6 0N 116 4 E
Jessheim, *Norway* **18 D8** 60 9N 11 10 E
Jessnitz, *Germany* **30 D8** 51 40N 12 18 E
Jessore, *Bangla.* **90 D2** 23 10N 89 10 E
Jessup L., *U.S.A.* **153 G8** 28 43N 81 14W
Jesup, *Ga., U.S.A.* **152 D8** 31 36N 81 53W
Jesup, *Iowa, U.S.A.* **156 B4** 42 29N 92 4W
Jesús, *Peru* **172 B2** 7 15 S 78 25W
Jesús Carranza, *Mexico* **163 D5** 17 28N 95 1W
Jesús María, *Argentina* **174 C3** 30 59 S 64 5W
Jetmore, *U.S.A.* **155 F5** 38 4N 99 54W
Jetpur, *India* **92 J4** 21 45N 70 10 E
Jeumont, *France* **27 B11** 50 18N 4 6 E
Jevnaker, *Norway* **15 F14** 60 15N 10 26 E
Jewell, *U.S.A.* **156 B3** 42 20N 93 38W
Jewett, *U.S.A.* **150 F3** 40 22N 81 2W
Jewett City, *U.S.A.* **151 E13** 41 36N 72 0W
Jeyḥūnābād, *Iran* **97 C6** 34 58N 48 59 E
Jeypore, *India* **94 E6** 18 50N 82 38 E
Jeziorak, Jezioro, *Poland* **54 E6** 53 40N 19 35 E
Jeziorany, *Poland* **54 E7** 53 58N 20 46 E
Jeziorka →, *Poland* **55 F8** 52 8N 21 9 E
Jha Jha, *India* **93 G12** 24 46N 86 22 E
Jhaarkand = Jharkhand □, *India* **93 H11** 24 0N 85 50 E
Jhabua, *India* **92 H6** 22 46N 74 36 E
Jhajjar, *India* **92 E7** 28 37N 76 42 E
Jhal, *Pakistan* **92 E2** 28 17N 67 27 E
Jhal Jhao, *Pakistan* **91 D2** 26 20N 65 35 E
Jhalakati, *Bangla.* **90 D3** 22 39N 90 12 E
Jhalawar, *India* **92 G7** 24 40N 76 10 E
Jhalida, *India* **93 H11** 23 22N 85 58 E
Jhalrapatan, *India* **92 G7** 24 33N 76 10 E
Jhang Maghiana, *Pakistan* **91 C4** 31 15N 72 22 E
Jhansi, *India* **93 G8** 25 30N 78 36 E
Jhargram, *India* **93 H12** 22 27N 86 59 E
Jharia, *India* **93 H12** 23 45N 86 26 E
Jharkhand □, *India* **93 H11** 24 0N 85 50 E
Jharsuguda, *India* **94 D7** 21 56N 84 5 E
Jhelum, *Pakistan* **91 B4** 33 0N 73 45 E
Jhelum →, *Pakistan* **92 D5** 31 20N 72 10 E
Jhilmilli, *India* **93 H10** 23 24N 82 51 E
Jhudo, *Pakistan* **92 G3** 24 58N 69 18 E
Jhunjhunu, *India* **92 E6** 28 10N 75 30 E
Ji-Paraná, *Brazil* **173 C5** 10 50 S 61 58W
Ji Xian, *Hebei, China* **74 F8** 37 35N 115 30 E
Ji Xian, *Henan, China* **74 G8** 35 22N 114 5 E
Ji Xian, *Shanxi, China* **74 F6** 36 7N 110 40 E
Jia Xian, *Henan, China* **74 H7** 33 59N 113 12 E
Jia Xian, *Shaanxi, China* **74 E6** 38 12N 110 28 E
Jiading, *China* **77 B13** 31 22N 121 15 E
Jiahe, *China* **77 E9** 25 38N 112 19 E
Jialing Jiang →, *China* **76 C6** 29 30N 106 20 E
Jiamusi, *China* **69 B8** 46 40N 130 26 E
Ji'an, *Jiangxi, China* **77 D10** 27 6N 114 59 E
Ji'an, *Jilin, China* **75 D14** 41 5N 126 10 E
Jianchang, *China* **75 D11** 40 55N 120 35 E
Jianchangying, *China* **75 D10** 40 10N 118 50 E
Jianchuan, *China* **76 D2** 26 38N 99 55 E
Jiande, *China* **77 C12** 29 23N 119 15 E
Jiang'an, *China* **76 C5** 28 40N 105 3 E
Jiangbei, *China* **76 C6** 29 40N 106 34 E
Jiangcheng, *China* **76 F3** 22 36N 101 52 E
Jiangchuan, *China* **76 E4** 24 8N 102 39 E
Jiangdi, *China* **76 D4** 26 57N 103 37 E
Jiangdu, *China* **77 A12** 32 27N 119 36 E
Jiange, *China* **76 A5** 32 4N 105 32 E
Jianghua, *China* **77 E8** 25 0N 111 47 E
Jiangjin, *China* **76 C6** 29 14N 106 14 E
Jiangkou, *China* **76 D7** 27 40N 108 49 E
Jiangle, *China* **77 D11** 26 42N 117 23 E
Jiangling, *China* **77 B9** 30 25N 112 12 E
Jiangmen, *China* **77 F9** 22 32N 113 0 E
Jiangning, *China* **77 B12** 31 55N 118 50 E
Jiangshan, *China* **77 C12** 28 40N 118 37 E
Jiangsu □, *China* **75 H11** 33 0N 120 0 E
Jiangxi □, *China* **77 D11** 27 30N 116 0 E
Jiangyan, *China* **77 A13** 32 30N 120 7 E
Jiangyin, *China* **77 B13** 31 54N 120 17 E
Jiangyong, *China* **77 E8** 25 20N 111 22 E
Jiangyou, *China* **76 B5** 31 44N 104 43 E
Jianhe, *China* **76 D7** 26 37N 108 31 E
Jianli, *China* **77 C9** 29 46N 112 56 E
Jianning, *China* **77 D11** 26 50N 116 50 E
Jian'ou, *China* **77 D12** 27 3N 118 17 E
Jianshi, *China* **76 B7** 30 37N 109 38 E
Jianshui, *China* **76 F4** 23 36N 102 43 E
Jianyang, *Fujian, China* **77 D12** 27 20N 118 5 E
Jianyang, *Sichuan, China* **76 B5** 30 24N 104 33 E
Jiao Xian = Jiaozhou, *China* **75 F11** 36 18N 120 1 E
Jiaohe, *Hebei, China* **74 E9** 38 2N 116 20 E
Jiaohe, *Jilin, China* **75 C14** 43 40N 127 22 E
Jiaojiang, *China* **77 C13** 28 40N 121 24 E
Jiaoling, *China* **77 E11** 24 41N 116 12 E
Jiaozhou, *China* **75 F11** 36 18N 120 1 E
Jiaozhou Wan, *China* **75 F11** 36 5N 120 10 E
Jiaozuo, *China* **74 G7** 35 16N 113 12 E
Jiashan, *China* **77 B13** 30 55N 120 55 E
Jiashi, *China* **65 D8** 39 29N 76 39 E
Jiawang, *China* **75 G9** 34 28N 117 26 E
Jiaxiang, *China* **74 G9** 35 25N 116 20 E
Jiaxing, *China* **77 B13** 30 49N 120 45 E
Jiayi = Chiai, *Taiwan* **77 F13** 23 29N 120 25 E
Jiayu, *China* **77 C9** 29 55N 113 55 E
Jibão, Serra do, *Brazil* **171 D3** 14 48 S 45 0W
Jibiya, *Nigeria* **113 C6** 13 5N 7 12 E
Jibou, *Romania* **53 C8** 47 15N 23 17 E
Jibuti = Djibouti ■, *Africa* **107 E5** 12 0N 43 0 E
Jicarón, I., *Panama* **164 E3** 7 10N 81 50W
Jičín, *Czech Rep.* **34 A8** 50 25N 15 28 E
Jiddah, *Si. Arabia* **98 B2** 21 29N 39 10 E
Jido, *India* **90 A5** 29 2N 94 58 E
Jieshou, *China* **74 H8** 33 18N 115 22 E
Jiexiu, *China* **74 F6** 37 2N 111 55 E
Jieyang, *China* **77 F11** 23 35N 116 21 E
Jigawa □, *Nigeria* **113 C6** 12 0N 9 45 E
Jiggalong, *Australia* **124 D3** 23 21 S 120 47 E
Jigni, *India* **93 G8** 25 45N 79 25 E
Jihlava, *Czech Rep.* **34 B8** 49 28N 15 35 E
Jihlava →, *Czech Rep.* **35 C9** 48 55N 16 36 E
Jihočeský □, *Czech Rep.* **34 B7** 49 8N 14 35 E
Jihomoravský □, *Czech Rep.* **35 B9** 49 5N 16 30 E
Jijel, *Algeria* **111 A6** 36 52N 5 50 E
Jijiga, *Ethiopia* **120 C2** 9 20N 42 50 E
Jikamshi, *Nigeria* **113 C6** 12 12N 7 45 E
Jikau, *Sudan* **107 F3** 8 28N 33 47 E
Jilib = Gelib, *Somali Rep.* **120 D2** 0 29N 42 46 E
Jilin, *China* **75 C14** 43 44N 126 30 E
Jilin □, *China* **75 C14** 44 0N 127 0 E
Jiloca →, *Spain* **40 D3** 41 21N 1 39W
Jilong = Chilung, *Taiwan* **77 E13** 25 3N 121 45 E
Jim Thorpe, *U.S.A.* **151 F9** 40 52N 75 44W
Jima, *Ethiopia* **107 F4** 7 40N 36 47 E
Jimbaran, Teluk, *Indonesia* **79 K18** 8 46 S 115 9 E
Jimbolia, *Romania* **52 E5** 45 47N 20 43 E
Jimena de la Frontera, *Spain* **43 J5** 36 27N 5 24W
Jiménez, *Mexico* **162 B4** 27 10N 104 54W
Jimenez, *Phil.* **81 G4** 8 20N 123 50 E
Jimo, *China* **75 F11** 36 23N 120 30 E
Jin, Kepulauan, *Indonesia* **83 C4** 6 50 S 134 40 E
Jin Jiang →, *China* **77 C10** 28 24N 115 48 E
Jin Xian = Jinzhou, *China* **74 E8** 38 2N 115 2 E
Jin Xian, *China* **75 E11** 38 55N 121 42 E
Jinan, *China* **74 F9** 36 38N 117 1 E
Jinchang, *China* **68 C5** 38 30N 102 10 E
Jincheng, *China* **74 G7** 35 29N 112 50 E
Jinchuan, *China* **76 B4** 31 30N 102 3 E
Jind, *India* **92 E7** 29 19N 76 22 E
Jindabyne, *Australia* **129 D8** 36 25 S 148 35 E
Jinding, *China* **69 G10** 22 22N 113 33 E
Jindřichův Hradec, *Czech Rep.* **34 B8** 49 10N 15 2 E
Jing He →, *China* **74 G5** 34 27N 109 4 E
Jing Shan, *China* **77 B8** 31 20N 111 35 E
Jing Xian, *China* **77 B12** 30 38N 118 25 E
Jing'an, *China* **77 C10** 28 50N 115 17 E
Jingbian, *China* **74 F5** 37 20N 108 30 E
Jingchuan, *China* **74 G4** 35 20N 107 20 E
Jingde, *China* **77 B12** 30 15N 118 27 E

Kai, Kepulauan 229

Jingdezhen, *China* 77 C11 29 20N 117 11 E
Jingdong, *China* 76 E3 24 23N 100 47 E
Jinggangshan, *China* 77 D10 26 58N 114 15 E
Jinggu, *China* 76 F3 23 35N 100 41 E
Jinghai, *China* 74 E9 38 55N 116 55 E
Jinghong, *China* 76 G3 22 0N 100 45 E
Jingjiang, *China* 77 A13 32 2N 120 16 E
Jingle, *China* 74 E6 38 20N 111 55 E
Jingmen, *China* 77 B9 31 0N 112 10 E
Jingning, *China* 74 G3 35 30N 105 43 E
Jingpo Hu, *China* 75 C15 43 55N 128 55 E
Jingshan, *China* 77 B9 31 1N 113 7 E
Jingtai, *China* 74 F3 37 10N 104 6 E
Jingxi, *China* 76 F6 23 8N 106 27 E
Jingxing, *China* 74 E8 38 2N 114 8 E
Jingyang, *China* 74 G5 34 30N 108 50 E
Jingyu, *China* 75 C14 42 25N 126 45 E
Jingyuan, *China* 74 F3 36 30N 104 40 E
Jingzhou, *China* 76 D7 26 33N 109 40 E
Jingziguan, *China* 74 H6 33 15N 111 0 E
Jinhua, *China* 77 C12 29 8N 119 38 E
Jining, *Nei Monggol Zizhiqu, China* 74 D7 41 5N 113 0 E
Jining, *Shandong, China* 74 G9 35 22N 116 34 E
Jinja, *Uganda* 118 B3 0 25N 33 12 E
Jinjang, *Malaysia* 87 L3 3 13N 101 39 E
Jinji, *China* 74 F4 37 58N 106 8 E
Jinjiang, *Fujian, China* 77 E12 24 43N 118 33 E
Jinjiang, *Yunnan, China* 76 D3 26 14N 100 34 E
Jinjini, *Ghana* 112 D4 7 26N 2 42W
Jinkou, *China* 77 B10 30 20N 114 8 E
Jinkouhe, *China* 76 C4 29 18N 103 4 E
Jinmen Dao, *China* 77 E12 24 25N 118 25 E
Jinning, *China* 76 E4 24 38N 102 38 E
Jinotega, *Nic.* 164 D2 13 6N 85 59W
Jinotepe, *Nic.* 164 D2 11 50N 86 10W
Jinping, *Guizhou, China* 76 D7 26 41N 109 10 E
Jinping, *Yunnan, China* 76 F4 22 45N 103 18 E
Jinsha, *China* 76 D6 27 29N 106 12 E
Jinsha Jiang →, *China* 76 C5 28 50N 104 36 E
Jinshan, *China* 77 B13 30 54N 121 10 E
Jinshi, *China* 77 C8 29 40N 111 50 E
Jintan, *China* 77 B12 31 42N 119 36 E
Jintotolo Channel, *Phil.* 81 F4 11 48N 123 5 E
Jintur, *India* 94 E3 19 37N 76 42 E
Jinxi, *Jiangxi, China* 77 D11 27 56N 116 45 E
Jinxi, *Liaoning, China* 75 D11 40 52N 120 50 E
Jinxian, *China* 77 C11 28 26N 116 17 E
Jinxiang, *China* 74 G9 35 5N 116 22 E
Jinyang, *China* 76 D4 27 28N 103 5 E
Jinyun, *China* 77 C13 28 35N 120 5 E
Jinzhai, *China* 77 B10 31 40N 115 53 E
Jinzhou, *Hebei, China* 74 E8 38 2N 115 2 E
Jinzhou, *Liaoning, China* 75 D11 41 5N 121 3 E
Jiparaná →, *Brazil* 173 B5 8 3 S 62 52W
Jipijapa, *Ecuador* 168 D1 1 0 S 80 40W
Jiquilpan, *Mexico* 162 D4 19 57N 102 42W
Jishan, *China* 74 G6 35 34N 110 58 E
Jishou, *China* 76 C7 28 21N 109 43 E
Jishui, *China* 77 D10 27 12N 115 8 E
Jisr ash Shughūr, *Syria* 100 E7 35 49N 36 18 E
Jitarning, *Australia* 125 F2 32 48 S 117 57 E
Jitra, *Malaysia* 87 J3 6 16N 100 25 E
Jiu →, *Romania* 53 G8 43 47N 23 48 E
Jiudengkou, *China* 74 E4 39 56N 106 40 E
Jiujiang, *Guangdong, China* 77 F9 22 50N 113 0 E
Jiujiang, *Jiangxi, China* 77 C10 29 42N 115 58 E
Jiuling Shan, *China* 77 C10 28 40N 114 40 E
Jiulong = Kowloon, *H.K.* 77 F10 22 19N 114 11 E
Jiulong, *China* 76 C3 28 57N 101 31 E
Jiutai, *China* 75 B13 44 10N 125 50 E
Jiuxincheng, *China* 74 E8 39 17N 115 59 E
Jiuyuhang, *China* 77 B12 30 18N 119 56 E
Jiwa, *U.A.E.* 99 B6 23 0N 54 10 E
Jiwani, Ras, *Pakistan* 91 D1 25 1N 61 44 E
Jixi, *Anhui, China* 77 B12 30 5N 118 34 E
Jixi, *Heilongjiang, China* 75 B16 45 20N 130 50 E
Jiyang, *China* 75 F9 37 0N 117 12 E
Jiyuan, *China* 74 G7 35 7N 112 57 E
Jiz', W. →, *Yemen* 99 C6 16 12N 52 14 E
Jīzān, *Si. Arabia* 98 C3 17 0N 42 20 E
Jize, *China* 74 F8 36 54N 114 56 E
Jizera →, *Czech Rep.* 34 A7 50 10N 14 43 E
Jizl, W. →, *Si. Arabia* 106 B4 25 39N 38 25 E
Jizl, Wādī al, *Si. Arabia* 96 E3 25 39N 38 25 E
Jizō-Zaki, *Japan* 72 B5 35 34N 133 20 E
Jizzakh, *Uzbekistan* 66 E7 40 6N 67 50 E
Joaçaba, *Brazil* 175 B5 27 5 S 51 31W
Joaíma, *Brazil* 171 E3 16 39 S 41 2W
Joal Fadiout, *Senegal* 112 C1 14 9N 16 50W
João Amaro, *Brazil* 171 D3 12 46 S 40 22W
João Câmara, *Brazil* 170 C4 5 32 S 35 48W
João Pessoa, *Brazil* 170 C5 7 10 S 34 52W
João Pinheiro, *Brazil* 171 E2 17 45 S 46 10W
Joaquim Távora, *Brazil* 171 F2 23 30 S 49 58W
Joaquín V. González, *Argentina* 174 B3 25 10 S 64 0W
Jobat, *India* 92 H6 22 25N 74 34 E
Jobourg, Nez de, *France* 26 C5 49 41N 1 57W
Jódar, *Spain* 43 H7 37 50N 3 21W
Jodhpur, *India* 92 F5 26 23N 73 8 E
Jodiya, *India* 92 H4 22 42N 70 18 E
Joensuu, *Finland* 56 B4 62 37N 29 49 E
Jōetsu, *Japan* 71 F9 37 12N 138 10 E
Jœuf, *France* 27 C12 49 12N 6 0 E
Jofane, *Mozam.* 117 C5 21 15 S 34 18 E
Jogbani, *India* 93 F12 26 25N 87 15 E
Jõgeva, *Estonia* 15 G22 58 45N 26 24 E
Jogjakarta = Yogyakarta, *Indonesia* 85 D4 7 49 S 110 22 E
Jōhana, *Japan* 73 A8 36 30N 136 57 E
Johannesburg, *S. Africa* 117 D4 26 10 S 28 2 E
Johannesburg, *U.S.A.* 161 K9 35 22N 117 38W
Johansfors, *Sweden* 17 H9 56 42N 15 32 E
Johilla →, *India* 93 H9 23 37N 81 14 E
John Crow Mts., *Jamaica* 164 a 18 5N 76 25W
John Day, *U.S.A.* 158 D4 44 25N 118 57W
John Day →, *U.S.A.* 158 D3 45 44N 120 39W
John D'Or Prairie, *Canada* 142 B5 58 30N 115 8W
John H. Kerr Reservoir, *U.S.A.* 149 G6 36 36N 78 18W
John o' Groats, *U.K.* 22 C5 58 38N 3 4W
Johnnie, *U.S.A.* 161 J10 36 25N 116 5W
Johns I., *U.S.A.* 152 C9 32 40N 80 10W
John's Ra., *Australia* 126 C1 21 55 S 133 23 E
Johnson, *Kans., U.S.A.* 155 G4 37 34N 101 45W
Johnson, *Vt., U.S.A.* 151 B12 44 38N 72 41W
Johnson City, *N.Y., U.S.A.* 151 D9 42 7N 75 58W
Johnson City, *Tenn., U.S.A.* 149 G4 36 19N 82 21W
Johnson City, *Tex., U.S.A.* 155 K5 30 17N 98 25W
Johnsonburg, *U.S.A.* 150 E6 41 29N 78 41W
Johnsondale, *U.S.A.* 161 K8 35 58N 118 32W
Johnson's Crossing, *Canada* 142 A2 60 29N 133 18W
Johnsonville, *N.Z.* 130 H3 41 13 S 174 48 E
Johnston, *U.S.A.* 152 B8 33 50N 81 48W
Johnston, L., *Australia* 125 F3 32 25 S 120 30 E
Johnston City, *U.S.A.* 156 G8 37 49N 88 56W
Johnston Falls = Mambilima Falls, *Zambia* 119 E2 10 31 S 28 45 E
Johnston I., *Pac. Oc.* 135 F11 17 10N 169 8W
Johnstone Str., *Canada* 142 C3 50 28N 126 0W
Johnstown, *N.Y., U.S.A.* 151 C10 43 0N 74 22W
Johnstown, *Ohio, U.S.A.* 150 F2 40 9N 82 41W
Johnstown, *Pa., U.S.A.* 150 F6 40 20N 78 55W
Johor □, *Malaysia* 84 B2 2 5N 103 20 E
Johor, Selat, *Asia* 87 d 1 28N 103 47 E
Johor Baharu, *Malaysia* 87 d 1 28N 103 46 E
Jõhvi, *Estonia* 15 G22 59 22N 27 27 E
Joigny, *France* 27 E10 47 58N 3 20 E
Joinville, *Brazil* 175 B6 26 15 S 48 55W
Joinville, *France* 27 D12 48 27N 5 10 E
Joinville I., *Antarctica* 7 C18 65 0 S 55 30W
Jojutla, *Mexico* 163 D5 18 37N 99 11W
Jokkmokk, *Sweden* 14 C18 66 35N 19 50 E
Jökulsá á Bru →, *Iceland* 11 B12 65 40N 14 16W
Jökulsá á Fjöllum →, *Iceland* 11 A10 66 10N 16 30W
Jolfā, *Āzarbājān-e Sharqī, Iran* 101 C11 38 57N 45 38 E
Jolfā, *Eşfahan, Iran* 97 C6 32 58N 51 37 E
Joliet, *U.S.A.* 157 C8 41 32N 88 5W
Joliette, *Canada* 140 C5 46 3N 73 24W
Jolo, *Phil.* 81 H3 6 0N 121 0 E
Jolo Group, *Phil.* 81 J3 6 0N 121 9 E
Jolon, *U.S.A.* 160 K5 35 58N 121 9W
Jølstravatnet, *Norway* 18 C3 61 32N 6 23 E
Jomalig I., *Phil.* 80 D4 14 42N 122 22 E
Jombang, *Indonesia* 85 D4 7 33 S 112 14 E
Jomda, *China* 76 B2 31 28N 98 12 E
Jona, *Switz.* 33 B7 47 14N 8 51 E
Jonava, *Lithuania* 15 J21 55 8N 24 12 E
Jondal, *Norway* 18 D3 60 16N 6 15 E
Jones, *Phil.* 80 C3 16 33N 121 42 E
Jones Sound, *Canada* 6 B3 76 0N 85 0W
Jonesboro, *Ark., U.S.A.* 155 H9 35 50N 90 42W
Jonesboro, *Ga., U.S.A.* 152 B5 33 31N 84 22W
Jonesboro, *La., U.S.A.* 155 J8 32 15N 92 43W
Jonesburg, *U.S.A.* 156 F5 38 51N 91 18W
Jonesville, *Ind., U.S.A.* 157 E11 39 5N 85 54W
Jonesville, *Mich., U.S.A.* 157 C12 41 59N 84 40W
Jong →, *S. Leone* 112 D2 7 32N 12 23W
Jonglei, *Sudan* 107 F3 6 25N 30 50 E
Jonglei □, *Sudan* 107 F3 7 30N 32 30 E
Joniškis, *Lithuania* 15 H20 56 13N 23 35 E
Jönköping, *Sweden* 17 G8 57 45N 14 8 E
Jönköpings län □, *Sweden* 17 G8 57 30N 14 30 E
Jonquière, *Canada* 141 C5 48 27N 71 14W
Jonsered, *Sweden* 17 G6 57 45N 12 10 E
Jonzac, *France* 28 C3 45 27N 0 28W
Joplin, *U.S.A.* 155 G7 37 6N 94 31W
Jora, *India* 92 F6 26 20N 77 49 E
Jordan, *Phil.* 81 F4 10 40N 122 35 E
Jordan, *Mont., U.S.A.* 158 C10 47 19N 106 55W
Jordan, *N.Y., U.S.A.* 151 C8 43 4N 76 29W
Jordan ■, *Asia* 103 E5 31 0N 36 0 E
Jordan →, *Asia* 103 D4 31 48N 35 32 E
Jordan Valley, *U.S.A.* 158 E5 42 59N 117 3W
Jordânia, *Brazil* 171 E3 15 55 S 40 11W
Jordanów, *Poland* 55 J6 49 41N 19 49 E
Jordet, *Norway* 18 C9 61 25N 12 8 E
Jorge, C., *Chile* 176 D1 51 40 S 75 35W
Jorgen Brønlund Fjord, *Greenland* 10 A8 82 30N 29 0W
Jorhat, *India* 90 B5 26 45N 94 12 E
Jorm, *Afghan.* 65 E5 36 50N 70 52 E
Jörn, *Sweden* 14 D19 65 4N 20 1 E
Jorong, *Indonesia* 85 C4 3 58 S 114 56 E
Jørpeland, *Norway* 15 G11 59 3N 6 1 E
Jorquera →, *Chile* 174 B2 28 3 S 69 58W
Jos, *Nigeria* 113 D6 9 53N 8 51 E
Jos Plateau, *Nigeria* 113 D6 9 55N 9 0 E
Jošanička Banja, *Serbia, Yug.* 50 C4 43 24N 20 47 E
Jose Abad Santos, *Phil.* 81 J5 5 55N 125 39 E
José Batlle y Ordóñez, *Uruguay* 175 C4 33 20 S 55 10W
José de San Martín, *Argentina* 176 B2 44 4 S 70 26W
Jose Panganiban, *Phil.* 80 D4 14 17N 122 41 E
Joseni, *Romania* 53 D10 46 42N 25 29 E
Joseph, L., *Nfld., Canada* 141 B6 52 45N 65 18W
Joseph, L., *Ont., Canada* 150 A5 45 10N 79 44W
Joseph Bonaparte G., *Australia* 124 B4 14 35 S 128 50 E
Joshinath, *India* 93 D8 30 34N 79 34 E
Joshua Tree, *U.S.A.* 161 L10 34 8N 116 19W
Joshua Tree Nat. Park, *U.S.A.* 161 M10 33 55N 116 0W
Josselin, *France* 26 E4 47 57N 2 33W
Jost Van Dyke, *Br. Virgin Is.* 165 e 18 29N 64 47W
Jostedal, *Norway* 18 C4 61 35N 7 15 E
Jostedalsbreen, *Norway* 15 F12 61 40N 6 59 E
Jotunheimen, *Norway* 15 F13 61 35N 8 25 E
Joubertberge, *Namibia* 116 B1 18 30 S 14 0 E
Joué-lès-Tours, *France* 26 E7 47 21N 0 40 E
Jourdanton, *U.S.A.* 155 L5 28 55N 98 33W
Joutseno, *Finland* 58 B5 61 7N 28 31 E
Jovellanos, *Cuba* 164 B3 22 40N 81 10W
Jovellar, *Phil.* 80 E4 13 4N 123 36 E
Jowai, *India* 90 C4 25 26N 92 12 E
Jowhar = Giohar, *Somali Rep.* 120 D3 2 48N 45 30 E
Jowzjān □, *Afghan.* 65 E3 36 10N 66 0 E
Joyeuse, *France* 29 D8 44 29N 4 16 E
Jōyō, *Japan* 73 C7 34 50N 135 47 E
Józefów, *Lubelskie, Poland* 55 H10 50 28N 23 2 E
Józefów, *Mazowieckie, Poland* 55 F8 52 10N 21 11 E
Ju Xian, *China* 75 F10 36 35N 118 20 E
Juan Aldama, *Mexico* 162 C4 24 20N 103 23W
Juan Bautista Alberdi, *Argentina* 174 C3 34 26 S 61 48W
Juan de Fuca Str., *Canada* 160 B3 48 15N 124 0W
Juan de Nova, *Ind. Oc.* 117 B7 17 3 S 43 45 E
Juan Fernández, Arch. de, *Pac. Oc.* 135 L20 33 50 S 80 0W
Juan José Castelli, *Argentina* 174 B3 25 27 S 60 57W
Juan L. Lacaze, *Uruguay* 174 C4 34 26 S 57 25W
Juanjuí, *Peru* 172 B2 7 10 S 76 45W
Juankoski, *Finland* 14 E23 63 3N 28 19 E
Juara, *Brazil* 173 C6 11 20 S 57 25W
Juárez, *Argentina* 174 D4 37 40 S 59 43W
Juárez, *Mexico* 161 N11 32 20N 115 57W
Juárez, Sierra de, *Mexico* 162 A1 32 0N 116 0W
Juatinga, Ponta de, *Brazil* 171 F3 23 17 S 44 30W
Juàzeiro, *Brazil* 170 C3 9 30 S 40 30W
Juàzeiro do Norte, *Brazil* 170 C4 7 10 S 39 18W
Juba = Giuba →, *Somali Rep.* 120 D2 1 30N 42 35 E
Juba, *Sudan* 107 G3 4 50N 31 35 E
Jubayl, *Lebanon* 103 A4 34 5N 35 39 E
Jubbah, *Si. Arabia* 96 D4 28 2N 40 56 E
Jubbal, *India* 92 D7 31 5N 77 40 E
Jubbulpore = Jabalpur, *India* 93 H8 23 9N 79 58 E
Jübek, *Germany* 30 A5 54 33N 9 22 E
Juba, *Russia* 61 H4 44 19N 38 48 E
Jubilee L., *Australia* 125 E4 29 0 S 126 50 E
Juby, C., *Morocco* 110 C2 28 0N 12 59W
Júcar = Xúquer →, *Spain* 41 F4 39 5N 0 10W
Júcaro, *Cuba* 164 B4 21 37N 78 51W
Juchitán, *Mexico* 163 D5 16 27N 95 5W
Judaberg, *Norway* 18 E2 59 10N 5 51 E
Judaea = Har Yehuda, *Israel* 103 D3 31 35N 34 57 E
Judenburg, *Austria* 34 D7 47 12N 14 38 E
Judith →, *U.S.A.* 158 C9 47 44N 109 39W
Judith, Pt., *U.S.A.* 151 E13 41 22N 71 29W
Judith Gap, *U.S.A.* 158 C9 46 41N 109 45W
Juelsminde, *Denmark* 17 J4 55 43N 10 1 E
Jufari →, *Brazil* 169 D5 1 13 S 62 0W
Jugoslavia = Yugoslavia ■, *Europe* 50 C4 43 20N 20 0 E
Juigalpa, *Nic.* 164 D2 12 6N 85 26W
Juillac, *France* 28 C5 45 20N 1 19 E
Juist, *Germany* 30 B2 53 40N 6 59 E
Juiz de Fora, *Brazil* 171 F3 21 43 S 43 19W
Jujuy □, *Argentina* 174 A2 23 20 S 65 40W
Julesburg, *U.S.A.* 154 E3 40 59N 102 16W
Juli, *Peru* 172 D4 16 10 S 69 25W
Julia Cr. →, *Australia* 126 C3 20 0 S 141 11 E
Julia Creek, *Australia* 126 C3 20 39 S 141 44 E
Juliaca, *Peru* 172 D3 15 25 S 70 10W
Julian, *U.S.A.* 161 M10 33 4N 116 38W
Julian Alps = Julijske Alpe, *Slovenia* 45 B11 46 15N 14 1 E
Julian L., *Canada* 140 B4 54 25N 77 57W
Julianatop, *Surinam* 169 C6 3 40N 56 30W
Julianehåb = Qaqortoq, *Greenland* 10 E6 60 43N 46 0W
Jülich, *Germany* 30 E2 50 55N 6 22 E
Julierpass, *Switz.* 33 D9 46 28N 9 32 E
Juliette, L., *U.S.A.* 152 B6 33 2N 83 50W
Julijske Alpe, *Slovenia* 45 B11 46 15N 14 1 E
Julimes, *Mexico* 162 B3 28 25N 105 27W
Jullundur, *India* 92 D6 31 20N 75 40 E
Julu, *China* 74 F8 37 15N 115 2 E
Jumbo, *Zimbabwe* 119 F3 17 30 S 30 58 E
Jumbo Pk., *U.S.A.* 161 J12 36 12N 114 11W
Jumentos Cays, *Bahamas* 164 B4 23 0N 75 40W
Jumilla, *Spain* 41 G3 38 28N 1 19W
Jumla, *Nepal* 93 E10 29 15N 82 13 E
Jumna = Yamuna →, *India* 93 G9 25 30N 81 53 E
Junagadh, *India* 92 J4 21 30N 70 30 E
Junction, *Tex., U.S.A.* 155 K5 30 29N 99 46W
Junction, *Utah, U.S.A.* 159 G7 38 14N 112 13W
Junction B., *Australia* 126 A1 11 52 S 133 55 E
Junction City, *Ga., U.S.A.* 152 C5 32 36N 84 28W
Junction City, *Kans., U.S.A.* 154 F6 39 2N 96 50W
Junction City, *Oreg., U.S.A.* 158 D2 44 13N 123 12W
Junction Pt., *Australia* 126 A1 11 45 S 133 50 E
Jundah, *Australia* 126 C3 24 46 S 143 2 E
Jundiaí, *Brazil* 175 A6 24 30 S 47 0W
Juneau, *U.S.A.* 142 B2 58 18N 134 25W
Junee, *Australia* 129 C7 34 53 S 147 35 E
Jungfrau, *Switz.* 32 C5 46 32N 7 58 E
Junggar Pendi, *China* 68 B3 44 30N 86 0 E
Jungsdalshytta, *Norway* 18 D4 60 49N 7 55 E
Jungshahi, *Pakistan* 92 G2 24 52N 67 44 E
Juniata →, *U.S.A.* 150 F7 40 30N 77 40W
Junín, *Argentina* 174 C3 34 33 S 60 57W
Junín, *Peru* 172 C2 11 12 S 76 0W
Junín □, *Peru* 172 C3 11 30 S 75 0W
Junín de los Andes, *Argentina* 176 A2 39 45 S 71 0W
Jūniyah, *Lebanon* 103 B4 33 59N 35 38 E
Junlian, *China* 76 C5 28 8N 104 29 E
Junnar, *India* 94 E1 19 12N 73 58 E
Juno Beach, *U.S.A.* 153 J9 26 52N 80 3W
Juntas, *Chile* 174 B2 28 24 S 69 58W
Juntura, *U.S.A.* 158 E4 43 45N 118 5W
Juparanã, L., *Brazil* 171 E3 19 16 S 40 8W
Jupiter, *U.S.A.* 153 J9 26 57N 80 6W
Juquiá, *Brazil* 171 F2 24 19 S 47 38W
Jur, Nahr el →, *Sudan* 107 F2 8 45N 29 15 E
Jura = Jura, Mts. du, *Europe* 27 F13 46 40N 6 5 E
Jura = Schwäbische Alb, *Germany* 31 G5 48 20N 9 30 E
Jura, *U.K.* 22 F3 56 0N 5 50W
Jura □, *France* 27 F12 46 47N 5 45 E
Jura □, *Switz.* 31 H3 47 20N 7 20 E
Jūra →, *Lithuania* 54 C9 55 3N 22 9 E
Jura, Mts. du, *Europe* 27 F13 46 40N 6 5 E
Jura, Sd. of, *U.K.* 22 F3 55 57N 5 45W
Jura Suisse, *Switz.* 32 B4 47 10N 7 0 E
Jurado, *Colombia* 168 B2 7 7N 77 46W
Jurbarkas, *Lithuania* 15 J20 55 4N 22 46 E
Jurien, *Australia* 125 F2 30 18 S 115 2 E
Jurilovca, *Romania* 53 F13 44 46N 28 52 E
Jūrmala, *Latvia* 15 H20 56 58N 23 34 E
Jurong, *China* 77 B12 31 57N 119 9 E
Jurong, *Singapore* 87 d 1 19N 103 42 E
Juruá, *Brazil* 168 D4 3 27 S 66 3W
Juruá →, *Brazil* 168 D4 2 37 S 65 44W
Juruena, *Brazil* 173 C6 13 0 S 58 10W
Juruena →, *Brazil* 173 B6 7 20 S 58 3W
Juruti, *Brazil* 169 D6 2 9 S 56 4W
Jussey, *France* 27 E12 47 50N 5 55 E
Justo Daract, *Argentina* 174 C2 33 52 S 65 12W
Jutaí, *Amazonas, Brazil* 168 D4 2 44 S 66 57W
Jutaí, *Amazonas, Brazil* 172 B4 5 11 S 68 54W
Jutaí →, *Brazil* 168 D4 2 43 S 66 57W
Jüterbog, *Germany* 30 D9 51 59N 13 5 E
Juticalpa, *Honduras* 164 D2 14 40N 86 12W
Jutland = Jylland, *Denmark* 17 H3 56 25N 9 30 E
Juventud, I. de la, *Cuba* 164 B3 21 40N 82 40W
Juvigny-sous-Andaine, *France* 26 D6 48 32N 0 30W
Jūy Zar, *Iran* 101 F12 33 50N 46 18 E
Juye, *China* 74 G9 35 22N 116 5 E
Juzennecourt, *France* 27 D11 48 10N 4 58 E
Jvari, *Georgia* 61 J6 42 42N 42 4 E
Jyderup, *Denmark* 17 J5 55 40N 11 26 E
Jylland, *Denmark* 17 H3 56 25N 9 30 E
Jyväskylä, *Finland* 15 E21 62 14N 25 50 E

K

K2, *Pakistan* 93 B7 35 58N 76 32 E
Ka →, *Nigeria* 113 C5 11 40N 4 10 E
Ka Lae, *U.S.A.* 145 E6 18 55N 155 41W
Kaaawa, *U.S.A.* 145 J14 21 33N 157 51W
Kaala, *U.S.A.* 145 J13 21 31N 158 9W
Kaala-Gomén, *N. Cal.* 133 T18 20 40 S 164 25 E
Kaalualu B., *U.S.A.* 145 E6 18 58N 155 37W
Kaap Plateau, *S. Africa* 116 D3 28 30 S 24 0 E
Kaapkruis, *Namibia* 116 C1 21 55 S 13 57 E
Kaapstad = Cape Town, *S. Africa* 116 E2 33 55 S 18 22 E
Kaataon, Mt., *Phil.* 81 G5 8 10N 124 52 E
Kaba, *Guinea* 112 C2 10 9N 11 40W
Kabacan, *Phil.* 81 H5 7 8N 124 49 E
Kabaena, *Indonesia* 82 C2 5 15 S 122 0 E
Kabala, *S. Leone* 112 D2 9 38N 11 37W
Kabale, *Uganda* 118 C3 1 15 S 30 0 E
Kabalebostuwmeer, *Surinam* 169 C6 4 45N 57 30W
Kabalo, *Dem. Rep. of the Congo* 118 D2 6 0 S 27 0 E
Kabambare, *Dem. Rep. of the Congo* 118 C2 4 41 S 27 39 E
Kabango, *Dem. Rep. of the Congo* 119 D2 8 35 S 28 30 E
Kabanjahe, *Indonesia* 84 B1 3 6N 98 30 E
Kabankalan, *Phil.* 81 G4 9 59N 122 49 E
Kabara, *Fiji* 133 B3 18 59 S 178 56W
Kabara, *Mali* 112 B4 16 40N 2 50W
Kabarai, *Indonesia* 83 B4 0 4 S 130 58 E
Kabardinka, *Russia* 59 K10 44 40N 37 57 E
Kabardino-Balkar Republic = Kabardino-Balkaria □, *Russia* 61 J6 43 30N 43 30 E
Kabardino-Balkaria □, *Russia* 61 J6 43 30N 43 30 E
Kabarega Falls = Murchison Falls, *Uganda* 118 B3 2 15N 31 30 E
Kabasalan, *Phil.* 81 H4 7 47N 122 44 E
Kabat, *Indonesia* 79 J17 8 16 S 114 19 E
Kabba, *Nigeria* 113 D6 7 50N 6 3 E
Kabbani →, *India* 95 H3 12 13N 76 54 E
Kabetogama, *U.S.A.* 154 A8 48 28N 92 59W
Kabi, *Niger* 113 C7 13 30N 12 35 E
Kabin Buri, *Thailand* 86 F3 13 57N 101 43 E
Kabinakagami L., *Canada* 140 C3 48 54N 84 25W
Kabinda, *Dem. Rep. of the Congo* 115 D4 6 10 S 24 29 E
Kabkabīyah, *Sudan* 109 F4 13 50N 24 0 E
Kablungu, C., *Papua N. G.* 132 B7 6 20 S 150 1 E
Kabna, *Sudan* 106 D3 19 6N 32 40 E
Kabo, *C.A.R.* 114 A3 7 35N 18 38 E
Kabompo, *Zambia* 119 E1 13 36 S 24 14 E
Kabompo →, *Zambia* 115 E4 14 11 S 23 11 E
Kabondo, *Dem. Rep. of the Congo* 119 D2 8 58 S 25 40 E
Kabongo, *Dem. Rep. of the Congo* 118 D2 7 22 S 25 33 E
Kabot, *Guinea* 112 C2 10 48N 14 57W
Kabou, *Togo* 113 D5 9 28N 0 55 E
Kaboudia, Rass, *Tunisia* 108 A2 35 13N 11 10 E
Kabr, *Sudan* 107 E2 10 54N 26 50 E
Kabrousse, *Senegal* 112 C1 12 25N 16 45W
Kabubu, *Dem. Rep. of the Congo* 115 D4 9 42 S 24 40 E
Kabūd Gonbad, *Iran* 97 B8 37 5N 59 45 E
Kabugao, *Phil.* 80 B3 18 2N 121 11 E
Kābul, *Afghan.* 91 B3 34 28N 69 11 E
Kābul □, *Afghan.* 91 B3 34 30N 69 0 E
Kābul →, *Pakistan* 91 B4 33 55N 72 14 E
Kabuli, *Papua N. G.* 132 B4 2 7 S 146 40 E
Kabunga, *Dem. Rep. of the Congo* 118 C2 1 38 S 28 3 E
Kaburuang, *Indonesia* 82 A3 3 50N 126 30 E
Kabushiya, *Sudan* 107 D3 16 54N 33 41 E
Kabwanga, *Dem. Rep. of the Congo* 115 D4 7 2 S 22 36 E
Kabwe, *Zambia* 119 E2 14 30 S 28 29 E
Kabwum, *Papua N. G.* 132 D4 6 11 S 147 15 E
Kačanik, *Kosovo, Yug.* 50 D5 42 13N 21 12 E
Kačerginė, *Lithuania* 54 D10 54 56N 23 42 E
Kachchh, Gulf of, *India* 92 H3 22 50N 69 15 E
Kachchh, Rann of, *India* 92 H4 24 0N 70 0 E
Kachchhidhana, *India* 93 J8 21 44N 78 46 E
Kachebera, *Zambia* 119 E3 13 50 S 32 50 E
Kachia, *Nigeria* 113 D6 9 50N 7 55 E
Kachikau, *Botswana* 116 B3 18 8 S 24 26 E
Kachin □, *Burma* 76 D1 26 0N 97 30 E
Kachira, L., *Uganda* 118 C3 0 40 S 31 7 E
Kachiry, *Kazakstan* 66 D8 53 10N 75 50 E
Kachisi, *Ethiopia* 107 F4 9 40N 37 50 E
Kachkanar, *Russia* 64 B7 58 42N 59 33 E
Kachnara, *India* 92 H6 23 50N 75 6 E
Kachot, *Cambodia* 87 G4 11 30N 103 3 E
Kaçkar, *Turkey* 101 B9 40 45N 41 10 E
Kada, *Chad* 109 E3 19 20N 19 39 E
Kadaingti, *Burma* 90 G6 17 37N 97 32 E
Kadaiyanallur, *India* 95 K3 9 3N 77 22 E
Kadan, *Czech Rep.* 34 A6 50 23N 13 16 E
Kadan Kyun, *Burma* 86 F2 12 30N 98 20 E
Kadanai →, *Afghan.* 92 D1 31 22N 65 45 E
Kadarkút, *Hungary* 52 D2 46 13N 17 39 E
Kadavu, *Fiji* 133 B2 19 0 S 178 15 E
Kadavu Passage, *Fiji* 133 B2 18 45 S 178 0 E
Kade, *Ghana* 113 D4 6 7N 0 56W
Kadei →, *C.A.R.* 114 B3 3 31N 16 3 E
Kadi, *India* 92 H5 23 18N 72 23 E
Kadina, *Australia* 128 B2 33 55 S 137 43 E
Kadınhanı, *Turkey* 100 C5 38 14N 32 13 E
Kadiolo, *Mali* 112 C3 10 35N 7 41W
Kadipur, *India* 93 F10 26 10N 82 23 E
Kadirabad, *India* 94 E2 19 51N 75 54 E
Kadiri, *India* 95 G4 14 12N 78 13 E
Kadirli, *Turkey* 100 D7 37 23N 36 5 E
Kadiyevka = Stakhanov, *Ukraine* 59 H10 48 35N 38 40 E
Kadja, O. →, *Chad* 109 F4 12 2N 22 28 E
Kadmat I., *India* 95 J1 11 14N 72 47 E
Kadodo, *Sudan* 107 E2 11 4N 29 31 E
Kadoka, *U.S.A.* 154 D4 43 50N 101 31W
Kadom, *Russia* 60 C6 54 37N 42 30 E
Kadoma, *Zimbabwe* 119 F2 18 20 S 29 52 E
Kâdugli, *Sudan* 107 E2 11 0N 29 45 E
Kaduna, *Nigeria* 113 C6 10 30N 7 21 E
Kaduna □, *Nigeria* 113 C6 11 0N 7 30 E
Kadur, *India* 95 H3 13 34N 76 1 E
Kaduy, *Russia* 58 C9 59 12N 37 9 E
Kaédi, *Mauritania* 112 B2 16 9N 13 28W
Kaélé, *Cameroon* 113 C7 10 7N 14 27 E
Kaelé, *Cent. Amer.* 109 F2 10 7N 14 27 E
Kaena Pt., *U.S.A.* 145 J13 21 35N 158 17W
Kaeng Khoï, *Thailand* 86 E3 14 35N 101 0 E
Kaeo, *N.Z.* 130 B2 35 6 S 173 49 E
Kaesŏng, *N. Korea* 75 F14 37 58N 126 35 E
Kāf, *Si. Arabia* 96 D3 31 25N 37 29 E
Kafakumba, *Dem. Rep. of the Congo* 115 D4 9 38 S 23 46 E
Kafan = Kapan, *Armenia* 101 C12 39 18N 46 27 E
Kafanchan, *Nigeria* 113 D6 9 40N 8 20 E
Kafareti, *Nigeria* 113 C7 10 25N 11 12 E
Kaffrine, *Senegal* 112 C1 14 8N 15 36W
Kafia Kingi, *Sudan* 114 A4 9 20N 24 25 E
Kafin, *Nigeria* 113 D6 9 30N 7 4 E
Kafin Madaki, *Nigeria* 113 C6 10 41N 9 46 E
Kafinda, *Zambia* 119 E3 12 32 S 30 20 E
Kafirévs, Ákra, *Greece* 48 C6 38 9N 24 38 E
Kafr el Battikh, *Egypt* 106 H7 31 25N 31 44 E
Kafr el Dauwâr, *Egypt* 106 H7 31 8N 30 8 E
Kafr el Sheikh, *Egypt* 106 H7 31 15N 30 50 E
Kafue, *Zambia* 119 F2 15 46 S 28 9 E
Kafue Flats, *Zambia* 119 F2 15 40 S 27 25 E
Kafue Nat. Park, *Zambia* 119 F2 15 12 S 25 38 E
Kafulwe, *Zambia* 119 D2 9 0 S 29 1 E
Kafumba, *Dem. Rep. of the Congo* 115 D3 5 23 S 18 55 E
Kaga, *Afghan.* 92 B4 34 14N 70 10 E
Kaga, *Japan* 73 A8 36 16N 136 15 E
Kaga Bandoro, *C.A.R.* 114 A3 7 0N 19 10 E
Kagamil I., *U.S.A.* 144 K5 53 0N 169 43W
Kagan, *Uzbekistan* 66 F7 39 43N 64 33 E
Kagarko, *Nigeria* 113 D6 9 28N 7 36 E
Kagawa □, *Japan* 72 C6 34 15N 134 0 E
Kagera = Ziwa Maghariba □, *Tanzania* 118 C3 2 0 S 31 30 E
Kagera →, *Uganda* 118 C3 0 57 S 31 47 E
Kağızman, *Turkey* 101 B10 40 5N 43 10 E
Kagmar, *Sudan* 107 E3 14 24N 30 25 E
Kagopal, *Chad* 109 G3 8 16N 16 23 E
Kagoshima, *Japan* 72 F2 31 35N 130 33 E
Kagoshima □, *Japan* 72 F2 31 30N 130 30 E
Kagoshima-Wan, *Japan* 72 F2 31 25N 130 40 E
Kagua, *Papua N. G.* 132 D2 6 26 S 143 48 E
Kagul = Cahul, *Moldova* 53 E13 45 50N 28 15 E
Kahak, *Iran* 97 B6 36 6N 49 46 E
Kahaluu, *U.S.A.* 145 K14 21 28N 157 50W
Kahama, *Tanzania* 118 C3 4 8 S 32 30 E
Kahan, *Pakistan* 92 E3 29 18N 68 54 E
Kahana, *U.S.A.* 145 J14 21 34N 157 53W
Kahana B., *U.S.A.* 145 J14 21 35N 157 50W
Kahang, *Malaysia* 87 L4 2 12N 103 32 E
Kahayan →, *Indonesia* 85 C4 3 40 S 114 0 E
Kahe, *Tanzania* 118 C4 3 30 S 37 25 E
Kahemba, *Dem. Rep. of the Congo* 115 D3 7 18 S 18 55 E
Kaherekoau Mts., *N.Z.* 131 F2 45 45 S 167 15 E
Kahil, Djebel bou, *Algeria* 111 B5 34 26N 4 0 E
Kahnūj, *Iran* 97 E8 27 55N 57 40 E
Kahoka, *U.S.A.* 156 D5 40 25N 91 44W
Kahoolawe, *U.S.A.* 145 C5 20 33N 156 37W
Kahramanmaraş, *Turkey* 100 D7 37 37N 36 53 E
Kâhta, *Turkey* 101 D8 37 46N 38 36 E
Kahuku, *U.S.A.* 145 J14 21 41N 157 57W
Kahuku Pt., *U.S.A.* 145 J14 21 43N 157 59W
Kahului, *U.S.A.* 145 C5 20 54N 156 28W
Kahurangi Nat. Park, *N.Z.* 131 B7 41 10 S 172 32 E
Kahurangi Pt., *N.Z.* 131 A7 40 50 S 172 10 E
Kahuta, *Pakistan* 92 C5 33 35N 73 24 E
Kahuzi-Biega, Parc Nat. du, *Dem. Rep. of the Congo* 118 C2 1 50 S 27 55 E
Kai, Kepulauan, *Indonesia* 83 C4 5 55 S 132 45 E

230 Kai Besar

Kai Besar, *Indonesia* **83 C4** 5 35 S 133 0 E
Kai Is. = Kai, Kepulauan, *Indonesia* **83 C4** 5 55 S 132 45 E
Kai Kecil, *Indonesia* **83 C4** 5 45 S 132 40 E
Kai Xian, *China* **76 B7** 31 11N 108 21 E
Kaiama, *Nigeria* **113 D5** 9 36N 4 1 E
Kaiapit, *Papua N. G.* **132 D4** 6 18 S 146 18 E
Kaiapoi, *N.Z.* **131 D7** 43 24 S 172 40 E
Kaieteur Falls, *Guyana* **169 B6** 5 1N 59 10W
Kaifeng, *China* **74 G8** 34 48N 114 21 E
Kaihua, *China* **77 C12** 29 12N 118 20 E
Kaijiang, *China* **76 B6** 31 7N 107 55 E
Kaikohe, *N.Z.* **130 B2** 35 25 S 173 49 E
Kaikoura, *N.Z.* **131 C8** 42 25 S 173 43 E
Kaikoura Pen., *N.Z.* **131 C8** 42 25 S 173 43 E
Kailahun, *S. Leone* **112 D2** 8 18N 10 39W
Kailashahar, *India* **90 C4** 24 19N 92 0 E
Kaileuna I., *Papua N. G.* **132 E6** 8 32 S 150 57 E
Kaili, *China* **76 D6** 26 33N 107 59 E
Kailu, *China* **75 C11** 43 38N 121 18 E
Kailua, *U.S.A.* **145 K14** 21 24N 157 44W
Kailua B., *U.S.A.* **145 K14** 21 25N 157 40W
Kailua Kona, *U.S.A.* **145 D6** 19 39N 155 59W
Kaim →, *Papua N. G.* **132 D1** 6 55 S 141 33 E
Kaima, *Indonesia* **83 C5** 5 32 S 138 48 E
Kaimana, *Indonesia* **83 B4** 3 39 S 133 45 E
Kaimanawa Mts., *N.Z.* **130 F4** 39 15 S 175 56 E
Kaimata, *N.Z.* **131 C6** 42 34 S 171 28 E
Kaimganj, *India* **93 F8** 27 33N 79 24 E
Kaimon-Dake, *Japan* **72 F2** 31 11N 130 32 E
Kaimuki, *U.S.A.* **145 K14** 21 17N 157 48W
Kaimur Hills, *India* **93 G10** 24 30N 82 0 E
Kainab →, *Namibia* **116 D2** 28 32 S 19 34 E
Kainan, *Japan* **73 C7** 34 9N 135 12 E
Kainantu, *Papua N. G.* **132 D3** 6 18 S 145 52 E
Kainji Dam, *Nigeria* **113 D5** 9 55N 4 35 E
Kainji Lake Nat. Park, *Nigeria* **113 C5** 10 5N 4 6 E
Kainji Res., *Nigeria* **113 C5** 10 1N 4 40 E
Kainuu, *Finland* **14 D23** 64 30N 29 7 E
Kaipara Harbour, *N.Z.* **130 C3** 36 25 S 174 14 E
Kaiping, *China* **77 F9** 22 23N 112 42 E
Kaipokok B., *Canada* **141 B8** 54 54N 59 47W
Kaira, *India* **92 H5** 22 45N 72 50 E
Kairana, *India* **92 E7** 29 24N 77 15 E
Kairiru I., *Papua N. G.* **132 B2** 3 21 S 143 34 E
Kaironi, *Indonesia* **83 B4** 0 47 S 133 40 E
Kairouan, *Tunisia* **108 A2** 35 45N 10 5 E
Kairuku, *Papua N. G.* **132 E4** 8 51 S 146 35 E
Kaiserslautern, *Germany* **31 F3** 49 26N 7 45 E
Kaiserstuhl, *Germany* **31 G3** 48 4N 7 40 E
Kaita, *Japan* **72 C4** 34 22N 132 32 E
Kaitaia, *N.Z.* **130 B2** 35 8 S 173 17 E
Kaitangata, *N.Z.* **131 G4** 46 17 S 169 51 E
Kaithal, *India* **92 E7** 29 48N 76 26 E
Kaitu →, *Pakistan* **92 C4** 33 10N 70 30 E
Kaiwi Channel, *U.S.A.* **145 K14** 21 15N 157 30W
Kaiyang, *China* **76 D6** 27 4N 106 59 E
Kaiyuan, *Liaoning, China* **75 C13** 42 28N 124 1 E
Kaiyuan, *Yunnan, China* **76 F4** 23 40N 103 12 E
Kaiyuh Mts., *U.S.A.* **144 D8** 64 30N 158 0W
Kajaani, *Finland* **14 D22** 64 17N 27 46 E
Kajabbi, *Australia* **126 C3** 20 0 S 140 1 E
Kajana = Kajaani, *Finland* **14 D22** 64 17N 27 46 E
Kajang, *Malaysia* **87 L3** 2 59N 101 48 E
Kajaran, *Armenia* **101 C12** 39 10N 46 7 E
Kajiado, *Kenya* **118 C4** 1 53 S 36 48 E
Kajo Kaji, *Sudan* **107 G3** 3 58N 31 40 E
Kajuru, *Nigeria* **113 C6** 10 15N 7 34 E
Kajy-Say, *Kyrgyzstan* **65 B8** 42 8N 77 10 E
Kaka, *Sudan* **107 E3** 10 38N 32 10 E
Kaka Pt., *U.S.A.* **145 C5** 20 31N 156 33W
Kakabeka Falls, *Canada* **140 C2** 48 24N 89 37W
Kakadu Nat. Park, *Australia* **124 B5** 12 0 S 132 3 E
Kakamas, *S. Africa* **116 D3** 28 45 S 20 33 E
Kakamega, *Kenya* **118 B3** 0 20N 34 46 E
Kakamigahara, *Japan* **73 B8** 35 28N 136 48 E
Kakana, *India* **95 K11** 9 7N 92 48 E
Kakanj, *Bos.-H.* **52 F3** 44 4N 18 4 E
Kakanui Mts., *N.Z.* **131 F5** 45 10 S 170 30 E
Kakata, *Liberia* **112 D2** 6 35N 10 20W
Kakdwip, *India* **93 J13** 21 53N 88 11 E
Kake, *Japan* **72 C4** 34 36N 132 19 E
Kake, *U.S.A.* **142 B2** 56 59N 133 57W
Kakegawa, *Japan* **73 C10** 34 45N 138 1 E
Kakeroma-Jima, *Japan* **71 K4** 28 8N 129 14 E
Kakhib, *Russia* **61 J8** 42 28N 46 34 E
Kakhonak, *U.S.A.* **144 G9** 59 26N 154 51W
Kakhovka, *Ukraine* **59 J7** 46 45N 33 30 E
Kakhovske Vdskh., *Ukraine* **59 J7** 47 5N 34 0 E
Kakinada, *India* **94 F6** 16 57N 82 11 E
Kakisa →, *Canada* **142 A5** 61 3N 118 10W
Kakisa L., *Canada* **142 A5** 60 56N 117 43W
Kakogawa, *Japan* **72 C6** 34 46N 134 51 E
Kaktovik, *U.S.A.* **144 A12** 70 8N 143 38W
Kakum Nat. Park, *Ghana* **113 D4** 5 24N 1 20W
Kakwa →, *Canada* **142 C5** 54 37N 118 28W
Kāl Gūsheh, *Iran* **97 D8** 30 59N 58 12 E
Kal Safīd, *Iran* **101 E12** 34 52N 47 23 E
Kala, *Nigeria* **113 C7** 12 2N 14 40 E
Kala Oya →, *Sri Lanka* **95 K4** 8 20N 79 45 E
Kalaa-Kebira, *Tunisia* **108 A2** 35 59N 10 32 E
Kalaallit Nunaat = Greenland ■, *N. Amer.* **10 D6** 66 0N 45 0W
Kalabagh, *Pakistan* **92 C4** 33 0N 71 28 E
Kalabahi, *Indonesia* **82 C2** 8 13 S 124 31 E
Kalabaka, *Greece* **48 B3** 39 42N 21 39 E
Kalabakan, *Malaysia* **85 B5** 4 25N 117 29 E
Kalabana, *Mali* **112 C3** 14 10N 8 35W
Kalabo, *Zambia* **115 E4** 14 58 S 22 40 E
Kalach, *Russia* **60 E5** 50 22N 41 0 E
Kalach na Donu, *Russia* **61 F6** 48 43N 43 32 E
Kaladan →, *Burma* **90 E4** 20 20N 93 5 E
Kaladar, *Canada* **140 D4** 44 37N 77 5W
Kalahari, *Africa* **116 C3** 24 0 S 21 30 E
Kalahari Gemsbok Nat. Park, *S. Africa* **116 D3** 25 30 S 20 30 E
Kalaheo, *U.S.A.* **145 B2** 21 56N 159 32W
Kalaikhum, *Tajikistan* **65 D5** 38 28N 70 46 E
Kalajoki, *Finland* **14 D20** 64 12N 24 10 E
Kālak, *Iran* **97 E8** 25 29N 59 22 E
Kalakamati, *Botswana* **117 C4** 20 40 S 27 25 E
Kalakan, *Russia* **67 D12** 55 15N 116 45 E
K'alak'unlun Shank'ou = Karakoram Pass, *Asia* **93 B7** 35 33N 77 50 E
Kalam, *Pakistan* **93 B5** 35 34N 72 30 E
Kalama, *Dem. Rep. of the Congo* **118 C2** 2 52 S 28 35 E
Kalama, *U.S.A.* **160 E4** 46 1N 122 51W
Kalámai, *Greece* **48 D4** 37 3N 22 10 E
Kalamaloué, Parc Nat. de, *Cameroon* **109 F2** 12 9N 14 58 E
Kalamansig, *Phil.* **81 H5** 6 33N 124 3 E
Kalamariá, *Greece* **50 F6** 40 33N 22 55 E
Kalamata = Kalámai, *Greece* **48 D4** 37 3N 22 10 E
Kalamazoo, *U.S.A.* **157 B11** 42 17N 85 35W
Kalamazoo →, *U.S.A.* **157 B10** 42 40N 86 10W
Kalamb, *India* **94 E2** 18 3N 74 48 E
Kalambo Falls, *Tanzania* **119 D3** 8 37 S 31 35 E
Kalamítsi, *Greece* **39 B2** 38 45N 20 36 E
Kalamnuri, *India* **94 E3** 19 40N 77 20 E
Kálamos, *Attikí, Greece* **48 C5** 38 17N 23 52 E
Kálamos, *Levkás, Greece* **39 B2** 38 37N 20 56 E
Kálamos Nisís, *Greece* **39 B2** 38 37N 20 55 E
Kalan, *Turkey* **96 B3** 39 7N 39 32 E
Kalangadoo, *Australia* **128 D4** 37 34 S 140 41 E
Kalankalan, *Guinea* **112 C3** 10 7N 8 54W
Kalannie, *Australia* **125 F2** 30 22 S 117 5 E
Kalāntarī, *Iran* **97 C7** 32 10N 54 8 E
Kalao, *Indonesia* **82 C2** 7 21 S 121 0 E
Kalaotoa, *Indonesia* **82 C2** 7 20 S 121 50 E
Kalapana, *U.S.A.* **145 D7** 19 21N 154 59W
Kälarne, *Sweden* **16 B10** 62 59N 16 5 E
Kalasin, *Thailand* **86 D4** 16 26N 103 30 E
Kalat, *Pakistan* **91 C2** 29 8N 66 31 E
Kalāteh, *Iran* **97 B7** 36 33N 55 41 E
Kalāteh-ye Ganj, *Iran* **97 E8** 27 31N 57 55 E
Kálathos, *Greece* **38 E12** 36 9N 28 8 E
Kalatungan Mt., *Phil.* **81 H5** 7 54N 124 50 E
Kalaupapa, *U.S.A.* **145 B5** 21 12N 156 59W
Kalaus →, *Russia* **61 H7** 45 40N 44 7 E
Kalávrita, *Greece* **48 C4** 38 3N 22 8 E
Kalaw, *Burma* **90 E6** 20 38N 96 34 E
Kalbān, *Oman* **99 B7** 20 18N 58 38 E
Kalbarri, *Australia* **125 E1** 27 40 S 114 10 E
Kalbarri Nat. Park, *Australia* **125 E1** 27 51 S 114 30 E
Kalce, *Slovenia* **36 F8** 45 54N 14 13 E
Kaldrananes, *Iceland* **11 B5** 65 45N 21 25W
Kale, *Antalya, Turkey* **49 E12** 36 14N 30 0 E
Kale, *Denizli, Turkey* **49 D10** 37 27N 28 49 E
Kalecik, *Turkey* **100 B5** 40 4N 33 26 E
Kalehe, *Dem. Rep. of the Congo* **118 C2** 2 6 S 28 50 E
Kalema, *Tanzania* **118 C3** 1 12 S 31 55 E
Kalemie, *Dem. Rep. of the Congo* **118 D2** 5 55 S 29 9 E
Kalemyo, *Burma* **90 D5** 23 11N 94 4 E
Kalety, *Poland* **55 H5** 50 35N 18 52 E
Kalewa, *Burma* **90 D5** 23 10N 94 15 E
Kaleybar, *Iran* **96 B5** 38 47N 47 2 E
Kálfafell, *Iceland* **11 D9** 63 57N 17 41W
Kalgan = Zhangjiakou, *China* **74 D8** 40 48N 114 55 E
Kalghatgi, *India* **95 G2** 15 11N 74 58 E
Kalgoorlie-Boulder, *Australia* **125 F3** 30 40 S 121 22 E
Kalhovd, *Norway* **18 D5** 60 4N 8 21 E
Kali →, *India* **93 F8** 27 6N 79 55 E
Kali Sindh →, *India* **92 G6** 25 32N 76 17 E
Kaliakra, Nos, *Bulgaria* **51 C12** 43 21N 28 30 E
Kalianda, *Indonesia* **84 D3** 5 50 S 105 45 E
Kalibo, *Phil.* **81 F4** 11 43N 122 22 E
Kaliganj, *Bangla.* **90 D2** 22 25N 89 8 E
Kalihi, *U.S.A.* **145 K14** 21 20N 157 53W
Kalima, *Dem. Rep. of the Congo* **118 C2** 2 33 S 26 32 E
Kalimantan □, *Indonesia* **85 C4** 0 0 114 0 E
Kalimantan Barat □, *Indonesia* **85 C4** 0 0 110 30 E
Kalimantan Selatan □, *Indonesia* **85 C5** 2 30 S 115 30 E
Kalimantan Tengah □, *Indonesia* **85 C4** 2 0 S 113 30 E
Kalimantan Timur □, *Indonesia* **85 B5** 1 30N 116 30 E
Kálimnos, *Greece* **49 D8** 37 0N 27 0 E
Kalimpong, *India* **90 B2** 27 4N 88 35 E
Kalinadi →, *India* **95 G2** 14 50N 74 7 E
Kalinga □, *Phil.* **80 C3** 17 30N 121 20 E
Kalinin = Tver, *Russia* **58 D8** 56 55N 35 55 E
Kaliningrad, *Russia* **15 J19** 54 42N 20 32 E
Kalininsk, *Russia* **60 E7** 51 30N 44 40 E
Kalininskoye = Kara-Balta, *Kyrgyzstan* **65 B6** 42 50N 73 49 E
Kalinkavichy, *Belarus* **59 F5** 52 12N 29 20 E
Kalinkovichi = Kalinkavichy, *Belarus* **59 F5** 52 12N 29 20 E
Kalinovik, *Bos.-H.* **50 C2** 43 31N 18 25 E
Kalipetrovo, *Bulgaria* **51 B11** 44 5N 27 14 E
Kaliro, *Uganda* **118 B3** 0 56N 33 30 E
Kalirrákhi, *Greece* **51 F8** 40 40N 24 35 E
Kalispell, *U.S.A.* **158 B6** 48 12N 114 19W
Kalisz, *Poland* **55 G5** 51 45N 18 8 E
Kalisz Pomorski, *Poland* **55 E2** 53 17N 15 55 E
Kaliua, *Tanzania* **118 D3** 5 5 S 31 48 E
Kaliveli Tank, *India* **95 H4** 12 5N 79 50 E
Kalívia Thorikoú, *Greece* **48 D5** 37 50N 23 55 E
Kalix, *Sweden* **14 D20** 65 53N 23 12 E
Kalix →, *Sweden* **14 D20** 65 50N 23 11 E
Kalka, *India* **92 D7** 30 46N 76 57 E
Kalkali Ghat, *India* **90 C4** 24 36N 92 20 E
Kalkan, *Turkey* **49 E11** 36 15N 29 23 E
Kalkarindji, *Australia* **124 C5** 17 30 S 130 47 E
Kalkaska, *U.S.A.* **148 C3** 44 44N 85 11W
Kalkfeld, *Namibia* **116 C2** 20 57 S 16 14 E
Kalkfontein, *Botswana* **116 C3** 22 4 S 20 57 E
Kalkım, *Turkey* **49 B9** 39 48N 27 13 E
Kalkrand, *Namibia* **116 C2** 24 1 S 17 35 E
Kallakkurichchi, *India* **95 J4** 11 44N 79 1 E
Kallam, *India* **94 E3** 18 36N 76 2 E
Källandsö, *Sweden* **17 F7** 58 40N 13 5 E
Kallavesi, *Finland* **14 E22** 62 58N 27 30 E
Kållby, *Sweden* **17 F7** 58 30N 13 8 E
Källered, *Sweden* **17 G6** 57 32N 12 4 E
Kallidaikurichi, *India* **95 K3** 8 38N 77 31 E
Kallimasiá, *Greece* **49 C8** 38 18N 26 6 E
Kallinge, *Sweden* **17 H9** 56 15N 15 18 E
Kallithéa, *Greece* **48 D5** 37 55N 23 41 E
Kallmet, *Albania* **50 E3** 41 51N 19 41 E
Kalloní, *Greece* **49 B8** 39 14N 26 12 E
Kallonís, Kólpos, *Greece* **49 B8** 39 10N 26 10 E
Kallsjön, *Sweden* **14 E15** 63 38N 13 0 E
Kalmalo, *Nigeria* **113 C6** 13 40N 5 20 E
Kalmanstunga, *Iceland* **11 C6** 64 44N 20 48W
Kalmar, *Sweden* **17 H10** 56 40N 16 20 E
Kalmar län □, *Sweden* **17 G10** 57 25N 16 0 E
Kalmar sund, *Sweden* **17 H10** 56 40N 16 25 E
Kalmunai, *Sri Lanka* **95 L5** 7 25N 81 49 E
Kalmyk Republic = Kalmykia □, *Russia* **61 G8** 46 5N 46 1 E
Kalmykia □, *Russia* **61 G8** 46 5N 46 1 E
Kalmykovo, *Kazakstan* **57 E9** 49 0N 51 47 E
Kalna, *India* **93 H13** 23 13N 88 25 E
Kalnai, *India* **93 H10** 22 46N 83 30 E
Kalni →, *Bangla.* **90 C3** 24 21N 91 13 E
Kalo, *Papua N. G.* **132 F4** 10 1 S 147 48 E
Kalocsa, *Hungary* **52 D4** 46 32N 19 0 E
Kalofer, *Bulgaria* **51 D8** 42 37N 24 59 E
Kalohi Channel, *U.S.A.* **145 C5** 21 0N 157 0W
Kalokhorio, *Cyprus* **39 F9** 34 51N 33 2 E
Kaloko, *Dem. Rep. of the Congo* **118 D2** 6 47 S 25 48 E
Kalol, *Gujarat, India* **92 H5** 22 37N 73 31 E
Kalol, *Gujarat, India* **92 H5** 23 15N 72 33 E
Kalolímnos, *Greece* **49 D9** 37 4N 27 5 E
Kalomo, *Zambia* **119 F2** 17 0 S 26 30 E
Kalona, *U.S.A.* **156 C5** 41 29N 91 43W
Kalonerón, *Greece* **48 D3** 37 20N 21 38 E
Kalpeni I., *India* **95 J1** 10 5N 73 38 E
Kalpi, *India* **93 F8** 26 8N 79 47 E
Kalpitiya, *Sri Lanka* **95 K4** 8 14N 79 46 E
Kalputhi I., *India* **95 J1** 10 49N 72 10 E
Kalrayan Hills, *India* **95 J4** 11 45N 78 40 E
Kalsubai, *India* **94 E1** 19 35N 73 45 E
Kaltag, *U.S.A.* **144 D8** 64 20N 158 43W
Kaltbrunn, *Switz.* **33 B8** 47 13N 9 2 E
Kaltern = Caldaro, *Italy* **45 B8** 46 25N 11 14 E
Kaltungo, *Nigeria* **113 D7** 9 48N 11 19 E
Kalu, *Pakistan* **92 G2** 25 5N 67 39 E
Kaluga, *Russia* **58 E9** 54 35N 36 10 E
Kalulong, Bukit, *Malaysia* **85 B4** 3 14N 114 39 E
Kalulushi, *Zambia* **119 E2** 12 50 S 28 3 E
Kalundborg, *Denmark* **17 J5** 55 41N 11 5 E
Kalush, *Ukraine* **59 H3** 49 3N 24 23 E
Kałuszyn, *Poland* **55 F8** 52 13N 21 52 E
Kalutara, *Sri Lanka* **95 L5** 6 35N 80 0 E
Kalvåg, *Norway* **18 C1** 61 46N 4 51 E
Kalvarija, *Lithuania* **54 D10** 54 24N 23 14 E
Kalwakurti, *India* **94 F4** 16 41N 78 30 E
Kalya, *Russia* **64 A7** 60 15N 59 59 E
Kalyan, *Maharashtra, India* **94 D2** 20 30N 74 3 E
Kalyan, *Maharashtra, India* **94 E1** 19 15N 73 9 E
Kalyandurg, *India* **95 G3** 14 33N 77 6 E
Kalyani, *India* **94 F3** 17 52N 76 57 E
Kalyansingapuram, *India* **94 E6** 19 30N 83 19 E
Kalyazin, *Russia* **58 D9** 57 15N 37 55 E
Kam, *Albania* **50 D4** 42 17N 20 18 E
Kam →, *Nigeria* **113 D7** 8 15N 1 10 E
Kama, *Burma* **90 F5** 19 1N 95 4 E
Kama, *Dem. Rep. of the Congo* **118 C2** 3 30 S 27 5 E
Kama →, *Russia* **64 C5** 55 45N 52 0 E
Kamachumu, *Tanzania* **118 C3** 1 37 S 31 37 E
Kamae, *Japan* **72 E3** 32 48N 131 56 E
Kamaing, *Burma* **90 C6** 25 26N 96 35 E
Kamaishi, *Japan* **70 E10** 39 16N 141 53 E
Kamakou, *U.S.A.* **145 B5** 21 7N 156 52W
Kamakura, *Japan* **73 B11** 35 19N 139 33 E
Kamalapuram, *India* **95 G4** 14 35N 78 39 E
Kamalété, *Gabon* **114 C2** 0 43 S 11 49 E
Kamalia, *Pakistan* **92 D5** 30 44N 72 42 E
Kaman, *India* **92 F6** 27 39N 77 16 E
Kaman, *Turkey* **100 C5** 39 22N 33 44 E
Kamana, *Dem. Rep. of the Congo* **115 D4** 5 59 S 24 58 E
Kamananui →, *U.S.A.* **145 J13** 21 38N 158 4W
Kamanjab, *Namibia* **116 B2** 19 35 S 14 51 E
Kamapanda, *Zambia* **119 E1** 12 5 S 24 0 E
Kamarān, *Yemen* **98 D3** 15 21N 42 35 E
Kamareddi, *India* **94 E4** 18 19N 78 21 E
Kamashi, *Uzbekistan* **65 D2** 38 51N 65 23 E
Kamativi, *Zimbabwe* **116 B4** 18 20 S 27 6 E
Kamba, *Dem. Rep. of the Congo* **115 C4** 4 0 S 22 22 E
Kamba, *Nigeria* **113 C5** 11 50N 3 45 E
Kambalda, *Australia* **125 F3** 31 10 S 121 37 E
Kambam, *India* **95 K3** 9 45N 77 16 E
Kambar, *Pakistan* **92 F3** 27 37N 68 1 E
Kambarka, *Russia* **64 C5** 56 15N 54 11 E
Kambia, *S. Leone* **112 D2** 9 3N 12 53W
Kambolé, *Togo* **113 D5** 8 43N 1 39 E
Kambolé, *Zambia* **119 D3** 8 47 S 30 48 E
Kambos, *Cyprus* **39 E8** 35 2N 32 44 E
Kambove, *Dem. Rep. of the Congo* **119 E2** 10 51 S 26 33 E
Kambuie, *Dem. Rep. of the Congo* **115 D4** 6 59 S 22 19 E
Kambwata, *Zambia* **115 E4** 14 3 S 23 43 E
Kamchatka, Poluostrov, *Russia* **67 D16** 57 0N 160 0 E
Kamchatka Pen. = Kamchatka, Poluostrov, *Russia* **67 D16** 57 0N 160 0 E
Kamchiya →, *Bulgaria* **51 C11** 43 4N 27 44 E
Kame Ruins, *Zimbabwe* **119 G2** 20 7 S 28 25 E
Kamehameha Heights, *U.S.A.* **145 K14** 21 21N 157 52W
Kamen, *Russia* **66 D9** 53 50N 81 30 E
Kamen-Rybolov, *Russia* **70 B6** 44 46N 132 2 E
Kamende, *Dem. Rep. of the Congo* **115 D4** 6 26 S 24 35 E
Kamenica, *Serbia, Yug.* **50 C6** 43 27N 22 27 E
Kamenica, *Serbia, Yug.* **50 B3** 44 25N 19 45 E
Kamenice nad Lipou, *Czech Rep.* **34 B8** 49 18N 15 2 E
Kamenjak, Rt, *Croatia* **45 D10** 44 47N 13 55 E
Kamenka = Kaminka, *Ukraine* **59 H7** 49 3N 32 6 E
Kamenka, *Kazakstan* **60 E10** 51 7N 50 19 E
Kamenka, *Arkhangelsk, Russia* **56 A7** 65 58N 44 0 E
Kamenka, *Penza, Russia* **60 D6** 53 10N 44 5 E
Kamenka, *Voronezh, Russia* **59 G10** 50 47N 39 20 E
Kamenka Bugskaya = Kamyanka-Buzka, *Ukraine* **59 G3** 50 8N 24 16 E
Kamenka Dneprovskaya = Kamyanka-Dniprovska, *Ukraine* **59 J8** 47 29N 34 28 E
Kamennomostskiy, *Russia* **61 H5** 44 18N 40 13 E
Kameno, *Bulgaria* **51 D11** 42 34N 27 18 E
Kamenolomini, *Russia* **61 G5** 47 40N 40 14 E
Kamensk-Shakhtinskiy, *Russia* **61 F5** 48 23N 40 20 E
Kamensk Uralskiy, *Russia* **64 C9** 56 25N 62 2 E
Kamenskiy, *Russia* **60 E7** 50 48N 45 25 E
Kamenskoye, *Russia* **67 C17** 62 45N 165 30 E
Kamenyak, *Bulgaria* **51 C10** 43 24N 26 57 E
Kamenz, *Germany* **30 D10** 51 15N 14 5 E
Kameoka, *Japan* **73 C7** 35 0N 135 35 E
Kameyama, *Japan* **73 C8** 34 51N 136 27 E
Kami-Jima, *Japan* **72 E2** 32 27N 130 20 E
Kami-Koshiki-Jima, *Japan* **72 F1** 31 50N 129 52 E
Kamiagata, *Japan* **72 C1** 34 47N 129 24 E
Kamiah, *U.S.A.* **158 C5** 46 14N 116 2W
Kamień Krajeński, *Poland* **54 E4** 53 32N 17 32 E
Kamień Pomorski, *Poland* **54 E1** 53 57N 14 43 E
Kamienna →, *Poland* **55 G8** 51 6N 21 47 E
Kamienna Góra, *Poland* **55 H3** 50 47N 16 2 E
Kamieńsk, *Poland* **55 G6** 51 12N 19 29 E
Kamieskroon, *S. Africa* **116 E2** 30 9 S 17 56 E
Kamilukuak, L., *Canada* **143 A8** 62 22N 101 40W
Kamin-Kashyrskyy, *Ukraine* **59 G3** 51 39N 24 56 E
Kamina, *Dem. Rep. of the Congo* **119 D2** 8 45 S 25 0 E
Kaminak L., *Canada* **143 A10** 62 10N 95 0W
Kaministiquia, *Canada* **140 C1** 48 32N 89 35W
Kaminka, *Ukraine* **59 H7** 49 3N 32 6 E
Kaminoyama, *Japan* **70 E10** 38 9N 140 17 E
Kamioka, *Japan* **73 A9** 36 25N 137 15 E
Kamiros, *Greece* **38 E11** 36 20N 27 56 E
Kamishak Bay, *U.S.A.* **144 G9** 59 15N 153 45W
Kamitsushima, *Japan* **72 C1** 34 50N 129 28 E
Kamituga, *Dem. Rep. of the Congo* **118 C2** 3 2 S 28 10 E
Kamla →, *India* **93 G12** 25 35N 86 36 E
Kamloops, *Canada* **142 C4** 50 40N 120 20W
Kamnik, *Slovenia* **45 B11** 46 14N 14 37 E
Kamo, *Armenia* **61 K7** 40 21N 45 7 E
Kamo, *Japan* **70 F9** 37 39N 139 3 E
Kamo, *N.Z.* **130 B3** 35 42 S 174 20 E
Kamoa Mts., *Guyana* **169 C6** 1 30N 59 0W
Kamogawa, *Japan* **73 B12** 35 5N 140 5 E
Kamojima, *Japan* **72 C6** 34 4N 134 21 E
Kamoke, *Pakistan* **92 C6** 32 4N 74 4 E
Kamooloa, *U.S.A.* **145 J13** 21 34N 158 7W
Kamp →, *Austria* **34 C8** 48 23N 15 42 E
Kampala, *Uganda* **118 B3** 0 20N 32 30 E
Kampang Chhnang, *Cambodia* **87 G5** 12 20N 104 35 E
Kampar, *Malaysia* **87 K3** 4 18N 101 9 E
Kampar →, *Indonesia* **84 B2** 0 30N 103 8 E
Kampen, *Neths.* **24 B5** 52 33N 5 53 E
Kamphaeng Phet, *Thailand* **86 D2** 16 28N 99 30 E
Kampolombo, L., *Zambia* **119 E2** 11 37 S 29 42 E
Kampong Pengerang, *Malaysia* **87 d** 1 22N 104 7 E
Kampong Punggai, *Malaysia* **87 d** 1 27N 104 18 E
Kampong Saom, *Cambodia* **87 G4** 10 38N 103 30 E
Kampong Saom, Chaak, *Cambodia* **87 G4** 10 50N 103 32 E
Kampong Tanjong Langsat, *Malaysia* **87 d** 1 28N 104 1 E
Kampong Telok Ramunia, *Malaysia* **87 d** 1 22N 104 15 E
Kampong To, *Thailand* **87 J3** 6 3N 101 13 E
Kampot, *Cambodia* **87 G5** 10 36N 104 10 E
Kampsville, *U.S.A.* **156 E6** 39 18N 90 37W
Kampti, *Burkina Faso* **112 C4** 10 7N 3 25W
Kampuchea = Cambodia ■, *Asia* **86 F5** 12 15N 105 0 E
Kampung Air Putih, *Malaysia* **87 K4** 4 15N 103 10 E
Kampung Jerangau, *Malaysia* **87 K4** 4 50N 103 10 E
Kampung Raja, *Malaysia* **87 K4** 5 45N 102 35 E
Kampungbaru = Tolitoli, *Indonesia* **82 A2** 1 5N 120 50 E
Kamrau, Teluk, *Indonesia* **83 B4** 3 30 S 133 36 E
Kamsack, *Canada* **143 C8** 51 34N 101 54W
Kamsar, *Guinea* **112 C2** 10 40N 14 36W
Kamskoye Ustye, *Russia* **60 C9** 55 10N 49 20 E
Kamskoye Vdkhr., *Russia* **64 B6** 58 41N 56 7 E
Kamthi, *India* **94 D4** 21 9N 79 19 E
Kamuchawie L., *Canada* **143 B8** 56 18N 101 59W
Kamuela, *U.S.A.* **145 C6** 20 1N 155 41W
Kamui-Misaki, *Japan* **70 C10** 43 20N 140 21 E
Kamundan →, *Indonesia* **83 B4** 2 17 S 132 39 E
Kamyanets-Podilskyy, *Ukraine* **59 H4** 48 45N 26 40 E
Kamyanka-Buzka, *Ukraine* **59 G3** 50 8N 24 16 E
Kamyanka-Dniprovska, *Ukraine* **59 J8** 47 29N 34 28 E
Kāmyārān, *Iran* **101 E12** 34 47N 46 56 E
Kamyshin, *Russia* **60 E7** 50 10N 45 24 E
Kamyshlov, *Russia* **64 C9** 56 50N 62 43 E
Kamyzyak, *Russia* **61 G9** 46 4N 48 10 E
Kan, *Burma* **90 D5** 22 25N 94 5 E
Kan, *Sudan* **107 F3** 9 1N 31 47 E
Kanaaupscow, *Canada* **140 B4** 54 2N 76 30W
Kanaaupscow →, *Canada* **139 C12** 53 39N 77 9W
Kanab, *U.S.A.* **159 H7** 37 3N 112 32W
Kanab →, *U.S.A.* **159 H7** 36 24N 112 38W
Kanacea, *Lau Group, Fiji* **133 A3** 17 15 S 179 6W
Kanacea, *Taveuni, Fiji* **133 A2** 16 59 S 179 56 E
Kanaga I., *U.S.A.* **144 L3** 51 45N 177 22W
Kanagawa □, *Japan* **73 B11** 35 20N 139 20 E
Kanagi, *Japan* **70 D10** 40 54N 140 27 E
Kanairiktok →, *Canada* **141 A7** 55 2N 60 18W
Kanakapura, *India* **95 H3** 12 33N 77 28 E
Kanália, *Greece* **48 B4** 39 30N 22 53 E
Kananga, *Dem. Rep. of the Congo* **115 D4** 5 55 S 22 18 E
Kanangra-Boyd Nat. Park, *Australia* **129 B9** 33 57 S 150 15 E
Kanash, *Russia* **60 C8** 55 30N 47 32 E
Kanaskat, *U.S.A.* **160 C5** 47 19N 121 54W
Kanastraíon, Ákra = Palioúrion, Ákra, *Greece* **50 G7** 39 57N 23 45 E
Kanawha →, *U.S.A.* **148 F4** 38 50N 82 9W
Kanazawa, *Japan* **73 A8** 36 30N 136 38 E
Kanbalu, *Burma* **90 D5** 23 12N 95 31 E
Kanchanaburi, *Thailand* **86 E2** 14 2N 99 31 E
Kanchenjunga, *Nepal* **93 F13** 27 50N 88 10 E
Kanchipuram, *India* **95 H4** 12 52N 79 45 E
Kańczuga, *Poland* **55 J9** 49 59N 22 25 E
Kanda Kanda, *Dem. Rep. of the Congo* **115 D4** 6 52 S 23 48 E
Kandaghat, *India* **92 D7** 30 59N 77 7 E
Kandahar = Qandahār, *Afghan.* **91 C2** 31 32N 65 43 E
Kandahar, *India* **94 E3** 18 52N 77 12 E
Kandala, *Dem. Rep. of the Congo* **115 D3** 6 20 S 19 40 E
Kandalaksha, *Russia* **56 A5** 67 9N 32 30 E
Kandalakshskiy Zaliv, *Russia* **56 A6** 66 0N 35 0 E
Kandangan, *Indonesia* **85 C5** 2 50 S 115 20 E
Kandanghaur, *Indonesia* **79 G13** 6 21 S 108 6 E
Kandanos, *Greece* **39 E4** 35 19N 23 44 E
Kandava, *Latvia* **54 A9** 57 2N 22 46 E
Kandavu = Kadavu, *Fiji* **133 B2** 19 0 S 178 15 E
Kandavu Passage = Kadavu Passage, *Fiji* **133 B2** 18 45 S 178 0 E
Kandep, *Papua N. G.* **132 C2** 5 54 S 143 32 E
Kander →, *Switz.* **32 C5** 46 33N 7 38 E
Kandersteg, *Switz.* **32 D5** 46 28N 7 40 E
Kandhíla, *Greece* **39 B2** 38 42N 20 56 E
Kandhíla, *Greece* **48 D4** 37 46N 22 22 E
Kandhkot, *Pakistan* **92 E3** 28 16N 69 8 E
Kandhla, *India* **92 E7** 29 18N 77 19 E
Kandi, *Benin* **113 C5** 11 7N 2 55 E
Kandi, *India* **93 H13** 23 58N 88 5 E
Kandiaro, *Pakistan* **92 F3** 27 4N 68 13 E
Kandıra, *Turkey* **100 B4** 41 4N 30 9 E
Kandla, *India* **92 H4** 23 0N 70 10 E
Kandor, O. →, *Chad* **109 E4** 17 13N 20 52 E
Kandos, *Australia* **129 B8** 32 45 S 149 58 E
Kandreho, *Madag.* **117 B8** 17 29 S 46 6 E
Kandrian, *Papua N. G.* **132 D5** 6 14 S 149 37 E
Kandy, *Sri Lanka* **95 L5** 7 18N 80 43 E
Kane, *U.S.A.* **150 E6** 41 40N 78 49W
Kane Basin, *Greenland* **10 B4** 79 1N 70 0W
Kaneilio Pt., *U.S.A.* **145 K13** 21 27N 158 12W
Kanel, *Senegal* **112 B2** 15 30N 13 18W
Kaneohe, *U.S.A.* **145 K14** 21 25N 157 48W
Kaneohe B., *U.S.A.* **145 K14** 21 30N 157 50W
Kanevskaya, *Russia* **61 G4** 46 3N 38 57 E
Kanfanar, *Croatia* **45 C10** 45 7N 13 50 E
Kang, *Botswana* **116 C3** 23 41 S 22 50 E
Kangaamiut, *Greenland* **10 D5** 65 50N 53 20W
Kangaba, *Mali* **112 C3** 11 56N 8 25W
Kangal, *Turkey* **100 C7** 39 14N 37 23 E
Kangān, *Fārs, Iran* **97 E7** 27 50N 52 3 E
Kangān, *Hormozgān, Iran* **97 E8** 25 48N 57 28 E
Kangar, *Malaysia* **87 J3** 6 27N 100 12 E
Kangaré, *Mali* **112 C3** 11 36N 8 4W
Kangaroo I., *Australia* **128 C2** 35 45 S 137 0 E
Kangaroo Mts., *Australia* **126 C3** 23 29 S 141 51 E
Kangasala, *Finland* **15 F21** 61 28N 24 4 E
Kangāvar, *Iran* **97 C6** 34 40N 48 0 E
Kangding, *China* **76 B3** 30 2N 101 57 E
Kangdong, *N. Korea* **75 E14** 39 9N 126 5 E
Kangean, Kepulauan, *Indonesia* **85 D5** 6 55 S 115 23 E
Kangean Is. = Kangean, Kepulauan, *Indonesia* **85 D5** 6 55 S 115 23 E
Kangen →, *Sudan* **107 F3** 6 47N 33 9 E
Kangerdlugssuak, *Greenland* **10 D7** 68 10N 32 20W
Kangerluarsoruseq, *Greenland* **10 E5** 63 45N 51 27W
Kangerluarsoruset = Kangerluarsoruseq, *Greenland* **10 E5** 63 45N 51 27W
Kangerlussuaq, *Greenland* **10 D5** 66 59N 50 40W
Kanggye, *N. Korea* **75 D14** 41 0N 126 35 E
Kanggyŏng, *S. Korea* **75 F14** 36 10N 127 0 E
Kanghwa, *S. Korea* **75 F14** 37 45N 126 30 E
Kangikajik, *Greenland* **10 C8** 70 7N 22 0W
Kangilinnguit, *Greenland* **10 E6** 61 20N 47 57W
Kangiqsliniq = Rankin Inlet, *Canada* **138 B10** 62 30N 93 0W
Kangiqsualujjuaq, *Canada* **139 C13** 58 30N 65 59W
Kangiqsujuaq, *Canada* **139 B12** 61 30N 72 0W
Kangiqtugaapik = Clyde River, *Canada* **139 A13** 70 30N 68 30W
Kangirsuk, *Canada* **139 B13** 60 0N 70 0W
Kangkar Chemaran, *Malaysia* **87 d** 1 34N 104 12 E
Kangkar Sungai Tiram, *Malaysia* **87 d** 1 35N 103 55 E
Kangkar Teberau, *Malaysia* **87 d** 1 32N 103 51 E
Kangnŭng, *S. Korea* **75 F15** 37 45N 128 54 E
Kango, *Gabon* **114 B2** 0 11N 10 5 E
Kangoya, *Dem. Rep. of the Congo* **115 D4** 9 55 S 22 48 E
Kangping, *China* **75 C12** 42 43N 123 18 E
Kangpokpi, *India* **90 C4** 25 8N 93 58 E
Kangra, *India* **92 C7** 32 6N 76 16 E
Kangyidaung, *Burma* **90 G5** 16 56N 94 54 E
Kanhan →, *India* **94 D4** 21 4N 79 34 E
Kanhangad, *India* **95 H2** 12 21N 74 58 E
Kanhar →, *India* **93 G10** 24 28N 83 8 E
Kanheri, *India* **94 E1** 19 13N 72 50 E
Kani, *Sagaing, Burma* **90 D5** 23 52N 95 22 E
Kani, *Sagaing, Burma* **90 D5** 22 26N 94 51 E
Kani, *Ivory C.* **112 D3** 8 29N 6 36W
Kaniama, *Dem. Rep. of the Congo* **118 D1** 7 30 S 24 12 E
Kaniapiskau = Caniapiscau →, *Canada* **141 A6** 56 40N 69 30W
Kaniapiskau, Res. = Caniapiscau, Rés. de, *Canada* **141 B6** 54 10N 69 55W

Kings Mountain 233

Kętrzyn, *Poland* **54 D8** 54 7N 21 22 E
Kettering, *U.K.* **21 E7** 52 24N 0 43W
Kettering, *U.S.A.* **157 E12** 39 41N 84 10W
Kettle →, *Canada* **143 B11** 56 40N 89 34W
Kettle Falls, *U.S.A.* **158 B4** 48 37N 118 3W
Kettle Pt., *Canada* **150 C2** 43 13N 82 1W
Kettleman City, *U.S.A.* **160 J7** 36 1N 119 58W
Kęty, *Poland* **55 J6** 49 51N 19 16 E
Keuka L., *U.S.A.* **150 D7** 42 30N 77 9W
Keuruu, *Finland* **15 E21** 62 16N 24 41 E
Kevelaer, *Germany* **30 D2** 51 36N 6 15 E
Kewanee, *U.S.A.* **156 C7** 41 14N 89 56W
Kewanna, *U.S.A.* **157 C10** 41 1N 86 25W
Kewaunee, *U.S.A.* **148 C2** 44 27N 87 31W
Keweenaw B., *U.S.A.* **148 B1** 47 0N 88 15W
Keweenaw Pen., *U.S.A.* **148 B2** 47 30N 88 0W
Keweenaw Pt., *U.S.A.* **148 B2** 47 25N 87 43W
Key Colony Beach, *U.S.A.* **153 L9** 24 45N 80 57W
Key Largo, *U.S.A.* **153 K9** 25 5N 80 27W
Key West, *U.S.A.* **153 L8** 24 33N 81 48W
Keyala, *Sudan* **107 G3** 4 27N 32 52 E
Keynsham, *U.K.* **21 F5** 51 24N 2 29W
Keyser, *U.S.A.* **148 F6** 39 26N 78 59W
Keytesville, *U.S.A.* **156 E4** 39 26N 92 56W
Kez, *Russia* **64 C4** 57 55N 53 46 E
Kezhma, *Russia* **67 D11** 58 59N 101 9 E
Kezi, *Zimbabwe* **117 C4** 20 58 S 28 32 E
Kežmarok, *Slovak Rep.* **35 B13** 49 10N 20 28 E
Kgalagadi Transfrontier Park,
Africa **116 D3** 25 10 S 21 0 E
Khabarovsk, *Russia* **67 E14** 48 30N 135 5 E
Khabr, *Iran* **97 D8** 28 51N 56 22 E
Khābūr →, *Syria* **101 E9** 35 17N 40 35 E
Khachmas = Xaçmaz, *Azerbaijan* **61 K9** 41 31N 48 42 E
Khachrod, *India* **92 H6** 23 25N 75 20 E
Khadari, W. el →, *Sudan* **107 E2** 10 29N 27 15 E
Khadro, *Pakistan* **92 F3** 26 11N 68 50 E
Khadyzhensk, *Russia* **61 H4** 44 26N 39 32 E
Khadzhilyangar, *China* **93 B8** 35 45N 79 20 E
Khaga, *India* **93 G9** 25 47N 81 7 E
Khagaria, *India* **93 G12** 25 30N 86 32 E
Khaipur, *Pakistan* **92 E5** 29 34N 72 17 E
Khair, *India* **92 F7** 27 57N 77 46 E
Khairabad, *India* **93 F9** 27 33N 80 47 E
Khairagarh, *India* **93 J9** 21 27N 81 2 E
Khairpur, *Pakistan* **91 D3** 27 32N 68 49 E
Khairpur Nathan Shah, *Pakistan* **92 F2** 27 6N 67 44 E
Khairwara, *India* **92 H5** 23 58N 73 38 E
Khaisor →, *Pakistan* **92 D3** 31 17N 68 59 E
Khajuri Kach, *Pakistan* **92 C3** 32 4N 69 51 E
Khāk Dow, *Afghan.* **91 B2** 34 57N 67 16 E
Khakassia □, *Russia* **66 D9** 53 0N 90 0 E
Khakhea, *Botswana* **116 C3** 24 48 S 23 22 E
Khalafābād, *Iran* **97 D6** 30 54N 49 24 E
Khalfallah, *Algeria* **111 B5** 34 20N 0 16 E
Khalfūt, *Yemen* **99 D6** 15 52N 52 10 E
Khalilabad, *India* **93 F10** 26 48N 83 5 E
Khalīlī, *Iran* **97 E7** 27 38N 53 17 E
Khalkhāl, *Iran* **97 B6** 37 37N 48 32 E
Khálki, *Dhodhekánisos, Greece* **49 E9** 36 17N 27 35 E
Khálki, *Thessalía, Greece* **48 B4** 39 36N 22 30 E
Khalkidhikí □, *Greece* **50 F7** 40 25N 23 20 E
Khalkís, *Greece* **48 C5** 38 27N 23 42 E
Khalmer-Sede = Tazovskiy, *Russia* **66 C8** 67 30N 78 44 E
Khalmer Yu, *Russia* **66 C7** 67 58N 65 1 E
Khalturin, *Russia* **64 B2** 58 40N 48 50 E
Khalūf, *Oman* **102 C6** 20 30N 58 13 E
Kham Keut, *Laos* **86 C5** 18 15N 104 43 E
Khamaria, *India* **93 H9** 23 5N 80 48 E
Khambhaliya, *India* **92 H3** 22 14N 69 41 E
Khambhat, *India* **92 H5** 22 23N 72 33 E
Khambhat, G. of, *India* **89 C6** 20 45N 72 30 E
Khamgaon, *India* **94 D3** 20 42N 76 37 E
Khamilonísion, *Greece* **49 F8** 35 50N 26 15 E
Khamīr, *Iran* **97 E7** 26 57N 55 36 E
Khamir, *Yemen* **98 C3** 16 2N 44 0 E
Khamīs Mushayţ, *Si. Arabia* **98 C3** 18 18N 42 44 E
Khammam, *India* **94 F5** 17 11N 80 6 E
Khamsa, *Egypt* **103 E1** 30 27N 32 23 E
Khamza, *Uzbekistan* **65 C5** 40 25N 71 29 E
Khan →, *Namibia* **116 C2** 22 37 S 14 56 E
Khān Abū Shāmat, *Syria* **103 B5** 33 39N 36 53 E
Khān Azād, *Iraq* **96 C5** 33 7N 44 22 E
Khān Mujiddah, *Iraq* **96 C4** 32 21N 43 48 E
Khān Shaykhūn, *Syria* **100 E7** 35 26N 36 38 E
Khān Yūnis, *Gaza Strip* **103 D3** 31 21N 34 18 E
Khānābād, *Afghan.* **65 E4** 36 45N 69 5 E
Khanabad, *Uzbekistan* **65 C6** 40 47N 73 0 E
Khanai, *Pakistan* **92 D2** 30 30N 67 8 E
Khānaqīn, *Iraq* **101 E11** 34 23N 45 25 E
Khānbāghī, *Iran* **97 B7** 36 10N 55 25 E
Khandrá, *Greece* **49 F8** 35 3N 26 8 E
Khandūd, *Afghan.* **65 E6** 36 57N 72 19 E
Khandwa, *India* **94 D3** 21 49N 76 22 E
Khandyga, *Russia* **67 C14** 62 42N 135 35 E
Khāneh, *Iran* **96 B5** 36 41N 45 8 E
Khanewal, *Pakistan* **91 C3** 30 20N 71 55 E
Khangah Dogran, *Pakistan* **92 D5** 31 50N 73 37 E
Khanh Duong, *Vietnam* **86 F7** 12 44N 108 44 E
Khaniá, *Greece* **39 E5** 35 30N 24 4 E
Khaniá □, *Greece* **39 E5** 35 30N 24 0 E
Khaniadhana, *India* **92 G8** 25 1N 78 8 E
Khaníon, Kólpos, *Greece* **39 E4** 35 33N 23 55 E
Khanka, L., *Asia* **67 E14** 45 0N 132 24 E
Khankendy = Xankändi,
Azerbaijan **101 C12** 39 52N 46 49 E
Khanna, *India* **92 D7** 30 42N 76 16 E
Khanozai, *Pakistan* **92 D2** 30 37N 67 19 E
Khanpur, *Pakistan* **91 C3** 28 42N 70 35 E
Khantaū, *Kazakstan* **65 A6** 44 13N 73 48 E
Khanty-Mansiysk, *Russia* **66 C7** 61 0N 69 0 E
Khao Phlu, *Thailand* **87 b** 9 29N 99 59 E
Khapalu, *Pakistan* **93 B7** 35 10N 76 20 E
Khapcheranga, *Russia* **67 E12** 49 42N 112 24 E
Kharabali, *Russia* **61 G8** 47 25N 47 15 E
Kharaghoda, *India* **92 H4** 23 11N 71 46 E
Kharagpur, *India* **93 H12** 22 20N 87 25 E
Khárakas, *Greece* **39 E6** 35 1N 25 7 E
Kharan Kalat, *Pakistan* **91 C2** 28 34N 65 21 E
Kharānaq, *Iran* **97 C7** 32 20N 54 45 E
Kharda, *India* **94 E2** 18 40N 75 34 E
Khardung La, *India* **93 B7** 34 20N 77 43 E
Khârga, El Wâhât-el, *Egypt* **106 B3** 25 10N 30 35 E
Khargon, *India* **94 D2** 21 45N 75 40 E
Khari →, *India* **92 G6** 25 54N 74 31 E
Kharian, *Pakistan* **92 C5** 32 49N 73 52 E
Khariar, *India* **94 D6** 20 17N 82 46 E
Kharit, Wadi el →, *Egypt* **106 C3** 24 26N 33 3 E
Khārk, Jazīreh-ye, *Iran* **97 D6** 29 15N 50 28 E
Kharkiv, *Ukraine* **59 H9** 49 58N 36 20 E
Kharkov = Kharkiv, *Ukraine* **59 H9** 49 58N 36 20 E
Kharmanli, *Bulgaria* **51 E9** 41 55N 25 55 E
Kharovsk, *Russia* **58 C11** 59 56N 40 13 E
Kharsawangarh, *India* **93 H11** 22 48N 85 50 E
Kharta, *Turkey* **100 B3** 40 55N 29 7 E
Khartoum = El Khartûm, *Sudan* **107 D3** 15 31N 32 35 E
Khasan, *Russia* **70 C5** 42 25N 130 40 E
Khasavyurt, *Russia* **61 J8** 43 16N 46 40 E
Khāsh, *Iran* **91 C1** 28 15N 61 15 E
Khāsh, Dasht-e, *Afghan.* **91 C1** 31 50N 62 30 E
Khashm el Girba, *Sudan* **107 E4** 14 59N 35 58 E
Khashum, *Sudan* **107 E2** 12 27N 28 2 E
Khashuri, *Georgia* **61 J6** 42 3N 43 35 E
Khasi Hills, *India* **90 C3** 25 30N 91 30 E
Khaskovo, *Bulgaria* **51 E9** 41 56N 25 30 E
Khaskovo □, *Bulgaria* **51 E9** 42 0N 25 40 E
Khatanga, *Russia* **67 B11** 72 0N 102 20 E
Khatanga →, *Russia* **67 B11** 72 55N 106 0 E
Khatauli, *India* **92 E7** 29 17N 77 43 E
Khatra, *India* **93 H12** 22 59N 86 51 E
Khātūnābād, *Iran* **97 D7** 30 1N 55 25 E
Khatyrka, *Russia* **67 C18** 62 3N 175 15 E
Khavast, *Uzbekistan* **65 C4** 40 10N 68 49 E
Khavda, *India* **92 H3** 23 51N 69 43 E
Khavdháta, *Greece* **39 D1** 38 12N 20 23 E
Khawlaf, Ra's, *Yemen* **99 D6** 12 40N 54 7 E
Khay', *Si. Arabia* **98 C3** 18 45N 41 24 E
Khaybar, Ḩarrat, *Si. Arabia* **96 E4** 25 45N 40 0 E
Khaydarken, *Kyrgyzstan* **65 D5** 39 57N 71 20 E
Khāzimiyah, *Iraq* **96 C4** 34 46N 43 37 E
Khazzān Jabal al Awliyā, *Sudan* **107 D3** 15 24N 32 20 E
Khe Bo, *Vietnam* **86 C5** 19 8N 104 41 E
Khe Long, *Vietnam* **86 B5** 21 29N 104 46 E
Khed, *Maharashtra, India* **94 F1** 17 43N 73 27 E
Khed, *Maharashtra, India* **94 E1** 18 51N 73 56 E
Khekra, *India* **92 E7** 28 52N 77 20 E
Khemarak Phouminville,
Cambodia **87 G4** 11 37N 102 59 E
Khemis Miliana, *Algeria* **111 A5** 36 11N 2 14 E
Khemisset, *Morocco* **110 B3** 33 50N 6 1W
Khemmarat, *Thailand* **86 D5** 16 10N 105 15 E
Khenāmān, *Iran* **97 D8** 30 27N 56 29 E
Khenchela, *Algeria* **111 A6** 35 28N 7 11 E
Khenifra, *Morocco* **110 B3** 32 58N 5 46W
Kherrata, *Algeria* **111 A6** 36 27N 5 13 E
Khersān →, *Iran* **97 D6** 31 33N 50 22 E
Khérson, *Greece* **50 E6** 41 5N 22 47 E
Kherson, *Ukraine* **59 J7** 46 35N 32 35 E
Khersónisos Akrotíri, *Greece* **39 E5** 35 30N 24 10 E
Kheta →, *Russia* **67 B11** 71 54N 102 6 E
Khewari, *Pakistan* **92 F3** 26 36N 68 52 E
Khilchipur, *India* **92 G7** 24 2N 76 34 E
Khiliomódhion, *Greece* **48 D4** 37 48N 22 51 E
Khilok, *Russia* **67 D12** 51 30N 110 45 E
Khimki, *Russia* **58 E9** 55 50N 37 20 E
Khíos, *Greece* **49 C8** 38 27N 26 9 E
Khíos □, *Greece* **49 C8** 38 27N 26 9 E
Khirsadoh, *India* **93 H8** 22 11N 78 47 E
Khiuma = Hiiumaa, *Estonia* **15 G20** 58 50N 22 45 E
Khiva, *Uzbekistan* **66 E7** 41 30N 60 18 E
Khīyāv, *Iran* **96 B5** 38 30N 47 45 E
Khlebarovo, *Bulgaria* **51 C10** 43 37N 26 15 E
Khlong Khlung, *Thailand* **86 D2** 16 12N 99 43 E
Khmelnik, *Ukraine* **59 H4** 49 33N 27 58 E
Khmelnitskiy = Khmelnytskyy,
Ukraine **59 H4** 49 23N 27 0 E
Khmelnytskyy, *Ukraine* **59 H4** 49 23N 27 0 E
Khmer Rep. = Cambodia ■, *Asia* **86 F5** 12 15N 105 0 E
Khoai, Hon, *Vietnam* **87 H5** 8 26N 104 50 E
Khodoriv, *Ukraine* **59 H3** 49 24N 24 19 E
Khodzent = Khŭjand, *Tajikistan* **66 E7** 40 17N 69 37 E
Khojak Pass, *Afghan.* **91 C2** 30 51N 66 34 E
Khok Kloi, *Thailand* **87 a** 8 17N 98 19 E
Khok Pho, *Thailand* **87 J3** 6 43N 101 6 E
Khokhropār, *Pakistan* **91 D3** 25 42N 70 12 E
Kholm, *Afghan.* **65 E3** 36 45N 67 40 E
Kholm, *Russia* **58 D6** 57 10N 31 15 E
Kholmsk, *Russia* **67 E15** 47 40N 142 5 E
Khomas Hochland, *Namibia* **116 C2** 22 40 S 16 0 E
Khombole, *Senegal* **112 C1** 14 43N 16 42W
Khomeyn, *Iran* **97 C6** 33 40N 50 7 E
Khomeynī Shahr, *Iran* **97 C6** 32 41N 51 31 E
Khomodino, *Botswana* **116 C3** 22 46 S 23 52 E
Khon Kaen, *Thailand* **86 D4** 16 30N 102 47 E
Khong →, *Cambodia* **86 F5** 13 32N 105 58 E
Khong Sedone, *Laos* **86 E5** 15 34N 105 49 E
Khonuu, *Russia* **67 C15** 66 30N 143 12 E
Khoper →, *Russia* **60 F6** 49 30N 42 20 E
Khor el 'Atash, *Sudan* **107 E3** 13 20N 34 15 E
Khóra, *Greece* **48 D3** 37 3N 21 42 E
Khóra Sfakíon, *Greece* **39 E5** 35 15N 24 9 E
Khorāsān □, *Iran* **97 C8** 34 0N 58 0 E
Khorat = Nakhon Ratchasima,
Thailand **86 E4** 14 59N 102 12 E
Khorat, Cao Nguyen, *Thailand* **86 E4** 15 30N 102 50 E
Khorb el Ethel, *Algeria* **110 C3** 28 30N 6 17W
Khorixas, *Namibia* **116 C1** 20 16 S 14 59 E
Khorol, *Ukraine* **59 H7** 49 48N 33 15 E
Khorramābād, *Khorāsān, Iran* **97 C8** 35 6N 57 57 E
Khorramābād, *Lorestān, Iran* **97 C6** 33 30N 48 25 E
Khorrāmshahr, *Iran* **97 D6** 30 29N 48 15 E
Khorugh, *Tajikistan* **66 F8** 37 30N 71 36 E
Khosravī, *Iran* **97 D6** 30 48N 51 28 E
Khosrowābād, *Khuzestān, Iran* **97 D6** 30 10N 48 25 E
Khosrowābād, *Kordestān, Iran* **101 E12** 35 31N 47 38 E
Khost, *Pakistan* **92 D2** 30 13N 67 35 E
Khosūyeh, *Iran* **97 D7** 28 32N 54 26 E
Khotyn, *Ukraine* **59 H4** 48 31N 26 27 E
Khouribga, *Morocco* **110 B3** 32 58N 6 57W
Khowai, *Bangla.* **90 C3** 24 5N 91 40 E
Khowst, *Afghan.* **91 B3** 33 22N 69 58 E
Khoyniki, *Belarus* **59 G5** 51 54N 29 55 E
Khrami →, *Georgia* **61 K7** 41 25N 45 0 E
Khrenovoye, *Russia* **60 E5** 51 4N 40 16 E
Khrisoúpolis, *Greece* **51 F8** 40 58N 24 42 E
Khristianá, *Greece* **49 E7** 36 14N 25 13 E
Khromtau, *Kazakstan* **64 F7** 50 17N 58 27 E
Khrysokhou B., *Cyprus* **39 E8** 35 6N 32 25 E
Khtapodhiá, *Greece* **49 D7** 37 24N 25 34 E
Khu Khan, *Thailand* **86 E5** 14 42N 104 12 E
Khuan Wa, *Thailand* **87 a** 7 53N 98 17 E
Khudrah, W. →, *Yemen* **99 C5** 18 10N 50 20 E
Khudzhand = Khŭjand, *Tajikistan* **66 E7** 40 17N 69 37 E
Khuff, *Si. Arabia* **96 E5** 24 55N 44 53 E
Khūgīānī, *Qandahar, Afghan.* **91 C2** 31 34N 66 32 E
Khūgīānī, *Qandahar, Afghan.* **91 C2** 31 37N 65 4 E
Khuis, *Botswana* **116 D3** 26 40 S 21 49 E
Khuiyala, *India* **92 F4** 27 9N 70 25 E
Khŭjand, *Tajikistan* **66 E7** 40 17N 69 37 E
Khujner, *India* **92 H7** 23 47N 76 36 E
Khulayş, *Si. Arabia* **98 B2** 22 9N 39 19 E
Khulna, *Bangla.* **90 D2** 22 45N 89 34 E
Khulna □, *Bangla.* **90 D2** 22 25N 89 35 E
Khulo, *Georgia* **61 K6** 41 33N 42 19 E
Khumago, *Botswana* **116 C3** 20 26 S 24 32 E
Khumrah, *Si. Arabia* **98 B2** 21 22N 39 13 E
Khūnsorkh, *Iran* **97 E8** 27 9N 56 7 E
Khunti, *India* **93 H11** 23 5N 85 17 E
Khūr, *Iran* **97 C8** 32 55N 58 18 E
Khurai, *India* **92 G8** 24 3N 78 23 E
Khuraydah, *Yemen* **99 D5** 15 33N 48 18 E
Khurayş, *Si. Arabia* **97 E6** 25 6N 48 2 E
Khurda, *India* **94 D7** 20 11N 85 37 E
Khureit, *Sudan* **107 E2** 13 59N 26 3 E
Khurīyā Murīyā, Ghubbat, *Oman* **99 C6** 17 40N 55 45 E
Khurīyā Murīyā, Jazā'ir, *Oman* **99 C6** 17 30N 55 58 E
Khurja, *India* **92 E7** 28 15N 77 58 E
Khūrmāl, *Iraq* **96 C5** 35 18N 46 2 E
Khurr, Wādī al, *Iraq* **96 C4** 32 3N 43 52 E
Khūsf, *Iran* **97 C8** 32 46N 58 53 E
Khushab, *Pakistan* **91 B4** 32 20N 72 20 E
Khust, *Ukraine* **59 H2** 48 10N 23 18 E
Khutse Game Reserve, *Botswana* **116 C3** 23 31 S 24 12 E
Khuzdar, *Pakistan* **91 D2** 27 52N 66 30 E
Khūzestān □, *Iran* **97 D6** 31 0N 49 0 E
Khvāf, *Iran* **97 C9** 34 33N 60 8 E
Khvājeh, *Iran* **96 B5** 38 9N 46 35 E
Khvājeh Moḩammad, Kūh-e,
Afghan. **65 E5** 36 22N 70 17 E
Khvalynsk, *Russia* **60 D9** 52 30N 48 2 E
Khvānsār, *Iran* **97 D7** 29 56N 54 8 E
Khvatovka, *Russia* **60 D8** 52 24N 46 32 E
Khvor, *Iran* **97 C7** 33 45N 55 0 E
Khvorgū, *Iran* **97 E8** 27 34N 56 27 E
Khvormūj, *Iran* **97 D6** 28 40N 51 30 E
Khvoy, *Iran* **101 C11** 38 35N 45 0 E
Khvoynaya, *Russia* **58 C8** 58 58N 34 28 E
Khyber Pass, *Afghan.* **91 B3** 34 10N 71 8 E
Kia, *Fiji* **133 A2** 16 16 S 179 8 E
Kia, *Solomon Is.* **133 L10** 7 32 S 158 26 E
Kiabukwa, *Dem. Rep. of the Congo* **119 D1** 8 40 S 24 48 E
Kiadho →, *India* **94 E3** 19 37N 77 40 E
Kiama, *Australia* **129 C9** 34 40 S 150 50 E
Kiamba, *Dem. Rep. of the Congo* **115 D3** 7 19 S 17 49 E
Kiamba, *Phil.* **81 H5** 6 2N 124 46 E
Kiambi, *Dem. Rep. of the Congo* **118 D2** 7 15 S 28 0 E
Kiambu, *Kenya* **118 C4** 1 8 S 36 50 E
Kiana, *U.S.A.* **144 C7** 66 58N 160 26W
Kiang West Nat. Park, *Gambia* **112 C1** 13 25N 15 50W
Kiangara, *Madag.* **117 B8** 17 58 S 47 2 E
Kiangsi = Jiangxi □, *China* **77 D11** 27 30N 116 0 E
Kiangsu = Jiangsu □, *China* **75 H11** 33 0N 120 0 E
Kiáton, *Greece* **48 C4** 38 1N 22 45 E
Kibæk, *Denmark* **17 H2** 56 2N 8 51 E
Kibale Nat. Park, *Uganda* **118 B3** 0 16N 30 18 E
Kibanga Port, *Uganda* **118 B3** 0 10N 32 58 E
Kibangou, *Congo* **114 C2** 3 26 S 12 22 E
Kibara, *Tanzania* **118 C3** 2 8 S 33 30 E
Kibare, Mts., *Dem. Rep. of*
the Congo **118 D2** 8 25 S 27 10 E
Kibawe, *Phil.* **81 H5** 7 34N 125 0 E
Kibenga, *Dem. Rep. of the Congo* **115 D3** 7 56 S 17 30 E
Kibira, Parc Nat. de, *Burundi* **118 C3** 3 6 S 30 24 E
Kibombo, *Dem. Rep. of the Congo* **118 C2** 3 57 S 25 53 E
Kibondo, *Tanzania* **118 C3** 3 35 S 30 45 E
Kibray, *Uzbekistan* **65 C4** 41 23N 69 27 E
Kibre Mengist, *Ethiopia* **107 F4** 5 54N 38 59 E
Kibumbu, *Burundi* **118 C2** 3 32 S 29 45 E
Kibungo, *Rwanda* **118 C3** 2 10 S 30 32 E
Kibuye, *Burundi* **118 C2** 3 39 S 29 59 E
Kibuye, *Rwanda* **118 C2** 2 3 S 29 21 E
Kibwesa, *Tanzania* **118 D2** 6 30 S 29 58 E
Kibwezi, *Kenya* **118 C4** 2 27 S 37 57 E
Kicasalih, *Turkey* **51 E10** 41 23N 26 48 E
Kičevo, *Macedonia* **50 E4** 41 34N 20 59 E
Kichha, *India* **93 E8** 28 53N 79 30 E
Kichha →, *India* **93 E8** 28 41N 79 18 E
Kichmengskiy Gorodok, *Russia* **56 B8** 59 59N 45 48 E
Kicking Horse Pass, *Canada* **142 C5** 51 28N 116 16W
Kidal, *Mali* **113 B5** 18 26N 1 22 E
Kidapawan, *Phil.* **81 H5** 7 1N 125 3 E
Kidderminster, *U.K.* **21 E5** 52 24N 2 15W
Kidepo Valley Nat. Park, *Uganda* **118 B3** 3 52N 33 50 E
Kidete, *Tanzania* **118 D4** 6 25 S 37 17 E
Kidira, *Senegal* **112 C2** 14 28N 12 13W
Kidnappers, C., *N.Z.* **130 F6** 39 38 S 177 5 E
Kidsgrove, *U.K.* **20 D5** 53 5N 2 14W
Kidston, *Australia* **126 B3** 18 52 S 144 8 E
Kidugallo, *Tanzania* **118 D4** 6 49 S 38 15 E
Kidurong, Tanjong, *Malaysia* **85 B4** 3 16N 113 3 E
Kiel, *Germany* **30 A6** 54 19N 10 8 E
Kiel Canal = Nord-Ostsee-Kanal,
Germany **30 A5** 54 12N 9 32 E
Kielce, *Poland* **55 H7** 50 52N 20 42 E
Kielder Water, *U.K.* **20 B5** 55 11N 2 31W
Kieler Bucht, *Germany* **30 A6** 54 35N 10 25 E
Kiembara, *Burkina Faso* **112 C4** 13 15N 2 44W
Kien Binh, *Vietnam* **87 H5** 9 55N 105 19 E
Kien Tan, *Vietnam* **87 G5** 10 7N 105 17 E
Kienge, *Dem. Rep. of the Congo* **119 E2** 10 30 S 27 30 E
Kiessé, *Niger* **113 C5** 13 29N 4 1 E
Kieta, *Papua N. G.* **132 D8** 6 12 S 155 36 E
Kiev = Kyyiv, *Ukraine* **59 G6** 50 30N 30 28 E
Kifaya, *Guinea* **112 C2** 12 10N 13 4W
Kiffa, *Mauritania* **112 B2** 16 37N 11 24W
Kifisiá, *Greece* **48 C5** 38 4N 23 49 E
Kifissós →, *Greece* **48 C5** 38 35N 23 20 E
Kifrī, *Iraq* **101 E11** 34 45N 45 0 E
Kigali, *Rwanda* **118 C3** 1 59 S 30 4 E
Kigarama, *Tanzania* **118 C3** 1 1 S 31 50 E
Kigelle, *Sudan* **107 F3** 8 40N 34 2 E
Kigezi Game Reserve, *Uganda* **118 C2** 0 34 S 29 55 E
Kigoma □, *Tanzania* **118 D3** 5 0 S 30 0 E
Kigoma-Ujiji, *Tanzania* **118 C2** 4 55 S 29 36 E
Kigomasha, Ras, *Tanzania* **118 C4** 4 58 S 38 58 E
Kığzı, *Turkey* **96 B4** 38 18N 43 25 E
Kihei, *U.S.A.* **145 C5** 20 47N 156 28W
Kihikihi, *N.Z.* **130 E4** 38 2 S 175 22 E
Kihnu, *Estonia* **15 G21** 58 9N 24 1 E
Kiholo B., *U.S.A.* **145 D6** 19 50N 155 55W
Kii-Hantō, *Japan* **73 D7** 34 0N 135 45 E
Kii-Nagashima, *Japan* **73 C8** 34 12N 136 20 E
Kii-Sanchi, *Japan* **73 C8** 34 20N 136 0 E
Kii-Suidō, *Japan* **72 D6** 33 40N 134 45 E
Kiire, *Japan* **72 F2** 31 22N 130 33 E
Kikaiga-Shima, *Japan* **71 K4** 28 19N 129 59 E
Kikinda, *Serbia, Yug.* **52 E5** 45 50N 20 30 E
Kikládhes, *Greece* **48 E6** 37 0N 24 30 E
Kikládhes □, *Greece* **48 D6** 37 0N 25 0 E
Kikoira, *Australia* **129 B7** 33 39 S 146 40 E
Kikombo, *Bandundu, Dem. Rep.*
of the Congo **115 D3** 5 37 S 18 50 E
Kikombo, *Bandundu, Dem. Rep.*
of the Congo **115 D3** 5 49 S 17 45 E
Kikongo, *Dem. Rep. of the Congo* **115 D3** 4 16 S 17 17 E
Kikori, *Papua N. G.* **132 D3** 7 25 S 144 15 E
Kikori →, *Papua N. G.* **132 D3** 7 38 S 144 20 E
Kikuchi, *Japan* **72 E2** 32 59N 130 47 E
Kikwit, *Dem. Rep. of the Congo* **115 D3** 5 0 S 18 45 E
Kil, *Sweden* **16 E7** 59 30N 13 20 E
Kilafors, *Sweden* **16 C10** 61 14N 16 36 E
Kilakkarai, *India* **95 K4** 9 12N 78 47 E
Kilar, *India* **92 C7** 33 6N 76 25 E
Kilauea, *U.S.A.* **145 A2** 22 13N 159 25W
Kilauea Crater, *U.S.A.* **145 D6** 19 25N 155 17W
Kilbrannan Sd., *U.K.* **22 F3** 55 37N 5 26W
Kilchberg, *Switz.* **33 B7** 47 18N 8 33 E
Kilchu, *N. Korea* **75 D15** 40 57N 129 25 E
Kilcoy, *Australia* **127 D5** 26 59 S 152 30 E
Kildare, *Ireland* **23 C5** 53 9N 6 55W
Kildare □, *Ireland* **23 C5** 53 10N 6 50W
Kileikli, *Sudan* **107 E2** 11 25N 25 31 E
Kilembe, *Dem. Rep. of the Congo* **115 D3** 5 42 S 19 55 E
Kilen, *Norway* **18 E5** 59 20N 8 49 E
Kilfinnane, *Ireland* **23 D3** 52 21N 8 28W
Kilgore, *U.S.A.* **155 J7** 32 23N 94 53W
Kilibo, *Benin* **113 D5** 8 32N 2 38 E
Kilifi, *Kenya* **118 C4** 3 40 S 39 48 E
Kilimanjaro, *Tanzania* **118 C4** 3 7 S 37 20 E
Kilimanjaro □, *Tanzania* **118 C4** 4 0 S 38 0 E
Kilimli, *Turkey* **100 B4** 41 28N 31 50 E
Kilinailau Is., *Papua N. G.* **132 C8** 4 45 S 155 20 E
Kilindini, *Kenya* **118 C4** 4 4 S 39 40 E
Kilis, *Turkey* **100 D7** 36 42N 37 6 E
Kiliya, *Ukraine* **59 K5** 45 28N 29 16 E
Kilkee, *Ireland* **23 D2** 52 41N 9 39W
Kilkeel, *U.K.* **23 B5** 54 4N 6 0W
Kilkenny, *Ireland* **23 D4** 52 39N 7 15W
Kilkenny □, *Ireland* **23 D4** 52 35N 7 15W
Kilkieran B., *Ireland* **23 C2** 53 20N 9 41W
Kilkís, *Greece* **50 F6** 40 58N 22 57 E
Kilkís □, *Greece* **50 E6** 41 5N 22 50 E
Killala, *Ireland* **23 B2** 54 13N 9 12W
Killala B., *Ireland* **23 B2** 54 16N 9 8W
Killaloe, *Ireland* **23 D3** 52 48N 8 28W
Killaloe Station, *Canada* **150 A7** 45 33N 77 25W
Killarney, *Australia* **127 D5** 28 20 S 152 18 E
Killarney, *Canada* **143 D9** 49 10N 99 40W
Killarney, *Ireland* **23 D2** 52 4N 9 30W
Killarney, L., *Bahamas* **9 b** 25 3N 77 27W
Killary Harbour, *Ireland* **23 C2** 53 38N 9 52W
Killdeer, *U.S.A.* **154 B3** 47 26N 102 48W
Killeberg, *Sweden* **17 H8** 56 29N 14 5 E
Killeen, *U.S.A.* **155 K6** 31 7N 97 44W
Killin, *U.K.* **22 E4** 56 28N 4 19W
Killíni, *Ilía, Greece* **39 D3** 37 55N 21 8 E
Killíni, *Korinthía, Greece* **48 D4** 37 54N 22 25 E
Killíni, Ákra, *Greece* **39 D3** 37 57N 21 8 E
Killorglin, *Ireland* **23 D2** 52 6N 9 47W
Killybegs, *Ireland* **23 B3** 54 38N 8 26W
Kilmarnock, *U.K.* **22 F4** 55 37N 4 29W
Kilmez, *Russia* **60 B10** 56 58N 50 55 E
Kilmez →, *Russia* **60 B10** 56 58N 50 28 E
Kilmore, *Australia* **129 D6** 37 25 S 144 53 E
Kilondo, *Tanzania* **119 D3** 9 45 S 34 20 E
Kilosa, *Tanzania* **118 D4** 6 48 S 37 0 E
Kilrush, *Ireland* **23 D2** 52 38N 9 29W
Kiltan I., *India* **95 J1** 11 29N 73 0 E
Kilwa Kisiwani, *Tanzania* **119 D4** 8 58 S 39 32 E
Kilwa Kivinje, *Tanzania* **119 D4** 8 45 S 39 25 E
Kilwa Masoko, *Tanzania* **119 D4** 8 55 S 39 30 E
Kilwinning, *U.K.* **22 F4** 55 39N 4 43W
Kim, *U.S.A.* **155 G3** 37 15N 103 21W
Kim →, *Cameroon* **113 D7** 5 28N 11 7 E
Kimaam, *Indonesia* **83 C5** 7 58 S 138 53 E
Kimamba, *Tanzania* **118 D4** 6 45 S 37 10 E
Kimba, *Australia* **128 B2** 33 8 S 136 23 E
Kimball, *Nebr., U.S.A.* **154 E3** 41 14N 103 40W
Kimball, *S. Dak., U.S.A.* **154 D5** 43 45N 98 57W
Kimbanda, *Dem. Rep. of*
the Congo **115 C3** 4 16 S 18 30 E
Kimbe, *Papua N. G.* **132 C6** 5 33 S 150 11 E
Kimbe B., *Papua N. G.* **132 C6** 5 15 S 150 30 E
Kimberley, *Australia* **124 C4** 16 20 S 127 0 E
Kimberley, *Canada* **142 D5** 49 40N 115 59W
Kimberley, *S. Africa* **116 D3** 28 43 S 24 46 E
Kimberly, *U.S.A.* **158 E6** 42 32N 114 22W
Kimbongo, *Dem. Rep. of*
the Congo **115 D3** 6 8 S 18 1 E
Kimch'aek, *N. Korea* **75 D15** 40 40N 129 10 E
Kimch'ŏn, *S. Korea* **75 F15** 36 11N 128 4 E
Kími, *Greece* **48 C6** 38 38N 24 6 E
Kimitsu, *Japan* **73 B10** 35 19N 139 54 E
Kimje, *S. Korea* **75 G14** 35 48N 126 45 E
Kimmirut, *Canada* **139 B13** 62 50N 69 50W
Kímolos, *Greece* **48 E6** 36 48N 24 37 E
Kimongo, *Congo* **115 C2** 4 27 S 12 53 E
Kimovsk, *Moskva, Russia* **58 E9** 55 21N 37 28 E
Kimovsk, *Tula, Russia* **58 E10** 54 0N 38 29 E
Kimpangu, *Dem. Rep. of*
the Congo **115 D3** 5 52 S 15 3 E
Kimparana, *Mali* **112 C4** 12 48N 5 0W
Kimry, *Russia* **58 D9** 56 55N 37 15 E
Kimstad, *Sweden* **17 F9** 58 35N 15 58 E
Kimvula, *Dem. Rep. of the Congo* **115 D3** 5 44 S 15 58 E
Kin, *Burma* **90 D5** 22 46N 94 42 E
Kin-u, *Burma* **90 D5** 22 46N 95 37 E
Kinabalu, Gunong, *Malaysia* **85 A5** 6 3N 116 14 E
Kinard, *U.S.A.* **152 E4** 30 16N 85 15W
Kínaros, *Greece* **49 E8** 36 59N 26 15 E
Kinaskan L., *Canada* **142 B2** 57 38N 130 8W
Kinbasket L., *Canada* **142 C5** 52 0N 118 10W
Kincaid, *U.S.A.* **156 E7** 39 35N 89 25W
Kincardine, *Canada* **140 D3** 44 10N 81 40W
Kinchafoonee Cr. →, *U.S.A.* **152 D5** 31 38N 84 10W
Kinchega Nat. Park, *Australia* **128 B5** 32 27 S 142 15 E
Kincolith, *Canada* **142 B3** 55 0N 129 57W
Kinda, *Kasai-Or., Dem. Rep. of*
the Congo **119 D2** 9 18 S 25 4 E
Kinda, *Katanga, Dem. Rep. of*
the Congo **115 C4** 4 47 S 21 48 E
Kindambi, *Dem. Rep. of the Congo* **115 D4** 5 6 S 18 14 E
Kindberg, *Austria* **34 D8** 47 30N 15 27 E
Kinde, *U.S.A.* **150 C2** 43 56N 83 0W
Kindele, *Dem. Rep. of the Congo* **115 D4** 8 39 S 24 10 E
Kinder Scout, *U.K.* **20 D6** 53 24N 1 52W
Kinderhook, *U.S.A.* **156 E5** 39 42N 91 10W
Kindersley, *Canada* **143 C7** 51 30N 109 10W
Kindia, *Guinea* **112 D2** 10 0N 12 52W
Kindley Field Airport, *Bermuda* **9 a** 32 22N 64 42W
Kindongo, *Dem. Rep. of the Congo* **114 C3** 3 58 S 17 30 E
Kindu, *Dem. Rep. of the Congo* **118 C2** 2 55 S 25 50 E
Kinel, *Russia* **60 D10** 53 15N 50 40 E
Kineshma, *Russia* **60 B6** 57 30N 42 5 E
Kinesi, *Tanzania* **118 C3** 1 25 S 33 50 E
King, L., *Australia* **125 F2** 33 10 S 119 35 E
King, Mt., *Australia* **126 D4** 25 10 S 147 30 E
King City, *Calif., U.S.A.* **160 J5** 36 13N 121 8W
King City, *Mo., U.S.A.* **156 D2** 40 3N 94 31W
King Cove, *U.S.A.* **144 J7** 55 3N 162 19W
King Cr. →, *Australia* **126 C2** 24 35 S 139 30 E
King Edward →, *Australia* **124 B4** 14 14 S 126 35 E
King Frederick VI Land = Kong
Frederik VI Kyst, *Greenland* **10 E6** 63 0N 43 0W
King George B., *Falk. Is.* **9 f** 51 30 S 60 30W
King George I., *Antarctica* **7 C18** 60 0 S 60 0W
King George Is., *Canada* **139 C11** 57 20N 80 30W
King I. = Kadan Kyun, *Burma* **86 F2** 12 30N 98 20 E
King I., *Australia* **127 F3** 39 50 S 144 0 E
King I., *Canada* **142 C3** 52 10N 127 40W
King Leopold Ranges, *Australia* **124 C4** 17 30 S 125 45 E
King of Prussia, *U.S.A.* **151 F9** 40 5N 75 23W
King Salmon, *U.S.A.* **144 G8** 58 42N 156 40W
King Sd., *Australia* **124 C3** 16 50 S 123 20 E
King William I., *Canada* **138 B10** 69 10N 97 25W
King William's Town, *S. Africa* **116 E4** 32 51 S 27 22 E
Kingaok = Bathurst Inlet, *Canada* **138 B9** 66 50N 108 1W
Kingaroy, *Australia* **127 D5** 26 32 S 151 51 E
Kingdom City, *U.S.A.* **156 F5** 38 57N 91 56W
Kingfisher, *U.S.A.* **155 H6** 35 52N 97 56W
Kingirbān, *Iraq* **96 C5** 34 40N 44 54 E
Kingisepp = Kuressaare, *Estonia* **15 G20** 58 15N 22 30 E
Kingisepp, *Russia* **58 C5** 59 25N 28 40 E
Kingking = Pantukan, *Phil.* **81 H5** 7 9N 125 54 E
Kinglake Nat. Park, *Australia* **129 D6** 37 30 S 145 22 E
Kingman, *Ariz., U.S.A.* **161 K12** 35 12N 114 4W
Kingman, *Ind., U.S.A.* **157 E9** 39 58N 87 18W
Kingman, *Kans., U.S.A.* **155 G5** 37 39N 98 7W
Kingoonya, *Australia* **127 E2** 30 55 S 135 19 E
Kingri, *Pakistan* **92 D3** 30 27N 69 49 E
Kings →, *U.S.A.* **160 J7** 36 3N 119 50W
Kings Canyon Nat. Park, *U.S.A.* **160 J8** 36 50N 118 40W
King's Lynn, *U.K.* **20 E8** 52 45N 0 24 E
Kings Mountain, *U.S.A.* **149 H5** 35 15N 81 20W

Kovur 235

Köksaray, *Kazakstan* **65 B4** 42 38N 68 9 E
Kökshetaū, *Kazakstan* **66 D7** 53 20N 69 25 E
Koksoak →, *Canada* **139 C13** 58 30N 68 10W
Kokstad, *S. Africa* **117 E4** 30 32 S 29 29 E
Köksū, *Kazakstan* **65 C4** 41 28N 68 1 E
Köktal, *Kazakstan* **65 B5** 43 16N 70 18 E
Kokubu, *Japan* **72 F2** 31 44N 130 46 E
Kokyar, *China* **65 E8** 37 23N 77 10 E
Kola, *Indonesia* **83 C4** 5 35 S 134 30 E
Kola, *Russia* **56 A5** 68 45N 33 8 E
Kola Pen. = Kolskiy Poluostrov, *Russia* **56 A6** 67 30N 38 0 E
Kolachel, *India* **95 K3** 8 10N 77 15 E
Kolachi →, *Pakistan* **92 F2** 27 8N 67 2 E
Kolahoi, *India* **93 B6** 34 12N 75 22 E
Kolahun, *Liberia* **112 D2** 8 15N 10 4W
Kolaka, *Indonesia* **82 B2** 4 3 S 121 46 E
Kolar, *India* **95 H4** 13 12N 78 15 E
Kolar Gold Fields, *India* **95 H4** 12 58N 78 16 E
Kolaras, *India* **92 G6** 25 14N 77 36 E
Kolari, *Finland* **14 C20** 67 20N 23 48 E
Kolárovo, *Slovak Rep.* **35 D10** 47 54N 18 0 E
Kolašin, *Montenegro, Yug.* **50 D3** 42 50N 19 31 E
Kolbäck, *Sweden* **16 E10** 59 34N 16 15 E
Kolbäcksån →, *Sweden* **16 E10** 59 36N 16 16 E
Kolbeinsstaðir, *Iceland* **11 C4** 64 59N 22 16W
Kolbermoor, *Germany* **31 H8** 47 51N 12 4 E
Kolbu, *Norway* **18 D7** 60 39N 10 45 E
Kolbuszowa, *Poland* **55 H8** 50 15N 21 46 E
Kolchugino = Leninsk-Kuznetskiy, *Russia* **66 D9** 54 44N 86 10 E
Kolchugino, *Russia* **58 D10** 56 17N 39 22 E
Kolda, *Senegal* **112 C2** 12 55N 14 57W
Koldegi, *Sudan* **107 E3** 12 3N 30 16 E
Kolding, *Denmark* **17 J3** 55 30N 9 29 E
Kole, *Dem. Rep. of the Congo* **114 C4** 3 16 S 22 42 E
Koléa, *Algeria* **111 A5** 36 38N 2 46 E
Kolepom = Dolak, Pulau, *Indonesia* **83 C5** 8 0 S 138 30 E
Kolguyev, Ostrov, *Russia* **56 A8** 69 20N 48 30 E
Kolhapur, *India* **94 F2** 16 43N 74 15 E
Kolia, *Ivory C.* **112 D3** 9 46N 6 28W
Koliganek, *U.S.A.* **144 G8** 59 48N 157 25W
Kolín, *Czech Rep.* **34 A8** 50 2N 15 9 E
Kolind, *Denmark* **17 H4** 56 21N 10 34 E
Kolkas rags, *Latvia* **15 H20** 57 46N 22 37 E
Kolkata, *India* **93 H13** 22 36N 88 24 E
Kolkhozobod, *Tajikistan* **65 E4** 37 35N 68 40 E
Kollam = Quilon, *India* **95 K3** 8 50N 76 38 E
Kölleda, *Germany* **30 D7** 51 11N 11 15 E
Kollegal, *India* **95 H3** 12 9N 77 9 E
Kolleru L., *India* **94 F5** 16 40N 81 10 E
Kollum, *Neths.* **24 A6** 53 17N 6 10 E
Kolmanskop, *Namibia* **116 D2** 26 45 S 15 14 E
Köln, *Germany* **30 E2** 50 56N 6 57 E
Kolno, *Poland* **54 E8** 53 25N 21 56 E
Koło, *Poland* **55 F5** 52 14N 18 40 E
Koloa, *U.S.A.* **145 B2** 21 55N 159 28W
Kołobrzeg, *Poland* **54 D2** 54 10N 15 35 E
Kolokani, *Mali* **112 C3** 13 35N 7 45W
Koloko, *Burkina Faso* **112 C3** 11 5N 5 19W
Kololo, *Ethiopia* **107 F5** 7 29N 41 58 E
Kolombangara, *Solomon Is.* **133 M9** 8 0 S 157 5 E
Kolomna, *Russia* **58 E10** 55 8N 38 45 E
Kolomyya, *Ukraine* **59 H3** 48 31N 25 2 E
Kolondiéba, *Mali* **112 C3** 11 5N 6 54W
Kolonodale, *Indonesia* **82 B2** 2 0 S 121 19 E
Kolonowskie, *Poland* **55 H5** 50 39N 18 22 E
Kolosib, *India* **90 C4** 24 15N 92 45 E
Kolpashevo, *Russia* **66 D9** 58 20N 83 5 E
Kolpino, *Russia* **58 C6** 59 44N 30 39 E
Kolpny, *Russia* **59 F9** 52 17N 37 1 E
Kolskiy Poluostrov, *Russia* **56 A6** 67 30N 38 0 E
Kolskiy Zaliv, *Russia* **56 A5** 69 23N 34 0 E
Kolsva, *Sweden* **16 E9** 59 36N 15 51 E
Kolubara →, *Serbia, Yug.* **50 B4** 44 35N 20 15 E
Koluszki, *Poland* **55 G6** 51 45N 19 46 E
Kolwezi, *Dem. Rep. of the Congo* **119 E2** 10 40 S 25 25 E
Kolyma →, *Russia* **67 C17** 69 30N 161 0 E
Kolymskoye Nagorye, *Russia* **67 C16** 63 0N 157 0 E
Kôm Hamâda, *Egypt* **106 H7** 30 46N 30 41 E
Kôm Ombo, *Egypt* **106 C3** 24 25N 32 52 E
Komadugu Gana →, *Nigeria* **113 C7** 13 5N 12 24 E
Komagane, *Japan* **73 B9** 35 44N 137 58 E
Komaki, *Japan* **73 B8** 35 17N 136 55 E
Komandorskiye Is. = Komandorskiye Ostrova, *Russia* **67 D17** 55 0N 167 0 E
Komandorskiye Ostrova, *Russia* **67 D17** 55 0N 167 0 E
Komárno, *Slovak Rep.* **35 D11** 47 49N 18 5 E
Komárom, *Hungary* **52 C3** 47 43N 18 7 E
Komárom-Esztergom □, *Hungary* **52 C3** 47 35N 18 20 E
Komatipoort, *S. Africa* **117 D5** 25 25 S 31 55 E
Komatou Yialou, *Cyprus* **39 E10** 35 25N 34 8 E
Komatsu, *Japan* **73 A8** 36 25N 136 30 E
Komatsushima, *Japan* **72 D6** 34 0N 134 35 E
Komba, *Dem. Rep. of the Congo* **114 B4** 2 52N 24 3 E
Kombissiri, *Burkina Faso* **113 C4** 12 4N 1 20W
Kombo, *Gabon* **114 C2** 0 20 S 12 22 E
Kombong, *India* **90 A5** 28 7N 94 51 E
Kombori, *Burkina Faso* **112 C4** 13 26N 3 56W
Kombóti, *Greece* **48 B3** 39 6N 21 5 E
Komen, *Slovenia* **45 C10** 45 49N 13 45 E
Komenda, *Ghana* **113 D4** 5 4N 1 28W
Komi □, *Russia* **56 B10** 64 0N 55 0 E
Komiža, *Croatia* **45 E13** 43 3N 16 11 E
Komló, *Hungary* **52 D3** 46 15N 18 16 E
Kommamur Canal, *India* **95 G5** 16 0N 80 25 E
Kommunarsk = Alchevsk, *Ukraine* **59 H10** 48 30N 38 45 E
Kommunizma, Pik, *Tajikistan* **66 F8** 39 0N 72 2 E
Komodo, *Indonesia* **82 C1** 8 37 S 119 20 E
Komoé →, *Ivory C.* **112 D4** 5 12N 3 44W
Komono, *Congo* **114 C2** 3 10 S 13 20 E
Komoran, Pulau, *Indonesia* **83 C5** 8 18 S 138 45 E
Komoro, *Japan* **73 A10** 36 19N 138 26 E
Komotini, *Greece* **51 E9** 41 9N 25 26 E
Komovi, *Montenegro, Yug.* **50 D3** 42 41N 19 39 E
Kompasberg, *S. Africa* **116 E3** 31 45 S 24 32 E
Kompong Bang, *Cambodia* **87 F5** 12 24N 104 40 E
Kompong Cham, *Cambodia* **87 F5** 12 0N 105 30 E
Kompong Chhnang = Kampang Chhnang, *Cambodia* **87 F5** 12 20N 104 35 E
Kompong Chikreng, *Cambodia* **86 F5** 13 5N 104 18 E
Kompong Kleang, *Cambodia* **86 F5** 13 6N 104 8 E
Kompong Luong, *Cambodia* **87 G5** 11 49N 104 48 E
Kompong Pranak, *Cambodia* **86 F5** 13 35N 104 55 E
Kompong Som = Kampong Saom, *Cambodia* **87 G4** 10 38N 103 30 E
Kompong Som, Chhung = Kampong Saom, Chaak, *Cambodia* **87 G4** 10 50N 103 32 E
Kompong Speu, *Cambodia* **87 G5** 11 26N 104 32 E
Kompong Sralao, *Cambodia* **86 E5** 14 5N 105 46 E
Kompong Thom, *Cambodia* **86 F5** 12 35N 104 51 E
Kompong Trabeck, *Cambodia* **86 F5** 13 6N 105 14 E
Kompong Trabeck, *Cambodia* **87 G5** 11 9N 105 28 E
Kompong Trach, *Cambodia* **87 G5** 11 25N 105 48 E
Kompong Tralach, *Cambodia* **87 G5** 11 54N 104 47 E
Komrat = Comrat, *Moldova* **53 D13** 46 18N 28 40 E
Komsberg, *S. Africa* **116 E3** 32 40 S 20 45 E
Komsomolabad, *Tajikistan* **65 D4** 38 50N 69 55 E
Komsomolets, *Kazakstan* **64 E9** 53 45N 62 2 E
Komsomolets, Ostrov, *Russia* **67 A10** 80 30N 95 0 E
Komsomolsk, *Amur, Russia* **67 D14** 50 30N 137 0 E
Komsomolsk, *Ivanovo, Russia* **58 D11** 57 2N 40 20 E
Komsomolsk, *Turkmenistan* **65 D1** 39 2N 63 36 E
Komsomolskiy, *Russia* **60 C7** 54 27N 45 33 E
Kömür Burnu, *Turkey* **49 C8** 38 39N 26 12 E
Kon Tum, *Vietnam* **86 E7** 14 24N 108 0 E
Kon Tum, Plateau du, *Vietnam* **86 E7** 14 30N 108 30 E
Kona, *Mali* **112 C4** 14 57N 3 53W
Konakovo, *Russia* **58 D9** 56 40N 36 51 E
Konarak, *India* **94 E8** 19 54N 86 7 E
Konarhā □, *Afghan.* **91 B3** 35 30N 71 3 E
Konārī, *Iran* **97 D6** 28 13N 51 36 E
Konch, *India* **93 G8** 26 0N 79 10 E
Konda, *Indonesia* **83 B4** 1 34 S 131 57 E
Kondagaon, *India* **94 E5** 19 35N 81 35 E
Konde, *Tanzania* **118 C4** 4 57 S 39 45 E
Kondiá, *Greece* **49 B7** 39 49N 25 10 E
Kondinin, *Australia* **125 F2** 32 34 S 118 8 E
Kondo, *Dem. Rep. of the Congo* **115 D2** 5 35 S 13 0 E
Kondoa, *Tanzania* **118 C4** 4 55 S 35 50 E
Kondókali, *Greece* **38 B9** 39 38N 19 51 E
Kondopaga, *Russia* **58 A8** 62 12N 34 17 E
Kondratyevo, *Russia* **67 D10** 57 22N 98 15 E
Kondrovo, *Russia* **58 E8** 54 48N 35 56 E
Konduga, *Nigeria* **113 C7** 11 35N 13 26 E
Kondukur, *India* **95 G4** 15 12N 79 57 E
Koné, *Cameroon* **114 A2** 8 50N 13 17 E
Koné, *N. Cal.* **133 U18** 21 4 S 164 52 E
Köneürgench, *Turkmenistan* **66 E6** 42 19N 59 10 E
Konevo, *Russia* **58 A10** 62 8N 39 20 E
Kong = Khong →, *Cambodia* **86 F5** 13 32N 105 58 E
Kong, *Ivory C.* **112 D4** 8 54N 4 36W
Kong, Koh, *Cambodia* **87 G4** 11 20N 103 0 E
Kong Christian IX Land, *Greenland* **10 D7** 68 0N 36 0W
Kong Christian X Land, *Greenland* **10 C8** 74 0N 29 0W
Kong Frederik IX Land, *Greenland* **10 D5** 67 0N 52 0W
Kong Frederik VI Kyst, *Greenland* **10 E6** 63 0N 43 0W
Kong Frederik VIII Land, *Greenland* **10 B8** 78 30N 26 0W
Kong Oscar Fjord, *Greenland* **10 C8** 72 20N 24 0W
Kongbo, *C.A.R.* **114 B4** 4 44N 21 23 E
Kongeå →, *Denmark* **17 J2** 55 23N 8 39 E
Kongerslev, *Denmark* **17 H4** 56 54N 10 6 E
Kongju, *S. Korea* **75 F14** 36 30N 127 0 E
Kongkemul, *Indonesia* **85 B4** 1 52N 112 11 E
Konglu, *Burma* **90 B6** 27 13N 97 57 E
Kongola, *Namibia* **116 B3** 17 45 S 23 20 E
Kongolo, *Kasai-Or., Dem. Rep. of the Congo* **118 D1** 5 26 S 24 49 E
Kongolo, *Katanga, Dem. Rep. of the Congo* **118 D2** 5 22 S 27 0 E
Kongor, *Sudan* **107 F3** 7 1N 31 27 E
Kongoulou, *Cameroon* **114 B2** 2 59N 11 7 E
Kongoussi, *Burkina Faso* **113 C4** 13 19N 1 32W
Kongsberg, *Norway* **15 G13** 59 39N 9 39 E
Kongsvinger, *Norway* **15 F15** 60 12N 12 2 E
Kongwa, *Tanzania* **118 D4** 6 11 S 36 26 E
Koni, *Dem. Rep. of the Congo* **119 E2** 10 40 S 27 11 E
Koni, Mts., *Dem. Rep. of the Congo* **119 E2** 10 36 S 27 10 E
Koniakari, *Mali* **112 C2** 14 35N 10 50W
Koniecpol, *Poland* **55 H6** 50 46N 19 40 E
Königs Wusterhausen, *Germany* **30 C9** 52 19N 13 38 E
Königsberg = Kaliningrad, *Russia* **15 J19** 54 42N 20 32 E
Königsbrunn, *Germany* **31 G6** 48 16N 10 54 E
Königslutter, *Germany* **30 C6** 52 15N 10 49 E
Konin, *Poland* **55 F5** 52 12N 18 15 E
Konispol, *Albania* **38 B10** 39 42N 20 10 E
Kónitsa, *Greece* **48 A2** 40 5N 20 48 E
Köniz, *Switz.* **32 C4** 46 56N 7 25 E
Konjic, *Bos.-H.* **52 G2** 43 42N 17 58 E
Konkiep, *Namibia* **116 D2** 26 49 S 17 15 E
Konkō, *Japan* **72 C4** 34 33N 133 36 E
Konkouré →, *Guinea* **112 D2** 9 50N 13 42W
Könnern, *Germany* **30 D7** 51 41N 11 47 E
Konnur, *India* **95 F2** 16 14N 74 49 E
Kono, *S. Leone* **112 D2** 8 30N 11 5W
Konogogo, *Papua N. G.* **132 B7** 3 29 S 152 10 E
Konolfingen, *Switz.* **32 C5** 46 54N 7 38 E
Konongo, *Ghana* **113 D4** 6 40N 1 15W
Konos, *Papua N. G.* **132 B6** 3 10 S 151 44 E
Konosha, *Russia* **58 B11** 61 0N 40 5 E
Kōnosu, *Japan* **73 A11** 36 3N 139 31 E
Konotop, *Ukraine* **59 G7** 51 12N 33 7 E
Konsankoro, *Guinea* **112 D3** 9 2N 9 0W
Końskie, *Poland* **55 G7** 51 15N 20 23 E
Konsmo, *Norway* **18 F4** 58 16N 7 23 E
Konstancin-Jeziorna, *Poland* **55 F8** 52 5N 21 7 E
Konstantinovka = Kostyantynivka, *Ukraine* **59 H9** 48 32N 37 39 E
Konstantinovsk, *Russia* **61 G5** 47 33N 41 10 E
Konstantynów Łódzki, *Poland* **55 G6** 51 45N 19 20 E
Konstanz, *Germany* **31 H5** 47 40N 9 10 E
Kont, *Iran* **97 E9** 26 55N 61 50 E
Konta, *India* **94 F5** 17 48N 81 23 E
Kontagora, *Nigeria* **113 C6** 10 23N 5 27 E
Kontcha, *Cameroon* **113 D7** 7 59N 12 15 E
Konya, *Turkey* **100 D5** 37 52N 32 35 E
Konya Ovası, *Turkey* **100 C5** 38 30N 33 5 E
Konyin, *Burma* **90 D5** 22 58N 94 42 E
Konz, *Germany* **31 F2** 49 42N 6 34 E
Konza, *Kenya* **118 C4** 1 45 S 37 7 E
Konzhakovskiy Kamen, Gora, *Russia* **64 B7** 59 38N 59 8 E
Koo-wee-rup, *Australia* **129 E6** 38 13 S 145 28 E
Koocanusa, L., *Canada* **158 B6** 49 20N 115 15W
Kookynie, *Australia* **125 E3** 29 17 S 121 22 E
Koolau Range, *U.S.A.* **145 J14** 21 35N 157 50W
Koolyanobbing, *Australia* **125 F2** 30 48 S 119 36 E
Koondrook, *Australia* **128 C6** 35 33 S 144 8 E
Koonibba, *Australia* **127 E1** 31 54 S 133 25 E
Koorawatha, *Australia* **129 C8** 34 2 S 148 33 E
Koorda, *Australia* **125 F2** 30 48 S 117 35 E
Kooskia, *U.S.A.* **158 C6** 46 9N 115 59W
Kootenay →, *U.S.A.* **142 D5** 49 19N 117 39W
Kootenay L., *Canada* **142 D5** 49 45N 116 50W
Kootenay Nat. Park, *Canada* **142 C5** 51 0N 116 0W
Kootingal, *Australia* **129 A9** 31 3 S 151 4 E
Kootjieskolk, *S. Africa* **116 E3** 31 15 S 20 21 E
Kopa = Qopa, *Kazakstan* **65 B7** 43 31N 75 50 E
Kopanovka, *Russia* **61 G8** 47 28N 46 50 E
Kopaonik, *Yugoslavia* **50 C4** 43 10N 20 50 E
Kópargaon, *India* **94 E2** 19 51N 74 28 E
Kópasker, *Iceland* **11 A10** 66 18N 16 27W
Kópavogur, *Iceland* **11 C5** 64 6N 21 55W
Koper, *Slovenia* **45 C10** 45 31N 13 44 E
Kopervik, *Norway* **15 G11** 59 17N 5 17 E
Kopet Dagh, *Asia* **97 B8** 38 0N 58 0 E
Kopeysk, *Russia* **64 D8** 55 7N 61 37 E
Kopi, *Australia* **127 E2** 33 24 S 135 40 E
Köping, *Sweden* **16 E10** 59 31N 16 3 E
Köpingsvik, *Sweden* **17 H10** 56 53N 16 43 E
Kopište, *Croatia* **45 F13** 42 48N 16 42 E
Koplik, *Albania* **50 D3** 42 15N 19 25 E
Köpmanholmen, *Sweden* **16 A12** 63 10N 18 35 E
Koppa, *India* **95 H2** 13 33N 75 21 E
Koppal, *India* **95 G3** 15 23N 76 5 E
Koppang, *Norway* **18 C8** 61 34N 11 3 E
Kopparberg, *Sweden* **16 E9** 59 52N 15 0 E
Koppeh Dāgh = Kopet Dagh, *Asia* **97 B8** 38 0N 58 0 E
Kopperå, *Norway* **18 A8** 63 24N 11 50 E
Koppies, *S. Africa* **117 D4** 27 20 S 27 30 E
Koppom, *Sweden* **16 E6** 59 43N 12 10 E
Koprivlen, *Bulgaria* **50 E7** 41 31N 23 53 E
Koprivnica, *Croatia* **45 B13** 46 12N 16 45 E
Kopřivnice, *Czech Rep.* **35 B11** 49 36N 18 9 E
Koprivshtitsa, *Bulgaria* **51 D8** 42 40N 24 19 E
Köprübaşı, *Turkey* **49 C10** 38 43N 28 23 E
Kopychyntsi, *Ukraine* **59 H3** 49 7N 25 58 E
Kora Nat. Park, *Kenya* **118 C4** 0 14 S 38 44 E
Korab, *Macedonia* **50 E4** 41 44N 20 40 E
Korakiána, *Greece* **38 B9** 39 42N 19 45 E
Koral, *India* **92 J5** 21 50N 73 12 E
Korangal, *India* **94 E3** 17 6N 77 38 E
Koraput, *India* **94 E6** 18 50N 82 40 E
Korarou, L., *Mali* **112 B4** 15 15N 3 15W
Korba, *India* **93 H10** 22 20N 82 45 E
Korbach, *Germany* **30 D4** 51 16N 8 52 E
Korbu, G., *Malaysia* **87 K3** 4 41N 101 18 E
Korce = Korçë, *Albania* **50 F4** 40 37N 20 50 E
Korçë, *Albania* **50 F4** 40 37N 20 50 E
Korčula, *Croatia* **45 F13** 42 56N 16 57 E
Korčulanski Kanal, *Croatia* **45 E13** 43 3N 16 40 E
Kord Kūy, *Iran* **97 B7** 36 48N 54 7 E
Kord Sheykh, *Iran* **97 D7** 28 31N 52 53 E
Korday, *Kazakstan* **65 B7** 43 3N 74 43 E
Kordestān □, *Iran* **96 C5** 36 0N 47 0 E
Koré Mayroua, *Niger* **113 C5** 13 18N 3 55 E
Korea, North ■, *Asia* **75 E14** 40 0N 127 0 E
Korea, South ■, *Asia* **75 G15** 36 0N 128 0 E
Korea Bay, *Korea* **75 E13** 39 0N 124 0 E
Korea Strait, *Asia* **75 H15** 34 0N 129 30 E
Koregaon, *India* **94 F2** 17 40N 74 10 E
Korem, *Ethiopia* **107 E4** 12 30N 39 32 E
Korenevo, *Russia* **59 G8** 51 27N 34 55 E
Korenovsk, *Russia* **61 H4** 45 30N 39 22 E
Korets, *Ukraine* **59 G4** 50 40N 27 5 E
Korfantów, *Poland* **55 H4** 50 29N 17 36 E
Korgan, *Turkey* **100 B7** 40 44N 37 13 E
Korgus, *Sudan* **106 D3** 19 16N 33 29 E
Korhogo, *Ivory C.* **112 D3** 9 29N 5 28W
Koribundu, *S. Leone* **112 D2** 7 41N 11 46W
Korienzé, *Mali* **112 B4** 15 22N 3 50W
Korim, *Indonesia* **83 B5** 0 58 S 136 10 E
Korinthía □, *Greece* **48 D4** 37 50N 22 35 E
Korinthiakós Kólpos, *Greece* **48 C4** 38 16N 22 30 E
Kórinthos, *Greece* **48 D4** 37 56N 22 55 E
Korioumé, *Mali* **112 B4** 16 35N 3 0W
Korissa, Límni, *Greece* **38 C9** 39 27N 19 53 E
Korithi, *Greece* **39 D2** 37 55N 20 42 E
Kōriyama, *Japan* **70 F10** 37 24N 140 23 E
Korkino, *Russia* **64 D8** 54 54N 61 23 E
Korkuteli, *Turkey* **49 D12** 37 4N 30 13 E
Korla, *China* **68 B3** 41 45N 86 4 E
Kormakiti, C., *Cyprus* **39 E8** 35 23N 32 56 E
Körmend, *Hungary* **52 C1** 47 5N 16 35 E
Kornat, *Croatia* **45 E12** 43 50N 15 20 E
Korneshty = Corneşti, *Moldova* **53 C13** 47 21N 28 1 E
Korneuburg, *Austria* **35 C9** 48 20N 16 20 E
Kórnik, *Poland* **55 F4** 52 15N 17 6 E
Kornsjø, *Norway* **18 F8** 58 57N 11 39 E
Koro, *Fiji* **133 A2** 17 19 S 179 23 E
Koro, *Ivory C.* **112 D3** 8 32N 7 30W
Koro, *Mali* **112 C4** 14 1N 2 58W
Koro Sea, *Fiji* **133 A3** 17 30 S 179 45W
Koro Toro, *Chad* **109 E3** 16 5N 18 30 E
Koroba, *Papua N. G.* **132 C2** 5 44 S 142 47 E
Korocha, *Russia* **59 G9** 50 54N 37 19 E
Köroğlu Dağları, *Turkey* **100 B5** 40 38N 33 0 E
Korogwe, *Tanzania* **118 D4** 5 5 S 38 25 E
Koroit, *Australia* **128 E5** 38 18 S 142 24 E
Korolevu, *Fiji* **133 B1** 18 12 S 177 46 E
Korona, *U.S.A.* **153 F8** 29 25N 81 12W
Koronadal, *Phil.* **81 H5** 6 12N 125 1 E
Korong Vale, *Australia* **128 D5** 36 22 S 143 45 E
Koroni, *Greece* **48 E3** 36 48N 21 57 E
Korónia, Límni, *Greece* **51 F7** 40 47N 23 10 E
Koronís, *Greece* **49 D7** 37 12N 25 35 E
Koronowo, *Poland* **55 E4** 53 19N 17 55 E
Koropelé, *C.A.R.* **114 B3** 4 44N 17 11 E
Koror, *Palau* **134 G5** 7 20N 134 28 E
Körös →, *Hungary* **52 D5** 46 43N 20 12 E
Körösstarcsa, *Hungary* **52 D6** 46 53N 21 3 E
Korosten, *Ukraine* **59 G5** 50 54N 28 36 E
Korostyshev, *Ukraine* **59 G5** 50 19N 29 4 E
Korotoyak, *Russia* **59 G10** 51 1N 39 2 E
Korovou, *Fiji* **133 A2** 17 47 S 178 32 E
Koroyanitu Nat. Heritage Park, *Fiji* **133 A1** 17 40 S 177 35 E
Korraraika, Helodranon' i, *Madag.* **117 B7** 17 45 S 43 57 E
Korsakov, *Russia* **67 E15** 46 36N 142 42 E
Korsberga, *Sweden* **17 G9** 57 19N 15 7 E
Korshunovo, *Russia* **67 D12** 58 37N 110 10 E
Korsør, *Denmark* **17 J5** 55 20N 11 9 E
Korsun Shevchenkovskiy, *Ukraine* **59 H6** 49 26N 31 16 E
Korsze, *Poland* **54 D8** 54 11N 21 9 E
Korti, *Sudan* **106 D3** 18 6N 31 33 E
Kortrijk, *Belgium* **24 D3** 50 50N 3 17 E
Korucu, *Turkey* **49 B9** 39 28N 27 22 E
Korumburra, *Australia* **129 E6** 38 26 S 145 50 E
Korup, Parc Nat. du, *Cameroon* **114 A1** 5 15N 9 2 E
Korwai, *India* **92 G8** 24 7N 78 5 E
Koryakskoye Nagorye, *Russia* **67 C18** 61 0N 171 0 E
Koryŏng, *S. Korea* **75 G15** 35 44N 128 15 E
Koryukovka, *Ukraine* **59 G7** 51 46N 32 16 E
Kos, *Greece* **49 E9** 36 50N 27 15 E
Kosa, *Ethiopia* **107 F4** 7 50N 36 50 E
Kosa, *Russia* **64 B5** 59 56N 55 0 E
Kosa →, *Russia* **64 A5** 60 11N 55 10 E
Kosai, *Japan* **73 C9** 34 42N 137 32 E
Kosaya Gora, *Russia* **58 E9** 54 10N 37 30 E
Koschagyl, *Kazakstan* **57 E9** 46 40N 54 0 E
Kościan, *Poland* **55 F3** 52 5N 16 40 E
Kościerzyna, *Poland* **54 D4** 54 8N 17 59 E
Kosciusko, *U.S.A.* **155 J10** 33 4N 89 35W
Kosciusko Nat. Park, *Australia* **129 D8** 36 30 S 148 20 E
Kosciuszko, Mt., *Australia* **129 D8** 36 27 S 148 16 E
Kösély →, *Hungary* **52 C6** 47 25N 21 5 E
Kosgi, *Andhra Pradesh, India* **94 F3** 16 58N 77 43 E
Kosgi, *Andhra Pradesh, India* **95 G3** 15 51N 77 16 E
Kosh-Döbö, *Kyrgyzstan* **65 C7** 41 5N 74 15 E
Kosha, *Sudan* **106 C3** 20 50N 30 30 E
Koshava, *Bulgaria* **50 B7** 44 4N 23 2 E
Koshigaya, *Japan* **73 B11** 35 54N 139 48 E
K'oshih = Kashi, *China* **65 D8** 39 30N 76 2 E
Koshiki-Rettō, *Japan* **72 F1** 31 45N 129 49 E
Koshkonong L., *U.S.A.* **157 B8** 42 52N 88 58W
Kōshoku, *Japan* **73 A10** 36 38N 138 6 E
Koshrabad, *Uzbekistan* **65 C3** 40 18N 66 32 E
Kosi, *India* **92 F7** 27 48N 77 29 E
Kosi →, *India* **93 E8** 28 41N 78 57 E
Košice, *Slovak Rep.* **35 C14** 48 42N 21 15 E
Košický □, *Slovak Rep.* **35 C14** 48 45N 21 0 E
Kosjerić, *Serbia, Yug.* **50 B3** 44 0N 19 55 E
Köşk, *Turkey* **49 D10** 37 50N 28 3 E
Koskinoú, *Greece* **38 E12** 36 23N 28 13 E
Koslan, *Russia* **56 B8** 63 34N 49 14 E
Kosŏng, *N. Korea* **75 E15** 38 40N 128 22 E
Kosovo □, *Yugoslavia* **50 D4** 42 30N 21 0 E
Kosovo Polje, *Kosovo, Yug.* **50 D5** 42 40N 21 5 E
Kosovska Kamenica, *Kosovo, Yug.* **50 D5** 42 35N 21 35 E
Kosovska Mitrovica, *Kosovo, Yug.* **50 D4** 42 54N 20 52 E
Kosrap, *China* **65 E8** 38 0N 76 12 E
Kossou, L. de, *Ivory C.* **112 D3** 6 59N 5 31W
Kosta, *Sweden* **17 H9** 56 50N 15 24 E
Kostajnica, *Croatia* **45 C13** 45 17N 16 30 E
Kostanjevica, *Slovenia* **45 C12** 45 51N 15 27 E
Kostenets, *Bulgaria* **50 D7** 42 15N 23 52 E
Koster, *S. Africa* **116 D4** 25 52 S 26 54 E
Kôstî, *Sudan* **107 E3** 13 8N 32 43 E
Kostinbrod, *Bulgaria* **50 D7** 42 49N 23 13 E
Kostolac, *Serbia, Yug.* **50 B5** 44 37N 21 15 E
Kostopil, *Ukraine* **59 G4** 50 51N 26 22 E
Kostroma, *Russia* **58 D11** 57 50N 40 58 E
Kostromskoye Vdkhr., *Russia* **58 D11** 57 52N 40 49 E
Kostrzyn, *Lubuskie, Poland* **55 F1** 52 35N 14 39 E
Kostrzyn, *Wielkopolskie, Poland* **55 F4** 52 24N 17 14 E
Kostyantynivka, *Ukraine* **59 H9** 48 32N 37 39 E
Kostyukovichi = Kastsyukovichy, *Belarus* **58 F7** 53 20N 32 4 E
Koszalin, *Poland* **54 D3** 54 11N 16 8 E
Kőszeg, *Hungary* **52 C1** 47 23N 16 33 E
Kot Addu, *Pakistan* **91 C3** 30 30N 71 0 E
Kot Kapura, *India* **92 D6** 30 35N 74 50 E
Kot Moman, *Pakistan* **92 C5** 32 13N 73 0 E
Kot Sultan, *Pakistan* **92 D4** 30 46N 70 56 E
Kota, *India* **92 G6** 25 14N 75 49 E
Kota Baharu, *Malaysia* **87 J4** 6 7N 102 14 E
Kota Barrage, *India* **92 G6** 25 6N 75 51 E
Kota Belud, *Malaysia* **85 A5** 6 21N 116 26 E
Kota Kinabalu, *Malaysia* **85 A5** 6 0N 116 4 E
Kota Kubu Baharu, *Malaysia* **87 L3** 3 34N 101 39 E
Kota Tinggi, *Malaysia* **87 M4** 1 44N 103 53 E
Kotaagung, *Indonesia* **84 D2** 5 38 S 104 29 E
Kotabaru, *Indonesia* **85 C5** 3 20 S 116 20 E
Kotabumi, *Indonesia* **84 C2** 4 49 S 104 54 E
Kotagede, *Indonesia* **85 D4** 7 54 S 110 26 E
Kotamobagu, *Indonesia* **82 A2** 0 57N 124 31 E
Kotapad, *India* **94 E6** 19 9N 82 21 E
Kotawaringin, *Indonesia* **85 C4** 2 28 S 111 27 E
Kotchandpur, *Bangla.* **90 D2** 23 24N 89 1 E
Kotcho L., *Canada* **142 B4** 59 7N 121 12W
Kotdwara, *India* **93 E8** 29 45N 78 32 E
Kotel, *Bulgaria* **51 D10** 42 52N 26 26 E
Kotelnich, *Russia* **60 A9** 58 22N 48 24 E
Kotelnikovo, *Russia* **61 G6** 47 38N 43 8 E
Kotelnyy, Ostrov, *Russia* **67 B14** 75 10N 139 0 E
Kothagudam, *India* **94 F5** 17 30N 80 40 E
Kothapet, *India* **94 E4** 19 21N 79 28 E
Kothari →, *India* **92 G6** 25 20N 75 4 E
Köthen, *Germany* **30 D7** 51 45N 11 59 E
Kothi, *Chhattisgarh, India* **93 H10** 23 21N 82 3 E
Kothi, *Mad. P., India* **93 G9** 24 45N 80 40 E
Kotiro, *Pakistan* **92 F2** 26 17N 67 13 E
Kotka, *Finland* **15 F22** 60 28N 26 58 E
Kotlas, *Russia* **56 B8** 61 17N 46 43 E
Kotlenska Planina, *Bulgaria* **51 D10** 42 56N 26 30 E
Kotli, *Pakistan* **92 C5** 33 30N 73 55 E
Kotlik, *U.S.A.* **144 E7** 63 2N 163 33W
Kotma, *India* **93 H9** 23 12N 81 58 E
Kotmul, *Pakistan* **93 B6** 35 32N 75 10 E
Kotohira, *Japan* **72 C5** 34 11N 133 49 E
Koton-Karifi, *Nigeria* **113 D6** 8 0N 6 48 E
Kotonkoro, *Nigeria* **113 C6** 11 3N 5 58 E
Kotor, *Montenegro, Yug.* **50 D2** 42 25N 18 47 E
Kotor Varoš, *Bos.-H.* **52 F2** 44 38N 17 22 E
Kotoriba, *Croatia* **45 B13** 46 23N 16 48 E
Kotovo, *Russia* **60 E7** 50 22N 44 45 E
Kotovsk, *Russia* **60 D5** 52 36N 41 32 E
Kotovsk, *Ukraine* **59 J5** 47 45N 29 35 E
Kotputli, *India* **92 F7** 27 43N 76 12 E
Kotri, *Pakistan* **91 D3** 25 22N 68 22 E
Kotri →, *India* **94 E5** 19 15N 80 35 E
Kótronas, *Greece* **48 E4** 36 38N 22 29 E
Kötschach-Mauthen, *Austria* **34 E6** 46 41N 13 1 E
Kottayam, *India* **95 K3** 9 35N 76 33 E
Kotto →, *C.A.R.* **114 B4** 4 14N 22 2 E
Kottur, *India* **95 J3** 10 34N 76 56 E
Kotu Group, *Tonga* **133 Q14** 20 0 S 173 25W
Kotuy →, *Russia* **67 B11** 71 54N 102 6 E
Kotzebue, *U.S.A.* **144 C7** 66 53N 162 39W
Kotzebue Sound, *U.S.A.* **144 C7** 66 20N 163 0W
Kouango, *C.A.R.* **114 B4** 5 0N 20 10 E
Koudougou, *Burkina Faso* **112 C4** 12 10N 2 20W
Koufonísi, *Greece* **39 F7** 34 56N 26 8 E
Koufonísia, *Greece* **49 E7** 36 57N 25 35 E
Kougaberge, *S. Africa* **116 E3** 33 48 S 23 50 E
Kouibli, *Ivory C.* **112 D3** 7 15N 7 14W
Kouilou →, *Congo* **115 C2** 4 10 S 12 5 E
Kouki, *C.A.R.* **114 A3** 7 22N 17 3 E
Koula Moutou, *Gabon* **114 C2** 1 15 S 12 25 E
Koulen = Kulen, *Cambodia* **86 F5** 13 50N 104 40 E
Koulikoro, *Mali* **112 C3** 12 40N 7 50W
Kouloúra, *Greece* **38 B9** 39 42N 19 54 E
Koúm-bournoú, Ákra, *Greece* **38 E12** 36 15N 28 11 E
Koumac, *N. Cal.* **133 T18** 20 33 S 164 17 E
Koumala, *Australia* **126 C4** 21 38 S 149 15 E
Koumameyong, *Gabon* **114 B2** 0 11N 11 51 E
Koumankou, *Mali* **112 C3** 11 58N 6 6W
Koumbia, *Burkina Faso* **112 C4** 11 10N 3 50W
Koumbia, *Guinea* **112 C2** 11 48N 13 29W
Koumboum, *Guinea* **112 C2** 10 25N 13 0W
Koumpenntoum, *Senegal* **112 C2** 13 59N 14 34W
Koumra, *Chad* **109 G3** 8 50N 17 35 E
Koun-Fao, *Ivory C.* **112 D4** 7 30N 3 15W
Koundara, *Guinea* **112 C2** 12 29N 13 18W
Koundé, *C.A.R.* **114 A2** 6 7N 14 38 E
Koundian, *Guinea* **112 C3** 13 10N 10 35W
Kounghheul, *Senegal* **112 C2** 14 0N 14 50W
Koungoulou, *Congo* **114 C2** 3 31 S 13 20 E
Kounradskiy, *Kazakstan* **66 E8** 46 59N 75 0 E
Kountze, *U.S.A.* **155 K7** 30 22N 94 19W
Koupéla, *Burkina Faso* **113 C4** 12 11N 0 21W
Kourémalé, *Mali* **112 C3** 11 59N 8 42W
Kouris →, *Cyprus* **39 F8** 34 38N 32 54 E
Kourizo, P. de, *Chad* **108 D3** 22 28N 15 27 E
Kourou, *Fr. Guiana* **169 B7** 5 9N 52 39W
Kourouba, *Mali* **112 C2** 13 22N 10 57W
Kouroukoto, *Mali* **112 C2** 13 10N 10 5W
Kourouma, *Burkina Faso* **112 C4** 11 35N 4 50W
Kourouninkoto, *Mali* **112 C3** 13 52N 9 35W
Kouroussa, *Guinea* **112 C3** 10 45N 9 45W
Koussanar, *Senegal* **112 C2** 13 52N 14 5W
Koussané, *Mali* **112 C2** 14 53N 11 14W
Koussane, *Senegal* **112 C2** 14 10N 12 22W
Kousseri, *Cameroon* **109 F2** 12 0N 14 55 E
Koutiala, *Mali* **112 C3** 12 25N 5 23W
Kouto, *Ivory C.* **112 D3** 9 53N 6 25W
Kouts, *U.S.A.* **157 C9** 41 19N 87 2W
Kouvé, *Togo* **113 D5** 6 25N 1 25 E
Kouvola, *Finland* **15 F22** 60 52N 26 43 E
Kouyi, *Congo* **114 C2** 2 29 S 12 55 E
Kouyou →, *Congo* **114 C3** 0 44 S 16 38 E
Kovačica, *Serbia, Yug.* **52 E5** 45 5N 20 38 E
Kovdor, *Russia* **56 A5** 67 34N 30 24 E
Kovel, *Ukraine* **59 G3** 51 11N 24 38 E
Kovilpatti, *India* **95 K3** 9 10N 77 50 E
Kovin, *Serbia, Yug.* **52 F5** 44 44N 20 59 E
Kovrov, *Russia* **60 B5** 56 25N 41 25 E
Kovur, *Andhra Pradesh, India* **94 F5** 17 3N 81 39 E

236 Kovur

Kovur, *Andhra Pradesh, India* **95 G5** 14 30N 80 1 E
Kowal, *Poland* **55 F6** 52 32N 19 7 E
Kowalewo Pomorskie, *Poland* **55 E5** 53 10N 18 52 E
Kowanyama, *Australia* **126 B3** 15 29 S 141 44 E
Kowlīnī, *Afghan.* **65 E2** 37 39N 65 58 E
Kowloon, *H.K.* **77 F10** 22 19N 114 11 E
Kowŏn, *N. Korea* **75 E14** 39 26N 127 14 E
Kōyama, *Japan* **72 F2** 31 20N 130 56 E
Köyceğiz, *Turkey* **49 E10** 36 57N 28 40 E
Köyceğiz Gölü, *Turkey* **49 E10** 36 56N 28 42 E
Koytash, *Uzbekistan* **65 C3** 40 11N 67 19 E
Koyuk, *U.S.A.* **144 D7** 64 56N 161 9W
Koyukuk, *U.S.A.* **144 D8** 64 53N 157 42W
Koyukuk →, *U.S.A.* **144 D8** 64 55N 157 32W
Koyulhisar, *Turkey* **100 B7** 40 20N 37 52 E
Koyunyeri, *Turkey* **51 F10** 40 50N 26 26 E
Koza, *Japan* **71 L3** 26 19N 127 46 E
Kozak, *Turkey* **49 B9** 39 15N 27 6 E
Kozan, *Turkey* **100 D6** 37 26N 35 50 E
Kozáni, *Greece* **50 F5** 40 19N 21 47 E
Kozáni □, *Greece* **50 F5** 40 18N 21 45 E
Kozara, *Bos.-H.* **45 D14** 45 0N 17 0 E
Kozarac, *Bos.-H.* **45 D13** 44 58N 16 48 E
Kozelets, *Ukraine* **59 G6** 50 55N 31 7 E
Kozelsk, *Russia* **58 E8** 54 2N 35 48 E
Kozhikode = Calicut, *India* **95 J2** 11 15N 75 43 E
Kozhva, *Russia* **56 A10** 65 10N 57 0 E
Koziegłowy, *Poland* **55 H6** 50 37N 19 8 E
Kozienice, *Poland* **55 G8** 51 35N 21 34 E
Kozje, *Slovenia* **45 B12** 46 5N 15 35 E
Kozloduy, *Bulgaria* **50 C7** 43 45N 23 42 E
Kozlovets, *Bulgaria* **51 C9** 43 30N 25 20 E
Kozlovka, *Russia* **60 C9** 55 52N 48 14 E
Kozlu, *Turkey* **100 B4** 41 26N 31 45 E
Kozluk, *Turkey* **101 C9** 38 11N 41 31 E
Koźmin, *Poland* **55 G4** 51 48N 17 27 E
Kozmodemyansk, *Russia* **60 B8** 56 20N 46 36 E
Kōzu-Shima, *Japan* **73 C11** 34 13N 139 10 E
Kożuchów, *Poland* **55 G2** 51 45N 15 31 E
Kozyatyn, *Ukraine* **59 H5** 49 45N 28 50 E
Kpabia, *Ghana* **113 D4** 9 10N 0 20W
Kpalimé, *Togo* **113 D5** 6 57N 0 44 E
Kpandae, *Ghana* **113 D4** 8 30N 0 2W
Kpessi, *Togo* **113 D5** 8 4N 1 16 E
Kra, Isthmus of = Kra, Kho Khot, *Thailand* **87 G2** 10 15N 99 30 E
Kra, Kho Khot, *Thailand* **87 G2** 10 15N 99 30 E
Kra Buri, *Thailand* **87 G2** 10 22N 98 46 E
Kraai →, *S. Africa* **116 E4** 30 40 S 26 45 E
Krabi, *Thailand* **87 H2** 8 4N 98 55 E
Kracheh, *Cambodia* **86 F6** 12 32N 106 10 E
Kragan, *Indonesia* **85 D4** 6 43 S 111 38 E
Kragerø, *Norway* **15 G13** 58 52N 9 25 E
Kragujevac, *Serbia, Yug.* **50 B4** 44 2N 20 56 E
Krajenka, *Poland* **55 E3** 53 18N 16 59 E
Krajina, *Bos.-H.* **45 D13** 44 45N 16 35 E
Krakatau = Rakata, Pulau, *Indonesia* **84 D3** 6 10 S 105 20 E
Krakatoa = Rakata, Pulau, *Indonesia* **84 D3** 6 10 S 105 20 E
Krakor, *Cambodia* **86 F5** 12 32N 104 12 E
Kraków, *Poland* **55 H6** 50 4N 19 57 E
Kraksaan, *Indonesia* **85 D4** 7 43 S 113 23 E
Kralanh, *Cambodia* **86 F4** 13 35N 103 25 E
Králíky, *Czech Rep.* **35 A9** 50 6N 16 45 E
Kraljevo, *Serbia, Yug.* **50 C4** 43 44N 20 41 E
Královský Chlmec, *Slovak Rep.* **35 C14** 48 27N 22 0 E
Kralupy nad Vltavou, *Czech Rep.* **34 A7** 50 13N 14 20 E
Kramatorsk, *Ukraine* **59 H9** 48 50N 37 30 E
Kramfors, *Sweden* **16 B11** 62 55N 17 48 E
Kramis, C., *Algeria* **111 A5** 36 26N 0 45 E
Kraniá, *Greece* **50 G5** 39 53N 21 18 E
Kranía Elassónas, *Greece* **48 B4** 39 57N 22 2 E
Kranídhion, *Greece* **48 D5** 37 20N 23 10 E
Kranj, *Slovenia* **45 B11** 46 16N 14 22 E
Kranjska Gora, *Slovenia* **45 B10** 46 29N 13 48 E
Krankskop, *S. Africa* **117 D5** 28 0 S 30 47 E
Krapina, *Croatia* **45 B12** 46 10N 15 52 E
Krapina →, *Croatia* **45 C12** 45 50N 15 50 E
Krapkowice, *Poland* **55 H4** 50 29N 17 56 E
Kras, *Croatia* **45 C10** 45 35N 14 0 E
Krasavino, *Russia* **56 B8** 60 58N 46 29 E
Krashyy Klyuch, *Russia* **64 D6** 55 23N 56 39 E
Kraskino, *Russia* **67 E14** 42 44N 130 48 E
Krāslava, *Latvia* **58 E4** 55 54N 27 10 E
Kraslice, *Czech Rep.* **34 A5** 50 19N 12 31 E
Krasnaya Gorbatka, *Russia* **60 C5** 55 52N 41 45 E
Krasnaya Polyana, *Russia* **61 J5** 43 40N 40 13 E
Kraśnik, *Poland* **55 H9** 50 55N 22 15 E
Krasnoarmeisk, *Ukraine* **59 H9** 48 18N 37 11 E
Krasnoarmeysk, *Russia* **60 E7** 51 0N 45 42 E
Krasnoarmeyskiy, *Russia* **61 G6** 47 0N 42 12 E
Krasnobrod, *Poland* **55 H10** 50 33N 23 12 E
Krasnodar, *Russia* **61 H4** 45 5N 39 0 E
Krasnodon, *Ukraine* **59 H10** 48 17N 39 44 E
Krasnogorskiy, *Russia* **60 B9** 56 10N 48 28 E
Krasnograd = Krasnohrad, *Ukraine* **59 H8** 49 27N 35 27 E
Krasnogvardeysk = Bulungur, *Uzbekistan* **65 D3** 39 46N 67 16 E
Krasnogvardeyskoye, *Russia* **61 H5** 45 52N 41 33 E
Krasnogvardyesk, *Ukraine* **59 K8** 45 32N 34 16 E
Krasnohrad, *Ukraine* **59 H8** 49 27N 35 27 E
Krasnokamsk, *Russia* **64 B5** 58 4N 55 48 E
Krasnokutsk, *Ukraine* **59 G8** 50 10N 34 50 E
Krasnolesnyy, *Russia* **59 G10** 51 53N 39 35 E
Krasnoperekopsk, *Ukraine* **59 J7** 46 0N 33 54 E
Krasnorechenskiy, *Russia* **70 B7** 44 41N 135 14 E
Krasnoselkup, *Russia* **66 C9** 65 20N 82 10 E
Krasnoslobodsk, *Mordvinia, Russia* **60 C6** 54 25N 43 45 E
Krasnoslobodsk, *Volgograd, Russia* **61 F7** 48 42N 44 33 E
Krasnoturinsk, *Russia* **64 B8** 59 46N 60 12 E
Krasnoufimsk, *Russia* **64 C6** 56 36N 57 38 E
Krasnouralsk, *Russia* **64 B8** 58 21N 60 3 E
Krasnousolskiy, *Russia* **64 E6** 53 54N 56 27 E
Krasnovishersk, *Russia* **64 A6** 60 23N 57 3 E
Krasnovodsk = Türkmenbashi, *Turkmenistan* **57 G9** 40 5N 53 5 E
Krasnoyarsk, *Russia* **67 D10** 56 8N 93 0 E
Krasnoyarskiy, *Russia* **64 F7** 51 58N 59 55 E
Krasnoye = Krasnyy, *Russia* **58 E6** 54 25N 31 30 E
Krasnoye, *Russia* **64 B1** 59 15N 47 40 E
Krasnozavodsk, *Russia* **58 D10** 56 27N 38 25 E
Krasny Sulin, *Russia* **59 J11** 47 52N 40 8 E
Krasnystaw, *Poland* **55 H10** 50 57N 23 5 E
Krasnyy, *Russia* **58 E6** 54 25N 31 30 E
Krasnyy Kholm, *Orenburg, Russia* **64 F5** 51 35N 54 9 E
Krasnyy Kholm, *Tver, Russia* **58 C9** 58 10N 37 10 E
Krasnyy Kut, *Russia* **60 E8** 50 50N 47 0 E
Krasnyy Liman, *Ukraine* **59 H9** 48 58N 37 50 E
Krasnýy Luch, *Ukraine* **59 H10** 48 13N 39 0 E
Krasnyy Profintern, *Russia* **58 D11** 57 45N 40 27 E
Krasnyy Yar, *Astrakhan, Russia* **61 G9** 46 43N 48 23 E
Krasnyy Yar, *Samara, Russia* **60 D10** 53 30N 50 22 E
Krasnyy Yar, *Volgograd, Russia* **60 E7** 50 42N 44 45 E
Krasnyye Baki, *Russia* **60 B7** 57 8N 45 10 E
Krasnyyoskolske Vdskh., *Ukraine* **59 H9** 49 27N 37 40 E
Kraszna →, *Hungary* **52 B7** 48 4N 22 20 E
Kratie = Kracheh, *Cambodia* **86 F6** 12 32N 106 10 E
Kratke Ra., *Papua N. G.* **132 D3** 6 45 S 146 0 E
Kratovo, *Macedonia* **50 D6** 42 6N 22 10 E
Krau, *Indonesia* **83 B6** 3 19 S 140 5 E
Kraulshavn = Nuussauq, *Greenland* **10 C5** 74 8N 57 3W
Kravanh, Chuor Phnum, *Cambodia* **87 G4** 12 0N 103 32 E
Kreb es Sefia, *Algeria* **110 C3** 27 12N 7 11W
Kreb n-Naga, *Algeria* **110 C3** 27 3N 7 9W
Kreb n-Neggar, *Algeria* **110 C3** 27 20N 7 15W
Krefeld, *Germany* **30 D2** 51 20N 6 33 E
Krémaston, Límni, *Greece* **48 C3** 38 52N 21 30 E
Kremen, *Croatia* **45 D12** 44 28N 15 53 E
Kremenchuk, *Ukraine* **59 H7** 49 5N 33 25 E
Kremenchuksk Vdskh., *Ukraine* **59 H7** 49 20N 32 30 E
Kremenets, *Ukraine* **59 G3** 50 8N 25 43 E
Kremennaya, *Ukraine* **59 H10** 49 1N 38 10 E
Kremges = Svitlovodsk, *Ukraine* **59 H7** 49 2N 33 13 E
Kremmen, *Germany* **30 C9** 52 45N 13 1 E
Kremmling, *U.S.A.* **158 F10** 40 4N 106 24W
Kremnica, *Slovak Rep.* **35 C11** 48 45N 18 50 E
Krems, *Austria* **34 C8** 48 25N 15 36 E
Kremsmünster, *Austria* **34 C7** 48 3N 14 8 E
Kretinga, *Lithuania* **15 J19** 55 53N 21 15 E
Krettamia, *Algeria* **110 C4** 28 47N 3 27W
Krettsy, *Russia* **58 C7** 58 15N 32 30 E
Kreuzberg, *Germany* **31 E5** 50 22N 9 58 E
Kreuzlingen, *Switz.* **33 A8** 47 38N 9 10 E
Kreuztal, *Germany* **30 E4** 50 57N 8 0 E
Kría Vrísi, *Greece* **50 F6** 40 41N 22 18 E
Kribi, *Cameroon* **113 E6** 2 57N 9 56 E
Krichem, *Bulgaria* **51 D8** 42 8N 24 28 E
Krichev = Krychaw, *Belarus* **58 F6** 53 40N 31 41 E
Kriens, *Switz.* **33 B6** 47 2N 8 17 E
Krim, *Slovenia* **45 C11** 45 53N 14 30 E
Krim-Krim, *Chad* **109 G3** 9 0N 15 24 E
Kriós, Ákra, *Greece* **39 E4** 35 13N 23 34 E
Krishna →, *India* **95 G5** 15 57N 80 59 E
Krishnagiri, *India* **95 H4** 12 32N 78 16 E
Krishnanagar, *India* **93 H13** 23 24N 88 33 E
Krishnaraja Sagara, *India* **95 H3** 12 20N 76 30 E
Kristdala, *Sweden* **17 G10** 57 24N 16 13 E
Kristiansand, *Norway* **15 G13** 58 8N 8 1 E
Kristianstad, *Sweden* **17 H8** 56 2N 14 9 E
Kristiansund, *Norway* **14 E12** 63 7N 7 45 E
Kristiinankaupunki, *Finland* **15 E19** 62 16N 21 21 E
Kristinehamn, *Sweden* **16 E8** 59 18N 14 7 E
Kristinestad = Kristiinankaupunki, *Finland* **15 E19** 62 16N 21 21 E
Krithotí, Ákra, *Greece* **39 B3** 38 30N 21 2 E
Kríti, *Greece* **39 E6** 35 15N 25 0 E
Kritsá, *Greece* **39 E6** 35 10N 25 41 E
Kriva →, *Macedonia* **50 D5** 42 5N 21 47 E
Kriva Palanka, *Macedonia* **50 D6** 42 11N 22 19 E
Krivaja →, *Bos.-H.* **52 F3** 44 27N 18 9 E
Krivelj, *Serbia, Yug.* **50 B6** 44 10N 22 5 E
Krivoy Rog = Kryvyy Rih, *Ukraine* **59 J7** 47 51N 33 20 E
Križevci, *Croatia* **45 B13** 46 3N 16 32 E
Krk, *Croatia* **45 C11** 45 8N 14 40 E
Krka →, *Slovenia* **45 C12** 45 50N 15 30 E
Krkonoše, *Czech Rep.* **34 A8** 50 50N 15 35 E
Krnov, *Czech Rep.* **35 A10** 50 5N 17 40 E
Krobia, *Poland* **55 G3** 51 47N 16 59 E
Krøderen, *Norway* **18 D6** 60 9N 9 49 E
Krokeaí, *Greece* **48 E4** 36 53N 22 32 E
Krokek, *Sweden* **17 F10** 58 40N 16 24 E
Krokodil →, *Mozam.* **117 D5** 25 14 S 32 18 E
Krokom, *Sweden* **16 A8** 63 20N 14 30 E
Krokowa, *Poland* **54 D5** 54 47N 18 9 E
Króksfjarðarnes, *Iceland* **11 B5** 65 27N 21 56W
Krokstadelva, *Norway* **18 E7** 59 56N 10 1 E
Krolevets, *Ukraine* **59 G7** 51 35N 33 20 E
Kroměříž, *Czech Rep.* **35 B10** 49 18N 17 21 E
Krompachy, *Slovak Rep.* **35 C13** 48 54N 20 52 E
Kromy, *Russia* **59 F8** 52 48N 35 48 E
Kronach, *Germany* **31 E7** 50 14N 11 19 E
Krong Kaoh Kong, *Cambodia* **78 B2** 11 35N 103 0 E
Kronobergs län □, *Sweden* **17 H8** 56 45N 14 30 E
Kronprins Christian Land, *Greenland* **10 A8** 80 30N 22 0W
Kronprins Frederik Land, *Greenland* **10 B5** 79 0N 55 0W
Kronprins Olav Kyst, *Antarctica* **7 C5** 69 0 S 42 0 E
Kronshtadt, *Russia* **58 C5** 59 57N 29 51 E
Kroonstad, *S. Africa* **116 D4** 27 43 S 27 19 E
Kröpelin, *Germany* **30 A7** 54 4N 11 47 E
Kropotkin, *Russia* **61 H5** 45 28N 40 28 E
Kropp, *Germany* **30 A5** 54 24N 9 31 E
Krosna, *Lithuania* **54 D10** 54 23N 23 33 E
Krośniewice, *Poland* **55 F6** 52 15N 19 11 E
Krosno, *Poland* **55 J8** 49 42N 21 46 E
Krosno Odrzańskie, *Poland* **55 F2** 52 3N 15 7 E
Krotoszyn, *Poland* **55 G4** 51 42N 17 23 E
Krotovka, *Russia* **60 D10** 53 18N 51 10 E
Kroussón, *Greece* **39 E5** 35 13N 24 59 E
Krrabë, *Albania* **50 E3** 41 13N 20 0 E
Krško, *Slovenia* **45 C12** 45 57N 15 30 E
Krstača, *Serbia, Yug.* **50 D4** 42 57N 20 8 E
Kruger Nat. Park, *S. Africa* **117 C5** 24 50 S 26 10 E
Krugersdorp, *S. Africa* **117 D4** 26 5 S 27 46 E
Kruisfontein, *S. Africa* **116 E3** 33 59 S 24 43 E
Krujë, *Albania* **50 E3** 41 32N 19 46 E
Krulevshchina = Krulyewshchyna, *Belarus* **58 E4** 55 5N 27 45 E
Krulyewshchyna, *Belarus* **58 E4** 55 5N 27 45 E
Krumbach, *Germany* **31 G6** 48 13N 10 22 E
Krumë, *Albania* **50 D4** 42 14N 20 28 E
Krumovgrad, *Bulgaria* **51 E9** 41 29N 25 38 E
Krung Thep = Bangkok, *Thailand* **86 F3** 13 45N 100 35 E
Krupanj, *Serbia, Yug.* **50 B3** 44 25N 19 22 E
Krupina, *Slovak Rep.* **35 C12** 48 22N 19 5 E
Krupinica →, *Slovak Rep.* **35 C11** 48 4N 18 55 E
Krupki, *Belarus* **58 E5** 54 19N 29 8 E
Krusenstern, C., *U.S.A.* **144 C7** 67 8N 163 45W
Kruševac, *Serbia, Yug.* **50 C5** 43 35N 21 28 E
Kruševo, *Macedonia* **50 E5** 41 23N 21 19 E
Kruszwica, *Poland* **55 F5** 52 40N 18 20 E
Krychaw, *Belarus* **58 F6** 53 40N 31 41 E
Krymsk, *Russia* **59 K10** 44 50N 38 0 E
Krymskiy Poluostrov = Krymskyy Pivostriv, *Ukraine* **59 K8** 45 0N 34 0 E
Krymskyy Pivostriv, *Ukraine* **59 K8** 45 0N 34 0 E
Krynica, *Poland* **55 J7** 49 25N 20 57 E
Krynica Morska, *Poland* **54 D6** 54 23N 19 28 E
Krynki, *Poland* **55 E10** 53 17N 23 43 E
Kryvyy Rih, *Ukraine* **59 J7** 47 51N 33 20 E
Krzepice, *Poland* **55 H5** 50 58N 18 50 E
Krzeszów, *Poland* **55 H9** 50 24N 22 21 E
Krzna →, *Poland* **55 F10** 52 8N 23 32 E
Krzywiń, *Poland* **55 G3** 51 58N 16 50 E
Krzyż Wielkopolski, *Poland* **55 F2** 52 52N 16 0 E
Ksabi, *Morocco* **110 B4** 32 51N 4 13W
Ksar Chellala, *Algeria* **111 A5** 35 13N 2 19 E
Ksar el Boukhari, *Algeria* **111 A5** 35 51N 2 52 E
Ksar el Kebir, *Morocco* **110 B3** 35 0N 6 0W
Ksar es Souk = Er Rachidia, *Morocco* **110 B4** 31 58N 4 20W
Ksar Rhilane, *Tunisia* **108 B1** 33 0N 9 39 E
Książ Wielkopolski, *Poland* **55 F4** 52 4N 17 14 E
Ksour, Mts. des, *Algeria* **111 B4** 32 45N 0 30W
Kstovo, *Russia* **60 B7** 56 12N 44 13 E
Ku, W. el →, *Sudan* **107 E2** 13 37N 25 15 E
Ku-Ring-Gai Chase Nat. Park, *Australia* **129 B9** 33 39 S 151 14 E
Ku Tree Reservoir, *U.S.A.* **145 K14** 21 30N 157 59W
Kuala, *Indonesia* **84 B3** 2 55N 105 47 E
Kuala Belait, *Malaysia* **85 B4** 4 35N 114 11 E
Kuala Berang, *Malaysia* **87 K4** 5 5N 103 1 E
Kuala Dungun = Dungun, *Malaysia* **87 K4** 4 45N 103 25 E
Kuala Kangsar, *Malaysia* **87 K3** 4 46N 100 56 E
Kuala Kelawang, *Malaysia* **87 L4** 2 56N 102 5 E
Kuala Kerai, *Malaysia* **87 K4** 5 30N 102 12 E
Kuala Kerian, *Malaysia* **87 c** 5 10N 100 25 E
Kuala Lipis, *Malaysia* **87 K4** 4 10N 102 3 E
Kuala Lumpur, *Malaysia* **87 L3** 3 9N 101 41 E
Kuala Nerang, *Malaysia* **87 J3** 6 16N 100 37 E
Kuala Pilah, *Malaysia* **87 L4** 2 45N 102 15 E
Kuala Rompin, *Malaysia* **87 L4** 2 49N 103 29 E
Kuala Selangor, *Malaysia* **87 L3** 3 20N 101 15 E
Kuala Sepetang, *Malaysia* **87 K3** 4 49N 100 28 E
Kuala Terengganu, *Malaysia* **87 K4** 5 20N 103 8 E
Kualajelai, *Indonesia* **85 C4** 2 58 S 110 46 E
Kualakapuas, *Indonesia* **85 C4** 2 55 S 114 20 E
Kualakurun, *Indonesia* **85 C4** 1 10 S 113 50 E
Kualapembuang, *Indonesia* **85 C4** 3 14 S 112 38 E
Kualapuu, *U.S.A.* **145 B4** 21 10N 157 2W
Kualasimpang, *Indonesia* **84 B1** 4 17N 98 3 E
Kualoa Pt., *U.S.A.* **145 J14** 21 31N 157 50W
Kuamat, *Malaysia* **85 A5** 5 13N 117 30 E
Kuancheng, *China* **75 D10** 40 37N 118 30 E
Kuandang, *Indonesia* **82 A2** 0 56N 123 1 E
Kuandian, *China* **75 D13** 40 45N 124 45 E
Kuangchou = Guangzhou, *China* **77 F9** 23 5N 113 10 E
Kuanshan, *Taiwan* **77 F13** 23 3N 121 9 E
Kuantan, *Malaysia* **87 L4** 3 49N 103 20 E
Kuapa Pond, *U.S.A.* **145 K14** 21 17N 157 43W
Kuba = Quba, *Azerbaijan* **61 K9** 41 21N 48 32 E
Kuban →, *Russia* **59 K9** 45 20N 37 30 E
Kubenskoye, Ozero, *Russia* **58 C10** 59 40N 39 25 E
Küblis, *Switz.* **33 C9** 46 54N 9 45 E
Kubokawa, *Japan* **72 D5** 33 12N 133 8 E
Kubor, Mt., *Papua N. G.* **132 D3** 6 10 S 144 44 E
Kubrat, *Bulgaria* **51 C10** 43 49N 26 31 E
Kubu, *Indonesia* **79 J18** 8 16 S 115 35 E
Kubutambahan, *Indonesia* **79 J18** 8 5 S 115 10 E
Kucar, Tanjung, *Indonesia* **79 K18** 8 39 S 114 34 E
Kučevo, *Serbia, Yug.* **50 B5** 44 30N 21 40 E
Kucha Gompa, *India* **93 B7** 34 25N 76 56 E
Kuchaman, *India* **92 F6** 27 13N 74 47 E
Kuchchaveli, *Sri Lanka* **95 K5** 8 49N 81 6 E
Kuchenspitze, *Austria* **34 D3** 47 7N 10 12 E
Kuchinda, *India* **93 J11** 21 44N 84 21 E
Kuching, *Malaysia* **85 B4** 1 33N 110 25 E
Kuchino-eruba-Jima, *Japan* **71 J5** 30 28N 130 12 E
Kuchino-Shima, *Japan* **71 K4** 29 57N 129 55 E
Kuchinotsu, *Japan* **72 E2** 32 36N 130 11 E
Kuchl, *Austria* **34 D6** 47 37N 13 9 E
Kūchnay Darvīshān, *Afghan.* **91 C2** 30 59N 64 10 E
Kucing = Kuching, *Malaysia* **85 B4** 1 33N 110 25 E
Kuçovë, *Albania* **50 F3** 40 47N 19 57 E
Küçükbahçe, *Turkey* **49 C8** 38 33N 26 24 E
Küçükköy, *Turkey* **49 B8** 39 16N 26 42 E
Küçükkuyu, *Turkey* **49 B8** 39 32N 26 36 E
Küçükmenderes →, *Turkey* **49 D9** 37 57N 27 16 E
Kud →, *Pakistan* **92 F2** 26 5N 66 20 E
Kudal, *India* **95 F1** 16 2N 73 41 E
Kudalier →, *India* **94 E4** 18 35N 79 48 E
Kudamatsu, *Japan* **72 D3** 34 0N 131 52 E
Kudara, *Tajikistan* **65 D6** 38 25N 72 39 E
Kudat, *Malaysia* **85 A5** 6 55N 116 55 E
Kudirkos Naumiestis, *Lithuania* **54 D9** 54 46N 22 53 E
Kudowa-Zdrój, *Poland* **55 H3** 50 27N 16 15 E
Kudremukh, *India* **95 H2** 13 15N 75 20 E
Kudus, *Indonesia* **85 D4** 6 48 S 110 51 E
Kudymkar, *Russia* **64 B5** 59 1N 54 39 E
Kueiyang = Guiyang, *China* **76 D6** 26 32N 106 40 E
Kufra Oasis = Al Kufrah, *Libya* **108 D4** 24 17N 23 15 E
Kufstein, *Austria* **34 D5** 47 35N 12 11 E
Kugluktuk, *Canada* **138 B8** 67 50N 115 5W
Kugong I., *Canada* **140 A4** 56 18N 79 50W
Kūhak, *Iran* **91 D1** 27 12N 63 10 E
Kuhan, *Pakistan* **92 E2** 28 19N 67 14 E
Kūhbonān, *Iran* **97 D8** 31 23N 56 19 E
Kūhestak, *Iran* **97 E8** 26 47N 57 2 E
Kūhestān, *Afghan.* **91 B1** 34 39N 61 12 E
Kuhin, *Iran* **97 B6** 36 22N 49 40 E
Kūhīrī, *Iran* **97 E9** 26 55N 61 2 E
Kuhnsdorf, *Austria* **34 E7** 46 37N 14 38 E
Kūhpāyeh, *Eşfahan, Iran* **97 C7** 32 44N 52 20 E
Kūhpāyeh, *Kermān, Iran* **97 D8** 30 35N 57 15 E
Kūhrān, Kūh-e, *Iran* **97 E8** 26 46N 58 12 E
Kui Buri, *Thailand* **87 F2** 12 3N 99 52 E
Kuichong, *China* **69 F11** 22 38N 114 25 E
Kuiseb →, *Namibia* **116 B2** 22 59 S 14 31 E
Kuito, *Angola* **115 E3** 12 22 S 16 55 E
Kuiu I., *U.S.A.* **142 B2** 57 45N 134 10W
Kujang, *N. Korea* **75 E14** 39 57N 126 1 E
Kujawsko-Pomorskie □, *Poland* **54 E5** 53 20N 18 30 E
Kuji, *Japan* **70 D10** 40 11N 141 46 E
Kujū-San, *Japan* **72 D3** 33 5N 131 15 E
Kukavica, *Serbia, Yug.* **50 D5** 42 48N 21 57 E
Kukawa, *Nigeria* **113 C7** 12 58N 13 27 E
Kukës, *Albania* **50 D4** 42 5N 20 27 E
Kuki, *Japan* **73 A11** 36 4N 139 40 E
Kukipi, *Papua N. G.* **132 E4** 8 10 S 146 6 E
Kukmor, *Russia* **60 B10** 56 11N 50 54 E
Kukuihaele, *U.S.A.* **145 C6** 20 5N 155 35W
Kukup, *Malaysia* **87 d** 1 20N 103 27 E
Kukup, Pulau, *Malaysia* **87 d** 1 18N 103 25 E
Kukvidze, *Russia* **60 E6** 50 40N 43 0 E
Kula, *Bulgaria* **50 C6** 43 52N 22 36 E
Kula, *Serbia, Yug.* **52 E4** 45 37N 19 32 E
Kula, *Turkey* **49 C10** 38 32N 28 40 E
Kula Gulf, *Solomon Is.* **133 M9** 8 5 S 157 18 E
Kulachi, *Pakistan* **92 D4** 31 56N 70 27 E
Kulai, *Malaysia* **87 M4** 1 44N 103 35 E
Kulal, Mt., *Kenya* **118 B4** 2 42N 36 57 E
Kulaly, Ostrov, *Kazakstan* **61 H10** 45 0N 50 0 E
Kulanak, *Kyrgyzstan* **65 C7** 41 22N 75 30 E
Kulasekarappattinam, *India* **95 K4** 8 20N 78 5 E
Kulassein I., *Phil.* **81 H3** 6 25N 120 41 E
Kulaura, *Bangla.* **90 C4** 24 32N 92 3 E
Kulautuva, *Lithuania* **54 D10** 54 56N 23 36 E
Kuldīga, *Latvia* **15 H19** 56 58N 21 59 E
Kuldīga □, *Latvia* **54 B8** 56 55N 22 0 E
Kuldja = Yining, *China* **66 E9** 43 58N 81 10 E
Kuldu, *Sudan* **107 E2** 12 50N 28 30 E
Kulebaki, *Russia* **60 C6** 55 22N 42 25 E
Kulen, *Cambodia* **86 F5** 13 50N 104 40 E
Kulen Vakuf, *Bos.-H.* **45 D13** 44 35N 16 2 E
Kulgam, *India* **93 C6** 33 36N 75 2 E
Kulgera, *Australia* **126 D1** 25 50 S 133 18 E
Kulim, *Malaysia* **87 K3** 5 22N 100 34 E
Kulin, *Australia* **125 F2** 32 40 S 118 2 E
Kulittalai, *India* **95 J4** 10 55N 78 25 E
Kullen, *Sweden* **17 H6** 56 18N 12 26 E
Kulmbach, *Germany* **31 E7** 50 6N 11 26 E
Kŭlob, *Tajikistan* **66 F7** 37 55N 69 50 E
Kulp, *Turkey* **101 C9** 38 29N 41 2 E
Kulpawn →, *Ghana* **113 D4** 10 20N 1 5W
Kulsary, *Kazakstan* **57 E9** 46 59N 54 1 E
Kulti, *India* **93 H12** 23 43N 86 50 E
Kulu, *India* **92 D7** 31 58N 77 6 E
Kulu, *Turkey* **100 C5** 39 5N 33 4 E
Kulumadau, *Papua N. G.* **132 E7** 9 3 S 152 43 E
Kulumbura, *Australia* **124 B4** 13 55 S 126 35 E
Kulunda, *Russia* **66 D8** 52 35N 78 57 E
Kulungar, *Afghan.* **92 C3** 34 0N 69 2 E
Kūlvand, *Iran* **97 D7** 31 21N 54 35 E
Kulwin, *Australia* **128 C5** 35 0 S 142 42 E
Kulyab = Kŭlob, *Tajikistan* **66 F7** 37 55N 69 50 E
Kuma, *Japan* **72 D4** 33 39N 132 54 E
Kuma →, *Russia* **61 H8** 44 55N 47 0 E
Kumafşarı, *Turkey* **49 D11** 37 19N 29 32 E
Kumaganum, *Nigeria* **113 C7** 13 8N 10 38 E
Kumagaya, *Japan* **73 A11** 36 9N 139 22 E
Kumai, *Indonesia* **85 C4** 2 44 S 111 43 E
Kumak, *Russia* **64 F8** 51 10N 60 8 E
Kumalar Dağı, *Turkey* **49 C12** 38 15N 30 20 E
Kumamba, Kepulauan, *Indonesia* **83 B5** 1 36 S 138 45 E
Kumamoto, *Japan* **72 E2** 32 45N 130 45 E
Kumamoto □, *Japan* **72 E2** 32 55N 130 55 E
Kumano, *Japan* **73 D8** 33 54N 136 5 E
Kumano-Nada, *Japan* **73 D8** 33 47N 136 20 E
Kumanovo, *Macedonia* **50 D5** 42 9N 21 42 E
Kumar →, *Afghan.* **91 B3** 34 30N 70 28 E
Kumara, *N.Z.* **131 C6** 42 37 S 171 12 E
Kumarina, *Australia* **125 D2** 24 41 S 119 32 E
Kumarkhali, *Bangla.* **90 D2** 23 51N 89 15 E
Kumasi, *Ghana* **112 D4** 6 41N 1 38W
Kumayri = Gyumri, *Armenia* **61 K6** 40 47N 43 50 E
Kumba, *Cameroon* **113 E6** 4 36N 9 24 E
Kumbağ, *Turkey* **51 F11** 40 51N 27 27 E
Kumbakonam, *India* **95 J4** 10 58N 79 25 E
Kumbarilla, *Australia* **127 D5** 27 15 S 150 55 E
Kumbe, *Indonesia* **83 C6** 8 21 S 140 13 E
Kumbhraj, *India* **92 G7** 24 22N 77 3 E
Kumbia, *Australia* **127 D5** 26 41 S 151 39 E
Kumbo, *Cameroon* **113 D7** 6 15N 10 36 E
Kumbukkan Oya →, *Sri Lanka* **95 L5** 6 35N 81 40 E
Kŭmch'ŏn, *N. Korea* **75 E14** 38 10N 126 29 E
Kumdah, *Si. Arabia* **98 B4** 20 23N 45 5 E
Kumdok, *India* **93 C8** 33 32N 78 10 E
Kume-Shima, *Japan* **71 L3** 26 20N 126 47 E
Kumeny, *Russia* **60 A9** 58 10N 49 47 E
Kumertau, *Russia* **64 E5** 52 45N 55 57 E
Kumharsain, *India* **92 D7** 31 19N 77 27 E
Kŭmhwa, *S. Korea* **75 E14** 38 17N 127 28 E
Kumi, *Uganda* **118 B3** 1 30N 33 58 E
Kumkale, *Turkey* **51 G10** 39 59N 26 11 E
Kumkurgan = Qumqŭrghan, *Uzbekistan* **65 E3** 37 49N 67 35 E
Kumla, *Sweden* **16 E9** 59 8N 15 10 E
Kumluca, *Turkey* **49 E12** 36 22N 30 20 E
Kummerower See, *Germany* **30 B8** 53 49N 12 51 E
Kumo, *Nigeria* **113 C7** 10 1N 11 12 E
Kumon Bum, *Burma* **90 B6** 26 30N 97 15 E
Kumotori-Yama, *Japan* **73 B10** 35 51N 138 57 E
Kumta, *India* **95 G2** 14 29N 74 25 E
Kumukahi, C., *U.S.A.* **145 D7** 19 31N 154 49W
Kumusi →, *Papua N. G.* **132 E5** 8 16 S 148 13 E
Kumylzhenskaya, *Russia* **60 F6** 49 51N 42 38 E
Kunágota, *Hungary* **52 D6** 46 26N 21 3 E
Kunak, *Malaysia* **85 B5** 4 41N 118 15 E
Kunashir, Ostrov, *Russia* **67 E15** 44 0N 146 0 E
Kunchaung, *Burma* **90 D6** 23 50N 96 35 E
Kunda, *Estonia* **15 G22** 59 30N 26 34 E
Kunda, *India* **93 G9** 25 43N 81 31 E
Kundar →, *Pakistan* **92 D3** 31 56N 69 19 E
Kundelungu, Parc Nat. de, *Dem. Rep. of the Congo* **119 E2** 10 30 S 27 40 E
Kundelungu Ouest, Parc Nat. de, *Dem. Rep. of the Congo* **119 D2** 9 55 S 27 17 E
Kundian, *Pakistan* **92 C4** 32 27N 71 28 E
Kundiawa, *Papua N. G.* **132 D3** 6 2 S 145 1 E
Kundla, *India* **92 J4** 21 21N 71 25 E
Kundur, *Indonesia* **84 C3** 3 8 S 107 48 E
Kung, Ao, *Thailand* **87 a** 8 5N 98 24 E
Kunga →, *Bangla.* **90 E2** 21 46N 89 30 E
Kungälv, *Sweden* **17 G5** 57 53N 11 59 E
Kunghit I., *Canada* **142 C2** 52 6N 131 3W
Kungrad = Qŭnghirot, *Uzbekistan* **66 E6** 43 6N 58 54 E
Kungsängen, *Sweden* **16 E11** 59 29N 17 45 E
Kungsbacka, *Sweden* **17 G6** 57 30N 12 5 E
Kungsgården, *Sweden* **16 D10** 60 37N 16 35 E
Kungshamn, *Sweden* **17 F5** 58 22N 11 15 E
Kungsör, *Sweden* **16 E10** 59 25N 16 5 E
Kungu, *Dem. Rep. of the Congo* **114 B3** 2 47N 19 12 E
Kungur, *Russia* **64 C6** 57 25N 56 57 E
Kungurri, *Australia* **126 K6** 21 4 S 148 45 E
Kungyangon, *Burma* **90 G6** 16 27N 96 20 E
Kunhar →, *Pakistan* **93 B5** 34 20N 73 30 E
Kunhegyes, *Hungary* **52 C5** 47 22N 20 36 E
Kunia, *U.S.A.* **145 K13** 21 28N 158 4W
Kunimi-Dake, *Japan* **72 E3** 32 33N 131 1 E
Kuningan, *Indonesia* **85 D3** 6 59 S 108 29 E
Kunisaki, *Japan* **72 D3** 33 33N 131 45 E
Kunjirap Daban, *Pakistan* **65 E7** 36 52N 75 27 E
Kunlara, *Australia* **128 C3** 34 54 S 139 55 E
Kunlong, *Burma* **76 F2** 23 20N 98 50 E
Kunlun Shan, *Asia* **68 C3** 36 0N 86 30 E
Kunmadaras, *Hungary* **52 C5** 47 28N 20 45 E
Kunming, *China* **76 E4** 25 1N 102 41 E
Kunnamkulam, *India* **95 J3** 10 38N 76 7 E
Kunów, *Poland* **55 H8** 50 57N 21 17 E
Kunsan, *S. Korea* **75 G14** 35 59N 126 45 E
Kunshan, *China* **77 B13** 31 22N 120 58 E
Kunszentmárton, *Hungary* **52 D5** 46 50N 20 20 E
Kunszentmiklós, *Hungary* **52 C4** 47 2N 19 8 E
Kuntaur, *Senegal* **112 C2** 13 40N 14 48W
Kunua, *Papua N. G.* **132 C8** 5 46 S 154 43 E
Kununurra, *Australia* **124 C4** 15 40 S 128 50 E
Kunwari →, *India* **93 F8** 26 26N 79 11 E
Kunya-Urgench = Köneürgench, *Turkmenistan* **66 E6** 42 19N 59 10 E
Künzelsau, *Germany* **31 F5** 49 17N 9 42 E
Kunzulu, *Dem. Rep. of the Congo* **114 C3** 3 28 S 16 12 E
Kuopio, *Finland* **14 E22** 62 53N 27 35 E
Kupa →, *Croatia* **45 C13** 45 28N 16 24 E
Kupang, *Indonesia* **82 D2** 10 19 S 123 39 E
Kupiano, *Papua N. G.* **132 F5** 10 4 S 148 14 E
Kupreanof I., *U.S.A.* **142 B2** 56 50N 133 30W
Kupres, *Bos.-H.* **52 G2** 43 56N 17 15 E
Kupyansk, *Ukraine* **59 H9** 49 52N 37 35 E
Kupyansk-Uzlovoi, *Ukraine* **59 H9** 49 40N 37 43 E
Kuqa, *China* **68 B3** 41 35N 82 30 E
Kur, *Indonesia* **83 C4** 5 20 S 132 0 E
Kür →, *Azerbaijan* **101 C13** 39 29N 49 15 E
Kur →, *Bhutan* **90 B3** 26 50N 91 0 E
Kür Dili, *Azerbaijan* **97 B6** 39 3N 49 13 E
Kura = Kür →, *Azerbaijan* **101 C13** 39 29N 49 15 E
Kurahashi-Jima, *Japan* **72 C4** 34 8N 132 31 E
Kuranda, *Australia* **126 B4** 16 48 S 145 35 E
Kuranga, *India* **92 H3** 22 4N 69 10 E
Kurashiki, *Japan* **72 C5** 34 40N 133 50 E
Kurayoshi, *Japan* **72 B5** 35 26N 133 50 E
Kürdämir, *Azerbaijan* **61 K9** 40 25N 48 3 E
Kurday = Qorday, *Kazakstan* **65 B7** 43 21N 74 59 E
Kurdistan, *Asia* **101 D10** 37 20N 43 30 E
Kurduvadi, *India* **94 E2** 18 8N 75 29 E
Kŭrdzhali, *Bulgaria* **51 E9** 41 38N 25 21 E
Kure, *Japan* **72 C4** 34 14N 132 32 E

La Souterraine 237

Küre, *Turkey* 100 B5 41 48N 33 43 E
Küre Dağları, *Turkey* 100 B6 41 50N 34 10 E
Kure I., *U.S.A.* 145 F8 28 25N 178 25W
Kuressaare, *Estonia* 15 G20 58 15N 22 30 E
Kurgan, *Russia* 66 D7 55 26N 65 18 E
Kurgan-Tyube = Qŭrghonteppa, *Tajikistan* 65 E4 37 50N 68 47 E
Kurganinsk, *Russia* 61 H5 44 54N 40 34 E
Kurgannaya = Kurganinsk, *Russia* 61 H5 44 54N 40 34 E
Kuri, *India* 92 F4 26 37N 70 43 E
Kuria Maria Is. = Khurīyā Murīyā, Jazā'ir, *Oman* 99 C6 17 30N 55 58 E
Kurichchi, *India* 95 J3 11 36N 77 35 E
Kuridala, *Australia* 126 C3 21 16 S 140 29 E
Kurigram, *Bangla.* 90 C2 25 49N 89 39 E
Kurik, *Indonesia* 83 C5 8 9 S 139 59 E
Kurikka, *Finland* 15 E20 62 36N 22 24 E
Kuril Is. = Kurilskiye Ostrova, *Russia* 67 E15 45 0N 150 0 E
Kuril Trench, *Pac. Oc.* 62 E19 44 0N 153 0 E
Kurilsk, *Russia* 67 E15 45 14N 147 53 E
Kurilskiye Ostrova, *Russia* 67 E15 45 0N 150 0 E
Kurino, *Japan* 72 F2 31 57N 130 43 E
Kurinskaya Kosa = Kür Dili, *Azerbaijan* 97 B6 39 3N 49 13 E
Kurkheda, *India* 94 D5 20 37N 80 12 E
Kurkur, *Egypt* 106 C3 23 50N 32 0 E
Kurla, *India* 94 E1 19 5N 72 52 E
Kurlovskiy, *Russia* 60 C5 55 25N 40 40 E
Kurmuk, *Sudan* 107 E3 10 33N 34 21 E
Kurnool, *India* 95 G4 15 45N 78 0 E
Kuro-Shima, *Kagoshima, Japan* 71 J4 30 50N 129 57 E
Kuro-Shima, *Okinawa, Japan* 71 M2 24 14N 124 1 E
Kurobe-Gawe →, *Japan* 73 A9 36 55N 137 25 E
Kurogi, *Japan* 72 D2 33 12N 130 40 E
Kuror, J., *Sudan* 106 C3 20 27N 31 30 E
Kurow, *N.Z.* 131 E5 44 44 S 170 29 E
Kurów, *Poland* 55 G9 51 23N 22 12 E
Kurrajong, *Australia* 129 B9 33 33 S 150 42 E
Kurram →, *Pakistan* 91 B3 32 36N 71 20 E
Kurri Kurri, *Australia* 129 B9 32 50 S 151 28 E
Kurrimine, *Australia* 126 B4 17 47 S 146 6 E
Kursavka, *Russia* 61 H6 44 29N 42 32 E
Kurse Korhi, *India* 94 D5 20 14N 80 46 E
Kurshskiy Zaliv, *Russia* 15 J19 55 9N 21 6 E
Kursk, *Russia* 59 G9 51 42N 36 11 E
Kuršumlija, *Serbia, Yug.* 50 C5 43 9N 21 19 E
Kuršumlijska Banja, *Serbia, Yug.* 50 C5 43 3N 21 11 E
Kurşunlu, *Bursa, Turkey* 51 F13 40 3N 29 40 E
Kurşunlu, *Çankırı, Turkey* 100 B5 40 51N 33 15 E
Kurtalan, *Turkey* 101 D9 37 56N 41 44 E
Kurtbey, *Turkey* 51 E10 41 9N 26 35 E
Kürti →, *Kazakstan* 65 A8 44 16N 76 42 E
Kurtistown, *U.S.A.* 145 D6 19 36N 155 4W
Kuru, *Sudan* 107 F2 7 43N 26 31 E
Kuru, Bahr el →, *Sudan* 107 F2 8 10N 26 50 E
Kurucaşile, *Turkey* 100 B5 41 49N 32 42 E
Kuruçay, *Turkey* 96 B3 39 39N 38 29 E
Kuruktag, *China* 68 B3 41 0N 89 0 E
Kuruman, *S. Africa* 116 D3 27 28 S 23 28 E
Kuruman →, *S. Africa* 116 D3 26 56 S 20 39 E
Kurume, *Japan* 72 D2 33 15N 130 30 E
Kurun →, *Sudan* 107 F3 5 30N 34 17 E
Kurunegala, *Sri Lanka* 95 L5 7 30N 80 23 E
Kurupukari, *Guyana* 169 C6 4 43N 58 37W
Kurya, *Russia* 56 B10 61 42N 57 9 E
Kus Gölü, *Turkey* 51 F11 40 10N 27 55 E
Kusa, *Russia* 64 D7 55 20N 59 29 E
Kuşadası, *Turkey* 100 D2 37 52N 27 15 E
Kuşadası Körfezi, *Turkey* 49 D8 37 56N 27 0 E
Kusamba, *Indonesia* 79 K18 8 34 S 115 27 E
Kusatsu, *Gumma, Japan* 73 A10 36 37N 138 36 E
Kusatsu, *Shiga, Japan* 73 C7 34 58N 135 57 E
Kusawa L., *Canada* 142 A1 60 20N 136 13W
Kusel, *Germany* 31 F3 49 32N 7 24 E
Kushaka, *Nigeria* 113 C6 10 32N 6 48 E
Kushalgarh, *India* 92 H6 23 10N 74 27 E
Kushalnagar, *India* 95 H2 12 14N 75 57 E
Kushchevskaya, *Russia* 61 G4 46 33N 39 35 E
Kusheriki, *Nigeria* 113 C6 10 33N 6 28 E
Kushikino, *Japan* 72 F2 31 44N 130 16 E
Kushima, *Japan* 72 F3 31 29N 131 14 E
Kushimoto, *Japan* 73 D7 33 28N 135 47 E
Kushiro, *Japan* 70 C12 43 0N 144 25 E
Kushiro-Gawa →, *Japan* 70 C12 42 59N 144 23 E
Kūshk, *Iran* 97 D8 28 46N 56 51 E
Kushka = Gushgy, *Turkmenistan* 66 F7 35 20N 62 18 E
Kūshkī, *Iran* 96 C5 33 31N 47 13 E
Kushnarenkovo, *Russia* 64 D5 55 6N 55 22 E
Kushol, *India* 93 C7 33 40N 76 36 E
Kushrabat = Koshrabad, *Uzbekistan* 65 C3 40 18N 66 32 E
Kushtia, *Bangla.* 90 D2 23 55N 89 5 E
Kushum →, *Kazakstan* 60 F10 49 20N 50 30 E
Kushva, *Russia* 64 B7 58 18N 59 45 E
Kuskokwim →, *U.S.A.* 144 F7 60 5N 162 25W
Kuskokwim B., *U.S.A.* 144 G7 59 45N 162 25W
Kuskokwim Mts., *U.S.A.* 144 E9 62 30N 156 0W
Kusmi, *India* 93 H10 23 17N 83 55 E
Küsnacht, *Switz.* 33 B7 47 19N 8 35 E
Kussharo-Ko, *Japan* 70 C12 43 38N 144 21 E
Küssnacht, *Switz.* 33 B6 47 5N 8 26 E
Kustanay = Qostanay, *Kazakstan* 66 D7 53 10N 63 35 E
Kusu, *Indonesia* 82 A3 0 53N 127 43 E
Kusu, *Japan* 72 D3 33 16N 131 9 E
Kut, Ko, *Thailand* 87 G4 11 40N 102 35 E
Kuta, *Indonesia* 79 K18 8 43 S 115 11 E
Kutacane, *Indonesia* 84 B1 3 50N 97 50 E
Kütahya, *Turkey* 49 B12 39 30N 30 2 E
Kütahya □, *Turkey* 49 B11 39 10N 29 30 E
Kutaisi, *Georgia* 61 J6 42 19N 42 40 E
Kutaraja = Banda Aceh, *Indonesia* 84 A1 5 35N 95 20 E
Kutch, Gulf of = Kachchh, Gulf of, *India* 92 H3 22 50N 69 15 E
Kutch, Rann of = Kachchh, Rann of, *India* 92 H4 24 0N 70 0 E
Kutina, *Croatia* 45 C13 45 29N 16 48 E
Kutiyana, *India* 92 J4 21 36N 70 2 E
Kutjevo, *Croatia* 52 E2 45 23N 17 55 E
Kutkai, *Burma* 90 D6 23 27N 97 56 E
Kutkashen, *Azerbaijan* 61 K8 40 58N 47 47 E
Kutná Hora, *Czech Rep.* 34 B8 49 57N 15 16 E
Kutno, *Poland* 55 F6 52 15N 19 23 E
Kutru, *India* 94 E5 19 5N 80 46 E
Kutse, *Botswana* 116 C3 21 7 S 22 16 E
Kuttabul, *Australia* 126 K6 21 1 S 148 54 E
Kutu, *Dem. Rep. of the Congo* 114 C3 2 40 S 18 11 E
Kutu Moke, *Dem. Rep. of the Congo* 114 C3 3 12 S 17 21 E
Kutum, *Sudan* 107 E1 14 10N 24 40 E
Küty, *Slovak Rep.* 35 C10 48 40N 17 3 E
Kuujjuaq, *Canada* 139 C13 58 6N 68 15W
Kuujjuarapik, *Canada* 140 A4 55 20N 77 35W
Kuŭp-tong, *N. Korea* 75 D14 40 45N 126 1 E
Kuusamo, *Finland* 14 D23 65 57N 29 8 E
Kuusankoski, *Finland* 15 F22 60 55N 26 38 E
Kuvandyk, *Russia* 64 F6 51 28N 57 21 E
Kuvango, *Angola* 115 E3 14 28 S 16 20 E
Kuvasay, *Uzbekistan* 65 C5 40 18N 71 59 E
Kuvshinovo, *Russia* 58 D8 57 2N 34 11 E
Kuwait = Al Kuwayt, *Kuwait* 96 D5 29 30N 48 0 E
Kuwait ■, *Asia* 96 D5 29 30N 47 30 E
Kuwana, *Japan* 73 B8 35 5N 136 43 E
Kuwana →, *India* 93 F10 26 25N 83 15 E
Kuybyshev = Samara, *Russia* 60 D10 53 8N 50 6 E
Kuybyshev, *Russia* 66 D8 55 27N 78 19 E
Kuybyshevo, *Ukraine* 59 J9 47 25N 36 40 E
Kuybyshevskiy, *Tajikistan* 65 E4 37 52N 68 44 E
Kuybyshevskoye Vdkhr., *Russia* 60 C9 55 2N 49 30 E
Kuye He →, *China* 74 E6 38 23N 110 46 E
Kūyeh, *Iran* 96 B5 38 45N 47 57 E
Kuylyuk, *Uzbekistan* 65 C4 41 14N 69 17 E
Kūysanjaq, *Iraq* 101 D11 36 5N 44 38 E
Kuyto, Ozero, *Russia* 56 B5 65 6N 31 20 E
Kuyucak, *Turkey* 49 D10 37 55N 28 28 E
Kuyumba, *Russia* 67 C10 60 58N 96 59 E
Kuzey Anadolu Dağları, *Turkey* 100 B7 41 30N 35 0 E
Kuzhitturai, *India* 95 K3 8 18N 77 11 E
Kuzino, *Russia* 64 C7 57 1N 59 27 E
Kuzitrin →, *U.S.A.* 144 D6 65 10N 165 25W
Kuzmin, *Serbia, Yug.* 52 E4 45 2N 19 25 E
Kuznetsk, *Russia* 60 D8 53 12N 46 40 E
Kuzomen, *Russia* 56 A6 66 22N 36 50 E
Kvænangen, *Norway* 14 A19 70 5N 21 15 E
Kværndrup, *Denmark* 17 J4 55 10N 10 31 E
Kvaløy, *Norway* 14 B18 69 40N 18 30 E
Kvam, *Norway* 18 C6 61 40N 9 42 E
Kvänum, *Sweden* 17 F7 58 18N 13 11 E
Kvareli = Qvareli, *Georgia* 61 K7 41 57N 45 47 E
Kvarner, *Croatia* 45 D11 44 50N 14 10 E
Kvarnerič, *Croatia* 45 D11 44 43N 14 37 E
Kvås, *Norway* 18 F4 58 16N 7 14 E
Kvernaland, *Norway* 18 F2 58 47N 5 45 E
Kvichak B., *U.S.A.* 144 G8 58 48N 157 30W
Kvicksund, *Sweden* 16 E10 59 27N 16 19 E
Kvikne, *Norway* 18 B7 62 35N 10 16 E
Kvillsfors, *Sweden* 17 G9 57 24N 15 29 E
Kvina →, *Norway* 18 F3 58 19N 6 55 E
Kvinlog, *Norway* 18 F3 58 31N 6 55 E
Kvismare kanal, *Sweden* 16 E9 59 11N 15 35 E
Kvissleby, *Sweden* 16 B11 62 18N 17 22 E
Kviteseid, *Norway* 18 E5 59 24N 8 29 E
Kwabhaca, *S. Africa* 117 E4 30 51 S 29 0 E
Kwakhanai, *Botswana* 116 C3 21 39 S 21 16 E
Kwakoegron, *Surinam* 169 B6 5 12N 55 25W
Kwale, *Kenya* 118 C4 4 15 S 39 31 E
Kwale, *Nigeria* 113 D6 5 46N 6 26 E
Kwamalasamutu, *Surinam* 169 C6 2 20N 56 47W
KwaMashu, *S. Africa* 117 D5 29 45 S 30 58 E
Kwamouth, *Dem. Rep. of the Congo* 114 C3 3 9 S 16 12 E
Kwando →, *Africa* 116 B3 18 27 S 23 32 E
Kwangdaeri, *N. Korea* 75 D14 40 31N 127 32 E
Kwangju, *S. Korea* 75 G14 35 9N 126 54 E
Kwango →, *Dem. Rep. of the Congo* 114 C3 3 14 S 17 22 E
Kwangsi-Chuang = Guangxi Zhuangzu Zizhiqu □, *China* 76 F7 24 0N 109 0 E
Kwangtung = Guangdong □, *China* 77 F9 23 0N 113 0 E
Kwara □, *Nigeria* 113 D6 8 45N 4 30 E
Kwataboahegan →, *Canada* 140 B3 51 9N 80 50W
Kwatisore, *Indonesia* 83 B4 3 18 S 134 50 E
KwaZulu Natal □, *S. Africa* 117 D5 29 0 S 30 0 E
Kweichow = Guizhou □, *China* 76 D6 27 0N 107 0 E
Kwekwe, *Zimbabwe* 119 F2 18 58 S 29 48 E
Kwenge →, *Dem. Rep. of the Congo* 115 C3 4 50 S 18 44 E
Kwethluk, *U.S.A.* 144 F7 60 49N 161 26W
Kwidzyn, *Poland* 54 E5 53 44N 18 55 E
Kwigillingok, *U.S.A.* 144 G7 59 51N 163 8W
Kwiguk, *U.S.A.* 144 E6 62 46N 164 30W
Kwiha, *Ethiopia* 107 E4 13 29N 39 32 E
Kwikila, *Papua N. G.* 132 E4 9 49 S 147 38 E
Kwilu →, *Dem. Rep. of the Congo* 115 C3 3 22 S 17 22 E
Kwinana New Town, *Australia* 125 F2 32 15 S 115 47 E
Kwinbet, *Burma* 90 G5 16 20N 94 14 E
Kwisa →, *Poland* 55 G2 51 34N 15 24 E
Kwoka, *Indonesia* 83 B4 0 31 S 132 27 E
Kwolla, *Nigeria* 113 D6 9 0N 9 15 E
Kwun Tong, *China* 69 G11 22 19N 114 13 E
Kya-in-Seikkyi, *Burma* 90 G7 16 2N 98 8 E
Kyabé, *Chad* 109 G3 9 30N 19 0 E
Kyabra Cr. →, *Australia* 127 D3 25 36 S 142 55 E
Kyabram, *Australia* 129 D6 36 19 S 145 4 E
Kyaikkami, *Burma* 90 G6 16 4N 97 34 E
Kyaiklat, *Burma* 90 G5 16 25N 95 40 E
Kyaikmaraw, *Burma* 90 G6 16 23N 97 44 E
Kyaikthin, *Burma* 90 D5 23 32N 95 40 E
Kyaikto, *Burma* 86 D1 17 20N 97 3 E
Kyakhta, *Russia* 67 D11 50 30N 106 25 E
Kyambura Game Reserve, *Uganda* 118 C3 0 7 S 30 9 E
Kyancutta, *Australia* 127 E2 33 8 S 135 33 E
Kyangin, *Burma* 90 F5 18 20N 95 20 E
Kyaukhnyat, *Burma* 90 F6 18 15N 97 31 E
Kyaukki, *Burma* 90 F6 18 27N 96 56 E
Kyaukkyi, *Burma* 90 F5 18 15N 94 29 E
Kyaukme, *Burma* 90 D6 22 32N 97 2 E
Kyaukpadaung, *Burma* 90 E5 20 52N 95 8 E
Kyaukpyu, *Burma* 90 F4 19 28N 93 30 E
Kyaukse, *Burma* 90 E6 21 36N 96 10 E
Kyauktaga, *Burma* 90 F6 18 10N 96 37 E
Kyauktan, *Burma* 90 G6 16 38N 96 19 E
Kyauktaw, *Burma* 90 E4 20 51N 92 59 E
Kyaunggon, *Burma* 90 G5 17 6N 95 11 E
Kyawkku, *Burma* 90 E6 21 48N 96 56 E
Kybartai, *Lithuania* 54 D9 54 39N 22 45 E
Kyburz, *U.S.A.* 160 G6 38 47N 120 18W
Kyeintali, *Burma* 90 G5 18 0N 94 29 E
Kyelang, *India* 92 C7 32 35N 77 2 E
Kyenjojo, *Uganda* 118 B3 0 40N 30 37 E
Kyidaunggan, *Burma* 90 F6 19 53N 96 12 E
Kyjov, *Czech Rep.* 35 B10 49 1N 17 7 E
Kyle, *Canada* 143 C7 50 50N 108 2W
Kyle Dam, *Zimbabwe* 119 G3 20 15 S 31 0 E
Kyle of Lochalsh, *U.K.* 22 D3 57 17N 5 44W
Kyll →, *Germany* 31 F2 49 48N 6 41 E
Kyllburg, *Germany* 31 E2 50 2N 6 34 E
Kymijoki →, *Finland* 15 F22 60 30N 26 55 E
Kyneton, *Australia* 128 D6 37 10 S 144 29 E
Kynuna, *Australia* 126 C3 21 37 S 141 55 E
Kyō-ga-Saki, *Japan* 73 B7 35 45N 135 15 E
Kyoga, L., *Uganda* 118 B3 1 35N 33 0 E
Kyogle, *Australia* 127 D5 28 40 S 153 0 E
Kyom →, *Sudan* 107 F2 8 58N 28 13 E
Kyongju, *S. Korea* 75 G15 35 51N 129 14 E
Kyŏngsŏng, *N. Korea* 75 D15 41 35N 129 36 E
Kyōto, *Japan* 73 C7 35 0N 135 45 E
Kyōto □, *Japan* 73 B7 35 15N 135 45 E
Kyparissovouno, *Cyprus* 39 E9 35 19N 33 10 E
Kyperounda, *Cyprus* 39 F8 34 56N 32 58 E
Kyrenia, *Cyprus* 39 E9 35 20N 33 20 E
Kyrgyzstan ■, *Asia* 66 E8 42 0N 75 0 E
Kyritz, *Germany* 30 C8 52 56N 12 24 E
Kyrkhult, *Sweden* 17 H8 56 22N 14 34 E
Kyrksæterøra, *Norway* 18 A6 63 18N 9 5 E
Kyrönjoki →, *Finland* 14 E19 63 14N 21 45 E
Kyshtym, *Russia* 64 D8 55 42N 60 34 E
Kystatyam, *Russia* 67 C13 67 20N 123 10 E
Kysucké Nové Mesto, *Slovak Rep.* 35 B11 49 18N 18 47 E
Kythréa, *Cyprus* 39 E9 35 15N 33 29 E
Kytlym, *Russia* 64 B7 59 30N 59 12 E
Kyu-hkok, *Burma* 90 C7 24 4N 98 4 E
Kyunhla, *Burma* 90 D5 23 25N 95 15 E
Kyuquot Sound, *Canada* 142 D3 50 2N 127 22W
Kyurdamir = Kürdämir, *Azerbaijan* 61 K9 40 25N 48 3 E
Kyūshū, *Japan* 72 E3 33 0N 131 0 E
Kyūshū □, *Japan* 72 E3 33 0N 131 0 E
Kyūshū-Sanchi, *Japan* 72 E3 32 35N 131 17 E
Kyustendil, *Bulgaria* 50 D6 42 16N 22 41 E
Kyusyur, *Russia* 67 B13 70 19N 127 30 E
Kywong, *Australia* 129 C7 34 58 S 146 44 E
Kyyiv, *Ukraine* 59 G6 50 30N 30 28 E
Kyyivske Vdskh., *Ukraine* 59 G6 51 0N 30 25 E
Kyzyl, *Russia* 67 D10 51 50N 94 30 E
Kyzyl-Adyr, *Kyrgyzstan* 65 B5 42 39N 71 35 E
Kyzyl Kum, *Uzbekistan* 66 E7 42 30N 65 0 E
Kyzyl-Kyya, *Kyrgyzstan* 66 E8 40 16N 72 8 E
Kyzyl-Suu, *Kyrgyzstan* 65 B9 42 20N 78 0 E
Kyzyl-Suu →, *Kyrgyzstan* 65 D6 38 50N 70 0 E
Kyzyltepa, *Uzbekistan* 65 C2 40 1N 64 51 E
Kzyl-Orda = Qyzylorda, *Kazakstan* 66 E7 44 48N 65 28 E

L

La Albuera, *Spain* 43 G4 38 45N 6 49W
La Alcarria, *Spain* 40 E2 40 31N 2 45W
La Almarcha, *Spain* 40 F2 39 41N 2 24W
La Almunia de Doña Godina, *Spain* 40 D3 41 29N 1 23W
La Asunción, *Venezuela* 169 A5 11 2N 63 53W
La Baie, *Canada* 141 C5 48 19N 70 53W
La Banda, *Argentina* 174 B3 27 45 S 64 10W
La Bañeza, *Spain* 42 C5 42 17N 5 54W
La Barca, *Mexico* 162 C4 20 20N 102 40W
La Barge, *U.S.A.* 158 E8 42 16N 110 12W
La Bastide-Puylaurent, *France* 28 D7 44 35N 3 55 E
La Baule-Escoubiac, *France* 26 E4 47 17N 2 24W
La Belle, *Fla., U.S.A.* 149 M5 26 46N 81 26W
La Belle, *Mo., U.S.A.* 156 D5 40 7N 91 55W
La Biche →, *Canada* 142 B4 59 57N 123 50W
La Biche, L., *Canada* 142 C6 54 50N 112 5W
La Bisbal d'Empordà, *Spain* 40 D8 41 58N 3 2 E
La Bomba, *Mexico* 162 A1 31 53N 115 2W
La Brea, *Trin. & Tob.* 169 F9 10 15N 61 37W
La Brède, *France* 28 D3 44 41N 0 32W
La Bresse, *France* 27 D13 48 2N 6 53 E
La Bureba, *Spain* 42 C7 42 36N 3 24W
La Cal →, *Bolivia* 173 D6 17 27 S 58 15W
La Calera, *Chile* 174 C1 32 50 S 71 10W
La Campiña, *Spain* 43 H6 37 45N 4 45W
La Canal = Sa Canal, *Spain* 38 D1 38 51N 1 23 E
La Cañiza = A Cañiza, *Spain* 42 C2 42 13N 8 16W
La Canourgue, *France* 28 D7 44 26N 3 13 E
La Capelle, *France* 27 C10 49 59N 3 50 E
La Carlota, *Argentina* 174 C3 33 30 S 63 20W
La Carlota, *Phil.* 81 F4 10 25N 122 55 E
La Carlota, *Spain* 43 H6 37 40N 4 56W
La Carolina, *Spain* 43 G7 38 17N 3 38W
La Castellana, *Phil.* 81 F4 10 20N 123 3 E
La Cavalerie, *France* 28 D7 44 1N 3 10 E
La Ceiba, *Honduras* 164 C2 15 40N 86 50W
La Ceiba, *Venezuela* 168 C3 9 28N 71 4W
La Chaise-Dieu, *France* 28 C7 45 18N 3 42 E
La Chapelle d'Angillon, *France* 27 E9 47 21N 2 25 E
La Chapelle-St-Luc, *France* 27 D11 48 20N 4 3 E
La Chapelle-sur-Erdre, *France* 26 E5 47 18N 1 34W
La Charité-sur-Loire, *France* 27 E10 47 10N 3 1 E
La Chartre-sur-le-Loir, *France* 26 E7 47 44N 0 34 E
La Châtaigneraie, *France* 28 B3 46 39N 0 44W
La Châtre, *France* 27 F9 46 35N 2 0 E
La Chaux-de-Fonds, *Switz.* 32 B3 47 7N 6 50 E
La Chorrera, *Colombia* 168 D3 0 44 S 73 1W
La Chorrera, *Panama* 164 E4 8 53N 79 47W
La Ciotat, *France* 29 E9 43 10N 5 37 E
La Clayette, *France* 27 F11 46 17N 4 19 E
La Cocha, *Argentina* 174 B2 27 50 S 65 40W
La Concepción = Ri-Aba, *Eq. Guin.* 113 E6 3 28N 8 40 E
La Concepción, *Panama* 164 E3 8 31N 82 37W
La Concepción, *Venezuela* 168 A3 10 30N 71 50W
La Concordia, *Mexico* 163 D6 16 8N 92 38W
La Coruña = A Coruña, *Spain* 42 B2 43 20N 8 25W
La Coruña □, *Spain* 42 B2 43 10N 8 30W
La Côte, *Switz.* 32 D2 46 25N 6 15 E
La Côte-St-André, *France* 29 C9 45 24N 5 15 E
La Courtine-le-Trucq, *France* 28 C6 45 41N 2 15 E
La Crau, *Bouches-du-Rhône, France* 29 E8 43 32N 4 40 E
La Crau, *Var, France* 29 E10 43 9N 6 4 E
La Crescent, *U.S.A.* 154 D9 43 50N 91 18W
La Crete, *Canada* 142 B5 58 11N 116 24W
La Crosse, *Fla., U.S.A.* 152 F7 29 51N 82 24W
La Crosse, *Kans., U.S.A.* 154 F5 38 32N 99 18W
La Crosse, *Wis., U.S.A.* 154 D9 43 48N 91 15W
La Cruz, *Costa Rica* 164 D2 11 4N 85 39W
La Cruz, *Mexico* 162 C3 23 55N 106 54W
La Cumbre, Volcán, *Ecuador* 172 a 0 21 S 91 32W
La Désirade, *Guadeloupe* 164 b 16 18N 61 3W
La Digue, *Seychelles* 121 b 4 20 S 55 51 E
La Dorada, *Colombia* 168 B3 5 30N 74 40W
La Ensenada, *Chile* 176 B2 41 12 S 72 33W
La Escondida, *Mexico* 162 C5 24 6N 99 55W
La Esmeralda, *Paraguay* 174 A3 22 16 S 62 33W
La Esperanza, *Argentina* 176 B3 40 26 S 68 32W
La Esperanza, *Cuba* 164 B3 22 46N 83 44W
La Esperanza, *Honduras* 164 D2 14 15N 88 10W
La Estrada = A Estrada, *Spain* 42 C2 42 43N 8 27W
La Faouët, *France* 26 D3 48 2N 3 30W
La Fayette, *U.S.A.* 149 H3 34 42N 85 17W
La Fé, *Cuba* 164 B3 22 2N 84 15W
La Fère, *France* 27 C10 49 39N 3 21 E
La Ferté-Bernard, *France* 26 D7 48 10N 0 40 E
La Ferté-Gaucher, *France* 27 D10 48 47N 3 19 E
La Ferté-Macé, *France* 26 D6 48 35N 0 22W
La Ferté-St-Aubin, *France* 27 E8 47 42N 1 57 E
La Ferté-sous-Jouarre, *France* 27 D10 48 56N 3 8 E
La Ferté-Vidame, *France* 26 D7 48 37N 0 53 E
La Flèche, *France* 26 E6 47 42N 0 4W
La Foa, *N. Cal.* 133 U19 21 43 S 165 50 E
La Follette, *U.S.A.* 149 G3 36 23N 84 7W
La Fontaine, *U.S.A.* 157 D11 40 40N 85 43W
La Fregeneda, *Spain* 42 E4 40 58N 6 54W
La Fría, *Venezuela* 168 B3 8 13N 72 15W
La Fuente de San Esteban, *Spain* 42 E4 40 49N 6 15W
La Gacilly, *France* 26 E4 47 45N 2 8W
La Gineta, *Spain* 41 F2 39 8N 2 1W
La Gloria, *Colombia* 168 B3 8 37N 73 48W
La Gran Sabana, *Venezuela* 169 B5 5 30N 61 30W
La Grand-Combe, *France* 29 D8 44 13N 4 2 E
La Grande, *U.S.A.* 158 D4 45 20N 118 5W
La Grande →, *Canada* 140 B5 53 50N 79 0W
La Grande Deux, Rés., *Canada* 140 B4 53 40N 76 55W
La Grande-Motte, *France* 29 E8 43 23N 4 5 E
La Grande Quatre, Rés., *Canada* 140 B5 54 0N 73 15W
La Grande Trois, Rés., *Canada* 140 B4 53 40N 75 10W
La Grange, *Calif., U.S.A.* 160 H6 37 42N 120 27W
La Grange, *Ga., U.S.A.* 153 B4 33 2N 85 2W
La Grange, *Ky., U.S.A.* 148 F3 38 25N 85 23W
La Grange, *Ky., U.S.A.* 157 F11 38 24N 85 22W
La Grange, *Mo., U.S.A.* 156 D5 40 3N 91 35W
La Grange, *Tex., U.S.A.* 155 L6 29 54N 96 52W
La Grave, *France* 29 C10 45 3N 6 18 E
La Grita, *Venezuela* 168 B3 8 8N 71 59W
La Guaira, *Venezuela* 168 A4 10 36N 66 56W
La Guardia = A Guarda, *Spain* 42 D2 41 56N 8 52W
La Gudiña = A Gudiña, *Spain* 42 C3 42 4N 7 8W
La Güera, *Mauritania* 110 D1 20 51N 17 0W
La Guerche-de-Bretagne, *France* 26 E5 47 57N 1 16W
La Guerche-sur-l'Aubois, *France* 27 F9 46 58N 2 56 E
La Habana, *Cuba* 164 B3 23 8N 82 22W
La Harpe, *U.S.A.* 156 D6 40 35N 90 58W
La Haye-du-Puits, *France* 26 C5 49 17N 1 33W
La Horqueta, *Venezuela* 169 B5 7 55N 60 20W
La Horra, *Spain* 42 D7 41 44N 3 53W
La Independencia, *Mexico* 163 D6 16 31N 91 47W
La Isabela, *Dom. Rep.* 165 C5 19 58N 71 2W
La Jonquera, *Spain* 40 C7 42 25N 2 53 E
La Joya, *Peru* 172 D3 16 43 S 71 52W
La Junta, *U.S.A.* 155 F3 37 59N 103 33W
La Laguna, *Canary Is.* 9 e1 28 28N 16 18W
La Libertad, *Guatemala* 164 C1 16 47N 90 7W
La Libertad, *Mexico* 162 B2 29 55N 112 41W
La Libertad □, *Peru* 172 B2 8 0 S 78 30W
La Ligua, *Chile* 174 C1 32 30 S 71 16W
La Línea de la Concepción, *Spain* 43 J5 36 15N 5 23W
La Loche, *Canada* 143 B7 56 29N 109 26W
La Londe-les-Maures, *France* 29 E10 43 8N 6 14 E
La Lora, *Spain* 42 C7 42 45N 4 0W
La Loupe, *France* 26 D8 48 29N 1 0 E
La Louvière, *Belgium* 24 D4 50 27N 4 10 E
La Lune, *Trin. & Tob.* 169 F9 10 3N 61 22W
La Machine, *France* 27 F10 46 54N 3 27 E
La Maddalena, *Italy* 46 A2 41 13N 9 24 E
La Malbaie, *Canada* 141 C5 47 40N 70 10W
La Mancha, *Spain* 41 F2 39 10N 2 54W
La Mariña, *Spain* 42 B3 43 30N 7 40W
La Martre, L., *Canada* 142 A5 63 15N 117 55W
La Mesa, *U.S.A.* 161 N9 32 46N 117 3W
La Misión, *Mexico* 162 A1 32 5N 116 50W
La Moille, *U.S.A.* 156 C7 41 32N 89 17W
La Moine →, *U.S.A.* 156 E6 39 59N 90 31W
La Monte, *U.S.A.* 156 F3 38 46N 93 26W
La Mothe-Achard, *France* 26 F5 46 37N 1 40W
La Motte, *France* 29 D10 44 20N 6 3 E
La Motte-Chalançon, *France* 29 D9 44 30N 5 21 E
La Motte-Servolex, *France* 29 C9 45 35N 5 53 E
La Moure, *U.S.A.* 154 B5 46 21N 98 18W
La Muela, *Spain* 40 D3 41 36N 1 7W
La Mure, *France* 29 D9 44 55N 5 48 E
La Negra, *Chile* 174 A1 23 46 S 70 18W
La Neuveville, *Switz.* 32 B4 47 4N 7 6 E
La Oliva, *Canary Is.* 9 e2 28 36N 13 57W
La Oraya, *Peru* 172 C2 11 32 S 75 54W
La Orotava, *Canary Is.* 9 e1 28 22N 16 31W
La Oroya, *Peru* 172 C2 11 32 S 75 54W
La Pacaudière, *France* 27 F10 46 11N 3 52 E
La Palma, *Canary Is.* 9 e1 28 40N 17 50W
La Palma, *Panama* 164 E4 8 15N 78 0W
La Palma del Condado, *Spain* 43 H4 37 21N 6 38W
La Paloma, *Chile* 174 C1 30 35 S 71 0W
La Pampa □, *Argentina* 174 D2 36 50 S 66 0W
La Paragua, *Venezuela* 169 B5 6 50N 63 20W
La Paz, *Entre Ríos, Argentina* 174 C4 30 50 S 59 45W
La Paz, *San Luis, Argentina* 174 C2 33 30 S 67 20W
La Paz, *Bolivia* 172 D4 16 20 S 68 10W
La Paz, *Honduras* 164 D2 14 20N 87 47W
La Paz, *Mexico* 162 C2 24 10N 110 20W
La Paz, *Abra, Phil.* 80 C3 17 40N 120 41 E
La Paz, *Tarlac, Phil.* 80 D3 15 26N 120 45 E
La Paz □, *Bolivia* 172 D4 15 30 S 68 0W
La Paz Centro, *Nic.* 164 D2 12 20N 86 41W
La Pedrera, *Colombia* 168 D4 1 18 S 69 43W
La Pérade, *Canada* 141 C5 46 35N 72 12W
La Perouse, Bahía, *Chile* 177 b 27 5 S 109 18W
La Perouse Str., *Asia* 70 B11 45 40N 142 0 E
La Pesca, *Mexico* 163 C5 23 46N 97 47W
La Piedad, *Mexico* 162 C4 20 20N 102 1W
La Pine, *U.S.A.* 158 E3 43 40N 121 30W
La Plata, *Argentina* 174 D4 35 0 S 57 55W
La Plata, *Colombia* 168 C2 2 23N 75 53W
La Plata, *U.S.A.* 156 D4 40 2N 92 29W
La Plata, L., *Argentina* 176 B2 44 55 S 71 50W
La Pobla de Lillet, *Spain* 40 C6 42 16N 1 59 E
La Pocatière, *Canada* 141 C5 47 22N 70 2W
La Pola de Gordón, *Spain* 42 C5 42 51N 5 41W
La Porta, *France* 29 F13 42 25N 9 21 E
La Porte, *Ind., U.S.A.* 157 C10 41 36N 86 43W
La Porte, *Tex., U.S.A.* 155 L7 29 39N 95 1W
La Porte City, *U.S.A.* 156 B4 42 19N 92 12W
La Presanella, *Italy* 44 B7 46 13N 10 40 E
La Puebla = Sa Pobla, *Spain* 38 B4 39 46N 3 1 E
La Puebla de Cazalla, *Spain* 43 H5 37 10N 5 20W
La Puebla de los Infantes, *Spain* 43 H5 37 47N 5 24W
La Puebla de Montalbán, *Spain* 42 F6 39 52N 4 22W
La Puebla del Río, *Spain* 43 H4 37 16N 6 3W
La Puerta de Segura, *Spain* 43 G8 38 22N 2 45W
La Punt, *Switz.* 33 C9 46 35N 9 56 E
La Purísima, *Mexico* 162 B2 26 10N 112 4W
La Push, *U.S.A.* 160 C2 47 55N 124 38W
La Quiaca, *Argentina* 174 A2 22 5 S 65 35W
La Réole, *France* 28 D3 44 35N 0 1W
La Restinga, *Canary Is.* 9 e1 27 38N 17 59W
La Rioja, *Argentina* 174 B2 29 20 S 67 0W
La Rioja □, *Argentina* 174 B2 29 30 S 67 0W
La Rioja □, *Spain* 40 C2 42 20N 2 20W
La Robla, *Spain* 42 C5 42 50N 5 41W
La Roche, *N. Cal.* 133 U22 21 26 S 168 2 E
La Roche, *Switz.* 32 C4 46 42N 7 7 E
La Roche-Bernard, *France* 26 E4 47 31N 2 19W
La Roche-Canillac, *France* 28 C5 45 12N 1 57 E
La Roche-en-Ardenne, *Belgium* 24 D7 50 11N 5 35 E
La Roche-sur-Foron, *France* 27 F13 46 4N 6 19 E
La Roche-sur-Yon, *France* 26 F5 46 40N 1 25W
La Rochefoucauld, *France* 28 C4 45 44N 0 24 E
La Rochelle, *France* 28 B2 46 10N 1 9W
La Roda, *Spain* 41 F2 39 13N 2 15W
La Roda de Andalucía, *Spain* 43 H6 37 12N 4 46W
La Romana, *Dom. Rep.* 165 C6 18 27N 68 57W
La Ronge, *Canada* 143 B7 55 5N 105 20W
La Rue, *U.S.A.* 157 D13 40 35N 83 23W
La Rumorosa, *Mexico* 161 N10 32 33N 116 4W
La Sabina = Sa Savina, *Spain* 38 D1 38 44N 1 25 E
La Sagra, *Spain* 41 H2 37 57N 2 35W
La Salle, *U.S.A.* 156 C7 41 20N 89 6W
La Sanabria, *Spain* 42 C4 42 0N 6 30W
La Santa, *Canary Is.* 9 e2 29 5N 13 40W
La Sarraz, *Switz.* 32 C3 46 38N 6 32 E
La Sarre, *Canada* 140 C4 48 45N 79 15W
La Scie, *Canada* 141 C8 49 57N 55 36W
La Selva, *Spain* 40 C7 42 0N 2 45 E
La Selva Beach, *U.S.A.* 160 J5 36 56N 121 51W
La Selva del Camp, *Spain* 40 D6 41 13N 1 8 E
La Serena, *Chile* 174 B1 29 55 S 71 10W
La Serena, *Spain* 43 G5 38 45N 5 40W
La Seu d'Urgell, *Spain* 40 C6 42 22N 1 23 E
La Seyne-sur-Mer, *France* 29 E9 43 7N 5 52 E
La Sila, *Italy* 47 C9 39 15N 16 35 E
La Solana, *Spain* 43 G7 38 59N 3 14W
La Soufrière, *St. Vincent* 165 D7 13 20N 61 11W
La Souterraine, *France* 27 F8 46 15N 1 30 E

Lyons 243

Lowa →, *Dem. Rep. of the Congo* **118 C2** 1 24 S 25 51 E
Lowden, *U.S.A.* **156 C6** 41 52N 90 56W
Lowell, *Ind., U.S.A.* **157 C9** 41 18N 87 25W
Lowell, *Mass., U.S.A.* **151 D13** 42 38N 71 19W
Lowell, *Mich., U.S.A.* **157 B11** 42 56N 85 20W
Lowellville, *U.S.A.* **150 E4** 41 2N 80 32W
Löwen →, *Namibia* **116 D2** 26 51 S 18 17 E
Lower Alkali L., *U.S.A.* **158 F3** 41 16N 120 2W
Lower Arrow L., *Canada* **142 D5** 49 40N 118 5W
Lower Austria = Niederösterreich □, *Austria* **34 C8** 48 25N 15 40 E
Lower California = Baja California, *Mexico* **162 A1** 31 10N 115 12W
Lower Glenelg Nat. Park, *Australia* **128 E4** 38 4 S 141 41 E
Lower Hutt, *N.Z.* **130 H3** 41 10 S 174 55 E
Lower Kalskag, *U.S.A.* **144 F7** 61 31N 160 22W
Lower Lake, *U.S.A.* **160 G4** 38 55N 122 37W
Lower Manitou L., *Canada* **143 D10** 49 15N 93 0W
Lower Paia, *U.S.A.* **145 C5** 20 55N 156 23W
Lower Post, *Canada* **142 B3** 59 58N 128 30W
Lower Red L., *U.S.A.* **154 B7** 47 58N 95 0W
Lower Saxony = Niedersachsen □, *Germany* **30 C4** 52 50N 9 0 E
Lower Tunguska = Tunguska, Nizhnyaya →, *Russia* **67 C9** 65 48N 88 4 E
Lower Zambezi Nat. Park, *Zambia* **119 F2** 15 25 S 29 40 E
Lowestoft, *U.K.* **21 E9** 52 29N 1 45 E
Lowgar □, *Afghan.* **91 B3** 34 0N 69 0 E
Łowicz, *Poland* **55 F6** 52 6N 19 55 E
Lowly, Pt., *Australia* **128 B2** 33 0 S 137 46 E
Lowry City, *U.S.A.* **156 F3** 38 8N 93 44W
Lowville, *U.S.A.* **151 C9** 43 47N 75 29W
Loxton, *Australia* **128 C4** 34 28 S 140 31 E
Loxton, *S. Africa* **116 E3** 31 30 S 22 22 E
Loyalton, *U.S.A.* **160 F6** 39 41N 120 14W
Loyalty Is. = Loyauté, Îs., *N. Cal.* **133 K4** 20 50 S 166 30 E
Loyang = Luoyang, *China* **74 G7** 34 40N 112 26 E
Loyauté, Îs., *N. Cal.* **133 K4** 20 50 S 166 30 E
Loyev = Loyew, *Belarus* **59 G6** 51 56N 30 46 E
Loyew, *Belarus* **59 G6** 51 56N 30 46 E
Loyoro, *Uganda* **118 B3** 3 22N 34 14 E
Lož, *Slovenia* **45 C11** 45 43N 14 30 E
Lozère □, *France* **28 D7** 44 35N 3 30 E
Loznica, *Serbia, Yug.* **50 B3** 44 32N 19 12 E
Lozova, *Ukraine* **59 H9** 49 0N 36 20 E
Lozva →, *Russia* **64 B9** 59 36N 62 20 E
Lu, *India* **90 B5** 26 58N 95 14 E
Lü Shan, *China* **77 C11** 29 30N 115 55 E
Lü-Tao, *Taiwan* **77 F13** 22 40N 121 30 E
Lu Verne, *U.S.A.* **156 B2** 42 55N 94 5W
Lu Wo, *China* **69 F11** 22 33N 114 6 E
Lua →, *Dem. Rep. of the Congo* **114 B3** 2 46N 18 26 E
Lua Makiki, *U.S.A.* **145 C5** 20 33N 156 37W
Luachimo, *Angola* **115 D4** 7 23 S 20 48 E
Luacono, *Angola* **115 E4** 11 15 S 21 37 E
Luajan →, *India* **93 G11** 24 44N 85 1 E
Lualaba →, *Dem. Rep. of the Congo* **118 B2** 0 26N 25 20 E
Luale, *Dem. Rep. of the Congo* **114 B4** 1 9N 23 5 E
Luampa, *Zambia* **119 F1** 15 4 S 24 20 E
Lu'an, *China* **77 B11** 31 45N 116 29 E
Luan Chau, *Vietnam* **76 G4** 21 38N 103 24 E
Luan He →, *China* **75 E10** 39 20N 119 5 E
Luan Xian, *China* **75 E10** 39 40N 118 40 E
Luancheng, *Guangxi Zhuangzu, China* **76 F7** 22 48N 108 55 E
Luancheng, *Hebei, China* **74 F8** 37 53N 114 40 E
Luanco, *Spain* **42 B5** 43 37N 5 48W
Luanda, *Angola* **115 D2** 8 50 S 13 15 E
Luando, Reserva Natural Integral do, *Angola* **115 E3** 11 0 S 17 32 E
Luang, Thale, *Thailand* **87 J3** 7 30N 100 15 E
Luang Prabang, *Laos* **76 H4** 19 52N 102 10 E
Luanginga →, *Zambia* **115 F4** 15 11 S 22 55 E
Luangwa, *Zambia* **119 F3** 15 35 S 30 16 E
Luangwa →, *Zambia* **119 E3** 14 25 S 30 25 E
Luangwa Valley, *Zambia* **119 E3** 13 30 S 31 30 E
Luania-Bubi, *Dem. Rep. of the Congo* **115 D4** 7 28 S 24 49 E
Luanne, *China* **75 D9** 40 55N 117 40 E
Luanping, *China* **75 D9** 40 53N 117 23 E
Luanshya, *Zambia* **119 E2** 13 3 S 28 28 E
Luapula □, *Zambia* **119 E2** 11 0 S 29 0 E
Luapula →, *Africa* **119 D2** 9 26 S 28 33 E
Luarca, *Spain* **42 B4** 43 32N 6 32W
Luashi, *Dem. Rep. of the Congo* **119 E1** 10 50 S 23 36 E
Luatamba, *Angola* **115 E4** 12 6 S 20 19 E
Luatira, *Angola* **115 E3** 12 52 S 17 14 E
Luau, *Angola* **115 E4** 10 40 S 22 10 E
Luba, *Phil.* **80 C3** 17 19N 120 42 E
Lubaczów, *Poland* **55 H10** 50 10N 23 8 E
Lubalo, *Angola* **115 D3** 9 10 S 19 15 E
Lubamiti, *Dem. Rep. of the Congo* **114 C3** 2 28 S 17 47 E
Lubań, *Poland* **55 G2** 51 5N 15 15 E
Lubana, Ozero = Lubānas Ezers, *Latvia* **15 H22** 56 45N 27 0 E
Lubānas Ezers, *Latvia* **15 H22** 56 45N 27 0 E
Lubang, *Phil.* **80 E3** 13 52N 120 7 E
Lubang Is., *Phil.* **80 E3** 13 50N 120 12 E
Lubango, *Angola* **115 E2** 14 55 S 13 30 E
Lubao, *Dem. Rep. of the Congo* **118 D2** 5 17 S 25 42 E
Lubartów, *Poland* **55 G9** 51 28N 22 42 E
Lubawa, *Poland* **54 E6** 53 30N 19 48 E
Lübbecke, *Germany* **30 C4** 52 18N 8 37 E
Lübben, *Germany* **30 D9** 51 56N 13 54 E
Lübbenau, *Germany* **30 D9** 51 52N 13 57 E
Lubbock, *U.S.A.* **155 J4** 33 35N 101 51W
Lübeck, *Germany* **30 B6** 53 52N 10 40 E
Lübecker Bucht, *Germany* **30 A6** 54 3N 10 54 E
Lubefu, *Dem. Rep. of the Congo* **118 C1** 4 47 S 24 27 E
Lubefu →, *Dem. Rep. of the Congo* **118 C1** 4 10 S 23 0 E
Lubelskie □, *Poland* **55 G9** 51 20N 22 50 E
Lubero = Luofu, *Dem. Rep. of the Congo* **118 C2** 0 10 S 29 15 E
Lubersac, *France* **28 C5** 45 26N 1 23 E
Lubicon L., *Canada* **142 B5** 56 23N 115 56W
Lubień Kujawski, *Poland* **55 F6** 52 23N 19 9 E
Lubilash →, *Dem. Rep. of the Congo* **115 D4** 6 2 S 23 45 E
Lubin, *Poland* **55 G3** 51 24N 16 11 E
Lublin, *Poland* **55 G9** 51 12N 22 38 E
Lubliniec, *Poland* **55 H5** 50 43N 18 45 E
Lubnān, Jabal, *Lebanon* **103 B4** 33 45N 35 40 E
Lubniewice, *Poland* **55 F2** 52 31N 15 15 E
Lubny, *Ukraine* **59 G7** 50 3N 32 58 E
Lubomierz, *Poland* **55 G2** 51 1N 15 31 E
Luboń, *Poland* **55 F3** 52 21N 16 51 E
Lubondaie, *Dem. Rep. of the Congo* **115 D4** 8 1 S 26 32 E
Lubongola, *Dem. Rep. of the Congo* **118 C2** 2 35 S 27 50 E
L'ubotín, *Slovak Rep.* **35 B13** 49 17N 20 53 E
Lubraniec, *Poland* **55 F5** 52 33N 18 50 E
Lubsko, *Poland* **55 G1** 51 45N 14 57 E
Lübtheen, *Germany* **30 B7** 53 18N 11 5 E
Lubuagan, *Phil.* **80 C3** 17 21N 121 10 E
Lubudi, *Dem. Rep. of the Congo* **115 D4** 6 51 S 21 18 E
Lubudi →, *Kasai-Occ., Dem. Rep. of the Congo* **115 C4** 4 19 S 20 23 E
Lubudi →, *Katanga, Dem. Rep. of the Congo* **119 D2** 9 0 S 25 35 E
Lubuklinggau, *Indonesia* **84 C2** 3 15 S 102 55 E
Lubuksikaping, *Indonesia* **84 B2** 0 10N 100 15 E
Lubumbashi, *Dem. Rep. of the Congo* **119 E2** 11 40 S 27 28 E
Lubunda, *Dem. Rep. of the Congo* **118 D2** 5 12 S 26 41 E
Lubungu, *Zambia* **119 E2** 14 35 S 26 24 E
Lubuskie □, *Poland* **55 F2** 52 10N 15 20 E
Lubutu, *Dem. Rep. of the Congo* **118 C2** 0 45 S 26 30 E
Luc An Chau, *Vietnam* **86 A5** 22 6N 104 43 E
Luc-en-Diois, *France* **29 D9** 44 36N 5 28 E
Lucala, *Angola* **115 D3** 9 7 S 15 58 E
Lucala →, *Angola* **115 D2** 9 38 S 14 14 E
Lucan, *Canada* **150 C3** 43 11N 81 24W
Lucania, Mt., *Canada* **138 B5** 61 1N 140 29W
Lucapa, *Angola* **115 D4** 8 25 S 20 45 E
Lucas, *U.S.A.* **156 C3** 41 2N 93 29W
Lucas Channel, *Canada* **150 A3** 45 21N 81 45W
Lucban, *Phil.* **80 D3** 14 6N 121 33 E
Lucca, *Italy* **44 E7** 43 50N 10 29 E
Lucé, *France* **26 D8** 48 26N 1 27 E
Luce Bay, *U.K.* **22 G4** 54 45N 4 48W
Lucea, *Jamaica* **164 a** 18 25N 78 10W
Lucedale, *U.S.A.* **149 K1** 30 56N 88 35W
Lucena, *Phil.* **80 E3** 13 56N 121 37 E
Lucena, *Spain* **43 H6** 37 27N 4 31W
Lučenec, *Slovak Rep.* **35 C12** 48 18N 19 42 E
Lucens, *Switz.* **32 C3** 46 43N 6 51 E
Lucera, *Italy* **47 A8** 41 30N 15 20 E
Lucerne = Luzern, *Switz.* **33 B6** 47 3N 8 18 E
Lucerne, *U.S.A.* **160 F4** 39 6N 122 48W
Lucerne Valley, *U.S.A.* **161 L10** 34 27N 116 57W
Lucero, *Mexico* **162 A3** 30 49N 106 30W
Luchena →, *Spain* **41 H3** 37 44N 1 50W
Lucheng, *China* **74 F7** 36 20N 113 11 E
Lucheringo →, *Mozam.* **119 E4** 11 43 S 36 17 E
Lüchow, *Germany* **30 C7** 52 58N 11 8 E
Luchuan, *China* **77 F8** 22 21N 110 12 E
Lucia, *U.S.A.* **160 J5** 36 2N 121 33W
Lucie →, *Surinam* **169 C6** 3 35N 57 38W
Lucinda, *Australia* **126 B4** 18 32 S 146 20 E
Lucindale, *Australia* **128 D4** 36 58 S 140 26 E
Lucira, *Angola* **115 E2** 14 0 S 12 35 E
Luciras, B. das, *Angola* **115 E2** 13 52 S 12 31 E
Luckau, *Germany* **30 D9** 51 50N 13 42 E
Luckenwalde, *Germany* **30 C9** 52 5N 13 10 E
Luckey, *U.S.A.* **157 C13** 41 27N 83 29W
Luckhoff, *S. Africa* **116 D3** 29 44 S 24 43 E
Lucknow, *Canada* **150 C3** 43 57N 81 31W
Lucknow, *India* **93 F9** 26 50N 81 0 E
Luçon, *France* **28 B2** 46 28N 1 10W
Lucusse, *Angola* **115 E4** 12 32 S 20 48 E
Lüda = Dalian, *China* **75 E11** 38 50N 121 40 E
Luda Kamchiya →, *Bulgaria* **51 C11** 43 3N 27 29 E
Ludbreg, *Croatia* **45 B13** 46 15N 16 38 E
Lüdenscheid, *Germany* **30 D3** 51 13N 7 37 E
Lüderitz, *Namibia* **116 D2** 26 41 S 15 8 E
Lüderitzbaai, *Namibia* **116 D2** 26 36 S 15 8 E
Ludhiana, *India* **92 D6** 30 57N 75 56 E
Ludian, *China* **76 D4** 27 10N 103 33 E
Luding Qiao, *China* **76 C4** 29 53N 102 12 E
Lüdinghausen, *Germany* **30 D3** 51 46N 7 27 E
Ludington, *U.S.A.* **148 D2** 43 57N 86 27W
Ludlow, *U.K.* **21 E5** 52 22N 2 42W
Ludlow, *Calif., U.S.A.* **161 L10** 34 43N 116 10W
Ludlow, *Pa., U.S.A.* **150 E6** 41 43N 78 56W
Ludlow, *Vt., U.S.A.* **151 C12** 43 24N 72 42W
Ludowici, *U.S.A.* **152 D8** 31 43N 81 45W
Luduş, *Romania* **53 D9** 46 29N 24 5 E
Ludvika, *Sweden* **16 D9** 60 8N 15 14 E
Ludwigsburg, *Germany* **31 G5** 48 53N 9 11 E
Ludwigsfelde, *Germany* **30 C9** 52 17N 13 17 E
Ludwigshafen, *Germany* **31 F4** 49 29N 8 26 E
Ludwigslust, *Germany* **30 B7** 53 19N 11 30 E
Ludza, *Latvia* **58 D4** 56 32N 27 43 E
Lue, *Australia* **129 B8** 32 38 S 149 50 E
Luebo, *Dem. Rep. of the Congo* **115 D4** 5 21 S 21 23 E
Lueki, *Dem. Rep. of the Congo* **118 C2** 3 20 S 25 48 E
Luena, *Angola* **115 E3** 12 13 S 19 51 E
Luena, *Dem. Rep. of the Congo* **119 D2** 9 28 S 25 43 E
Luena, *Zambia* **119 E3** 10 40 S 30 25 E
Luena →, *Angola* **115 E4** 12 30 S 22 34 E
Luena →, *Zambia* **115 E4** 14 46 S 23 30 E
Luena Flats, *Zambia* **115 E4** 14 47 S 23 17 E
Luengué, Coutada Pública do, *Angola* **115 F3** 16 55 S 19 55 E
Luepa, *Venezuela* **169 B5** 5 43N 61 31W
Lueta →, *Dem. Rep. of the Congo* **115 D4** 7 4 S 21 40 E
Luete →, *Zambia* **115 F4** 15 46 S 23 10 E
Lüeyang, *China* **74 H4** 33 22N 106 10 E
Lufeng, *Guangdong, China* **77 F10** 22 57N 115 38 E
Lufeng, *Yunnan, China* **76 E4** 25 0N 102 5 E
Lufico, *Angola* **115 D2** 6 24 S 13 23 E
Lufira →, *Dem. Rep. of the Congo* **119 D2** 9 30 S 27 0 E
Lufkin, *U.S.A.* **155 K7** 31 21N 94 44W
Lufupa, *Dem. Rep. of the Congo* **119 E1** 10 37 S 24 56 E
Luga, *Russia* **58 C5** 58 40N 29 55 E
Luga →, *Russia* **58 C5** 59 40N 28 18 E
Lugano, *Switz.* **33 E7** 46 1N 8 57 E
Lugano, L. di, *Switz.* **33 E8** 46 0N 9 0 E
Lugansk = Luhansk, *Ukraine* **59 H10** 48 38N 39 15 E
Luganville, *Vanuatu* **133 E5** 15 27 S 167 10 E
Lugard's Falls, *Kenya* **118 C4** 3 6 S 38 41 E
Lugela, *Mozam.* **119 F4** 16 25 S 36 43 E
Lugenda →, *Mozam.* **119 E4** 11 25 S 38 33 E
Lugh Ganana, *Somali Rep.* **120 D2** 3 48N 42 34 E
Lugnaquilla, *Ireland* **23 D5** 52 58N 6 28W
Lugo, *Italy* **45 D8** 44 25N 11 54 E
Lugo, *Spain* **42 B3** 43 2N 7 35W
Lugo □, *Spain* **42 C3** 43 0N 7 30W
Lugoj, *Romania* **52 E6** 45 42N 21 57 E
Lugovoy = Qulan, *Kazakstan* **66 E8** 42 55N 72 43 E
Lugus I., *Phil.* **81 J3** 5 41N 120 50 E
Luhansk, *Ukraine* **59 H10** 48 38N 39 15 E
Luhe, *China* **77 A12** 32 19N 118 50 E
Luhe →, *Germany* **30 B6** 53 23N 10 13 E
Luhit →, *India* **90 B5** 27 48N 95 28 E
Luhuo, *China* **76 B3** 31 21N 100 48 E
Lui →, *Angola* **115 D3** 8 21 S 17 33 E
Lui →, *Zambia* **115 F4** 16 18 S 23 17 E
Luia, *Angola* **115 D4** 8 10 S 21 32 E
Luia →, *Angola* **115 D4** 8 32 S 21 47 E
Luiana, *Angola* **116 B3** 17 25 S 22 59 E
Luiana →, *Angola* **115 F4** 17 24 S 23 3 E
Luiana, Coutada Pública do, *Angola* **115 F4** 16 55 S 22 20 E
Luilaka →, *Dem. Rep. of the Congo* **114 C4** 0 52 S 20 12 E
Luimneach = Limerick, *Ireland* **23 D3** 52 40N 8 37W
Luing, *U.K.* **22 E3** 56 14N 5 39W
Luino, *Italy* **44 C5** 45 59N 8 44 E
Luio →, *Angola* **115 E4** 13 17 S 21 37 E
Luís Correia, *Brazil* **170 B3** 3 0 S 41 35W
Luís Gonçalves, *Brazil* **170 C1** 5 37 S 50 25W
Luitpold Coast, *Antarctica* **7 D1** 78 30 S 32 0W
Luiza, *Dem. Rep. of the Congo* **115 D4** 7 40 S 22 30 E
Luizi, *Dem. Rep. of the Congo* **118 D2** 6 0 S 27 25 E
Luján, *Argentina* **174 C4** 34 45 S 59 5W
Lujiang, *China* **77 B11** 31 20N 117 15 E
Lukala, *Dem. Rep. of the Congo* **115 D2** 5 31 S 14 32 E
Lukang, *Taiwan* **77 E13** 24 1N 120 22 E
Lukanga, *Bandundu, Dem. Rep. of the Congo* **114 C3** 1 41 S 18 9 E
Lukanga, *Équateur, Dem. Rep. of the Congo* **114 C3** 1 0 S 18 8 E
Lukanga Swamp, *Zambia* **119 E2** 14 30 S 27 40 E
Lukavac, *Bos.-H.* **52 F3** 44 33N 18 32 E
Lukenie →, *Dem. Rep. of the Congo* **114 C3** 3 0 S 18 50 E
Lukhisaral, *India* **93 G12** 25 11N 86 5 E
Lŭki, *Bulgaria* **51 E8** 41 50N 24 43 E
Lukk, *Libya* **108 B4** 32 1N 24 46 E
Lukolela, *Équateur, Dem. Rep. of the Congo* **114 C3** 1 10 S 17 12 E
Lukolela, *Kasai-Or., Dem. Rep. of the Congo* **118 D1** 5 23 S 24 32 E
Lukosi, *Zimbabwe* **119 F2** 18 30 S 26 30 E
Lukovë, *Albania* **50 G3** 39 59N 19 54 E
Lukovit, *Bulgaria* **51 C8** 43 13N 24 11 E
Łuków, *Poland* **55 G9** 51 55N 22 23 E
Lukoyanov, *Russia* **60 C7** 55 2N 44 29 E
Luksefjell, *Norway* **18 E6** 59 23N 9 34 E
Lukuni, *Dem. Rep. of the Congo* **115 D3** 5 50 S 17 16 E
Lukusuzi Nat. Park, *Zambia* **119 E3** 12 43 S 32 36 E
Lula, *Dem. Rep. of the Congo* **115 D3** 5 22 S 16 2 E
Lule älv →, *Sweden* **14 D19** 65 35N 22 10 E
Luleå, *Sweden* **14 D20** 65 35N 22 10 E
Lüleburgaz, *Turkey* **51 E11** 41 23N 27 22 E
Luliang, *China* **76 E4** 25 0N 103 40 E
Luling, *U.S.A.* **155 L6** 29 41N 97 39W
Lulong, *China* **75 E10** 39 53N 118 51 E
Lulonga →, *Dem. Rep. of the Congo* **114 B3** 1 0N 18 10 E
Lulu, *U.S.A.* **152 E7** 30 7N 82 29W
Lulu →, *Dem. Rep. of the Congo* **114 B4** 1 18N 23 42 E
Lulua →, *Dem. Rep. of the Congo* **115 C4** 4 30 S 20 30 E
Luma, *Amer. Samoa* **133 X25** 14 16 S 169 33W
Lumai, *Angola* **115 E4** 13 13 S 21 25 E
Lumajang, *Indonesia* **85 D4** 8 8 S 113 13 E
Lumaku, Gunong, *Malaysia* **85 B5** 4 52N 115 38 E
Lumbala →, *Angola* **115 E4** 12 39 S 22 35 E
Lumbala Kaquengue, *Angola* **115 E4** 12 39 S 22 34 E
Lumbala N'guimbo, *Angola* **115 E4** 14 18 S 21 18 E
Lumbe →, *Zambia* **115 F4** 16 44 S 23 41 E
Lumber City, *U.S.A.* **152 D7** 31 56N 82 41W
Lumberton, *U.S.A.* **149 H6** 34 37N 79 0W
Lumbwa, *Kenya* **118 C4** 0 12 S 35 28 E
Lumding, *India* **90 C4** 25 46N 93 10 E
Lumi, *Papua N. G.* **132 B2** 3 30 S 142 2 E
Lumpkin, *U.S.A.* **152 C5** 32 3N 84 48W
Lumsden, *Canada* **143 C8** 50 39N 104 52W
Lumsden, *N.Z.* **131 F3** 45 44 S 168 27 E
Lumut, *Malaysia* **87 K3** 4 13N 100 37 E
Lumut, Tanjung, *Indonesia* **84 C3** 3 50 S 105 58 E
Luna, *India* **92 H3** 23 43N 69 16 E
Luna, *Phil.* **80 B3** 18 18N 121 21 E
Lunan, *China* **76 E4** 24 40N 103 18 E
Lunavada, *India* **92 H5** 23 8N 73 37 E
Lunca, *Romania* **53 C10** 47 22N 25 1 E
Lunca Corbului, *Romania* **53 F9** 44 42N 24 45 E
Lund, *Sweden* **17 J7** 55 44N 13 12 E
Lunda Norte □, *Angola* **115 D3** 8 0 S 20 0 E
Lunda Sul □, *Angola* **115 D4** 10 0 S 20 0 E
Lundamo, *Norway* **18 A7** 63 9N 10 19 E
Lundazi, *Zambia* **119 E3** 12 20 S 33 7 E
Lunderskov, *Denmark* **17 J3** 55 29N 9 19 E
Lundi →, *Zimbabwe* **117 C5** 21 43 S 32 34 E
Lundu, *Malaysia* **85 B3** 1 40N 109 50 E
Lundy, *U.K.* **21 F3** 51 10N 4 41W
Lune →, *U.K.* **20 C5** 54 0N 2 51W
Lüneburg, *Germany* **30 B6** 53 15N 10 24 E
Lüneburg Heath = Lüneburger Heide, *Germany* **30 B6** 53 10N 10 12 E
Lüneburger Heide, *Germany* **30 B6** 53 10N 10 12 E
Lunel, *France* **29 E8** 43 39N 4 9 E
Lünen, *Germany* **30 D3** 51 37N 7 32 E
Lunenburg, *Canada* **141 D7** 44 22N 64 18W
Lunéville, *France* **27 D13** 48 36N 6 30 E
Lunga, *Dem. Rep. of the Congo* **115 C4** 5 46 S 21 12 E
Lunga →, *Zambia* **119 E2** 14 34 S 26 25 E
Lunge, *Angola* **115 E3** 12 13 S 16 7 E
Lungern, *Switz.* **32 C6** 46 48N 8 10 E
Lungga, *Solomon Is.* **133 M11** 9 25 S 160 3 E
Lungi Airport, *S. Leone* **112 D2** 8 40N 13 17W
Lunglei, *India* **90 D4** 22 55N 92 45 E
Lungngo, *Burma* **90 E4** 21 57N 93 36 E
Lungwebungu →, *Zambia* **115 E4** 14 19 S 23 14 E
Luni, *India* **92 G5** 26 0N 73 6 E
Luni →, *India* **92 G4** 24 41N 71 14 E
Luninets = Luninyets, *Belarus* **59 F4** 52 15N 26 50 E
Luning, *U.S.A.* **158 G4** 38 30N 118 11W
Lunino, *Russia* **60 D7** 53 38N 45 18 E
Luninyets, *Belarus* **59 F4** 52 15N 26 50 E
Lunkaransar, *India* **92 E5** 28 29N 73 44 E
Lunner, *Norway* **18 D7** 60 19N 10 35 E
Lunsemfwa →, *Zambia* **119 E3** 14 54 S 30 12 E
Lunsemfwa Falls, *Zambia* **119 E2** 14 30 S 29 6 E
Luo He →, *China* **74 G6** 34 35N 110 20 E
Luocheng, *China* **76 E7** 24 48N 108 53 E
Luochuan, *China* **74 G5** 35 45N 109 26 E
Luoci, *China* **76 E4** 25 19N 102 18 E
Luodian, *China* **76 E6** 25 24N 106 43 E
Luoding, *China* **77 F8** 22 45N 111 40 E
Luofu, *Dem. Rep. of the Congo* **118 C2** 0 10 S 29 15 E
Luohe, *China* **74 H8** 33 32N 114 2 E
Luojiang, *China* **76 B5** 31 18N 104 33 E
Luonan, *China* **74 G6** 34 5N 110 10 E
Luoning, *China* **74 G6** 34 35N 111 40 E
Luoshan, *China* **77 A10** 32 13N 114 30 E
Luotian, *China* **77 B10** 30 46N 115 22 E
Luoxiao Shan, *China* **77 D10** 26 30N 114 1 E
Luoyang, *China* **74 G7** 34 40N 112 26 E
Luoyuan, *China* **77 D12** 26 28N 119 30 E
Luozi, *Dem. Rep. of the Congo* **115 C2** 4 54 S 14 0 E
Luozigou, *China* **75 C16** 43 42N 130 18 E
Lupanshui, *China* **76 D5** 26 38N 104 48 E
Lupeni, *Romania* **53 E8** 45 21N 23 13 E
Lupilichi, *Mozam.* **119 E4** 11 47 S 35 13 E
Lupire, *Angola* **115 E3** 14 36 S 19 29 E
Łupków, *Poland* **55 J9** 49 15N 22 4 E
Lupoing, *China* **76 E5** 24 53N 104 21 E
Lupon, *Phil.* **81 H6** 6 54N 126 0 E
Luputa, *Dem. Rep. of the Congo* **115 D4** 7 7 S 23 43 E
Luqa, *Malta* **38 F7** 35 52N 14 29 E
Luquan, *China* **76 E4** 25 35N 102 25 E
Luque, *Paraguay* **174 B4** 25 19 S 57 25W
Luquembo, *Angola* **115 E3** 10 44 S 17 43 E
Lúras, *Italy* **46 B2** 40 56N 9 10 E
Luray, *U.S.A.* **148 F6** 38 40N 78 28W
Lure, *France* **27 E13** 47 40N 6 30 E
Luremo, *Angola* **115 D3** 8 30 S 17 50 E
Lurgan, *U.K.* **23 B5** 54 28N 6 19W
Luribay, *Bolivia* **172 D4** 17 6 S 67 39W
Lurín, *Peru* **172 C2** 12 17 S 76 52W
Lusaka, *Zambia* **119 F2** 15 28 S 28 16 E
Lusambo, *Dem. Rep. of the Congo* **118 C1** 4 58 S 23 28 E
Lusancay Is. and Reefs, *Papua N. G.* **132 E6** 8 30 S 150 30 E
Lusangaye, *Dem. Rep. of the Congo* **118 C2** 4 54 S 26 0 E
Luseland, *Canada* **143 C7** 52 5N 109 24W
Lusenga Plain Nat. Park, *Zambia* **119 D2** 9 22 S 29 14 E
Lusengo, *Dem. Rep. of the Congo* **114 B3** 1 47N 19 31 E
Lushan, *Henan, China* **74 H7** 33 45N 112 55 E
Lushan, *Sichuan, China* **76 B4** 30 12N 102 52 E
Lushi, *China* **74 G6** 34 3N 111 3 E
Lushnjë, *Albania* **50 F3** 40 55N 19 41 E
Lushoto, *Tanzania* **118 C4** 4 47 S 38 20 E
Lushui, *China* **76 E2** 25 58N 98 44 E
Lüshun, *China* **75 E11** 38 45N 121 15 E
Lusignan, *France* **28 B4** 46 26N 0 8 E
Lusigny-sur-Barse, *France* **27 D11** 48 16N 4 15 E
Lusiye, *Zambia* **115 F4** 16 30 S 27 57 E
Lusk, *U.S.A.* **154 D2** 42 46N 104 27W
Lussac-les-Châteaux, *France* **28 B4** 46 24N 0 43 E
Lustenau, *Austria* **34 D2** 47 26N 9 39 E
Lustrafjorden, *Norway* **18 C4** 61 23N 7 25 E
Lūt, Dasht-e, *Iran* **97 D8** 31 30N 58 0 E
Luta = Dalian, *China* **75 E11** 38 50N 121 40 E
Lutembo, *Angola* **115 E4** 13 26 S 21 16 E
Lutherstadt Wittenberg, *Germany* **30 D8** 51 53N 12 39 E
Luthersville, *U.S.A.* **152 B5** 33 13N 84 45W
Luti, *Solomon Is.* **133 L9** 7 14 S 157 0 E
Luton, *U.K.* **21 F7** 51 53N 0 24W
Luton □, *U.K.* **21 F7** 51 53N 0 24W
Lutong, *Malaysia* **85 B4** 4 28N 114 0 E
Lutry, *Switz.* **32 C3** 46 31N 6 42 E
Lutselke, *Canada* **143 A6** 62 24N 110 44W
Lutshima →, *Dem. Rep. of the Congo* **115 D3** 5 22 S 18 59 E
Lutsk, *Ukraine* **59 G3** 50 50N 25 15 E
Lutuai, *Angola* **115 E4** 12 41 S 20 7 E
Lutz, *U.S.A.* **153 G7** 28 9N 82 28W
Lützow Holmbukta, *Antarctica* **7 C4** 69 10 S 37 30 E
Lutzputs, *S. Africa* **116 D3** 28 3 S 20 40 E
Luuk, *Phil.* **81 J3** 5 58N 121 18 E
Luuq = Lugh Ganana, *Somali Rep.* **120 D2** 3 48N 42 34 E
Luverne, *Ala., U.S.A.* **152 D3** 31 43N 86 16W
Luverne, *Minn., U.S.A.* **154 D6** 43 39N 96 13W
Luvo, *Angola* **115 D2** 5 51 S 14 5 E
Lúvua, *Angola* **115 E4** 8 49 S 25 19 E
Luvua, *Dem. Rep. of the Congo* **119 D2** 8 48 S 25 17 E
Luvua →, *Dem. Rep. of the Congo* **118 D2** 6 50 S 27 30 E
Luvuvhu →, *S. Africa* **117 C5** 22 25 S 31 18 E
Luwegu →, *Tanzania* **119 D4** 8 31 S 37 23 E
Luwuk, *Indonesia* **82 B2** 0 56 S 122 47 E
Luxembourg, *Lux.* **24 E6** 49 37N 6 9 E
Luxembourg □, *Belgium* **24 E5** 49 58N 5 30 E
Luxembourg ■, *Europe* **25 B7** 49 45N 6 0 E
Luxemburg, *U.S.A.* **156 B5** 42 36N 91 5W
Luxeuil-les-Bains, *France* **27 E13** 47 49N 6 24 E
Luxi, *Hunan, China* **77 C8** 28 20N 110 7 E
Luxi, *Yunnan, China* **76 E4** 24 40N 103 55 E
Luxi, *Yunnan, China* **76 E2** 24 27N 98 36 E
Luxor = El Uqsur, *Egypt* **106 B3** 25 41N 32 38 E
Luy-de-Béarn →, *France* **28 E3** 43 39N 0 48W
Luy-de-France →, *France* **28 E3** 43 39N 0 48W
Luyi, *China* **74 H8** 33 50N 115 35 E
Luz, *Azores* **9 d1** 39 1N 28 0W
Luz-St-Sauveur, *France* **28 F4** 42 53N 0 0W
Luza, *Russia* **56 B8** 60 39N 47 10 E
Luzern, *Switz.* **33 B6** 47 3N 8 18 E
Luzern □, *Switz.* **32 B5** 47 2N 7 55 E
Luzhai, *China* **76 E7** 24 29N 109 42 E
Luzhi, *China* **76 D5** 26 21N 105 16 E
Luzhou, *China* **76 C5** 28 52N 105 20 E
Luziânia, *Brazil* **171 E2** 16 20 S 48 0W
Luzilândia, *Brazil* **170 B3** 3 28 S 42 22W
Lužnice →, *Czech Rep.* **34 B7** 49 14N 14 23 E
Luzon, *Phil.* **80 C3** 16 0N 121 0 E
Luzy, *France* **27 F10** 46 47N 3 58 E
Luzzi, *Italy* **47 C9** 39 27N 16 17 E
Lviv, *Ukraine* **59 H3** 49 50N 24 0 E
Lvov = Lviv, *Ukraine* **59 H3** 49 50N 24 0 E
Lwówek, *Poland* **55 F3** 52 28N 16 10 E
Lwówek Śląski, *Poland* **55 G2** 51 7N 15 38 E
Lyakhavichy, *Belarus* **59 F4** 53 2N 26 32 E
Lyakhovskiye, Ostrova, *Russia* **67 B15** 73 40N 141 0 E
Lyaki = Läki, *Azerbaijan* **61 K8** 40 34N 47 22 E
Lyal I., *Canada* **150 B3** 44 57N 81 24W
Lyall, Mt., *N.Z.* **131 F2** 45 16 S 167 32 E
Lyallpur = Faisalabad, *Pakistan* **91 C4** 31 30N 73 5 E
Lyalya →, *Russia* **64 B8** 59 9N 61 29 E
Lyangar, *Tajikistan* **65 E6** 37 3N 72 40 E
Lyaskovets, *Bulgaria* **51 C9** 43 6N 25 44 E
Lybster, *U.K.* **22 C5** 58 18N 3 15W
Lycaonia, *Turkey* **100 D5** 38 0N 33 0 E
Lychen, *Germany* **30 B9** 53 12N 13 18 E
Lychkova, *Russia* **58 D7** 57 55N 32 24 E
Lycia, *Turkey* **49 E11** 36 30N 29 30 E
Lyckebyån →, *Sweden* **17 H9** 56 12N 15 39 E
Lycksele, *Sweden* **14 D18** 64 38N 18 40 E
Lycosura, *Greece* **48 D4** 37 20N 22 3 E
Lydda = Lod, *Israel* **103 D3** 31 57N 34 54 E
Lydenburg, *S. Africa* **117 D5** 25 10 S 30 29 E
Lydia, *Turkey* **49 C10** 38 48N 28 19 E
Łydynia →, *Poland* **55 F7** 52 43N 20 26 E
Lyell, *N.Z.* **131 B7** 41 48 S 172 4 E
Lyell I., *Canada* **142 C2** 52 40N 131 35W
Lyepyel, *Belarus* **58 E5** 54 50N 28 40 E
Lyford Cay, *Bahamas* **9 b** 25 2N 77 33W
Lygnern, *Sweden* **17 G6** 57 30N 12 15 E
Lykens, *U.S.A.* **151 F8** 40 34N 76 42W
Lyman, *Iowa, U.S.A.* **156 C2** 30 29N 94 59W
Lyman, *Wyo., U.S.A.* **158 F8** 41 20N 110 18W
Lyme B., *U.K.* **21 G4** 50 42N 2 53W
Lyme Regis, *U.K.* **21 G5** 50 43N 2 57W
Lymington, *U.K.* **21 G6** 50 45N 1 32W
Łyna →, *Poland* **15 J19** 54 37N 21 14 E
Lynchburg, *Ohio, U.S.A.* **157 E13** 39 15N 83 48W
Lynchburg, *S.C., U.S.A.* **152 A9** 34 3N 80 4W
Lynchburg, *Va., U.S.A.* **148 G6** 37 25N 79 9W
Lynd →, *Australia* **126 B3** 16 28 S 143 18 E
Lynd Ra., *Australia* **127 D4** 25 30 S 149 20 E
Lynden, *Canada* **150 C4** 43 14N 80 9W
Lynden, *U.S.A.* **160 B4** 48 57N 122 27W
Lyndhurst, *Australia* **127 E2** 30 15 S 138 18 E
Lyndon →, *Australia* **125 D1** 23 29 S 114 6 E
Lyndonville, *N.Y., U.S.A.* **150 C6** 43 20N 78 23W
Lyndonville, *Vt., U.S.A.* **151 B12** 44 31N 72 1W
Lyngdal, *Buskerud, Norway* **18 E6** 59 54N 9 32 E
Lyngdal, *Vest-Agder, Norway* **18 F4** 58 8N 7 7 E
Lyngen, *Norway* **14 B19** 69 45N 20 30 E
Lyngør, *Norway* **18 F6** 58 38N 9 8 E
Lynher Reef, *Australia* **124 C3** 15 27 S 121 55 E
Lynn, *Ind., U.S.A.* **157 D12** 40 3N 84 56W
Lynn, *Mass., U.S.A.* **151 D14** 42 28N 70 57W
Lynn Canal, *U.S.A.* **144 G14** 58 50N 135 15W
Lynn Haven, *U.S.A.* **152 E4** 30 15N 85 39W
Lynn Lake, *Canada* **143 B8** 56 51N 101 3W
Lynne, *U.S.A.* **153 F8** 29 12N 81 55W
Lynnville, *U.S.A.* **157 F9** 38 12N 87 19W
Lynnwood, *U.S.A.* **160 C4** 47 49N 122 19W
Lynton, *U.K.* **21 F4** 51 13N 3 50W
Lyntupy, *Belarus* **15 J22** 55 4N 26 23 E
Lynx L., *Canada* **143 A7** 62 25N 106 15W
Lyon, *France* **29 C8** 45 46N 4 50 E
Lyonnais, *France* **29 C8** 45 45N 4 15 E
Lyons = Lyon, *France* **29 C8** 45 46N 4 50 E
Lyons, *Ga., U.S.A.* **152 C7** 32 12N 82 19W
Lyons, *Kans., U.S.A.* **154 F5** 38 21N 98 12W
Lyons, *N.Y., U.S.A.* **150 C8** 43 5N 77 0W

244 Lyons

Lyons →, *Australia* **125 E2** 25 2 S 115 9 E
Lyons Falls, *U.S.A.* **151 C9** 43 37N 75 22W
Lyozna, *Belarus* **58 E6** 55 0N 30 50 E
Lyra Reef, *Papua N. G.* **132 A7** 1 50 S 153 35 E
Lys = Leie →, *Belgium* **24 C3** 51 2N 3 45 E
Lysá nad Labem, *Czech Rep.* **34 A7** 50 11N 14 51 E
Lysebotn, *Norway* **18 E3** 59 3N 6 37 E
Lysefjorden, *Norway* **18 E3** 59 0N 6 23 E
Lysekil, *Sweden* **17 F5** 58 17N 11 26 E
Lyskovo, *Russia* **60 B7** 56 0N 45 3 E
Lyss, *Switz.* **32 B4** 47 4N 7 19 E
Lystrup, *Denmark* **17 H4** 56 14N 10 14 E
Lysva, *Russia* **64 B6** 58 7N 57 49 E
Lysvik, *Sweden* **16 D7** 60 1N 13 9 E
Lysychansk, *Ukraine* **59 H10** 48 55N 38 30 E
Lytham St. Anne's, *U.K.* **20 D4** 53 45N 3 0W
Lyttelton, *N.Z.* **131 D7** 43 35 S 172 44 E
Lytton, *Canada* **142 C4** 50 13N 121 31W
Lyuban, *Russia* **58 C6** 59 16N 31 18 E
Lyubertsy, *Russia* **58 E9** 55 39N 37 50 E
Lyubim, *Russia* **58 C11** 58 20N 40 39 E
Lyubimets, *Bulgaria* **51 E10** 41 50N 26 5 E
Lyuboml, *Ukraine* **59 G3** 51 11N 24 4 E
Lyubotyn, *Ukraine* **59 H8** 50 0N 36 0 E
Lyubytino, *Russia* **58 C7** 58 50N 33 16 E
Lyudinovo, *Russia* **58 F8** 53 52N 34 28 E

M

M.R. Gomez, Presa, *Mexico* **163 B5** 26 10N 99 0W
Ma →, *Vietnam* **76 H5** 19 47N 105 56 E
Ma, O. el →, *Algeria* **110 C3** 27 45N 7 52W
Ma-ubin, *Burma* **90 G5** 16 44N 95 39 E
Ma'adaba, *Jordan* **103 E4** 30 43N 35 47 E
Maamba, *Zambia* **116 B4** 17 17 S 26 28 E
Ma'ān, *Jordan* **103 E4** 30 12N 35 44 E
Ma'ān □, *Jordan* **103 F5** 30 0N 36 0 E
Maana'oba, *Solomon Is.* **133 M11** 8 17 S 160 50 E
Maanselkä, *Finland* **14 C23** 63 52N 28 32 E
Ma'anshan, *China* **77 B12** 31 44N 118 29 E
Maarianhamina, *Finland* **15 F18** 60 5N 19 55 E
Maarmorilik, *Greenland* **10 C5** 71 3N 51 0W
Ma'arrat an Nu'mān, *Syria* **100 E7** 35 43N 36 43 E
Maas →, *Neths.* **24 C4** 51 45N 4 32 E
Maaseik, *Belgium* **24 C5** 51 6N 5 45 E
Maasim, *Phil.* **81 J5** 5 52N 125 0 E
Maasin, *Phil.* **79 B6** 10 8N 124 50 E
Maastricht, *Neths.* **24 D5** 50 50N 5 40 E
Maasupa, *Solomon Is.* **133 M11** 9 16 S 161 17 E
Maave, *Mozam.* **117 C5** 21 4 S 34 47 E
Mababe Depression, *Botswana* **116 B3** 18 50 S 24 15 E
Mabaia, *Angola* **115 D2** 7 12 S 14 2 E
Mabalane, *Mozam.* **117 C5** 23 37 S 32 31 E
Mabanga, *Dem. Rep. of the Congo* **114 B3** 1 30N 19 6 E
Ma'bar, *Yemen* **98 D4** 14 48N 44 17 E
Mabaruma, *Guyana* **169 B6** 8 10N 59 50W
Mabein, *Burma* **90 D6** 23 29N 96 37 E
Mabel L., *Canada* **142 C5** 50 35N 118 43W
Mabenga, *Dem. Rep. of the Congo* **114 C3** 3 39 S 18 40 E
Mabenge, *Dem. Rep. of the Congo* **118 B1** 4 15N 24 12 E
Maberly, *Canada* **151 B8** 44 50N 76 32W
Mabian, *China* **76 C4** 28 47N 103 37 E
Mabil, *Ethiopia* **107 E4** 10 26N 36 52 E
Mabinay, *Phil.* **81 G4** 9 48N 122 54 E
Mabirou, *Congo* **114 C3** 1 3 S 15 42 E
Mablethorpe, *U.K.* **20 D8** 53 20N 0 15 E
Mableton, *U.S.A.* **152 B5** 33 49N 84 35W
Mably, *France* **27 F11** 46 5N 4 4 E
Maboma, *Dem. Rep. of the Congo* **118 B2** 2 30N 28 10 E
Mabonto, *S. Leone* **112 D2** 8 53N 11 50W
Maboukou, *Congo* **114 C2** 3 39 S 12 31 E
Mabrouk, *Mali* **113 B4** 19 29N 1 15W
Mabrous, *Niger* **109 D2** 21 14N 13 35 E
Mabuasehube Game Reserve,
Botswana **116 D3** 25 5 S 21 10 E
Mabungo, *Somali Rep.* **120 D2** 0 49N 42 35 E
Mac Bac, *Vietnam* **87 H6** 9 46N 106 7 E
Macachín, *Argentina* **174 D3** 37 10 S 63 43W
Macaé, *Brazil* **171 F3** 22 20 S 41 43W
Macael, *Spain* **41 H2** 37 20N 2 18W
Macaíba, *Brazil* **170 C4** 5 51 S 35 21W
Macajuba, *Brazil* **171 D3** 12 9 S 40 22W
McAlester, *U.S.A.* **155 H7** 34 56N 95 46W
McAllen, *U.S.A.* **155 M5** 26 12N 98 14W
McAlpin, *U.S.A.* **152 E7** 30 8N 82 57W
MacAlpine L., *Canada* **138 B9** 66 40N 102 50W
Macamic, *Canada* **140 C4** 48 45N 79 0W
Macao = Macau, *China* **77 F9** 22 12N 113 33 E
Macão, *Portugal* **43 F3** 39 35N 7 59W
Macapá, *Brazil* **169 C7** 0 5N 51 4W
Macará, *Ecuador* **168 D2** 4 23 S 79 57W
Macarani, *Brazil* **171 E3** 15 33 S 40 24W
Macarena, Serranía de la,
Colombia **168 C3** 2 45N 73 55W
Macareo, Caño →, *Venezuela* **169 B5** 9 47N 61 36W
Macarthur, *Australia* **128 E5** 38 5 S 142 0 E
McArthur →, *Australia* **126 B2** 15 54 S 136 40 E
McArthur, Port, *Australia* **126 B2** 16 4 S 136 23 E
Macas, *Ecuador* **168 D2** 2 19 S 78 7W
Macate, *Peru* **172 B2** 8 48 S 78 7W
Macau, *Brazil* **170 C4** 5 15 S 36 40W
Macau, *China* **77 F9** 22 12N 113 33 E
Macaúbas, *Brazil* **171 D3** 13 2 S 42 42W
Macaya →, *Colombia* **168 C3** 0 59N 72 20W
McBride, *Canada* **142 C4** 53 20N 120 19W
McCall, *U.S.A.* **158 D5** 44 55N 116 6W
McCamey, *U.S.A.* **155 K3** 31 8N 102 14W
McCammon, *U.S.A.* **158 E7** 42 39N 112 12W
McCarthy, *U.S.A.* **144 F12** 61 26N 142 56W
McCauley I., *Canada* **142 C2** 53 40N 130 15W
McCleary, *U.S.A.* **160 C3** 47 3N 123 16W
Macclenny, *U.S.A.* **152 E7** 30 17N 82 7W
Macclesfield, *U.K.* **20 D5** 53 15N 2 8W
M'Clintock Chan., *Canada* **138 A9** 72 0N 102 0W
McClintock Ra., *Australia* **124 C4** 18 44 S 127 38 E
McCloud, *U.S.A.* **158 F2** 41 15N 122 8W
McCluer I., *Australia* **124 B5** 11 5 S 133 0 E
McClure, *U.S.A.* **150 F7** 40 42N 77 19W
McClure, L., *U.S.A.* **160 H6** 37 35N 120 16W
M'Clure Str., *Canada* **6 B2** 75 0N 119 0W
McClusky, *U.S.A.* **154 B4** 47 29N 100 27W
McComb, *U.S.A.* **155 K9** 31 15N 90 27W
McConaughy, L., *U.S.A.* **154 E4** 41 14N 101 40W
McCook, *U.S.A.* **154 E4** 40 12N 100 38W
McCormick, *U.S.A.* **152 B7** 33 55N 82 17W
McCreary, *Canada* **143 C9** 50 47N 99 29W
McCullough Mt., *U.S.A.* **161 K11** 35 35N 115 13W
McCusker →, *Canada* **143 B7** 55 32N 108 39W
McDame, *Canada* **142 B3** 59 44N 128 59W
McDavid, *U.S.A.* **153 E2** 30 52N 87 19W
McDermitt, *U.S.A.* **158 F5** 41 59N 117 43W
McDonald, *U.S.A.* **150 F4** 40 22N 80 14W
Macdonald, L., *Australia* **124 D4** 23 30 S 129 0 E
Macdonald, Mt., *Vanuatu* **133 G6** 17 36 S 168 23 E
McDonald Is., *Ind. Oc.* **121 K6** 53 0 S 73 0 E
MacDonnell Ranges, *Australia* **124 D5** 23 40 S 133 0 E
McDonough, *U.S.A.* **152 B5** 33 27N 84 9W
McDougalls Well, *Australia* **128 A4** 31 8 S 141 15 E
MacDowell L., *Canada* **140 B1** 52 15N 92 45W
Macduff, *U.K.* **22 D6** 57 40N 2 31W
Maceda, *Spain* **42 C3** 42 16N 7 39W
Macedonia, *U.S.A.* **150 E3** 41 19N 81 31W
Macedonia ■, *Europe* **50 E5** 41 53N 21 40 E
Maceió, *Brazil* **170 C4** 9 40 S 35 41W
Maceira, *Portugal* **42 F2** 39 41N 8 55W
Macenta, *Guinea* **112 D3** 8 35N 9 32W
Macerata, *Italy* **45 E10** 43 18N 13 27 E
McFarland, *U.S.A.* **161 K7** 35 41N 119 14W
McFarlane →, *Canada* **143 B7** 59 12N 107 58W
Macfarlane, L., *Australia* **128 B2** 32 0 S 136 40 E
McGehee, *U.S.A.* **155 J9** 33 38N 91 24W
McGill, *U.S.A.* **158 G6** 39 23N 114 47W
Macgillycuddy's Reeks, *Ireland* **23 E2** 51 58N 9 45W
McGrath, *U.S.A.* **144 E9** 62 58N 155 36W
McGraw, *U.S.A.* **151 D8** 42 36N 76 8W
McGregor, *U.S.A.* **156 A5** 43 1N 91 11W
McGregor Ra., *Australia* **127 D3** 27 0 S 142 45 E
McGuire, Mt, *Australia* **126 J6** 20 18 S 148 23 E
Māch Kowr, *Iran* **97 E9** 25 48N 61 28 E
Machacalis, *Brazil* **171 E3** 17 5 S 40 45W
Machado = Jiparaná →, *Brazil* **173 B5** 8 3 S 62 52W
Machagai, *Argentina* **174 B3** 26 56 S 60 2W
Machakos, *Kenya* **118 C4** 1 30 S 37 15 E
Machala, *Ecuador* **168 D2** 3 20 S 79 57W
Machanga, *Mozam.* **117 C6** 20 59 S 35 0 E
Machattie, L., *Australia* **126 C2** 24 50 S 139 48 E
Machault, *France* **27 C11** 49 21N 4 29 E
Machava, *Mozam.* **117 D5** 25 54 S 32 28 E
Machece, *Mozam.* **119 F4** 19 15 S 35 32 E
Machecoul, *France* **26 F5** 47 0N 1 49W
Macheke, *Zimbabwe* **117 B5** 18 5 S 31 51 E
Macheng, *China* **77 B10** 31 12N 115 2 E
McHenry, *U.S.A.* **157 B8** 42 21N 88 16W
Macherla, *India* **94 F4** 16 29N 79 26 E
Machero, *Spain* **43 F6** 39 21N 4 20W
Machgaon, *India* **94 D8** 20 5N 86 17 E
Machhu →, *India* **92 H4** 23 6N 70 46 E
Machias, *Maine, U.S.A.* **149 C12** 44 43N 67 28W
Machias, *N.Y., U.S.A.* **150 D6** 42 25N 78 30W
Machichi →, *Canada* **143 B10** 57 3N 92 6W
Machico, *Madeira* **9 c** 32 43N 16 44W
Machida, *Japan* **73 B11** 35 28N 139 23 E
Machilipatnam, *India* **95 F5** 16 12N 81 8 E
Machiques, *Venezuela* **168 A3** 10 4N 72 34W
Machupicchu, *Peru* **172 C3** 13 8 S 72 30W
Machynlleth, *U.K.* **21 E4** 52 35N 3 50W
Macia, *Mozam.* **117 D5** 25 2 S 33 8 E
Maciejowice, *Poland* **55 G8** 51 36N 21 26 E
McIlwraith Ra., *Australia* **126 A3** 13 50 S 143 20 E
Măcin, *Romania* **53 E13** 45 16N 28 8 E
Macina, *Mali* **112 C4** 14 50N 5 0W
McInnes L., *Canada* **143 C10** 52 13N 93 45W
McIntosh, *U.S.A.* **154 C4** 45 55N 101 21W
McIntosh L., *Canada* **143 B8** 55 45N 105 0W
Macintosh Ra., *Australia* **125 E4** 27 39 S 125 32 E
Macintyre →, *Australia* **127 D5** 28 37 S 150 47 E
Macizo Galaico, *Spain* **42 C3** 42 30N 7 30W
Mackay, *Australia* **126 K7** 21 8 S 149 11 E
Mackay, *U.S.A.* **158 E7** 43 55N 113 37W
MacKay →, *Canada* **142 B6** 57 10N 111 38W
Mackay, L., *Australia* **124 D4** 22 30 S 129 0 E
McKay Ra., *Australia* **124 D3** 23 0 S 122 30 E
McKeesport, *U.S.A.* **150 F5** 40 21N 79 52W
McKellar, *Canada* **150 A5** 45 30N 79 55W
McKenna, *U.S.A.* **160 D4** 46 56N 122 33W
Mackenzie, *Canada* **142 B4** 55 20N 123 5W
Mackenzie, *Guyana* **169 B6** 6 0N 58 17W
McKenzie, *U.S.A.* **149 G1** 36 8N 88 31W
Mackenzie →, *Australia* **126 C4** 23 38 S 149 46 E
Mackenzie →, *Canada* **138 B6** 69 10N 134 20W
McKenzie →, *U.S.A.* **158 D2** 44 7N 123 6W
Mackenzie Bay, *Canada* **6 B1** 69 0N 137 30W
Mackenzie City = Linden, *Guyana* **169 B6** 6 0N 58 10W
Mackenzie Mts., *Canada* **138 B6** 64 0N 130 0W
Mackenzie Plains, *N.Z.* **131 E5** 44 10 S 170 25 E
McKerrow, L., *N.Z.* **131 E3** 44 25 S 168 5 E
Mackinaw, *U.S.A.* **156 D7** 40 32N 89 21W
Mackinaw →, *U.S.A.* **156 D7** 40 33N 89 44W
Mackinaw City, *U.S.A.* **148 C3** 45 47N 84 44W
McKinlay, *Australia* **126 C3** 21 16 S 141 18 E
McKinlay →, *Australia* **126 C3** 20 50 S 141 28 E
McKinley, Mt., *U.S.A.* **144 E10** 63 4N 151 0W
McKinley Park, *U.S.A.* **144 E10** 63 44N 148 55W
McKinley Sea, *Arctic* **10 A11** 82 0N 0 0W
McKinney, *U.S.A.* **155 J6** 33 12N 96 37W
Mackinnon Road, *Kenya* **118 C4** 3 40 S 39 1 E
McKittrick, *Calif., U.S.A.* **161 K7** 35 18N 119 37W
McKittrick, *Mo., U.S.A.* **156 F5** 38 44N 91 27W
Macklin, *Canada* **143 C7** 52 20N 109 56W
Macksville, *Australia* **129 A10** 30 40 S 152 56 E
McLaren Vale, *Australia* **128 C3** 35 13 S 138 31 E
McLaughlin, *U.S.A.* **154 C4** 45 49N 100 49W
Maclean, *Australia* **127 D5** 29 26 S 153 16 E
McLean, *Ill., U.S.A.* **156 D7** 40 19N 89 10W
McLean, *Tex., U.S.A.* **155 H4** 35 14N 100 36W
McLeansboro, *U.S.A.* **154 F10** 38 6N 88 32W
Maclear, *S. Africa* **117 E4** 31 2 S 28 23 E
Maclear, C., *Malawi* **119 E3** 13 58 S 34 49 E
Macleay →, *Australia* **129 A10** 30 56 S 153 0 E
McLennan, *Canada* **142 B5** 55 42N 116 50W
McLeod →, *Canada* **142 C5** 54 9N 115 44W
MacLeod, B., *Canada* **143 A7** 62 53N 110 0W
McLeod, L., *Australia* **125 D1** 24 9 S 113 47 E
MacLeod Lake, *Canada* **142 C4** 54 58N 123 0W
McLoughlin, Mt., *U.S.A.* **158 E2** 42 27N 122 19W
McMechen, *U.S.A.* **150 G4** 39 57N 80 44W
McMinnville, *Oreg., U.S.A.* **158 D2** 45 13N 123 12W
McMinnville, *Tenn., U.S.A.* **149 H3** 35 41N 85 46W
McMurdo Sd., *Antarctica* **7 D11** 77 0 S 170 0 E
McMurray = Fort McMurray,
Canada **142 B6** 56 44N 111 7W
McMurray, *U.S.A.* **160 B4** 48 19N 122 14W
Maco, *Phil.* **81 H5** 7 20N 125 50 E
Macocolo, *Angola* **115 D3** 6 47 S 16 8 E
Macodoene, *Mozam.* **117 C6** 23 32 S 35 5 E
Macolo, *Angola* **115 D3** 7 5 S 16 42 E
Macomb, *U.S.A.* **156 D6** 40 27N 90 40W
Macomer, *Italy* **46 B1** 40 16N 8 47 E
Mâcon, *France* **27 F11** 46 19N 4 50 E
Macon, *Ga., U.S.A.* **152 C6** 32 51N 83 38W
Macon, *Ill., U.S.A.* **156 E8** 39 43N 89 0W
Macon, *Miss., U.S.A.* **149 J1** 33 7N 88 34W
Macon, *Mo., U.S.A.* **156 E4** 39 44N 92 28W
Macondo, *Angola* **115 E4** 12 37 S 23 46 E
Macossa, *Mozam.* **119 F3** 17 55 S 33 56 E
Macoun L., *Canada* **143 B8** 56 32N 103 40W
Macoupin Cr. →, *U.S.A.* **156 F6** 39 11N 90 38W
Macovane, *Mozam.* **117 C6** 21 30 S 35 2 E
McPherson, *U.S.A.* **154 F6** 38 22N 97 40W
McPherson Pk., *U.S.A.* **161 L7** 34 53N 119 53W
McPherson Ra., *Australia* **127 D5** 28 15 S 153 15 E
Macquarie →, *N.S.W., Australia* **127 E4** 30 5 S 147 30 E
Macquarie →, *N.S.W., Australia* **129 A7** 30 7 S 147 24 E
Macquarie Harbour, *Australia* **127 G4** 42 15 S 145 23 E
Macquarie Is., *Pac. Oc.* **134 N7** 54 36 S 158 55 E
McRae, *U.S.A.* **152 C7** 32 4N 82 54W
MacRobertson Land, *Antarctica* **7 D6** 71 0S 64 0 E
Macroom, *Ireland* **23 E3** 51 54N 8 57W
MacTier, *Canada* **150 A5** 45 9N 79 46W
Macubela, *Mozam.* **119 F4** 16 53 S 37 49 E
Macugnaga, *Italy* **44 C4** 45 58N 7 58 E
Macuiza, *Mozam.* **119 F3** 18 7 S 34 29 E
Macujer, *Colombia* **168 C3** 0 24N 73 10W
Macuro, *Venezuela* **169 F9** 10 42N 61 55W
Macusani, *Peru* **172 C3** 14 4 S 70 29W
Macuse, *Mozam.* **119 F4** 17 45 S 37 10 E
Macuspana, *Mexico* **163 D6** 17 46N 92 36W
Macusse, *Angola* **116 B3** 17 48 S 20 23 E
Mada →, *Nigeria* **113 D6** 7 59N 7 55 E
Madadeni, *S. Africa* **117 D5** 27 43 S 30 3 E
Madadi, *Chad* **109 E4** 18 28N 20 45 E
Madagali, *Nigeria* **113 C7** 10 56N 13 33 E
Madagascar ■, *Africa* **117 C8** 20 0 S 47 0 E
Madā'in Sālih, *Si. Arabia* **96 E3** 26 46N 37 57 E
Madakasira, *India* **95 H3** 13 56N 77 16 E
Madalena, *Azores* **9 d1** 38 32N 28 32W
Madama, *Niger* **109 D2** 22 0N 13 40 E
Madame I., *Canada* **141 C7** 45 30N 60 58W
Madan, *Bulgaria* **51 E8** 41 30N 24 57 E
Madanapalle, *India* **95 H4** 13 33N 78 28 E
Madang, *Papua N. G.* **132 C3** 5 12 S 145 49 E
Madang □, *Papua N. G.* **132 C3** 5 0 S 145 30 E
Madaoua, *Niger* **113 C6** 14 5N 6 27 E
Madara, *Nigeria* **113 C7** 11 45N 10 35 E
Madaripur, *Bangla.* **90 C3** 23 19N 90 15 E
Madau I., *Papua N. G.* **132 E7** 8 58 S 152 28 E
Madauk, *Burma* **90 G6** 17 56N 96 52 E
Madawaska, *Canada* **150 A7** 45 30N 78 0W
Madawaska →, *Canada* **140 C4** 45 27N 76 21W
Madaya, *Burma* **90 D6** 22 12N 96 10 E
Madbar, *Sudan* **107 F3** 6 17N 30 45 E
Maddalena, *Italy* **46 A2** 41 16N 9 23 E
Maddaloni, *Italy* **47 A7** 41 2N 14 23 E
Maddela, *Phil.* **80 C3** 16 21N 121 41 E
Maddur, *India* **95 H3** 12 36N 77 4 E
Madeira, *Atl. Oc.* **9 c** 32 50N 17 0W
Madeira, *U.S.A.* **157 E12** 39 11N 84 22W
Madeira →, *Brazil* **169 D6** 3 22 S 58 45W
Mädelegabel, *Germany* **33 B10** 47 18N 10 18 E
Madeleine, Îs. de la, *Canada* **141 C7** 47 30N 61 40W
Maden, *Turkey* **101 C8** 38 23N 39 40 E
Madera, *Mexico* **162 B3** 29 12N 108 7W
Madera, *Calif., U.S.A.* **160 J6** 36 57N 120 3W
Madera, *Pa., U.S.A.* **150 F6** 40 49N 78 26W
Madgaon, *India* **95 G1** 15 12N 73 58 E
Madha, *India* **94 F2** 18 0N 75 30 E
Madhavpur, *India* **92 J3** 21 15N 69 58 E
Madhepura, *India* **93 F12** 26 11N 86 23 E
Madhira, *India* **94 F5** 16 55N 80 22 E
Madhubani, *India* **93 F12** 26 21N 86 7 E
Madhugiri, *India* **95 H3** 13 40N 77 12 E
Madhumati →, *Bangla.* **90 D2** 22 53N 89 52 E
Madhupur, *Bangla.* **90 C3** 24 37N 90 2 E
Madhupur, *India* **93 G12** 24 16N 86 39 E
Madhya Pradesh □, *India* **92 J8** 22 50N 78 0 E
Madidi →, *Bolivia* **172 C4** 12 32 S 66 52W
Madikeri, *India* **95 H2** 12 30N 75 45 E
Madikwe Game Reserve, *S. Africa* **117 D5** 27 38 S 32 15 E
Madill, *U.S.A.* **155 H6** 34 6N 96 46W
Madimba, *Angola* **115 D2** 6 36 S 14 23 E
Madimba, *Dem. Rep. of the Congo* **114 C3** 4 58 S 15 5 E
Ma'din, *Syria* **101 E8** 35 45N 39 36 E
Madina, *Mali* **112 C3** 13 25N 8 50W
Madinani, *Ivory C.* **112 D3** 9 37N 6 57W
Madīnat ash Sha'b, *Yemen* **98 D4** 12 50N 45 0 E
Madingo, *Congo* **114 C2** 4 5 S 11 24 E
Madingou, *Congo* **114 C2** 4 10 S 13 33 E
Madirovalo, *Madag.* **117 B8** 16 26 S 46 32 E
Madison, *Calif., U.S.A.* **160 G5** 38 41N 121 59W
Madison, *Fla., U.S.A.* **152 E6** 30 28N 83 25W
Madison, *Ga., U.S.A.* **152 B6** 33 36N 83 28W
Madison, *Ind., U.S.A.* **157 F11** 38 44N 85 23W
Madison, *Mo., U.S.A.* **156 E4** 39 28N 92 13W
Madison, *Nebr., U.S.A.* **154 E6** 41 50N 97 27W
Madison, *Ohio, U.S.A.* **150 E3** 41 46N 81 3W
Madison, *S. Dak., U.S.A.* **154 D6** 44 0N 97 7W
Madison, *Wis., U.S.A.* **156 A7** 43 4N 89 24W
Madison →, *U.S.A.* **158 D8** 45 56N 111 31W
Madison Heights, *U.S.A.* **148 G6** 37 25N 79 8W
Madisonville, *Ky., U.S.A.* **148 G2** 37 20N 87 30W
Madisonville, *Tex., U.S.A.* **155 K7** 30 57N 95 55W
Madista, *Botswana* **116 C4** 21 15 S 25 6 E
Madiun, *Indonesia* **85 D4** 7 38 S 111 32 E
Madjingo, *Gabon* **114 B2** 1 20N 14 4 E
Madoc, *Canada* **150 B7** 44 30N 77 28W
Madol, *Sudan* **107 F2** 9 3N 27 45 E
Madon →, *France* **27 D13** 48 36N 6 6 E
Madona, *Latvia* **15 H22** 56 53N 26 5 E
Madonie, *Italy* **46 E6** 37 50N 13 50 E
Madonna di Campíglio, *Italy* **44 B7** 46 14N 10 49 E
Madra Dağı, *Turkey* **49 B9** 39 23N 27 12 E
Madrakah, Ra's al, *Oman* **99 C7** 19 0N 57 50 E
Madras = Chennai, *India* **95 H5** 13 8N 80 19 E
Madras = Tamil Nadu □, *India* **95 J3** 11 0N 77 0 E
Madras, *U.S.A.* **158 D3** 44 38N 121 8W
Madre, Laguna, *U.S.A.* **155 M6** 27 0N 97 30W
Madre, Sierra, *Phil.* **80 C4** 17 0N 122 0 E
Madre de Dios □, *Peru* **172 C3** 12 0 S 70 15W
Madre de Dios →, *Bolivia* **172 C4** 10 59 S 66 8W
Madre de Dios, I., *Chile* **176 D1** 50 20 S 75 10W
Madre del Sur, Sierra, *Mexico* **163 D5** 17 30N 100 0W
Madre Occidental, Sierra, *Mexico* **162 B3** 27 0N 107 0W
Madre Oriental, Sierra, *Mexico* **162 C5** 25 0N 100 0W
Madri, *India* **92 G5** 24 16N 73 32 E
Madrid, *Spain* **42 E7** 40 25N 3 45W
Madrid, *Ala., U.S.A.* **152 D4** 31 2N 85 24W
Madrid, *Iowa, U.S.A.* **156 C3** 41 53N 93 49W
Madrid, *N.Y., U.S.A.* **151 B9** 44 45N 75 8W
Madrid □, *Spain* **42 E7** 40 30N 3 45W
Madridejos, *Spain* **43 F7** 39 28N 3 33W
Madrigal de las Altas Torres, *Spain* **42 D6** 41 5N 5 0W
Madrona, Sierra, *Spain* **43 G6** 38 27N 4 16W
Madroñera, *Spain* **43 F5** 39 26N 5 42W
Madrusah, *Libya* **108 D2** 24 48N 14 32 E
Madu, *Sudan* **107 E2** 14 37N 26 4 E
Maduo, *Dem. Rep. of the Congo* **114 C4** 1 24 S 20 44 E
Madura, *Australia* **125 F4** 31 55 S 127 0 E
Madura, *Indonesia* **79 G15** 7 30 S 114 0 E
Madura, Selat, *Indonesia* **85 D4** 7 30 S 113 20 E
Madurai, *India* **95 K4** 9 55N 78 10 E
Madurantakam, *India* **95 H4** 12 30N 79 50 E
Madzhalis, *Russia* **61 J8** 42 9N 47 47 E
Mae Chan, *Thailand* **86 B2** 20 9N 99 52 E
Mae Hong Son, *Thailand* **86 C2** 19 16N 97 56 E
Mae Khlong →, *Thailand* **86 F3** 13 24N 100 0 E
Mae Phrik, *Thailand* **86 D2** 17 27N 99 7 E
Mae Ramat, *Thailand* **86 D2** 16 58N 98 31 E
Mae Rim, *Thailand* **86 C2** 18 54N 98 57 E
Mae Sot, *Thailand* **86 D2** 16 43N 98 34 E
Mae Suai, *Thailand* **76 H2** 19 39N 99 33 E
Mae Tha, *Thailand* **86 C2** 18 28N 99 8 E
Maebaru, *Japan* **72 D2** 33 33N 130 12 E
Maebashi, *Japan* **73 A11** 36 24N 139 4 E
Maella, *Spain* **40 D5** 41 8N 0 7 E
Maesteg, *U.K.* **21 F4** 51 36N 3 40W
Maestra, Sierra, *Cuba* **164 B4** 20 15N 77 0W
Maestre de Campo I., *Phil.* **80 E3** 12 56N 121 42 E
Maetambe, Mt., *Solomon Is.* **133 L9** 7 3 S 157 1 E
Maevatanana, *Madag.* **117 B8** 16 56 S 46 49 E
Maéwo, *Vanuatu* **133 E6** 15 10 S 168 10 E
Mafa, *Indonesia* **82 A3** 0 3N 127 53 E
Ma'fan, *Libya* **108 C2** 25 56N 14 29 E
Mafeking = Mafikeng, *S. Africa* **116 D4** 25 50 S 25 38 E
Mafeking, *Canada* **143 C8** 52 40N 101 10W
Maféré, *Ivory C.* **112 D4** 5 30N 3 2W
Mafeteng, *Lesotho* **116 D4** 29 51 S 27 15 E
Maffra, *Australia* **129 D7** 37 53 S 146 58 E
Mafia I., *Tanzania* **118 D4** 7 45 S 39 50 E
Mafikeng, *S. Africa* **116 D4** 25 50 S 25 38 E
Mafra, *Brazil* **175 B6** 26 10 S 49 55W
Mafra, *Portugal* **43 G1** 38 55N 9 20W
Mafungabusi Plateau, *Zimbabwe* **119 F2** 18 30 S 29 8 E
Magadan, *Russia* **67 D16** 59 38N 150 50 E
Magadi, *India* **95 H3** 12 58N 77 14 E
Magadi, *Kenya* **118 C4** 1 54 S 36 19 E
Magadi, L., *Kenya* **118 C4** 1 54 S 36 19 E
Magaliesburg, *S. Africa* **117 D4** 26 0 S 27 32 E
Magallanes, *Phil.* **80 E4** 12 50N 123 50 E
Magallanes □, *Chile* **176 D2** 52 0 S 72 0W
Magallanes, Estrecho de, *Chile* **176 D2** 52 30 S 75 0W
Magaluf, *Spain* **38 B3** 39 29N 2 32 E
Magangué, *Colombia* **168 B3** 9 14N 74 45W
Maganoy, *Phil.* **81 H5** 6 51N 124 31 E
Magaria, *Niger* **113 C6** 13 4N 9 5 E
Magarida, *Papua N. G.* **132 F5** 10 18 S 149 20 E
Magburaka, *S. Leone* **112 D2** 8 47N 12 0W
Magdalen Is. = Madeleine, Îs. de
la, *Canada* **141 C7** 47 30N 61 40W
Magdalena, *Argentina* **174 D4** 35 5 S 57 30W
Magdalena, *Bolivia* **173 C5** 13 13 S 63 57W
Magdalena, *Malaysia* **83 B5** 4 25N 117 55 E
Magdalena, *Mexico* **162 A2** 30 50N 112 0W
Magdalena, *U.S.A.* **159 J10** 34 7N 107 15W
Magdalena □, *Colombia* **168 A3** 10 0N 74 0W
Magdalena →, *Colombia* **168 A3** 11 6N 74 51W
Magdalena →, *Mexico* **162 A2** 30 40N 112 25W
Magdalena, B., *Mexico* **162 C2** 24 30N 112 10W
Magdalena, I., *Chile* **176 B2** 44 40 S 73 0W
Magdalena, Llano de la, *Mexico* **162 C2** 25 0N 111 30W
Magdeburg, *Germany* **30 C7** 52 7N 11 38 E
Magdelaine Cays, *Australia* **126 B5** 16 33 S 150 18 E
Magdub, *Sudan* **107 E2** 13 42N 25 5 E
Magee, *U.S.A.* **155 K10** 31 52N 89 44W
Magelang, *Indonesia* **85 D4** 7 29 S 110 13 E
Magellan's Str. = Magallanes,
Estrecho de, *Chile* **176 D2** 52 30 S 75 0W
Magenta, *Italy* **44 C5** 45 28N 8 53 E
Magenta, L., *Australia* **125 F2** 33 30 S 119 2 E
Magerøya, *Norway* **14 A21** 71 3N 25 40 E
Maggea, *Australia* **128 C4** 34 28 S 140 2 E
Maggia, *Switz.* **33 D7** 46 15N 8 42 E
Maggia →, *Switz.* **33 D7** 46 18N 8 36 E
Maggiorasca, Mte., *Italy* **44 D6** 44 33N 9 29 E
Maggiore, Lago, *Italy* **44 C5** 45 57N 8 39 E
Maggotty, *Jamaica* **164 a** 18 9N 77 46W
Maghâgha, *Egypt* **106 B3** 28 38N 30 50 E
Maghama, *Mauritania* **112 B2** 15 32N 12 57W
Magherafelt, *U.K.* **23 B5** 54 45N 6 37W
Maghnia, *Algeria* **111 B4** 34 50N 1 43W
Magione, *Italy* **45 E9** 43 8N 12 12 E
Magistralnyy, *Russia* **67 D11** 56 16N 107 36 E
Maglaj, *Bos.-H.* **52 F3** 44 33N 18 7 E
Magliano in Toscana, *Italy* **45 F8** 42 36N 11 17 E
Máglie, *Italy* **47 B11** 40 7N 18 18 E
Magnac-Laval, *France* **28 B5** 46 13N 1 11 E
Magnetic Pole (North) = North
Magnetic Pole, *Canada* **6 B2** 77 58N 102 8W
Magnetic Pole (South) = South
Magnetic Pole, *Antarctica* **7 C9** 64 8 S 138 8 E
Magnisía □, *Greece* **48 B5** 39 15N 23 0 E
Magnitogorsk, *Russia* **64 E7** 53 27N 59 4 E
Magnolia, *Ark., U.S.A.* **155 J8** 33 16N 93 14W
Magnolia, *Miss., U.S.A.* **155 K9** 31 9N 90 28W
Magnor, *Norway* **18 E9** 59 56N 12 15 E
Magny-en-Vexin, *France* **27 C8** 49 9N 1 47 E
Mago, *Fiji* **133 A3** 17 26 S 179 8W
Mago Nat. Park, *Ethiopia* **107 F4** 5 40N 36 18 E
Magog, *Canada* **141 C5** 45 18N 72 9W
Magoro, *Uganda* **118 B3** 1 45N 34 12 E
Magosa = Famagusta, *Cyprus* **39 E9** 35 8N 33 55 E
Magouládhes, *Greece* **38 B9** 39 45N 19 42 E
Magoye, *Zambia* **119 F2** 16 1 S 27 30 E
Magozal, *Mexico* **163 C5** 21 34N 97 59W
Magpie, L., *Canada* **141 B7** 51 0N 64 41W
Magrath, *Canada* **142 D6** 49 25N 112 50W
Magre →, *Spain* **41 F4** 39 11N 0 15W
Magrur, *Sudan* **107 E3** 14 1N 30 27 E
Magrur, Wadi →, *Sudan* **107 D2** 16 5N 26 30 E
Magsingal, *Phil.* **80 C3** 17 41N 120 25 E
Magta Lahjar, *Mauritania* **112 B2** 17 28N 13 17W
Maguan, *China* **76 F5** 23 0N 104 21 E
Maguarinho, C., *Brazil* **170 B2** 0 15 S 48 30W
Magude, *Mozam.* **117 D5** 25 2 S 32 40 E
Maguindanao □, *Phil.* **81 H5** 7 5N 124 0 E
Mağusa = Famagusta, *Cyprus* **39 E9** 35 8N 33 55 E
Maguse L., *Canada* **143 A9** 61 40N 95 10W
Maguse Pt., *Canada* **143 A10** 61 20N 93 50W
Magvana, *India* **92 H3** 23 13N 69 22 E
Magwe, *Burma* **90 E5** 20 10N 95 0 E
Magwe, *Sudan* **107 G3** 4 8N 32 17 E
Magwe □, *Burma* **90 F5** 20 0N 95 0 E
Maha Oya, *Sri Lanka* **95 L5** 7 31N 81 22 E
Maha Sarakham, *Thailand* **86 D4** 16 12N 103 16 E
Mahābād, *Iran* **101 D11** 36 50N 45 45 E
Mahabaleshwar, *India* **94 F1** 17 58N 73 43 E
Mahabharat Lekh, *Nepal* **93 E10** 28 30N 82 0 E
Mahabo, *Madag.* **117 C7** 20 23 S 44 40 E
Mahad, *India* **94 E1** 18 6N 73 29 E
Mahaddei Uen, *Somali Rep.* **120 D3** 2 58N 45 32 E
Mahadeo Hills, *India* **93 H8** 22 20N 78 30 E
Mahadeopur, *India* **94 E5** 18 48N 80 0 E
Mahaffey, *U.S.A.* **150 F6** 40 53N 78 44W
Mahagi, *Dem. Rep. of the Congo* **118 B3** 2 20N 31 0 E
Mahaicony, *Guyana* **169 B6** 6 36N 57 48W
Mahajamba →, *Madag.* **117 B8** 15 33 S 47 8 E
Mahajamba, Helodranon' i,
Madag. **117 B8** 15 24 S 47 5 E
Mahajan, *India* **92 E5** 28 48N 73 56 E
Mahajanga, *Madag.* **117 B8** 15 40 S 46 25 E
Mahajanga □, *Madag.* **117 B8** 17 0 S 47 0 E
Mahajilo →, *Madag.* **117 B8** 19 42 S 45 22 E
Mahakam →, *Indonesia* **85 C5** 0 35 S 117 17 E
Mahalapye, *Botswana* **116 C4** 23 1 S 26 51 E
Mahalchhar, *Bangla.* **90 D4** 22 55N 92 2 E
Mahale Mountains Nat. Park,
Tanzania **118 D2** 6 10 S 29 50 E
Mahale Mts., *Tanzania* **118 D3** 6 20 S 30 0 E
Maḥallāt, *Iran* **97 C6** 33 55N 50 30 E
Māhān, *Iran* **97 D8** 30 5N 57 18 E
Mahan →, *India* **93 H10** 23 30N 82 50 E
Mahanadi →, *India* **94 D8** 20 20N 86 25 E
Mahananda →, *India* **93 G12** 25 12N 87 52 E
Mahanoro, *Madag.* **117 B8** 19 54 S 48 48 E
Mahanoy City, *U.S.A.* **151 F8** 40 49N 76 9W
Mahaplag, *Phil.* **81 F5** 10 35N 124 57 E
Maharashtra □, *India* **94 D2** 20 30N 75 30 E
Maharès, *Tunisia* **108 B2** 34 32N 10 29 E
Mahasamund, *India* **94 D6** 21 6N 82 6 E
Mahasham, W. →, *Egypt* **103 E3** 30 15N 34 10 E
Mahasoa, *Madag.* **117 C8** 22 12 S 46 6 E
Mahasolo, *Madag.* **117 B8** 19 7 S 46 22 E
Mahattat ash Shīdīyah, *Jordan* **103 F4** 29 55N 35 55 E

Manaravolo 245

Mahattat 'Unayzah, Jordan 103 E4 30 30N 35 47 E
Mahavavy →, Madag. 117 B8 15 57 S 45 54 E
Mahaweli Ganga →, Sri Lanka 95 K5 8 27N 81 13 E
Mahaxay, Laos 86 D5 17 22N 105 12 E
Mahbubabad, India 94 F5 17 42N 80 2 E
Mahbubnagar, India 94 F3 16 45N 77 59 E
Mahd adh Dhahab, Si. Arabia 98 B3 23 30N 40 52 E
Mahdah, Oman 97 E7 24 24N 55 59 E
Mahdia, Guyana 169 B6 5 13N 59 8W
Mahdia, Tunisia 108 A2 35 28N 11 0 E
Mahe, Jammu & Kashmir, India 93 C8 33 10N 78 32 E
Mahé, Pondicherry, India 95 J2 11 42N 75 34 E
Mahé, Seychelles 121 b 5 0 S 55 30 E
Mahebourg, Mauritius 121 d 20 24 S 57 42 E
Mahendra Giri, India 95 K3 8 20N 77 30 E
Mahendraganj, India 90 C2 25 20N 89 45 E
Mahendragarh, India 92 E7 28 17N 76 14 E
Mahenge, Tanzania 119 D4 8 45 S 36 41 E
Maheno, N.Z. 131 F5 45 10 S 170 50 E
Mahesana, India 92 H5 23 39N 72 26 E
Maheshwar, India 92 H6 22 11N 75 35 E
Mahgawan, India 93 F8 26 29N 78 37 E
Mahi →, India 92 H5 22 15N 72 55 E
Mahia Pen., N.Z. 130 F6 39 9 S 177 55 E
Mahighe, Solomon Is. 133 M10 8 30 S 159 58 E
Mahilyow, Belarus 58 F6 53 55N 30 18 E
Mahim, India 94 E1 19 39N 72 44 E
Mahina, Tahiti 133 S16 17 30 S 149 27W
Mahirija, Morocco 111 B4 34 0N 3 16W
Mahlaing, Burma 90 E5 21 6N 95 39 E
Mahmiya, Sudan 107 D3 17 12N 33 43 E
Mahmud Kot, Pakistan 92 D4 30 16N 71 0 E
Mahmudia, Romania 53 E14 45 5N 29 5 E
Mahmudiye, Turkey 49 B12 39 48N 30 15 E
Mahmutbey, Turkey 51 E12 41 3N 28 49 E
Mahnomen, U.S.A. 154 B7 47 19N 95 58W
Maho, Sri Lanka 95 L5 7 49N 80 16 E
Mahoba, India 93 G8 25 15N 79 55 E
Mahomet, U.S.A. 157 D8 40 12N 88 24W
Mahón = Maó, Spain 38 B5 39 53N 4 16 E
Mahone Bay, Canada 141 D7 44 30N 64 20W
Mahopac, U.S.A. 151 E11 41 22N 73 45W
Mahoua, Chad 109 F3 11 49N 18 26 E
Mahuta, Nigeria 113 C5 11 32N 4 58 E
Mahuva, India 92 J4 21 5N 71 48 E
Mahya Dağı, Turkey 51 E11 41 47N 27 36 E
Mai-Ndombe, L., Dem. Rep. of the Congo 114 C3 2 0 S 18 20 E
Mai-Sai, Thailand 76 G2 20 20N 99 55 E
Mai Thon, Ko, Thailand 87 a 7 40N 98 28 E
Maia, Azores 9 d4 36 56N 25 1W
Maia, Portugal 42 D2 41 14N 8 37W
Maia, Spain 40 B3 43 12N 1 29W
Maials, Spain 40 D5 41 22N 0 30 E
Maibong, India 90 C4 25 18N 93 10 E
Maicao, Colombia 168 A3 11 23N 72 13W
Maîche, France 27 E13 47 16N 6 48 E
Maici →, Brazil 173 B5 6 30 S 61 43W
Maicurú →, Brazil 169 D7 2 14 S 54 17W
Màida, Italy 47 D9 38 51N 16 22 E
Maidan Khula, Afghan. 91 B3 33 36N 69 50 E
Maidenhead, U.K. 21 F7 51 31N 0 42W
Maidstone, Canada 143 C7 53 5N 109 20W
Maidstone, U.K. 21 F8 51 16N 0 32 E
Maiduguri, Nigeria 113 C7 12 0N 13 20 E
Măieruş, Romania 53 E10 45 53N 25 31 E
Maigatari, Nigeria 113 C6 12 46N 9 27 E
Maignelay Montigny, France 27 C9 49 32N 2 30 E
Maigo, Phil. 81 G4 8 10N 123 57 E
Maigualida, Sierra, Venezuela 169 B4 5 30N 65 10W
Maigudo, Ethiopia 107 F4 7 30N 37 8 E
Maihar, India 93 G9 24 16N 80 45 E
Maihara, Japan 73 B8 35 19N 136 17 E
Maijdi, Bangla. 90 D3 22 48N 91 10 E
Maikala Ra., India 94 D5 22 0N 81 0 E
Maiko, Parc Nat. de la, Dem. Rep. of the Congo 118 C2 0 30 S 27 50 E
Maikoor, Indonesia 83 C4 6 8 S 134 6 E
Mailani, India 93 E9 28 17N 80 21 E
Maili, U.S.A. 145 K13 21 25N 158 11W
Maili Pt., U.S.A. 145 K13 21 24N 158 11W
Maillezais, France 28 B3 46 22N 0 45W
Mailsi, Pakistan 92 E5 29 48N 72 15 E
Maimbung, Phil. 81 J3 5 56N 121 2 E
Main →, Germany 31 F4 50 0N 8 18 E
Main →, U.K. 23 B5 54 48N 6 18W
Main Range Nat. Park, Australia 127 D5 28 11 S 152 27 E
Main Ridge, Trin. & Tob. 169 E10 11 16N 60 40W
Mainburg, Germany 31 G7 48 38N 11 47 E
Maindargi, India 94 F3 17 28N 76 18 E
Maine, France 26 D6 48 20N 0 15W
Maine ☐, U.S.A. 149 C11 45 20N 69 0W
Maine →, Ireland 23 D2 52 9N 9 45W
Maine-et-Loire ☐, France 26 E6 47 31N 0 30W
Maïne-Soroa, Niger 113 C7 13 13N 12 2 E
Maingkaing, Burma 90 C5 24 48N 95 16 E
Maingkwan, Burma 90 B6 26 15N 96 37 E
Mainit, Phil. 81 G5 9 32N 125 32 E
Mainit, L., Phil. 81 G5 9 31N 125 30 E
Mainland, Orkney, U.K. 22 C5 58 59N 3 8W
Mainland, Shet., U.K. 22 A7 60 15N 1 22W
Mainoru, Australia 126 A1 14 0 S 134 6 E
Mainpuri, India 93 F8 27 18N 79 4 E
Maintal, Germany 31 E4 50 7N 8 52 E
Maintenon, France 27 D8 48 35N 1 35 E
Maintirano, Madag. 117 B7 18 3 S 44 1 E
Mainz, Germany 31 E4 50 1N 8 14 E
Maio, C. Verde Is. 9 j 15 10N 23 10W
Maipú, Argentina 174 D4 36 52 S 57 50W
Maiquetía, Venezuela 168 A4 10 36N 66 57W
Màira →, Italy 44 D4 44 49N 7 38 E
Mairabari, India 90 B4 26 30N 92 22 E
Mairipotaba, Brazil 171 E2 17 18 S 49 28W
Maisí, Cuba 165 B5 20 17N 74 9W
Maisí, Pta. de, Cuba 165 B5 20 10N 74 10W
Maitland, N.S.W., Australia 129 B9 32 33 S 151 36 E
Maitland, S. Austral., Australia 128 C2 34 23 S 137 40 E
Maitland →, Canada 150 C3 43 45N 81 43W
Maitland, Banjaran, Malaysia 85 B5 4 55N 116 37 E
Maitum, Phil. 81 H5 6 2N 124 30 E
Maiyema, Nigeria 113 C5 12 5N 4 25 E
Maiyuan, China 77 E11 25 34N 117 28 E
Maiz, Is. del, Nic. 164 D3 12 15N 83 4W
Maizuru, Japan 73 B7 35 25N 135 22 E
Majagual, Colombia 168 B3 8 33N 74 38W
Majalengka, Indonesia 85 D3 6 50 S 108 13 E
Majari →, Brazil 169 C5 3 29N 60 58W
Majdūl, Libya 108 C3 25 51N 15 7 E
Majene, Indonesia 82 B1 3 38 S 118 57 E
Majes →, Peru 172 D3 16 40 S 72 44W
Majete Game Reserve, Malawi 119 F3 15 54 S 34 34 E
Majevica, Bos.-H. 52 F3 44 45N 18 50 E
Maji, Ethiopia 107 F4 6 12N 35 30 E
Majiang, China 76 D6 26 28N 107 32 E
Majorca = Mallorca, Spain 38 B4 39 30N 3 0 E
Majors Creek, Australia 129 C8 35 33 S 149 45 E
Majuriã, Brazil 173 B5 7 30 S 64 55W
Maka, Senegal 112 C2 13 40N 14 10W
Makaha, U.S.A. 145 K13 21 29N 158 13W
Makaha, Zimbabwe 117 B5 17 20 S 32 39 E
Makahoa Pt., U.S.A. 145 J14 21 41N 157 56W
Makahuena Pt., U.S.A. 145 B2 21 52N 159 27W
Makak, Cameroon 113 E7 3 36N 11 0 E
Makakilo City, U.S.A. 145 K13 21 22N 158 5W
Makakou, Gabon 114 C2 0 11 S 12 12 E
Makalamabedi, Botswana 116 C3 20 19 S 23 51 E
Makale, Indonesia 82 B1 3 6 S 119 51 E
Makamba, Burundi 118 C2 4 8 S 29 49 E
Makapuu Pt., U.S.A. 145 K14 21 19N 157 39W
Makarewa, N.Z. 131 G3 46 20 S 168 21 E
Makari, Cameroon 113 C7 12 35N 10 27 E
Makari, Cent. Amer. 109 F2 12 35N 10 27 E
Makarikari = Makgadikgadi Salt Pans, Botswana 116 C4 20 40 S 25 45 E
Makarovo, Russia 67 D11 57 40N 107 45 E
Makarska, Croatia 45 E14 43 20N 17 2 E
Makaryev, Russia 60 B6 57 52N 43 50 E
Makasar = Ujung Pandang, Indonesia 82 C1 5 10 S 119 20 E
Makasar, Selat, Indonesia 85 C5 1 0 S 118 20 E
Makasar, Str. of = Makasar, Selat, Indonesia 85 C5 1 0 S 118 20 E
Makat, Kazakstan 57 E9 47 39N 53 19 E
Makaw, Dem. Rep. of the Congo 114 C3 3 29 S 18 20 E
Makawao, U.S.A. 145 C5 20 52N 156 17W
Makaya, Dem. Rep. of the Congo 114 C3 3 21 S 18 1 E
Makbon, Indonesia 83 B4 0 45 S 131 32 E
Makedonija = Macedonia ■, Europe 50 E5 41 53N 21 40 E
Makeni, S. Leone 112 D2 8 55N 12 5W
Makeyevka = Makiyivka, Ukraine 59 H9 48 0N 38 0 E
Makgadikgadi Nat. Park, Botswana 116 C3 20 27 S 24 47 E
Makgadikgadi Salt Pans, Botswana 116 C4 20 40 S 25 45 E
Makhachkala, Russia 61 J8 43 0N 47 30 E
Makhairádhon, Greece 39 D2 37 46N 20 49 E
Makharadze = Ozurgeti, Georgia 61 K5 41 55N 42 2 E
Makhmūr, Iraq 101 E10 35 46N 43 35 E
Makhtal, India 95 E3 16 30N 77 31 E
Makhyah, W. →, Yemen 99 C5 17 40N 49 1 E
Makian, Indonesia 82 A3 0 20N 127 20 E
Makina, Solomon Is. 133 M11 9 50 S 160 50 E
Makindu, Kenya 118 C4 2 18 S 37 50 E
Makinsk, Kazakstan 66 D8 52 37N 70 26 E
Makiyivka, Ukraine 59 H9 48 0N 38 0 E
Makkah, Si. Arabia 98 B2 21 30N 39 54 E
Makkovik, Canada 141 A8 55 10N 59 10W
Makó, Hungary 52 D5 46 14N 20 33 E
Mako, Senegal 112 C2 12 52N 12 20W
Makogai, Fiji 133 A2 17 28 S 179 0 E
Makok, Gabon 114 C1 0 1 S 9 35 E
Makokou, Gabon 114 B2 0 40N 12 50 E
Makongo, Dem. Rep. of the Congo 118 B2 3 25N 26 17 E
Makoro, Dem. Rep. of the Congo 118 B2 3 10N 29 59 E
Makoua, Congo 114 C3 0 5 S 15 50 E
Maków Mazowiecki, Poland 55 F8 52 52N 21 6 E
Maków Podhalański, Poland 55 J6 49 43N 19 45 E
Makrá, Greece 49 E7 36 15N 25 54 E
Makran, Asia 91 D1 26 13N 61 30 E
Makran Coast Range, Pakistan 91 D2 25 40N 64 0 E
Makrana, India 92 F6 27 2N 74 46 E
Mákri, Greece 51 F9 40 52N 25 40 E
Makri, India 94 E5 19 46N 81 55 E
Makriyialos, Greece 39 E6 35 2N 25 59 E
Maktar, Tunisia 108 A1 35 48N 9 12 E
Mākū, Iran 101 C11 39 15N 44 31 E
Makum, India 90 B5 27 30N 95 23 E
Makumbi, Dem. Rep. of the Congo 115 D4 5 50 S 20 43 E
Makunda, Botswana 116 C3 22 30 S 20 7 E
Makung, Taiwan 77 F12 23 34N 119 34 E
Makunza, Dem. Rep. of the Congo 115 D4 8 52 S 24 19 E
Makurazaki, Japan 72 F2 31 15N 130 20 E
Makurdi, Nigeria 113 D6 7 43N 8 35 E
Makushin Volcano, U.S.A. 144 K6 53 53N 166 55W
Makūyeh, Iran 97 D7 28 7N 53 9 E
Makwassie, S. Africa 116 D4 27 17 S 26 0 E
Makwiro, Zimbabwe 117 B5 17 58 S 30 25 E
Mal, India 90 B2 26 51N 88 45 E
Mâl, Mauritania 112 B2 16 58N 13 23W
Mal B., Ireland 23 D2 52 50N 9 30W
Mala, Peru 172 C2 12 40 S 76 38W
Mala, Pta., Panama 164 E3 7 28N 80 2W
Mala Belozërka, Ukraine 59 J8 47 12N 34 56 E
Mala Kapela, Croatia 45 D12 44 45N 15 30 E
Mała Panew →, Poland 55 H4 50 43N 17 54 E
Mala Vyska, Ukraine 59 H6 48 39N 31 36 E
Malabang, Phil. 81 H5 7 36N 124 3 E
Malabar, U.S.A. 153 H9 28 0N 80 34W
Malabar Coast, India 95 J2 11 0N 75 0 E
Malabo = Rey Malabo, Eq. Guin. 113 E6 3 45N 8 50 E
Malabon, Phil. 80 D3 14 21N 121 0 E
Malabrigo Pt., Phil. 80 E3 13 36N 121 15 E
Malabu, Nigeria 113 D7 9 32N 12 48 E
Malabuñgan, Phil. 81 G1 9 3N 117 38 E
Malacca, Str. of, Indonesia 87 L3 3 0N 101 0 E
Malacky, Slovak Rep. 35 C10 48 27N 17 0 E
Malad City, U.S.A. 158 E7 42 12N 112 15W
Maladeta, Spain 40 C5 42 39N 0 39 E
Maladzyechna, Belarus 58 E4 54 20N 26 50 E
Malae Pt., U.S.A. 145 C6 20 7N 155 53W
Málaga, Colombia 168 B3 6 42N 72 44W
Málaga, Spain 43 J6 36 43N 4 23W
Málaga ☐, Spain 43 J6 36 38N 4 58W
Malagarasi, Tanzania 118 D3 5 5 S 30 50 E
Malagarasi →, Tanzania 118 D2 5 12 S 29 47 E
Malagasy Rep. = Madagascar ■, Africa 117 C8 20 0 S 47 0 E
Malagón, Spain 43 F7 39 11N 3 52W
Malagón →, Spain 43 H3 37 35N 7 29W
Malahide, Ireland 23 C5 53 26N 6 9W
Malaimbandy, Madag. 117 C8 20 20 S 45 36 E
Malaita, Solomon Is. 133 M11 9 0 S 161 0 E
Malakâl, Sudan 107 F3 9 33N 31 40 E
Malakanagiri, India 94 E5 18 21N 81 54 E
Malakand, Pakistan 91 B3 34 40N 71 55 E
Malakula, Vanuatu 133 F5 16 15 S 167 30 E
Malakwal, Pakistan 92 C5 32 34N 73 13 E
Malalag, Phil. 81 H5 6 36N 125 24 E
Malalaua, Papua N. G. 132 E4 8 4 S 146 10 E
Malam, Chad 109 F4 11 27N 20 59 E
Malamala, Indonesia 82 B2 3 21 S 120 55 E
Malanda, Australia 126 B4 17 22 S 145 35 E
Malang, Indonesia 85 D4 7 59 S 112 45 E
Malangas, Phil. 81 H4 7 37N 123 1 E
Malange ☐, Angola 115 D3 9 30 S 16 0 E
Malangen, Norway 14 B18 69 24N 18 37 E
Malanje, Angola 115 D3 9 36 S 16 17 E
Malapatan, Phil. 81 J5 5 59N 125 18 E
Mälaren, Sweden 16 E11 59 30N 17 10 E
Malargüe, Argentina 174 D2 35 32 S 69 30W
Malartic, Canada 140 C4 48 9N 78 9W
Malaryta, Belarus 59 G3 51 50N 24 3 E
Malaspina Glacier, U.S.A. 144 G12 59 50N 140 30W
Malatya, Turkey 101 C8 38 25N 38 20 E
Malawali, Malaysia 85 A5 7 3N 117 18 E
Malawi ■, Africa 119 E3 11 55 S 34 0 E
Malawi, L. = Nyasa, L., Africa 119 E3 12 30 S 34 30 E
Malay, Phil. 81 F4 11 54N 121 55 E
Malay Pen., Asia 87 J3 7 25N 100 0 E
Malaya Belozërka = Mala Belozërka, Ukraine 59 J8 47 12N 34 56 E
Malaya Vishera, Russia 58 C7 58 55N 32 25 E
Malaya Viska = Mala Vyska, Ukraine 59 H6 48 39N 31 36 E
Malaybalay, Phil. 81 G5 8 5N 125 7 E
Malāyer, Iran 97 C6 34 19N 48 51 E
Malaysia ■, Asia 81 J1 5 0N 110 0 E
Malazgirt, Turkey 101 C10 39 10N 42 33 E
Malbaza, Niger 113 C6 13 59N 5 38 E
Malbon, Australia 126 C3 21 5 S 140 17 E
Malbooma, Australia 127 E1 30 41 S 134 11 E
Malbork, Poland 54 D6 54 3N 19 1 E
Malca Dube, Ethiopia 120 C2 6 47N 42 4 E
Malcésine, Italy 44 C7 45 46N 10 48 E
Malchin, Germany 30 B8 53 44N 12 44 E
Malchow, Germany 30 B8 53 28N 12 25 E
Malcolm, Australia 125 E3 28 51 S 121 25 E
Malcolm, Pt., Australia 125 F3 33 48 S 123 45 E
Malczyce, Poland 55 G3 51 14N 16 29 E
Maldah, India 93 G13 25 2N 88 9 E
Maldegem, Belgium 24 C3 51 14N 3 26 E
Malden, Mass., U.S.A. 151 D13 42 26N 71 4W
Malden, Mo., U.S.A. 155 G10 36 34N 89 57W
Malden I., Kiribati 135 H12 4 3 S 155 1W
Maldives ■, Ind. Oc. 62 J11 5 0N 73 0 E
Maldon, Australia 128 D6 37 0 S 144 6 E
Maldonado, Uruguay 175 C5 34 59 S 55 0W
Maldonado, Punta, Mexico 163 D5 16 19N 98 35W
Malè, Italy 44 B7 46 21N 10 55 E
Malé, Maldives 63 J11 4 0N 73 28 E
Malé Karpaty, Slovak Rep. 35 C10 48 30N 17 20 E
Maléa, Akra, Greece 48 E5 36 28N 23 7 E
Malebo, Pool, Africa 115 C3 4 17 S 15 20 E
Malegaon, India 94 D2 20 30N 74 38 E
Malei, Mozam. 119 F4 17 12 S 36 58 E
Malek, Sudan 107 F3 6 4N 31 36 E
Malek Kandī, Iran 101 D12 37 9N 46 6 E
Malela, Bas-Congo, Dem. Rep. of the Congo 115 D2 5 59 S 12 37 E
Malela, Maniema, Dem. Rep. of the Congo 118 C2 4 22 S 26 8 E
Malema, Mozam. 119 E4 14 57 S 37 20 E
Máleme, Greece 39 E4 35 31N 23 49 E
Malendok I., Papua N. G. 132 B7 3 28 S 153 13 E
Maleny, Australia 127 D5 26 45 S 152 52 E
Mālerås, Sweden 17 H9 56 54N 15 34 E
Malerkotla, India 92 D6 30 32N 75 58 E
Máles, Greece 39 E6 35 6N 25 35 E
Malesherbes, France 27 D9 48 15N 2 24 E
Maleshevska Planina, Europe 50 E7 41 38N 23 7 E
Malesína, Greece 48 C5 38 37N 23 14 E
Malestroit, France 26 E4 47 49N 2 25W
Malfa, Italy 47 D7 38 35N 14 50 E
Malgobek, Russia 61 J7 43 30N 44 34 E
Malgomaj, Sweden 14 D17 64 40N 16 30 E
Malgrat = Malgrat de Mar, Spain 40 D7 41 39N 2 46 E
Malgrat de Mar, Spain 40 D7 41 39N 2 46 E
Malha, Sudan 107 D2 15 8N 25 10 E
Malhada, Brazil 171 D3 14 21 S 43 47W
Malhargarh, India 92 G6 24 17N 74 59 E
Malheur →, U.S.A. 158 D5 44 4N 116 59W
Malheur L., U.S.A. 158 E4 43 20N 118 48W
Mali, Guinea 112 C2 12 10N 12 20W
Mali ■, Africa 112 B4 17 0N 3 0W
Mali →, Burma 90 C6 25 42N 97 30 E
Mali Kanal, Serbia, Yug. 52 E4 45 36N 19 24 E
Mali Kyun, Burma 86 F2 13 0N 98 20 E
Malibu, U.S.A. 161 L8 34 2N 118 41W
Maligaya = Gloria, Phil. 80 E3 12 59N 121 30 E
Maliku, Indonesia 82 B2 0 39 S 123 16 E
Malili, Indonesia 82 B2 2 42 S 121 6 E
Mälilla, Sweden 17 G9 57 23N 15 48 E
Malimba, Mts., Dem. Rep. of the Congo 118 D2 7 30 S 29 30 E
Malin Hd., Ireland 23 A4 55 23N 7 23W
Malin Pen., Ireland 23 A4 55 20N 7 17W
Malindang, Mt., Phil. 81 G4 8 13N 123 38 E
Malindi, Kenya 118 C5 3 12 S 40 5 E
Malines = Mechelen, Belgium 24 C4 51 2N 4 29 E
Malino, Indonesia 82 A2 1 0N 121 0 E
Malinyi, Tanzania 119 D4 8 56 S 36 0 E
Malipo, China 76 F5 23 7N 104 42 E
Maliq, Albania 50 F4 40 45N 20 48 E
Malita, Phil. 81 H5 6 19N 125 39 E
Maliwun, Burma 78 B1 10 17N 98 40 E
Maliya, India 92 H4 23 5N 70 46 E
Maljenik, Serbia, Yug. 50 C5 43 54N 21 43 E
Malka Mari Nat. Park, Kenya 118 B5 4 11N 40 46 E
Malkapur, India 94 D1 20 53N 73 58 E
Malkara, Turkey 51 F10 40 53N 26 53 E
Małkinia Górna, Poland 55 F9 52 42N 22 5 E
Malko Tŭrnovo, Bulgaria 51 E11 41 59N 27 31 E
Mallacoota, Australia 129 D8 37 40 S 149 40 E
Mallacoota Inlet, Australia 129 D8 37 34 S 149 40 E
Mallaig, U.K. 22 D3 57 0N 5 50W
Mallala, Australia 128 C3 34 26 S 138 30 E
Mallaoua, Niger 113 C6 13 2N 9 36 E
Mallard, U.S.A. 156 B2 42 56N 94 41W
Mallawan, India 93 F9 27 4N 80 12 E
Mallawi, Egypt 106 B3 27 44N 30 44 E
Mallee Cliffs Nat. Park, Australia 128 C5 34 16 S 142 32 E
Mallembe, Gabon 114 C2 3 34 S 10 53 E
Mallemort, France 29 E9 43 43N 5 11 E
Málles Venosta, Italy 44 B7 46 41N 10 32 E
Mállia, Greece 39 E6 35 17N 25 32 E
Mallicolo = Malakula, Vanuatu 133 E5 16 15 S 167 30 E
Mallión, Kólpos, Greece 39 E6 35 19N 25 27 E
Mallorca, Spain 38 B4 39 30N 3 0 E
Mallorytown, Canada 151 B9 44 29N 75 53W
Mallow, Ireland 23 D3 52 8N 8 39W
Malmbäck, Sweden 17 G8 57 34N 14 28 E
Malmberget, Sweden 14 C19 67 11N 20 40 E
Malmédy, Belgium 24 D6 50 25N 6 2 E
Malmesbury, S. Africa 116 E2 33 28 S 18 41 E
Malmköping, Sweden 16 E10 59 8N 16 44 E
Malmö, Sweden 17 J6 55 36N 12 59 E
Malmslätt, Sweden 17 F9 58 27N 15 33 E
Malmyzh, Russia 60 B10 56 31N 50 41 E
Malnaş, Romania 53 D10 46 2N 25 49 E
Malo, Vanuatu 133 E5 15 40 S 167 11 E
Malo Konare, Bulgaria 51 D8 42 12N 24 24 E
Maloarkhangelsk, Russia 59 F9 52 28N 36 30 E
Maloca, Brazil 169 C6 0 43N 55 57W
Maloja, Switz. 33 D9 46 25N 9 35 E
Malojapass, Switz. 33 D9 46 23N 9 42 E
Malolo, Fiji 133 A1 17 45 S 177 11 E
Malolos, Phil. 80 D3 14 50N 120 49 E
Malolotja Nature Reserve, Swaziland 117 D5 26 4 S 31 6 E
Malombe L., Malawi 119 E4 14 40 S 35 15 E
Małomice, Poland 55 G2 51 34N 15 29 E
Malomir, Bulgaria 51 D10 42 16N 26 32 E
Malone, Fla., U.S.A. 152 E4 30 57N 85 10W
Malone, N.Y., U.S.A. 151 B10 44 51N 74 18W
Malong, China 76 E4 25 24N 103 34 E
Malonga, Dem. Rep. of the Congo 115 E4 10 24 S 23 10 E
Malonno, Italy 33 D10 46 7N 10 18 E
Małopolskie ☐, Poland 55 J7 49 50N 20 20 E
Malorad, Bulgaria 50 C7 43 28N 23 41 E
Måløy, Norway 15 F11 61 57N 5 6 E
Maloyaroslovets, Russia 58 E9 55 2N 36 20 E
Malpartida, Spain 43 F4 39 26N 6 30W
Malpaso, Canary Is. 9 e1 27 43N 18 3W
Malpelo, I. de, Colombia 135 G19 4 3N 81 35W
Malpica de Bergantiños, Spain 42 B2 43 19N 8 50W
Malprabha →, India 95 F3 16 20N 76 5 E
Malpur, India 92 H5 23 21N 73 27 E
Malpura, India 92 F6 26 17N 75 23 E
Mals = Málles Venosta, Italy 44 B7 46 41N 10 32 E
Malsiras, India 94 F2 17 52N 74 55 E
Malta, Brazil 170 C4 6 54 S 37 31W
Malta, Idaho, U.S.A. 158 E7 42 18N 113 22W
Malta, Mont., U.S.A. 158 B10 48 21N 107 52W
Malta ■, Europe 38 F7 35 55N 14 26 E
Maltahöhe, Namibia 116 C2 24 55 S 17 0 E
Maltepe, Turkey 51 F13 40 55N 29 8 E
Malters, Switz. 32 B6 47 3N 8 11 E
Malton, Canada 150 C5 43 42N 79 38W
Malton, U.K. 20 C7 54 8N 0 49W
Malu'a, Solomon Is. 133 M11 8 20 S 160 38 E
Maluku, Dem. Rep. of the Congo 114 C3 4 3 S 15 34 E
Maluku, Indonesia 79 E7 1 0 S 127 0 E
Maluku ☐, Indonesia 82 B3 3 0 S 128 0 E
Maluku Sea = Molucca Sea, Indonesia 82 A3 0 0 125 0 E
Malumfashi, Nigeria 113 C6 11 48N 7 39 E
Malunda, Indonesia 82 B1 3 0 S 118 50 E
Malundo, Angola 115 E4 14 51 S 22 0 E
Malung, Sweden 16 D7 60 42N 13 44 E
Malungon, Phil. 81 H5 6 16N 125 14 E
Malungsfors, Sweden 16 D7 60 44N 13 33 E
Malur, India 95 H3 13 0N 77 55 E
Maluso, Phil. 81 H3 6 33N 121 53 E
Maluwe, Ghana 112 D4 8 40N 2 17W
Malvaglia, Switz. 33 D7 46 24N 8 59 E
Malvalli, India 95 H3 12 28N 77 8 E
Malvan, India 95 F1 16 2N 73 30 E
Malvern, U.S.A. 155 H8 34 22N 92 49W
Malvern Hills, U.K. 21 E5 52 0N 2 19W
Malvik, Norway 18 A7 63 25N 10 40 E
Malvinas, Is. = Falkland Is. ☐, Atl. Oc. 9 f 51 30 S 59 0W
Malý Dunaj →, Slovak Rep. 35 D11 47 45N 18 9 E
Malya, Tanzania 118 C3 3 5 S 33 38 E
Malybay, Kazakstan 65 B9 43 30N 78 25 E
Malyn, Ukraine 59 G5 50 46N 29 3 E
Malyy Lyakhovskiy, Ostrov, Russia 67 B15 74 7N 140 36 E
Mama, Russia 67 D12 58 18N 112 54 E
Mamadysh, Russia 60 C10 55 44N 51 23 E
Mamaku, N.Z. 130 E5 38 5 S 176 8 E
Mamala B., U.S.A. 145 K14 21 15N 157 55W
Mamanguape, Brazil 170 C4 6 50 S 35 4W
Mamanuca Group, Fiji 133 A1 17 35 S 177 5 E
Mamanutha Group, Fiji 133 A1 17 34 S 177 4 E
Mamarr Mitlā, Egypt 103 E1 30 2N 32 54 E
Mamasa, Indonesia 82 B1 2 55 S 119 20 E
Mambajao, Phil. 81 G5 9 15N 124 43 E
Mambasa, Dem. Rep. of the Congo 118 B2 1 22N 29 3 E
Mamberamo →, Indonesia 83 B5 2 0 S 137 50 E
Mambéré →, C.A.R. 114 B3 3 31N 16 3 E
Mambili →, Congo 114 B3 0 6N 16 5 E
Mambilima Falls, Zambia 119 E2 10 31 S 28 45 E
Mambirima, Dem. Rep. of the Congo 119 E2 11 25 S 27 33 E
Mambo, Tanzania 118 C4 4 52 S 38 22 E
Mambrui, Kenya 118 C5 3 5 S 40 5 E
Mamburao, Phil. 80 E3 13 13N 120 39 E
Mameigwess L., Canada 140 B2 52 35N 87 50W
Mamers, France 26 D7 48 21N 0 22 E
Mamfé, Cameroon 113 D6 5 50N 9 15 E
Māmī, Ra's, Yemen 99 D6 12 32N 54 30 E
Mamiña, Chile 172 E4 20 5 S 69 14W
Mammoth, U.S.A. 159 K8 32 43N 110 39W
Mammoth Cave Nat. Park, U.S.A. 148 G3 37 8N 86 13W
Mamoré →, Bolivia 173 C4 10 23 S 65 53W
Mamou, Guinea 112 C2 10 15N 12 0W
Mamoudzou, Mayotte 105 H8 12 48 S 45 14 E
Mampatá, Guinea-Biss. 112 C2 11 54N 14 53W
Mampikony, Madag. 117 B8 16 6 S 47 38 E
Mampoko, Dem. Rep. of the Congo 114 B3 0 51N 18 42 E
Mampong, Ghana 113 D4 7 6N 1 26W
Mamry, Jezioro, Poland 54 D8 54 5N 21 50 E
Mamuil Malal, Paso, S. Amer. 176 A2 39 35 S 71 28W
Mamuju, Indonesia 82 B1 2 41 S 118 50 E
Ma'mūl, Oman 99 C6 18 8N 55 16 E
Mamuno, Botswana 116 C3 22 16 S 20 1 E
Mamuras, Albania 50 E3 41 34N 19 41 E
Man, Ivory C. 112 D3 7 30N 7 40W
Man →, India 94 F2 17 31N 75 32 E
Man, I. of, India 95 K11 8 28N 93 36 E
Man, I. of, U.K. 20 C3 54 15N 4 30W
Man-Bazar, India 93 H12 23 4N 86 39 E
Mān Kat, Burma 90 D7 22 5N 98 1 E
Man Na, Burma 90 D6 23 27N 97 19 E
Man Tun, Burma 90 D7 23 52N 98 38 E
Mana, Fr. Guiana 169 B7 5 45N 53 55W
Mana, U.S.A. 145 A2 22 2N 159 47W
Mana →, Fr. Guiana 169 B7 5 45N 53 55W
Mana Pools Nat. Park, Zimbabwe 119 F2 15 56 S 29 25 E
Manaar, G. of = Mannar, G. of, Asia 95 K4 8 30N 79 0 E
Manabí ☐, Ecuador 168 D1 0 40 S 80 5W
Manacacías →, Colombia 168 C3 4 23N 72 4W
Manacapuru, Brazil 169 D5 3 16 S 60 37W
Manacapuru →, Brazil 169 D5 3 18 S 60 37W
Manacor, Spain 38 B4 39 34N 3 13 E
Manadas, Azores 9 d1 38 38N 28 6W
Manado, Indonesia 82 A2 1 29N 124 51 E
Managua, Nic. 164 D2 12 6N 86 20W
Managua, L. de, Nic. 164 D2 12 20N 86 30W
Manaia, N.Z. 130 F3 39 33 S 174 8 E
Manakara, Madag. 117 C8 22 8 S 48 1 E
Manakau, N.Z. 131 C8 42 15 S 173 42 E
Manākhah, Yemen 98 D3 15 5N 43 44 E
Manali, India 92 C7 32 16N 77 10 E
Manam I., Papua N. G. 132 C3 4 5 S 145 0 E
Manama = Al Manāmah, Bahrain 97 E6 26 10N 50 30 E
Manambao →, Madag. 117 B7 17 35 S 44 0 E
Manambato, Madag. 117 A8 13 43 S 49 7 E
Manambolo →, Madag. 117 B7 19 18 S 44 22 E
Manambolosy, Madag. 117 B8 16 2 S 49 40 E
Mánamo, Caño →, Venezuela 169 B5 9 55N 62 16W
Manana I., U.S.A. 145 K14 21 20N 157 40W
Mananara, Madag. 117 B8 16 10 S 49 46 E
Mananara →, Madag. 117 C8 23 21 S 47 42 E
Mananara, Réserve Naturelle Intégrale de, Madag. 117 B8 16 14 S 49 45 E
Manangatang, Australia 128 C5 35 5 S 142 54 E
Mananjary, Madag. 117 C8 21 13 S 48 20 E
Manankoro, Mali 112 C3 10 28N 7 25W
Manantavadi, India 95 J3 11 49N 76 1 E
Manantenina, Madag. 117 C8 24 17 S 47 19 E
Manaos = Manaus, Brazil 169 D6 3 0 S 60 0W
Manapala, Phil. 81 F4 10 58N 123 5 E
Manapire →, Venezuela 168 B4 7 42N 66 7W
Manapouri, N.Z. 131 F2 45 34 S 167 39 E
Manapouri, L., N.Z. 131 F2 45 32 S 167 32 E
Manapparai, India 95 J4 10 36N 78 25 E
Manaqil, Sudan 107 E3 14 15N 32 59 E
Manar →, India 94 E3 18 50N 77 20 E
Manār, Jabal, Yemen 98 D4 14 2N 44 17 E
Manaravolo, Madag. 117 C8 23 59 S 45 39 E

246 Manas

Manas, *China* **68 B3** 44 17N 85 56 E
Manas, *Somali Rep.* **120 D2** 2 57N 43 28 E
Manas ➝, *India* **90 B3** 26 12N 90 40 E
Manas, Gora, *Kyrgyzstan* **65 B5** 42 22N 71 2 E
Manaslu, *Nepal* **93 E11** 28 33N 84 33 E
Manasquan, *U.S.A.* **151 F10** 40 8N 74 3W
Manassa, *U.S.A.* **159 H11** 37 11N 105 56W
Manatí, *Puerto Rico* **165 d** 18 26N 66 29W
Manati B., *St. Helena* **9 h** 16 0S 5 46W
Manatuto, *E. Timor* **82 C3** 8 30 S 126 1 E
Manau, *Papua N. G.* **132 E4** 8 4 S 148 0 E
Manaung, *Burma* **90 F4** 18 45N 93 40 E
Manaus, *Brazil* **169 D6** 3 0S 60 0W
Manavgat, *Turkey* **100 D4** 36 47N 31 26 E
Manawan L., *Canada* **143 B8** 55 24N 103 14W
Manawatu ➝, *N.Z.* **130 G4** 40 28 S 175 12 E
Manawatu-Wanganui □, *N.Z.* **130 F4** 39 50 S 175 30 E
Manay, *Phil.* **81 H6** 7 17N 126 33 E
Manbij, *Syria* **100 D7** 36 31N 37 57 E
Mancha Real, *Spain* **43 H7** 37 48N 3 39W
Manche □, *France* **26 C5** 49 10N 1 20W
Manchegorsk, *Russia* **66 C4** 67 54N 32 58 E
Manchester, *U.K.* **20 D5** 53 29N 2 12W
Manchester, *Calif., U.S.A.* **160 G3** 38 58N 123 41W
Manchester, *Conn., U.S.A.* **151 E12** 41 47N 72 31W
Manchester, *Ga., U.S.A.* **152 C5** 32 51N 84 37W
Manchester, *Iowa, U.S.A.* **156 B5** 42 29N 91 27W
Manchester, *Ky., U.S.A.* **148 G4** 37 9N 83 46W
Manchester, *Mich., U.S.A.* **157 B12** 42 9N 84 2W
Manchester, *N.H., U.S.A.* **151 D13** 42 59N 71 28W
Manchester, *N.Y., U.S.A.* **150 D7** 42 56N 77 16W
Manchester, *Ohio, U.S.A.* **157 F13** 38 41N 83 36W
Manchester, *Pa., U.S.A.* **151 F8** 40 4N 76 43W
Manchester, *Tenn., U.S.A.* **149 H2** 35 29N 86 5W
Manchester, *Vt., U.S.A.* **151 C11** 43 10N 73 5W
Manchester L., *Canada* **143 A7** 61 28N 107 29W
Manchhar L., *Pakistan* **92 F2** 26 25N 67 39 E
Manchuria = Dongbei, *China* **75 D13** 45 0N 125 0 E
Manchurian Plain, *China* **62 E16** 47 0N 124 0 E
Manciano, *Italy* **45 F8** 42 35N 11 31 E
Mancifa, *Ethiopia* **107 F5** 6 53N 41 50 E
Mancora, *Peru* **172 A1** 4 9S 81 1W
Mand ➝, *India* **93 J10** 21 42N 83 15 E
Mand ➝, *Iran* **97 D7** 28 20N 52 30 E
Manda, *Ludewe, Tanzania* **119 E3** 10 30 S 34 40 E
Manda, *Mbeya, Tanzania* **118 D3** 7 58 S 32 29 E
Manda, *Mbeya, Tanzania* **119 D3** 8 30 S 32 49 E
Manda, Parc Nat. de, *Chad* **109 G3** 9 45N 17 52 E
Mandabé, *Madag.* **117 C7** 21 0S 44 55 E
Mandaguari, *Brazil* **175 A5** 23 32 S 51 42W
Mandah = Töhöm, *Mongolia* **74 B5** 44 27N 108 2 E
Mandal, *Norway* **15 G12** 58 2N 7 25 E
Mandala, Puncak, *Indonesia* **83 B6** 4 44 S 140 20 E
Mandalay, *Burma* **90 D6** 22 0N 96 4 E
Mandalay □, *Burma* **90 E5** 22 0N 96 5 E
Mandale = Mandalay, *Burma* **90 D6** 22 0N 96 4 E
Mandalgarh, *India* **92 G6** 25 12N 75 6 E
Mandalgovi, *Mongolia* **74 B4** 45 45N 106 10 E
Mandali, *Iraq* **101 F11** 33 43N 45 28 E
Mandan, *U.S.A.* **154 B4** 46 50N 100 54W
Mandaon, *Phil.* **80 E4** 12 13N 123 17 E
Mandar, Teluk, *Indonesia* **82 B1** 3 35 S 119 15 E
Mandara Mts., *Nigeria* **109 F2** 10 40N 13 40 E
Mándas, *Italy* **46 C2** 39 40N 9 8 E
Mandaue, *Phil.* **81 F4** 10 20N 123 56 E
Mandelieu-la-Napoule, *France* **29 E10** 43 34N 6 57 E
Mandera, *Kenya* **118 B5** 3 55N 41 53 E
Mandeville, *Jamaica* **164 a** 18 2N 77 31W
Mandi, *India* **92 D7** 31 39N 76 58 E
Mandi Dabwali, *India* **92 E6** 29 58N 74 42 E
Mandiana, *Guinea* **112 C3** 10 37N 8 39W
Mandimba, *Mozam.* **119 E4** 14 20 S 35 40 E
Mandioli, *Indonesia* **82 B3** 0 40 S 127 20 E
Mandioré, L., *S. Amer.* **173 D6** 18 8 S 57 33W
Mandla, *India* **93 H9** 22 39N 80 30 E
Mandø, *Denmark* **17 J2** 55 18N 8 33 E
Mandorah, *Australia* **124 B5** 12 32 S 130 42 E
Mandoto, *Madag.* **117 B8** 19 34 S 46 17 E
Mandoúdhion, *Greece* **48 C5** 38 48N 23 29 E
Mándra, *Greece* **48 C5** 38 4N 23 30 E
Mandra, *Pakistan* **92 C5** 33 23N 73 12 E
Mandrákhi, *Greece* **49 E9** 36 36N 27 11 E
Mandrare ➝, *Madag.* **117 D8** 25 10 S 46 30 E
Mandritsara, *Madag.* **117 B8** 15 50 S 48 49 E
Mandronarivo, *Madag.* **117 C8** 21 7 S 45 38 E
Mandsaur, *India* **92 G6** 24 3N 75 8 E
Mandurah, *Australia* **125 F2** 32 36 S 115 48 E
Mandúria, *Italy* **47 B10** 40 24N 17 38 E
Mandvi, *India* **92 H3** 22 51N 69 22 E
Mandya, *India* **95 H3** 12 30N 77 0 E
Mandzai, *Pakistan* **92 D2** 30 55N 67 6 E
Mané, *Burkina Faso* **113 C4** 12 59N 1 21W
Maneh, *Iran* **97 B8** 37 39N 57 7 E
Manengouba, Mts., *Cameroon* **113 E6** 5 0N 9 50 E
Maner ➝, *India* **94 E4** 18 30N 79 40 E
Manera, *Madag.* **117 C7** 22 55 S 44 20 E
Manérbio, *Italy* **44 C7** 45 21N 10 8 E
Maneroo Cr. ➝, *Australia* **126 C3** 23 21 S 143 53 E
Manfalût, *Egypt* **106 B3** 27 20N 30 52 E
Manfred, *Australia* **128 B5** 33 19 S 143 45 E
Manfredónia, *Italy* **45 G12** 41 38N 15 55 E
Manfredónia, G. di, *Italy* **45 G13** 41 35N 16 5 E
Manga, *Brazil* **171 D3** 14 46 S 43 56W
Manga, *Burkina Faso* **113 C4** 11 40N 1 4W
Manga, *Congo* **114 C3** 0 13 S 16 5 E
Manga, *Niger* **113 C7** 15 0N 14 0 E
Mangabeiras, Chapada das, *Brazil* **170 D2** 10 0S 46 30W
Mangai, *Dem. Rep. of the Congo* **115 C3** 4 2S 19 33 E
Mangakino, *N.Z.* **130 E4** 38 22 S 175 47 E
Mangal, *Phil.* **81 H3** 6 25N 121 58 E
Mangalagiri, *India* **95 F5** 16 26N 80 36 E
Mangaldai, *India* **90 B4** 26 26N 92 2 E
Mangaldan, *Phil.* **80 C3** 16 4N 120 24 E
Mangalia, *Romania* **53 G13** 43 50N 28 35 E
Mangalmé, *Chad* **109 F3** 12 26N 19 37 E
Mangalore, *India* **95 H2** 12 55N 74 47 E
Mangalvedha, *India* **94 F2** 17 31N 75 28 E
Mangan, *India* **90 B2** 27 31N 88 32 E
Mangaon, *India* **94 E1** 18 15N 73 20 E
Mangawan, *India* **93 G9** 24 41N 81 33 E
Mangaweka, *N.Z.* **130 F4** 39 48 S 175 47 E
Mangaweka, Mt., *N.Z.* **130 F5** 39 49 S 176 5 E
Mange, *Dem. Rep. of the Congo* **114 B4** 0 54N 20 30 E
Manger, *Norway* **18 D2** 60 38N 5 3 E
Manggar, *Indonesia* **85 C3** 2 50 S 108 10 E
Manggawitu, *Indonesia* **83 B4** 4 8 S 133 32 E
Manggis, *Indonesia* **79 J18** 8 29 S 115 31 E
Mangin Taungdan, *Burma* **90 C5** 24 15N 95 45 E
Mangindrano, *Madag.* **117 A8** 14 17 S 48 58 E
Mangkalihat, Tanjung, *Indonesia* **85 B5** 1 2N 118 59 E
Mangla, *Pakistan* **92 C5** 33 7N 73 39 E
Mangla Dam, *Pakistan* **93 C5** 33 9N 73 44 E
Manglares, C., *Colombia* **168 C2** 1 36N 79 2W
Manglaur, *India* **92 E7** 29 44N 77 49 E
Mangnai, *China* **68 C4** 37 52N 91 43 E
Mango, *Togo* **113 C5** 10 20N 0 30 E
Mango, *Tonga* **133 Q14** 20 17 S 173 25W
Mangoche, *Malawi* **119 E4** 14 25 S 35 16 E
Mangoky ➝, *Madag.* **117 C7** 21 29 S 43 41 E
Mangole, *Indonesia* **82 B3** 1 50 S 125 55 E
Mangombe, *Dem. Rep. of the Congo* **118 C2** 1 20 S 26 48 E
Mangonui, *N.Z.* **130 B2** 35 1 S 173 32 E
Mangoro ➝, *Madag.* **117 B8** 20 0S 48 45 E
Mangrol, *Mad. P., India* **92 J4** 21 7N 70 7 E
Mangrol, *Raj., India* **92 G6** 25 20N 76 31 E
Mangrul Pir, *India* **94 D3** 20 19N 77 21 E
Mangualde, *Portugal* **42 E3** 40 38N 7 48W
Mangueigne, *Chad* **109 F4** 10 30N 21 15 E
Mangueira, L. da, *Brazil* **175 C5** 33 0S 52 50W
Manguéni, Hamada, *Niger* **108 D2** 22 35N 12 40 E
Mangum, *U.S.A.* **155 H5** 34 53N 99 30W
Mangungu, *Dem. Rep. of the Congo* **115 D3** 5 16 S 19 36 E
Mangyshlak Poluostrov, *Kazakstan* **66 E6** 44 30N 52 30 E
Manhattan, *U.S.A.* **154 F6** 39 11N 96 35W
Manhatten, *U.S.A.* **157 C9** 41 26N 87 59W
Manhiça, *Mozam.* **117 D5** 25 23 S 32 49 E
Manhuaçu, *Brazil* **171 F3** 20 15 S 42 2W
Manhumirim, *Brazil* **171 F3** 20 22 S 41 57W
Maní, *Colombia* **168 C3** 4 49N 72 17W
Mania ➝, *Madag.* **117 B8** 19 42 S 45 22 E
Maniago, *Italy* **45 B9** 46 10N 12 43 E
Manica, *Mozam.* **117 B5** 18 58 S 32 59 E
Manica □, *Mozam.* **117 B5** 19 10 S 33 45 E
Manicaland □, *Zimbabwe* **117 B5** 19 0S 32 30 E
Manicoré, *Brazil* **173 B5** 5 48 S 61 16W
Manicoré ➝, *Brazil* **173 B5** 5 51 S 61 19W
Manicouagan ➝, *Canada* **141 C6** 49 30N 68 30W
Manicouagan, Rés., *Canada* **141 B6** 51 5N 68 40W
Maniema □, *Dem. Rep. of the Congo* **118 C2** 3 0S 26 0 E
Manīfah, *Si. Arabia* **97 E6** 27 44N 49 0 E
Manifold, C., *Australia* **126 C5** 22 41 S 150 50 E
Maniganggo, *China* **76 B2** 31 56N 99 10 E
Manigotagan, *Canada* **143 C9** 51 6N 96 18W
Manigotagan ➝, *Canada* **143 C9** 51 7N 96 20W
Manihari, *India* **93 G12** 25 21N 87 38 E
Manihiki, *Cook Is.* **135 J11** 10 24 S 161 1W
Maniitsoq, *Greenland* **10 D5** 65 26N 52 55W
Manika, Plateau de la, *Dem. Rep. of the Congo* **119 E2** 10 0S 25 5 E
Manikchhari, *Bangla.* **90 D3** 22 51N 91 50 E
Manikganj, *Bangla.* **90 D3** 23 52N 90 0 E
Manikpur, *India* **93 G9** 25 4N 81 7 E
Manila, *Phil.* **80 D3** 14 40N 121 3 E
Manila, *U.S.A.* **158 F9** 40 59N 109 43W
Manila B., *Phil.* **80 D3** 14 40N 120 35 E
Manildra, *Australia* **129 B8** 33 11 S 148 41 E
Manilla, *Australia* **129 A9** 30 45 S 150 43 E
Manimpé, *Mali* **112 C3** 14 11N 5 28W
Maningrida, *Australia* **126 A1** 12 3 S 134 13 E
Maninian, *Ivory C.* **112 C3** 10 3N 7 52W
Maninjau, Danau, *Indonesia* **82 B3** 3 17 S 127 35 E
Manipur □, *India* **90 C4** 25 0N 94 0 E
Manipur ➝, *Burma* **90 D5** 23 45N 94 20 E
Manisa, *Turkey* **49 C9** 38 38N 27 30 E
Manisa □, *Turkey* **49 C9** 38 40N 28 0 E
Manistee, *U.S.A.* **148 C2** 44 15N 86 19W
Manistee ➝, *U.S.A.* **148 C2** 44 15N 86 21W
Manistique, *U.S.A.* **148 C2** 45 57N 86 15W
Manito, *U.S.A.* **156 D7** 40 26N 89 47W
Manito L., *Canada* **143 C7** 52 43N 109 43W
Manitoba □, *Canada* **143 B9** 55 30N 97 0W
Manitoba, L., *Canada* **143 C9** 51 0N 98 45W
Manitou, *Canada* **143 D9** 49 15N 98 32W
Manitou, L., *Canada* **141 B6** 50 55N 65 17W
Manitou Beach, *U.S.A.* **157 C12** 41 58N 84 19W
Manitou Is., *U.S.A.* **148 C3** 45 8N 86 0W
Manitou Springs, *U.S.A.* **154 F2** 38 52N 104 55W
Manitoulin I., *Canada* **140 C3** 45 40N 82 30W
Manitouwadge, *Canada* **140 C2** 49 8N 85 48W
Manitowoc, *U.S.A.* **148 C2** 44 5N 87 40W
Manitsauá-Missu ➝, *Brazil* **173 C7** 10 58 S 53 20W
Maniyachi, *India* **95 K3** 8 51N 77 55 E
Manizales, *Colombia* **168 B2** 5 5N 75 32W
Manja, *Madag.* **117 C7** 21 26 S 44 20 E
Manjacaze, *Mozam.* **117 C5** 24 45 S 34 0 E
Manjakandriana, *Madag.* **117 B8** 18 55 S 47 47 E
Manjeri, *India* **95 J3** 11 7N 76 11 E
Manjhand, *Pakistan* **91 D3** 25 50N 68 10 E
Manjil, *Iran* **97 B6** 36 46N 49 30 E
Manjimup, *Australia* **125 F2** 34 15 S 116 6 E
Manjlegaon, *India* **94 E3** 19 9N 76 14 E
Manjra ➝, *India* **94 E3** 18 49N 77 52 E
Mankato, *Kans., U.S.A.* **154 F5** 39 47N 98 13W
Mankato, *Minn., U.S.A.* **154 C8** 44 10N 94 0W
Mankayan, *Phil.* **80 C3** 16 52N 120 47 E
Mankayane, *Swaziland* **117 D5** 26 40 S 31 4 E
Mankera, *Pakistan* **92 D4** 31 23N 71 26 E
Mankim, *Cameroon* **113 D7** 5 6N 12 3 E
Mankono, *Ivory C.* **112 D3** 8 1N 6 10W
Mankota, *Canada* **143 D7** 49 25N 107 5W
Mankulam, *Sri Lanka* **95 K5** 9 8N 80 26 E
Manlay = Üydzin, *Mongolia* **74 B4** 44 9N 107 0 E
Manley Hot Springs, *U.S.A.* **144 D10** 65 0N 150 38W
Manlleu, *Spain* **40 C7** 42 2N 2 17 E
Manly, *Australia* **129 B9** 33 48 S 151 17 E
Manmad, *India* **94 D2** 20 18N 74 28 E
Mann Ranges, *Australia* **125 E5** 26 6 S 130 5 E
Manna, *Indonesia* **84 C2** 4 25 S 102 55 E
Mannahill, *Australia* **128 B4** 32 25 S 140 0 E
Mannar, *Sri Lanka* **95 K4** 9 1N 79 54 E
Mannar, G. of, *Asia* **95 K4** 8 30N 79 0 E
Mannar I., *Sri Lanka* **95 K4** 9 5N 79 45 E
Mannargudi, *India* **95 J4** 10 45N 79 51 E
Männedorf, *Switz.* **33 B7** 47 15N 8 43 E
Mannheim, *Germany* **31 F4** 49 29N 8 29 E
Manning, *Canada* **142 B5** 56 53N 117 39W
Manning, *Oreg., U.S.A.* **160 E3** 45 45N 123 13W
Manning, *S.C., U.S.A.* **152 B9** 33 42N 80 13W
Manning ➝, *Australia* **129 A10** 31 52 S 152 43 E
Manning Prov. Park, *Canada* **142 D4** 49 5N 120 45W
Manning Str., *Solomon Is.* **133 L10** 7 30 S 158 0 E
Mannu ➝, *Italy* **46 C2** 39 16N 9 0 E
Mannu, C., *Italy* **46 B1** 40 3N 8 21 E
Mannum, *Australia* **128 C3** 34 50 S 139 20 E
Mano, *S. Leone* **112 D2** 8 3N 12 2W
Mano ➝, *Liberia* **112 D2** 6 56N 11 30W
Mano River, *Liberia* **112 D2** 7 20N 11 6W
Manoa, *Bolivia* **173 B4** 9 40 S 65 27W
Manoharpur, *India* **93 H11** 22 23N 85 12 E
Manokotak, *U.S.A.* **144 G8** 58 58N 159 3W
Manokwari, *Indonesia* **83 B4** 0 54 S 134 0 E
Manolás, *Greece* **48 C3** 38 4N 21 21 E
Manolo Fortich, *Phil.* **81 G5** 8 28N 124 50 E
Manombo, *Madag.* **117 C7** 22 57 S 43 28 E
Manono, *Dem. Rep. of the Congo* **118 D2** 7 15 S 27 25 E
Manono, *Samoa* **133 W23** 13 50 S 172 5W
Manoppello, *Italy* **45 F11** 42 15N 14 3 E
Manosque, *France* **29 E9** 43 49N 5 47 E
Manotick, *Canada* **151 A9** 45 13N 75 41W
Manouane ➝, *Canada* **141 C5** 49 30N 71 10W
Manouane, L., *Canada* **141 B5** 50 45N 70 45W
Manovo-Gounda Saint Floris, Parc Nat. du, *C.A.R.* **114 A4** 9 30N 21 25 E
Manp'o, *N. Korea* **75 D14** 41 6N 126 24 E
Manpojin = Manp'o, *N. Korea* **75 D14** 41 6N 126 24 E
Manpur, *Chhattisgarh, India* **93 H10** 23 17N 83 35 E
Manpur, *Chhattisgarh, India* **94 D5** 20 22N 80 43 E
Manpur, *Mad. P., India* **92 H6** 22 26N 75 37 E
Manresa, *Spain* **40 D6** 41 48N 1 50 E
Mansa, *Gujarat, India* **92 H5** 23 27N 72 45 E
Mansa, *Punjab, India* **92 E6** 30 0N 75 27 E
Mansa, *Zambia* **119 E2** 11 13 S 28 55 E
Mansalay, *Phil.* **80 E3** 12 31N 121 26 E
Månsåsen, *Sweden* **16 A8** 63 5N 14 18 E
Mansehra, *Pakistan* **92 B5** 34 20N 73 15 E
Mansel I., *Canada* **139 B11** 62 0N 80 0W
Mansfield, *Australia* **129 D7** 37 4 S 146 6 E
Mansfield, *U.K.* **20 D6** 53 9N 1 11W
Mansfield, *Ga., U.S.A.* **152 B6** 33 31N 83 44W
Mansfield, *La., U.S.A.* **155 J8** 32 2N 93 43W
Mansfield, *Mass., U.S.A.* **151 D13** 42 2N 71 13W
Mansfield, *Ohio, U.S.A.* **150 F2** 40 45N 82 31W
Mansfield, *Pa., U.S.A.* **150 E7** 41 48N 77 5W
Mansfield, Mt., *U.S.A.* **151 B12** 44 33N 72 49W
Mansi, *Burma* **90 C5** 24 48N 95 52 E
Mansidão, *Brazil* **170 D3** 10 43 S 44 2W
Mansilla de las Mulas, *Spain* **42 C5** 42 30N 5 25W
Mansle, *France* **28 C4** 45 52N 0 12 E
Manso ➝, *Brazil* **171 D2** 13 50 S 47 0W
Mansoa, *Guinea-Biss.* **112 C1** 12 0N 15 20W
Manson, *U.S.A.* **156 B2** 42 32N 94 32W
Manson Creek, *Canada* **142 B4** 55 37N 124 32W
Mansoura, *Algeria* **111 A5** 36 1N 4 31 E
Manta, *Ecuador* **168 D1** 1 0S 80 40W
Manta, B. de, *Ecuador* **168 D1** 0 54 S 80 44W
Mantadia, Parc Nat. de, *Madag.* **117 B8** 18 54 S 48 21 E
Mantalingajan, Mt., *Phil.* **81 G1** 8 55N 117 45 E
Mantantale, *Dem. Rep. of the Congo* **114 C4** 2 10 S 20 11 E
Mantare, *Tanzania* **118 C3** 2 42 S 33 13 E
Mantaro ➝, *Peru* **172 C3** 12 16 S 73 57W
Manteca, *U.S.A.* **160 H5** 37 48N 121 13W
Mantecal, *Venezuela* **168 B4** 7 34N 69 17W
Mantena, *Brazil* **171 E3** 18 47 S 40 59W
Manteno, *U.S.A.* **157 C9** 41 15N 87 50W
Manteo, *U.S.A.* **149 H8** 35 55N 75 40W
Mantes-la-Jolie, *France* **27 D8** 48 58N 1 41 E
Mantha, *India* **94 E3** 19 40N 76 23 E
Manthani, *India* **94 E4** 18 40N 79 35 E
Manti, *U.S.A.* **158 G8** 39 16N 111 38W
Mantiqueira, Serra da, *Brazil* **171 F3** 22 0S 44 0W
Manton, *U.S.A.* **148 C3** 44 25N 85 24W
Mantorp, *Sweden* **17 F9** 58 21N 15 20 E
Mántova, *Italy* **44 C7** 45 9N 10 48 E
Mänttä, *Finland* **15 E21** 62 0N 24 40 E
Mantua = Mántova, *Italy* **44 C7** 45 9N 10 48 E
Mantung, *Australia* **128 C4** 34 35 S 140 3 E
Manturovo, *Russia* **60 A7** 58 23N 44 45 E
Manu, *Peru* **172 C3** 12 10 S 70 51W
Manu ➝, *Peru* **172 C3** 12 16 S 70 55W
Manu'a Is., *Amer. Samoa* **133 X25** 14 13 S 169 35W
Manuel Alves ➝, *Brazil* **171 D2** 11 19 S 48 28W
Manuel Alves Grande ➝, *Brazil* **170 C2** 7 27 S 47 35W
Manuel Urbano, *Brazil* **172 B4** 8 53 S 69 18W
Manui, *Indonesia* **82 B2** 3 35 S 123 5 E
Manukan, *Phil.* **81 G4** 8 32N 123 12 E
Manukau, *N.Z.* **130 D3** 37 0S 174 52 E
Manukau Harbour, *N.Z.* **130 D3** 37 3 S 174 45 E
Manunui, *N.Z.* **130 E4** 38 54 S 175 21 E
Manuoha, *N.Z.* **130 E6** 38 39 S 177 7 E
Manuripi ➝, *Bolivia* **172 C4** 11 6S 67 36W
Manus □, *Papua N. G.* **132 B4** 2 0S 147 0 E
Manus I., *Papua N. G.* **132 B4** 2 0S 147 0 E
Manvi, *India* **95 G3** 15 57N 76 59 E
Manwath, *India* **94 E3** 19 19N 76 32 E
Many, *U.S.A.* **155 K8** 31 34N 93 29W
Manyara, L., *Tanzania* **118 C4** 3 40 S 35 50 E
Manyas, *Turkey* **51 F11** 40 2N 27 59 E
Manych ➝, *Russia* **61 G5** 47 13N 40 40 E
Manych-Gudilo, Ozero, *Russia* **61 G6** 46 24N 42 38 E
Manyonga ➝, *Tanzania* **118 C3** 4 10 S 34 15 E
Manyoni, *Tanzania* **118 D3** 5 45 S 34 55 E
Manzai, *Pakistan* **92 C4** 32 12N 70 15 E
Manzala, Bahra el, *Egypt* **106 H7** 31 10N 31 56 E
Manzanares, *Spain* **43 F7** 39 2N 3 22W
Manzaneda, *Spain* **42 C3** 42 12N 7 15W
Manzanillo, *Cuba* **164 B4** 20 20N 77 31W
Manzanillo, *Mexico* **162 D4** 19 0N 104 20W
Manzanillo, Pta., *Panama* **164 E4** 9 30N 79 40W
Manzano Mts., *U.S.A.* **159 J10** 34 40N 106 20W
Manzarīyeh, *Iran* **97 C6** 34 53N 50 50 E
Manzhouli, *China* **69 B6** 49 35N 117 25 E
Manzini, *Swaziland* **117 D5** 26 30 S 31 25 E
Mao, *Chad* **109 F3** 14 4N 15 19 E
Maó, *Spain* **38 B5** 39 53N 4 16 E
Maoke, Pegunungan, *Indonesia* **83 B5** 3 40 S 137 30 E
Maolin, *China* **75 C12** 43 58N 123 30 E
Maoming, *China* **77 G8** 21 50N 110 54 E
Maopi T'ou, *China* **77 G13** 21 56N 120 43 E
Maouri, Dallol ➝, *Niger* **113 C5** 12 5N 3 30 E
Maoxian, *China* **76 B4** 31 41N 103 49 E
Maoxing, *China* **75 B13** 45 28N 124 40 E
Mapalma, *Dem. Rep. of the Congo* **114 B4** 2 3N 24 30 E
Mapam Yumco, *China* **68 C3** 30 45N 81 28 E
Mapastepec, *Mexico* **163 D6** 15 26N 92 54W
Mapfongui, *Gabon* **114 C2** 1 15 S 12 59 E
Maphrao, Ko, *Thailand* **87 a** 7 56N 98 26 E
Mapi ➝, *Indonesia* **83 C5** 6 55 S 139 14 E
Mapia, Kepulauan, *Indonesia* **83 A4** 0 50N 134 20 E
Mapimí, *Mexico* **162 B4** 25 50N 103 50W
Mapimí, Bolsón de, *Mexico* **162 B4** 27 30N 104 15W
Maping, *China* **77 B9** 31 34N 113 32 E
Mapinga, *Tanzania* **118 D4** 6 40 S 39 12 E
Mapinhane, *Mozam.* **117 C6** 22 20 S 35 0 E
Mapire, *Venezuela* **169 B5** 7 45N 64 42W
Maple ➝, *U.S.A.* **157 B12** 42 59N 84 57W
Maple Creek, *Canada* **143 D7** 49 55N 109 29W
Maple Valley, *U.S.A.* **160 C4** 47 25N 122 3W
Mapleton, *U.S.A.* **158 D2** 44 2N 123 52W
Mapourika, L., *N.Z.* **131 D5** 43 16 S 170 12 E
Maprik, *Papua N. G.* **132 B2** 3 44 S 143 3 E
Mapuca, *India* **95 G1** 15 36N 73 46 E
Mapuera ➝, *Brazil* **169 D6** 1 5S 57 2W
Mapulanguene, *Mozam.* **117 C5** 24 29 S 32 6 E
Maputo, *Mozam.* **117 D5** 25 58 S 32 32 E
Maputo □, *Mozam.* **117 D5** 26 0S 32 25 E
Maputo, B. de, *Mozam.* **117 D5** 25 50 S 32 45 E
Maqiaohe, *China* **75 B16** 44 40N 130 30 E
Maqnā, *Si. Arabia* **96 D2** 28 25N 34 50 E
Maqran, W. ➝, *Si. Arabia* **96 B4** 20 55N 47 12 E
Maqteïr, *Mauritania* **110 D2** 21 50N 11 40W
Maqueda, *Spain* **42 E6** 40 4N 4 22W
Maqueda Channel, *Phil.* **80 E5** 13 42N 124 1 E
Maquela do Zombo, *Angola* **115 D3** 6 0S 15 15 E
Maquinchao, *Argentina* **176 B3** 41 15 S 68 50W
Maquoketa, *U.S.A.* **156 B6** 42 4N 90 40W
Mar, Serra do, *Brazil* **175 B6** 25 30 S 49 0W
Mar Chiquita, L., *Argentina* **174 C3** 30 40 S 62 50W
Mar del Plata, *Argentina* **174 D4** 38 0S 57 30W
Mar Menor, *Spain* **41 H4** 37 40N 0 45W
Mara, *Guyana* **169 B6** 6 0N 57 36W
Mara, *India* **90 A5** 28 11N 94 14 E
Mara, *Tanzania* **118 C3** 1 30 S 34 32 E
Mara □, *Tanzania* **118 C3** 1 45 S 34 20 E
Maraã, *Brazil* **168 D4** 1 52 S 65 25W
Marabá, *Brazil* **170 C2** 5 20 S 49 5W
Maracá, I. de, *Brazil* **169 C7** 2 10N 50 30W
Maracaibo, *Venezuela* **168 A3** 10 40N 71 37W
Maracaibo, L. de, *Venezuela* **168 B3** 9 40N 71 30W
Maracaju, *Brazil* **175 A4** 21 38 S 55 9W
Maracajú, Serra de, *Brazil* **173 E6** 23 57 S 55 1W
Maracanã, *Brazil* **170 B2** 0 46 S 47 27W
Maracás, *Brazil* **171 D3** 13 26 S 40 18W
Maracas Bay Village, *Trin. & Tob.* **169 F9** 10 46N 61 28W
Maracay, *Venezuela* **168 A4** 10 15N 67 28W
Maracena, *Spain* **43 H7** 37 12N 3 38W
Marādah, *Libya* **108 C3** 29 15N 19 15 E
Maradi, *Niger* **113 C6** 13 29N 7 20 E
Maraetiria, Pte., *Tahiti* **133 S16** 17 51 S 149 10W
Marāgheh, *Iran* **101 D12** 37 30N 46 12 E
Maragogipe, *Brazil* **171 D4** 12 46 S 38 55W
Marāh, *Si. Arabia* **96 E5** 25 0N 45 35 E
Marahoue, Parc Nat. de la, *Ivory C.* **112 D3** 8 0N 7 8W
Marajó, B. de, *Brazil* **170 B2** 1 0S 48 30W
Marajó, I. de, *Brazil* **170 B2** 1 0S 49 30W
Marākand, *Iran* **96 B5** 38 51N 45 16 E
Marakele Nat. Park, *S. Africa* **117 E4** 32 14 S 25 27 E
Maralal, *Kenya* **118 B4** 1 0N 36 38 E
Maralinga, *Australia* **125 F5** 30 13 S 131 32 E
Maram, *India* **90 C5** 25 25N 94 6 E
Marama, *Australia* **128 C4** 35 10 S 140 10 E
Maramag, *Phil.* **81 H5** 7 46N 125 0 E
Maramaraereğlisi, *Turkey* **51 F11** 40 57N 27 57 E
Maramasike, *Solomon Is.* **133 M11** 9 30 S 161 25 E
Marampa, *S. Leone* **112 D2** 8 45N 12 28W
Maramureș □, *Romania* **53 C9** 47 45N 24 0 E
Maran, *Malaysia* **87 L4** 3 35N 102 45 E
Marana, *U.S.A.* **159 K8** 32 27N 111 13W
Maranboy, *Australia* **124 B5** 14 40 S 132 39 E
Maranchón, *Spain* **40 D2** 41 6N 2 15W
Marand, *Iran* **101 C11** 38 30N 45 45 E
Marandokhóri, *Greece* **39 B2** 38 38N 20 39 E
Marang, *Malaysia* **87 K4** 5 12N 103 13 E
Maranguape, *Brazil* **170 B4** 3 55 S 38 50W
Maranhão = São Luís, *Brazil* **170 B3** 2 39 S 44 15W
Maranhão □, *Brazil* **170 B2** 5 0S 46 0W
Marano, L. di, *Italy* **45 C10** 45 44N 13 10 E
Maranoa ➝, *Australia* **127 D4** 27 50 S 148 37 E
Marañón ➝, *Peru* **172 A3** 4 30 S 73 35W
Marão, *Mozam.* **117 C5** 24 18 S 34 2 E
Marapi ➝, *Brazil* **169 C6** 0 37N 55 58W
Marari, *Brazil* **172 B4** 5 43 S 67 47W
Maraş = Kahramanmaraş, *Turkey* **100 D7** 37 37N 36 53 E
Mărășești, *Romania* **53 E12** 45 52N 27 14 E
Maratea, *Italy* **47 C8** 39 59N 15 43 E
Marateca, *Portugal* **43 G2** 38 34N 8 40W
Marathasa, *Cyprus* **39 F8** 34 59N 32 51 E
Marathiás, Ákra, *Greece* **39 D2** 37 39N 20 50 E
Marathókambos, *Greece* **49 D8** 37 43N 26 42 E
Marathon, *Australia* **126 C3** 20 51 S 143 32 E
Marathon, *Canada* **140 C2** 48 44N 86 23W
Marathón, *Greece* **48 C5** 38 11N 23 58 E
Marathon, *Fla., U.S.A.* **153 L8** 24 43N 81 5W
Marathon, *N.Y., U.S.A.* **151 D8** 42 27N 76 2W
Marathon, *Tex., U.S.A.* **155 K3** 30 12N 103 15W
Marathóvouno, *Cyprus* **39 E9** 35 13N 33 37 E
Maratua, *Indonesia* **85 B5** 2 10N 118 35 E
Maraú, *Brazil* **171 D4** 14 6S 39 0W
Marau, *Solomon Is.* **133 N11** 10 31 S 161 31 E
Maraval, *Trin. & Tob.* **169 F9** 10 43N 61 32W
Maravari, *Solomon Is.* **133 L9** 7 50 S 156 42 E
Maravatío, *Mexico* **162 D4** 19 51N 100 25W
Marawi City, *Phil.* **81 G5** 8 0N 124 21 E
Marāwih, *U.A.E.* **97 E7** 24 18N 53 18 E
Marbach, *Switz.* **32 C5** 46 51N 7 53 E
Marbella, *Spain* **43 J6** 36 30N 4 57W
Marble Bar, *Australia* **124 D2** 21 9 S 119 44 E
Marble Falls, *U.S.A.* **155 K5** 30 35N 98 16W
Marblehead, *U.S.A.* **151 D14** 42 30N 70 51W
Mârbu, *Norway* **18 D5** 60 11N 8 9 E
Marburg, *Germany* **30 E4** 50 47N 8 46 E
Marcal ➝, *Hungary* **52 C2** 47 41N 17 40 E
Marcali, *Hungary* **52 D2** 46 35N 17 25 E
Marcapata, *Peru* **172 C3** 13 31 S 70 52W
Marcaria, *Italy* **44 C7** 45 7N 10 32 E
Mărcăuți, *Moldova* **53 B12** 48 20N 27 14 E
Marceline, *U.S.A.* **156 E4** 39 43N 92 57W
March, *U.K.* **21 E8** 52 33N 0 5 E
Marchal, *Dem. Rep. of the Congo* **115 D2** 5 16 S 14 58 E
Marchand = Rommani, *Morocco* **110 B3** 33 31N 6 40W
Marche, *France* **28 B5** 46 5N 1 20 E
Marche □, *Italy* **45 E10** 43 30N 13 15 E
Marche-en-Famenne, *Belgium* **24 D5** 50 14N 5 19 E
Marchena, *Spain* **43 H5** 37 18N 5 23W
Marchena, Canal de, *Ecuador* **172 a** 0 19N 90 12W
Marchena, I., *Ecuador* **172 a** 0 19N 90 29W
Marches = Marche □, *Italy* **45 E10** 43 30N 13 15 E
Marciana Marina, *Italy* **44 F7** 42 48N 10 12 E
Marcianise, *Italy* **47 A7** 41 2N 14 17 E
Marcigny, *France* **27 F11** 46 17N 4 2 E
Marcillat-en-Combraille, *France* **27 F9** 46 12N 2 38 E
Marck, *France* **27 B8** 50 57N 1 57 E
Marckolsheim, *France* **27 D14** 48 10N 7 30 E
Marco, *U.S.A.* **153 K8** 25 58N 81 44W
Marco Rondon, *Brazil* **173 C5** 12 0S 60 56W
Marcona, *Peru* **172 D2** 15 10 S 75 0W
Marcos Juárez, *Argentina* **174 C3** 32 42 S 62 5W
Mărculești, *Moldova* **53 C13** 47 52N 28 14 E
Marcus Baker, Mt., *U.S.A.* **144 F11** 61 26N 147 45W
Marcus I. = Minami-Tori-Shima, *Pac. Oc.* **134 E7** 24 20N 153 58 E
Marcus Necker Ridge, *Pac. Oc.* **134 F9** 20 0N 175 0 E
Marcy, Mt., *U.S.A.* **151 B11** 44 7N 73 56W
Mardan, *Pakistan* **91 B4** 34 20N 72 0 E
Mardin, *Turkey* **101 D9** 37 20N 40 43 E
Mårdsjön, *Sweden* **16 A9** 63 18N 15 35 E
Maré, Î., *N. Cal.* **133 U22** 21 30 S 168 0 E
Marécchia ➝, *Italy* **45 D9** 44 4N 12 34 E
Marechal Deodoro, *Brazil* **170 C4** 9 43 S 35 54W
Maree, L., *U.K.* **22 D3** 57 40N 5 26W
Mareeba, *Australia* **126 B4** 16 59 S 145 28 E
Mareetsane, *S. Africa* **116 D4** 26 9 S 25 25 E
Marek, *Indonesia* **82 B2** 4 41 S 120 24 E
Maremma, *Italy* **45 F8** 42 30N 11 30 E
Maréna, *Kayes, Mali* **112 C2** 14 36N 10 45W
Maréna, *Koulikoro, Mali* **112 C3** 13 55N 7 20W
Marengo, *Ind., U.S.A.* **157 F10** 38 22N 86 21W
Marengo, *Iowa, U.S.A.* **156 C4** 41 48N 92 4W
Marennes, *France* **28 C2** 45 49N 1 7W
Marenyi, *Kenya* **118 C4** 4 22 S 39 8 E
Marerano, *Madag.* **117 C7** 21 23 S 44 52 E
Marèttimo, *Italy* **46 E5** 37 58N 12 4 E
Mareuil, *France* **28 C4** 45 26N 0 29 E
Marfa, *U.S.A.* **155 K2** 30 19N 104 1W
Marganets = Marhanets, *Ukraine* **59 J8** 47 40N 34 40 E
Margaret ➝, *Australia* **124 C4** 18 9 S 125 41 E
Margaret Bay, *Canada* **142 C3** 51 20N 127 35W
Margaret L., *Canada* **142 B5** 58 56N 115 25W
Margaret River, *Australia* **125 F2** 33 57 S 115 4 E
Margarita, I. de, *Venezuela* **169 A5** 11 0N 64 0W
Margaritíon, *Greece* **48 B2** 39 22N 20 26 E
Margaritovo, *Russia* **70 C7** 43 25N 134 45 E
Margate, *S. Africa* **117 E5** 30 50 S 30 20 E
Margate, *U.K.* **21 F9** 51 23N 1 23 E
Margate, *U.S.A.* **153 J9** 26 15N 80 12W
Margeride, Mts. de la, *France* **28 D7** 44 43N 3 38 E
Margherita, *India* **90 B5** 27 16N 95 40 E
Margherita di Savóia, *Italy* **47 A9** 41 22N 16 9 E
Margherita Pk., *Uganda* **118 B3** 0 22N 29 51 E

248 Mateira

Mateira, *Brazil* **171 E1** 18 54 S 50 30W
Mateke, *Dem. Rep. of the Congo* **114 C3** 4 52 S 24 25 E
Mateke Hills, *Zimbabwe* **119 G3** 21 48 S 31 0 E
Matelot, *Trin. & Tob.* **169 F9** 10 50N 61 7W
Matera, *Italy* **47 B9** 40 40N 16 36 E
Matese, Monti del, *Italy* **47 A7** 41 27N 14 22 E
Mátészalka, *Hungary* **52 C7** 47 58N 22 20 E
Matetsi, *Zimbabwe* **119 F2** 18 12 S 26 0 E
Mateur, *Tunisia* **108 A1** 37 0N 9 40 E
Matfors, *Sweden* **16 B11** 62 21N 17 2 E
Matha, *France* **28 C3** 45 52N 0 20W
Matheniko Game Reserve, *Uganda* **118 B3** 2 49N 34 27 E
Mathis, *U.S.A.* **155 L6** 28 6N 97 50W
Mathoura, *Australia* **129 C6** 35 50 S 144 55 E
Mathráki, *Greece* **38 B9** 39 48N 19 31 E
Mathura, *India* **92 F7** 27 30N 77 40 E
Mati, *Phil.* **81 H6** 6 55N 126 15 E
Matiakoali, *Burkina Faso* **113 C5** 12 28N 1 2 E
Matiali, *India* **93 F13** 26 56N 88 49 E
Matías Romero, *Mexico* **163 D5** 16 53N 95 2W
Matibane, *Mozam.* **119 E5** 14 49 S 40 45 E
Matima, *Botswana* **116 C3** 20 15 S 24 26 E
Matinhos, *Brazil* **171 G2** 25 49 S 48 32W
Matiri Ra., *N.Z.* **131 B7** 41 38 S 172 20 E
Matjiesfontein, *S. Africa* **116 E3** 33 14 S 20 35 E
Matla →, *India* **93 J13** 21 40N 88 40 E
Matlamanyane, *Botswana* **116 B4** 19 33 S 25 57 E
Matli, *Pakistan* **92 G3** 25 2N 68 39 E
Matlock, *U.K.* **20 D6** 53 9N 1 33W
Matmata, *Tunisia* **108 B1** 33 37N 9 59 E
Matna, *Sudan* **107 E4** 13 49N 35 10 E
Matnog, *Phil.* **80 E5** 12 35N 124 5 E
Mato, *Dem. Rep. of the Congo* **115 D4** 8 1 S 24 24 E
Mato →, *Venezuela* **169 B4** 7 9N 65 7W
Mato, Serrania de, *Venezuela* **168 B4** 6 25N 65 25W
Mato Grosso □, *Brazil* **173 C6** 14 0 S 55 0W
Mato Grosso, Planalto do, *Brazil* **173 C7** 15 0 S 55 0W
Mato Grosso do Sul □, *Brazil* **173 D7** 18 0 S 55 0W
Mato Verde, *Brazil* **171 D1** 11 13 S 50 40W
Matochkin Shar, *Russia* **66 B6** 73 10N 56 40 E
Matong, *Papua N. G.* **132 C6** 5 36 S 151 50 E
Matopo Hills, *Zimbabwe* **119 G2** 20 36 S 28 20 E
Matopos, *Zimbabwe* **119 G2** 20 20 S 28 29 E
Matosinhos, *Portugal* **42 D2** 41 11N 8 42W
Matour, *France* **27 F11** 46 19N 4 29 E
Matroosberg, *S. Africa* **116 E2** 33 23 S 19 40 E
Maţruḩ, *Oman* **99 B7** 23 37N 58 30 E
Matsena, *Nigeria* **113 C7** 13 5N 10 5 E
Matsesta, *Russia* **61 J4** 43 34N 39 51 E
Matsu Tao, *Taiwan* **77 E13** 26 9N 119 56 E
Matsudo, *Japan* **73 B11** 35 47N 139 54 E
Matsue, *Japan* **72 B5** 35 25N 133 10 E
Matsum, Ko, *Thailand* **87 b** 9 22N 99 59 E
Matsumae, *Japan* **70 D10** 41 26N 140 7 E
Matsumoto, *Japan* **73 A10** 36 15N 138 0 E
Matsusaka, *Japan* **73 C8** 34 34N 136 32 E
Matsushima, *Japan* **72 E2** 32 30N 130 25 E
Matsuura, *Japan* **72 D1** 33 20N 129 49 E
Matsuyama, *Japan* **72 D4** 33 45N 132 45 E
Matsuzaki, *Japan* **73 C10** 34 43N 138 50 E
Mattagami →, *Canada* **140 B3** 50 43N 81 29W
Mattancheri, *India* **95 K3** 9 50N 76 15 E
Mattawa, *Canada* **140 C4** 46 20N 78 45W
Matterhorn, *Switz.* **32 E5** 45 58N 7 39 E
Mattersburg, *Austria* **35 D9** 47 44N 16 24 E
Matteson, *U.S.A.* **157 C9** 41 30N 87 42W
Matthew, I., *N. Cal.* **123 E13** 22 29 S 171 15 E
Matthew Town, *Bahamas* **165 B5** 20 57N 73 40W
Matthews, *U.S.A.* **157 D11** 40 23N 85 30W
Matthew's Ridge, *Guyana* **169 B5** 7 37N 60 10W
Mattice, *Canada* **140 C3** 49 40N 83 20W
Mattili, *India* **94 E6** 18 33N 82 12 E
Mattituck, *U.S.A.* **151 F12** 40 59N 72 32W
Mattō, *Japan* **73 A8** 36 31N 136 34 E
Mattoon, *U.S.A.* **154 F10** 39 29N 88 23W
Matuba, *Mozam.* **117 C5** 24 28 S 32 49 E
Matucana, *Peru* **172 C2** 11 55 S 76 25W
Matugama, *Sri Lanka* **95 L5** 6 31N 80 7 E
Matuka, *Papua N. G.* **132 C3** 4 54 S 145 47 E
Matuku, *Fiji* **133 B2** 19 10 S 179 44 E
Matūn = Khowst, *Afghan.* **91 B3** 33 22N 69 58 E
Matura B., *Trin. & Tob.* **169 F10** 10 39N 61 1W
Maturín, *Venezuela* **169 B5** 9 45N 63 11W
Matusadona Nat. Park, *Zimbabwe* **119 F2** 16 58 S 28 42 E
Matutum, Mt., *Phil.* **81 H5** 6 22N 125 5 E
Matveyev Kurgan, *Russia* **59 J10** 47 35N 38 57 E
Matxitxako, C., *Spain* **40 B2** 43 28N 2 47W
Mau, *Mad. P., India* **93 F8** 26 17N 78 41 E
Mau, *Ut. P., India* **93 G10** 25 56N 83 33 E
Mau, *Ut. P., India* **93 G9** 25 17N 81 23 E
Mau Escarpment, *Kenya* **118 C4** 0 40 S 36 0 E
Mau Ranipur, *India* **93 G8** 25 16N 79 8 E
Mauban, *Phil.* **80 D3** 14 12N 121 44 E
Maubeuge, *France* **27 B10** 50 17N 3 57 E
Maubourguet, *France* **28 E4** 43 29N 0 1 E
Maud, Pt., *Australia* **124 D1** 23 6 S 113 45 E
Maude, *Australia* **128 C6** 34 29 S 144 18 E
Maudin Sun, *Burma* **90 G5** 16 0N 94 12 E
Maués, *Brazil* **169 D6** 3 20 S 57 45W
Maués-Acu →, *Brazil* **169 D6** 3 22 S 57 44W
Maughold Hd., *U.K.* **20 C3** 54 18N 4 18W
Mauguio, *France* **28 E7** 43 37N 4 1 E
Maui, *U.S.A.* **145 C5** 20 48N 156 20W
Maulamyaing = Moulmein, *Burma* **90 G6** 16 30N 97 40 E
Maule □, *Chile* **174 D1** 36 5 S 72 30W
Mauléon-Licharre, *France* **28 E3** 43 14N 0 54W
Maullín, *Chile* **176 B2** 41 38 S 73 37W
Maulvibazar, *Bangla.* **90 C3** 24 29N 91 42 E
Maumee, *U.S.A.* **157 C13** 41 34N 83 39W
Maumee →, *U.S.A.* **157 C13** 41 42N 83 28W
Maumere, *Indonesia* **82 C2** 8 38 S 122 13 E
Maumusson, Pertuis de, *France* **28 C2** 45 48N 1 14W
Maun, *Botswana* **116 C3** 20 0 S 23 26 E
Mauna Kea, *U.S.A.* **145 D6** 19 50N 155 28W
Mauna Loa, *U.S.A.* **145 D6** 19 30N 155 35W
Maunaloa, *U.S.A.* **145 B4** 21 8N 157 13W
Maunalua B., *U.S.A.* **145 K14** 21 15N 157 45W
Maunawili, *U.S.A.* **145 K14** 21 23N 157 46W
Maunga Orito, *Chile* **172 b** 27 10 S 109 25W
Maunga Puakatiki, *Chile* **172 b** 27 6 S 109 15W
Maunga Terevaka, *Chile* **172 b** 27 5 S 109 23W
Maungaturoto, *N.Z.* **130 C3** 36 6 S 174 23 E
Maungdow, *Burma* **90 E4** 20 50N 92 21 E
Maungmagan Kyunzu, *Burma* **86 E1** 14 0N 97 48 E
Maupin, *U.S.A.* **158 D3** 45 11N 121 5W
Maure-de-Bretagne, *France* **26 E5** 47 59N 1 58W
Maurepas, L., *U.S.A.* **155 K9** 30 15N 90 30W
Maures, *France* **29 E10** 43 15N 6 15 E
Mauriac, *France* **28 C6** 45 13N 2 19 E
Maurice, L., *Australia* **125 E5** 29 30 S 131 0 E
Mauriceville, *N.Z.* **130 G4** 40 45 S 175 42 E
Mauricie, Parc Nat. de la, *Canada* **140 C5** 46 45N 73 0W
Maurienne, *France* **29 C10** 45 13N 6 30 E
Mauritania ■, *Africa* **110 D3** 20 50N 10 0W
Mauritius ■, *Ind. Oc.* **105 J9** 20 0 S 57 0 E
Mauron, *France* **26 D4** 48 9N 2 18W
Maurs, *France* **28 D6** 44 43N 2 12 E
Mauston, *U.S.A.* **154 D9** 43 48N 90 5W
Mauterndorf, *Austria* **34 D6** 47 9N 13 40 E
Mauthen, *Austria* **34 E6** 46 40N 13 0 E
Mauvezin, *France* **28 E4** 43 44N 0 53 E
Mauvoisin, Barr. de, *Switz.* **32 E4** 45 58N 7 20 E
Mauzé-sur-le-Mignon, *France* **28 B3** 46 12N 0 41W
Mavaca →, *Venezuela* **169 C4** 2 31N 65 11W
Mavinga, *Angola* **115 F4** 15 50 S 20 21 E
Mavli, *India* **92 G5** 24 45N 73 55 E
Mavráta, *Greece* **39 C2** 38 4N 20 44 E
Mavrovë, *Albania* **50 F3** 40 26N 19 32 E
Mavuradonha Mts., *Zimbabwe* **119 F3** 16 30 S 31 30 E
Mawa, *Dem. Rep. of the Congo* **118 B2** 2 45N 26 40 E
Mawai, *India* **93 H9** 22 30N 81 4 E
Mawana, *India* **92 E7** 29 6N 77 58 E
Mawand, *Pakistan* **92 E3** 29 33N 68 38 E
Mawasangka, *Indonesia* **82 C2** 5 17 S 122 18 E
Mawk Mai, *Burma* **90 E6** 20 14N 97 37 E
Mawlaik, *Burma* **90 D5** 23 40N 94 26 E
Mawlamyine = Moulmein, *Burma* **90 G6** 16 30N 97 40 E
Mawlawkho, *Burma* **90 G6** 17 50N 97 38 E
Mawqaq, *Si. Arabia* **96 E4** 27 25N 41 8 E
Mawshij, *Yemen* **98 D3** 13 43N 43 17 E
Mawson Coast, *Antarctica* **7 C6** 68 30 S 63 0 E
Max, *U.S.A.* **154 B4** 47 49N 101 18W
Maxcanú, *Mexico* **163 C6** 20 40N 92 0W
Maxesibeni, *S. Africa* **117 E4** 30 49 S 29 23 E
Maxeys, *U.S.A.* **152 B6** 33 45N 83 11W
Maxhamish L., *Canada* **142 B4** 59 50N 123 17W
Maxixe, *Mozam.* **117 C6** 23 54 S 35 17 E
Maxville, *Canada* **151 A10** 45 17N 74 51W
Maxwell, *N.Z.* **130 F3** 39 51 S 174 49 E
Maxwell, *U.S.A.* **160 F4** 39 17N 122 11W
Maxwelton, *Australia* **126 C3** 20 43 S 142 41 E
May, C., *U.S.A.* **148 F8** 38 56N 74 58W
May Jirgui, *Niger* **109 F1** 13 44N 8 8 E
May Pen, *Jamaica* **164 a** 17 58N 77 15W
May River, *Papua N. G.* **132 C1** 4 19 S 141 58 E
Maya, *Indonesia* **85 C3** 1 10 S 109 35 E
Maya →, *Russia* **67 D14** 60 28N 134 28 E
Maya Mts., *Belize* **163 D7** 16 30N 89 0W
Mayabandar, *India* **95 H11** 12 56N 92 56 E
Mayaguana, *Bahamas* **165 B5** 22 30N 72 44W
Mayagüez, *Puerto Rico* **165 d** 18 12N 67 9W
Mayahi, *Niger* **113 C6** 13 58N 7 40 E
Mayals = Maials, *Spain* **40 D5** 41 22N 0 30 E
Mayama, *Congo* **114 C2** 3 51 S 14 54 E
Mayāmey, *Iran* **97 B7** 36 24N 55 42 E
Mayang, *China* **76 D7** 27 53N 109 49 E
Mayanup, *Australia* **125 F2** 33 57 S 116 27 E
Mayapan, *Mexico* **163 C7** 20 30N 89 25W
Mayaqum, *Kazakstan* **65 B4** 42 51N 68 3 E
Mayarí, *Cuba* **165 B4** 20 40N 75 41W
Mayaro B., *Trin. & Tob.* **169 F10** 10 14N 61 0W
Mayavaram = Mayuram, *India* **95 J4** 11 3N 79 42 E
Maybell, *U.S.A.* **158 F9** 40 31N 108 5W
Maybole, *U.K.* **22 F4** 55 21N 4 42W
Maychew, *Ethiopia* **107 E4** 12 50N 39 31 E
Maydān, *Iraq* **101 E11** 34 55N 45 37 E
Maydena, *Australia* **127 G4** 42 45 S 146 30 E
Maydī, *Yemen* **98 C3** 16 19N 42 48 E
Mayen, *Germany* **31 E3** 50 19N 7 13 E
Mayenne, *France* **26 D6** 48 20N 0 38W
Mayenne □, *France* **26 D6** 48 10N 0 40W
Mayenne →, *France* **26 E6** 47 30N 0 32W
Mayer, *U.S.A.* **159 J7** 34 24N 112 14W
Mayerthorpe, *Canada* **142 C5** 53 57N 115 8W
Mayesville, *U.S.A.* **152 A9** 34 0N 80 12W
Mayfield, *Ky., U.S.A.* **149 G1** 36 44N 88 38W
Mayfield, *N.Y., U.S.A.* **151 C10** 43 6N 74 16W
Mayhill, *U.S.A.* **159 K11** 32 53N 105 29W
Maykop, *Russia* **61 H5** 44 35N 40 10 E
Mayli-Say = Mayluu-Suu, *Kyrgyzstan* **65 C6** 41 17N 72 24 E
Mayluu-Suu, *Kyrgyzstan* **65 C6** 41 17N 72 24 E
Maymak, *Kyrgyzstan* **65 B5** 42 42N 71 13 E
Maymyo, *Burma* **86 A1** 22 2N 96 28 E
Maynard, *Mass., U.S.A.* **151 D13** 42 26N 71 27W
Maynard, *Wash., U.S.A.* **160 C4** 47 59N 122 55W
Maynard Hills, *Australia* **125 E2** 28 28 S 119 49 E
Mayne →, *Australia* **126 C3** 23 40 S 141 55 E
Maynooth, *Ireland* **23 C5** 53 23N 6 34W
Mayo, *Canada* **138 B6** 63 38N 135 57W
Mayo, *U.S.A.* **152 E6** 30 3N 83 10W
Mayo □, *Ireland* **23 C2** 53 53N 9 3W
Mayo →, *Argentina* **176 C3** 45 45 S 69 45W
Mayo →, *Peru* **172 B2** 6 38 S 76 15W
Mayo Bay, *Phil.* **81 H6** 6 56N 126 22 E
Mayo Daga, *Nigeria* **113 D7** 6 59N 11 25 E
Mayo Faran, *Nigeria* **113 D7** 8 57N 12 4 E
Mayoko, *Congo* **114 C2** 2 18 S 12 49 E
Mayoko, *Dem. Rep. of the Congo* **114 C4** 1 6 S 23 50 E
Mayon Volcano, *Phil.* **80 E4** 13 15N 123 41 E
Mayor Buratovich, *Argentina* **176 A4** 39 15 S 62 37W
Mayor I., *N.Z.* **130 D5** 37 16 S 176 17 E
Mayorga, *Spain* **42 C5** 42 10N 5 16W
Mayotte, *Ind. Oc.* **105 H8** 12 50 S 45 10 E
Mayoyao, *Phil.* **80 C3** 16 59N 121 14 E
Mayraira Pt., *Phil.* **80 B3** 18 39N 120 51 E
Mayskiy, *Russia* **61 J7** 43 47N 44 2 E
Maysville, *Ky., U.S.A.* **157 F13** 38 39N 83 46W
Maysville, *Mo., U.S.A.* **156 E2** 39 53N 94 22W
Mayu, *Indonesia* **82 A3** 1 30N 126 30 E
Mayumba, *Gabon* **114 C2** 3 25 S 10 39 E
Mayuram, *India* **95 J4** 11 3N 79 42 E
Mayville, *N. Dak., U.S.A.* **154 B6** 47 30N 97 20W
Mayville, *N.Y., U.S.A.* **150 D5** 42 15N 79 30W
Mayya, *Russia* **67 C14** 61 44N 130 18 E
Mazabuka, *Zambia* **119 F2** 15 52 S 27 44 E
Mazagán = El Jadida, *Morocco* **110 B3** 33 11N 8 17W
Mazagão, *Brazil* **169 D7** 0 7 S 51 16W
Mazamet, *France* **28 E6** 43 30N 2 20 E
Mazán, *Peru* **168 D3** 3 30 S 73 0W
Māzandarān □, *Iran* **97 B7** 36 30N 52 0 E
Mazapil, *Mexico* **162 C4** 24 38N 101 34W
Mazar, *China* **65 E8** 36 32N 77 1 E
Mazar, O. →, *Algeria* **111 B5** 31 50N 1 36 E
Mazār-e Sharīf, *Afghan.* **65 E3** 36 41N 67 0 E
Mazara del Vallo, *Italy* **46 E5** 37 39N 12 35 E
Mazarredo, *Argentina* **176 C3** 47 10 S 66 50W
Mazarrón, *Spain* **41 H3** 37 38N 1 19W
Mazarrón, G. de, *Spain* **41 H3** 37 27N 1 19W
Mazaruni →, *Guyana* **169 B6** 6 25N 58 35W
Mazatán, *Mexico* **162 B2** 29 0N 110 8W
Mazatenango, *Guatemala* **164 D1** 14 35N 91 30W
Mazatlán, *Mexico* **162 C3** 23 13N 106 25W
Mažeikiai, *Lithuania* **15 H20** 56 20N 22 20 E
Māzhān, *Iran* **97 C8** 32 30N 59 0 E
Mazīnān, *Iran* **97 B8** 36 19N 56 56 E
Mazo Cruz, *Peru* **172 D4** 16 45 S 69 44W
Mazoe, *Mozam.* **119 F3** 16 42 S 33 7 E
Mazoe →, *Mozam.* **119 F3** 16 20 S 33 30 E
Mazomanie, *U.S.A.* **156 A7** 43 11N 89 48W
Mazon, *U.S.A.* **157 C8** 41 14N 88 25W
Mazowe, *Zimbabwe* **119 F3** 17 28 S 30 58 E
Mazowieckie □, *Poland* **55 F8** 52 40N 21 0 E
Mazrûb, *Sudan* **107 E2** 14 0N 29 20 E
Mazu Dao, *China* **77 D12** 26 10N 119 55 E
Mazurian Lakes = Mazurski, Pojezierze, *Poland* **54 E7** 53 50N 21 0 E
Mazurski, Pojezierze, *Poland* **54 E7** 53 50N 21 0 E
Mazyr, *Belarus* **59 F5** 51 59N 29 15 E
Mba, *Fiji* **133 A1** 17 33 S 177 41 E
Mbaba, *Senegal* **112 C1** 14 59N 16 44W
Mbabane, *Swaziland* **117 D5** 26 18 S 31 6 E
Mbaéré →, *C.A.R.* **114 B3** 3 47N 17 31 E
Mbagne, *Mauritania* **112 B2** 16 6N 14 47W
M'bahiakro, *Ivory C.* **112 D4** 7 33N 4 19W
Mbaïki, *C.A.R.* **114 B3** 3 53N 18 1 E
Mbakana, Mt. de, *Cameroon* **114 A3** 7 57N 15 6 E
Mbala, *Zambia* **119 D3** 8 46 S 31 24 E
Mbalabala, *Zimbabwe* **117 C4** 20 27 S 29 3 E
Mbale, *Uganda* **118 B3** 1 8N 34 12 E
Mbali →, *C.A.R.* **114 B3** 4 27N 18 20 E
Mbalmayo, *Cameroon* **113 E7** 3 33N 11 33 E
Mbam →, *Cameroon* **113 E7** 4 24N 11 17 E
Mbamba Bay, *Tanzania* **119 E3** 11 13 S 34 49 E
Mbandaka, *Dem. Rep. of the Congo* **114 B3** 0 1N 18 18 E
Mbanga, *Cameroon* **113 E6** 4 30N 9 33 E
Mbanika, *Solomon Is.* **133 M10** 9 3 S 159 13 E
M'Banio, Lagune, *Gabon* **114 C2** 3 35 S 11 0 E
Mbanza Congo, *Angola* **115 D2** 6 18 S 14 16 E
Mbanza Ngungu, *Dem. Rep. of the Congo* **115 D2** 5 12 S 14 53 E
Mbarangandu, *Tanzania* **119 D4** 10 11 S 36 48 E
Mbarara, *Uganda* **118 C3** 0 35 S 30 40 E
Mbari →, *C.A.R.* **114 B4** 4 34N 22 43 E
Mbashe →, *S. Africa* **117 E4** 32 15 S 28 54 E
Mbatto, *Ivory C.* **112 D4** 6 28N 4 22W
Mbava, *Solomon Is.* **133 L9** 7 47 S 156 33 E
Mbé, *Congo* **114 C3** 3 14 S 15 50 E
Mbe, *Eq. Guin.* **114 B1** 1 47N 9 56 E
Mbengga = Beqa, *Fiji* **133 B2** 18 23 S 178 8 E
Mbengué, *Gabon* **114 C2** 2 2 S 11 7 E
Mbengui, *Gabon* **114 C2** 2 3 S 10 4 E
Mbenkuru →, *Tanzania* **119 D4** 9 25 S 39 50 E
Mbéré →, *Cameroon* **114 A3** 7 45N 15 36 E
Mberengwa, *Zimbabwe* **119 G2** 20 29 S 29 57 E
Mberengwa, Mt., *Zimbabwe* **119 G2** 20 37 S 29 55 E
Mberubu, *Nigeria* **113 D6** 6 10N 7 38 E
Mbesuma, *Zambia* **119 E3** 10 0 S 32 2 E
Mbeya, *Tanzania* **119 D3** 8 54 S 33 29 E
Mbeya □, *Tanzania* **118 D3** 8 15 S 33 30 E
Mbigou, *Gabon* **114 C2** 1 53 S 11 56 E
M'bili, *Sudan* **107 F2** 7 35N 28 15 E
Mbinga, *Tanzania* **119 E4** 10 50 S 35 0 E
Mbini = Río Muni □, *Eq. Guin.* **114 B2** 1 30N 10 0 E
Mbini, *Eq. Guin.* **114 B1** 1 35N 9 37 E
Mboi, *Dem. Rep. of the Congo* **115 D4** 6 57 S 21 54 E
Mboki, *C.A.R.* **107 F2** 5 19N 25 58 E
Mbokonimbeti, *Solomon Is.* **133 M11** 8 57 S 160 7 E
Mboli, *Dem. Rep. of the Congo* **114 B4** 4 8N 23 9 E
M'bonge, *Cameroon* **113 E6** 4 33N 9 5 E
Mboro, *Senegal* **112 B1** 15 9N 16 54W
Mboua, *Cameroon* **114 A2** 4 25N 14 16 E
M'boukou, Rés. de, *Cameroon* **113 D7** 6 23N 12 50 E
Mboune, *Senegal* **112 C2** 14 42N 13 34W
Mbouoma, *Congo* **114 C3** 0 52 S 15 4 E
Mbour, *Senegal* **112 C1** 14 22N 16 54W
Mbout, *Mauritania* **112 B2** 16 1N 12 38W
Mbrés, *C.A.R.* **114 A3** 6 40N 19 48 E
M'Bridge →, *Angola* **115 D2** 7 12 S 12 51 E
Mbuji-Mayi, *Dem. Rep. of the Congo* **118 D1** 6 9 S 23 40 E
Mbulu, *Tanzania* **118 C4** 3 45 S 35 30 E
Mbuma, *Dem. Rep. of the Congo* **114 C4** 3 32N 24 50 E
Mbuma, *Solomon Is.* **133 M11** 8 59 S 160 46 E
Mburucuyá, *Argentina* **174 B4** 28 1 S 58 14W
M'bwat, *Cameroon* **114 A2** 6 29N 10 45 E
Mcherrah, *Algeria* **110 C4** 27 0N 4 30W
Mchinja, *Tanzania* **119 D4** 9 44 S 39 45 E
Mchinji, *Malawi* **119 E3** 13 47 S 32 58 E
Mdennah, *Mauritania* **110 D3** 24 37N 6 0W
Mé Maoya, *N. Cal.* **133 U19** 21 22 S 165 22 E
Mead, L., *U.S.A.* **161 J12** 36 1N 114 44W
Meade, *U.S.A.* **155 G4** 37 17N 100 20W
Meade →, *U.S.A.* **144 A9** 70 52N 155 55W
Meade River, *U.S.A.* **144 A8** 70 28N 157 24W
Meadow Lake, *Canada* **143 C7** 54 10N 108 26W
Meadow Lake Prov. Park, *Canada* **143 C7** 54 27N 109 0W
Meadow Valley Wash →, *U.S.A.* **161 J12** 36 40N 114 34W
Meadville, *Mo., U.S.A.* **156 E3** 39 47N 93 18W
Meadville, *Pa., U.S.A.* **150 E4** 41 39N 80 9W
Meaford, *Canada* **140 D3** 44 36N 80 35W
Mealhada, *Portugal* **42 E2** 40 22N 8 27W
Mealy Mts., *Canada* **141 B8** 53 10N 58 0W
Meander River, *Canada* **142 B5** 59 2N 117 42W
Meares, C., *U.S.A.* **158 D2** 45 37N 124 0W
Mearim →, *Brazil* **170 B3** 3 4 S 44 35W
Meath □, *Ireland* **23 C5** 53 40N 6 57W
Meath Park, *Canada* **143 C7** 53 27N 105 22W
Meaulne, *France* **27 F9** 46 36N 2 36 E
Meaux, *France* **27 D9** 48 58N 2 50 E
Mebechi-Gawa →, *Japan* **70 D10** 40 31N 141 31 E
Mebonden, *Norway* **18 A8** 63 13N 11 2 E
Mebulu, Tanjung, *Indonesia* **79 K18** 8 50 S 115 5 E
Mecanhelas, *Mozam.* **119 F4** 15 12 S 35 54 E
Mecaya →, *Colombia* **168 C2** 0 29N 75 11W
Mecca = Makkah, *Si. Arabia* **98 B2** 21 30N 39 54 E
Mecca, *U.S.A.* **161 M10** 33 34N 116 5W
Mechanicsburg, *Ohio, U.S.A.* **157 D13** 40 4N 83 33W
Mechanicsburg, *Pa., U.S.A.* **150 F8** 40 13N 77 1W
Mechanicsville, *U.S.A.* **156 C5** 41 54N 91 16W
Mechanicville, *U.S.A.* **151 D11** 42 54N 73 41W
Mechara, *Ethiopia* **107 F5** 8 36N 40 20 E
Mechelen, *Belgium* **24 C4** 51 2N 4 29 E
Mecheria, *Algeria* **111 B4** 33 35N 0 18W
Mechernich, *Germany* **30 E2** 50 35N 6 39 E
Mechetinskaya, *Russia* **61 G5** 46 45N 40 32 E
Mechra Bel Ksiri, *Morocco* **110 B3** 34 34N 5 57W
Mechra Benâbbou, *Morocco* **110 B3** 32 39N 7 48W
Mecidiye, *Turkey* **51 F10** 40 38N 26 32 E
Mecitözü, *Turkey* **100 B6** 40 32N 35 17 E
Mecklenburg, *Germany* **30 C6** 53 33N 11 40 E
Mecklenburg-Vorpommern □, *Germany* **30 B8** 53 45N 12 15 E
Mecklenburger Bucht, *Germany* **30 A7** 54 20N 11 40 E
Meconta, *Mozam.* **119 E4** 14 59 S 39 50 E
Mecsek, *Hungary* **52 D3** 46 10N 18 18 E
Meda, *Portugal* **42 E3** 40 57N 7 18W
Medak, *India* **94 E4** 18 1N 78 15 E
Medan, *Indonesia* **84 B1** 3 40N 98 38 E
Médanos, *Argentina* **176 A4** 38 50 S 62 42W
Médanos de Coro, Pta., *Argentina* **176 C3** 48 8 S 66 0W
Medart, *U.S.A.* **152 E5** 30 5N 84 23W
Medaryville, *U.S.A.* **157 C10** 41 5N 86 55W
Medawachchiya, *Sri Lanka* **95 K5** 8 30N 80 30 E
Medchal, *India* **94 F4** 17 37N 78 29 E
Mede, *Italy* **44 C5** 45 6N 8 44 E
Médéa, *Algeria* **111 A5** 36 12N 2 50 E
Mededa, *Bos.-H.* **52 G4** 43 44N 19 10 E
Médégué, *Gabon* **114 B2** 0 37N 10 8 E
Medeiros Neto, *Brazil* **171 E3** 17 20 S 40 14W
Medel, Pic, *Switz.* **33 C7** 46 34N 8 55 E
Medellín, *Colombia* **168 B2** 6 15N 75 35W
Medelpad, *Sweden* **16 B10** 62 33N 16 30 E
Medemblik, *Neths.* **24 B5** 52 46N 5 8 E
Médenine, *Tunisia* **108 B2** 33 21N 10 30 E
Mederdra, *Mauritania* **112 B1** 17 0N 15 38W
Medford, *Mass., U.S.A.* **151 D13** 42 25N 71 7W
Medford, *Oreg., U.S.A.* **158 E2** 42 19N 122 52W
Medford, *Wis., U.S.A.* **154 C9** 45 9N 90 20W
Medgidia, *Romania* **53 F13** 44 15N 28 19 E
Medi, *Sudan* **107 F3** 5 4N 30 42 E
Media Agua, *Argentina* **174 C2** 31 58 S 68 25W
Media Luna, *Argentina* **174 C2** 34 45 S 66 44W
Medianeira, *Brazil* **175 B5** 25 17 S 54 5W
Mediapolis, *U.S.A.* **156 D5** 41 0N 91 10W
Mediaş, *Romania* **53 D9** 46 9N 24 22 E
Medicilândia, *Brazil* **169 D7** 3 33 S 53 8W
Medicina, *Italy* **45 D8** 44 28N 11 38 E
Medicine Bow, *U.S.A.* **158 F10** 41 54N 106 12W
Medicine Bow Pk., *U.S.A.* **158 F10** 41 21N 106 19W
Medicine Bow Ra., *U.S.A.* **158 F10** 41 10N 106 25W
Medicine Hat, *Canada* **143 D6** 50 0N 110 45W
Medicine Lake, *U.S.A.* **154 A2** 48 30N 104 30W
Medicine Lodge, *U.S.A.* **155 G5** 37 17N 98 35W
Medina = Al Madīnah, *Si. Arabia* **96 E3** 24 35N 39 52 E
Medina, *Brazil* **171 E3** 16 15 S 41 29W
Medina, *Colombia* **168 C3** 4 30N 73 21W
Medina, *Phil.* **81 G5** 8 55N 125 0 E
Medina, *N. Dak., U.S.A.* **154 B5** 46 54N 99 18W
Medina, *N.Y., U.S.A.* **150 C6** 43 13N 78 23W
Medina, *Ohio, U.S.A.* **150 E3** 41 8N 81 52W
Medina →, *U.S.A.* **155 L5** 29 16N 98 29W
Medina de Pomar, *Spain* **42 C7** 42 56N 3 29W
Medina de Ríoseco, *Spain* **42 D5** 41 53N 5 3W
Medina del Campo, *Spain* **42 D6** 41 18N 4 55W
Medina L., *U.S.A.* **155 L5** 29 32N 98 56W
Medina Sidonia, *Spain* **43 J5** 36 28N 5 57W
Medinaceli, *Spain* **40 D2** 41 12N 2 30W
Medinipur, *India* **93 H12** 22 25N 87 21 E
Mediterranean Sea, *Europe* **12 H7** 35 0N 15 0 E
Medjerda, O. →, *Tunisia* **108 A2** 37 7N 10 13 E
Mednogorsk, *Russia* **64 F6** 51 24N 57 37 E
Médoc, *France* **28 C3** 45 10N 0 50W
Medora, *U.S.A.* **157 F10** 38 49N 86 10W
Médouneu, *Gabon* **114 B2** 0 57N 10 47 E
Medulin, *Croatia* **45 D10** 44 49N 13 55 E
Medveđa, *Serbia, Yug.* **50 D5** 42 50N 21 32 E
Medvedevo, *Russia* **60 B8** 56 37N 47 47 E
Medveditsa →, *Tver, Russia* **58 D9** 57 5N 37 30 E
Medveditsa →, *Volgograd, Russia* **60 F6** 49 35N 42 41 E
Medvedok, *Russia* **60 B10** 57 20N 50 1 E
Medvezhi, Ostrava, *Russia* **67 B17** 71 0N 161 0 E
Medvezhyegorsk, *Russia* **56 B5** 63 0N 34 25 E
Medway □, *U.K.* **21 F8** 51 25N 0 32 E
Medway →, *U.K.* **21 F8** 51 27N 0 46 E
Medzev, *Slovak Rep.* **35 C13** 48 43N 20 55 E
Medzilaborce, *Slovak Rep.* **35 B14** 49 17N 21 52 E
Medžitlija, *Macedonia* **50 F5** 40 56N 21 26 E
Meekatharra, *Australia* **125 E2** 26 32 S 118 29 E
Meeker, *U.S.A.* **158 F10** 40 2N 107 55W
Meelpaeg Res., *Canada* **141 C8** 48 15N 56 33W
Meeniyan, *Australia* **129 E7** 38 35 S 146 0 E
Meersburg, *Germany* **31 H5** 47 41N 9 16 E
Meerut, *India* **92 E7** 29 1N 77 42 E
Meeteetse, *U.S.A.* **158 D9** 44 9N 108 52W
Mega, *Ethiopia* **107 G4** 3 57N 38 19 E
Megálo Khorío, *Greece* **49 E9** 36 27N 27 24 E
Megálo Petalí, *Greece* **48 D6** 38 0N 24 15 E
Megalópolis, *Greece* **48 D4** 37 25N 22 7 E
Meganísi Nisís, *Greece* **39 B2** 38 38N 20 46 E
Mégara, *Greece* **48 D5** 37 58N 23 22 E
Megasini, *India* **93 J12** 21 38N 86 21 E
Megdhova →, *Greece* **48 B3** 39 10N 21 45 E
Megève, *France* **29 C10** 45 51N 6 37 E
Meghalaya □, *India* **90 C3** 25 50N 91 0 E
Meghezez, *Ethiopia* **107 F4** 9 18N 39 26 E
Meghna →, *Bangla.* **90 D3** 22 50N 90 50 E
Mégiscane, L., *Canada* **140 C4** 48 35N 75 55W
Megiste, *Greece* **49 E11** 36 8N 29 34 E
Megra, *Russia* **58 B9** 60 11N 37 14 E
Mehadia, *Romania* **52 F7** 44 56N 22 23 E
Mehaïguene, O. →, *Algeria* **111 B5** 32 15N 2 59 E
Meharry, Mt., *Australia* **124 D2** 22 59 S 118 35 E
Mehedeby, *Sweden* **16 D11** 60 27N 17 25 E
Mehedinţi □, *Romania* **52 F7** 44 40N 22 45 E
Meheisa, *Sudan* **106 D3** 19 38N 32 57 E
Mehekar, *India* **94 D3** 20 9N 76 34 E
Mehlville, *U.S.A.* **154 F9** 38 30N 90 19W
Mehndawal, *India* **93 F10** 26 58N 83 5 E
Mehr Jān, *Iran* **97 C7** 33 50N 55 6 E
Mehrābād, *Iran* **101 D12** 36 53N 47 55 E
Mehrān, *Iran* **101 F12** 33 7N 46 10 E
Mehrīz, *Iran* **97 D7** 31 35N 54 28 E
Mehun-sur-Yèvre, *France* **27 E9** 47 10N 2 13 E
Mei Jiang →, *China* **77 E11** 24 25N 116 35 E
Mei Xian, *China* **74 G4** 34 18N 107 55 E
Meia Ponte →, *Brazil* **171 E2** 18 32 S 49 36W
Meicheng, *China* **77 C12** 29 29N 119 16 E
Meichengzhen, *China* **77 C8** 28 9N 111 40 E
Meichuan, *China* **77 B10** 30 8N 115 31 E
Meiganga, *Cameroon* **114 A2** 6 30N 14 25 E
Meigs, *U.S.A.* **152 D5** 31 4N 84 6W
Meigu, *China* **76 C4** 28 16N 103 20 E
Meiktila, *Burma* **90 E5** 20 53N 95 54 E
Meilen, *Switz.* **33 B7** 47 16N 8 39 E
Meinerzhagen, *Germany* **30 D3** 51 6N 7 38 E
Meiningen, *Germany* **30 E6** 50 34N 10 25 E
Meio →, *Brazil* **171 D3** 13 36 S 44 7W
Meira, Serra de, *Spain* **42 B3** 43 15N 7 15W
Meiringen, *Switz.* **32 C6** 46 43N 8 12 E
Meishan, *China* **76 B4** 30 3N 103 23 E
Meissen, *Germany* **30 D9** 51 9N 13 29 E
Meissner, *Germany* **30 D5** 51 14N 9 50 E
Meitan, *China* **76 D6** 27 45N 107 29 E
Meizhou, *China* **77 E11** 24 16N 116 6 E
Meja, *India* **93 G10** 25 9N 82 7 E
Mejillones, *Chile* **174 A1** 23 10 S 70 30W
Mékambo, *Gabon* **114 B2** 1 2N 13 50 E
Mekdela, *Ethiopia* **107 E4** 11 24N 39 10 E
Mekele, *Ethiopia* **107 E4** 13 33N 39 30 E
Mekerghene, Sebkra, *Algeria* **111 C5** 26 21N 1 30 E
Mekhtar, *Pakistan* **91 C3** 30 30N 69 15 E
Meknès, *Morocco* **110 B3** 33 57N 5 33W
Meko, *Nigeria* **113 D5** 7 27N 2 52 E
Mekong →, *Asia* **87 H6** 9 30N 106 15 E
Mekongga, *Indonesia* **82 B2** 3 39 S 121 15 E
Mekoryuk, *U.S.A.* **144 F6** 60 23N 166 11W
Mekrou →, *Benin* **113 C5** 12 25N 2 50 E
Mekvari = Kür →, *Azerbaijan* **101 C13** 39 29N 49 15 E
Mel, *Italy* **45 B9** 46 4N 12 5 E
Melagiri Hills, *India* **95 H3** 12 20N 77 30 E
Melah, Oued el →, *Algeria* **111 C6** 32 20N 2 28 E
Melah, Sebkhet el, *Algeria* **111 C4** 29 20N 1 30W
Melaka, *Malaysia* **87 L4** 2 15N 102 15 E
Melaka □, *Malaysia* **84 B2** 2 15N 102 15 E
Melalap, *Malaysia* **78 C5** 5 10N 116 5 E
Mélambes, *Greece* **39 E5** 35 8N 24 40 E
Melanesia, *Pac. Oc.* **134 H7** 4 0 S 155 0 E
Melapalaiyam, *India* **95 K3** 8 39N 77 44 E
Melawi →, *Indonesia* **85 B4** 0 5 S 111 29 E
Melaya, *Indonesia* **79 J17** 8 17 S 114 30 E
Melbourne, *Australia* **129 D6** 37 50 S 145 0 E
Melbourne, *Fla., U.S.A.* **149 L5** 28 5N 80 37W
Melbourne, *Iowa, U.S.A.* **156 C3** 41 57N 93 6W
Melcher-Dallas, *U.S.A.* **156 C3** 41 14N 93 15W
Melchor Múzquiz, *Mexico* **162 B4** 27 50N 101 30W
Melchor Ocampo, *Mexico* **162 C4** 24 52N 101 40W
Meldal, *Norway* **18 A6** 63 3N 9 44 E
Méldola, *Italy* **45 D9** 44 7N 12 5 E
Meldorf, *Germany* **30 A5** 54 5N 9 5 E
Mélé, *C.A.R.* **114 A4** 9 46N 21 33 E
Mele B., *Vanuatu* **133 G6** 17 44 S 168 14 E

Meleden, *Somali Rep.* **120 B3** 10 25N 49 51 E
Melegnano, *Italy* **44 C6** 45 21N 9 19 E
Meleizem, *Mauritania* **110 D2** 22 19N 11 24W
Melenci, *Serbia, Yug.* **52 E5** 45 32N 20 20 E
Melenki, *Russia* **60 C5** 55 20N 41 37 E
Meleuz, *Russia* **64 E6** 52 58N 55 55 E
Mélèzes →, *Canada* **140 A5** 57 40N 69 29W
Melfi, *Chad* **109 F3** 11 0N 17 59 E
Melfi, *Italy* **47 B8** 41 0N 15 39 E
Melfort, *Canada* **143 C8** 52 50N 104 37W
Melfort, *Zimbabwe* **119 F3** 18 0 S 31 25 E
Melgaço, *Portugal* **42 C2** 42 7N 8 15W
Melgar de Fernamental, *Spain* **42 C6** 42 27N 4 17W
Melgraseyri, *Iceland* **11 A4** 66 1N 22 27W
Melhus, *Norway* **14 E14** 63 17N 10 18 E
Melide, *Spain* **42 C2** 42 55N 8 1W
Melide, *Switz.* **33 E7** 45 57N 8 57 E
Meligalá, *Greece* **48 D3** 37 15N 21 59 E
Melilla, *N. Afr.* **111 A4** 35 21N 2 57W
Melilli, *Italy* **47 E8** 37 11N 15 7 E
Melipilla, *Chile* **174 C1** 33 42 S 71 15W
Mélissa, Ákra, *Greece* **39 E5** 35 6N 24 33 E
Mélissa Óros, *Greece* **49 D8** 37 32N 26 4 E
Melissani Cave, *Greece* **39 C2** 38 15N 20 38 E
Melita, *Canada* **143 D8** 49 15N 101 0W
Mélito di Porto Salvo, *Italy* **47 E8** 37 55N 15 47 E
Melitopol, *Ukraine* **59 J8** 46 50N 35 22 E
Melk, *Austria* **34 C8** 48 13N 15 20 E
Mellan Fryken, *Sweden* **16 E7** 59 45N 13 10 E
Mellansel, *Sweden* **14 E18** 63 25N 18 17 E
Mellbystrand, *Sweden* **17 H6** 56 30N 12 56 E
Melle, *France* **28 B3** 46 14N 0 10W
Melle, *Germany* **30 C4** 52 12N 8 20 E
Mellègue, O. →, *Tunisia* **108 A1** 36 36N 9 14 E
Mellen, *U.S.A.* **154 B9** 46 20N 90 40W
Mellerud, *Sweden* **17 F6** 58 41N 12 28 E
Mellette, *U.S.A.* **154 C5** 45 9N 98 30W
Mellid = Melide, *Spain* **42 C2** 42 55N 8 1W
Mellieha, *Malta* **38 F7** 35 57N 14 22 E
Mellieha Bay, *Malta* **38 F7** 35 59N 14 22 E
Mellit, *Sudan* **107 E2** 14 7N 25 34 E
Mellizo Sur, Cerro, *Chile* **176 C2** 48 33 S 73 10W
Mellrichstadt, *Germany* **30 E6** 50 25N 10 17 E
Melnik, *Bulgaria* **50 E7** 41 30N 23 25 E
Mělník, *Czech Rep.* **34 A7** 50 22N 14 23 E
Melo, *Uruguay* **175 C5** 32 20 S 54 10W
Melolo, *Indonesia* **82 C2** 9 53 S 120 40 E
Meloupres, *Cambodia* **86 F5** 13 48N 105 16 E
Melrhir, Chott, *Algeria* **111 B6** 34 13N 6 30 E
Melrose, *Australia* **129 B7** 32 42 S 146 57 E
Melrose, *U.K.* **22 F6** 55 36N 2 43W
Melrose, *Minn., U.S.A.* **154 C7** 45 40N 94 49W
Melrose, *N. Mex., U.S.A.* **155 H3** 34 26N 103 38W
Mels, *Switz.* **33 B8** 47 3N 9 25 E
Melsisi, *Vanuatu* **133 E6** 15 46 S 168 10 E
Melstone, *U.S.A.* **158 C10** 46 36N 107 52W
Melsungen, *Germany* **30 D5** 51 7N 9 32 E
Melton, *Australia* **128 D6** 37 41 S 144 35 E
Melton Mowbray, *U.K.* **20 E7** 52 47N 0 54W
Melun, *France* **27 D9** 48 32N 2 39 E
Melur, *India* **95 J4** 10 2N 78 23 E
Melut, *Sudan* **107 E3** 10 30N 32 13 E
Melville, *Canada* **143 C8** 50 55N 102 50W
Melville, C., *Australia* **126 A3** 14 11 S 144 30 E
Melville, C., *Phil.* **81 H1** 7 49N 117 0 E
Melville, L., *Canada* **141 B8** 53 30N 60 0W
Melville B., *Australia* **126 A2** 12 0 S 136 45 E
Melville B., *Greenland* **10 B4** 75 30N 63 0W
Melville I., *Australia* **124 B5** 11 30 S 131 0 E
Melville I., *Canada* **6 B2** 75 30N 112 0W
Melville Pen., *Canada* **139 B11** 68 0N 84 0W
Mélykút, *Hungary* **52 D4** 46 11N 19 25 E
Memaliaj, *Albania* **50 F3** 40 25N 19 56 E
Memba, *Mozam.* **119 E5** 14 11 S 40 30 E
Memboro, *Indonesia* **82 C1** 9 30 S 119 30 E
Membrilla, *Spain* **43 G7** 38 59N 3 21W
Memel = Klaipėda, *Lithuania* **15 J19** 55 43N 21 10 E
Memel, *S. Africa* **117 D4** 27 38 S 29 36 E
Memmingen, *Germany* **31 H6** 47 58N 10 10 E
Mempawah, *Indonesia* **85 B3** 0 30N 109 5 E
Memphis, *Egypt* **106 J7** 29 52N 31 12 E
Memphis, *Mich., U.S.A.* **150 D2** 42 54N 82 46W
Memphis, *Mo., U.S.A.* **156 D4** 40 28N 92 10W
Memphis, *Tenn., U.S.A.* **155 H10** 35 8N 90 3W
Memphis, *Tex., U.S.A.* **155 H4** 34 44N 100 33W
Memphremagog, L., *U.S.A.* **151 B12** 45 0N 72 12W
Mena, *Ukraine* **59 G7** 51 31N 32 13 E
Mena, *U.S.A.* **155 H7** 34 35N 94 15W
Mena →, *Ethiopia* **107 F5** 5 40N 40 50 E
Menai Strait, *U.K.* **20 D3** 53 11N 4 13W
Ménaka, *Mali* **113 B5** 15 59N 2 18 E
Menan = Chao Phraya →, *Thailand* **86 F3** 13 32N 100 36 E
Menarandra →, *Madag.* **117 D7** 25 17 S 44 30 E
Menard, *U.S.A.* **155 K5** 30 55N 99 47W
Menate, *Indonesia* **85 C4** 0 12 S 113 3 E
Menawashei, *Sudan* **107 E1** 12 41N 24 59 E
Mendawai →, *Indonesia* **85 C4** 3 30 S 113 0 E
Mende, *France* **28 D7** 44 31N 3 30 E
Mendebo, *Ethiopia* **107 F4** 7 0N 39 22 E
Menden, *Germany* **30 D3** 51 26N 7 47 E
Mendenhall, C., *U.S.A.* **144 G6** 59 45N 166 10W
Menderes, *Turkey* **49 C9** 38 14N 27 8 E
Mendez, *Mexico* **163 B5** 25 7N 98 34W
Mendhar, *India* **93 C6** 33 35N 74 10 E
Mendi, *Ethiopia* **107 F4** 9 47N 35 4 E
Mendi, *Papua N. G.* **132 D2** 6 11 S 143 39 E
Mendip Hills, *U.K.* **21 F5** 51 17N 2 40W
Mendocino, *U.S.A.* **158 G2** 39 19N 123 48W
Mendocino, C., *U.S.A.* **158 F1** 40 26N 124 25W
Mendon, *U.S.A.* **157 B11** 42 0N 85 27W
Mendooran, *Australia* **129 A8** 31 50 S 149 6 E
Mendota, *Calif., U.S.A.* **160 J6** 36 45N 120 23W
Mendota, *Ill., U.S.A.* **156 C7** 41 33N 89 7W
Mendoyo, *Indonesia* **79 J17** 8 23 S 114 42 E
Mendoza, *Argentina* **174 C2** 32 50 S 68 52W
Mendoza □, *Argentina* **174 C2** 33 0 S 69 0W
Mendrisio, *Switz.* **33 E7** 45 52N 8 59 E
Mene Grande, *Venezuela* **168 B3** 9 49N 70 56W
Menemen, *Turkey* **49 C9** 38 34N 27 3 E
Menen, *Belgium* **24 D3** 50 47N 3 7 E
Menéndez, L., *Argentina* **176 B2** 42 40 S 71 51W
Menfi, *Italy* **46 E5** 37 36N 12 58 E
Mengdingjie, *China* **76 F2** 23 31N 98 58 E
Mengeš, *Slovenia* **45 B11** 46 10N 14 35 E
Menggala, *Indonesia* **84 C3** 4 30 S 105 15 E
Menghai, *China* **76 G3** 21 49N 100 55 E
Mengíbar, *Spain* **43 H7** 37 58N 3 48W
Mengjin, *China* **74 G7** 34 55N 112 45 E
Mengla, *China* **76 G3** 21 20N 101 25 E
Menglian, *China* **76 F2** 22 21N 99 27 E
Mengoub, *Algeria* **110 C3** 29 49N 5 26W
Mengshan, *China* **77 E8** 24 14N 110 55 E
Mengyin, *China* **75 G9** 35 40N 117 58 E
Mengzhe, *China* **76 F3** 22 2N 100 15 E
Mengzi, *China* **76 F4** 23 20N 103 22 E
Menihek, *Canada* **141 B6** 54 28N 56 36W
Menihek L., *Canada* **141 B6** 54 0N 67 0W
Menin = Menen, *Belgium* **24 D3** 50 47N 3 7 E
Menindee, *Australia* **128 B5** 32 20 S 142 25 E
Menindee L., *Australia* **128 B5** 32 20 S 142 25 E
Meningie, *Australia* **128 C3** 35 50 S 139 18 E
Menjangan, Pulau, *Indonesia* **79 J17** 8 7 S 114 31 E
Menkrour, *Algeria* **111 C6** 26 27N 8 9 E
Menlo Park, *U.S.A.* **160 H4** 37 27N 122 12W
Menominee, *U.S.A.* **148 C2** 45 6N 87 37W
Menominee →, *U.S.A.* **148 C2** 45 6N 87 36W
Menomonee Falls, *U.S.A.* **157 A8** 43 11N 88 7W
Menomonie, *U.S.A.* **154 C9** 44 53N 91 55W
Menongue, *Angola* **115 E3** 14 48 S 17 52 E
Menorca, *Spain* **38 B5** 40 0N 4 0 E
Mentakab, *Malaysia* **87 L4** 3 29N 102 21 E
Mentasta Lake, *U.S.A.* **144 E12** 62 55N 143 45W
Mentawai, Kepulauan, *Indonesia* **84 C1** 2 0 S 99 0 E
Menton, *France* **29 E11** 43 50N 7 29 E
Mentone, *U.S.A.* **157 C10** 41 10N 86 2W
Mentor, *U.S.A.* **150 E3** 41 40N 81 21W
Menyamya, *Papua N. G.* **132 D3** 7 10 S 145 59 E
Menzel-Bourguiba, *Tunisia* **108 A1** 37 9N 9 49 E
Menzel-Chaker, *Tunisia* **108 B2** 35 0N 10 26 E
Menzel-Temime, *Tunisia* **108 A2** 36 46N 11 0 E
Menzelinsk, *Russia* **64 D4** 55 47N 53 11 E
Menzies, *Australia* **125 E3** 29 40 S 121 2 E
Meob B., *Namibia* **116 B2** 24 25 S 14 34 E
Me'ona, *Israel* **103 B4** 33 1N 35 15 E
Meoqui, *Mexico* **162 B3** 28 17N 105 29W
Mepaco, *Mozam.* **119 F3** 15 57 S 30 48 E
Meppel, *Neths.* **24 B6** 52 42N 6 12 E
Meppen, *Germany* **30 C3** 52 42N 7 17 E
Mequinenza, *Spain* **40 D5** 41 22N 0 17 E
Mequinenza, Embalse de, *Spain* **40 D5** 41 25N 0 15 E
Mequon, *U.S.A.* **157 A9** 43 14N 87 59W
Mer, *France* **26 E8** 47 42N 1 30 E
Merabéllou, Kólpos, *Greece* **39 E6** 35 10N 25 50 E
Merai, *Papua N. G.* **132 C7** 4 52 S 152 19 E
Merak, *Indonesia* **79 F12** 6 10N 106 26 E
Meråker, *Norway* **18 A8** 63 25N 11 46 E
Meramangye, L., *Australia* **125 E5** 28 25 S 132 13 E
Meramec →, *U.S.A.* **156 F6** 38 24N 90 21W
Meran = Merano, *Italy* **45 B8** 46 40N 11 9 E
Merano, *Italy* **45 B8** 46 40N 11 9 E
Merate, *Italy* **44 C6** 45 42N 9 25 E
Merauke, *Indonesia* **83 C6** 8 29 S 140 24 E
Merauke →, *Indonesia* **83 C6** 8 30 S 140 24 E
Merbabu, *Indonesia* **85 D4** 7 30 S 110 40 E
Merbein, *Australia* **128 C5** 34 10 S 142 2 E
Merbuk, Gunung, *Indonesia* **79 J17** 8 13 S 114 39 E
Merca, *Somali Rep.* **120 D2** 1 48N 44 50 E
Mercato Saraceno, *Italy* **45 E9** 43 57N 12 12 E
Merced, *U.S.A.* **160 H6** 37 18N 120 29W
Merced →, *U.S.A.* **160 H6** 37 21N 120 59W
Merced Pk., *U.S.A.* **160 H7** 37 36N 119 24W
Mercedes, *Buenos Aires, Argentina* **174 C4** 34 40 S 59 30W
Mercedes, *Corrientes, Argentina* **174 B4** 29 10 S 58 5W
Mercedes, *San Luis, Argentina* **174 C2** 33 40 S 65 21W
Mercedes, *Phil.* **80 D4** 14 7N 123 1 E
Mercedes, *Uruguay* **174 C4** 33 12 S 58 0W
Mercedes, *U.S.A.* **155 M6** 26 9N 97 55W
Merceditas, *Chile* **174 B1** 28 20 S 70 35W
Mercer, *N.Z.* **130 D4** 37 16 S 175 5 E
Mercer, *Mo., U.S.A.* **156 D3** 40 31N 93 32W
Mercer, *Pa., U.S.A.* **150 E4** 41 14N 80 15W
Mercer Island, *U.S.A.* **160 C4** 47 35N 122 15W
Mercier, *Bolivia* **172 C4** 10 42 S 68 5W
Mercury, *U.S.A.* **161 J11** 36 40N 115 58W
Mercury B., *N.Z.* **130 C4** 36 48 S 175 45 E
Mercury Is., *N.Z.* **130 C4** 36 37 S 175 52 E
Mercy C., *Canada* **139 B13** 65 0N 63 30W
Merdrignac, *France* **26 D4** 48 11N 2 27W
Mere, *U.K.* **21 F5** 51 6N 2 16W
Mere Lava, *Vanuatu* **133 D6** 14 25 S 168 3 E
Meredith, *Australia* **128 D6** 37 49 S 144 5 E
Meredith, C., *Falk. Is.* **9 f** 52 15 S 60 40W
Meredith, L., *U.S.A.* **155 H4** 35 43N 101 33W
Meredosia, *U.S.A.* **156 E6** 39 50N 90 34W
Merefa, *Ukraine* **59 H9** 49 48N 36 3 E
Meregh, *Somali Rep.* **120 D3** 3 46N 47 18 E
Merei, *Romania* **53 E11** 45 7N 26 43 E
Merga = Nukheila, *Sudan* **106 D2** 19 1N 26 21 E
Mergui, *Burma* **86 F2** 12 26N 98 34 E
Mergui Arch. = Myeik Kyunzu, *Burma* **87 G1** 11 30N 97 30 E
Meribah, *Australia* **128 C4** 34 43 S 140 51 E
Meriç, *Turkey* **51 E10** 41 11N 26 25 E
Meriç →, *Turkey* **51 F10** 40 52N 26 12 E
Mérida, *Mexico* **163 C7** 20 58N 89 37W
Mérida, *Phil.* **81 F5** 10 55N 124 32 E
Mérida, *Spain* **43 G4** 38 55N 6 25W
Mérida, *Venezuela* **168 B3** 8 24N 71 8W
Mérida □, *Venezuela* **168 B3** 8 30N 71 10W
Mérida, Cord. de, *Venezuela* **168 B3** 9 0N 71 0W
Meriden, *U.K.* **21 E6** 52 26N 1 38W
Meriden, *U.S.A.* **151 E12** 41 32N 72 48W
Meridian, *Calif., U.S.A.* **160 F5** 39 9N 121 55W
Meridian, *Ga., U.S.A.* **152 D8** 31 27N 81 23W
Meridian, *Idaho, U.S.A.* **158 E5** 43 37N 116 24W
Meridian, *Miss., U.S.A.* **153 J1** 32 22N 88 42W
Mérignac, *France* **28 D3** 44 51N 0 39W
Merimbula, *Australia* **129 D8** 36 53 S 149 54 E
Mérinaghène, *Senegal* **112 B1** 15 57N 15 55W
Merinda, *Australia* **126 C4** 20 2 S 148 11 E
Mering, *Germany* **31 G6** 48 16N 10 59 E
Meringa, *Nigeria* **113 C7** 10 44N 12 9 E
Meringur, *Australia* **128 C4** 34 20 S 141 19 E
Merir, *Pac. Oc.* **79 D8** 4 10N 132 30 E
Merirumã, *Brazil* **169 C7** 1 15N 54 50W
Merke, *Kazakstan* **65 B6** 42 52N 73 11 E
Merkel, *U.S.A.* **155 J5** 32 28N 100 1W
Mermaid Reef, *Australia* **124 C2** 17 6 S 119 36 E
Meroe, *India* **95 L11** 7 33N 93 33 E
Merowe, *Sudan* **106 D3** 18 29N 31 46 E
Merredin, *Australia* **125 F2** 31 28 S 118 18 E
Merrick, *U.K.* **22 F4** 55 8N 4 28W
Merrickville, *Canada* **151 B9** 44 55N 75 50W
Merrill, *Oreg., U.S.A.* **158 E3** 42 1N 121 36W
Merrill, *Wis., U.S.A.* **154 C10** 45 11N 89 41W
Merrillville, *U.S.A.* **157 C9** 41 29N 87 20W
Merrimack →, *U.S.A.* **151 D14** 42 49N 70 49W
Merriman, *U.S.A.* **154 D4** 42 55N 101 42W
Merritt, *Canada* **142 C4** 50 10N 120 45W
Merritt Island, *U.S.A.* **153 G9** 28 21N 80 42W
Merriwa, *Australia* **129 B9** 32 6 S 150 22 E
Merriwagga, *Australia* **129 B6** 33 47 S 145 43 E
Merry I., *Canada* **140 A4** 55 29N 77 31W
Merrygoen, *Australia* **129 A8** 31 51 S 149 12 E
Merryville, *U.S.A.* **155 K8** 30 45N 93 33W
Mersa Fatma, *Eritrea* **107 E5** 14 57N 40 17 E
Mersch, *Lux.* **24 E6** 49 44N 6 7 E
Merse →, *Italy* **45 E8** 43 5N 11 22 E
Mersea I., *U.K.* **21 F8** 51 47N 0 58 E
Merseburg, *Germany* **30 D7** 51 22N 11 59 E
Mersey →, *U.K.* **20 D4** 53 25N 3 1W
Merseyside □, *U.K.* **20 D4** 53 31N 3 2W
Mersin, *Turkey* **100 D6** 36 51N 34 36 E
Mersing, *Malaysia* **87 L4** 2 25N 103 50 E
Merta, *India* **92 F6** 26 39N 74 4 E
Merta Road, *India* **92 F5** 26 43N 73 55 E
Merthyr Tydfil, *U.K.* **21 F4** 51 45N 3 22W
Merthyr Tydfil □, *U.K.* **21 F4** 51 46N 3 21W
Mértola, *Portugal* **43 H3** 37 40N 7 40W
Mertzon, *U.S.A.* **155 K4** 31 16N 100 49W
Méru, *France* **27 C9** 49 13N 2 8 E
Meru, *Kenya* **118 B4** 0 3N 37 40 E
Meru, *Tanzania* **118 C4** 3 15 S 36 46 E
Meru Nat. Park, *Kenya* **118 B4** 0 5N 38 10 E
Merville, *France* **27 B9** 50 38N 2 38 E
Méry-sur-Seine, *France* **27 D10** 48 31N 3 54 E
Merzifon, *Turkey* **100 B6** 40 53N 35 32 E
Merzig, *Germany* **31 F2** 49 26N 6 38 E
Merzouga, Erg Tin, *Algeria* **111 D7** 24 0N 11 4 E
Mesa, *U.S.A.* **159 K8** 33 25N 111 50W
Mesa Verde Nat. Park, *U.S.A.* **159 H9** 37 11N 108 29W
Mesach Mellet, *Libya* **108 D2** 24 30N 11 30 E
Mesagne, *Italy* **47 B10** 40 34N 17 48 E
Mesanagrós, *Greece* **38 E11** 36 1N 27 49 E
Mesaoría, *Cyprus* **39 E9** 35 12N 33 14 E
Mesarás, Kólpos, *Greece* **39 E5** 35 6N 24 47 E
Meschede, *Germany* **30 D4** 51 20N 8 18 E
Mescit, *Turkey* **101 B9** 40 21N 41 11 E
Mesfinto, *Ethiopia* **107 E4** 13 20N 37 22 E
Mesgouez, L., *Canada* **140 B5** 51 20N 75 0W
Meshchovsk, *Russia* **58 E8** 54 22N 35 17 E
Meshed = Mashhad, *Iran* **97 B8** 36 20N 59 35 E
Meshoppen, *U.S.A.* **151 E8** 41 36N 76 3W
Meshra er Req, *Sudan* **107 F2** 8 25N 29 18 E
Mesilinka →, *Canada* **142 B4** 56 6N 124 30W
Mesilla, *U.S.A.* **159 K10** 32 16N 106 48W
Meslay-du-Maine, *France* **26 E6** 47 58N 0 33W
Mesocco, *Switz.* **33 D8** 46 23N 9 12 E
Mesolóngion, *Greece* **48 C3** 38 21N 21 28 E
Mesopotamia = Al Jazirah, *Iraq* **101 E10** 33 30N 44 0 E
Mesopotamia, *U.S.A.* **150 E4** 41 27N 80 57W
Mesopótamon, *Greece* **48 B2** 39 14N 20 32 E
Mesoraca, *Italy* **47 C9** 39 5N 16 48 E
Mésou Volímais = Volímai, *Greece* **39 D2** 37 52N 20 39 E
Mesquite, *U.S.A.* **159 H6** 36 47N 114 6W
Messaad, *Algeria* **111 B5** 34 8N 3 30 E
Messac, *France* **26 E5** 47 49N 1 50W
Messalo →, *Mozam.* **119 E4** 12 25 S 39 15 E
Méssaména, *Cameroon* **113 E7** 3 48N 12 49 E
Messeue, *Greece* **48 D3** 37 12N 21 58 E
Messier, Canal, *Chile* **176 C2** 48 20 S 74 33W
Messina, *Italy* **47 D8** 38 11N 15 34 E
Messina, *S. Africa* **117 C5** 22 20 S 30 5 E
Messina, Str. di, *Italy* **47 D8** 38 15N 15 35 E
Messíni, *Greece* **48 D3** 37 4N 22 1 E
Messinía □, *Greece* **48 D3** 37 10N 22 0 E
Messiniakós Kólpos, *Greece* **48 E4** 36 45N 22 5 E
Messkirch, *Germany* **31 H5** 47 59N 9 7 E
Messonghi, *Greece* **38 C9** 39 29N 19 56 E
Mesta →, *Bulgaria* **50 E7** 40 54N 24 49 E
Mestá, Ákra, *Greece* **49 C7** 38 16N 25 53 E
Mestanza, *Spain* **43 G6** 38 35N 4 4W
Mestersvig, *Greenland* **10 C8** 72 10N 23 40W
Mestre, *Italy* **45 C9** 45 29N 12 15 E
Mestre, Espigão, *Brazil* **171 D2** 12 30 S 46 10W
Mesudiye, *Turkey* **100 B7** 40 28N 37 46 E
Meta, *U.S.A.* **156 F4** 38 19N 92 10W
Meta □, *Colombia* **168 C3** 3 30N 73 0W
Meta →, *S. Amer.* **168 B4** 6 12N 67 28W
Meta Incognita Peninsula, *Canada* **139 B13** 62 40N 68 0W
Metabetchouan, *Canada* **141 C5** 48 26N 71 52W
Metairie, *U.S.A.* **155 L9** 29 58N 90 10W
Metalici, Munţii, *Romania* **52 D7** 46 15N 22 50 E
Metaline Falls, *U.S.A.* **158 B5** 48 52N 117 22W
Metallifere, Colline, *Italy* **44 E8** 43 10N 11 0 E
Metamora, *U.S.A.* **156 D7** 40 47N 89 22W
Metán, *Argentina* **174 B3** 25 30 S 65 0W
Metangula, *Mozam.* **119 E3** 12 40 S 34 50 E
Metauro →, *Italy* **45 E10** 43 50N 13 3 E
Metcalf, *U.S.A.* **152 E6** 30 43N 83 59W
Metema, *Ethiopia* **107 E4** 12 56N 36 13 E
Metengobalame, *Mozam.* **119 E3** 14 49 S 34 30 E
Méthana, *Greece* **48 D5** 37 35N 23 23 E
Methóni, *Greece* **48 E3** 36 49N 21 42 E
Methven, *N.Z.* **131 D6** 43 38 S 171 40 E
Metil, *Mozam.* **119 F4** 16 24 S 39 0 E
Metkovets, *Bulgaria* **50 C7** 43 37N 23 10 E
Metković, *Croatia* **45 E14** 43 6N 17 39 E
Metlakatla, *U.S.A.* **144 J15** 55 8N 131 35W
Metlaoui, *Tunisia* **108 B1** 34 24N 8 24 E
Metlik, *Papua N. G.* **132 C7** 4 46 S 152 55 E
Metlika, *Slovenia* **45 C12** 45 40N 15 20 E
Metro, *Indonesia* **84 D3** 5 5 S 105 20 E
Metropolis, *U.S.A.* **155 G10** 37 9N 88 44W
Métsovon, *Greece* **48 B3** 39 48N 21 12 E
Metter, *U.S.A.* **152 C7** 32 24N 82 3W
Mettuppalaiyam, *India* **95 J3** 11 18N 76 59 E
Mettur, *India* **95 J3** 11 48N 77 47 E
Metu, *Ethiopia* **107 F4** 8 18N 35 35 E
Metz, *France* **27 C13** 49 8N 6 10 E
Metzingen, *Germany* **31 G5** 48 31N 9 17 E
Meulaboh, *Indonesia* **84 B1** 4 11N 96 3 E
Meung-sur-Loire, *France* **27 E8** 47 50N 1 40 E
Meurcourt, *France* **32 A2** 47 46N 6 4 E
Meureudu, *Indonesia* **84 A1** 5 19N 96 10 E
Meurthe →, *France* **27 D13** 48 47N 6 9 E
Meurthe-et-Moselle □, *France* **27 D13** 48 52N 6 0 E
Meuse □, *France* **27 C12** 49 8N 5 25 E
Meuse →, *Europe* **24 D5** 50 45N 5 41 E
Meuselwitz, *Germany* **30 D8** 51 2N 12 17 E
Meutapok, Mt., *Malaysia* **85 A5** 5 40N 117 0 E
Mexia, *U.S.A.* **155 K6** 31 41N 96 29W
Mexiana, I., *Brazil* **170 A2** 0 0 49 30W
Mexicali, *Mexico* **161 N11** 32 40N 115 30W
Mexican Plateau, *Mexico* **136 G9** 25 0N 104 0W
Mexican Water, *U.S.A.* **159 H9** 36 57N 109 32W
México, *Mexico* **163 D5** 19 20N 99 10W
Mexico, *Maine, U.S.A.* **151 B14** 44 34N 70 33W
Mexico, *Mo., U.S.A.* **156 E5** 39 10N 91 53W
Mexico, *N.Y., U.S.A.* **151 C8** 43 28N 76 18W
México □, *Mexico* **163 D5** 19 20N 99 10W
Mexico ■, *Cent. Amer.* **162 C4** 25 0N 105 0W
Mexico, G. of, *Cent. Amer.* **163 C7** 25 0N 90 0W
Mexico B., *U.S.A.* **151 C8** 43 35N 76 20W
Mexico Beach, *U.S.A.* **152 F4** 29 57N 85 25W
Meydān-e Naftūn, *Iran* **97 D6** 31 56N 49 18 E
Meydani, Ra's-e, *Iran* **97 E8** 25 24N 59 6 E
Meyenburg, *Germany* **30 B8** 53 18N 12 14 E
Meyers Chuck, *U.S.A.* **144 J14** 55 45N 132 15W
Meymac, *France* **28 C6** 45 32N 2 10 E
Meymaneh, *Afghan.* **91 B2** 35 53N 64 38 E
Meyo, *Cameroon* **114 B2** 2 50N 11 1 E
Meyrueis, *France* **28 D7** 44 12N 3 27 E
Meyssac, *France* **28 C5** 45 3N 1 40 E
Meyzieu, *France* **29 C8** 45 46N 4 59 E
Mezdra, *Bulgaria* **50 C7** 43 12N 23 42 E
Mèze, *France* **28 E7** 43 27N 3 36 E
Mezen, *Russia* **56 A7** 65 50N 44 20 E
Mezen →, *Russia* **56 A7** 65 44N 44 22 E
Mézenc, Mt., *France* **29 D8** 44 54N 4 11 E
Mezeș, Munţii, *Romania* **52 C8** 47 5N 23 5 E
Mezha →, *Russia* **58 E6** 55 44N 31 33 E
Mezhdurechenskiy, *Russia* **66 D7** 59 36N 65 56 E
Mézidon-Canon, *France* **26 C6** 49 5N 0 1W
Mézières-en-Brenne, *France* **28 B5** 46 49N 1 13 E
Mézilhac, *France* **29 D8** 44 49N 4 21 E
Mézin, *France* **28 D4** 44 4N 0 16 E
Mezöberény, *Hungary* **52 D6** 46 49N 21 3 E
Mezőfalva, *Hungary* **52 D3** 46 55N 18 49 E
Mezőhegyes, *Hungary* **52 D5** 46 19N 20 49 E
Mezőkövácsháza, *Hungary* **52 D5** 46 25N 20 57 E
Mezökövesd, *Hungary* **52 C5** 47 49N 20 35 E
Mézos, *France* **28 D2** 44 5N 1 10W
Mezőtúr, *Hungary* **52 C5** 47 1N 20 41 E
Mezquital, *Mexico* **162 C4** 23 29N 104 23W
Mezzolombardo, *Italy* **44 B8** 46 13N 11 5 E
Mfolozi →, *S. Africa* **117 D5** 28 25 S 32 26 E
Mgarr, *Malta* **38 F7** 35 55N 14 22 E
Mgarr, *Gozo, Malta* **38 E7** 36 2N 14 18 E
Mgeta, *Tanzania* **119 D4** 8 22 S 36 6 E
Mglin, *Russia* **59 F7** 53 2N 32 50 E
Mhlaba Hills, *Zimbabwe* **119 F3** 18 30 S 30 30 E
Mhow, *India* **92 H6** 22 33N 75 50 E
Mi-Shima, *Japan* **72 C3** 34 46N 131 9 E
Miagao, *Phil.* **81 F4** 10 39N 122 14 E
Miahuatlán, *Mexico* **163 D5** 16 21N 96 36W
Miajadas, *Spain* **43 F5** 39 9N 5 54W
Miami, *Fla., U.S.A.* **149 N5** 25 47N 80 11W
Miami, *Okla., U.S.A.* **155 G7** 36 53N 94 53W
Miami, *Tex., U.S.A.* **155 H4** 35 42N 100 38W
Miami Beach, *U.S.A.* **149 N5** 25 47N 80 8W
Miami Canal, *U.S.A.* **153 J9** 26 30N 80 45W
Miami Shores, *U.S.A.* **153 K9** 25 52N 80 12W
Miami Springs, *U.S.A.* **153 K9** 25 49N 80 17W
Miamisburg, *U.S.A.* **157 E12** 39 38N 84 17W
Mian Xian, *China* **74 H4** 33 10N 106 32 E
Mianchi, *China* **74 G6** 34 48N 111 48 E
Mīāndarreh, *Iran* **97 C7** 35 37N 53 39 E
Mīāndowāb, *Iran* **101 D12** 37 0N 46 5 E
Miandrivazo, *Madag.* **117 B8** 19 31 S 45 29 E
Mīāneh, *Iran* **101 D12** 37 30N 47 40 E
Mianning, *China* **76 C4** 28 32N 102 9 E
Mianwali, *Pakistan* **91 B3** 32 38N 71 28 E
Mianyang, *China* **76 B5** 31 22N 104 47 E
Mianzhu, *China* **76 B5** 31 22N 104 7 E
Miaoli, *Taiwan* **77 E13** 24 37N 120 49 E
Miarinarivo, *Antananarivo, Madag.* **117 B8** 18 57 S 46 55 E
Miarinarivo, *Toamasina, Madag.* **117 B8** 16 38 S 48 15 E
Miariravaratra, *Madag.* **117 C8** 20 13 S 47 31 E
Miass, *Russia* **64 D8** 54 59N 60 6 E
Miasteczko Krajeńskie, *Poland* **55 E4** 53 7N 17 1 E
Miastko, *Poland* **54 E3** 54 0N 16 58 E
Mica, *S. Africa* **117 C5** 24 10 S 30 48 E
Micanopy, *U.S.A.* **153 F7** 29 30N 82 17W
Micăsasa, *Romania* **53 D9** 46 7N 24 7 E
Micco, *U.S.A.* **153 H9** 27 53N 80 30W
Miccosukee, *U.S.A.* **152 E5** 30 36N 84 3W
Miccosukee, L., *U.S.A.* **152 E6** 30 33N 83 53W
Michael, Mt., *Papua N. G.* **132 D3** 6 27 S 145 22 E
Michalovce, *Slovak Rep.* **35 C14** 48 47N 21 58 E
Michigan □, *U.S.A.* **148 C3** 44 0N 85 0W
Michigan, L., *U.S.A.* **157 B9** 44 0N 87 0W
Michigan Center, *U.S.A.* **157 B12** 42 14N 84 20W
Michigan City, *U.S.A.* **157 C10** 41 43N 86 54W
Michika, *Nigeria* **113 C7** 10 36N 13 23 E
Michipicoten I., *Canada* **140 C2** 47 40N 85 40W
Michoacan □, *Mexico* **162 D4** 19 0N 102 0W
Michurin, *Bulgaria* **51 D11** 42 9N 27 51 E
Michurinsk, *Russia* **60 D5** 52 58N 40 27 E
Mico, Pta., *Nic.* **164 D3** 12 0N 83 30W
Miconje, *Angola* **115 C2** 4 26 S 12 48 E
Micoud, *St. Lucia* **165 f** 13 49N 60 54W
Micronesia, *Pac. Oc.* **134 G7** 11 0N 160 0 E
Micronesia, Federated States of ■, *Pac. Oc.* **134 G7** 9 0N 150 0 E
Mid-Indian Ridge, *Ind. Oc.* **121 H6** 30 0 S 75 0 E
Midai, *Indonesia* **85 B3** 3 0N 107 47 E
Midale, *Canada* **143 D8** 49 25N 103 20W
Middelburg, *Neths.* **24 C3** 51 30N 3 36 E
Middelburg, *Eastern Cape, S. Africa* **116 E4** 31 30 S 25 0 E
Middelburg, *Mpumalanga, S. Africa* **117 D4** 25 49 S 29 28 E
Middelfart, *Denmark* **17 J3** 55 30N 9 43 E
Middelpos, *S. Africa* **116 E3** 31 55 S 20 13 E
Middelwit, *S. Africa* **116 C4** 24 51 S 27 3 E
Middle →, *U.S.A.* **156 C3** 41 26N 93 30W
Middle Alkali L., *U.S.A.* **158 F3** 41 27N 120 5W
Middle Andaman I., *India* **95 H11** 12 30N 92 50 E
Middle Bass I., *U.S.A.* **150 E2** 41 41N 82 49W
Middle East, *Asia* **62 F7** 38 0N 40 0 E
Middle Fork Feather →, *U.S.A.* **160 F5** 38 33N 121 30W
Middle I., *Australia* **125 F3** 34 6 S 123 11 E
Middle Loup →, *U.S.A.* **154 E5** 41 17N 98 24W
Middle Raccoon →, *U.S.A.* **156 C3** 41 35N 93 35W
Middle Sackville, *Canada* **141 D7** 44 47N 63 42W
Middleboro, *U.S.A.* **151 E14** 41 54N 70 55W
Middleburg, *Fla., U.S.A.* **152 E8** 30 4N 81 52W
Middleburg, *N.Y., U.S.A.* **151 D10** 42 36N 74 20W
Middleburg, *Pa., U.S.A.* **150 F7** 40 47N 77 3W
Middlebury, *Ind., U.S.A.* **157 C11** 41 41N 85 42W
Middlebury, *Vt., U.S.A.* **151 B11** 44 1N 73 10W
Middlemarch, *N.Z.* **131 F5** 45 30 S 170 9 E
Middlemount, *Australia* **126 C4** 22 50 S 148 40 E
Middleport, *N.Y., U.S.A.* **150 C6** 43 13N 78 29W
Middleport, *Ohio, U.S.A.* **148 F4** 39 0N 82 3W
Middlesboro, *U.S.A.* **149 G4** 36 36N 83 43W
Middlesbrough, *U.K.* **20 C6** 54 35N 1 13W
Middlesbrough □, *U.K.* **20 C6** 54 28N 1 13W
Middlesex, *Belize* **164 C2** 17 2N 88 31W
Middlesex, *N.J., U.S.A.* **151 F10** 40 36N 74 30W
Middlesex, *N.Y., U.S.A.* **150 D7** 42 42N 77 16W
Middleton, *Australia* **126 C3** 22 22 S 141 32 E
Middleton, *Canada* **141 D6** 44 57N 65 4W
Middleton, *U.S.A.* **156 A7** 43 6N 89 30W
Middleton Cr. →, *Australia* **126 C3** 22 35 S 141 51 E
Middleton I., *U.S.A.* **144 G11** 59 26N 146 20W
Middletown, *U.K.* **23 B5** 54 17N 6 51W
Middletown, *Calif., U.S.A.* **160 G4** 38 45N 122 37W
Middletown, *Conn., U.S.A.* **151 E12** 41 34N 72 39W
Middletown, *Ky., U.S.A.* **157 F11** 38 14N 85 32W
Middletown, *N.Y., U.S.A.* **151 E10** 41 27N 74 25W
Middletown, *Ohio, U.S.A.* **157 E12** 39 31N 84 24W
Middletown, *Pa., U.S.A.* **151 F8** 40 12N 76 44W
Middleville, *U.S.A.* **157 B11** 42 43N 85 28W
Midelt, *Morocco* **110 B4** 32 46N 4 44W
Midge Point, *Australia* **126 J6** 20 39 S 148 43 E
Midhirst, *N.Z.* **130 F3** 39 17 S 174 18 E
Miðsandur, *Iceland* **11 C5** 64 24N 21 28W
Midhurst, *U.K.* **21 G7** 50 59N 0 44W
Midī, *Yemen* **107 D5** 16 20N 42 45 E
Midi, Canal du →, *France* **28 E5** 43 45N 1 21 E
Midi d'Ossau, Pic du, *France* **28 F3** 42 50N 0 26W
Midi-Pyrénées □, *France* **28 E5** 43 55N 1 45 E
Midland, *Canada* **140 D4** 44 45N 79 50W
Midland, *Calif., U.S.A.* **161 M12** 33 52N 114 48W
Midland, *Mich., U.S.A.* **148 D3** 43 37N 84 14W
Midland, *Pa., U.S.A.* **150 F4** 40 39N 80 27W
Midland, *Tex., U.S.A.* **155 K3** 32 0N 102 3W
Midlands □, *Zimbabwe* **119 F2** 19 40 S 29 0 E
Midleton, *Ireland* **23 E3** 51 55N 8 10W
Midlothian, *U.S.A.* **155 J6** 32 30N 97 0W
Midlothian □, *U.K.* **22 F5** 55 51N 3 5W
Midongy, Tangorombohitr' i, *Madag.* **117 C8** 23 30 S 47 0 E
Midongy Atsimo, *Madag.* **117 C8** 23 35 S 47 1 E
Midou →, *France* **28 E3** 43 54N 0 30W
Midouze →, *France* **28 E3** 43 48N 0 51W
Midsayap, *Phil.* **81 H5** 7 12N 124 32 E
Midsund, *Norway* **18 B3** 62 41N 6 40 E
Midtgulen, *Norway* **18 C2** 61 44N 5 11 E
Midu, *China* **76 E3** 25 18N 100 32 E

250 Midville

Midville, U.S.A. 152 C7 32 49N 82 14W
Midway, Ala., U.S.A. 152 C4 32 5N 85 31W
Midway, Fla., U.S.A. 152 E5 30 30N 84 27W
Midway Is., Pac. Oc. 134 E10 28 13N 177 22W
Midway Is., U.S.A. 145 F8 28 13N 177 22W
Midway Wells, U.S.A. 161 N11 32 41N 115 7W
Midwest, U.S.A. 158 E10 43 25N 106 16W
Midwest City, U.S.A. 155 H6 35 27N 97 24W
Midyat, Turkey 101 D9 37 25N 41 23 E
Midzŏr, Bulgaria 50 C6 43 24N 22 40 E
Mie, Japan 72 E3 32 58N 131 35 E
Mie □, Japan 73 C8 34 30N 136 10 E
Miechów, Poland 55 H7 50 21N 20 5 E
Miedwie, Jezioro, Poland 55 E1 53 17N 14 54 E
Międzybórz, Poland 55 G4 51 25N 17 34 E
Międzychód, Poland 55 F2 52 35N 15 53 E
Międzylesie, Poland 55 H3 50 8N 16 40 E
Międzyrzec Podlaski, Poland 55 G9 51 58N 22 45 E
Międzyrzecz, Poland 55 F2 52 26N 15 35 E
Międzyzdroje, Poland 54 E1 53 56N 14 26 E
Miejska Górka, Poland 55 G3 51 39N 16 58 E
Miélan, France 28 E4 43 27N 0 19 E
Mielec, Poland 55 H8 50 15N 21 25 E
Mienga, Angola 116 B2 17 12 S 19 48 E
Miercurea-Ciuc, Romania 53 D10 46 21N 25 48 E
Miercurea Sibiului, Romania 53 E8 45 53N 23 48 E
Mieres, Spain 42 B5 43 18N 5 48W
Mieroszów, Poland 55 H3 50 40N 16 11 E
Mieso, Ethiopia 107 F5 9 15N 40 43 E
Mieszkowice, Poland 55 F1 52 47N 14 30 E
Mifflintown, U.S.A. 150 F7 40 34N 77 24W
Mifraz Hefa, Israel 103 C4 32 52N 35 0 E
Migennes, France 27 E10 47 58N 3 31 E
Migliarino, Italy 45 D8 44 46N 11 56 E
Miguel Alemán, Presa, Mexico 163 D5 18 15N 96 40W
Miguel Alves, Brazil 170 B3 4 11 S 42 55W
Miguel Calmon, Brazil 170 D3 11 26 S 40 36W
Miguelturra, Spain 43 G7 38 58N 3 53W
Mihăileni, Romania 53 C11 47 58N 26 9 E
Mihăilești, Romania 53 F10 44 20N 25 54 E
Mihailovca, Moldova 53 D13 46 33N 28 56 E
Mihalgazi, Turkey 49 A12 40 2N 30 34 E
Mihaliççık, Turkey 100 C4 39 53N 31 30 E
Mihara, Japan 72 C5 34 24N 133 5 E
Mihara-Yama, Japan 73 C11 34 43N 139 23 E
Miheșu de Cîmpie, Romania 53 D9 46 41N 24 9 E
Mijas, Spain 43 J6 36 36N 4 40W
Mikese, Tanzania 118 D4 6 48 S 37 55 E
Mikha-Tskhakaya = Senaki, Georgia 61 J6 42 15N 42 7 E
Mikhailovka = Mykhaylivka, Ukraine 59 J8 47 12N 35 15 E
Mikhaylov, Russia 58 E10 54 14N 39 0 E
Mikhaylovgrad = Montana, Bulgaria 50 C7 43 27N 23 16 E
Mikhaylovka, Kyrgyzstan 65 B9 42 37N 78 20 E
Mikhaylovka, Russia 60 E6 50 3N 43 5 E
Mikhaylovski, Russia 64 C7 56 27N 59 7 E
Mikhnevo, Russia 58 E9 55 4N 37 59 E
Miki, Hyōgo, Japan 72 C6 34 48N 134 59 E
Miki, Kagawa, Japan 72 C6 34 12N 134 7 E
Mikínai, Greece 48 D4 37 43N 22 46 E
Mikir Hills, India 90 B4 26 10N 93 30 E
Mikkeli, Finland 15 F22 61 43N 27 15 E
Mikkwa →, Canada 142 B6 58 25N 114 46W
Mikniya, Sudan 107 D3 17 0N 33 45 E
Mikołajki, Poland 54 E8 53 49N 21 37 E
Míkonos, Greece 49 D7 37 30N 25 25 E
Mikope, Dem. Rep. of the Congo 115 C4 4 58 S 20 43 E
Mikrí Préspa, Límni, Greece 50 F5 40 47N 21 3 E
Mikrón Dhérion, Greece 51 E10 41 19N 26 6 E
Mikstat, Poland 55 G4 51 32N 17 59 E
Mikulov, Czech Rep. 35 C9 48 48N 16 39 E
Mikumi, Tanzania 118 D4 7 26 S 37 0 E
Mikumi Nat. Park, Tanzania 118 D4 7 35 S 37 15 E
Mikun, Russia 56 B9 62 20N 50 0 E
Mikuni, Japan 73 A8 36 13N 136 9 E
Mikuni-Tōge, Japan 73 A10 36 50N 138 50 E
Mikura-Jima, Japan 73 D11 33 52N 139 36 E
Milaca, U.S.A. 154 C8 45 45N 93 39W
Milagro, Ecuador 168 D2 2 11 S 79 36W
Milagros, Phil. 80 E4 12 13N 123 30 E
Milan = Milano, Italy 44 C6 45 28N 9 12 E
Milan, Ga., U.S.A. 152 C6 32 1N 83 4W
Milan, Ill., U.S.A. 156 C6 41 27N 90 34W
Milan, Mich., U.S.A. 157 B13 42 5N 83 41W
Milan, Mo., U.S.A. 156 D3 40 12N 93 7W
Milan, Tenn., U.S.A. 149 H1 35 55N 88 46W
Miland, Norway 18 E5 59 54N 8 45 E
Milando, Angola 115 D3 8 45 S 17 36 E
Milando, Reserva Parcial de, Angola 115 D3 8 45 S 17 10 E
Milang, Australia 128 C3 35 24 S 138 58 E
Milange, Mozam. 119 F4 16 3 S 35 45 E
Milano, Italy 44 C6 45 28N 9 12 E
Milanoa, Madag. 117 A8 13 35 S 49 47 E
Milâs, Turkey 49 D9 37 20N 27 50 E
Milatos, Greece 39 E6 35 18N 25 34 E
Milazzo, Italy 47 D8 38 13N 15 15 E
Milbank, U.S.A. 154 C6 45 13N 96 38W
Milbanke Sd., Canada 142 C3 52 15N 128 35W
Milden, Canada 143 C7 51 29N 107 32W
Mildenhall, U.K. 21 E8 52 21N 0 32 E
Mildmay, Canada 150 B3 44 3N 81 7W
Mildura, Australia 128 C5 34 13 S 142 9 E
Mile, China 76 E4 24 28N 103 20 E
Miléai, Greece 48 B5 39 20N 23 9 E
Miles, Australia 127 D5 26 40 S 150 9 E
Miles City, U.S.A. 154 B2 46 25N 105 51W
Mileşti, Moldova 53 C13 47 13N 28 3 E
Milestone, Canada 143 D8 49 59N 104 31W
Mileto, Italy 47 D9 38 36N 16 4 E
Miletto, Mte., Italy 47 A7 41 27N 14 22 E
Miletus, Turkey 49 D9 37 30N 27 18 E
Milevsko, Czech Rep. 34 B7 49 27N 14 21 E
Milford, Calif., U.S.A. 160 E6 40 10N 120 22W
Milford, Conn., U.S.A. 151 E11 41 14N 73 3W
Milford, Del., U.S.A. 148 F8 38 55N 75 26W
Milford, Ill., U.S.A. 157 D9 40 38N 87 42W
Milford, Mass., U.S.A. 151 D13 42 8N 71 31W
Milford, Mich., U.S.A. 157 B13 42 35N 83 36W
Milford, N.H., U.S.A. 151 D13 42 50N 71 39W
Milford, Pa., U.S.A. 151 E10 41 19N 74 48W
Milford, Utah, U.S.A. 159 G7 38 24N 113 1W
Milford Haven, U.K. 21 F2 51 42N 5 7W
Milford Sd., N.Z. 131 E2 44 41 S 167 47 E
Milh, Bahr al, Iraq 101 F10 32 40N 43 35 E
Miliana, Aïn Salah, Algeria 111 C5 27 20N 2 32 E
Miliana, Médéa, Algeria 111 A5 36 20N 2 15 E
Milicz, Poland 55 G4 51 31N 17 19 E
Milikapiti, Australia 124 B5 11 26 S 130 40 E
Mililani Town, U.S.A. 145 K13 21 28N 158 1W
Miling, Australia 125 F2 30 30 S 116 17 E
Militello in Val di Catánia, Italy 47 E7 37 16N 14 48 E
Milk →, U.S.A. 158 B10 48 4N 106 19W
Milk, Wadi el →, Sudan 106 D3 17 55N 30 20 E
Milk River, Canada 142 D6 49 10N 112 5W
Mill I., Antarctica 7 C8 66 0 S 101 30 E
Mill Shoals, U.S.A. 157 F8 38 15N 88 21W
Mill Valley, U.S.A. 160 H4 37 54N 122 32W
Millárs →, Spain 40 F4 39 55N 0 1W
Millau, France 28 D7 44 8N 3 4 E
Millbridge, Canada 150 B7 44 41N 77 36W
Millbrook, Canada 150 B6 44 10N 78 29W
Millbrook, U.S.A. 151 E11 41 47N 73 42W
Mille Lacs, L. des, Canada 140 C1 48 45N 90 35W
Mille Lacs L., U.S.A. 154 B8 46 15N 93 39W
Milledgeville, Ga., U.S.A. 152 B6 33 5N 83 14W
Milledgeville, Ill., U.S.A. 156 C7 41 58N 89 46W
Millen, U.S.A. 152 C8 32 48N 81 57W
Millennium I. = Caroline I., Kiribati 135 H12 9 58 S 150 13W
Miller, U.S.A. 154 C5 44 31N 98 59W
Millerovo, Russia 61 F5 48 57N 40 28 E
Miller's Flat, N.Z. 131 F4 45 39 S 169 23 E
Millersburg, Ind., U.S.A. 157 C11 41 32N 85 42W
Millersburg, Ohio, U.S.A. 150 F3 40 33N 81 55W
Millersburg, Pa., U.S.A. 150 F8 40 32N 76 58W
Millerton, N.Z. 131 B6 41 39 S 171 54 E
Millerton, U.S.A. 151 E11 41 57N 73 31W
Millerton L., U.S.A. 160 J7 37 1N 119 41W
Millet, St. Lucia 165 f 13 55N 60 59W
Millevaches, Plateau de, France 28 C6 45 45N 2 0 E
Millheim, U.S.A. 150 F7 40 54N 77 29W
Millicent, Australia 128 D4 37 34 S 140 21 E
Milligan, U.S.A. 153 E3 30 45N 86 38W
Millington, U.S.A. 155 H10 35 20N 89 53W
Millinocket, U.S.A. 149 C11 45 39N 68 43W
Millmerran, Australia 127 D5 27 53 S 151 16 E
Millom, U.K. 20 C4 54 13N 3 16W
Mills L., Canada 142 A5 61 30N 118 20W
Millsboro, U.S.A. 150 G5 40 0N 80 0W
Millstream-Chichester Nat. Park, Australia 124 D2 21 35 S 117 6 E
Millthorpe, Australia 129 B8 33 26 S 149 12 E
Milltown Malbay, Ireland 23 D2 52 52N 9 24W
Millville, N.J., U.S.A. 148 F8 39 24N 75 2W
Millville, Pa., U.S.A. 151 E8 41 7N 76 32W
Millwood L., U.S.A. 155 J8 33 42N 93 58W
Milna, Croatia 45 E13 43 20N 16 28 E
Milne →, Australia 126 C2 21 10 S 137 33 E
Milne Bay □, Papua N. G. 132 E7 10 0 S 152 30 E
Milne Land, Greenland 10 C8 70 40N 26 30W
Milo, U.S.A. 149 C11 45 15N 68 59W
Milolii, U.S.A. 145 D6 19 11N 155 55W
Milos, Greece 49 E6 36 44N 24 25 E
Miłosław, Poland 55 F4 52 12N 17 32 E
Milot, Albania 50 E3 41 41N 19 43 E
Milparinka, Australia 127 D3 29 46 S 141 57 E
Milroy, U.S.A. 157 E11 39 30N 85 28W
Miltenberg, Germany 31 F5 49 41N 9 16 E
Milton, Australia 129 C9 35 20 S 150 27 E
Milton, N.S., Canada 141 D7 44 4N 64 45W
Milton, Ont., Canada 150 C5 43 31N 79 53W
Milton, N.Z. 131 G4 46 7 S 169 59 E
Milton, Calif., U.S.A. 160 G6 38 3N 120 51W
Milton, Fla., U.S.A. 153 E3 30 38N 87 3W
Milton, Iowa, U.S.A. 156 D4 40 41N 92 10W
Milton, Pa., U.S.A. 150 F8 41 1N 76 51W
Milton, Vt., U.S.A. 151 B11 44 38N 73 7W
Milton, Wis., U.S.A. 157 B8 42 47N 88 56W
Milton-Freewater, U.S.A. 158 D4 45 56N 118 23W
Milton Keynes, U.K. 21 E7 52 1N 0 44W
Milton Keynes □, U.K. 21 E7 52 1N 0 44W
Miltou, Chad 109 F3 10 14N 17 26 E
Miluo, China 77 C9 29 0N 112 59 E
Milverton, Canada 150 C4 43 34N 80 55W
Milwaukee, U.S.A. 157 A9 43 2N 87 55W
Milwaukee Deep, Atl. Oc. 165 C6 19 50N 68 0W
Milwaukie, U.S.A. 160 E4 45 27N 122 38W
Mim, Ghana 112 D4 6 57N 2 33W
Mimizan, France 28 D2 44 12N 1 13W
Mimoň, Czech Rep. 34 A7 50 38N 14 43 E
Mimongo, Gabon 114 C2 1 11 S 11 36 E
Mimoso, Brazil 171 E2 15 10 S 48 5W
Mims, U.S.A. 153 G9 28 40N 80 51W
Min Jiang →, Fujian, China 77 E12 26 0N 119 35 E
Min Jiang →, Sichuan, China 76 C5 28 45N 104 40 E
Min Xian, China 74 G3 34 25N 104 5 E
Mina Pirquitas, Argentina 174 A2 22 40 S 66 30W
Mīnā Su'ud, Si. Arabia 97 D6 28 45N 48 28 E
Mīnā'al Aḩmadī, Kuwait 97 D6 29 5N 48 10 E
Minago →, Canada 143 C9 54 33N 98 59W
Minakami, Japan 73 A10 36 49N 138 59 E
Minaki, Canada 143 D10 49 59N 94 40W
Minakuchi, Japan 73 C8 34 58N 136 10 E
Minamata, Japan 72 E2 32 10N 130 30 E
Minami-Tori-Shima, Pac. Oc. 134 E7 24 20N 153 58 E
Minas, Uruguay 175 C4 34 20 S 55 10W
Minas, Sierra de las, Guatemala 164 C2 15 9N 89 31W
Minas Basin, Canada 141 C7 45 20N 64 12W
Minas de Rio Tinto = Minas de Riotinto, Spain 43 H4 37 42N 6 35W
Minas de Riotinto, Spain 43 H4 37 42N 6 35W
Minas Gerais □, Brazil 171 E2 18 50 S 46 0W
Minas Novas, Brazil 171 E3 17 15 S 42 36W
Minatitlán, Mexico 163 D6 17 59N 94 31W
Minbu, Burma 90 E5 20 10N 94 52 E
Minbya, Burma 90 E4 20 22N 93 16 E
Minchinabad, Pakistan 92 D5 30 10N 73 34 E
Mincio →, Italy 44 C7 45 4N 10 59 E
Minčol, Slovak Rep. 35 B13 49 15N 20 58 E
Mindanao, Phil. 81 H5 8 0N 125 0 E
Mindanao Sea = Bohol Sea, Phil. 81 G5 9 0N 124 0 E
Mindanao Trench, Pac. Oc. 80 E5 12 0N 126 6 E
Mindel →, Germany 31 G6 48 31N 10 23 E
Mindelheim, Germany 31 G6 48 3N 10 29 E
Mindelo, C. Verde Is. 9 j 16 24N 25 0W
Minden, Canada 150 B6 44 55N 78 43W
Minden, Germany 30 C4 52 17N 8 55 E
Minden, La., U.S.A. 155 J8 32 37N 93 17W
Minden, Nev., U.S.A. 160 G7 38 57N 119 46W
Mindiptana, Indonesia 83 C6 5 55 S 140 22 E
Mindon, Burma 90 F5 19 21N 94 44 E
Mindona L., Australia 128 B5 33 6 S 142 6 E
Mindoro, Phil. 80 E3 13 0N 121 0 E
Mindoro Occidental □, Phil. 80 E3 13 0N 120 55 E
Mindoro Oriental □, Phil. 80 E3 13 0N 121 5 E
Mindoro Str., Phil. 80 E3 12 30N 120 30 E
Mindouli, Congo 115 C2 4 12 S 14 28 E
Mindourou, Cameroon 114 B2 3 29N 13 26 E
Mine, Japan 72 C3 34 12N 131 7 E
Minehead, U.K. 21 F4 51 12N 3 29W
Mineiros, Brazil 173 D7 17 34 S 52 34W
Mineola, N.Y., U.S.A. 151 F11 40 45N 73 39W
Mineola, Tex., U.S.A. 155 J7 32 40N 95 29W
Mineral King, U.S.A. 160 J8 36 27N 118 36W
Mineral Point, U.S.A. 156 B6 42 52N 90 11W
Mineral Wells, U.S.A. 155 J5 32 48N 98 7W
Mineralnyye Vody, Russia 61 H6 44 15N 43 8 E
Minersville, U.S.A. 151 F8 40 41N 76 16W
Minerva, U.S.A. 150 F3 40 44N 81 6W
Minervino Murge, Italy 47 A9 41 5N 16 5 E
Minetto, U.S.A. 151 C8 43 24N 76 28W
Ming-Kush, Kyrgyzstan 65 C7 41 40N 74 28 E
Mingäçevir, Azerbaijan 61 K8 40 45N 47 0 E
Mingäçevir Su Anbarı, Azerbaijan 61 K8 40 57N 46 50 E
Mingala, C.A.R. 114 A4 5 6N 21 49 E
Mingan, Canada 141 B7 50 20N 64 0W
Mingary, Australia 128 B4 32 8 S 140 45 E
Mingechaur = Mingäçevir, Azerbaijan 61 K8 40 45N 47 0 E
Mingechaurskoye Vdkhr. = Mingäçevir Su Anbarı, Azerbaijan 61 K8 40 57N 46 50 E
Mingela, Australia 126 B4 19 52 S 146 38 E
Mingenew, Australia 125 E2 29 12 S 115 21 E
Mingera Cr. →, Australia 126 C2 20 38 S 137 45 E
Minggang, China 77 A10 32 24N 114 3 E
Mingguang, China 77 A11 32 46N 117 59 E
Mingin, Burma 90 D5 22 50N 94 30 E
Mingir, Moldova 53 D13 46 40N 28 20 E
Minglanilla, Spain 41 F3 39 34N 1 38W
Minglun, China 76 E7 25 10N 108 21 E
Mingo, Congo 114 C3 1 55 S 15 1 E
Mingo Junction, U.S.A. 150 F4 40 19N 80 37W
Mingorria, Spain 42 E6 40 45N 4 40W
Mingshan, China 76 B4 30 6N 103 10 E
Mingteke, China 65 E7 37 7N 75 4 E
Mingteke Daban = Mintaka Pass, Pakistan 65 E7 37 0N 74 58 E
Mingxi, China 77 D11 26 18N 117 12 E
Mingyuegue, China 75 C15 43 2N 128 50 E
Minhla, Magwe, Burma 90 F5 19 58N 95 3 E
Minhla, Pegu, Burma 90 G5 17 59N 95 43 E
Minho = Miño →, Spain 42 D2 41 52N 8 40W
Minhou, China 77 E12 26 0N 119 15 E
Miničevo, Serbia, Yug. 52 G7 43 42N 22 18 E
Minicoy I., India 95 K1 8 17N 73 2 E
Minidoka, U.S.A. 158 E7 42 45N 113 29W
Minier, U.S.A. 156 D7 40 26N 89 19W
Minigwal, L., Australia 125 E3 29 31 S 123 14 E
Minilya →, Australia 125 D1 23 45 S 114 0 E
Minilya Roadhouse, Australia 125 D1 23 55 S 114 0 E
Mininera, Australia 128 D5 37 37 S 142 58 E
Minipi L., Canada 141 B7 52 25N 60 45W
Minj, Papua N. G. 132 C3 5 54 S 144 37 E
Mink L., Canada 142 A5 61 54N 117 40W
Minkammen, Sudan 107 F3 6 3N 31 32 E
Minkebé, Gabon 114 B2 1 45N 12 45 E
Minlaton, Australia 128 C2 34 45 S 137 35 E
Minna, Nigeria 113 D6 9 37N 6 30 E
Minneapolis, Kans., U.S.A. 154 F6 39 8N 97 42W
Minneapolis, Minn., U.S.A. 154 C8 44 59N 93 16W
Minnedosa, Canada 143 C9 50 14N 99 50W
Minnesota □, U.S.A. 154 B8 46 0N 94 15W
Minnesota →, U.S.A. 154 C8 44 54N 93 9W
Minnesund, Norway 18 D8 60 23N 11 14 E
Minnewaukan, U.S.A. 154 A5 48 4N 99 15W
Minnipa, Australia 127 E2 32 51 S 135 9 E
Minnitaki L., Canada 140 C1 49 57N 92 10W
Mino, Japan 73 B8 35 32N 136 55 E
Miño, Spain 42 B2 43 21N 8 12W
Miño →, Spain 42 D2 41 52N 8 40W
Mino-Kamo, Japan 73 B9 35 23N 137 2 E
Mino-Mikawa-Kōgen, Japan 73 B9 35 10N 137 23 E
Minoa, Greece 49 F7 35 6N 25 45 E
Minobu, Japan 73 B10 35 22N 138 26 E
Minobu-Sanchi, Japan 73 B10 35 14N 138 20 E
Minonk, U.S.A. 156 D7 40 54N 89 2W
Minooka, U.S.A. 157 C8 41 27N 88 16W
Minorca = Menorca, Spain 38 B5 40 0N 4 0 E
Minore, Australia 129 B8 32 14 S 148 27 E
Minot, U.S.A. 154 A4 48 14N 101 18W
Minqin, China 74 E2 38 38N 103 20 E
Minqing, China 77 D12 26 15N 118 50 E
Minsen, Germany 30 B3 53 41N 7 58 E
Minsk, Belarus 58 F4 53 52N 27 30 E
Mińsk Mazowiecki, Poland 55 F8 52 10N 21 33 E
Minster, U.S.A. 157 D12 40 24N 84 23W
Mintabie, Australia 127 D1 27 15 S 133 7 E
Mintaka Pass, Pakistan 65 E7 37 0N 74 58 E
Minthami, Burma 90 D5 23 55N 94 16 E
Minto, Canada 141 C6 46 5N 66 5W
Minto, U.S.A. 144 D10 64 53N 149 11W
Minto, L., Canada 140 A5 57 13N 75 0W
Minton, Canada 143 D8 49 10N 104 35W
Mintom, Gabon 114 B2 0 27N 12 16 E
Minturn, U.S.A. 158 G10 39 35N 106 26W
Minturno, Italy 46 A6 41 15N 13 45 E
Minûf, Egypt 106 H7 30 26N 30 52 E
Minusinsk, Russia 67 D10 53 43N 91 20 E
Minusio, Switz. 33 D7 46 11N 8 49 E
Minutang, India 90 A6 28 15N 96 30 E
Minvoul, Gabon 114 B2 2 9N 12 8 E
Minwakh, Yemen 99 C5 16 48N 48 6 E
Minya el Qamh, Egypt 106 H7 30 31N 31 21 E
Minyar, Russia 64 D6 55 4N 57 33 E
Minyip, Australia 128 D5 36 29 S 142 36 E
Minzhong, China 69 F10 22 37N 113 30 E
Mionica, Bos.-H. 52 F3 44 51N 18 29 E
Mionica, Serbia, Yug. 50 B4 44 14N 20 6 E
Miquelon, Canada 140 C4 49 25N 76 27W
Miquelon, St- P. & M. 141 C8 47 8N 56 22W
Mir, Niger 113 C7 14 5N 11 59 E
Mīr Kūh, Iran 97 E8 26 22N 58 55 E
Mīr Shahdād, Iran 97 E8 26 15N 58 29 E
Mira, Italy 45 C9 45 26N 12 8 E
Mira, Portugal 42 E2 40 26N 8 44W
Mira →, Colombia 168 C2 1 36N 79 1W
Mira →, Portugal 43 H2 37 43N 8 47W
Mira por vos Cay, Bahamas 165 B5 22 9N 74 30W
Mirābād, Afghan. 91 C1 30 25N 61 50 E
Mirabella Eclano, Italy 47 A7 41 2N 14 59 E
Miracema do Norte, Brazil 170 C2 9 33 S 48 24W
Mirador, Brazil 170 C3 6 22 S 44 22W
Miraflores, Colombia 168 C3 1 25N 72 13W
Miraj, India 94 F2 16 50N 74 45 E
Miram Shah, Pakistan 91 B3 33 0N 70 2 E
Miramar, Argentina 174 D4 38 15 S 57 50W
Miramar, Mozam. 117 C6 23 50 S 35 35 E
Miramas, France 29 E8 43 33N 4 59 E
Mirambeau, France 28 C3 45 23N 0 35W
Miramichi, Canada 141 C6 47 2N 65 28W
Miramichi B., Canada 141 C7 47 15N 65 0W
Miramont-de-Guyenne, France 28 D4 44 37N 0 21 E
Miranda, Brazil 173 E6 20 10 S 56 15W
Miranda □, Venezuela 168 A4 10 15N 66 25W
Miranda →, Brazil 173 D6 19 25 S 57 20W
Miranda de Ebro, Spain 40 C2 42 41N 2 57W
Miranda do Corvo, Portugal 42 E2 40 6N 8 20W
Miranda do Douro, Portugal 42 D4 41 30N 6 16W
Mirande, France 28 E4 43 31N 0 25 E
Mirandela, Portugal 42 D3 41 32N 7 10W
Mirándola, Italy 44 D8 44 53N 11 4 E
Mirandópolis, Brazil 175 A5 21 9 S 51 6W
Mirango, Malawi 119 E3 13 32 S 34 58 E
Mirani, Australia 126 K6 21 8 S 148 53 E
Mirano, Italy 45 C9 45 30N 12 7 E
Miras, Albania 50 F4 40 30N 20 56 E
Mirassol, Brazil 175 A6 20 46 S 49 28W
Mirbāţ, Oman 99 C6 17 0N 54 45 E
Mirboo North, Australia 129 E7 38 24 S 146 10 E
Mirear, Egypt 106 C4 23 15N 35 41 E
Mirebeau, Côte-d'Or, France 27 E12 47 25N 5 20 E
Mirebeau, Vienne, France 26 F7 46 49N 0 10 E
Mirecourt, France 27 D13 48 20N 6 10 E
Mirgorod = Myrhorod, Ukraine 59 H7 49 58N 33 37 E
Miri, Malaysia 85 B4 4 23N 113 59 E
Miriałguda, India 94 F4 16 52N 79 35 E
Miriam Vale, Australia 126 C5 24 20 S 151 33 E
Miribel, France 27 G11 45 50N 4 57 E
Mirigama, Sri Lanka 95 L5 7 15N 80 8 E
Mirim, L., S. Amer. 175 C5 32 45 S 52 50W
Mirimire, Venezuela 168 A4 11 10N 68 43W
Miriti, Brazil 173 B6 6 15 S 59 0W
Mirnyy, Russia 67 C12 62 33N 113 53 E
Miroč, Serbia, Yug. 50 B6 44 32N 22 16 E
Mirokhan, Pakistan 92 F3 27 46N 68 6 E
Mirond L., Canada 143 B8 55 6N 102 47W
Mirosławiec, Poland 54 E3 53 20N 16 5 E
Mirpur, Pakistan 93 C5 33 32N 73 56 E
Mirpur Batoro, Pakistan 92 G3 24 44N 68 16 E
Mirpur Bibiwari, Pakistan 92 E2 28 33N 67 44 E
Mirpur Khas, Pakistan 91 D3 25 30N 69 0 E
Mirpur Sakro, Pakistan 92 G2 24 33N 67 41 E
Mirria, Niger 113 C6 13 43N 9 7 E
Mirrool, Australia 129 C7 34 19 S 147 10 E
Mirs Bay = Tai Pang Wan, H.K. 69 F11 22 33N 114 24 E
Mirsk, Poland 55 H2 50 58N 15 23 E
Mirtağ, Turkey 96 B4 38 23N 41 56 E
Mírtou, Kólpos, Greece 39 C1 38 20N 20 27 E
Miryang, S. Korea 75 G15 35 31N 128 44 E
Mirzaani, Georgia 61 K8 41 24N 46 5 E
Mirzapur, India 93 G10 25 10N 82 34 E
Mirzapur-cum-Vindhyachal = Mirzapur, India 93 G10 25 10N 82 34 E
Misaki, Japan 73 C7 34 18N 135 9 E
Misamis Occidental □, Phil. 81 G4 8 20N 123 42 E
Misamis Oriental □, Phil. 81 G5 8 45N 125 0 E
Misantla, Mexico 163 D5 19 56N 96 50W
Misawa, Japan 70 D10 40 41N 141 24 E
Miscou I., Canada 141 C7 47 57N 64 31W
Misha, India 95 L10 7 59N 93 20 E
Mish'āb, Ra's al, Si. Arabia 97 D6 28 15N 48 43 E
Mishagua →, Peru 172 C3 11 12 S 72 58W
Mishan, China 69 B8 45 37N 131 48 E
Mishawaka, U.S.A. 157 C10 41 40N 86 11W
Mishbih, Gebel, Egypt 106 C3 22 38N 34 44 E
Mishima, Japan 73 B10 35 10N 138 52 E
Mishmi Hills, India 90 A5 29 0N 96 0 E
Mishō, Japan 72 E4 32 57N 132 35 E
Misima I., Papua N. G. 132 F7 10 40 S 152 45 E
Misión, Mexico 161 N10 32 6N 116 53W
Misión Fagnano, Argentina 176 D3 54 32 S 67 17W
Misiones □, Argentina 175 B5 27 0 S 55 0W
Misiones □, Paraguay 174 B4 27 0 S 56 0W
Miskah, Si. Arabia 96 E4 24 49N 42 56 E
Miski, E. →, Chad 109 E3 20 0N 17 55 E
Miskitos, Cayos, Nic. 164 D3 14 26N 82 50W
Miskolc, Hungary 52 B5 48 7N 20 50 E
Misoke, Dem. Rep. of the Congo 118 C2 0 42 S 28 2 E
Misool, Indonesia 83 B4 1 52 S 130 10 E
Mişrātah, Libya 108 B3 32 24N 15 3 E
Mişrātah □, Libya 108 C3 33 30N 15 0 E
Missanabie, Canada 140 C3 48 20N 84 6W
Missão Catrimani, Brazil 169 C5 2 48N 62 18W
Missão Velha, Brazil 170 C4 7 15 S 39 10W
Missinaibi →, Canada 140 B3 50 43N 81 29W
Missinaibi L., Canada 140 C3 48 23N 83 40W
Mission, Canada 142 D4 49 10N 122 15W
Mission, S. Dak., U.S.A. 154 D4 43 18N 100 39W
Mission, Tex., U.S.A. 155 M5 26 13N 98 20W
Mission Beach, Australia 126 B4 17 53 S 146 6 E
Mission Viejo, U.S.A. 161 M9 33 36N 117 40W
Missirah, Senegal 112 C1 13 40N 16 30W
Missisa L., Canada 140 B2 52 20N 85 7W
Missisicabi →, Canada 140 B4 51 14N 79 31W
Mississagi →, Canada 140 C3 46 15N 83 9W
Mississauga, Canada 150 C5 43 32N 79 35W
Mississinewa L., U.S.A. 157 D10 40 46N 86 3W
Mississippi □, U.S.A. 155 J10 33 0N 90 0W
Mississippi →, U.S.A. 155 L10 29 9N 89 15W
Mississippi L., Canada 151 A8 45 5N 76 10W
Mississippi River Delta, U.S.A. 155 L9 29 10N 89 15W
Mississippi Sd., U.S.A. 155 K10 30 20N 89 0W
Missoula, U.S.A. 158 C7 46 52N 114 1W
Missour, Morocco 110 B4 33 3N 4 0W
Missouri □, U.S.A. 156 E3 38 25N 92 30W
Missouri →, U.S.A. 156 F6 38 49N 90 7W
Missouri City, U.S.A. 155 L7 29 37N 95 32W
Missouri Valley, U.S.A. 154 E7 41 34N 95 53W
Mist, U.S.A. 160 E3 45 59N 123 15W
Mistassibi →, Canada 141 B5 48 53N 72 13W
Mistassini, Canada 141 C5 48 53N 72 12W
Mistassini →, Canada 141 C5 48 42N 72 20W
Mistassini, L., Canada 140 B5 51 0N 73 30W
Mistastin L., Canada 141 A7 55 57N 63 20W
Mistelbach, Austria 35 C9 48 34N 16 34 E
Misterbianco, Italy 47 E8 37 31N 15 1 E
Misti, Volcán, Peru 172 D3 16 18 S 71 24W
Mistinibi, L., Canada 141 A7 55 56N 64 17W
Mistretta, Italy 47 E7 37 56N 14 22 E
Misty L., Canada 143 B8 58 53N 101 40W
Misugi, Japan 73 C8 34 31N 136 16 E
Misumi, Japan 72 E2 32 37N 130 27 E
Misurata = Mişrātah, Libya 108 B3 32 24N 15 3 E
Mît Ghamr, Egypt 106 H7 30 42N 31 12 E
Mitaka, Japan 73 B11 35 40N 139 33 E
Mitatib, Sudan 107 D4 15 59N 36 12 E
Mitchell, Australia 127 D4 26 29 S 147 58 E
Mitchell, Canada 150 C3 43 28N 81 12W
Mitchell, Ga., U.S.A. 152 B7 33 13N 82 42W
Mitchell, Ind., U.S.A. 157 F10 38 44N 86 28W
Mitchell, Nebr., U.S.A. 154 E3 41 57N 103 49W
Mitchell, Oreg., U.S.A. 158 D3 44 34N 120 9W
Mitchell, S. Dak., U.S.A. 154 D6 43 43N 98 2W
Mitchell →, Australia 126 B3 15 12 S 141 35 E
Mitchell, Mt., U.S.A. 149 H4 35 46N 82 16W
Mitchell and Alice Rivers Nat. Park, Australia 126 B3 15 28 S 142 5 E
Mitchell Ranges, Australia 126 A2 12 49 S 135 36 E
Mitchell River Nat. Park, Australia 129 D7 37 37 S 147 22 E
Mitchelstown, Ireland 23 D3 52 15N 8 16W
Mitha Tiwana, Pakistan 92 C5 32 13N 72 6 E
Mithi, Pakistan 92 G3 24 44N 69 48 E
Míthimna, Greece 49 B8 39 20N 26 12 E
Mithrao, Pakistan 92 F3 27 28N 69 40 E
Mitiamo, Australia 128 D6 36 12 S 144 15 E
Mítikas, Greece 39 B2 38 40N 20 56 E
Mítikas, Greece 39 B2 39 0N 20 42 E
Mitilíni, Greece 49 B8 39 6N 26 35 E
Mitilinoí, Greece 49 D8 37 42N 26 56 E
Mito, Japan 73 A12 36 20N 140 30 E
Mitra, Mt., Eq. Guin. 114 B1 1 23N 9 19 E
Mitre, Mt., N.Z. 130 G4 40 50 S 175 30 E
Mitrofanovka, Russia 59 H10 49 58N 39 42 E
Mitrovica = Kosovska Mitrovica, Kosovo, Yug. 50 D4 42 54N 20 52 E
Mitsamiouli, Comoros Is. 121 a 11 20 S 43 16 E
Mitsang, Gabon 114 B2 0 42N 12 33 E
Mitsinjo, Madag. 117 B8 16 1 S 45 52 E
Mitsiwa, Eritrea 107 D4 15 35N 39 25 E
Mitsiwa Channel, Eritrea 107 D5 15 30N 40 0 E
Mitsukaidō, Japan 73 A11 36 1N 139 59 E
Mitsushima, Japan 72 C1 34 15N 129 20 E
Mittagong, Australia 129 C9 34 28 S 150 29 E
Mittelberg, Tirol, Austria 33 C11 46 57N 10 53 E
Mittelberg, Vorarlberg, Austria 33 B10 47 20N 10 9 E
Mittelberg, Germany 33 A10 47 38N 10 26 E
Mittelfranken □, Germany 31 F6 49 25N 10 40 E
Mittelland, Switz. 32 C4 46 50N 7 23 E
Mittellandkanal →, Germany 30 C4 52 16N 8 28 E
Mittenwalde, Germany 30 C9 52 15N 13 31 E

Mittersill, Austria — 34 D5 47 16N 12 29 E
Mitterteich, Germany — 31 F8 49 57N 12 14 E
Mittimatalik = Pond Inlet, Canada 139 A12 72 40N 77 0W
Mittweida, Germany — 30 E8 50 59N 12 59 E
Mitú, Colombia — 168 C3 1 15N 70 13W
Mituas, Colombia — 168 C4 3 52N 68 49W
Mitumba, Tanzania — 118 D3 7 8S 31 2 E
Mitumba, Mts., Dem. Rep. of the Congo — 118 D2 7 0S 27 30 E
Mitwaba, Dem. Rep. of the Congo 119 D2 8 2S 27 17 E
Mityana, Uganda — 118 B3 0 23N 32 2 E
Mitzic, Gabon — 114 B2 0 45N 11 40 E
Miura, Japan — 73 B11 35 12N 139 40 E
Mixteco →, Mexico — 163 D5 18 11N 98 30W
Miyagi □, Japan — 70 E10 38 15N 140 45 E
Miyah, W. el →, Egypt — 106 C3 25 0N 33 23 E
Miyah, W. el →, Syria — 96 C3 34 44N 39 57 E
Miyake-Jima, Japan — 73 C11 34 5N 139 30 E
Miyako, Japan — 70 E10 39 40N 141 59 E
Miyako-Jima, Japan — 71 M2 24 45N 125 20 E
Miyako-Rettō, Japan — 71 M2 24 24N 125 0 E
Miyakonojō, Japan — 72 F3 31 40N 131 5 E
Miyani, India — 92 J3 21 50N 69 26 E
Miyanojō, Japan — 72 F2 31 54N 130 27 E
Miyata, Japan — 72 D2 33 49N 130 42 E
Miyazaki, Japan — 72 F3 31 56N 131 30 E
Miyazaki □, Japan — 72 E3 32 30N 131 30 E
Miyazu, Japan — 73 B7 35 35N 135 10 E
Miyet, Bahr el = Dead Sea, Asia 103 D4 31 30N 35 30 E
Miyi, China — 76 D4 26 47N 102 9 E
Miyoshi, Japan — 72 C4 34 48N 132 51 E
Miyun, China — 74 D9 40 28N 116 50 E
Miyun Shuiku, China — 75 D9 40 30N 117 0 E
Mizan Teferi, Ethiopia — 107 F4 6 57N 35 3 E
Mizdah, Libya — 108 B2 31 30N 13 0 E
Mizen Hd., Cork, Ireland — 23 E2 51 27N 9 50W
Mizen Hd., Wick., Ireland — 23 D5 52 51N 6 4W
Mizhi, China — 74 F6 37 47N 110 12 E
Mizil, Romania — 53 F11 44 59N 26 29 E
Mizoram □, India — 90 D4 23 30N 92 40 E
Mizpe Ramon, Israel — 103 E3 30 34N 34 49 E
Mizuho, Japan — 73 B7 35 6N 135 17 E
Mizunami, Japan — 73 B9 35 22N 137 15 E
Mizusawa, Japan — 70 E10 39 8N 141 8 E
Mjällby, Sweden — 17 H8 56 3N 14 40 E
Mjöbäck, Sweden — 17 G6 57 28N 12 53 E
Mjölby, Sweden — 17 F9 58 20N 15 10 E
Mjølfjell, Norway — 18 D3 60 41N 6 55 E
Mjømna, Norway — 18 D1 60 55N 4 55 E
Mjörn, Sweden — 17 G6 57 55N 12 25 E
Mjøsa, Norway — 15 F14 60 40N 11 0 E
Mkata, Tanzania — 118 D4 5 45S 38 20 E
Mkhaya Nature Reserve, Swaziland — 117 D5 26 34S 34 45 E
Mkokotoni, Tanzania — 118 D4 5 55S 39 15 E
Mkomazi, Tanzania — 118 C4 4 40S 38 7 E
Mkomazi →, S. Africa — 117 E5 30 12S 30 50 E
Mkomazi Game Reserve, Tanzania — 118 C3 4 4S 30 2 E
Mkulwe, Tanzania — 119 D3 8 37S 32 20 E
Mkumbi, Ras, Tanzania — 118 D4 7 38S 39 55 E
Mkushi, Zambia — 119 E2 14 25S 29 15 E
Mkushi River, Zambia — 119 E2 13 32S 29 45 E
Mkuze, S. Africa — 117 D5 27 10S 32 0 E
Mkuze Game Reserve, S. Africa 117 D4 29 27S 29 30 E
Mladá Boleslav, Czech Rep. — 34 A7 50 27N 14 53 E
Mladenovac, Serbia, Yug. — 50 B4 44 28N 20 44 E
Mlala Hills, Tanzania — 118 D3 6 50S 31 40 E
Mlange = Mulanje, Malawi — 119 F4 16 2S 35 33 E
Mlava →, Serbia, Yug. — 50 B5 44 45N 21 13 E
Mława, Poland — 55 E7 53 9N 20 25 E
Mlawula Nature Reserve, Swaziland — 117 D5 26 12S 32 2 E
Mlinište, Bos.-H. — 45 D13 44 15N 16 50 E
Mljet, Croatia — 45 F14 42 43N 17 30 E
Mljetski Kanal, Croatia — 45 F14 42 48N 17 35 E
Młynary, Poland — 54 D6 54 12N 19 46 E
Mmabatho, S. Africa — 116 D4 25 49S 25 30 E
Mme, Cameroon — 113 D7 6 18N 10 14 E
Mnichovo Hradiště, Czech Rep. — 34 A7 50 27N 14 59 E
Mo, Hordaland, Norway — 18 D2 60 49N 5 48 E
Mo, Møre og Romsdal, Norway 18 A5 63 0N 8 59 E
Mo, Telemark, Norway — 18 E4 59 28N 7 50 E
Mo i Rana, Norway — 14 C16 66 20N 14 7 E
Moa, Cuba — 165 B4 20 40N 74 56W
Moa, Indonesia — 82 C3 8 0S 128 0 E
Moa →, S. Leone — 112 D2 6 59N 11 36W
Moa, I., Papua N. G. — 132 F2 10 10S 142 15 E
Moab, U.S.A. — 159 G9 38 35N 109 33W
Moabi, Gabon — 114 C2 2 24S 10 59 E
Moaco →, Brazil — 172 B4 7 41S 68 18W
Moala, Fiji — 133 B2 18 36S 179 53 E
Moama, Australia — 127 F3 36 7S 144 46 E
Moamba, Mozam. — 117 D5 25 36S 32 15 E
Moapa, U.S.A. — 161 J12 36 40N 114 37W
Moate, Ireland — 23 C4 53 24N 7 44W
Moba, Dem. Rep. of the Congo — 118 D2 7 0S 29 48 E
Mobara, Japan — 73 B12 35 25N 140 18 E
Mobārakābād, Iran — 97 D7 28 24N 53 20 E
Mobaye, C.A.R. — 114 B4 4 25N 21 5 E
Mobayi, Dem. Rep. of the Congo 114 B4 4 15N 21 8 E
Mobeka, Dem. Rep. of the Congo 114 B3 1 52N 19 49 E
Mobenzélé, Congo — 114 B3 0 56N 17 50 E
Moberley Lake, Canada — 142 B4 55 50N 121 44W
Moberly, U.S.A. — 156 F8 39 25N 92 26W
Mobile, U.S.A. — 149 K1 30 41N 88 3W
Mobile B., U.S.A. — 149 K2 30 30N 88 0W
Mobridge, U.S.A. — 154 C4 45 32N 100 26W
Mobutu Sese Seko, L. = Albert, L., Africa — 118 B3 1 30N 31 0 E
Moc Chau, Vietnam — 86 B5 20 50N 104 38 E
Moc Hoa, Vietnam — 87 G5 10 46N 105 56 E
Mocaba, Sa. de, Angola — 115 D3 7 12S 15 0 E
Mocabe Kasari, Dem. Rep. of the Congo — 119 D2 9 58S 26 12 E
Mocajuba, Brazil — 170 B2 2 35S 49 30W
Moçambique, Mozam. — 119 F5 15 3S 40 42 E
Moçâmedes = Namibe, Angola — 115 F2 15 7S 12 11 E
Mocanaqua, U.S.A. — 151 E8 41 9N 76 8W
Mocapra →, Venezuela — 168 B4 7 56N 66 46W
Moce, Fiji — 133 B3 18 40S 178 29W
Mochudi, Botswana — 116 C4 24 27S 26 7 E
Mocimboa da Praia, Mozam. — 119 E5 11 25S 40 20 E
Mociu, Romania — 53 D9 46 46N 24 3 E
Möckeln, Sweden — 17 H8 56 40N 14 15 E
Mockfjärd, Sweden — 16 F10 60 29N 14 53 E
Moclips, U.S.A. — 160 C2 47 14N 124 13W
Mocoa, Colombia — 168 C2 1 7N 76 35W
Mococa, Brazil — 175 A6 21 28S 47 0W
Mocorito, Mexico — 162 B3 25 30N 107 53W
Moctezuma, Mexico — 162 B3 29 50N 109 0W
Moctezuma →, Mexico — 163 C5 21 59N 98 34W
Mocuba, Mozam. — 119 F4 16 54S 36 57 E
Mocúzari, Presa, Mexico — 162 B3 27 10N 109 10W
Moda, Burma — 90 C6 24 22N 96 29 E
Modane, France — 29 C10 45 12N 6 40 E
Modasa, India — 92 H5 23 30N 73 21 E
Modder →, S. Africa — 116 D3 29 2S 24 37 E
Modderrivier, S. Africa — 116 D3 29 2S 24 38 E

Módena, Italy — 44 D7 44 40N 10 55 E
Modena, U.S.A. — 159 H7 37 48N 113 56W
Modesto, U.S.A. — 160 H6 37 39N 121 0W
Möðrudalur, Iceland — 11 B11 65 22N 15 53W
Möðruvellir, Iceland — 11 B8 65 46N 18 15W
Módica, Italy — 47 F7 36 52N 14 46 E
Modjamboli, Dem. Rep. of the Congo — 114 B4 2 28N 22 6 E
Mödling, Austria — 35 C9 48 5N 16 17 E
Modo, Sudan — 107 F3 5 31N 30 33 E
Modoc, U.S.A. — 152 B7 33 44N 82 13W
Modowi, Indonesia — 83 B4 4 5S 134 39 E
Modra, Slovak Rep. — 35 C10 48 19N 17 20 E
Modriča, Bos.-H. — 52 F3 44 57N 18 17 E
Moe, Australia — 129 E7 38 12S 146 19 E
Moebase, Mozam. — 119 F4 17 3S 38 41 E
Moëlan-sur-Mer, France — 26 E3 47 49N 3 38W
Moelv, Norway — 18 D7 60 56N 10 43 E
Moengo, Surinam — 169 B7 5 45N 54 20W
Moerewa, N.Z. — 130 B3 35 8S 174 1 E
Moësa →, Switz. — 33 D8 46 12N 9 10 E
Moffat, U.K. — 22 F5 55 21N 3 27W
Moga, India — 92 D6 30 48N 75 8 E
Mogadishu = Muqdisho, Somali Rep. — 120 D3 2 2N 45 25 E
Mogador = Essaouira, Morocco — 110 B3 31 32N 9 42W
Mogadouro, Portugal — 42 D4 41 22N 6 47W
Mogalakwena →, S. Africa — 117 C4 22 38S 28 40 E
Mogami →, Japan — 70 E10 38 45N 140 0 E
Mogán, Canary Is. — 9 e1 27 53N 15 43W
Mogandjo, Dem. Rep. of the Congo 114 B4 1 23N 24 15 E
Mogaung, Burma — 90 C6 25 20N 97 0 E
Mogen, Norway — 18 D4 60 2N 7 52 E
Mogente = Moixent, Spain — 41 G4 38 52N 0 45W
Mogho, Ethiopia — 107 G5 4 54N 40 16 E
Mogi das Cruzes, Brazil — 175 A6 23 31S 46 11W
Mogi-Guaçu →, Brazil — 175 A6 20 53S 48 10W
Mogi-Mirim, Brazil — 175 A6 22 29S 47 0W
Mogielnica, Poland — 55 G7 51 42N 20 41 E
Mogige, Ethiopia — 107 F4 5 24N 36 14 E
Mogilev = Mahilyow, Belarus — 58 F6 53 55N 30 18 E
Mogilev-Podolskiy = Mohyliv-Podilskyy, Ukraine — 59 H4 48 26N 27 48 E
Mogilno, Poland — 55 F4 52 39N 17 55 E
Mogincual, Mozam. — 119 F5 15 35S 40 25 E
Mogliano Véneto, Italy — 45 C9 45 33N 12 14 E
Mogocha, Russia — 67 D12 53 40N 119 50 E
Mogoi, Indonesia — 83 B4 1 55S 133 10 E
Mogok, Burma — 90 D6 23 0N 96 40 E
Mogollon Rim, U.S.A. — 159 J8 34 10N 110 50W
Mógoro, Italy — 46 C1 39 41N 8 47 E
Mograt, Sudan — 109 D3 19 28N 33 16 E
Mogroum, Chad — 109 F3 11 6N 15 25 E
Moguer, Spain — 43 H4 37 15N 6 52W
Mogumber, Australia — 125 F2 31 2S 116 3 E
Mohács, Hungary — 52 E3 45 58N 18 41 E
Mohaka →, N.Z. — 130 F6 39 7S 177 12 E
Mohales Hoek, Lesotho — 116 E4 30 7S 27 26 E
Mohall, U.S.A. — 154 A4 48 46N 101 31W
Moḥammadābād, Iran — 97 B8 37 52N 59 5 E
Mohammadia, Algeria — 111 A5 35 33N 0 3 E
Mohammedia, Morocco — 110 B3 33 44N 7 21W
Mohana, India — 94 E7 19 27N 84 16 E
Mohana →, India — 93 G11 24 43N 85 0 E
Mohanganj, Bangla. — 90 C3 24 54N 90 59 E
Mohanlalganj, India — 93 F9 26 41N 80 58 E
Mohave, L., U.S.A. — 161 K12 35 12N 114 34W
Mohawk →, U.S.A. — 151 D11 42 47N 73 41W
Moheda, Sweden — 17 G8 57 1N 14 35 E
Mohéli, Comoros Is. — 121 a 12 20S 43 40 E
Mohenjodaro, Pakistan — 91 D3 27 19N 68 7 E
Mohican, C., U.S.A. — 144 F6 60 12N 167 25W
Mohicanville Reservoir, U.S.A. — 150 F3 40 45N 82 0W
Mohlin, Switz. — 32 A5 47 33N 7 51 E
Möhne →, Germany — 30 D3 51 29N 7 57 E
Mohnyin, Burma — 90 C6 24 47N 96 22 E
Mohoro, Tanzania — 118 D4 8 6S 39 8 E
Mohyliv-Podilskyy, Ukraine — 59 H4 48 26N 27 48 E
Moi, Norway — 18 F3 58 27N 6 32 E
Moia, Sudan — 107 F2 5 3N 28 2 E
Moidart, U.K. — 22 E3 56 47N 5 52W
Moinabad, India — 94 F3 17 44N 77 16 E
Moindou, N. Cal. — 133 U19 21 42S 165 41 E
Moineşti, Romania — 53 D11 46 28N 26 31 E
Moira →, Canada — 150 B7 44 21N 77 24W
Moirang, India — 90 C4 24 30N 93 46 E
Moirans, France — 29 C9 45 20N 5 33 E
Moirans-en-Montagne, France — 27 F12 46 26N 5 43 E
Moíres, Greece — 39 E5 35 4N 24 56 E
Moisaküla, Estonia — 15 G21 58 3N 25 12 E
Moisie, Canada — 141 B6 50 12N 66 1W
Moisie →, Canada — 141 B6 50 14N 66 5W
Moissac, France — 28 D5 44 7N 1 5 E
Moïssala, Chad — 109 G3 8 21N 17 46 E
Moita, Portugal — 43 G2 38 38N 8 58W
Moixent, Spain — 41 G4 38 52N 0 45W
Möja, Sweden — 16 E12 59 26N 18 55 E
Mojácar, Spain — 41 H3 37 6N 1 55W
Mojados, Spain — 42 D6 41 26N 4 40W
Mojave, U.S.A. — 161 K8 35 3N 118 10W
Mojave Desert, U.S.A. — 161 L10 35 0N 116 30W
Moji, China — 65 D7 23 37N 101 35 E
Mojiang, China — 76 F3 23 37N 101 35 E
Mojjo →, Ethiopia — 107 F5 7 55N 42 0 E
Mojkovac, Montenegro, Yug. — 50 D3 42 58N 19 35 E
Mojo, Bolivia — 174 A2 21 48S 65 33W
Mojo, Ethiopia — 107 F4 8 35N 39 5 E
Mojokerto, Indonesia — 85 D4 7 28S 112 26 E
Mojos, Llanos de, Bolivia — 173 D5 15 10S 65 0W
Moju, Brazil — 170 B2 1 45S 48 45W
Moju →, Brazil — 170 B2 1 40S 48 25W
Mokai, N.Z. — 130 E3 38 32S 175 56 E
Mokambo, Dem. Rep. of the Congo — 119 E2 12 25S 28 20 E
Mokameh, India — 93 G11 25 24N 85 55 E
Mokane, U.S.A. — 156 F5 38 41N 91 53W
Mokapu Peninsula, U.S.A. — 145 K14 21 25N 157 45W
Mokau, N.Z. — 130 E3 38 35S 174 35 E
Mokau →, N.Z. — 130 E3 38 35S 174 35 E
Mokelumne →, U.S.A. — 160 G5 38 13N 121 28W
Mokelumne Hill, U.S.A. — 160 G6 38 18N 120 43W
Mokhós, Greece — 39 E6 35 16N 25 27 E
Mokhotlong, Lesotho — 117 D4 29 22S 29 2 E
Mokihinui →, N.Z. — 131 B6 41 33S 171 58 E
Möklinta, Sweden — 16 D10 60 4N 16 33 E
Moknine, Tunisia — 108 A2 35 35N 10 58 E
Mokoan, L., Australia — 129 D7 36 27S 146 5 E
Mokokchung, India — 90 B5 26 15N 94 30 E
Mokolea Rock, U.S.A. — 145 K14 21 27N 157 44W
Mokolo, Cameroon — 113 C7 10 50N 13 55 E
Mokolo →, Cent. Amer. — 109 F3 10 49N 13 54 E
Mokolo, Dem. Rep. of the Congo 114 B3 1 35S 18 6 E
Mokolo →, S. Africa — 117 C4 23 14S 27 43 E
Mokp'o, S. Korea — 75 G14 34 50N 126 25 E
Mokra Gora, Yugoslavia — 50 D4 42 50N 20 18 E
Mokronog, Slovenia — 45 C12 45 57N 15 9 E

Moksha →, Russia — 60 C6 54 45N 41 53 E
Mokshan, Russia — 60 D7 53 25N 44 35 E
Mokuaeae I., U.S.A. — 145 A2 22 14N 159 25W
Mokuauia I., U.S.A. — 145 J14 21 40N 157 56W
Mokulua Is., U.S.A. — 145 K14 21 26N 157 42W
Mokwa, Nigeria — 113 D6 9 19N 5 0 E
Mol, Belgium — 24 C5 51 11N 5 5 E
Mola di Bari, Italy — 47 A10 41 4N 17 5 E
Molakalmuru, India — 95 G3 14 55N 76 50 E
Molale, Ethiopia — 107 E4 10 10N 39 41 E
Molanda, Dem. Rep. of the Congo 114 B4 2 28N 20 48 E
Moláoi, Greece — 48 E4 36 49N 22 56 E
Molara, Italy — 46 B2 40 52N 9 43 E
Molat, Croatia — 45 D11 44 15N 14 50 E
Molave, Phil. — 81 G4 8 5N 123 30 E
Molchanovo, Russia — 66 D9 57 40N 83 50 E
Mold, U.K. — 20 D4 53 9N 3 8W
Moldava nad Bodvou, Slovak Rep. 35 C14 48 38N 21 0 E
Moldavia = Moldova ■, Europe — 53 C13 47 0N 28 0 E
Moldavia, Romania — 53 D12 46 30N 27 0 E
Molde, Norway — 14 E12 62 45N 7 9 E
Moldo Too, Kyrgyzstan — 65 C7 41 35N 75 0 E
Moldotau = Moldo Too, Kyrgyzstan — 65 C7 41 35N 75 0 E
Moldova ■, Europe — 53 C13 47 0N 28 0 E
Moldova Nouă, Romania — 52 F6 44 45N 21 41 E
Moldoveanu, Vf., Romania — 53 E9 45 36N 24 45 E
Moldovița, Romania — 53 C10 47 41N 25 32 E
Mole →, U.K. — 21 F7 51 24N 0 21W
Mole Creek, Australia — 127 G4 41 34S 146 24 E
Mole Nat. Park, Ghana — 113 D4 9 43N 1 44W
Molegbwe, Dem. Rep. of the Congo — 114 B4 1 42N 20 53 E
Molepolole, Botswana — 116 C4 24 28S 25 28 E
Molesworth, N.Z. — 131 C8 42 5S 173 16 E
Molfetta, Italy — 47 A9 41 12N 16 36 E
Molii Pond, U.S.A. — 145 J14 21 33N 157 51W
Molina de Aragón, Spain — 40 E3 40 46N 1 52W
Molina de Segura, Spain — 41 G3 38 3N 1 7W
Moline, U.S.A. — 156 C6 41 30N 90 31W
Molinella, Italy — 45 D8 44 37N 11 40 E
Molino, U.S.A. — 153 E2 30 43N 87 20W
Molinos, Argentina — 174 B2 25 28S 66 15W
Moliro, Dem. Rep. of the Congo — 118 D3 8 12S 30 30 E
Moliterno, Italy — 47 B8 40 14N 15 52 E
Molkom, Sweden — 16 E7 59 37N 13 44 E
Mölle, Sweden — 17 H6 56 17N 12 31 E
Molledo, Spain — 42 B6 43 8N 4 6W
Mollendo, Peru — 172 D3 17 0S 72 0W
Mollerin, L., Australia — 125 F2 30 30S 117 35 E
Mollerussa, Spain — 40 D5 41 37N 0 54 E
Mollina, Spain — 43 H6 37 8N 4 38W
Mölln, Germany — 30 B6 53 37N 10 41 E
Mölltorp, Sweden — 17 F8 58 30N 14 26 E
Mölnlycke, Sweden — 17 G6 57 40N 12 8 E
Molo, Burma — 90 D6 23 22N 96 53 E
Molochansk, Ukraine — 59 J8 47 15N 35 35 E
Molochnoye, Ozero, Ukraine — 59 J8 46 30N 35 20 E
Molodechno = Maladzyechna, Belarus — 58 E4 54 20N 26 50 E
Molokai, U.S.A. — 145 B5 21 8N 157 0W
Molokini I., U.S.A. — 145 C5 20 38N 156 30W
Moloma →, Russia — 64 B8 58 20N 48 15 E
Molong, Australia — 129 B8 33 5S 148 54 E
Molopo →, Africa — 116 D3 27 30S 20 13 E
Mólos, Greece — 48 C4 38 47N 22 37 E
Molotov = Perm, Russia — 64 C6 58 0N 56 10 E
Moloundou, Cameroon — 114 B2 2 8N 15 15 E
Molowaie, Dem. Rep. of the Congo 115 D4 5 47S 23 18 E
Molsheim, France — 27 D14 48 33N 7 29 E
Molson L., Canada — 143 C9 54 22N 96 40W
Molteno, S. Africa — 116 E4 31 22S 26 22 E
Moltrásio, Italy — 33 E8 45 52N 9 6 E
Molu, Indonesia — 83 C4 6 45S 131 40 E
Molucca Sea, Indonesia — 82 A3 0 0 125 0 E
Moluccas = Maluku, Indonesia — 79 E7 1 0S 127 0 E
Molundo, Phil. — 81 H5 7 5N 124 23 E
Moma, Dem. Rep. of the Congo — 114 B4 1 35S 23 52 E
Moma, Mozam. — 119 F4 16 47S 39 4 E
Momba, Australia — 128 A5 30 58S 144 30 E
Mombaça, Brazil — 170 C4 5 43S 39 45W
Mombango, Dem. Rep. of the Congo — 114 B4 1 45N 24 26 E
Mombasa, Kenya — 118 C4 4 2S 39 43 E
Mombetsu, Japan — 70 B11 44 21N 143 22 E
Mombil, Burma — 90 B7 27 46N 98 6 E
Momboyo →, Dem. Rep. of the Congo — 114 C3 0 16S 19 0 E
Mombuey, Spain — 42 C4 42 3N 6 20W
Momchilgrad, Bulgaria — 51 E9 41 33N 25 23 E
Momence, U.S.A. — 157 C9 41 10N 87 40W
Momi, Dem. Rep. of the Congo — 118 C2 1 42S 27 0 E
Momote, Papua N. G. — 132 B4 2 4S 147 27 E
Mompog Pass, Phil. — 80 E4 13 34N 122 13 E
Mompós, Colombia — 168 B3 9 14N 74 26W
Møn, Denmark — 17 K6 54 57N 12 20 E
Mon □, Burma — 90 G6 16 0N 97 30 E
Mona, Canal de la, W. Indies — 165 C6 18 30N 67 45W
Mona, Isla, Puerto Rico — 164 C3 18 5N 67 54W
Mona, Pta., Costa Rica — 164 E3 9 37N 82 36W
Mona Quimbundo, Angola — 115 D4 11 45S 20 30 E
Monaca, U.S.A. — 150 F4 40 41N 80 17W
Monachil, Spain — 43 H7 37 8N 3 30W
Monaco ■, Europe — 29 E11 43 46N 7 23 E
Monadhliath Mts., U.K. — 22 D4 57 10N 4 4W
Monadnock, Mt., U.S.A. — 151 D12 42 52N 72 7W
Monagas □, Venezuela — 169 B5 9 20N 63 0W
Monaghan, Ireland — 23 B5 54 15N 6 57W
Monaghan □, Ireland — 23 B5 54 11N 6 56W
Monahans, U.S.A. — 155 K3 31 36N 102 54W
Monapo, Mozam. — 119 E5 14 56S 40 19 E
Monar, L., U.K. — 22 D3 57 26N 5 8W
Monaragala, Sri Lanka — 95 L5 6 52N 81 22 E
Monarch Mt., Canada — 142 C3 51 55N 125 57W
Monashee Mts., Canada — 142 C5 51 0N 118 43W
Monasterevin, Ireland — 23 C4 53 8N 7 4W
Monastir = Bitola, Macedonia — 50 F5 41 1N 21 20 E
Monastir, Tunisia — 108 A2 35 50N 10 49 E
Moncada, Phil. — 80 D3 15 44N 120 34 E
Moncalieri, Italy — 44 D4 45 0N 7 41 E
Moncalvo, Italy — 44 D5 45 3N 8 16 E
Monção, Portugal — 42 C2 42 4N 8 27W
Moncarapacho, Portugal — 43 H3 37 5N 7 46W
Moncayo, Sierra del, Spain — 40 D3 41 48N 1 50W
Monchegorsk, Russia — 56 A5 67 54N 32 58 E
Mönchengladbach, Germany — 30 D2 51 11N 6 27 E
Monchique, Portugal — 43 H2 37 19N 8 38W
Moncks Corner, U.S.A. — 152 B9 33 12N 80 1W
Monclova, Mexico — 162 B4 26 50N 101 30W
Moncontour, France — 26 D4 48 22N 2 38W
Moncton, Canada — 141 C7 46 7N 64 51W
Mondariz, Spain — 42 C2 42 14N 8 27W
Mondego →, Portugal — 42 E2 40 9N 8 52W
Mondego, C., Portugal — 42 E2 40 11N 8 54W
Mondeodo, Indonesia — 83 B2 3 34S 122 9 E
Mondeville, France — 26 C6 49 10N 0 18W
Mondimbi, Dem. Rep. of the Congo — 114 B4 1 48N 22 46 E
Mondjuku, Dem. Rep. of the Congo — 114 C4 1 59S 23 48 E
Mondo, Chad — 109 F3 13 47N 15 32 E
Mondolfo, Italy — 45 E10 43 45N 13 6 E

Mondoñedo, Spain — 42 B3 43 25N 7 23W
Mondovì, Italy — 44 D4 44 23N 7 49 E
Mondragon, Phil. — 80 E5 12 31N 124 45 E
Mondragone, Italy — 46 A6 41 7N 13 53 E
Mondrain I., Australia — 125 F3 34 9S 122 14 E
Moneague, Jamaica — 164 a 18 16N 77 7W
Monemvasía, Greece — 48 E5 36 41N 23 3 E
Monessen, U.S.A. — 150 F5 40 9N 79 54W
Monesterio, Spain — 43 G4 38 6N 6 15W
Monestier-de-Clermont, France — 29 D9 44 55N 5 38 E
Monett, U.S.A. — 155 G8 36 55N 93 55W
Moneymore, U.K. — 23 B5 54 41N 6 40W
Monfalcone, Italy — 45 C10 45 49N 13 32 E
Monflanquin, France — 28 D4 44 32N 0 47 E
Monforte, Portugal — 43 F3 39 6N 7 25W
Monforte de Lemos, Spain — 42 C3 42 31N 7 33W
Möng Hsu, Burma — 76 G2 21 54N 98 30 E
Mong Hta, Burma — 90 F7 19 50N 98 35 E
Mong Ket, Burma — 90 D7 23 8N 98 22 E
Mong Kung, Burma — 90 E6 21 35N 97 35 E
Mong Kyawt, Burma — 90 F7 19 56N 98 45 E
Möng Long, Burma — 90 D6 22 47N 96 32 E
Möng Mit, Burma — 90 D6 23 7N 96 41 E
Mong Nai, Burma — 90 E6 20 32N 97 46 E
Möng Pan, Burma — 90 E7 20 19N 98 22 E
Möng Ping, Burma — 76 G2 21 22N 99 2 E
Mong Pu, Burma — 90 F7 20 55N 98 44 E
Möng Ton, Burma — 90 D6 22 21N 97 41 E
Mong Yang, Burma — 90 D6 22 2N 97 41 E
Mong Yai, Burma — 90 D7 22 21N 98 3 E
Möng Yu, Burma — 90 D6 23 30N 97 51 E
Monga, Dem. Rep. of the Congo 114 B4 4 12N 22 49 E
Mongala →, Dem. Rep. of the Congo — 114 B3 1 53N 19 46 E
Mongalla, Sudan — 107 F3 5 8N 31 42 E
Mongandi, Congo — 114 B3 0 45N 17 11 E
Mongers, L., Australia — 125 E2 29 25S 117 5 E
Mongga, Solomon Is. — 133 L9 7 52S 157 0 E
Monghyr = Munger, India — 93 G12 25 23N 86 30 E
Mongibello = Etna, Italy — 47 E7 37 50N 14 55 E
Mongla, Bangla. — 90 D2 22 8N 89 35 E
Mongngaw, Burma — 90 D6 22 47N 96 59 E
Mongo, Chad — 109 F3 12 14N 18 43 E
Mongó, Eq. Guin. — 114 B2 1 52N 10 10 E
Mongo →, S. Leone — 112 D2 9 35N 12 10W
Mongolia ■, Asia — 67 E10 47 0N 103 0 E
Mongomo, Eq. Guin. — 114 B2 1 38N 11 19 E
Mongonu, Nigeria — 113 C7 12 40N 13 32 E
Mongororo, Chad — 109 F4 12 3N 22 26 E
Mongstad, Norway — 18 D2 60 49N 5 2 E
Mongu, Zambia — 115 F4 15 16S 23 12 E
Môngua, Angola — 116 B2 16 43S 15 20 E
Moniac, U.S.A. — 153 F5 30 31N 82 14W
Monifieth, U.K. — 22 E6 56 30N 2 48W
Monistrol-sur-Loire, France — 29 C8 45 17N 4 11 E
Monkayo, Phil. — 81 H6 7 50N 126 5 E
Monkey Bay, Malawi — 119 E4 14 7S 35 1 E
Monkey Mia, Australia — 125 E1 25 48S 113 43 E
Monkey River, Belize — 163 D7 16 22N 88 29W
Mońki, Poland — 54 E9 53 23N 22 48 E
Monkoto, Dem. Rep. of the Congo 114 C4 1 38S 20 35 E
Monkton, Canada — 150 C3 43 35N 81 5W
Monmouth, U.K. — 21 F5 51 48N 2 42W
Monmouth, Ill., U.S.A. — 156 D6 40 55N 90 39W
Monmouth, Oreg., U.S.A. — 158 D2 44 51N 123 14W
Monmouthshire □, U.K. — 21 F5 51 48N 2 54W
Mono, Solomon Is. — 133 L8 7 20S 155 35 E
Mono L., U.S.A. — 160 H7 38 1N 119 1W
Monolith, U.S.A. — 161 K8 35 7N 118 22W
Monólithos, Greece — 38 E11 36 7N 27 45 E
Monon, U.S.A. — 157 D10 40 52N 86 53W
Monona, Iowa, U.S.A. — 156 A5 43 3N 91 23W
Monona, Wis., U.S.A. — 156 A7 43 4N 89 20W
Monongahela, U.S.A. — 150 F5 40 12N 79 56W
Monópoli, Italy — 47 B10 40 57N 17 18 E
Monor, Hungary — 52 C4 47 21N 19 27 E
Monos I., Trin. & Tob. — 169 D7 10 42N 61 44W
Monóvar, Spain — 41 G4 38 28N 0 53W
Monowai, N.Z. — 131 F2 45 53S 167 31 E
Monowai, L., N.Z. — 131 F2 45 53S 167 25 E
Monqoumba, C.A.R. — 114 B3 3 33N 18 40 E
Monreal del Campo, Spain — 40 E3 40 47N 1 20W
Monreale, Italy — 46 D6 38 5N 13 17 E
Monroe, Ga., U.S.A. — 152 B6 33 47N 83 43W
Monroe, Iowa, U.S.A. — 156 C3 41 31N 93 6W
Monroe, La., U.S.A. — 155 J8 32 30N 92 7W
Monroe, Mich., U.S.A. — 157 C13 41 55N 83 24W
Monroe, N.C., U.S.A. — 149 H5 34 59N 80 33W
Monroe, N.Y., U.S.A. — 151 E10 41 20N 74 11W
Monroe, Ohio, U.S.A. — 157 E12 39 27N 84 22W
Monroe, Utah, U.S.A. — 159 G7 38 38N 112 7W
Monroe, Wash., U.S.A. — 160 C5 47 51N 121 58W
Monroe, Wis., U.S.A. — 156 B7 42 36N 89 38W
Monroe, L., Ind., U.S.A. — 153 G8 28 50N 81 19W
Monroe City, Ind., U.S.A. — 157 F9 38 37N 87 21W
Monroe City, Mo., U.S.A. — 156 F9 39 39N 91 44W
Monroe L., U.S.A. — 157 F9 39 1N 86 31W
Monroeton, U.S.A. — 151 E8 41 43N 76 29W
Monroeville, Ala., U.S.A. — 149 K2 31 31N 87 20W
Monroeville, Pa., U.S.A. — 150 F5 40 26N 79 45W
Monrovia, Liberia — 112 D2 6 18N 10 47W
Mons, Belgium — 24 D3 50 27N 3 58 E
Møns Klint, Denmark — 17 K6 54 57N 12 33 E
Monsaraz, Portugal — 43 G3 38 28N 7 22W
Monse, Indonesia — 82 B2 4 7S 123 15 E
Monsefú, Peru — 172 B2 6 52S 79 52W
Monségur, France — 28 D4 44 38N 0 4 E
Monsélice, Italy — 45 C8 45 14N 11 45 E
Mønshaug, Norway — 18 D3 60 37N 6 31 E
Mönsterås, Sweden — 17 G10 57 3N 16 26 E
Mont Cenis, Col du, France — 29 C10 45 15N 6 55 E
Mont-de-Marsan, France — 28 E3 43 54N 0 31W
Mont-Dore, N. Cal. — 133 V20 22 16S 166 34 E
Mont Fouari, Réserve du, Congo — 114 C2 2 52S 11 32 E
Mont-Joli, Canada — 141 C6 48 37N 68 10W
Mont-Laurier, Canada — 140 C4 46 35N 75 30W
Mont-Louis, Canada — 141 C6 49 15N 65 44W
Mont Peko, Parc Nat. du, Ivory C. 112 D3 7 9N 7 15W
Mont-roig del Camp, Spain — 40 D5 41 9N 0 57 E
Mont-St-Michel, Le = Le Mont-St-Michel, France — 26 D5 48 40N 1 30W
Mont Sangbe, Parc Nat. du, Ivory C. — 112 D3 8 0N 7 17W
Mont Tremblant, Parc Recr. du, Canada — 140 C5 46 30N 74 30W
Montabaur, Germany — 30 E3 50 26N 7 50 E
Montagnac, France — 29 E7 43 29N 3 28 E
Montagnana, Italy — 45 C8 45 14N 11 28 E
Montagne d'Ambre, Parc Nat. de la, Madag. — 117 A8 12 37S 49 8 E
Montagu, S. Africa — 116 E3 33 45S 20 8 E
Montagu I., Antarctica — 7 B1 58 25S 26 20W
Montague, Canada — 141 C7 46 10N 62 39W
Montague, I., Mexico — 162 A2 31 40N 114 56W
Montague I., Australia — 129 D9 36 16S 150 13 E
Montague I., U.S.A. — 144 G11 60 0N 147 30W
Montague Ra., Australia — 125 E2 27 15S 119 30 E
Montague Sd., Australia — 124 B4 14 28S 125 20 E
Montaigu, France — 26 F5 46 59N 1 18W
Montalbán, Spain — 40 E4 40 50N 0 45W

254 Mungaoli

Mungaoli, *India* **92 G8** 24 24N 78 7 E
Mungari, *Mozam.* **119 F3** 17 12 S 33 30 E
Mungbere, *Dem. Rep. of the Congo* **118 B2** 2 36N 28 28 E
Mungeli, *India* **93 H9** 22 4N 81 41 E
Munger, *India* **93 G12** 25 23N 86 30 E
Mungkan Kandju Nat. Park, *Australia* **126 A3** 13 35 S 142 52 E
Mungo, *Angola* **115 E3** 11 49 S 16 16 E
Mungo, L., *Australia* **128 B5** 33 45 S 143 0 E
Mungo Nat. Park, *Australia* **128 B5** 33 44 S 143 6 E
Munhango, *Angola* **115 E3** 12 10 S 18 38 E
Munhango →, *Angola* **115 E4** 11 17 S 19 44 E
Munich = München, *Germany* **31 G7** 48 8N 11 34 E
Munirabad, *India* **95 F3** 15 20N 76 20 E
Munising, *U.S.A.* **148 B2** 46 25N 86 40W
Munka-Ljungby, *Sweden* **17 H6** 56 16N 12 58 E
Munkebo, *Denmark* **17 J4** 55 27N 10 34 E
Munkedal, *Sweden* **17 F5** 58 28N 11 40 E
Munkfors, *Sweden* **16 E7** 59 47N 13 30 E
Munku-Sardyk, *Russia* **67 D11** 51 45N 100 20 E
Münnerstadt, *Germany* **31 E6** 50 14N 10 12 E
Munoz, *Phil.* **80 D3** 15 43N 120 54 E
Muñoz Gamero, Pen., *Chile* **176 D2** 52 30 S 73 5W
Munroe L., *Canada* **143 B9** 59 13N 98 35W
Munsan, *S. Korea* **75 F14** 37 51N 126 48 E
Munshiganj, *Bangla.* **90 D3** 23 33N 90 32 E
Münsingen, *Switz.* **32 C5** 46 52N 7 32 E
Munson, *U.S.A.* **153 E3** 30 52N 86 52W
Munster, *France* **27 D14** 48 2N 7 8 E
Munster, *Niedersachsen, Germany* **30 C6** 52 58N 10 5 E
Münster, *Nordrhein-Westfalen, Germany* **30 D3** 51 58N 7 37 E
Münster, *Switz.* **33 D6** 46 29N 8 17 E
Munster □, *Ireland* **23 D3** 52 18N 8 44W
Muntadgin, *Australia* **125 F2** 31 45 S 118 33 E
Muntele Mare, Vf., *Romania* **53 D8** 46 30N 23 12 E
Muntok, *Indonesia* **84 C3** 2 5 S 105 10 E
Munyama, *Zambia* **119 F2** 16 5 S 28 31 E
Munzur Dağları, *Turkey* **101 C8** 39 30N 39 10 E
Muong Beng, *Laos* **76 G3** 20 23N 101 46 E
Muong Boum, *Vietnam* **76 F4** 22 24N 102 49 E
Muong Et, *Laos* **86 B5** 20 49N 104 1 E
Muong Hai, *Laos* **76 G3** 21 3N 101 49 E
Muong Hiem, *Laos* **86 B4** 20 5N 103 22 E
Muong Houn, *Laos* **76 G3** 20 8N 101 23 E
Muong Hung, *Vietnam* **76 G4** 20 56N 103 53 E
Muong Kau, *Laos* **86 E5** 15 6N 105 47 E
Muong Khao, *Laos* **86 C4** 19 38N 103 32 E
Muong Khoua, *Laos* **76 G4** 21 5N 102 31 E
Muong Liep, *Laos* **86 C3** 18 29N 101 40 E
Muong May, *Laos* **86 E6** 14 49N 106 56 E
Muong Ngeun, *Laos* **76 G3** 20 36N 101 3 E
Muong Ngoi, *Laos* **76 G4** 20 43N 102 41 E
Muong Nhie, *Vietnam* **76 F4** 22 12N 102 28 E
Muong Nong, *Laos* **86 D6** 16 22N 106 30 E
Muong Ou Tay, *Laos* **76 F3** 22 7N 101 48 E
Muong Oua, *Laos* **86 C3** 18 18N 101 20 E
Muong Peun, *Laos* **76 G4** 20 13N 103 52 E
Muong Phalane, *Laos* **86 D5** 16 39N 105 34 E
Muong Phieng, *Laos* **86 C3** 19 6N 101 32 E
Muong Phine, *Laos* **86 D6** 16 32N 106 2 E
Muong Sai, *Laos* **76 G3** 20 42N 101 59 E
Muong Saiapoun, *Laos* **86 C3** 18 24N 101 31 E
Muong Sen, *Vietnam* **86 C5** 19 24N 104 8 E
Muong Sing, *Laos* **76 G3** 21 11N 101 9 E
Muong Son, *Laos* **76 G4** 20 27N 103 19 E
Muong Soui, *Laos* **86 C4** 19 33N 102 52 E
Muong Va, *Laos* **76 G4** 21 53N 102 19 E
Muong Xia, *Vietnam* **86 B5** 20 19N 104 50 E
Muonio, *Finland* **14 C20** 67 57N 23 40 E
Muonionjoki →, *Finland* **14 C20** 67 11N 23 34 E
Muotathal, *Switz.* **33 C7** 46 58N 8 46 E
Mupa, *Angola* **115 F3** 16 5 S 15 50 E
Mupa, Parque Nacional da, *Angola* **115 F3** 15 55 S 15 35 E
Muping, *China* **75 F11** 37 22N 121 36 E
Mupoi, *Sudan* **107 F2** 5 28N 27 40 E
Muqaddam, Wadi →, *Sudan* **106 D3** 18 4N 31 30 E
Muqdisho, *Somali Rep.* **120 D3** 2 2N 45 25 E
Muqshin, W. →, *Oman* **99 C6** 19 44N 55 14 E
Muquequete, *Angola* **115 E2** 14 50 S 14 16 E
Mur →, *Austria* **35 E9** 46 18N 16 52 E
Mur-de-Bretagne, *France* **26 D4** 48 12N 3 0W
Muradiye, *Manisa, Turkey* **49 C9** 38 39N 27 21 E
Muradiye, *Van, Turkey* **101 C10** 39 0N 43 44 E
Murakami, *Japan* **70 E9** 38 14N 139 29 E
Murallón, Cerro, *Chile* **176 C2** 49 48 S 73 30W
Muranda, *Rwanda* **118 C2** 1 52 S 29 20 E
Murang'a, *Kenya* **118 C4** 0 45 S 37 9 E
Murashi, *Russia* **64 B2** 59 30N 49 0 E
Murat, *France* **28 C6** 45 7N 2 53 E
Murat →, *Turkey* **101 C9** 38 46N 40 0 E
Murat Dağı, *Turkey* **49 C11** 38 55N 29 43 E
Muratlı, *Turkey* **51 E11** 41 10N 27 29 E
Murato, *France* **29 F13** 42 35N 9 20 E
Murau, *Austria* **34 D7** 47 6N 14 10 E
Muravera, *Italy* **46 C2** 39 25N 9 34 E
Murayama, *Japan* **70 E10** 38 30N 140 25 E
Murça, *Portugal* **42 D3** 41 24N 7 28W
Murchison, *N.Z.* **131 B7** 41 49 S 172 21 E
Murchison →, *Australia* **125 E1** 27 45 S 114 0 E
Murchison, Mt., *Antarctica* **7 D11** 73 0 S 168 0 E
Murchison, Mt., *N.Z.* **131 D6** 43 0 S 171 22 E
Murchison Falls, *Uganda* **118 B3** 2 15N 31 30 E
Murchison Falls Nat. Park, *Uganda* **118 B3** 2 17N 31 48 E
Murchison Mts., *N.Z.* **131 F2** 45 13 S 167 23 E
Murchison Ra., *Australia* **126 C1** 20 0 S 134 10 E
Murchison Rapids, *Malawi* **119 F3** 15 55 S 34 35 E
Murcia, *Spain* **41 G3** 38 5N 1 10W
Murcia □, *Spain* **41 H3** 37 50N 1 30W
Murdo, *U.S.A.* **154 D4** 43 53N 100 43W
Murdoch Pt., *Australia* **126 A3** 14 37 S 144 55 E
Mürefte, *Turkey* **51 F11** 40 40N 27 14 E
Mureş □, *Romania* **53 D9** 46 45N 24 40 E
Mureş →, *Romania* **52 D5** 46 15N 20 13 E
Mureşul = Mureş →, *Romania* **52 D5** 46 15N 20 13 E
Muret, *France* **28 E5** 43 30N 1 20 E
Murewa, *Zimbabwe* **117 B5** 17 39 S 31 47 E
Murfreesboro, *N.C., U.S.A.* **149 G7** 36 27N 77 6W
Murfreesboro, *Tenn., U.S.A.* **149 H2** 35 51N 86 24W
Murg, *Switz.* **33 B8** 47 6N 9 13 E
Murgab = Murghob, *Tajikistan* **66 F8** 38 10N 74 2 E
Murgab →, *Turkmenistan* **97 B9** 38 18N 61 12 E
Murgenella, *Australia* **124 B5** 11 34 S 132 56 E
Murgeni, *Romania* **53 D13** 46 12N 28 1 E
Murgenthal, *Switz.* **32 B5** 47 16N 7 50 E
Murgha Kibzai, *Pakistan* **92 D3** 30 44N 69 25 E
Murghob, *Tajikistan* **66 F8** 38 10N 74 2 E
Murgon, *Australia* **127 D5** 26 15 S 151 54 E
Muri, *India* **93 H11** 23 22N 85 52 E
Muri, *Switz.* **33 B6** 47 17N 8 21 E
Muria, *Indonesia* **85 D4** 6 36 S 110 53 E
Muriaé, *Brazil* **171 F3** 21 8 S 42 23W
Murias de Paredes, *Spain* **42 C4** 42 52N 6 11W
Murici, *Brazil* **170 C4** 9 19 S 35 56W
Muriége, *Angola* **115 D4** 9 58 S 21 11 E
Muriel Mine, *Zimbabwe* **119 F3** 17 14 S 30 40 E
Murila, *Angola* **115 E4** 10 44 S 20 20 E
Müritz, *Germany* **30 B8** 53 25N 12 42 E
Murka, *Kenya* **118 C4** 3 27 S 38 0 E
Murkong Selek, *India* **90 B5** 27 44N 95 18 E
Murliganj, *India* **93 G12** 25 54N 86 59 E
Murmansk, *Russia* **56 A5** 68 57N 33 10 E
Murnau, *Germany* **31 H7** 47 40N 11 12 E
Muro, *France* **29 F12** 42 34N 8 54 E
Muro, *Spain* **38 B4** 39 44N 3 3 E
Muro, C. de, *France* **29 G12** 41 44N 8 37 E
Muro de Alcoy, *Spain* **41 G4** 38 46N 0 26W
Muro Lucano, *Italy* **47 B8** 40 45N 15 29 E
Murom, *Russia* **60 C6** 55 35N 42 3 E
Muroran, *Japan* **70 C10** 42 25N 141 0 E
Muros, *Spain* **42 C1** 42 45N 9 5W
Muros y de Noya, Ría de, *Spain* **42 C1** 42 45N 9 0W
Muroto, *Japan* **72 D6** 33 18N 134 9 E
Muroto-Misaki, *Japan* **72 D6** 33 15N 134 10 E
Murowana Goślina, *Poland* **55 F3** 52 35N 17 0 E
Murphy, *U.S.A.* **158 E5** 43 13N 116 33W
Murphys, *U.S.A.* **160 G6** 38 8N 120 28W
Murphysboro, *U.S.A.* **156 G7** 37 46N 89 20W
Murrat, *Sudan* **106 D2** 18 51N 29 33 E
Murrat Wells, *Sudan* **106 C3** 21 3N 32 55 E
Murray, *Iowa, U.S.A.* **156 C3** 41 3N 93 57W
Murray, *Ky., U.S.A.* **149 G1** 36 37N 88 19W
Murray, *Utah, U.S.A.* **158 F8** 40 40N 111 53W
Murray →, *Australia* **128 C3** 35 20 S 139 22 E
Murray, L., *Papua N. G.* **132 D1** 7 0 S 141 35 E
Murray, L., *U.S.A.* **152 A8** 34 3N 81 13W
Murray Bridge, *Australia* **128 C3** 35 6 S 139 14 E
Murray Harbour, *Canada* **141 C7** 46 0N 62 28W
Murray River Nat. Park, *Australia* **127 E3** 34 23 S 140 32 E
Murray-Sunset Nat. Park, *Australia* **128 C4** 34 45 S 141 30 E
Murraysburg, *S. Africa* **116 E3** 31 58 S 23 47 E
Murrayville, *Ill., U.S.A.* **156 E6** 39 35N 90 15W
Murrayville, *Ill., U.S.A.* **156 E6** 39 35N 90 15W
Murree, *Pakistan* **92 C5** 33 56N 73 28 E
Murren, *Switz.* **32 C5** 46 34N 7 53 E
Murrieta, *U.S.A.* **161 M9** 33 33N 117 13W
Murro di Porco, Capo, *Italy* **47 F8** 37 0N 15 20 E
Murrumbateman, *Australia* **129 C8** 34 58 S 149 0 E
Murrumbidgee →, *Australia* **128 C5** 34 43 S 143 12 E
Murrumburrah, *Australia* **129 C8** 34 32 S 148 22 E
Murrurundi, *Australia* **129 A9** 31 42 S 150 51 E
Murshid, *Sudan* **106 C3** 21 40N 31 10 E
Murshidabad, *India* **93 G13** 24 11N 88 19 E
Murska Sobota, *Slovenia* **45 B13** 46 39N 16 12 E
Murtazapur, *India* **94 D3** 20 40N 77 25 E
Murten, *Switz.* **32 C4** 46 56N 7 4 E
Murtensee, *Switz.* **32 C4** 46 56N 7 7 E
Murtle L., *Canada* **142 C5** 52 8N 119 38W
Murtoa, *Australia* **128 D5** 36 35 S 142 28 E
Murtosa, *Portugal* **42 E2** 40 44N 8 40W
Muru →, *Brazil* **172 B3** 8 9 S 70 45W
Murud, *India* **94 E1** 18 19N 72 58 E
Murungu, *Tanzania* **118 C3** 4 12 S 31 10 E
Muruntau, *Uzbekistan* **65 C2** 41 30N 64 37 E
Murupara, *N.Z.* **130 E5** 38 28 S 176 42 E
Mururoa, *Pac. Oc.* **135 K14** 21 52 S 138 55W
Murwara, *India* **93 H9** 23 46N 80 28 E
Murwillumbah, *Australia* **127 D5** 28 18 S 153 27 E
Mürz →, *Austria* **34 D8** 47 30N 15 25 E
Mürzzuschlag, *Austria* **34 D8** 47 36N 15 41 E
Mus, *India* **95 K11** 9 14N 92 47 E
Muş, *Turkey* **101 C9** 38 45N 41 30 E
Musa, *Dem. Rep. of the Congo* **114 B3** 2 40N 19 18 E
Musa →, *Papua N. G.* **132 E5** 9 3 S 148 55 E
Mûsa, Gebel, *Egypt* **96 D2** 28 33N 33 59 E
Musa Khel, *Pakistan* **92 D3** 30 59N 69 52 E
Mūsá Qal'eh, *Afghan.* **91 B2** 32 20N 64 50 E
Musadi, *Dem. Rep. of the Congo* **114 C4** 2 31 S 22 50 E
Musafirkhana, *India* **93 F9** 26 22N 81 48 E
Musala, *Bulgaria* **50 D7** 42 13N 23 37 E
Musala, *Indonesia* **84 B1** 1 41N 98 28 E
Musan, *N. Korea* **75 C15** 42 12N 129 12 E
Musandam, Ra's, *Oman* **99 A7** 26 20N 56 20 E
Musangu, *Dem. Rep. of the Congo* **119 E1** 10 28 S 23 55 E
Musasa, *Tanzania* **118 C3** 3 25 S 31 30 E
Musashino, *Japan* **73 B11** 35 42N 139 34 E
Musay'id, *Qatar* **97 E6** 25 0N 51 33 E
Musaymir, *Yemen* **98 D4** 13 27N 44 37 E
Muscat = Masqat, *Oman* **99 B7** 23 37N 58 36 E
Muscat & Oman = Oman ■, *Asia* **99 B7** 23 0N 58 0 E
Muscatatuc →, *U.S.A.* **157 F10** 38 47N 86 9W
Muscatine, *U.S.A.* **156 C5** 41 25N 91 3W
Muschu I., *Papua N. G.* **132 B2** 3 25 S 143 35 E
Muscoda, *U.S.A.* **156 A6** 43 11N 90 27W
Musgrave Harbour, *Canada* **141 C9** 49 27N 53 58W
Musgrave Ranges, *Australia* **125 E5** 26 0 S 132 0 E
Mushie, *Dem. Rep. of the Congo* **114 C3** 2 56 S 16 55 E
Mushima, *Zambia* **115 E4** 14 10 S 24 56 E
Mushin, *Nigeria* **113 D5** 6 32N 3 21 E
Musi →, *India* **94 F4** 16 41N 79 40 E
Musi →, *Indonesia* **84 C2** 2 20 S 104 56 E
Musiri, *India* **95 J4** 10 56N 78 27 E
Muskeg →, *Canada* **142 A4** 60 20N 123 20W
Muskego, *U.S.A.* **157 B8** 42 55N 88 8W
Muskegon, *U.S.A.* **157 A10** 43 14N 86 16W
Muskegon →, *U.S.A.* **148 D2** 43 14N 86 21W
Muskegon Heights, *U.S.A.* **157 A10** 43 12N 86 16W
Muskogee, *U.S.A.* **155 H7** 35 45N 95 22W
Muskoka, L., *Canada* **150 B5** 45 0N 79 25W
Muskwa →, *Canada* **142 B4** 58 47N 122 48W
Muslimiyah, *Syria* **96 B3** 36 19N 37 12 E
Musmar, *Sudan* **106 D4** 18 13N 35 40 E
Musofu, *Zambia* **119 E2** 13 30 S 29 0 E
Musoma, *Tanzania* **118 C3** 1 30 S 33 48 E
Musquaro, L., *Canada* **141 B7** 50 38N 61 5W
Musquodoboit Harbour, *Canada* **141 D7** 44 50N 63 9W
Mussau I., *Papua N. G.* **132 A5** 1 30 S 149 40 E
Musselburgh, *U.K.* **22 F5** 55 57N 3 2W
Musselshell →, *U.S.A.* **158 C10** 47 21N 107 57W
Mussende, *Angola* **115 E3** 10 32 S 16 5 E
Mussidan, *France* **28 C4** 45 2N 0 22 E
Mussolo, *Angola* **115 D3** 9 59 S 17 19 E
Mussomeli, *Italy* **46 E6** 37 35N 13 45 E
Mussoorie, *India* **92 D8** 30 27N 78 6 E
Mussuco, *Angola* **116 B2** 17 2 S 19 3 E
Mustafakemalpaşa, *Turkey* **51 F12** 40 2N 28 24 E
Mustahil, *Ethiopia* **120 C2** 5 16N 44 45 E
Mustang, *Nepal* **93 E10** 29 10N 83 55 E
Musters, L., *Argentina* **176 C3** 45 20 S 69 25W
Musudan, *N. Korea* **75 D15** 40 50N 129 43 E
Muswellbrook, *Australia* **129 B9** 32 16 S 150 56 E
Muszyna, *Poland* **55 J7** 49 22N 20 55 E
Mût, *Egypt* **106 B2** 25 28N 28 58 E
Mut, *Turkey* **100 D5** 36 40N 33 28 E
Mutanda, *Dem. Rep. of the Congo* **115 D3** 5 17 S 16 34 E
Mutanda, *Mozam.* **117 C5** 21 0 S 33 34 E
Mutanda, *Zambia* **119 E2** 12 24 S 26 13 E
Mutare, *Zimbabwe* **119 F3** 18 58 S 32 38 E
Muting, *Indonesia* **83 C6** 7 23 S 140 20 E
Mutis, *Indonesia* **82 C2** 9 30 S 124 14 E
Mutoko, *Zimbabwe* **117 B5** 17 24 S 32 13 E
Mutoray, *Russia* **67 C11** 60 56N 101 0 E
Mutoto, *Dem. Rep. of the Congo* **115 D4** 5 42 S 22 42 E
Mutoxo, *Angola* **115 E4** 12 17 S 21 40 E
Mutshatsha, *Dem. Rep. of the Congo* **119 E1** 10 35 S 24 20 E
Mutsu, *Japan* **70 D10** 41 5N 140 55 E
Mutsu-Wan, *Japan* **70 D10** 41 5N 140 55 E
Muttaburra, *Australia* **126 C3** 22 38 S 144 29 E
Muttalip, *Turkey* **49 B12** 39 50N 30 32 E
Mutton I., *Ireland* **23 D2** 52 49N 9 32W
Muttukuru, *India* **95 G5** 14 16N 80 6 E
Mutuáli, *Mozam.* **119 E4** 14 55 S 37 0 E
Mutum Biyu, *Nigeria* **113 D7** 8 40N 10 50 E
Mutunópolis, *Brazil* **171 D2** 13 40 S 49 15W
Mutur, *Sri Lanka* **95 K5** 8 27N 81 16 E
Muweilih, *Egypt* **103 E3** 30 42N 34 19 E
Muxaluando, *Angola* **115 D2** 8 8 S 14 18 E
Muxía, *Spain* **42 B1** 43 3N 9 10W
Muxima, *Angola* **115 D2** 9 33 S 13 58 E
Muy Muy, *Nic.* **164 D2** 12 39N 85 36W
Muyinga, *Burundi* **118 C3** 3 14 S 30 33 E
Muynak, *Uzbekistan* **66 E6** 43 44N 59 10 E
Muyunkum, Peski, *Kazakstan* **65 A4** 44 12N 71 0 E
Muzaffarabad, *Pakistan* **93 B5** 34 25N 73 30 E
Muzaffargarh, *Pakistan* **91 C3** 30 5N 71 14 E
Muzaffarnagar, *India* **92 E7** 29 26N 77 40 E
Muzaffarpur, *India* **93 F11** 26 7N 85 23 E
Muzafirpur, *Pakistan* **92 D3** 30 58N 69 9 E
Muzeze, *Angola* **115 F3** 15 3 S 17 43 E
Muzhi, *Russia* **56 A11** 65 25N 64 40 E
Muzillac, *France* **26 E4** 47 35N 2 30W
Muzon, C., *U.S.A.* **144 J14** 54 40N 132 42W
Muztagh-Ata, *China* **65 D7** 38 17N 75 7 E
Muzūra, *Egypt* **106 J7** 28 53N 30 48 E
Mvadhi-Ousyé, *Gabon* **114 B2** 1 13N 13 12 E
Mvam, *Gabon* **114 C1** 0 13 S 9 39 E
Mvangan, *Cameroon* **114 B2** 2 17N 11 43 E
Mvôlô, *Sudan* **107 F2** 6 2N 29 53 E
Mvuma, *Zimbabwe* **119 F3** 19 16 S 30 30 E
Mvurwi, *Zimbabwe* **119 F3** 17 0 S 30 57 E
Mwabvi Game Reserve, *Malawi* **119 F3** 16 42 S 35 0 E
Mwadi-Kalumbu, *Dem. Rep. of the Congo* **115 D3** 7 53 S 18 43 E
Mwadui, *Tanzania* **118 C3** 3 26 S 33 32 E
Mwali = Mohéli, *Comoros Is.* **121 a** 12 20 S 43 40 E
Mwambo, *Tanzania* **119 E5** 10 30 S 40 22 E
Mwandi, *Zambia* **119 F1** 17 30 S 24 51 E
Mwanza, *Dem. Rep. of the Congo* **118 D2** 7 55 S 26 43 E
Mwanza, *Tanzania* **118 C3** 2 30 S 32 58 E
Mwanza, *Zambia* **119 F1** 16 58 S 24 28 E
Mwanza □, *Tanzania* **118 C3** 2 0 S 33 0 E
Mwaya, *Tanzania* **119 D3** 9 32 S 33 55 E
Mweelrea, *Ireland* **23 C2** 53 39N 9 49W
Mweka, *Dem. Rep. of the Congo* **115 C4** 4 50 S 21 34 E
Mwendjila, *Dem. Rep. of the Congo* **115 D3** 7 12 S 18 51 E
Mwene-Ditu, *Dem. Rep. of the Congo* **115 D4** 6 35 S 22 27 E
Mwenezi, *Zimbabwe* **119 G3** 21 15 S 30 48 E
Mwenezi →, *Mozam.* **119 G3** 22 40 S 31 50 E
Mwenga, *Dem. Rep. of the Congo* **118 C2** 3 1 S 28 28 E
Mweru, L., *Zambia* **119 D2** 9 0 S 28 40 E
Mwetshi, *Dem. Rep. of the Congo* **115 C4** 4 50 S 22 38 E
Mweza Range, *Zimbabwe* **119 G3** 21 0 S 30 0 E
Mwilambwe, *Dem. Rep. of the Congo* **118 D2** 8 7 S 25 5 E
Mwimbi, *Tanzania* **119 D3** 8 38 S 31 39 E
Mwinilunga, *Zambia* **119 E1** 11 43 S 24 25 E
My Tho, *Vietnam* **87 G6** 10 29N 106 23 E
Mya, O. →, *Algeria* **111 B5** 30 46N 4 54 E
Myajlar, *India* **92 F4** 26 15N 70 20 E
Myakka →, *U.S.A.* **153 J7** 26 56N 82 11W
Myall Lakes Nat. Park, *Australia* **129 B10** 32 25 S 152 30 E
Myanaung, *Burma* **90 F5** 18 18N 95 22 E
Myanmar = Burma ■, *Asia* **90 E6** 21 0N 96 30 E
Myaung, *Burma* **90 E5** 21 50N 95 23 E
Myaungmya, *Burma* **90 G5** 16 30N 94 40 E
Myebon, *Burma* **90 E4** 20 3N 93 22 E
Myeik Kyunzu, *Burma* **87 G1** 11 30N 97 30 E
Myers Chuck, *U.S.A.* **142 B2** 55 44N 132 11W
Myerstown, *U.S.A.* **151 F8** 40 22N 76 19W
Myingyan, *Burma* **90 E5** 21 30N 95 20 E
Myitkyina, *Burma* **90 C6** 25 24N 97 26 E
Myitson, *Burma* **90 D6** 23 16N 96 34 E
Myittha, *Burma* **90 E6** 21 25N 96 8 E
Myittha →, *Burma* **90 D5** 23 12N 94 17 E
Myjava, *Slovak Rep.* **35 C10** 48 41N 17 37 E
Mykhaylivka, *Ukraine* **59 J8** 47 12N 35 15 E
Mykines, *Færoe Is.* **14 E9** 62 7N 7 35W
Myking, *Norway* **18 D2** 60 41N 5 19 E
Mykolayiv, *Ukraine* **59 J7** 46 58N 32 0 E
Mylius Erichsen Land, *Greenland* **10 A8** 81 30N 27 0W
Mymensingh, *Bangla.* **90 C3** 24 45N 90 24 E
Mynydd Du, *U.K.* **21 F4** 51 52N 3 50W
Myo-gyi, *Burma* **90 E6** 21 27N 96 22 E
Myohaung, *Burma* **90 E4** 20 35N 93 11 E
Myohla, *Burma* **90 F5** 19 16N 95 25 E
Myotha, *Burma* **90 E5** 21 41N 95 43 E
Myothit, *Kachin, Burma* **90 C6** 24 24N 97 24 E
Myothit, *Magwe, Burma* **90 E5** 20 12N 95 27 E
Myrasýsla □, *Iceland* **11 C5** 64 45N 21 30W
Mýrdalsjökull, *Iceland* **11 D7** 63 40N 19 6W
Myrhorod, *Ukraine* **59 H7** 49 58N 33 37 E
Mýri, *Iceland* **11 B9** 65 23N 17 23W
Myrtle Beach, *U.S.A.* **149 J6** 33 42N 78 53W
Myrtle Creek, *U.S.A.* **158 E2** 43 1N 123 17W
Myrtle Grove, *U.S.A.* **153 E2** 30 23N 87 17W
Myrtle Point, *U.S.A.* **158 E1** 43 4N 124 8W
Myrtleford, *Australia* **129 D7** 36 34 S 146 44 E
Myrtou, *Cyprus* **39 E9** 35 18N 33 4 E
Myrzakent, *Kazakstan* **65 C4** 40 40N 68 32 E
Mysen, *Norway* **18 E8** 59 33N 11 20 E
Mysia, *Turkey* **51 G11** 39 50N 27 0 E
Myślenice, *Poland* **55 J6** 49 51N 19 57 E
Myślibórz, *Poland* **55 F1** 52 55N 14 50 E
Mysłowice, *Poland* **55 H6** 50 15N 19 12 E
Mysore = Karnataka □, *India* **95 H3** 13 15N 77 0 E
Mysore, *India* **95 H3** 12 17N 76 41 E
Mystic, *Conn., U.S.A.* **151 E13** 41 21N 71 58W
Mystic, *Iowa, U.S.A.* **156 D4** 40 47N 92 57W
Myszków, *Poland* **55 H6** 50 45N 19 22 E
Myszyniec, *Poland* **54 E8** 53 23N 21 21 E
Mythen, *Switz.* **33 B7** 47 2N 8 42 E
Mytishchi, *Russia* **59 E5** 55 50N 37 50 E
Mývatn, *Iceland* **11 B10** 65 36N 17 0W
Mzab, Oued en →, *Algeria* **111 B6** 32 15N 5 0 E
Mže →, *Czech Rep.* **34 B6** 49 46N 13 24 E
Mzimba, *Malawi* **119 E3** 11 55 S 33 39 E
Mzimkulu →, *S. Africa* **117 E5** 30 44 S 30 28 E
Mzimvubu →, *S. Africa* **117 E4** 31 38 S 29 33 E
Mzuzu, *Malawi* **119 E3** 11 30 S 33 55 E

N

Na Hearadh = Harris, *U.K.* **22 D2** 57 50N 6 55W
Na-lang, *Burma* **90 D6** 22 42N 97 33 E
Na Noi, *Thailand* **86 C3** 18 19N 100 43 E
Na Phao, *Laos* **86 D5** 17 35N 105 44 E
Na Sam, *Vietnam* **76 F6** 22 3N 106 37 E
Na San, *Vietnam* **86 B5** 21 12N 104 2 E
Na Thon, *Thailand* **87 b** 9 32N 99 56 E
Naab →, *Germany* **31 F8** 49 1N 12 2 E
Naalehu, *U.S.A.* **145 D6** 19 4N 155 35W
Na'am, *Sudan* **107 F2** 9 42N 28 27 E
Na'am →, *Sudan* **107 F2** 6 48N 29 57 E
Naantali, *Finland* **15 F19** 60 29N 22 2 E
Naas, *Ireland* **23 C5** 53 12N 6 40W
Nababeep, *S. Africa* **116 D2** 29 36 S 17 46 E
Nabadwip = Navadwip, *India* **93 H13** 23 34N 88 20 E
Nabari, *Japan* **73 C8** 34 37N 136 5 E
Nabawa, *Australia* **125 E1** 28 30 S 114 48 E
Nabberu, L., *Australia* **125 E3** 25 50 S 120 30 E
Nabburg, *Germany* **31 F8** 49 27N 12 11 E
Naberezhnyye Chelny, *Russia* **60 C11** 55 42N 52 19 E
Nabesna, *U.S.A.* **144 E12** 62 22N 143 0W
Nabeul, *Tunisia* **108 A2** 36 30N 10 44 E
Nabha, *India* **92 D7** 30 26N 76 14 E
Nabīd, *Iran* **97 D8** 29 40N 57 38 E
Nabire, *Indonesia* **83 B5** 3 15 S 135 26 E
Nabisar, *Pakistan* **92 G3** 25 8N 69 40 E
Nabisipi →, *Canada* **141 B7** 50 14N 62 13W
Nabiswera, *Uganda* **118 B3** 1 27N 32 15 E
Nablus = Nābulus, *West Bank* **103 C4** 32 14N 35 15 E
Naboomspruit, *S. Africa* **117 C4** 24 32 S 28 40 E
Nabou, *Burkina Faso* **112 C4** 11 25N 2 50W
Nabouwalu, *Fiji* **133 A2** 17 0 S 178 45 E
Nabua, *Phil.* **80 E4** 13 24N 123 22 E
Nābulus, *West Bank* **103 C4** 32 14N 35 15 E
Nabunturan, *Phil.* **81 H5** 7 35N 125 58 E
Nacala, *Mozam.* **119 E5** 14 31 S 40 34 E
Nacala-Velha, *Mozam.* **119 E5** 14 32 S 40 34 E
Nacaome, *Honduras* **164 D2** 13 31N 87 30W
Nacaroa, *Mozam.* **119 E4** 14 22 S 39 56 E
Naches, *U.S.A.* **158 C3** 46 44N 120 42W
Naches →, *U.S.A.* **160 D6** 46 38N 120 31W
Nachicapau, L., *Canada* **141 A6** 56 40N 68 5W
Nachikatsuura, *Japan* **73 D7** 33 33N 135 58 E
Nachingwea, *Tanzania* **119 E4** 10 23 S 38 49 E
Nachna, *India* **92 F4** 27 34N 71 41 E
Náchod, *Czech Rep.* **34 A9** 50 25N 16 8 E
Nachuge, *India* **95 J11** 10 47N 92 21 E
Nacimiento L., *U.S.A.* **160 K6** 35 46N 120 53W
Nackara, *Australia* **128 B3** 32 48 S 139 12 E
Naco, *Mexico* **162 A3** 31 20N 109 56W
Nacogdoches, *U.S.A.* **155 K7** 31 36N 94 39W
Nácori Chico, *Mexico* **162 B3** 29 39N 109 1W
Nacozari, *Mexico* **162 A3** 30 24N 109 39W
Nacula, *Fiji* **133 A1** 16 54 S 177 27 E
Nadi, *Fiji* **133 A1** 17 42 S 177 20 E
Nadi, *Sudan* **106 D3** 18 40N 33 41 E
Nadiad, *India* **92 H5** 22 41N 72 56 E
Nădlac, *Romania* **52 D5** 46 10N 20 50 E
Nador, *Morocco* **111 A4** 35 14N 2 58W
Nadur, *Malta* **38 F7** 35 54N 14 22 E
Nadur, *Gozo, Malta* **38 E7** 36 2N 14 18 E
Nadūshan, *Iran* **97 C7** 32 2N 53 35 E
Nadvirna, *Ukraine* **59 H3** 48 37N 24 30 E
Nadvoitsy, *Russia* **56 B5** 63 52N 34 14 E
Nadvornaya = Nadvirna, *Ukraine* **59 H3** 48 37N 24 30 E
Nadym, *Russia* **66 C8** 65 35N 72 42 E
Nadym →, *Russia* **66 C8** 66 12N 72 0 E
Nærbø, *Norway* **15 G11** 58 40N 5 39 E
Næstved, *Denmark* **17 J5** 55 13N 11 44 E
Nafada, *Nigeria* **113 C7** 11 8N 11 20 E
Näfels, *Switz.* **33 B8** 47 6N 9 4 E
Naft-e Safīd, *Iran* **97 D6** 31 40N 49 17 E
Naftshahr, *Iran* **101 E11** 34 0N 45 30 E
Nafud Desert = An Nafūd, *Si. Arabia* **96 D4** 28 15N 41 0 E
Nafūsah, Jabal, *Libya* **108 B2** 32 12N 12 30 E
Nag Hammâdi, *Egypt* **106 B3** 26 2N 32 18 E
Naga, *Camarines S., Phil.* **80 E4** 13 38N 123 15 E
Naga, *Cebu, Phil.* **81 F4** 10 13N 123 45 E
Naga, *Zamboanga del S., Phil.* **81 H4** 7 46N 122 45 E
Naga, Kreb en, *Africa* **110 D3** 24 12N 6 0W
Naga-Shima, *Kagoshima, Japan* **72 E2** 32 10N 130 9 E
Naga-Shima, *Yamaguchi, Japan* **72 D4** 33 49N 132 5 E
Nagahama, *Ehime, Japan* **72 D4** 33 36N 132 29 E
Nagahama, *Shiga, Japan* **73 B8** 35 23N 136 16 E
Nagai, *Japan* **70 E10** 38 6N 140 2 E
Nagai I., *U.S.A.* **144 J8** 55 5N 160 0W
Nagaland □, *India* **90 B5** 26 0N 94 30 E
Nagambie, *Australia* **129 D6** 36 47 S 145 10 E
Nagano, *Japan* **73 A10** 36 40N 138 10 E
Nagano □, *Japan* **73 A10** 36 15N 138 0 E
Nagaoka, *Japan* **71 F9** 37 27N 138 51 E
Nagappattinam, *India* **95 J4** 10 46N 79 51 E
Nagar →, *Bangla.* **90 C2** 24 27N 89 12 E
Nagar Karnul, *India* **95 F4** 16 29N 78 20 E
Nagar Parkar, *Pakistan* **92 G4** 24 28N 70 46 E
Nagara-Gawa →, *Japan* **73 B8** 35 4N 136 43 E
Nagaram, *India* **94 E5** 18 21N 80 26 E
Nagari Hills, *India* **95 H4** 13 3N 79 45 E
Nagasaki, *Japan* **72 E1** 32 47N 129 50 E
Nagasaki □, *Japan* **72 E1** 32 50N 129 40 E
Nagato, *Japan* **72 C3** 34 19N 131 5 E
Nagaur, *India* **92 F5** 27 15N 73 45 E
Nagbhir, *India* **94 D4** 20 34N 79 55 E
Nagda, *India* **92 H6** 23 27N 75 25 E
Nagercoil, *India* **95 K3** 8 12N 77 26 E
Nagina, *India* **93 E8** 29 30N 78 30 E
Nagīneh, *Iran* **97 C8** 34 20N 57 15 E
Naginimara, *India* **90 B5** 26 49N 94 50 E
Nagir, *Pakistan* **93 A6** 36 12N 74 42 E
Naglarby, *Sweden* **16 D9** 60 25N 15 34 E
Nagod, *India* **93 G9** 24 34N 80 36 E
Nagold, *Germany* **31 G4** 48 32N 8 43 E
Nagold →, *Germany* **31 G4** 48 52N 8 42 E
Nagoorin, *Australia* **126 C5** 24 17 S 151 15 E
Nagorno-Karabakh, *Azerbaijan* **101 C12** 39 55N 46 45 E
Nagornyy, *Russia* **67 D13** 55 58N 124 57 E
Nagorsk, *Russia* **64 B3** 59 18N 50 48 E
Nagoya, *Japan* **73 B8** 35 10N 136 50 E
Nagpur, *India* **94 D4** 21 8N 79 10 E
Nagua, *Dom. Rep.* **165 C6** 19 23N 69 50W
Naguabo, *Puerto Rico* **165 d** 18 13N 65 44W
Nagyatád, *Hungary* **52 D2** 46 14N 17 22 E
Nagyecsed, *Hungary* **52 C7** 47 53N 22 24 E
Nagykálló, *Hungary* **52 C6** 47 53N 21 51 E
Nagykanizsa, *Hungary* **52 D2** 46 28N 17 0 E
Nagykáta, *Hungary* **52 C4** 47 25N 19 45 E
Nagykőrös, *Hungary* **52 C4** 47 5N 19 48 E
Naha, *Japan* **71 L3** 26 13N 127 42 E
Nahan, *India* **92 D7** 30 33N 77 18 E
Nahanni Butte, *Canada* **142 A4** 61 2N 123 31W
Nahanni Nat. Park, *Canada* **142 A4** 61 15N 125 0W
Nahargarh, *Mad. P., India* **92 G6** 24 10N 75 14 E
Nahargarh, *Raj., India* **92 G7** 24 55N 76 50 E
Nahariyya, *Israel* **100 F6** 33 1N 35 5 E
Nahāvand, *Iran* **97 C6** 34 10N 48 22 E
Nahe →, *Germany* **31 F3** 49 58N 7 54 E
Nahîya, W. →, *Egypt* **106 B3** 28 55N 31 0 E
Nahuel Huapi, L., *Argentina* **176 B2** 41 0 S 71 32W
Nahunta, *U.S.A.* **152 D8** 31 12N 81 59W
Nai Yong, *Thailand* **87 a** 8 14N 98 22 E
Naic, *Phil.* **80 D3** 14 19N 120 46 E
Naicá, *Mexico* **162 B3** 27 53N 105 31W
Naicam, *Canada* **143 C8** 52 30N 104 30W
Naikliu, *Indonesia* **82 C2** 9 30 S 123 50 E
Naikoon Prov. Park, *Canada* **142 C2** 53 55N 131 55W
Naikul, *India* **94 D7** 21 20N 84 58 E
Naila, *Germany* **31 E7** 50 19N 11 42 E
Naimisharanya, *India* **93 F9** 27 21N 80 30 E
Nain, *Canada* **141 A7** 56 34N 61 40W
Nā'īn, *Iran* **97 C7** 32 54N 53 0 E
Naini Tal, *India* **93 E8** 29 30N 79 30 E
Naintré, *France* **26 F7** 46 46N 0 29 E
Nainwa, *India* **92 G6** 25 46N 75 51 E
Naipu, *Romania* **53 F10** 44 12N 25 47 E

Nawoiy 255

Nairai, Fiji 133 A2 17 49 S 179 15 E
Nairn, U.K. 22 D5 57 35N 3 53W
Nairobi, Kenya 118 C4 1 17 S 36 48 E
Nairobi Nat. Park, Kenya 118 C4 1 22 S 36 50 E
Naissaar, Estonia 15 G21 59 34N 24 29 E
Naita, Mt., Ethiopia 107 F4 5 30N 35 18 E
Naitaba, Fiji 133 A3 17 0 S 179 16W
Naivasha, Kenya 118 C4 0 40 S 36 30 E
Naivasha, L., Kenya 118 C4 0 48 S 36 20 E
Najac, France 28 D5 44 14N 1 58 E
Najafābād, Iran 97 C6 32 40N 51 15 E
Najd, Si. Arabia 102 B3 26 30N 42 0 E
Nájera, Spain 40 C2 42 26N 2 48W
Najerilla →, Spain 40 C2 42 32N 2 48W
Najibabad, India 92 E8 29 40N 78 20 E
Najin, N. Korea 75 C16 42 12N 130 15 E
Najmah, Si. Arabia 97 E6 26 42N 50 6 E
Najrān, Si. Arabia 98 C4 17 34N 44 18 E
Naju, S. Korea 75 G14 35 3N 126 43 E
Naka-Gawa →, Japan 73 A12 36 20N 140 36 E
Nakadōri-Shima, Japan 71 H4 32 57N 129 4 E
Nakalagba, Dem. Rep. of the Congo 118 B2 2 50N 27 58 E
Nakalele Pt., U.S.A. 145 B5 21 2N 156 35W
Nakama, Japan 72 D2 33 56N 130 43 E
Nakaminato, Japan 73 A12 36 21N 140 36 E
Nakamura, Japan 72 E4 32 59N 132 56 E
Nakanai Mts., Papua N. G. 132 C6 5 40 S 151 0 E
Nakano, Japan 73 A10 36 45N 138 22 E
Nakano-Shima, Japan 71 K4 29 51N 129 52 E
Nakanojō, Japan 73 A10 36 35N 138 51 E
Nakashibetsu, Japan 70 C12 43 33N 144 59 E
Nakatsu, Japan 72 D3 33 34N 131 15 E
Nakatsugawa, Japan 73 B9 35 29N 137 30 E
Nakfa, Eritrea 107 D4 16 40N 38 32 E
Nakfa Wildlife Reserve, Eritrea 107 D4 17 28N 38 55 E
Nakha Yai, Ko, Thailand 87 a 8 3N 98 28 E
Nakhfar al Buşayyah, Iraq 96 D5 30 0N 46 10 E
Nakhichevan = Naxçıvan, Azerbaijan 101 C11 39 12N 45 15 E
Nakhichevan Republic = Naxçıvan □, Azerbaijan 101 C11 39 25N 45 26 E
Nakhl, Egypt 103 F2 29 55N 33 43 E
Nakhl-e Taqī, Iran 97 E7 27 28N 52 36 E
Nakhodka, Russia 67 E14 42 53N 132 54 E
Nakhon Nayok, Thailand 86 E3 14 12N 101 13 E
Nakhon Pathom, Thailand 86 F3 13 49N 100 3 E
Nakhon Phanom, Thailand 86 D5 17 23N 104 43 E
Nakhon Ratchasima, Thailand 86 E4 14 59N 102 12 E
Nakhon Sawan, Thailand 86 E3 15 35N 100 10 E
Nakhon Si Thammarat, Thailand 87 H3 8 29N 100 0 E
Nakhon Thai, Thailand 86 D3 17 5N 100 44 E
Nakhtarana, India 92 H3 23 20N 69 15 E
Nakina, Canada 140 B2 50 10N 86 40W
Nakło nad Notecią, Poland 55 E4 53 9N 17 38 E
Naknek, U.S.A. 144 G8 58 44N 157 1W
Nako, Burkina Faso 112 C4 10 40N 3 4W
Nakodar, India 92 D6 31 8N 75 31 E
Nakskov, Denmark 17 K5 54 50N 11 8 E
Naktong →, S. Korea 75 G15 35 7N 128 57 E
Nakuru, Kenya 118 C4 0 15 S 36 4 E
Nakuru, L., Kenya 118 C4 0 23 S 36 5 E
Nakusp, Canada 142 C5 50 20N 117 45W
Nal, Pakistan 92 F2 27 40N 66 12 E
Nal →, Pakistan 91 D2 25 20N 65 30 E
Nalázi, Mozam. 117 C5 24 3 S 33 20 E
Nalchik, Russia 61 J6 43 30N 43 33 E
Nałęczów, Poland 55 G9 51 17N 22 9 E
Nalerigu, Ghana 113 C4 10 35N 0 25W
Nalgonda, India 94 F4 17 6N 79 15 E
Nalhati, India 93 G12 24 17N 87 52 E
Naliya, India 92 H3 23 16N 68 50 E
Nallamalai Hills, India 95 G4 15 30N 78 50 E
Nallıhan, Turkey 100 B4 40 11N 31 20 E
Nalolo, Zambia 115 F4 15 33 S 23 7 E
Nalón →, Spain 42 B4 43 32N 6 4W
Nalong, Burma 90 C6 24 44N 97 28 E
Nālūt, Libya 108 B2 31 54N 11 0 E
Nam Can, Vietnam 87 H5 8 46N 104 59 E
Nam-ch'on, N. Korea 75 E14 38 15N 126 26 E
Nam Co, China 68 C4 30 30N 90 45 E
Nam Dinh, Vietnam 76 G6 20 25N 106 5 E
Nam Du, Hon, Vietnam 87 H5 9 41N 104 21 E
Nam Ngum Dam, Laos 86 C4 18 35N 102 34 E
Nam-Phan, Vietnam 87 G6 10 30N 106 0 E
Nam Phong, Thailand 86 D4 16 42N 102 52 E
Nam Tha, Laos 76 G3 20 58N 101 30 E
Nam Tok, Thailand 86 E2 14 21N 99 4 E
Namachire, Angola 115 E4 11 26 S 22 43 E
Namacunde, Angola 116 B2 17 18 S 15 50 E
Namacurra, Mozam. 117 B6 17 30 S 36 50 E
Namadgi Nat. Park, Australia 129 C8 35 42 S 149 0 E
Namak, Daryācheh-ye, Iran 97 C7 34 30N 52 0 E
Namak, Kavir-e, Iran 97 C8 34 30N 57 30 E
Namakkal, India 95 J4 11 13N 78 13 E
Namakzār, Daryācheh-ye, Iran 91 B1 34 0N 60 30 E
Namaland, Namibia 116 C2 26 0 S 17 0 E
Namangan, Uzbekistan 66 E8 41 0N 71 40 E
Namapa, Mozam. 119 E4 13 43 S 39 50 E
Namaqualand, S. Africa 116 E2 30 0 S 17 25 E
Namasagali, Uganda 118 B3 1 2N 33 0 E
Namatanai, Papua N. G. 132 B7 3 40 S 152 29 E
Namber, Indonesia 83 B4 1 2 S 134 49 E
Nambour, Australia 127 D5 26 32 S 152 58 E
Nambouwalu = Nabouwalu, Fiji 133 A2 17 0 S 178 45 E
Nambuangongo, Angola 115 D2 8 1 S 14 12 E
Nambucca Heads, Australia 129 A10 30 37 S 153 0 E
Nambung Nat. Park, Australia 125 F2 30 30 S 115 5 E
Namcha Barwa, China 68 D4 29 40N 95 10 E
Namche Bazar, Nepal 93 F12 27 51N 86 47 E
Namchonjŏm = Nam-ch'on, N. Korea 75 E14 38 15N 126 26 E
Namecunda, Mozam. 119 E4 14 54 S 37 37 E
Nameh, Indonesia 85 B5 2 34N 116 21 E
Namenalala, Fiji 133 A2 17 8 S 179 9 E
Nameponda, Mozam. 119 F4 15 50 S 39 50 E
Namerikawa, Japan 73 A9 36 46N 137 20 E
Náměšť nad Oslavou, Czech Rep. 35 B9 49 12N 16 10 E
Námestovo, Slovak Rep. 35 B12 49 24N 19 25 E
Nametil, Mozam. 119 F4 15 40 S 39 21 E
Namew L., Canada 143 C8 54 14N 101 56W
Namgia, India 93 D8 31 48N 78 40 E
Namhkam, Burma 76 E1 23 50N 97 41 E
Namho, Burma 90 D7 22 4N 99 1 E
Namhsan, Burma 90 D6 22 48N 97 2 E
Namib Desert, Namibia 116 C2 22 30 S 15 0 E
Namib-Naukluft Park, Namibia 116 C2 24 40 S 15 16 E
Namibe, Angola 115 F2 15 7 S 12 11 E
Namibe □, Angola 116 B1 16 35 S 12 30 E
Namibe, Reserva Parcial de, Angola 115 F2 16 35 S 12 20 E
Namibia ■, Africa 116 C2 22 0 S 18 9 E
Namibwoestyn = Namib Desert, Namibia 116 C2 22 30 S 15 0 E
Namīn, Iran 101 C13 38 25N 48 30 E
Namlan, Burma 90 D6 22 15N 97 24 E
Namlea, Indonesia 82 B3 3 18 S 127 5 E
Namoi →, N.S.W., Australia 129 A8 30 12 S 149 30 E
Namoi →, N.S.W., Australia 129 A9 30 0 S 148 7 E
Namous, O. en →, Algeria 111 B4 31 0N 0 15W
Nampa, U.S.A. 158 E5 43 34N 116 34W
Nampala, Mali 112 B3 15 20N 5 30W
Namp'o, N. Korea 75 E13 38 52N 125 10 E
Nampō-Shotō, Japan 71 J10 32 0N 140 0 E
Nampula, Mozam. 119 F4 15 6 S 39 15 E
Namrole, Indonesia 82 B3 3 46 S 126 46 E
Namsang, Burma 90 E6 20 53N 97 43 E
Namsen →, Norway 14 D14 64 28N 11 37 E
Namsos, Norway 14 D14 64 29N 11 30 E
Namtsy, Russia 67 C13 62 43N 129 37 E
Namtu, Burma 90 D6 23 5N 97 28 E
Namtumbo, Tanzania 119 E4 10 30 S 36 4 E
Namu, Canada 142 C3 51 52N 127 50W
Namuka-i-Lau, Fiji 133 B3 18 53 S 178 37W
Namumea, Tuvalu 123 B14 5 41 S 176 9 E
Namur, Belgium 24 D4 50 27N 4 52 E
Namur □, Belgium 24 D4 50 17N 5 0 E
Namutoni, Namibia 116 B2 18 49 S 16 55 E
Namwala, Zambia 119 F2 15 44 S 26 30 E
Namwŏn, S. Korea 75 G14 35 23N 127 23 E
Namysłów, Poland 55 G4 51 6N 17 42 E
Nan, Thailand 86 C3 18 48N 100 46 E
Nan →, Thailand 86 E3 15 42N 100 9 E
Nan-ch'ang = Nanchang, China 77 C10 28 42N 115 55 E
Nan Ling, China 77 E8 25 0N 112 30 E
Nan Xian, China 77 C9 29 20N 112 22 E
Nana, C.A.R. 114 A3 5 0N 15 50 E
Nana, Romania 53 F11 44 17N 26 34 E
Nana-Barya, Réserve de Faune de la, C.A.R. 114 A3 7 40N 17 29 E
Nana Kru, Liberia 112 E3 4 55N 8 45W
Nanaimo, Canada 142 D4 49 10N 124 0W
Nanakuli, U.S.A. 145 K13 21 24N 158 9W
Nanam, N. Korea 75 D15 41 44N 129 40 E
Nanan, China 77 E12 24 59N 118 21 E
Nanango, Australia 127 D5 26 40 S 152 0 E
Nan'ao, China 77 F11 23 28N 117 5 E
Nanao, Japan 71 F8 37 0N 137 0 E
Nanbu, China 76 B6 31 18N 106 3 E
Nanchang, Jiangxi, China 77 C10 28 42N 115 55 E
Nanchang, Kiangsi, China 77 C10 28 34N 115 48 E
Nancheng, China 77 D11 27 33N 116 35 E
Nanching = Nanjing, China 77 A12 32 2N 118 47 E
Nanchong, China 76 B6 30 43N 106 2 E
Nanchuan, China 76 C6 29 9N 107 6 E
Nancowry, India 95 L11 7 59N 93 32 E
Nancy, France 27 D13 48 42N 6 12 E
Nanda Devi, India 93 D8 30 23N 79 59 E
Nanda Kot, India 93 D9 30 17N 80 5 E
Nandan, China 76 E6 24 58N 107 29 E
Nandan, Japan 72 C6 34 10N 134 42 E
Nanded, India 94 E3 19 10N 77 20 E
Nandewar Ra., Australia 127 E5 30 15 S 150 35 E
Nandgaon, India 94 D2 20 19N 74 39 E
Nandi = Nadi, Fiji 133 A1 17 42 S 177 20 E
Nandiarane, Pte., N. Cal. 133 T18 20 14 S 164 19 E
Nandigama, India 94 F5 16 47N 80 18 E
Nandigram, India 93 H12 22 1N 87 58 E
Nandikotkur, India 95 G4 15 52N 78 18 E
Nandura, India 94 D3 20 52N 76 25 E
Nandurbar, India 94 D2 21 20N 74 15 E
Nandyal, India 95 G4 15 30N 78 30 E
Nanfeng, Guangdong, China 77 F8 23 45N 111 47 E
Nanfeng, Jiangxi, China 77 D11 27 12N 116 28 E
Nanga-Eboko, Cameroon 113 E7 4 41N 12 22 E
Nanga Parbat, Pakistan 93 B6 35 10N 74 35 E
Nangade, Mozam. 119 E4 11 5 S 39 36 E
Nangapinoh, Indonesia 85 C4 0 20 S 111 44 E
Nangarhār □, Afghan. 91 B3 34 20N 70 0 E
Nangatayap, Indonesia 85 C4 1 32 S 110 34 E
Nangeya Mts., Uganda 118 B3 3 30N 33 30 E
Nangis, France 27 D10 48 33N 3 1 E
Nangong, China 74 F8 37 23N 115 22 E
Nangtud, Mt., Phil. 81 F4 11 17N 122 11 E
Nanguneri, India 95 K3 8 29N 77 40 E
Nangwarry, Australia 128 D4 37 33 S 140 48 E
Nanhua, China 76 E3 25 13N 101 21 E
Nanhuang, China 75 F11 36 58N 121 48 E
Nanhui, China 77 B13 31 5N 121 44 E
Nanjangud, India 95 H3 12 6N 76 43 E
Nanjeko, Zambia 119 F1 15 31 S 23 30 E
Nanji Shan, China 77 D13 27 27N 121 4 E
Nanjian, China 76 E3 25 2N 100 25 E
Nanjiang, China 76 A6 32 28N 106 51 E
Nanjing, Fujian, China 77 E11 24 25N 117 20 E
Nanjing, Jiangsu, China 77 A12 32 2N 118 47 E
Nanjirinji, Tanzania 119 D4 9 41 S 39 5 E
Nankana Sahib, Pakistan 92 D5 31 27N 73 38 E
Nankang, China 77 E10 25 40N 114 45 E
Nanking = Nanjing, China 77 A12 32 2N 118 47 E
Nankoku, Japan 72 D5 33 39N 133 44 E
Nanlang, China 69 G10 22 30N 113 32 E
Nanling, China 77 B12 30 55N 118 20 E
Nannial, India 94 E4 19 4N 79 38 E
Nanning, China 76 F7 22 48N 108 20 E
Nannup, Australia 125 F2 33 59 S 115 48 E
Nanortalik, Greenland 10 E6 60 10N 45 17W
Nanpan Jiang →, China 76 E6 25 10N 106 5 E
Nanpara, India 93 F9 27 52N 81 33 E
Nanpi, China 74 E9 38 2N 116 45 E
Nanping, Fujian, China 77 D12 26 38N 118 10 E
Nanping, Henan, China 77 C9 29 55N 112 3 E
Nanri Dao, China 77 E12 25 15N 119 25 E
Nanripe, Mozam. 119 E4 13 52 S 38 52 E
Nansei-Shotō = Ryūkyū-rettō, Japan 71 M3 26 0N 126 0 E
Nansen Land, Greenland 10 A6 83 0N 43 0W
Nansen Sd., Canada 6 A3 81 0N 91 0W
Nansha, China 69 F10 22 45N 113 34 E
Nanshan I., S. China Sea 78 B5 10 45N 115 49 E
Nansio, Tanzania 118 C3 2 3 S 33 4 E
Nant, France 28 D7 44 1N 3 18 E
Nanterre, France 27 D9 48 53N 2 13 E
Nantes, France 26 E5 47 12N 1 33W
Nantiat, France 28 B5 46 1N 1 11 E
Nanticoke, U.S.A. 151 E8 41 12N 76 0W
Nanton, Canada 142 C6 50 21N 113 46W
Nantong, China 77 A13 32 1N 120 52 E
Nantou, China 69 F10 22 32N 113 55 E
Nantou, Taiwan 77 F13 23 57N 120 35 E
Nantua, France 27 F12 46 10N 5 35 E
Nantucket I., U.S.A. 148 E10 41 16N 70 5W
Nantwich, U.K. 20 D5 53 4N 2 31W
Nanty Glo, U.S.A. 150 F6 40 28N 78 50W
Nanuku Passage, Fiji 133 A3 16 45 S 179 15W
Nanuque, Brazil 171 E3 17 50 S 40 21W
Nanusa, Kepulauan, Indonesia 79 D7 4 45N 127 1 E
Nanutarra Roadhouse, Australia 124 D2 22 32 S 115 30 E
Nanxi, China 76 C5 28 54N 104 59 E
Nanxiong, China 77 E10 25 6N 114 15 E
Nanyang, China 74 H7 33 11N 112 30 E
Nanyi Hu, China 77 B12 31 5N 119 0 E
Nanyuki, Kenya 118 B4 0 2N 37 4 E
Nanzhang, China 77 B8 31 45N 111 50 E
Nao, C. de la, Spain 41 G5 38 44N 0 14 E
Naococane, L., Canada 141 B5 52 50N 70 45W
Naogaon, Bangla. 90 C2 24 52N 88 52 E
Naoné, Vanuatu 133 E6 15 0 S 168 8 E
Náousa, Imathía, Greece 50 F6 40 42N 22 9 E
Náousa, Kikládhes, Greece 49 D7 37 7N 25 14 E
Naozhou Dao, China 77 G8 20 55N 110 20 E
Napa, U.S.A. 160 G4 38 18N 122 17W
Napa →, U.S.A. 160 G4 38 10N 122 19W
Napakiak, U.S.A. 144 F7 60 42N 161 57W
Napamute, U.S.A. 144 F8 61 33N 158 42W
Napanee, Canada 140 D4 44 15N 77 0W
Napanoch, U.S.A. 151 E10 41 44N 74 22W
Napanwainami, Indonesia 83 B5 3 3 S 135 45 E
Napaskiak, U.S.A. 144 F7 60 43N 161 55W
Nape, Laos 86 C5 18 18N 105 6 E
Nape Pass = Keo Neua, Deo, Vietnam 86 C5 18 23N 105 10 E
Naperville, U.S.A. 157 C8 41 46N 88 9W
Napf, Switz. 32 B5 47 1N 7 56 E
Napier, N.Z. 130 F5 39 30 S 176 56 E
Napier Broome B., Australia 124 B4 14 2 S 126 37 E
Napier Pen., Australia 126 A2 12 4 S 135 43 E
Napierville, Canada 151 A11 45 11N 73 25W
Naples = Nápoli, Italy 47 B7 40 50N 14 15 E
Naples, U.S.A. 149 M5 26 8N 81 48W
Naples Park, U.S.A. 153 J8 26 17N 81 46W
Napo, China 76 F5 23 22N 105 50 E
Napo □, Ecuador 168 D2 0 30 S 77 0W
Napo →, Peru 168 D3 3 20 S 72 40W
Napoleon, N. Dak., U.S.A. 154 B5 46 30N 99 46W
Napoleon, Ohio, U.S.A. 157 C12 41 23N 84 8W
Napoleon's Tomb, St. Helena 9 h 15 56 S 5 42W
Nápoli, Italy 47 B7 40 50N 14 15 E
Nápoli, G. di, Italy 47 B7 40 43N 14 10 E
Napopo, Dem. Rep. of the Congo 118 B2 4 15N 28 0 E
Nappanee, U.S.A. 157 C11 41 27N 86 0W
Napperby, Australia 128 B3 33 9 S 138 7 E
Naqâda, Egypt 106 B3 25 53N 32 42 E
Naqadeh, Iran 101 D11 36 57N 45 23 E
Naqb, Ra's an, Jordan 103 F4 30 0N 35 29 E
Naqqāsh, Iran 97 C6 35 40N 49 6 E
Nara, Japan 73 C7 34 40N 135 49 E
Nara, Mali 112 B3 15 10N 7 20W
Nara □, Japan 73 C8 34 30N 136 0 E
Nara Canal, Pakistan 92 G3 24 30N 69 20 E
Nara Visa, U.S.A. 155 H3 35 37N 103 6W
Naracoorte, Australia 128 D4 36 58 S 140 45 E
Naradhan, Australia 129 B7 33 34 S 146 17 E
Naraini, India 93 G9 25 11N 80 29 E
Narasannapeta, India 94 E7 18 25N 84 3 E
Narasapur, India 95 F5 16 26N 81 40 E
Narasaropet, India 95 F5 16 14N 80 4 E
Narathiwat, Thailand 87 J3 6 30N 101 48 E
Narayanapatnam, India 94 E6 18 53N 83 10 E
Narayanganj, Bangla. 90 D3 23 40N 90 33 E
Narayanpet, India 94 F3 16 45N 77 30 E
Narbonne, France 28 E7 43 11N 3 0 E
Narbuvollen, Norway 18 B8 62 21N 11 27 E
Narcea →, Spain 42 B4 43 33N 6 44W
Narcondam I., India 95 H12 13 20N 94 16 E
Nardīn, Iran 97 B7 37 3N 55 59 E
Nardò, Italy 47 B11 40 11N 18 2 E
Narembeen, Australia 125 F2 32 7 S 118 24 E
Narendranagar, India 92 D8 30 10N 78 18 E
Nares Str., Arctic 10 B3 80 0N 70 0W
Naretha, Australia 125 F3 31 0 S 124 45 E
Narew →, Poland 55 F7 52 26N 20 41 E
Nari →, Pakistan 92 F2 28 0N 67 40 E
Narin, Afghan. 91 A3 36 5N 69 0 E
Narindra, Helodranon' i, Madag. 117 A8 14 55 S 47 30 E
Narino □, Colombia 168 C2 1 30N 78 0W
Narita, Japan 73 B12 35 47N 140 19 E
Nariva Swamp, Trin. & Tob. 169 F9 10 26N 61 4W
Närke, Sweden 16 E8 59 10N 15 0 E
Narmada →, India 92 J5 21 38N 72 36 E
Narman, Turkey 101 B9 40 26N 41 57 E
Narmland, Sweden 15 F15 60 0N 13 30 E
Narnaul, India 92 E7 28 5N 76 11 E
Narni, Italy 45 F9 42 30N 12 30 E
Naro, Ghana 112 C4 10 22N 2 27W
Naro Fominsk, Russia 58 E9 55 23N 36 43 E
Narodnaya, Russia 56 A10 65 5N 59 58 E
Narok, Kenya 118 C4 1 55 S 35 52 E
Narón, Spain 42 B2 43 32N 8 9W
Narooma, Australia 129 D9 36 14 S 150 4 E
Narowal, Pakistan 91 B4 32 6N 74 52 E
Narra, Phil. 81 G2 9 18N 118 28 E
Narrabri, Australia 127 E4 30 19 S 149 46 E
Narran →, Australia 127 D4 28 37 S 148 12 E
Narrandera, Australia 129 C7 34 42 S 146 31 E
Narrogin, Australia 125 F2 32 58 S 117 14 E
Narromine, Australia 129 B8 32 12 S 148 12 E
Narrow Hills Prov. Park, Canada 143 C8 54 0N 104 37W
Narsampet, India 94 F4 17 57N 79 58 E
Narsaq, Greenland 10 E6 60 57N 46 4W
Narsimhapur, India 93 H8 22 54N 79 14 E
Narsinghgarh, India 92 H7 23 45N 76 40 E
Narsinghpur, India 94 D7 20 28N 85 5 E
Narsipatnam, India 94 F6 17 40N 82 37 E
Nartes, L. e, Albania 50 F3 40 32N 19 25 E
Nartkala, Russia 61 J6 43 33N 43 51 E
Naruto, Kantō, Japan 73 B12 34 11N 134 37 E
Naruto, Shikoku, Japan 73 B12 35 36N 140 25 E
Naruto-Kaikyō, Japan 72 C6 34 14N 134 39 E
Narva, Estonia 58 C5 59 23N 28 12 E
Narva →, Russia 15 G22 59 27N 28 2 E
Narva Bay, Estonia 15 G19 59 35N 27 35 E
Narvacan, Phil. 80 C3 17 25N 120 28 E
Narvik, Norway 14 B17 68 28N 17 26 E
Narvskoye Vdkhr., Russia 58 C5 59 18N 28 14 E
Narwana, India 92 E7 29 39N 76 6 E
Naryan-Mar, Russia 56 A9 67 42N 53 12 E
Narym, Russia 66 D9 59 0N 81 30 E
Naryn, Kyrgyzstan 66 E8 41 26N 75 58 E
Naryn →, Uzbekistan 65 C5 40 52N 71 36 E
Nasa, Norway 14 C16 66 29N 15 23 E
Nasau, Fiji 133 A2 17 19 S 179 27 E
Năsăud, Romania 53 C9 47 19N 24 29 E
Nasawa, Vanuatu 133 E6 15 12 S 168 9 E
Naseby, N.Z. 131 F5 45 1 S 170 10 E
Naselle, U.S.A. 160 D3 46 22N 123 49W
Naser, Buheirat en, Egypt 106 C3 23 0N 32 30 E
Nashua, Iowa, U.S.A. 156 B4 42 57N 92 32W
Nashua, Mont., U.S.A. 158 B10 48 8N 106 22W
Nashua, N.H., U.S.A. 151 D13 42 45N 71 28W
Nashville, Ark., U.S.A. 155 J8 33 57N 93 51W
Nashville, Ga., U.S.A. 152 D6 31 12N 83 15W
Nashville, Ill., U.S.A. 156 F7 38 21N 89 23W
Nashville, Ind., U.S.A. 157 E10 39 12N 86 15W
Nashville, Mich., U.S.A. 157 B11 42 36N 85 5W
Nashville, Tenn., U.S.A. 149 G2 36 10N 86 47W
Našice, Croatia 52 E3 45 32N 18 4 E
Nasielsk, Poland 55 F7 52 35N 20 50 E
Nasik, India 94 E1 19 58N 73 50 E
Nasipit, Phil. 81 G5 8 57N 125 19 E
Nasir, Sudan 107 F3 8 36N 33 4 E
Nasirabad, India 92 F6 26 15N 74 45 E
Nasirabad, Pakistan 92 E3 28 23N 68 24 E
Naskaupi →, Canada 141 B7 53 47N 60 51W
Naso, Italy 47 D7 38 7N 14 47 E
Naso Pt., Phil. 81 F3 10 25N 121 57 E
Naşrābād, Iran 97 C6 34 8N 51 26 E
Naşriān-e Pā'īn, Iran 96 C5 32 52N 46 52 E
Nass →, Canada 142 C3 55 0N 129 40W
Nassarawa, Nigeria 113 D6 8 32N 7 41 E
Nassarawa □, Nigeria 113 D6 8 35N 8 20 E
Nassau, Bahamas 9 b 25 5N 77 20W
Nassau, U.S.A. 151 D11 42 31N 73 37W
Nassau, B., Chile 176 E3 55 20 S 68 0W
Nasser, L. = Naser, Buheirat en, Egypt 106 C3 23 0N 32 30 E
Nasser City = Kôm Ombo, Egypt 106 C3 24 25N 32 52 E
Nassereith, Austria 33 B11 47 19N 10 50 E
Nassian, Ivory C. 112 D4 8 28N 3 28W
Nässjö, Sweden 17 G8 57 39N 14 42 E
Nastapoka →, Canada 140 A4 56 55N 76 33W
Nastapoka, Is., Canada 140 A4 56 55N 76 50W
Nasugbu, Phil. 80 D3 14 5N 120 38 E
Näsum, Sweden 17 H8 56 10N 14 29 E
Näsviken, Sweden 16 C10 61 46N 16 52 E
Nata, Botswana 116 C4 20 12 S 26 12 E
Nata →, Botswana 116 C4 20 14 S 26 10 E
Natagaima, Colombia 168 C2 3 37N 75 6W
Natal, Brazil 170 C4 5 47 S 35 13W
Natal, Indonesia 84 B1 0 35N 99 7 E
Natal Drakensberg Park, S. Africa 117 D4 29 27 S 29 30 E
Natalinci, Serbia, Yug. 52 F5 44 15N 20 49 E
Naṭanz, Iran 97 C6 33 30N 51 55 E
Natashquan, Canada 141 B7 50 14N 61 46W
Natashquan →, Canada 141 B7 50 7N 61 50W
Natchez, U.S.A. 155 K9 31 34N 91 24W
Natchitoches, U.S.A. 155 K8 31 46N 93 5W
Naters, Switz. 32 D5 46 19N 7 58 E
Natewa B., Fiji 133 A2 16 35 S 179 40 E
Nathalia, Australia 129 D6 36 1 S 145 13 E
Nathdwara, India 92 G5 24 55N 73 50 E
Nati, Pta., Spain 38 A4 40 3N 3 50 E
Natimuk, Australia 128 D5 36 42 S 142 0 E
Nation →, Canada 142 B4 55 30N 123 32W
National Capital District □, Papua N. G. 132 E4 9 25 S 147 10 E
National City, U.S.A. 161 N9 32 41N 117 6W
National West Coast Tourist Recr. Area, Namibia 116 C1 21 53 S 14 14 E
Natitingou, Benin 113 C5 10 20N 1 26 E
Natividad, I., Mexico 162 B1 27 50N 115 10W
Natividade, Brazil 171 D2 11 43 S 47 47W
Natkyizin, Burma 86 E1 14 57N 97 59 E
Natmauk, Burma 90 E5 20 20N 95 24 E
Natogyi, Burma 90 E5 21 25N 95 39 E
Natonin, Phil. 80 C3 17 6N 121 18 E
Natron, L., Tanzania 118 C4 2 20 S 36 0 E
Natrona Heights, U.S.A. 150 F5 40 37N 79 44W
Natrūn, W. el →, Egypt 106 H7 30 25N 30 13 E
Nattai Nat. Park, Australia 129 C9 34 12 S 150 22 E
Nättraby, Sweden 17 H9 56 13N 15 31 E
Natukanaoka Pan, Namibia 116 B2 18 40 S 15 45 E
Natuna Besar, Kepulauan, Indonesia 84 B3 4 0N 108 15 E
Natuna Is. = Natuna Besar, Kepulauan, Indonesia 84 B3 4 0N 108 15 E
Natuna Selatan, Kepulauan, Indonesia 85 B3 2 45N 109 0 E
Natural Bridge, U.S.A. 151 B9 44 5N 75 30W
Naturaliste, C., Australia 127 G4 40 50 S 148 15 E
Nau, Tajikistan 65 C4 40 9N 69 22 E
Nau Qala, Afghan. 92 B3 34 5N 68 5 E
Naucelle, France 28 D6 44 13N 2 20 E
Nauders, Austria 34 E3 46 54N 10 30 E
Nauen, Germany 30 C8 52 36N 12 52 E
Naugatuck, U.S.A. 151 E11 41 30N 73 3W
Naujaat = Repulse Bay, Canada 139 B11 66 30N 86 30W
Naujan, Phil. 80 E3 13 20N 121 18 E
Naujoji Akmenė, Lithuania 54 B9 56 19N 22 54 E
Naulila, Angola 115 F2 17 13 S 14 39 E
Naumburg, Germany 30 D7 51 9N 11 47 E
Naupada, India 94 E7 18 34N 84 18 E
Nā'ūr at Tunayb, Jordan 103 D4 31 48N 35 57 E
Nauru ■, Pac. Oc. 134 H8 1 0 S 166 0 E
Naushahra = Nowshera, Pakistan 91 B3 34 0N 72 0 E
Naushahro, Pakistan 92 F3 26 50N 68 7 E
Naushon I., U.S.A. 151 E14 41 29N 70 45W
Nausori, Fiji 133 B2 18 2 S 178 32 E
Naustdal, Norway 18 C2 61 31N 5 43 E
Nauta, Peru 168 D3 4 31 S 73 35W
Naute Recreational Resort, Namibia 116 D2 26 55 S 17 57 E
Nautla, Mexico 163 C5 20 20N 96 50W
Nauvoo, U.S.A. 156 D5 40 33N 91 23W
Nava, Mexico 162 B4 28 25N 100 46W
Nava, Spain 42 B5 43 21N 5 31W
Nava del Rey, Spain 42 D5 41 22N 5 6W
Navadwip, India 93 H13 23 34N 88 20 E
Navahermosa, Spain 43 F6 39 41N 4 28W
Navahrudak, Belarus 58 F3 53 40N 25 50 E
Navai, Fiji 133 A1 17 36 S 177 57 E
Navajo Reservoir, U.S.A. 159 H10 36 48N 107 36W
Naval, Phil. 81 F5 11 34N 124 23 E
Navalcarnero, Spain 42 E6 40 17N 4 5W
Navalgund, India 95 G2 15 34N 75 22 E
Navalmoral de la Mata, Spain 42 F5 39 52N 5 33W
Navalvillar de Pela, Spain 43 F5 39 9N 5 24W
Navan = An Uaimh, Ireland 23 C5 53 39N 6 41W
Navapolatsk, Belarus 58 E5 55 32N 28 37 E
Navarino, I., Chile 176 E3 55 0 S 67 40W
Navarra □, Spain 40 C3 42 40N 1 40W
Navarre, Fla., U.S.A. 153 E3 30 24N 86 52W
Navarre, Ohio, U.S.A. 150 F3 40 43N 81 31W
Navarro →, U.S.A. 160 F3 39 11N 123 45W
Navas de San Juan, Spain 43 G7 38 30N 3 19W
Navasota, U.S.A. 155 K6 30 23N 96 5W
Navassa I., W. Indies 165 C5 18 30N 75 0W
Nävekvarn, Sweden 17 F10 58 38N 16 49 E
Naver →, U.K. 22 C4 58 32N 4 14W
Navia, Spain 42 B4 43 35N 6 42W
Navia →, Spain 42 B4 43 15N 6 50W
Navia de Suarna, Spain 42 C3 42 58N 7 3W
Navibandar, India 92 J3 21 26N 69 48 E
Navidad, Chile 174 C1 33 57 S 71 50W
Naviraí, Brazil 175 A5 23 8 S 54 13W
Naviti, Fiji 133 A1 17 7 S 177 15 E
Navlakhi, India 92 H4 22 58N 70 28 E
Navlya, Russia 59 F8 52 53N 34 30 E
Năvodari, Romania 53 F13 44 19N 28 36 E
Navoi = Nawoiy, Uzbekistan 66 E7 40 9N 65 22 E
Navojoa, Mexico 162 B3 27 0N 109 30W
Navolato, Mexico 162 C3 24 47N 107 42W
Návpaktos, Greece 48 C3 38 24N 21 50 E
Návplion, Greece 48 D4 37 33N 22 50 E
Navrongo, Ghana 113 C4 10 51N 1 3W
Navsari, India 94 D1 20 57N 72 59 E
Navua, Fiji 133 B2 18 12 S 178 11 E
Nawa Kot, Pakistan 92 E4 28 21N 71 24 E
Nawab Khan, Pakistan 92 D3 30 17N 69 12 E
Nawabganj, Bangla. 90 C2 24 35N 88 14 E
Nawabganj, Ut. P., India 93 F9 26 56N 81 14 E
Nawabganj, Ut. P., India 93 E8 28 32N 79 40 E
Nawabshah, Pakistan 91 D3 26 15N 68 25 E
Nawada, India 93 G11 24 50N 85 33 E
Nāwah, Afghan. 91 B2 32 19N 67 53 E
Nawakot, Nepal 93 F11 27 55N 85 10 E
Nawalgarh, India 92 F6 27 50N 75 15 E
Nawanshahr, India 93 C6 32 33N 74 48 E
Nawapara, India 94 D6 20 46N 82 33 E
Nawar, Dasht-i-, Afghan. 91 B2 33 52N 68 0 E
Nawāsīf, Ḩarrat, Si. Arabia 98 B3 21 20N 42 10 E
Nawi, Sudan 106 D3 18 32N 30 50 E
Nawng Hpa, Burma 90 D7 22 30N 98 30 E
Nawoiy, Uzbekistan 66 E7 40 9N 65 22 E

Nawş, Ra's, *Oman* **99 C6** 17 15N 55 16 E
Naxçıvan, *Azerbaijan* **101 C11** 39 12N 45 15 E
Naxçıvan □, *Azerbaijan* **101 C11** 39 25N 45 26 E
Náxos, *Greece* **49 D7** 37 8N 25 25 E
Naxxar, *Malta* **38 F7** 35 55N 14 27 E
Nay, *France* **28 E3** 43 10N 0 18W
Nay, Mui, *Vietnam* **78 B3** 12 55N 109 23 E
Nāy Band, *Būshehr, Iran* **97 E7** 27 20N 52 40 E
Nāy Band, *Khorāsān, Iran* **97 C8** 32 20N 57 34 E
Naya →, *Colombia* **168 C2** 3 13N 77 22W
Nayagarh, *India* **94 D7** 20 8N 85 6 E
Nayakhan, *Russia* **67 C16** 61 56N 159 0 E
Nayarit □, *Mexico* **162 C4** 22 0N 105 0W
Nayau, *Fiji* **133 B2** 18 6 S 178 10 E
Nayé, *Senegal* **112 C2** 14 28N 12 12W
Nayong, *China* **76 D5** 26 50N 105 20 E
Nayoro, *Japan* **70 B11** 44 21N 142 28 E
Nayudupeta, *India* **95 H4** 13 54N 79 54 E
Nayyāl, W. →, *Si. Arabia* **96 D3** 28 35N 39 4 E
Nazaré, *Bahia, Brazil* **171 D4** 13 2 S 39 0W
Nazaré, *Pará, Brazil* **173 B7** 6 25 S 52 29W
Nazaré, *Tocantins, Brazil* **170 C2** 6 23 S 47 40W
Nazaré, *Portugal* **43 F1** 39 36N 9 4W
Nazareth = Nazerat, *Israel* **103 C4** 32 42N 35 17 E
Nazareth, *U.S.A.* **151 F9** 40 44N 75 19W
Nazas, *Mexico* **162 B4** 25 10N 104 6W
Nazas →, *Mexico* **162 B4** 25 35N 103 25W
Nazca, *Peru* **172 C3** 14 50 S 74 57W
Naze, The, *U.K.* **21 F9** 51 53N 1 18 E
Nazerat, *Israel* **103 C4** 32 42N 35 17 E
Nāzīk, *Iran* **101 C11** 39 1N 45 4 E
Nazilli, *Turkey* **49 D10** 37 55N 28 15 E
Nazir Hat, *Bangla.* **90 D3** 22 35N 91 49 E
Nazko, *Canada* **142 C4** 53 1N 123 37W
Nazko →, *Canada* **142 C4** 53 7N 123 34W
Nazret, *Ethiopia* **107 F4** 8 32N 39 22 E
Nazwa, *Oman* **99 B7** 22 56N 57 32 E
Ncama, *Eq. Guin.* **114 B2** 1 55N 10 56 E
Nchanga, *Zambia* **119 E2** 12 30 S 27 49 E
Ncheu, *Malawi* **119 E3** 14 50 S 34 47 E
Ndala, *Tanzania* **118 C3** 4 45 S 33 15 E
Ndalatando, *Angola* **115 D2** 9 12 S 14 48 E
Ndali, *Benin* **113 D5** 9 50N 2 46 E
Ndareda, *Tanzania* **118 C4** 4 12 S 35 30 E
Ndélé, *C.A.R.* **114 A4** 8 25N 20 36 E
Ndendé, *Gabon* **114 C2** 2 22 S 11 23 E
Ndiael, Réserve de Faune du, *Senegal* **112 B1** 16 15N 16 0W
Ndikinimeki, *Cameroon* **113 E7** 4 46N 10 50 E
Ndindi, *Gabon* **114 C2** 3 46 S 11 9 E
N'Dioum, *Senegal* **112 B2** 16 31N 14 39W
Ndjamena, *Chad* **109 F2** 12 10N 14 59 E
Ndjolé, *Gabon* **114 C2** 0 10 S 10 45 E
Ndogo, Lagune, *Gabon* **114 C2** 2 35 S 10 0 E
Ndoki-Nouabalé, Réserve de Faune de, *Congo* **114 B3** 2 32N 16 32 E
Ndola, *Zambia* **119 E2** 13 0 S 28 34 E
Ndoto Mts., *Kenya* **118 B4** 2 0N 37 0 E
Ndoua, C., *N. Cal.* **133 V20** 22 24 S 166 56 E
Ndouba, *Congo* **114 C2** 0 9 S 14 4 E
Nduguti, *Tanzania* **118 C3** 4 18 S 34 41 E
Ndumu Game Reserve, *S. Africa* **117 D5** 26 52 S 32 15 E
Nea →, *Norway* **18 A8** 63 15N 11 0 E
Néa Alikarnassós, *Greece* **49 F7** 35 18N 25 13 E
Néa Ankhíalos, *Greece* **48 B4** 39 16N 22 49 E
Néa Epídhavros, *Greece* **48 D5** 37 40N 23 7 E
Néa Flippiás, *Greece* **48 B2** 39 12N 20 53 E
Néa Ionia, *Greece* **48 B4** 39 22N 22 56 E
Néa Kallikrátia, *Greece* **50 F7** 40 21N 23 3 E
Néa Mákri, *Greece* **48 C5** 38 5N 23 59 E
Néa Moudhaniá, *Greece* **50 F7** 40 15N 23 17 E
Néa Péramos, *Attikí, Greece* **48 C5** 38 0N 23 26 E
Néa Péramos, *Kavállla, Greece* **51 F8** 40 50N 24 18 E
Néa Víssi, *Greece* **51 E10** 41 34N 26 33 E
Néa Zíkhna, *Greece* **50 E7** 41 2N 23 49 E
Neagari, *Japan* **73 A8** 36 26N 136 25 E
Neagh, Lough, *U.K.* **23 B5** 54 37N 6 25W
Neah Bay, *U.S.A.* **160 B2** 48 22N 124 37W
Neale, L., *Australia* **124 D5** 24 15 S 130 0 E
Neamati, *India* **90 B5** 26 50N 94 20 E
Neamţ □, *Romania* **53 C11** 47 0N 26 20 E
Neápolis, *Kozáni, Greece* **50 F5** 40 20N 21 24 E
Neápolis, *Kríti, Greece* **39 E6** 35 15N 25 37 E
Neápolis, *Lakonía, Greece* **48 E5** 36 27N 23 8 E
Near Is., *U.S.A.* **144 K1** 52 30N 174 0 E
Neath, *U.K.* **21 F4** 51 39N 3 48W
Neath Port Talbot □, *U.K.* **21 F4** 51 42N 3 45W
Neba, Î., *N. Cal.* **133 T17** 20 10 S 163 57 E
Nebbou, *Burkina Faso* **113 C4** 11 9N 1 51W
Nebelat el Hagana, *Sudan* **107 E2** 13 13N 29 2 E
Nebine Cr. →, *Australia* **127 D4** 29 27 S 146 56 E
Nebitdag, *Turkmenistan* **57 G9** 39 30N 54 22 E
Nebka, *Algeria* **110 C4** 27 28N 3 12W
Nebo, *Australia* **126 C4** 21 42 S 148 42 E
Nebolchy, *Russia* **58 C7** 59 8N 33 18 E
Nebraska □, *U.S.A.* **154 E5** 41 30N 99 30W
Nebraska City, *U.S.A.* **154 E7** 40 41N 95 52W
Nébrodi, Monti, *Italy* **47 E7** 37 54N 14 35 E
Necedah, *U.S.A.* **154 C9** 44 2N 90 4W
Nechako →, *Canada* **142 C4** 53 30N 122 44W
Neches →, *U.S.A.* **155 L8** 29 58N 93 51W
Nechisar Nat. Park, *Ethiopia* **107 F4** 5 58N 37 55 E
Neckar →, *Germany* **31 F4** 49 27N 8 29 E
Necker I., *U.S.A.* **145 G11** 23 35N 164 42W
Necochea, *Argentina* **174 D4** 38 30 S 58 50W
Nectar Brook, *Australia* **128 B2** 32 43 S 137 57 E
Neda, *Spain* **42 B2** 43 30N 8 9W
Nedalshytta, *Norway* **18 B9** 62 59N 12 3 E
Nedelino, *Bulgaria* **51 E9** 41 27N 25 3 E
Nedelišće, *Croatia* **45 B13** 46 23N 16 22 E
Nédha →, *Greece* **48 D3** 37 25N 21 45 E
Nedreberg, *Norway* **18 D8** 60 59N 11 41 E
Nedroma, *Algeria* **111 A4** 35 1N 1 45W
Nedstrand, *Norway* **18 E2** 59 21N 5 49 E
Needles, *Canada* **142 D5** 49 53N 118 7W
Needles, *U.S.A.* **161 L12** 34 51N 114 37W
Needles, The, *U.K.* **21 G6** 50 39N 1 35W
Needles Pt., *N.Z.* **130 C4** 36 3 S 175 25 E
Neely Henry L., *U.S.A.* **152 B3** 33 55N 86 2W
Ñeembucú □, *Paraguay* **174 B4** 27 0 S 58 0W
Neemuch = Nimach, *India* **92 G6** 24 30N 74 56 E
Neenah, *U.S.A.* **148 C1** 44 11N 88 28W
Neepawa, *Canada* **143 C9** 50 15N 99 30W
Neeses, *U.S.A.* **152 B8** 33 33N 81 7W
Nefta, *Tunisia* **108 B1** 33 53N 7 50 E
Neftah Sidi Boubekeur, *Algeria* **111 A5** 35 1N 0 4 E
Neftçala, *Azerbaijan* **97 B6** 39 19N 49 12 E
Neftegorsk, *Russia* **61 H4** 44 25N 39 45 E
Neftekamsk, *Russia* **64 C5** 56 6N 54 17 E
Neftekumsk, *Russia* **61 H7** 44 46N 44 50 E
Neftenbach, *Switz.* **33 A7** 47 32N 8 41 E
Nefyn, *U.K.* **20 E3** 52 56N 4 31W
Négala, *Mali* **112 C3** 12 52N 8 30W
Negapatam = Nagappattinam, *India* **95 J4** 10 46N 79 51 E
Negara, *Indonesia* **79 J17** 8 22 S 114 37 E
Negaunee, *U.S.A.* **148 B2** 46 30N 87 36W
Negele, *Ethiopia* **107 F4** 5 20N 39 36 E
Negeri Sembilan □, *Malaysia* **84 B2** 2 45N 102 10 E
Negev Desert = Hanegev, *Israel* **103 E4** 30 50N 35 0 E
Negoiul, Vf., *Romania* **53 E9** 45 38N 24 35 E
Negombo, *Sri Lanka* **95 L4** 7 12N 79 50 E
Negotin, *Serbia, Yug.* **50 B6** 44 16N 22 37 E
Negotino, *Macedonia* **50 E6** 41 29N 22 7 E
Negra, Peña, *Spain* **42 C4** 42 11N 6 30W
Negra, Pta., *Mauritania* **110 D1** 22 54N 16 18W
Negra, Pta., *Peru* **172 B1** 6 6 S 81 10W
Negra Pt., *Phil.* **80 B3** 18 40N 120 50 E
Negrais C. = Maudin Sun, *Burma* **90 G5** 16 0N 94 12 E
Negreşti, *Romania* **53 D12** 46 50N 27 30 E
Negreşti-Oaş, *Romania* **53 C8** 47 52N 23 26 E
Negril, *Jamaica* **164 a** 18 22N 78 20W
Négrine, *Algeria* **111 B6** 34 30N 7 30 E
Negro →, *Argentina* **176 B4** 41 2 S 62 47W
Negro →, *Bolivia* **173 C5** 14 11 S 63 7W
Negro →, *Brazil* **169 D6** 3 0 S 60 0W
Negro →, *Uruguay* **175 C4** 33 24 S 58 22W
Negros, *Phil.* **81 G4** 9 30N 122 40 E
Negros Occidental □, *Phil.* **81 F4** 10 0N 122 55 E
Negros Oriental □, *Phil.* **81 G4** 9 45N 123 0 E
Negru Vodă, *Romania* **53 G13** 43 47N 28 21 E
Neguac, *Canada* **141 C6** 47 15N 65 5W
Nehalem →, *U.S.A.* **160 E3** 45 40N 123 56W
Nehāvand, *Iran* **97 C6** 35 56N 49 31 E
Nehbandān, *Iran* **97 D9** 31 35N 60 5 E
Nehoiu, *Romania* **53 E11** 45 24N 26 20 E
Nei Monggol Zizhiqu □, *China* **74 D7** 42 0N 112 0 E
Neiafu, *Tonga* **133 P14** 18 39 S 173 59W
Neiges, Piton des, *Réunion* **121 c** 21 5 S 55 29 E
Neijiang, *China* **76 C5** 29 35N 104 55 E
Neilingding Dao, *China* **69 G10** 22 25N 113 48 E
Neill I., *India* **95 J11** 11 50N 93 3 E
Neillsville, *U.S.A.* **154 C9** 44 34N 90 36W
Neilton, *U.S.A.* **158 C2** 47 25N 123 53W
Neiqiu, *China* **74 F8** 37 15N 114 30 E
Neiva, *Colombia* **168 C2** 2 56N 75 18W
Neixiang, *China* **74 H6** 33 10N 111 52 E
Nejanilini L., *Canada* **143 B9** 59 33N 97 48W
Nejd = Najd, *Si. Arabia* **102 B3** 26 30N 42 0 E
Nejo, *Ethiopia* **107 F4** 9 30N 35 28 E
Nekā, *Iran* **97 B7** 36 39N 53 19 E
Nekemte, *Ethiopia* **107 F4** 9 4N 36 30 E
Nêkheb, *Egypt* **106 B3** 25 10N 32 48 E
Neksø, *Denmark* **17 J9** 55 4N 15 8 E
Nelamangala, *India* **95 H3** 13 6N 77 24 E
Nelas, *Portugal* **42 E3** 40 32N 7 52W
Nelaug, *Norway* **18 F5** 58 39N 8 40 E
Nelia, *Australia* **126 C3** 20 39 S 142 12 E
Nelidovo, *Russia* **58 D7** 56 13N 32 49 E
Neligh, *U.S.A.* **154 D5** 42 8N 98 2W
Nelkan, *Russia* **67 D14** 57 40N 136 4 E
Nellikuppam, *India* **95 J4** 11 46N 79 43 E
Nellore, *India* **95 G4** 14 27N 79 59 E
Nelson, *Canada* **142 D5** 49 30N 117 20W
Nelson, *N.Z.* **131 B8** 41 18 S 173 16 E
Nelson, *U.K.* **20 D5** 53 50N 2 13W
Nelson, *Ariz., U.S.A.* **159 J7** 35 31N 113 19W
Nelson, *Nev., U.S.A.* **161 K12** 35 42N 114 50W
Nelson □, *N.Z.* **131 B8** 41 20 S 173 20 E
Nelson →, *Canada* **143 C9** 54 33N 98 2W
Nelson, C., *Australia* **128 E4** 38 26 S 141 32 E
Nelson, C., *Papua N. G.* **132 E5** 9 0 S 149 20 E
Nelson, Estrecho, *Chile* **176 D2** 51 30 S 75 0W
Nelson Bay, *Australia* **129 B10** 32 43 S 152 9 E
Nelson Forks, *Canada* **142 B4** 59 30N 124 0W
Nelson House, *Canada* **143 B9** 55 47N 98 51W
Nelson L., *Canada* **143 B8** 55 48N 100 7W
Nelson Lakes Nat. Park, *N.Z.* **131 B7** 41 55 S 172 44 E
Nelspoort, *S. Africa* **116 E3** 32 7 S 23 0 E
Nelspruit, *S. Africa* **117 D5** 25 29 S 30 59 E
Néma, *Mauritania* **112 B3** 16 40N 7 15W
Neman, *Russia* **15 J20** 55 2N 22 2 E
Neman →, *Lithuania* **15 J19** 55 25N 21 10 E
Nembrala, *Indonesia* **82 D2** 10 53 S 122 50 E
Neméa, *Greece* **48 D4** 37 49N 22 40 E
Nemeiben L., *Canada* **143 B7** 55 20N 105 20W
Nemërçkë, Mal, *Albania* **50 F4** 40 15N 20 15 E
Nemira, Vf., *Romania* **53 D11** 46 17N 26 19 E
Némiscau, *Canada* **140 B4** 51 18N 76 54W
Némiscau, L., *Canada* **140 B4** 51 25N 76 40W
Nemours, *France* **27 D9** 48 16N 2 40 E
Nemšová, *Slovak Rep.* **35 C11** 48 58N 18 7 E
Nemunas = Neman →, *Lithuania* **15 J19** 55 25N 21 10 E
Nemuro, *Japan* **70 C12** 43 20N 145 35 E
Nemuro-Kaikyō, *Japan* **70 C12** 43 30N 145 30 E
Nen Jiang →, *China* **75 B13** 45 28N 124 30 E
Nenagh, *Ireland* **23 D3** 52 52N 8 11W
Nenana, *U.S.A.* **144 D10** 64 34N 149 5W
Nenasi, *Malaysia* **87 L4** 3 9N 103 23 E
Nene →, *U.K.* **21 E8** 52 49N 0 11 E
Nénita, *Greece* **49 C8** 38 14N 26 6 E
Nenjiang, *China* **69 B7** 49 10N 125 10 E
Neno, *Malawi* **119 F3** 15 25 S 34 40 E
Nenzing, *Austria* **34 D2** 47 11N 9 42 E
Neodesha, *U.S.A.* **155 G7** 37 25N 95 41W
Neoga, *U.S.A.* **157 E8** 39 19N 88 27W
Neokhórion, *Aitolía kai Akarnanía, Greece* **48 C3** 38 25N 21 17 E
Neokhórion, *Árta, Greece* **48 B2** 39 4N 21 0 E
Néon Karlovásion, *Greece* **49 D8** 37 45N 26 42 E
Néon Petrítsi, *Greece* **50 E7** 41 16N 23 15 E
Neópolis, *Brazil* **170 D4** 10 18 S 36 35W
Neosho, *U.S.A.* **155 G7** 36 52N 94 22W
Neosho →, *U.S.A.* **155 H7** 36 48N 95 18W
Nepal ■, *Asia* **93 F11** 28 0N 84 30 E
Nepalganj, *Nepal* **93 E9** 28 5N 81 40 E
Nepalganj Road, *India* **93 E9** 28 1N 81 41 E
Nepean B., *Australia* **128 C2** 35 42 S 137 37 E
Nephi, *U.S.A.* **158 G8** 39 43N 111 50W
Nephin, *Ireland* **23 B2** 54 1N 9 22W
Nepi, *Italy* **45 F9** 42 14N 12 21 E
Nepomuk, *Czech Rep.* **34 B6** 49 29N 13 35 E
Neptune, *U.S.A.* **151 F10** 40 13N 74 2W
Neptune Is., *Australia* **128 C2** 35 17 S 136 10 E
Nera →, *Italy* **45 F9** 42 26N 12 24 E
Nera →, *Romania* **52 F6** 44 48N 21 25 E
Nérac, *France* **28 D4** 44 8N 0 21 E
Nerang, *Australia* **127 D5** 27 58 S 153 20 E
Nerastro, Sarīr, *Libya* **108 D4** 24 20N 20 37 E
Neratovice, *Czech Rep.* **34 A7** 50 16N 14 31 E
Nerchinsk, *Russia* **67 D12** 52 0N 116 39 E
Nereju, *Romania* **53 E11** 45 43N 26 43 E
Nerekhta, *Russia* **58 D11** 57 26N 40 38 E
Néret, L., *Canada* **141 B5** 54 45N 70 44W
Neretvanski Kanal, *Croatia* **45 E14** 43 7N 17 10 E
Neringa, *Lithuania* **15 J19** 55 20N 21 5 E
Nerja, *Spain* **43 J7** 36 43N 3 55W
Nerl →, *Russia* **58 D11** 56 11N 40 34 E
Nerpio, *Spain* **41 G2** 38 11N 2 16W
Nerva, *Spain* **43 H4** 37 42N 6 30W
Nervi, *Italy* **44 D6** 44 23N 9 2 E
Neryungri, *Russia* **67 D13** 57 38N 124 28 E
Nes, *Iceland* **11 B9** 65 53N 17 24W
Nes, *Norway* **18 D6** 60 34N 9 59 E
Nesbyen, *Norway* **18 D6** 60 34N 9 8 E
Nescopeck, *U.S.A.* **151 E8** 41 3N 76 12W
Nesebŭr, *Bulgaria* **51 D11** 42 41N 27 46 E
Neset, *Norway* **18 C7** 61 53N 10 7 E
Nesflaten, *Norway* **18 E3** 59 38N 6 48 E
Neskaupstaður, *Iceland* **11 B13** 65 9N 13 42W
Nesland, *Norway* **18 E4** 59 31N 7 59 E
Neslandsvatn, *Norway* **18 F6** 58 57N 9 10 E
Nesoddtangen, *Norway* **18 E7** 59 48N 10 40 E
Ness, L., *U.K.* **22 D4** 57 15N 4 32W
Ness City, *U.S.A.* **154 F5** 38 27N 99 54W
Nesslau, *Switz.* **33 B8** 47 14N 9 13 E
Nesterov, *Poland* **59 G2** 50 4N 23 58 E
Nestórion, *Greece* **50 F5** 40 24N 21 5 E
Néstos →, *Greece* **51 E8** 41 20N 24 35 E
Nesttun, *Norway* **18 D2** 60 19N 5 20 E
Nesvady, *Slovak Rep.* **35 D11** 47 56N 18 7 E
Nesvizh = Nyasvizh, *Belarus* **59 F4** 53 14N 26 38 E
Netanya, *Israel* **103 C3** 32 20N 34 51 E
Netarhat, *India* **93 H11** 23 29N 84 16 E
Nete →, *Belgium* **24 C4** 51 7N 4 14 E
Netherdale, *Australia* **126 K6** 21 10 S 148 33 E
Netherlands ■, *Europe* **24 C5** 52 0N 5 30 E
Netherlands Antilles ■, *W. Indies* **168 A4** 12 15N 69 0W
Neto →, *Italy* **47 C10** 39 12N 17 9 E
Netrakona, *Bangla.* **90 C3** 24 53N 90 47 E
Netrang, *India* **92 J5** 21 39N 73 21 E
Netstal, *Switz.* **33 B8** 47 3N 9 3 E
Nettancourt, *France* **27 D11** 48 51N 4 57 E
Nettetal, *Germany* **30 D2** 51 19N 6 12 E
Nettilling L., *Canada* **139 B12** 66 30N 71 0W
Nettuno, *Italy* **46 A5** 41 27N 12 39 E
Netzahualcoyotl, Presa, *Mexico* **163 D6** 17 10N 93 30W
Neu-Isenburg, *Germany* **31 E4** 50 3N 8 42 E
Neu-Ulm, *Germany* **31 G6** 48 22N 10 0 E
Neubrandenburg, *Germany* **30 B9** 53 33N 13 15 E
Neubukow, *Germany* **30 A7** 54 2N 11 39 E
Neuburg, *Germany* **31 G7** 48 44N 11 11 E
Neuchâtel, *Switz.* **32 C3** 47 0N 6 55 E
Neuchâtel □, *Switz.* **32 C3** 47 0N 6 55 E
Neuchâtel, Lac de, *Switz.* **32 C3** 46 53N 6 50 E
Neudau, *Austria* **34 D9** 47 11N 16 6 E
Neuenegg, *Switz.* **32 C4** 46 54N 7 18 E
Neuenhagen, *Germany* **30 C9** 52 30N 13 38 E
Neuenhaus, *Germany* **30 C2** 52 30N 6 58 E
Neuenhof, *Switz.* **33 B6** 47 27N 8 19 E
Neuf-Brisach, *France* **27 D14** 48 1N 7 30 E
Neufahrn, *Bayern, Germany* **31 G8** 48 41N 12 11 E
Neufahrn, *Bayern, Germany* **31 G7** 48 18N 11 40 E
Neufchâteau, *Belgium* **24 E5** 49 50N 5 25 E
Neufchâteau, *France* **27 D12** 48 21N 5 40 E
Neufchâtel-en-Bray, *France* **26 C8** 49 44N 1 26 E
Neufchâtel-sur-Aisne, *France* **27 C11** 49 26N 4 1 E
Neuhaus, *Germany* **30 B6** 53 17N 10 56 E
Neuhausen, *Switz.* **33 A7** 47 41N 8 37 E
Neuillé-Pont-Pierre, *France* **26 E7** 47 33N 0 33 E
Neuilly-St-Front, *France* **27 C10** 49 10N 3 15 E
Neukalen, *Germany* **30 B8** 53 49N 12 46 E
Neumarkt, *Germany* **31 F7** 49 26N 11 27 E
Neumünster, *Germany* **30 A5** 54 4N 9 58 E
Neung-sur-Beuvron, *France* **27 E8** 47 30N 1 50 E
Neunkirch, *Switz.* **33 A7** 47 42N 8 30 E
Neunkirchen, *Austria* **34 D9** 47 43N 16 4 E
Neunkirchen, *Germany* **31 F3** 49 20N 7 9 E
Neuquén, *Argentina* **176 A3** 38 55 S 68 0W
Neuquén □, *Argentina* **174 D2** 38 0 S 69 50W
Neuquén →, *Argentina* **176 A3** 38 59 S 68 0W
Neuruppin, *Germany* **30 C8** 52 55N 12 48 E
Neusäss, *Germany* **31 G6** 48 24N 10 50 E
Neuse →, *U.S.A.* **149 H7** 35 6N 76 29W
Neusiedl, *Austria* **35 D9** 47 57N 16 50 E
Neusiedler See, *Austria* **35 D9** 47 50N 16 47 E
Neuss, *Germany* **30 D2** 51 11N 6 42 E
Neussargues-Moissac, *France* **28 C7** 45 9N 3 0 E
Neustadt, *Bayern, Germany* **31 F8** 49 44N 12 10 E
Neustadt, *Bayern, Germany* **31 G7** 48 48N 11 46 E
Neustadt, *Bayern, Germany* **31 F6** 49 34N 10 37 E
Neustadt, *Bayern, Germany* **31 E7** 50 19N 11 7 E
Neustadt, *Brandenburg, Germany* **30 C8** 52 50N 12 27 E
Neustadt, *Hessen, Germany* **30 E5** 50 51N 9 9 E
Neustadt, *Niedersachsen, Germany* **30 C5** 52 30N 9 30 E
Neustadt, *Rhld-Pfz., Germany* **31 F4** 49 21N 8 10 E
Neustadt, *Sachsen, Germany* **30 D10** 51 2N 14 12 E
Neustadt, *Schleswig-Holstein, Germany* **30 A6** 54 6N 10 49 E
Neustadt, *Thüringen, Germany* **30 E7** 50 45N 11 43 E
Neustrelitz, *Germany* **30 B9** 53 21N 13 4 E
Neuvic, *France* **28 C6** 45 23N 2 16 E
Neuville-sur-Saône, *France* **29 C8** 45 52N 4 51 E
Neuvy-le-Roi, *France* **26 E7** 47 36N 0 36 E
Neuvy-St-Sépulchre, *France* **27 F8** 46 35N 1 48 E
Neuvy-sur-Barangeon, *France* **27 E9** 47 20N 2 15 E
Neuwerk, *Germany* **30 B4** 53 55N 8 30 E
Neuwied, *Germany* **30 E3** 50 26N 7 29 E
Neva →, *Russia* **58 C6** 59 50N 30 30 E
Nevada, *Iowa, U.S.A.* **156 B3** 42 1N 93 27W
Nevada, *Mo., U.S.A.* **155 G7** 37 51N 94 22W
Nevada □, *U.S.A.* **158 G5** 39 0N 117 0W
Nevada City, *U.S.A.* **160 F6** 39 16N 121 1W
Nevado, Cerro, *Argentina* **174 D2** 35 30 S 68 32W
Nevasa, *India* **94 E2** 19 34N 75 0 E
Neve, Sa. da, *Angola* **115 E2** 13 43 S 13 10 E
Nevel, *Russia* **58 D5** 56 0N 29 55 E
Nevers, *France* **27 F10** 47 0N 3 9 E
Nevertire, *Australia* **129 A7** 31 50 S 147 44 E
Nevesinje, *Bos.-H.* **50 C2** 43 14N 18 6 E
Neville, *Canada* **143 D7** 49 58N 107 39W
Nevinnomyssk, *Russia* **61 H6** 44 40N 42 0 E
Nevis, *St. Kitts & Nevis* **165 C7** 17 0N 62 30W
Nevlunghavn, *Norway* **18 F6** 58 58N 9 53 E
Nevrokop = Gotse Delchev, *Bulgaria* **50 E7** 41 36N 23 46 E
Nevşehir, *Turkey* **100 C6** 38 33N 34 40 E
Nevyansk, *Russia* **64 C8** 57 30N 60 13 E
New →, *Guyana* **169 C6** 3 20N 57 37W
New →, *U.S.A.* **148 F5** 38 10N 81 12W
New Aiyansh, *Canada* **142 B3** 55 12N 129 4W
New Albany, *Ind., U.S.A.* **157 F11** 38 18N 85 49W
New Albany, *Miss., U.S.A.* **155 H10** 34 29N 89 0W
New Albany, *Pa., U.S.A.* **151 E8** 41 36N 76 27W
New Amsterdam, *Guyana* **169 B6** 6 15N 57 36W
New Angledool, *Australia* **127 D4** 29 5 S 147 55 E
New Athens, *U.S.A.* **156 F7** 38 19N 89 53W
New Baltimore, *U.S.A.* **150 D2** 42 41N 82 44W
New Bedford, *U.S.A.* **151 E14** 41 38N 70 56W
New Berlin, *Ill., U.S.A.* **156 E7** 39 44N 89 55W
New Berlin, *N.Y., U.S.A.* **151 D9** 42 37N 75 20W
New Berlin, *Pa., U.S.A.* **150 F8** 40 50N 76 57W
New Berlin, *Wis., U.S.A.* **157 B8** 42 59N 88 6W
New Bern, *U.S.A.* **149 H7** 35 7N 77 3W
New Bethlehem, *U.S.A.* **150 F5** 41 0N 79 20W
New Bloomfield, *U.S.A.* **150 F7** 40 25N 77 11W
New Boston, *U.S.A.* **155 J7** 33 28N 94 25W
New Braunfels, *U.S.A.* **155 L5** 29 42N 98 8W
New Brighton, *N.Z.* **131 D7** 43 29 S 172 43 E
New Brighton, *U.S.A.* **150 F4** 40 42N 80 19W
New Britain, *Papua N. G.* **132 C6** 5 50 S 150 20 E
New Britain, *U.S.A.* **151 E12** 41 40N 72 47W
New Brockton, *U.S.A.* **152 D4** 31 23N 85 56W
New Brunswick, *U.S.A.* **151 F10** 40 30N 74 27W
New Brunswick □, *Canada* **141 C6** 46 50N 66 30W
New Buffalo, *U.S.A.* **157 C10** 41 47N 86 45W
New Bussa, *Nigeria* **113 D5** 9 53N 4 31 E
New Caledonia ■, *Pac. Oc.* **133 U19** 21 0 S 165 0 E
New Carlisle, *Ind., U.S.A.* **157 C10** 41 45N 86 32W
New Carlisle, *Ohio, U.S.A.* **157 E12** 39 56N 84 2W
New Castile = Castilla-La Mancha □, *Spain* **12 H5** 39 30N 3 30W
New Castle, *Ind., U.S.A.* **157 E11** 39 55N 85 22W
New Castle, *Ky., U.S.A.* **157 F11** 38 26N 85 10W
New Castle, *Pa., U.S.A.* **150 F4** 41 0N 80 21W
New City, *U.S.A.* **151 E11** 41 9N 73 59W
New Concord, *U.S.A.* **150 G3** 39 59N 81 54W
New Cumberland, *U.S.A.* **150 F4** 40 30N 80 36W
New Cuyama, *U.S.A.* **161 L7** 34 57N 119 38W
New Delhi, *India* **92 E7** 28 37N 77 13 E
New Denver, *Canada* **142 D5** 50 0N 117 25W
New Don Pedro Reservoir, *U.S.A.* **160 H6** 37 43N 120 24W
New Ellenton, *U.S.A.* **152 B8** 33 28N 81 41W
New England, *U.S.A.* **154 B3** 46 32N 102 52W
New England Nat. Park, *Australia* **129 A10** 30 25 S 152 30 E
New England Ra., *Australia* **127 E5** 30 20 S 151 45 E
New Forest, *U.K.* **21 G6** 50 53N 1 34W
New Franklin, *U.S.A.* **156 E4** 39 1N 92 44W
New Galloway, *U.K.* **22 F4** 55 5N 4 9W
New Georgia Is., *Solomon Is.* **133 M9** 8 15 S 157 30 E
New Georgia Sound, *Solomon Is.* **133 L9** 8 0 S 158 20 E
New Glarus, *U.S.A.* **156 B7** 42 49N 89 38W
New Glasgow, *Canada* **141 C7** 45 35N 62 36W
New Guinea, *Oceania* **132 C1** 4 0 S 136 0 E
New Hamburg, *Canada* **150 C4** 43 23N 80 42W
New Hampshire □, *U.S.A.* **151 C13** 44 0N 71 30W
New Hampton, *U.S.A.* **156 A4** 43 3N 92 19W
New Hanover, *Papua N. G.* **132 B6** 2 30 S 150 10 E
New Hanover, *S. Africa* **117 D5** 29 22 S 30 31 E
New Harmony, *U.S.A.* **157 F9** 38 8N 87 56W
New Hartford, *U.S.A.* **151 C9** 43 4N 75 18W
New Haven, *Conn., U.S.A.* **151 E12** 41 18N 72 55W
New Haven, *Ill., U.S.A.* **157 G8** 37 55N 88 8W
New Haven, *Ind., U.S.A.* **157 C11** 41 4N 85 1W
New Haven, *Mich., U.S.A.* **150 D2** 42 44N 82 48W
New Haven, *Mo., U.S.A.* **156 F5** 38 37N 91 13W
New Hazelton, *Canada* **142 B3** 55 20N 127 30W
New Hebrides = Vanuatu ■, *Pac. Oc.* **133 E6** 15 0 S 168 0 E
New Hebrides, *Vanuatu* **133 D6** 15 0 S 168 0 E
New Holland, *U.S.A.* **151 F8** 40 6N 76 5W
New Iberia, *U.S.A.* **155 K9** 30 1N 91 49W
New Ireland, *Papua N. G.* **132 B6** 3 20 S 151 50 E
New Ireland □, *Papua N. G.* **132 B6** 3 0 S 151 30 E
New Jersey □, *U.S.A.* **148 E8** 40 0N 74 30W
New Kensington, *U.S.A.* **150 F5** 40 34N 79 46W
New Lexington, *U.S.A.* **148 F4** 39 43N 82 13W
New Liskeard, *Canada* **140 C4** 47 31N 79 41W
New London, *Conn., U.S.A.* **151 E12** 41 22N 72 6W
New London, *Iowa, U.S.A.* **156 D5** 40 55N 91 24W
New London, *Mo., U.S.A.* **156 E5** 39 35N 91 24W
New London, *Ohio, U.S.A.* **150 E2** 41 5N 82 24W
New London, *Wis., U.S.A.* **154 C10** 44 23N 88 45W
New Madrid, *U.S.A.* **155 G10** 36 36N 89 32W
New Martinsville, *U.S.A.* **148 F5** 39 39N 80 52W
New Meadows, *U.S.A.* **158 D5** 44 58N 116 18W
New Melones L., *U.S.A.* **160 H6** 37 57N 120 31W
New Mexico □, *U.S.A.* **159 J10** 34 30N 106 0W
New Miami, *U.S.A.* **157 E12** 39 26N 84 32W
New Milford, *Conn., U.S.A.* **151 E11** 41 35N 73 25W
New Milford, *Pa., U.S.A.* **151 E9** 41 52N 75 44W
New Norcia, *Australia* **125 F2** 30 57 S 116 13 E
New Norfolk, *Australia* **127 G4** 42 46 S 147 2 E
New Orleans, *U.S.A.* **155 L9** 29 58N 90 4W
New Palestine, *U.S.A.* **157 E11** 39 45N 85 52W
New Panamao, *Phil.* **81 J3** 5 59N 121 13 E
New Paris, *U.S.A.* **157 E12** 39 51N 84 48W
New Pekin, *U.S.A.* **157 F10** 38 31N 86 2W
New Philadelphia, *U.S.A.* **150 F3** 40 30N 81 27W
New Plymouth, *N.Z.* **130 F3** 39 4 S 174 5 E
New Plymouth, *U.S.A.* **158 E5** 43 58N 116 49W
New Port Richey, *U.S.A.* **153 G7** 28 16N 82 43W
New Providence, *Bahamas* **164 A4** 25 25N 78 35W
New Providence I., *Bahamas* **9 b** 25 3N 77 25W
New Quay, *U.K.* **21 E3** 52 13N 4 21W
New Radnor, *U.K.* **21 E4** 52 15N 3 9W
New Richmond, *Canada* **141 C6** 48 15N 65 45W
New Richmond, *Ohio, U.S.A.* **157 F12** 38 57N 84 17W
New Richmond, *Wis., U.S.A.* **154 C8** 45 7N 92 32W
New Roads, *U.S.A.* **155 K9** 30 42N 91 26W
New Rochelle, *U.S.A.* **151 F11** 40 55N 73 47W
New Rockford, *U.S.A.* **154 B5** 47 41N 99 8W
New Romney, *U.K.* **21 G8** 50 59N 0 57 E
New Ross, *Ireland* **23 D5** 52 23N 6 57W
New Salem, *U.S.A.* **154 B4** 46 51N 101 25W
New Scone, *U.K.* **22 E5** 56 25N 3 24W
New Sharon, *U.S.A.* **156 C4** 41 28N 92 39W
New Siberian I. = Novaya Sibir, Ostrov, *Russia* **67 B16** 75 10N 150 0 E
New Siberian Is. = Novosibirskiye Ostrova, *Russia* **67 B15** 75 0N 142 0 E
New Smyrna Beach, *U.S.A.* **149 L5** 29 1N 80 56W
New South Wales □, *Australia* **129 B7** 33 0 S 146 0 E
New Stuyahok, *U.S.A.* **144 G8** 59 29N 157 20W
New Town, *U.S.A.* **154 B3** 47 59N 102 30W
New Tredegar, *U.K.* **21 F4** 51 44N 3 16W
New Ulm, *U.S.A.* **154 C7** 44 19N 94 28W
New Vienna, *U.S.A.* **157 E13** 39 19N 83 42W
New Washington, *Phil.* **81 F4** 11 39N 122 26 E
New Waterford, *Canada* **141 C7** 46 13N 60 4W
New Westminster, *Canada* **160 A4** 49 13N 122 55W
New York, *U.S.A.* **151 F11** 40 45N 74 0W
New York □, *U.S.A.* **151 D9** 43 0N 75 0W
New York Mts., *U.S.A.* **159 J6** 35 0N 115 20W
New Zealand ■, *Oceania* **130 G5** 40 0 S 176 0 E
Newaj →, *India* **92 G7** 24 24N 76 49 E
Newala, *Tanzania* **119 E4** 10 58 S 39 18 E
Newark, *Del., U.S.A.* **148 F8** 39 41N 75 46W
Newark, *N.J., U.S.A.* **151 F10** 40 44N 74 10W
Newark, *N.Y., U.S.A.* **150 C7** 43 3N 77 6W
Newark, *Ohio, U.S.A.* **150 F2** 40 3N 82 24W
Newark-on-Trent, *U.K.* **20 D7** 53 5N 0 48W
Newark Valley, *U.S.A.* **151 D8** 42 14N 76 11W
Newberg, *Mo., U.S.A.* **156 G5** 37 55N 91 54W
Newberg, *Oreg., U.S.A.* **158 D2** 45 18N 122 58W
Newberry, *Fla., U.S.A.* **153 F7** 29 39N 82 37W
Newberry, *Mich., U.S.A.* **148 B3** 46 21N 85 30W
Newberry, *S.C., U.S.A.* **149 H5** 34 17N 81 37W
Newberry Springs, *U.S.A.* **161 L10** 34 50N 116 41W
Newboro L., *Canada* **151 B8** 44 38N 76 20W
Newbridge = Droichead Nua, *Ireland* **23 C5** 53 11N 6 48W
Newburgh, *Canada* **150 B8** 44 19N 76 52W
Newburgh, *Ind., U.S.A.* **157 G9** 37 57N 87 24W
Newburgh, *N.Y., U.S.A.* **151 E10** 41 30N 74 1W
Newbury, *U.K.* **21 F6** 51 24N 1 20W
Newbury, *N.H., U.S.A.* **151 B12** 43 19N 72 3W
Newbury, *Vt., U.S.A.* **151 B12** 44 5N 72 4W
Newburyport, *U.S.A.* **149 D10** 42 49N 70 53W
Newcastle, *Australia* **129 B9** 33 0 S 151 46 E
Newcastle, *N.B., Canada* **141 C6** 47 1N 65 38W
Newcastle, *Ont., Canada* **140 D4** 43 55N 78 35W
Newcastle, *S. Africa* **117 D4** 27 45 S 29 58 E
Newcastle, *U.K.* **23 B6** 54 13N 5 54W
Newcastle, *Calif., U.S.A.* **160 G5** 38 53N 121 8W
Newcastle, *Wyo., U.S.A.* **154 D2** 43 50N 104 11W
Newcastle Emlyn, *U.K.* **21 E3** 52 2N 4 28W
Newcastle Ra., *Australia* **124 C5** 15 45 S 130 15 E
Newcastle-under-Lyme, *U.K.* **20 D5** 53 1N 2 14W
Newcastle-upon-Tyne, *U.K.* **20 C6** 54 58N 1 36W
Newcastle Waters, *Australia* **126 B1** 17 30 S 133 28 E
Newcastle West, *Ireland* **23 D2** 52 27N 9 3W
Newcomb, *U.S.A.* **151 C10** 43 58N 74 10W
Newcomerstown, *U.S.A.* **150 F3** 40 16N 81 36W

Nonancourt 257

Newdegate, *Australia* .... **125 F2** 33 6 S 119 0 E
Newell, *Australia* .... **126 B4** 16 20 S 145 16 E
Newell, *Iowa, U.S.A.* **156 B1** 42 36N 95 0W
Newell, *S. Dak., U.S.A.* **154 C3** 44 43N 103 25W
Newenham, C., *U.S.A.* **144 G7** 58 39N 162 11W
Newfane, *U.S.A.* **150 C6** 43 17N 78 43W
Newfield, *U.S.A.* **151 D8** 42 18N 76 33W
Newfound L., *U.S.A.* **151 C13** 43 40N 71 47W
Newfoundland, *Canada* **136 E14** 49 0N 55 0W
Newfoundland, *U.S.A.* **151 E9** 41 18N 75 19W
Newfoundland □, *Canada* **141 B8** 53 0N 58 0W
Newhalen, *U.S.A.* **144 G9** 59 43N 154 54W
Newhall, *U.S.A.* **161 L8** 34 23N 118 32W
Newhaven, *U.K.* .... **21 G8** 50 47N 0 3 E
Newington, *U.S.A.* **152 C8** 32 35N 81 30W
Newkirk, *U.S.A.* **155 G6** 36 53N 97 3W
Newlyn, *U.K.* **21 G2** 50 6N 5 34W
Newman, *Australia* .... **124 D2** 23 18 S 119 45 E
Newman, *Calif., U.S.A.* **160 H5** 37 19N 121 1W
Newman, *Ill., U.S.A.* **157 E9** 39 48N 87 59W
Newmarket, *Canada* **150 B5** 44 3N 79 28W
Newmarket, *Ireland* **23 D2** 52 13N 9 0W
Newmarket, *U.K.* .... **21 E8** 52 15N 0 25 E
Newmarket, *U.S.A.* **151 C14** 43 4N 70 56W
Newnan, *U.S.A.* **152 B5** 33 23N 84 48W
Newport, *Ireland* **23 C2** 53 53N 9 33W
Newport, *I. of W., U.K.* **21 G6** 50 42N 1 17W
Newport, *Newp., U.K.* **21 F5** 51 35N 3 0W
Newport, *Ark., U.S.A.* **155 H9** 35 37N 91 16W
Newport, *Ind., U.S.A.* **157 E9** 39 53N 87 25W
Newport, *Ky., U.S.A.* **157 E12** 39 5N 84 30W
Newport, *N.H., U.S.A.* **151 C12** 43 22N 72 10W
Newport, *N.Y., U.S.A.* **151 C9** 43 11N 75 1W
Newport, *Oreg., U.S.A.* **158 D1** 44 39N 124 3W
Newport, *Pa., U.S.A.* **150 F7** 40 29N 77 8W
Newport, *R.I., U.S.A.* **151 E13** 41 29N 71 19W
Newport, *Tenn., U.S.A.* **149 H4** 35 58N 83 11W
Newport, *Vt., U.S.A.* **151 B12** 44 56N 72 13W
Newport, *Wash., U.S.A.* **158 B5** 48 11N 117 3W
Newport □, *U.K.* **21 F4** 51 33N 3 1W
Newport Beach, *U.S.A.* **161 M9** 33 37N 117 56W
Newport News, *U.S.A.* **148 G7** 36 59N 76 25W
Newport Pagnell, *U.K.* **21 E7** 52 5N 0 43W
Newquay, *U.K.* **21 G2** 50 25N 5 6W
Newry, *U.K.* **23 B5** 54 11N 6 21W
Newtok, *U.S.A.* **144 F6** 60 56N 164 38W
Newton, *Ga., U.S.A.* **152 D5** 31 19N 84 20W
Newton, *Ill., U.S.A.* **154 F10** 38 59N 88 10W
Newton, *Iowa, U.S.A.* **156 C3** 41 42N 93 3W
Newton, *Kans., U.S.A.* **155 F6** 38 3N 97 21W
Newton, *Mass., U.S.A.* **151 D13** 42 21N 71 12W
Newton, *Miss., U.S.A.* **155 J10** 32 19N 89 10W
Newton, *N.C., U.S.A.* **149 H5** 35 40N 81 13W
Newton, *N.J., U.S.A.* **151 E10** 41 3N 74 45W
Newton, *Tex., U.S.A.* **155 K8** 30 51N 93 46W
Newton Abbot, *U.K.* **21 G4** 50 32N 3 37W
Newton Aycliffe, *U.K.* **20 C6** 54 37N 1 34W
Newton Falls, *U.S.A.* **150 E4** 41 11N 80 59W
Newton L., *U.S.A.* **157 F8** 38 55N 88 15W
Newton Stewart, *U.K.* **22 G4** 54 57N 4 30W
Newtonmore, *U.K.* **22 D4** 57 4N 4 8W
Newtown, *U.K.* **21 E4** 52 31N 3 19W
Newtown, *Ind., U.S.A.* **157 D9** 40 13N 87 9W
Newtown, *Mo., U.S.A.* **156 D3** 40 22N 93 20W
Newtownabbey, *U.K.* **23 B6** 54 40N 5 56W
Newtownards, *U.K.* **23 B6** 54 36N 5 42W
Newtownbarry = Bunclody, *Ireland* **23 D5** 52 39N 6 40W
Newtownstewart, *U.K.* **23 B4** 54 43N 7 23W
Newville, *U.S.A.* **150 F7** 40 10N 77 24W
Nexon, *France* .... **28 C5** 45 41N 1 11 E
Neya, *Russia* .... **60 A6** 58 21N 43 49 E
Neyrīz, *Iran* .... **97 D7** 29 15N 54 19 E
Nëyruz, *Switz.* .... **32 C4** 46 47N 7 4 E
Neyshābūr, *Iran* .... **97 B8** 36 10N 58 50 E
Neyyattinkara, *India* .... **95 K3** 8 26N 77 5 E
Nezhin = Nizhyn, *Ukraine* .... **59 G6** 51 5N 31 55 E
Nezperce, *U.S.A.* **158 C5** 46 14N 116 14W
Ngabang, *Indonesia* .... **85 B3** 0 23N 109 55 E
Ngabe, *Congo* .... **114 C3** 3 12 S 16 12 E
Ngabordamlu, Tanjung, *Indonesia* .... **83 C4** 6 56 S 134 11 E
N'Gage, *Angola* .... **115 D3** 7 46 S 15 15 E
Ngaiphaipi, *Burma* .... **90 D4** 22 14N 93 15 E
Ngala, *Nigeria* .... **113 C7** 12 20N 14 11 E
Ngama, *Chad* .... **109 F3** 11 45N 17 6 E
Ngambé, *Centre, Cameroon* .... **113 D7** 5 48N 11 29 E
Ngambé, *Littoral, Cameroon* .... **113 E7** 4 21N 10 40 E
Ngami Depression, *Botswana* .... **116 C3** 20 30 S 22 46 E
Ngamo, *Zimbabwe* .... **119 F2** 19 3 S 27 32 E
Ngangala, *Sudan* .... **107 G3** 4 42N 31 55 E
Nganjuk, *Indonesia* .... **85 D4** 7 32 S 111 55 E
Ngao, *Thailand* .... **86 C2** 18 46N 99 59 E
Ngaoundéré, *Cameroon* .... **114 A2** 7 15N 13 35 E
Ngapara, *N.Z.* .... **131 F5** 44 57 S 170 46 E
Ngape, *Burma* .... **90 E5** 20 2N 94 28 E
Ngara, *Tanzania* .... **118 C3** 2 29 S 30 40 E
Ngaruawahia, *N.Z.* .... **130 D4** 37 42 S 175 11 E
Ngaruroro →, *N.Z.* .... **130 F5** 39 34 S 176 55 E
Ngatapa, *N.Z.* .... **130 E6** 38 32 S 177 45 E
Ngathainggyaung, *Burma* .... **90 G5** 17 24N 95 5 E
Ngauruhoe, Mt., *N.Z.* .... **130 F4** 39 13 S 175 45 E
Ngawi, *Indonesia* .... **85 D4** 7 24 S 111 26 E
Ngele, *Dem. Rep. of the Congo* .... **114 C4** 0 30 S 20 22 E
Ngelebok, *Cameroon* .... **114 B2** 4 16N 14 3 E
Nggatokae, *Solomon Is.* .... **133 M10** 8 45 S 158 15 E
Nggela, *Solomon Is.* .... **133 M11** 9 5 S 160 15 E
Nggela Pile, *Solomon Is.* .... **133 M11** 9 5 S 160 20 E
Nggela Sule, *Solomon Is.* .... **133 M11** 9 2 S 160 12 E
Nghia Lo, *Vietnam* .... **76 G5** 21 33N 104 28 E
Ngidinga, *Dem. Rep. of the Congo* .... **115 D3** 5 37 S 15 17 E
Ngo, *Congo* .... **114 C3** 2 29 S 15 45 E
Ngoap, *Cameroon* .... **114 B2** 4 9N 12 51 E
Ngoboli, *Sudan* .... **107 G3** 4 57N 32 37 E
N'Gola, *Angola* .... **115 E2** 14 10 S 14 30 E
Ngoma, *Malawi* .... **119 E3** 13 8 S 33 45 E
Ngomahura, *Zimbabwe* .... **119 G3** 20 26 S 30 43 E
Ngomba, *Tanzania* .... **119 D3** 8 20 S 32 53 E
Ngongotaha, *N.Z.* .... **130 E5** 38 5 S 176 12 E
Ngop, *Sudan* .... **107 F3** 6 17N 30 9 E
Ngoring Hu, *China* .... **68 C4** 34 55N 97 5 E
Ngorkou, *Mali* **112 B4** 15 40N 3 41W
Ngorongoro, *Tanzania* .... **118 C4** 3 11 S 35 32 E
Ngorongoro Conservation Area, *Tanzania* .... **118 C4** 2 40 S 35 30 E
Ngoto, *C.A.R.* .... **114 B3** 3 59N 17 19 E
Ngouo, Dj., *C.A.R.* .... **114 A4** 7 55N 24 38 E
Ngoura, *Chad* .... **109 F3** 12 44N 16 21 E
Ngouri, *Chad* .... **109 F3** 13 38N 15 22 E
Ngourti, *Niger* .... **109 E2** 15 19N 13 12 E
Ngoussou, *Gabon* .... **114 C2** 3 0 S 11 7 E
Ngozi, *Burundi* .... **118 C2** 2 54 S 29 50 E
Ngudu, *Tanzania* .... **118 C3** 2 58 S 33 25 E
Nguigmi, *Niger* .... **109 F2** 14 20N 13 20 E
Nguila, *Cameroon* .... **113 E7** 4 41N 11 43 E
Nguiu, *Australia* .... **124 B5** 11 46 S 130 38 E
Ngukurr, *Australia* .... **126 A1** 14 44 S 134 44 E
Nguna, *Vanuatu* .... **133 G6** 17 26 S 168 22 E
Ngunga, *Tanzania* .... **118 C3** 3 37 S 33 37 E
Nguru, *Nigeria* .... **113 C7** 12 56N 10 29 E
Nguru Mts., *Tanzania* .... **118 D4** 6 0 S 37 30 E
Ngusi, *Malawi* .... **119 E3** 14 0 S 34 50 E
Nguyen Binh, *Vietnam* .... **76 F5** 22 39N 105 56 E
Ngwedaung, *Burma* .... **90 F6** 19 31N 97 9 E
Nha Trang, *Vietnam* .... **87 F7** 12 16N 109 10 E
Nhacoongo, *Mozam.* .... **117 C6** 24 18 S 35 14 E
Nhamaabué, *Mozam.* .... **119 F4** 17 25 S 35 5 E
Nhambiquara, *Brazil* .... **173 C6** 12 50 S 59 49W
Nhamundá, *Brazil* .... **169 D6** 2 14 S 56 43W
Nhamundá →, *Brazil* .... **169 D6** 2 12 S 56 41W
Nhangulaze, L., *Mozam.* .... **117 C5** 24 0 S 34 30 E
Nharêa, *Angola* .... **115 E3** 11 38 S 16 58 E
Nhecolândia, *Brazil* .... **173 D6** 19 17 S 56 58W
Nhill, *Australia* .... **128 D4** 36 18 S 141 40 E
Nho Quan, *Vietnam* .... **76 G5** 20 18N 105 45 E
Nhulunbuy, *Australia* .... **126 A2** 12 10 S 137 20 E
Nhundo, *Angola* .... **115 E4** 14 25 S 21 23 E
Nia-nia, *Dem. Rep. of the Congo* .... **118 B2** 1 30N 27 40 E
Niafounké, *Mali* **112 B4** 16 0N 4 5W
Niagara Falls, *Canada* **140 D4** 43 7N 79 5W
Niagara Falls, *U.S.A.* **150 C6** 43 5N 79 4W
Niagara-on-the-Lake, *Canada* **150 C5** 43 15N 79 4W
Niah, *Malaysia* .... **85 B4** 3 58N 113 46 E
Nialaha'u Pt., *Solomon Is.* .... **133 M11** 9 47 S 161 34 E
Niamey, *Niger* .... **113 C5** 13 27N 2 6 E
Niandan-Koro, *Guinea* **112 C3** 11 5N 9 15W
Nianforando, *Guinea* **112 D2** 9 37N 10 36W
Niangara, *Dem. Rep. of the Congo* .... **118 B2** 3 42N 27 50 E
Niangbo, *Ivory C.* **112 D3** 8 49N 5 10W
Niangoloko, *Burkina Faso* **112 C4** 10 15N 4 55W
Niangua →, *U.S.A.* **156 G4** 38 0N 92 48W
Niantic, *U.S.A.* **151 E12** 41 20N 72 11W
Niari, *Congo* .... **114 C2** 4 9 S 14 9 E
Niaro, *Sudan* .... **107 E3** 10 38N 31 31 E
Nias, *Indonesia* .... **84 B1** 1 0N 97 30 E
Niassa □, *Mozam.* .... **119 E4** 13 30 S 36 0 E
Niassa, Reserva do, *Mozam.* .... **119 E4** 12 4 S 36 57 E
Nibāk, *Si. Arabia* .... **97 E7** 24 25N 50 50 E
Nibe, *Denmark* .... **17 H3** 56 59N 9 38 E
Nicaragua ■, *Cent. Amer.* **164 D2** 11 40N 85 30W
Nicaragua, L. de, *Nic.* **164 D2** 12 0N 85 30W
Nicastro, *Italy* .... **47 D9** 38 59N 16 19 E
Nice, *France* .... **29 E11** 43 42N 7 14 E
Niceville, *U.S.A.* **149 K2** 30 31N 86 30W
Nichicun, L., *Canada* **141 B5** 53 5N 71 0W
Nichinan, *Japan* .... **72 F3** 31 38N 131 23 E
Nicholás, Canal, *W. Indies* **164 B3** 23 30N 80 5W
Nicholasville, *U.S.A.* **157 G12** 37 53N 84 34W
Nicholls, *U.S.A.* **152 D7** 31 31N 82 38W
Nichols, *U.S.A.* **151 D8** 42 1N 76 22W
Nicholson, *Australia* .... **124 C4** 18 2 S 128 54 E
Nicholson, *U.S.A.* **151 E9** 41 37N 75 47W
Nicholson →, *Australia* .... **126 B2** 17 31 S 139 36 E
Nicholson L., *Canada* **143 A8** 62 40N 102 40W
Nicholson Ra., *Australia* .... **125 E2** 27 15 S 116 45 E
Nicholville, *U.S.A.* **151 B10** 44 41N 74 39W
Nickerie →, *Surinam* **169 B6** 5 58N 57 0W
Nicobar Is., *Ind. Oc.* .... **95 L11** 8 0N 93 30 E
Nicola, *Canada* **142 C4** 50 12N 120 40W
Nicolls Town, *Bahamas* **164 A4** 25 8N 78 0W
Nicopolis, *Greece* .... **49 B3** 39 5N 20 43 E
Nicosia, *Cyprus* .... **39 E9** 35 10N 33 25 E
Nicosia, *Italy* .... **47 E7** 37 45N 14 24 E
Nicótera, *Italy* .... **47 D8** 38 33N 15 56 E
Nicoya, *Costa Rica* **164 D2** 10 9N 85 27W
Nicoya, G. de, *Costa Rica* **164 E3** 10 0N 85 0W
Nicoya, Pen. de, *Costa Rica* **164 E2** 9 45N 85 40W
Nidau, *Switz.* .... **32 B4** 47 7N 7 15 E
Nidd →, *U.K.* **20 D6** 53 59N 1 23W
Nidda, *Germany* .... **31 E5** 50 23N 9 1 E
Nidda →, *Germany* .... **31 E4** 50 17N 8 48 E
Nidri, *Greece* .... **49 B2** 38 43N 20 42 E
Nidwalden □, *Switz.* .... **33 C6** 46 50N 8 25 E
Nidzica, *Poland* .... **55 E7** 53 25N 20 28 E
Niē, Î., *N. Cal.* .... **133 U21** 21 8 S 167 35 E
Niebüll, *Germany* .... **30 A4** 54 46N 8 48 E
Nied →, *Germany* .... **27 C13** 49 23N 6 40 E
Niederaula, *Germany* .... **30 E5** 50 47N 9 36 E
Niederbayern □, *Germany* .... **31 G8** 48 40N 12 50 E
Niederbipp, *Switz.* .... **32 B5** 47 16N 7 42 E
Niederbronn-les-Bains, *France* .... **27 D14** 48 57N 7 39 E
Niedere Tauern, *Austria* .... **34 D7** 47 20N 14 0 E
Niederlausitz, *Germany* .... **30 D9** 51 42N 13 59 E
Niederösterreich □, *Austria* .... **34 C8** 48 25N 15 40 E
Niedersachsen □, *Germany* .... **30 C4** 52 50N 9 0 E
Niefang, *Eq. Guin.* .... **114 B2** 1 50N 10 14 E
Niekerkshoop, *S. Africa* .... **116 D3** 29 19 S 22 51 E
Niellé, *Ivory C.* **112 C3** 10 5N 5 38W
Niellim, *Chad* .... **109 G3** 9 42N 17 49 E
Niem, *C.A.R.* .... **114 A3** 6 12N 15 14 E
Niemba, *Dem. Rep. of the Congo* .... **118 D2** 5 58 S 28 24 E
Niemen = Neman →, *Lithuania* .... **15 J19** 55 25N 21 10 E
Niemodlin, *Poland* .... **55 H4** 50 38N 17 38 E
Niemur, *Australia* .... **128 C6** 35 17 S 144 9 E
Nienburg, *Germany* .... **30 C5** 52 39N 9 13 E
Niepołomice, *Poland* .... **55 H7** 50 3N 20 13 E
Niers →, *Germany* .... **30 D1** 51 43N 5 57 E
Niesen, *Switz.* .... **32 C5** 46 38N 7 39 E
Niesky, *Germany* .... **30 D10** 51 17N 14 49 E
Nieszawa, *Poland* .... **55 F5** 52 52N 18 50 E
Nieu Bethesda, *S. Africa* .... **116 E3** 31 51 S 24 34 E
Nieuw Amsterdam, *Surinam* **169 B6** 5 53N 55 5W
Nieuw Nickerie, *Surinam* **169 B6** 6 0N 56 59W
Nieuwoudtville, *S. Africa* .... **116 E2** 31 23 S 19 7 E
Nieuwpoort, *Belgium* .... **24 C2** 51 8N 2 45 E
Nieves, Pico de las, *Canary Is.* **9 e1** 27 57N 15 35W
Nièvre □, *France* .... **27 E10** 47 10N 3 40 E
Niga, *Mali* **112 C3** 13 38N 5 27W
Niğde, *Turkey* .... **100 D6** 37 58N 34 40 E
Nigel, *S. Africa* .... **117 D4** 26 27 S 28 25 E
Niger □, *Nigeria* .... **113 D6** 10 0N 5 50 E
Niger ■, *W. Afr.* .... **113 B7** 17 30N 10 0 E
Niger →, *W. Afr.* .... **113 D6** 5 33N 6 33 E
Niger Delta, *Africa* .... **113 E6** 5 0N 6 0 E
Nigeria ■, *W. Afr.* .... **113 D6** 8 30N 8 0 E
Nighasin, *India* .... **93 E9** 28 14N 80 52 E
Nightcaps, *N.Z.* .... **131 F3** 45 57 S 168 2 E
Nightmute, *U.S.A.* **144 F6** 60 29N 164 44W
Nigríta, *Greece* .... **50 F7** 40 56N 23 29 E
Nihoa, *U.S.A.* **145 G11** 23 6N 161 58W
Nii-Jima, *Japan* .... **73 C11** 34 20N 139 15 E
Niigata, *Japan* .... **70 F9** 37 58N 139 0 E
Niigata □, *Japan* .... **71 F9** 37 15N 138 45 E
Niihama, *Japan* .... **72 D5** 33 55N 133 16 E
Niihau, *U.S.A.* **145 B1** 21 54N 160 9W
Niimi, *Japan* .... **72 C5** 34 59N 133 28 E
Niitsu, *Japan* .... **70 F9** 37 48N 139 7 E
Nij Laluk, *India* .... **95 H9** 26 52N 93 56 E
Nījar, *Spain* **41 J2** 36 53N 2 15W
Nijil, *Jordan* .... **103 E4** 30 32N 35 33 E
Nijkerk, *Neths.* .... **24 B5** 52 13N 5 30 E
Nijmegen, *Neths.* .... **24 C5** 51 50N 5 52 E
Nijverdal, *Neths.* .... **24 B6** 52 22N 6 28 E
Nīk Pey, *Iran* .... **97 B6** 36 50N 48 10 E
Nikaweratiya, *Sri Lanka* .... **95 L5** 7 45N 80 7 E
Nike, *Nigeria* .... **113 D6** 6 26N 7 29 E
Nikiniki, *Indonesia* .... **82 C2** 9 49 S 124 30 E
Nikísiani, *Greece* .... **51 F8** 40 57N 24 9 E
Nikitas, *Greece* .... **50 F7** 40 13N 23 43 E
Nikki, *Benin* .... **113 D5** 9 58N 3 12 E
Nikkō, *Japan* .... **73 A11** 36 45N 139 35 E
Nikolai, *U.S.A.* **144 E9** 62 58N 154 10W
Nikolayev = Mykolayiv, *Ukraine* .... **59 J7** 46 58N 32 0 E
Nikolayevsk, *Russia* .... **60 E7** 50 0N 45 35 E
Nikolayevsk-na-Amur, *Russia* .... **67 D15** 53 8N 140 44 E
Nikolsk, *Russia* .... **60 D8** 53 49N 46 4 E
Nikolski, *U.S.A.* **144 K5** 52 56N 168 52W
Nikolskoye, *Russia* .... **67 D17** 55 12N 166 0 E
Nikopol, *Bulgaria* .... **51 C8** 43 43N 24 54 E
Nikopol, *Ukraine* .... **59 J8** 47 35N 34 25 E
Niksar, *Turkey* .... **100 B7** 40 31N 37 2 E
Nīkshahr, *Iran* .... **97 E9** 26 15N 60 10 E
Nikšić, *Montenegro, Yug.* .... **50 D2** 42 50N 18 57 E
Nîl, Nahr en →, *Africa* .... **106 H7** 30 10N 31 6 E
Nîl el Abyad →, *Sudan* .... **107 D3** 15 38N 32 31 E
Nîl el Azraq →, *Sudan* .... **107 D3** 15 38N 32 31 E
Nila, *Indonesia* .... **83 C3** 6 44 S 129 31 E
Nilakkottai, *India* .... **95 J3** 10 10N 77 52 E
Niland, *U.S.A.* **161 M11** 33 14N 115 31W
Nilanga, *India* .... **94 E3** 18 6N 76 46 E
Nile = Nîl, Nahr en →, *Africa* .... **106 H7** 30 10N 31 6 E
Niles, *Mich., U.S.A.* **157 C10** 41 50N 86 15W
Niles, *Ohio, U.S.A.* **150 E4** 41 11N 80 46W
Nileshwar, *India* .... **95 H2** 12 15N 75 6 E
Nilgiri Hills, *India* .... **95 J3** 11 30N 76 30 E
Nilo Peçanha, *Brazil* .... **171 D4** 13 37 S 39 6W
Nilsebu, *Norway* .... **18 E3** 59 11N 6 39 E
Nilüfer →, *Turkey* .... **51 F12** 40 18N 28 27 E
Nim Ka Thana, *India* .... **92 F6** 27 44N 75 48 E
Nimach, *India* .... **92 G6** 24 30N 74 56 E
Nimbahera, *India* .... **92 G6** 24 37N 74 45 E
Nîmes, *France* .... **29 E8** 43 50N 4 23 E
Nimfaíon, Ákra = Pínnes, Ákra, *Greece* .... **51 F8** 40 5N 24 20 E
Nimmitabel, *Australia* .... **129 D8** 36 29 S 149 15 E
Nīmrūz □, *Afghan.* .... **91 C1** 30 0N 62 0 E
Nimule, *Sudan* .... **107 G3** 3 32N 32 3 E
Nimule Nat. Park, *Sudan* .... **107 G3** 3 38N 32 2 E
Nin, *Croatia* .... **45 D12** 44 16N 15 12 E
Nīnawá, *Iraq* .... **101 D10** 36 25N 43 10 E
Ninda, *Angola* .... **115 E4** 14 47 S 21 24 E
Nindigully, *Australia* .... **127 D4** 28 21 S 148 50 E
Nine Degree Channel, *India* .... **95 K1** 9 0N 73 0 E
Ninepin Group, *China* .... **69 G11** 22 16N 114 21 E
Ninety East Ridge, *Ind. Oc.* .... **121 E7** 1 0 S 90 0 E
Ninety Mile Beach, *N.Z.* .... **130 A1** 34 48 S 173 0 E
Ninety Mile Beach, The, *Australia* .... **129 E7** 38 15 S 147 24 E
Ninety Six, *U.S.A.* **152 A7** 34 11N 82 1W
Nineveh = Nīnawá, *Iraq* .... **101 D10** 36 25N 43 10 E
Ning Xian, *China* .... **74 G4** 35 30N 107 58 E
Ningaloo Marine Park, *Australia* .... **124 D1** 22 23 S 113 32 E
Ning'an, *China* .... **75 B15** 44 22N 129 20 E
Ningbo, *China* .... **77 C13** 29 51N 121 28 E
Ningcheng, *China* .... **75 D10** 41 32N 119 53 E
Ningde, *China* .... **77 D12** 26 38N 119 23 E
Ningdu, *China* .... **77 D10** 26 25N 115 59 E
Ningerum, *Papua N. G.* .... **132 C1** 5 41 S 141 8 E
Ninggang, *China* .... **77 D9** 26 42N 113 55 E
Ningguo, *China* .... **77 B12** 30 35N 119 0 E
Ninghai, *China* .... **77 C13** 29 15N 121 27 E
Ninghua, *China* .... **77 D11** 26 14N 116 45 E
Ningi, *Nigeria* .... **113 C6** 10 55N 9 30 E
Ningjin, *China* .... **74 F8** 37 35N 114 57 E
Ningjing Shan, *China* .... **76 C2** 30 0N 98 20 E
Ninglang, *China* .... **76 D3** 27 20N 100 55 E
Ningling, *China* .... **74 G8** 34 25N 115 22 E
Ningming, *China* .... **76 F6** 22 8N 107 4 E
Ningnan, *China* .... **76 D4** 27 5N 102 36 E
Ningpo = Ningbo, *China* .... **77 C13** 29 51N 121 28 E
Ningqiang, *China* .... **74 H4** 32 47N 106 15 E
Ningshan, *China* .... **74 H5** 33 21N 108 21 E
Ningsia Hui A.R. = Ningxia Huizu Zizhiqu □, *China* .... **74 F4** 38 0N 106 0 E
Ningwu, *China* .... **74 E7** 39 0N 112 18 E
Ningxia Huizu Zizhiqu □, *China* .... **74 F4** 38 0N 106 0 E
Ningxiang, *China* .... **77 C9** 28 15N 112 30 E
Ningyang, *China* .... **74 G9** 35 47N 116 45 E
Ningyuan, *China* .... **77 E8** 25 37N 111 57 E
Ninh Binh, *Vietnam* .... **76 G5** 20 15N 105 55 E
Ninh Giang, *Vietnam* .... **86 B6** 20 44N 106 24 E
Ninh Hoa, *Vietnam* .... **86 F7** 12 30N 109 7 E
Ninh Ma, *Vietnam* .... **86 F7** 12 48N 109 21 E
Nini-Suhien Nat. Park, *Ghana* **112 D4** 5 20N 2 34W
Ninigo Group, *Papua N. G.* .... **132 A3** 1 22 S 144 17 E
Ninini Pt., *U.S.A.* **145 B2** 21 58N 159 20W
Ninove, *Belgium* .... **24 D4** 50 51N 4 2 E
Nioaque, *Brazil* .... **175 A4** 21 5 S 55 50W
Niobrara, *U.S.A.* **154 D6** 42 45N 98 2W
Niobrara →, *U.S.A.* **154 D6** 42 46N 98 3W
Nioki, *Dem. Rep. of the Congo* .... **114 C3** 2 47 S 17 40 E
Niokolo-Koba, Parc Nat. du, *Senegal* **112 C2** 13 3N 13 2W
Niono, *Mali* **112 C3** 14 15N 6 0W
Nionsamoridougou, *Guinea* **112 D3** 8 45N 8 50W
Nioro du Rip, *Senegal* **112 C1** 13 40N 15 50W
Nioro du Sahel, *Mali* **112 B3** 15 15N 9 30W
Niort, *France* **28 B3** 46 19N 0 29W
Nipa, *Papua N. G.* .... **132 D2** 6 9 S 143 29 E
Nipani, *India* .... **95 F2** 16 20N 74 25 E
Nipawin, *Canada* **143 C8** 53 20N 104 0W
Nipfjället, *Sweden* .... **16 C6** 61 59N 12 50 E
Nipigon, *Canada* **140 C2** 49 0N 88 17W
Nipigon, L., *Canada* **140 C2** 49 50N 88 30W
Nipishish L., *Canada* **141 B7** 54 12N 60 45W
Nipissing, L., *Canada* **140 C4** 46 20N 80 0W
Nipomo, *U.S.A.* **161 K6** 35 3N 120 29W
Nipton, *U.S.A.* **161 K11** 35 28N 115 16W
Niquelândia, *Brazil* .... **171 D2** 14 33 S 48 23W
Nīr, *Iran* .... **101 C12** 38 2N 47 59 E
Nira →, *India* .... **94 F2** 17 58N 75 8 E
Nirasaki, *Japan* .... **73 B10** 35 42N 138 27 E
Nirmal, *India* .... **94 E4** 19 3N 78 20 E
Nirmali, *India* .... **93 F12** 26 20N 86 35 E
Niš, *Serbia, Yug.* .... **50 C5** 43 19N 21 58 E
Nisa, *Portugal* **43 F3** 39 30N 7 41W
Nişāb, *Si. Arabia* .... **96 D5** 29 11N 44 43 E
Nişāb, *Yemen* .... **98 D4** 14 25N 46 29 E
Nišava →, *Serbia, Yug.* .... **50 C5** 43 20N 21 46 E
Niscemi, *Italy* .... **47 E7** 37 9N 14 23 E
Nishi-Sonogi-Hantō, *Japan* .... **72 E1** 32 55N 129 45 E
Nishi-Tosa, *Japan* .... **72 D4** 33 13N 132 46 E
Nishinomiya, *Japan* .... **73 C7** 34 45N 135 20 E
Nishino'omote, *Japan* .... **71 J5** 30 43N 130 59 E
Nishio, *Japan* .... **73 C9** 34 52N 137 3 E
Nishiwaki, *Japan* .... **72 C6** 34 59N 134 58 E
Nísíros, *Greece* .... **49 E9** 36 35N 27 12 E
Niška Banja, *Serbia, Yug.* .... **50 C6** 43 18N 22 1 E
Niskibi →, *Canada* **140 A2** 56 29N 88 9W
Nisko, *Poland* .... **55 H9** 50 35N 22 7 E
Nisporeni, *Moldova* .... **53 C13** 47 4N 28 10 E
Nisqually →, *U.S.A.* **160 C4** 47 6N 122 42W
Nissáki, *Greece* .... **38 B9** 39 43N 19 52 E
Nissan →, *Sweden* .... **17 H6** 56 40N 12 51 E
Nissedal, *Norway* .... **18 E5** 59 10N 8 30 E
Nisser, *Norway* .... **18 E5** 59 7N 8 28 E
Nissum Bredning, *Denmark* .... **17 H2** 56 40N 8 20 E
Nissum Fjord, *Denmark* .... **17 H2** 56 20N 8 11 E
Nistru = Dnister →, *Europe* .... **59 J6** 46 18N 30 17 E
Nisutlin →, *Canada* **142 A2** 60 14N 132 34W
Nitchequon, *Canada* **141 B5** 53 10N 70 58W
Niterói, *Brazil* .... **171 F3** 22 52 S 43 0W
Nith →, *Canada* **150 C4** 43 12N 80 23W
Nith →, *U.K.* **22 F5** 55 14N 3 33W
Nitmiluk Nat. Park, *Australia* .... **124 B5** 14 6 S 132 15 E
Nitra, *Slovak Rep.* .... **35 C11** 48 19N 18 4 E
Nitra →, *Slovak Rep.* .... **35 D11** 47 46N 18 10 E
Nitriansky □, *Slovak Rep.* .... **35 C11** 48 10N 18 30 E
Nittenau, *Germany* .... **31 F8** 49 12N 12 16 E
Niu, *U.S.A.* **145 K14** 21 19N 157 44W
Niuafo'ou, *Tonga* .... **123 D15** 15 30 S 175 58W
Niue, *Cook Is.* .... **135 J11** 19 2 S 169 54W
Niulan Jiang →, *China* .... **76 D4** 27 30N 103 5 E
Niut, *Indonesia* .... **85 B4** 0 55N 110 6 E
Niutou Shan, *China* .... **77 C13** 29 5N 121 59 E
Niuzhuang, *China* .... **75 D12** 40 58N 122 28 E
Nivala, *Finland* .... **14 E21** 63 56N 24 57 E
Nivelles, *Belgium* .... **24 D4** 50 35N 4 20 E
Nivernais, *France* .... **27 E10** 47 15N 3 30 E
Niwas, *India* .... **93 H9** 23 3N 80 26 E
Nixon, *U.S.A.* **155 L6** 29 16N 97 46W
Nizam Sagar, *India* .... **94 E3** 18 10N 77 58 E
Nizamabad, *India* .... **94 E4** 18 45N 78 7 E
Nizamghat, *India* .... **90 A5** 28 20N 95 45 E
Nizhne Kolymsk, *Russia* .... **67 C17** 68 34N 160 55 E
Nizhnegorskiy = Nyzhnohirskyy, *Ukraine* .... **59 K8** 45 27N 34 38 E
Nizhnekamsk, *Russia* .... **60 C10** 55 38N 51 49 E
Nizhnekamskoye Vdkhr., *Russia* .... **64 D4** 55 56N 52 56 E
Nizhneudinsk, *Russia* .... **67 D10** 54 54N 99 3 E
Nizhnevartovsk, *Russia* .... **66 C8** 60 56N 76 38 E
Nizhniy Chir, *Russia* .... **61 F6** 48 22N 43 5 E
Nizhniy Lomov, *Russia* .... **60 D6** 53 34N 43 38 E
Nizhniy Novgorod, *Russia* .... **60 B7** 56 20N 44 0 E
Nizhniy Tagil, *Russia* .... **64 C7** 57 55N 59 57 E
Nizhniye Sergi, *Russia* .... **64 C7** 56 40N 59 18 E
Nizhnyaya Salda, *Russia* .... **64 B8** 58 8N 60 42 E
Nizhyn, *Ukraine* .... **59 G6** 51 5N 31 55 E
Nizina Mazowiecka, *Poland* .... **55 F8** 52 30N 21 0 E
Nizip, *Turkey* .... **100 D7** 37 5N 37 50 E
Nízké Tatry, *Slovak Rep.* .... **35 C12** 48 55N 19 30 E
Nízký Jeseník, *Czech Rep.* .... **35 B10** 49 50N 17 30 E
Nizza Monferrato, *Italy* .... **44 D5** 44 46N 8 21 E
Njakwa, *Malawi* .... **119 E3** 11 1 S 33 56 E
Njanji, *Zambia* .... **119 E3** 14 25 S 31 46 E
Njarðvíkur, *Iceland* **11 D4** 63 59N 22 32W
Njazidja = Grande Comore, *Comoros Is.* .... **121 a** 11 35 S 43 20 E
Njegoš, *Montenegro, Yug.* .... **50 D2** 42 53N 18 45 E
Njinjo, *Tanzania* .... **119 D4** 8 48 S 38 54 E
Njoko →, *Zambia* .... **115 F4** 17 8 S 24 4 E
Njombe, *Tanzania* .... **119 D3** 9 20 S 34 50 E
Njombe →, *Tanzania* .... **118 D4** 6 56 S 35 6 E
Njurundabommen, *Sweden* .... **16 B11** 62 15N 17 25 E
Nkambe, *Cameroon* .... **113 D7** 6 35N 10 40 E
Nkana, *Zambia* .... **119 E2** 12 50 S 28 8 E
Nkandla, *S. Africa* .... **117 D5** 28 37 S 31 5 E
Nkawkaw, *Ghana* **113 D4** 6 36N 0 49W
Nkayi, *Zimbabwe* .... **119 F2** 19 41 S 29 20 E
Nkhotakota, *Malawi* .... **119 E3** 12 56 S 34 15 E
Nkhotakota Game Reserve, *Malawi* .... **119 E3** 12 50 S 34 0 E
Nkolabona, *Gabon* .... **114 B2** 1 14N 11 43 E
Nkomi, Lagune, *Gabon* .... **114 C1** 1 35 S 9 17 E
Nkone, *Dem. Rep. of the Congo* .... **114 C4** 1 2 S 22 20 E
Nkongsamba, *Cameroon* .... **113 E6** 4 55N 9 55 E
Nkunga, *Dem. Rep. of the Congo* .... **115 C3** 4 41 S 18 34 E
Nkurenkuru, *Namibia* .... **116 B2** 17 42 S 18 32 E
Nkwanta, *Ghana* **112 D4** 6 10N 2 10W
Nmai →, *Burma* .... **76 F2** 25 30N 97 25 E
Noakhali = Maijdi, *Bangla.* .... **90 D3** 22 48N 91 10 E
Noatak, *U.S.A.* **144 C7** 67 34N 162 58W
Nobel, *Canada* **150 A4** 45 25N 80 6W
Nobeoka, *Japan* .... **72 E3** 32 36N 131 41 E
Noble, *U.S.A.* **157 F8** 38 42N 88 14W
Noblejas, *Spain* **42 F7** 39 58N 3 26W
Noblesville, *U.S.A.* **157 D11** 40 3N 86 1W
Nocatee, *U.S.A.* **153 H8** 27 10N 81 53W
Noce →, *Italy* .... **44 B8** 46 9N 11 4 E
Nocera Inferiore, *Italy* .... **47 B7** 40 44N 14 38 E
Nocera Umbra, *Italy* .... **45 E9** 43 8N 12 47 E
Noci, *Italy* .... **47 B10** 40 48N 17 7 E
Nocona, *U.S.A.* **155 J6** 33 47N 97 44W
Nocrich, *Romania* .... **53 E9** 45 55N 24 26 E
Noda, *Japan* .... **73 B11** 35 56N 139 52 E
Nodeland, *Norway* .... **18 F4** 58 8N 7 51 E
Nogal Valley = Nugaaleed, Dooxo, *Somali Rep.* .... **120 C3** 8 35N 48 35 E
Nogales, *Mexico* **162 A2** 31 20N 110 56W
Nogales, *U.S.A.* **159 L8** 31 20N 110 56W
Nogaro, *France* **28 E3** 43 45N 0 2W
Nogat →, *Poland* .... **54 D6** 54 17N 19 17 E
Nōgata, *Japan* .... **72 D2** 33 48N 130 44 E
Nogent, *France* .... **27 D12** 48 1N 5 20 E
Nogent-le-Rotrou, *France* .... **26 D7** 48 20N 0 50 E
Nogent-sur-Seine, *France* .... **27 D10** 48 30N 3 30 E
Noggerup, *Australia* .... **125 F2** 33 32 S 116 5 E
Noginsk, *Moskva, Russia* .... **58 E10** 55 50N 38 25 E
Noginsk, *Tunguska, Russia* .... **67 C10** 64 30N 90 50 E
Nogoa →, *Australia* .... **126 C4** 23 40 S 147 55 E
Nogoyá, *Argentina* .... **174 C4** 32 24 S 59 48W
Nógrád □, *Hungary* .... **52 C4** 48 0N 19 30 E
Noguera Pallaresa →, *Spain* .... **40 D5** 41 55N 0 55 E
Noguera Ribagorzana →, *Spain* .... **40 D5** 41 40N 0 43 E
Nohar, *India* .... **92 E6** 29 11N 74 49 E
Nohfelden, *Germany* .... **31 F3** 49 35N 7 7 E
Nohili Pt., *U.S.A.* **145 A2** 22 4N 159 47W
Nohta, *India* .... **93 H8** 23 40N 79 34 E
Noia, *Spain* **42 C2** 42 48N 8 53W
Noichi, *Japan* .... **72 D5** 33 33N 133 42 E
Noing, *Phil.* .... **81 J5** 5 40N 125 28 E
Noipuos, *Papua N. G.* .... **132 B6** 2 25 S 150 7 E
Noire, Montagne, *France* .... **28 E6** 43 28N 2 18 E
Noires, Mts., *France* **26 D3** 48 11N 3 40W
Noirétable, *France* .... **28 C7** 45 48N 3 46 E
Noirmoutier, Î. de, *France* **26 F4** 46 58N 2 10W
Noirmoutier-en-l'Île, *France* **26 F4** 47 0N 2 14W
Nojane, *Botswana* .... **116 C3** 23 15 S 20 14 E
Nojima-Zaki, *Japan* .... **73 C11** 34 54N 139 53 E
Nok Kundi, *Pakistan* .... **91 C1** 28 50N 62 45 E
Nok Ta Phao, Ko, *Thailand* .... **87 b** 9 23N 99 40 E
Nokaneng, *Botswana* .... **116 B3** 19 40 S 22 17 E
Nokia, *Finland* .... **15 F20** 61 30N 23 30 E
Nokomis, *Canada* **143 C8** 51 35N 105 0W
Nokomis, *Fla., U.S.A.* **153 H7** 27 7N 82 27W
Nokomis, *Ill., U.S.A.* **156 E7** 39 18N 89 18W
Nokomis L., *Canada* **143 B8** 57 0N 103 0W
Nokou, *Chad* .... **109 F2** 14 35N 14 47 E
Nokuku, *Vanuatu* .... **133 D4** 14 54 S 166 35 E
Nol, *Sweden* .... **17 G6** 57 56N 12 5 E
Nola, *C.A.R.* .... **114 B3** 3 35N 16 4 E
Nola, *Italy* .... **47 B7** 40 55N 14 33 E
Nolay, *France* .... **27 F11** 46 58N 4 35 E
Noli, C. di, *Italy* .... **44 D5** 44 12N 8 25 E
Nolinsk, *Russia* .... **60 B9** 57 28N 49 57 E
Noma, *U.S.A.* **152 E4** 30 59N 85 37W
Noma Omuramba →, *Namibia* .... **116 B3** 18 52 S 20 53 E
Noma-Saki, *Japan* .... **72 F2** 31 25N 130 7 E
Nomad, *Papua N. G.* .... **132 D2** 6 19 S 142 13 E
Nombre de Dios, *Panama* **164 E4** 9 34N 79 28W
Nome, *U.S.A.* **144 D6** 64 30N 165 25W
Nomo-Zaki, *Japan* .... **72 E1** 32 35N 129 44 E
Nomuka, *Tonga* .... **133 Q13** 20 17 S 174 48W
Nomuka Group, *Tonga* .... **133 Q13** 20 20 S 174 48W
Nonacho L., *Canada* **143 A7** 61 42N 109 40W
Nonancourt, *France* .... **26 D8** 48 47N 1 11 E

258 Nonda

Nonda, *Australia* **126 C3** 20 40 S 142 28 E
Nondalton, *U.S.A.* **144 G9** 60 0N 154 51W
None, *Italy* **44 D4** 44 56N 7 32 E
Nong Chang, *Thailand* **86 E2** 15 23N 99 51 E
Nong Het, *Laos* **86 C4** 19 29N 103 59 E
Nong Khai, *Thailand* **86 D4** 17 50N 102 46 E
Nong'an, *China* **75 B13** 44 25N 125 5 E
Nongjrong, *India* **90 C4** 25 29N 92 6 E
Nongoma, *S. Africa* **117 D5** 27 58 S 31 35 E
Nongsa, *Indonesia* **87 d** 1 11N 104 8 E
Nongstoin, *India* **90 C3** 25 31N 91 16 E
Nonoava, *Mexico* **162 B3** 27 28N 106 44W
Nonoava →, *Mexico* **162 B3** 27 29N 106 45W
Nonoc I., *Phil.* **81 G5** 9 51N 125 37 E
Nonthaburi, *Thailand* **86 F3** 13 51N 100 34 E
Nontron, *France* **28 C4** 45 31N 0 40 E
Nonza, *France* **29 F13** 42 47N 9 21 E
Noonamah, *Australia* **124 B5** 12 40 S 131 4 E
Noord Brabant □, *Neths.* **24 C5** 51 40N 5 0 E
Noord Holland □, *Neths.* **24 B4** 52 30N 4 45 E
Noordbeveland, *Neths.* **24 C3** 51 35N 3 50 E
Noordoostpolder, *Neths.* **24 B5** 52 45N 5 45 E
Noordwijk, *Neths.* **24 B4** 52 14N 4 26 E
Noorvik, *U.S.A.* **144 C7** 66 50N 161 3W
Nootka I., *Canada* **142 D3** 49 32N 126 42W
Nopiming Prov. Park, *Canada* **143 C9** 50 30N 95 37W
Nóqui, *Angola* **115 D2** 5 55 S 13 30 E
Nora, *Eritrea* **107 D5** 16 6N 40 4 E
Nora, *Sweden* **16 E9** 59 32N 15 2 E
Nora Springs, *U.S.A.* **156 A4** 43 9N 93 0W
Norala, *Phil.* **81 H5** 6 32N 124 40 E
Noralee, *Canada* **142 C3** 53 59N 126 26W
Noranda = Rouyn-Noranda, *Canada* **140 C4** 48 20N 79 0W
Norberg, *Sweden* **16 D9** 60 4N 15 56 E
Norborne, *U.S.A.* **156 E3** 39 18N 93 40W
Nórcia, *Italy* **45 F10** 42 48N 13 5 E
Norco, *U.S.A.* **161 M9** 33 56N 117 33W
Norcross, *U.S.A.* **152 B5** 33 56N 84 13W
Nord □, *France* **27 B10** 50 15N 3 30 E
Nord-Kivu □, *Dem. Rep. of the Congo* **118 C2** 1 0 S 29 0 E
Nord-Ostsee-Kanal, *Germany* **30 A5** 54 12N 9 32 E
Nord-Pas-de-Calais □, *France* **27 B9** 50 30N 2 50 E
Nordagutu, *Norway* **18 E6** 59 25N 9 20 E
Nordaustlandet, *Svalbard* **6 B9** 79 14N 23 0 E
Nordberg, *Norway* **18 C5** 61 54N 8 10 E
Nordborg, *Denmark* **17 J3** 55 5N 9 50 E
Nordby, *Denmark* **17 J2** 55 27N 8 24 E
Norddeich, *Germany* **30 B3** 53 36N 7 9 E
Nordegg, *Canada* **142 C5** 52 29N 116 5W
Norden, *Germany* **30 B3** 53 35N 7 12 E
Nordenham, *Germany* **30 B4** 53 30N 8 30 E
Norderhov, *Norway* **18 D7** 60 7N 10 17 E
Norderney, *Germany* **30 B3** 53 42N 7 9 E
Norderstedt, *Germany* **30 B6** 53 42N 10 1 E
Nordeste, *Azores* **9 d3** 37 50N 25 10W
Nordfjord, *Norway* **15 F11** 61 55N 5 30 E
Nordfjordeid, *Norway* **18 C2** 61 54N 6 0 E
Nordfriesische Inseln, *Germany* **30 A4** 54 40N 8 20 E
Nordgrønland = Avannaarsua □, *Greenland* **10 B5** 80 0N 55 0W
Nordhausen, *Germany* **30 D6** 51 30N 10 47 E
Nordhorn, *Germany* **30 C3** 52 26N 7 4 E
Norðoyar, *Færoe Is.* **14 E9** 62 17N 6 35W
Norðtunga, *Iceland* **11 C5** 64 44N 21 24W
Norður-múlasýsla □, *Iceland* **11 B11** 65 30N 15 0W
Norðurbotn, *Iceland* **11 B3** 65 36N 23 46W
Nordingrå, *Sweden* **16 B12** 62 56N 18 17 E
Nordjyllands Amtskommune □, *Denmark* **17 G4** 57 20N 10 0 E
Nordkapp, *Norway* **14 A21** 71 10N 25 50 E
Nordkapp, *Svalbard* **6 A9** 80 31N 20 0 E
Nordkinn = Kinnarodden, *Norway* **12 A11** 71 8N 27 40 E
Nordkinn-halvøya, *Norway* **14 A22** 70 55N 27 40 E
Nördlingen, *Germany* **31 G6** 48 48N 10 30 E
Nordmøre, *Norway* **18 B4** 63 6N 8 15 E
Nordostrundingen, *Greenland* **10 A9** 81 22N 11 40W
Nordøyane, *Norway* **18 B3** 62 40N 6 0 E
Nordre Osen, *Norway* **18 C8** 61 18N 11 45 E
Nordre Strømfjord, *Greenland* **10 D5** 67 10N 53 35W
Nordrhein-Westfalen □, *Germany* **30 D3** 51 45N 7 30 E
Nordsinni, *Norway* **18 D6** 60 50N 9 57 E
Nørdstedalsseter, *Norway* **18 C4** 61 40N 7 48 E
Nordstrand, *Germany* **30 A4** 54 30N 8 52 E
Nordvik, *Russia* **67 B12** 74 2N 111 32 E
Nore →, *Ireland* **23 D4** 52 25N 6 58W
Norefjell, *Norway* **18 D6** 60 16N 9 29 E
Noresund, *Norway* **18 D6** 60 11N 9 37 E
Norfolk, *Nebr., U.S.A.* **154 D6** 42 2N 97 25W
Norfolk, *Va., U.S.A.* **148 G7** 36 51N 76 17W
Norfolk □, *U.K.* **21 E8** 52 39N 0 54 E
Norfolk I., *Pac. Oc.* **134 K8** 28 58 S 168 3 E
Norfork L., *U.S.A.* **155 G8** 36 15N 92 14W
Norheimsund, *Norway* **18 D3** 60 23N 6 6 E
Norilsk, *Russia* **67 C9** 69 20N 88 6 E
Norma, Mt., *Australia* **126 C3** 20 55 S 140 42 E
Normal, *U.S.A.* **156 D8** 40 31N 88 59W
Norman, *U.S.A.* **155 H6** 35 13N 97 26W
Norman →, *Australia* **126 B3** 19 18 S 141 51 E
Norman Park, *U.S.A.* **152 D6** 31 16N 83 41W
Norman Wells, *Canada* **138 B7** 65 17N 126 51W
Normanby, *N.Z.* **130 F3** 39 32 S 174 18 E
Normanby →, *Australia* **126 A3** 14 23 S 144 10 E
Normanby I., *Papua N. G.* **132 F6** 10 55 S 151 5 E
Normandie, *France* **26 D7** 48 45N 0 10 E
Normandin, *Canada* **140 C5** 48 49N 72 31W
Normandy = Normandie, *France* **25 B4** 48 45N 0 10 E
Normanhurst, Mt., *Australia* **125 E3** 25 4 S 122 30 E
Normanton, *Australia* **126 B3** 17 40 S 141 10 E
Normanville, *Australia* **128 C3** 35 27 S 138 18 E
Normétal, *Canada* **140 C4** 49 0N 79 22W
Norquay, *Canada* **143 C8** 51 53N 102 5W
Norquinco, *Argentina* **176 B2** 41 51 S 70 55W
Norra Dellen, *Sweden* **16 C10** 61 53N 16 43 E
Norra Ulvön, *Sweden* **16 A12** 63 3N 18 40 E
Norrahammar, *Sweden* **17 G8** 57 43N 14 7 E
Norrbotten □, *Sweden* **14 C19** 66 30N 22 30 E
Nørre Åby, *Denmark* **17 J3** 55 27N 9 52 E
Nørre Alslev, *Denmark* **17 K5** 54 54N 11 52 E
Nørresundby, *Denmark* **17 G3** 57 5N 9 52 E
Norrhult, *Sweden* **17 G9** 57 7N 15 10 E
Norris City, *U.S.A.* **157 G8** 37 59N 88 20W
Norris Point, *Canada* **141 C8** 49 31N 57 53W
Norristown, *Ga., U.S.A.* **152 C7** 32 30N 82 30W
Norristown, *Pa., U.S.A.* **151 F9** 40 7N 75 21W
Norrköping, *Sweden* **17 F10** 58 37N 16 11 E
Norrland, *Sweden* **15 E16** 62 15N 15 45 E
Norrsundet, *Sweden* **16 D11** 60 56N 17 8 E
Norrtälje, *Sweden* **16 E12** 59 46N 18 42 E
Norseman, *Australia* **125 F3** 32 8 S 121 43 E
Norsewood, *N.Z.* **130 G5** 40 3 S 176 13 E
Norsjø, *Norway* **18 E6** 59 18N 9 20 E
Norsk, *Russia* **67 D14** 52 30N 130 5 E
Norsup, *Vanuatu* **133 F5** 16 3 S 167 24 E
Norte, C., *Chile* **172 b** 27 3 S 109 24W
Norte, Canal do →, *Brazil* **169 C7** 0 40N 50 20W
Norte, Pta., *Argentina* **176 B4** 42 5 S 63 46W
Norte, Pta. del, *Canary Is.* **9 e1** 27 51N 17 57W
Norte, Pta. do, *Azores* **9 d4** 37 1N 25 4W
Norte, Serra do, *Brazil* **173 C6** 11 20 S 59 0W
Norte de Santander □, *Colombia* **168 B3** 8 0N 73 0W
Norte Grande, *Azores* **9 d1** 38 40N 28 4W
Nortelândia, *Brazil* **173 C6** 14 25 S 56 48W
North, *U.S.A.* **152 B8** 33 37N 81 6W
North, C., *Canada* **141 C7** 47 2N 60 20W
North Adams, *U.S.A.* **151 D11** 42 42N 73 7W
North Andaman I., *India* **95 H11** 13 15N 92 55 E
North Arm, *Canada* **142 A5** 62 0N 114 30W
North Atlantic Ocean, *Atl. Oc.* **8 C7** 30 0N 50 0W
North Augusta, *U.S.A.* **152 B8** 33 30N 81 59W
North Ayrshire □, *U.K.* **22 F4** 55 45N 4 44W
North Baltimore, *U.S.A.* **157 C13** 41 11N 83 41W
North Bass I., *U.S.A.* **150 E2** 41 44N 82 53W
North Battleford, *Canada* **143 C7** 52 50N 108 17W
North Bay, *Canada* **140 C4** 46 20N 79 30W
North Belcher Is., *Canada* **140 A4** 56 50N 79 50W
North Bend, *Oreg., U.S.A.* **158 E1** 43 24N 124 14W
North Bend, *Pa., U.S.A.* **150 E7** 41 20N 77 42W
North Bend, *Wash., U.S.A.* **160 C5** 47 30N 121 47W
North Bennington, *U.S.A.* **151 D11** 42 56N 73 15W
North Berwick, *U.K.* **22 E6** 56 4N 2 42W
North Berwick, *U.S.A.* **151 C14** 43 18N 70 44W
North Brother I., *India* **95 J11** 10 59N 92 40 E
North C., *Canada* **141 C7** 47 5N 64 0W
North C., *N.Z.* **130 A2** 34 23 S 173 4 E
North C., *Papua N. G.* **132 B6** 2 32 S 150 50 E
North Canadian →, *U.S.A.* **155 H7** 35 16N 95 31W
North Canton, *U.S.A.* **150 F3** 40 53N 81 24W
North Cape = Nordkapp, *Norway* **14 A21** 71 10N 25 50 E
North Cape = Nordkapp, *Svalbard* **6 A9** 80 31N 20 0 E
North Caribou L., *Canada* **140 B1** 52 50N 90 40W
North Carolina □, *U.S.A.* **149 H6** 35 30N 80 0W
North Cascades Nat. Park, *U.S.A.* **158 B3** 48 45N 121 10W
North Cay, *Bahamas* **9 b** 25 6N 77 26W
North Channel, *Canada* **140 C3** 46 0N 83 0W
North Channel, *U.K.* **22 F3** 55 13N 5 52W
North Charleston, *U.S.A.* **152 C10** 32 53N 79 58W
North Chicago, *U.S.A.* **157 B9** 42 19N 87 51W
North College Hill, *U.S.A.* **157 E12** 39 13N 84 33W
North Comino Channel, *Malta* **38 E7** 36 1N 14 20 E
North Creek, *U.S.A.* **151 C11** 43 41N 73 59W
North Dakota □, *U.S.A.* **154 B5** 47 30N 100 15W
North Downs, *U.K.* **21 F8** 51 19N 0 21 E
North East, *U.S.A.* **150 D5** 42 13N 79 50W
North East B., *Ascension I.* **9 g** 7 55 S 14 21W
North East Frontier Agency = Arunachal Pradesh □, *India* **90 A5** 28 0N 95 0 E
North East Lincolnshire □, *U.K.* **20 D7** 53 34N 0 2W
North Eastern □, *Kenya* **118 B5** 1 30N 40 0 E
North Esk →, *U.K.* **22 E6** 56 46N 2 24W
North European Plain, *Europe* **12 E10** 55 0N 25 0 E
North Fabius →, *U.S.A.* **156 E5** 39 54N 91 30W
North Foreland, *U.K.* **21 F9** 51 22N 1 28 E
North Fork, *U.S.A.* **160 H7** 37 14N 119 21W
North Fork, Salt →, *U.S.A.* **156 E5** 39 26N 91 53W
North Fork American →, *U.S.A.* **160 G5** 38 57N 120 59W
North Fork Edisto →, *U.S.A.* **152 B9** 33 16N 80 54W
North Fork Feather →, *U.S.A.* **160 F5** 38 33N 121 30W
North Fork Grand →, *U.S.A.* **154 C3** 45 47N 102 16W
North Fork Red →, *U.S.A.* **155 H5** 34 24N 99 14W
North Fort Myers, *U.S.A.* **153 J8** 26 41N 81 53W
North Frisian Is. = Nordfriesische Inseln, *Germany* **30 A4** 54 40N 8 20 E
North Gower, *Canada* **151 A9** 45 8N 75 43W
North Hd., *Australia* **125 F1** 30 14 S 114 59 E
North Henik L., *Canada* **143 A9** 61 45N 97 40W
North Highlands, *U.S.A.* **160 G5** 38 40N 121 23W
North Horr, *Kenya* **118 B4** 3 20N 37 8 E
North I., *India* **95 J1** 10 8N 72 20 E
North I., *Kenya* **118 B4** 4 5N 36 5 E
North I., *N.Z.* **130 E4** 38 0 S 175 0 E
North I., *Seychelles* **121 b** 4 25 S 55 13 E
North Judson, *U.S.A.* **157 C10** 41 13N 86 46W
North Kingsville, *U.S.A.* **150 E4** 41 54N 80 42W
North Kitui Nat. Reserve, *Kenya* **118 C4** 0 15 S 38 29 E
North Knife →, *Canada* **143 B10** 58 53N 94 45W
North Koel →, *India* **93 G10** 24 45N 83 50 E
North Korea ■, *Asia* **75 E14** 40 0N 127 0 E
North L., *Australia* **128 B5** 32 30 S 143 5 E
North Lakhimpur, *India* **90 B5** 27 14N 94 7 E
North Lanarkshire □, *U.K.* **22 F5** 55 52N 3 56W
North Las Vegas, *U.S.A.* **161 J11** 36 12N 115 7W
North Liberty, *U.S.A.* **157 C10** 41 32N 86 26W
North Lincolnshire □, *U.K.* **20 D7** 53 36N 0 30W
North Little Rock, *U.S.A.* **155 H8** 34 45N 92 16W
North Loup →, *U.S.A.* **154 E5** 41 17N 98 24W
North Luangwa Nat. Park, *Zambia* **119 E3** 11 49 S 32 9 E
North Magnetic Pole, *Canada* **6 B2** 77 58N 102 8W
North Manchester, *U.S.A.* **157 D11** 41 0N 85 46W
North Miami Beach, *U.S.A.* **153 K9** 25 56N 80 10W
North Minch, *U.K.* **22 C3** 58 5N 5 55W
North Moose L., *Canada* **143 C8** 54 11N 100 6W
North Myrtle Beach, *U.S.A.* **149 J6** 33 48N 78 42W
North Nahanni →, *Canada* **142 A4** 62 15N 123 20W
North Naples, *U.S.A.* **153 J8** 26 12N 81 48W
North New River Canal, *U.S.A.* **153 J9** 26 30N 80 30W
North Olmsted, *U.S.A.* **150 E3** 41 25N 81 56W
North Ossetia □, *Russia* **61 J7** 43 30N 44 30 E
North Pagai, I. = Pagai Utara, Pulau, *Indonesia* **84 C2** 2 35 S 100 0 E
North Palisade, *U.S.A.* **160 H8** 37 6N 118 31W
North Platte, *U.S.A.* **154 E4** 41 8N 100 46W
North Platte →, *U.S.A.* **154 E4** 41 7N 100 42W
North Pole, *Arctic* **6 A** 90 0N 0 0W
North Pole, *U.S.A.* **144 D11** 64 45N 147 21W
North Portal, *Canada* **143 D8** 49 0N 102 33W
North Powder, *U.S.A.* **158 D5** 45 2N 117 55W
North Pt., *Ascension I.* **9 g** 7 53 S 14 23W
North Pt., *Barbados* **165 g** 13 20N 59 37W
North Pt., *Trin. & Tob.* **169 E10** 11 21N 60 31W
North Pt., *U.S.A.* **150 A1** 45 2N 83 16W
North Pt., *Vanuatu* **133 D6** 14 56 S 168 6 E
North Reef I., *India* **95 H11** 13 5N 92 43 E
North Rhine Westphalia = Nordrhein-Westfalen □, *Germany* **30 D3** 51 45N 7 30 E
North River, *Canada* **141 B8** 53 49N 57 6W
North Ronaldsay, *U.K.* **22 B6** 59 22N 2 26W
North Salem, *U.S.A.* **157 E10** 39 52N 86 39W
North Saskatchewan →, *Canada* **143 C7** 53 15N 105 5W
North Sea, *Europe* **19 C7** 56 0N 4 0 E
North Seal →, *Canada* **143 B9** 58 50N 98 7W
North Sentinel I., *India* **95 J11** 11 33N 92 15 E
North Shields, *Australia* **128 C1** 34 38 S 135 52 E
North Solomons □, *Papua N. G.* **132 B8** 4 0 S 155 0 E
North Somerset □, *U.K.* **21 F5** 51 24N 2 45W
North Sporades = Vóriai Sporádhes, *Greece* **48 B5** 39 15N 23 30 E
North Sydney, *Canada* **141 C7** 46 12N 60 15W
North Syracuse, *U.S.A.* **151 C8** 43 8N 76 7W
North Taranaki Bight, *N.Z.* **130 E3** 38 50 S 174 15 E
North Thompson →, *Canada* **142 C4** 50 40N 120 20W
North Tonawanda, *U.S.A.* **150 C6** 43 2N 78 53W
North Troy, *U.S.A.* **151 B12** 45 0N 72 24W
North Truchas Pk., *U.S.A.* **159 J11** 36 0N 105 30W
North Twin I., *Canada* **140 B4** 53 20N 80 0W
North Tyne →, *U.K.* **20 B5** 55 0N 2 8W
North Ubian I., *Phil.* **81 H3** 6 9N 120 27 E
North Uist, *U.K.* **22 D1** 57 40N 7 15W
North Vancouver, *Canada* **142 D4** 49 19N 123 4W
North Vernon, *U.S.A.* **157 F11** 39 0N 85 38W
North Wabasca L., *Canada* **142 B6** 56 0N 113 55W
North Walsham, *U.K.* **20 E9** 52 50N 1 22 E
North Webster, *U.S.A.* **157 C11** 41 25N 85 48W
North-West □, *S. Africa* **116 D4** 27 0 S 25 0 E
North West C., *Australia* **124 D1** 21 45 S 114 9 E
North West Christmas I. Ridge, *Pac. Oc.* **135 G11** 6 30N 165 0W
North West Frontier □, *Pakistan* **91 B3** 34 0N 72 0 E
North West Highlands, *U.K.* **22 D4** 57 33N 4 58W
North West River, *Canada* **141 B7** 53 30N 60 10W
North Western □, *Zambia* **119 E2** 13 30 S 25 30 E
North Wildwood, *U.S.A.* **148 F8** 39 0N 74 48W
North York Moors, *U.K.* **20 C7** 54 23N 0 53W
North Yorkshire □, *U.K.* **20 C6** 54 15N 1 25W
Northallerton, *U.K.* **20 C6** 54 20N 1 26W
Northam, *Australia* **125 F2** 31 35 S 116 42 E
Northam, *S. Africa* **116 C4** 24 56 S 27 18 E
Northampton, *Australia* **125 E1** 28 27 S 114 33 E
Northampton, *U.K.* **21 E7** 52 15N 0 53W
Northampton, *Mass., U.S.A.* **151 D12** 42 19N 72 38W
Northampton, *Pa., U.S.A.* **151 F9** 40 41N 75 30W
Northamptonshire □, *U.K.* **21 E7** 52 16N 0 55W
Northbridge, *U.S.A.* **151 D13** 42 9N 71 39W
Northcliffe, *Australia* **125 F2** 34 39 S 116 7 E
Northeast C., *U.S.A.* **144 E5** 63 18N 168 42W
Northeast Providence Chan., *W. Indies* **164 A4** 26 0N 76 0W
Northeim, *Germany* **30 D6** 51 42N 10 0 E
Northern □, *Ghana* **113 D4** 9 30N 1 0W
Northern □, *Malawi* **119 E3** 11 0 S 34 0 E
Northern □, *Papua N. G.* **132 E5** 9 0 S 148 30 E
Northern □, *Zambia* **119 E3** 10 30 S 31 0 E
Northern Areas □, *Pakistan* **93 A5** 36 30N 73 0 E
Northern Cape □, *S. Africa* **116 D3** 30 0 S 20 0 E
Northern Circars, *India* **94 F6** 17 30N 82 30 E
Northern Indian L., *Canada* **143 B9** 57 20N 97 20W
Northern Ireland □, *U.K.* **23 B5** 54 45N 7 0W
Northern Lau Group, *Fiji* **133 A3** 17 30 S 178 59W
Northern Light L., *Canada* **140 C1** 48 15N 90 39W
Northern Marianas ■, *Pac. Oc.* **134 F6** 17 0N 145 0 E
Northern Mid-Atlantic Ridge, *Atl. Oc.* **8 C8** 35 0N 35 0W
Northern Province □, *S. Leone* **112 D2** 9 15N 11 30W
Northern Province □, *S. Africa* **117 C4** 24 0 S 29 0 E
Northern Range, *Trin. & Tob.* **169 F9** 10 46N 61 15W
Northern Samar □, *Phil.* **80 E5** 12 30N 124 40 E
Northern Territory □, *Australia* **124 D5** 20 0 S 133 0 E
Northfield, *Minn., U.S.A.* **154 C8** 44 27N 93 9W
Northfield, *Vt., U.S.A.* **151 B12** 44 9N 72 40W
Northland □, *N.Z.* **130 B2** 35 30 S 173 30 E
Northome, *U.S.A.* **154 B7** 47 52N 94 17W
Northport, *Ala., U.S.A.* **149 J2** 33 14N 87 35W
Northport, *Wash., U.S.A.* **158 B5** 48 55N 117 48W
Northumberland □, *U.K.* **20 B6** 55 12N 2 0W
Northumberland, C., *Australia* **128 E4** 38 5 S 140 40 E
Northumberland Is., *Australia* **126 C4** 21 30 S 149 50 E
Northumberland Str., *Canada* **141 C7** 46 20N 64 0W
Northville, *U.S.A.* **151 C10** 43 13N 74 11W
Northway, *U.S.A.* **144 E12** 62 58N 141 56W
Northwest Providence Channel, *W. Indies* **164 A4** 26 0N 78 0W
Northwest Pt., *Bahamas* **9 b** 25 4N 77 31W
Northwest Territories □, *Canada* **138 B9** 63 0N 118 0W
Northwood, *Iowa, U.S.A.* **154 D8** 43 27N 93 13W
Northwood, *N. Dak., U.S.A.* **154 B6** 47 44N 97 34W
Norton, *U.S.A.* **154 F5** 39 50N 99 53W
Norton, *Zimbabwe* **119 F3** 17 52 S 30 40 E
Norton B., *U.S.A.* **144 D7** 64 45N 161 15W
Norton Sd., *U.S.A.* **144 E7** 63 50N 164 0W
Norton Shores, *U.S.A.* **157 A10** 43 8N 86 15W
Nortorf, *Germany* **30 A5** 54 10N 9 50 E
Norwalk, *Calif., U.S.A.* **161 M8** 33 54N 118 5W
Norwalk, *Conn., U.S.A.* **151 E11** 41 7N 73 22W
Norwalk, *Iowa, U.S.A.* **156 C3** 41 29N 93 41W
Norwalk, *Ohio, U.S.A.* **150 E2** 41 15N 82 37W
Norway, *Maine, U.S.A.* **149 C10** 44 13N 70 32W
Norway, *Mich., U.S.A.* **148 C2** 45 47N 87 55W
Norway ■, *Europe* **14 E14** 63 0N 11 0 E
Norway House, *Canada* **143 C9** 53 59N 97 50W
Norwegian Sea, *Atl. Oc.* **18 A1** 66 0N 1 0 E
Norwich, *Canada* **150 D4** 42 59N 80 36W
Norwich, *U.K.* **21 E9** 52 38N 1 18 E
Norwich, *Conn., U.S.A.* **151 E12** 41 31N 72 5W
Norwich, *N.Y., U.S.A.* **151 D9** 42 32N 75 32W
Norwood, *Canada* **150 B7** 44 23N 77 59W
Norwood, *N.Y., U.S.A.* **151 B10** 44 45N 75 0W
Norwood, *Ohio, U.S.A.* **157 E12** 39 10N 84 27W
Noshiro, *Japan* **70 D10** 40 12N 140 0 E
Nosivka, *Ukraine* **59 G6** 50 50N 31 37 E
Nosovka = Nosivka, *Ukraine* **59 G6** 50 50N 31 37 E
Noşratābād, *Iran* **97 D8** 29 55N 60 0 E
Noss Hd., *U.K.* **22 C5** 58 28N 3 3W
Nossa Senhora da Glória, *Brazil* **170 D4** 10 14 S 37 25W
Nossa Senhora das Dores, *Brazil* **170 D4** 10 29 S 37 13W
Nossa Senhora do Livramento, *Brazil* **173 D6** 15 48 S 56 22W
Nossebro, *Sweden* **17 F6** 58 12N 12 43 E
Nossob →, *S. Africa* **116 D3** 26 55 S 20 45 E
Nossombougou, *Mali* **112 C3** 13 5N 7 55W
Nosy Boraha, *Madag.* **117 B8** 16 50 S 49 55 E
Nosy Lava, *Madag.* **117 A8** 14 33 S 47 36 E
Nosy Varika, *Madag.* **117 C8** 20 35 S 48 32 E
Notasulga, *U.S.A.* **152 C4** 32 34N 85 41W
Noteć →, *Poland* **55 F2** 52 44N 15 26 E
Notikewin →, *Canada* **142 B5** 57 2N 117 38W
Notio Aigaio = Notios Aiyaíon □ **49 E7** 36 52N 25 34 E
Notios Aiyaíon □ **49 E7** 36 52N 25 34 E
Notios Evvoïkos Kólpos, *Greece* **48 C5** 38 20N 24 0 E
Noto, *Italy* **47 F8** 36 53N 15 4 E
Noto, G. di, *Italy* **47 F8** 36 50N 15 12 E
Notodden, *Norway* **15 G13** 59 35N 9 17 E
Notre Dame B., *Canada* **141 C8** 49 45N 55 30W
Notre Dame de Koartac = Quaqtaq, *Canada* **139 B13** 60 55N 69 40W
Notre-Dame-des-Bois, *Canada* **151 A13** 45 24N 71 4W
Notre Dame d'Ivugivic = Ivujivik, *Canada* **139 B12** 62 24N 77 55W
Notre-Dame-du-Nord, *Canada* **140 C4** 47 36N 79 30W
Notsé, *Togo* **113 D5** 7 0N 1 17 E
Nottawasaga B., *Canada* **150 B4** 44 35N 80 15W
Nottaway →, *Canada* **140 B4** 51 22N 78 55W
Nottingham, *U.K.* **20 E6** 52 58N 1 10W
Nottingham, City of □, *U.K.* **20 E6** 52 58N 1 10W
Nottingham I., *Canada* **139 B12** 63 20N 77 55W
Nottinghamshire □, *U.K.* **20 D6** 53 10N 1 3W
Nottoway →, *U.S.A.* **148 G7** 36 33N 76 55W
Notwane →, *Botswana* **116 C4** 23 35 S 26 58 E
Nouâdhibou, *Mauritania* **110 D1** 20 54N 17 0W
Nouâdhibou, Dakhlet, *Mauritania* **110 D1** 20 55N 16 52W
Nouâdhibou, Ras, *Mauritania* **110 D1** 20 50N 17 0W
Nouakchott, *Mauritania* **112 B1** 18 9N 15 58W
Nouâmghâr, *Mauritania* **112 B1** 19 20N 16 20W
Nouméa, *N. Cal.* **133 V20** 22 17 S 166 30 E
Nouna, *Burkina Faso* **112 C4** 12 45N 3 52W
Noupoort, *S. Africa* **116 E3** 31 10 S 24 57 E
Nouveau Comptoir = Wemindji, *Canada* **140 B4** 53 0N 78 49W
Nouvelle-Amsterdam, I., *Ind. Oc.* **121 H6** 38 30 S 77 30 E
Nouvelle-Calédonie = New Caledonia ■, *Pac. Oc.* **133 U19** 21 0 S 165 0 E
Nouzonville, *France* **27 C11** 49 48N 4 44 E
Nov = Nau, *Tajikistan* **65 C4** 40 9N 69 22 E
Nova Aripuanã, *Brazil* **169 E5** 5 8 S 60 22W
Nová Baňa, *Slovak Rep.* **35 C11** 48 28N 18 39 E
Nová Bystřice, *Czech Rep.* **34 B8** 49 2N 15 8 E
Nova Casa Nova, *Brazil* **170 C3** 9 25 S 41 5W
Nova Cruz, *Brazil* **170 C4** 6 28 S 35 25W
Nova Era, *Brazil* **171 E3** 19 45 S 43 3W
Nova Esperança, *Brazil* **175 A5** 23 8 S 52 24W
Nova Friburgo, *Brazil* **171 F3** 22 16 S 42 30W
Nova Gaia = Cambundi-Catembo, *Angola* **115 E3** 10 10 S 17 35 E
Nova Gorica, *Slovenia* **45 C10** 45 7N 13 39 E
Nova Gradiška, *Croatia* **52 E2** 45 17N 17 28 E
Nova Granada, *Brazil* **171 F2** 20 30 S 49 20W
Nova Iguaçu, *Brazil* **171 F3** 22 45 S 43 28W
Nova Iorque, *Brazil* **170 C3** 7 0 S 44 5W
Nova Kakhovka, *Ukraine* **59 J7** 46 42N 33 27 E
Nova Lamego, *Guinea-Biss.* **112 C2** 12 19N 14 11W
Nova Lima, *Brazil* **175 A7** 19 59 S 43 51W
Nova Lisboa = Huambo, *Angola* **115 E3** 12 42 S 15 54 E
Nova Lusitânia, *Mozam.* **119 F3** 19 50 S 34 34 E
Nova Mambone, *Mozam.* **117 C6** 21 0 S 35 3 E
Nova Odesa, *Ukraine* **59 J6** 47 19N 31 47 E
Nova Olinda do Norte, *Brazil* **169 D6** 3 45 S 59 3W
Nová Paka, *Czech Rep.* **34 A8** 50 29N 15 30 E
Nova Pavova, *Serbia, Yug.* **52 F5** 44 56N 20 14 E
Nova Ponte, *Brazil* **171 E2** 19 8 S 47 41W
Nova Scotia □, *Canada* **141 C7** 45 10N 63 0W
Nova Siri, *Italy* **47 B9** 40 10N 16 35 E
Nova Sofala, *Mozam.* **117 C5** 20 7 S 34 42 E
Nova Varoš, *Serbia, Yug.* **50 C3** 43 29N 19 48 E
Nova Venécia, *Brazil* **171 E3** 18 45 S 40 24W
Nova Vida, *Brazil* **173 C5** 10 11 S 62 47W
Nova Zagora, *Bulgaria* **51 D10** 42 32N 26 1 E
Novaci, *Macedonia* **50 E5** 41 5N 21 29 E
Novaci, *Romania* **53 E8** 45 10N 23 42 E
Novafeltria, *Italy* **45 E9** 43 53N 12 17 E
Novaleksandrovskaya = Novoaleksandrovsk, *Russia* **61 H5** 45 29N 41 17 E
Novannenskiy = Novoannenskiy, *Russia* **60 E6** 50 32N 42 39 E
Novar, *Canada* **150 A5** 45 27N 79 15W
Novara, *Italy* **44 C5** 45 28N 8 38 E
Novato, *U.S.A.* **160 G4** 38 6N 122 35W
Novaya Kakhovka = Nova Kakhovka, *Ukraine* **59 J7** 46 42N 33 27 E
Novaya Kazanka, *Kazakstan* **61 F9** 48 56N 49 36 E
Novaya Ladoga, *Russia* **58 B7** 60 7N 32 16 E
Novaya Lyalya, *Russia* **64 B8** 59 4N 60 45 E
Novaya Sibir, Ostrov, *Russia* **67 B16** 75 10N 150 0 E
Novaya Zemlya, *Russia* **66 B6** 75 0N 56 0 E
Nové Město, *Slovak Rep.* **35 C10** 48 45N 17 50 E
Nové Město na Moravě, *Czech Rep.* **34 B9** 49 34N 16 5 E
Nové Město nad Metují, *Czech Rep.* **35 A9** 50 20N 16 10 E
Nové Zámky, *Slovak Rep.* **35 C11** 48 2N 18 8 E
Novelda, *Spain* **41 G4** 38 24N 0 45W
Novellara, *Italy* **44 D7** 44 51N 10 44 E
Novelty, *U.S.A.* **156 D4** 40 1N 92 12W
Noventa Vicentina, *Italy* **45 C8** 45 17N 11 32 E
Novgorod, *Russia* **58 C6** 58 30N 31 25 E
Novgorod-Severskiy = Novhorod-Siverskyy, *Ukraine* **59 G7** 52 2N 33 10 E
Novhorod-Siverskyy, *Ukraine* **59 G7** 52 2N 33 10 E
Novi Bečej, *Serbia, Yug.* **52 E5** 45 36N 20 10 E
Novi Iskar, *Bulgaria* **50 D7** 42 48N 23 21 E
Novi Kneževac, *Serbia, Yug.* **52 D5** 46 4N 20 8 E
Novi Lígure, *Italy* **44 D5** 44 46N 8 47 E
Novi Pazar, *Bulgaria* **51 C11** 43 25N 27 15 E
Novi Pazar, *Serbia, Yug.* **50 C4** 43 12N 20 28 E
Novi Sad, *Serbia, Yug.* **52 E4** 45 18N 19 52 E
Novi Slankamen, *Serbia, Yug.* **52 E5** 45 8N 20 15 E
Novi Travnik, *Bos.-H.* **52 F2** 44 10N 17 40 E
Novi Vinodolski, *Croatia* **45 C11** 45 10N 14 48 E
Novigrad, *Istra, Croatia* **45 C10** 45 19N 13 33 E
Novigrad, *Zadar, Croatia* **45 D12** 44 10N 15 32 E
Novigradsko More, *Croatia* **45 D12** 44 12N 15 24 E
Novinger, *U.S.A.* **156 D4** 40 14N 92 43W
Novo Acôrdo, *Brazil* **170 D2** 10 10 S 46 48W
Novo Airão, *Brazil* **169 D5** 2 40 S 60 59W
Novo Aripuanã, *Brazil* **169 E5** 5 8 S 60 22W
Novo Cruzeiro, *Brazil* **171 E3** 17 29 S 41 53W
Novo Hamburgo, *Brazil* **175 B5** 29 37 S 51 7W
Novo Horizonte, *Brazil* **171 F2** 21 25 S 49 10W
Novo Mesto, *Slovenia* **45 C12** 45 47N 15 12 E
Novo Miloševo, *Serbia, Yug.* **52 E5** 45 43N 20 20 E
Novo Paraiso, *Brazil* **169 C5** 1 17N 60 28W
Novo Remanso, *Brazil* **170 C3** 9 41 S 42 4W
Novo-Sergiyevskiy, *Russia* **64 E4** 52 5N 53 38 E
Novoaleksandrovsk, *Russia* **61 H5** 45 29N 41 17 E
Novoalekseyevka, *Kazakstan* **64 F5** 50 8N 55 39 E
Novoannenskiy, *Russia* **60 E6** 50 32N 42 39 E
Novoataysk, *Russia* **66 D9** 53 30N 84 0 E
Novoazovsk, *Ukraine* **59 J10** 47 15N 38 4 E
Novocheboksarsk, *Russia* **60 B8** 56 5N 47 27 E
Novocherkassk, *Russia* **61 G5** 47 27N 40 15 E
Novodevichye, *Russia* **60 D9** 53 37N 48 50 E
Novogrudok = Navahrudak, *Belarus* **58 F3** 53 40N 25 50 E
Novohrad-Volynskyy, *Ukraine* **59 G4** 50 34N 27 35 E
Novokachalinsk, *Russia* **70 B6** 45 5N 132 0 E
Novokazalinsk = Zhangaqazaly, *Kazakstan* **66 E7** 45 48N 62 6 E
Novokhopersk, *Russia* **60 E5** 51 5N 41 39 E
Novokuybyshevsk, *Russia* **60 D9** 53 7N 49 58 E
Novokuznetsk, *Russia* **66 D9** 53 45N 87 10 E
Novomirgorod, *Ukraine* **59 H6** 48 45N 31 33 E
Novomoskovsk, *Russia* **58 E10** 54 5N 38 15 E
Novomoskovsk, *Ukraine* **59 H8** 48 33N 35 17 E
Novoorsk, *Russia* **64 F7** 51 21N 59 2 E
Novopolotsk = Navapolatsk, *Belarus* **58 E5** 55 32N 28 37 E
Novorossiysk, *Russia* **59 K9** 44 43N 37 46 E
Novorossiyskoye, *Kazakstan* **64 F7** 50 13N 58 0 E
Novorybnoye, *Russia* **67 B11** 72 50N 105 50 E
Novorzhev, *Russia* **58 D5** 57 3N 29 25 E
Novosej, *Albania* **50 E4** 41 56N 20 35 E
Novoselytsya, *Ukraine* **59 H4** 48 14N 26 15 E
Novoshakhtinsk, *Russia* **59 J10** 47 46N 39 58 E
Novosibirsk, *Russia* **66 D9** 55 0N 83 5 E
Novosibirskiye Ostrova, *Russia* **67 B15** 75 0N 142 0 E
Novosil, *Russia* **59 F9** 52 59N 37 2 E
Novosinеglazovskiy, *Russia* **64 D8** 55 2N 61 21 E
Novosokolniki, *Russia* **58 D6** 56 20N 30 2 E
Novotitarovskaya, *Russia* **61 H4** 45 17N 39 2 E
Novotroitsk, *Russia* **64 F7** 51 10N 58 15 E
Novotroitskoye = Tōle Bī, *Kazakstan* **65 B6** 43 42N 73 46 E
Novoukrayinka, *Ukraine* **59 H6** 48 25N 31 30 E
Novouljanovsk, *Russia* **60 C9** 54 8N 48 24 E
Novouzensk, *Russia* **60 E9** 50 32N 48 17 E
Novovolynsk, *Ukraine* **59 G3** 50 45N 24 4 E
Novovoronezhskiy, *Russia* **59 G10** 51 19N 39 13 E
Novovoznesenovka, *Kyrgyzstan* **65 B9** 42 36N 78 44 E
Novoyatsk, *Russia* **64 B2** 58 24N 49 45 E
Novozybkov, *Russia* **59 F6** 52 30N 32 0 E

Ogallala 259

Novska, *Croatia* 45 C14 45 19N 17 0 E
Novvy Urengoy, *Russia* 66 C8 65 48N 76 52 E
Nový Bor, *Czech Rep.* 34 A7 50 46N 14 35 E
Novy Bug = Novyy Buh, *Ukraine* 59 J7 47 34N 32 29 E
Nový Bydžov, *Czech Rep.* 34 A8 50 14N 15 29 E
Nowy Dwór Mazowiecki, *Poland* 55 F7 52 26N 20 44 E
Nový Jičín, *Czech Rep.* 35 B11 49 30N 18 2 E
Novyy Afon, *Georgia* 61 J5 43 7N 40 50 E
Novyy Bor, *Russia* 56 A9 66 43N 52 19 E
Novyy Buh, *Ukraine* 59 J7 47 34N 32 29 E
Novyy Oskol, *Russia* 59 G9 50 44N 37 55 E
Novyy Port, *Russia* 66 C8 67 40N 72 30 E
Now Shahr, *Iran* 97 B6 36 40N 51 30 E
Nowa Deba, *Poland* 55 H8 50 26N 21 41 E
Nowa Nowa, *Australia* 129 D8 37 44 S 148 3 E
Nowa Ruda, *Poland* 55 H3 50 35N 16 30 E
Nowa Sarzyna, *Poland* 55 H9 50 21N 22 21 E
Nowa Sól, *Poland* 55 G2 51 48N 15 44 E
Nowata, *U.S.A.* 155 G7 36 42N 95 38W
Nowbarān, *Iran* 97 C6 35 8N 49 42 E
Nowe, *Poland* 54 E5 53 41N 18 44 E
Nowe Miasteczko, *Poland* 55 G2 51 42N 15 42 E
Nowe Miasto, *Poland* 55 G7 51 38N 20 34 E
Nowe Miasto Lubawskie, *Poland* 54 E6 53 27N 19 33 E
Nowe Skalmierzyce, *Poland* 55 G4 51 43N 18 0 E
Nowe Warpno, *Poland* 54 E1 53 42N 14 18 E
Nowendoc, *Australia* 129 A9 31 32 S 151 44 E
Nowghāb, *Iran* 97 C8 33 53N 59 4 E
Nowgong, *Assam, India* 90 B4 26 20N 92 50 E
Nowgong, *Mad. P., India* 93 G8 25 4N 79 27 E
Nowogard, *Poland* 54 E2 53 41N 15 10 E
Nowogród, *Poland* 55 E8 53 14N 21 53 E
Nowogród Bobrzanski, *Poland* 55 G2 51 48N 15 15 E
Nowogrodziec, *Poland* 55 G2 51 12N 15 24 E
Nowra, *Australia* 129 C9 34 53 S 150 35 E
Nowrangapur, *India* 94 E6 19 14N 82 33 E
Nowshera, *Pakistan* 91 B3 34 0N 72 0 E
Nowy Dwór Gdański, *Poland* 54 D6 54 13N 19 7 E
Nowy Sącz, *Poland* 55 J7 49 40N 20 41 E
Nowy Staw, *Poland* 54 D6 54 13N 19 2 E
Nowy Targ, *Poland* 55 J7 49 29N 20 2 E
Nowy Tomyśl, *Poland* 55 F3 52 19N 16 10 E
Nowy Wiśnicz, *Poland* 55 J7 49 55N 20 28 E
Noxen, *U.S.A.* 151 E8 41 25N 76 4W
Noxon, *U.S.A.* 158 C6 48 0N 115 43W
Noyabr'sk, *Russia* 66 C8 64 34N 76 21 E
Noyant, *France* 26 E7 47 30N 0 6 E
Noyers, *France* 27 E10 47 40N 4 0 E
Noyon, *France* 27 C9 49 34N 2 59 E
Noyon, *Mongolia* 74 C2 43 2N 102 4 E
Nozay, *France* 26 E5 47 34N 1 38W
Nqutu, *S. Africa* 117 D5 28 13 S 30 32 E
Nsa, *Congo* 114 C3 2 22 S 15 19 E
Nsa, O. en →, *Algeria* 111 B6 32 28N 5 24 E
Nsa, Plateau de, *Congo* 114 C3 2 26 S 15 20 E
Nsanje, *Malawi* 119 F4 16 55 S 35 12 E
Nsawam, *Ghana* 113 D4 5 50N 0 24W
Nsok, *Eq. Guin.* 114 B2 1 10N 11 19 E
Nsomba, *Zambia* 119 E2 10 45 S 29 51 E
Nsontin, *Dem. Rep. of the Congo* 114 C3 3 7 S 17 56 E
Nsopzup, *Burma* 90 C6 25 51N 97 30 E
Nsukka, *Nigeria* 113 D6 6 51N 7 29 E
Ntem →, *Cameroon* 114 B2 2 21N 9 49 E
Ntoum, *Gabon* 114 B1 0 22N 9 47 E
N'Tsama, *Congo* 114 C2 0 53 S 14 44 E
Ntui, *Cameroon* 113 E7 4 27N 11 38 E
Nu Jiang →, *China* 76 E2 29 58N 97 25 E
Nu Shan, *China* 76 E2 26 0N 99 20 E
Nuakata I., *Papua N. G.* 132 F6 10 17 S 151 2 E
Nuba Mts. = Nubah, Jibalan, *Sudan* 107 E3 12 0N 31 0 E
Nubah, Jibalan, *Sudan* 107 E3 12 0N 31 0 E
Nubia, *Africa* 104 D7 21 0N 32 0 E
Nubian Desert = Nûbîya, Es Sahrâ en, *Sudan* 106 C3 21 30N 33 30 E
Nûbîya, Es Sahrâ en, *Sudan* 106 C3 21 30N 33 30 E
Nubledo, *Spain* 42 B5 43 31N 5 52W
Nuboai, *Indonesia* 83 B5 2 10 S 136 30 E
Nubra →, *India* 93 B7 34 35N 77 35 E
Nucet, *Romania* 52 D7 46 28N 22 35 E
Nueces →, *U.S.A.* 155 M6 27 51N 97 30W
Nueltin L., *Canada* 143 A9 60 30N 99 30W
Nueva, I., *Chile* 176 E3 55 13 S 66 30W
Nueva Antioquia, *Colombia* 168 B4 6 5N 69 26W
Nueva Asunción □, *Paraguay* 174 A3 21 0 S 61 0W
Nueva Carteya, *Spain* 43 H6 37 35N 4 28W
Nueva Ecija □, *Phil.* 80 D3 15 35N 121 0 E
Nueva Esparta □, *Venezuela* 169 A5 11 0N 64 0W
Nueva Gerona, *Cuba* 164 B3 21 53N 82 49W
Nueva Imperial, *Chile* 176 A2 38 45 S 72 58W
Nueva Palmira, *Uruguay* 174 C4 33 52 S 58 20W
Nueva Rosita, *Mexico* 162 B4 28 0N 101 11W
Nueva San Salvador, *El Salv.* 164 D2 13 40N 89 18W
Nueva Tabarca, *Spain* 41 G4 38 17N 0 30W
Nueva Vizcaya □, *Phil.* 80 C3 16 20N 121 20 E
Nuéve de Julio, *Argentina* 174 D3 35 30 S 61 0W
Nuevitas, *Cuba* 164 B4 21 30N 77 20W
Nuevo, G., *Argentina* 176 B4 43 0 S 64 30W
Nuevo Casas Grandes, *Mexico* 162 A3 30 22N 108 0W
Nuevo Guerrero, *Mexico* 163 B5 26 34N 99 15W
Nuevo Laredo, *Mexico* 163 B5 27 30N 99 30W
Nuevo León □, *Mexico* 162 C5 25 0N 100 0W
Nuevo Mundo, Cerro, *Bolivia* 172 E4 21 55 S 66 53W
Nuevo Rocafuerte, *Ecuador* 168 D2 0 55 S 75 27W
Nugaaleed, Dooxo, *Somali Rep.* 120 C3 8 35N 48 35 E
Nugget Pt., *N.Z.* 131 G4 46 27 S 169 50 E
Nugrus, Gebel, *Egypt* 106 C3 24 47N 34 35 E
Nuguria Is., *Papua N. G.* 132 B8 3 20 S 154 45 E
Nuhaka, *N.Z.* 130 F6 39 3 S 177 45 E
Nuits-St-Georges, *France* 27 E11 47 10N 4 56 E
Nukey Bluff, *Australia* 127 E2 32 26 S 135 29 E
Nukheila, *Sudan* 106 D2 19 1N 26 21 E
Nukhuyb, *Iraq* 101 F10 32 4N 42 3 E
Nukiki, *Solomon Is.* 133 L9 6 46 S 156 35 E
Nuku, *Papua N. G.* 132 B2 3 41 S 142 28 E
Nuku'alofa, *Tonga* 133 Q14 21 10 S 174 0W
Nukuhu, *Papua N. G.* 132 C5 5 34 S 149 22 E
Nukulaelae, *Tuvalu* 123 B14 9 23 S 179 52 E
Nukus, *Uzbekistan* 66 E6 42 27N 59 41 E
Nulato, *U.S.A.* 144 D8 64 43N 158 6W
Nules, *Spain* 40 F4 39 51N 0 9W
Nullagine, *Australia* 124 D3 21 53 S 120 7 E
Nullagine →, *Australia* 124 D3 21 20 S 120 20 E
Nullarbor, *Australia* 125 F5 31 28 S 130 55 E
Nullarbor Nat. Park, *Australia* 125 F2 32 39 S 115 37 E
Nullarbor Plain, *Australia* 125 F4 31 10 S 129 0 E
Num, *Indonesia* 83 B5 1 30 S 135 13 E
Numalla, L., *Australia* 127 D3 28 43 S 144 20 E
Numan, *Nigeria* 113 D7 9 29N 12 3 E
Numanuma, *Papua N. G.* 132 E6 9 41 S 150 55 E
Numata, *Japan* 73 A11 36 45N 139 4 E
Numatinna →, *Sudan* 107 F2 7 38N 27 20 E
Numazu, *Japan* 73 B10 35 7N 138 51 E
Numbulwar, *Australia* 126 A2 14 15 S 135 45 E
Numedal, *Norway* 18 D6 60 6N 9 6 E
Numfoor, *Indonesia* 83 B4 1 0 S 134 50 E
Numurkah, *Australia* 129 D6 36 5 S 145 26 E
Nunaksaluk I., *Canada* 141 A7 55 49N 60 20W
Nunap Isua, *Greenland* 10 F6 59 48N 43 55W
Nunavut □, *Canada* 139 B11 66 0N 85 0W
Nunda, *U.S.A.* 150 D7 42 35N 77 56W
Nuneaton, *U.K.* 19 E6 52 32N 1 27W
Nungarin, *Australia* 125 F2 31 12 S 118 6 E
Nungo, *Mozam.* 119 E4 13 23 S 37 43 E
Nungwe, *Tanzania* 118 C3 2 48 S 32 2 E
Nunivak I., *U.S.A.* 144 F6 60 10N 166 30W
Nunkun, *India* 93 C7 33 57N 76 2 E
Nùoro, *Italy* 46 B2 40 20N 9 20 E
Núpur, *Iceland* 11 B3 65 56N 23 36W
Nuqayy, Jabal, *Libya* 108 D3 23 11N 19 30 E
Nuqūb, *Yemen* 98 D4 14 59N 45 48 E
Nuquí, *Colombia* 168 B2 5 42N 77 17W
Nūrābād, *Iran* 97 E8 27 47N 57 12 E
Nurabad, *Uzbekistan* 65 D3 39 36N 66 17 E
Nurata, *Uzbekistan* 65 C2 40 33N 65 41 E
Nurata Tizmasi, *Uzbekistan* 65 C3 40 40N 66 30 E
Nure →, *Italy* 44 C6 45 3N 9 49 E
Nurek, *Tajikistan* 65 D4 38 23N 69 19 E
Nuremberg = Nürnberg, *Germany* 31 F7 49 27N 11 3 E
Nuri, *Mexico* 162 B3 28 2N 109 22W
Nuri, *Sudan* 106 D3 18 29N 31 53 E
Nuriootpa, *Australia* 128 C3 34 27 S 139 0 E
Nurlat, *Russia* 60 C10 54 29N 50 45 E
Nurmes, *Finland* 14 E23 63 33N 29 10 E
Nürnberg, *Germany* 31 F7 49 27N 11 3 E
Nurpur, *Pakistan* 92 D4 31 53N 71 54 E
Nurra, La, *Italy* 46 B1 40 45N 8 15 E
Nurran, L. = Terewah, L., *Australia* 127 D4 29 52 S 147 35 E
Nurrari Lakes, *Australia* 125 E5 29 1 S 130 5 E
Nurri, *Italy* 46 C2 39 43N 9 14 E
Nürtingen, *Germany* 31 G5 48 37N 9 19 E
Nurzec →, *Poland* 55 F9 52 37N 22 25 E
Nus, *Italy* 44 C4 45 45N 7 28 E
Nusa Barung, *Indonesia* 83 D4 8 30 S 113 30 E
Nusa Dua, *Indonesia* 79 K18 8 48 S 115 14 E
Nusa Kambangan, *Indonesia* 85 D3 7 40 S 108 10 E
Nusa Tenggara Barat □, *Indonesia* 85 D5 8 50 S 117 30 E
Nusa Tenggara Timur □, *Indonesia* 82 C2 9 30 S 122 0 E
Nusaybin, *Turkey* 101 D9 37 3N 41 10 E
Nushki, *Pakistan* 91 C2 29 35N 66 0 E
Nuuk, *Greenland* 10 E5 64 10N 51 35W
Nuussauq, *Greenland* 10 C5 74 8N 57 3W
Nuwakot, *Nepal* 93 E10 28 10N 83 55 E
Nuwara Eliya, *Sri Lanka* 95 L5 6 58N 80 48 E
Nuweiba', *Egypt* 96 D2 28 59N 34 39 E
Nuwerus, *S. Africa* 116 E2 31 8 S 18 24 E
Nuweveldberge, *S. Africa* 116 E3 32 10 S 21 45 E
Nuyts, C., *Australia* 125 F5 32 2 S 132 21 E
Nuyts, Pt., *Australia* 125 G2 35 4 S 116 38 E
Nuyts Arch., *Australia* 127 E1 32 35 S 133 20 E
Nuzvid, *India* 94 F5 16 47N 80 53 E
N'Vinda, *Angola* 115 E3 13 8 S 19 2 E
Nxai Pan Nat. Park, *Botswana* 116 B3 19 50 S 24 46 E
Nxau-Nxau, *Botswana* 116 B3 18 57 S 21 4 E
Nyaake, *Liberia* 112 E3 4 52N 7 37W
Nyabessan, *Cameroon* 114 B2 2 28N 10 24 E
Nyabing, *Australia* 125 F2 33 33 S 118 9 E
Nyack, *U.S.A.* 151 E11 41 5N 73 55W
Nyagan, *Russia* 66 C7 62 30N 65 38 E
Nyah West, *Australia* 128 C5 35 16 S 143 21 E
Nyahanga, *Tanzania* 118 C3 2 20 S 33 37 E
Nyahua, *Tanzania* 118 D3 5 25 S 33 23 E
Nyahururu, *Kenya* 118 B4 0 2N 36 27 E
Nyainqentanglha Shan, *China* 68 D4 30 0N 90 0 E
Nyakanazi, *Tanzania* 118 C3 3 2 S 31 10 E
Nyakrom, *Ghana* 113 D4 5 40N 0 50W
Nyâlâ, *Sudan* 107 E1 12 2N 24 58 E
Nyamandhlovu, *Zimbabwe* 119 F2 19 55 S 28 16 E
Nyambiti, *Tanzania* 118 C3 2 48 S 33 27 E
Nyamlell, *Sudan* 107 F2 9 7N 26 59 E
Nyamwaga, *Tanzania* 118 C3 1 27 S 34 33 E
Nyandekwa, *Tanzania* 118 C3 3 57 S 32 32 E
Nyanding →, *Sudan* 107 F3 8 40N 32 41 E
Nyandoma, *Russia* 58 B11 61 40N 40 12 E
Nyanga →, *Gabon* 114 C2 2 58 S 10 15 E
Nyanga Nat. Park, *Zimbabwe* 119 F3 18 17 S 32 46 E
Nyangana, *Namibia* 116 B3 18 0 S 20 40 E
Nyanguge, *Tanzania* 118 C3 2 30 S 33 12 E
Nyankpala, *Ghana* 113 D4 9 21N 0 58W
Nyanza, *Rwanda* 118 C2 2 20 S 29 42 E
Nyanza □, *Kenya* 118 C3 0 10 S 34 15 E
Nyanza-Lac, *Burundi* 118 C2 4 21 S 29 36 E
Nyaponges, *Sudan* 107 F3 5 5N 33 45 E
Nyasa, L., *Africa* 119 E3 12 30 S 34 30 E
Nyasvizh, *Belarus* 59 F4 53 14N 26 38 E
Nyaunglebin, *Burma* 90 G6 17 52N 96 42 E
Nyazepetrovsk, *Russia* 64 C7 56 3N 59 36 E
Nyazura, *Zimbabwe* 119 F3 18 40 S 32 16 E
Nyazwidzi →, *Zimbabwe* 119 G3 20 0 S 31 17 E
Nybergsund, *Norway* 18 C9 61 15N 12 19 E
Nyborg, *Denmark* 17 J4 55 18N 10 47 E
Nybro, *Sweden* 17 H9 56 44N 15 55 E
Nyda, *Russia* 66 C8 66 40N 72 58 E
Nyeboe Land, *Greenland* 10 A5 82 0N 57 0W
Nyengo Swamp, *Zambia* 115 E4 14 51 S 22 7 E
Nyeri, *Kenya* 118 C4 0 23 S 36 56 E
Nyerol, *Sudan* 107 F3 8 41N 32 1 E
Nyhammar, *Sweden* 16 D8 60 17N 14 58 E
Nyika Nat. Park, *Malawi* 119 E3 10 30 S 33 53 E
Nyinahin, *Ghana* 112 D4 6 43N 2 3W
Nyíradony, *Hungary* 52 C6 47 41N 21 55 E
Nyírbátor, *Hungary* 52 C7 47 49N 22 9 E
Nyíregyháza, *Hungary* 52 C6 47 58N 21 47 E
Nykirke, *Norway* 18 D7 60 54N 10 19 E
Nykøbing, *Storstrøm, Denmark* 17 K5 54 56N 11 52 E
Nykøbing, *Vestsjælland, Denmark* 17 J5 55 55N 11 40 E
Nykøbing, *Viborg, Denmark* 17 H2 56 48N 8 51 E
Nyköping, *Sweden* 17 F11 58 45N 17 1 E
Nykroppa, *Sweden* 16 E8 59 37N 14 18 E
Nykvarn, *Sweden* 16 E11 59 11N 17 25 E
Nyland, *Sweden* 16 A11 63 1N 17 45 E
Nylstroom, *S. Africa* 117 C4 24 42 S 28 22 E
Nymagee, *Australia* 129 B7 32 7 S 146 20 E
Nymboida Nat. Park, *Australia* 127 D5 29 38 S 152 26 E
Nymburk, *Czech Rep.* 34 A8 50 10N 15 1 E
Nynäshamn, *Sweden* 17 F11 58 54N 17 57 E
Nyngan, *Australia* 129 A7 31 30 S 147 8 E
Nyoma Rap, *India* 93 C8 33 10N 78 40 E
Nyoman = Neman →, *Lithuania* 15 J19 55 25N 21 10 E
Nyon, *Switz.* 32 D2 46 23N 6 14 E
Nyong →, *Cameroon* 113 E6 3 17N 9 54 E
Nyons, *France* 29 D9 44 22N 5 10 E
Nyou, *Burkina Faso* 113 C4 12 42N 2 1W
Nýrsko, *Czech Rep.* 34 B6 49 18N 13 9 E
Nysa, *Poland* 55 H4 50 30N 17 22 E
Nysa →, *Europe* 30 C10 52 4N 14 46 E
Nysa Kłodzka →, *Poland* 55 H4 50 49N 17 40 E
Nysäter, *Sweden* 16 E6 59 17N 12 47 E
Nyseter, *Norway* 18 B5 62 6N 8 50 E
Nyssa, *U.S.A.* 158 E5 43 53N 117 0W
Nysted, *Denmark* 17 K5 54 40N 11 44 E
Nytva, *Russia* 64 C5 57 56N 55 20 E
Nyunzu, *Dem. Rep. of the Congo* 118 D2 5 57 S 27 58 E
Nyurba, *Russia* 67 C12 63 17N 118 28 E
Nyzhnohirskyy, *Ukraine* 59 K8 45 27N 34 38 E
Nzébéla, *Guinea* 112 D3 8 9N 9 7W
Nzega, *Tanzania* 118 C3 4 10 S 33 12 E
Nzérékoré, *Guinea* 112 D3 7 49N 8 48W
Nzeto, *Angola* 115 D2 7 10 S 12 52 E
Nzilo, Chutes de, *Dem. Rep. of the Congo* 119 E2 10 18 S 25 27 E
Nzo →, *Ivory C.* 112 D3 6 15N 7 3W
N'Zo, Réserve de Faune du, *Ivory C.* 112 D3 6 15N 7 15W
Nzubuka, *Tanzania* 118 C3 4 45 S 32 50 E
Nzwani = Anjouan, *Comoros Is.* 121 a 12 15 S 44 20 E

O

O Barco, *Spain* 42 C4 42 23N 6 58W
O Carballiño, *Spain* 42 C2 42 26N 8 5W
O Corgo, *Spain* 42 C3 42 56N 7 25W
O Le Pupū Pu'e Nat. Park, *Samoa* 133 W24 13 59 S 171 43W
O Pino, *Spain* 42 C2 42 56N 8 20W
O Porriño, *Spain* 42 C2 42 10N 8 37W
Ō-Shima, *Fukuoka, Japan* 72 D2 30 53N 130 28 E
Ō-Shima, *Nagasaki, Japan* 72 C1 33 29N 129 33 E
Ō-Shima, *Shizuoka, Japan* 73 C11 34 44N 139 24 E
Oa, Mull of, *U.K.* 22 F2 55 35N 6 20W
Oacoma, *U.S.A.* 154 D5 43 48N 99 24W
Oahe, L., *U.S.A.* 154 C4 44 27N 100 24W
Oahe Dam, *U.S.A.* 154 C4 44 27N 100 24W
Oahu, *U.S.A.* 145 K14 21 28N 157 58W
Oak Creek, *U.S.A.* 157 B9 42 52N 87 55W
Oak Harbor, *U.S.A.* 160 B4 48 18N 122 39W
Oak Hill, *Fla., U.S.A.* 153 G9 28 52N 80 51W
Oak Hill, *W. Va., U.S.A.* 148 G5 37 59N 81 9W
Oak Lawn, *U.S.A.* 157 C9 41 43N 87 44W
Oak Park, *Ga., U.S.A.* 152 C7 32 22N 82 19W
Oak Park, *Ill., U.S.A.* 157 C9 41 53N 87 47W
Oak Ridge, *U.S.A.* 149 G3 36 1N 84 16W
Oak View, *U.S.A.* 161 L7 34 24N 119 18W
Oakan-Dake, *Japan* 70 C12 43 27N 144 10 E
Oakbank, *Australia* 128 B4 33 4 S 140 33 E
Oakdale, *Calif., U.S.A.* 160 H6 37 46N 120 51W
Oakdale, *La., U.S.A.* 155 K8 30 49N 92 40W
Oakes, *U.S.A.* 154 B5 46 8N 98 6W
Oakesdale, *U.S.A.* 158 C5 47 8N 117 15W
Oakey, *Australia* 127 D5 27 25 S 151 43 E
Oakfield, *Ga., U.S.A.* 152 D6 31 47N 83 58W
Oakfield, *N.Y., U.S.A.* 150 C6 43 4N 78 16W
Oakford, *U.S.A.* 156 D7 40 6N 89 58W
Oakham, *U.K.* 21 E7 52 40N 0 43W
Oakhurst, *U.S.A.* 160 H7 37 19N 119 40W
Oakland, *Calif., U.S.A.* 160 H4 37 49N 122 16W
Oakland, *Ill., U.S.A.* 157 E8 39 39N 88 2W
Oakland City, *U.S.A.* 157 F9 38 20N 87 21W
Oaklands, *Australia* 129 C7 35 34 S 146 10 E
Oakley, *Idaho, U.S.A.* 158 E7 42 15N 113 53W
Oakley, *Kans., U.S.A.* 154 F4 39 8N 100 51W
Oakover →, *Australia* 124 D3 21 0 S 120 40 E
Oakridge, *U.S.A.* 158 E2 43 45N 122 28W
Oaktown, *U.S.A.* 157 F9 38 52N 87 27W
Oakville, *Canada* 150 C5 43 27N 79 41W
Oakville, *U.S.A.* 160 D3 46 51N 123 14W
Oakwood, *U.S.A.* 157 C12 41 6N 84 23W
Oamaru, *N.Z.* 131 F5 45 5 S 170 59 E
Ōamishirasato, *Japan* 73 B12 35 31N 140 18 E
Oancea, *Romania* 53 E12 45 21N 27 42 E
Oarai, *Japan* 73 A12 36 21N 140 34 E
Oasis, *Calif., U.S.A.* 161 M10 33 28N 116 6W
Oasis, *Nev., U.S.A.* 160 H9 37 29N 117 55W
Oates Land, *Antarctica* 7 C11 69 0 S 160 0 E
Oatlands, *Australia* 127 G4 42 17 S 147 21 E
Oatman, *U.S.A.* 161 K12 35 1N 114 19W
Oaxaca, *Mexico* 163 D5 17 2N 96 40W
Oaxaca □, *Mexico* 163 D5 17 0N 97 0W
Ob →, *Russia* 66 C7 66 45N 69 30 E
Oba, *Canada* 140 C3 49 4N 84 7W
Obala, *Cameroon* 113 E7 4 9N 11 32 E
Obama, *Fukui, Japan* 73 B7 35 30N 135 45 E
Obama, *Nagasaki, Japan* 72 E2 32 43N 130 13 E
Oban, *Nigeria* 113 D6 5 17N 8 33 E
Oban, *U.K.* 22 E3 56 25N 5 29W
Obbia, *Somali Rep.* 120 C3 5 25N 48 30 E
Ober-Aargau, *Switz.* 32 B5 47 10N 7 45 E
Ober-engadin, *Switz.* 33 C9 46 35N 9 55 E
Obera, *Argentina* 175 B4 27 21 S 55 2W
Oberalppass, *Switz.* 33 C7 46 39N 8 35 E
Oberalpstock, *Switz.* 33 C7 46 45N 8 47 E
Oberammergau, *Germany* 31 H7 47 36N 11 4 E
Oberasbach, *Germany* 31 F6 49 25N 10 57 E
Oberbayern □, *Germany* 31 G7 48 5N 11 50 E
Oberdiessbach, *Switz.* 32 C5 46 51N 7 40 E
Oberdrauburg, *Austria* 34 E5 46 44N 12 58 E
Oberentfelden, *Switz.* 32 B6 47 21N 8 2 E
Oberfranken □, *Germany* 31 E7 50 10N 11 20 E
Oberhausen, *Germany* 30 D2 51 28N 6 51 E
Oberkirch, *Germany* 31 G4 48 31N 8 4 E
Oberland, *Switz.* 32 C5 46 35N 7 38 E
Oberlausitz, *Germany* 30 D10 51 16N 14 18 E
Oberlin, *Kans., U.S.A.* 154 F4 39 49N 100 32W
Oberlin, *La., U.S.A.* 155 K8 30 37N 92 46W
Oberlin, *Ohio, U.S.A.* 150 E2 41 18N 82 13W
Obernai, *France* 27 D14 48 28N 7 30 E
Oberndorf, *Germany* 31 G4 48 17N 8 34 E
Oberon, *Australia* 129 B8 33 45 S 149 52 E
Oberösterreich □, *Austria* 34 C7 48 10N 14 0 E
Oberpfalz □, *Germany* 31 F8 49 20N 12 10 E
Oberpfälzer Wald, *Germany* 31 F8 49 30N 12 30 E
Oberriet, *Switz.* 33 B9 47 19N 9 34 E
Obersiggenthal, *Switz.* 33 B6 47 29N 8 18 E
Oberstdorf, *Germany* 31 H6 47 24N 10 15 E
Oberting, *Gabon* 114 C1 0 22 S 9 46 E
Oberursel, *Germany* 31 E4 50 11N 8 35 E
Oberwart, *Austria* 35 D9 47 17N 16 12 E
Oberwil, *Switz.* 32 A5 47 32N 7 33 E
Obi, *Indonesia* 82 B3 1 23 S 127 45 E
Obiaruku, *Nigeria* 113 D6 5 51N 6 9 E
Óbidos, *Brazil* 169 D6 1 50 S 55 30W
Óbidos, *Portugal* 43 F1 39 19N 9 10W
Obigarm, *Tajikistan* 65 D4 38 43N 69 42 E
Obihiro, *Japan* 70 C11 42 56N 143 12 E
Obikiik, *Tajikistan* 65 D4 38 9N 68 39 E
Obilatu, *Indonesia* 82 B3 1 25 S 127 20 E
Obilnoye, *Russia* 61 G7 47 32N 44 30 E
Obing, *Germany* 31 G8 48 0N 12 24 E
Objat, *France* 28 C5 45 16N 1 24 E
Oblong, *U.S.A.* 157 F9 39 0N 87 55W
Obluchye, *Russia* 67 E14 49 1N 131 4 E
Obninsk, *Russia* 58 E9 55 8N 36 37 E
Obo, *C.A.R.* 118 A2 5 20N 26 32 E
Oboa, Mt., *Uganda* 118 B3 1 45N 34 45 E
Obock, *Djibouti* 107 E5 12 0N 43 20 E
Oborniki, *Poland* 55 F3 52 39N 16 50 E
Oborniki Śląskie, *Poland* 55 G3 51 17N 16 53 E
Obouya, *Congo* 114 C3 0 56 S 15 43 E
Oboyan, *Russia* 59 G9 51 15N 36 21 E
Obozerskaya = Obozerskiy, *Russia* 56 B7 63 34N 40 21 E
Obozerskiy, *Russia* 56 B7 63 34N 40 21 E
Obrenovac, *Serbia, Yug.* 50 B4 44 40N 20 11 E
O'Brien, *U.S.A.* 152 E7 30 2N 82 57W
Obrovac, *Croatia* 45 D12 44 11N 15 41 E
Obruk, *Turkey* 100 C5 38 7N 33 12 E
Obrzycko, *Poland* 55 F3 52 42N 16 32 E
Observatory Inlet, *Canada* 142 B3 55 10N 129 54W
Obshchi Syrt, *Russia* 64 E4 52 0N 53 0 E
Obskaya Guba, *Russia* 66 C8 69 0N 73 0 E
Obuasi, *Ghana* 113 D4 6 17N 1 40W
Obubra, *Nigeria* 113 D6 6 8N 8 20 E
Obudu, *Nigeria* 113 D6 6 38N 9 5 E
Obura, *Papua N. G.* 132 D3 6 33 S 145 58 E
Obwalden □, *Switz.* 32 C6 46 55N 8 15 E
Obzor, *Bulgaria* 51 D11 42 50N 27 52 E
Ocala, *U.S.A.* 149 L4 29 11N 82 8W
Ocamo →, *Venezuela* 169 C4 2 48N 65 14W
Ocampo, *Chihuahua, Mexico* 162 B3 28 9N 108 24W
Ocampo, *Tamaulipas, Mexico* 163 C5 22 50N 99 20W
Ocaña, *Colombia* 168 B3 8 15N 73 20W
Ocaña, *Spain* 42 F7 39 55N 3 30W
Ocanomowoc, *U.S.A.* 154 D10 43 7N 88 30W
Occidental, Cordillera, *Colombia* 168 C3 5 0N 76 0W
Occidental, Cordillera, *Peru* 172 C3 14 0 S 74 0W
Occidental, Grand Erg, *Algeria* 111 B5 30 20N 1 0 E
Ocean City, *Md., U.S.A.* 148 F8 38 20N 75 5W
Ocean City, *N.J., U.S.A.* 148 F8 39 17N 74 35W
Ocean City, *Wash., U.S.A.* 160 C2 47 4N 124 10W
Ocean Falls, *Canada* 142 C3 52 18N 127 48W
Ocean I. = Banaba, *Kiribati* 134 H8 0 45 S 169 50 E
Ocean Park, *U.S.A.* 160 D2 46 30N 124 3W
Oceano, *U.S.A.* 161 K6 35 6N 120 37W
Oceanport, *U.S.A.* 151 F10 40 19N 74 3W
Oceanside, *U.S.A.* 161 M9 33 12N 117 23W
Ochagavía, *Spain* 40 C3 42 55N 1 5W
Ochakiv, *Ukraine* 59 J6 46 37N 31 33 E
Ochamchira, *Georgia* 61 J5 42 46N 41 32 E
Ocher, *Russia* 64 C5 57 53N 54 42 E
Ochiai, *Japan* 72 B5 35 1N 133 45 E
Ochil Hills, *U.K.* 22 E5 56 14N 3 40W
Ochlocknee, *U.S.A.* 152 E5 30 58N 84 3W
Ochlockonee →, *U.S.A.* 152 F5 29 59N 84 26W
Ocho Rios, *Jamaica* 164 a 18 24N 77 6W
Ochopee, *U.S.A.* 153 K8 25 54N 81 18W
Ochsenfurt, *Germany* 31 F6 49 40N 10 4 E
Ochsenhausen, *Germany* 31 G5 48 4N 9 57 E
Ocilla, *U.S.A.* 152 D6 31 36N 83 15W
Ockelbo, *Sweden* 16 D10 60 54N 16 45 E
Ocmulgee →, *U.S.A.* 152 D7 31 58N 82 33W
Ocna Mureş, *Romania* 53 D8 46 23N 23 55 E
Ocna Sibiului, *Romania* 53 E9 45 52N 24 2 E
Ocnele Mari, *Romania* 53 E9 45 8N 24 18 E
Ocniţa, *Moldova* 53 B12 48 25N 27 30 E
Ocoee, *U.S.A.* 153 G8 28 34N 81 33W
Ocoña, *Peru* 172 D3 16 26 S 73 8W
Ocoña →, *Peru* 172 D3 16 28 S 73 8W
Oconee →, *U.S.A.* 152 D7 31 58N 82 33W
Oconee, L., *U.S.A.* 152 B6 33 28N 83 15W
Oconomowoc, *U.S.A.* 157 A8 43 7N 88 30W
Oconto, *U.S.A.* 148 C2 44 53N 87 52W
Oconto Falls, *U.S.A.* 148 C1 44 52N 88 9W
Ocosingo, *Mexico* 163 D6 17 10N 92 15W
Ocotal, *Nic.* 164 D2 13 41N 86 31W
Ocotlán, *Mexico* 162 C4 20 21N 102 42W
Ocotlán de Morelos, *Mexico* 163 D5 16 48N 96 40W
Ocreza →, *Portugal* 43 F3 39 32N 7 50W
Öcsa, *Hungary* 52 C4 47 17N 19 15 E
Octeville, *France* 26 C5 49 38N 1 40W
Ocumare del Tuy, *Venezuela* 168 A4 10 7N 66 46W
Ocuri, *Bolivia* 173 D4 18 45 S 65 50W
Oda, *Ghana* 113 D4 5 50N 0 51W
Ōda, *Japan* 72 B4 35 11N 132 30 E
Oda, J., *Sudan* 106 C4 20 21N 36 39 E
Ódáðahraun, *Iceland* 11 B9 65 5N 17 0W
Ödåkra, *Sweden* 17 H6 56 7N 12 45 E
Odammun →, *Indonesia* 83 C5 4 50 S 138 45 E
Odate, *Japan* 70 D10 40 16N 140 34 E
Odawara, *Japan* 73 B11 35 20N 139 6 E
Odda, *Norway* 15 F12 60 3N 6 35 E
Odder, *Denmark* 17 J4 55 58N 10 10 E
Oddur, *Somali Rep.* 120 D2 4 11N 43 52 E
Odei →, *Canada* 143 B9 56 6N 96 54W
Odell, *U.S.A.* 157 C8 41 0N 88 31W
Odemira, *Portugal* 43 H2 37 35N 8 40W
Ödemiş, *Turkey* 49 C9 38 15N 28 0 E
Odendaalsrus, *S. Africa* 116 D4 27 48 S 26 45 E
Odensbacken, *Sweden* 16 E9 59 10N 15 32 E
Odense, *Denmark* 17 J4 55 22N 10 23 E
Odenwald, *Germany* 31 F5 49 35N 9 0 E
Oder →, *Europe* 30 B10 53 33N 14 38 E
Oder-Havel Kanal, *Germany* 30 C10 52 52N 14 2 E
Oderzo, *Italy* 45 C9 45 47N 12 29 E
Odesa, *Ukraine* 59 J6 46 30N 30 45 E
Ödeshög, *Sweden* 17 F8 58 14N 14 39 E
Odessa = Odesa, *Ukraine* 59 J6 46 30N 30 45 E
Odessa, *Canada* 151 B8 44 17N 76 43W
Odessa, *Mo., U.S.A.* 156 F3 39 0N 93 57W
Odessa, *Tex., U.S.A.* 155 K3 31 52N 102 23W
Odessa, *Wash., U.S.A.* 158 C4 47 20N 118 41W
Odiakwe, *Botswana* 116 C4 20 12 S 25 17 E
Odiel →, *Spain* 43 H4 37 10N 6 55W
Odienné, *Ivory C.* 112 D3 9 30N 7 34W
Odimba, *Gabon* 114 C2 2 2 S 9 33 E
Odintsovo, *Russia* 58 E9 55 39N 37 15 E
Odiongan, *Phil.* 80 E3 12 24N 121 59 E
Odobeşti, *Romania* 53 E12 45 43N 27 4 E
Odolanów, *Poland* 55 G4 51 34N 17 40 E
O'Donnell, *U.S.A.* 155 J4 32 58N 101 50W
Odorheiu Secuiesc, *Romania* 53 D10 46 21N 25 21 E
Odoyevo, *Russia* 58 F9 53 56N 36 42 E
Odra = Oder →, *Europe* 30 B10 53 33N 14 38 E
Odra →, *Spain* 42 C6 42 14N 4 17W
Odum, *U.S.A.* 152 D7 31 40N 82 2W
Odweina, *Somali Rep.* 120 C3 9 25N 45 4 E
Odžaci, *Serbia, Yug.* 52 E4 45 30N 19 17 E
Odžak, *Bos.-H.* 52 E3 45 3N 18 18 E
Odzala, *Congo* 114 B2 0 37N 14 37 E
Odzala, Parc Nat. d', *Congo* 114 B2 0 55N 14 55 E
Odzi, *Zimbabwe* 117 B5 19 0 S 32 20 E
Odzi →, *Zimbabwe* 117 B5 19 45 S 32 23 E
Oebisfelde, *Germany* 30 C6 52 27N 10 57 E
Oeiras, *Brazil* 170 C3 7 0 S 42 8W
Oeiras, *Portugal* 43 G1 38 41N 9 18W
Oeiras do Para, *Brazil* 169 D8 1 58 S 49 51W
Oelrichs, *U.S.A.* 154 D3 43 11N 103 14W
Oelsnitz, *Germany* 31 E8 50 24N 12 10 E
Oelwein, *U.S.A.* 156 B5 42 41N 91 55W
Oenpelli, *Australia* 124 B5 12 20 S 133 4 E
Oetz, *Austria* 34 D3 47 13N 10 53 E
Of, *Turkey* 101 B9 40 59N 40 23 E
O'Fallon, *U.S.A.* 156 F6 38 49N 90 42W
Ofanto →, *Italy* 47 A9 41 22N 16 13 E
Offa, *Nigeria* 113 D5 8 13N 4 42 E
Offaly □, *Ireland* 23 C4 53 15N 7 30W
Offenbach, *Germany* 31 E4 50 6N 8 44 E
Offenburg, *Germany* 31 G3 48 28N 7 56 E
Offida, *Italy* 45 F10 42 56N 13 41 E
Offoué →, *Gabon* 114 C2 0 4 S 11 44 E
Ofidhousa, *Greece* 49 E8 36 33N 26 8 E
Ofir, *Portugal* 42 D2 41 31N 8 47W
Ofolanga, *Tonga* 133 P14 19 38 S 174 27W
Ofotfjorden, *Norway* 14 B17 68 27N 17 0 E
Ofte, *Norway* 18 E5 59 30N 8 12 E
Ofu, *Amer. Samoa* 133 X25 14 11 S 169 41W
Ōfunato, *Japan* 70 E10 39 4N 141 43 E
Oga, *Japan* 70 E9 39 55N 139 50 E
Oga-Hantō, *Japan* 70 E9 39 58N 139 47 E
Ogaden, *Ethiopia* 120 C3 7 30N 45 30 E
Ōgaki, *Japan* 73 B8 35 21N 136 37 E
Ogallala, *U.S.A.* 154 E4 41 8N 101 43W

Oualâta 261

Oppdal, *Norway* **15 E13** 62 35N 9 41 E
Óppido Mamertina, *Italy* **47 D8** 38 16N 15 59 E
Oppland □, *Norway* **18 C6** 61 15N 9 40 E
Opportunity, *U.S.A.* **158 C5** 47 39N 117 15W
Oprişor, *Romania* **52 F8** 44 17N 23 5 E
Oprtalj, *Croatia* **45 C10** 45 23N 13 50 E
Opua, *N.Z.* **130 B3** 35 19 S 174 9 E
Opunake, *N.Z.* **130 F2** 39 26 S 173 52 E
Opuwo, *Namibia* **116 B1** 18 3 S 13 45 E
Opuzen, *Croatia* **45 E14** 43 1N 17 34 E
Oquawka, *U.S.A.* **156 D6** 40 56N 90 57W
Ora, *Cyprus* **39 F9** 34 51N 33 12 E
Oracle, *U.S.A.* **159 K8** 32 37N 110 46W
Oracuzar, *Peru* **168 D2** 4 42 S 78 6W
Oradea, *Romania* **52 C6** 47 2N 21 58 E
Öræfajökull, *Iceland* **11 C10** 64 2N 16 39W
Orahovac, *Kosovo, Yug.* **50 D4** 42 24N 20 40 E
Orahovica, *Croatia* **52 E2** 45 35N 17 52 E
Orai, *India* **93 G8** 25 58N 79 30 E
Oraison, *France* **29 E9** 43 55N 5 55 E
Oral = Zhayyq →, *Kazakstan* **57 E9** 47 0N 51 48 E
Oral, *Kazakstan* **60 E10** 51 20N 51 20 E
Oran, *Algeria* **111 A4** 35 45N 0 39W
Orange, *Australia* **129 B8** 33 15 S 149 7 E
Orange, *France* **29 D8** 44 8N 4 47 E
Orange, *Calif., U.S.A.* **161 M9** 33 47N 117 51W
Orange, *Mass., U.S.A.* **151 D12** 42 35N 72 19W
Orange, *Tex., U.S.A.* **155 K8** 30 6N 93 44W
Orange, *Va., U.S.A.* **148 F6** 38 15N 78 7W
Orange →, *S. Africa* **116 D2** 28 41 S 16 28 E
Orange, C., *Brazil* **169 C7** 4 20N 51 30W
Orange City, *U.S.A.* **153 G8** 28 57N 81 18W
Orange Cove, *U.S.A.* **160 J7** 36 38N 119 19W
Orange Free State = Free State □, *S. Africa* **116 D4** 28 30 S 27 0 E
Orange Grove, *U.S.A.* **155 M6** 27 58N 97 56W
Orange L., *U.S.A.* **153 F7** 29 25N 82 13W
Orange Park, *U.S.A.* **152 E8** 30 10N 81 42W
Orange Walk, *Belize* **163 D7** 18 6N 88 33W
Orangeburg, *U.S.A.* **152 B9** 33 30N 80 52W
Orangeville, *Canada* **140 D3** 43 55N 80 5W
Orangeville, *U.S.A.* **156 B7** 42 28N 89 39W
Orango, *Guinea-Biss.* **112 C1** 11 5N 16 0W
Orani, *Phil.* **80 D3** 14 49N 120 32 E
Oranienburg, *Germany* **30 C9** 52 45N 13 14 E
Oranje = Orange →, *S. Africa* **116 D2** 28 41 S 16 28 E
Oranje Vrystaat = Free State □, *S. Africa* **116 D4** 28 30 S 27 0 E
Oranjemund, *Namibia* **116 D2** 28 38 S 16 29 E
Oranjerivier, *S. Africa* **116 D3** 29 40 S 24 12 E
Oranjestad, *Aruba* **165 D5** 12 32N 70 2W
Orap, *Vanuatu* **133 E5** 15 58 S 167 20 E
Orarak, *Sudan* **107 F3** 6 15N 32 23 E
Oras, *Phil.* **80 E5** 12 9N 125 28 E
Orašje, *Bos.-H.* **52 E3** 45 1N 18 42 E
Orăştie, *Romania* **53 E8** 45 50N 23 10 E
Oraşul Stalin = Braşov, *Romania* **53 E10** 45 38N 25 35 E
Orava →, *Slovak Rep.* **35 B12** 49 9N 19 8 E
Orava, Vodna nádrž, *Slovak Rep.* **35 B12** 49 25N 19 35 E
Oraviţa, *Romania* **52 E6** 45 2N 21 43 E
Orawia, *N.Z.* **131 G2** 46 1 S 167 50 E
Orb →, *France* **28 E7** 43 15N 3 18 E
Orba →, *Italy* **44 D5** 44 53N 8 37 E
Ørbæk, *Denmark* **17 J4** 55 17N 10 39 E
Orbe, *Switz.* **32 C3** 46 43N 6 32 E
Orbec, *France* **26 C7** 49 1N 0 23 E
Orbetello, *Italy* **45 F8** 42 27N 11 13 E
Órbigo →, *Spain* **42 C5** 42 5N 5 42W
Orbisonia, *U.S.A.* **150 F7** 40 15N 77 54W
Orbost, *Australia* **129 D8** 37 40 S 148 29 E
Örbyhus, *Sweden* **16 D11** 60 15N 17 43 E
Orcas I., *U.S.A.* **160 B4** 48 42N 122 56W
Orce, *Spain* **41 H2** 37 44N 2 28W
Orce →, *Spain* **41 H2** 37 44N 2 28W
Orchard City, *U.S.A.* **159 G10** 38 50N 107 58W
Orchies, *France* **27 B10** 50 28N 3 14 E
Orchila, I., *Venezuela* **165 D6** 11 48N 66 10W
Órcia →, *Italy* **45 F8** 42 58N 11 21 E
Orco →, *Italy* **44 C4** 45 10N 7 52 E
Orcopampa, *Peru* **172 D3** 15 20 S 72 23W
Orcutt, *U.S.A.* **161 L6** 34 52N 120 27W
Ord, *U.S.A.* **154 E5** 41 36N 98 56W
Ord →, *Australia* **124 C4** 15 33 S 128 15 E
Ord, Mt., *Australia* **124 C4** 17 20 S 125 34 E
Ordenes = Ordes, *Spain* **42 B2** 43 5N 8 29W
Orderville, *U.S.A.* **159 H7** 37 17N 112 38W
Ordes, *Spain* **42 B2** 43 5N 8 29W
Ording = St-Peter-Ording, *Germany* **30 A4** 54 20N 8 36 E
Ordos = Mu Us Shamo, *China* **74 E5** 39 0N 109 0 E
Ordu, *Turkey* **100 B7** 40 55N 37 53 E
Ordubad, *Azerbaijan* **101 C12** 38 54N 46 1 E
Orduña, *Álava, Spain* **40 C2** 42 58N 2 58W
Orduña, *Granada, Spain* **43 H7** 37 20N 3 30W
Ordway, *U.S.A.* **154 F3** 38 13N 103 46W
Ordzhonikidze = Vladikavkaz, *Russia* **61 J7** 43 0N 44 35 E
Ordzhonikidze, *Kazakstan* **64 E8** 52 27N 61 39 E
Ordzhonikidze, *Ukraine* **59 J8** 47 39N 34 3 E
Ordzhonikidzeabad = Kofarnikhon, *Tajikistan* **65 D4** 38 34N 69 1 E
Ore, *Dem. Rep. of the Congo* **118 B2** 3 17N 29 30 E
Ore Mts. = Erzgebirge, *Germany* **30 E8** 50 27N 12 55 E
Orealla, *Guyana* **169 B6** 5 15N 57 23W
Orebić, *Croatia* **45 F14** 43 0N 17 11 E
Örebro, *Sweden* **16 E9** 59 20N 15 18 E
Örebro län □, *Sweden* **16 E8** 59 27N 15 0 E
Oregon, *Ill., U.S.A.* **156 B7** 42 1N 89 20W
Oregon, *Ohio, U.S.A.* **157 C13** 41 38N 83 25W
Oregon, *Wis., U.S.A.* **156 B7** 42 56N 89 23W
Oregon □, *U.S.A.* **158 E3** 44 0N 121 0W
Oregon City, *U.S.A.* **160 E4** 45 21N 122 36W
Öregrund, *Sweden* **16 D12** 60 21N 18 30 E
Öregrundsgrepen, *Sweden* **16 D12** 60 25N 18 15 E
Orekhov = Orikhiv, *Ukraine* **59 J8** 47 30N 35 48 E
Orekhovo-Zuyevo, *Russia* **58 E10** 55 50N 38 55 E
Orel, *Russia* **59 F9** 52 57N 36 3 E
Orel →, *Ukraine* **59 H8** 48 40N 34 39 E
Orellana, *Spain* **43 F5** 39 1N 5 32W
Orellana, Canal de, *Spain* **43 F5** 39 2N 6 0W
Orellana, Embalse de, *Spain* **43 F5** 39 5N 5 10W
Orem, *U.S.A.* **158 F8** 40 19N 111 42W
Ören, *Turkey* **49 D9** 37 3N 27 57 E
Orenburg, *Russia* **64 F5** 51 45N 55 6 E
Örencik, *Turkey* **49 B11** 39 16N 29 33 E
Orense = Ourense, *Spain* **42 C3** 42 19N 7 55W
Orense □, *Spain* **42 C3** 42 15N 7 51W
Orepuki, *N.Z.* **131 G2** 46 19 S 167 46 E
Orestiás, *Greece* **51 E10** 41 30N 26 33 E
Orestos Pereyra, *Mexico* **162 B3** 26 31N 105 40W
Øresund, *Europe* **17 J6** 55 45N 12 45 E
Oreti →, *N.Z.* **131 G3** 46 28 S 168 14 E
Orford Ness, *U.K.* **21 E9** 52 5N 1 35 E
Organà = Organyà, *Spain* **40 C6** 42 13N 1 20 E
Organos, Pta. de los, *Canary Is.* **9 e1** 28 12N 17 17W
Organyà, *Spain* **40 C6** 42 13N 1 20 E
Orgaz, *Spain* **43 F7** 39 39N 3 53W
Ørgenvika, *Norway* **18 D6** 60 17N 9 42 E
Orgeyev = Orhei, *Moldova* **53 C13** 47 24N 28 50 E
Orgūn, *Afghan.* **91 B3** 32 55N 69 12 E
Orhaneli, *Turkey* **51 G12** 39 54N 28 59 E
Orhaneli →, *Turkey* **51 G12** 39 50N 28 55 E
Orhangazi, *Turkey* **51 F13** 40 29N 29 18 E
Orhei, *Moldova* **53 C13** 47 24N 28 50 E
Orhon Gol →, *Mongolia* **68 A5** 50 21N 106 0 E
Ória, *Italy* **47 B10** 40 30N 17 38 E
Orida, *Niger* **111 D7** 21 20N 12 15 E
Oriental, Cordillera, *Bolivia* **173 D4** 17 0 S 66 0W
Oriental, Cordillera, *Colombia* **168 B3** 6 0N 73 0W
Oriental, Grand Erg, *Algeria* **111 C6** 30 0N 6 30 E
Orientale □, *Dem. Rep. of the Congo* **118 B2** 2 20N 26 0 E
Oriente, *Argentina* **174 D3** 38 44 S 60 37W
Orihuela, *Spain* **41 G4** 38 7N 0 55W
Orihuela del Tremedal, *Spain* **40 E3** 40 33N 1 39W
Orikhiv, *Ukraine* **59 J8** 47 30N 35 48 E
Orikum, *Albania* **50 F3** 40 20N 19 26 E
Orillia, *Canada* **140 D4** 44 40N 79 24W
Orinduik, *Guyana* **169 C5** 4 40N 60 3W
Orinoco →, *Venezuela* **169 B5** 9 15N 61 30W
Orion, *Canada* **143 D6** 49 27N 110 49W
Orion, *Ala., U.S.A.* **152 D4** 31 58N 86 0W
Orion, *Ill., U.S.A.* **156 C6** 41 21N 90 23W
Oriskany, *U.S.A.* **151 C9** 43 10N 75 20W
Orissa □, *India* **94 E7** 20 0N 84 0 E
Orissaare, *Estonia* **15 G20** 58 34N 23 5 E
Oristano, *Italy* **46 C1** 39 54N 8 36 E
Oristano, G. di, *Italy* **46 C1** 39 50N 8 29 E
Orituco →, *Venezuela* **168 B4** 8 45N 67 27W
Oriximina, *Brazil* **169 D6** 1 45 S 55 52W
Orizaba, *Mexico* **163 D5** 18 51N 97 6W
Orizare, *Bulgaria* **51 D11** 42 44N 27 39 E
Orizona, *Brazil* **171 E2** 17 3 S 48 18W
Ørje, *Norway* **18 E8** 59 29N 11 39 E
Orjen, *Bos.-H.* **50 D2** 42 35N 18 34 E
Orjiva, *Spain* **43 J7** 36 53N 3 24W
Orkanger, *Norway* **14 E13** 63 18N 9 52 E
Örkelljunga, *Sweden* **17 H7** 56 17N 13 17 E
Örken, *Sweden* **17 G9** 57 6N 15 1 E
Örkény, *Hungary* **52 C4** 47 9N 19 26 E
Orkla →, *Norway* **14 E13** 63 18N 9 51 E
Orkney, *S. Africa* **116 D4** 26 58 S 26 40 E
Orkney □, *U.K.* **22 B5** 59 2N 3 13W
Orkney Is., *U.K.* **22 B6** 59 0N 3 0W
Orland, *Calif., U.S.A.* **160 F4** 39 45N 122 12W
Orland, *Ind., U.S.A.* **157 C11** 41 47N 85 12W
Orlando, *U.S.A.* **149 L5** 28 33N 81 23W
Orlando, C. d', *Italy* **47 D7** 38 10N 14 43 E
Orléanais, *France* **27 E9** 48 0N 2 0 E
Orléans, *France* **27 E8** 47 54N 1 52 E
Orleans, *Ind., U.S.A.* **157 F10** 38 40N 86 27W
Orleans, *Vt., U.S.A.* **151 B12** 44 49N 72 12W
Orléans, I. d', *Canada* **141 C5** 46 54N 70 58W
Orlice →, *Czech Rep.* **34 A8** 50 13N 15 50 E
Orlov, *Slovak Rep.* **35 B13** 49 17N 20 51 E
Orlov Gay, *Russia* **60 E9** 50 56N 48 19 E
Orlová, *Czech Rep.* **35 B11** 49 51N 18 26 E
Orlovat, *Serbia, Yug.* **52 E5** 45 14N 20 33 E
Orlovka, *Kyrgyzstan* **65 B7** 42 45N 75 36 E
Ormara, *Pakistan* **91 D2** 25 16N 64 33 E
Ormea, *Italy* **44 D4** 44 9N 7 54 E
Ormília, *Greece* **50 F7** 40 16N 23 39 E
Ormoc, *Phil.* **81 F5** 11 0N 124 37 E
Ormond, *N.Z.* **130 E6** 38 33 S 177 56 E
Ormond Beach, *U.S.A.* **149 L5** 29 17N 81 3W
Ormond by the Sea, *U.S.A.* **153 F8** 29 21N 81 4W
Ormondville, *N.Z.* **130 G5** 40 5 S 176 19 E
Órmos Keríou, *Greece* **39 D2** 37 42N 20 53 E
Ormož, *Slovenia* **45 B13** 46 25N 16 10 E
Ormskirk, *U.K.* **20 D5** 53 35N 2 54W
Ormstown, *Canada* **151 A11** 45 8N 74 0W
Ornans, *France* **27 E13** 47 7N 6 10 E
Ornavasso, *Italy* **33 E6** 45 58N 8 24 E
Orne □, *France* **26 D7** 48 40N 0 5 E
Orne →, *France* **26 C6** 49 18N 0 15W
Orneta, *Poland* **54 D7** 54 8N 20 9 E
Ornö, *Sweden* **16 E12** 59 4N 18 24 E
Örnsköldsvik, *Sweden* **16 A12** 63 17N 18 40 E
Oro, *N. Korea* **75 D14** 40 1N 127 27 E
Oro →, *Mexico* **162 B3** 25 35N 105 2W
Oro Grande, *U.S.A.* **161 L9** 34 36N 117 20W
Oro Valley, *U.S.A.* **159 K8** 32 26N 110 58W
Orobie, Alpi, *Italy* **44 B6** 46 7N 10 0 E
Orocué, *Colombia* **168 C3** 4 48N 71 20W
Orodara, *Burkina Faso* **112 C4** 11 0N 4 55W
Orodo, *Nigeria* **113 D6** 5 34N 7 4 E
Orofino, *U.S.A.* **158 C5** 46 29N 116 15W
Orohena, Mt., *Tahiti* **133 S16** 17 37 S 149 28W
Orol Dengizi = Aral Sea, *Asia* **66 E7** 44 30N 60 0 E
Oromocto, *Canada* **141 C6** 45 54N 66 29W
Oron, *Nigeria* **113 E6** 4 48N 8 14 E
Oron, *Switz.* **32 C3** 46 34N 6 50 E
Orongo, *Chile* **172 b** 27 11 S 109 27W
Orono, *Canada* **150 C6** 43 59N 78 37W
Orono, *U.S.A.* **149 C11** 44 53N 68 40W
Oronsay, *U.K.* **22 E2** 56 1N 6 15W
Oropesa, *Spain* **42 F5** 39 57N 5 10W
Oroqen Zizhiqi, *China* **69 A7** 50 34N 123 43 E
Oroquieta, *Phil.* **81 G4** 8 32N 123 44 E
Orós, *Brazil* **170 C4** 6 15 S 38 55W
Orosei, *Italy* **46 B2** 40 23N 9 42 E
Orosei, G. di, *Italy* **46 B2** 40 15N 9 44 E
Orosháza, *Hungary* **52 D5** 46 32N 20 42 E
Oroszlány, *Hungary* **52 C3** 47 29N 18 19 E
Orote Pen., *Guam* **133 R15** 13 26N 144 38 E
Orotukan, *Russia* **67 C16** 62 16N 151 42 E
Oroville, *Calif., U.S.A.* **160 F5** 39 31N 121 33W
Oroville, *Wash., U.S.A.* **158 B4** 48 56N 119 26W
Oroville, L., *U.S.A.* **160 F5** 39 33N 121 29W
Orrefors, *Sweden* **17 H9** 56 50N 15 45 E
Orrick, *U.S.A.* **156 E2** 39 13N 94 7W
Orroroo, *Australia* **128 B3** 32 43 S 138 38 E
Orrviken, *Sweden* **16 A8** 63 6N 14 26 E
Orrville, *U.S.A.* **150 F3** 40 50N 81 46W
Orsa, *Sweden* **16 C8** 61 7N 14 37 E
Orsara di Púglia, *Italy* **47 A8** 41 17N 15 16 E
Orsasjön, *Sweden* **16 C8** 61 7N 14 37 E
Orsha, *Belarus* **58 E6** 54 30N 30 25 E
Orsières, *Switz.* **32 D4** 46 2N 7 9 E
Örsjö, *Sweden* **17 H9** 56 42N 15 45 E
Orsk, *Russia* **64 F7** 51 12N 58 34 E
Orşova, *Romania* **52 F7** 44 41N 22 25 E
Ørsta, *Norway* **18 B3** 62 13N 6 8 E
Ørsted, *Denmark* **17 H4** 56 30N 10 20 E
Örsundsbro, *Sweden* **16 E11** 59 44N 17 18 E
Orta, L. d', *Italy* **44 C5** 45 49N 8 24 E
Orta Nova, *Italy* **47 A8** 41 19N 15 42 E
Ortaca, *Turkey* **49 E10** 36 49N 28 45 E
Ortakent, *Turkey* **49 D9** 37 5N 27 21 E
Ortaklar, *Turkey* **49 D9** 37 53N 27 30 E
Ortaköy, *Çorum, Turkey* **100 B6** 40 16N 35 15 E
Ortaköy, *Niğde, Turkey* **100 C6** 38 44N 34 3 E
Orte, *Italy* **45 F9** 42 27N 12 23 E
Ortegal, C., *Spain* **42 B3** 43 43N 7 52W
Orteguaza →, *Colombia* **168 C2** 0 43N 75 16W
Orthez, *France* **28 E3** 43 29N 0 48W
Ortigueira, *Spain* **42 B3** 43 40N 7 50W
Orting, *U.S.A.* **160 C4** 47 6N 122 12W
Ortisei, *Italy* **45 B8** 46 34N 11 40 E
Ortles, *Italy* **44 B7** 46 31N 10 33 E
Ortnevik, *Norway* **18 C3** 61 6N 6 7 E
Orto-Tokoy, *Kyrgyzstan* **65 B8** 42 20N 76 1 E
Ortón →, *Bolivia* **172 C4** 10 50 S 67 0W
Ortona, *Italy* **45 F11** 42 21N 14 24 E
Ortonville, *U.S.A.* **154 C6** 45 19N 96 27W
Orūmīyeh, *Iran* **101 D11** 37 40N 45 0 E
Orūmīyeh, Daryācheh-ye, *Iran* **101 D11** 37 50N 45 30 E
Orune, *Italy* **46 B2** 40 24N 9 22 E
Oruro, *Bolivia* **172 D4** 18 0 S 67 9W
Oruro □, *Bolivia* **172 D4** 18 40 S 67 30W
Orust, *Sweden* **17 F5** 58 10N 11 40 E
Oruzgān □, *Afghan.* **91 B2** 33 30N 66 0 E
Orvault, *France* **26 E5** 47 17N 1 38W
Orvieto, *Italy* **45 F9** 42 43N 12 7 E
Orwell, *N.Y., U.S.A.* **151 C9** 43 35N 75 50W
Orwell, *Ohio, U.S.A.* **150 E4** 41 32N 80 52W
Orwell →, *U.K.* **21 F9** 51 59N 1 18 E
Orwigsburg, *U.S.A.* **151 F8** 40 38N 76 6W
Oryakhovo, *Bulgaria* **50 C7** 43 40N 23 57 E
Orzinuovi, *Italy* **44 C6** 45 24N 9 55 E
Orzyc →, *Poland* **55 F8** 52 46N 21 14 E
Orzysz, *Poland* **54 E8** 53 50N 21 58 E
Os, *Norway* **18 B8** 62 30N 11 14 E
Osa, *Russia* **64 C5** 57 17N 55 26 E
Osa →, *Norway* **18 C8** 61 18N 11 46 E
Osa →, *Poland* **54 E5** 53 33N 18 46 E
Osa, Pen. de, *Costa Rica* **164 E3** 8 0N 84 0W
Osage, *U.S.A.* **154 D8** 43 17N 92 49W
Osage →, *U.S.A.* **156 F5** 38 35N 91 57W
Osage City, *U.S.A.* **154 F7** 38 38N 95 50W
Ōsaka, *Japan* **73 C7** 34 40N 135 30 E
Ōsaka □, *Japan* **73 C7** 34 30N 135 30 E
Ōsaka-Wan, *Japan* **73 C7** 34 30N 135 18 E
Osaki, *Japan* **72 F3** 31 25N 131 2 E
Osan, *S. Korea* **75 F14** 37 11N 127 4 E
Osawatomie, *U.S.A.* **154 F7** 38 31N 94 57W
Osborne, *U.S.A.* **154 F5** 39 26N 98 42W
Osby, *Sweden* **17 H7** 56 23N 13 59 E
Osceola, *Ark., U.S.A.* **155 H10** 35 42N 89 58W
Osceola, *Iowa, U.S.A.* **156 C3** 41 2N 93 46W
Osceola, *Mo., U.S.A.* **156 F3** 38 3N 93 42W
Oschatz, *Germany* **30 D9** 51 17N 13 6 E
Oschersleben, *Germany* **30 C7** 52 2N 11 14 E
Öschiri, *Italy* **46 B2** 40 43N 9 6 E
Oscoda, *U.S.A.* **150 B1** 44 26N 83 20W
Osečina, *Serbia, Yug.* **50 B3** 44 23N 19 34 E
Ösel = Saaremaa, *Estonia* **15 G20** 58 30N 22 30 E
Osensjøen, *Norway* **18 C8** 61 13N 11 50 E
Osery, *Russia* **58 E10** 54 52N 38 28 E
Osgood, *U.S.A.* **157 E11** 39 8N 85 18W
Osgoode, *Canada* **151 A9** 45 8N 75 36W
Osh, *Kyrgyzstan* **66 E8** 40 37N 72 49 E
Oshawa, *Canada* **140 D4** 43 50N 78 50W
Oshigambo, *Namibia* **116 B2** 17 45 S 16 5 E
Oshkosh, *Nebr., U.S.A.* **154 E3** 41 24N 102 21W
Oshkosh, *Wis., U.S.A.* **154 C10** 44 1N 88 33W
Oshmyany = Ashmyany, *Belarus* **15 J21** 54 26N 25 52 E
Oshnovīyeh, *Iran* **96 B5** 37 2N 45 6 E
Oshogbo, *Nigeria* **113 D5** 7 48N 4 37 E
Oshtorīnān, *Iran* **97 C6** 34 1N 48 38 E
Oshwe, *Dem. Rep. of the Congo* **114 C3** 3 25 S 19 28 E
Osi, *Nigeria* **113 D6** 8 8N 5 14 E
Osieczna, *Poland* **55 G3** 51 55N 16 40 E
Osijek, *Croatia* **52 E3** 45 34N 18 41 E
Ósilo, *Italy* **46 B1** 40 45N 8 40 E
Ósimo, *Italy* **45 E10** 43 28N 13 30 E
Osintorf, *Belarus* **58 E6** 54 40N 30 39 E
Osipenko = Berdyansk, *Ukraine* **59 J9** 46 45N 36 50 E
Osipovichi = Asipovichy, *Belarus* **58 F5** 53 19N 28 33 E
Osiyan, *India* **92 F5** 26 43N 72 55 E
Osizweni, *S. Africa* **117 D5** 27 49 S 30 7 E
Oskaloosa, *U.S.A.* **156 C4** 41 18N 92 39W
Oskarshamn, *Sweden* **17 G10** 57 15N 16 27 E
Oskarström, *Sweden* **17 H6** 56 48N 12 58 E
Oskélanéo, *Canada* **140 C4** 48 5N 75 15W
Öskemen, *Kazakstan* **66 E9** 50 0N 82 36 E
Oskol →, *Ukraine* **59 H9** 49 6N 37 25 E
Oslo, *Norway* **15 G14** 59 55N 10 45 E
Oslo □, *Norway* **18 D7** 59 54N 10 43 E
Oslob, *Phil.* **81 G4** 9 31N 123 26 E
Oslofjorden, *Norway* **15 G14** 59 20N 10 35 E
Osmanabad, *India* **94 E3** 18 5N 76 10 E
Osmancık, *Turkey* **100 B6** 40 58N 34 47 E
Osmaniye, *Turkey* **100 D7** 37 5N 36 10 E
Osmanlı, *Turkey* **51 E10** 41 35N 26 51 E
Osmannagar, *India* **94 E4** 18 32N 79 20 E
Ösmo, *Sweden* **16 F11** 58 58N 17 55 E
Osnabrück, *Germany* **30 C4** 52 17N 8 3 E
Ośno Lubuskie, *Poland* **55 F1** 52 28N 14 51 E
Osoblaha, *Czech Rep.* **35 A10** 50 17N 17 44 E
Osogovska Planina, *Macedonia* **50 D6** 42 10N 22 30 E
Osor, *Italy* **45 D11** 44 42N 14 24 E
Osorio, *Brazil* **175 B5** 29 53 S 50 17W
Osório da Fonseca, *Brazil* **169 D6** 3 52 S 58 14W
Osorno, *Chile* **176 B2** 40 25 S 73 0W
Osorno, *Spain* **42 C6** 42 24N 4 22W
Osorno □, *Chile* **176 B2** 40 34 S 73 9W
Osorno, Vol., *Chile* **176 B2** 41 0 S 72 30W
Osoyoos, *Canada* **142 D5** 49 0N 119 30W
Osøyro, *Norway* **15 F11** 60 9N 5 30 E
Ospakseyri, *Iceland* **11 B5** 65 27N 21 26W
Ospika →, *Canada* **142 B4** 56 20N 124 0W
Osprey, *U.S.A.* **153 H7** 27 12N 82 29W
Osprey Reef, *Australia* **126 A4** 13 52 S 146 36 E
Oss, *Neths.* **24 C5** 51 46N 5 32 E
Ossa, Mt., *Australia* **127 G4** 41 52 S 146 3 E
Óssa, Óros, *Greece* **48 B4** 39 47N 22 42 E
Ossa de Montiel, *Spain* **41 G2** 38 58N 2 45W
Ossabaw I., *U.S.A.* **152 D8** 31 50N 81 5W
Ossabaw Sd., *U.S.A.* **152 D8** 31 50N 81 6W
Osse →, *France* **28 D4** 44 7N 0 17 E
Osse →, *Nigeria* **113 D6** 6 10N 5 20 E
Ossi, *Italy* **46 B1** 40 40N 8 35 E
Ossining, *U.S.A.* **151 E11** 41 10N 73 55W
Ossipee, *U.S.A.* **151 C13** 43 41N 71 7W
Ossokmanuan L., *Canada* **141 B7** 53 25N 65 0W
Ossora, *Russia* **67 D17** 59 20N 163 13 E
Ostashkov, *Russia* **58 D7** 57 4N 33 2 E
Östavall, *Sweden* **16 B9** 62 26N 15 29 E
Østby, *Norway* **18 C9** 61 15N 12 33 E
Oste →, *Germany* **30 B5** 53 49N 9 2 E
Ostend = Oostende, *Belgium* **24 C2** 51 15N 2 54 E
Ostend, *N.Z.* **130 C4** 36 48 S 175 2 E
Oster, *Ukraine* **59 G6** 50 57N 30 53 E
Osterburg, *Germany* **30 C7** 52 47N 11 45 E
Osterburg, *U.S.A.* **150 F6** 40 16N 78 31W
Osterburken, *Germany* **31 F5** 49 25N 9 26 E
Österbybruk, *Sweden* **16 D11** 60 13N 17 55 E
Österbymo, *Sweden* **17 G9** 57 49N 15 15 E
Österdalälven, *Sweden* **16 C7** 61 30N 13 45 E
Østerdalen, *Norway* **15 F14** 61 40N 10 50 E
Österfärnebo, *Sweden* **16 D10** 60 19N 16 48 E
Österforse, *Sweden* **16 A11** 63 9N 17 3 E
Östergötlands län □, *Sweden* **17 F9** 58 35N 15 45 E
Osterholz-Scharmbeck, *Germany* **30 B4** 53 13N 8 47 E
Østerild, *Denmark* **17 G2** 57 2N 8 51 E
Ostermundigen, *Switz.* **32 C4** 46 58N 7 27 E
Osterode, *Germany* **30 D6** 51 43N 10 15 E
Östersund, *Sweden* **16 A8** 63 10N 14 38 E
Östervåla, *Sweden* **16 D11** 60 11N 17 11 E
Østfold □, *Norway* **18 E8** 59 25N 11 25 E
Ostfriesische Inseln, *Germany* **30 B3** 53 42N 7 0 E
Ostfriesland, *Germany* **30 B3** 53 20N 7 30 E
Östhammar, *Sweden* **16 D12** 60 16N 18 22 E
Óstia, Lido di, *Italy* **45 G9** 41 43N 12 17 E
Ostíglia, *Italy* **45 C8** 45 4N 11 8 E
Östmark, *Sweden* **16 D6** 60 17N 12 45 E
Östra Husby, *Sweden* **17 F10** 58 35N 16 33 E
Ostrava, *Czech Rep.* **35 B11** 49 51N 18 18 E
Ostróda, *Poland* **54 E6** 53 42N 19 58 E
Ostrogozhsk, *Russia* **59 G10** 50 55N 39 7 E
Ostroh, *Ukraine* **59 G4** 50 20N 26 30 E
Ostrołęka, *Poland* **55 E8** 53 4N 21 32 E
Ostrov, *Bulgaria* **51 C8** 43 40N 24 9 E
Ostrov, *Czech Rep.* **34 A5** 50 18N 12 57 E
Ostrov, *Romania* **53 F12** 44 6N 27 24 E
Ostrov, *Russia* **58 D5** 57 25N 28 20 E
Ostrów Lubelski, *Poland* **55 G9** 51 29N 22 51 E
Ostrów Mazowiecka, *Poland* **55 F8** 52 50N 21 51 E
Ostrów Wielkopolski, *Poland* **55 G4** 51 36N 17 44 E
Ostrowiec-Świętokrzyski, *Poland* **55 H8** 50 55N 21 22 E
Ostrožac, *Bos.-H.* **52 G2** 43 43N 17 49 E
Ostrzeszów, *Poland* **55 G4** 51 25N 17 52 E
Ostseebad Kühlungsborn, *Germany* **30 A7** 54 8N 11 44 E
Osttirol □, *Austria* **34 E5** 46 50N 12 30 E
Ostuni, *Italy* **47 B10** 40 44N 17 35 E
Osum →, *Albania* **50 F4** 40 40N 20 10 E
Osŭm →, *Bulgaria* **51 C8** 43 40N 24 50 E
Ōsumi-Hantō, *Japan* **72 F2** 31 20N 130 55 E
Ōsumi-Kaikyō, *Japan* **71 J5** 30 55N 131 0 E
Ōsumi-Shotō, *Japan* **71 J5** 30 30N 130 0 E
Osun □, *Nigeria* **113 D5** 7 30N 4 30 E
Osuna, *Spain* **43 H5** 37 14N 5 8W
Oswegatchie →, *U.S.A.* **151 B9** 44 42N 75 30W
Oswego, *U.S.A.* **151 C8** 43 27N 76 31W
Oswego →, *U.S.A.* **151 C8** 43 27N 76 30W
Oswestry, *U.K.* **20 E4** 52 52N 3 3W
Oświęcim, *Poland* **55 H6** 50 2N 19 11 E
Ōta, *Fukui, Japan* **73 B8** 35 57N 136 3 E
Ōta, *Gumma, Japan* **73 A11** 36 18N 139 22 E
Ōta-Gawa →, *Japan* **72 C4** 34 21N 132 18 E
Otaci, *Moldova* **53 B12** 48 27N 27 47 E
Otago □, *N.Z.* **131 E4** 45 15 S 170 0 E
Otago Harbour, *N.Z.* **131 F5** 45 47 S 170 42 E
Otago Pen., *N.Z.* **131 F5** 45 48 S 170 39 E
Otaheite B., *Trin. & Tob.* **169 F9** 10 20N 61 30W
Otahuhu, *N.Z.* **130 C3** 36 56 S 174 51 E
Ōtake, *Japan* **72 C4** 34 12N 132 13 E
Ōtaki, *Japan* **73 B12** 35 17N 140 15 E
Otaki, *N.Z.* **130 G4** 40 45 S 175 10 E
Otane, *N.Z.* **130 F5** 39 54 S 176 39 E
Otar, *Kazakstan* **65 B7** 43 32N 75 12 E
Otaru, *Japan* **70 C10** 43 10N 141 0 E
Otaru-Wan = Ishikari-Wan, *Japan* **70 C10** 43 25N 141 1 E
Otautau, *N.Z.* **131 G3** 46 9 S 168 1 E
Otava →, *Czech Rep.* **34 B7** 49 26N 14 12 E
Otavalo, *Ecuador* **168 C2** 0 13N 78 20W
Otavi, *Namibia* **116 B2** 19 40 S 17 24 E
Otchinjau, *Angola* **116 B1** 16 30 S 13 56 E
Otelec, *Romania* **52 E5** 45 36N 20 50 E
Otelnuk L., *Canada* **141 A6** 56 9N 68 12W
Oţelu Roşu, *Romania* **52 E7** 45 32N 22 22 E
Otero de Rey = Outeiro de Rei, *Spain* **42 B3** 43 6N 7 36W
Othello, *U.S.A.* **158 C4** 46 50N 119 10W
Othonoí, *Greece* **38 B9** 39 52N 19 22 E
Óthris, Óros, *Greece* **48 B4** 39 2N 22 37 E
Oti, Réserve de Faune de l', *Togo* **113 C5** 10 40N 0 35 E
Otira, *N.Z.* **131 C6** 42 49 S 171 35 E
Otira Gorge, *N.Z.* **131 C6** 42 53 S 171 33 E
Otjiwarongo, *Namibia* **116 C2** 20 30 S 16 33 E
Otmök, *Kyrgyzstan* **65 B6** 42 20N 73 10 E
Otmuchów, *Poland* **55 H4** 50 28N 17 10 E
Oto Tolu Group, *Tonga* **133 Q13** 20 21 S 174 32W
Otočac, *Croatia* **45 D12** 44 53N 15 12 E
Otoineppu, *Japan* **70 B11** 44 44N 142 16 E
Otok, *Croatia* **45 E13** 43 42N 16 44 E
Oton, *Phil.* **81 F4** 10 42N 122 29 E
Otorohanga, *N.Z.* **130 E4** 38 12 S 175 14 E
Otoskwin →, *Canada* **140 B2** 52 13N 88 6W
Ōtoyo, *Japan* **72 D5** 33 43N 133 45 E
Otra →, *Norway* **15 G13** 58 9N 8 1 E
Otradnyy, *Russia* **60 D10** 53 22N 51 21 E
Otranto, *Italy* **47 B11** 40 9N 18 28 E
Otranto, C. d', *Italy* **47 B11** 40 7N 18 30 E
Otranto, Str. of, *Italy* **47 B11** 40 15N 18 40 E
Otrokovice, *Czech Rep.* **35 B10** 49 12N 17 32 E
Otse, *S. Africa* **116 D4** 25 2 S 25 45 E
Otsego, *U.S.A.* **157 B11** 42 27N 85 42W
Ōtsu, *Japan* **73 C7** 35 0N 135 50 E
Ōtsuki, *Japan* **73 B10** 35 36N 138 57 E
Otta, *Norway* **18 C6** 61 46N 9 32 E
Otta →, *Norway* **18 C6** 61 46N 9 31 E
Ottapalam, *India* **95 J3** 10 46N 76 23 E
Ottawa = Outaouais →, *Canada* **140 C5** 45 27N 74 8W
Ottawa, *Canada* **140 C4** 45 27N 75 42W
Ottawa, *Ill., U.S.A.* **154 E10** 41 21N 88 51W
Ottawa, *Kans., U.S.A.* **154 F7** 38 37N 95 16W
Ottawa, *Ohio, U.S.A.* **157 C12** 41 1N 84 3W
Ottawa Is., *Canada* **139 C11** 59 35N 80 10W
Ottélé, *Cameroon* **113 E7** 3 38N 11 19 E
Ottensheim, *Austria* **34 C7** 48 21N 14 12 E
Otter Cr. →, *U.S.A.* **151 B11** 44 13N 73 17W
Otter Creek, *U.S.A.* **153 F7** 29 19N 82 46W
Otter L., *Canada* **143 B8** 55 35N 104 39W
Otterbein, *U.S.A.* **157 D9** 40 29N 87 6W
Otterndorf, *Germany* **30 B4** 53 48N 8 53 E
Otterøya, *Norway* **18 B3** 62 45N 6 50 E
Otterup, *Denmark* **17 J4** 55 30N 10 22 E
Otterville, *Canada* **150 D4** 42 55N 80 36W
Otterville, *U.S.A.* **156 F4** 38 42N 93 0W
Ottery St. Mary, *U.K.* **21 G4** 50 44N 3 17W
Ottilien Reef, *Papua N. G.* **132 C5** 4 33 S 148 49 E
Otto Beit Bridge, *Zimbabwe* **119 F2** 15 59 S 28 56 E
Ottosdal, *S. Africa* **116 D4** 26 46 S 25 59 E
Ottoville, *U.S.A.* **157 D12** 40 57N 84 22W
Ottumwa, *U.S.A.* **156 D4** 41 1N 92 25W
Otu, *Nigeria* **113 D5** 8 14N 3 22 E
Otukpa, *Nigeria* **113 D6** 7 9N 7 41 E
Oturkpo, *Nigeria* **113 D6** 7 16N 8 8 E
Otway, B., *Chile* **176 D2** 53 30 S 74 0W
Otway, C., *Australia* **128 E5** 38 52 S 143 30 E
Otway, Seno de, *Chile* **176 D2** 53 0 S 71 30W
Otway Nat. Park, *Australia* **128 E5** 38 47 S 143 34 E
Otwock, *Poland* **55 F8** 52 5N 21 20 E
Ötztaler Ache →, *Austria* **34 D3** 47 14N 10 50 E
Ötztaler Alpen, *Austria* **34 E3** 46 56N 11 0 E
Ou →, *Laos* **86 B4** 20 4N 102 13 E
Ou Neua, *Laos* **76 F3** 22 18N 101 48 E
Ou-Sammyaku, *Japan* **70 E10** 39 20N 140 35 E
Ouachita →, *U.S.A.* **155 K9** 31 38N 91 49W
Ouachita, L., *U.S.A.* **155 H8** 34 34N 93 12W
Ouachita Mts., *U.S.A.* **155 H7** 34 40N 94 25W
Ouaco, *N. Cal.* **133 T18** 20 50 S 164 29 E
Ouadâne, *Mauritania* **110 D3** 20 50N 11 40W
Ouadda, *C.A.R.* **114 A4** 8 15N 22 20 E
Ouagadougou, *Burkina Faso* **113 C4** 12 25N 1 30W
Ouagam, *Chad* **109 F2** 14 22N 14 42 E
Ouahan →, *C.A.R.* **114 A3** 6 35N 15 12 E
Ouahigouya, *Burkina Faso* **112 C4** 13 31N 2 25W
Ouahila, *Algeria* **110 C4** 27 50N 5 0W
Ouahran = Oran, *Algeria* **111 A4** 35 45N 0 39W
Oualâta, *Mauritania* **112 B3** 17 20N 6 55W

Paso de los Toros 263

Palma Nova, *Spain* **38 B3** 39 32N 2 34 E
Palma Soriano, *Cuba* **164 B4** 20 15N 76 0W
Palmaner, *India* **95 H4** 13 12N 78 45 E
Palmares, *Brazil* **170 C4** 8 41 S 35 28W
Palmarito, *Venezuela* **168 B3** 7 37N 70 10W
Palmarola, *Italy* **46 B5** 40 56N 12 51 E
Palmas, *Brazil* **175 B5** 26 29 S 52 0W
Palmas, C., *Liberia* **112 E3** 4 27N 7 46W
Pálmas, G. di, *Italy* **46 D1** 39 0N 8 30 E
Palmas de Monte Alto, *Brazil* **171 D3** 14 16 S 43 10W
Palmdale, *Calif., U.S.A.* **161 L8** 34 35N 118 7W
Palmdale, *Fla., U.S.A.* **153 J8** 26 57N 81 19W
Palmeira, *Brazil* **171 G2** 25 25 S 50 0W
Palmeira das Missões, *Brazil* **175 B5** 27 55 S 53 17W
Palmeira dos Índios, *Brazil* **170 C4** 9 25 S 36 37W
Palmeirais, *Brazil* **170 C3** 6 0 S 43 0W
Palmeiras, *Brazil* **171 D3** 12 31 S 41 34W
Palmeiras →, *Brazil* **171 D2** 12 22 S 47 8W
Palmeirinhas, Pta. das, *Angola* **115 D2** 9 2 S 12 57 E
Palmela, *Portugal* **43 G2** 38 32N 8 57W
Palmelo, *Brazil* **171 E2** 17 20 S 48 27W
Palmer, *U.S.A.* **144 F10** 61 36N 149 7W
Palmer →, *Australia* **126 B3** 16 0 S 142 26 E
Palmer Arch., *Antarctica* **7 C17** 64 15 S 65 0W
Palmer Lake, *U.S.A.* **154 F2** 39 7N 104 55W
Palmer Land, *Antarctica* **7 D18** 73 0 S 63 0W
Palmerston, *Canada* **150 C4** 43 50N 80 51W
Palmerston, *N.Z.* **131 F5** 45 29 S 170 43 E
Palmerston North, *N.Z.* **130 G4** 40 21 S 175 39 E
Palmerton, *U.S.A.* **151 F9** 40 48N 75 37W
Palmetto, *Fla., U.S.A.* **149 M4** 27 31N 82 34W
Palmetto, *Ga., U.S.A.* **152 B5** 33 31N 84 40W
Palmi, *Italy* **47 D8** 38 21N 15 51 E
Palmira, *Argentina* **174 C2** 32 59 S 68 34W
Palmira, *Colombia* **168 C2** 3 32N 76 16W
Palmyra = Tudmur, *Syria* **101 E8** 34 36N 38 15 E
Palmyra, *Ill., U.S.A.* **156 E7** 39 26N 90 0W
Palmyra, *Mo., U.S.A.* **156 E5** 39 48N 91 32W
Palmyra, *N.J., U.S.A.* **151 F9** 40 1N 75 1W
Palmyra, *N.Y., U.S.A.* **150 C7** 43 5N 77 18W
Palmyra, *Pa., U.S.A.* **151 F8** 40 18N 76 36W
Palmyra, *Wis., U.S.A.* **157 B8** 42 52N 88 36W
Palmyra Is., *Pac. Oc.* **135 G11** 5 52N 162 5W
Palmyras Pt., *India* **94 D8** 20 46N 87 1 E
Palo, *Phil.* **81 F5** 11 10N 124 59 E
Palo Alto, *U.S.A.* **160 H4** 37 27N 122 10W
Palo Seco, *Trin. & Tob.* **169 F9** 10 4N 61 36W
Palo Verde, *U.S.A.* **161 M12** 33 26N 114 44W
Paloich, *Sudan* **107 E3** 10 28N 32 32 E
Palompon, *Phil.* **81 F5** 11 3N 124 23 E
Palopo, *Indonesia* **82 B2** 3 0 S 120 16 E
Palos, C. de, *Spain* **41 H4** 37 38N 0 40W
Palos de la Frontera, *Spain* **43 H4** 37 14N 6 53W
Palos Verdes, *U.S.A.* **161 M8** 33 48N 118 23W
Palos Verdes, Pt., *U.S.A.* **161 M8** 33 43N 118 26W
Palpa, *Peru* **172 C2** 14 30 S 75 15W
Pålsboda, *Sweden* **16 E9** 59 3N 15 22 E
Palu, *Indonesia* **82 B1** 1 0 S 119 52 E
Palu, *Turkey* **101 C9** 38 45N 40 0 E
Paluan, *Phil.* **80 E3** 13 26N 120 29 E
Paluke, *Liberia* **112 D3** 5 2N 8 5W
Paluzza, *Italy* **45 B10** 46 32N 13 1 E
Palwal, *India* **92 E7** 28 8N 77 19 E
Pama, *Burkina Faso* **113 C5** 11 19N 0 44 E
Pama →, *C.A.R.* **114 B3** 4 23N 18 43 E
Pama, Réserve de, *Burkina Faso* **113 C5** 11 27N 0 40 E
Pamanukan, *Indonesia* **85 D3** 6 16 S 107 49 E
Pamban I., *India* **95 K4** 9 15N 79 20 E
Pamekasan, *Indonesia* **85 D4** 7 10 S 113 28 E
Pamenang, *Indonesia* **79 J19** 8 24 S 116 6 E
Pamiers, *France* **28 E5** 43 7N 1 39 E
Pamir, *Tajikistan* **66 F8** 37 40N 73 0 E
Pamir →, *Tajikistan* **65 E6** 37 1N 72 41 E
Pamlico →, *U.S.A.* **149 H7** 35 20N 76 28W
Pamlico Sd., *U.S.A.* **149 H8** 35 20N 76 0W
Pampa, *U.S.A.* **155 H4** 35 32N 100 58W
Pampa de Agma, *Argentina* **176 B3** 43 45 S 69 40W
Pampa de las Salinas, *Argentina* **174 C2** 32 1 S 66 58W
Pampa Grande, *Bolivia* **173 D5** 18 5 S 64 6W
Pampa Hermosa, *Peru* **172 B2** 7 7 S 75 4W
Pampanga □, *Phil.* **80 D3** 15 4N 120 40 E
Pampanua, *Indonesia* **82 B2** 4 16 S 120 8 E
Pampas, *Argentina* **174 D3** 35 0 S 63 0W
Pampas, *Peru* **172 C3** 12 20 S 74 50W
Pampas →, *Peru* **172 C3** 13 24 S 73 12W
Pamphylia, *Turkey* **100 D4** 37 0N 31 20 E
Pamplona, *Colombia* **168 B3** 7 23N 72 39W
Pamplona, *Phil.* **80 B3** 18 31N 121 20 E
Pamplona, *Spain* **40 C3** 42 48N 1 38W
Pampoenpoort, *S. Africa* **116 E3** 31 3 S 22 40 E
Pamukçu, *Turkey* **49 B9** 39 30N 27 54 E
Pamukkale, *Turkey* **49 D11** 37 55N 29 8 E
Pan Xian, *China* **76 E5** 25 46N 104 38 E
Pana, *U.S.A.* **156 E7** 39 23N 89 5W
Panabo, *Phil.* **81 H5** 7 19N 125 42 E
Panaca, *U.S.A.* **159 H6** 37 47N 114 23W
Panacea, *U.S.A.* **152 E5** 30 2N 84 23W
Panagyurishte, *Bulgaria* **51 D8** 42 30N 24 15 E
Panaitan, *Indonesia* **84 D3** 6 36 S 105 12 E
Panaji, *India* **95 G1** 15 25N 73 50 E
Panamá, *Panama* **164 E4** 9 0N 79 25W
Panama, *Sri Lanka* **95 L5** 6 45N 81 48 E
Panama ■, *Cent. Amer.* **164 E4** 8 48N 79 55W
Panamá, G. de, *Panama* **164 E4** 8 4N 79 20W
Panama Canal, *Panama* **164 E4** 9 10N 79 37W
Panama City, *U.S.A.* **152 E4** 30 10N 85 40W
Panama City Beach, *U.S.A.* **152 E4** 30 11N 85 48W
Panamint Range, *U.S.A.* **161 J9** 36 20N 117 20W
Panamint Springs, *U.S.A.* **161 J9** 36 20N 117 28W
Panão, *Peru* **172 B2** 9 55 S 75 55W
Panaon I., *Phil.* **81 F5** 10 3N 125 13 E
Panare, *Thailand* **87 J3** 6 51N 101 30 E
Panarea, *Italy* **47 D8** 38 38N 15 4 E
Panaro →, *Italy* **45 D8** 44 55N 11 25 E
Panarukan, *Indonesia* **85 D4** 7 42 S 113 56 E
Panay, *Phil.* **81 F4** 11 10N 122 30 E
Panay, G., *Phil.* **79 B6** 11 0N 122 30 E
Pančevo, *Serbia, Yug.* **52 F5** 44 52N 20 41 E
Panch'iao, *Taiwan* **77 E13** 25 1N 121 27 E
Panciu, *Romania* **53 E12** 45 54N 27 8 E
Pancol, *Phil.* **81 F2** 10 52N 119 25 E
Pancorbo, Desfiladero, *Spain* **42 C7** 42 32N 3 5W
Pâncota, *Romania* **52 D6** 46 20N 21 45 E
Panda, *Mozam.* **117 C5** 24 2 S 34 45 E
Pandan, *Malaysia* **87 d** 1 32N 103 46 E
Pandan, *Antique, Phil.* **81 F4** 11 45N 122 10 E
Pandan, *Catanduanes, Phil.* **80 D5** 14 3N 124 10 E
Pandan, Selat, *Singapore* **87 d** 1 15N 103 44 E
Pandan Bay, *Phil.* **81 F4** 11 43N 122 0 E
Pandegelang, *Indonesia* **84 D3** 6 25 S 106 5 E
Pandhana, *India* **92 J7** 21 42N 76 13 E
Pandharkawada, *India* **94 D4** 20 1N 78 32 E
Pandharpur, *India* **94 F2** 17 41N 75 20 E
Pandhurna, *India* **94 D4** 21 36N 78 35 E
Pando, *Uruguay* **175 C4** 34 44 S 56 0W
Pando □, *Bolivia* **172 C4** 11 20 S 67 40W
Pando, L. = Hope, L., *Australia* **127 D2** 28 24 S 139 18 E
Pandokrátor, *Greece* **38 B9** 39 45N 19 50 E
Pandora, *Costa Rica* **164 E3** 9 43N 83 3W
Pandrup, *Denmark* **17 G3** 57 14N 9 40 E
Pandu, *Dem. Rep. of the Congo* **114 B3** 4 59N 19 16 E
Panevėžys, *Lithuania* **15 J21** 55 42N 24 25 E
Panfilov, *Kazakstan* **66 E8** 44 10N 80 0 E
Panfilov Atyndaghy, *Kazakstan* **65 B8** 43 23N 77 7 E
Panfilovo, *Russia* **60 E6** 50 25N 42 46 E
Panga, *Dem. Rep. of the Congo* **118 B2** 1 52N 26 18 E
Pangaíon Óros, *Greece* **51 F8** 40 50N 24 0 E
Pangala, *Congo* **114 C2** 3 16 S 14 34 E
Pangalanes, Canal des = Ampangalana, Lakandranon', *Madag.* **117 C8** 22 48 S 47 50 E
Pangani, *Tanzania* **118 D4** 5 25 S 38 58 E
Pangani →, *Tanzania* **118 D4** 5 26 S 38 58 E
Pangantocan, *Phil.* **81 H5** 7 50N 124 49 E
Pangar Djérem, Réserve de, *Cameroon* **114 A2** 5 50N 13 10 E
Pangasinan □, *Phil.* **80 D3** 15 55N 120 20 E
Pangfou = Bengbu, *China* **75 H9** 32 58N 117 20 E
Pangil, *Dem. Rep. of the Congo* **118 C2** 3 10 S 26 35 E
Pangkah, Tanjung, *Indonesia* **85 D4** 6 51 S 112 33 E
Pangkai, *Burma* **90 D7** 22 40N 98 40 E
Pangkajene, *Indonesia* **82 B1** 4 46 S 119 34 E
Pangkalanbrandan, *Indonesia* **84 B1** 4 1N 98 20 E
Pangkalanbuun, *Indonesia* **85 C4** 2 41 S 111 37 E
Pangkalansusu, *Indonesia* **84 B1** 4 2N 98 13 E
Pangkalpinang, *Indonesia* **84 C3** 2 0 S 106 0 E
Pangkoh, *Indonesia* **85 C4** 3 5 S 114 8 E
Panglao, *Phil.* **81 G4** 9 35N 123 45 E
Panglao I., *Phil.* **81 G4** 9 35N 123 45 E
Pangnirtung, *Canada* **139 B13** 66 8N 65 54W
Pango Alucuem, *Angola* **115 D2** 8 43 S 14 33 E
Pangong Tso, *India* **92 B8** 34 40N 78 40 E
Pangrango, *Indonesia* **84 D3** 6 46 S 107 1 E
Pangsau Pass, *Burma* **90 B6** 27 15N 96 10 E
Pangtara, *Burma* **90 E6** 20 57N 96 40 E
Panguipulli, *Chile* **176 A2** 39 38 S 72 20W
Panguitch, *U.S.A.* **159 H7** 37 50N 112 26W
Panguna, *Papua N. G.* **132 D8** 6 21 S 155 25 E
Pangutaran, *Phil.* **81 H3** 6 18N 120 35 E
Pangutaran Group, *Phil.* **81 H3** 6 18N 120 34 E
Panhala, *India* **94 F2** 16 49N 74 7 E
Panhandle, *U.S.A.* **155 H4** 35 21N 101 23W
Pani Mines, *India* **92 H5** 22 29N 73 50 E
Pania-Mutombo, *Dem. Rep. of the Congo* **118 D1** 5 11 S 23 51 E
Paniau, *U.S.A.* **145 B1** 21 56N 160 5W
Panié, Mt., *N. Cal.* **133 T18** 20 36 S 164 46 E
Panikota I., *India* **92 J4** 20 46N 71 21 E
Panipat, *India* **92 E7** 29 25N 77 2 E
Panitan, *Phil.* **81 F4** 11 28N 122 46 E
Panj = Pyandzh, *Tajikistan* **65 E4** 37 14N 69 6 E
Panj = Pyandzh →, *Asia* **65 E4** 37 6N 68 20 E
Panjab, *Afghan.* **91 B2** 34 23N 67 1 E
Panjakent = Pendzhikent, *Tajikistan* **65 D3** 39 29N 67 37 E
Panjal Range = Pir Panjal Range, *India* **92 C7** 32 30N 76 50 E
Panjang, Hon, *Vietnam* **87 H4** 9 20N 103 28 E
Panjgur, *Pakistan* **91 D2** 27 0N 64 5 E
Panjhra →, *India* **94 D2** 21 13N 74 57 E
Panji Poyon, *Tajikistan* **65 E4** 37 12N 68 35 E
Panjim = Panaji, *India* **95 G1** 15 25N 73 50 E
Panjin, *China* **75 D12** 41 3N 122 2 E
Panjnad →, *Pakistan* **92 E4** 28 57N 70 30 E
Panjwai, *Afghan.* **91 C2** 31 26N 65 27 E
Pankshin, *Nigeria* **113 D6** 9 16N 9 25 E
Panmunjŏm, *N. Korea* **75 F14** 37 59N 126 38 E
Panna, *India* **93 G9** 24 40N 80 15 E
Panna Hills, *India* **93 G9** 24 40N 81 15 E
Pannawonica, *Australia* **124 D2** 21 39 S 116 19 E
Pannga, Tanjung, *Indonesia* **79 K19** 8 54 S 116 2 E
Panngi, *Vanuatu* **133 E6** 15 58 S 168 12 E
Pannirtuuq = Pangnirtung, *Canada* **139 B13** 66 8N 65 54W
Pano Akil, *Pakistan* **92 F3** 27 51N 69 7 E
Pano Lefkara, *Cyprus* **39 F9** 34 53N 33 20 E
Pano Panayia, *Cyprus* **39 F8** 34 55N 32 38 E
Panora, *U.S.A.* **156 C2** 41 42N 94 22W
Panorama, *Brazil* **175 A5** 21 21 S 51 51W
Pánormon, *Greece* **39 E5** 35 25N 24 41 E
Panruti, *India* **95 J4** 11 46N 79 35 E
Pansemal, *India* **92 J6** 21 39N 74 42 E
Panshan = Panjin, *China* **75 D12** 41 3N 122 2 E
Panshi, *China* **75 C14** 42 58N 126 5 E
Pantanaw, *Burma* **90 G5** 16 59N 95 28 E
Pantar, *Indonesia* **82 C2** 8 28 S 124 10 E
Pante Macassar, *E. Timor* **82 C2** 9 30 S 123 58 E
Pante Makasar = Pante Macassar, *E. Timor* **82 C2** 9 30 S 123 58 E
Pantelleria, *Italy* **46 F4** 36 50N 11 57 E
Pantin Sakan, *Burma* **90 F6** 18 38N 97 33 E
Pantoja, *Peru* **168 D2** 0 58 S 75 10W
Pantón, *Spain* **42 C3** 42 31N 7 37W
Pantukan, *Phil.* **81 H5** 7 9N 125 54 E
Panu, *Dem. Rep. of the Congo* **114 C3** 3 50 S 19 10 E
Pánuco, *Mexico* **163 C5** 22 0N 98 15W
Panukulan, *Phil.* **80 D3** 14 56N 121 49 E
Panvel, *India* **94 E1** 18 59N 73 4 E
Panyam, *Nigeria* **113 D6** 9 27N 9 8 E
Panyu, *China* **77 F9** 22 51N 113 20 E
Panzhihua, *China* **76 D3** 26 33N 101 44 E
Panzi, *Dem. Rep. of the Congo* **115 D3** 7 17 S 18 1 E
Pao →, *Anzoátegui, Venezuela* **169 B5** 8 6N 64 17W
Pao →, *Apure, Venezuela* **168 B4** 8 33N 68 1W
Páola, *Italy* **47 C9** 39 21N 16 2 E
Paola, *Malta* **38 F8** 35 52N 14 30 E
Paola, *U.S.A.* **154 F7** 38 35N 94 53W
Paoli, *U.S.A.* **157 F10** 38 33N 86 28W
Paonia, *U.S.A.* **159 G10** 38 52N 107 36W
Paoting = Baoding, *China* **74 E8** 38 50N 115 28 E
Paot'ou = Baotou, *China* **74 D6** 40 32N 110 2 E
Paoua, *C.A.R.* **114 A3** 7 9N 16 20 E
Pap, *Uzbekistan* **65 C5** 40 52N 71 6 E
Pápa, *Hungary* **52 C2** 47 22N 17 30 E
Papa, *U.S.A.* **145 D6** 19 13N 155 52W
Papa Stour, *U.K.* **22 A7** 60 20N 1 42W
Papa Westray, *U.K.* **22 B6** 59 20N 2 55W
Papaaloa, *U.S.A.* **145 D6** 19 59N 155 13W
Papagayo →, *Mexico* **163 D5** 16 36N 99 43W
Papagayo, G. de, *Costa Rica* **164 D2** 10 30N 85 50W
Papagni →, *India* **95 G3** 15 35N 77 45 E
Papaichton, *Fr. Guiana* **169 C7** 3 48N 54 10W
Papaikou, *U.S.A.* **145 D6** 19 47N 155 6W
Papakura, *N.Z.* **130 D3** 37 4 S 174 59 E
Papantla, *Mexico* **163 C5** 20 30N 97 30W
Papar, *Malaysia* **78 C5** 5 45N 116 0 E
Papara, *Tahiti* **133 S16** 17 43 S 149 22W
Paparoa, *N.Z.* **130 C3** 36 6 S 174 16 E
Paparoa Nat. Park, *N.Z.* **131 C6** 42 7 S 171 26 E
Paparoa Ra., *N.Z.* **131 C6** 42 5 S 171 35 E
Pápas, Ákra, *Greece* **48 C3** 38 13N 21 20 E
Papatoetoe, *N.Z.* **130 C3** 36 59 S 174 51 E
Papatura, *Solomon Is.* **133 L10** 7 32 S 158 47 E
Papawai Pt., *U.S.A.* **145 C5** 20 47N 156 32W
Papeete, *Tahiti* **133 S16** 17 32 S 149 34W
Papenburg, *Germany* **30 B3** 53 5N 7 23 E
Papetoai, *Tahiti* **133 S16** 17 29 S 149 52W
Paphlagonia, *Turkey* **100 B5** 41 30N 33 0 E
Paphos, *Cyprus* **39 F8** 34 46N 32 25 E
Papien Chiang = Da →, *Vietnam* **76 G5** 21 15N 105 20 E
Papigochic →, *Mexico* **162 B3** 29 9N 109 40W
Paposo, *Chile* **174 B1** 25 0 S 70 30W
Papoutsa, *Cyprus* **39 F9** 34 54N 33 4 E
Papua, G. of, *Papua N. G.* **132 E3** 9 0 S 144 50 E
Papua New Guinea ■, *Oceania* **132 D3** 8 0 S 145 0 E
Papudo, *Chile* **174 C1** 32 29 S 71 27W
Papuk, *Croatia* **52 E2** 45 30N 17 30 E
Papun, *Burma* **90 F6** 18 2N 97 30 E
Papunya, *Australia* **124 D5** 23 15 S 131 54 E
Pará = Belém, *Brazil* **170 B2** 1 20 S 48 30W
Pará □, *Brazil* **173 A7** 3 20 S 52 0W
Paraburdoo, *Australia* **124 D2** 23 14 S 117 32 E
Paracale, *Phil.* **80 D4** 14 17N 122 48 E
Paracas, Pen., *Peru* **172 C2** 13 53 S 76 20W
Paracatu, *Brazil* **171 E2** 17 10 S 46 50W
Paracatu →, *Brazil* **171 E2** 16 30 S 45 4W
Paracel Is., *S. China Sea* **78 A4** 15 50N 112 0 E
Parachilna, *Australia* **128 A3** 31 10 S 138 21 E
Parachinar, *Pakistan* **91 B3** 33 55N 70 5 E
Paraćin, *Serbia, Yug.* **50 C5** 43 54N 21 27 E
Paracuru, *Brazil* **170 B4** 3 24 S 39 4W
Parada, Punta, *Peru* **172 D2** 15 22 S 75 11W
Paradas, *Spain* **43 H5** 37 18N 5 29W
Paradela, *Spain* **42 C3** 42 44N 7 37W
Paradhísi, *Greece* **38 E12** 36 18N 28 7 E
Paradip, *India* **94 D8** 20 15N 86 35 E
Paradise, *Calif., U.S.A.* **160 F5** 39 46N 121 37W
Paradise, *Nev., U.S.A.* **161 J11** 36 9N 115 10W
Paradise →, *Canada* **143 B8** 53 27N 57 19W
Paradise Hill, *Canada* **143 C7** 53 32N 109 28W
Paradise I., *Bahamas* **9 b** 25 6N 77 19W
Paradise River, *Canada* **141 B8** 53 27N 57 17W
Paradise Valley, *U.S.A.* **158 F5** 41 30N 117 32W
Parado, *Indonesia* **85 D5** 8 42 S 118 30 E
Paragould, *U.S.A.* **155 G9** 36 3N 90 29W
Paraguá →, *Bolivia* **173 C5** 13 34 S 61 53W
Paragua →, *Venezuela* **169 B5** 6 55N 62 55W
Paraguaçu →, *Brazil* **171 D4** 12 45 S 38 54W
Paraguaçu Paulista, *Brazil* **175 A5** 22 22 S 50 35W
Paraguaipoa, *Venezuela* **168 A3** 11 21N 71 57W
Paraguaná, Pen. de, *Venezuela* **168 A3** 12 0N 70 0W
Paraguarí, *Paraguay* **174 B4** 25 36 S 57 0W
Paraguarí □, *Paraguay* **174 B4** 26 0 S 57 10W
Paraguay ■, *S. Amer.* **174 A4** 23 0 S 57 0W
Paraguay →, *Paraguay* **174 B4** 27 18 S 58 38W
Paraíba = João Pessoa, *Brazil* **170 C5** 7 10 S 34 52W
Paraíba □, *Brazil* **170 C4** 7 0 S 36 0W
Paraíba do Sul →, *Brazil* **171 F3** 21 37 S 41 3W
Parainen, *Finland* **15 F20** 60 18N 22 18 E
Paraiso, *Brazil* **173** 19 3 S 52 59W
Paraiso, *Mexico* **163 D6** 18 24N 93 14W
Parak, *Iran* **97 E7** 27 38N 52 25 E
Parakhino Paddubye, *Russia* **58 C7** 58 26N 33 10 E
Parakou, *Benin* **113 D5** 9 25N 2 40 E
Parakylia, *Australia* **128 A2** 30 24 S 136 25 E
Paralimni, *Cyprus* **39 E9** 35 2N 33 58 E
Parálion-Astrous, *Greece* **48 D4** 37 25N 22 45 E
Paralkote, *India* **94 E5** 19 47N 80 41 E
Parama I., *Papua N. G.* **132 E2** 9 0 S 143 25 E
Paramaribo, *Surinam* **169 B6** 5 50N 55 10W
Parambu, *Brazil* **170 C3** 6 13 S 40 43W
Paramillo, Nudo del, *Colombia* **168 B2** 7 4N 75 55W
Paramirim, *Brazil* **171 D3** 13 26 S 42 15W
Paramirim →, *Brazil* **171 D3** 11 34 S 43 18W
Paramithiá, *Greece* **48 B2** 39 30N 20 35 E
Paramushir, Ostrov, *Russia* **67 D16** 50 24N 156 0 E
Paran →, *Israel* **103 E4** 30 20N 35 10 E
Paraná, *Argentina* **174 C3** 31 45 S 60 30W
Paraná, *Brazil* **171 D2** 12 30 S 47 48W
Paraná □, *Brazil* **175 A5** 24 30 S 51 0W
Paraná →, *Argentina* **174 C4** 33 43 S 59 15W
Paranã →, *Brazil* **171 D2** 12 30 S 48 14W
Paranaguá, *Brazil* **175 B6** 25 30 S 48 30W
Paranaíba, *Brazil* **173 D7** 19 40 S 51 11W
Paranaíba →, *Brazil* **171 F1** 20 6 S 51 4W
Paranapanema →, *Brazil* **175 A5** 22 40 S 53 9W
Paranapiacaba, Serra do, *Brazil* **175 A6** 24 31 S 48 35W
Paranas, *Phil.* **81 F5** 11 42N 125 2 E
Paranavaí, *Brazil* **175 A5** 23 4 S 52 56W
Parang, *Maguindanao, Phil.* **81 H5** 7 23N 124 16 E
Parang, *Sulu, Phil.* **81 J3** 5 55N 120 54 E
Parangaba, *Brazil* **170 B4** 3 45 S 38 33W
Parangippettai, *India* **95 J4** 11 30N 79 38 E
Parângul Mare, Vf., *Romania* **53 E8** 45 20N 23 37 E
Paranthan, *Sri Lanka* **95 K5** 9 26N 80 24 E
Paraparaumu, *N.Z.* **130 G4** 40 57 S 175 3 E
Parapetí →, *Bolivia* **173 D5** 18 58 S 62 21W
Parapóla, *Greece* **48 E5** 36 55N 23 27 E
Paraspóri, Ákra, *Greece* **49 F9** 35 55N 27 15 E
Paratinga, *Brazil* **171 D3** 12 40 S 43 10W
Paratoo, *Australia* **128 B3** 32 42 S 139 20 E
Paraúna, *Brazil* **171 E1** 16 55 S 50 26W
Paray-le-Monial, *France* **27 F11** 46 27N 4 7 E
Parbati →, *Mad. P., India* **92 G7** 25 50N 76 30 E
Parbati →, *Raj., India* **92 F7** 26 54N 77 53 E
Parbatipur, *Bangla.* **90 C2** 25 39N 88 55 E
Parbhani, *India* **94 E3** 19 8N 76 52 E
Parchim, *Germany* **30 B7** 53 26N 11 52 E
Parczew, *Poland* **55 G9** 51 40N 22 52 E
Pardes Hanna-Karkur, *Israel* **103 C3** 32 28N 34 57 E
Pardilla, *Spain* **42 D7** 41 33N 3 43W
Pardo →, *Bahia, Brazil* **171 E4** 15 40 S 39 0W
Pardo →, *Mato Grosso, Brazil* **175 A5** 21 46 S 52 9W
Pardo →, *Minas Gerais, Brazil* **171 E3** 15 48 S 44 48W
Pardo →, *São Paulo, Brazil* **171 F2** 20 10 S 48 38W
Pardubice, *Czech Rep.* **34 A8** 50 3N 15 45 E
Pare, *Indonesia* **85 D4** 7 43 S 112 12 E
Pare Mts., *Tanzania* **118 C4** 4 0 S 37 45 E
Parecis, Serra dos, *Brazil* **173 C6** 13 0 S 60 0W
Paredes de Nava, *Spain* **42 C6** 42 9N 4 42W
Parelhas, *Brazil* **170 C4** 6 41 S 36 39W
Paren, *Russia* **67 C17** 62 30N 163 15 E
Parenda, *India* **94 E2** 18 16N 75 28 E
Parengarenga Harbour, *N.Z.* **130 A1** 34 31 S 173 0 E
Parent, *Canada* **140 C5** 47 55N 74 35W
Parent, L., *Canada* **140 C4** 48 31N 77 1W
Parentis-en-Born, *France* **28 D2** 44 21N 1 4W
Parepare, *Indonesia* **82 B1** 4 0 S 119 40 E
Parfino, *Russia* **58 D6** 57 59N 31 34 E
Párga, *Greece* **48 B2** 39 15N 20 29 E
Pargi, *India* **94 E3** 17 11N 77 53 E
Pargo, Pta. do, *Madeira* **9 c** 32 49N 17 17W
Paria, G. de, *Venezuela* **169 A5** 10 20N 62 0W
Paria, Pen. de, *Venezuela* **169 A5** 10 50N 62 30W
Pariaguán, *Venezuela* **169 B5** 8 51N 64 34W
Pariaman, *Indonesia* **84 C2** 0 47 S 100 11 E
Paricatuba, *Brazil* **169 D5** 4 26 S 61 53W
Paricutín, Cerro, *Mexico* **162 D4** 19 28N 102 15W
Parigi, *Java, Indonesia* **85 D3** 7 42 S 108 29 E
Parigi, *Sulawesi, Indonesia* **82 B2** 0 50 S 120 5 E
Parika, *Guyana* **169 B6** 6 50N 58 20W
Parikkala, *Finland* **58 B5** 61 33N 29 31 E
Parima, Serra, *Brazil* **169 C5** 2 30N 64 0W
Parinari, *Peru* **172 A3** 4 35 S 74 25W
Pariñas, Pta., *S. Amer.* **166 D2** 4 30 S 82 0W
Parincea, *Romania* **53 D12** 46 27N 27 9 E
Paringa, *Australia* **128 C4** 34 10 S 140 46 E
Parintins, *Brazil* **169 D6** 2 40 S 56 50W
Paris, *Canada* **150 C4** 43 12N 80 25W
Paris, *France* **27 D9** 48 50N 2 20 E
Paris, *Idaho, U.S.A.* **158 E8** 42 14N 111 24W
Paris, *Ill., U.S.A.* **157 E9** 39 36N 87 42W
Paris, *Ky., U.S.A.* **157 F12** 38 13N 84 15W
Paris, *Mo., U.S.A.* **156 E5** 39 29N 92 0W
Paris, *Tenn., U.S.A.* **149 G1** 36 18N 88 19W
Paris, *Tex., U.S.A.* **155 J7** 33 40N 95 33W
Paris, Ville de □, *France* **27 D9** 48 50N 2 20 E
Parish, *U.S.A.* **151 C8** 43 25N 76 8W
Parishville, *U.S.A.* **151 B10** 44 38N 74 49W
Pariti, *Indonesia* **82 D2** 10 1 S 123 45 E
Park, *U.S.A.* **160 B4** 48 45N 122 18W
Park City, *U.S.A.* **155 G6** 37 48N 97 20W
Park Falls, *U.S.A.* **154 C9** 45 56N 90 27W
Park Forest, *U.S.A.* **157 C9** 41 29N 87 40W
Park Head, *Canada* **150 B3** 44 36N 81 9W
Park Hills, *Mo., U.S.A.* **155 G9** 37 53N 90 28W
Park Hills, *Mo., U.S.A.* **156 G6** 37 51N 90 31W
Park Range, *U.S.A.* **158 G10** 40 0N 106 30W
Park Rapids, *U.S.A.* **154 B7** 46 55N 95 4W
Park Ridge, *U.S.A.* **157 B9** 42 2N 87 51W
Park River, *U.S.A.* **154 A6** 48 24N 97 45W
Park Rynie, *S. Africa* **117 E5** 30 25 S 30 45 E
Parkā Bandar, *Iran* **97 E8** 25 55N 59 35 E
Parkal, *India* **94 E4** 18 12N 79 43 E
Parkano, *Finland* **15 E20** 62 1N 23 0 E
Parkent, *Uzbekistan* **65 C4** 41 18N 69 40 E
Parker, *Ariz., U.S.A.* **161 L12** 34 9N 114 17W
Parker, *Pa., U.S.A.* **150 E5** 41 5N 79 41W
Parker Dam, *U.S.A.* **161 L12** 34 18N 114 8W
Parkersburg, *Iowa, U.S.A.* **156 B4** 42 35N 92 47W
Parkersburg, *W. Va., U.S.A.* **148 F5** 39 16N 81 34W
Parkes, *Australia* **129 B8** 33 9 S 148 11 E
Parkfield, *U.S.A.* **160 K6** 35 54N 120 26W
Parkhar, *Tajikistan* **65 E4** 37 30N 69 34 E
Parkhill, *Canada* **150 C3** 43 15N 81 38W
Parkland, *U.S.A.* **160 C4** 47 9N 122 26W
Parkston, *U.S.A.* **154 D6** 43 24N 97 59W
Parksville, *Canada* **142 D4** 49 20N 124 21W
Parla, *Spain* **42 E7** 40 14N 3 46W
Parlakimidi, *India* **94 E7** 18 45N 84 5 E
Parli, *India* **94 E3** 18 50N 76 35 E
Pârliţa, *Moldova* **53 C12** 47 19N 27 52 E
Parma, *Italy* **44 D7** 44 48N 10 20 E
Parma, *Idaho, U.S.A.* **158 E5** 43 47N 116 57W
Parma, *Ohio, U.S.A.* **150 E3** 41 23N 81 43W
Parma →, *Italy* **44 D7** 44 56N 10 26 E
Parnaguá, *Brazil* **170 D3** 10 10 S 44 38W
Parnaíba, *Piauí, Brazil* **170 B3** 2 54 S 41 47W
Parnaíba, *São Paulo, Brazil* **173 D7** 19 34 S 51 14W
Parnaíba →, *Brazil* **170 B3** 3 0 S 41 50W
Parnamirim, *Brazil* **170 C4** 8 5 S 39 34W
Parnarama, *Brazil* **170 C3** 5 31 S 43 6W
Parnassós, *Greece* **48 C4** 38 35N 22 30 E
Parnassus, *N.Z.* **131 C8** 42 42 S 173 23 E
Parndana, *Australia* **128 C2** 35 48 S 137 12 E
Parner, *India* **94 E2** 19 0N 74 26 E
Párnis, *Greece* **48 C5** 38 14N 23 45 E
Párnon Óros, *Greece* **48 D4** 37 15N 22 45 E
Pärnu, *Estonia* **15 G21** 58 28N 24 33 E
Parola, *India* **94 D2** 20 47N 75 7 E
Paroo →, *Australia* **128 A5** 31 28 S 143 32 E
Páros, *Greece* **49 D7** 37 5N 25 12 E
Parowan, *U.S.A.* **159 H7** 37 51N 112 50W
Parpaillon, *France* **29 D10** 44 30N 6 40 E
Parral, *Chile* **174 D1** 36 10 S 71 52W
Parramatta, *Australia* **129 B9** 33 48 S 151 1 E
Parras, *Mexico* **162 B4** 25 30N 102 20W
Parrett →, *U.K.* **21 F4** 51 12N 3 1W
Parris I., *U.S.A.* **152 C9** 32 20N 80 41W
Parrish, *U.S.A.* **153 H7** 27 35N 82 26W
Parrott, *U.S.A.* **152 D5** 31 54N 84 31W
Parrsboro, *Canada* **141 C7** 45 30N 64 25W
Parry I., *Canada* **150 A4** 45 18N 80 10W
Parry Is., *Canada* **6 B2** 77 0N 110 0W
Parry Sound, *Canada* **140 C4** 45 20N 80 0W
Parsberg, *Germany* **31 F7** 49 10N 11 43 E
Parseier Spitze, *Austria* **33 B10** 47 10N 10 28 E
Parsęta →, *Poland* **54 D2** 54 11N 15 34 E
Parsnip →, *Canada* **142 B4** 55 10N 123 2W
Parsons, *U.S.A.* **155 G7** 37 20N 95 16W
Parsons Ra., *Australia* **126 A2** 13 30 S 135 15 E
Partabpur, *India* **94 E5** 20 0N 80 42 E
Partanna, *Italy* **46 E5** 37 43N 12 53 E
Parthenay, *France* **26 F6** 46 38N 0 16W
Partinico, *Italy* **46 D6** 38 3N 13 7 E
Partizánske, *Slovak Rep.* **35 C11** 48 38N 18 23 E
Partridge I., *Canada* **140 A2** 55 59N 87 37W
Partur, *India* **94 E3** 19 40N 76 14 E
Paru →, *Brazil* **169 D7** 1 33 S 52 38W
Parú →, *Venezuela* **168 C4** 4 20N 66 27W
Paru de Oeste →, *Brazil* **169 C6** 1 30N 56 0W
Parucito →, *Venezuela* **168 B4** 5 18N 65 59W
Parur, *India* **95 J3** 10 13N 76 14 E
Paruro, *Peru* **172 C3** 13 45 S 71 50W
Parvān □, *Afghan.* **91 B3** 35 0N 69 0 E
Parvatipuram, *India* **94 E6** 18 50N 83 25 E
Parvatsar, *India* **92 F6** 26 52N 74 49 E
Påryd, *Sweden* **17 H9** 56 34N 15 55 E
Parys, *S. Africa* **116 D4** 26 52 S 27 29 E
Pas, Pta. des, *Spain* **38 D1** 38 46N 1 26 E
Pas-de-Calais □, *France* **27 B9** 50 30N 2 10 E
Pasada, *Spain* **42 B5** 43 23N 5 40W
Pasadena, *Canada* **141 C8** 49 1N 57 36W
Pasadena, *Calif., U.S.A.* **161 L8** 34 9N 118 9W
Pasadena, *Tex., U.S.A.* **155 L7** 29 43N 95 13W
Pasaje, *Ecuador* **168 D2** 3 23 S 79 50W
Pasaje →, *Argentina* **174 B3** 25 39 S 63 56W
Paşalimanı, *Turkey* **51 F11** 40 29N 27 36 E
Pasar, *Indonesia* **79 J17** 8 27 S 114 54 E
Pasay, *Phil.* **80 D3** 14 33N 121 0 E
Pascagoula, *U.S.A.* **155 K10** 30 21N 88 33W
Pascagoula →, *U.S.A.* **155 K10** 30 23N 88 37W
Paşcani, *Romania* **53 C11** 47 14N 26 45 E
Pasco, *U.S.A.* **158 C4** 46 14N 119 6W
Pasco □, *Peru* **172 C2** 10 40 S 75 0W
Pasco, Cerro de, *Peru* **172 C2** 10 45 S 76 10W
Pasco I., *Australia* **124 D2** 20 57 S 115 20 E
Pascoag, *U.S.A.* **151 E13** 41 57N 71 42W
Pascua, I. de, *Chile* **172 b** 27 7 S 109 23W
Pasewalk, *Germany* **30 B9** 53 30N 13 58 E
Pasfield L., *Canada* **143 B7** 58 24N 105 20W
Pasha →, *Russia* **58 B7** 60 29N 32 55 E
Pashiya, *Russia* **64 B7** 58 33N 58 26 E
Pashmakli = Smolyan, *Bulgaria* **51 E8** 41 36N 24 38 E
Pasig, *Phil.* **80 D3** 14 35N 121 5 E
Pasighat, *India* **90 A5** 28 4N 95 21 E
Pasinler, *Turkey* **101 C9** 39 59N 41 41 E
Pasir Mas, *Malaysia* **87 J4** 6 2N 102 8 E
Pasir Panjang, *Singapore* **87 d** 1 18N 103 46 E
Pasir Putih, *Malaysia* **87 K4** 5 50N 102 24 E
Pasirian, *Indonesia* **85 D4** 8 13 S 113 8 E
Pasirkuning, *Indonesia* **84 C2** 0 30 S 104 33 E
Påskallavik, *Sweden* **17 G10** 57 10N 16 26 E
Paskūh, *Iran* **97 E9** 27 34N 61 39 E
Pasłęk, *Poland* **54 D6** 54 3N 19 41 E
Pasłęka →, *Poland* **54 D6** 54 26N 19 46 E
Pasley, C., *Australia* **125 F3** 33 52 S 123 35 E
Pašman, *Croatia* **45 E12** 43 58N 15 20 E
Pasmore →, *Australia* **128 A3** 31 5 S 139 49 E
Pasni, *Pakistan* **91 D1** 25 15N 63 27 E
Paso Cantinela, *Mexico* **161 N11** 32 33N 115 47W
Paso de Indios, *Argentina* **176 B3** 43 55 S 69 0W
Paso de los Indios, *Argentina* **176 B3** 38 32 S 69 25W
Paso de los Libres, *Argentina* **174 B4** 29 44 S 57 10W
Paso de los Toros, *Uruguay* **174 C4** 32 45 S 56 30W

Posada 267

Polillo Is., Phil. 80 D4 14 56N 122 0 E
Polillo Strait, Phil. 80 D3 14 44N 121 51 E
Polis, Cyprus 39 E8 35 2N 32 26 E
Polístena, Italy 47 D9 38 24N 16 4 E
Políyiros, Greece 50 F7 40 23N 23 25 E
Polk, U.S.A. 150 E5 41 22N 79 56W
Polkowice, Poland 55 G3 51 29N 16 3 E
Polla, Italy 47 B8 40 31N 15 29 E
Pollachi, India 95 J3 10 35N 77 0 E
Pollença, Spain 38 B4 39 54N 3 1 E
Pollença, B. de, Spain 38 B4 39 53N 3 8 E
Pollfoss, Norway 18 C4 61 58N 7 54 E
Póllica, Italy 47 B8 40 11N 15 3 E
Pollino, Mte., Italy 47 C9 39 55N 16 11 E
Polna, Russia 58 C5 58 31N 28 5 E
Polnovat, Russia 66 C7 63 50N 65 54 E
Polo, Ill., U.S.A. 156 C7 41 59N 89 35W
Polo, Mo., U.S.A. 156 E2 39 33N 94 3W
Pology, Ukraine 59 J9 47 29N 36 15 E
Polonnaruwa, Sri Lanka 95 L5 7 56N 81 0 E
Polonne, Ukraine 59 G4 50 6N 27 30 E
Polonnoye = Polonne, Ukraine 59 G4 50 6N 27 30 E
Polski Trŭmbesh, Bulgaria 51 C9 43 20N 25 38 E
Polsko Kosovo, Bulgaria 51 C9 43 23N 25 38 E
Polson, U.S.A. 158 C6 47 41N 114 9W
Poltár, Slovak Rep. 35 C12 48 26N 19 48 E
Poltava, Ukraine 59 H8 49 35N 34 35 E
Põltsamaa, Estonia 15 G21 58 41N 25 58 E
Polunochnoye, Russia 66 C7 60 52N 60 25 E
Polur, India 95 H4 12 32N 79 11 E
Põlva, Estonia 15 G22 58 3N 27 3 E
Polyarny, Russia 56 A5 69 8N 33 20 E
Polynesia, Pac. Oc. 135 J11 10 0 S 162 0W
Polynésie française = French Polynesia ■, Pac. Oc. 135 K13 20 0 S 145 0W
Pomabamba, Peru 172 B2 8 50 S 77 28W
Pomarance, Italy 44 E7 43 18N 10 52 E
Pomaro, Mexico 162 D4 18 20N 103 18W
Pombal, Brazil 170 C4 6 45 S 37 50W
Pombal, Portugal 42 F2 39 55N 8 40W
Pómbia, Greece 39 F5 35 0N 24 51 E
Pombos, B. dos, Angola 115 E2 11 40 S 13 47 E
Pomene, Mozam. 117 C6 22 53 S 35 33 E
Pomeroy, Ohio, U.S.A. 148 F4 39 2N 82 2W
Pomeroy, Wash., U.S.A. 158 C5 46 28N 117 36W
Pomézia, Italy 46 A5 41 40N 12 30 E
Pomichna, Ukraine 59 H6 48 13N 31 36 E
Pomio, Papua N. G. 132 C6 5 32 S 151 33 E
Pomme de Terre L., U.S.A. 156 G3 37 54N 93 19W
Pomona, Australia 127 D5 26 22 S 152 52 E
Pomona, U.S.A. 161 L9 34 4N 117 45W
Pomona Park, U.S.A. 153 F8 29 30N 81 36W
Pomorie, Bulgaria 51 D11 42 32N 27 41 E
Pomorskie □, Poland 54 D5 54 30N 18 0 E
Pomorskie, Pojezierze, Poland 54 E3 53 40N 16 37 E
Pomos, Cyprus 39 E8 35 9N 32 33 E
Pomos, C., Cyprus 39 E8 35 10N 32 33 E
Pompano Beach, U.S.A. 149 M5 26 14N 80 8W
Pompei, Italy 47 B7 40 45N 14 30 E
Pompey, France 27 D13 48 46N 6 6 E
Pompeys Pillar, U.S.A. 158 D10 45 59N 107 57W
Pompton Lakes, U.S.A. 151 F10 41 0N 74 17W
Ponape = Pohnpei, Micronesia 134 G7 6 55N 158 10 E
Ponask L., Canada 140 B1 54 0N 92 41W
Ponca, U.S.A. 154 D6 42 34N 96 43W
Ponca City, U.S.A. 155 G6 36 42N 97 5W
Ponce, Puerto Rico 165 d 18 1N 66 37W
Ponce de Leon, U.S.A. 152 E4 30 44N 85 56W
Ponce de Leon B., U.S.A. 153 K8 25 15N 81 10W
Ponchatoula, U.S.A. 155 K9 30 26N 90 26W
Poncheville, L., Canada 140 B4 50 10N 76 55W
Pond, U.S.A. 161 K7 35 43N 119 20W
Pond Inlet, Canada 139 A12 72 40N 77 0W
Pondicherry, India 95 J4 11 59N 79 50 E
Pondo, Papua N. G. 132 C6 4 33 S 151 38 E
Ponds, I. of, Canada 141 B8 53 27N 55 52W
Ponérihouen, N. Cal. 133 U19 21 5 S 165 24 E
Ponferrada, Spain 42 C4 42 32N 6 35W
Pongo, Wadi →, Sudan 107 F2 8 42N 27 40 E
Poniatowa, Poland 55 G9 51 11N 22 3 E
Poniec, Poland 55 G3 51 48N 16 50 E
Ponikva, Slovenia 45 B12 46 16N 15 26 E
Ponnaiyar →, India 95 J4 11 50N 79 45 E
Ponnani, India 95 J2 10 45N 75 59 E
Ponneri, India 95 H5 13 20N 80 15 E
Ponnuru, India 95 F5 16 5N 80 34 E
Ponoka, Canada 142 C6 52 42N 113 40W
Ponomarevka, Russia 64 E5 53 19N 54 8 E
Ponorogo, Indonesia 85 D4 7 52 S 111 27 E
Ponot, Phil. 81 G4 8 25N 123 0 E
Ponoy, Russia 56 A7 67 0N 41 13 E
Ponoy →, Russia 56 A7 66 59N 41 17 E
Pons = Ponts, Spain 40 D6 41 55N 1 12 E
Pons, France 28 C3 45 35N 0 34W
Ponsul →, Portugal 42 F3 39 40N 7 31W
Pont-à-Mousson, France 27 D13 48 54N 6 1 E
Pont-Audemer, France 26 C7 49 21N 0 30 E
Pont-Aven, France 26 E3 47 51N 3 47W
Pont Canavese, Italy 44 C4 45 25N 7 36 E
Pont-d'Ain, France 27 F12 46 3N 5 21 E
Pont-de-Roide, France 27 E13 47 23N 6 45 E
Pont-de-Salars, France 28 D6 44 18N 2 44 E
Pont-de-Vaux, France 27 F11 46 26N 4 56 E
Pont-de-Veyle, France 27 F11 46 17N 4 53 E
Pont-du-Château, France 27 G10 45 47N 3 15 E
Pont-l'Abbé, France 26 E2 47 52N 4 15W
Pont-l'Évêque, France 26 C7 49 18N 0 11 E
Pont-St-Esprit, France 29 D8 44 16N 4 40 E
Pont-St-Martin, Italy 44 C4 45 36N 7 48 E
Pont-Ste-Maxence, France 27 C9 49 18N 2 35 E
Pont-sur-Yonne, France 27 D10 48 18N 3 10 E
Ponta de Pedras, Brazil 170 B2 1 23 S 48 52W
Ponta Delgada, Flores, Azores 9 d2 39 31N 31 13W
Ponta Delgada, São Miguel, Azores 9 d3 37 44N 25 40W
Ponta do Sol, Madeira 9 c 32 42N 17 7W
Ponta Grossa, Brazil 175 B5 25 7 S 50 10W
Ponta Pora, Brazil 175 A4 22 20 S 55 35W
Pontacq, France 28 E3 43 11N 0 8W
Pontailler-sur-Saône, France 27 E12 47 13N 5 25 E
Pontal →, Brazil 170 C3 9 8 S 40 12W
Pontalina, Brazil 171 E2 17 31 S 49 27W
Pontarlier, France 27 F13 46 54N 6 20 E
Pontassieve, Italy 45 E8 43 46N 11 26 E
Pontaumur, France 28 C6 45 52N 2 40 E
Pontcharra, France 29 C10 45 26N 6 1 E
Pontchartrain L., U.S.A. 155 K10 30 5N 90 5W
Pontchâteau, France 26 E4 47 25N 2 5W
Ponte Alta, Serra do, Brazil 171 E2 19 42 S 47 40W
Ponte Alta do Norte, Brazil 170 D2 10 45 S 47 34W
Ponte Branca, Brazil 173 D7 16 27 S 52 40W
Ponte da Barca, Portugal 42 D2 41 48N 8 25W
Ponte de Sor, Portugal 43 F2 39 17N 8 1W
Ponte dell'Ólio, Italy 44 D6 44 52N 9 39 E
Ponte di Legno, Italy 44 B7 46 16N 10 31 E
Ponte do Lima, Portugal 42 D2 41 46N 8 35W
Ponte do Pungué, Mozam. 119 F3 19 30 S 34 33 E
Ponte-Leccia, France 29 F13 42 28N 9 13 E
Ponte nelle Alpi, Italy 45 B9 46 11N 12 16 E
Ponte Nova, Brazil 171 F3 20 25 S 42 54W
Ponte Tresa, Italy 33 E7 45 58N 8 51 E
Ponte Vedra Beach, U.S.A. 152 E8 30 15N 81 23W
Ponteareas, Spain 42 C2 42 10N 8 28W
Pontebba, Italy 45 B10 46 30N 13 18 E
Ponteceso, Spain 42 B2 43 15N 8 54W
Pontecorvo, Italy 46 A6 41 27N 13 40 E
Pontedeume, Spain 42 B2 43 24N 8 10W
Ponteix, Canada 143 D7 49 46N 107 29W
Pontes e Lacerda, Brazil 173 D6 15 12 S 59 22W
Pontevedra, Capiz, Phil. 81 F4 11 29N 122 50 E
Pontevedra, Neg. Occ., Phil. 81 F4 10 22N 122 52 E
Pontevedra, Spain 42 C2 42 26N 8 40W
Pontevedra □, Spain 42 C2 42 25N 8 39W
Pontevedra, R. de →, Spain 42 C2 42 22N 8 45W
Pontevico, Italy 44 C7 45 16N 10 5 E
Pontiac, Ill., U.S.A. 154 E10 40 53N 88 38W
Pontiac, Mich., U.S.A. 157 B13 42 38N 83 18W
Pontian Kecil, Malaysia 87 d 1 29N 103 23 E
Pontianak, Indonesia 85 C3 0 3 S 109 15 E
Pontine Is. = Ponziane, Ísole, Italy 46 B5 40 55N 12 57 E
Pontine Mts. = Kuzey Anadolu Dağları, Turkey 100 B7 41 30N 35 0 E
Pontínia, Italy 46 A6 41 25N 13 2 E
Pontivy, France 26 D4 48 5N 2 58W
Pontoise, France 27 C9 49 3N 2 5 E
Ponton →, Canada 142 B5 58 27N 116 11W
Pontorson, France 26 D5 48 34N 1 30W
Pontrémoli, Italy 44 D6 44 22N 9 53 E
Pontresina, Switz. 33 D9 46 29N 9 48 E
Pontrieux, France 26 D3 48 42N 3 10W
Ponts, Spain 40 D6 41 55N 1 12 E
Pontypool, Canada 150 B6 44 6N 78 38W
Pontypool, U.K. 21 F4 51 42N 3 2W
Ponza, Italy 46 B5 40 54N 12 58 E
Ponziane, Ísole, Italy 46 B5 40 55N 12 57 E
Poochera, Australia 127 E1 32 43 S 134 51 E
Poole, U.K. 21 G6 50 43N 1 59W
Poole □, U.K. 21 G6 50 43N 1 59W
Pooler, U.S.A. 152 C8 32 7N 81 15W
Poona = Pune, India 94 E1 18 29N 73 57 E
Poonamallee, India 95 H5 13 3N 80 10 E
Pooncarie, Australia 128 B5 33 22 S 142 31 E
Poopelloe L., Australia 128 A6 31 40 S 144 0 E
Poopó, Bolivia 172 D4 18 23 S 66 59W
Poopó, L. de, Bolivia 172 D4 18 30 S 67 35W
Poor Knights Is., N.Z. 130 B3 35 29 S 174 43 E
Popa, Gabon 114 C2 1 35 S 12 32 E
Popayán, Colombia 168 C2 2 27N 76 36W
Poperinge, Belgium 24 D2 50 51N 2 42 E
Popilta L., Australia 128 B4 33 10 S 141 42 E
Popina, Bulgaria 51 B10 44 7N 26 57 E
Popio L., Australia 128 B4 33 10 S 141 52 E
Poplar, U.S.A. 154 A2 48 7N 105 12W
Poplar →, Canada 143 C9 53 0N 97 19W
Poplar Bluff, U.S.A. 155 G9 36 46N 90 24W
Poplarville, U.S.A. 155 K10 30 51N 89 32W
Popocatépetl, Volcán, Mexico 163 D5 19 2N 98 38W
Popokabaka, Dem. Rep. of the Congo 115 D3 5 41 S 16 40 E
Pópoli, Italy 45 F10 42 10N 13 50 E
Popolo, Dem. Rep. of the Congo 114 B4 2 22N 21 8 E
Popomanaseu, Mt., Solomon Is. 133 M11 9 40 S 160 1 E
Popondetta, Papua N. G. 132 E5 8 48 S 148 17 E
Popovača, Croatia 45 C13 45 30N 16 41 E
Popovo, Bulgaria 51 C10 43 21N 26 18 E
Poppberg, Germany 31 F7 49 26N 11 37 E
Poppi, Italy 45 E8 43 43N 11 46 E
Poprad, Slovak Rep. 35 B13 49 3N 20 18 E
Poprad →, Slovak Rep. 35 B13 49 38N 20 42 E
Poradaha, Bangla. 90 D2 23 51N 89 1 E
Porali →, Pakistan 91 D2 25 58N 66 26 E
Porangaba, Brazil 172 B3 8 48 S 70 36W
Porangahau, N.Z. 130 G5 40 17 S 176 37 E
Porangatu, Brazil 171 D2 13 26 S 49 10W
Porbandar, India 92 J3 21 44N 69 43 E
Porce →, Colombia 168 B3 7 28N 74 53W
Porcher I., Canada 142 C2 53 50N 130 30W
Porco, Bolivia 173 D4 19 50 S 65 59W
Porcos →, Brazil 171 D2 12 42 S 45 7W
Porcuna, Spain 43 H6 37 52N 4 11W
Porcupine →, Canada 143 B8 59 11N 104 46W
Porcupine →, U.S.A. 144 C11 66 34N 145 19W
Porcupine Gorge Nat. Park, Australia 126 C3 20 22 S 144 26 E
Pordenone, Italy 45 C9 45 57N 12 39 E
Pordim, Bulgaria 51 C8 43 23N 24 51 E
Pore, Colombia 168 B3 5 43N 72 0W
Poreč, Croatia 45 C10 45 14N 13 36 E
Porecatu, Brazil 171 F1 22 43 S 51 24W
Poretskoye, Russia 60 C8 55 9N 46 21 E
Porgera, Papua N. G. 132 C2 5 28 S 143 12 E
Pori, Finland 15 F19 61 29N 21 48 E
Porí, Greece 48 F5 35 58N 23 13 E
Porkhov, Russia 58 D5 57 45N 29 38 E
Porlamar, Venezuela 169 A5 10 57N 63 51W
Porlezza, Italy 44 B6 46 2N 9 7 E
Porma →, Spain 42 C5 42 49N 5 28W
Pornic, France 26 E4 47 7N 2 5W
Poronaysk, Russia 67 E15 49 13N 143 0 E
Póros 39 C2 38 9N 20 47 E
Póros, Attikí, Greece 48 D5 37 30N 23 30 E
Póros, Levkás, Greece 39 B2 38 38N 20 43 E
Poroshiri-Dake, Japan 70 C11 42 41N 142 52 E
Poroszló, Hungary 52 C5 47 39N 20 40 E
Poroto Mts., Tanzania 119 D3 9 0 S 33 30 E
Porpoise B., Antarctica 7 C9 66 0 S 127 0 E
Porpoise Pt., Ascension I. 9 g 7 54 S 14 21W
Porquerolles, Î. de, France 29 F10 43 0N 6 13 E
Porrentruy, Switz. 32 B4 47 25N 7 6 E
Porreres, Spain 38 B4 39 31N 3 2 E
Porsangen, Norway 14 A21 70 40N 25 40 E
Porsgrunn, Norway 15 G13 59 10N 9 40 E
Port Adelaide, Australia 128 C3 34 46 S 138 30 E
Port Alberni, Canada 142 D4 49 14N 124 50W
Port Albert, Australia 129 E7 38 42 S 146 42 E
Port Alexander, U.S.A. 144 H14 56 15N 134 38W
Port Alfred, S. Africa 116 E4 33 36 S 26 55 E
Port Alice, Canada 142 C3 50 20N 127 25W
Port Allegany, U.S.A. 150 E6 41 48N 78 17W
Port Allen, U.S.A. 155 K9 30 27N 91 12W
Port Alma, Australia 126 C5 23 38 S 150 53 E
Port Angeles, U.S.A. 160 B3 48 7N 123 27W
Port Antonio, Jamaica 164 a 18 10N 76 30W
Port Aransas, U.S.A. 155 M6 27 50N 97 4W
Port Arthur = Lüshun, China 75 E11 38 45N 121 15 E
Port Arthur, Australia 127 G4 43 7 S 147 50 E
Port Arthur, U.S.A. 155 L8 29 54N 93 56W
Port au Choix, Canada 141 B8 50 43N 57 22W
Port au Port B., Canada 141 C8 48 40N 58 50W
Port-au-Prince, Haiti 165 C5 18 40N 72 20W
Port Augusta, Australia 128 B2 32 30 S 137 50 E
Port Austin, U.S.A. 150 B2 44 3N 83 1W
Port Bell, Uganda 118 B3 0 18N 32 35 E
Port Bergé Vaovao, Madag. 117 B8 15 33 S 47 40 E
Port Blair, India 95 J11 11 40N 92 45 E
Port Blandford, Canada 141 C9 48 20N 54 10W
Port-Bouët, Ivory C. 112 D4 5 16N 3 57W
Port Bradshaw, Australia 126 A2 12 30 S 137 20 E
Port Broughton, Australia 128 B2 33 37 S 137 56 E
Port Burwell, Canada 150 D4 42 40N 80 48W
Port Byron, U.S.A. 156 C6 41 37N 90 19W
Port Campbell, Australia 128 E5 38 37 S 143 1 E
Port Campbell, India 95 J11 11 56N 92 37 E
Port Campbell Nat. Park, Australia 128 E5 38 8 S 143 6 E
Port Canning, India 93 H13 22 23N 88 40 E
Port-Cartier, Canada 141 B6 50 2N 66 50W
Port Chalmers, N.Z. 131 F5 45 49 S 170 30 E
Port Charles, N.Z. 130 C4 36 33 S 175 30 E
Port Charlotte, U.S.A. 153 J7 26 59N 82 6W
Port Chester, U.S.A. 151 F11 41 0N 73 40W
Port Clements, Canada 142 C2 53 40N 132 10W
Port Clinton, U.S.A. 157 C14 41 31N 82 56W
Port Colborne, Canada 140 D4 42 50N 79 10W
Port Coquitlam, Canada 142 D4 49 15N 122 45W
Port Cornwallis, India 95 H11 13 17N 93 5 E
Port Credit, Canada 150 C5 43 33N 79 35W
Port Curtis, Australia 126 C5 23 57 S 151 20 E
Port d'Alcúdia, Spain 38 B4 39 50N 3 7 E
Port Dalhousie, Canada 150 C5 43 13N 79 16W
Port d'Andratx, Spain 38 B3 39 32N 2 23 E
Port Darwin, Australia 124 B5 12 24 S 130 45 E
Port Darwin, Falk. Is. 9 f 51 50 S 59 0W
Port Davey, Australia 127 G4 43 16 S 145 55 E
Port-de-Bouc, France 29 E8 43 24N 4 59 E
Port-de-Paix, Haiti 165 C5 19 50N 72 50W
Port de Pollença, Spain 38 B4 39 54N 3 4 E
Port de Sóller, Spain 38 B3 39 48N 2 42 E
Port Dickson, Malaysia 87 L3 2 30N 101 49 E
Port Douglas, Australia 126 B4 16 30 S 145 30 E
Port Dover, Canada 150 D4 42 47N 80 12W
Port Edward, Canada 142 C2 54 12N 130 10W
Port Elgin, Canada 140 D3 44 25N 81 25W
Port Elizabeth, S. Africa 116 E4 33 58 S 25 40 E
Port Ellen, U.K. 22 F2 55 38N 6 11W
Port Elliot, Australia 128 C3 35 32 S 138 41 E
Port-en-Bessin, France 26 C6 49 21N 0 45W
Port Erin, U.K. 20 C3 54 5N 4 45W
Port Essington, Australia 124 B5 11 15 S 132 10 E
Port Etienne = Nouâdhibou, Mauritania 110 D1 20 54N 17 0W
Port Ewen, U.S.A. 151 E11 41 54N 73 59W
Port Fairy, Australia 128 E5 38 22 S 142 12 E
Port Fitzroy, N.Z. 130 C4 36 8 S 175 20 E
Port Fouâd = Bûr Fuad, Egypt 106 H8 31 15N 32 20 E
Port Gamble, U.S.A. 160 C4 47 51N 122 35W
Port-Gentil, Gabon 114 C1 0 40 S 8 50 E
Port Germein, Australia 127 E2 33 1 S 138 1 E
Port Gibson, U.S.A. 155 K9 31 58N 90 59W
Port Glasgow, U.K. 22 F4 55 56N 4 41W
Port Harcourt, Nigeria 113 E6 4 40N 7 10 E
Port Hardy, Canada 142 C3 50 41N 127 30W
Port Harrison = Inukjuak, Canada 139 C12 58 25N 78 15W
Port Hawkesbury, Canada 141 C7 45 36N 61 22W
Port Hedland, Australia 124 D2 20 25 S 118 35 E
Port Heiden, U.S.A. 144 H8 56 55N 158 41W
Port Henry, U.S.A. 151 B11 44 3N 73 28W
Port Hood, Canada 141 C7 46 0N 61 32W
Port Hope, Canada 140 D4 43 56N 78 20W
Port Hope, U.S.A. 150 C2 43 57N 82 43W
Port Hope Simpson, Canada 141 B8 52 33N 56 18W
Port Hueneme, U.S.A. 161 L7 34 7N 119 12W
Port Huron, U.S.A. 150 D2 42 58N 82 26W
Port Ilıç, Azerbaijan 101 C13 38 53N 48 47 E
Port Jefferson, U.S.A. 151 F11 40 57N 73 3W
Port Jervis, U.S.A. 151 E10 41 22N 74 41W
Port-Joinville, France 26 F4 46 45N 2 23W
Port Katon, Russia 59 J10 46 52N 38 46 E
Port Kelang = Pelabuhan Kelang, Malaysia 87 L3 3 0N 101 23 E
Port Kembla, Australia 129 C9 34 52 S 150 49 E
Port Kenny, Australia 127 E1 33 10 S 134 41 E
Port-la-Nouvelle, France 28 E7 43 1N 3 3 E
Port Lairge = Waterford, Ireland 23 D4 52 15N 7 8W
Port Laoise, Ireland 23 C4 53 2N 7 18W
Port Lavaca, U.S.A. 155 L6 28 37N 96 38W
Port Leyden, U.S.A. 151 C9 43 35N 75 21W
Port Lincoln, Australia 128 C1 34 42 S 135 52 E
Port Lions, U.S.A. 144 H9 57 52N 152 53W
Port Loko, S. Leone 112 D2 8 48N 12 46W
Port Louis, France 26 E3 47 42N 3 22W
Port-Louis, Guadeloupe 164 b 16 28N 61 32W
Port Louis, Mauritius 105 H9 20 10 S 57 30 E
Port MacDonnell, Australia 128 E4 38 5 S 140 48 E
Port McNeill, Canada 142 C3 50 35N 127 6W
Port Macquarie, Australia 129 A10 31 25 S 152 25 E
Port Maria, Jamaica 164 a 18 25N 76 55W
Port Matilda, U.S.A. 150 F6 40 48N 78 3W
Port Mayaca, U.S.A. 153 J9 26 59N 80 36W
Port Mellon, Canada 142 D4 49 32N 123 31W
Port-Menier, Canada 141 C7 49 51N 64 15W
Port Moller, U.S.A. 144 J7 55 59N 160 34W
Port Moody, Canada 160 A4 49 17N 122 51W
Port Morant, Jamaica 164 a 17 54N 76 19W
Port Moresby, Papua N. G. 132 E4 9 24 S 147 8 E
Port Mourant, Guyana 169 B6 6 15N 57 20W
Port Musgrave, Australia 126 A3 11 55 S 141 50 E
Port Narevin, Vanuatu 133 H7 18 45 S 169 10 E
Port-Navalo, France 26 E4 47 34N 2 54W
Port Neches, U.S.A. 155 L8 30 0N 93 59W
Port Nicholson, N.Z. 130 H3 41 20 S 174 52 E
Port Nolloth, S. Africa 116 D2 29 17 S 16 52 E
Port Nouveau-Québec = Kangiqsualujjuaq, Canada 139 C13 58 30N 65 59W
Port of Spain, Trin. & Tob. 165 D7 10 40N 61 31W
Port Olry, Vanuatu 133 E5 15 1 S 167 4 E
Port Orange, U.S.A. 153 F9 29 9N 80 59W
Port Orchard, U.S.A. 160 C4 47 32N 122 38W
Port Orford, U.S.A. 158 E1 42 45N 124 30W
Port Pegasus, N.Z. 131 H2 47 12 S 167 41 E
Port Perry, Canada 140 D4 44 6N 78 56W
Port Phillip B., Australia 129 E6 38 10 S 144 50 E
Port Pirie, Australia 128 B3 33 10 S 138 1 E
Port Radium = Echo Bay, Canada 138 B8 66 5N 117 55W
Port Renfrew, Canada 142 D4 48 30N 124 20W
Port Roper, Australia 126 A2 14 45 S 135 25 E
Port Rowan, Canada 150 D4 42 40N 80 30W
Port Royal Sd., U.S.A. 152 C9 32 15N 80 40W
Port Safaga = Bûr Safâga, Egypt 96 E2 26 43N 33 57 E
Port Said = Bûr Sa'îd, Egypt 106 H8 31 16N 32 18 E
Port St. Joe, U.S.A. 152 F4 29 49N 85 18W
Port St. Johns = Umzimvubu, S. Africa 117 E4 31 38 S 29 33 E
Port-St-Louis-du-Rhône, France 29 E8 43 23N 4 49 E
Port St. Lucie, U.S.A. 149 M5 27 20N 80 20W
Port-Ste-Marie, France 28 D4 44 15N 0 25 E
Port Salerno, U.S.A. 153 H9 27 9N 80 12W
Port Sanilac, U.S.A. 150 C2 43 26N 82 33W
Port Severn, Canada 150 B5 44 48N 79 43W
Port Shepstone, S. Africa 117 E5 30 44 S 30 28 E
Port Simpson, Canada 142 C2 54 30N 130 20W
Port Stanley = Stanley, Falk. Is. 9 f 51 40 S 59 51W
Port Stanley, Canada 140 D3 42 40N 81 10W
Port Sudan = Bûr Sûdân, Sudan 106 D4 19 32N 37 9 E
Port Sulphur, U.S.A. 155 L10 29 29N 89 42W
Port-sur-Saône, France 27 E13 47 42N 6 2 E
Port Talbot, U.K. 21 F4 51 35N 3 47W
Port Taufîq = Bûr Taufiq, Egypt 106 J8 29 54N 32 32 E
Port Townsend, U.S.A. 160 B4 48 7N 122 45W
Port-Vato, Vanuatu 133 F6 16 25 S 168 1 E
Port-Vendres, France 28 F7 42 32N 3 8 E
Port Victoria, Australia 128 C2 34 30 S 137 29 E
Port Vila, Vanuatu 133 G6 17 45 S 168 18 E
Port Vladimir, Russia 56 A5 69 25N 33 6 E
Port Wakefield, Australia 128 C3 34 12 S 138 10 E
Port Washington, U.S.A. 148 D2 43 23N 87 53W
Port Weld = Kuala Sepetang, Malaysia 87 K3 4 49N 100 28 E
Port Wentworth, U.S.A. 152 C8 32 9N 81 10W
Porta Orientalis, Romania 37 F12 45 6N 22 18 E
Portachuelo, Bolivia 173 D5 17 10 S 63 20W
Portadown, U.K. 23 B5 54 25N 6 27W
Portaferry, U.K. 23 B6 54 23N 5 33W
Portage, Mich., U.S.A. 157 B11 42 12N 85 35W
Portage, Pa., U.S.A. 150 F6 40 23N 78 41W
Portage, Wis., U.S.A. 154 D10 43 33N 89 28W
Portage →, U.S.A. 157 C14 41 31N 83 5W
Portage La Prairie, Canada 143 D9 49 58N 98 18W
Portageville, U.S.A. 155 G10 36 26N 89 42W
Portal, U.S.A. 152 C8 32 33N 81 56W
Portalegre, Portugal 43 F3 39 19N 7 25W
Portalegre □, Portugal 43 F3 39 20N 7 40W
Portales, U.S.A. 155 H3 34 11N 103 20W
Portarlington, Ireland 23 C4 53 9N 7 14W
Portbou, Spain 40 C8 42 25N 3 9 E
Porteira, Brazil 169 D6 1 5 S 57 4W
Porteirinha, Brazil 171 E3 15 44 S 43 2W
Portel, Brazil 170 B1 1 57 S 50 49W
Portel, Portugal 43 G3 38 19N 7 41W
Porter, U.S.A. 157 C9 41 36N 87 4W
Porter L., N.W.T., Canada 143 A7 61 41N 108 5W
Porter L., Sask., Canada 143 B7 56 20N 107 20W
Porterville, S. Africa 116 E2 33 0 S 19 0 E
Porterville, U.S.A. 160 J8 36 4N 119 1W
Portes-lès-Valence, France 29 D8 44 52N 4 54 E
Porthcawl, U.K. 21 F4 51 29N 3 42W
Porthill, U.S.A. 158 B5 48 59N 116 30W
Porthmadog, U.K. 20 E3 52 55N 4 8W
Portile de Fier, Europe 52 F7 44 44N 22 30 E
Portimão, Portugal 43 H2 37 8N 8 32W
Portishead, U.K. 21 F5 51 29N 2 46W
Portiţei, Gura, Romania 53 F14 44 41N 29 0 E
Portknockie, U.K. 22 D6 57 42N 2 51W
Portland, N.S.W., Australia 129 B9 33 20 S 150 0 E
Portland, Vic., Australia 128 E4 38 20 S 141 35 E
Portland, Canada 151 B8 44 42N 76 12W
Portland, Conn., U.S.A. 151 E12 41 34N 72 38W
Portland, Fla., U.S.A. 152 E3 30 31N 86 12W
Portland, Ind., U.S.A. 157 D12 40 26N 84 59W
Portland, Maine, U.S.A. 139 D12 43 39N 70 16W
Portland, Mich., U.S.A. 157 B12 42 52N 84 54W
Portland, Oreg., U.S.A. 160 E4 45 32N 122 37W
Portland, Pa., U.S.A. 151 F9 40 55N 75 6W
Portland, Tex., U.S.A. 155 M6 27 53N 97 20W
Portland, I. of, U.K. 21 G5 50 33N 2 26W
Portland B., Australia 128 E4 38 15 S 141 45 E
Portland Bight, Jamaica 164 a 17 52N 77 5W
Portland Bill, U.K. 21 G5 50 31N 2 28W
Portland Canal, U.S.A. 142 B2 55 56N 130 0W
Portland Pt., N.Z. 130 F6 39 20 S 177 51 E
Portland Pt., Ascension I. 9 g 7 59 S 14 25W
Portland Pt., Jamaica 164 a 17 42N 77 11W
Portmadoc = Porthmadog, U.K. 20 E3 52 55N 4 8W
Portmore, Jamaica 164 a 17 53N 77 33W
Pôrto, Brazil 170 B3 3 54 S 42 42W
Porto, France 29 F12 42 16N 8 42 E
Porto, Portugal 42 D2 41 8N 8 40W
Porto □, Portugal 42 D2 41 8N 8 20W
Porto, G. de, France 29 F12 42 17N 8 34 E
Pôrto Acre, Brazil 172 B4 9 34 S 67 31W
Pôrto Alegre, Pará, Brazil 169 D7 4 22 S 52 44W
Pôrto Alegre, Rio Grande do S., Brazil 175 C5 30 5 S 51 10W
Porto Alegre, São Tomé & Principe 115 G6 0 2N 6 32 E
Porto Amboim = Gunza, Angola 115 E2 10 50 S 13 50 E
Porto Azzurro, Italy 44 F7 42 46N 10 24 E
Pôrto Cajueiro, Brazil 173 C6 11 3 S 55 53W
Porto Cristo, Spain 38 B4 39 33N 3 20 E
Pôrto da Fôlha, Brazil 170 C4 9 55 S 37 17W
Pôrto de Móz, Brazil 169 D7 1 41 S 52 13W
Pôrto de Pedras, Brazil 170 C4 9 10 S 35 17W
Pôrto des Meinacos, Brazil 173 C7 12 33 S 53 7W
Pôrto dos Gaúchos, Brazil 173 C6 11 32 S 57 16W
Porto Empédocle, Italy 46 E6 37 17N 13 32 E
Pôrto Esperança, Brazil 173 D6 19 37 S 57 29W
Pôrto Esperidão, Brazil 173 D6 15 51 S 58 28W
Pôrto Formoso, Azores 9 d3 37 49N 25 25W
Pôrto Franco, Brazil 170 C2 6 20 S 47 24W
Pôrto Grande, Brazil 169 C7 0 42N 51 24W
Porto Inglês, C. Verde Is. 9 j 15 21N 23 10W
Pôrto Jofre, Brazil 173 D6 17 20 S 56 48W
Pórto Lágos, Greece 51 E9 41 1N 25 6 E
Pôrto Mendes, Brazil 175 A5 24 30 S 54 15W
Porto Moniz, Madeira 9 c 32 52N 17 11W
Pôrto Murtinho, Brazil 173 E6 21 45 S 57 55W
Pôrto Nacional, Brazil 170 D2 10 40 S 48 30W
Porto-Novo, Benin 113 D5 6 23N 2 42 E
Porto Petro, Spain 38 B4 39 22N 3 13 E
Porto San Giórgio, Italy 45 E10 43 11N 13 48 E
Porto Sant' Elpídio, Italy 45 E10 43 15N 13 43 E
Pôrto Santana, Brazil 169 D7 0 3 S 51 11W
Porto Santo, I. de, Madeira 110 B1 33 45N 16 25W
Porto Santo Stéfano, Italy 44 F8 42 26N 11 7 E
Pôrto São José, Brazil 175 A5 22 43 S 53 10W
Pôrto Seguro, Brazil 171 E4 16 26 S 39 5W
Porto Tolle, Italy 45 D9 44 56N 12 22 E
Porto Tórres, Italy 46 B1 40 50N 8 24 E
Pôrto União, Brazil 175 B5 26 10 S 51 10W
Pôrto Válter, Brazil 172 B3 8 15 S 72 40W
Porto-Vecchio, France 29 G13 41 35N 9 16 E
Pôrto Velho, Brazil 173 B5 8 46 S 63 54W
Portobelo, Panama 164 E4 9 35N 79 42W
Portoferráio, Italy 44 F7 42 48N 10 20 E
Portogruaro, Italy 45 C9 45 47N 12 50 E
Portola, U.S.A. 160 F6 39 49N 120 28W
Portomaggiore, Italy 45 D8 44 42N 11 48 E
Portør, Norway 18 F6 58 48N 9 28 E
Portoscuso, Italy 46 C1 39 12N 8 24 E
Portovénere, Italy 44 D6 44 3N 9 51 E
Portoviejo, Ecuador 168 D1 1 7 S 80 28W
Portpatrick, U.K. 22 G3 54 51N 5 7W
Portree, U.K. 22 D2 57 25N 6 12W
Portrush, U.K. 23 A5 55 12N 6 40W
Portsmouth, Domin. 165 C7 15 34N 61 27W
Portsmouth, U.K. 21 G6 50 48N 1 6W
Portsmouth, N.H., U.S.A. 149 D10 43 5N 70 45W
Portsmouth, Ohio, U.S.A. 148 F4 38 44N 82 57W
Portsmouth, R.I., U.S.A. 151 E13 41 36N 71 15W
Portsmouth, Va., U.S.A. 148 G7 36 50N 76 18W
Portsmouth □, U.K. 21 G6 50 48N 1 6W
Portsoy, U.K. 22 D6 57 41N 2 41W
Portstewart, U.K. 23 A5 55 11N 6 43W
Porttipahtan tekojärvi, Finland 14 B22 68 5N 26 40 E
Portugal ■, Europe 42 F3 40 0N 8 0W
Portugalete, Spain 40 B1 43 19N 3 4W
Portuguesa □, Venezuela 168 B4 9 10N 69 15W
Portumna, Ireland 23 C3 53 6N 8 14W
Portville, U.S.A. 150 D6 42 3N 78 20W
Porvenir, Bolivia 172 C4 11 10 S 68 50W
Porvenir, Chile 176 D2 53 10 S 70 16W
Porvoo, Finland 15 F21 60 24N 25 40 E
Porzuna, Spain 43 F6 39 9N 4 9W
Posada, Italy 46 B2 40 38N 9 43 E
Posada →, Italy 46 B2 40 39N 9 45 E

Quedlinburg 269

Puerto Deseado, *Argentina* **176 C3** 47 55 S 66 0W
Puerto Escondido, *Mexico* **163 D5** 15 50N 97 3W
Puerto Gaitán, *Colombia* **168 C3** 4 19N 72 4W
Puerto Guaraní, *Paraguay* **173 E6** 21 18 S 57 55W
Puerto Heath, *Bolivia* **172 C4** 12 34 S 68 39W
Puerto Huitoto, *Colombia* **168 C3** 0 18N 74 3W
Puerto Inca, *Peru* **172 B3** 9 22 S 74 54W
Puerto Inírida, *Colombia* **168 C4** 3 53N 67 52W
Puerto Juárez, *Mexico* **163 C7** 21 11N 86 49W
Puerto La Cruz, *Venezuela* **169 A5** 10 13N 64 38W
Puerto Leguízamo, *Colombia* **168 D3** 0 12 S 74 46W
Puerto Limón, *Colombia* **168 C3** 3 23N 73 30W
Puerto Lobos, *Argentina* **176 B3** 42 0 S 65 3W
Puerto López, *Colombia* **168 C3** 4 5N 72 58W
Puerto Lumbreras, *Spain* **41 H3** 37 34N 1 48W
Puerto Madryn, *Argentina* **176 B3** 42 48 S 65 4W
Puerto Maldonado, *Peru* **172 C4** 12 30 S 69 10W
Puerto Manotí, *Cuba* **164 B4** 21 22N 76 50W
Puerto Mariti, *Colombia* **168 D4** 1 10 S 69 59W
Puerto Mercedes, *Colombia* **168 C3** 1 11N 72 53W
Puerto Miraña, *Colombia* **168 D3** 1 20 S 70 19W
Puerto Montt, *Chile* **176 B2** 41 28 S 73 0W
Puerto Morazán, *Nic.* **164 D2** 12 51N 87 11W
Puerto Morelos, *Mexico* **163 C7** 20 49N 86 52W
Puerto Mutis, *Colombia* **168 B2** 6 14N 77 25W
Puerto Nariño, *Colombia* **168 C4** 4 56N 67 48W
Puerto Natales, *Chile* **176 D2** 51 45 S 72 15W
Puerto Nuevo, *Colombia* **168 B4** 5 53N 69 56W
Puerto Nutrias, *Venezuela* **168 B4** 8 5N 69 18W
Puerto Ordaz, *Venezuela* **169 B5** 8 16N 62 44W
Puerto Padre, *Cuba* **164 B4** 21 13N 76 35W
Puerto Páez, *Venezuela* **168 B4** 6 13N 67 28W
Puerto Peñasco, *Mexico* **162 A2** 31 20N 113 33W
Puerto Pinasco, *Paraguay* **174 A4** 22 36 S 57 50W
Puerto Pirámides, *Argentina* **176 B4** 42 35 S 64 20W
Puerto Piritu, *Venezuela* **169 A4** 10 4N 65 3W
Puerto Plata, *Dom. Rep.* **165 C5** 19 48N 70 45W
Puerto Pollensa = Port de Pollença, *Spain* **38 B4** 39 54N 3 4 E
Puerto Portillo, *Peru* **172 B3** 9 45 S 72 42W
Puerto Princesa, *Phil.* **81 G2** 9 46N 118 45 E
Puerto Quellón, *Chile* **176 B2** 43 7 S 73 37W
Puerto Quepos, *Costa Rica* **164 E3** 9 29N 84 6W
Puerto Real, *Spain* **43 J4** 36 33N 6 12W
Puerto Rico, *Bolivia* **172 C4** 11 5 S 67 38W
Puerto Rico, *Canary Is.* **9 e1** 27 47N 15 42W
Puerto Rico ■, *W. Indies* **165 d** 18 15N 66 45W
Puerto Rico Trench, *Atl. Oc.* **165 C6** 19 50N 66 0W
Puerto Rondón, *Colombia* **168 B3** 6 17N 71 6W
Puerto Saavedra, *Chile* **176 A2** 38 47 S 73 24W
Puerto Sastre, *Paraguay* **174 A4** 22 2 S 57 55W
Puerto Serrano, *Spain* **43 J5** 36 56N 5 33W
Puerto Siles, *Bolivia* **173 C4** 12 48 S 65 5W
Puerto Suárez, *Bolivia* **173 D6** 18 58 S 57 52W
Puerto Tejada, *Colombia* **168 C2** 3 14N 76 24W
Puerto Umbría, *Colombia* **168 C2** 0 52N 76 33W
Puerto Vallarta, *Mexico* **162 C3** 20 36N 105 15W
Puerto Varas, *Chile* **176 B2** 41 19 S 72 59W
Puerto Velasco Ibarra, *Ecuador* **172 a** 1 17 S 90 29W
Puerto Villamil, *Ecuador* **172 a** 0 56 S 91 1W
Puerto Villazón, *Bolivia* **173 C5** 13 32 S 61 57W
Puerto Wilches, *Colombia* **168 B3** 7 21N 73 54W
Puertollano, *Spain* **43 G6** 38 43N 4 7W
Puesto Cunambo, *Peru* **168 D2** 2 10 S 76 0W
Pueyrredón, L., *Argentina* **176 C2** 47 20 S 72 0W
Puffin I., *Ireland* **23 E1** 51 50N 10 24W
Pugachev, *Russia* **60 D9** 52 0N 48 49 E
Pugal, *India* **92 E5** 28 30N 72 48 E
Puge, *China* **76 D4** 27 20N 102 31 E
Puge, *Tanzania* **118 C3** 4 45 S 33 11 E
Puget Sound, *U.S.A.* **158 C2** 47 50N 122 30W
Puget-Théniers, *France* **29 E10** 43 58N 6 53 E
Púglia □, *Italy* **47 A9** 41 15N 16 15 E
Pugŏdong, *N. Korea* **75 C16** 42 5N 130 0 E
Pugu, *Tanzania* **118 D4** 6 55 S 39 4 E
Pūgūnzī, *Iran* **97 E8** 25 49N 59 10 E
Puha, *N.Z.* **130 E6** 38 30 S 177 50 E
Pui, *Romania* **52 E8** 45 30N 23 4 E
Puica, *Peru* **172 C3** 15 0 S 72 33W
Puieşti, *Romania* **53 D12** 46 25N 27 33 E
Puig Major, *Spain* **38 B3** 39 48N 2 47 E
Puigcerdà, *Spain* **40 C6** 42 24N 1 50 E
Puigmal, *Spain* **40 C7** 42 23N 2 7 E
Puigpunyent, *Spain* **38 B3** 39 38N 2 32 E
Puijiang, *China* **76 B4** 30 14N 103 30 E
Puisaye, Collines de la, *France* **27 E10** 47 37N 3 20 E
Puiseaux, *France* **27 D9** 48 11N 2 30 E
Pujehun, *S. Leone* **112 D2** 7 23N 11 45W
Pujiang, *China* **77 C12** 29 29N 119 54 E
Pujilí, *Ecuador* **168 D2** 0 57 S 78 41W
Pujols, *France* **28 D3** 44 48N 0 2W
Pujon-chŏsuji, *N. Korea* **75 D14** 40 35N 127 35 E
Pukaki, L., *N.Z.* **131 E5** 44 4 S 170 1 E
Pukalani, *U.S.A.* **145 C5** 20 51N 156 20W
Pukapuka, *Cook Is.* **135 J11** 10 53 S 165 49W
Pukaskwa Nat. Park, *Canada* **140 C2** 48 20N 86 0W
Pukatawagan, *Canada* **143 B8** 55 45N 101 20W
Pukchin, *N. Korea* **75 D13** 40 12N 125 45 E
Pukch'ŏng, *N. Korea* **75 D15** 40 14N 128 10 E
Pukë, *Albania* **50 D3** 42 2N 19 53 E
Pukearuhe, *N.Z.* **130 E3** 38 55 S 174 31 E
Pukekohe, *N.Z.* **130 D3** 37 12 S 174 55 E
Puketeraki Ra., *N.Z.* **131 C7** 42 58 S 172 13 E
Puketoi Ra., *N.Z.* **130 G5** 40 30 S 176 5 E
Pukeuri, *N.Z.* **131 F6** 45 4 S 171 2 E
Pukhrayan, *India* **93 F8** 26 14N 79 51 E
Pukoo, *U.S.A.* **145 B5** 21 4N 156 48W
Pukou, *China* **77 A12** 32 7N 118 38 E
Pula, *Croatia* **45 D10** 44 54N 13 57 E
Pula, *Italy* **46 C1** 39 1N 9 0 E
Pulacayo, *Bolivia* **172 E4** 20 25 S 66 41W
Pulai, *Malaysia* **87 d** 1 20N 103 31 E
Pulandian, *China* **75 E11** 39 25N 121 58 E
Pularumpi, *Australia* **124 B5** 11 24 S 130 26 E
Pulaski, *N.Y., U.S.A.* **151 C8** 43 34N 76 8W
Pulaski, *Tenn., U.S.A.* **149 H2** 35 12N 87 2W
Pulaski, *Va., U.S.A.* **148 G5** 37 3N 80 47W
Pulau →, *Indonesia* **83 C5** 5 50 S 138 15 E
Pulau Miangas, *Indonesia* **81 J6** 5 35N 126 34 E
Puławy, *Poland* **55 G8** 51 23N 21 59 E
Pulga, *U.S.A.* **160 F5** 39 48N 121 29W
Pulgaon, *India* **94 D4** 20 44N 78 21 E
Pulicat, *India* **95 H5** 13 25N 80 19 E
Pulicat L., *India* **95 H5** 13 40N 80 15 E
Pulivendla, *India* **95 G4** 14 25N 78 14 E
Puliyangudi, *India* **95 K3** 9 11N 77 24 E
Pullman, *U.S.A.* **158 C5** 46 44N 117 10W
Pulog, Mt., *Phil.* **80 C3** 16 40N 120 50 E
Púlpito do Sul, *Angola* **115 F2** 15 46 S 12 0 E
Pułtusk, *Poland* **55 F8** 52 43N 21 6 E
Pülümür, *Turkey* **101 C8** 39 30N 39 51 E
Pumlumon Fawr, *U.K.* **21 E4** 52 28N 3 46W
Puna, *Bolivia* **173 D4** 19 45 S 65 28W
Puná, I., *Ecuador* **168 D1** 2 55 S 80 5W
Punaauia, *Tahiti* **133 S16** 17 37 S 149 34W
Punakha, *Bhutan* **90 B2** 27 42N 89 52 E
Punalur, *India* **95 K3** 9 0N 76 56 E
Punaluu, *U.S.A.* **145 J14** 21 35N 157 53W
Punasar, *India* **92 F5** 27 6N 73 6 E
Punata, *Bolivia* **173 D4** 17 32 S 65 50W
Punch, *India* **93 C6** 33 48N 74 4 E
Punch →, *Pakistan* **92 C5** 33 12N 73 40 E
Punda Maria, *S. Africa* **117 C5** 22 40 S 31 5 E
Pune, *India* **94 E1** 18 29N 73 57 E
Pungo Andongo, *Angola* **115 D3** 9 44 S 15 35 E
P'ungsan, *N. Korea* **75 D15** 40 50N 128 9 E
Pungue, Ponte de, *Mozam.* **119 F3** 19 0 S 34 0 E
Puning, *China* **77 F11** 23 20N 116 12 E
Punjab □, *India* **92 D7** 31 0N 76 0 E
Punjab □, *Pakistan* **91 C4** 32 0N 72 30 E
Puno, *Peru* **172 D3** 15 55 S 70 3W
Punpun →, *India* **93 G11** 25 31N 85 18 E
Punta, Cerro de, *Puerto Rico* **165 d** 18 10N 66 37W
Punta Alta, *Argentina* **176 A4** 38 53 S 62 4W
Punta Arenas, *Chile* **176 D2** 53 10 S 71 0W
Punta Cardón, *Venezuela* **168 A3** 11 38N 70 14W
Punta Coles, *Peru* **172 D3** 17 43 S 71 23W
Punta de Bombón, *Peru* **172 D3** 17 10 S 71 48W
Punta de Díaz, *Chile* **174 B1** 28 0 S 70 45W
Punta del Hidalgo, *Canary Is.* **9 e1** 28 33N 16 19W
Punta Delgado, *Argentina* **176 B4** 42 43 S 63 38W
Punta Gorda, *Belize* **163 D7** 16 10N 88 45W
Punta Gorda, *U.S.A.* **149 M5** 26 56N 82 3W
Punta Prieta, *Mexico* **162 B2** 28 58N 114 17W
Punta Prima, *Spain* **38 B5** 39 48N 4 16 E
Punta Umbría, *Spain* **43 H4** 37 10N 6 56W
Puntarenas, *Costa Rica* **164 E3** 10 0N 84 50W
Punto Fijo, *Venezuela* **168 A3** 11 50N 70 13W
Punxsatawney, *U.S.A.* **150 F6** 40 57N 78 59W
Puolo Pt., *U.S.A.* **145 B2** 21 54N 159 36W
Pupuan, *Indonesia* **79 J18** 8 19 S 115 0 E
Puqi, *China* **77 C9** 29 40N 113 50 E
Puquio, *Peru* **172 C3** 14 45 S 74 10W
Pur →, *Russia* **66 C8** 67 31N 77 55 E
Purace, Vol., *Colombia* **168 C2** 2 21N 76 23W
Puračić, *Bos.-H.* **52 F3** 44 33N 18 28 E
Puralia = Puruliya, *India* **93 H12** 23 17N 86 24 E
Puranpur, *India* **93 E9** 28 31N 80 9 E
Purari →, *Papua N. G.* **132 D3** 7 49 S 145 0 E
Purbeck, Isle of, *U.K.* **21 G6** 50 39N 1 59W
Purcell, *U.S.A.* **155 H6** 35 1N 97 22W
Purcell Mts., *Canada* **142 D5** 49 55N 116 15W
Puri, *India* **94 E7** 19 50N 85 58 E
Purificación, *Colombia* **168 C3** 3 51N 74 55W
Purmerend, *Neths.* **24 B4** 52 32N 4 58 E
Purna →, *India* **94 E3** 19 6N 77 2 E
Purnia, *India* **93 G12** 25 45N 87 31 E
Pursat = Pouthisat, *Cambodia* **86 F4** 12 34N 103 50 E
Purukcahu, *Indonesia* **82 C4** 0 35 S 114 35 E
Puruliya, *India* **93 H12** 23 17N 86 24 E
Purus →, *Brazil* **169 D5** 3 42 S 61 28W
Purutu I., *Papua N. G.* **132 E2** 8 24 S 143 27 E
Puruvesi, *Finland* **58 B5** 61 50N 29 30 E
Purvis, *U.S.A.* **155 K10** 31 9N 89 25W
Pŭrvomay, *Bulgaria* **51 D9** 42 8N 25 17 E
Purwa, *India* **93 F9** 26 28N 80 47 E
Purwakarta, *Indonesia* **85 D3** 6 35 S 107 29 E
Purwo, Tanjung, *Indonesia* **79 K18** 8 44 S 114 21 E
Purwodadi, *Jawa, Indonesia* **85 D4** 7 7 S 110 55 E
Purwodadi, *Jawa, Indonesia* **85 D3** 7 51 S 110 0 E
Purwokerto, *Indonesia* **85 D3** 7 25 S 109 14 E
Purworejo, *Indonesia* **85 D4** 7 43 S 110 2 E
Puryŏng, *N. Korea* **75 C15** 42 5N 129 43 E
Pus →, *India* **94 E3** 19 55N 77 55 E
Pusa, *India* **93 G11** 25 59N 85 41 E
Pusad, *India* **94 E3** 19 56N 77 36 E
Pusan, *S. Korea* **75 G15** 35 5N 129 0 E
Pushkin, *Russia* **58 C6** 59 45N 30 25 E
Pushkino, *Moskva, Russia* **58 D9** 56 2N 37 49 E
Pushkino, *Saratov, Russia* **60 E8** 51 16N 47 0 E
Püspökladány, *Hungary* **52 C6** 47 19N 21 6 E
Pustoshka, *Russia* **58 D5** 56 20N 29 30 E
Puszczykowo, *Poland* **55 F3** 52 18N 16 49 E
Putahow L., *Canada* **143 B8** 59 54N 100 40W
Putao, *Burma* **90 B6** 27 28N 97 30 E
Putaruru, *N.Z.* **130 E4** 38 2 S 175 50 E
Putbus, *Germany* **30 A9** 54 22N 13 28 E
Putian, *China* **77 E12** 25 23N 119 0 E
Putignano, *Italy* **47 B10** 40 51N 17 7 E
Putina, *Peru* **172 C4** 14 55 S 69 55W
Puting, Tanjung, *Indonesia* **85 C4** 3 31 S 111 46 E
Putlitz, *Germany* **30 B8** 53 15N 12 2 E
Putna, *Romania* **53 C10** 47 50N 25 33 E
Putna →, *Romania* **53 E12** 45 42N 27 26 E
Putnam, *U.S.A.* **151 E13** 41 55N 71 55W
Putney, *U.S.A.* **152 D5** 31 29N 84 8W
Putnok, *Hungary* **52 B5** 48 18N 20 26 E
Putorana, Gory, *Russia* **67 C10** 69 0N 95 0 E
Putorino, *N.Z.* **130 F5** 39 4 S 176 58 E
Putre, *Chile* **172 D4** 18 12 S 69 35W
Puttalam, *Sri Lanka* **95 K5** 8 1N 79 55 E
Puttalam Lagoon, *Sri Lanka* **95 K4** 8 15N 79 45 E
Puttgarden, *Germany* **30 A7** 54 30N 11 10 E
Püttlingen, *Germany* **31 F2** 49 17N 6 53 E
Puttur, *Andhra Pradesh, India* **95 H4** 13 27N 79 33 E
Puttur, *Karnataka, India* **95 H2** 12 46N 75 12 E
Putty, *Australia* **129 B9** 32 57 S 150 42 E
Putumayo →, *S. Amer.* **168 D4** 3 7 S 67 58W
Putuo, *China* **77 C14** 29 56N 122 20 E
Putussibau, *Indonesia* **85 B4** 0 50N 112 56 E
Pututahi, *N.Z.* **130 E6** 38 39 S 177 53 E
Puu Kaaumakua, *U.S.A.* **145 K14** 21 30N 157 54W
Puu Keahiakahoe, *U.S.A.* **145 K14** 21 23N 157 49W
Puu o Keokeo, *U.S.A.* **145 D6** 19 13N 155 44W
Puuanahulu, *U.S.A.* **145 D6** 19 49N 155 51W
Puukolii, *U.S.A.* **145 B5** 20 56N 156 41W
Puunene, *U.S.A.* **145 C5** 20 53N 156 23W
Puuwai, *U.S.A.* **145 B1** 21 54N 160 12W
Puvirnituq, *Canada* **139 B12** 60 2N 77 10W
Puy-de-Dôme, *France* **28 C6** 45 46N 2 57 E
Puy-de-Dôme □, *France* **28 C7** 45 40N 3 5 E
Puy-l'Évêque, *France* **28 D5** 44 31N 1 9 E
Puyallup, *U.S.A.* **160 C4** 47 12N 122 18W
Puyang, *China* **74 G8** 35 40N 115 1 E
Puyehue, *Chile* **176 B2** 40 40 S 72 37W
Puylaurens, *France* **28 E6** 43 35N 2 0 E
Puyo, *Ecuador* **168 D2** 1 28 S 77 59W
Puysegur Pt., *N.Z.* **131 G1** 46 9 S 166 37 E
Pūzeh Rīg, *Iran* **97 E8** 27 20N 58 40 E
Pwani □, *Tanzania* **118 D4** 7 0 S 39 0 E
Pweto, *Dem. Rep. of the Congo* **119 D2** 8 25 S 28 51 E
Pwinbyu, *Burma* **90 E5** 20 23N 94 40 E
Pwllheli, *U.K.* **20 E3** 52 53N 4 25W
Pya-ozero, *Russia* **56 A5** 66 5N 30 58 E
Pyana →, *Russia* **60 C8** 55 43N 46 1 E
Pyandzh, *Tajikistan* **65 E4** 37 14N 69 6 E
Pyandzh →, *Asia* **65 E4** 37 6N 68 20 E
Pyapon, *Burma* **90 G5** 16 20N 95 40 E
Pyasina →, *Russia* **67 B9** 73 30N 87 0 E
Pyatigorsk, *Russia* **61 H6** 44 2N 43 6 E
Pyatykhatky, *Ukraine* **59 H7** 48 28N 33 38 E
Pyawbwe, *Burma* **90 E6** 20 35N 96 4 E
Pyaye, *Burma* **90 F5** 19 12N 95 10 E
Pydna, *Greece* **50 F6** 40 20N 22 34 E
Pyè = Prome, *Burma* **90 F5** 18 49N 95 13 E
Pyetrikaw, *Belarus* **59 F5** 52 11N 28 29 E
Pyhäjoki, *Finland* **14 D21** 64 28N 24 14 E
Pyinbauk, *Burma* **90 F5** 19 10N 95 12 E
Pyingaing, *Burma* **90 D5** 23 9N 94 50 E
Pyinkayaing, *Burma* **90 H5** 15 58N 94 24 E
Pyinmana, *Burma* **90 F6** 19 45N 96 12 E
Pyinyaung, *Burma* **90 E6** 20 49N 96 25 E
Pyla, C., *Cyprus* **39 F9** 34 56N 33 51 E
Pymatuning Reservoir, *U.S.A.* **150 E4** 41 30N 80 28W
Pyŏktong, *N. Korea* **75 D13** 40 50N 125 50 E
Pyŏnggang, *N. Korea* **75 E14** 38 24N 127 17 E
P'yŏngt'aek, *S. Korea* **75 F14** 37 1N 127 4 E
P'yŏngyang, *N. Korea* **75 E13** 39 0N 125 30 E
Pyote, *U.S.A.* **155 K3** 31 32N 103 8W
Pyramid L., *U.S.A.* **158 G4** 40 1N 119 35W
Pyramid Pk., *U.S.A.* **161 J10** 36 25N 116 37W
Pyramid Pt., *Ascension I.* **9 g** 7 55 S 14 24W
Pyramids, *Egypt* **106 J7** 29 58N 31 9 E
Pyrénées, *Europe* **28 F4** 42 45N 0 18 E
Pyrénées-Atlantiques □, *France* **28 E3** 43 10N 0 50W
Pyrénées-Orientales □, *France* **28 F6** 42 35N 2 26 E
Pyryatyn, *Ukraine* **59 G7** 50 15N 32 25 E
Pyrzyce, *Poland* **55 E1** 53 10N 14 55 E
Pyskowice, *Poland* **55 H5** 50 24N 18 38 E
Pytalovo, *Russia* **58 D4** 57 5N 27 55 E
Pyttegga, *Norway* **18 B4** 62 13N 7 42 E
Pyu, *Burma* **90 F6** 18 30N 96 28 E
Pyzdry, *Poland* **55 F4** 52 11N 17 42 E

Q

Qaanaaq, *Greenland* **10 B4** 77 40N 69 0W
Qabirri →, *Azerbaijan* **61 K8** 41 3N 46 17 E
Qabr Hūd, *Yemen* **99 C5** 16 9N 49 34 E
Qachasnek, *S. Africa* **117 E4** 30 6 S 28 42 E
Qādib, *Yemen* **99 D6** 12 37N 53 57 E
Qa'el Jafr, *Jordan* **103 E5** 30 20N 36 25 E
Qa'emābād, *Iran* **97 D9** 31 44N 60 2 E
Qā'emshahr, *Iran* **97 B7** 36 30N 52 53 E
Qagan Nur, *China* **74 C8** 43 30N 114 55 E
Qahar Youyi Zhongqi, *China* **74 D7** 41 12N 112 40 E
Qahremānshahr = Bākhtarān, *Iran* **101 E12** 34 23N 47 0 E
Qaidam Pendi, *China* **68 C4** 37 0N 95 0 E
Qajarīyeh, *Iran* **97 D6** 31 1N 48 22 E
Qala, *Malta* **38 E7** 36 2N 14 19 E
Qala, Ras il, *Malta* **38 E7** 36 2N 14 20 E
Qala-i-Jadid = Spīn Būldak, *Afghan.* **91 C2** 31 1N 66 25 E
Qala Point = Qala, Ras il, *Malta* **38 E7** 36 2N 14 20 E
Qala Viala, *Pakistan* **92 D2** 30 49N 67 17 E
Qala Yangi, *Afghan.* **92 B2** 34 20N 66 30 E
Qalācheh, *Afghan.* **91 B2** 35 30N 67 43 E
Qalaikhum = Kalaikhum, *Tajikistan* **65 D5** 38 28N 70 46 E
Qalansīyah, *Yemen* **99 D6** 12 41N 53 29 E
Qal'at al Akhḑar, *Si. Arabia* **96 E3** 28 0N 37 10 E
Qal'at Bīshah, *Si. Arabia* **98 C3** 20 0N 42 36 E
Qal'at Dīzah, *Iraq* **101 D11** 36 11N 45 7 E
Qalāt-i-Ghilzai, *Afghan.* **91 B2** 32 15N 66 58 E
Qal'at Şaliḩ, *Iraq* **96 D5** 31 31N 47 16 E
Qal'at Sukkar, *Iraq* **101 G12** 31 51N 46 5 E
Qal'eh-ye Bost, *Afghan.* **91 C2** 31 30N 64 21 E
Qal'eh-ye Now, *Afghan.* **91 B1** 35 0N 63 5 E
Qal'eh-ye Panjeh, *Afghan.* **65 E6** 37 0N 72 35 E
Qal'eh-ye Sarkari, *Afghan.* **91 B2** 35 54N 67 17 E
Qal'eh-ye Valī, *Afghan.* **91 B1** 35 46N 63 45 E
Qalyūb, *Egypt* **106 H7** 30 12N 31 11 E
Qamani'tuaq = Baker Lake, *Canada* **138 B10** 64 20N 96 3W
Qamar, Ghubbat al, *Yemen* **99 C6** 16 20N 52 30 E
Qamar, Jabal al, *Oman* **99 C6** 16 48N 53 15 E
Qamashi, *Uzbekistan* **65 D3** 38 49N 66 28 E
Qamdo, *China* **76 B1** 31 15N 97 6 E
Qamea, *Fiji* **133 A3** 16 45 S 179 45W
Qammieh Point, *Malta* **38 F7** 35 58N 14 19 E
Qamruddin Karez, *Pakistan* **91 C3** 31 45N 68 20 E
Qandahār, *Afghan.* **91 C2** 31 32N 65 43 E
Qandahār □, *Afghan.* **91 C2** 31 0N 65 0 E
Qanshenggel, *Kazakstan* **65 A7** 44 19N 75 33 E
Qapān, *Iran* **97 B7** 37 40N 55 47 E
Qapshaghay, *Kazakstan* **66 E8** 43 51N 77 14 E
Qapshaghay Bögeni, *Kazakstan* **65 B8** 43 45N 77 50 E
Qaqortoq, *Greenland* **10 E6** 60 43N 46 0W
Qâra, *Egypt* **106 B2** 29 38N 26 30 E
Qarā', Jabal al, *Oman* **99 C6** 17 15N 54 15 E
Qara Qash →, *China* **93 B8** 35 0N 78 30 E
Qarabulaq, *Kazakstan* **65 A9** 44 54N 78 30 E
Qarabulaq, *Kazakstan* **65 B4** 42 31N 69 46 E
Qarabulaq, *Kazakstan* **65 A10** 44 59N 60 14 E
Qaraçala, *Azerbaijan* **61 L9** 39 45N 48 53 E
Qaradarya →, *Uzbekistan* **65 C2** 39 0N 63 35 E
Qaraghandy, *Kazakstan* **66 E8** 49 50N 73 10 E
Qārah, *Si. Arabia* **96 D4** 29 55N 40 3 E
Qarak, *China* **65 D8** 38 25N 77 0 E
Qarataū, *Kazakstan* **66 E8** 43 10N 70 28 E
Qarataū, *Kazakstan* **66 E7** 43 30N 69 30 E
Qaraturyq, *Kazakstan* **65 B8** 43 35N 77 50 E
Qarāvol, *Afghan.* **65 E4** 37 14N 68 46 E
Qardho = Gardo, *Somali Rep.* **120 C3** 9 30N 49 6 E
Qardud, *Sudan* **107 E2** 10 20N 29 56 E
Qareh →, *Iran* **101 C12** 39 25N 47 22 E
Qareh Tekān, *Iran* **97 B6** 36 38N 49 29 E
Qarqan He →, *China* **68 C3** 39 30N 88 30 E
Qarqaraly, *Kazakstan* **66 E8** 49 26N 75 30 E
Qarqin, *Afghan.* **65 E3** 37 24N 66 4 E
Qarrasa, *Sudan* **107 E3** 14 38N 32 5 E
Qarshi, *Uzbekistan* **66 F7** 38 53N 65 48 E
Qartabā, *Lebanon* **103 A4** 34 4N 35 50 E
Qaryat al Gharab, *Iraq* **96 D5** 31 27N 44 48 E
Qaryat al 'Ulyā, *Si. Arabia* **96 E5** 27 33N 47 42 E
Qasigianguit, *Greenland* **10 D5** 68 50N 51 18W
Qaskeleng, *Kazakstan* **65 B8** 43 20N 76 35 E
Qasr 'Amra, *Jordan* **96 D3** 31 48N 36 35 E
Qaşr Bū Hadi, *Libya* **108 B3** 31 1N 16 45 E
Qaşr-e Qand, *Iran* **97 E9** 26 15N 60 45 E
Qasr Farâfra, *Egypt* **106 B2** 27 0N 28 1 E
Qa'ṭabah, *Yemen* **98 D4** 13 51N 44 42 E
Qatanā, *Syria* **103 B5** 33 26N 36 4 E
Qaţānan, Ra's, *Yemen* **99 D6** 12 21N 53 33 E
Qatar ■, *Asia* **97 E6** 25 30N 51 15 E
Qatlīsh, *Iran* **97 B8** 37 50N 57 19 E
Qattâra, *Egypt* **106 A2** 30 12N 27 3 E
Qattâra, Munkhafed el, *Egypt* **106 B2** 29 30N 27 30 E
Qattâra Depression = Qattâra, Munkhafed el, *Egypt* **106 B2** 29 30N 27 30 E
Qawām al Ḩamzah, *Iraq* **96 D5** 31 43N 44 58 E
Qawra Point, *Malta* **38 F7** 35 58N 14 26 E
Qāyen, *Iran* **97 C8** 33 40N 59 10 E
Qazaqstan = Kazakstan ■, *Asia* **66 E7** 50 0N 70 0 E
Qazimämmäd, *Azerbaijan* **61 K9** 40 3N 49 0 E
Qazvin, *Iran* **97 B6** 36 15N 50 0 E
Qazyghurt, *Kazakstan* **65 C4** 41 45N 69 23 E
Qeissan, *Sudan* **107 E3** 10 43N 34 40 E
Qena, *Egypt* **106 B3** 26 10N 32 43 E
Qena, W. →, *Egypt* **106 B3** 26 12N 32 44 E
Qeqertarsuaq, *Greenland* **10 D5** 69 45N 53 30W
Qeqertarsuaq, *Greenland* **10 D5** 69 15N 53 38W
Qeqertarsuatsiaat, *Greenland* **10 E5** 63 5N 50 45W
Qeshlāq, *Iran* **101 E12** 34 55N 46 28 E
Qeshm, *Iran* **97 E8** 26 55N 56 10 E
Qeys, *Iran* **97 E7** 26 32N 53 58 E
Qezel Owzen →, *Iran* **97 B6** 36 45N 49 22 E
Qezi'ot, *Israel* **103 E3** 30 52N 34 26 E
Qi Xian, *China* **74 G8** 34 40N 114 48 E
Qian Gorlos, *China* **75 B13** 45 5N 124 42 E
Qian Hai, *China* **69 F10** 22 32N 113 54 E
Qian Xian, *China* **74 G5** 34 31N 108 15 E
Qiancheng, *China* **76 D7** 27 12N 109 50 E
Qianjiang, *Guangxi Zhuangzu, China* **76 F7** 23 38N 108 58 E
Qianjiang, *Hubei, China* **77 B9** 30 24N 112 55 E
Qianjiang, *Sichuan, China* **76 C7** 29 33N 108 47 E
Qianshan, *Anhui, China* **77 B11** 30 37N 116 35 E
Qianshan, *Guangdong, China* **69 G10** 22 15N 113 31 E
Qianwei, *China* **76 C4** 29 13N 103 56 E
Qianxi, *China* **76 D6** 27 3N 106 3 E
Qianyang, *Hunan, China* **77 D8** 27 18N 110 10 E
Qianyang, *Shaanxi, China* **74 G4** 34 40N 107 8 E
Qianyang, *Zhejiang, China* **77 B12** 30 11N 119 25 E
Qi'ao, *China* **69 G10** 22 25N 113 39 E
Qi'ao Dao, *China* **69 G10** 22 25N 113 38 E
Qiaojia, *China* **76 D4** 26 56N 102 58 E
Qichun, *China* **77 B10** 30 18N 115 25 E
Qidong, *Hunan, China* **77 D9** 26 49N 112 7 E
Qidong, *Jiangsu, China* **77 B13** 31 48N 121 38 E
Qijiang, *China* **76 C6** 28 57N 106 35 E
Qikiqtarjuaq, *Canada* **139 B13** 67 33N 63 0W
Qila Safed, *Pakistan* **91 C1** 29 0N 61 30 E
Qila Saifullāh, *Pakistan* **91 C3** 30 45N 68 17 E
Qilian Shan, *China* **68 C4** 38 30N 96 0 E
Qimen, *China* **77 C11** 29 50N 117 42 E
Qin He →, *China* **74 G7** 35 1N 113 22 E
Qin Jiang →, *Guangxi Zhuangzu, China* **76 F7** 21 53N 108 35 E
Qin Jiang →, *Jiangxi, China* **77 D10** 26 15N 115 55 E
Qin Ling = Qinling Shandi, *China* **74 H5** 33 50N 108 10 E
Qinā, W. →, *Yemen* **99 C5** 17 55N 49 59 E
Qin'an, *China* **74 G3** 34 48N 105 40 E
Qing Xian, *China* **74 E9** 38 35N 116 45 E
Qingcheng, *China* **75 F9** 37 15N 117 40 E
Qingdao, *China* **75 F11** 36 5N 120 20 E
Qingfeng, *China* **74 G8** 35 52N 115 8 E
Qinghai □, *China* **68 C4** 36 0N 98 0 E
Qinghai Hu, *China* **68 C5** 36 40N 100 10 E
Qinghecheng, *China* **75 D13** 41 28N 124 15 E
Qinghemen, *China* **75 D11** 41 48N 121 25 E
Qingjian, *China* **74 F6** 37 8N 110 8 E
Qingjiang = Huaiyin, *China* **75 H10** 33 30N 119 2 E
Qingliu, *China* **77 D11** 26 11N 116 48 E
Qinglong, *China* **76 E5** 25 49N 105 12 E
Qingping, *China* **76 D6** 26 39N 107 47 E
Qingpu, *China* **77 B13** 31 10N 121 6 E
Qingshui, *China* **74 G4** 34 48N 106 8 E
Qingshuihe, *China* **74 E6** 39 55N 111 35 E
Qingtian, *China* **77 C13** 28 12N 120 15 E
Qingtongxia Shuiku, *China* **74 F3** 37 50N 105 58 E
Qingxi, *China* **76 D7** 27 8N 108 43 E
Qingxu, *China* **74 F7** 37 34N 112 22 E
Qingyang, *Anhui, China* **77 B11** 30 38N 117 50 E
Qingyang, *Gansu, China* **74 F4** 36 2N 107 55 E
Qingyi Jiang →, *China* **76 C4** 29 32N 103 44 E
Qingyuan, *Guangdong, China* **77 F9** 23 40N 112 59 E
Qingyuan, *Liaoning, China* **75 C13** 42 10N 124 55 E
Qingyuan, *Zhejiang, China* **77 D12** 27 36N 119 3 E
Qingyun, *China* **75 F9** 37 45N 117 20 E
Qingzhen, *China* **76 D6** 26 31N 106 25 E
Qinhuangdao, *China* **75 E10** 39 56N 119 30 E
Qinling Shandi, *China* **74 H5** 33 50N 108 10 E
Qinshui, *China* **74 G7** 35 40N 112 8 E
Qinyang = Jiyuan, *China* **74 G7** 35 7N 112 57 E
Qinyuan, *China* **74 F7** 36 29N 112 20 E
Qinzhou, *China* **76 G7** 21 58N 108 38 E
Qionghai, *China* **86 C8** 19 15N 110 26 E
Qionglai, *China* **76 B4** 30 25N 103 31 E
Qionglai Shan, *China* **76 B4** 31 0N 102 30 E
Qiongzhou Haixia, *China* **86 B8** 20 10N 110 15 E
Qiqihar, *China* **67 E13** 47 26N 124 0 E
Qiraîya, W. →, *Egypt* **103 E3** 30 27N 34 0 E
Qiryat Ata, *Israel* **103 C4** 32 47N 35 6 E
Qiryat Gat, *Israel* **103 D3** 31 32N 34 46 E
Qiryat Mal'akhi, *Israel* **103 D3** 31 44N 34 44 E
Qiryat Shemona, *Israel* **103 B4** 33 13N 35 35 E
Qiryat Yam, *Israel* **103 C4** 32 51N 35 4 E
Qirzah, W. →, *Libya* **108 B2** 30 56N 14 31 E
Qishan, *China* **74 G4** 34 25N 107 38 E
Qishn, *Yemen* **99 D5** 15 26N 51 40 E
Qitai, *China* **68 B3** 44 2N 89 35 E
Qitbīt, W. →, *Oman* **99 C6** 19 15N 54 23 E
Qiubei, *China* **76 E5** 24 2N 104 12 E
Qixia, *China* **75 F11** 37 17N 120 52 E
Qiyang, *China* **77 D8** 26 35N 111 50 E
Qızılağac Körfäzi, *Azerbaijan* **97 B6** 39 9N 49 0 E
Qoghaly, *Kazakstan* **65 A9** 44 29N 78 39 E
Qojūr, *Iran* **96 B5** 36 12N 47 55 E
Qom, *Iran* **97 C6** 34 40N 51 0 E
Qomolangma Feng = Everest, Mt., *Nepal* **93 E12** 28 5N 86 58 E
Qomsheh, *Iran* **97 D6** 32 0N 51 55 E
Qondūz, *Afghan.* **65 E4** 36 50N 68 50 E
Qondūz □, *Afghan.* **65 E4** 36 50N 68 50 E
Qondūz →, *Afghan.* **91 A3** 37 0N 68 16 E
Qopa, *Kazakstan* **65 B7** 43 31N 75 50 E
Qoraqalpoghistan □, *Uzbekistan* **66 E6** 43 0N 58 0 E
Qorday, *Kazakstan* **65 B7** 43 21N 74 59 E
Qormi, *Malta* **38 F7** 35 53N 14 28 E
Qorveh, *Iran* **101 E12** 35 10N 47 48 E
Qosqudyq, *Kazakstan* **65 A8** 44 10N 77 18 E
Qostanay, *Kazakstan* **66 D7** 53 10N 63 35 E
Qoţūr, *Iran* **101 C11** 38 28N 44 25 E
Qoz Salsilgo, *C.A.R.* **114 A4** 10 45N 22 54 E
Qrejten Point, *Malta* **38 F7** 35 57N 14 27 E
Qu Jiang →, *China* **76 B6** 30 1N 106 24 E
Qu Xian, *China* **76 B6** 30 48N 106 58 E
Quabbin Reservoir, *U.S.A.* **151 D12** 42 20N 72 20W
Quairading, *Australia* **125 F2** 32 0 S 117 21 E
Quakenbrück, *Germany* **30 C3** 52 41N 7 57 E
Quakertown, *U.S.A.* **151 F9** 40 26N 75 21W
Qualicum Beach, *Canada* **142 D4** 49 22N 124 26W
Quambatook, *Australia* **128 C5** 35 49 S 143 34 E
Quambone, *Australia* **129 A7** 30 57 S 147 53 E
Quamby, *Australia* **126 C3** 20 22 S 140 17 E
Quan Long = Ca Mau, *Vietnam* **87 H5** 9 7N 105 8 E
Quanah, *U.S.A.* **155 H5** 34 18N 99 44W
Quandialla, *Australia* **129 C7** 34 1 S 147 47 E
Quang Ngai, *Vietnam* **86 E7** 15 13N 108 58 E
Quang Tri, *Vietnam* **86 D6** 16 45N 107 13 E
Quang Yen, *Vietnam* **76 G6** 20 56N 106 52 E
Quannan, *China* **77 E10** 24 45N 114 33 E
Quantock Hills, *U.K.* **21 F4** 51 8N 3 10W
Quanzhou, *Fujian, China* **77 E12** 24 55N 118 34 E
Quanzhou, *Guangxi Zhuangzu, China* **77 E8** 25 57N 111 5 E
Qu'Appelle, *Canada* **143 C8** 50 33N 103 53W
Quaqtaq, *Canada* **139 B13** 60 55N 69 40W
Quaraí, *Brazil* **174 C4** 30 15 S 56 20W
Quarré-les-Tombes, *France* **27 E11** 47 21N 4 0 E
Quarteira, *Portugal* **43 H2** 37 4N 8 6W
Quartu Sant'Élena, *Italy* **46 C2** 39 15N 9 10 E
Quartzsite, *U.S.A.* **161 M12** 33 40N 114 13W
Quatre Bornes, *Mauritius* **121 d** 20 15 S 57 28 E
Quatsino Sd., *Canada* **142 C3** 50 25N 127 58W
Quba, *Azerbaijan* **61 K9** 41 21N 48 32 E
Qūchān, *Iran* **97 B8** 37 10N 58 27 E
Queanbeyan, *Australia* **129 C8** 35 17 S 149 14 E
Québec, *Canada* **141 C5** 46 52N 71 13W
Québec □, *Canada* **141 C6** 48 0N 74 0W
Quedlinburg, *Germany* **30 D7** 51 47N 11 8 E

270 Queen Alexandra Ra.

Queen Alexandra Ra., *Antarctica* **7 E11** 85 0 S 170 0 E
Queen Charlotte B., *Falk. Is.* **9 f** 51 50 S 60 40W
Queen Charlotte City, *Canada* **142 C2** 53 15N 132 2W
Queen Charlotte Is., *Canada* **142 C2** 53 20N 132 10W
Queen Charlotte Sd., *Canada* **142 C3** 51 0N 128 0W
Queen Charlotte Sd., *N.Z.* **131 B9** 41 10 S 174 15 E
Queen Charlotte Strait, *Canada* **142 C3** 50 45N 127 10W
Queen City, *U.S.A.* **156 D4** 40 25N 92 34W
Queen Elizabeth Is., *Canada* **136 B10** 76 0N 95 0W
Queen Elizabeth Nat. Park, *Uganda* **118 C3** 0 0 30 0 E
Queen Mary Land, *Antarctica* **7 D7** 70 0 S 95 0 E
Queen Maud G., *Canada* **138 B9** 68 15N 102 30W
Queen Maud Land, *Antarctica* **7 D3** 72 30 S 12 0 E
Queen Maud Mts., *Antarctica* **7 E13** 86 0 S 160 0W
Queens Chan., *Australia* **124 C4** 15 0 S 129 30 E
Queenscliff, *Australia* **128 E6** 38 16 S 144 39 E
Queensland, *U.S.A.* **152 D6** 31 46N 83 14W
Queensland □, *Australia* **126 C3** 22 0 S 142 0 E
Queenstown, *Australia* **127 G4** 42 4 S 145 35 E
Queenstown, *N.Z.* **131 F3** 45 1 S 168 40 E
Queenstown, *Singapore* **87 d** 1 18N 103 48 E
Queenstown, *S. Africa* **116 E4** 31 52 S 26 52 E
Queets, *U.S.A.* **160 C2** 47 32N 124 20W
Queguay Grande →, *Uruguay* **174 C4** 32 9 S 58 9W
Queimada, Pta. da, *Azores* **9 d1** 38 23N 28 14W
Queimadas, *Brazil* **170 D4** 11 0 S 39 38W
Queiros, C., *Vanuatu* **133 D5** 14 55 S 167 1 E
Quela, *Angola* **115 D3** 9 10 S 16 56 E
Quelimane, *Mozam.* **119 F4** 17 53 S 36 58 E
Quelo, *Angola* **115 D2** 6 29 S 12 36 E
Quelpart = Cheju do, *S. Korea* **75 H14** 33 29N 126 34 E
Queluz, *Portugal* **43 G1** 38 45N 9 15W
Quemado, *N. Mex., U.S.A.* **159 J9** 34 20N 108 30W
Quemado, *Tex., U.S.A.* **155 L4** 28 58N 100 35W
Quemoy = Chinmen, *Taiwan* **77 E13** 24 26N 118 19 E
Quemú-Quemú, *Argentina* **174 D3** 36 3 S 63 36W
Quepem, *India* **95 G2** 15 13N 74 3 E
Quequén, *Argentina* **174 D4** 38 30 S 58 30W
Querco, *Peru* **172 C3** 13 50 S 74 52W
Querétaro, *Mexico* **162 C4** 20 36N 100 23W
Querétaro □, *Mexico* **162 C5** 20 30N 100 0W
Querfurt, *Germany* **30 D7** 51 23N 11 35 E
Quérigut, *France* **28 F6** 42 42N 2 6 E
Querqueville, *France* **26 C5** 49 40N 1 42W
Quesada, *Spain* **43 H7** 37 51N 3 4W
Queshan, *China* **74 H8** 32 55N 114 2 E
Quesnel, *Canada* **142 C4** 53 0N 122 30W
Quesnel →, *Canada* **142 C4** 52 58N 122 29W
Quesnel L., *Canada* **142 C4** 52 30N 121 20W
Questa, *U.S.A.* **159 H11** 36 42N 105 36W
Questembert, *France* **26 E4** 47 40N 2 28W
Quetena, *Bolivia* **172 E4** 22 10 S 67 25W
Quetico Prov. Park, *Canada* **140 C1** 48 30N 91 45W
Quetrequile, *Argentina* **176 B3** 41 33 S 69 22W
Quetta, *Pakistan* **91 C2** 30 15N 66 55 E
Quevedo, *Ecuador* **168 D2** 1 2 S 79 29W
Quezaltenango, *Guatemala* **164 D1** 14 50N 91 30W
Quezon, *Phil.* **81 G1** 9 15N 117 59 E
Quezon □, *Phil.* **80 D3** 14 40N 121 30 E
Quezon City, *Phil.* **80 D3** 14 38N 121 0 E
Qufār, *Si. Arabia* **96 E4** 27 26N 41 37 E
Qui Nhon, *Vietnam* **86 F7** 13 40N 109 13 E
Quibala, *Angola* **115 E2** 10 46 S 14 59 E
Quibaxe, *Angola* **115 D2** 8 24 S 14 27 E
Quibdo, *Colombia* **168 B2** 5 42N 76 40W
Quiberon, *France* **26 E3** 47 29N 3 9W
Quiberon, Presqu'île de, *France* **26 E3** 47 30N 3 8W
Quiçama, Parque Nacional da, *Angola* **115 D2** 9 41 S 13 35 E
Quickborn, *Germany* **30 B5** 53 42N 9 52 E
Quiet L., *Canada* **142 A2** 61 5N 133 5W
Quiindy, *Paraguay* **174 B4** 25 58 S 57 14W
Quila, *Mexico* **162 C3** 24 23N 107 13W
Quilán, C., *Chile* **176 B2** 43 15 S 74 30W
Quilcene, *U.S.A.* **160 C4** 47 49N 122 53W
Quilenda, *Angola* **115 E2** 10 39 S 14 23 E
Quilengues, *Angola* **115 E2** 14 12 S 14 12 E
Quilimarí, *Chile* **174 C1** 32 5 S 71 30W
Quilino, *Argentina* **174 C3** 30 14 S 64 29W
Quill Lakes, *Canada* **143 C8** 51 55N 104 13W
Quillabamba, *Peru* **172 C3** 12 50 S 72 50W
Quillacollo, *Bolivia* **172 D4** 17 26 S 66 17W
Quillagua, *Chile* **174 A2** 21 40 S 69 40W
Quillaicillo, *Chile* **174 C1** 31 17 S 71 40W
Quillan, *France* **28 F6** 42 53N 2 10 E
Quillota, *Chile* **174 C1** 32 54 S 71 16W
Quilmes, *Argentina* **174 C4** 34 43 S 58 15W
Quilon, *India* **95 K3** 8 50N 76 38 E
Quilpie, *Australia* **127 D3** 26 35 S 144 11 E
Quilpué, *Chile* **174 C1** 33 5 S 71 33W
Quilua, *Mozam.* **119 F4** 16 17 S 39 54 E
Quimbele, *Angola* **115 D3** 6 17 S 16 41 E
Quimbo, *Angola* **115 E3** 14 4 S 16 11 E
Quimbonge, *Angola* **115 D3** 8 36 S 18 30 E
Quime, *Bolivia* **172 D4** 17 2 S 67 15W
Quimilí, *Argentina* **174 B3** 27 40 S 62 30W
Quimper, *France* **26 E2** 48 0N 4 9W
Quimperlé, *France* **26 E3** 47 53N 3 33W
Quinault →, *U.S.A.* **160 C2** 47 21N 124 18W
Quincemil, *Peru* **172 C3** 13 15 S 70 40W
Quincy, *Calif., U.S.A.* **160 F6** 39 56N 120 57W
Quincy, *Fla., U.S.A.* **152 E5** 30 35N 84 34W
Quincy, *Ill., U.S.A.* **156 E5** 39 56N 91 23W
Quincy, *Mass., U.S.A.* **151 D14** 42 15N 71 0W
Quincy, *Mich., U.S.A.* **157 C12** 41 57N 84 53W
Quincy, *Wash., U.S.A.* **158 C4** 47 22N 119 56W
Quines, *Argentina* **174 C2** 32 13 S 65 48W
Quinga, *Mozam.* **119 F5** 15 49 S 40 15 E
Quingey, *France* **27 E12** 47 7N 5 52 E
Quingombe, *Angola* **115 D2** 6 38 S 13 1 E
Quinhagak, *U.S.A.* **144 G7** 59 45N 161 54W
Quiniluban Group, *Phil.* **81 F3** 11 27N 120 48 E
Quinns Rocks, *Australia* **125 F2** 31 40 S 115 42 E
Quintana de la Serena, *Spain* **43 G5** 38 45N 5 40W
Quintana Roo □, *Mexico* **163 D7** 19 0N 88 0W
Quintanar de la Orden, *Spain* **43 F7** 39 36N 3 5W
Quintanar de la Sierra, *Spain* **40 D2** 41 57N 2 55W
Quintanar del Rey, *Spain* **41 F3** 39 21N 1 56W
Quintero, *Chile* **174 C1** 32 45 S 71 30W
Quintin, *France* **26 D4** 48 26N 2 56W
Quinto, *Spain* **40 D4** 41 25N 0 32W
Quinzáu, *Angola* **115 D2** 6 51 S 12 44 E
Quípar →, *Spain* **41 G3** 38 15N 1 40W
Quipeio, *Angola* **115 E3** 12 27 S 15 30 E
Quirihue, *Chile* **174 D1** 36 15 S 72 35W
Quirima, *Angola* **115 E3** 10 47 S 18 6 E
Quirimbo, *Angola* **115 E2** 10 36 S 14 12 E
Quirindi, *Australia* **129 A9** 31 28 S 150 40 E
Quirino □, *Phil.* **80 C3** 16 15N 121 40 E
Quirinopolis, *Brazil* **171 E1** 18 32 S 50 30W
Quiroga, *Spain* **42 C3** 42 28N 7 18W
Quiruvilca, *Peru* **172 B2** 8 1 S 78 19W
Quissac, *France* **29 E8** 43 55N 4 0 E
Quissanga, *Mozam.* **119 E5** 12 24 S 40 28 E
Quissico, *Mozam.* **117 C5** 24 42 S 34 44 E
Quitapa, *Angola* **115 E3** 10 20 S 18 19 E
Quitilipi, *Argentina* **174 B3** 26 50 S 60 13W
Quitman, *U.S.A.* **152 E6** 30 47N 83 34W
Quito, *Ecuador* **168 D2** 0 15 S 78 35W
Quixadá, *Brazil* **170 B4** 4 55 S 39 0W
Quixaxe, *Mozam.* **119 F5** 15 17 S 40 4 E
Quixeramobim, *Brazil* **170 C4** 5 12 S 39 17W
Quixico, *Angola* **115 D2** 7 59 S 14 25 E
Quixinge, *Angola* **115 D2** 9 52 S 14 23 E
Quizenga, *Angola* **115 D3** 9 21 S 15 28 E
Qujing, *China* **76 E4** 25 32N 103 41 E
Qulan, *Kazakstan* **66 E8** 42 55N 72 43 E
Qul'ân, Jazâ'ir, *Egypt* **96 E2** 24 22N 35 31 E
Qumbu, *S. Africa* **117 E4** 31 10 S 28 48 E
Qumqŭrghan, *Uzbekistan* **65 E3** 37 49N 67 35 E
Quneitra, *Syria* **103 B4** 33 7N 35 48 E
Qŭnghirot, *Uzbekistan* **66 E6** 43 6N 58 54 E
Qu'nyido, *China* **76 B2** 31 15N 98 6 E
Quoin I., *Australia* **124 B4** 14 54 S 129 32 E
Quoin Pt., *S. Africa* **116 E2** 34 46 S 19 37 E
Quorn, *Australia* **128 B3** 32 25 S 138 5 E
Qŭqon, *Uzbekistan* **66 E8** 40 30N 70 57 E
Qurein, *Sudan* **107 E3** 13 30N 34 50 E
Qŭrghonteppa, *Tajikistan* **65 E4** 37 50N 68 47 E
Qurnat as Sawdā', *Lebanon* **103 A5** 34 18N 36 6 E
Qûs, *Egypt* **106 B3** 25 55N 32 50 E
Qusar, *Azerbaijan* **61 K9** 41 25N 48 26 E
Quşaybā', *Si. Arabia* **96 E4** 26 53N 43 35 E
Qusaybah, *Iraq* **101 E9** 34 24N 40 59 E
Quşay'ir, *Yemen* **99 D5** 14 55N 50 20 E
Quseir, *Egypt* **96 E2** 26 7N 34 16 E
Qūshchī, *Iran* **101 D11** 37 59N 45 3 E
Quthing, *Lesotho* **117 E4** 30 25 S 27 36 E
Qūţīābād, *Iran* **97 C6** 35 47N 48 30 E
Quwo, *China* **74 G6** 35 38N 111 25 E
Quyang, *China* **74 E8** 38 35N 114 40 E
Quynh Nhai, *Vietnam* **86 B4** 21 49N 103 33 E
Quyon, *Canada* **151 A8** 45 31N 76 14W
Quzhou, *China* **77 C12** 28 57N 118 54 E
Quzi, *China* **74 F4** 36 20N 107 20 E
Qvareli, *Georgia* **61 K7** 41 57N 45 47 E
Qytet Stalin = Kuçovë, *Albania* **50 F3** 40 47N 19 57 E
Qyzylorda, *Kazakstan* **66 E7** 44 48N 65 28 E

R

Ra, Ko, *Thailand* **87 H2** 9 13N 98 16 E
Raab, *Austria* **34 C6** 48 21N 13 39 E
Raahe, *Finland* **14 D21** 64 40N 24 28 E
Raalte, *Neths.* **24 B6** 52 23N 6 16 E
Raasay, *U.K.* **22 D2** 57 25N 6 4W
Raasay, Sd. of, *U.K.* **22 D2** 57 30N 6 8W
Rab, *Croatia* **45 D11** 44 45N 14 45 E
Raba, *Indonesia* **85 D5** 8 36 S 118 55 E
Rába →, *Hungary* **52 C2** 47 38N 17 38 E
Raba →, *Poland* **55 H7** 50 8N 20 30 E
Rabaçal →, *Portugal* **42 D3** 41 30N 7 12W
Rabah, *Nigeria* **113 C6** 13 5N 5 30 E
Rabai, *Kenya* **118 C4** 3 50 S 39 31 E
Rabak, *Sudan* **107 E3** 13 9N 32 44 E
Rabaraba, *Papua N. G.* **132 E5** 9 58 S 149 49 E
Rabastens, *France* **28 E5** 43 50N 1 43 E
Rabastens-de-Bigorre, *France* **28 E4** 43 23N 0 9 E
Rabat = Victoria, *Malta* **38 E6** 36 3N 14 14 E
Rabat, *Kazakstan* **65 B4** 42 2N 69 31 E
Rabat, *Malta* **38 F7** 35 53N 14 24 E
Rabat, *Morocco* **110 B3** 34 2N 6 48W
Rabaul, *Papua N. G.* **132 C7** 4 24 S 152 18 E
Rabi, *Fiji* **133 A3** 16 30 S 179 59W
Rābigh, *Si. Arabia* **98 B2** 22 50N 39 5 E
Rabka, *Poland* **55 J6** 49 37N 19 59 E
Râbniţa, *Moldova* **53 C14** 47 45N 29 0 E
Rābor, *Iran* **97 D8** 29 17N 56 55 E
Rabyānah, *Libya* **108 D4** 24 15N 22 0 E
Rača, *Serbia, Yug.* **50 B4** 44 14N 21 0 E
Răcăciuni, *Romania* **53 D11** 46 20N 26 59 E
Răcăşdia, *Romania* **52 F6** 44 59N 21 36 E
Racconigi, *Italy* **44 D4** 44 46N 7 46 E
Raccoon →, *U.S.A.* **156 C3** 41 35N 93 37W
Raccoon Cr. →, *U.S.A.* **157 E9** 39 47N 87 23W
Race, C., *Canada* **141 C9** 46 40N 53 5W
Rach Gia, *Vietnam* **87 G5** 10 5N 105 5 E
Rachid, *Mauritania* **112 B2** 18 45N 11 35W
Raciąż, *Poland* **55 F7** 52 46N 20 10 E
Racibórz, *Poland* **55 H5** 50 7N 18 18 E
Racine, *U.S.A.* **157 B9** 42 41N 87 51W
Rackerby, *U.S.A.* **160 F5** 39 26N 121 22W
Radama, Nosy, *Madag.* **117 A8** 14 0 S 47 47 E
Radama, Saikanosy, *Madag.* **117 A8** 14 16 S 47 53 E
Radan, *Serbia, Yug.* **50 D5** 42 59N 21 29 E
Rădăuţi, *Romania* **53 C10** 47 50N 25 59 E
Rădăuţi-Prut, *Romania* **53 B11** 48 14N 26 48 E
Radbuza →, *Czech Rep.* **34 B6** 49 45N 13 22 E
Radcliff, *U.S.A.* **157 G11** 37 51N 85 57W
Radeberg, *Germany* **30 D9** 51 7N 13 53 E
Radebeul, *Germany* **30 D9** 51 6N 13 39 E
Radeče, *Slovenia* **45 B12** 46 5N 15 14 E
Radekhiv, *Ukraine* **59 G3** 50 25N 24 32 E
Radekhov = Radekhiv, *Ukraine* **59 G3** 50 25N 24 32 E
Radenthein, *Austria* **34 E6** 46 48N 13 43 E
Radew →, *Poland* **54 D2** 54 2N 15 52 E
Radford, *U.S.A.* **148 G5** 37 8N 80 34W
Radhanpur, *India* **92 H4** 23 50N 71 38 E
Radhwa, Jabal, *Si. Arabia* **96 E3** 24 34N 38 18 E
Radika →, *Macedonia* **50 E4** 41 38N 20 37 E
Radisson, *Qué., Canada* **140 B4** 53 47N 77 37W
Radisson, *Sask., Canada* **143 C7** 52 30N 107 20W
Radium Hot Springs, *Canada* **142 C5** 50 35N 116 2W
Radlje ob Dravi, *Slovenia* **45 B12** 46 38N 15 13 E
Radnevo, *Bulgaria* **51 D9** 42 17N 25 58 E
Radnice, *Czech Rep.* **34 B6** 49 51N 13 35 E
Radnor Forest, *U.K.* **21 E4** 52 17N 3 10W
Radolfzell, *Germany* **31 H4** 47 39N 8 59 E
Radom, *Poland* **55 G8** 51 23N 21 12 E
Radom Nat. Park, *Sudan* **114 A4** 9 20N 23 50 E
Radomir, *Bulgaria* **50 D6** 42 37N 22 59 E
Radomka →, *Poland* **55 G8** 51 43N 21 28 E
Radomsko, *Poland* **55 G6** 51 5N 19 28 E
Radomyshl, *Ukraine* **59 G5** 50 30N 29 12 E
Radomyśl Wielki, *Poland* **55 H8** 50 14N 21 15 E
Radoszyce, *Poland* **55 G7** 51 4N 20 15 E
Radoviš, *Macedonia* **50 E6** 41 38N 22 28 E
Radovljica, *Slovenia* **45 B11** 46 22N 14 12 E
Radstadt, *Austria* **34 D6** 47 24N 13 28 E
Radstock, C., *Australia* **127 E1** 33 12 S 134 20 E
Răducăneni, *Romania* **53 D12** 46 58N 27 54 E
Raduša, *Macedonia* **50 D5** 42 7N 21 15 E
Radviliškis, *Lithuania* **15 J20** 55 49N 23 33 E
Radville, *Canada* **143 D8** 49 30N 104 15W
Raḑwá, J., *Si. Arabia* **106 C4** 24 34N 38 18 E
Radymno, *Poland* **55 J9** 49 59N 22 52 E
Radzanów, *Poland* **55 F7** 52 56N 20 8 E
Radziejów, *Poland* **55 F5** 52 40N 18 30 E
Radzyń Chełmiński, *Poland* **54 E5** 53 23N 18 55 E
Radzyń Podlaski, *Poland* **55 G9** 51 47N 22 37 E
Rae, *Canada* **142 A5** 62 50N 116 3W
Rae Bareli, *India* **93 F9** 26 18N 81 20 E
Rae Isthmus, *Canada* **139 B11** 66 40N 87 30W
Raeren, *Belgium* **24 D6** 50 41N 6 7 E
Raeside, L., *Australia* **125 E3** 29 20 S 122 0 E
Raetihi, *N.Z.* **130 F4** 39 25 S 175 17 E
Rafaela, *Argentina* **174 C3** 31 10 S 61 30W
Rafah, *Gaza Strip* **103 D3** 31 18N 34 14 E
Rafai, *C.A.R.* **118 B1** 4 59N 23 58 E
Raffadali, *Italy* **46 E6** 37 24N 13 32 E
Raffili, *Sudan* **107 F2** 6 50N 28 0 E
Rafḩā, *Si. Arabia* **96 D4** 29 35N 43 35 E
Rafsanjān, *Iran* **97 D8** 30 30N 56 5 E
Raft Pt., *Australia* **124 C3** 16 4 S 124 26 E
Râgâ, *Sudan* **107 F2** 8 28N 25 41 E
Raga →, *Sudan* **107 F2** 8 41N 25 52 E
Ragachow, *Belarus* **59 F6** 53 8N 30 5 E
Ragag, *Sudan* **107 E1** 10 59N 24 40 E
Ragang, Mt., *Phil.* **81 H5** 7 43N 124 32 E
Ragay, *Phil.* **80 E4** 13 49N 122 47 E
Ragay G., *Phil.* **80 E4** 13 30N 122 45 E
Ragged, Mt., *Australia* **125 F3** 33 27 S 123 25 E
Ragged Pt., *Barbados* **165 g** 13 10N 59 10W
Rāgh, *Afghan.* **65 E5** 37 32N 70 27 E
Raghunathpalli, *India* **93 H11** 22 14N 84 48 E
Raghunathpur, *India* **93 H12** 23 33N 86 40 E
Raglan, *N.Z.* **130 D3** 37 55 S 174 55 E
Raglan Harbour, *N.Z.* **130 D3** 37 47 S 174 50 E
Ragland, *U.S.A.* **152 B3** 33 45N 86 9W
Ragusa, *Italy* **47 F7** 36 55N 14 44 E
Raha, *Indonesia* **82 B2** 4 55 S 123 0 E
Rahad, Nahr ed →, *Sudan* **107 E3** 14 28N 33 31 E
Rahad al Bardī, *Sudan* **109 F4** 11 20N 23 40 E
Rahaeng = Tak, *Thailand* **86 D2** 16 52N 99 8 E
Rahatgarh, *India* **93 H8** 23 47N 78 22 E
Rahden, *Germany* **30 C4** 52 26N 8 36 E
Raheb, Ras ir-, *Malta* **38 F7** 35 54N 14 20 E
Raheita, *Eritrea* **107 E5** 12 46N 43 4 E
Rahimyar Khan, *Pakistan* **91 C3** 28 30N 70 25 E
Rāhjerd, *Iran* **97 C6** 34 22N 50 22 E
Rahole Nat. Reserve, *Kenya* **118 B4** 0 5N 38 57 E
Råholt, *Norway* **18 D8** 60 16N 11 11 E
Rahon, *India* **92 D7** 31 3N 76 7 E
Rahotu, *N.Z.* **130 F2** 39 20 S 173 49 E
Rahuri, *India* **94 E2** 19 23N 74 39 E
Raichur, *India* **95 F3** 16 10N 77 20 E
Raiford, *U.S.A.* **152 E7** 30 4N 82 14W
Raiganj, *India* **93 G13** 25 37N 88 10 E
Raigarh, *India* **94 D6** 21 56N 83 25 E
Raighar, *India* **94 E6** 19 51N 82 6 E
Raijua, *Indonesia* **82 D2** 10 37 S 121 36 E
Raikot, *India* **92 D6** 30 41N 75 42 E
Railton, *Australia* **127 G4** 41 25 S 146 28 E
Rainbow City, *U.S.A.* **152 B3** 33 57N 86 5W
Rainbow Lake, *Canada* **142 B5** 58 30N 119 23W
Rainier, *U.S.A.* **160 D4** 46 53N 122 41W
Rainier, Mt., *U.S.A.* **160 D5** 46 52N 121 46W
Rainy L., *Canada* **143 D10** 48 42N 93 10W
Rainy River, *Canada* **143 D10** 48 43N 94 29W
Raippaluoto, *Finland* **14 E19** 63 13N 21 14 E
Raipur, *India* **94 D5** 21 17N 81 45 E
Rairakhol, *India* **94 D7** 21 4N 84 21 E
Ra'is, *Si. Arabia* **106 C4** 23 33N 38 43 E
Raisen, *India* **92 H8** 23 20N 77 48 E
Raisio, *Finland* **15 F20** 60 28N 22 11 E
Raj Nandgaon, *India* **94 D5** 21 5N 81 5 E
Raj Nilgiri, *India* **93 J12** 21 28N 86 46 E
Raja, Ujung, *Indonesia* **84 B1** 3 40N 96 25 E
Raja Ampat, Kepulauan, *Indonesia* **83 B4** 0 30 S 130 0 E
Rajahmundry, *India* **94 F5** 17 1N 81 48 E
Rajampet, *India* **95 G4** 14 11N 79 10 E
Rajang →, *Malaysia* **85 B4** 2 30N 112 0 E
Rajanpur, *Pakistan* **92 E4** 29 6N 70 19 E
Rajapalaiyam, *India* **95 K3** 9 25N 77 35 E
Rajapur, *India* **94 F1** 16 40N 73 31 E
Rajasthan □, *India* **92 F5** 26 45N 73 30 E
Rajasthan Canal, *India* **92 F5** 28 0N 72 0 E
Rajauri, *India* **93 C6** 33 25N 74 21 E
Rajbari, *Bangla.* **90 D2** 23 47N 89 41 E
Rajgarh, *Mad. P., India* **92 G7** 24 2N 76 45 E
Rajgarh, *Raj., India* **92 F7** 27 14N 76 38 E
Rajgarh, *Raj., India* **92 E6** 28 40N 75 25 E
Rajgir, *India* **93 G11** 25 2N 85 25 E
Rajgród, *Poland* **54 E9** 53 42N 22 42 E
Rajim, *India* **94 D5** 20 58N 81 53 E
Rajkot, *India* **92 H4** 22 15N 70 56 E
Rajmahal Hills, *India* **93 G12** 24 30N 87 30 E
Rajpipla, *India* **94 D1** 21 50N 73 30 E
Rajpur, *India* **92 H6** 22 18N 74 21 E
Rajpura, *India* **92 D7** 30 25N 76 32 E
Rajshahi, *Bangla.* **90 C2** 24 22N 88 39 E
Rajshahi □, *Bangla.* **90 C2** 25 0N 89 0 E
Rajula, *India* **92 J4** 21 3N 71 26 E
Rajur, *India* **94 D4** 20 7N 78 55 E
Rajura, *India* **94 E4** 19 47N 79 22 E
Rakaia, *N.Z.* **131 D7** 43 45 S 172 1 E
Rakaia →, *N.Z.* **131 D7** 43 36 S 172 15 E
Rakan, Ra's, *Qatar* **97 E6** 26 10N 51 20 E
Rakaposhi, *Pakistan* **93 A6** 36 10N 74 25 E
Rakata, Pulau, *Indonesia* **84 D3** 6 10 S 105 20 E
Rakhiv, *Ukraine* **59 H3** 48 3N 24 12 E
Rakhni, *Pakistan* **92 D3** 30 4N 69 56 E
Rakhni →, *Pakistan* **92 E3** 29 31N 69 36 E
Rakhyūt, *Oman* **99 C6** 16 44N 53 20 E
Rakiraki, *Fiji* **133 A2** 17 22 S 178 11 E
Rakitnoye, *Russia* **70 B7** 45 36N 134 17 E
Rakitovo, *Bulgaria* **51 E8** 41 59N 24 5 E
Rakkestad, *Norway* **18 E8** 59 25N 11 21 E
Rakoniewice, *Poland* **55 F3** 52 10N 16 16 E
Rakops, *Botswana* **116 C3** 21 1 S 24 28 E
Rakovica, *Croatia* **45 D12** 44 59N 15 38 E
Rakovník, *Czech Rep.* **34 A6** 50 6N 13 42 E
Rakovski, *Bulgaria* **51 D8** 42 21N 24 57 E
Rakshan →, *Pakistan* **91 D1** 27 10N 63 25 E
Rakvere, *Estonia* **15 G22** 59 20N 26 25 E
Raleigh, *Fla., U.S.A.* **153 F7** 29 25N 82 32W
Raleigh, *N.C., U.S.A.* **149 H6** 35 47N 78 39W
Rali Salem, *Algeria* **111 D5** 21 3N 1 9 E
Ralja, *Serbia, Yug.* **50 B4** 44 33N 20 34 E
Ralls, *U.S.A.* **155 J4** 33 41N 101 24W
Ralston, *U.S.A.* **150 E8** 41 30N 76 57W
Ram →, *Canada* **142 A4** 62 1N 123 41W
Rām Allāh, *West Bank* **103 D4** 31 55N 35 10 E
Rama, *Nic.* **164 D3** 12 9N 84 15W
Ramacca, *Italy* **47 E7** 37 23N 14 42 E
Ramachandrapuram, *India* **94 F6** 16 50N 82 4 E
Ramagiri Udayagiri, *India* **94 E7** 19 5N 84 18 E
Ramakona, *India* **93 J8** 21 43N 78 50 E
Ramales de la Victoria, *Spain* **42 B7** 43 15N 3 28W
Ramalho, Serra do, *Brazil* **171 D3** 13 45 S 44 0W
Raman, *Thailand* **87 J3** 6 29N 101 18 E
Ramanathapuram, *India* **95 K4** 9 25N 78 55 E
Ramanetaka, B. de, *Madag.* **117 A8** 14 13 S 47 52 E
Ramanujganj, *India* **93 H10** 23 48N 83 42 E
Ramas C., *India* **95 G1** 15 5N 73 55 E
Ramat Gan, *Israel* **103 C3** 32 4N 34 48 E
Ramatlhabama, *S. Africa* **116 D4** 25 37 S 25 33 E
Ramban, *India* **93 C6** 33 14N 75 12 E
Rambervillers, *France* **27 D13** 48 20N 6 38 E
Rambi = Rabi, *Fiji* **133 A3** 16 30 S 179 59W
Rambipuji, *Indonesia* **85 D4** 8 12 S 113 37 E
Rambouillet, *France* **27 D8** 48 39N 1 50 E
Rambrai, *India* **90 C3** 25 40N 91 19 E
Rambutyo I., *Papua N. G.* **132 B4** 2 18 S 147 49 E
Ramdurg, *India* **95 G2** 15 58N 75 22 E
Rame Hd., *Australia* **129 D8** 37 47 S 149 30 E
Ramechhap, *Nepal* **93 F12** 27 25N 86 10 E
Ramenskoye, *Russia* **58 E10** 55 32N 38 15 E
Ramer, *U.S.A.* **152 C3** 32 3N 86 13W
Rameswaram, *India* **95 K4** 9 17N 79 18 E
Ramganga →, *India* **93 F8** 27 5N 79 58 E
Ramgarh, *Bangla.* **90 D3** 22 59N 91 44 E
Ramgarh, *Jharkhand, India* **93 H11** 23 40N 85 35 E
Ramgarh, *Raj., India* **92 F6** 27 16N 75 14 E
Ramgarh, *Raj., India* **92 F4** 27 30N 70 36 E
Rāmhormoz, *Iran* **97 D6** 31 15N 49 35 E
Ramīān, *Iran* **97 B7** 37 3N 55 16 E
Ramingining, *Australia* **126 A2** 12 19 S 135 3 E
Ramla, *Israel* **103 D3** 31 55N 34 52 E
Ramlat Zalţan, *Libya* **108 C3** 28 30N 19 30 E
Ramlu, *Eritrea* **107 E5** 13 32N 41 40 E
Ramm, Jabal, *Jordan* **103 F4** 29 35N 35 24 E
Râmna →, *Romania* **53 E12** 45 36N 27 3 E
Ramnad = Ramanathapuram, *India* **95 K4** 9 25N 78 55 E
Ramnagar, *Jammu & Kashmir, India* **93 C6** 32 47N 75 18 E
Ramnagar, *Uttaranchal, India* **93 E8** 29 24N 79 7 E
Ramnäs, *Sweden* **16 E10** 59 46N 16 12 E
Râmnicu Sărat, *Romania* **53 E12** 45 26N 27 3 E
Râmnicu Vâlcea, *Romania* **53 E9** 45 9N 24 21 E
Ramon, *Phil.* **80 C3** 16 50N 121 31 E
Ramon, *Russia* **59 G10** 51 55N 39 21 E
Ramona, *U.S.A.* **161 M10** 33 2N 116 52W
Ramonville-St-Agne, *France* **28 E5** 43 33N 1 28 E
Ramore, *Canada* **140 C3** 48 30N 80 25W
Ramos →, *Nigeria* **113 D6** 5 8N 5 22 E
Ramotswa, *Botswana* **116 C4** 24 50 S 25 52 E
Rampart, *U.S.A.* **144 D10** 65 30N 150 10W
Rampur, *H.P., India* **92 D7** 31 26N 77 43 E
Rampur, *Mad. P., India* **92 H5** 23 25N 73 53 E
Rampur, *Orissa, India* **94 D6** 21 48N 83 58 E
Rampur, *Ut. P., India* **93 E8** 28 50N 79 5 E
Rampur Hat, *India* **93 G12** 24 10N 87 50 E
Rampura, *India* **92 G6** 24 30N 75 27 E
Ramrama Tola, *India* **93 J8** 21 52N 79 55 E
Ramree I., *Burma* **90 F5** 19 0N 93 40 E
Rāmsar, *Iran* **97 B6** 36 53N 50 41 E
Ramsey, *U.K.* **20 C3** 54 20N 4 22W
Ramsey, *Ill., U.S.A.* **156 E7** 39 8N 89 7W
Ramsey, *N.J., U.S.A.* **151 E10** 41 4N 74 9W
Ramsey L., *Canada* **140 C3** 47 13N 82 15W
Ramsgate, *U.K.* **21 F9** 51 20N 1 25 E
Ramshai, *India* **90 B2** 26 44N 88 51 E
Ramsjö, *Sweden* **16 B9** 62 11N 15 37 E
Ramstein, *Germany* **31 F3** 49 27N 7 32 E
Ramtek, *India* **94 D4** 21 20N 79 15 E
Ramu →, *Papua N. G.* **132 C3** 4 0 S 144 41 E
Ramvik, *Sweden* **16 B11** 62 49N 17 51 E
Rana Pratap Sagar Dam, *India* **92 G6** 24 58N 75 38 E
Ranaghat, *India* **93 H13** 23 15N 88 35 E
Ranahu, *Pakistan* **92 G3** 25 55N 69 45 E
Ranau, *Malaysia* **78 C5** 6 2N 116 40 E
Rancagua, *Chile* **174 C1** 34 10 S 70 50W
Rance →, *France* **26 D5** 48 34N 1 59W
Rancharia, *Brazil* **171 F1** 22 15 S 50 55W
Rancheria →, *Canada* **142 A3** 60 13N 129 7W
Ranchester, *U.S.A.* **158 D10** 44 54N 107 10W
Ranchi, *India* **93 H11** 23 19N 85 27 E
Rancho Cucamonga, *U.S.A.* **161 L9** 34 10N 117 30W
Ranco, L., *Chile* **176 B2** 40 15 S 72 25W
Rand, *Australia* **129 C7** 35 33 S 146 32 E
Randaberg, *Norway* **18 E2** 59 1N 5 36 E
Randabygd, *Norway* **18 C3** 61 51N 6 20 E
Randalstown, *U.K.* **23 B5** 54 45N 6 19W
Randan, *France* **27 F10** 46 2N 3 21 E
Randazzo, *Italy* **47 E7** 37 53N 14 57 E
Rander, *India* **94 D1** 21 14N 72 47 E
Randers, *Denmark* **17 H4** 56 29N 10 1 E
Randers Fjord, *Denmark* **17 H4** 56 37N 10 20 E
Randfontein, *S. Africa* **117 D4** 26 8 S 27 45 E
Randle, *U.S.A.* **160 D5** 46 32N 121 57W
Randolph, *Mass., U.S.A.* **151 D13** 42 10N 71 2W
Randolph, *N.Y., U.S.A.* **150 D6** 42 10N 78 59W
Randolph, *Utah, U.S.A.* **158 F8** 41 40N 111 11W
Randolph, *Vt., U.S.A.* **151 C12** 43 55N 72 40W
Randsburg, *U.S.A.* **161 K9** 35 22N 117 39W
Randsfjorden, *Norway* **18 D7** 60 25N 10 24 E
Randsverk, *Norway* **18 C6** 61 44N 9 3 E
Råne älv →, *Sweden* **14 D20** 65 50N 22 20 E
Ranfurly, *N.Z.* **131 F5** 45 7 S 170 6 E
Rangae, *Thailand* **87 J3** 6 19N 101 44 E
Rangamati, *Bangla.* **90 D4** 22 38N 92 12 E
Rangapara, *India* **90 B4** 26 49N 92 39 E
Rangárvallasýsla □, *Iceland* **11 D7** 63 55N 20 0W
Rangataua, *N.Z.* **130 F4** 39 26 S 175 28 E
Rangaunu B., *N.Z.* **130 A2** 34 51 S 173 15 E
Rangeley, *U.S.A.* **151 B14** 44 58N 70 39W
Rangeley L., *U.S.A.* **151 B14** 44 55N 70 43W
Rangely, *U.S.A.* **158 F9** 40 5N 108 48W
Ranger, *U.S.A.* **155 J5** 32 28N 98 41W
Rangia, *India* **90 B3** 26 28N 91 38 E
Rangiora, *N.Z.* **131 D7** 43 19 S 172 36 E
Rangitaiki, *N.Z.* **130 E5** 38 52 S 176 24 E
Rangitaiki →, *N.Z.* **130 D5** 37 54 S 176 49 E
Rangitata →, *N.Z.* **131 D6** 43 45 S 171 15 E
Rangitikei →, *N.Z.* **130 G4** 40 17 S 175 15 E
Rangitoto Ra., *N.Z.* **130 E4** 38 25 S 175 35 E
Rangkasbitung, *Indonesia* **84 D3** 6 21 S 106 15 E
Rangoon, *Burma* **90 G6** 16 45N 96 20 E
Rangpur, *Bangla.* **90 C2** 25 42N 89 22 E
Rangsang, *Indonesia* **84 B2** 1 20N 103 30 E
Rangsit, *Thailand* **86 F3** 13 59N 100 37 E
Ranheim, *Norway* **18 A7** 63 26N 10 32 E
Ranibennur, *India* **95 G2** 14 35N 75 30 E
Raniganj, *India* **93 F9** 27 3N 82 13 E
Ranikhet, *India* **93 E8** 29 39N 79 25 E
Ranippettai, *India* **95 H4** 12 56N 79 23 E
Rāniyah, *Iraq* **96 B5** 36 15N 44 53 E
Ranka, *India* **93 H10** 23 59N 83 47 E
Ranken →, *Australia* **126 C2** 20 31 S 137 36 E
Rankin, *Ill., U.S.A.* **157 D9** 40 28N 87 54W
Rankin, *Tex., U.S.A.* **155 K4** 31 13N 101 56W
Rankin Inlet, *Canada* **138 B10** 62 30N 93 0W
Rankins Springs, *Australia* **129 B7** 33 49 S 146 14 E
Rankweil, *Austria* **34 D2** 47 17N 9 39 E
Rannoch, L., *U.K.* **22 E4** 56 41N 4 20W
Rannoch Moor, *U.K.* **22 E4** 56 38N 4 48W
Rano Kau, *Chile* **172 b** 27 11 S 109 26W
Rano Raraku, Volcán, *Chile* **172 b** 27 7 S 109 17W
Ranobe, Helodranon' i, *Madag.* **117 C7** 23 3 S 43 33 E
Ranohira, *Madag.* **117 C8** 22 29 S 45 24 E
Ranomafana, *Toamasina, Madag.* **117 B8** 18 57 S 48 50 E
Ranomafana, *Toliara, Madag.* **117 C8** 24 34 S 47 0 E
Ranomafana, Parc Nat. de, *Madag.* **117 C8** 21 16 S 47 25 E
Ranomena, *Madag.* **117 C8** 23 25 S 47 17 E
Ranon, *Vanuatu* **133 F6** 16 8 S 168 7 E
Ranong, *Thailand* **87 H2** 9 56N 98 40 E
Ranongga, *Solomon Is.* **133 M9** 8 5 S 156 35 E
Ranotsara Nord, *Madag.* **117 C8** 22 48 S 46 36 E
Ranpur, *India* **94 D7** 20 5N 85 20 E
Rānsa, *Iran* **97 C6** 33 39N 48 18 E
Ransiki, *Indonesia* **83 B4** 1 30 S 134 10 E
Ransom, *U.S.A.* **157 C8** 41 9N 88 39W
Rantabe, *Madag.* **117 B8** 15 42 S 49 39 E
Rantau, *Indonesia* **85 C5** 2 56 S 115 9 E
Rantauprapat, *Indonesia* **84 B1** 2 15N 99 50 E
Rantemario, *Indonesia* **82 B1** 3 15 S 119 57 E
Rantoul, *U.S.A.* **157 D8** 40 19N 88 9W
Ranum, *Denmark* **17 H3** 56 54N 9 14 E

Riansáres 271

Ranyah, W. →, Si. Arabia 98 B3 21 18N 43 20 E
Raon l'Étape, France 27 D13 48 24N 6 50 E
Raoping, China 77 F11 23 42N 117 1 E
Raoui, Erg er, Algeria 111 C4 29 0N 2 0W
Raoyang, China 74 E8 38 15N 115 45 E
Rap, Ko, Thailand 87 b 9 19N 99 58 E
Rapa, Pac. Oc. 135 K13 27 35 S 144 20W
Rapa Nui = Pascua, I. de, Chile 172 b 27 7 S 109 23W
Rapallo, Italy 44 D6 44 21N 9 14 E
Rapang, Indonesia 82 B1 3 50 S 119 48 E
Rapar, India 92 H4 23 34N 70 38 E
Rāpch, Iran 97 E8 25 40N 59 15 E
Raper, C., Canada 139 B13 69 44N 67 6W
Rapid City, U.S.A. 154 D3 44 5N 103 14W
Rapid River, U.S.A. 148 C2 45 55N 86 58W
Rapla, Estonia 15 G21 59 1N 24 52 E
Rapperswil, Switz. 33 B7 47 14N 8 45 E
Rapti →, India 93 F10 26 18N 83 41 E
Rapu Rapu I., Phil. 80 E5 13 12N 124 9 E
Raqaba ez Zarqa →, Sudan 107 F2 9 14N 29 44 E
Rāqūbah, Libya 108 C3 28 58N 19 2 E
Raquette →, U.S.A. 151 B10 45 0N 74 42W
Raquette Lake, U.S.A. 151 C10 43 49N 74 40W
Rarotonga, Cook Is. 135 K12 21 30 S 160 0W
Ra's al 'Ayn, Syria 101 D9 36 45N 40 12 E
Ra's al Khaymah, U.A.E. 97 E7 25 50N 55 59 E
Ras el Ma, Algeria 111 B4 34 26N 0 50W
Ras el Mâ, Mali 112 B4 16 35N 4 30W
Râs Ghârib, Egypt 106 B3 28 6N 33 18 E
Rās Kōh, Pakistan 91 C2 28 43N 64 55 E
Ra's Lānūf, Libya 108 B3 30 46N 18 11 E
Râs Mallap, Egypt 106 B3 29 18N 32 50 E
Râs Muhammad Nat. Park, Egypt 106 B3 27 45N 34 16 E
Rasa, Punta, Argentina 176 B4 40 50 S 62 15W
Rasca, Pta. de la, Canary Is. 9 e1 27 59N 16 41W
Rășcani, Moldova 53 C12 47 58N 27 33 E
Raseiniai, Lithuania 15 J20 55 25N 23 5 E
Rashad, Sudan 107 E3 11 55N 31 0 E
Rashîd, Egypt 106 H7 31 21N 30 22 E
Rashîd, Masabb, Egypt 106 H7 31 22N 30 17 E
Rashmi, India 92 G6 25 4N 74 22 E
Rasht, Iran 97 B6 37 20N 49 40 E
Rasi Salai, Thailand 86 E5 15 20N 104 9 E
Rasipuram, India 95 J4 11 30N 78 15 E
Raška, Serbia, Yug. 50 C4 43 19N 20 39 E
Râsnov, Romania 53 E10 45 35N 25 27 E
Rason L., Australia 125 E3 28 45 S 124 25 E
Rașova, Romania 53 F12 44 15N 27 55 E
Rasovo, Bulgaria 50 C7 43 42N 23 17 E
Rasra, India 93 G10 25 50N 83 50 E
Rass el Oued, Algeria 111 A6 35 57N 5 2 E
Rasskazovo, Russia 60 D5 52 35N 41 50 E
Rast, Romania 53 G8 43 53N 23 16 E
Rastatt, Germany 31 G4 48 50N 8 11 E
Rastede, Germany 30 B4 53 15N 8 12 E
Răstolița, Romania 53 D9 46 59N 24 58 E
Rasul, Pakistan 92 C5 32 42N 73 34 E
Raszków, Poland 55 G4 51 43N 17 40 E
Rat Buri, Thailand 86 F2 13 30N 99 54 E
Rat Islands, U.S.A. 144 L2 52 0N 178 0 E
Rat L., Canada 143 B9 56 10N 99 40W
Ratangarh, India 92 E6 28 5N 74 35 E
Rätansbyn, Sweden 16 B8 62 29N 14 33 E
Raṭāwī, Iraq 96 D5 30 38N 47 13 E
Ratcatchers L., Australia 128 B5 32 38 S 143 12 E
Rath, India 93 G8 25 36N 79 37 E
Rath Luirc, Ireland 23 D3 52 21N 8 40W
Rathbun L., U.S.A. 156 D4 40 49N 92 53W
Rathdrum, Ireland 23 D5 52 56N 6 14W
Rathedaung, Burma 90 E4 20 29N 92 45 E
Rathenow, Germany 30 C8 52 37N 12 19 E
Rathkeale, Ireland 23 D3 52 32N 8 56W
Rathlin I., U.K. 23 A5 55 18N 6 14W
Rathmelton, Ireland 23 A4 55 2N 7 38W
Ratibor = Racibórz, Poland 55 H5 50 7N 18 18 E
Rätikon, Austria 33 B9 47 0N 9 55 E
Ratingen, Germany 30 D2 51 18N 6 52 E
Ratlam, India 92 H6 23 20N 75 0 E
Ratnagiri, India 94 F1 16 57N 73 18 E
Ratnapura, Sri Lanka 95 L5 6 40N 80 20 E
Ratodero, Pakistan 92 F3 27 48N 68 18 E
Raton, U.S.A. 155 G2 36 54N 104 24W
Rattaphum, Thailand 87 J3 7 8N 100 16 E
Ratten, Austria 34 D8 47 28N 15 44 E
Rattray Hd., U.K. 22 D7 57 38N 1 50W
Rättvik, Sweden 16 D9 60 52N 15 7 E
Ratz, Mt., Canada 142 B2 57 23N 132 12W
Ratzeburg, Germany 30 B6 53 40N 10 46 E
Rau, Indonesia 82 A3 2 20N 128 10 E
Raub, Malaysia 87 L3 3 47N 101 52 E
Rauch, Argentina 174 D4 36 45 S 59 5W
Raudales de Malpaso, Mexico 163 D6 17 30N 93 30W
Raudeberg, Norway 18 C2 61 59N 5 7 E
Raufarhöfn, Iceland 11 A11 66 27N 15 57W
Raufoss, Norway 15 F14 60 44N 10 37 E
Rauhellern, Norway 18 D4 60 15N 7 50 E
Raukumara Ra., N.Z. 130 E6 38 5 S 177 55 E
Raul Soares, Brazil 171 F3 20 5 S 42 22W
Rauma, Finland 15 F19 61 10N 21 30 E
Rauma →, Norway 18 B4 62 34N 7 43 E
Raung, Gunung, Indonesia 79 J17 8 8 S 114 3 E
Raurkela, India 93 H11 22 14N 84 50 E
Rausu-Dake, Japan 70 B12 44 4N 145 7 E
Răut →, Moldova 53 C14 47 15N 29 9 E
Rava-Ruska, Poland 59 G2 50 15N 23 42 E
Rava Russkaya = Rava-Ruska, Poland 59 G2 50 15N 23 42 E
Ravalli, U.S.A. 158 C6 47 17N 114 11W
Ravānsar, Iran 101 E12 34 43N 46 40 E
Ravanusa, Italy 46 E6 37 16N 13 58 E
Rāvar, Iran 97 D8 31 20N 56 51 E
Ravena, U.S.A. 151 D11 42 28N 73 49W
Ravenel, U.S.A. 152 C9 32 46N 80 15W
Ravenna, Italy 45 D9 44 25N 12 12 E
Ravenna, Ky., U.S.A. 157 G13 37 42N 83 55W
Ravenna, Nebr., U.S.A. 154 E5 41 1N 98 55W
Ravenna, Ohio, U.S.A. 150 E3 41 9N 81 15W
Ravensburg, Germany 31 H5 47 46N 9 36 E
Ravenshoe, Australia 126 B4 17 37 S 145 29 E
Ravensthorpe, Australia 125 F3 33 35 S 120 2 E
Ravenswood, Australia 126 C4 20 6 S 146 54 E
Ravenswood, U.S.A. 148 F5 38 57N 81 46W
Ravensworth, Australia 129 B9 32 26 S 151 4 E
Ravenwood, U.S.A. 156 D2 40 22N 94 41W
Raver, India 94 D3 21 15N 76 2 E
Ravi →, Pakistan 92 D4 30 35N 71 49 E
Ravna Gora, Croatia 45 C11 45 24N 14 50 E
Ravna Reka, Serbia, Yug. 50 B5 44 1N 21 35 E
Ravne na Koroškem, Slovenia 45 B11 46 36N 14 59 E
Rawa Mazowiecka, Poland 55 G7 51 46N 20 12 E
Rawalpindi, Pakistan 91 B4 33 38N 73 8 E
Rawāndūz, Iraq 101 D11 36 40N 44 30 E
Rawang, Malaysia 87 L3 3 20N 101 35 E
Rawene, N.Z. 130 B2 35 25 S 173 32 E
Rawicz, Poland 55 G3 51 36N 16 52 E
Rawka →, Poland 55 F7 52 9N 20 8 E
Rawlinna, Australia 125 F4 30 58 S 125 28 E
Rawlins, U.S.A. 158 F10 41 47N 107 14W
Rawlinson Ra., Australia 125 D4 24 40 S 128 30 E
Rawson, Argentina 176 B3 43 15 S 65 5W
Raxaul, India 93 F11 26 59N 84 51 E
Ray, U.S.A. 154 A3 48 21N 103 10W
Ray, C., Canada 141 C8 47 33N 59 15W
Ray City, U.S.A. 152 D6 31 5N 83 11W
Ray Mts., U.S.A. 144 D10 66 0N 152 0W
Raya Ring, Ko, Thailand 87 a 8 18N 98 29 E
Rayachoti, India 95 G4 14 4N 78 50 E
Rayadurg, India 95 G3 14 40N 76 50 E
Rayagada, India 94 E6 19 15N 83 20 E
Raychikhinsk, Russia 67 E13 49 46N 129 25 E
Rāyen, Iran 97 D8 29 34N 57 26 E
Rayevskiy, Russia 64 D5 54 4N 54 56 E
Rayle, U.S.A. 152 B7 33 48N 82 54W
Rayleigh, U.K. 21 F8 51 36N 0 37 E
Raymond, Canada 142 D6 49 30N 112 35W
Raymond, Calif., U.S.A. 160 H7 37 13N 119 54W
Raymond, Ill., U.S.A. 156 E7 39 19N 89 34W
Raymond, N.H., U.S.A. 151 C13 43 2N 71 11W
Raymond, Wash., U.S.A. 160 D3 46 41N 123 44W
Raymond Terrace, Australia 129 B9 32 45 S 151 44 E
Raymondville, U.S.A. 155 M6 26 29N 97 47W
Raymore, Canada 143 C8 51 25N 104 31W
Rayón, Mexico 162 B2 29 43N 110 35W
Rayong, Thailand 86 F3 12 40N 101 20 E
Raytown, U.S.A. 156 E2 39 1N 94 28W
Rayville, U.S.A. 155 J9 32 29N 91 46W
Raz, Pte. du, France 26 D2 48 2N 4 47W
Razan, Iran 97 C6 35 23N 49 2 E
Ražana, Serbia, Yug. 50 B3 44 6N 19 55 E
Ražanj, Serbia, Yug. 50 C5 43 40N 21 31 E
Razdelna, Bulgaria 51 C11 43 13N 27 41 E
Razdel'naya = Rozdilna, Ukraine 59 J6 46 50N 30 2 E
Razdolnoye, Russia 70 C5 43 30N 131 52 E
Razdolnoye, Ukraine 59 K7 45 46N 33 29 E
Razeh, Iran 97 C6 32 47N 48 9 E
Razgrad, Bulgaria 51 C10 43 33N 26 34 E
Razim, Lacul, Romania 53 F14 44 50N 29 0 E
Razlog, Bulgaria 50 E7 41 53N 23 28 E
Razmak, Pakistan 91 B3 32 45N 69 50 E
Ré, Î. de, France 28 B2 46 12N 1 30W
Reading, U.K. 21 F7 51 27N 0 58W
Reading, Mich., U.S.A. 157 C12 41 50N 84 45W
Reading, Ohio, U.S.A. 157 E12 39 13N 84 26W
Reading, Pa., U.S.A. 151 F9 40 20N 75 56W
Reading □, U.K. 21 F7 51 27N 0 58W
Real, Cordillera, Bolivia 172 D4 17 0 S 67 10W
Realicó, Argentina 174 D3 35 0 S 64 15W
Réalmont, France 28 E6 43 48N 2 10 E
Realp, Switz. 33 C6 46 36N 8 30 E
Ream, Cambodia 87 G4 10 34N 103 39 E
Reata, Mexico 162 B4 26 8N 101 5W
Reay Forest, U.K. 22 C4 58 22N 4 55W
Rebais, France 27 D10 48 50N 3 10 E
Rebi, Indonesia 83 C4 6 23 S 134 7 E
Rebiana, Libya 108 D4 24 12N 22 10 E
Rebiana, Sahrâ, Libya 108 D3 24 0N 23 0 E
Rebun-Tō, Japan 70 B10 45 23N 141 2 E
Recanati, Italy 45 E10 43 24N 13 32 E
Recaş, Romania 52 E6 45 46N 21 30 E
Recco, Italy 44 D6 44 22N 9 9 E
Recherche, Arch. of the, Australia 125 F3 34 15 S 122 50 E
Rechna Doab, Pakistan 92 D5 31 35N 73 30 E
Rechytsa, Belarus 59 F6 52 21N 30 24 E
Recife, Brazil 170 C5 8 0 S 35 0W
Recife, Seychelles 121 b 4 36 S 55 42 E
Recklinghausen, Germany 24 C7 51 37N 7 12 E
Reconquista, Argentina 174 B4 29 10 S 59 45W
Recreio, Brazil 173 B6 8 0 S 58 25W
Recreo, Argentina 174 B2 29 25 S 65 10W
Recuay, Peru 172 B2 9 43 S 77 28W
Recz, Poland 55 E2 53 16N 15 31 E
Red →, La., U.S.A. 155 K9 31 1N 91 45W
Red →, N. Dak., U.S.A. 138 C10 49 0N 97 15W
Red Bank, U.S.A. 151 F10 40 21N 74 5W
Red Bay, Canada 141 B8 51 44N 56 25W
Red Bluff, U.S.A. 158 F2 40 11N 122 15W
Red Bluff L., U.S.A. 155 K3 31 54N 103 55W
Red Bud, U.S.A. 156 F7 38 13N 89 59W
Red Cliffs, Australia 128 C5 34 19 S 142 11 E
Red Cloud, U.S.A. 154 E5 40 5N 98 32W
Red Creek, U.S.A. 151 C8 43 14N 76 45W
Red Deer, Canada 142 C6 52 20N 113 50W
Red Deer →, Alta., Canada 143 C7 50 58N 110 0W
Red Deer →, Man., Canada 143 C8 52 53N 101 1W
Red Deer L., Canada 143 C8 52 55N 101 20W
Red Devil, U.S.A. 144 F8 61 46N 157 19W
Red Hook, U.S.A. 151 E11 41 55N 73 53W
Red Indian L., Canada 141 C8 48 35N 57 0W
Red L., Canada 143 C10 51 3N 93 49W
Red Lake, Canada 143 C10 51 3N 93 49W
Red Lake Falls, U.S.A. 154 B6 47 53N 96 16W
Red Lake Road, Canada 143 C10 49 59N 93 25W
Red Lodge, U.S.A. 158 D9 45 11N 109 15W
Red Mountain, U.S.A. 161 K9 35 37N 117 38W
Red Oak, U.S.A. 154 E7 41 1N 95 14W
Red Rock, Canada 140 C2 48 55N 88 15W
Red Rock, L., U.S.A. 156 C3 41 22N 92 59W
Red Rocks Pt., Australia 125 F4 32 13 S 127 32 E
Red Sea, Asia 102 C2 25 0N 36 0 E
Red Slate Mt., U.S.A. 160 H8 37 31N 118 52W
Red Sucker L., Canada 140 B1 54 9N 93 40W
Red Tower Pass = Turnu Roşu, P., Romania 53 E9 45 33N 24 17 E
Red Wing, U.S.A. 154 C8 44 34N 92 31W
Reda, Poland 54 D5 54 40N 18 19 E
Redang, Malaysia 78 C2 5 49N 103 2 E
Redange, Lux. 24 E5 49 46N 5 52 E
Redcar, U.K. 20 C6 54 37N 1 4W
Redcar & Cleveland □, U.K. 20 C7 54 29N 1 0W
Redcliff, Canada 143 C6 50 10N 110 50W
Redcliffe, Australia 127 D5 27 12 S 153 0 E
Redcliffe, Mt., Australia 125 E3 28 30 S 121 30 E
Reddersburg, S. Africa 116 D4 29 41 S 26 10 E
Reddick, Fla., U.S.A. 153 F7 29 22N 82 12W
Reddick, Ill., U.S.A. 157 C8 41 6N 88 15W
Redding, Calif., U.S.A. 158 F2 40 35N 122 24W
Redding, Iowa, U.S.A. 156 D2 40 36N 94 23W
Redditch, U.K. 21 E6 52 18N 1 55W
Redenção, Brazil 170 B4 4 13 S 38 43W
Redfield, U.S.A. 154 C5 44 53N 98 31W
Redford, U.S.A. 151 B11 44 38N 73 48W
Redhead, Trin. & Tob. 169 F10 10 48N 60 3W
Redkey, U.S.A. 157 D11 40 21N 85 9W
Redkino, Russia 58 D9 56 39N 36 16 E
Redlands, U.S.A. 161 M9 34 4N 117 11W
Redmond, Oreg., U.S.A. 158 D3 44 17N 121 11W
Redmond, Wash., U.S.A. 160 C4 47 41N 122 7W
Redon, France 26 E4 47 40N 2 6W
Redonda, Antigua 165 C7 16 58N 62 19W
Redonda, Pta., Chile 172 b 27 10 S 109 22W
Redondela, Spain 42 C2 42 15N 8 38W
Redondo, Portugal 43 G3 38 39N 7 37W
Redondo Beach, U.S.A. 161 M8 33 50N 118 23W
Redoubt Volcano, U.S.A. 144 F9 60 29N 152 45W
Redruth, U.K. 21 G2 50 14N 5 14W
Redvers, Canada 143 D8 49 35N 101 40W
Redwater, Canada 142 C6 53 55N 113 6W
Redwood, U.S.A. 151 B9 44 18N 75 48W
Redwood City, U.S.A. 160 H4 37 30N 122 15W
Redwood Falls, U.S.A. 154 C7 44 32N 95 7W
Redwood Nat. Park, U.S.A. 158 F1 41 40N 124 5W
Ree, L., Ireland 23 C3 53 35N 8 0W
Reed, L., Canada 143 C8 54 38N 100 30W
Reed City, U.S.A. 148 D3 43 53N 85 31W
Reedley, U.S.A. 160 J7 36 36N 119 27W
Reedsburg, U.S.A. 154 D9 43 32N 90 0W
Reedsport, U.S.A. 158 E1 43 42N 124 6W
Reedsville, U.S.A. 150 F7 40 39N 77 35W
Reedy Creek, Australia 128 D4 36 58 S 140 2 E
Reefton, N.Z. 131 C6 42 6 S 171 51 E
Rees, Germany 30 D2 51 46N 6 24 E
Reese →, U.S.A. 158 F5 40 48N 117 4W
Refahiye, Turkey 101 C8 39 54N 38 47 E
Reftele, Sweden 17 G7 57 11N 13 35 E
Refugio, U.S.A. 155 L6 28 18N 97 17W
Rega →, Poland 54 D2 54 10N 15 18 E
Regalbuto, Italy 47 E7 37 39N 14 38 E
Regen, Germany 31 G9 48 58N 13 8 E
Regen →, Germany 31 F8 49 1N 12 6 E
Regeneração, Brazil 170 C3 6 15 S 42 41W
Regensburg, Germany 31 F8 49 1N 12 6 E
Regensdorf, Switz. 33 B6 47 26N 8 28 E
Regenstauf, Germany 31 F8 49 7N 12 8 E
Reggâne = Zaouiet Reggâne, Algeria 111 C5 26 32N 0 3 E
Reggello, Italy 45 E8 43 41N 11 32 E
Réggio di Calábria, Italy 47 D8 38 6N 15 39 E
Réggio nell'Emília, Italy 44 D7 44 43N 10 36 E
Reghin, Romania 53 D9 46 46N 24 42 E
Regina, Canada 143 C8 50 27N 104 35W
Régina, Fr. Guiana 169 C7 4 19N 52 8W
Regina Beach, Canada 143 C8 50 47N 105 0W
Register, U.S.A. 152 C8 32 22N 81 53W
Registro, Brazil 175 A6 24 29 S 47 49W
Reguengos de Monsaraz, Portugal 43 G3 38 25N 7 32W
Reh, Erg er, Algeria 111 C5 27 48N 4 30 E
Rehar →, India 93 H10 23 55N 82 40 E
Rehli, India 93 H8 23 38N 79 5 E
Rehoboth, Namibia 116 C2 23 15 S 17 4 E
Rehovot, Israel 103 D3 31 54N 34 48 E
Reichenbach, Germany 30 E8 50 37N 12 17 E
Reichenbach, Switz. 32 C5 46 38N 7 42 E
Reid, Australia 125 F4 30 49 S 128 26 E
Reiden, Switz. 32 B5 47 14N 7 59 E
Reidsville, Ga., U.S.A. 152 C7 32 6N 82 7W
Reidsville, N.C., U.S.A. 149 G6 36 21N 79 40W
Reigate, U.K. 21 F7 51 14N 0 12W
Reillo, Spain 40 F3 39 54N 1 53W
Reims, France 27 C11 49 15N 4 1 E
Reina Adelaida, Arch., Chile 176 D2 52 20 S 74 0W
Reinach, Aargau, Switz. 32 B6 47 14N 8 11 E
Reinach, Basel, Switz. 32 B5 47 29N 7 35 E
Reinbeck, U.S.A. 156 B4 42 19N 92 36W
Reinbek, Germany 30 B6 53 30N 10 16 E
Reindeer →, Canada 143 B8 55 36N 103 11W
Reindeer I., Canada 143 C9 52 30N 98 0W
Reindeer L., Canada 143 B8 57 15N 102 15W
Reinga, C., N.Z. 130 A1 34 25 S 172 43 E
Reinosa, Spain 42 B6 43 2N 4 15W
Reinsvoll, Norway 18 D7 60 40N 10 38 E
Reitan, Norway 18 B8 62 49N 11 22 E
Reitz, S. Africa 117 D4 27 48 S 28 29 E
Reivilo, S. Africa 116 D3 27 36 S 24 8 E
Rejaf, Sudan 107 G3 4 45N 31 35 E
Rejmyre, Sweden 17 F9 58 50N 15 55 E
Rejowiec Fabryczny, Poland 55 G10 51 5N 23 17 E
Reka →, Slovenia 45 C11 45 40N 14 0 E
Rekovac, Serbia, Yug. 50 C5 43 51N 21 3 E
Reliance, Canada 143 A7 63 0N 109 20W
Relizane, Algeria 111 A5 35 44N 0 31 E
Remad, Oued →, Algeria 111 B4 33 28N 1 20W
Rémalard, France 26 D7 48 26N 0 47 E
Remarkable, Mt., Australia 128 B3 32 48 S 138 10 E
Rembang, Indonesia 85 D4 6 42 S 111 21 E
Rembau, Malaysia 84 B2 2 35N 102 6 E
Rembert, U.S.A. 152 A9 34 6N 80 32W
Remchi, Algeria 111 A4 35 2N 1 26W
Remedios, Colombia 168 B3 7 2N 74 41W
Remedios, Panama 164 E3 8 15N 81 50W
Remeshk, Iran 97 E8 26 55N 58 50 E
Remetea, Romania 53 D10 46 45N 25 29 E
Remich, Lux. 24 E6 49 32N 6 22 E
Remington, U.S.A. 157 D9 40 46N 87 9W
Rémire, Fr. Guiana 169 C7 4 53N 52 17W
Remiremont, France 27 D13 48 2N 6 36 E
Remo, Ethiopia 107 F5 6 48N 41 20 E
Remontnoye, Russia 61 G6 46 34N 43 37 E
Remoulins, France 29 E8 43 55N 4 35 E
Remscheid, Germany 24 C7 51 11N 7 12 E
Ren Xian, China 74 F8 37 8N 114 40 E
Rena, Norway 18 C8 61 8N 11 20 E
Rena →, Norway 18 C8 61 8N 11 23 E
Renascença, Brazil 168 D4 3 50 S 66 21W
Rend Lake, U.S.A. 156 F8 38 2N 88 58W
Rendang, Indonesia 79 J18 8 26 S 115 25 E
Rende, Italy 47 C9 39 20N 16 11 E
Rendína, Greece 48 B3 39 4N 21 58 E
Rendova, Solomon Is. 133 M9 8 33 S 157 17 E
Rendsburg, Germany 30 A5 54 17N 9 39 E
Renens, Switz. 32 C3 46 32N 6 35 E
Renfrew, Canada 140 C4 45 30N 76 40W
Renfrewshire □, U.K. 22 F4 55 49N 4 38W
Renfroe, U.S.A. 152 C5 32 14N 84 43W
Rengat, Indonesia 84 C2 0 30 S 102 45 E
Rengo, Chile 174 C1 34 24 S 70 50W
Renhua, China 77 E9 25 5N 113 40 E
Renhuai, China 76 D6 27 48N 106 24 E
Reni, Ukraine 59 K5 45 28N 28 15 E
Renigunta, India 95 H4 13 38N 79 30 E
Renk, Sudan 107 E3 11 50N 32 50 E
Renland, Greenland 10 C8 71 10N 26 30W
Renmark, Australia 128 C4 34 11 S 140 43 E
Rennebu, Norway 18 B6 62 52N 9 49 E
Rennell, Solomon Is. 133 N11 11 40 S 160 10 E
Rennell Sd., Canada 142 C2 53 23N 132 35W
Renner Springs, Australia 126 B1 18 20 S 133 47 E
Rennes, France 26 D5 48 7N 1 41W
Rennie L., Canada 143 A7 61 32N 105 35W
Reno, U.S.A. 160 F7 39 31N 119 48W
Reno →, Italy 45 D9 44 38N 12 16 E
Renovo, U.S.A. 150 E7 41 20N 77 45W
Renqiu, China 74 E9 38 43N 116 5 E
Rens, Denmark 17 K3 54 54N 9 5 E
Renshou, China 76 C5 30 0N 104 9 E
Rensselaer, Ind., U.S.A. 157 D9 40 57N 87 9W
Rensselaer, N.Y., U.S.A. 151 D11 42 38N 73 45W
Rentería, Spain 40 B3 43 19N 1 54W
Renton, U.S.A. 160 C4 47 29N 122 12W
Renwick, N.Z. 131 B8 41 30 S 173 51 E
Réo, Burkina Faso 112 C4 12 28N 2 35W
Reo, Indonesia 82 C2 8 19 S 120 30 E
Reocín, Spain 42 B6 43 21N 4 5W
Reotipur, India 93 G10 25 33N 83 45 E
Repalle, India 95 F5 16 2N 80 45 E
Répcelak, Hungary 52 C2 47 24N 17 1 E
Republic, Mo., U.S.A. 155 G8 37 7N 93 29W
Republic, Wash., U.S.A. 158 B4 48 39N 118 44W
Republican →, U.S.A. 154 F6 39 4N 96 48W
Republiek, Surinam 169 B6 5 30N 55 13W
Repulse B., Australia 126 J6 20 35 S 148 46 E
Repulse Bay, Canada 139 B11 66 30N 86 30W
Requena, Peru 172 B3 5 5 S 73 52W
Requena, Spain 41 F3 39 30N 1 4W
Réquista, France 28 D6 44 1N 2 32 E
Reşadiye = Datça, Turkey 49 E9 36 46N 27 40 E
Reşadiye, Turkey 100 B7 40 23N 37 20 E
Reşadiye Yarımadası, Turkey 49 E9 36 40N 27 45 E
Resavica, Serbia, Yug. 50 B5 44 4N 21 31 E
Resen, Macedonia 50 E5 41 5N 21 0 E
Reserve, U.S.A. 159 K9 33 43N 108 45W
Resht = Rasht, Iran 97 B6 37 20N 49 40 E
Résia, Italy 33 C11 46 50N 10 31 E
Resistencia, Argentina 174 B4 27 30 S 59 0W
Reşiţa, Romania 52 E6 45 18N 21 53 E
Resko, Poland 54 E2 53 47N 15 25 E
Resolution I., Canada 139 B13 61 30N 65 0W
Resolution I., N.Z. 131 F1 45 40 S 166 40 E
Resplandes, Brazil 170 C2 6 17 S 45 13W
Resplendor, Brazil 171 E3 19 20 S 41 15W
Ressano Garcia, Mozam. 117 D5 25 25 S 32 0 E
Reston, Canada 143 D8 49 33N 101 6W
Reszel, Poland 54 D8 54 4N 21 10 E
Retalhuleu, Guatemala 164 D1 14 33N 91 46W
Retenue, L. de, Dem. Rep. of the Congo 119 E2 11 0 S 27 0 E
Retezat, Munţii, Romania 52 E8 45 25N 23 0 E
Retford, U.K. 20 D7 53 19N 0 56W
Rethel, France 27 C11 49 30N 4 20 E
Rethem, Germany 30 C5 52 47N 9 22 E
Réthímnon, Greece 39 E5 35 18N 24 30 E
Réthímnon □, Greece 39 E5 35 23N 24 28 E
Reti, Pakistan 92 E3 28 5N 69 48 E
Retiche, Alpi, Switz. 33 D10 46 30N 10 0 E
Retiers, France 26 E5 47 55N 1 23W
Retortillo, Spain 42 E4 40 48N 6 21W
Retournac, France 29 C8 45 12N 4 2 E
Rétság, Hungary 52 C4 47 58N 19 10 E
Rettenberg, Germany 33 A10 47 35N 10 18 E
Réunion ■, Ind. Oc. 105 J9 21 0 S 56 0 E
Reus, Spain 40 D6 41 10N 1 5 E
Reuss →, Switz. 33 B6 47 16N 8 24 E
Reuterstadt Stavenhagen, Germany 30 B8 53 42N 12 54 E
Reutlingen, Germany 31 G5 48 29N 9 12 E
Reutte, Austria 34 D3 47 29N 10 42 E
Reval = Tallinn, Estonia 15 G21 59 22N 24 48 E
Revda, Russia 64 C7 56 48N 59 57 E
Revel, France 28 E6 43 28N 2 1 E
Revelganj, India 93 G11 25 50N 84 40 E
Revelstoke, Canada 142 C5 51 0N 118 10W
Reventazón, Peru 172 B1 6 10 S 80 58W
Revigny-sur-Ornain, France 27 D11 48 49N 4 59 E
Revillagigedo, Is. de, Pac. Oc. 162 D2 18 40N 112 0W
Revin, France 27 C11 49 55N 4 39 E
Revolyutsii, Pik, Tajikistan 65 D6 38 31N 72 21 E
Revolyutsiya, Qullai = Revolyutsii, Pik, Tajikistan 65 D6 38 31N 72 21 E
Revúca, Slovak Rep. 35 C13 48 41N 20 7 E
Revuè →, Mozam. 119 F3 19 50 S 34 0 E
Rewa, India 93 G9 24 33N 81 25 E
Rewa →, Guyana 169 C6 3 19N 58 42W
Rewari, India 92 E7 28 15N 76 40 E
Rexburg, U.S.A. 158 E8 43 49N 111 47W
Rey, Iran 97 C6 35 35N 51 25 E
Rey, I. del, Panama 164 E4 8 20N 78 30W
Rey, Mayo →, Cameroon 114 A2 8 47N 14 1 E
Rey, Rio-del-→, Cameroon 114 B1 4 31N 8 45 E
Rey Bouba, Cameroon 114 A2 8 40N 14 15 E
Rey Malabo, Eq. Guin. 113 E6 3 45N 8 50 E
Reyðarfjörður, Iceland 11 B12 65 2N 14 13W
Reyes, Bolivia 172 C4 14 19 S 67 23W
Reyes, Pt., U.S.A. 160 H3 38 0N 123 0W
Reyhanlı, Turkey 100 D7 36 16N 36 35 E
Reykholt, Árnessýsla, Iceland 11 C5 64 40N 21 18W
Reykholt, Borgarfjarðarsýsla, Iceland 11 C6 64 10N 20 25W
Reykjahlið, Iceland 11 B10 65 40N 16 55W
Reykjanes, Iceland 11 D4 63 48N 22 40W
Reykjavík, Iceland 11 C5 64 10N 21 57W
Reynolds, Ga., U.S.A. 152 C5 32 33N 84 6W
Reynolds, Ill., U.S.A. 156 C6 41 20N 90 40W
Reynolds Ra., Australia 124 D5 22 30 S 133 0 E
Reynoldsville, Ga., U.S.A. 152 E5 30 51N 84 47W
Reynoldsville, Pa., U.S.A. 150 E6 41 5N 78 58W
Reynosa, Mexico 163 B5 26 5N 98 18W
Rēzekne, Latvia 15 H22 56 30N 27 17 E
Rezh, Russia 64 C8 57 23N 61 24 E
Rezina, Moldova 53 C13 47 45N 28 58 E
Rezovo, Bulgaria 51 D12 42 0N 28 0 E
Rezvān, Iran 97 E8 27 34N 56 6 E
Rgotina, Serbia, Yug. 50 B6 44 1N 22 17 E
Rhamnus, Greece 48 C6 38 12N 24 3 E
Rharbi, Zahrez, Algeria 111 B5 34 50N 2 55 E
Rharis, O. →, Algeria 111 C6 26 0N 5 4 E
Rhayader, U.K. 21 E4 52 18N 3 29W
Rheda-Wiedenbrück, Germany 30 D4 51 50N 8 20 E
Rhede, Germany 30 D2 51 50N 6 42 E
Rhein →, Europe 24 C6 51 52N 6 2 E
Rhein-Main-Donau-Kanal, Germany 31 F7 49 1N 11 27 E
Rheinbach, Germany 30 E2 50 38N 6 57 E
Rheine, Germany 30 C3 52 17N 7 26 E
Rheineck, Switz. 33 B9 47 28N 9 31 E
Rheinfelden, Germany 31 H3 47 33N 7 47 E
Rheinfelden, Switz. 32 A5 47 32N 7 47 E
Rheinhessen-Pfalz □, Germany 31 F3 49 20N 8 0 E
Rheinland-Pfalz □, Germany 31 E2 50 0N 7 0 E
Rheinsberg, Germany 30 B8 53 6N 12 54 E
Rheinwaldhorn, Switz. 33 D8 46 30N 9 3 E
Rheris, Oued →, Morocco 110 B4 30 50N 4 34W
Rhin = Rhein →, Europe 24 C6 51 52N 6 2 E
Rhine = Rhein →, Europe 24 C6 51 52N 6 2 E
Rhine, U.S.A. 152 D6 31 59N 83 12W
Rhinebeck, U.S.A. 151 E11 41 56N 73 55W
Rhineland-Palatinate = Rheinland-Pfalz □, Germany 31 E2 50 0N 7 0 E
Rhinelander, U.S.A. 154 C10 45 38N 89 25W
Rhinns Pt., U.K. 22 F2 55 40N 6 29W
Rhino Camp, Uganda 118 B3 3 0N 31 22 E
Rhir, Cap, Morocco 110 B3 30 38N 9 54W
Rho, Italy 44 C6 45 32N 9 2 E
Rhode Island □, U.S.A. 151 E13 41 40N 71 30W
Rhodes = Ródhos, Greece 38 E12 36 15N 28 10 E
Rhodesia = Zimbabwe ■, Africa 119 F3 19 0 S 30 0 E
Rhodope Mts. = Rhodopi Planina, Bulgaria 51 E8 41 40N 24 20 E
Rhodopi Planina, Bulgaria 51 E8 41 40N 24 20 E
Rhön, Germany 30 E5 50 24N 9 58 E
Rhondda, U.K. 21 F4 51 39N 3 31W
Rhondda Cynon Taff □, U.K. 21 F4 51 42N 3 27W
Rhône □, France 29 C8 45 54N 4 35 E
Rhône →, France 29 E8 43 28N 4 42 E
Rhône-Alpes □, France 29 C9 45 40N 6 0 E
Rhum, U.K. 22 E2 57 0N 6 20W
Rhyl, U.K. 20 D4 53 20N 3 29W
Ri-Aba, Eq. Guin. 113 E6 3 28N 8 40 E
Riachão, Brazil 170 C2 7 20 S 46 37W
Riacho de Santana, Brazil 171 D3 13 37 S 42 57W
Rialma, Brazil 171 E2 15 18 S 49 34W
Riang, India 90 B4 27 31N 92 56 E
Riangnom, Sudan 107 F3 9 55N 30 1 E
Riaño, Spain 42 C6 42 59N 4 59W
Rians, France 29 E9 43 37N 5 44 E
Riansáres →, Spain 43 F7 39 32N 3 18W

272 Riasi

Riasi, India 93 C6 33 10N 74 50 E
Riau □, Indonesia 84 B2 0 0 102 35 E
Riau, Kepulauan, Indonesia 84 B2 0 30N 104 20 E
Riau Arch. = Riau, Kepulauan, Indonesia 84 B2 0 30N 104 20 E
Riaza, Spain 42 D7 41 18N 3 30W
Riaza →, Spain 42 D7 41 42N 3 55W
Riba de Saelices, Spain 40 E2 40 55N 2 17W
Riba-Roja de Turia, Spain 41 F4 39 33N 0 34W
Ribadavia, Spain 42 C2 42 17N 8 8W
Ribadeo, Spain 42 B3 43 35N 7 5W
Ribadesella, Spain 42 B5 43 30N 5 7W
Ribado, Nigeria 113 D7 9 16N 12 47 E
Ribamar, Brazil 170 B3 2 33 S 44 3W
Ribao, Cameroon 113 D7 6 32N 11 30 E
Ribas = Ribes de Freser, Spain 40 C7 42 19N 2 15 E
Ribas do Rio Pardo, Brazil 173 E7 20 27 S 53 46W
Ribauè, Mozam. 119 E4 14 57 S 38 17 E
Ribble →, U.K. 20 D5 53 52N 2 25W
Ribe, Denmark 17 J2 55 19N 8 44 E
Ribe Amtskommune □, Denmark 17 J2 55 35N 8 45 E
Ribeauvillé, France 27 D14 48 10N 7 20 E
Ribécourt-Dreslincourt, France 27 C9 49 30N 2 55 E
Ribeira = Santa Uxía, Spain 42 C2 42 36N 8 58W
Ribeira Brava, Madeira 9 c 32 41N 17 4W
Ribeira do Pombal, Brazil 170 D4 10 50 S 38 32W
Ribeira Grande, Azores 9 d3 37 49N 25 31W
Ribeira Grande, C. Verde Is. 9 j 17 0N 25 4W
Ribeirão, Brazil 170 C4 8 31 S 35 23W
Ribeirão Prêto, Brazil 175 A6 21 10 S 47 50W
Ribeiro Gonçalves, Brazil 170 C2 7 32 S 45 14W
Ribemont, France 27 C10 49 47N 3 27 E
Ribera, Italy 46 E6 37 30N 13 16 E
Ribérac, France 28 C4 45 15N 0 20 E
Riberalta, Bolivia 173 C4 11 0 S 66 0W
Ribes de Freser, Spain 40 C7 42 19N 2 15 E
Ribnica, Slovenia 45 C11 45 45N 14 45 E
Ribnitz-Damgarten, Germany 30 A8 54 15N 12 27 E
Ričany, Czech Rep. 34 B7 50 0N 14 40 E
Riccarton, N.Z. 131 D7 43 32 S 172 37 E
Ríccia, Italy 47 A7 41 30N 14 50 E
Riccione, Italy 45 E9 43 59N 12 39 E
Rice, U.S.A. 161 L12 34 5N 114 51W
Rice L., Canada 150 B6 44 12N 78 10W
Rice Lake, U.S.A. 154 C9 45 30N 91 44W
Riceboro, U.S.A. 152 D8 31 44N 81 26W
Rich, Morocco 110 B4 32 16N 4 30W
Rich, C., Canada 150 B4 44 43N 80 38W
Richard Toll, Senegal 112 B1 16 25N 15 42W
Richards Bay, S. Africa 117 D5 28 48 S 32 6 E
Richardson →, Canada 143 B6 58 25N 111 14W
Richardson Lakes, U.S.A. 148 C10 44 46N 70 58W
Richardson Mts., N.Z. 131 E3 44 49 S 168 34 E
Richardson Springs, U.S.A. 160 F5 39 51N 121 46W
Riche, C., Australia 125 F2 34 36 S 118 47 E
Richelieu, France 26 E7 47 1N 0 20 E
Richey, U.S.A. 154 B2 47 39N 105 4W
Richfield, U.S.A. 159 G8 38 46N 112 5W
Richfield Springs, U.S.A. 151 D10 42 51N 74 59W
Richford, U.S.A. 151 B12 45 0N 72 40W
Richibucto, Canada 141 C7 46 42N 64 54W
Richland, Ga., U.S.A. 152 C5 32 5N 84 40W
Richland, Iowa, U.S.A. 156 C5 41 13N 92 0W
Richland, Mo., U.S.A. 156 G4 37 51N 92 26W
Richland, Wash., U.S.A. 158 C4 46 17N 119 18W
Richland Center, U.S.A. 154 D9 43 21N 90 23W
Richlands, U.S.A. 148 G5 37 6N 81 48W
Richmond, N.S.W., Australia 129 B9 33 35 S 150 42 E
Richmond, Queens., Australia 126 C3 20 43 S 143 8 E
Richmond, N.Z. 131 B8 41 20 S 173 12 E
Richmond, U.K. 20 C6 54 25N 1 43W
Richmond, Calif., U.S.A. 160 H4 37 56N 122 21W
Richmond, Ind., U.S.A. 157 E12 39 50N 84 53W
Richmond, Ky., U.S.A. 157 G12 37 45N 84 18W
Richmond, Mich., U.S.A. 150 D2 42 49N 82 45W
Richmond, Mo., U.S.A. 156 E3 39 17N 93 58W
Richmond, Tex., U.S.A. 155 L7 29 35N 95 46W
Richmond, Utah, U.S.A. 158 F8 41 56N 111 48W
Richmond, Va., U.S.A. 148 G7 37 33N 77 27W
Richmond, Vt., U.S.A. 151 B12 44 24N 72 59W
Richmond, Mt., N.Z. 131 B8 41 32 S 173 22 E
Richmond Hill, Canada 150 C5 43 52N 79 27W
Richmond Hill, U.S.A. 152 D8 31 56N 81 18W
Richmond Ra., Australia 127 D5 29 0 S 152 45 E
Richmond Ra., N.Z. 131 B8 41 32 S 173 22 E
Richtersveld Nat. Park, S. Africa 116 D2 28 15 S 17 10 E
Richterswil, Switz. 33 B7 47 13N 8 43 E
Richwood, Ohio, U.S.A. 157 D13 40 26N 83 18W
Richwood, W. Va., U.S.A. 148 F5 38 14N 80 32W
Ricla, Spain 40 D3 41 31N 1 24W
Ricupe, Angola 115 E4 14 37 S 21 25 E
Ridā', Yemen 98 D4 14 25N 44 50 E
Ridder = Leninogorsk, Kazakstan 66 D9 50 20N 83 30 E
Riddes, Switz. 32 D4 46 11N 7 14 E
Riddlesburg, U.S.A. 150 F6 40 9N 78 15W
Ridge Farm, U.S.A. 157 E9 39 54N 87 39W
Ridge Spring, U.S.A. 152 B8 33 51N 81 40W
Ridgecrest, U.S.A. 161 K9 35 38N 117 40W
Ridgefield, Conn., U.S.A. 151 E11 41 17N 73 30W
Ridgefield, Wash., U.S.A. 160 E4 45 49N 122 45W
Ridgeland, U.S.A. 152 C9 32 29N 80 59W
Ridgetown, Canada 140 D3 42 26N 81 52W
Ridgeville, Ind., U.S.A. 157 D11 40 18N 85 2W
Ridgeville, S.C., U.S.A. 152 B9 33 6N 80 19W
Ridgewood, U.S.A. 151 F10 40 59N 74 7W
Ridgway, Ill., U.S.A. 157 G8 37 48N 88 16W
Ridgway, Pa., U.S.A. 150 E6 41 25N 78 44W
Riding Mountain Nat. Park, Canada 143 C9 50 50N 100 0W
Ridley, Mt., Australia 125 F3 33 12 S 122 7 E
Riebeek-Oos, S. Africa 116 E4 33 10 S 26 10 E
Ried, Austria 34 C6 48 14N 13 30 E
Riedlingen, Germany 31 G5 48 9N 9 28 E
Riedstadt, Germany 31 F4 49 45N 8 30 E
Riehen, Switz. 32 A5 47 37N 7 38 E
Rienza →, Italy 45 B8 46 49N 11 47 E
Riesa, Germany 30 D9 51 17N 13 17 E
Riesco, I., Chile 176 D2 52 55 S 72 40W
Riesi, Italy 47 E7 37 17N 14 5 E
Riet →, S. Africa 116 D3 29 0 S 23 54 E
Rietavas, Lithuania 54 C8 55 44N 21 56 E
Rietbron, S. Africa 116 E3 32 54 S 23 10 E
Rietfontein, Namibia 116 C3 21 58 S 20 58 E
Rieti, Italy 45 F9 42 24N 12 51 E
Rieupeyroux, France 28 D6 44 19N 2 12 E
Riez, France 29 E10 43 49N 6 6 E
Rif, Er = Er Rif, Morocco 111 A4 35 1N 4 1W
Riffe L., U.S.A. 160 D4 46 32N 122 26W
Rifle, U.S.A. 158 G10 39 32N 107 47W
Rift Valley □, Kenya 118 B4 0 20N 36 0 E
Rig Rig, Chad 109 F2 14 13N 14 25 E
Riga, India 90 A5 28 26N 95 2 E
Rīga, Latvia 15 H21 56 53N 24 8 E
Riga, G. of, Latvia 15 H20 57 40N 23 45 E
Rigacikun, Nigeria 113 C6 10 40N 7 28 E
Rīgān, Iran 97 D8 28 37N 58 58 E
Rīgas Jūras Līcis = Riga, G. of, Latvia 15 H20 57 40N 23 45 E
Rigaud, Canada 151 A10 45 29N 74 18W
Rigby, U.S.A. 158 E8 43 40N 111 55W
Rīgestān, Afghan. 91 C2 30 15N 65 0 E
Riggins, U.S.A. 158 D5 45 25N 116 19W
Rignac, France 28 D6 44 25N 2 16 E
Rigolet, Canada 141 B8 54 10N 58 23W
Rihand Dam, India 93 G10 24 9N 83 2 E
Riihimäki, Finland 15 F21 60 45N 24 48 E
Riiser-Larsen-halvøya, Antarctica 7 C4 68 0 S 35 0 E
Rijau, Nigeria 113 C6 11 8N 5 17 E
Rijeka, Croatia 45 C11 45 20N 14 21 E
Rijeka Crnojevića, Montenegro, Yug. 50 D3 42 24N 19 1 E
Rijssen, Neths. 24 B6 52 19N 6 31 E
Rikā', W. ar →, Si. Arabia 98 B4 22 25N 44 50 E
Rike, Ethiopia 107 E4 10 50N 39 53 E
Rikuzentakada, Japan 70 E10 39 0N 141 40 E
Rila, Bulgaria 50 D7 42 7N 23 7 E
Rila Planina, Bulgaria 50 D7 42 10N 23 20 E
Riley, U.S.A. 158 E4 43 32N 119 28W
Rima →, Nigeria 113 C6 13 4N 5 10 E
Rimah, Wadi ar →, Si. Arabia 96 E4 26 5N 41 30 E
Rimau, Pulau, Malaysia 87 c 5 15N 100 16 E
Rimavská Sobota, Slovak Rep. 35 C13 48 22N 20 2 E
Rimbey, Canada 142 C6 52 35N 114 15W
Rimbo, Sweden 16 E12 59 44N 18 21 E
Rimersburg, U.S.A. 150 E5 41 3N 79 30W
Rimforsa, Sweden 17 F9 58 6N 15 43 E
Rimi, Nigeria 113 C6 12 58N 7 43 E
Rímini, Italy 45 D9 44 3N 12 33 E
Rimouski, Canada 141 C6 48 27N 68 30W
Rimrock, U.S.A. 160 D5 46 38N 121 10W
Rinca, Indonesia 82 C1 8 45 S 119 35 E
Rincon, U.S.A. 152 C8 32 18N 81 14W
Rincón de la Victoria, Spain 43 J6 36 43N 4 18W
Rincón de Romos, Mexico 162 C4 22 14N 102 18W
Rinconada, Argentina 174 A2 22 26 S 66 10W
Rind →, India 93 G9 25 53N 80 33 E
Rindal, Norway 18 A6 63 3N 9 13 E
Ringarum, Sweden 17 F10 58 21N 16 26 E
Ringas, India 92 F6 27 21N 75 34 E
Ringdove, Vanuatu 133 F6 16 40 S 168 10 E
Ringe, Denmark 17 J4 55 13N 10 28 E
Ringebu, Norway 18 C7 61 32N 10 7 E
Ringgi, Solomon Is. 133 M9 8 5 S 157 10 E
Ringgold Is., Fiji 133 A3 16 15 S 179 25W
Ringim, Nigeria 113 C6 12 13N 9 10 E
Ringkøbing, Denmark 17 H2 56 5N 8 15 E
Ringkøbing Amtskommune □, Denmark 17 H2 56 10N 8 45 E
Ringkøbing Fjord, Denmark 17 H2 56 0N 8 15 E
Ringoma, Angola 115 E3 12 25 S 17 32 E
Ringsaker, Norway 18 D7 60 54N 10 45 E
Ringsjön, Sweden 17 J7 55 55N 13 30 E
Ringsted, Denmark 17 J5 55 25N 11 46 E
Ringvassøy, Norway 14 B18 69 56N 19 15 E
Ringwood, U.S.A. 151 E10 41 7N 74 15W
Rinía, Greece 49 D7 37 23N 25 13 E
Rinjani, Indonesia 85 D5 8 24 S 116 28 E
Rinteln, Germany 30 C5 52 10N 9 8 E
Río, Punta del, Spain 41 J2 36 49N 2 24W
Rio Branco, Brazil 172 B4 9 58 S 67 49W
Río Branco, Uruguay 175 C5 32 40 S 53 40W
Río Bravo del Norte →, Mexico 163 B5 25 57N 97 9W
Rio Brilhante, Brazil 175 A5 21 48 S 54 33W
Río Bueno, Chile 176 B2 40 19 S 72 58W
Río Caribe, Venezuela 169 A5 10 42N 63 7W
Río Chico, Venezuela 168 A4 10 19N 65 59W
Rio Claro, Brazil 175 A6 22 19 S 47 35W
Rio Claro, Trin. & Tob. 165 D7 10 20N 61 25W
Río Colorado, Argentina 176 A4 39 0 S 64 0W
Río Cuarto, Argentina 174 C3 33 10 S 64 25W
Rio das Pedras, Mozam. 117 C6 23 8 S 35 28 E
Rio de Contas, Brazil 171 D3 13 36 S 41 48W
Rio de Janeiro, Brazil 171 F3 23 0 S 43 12W
Rio de Janeiro □, Brazil 171 F3 22 50 S 43 0W
Río de Oro, B. de, W. Sahara 110 D1 23 45N 15 50W
Rio do Prado, Brazil 171 E3 16 35 S 40 34W
Rio do Sul, Brazil 175 B6 27 13 S 49 37W
Río Gallegos, Argentina 176 D3 51 35 S 69 15W
Rio Grande = Grande, Rio →, U.S.A. 155 N6 25 58N 97 9W
Río Grande, Argentina 176 D3 53 50 S 67 45W
Río Grande, Bolivia 172 E4 20 51 S 67 17W
Rio Grande, Brazil 175 C5 32 0 S 52 20W
Río Grande, Mexico 162 C4 23 50N 103 2W
Río Grande, Nic. 164 D3 12 54N 83 33W
Río Grande, Puerto Rico 165 d 18 23N 65 50W
Rio Grande City, U.S.A. 155 M5 26 23N 98 49W
Río Grande de Santiago →, Mexico 162 C3 21 36N 105 26W
Rio Grande do Norte □, Brazil 170 C4 5 40 S 36 0W
Rio Grande do Sul □, Brazil 175 C5 30 0 S 53 0W
Río Hato, Panama 164 E3 8 22N 80 10W
Río Lagartos, Mexico 163 C7 21 36N 88 10W
Rio Largo, Brazil 170 C4 9 28 S 35 50W
Rio Maior, Portugal 43 F2 39 19N 8 57W
Rio Marina, Italy 44 F7 42 49N 10 25 E
Rio Mayo, Argentina 176 C2 45 40 S 70 15W
Rio Mulatos, Bolivia 172 D4 19 40 S 66 50W
Río Muni □, Eq. Guin. 114 B2 1 30N 10 0 E
Rio Negro, Brazil 175 B6 26 0 S 49 55W
Río Negro, Chile 176 B2 40 47 S 73 14W
Rio Negro, Pantanal do, Brazil 173 D6 19 0 S 56 0W
Rio Pardo, Brazil 175 C5 30 0 S 52 30W
Río Pico, Argentina 176 B2 44 0 S 70 22W
Rio Preto da Eva, Brazil 169 D6 2 46 S 59 41W
Rio Rancho, U.S.A. 159 J10 35 14N 106 38W
Rio Real, Brazil 171 D4 11 28 S 37 56W
Río Segundo, Argentina 174 C3 31 40 S 63 59W
Río Tercero, Argentina 174 C3 32 15 S 64 8W
Rio Tinto, Brazil 170 C4 6 48 S 35 5W
Rio Tinto, Portugal 42 D2 41 11N 8 34W
Río Turbio, Argentina 176 D2 51 32 S 72 18W
Rio Verde, Brazil 171 E1 17 50 S 51 0W
Río Verde, Mexico 163 C5 21 56N 99 59W
Rio Verde de Mato Grosso, Brazil 173 D7 18 56 S 54 52W
Rio Vista, U.S.A. 160 G5 38 10N 121 42W
Ríobamba, Ecuador 168 D2 1 50 S 78 45W
Ríohacha, Colombia 168 A3 11 33N 72 55W
Rioja, Peru 172 B2 6 11 S 77 5W
Riom, France 28 C7 45 54N 3 7 E
Riom-ès-Montagnes, France 28 C6 45 17N 2 39 E
Rion-des-Landes, France 28 E3 43 55N 0 56W
Rionegro, Antioquia, Colombia 168 B2 6 9N 75 22W
Rionegro, Santander, Colombia 168 B3 7 15N 73 9W
Rionero in Vúlture, Italy 47 B8 40 55N 15 40 E
Rioni →, Georgia 61 J5 42 14N 41 44 E
Riós, Spain 42 D3 41 58N 7 16W
Riosinho →, Brazil 173 B7 7 7 S 51 39W
Ríosucio, Caldas, Colombia 168 B2 5 30N 75 40W
Ríosucio, Choco, Colombia 168 B2 7 27N 77 7W
Riou L., Canada 143 B7 59 7N 106 25W
Rioz, France 27 E13 47 26N 6 5 E
Riozinho →, Brazil 168 D4 2 55 S 67 7W
Ripatransone, Italy 45 F10 42 59N 13 46 E
Ripley, Canada 150 B3 44 4N 81 35W
Ripley, Calif., U.S.A. 161 M12 33 32N 114 39W
Ripley, N.Y., U.S.A. 150 D5 42 16N 79 43W
Ripley, Ohio, U.S.A. 157 F13 38 45N 83 51W
Ripley, Tenn., U.S.A. 155 H10 35 45N 89 32W
Ripley, W. Va., U.S.A. 148 F5 38 49N 81 43W
Ripoll, Spain 40 C7 42 15N 2 13 E
Ripon, U.K. 20 C6 54 9N 1 31W
Ripon, Calif., U.S.A. 160 H5 37 44N 121 7W
Ripon, Wis., U.S.A. 148 D1 43 51N 88 50W
Riposto, Italy 47 E8 37 44N 15 12 E
Risan, Montenegro, Yug. 50 D2 42 32N 18 42 E
Risaralda □, Colombia 168 B2 5 0N 76 10W
Riscle, France 28 E3 43 39N 0 5W
Rishā', W. ar →, Si. Arabia 96 E5 25 33N 44 5 E
Rishiri-Tō, Japan 70 B10 45 11N 141 15 E
Rishon le Ẕiyyon, Israel 103 D3 31 58N 34 48 E
Rishtan, Uzbekistan 65 C5 40 20N 71 15 E
Rising Sun, U.S.A. 157 F12 38 57N 84 51W
Risle →, France 26 C7 49 26N 0 23 E
Rison, U.S.A. 155 J8 33 58N 92 11W
Risør, Norway 15 G13 58 43N 9 13 E
Rissani, Morocco 110 B4 31 18N 4 12W
Rita Blanca Cr. →, U.S.A. 155 H3 35 40N 102 29W
Ritchie's Arch., India 95 H11 12 14N 93 10 E
Riti, Nigeria 113 D6 7 57N 9 41 E
Ritidian Pt., Guam 133 R15 13 39N 144 51 E
Ritter, Mt., U.S.A. 160 H7 37 41N 119 12W
Rittman, U.S.A. 150 F3 40 58N 81 47W
Ritzville, U.S.A. 158 C4 47 8N 118 23W
Riu, India 90 A5 28 19N 95 3 E
Riva del Garda, Italy 44 C7 45 53N 10 50 E
Riva Lígure, Italy 44 E4 43 50N 7 50 E
Rivadavia, Buenos Aires, Argentina 174 D3 35 29 S 62 59W
Rivadavia, Mendoza, Argentina 174 C2 33 13 S 68 30W
Rivadavia, Salta, Argentina 174 A3 24 5 S 62 54W
Rivadavia, Chile 174 B1 29 57 S 70 35W
Rivarolo Canavese, Italy 44 C4 45 19N 7 43 E
Rivas, Nic. 164 D2 11 30N 85 50W
Rive-de-Gier, France 29 C8 45 32N 4 37 E
River Cess, Liberia 112 D3 5 30N 9 32W
River Jordan, Canada 160 B2 48 26N 124 3W
Rivera, Argentina 174 D3 37 12 S 63 14W
Rivera, Uruguay 175 C4 31 0 S 55 50W
Riverbank, U.S.A. 160 H6 37 44N 120 56W
Riverdale, Calif., U.S.A. 160 J7 36 26N 119 52W
Riverdale, Ga., U.S.A. 152 B5 33 34N 84 25W
Riverhead, U.S.A. 151 F12 40 55N 72 40W
Riverhurst, Canada 143 C7 50 55N 106 50W
Rivers, Canada 143 C8 50 2N 100 14W
Rivers □, Nigeria 113 E6 4 30N 7 10 E
Rivers Inlet, Canada 142 C3 51 42N 127 15W
Riversdale, N.Z. 131 F3 45 54 S 168 44 E
Riversdale, S. Africa 116 E3 34 7 S 21 15 E
Riverside, U.S.A. 161 M9 33 59N 117 22W
Riverton, Australia 128 C3 34 10 S 138 46 E
Riverton, Canada 143 C9 51 1N 97 0W
Riverton, N.Z. 131 G2 46 21 S 168 0 E
Riverton, Ill., U.S.A. 156 E7 39 51N 89 33W
Riverton, Wyo., U.S.A. 158 E9 43 2N 108 23W
Riverton Heights, U.S.A. 160 C4 47 28N 122 17W
Riverview, U.S.A. 153 H7 27 52N 82 20W
Rives, France 29 C9 45 21N 5 31 E
Rivesaltes, France 28 F6 42 47N 2 50 E
Riviera, U.S.A. 161 K12 35 4N 114 35W
Riviera Beach, U.S.A. 153 J9 26 47N 80 3W
Riviera di Levante, Italy 44 D6 44 15N 9 30 E
Riviera di Ponente, Italy 44 D5 44 10N 8 20 E
Rivière-au-Renard, Canada 141 C7 48 59N 64 23W
Rivière Bleue, Parc Territorial de la, N. Cal. 133 V20 22 6 S 166 38 E
Rivière-du-Loup, Canada 141 C6 47 50N 69 30W
Rivière-Pentecôte, Canada 141 C6 49 57N 67 1W
Rivière-Pilote, Martinique 164 c 14 26N 60 53W
Rivière St. Paul, Canada 141 B8 51 28N 57 45W
Rivière-Salée, Martinique 164 c 14 31N 61 0W
Rivne, Ukraine 59 G4 50 40N 26 10 E
Rívoli, Italy 44 C4 45 3N 7 31 E
Rivoli B., Australia 128 D4 37 32 S 140 3 E
Riwaka, N.Z. 131 B7 41 5 S 172 59 E
Rixheim, France 27 E14 47 40N 7 24 E
Riyadh = Ar Riyāḍ, Si. Arabia 96 E5 24 41N 46 42 E
Rizal, Cagayan, Phil. 80 C3 17 51N 121 21 E
Rizal, Nueva Ecija, Phil. 80 D3 15 43N 121 6 E
Rizal, Zamboanga del N., Phil. 81 G4 8 35N 123 26 E
Rize, Turkey 101 B9 41 0N 40 30 E
Rizhao, China 75 G10 35 25N 119 30 E
Rizokarpaso, Cyprus 39 E10 35 36N 34 23 E
Rizzuto, C., Italy 47 D10 38 53N 17 5 E
Rjukan, Norway 15 G13 59 54N 8 33 E
Rjuven, Norway 18 E4 59 9N 7 8 E
Ro, Greece 49 E11 36 9N 29 33 E
Rô, N. Cal. 133 U21 21 22 S 167 50 E
Roa, Dem. Rep. of the Congo 114 B4 3 49N 24 56 E
Roa, Norway 18 D7 60 17N 10 37 E
Roa, Spain 42 D7 41 41N 3 56W
Roachdale, U.S.A. 157 E10 39 51N 86 48W
Road Town, Br. Virgin Is. 165 e 18 27N 64 37W
Roan Plateau, U.S.A. 158 G9 39 20N 109 20W
Roanne, France 27 F11 46 3N 4 4 E
Roanoke, Ala., U.S.A. 152 B4 33 9N 85 22W
Roanoke, Ind., U.S.A. 157 D11 40 58N 85 22W
Roanoke, Va., U.S.A. 148 G6 37 16N 79 56W
Roanoke →, U.S.A. 149 H7 35 57N 76 42W
Roanoke I., U.S.A. 149 H8 35 55N 75 40W
Roanoke Rapids, U.S.A. 149 G7 36 28N 77 40W
Roatán, Honduras 164 C2 16 18N 86 35W
Rob Roy, Solomon Is. 133 L9 7 23 S 157 36 E
Robāt Sang, Iran 97 C8 35 35N 59 10 E
Robbins I., Australia 127 G4 40 42 S 145 0 E
Róbbio, Italy 44 C5 45 17N 8 35 E
Robe, Australia 128 D3 37 11 S 139 45 E
Robe →, Australia 124 D2 21 42 S 116 15 E
Röbel, Germany 30 B8 53 22N 12 35 E
Robert Lee, U.S.A. 155 K4 31 54N 100 29W
Roberta, U.S.A. 152 C5 32 43N 84 1W
Roberts, U.S.A. 157 D8 40 37N 88 11W
Robertsdale, U.S.A. 150 F6 40 11N 78 6W
Robertsganj, India 93 G10 24 44N 83 4 E
Robertson, S. Africa 116 E2 33 46 S 19 50 E
Robertson I., Antarctica 7 C18 65 15 S 59 30W
Robertson Ra., Australia 124 D3 23 15 S 121 0 E
Robertsport, Liberia 112 D2 6 45N 11 26W
Robertstown, Australia 128 B3 33 58 S 139 5 E
Roberval, Canada 141 C5 48 32N 72 15W
Robeson Chan., Greenland 10 A4 82 0N 61 30W
Robesonia, U.S.A. 151 F8 40 21N 76 8W
Robi, Ethiopia 107 F4 7 52N 39 38 E
Robinson, U.S.A. 157 F9 39 0N 87 44W
Robinson →, Australia 126 B2 16 3 S 137 16 E
Robinson Ra., Australia 125 E2 25 40 S 119 0 E
Robinvale, Australia 128 C5 34 40 S 142 45 E
Robledo, Spain 41 G2 38 46N 2 26W
Roblin, Canada 143 C8 51 14N 101 21W
Roboré, Bolivia 173 D6 18 10 S 59 45W
Robson, Canada 142 D5 49 20N 117 41W
Robson, Mt., Canada 142 C5 53 10N 119 10W
Robstown, U.S.A. 155 M6 27 47N 97 40W
Roca, C. da, Portugal 43 G1 38 40N 9 31W
Roca Partida, I., Mexico 162 D2 19 1N 112 2W
Rocamadour, France 28 D5 44 48N 1 37 E
Rocca San Casciano, Italy 45 D8 44 3N 11 50 E
Roccadáspide, Italy 47 B8 40 27N 15 10 E
Roccastrada, Italy 45 F8 43 0N 11 10 E
Roccella Iónica, Italy 47 D9 38 19N 16 24 E
Rocha, Uruguay 175 C5 34 30 S 54 25W
Rochdale, U.K. 20 D5 53 38N 2 9W
Rochechouart, France 28 C4 45 50N 0 49 E
Rochedo, Brazil 173 D7 19 57 S 54 52W
Rochefort, Belgium 24 D5 50 9N 5 12 E
Rochefort, France 28 C3 45 56N 0 57W
Rochefort-en-Terre, France 26 E4 47 42N 2 22W
Rochelle, Ga., U.S.A. 152 D6 31 57N 83 27W
Rochelle, Ill., U.S.A. 156 C7 41 56N 89 4W
Rocher River, Canada 142 A6 61 23N 112 44W
Rocheservière, France 26 F5 46 57N 1 30W
Rochester, Australia 128 D6 36 22 S 144 41 E
Rochester, U.K. 21 F8 51 23N 0 31 E
Rochester, Ind., U.S.A. 157 C10 41 4N 86 13W
Rochester, Minn., U.S.A. 154 C8 44 1N 92 28W
Rochester, N.H., U.S.A. 151 C14 43 18N 70 59W
Rochester, N.Y., U.S.A. 150 C7 43 10N 77 37W
Rochester Hills, U.S.A. 157 B13 42 41N 83 8W
Rociu, Romania 53 F10 44 43N 25 2 E
Rock →, Canada 142 A3 60 7N 127 7W
Rock →, U.S.A. 156 C6 41 29N 90 37W
Rock Creek, U.S.A. 150 E4 41 40N 80 52W
Rock Falls, U.S.A. 156 C7 41 47N 89 41W
Rock Flat, Australia 129 D8 36 21 S 149 13 E
Rock Hill, U.S.A. 149 H5 34 56N 81 1W
Rock Island, U.S.A. 156 C6 41 30N 90 34W
Rock Rapids, U.S.A. 154 D6 43 26N 96 10W
Rock Sound, Bahamas 164 B4 24 54N 76 12W
Rock Springs, Mont., U.S.A. 158 C10 46 49N 106 15W
Rock Springs, Wyo., U.S.A. 158 F9 41 35N 109 14W
Rock Valley, U.S.A. 154 D6 43 12N 96 18W
Rockall, Atl. Oc. 8 A10 57 37N 13 42W
Rockdale, Tex., U.S.A. 155 K6 30 39N 97 0W
Rockdale, Wash., U.S.A. 160 C5 47 22N 121 28W
Rockefeller Plateau, Antarctica 7 E14 80 0 S 140 0W
Rockford, Ala., U.S.A. 152 C3 32 53N 86 13W
Rockford, Ill., U.S.A. 156 B7 42 16N 89 6W
Rockford, Iowa, U.S.A. 156 A4 43 3N 92 57W
Rockford, Mich., U.S.A. 157 A11 43 7N 85 34W
Rockford, Ohio, U.S.A. 157 D12 40 41N 84 39W
Rockglen, Canada 143 D7 49 11N 105 57W
Rockhampton, Australia 126 C5 23 22 S 150 32 E
Rockingham, Australia 125 F2 32 15 S 115 38 E
Rockingham, U.S.A. 149 H6 34 57N 79 46W
Rockingham B., Australia 126 B4 18 5 S 146 10 E
Rocklake, U.S.A. 154 A5 48 47N 99 15W
Rockland, Canada 151 A9 45 33N 75 17W
Rockland, Idaho, U.S.A. 158 E7 42 34N 112 53W
Rockland, Maine, U.S.A. 149 C11 44 6N 69 7W
Rockland, Mich., U.S.A. 154 B10 46 44N 89 11W
Rocklands Reservoir, Australia 128 D5 37 15 S 142 5 E
Rockledge, U.S.A. 153 G9 28 20N 80 43W
Rocklin, U.S.A. 160 G5 38 48N 121 14W
Rockly B., Trin. & Tob. 169 E10 11 9N 60 46W
Rockmart, U.S.A. 149 H3 34 0N 85 3W
Rockport, Ind., U.S.A. 157 G9 37 53N 87 3W
Rockport, Mass., U.S.A. 151 D14 42 39N 70 37W
Rockport, Mo., U.S.A. 154 E7 40 25N 95 31W
Rockport, Tex., U.S.A. 155 L6 28 2N 97 3W
Rocksprings, U.S.A. 155 K4 30 1N 100 13W
Rockstone, Guyana 169 B6 5 59N 58 33W
Rockville, Conn., U.S.A. 151 E12 41 52N 72 28W
Rockville, Ind., U.S.A. 157 E9 39 46N 87 14W
Rockville, Md., U.S.A. 148 F7 39 5N 77 9W
Rockwall, U.S.A. 155 J6 32 56N 96 28W
Rockwell City, U.S.A. 156 B2 42 24N 94 38W
Rockwood, Canada 150 C4 43 37N 80 8W
Rockwood, Maine, U.S.A. 149 C11 45 41N 69 45W
Rockwood, Tenn., U.S.A. 149 H3 35 52N 84 41W
Rocky Ford, U.S.A. 154 F3 38 3N 103 43W
Rocky Fork Lake, U.S.A. 157 E13 39 12N 83 23W
Rocky Gully, Australia 125 F2 34 30 S 116 57 E
Rocky Harbour, Canada 141 C8 49 36N 57 55W
Rocky Island L., Canada 140 C3 46 55N 83 0W
Rocky Lane, Canada 142 B5 58 31N 116 22W
Rocky Mount, U.S.A. 149 H7 35 57N 77 48W
Rocky Mountain House, Canada 142 C6 52 22N 114 55W
Rocky Mountain Nat. Park, U.S.A. 158 F11 40 25N 105 45W
Rocky Mts., N. Amer. 158 G10 49 0N 115 0W
Rocky Point, Namibia 116 B2 19 3 S 12 30 E
Rocroi, France 27 C11 49 55N 4 30 E
Rod, Pakistan 91 C1 28 10N 63 5 E
Rødberg, Norway 18 D5 60 17N 8 56 E
Rødby, Denmark 17 K5 54 41N 11 23 E
Rødbyhavn, Denmark 17 K5 54 39N 11 22 E
Roddickton, Canada 141 B8 50 51N 56 8W
Rødding, Denmark 17 J3 55 23N 9 3 E
Rödeby, Sweden 17 H9 56 15N 15 37 E
Rødekro, Denmark 17 J3 55 4N 9 20 E
Rodenkirchen, Germany 30 B4 53 23N 8 26 E
Rodez, France 28 D6 44 21N 2 33 E
Rodholívas, Greece 50 F7 40 55N 24 0 E
Rodhópi □, Greece 51 E9 41 5N 25 30 E
Rodhopoú, Greece 39 E4 35 34N 23 45 E
Ródhos, Greece 38 E12 36 15N 28 10 E
Rodi Gargánico, Italy 45 G12 41 55N 15 53 E
Rodna, Romania 53 C9 47 25N 24 50 E
Rodnei, Munții, Romania 53 C9 47 35N 24 35 E
Rodney, Canada 150 D3 42 34N 81 41W
Rodney, C., N.Z. 130 C3 36 17 S 174 50 E
Rodniki, Russia 60 B5 57 7N 41 47 E
Rodonit, Kepi i, Albania 50 E3 41 35N 19 27 E
Rodriguez, Ind. Oc. 121 F5 19 45 S 63 20 E
Roe →, U.K. 23 A5 55 6N 6 59W
Roebling, U.S.A. 151 F10 40 7N 74 47W
Roebourne, Australia 124 D2 20 44 S 117 9 E
Roebuck B., Australia 124 C3 18 5 S 122 20 E
Roermond, Neths. 24 C6 51 12N 6 0 E
Roes Welcome Sd., Canada 139 B11 65 0N 87 0W
Roeselare, Belgium 24 D3 50 57N 3 7 E
Rogachev = Ragachow, Belarus 59 F6 53 8N 30 5 E
Rogačica, Serbia, Yug. 50 B3 44 4N 19 40 E
Rogagua, L., Bolivia 172 C4 13 43 S 66 50W
Rogaland □, Norway 18 E3 59 12N 6 20 E
Rogaška Slatina, Slovenia 45 B12 46 15N 15 42 E
Rogatec, Slovenia 45 B12 46 15N 15 46 E
Rogatica, Bos.-H. 52 G4 43 47N 19 0 E
Rogatyn, Ukraine 59 H3 49 24N 24 36 E
Rogdhia, Greece 39 E6 35 22N 25 1 E
Rogers, U.S.A. 155 G7 36 20N 94 7W
Rogers City, U.S.A. 148 C4 45 25N 83 49W
Rogersville, Canada 141 C6 46 44N 65 26W
Roggan →, Canada 140 B4 54 24N 79 25W
Roggan L., Canada 140 B4 54 8N 77 50W
Roggeveldberge, S. Africa 116 E3 32 10 S 20 10 E
Roggiano Gravina, Italy 47 C9 39 37N 16 9 E
Rogliano, France 29 F13 42 57N 9 30 E
Rogliano, Italy 47 C9 39 10N 16 19 E
Rogoaguado, L., Bolivia 173 C4 13 0 S 65 30W
Rogojampi, Indonesia 79 J17 8 19 S 114 17 E
Rogoźno, Poland 55 F3 52 45N 16 59 E
Rogue →, U.S.A. 158 E1 42 26N 124 26W
Roha, India 94 E1 18 26N 73 7 E
Rohan, France 26 D4 48 4N 2 45W
Róhda, Greece 38 B9 39 48N 19 46 E
Rohnert Park, U.S.A. 160 G4 38 16N 122 40W
Rohri, Pakistan 91 D3 27 45N 68 51 E
Rohri Canal, Pakistan 92 F3 26 15N 68 27 E
Rohtak, India 92 E7 28 55N 76 43 E
Roi Et, Thailand 86 D4 16 4N 103 40 E
Roja, Latvia 15 H20 57 29N 22 43 E
Rojas, Argentina 174 C3 34 10 S 60 45W
Rojiște, Romania 53 F8 44 4N 23 56 E
Rojo, C., Mexico 163 C5 21 33N 97 20W

Rokan →, *Indonesia* **84 B2** 2 0N 100 50 E
Rokel →, *S. Leone* **112 D2** 8 30N 12 48W
Rokiškis, *Lithuania* **15 J21** 55 55N 25 35 E
Rokitno, *Russia* **59 G8** 50 57N 35 56 E
Rokycany, *Czech Rep.* **34 B6** 49 43N 13 35 E
Rolândia, *Brazil* **175 A5** 23 18 S 51 23W
Røldal, *Norway* **18 E3** 59 47N 6 50 E
Rolfe, *U.S.A.* **156 B2** 42 49N 94 31W
Rolla, *U.S.A.* **155 G9** 37 57N 91 46W
Rolle, *Switz.* **32 D2** 46 28N 6 20 E
Rolleston, *Australia* **126 C4** 24 28 S 148 35 E
Rolleston, *N.Z.* **131 D7** 43 35 S 172 24 E
Rolling Fork →, *U.S.A.* **157 G11** 37 55N 85 50W
Rollingstone, *Australia* **126 B4** 19 2 S 146 24 E
Rom, *Norway* **18 F4** 58 8N 7 5 E
Rom, *Sudan* **107 F3** 9 54N 32 16 E
Roma, *Australia* **127 D4** 26 32 S 148 49 E
Roma, *Italy* **45 G9** 41 54N 12 29 E
Roma, *Sweden* **17 G12** 57 32N 18 26 E
Roma, *U.S.A.* **155 M5** 26 25N 99 1W
Romain C., *U.S.A.* **149 J6** 33 0N 79 22W
Romaine, *Canada* **141 B7** 50 13N 60 40W
Romaine →, *Canada* **141 B7** 50 18N 63 47W
Roman, *Bulgaria* **50 C7** 43 8N 23 57 E
Roman, *Romania* **53 D11** 46 57N 26 55 E
Roman-Kosh, Gora, *Ukraine* **59 K8** 44 37N 34 15 E
Romanche →, *France* **29 C9** 45 5N 5 43 E
Romang, *Indonesia* **82 C3** 7 30 S 127 20 E
Români, *Egypt* **103 E1** 30 59N 32 38 E
Romania ■, *Europe* **53 D10** 46 0N 25 0 E
Romanija, *Bos.-H.* **52 G3** 43 50N 18 45 E
Romano, C., *U.S.A.* **153 K8** 25 51N 81 41W
Romano, Cayo, *Cuba* **164 B4** 22 0N 77 30W
Romanovka = Basarabeasca, *Moldova* **53 D13** 46 21N 28 58 E
Romans-sur-Isère, *France* **29 C9** 45 3N 5 3 E
Romanshorn, *Switz.* **33 A8** 47 33N 9 22 E
Romanzof C., *U.S.A.* **144 F6** 61 49N 166 6W
Rombari, *Sudan* **107 G3** 4 33N 31 2 E
Rombebai, Danau, *Indonesia* **83 B5** 1 50 S 137 53 E
Romblon, *Phil.* **80 E4** 12 33N 122 17 E
Romblon □, *Phil.* **80 E4** 12 30N 122 15 E
Romblon Pass, *Phil.* **80 E4** 12 27N 122 12 E
Rome = Roma, *Italy* **45 G9** 41 54N 12 29 E
Rome, *Ga., U.S.A.* **149 H3** 34 15N 85 10W
Rome, *N.Y., U.S.A.* **151 C9** 43 13N 75 27W
Rome, *Pa., U.S.A.* **151 E8** 41 51N 76 21W
Romeoville, *U.S.A.* **157 C8** 41 39N 88 3W
Rometta, *Italy* **47 D8** 38 10N 15 25 E
Romilly-sur-Seine, *France* **27 D10** 48 31N 3 44 E
Romitan, *Uzbekistan* **65 D2** 39 56N 64 23 E
Rommani, *Morocco* **110 B3** 33 31N 6 40W
Romney, *U.S.A.* **148 F6** 39 21N 78 45W
Romney Marsh, *U.K.* **21 F8** 51 2N 0 54 E
Romny, *Ukraine* **59 G7** 50 48N 33 28 E
Rømø, *Denmark* **17 J2** 55 10N 8 30 E
Romodan, *Ukraine* **59 G7** 49 55N 33 15 E
Romodanovo, *Russia* **60 C7** 54 26N 45 23 E
Romont, *Switz.* **32 C3** 46 42N 6 54 E
Romorantin-Lanthenay, *France* **27 E8** 47 21N 1 45 E
Rompin →, *Malaysia* **84 B2** 2 49N 103 29 E
Romsdalen, *Norway* **15 E12** 62 25N 7 52 E
Romsdalsfjorden, *Norway* **18 B4** 62 38N 7 20 E
Romsey, *U.K.* **21 G6** 51 0N 1 29W
Ron, *India* **95 G2** 15 40N 75 44 E
Ron, *Vietnam* **86 D6** 17 53N 106 27 E
Rona, *U.K.* **22 D3** 57 34N 5 59W
Ronan, *U.S.A.* **158 C6** 47 32N 114 6W
Roncador, Cayos, *Colombia* **164 D3** 13 32N 80 4W
Roncador, Serra do, *Brazil* **171 D1** 12 30 S 52 30W
Ronciglione, *Italy* **45 F9** 42 17N 12 13 E
Ronco →, *Italy* **45 D9** 44 24N 12 12 E
Ronda, *Spain* **43 J5** 36 46N 5 12W
Ronda, Serranía de, *Spain* **43 J5** 36 44N 5 3W
Rondane, *Norway* **15 F13** 61 57N 9 50 E
Rondón, *Colombia* **168 B3** 6 17N 71 6W
Rondônia, *Brazil* **173 C5** 10 52 S 61 57W
Rondônia □, *Brazil* **173 C5** 11 0 S 63 0W
Rondonópolis, *Brazil* **173 D7** 16 28 S 54 38W
Rondslottet, *Norway* **18 C6** 61 55N 9 45 E
Rong, Koh, *Cambodia* **87 G4** 10 45N 103 15 E
Rong Jiang →, *China* **76 E7** 24 35N 109 20 E
Rong Xian, *Guangxi Zhuangzu, China* **77 F8** 22 50N 110 31 E
Rong Xian, *Sichuan, China* **76 C5** 29 23N 104 22 E
Rong'an, *China* **76 E7** 25 14N 109 22 E
Rongchang, *China* **76 C5** 29 20N 105 32 E
Ronge, L. la, *Canada* **143 B7** 55 6N 105 17W
Rongjiang, *China* **76 E7** 25 57N 108 28 E
Rongotea, *N.Z.* **130 G4** 40 19 S 175 25 E
Rongshui, *China* **76 E7** 25 5N 109 12 E
Rønne, *Denmark* **17 J8** 55 6N 14 43 E
Ronne Ice Shelf, *Antarctica* **7 D18** 78 0 S 60 0W
Ronneby, *Sweden* **17 H9** 56 12N 15 17 E
Ronnebyån →, *Sweden* **17 H9** 56 11N 15 18 E
Rönneshytta, *Sweden* **17 F9** 58 56N 15 2 E
Ronsard, C., *Australia* **125 D1** 24 46 S 113 10 E
Ronse, *Belgium* **24 D3** 50 45N 3 35 E
Ronuro →, *Brazil* **173 C7** 11 56 S 53 33W
Roodepoort, *S. Africa* **117 D4** 26 11 S 27 54 E
Roodhouse, *U.S.A.* **156 E6** 39 29N 90 24W
Roof Butte, *U.S.A.* **159 H9** 36 28N 109 5W
Rooiboklaagte →, *Namibia* **116 C3** 20 50 S 21 0 E
Roon, *Indonesia* **83 B4** 2 23 S 134 33 E
Rooniu, Mt., *Tahiti* **133 S16** 17 49 S 149 12W
Roopville, *U.S.A.* **152 B4** 33 27N 85 8W
Roorkee, *India* **92 E7** 29 52N 77 59 E
Roosendaal, *Neths.* **24 C4** 51 32N 4 29 E
Roosevelt, *U.S.A.* **158 F8** 40 18N 109 59W
Roosevelt →, *Brazil* **173 B5** 7 35 S 60 20W
Roosevelt, Mt., *Canada* **142 B3** 58 26N 125 20W
Roosevelt I., *Antarctica* **7 D12** 79 30 S 162 0W
Root, *Switz.* **33 B6** 47 5N 8 23 E
Ropczyce, *Poland* **55 H8** 50 4N 21 38 E
Roper →, *Australia* **126 A2** 14 43 S 135 27 E
Roper Bar, *Australia* **126 A1** 14 44 S 134 44 E
Roque Pérez, *Argentina* **174 D4** 35 25 S 59 24W
Roquefort, *France* **28 D3** 44 2N 0 20W
Roquemaure, *France* **29 D8** 44 3N 4 48 E
Roquetas de Mar, *Spain* **41 J2** 36 46N 2 36W
Roquetes, *Spain* **40 E5** 40 50N 0 30 E
Roquevaire, *France* **29 E9** 43 20N 5 36 E
Roraima □, *Brazil* **169 C5** 2 0N 61 30W
Roraima, Mt., *Venezuela* **169 B5** 5 10N 60 40W
Røros, *Norway* **15 E14** 62 35N 11 23 E
Rorschach, *Switz.* **33 B8** 47 28N 9 28 E
Rosa, *Zambia* **119 D3** 9 33 S 31 15 E
Rosa, C., *Algeria* **111 A6** 37 0N 8 16 E
Rosa, C., *Ecuador* **172 a** 1 4 S 91 10W
Rosa, L., *Bahamas* **165 B5** 21 0N 73 30W
Rosa, Monte, *Europe* **32 E5** 45 57N 7 53 E
Rosais, Pta. dos, *Azores* **9 d1** 38 45N 28 19W
Rosal de la Frontera, *Spain* **43 H3** 37 59N 7 13W
Rosales, *Phil.* **80 D3** 15 54N 120 38 E
Rosalia, *U.S.A.* **158 C5** 47 14N 117 22W
Rosamond, *U.S.A.* **161 L8** 34 52N 118 10W
Rosans, *France* **29 D9** 44 24N 5 29 E
Rosario, *Argentina* **174 C3** 33 0 S 60 40W
Rosário, *Brazil* **170 B3** 3 0 S 44 15W
Rosario, *Baja Calif., Mexico* **162 B1** 30 0N 115 50W
Rosario, *Sinaloa, Mexico* **162 C3** 23 0N 105 52W
Rosario, *Paraguay* **174 A4** 24 30 S 57 35W
Rosario, *Phil.* **81 G5** 8 24N 125 59 E
Rosario, Villa del, *Venezuela* **168 A3** 10 19N 72 19W
Rosario de la Frontera, *Argentina* **174 B3** 25 50 S 65 0W
Rosario de Lerma, *Argentina* **174 A2** 24 59 S 65 35W
Rosario del Tala, *Argentina* **174 C4** 32 20 S 59 10W
Rosário do Sul, *Brazil* **175 C5** 30 15 S 54 55W
Rosário Oeste, *Brazil* **173 C6** 14 50 S 56 25W
Rosarito, *Mexico* **161 N9** 32 18N 117 4W
Rosarno, *Italy* **47 D8** 38 29N 15 58 E
Rosas = Roses, *Spain* **40 C8** 42 19N 3 10 E
Roscoe, *Miss., U.S.A.* **156 G3** 37 58N 93 48W
Roscoe, *N.Y., U.S.A.* **151 E10** 41 56N 74 55W
Roscoff, *France* **26 D3** 48 44N 3 58W
Roscommon, *Ireland* **23 C3** 53 38N 8 11W
Roscommon □, *Ireland* **23 C3** 53 49N 8 23W
Roscrea, *Ireland* **23 D4** 52 57N 7 49W
Rose →, *Australia* **126 A2** 14 16 S 135 45 E
Rose Belle, *Mauritius* **121 d** 20 24 S 57 36 E
Rose Blanche, *Canada* **141 C8** 47 38N 58 45W
Rose Hill, *Mauritius* **121 d** 20 14 S 57 27 E
Rose Pt., *Canada* **142 C2** 54 11N 131 39W
Rose Valley, *Canada* **143 C8** 52 19N 103 49W
Roseau, *Domin.* **165 C7** 15 20N 61 24W
Roseau, *U.S.A.* **154 A7** 48 51N 95 46W
Rosebery, *Australia* **127 G4** 41 46 S 145 33 E
Rosebud, *Australia* **128 E6** 38 21 S 144 54 E
Rosebud, *S. Dak., U.S.A.* **154 D4** 43 14N 100 51W
Rosebud, *Tex., U.S.A.* **155 K6** 31 4N 96 59W
Roseburg, *U.S.A.* **158 E2** 43 13N 123 20W
Rosedale, *U.S.A.* **155 J9** 33 51N 91 2W
Roseland, *U.S.A.* **160 G4** 38 25N 122 43W
Rosemary, *Canada* **142 C6** 50 46N 112 5W
Rosenberg, *U.S.A.* **155 L7** 29 34N 95 49W
Rosendaël, *France* **27 A9** 51 3N 2 24 E
Rosendal, *Norway* **18 E3** 59 59N 6 0 E
Rosendale, *U.S.A.* **156 D2** 40 4N 94 51W
Rosenheim, *Germany* **31 H8** 47 51N 12 7 E
Roses, *Spain* **40 C8** 42 19N 3 10 E
Roses, G. de, *Spain* **40 C8** 42 10N 3 15 E
Roseto degli Abruzzi, *Italy* **45 F11** 42 41N 14 1 E
Rosetown, *Canada* **143 C7** 51 35N 107 59W
Rosetta = Rashîd, *Egypt* **106 H7** 31 21N 30 22 E
Roseville, *Calif., U.S.A.* **160 G5** 38 45N 121 17W
Roseville, *Ill., U.S.A.* **156 D6** 40 44N 90 40W
Roseville, *Mich., U.S.A.* **150 D2** 42 30N 82 56W
Rosewood, *Australia* **127 D5** 27 38 S 152 36 E
Roshkhvār, *Iran* **97 C8** 34 58N 59 37 E
Roshtqala, *Tajikistan* **65 E5** 37 16N 71 49 E
Rosières-en-Santerre, *France* **27 C9** 49 49N 2 42 E
Rosignano Maríttimo, *Italy* **44 E7** 43 24N 10 28 E
Rosignol, *Guyana* **169 B6** 6 15N 57 30W
Roşiori de Vede, *Romania* **53 F10** 44 9N 25 0 E
Rositsa, *Bulgaria* **51 C11** 43 57N 27 57 E
Rositsa →, *Bulgaria* **51 C9** 43 10N 25 30 E
Roskilde, *Denmark* **17 J6** 55 38N 12 3 E
Roskilde Amtskommune □, *Denmark* **17 J6** 55 35N 12 5 E
Roskovec, *Albania* **50 F3** 40 44N 19 43 E
Roslavl, *Russia* **58 F7** 53 57N 32 55 E
Rosmaninhal, *Portugal* **42 F3** 39 44N 7 5W
Rosmead, *S. Africa* **116 E4** 31 29 S 25 8 E
Røsnæs, *Denmark* **17 J4** 55 44N 10 55 E
Rosolini, *Italy* **47 F7** 36 49N 14 57 E
Rosporden, *France* **26 E3** 47 57N 3 50W
Ross, *Australia* **127 G4** 42 2 S 147 30 E
Ross, *N.Z.* **131 C5** 42 53 S 170 49 E
Ross Béthio, *Mauritania* **112 B1** 16 15N 16 8W
Ross I., *Antarctica* **7 D11** 77 30 S 168 0 E
Ross Ice Shelf, *Antarctica* **7 E12** 80 0 S 180 0 E
Ross L., *U.S.A.* **158 B3** 48 44N 121 4W
Ross-on-Wye, *U.K.* **21 F5** 51 54N 2 34W
Ross River, *Australia* **126 C1** 23 44 S 134 30 E
Ross River, *Canada* **142 A2** 62 30N 131 30W
Ross Sea, *Antarctica* **7 D11** 74 0 S 178 0 E
Rossa, *Switz.* **33 D8** 46 23N 9 8 E
Rossall Pt., *U.K.* **20 D4** 53 55N 3 3W
Rossan Pt., *Ireland* **23 B3** 54 42N 8 47W
Rossano, *Italy* **47 C9** 39 36N 16 39 E
Rossburn, *Canada* **143 C8** 50 40N 100 49W
Rosseau, *Canada* **150 A5** 45 16N 79 39W
Rosseau L., *Canada* **150 A5** 45 10N 79 35W
Rossel, C., *Vanuatu* **133 K4** 20 23 S 166 36 E
Rossel I., *Papua N. G.* **132 F8** 11 21 S 154 9 E
Rossens, *Switz.* **32 C4** 46 43N 7 7 E
Rosses, The, *Ireland* **23 A3** 55 2N 8 20W
Rossford, *U.S.A.* **157 C13** 41 36N 83 34W
Rossignol, L., *Canada* **140 B5** 52 43N 73 40W
Rossignol Res., *Canada* **141 D6** 44 12N 65 10W
Rosskreppfjorden, *Norway* **18 E4** 59 4N 7 10 E
Rossland, *Canada* **142 D5** 49 6N 117 50W
Rosslare, *Ireland* **23 D5** 52 17N 6 24W
Rosslau, *Germany* **30 D8** 51 52N 12 15 E
Rosso, *Mauritania* **112 B1** 16 40N 15 45W
Rosso, C., *France* **29 F12** 42 13N 8 32 E
Rossosh, *Russia* **59 G10** 50 15N 39 28 E
Røssvatnet, *Norway* **14 D16** 65 45N 14 5 E
Rossville, *Ill., U.S.A.* **157 D9** 40 23N 87 40W
Rossville, *Ind., U.S.A.* **157 D10** 40 25N 86 36W
Røst, *Norway* **14 C15** 67 32N 12 0 E
Rostāq, *Afghan.* **65 E4** 37 7N 69 49 E
Rosthern, *Canada* **143 C7** 52 40N 106 20W
Rostock, *Germany* **30 A8** 54 5N 12 8 E
Rostov, *Don, Russia* **59 J10** 47 15N 39 45 E
Rostov, *Yaroslavl, Russia* **58 D10** 57 14N 39 25 E
Rostrenen, *France* **26 D3** 48 14N 3 21W
Roswell, *Ga., U.S.A.* **152 A5** 34 2N 84 22W
Roswell, *N. Mex., U.S.A.* **155 J2** 33 24N 104 32W
Rota, *Spain* **43 J4** 36 37N 6 20W
Rotan, *U.S.A.* **155 J4** 32 51N 100 28W
Rote Wand, *Austria* **33 B9** 47 11N 9 59 E
Rotenburg, *Hessen, Germany* **30 E5** 50 59N 9 44 E
Rotenburg, *Niedersachsen, Germany* **30 B5** 53 6N 9 25 E
Roth, *Germany* **31 F7** 49 15N 11 5 E
Rothaargebirge, *Germany* **30 D4** 51 2N 8 13 E
Rothenburg, *Switz.* **33 B6** 47 6N 8 16 E
Rothenburg ob der Tauber, *Germany* **31 F6** 49 23N 10 11 E
Rother →, *U.K.* **21 G8** 50 59N 0 45 E
Rotherham, *U.K.* **20 D6** 53 26N 1 20W
Rothes, *U.K.* **22 D5** 57 32N 3 13W
Rothesay, *Canada* **141 C6** 45 23N 66 0W
Rothesay, *U.K.* **22 F3** 55 50N 5 3W
Rothrist, *Switz.* **32 B5** 47 18N 7 54 E
Roti, *Indonesia* **82 D2** 10 50 S 123 0 E
Rotja, Pta., *Spain* **38 D2** 38 38N 1 35 E
Rotnes, *Norway* **18 D7** 60 3N 10 51 E
Roto, *Australia* **129 B6** 33 0 S 145 30 E
Rotoaira, L., *N.Z.* **130 F4** 39 3 S 175 45 E
Rotoehu, L., *N.Z.* **130 E5** 38 1 S 176 32 E
Rotoiti, L., *Bay of Plenty, N.Z.* **130 E5** 38 2 S 176 26 E
Rotoiti, L., *W. Coast, N.Z.* **131 B7** 41 51 S 172 49 E
Rotoma, L., *N.Z.* **130 E5** 38 2 S 176 35 E
Rotondo, Mte., *France* **29 F13** 42 14N 9 8 E
Rotoroa, L., *N.Z.* **131 B7** 41 55 S 172 39 E
Rotorua, *N.Z.* **130 E5** 38 9 S 176 16 E
Rotorua, L., *N.Z.* **130 E5** 38 5 S 176 18 E
Rott →, *Germany* **31 G9** 48 27N 13 25 E
Rotten →, *Switz.* **32 D5** 46 18N 7 36 E
Rottenburg, *Germany* **31 G4** 48 28N 8 55 E
Rottenmann, *Austria* **34 D7** 47 31N 14 22 E
Rotterdam, *Neths.* **24 C4** 51 55N 4 30 E
Rotterdam, *U.S.A.* **151 D10** 42 48N 74 1W
Rottne, *Sweden* **17 G8** 57 1N 14 54 E
Rottnest I., *Australia* **125 F2** 32 0 S 115 27 E
Rottumeroog, *Neths.* **24 A6** 53 33N 6 34 E
Rottweil, *Germany* **31 G4** 48 9N 8 37 E
Rotuma, *Fiji* **134 J9** 12 25 S 177 5 E
Roubaix, *France* **27 B10** 50 40N 3 10 E
Roudnice nad Labem, *Czech Rep.* **34 A7** 50 25N 14 15 E
Rouen, *France* **26 C8** 49 27N 1 4 E
Rouergue, *France* **28 D5** 44 15N 2 0 E
Rough Ridge, *N.Z.* **131 F4** 45 10 S 169 55 E
Rouillac, *France* **28 C3** 45 47N 0 4W
Rouleau, *Canada* **143 C8** 50 10N 104 56W
Round I., *Mauritius* **121 d** 19 51 S 57 45 E
Round Mountain, *U.S.A.* **158 G5** 38 43N 117 4W
Round Mt., *N.S.W., Australia* **127 E5** 30 26 S 152 16 E
Round Mt., *N.S.W., Australia* **129 A9** 30 15 S 152 15 E
Round Rock, *U.S.A.* **155 K6** 30 31N 97 41W
Roundup, *U.S.A.* **158 C9** 46 27N 108 33W
Roura, *Fr. Guiana* **169 C7** 4 44N 52 20W
Rousay, *U.K.* **22 B5** 59 10N 3 2W
Rouses Point, *U.S.A.* **151 B11** 44 59N 73 22W
Rouseville, *U.S.A.* **150 E5** 41 28N 79 42W
Roussillon, *Isère, France* **29 C8** 45 24N 4 49 E
Roussillon, *Pyrénées-Or., France* **28 F6** 42 30N 2 35 E
Roussin, C., *N. Cal.* **133 U21** 21 20 S 167 59 E
Rouxville, *S. Africa* **116 E4** 30 25 S 26 50 E
Rouyn-Noranda, *Canada* **140 C4** 48 20N 79 0W
Rovaniemi, *Finland* **14 C21** 66 29N 25 41 E
Rovato, *Italy* **44 C7** 45 34N 10 0 E
Rovenki, *Ukraine* **59 H10** 48 5N 39 21 E
Rovereto, *Italy* **44 C8** 45 53N 11 3 E
Roverud, *Norway* **18 D9** 60 15N 12 3 E
Rovigo, *Italy* **45 C8** 45 4N 11 47 E
Rovinj, *Croatia* **45 C10** 45 5N 13 40 E
Rovìra, *Colombia* **168 C2** 4 15N 75 20W
Rovno = Rivne, *Ukraine* **59 G4** 50 40N 26 10 E
Rovnoye, *Russia* **60 E8** 50 52N 46 3 E
Rovuma = Ruvuma →, *Tanzania* **119 E5** 10 29 S 40 28 E
Row'ān, *Iran* **97 C6** 35 8N 48 51 E
Rowena, *Australia* **127 D4** 29 48 S 148 55 E
Rowley Shoals, *Australia* **124 C2** 17 30 S 119 0 E
Roxa, *Guinea-Biss.* **112 C1** 11 15N 15 45W
Roxas, *Capiz, Phil.* **81 F4** 11 36N 122 49 E
Roxas, *Isabela, Phil.* **80 C3** 17 8N 121 36 E
Roxas, *Mind. Or., Phil.* **80 E3** 12 35N 121 31 E
Roxas, *Palawan, Phil.* **81 F2** 10 20N 119 21 E
Roxboro, *U.S.A.* **149 G6** 36 24N 78 59W
Roxborough, *Trin. & Tob.* **169 E10** 11 15N 60 35W
Roxburgh, *N.Z.* **131 F4** 45 33 S 169 19 E
Roxbury, *U.S.A.* **150 F7** 40 6N 77 39W
Roxen, *Sweden* **17 F9** 58 30N 15 40 E
Roy, *Mont., U.S.A.* **158 C9** 47 20N 108 58W
Roy, *N. Mex., U.S.A.* **155 H2** 35 57N 104 12W
Roy, *Utah, U.S.A.* **158 F7** 41 10N 112 2W
Royal Canal, *Ireland* **23 C4** 53 30N 7 13W
Royal Center, *U.S.A.* **157 D10** 40 52N 86 30W
Royal Leamington Spa, *U.K.* **21 E6** 52 18N 1 31W
Royal Nat. Park, *Australia* **129 C9** 34 5 S 151 5 E
Royal Natal Nat. Park, *S. Africa* **117 D4** 28 43 S 28 51 E
Royal Oak, *U.S.A.* **157 B13** 42 30N 83 9W
Royal Tunbridge Wells, *U.K.* **21 F8** 51 7N 0 16 E
Royale, Isle, *U.S.A.* **154 B10** 48 0N 88 54W
Royalla, *Australia* **129 C8** 35 30 S 149 9 E
Royan, *France* **28 C2** 45 37N 1 2W
Roye, *France* **27 C9** 49 42N 2 48 E
Royston, *U.K.* **21 E7** 52 3N 0 0W
Rožaj, *Montenegro, Yug.* **50 D4** 42 50N 20 11 E
Różan, *Poland* **55 F8** 52 52N 21 25 E
Rozay-en-Brie, *France* **27 D9** 48 41N 2 58 E
Rozdilna, *Ukraine* **59 J6** 46 50N 30 2 E
Rozhyshche, *Ukraine* **59 G3** 50 54N 25 15 E
Rožmitál pod Třemšínem, *Czech Rep.* **34 B6** 49 36N 13 53 E
Rožňava, *Slovak Rep.* **35 C13** 48 37N 20 35 E
Rozogi, *Poland* **54 E8** 53 28N 21 19 E
Rozoy-sur-Serre, *France* **27 C11** 49 40N 4 8 E
Rozzano, *Italy* **44 C6** 45 22N 9 10 E
Rrëshen, *Albania* **50 E3** 41 47N 19 49 E
Rrogozhine, *Albania* **50 E3** 41 4N 19 50 E
Rtanj, *Serbia, Yug.* **50 C5** 43 45N 21 50 E
Rtem, O. el →, *Algeria* **111 B6** 33 29N 5 38 E
Rtishchevo, *Russia* **60 D6** 52 18N 43 46 E
Rúa = A Rúa, *Spain* **42 C3** 42 24N 7 6W
Ruacaná, *Namibia* **116 B1** 17 27 S 14 21 E
Ruaha Nat. Park, *Tanzania* **118 D3** 7 41 S 34 30 E
Ruahine Ra., *N.Z.* **130 F5** 39 55 S 176 2 E
Ruamahanga →, *N.Z.* **130 H4** 41 24 S 175 8 E
Ruapehu, *N.Z.* **130 F4** 39 17 S 175 35 E
Ruapuke I., *N.Z.* **131 G3** 46 46 S 168 31 E
Ruâq, W. →, *Egypt* **103 F2** 30 0N 33 49 E
Ruatoria, *N.Z.* **130 D7** 37 55 S 178 20 E
Ruavatu, *Solomon Is.* **133 M11** 9 26 S 160 26 E
Ruawai, *N.Z.* **130 C2** 36 8 S 173 59 E
Rub' al Khālī, *Si. Arabia* **99 C5** 19 0N 48 0 E
Rubeho Mts., *Tanzania* **118 D4** 6 50 S 36 25 E
Rubezhnoye = Rubizhne, *Ukraine* **59 H10** 49 6N 38 25 E
Rubh a' Mhail, *U.K.* **22 F2** 55 56N 6 8W
Rubha Hunish, *U.K.* **22 D2** 57 42N 6 20W
Rubha Robhanais = Lewis, Butt of, *U.K.* **22 C2** 58 31N 6 16W
Rubi, *Spain* **40 D7** 41 29N 2 2 E
Rubiataba, *Brazil* **171 E2** 15 8 S 49 48W
Rubicon →, *U.S.A.* **160 G5** 38 53N 121 4W
Rubicone →, *Italy* **45 D9** 44 8N 12 28 E
Rubik, *Albania* **50 E3** 41 46N 19 47 E
Rubinéia, *Brazil* **171 F1** 20 13 S 51 2W
Rubino, *Ivory C.* **112 D4** 6 4N 4 18W
Rubio, *Venezuela* **168 B3** 7 43N 72 22W
Rubizhne, *Ukraine* **59 H10** 49 6N 38 25 E
Rubondo Nat. Park, *Tanzania* **118 C3** 2 18 S 31 58 E
Rubtsovsk, *Russia* **66 D9** 51 30N 81 10 E
Ruby, *U.S.A.* **144 D9** 64 45N 155 30W
Ruby L., *U.S.A.* **158 F6** 40 10N 115 28W
Ruby Mts., *U.S.A.* **158 F6** 40 30N 115 20W
Rubyvale, *Australia* **126 C4** 23 25 S 147 42 E
Rucheng, *China* **77 E9** 25 33N 113 38 E
Ruciane-Nida, *Poland* **54 E8** 53 40N 21 32 E
Rūd Sar, *Iran* **97 B6** 37 8N 50 18 E
Ruda, *Sweden* **17 G10** 57 6N 16 7 E
Ruda Śląska, *Poland* **55 H5** 50 16N 18 50 E
Rudall, *Australia* **128 B2** 33 43 S 136 17 E
Rudall →, *Australia* **124 D3** 22 34 S 122 13 E
Rudall River Nat. Park, *Australia* **124 D3** 22 38 S 122 30 E
Rūdbār, *Afghan.* **91 C1** 30 9N 62 36 E
Rüdersdorf, *Germany* **30 C9** 52 27N 13 47 E
Rudewa, *Tanzania* **119 E3** 10 7 S 34 40 E
Rudkøbing, *Denmark* **17 K4** 54 56N 10 41 E
Rudna, *Poland* **55 G3** 51 30N 16 17 E
Rūdnīchnyy, *Kazakstan* **65 A9** 44 40N 78 54 E
Rudnik, *Bulgaria* **51 D11** 42 36N 27 30 E
Rudnik, *Poland* **55 H9** 50 26N 22 15 E
Rudnik, *Serbia, Yug.* **50 B4** 44 7N 20 35 E
Rudnya, *Russia* **58 E6** 54 55N 31 7 E
Rudnyy, *Kazakstan* **64 E9** 52 57N 63 7 E
Rudo, *Bos.-H.* **52 G4** 43 41N 19 23 E
Rudolfa, Ostrov, *Russia* **66 A6** 81 45N 58 30 E
Rudolstadt, *Germany* **30 E7** 50 44N 11 19 E
Rudong, *China* **77 A13** 32 20N 121 12 E
Rudozem, *Bulgaria* **51 E8** 41 29N 24 51 E
Rudyard, *U.S.A.* **148 B3** 46 14N 84 36W
Rue, *France* **27 B8** 50 15N 1 40 E
Ruenya →, *Africa* **119 F3** 16 24 S 33 48 E
Rufa'a, *Sudan* **107 E3** 14 44N 33 22 E
Rufflin, *U.S.A.* **152 B9** 33 0N 80 49W
Rufiji →, *Tanzania* **118 D4** 7 50 S 39 15 E
Rufino, *Argentina* **174 C3** 34 20 S 62 50W
Rufisque, *Senegal* **112 C1** 14 40N 17 15W
Rufling Pt., *Br. Virgin Is.* **165 e** 18 44N 64 27W
Rufunsa, *Zambia* **119 F2** 15 4 S 29 34 E
Rugao, *China* **77 A13** 32 23N 120 31 E
Rugby, *U.K.* **21 E6** 52 23N 1 16W
Rugby, *U.S.A.* **154 A5** 48 22N 100 0W
Rügen, *Germany* **30 A9** 54 22N 13 24 E
Rugles, *France* **26 D7** 48 50N 0 40 E
Ruhea, *Bangla.* **90 B2** 26 10N 88 25 E
Ruhengeri, *Rwanda* **118 C2** 1 30 S 29 36 E
Ruhla, *Germany* **30 E6** 50 54N 10 23 E
Ruhland, *Germany* **30 D9** 51 27N 13 51 E
Ruhnu, *Estonia* **15 H20** 57 48N 23 15 E
Ruhr →, *Germany* **30 D2** 51 27N 6 43 E
Ruhuhu →, *Tanzania* **119 E3** 10 31 S 34 34 E
Rui Barbosa, *Brazil* **171 D3** 12 18 S 40 27W
Rui'an, *China* **77 D13** 27 47N 120 40 E
Ruichang, *China* **77 C10** 29 40N 115 39 E
Ruidoso, *U.S.A.* **159 K11** 33 20N 105 41W
Ruijin, *China* **77 E10** 25 48N 116 0 E
Ruili, *China* **76 E1** 24 1N 97 43 E
Ruivo, Pico, *Madeira* **9 c** 32 45N 16 56W
Ruj, *Bulgaria* **50 D6** 42 52N 22 34 E
Rujen, *Macedonia* **50 D6** 42 9N 22 30 E
Rujm Tal'at al Jamā'ah, *Jordan* **103 E4** 30 24N 35 30 E
Ruk, *Pakistan* **92 F3** 27 50N 68 42 E
Rukhla, *Pakistan* **92 C4** 32 27N 71 57 E
Rukwa □, *Tanzania* **118 D3** 7 0 S 31 30 E
Rukwa, L., *Tanzania* **118 D3** 8 0 S 32 20 E
Rulhieres, C., *Australia* **124 B4** 13 56 S 127 22 E
Rum = Rhum, *U.K.* **22 E2** 57 0N 6 20W
Rum Cay, *Bahamas* **165 B5** 23 40N 74 58W
Rum Jungle, *Australia* **124 B5** 13 0 S 130 59 E
Ruma, *Serbia, Yug.* **52 E4** 45 0N 19 50 E
Ruma Nat. Park, *Kenya* **118 C3** 0 39 S 34 18 E
Rumāḩ, *Si. Arabia* **96 E5** 25 29N 47 10 E
Rumania = Romania ■, *Europe* **53 D10** 46 0N 25 0 E
Rumaylah, *Iraq* **96 D5** 30 47N 47 37 E
Rumbêk, *Sudan* **107 F2** 6 54N 29 37 E
Rumberpon, *Indonesia* **83 B4** 1 50 S 134 15 E
Rumburk, *Czech Rep.* **34 A7** 50 57N 14 32 E
Rumford, *U.S.A.* **149 C10** 44 33N 70 33W
Rumia, *Poland* **54 D5** 54 37N 18 25 E
Rumilly, *France* **29 C9** 45 53N 5 56 E
Rumoi, *Japan* **70 C10** 43 56N 141 39 E
Rumonge, *Burundi* **118 C2** 3 59 S 29 26 E
Rumson, *U.S.A.* **151 F11** 40 23N 74 0W
Rumuruti, *Kenya* **118 B4** 0 17N 36 32 E
Runan, *China* **74 H8** 33 0N 114 30 E
Runanga, *N.Z.* **131 C6** 42 25 S 171 15 E
Runaway, C., *N.Z.* **130 D6** 37 32 S 177 59 E
Runaway Bay, *Jamaica* **164 a** 18 27N 77 20W
Runcorn, *U.K.* **20 D5** 53 21N 2 44W
Rundu, *Namibia* **116 B2** 17 52 S 19 43 E
Rungwa, *Tanzania* **118 D3** 6 55 S 33 32 E
Rungwa →, *Tanzania* **118 D3** 7 36 S 31 50 E
Rungwa Game Reserve, *Tanzania* **118 D3** 6 53 S 34 2 E
Rungwe, *Tanzania* **119 D3** 9 11 S 33 32 E
Runka, *Nigeria* **113 C6** 12 28N 7 20 E
Runn, *Sweden* **16 D9** 60 30N 15 40 E
Runton Ra., *Australia* **124 D3** 23 31 S 123 6 E
Ruokolahti, *Finland* **58 B5** 61 17N 28 50 E
Ruoqiang, *China* **68 C3** 38 55N 88 10 E
Rupa, *India* **90 B4** 27 15N 92 21 E
Rupar, *India* **92 D7** 31 2N 76 38 E
Rupat, *Indonesia* **84 B2** 1 45N 101 40 E
Rupea, *Romania* **53 D10** 46 2N 25 13 E
Rupen →, *India* **92 H4** 23 28N 71 31 E
Rupert, *U.S.A.* **158 E7** 42 37N 113 41W
Rupert →, *Canada* **140 B4** 51 29N 78 45W
Rupert B., *Canada* **140 B4** 51 35N 79 0W
Rupert House = Waskaganish, *Canada* **140 B4** 51 30N 78 40W
Rupsa, *India* **93 J12** 21 37N 87 1 E
Rupununi →, *Guyana* **169 C6** 4 3N 58 35W
Rur →, *Germany* **30 D1** 51 11N 5 59 E
Rurópolis, *Brazil* **169 D7** 4 3 S 54 59W
Rurrenabaque, *Bolivia* **172 C4** 14 30 S 67 32W
Rus →, *Spain* **41 F2** 39 30N 2 30W
Rusambo, *Zimbabwe* **119 F3** 16 30 S 32 4 E
Rusape, *Zimbabwe* **119 F3** 18 35 S 32 8 E
Ruschuk = Ruse, *Bulgaria* **51 C9** 43 48N 25 59 E
Ruse, *Bulgaria* **51 C9** 43 48N 25 59 E
Ruse □, *Bulgaria* **51 C10** 43 35N 26 20 E
Ruşeţu, *Romania* **53 F12** 44 57N 27 14 E
Rush, *Ireland* **23 C5** 53 31N 6 6W
Rushan, *China* **75 F11** 36 56N 121 30 E
Rushden, *U.K.* **21 E7** 52 18N 0 35W
Rushikulya →, *India* **94 E7** 19 23N 85 5 E
Rushmore, Mt., *U.S.A.* **154 D3** 43 53N 103 28W
Rushon, *Tajikistan* **65 E5** 37 57N 71 33 E
Rushville, *Ill., U.S.A.* **156 D6** 40 7N 90 34W
Rushville, *Ind., U.S.A.* **157 E11** 39 37N 85 27W
Rushville, *Nebr., U.S.A.* **154 D3** 42 43N 102 28W
Rushworth, *Australia* **129 D6** 36 32 S 145 1 E
Ruskin, *U.S.A.* **153 H7** 27 43N 82 26W
Russas, *Brazil* **170 B4** 4 55 S 37 50W
Russell, *Canada* **143 C8** 50 50N 101 20W
Russell, *N.Z.* **130 B3** 35 16 S 174 10 E
Russell, *Fla., U.S.A.* **152 E8** 30 3N 81 45W
Russell, *Kans., U.S.A.* **154 F5** 38 54N 98 52W
Russell, *N.Y., U.S.A.* **151 B9** 44 27N 75 9W
Russell, *Pa., U.S.A.* **150 E5** 41 56N 79 8W
Russell Is., *Solomon Is.* **133 M10** 9 4 S 159 12 E
Russell L., *Man., Canada* **143 B8** 56 15N 101 30W
Russell L., *N.W.T., Canada* **142 A5** 63 5N 115 44W
Russellkonda, *India* **94 E7** 19 57N 84 42 E
Russells Point, *U.S.A.* **157 D13** 40 28N 83 54W
Russellville, *Ala., U.S.A.* **149 H2** 34 30N 87 44W
Russellville, *Ark., U.S.A.* **155 H8** 35 17N 93 8W
Russellville, *Ky., U.S.A.* **149 G2** 36 51N 86 53W
Rüsselsheim, *Germany* **31 F4** 49 59N 8 23 E
Russi, *Italy* **45 D9** 44 22N 12 2 E
Russia ■, *Eurasia* **67 C11** 62 0N 105 0 E
Russian →, *U.S.A.* **160 G3** 38 27N 123 8W
Russian Mission, *U.S.A.* **144 F7** 61 47N 161 19W
Russiaville, *U.S.A.* **157 D10** 40 25N 86 16W
Russkoye Ustie, *Russia* **6 B15** 71 0N 149 0 E
Rust, *Austria* **35 D9** 47 49N 16 42 E
Rustam, *Pakistan* **92 B5** 34 25N 72 13 E
Rustam Shahr, *Pakistan* **92 F2** 26 58N 66 6 E
Rustavi, *Georgia* **61 K7** 41 30N 45 0 E
Rustenburg, *S. Africa* **116 D4** 25 41 S 27 14 E
Ruston, *U.S.A.* **155 J8** 32 32N 92 38W
Ruswil, *Switz.* **32 B6** 47 5N 8 8 E
Rutana, *Burundi* **118 C3** 3 55 S 30 0 E
Rute, *Spain* **43 H6** 37 19N 4 23W
Ruteng, *Indonesia* **82 C2** 8 35 S 120 30 E
Ruth, *U.S.A.* **150 C2** 43 42N 82 45W
Rutherford, *U.S.A.* **160 G4** 38 26N 122 24W
Rutherglen, *Australia* **129 D7** 36 5 S 146 29 E
Rüti, *Switz.* **33 B7** 47 16N 8 51 E

274 Rutland

Rutland, U.S.A. 151 C12 43 37N 72 58W
Rutland □, U.K. 21 E7 52 38N 0 40W
Rutland I., India 95 J11 11 25N 92 10 E
Rutland Water, U.K. 21 E7 52 39N 0 38W
Rutledal, Norway 18 C2 61 4N 5 10 E
Rutledge, U.S.A. 152 B6 33 38N 83 37W
Rutledge →, Canada 143 A6 61 4N 112 0W
Rutledge L., Canada 143 A6 61 33N 110 47W
Rutqa, W. →, Syria 101 E9 34 30N 41 3 E
Rutshuru, Dem. Rep. of the Congo 118 C2 1 13 S 29 25 E
Ruvo di Púglia, Italy 47 A9 41 7N 16 29 E
Ruvu, Tanzania 118 D4 6 49 S 38 43 E
Ruvu →, Tanzania 118 D4 6 23 S 38 52 E
Ruvuba, Parc Nat. de, Burundi 118 C2 3 3 S 29 33 E
Ruvuma □, Tanzania 119 E4 10 20 S 36 0 E
Ruvuma →, Tanzania 119 E5 10 29 S 40 28 E
Ruwais, U.A.E. 97 E7 24 5N 52 50 E
Ruwenzori, Africa 118 B2 0 30N 29 55 E
Ruwenzori Nat. Park, Uganda 118 B2 0 20 S 30 0 E
Ruya →, Zimbabwe 117 B5 16 27 S 32 5 E
Ruyigi, Burundi 118 C3 3 29 S 30 15 E
Ruyuan, China 77 E9 24 46N 113 16 E
Ruzayevka, Russia 60 C7 54 4N 45 0 E
Rŭzhevo Konare, Bulgaria 51 D8 42 23N 24 46 E
Ružomberok, Slovak Rep. 35 B12 49 3N 19 17 E
Rwanda ■, Africa 118 C3 2 0 S 30 0 E
Ryakhovo, Bulgaria 51 C10 43 58N 26 18 E
Ryan, L., U.K. 22 G3 55 0N 5 2W
Ryazan, Russia 58 E10 54 40N 39 40 E
Ryazhsk, Russia 58 F11 53 45N 40 3 E
Rybache = Rybachye, Kazakstan 66 E9 46 40N 81 20 E
Rybachiy Poluostrov, Russia 56 A5 69 43N 32 0 E
Rybachye = Balykchy, Kyrgyzstan 65 B8 42 26N 76 12 E
Rybachye, Kazakstan 66 E9 46 40N 81 20 E
Rybinsk, Russia 58 C10 58 5N 38 50 E
Rybinskoye Vdkhr., Russia 58 C10 58 30N 38 25 E
Rybnik, Poland 55 H5 50 6N 18 32 E
Rybnitsa = Râbniţa, Moldova 53 C14 47 45N 29 0 E
Rybnoye, Russia 58 E10 54 45N 39 30 E
Rychnov nad Kněžnou, Czech Rep. 35 A9 50 10N 16 17 E
Rychwał, Poland 55 F5 52 4N 18 10 E
Rycroft, Canada 142 B5 55 45N 118 40W
Ryd, Sweden 17 H8 56 27N 14 42 E
Rydaholm, Sweden 17 H8 56 59N 14 18 E
Ryde, U.K. 21 G6 50 43N 1 9W
Ryderwood, U.S.A. 160 D3 46 23N 123 3W
Rydzyna, Poland 55 G3 51 47N 16 39 E
Rye, U.K. 21 G8 50 57N 0 45 E
Rye →, U.K. 20 C7 54 11N 0 44W
Rye Bay, U.K. 21 G8 50 52N 0 49 E
Rye Patch Reservoir, U.S.A. 158 F4 40 28N 118 19W
Ryegate, U.S.A. 158 C9 46 18N 109 15W
Ryfylke, Norway 18 E3 59 25N 6 25 E
Rykene, Norway 18 F5 58 24N 8 37 E
Ryki, Poland 55 G8 51 38N 21 56 E
Ryley, Canada 142 C6 53 17N 112 26W
Rylsk, Russia 59 G8 51 36N 34 43 E
Rylstone, Australia 129 B8 32 46 S 149 58 E
Rymanów, Poland 55 J8 49 35N 21 51 E
Ryn, Poland 54 E8 53 57N 21 34 E
Ryn Peski, Kazakstan 61 G9 47 30N 49 0 E
Ryōhaku-Sanchi, Japan 73 A8 36 9N 136 49 E
Ryōtsu, Japan 70 E9 38 5N 138 26 E
Rypin, Poland 55 E6 53 3N 19 25 E
Ryssby, Sweden 17 H8 56 52N 14 10 E
Ryūgasaki, Japan 73 B12 35 54N 140 11 E
Ryūkyū Is. = Ryūkyū-rettō, Japan 71 M3 26 0N 126 0 E
Ryūkyū-rettō, Japan 71 M3 26 0N 126 0 E
Rzepin, Poland 55 F1 52 20N 14 49 E
Rzeszów, Poland 55 H8 50 5N 21 58 E
Rzhev, Russia 58 D8 56 20N 34 20 E

S

Sa, Thailand 86 C3 18 34N 100 45 E
Sa Canal, Spain 38 D1 38 51N 1 23 E
Sa Conillera, Spain 38 D1 38 59N 1 13 E
Sa Dec, Vietnam 87 G5 10 20N 105 46 E
Sa Dragonera, Spain 38 B3 39 35N 2 19 E
Sa-koi, Burma 90 F6 19 54N 97 3 E
Sa Mesquida, Spain 38 B5 39 55N 4 16 E
Sa Pobla, Spain 38 B4 39 46N 3 1 E
Sa Savina, Spain 38 D1 38 44N 1 25 E
Sa'a, Solomon Is. 133 M11 9 43 S 161 35 E
Sa'ādatābād, Fārs, Iran 97 D7 30 10N 53 5 E
Sa'ādatābād, Hormozgān, Iran 97 D7 28 3N 55 53 E
Sa'ādatābād, Kermān, Iran 97 D7 29 40N 55 51 E
Saale →, Germany 30 D7 51 56N 11 54 E
Saaler Bodden, Germany 30 A8 54 20N 12 27 E
Saalfeld, Germany 30 E7 50 38N 11 21 E
Saalfelden, Austria 34 D5 47 25N 12 51 E
Saane →, Switz. 32 B4 47 8N 7 10 E
Saanen, Switz. 32 D4 46 29N 7 15 E
Saar →, Europe 24 E6 49 41N 6 32 E
Saarbrücken, Germany 31 F2 49 14N 6 59 E
Saarburg, Germany 31 F2 49 36N 6 32 E
Saaremaa, Estonia 15 G20 58 30N 22 30 E
Saarijärvi, Finland 15 E21 62 43N 25 16 E
Saariselkä, Finland 14 B23 68 16N 28 15 E
Saarland □, Germany 31 F2 49 20N 7 0 E
Saarlouis, Germany 31 F2 49 18N 6 45 E
Saas Fee, Switz. 32 D5 46 7N 7 56 E
Sab 'Ābar, Syria 100 F7 33 46N 37 41 E
Saba, W. Indies 165 C7 17 42N 63 26W
Šabac, Serbia, Yug. 50 B3 44 48N 19 42 E
Sabadell, Spain 40 D7 41 28N 2 7 E
Sabae, Japan 73 B8 35 57N 136 11 E
Sabah □, Malaysia 85 A5 6 0N 117 0 E
Sabak Bernam, Malaysia 87 L3 3 46N 100 58 E
Sabalān, Kūhhā-ye, Iran 101 C12 38 15N 47 45 E
Sabalana, Kepulauan, Indonesia 82 C1 6 45 S 118 50 E
Sábana de la Mar, Dom. Rep. 165 C6 19 7N 69 24W
Sábanalarga, Colombia 168 A3 10 38N 74 55W
Sabang, Indonesia 84 A1 5 50N 95 15 E
Săbăoani, Romania 53 C11 47 1N 26 51 E
Sabará, Brazil 171 E3 19 55 S 43 46W
Sabari →, India 94 F5 17 35N 81 16 E
Sabarmati →, India 92 H5 22 18N 72 22 E
Sab'atayn, Ramlat as, Yemen 98 D4 15 30N 46 10 E
Sabattis, U.S.A. 151 B10 44 6N 74 40W
Sabáudia, Italy 46 A6 41 18N 13 1 E
Sabaya, Bolivia 172 D4 19 1 S 68 23W
Şābāyā, Jaza'ir, Si. Arabia 98 C3 18 35N 41 3 E
Sabbio Chiese, Italy 33 E10 45 39N 10 25 E
Saberania, Indonesia 83 B5 2 5 S 138 18 E
Sabhah, Libya 108 C2 27 9N 14 29 E
Sabhah □, Libya 108 C2 26 0N 14 0 E
Sabi →, India 92 E7 28 29N 76 44 E
Sabidana, J., Sudan 106 D4 18 4N 36 50 E
Sabie, S. Africa 117 D5 25 10 S 30 48 E
Sabina, U.S.A. 157 E13 39 29N 83 38W
Sabinal, Mexico 162 A3 30 58N 107 25W
Sabinal, U.S.A. 155 L5 29 19N 99 28W
Sabiñánigo, Spain 40 C4 42 31N 0 22W
Sabinar, Punta del, Spain 41 J2 36 43N 2 44W
Sabinas, Mexico 162 B4 27 50N 101 10W
Sabinas →, Mexico 162 B4 27 37N 100 42W
Sabinas Hidalgo, Mexico 162 B4 26 33N 100 10W
Sabine →, U.S.A. 155 L8 29 59N 93 47W
Sabine L., U.S.A. 155 L8 29 53N 93 51W
Sabine Pass, U.S.A. 155 L8 29 44N 93 54W
Sabinópolis, Brazil 171 E3 18 40 S 43 6W
Sabinov, Slovak Rep. 35 B14 49 6N 21 5 E
Sabinsville, U.S.A. 150 E7 41 52N 77 31W
Sabirabad, Azerbaijan 61 K9 40 5N 48 30 E
Sabka, Chad 109 E3 19 15N 16 35 E
Sablayan, Phil. 80 E3 12 50N 120 50 E
Sable, Canada 141 A6 55 30N 68 21W
Sable, C., Canada 141 D6 43 29N 65 38W
Sable, C., U.S.A. 153 K8 25 9N 81 8W
Sable I., Canada 141 D8 44 0N 60 0W
Sable I., Papua N. G. 132 B8 3 38 S 154 42 E
Sablé-sur-Sarthe, France 26 E6 47 50N 0 20W
Saboeiro, Brazil 170 C4 6 32 S 39 54W
Sabonkafi, Niger 113 C6 14 40N 8 45 E
Sabor →, Portugal 42 D3 41 10N 7 7W
Sabou, Burkina Faso 112 C4 12 1N 2 15W
Şabrātah, Libya 108 B2 32 47N 12 29 E
Sabres, France 28 D3 44 9N 0 43W
Sabria, Tunisia 108 B1 33 22N 8 45 E
Sabrina Coast, Antarctica 7 C9 68 0 S 120 0 E
Sabtang I., Phil. 80 A3 20 19N 121 52 E
Sabugal, Portugal 42 E3 40 20N 7 5W
Sabula, U.S.A. 156 B6 42 4N 90 10W
Sabulubbek, Indonesia 84 C1 1 36 S 98 40 E
Sabuncu, Turkey 49 B12 39 33N 30 12 E
Şabyā, Si. Arabia 98 C3 17 9N 42 37 E
Sabzevār, Iran 97 B8 36 15N 57 40 E
Sabzvārān, Iran 97 D8 28 45N 57 50 E
Sac City, U.S.A. 156 B2 42 25N 95 0W
Sacaolo, Angola 115 E4 12 58 S 22 28 E
Sacatengo, Angola 115 E4 13 16 S 21 20 E
Sacedón, Spain 40 E2 40 29N 2 41W
Săcele, Romania 53 E10 45 37N 25 41 E
Sachigo →, Canada 140 A2 55 6N 88 58W
Sachigo, L., Canada 140 B1 53 50N 92 12W
Sachimbo, Angola 115 D4 9 14 S 20 16 E
Sachin, India 94 D1 21 5N 72 53 E
Sachkhere, Georgia 61 J6 42 25N 43 28 E
Sachseln, Switz. 33 C6 46 52N 8 15 E
Sachsen □, Germany 30 E9 50 55N 13 10 E
Sachsen-Anhalt □, Germany 30 D7 52 0N 12 0 E
Sacile, Italy 45 C9 45 57N 12 30 E
Sackets Harbor, U.S.A. 151 C8 43 57N 76 7W
Sackville, Canada 141 C7 45 54N 64 22W
Saco, Maine, U.S.A. 149 D10 43 30N 70 27W
Saco, Mont., U.S.A. 158 B10 48 28N 107 21W
Sacramento, Brazil 171 E2 19 53 S 47 27W
Sacramento, U.S.A. 160 G5 38 35N 121 29W
Sacramento →, U.S.A. 160 G5 38 3N 121 56W
Sacramento Mts., U.S.A. 159 K11 32 30N 105 30W
Sacramento Valley, U.S.A. 160 G5 39 30N 122 0W
Sacratif, C., Spain 43 J7 36 42N 3 28W
Săcueni, Romania 52 C7 47 20N 22 5 E
Sada, Spain 42 B2 43 22N 8 15W
Sada-Misaki, Japan 71 H6 33 20N 132 1 E
Sada-Misaki-Hantō, Japan 72 D4 33 22N 132 1 E
Sádaba, Spain 40 C3 42 19N 1 12W
Sadabad, India 92 F8 27 27N 78 3 E
Şa'dah, Yemen 98 C3 16 15N 43 37 E
Sadani, Tanzania 118 D4 5 58 S 38 35 E
Sadao, Thailand 87 J3 6 38N 100 26 E
Sadaseopet, India 94 F3 17 38N 77 59 E
Sadd el Aali, Egypt 106 C3 23 54N 32 54 E
Saddle Mt., U.S.A. 160 E3 45 58N 123 41W
Saddle Pk., India 95 H11 13 9N 93 1 E
Saddle Pt., St. Helena 9 h 15 57 S 5 38W
Sade, Nigeria 113 C7 11 22N 10 45 E
Şadh, Oman 99 C6 17 3N 55 4 E
Sadimi, Dem. Rep. of the Congo 119 D1 9 25 S 23 32 E
Sadiola, Mali 112 C2 13 50N 11 40W
Sadiya, India 90 B5 27 50N 95 40 E
Sa'dīyah, Hawr as, Iraq 101 F12 32 15N 46 30 E
Sado, Japan 70 F9 38 0N 138 25 E
Sado →, Portugal 43 G2 38 29N 8 55W
Sadon, Russia 61 J6 42 52N 43 58 E
Sadowara, Japan 72 E3 32 2N 131 26 E
Sadra, India 92 H5 23 21N 72 43 E
Sadri, India 92 G5 25 11N 73 26 E
Sæbøvik, Norway 18 E2 59 47N 5 40 E
Sæby, Denmark 17 G4 57 21N 10 30 E
Saegertown, U.S.A. 150 E4 41 43N 80 9W
Saelices, Spain 40 F2 39 55N 2 49W
Sætre, Norway 18 E7 59 41N 10 33 E
Sævareid, Norway 18 D2 60 11N 5 46 E
Safaalan, Turkey 51 E12 41 26N 28 6 E
Safaga, Egypt 106 B3 26 42N 34 0 E
Şafājah, Si. Arabia 96 E3 26 25N 39 0 E
Šafárikovo = Tornal'a, Slovak Rep. 35 C13 48 25N 20 20 E
Safata B., Samoa 133 X24 14 0 S 171 50W
Safed Koh, Afghan. 91 B3 34 0N 70 0 E
Säffle, Sweden 16 E6 59 8N 12 55 E
Safford, U.S.A. 159 K9 32 50N 109 43W
Saffron Walden, U.K. 21 E8 52 1N 0 16 E
Safi, Morocco 110 B3 32 18N 9 20W
Safia, Papua N. G. 132 E5 9 35 S 148 38 E
Safia, Hamada, Mali 110 D4 23 10N 4 15W
Şafīābād, Iran 97 B8 36 45N 57 58 E
Safīd Dasht, Iran 97 C6 33 27N 48 11 E
Safīd Kūh, Afghan. 91 B1 34 45N 63 0 E
Safīd Rūd →, Iran 97 B6 37 23N 50 11 E
Safipur, India 93 F9 26 44N 80 21 E
Safonovo, Russia 58 E7 55 4N 33 16 E
Safranbolu, Turkey 100 B5 41 15N 32 41 E
Saft Rashîn, Egypt 106 J7 28 58N 30 55 E
Safune, Samoa 133 W23 13 25 S 172 21W
Safwān, Iraq 96 D5 30 7N 47 43 E
Sag Harbor, U.S.A. 151 F12 41 0N 72 18W
Sag Sag, Papua N. G. 132 C5 5 32 S 148 23 E
Saga, Indonesia 83 B4 2 40 S 132 55 E
Saga, Kōchi, Japan 72 D5 33 5N 133 6 E
Saga, Saga, Japan 72 D2 33 15N 130 16 E
Saga □, Japan 72 D2 33 15N 130 20 E
Sagae, Japan 70 E10 38 22N 140 17 E
Sagaing, Burma 90 E5 21 52N 95 59 E
Sagaing □, Burma 90 D5 23 55N 95 56 E
Sagala, Mali 112 C3 14 9N 6 38W
Sagami-Nada, Japan 73 C11 34 58N 139 30 E
Sagami-Wan, Japan 73 B11 35 15N 139 25 E
Sagamihara, Japan 73 B11 35 33N 139 25 E
Sagamore, U.S.A. 150 F5 40 46N 79 14W
Saganoseki, Japan 72 D3 33 15N 131 53 E
Sagar, Karnataka, India 94 F3 16 38N 76 48 E
Sagar, Karnataka, India 95 G2 14 14N 75 6 E
Sagar, Mad. P., India 93 H8 23 50N 78 44 E
Sagara, Japan 73 C10 34 41N 138 12 E
Sagara, L., Tanzania 118 D3 5 20 S 31 0 E
Sagavanirktok →, U.S.A. 144 A11 70 19N 147 53W
Sagay, Phil. 81 F4 10 57N 123 25 E
Saginaw, U.S.A. 148 D4 43 26N 83 56W
Saginaw →, U.S.A. 148 D4 43 39N 83 51W
Saginaw B., U.S.A. 148 D4 43 50N 83 40W
Sagleipie, Liberia 112 D3 7 0N 8 52W
Saglouc = Salluit, Canada 139 B12 62 14N 75 38W
Sagŏ-ri, S. Korea 75 G14 35 25N 126 49 E
Sagone, France 29 F12 42 7N 8 42 E
Sagone, G. de, France 29 F12 42 4N 8 40 E
Sagres, Portugal 43 J2 37 0N 8 58W
Sagu, Burma 90 E5 20 13N 94 46 E
Sagua la Grande, Cuba 164 B3 22 50N 80 10W
Saguache, U.S.A. 159 G10 38 5N 106 8W
Saguaro Nat. Park, U.S.A. 159 K8 32 12N 110 38W
Saguenay →, Canada 141 C5 48 22N 71 0W
Saguia el Hamra →, W. Sahara 110 C2 27 24N 13 43W
Sagunt, Spain 40 F4 39 42N 0 18W
Sagunto = Sagunt, Spain 40 F4 39 42N 0 18W
Sagvåg, Norway 18 E2 59 46N 5 25 E
Sagwara, India 92 H6 23 41N 74 1 E
Sahaba, Sudan 106 D3 18 57N 30 25 E
Sahagún, Colombia 168 B2 8 57N 75 27W
Sahagún, Spain 42 C5 42 18N 5 2W
Saḩam al Jawlān, Syria 103 C4 32 45N 35 55 E
Sahamandrevo, Madag. 117 C8 23 15 S 45 35 E
Sahand, Kūh-e, Iran 101 D12 37 44N 46 27 E
Sahara, Africa 104 D4 23 0N 5 0 E
Saharan Atlas = Saharien, Atlas, Algeria 111 B5 33 30N 1 0 E
Saharanpur, India 92 E7 29 58N 77 33 E
Saharien, Atlas, Algeria 111 B5 33 30N 1 0 E
Saharsa, India 93 G12 25 53N 86 36 E
Sahasinaka, Madag. 117 C8 21 49 S 47 49 E
Sahaswan, India 93 E8 28 5N 78 45 E
Sahel, Canal du, Mali 112 C3 14 20N 6 0W
Sahibganj, India 93 G12 25 12N 87 40 E
Sāḩilīyah, Iraq 101 F10 33 43N 42 42 E
Sahiwal, Pakistan 91 C4 30 45N 73 8 E
Şaḩneh, Iran 101 E12 34 29N 47 41 E
Sahuaripa, Mexico 162 B3 29 0N 109 13W
Sahuarita, U.S.A. 159 L8 31 57N 110 58W
Sahuayo, Mexico 162 C4 20 4N 102 43W
Šahy, Slovak Rep. 35 C11 48 4N 18 55 E
Sai →, India 93 G10 25 39N 82 47 E
Sai Buri, Thailand 87 J3 6 43N 101 45 E
Sai-Cinza, Brazil 173 B6 6 17 S 57 42W
Sai Kung, China 69 G11 22 23N 114 16 E
Saibai I., Australia 132 E2 9 25 S 142 40 E
Sa'id Bundas, Sudan 109 G4 8 24N 24 48 E
Saïda, Algeria 111 B5 34 50N 0 11 E
Sa'īdābād, Kermān, Iran 97 D7 29 30N 55 45 E
Sa'īdābād, Semnān, Iran 97 B7 36 8N 54 11 E
Saidaiji, Japan 72 C6 34 39N 134 2 E
Saïdia, Morocco 111 A4 35 5N 2 14W
Sa'īdīyeh, Iran 97 B6 36 20N 48 55 E
Saidor, Papua N. G. 132 C4 5 40 S 146 29 E
Saidpur, Bangla. 90 C2 25 48N 89 0 E
Saidpur, India 93 G10 25 33N 83 11 E
Saidu, Pakistan 93 B5 34 43N 72 24 E
Saignelégier, Switz. 32 B4 47 15N 7 0 E
Saignes, France 28 C6 45 20N 2 31 E
Saigō, Japan 72 A5 36 12N 133 20 E
Saigon = Thanh Pho Ho Chi Minh, Vietnam 87 G6 10 58N 106 40 E
Saijō, Japan 72 D5 33 55N 133 11 E
Saikanosy Masoala, Madag. 117 B9 15 45 S 50 10 E
Saikhoa Ghat, India 90 B5 27 50N 95 40 E
Saiki, Japan 72 E3 32 58N 131 51 E
Sailana, India 92 H6 23 28N 74 55 E
Saillans, France 29 D9 44 42N 5 12 E
Sailolof, Indonesia 83 B4 1 15 S 130 46 E
Sailu, India 94 E3 19 29N 76 28 E
Saimaa, Finland 15 F23 61 15N 28 15 E
Saimbeyli, Turkey 100 D7 37 59N 36 6 E
Şa'in Dezh, Iran 101 D12 36 40N 46 25 E
St. Abb's Head, U.K. 22 F6 55 55N 2 8W
St-Affrique, France 28 E6 43 57N 2 53 E
St-Agrève, France 29 C8 45 0N 4 23 E
St-Aignan, France 26 E8 47 16N 1 22 E
St. Alban's, Canada 141 C8 47 51N 55 50W
St. Albans, U.K. 21 F7 51 45N 0 19W
St. Albans, Vt., U.S.A. 151 B11 44 49N 73 5W
St. Albans, W. Va., U.S.A. 148 F5 38 23N 81 50W
St. Alban's Head, U.K. 21 G5 50 34N 2 4W
St. Albert, Canada 142 C6 53 37N 113 32W
St-Amand-en-Puisaye, France 27 E10 47 32N 3 5 E
St-Amand-les-Eaux, France 27 B10 50 27N 3 25 E
St-Amand-Montrond, France 27 F9 46 43N 2 30 E
St-Amarin, France 27 E14 47 54N 7 2 E
St-Amour, France 27 F12 46 26N 5 21 E
St-André, Réunion 121 c 20 57 S 55 39 E
St-André-de-Cubzac, France 28 D3 44 59N 0 26W
St-André-les-Alpes, France 29 E10 43 58N 6 30 E
St. Andrew Sd., U.S.A. 152 E8 31 0N 81 25W
St. Andrew's, Canada 141 C8 47 45N 59 15W
St. Andrews, N.Z. 131 E6 44 33 S 171 10 E
St. Andrews, U.K. 22 E6 56 20N 2 47W
St. Andrews, U.S.A. 152 C9 32 47N 80 0W
St-Anicet, Canada 151 A10 45 8N 74 22W
St. Ann B., Canada 141 C7 46 22N 60 25W
St. Anne, U.S.A. 157 C9 41 1N 87 43W
St. Ann's Bay, Jamaica 164 a 18 26N 77 15W
St. Anthony, Canada 141 B8 51 22N 55 35W
St. Anthony, U.S.A. 158 E8 43 58N 111 41W
St. Antoine, Canada 141 C7 46 22N 64 45W
St. Anton am Arlberg, Austria 33 B10 47 8N 10 16 E
St-Antonin-Noble-Val, France 28 D5 44 10N 1 45 E
St. Arnaud, Australia 128 D5 36 40 S 143 16 E
St. Arnaud Ra., N.Z. 131 C7 42 1 S 172 53 E
St-Astier, France 28 C4 45 8N 0 31 E
St-Aubin, Switz. 32 C3 46 54N 6 47 E
St-Aubin-du-Cormier, France 26 D5 48 15N 1 26W
St-Augustin →, Canada 141 B8 51 16N 58 40W
St-Augustin-Saguenay, Canada 141 B8 51 13N 58 38W
St. Augustine, U.S.A. 152 F8 29 54N 81 19W
St. Augustine Beach, U.S.A. 152 F8 29 51N 81 16W
St-Aulaye, France 28 C4 45 12N 0 9 E
St. Austell, U.K. 21 G3 50 20N 4 47W
St-Avold, France 27 C13 49 6N 6 43 E
St. Barbe, Canada 141 B8 51 12N 56 46W
St-Barthélemy, W. Indies 165 C7 17 50N 62 50W
St. Bathans, N.Z. 131 E4 44 53 S 169 50 E
St. Bathan's, Mt., N.Z. 131 E4 44 45 S 169 45 E
St-Béat, France 28 F4 42 55N 0 41 E
St. Bees Hd., U.K. 20 C4 54 31N 3 38W
St. Bees I., Australia 126 J7 20 56 S 149 26 E
St-Benoît, Réunion 121 c 21 2 S 55 43 E
St-Benoît-du-Sault, France 28 B5 46 26N 1 24 E
St-Bernard, Col du Grand, Europe 32 E4 45 53N 7 11 E
St-Blaise, Switz. 32 B3 47 1N 6 59 E
St-Bonnet, France 29 D10 44 40N 6 5 E
St-Brévin-les-Pins, France 26 E4 47 14N 2 10W
St-Brice-en-Coglès, France 26 D5 48 25N 1 22W
St. Bride's, Canada 141 C9 46 56N 54 10W
St. Brides B., U.K. 21 F2 51 49N 5 9W
St-Brieuc, France 26 D4 48 30N 2 46W
St-Calais, France 26 E7 47 55N 0 45 E
St-Cast-le-Guildo, France 26 D4 48 37N 2 18W
St. Catharines, Canada 140 D4 43 10N 79 15W
St. Catherine Pt., Bermuda 9 a 32 23N 64 40W
St. Catherines I., U.S.A. 152 D8 31 40N 81 10W
St. Catherine's Monastery, Egypt 110 B3 28 30N 33 58 E
St. Catherine's Pt., U.K. 21 G6 50 34N 1 18W
St-Céré, France 28 D5 44 51N 1 54 E
St-Cergue, Switz. 32 D2 46 27N 6 10 E
St-Cernin, France 28 C6 45 5N 2 25 E
St-Chamond, France 29 C8 45 28N 4 31 E
St. Charles, Ill., U.S.A. 157 C8 41 54N 88 19W
St. Charles, Mo., U.S.A. 156 F6 38 47N 90 29W
St. Charles, Va., U.S.A. 148 F7 36 48N 83 4W
St-Chély-d'Apcher, France 28 D7 44 48N 3 17 E
St-Chinian, France 28 E6 43 25N 2 56 E
St. Christopher-Nevis = St. Kitts & Nevis ■, W. Indies 165 C7 17 20N 62 40W
St-Ciers-sur-Gironde, France 28 C3 45 17N 0 37W
St. Clair, Ga., U.S.A. 152 B7 33 9N 82 13W
St. Clair, Mich., U.S.A. 150 D2 42 50N 82 30W
St. Clair, Mo., U.S.A. 156 F6 38 21N 90 59W
St. Clair, Pa., U.S.A. 151 F8 40 43N 76 12W
St. Clair →, U.S.A. 150 D2 42 38N 82 31W
St. Clair, L., Australia 128 D3 37 20 S 139 55 E
St. Clair, L., Canada 140 D3 42 30N 82 45W
St. Clair, L., U.S.A. 150 D2 42 27N 82 39W
St. Clair Shores, U.S.A. 157 B14 42 30N 82 53W
St. Clairsville, U.S.A. 150 F4 40 5N 80 54W
St-Claud, France 28 C4 45 54N 0 28 E
St. Claude, Canada 143 D9 49 40N 98 20W
St-Claude, France 27 F12 46 22N 5 52 E
St-Clet, Canada 151 A10 45 21N 74 13W
St. Cloud, Fla., U.S.A. 149 L5 28 15N 81 17W
St. Cloud, Minn., U.S.A. 154 C7 45 34N 94 10W
St. Cricq, C., Australia 125 E1 25 17 S 113 6 E
St. Croix, U.S. Virgin Is. 165 C7 17 45N 64 45W
St. Croix →, U.S.A. 154 C8 44 45N 92 48W
St. Croix Falls, U.S.A. 154 C8 45 24N 92 38W
St-Cyprien, France 28 F7 42 37N 3 2 E
St-Cyr-sur-Mer, France 29 E9 43 11N 5 43 E
St. David, U.S.A. 156 D6 40 30N 90 3W
St. David's, Canada 141 C8 48 12N 58 52W
St. David's, U.K. 21 F2 51 53N 5 16W
St. David's Head, U.K. 21 F2 51 54N 5 19W
St. David's I., Bermuda 9 a 32 21N 64 39W
St-Denis, France 27 D9 48 56N 2 22 E
St-Denis, Réunion 121 c 20 52 S 55 27 E
St-Dié, France 27 D13 48 17N 6 56 E
St-Dizier, France 27 D11 48 38N 4 56 E
St-Égrève, France 29 C9 45 14N 5 41 E
St. Elias, Mt., U.S.A. 144 F12 60 18N 140 56W
St. Elias Mts., Canada 142 A1 60 33N 139 28W
St. Elias Mts., U.S.A. 144 G13 60 0N 138 0W
St.-Élie, Fr. Guiana 169 C7 4 49N 53 17W
St. Elmo, U.S.A. 157 E8 39 2N 88 51W
St-Éloy-les-Mines, France 27 F9 46 10N 2 51 E
St-Émilion, France 28 D3 44 53N 0 9W
St-Étienne, France 29 C8 45 27N 4 22 E
St-Étienne-de-Tinée, France 29 D10 44 16N 6 56 E
St-Étienne-du-Rouvray, France 26 C8 49 23N 1 6 E
St. Eugène, Canada 151 A10 45 30N 74 28W
St. Eustatius, W. Indies 165 C7 17 20N 63 0W
St-Fargeau, France 27 E10 47 39N 3 4 E
St-Félicien, Canada 140 C5 48 40N 72 25W
St-Florent, France 29 F13 42 41N 9 18 E
St-Florent, G. de, France 29 F13 42 47N 9 12 E
St-Florent-sur-Cher, France 27 F9 46 59N 2 15 E
St-Florentin, France 27 E10 48 0N 3 45 E
St-Flour, France 28 C7 45 2N 3 6 E
St. Francis, U.S.A. 154 F4 39 47N 101 48W
St. Francis →, U.S.A. 155 H9 34 38N 90 36W
St. Francis, C., S. Africa 116 E3 34 14 S 24 49 E
St. Francisville, Ill., U.S.A. 157 F9 38 36N 87 39W
St. Francisville, La., U.S.A. 155 K9 30 47N 91 23W
St-François, L., Canada 151 A10 45 10N 74 22W
St-Fulgent, France 26 F5 46 50N 1 10W
St-Gabriel, Canada 140 C5 46 17N 73 24W
St. Gallen = Sankt Gallen, Switz. 33 B8 47 26N 9 22 E
St. Gallenkirch, Austria 33 B9 47 1N 9 58 E
St-Galmier, France 27 G11 45 35N 4 19 E
St-Gaudens, France 28 E4 43 6N 0 44 E
St-Gaultier, France 26 F8 46 39N 1 26 E
St-Gengoux-le-National, France 27 F11 46 37N 4 40 E
St-Geniez-d'Olt, France 28 D6 44 27N 2 58 E
St. George, Australia 127 D4 28 1 S 148 30 E
St. George, Bermuda 9 a 32 22N 64 40W
St. George, Canada 141 C6 45 11N 66 50W
St. George, Ga., U.S.A. 152 E7 30 31N 82 2W
St. George, S.C., U.S.A. 152 B9 33 11N 80 35W
St. George, Utah, U.S.A. 159 H7 37 6N 113 35W
St. George, C., Canada 141 C8 48 30N 59 16W
St. George, C., Papua N. G. 132 C7 4 49 S 152 53 E
St. George, C., U.S.A. 149 L3 29 40N 85 5W
St. George I., Alaska, U.S.A. 144 H5 56 35N 169 35W
St. George I., Fla., U.S.A. 152 F5 29 35N 84 55W
St. George Ra., Australia 124 C4 18 40 S 125 0 E
St. George's, Canada 141 C8 48 26N 58 31W
St-Georges, Canada 141 C5 46 8N 70 40W
St-Georges, Fr. Guiana 169 C7 4 0N 52 0W
St. George's, Grenada 165 D7 12 5N 61 43W
St. George's B., Canada 141 C8 48 24N 58 53W
St. Georges Basin, N.S.W., Australia 127 F5 35 7 S 150 36 E
St. Georges Basin, N.S.W., Australia 129 C9 35 7 S 150 36 E
St. Georges Basin, W. Austral., Australia 124 C4 15 23 S 125 2 E
St. George's Channel, Europe 23 E6 52 0N 6 0W
St. George's Channel, India 95 L11 7 15N 93 43 E
St. George's Channel, Papua N. G. 132 C7 4 10 S 152 20 E
St. Georges Hd., Australia 129 C9 35 12 S 150 42 E
St. Georges I., Bermuda 9 a 32 23N 64 40W
St-Georges-lès-Baillargeaux, France 28 B4 46 41N 0 22 E
St-Germain-de-Calberte, France 28 D7 44 13N 3 48 E
St-Germain-en-Laye, France 27 D9 48 54N 2 6 E
St-Germain-Lembron, France 28 C7 45 27N 3 14 E
St-Gervais-d'Auvergne, France 27 F9 46 4N 2 50 E
St-Gervais-les-Bains, France 29 C10 45 53N 6 42 E
St-Gildas, Pte. de, France 26 E4 47 8N 2 14W
St-Gilles, France 29 E8 43 40N 4 26 E
St-Gingolph, Switz. 32 D3 46 24N 6 48 E
St-Girons, Ariège, France 28 F5 42 59N 1 8 E
St-Girons, Landes, France 28 E2 43 56N 1 18W
St. Gotthard P. = San Gottardo, P. del, Switz. 33 C7 46 33N 8 33 E
St. Helena, Atl. Oc. 9 h 15 58 S 5 42W
St. Helena, U.S.A. 158 G2 38 30N 122 28W
St. Helena, Mt., U.S.A. 160 G4 38 40N 122 36W
St. Helena B., S. Africa 116 E2 32 40 S 18 10 E
St. Helena Sd., U.S.A. 152 C9 32 15N 80 25W
St. Helens, Australia 127 G4 41 20 S 148 15 E
St. Helens, U.K. 20 D5 53 27N 2 44W
St. Helens, U.S.A. 160 E4 45 52N 122 48W
St. Helens, Mt., U.S.A. 160 D4 46 12N 122 12W
St. Helier, U.K. 21 H5 49 10N 2 7W
St-Herblain, France 26 E5 47 13N 1 40W
St-Hilaire-du-Harcouët, France 26 D5 48 35N 1 5W
St-Hippolyte, France 27 E13 47 19N 6 50 E
St-Hippolyte-du-Fort, France 28 E7 43 58N 3 52 E
St-Honoré-les-Bains, France 27 F10 46 54N 3 50 E
St-Hubert, Belgium 24 D5 50 2N 5 23 E
St-Hyacinthe, Canada 140 C5 45 40N 72 58W
St. Ignace, U.S.A. 148 C3 45 52N 84 44W
St. Ignace I., Canada 140 C2 48 45N 88 0W
St. Ignatius, U.S.A. 158 C6 47 19N 114 6W
St-Imier, Switz. 32 B3 47 9N 6 58 E
St. Ives, U.K. 21 G2 50 12N 5 30W
St. James, France 26 D5 48 31N 1 20W
St. James, Minn., U.S.A. 154 D7 43 59N 94 38W
St. James, Mo., U.S.A. 156 G5 38 0N 91 37W
St-Jean →, Canada 141 B7 50 17N 64 20W
St-Jean, L., Canada 141 C5 48 40N 72 0W
St-Jean-d'Angély, France 28 C3 45 57N 0 31W
St-Jean-de-Braye, France 27 E8 47 53N 1 58 E
St-Jean-de-Luz, France 28 E2 43 23N 1 39W

St-Jean-de-Maurienne, France 29 C10 45 16N 6 21 E
St-Jean-de-Monts, France 26 F4 46 47N 2 4W
St-Jean-du-Gard, France 28 D7 44 7N 3 52 E
St-Jean-en-Royans, France 29 C9 45 1N 5 18 E
St-Jean-Pied-de-Port, France 28 E2 43 10N 1 14W
St-Jean-Port-Joli, Canada 141 C5 47 15N 70 13W
St-Jean-sur-Richelieu, Canada 140 C5 45 20N 73 20W
St-Jérôme, Canada 140 C5 45 47N 74 0W
St. Joe, U.S.A. 157 C12 41 19N 84 54W
St. John, Canada 141 C6 45 20N 66 8W
St. John, U.S.A. 155 G5 38 0N 98 46W
St. John →, Liberia 112 D2 6 40N 9 10W
St. John →, U.S.A. 149 C12 45 12N 66 5W
St. John, C., Canada 141 C8 50 0N 55 32W
St. John I., U.S. Virgin Is. 165 e 18 20N 64 42W
St. John's, Antigua 165 C7 17 6N 61 51W
St. John's, Canada 141 C9 47 35N 52 40W
St. Johns, Ariz., U.S.A. 159 J9 34 30N 109 22W
St. Johns, Mich., U.S.A. 157 B12 43 0N 84 33W
St. Johns →, U.S.A. 152 E8 30 24N 81 24W
St. John's Pt., Ireland 23 B3 54 34N 8 27W
St. Johnsbury, U.S.A. 151 B12 44 25N 72 1W
St. Johnsville, U.S.A. 151 D10 43 0N 74 43W
St-Joseph, Martinique 164 c 14 39N 61 4W
St-Joseph, N. Cal. 133 K4 20 27 S 166 36 E
St-Joseph, Réunion 121 c 21 22 S 55 37 E
St. Joseph, Ill., U.S.A. 157 D8 40 7N 88 2W
St. Joseph, La., U.S.A. 155 K9 31 55N 91 14W
St. Joseph, Mich., U.S.A. 157 B10 42 6N 86 29W
St. Joseph, Mo., U.S.A. 156 E2 39 46N 94 50W
St. Joseph →, U.S.A. 157 B10 42 7N 86 29W
St. Joseph, I., Canada 140 C3 46 12N 83 58W
St. Joseph, L., Canada 140 B1 51 10N 90 35W
St. Joseph Pt., U.S.A. 152 F4 29 52N 85 24W
St-Jovite, Canada 140 C5 46 8N 74 38W
St-Juéry, France 28 E6 43 57N 2 12 E
St. Julian's, Malta 38 F7 35 55N 14 29 E
St-Julien-Chapteuil, France 29 C8 45 2N 4 4 E
St-Julien-de-Vouvantes, France 26 E5 47 38N 1 13W
St-Julien-en-Genevois, France 27 F13 46 9N 6 5 E
St-Junien, France 28 C4 45 53N 0 55 E
St-Just-en-Chaussée, France 27 C9 49 30N 2 25 E
St-Just-en-Chevalet, France 28 C7 45 55N 3 50 E
St. Kilda, N.Z. 131 F5 45 53 S 170 31 E
St. Kilda, U.K. 19 C2 57 49N 8 34W
St. Kitts & Nevis ■, W. Indies 165 C7 17 20N 62 40W
St. Laurent, Canada 143 C9 50 25N 97 58W
St-Laurent, Fr. Guiana 169 B7 5 29N 54 3W
St-Laurent-de-la-Salanque, France 28 F6 42 46N 2 59 E
St-Laurent-du-Pont, France 29 C9 45 23N 5 45 E
St-Laurent-en-Grandvaux, France 27 F12 46 35N 5 58 E
St-Laurent-Médoc, France 28 C3 45 8N 0 49W
St. Lawrence, Australia 126 C4 22 16 S 149 31 E
St. Lawrence, Canada 141 C8 46 54N 55 23W
St. Lawrence →, Canada 141 C6 49 30N 66 0W
St. Lawrence, Gulf of, Canada 141 C7 48 25N 62 0W
St. Lawrence I., U.S.A. 144 E5 63 30N 170 30W
St. Leonard, Canada 141 C6 47 12N 67 58W
St-Léonard-de-Noblat, France 28 C5 45 49N 1 29 E
St. Leonhard im Pitztal, Austria 33 B11 47 4N 10 51 E
St-Leu, Réunion 121 c 21 9 S 55 18 E
St. Lewis →, Canada 141 B8 52 26N 56 11W
St-Lô, France 26 C5 49 7N 1 5W
St-Louis, France 27 E14 47 30N 7 34 E
St.-Louis, Guadeloupe 164 b 15 56N 61 19W
St-Louis, Réunion 121 c 21 16 S 55 25 E
St. Louis, Senegal 112 B1 16 8N 16 27W
St. Louis, U.S.A. 156 F6 38 37N 90 12W
St. Louis →, U.S.A. 154 B8 47 15N 92 45W
St-Loup-sur-Semouse, France 27 E13 47 53N 6 16 E
St. Lucia ■, W. Indies 165 f 14 0N 60 50W
St. Lucia, L., S. Africa 117 D5 28 5 S 32 30 E
St. Lucia Channel, W. Indies 165 D7 14 15N 61 0W
St. Lucie, U.S.A. 153 H9 27 29N 80 20W
St. Lucie Canal, U.S.A. 153 H9 27 10N 80 18W
St. Maarten, W. Indies 165 C7 18 0N 63 5W
St. Magnus B., U.K. 22 A7 60 25N 1 35W
St-Maixent-l'École, France 28 B3 46 24N 0 12W
St-Malo, France 26 D4 48 39N 2 1W
St-Malo, G. de, France 26 D4 48 50N 2 30W
St-Mandrier-sur-Mer, France 29 E9 43 4N 5 57 E
St-Marc, Haiti 165 C5 19 10N 72 41W
St-Marcellin, France 29 C9 45 9N 5 20 E
St-Marcouf, Îs., France 26 C5 49 30N 1 10W
St. Maries, U.S.A. 158 C5 47 19N 116 35W
St. Marks, U.S.A. 152 E5 30 9N 84 12W
St-Martin, W. Indies 165 C7 18 0N 63 0W
St-Martin, C., Martinique 164 c 14 52N 61 14W
St. Martin, L., Canada 143 C9 51 40N 98 30W
St-Martin-de-Crau, France 29 E8 43 38N 4 48 E
St-Martin-de-Ré, France 28 B2 46 12N 1 21W
St-Martin-d'Hères, France 29 C9 45 9N 5 45 E
St-Martin-Vésubie, France 29 D11 44 4N 7 15 E
St. Martins, Barbados 165 g 13 5N 59 28W
St-Martory, France 28 E4 43 9N 0 56 E
St. Mary, U.S.A. 156 G7 37 53N 89 57W
St. Mary, Mt., Papua N. G. 132 E4 8 8 S 147 2 E
St. Mary Is., India 95 H2 13 20N 74 35 E
St. Mary Pk., Australia 128 A3 31 32 S 138 34 E
St. Marys, Australia 127 G4 41 35 S 148 11 E
St. Marys, Canada 150 C3 43 20N 81 10W
St. Mary's, Corn., U.K. 21 H1 49 55N 6 18W
St. Mary's, Orkney, U.K. 22 C6 58 54N 2 54W
St. Mary's, Alaska, U.S.A. 144 E7 62 4N 163 10W
St. Marys, Ga., U.S.A. 152 E8 30 44N 81 33W
St. Marys, Ohio, U.S.A. 157 D12 40 33N 84 24W
St. Marys, Pa., U.S.A. 150 E6 41 26N 78 34W
St. Marys →, U.S.A. 152 E8 30 43N 81 27W
St. Mary's, C., Canada 141 C9 46 50N 54 12W
St. Mary's B., Canada 141 C9 46 50N 53 50W
St. Marys Bay, Canada 141 D6 44 25N 66 10W
St-Mathieu, Pte., France 26 D2 48 20N 4 45W
St. Matthew I., U.S.A. 144 F4 60 24N 172 42W
St. Matthews, Ky., U.S.A. 157 F11 38 15N 85 39W
St. Matthews, S.C., U.S.A. 152 B9 33 40N 80 46W
St. Matthews, I. = Zadetkyi Kyun, Burma 87 G1 10 0N 98 25 E
St. Matthias Group, Papua N. G. 132 A5 1 30 S 150 0 E
St-Maurice, Switz. 32 D4 46 13N 7 0 E
St-Maurice →, Canada 140 C5 46 21N 72 31W
St-Maximin-la-Ste-Baume, France 29 E9 43 27N 5 52 E
St-Médard-en-Jalles, France 28 D3 44 53N 0 43W
St-Méen-le-Grand, France 26 D4 48 11N 2 12W
St. Meinrad, U.S.A. 157 F10 38 10N 86 49W
St. Michael, U.S.A. 144 E7 63 29N 162 2W
St-Mihiel, France 27 D12 48 54N 5 32 E
St. Moritz, Switz. 31 J5 46 30N 9 51 E
St-Nazaire, France 26 E4 47 17N 2 12W
St. Neots, U.K. 21 E7 52 14N 0 15W
St-Nicolas-de-Port, France 27 D13 48 38N 6 18 E
St. Niklaas, Belgium 24 C4 51 10N 4 8 E
St. Niklaus, Switz. 32 D5 46 10N 7 49 E
St-Omer, France 27 B9 50 45N 2 15 E
St-Palais-sur-Mer, France 28 C2 45 38N 1 5W
St-Pamphile, Canada 141 C6 46 58N 69 48W
St-Pardoux-la-Rivière, France 28 C4 45 29N 0 45 E
St. Paris, U.S.A. 157 D13 40 8N 83 58W
St. Pascal, Canada 141 C6 47 32N 69 48W
St. Paul, Canada 142 C6 54 0N 111 17W
St-Paul, France 29 D10 44 31N 6 45 E
St-Paul, Réunion 121 c 20 59 S 55 17 E
St. Paul, Alaska, U.S.A. 144 H5 57 7N 170 17W
St. Paul, Ind., U.S.A. 157 E11 39 26N 85 38W
St. Paul, Minn., U.S.A. 154 C8 44 57N 93 6W
St. Paul, Nebr., U.S.A. 154 E5 41 13N 98 27W
St-Paul →, Canada 141 B8 51 27N 57 42W
St. Paul →, Liberia 112 D2 6 25N 10 48W
St. Paul, I., Ind. Oc. 121 H6 38 55 S 77 34 E
St-Paul-de-Fenouillet, France 28 F6 42 48N 2 30 E
St. Paul I., Canada 141 C7 47 12N 60 9W
St. Paul I., U.S.A. 144 H5 57 10N 170 15W
St-Paul-lès-Dax, France 28 E2 43 44N 1 3W
St. Paul's Bay, Malta 38 F7 35 57N 14 24 E
St-Péray, France 29 D8 44 57N 4 50 E
St. Peter, U.S.A. 154 C8 44 20N 93 57W
St. Peter-Ording, Germany 30 A4 54 20N 8 36 E
St. Peter Port, U.K. 21 H5 49 26N 2 33W
St. Peters, N.S., Canada 141 C7 45 40N 60 53W
St. Peters, P.E.I., Canada 141 C7 46 25N 62 35W
St. Petersburg = Sankt-Peterburg, Russia 58 C6 59 55N 30 20 E
St. Petersburg, U.S.A. 149 M4 27 46N 82 39W
St. Petersburg Beach, U.S.A. 153 H7 27 45N 82 45W
St-Philbert-de-Grand-Lieu, France 26 E5 47 2N 1 39W
St-Phillippe, Réunion 121 c 21 21 S 55 44 E
St-Pie, Canada 151 A12 45 30N 72 54W
St-Pierre, Martinique 164 c 14 45N 61 10W
St-Pierre, Réunion 121 c 21 19 S 55 28 E
St-Pierre, St- P. & M. 141 C8 46 46N 56 12W
St. Pierre, Seychelles 121 E3 9 20 S 46 0 E
St-Pierre, L., Canada 140 C5 46 12N 72 52W
St-Pierre-d'Oléron, France 28 C2 45 57N 1 19W
St-Pierre-en-Port, France 26 C7 49 48N 0 30 E
St-Pierre et Miquelon □, St- P. & M. 141 C8 46 55N 56 10W
St-Pierre-le-Moûtier, France 27 F10 46 47N 3 7 E
St-Pierre-sur-Dives, France 26 C6 49 2N 0 1W
St-Pol-de-Léon, France 26 D3 48 41N 4 0W
St-Pol-sur-Mer, France 27 A9 51 1N 2 20 E
St-Pol-sur-Ternoise, France 27 B9 50 23N 2 20 E
St-Pons, France 28 E6 43 30N 2 45 E
St-Pourçain-sur-Sioule, France 27 F10 46 18N 3 18 E
St-Priest, France 29 C8 45 42N 4 57 E
St-Quay-Portrieux, France 26 D4 48 39N 2 51W
St. Quentin, Canada 141 C6 47 30N 67 23W
St-Quentin, France 27 C10 49 50N 3 16 E
St-Rambert-d'Albon, France 29 C8 45 17N 4 49 E
St-Raphaël, France 29 E10 43 25N 6 46 E
St. Regis, U.S.A. 158 C6 47 18N 115 6W
St-Renan, France 26 D2 48 26N 4 37W
St. Robert, U.S.A. 156 G4 37 48N 92 9W
St-Saëns, France 26 C8 49 41N 1 16 E
St-Savin, France 28 B4 46 34N 0 53 E
St-Savinien, France 28 C3 45 53N 0 42W
St. Sebastien, Tanjon' i, Madag. 117 A8 12 26 S 48 44 E
St-Seine-l'Abbaye, France 27 E11 47 26N 4 47 E
St-Sernin-sur-Rance, France 28 E6 43 54N 2 35 E
St-Sever, France 28 E3 43 45N 0 35W
St-Siméon, Canada 141 C6 47 51N 69 54W
St. Simons I., U.S.A. 152 D8 31 12N 81 15W
St. Simons Island, U.S.A. 149 K5 31 9N 81 22W
St. Stephen, Canada 141 C6 45 16N 67 17W
St. Stephen, U.S.A. 152 B10 33 24N 79 55W
St-Sulpice, France 28 E5 43 46N 1 41 E
St-Sulpice-Laurière, France 28 B5 46 3N 1 29 E
St-Sulpice-les-Feuilles, France 28 B5 46 19N 1 21 E
St-Syprien = St-Cyprien, France 28 F7 42 37N 3 2 E
St-Thégonnec, France 26 D3 48 31N 3 57W
St. Thomas, Canada 140 D3 42 45N 81 10W
St. Thomas Bay, Malta 38 F8 35 51N 14 34 E
St. Thomas I., U.S. Virgin Is. 165 e 18 20N 64 55W
St-Tite, Canada 140 C5 46 45N 72 34W
St-Tropez, France 29 E10 43 17N 6 38 E
St. Troud = St. Truiden, Belgium 24 D5 50 48N 5 10 E
St. Truiden, Belgium 24 D5 50 48N 5 10 E
St-Vaast-la-Hougue, France 26 C5 49 35N 1 17W
St-Valery-en-Caux, France 26 C7 49 52N 0 43 E
St-Valéry-sur-Somme, France 27 B8 50 11N 1 38 E
St-Vallier, France 27 F11 46 38N 4 22 E
St-Vallier-de-Thiey, France 29 E10 43 42N 6 51 E
St-Varent, France 26 F6 46 53N 0 13W
St-Vaury, France 28 B5 46 12N 1 46 E
St. Vincent = São Vicente, C. Verde Is. 9 j 17 0N 25 0W
St. Vincent, Italy 44 C4 45 45N 7 39 E
St. Vincent, G., Australia 128 C3 35 0 S 138 0 E
St. Vincent & the Grenadines ■, W. Indies 165 D7 13 0N 61 10W
St-Vincent-de-Tyrosse, France 28 E2 43 39N 1 19W
St. Vincent Passage, W. Indies 165 D7 13 30N 61 0W
St-Vith, Belgium 24 D6 50 17N 6 9 E
St-Vivien-de-Médoc, France 28 C2 45 25N 1 2W
St. Walburg, Canada 143 C7 53 39N 109 12W
St-Yrieix-la-Perche, France 28 C5 45 31N 1 12 E
Saintala, India 94 D6 20 26N 83 20 E
Ste-Adresse, France 26 C7 49 31N 0 5 E
Ste-Agathe-des-Monts, Canada 140 C5 46 3N 74 17W
Ste-Anne, Guadeloupe 164 b 16 13N 61 24W
Ste Anne, Seychelles 121 b 4 36 S 55 1 E
Ste-Anne, L., Canada 141 B6 50 0N 67 42W
Ste-Anne-des-Monts, Canada 141 C6 49 8N 66 30W
Ste-Croix, Switz. 32 C3 46 49N 6 34 E
Ste-Enimie, France 28 D7 44 22N 3 26 E
Ste-Foy-la-Grande, France 28 D4 44 50N 0 13 E
Ste. Genevieve, U.S.A. 156 G6 37 59N 90 2W
Ste-Hermine, France 28 B2 46 32N 1 4W
Ste-Livrade-sur-Lot, France 28 D4 44 24N 0 36 E
Ste-Marguerite →, Canada 141 B6 50 9N 66 36W
Ste. Marie, Gabon 114 C2 3 48 S 11 1 E
Ste-Marie, Martinique 164 c 14 48N 61 1W
Ste-Marie, Réunion 121 c 20 53 S 55 33 E
Ste-Marie-aux-Mines, France 27 D14 48 15N 7 12 E
Ste-Marie de la Madeleine, Canada 141 C5 46 26N 71 0W
Ste-Maure-de-Touraine, France 26 E7 47 7N 0 37 E
Ste-Maxime, France 29 E10 43 19N 6 39 E
Ste-Menehould, France 27 C11 49 5N 4 54 E
Ste-Mère-Église, France 26 C5 49 24N 1 19W
Ste-Rose, Guadeloupe 164 b 16 20N 61 45W
Ste-Rose, Réunion 121 c 21 8 S 55 45 E
Ste. Rose du Lac, Canada 143 C9 51 4N 99 30W
Ste-Savine, France 27 D11 48 18N 4 3 E
Ste-Sigolène, France 29 C8 45 15N 4 14 E
Saintes, France 28 C3 45 45N 0 37W
Saintes, I. des, Guadeloupe 164 b 15 50N 61 35W
Stes-Maries-de-la-Mer, France 29 E8 43 26N 4 26 E
Saintfield, U.K. 23 B6 54 28N 5 49W
Saintonge, France 28 C3 45 40N 0 50W
Saipan, Pac. Oc. 134 F6 15 12N 145 45 E
Sairang, India 90 D4 23 50N 92 45 E
Sairecábur, Cerro, Bolivia 174 A2 22 43 S 67 54W
Saitama □, Japan 73 A11 36 25N 139 30 E
Saiteli = Kadınhanı, Turkey 100 C5 38 14N 32 13 E
Saiți, Moldova 53 D14 46 30N 29 24 E
Saito, Japan 72 E3 32 3N 131 24 E
Saiyid, Pakistan 92 C5 33 7N 73 2 E
Sajama, Bolivia 172 D4 18 7 S 69 0W
Sajama, Nevado, Bolivia 172 D4 18 6 S 68 54W
Sajan, Serbia, Yug. 52 E5 45 50N 20 20 E
Sajó →, Hungary 52 C6 47 56N 21 7 E
Sajószentpéter, Hungary 52 B5 48 12N 20 44 E
Sajum, India 93 C8 33 20N 79 0 E
Sak →, S. Africa 116 E3 30 52 S 20 25 E
Saka Kalat, Pakistan 91 D2 27 3N 65 3 E
Sakaba, Nigeria 113 C6 11 4N 5 35 E
Sakai, Japan 73 C7 34 30N 135 30 E
Sakaide, Japan 72 C5 34 19N 133 50 E
Sakaiminato, Japan 72 B5 35 38N 133 11 E
Sakākah, Si. Arabia 96 D4 30 0N 40 8 E
Sakakawea, L., U.S.A. 154 B4 47 30N 101 25W
Sakami →, Canada 140 B4 53 40N 76 40W
Sakami, L., Canada 140 B4 53 15N 77 0W
Sâkâne, 'Erg i-n, Mali 113 A4 20 30N 1 30W
Sakania, Dem. Rep. of the Congo 119 E2 12 43 S 28 30 E
Sakar I., Papua N. G. 132 C5 5 25 S 148 6 E
Sakaraha, Madag. 117 C7 22 55 S 44 32 E
Sakarya, Turkey 100 B4 40 48N 30 25 E
Sakarya →, Turkey 100 B4 41 7N 30 39 E
Sakashima-Guntō, Japan 71 M2 24 46N 124 0 E
Sakassou, Ivory C. 112 D3 7 29N 5 19W
Sakata, Japan 70 E9 38 55N 139 50 E
Sakawa, Japan 72 D5 33 28N 133 11 E
Sakchu, N. Korea 75 D13 40 23N 125 2 E
Sakeny →, Madag. 117 C8 20 0 S 45 25 E
Sakété, Benin 113 D5 6 40N 2 45 E
Sakha □, Russia 67 C13 66 0N 130 0 E
Sakhalin, Russia 67 D15 51 0N 143 0 E
Sakhalinskiy Zaliv, Russia 67 D15 54 0N 141 0 E
Sakhi Gopal, India 94 E7 19 58N 85 50 E
Şaki, Azerbaijan 61 K8 41 10N 47 5 E
Šakiai, Lithuania 15 J20 54 59N 23 2 E
Sakmara →, Russia 64 F5 51 46N 55 1 E
Sakoli, India 94 D4 21 5N 79 59 E
Sakon Nakhon, Thailand 86 D5 17 10N 104 9 E
Sakrand, Pakistan 92 F3 26 10N 68 15 E
Sakri, Maharashtra, India 93 F12 26 13N 86 5 E
Sakri, Maharashtra, India 94 D2 21 2N 74 20 E
Sakrivier, S. Africa 116 E3 30 54 S 20 28 E
Sakskøbing, Denmark 17 K5 54 49N 11 39 E
Sakti, India 93 H10 22 2N 82 58 E
Saku, Japan 73 A10 36 17N 138 31 E
Sakuma, Japan 73 B9 35 3N 137 49 E
Sakura, Japan 73 B12 35 43N 140 14 E
Sakurai, Japan 73 C7 34 30N 135 51 E
Saky, Ukraine 59 K7 45 9N 33 34 E
Sal →, Russia 61 G5 47 31N 40 45 E
Sal Rei, C. Verde Is. 9 j 16 11N 22 53W
Sala, Eritrea 107 D4 16 53N 37 36 E
Šal'a, Slovak Rep. 35 C10 48 10N 17 50 E
Sala, Sweden 16 E10 59 58N 16 35 E
Sala →, Eritrea 107 D4 16 53N 37 36 E
Sala, O. →, Chad 109 E4 17 0N 20 53 E
Sala Consilina, Italy 47 B8 40 23N 15 36 E
Sala-y-Gómez, Pac. Oc. 135 K17 26 28 S 105 28W
Salaberry-de-Valleyfield, Canada 140 C5 45 15N 74 8W
Saladas, Argentina 174 B4 28 15 S 58 40W
Saladillo, Argentina 174 D4 35 40 S 59 55W
Salado →, Buenos Aires, Argentina 174 D4 35 44 S 57 22W
Salado →, La Pampa, Argentina 176 A3 37 30 S 67 0W
Salado →, Río Negro, Argentina 176 B3 41 34 S 65 3W
Salado →, Santa Fe, Argentina 174 C3 31 40 S 60 41W
Salado →, Mexico 155 M5 26 52N 99 19W
Salaga, Ghana 113 D4 8 31N 0 31W
Sālah, Syria 103 C5 32 40N 36 45 E
Sălaj □, Romania 52 C8 47 15N 23 0 E
Sálakhos, Greece 38 E11 36 17N 27 57 E
Salal, Chad 109 F3 14 48N 17 12 E
Salala, Liberia 112 D2 6 42N 10 7W
Salala, Sudan 106 C4 21 17N 36 16 E
Salālah, Oman 99 C6 16 56N 53 59 E
Salamanca, Chile 174 C1 31 46 S 70 59W
Salamanca, Spain 42 E5 40 58N 5 39W
Salamanca, U.S.A. 150 D6 42 10N 78 43W
Salamanca □, Spain 42 E5 40 57N 5 40W
Salamat, Bahr →, Chad 109 G3 9 20N 18 0 E
Salāmatābād, Iran 96 C5 35 39N 47 50 E
Salamina, Colombia 168 B2 5 25N 75 29W
Salamis, Cyprus 39 E9 35 11N 33 54 E
Salamís, Greece 48 D5 37 56N 23 30 E
Salamonie L., U.S.A. 157 D11 40 46N 85 37W
Salaóra, Greece 39 A2 39 2N 20 52 E
Salar de Atacama, Chile 174 A2 23 30 S 68 25W
Salar de Uyuni, Bolivia 172 E4 20 30 S 67 45W
Sălard, Romania 52 C7 47 12N 22 3 E
Salas, Spain 42 B4 43 25N 6 15W
Salas de los Infantes, Spain 42 C7 42 2N 3 17W
Salatiga, Indonesia 85 D4 7 19 S 110 30 E
Salavat, Russia 64 E5 53 21N 55 55 E
Salaverry, Peru 172 B2 8 15 S 79 0W
Salawati, Indonesia 83 B4 1 7 S 130 52 E
Salaya, India 92 H3 22 19N 69 35 E
Salayar, Indonesia 82 C2 6 7 S 120 30 E
Salazar →, Spain 40 C3 42 40N 1 20W
Salbris, France 27 E9 47 25N 2 3 E
Salcedo, Phil. 81 F5 11 9N 125 40 E
Salcia, Romania 53 G9 43 56N 24 55 E
Sălciua, Romania 53 D8 46 24N 23 26 E
Salcombe, U.K. 21 G4 50 14N 3 47W
Saldaña, Spain 42 C6 42 32N 4 48W
Saldanha, S. Africa 116 E2 33 0 S 17 58 E
Saldanha B., S. Africa 116 E2 33 6 S 18 0 E
Saldus, Latvia 15 H20 56 38N 22 30 E
Saldus □, Latvia 54 B9 56 35N 22 30 E
Sale, Australia 129 E7 38 6 S 147 6 E
Sale, Burma 90 E5 20 50N 94 45 E
Sale, Italy 44 D5 44 59N 8 48 E
Salé, Morocco 110 B3 34 3N 6 48W
Sale, U.K. 20 D5 53 26N 2 19W
Sale City, U.S.A. 152 D5 31 16N 84 1W
Salekhard, Russia 66 C7 66 30N 66 35 E
Salelologa, Samoa 133 W23 13 41 S 172 11W
Salem, India 95 J4 11 40N 78 11 E
Salem, Fla., U.S.A. 152 F6 29 53N 83 25W
Salem, Ill., U.S.A. 156 F8 38 38N 88 57W
Salem, Ind., U.S.A. 157 F10 38 36N 86 6W
Salem, Mass., U.S.A. 151 D14 42 31N 70 53W
Salem, Mo., U.S.A. 155 G9 37 39N 91 32W
Salem, N.H., U.S.A. 151 D13 42 45N 71 12W
Salem, N.J., U.S.A. 148 F8 39 34N 75 28W
Salem, N.Y., U.S.A. 151 C11 43 10N 73 20W
Salem, Ohio, U.S.A. 150 F4 40 54N 80 52W
Salem, Oreg., U.S.A. 158 D2 44 56N 123 2W
Salem, S. Dak., U.S.A. 154 D6 43 44N 97 23W
Salem, Va., U.S.A. 148 G5 37 18N 80 3W
Salemi, Italy 46 E5 37 49N 12 48 E
Sälen, Sweden 16 C7 61 15N 13 22 E
Salernes, France 29 E10 43 34N 6 15 E
Salerno, Italy 47 B7 40 41N 14 47 E
Salerno, G. di, Italy 47 B7 40 32N 14 42 E
Sales, Brazil 169 D5 4 2 S 63 40W
Salford, U.K. 20 D5 53 30N 2 18W
Salgir →, Ukraine 59 K8 45 38N 35 1 E
Salgótarján, Hungary 52 B4 48 5N 19 47 E
Salgueiro, Brazil 170 C4 8 4 S 39 6W
Salher, India 94 D1 20 40N 73 55 E
Salhus, Norway 18 D2 60 30N 5 15 E
Salibabu, Indonesia 79 D7 3 51N 126 40 E
Salibea, Trin. & Tob. 169 K9 10 43N 61 2W
Salida, U.S.A. 146 C5 38 32N 106 0W
Salies-de-Béarn, France 28 E3 43 28N 0 56W
Şalif, Yemen 98 D3 15 18N 42 41 E
Salihli, Turkey 100 C3 38 28N 28 8 E
Salihorsk, Belarus 59 F4 52 51N 27 27 E
Salin, Burma 90 E5 20 35N 94 40 E
Salina, Italy 47 D7 38 34N 14 50 E
Salina, Kans., U.S.A. 154 F6 38 50N 97 37W
Salina, Utah, U.S.A. 159 G8 38 58N 111 51W
Salina Cruz, Mexico 163 D5 16 10N 95 10W
Salinas, Brazil 171 E3 16 10 S 42 10W
Salinas, Chile 174 A2 23 31 S 69 29W
Salinas, Ecuador 168 D1 2 10 S 80 58W
Salinas, U.S.A. 160 J5 36 40N 121 39W
Salinas →, Guatemala 163 D6 16 28N 90 31W
Salinas →, U.S.A. 160 J5 36 45N 121 48W
Salinas, B. das, Angola 115 E2 14 11 S 12 21 E
Salinas, B. de, Nic. 164 D2 11 4N 85 45W
Salinas, Pampa de las, Argentina 174 C2 31 58 S 66 42W
Salinas Ambargasta, Argentina 174 B3 29 0 S 65 0W
Salinas de Hidalgo, Mexico 162 C4 22 30N 101 40W
Salinas Grandes, Argentina 174 C3 30 0 S 65 0W
Saline, U.S.A. 157 B13 42 10N 83 47W
Saline →, Ark., U.S.A. 155 J8 33 10N 92 8W
Saline →, Kans., U.S.A. 154 F6 38 52N 97 30W
Salines, C. de ses, Spain 38 B4 39 16N 3 4 E
Salinópolis, Brazil 170 B2 0 40 S 47 20W
Salins-les-Bains, France 27 F12 46 58N 5 52 E
Salir, Portugal 43 H2 37 14N 8 2W
Salisbury = Harare, Zimbabwe 119 F3 17 43 S 31 2 E
Salisbury, U.K. 21 F6 51 4N 1 47W
Salisbury, Md., U.S.A. 148 F8 38 22N 75 36W
Salisbury, Mo., U.S.A. 156 E4 39 25N 92 48W
Salisbury, N.C., U.S.A. 149 H5 35 40N 80 29W
Salisbury I., Canada 139 B12 63 30N 77 0W
Salisbury Plain, U.K. 21 F6 51 14N 1 55W
Săliște, Romania 53 E8 45 45N 23 56 E
Salitre →, Brazil 170 C3 9 29 S 40 39W
Salka, Nigeria 113 C5 10 20N 4 58 E
Salkehatchie →, U.S.A. 152 C9 32 37N 80 53W
Şalkhad, Syria 103 C5 32 29N 36 43 E
Salla, Finland 14 C23 66 50N 28 49 E
Sallanches, France 29 C10 45 55N 6 38 E
Sallent, Spain 40 D6 41 49N 1 54 E
Salles, France 28 D3 44 33N 0 52W
Salles-Curan, France 28 D6 44 11N 2 48 E
Salling, Denmark 17 H2 56 40N 8 55 E
Salliq, Canada 139 B11 64 8N 83 10W
Sallisaw, U.S.A. 155 H7 35 28N 94 47W
Sallom Junction, Sudan 106 D4 19 17N 37 6 E
Salluit, Canada 139 B12 62 14N 75 38W
Salmās, Iran 101 C11 38 11N 44 47 E
Salmerón, Spain 40 E2 40 33N 2 29W
Salmo, Canada 142 D5 49 10N 117 20W
Salmon, U.S.A. 158 D7 45 11N 113 54W
Salmon →, Canada 142 C4 54 3N 122 40W
Salmon →, U.S.A. 158 D5 45 51N 116 47W
Salmon Arm, Canada 142 C5 50 40N 119 15W
Salmon Gums, Australia 125 F3 32 59 S 121 38 E
Salmon River Mts., U.S.A. 158 D6 45 0N 114 30W
Salo, C.A.R. 114 B3 3 10N 16 8 E
Salo, Finland 15 F20 60 22N 23 10 E
Salò, Italy 44 C7 45 36N 10 31 E
Salobreña, Spain 43 J7 36 44N 3 35W
Salome, U.S.A. 161 M13 33 47N 113 37W
Salon, India 93 F9 26 2N 81 27 E
Salon-de-Provence, France 29 E9 43 39N 5 6 E
Salonga →, Dem. Rep. of the Congo 114 C4 0 10 S 19 50 E
Salonga-Nord, Parc Nat. de la, Dem. Rep. of the Congo 114 C4 1 55 S 21 45 E
Salonga-Sud, Parc Nat. de la, Dem. Rep. of the Congo 114 C4 2 25 S 21 0 E
Salonica = Thessaloníki, Greece 50 F6 40 38N 22 58 E
Salonta, Romania 52 D6 46 49N 21 42 E
Salor →, Spain 43 F3 39 39N 7 3W
Salou, Spain 40 D6 41 4N 1 8 E
Salou, C. de, Spain 40 D6 41 3N 1 10 E
Saloum →, Senegal 112 C1 13 50N 16 45W
Salpausselkä, Finland 15 F22 61 0N 27 0 E
Salsacate, Argentina 174 C2 31 20 S 65 5W
Salses, France 28 F6 42 50N 2 55 E
Salsette I., India 94 E1 19 5N 72 50 E
Salsk, Russia 61 G5 46 28N 41 30 E
Salso →, Italy 46 E6 37 6N 13 57 E
Salsomaggiore Terme, Italy 44 D6 44 49N 9 59 E
Salt, Spain 40 D7 41 59N 2 47 E
Salt →, Canada 142 B6 60 0N 112 25W
Salt →, Ariz., U.S.A. 159 K7 33 23N 112 19W
Salt →, Mo., U.S.A. 156 E5 39 28N 91 4W
Salt Cay, Bahamas 9 b 26 6N 77 18W
Salt L., U.S.A. 145 K14 21 21N 157 55W
Salt Lake City, U.S.A. 158 F8 40 45N 111 53W
Salt Range, Pakistan 92 C5 32 30N 72 25 E
Salt Springs, U.S.A. 153 F8 29 21N 81 44W
Salta, Argentina 174 A2 24 57 S 65 25W
Salta □, Argentina 174 A2 24 48 S 65 30W
Saltara, Italy 45 E9 43 45N 12 50 E
Saltash, U.K. 21 G3 50 24N 4 14W
Saltburn by the Sea, U.K. 20 C7 54 35N 0 58W
Saltcoats, U.K. 22 F4 55 38N 4 47W
Saltee Is., Ireland 23 D5 52 7N 6 37W
Salters, U.S.A. 152 B10 33 36N 79 51W
Saltfjellet, Norway 14 C16 66 40N 15 15 E
Saltfjorden, Norway 14 C16 67 15N 14 10 E
Saltholm, Denmark 17 J6 55 38N 12 43 E
Salthólmavík, Iceland 11 B5 65 24N 21 57W
Saltillo, Mexico 162 B4 25 25N 101 0W
Salto, Argentina 174 C3 34 20 S 60 15W
Salto, Uruguay 174 C4 31 27 S 57 50W
Salto da Divisa, Brazil 171 E4 16 0 S 39 57W
Salto del Guaíra, Paraguay 175 A5 24 3 S 54 17W
Salton City, U.S.A. 161 M11 33 29N 115 51W
Salton Sea, U.S.A. 161 M11 33 15N 115 45W
Saltpond, Ghana 113 D4 5 15N 1 3W
Saltrød, Norway 18 F5 58 30N 8 49 E
Saltsburg, U.S.A. 150 F5 40 29N 79 27W
Saltsjöbaden, Sweden 16 E12 59 15N 18 20 E
Saluda, U.S.A. 152 A8 34 0N 81 46W
Saluda →, U.S.A. 149 J5 34 1N 81 4W
Salug, Phil. 81 G4 8 7N 122 47 E
Salûm, Egypt 106 A2 31 31N 25 7 E
Salûm, Khâlig el, Egypt 106 A2 31 35N 25 24 E
Salur, India 94 E6 18 27N 83 18 E
Salut, Is. du, Fr. Guiana 169 B7 5 15N 52 35W
Saluzzo, Italy 44 D4 44 39N 7 29 E
Salvación, B., Chile 176 D1 50 50 S 75 10W
Salvador, Brazil 171 D4 13 0 S 38 30W
Salvador, Canada 143 C7 52 10N 109 32W
Salvador, L., U.S.A. 155 L9 29 43N 90 15W
Salvaterra, Brazil 170 B2 0 46 S 48 31W
Salvaterra de Magos, Portugal 43 F2 39 1N 8 47W
Salvisa, U.S.A. 157 G12 37 54N 84 51W
Sálvora, I. de, Spain 42 C2 42 30N 8 58W
Salween →, Burma 90 G6 16 31N 97 37 E
Salyan, Azerbaijan 101 C13 39 33N 48 59 E
Salza →, Austria 34 D7 47 40N 14 43 E
Salzach →, Austria 34 C5 48 12N 12 56 E
Salzburg, Austria 34 D6 47 48N 13 2 E
Salzburg □, Austria 34 D6 47 15N 13 0 E
Salzgitter, Germany 30 C6 52 9N 10 19 E
Salzkotten, Germany 30 D4 51 40N 8 37 E
Salzwedel, Germany 30 C7 52 52N 11 10 E
Sam, Gabon 114 B2 0 58N 11 16 E

Sam, *India* **92 F4** 26 50N 70 31 E
Sam Neua, *Laos* **76 G5** 20 29N 104 5 E
Sam Ngao, *Thailand* **86 D2** 17 18N 99 0 E
Sam Rayburn Reservoir, *U.S.A.* **155 K7** 31 4N 94 5W
Sam Son, *Vietnam* **86 C5** 19 44N 105 54 E
Sam Teu, *Laos* **86 C5** 19 59N 104 38 E
Sama de Langreo = Langreo, *Spain* **42 B5** 43 18N 5 40W
Samacimbo, *Angola* **115 E3** 13 33 S 16 59 E
Samagaltay, *Russia* **67 D10** 50 36N 95 3 E
Samā'il, *Oman* **99 B7** 23 40N 57 50 E
Samaipata, *Bolivia* **173 D5** 18 9 S 63 52W
Samal, *Phil.* **81 H5** 7 5N 125 42 E
Samal I., *Phil.* **81 H5** 7 3N 125 44 E
Samales Group, *Phil.* **81 J3** 6 0N 122 0 E
Samalkot, *India* **94 F6** 17 3N 82 13 E
Samâlût, *Egypt* **106 B3** 28 20N 30 42 E
Samana, *India* **92 D7** 30 10N 76 13 E
Samana Cay, *Bahamas* **165 B5** 23 3N 73 45W
Samandağı, *Turkey* **100 D6** 36 5N 35 59 E
Samandıra, *Turkey* **51 F13** 40 59N 29 13 E
Samanga, *Tanzania* **119 D4** 8 20 S 39 13 E
Samangān □, *Afghan.* **91 A3** 36 15N 68 3 E
Samangwa, *Dem. Rep. of the Congo* **118 C1** 4 23 S 24 10 E
Samani, *Japan* **70 C11** 42 7N 142 56 E
Samanli Dağları, *Turkey* **51 F13** 40 32N 29 10 E
Samar, *Phil.* **81 E5** 12 0N 125 0 E
Samar □, *Phil.* **81 F5** 11 50N 125 0 E
Samar Sea, *Phil.* **80 E5** 12 0N 124 15 E
Samara, *Russia* **60 D10** 53 8N 50 6 E
Samara →, *Russia* **60 D10** 53 10N 50 4 E
Samara →, *Ukraine* **59 H8** 48 28N 35 7 E
Samarai, *Papua N. G.* **132 F6** 10 39 S 150 41 E
Samaria = Shōmrōn, *West Bank* **103 C4** 32 15N 35 13 E
Samariá, *Greece* **39 E4** 35 17N 23 58 E
Samariapo, *Venezuela* **168 B4** 5 15N 67 48W
Samarinda, *Indonesia* **85 C5** 0 30 S 117 9 E
Samarkand = Samarqand, *Uzbekistan* **66 F7** 39 40N 66 55 E
Samarqand, *Uzbekistan* **66 F7** 39 40N 66 55 E
Sāmarrā, *Iraq* **101 E10** 34 12N 43 52 E
Samastipur, *India* **93 G11** 25 50N 85 50 E
Samate, *Indonesia* **83 B4** 0 58 S 131 4 E
Samaúma, *Brazil* **173 B5** 7 50 S 60 2W
Şamaxi, *Azerbaijan* **61 K9** 40 38N 48 37 E
Samba, *Équateur, Dem. Rep. of the Congo* **114 B4** 0 13N 21 25 E
Samba, *Maniema, Dem. Rep. of the Congo* **118 C2** 4 38 S 26 22 E
Samba, *India* **93 C6** 32 32N 75 10 E
Samba Caju, *Angola* **115 D3** 8 46 S 15 24 E
Sambaíba, *Brazil* **170 C2** 7 8 S 45 21W
Sambalpur, *India* **94 D7** 21 28N 84 4 E
Sambar, Tanjung, *Indonesia* **85 C4** 2 59 S 110 19 E
Sambas, *Indonesia* **85 B3** 1 20N 109 20 E
Sambava, *Madag.* **117 A9** 14 16 S 50 10 E
Sambawizi, *Zimbabwe* **119 F2** 18 24 S 26 13 E
Sambhal, *India* **93 E8** 28 35N 78 37 E
Sambhar, *India* **92 F6** 26 52N 75 6 E
Sambhar L., *India* **92 F6** 26 55N 75 12 E
Sambiase, *Italy* **47 D9** 38 58N 16 17 E
Sambir, *Ukraine* **59 H2** 49 30N 23 10 E
Sambo, *Angola* **115 E3** 13 3 S 16 8 E
Sambor, *Cambodia* **86 F6** 12 46N 106 0 E
Samborombón, B., *Argentina* **174 D4** 36 5 S 57 20W
Sambuca di Sicília, *Italy* **46 E6** 37 39N 13 7 E
Samburu Nat. Reserve, *Kenya* **118 B4** 0 37N 37 31 E
Samch'ŏk, *S. Korea* **75 F15** 37 30N 129 10 E
Samch'onp'o, *S. Korea* **75 G15** 35 0N 128 6 E
Same, *Tanzania* **118 C4** 4 2 S 37 38 E
Samedan, *Switz.* **33 C9** 46 32N 9 52 E
Samer, *France* **27 B8** 50 38N 1 44 E
Samfya, *Zambia* **119 E2** 11 22 S 29 31 E
Samḩān, Jabal, *Oman* **99 C6** 17 12N 54 55 E
Sámi, *Greece* **39 C2** 38 15N 20 39 E
Samka, *Burma* **90 E6** 20 9N 96 57 E
Şämkir, *Azerbaijan* **61 K8** 40 50N 46 0 E
Şamlı, *Turkey* **49 B9** 39 48N 27 51 E
Sammanturai, *Sri Lanka* **95 L5** 7 36N 81 39 E
Samnah, *Si. Arabia* **96 E3** 25 10N 37 15 E
Samnaun, *Switz.* **33 C10** 46 57N 10 22 E
Samnū, *Libya* **108 C2** 27 15N 14 55 E
Samo Alto, *Chile* **174 C1** 30 22 S 71 0W
Samoa ■, *Pac. Oc.* **133 X24** 14 0 S 172 0W
Samoan Is., *Pac. Oc.* **133 X24** 14 0 S 171 0W
Samobor, *Croatia* **45 C12** 45 47N 15 44 E
Samoëns, *France* **27 F13** 46 5N 6 45 E
Samokov, *Bulgaria* **50 D7** 42 18N 23 35 E
Šamorín, *Slovak Rep.* **35 C10** 48 2N 17 19 E
Samorogouan, *Burkina Faso* **112 C4** 11 21N 4 57W
Sámos, *Greece* **49 D8** 37 45N 26 50 E
Samoš, *Serbia, Yug.* **52 E5** 45 13N 20 46 E
Samos, *Spain* **42 C3** 42 44N 7 20W
Sámos □, *Greece* **49 D8** 37 45N 26 50 E
Samoset, *U.S.A.* **153 H7** 27 28N 82 33W
Samosir, *Indonesia* **84 B1** 2 55N 98 50 E
Samothráki = Mathráki, *Greece* **38 B9** 39 48N 19 31 E
Samothráki, *Évros, Greece* **51 F9** 40 28N 25 28 E
Samothráki, *Évros, Greece* **51 F9** 40 28N 25 28 E
Samoylovka, *Russia* **60 E6** 51 12N 43 43 E
Sampa, *Angola* **115 E3** 10 38 S 18 56 E
Sampa, *Ghana* **112 D4** 8 0N 2 36W
Sampacho, *Argentina* **174 C3** 33 20 S 64 50W
Sampalan, *Indonesia* **79 K18** 8 41 S 115 34 E
Sampang, *Indonesia* **85 D4** 7 11 S 113 13 E
Samper de Calanda, *Spain* **40 D4** 41 11N 0 28W
Sampéyre, *Italy* **44 D4** 44 34N 7 11 E
Sampit, *Indonesia* **85 C4** 2 34 S 113 0 E
Sampit →, *Indonesia* **85 C4** 2 44 S 112 54 E
Sampit, Teluk, *Indonesia* **85 C4** 3 5 S 113 3 E
Sampsoús, *Greece* **39 A2** 39 5N 20 45 E
Sampun, *Papua N. G.* **132 C7** 5 21 S 152 8 E
Samrong, *Cambodia* • **86 E4** 14 15N 103 30 E
Samrong, *Thailand* **86 E3** 15 10N 100 40 E
Samsø, *Denmark* **17 J4** 55 50N 10 35 E
Samsø Bælt, *Denmark* **17 J4** 55 45N 10 45 E
Samson, *U.S.A.* **152 D3** 31 7N 86 3W
Samsun, *Turkey* **100 B7** 41 15N 36 22 E
Samtredia, *Georgia* **61 J6** 42 7N 42 24 E
Samui, Ko, *Thailand* **87 b** 9 30N 100 0 E
Samur →, *Russia* **61 K9** 41 53N 48 32 E
Samurskiy Khrebet, *Russia* **61 K8** 41 55N 47 11 E
Samusole, *Dem. Rep. of the Congo* **119 E1** 10 2 S 24 0 E
Samut Prakan, *Thailand* **86 F3** 13 32N 100 40 E
Samut Songkhram →, *Thailand* **78 B1** 13 24N 100 1 E
Samwari, *Pakistan* **92 E2** 28 30N 66 46 E
San, *Mali* **112 C4** 13 15N 4 57W
San →, *Cambodia* **86 F5** 13 32N 105 57 E
San →, *Poland* **55 H8** 50 45N 21 51 E
San Adrián, *Spain* **40 C3** 42 20N 1 56W
San Adrián, C. de, *Spain* **42 B2** 43 21N 8 50W
San Agustín, *Colombia* **168 C2** 1 53N 76 16W
San Agustin, *Phil.* **80 E4** 12 34N 122 6 E
San Agustin, C., *Phil.* **81 H6** 6 20N 126 13 E
San Agustín de Valle Fértil, *Argentina* **174 C2** 30 35 S 67 30W
San Ambrosio, *Pac. Oc.* **135 K20** 26 28 S 79 53W
San Andreas, *U.S.A.* **160 G6** 38 12N 120 41W
San Andres, *Catanduanes, Phil.* **80 E5** 13 36N 124 6 E
San Andres, *Romblon, Phil.* **80 E4** 13 19N 122 41 E
San Andres, *Romblon, Phil.* **80 E4** 12 31N 122 2 E
San Andrés, I. de, *Caribbean* **164 D3** 12 42N 81 46W
San Andrês del Rabanedo, *Spain* **42 C5** 42 37N 5 36W
San Andres Mts., *U.S.A.* **159 K10** 33 0N 106 30W
San Andrés Tuxtla, *Mexico* **163 D5** 18 30N 95 20W
San Angelo, *U.S.A.* **155 K4** 31 28N 100 26W
San Anselmo, *U.S.A.* **160 H4** 37 59N 122 34W
San Antonio, *Belize* **163 D7** 16 15N 89 2W
San Antonio, *Chile* **174 C1** 33 40 S 71 40W
San Antonio, *Phil.* **80 D3** 14 57N 120 5 E
San Antonio, *N. Mex., U.S.A.* **159 K10** 33 55N 106 52W
San Antonio, *Tex., U.S.A.* **155 L5** 29 25N 98 30W
San Antonio, *Venezuela* **168 C4** 3 30N 66 44W
San Antonio →, *U.S.A.* **155 L6** 28 30N 96 54W
San Antonio, C., *Argentina* **174 D4** 36 15 S 56 40W
San Antonio, C., *Cuba* **164 B3** 21 50N 84 57W
San Antonio, C. de, *Spain* **41 G5** 38 48N 0 12 E
San Antonio, Mt., *U.S.A.* **161 L9** 34 17N 117 38W
San Antonio Bay, *Phil.* **81 G1** 8 38N 117 35 E
San Antonio de los Baños, *Cuba* **164 B3** 22 54N 82 31W
San Antonio de los Cobres, *Argentina* **174 A2** 24 10 S 66 17W
San Antonio Oeste, *Argentina* **176 B4** 40 40 S 65 0W
San Arcángelo, *Italy* **47 B9** 40 14N 16 14 E
San Ardo, *U.S.A.* **160 J6** 36 1N 120 54W
San Augustín, *Canary Is.* **9 e1** 27 47N 15 32W
San Augustine, *U.S.A.* **155 K7** 31 30N 94 7W
San Bartolomé, *Canary Is.* **9 e2** 28 59N 13 37W
San Bartolomé de Tirajana, *Canary Is.* **9 e1** 27 54N 15 34W
San Bartolomeo in Galdo, *Italy* **47 A8** 41 24N 15 1 E
San Benedetto del Tronto, *Italy* **45 F10** 42 57N 13 53 E
San Benedetto Po, *Italy* **44 C7** 45 2N 10 55 E
San Benedicto, I., *Mexico* **162 D2** 19 18N 110 49W
San Benito, *U.S.A.* **155 M6** 26 8N 97 38W
San Benito →, *U.S.A.* **160 J5** 36 53N 121 34W
San Benito Mt., *U.S.A.* **160 J6** 36 22N 120 37W
San Bernadino, *Switz.* **33 D8** 46 27N 9 12 E
San Bernardino, *U.S.A.* **161 L9** 34 7N 117 19W
San Bernardino, Paso del, *Switz.* **33 D8** 46 28N 9 11 E
San Bernardino Mts., *U.S.A.* **161 L10** 34 10N 116 45W
San Bernardino Str., *Phil.* **80 E5** 13 0N 125 0 E
San Bernardo, *Chile* **174 C1** 33 40 S 70 50W
San Bernardo, I. de, *Colombia* **168 B2** 9 45N 75 50W
San Blas, *Mexico* **162 B3** 26 4N 108 46W
San Blas, Arch. de, *Panama* **164 E4** 9 50N 78 31W
San Blas, C., *U.S.A.* **152 F4** 29 40N 85 21W
San Bonifacio, *Italy* **45 C8** 45 24N 11 16 E
San Borja, *Bolivia* **172 C4** 14 50 S 66 52W
San Buenaventura, *Bolivia* **172 C4** 14 28 S 67 35W
San Buenaventura, *Mexico* **162 B4** 27 5N 101 32W
San Carlos = Butuku-Luba, *Eq. Guin.* **113 E6** 3 29N 8 33 E
San Carlos = Sant Carles, *Spain* **38 C2** 39 3N 1 34 E
San Carlos, *Argentina* **174 C2** 33 50 S 69 0W
San Carlos, *Bolivia* **173 D5** 17 24 S 63 45W
San Carlos, *Chile* **174 D1** 36 10 S 72 0W
San Carlos, *Baja Calif. S., Mexico* **162 C2** 24 47N 112 6W
San Carlos, *Coahuila, Mexico* **162 B4** 29 0N 100 54W
San Carlos, *Nic.* **164 D3** 11 12N 84 50W
San Carlos, *Neg. Occ., Phil.* **81 F4** 10 29N 123 25 E
San Carlos, *Pangasinan, Phil.* **80 D3** 15 55N 120 20 E
San Carlos, *Uruguay* **175 C5** 34 46 S 54 58W
San Carlos, *U.S.A.* **159 K8** 33 21N 110 27W
San Carlos, *Amazonas, Venezuela* **168 C4** 1 55N 67 4W
San Carlos, *Cojedes, Venezuela* **168 B4** 9 40N 68 36W
San Carlos de Bariloche, *Argentina* **176 B2** 41 10 S 71 25W
San Carlos de la Rápita = Sant Carles de la Ràpita, *Spain* **40 E5** 40 37N 0 35 E
San Carlos de Río Negro, *Venezuela* **168 C4** 1 55N 67 4W
San Carlos del Zulia, *Venezuela* **168 B3** 9 1N 71 55W
San Carlos L., *U.S.A.* **159 K8** 33 11N 110 32W
San Cataldo, *Italy* **46 E6** 37 29N 13 59 E
San Celoni = Sant Celoni, *Spain* **40 D7** 41 42N 2 30 E
San Clemente, *Chile* **174 D1** 35 30 S 71 29W
San Clemente, *Spain* **41 F2** 39 24N 2 25W
San Clemente, *U.S.A.* **161 M9** 33 26N 117 37W
San Clemente I., *U.S.A.* **161 N8** 32 53N 118 29W
San Cristóbal = Es Migjorn Gran, *Spain* **38 B5** 39 57N 4 3 E
San Cristóbal, *Argentina* **174 C3** 30 20 S 61 10W
San Cristóbal, *Colombia* **168 D3** 2 18 S 73 2W
San Cristóbal, *Dom. Rep.* **165 C5** 18 25N 70 6W
San Cristóbal, *Solomon Is.* **133 N11** 10 30 S 161 0 E
San Cristóbal, *Venezuela* **168 B3** 7 46N 72 14W
San Cristóbal, I., *Ecuador* **172 a** 0 50 S 89 26W
San Cristóbal de la Casas, *Mexico* **163 D6** 16 50N 92 33W
San Damiano d'Asti, *Italy* **44 D5** 44 50N 8 4 E
San Daniele del Friuli, *Italy* **45 B10** 46 9N 13 1 E
San Diego, *Calif., U.S.A.* **161 N9** 32 43N 117 9W
San Diego, *Tex., U.S.A.* **155 M5** 27 46N 98 14W
San Diego, C., *Argentina* **176 D3** 54 40 S 65 10W
San Diego de la Unión, *Mexico* **162 C4** 21 28N 100 52W
San Dimitri, Ras, *Malta* **38 E6** 36 4N 14 11 E
San Dimitri Point = San Dimitri, Ras, *Malta* **38 E6** 36 4N 14 11 E
San Donà di Piave, *Italy* **45 C9** 45 38N 12 34 E
San Estanislao, *Paraguay* **174 A4** 24 39 S 56 26W
San Esteban de Gormaz, *Spain* **40 D1** 41 34N 3 13W
San Felice Circeo, *Italy* **46 A6** 41 14N 13 5 E
San Felice sul Panaro, *Italy* **45 D8** 44 50N 11 8 E
San Felipe, *Chile* **174 C1** 32 43 S 70 42W
San Felipe, *Colombia* **168 C4** 1 55N 67 6W
San Felipe, *Mexico* **162 A2** 31 0N 114 52W
San Felipe, *Phil.* **80 D3** 15 4N 120 4 E
San Felipe, *Venezuela* **168 A4** 10 20N 68 44W
San Felipe →, *U.S.A.* **161 M11** 33 12N 115 49W
San Félix, *Chile* **174 B1** 28 56 S 70 28W
San Félix, *Pac. Oc.* **135 K20** 26 23 S 80 0W
San Fernando = Sant Ferran, *Spain* **38 D1** 38 42N 1 28 E
San Fernando, *Chile* **174 C1** 34 30 S 71 0W
San Fernando, *Baja Calif., Mexico* **162 B1** 29 55N 115 10W
San Fernando, *Tamaulipas, Mexico* **163 C5** 24 51N 98 10W
San Fernando, *Cebu, Phil.* **81 F4** 10 10N 123 42 E
San Fernando, *La Union, Phil.* **80 C3** 16 40N 120 23 E
San Fernando, *Pampanga, Phil.* **80 D3** 15 5N 120 37 E
San Fernando, *Romblon, Phil.* **80 E4** 12 18N 122 36 E
San Fernando, *Spain* **43 J4** 36 28N 6 17W
San Fernando, *Trin. & Tob.* **165 D7** 10 20N 61 30W
San Fernando, *U.S.A.* **161 L8** 34 17N 118 26W
San Fernando de Apure, *Venezuela* **168 B4** 7 54N 67 15W
San Fernando de Atabapo, *Venezuela* **168 C4** 4 3N 67 42W
San Fernando di Púglia, *Italy* **47 A9** 41 18N 16 5 E
San Francisco, *Argentina* **174 C3** 31 30 S 62 5W
San Francisco, *Bolivia* **173 D4** 15 16 S 65 31W
San Francisco, *Peru* **172 C3** 12 36 S 73 49W
San Francisco, *Agusan del S., Phil.* **81 G5** 8 30N 125 56 E
San Francisco, *Cebu, Phil.* **81 F5** 10 39N 124 23 E
San Francisco, *Quezon, Phil.* **80 E4** 13 21N 122 31 E
San Francisco, *S. Leyte, Phil.* **81 F5** 10 4N 125 9 E
San Francisco, *U.S.A.* **160 H4** 37 47N 122 25W
San Francisco →, *U.S.A.* **159 K9** 32 59N 109 22W
San Francisco, Paso de, *S. Amer.* **174 B2** 27 0 S 68 0W
San Francisco de Macorís, *Dom. Rep.* **165 C5** 19 19N 70 15W
San Francisco del Monte de Oro, *Argentina* **174 C2** 32 36 S 66 8W
San Francisco del Oro, *Mexico* **162 B3** 26 52N 105 50W
San Francisco Javier = Sant Francesc de Formentera, *Spain* **38 D1** 38 42N 1 26 E
San Francisco Solano, Pta., *Colombia* **168 B2** 6 18N 77 29W
San Fratello, *Italy* **47 D7** 38 1N 14 36 E
San Gabriel, *Chile* **174 C1** 33 47 S 70 15W
San Gabriel, *Ecuador* **168 C2** 0 36N 77 49W
San Gabriel Mts., *U.S.A.* **161 L9** 34 20N 118 0W
San Gavino Monreale, *Italy* **46 C1** 39 33N 8 47 E
San German, *Puerto Rico* **165 d** 18 4N 67 4W
San Gil, *Colombia* **168 B3** 6 33N 73 8W
San Gimignano, *Italy* **44 E8** 43 28N 11 2 E
San Giórgio di Nogaro, *Italy* **45 C10** 45 50N 13 13 E
San Giórgio Iónico, *Italy* **47 B10** 40 27N 17 23 E
San Giovanni Bianco, *Italy* **44 C6** 45 52N 9 39 E
San Giovanni in Fiore, *Italy* **47 C9** 39 15N 16 42 E
San Giovanni in Persiceto, *Italy* **45 D8** 44 38N 11 11 E
San Giovanni Rotondo, *Italy* **45 G12** 41 42N 15 44 E
San Giovanni Valdarno, *Italy* **45 E8** 43 34N 11 32 E
San Giuliano Terme, *Italy* **44 E7** 43 46N 10 26 E
San Gorgonio Mt., *U.S.A.* **161 L10** 34 7N 116 51W
San Gottardo, P. del, *Switz.* **33 C7** 46 33N 8 33 E
San Gregorio, *Uruguay* **175 C4** 32 37 S 55 40W
San Gregorio, *U.S.A.* **160 H4** 37 20N 122 23W
San Guiseppe Jato, *Italy* **46 E6** 37 57N 13 11 E
San Ignacio, *Belize* **163 D7** 17 10N 89 0W
San Ignacio, *Beni, Bolivia* **173 C4** 14 53 S 65 36W
San Ignacio, *Santa Cruz, Bolivia* **173 D5** 16 20 S 60 55W
San Ignacio, *Mexico* **162 B2** 27 27N 113 0W
San Ignacio, *Paraguay* **164 C2** 26 52 S 57 3W
San Ignacio, *Peru* **172 B2** 5 8 S 78 59W
San Ignacio, L., *Mexico* **162 B2** 26 50N 113 11W
San Ildefonso, C., *Phil.* **80 C4** 16 0N 122 1 E
San Isidro, *Argentina* **174 C4** 34 29 S 58 31W
San Isidro, *Phil.* **81 H6** 6 50N 126 5 E
San Jacinto, *Colombia* **168 B2** 9 50N 75 8W
San Jacinto, *Phil.* **80 E4** 12 34N 123 44 E
San Jacinto, *U.S.A.* **161 M10** 33 47N 116 57W
San Jaime = Sant Jaume, *Spain* **38 B5** 39 54N 4 4 E
San Javier, *Misiones, Argentina* **175 B4** 27 55 S 55 5W
San Javier, *Santa Fe, Argentina* **174 C4** 30 40 S 59 55W
San Javier, *Beni, Bolivia* **173 C5** 14 34 S 64 42W
San Javier, *Santa Cruz, Bolivia* **173 D5** 16 18 S 62 30W
San Javier, *Chile* **174 D1** 35 40 S 71 45W
San Javier, *Spain* **41 H4** 37 49N 0 50W
San Jeronimo Taviche, *Mexico* **163 D5** 16 38N 96 32W
San Joaquín, *Bolivia* **173 C5** 13 4 S 64 49W
San Joaquin, *Phil.* **81 F4** 10 35N 122 8 E
San Joaquin, *U.S.A.* **160 J6** 36 36N 120 11W
San Joaquín →, *Bolivia* **173 C5** 13 8 S 63 41W
San Joaquin →, *U.S.A.* **160 G5** 38 4N 121 51W
San Joaquín, Cerro, *Ecuador* **172 a** 0 53 S 89 30W
San Joaquin Valley, *U.S.A.* **160 J6** 37 20N 121 0W
San Jon, *U.S.A.* **155 H3** 35 6N 103 20W
San Jordi = Sant Jordi, *Spain* **38 B3** 39 33N 2 46 E
San Jorge, *Argentina* **174 C3** 31 54 S 61 50W
San Jorge, *Solomon Is.* **133 M10** 8 28 S 159 38 E
San Jorge, B. de, *Mexico* **162 A2** 31 20N 113 20W
San Jorge, G., *Argentina* **176 C3** 46 0 S 66 0W
San José = San Josep, *Spain* **38 D1** 38 55N 1 18 E
San José, *Costa Rica* **164 E3** 9 55N 84 2W
San José, *Guatemala* **164 D1** 14 0N 90 50W
San José, *Mexico* **162 C2** 25 0N 110 50W
San Jose, *Mind. Occ., Phil.* **80 E3** 12 27N 121 4 E
San Jose, *Nueva Ecija, Phil.* **80 D3** 15 45N 120 55 E
San Jose, *Calif., U.S.A.* **160 H5** 37 20N 121 53W
San Jose, *Ill., U.S.A.* **156 D7** 40 18N 89 36W
San Jose →, *U.S.A.* **159 J10** 34 25N 106 45W
San José, Golfo, *Argentina* **176 B4** 42 20 S 64 18W
San Jose de Buenavista, *Phil.* **79 B6** 10 45N 121 56 E
San José de Chiquitos, *Bolivia* **173 D5** 17 53 S 60 50W
San José de Feliciano, *Argentina* **174 C4** 30 26 S 58 46W
San José de Jáchal, *Argentina* **174 C2** 30 15 S 68 46W
San José de Mayo, *Uruguay* **174 C4** 34 27 S 56 40W
San José de Ocune, *Colombia* **168 C3** 4 15N 70 20W
San José de Uchapiamonas, *Bolivia* **172 C4** 14 13 S 68 5W
San José del Cabo, *Mexico* **162 C3** 23 0N 109 40W
San José del Guaviare, *Colombia* **168 C3** 2 35N 72 38W
San Jose del Monte, *Phil.* **80 D3** 14 49N 121 3 E
San José do Anauá, *Brazil* **169 C5** 0 58N 61 22W
San Josep, *Spain* **38 D1** 38 55N 1 18 E
San Juan, *Argentina* **174 C2** 31 30 S 68 30W
San Juan, *Colombia* **168 B2** 8 46N 76 32W
San Juan, *Mexico* **162 C4** 21 20N 102 50W
San Juan, *Ica, Peru* **172 D2** 15 22 S 75 7W
San Juan, *Puno, Peru* **172 C4** 14 2 S 69 19W
San Juan, *Batangas, Phil.* **80 E3** 13 50N 121 24 E
San Juan, *S. Leyte, Phil.* **81 F5** 10 16N 125 10 E
San Juan, *Puerto Rico* **165 d** 18 28N 66 7W
San Juan, *Trin. & Tob.* **169 F9** 10 39N 61 29W
San Juan □, *Argentina* **174 C2** 31 9 S 69 0W
San Juan →, *Argentina* **174 C2** 32 20 S 67 25W
San Juan →, *Bolivia* **173 E4** 21 2 S 65 19W
San Juan →, *Colombia* **168 C2** 4 3N 77 27W
San Juan →, *Nic.* **164 D3** 10 56N 83 42W
San Juan →, *U.S.A.* **159 H8** 37 16N 110 26W
San Juan →, *Venezuela* **169 A5** 10 14N 62 38W
San Juan, C., *Eq. Guin.* **114 B1** 1 5N 9 20 E
San Juan Bautista = Sant Joan Baptista, *Spain* **38 C2** 39 5N 1 31 E
San Juan Bautista, *Paraguay* **174 B4** 26 37 S 57 6W
San Juan Bautista, *U.S.A.* **160 J5** 36 51N 121 32W
San Juan Bautista Valle Nacional, *Mexico* **163 D5** 17 47N 96 19W
San Juan Capistrano, *U.S.A.* **161 M9** 33 30N 117 40W
San Juan Cr. →, *U.S.A.* **160 J5** 35 40N 120 22W
San Juan de Alicante, *Spain* **41 G4** 38 24N 0 26W
San Juan de Guadalupe, *Mexico* **162 C4** 24 38N 102 44W
San Juan de Guía, Cabo de, *Colombia* **168 A3** 11 21N 73 59W
San Juan de la Costa, *Mexico* **162 C2** 24 23N 110 45W
San Juan de los Morros, *Venezuela* **168 B4** 9 55N 67 21W
San Juan de Manapiare, *Venezuela* **168 B4** 5 15N 66 5W
San Juan del César, *Colombia* **168 A3** 10 46N 73 1W
San Juan del Norte, *Nic.* **164 D3** 10 58N 83 40W
San Juan del Norte, B. de, *Nic.* **164 D3** 11 0N 83 40W
San Juan del Río, *Mexico* **163 C5** 20 25N 100 0W
San Juan del Sur, *Nic.* **164 D2** 11 20N 85 51W
San Juan I., *U.S.A.* **160 B3** 48 32N 123 5W
San Juan Mts., *U.S.A.* **159 H10** 37 30N 107 0W
San Julián, *Argentina* **176 C3** 49 15 S 67 45W
San Julian, *Phil.* **81 F5** 11 45N 125 27 E
San Just, Sierra de, *Spain* **40 E4** 40 45N 0 49W
San Justo, *Argentina* **174 C3** 30 47 S 60 30W
San Kamphaeng, *Thailand* **86 C2** 18 45N 99 8 E
San Lázaro, C., *Mexico* **162 C2** 24 50N 112 18W
San Lázaro, Sa., *Mexico* **162 C3** 23 25N 110 0W
San Leandro, *U.S.A.* **160 H4** 37 44N 122 9W
San Leonardo de Yagüe, *Spain* **40 D1** 41 51N 3 5W
San Lorenzo = Sant Llorenç des Cardassar, *Spain* **38 B4** 39 37N 3 17 E
San Lorenzo, *Argentina* **174 C3** 32 45 S 60 45W
San Lorenzo, *Beni, Bolivia* **173 D4** 15 22 S 65 48W
San Lorenzo, *Tarija, Bolivia* **173 E5** 21 26 S 64 47W
San Lorenzo, *Ecuador* **168 C2** 1 15N 78 50W
San Lorenzo, *Paraguay* **174 B4** 25 20 S 57 32W
San Lorenzo →, *Mexico* **162 C3** 24 15N 107 24W
San Lorenzo, I., *Mexico* **162 B2** 28 35N 112 50W
San Lorenzo, I., *Peru* **172 C2** 12 7 S 77 15W
San Lorenzo, Mte., *Argentina* **176 C2** 47 40 S 72 20W
San Lorenzo de la Parrilla, *Spain* **40 F2** 39 51N 2 22W
San Lorenzo de Morunys = Sant Llorenç de Morunys, *Spain* **40 C6** 42 8N 1 35 E
San Lucas, *Bolivia* **173 E4** 20 5 S 65 7W
San Lucas, *Baja Calif. S., Mexico* **162 C3** 22 53N 109 54W
San Lucas, *Baja Calif. S., Mexico* **162 B2** 27 10N 112 14W
San Lucas, *U.S.A.* **160 J5** 36 8N 121 1W
San Lucas, C., *Mexico* **162 C3** 22 50N 110 0W
San Lúcido, *Italy* **47 C9** 39 18N 16 3 E
San Luis, *Argentina* **174 C2** 33 20 S 66 20W
San Luis, *Cuba* **164 B3** 22 17N 83 46W
San Luis, *Guatemala* **164 C2** 16 14N 89 27W
San Luis, *Ariz., U.S.A.* **159 K6** 32 29N 114 47W
San Luis, *Colo., U.S.A.* **159 H11** 37 12N 105 25W
San Luis □, *Argentina* **174 C2** 34 0 S 66 0W
San Luis, I., *Mexico* **162 B2** 29 58N 114 26W
San Luis, L. de, *Bolivia* **173 C5** 13 45 S 64 0W
San Luis, Sierra de, *Argentina* **174 C2** 32 30 S 66 10W
San Luis de la Paz, *Mexico* **162 C4** 21 19N 100 32W
San Luis Obispo, *U.S.A.* **161 K6** 35 17N 120 40W
San Luis Potosí, *Mexico* **162 C4** 22 9N 100 59W
San Luis Potosí □, *Mexico* **162 C4** 22 10N 101 0W
San Luis Reservoir, *U.S.A.* **160 H5** 37 4N 121 5W
San Luis Río Colorado, *Mexico* **162 A2** 32 29N 114 58W
San Manuel, *Phil.* **80 C3** 16 4N 120 40 E
San Manuel, *U.S.A.* **159 K8** 32 36N 110 38W
San Marco, C., *Italy* **46 C1** 39 51N 8 26 E
San Marco Argentano, *Italy* **47 C9** 39 33N 16 7 E
San Marco in Lámis, *Italy* **45 G12** 41 43N 15 38 E
San Marcos, *Colombia* **168 B2** 8 39N 75 8W
San Marcos, *Guatemala* **164 D1** 14 59N 91 52W
San Marcos, *Mexico* **162 B2** 27 13N 112 6W
San Marcos, *Calif., U.S.A.* **161 M9** 33 9N 117 10W
San Marcos, *Tex., U.S.A.* **155 L6** 29 53N 97 56W
San Mariano, *Phil.* **80 C4** 17 0N 122 2 E
San Marino, *San Marino* **45 E9** 43 55N 12 30 E
San Marino ■, *Europe* **45 E9** 43 56N 12 25 E
San Martín, *Argentina* **174 C2** 33 5 S 68 28W
San Martín, *Colombia* **168 C3** 3 42N 73 42W
San Martín □, *Peru* **172 B2** 7 0 S 76 50W
San Martín →, *Bolivia* **173 C5** 13 8 S 63 43W
San Martín, L., *Argentina* **176 C2** 48 50 S 72 50W
San Martín de la Vega, *Spain* **42 E7** 40 13N 3 34W
San Martín de los Andes, *Argentina* **176 B2** 40 10 S 71 20W
San Martín de Valdeiglesias, *Spain* **42 E6** 40 21N 4 24W
San Mateo = Sant Mateu, *Baleares, Spain* **38 C1** 39 3N 1 23 E
San Mateo = Sant Mateu, *Valencia, Spain* **40 E5** 40 28N 0 10 E
San Mateo, *Phil.* **80 C3** 16 54N 121 33 E
San Mateo, *U.S.A.* **160 H4** 37 34N 122 19W
San Matías, *Bolivia* **173 D6** 16 25 S 58 20W
San Matías, G., *Argentina* **176 B4** 41 30 S 64 0W
San Miguel = Linapacan, *Phil.* **81 F2** 11 30N 119 52 E
San Miguel = Sant Miguel, *Spain* **38 C1** 39 3N 1 26 E
San Miguel, *Bolivia* **173 C5** 16 42 S 61 1W
San Miguel, *El Salv.* **164 D2** 13 30N 88 12W
San Miguel, *Panama* **164 E4** 8 27N 78 55W
San Miguel, *Bulacan, Phil.* **80 D3** 15 9N 120 59 E
San Miguel, *Palawan, Phil.* **81 F2** 11 30N 119 51 E
San Miguel, *Surigao S., Phil.* **81 G5** 9 3N 125 59 E
San Miguel, *U.S.A.* **160 K6** 35 45N 120 42W
San Miguel →, *Bolivia* **173 C5** 13 52 S 63 56W
San Miguel →, *S. Amer.* **168 C2** 0 25N 76 30W
San Miguel, Golfo de, *Panama* **168 B2** 8 22N 78 17W
San Miguel de Huachi, *Bolivia* **172 D4** 15 40 S 67 15W
San Miguel de Tucumán, *Argentina* **174 B2** 26 50 S 65 20W
San Miguel del Monte, *Argentina* **174 D4** 35 23 S 58 50W
San Miguel I., *U.S.A.* **161 L6** 34 2N 120 23W
San Miguel Is., *Phil.* **81 H2** 7 45N 118 28 E
San Miniato, *Italy* **44 E7** 43 41N 10 51 E
San Narciso, *Phil.* **80 E4** 13 34N 122 34 E
San Nicolás, *Canary Is.* **9 e1** 27 58N 15 47W
San Nicolas, *Phil.* **80 B3** 18 10N 120 36 E
San Nicolás de los Arroyas, *Argentina* **174 C3** 33 25 S 60 10W
San Nicolas I., *U.S.A.* **161 M7** 33 15N 119 30W
San Onofre, *Colombia* **168 B2** 9 44N 75 32W
San Onofre, *U.S.A.* **161 M9** 33 22N 117 34W
San Pablo, *Bolivia* **174 A2** 21 43 S 66 38W
San Pablo, *Isabela, Phil.* **80 C3** 17 27N 121 48 E
San Pablo, *Laguna, Phil.* **80 D3** 14 11N 121 31 E
San Pablo, *U.S.A.* **160 H4** 37 58N 122 21W
San Páolo di Civitate, *Italy* **45 G12** 41 44N 15 15 E
San Pascual, *Phil.* **80 E4** 13 8N 122 59 E
San Pedro, *Buenos Aires, Argentina* **174 C4** 33 40 S 59 40W
San Pedro, *Misiones, Argentina* **175 B5** 26 30 S 54 10W
San Pedro, *Chile* **174 C1** 33 54 S 71 28W
San Pedro, *Colombia* **168 C3** 4 56N 71 53W
San Pédro, *Ivory C.* **112 E3** 4 50N 6 33W
San Pedro, *Mexico* **162 C2** 23 55N 110 17W
San Pedro, *Peru* **172 C3** 14 49 S 74 5W
San Pedro □, *Paraguay* **174 A4** 24 0 S 57 0W
San Pedro →, *Chihuahua, Mexico* **162 B3** 28 20N 106 10W
San Pedro →, *Nayarit, Mexico* **162 C3** 21 45N 105 30W
San Pedro →, *U.S.A.* **159 K8** 32 59N 110 47W
San Pedro, Pta., *Chile* **174 B1** 25 30 S 70 38W
San Pedro, Sierra de, *Spain* **43 F4** 39 18N 6 40W
San Pedro Channel, *U.S.A.* **161 M8** 33 30N 118 25W
San Pedro de Arimena, *Colombia* **168 C3** 4 37N 71 42W
San Pedro de Atacama, *Chile* **174 A2** 22 55 S 68 15W
San Pedro de Jujuy, *Argentina* **174 A3** 24 12 S 64 55W
San Pedro de las Colonias, *Mexico* **162 B4** 25 50N 102 59W
San Pedro de Lloc, *Peru* **172 B2** 7 15 S 79 28W
San Pedro de Macorís, *Dom. Rep.* **165 C6** 18 30N 69 18W
San Pedro del Norte, *Nic.* **164 D3** 13 4N 84 33W
San Pedro del Paraná, *Paraguay* **174 B4** 26 43 S 56 13W
San Pedro del Pinatar, *Spain* **41 H4** 37 50N 0 50W
San Pedro Mártir, Sierra, *Mexico* **162 A1** 31 0N 115 30W
San Pedro Mixtepec, *Mexico* **163 D5** 16 2N 97 7W
San Pedro Ocampo = Melchor Ocampo, *Mexico* **162 C4** 24 52N 101 40W
San Pedro Sula, *Honduras* **164 C2** 15 30N 88 0W
San Pietro, *Italy* **46 C1** 39 8N 8 17 E
San Pietro Vernótico, *Italy* **47 B11** 40 29N 18 0 E
San Quintín, *Mexico* **162 A1** 30 29N 115 57W
San Rafael, *Argentina* **174 C2** 34 40 S 68 21W
San Rafael, *Bolivia* **173 D5** 16 45 S 60 34W
San Rafael, *Calif., U.S.A.* **160 H4** 37 58N 122 32W
San Rafael, *N. Mex., U.S.A.* **159 J10** 35 7N 107 53W
San Rafael, *Venezuela* **168 A3** 10 58N 71 46W
San Rafael Mt., *U.S.A.* **161 L7** 34 41N 119 52W
San Rafael Mts., *U.S.A.* **161 L7** 34 40N 119 50W
San Ramón, *Bolivia* **173 C5** 13 17 S 64 43W
San Ramón, *Peru* **172 C2** 11 8 S 75 20W
San Ramón de la Nueva Orán, *Argentina* **174 A3** 23 10 S 64 20W
San Remo, *Australia* **129 E6** 38 33 S 145 22 E
San Remo, *Italy* **44 E4** 43 49N 7 46 E
San Román, C., *Venezuela* **168 A3** 12 12N 70 0W
San Roque, *Argentina* **174 B4** 28 25 S 58 45W
San Roque, *Phil.* **80 E5** 12 37N 124 52 E
San Roque, *Spain* **43 J5** 36 17N 5 21W
San Rosendo, *Chile* **174 D1** 37 16 S 72 43W
San Saba, *U.S.A.* **155 K5** 31 12N 98 43W
San Salvador, *El Salv.* **164 D2** 13 40N 89 10W
San Salvador, *Spain* **38 B4** 39 27N 3 11 E
San Salvador, Canal de, *Ecuador* **172 a** 0 25 S 90 30W

Santiago de los Cabelleros 277

San Salvador, I., *Ecuador* **172 a** 0 16 S 90 42W
San Salvador de Jujuy, *Argentina* **174 A3** 24 10 S 64 48W
San Salvador I., *Bahamas* **165 B5** 24 0N 74 40W
San Salvo, *Italy* **45 F11** 42 3N 14 44 E
San Sebastián = Donostia-San Sebastián, *Spain* **40 B3** 43 17N 1 58W
San Sebastián, *Argentina* **176 D3** 53 10 S 68 30W
San Sebastian, *Puerto Rico* **165 d** 18 20N 66 59W
San Sebastián de la Gomera, *Canary Is.* **9 e1** 28 5N 17 7W
San Serra = Son Serra, *Spain* **38 B4** 39 43N 3 13 E
San Serverino Marche, *Italy* **45 E10** 43 13N 13 10 E
San Severo, *Italy* **45 G12** 41 41N 15 23 E
San Simeon, *U.S.A.* **160 K5** 35 39N 121 11W
San Simon, *U.S.A.* **159 K9** 32 16N 109 14W
San Stéfano di Cadore, *Italy* **45 B9** 46 34N 12 33 E
San Stino di Livenza, *Italy* **45 C9** 45 44N 12 41 E
San Telmo = Sant Telm, *Spain* **38 B3** 39 35N 2 21 E
San Telmo, *Mexico* **162 A1** 30 58N 116 6W
San Teodoro, *Phil.* **80 E3** 13 26N 121 1 E
San Tiburcio, *Mexico* **162 C4** 24 8N 101 32W
San Valentin, Mte., *Chile* **176 C2** 46 30 S 73 30W
San Vicente de Alcántara, *Spain* **43 F3** 39 22N 7 8W
San Vicente de la Barquera, *Spain* **42 B6** 43 23N 4 29W
San Vicente del Caguán, *Colombia* **168 C3** 2 7N 74 46W
San Vincente del Raspeig, *Spain* **41 G4** 38 24N 0 31W
San Vincenzo, *Italy* **44 E7** 43 6N 10 32 E
San Vito, *Costa Rica* **164 E3** 8 50N 82 58W
San Vito, *Italy* **46 C2** 39 26N 9 32 E
San Vito, C., *Italy* **46 D5** 38 11N 12 41 E
San Vito al Tagliamento, *Italy* **45 C9** 45 54N 12 52 E
San Vito Chietino, *Italy* **45 F11** 42 18N 14 27 E
San Vito dei Normanni, *Italy* **47 B10** 40 39N 17 42 E
San Yanaro, *Colombia* **168 C4** 2 47N 69 42W
Saña, *Peru* **172 B2** 6 54 S 79 36W
Sana', *Yemen* **98 D4** 15 27N 44 12 E
Sana →, *Bos.-H.* **45 C13** 45 3N 16 23 E
Sanaba, *Burkina Faso* **112 C4** 12 25N 3 47W
Şanāfīr, *Si. Arabia* **106 B3** 27 56N 34 42 E
Sanaga →, *Cameroon* **113 E6** 3 35N 9 38 E
Sanak I., *U.S.A.* **144 J7** 54 25N 162 40W
Sanaloa, Presa, *Mexico* **162 C3** 24 50N 107 20W
Sanām, *Si. Arabia* **98 B4** 23 40N 44 45 E
Sanana, *Indonesia* **82 B3** 2 4 S 125 58 E
Sanand, *India* **92 H5** 22 59N 72 25 E
Sanandaj, *Iran* **101 E12** 35 18N 47 1 E
Sanandita, *Bolivia* **174 A3** 21 40 S 63 45W
Sanaroa I., *Papua N. G.* **132 E6** 9 37 S 151 0 E
Sanary-sur-Mer, *France* **29 E9** 43 7N 5 49 E
Sanāw, *Yemen* **99 C5** 17 50N 51 5 E
Sanawad, *India* **92 H7** 22 11N 76 5 E
Sanbe-San, *Japan* **72 B4** 35 6N 132 38 E
Sancellas = Sencelles, *Spain* **38 B3** 39 39N 2 54 E
Sancergues, *France* **27 E9** 47 10N 2 54 E
Sancerre, *France* **27 E9** 47 20N 2 50 E
Sancerrois, Collines du, *France* **27 E9** 47 20N 2 40 E
Sancha He →, *China* **76 D6** 26 48N 106 7 E
Sanchahe, *China* **75 B14** 44 50N 126 2 E
Sanchakou, *China* **65 D9** 39 47N 78 20 E
Sánchez, *Dom. Rep.* **165 C6** 19 15N 69 36W
Sanchez-Mira, *Phil.* **80 B3** 18 34N 121 14 E
Sanchor, *India* **92 G4** 24 45N 71 55 E
Sanco Pt., *Phil.* **81 G6** 8 15N 126 27 E
Sancoins, *France* **27 F9** 46 47N 2 55 E
Sancti Spíritus, *Cuba* **164 B4** 21 52N 79 33W
Sancy, Puy de, *France* **28 C6** 45 32N 2 50 E
Sand, *Norway* **18 E3** 59 29N 6 16 E
Sand →, *S. Africa* **117 C5** 22 25 S 30 5 E
Sand Cr. →, *U.S.A.* **157 E11** 39 3N 85 51W
Sand Hills, *Guyana* **169 B6** 6 27N 58 19W
Sand Hills, *U.S.A.* **154 D4** 42 10N 101 30W
Sand I., *U.S.A.* **145 K14** 21 19N 157 53W
Sand Point, *U.S.A.* **144 J7** 55 20N 160 30W
Sand Springs, *U.S.A.* **155 G6** 36 9N 96 7W
Sanda, *Japan* **73 C7** 34 53N 135 14 E
Sandakan, *Malaysia* **85 A5** 5 53N 118 4 E
Sandalwood, *Australia* **128 C4** 34 55 S 140 9 E
Sandan = Sambor, *Cambodia* **86 F6** 12 46N 106 0 E
Sandane, *Norway* **18 C3** 61 46N 6 13 E
Sandanski, *Bulgaria* **50 E7** 41 35N 23 16 E
Sandaré, *Mali* **112 C2** 14 40N 10 15W
Sandared, *Sweden* **17 G6** 57 43N 12 47 E
Sandarne, *Sweden* **16 C11** 61 16N 17 9 E
Sanday, *U.K.* **22 B6** 59 16N 2 31W
Sande, *Møre og Romsdal, Norway* **18 B2** 62 15N 5 27 E
Sande, *Sogn og Fjordane, Norway* **18 C2** 61 20N 5 47 E
Sande, *Vestfold, Norway* **18 E7** 59 36N 10 12 E
Sandefjord, *Norway* **15 G14** 59 10N 10 15 E
Sandeid, *Norway* **18 E2** 59 33N 5 52 E
Sanders, *Ariz., U.S.A.* **159 J9** 35 13N 109 20W
Sanders, *Ky., U.S.A.* **157 F12** 38 40N 84 56W
Sanderson, *Fla., U.S.A.* **152 E7** 30 15N 82 16W
Sanderson, *Tex., U.S.A.* **155 K3** 30 9N 102 24W
Sandersville, *U.S.A.* **152 C7** 32 59N 82 48W
Sandfire Roadhouse, *Australia* **124 C3** 19 45 S 121 15 E
Sandfloegga, *Norway* **18 E4** 59 58N 7 10 E
Sandfly L., *Canada* **143 B7** 55 43N 106 6W
Sandfontein, *Namibia* **116 C2** 23 48 S 29 1 E
Sandhammaren, C., *Sweden* **17 J8** 55 23N 14 14 E
Sandía, *Peru* **172 C4** 14 10 S 69 30W
Sandıklı, *Turkey* **49 C12** 38 28N 30 17 E
Sandila, *India* **93 F9** 27 5N 80 31 E
Sandilands, *Bahamas* **9 b** 25 3N 77 19W
Sandnes, *Aust-Agder, Norway* **18 F4** 58 53N 7 45 E
Sandnes, *Rogaland, Norway* **15 G11** 58 50N 5 45 E
Sandnessjøen, *Norway* **14 C15** 66 2N 12 38 E
Sandoa, *Dem. Rep. of the Congo* **115 D4** 9 41 S 23 0 E
Sandomierz, *Poland* **55 H8** 50 40N 21 43 E
Sândominic, *Romania* **53 D10** 46 35N 25 47 E
Sandona, *Colombia* **168 C2** 1 17N 77 28W
Sandongo, *Angola* **115 F4** 15 30 S 21 28 E
Sandoval, *U.S.A.* **156 F7** 38 37N 89 7W
Sandover →, *Australia* **126 C2** 21 43 S 136 32 E
Sandoway, *Burma* **90 F5** 18 20N 94 30 E
Sandoy, *Færoe Is.* **14 F9** 61 52N 6 46W
Sandpoint, *U.S.A.* **158 B5** 48 17N 116 33W
Sandray, *U.K.* **22 E1** 56 53N 7 31W
Sandringham, *U.K.* **20 E8** 52 51N 0 31 E
Sandstone, *Australia* **125 E2** 27 59 S 119 16 E
Sandu, *China* **76 E6** 26 0N 107 52 E
Sandumba, *Angola* **115 E3** 13 45 S 17 34 E
Sandur, *India* **95 F3** 15 6N 76 33 E
Sandusky, *Mich., U.S.A.* **150 C2** 43 25N 82 50W
Sandusky, *Ohio, U.S.A.* **150 E2** 41 27N 82 42W
Sandusky →, *U.S.A.* **157 C14** 41 27N 83 0W
Sandvig, *Sweden* **17 J8** 55 18N 14 47 E
Sandvika, *Norway* **18 E7** 59 54N 10 31 E
Sandviken, *Sweden* **16 D10** 60 38N 16 46 E
Sandwich, *U.S.A.* **157 C8** 41 39N 88 37W
Sandwich, C., *Australia* **126 B4** 18 14 S 146 18 E
Sandwich B., *Canada* **141 B8** 53 40N 57 15W
Sandwich B., *Namibia* **116 C1** 23 25 S 14 20 E
Sandwip I., *Bangla.* **90 D3** 22 30N 91 25 E
Sandy, *Oreg., U.S.A.* **160 E4** 45 24N 122 16W
Sandy, *Pa., U.S.A.* **150 E6** 41 6N 78 46W
Sandy, *Utah, U.S.A.* **158 F8** 40 35N 111 50W
Sandy Bay, *St. Helena* **9 h** 16 0 S 5 43W
Sandy Bay, *Canada* **143 B8** 55 31N 102 19W
Sandy Bight, *Australia* **125 F3** 33 50 S 123 20 E
Sandy C., *Queens., Australia* **126 C5** 24 42 S 153 15 E
Sandy C., *Tas., Australia* **127 G3** 41 25 S 144 45 E
Sandy Cay, *Bahamas* **165 B4** 23 13N 75 18W
Sandy Cr. →, *U.S.A.* **158 F9** 41 51N 109 47W
Sandy L., *Canada* **140 B1** 53 2N 93 0W
Sandy Lake, *Canada* **140 B1** 53 0N 93 15W
Sandy Point, *India* **95 J11** 10 32N 92 22 E
Sandy Springs, *U.S.A.* **152 B5** 33 56N 84 23W
Sandy Valley, *U.S.A.* **161 K11** 35 49N 115 36W
Sanford, *Fla., U.S.A.* **149 L5** 28 48N 81 16W
Sanford, *Maine, U.S.A.* **149 D10** 43 27N 70 47W
Sanford, *N.C., U.S.A.* **149 H6** 35 29N 79 10W
Sanford →, *Australia* **125 E2** 27 22 S 115 53 E
Sanford, Mt., *U.S.A.* **144 E11** 62 13N 144 8W
Sang-i-Masha, *Afghan.* **92 C2** 33 8N 67 27 E
Sanga, *Angola* **115 E3** 11 9 S 15 21 E
Sanga, *Mozam.* **119 E4** 12 22 S 35 21 E
Sanga →, *Congo* **114 C3** 1 5 S 17 0 E
Sangaie, *Dem. Rep. of the Congo* **115 D4** 6 48 S 22 46 E
Sangamner, *India* **94 E2** 19 37N 74 15 E
Sangamon →, *U.S.A.* **156 D6** 40 7N 90 20W
Sanganeb Atoll Marine Nat. Park, *Sudan* **106 D4** 19 33N 37 11 E
Sangar, *Afghan.* **92 C1** 32 56N 65 30 E
Sangar, *Russia* **67 C13** 64 2N 127 31 E
Sangar Sarai, *Afghan.* **92 B4** 34 27N 70 35 E
Sangareddi, *India* **94 F4** 17 38N 78 7 E
Sangaredi, *Guinea* **112 C2** 11 7N 13 52W
Sangarh →, *Pakistan* **92 D4** 30 43N 70 44 E
Sangasangadalam, *Indonesia* **85 C5** 0 36 S 117 13 E
Sangasso, *Mali* **112 C3** 12 5N 5 35W
Sangatte, *France* **27 B8** 50 56N 1 44 E
Sangay, *Ecuador* **168 D2** 2 0 S 78 20W
Sangchris L., *U.S.A.* **156 E7** 39 35N 89 30W
Sange, *Dem. Rep. of the Congo* **118 D2** 6 58 S 28 21 E
Sangeang, *Indonesia* **85 D5** 8 12 S 119 6 E
Sângeorz-Băi, *Romania* **53 C9** 47 22N 24 41 E
Sanger, *U.S.A.* **160 J7** 36 42N 119 33W
Sângera, *Moldova* **53 D13** 46 55N 28 58 E
Sangerhausen, *Germany* **30 D7** 51 28N 11 18 E
Sanggan He →, *China* **74 E9** 38 12N 117 15 E
Sanggau, *Indonesia* **85 B4** 0 5N 110 30 E
Sanghar, *Pakistan* **92 F3** 26 2N 68 57 E
Sangihe, Kepulauan, *Indonesia* **82 A3** 3 0N 125 30 E
Sangihe, Pulau, *Indonesia* **82 A3** 3 35N 125 30 E
Sangju, *S. Korea* **75 F15** 36 25N 128 10 E
Sangkapura, *Indonesia* **85 D4** 5 52 S 112 40 E
Sangkhla, *Thailand* **86 E2** 14 57N 98 28 E
Sangkulirang, *Indonesia* **83 B5** 0 59N 117 58 E
Sangla, *Pakistan* **92 D5** 31 43N 73 23 E
Sangli, *India* **94 F2** 16 55N 74 33 E
Sangmélima, *Cameroon* **113 E7** 2 57N 12 1 E
Sango, *Angola* **115 D2** 9 51 S 15 44 E
Sangod, *India* **92 G7** 24 55N 76 17 E
Sangole, *India* **94 F2** 17 26N 75 12 E
Sangpang Bum, *Burma* **90 B5** 26 30N 95 50 E
Sangre de Cristo Mts., *U.S.A.* **155 G2** 37 30N 105 20W
Sangre Grande, *Trin. & Tob.* **169 F9** 10 35N 61 8W
Sangro →, *Italy* **45 F11** 42 14N 14 32 E
Sangrur, *India* **92 D6** 30 14N 75 50 E
Sangudo, *Canada* **142 C6** 53 50N 114 54W
Sangue →, *Brazil* **173 C6** 11 1 S 58 39W
Sangüesa, *Spain* **40 C3** 42 37N 1 17W
Sanguinaires, Îs., *France* **29 G12** 41 51N 8 36 E
Sangzhi, *China* **77 C8** 29 25N 110 12 E
Sanhala, *Ivory C.* **112 C3** 10 3N 6 51W
Sanibel, *U.S.A.* **149 M4** 26 26N 82 1W
Sanibel I., *U.S.A.* **153 J7** 26 26N 82 6W
Sanirajak, *Canada* **139 B11** 68 46N 81 12W
Sanjawi, *Pakistan* **92 D3** 30 17N 68 21 E
Sanje, *Uganda* **118 C3** 0 49 S 31 30 E
Sanjiang, *China* **76 E7** 25 48N 109 37 E
Sanjo, *Japan* **70 F9** 37 37N 138 57 E
Sankarankovil, *India* **95 K3** 9 10N 77 35 E
Sankeshwar, *India* **95 F2** 16 23N 74 32 E
Sankh →, *India* **93 H11** 22 15N 84 48 E
Sankosh →, *India* **90 B2** 26 24N 89 47 E
Sankt Andrä, *Austria* **34 E7** 46 46N 14 50 E
Sankt Antönien, *Switz.* **33 C9** 46 58N 9 48 E
Sankt Augustin, *Germany* **30 E3** 50 45N 7 10 E
Sankt Blasien, *Germany* **31 H4** 47 47N 8 7 E
Sankt Gallen, *Switz.* **33 B8** 47 26N 9 22 E
Sankt Gallen □, *Switz.* **33 B8** 47 25N 9 22 E
Sankt Goar, *Germany* **31 E3** 50 12N 7 43 E
Sankt Ingbert, *Germany* **31 F3** 49 16N 7 6 E
Sankt Johann im Pongau, *Austria* **34 D6** 47 22N 13 12 E
Sankt Johann in Tirol, *Austria* **34 D5** 47 30N 12 25 E
Sankt Margrethen, *Switz.* **33 B9** 47 28N 9 37 E
Sankt Moritz, *Switz.* **33 D9** 46 30N 9 50 E
Sankt-Peterburg, *Russia* **58 C6** 59 55N 30 20 E
Sankt Pölten, *Austria* **34 C8** 48 12N 15 38 E
Sankt Ulrich = Ortisei, *Italy* **45 B8** 46 34N 11 40 E
Sankt Valentin, *Austria* **34 C7** 48 11N 14 33 E
Sankt Veit an der Glan, *Austria* **34 E7** 46 47N 14 22 E
Sankt Wendel, *Germany* **31 F3** 49 27N 7 9 E
Sankt Wolfgang, *Austria* **34 D6** 47 43N 13 27 E
Sankuru →, *Dem. Rep. of the Congo* **115 C4** 4 17 S 20 25 E
Sanliurfa, *Turkey* **101 D8** 37 12N 38 50 E
Sanlúcar de Barrameda, *Spain* **43 J4** 36 46N 6 21W
Sanluri, *Italy* **46 C1** 39 34N 8 54 E
Sânmartin, *Romania* **53 D10** 46 19N 25 58 E
Sanmen, *China* **77 C13** 29 5N 121 35 E
Sanmenxia, *China* **74 G6** 34 47N 111 12 E
Sanming, *China* **77 D11** 26 15N 117 40 E
Sannan, *Japan* **73 B7** 35 2N 135 1 E
Sannaspos, *S. Africa* **116 D4** 29 6 S 26 34 E
Sannat, *Malta* **38 E6** 36 1N 14 15 E
Sannicandro Garganico, *Italy* **45 G12** 41 50N 15 34 E
Sânnicolau Mare, *Romania* **52 D5** 46 5N 20 39 E
Sannieshof, *S. Africa* **116 D4** 26 30 S 25 47 E
Sannīn, J., *Lebanon* **103 B4** 33 57N 35 52 E
Sanniquellie, *Liberia* **112 D3** 7 19N 8 38W
Sannûr, W. →, *Egypt* **106 B3** 28 59N 31 3 E
Sano, *Japan* **73 A11** 36 19N 139 35 E
Sanok, *Poland* **55 J9** 49 35N 22 10 E
Sanquhar, *U.K.* **22 F5** 55 22N 3 54W
Sans Souci, *Trin. & Tob.* **169 F9** 10 50N 61 0W
Sansanding, *Mali* **112 C3** 13 48N 6 0W
Sansepolcro, *Italy* **45 E9** 43 34N 12 8 E
Sansha, *China* **77 D13** 26 58N 120 12 E
Sanshui, *China* **77 F9** 23 10N 112 56 E
Sanski Most, *Bos.-H.* **45 D13** 44 46N 16 40 E
Sansui, *China* **76 D7** 26 58N 108 39 E
Sant Antoni Abat, *Spain* **38 D1** 38 59N 1 19 E
Sant Boi de Llobregat, *Spain* **40 D7** 41 21N 2 2 E
Sant Carles, *Spain* **38 C2** 39 3N 1 34 E
Sant Carles de la Ràpita, *Spain* **40 E5** 40 37N 0 35 E
Sant Celoni, *Spain* **40 D7** 41 42N 2 30 E
Sant Feliu de Guíxols, *Spain* **40 D8** 41 45N 3 1 E
Sant Feliu de Llobregat, *Spain* **40 D7** 41 23N 2 2 E
Sant Ferran, *Spain* **38 D1** 38 42N 1 28 E
Sant Francesc de Formentera, *Spain* **38 D1** 38 42N 1 26 E
Sant Jaume, *Spain* **38 B5** 39 54N 4 4 E
Sant Joan Baptista, *Spain* **38 C2** 39 5N 1 31 E
Sant Jordi, *Ibiza, Spain* **38 D1** 38 53N 1 24 E
Sant Jordi, *Mallorca, Spain* **38 B3** 39 33N 2 46 E
Sant Jordi, G. de, *Spain* **40 E6** 40 53N 1 2 E
Sant Llorenç de Morunys, *Spain* **40 C6** 42 8N 1 35 E
Sant Llorenç des Cardassar, *Spain* **38 B4** 39 37N 3 17 E
Sant Mateu, *Baleares, Spain* **38 C1** 39 3N 1 23 E
Sant Mateu, *Valencia, Spain* **40 E5** 40 28N 0 10 E
Sant Miguel, *Spain* **38 C1** 39 3N 1 26 E
Sant Telm, *Spain* **38 B3** 39 35N 2 21 E
Santa, *Peru* **172 B2** 8 59 S 78 40W
Sant' Ágata Militello, *Italy* **47 D7** 38 2N 14 8 E
Santa Agnés, *Spain* **38 C1** 39 3N 1 21 E
Santa Ana, *Beni, Bolivia* **173 C4** 13 50 S 65 40W
Santa Ana, *La Paz, Bolivia* **172 D4** 15 31 S 67 30W
Santa Ana, *Santa Cruz, Bolivia* **173 D6** 18 43 S 58 44W
Santa Ana, *Santa Cruz, Bolivia* **173 D5** 16 37 S 60 43W
Santa Ana, *Ecuador* **168 D1** 1 16 S 80 20W
Santa Ana, *El Salv.* **164 D2** 14 0N 89 31W
Santa Ana, *Mexico* **162 A2** 30 31N 111 8W
Santa Ana, *Phil.* **80 B4** 18 28N 122 20 E
Santa Ana, *Solomon Is.* **133 N12** 10 50 S 162 30 E
Santa Ana, *U.S.A.* **161 M9** 33 46N 117 52W
Santa Ana →, *Venezuela* **168 B3** 9 30N 71 57W
Sant' Ángelo Lodigiano, *Italy* **44 C6** 45 14N 9 25 E
Sant' Antíoco, *Italy* **46 C1** 39 4N 8 27 E
Santa Bárbara, *Santa Maria, Azores* **9 d4** 36 59N 25 4W
Santa Bárbara, *Terceira, Azores* **9 d1** 38 41N 27 20W
Santa Bárbara, *Chile* **174 D1** 37 40 S 72 1W
Santa Bárbara, *Colombia* **168 B2** 5 53N 75 35W
Santa Bárbara, *Honduras* **164 D2** 14 53N 88 14W
Santa Bárbara, *Mexico* **162 B3** 26 48N 105 50W
Santa Barbara, *Phil.* **81 F4** 10 50N 122 32 E
Santa Bárbara, *Spain* **40 E5** 40 42N 0 29 E
Santa Barbara, *U.S.A.* **161 L7** 34 25N 119 42W
Santa Bárbara, *Amazonas, Venezuela* **168 C4** 3 57N 67 6W
Santa Bárbara, *Barinas, Venezuela* **168 B3** 7 47N 71 10W
Santa Bárbara, Mt., *Spain* **41 H2** 37 23N 2 50W
Santa Bárbara, Serra de, *Azores* **9 d1** 38 44N 27 19W
Santa Barbara Channel, *U.S.A.* **161 L7** 34 15N 120 0W
Santa Barbara I., *U.S.A.* **161 M7** 33 29N 119 2W
Santa Catalina, *Colombia* **168 A2** 10 36N 75 17W
Santa Catalina, *Phil.* **81 G4** 9 20N 122 52 E
Santa Catalina, *Solomon Is.* **133 N12** 10 53 S 162 29 E
Santa Catalina, Gulf of, *U.S.A.* **161 N9** 33 10N 117 50W
Santa Catalina, I., *Mexico* **162 B2** 25 40N 110 50W
Santa Catalina I., *U.S.A.* **161 M8** 33 23N 118 25W
Santa Catarina □, *Brazil* **175 B6** 27 25 S 48 30W
Santa Catarina, I. de, *Brazil* **175 B6** 27 30 S 48 40W
Santa Caterina di Pittinuri, *Italy* **46 B1** 40 6N 8 27 E
Santa Caterina Villarmosa, *Italy* **47 E7** 37 35N 14 2 E
Santa Cecília, *Brazil* **175 B5** 26 56 S 50 18W
Santa Clara, *Cuba* **164 B4** 22 20N 80 0W
Santa Clara, *Calif., U.S.A.* **160 H5** 37 21N 121 57W
Santa Clara, *Utah, U.S.A.* **159 H7** 37 8N 113 39W
Santa Clara, El Golfo de, *Mexico* **162 A2** 31 42N 114 30W
Santa Clara de Olimar, *Uruguay* **175 C5** 32 50 S 54 54W
Santa Clarita, *U.S.A.* **161 L8** 34 24N 118 30W
Santa Clotilde, *Peru* **168 D3** 2 33 S 73 45W
Santa Coloma de Farners, *Spain* **40 D7** 41 50N 2 39 E
Santa Coloma de Gramenet, *Spain* **40 D7** 41 27N 2 13 E
Santa Comba, *Spain* **42 B2** 43 2N 8 49W
Santa Croce Camerina, *Italy* **47 F7** 36 50N 14 31 E
Santa Croce di Magliano, *Italy* **45 G11** 41 42N 14 59 E
Santa Cruz, *Argentina* **176 D3** 50 0 S 68 32W
Santa Cruz, *Bolivia* **173 D5** 17 43 S 63 10W
Santa Cruz, *Brazil* **170 C4** 6 13 S 36 1W
Santa Cruz, *Chile* **174 C1** 34 38 S 71 27W
Santa Cruz, *Costa Rica* **164 D2** 10 15N 85 35W
Santa Cruz, *Madeira* **9 c** 32 42N 16 46W
Santa Cruz, *Peru* **172 B2** 5 40 S 75 56W
Santa Cruz, *Davao del S., Phil.* **81 H5** 6 50N 125 25 E
Santa Cruz, *Laguna, Phil.* **80 D3** 14 20N 121 24 E
Santa Cruz, *Marinduque, Phil.* **80 E4** 13 28N 122 2 E
Santa Cruz, *Mind. Occ., Phil.* **80 E3** 13 4N 120 43 E
Santa Cruz, *Zambales, Phil.* **80 D2** 15 46N 119 55 E
Santa Cruz, *U.S.A.* **160 J4** 36 58N 122 1W
Santa Cruz, *Venezuela* **169 B5** 8 3N 64 27W
Santa Cruz □, *Argentina* **176 C3** 49 0 S 70 0W
Santa Cruz □, *Bolivia* **173 D5** 17 43 S 63 10W
Santa Cruz →, *Argentina* **176 D3** 50 10 S 68 20W
Santa Cruz, I., *Ecuador* **172 a** 0 38 S 90 23W
Santa Cruz Cabrália, *Brazil* **171 E4** 16 17 S 39 2W
Santa Cruz da Graciosa, *Azores* **9 d1** 39 5N 28 1W
Santa Cruz das Flores, *Azores* **9 d2** 39 27N 31 7W
Santa Cruz de la Palma, *Canary Is.* **9 e1** 28 41N 17 46W
Santa Cruz de Mudela, *Spain* **43 G7** 38 39N 3 28W
Santa Cruz de Tenerife, *Canary Is.* **9 e1** 28 28N 16 15W
Santa Cruz del Norte, *Cuba* **164 B3** 23 9N 81 55W
Santa Cruz del Retamar, *Spain* **42 E6** 40 8N 4 14W
Santa Cruz del Sur, *Cuba* **164 B4** 20 44N 78 0W
Santa Cruz do Rio Pardo, *Brazil* **175 A6** 22 54 S 49 37W
Santa Cruz do Sul, *Brazil* **175 B5** 29 42 S 52 25W
Santa Cruz I., *U.S.A.* **161 M7** 34 1N 119 43W
Santa Cruz Is., *Solomon Is.* **134 J8** 10 30 S 166 0 E
Santa Cruz Mts., *Jamaica* **164 a** 17 58N 77 43W
Santa Domingo, Cay, *Bahamas* **164 B4** 21 25N 75 15W
Sant' Egídio alla Vibrata, *Italy* **45 F10** 42 49N 13 42 E
Santa Elena, *Argentina* **174 C4** 30 58 S 59 47W
Santa Elena, *Ecuador* **168 D1** 2 16 S 80 52W
Santa Elena, *Phil.* **80 D4** 14 12N 122 24 E
Santa Elena, C., *Costa Rica* **164 D2** 10 54N 85 56W
Sant' Eufémia, G. di, *Italy* **47 D9** 38 51N 16 4 E
Santa Eulàlia des Riu, *Spain* **38 D2** 38 59N 1 32 E
Santa Fe, *Argentina* **174 C3** 31 35 S 60 41W
Santa Fe, *Nueva Vizcaya, Phil.* **80 C3** 16 10N 120 57 E
Santa Fe, *Romblon, Phil.* **80 E4** 12 10N 122 0 E
Santa Fe, *Spain* **43 H7** 37 11N 3 43W
Santa Fe, *U.S.A.* **159 J11** 35 41N 105 57W
Santa Fé □, *Argentina* **174 C3** 31 50 S 60 55W
Santa Fé, Canal de, *Ecuador* **172 a** 0 48 S 89 55W
Santa Fé, I., *Ecuador* **172 a** 0 49 S 90 5W
Santa Fé do Sul, *Brazil* **171 F1** 20 13 S 50 56W
Santa Filomena, *Brazil* **170 C2** 9 6 S 45 50W
Santa Fiora, *Italy* **45 F8** 42 50N 11 35 E
Santa Gertrudis, *Spain* **38 C1** 39 0N 1 26 E
Santa Giustina, *Italy* **45 B9** 46 10N 12 5 E
Santa Helena, *Brazil* **170 B2** 2 14 S 45 18W
Santa Helena de Goiás, *Brazil* **171 E1** 17 53 S 50 35W
Santa Inês, *Bahia, Brazil* **171 D4** 13 17 S 39 48W
Santa Inês, *Maranhão, Brazil* **170 B2** 3 39 S 45 20W
Santa Inés, *Spain* **43 G5** 38 32N 5 37W
Santa Inés, I., *Chile* **176 D2** 54 0 S 73 0W
Santa Isabel = Rey Malabo, *Eq. Guin.* **113 E6** 3 45N 8 50 E
Santa Isabel, *Argentina* **174 D2** 36 10 S 66 54W
Santa Isabel, *Solomon Is.* **133 M10** 8 0 S 159 0 E
Santa Isabel, Pico, *Eq. Guin.* **113 E6** 3 36N 8 49 E
Santa Isabel do Araguaia, *Brazil* **170 C2** 6 7 S 48 19W
Santa Isabel do Morro, *Brazil* **171 D1** 11 34 S 50 40W
Santa Isabel do Río Negro, *Brazil* **169 D4** 0 24 S 65 2W
Santa Lucía, *Corrientes, Argentina* **174 B4** 28 58 S 59 5W
Santa Lucía, *San Juan, Argentina* **174 C2** 31 30 S 68 30W
Santa Lucia, *Phil.* **80 C3** 17 7N 120 27 E
Santa Lucía, *Spain* **41 H4** 37 35N 0 58W
Santa Lucia, *Uruguay* **174 C4** 34 27 S 56 24W
Santa Lucia Range, *U.S.A.* **160 K5** 36 0N 121 20W
Santa Luzia, *C. Verde Is.* **9 j** 16 50N 24 35W
Santa Magdalena, I., *Mexico* **162 C2** 24 40N 112 15W
Santa Margarita, *Argentina* **174 D3** 38 28 S 61 35W
Santa Margarita, *Spain* **38 B4** 39 42N 3 6 E
Santa Margarita, *U.S.A.* **160 K6** 35 23N 120 37W
Santa Margarita →, *U.S.A.* **161 M9** 33 13N 117 23W
Santa Margarita, I., *Mexico* **162 C2** 24 30N 111 50W
Santa Margherita, *Italy* **46 D1** 38 58N 8 58 E
Santa Margherita Ligure, *Italy* **44 D6** 44 20N 9 11 E
Santa María, *Argentina* **174 B2** 26 40 S 66 0W
Santa Maria, *Azores* **9 d4** 36 58N 25 6W
Santa Maria, *Brazil* **175 B5** 29 40 S 53 48W
Santa Maria, *C. Verde Is.* **9 j** 16 31N 22 53W
Santa Maria, *Ilocos S., Phil.* **80 C3** 17 22N 120 29 E
Santa Maria, *Isabela, Phil.* **80 C3** 17 28N 121 45 E
Santa Maria, *Switz.* **33 C10** 46 36N 10 25 E
Santa Maria, *U.S.A.* **161 L6** 34 57N 120 26W
Santa María →, *Mexico* **162 A3** 31 0N 107 14W
Santa María, B. de, *Mexico* **162 B3** 25 10N 108 40W
Santa Maria, C. de, *Portugal* **43 J3** 36 58N 7 53W
Santa María, I., *Ecuador* **172 a** 1 17 S 90 26W
Santa Maria Cápua Vétere, *Italy* **47 A7** 41 5N 14 15 E
Santa Maria da Feira, *Portugal* **42 E2** 40 55N 8 35W
Santa Maria da Vitória, *Brazil* **171 D3** 13 24 S 44 12W
Santa María de Ipire, *Venezuela* **169 B4** 8 49N 65 19W
Santa Maria del Camí, *Spain* **38 B3** 39 38N 2 47 E
Santa Maria di Léuca, C., *Italy* **47 C11** 39 47N 18 22 E
Santa Maria do Boiaçu, *Brazil* **169 D5** 0 25 S 61 48W
Santa Maria do Suaçuí, *Brazil* **171 E3** 18 12 S 42 25W
Santa Maria dos Marmelos, *Brazil* **173 B5** 6 7 S 61 51W
Santa María la Real de Nieva, *Spain* **42 D6** 41 4N 4 24W
Santa Marinella, *Italy* **45 F8** 42 2N 11 52 E
Santa Marta, *Colombia* **168 A3** 11 15N 74 13W
Santa Marta, Sierra Nevada de, *Colombia* **168 A3** 10 55N 73 50W
Santa Marta de Tormes, *Spain* **42 E5** 40 57N 5 38W
Santa Marta Grande, C., *Brazil* **175 B6** 28 43 S 48 50W
Santa Marta Ortigueira, Ría de, *Spain* **42 B3** 43 44N 7 45W
Santa Maura = Levkás, *Greece* **39 B2** 38 40N 20 43 E
Santa Monica, *U.S.A.* **161 M8** 34 1N 118 29W
Santa Olalla, *Huelva, Spain* **43 H4** 37 54N 6 14W
Santa Olalla, *Toledo, Spain* **42 E6** 40 2N 4 25W
Santa Paula, *U.S.A.* **161 L7** 34 21N 119 4W
Santa Pola, *Spain* **41 G4** 38 13N 0 35W
Santa Ponça, *Spain* **38 B3** 39 30N 2 28 E
Santa Quitéria, *Brazil* **170 B3** 4 20 S 40 10W
Santa Rita, *Brazil* **168 D4** 3 29 S 69 19W
Santa Rita, *Colombia* **168 C4** 4 53N 68 24W
Santa Rita, *Phil.* **81 F5** 11 27N 124 56 E
Santa Rita, *U.S.A.* **159 K10** 32 48N 108 4W
Santa Rita, *Venezuela* **168 A3** 10 32N 71 32W
Santa Rita do Araquaia, *Brazil* **173 D7** 17 20 S 53 12W
Santa Rosa, *La Pampa, Argentina* **174 D3** 36 40 S 64 17W
Santa Rosa, *San Luis, Argentina* **174 C2** 32 21 S 65 10W
Santa Rosa, *Beni, Bolivia* **172 C4** 14 10 S 66 53W
Santa Rosa, *Pando, Bolivia* **172 C4** 10 36 S 67 20W
Santa Rosa, *Santa Cruz, Bolivia* **173 D5** 17 7 S 63 35W
Santa Rosa, *Brazil* **175 B5** 27 52 S 54 29W
Santa Rosa, *Colombia* **168 C4** 3 32N 69 48W
Santa Rosa, *El Oro, Ecuador* **168 D2** 3 27 S 79 58W
Santa Rosa, *Galápagos Is., Ecuador* **172 a** 0 40 S 90 25W
Santa Rosa, *Puno, Peru* **172 C3** 14 30 S 70 50W
Santa Rosa, *San Martin, Peru* **172 B2** 6 41 S 76 37W
Santa Rosa, *Phil.* **80 D3** 15 25N 120 57 E
Santa Rosa, *Calif., U.S.A.* **160 G4** 38 26N 122 43W
Santa Rosa, *N. Mex., U.S.A.* **155 H2** 34 57N 104 41W
Santa Rosa, *Venezuela* **168 C4** 1 29N 66 55W
Santa Rosa Beach, *U.S.A.* **152 E3** 30 22N 86 14W
Santa Rosa de Amanadona, *Venezuela* **168 C4** 1 29N 66 55W
Santa Rosa de Cabal, *Colombia* **168 C2** 4 52N 75 38W
Santa Rosa de Copán, *Honduras* **164 D2** 14 47N 88 46W
Santa Rosa de la Roca, *Bolivia* **173 D5** 16 3 S 61 34W
Santa Rosa de Osos, *Colombia* **168 B2** 6 39N 75 28W
Santa Rosa de Río Primero, *Argentina* **174 C3** 31 8 S 63 20W
Santa Rosa de Viterbo, *Colombia* **168 B3** 5 53N 72 59W
Santa Rosa del Palmar, *Bolivia* **173 D5** 16 54 S 62 24W
Santa Rosa I., *Calif., U.S.A.* **161 M6** 33 58N 120 6W
Santa Rosa I., *Fla., U.S.A.* **149 K2** 30 20N 86 50W
Santa Rosa Range, *U.S.A.* **158 F5** 41 45N 117 40W
Santa Rosalía, *Mexico* **162 B2** 27 20N 112 20W
Santa Sylvina, *Argentina* **174 B3** 27 50 S 61 10W
Santa Tecla = Nueva San Salvador, *El Salv.* **164 D2** 13 40N 89 18W
Santa Teresa, *Argentina* **174 C3** 33 25 S 60 47W
Santa Teresa, *Australia* **126 C1** 24 8 S 134 22 E
Santa Teresa, *Brazil* **171 E3** 19 55 S 40 36W
Santa Teresa, *Mexico* **163 B5** 25 17N 97 51W
Santa Teresa, *Venezuela* **169 C5** 4 43N 61 4W
Santa Teresa di Riva, *Italy* **47 E8** 37 57N 15 22 E
Santa Teresa Gallura, *Italy* **46 A2** 41 14N 9 11 E
Santa Teresinha, *Brazil* **170 D1** 10 28 S 50 31W
Santa Uxía, *Spain* **42 C2** 42 36N 8 58W
Santa Vitória, *Brazil* **171 E1** 18 50 S 50 8W
Santa Vitória do Palmar, *Brazil* **175 C5** 33 32 S 53 25W
Santa Ynez →, *U.S.A.* **161 L6** 35 41N 120 36W
Santa Ynez Mts., *U.S.A.* **161 L6** 34 30N 120 0W
Santa Ysabel, *U.S.A.* **161 M10** 33 7N 116 40W
Santadi, *Italy* **46 C1** 39 5N 8 43 E
Santaella, *Spain* **43 H6** 37 34N 4 51W
Santahar, *Bangla.* **90 C2** 24 48N 88 59 E
Santai, *China* **76 B5** 31 5N 104 58 E
Santaluz, *Brazil* **170 D4** 11 15 S 39 22W
Santana, *Brazil* **171 D3** 13 2 S 44 5W
Santana, *Madeira* **9 c** 32 48N 16 52W
Sântana, *Romania* **52 D6** 46 20N 21 30 E
Santana, Coxilha de, *Brazil* **175 C4** 30 50 S 55 35W
Santana do Ipanema, *Brazil* **170 C4** 9 22 S 37 14W
Santana do Livramento, *Brazil* **175 C5** 30 55 S 55 30W
Santander, *Colombia* **168 C2** 3 1N 76 28W
Santander, *Phil.* **81 G4** 9 25N 123 20 E
Santander, *Spain* **42 B7** 43 27N 3 51W
Santander □, *Colombia* **168 B3** 7 0N 73 15W
Santander Jiménez, *Mexico* **163 C5** 24 11N 98 29W
Santanilla, Is., *Honduras* **164 C3** 17 22N 83 57W
Santanyí, *Spain* **38 B4** 39 20N 3 5 E
Santaquin, *U.S.A.* **158 G8** 39 59N 111 47W
Santarcángelo di Romagna, *Italy* **45 D9** 44 4N 12 26 E
Santarém, *Brazil* **169 D7** 2 25 S 54 42W
Santarém, *Portugal* **43 F2** 39 12N 8 42W
Santarém □, *Portugal* **43 F2** 39 10N 8 40W
Santaren Channel, *W. Indies* **164 B4** 24 0N 79 30W
Santee, *U.S.A.* **161 N10** 32 50N 116 58W
Santee →, *U.S.A.* **149 J6** 33 7N 79 17W
Santéramo in Colle, *Italy* **47 B9** 40 49N 16 45 E
Santerno →, *Italy* **45 D8** 44 34N 11 58 E
Santhià, *Italy* **44 C5** 45 22N 8 10 E
Santi-Quaranta = Sarandë, *Albania* **38 B9** 39 52N 19 55 E
Santiago = São Tiago, *C. Verde Is.* **9 j** 15 0N 23 40W
Santiago, *Bolivia* **173 D6** 18 19 S 59 34W
Santiago, *Brazil* **175 B5** 29 11 S 54 52W
Santiago, *Chile* **174 C1** 33 24 S 70 40W
Santiago, *Panama* **164 E3** 8 0N 81 0W
Santiago, *Peru* **172 C2** 14 11 S 75 43W
Santiago, *Ilocos S., Phil.* **80 C3** 17 18N 120 27 E
Santiago, *Isabela, Phil.* **80 C3** 16 41N 121 33 E
Santiago □, *Chile* **174 C1** 33 30 S 70 50W
Santiago →, *Mexico* **136 G9** 25 11N 105 26W
Santiago →, *Peru* **168 D2** 4 27 S 77 38W
Santiago, C., *Chile* **176 D1** 50 46 S 75 27W
Santiago, Punta de, *Eq. Guin.* **113 E6** 3 12N 8 40 E
Santiago, Serranía de, *Bolivia* **173 D6** 18 25 S 59 25W
Santiago de Chuco, *Peru* **172 B2** 8 9 S 78 11W
Santiago de Compostela, *Spain* **42 C2** 42 52N 8 37W
Santiago de Cuba, *Cuba* **164 C4** 20 0N 75 49W
Santiago de los Cabelleros, *Dom. Rep.* **165 C5** 19 30N 70 40W

278 Santiago del Estero

Santiago del Estero, *Argentina* **174 B3** 27 50 S 64 15W
Santiago del Estero □, *Argentina* **174 B3** 27 40 S 63 15W
Santiago del Teide, *Canary Is.* **9 e1** 28 17N 16 48W
Santiago do Cacém, *Portugal* **43 G2** 38 1N 8 42W
Santiago Ixcuintla, *Mexico* **162 C3** 21 50N 105 11W
Santiago Papasquiaro, *Mexico* **162 C3** 25 0N 105 20W
Santiaguillo, L. de, *Mexico* **162 C4** 24 50N 104 50W
Santiguila, *Mali* **112 C3** 12 42N 7 25W
Santillana, *Spain* **42 B6** 43 24N 4 6W
Säntis, *Switz.* **33 B8** 47 15N 9 22 E
Santisteban del Puerto, *Spain* **43 G7** 38 17N 3 15W
Santo →, *Peru* **172 B2** 8 56 S 78 37W
Santo Amaro, *Brazil* **171 D4** 12 30 S 38 43W
Santo Anastácio, *Brazil* **175 A5** 21 58 S 51 39W
Santo André, *Brazil* **175 A6** 23 39 S 46 29W
Santo Ângelo, *Brazil* **175 B5** 28 15 S 54 15W
Santo Antão, *C. Verde Is.* **9 j** 16 52N 25 10W
Santo António, *São Tomé & Principe* **115 G6** 1 37N 7 27 E
Santo Antonio, *Brazil* **169 D5** 2 24 S 60 58W
Santo Antônio de Jesus, *Brazil* **171 D4** 12 58 S 39 16W
Santo Antônio do Içá, *Brazil* **168 D4** 3 5 S 67 57W
Santo Antônio do Leverger, *Brazil* **173 D6** 15 52 S 56 5W
Santo Corazón, *Bolivia* **173 D6** 18 0 S 58 45W
Santo Domingo, *Dom. Rep.* **165 C6** 18 30N 69 59W
Santo Domingo, *Baja Calif., Mexico* **162 A1** 30 43N 116 2W
Santo Domingo, *Baja Calif. S., Mexico* **162 B2** 25 32N 112 2W
Santo Domingo, *Nic.* **164 D3** 12 14N 84 59W
Santo Domingo de la Calzada, *Spain* **40 C2** 42 26N 2 57W
Santo Domingo de los Colorados, *Ecuador* **168 D2** 0 15 S 79 9W
Santo Domingo Pueblo, *U.S.A.* **159 J10** 35 31N 106 22W
Santo Stéfano di Camastro, *Italy* **47 D7** 38 1N 14 22 E
Santo Tirso, *Portugal* **42 D2** 41 21N 8 28W
Santo Tomás, *Ecuador* **172 a** 0 51 S 91 2W
Santo Tomás, *Mexico* **162 A1** 31 33N 116 24W
Santo Tomás, *Peru* **172 C3** 14 26 S 72 8W
Santo Tomás, Volcán, *Ecuador* **172 a** 0 48 S 91 7W
Santo Tomé, *Argentina* **175 B4** 28 40 S 56 5W
Santo Tomé de Guayana = Ciudad Guayana, *Venezuela* **169 B5** 8 0N 62 30W
Santomera, *Spain* **41 G3** 38 4N 1 3W
Santoña, *Spain* **42 B7** 43 29N 3 27W
Santoríni = Thíra, *Greece* **49 E7** 36 23N 25 27 E
Santos, *Brazil* **175 A6** 24 0 S 46 20W
Santos, Sierra de los, *Spain* **43 G5** 38 7N 5 12W
Santos Dumont, *Brazil* **171 F3** 22 55 S 43 10W
Sanur, *Indonesia* **79 K18** 8 41 S 115 15 E
Sanwer, *India* **92 H6** 22 59N 75 50 E
Sanxenxo, *Spain* **42 C2** 42 24N 8 49W
Sanxiang, *China* **69 G9** 22 21N 113 25 E
San'yō, *Japan* **72 C3** 34 2N 131 5 E
Sanyuan, *China* **74 G5** 34 35N 108 58 E
Sanyuki-Sammyaku, *Japan* **72 C6** 34 5N 134 0 E
Sanza Pombo, *Angola* **115 D3** 7 18 S 15 56 E
São Bartolomeu de Messines, *Portugal* **43 H2** 37 15N 8 17W
São Benedito, *Brazil* **170 B3** 4 3 S 40 53W
São Benedito →, *Brazil* **170 D3** 9 11 S 57 2W
São Bento, *Brazil* **170 B3** 2 42 S 44 50W
São Bento do Norte, *Brazil* **170 C4** 5 4 S 36 2W
São Bernardo do Campo, *Brazil* **171 F2** 23 45 S 46 34W
São Borja, *Brazil* **175 B4** 28 39 S 56 0W
São Brás de Alportel, *Portugal* **43 H3** 37 8N 7 37W
São Braz, C. de, *Angola* **115 D2** 9 58 S 13 19 E
São Caitano, *Brazil* **170 C4** 8 21 S 36 6W
São Carlos, *Brazil* **175 A6** 22 0 S 47 50W
São Cristóvão, *Brazil* **170 D4** 11 1 S 37 15W
São Domingos, *Brazil* **171 D2** 13 25 S 46 19W
São Domingos, *Guinea-Biss.* **112 C1** 12 19N 16 13 E
São Domingos do Maranhão, *Brazil* **170 C3** 5 42 S 44 22W
São Félix, *Brazil* **171 D1** 11 36 S 50 39W
São Felix do Xingu, *Brazil* **173 B7** 6 38 S 51 59W
São Filipe, *C. Verde Is.* **9 j** 15 2N 24 30W
São Francisco, *Brazil* **171 E3** 16 0 S 44 50W
São Francisco →, *Brazil* **170 D4** 10 30 S 36 24W
São Francisco do Maranhão, *Brazil* **170 C3** 6 15 S 42 52W
São Francisco do Sul, *Brazil* **175 B6** 26 15 S 48 36W
São Gabriel, *Brazil* **175 C5** 30 20 S 54 20W
São Gabriel da Cachoeira, *Brazil* **168 D4** 0 8 S 67 5W
São Gabriel da Palha, *Brazil* **171 E3** 18 47 S 40 39W
São Gonçalo, *Brazil* **171 F3** 22 48 S 43 5W
São Gotardo, *Brazil* **171 E2** 19 19 S 46 3W
Sao Hill, *Tanzania* **119 D4** 8 20 S 35 12 E
São João, *Guinea-Biss.* **112 C1** 11 32N 15 25W
São João da Baliza, *Brazil* **169 C6** 0 52N 59 52W
São João da Boa Vista, *Brazil* **175 A6** 22 0 S 46 52W
São João da Madeira, *Portugal* **42 E2** 40 54N 8 30W
São João da Pesqueira, *Portugal* **42 D3** 41 8N 7 24W
São João da Ponte, *Brazil* **171 E3** 15 56 S 44 1W
São João del Rei, *Brazil* **171 F3** 21 8 S 44 15W
São João do Araguaia, *Brazil* **170 C2** 5 23 S 48 46W
São João do Paraíso, *Brazil* **171 E3** 15 19 S 42 1W
São João do Piauí, *Brazil* **170 C3** 8 21 S 42 15W
São João dos Patos, *Brazil* **170 C3** 6 30 S 43 42W
São Joaquim, *Amazonas, Brazil* **168 D4** 0 1 S 67 16W
São Joaquim, *Sta. Catarina, Brazil* **175 B6** 28 18 S 49 56W
São Joaquim da Barra, *Brazil* **171 F2** 20 35 S 47 53W
São Jorge, *Azores* **9 d1** 38 38N 28 3W
São Jorge, Canal de, *Azores* **9 d1** 38 30N 28 0W
São Jorge, Pta. de, *Azores* **9 d1** 38 42N 27 34W
São Jorge, Pta. de, *Madeira* **9 c** 32 50N 16 53W
São José, *Brazil* **175 B5** 27 38 S 48 39W
São José, B. de, *Brazil* **170 B3** 2 38 S 44 4W
São José da Laje, *Brazil* **170 C4** 9 1 S 36 3W
São José de Mipibu, *Brazil* **170 C4** 6 5 S 35 15W
São José do Norte, *Brazil* **175 C5** 32 1 S 52 3W
São José do Peixe, *Brazil* **170 C3** 7 24 S 42 34W
São José do Rio Prêto, *Brazil* **175 A6** 20 50 S 49 20W
São José dos Campos, *Brazil* **175 A6** 23 7 S 45 52W
São Leopoldo, *Brazil* **175 B5** 29 50 S 51 10W
São Lourenço, *Brazil* **171 F2** 22 7 S 45 3W
São Lourenço →, *Brazil* **173 D6** 17 53 S 57 27W
São Lourenço, Pantanal do, *Brazil* **173 D6** 17 30 S 56 20W
São Lourenço, Pta. de, *Madeira* **9 c** 32 44N 16 39W
São Lourenço do Sul, *Brazil* **175 C5** 31 22 S 51 58W
São Luís, *Brazil* **170 B3** 2 39 S 44 15W
São Luís do Curu, *Brazil* **170 B4** 3 40 S 39 14W
São Luís do Tapajós, *Brazil* **169 D6** 4 25 S 56 12W
São Luís Gonzaga, *Brazil* **175 B5** 28 25 S 55 0W
São Marcos →, *Brazil* **171 E2** 18 15 S 47 37W
São Marcos, B. de, *Brazil* **170 B3** 2 0 S 44 0W
São Martinho da Cortiça, *Portugal* **42 E2** 40 18N 8 8W
São Mateus, *Azores* **9 d1** 38 26N 28 27W
São Mateus, *Brazil* **171 E4** 18 44 S 39 50W
São Mateus →, *Brazil* **171 E4** 18 35 S 39 44W
São Mateus do Sul, *Brazil* **175 B5** 25 52 S 50 23W
São Miguel, *Azores* **9 d3** 37 47N 25 30W
São Miguel do Araguaia, *Brazil* **171 D1** 13 19 S 50 13W
São Miguel do Oeste, *Brazil* **175 B5** 26 45 S 53 34W
São Miguel dos Campos, *Brazil* **170 C4** 9 47 S 36 5W
São Nicolau, *C. Verde Is.* **9 j** 16 20N 24 20W
São Nicolau →, *Angola* **115 E2** 14 16 S 12 22 E
São Nicolau →, *Brazil* **170 C3** 5 45 S 42 2W
São Paulo, *Brazil* **175 A6** 23 32 S 46 37W
São Paulo □, *Brazil* **175 A6** 22 0 S 49 0W
São Paulo, I., *Atl. Oc.* **8 F9** 0 50N 31 40W
São Paulo de Olivença, *Brazil* **168 D4** 3 27 S 68 48W
São Pedro do Sul, *Portugal* **42 E2** 40 46N 8 4W
São Rafael, *Brazil* **170 C4** 5 47 S 36 55W
São Raimundo das Mangabeiras, *Brazil* **170 C2** 7 1 S 45 29W
São Raimundo Nonato, *Brazil* **170 C3** 9 1 S 42 42W
São Romão, *Brazil* **171 E2** 16 22 S 45 4W
São Roque, *Madeira* **9 c** 32 46N 16 48W
São Roque, C. de, *Brazil* **170 C4** 5 30 S 35 16W
São Roque do Pico, *Azores* **9 d1** 38 31N 28 19W
São Sebastião, *Azores* **9 d1** 38 39N 27 6W
São Sebastião, I. de, *Brazil* **175 A6** 23 50 S 45 18W
São Sebastião do Paraíso, *Brazil* **175 A6** 20 54 S 46 59W
São Simão, *Brazil* **171 E1** 18 56 S 50 30W
São Teotónio, *Portugal* **43 H2** 37 30N 8 42W
São Tiago, *C. Verde Is.* **9 j** 15 0N 23 40W
São Tomé, *Brazil* **170 C4** 5 58 S 36 4W
São Tomé, *São Tomé & Principe* **115 G6** 0 10N 6 39 E
São Tomé, C. de, *Brazil* **171 F3** 22 0 S 40 59W
São Tomé, Pico de, *São Tomé & Principe* **115 G6** 0 16N 6 33 E
São Tomé & Principe ■, *Africa* **115 G6** 0 12N 6 39 E
São Vicente, *Brazil* **175 A6** 23 57 S 46 23W
São Vicente, *C. Verde Is.* **9 j** 17 0N 25 0W
São Vicente, *Madeira* **9 c** 32 48N 17 3W
São Vicente, C. de, *Portugal* **43 H1** 37 0N 9 0W
Saona, I., *Dom. Rep.* **165 C6** 18 10N 68 40W
Saône →, *France* **27 G11** 45 44N 4 50 E
Saône-et-Loire □, *France* **27 F11** 46 30N 4 50 E
Saonek, *Indonesia* **83 B4** 0 22 S 130 55 E
Saoura, O. →, *Algeria* **111 C4** 29 0N 0 55W
Sápai, *Greece* **51 E9** 41 2N 25 43 E
Sapam, Ao, *Thailand* **87 a** 8 0N 98 26 E
Sapanca, *Turkey* **100 B4** 40 41N 30 16 E
Sapão →, *Brazil* **170 D2** 11 1 S 45 32W
Saparua, *Indonesia* **82 B3** 3 33 S 128 40 E
Sapé, *Brazil* **170 C4** 7 6 S 35 13W
Sape, *Indonesia* **85 D5** 8 34 S 118 59 E
Sapele, *Nigeria* **113 D6** 5 50N 5 40 E
Sapelo I., *U.S.A.* **152 D8** 31 25N 81 12W
Sapelo Sound, *U.S.A.* **152 D8** 31 30N 81 10W
Şaphane, *Turkey* **49 B11** 39 1N 29 13 E
Sapi Safari Area, *Zimbabwe* **119 F2** 15 48 S 29 42 E
Sapiéntza, *Greece* **48 E3** 36 45N 21 43 E
Sapindji, *Dem. Rep. of the Congo* **115 D4** 9 39 S 23 12 E
Sapo Nat. Park, *Liberia* **112 D3** 5 15N 8 30W
Sapone, *Burkina Faso* **113 C4** 12 3N 1 35W
Saposoa, *Peru* **172 B2** 6 55 S 76 45W
Sapouy, *Burkina Faso* **113 C4** 11 34N 1 44W
Sapozhok, *Russia* **60 D5** 53 59N 40 41 E
Sapphire, *Australia* **126 C4** 23 28 S 147 43 E
Sappho, *U.S.A.* **160 B2** 48 4N 124 16W
Sapporo, *Japan* **70 C10** 43 0N 141 21 E
Sapri, *Italy* **47 B8** 40 4N 15 38 E
Sapu, *Angola* **115 E3** 12 28 S 19 26 E
Sapudi, *Indonesia* **85 D4** 7 6 S 114 20 E
Sapulpa, *U.S.A.* **155 H6** 35 59N 96 5W
Saqqez, *Iran* **101 D12** 36 15N 46 20 E
Sar Dasht, *Iran* **97 C6** 32 32N 48 52 E
Sar-e Pol, *Afghan.* **91 A2** 36 10N 66 0 E
Sar-e Pol □, *Afghan.* **91 A2** 36 20N 65 50 E
Sar Gachīneh = Yāsūj, *Iran* **97 D6** 30 31N 51 31 E
Sar Planina, *Macedonia* **50 E4** 42 0N 21 0 E
Sara, *Burkina Faso* **112 C4** 11 40N 3 53W
Sara, *Niger* **109 D2** 20 46N 12 35 E
Sara, *Phil.* **81 F4** 11 16N 123 1 E
Sara Buri = Saraburi, *Thailand* **86 E3** 14 30N 100 55 E
Sarāb, *Iran* **101 D12** 37 55N 47 40 E
Sarabadi, *Iraq* **96 C5** 33 1N 44 48 E
Saraburi, *Thailand* **86 E3** 14 30N 100 55 E
Saradiya, *India* **92 J4** 21 34N 70 2 E
Saraféré, *Mali* **112 B4** 15 50N 3 40W
Saragossa = Zaragoza, *Spain* **40 D4** 41 39N 0 53W
Saraguro, *Ecuador* **168 D2** 3 35 S 79 16W
Sarai Naurang, *Pakistan* **92 C4** 32 50N 70 47 E
Saraikela, *India* **93 H11** 22 42N 85 56 E
Saraipali, *India* **94 D6** 21 20N 82 59 E
Saraiu, *Romania* **53 F13** 44 43N 28 10 E
Sarajevo, *Bos.-H.* **52 G3** 43 52N 18 26 E
Sarakhs, *Turkmenistan* **97 B9** 36 32N 61 13 E
Saraktash, *Russia* **64 F6** 51 47N 56 22 E
Saramacca →, *Surinam* **169 B6** 5 50N 55 55W
Saramati, *Burma* **90 C5** 25 44N 95 2 E
Saran, Gunung, *Indonesia* **85 C4** 0 30 S 111 25 E
Saranac, *U.S.A.* **157 B11** 42 56N 85 13W
Saranac L., *U.S.A.* **151 B10** 44 20N 74 10W
Saranac Lake, *U.S.A.* **151 B10** 44 20N 74 8W
Saranda, *Tanzania* **118 D3** 5 45 S 34 59 E
Sarandë, *Albania* **38 B9** 39 52N 19 55 E
Sarandí del Yi, *Uruguay* **175 C4** 33 18 S 55 38W
Sarandí Grande, *Uruguay* **174 C4** 33 44 S 56 20W
Sarangani □, *Phil.* **81 J5** 5 45N 125 20 E
Sarangani B., *Phil.* **81 J5** 6 0N 125 13 E
Sarangani Is., *Phil.* **81 J5** 5 25N 125 25 E
Sarangarh, *India* **94 D6** 21 30N 83 5 E
Saransk, *Russia* **60 C7** 54 10N 45 10 E
Sarapul, *Russia* **64 C4** 56 28N 53 48 E
Sarar Plain = Bannaanka Saraar, *Somali Rep.* **120 C3** 9 25N 46 17 E
Sarasota, *U.S.A.* **149 M4** 27 20N 82 32W
Saratoga, *Calif., U.S.A.* **160 H4** 37 16N 122 2W
Saratoga, *Wyo., U.S.A.* **158 F10** 41 27N 106 49W
Saratoga Springs, *U.S.A.* **151 C11** 43 5N 73 47W
Saratok, *Malaysia* **78 D4** 1 55N 111 17 E
Saratov, *Russia* **60 E7** 51 30N 46 2 E
Saravane, *Laos* **86 E6** 15 43N 106 25 E
Sarawak □, *Malaysia* **85 B4** 2 0N 113 0 E
Saray, *Tekirdağ, Turkey* **51 E11** 41 26N 27 55 E
Saray, *Van, Turkey* **101 C11** 38 38N 44 9 E
Saraya, *Guinea* **112 C2** 12 50N 11 45W
Saraya, *Senegal* **112 C2** 12 50N 11 45W
Saraycık, *Turkey* **49 B11** 39 1N 29 49 E
Sarayköy, *Turkey* **49 D10** 37 55N 28 54 E
Saraylar, *Turkey* **51 F11** 40 39N 27 40 E
Sarayönü, *Turkey* **100 C5** 38 16N 32 24 E
Sarbāz, *Iran* **97 E9** 26 38N 61 19 E
Sarbīsheh, *Iran* **97 C8** 32 30N 59 40 E
Sárbogárd, *Hungary* **52 D3** 46 50N 18 40 E
Sarca →, *Italy* **44 C7** 45 52N 10 52 E
Sarcelles, *France* **27 D9** 48 59N 2 23 E
Sardalas, *Libya* **108 C2** 25 50N 10 34 E
Sardarshahr, *India* **92 E6** 28 30N 74 29 E
Sardegna □, *Italy* **46 B1** 40 0N 9 0 E
Sardhana, *India* **92 E7** 29 9N 77 39 E
Sardina, Pta., *Canary Is.* **9 e1** 28 9N 15 44W
Sardinata, *Colombia* **168 B3** 8 5N 72 48W
Sardinia = Sardegna □, *Italy* **46 B1** 40 0N 9 0 E
Sardinia, *U.S.A.* **157 F13** 39 0N 83 49W
Sardis, *Turkey* **49 C10** 38 28N 28 2 E
Sardis, *U.S.A.* **152 C8** 32 58N 81 46W
Sārdūīyeh = Dar Mazār, *Iran* **97 D8** 29 14N 57 20 E
Saren, *Indonesia* **79 J18** 8 26 S 115 34 E
S'Arenal, *Spain* **38 B3** 39 30N 2 45 E
Sarentino, *Italy* **45 B8** 46 38N 11 21 E
Saréyamou, *Mali* **112 B4** 16 7N 3 10W
Sargans, *Switz.* **33 B8** 47 3N 9 15 E
Sargasso Sea, *Atl. Oc.* **8 D4** 27 0N 72 0W
Sargent, *U.S.A.* **152 B5** 33 26N 84 52W
Sargodha, *Pakistan* **91 B4** 32 10N 72 40 E
Sarh, *Chad* **109 G8** 9 5N 18 23 E
Sarhala, *Ivory C.* **112 D3** 8 22N 6 8W
Sarhro, Jebel, *Morocco* **110 B4** 31 6N 5 0W
Sārī, *Iran* **97 B7** 36 30N 53 4 E
Sari d'Orcino, *France* **29 F12** 42 3N 8 49 E
Sária, *Greece* **49 F9** 35 54N 27 17 E
Saria, *India* **93 J10** 21 38N 83 22 E
Sariab, *Pakistan* **92 D2** 30 6N 66 59 E
Sarıbeyler, *Turkey* **49 B9** 39 24N 27 35 E
Saricumbe, *Angola* **115 E3** 12 12 S 19 46 E
Sarıgöl, *Turkey* **100 C3** 38 14N 28 41 E
Sarikamiş, *Turkey* **101 B10** 40 22N 42 35 E
Sarıkaya, *Turkey* **100 C6** 39 29N 35 22 E
Sarikei, *Malaysia* **85 B4** 2 8N 111 30 E
Sarıköy, *Turkey* **51 F11** 40 12N 27 37 E
Sarila, *India* **93 G8** 25 46N 79 41 E
Sarina, *Australia* **126 C4** 21 22 S 149 13 E
Sariñena, *Spain* **40 D4** 41 47N 0 10W
Sariri, *Papua N. G.* **132 E5** 9 11 S 148 35 E
Sarita, *U.S.A.* **155 M6** 27 13N 97 47W
Sariwŏn, *N. Korea* **75 E13** 38 31N 125 46 E
Sariyar Barajı, *Turkey* **100 B4** 40 2N 31 33 E
Sariyer, *Turkey* **51 E13** 41 10N 29 3 E
Sarju →, *India* **93 F9** 27 21N 81 23 E
Sark, *U.K.* **21 H5** 49 25N 2 22W
Sarkad, *Hungary* **52 D6** 46 47N 21 23 E
Sarkari Tala, *India* **92 F4** 27 39N 70 52 E
Şarkışla, *Turkey* **100 C7** 39 21N 36 25 E
Şarköy, *Turkey* **51 F11** 40 36N 27 6 E
Sarlat-la-Canéda, *France* **28 D5** 44 54N 1 13 E
Sărmăşag, *Romania* **52 C7** 47 21N 22 50 E
Sărmaşu, *Romania* **53 D9** 46 45N 24 13 E
Sarmi, *Indonesia* **83 B5** 1 49 S 138 44 E
Sarmiento, *Argentina* **176 C3** 45 35 S 69 5W
Sarmizegetusa, *Romania* **52 E7** 45 31N 22 47 E
Särna, *Sweden* **16 C7** 61 41N 13 8 E
Sarnano, *Italy* **45 E10** 43 2N 13 18 E
Sarnen, *Switz.* **32 C6** 46 53N 8 13 E
Sarnia, *Canada* **140 D3** 42 58N 82 23W
Sarno, *Italy* **47 B7** 40 49N 14 37 E
Sarnthein = Sarentino, *Italy* **45 B8** 46 38N 11 21 E
Särö, *Sweden* **17 G5** 57 31N 11 57 E
Saroako, *Indonesia* **82 B2** 2 31 S 121 22 E
Sarolangun, *Indonesia* **84 C2** 2 19 S 102 42 E
Saronikós Kólpos, *Greece* **48 D5** 37 45N 23 45 E
Saronno, *Italy* **44 C6** 45 38N 9 2 E
Saros Körfezi, *Turkey* **51 F10** 40 30N 26 15 E
Sárospatak, *Hungary* **52 B6** 48 18N 21 33 E
Sarowbī, *Afghan.* **91 B3** 34 36N 69 44 E
Sarpsborg, *Norway* **15 G14** 59 16N 11 7 E
Sarracín, *Spain* **42 C7** 42 15N 3 45W
Sarralbe, *France* **27 D14** 49 0N 7 1 E
Sarrat, *Phil.* **80 B3** 18 9N 120 39 E
Sarre = Saar →, *Europe* **24 E6** 49 41N 6 32 E
Sarre, *Italy* **44 C4** 45 40N 7 15 E
Sarre-Union, *France* **27 D14** 48 57N 7 4 E
Sarrebourg, *France* **27 D14** 48 43N 7 3 E
Sarreguemines, *France* **27 C14** 49 5N 7 4 E
Sarria, *Spain* **42 C3** 42 49N 7 29W
Sarrión, *Spain* **40 E4** 40 9N 0 49W
Sarro, *Mali* **112 C3** 13 40N 5 15W
Sarstedt, *Germany* **30 C5** 52 14N 9 52 E
Sartène, *France* **29 G12** 41 38N 8 58 E
Sarthe □, *France* **26 D7** 48 10N 0 10 E
Sarthe →, *France* **26 E6** 47 33N 0 31W
Sartilly, *France* **26 D5** 48 45N 1 28W
Saruhanlı, *Turkey* **49 C9** 38 44N 27 36 E
Sărulești, *Romania* **53 F11** 44 25N 26 39 E
Saruna →, *Pakistan* **92 F2** 26 31N 67 7 E
Sarupeta, *India* **90 B3** 26 30N 91 5 E
Saruwaged Ra., *Papua N. G.* **132 D4** 6 13 S 146 45 E
Sárvár, *Hungary* **52 C1** 47 15N 16 56 E
Sarvar, *India* **92 F6** 26 4N 75 0 E
Sarvestān, *Iran* **97 D7** 29 20N 53 10 E
Särvfjället, *Sweden* **16 B7** 62 42N 13 30 E
Sárvíz →, *Hungary* **52 D3** 46 24N 18 41 E
Sary-Tash, *Kyrgyzstan* **66 F8** 39 44N 73 15 E
Saryaghash, *Kazakstan* **65 C4** 41 27N 69 9 E
Sarybulaq, *Kazakstan* **65 B5** 43 23N 71 29 E
Sarych, Mys, *Ukraine* **59 K7** 44 25N 33 45 E
Sarykemer, *Kazakstan* **65 B5** 43 0N 71 30 E
Sarykolskiy Khrebet, *Tajikistan* **65 D7** 38 30N 74 30 E
Saryözek, *Kazakstan* **65 A8** 44 22N 77 59 E
Saryshagan, *Kazakstan* **66 E8** 46 12N 73 38 E
Sarzana, *Italy* **44 D6** 44 7N 9 58 E
Sarzeau, *France* **26 E4** 47 31N 2 48W
Sasabeneh, *Ethiopia* **120 C2** 7 59N 44 43 E
Sasamungga, *Solomon Is.* **133 L9** 7 0 S 156 50 E
Sasan Gir, *India* **92 J4** 21 10N 70 36 E
Sasaram, *India* **93 G11** 24 57N 84 5 E
Sasari, Mt., *Solomon Is.* **133 M10** 8 10 S 159 30 E
Sasayama, *Japan* **73 B7** 35 4N 135 13 E
Sasebo, *Japan* **72 D1** 33 10N 129 43 E
Saser, *India* **93 B7** 34 50N 77 50 E
Saskatchewan □, *Canada* **143 C7** 54 40N 106 0W
Saskatchewan →, *Canada* **143 C8** 53 37N 100 40W
Saskatoon, *Canada* **143 C7** 52 10N 106 38W
Saskylakh, *Russia* **67 B12** 71 55N 114 1 E
Sasolburg, *S. Africa* **117 D4** 26 46 S 27 49 E
Sasovo, *Russia* **60 C5** 54 25N 41 55 E
Sassandra, *Ivory C.* **112 E3** 4 55N 6 8W
Sassandra →, *Ivory C.* **112 E3** 4 58N 6 5W
Sássari, *Italy* **46 B1** 40 43N 8 34 E
Sassnitz, *Germany* **30 A9** 54 29N 13 39 E
Sasso Marconi, *Italy* **45 D8** 44 24N 11 15 E
Sassocorvaro, *Italy* **45 E9** 43 47N 12 30 E
Sassoferrato, *Italy* **45 E9** 43 26N 12 51 E
Sasstown, *Liberia* **112 E3** 4 45N 8 27W
Sassuolo, *Italy* **44 D7** 44 33N 10 47 E
Sástago, *Spain* **40 D4** 41 19N 0 21W
Sastöbe, *Kazakstan* **65 B4** 42 33N 70 0 E
Sasumua Dam, *Kenya* **118 C4** 0 45 S 36 40 E
Sasvad, *India* **94 E2** 18 20N 74 2 E
Sasyk, Ozero, *Ukraine* **59 K5** 45 45N 29 20 E
Sata-Misaki, *Japan* **72 F2** 31 0N 130 40 E
Satadougou, *Mali* **112 C2** 12 25N 11 25W
Satakunta, *Finland* **15 F20** 61 45N 23 0 E
Satama-Soukoura, *Ivory C.* **112 D4** 7 55N 4 27W
Satara, *India* **94 F1** 17 44N 73 58 E
Satara, *S. Africa* **117 C5** 24 29 S 31 47 E
Satbarwa, *India* **93 H11** 23 55N 84 16 E
Satellite Beach, *U.S.A.* **153 G9** 28 10N 80 36W
Sätenäs, *Sweden* **17 F6** 58 27N 12 41 E
Säter, *Sweden* **16 D9** 60 21N 15 45 E
Satevó, *Mexico* **162 B3** 27 57N 106 7W
Satilla →, *U.S.A.* **152 E8** 30 59N 81 29W
Satipo, *Peru* **172 C3** 11 15 S 74 25W
Satka, *Russia* **64 D7** 55 3N 59 1 E
Satkania, *Bangla.* **90 D4** 22 4N 92 3 E
Satkhira, *Bangla.* **90 D2** 22 43N 89 8 E
Satmala Hills, *Andhra Pradesh, India* **94 E4** 19 45N 78 45 E
Satmala Hills, *Maharashtra, India* **94 D2** 20 15N 74 40 E
Satna, *India* **93 G9** 24 35N 80 50 E
Šator, *Bos.-H.* **45 D13** 44 11N 16 37 E
Sátoraljaújhely, *Hungary* **52 B6** 48 25N 21 41 E
Satpura Ra., *India* **94 D3** 21 25N 76 10 E
Satrup, *Germany* **30 A5** 54 41N 9 36 E
Satsuma-Hantō, *Japan* **72 F2** 31 25N 130 25 E
Satsuna-Shotō, *Japan* **71 K5** 30 0N 130 0 E
Sattahip, *Thailand* **86 F3** 12 41N 100 54 E
Sattenapalle, *India* **95 F5** 16 25N 80 6 E
Satu Mare, *Romania* **52 C7** 47 46N 22 55 E
Satu Mare □, *Romania* **52 C8** 47 45N 23 0 E
Satui, *Indonesia* **85 C5** 3 50 S 115 27 E
Satun, *Thailand* **87 J3** 6 43N 100 2 E
Satupa'itea, *Samoa* **133 W23** 13 45 S 172 18W
Saturnina →, *Brazil* **173 C6** 12 15 S 58 10W
Sauce, *Argentina* **174 C4** 30 5 S 58 46W
Sauceda, *Mexico* **162 B4** 25 55N 101 18W
Saucillo, *Mexico* **162 B3** 28 1N 105 17W
Sauda, *Norway* **15 G12** 59 40N 6 20 E
Saūdakent, *Kazakstan* **65 B4** 43 48N 69 58 E
Saudasjøen, *Norway* **18 E3** 59 38N 6 17 E
Saúde, *Brazil* **170 D3** 10 56 S 40 24W
Sauðarkrókur, *Iceland* **11 B7** 65 45N 19 40W
Saudi Arabia ■, *Asia* **96 B3** 26 0N 44 0 E
Sauerland, *Germany* **36 C4** 51 12N 7 59 E
Saugatuck, *U.S.A.* **157 B10** 42 40N 86 12W
Saugeen →, *Canada* **150 B3** 44 30N 81 22W
Saugerties, *U.S.A.* **151 D11** 42 5N 73 57W
Saugues, *France* **28 D7** 44 58N 3 32 E
Saugus, *U.S.A.* **161 L8** 34 25N 118 32W
Saujon, *France* **28 C3** 45 41N 0 55W
Sauk Centre, *U.S.A.* **154 C7** 45 44N 94 57W
Sauk City, *U.S.A.* **156 A7** 43 17N 89 43W
Sauk Rapids, *U.S.A.* **154 C7** 45 35N 94 10W
Saül, *Fr. Guiana* **169 C7** 3 37N 53 12W
Sauland, *Norway* **18 E5** 59 37N 8 56 E
Saulgau, *Germany* **31 G5** 48 1N 9 29 E
Saulieu, *France* **27 E11** 47 17N 4 14 E
Sault, *France* **29 D9** 44 6N 5 24 E
Sault Ste. Marie, *Canada* **140 C3** 46 30N 84 20W
Sault Ste. Marie, *U.S.A.* **139 D11** 46 30N 84 21W
Saumlaki, *Indonesia* **83 C4** 7 55 S 131 20 E
Saumur, *France* **26 E6** 47 15N 0 5W
Saundatti, *India* **95 G2** 15 47N 75 7 E
Saunders, C., *N.Z.* **131 F5** 45 53 S 170 45 E
Saunders I., *Antarctica* **7 B1** 57 48 S 26 28W
Saunders Point, *Australia* **125 E4** 27 52 S 125 38 E
Saunemin, *U.S.A.* **157 D8** 40 54N 88 24W
Saupite, *Angola* **115 E3** 13 54 S 17 43 E
Saurbær, *Borgarfjarðarsýsla, Iceland* **11 C5** 64 24N 21 35W
Saurbær, *Eyjafjarðarsýsla, Iceland* **11 B8** 65 27N 18 13W
Sauri, *Nigeria* **113 C6** 11 42N 6 44 E
Saurimo, *Angola* **115 D4** 9 40 S 20 12 E
Sausalito, *U.S.A.* **160 H4** 37 51N 122 29W
Sausapor, *Indonesia* **83 B4** 0 31 S 132 4 E
Sautatá, *Colombia* **168 B2** 7 50N 77 4W
Sauveterre-de-Béarn, *France* **28 E3** 43 24N 0 57W
Sauzé-Vaussais, *France* **28 B4** 46 8N 0 8 E
Savá, *Honduras* **164 C2** 15 32N 86 15W
Sava, *Italy* **47 B10** 40 24N 17 33 E
Sava →, *Serbia, Yug.* **52 F5** 44 50N 20 26 E
Savage, *U.S.A.* **154 B2** 47 27N 104 21W
Savage I. = Niue, *Cook Is.* **135 J11** 19 2 S 169 54W
Savage River, *Australia* **127 G4** 41 31 S 145 14 E
Savai'i, *Samoa* **133 W23** 13 28 S 172 24W
Savalou, *Benin* **113 D5** 7 57N 1 58 E
Savane, *Mozam.* **119 F4** 19 37 S 35 8 E
Savanna, *U.S.A.* **156 B6** 42 5N 90 8W
Savanna-la-Mar, *Jamaica* **164 a** 18 10N 78 10W
Savannah, *Ga., U.S.A.* **152 C8** 32 5N 81 6W
Savannah, *Mo., U.S.A.* **156 E2** 39 56N 94 50W
Savannah, *Tenn., U.S.A.* **149 H1** 35 14N 88 15W
Savannah →, *U.S.A.* **152 C9** 32 2N 80 53W
Savannah Beach = Tybee Island, *U.S.A.* **152 C9** 32 1N 80 51W
Savannakhet, *Laos* **86 D5** 16 30N 104 49 E
Savant L., *Canada* **140 B1** 50 16N 90 44W
Savant Lake, *Canada* **140 B1** 50 14N 90 40W
Savantvadi, *India* **95 G1** 15 55N 73 54 E
Savanur, *India* **95 G2** 14 59N 75 21 E
Săvârşin, *Romania* **52 D7** 46 1N 22 14 E
Savaştepe, *Turkey* **49 B9** 39 22N 27 42 E
Savda, *India* **94 D2** 21 9N 75 56 E
Savé, *Benin* **113 D5** 8 2N 2 29 E
Save →, *France* **28 E5** 43 47N 1 17 E
Save →, *Mozam.* **117 C5** 21 16 S 34 0 E
Sāveh, *Iran* **97 C6** 35 2N 50 20 E
Savelugu, *Ghana* **113 D4** 9 38N 0 54W
Savenay, *France* **26 E5** 47 20N 1 55W
Săveni, *Romania* **53 C11** 47 57N 26 52 E
Saverdun, *France* **28 E5** 43 14N 1 34 E
Saverne, *France* **27 D14** 48 43N 7 20 E
Savièse, *Switz.* **32 D4** 46 17N 7 22 E
Savigliano, *Italy* **44 D4** 44 38N 7 40 E
Savigny-sur-Braye, *France* **26 E7** 47 53N 0 49 E
Sávio →, *Italy* **45 D9** 44 19N 12 20 E
Šavnik, *Montenegro, Yug.* **50 D3** 42 59N 19 10 E
Savo, *Finland* **14 E22** 62 45N 27 30 E
Savo, *Solomon Is.* **133 M10** 9 8 S 159 48 E
Savognin, *Switz.* **33 C9** 46 36N 9 37 E
Savoie □, *France* **29 C10** 45 26N 6 25 E
Savona, *Italy* **44 D5** 44 17N 8 30 E
Savona, *U.S.A.* **150 D7** 42 17N 77 13W
Savonlinna, *Finland* **58 B5** 61 52N 28 53 E
Savoonga, *U.S.A.* **144 E5** 63 42N 170 29W
Savoy = Savoie □, *France* **29 C10** 45 26N 6 25 E
Şavşat, *Turkey* **101 B10** 41 15N 42 20 E
Sävsjö, *Sweden* **17 G8** 57 20N 14 40 E
Savur, *Turkey* **96 B4** 37 34N 40 53 E
Savusavu, *Fiji* **133 A2** 16 34 S 179 15 E
Savusavu B., *Fiji* **133 A2** 16 45 S 179 15 E
Sawahlunto, *Indonesia* **84 C2** 0 40 S 100 52 E
Sawai, *Indonesia* **83 B3** 3 0 S 129 5 E
Sawai Madhopur, *India* **92 G7** 26 0N 76 25 E
Sawaleke, *Fiji* **133 A2** 17 59 S 179 18 E
Sawang Daen Din, *Thailand* **86 D4** 17 28N 103 28 E
Sawankhalok, *Thailand* **86 D2** 17 19N 99 50 E
Sawara, *Japan* **73 B12** 35 55N 140 30 E
Sawatch Range, *U.S.A.* **159 G10** 38 30N 106 30W
Sawdā', Jabal as, *Libya* **108 C3** 28 51N 15 12 E
Sawel Mt., *U.K.* **23 B4** 54 50N 7 2W
Sawfajjin □, *Libya* **108 B3** 31 0N 15 0 E
Sawfajjin, W. →, *Libya* **108 B2** 31 41N 14 44 E
Sawi, *Thailand* **87 G2** 10 14N 99 5 E
Sawla, *Ghana* **112 D4** 9 17N 2 25W
Sawmills, *Zimbabwe* **119 F2** 19 30 S 28 2 E
Şawqirah, *Oman* **99 C7** 18 7N 56 32 E
Şawqirah, Ghubbat, *Oman* **99 C7** 18 35N 57 0 E
Sawtell, *Australia* **129 A10** 30 19 S 153 6 E
Sawtooth Range, *U.S.A.* **158 E6** 44 3N 114 58W
Sawu, *Indonesia* **82 C2** 10 35 S 121 50 E
Sawu Sea, *Indonesia* **82 C2** 9 30 S 121 50 E
Saxby →, *Australia* **126 B3** 18 25 S 140 53 E
Saxmundham, *U.K.* **21 E9** 52 13N 1 30 E
Saxon, *Switz.* **32 D4** 46 9N 7 11 E
Saxony = Sachsen □, *Germany* **30 E9** 50 55N 13 10 E
Saxony, Lower = Niedersachsen □, *Germany* **30 C4** 52 50N 9 0 E
Saxton, *U.S.A.* **150 F6** 40 13N 78 15W
Say, *Mali* **112 C4** 13 50N 4 57W
Say, *Niger* **113 C5** 13 8N 2 22 E
Saya, *Nigeria* **113 D5** 9 30N 3 18 E
Sayabec, *Canada* **141 C6** 48 35N 67 41W
Sayaboury, *Laos* **86 C3** 19 15N 101 45 E
Sayán, *Peru* **172 C2** 11 8 S 77 12W
Sayan, Vostochnyy, *Russia* **67 D10** 54 0N 96 0 E
Sayan, Zapadnyy, *Russia* **67 D10** 52 30N 94 0 E
Saydā, *Lebanon* **103 B4** 33 35N 35 25 E
Sayghān, *Afghan.* **91 B2** 35 10N 67 55 E
Sayhandulaan = Oldziyt, *Mongolia* **74 B5** 44 40N 109 1 E

Sayhūt, Yemen 99 D5 15 12N 51 10 E
Sayiádha, Greece 38 B10 39 38N 20 12 E
Saykhin, Kazakstan 61 F8 48 50N 46 47 E
Saylac = Zeila, Somali Rep. 120 B2 11 21N 43 30 E
Saylorville L., U.S.A. 156 C3 41 48N 93 46W
Saynshand, Mongolia 69 B6 44 55N 110 11 E
Sayō, Japan 72 C6 34 59N 134 22 E
Sayre, Okla., U.S.A. 155 H5 35 18N 99 38W
Sayre, Pa., U.S.A. 151 E8 41 59N 76 32W
Sayreville, U.S.A. 151 F10 40 28N 74 22W
Sayula, Mexico 162 D4 19 50N 103 40W
Sayward, Canada 142 C3 50 21N 125 55W
Saywūn, Yemen 99 D5 15 56N 48 47 E
Saza, Japan 72 D1 33 14N 129 39 E
Sazanit, Albania 50 F3 40 30N 19 20 E
Sázava →, Czech Rep. 34 B7 49 53N 14 24 E
Sazin, Pakistan 93 B5 35 35N 73 30 E
Sazlika →, Bulgaria 51 E9 41 59N 25 50 E
Sbeïtla, Tunisia 108 A1 35 12N 9 7 E
Scaër, France 26 D3 48 2N 3 42W
Scafell Pike, U.K. 20 C4 54 27N 3 14W
Scalea, Italy 47 C8 39 49N 15 47 E
Scalloway, U.K. 22 A7 60 9N 1 17W
Scalpay, U.K. 22 D3 57 18N 6 0W
Scammon Bay, U.S.A. 144 F6 61 51N 165 35W
Scandia, Canada 142 C6 50 20N 112 0W
Scandiano, Italy 44 D7 44 36N 10 43 E
Scandicci, Italy 45 E8 43 45N 11 11 E
Scandinavia, Europe 14 E16 64 0N 12 0 E
Scansano, Italy 45 F8 42 41N 11 20 E
Scapa Flow, U.K. 22 C5 58 53N 3 3W
Scappoose, U.S.A. 160 E4 45 45N 122 53W
Scarámia, Capo, Italy 47 F7 36 47N 14 29 E
Scarba, U.K. 22 E3 56 11N 5 43W
Scarborough, Trin. & Tob. 165 D7 11 11N 60 42W
Scarborough, U.K. 20 C7 54 17N 0 24W
Scargill, N.Z. 131 C7 42 56 S 172 58 E
Scariff I., Ireland 23 E1 51 44N 10 15W
Scarp, U.K. 22 C1 58 1N 7 8W
Scarsdale, Australia 128 D5 37 41 S 143 39 E
Scebeli, Wabi →, Somali Rep. 120 D2 2 0N 44 0 E
Šćedro, Croatia 45 E13 43 6N 16 43 E
Schaal See, Germany 30 B6 53 36N 10 55 E
Schaan, Liech. 33 B9 47 10N 9 31 E
Schaffhausen, Switz. 33 A7 47 42N 8 39 E
Schaffhausen □, Switz. 33 A7 47 42N 8 36 E
Schagen, Neths. 24 B4 52 49N 4 48 E
Schaghticoke, U.S.A. 151 D11 42 54N 73 35W
Schangnau, Switz. 32 C5 46 50N 7 47 E
Schänis, Switz. 33 B8 47 10N 9 3 E
Schärding, Austria 34 C6 48 27N 13 27 E
Scharhörn, Germany 30 B4 53 57N 8 24 E
Scheessel, Germany 30 B5 53 10N 9 29 E
Schefferville, Canada 141 B6 54 48N 66 50W
Scheibbs, Austria 34 C8 48 1N 15 9 E
Schelde →, Belgium 24 C4 51 15N 4 16 E
Schell City, U.S.A. 156 F2 38 1N 94 7W
Schell Creek Ra., U.S.A. 158 G6 39 15N 114 30W
Schellsburg, U.S.A. 150 F6 40 3N 78 39W
Schenectady, U.S.A. 151 D11 42 49N 73 57W
Schenevus, U.S.A. 151 D10 42 33N 74 50W
Scherfede, Germany 30 D5 51 32N 9 2 E
Schesaplana, Switz. 33 B9 47 5N 9 43 E
Schesslitz, Germany 31 F7 49 58N 11 1 E
Schiedam, Neths. 24 C4 51 55N 4 25 E
Schiermonnikoog, Neths. 24 A6 53 30N 6 15 E
Schiers, Switz. 33 C9 46 58N 9 41 E
Schiltigheim, France 27 D14 48 35N 7 45 E
Schio, Italy 45 C8 45 43N 11 21 E
Schladming, Austria 34 D6 47 23N 13 41 E
Schlanders = Silandro, Italy 44 B7 46 38N 10 46 E
Schlei →, Germany 30 A5 54 40N 10 0 E
Schleiden, Germany 30 E2 50 31N 6 28 E
Schleinitz Ra., Papua N. G. 132 B6 3 0 S 151 30 E
Schleiz, Germany 30 E7 50 35N 11 49 E
Schleswig, Germany 30 A5 54 31N 9 34 E
Schleswig-Holstein □, Germany 30 A5 54 30N 9 30 E
Schlieren, Switz. 33 B6 47 26N 8 27 E
Schlüchtern, Germany 31 E5 50 20N 9 32 E
Schmalkalden, Germany 30 E6 50 44N 10 26 E
Schmölln, Germany 30 E8 50 54N 12 19 E
Schneeberg, Austria 34 D8 47 47N 15 48 E
Schneeberg, Germany 30 E8 50 35N 12 38 E
Schneider, U.S.A. 157 C9 41 13N 87 28W
Schneverdingen, Germany 30 B5 53 7N 9 48 E
Schœlcher, Martinique 164 c 14 36N 61 7W
Schoharie, U.S.A. 151 D10 42 40N 74 19W
Schoharie →, U.S.A. 151 D10 42 57N 74 18W
Scholls, U.S.A. 160 E4 45 24N 122 56W
Schönberg, Mecklenburg-Vorpommern, Germany 30 B6 53 52N 10 56 E
Schönberg, Schleswig-Holstein, Germany 30 A6 54 23N 10 21 E
Schönebeck, Germany 30 C7 52 2N 11 44 E
Schönenwerd, Switz. 32 B6 47 23N 8 0 E
Schongau, Germany 31 H6 47 47N 10 53 E
Schöningen, Germany 30 C6 52 8N 10 56 E
Schoolcraft, U.S.A. 157 B11 42 7N 85 38W
Schopfheim, Germany 31 H3 47 38N 7 50 E
Schorndorf, Germany 31 G5 48 47N 9 32 E
Schortens, Germany 30 B3 53 31N 7 56 E
Schouten I., Australia 127 G4 42 20 S 148 20 E
Schouten Is. = Supiori, Indonesia 83 B5 1 0 S 136 0 E
Schouten Is., Papua N. G. 132 B3 3 30 S 144 30 E
Schouwen, Neths. 24 C3 51 43N 3 45 E
Schramberg, Germany 31 G4 48 13N 8 22 E
Schrankogel, Austria 34 D4 47 3N 11 7 E
Schreckhorn, Switz. 32 C6 46 36N 8 7 E
Schreiber, Canada 140 C2 48 45N 87 20W
Schrems, Austria 34 C8 48 47N 15 4 E
Schrobenhausen, Germany 31 G7 48 34N 11 16 E
Schröcken, Austria 33 B10 47 17N 10 5 E
Schroffenstein, Namibia 116 D2 27 11 S 18 42 E
Schroon Lake, U.S.A. 151 C11 43 50N 73 46W
Schruns, Austria 34 D2 47 5N 9 56 E
Schuler, Canada 143 C6 50 20N 110 6W
Schuls, Switz. 33 C10 46 48N 10 18 E
Schumacher, Canada 140 C3 48 30N 81 16W
Schüpfen, Switz. 32 B4 47 2N 7 24 E
Schüpfheim, Switz. 32 C6 46 57N 8 2 E
Schurz, U.S.A. 158 G4 38 57N 118 49W
Schuyler, U.S.A. 154 E6 41 27N 97 4W
Schuylerville, U.S.A. 151 C11 43 6N 73 35W
Schuylkill →, U.S.A. 151 G9 39 53N 75 12W
Schuylkill Haven, U.S.A. 151 F8 40 37N 76 11W
Schwabach, Germany 31 F7 49 19N 11 2 E
Schwaben □, Germany 31 G6 48 15N 10 30 E
Schwäbisch Gmünd, Germany 31 G5 48 48N 9 47 E
Schwäbisch Hall, Germany 31 F5 49 6N 9 44 E
Schwäbische Alb, Germany 31 G5 48 20N 9 30 E
Schwabmünchen, Germany 31 G6 48 10N 10 46 E
Schwalmstadt, Germany 30 E5 50 55N 9 10 E
Schwanden, Switz. 33 C8 46 58N 9 5 E
Schwandorf, Germany 31 F8 49 20N 12 7 E
Schwaner, Pegunungan, Indonesia 85 C4 1 0 S 112 30 E
Schwanewede, Germany 30 B4 53 14N 8 35 E
Schwarmstedt, Germany 30 C5 52 39N 9 38 E
Schwarze Elster →, Germany 30 D8 51 48N 12 50 E
Schwarzenberg, Germany 30 E8 50 32N 12 47 E
Schwarzenburg, Switz. 32 C4 46 49N 7 20 E
Schwarzrand, Namibia 116 D2 25 37 S 16 50 E
Schwarzwald, Germany 31 G4 48 30N 8 20 E
Schwatka Mts., U.S.A. 144 C8 67 20N 156 30W
Schwaz, Austria 34 D4 47 20N 11 44 E
Schwechat, Austria 35 C9 48 8N 16 28 E
Schwedt, Germany 30 B10 53 3N 14 16 E
Schweinfurt, Germany 31 E6 50 3N 10 14 E
Schweizer Mittelland, Switz. 32 C4 47 0N 7 15 E
Schweizer-Reneke, S. Africa 116 D4 27 11 S 25 18 E
Schwenningen = Villingen-Schwenningen, Germany 31 G4 48 3N 8 26 E
Schwerin, Germany 30 B7 53 36N 11 22 E
Schweriner See, Germany 30 B7 53 43N 11 28 E
Schwetzingen, Germany 31 F4 49 23N 8 35 E
Schwyz, Switz. 33 B7 47 2N 8 39 E
Schwyz □, Switz. 33 B7 47 2N 8 39 E
Sciacca, Italy 46 E6 37 31N 13 3 E
Sciao, Somali Rep. 120 D3 3 26N 45 21 E
Scicli, Italy 47 F7 36 47N 14 42 E
Scilla, Italy 47 D8 38 15N 15 43 E
Scilly, Isles of, U.K. 21 H1 49 56N 6 22W
Ścinawa, Poland 55 G3 51 25N 16 26 E
Scione, Greece 50 G7 39 57N 23 36 E
Scioto →, U.S.A. 157 D13 38 44N 83 1W
Scituate, U.S.A. 151 D14 42 12N 70 44W
Scobey, U.S.A. 154 A2 48 47N 105 25W
Scone, Australia 129 B9 32 5 S 150 52 E
Scordia, Italy 47 E7 37 18N 14 51 E
Scoresby Sund, Greenland 10 C8 70 28N 21 46W
Scoresbysund = Ittoqqortoormiit, Greenland 10 C8 70 20N 23 0W
Scornicești, Romania 53 F9 44 34N 24 33 E
Scotia, Calif., U.S.A. 158 F1 40 29N 124 6W
Scotia, N.Y., U.S.A. 151 D11 42 50N 73 58W
Scotia Sea, Antarctica 7 B18 56 5 S 56 0W
Scotland, Canada 150 C4 43 1N 80 22W
Scotland □, U.K. 22 E5 57 0N 4 0W
Scott, C., Australia 124 B4 13 30 S 129 49 E
Scott City, U.S.A. 154 F4 38 29N 100 54W
Scott Glacier, Antarctica 7 C8 66 15 S 100 5 E
Scott I., Antarctica 7 C11 67 0 S 179 0 E
Scott Is., Canada 142 C3 50 48N 128 40W
Scott L., Canada 143 B7 59 55N 106 18W
Scott Reef, Australia 124 B3 14 0 S 121 50 E
Scottburgh, S. Africa 117 E5 30 15 S 30 47 E
Scottdale, U.S.A. 150 F5 40 6N 79 35W
Scottish Borders □, U.K. 22 F6 55 35N 2 50W
Scotts Head, Australia 129 A10 30 45 S 153 0 E
Scottsbluff, U.S.A. 154 E3 41 52N 103 40W
Scottsboro, U.S.A. 149 H3 34 40N 86 2W
Scottsburg, U.S.A. 157 F11 38 41N 85 47W
Scottsdale, Australia 127 G4 41 9 S 147 31 E
Scottsdale, U.S.A. 159 K7 33 29N 111 56W
Scottsville, Ky., U.S.A. 149 G2 36 45N 86 11W
Scottsville, N.Y., U.S.A. 150 C7 43 2N 77 47W
Scottville, U.S.A. 148 D2 43 58N 86 17W
Scranton, U.S.A. 151 E9 41 25N 75 40W
Screven, U.S.A. 152 D7 31 29N 82 1W
Scugog, L., Canada 150 B6 44 10N 78 55W
Sculeni, Moldova 53 C12 47 20N 27 37 E
Scunthorpe, U.K. 20 D7 53 36N 0 39W
Scuol Schuls, Switz. 33 C10 46 48N 10 17 E
Scusciuban, Somali Rep. 120 B4 10 18N 50 12 E
Scutari = Shkodër, Albania 50 D3 42 4N 19 32 E
Scutari = Üsküdar, Turkey 51 F13 41 0N 29 5 E
Sea Lake, Australia 128 C5 35 28 S 142 55 E
Seabra, Brazil 171 D3 12 25 S 41 46W
Seabrook, L., Australia 125 F2 30 55 S 119 40 E
Seaford, U.K. 21 G8 50 47N 0 7 E
Seaford, U.S.A. 148 F8 38 39N 75 37W
Seaforth, Australia 126 J6 20 55 S 148 57 E
Seaforth, Canada 150 C3 43 35N 81 25W
Seaforth, L., U.K. 22 D2 57 52N 6 36W
Seagraves, U.S.A. 155 J3 32 57N 102 34W
Seaham, U.K. 20 C6 54 50N 1 20W
Seal →, Canada 143 B10 59 4N 94 48W
Seal L., Canada 141 B7 54 20N 61 30W
Seale, U.S.A. 152 C4 32 18N 85 10W
Sealy, U.S.A. 155 L6 29 47N 96 9W
Seaman, U.S.A. 157 F13 38 57N 83 34W
Searchlight, U.S.A. 161 K12 35 28N 114 55W
Searcy, U.S.A. 155 H9 35 15N 91 44W
Searles L., U.S.A. 161 K9 35 44N 117 21W
Seascale, U.K. 20 C4 54 24N 3 29W
Seaside, Calif., U.S.A. 160 J5 36 37N 121 50W
Seaside, Oreg., U.S.A. 160 E3 46 0N 123 56W
Seaspray, Australia 129 E7 38 25 S 147 15 E
Seattle, U.S.A. 160 C4 47 36N 122 20W
Seaview Ra., Australia 126 B4 18 40 S 145 45 E
Seaward Kaikoura Ra., N.Z. 131 C8 42 10 S 173 44 E
Seba, Indonesia 82 D2 10 29 S 121 50 E
Sebago L., U.S.A. 151 C14 43 52N 70 34W
Sebago Lake, U.S.A. 151 C14 43 51N 70 34W
Sebangka, Indonesia 84 B2 0 7N 104 36 E
Sebastian, U.S.A. 153 H9 27 49N 80 28W
Sebastián Vizcaíno, B., Mexico 162 B2 28 0N 114 30W
Sebastopol = Sevastopol, Ukraine 59 K7 44 35N 33 30 E
Sebastopol, U.S.A. 160 G4 38 24N 122 49W
Sebba, Burkina Faso 113 C5 13 35N 0 32 E
Sebderat, Eritrea 107 D4 15 26N 36 42 E
Sebdou, Algeria 111 B4 34 38N 1 19W
Sébé →, Gabon 114 C2 1 2S 13 6 E
Sébékoro, Mali 112 C3 12 58N 9 0W
Seben, Turkey 100 B4 40 24N 31 34 E
Sebeș, Romania 53 E8 45 58N 23 34 E
Sebeșului, Munții, Romania 53 E8 45 36N 23 40 E
Sebewaing, U.S.A. 148 D4 43 44N 83 27W
Sebezh, Russia 58 D5 56 14N 28 22 E
Sebha = Sabhah, Libya 108 C2 27 9N 14 29 E
Sébi, Mali 112 B4 15 50N 4 12W
Şebinkarahisar, Turkey 101 B8 40 22N 38 28 E
Sebiș, Romania 52 D7 46 23N 22 13 E
Seblat, Indonesia 84 C2 3 14 S 101 38 E
Sebnitz, Germany 30 E10 50 58N 14 15 E
Sebou, Oued →, Morocco 110 B3 34 16N 6 40W
Sebring, Fla., U.S.A. 149 M5 27 30N 81 27W
Sebring, Ohio, U.S.A. 150 F3 40 55N 81 2W
Sebringville, Canada 150 C3 43 24N 81 4W
Sebta = Ceuta, N. Afr. 110 A3 35 52N 5 18W
Sebuku, Indonesia 85 C5 3 30 S 116 25 E
Sebuku, Teluk, Malaysia 85 B5 4 0N 118 10 E
Sečanj, Serbia, Yug. 52 E5 45 25N 20 47 E
Secchia →, Italy 44 C8 45 4N 11 0 E
Sechelt, Canada 142 D4 49 25N 123 42W
Sechura, Peru 172 B1 5 39 S 80 50W
Sechura, Desierto de, Peru 172 B1 6 0S 80 30W
Seclin, France 27 B10 50 33N 3 2 E
Secondigny, France 26 F6 46 37N 0 26W
Sečovce, Slovak Rep. 35 C14 48 42N 21 40 E
Secretary I., N.Z. 131 F1 45 15 S 166 56 E
Secunderabad, India 94 F4 17 28N 78 30 E
Sécure →, Bolivia 173 D5 15 10 S 64 52W
Security-Widefield, U.S.A. 154 F2 38 45N 104 45W
Sedalia, U.S.A. 156 F3 38 42N 93 14W
Sedam, India 94 E3 17 11N 77 17 E
Sedan, Australia 128 C3 34 34 S 139 19 E
Sedan, France 27 C11 49 43N 4 57 E
Sedan, U.S.A. 155 G6 37 8N 96 11W
Sedano, Spain 42 C7 42 43N 3 49W
Sedaw, Burma 90 D6 22 19N 96 19 E
Seddon, N.Z. 131 B9 41 40 S 174 7 E
Seddonville, N.Z. 131 B7 41 33 S 172 1 E
Sedé Boqér, Israel 103 E3 30 52N 34 47 E
Sedeh, Fārs, Iran 97 D7 30 45N 52 11 E
Sedeh, Khorāsān, Iran 97 C8 33 20N 59 14 E
Séderon, France 29 D9 44 12N 5 32 E
Sederot, Israel 103 D3 31 32N 34 37 E
Sédhiou, Senegal 112 C1 12 44N 15 30W
Sedico, Italy 45 B9 46 8N 12 6 E
Sedlčany, Czech Rep. 34 B7 49 40N 14 25 E
Sedley, Canada 143 C8 50 10N 104 0W
Sedona, U.S.A. 159 J8 34 52N 111 46W
Sedova, Pik, Russia 66 B6 73 29N 54 58 E
Sedrata, Algeria 111 A6 36 7N 7 31 E
Sedro Woolley, U.S.A. 160 B4 48 30N 122 14W
Sedrun, Switz. 33 C7 46 36N 8 47 E
Šeduva, Lithuania 54 C10 55 45N 23 45 E
Sędziszów, Poland 55 H7 50 35N 20 4 E
Sędziszów Małapolski, Poland 55 H8 50 5N 21 45 E
Seebad Ahlbeck, Germany 30 B10 53 56N 14 10 E
Seefeld in Tirol, Austria 34 D4 47 19N 11 13 E
Seehausen, Germany 30 C7 52 54N 11 45 E
Seeheim, Namibia 116 D2 26 50 S 17 45 E
Seeheim-Jugenheim, Germany 31 F4 49 49N 8 40 E
Seeis, Namibia 116 C2 22 29 S 17 39 E
Seekoei →, S. Africa 116 E4 30 18 S 25 1 E
Seeley's Bay, Canada 151 B8 44 29N 76 14W
Seelow, Germany 30 C10 52 32N 14 23 E
Sées, France 26 D7 48 38N 0 10 E
Seesen, Germany 30 D6 51 54N 10 10 E
Seevetal, Germany 30 B6 53 26N 10 1 E
Sefadu, S. Leone 112 D2 8 35N 10 58W
Seferihisar, Turkey 49 C8 38 10N 26 50 E
Séfeto, Mali 112 C3 14 8N 9 49W
Sefrou, Morocco 110 B4 33 52N 4 52W
Sefton, N.Z. 131 D7 43 15 S 172 41 E
Sefuri-San, Japan 72 D2 33 28N 130 18 E
Sefwi Bekwai, Ghana 112 D4 6 10N 2 25W
Seg-ozero, Russia 56 B5 63 20N 33 46 E
Segaf, Kepulauan, Indonesia 83 B4 2 10 S 130 28 E
Segag, Ethiopia 120 C2 7 39N 42 50 E
Segamat, Malaysia 87 L4 2 30N 102 50 E
Şegarcea, Romania 53 F8 44 6N 23 43 E
Ségbana, Benin 113 C5 10 55N 3 42 E
Segbwema, S. Leone 112 D2 8 0N 11 0W
Seget, Indonesia 83 B4 1 24 S 130 58 E
Segezha, Russia 56 B5 63 44N 34 19 E
Segguer, O. →, Algeria 111 B5 32 14N 1 48 E
Seghe, Solomon Is. 133 M9 8 32 S 157 54 E
Segonzac, France 28 C3 45 36N 0 14W
Segorbe, Spain 40 F4 39 50N 0 30W
Ségou, Mali 112 C3 13 30N 6 16W
Segovia = Coco →, Cent. Amer. 164 D3 15 0N 83 8W
Segovia, Colombia 168 B3 7 7N 74 42W
Segovia, Spain 42 E6 40 57N 4 10W
Segovia □, Spain 42 E6 40 55N 4 10W
Segré, France 26 E6 47 40N 0 52W
Segre →, Spain 40 D5 41 40N 0 43 E
Seguam I., U.S.A. 144 K4 52 19N 172 30W
Seguam Pass, U.S.A. 144 L4 52 0N 172 30W
Séguédine, Niger 109 D2 20 9N 12 55 E
Séguéla, Ivory C. 112 D3 7 55N 6 40W
Séguénéga, Burkina Faso 113 C4 13 25N 1 58W
Seguin, U.S.A. 155 L6 29 34N 97 58W
Segundo →, Argentina 174 C3 30 53 S 62 44W
Segura →, Spain 41 G4 38 3N 0 44W
Segura, Sierra de, Spain 41 G2 38 5N 2 45W
Seh Konj, Kūh-e, Iran 97 D8 30 6N 57 30 E
Seh Qal'eh, Iran 97 C8 33 40N 58 24 E
Sehitwa, Botswana 116 C3 20 30 S 22 30 E
Sehlabathebe Nat. Park, Lesotho 117 D4 29 53 S 29 7 E
Sehore, India 92 H7 23 10N 77 5 E
Sehulea, Papua N. G. 132 E6 9 58 S 151 10 E
Sehwan, Pakistan 91 D2 26 28N 67 53 E
Şeica Mare, Romania 53 D9 46 1N 24 7 E
Seikpyu, Burma 90 E5 20 54N 94 48 E
Seil, U.K. 22 E3 56 18N 5 38W
Seiland, Norway 14 A20 70 25N 23 15 E
Seilhac, France 28 C5 45 22N 1 43 E
Seiling, U.S.A. 155 G5 36 9N 98 56W
Seille →, Moselle, France 27 C13 49 7N 6 11 E
Seille →, Saône-et-Loire, France 27 F11 46 31N 4 57 E
Sein, Î. de, France 26 D2 48 2N 4 52W
Seinäjoki, Finland 15 E20 62 40N 22 51 E
Seine →, France 26 C7 49 26N 0 26 E
Seine, B. de la, France 26 C6 49 40N 0 40W
Seine-et-Marne □, France 27 D10 48 45N 3 0 E
Seine-Maritime □, France 26 C7 49 40N 1 0 E
Seine-St-Denis □, France 27 D9 48 58N 2 24 E
Seini, Romania 53 C8 47 44N 23 21 E
Seirijai, Lithuania 54 D10 54 14N 23 49 E
Seistan = Sīstān, Asia 97 D9 30 50N 61 0 E
Seistan, Daryācheh-ye = Sīstān, Daryācheh-ye, Iran 97 D9 31 0N 61 0 E
Sejerø, Denmark 17 J5 55 54N 11 9 E
Sejerø Bugt, Denmark 17 J5 55 53N 11 15 E
Sejny, Poland 54 D10 54 6N 23 21 E
Seka, Ethiopia 107 F4 8 10N 36 52 E
Sekayu, Indonesia 84 C2 2 51 S 103 51 E
Seke, Tanzania 118 C3 3 20 S 33 31 E
Seke-Banza, Dem. Rep. of the Congo 115 D2 5 20 S 13 16 E
Sekenke, Tanzania 118 C3 4 18 S 34 11 E
Sekhira, Tunisia 108 B2 34 20N 10 5 E
Seki, Japan 73 B8 35 29N 136 55 E
Seki, Turkey 49 E11 36 48N 29 33 E
Sekigahara, Japan 73 B8 35 22N 136 28 E
Sekondi-Takoradi, Ghana 112 E4 4 58N 1 45W
Sekota, Ethiopia 107 E4 12 40N 39 2 E
Seksna, Russia 58 C10 59 13N 38 30 E
Sekudai, Malaysia 87 d 1 32N 103 39 E
Sekuma, Botswana 116 C3 24 36 S 23 50 E
Selah, U.S.A. 158 C3 46 39N 120 32W
Selama, Malaysia 87 K3 5 12N 100 42 E
Selangor □, Malaysia 84 B2 3 10N 101 30 E
Selárgius, Italy 46 C2 39 16N 9 10 E
Selaru, Indonesia 83 C4 8 9 S 131 0 E
Selatan, Selat, Malaysia 87 c 5 15N 100 20 E
Selawik, U.S.A. 144 C8 66 36N 160 0W
Selawik L., U.S.A. 144 C7 66 30N 160 45W
Selb, Germany 31 E8 50 10N 12 7 E
Selbusjøen, Norway 18 A7 63 15N 10 50 E
Selby, U.K. 20 D6 53 47N 1 5W
Selby, U.S.A. 154 C4 45 31N 100 2W
Selca, Croatia 45 E13 43 20N 16 50 E
Selçuk, Turkey 49 D9 37 56N 27 22 E
Selden, U.S.A. 154 F4 39 33N 100 34W
Seldovia, U.S.A. 144 G10 59 26N 151 43W
Sele →, Italy 47 B7 40 29N 14 56 E
Selebi-Pikwe, Botswana 117 C4 21 58 S 27 48 E
Selemdzha →, Russia 67 D13 51 42N 128 53 E
Selendi, Manisa, Turkey 49 C10 38 43N 28 50 E
Selendi, Manisa, Turkey 49 C9 38 46N 27 53 E
Selenga = Selenge Mörön →, Asia 68 A5 52 16N 106 16 E
Selenge, Dem. Rep. of the Congo 114 C3 1 58 S 18 11 E
Selenge Mörön →, Asia 68 A5 52 16N 106 16 E
Selenicë, Albania 50 F3 40 33N 19 39 E
Selenter See, Germany 30 A6 54 18N 10 26 E
Sélestat, France 27 D14 48 16N 7 26 E
Seletan, Tanjung, Indonesia 85 C4 4 10 S 114 40 E
Selevac, Serbia, Yug. 50 B4 44 28N 20 52 E
Selfoss, Iceland 11 D6 63 56N 21 0W
Sélibabi, Mauritania 112 B2 15 10N 12 15W
Seliger, Ozero, Russia 58 D7 57 15N 33 0 E
Seligman, U.S.A. 159 J7 35 20N 112 53W
Şelim, Turkey 101 B10 40 30N 42 46 E
Selîma, El Wâhât el, Sudan 106 C2 21 22N 29 19 E
Selimiye, Turkey 49 D9 37 24N 27 40 E
Selinda Spillway →, Botswana 116 B3 18 35 S 23 10 E
Selinoús, Greece 48 D3 37 35N 21 37 E
Selinsgrove, U.S.A. 150 F8 40 48N 76 52W
Selizharovo, Russia 58 D7 56 51N 33 27 E
Selje, Norway 18 B2 62 3N 5 22 E
Seljord, Norway 18 E5 59 30N 8 40 E
Selkirk, Canada 143 C9 50 10N 96 55W
Selkirk, U.K. 22 F6 55 33N 2 50W
Selkirk I., Canada 143 C9 53 20N 99 6W
Selkirk Mts., Canada 138 C8 51 15N 117 40W
Sellama, Sudan 107 E2 12 51N 29 46 E
Selliá, Greece 39 E5 35 12N 24 23 E
Sellières, France 27 F12 46 50N 5 32 E
Sells, U.S.A. 159 L8 31 55N 111 53W
Sellye, Hungary 52 E2 45 52N 17 51 E
Selma, Ala., U.S.A. 149 J2 32 25N 87 1W
Selma, Calif., U.S.A. 160 J7 36 34N 119 37W
Selma, N.C., U.S.A. 149 H6 35 32N 78 17W
Selmer, U.S.A. 149 H1 35 10N 88 36W
Selong, Indonesia 85 D5 8 39 S 116 32 E
Selongey, France 27 E12 47 36N 5 11 E
Selouane, Morocco 111 A4 35 7N 2 57W
Selous Game Reserve, Tanzania 119 D4 8 37 S 37 42 E
Selowandoma Falls, Zimbabwe 119 G3 21 15 S 31 50 E
Selpele, Indonesia 83 B4 0 1 S 130 5 E
Selsey Bill, U.K. 21 G7 50 43N 0 47W
Seltso, Russia 58 F8 53 22N 34 4 E
Seltz, France 27 D15 48 54N 8 4 E
Selu, Indonesia 83 C4 7 32 S 130 55 E
Sélune →, France 26 D5 48 38N 1 22W
Selva = La Selva del Camp, Spain 40 D6 41 13N 1 8 E
Selva, Argentina 174 B3 29 50 S 62 0W
Selvagens, Ilhas, Madeira 110 B1 30 5N 15 55W
Selvas, Brazil 172 B4 6 30 S 67 0W
Selwyn L., Canada 143 B8 60 0N 104 30W
Selwyn Mts., Canada 138 B6 63 0N 130 0W
Selwyn Passage, Vanuatu 133 F6 16 3 S 168 12 E
Selwyn Ra., Australia 126 C3 21 10 S 140 0 E
Sem, Norway 18 E7 59 14N 10 17 E
Seman →, Albania 50 F3 40 47N 19 30 E
Semara, W. Sahara 110 C2 26 48N 11 41W
Semarang, Indonesia 85 D4 7 0 S 110 26 E
Sematan, Malaysia 85 B3 1 48N 109 46 E
Semau, Indonesia 82 D2 10 13 S 123 22 E
Sembabule, Uganda 118 C3 0 4 S 31 25 E
Sembawang, Singapore 87 d 1 27N 103 50 E
Sembé, Congo 114 B2 1 39N 14 36 E
Sembung, Indonesia 79 J18 8 28 S 115 11 E
Şemdinli, Turkey 101 D11 37 18N 44 35 E
Sémé, Senegal 112 B2 15 4N 13 41W
Semeih, Sudan 107 E3 12 43N 30 53 E
Semenanjung Blambangan, Indonesia 79 K17 8 42 S 114 29 E
Semendua, Dem. Rep. of the Congo 114 C3 3 10 S 18 6 E
Semenov, Russia 60 B7 56 43N 44 30 E
Semenovka, Chernihiv, Ukraine 59 F7 52 8N 32 36 E
Semenovka, Kremenchuk, Ukraine 59 H7 49 37N 33 10 E
Semeru, Indonesia 85 D4 8 4 S 112 55 E
Semey, Kazakstan 66 D9 50 30N 80 10 E
Semichi Is., U.S.A. 144 K1 52 42N 174 0 E
Semikarakorskiy, Russia 61 G5 47 31N 40 48 E
Semiluki, Russia 59 G10 51 41N 39 2 E
Seminoe Reservoir, U.S.A. 158 F10 42 9N 106 55W
Seminole, Fla., U.S.A. 153 H7 27 50N 82 47W
Seminole, Okla., U.S.A. 155 H6 35 14N 96 41W
Seminole, Tex., U.S.A. 155 J3 32 43N 102 39W
Seminole L., U.S.A. 152 E5 30 43N 84 52W
Seminole Draw →, U.S.A. 155 J3 32 27N 102 20W
Semipalatinsk = Semey, Kazakstan 66 D9 50 30N 80 10 E
Semirara I., Phil. 80 E3 12 4N 121 23 E
Semirara Is., Phil. 81 F3 12 0N 121 20 E
Semisopochnoi I., U.S.A. 144 L2 51 55N 179 36 E
Semitau, Indonesia 85 B4 0 29N 111 57 E
Semiyarka, Kazakstan 66 D8 50 55N 78 23 E
Semiyarskoye = Semiyarka, Kazakstan 66 D8 50 55N 78 23 E
Semmering P., Austria 34 D8 47 41N 15 45 E
Semnān, Iran 97 C7 35 40N 53 23 E
Semnān □, Iran 97 C7 36 0N 54 0 E
Sempang Mengayou, Tanjong, Malaysia 85 A5 7 0N 116 40 E
Semporna, Malaysia 85 B5 4 30N 118 33 E
Semuda, Indonesia 85 C4 2 51 S 112 58 E
Semur-en-Auxois, France 27 E11 47 30N 4 20 E
Sen →, Cambodia 78 B3 13 45N 105 12 E
Sena, Bolivia 172 C4 11 32 S 67 11W
Senā, Iran 97 D6 28 27N 51 36 E
Sena, Mozam. 119 F4 17 25 S 35 0 E
Sena →, Bolivia 172 C4 11 31 S 67 11W
Sena Madureira, Brazil 172 B4 9 5 S 68 45W
Senachwine L., U.S.A. 156 C7 41 10N 89 18W
Senador José Porfírio, Brazil 169 D7 2 35 S 51 55W
Senador Pompeu, Brazil 170 C4 5 40 S 39 20W
Senaja, Malaysia 85 A5 6 45N 117 3 E
Senaki, Georgia 61 J6 42 15N 42 7 E
Senang, Pulau, Singapore 87 d 1 10N 103 44 E
Senanga, Zambia 115 F4 16 7 S 23 16 E
Senatobia, U.S.A. 155 H10 34 37N 89 58W
Sencelles, Spain 38 B3 39 39N 2 54 E
Sendafa, Ethiopia 107 F4 9 11N 39 3 E
Sendai, Kagoshima, Japan 72 F2 31 50N 130 20 E
Sendai, Miyagi, Japan 70 E10 38 15N 140 53 E
Sendai-Wan, Japan 70 E10 38 15N 141 0 E
Senden, Bayern, Germany 31 G6 48 19N 10 4 E
Senden, Nordrhein-Westfalen, Germany 30 D3 51 52N 7 22 E
Sendhwa, India 92 J6 21 41N 75 6 E
Sendurjana, India 94 D4 21 32N 78 17 E
Sene →, Ghana 113 D4 7 30N 0 33W
Senec, Slovak Rep. 35 C10 48 12N 17 23 E
Seneca, Ill., U.S.A. 157 C8 41 19N 88 37W
Seneca, S.C., U.S.A. 149 H4 34 41N 82 57W
Seneca Falls, U.S.A. 151 D8 42 55N 76 48W
Seneca L., U.S.A. 150 D8 42 40N 76 54W
Senecaville L., U.S.A. 150 G3 39 55N 81 25W
Senegal ■, W. Afr. 112 C2 14 30N 14 30W
Sénégal →, W. Afr. 112 B1 15 48N 16 32W
Senegambia, Africa 104 E2 12 45N 12 0W
Senekal, S. Africa 117 D4 28 20 S 27 36 E
Senftenberg, Germany 30 D10 51 32N 14 0 E
Senga Hill, Zambia 119 D3 9 19 S 31 11 E
Senge Khambab = Indus →, Pakistan 91 D2 24 20N 67 47 E
Sengiley, Russia 60 D9 53 58N 48 46 E
Sengua →, Zimbabwe 119 F2 17 7 S 28 5 E
Senguerr →, Argentina 176 C3 45 35 S 68 50W
Senhor-do-Bonfim, Brazil 170 D3 10 30 S 40 10W
Senica, Slovak Rep. 35 C10 48 41N 17 25 E
Senigállia, Italy 45 E10 43 43N 13 13 E
Seniku, Burma 90 C6 25 32N 97 48 E
Senio →, Italy 45 D9 44 35N 12 15 E
Senirkent, Turkey 49 C12 38 6N 30 33 E
Senise, Italy 47 B9 40 9N 16 17 E
Senj, Croatia 45 D11 45 0N 14 58 E

280 Senja

Senja, *Norway* **14 B17** 69 25N 17 30 E
Senkaku-Shotō, *Japan* **71 L1** 25 45N 124 0 E
Senkuang, *Indonesia* **87 d** 1 11N 104 2 E
Senlis, *France* **27 C9** 49 13N 2 35 E
Senmonorom, *Cambodia* **86 F6** 12 27N 107 12 E
Sennâr, *Sudan* **107 E3** 13 30N 33 35 E
Sennar □, *Sudan* **107 E3** 13 0N 34 0 E
Senneterre, *Canada* **140 C4** 48 25N 77 15W
Senno, *Belarus* **58 E5** 54 45N 29 43 E
Sénnori, *Italy* **46 B1** 40 47N 8 35 E
Seno, *Laos* **86 D5** 16 35N 104 50 E
Senoia, *U.S.A.* **152 B5** 33 18N 84 33W
Senonches, *France* **26 D8** 48 34N 1 2 E
Senorbì, *Italy* **46 C2** 39 32N 9 8 E
Senožeče, *Slovenia* **45 C11** 45 43N 14 3 E
Sens, *France* **27 D10** 48 11N 3 15 E
Senta, *Serbia, Yug.* **52 E5** 45 55N 20 3 E
Sentani, *Indonesia* **83 B6** 2 36 S 140 37 E
Sentani, Danau, *Indonesia* **83 B6** 2 36 S 140 34 E
Sentery = Lubao, *Dem. Rep. of the Congo* **118 D2** 5 17 S 25 42 E
Sentinel, *U.S.A.* **159 K7** 32 52N 113 13W
Šentjur, *Slovenia* **45 B12** 46 14N 15 24 E
Sentolo, *Indonesia* **85 D4** 7 55 S 110 13 E
Sentosa, *Singapore* **87 d** 1 15N 103 50 E
Senya Beraku, *Ghana* **113 D4** 5 28N 0 31W
Seo de Urgel = La Seu d'Urgell, *Spain* **40 C6** 42 22N 1 23 E
Seohara, *India* **93 E8** 29 15N 78 33 E
Seonath →, *India* **93 J10** 21 44N 82 28 E
Seondha, *India* **93 F8** 26 9N 78 48 E
Seoni, *India* **93 H8** 22 5N 79 30 E
Seoni Malwa, *India* **92 H8** 22 27N 77 28 E
Seoriuarayan, *India* **94 D6** 21 45N 82 34 E
Seoul = Sŏul, *S. Korea* **75 F14** 37 31N 126 58 E
Separation Pt., *N.Z.* **131 A7** 40 47 S 172 59 E
Sepatini →, *Brazil* **172 B4** 7 36 S 65 24W
Sepi, *Solomon Is.* **133 M10** 8 31 S 159 52 E
Sepīdān, *Iran* **97 D7** 30 20N 52 5 E
Sepik →, *Papua N. G.* **132 B3** 3 49 S 144 30 E
Sepo-ri, *N. Korea* **75 E14** 38 57N 127 25 E
Sępólno Krajeńskie, *Poland* **54 E4** 53 26N 17 30 E
Sepone, *Laos* **86 D6** 16 45N 106 13 E
Sępopol, *Poland* **54 D8** 54 16N 21 2 E
Sept-Îles, *Canada* **141 B6** 50 13N 66 22W
Septemvri, *Bulgaria* **51 D8** 42 13N 24 6 E
Sepúlveda, *Spain* **42 D7** 41 18N 3 45W
Sequeros, *Spain* **42 E4** 40 31N 6 2W
Sequim, *U.S.A.* **160 B3** 48 5N 123 6W
Sequoia Nat. Park, *U.S.A.* **160 J8** 36 30N 118 30W
Sera, *Indonesia* **83 C4** 7 40 S 131 5 E
Serafimovich, *Russia* **60 F6** 49 36N 42 43 E
Seraing, *Belgium* **24 D5** 50 35N 5 32 E
Serakhis →, *Cyprus* **39 E8** 35 13N 32 55 E
Seram, *Indonesia* **83 B3** 3 10 S 129 0 E
Seram Sea, *Indonesia* **82 B3** 2 30 S 128 30 E
Seranantsara, *Madag.* **117 B8** 18 30 S 49 5 E
Serang, *Indonesia* **84 D3** 6 8 S 106 10 E
Serangoon, *Singapore* **87 d** 1 23N 103 54 E
Serasan, *Indonesia* **85 B3** 2 29N 109 4 E
Seravezza, *Italy* **44 E7** 43 59N 10 13 E
Şerbettar, *Turkey* **51 E10** 41 27N 26 46 E
Serbia □, *Yugoslavia* **50 C5** 43 30N 21 0 E
Şercaia, *Romania* **53 E10** 45 49N 25 9 E
Serdo, *Ethiopia* **107 E5** 11 56N 41 14 E
Serdobsk, *Russia* **60 D7** 52 28N 44 10 E
Sered', *Slovak Rep.* **35 C10** 48 17N 17 44 E
Seredka, *Russia* **58 C5** 58 12N 28 10 E
Şereflikoçhisar, *Turkey* **100 C5** 38 56N 33 32 E
Seregno, *Italy* **44 C6** 45 39N 9 12 E
Seremban, *Malaysia* **87 L3** 2 43N 101 53 E
Serengeti Nat. Park, *Tanzania* **118 C3** 2 11 S 35 0 E
Serengeti Plain, *Tanzania* **118 C4** 2 40 S 35 0 E
Serenje, *Zambia* **119 E3** 13 14 S 30 15 E
Sereth = Siret →, *Romania* **53 E12** 45 24N 28 1 E
Sergach, *Russia* **60 C7** 55 30N 45 30 E
Sergen, *Turkey* **51 E11** 41 41N 27 42 E
Sergino, *Russia* **66 C7** 62 25N 65 12 E
Sergipe □, *Brazil* **170 D4** 10 30 S 37 30W
Sergiyev Posad, *Russia* **58 D10** 56 20N 38 10 E
Seria, *Brunei* **85 B4** 4 37N 114 23 E
Serian, *Malaysia* **85 B4** 1 10N 110 31 E
Seriate, *Italy* **44 C6** 45 41N 9 43 E
Seribu, Kepulauan, *Indonesia* **84 D3** 5 36 S 106 33 E
Sérifontaine, *France* **27 C8** 49 20N 1 45 E
Sérifos, *Greece* **48 D6** 37 9N 24 30 E
Sérignan, *France* **28 E7** 43 17N 3 17 E
Sérigny →, *Canada* **141 A6** 56 47N 66 0W
Serik, *Turkey* **100 D4** 36 55N 31 7 E
Serikbuya, *China* **65 D8** 39 21N 77 50 E
Seringapatam Reef, *Australia* **124 B3** 13 38 S 122 5 E
Serinhisar, *Turkey* **49 D11** 37 36N 29 18 E
Seririt, *Indonesia* **79 J17** 8 12 S 114 56 E
Sermaize-les-Bains, *France* **27 D11** 48 47N 4 54 E
Sermata, *Indonesia* **83 C3** 8 15 S 128 50 E
Sérmide, *Italy* **45 D8** 45 0N 11 18 E
Sernovodsk, *Russia* **60 D10** 53 54N 51 16 E
Sernur, *Russia* **60 B9** 56 52N 49 2 E
Serock, *Poland* **55 F8** 52 31N 21 4 E
Serón, *Spain* **41 H2** 37 20N 2 29W
Seròs, *Spain* **40 D5** 41 27N 0 24 E
Serouenout, *Algeria* **111 D6** 24 18N 7 25 E
Serov, *Russia* **64 B8** 59 29N 60 35 E
Serowe, *Botswana* **116 C4** 22 25 S 26 43 E
Serpa, *Portugal* **43 H3** 37 57N 7 38W
Serpeddí, Punta, *Italy* **46 C2** 39 22N 9 18 E
Serpentara, *Italy* **46 C2** 39 8N 9 36 E
Serpentine Lakes, *Australia* **125 E4** 28 30 S 129 10 E
Serpis →, *Spain* **41 G4** 38 59N 0 9W
Serpukhov, *Russia* **58 E9** 54 55N 37 28 E
Serra de Outes, *Spain* **42 C2** 42 52N 8 55W
Serra do Navio, *Brazil* **169 C7** 0 59N 52 3W
Serra do Salitre, *Brazil* **171 E2** 19 6 S 46 41W
Serra San Bruno, *Italy* **47 D9** 38 35N 16 20 E
Serra Talhada, *Brazil* **170 C4** 7 59 S 38 18W
Serradilla, *Spain* **42 F4** 39 50N 6 9W
Sérrai, *Greece* **50 E7** 41 5N 23 31 E
Sérrai □, *Greece* **50 E7** 41 5N 23 37 E
Serramanna, *Italy* **46 C1** 39 25N 8 55 E
Serranópolis, *Brazil* **173** 18 16 S 52 0W
Serrat, C., *Tunisia* **108 A1** 37 14N 9 10 E
Serravalle, *Italy* **33 E6** 45 41N 8 18 E
Serravalle Scrívia, *Italy* **44 D5** 44 43N 8 51 E
Serre-Ponçon, L. de, *France* **29 D10** 44 22N 6 20 E
Serres, *France* **29 D9** 44 26N 5 43 E
Serrezuela, *Argentina* **174 C2** 30 40 S 65 20W
Serrinha, *Brazil* **171 D4** 11 39 S 39 0W
Serrita, *Brazil* **170 C4** 7 56 S 39 19W
Sersale, *Italy* **47 C9** 39 1N 16 43 E
Sertã, *Portugal* **42 F2** 39 48N 8 6W
Sertânia, *Brazil* **170 C4** 8 5 S 37 20W
Sertanópolis, *Brazil* **175 A5** 23 4 S 51 2W
Sêrtar, *China* **76 A3** 32 20N 100 41 E
Sertig, *Switz.* **33 C9** 46 44N 9 52 E
Serua, *Indonesia* **83 C4** 6 18 S 130 1 E
Serui, *Indonesia* **83 B5** 1 53 S 136 10 E
Serule, *Botswana* **116 C4** 21 57 S 27 20 E
Sérvia, *Greece* **50 F6** 40 11N 22 0 E
Serzedelo, *Portugal* **42 D2** 41 24N 8 14W
Ses Salines, *Spain* **38 B4** 39 21N 3 3 E
Sesayap →, *Indonesia* **85 B5** 3 36N 117 15 E
Sese Is., *Uganda* **118 C3** 0 20 S 32 20 E
Sesepe, *Indonesia* **82 B3** 1 30 S 127 59 E
Sesfontein, *Namibia* **116 B1** 19 7 S 13 39 E
Sesheke, *Zambia* **116 B3** 17 29 S 24 13 E
Sésia →, *Italy* **44 C5** 45 5N 8 37 E
Sesimbra, *Portugal* **43 G1** 38 28N 9 6W
S'Espalmador, *Spain* **38 D1** 38 47N 1 26 E
S'Espardell, *Spain* **38 D1** 38 48N 1 29 E
Sessa, *Angola* **115 E4** 13 56 S 20 38 E
Sessa Aurunca, *Italy* **46 A6** 41 14N 13 56 E
Sesser, *U.S.A.* **156 F7** 38 5N 89 1W
S'Estanyol, *Spain* **38 B3** 39 22N 2 54 E
Sestao, *Spain* **40 B2** 43 18N 3 0W
Sesto Calende, *Italy* **44 C5** 45 44N 8 37 E
Sesto San Giovanni, *Italy* **44 C6** 45 32N 9 14 E
Sestri Levante, *Italy* **44 D6** 44 16N 9 24 E
Sestriere, *Italy* **44 D3** 44 57N 6 53 E
Sestroretsk, *Russia* **58 B6** 60 5N 29 58 E
Sestrunj, *Croatia* **45 D11** 44 10N 15 0 E
Sestu, *Italy* **46 C2** 39 18N 9 5 E
Sesvenna, *Switz.* **33 C10** 46 42N 10 25 E
Setaka, *Japan* **72 D2** 33 9N 130 28 E
Setana, *Japan* **70 C9** 42 26N 139 51 E
Sète, *France* **28 E7** 43 25N 3 42 E
Sete Lagôas, *Brazil* **171 E3** 19 27 S 44 16W
Setesdalsheiene, *Norway* **18 E3** 59 28N 7 10 E
Sétif, *Algeria* **111 A6** 36 9N 5 26 E
Seto, *Japan* **73 B9** 35 14N 137 6 E
Setonaikai, *Japan* **72 C5** 34 20N 133 30 E
Setsan, *Burma* **90 G5** 16 3N 95 23 E
Settat, *Morocco* **110 B3** 33 0N 7 40W
Setté-Cama, *Gabon* **114 C1** 2 32 S 9 45 E
Séttimo Torinese, *Italy* **44 C4** 45 9N 7 46 E
Setting L., *Canada* **143 C9** 55 0N 98 38W
Settle, *U.K.* **20 C5** 54 5N 2 16W
Settlement Pt., *Bahamas* **149 M6** 26 40N 79 0W
Settlers, *S. Africa* **117 C4** 25 2 S 28 30 E
Setúbal, *Portugal* **43 G2** 38 30N 8 58W
Setúbal □, *Portugal* **43 G2** 38 25N 8 35W
Setúbal, B. de, *Portugal* **43 G2** 38 40N 8 56W
Seugne →, *France* **28 C3** 45 42N 0 32W
Seul, Lac, *Canada* **140 B1** 50 20N 92 30W
Seulimeum, *Indonesia* **84 A1** 5 27N 95 15 E
Seurre, *France* **27 F12** 47 0N 5 8 E
Seuzach, *Switz.* **33 A7** 47 32N 8 49 E
Sevan, *Armenia* **61 K7** 40 33N 44 56 E
Sevan, Ozero = Sevana Lich, *Armenia* **61 K7** 40 30N 45 20 E
Sevana Lich, *Armenia* **61 K7** 40 30N 45 20 E
Sevastopol, *Ukraine* **59 K7** 44 35N 33 30 E
Sevelen, *Switz.* **33 B8** 47 7N 9 28 E
Seven Sisters, *Canada* **142 C3** 54 56N 128 10W
Sever →, *Spain* **43 F3** 39 40N 7 32W
Sévérac-le-Château, *France* **28 D7** 44 20N 3 5 E
Severn →, *Canada* **140 A2** 56 2N 87 36W
Severn →, *U.K.* **21 F5** 51 35N 2 40W
Severn L., *Canada* **140 B1** 53 54N 90 48W
Severnaya Zemlya, *Russia* **67 B10** 79 0N 100 0 E
Severnyye Uvaly, *Russia* **64 B2** 60 0N 50 0 E
Severo-Kurilsk, *Russia* **67 D16** 50 40N 156 8 E
Severo-Yeniseyskiy, *Russia* **67 C10** 60 22N 93 1 E
Severočeský □, *Czech Rep.* **34 A7** 50 30N 14 0 E
Severodonetsk = Syeverodonetsk, *Ukraine* **59 H10** 48 58N 38 35 E
Severodvinsk, *Russia* **56 B6** 64 27N 39 58 E
Severomoravský □, *Czech Rep.* **35 B10** 49 38N 17 40 E
Severomorsk, *Russia* **56 A5** 69 5N 33 27 E
Severouralsk, *Russia* **64 A7** 60 9N 59 57 E
Sevier, *U.S.A.* **159 G7** 38 39N 112 11W
Sevier →, *U.S.A.* **159 G7** 39 4N 113 6W
Sevier Desert, *U.S.A.* **158 G7** 39 40N 112 45W
Sevier L., *U.S.A.* **158 G7** 38 54N 113 9W
Sevilla, *Colombia* **168 C2** 4 16N 75 57W
Sevilla, *Spain* **43 H5** 37 23N 5 58W
Sevilla □, *Spain* **43 H5** 37 25N 5 30W
Seville = Sevilla, *Spain* **43 H5** 37 23N 5 58W
Seville, *Fla., U.S.A.* **153 F8** 29 19N 81 30W
Seville, *Ga., U.S.A.* **152 D6** 31 58N 83 36W
Sevlievo, *Bulgaria* **51 C9** 43 2N 25 6 E
Sevnica, *Slovenia* **45 B12** 46 2N 15 19 E
Sèvre-Nantaise →, *France* **26 E5** 47 12N 1 33W
Sèvre-Niortaise →, *France* **28 B3** 46 28N 0 50W
Sevsk, *Russia* **59 F8** 52 10N 34 30 E
Sewa →, *S. Leone* **112 D2** 7 20N 12 10W
Sewani, *India* **92 E6** 28 58N 75 39 E
Seward, *Alaska, U.S.A.* **144 F10** 60 7N 149 27W
Seward, *Nebr., U.S.A.* **154 E6** 40 55N 97 6W
Seward, *Pa., U.S.A.* **150 F5** 40 25N 79 1W
Seward Peninsula, *U.S.A.* **144 D6** 65 30N 166 0W
Sewell, *Chile* **174 C1** 34 10 S 70 23W
Sewer, *Indonesia* **83 C4** 5 53 S 134 40 E
Sewickley, *U.S.A.* **150 F4** 40 32N 80 12W
Sexsmith, *Canada* **142 B5** 55 21N 118 47W
Seychelles ■, *Ind. Oc.* **62 K9** 5 0 S 56 0 E
Seyðisfjörður, *Iceland* **11 B13** 65 16N 13 57W
Seydişehir, *Turkey* **100 D4** 37 25N 31 51 E
Seydvān, *Iran* **101 C11** 38 34N 45 2 E
Seyhan →, *Turkey* **100 D6** 36 43N 34 53 E
Seyhan Barajı, *Turkey* **100 D6** 37 2N 35 18 E
Seyitgazi, *Turkey* **49 B12** 39 27N 30 43 E
Seyitömer, *Turkey* **49 B11** 39 34N 29 52 E
Seym →, *Ukraine* **59 G7** 51 27N 32 34 E
Seymen, *Turkey* **51 E11** 41 6N 27 57 E
Seymour, *Australia* **129 D6** 37 0 S 145 10 E
Seymour, *S. Africa* **117 E4** 32 33 S 26 46 E
Seymour, *Conn., U.S.A.* **151 E11** 41 24N 73 4W
Seymour, *Ind., U.S.A.* **157 F11** 38 58N 85 53W
Seymour, *Tex., U.S.A.* **155 J5** 33 35N 99 16W
Seyne, *France* **29 D10** 44 21N 6 22 E
Seyssel, *France* **29 C9** 45 57N 5 50 E
Sežana, *Slovenia* **45 C10** 45 43N 13 41 E
Sézanne, *France* **27 D10** 48 40N 3 40 E
Sezze, *Italy* **46 A6** 41 30N 13 3 E
Sfântu Gheorghe, *Covasna, Romania* **53 E10** 45 52N 25 48 E
Sfântu Gheorghe, *Tulcea, Romania* **53 F14** 44 53N 29 36 E
Sfântu Gheorghe, Braţul →, *Romania* **53 F14** 44 51N 29 36 E
Sfax, *Tunisia* **108 B2** 34 49N 10 48 E
Sha Tau Kok, *China* **69 F11** 22 33N 114 13 E
Sha Tin, *China* **69 G11** 22 23N 114 12 E
Sha Xi →, *China* **77 D12** 26 35N 118 0 E
Sha Xian, *China* **77 D11** 26 23N 117 45 E
Shaanxi □, *China* **74 G5** 35 0N 109 0 E
Shaartuz, *Tajikistan* **65 E4** 37 16N 68 8 E
Shaba = Katanga □, *Dem. Rep. of the Congo* **118 D2** 8 0 S 25 0 E
Shaba Nat. Reserve, *Kenya* **118 B4** 0 38N 37 48 E
Shaballe = Scebeli, Wabi →, *Somali Rep.* **120 D2** 2 0N 44 0 E
Shabla, *Bulgaria* **51 C12** 43 31N 28 32 E
Shabogamo L., *Canada* **141 B6** 53 15N 66 30W
Shabunda, *Dem. Rep. of the Congo* **118 C2** 2 40 S 27 16 E
Shabwah, *Yemen* **98 D4** 15 22N 47 1 E
Shache, *China* **65 D8** 38 20N 77 10 E
Shackleton Ice Shelf, *Antarctica* **7 C8** 66 0 S 100 0 E
Shackleton Inlet, *Antarctica* **7 E11** 83 0 S 160 0 E
Shādegān, *Iran* **97 D6** 30 40N 48 38 E
Shadi, *China* **77 D10** 26 7N 114 47 E
Shadi, *India* **93 C7** 33 24N 77 14 E
Shadrinsk, *Russia* **64 C9** 56 5N 63 32 E
Shady Dale, *U.S.A.* **152 B6** 33 24N 83 36W
Shady Grove, *U.S.A.* **152 E6** 30 17N 83 38W
Shadyside, *U.S.A.* **150 G4** 39 58N 80 45W
Shafer, L., *U.S.A.* **157 D10** 40 46N 86 46W
Shaffa, *Nigeria* **113 C7** 10 30N 12 6 E
Shafter, *U.S.A.* **161 K7** 35 30N 119 16W
Shaftesbury, *U.K.* **21 F5** 51 0N 2 11W
Shag Pt., *N.Z.* **131 F5** 45 29 S 170 52 E
Shag Rocks, *Atl. Oc.* **8 M7** 53 0 S 41 0W
Shagamu, *Nigeria* **113 D5** 6 51N 3 39 E
Shageluk, *U.S.A.* **144 E8** 62 41N 159 34W
Shaghan, *Kazakstan* **65 A2** 44 53N 64 57 E
Shagram, *Pakistan* **93 A5** 36 24N 72 20 E
Shah Alam, *Malaysia* **84 B2** 3 5N 101 30 E
Shah Alizai, *Pakistan* **92 E2** 29 25N 66 33 E
Shah Bunder, *Pakistan* **92 G2** 24 13N 67 56 E
Shāh Jūy, *Afghan.* **91 B2** 32 31N 67 25 E
Shahabad, *Andhra Pradesh, India* **94 F4** 17 10N 78 7 E
Shahabad, *Karnataka, India* **94 F3** 17 10N 76 54 E
Shahabad, *Punjab, India* **92 D7** 30 10N 76 55 E
Shahabad, *Raj., India* **92 G7** 25 15N 77 11 E
Shahabad, *Ut. P., India* **93 F8** 27 36N 79 56 E
Shahada, *India* **94 D2** 21 33N 74 30 E
Shahadpur, *Pakistan* **92 G3** 25 55N 68 35 E
Shahapur, *India* **95 G2** 15 50N 74 34 E
Shahba, *Syria* **103 C5** 32 52N 36 38 E
Shahbazpur I., *Bangla.* **90 D3** 22 30N 90 45 E
Shahdād, *Iran* **97 D8** 30 30N 57 40 E
Shahdād, Namakzār-e, *Iran* **97 D8** 30 20N 58 20 E
Shahdadkot, *Pakistan* **91 D2** 27 50N 67 55 E
Shahdol, *India* **93 H9** 23 19N 81 26 E
Shahe, *China* **74 F8** 37 0N 114 32 E
Shahganj, *India* **93 F10** 26 3N 82 44 E
Shaḩḩāt, *Libya* **108 B4** 32 48N 21 54 E
Shahīdān, *Afghan.* **91 A2** 36 42N 67 49 E
Shahjahanpur, *India* **93 F8** 27 54N 79 57 E
Shahpur, *Karnataka, India* **94 F3** 16 40N 76 48 E
Shahpur, *Mad. P., India* **92 H7** 22 12N 77 58 E
Shahpur, *Baluchistan, Pakistan* **92 E3** 28 46N 68 27 E
Shahpur, *Punjab, Pakistan* **92 C5** 32 17N 72 26 E
Shahpur Chakar, *Pakistan* **92 F3** 26 9N 68 39 E
Shahpura, *Mad. P., India* **93 H9** 23 10N 80 45 E
Shahpura, *Raj., India* **92 G6** 25 38N 74 56 E
Shahr-e Bābak, *Iran* **97 D7** 30 7N 55 9 E
Shahr-e Kord, *Iran* **97 C6** 32 15N 50 55 E
Shāhrakht, *Iran* **97 C9** 33 38N 60 16 E
Shahrig, *Pakistan* **91 C2** 30 15N 67 40 E
Shahukou, *China* **74 D7** 40 20N 112 18 E
Shaikhabad, *Afghan.* **91 B3** 34 2N 68 45 E
Shajapur, *India* **92 H7** 23 27N 76 21 E
Shajing, *China* **69 F10** 22 44N 113 48 E
Shakargarh, *Pakistan* **92 C6** 32 17N 75 10 E
Shakawe, *Botswana* **116 B3** 18 28 S 21 49 E
Shakenge, *Dem. Rep. of the Congo* **115 D3** 6 14 S 18 41 E
Shaker Heights, *U.S.A.* **150 E3** 41 29N 81 32W
Shakhrikhan, *Uzbekistan* **65 C6** 40 42N 72 3 E
Shakhrisabz, *Uzbekistan* **65 D3** 39 3N 66 50 E
Shakhristan, *Tajikistan* **65 D4** 39 47N 68 49 E
Shakhty, *Russia* **61 G5** 47 40N 40 16 E
Shakhunya, *Russia* **60 B8** 57 40N 46 46 E
Shaki, *Nigeria* **113 D5** 8 41N 3 21 E
Shākir, *Egypt* **106 B3** 27 30N 33 59 E
Shakpak, *Kazakstan* **65 B4** 43 15N 69 20 E
Shaktoolik, *U.S.A.* **144 D7** 64 20N 161 9W
Shala, L., *Ethiopia* **107 F4** 7 30N 38 30 E
Shali, *Russia* **61 J7** 43 9N 45 55 E
Shalkar, *Kazakstan* **64 F3** 50 40N 51 53 E
Shalkar, Ozero, *Kazakstan* **64 F3** 50 35N 51 47 E
Shallow Lake, *Canada* **150 B3** 44 36N 81 5W
Shalqar, *Kazakstan* **66 E6** 47 48N 59 39 E
Shalskiy, *Russia* **58 B8** 61 48N 35 58 E
Shaluli Shan, *China* **76 B2** 30 40N 99 55 E
Shām, *Iran* **97 E8** 26 39N 57 21 E
Shām, Bādiyat ash, *Asia* **96 C3** 32 0N 40 0 E
Shām, J. ash, *Oman* **99 B7** 23 10N 57 5 E
Shamâl Bahr el Ghazal □, *Sudan* **107 F2** 8 0N 27 30 E
Shamâl Dârfûr □, *Sudan* **107 E2** 15 0N 25 0 E
Shamâl Kordofân □, *Sudan* **107 E3** 15 0N 30 0 E
Shamaldy-Say, *Kyrgyzstan* **65 C6** 41 12N 72 11 E
Shamattawa, *Canada* **140 A1** 55 51N 92 5W
Shamattawa →, *Canada* **140 A2** 55 1N 85 23W
Shambe, *Sudan* **107 F3** 7 8N 30 46 E
Shambe Nat. Park, *Sudan* **107 F3** 6 57N 30 50 E
Shambu, *Ethiopia* **107 F4** 9 32N 37 3 E
Shamgong Dzong, *Bhutan* **90 B3** 27 13N 90 35 E
Shamīl, *Iran* **97 E8** 27 30N 56 55 E
Shamkhor = Şämkir, *Azerbaijan* **61 K8** 40 50N 46 0 E
Shāmkūh, *Iran* **97 C8** 35 47N 57 50 E
Shamli, *India* **92 E7** 29 32N 77 18 E
Shammar, Jabal, *Si. Arabia* **96 E4** 27 40N 41 0 E
Shamo = Gobi, *Asia* **74 C6** 44 0N 110 0 E
Shamo, L., *Ethiopia* **107 F4** 5 45N 37 30 E
Shamokin, *U.S.A.* **151 F8** 40 47N 76 34W
Shamrock, *U.S.A.* **155 H4** 35 13N 100 15W
Shamshabad, *India* **94 F4** 17 15N 78 25 E
Shamva, *Zimbabwe* **119 F3** 17 20 S 31 32 E
Shan □, *Burma* **90 E7** 21 30N 98 30 E
Shan Xian, *China* **74 G9** 34 50N 116 5 E
Shanan →, *Ethiopia* **107 F5** 8 0N 40 20 E
Shanchengzhen, *China* **75 C13** 42 20N 125 20 E
Shāndak, *Iran* **97 D9** 28 28N 60 27 E
Shandon, *U.S.A.* **160 K6** 35 39N 120 23W
Shandong □, *China* **75 G10** 36 0N 118 0 E
Shandong Bandao, *China* **75 F11** 37 0N 121 0 E
Shang Xian = Shangzhou, *China* **74 H5** 33 50N 109 58 E
Shangalowe, *Dem. Rep. of the Congo* **119 E2** 10 50 S 26 30 E
Shangani, *Zimbabwe* **117 B4** 19 41 S 29 20 E
Shangani →, *Zimbabwe* **119 F2** 18 41 S 27 10 E
Shangbancheng, *China* **75 D10** 40 50N 118 1 E
Shangcheng, *China* **77 B10** 31 47N 115 26 E
Shangchuan Dao, *China* **77 G9** 21 40N 112 50 E
Shangdu, *China* **74 D7** 41 30N 113 30 E
Shanggao, *China* **77 C10** 28 17N 114 55 E
Shanghai, *China* **77 B13** 31 15N 121 26 E
Shanghai Shi □, *China* **77 B13** 31 0N 121 30 E
Shanghang, *China* **77 E11** 25 2N 116 23 E
Shanghe, *China* **75 F9** 37 20N 117 10 E
Shanglin, *China* **76 F7** 23 27N 108 33 E
Shangnan, *China* **74 H6** 33 32N 110 50 E
Shangqiu, *China* **74 G8** 34 26N 115 36 E
Shangrao, *China* **77 C11** 28 25N 117 59 E
Shangshui, *China* **69 C6** 33 42N 114 35 E
Shangsi, *China* **76 F6** 22 8N 107 58 E
Shangyou, *China* **77 E10** 25 48N 114 32 E
Shangyu, *China* **77 B13** 30 3N 120 52 E
Shangzhi, *China* **75 B14** 45 22N 127 56 E
Shangzhou, *China* **74 H5** 33 50N 109 58 E
Shanhetun, *China* **75 B14** 44 33N 127 15 E
Shani, *Nigeria* **113 C7** 10 14N 12 2 E
Shannon, *Greenland* **10 B9** 75 10N 18 30W
Shannon, *N.Z.* **130 G4** 40 33 S 175 25 E
Shannon →, *Ireland* **23 D2** 52 35N 9 30W
Shannon, Mouth of the, *Ireland* **23 D2** 52 30N 9 55W
Shannon Airport, *Ireland* **23 D3** 52 42N 8 57W
Shannon Nat. Park, *Australia* **125 F2** 31 55 S 117 51 E
Shannontown, *U.S.A.* **152 B9** 33 53N 80 21W
Shansi = Shanxi □, *China* **74 F7** 37 0N 112 0 E
Shantar, Ostrov Bolshoy, *Russia* **67 D14** 55 9N 137 40 E
Shantipur, *India* **93 H13** 23 17N 88 25 E
Shantou, *China* **77 F11** 23 18N 116 40 E
Shantung = Shandong □, *China* **75 G10** 36 0N 118 0 E
Shanwei, *China* **77 F10** 22 48N 115 22 E
Shanxi □, *China* **74 F7** 37 0N 112 0 E
Shanyang, *China* **74 H5** 33 31N 109 55 E
Shanyin, *China* **74 E7** 39 25N 112 56 E
Shaodong, *China* **77 D8** 27 15N 111 43 E
Shaoguan, *China* **77 E9** 24 48N 113 35 E
Shaoshan, *China* **77 D9** 27 55N 112 33 E
Shaowu, *China* **77 D11** 27 22N 117 28 E
Shaoxing, *China* **77 C13** 30 0N 120 35 E
Shaoyang, *Hunan, China* **77 D8** 26 59N 111 20 E
Shaoyang, *Hunan, China* **77 D8** 27 14N 111 25 E
Shap, *U.K.* **20 C5** 54 32N 2 40W
Shapinsay, *U.K.* **22 B6** 59 3N 2 51W
Shaqq el Gi'eifer →, *Sudan* **107 D2** 15 16N 26 0 E
Shaqra', *Si. Arabia* **96 E5** 25 15N 45 16 E
Shaqrā', *Yemen* **98 D4** 13 22N 45 44 E
Sharafa, *Sudan* **107 E2** 11 59N 27 7 E
Sharafkhāneh, *Iran* **101 C11** 38 11N 45 29 E
Sharavati →, *India* **95 G2** 14 20N 74 25 E
Sharbatāt, Ra's ash, *Oman* **99 C7** 17 56N 56 21 E
Sharbot Lake, *Canada* **151 B8** 44 46N 76 41W
Shardara, *Kazakstan* **65 C3** 41 15N 67 0 E
Shardara, Step, *Kazakstan* **65 C3** 42 20N 68 0 E
Shardara Bögeni, *Kazakstan* **65 C4** 41 10N 68 15 E
Shargun, *Uzbekistan* **65 D3** 38 35N 67 58 E
Shari, *Japan* **70 C12** 43 55N 144 40 E
Sharjah = Ash Shāriqah, *U.A.E.* **97 E7** 25 23N 55 26 E
Shark B., *Australia* **125 E1** 25 30 S 113 32 E
Shark Bay Marine Nature Reserve, *Australia* **125 F2** 32 49 S 118 49 E
Sharm el Sheikh, *Egypt* **106 B3** 27 53N 34 18 E
Sharon, *Mass., U.S.A.* **151 D13** 42 7N 71 11W
Sharon, *Pa., U.S.A.* **150 E4** 41 14N 80 31W
Sharon, *Wis., U.S.A.* **157 B8** 42 30N 88 44W
Sharon Springs, *Kans., U.S.A.* **154 F4** 38 54N 101 45W
Sharon Springs, *N.Y., U.S.A.* **151 D10** 42 48N 74 37W
Sharonville, *U.S.A.* **157 E12** 39 16N 84 25W
Sharp Pk., *Phil.* **81 J5** 5 58N 125 31 E
Sharp Pt., *Australia* **126 A3** 10 58 S 142 43 E
Sharpe L., *Canada* **140 B1** 54 24N 93 40W
Sharpes, *U.S.A.* **153 G9** 28 26N 80 46W
Sharpsville, *U.S.A.* **150 E4** 41 15N 80 29W
Sharq el Istiwa'iya □, *Sudan* **107 G3** 5 0N 33 0 E
Sharya, *Russia* **60 A7** 58 22N 45 20 E
Shasha, *Ethiopia* **107 F4** 6 29N 35 59 E
Shashemene, *Ethiopia* **107 F4** 7 13N 38 33 E
Shashi, *Botswana* **117 C4** 21 15 S 27 27 E
Shashi, *China* **77 B9** 30 25N 112 14 E
Shashi →, *Africa* **119 G2** 21 14 S 29 20 E
Shasta, Mt., *U.S.A.* **158 F2** 41 25N 122 12W
Shasta L., *U.S.A.* **158 F2** 40 43N 122 25W
Shatawi, *Sudan* **107 E3** 14 39N 32 6 E
Shāţi', Wādī ash →, *Libya* **108 C3** 27 30N 15 0 E
Shatsk, *Russia* **60 C5** 54 5N 41 45 E
Shatt al Arab = Arab, Shatt al →, *Asia* **97 D6** 30 0N 48 31 E
Shatura, *Russia* **58 E10** 55 33N 39 21 E
Shäüildir, *Kazakstan* **65 B4** 42 47N 68 3 E
Shaumyani = Shulaveri, *Georgia* **61 K7** 41 22N 44 45 E
Shaunavon, *Canada* **143 D7** 49 35N 108 25W
Shaver L., *U.S.A.* **160 H7** 37 9N 119 18W
Shaw →, *Australia* **124 D2** 20 21 S 119 17 E
Shaw I., *Australia* **126 J7** 20 30 S 149 2 E
Shawanaga, *Canada* **150 A4** 45 31N 80 17W
Shawangunk Mts., *U.S.A.* **151 E10** 41 35N 74 30W
Shawano, *U.S.A.* **148 C1** 44 47N 88 36W
Shawinigan, *Canada* **140 C5** 46 35N 72 50W
Shawnee, *Ga., U.S.A.* **152 C8** 32 29N 81 25W
Shawnee, *Kans., U.S.A.* **156 E2** 39 1N 94 43W
Shawnee, *Okla., U.S.A.* **155 H6** 35 20N 96 55W
Shay Gap, *Australia* **124 D3** 20 30 S 120 10 E
Shayan, *Kazakstan* **65 B4** 43 5N 69 25 E
Shayang, *China* **77 B9** 30 42N 112 29 E
Shaybārā, *Si. Arabia* **96 E3** 25 26N 36 47 E
Shayib el Banat, Gebel, *Egypt* **106 B3** 26 59N 33 29 E
Shaykh, J. ash, *Lebanon* **103 B4** 33 25N 35 50 E
Shaykh Miskīn, *Syria* **103 C5** 32 49N 36 9 E
Shaykh Sa'īd, *Iraq* **101 F12** 32 34N 46 17 E
Shaykh 'Uthmān, *Yemen* **98 D4** 12 52N 44 59 E
Shaymak, *Tajikistan* **65 E7** 37 33N 74 50 E
Shazud, *Tajikistan* **65 E6** 37 45N 72 25 E
Shchekino, *Russia* **58 E9** 54 1N 37 34 E
Shcherbakov = Rybinsk, *Russia* **58 C10** 58 5N 38 50 E
Shchigry, *Russia* **59 G9** 51 55N 36 58 E
Shchors, *Ukraine* **59 G6** 51 48N 31 56 E
Shchuchinsk, *Kazakstan* **66 D8** 52 56N 70 12 E
Shchuchye, *Russia* **64 D9** 55 12N 62 46 E
She Xian, *Anhui, China* **77 C12** 29 50N 118 25 E
She Xian, *Hebei, China* **74 F7** 36 30N 113 40 E
Shea, *Guyana* **169 C6** 2 48N 59 4W
Shebekino, *Russia* **59 G9** 50 28N 36 54 E
Shebele = Scebeli, Wabi →, *Somali Rep.* **120 D2** 2 0N 44 0 E
Sheberghān, *Afghan.* **65 E2** 36 40N 65 45 E
Sheboygan, *U.S.A.* **148 D2** 43 46N 87 45W
Shebshi Mts., *Nigeria* **113 D7** 8 30N 12 0 E
Shediac, *Canada* **141 C7** 46 14N 64 32W
Sheelin, L., *Ireland* **23 C4** 53 48N 7 20W
Sheenjek →, *U.S.A.* **144 C11** 66 45N 144 33W
Sheep Haven, *Ireland* **23 A4** 55 11N 7 52W
Sheerness, *U.K.* **21 F8** 51 26N 0 47 E
Sheet Harbour, *Canada* **141 D7** 44 56N 62 31W
Sheffield, *N.Z.* **131 D7** 43 23 S 172 1 E
Sheffield, *U.K.* **20 D6** 53 23N 1 28W
Sheffield, *Ala., U.S.A.* **149 H2** 34 46N 87 41W
Sheffield, *Ill., U.S.A.* **156 C7** 41 21N 89 44W
Sheffield, *Iowa, U.S.A.* **156 B3** 42 54N 93 13W
Sheffield, *Mass., U.S.A.* **151 D11** 42 5N 73 21W
Sheffield, *Pa., U.S.A.* **150 E5** 41 42N 79 3W
Shegaon, *India* **94 D3** 20 48N 76 47 E
Sheghnān, *Afghan.* **65 E5** 37 37N 71 36 E
Shehojele, *Ethiopia* **107 E4** 10 40N 35 9 E
Shehong, *China* **76 B5** 30 54N 105 18 E
Shehuen →, *Argentina* **176 C3** 49 35 S 69 34W
Sheikh Idris, *Sudan* **107 E3** 11 43N 33 30 E
Sheikhpura, *India* **93 G11** 25 9N 85 53 E
Shek Hasan, *Ethiopia* **107 E4** 12 5N 35 58 E
Shekhupura, *Pakistan* **91 C4** 31 42N 73 58 E
Sheki = Şaki, *Azerbaijan* **61 K8** 41 10N 47 5 E
Shekou, *China* **69 G10** 22 30N 113 55 E
Shelbina, *U.S.A.* **156 E4** 39 47N 92 2W
Shelburn, *U.S.A.* **157 E9** 39 11N 87 24W
Shelburne, *N.S., Canada* **141 D6** 43 47N 65 20W
Shelburne, *Ont., Canada* **140 D3** 44 4N 80 15W
Shelburne, *U.S.A.* **151 B11** 44 23N 73 14W
Shelburne B., *Australia* **126 A3** 11 50 S 142 50 E
Shelburne Falls, *U.S.A.* **151 D12** 42 36N 72 45W
Shelby, *Mich., U.S.A.* **148 D2** 43 37N 86 22W
Shelby, *Miss., U.S.A.* **155 J9** 33 57N 90 46W
Shelby, *Mont., U.S.A.* **158 B8** 48 30N 111 51W
Shelby, *N.C., U.S.A.* **149 H5** 35 17N 81 32W
Shelby, *Ohio, U.S.A.* **150 F2** 40 53N 82 40W
Shelbyville, *Ill., U.S.A.* **154 F10** 39 24N 88 48W
Shelbyville, *Ind., U.S.A.* **157 E11** 39 31N 85 47W
Shelbyville, *Ky., U.S.A.* **157 F11** 38 13N 85 14W
Shelbyville, *Mo., U.S.A.* **156 E4** 39 48N 92 2W
Shelbyville, *Tenn., U.S.A.* **149 H2** 35 29N 86 28W
Shelbyville, L., *U.S.A.* **157 E8** 39 26N 88 46W
Sheldon, *Ill., U.S.A.* **157 D9** 40 46N 87 34W
Sheldon, *Iowa, U.S.A.* **154 D7** 43 11N 95 51W

282 Sikhote Alin Ra.

Sikhote Alin Ra. = Sikhote Alin, Khrebet, *Russia* **67 E14** 45 0N 136 0 E
Sikiá., *Greece* **50 F7** 40 2N 23 56 E
Síkinos, *Greece* **49 E7** 36 40N 25 8 E
Sikkani Chief →, *Canada* **142 B4** 57 47N 122 15W
Sikkim □, *India* **90 B2** 27 50N 88 30 E
Siklós, *Hungary* **52 E3** 45 50N 18 19 E
Sikotu-Ko, *Japan* **70 C10** 42 45N 141 25 E
Sil →, *Spain* **42 C3** 42 27N 7 43W
Silacayoapan, *Mexico* **163 D5** 17 30N 98 9W
Šilalė, *Lithuania* **54 C9** 55 28N 22 12 E
Silam, *Malaysia* **81 J2** 4 59N 118 12 E
Silandro, *Italy* **44 B7** 46 38N 10 46 E
Silang, *Phil.* **80 D3** 14 14N 120 58 E
Silawad, *India* **92 J6** 21 54N 74 54 E
Silay, *Phil.* **81 F4** 10 47N 122 58 E
Silba, *Croatia* **45 D11** 44 24N 14 41 E
Silchar, *India* **90 C4** 24 49N 92 48 E
Sildegapet, *Norway* **18 B2** 62 5N 5 0 E
Şile, *Turkey* **51 E13** 41 10N 29 37 E
Siler City, *U.S.A.* **149 H6** 35 44N 79 28W
Sileru →, *India* **94 F5** 17 49N 81 24 E
Silesia = Śląsk, *Poland* **36 C9** 51 0N 16 30 E
Silet, *Algeria* **111 D5** 22 44N 4 37 E
Silgarhi Doti, *Nepal* **93 E9** 29 15N 81 0 E
Silghat, *India* **90 B4** 26 35N 93 0 E
Silhouette, *Seychelles* **121 b** 4 29 S 55 12 E
Sili, *Burkina Faso* **112 C4** 11 37N 2 30W
Silifke, *Turkey* **100 D5** 36 22N 33 58 E
Siliguri = Shiliguri, *India* **90 B2** 26 45N 88 25 E
Siling Co, *China* **68 C3** 31 50N 89 20 E
Silistea Nouă, *Romania* **53 F10** 44 23N 25 1 E
Silistra, *Bulgaria* **51 B11** 44 6N 27 19 E
Silivri, *Turkey* **51 E12** 41 4N 28 14 E
Siljan, *Norway* **18 E6** 59 18N 9 42 E
Siljan, *Sweden* **16 D8** 60 55N 14 45 E
Siljansnäs, *Sweden* **16 D8** 60 47N 14 52 E
Silkeborg, *Denmark* **17 H3** 56 10N 9 32 E
Silkwood, *Australia* **126 B4** 17 45 S 146 2 E
Silla, *Spain* **41 F4** 39 22N 0 25W
Sillajhuay, Cordillera, *Chile* **172 D4** 19 46 S 68 40W
Sillamäe, *Estonia* **15 G22** 59 24N 27 45 E
Sillé-le-Guillaume, *France* **26 D6** 48 10N 0 8W
Silleda, *Spain* **42 C2** 42 42N 8 14W
Sillod, *India* **94 D2** 20 18N 75 39 E
Silloth, *U.K.* **20 C4** 54 52N 3 23W
Sillustani, *Peru* **172 D3** 15 50 S 70 7W
Sílo, *Greece* **51 E9** 41 10N 25 53 E
Siloam Springs, *U.S.A.* **155 G7** 36 11N 94 32W
Silopi, *Turkey* **101 D10** 37 15N 42 27 E
Silsbee, *U.S.A.* **155 K7** 30 21N 94 11W
Siltou, *Chad* **109 E3** 16 46N 15 33 E
Siluko, *Nigeria* **113 D6** 6 35N 5 10 E
Šilutė, *Lithuania* **15 J19** 55 21N 21 33 E
Silva Porto = Kuito, *Angola* **115 E3** 12 22 S 16 55 E
Silvan, *Turkey* **101 C9** 38 7N 41 2 E
Silvani, *India* **93 H8** 23 18N 78 25 E
Silvaplana, *Switz.* **33 D9** 46 28N 9 48 E
Silver City, *U.S.A.* **159 K9** 32 46N 108 17W
Silver Cr. →, *U.S.A.* **158 E4** 43 16N 119 13W
Silver Creek, *U.S.A.* **150 D5** 42 33N 79 10W
Silver Grove, *U.S.A.* **157 E12** 39 2N 84 24W
Silver L., *U.S.A.* **160 G6** 38 39N 120 6W
Silver Lake, *Calif., U.S.A.* **161 K10** 35 21N 116 7W
Silver Lake, *Ind., U.S.A.* **157 C11** 41 4N 85 53W
Silver Lake, *Oreg., U.S.A.* **158 E3** 43 8N 121 3W
Silver Lake, *Wis., U.S.A.* **157 B8** 42 33N 88 13W
Silver Springs, *U.S.A.* **153 F7** 29 13N 82 3W
Silverdalen, *Sweden* **17 G9** 57 32N 15 45 E
Silverton, *Australia* **128 A4** 31 52 S 141 10 E
Silverton, *Colo., U.S.A.* **159 H10** 37 49N 107 40W
Silverton, *Tex., U.S.A.* **155 H4** 34 28N 101 19W
Silves, *Brazil* **169 D6** 2 54 S 58 27W
Silves, *Portugal* **43 H2** 37 11N 8 26W
Silvi Marina, *Italy* **45 F11** 42 34N 14 5 E
Silvia, *Colombia* **168 C2** 2 37N 76 21W
Silvies →, *U.S.A.* **158 E4** 43 34N 119 2W
Silvrettahorn, *Switz.* **33 C10** 46 50N 10 6 E
Silwa Bahari, *Egypt* **106 C3** 24 45N 32 55 E
Silz, *Austria* **34 D3** 47 16N 10 56 E
Sim, C., *Morocco* **110 B3** 31 26N 9 51W
Simakumba, *Zambia* **115 E4** 14 12 S 23 16 E
Simaltala, *India* **93 G12** 24 43N 86 33 E
Simaluguri, *India* **90 B5** 26 55N 94 46 E
Simanggang = Bandar Sri Aman, *Malaysia* **85 B4** 1 15N 111 32 E
Simao, *China* **76 F3** 22 47N 101 5 E
Simão Dias, *Brazil* **170 D4** 10 44 S 37 49W
Simara I., *Phil.* **80 E4** 12 48N 122 3 E
Simard, L., *Canada* **140 C4** 47 40N 78 40W
Şīmareh →, *Iran* **101 F12** 33 9N 47 41 E
Simav, *Turkey* **49 B10** 39 4N 28 58 E
Simav →, *Turkey* **51 F12** 40 23N 28 31 E
Simav Dağları, *Turkey* **49 B10** 39 10N 28 30 E
Simba, *Dem. Rep. of the Congo* **114 B4** 0 38N 22 59 E
Simba, *Tanzania* **118 C4** 2 10 S 37 36 E
Simbach, *Germany* **31 G9** 48 16N 13 2 E
Simberi I., *Papua N. G.* **132 B7** 2 38 S 152 0 E
Simbirsk, *Russia* **60 C9** 54 20N 48 25 E
Simbo, *Solomon Is.* **133 M9** 8 16 S 156 33 E
Simbo, *Tanzania* **118 C2** 4 51 S 29 41 E
Simcoe, *Canada* **140 D3** 42 50N 80 20W
Simcoe, L., *Canada* **140 D4** 44 25N 79 20W
Simdega, *India* **93 H11** 22 37N 84 31 E
Simeonovgrad, *Bulgaria* **51 D9** 42 1N 25 50 E
Simeria, *Romania* **52 E8** 45 51N 23 1 E
Simeto →, *Italy* **47 E8** 37 24N 15 6 E
Simeulue, *Indonesia* **84 B1** 2 45N 95 45 E
Simferopol, *Ukraine* **59 K8** 44 55N 34 3 E
Sími, *Greece* **49 E9** 36 35N 27 50 E
Simi Valley, *U.S.A.* **161 L8** 34 16N 118 47W
Simien Mountains Nat. Park, *Ethiopia* **107 E4** 13 19N 38 0 E
Simikot, *Nepal* **93 E9** 30 0N 81 50 E
Simití, *Colombia* **168 B3** 7 58N 73 57W
Simitli, *Bulgaria* **50 E7** 41 52N 23 7 E
Simla, *India* **92 D7** 31 2N 77 9 E
Simlångsdalen, *Sweden* **17 H7** 56 43N 13 6 E
Şimleu-Silvaniei, *Romania* **52 C7** 47 17N 22 50 E
Simme →, *Switz.* **32 C4** 46 38N 7 25 E
Simmern, *Germany* **31 F3** 49 58N 7 30 E
Simmie, *Canada* **143 D7** 49 56N 108 6W
Simmler, *U.S.A.* **161 K7** 35 21N 119 59W
Simnas, *Lithuania* **54 D10** 54 24N 23 39 E
Simões, *Brazil* **170 C3** 7 36 S 40 49W
Simojoki →, *Finland* **14 D21** 65 35N 25 1 E
Simojovel, *Mexico* **163 D6** 17 12N 92 38W
Simonette →, *Canada* **142 B5** 55 9N 118 15W
Simonstown, *S. Africa* **116 E2** 34 14 S 18 26 E
Simontornya, *Hungary* **52 D3** 46 45N 18 33 E
Simpang Empat, *Malaysia* **87 c** 5 27N 100 29 E
Simpangkiri →, *Indonesia* **84 B1** 2 50N 97 40 E
Simplício Mendes, *Brazil* **170 C3** 7 51 S 41 54W
Simplon, *Switz.* **32 D6** 46 12N 8 4 E
Simplonpass, *Switz.* **32 D6** 46 15N 8 3 E
Simplontunnel, *Switz.* **32 D6** 46 15N 8 7 E
Simpson, Mt., *Papua N. G.* **132 F5** 10 2 S 149 34 E
Simpson Desert, *Australia* **126 D2** 25 0 S 137 0 E
Simpson Desert Nat. Park, *Australia* **126 C2** 24 59 S 138 21 E
Simpson Pen., *Canada* **139 B11** 68 34N 88 45W
Simpungdong, *N. Korea* **75 D15** 40 56N 129 29 E
Simrishamn, *Sweden* **17 J8** 55 33N 14 22 E
Simsbury, *U.S.A.* **151 E12** 41 53N 72 48W
Simunjan, *Malaysia* **85 B4** 1 25N 110 45 E
Simunul, *Phil.* **81 J2** 4 54N 119 51 E
Simushir, Ostrov, *Russia* **67 E16** 46 50N 152 30 E
Sin Cowe I., *S. China Sea* **78 C4** 9 53N 114 19 E
Sînâ' □, *Egypt* **103 F3** 30 0N 34 0 E
Sina →, *India* **94 F2** 17 30N 75 55 E
Sinabang, *Indonesia* **84 B1** 2 30N 96 24 E
Sinadogo, *Somali Rep.* **120 C3** 5 50N 47 0 E
Sinai = Es Sînâ', *Egypt* **103 F3** 29 0N 34 0 E
Sinai, Mt. = Mûsa, Gebel, *Egypt* **96 D2** 28 33N 33 59 E
Sinai Peninsula, *Egypt* **103 F3** 29 30N 34 0 E
Sinaia, *Romania* **53 E10** 45 21N 25 38 E
Sinait, *Phil.* **80 C3** 17 52N 120 27 E
Sinako, Mt., *Phil.* **81 H5** 7 30N 125 17 E
Sinaloa □, *Mexico* **162 C3** 25 0N 107 30W
Sinaloa de Leyva, *Mexico* **162 B3** 25 50N 108 20W
Sinalunga, *Italy* **45 E8** 43 12N 11 44 E
Sinan, *China* **76 D7** 27 56N 108 13 E
Sînandrei, *Romania* **52 E6** 45 52N 21 13 E
Sinarádhes, *Greece* **38 B9** 39 34N 19 51 E
Sīnāwan, *Libya* **108 B2** 31 0N 10 37 E
Sinbaungwe, *Burma* **90 F5** 19 43N 95 10 E
Sinbo, *Burma* **90 C6** 24 46N 97 3 E
Sincan, *Turkey* **100 B5** 39 58N 32 36 E
Sincanlı, *Turkey* **49 C12** 38 45N 30 15 E
Sincé, *Colombia* **168 B2** 9 15N 75 9W
Sincelejo, *Colombia* **168 B2** 9 18N 75 24W
Sinch'ang, *N. Korea* **75 D15** 40 7N 128 28 E
Sinchang-ni, *N. Korea* **75 E14** 39 24N 126 8 E
Sinclair, *U.S.A.* **158 F10** 41 47N 107 7W
Sinclair, L., *U.S.A.* **152 B6** 33 8N 83 12W
Sinclair Mills, *Canada* **142 C4** 54 5N 121 40W
Sinclair's B., *U.K.* **22 C5** 58 31N 3 5W
Sinclairville, *U.S.A.* **150 D5** 42 16N 79 16W
Sind, *Pakistan* **92 G3** 26 0N 68 30 E
Sind □, *Pakistan* **91 D3** 26 0N 69 0 E
Sind →, *Jammu & Kashmir, India* **93 B6** 34 18N 74 45 E
Sind →, *Mad. P., India* **93 F8** 26 26N 79 13 E
Sind Sagar Doab, *Pakistan* **92 D4** 32 0N 71 30 E
Sindal, *Denmark* **17 G4** 57 28N 10 10 E
Sindangan, *Phil.* **81 G4** 8 10N 123 5 E
Sindangan Bay, *Phil.* **81 G4** 8 11N 122 50 E
Sindangbarang, *Indonesia* **85 D3** 7 27 S 107 1 E
Sindara, *Gabon* **114 C2** 1 7 S 10 41 E
Sinde, *Zambia* **119 F2** 17 28 S 25 51 E
Sindelfingen, *Germany* **31 G4** 48 42N 9 0 E
Sindewahi, *India* **94 D4** 20 17N 79 39 E
Sindgi, *India* **94 F3** 16 55N 76 14 E
Sindh = Sind □, *Pakistan* **91 D3** 26 0N 69 0 E
Sindhnur, *India* **95 F3** 15 47N 76 46 E
Sindi, *India* **94 D4** 20 48N 78 52 E
Sındırgı, *Turkey* **49 B10** 39 13N 28 10 E
Sindou, *Burkina Faso* **112 C3** 10 35N 5 4W
Sindri, *India* **93 H12** 23 45N 86 42 E
Sine →, *Senegal* **112 C1** 14 10N 16 28W
Sinegorskiy, *Russia* **61 G5** 47 55N 40 52 E
Sinekli, *Turkey* **51 E12** 41 14N 28 12 E
Sinelnikovo = Synelnykove, *Ukraine* **59 H8** 48 25N 35 30 E
Sinendé, *Benin* **113 C5** 10 20N 2 22 E
Sines, *Portugal* **43 H2** 37 56N 8 51W
Sines, C. de, *Portugal* **43 H2** 37 58N 8 53W
Sineu, *Spain* **38 B4** 39 38N 3 1 E
Sinewit, Mt., *Papua N. G.* **132 C7** 4 44 S 152 2 E
Sinfra, *Ivory C.* **112 D3** 6 35N 5 56W
Sing Buri, *Thailand* **86 E3** 14 53N 100 25 E
Singa, *Sudan* **107 E3** 13 10N 33 57 E
Singako, *Chad* **109 G3** 9 50N 19 24 E
Singanallur, *India* **95 J3** 11 2N 77 1 E
Singapore ■, *Asia* **87 d** 1 17N 103 51 E
Singapore, Straits of, *Asia* **87 d** 1 15N 104 0 E
Singaraja, *Indonesia* **85 D5** 8 7 S 115 6 E
Singatoka = Sigatoka, *Fiji* **133 B1** 18 8 S 177 30 E
Singen, *Germany* **31 H4** 47 45N 8 50 E
Singida, *Tanzania* **118 C3** 4 49 S 34 48 E
Singida □, *Tanzania* **118 D3** 6 0 S 34 30 E
Singitikós Kólpos, *Greece* **50 F7** 40 6N 24 0 E
Singkaling Hkamti, *Burma* **90 C5** 26 0N 95 39 E
Singkang, *Indonesia* **82 B2** 4 8 S 120 1 E
Singkawang, *Indonesia* **85 B3** 1 0N 108 57 E
Singkep, *Indonesia* **78 E2** 0 30 S 104 25 E
Singleton, *Australia* **129 B9** 32 33 S 151 0 E
Singleton, Mt., *N. Terr., Australia* **124 D5** 22 0 S 130 46 E
Singleton, Mt., *W. Austral., Australia* **125 E2** 29 27 S 117 15 E
Singö, *Sweden* **16 D12** 60 12N 18 45 E
Singoli, *India* **92 G6** 25 0N 75 22 E
Singora = Songkhla, *Thailand* **87 J3** 7 13N 100 37 E
Singosan, *N. Korea* **75 E14** 38 52N 127 25 E
Singri, *India* **90 B4** 26 36N 92 29 E
Singsås, *Norway* **18 B7** 62 56N 10 37 E
Singu, *Burma* **90 D6** 22 33N 96 0 E
Sinhgarh, *India* **94 E1** 18 22N 73 45 E
Sinhung, *N. Korea* **75 D14** 40 11N 127 34 E
Siniátsikon, Óros, *Greece* **50 F5** 40 25N 21 35 E
Siniloan, *Phil.* **80 D3** 14 25N 121 27 E
Siniscóla, *Italy* **46 B2** 40 34N 9 41 E
Sinj, *Croatia* **45 E13** 43 42N 16 39 E
Sinjai, *Indonesia* **82 C2** 5 7 S 120 20 E
Sinjajevina, *Montenegro, Yug.* **50 D3** 42 57N 19 22 E
Sinjār, *Iraq* **101 D9** 36 19N 41 52 E
Sinkat, *Sudan* **106 D4** 18 55N 36 49 E
Sinkiang Uighur = Xinjiang Uygur Zizhiqu □, *China* **68 C3** 42 0N 86 0 E
Sinlumkaba, *Burma* **90 C6** 24 16N 97 31 E
Sinmak, *N. Korea* **75 E14** 38 25N 126 14 E
Sínnai, *Italy* **46 C2** 39 18N 9 13 E
Sinnar, *India* **94 E2** 19 48N 74 0 E
Sinni →, *Italy* **47 B9** 40 8N 16 41 E
Sinnuris, *Egypt* **106 J7** 29 26N 30 31 E
Sinoie, Lacul, *Romania* **53 F13** 44 35N 28 50 E
Sinop, *Turkey* **100 A6** 42 1N 35 11 E
Sinor, *India* **92 J5** 21 55N 73 20 E
Sinp'o, *N. Korea* **75 E15** 40 0N 128 13 E
Sins, *Switz.* **33 B6** 47 12N 8 24 E
Sinsheim, *Germany* **31 F4** 49 15N 8 52 E
Sinsk, *Russia* **67 C13** 61 8N 126 48 E
Sintang, *Indonesia* **85 B4** 0 5N 111 35 E
Sinton, *U.S.A.* **155 L6** 28 2N 97 31W
Sintra, *Portugal* **43 G1** 38 47N 9 25W
Sinugif, *Somali Rep.* **120 C3** 8 33N 48 59 E
Sinŭiju, *N. Korea* **75 D13** 40 5N 124 24 E
Sinyukha →, *Ukraine* **59 H6** 48 3N 30 51 E
Sinzig, *Germany* **30 E3** 50 32N 7 14 E
Sio →, *Hungary* **52 D3** 46 20N 18 53 E
Siocon, *Phil.* **81 H4** 7 40N 122 10 E
Siófok, *Hungary* **52 D3** 46 54N 18 3 E
Sioma, *Zambia* **115 F4** 16 40 S 23 32 E
Sioma Ngwezi Nat. Park, *Zambia* **115 F4** 17 14 S 23 26 E
Sion, *Switz.* **32 D4** 46 14N 7 20 E
Sion Mills, *U.K.* **23 B4** 54 48N 7 29W
Sioux City, *U.S.A.* **154 D6** 42 30N 96 24W
Sioux Falls, *U.S.A.* **154 D6** 43 33N 96 44W
Sioux Lookout, *Canada* **140 B1** 50 10N 91 50W
Sioux Narrows, *Canada* **143 D10** 49 25N 94 10W
Sipalay, *Phil.* **81 G4** 9 45N 122 24 E
Šipan, *Croatia* **50 D1** 42 45N 17 52 E
Sipang, Tanjong, *Malaysia* **85 B4** 1 48N 110 20 E
Siparia, *Trin. & Tob.* **169 F9** 10 8N 61 31W
Siping, *China* **75 C13** 43 8N 124 21 E
Sipiwesk L., *Canada* **143 B9** 55 5N 97 35W
Sipocot, *Phil.* **80 E4** 13 46N 122 58 E
Šipovo, *Bos.-H.* **52 F2** 44 16N 17 6 E
Sipra →, *India* **92 H6** 23 55N 75 28 E
Sipur, *India* **94 D7** 21 11N 85 9 E
Sipura, *Indonesia* **84 C1** 2 18 S 99 40 E
Siquia →, *Nic.* **164 D3** 12 10N 84 20W
Siquijor, *Phil.* **81 G4** 9 12N 123 35 E
Siquijor □, *Phil.* **81 G4** 9 11N 123 35 E
Siquirres, *Costa Rica* **164 D3** 10 6N 83 30W
Siquisique, *Venezuela* **168 A4** 10 34N 69 42W
Şīr Banī Yās, *U.A.E.* **97 E7** 24 19N 52 37 E
Sir Edward Pellew Group, *Australia* **126 B2** 15 40 S 137 10 E
Sir Graham Moore Is., *Australia* **124 B4** 13 53 S 126 34 E
Sir James MacBrien, Mt., *Canada* **138 B7** 62 8N 127 40W
Sir Joseph Banks Group, *Australia* **128 C2** 34 36 S 136 16 E
Sira, *India* **95 H3** 13 41N 76 49 E
Sira, *Norway* **18 F3** 58 24N 6 40 E
Sira →, *Norway* **15 G12** 58 23N 6 34 E
Siracusa, *Italy* **47 E8** 37 4N 15 17 E
Sirajganj, *Bangla.* **90 C2** 24 25N 89 47 E
Sirakoro, *Mali* **112 C3** 12 41N 9 14W
Şiran, *Turkey* **101 B8** 40 11N 39 7 E
Sirasso, *Ivory C.* **112 D3** 9 16N 6 6W
Sirathu, *India* **93 G9** 25 39N 81 19 E
Sirawai, *Phil.* **81 H4** 7 34N 122 8 E
Sirdalsvatnet, *Norway* **18 F3** 58 34N 6 43 E
Sīrdān, *Iran* **97 B6** 36 39N 49 12 E
Sirdaryo = Syrdarya, *Uzbekistan* **65 C4** 40 50N 68 40 E
Sirdaryo = Syrdarya →, *Kazakstan* **66 E7** 46 3N 61 0 E
Sire, *Ethiopia* **107 F4** 6 55N 35 36 E
Siren, *U.S.A.* **154 C8** 45 47N 92 24W
Sirer, *Spain* **38 D1** 38 56N 1 22 E
Siret, *Romania* **53 C11** 47 55N 26 5 E
Siret →, *Romania* **53 E12** 45 24N 28 1 E
Sirevåg, *Norway* **18 F2** 58 30N 5 48 E
Sirghāyā, *Syria* **103 B5** 33 51N 36 8 E
Şiria, *Romania* **52 D6** 46 16N 21 38 E
Sirik, Tanjong, *Malaysia* **85 B4** 2 47N 111 15 E
Sirino, Mte., *Italy* **47 B8** 40 7N 15 50 E
Sirkali = Sirkazhi, *India* **95 J4** 11 15N 79 41 E
Sirkazhi, *India* **95 J4** 11 15N 79 41 E
Sirmans, *U.S.A.* **152 E6** 30 21N 83 39W
Sirmaur, *India* **93 G9** 24 51N 81 23 E
Sírna, *Greece* **49 E8** 36 22N 26 42 E
Sirnach, *Switz.* **33 B7** 47 28N 8 59 E
Şırnak, *Turkey* **101 D10** 37 32N 42 28 E
Sirohi, *India* **92 G5** 24 52N 72 53 E
Sironj, *India* **92 G7** 24 5N 77 39 E
Síros, *Greece* **48 D6** 37 28N 24 57 E
Sirpur, *India* **94 E4** 19 29N 79 36 E
Sirrayn, *Si. Arabia* **98 C3** 19 38N 40 36 E
Sirretta Pk., *U.S.A.* **161 K8** 35 56N 118 19W
Sīrrī, *Iran* **97 E7** 25 55N 54 32 E
Sirsa, *India* **92 E6** 29 33N 75 4 E
Sirsa →, *India* **93 F8** 26 51N 79 4 E
Sirsi, *India* **95 G2** 14 40N 74 49 E
Sirsilla, *India* **94 E4** 18 23N 78 50 E
Siruela, *Spain* **43 G5** 38 58N 5 3W
Siruguppa, *India* **95 F3** 15 38N 76 54 E
Sirur, *India* **94 E2** 18 50N 74 23 E
Sisak, *Croatia* **45 C13** 45 30N 16 21 E
Sisaket, *Thailand* **86 E5** 15 8N 104 23 E
Sisante, *Spain* **41 F2** 39 25N 2 12W
Sisargas, Is., *Spain* **42 B2** 43 21N 8 50W
Sishen, *S. Africa* **116 D3** 27 47 S 22 59 E
Sishui, *Henan, China* **74 G7** 34 48N 113 15 E
Sishui, *Shandong, China* **75 G9** 35 42N 117 18 E
Sisiga, *Solomon Is.* **133 L10** 7 54 S 159 10 E
Sisimiut, *Greenland* **10 D5** 66 40N 53 30W
Sisipuk L., *Canada* **143 B8** 55 45N 101 50W
Sisophon, *Cambodia* **86 F4** 13 38N 102 59 E
Sissach, *Switz.* **32 B5** 47 27N 7 48 E
Sissano, *Papua N. G.* **132 B2** 3 0 S 142 3 E
Sisseton, *U.S.A.* **154 C6** 45 40N 97 3W
Sissonne, *France* **27 C10** 49 34N 3 51 E
Sīstān, *Asia* **97 D9** 30 50N 61 0 E
Sīstān, Daryācheh-ye, *Iran* **97 D9** 31 0N 61 0 E
Sīstān va Balūchestān □, *Iran* **97 E9** 27 0N 62 0 E
Sisteron, *France* **29 D9** 44 12N 5 57 E
Sisters, *U.S.A.* **158 D3** 44 18N 121 33W
Sisters Pk., *Ascension I.* **9 g** 7 56 S 14 22W
Siswa Bazar, *India* **93 F10** 27 9N 83 46 E
Sitakili, *Mali* **112 C2** 13 7N 11 14W
Sitakunda, *Bangla.* **90 D3** 22 37N 91 39 E
Sitamarhi, *India* **93 F11** 26 37N 85 30 E
Sitampiky, *Madag.* **117 B8** 16 41 S 46 6 E
Sitangkai, *Phil.* **81 J2** 4 40N 119 24 E
Sitapur, *India* **93 F9** 27 38N 80 45 E
Siteki, *Swaziland* **117 D5** 26 32 S 31 58 E
Sitges, *Spain* **40 D6** 41 17N 1 47 E
Sithoniá, *Greece* **50 F7** 40 0N 23 45 E
Sitía, *Greece* **39 E7** 35 13N 26 6 E
Sítio da Abadia, *Brazil* **171 D2** 14 48 S 46 16W
Sitka, *U.S.A.* **142 B1** 57 3N 135 20W
Sitkinak I., *U.S.A.* **144 H9** 56 33N 154 10W
Sitoti, *Botswana* **116 C3** 23 15 S 23 40 E
Sitra, *Egypt* **106 B2** 28 40N 26 53 E
Sittang Myit →, *Burma* **90 G6** 17 20N 96 45 E
Sittard, *Neths.* **24 C5** 51 0N 5 52 E
Sittaung, *Burma* **90 C5** 24 10N 94 35 E
Sittensen, *Germany* **30 B5** 53 17N 9 32 E
Sittingbourne, *U.K.* **21 F8** 51 21N 0 45 E
Sittona, *Eritrea* **107 E4** 14 25N 37 23 E
Sittoung = Sittang Myit →, *Burma* **90 G6** 17 20N 96 45 E
Sittwe, *Burma* **90 E4** 20 18N 92 45 E
Situbondo, *Indonesia* **79 G16** 7 42 S 114 0 E
Si'umu, *Samoa* **133 X24** 14 1 S 171 48W
Siuna, *Nic.* **164 D3** 13 37N 84 45W
Siuri, *India* **93 H12** 23 50N 87 34 E
Siutghiol, Lacul, *Romania* **53 F13** 44 15N 28 35 E
Sivaganga, *India* **95 K4** 9 50N 78 28 E
Sivagiri, *India* **95 K3** 9 16N 77 26 E
Sivakasi, *India* **95 K3** 9 24N 77 47 E
Sīvand, *Iran* **97 D7** 30 5N 52 55 E
Sivas, *Turkey* **100 C7** 39 43N 36 58 E
Sivasamudram, *India* **95 H3** 12 16N 77 10 E
Sivaslı, *Turkey* **49 C11** 38 31N 29 42 E
Siverek, *Turkey* **101 D8** 37 50N 39 19 E
Sivomaskinskiy, *Russia* **56 A11** 66 40N 62 35 E
Sívota, *Greece* **38 C10** 39 24N 20 13 E
Sivrihisar, *Turkey* **100 C4** 39 30N 31 35 E
Sívros, *Greece* **39 B2** 38 40N 20 39 E
Sîwa, *Egypt* **106 B2** 29 11N 25 31 E
Sīwa, El Wâhât es, *Egypt* **106 B2** 29 10N 25 30 E
Siwa Oasis = Sīwa, El Wâhât es, *Egypt* **106 B2** 29 10N 25 30 E
Siwalik Range, *Nepal* **93 F10** 28 0N 83 0 E
Siwan, *India* **93 F11** 26 13N 84 21 E
Siwana, *India* **92 G5** 25 38N 72 25 E
Six Cross Roads, *Barbados* **165 g** 13 10N 59 28W
Sixmilebridge, *Ireland* **23 D3** 52 44N 8 46W
Sixth Cataract, *Sudan* **107 D3** 16 20N 32 42 E
Siyāh Kuh, *Afghan.* **91 B2** 34 7N 64 10 E
Siyâl, Jazâ'ir, *Egypt* **106 C4** 22 49N 36 12 E
Siyäzän, *Azerbaijan* **61 K9** 41 3N 49 10 E
Siziwang Qi, *China* **74 D6** 41 25N 111 40 E
Sjælland, *Denmark* **17 J5** 55 30N 11 30 E
Sjællands Odde, *Denmark* **17 J5** 55 58N 11 24 E
Sjenica, *Serbia, Yug.* **50 C3** 43 16N 20 0 E
Sjoa, *Norway* **18 C6** 61 41N 9 33 E
Sjöbo, *Sweden* **17 J7** 55 37N 13 45 E
Sjøholt, *Norway* **18 B3** 62 27N 6 52 E
Sjøli, *Norway* **18 C8** 61 29N 11 18 E
Sjötofta, *Sweden* **17 G7** 57 22N 13 17 E
Sjötorp, *Sweden* **17 F8** 58 50N 14 0 E
Sjumen = Shumen, *Bulgaria* **51 C10** 43 18N 26 55 E
Sjuntorp, *Sweden* **17 F6** 58 12N 12 13 E
Skåbu, *Norway* **18 C6** 61 32N 9 24 E
Skadarsko Jezero, *Montenegro, Yug.* **50 D3** 42 10N 19 20 E
Skadovsk, *Ukraine* **59 J7** 46 17N 32 52 E
Skælskør, *Denmark* **17 J5** 55 15N 11 18 E
Skærbæk, *Denmark* **17 J2** 55 9N 8 45 E
Skaftafell, *Iceland* **11 C9** 64 1N 17 0W
Skagafjarðarsýsla □, *Iceland* **11 B7** 65 30N 19 0W
Skagafjörður, *Iceland* **11 B7** 65 54N 19 35W
Skagastølstindane, *Norway* **15 F12** 61 28N 7 52 E
Skagaströnd, *Iceland* **11 B6** 65 50N 20 19W
Skagatá, *Iceland* **11 A6** 66 7N 20 6W
Skagen, *Denmark* **17 G4** 57 43N 10 35 E
Skagern, *Sweden* **16 F8** 59 0N 14 20 E
Skagerrak, *Denmark* **17 G2** 57 30N 9 0 E
Skagit →, *U.S.A.* **160 B4** 48 23N 122 22W
Skagway, *U.S.A.* **144 G14** 59 28N 135 19W
Skála **39 C2** 38 5N 20 47 E
Skala-Podilska, *Ukraine* **59 H4** 48 50N 26 15 E
Skala Podolskaya = Skala-Podilska, *Ukraine* **59 H4** 48 50N 26 15 E
Skalat, *Ukraine* **59 H3** 49 23N 25 55 E
Skálavík, *Iceland* **11 A3** 66 11N 23 29W
Skalbmierz, *Poland* **55 H7** 50 20N 20 25 E
Skälderviken, *Sweden* **17 H6** 56 22N 12 30 E
Skålevik, *Norway* **18 F5** 58 5N 8 1 E
Skalica, *Slovak Rep.* **35 C10** 48 50N 17 15 E
Skallingen, *Denmark* **17 J2** 55 32N 8 13 E
Skalni Dol = Kamenyak, *Bulgaria* **51 C10** 43 24N 26 57 E
Skanderborg, *Denmark* **17 H3** 56 2N 9 55 E
Skåne, *Sweden* **17 J7** 55 59N 13 30 E
Skåne län □, *Sweden* **17 H7** 56 15N 14 0 E
Skaneateles, *U.S.A.* **151 D8** 42 57N 76 26W
Skaneateles L., *U.S.A.* **151 D8** 42 51N 76 22W
Skånevik, *Norway* **18 E2** 59 43N 5 53 E
Skänninge, *Sweden* **17 F9** 58 24N 15 5 E
Skanör med Falsterbo, *Sweden* **17 J6** 55 24N 12 50 E
Skantzoúra, *Greece* **48 B6** 39 5N 24 6 E
Skara, *Sweden* **17 F7** 58 25N 13 30 E
Skärblacka, *Sweden* **17 F9** 58 35N 15 54 E
Skarð, *Iceland* **11 B4** 65 17N 22 19W
Skardu, *Pakistan* **93 B6** 35 20N 75 44 E
Skare, *Norway* **18 E3** 59 55N 6 36 E
Skåre, *Sweden* **16 E7** 59 26N 13 26 E
Skärhamn, *Sweden* **17 G5** 57 59N 11 34 E
Skarnes, *Norway* **18 D8** 60 15N 11 41 E
Skarszewy, *Poland* **54 D5** 54 4N 18 25 E
Skaryszew, *Poland* **55 G8** 51 19N 21 15 E
Skarżysko-Kamienna, *Poland* **55 G7** 51 7N 20 52 E
Skattkärr, *Sweden* **16 E7** 59 25N 13 40 E
Skattungbyn, *Sweden* **16 C8** 61 10N 14 56 E
Skawina, *Poland* **55 J6** 49 59N 19 50 E
Skebobruk, *Sweden* **16 E12** 59 58N 18 36 E
Skeena →, *Canada* **142 C2** 54 9N 130 5W
Skeena Mts., *Canada* **142 B3** 56 40N 128 30W
Skegness, *U.K.* **20 D8** 53 9N 0 20 E
Skei, *Norway* **18 C3** 61 34N 6 28 E
Skeiðarársandur, *Iceland* **11 D9** 63 54N 17 14W
Skeiðflötur, *Iceland* **11 D7** 63 26N 19 11W
Skeldon, *Guyana* **169 B6** 5 55N 57 20W
Skeleton Coast Park, *Namibia* **116 C1** 20 0 S 13 20 E
Skellefte älv →, *Sweden* **14 D19** 64 45N 21 10 E
Skellefteå, *Sweden* **14 D19** 64 45N 20 50 E
Skelleftehamn, *Sweden* **14 D19** 64 40N 21 9 E
Skender Vakuf, *Bos.-H.* **52 F2** 44 29N 17 22 E
Skerries, The, *U.K.* **20 D3** 53 25N 4 36W
Skhíza, *Greece* **48 E3** 36 41N 21 40 E
Skhoinoúsa, *Greece* **49 E7** 36 53N 25 31 E
Ski, *Norway* **15 G14** 59 43N 10 52 E
Skíathos, *Greece* **48 B5** 39 12N 23 30 E
Skibbereen, *Ireland* **23 E2** 51 33N 9 16W
Skiddaw, *U.K.* **20 C4** 54 39N 3 9W
Skidegate, *Canada* **142 C2** 53 15N 132 1W
Skídhra, *Greece* **50 F6** 40 46N 22 10 E
Skien, *Norway* **15 G13** 59 12N 9 35 E
Skierniewice, *Poland* **55 G7** 51 58N 20 10 E
Skikda, *Algeria* **111 A6** 36 50N 6 58 E
Skillet →, *U.S.A.* **157 F8** 38 5N 88 5W
Skillingaryd, *Sweden* **17 G8** 57 27N 14 5 E
Skillinge, *Sweden* **17 J8** 55 30N 14 16 E
Skilloura, *Cyprus* **39 E9** 35 14N 33 10 E
Skinári, Ákra, *Greece* **39 D2** 37 56N 20 42 E
Skinnastaður, *Iceland* **11 A10** 66 4N 16 27W
Skinnskatteberg, *Sweden* **16 E9** 59 50N 15 42 E
Skipton, *Australia* **128 D5** 37 39 S 143 40 E
Skipton, *U.K.* **20 D5** 53 58N 2 3W
Skiptvet, *Norway* **18 E8** 59 28N 11 11 E
Skiring, C., *Senegal* **112 C1** 12 26N 16 46W
Skirmish Pt., *Australia* **126 A1** 11 59 S 134 17 E
Skiropoúla, *Greece* **48 C6** 38 50N 24 21 E
Skíros, *Greece* **48 C6** 38 55N 24 34 E
Skivarp, *Sweden* **17 J7** 55 26N 13 34 E
Skive, *Denmark* **17 H3** 56 33N 9 2 E
Skjærhalden, *Norway* **18 E8** 59 2N 11 2 E
Skjálfandafljót →, *Iceland* **11 B9** 65 59N 17 25W
Skjálfandi, *Iceland* **11 A9** 66 5N 17 30W
Skjeberg, *Norway* **18 E8** 59 12N 11 12 E
Skjern, *Denmark* **17 J2** 55 57N 8 30 E
Skjold, *Norway* **18 E2** 59 31N 5 34 E
Skjolden, *Norway* **18 C4** 61 29N 7 36 E
Skjöldólfsstaðir, *Iceland* **11 B11** 65 19N 15 7W
Skjønhaug, *Norway* **18 E8** 59 39N 11 19 E
Skobeleva, Pik, *Kyrgyzstan* **65 D6** 39 48N 72 36 E
Skoczów, *Poland* **55 J5** 49 49N 18 45 E
Skodje, *Norway* **18 B3** 62 30N 6 43 E
Škofja Loka, *Slovenia* **45 B11** 46 9N 14 19 E
Skógar, *Iceland* **11 D7** 63 32N 19 28W
Skógarnes, *Iceland* **11 C4** 64 46N 22 34W
Skoghall, *Sweden* **16 E7** 59 20N 13 30 E
Skogstorp, *Sweden* **16 E10** 59 19N 16 29 E
Skoki, *Poland* **55 F4** 52 40N 17 11 E
Skokie, *U.S.A.* **157 B9** 42 3N 87 45W
Skole, *Ukraine* **59 H2** 49 3N 23 30 E
Skollenborg, *Norway* **18 E6** 59 38N 9 43 E
Skópelos, *Greece* **48 B5** 39 9N 23 47 E
Skopí, *Greece* **39 E7** 35 11N 26 2 E
Skopin, *Russia* **58 F10** 53 55N 39 32 E
Skopje, *Macedonia* **50 D5** 42 1N 21 26 E
Skoppum, *Norway* **18 E7** 59 23N 10 26 E
Skórcz, *Poland* **54 E5** 53 47N 18 30 E
Skørping, *Denmark* **17 H3** 56 50N 9 53 E
Skotfoss, *Norway* **18 E6** 59 12N 9 30 E
Skotterud, *Norway* **18 D9** 60 0N 12 7 E
Skövde, *Sweden* **17 F7** 58 24N 13 50 E
Skovorodino, *Russia* **67 D13** 54 0N 124 0 E
Skowhegan, *U.S.A.* **149 C11** 44 46N 69 43W
Skradin, *Croatia* **45 E12** 43 52N 15 53 E
Skrea, *Sweden* **17 H6** 56 53N 12 34 E
Skreia, *Norway* **18 D7** 60 40N 10 56 E
Skrim, *Norway* **18 E6** 59 31N 9 38 E
Skrunda, *Latvia* **54 B9** 56 41N 22 1 E

Skrwa →, *Poland* 55 F6 52 35N 19 32 E
Skudeneshavn, *Norway* 18 E2 59 10N 5 10 E
Skull, *Ireland* 23 E2 51 32N 9 34W
Skultorp, *Sweden* 17 F7 58 24N 13 51 E
Skultuna, *Sweden* 16 E10 59 43N 16 25 E
Skunk →, *U.S.A.* 156 D5 40 42N 91 7W
Skuodas, *Lithuania* 15 H19 56 16N 21 33 E
Skurup, *Sweden* 17 J7 55 28N 13 30 E
Skutskär, *Sweden* 16 D11 60 37N 17 25 E
Skútustaðir, *Iceland* 11 B9 65 34N 17 2W
Skvyra, *Ukraine* 59 H5 49 44N 29 40 E
Skwierzyna, *Poland* 55 F2 52 33N 15 30 E
Skye, *U.K.* 22 D2 57 15N 6 10W
Skykomish, *U.S.A.* 158 C3 47 42N 121 22W
Skyring, Seno, *Chile* 176 D3 52 35 S 72 0W
Skyros = Skíros, *Greece* 48 C6 38 55N 24 34 E
Skyttorp, *Sweden* 16 D11 60 5N 17 44 E
Slade Pt., *Australia* 126 K7 21 5 S 149 13 E
Slættaratindur, *Færoe Is.* 14 E9 62 18N 7 1W
Slagelse, *Denmark* 17 J5 55 23N 11 19 E
Slamet, *Indonesia* 85 D3 7 16 S 109 8 E
Slaney →, *Ireland* 23 D5 52 26N 6 33W
Slangberge, *S. Africa* 116 E3 31 32 S 20 48 E
Slănic, *Romania* 53 E10 45 14N 25 58 E
Slano, *Croatia* 50 D1 42 48N 17 53 E
Slantsy, *Russia* 58 C5 59 7N 28 5 E
Slaný, *Czech Rep.* 34 A7 50 13N 14 6 E
Śląsk, *Poland* 36 C9 51 0N 16 30 E
Śląskie □, *Poland* 55 H6 50 30N 19 0 E
Slätbaken, *Sweden* 17 F10 58 25N 16 45 E
Slate Is., *Canada* 140 C2 48 40N 87 0W
Slater, *U.S.A.* 156 E3 39 13N 93 4W
Slatina, *Croatia* 52 E2 45 42N 17 45 E
Slatina, *Romania* 53 F9 44 28N 24 22 E
Slatina Timiş, *Romania* 52 E7 45 15N 22 17 E
Slatington, *U.S.A.* 151 F9 40 45N 75 37W
Slaton, *U.S.A.* 155 J4 33 26N 101 39W
Slave →, *Canada* 142 A6 61 18N 113 39W
Slave Coast, *W. Afr.* 113 D5 6 0N 2 30 E
Slave Lake, *Canada* 142 B6 55 17N 114 43W
Slave Pt., *Canada* 142 A5 61 11N 115 56W
Slavgorod, *Russia* 66 D8 53 1N 78 37 E
Slavinja, *Serbia, Yug.* 50 C6 43 9N 22 50 E
Slavkov u Brna, *Czech Rep.* 35 B9 49 10N 16 52 E
Slavonija, *Europe* 52 E2 45 20N 17 40 E
Slavonski Brod, *Croatia* 52 E3 45 11N 18 1 E
Slavuta, *Ukraine* 59 G4 50 15N 27 2 E
Slavyanka, *Russia* 70 C5 42 53N 131 21 E
Slavyanovo, *Bulgaria* 51 C8 43 28N 24 52 E
Slavyansk = Slovyansk, *Ukraine* 59 H9 48 55N 37 36 E
Slavyansk-na-Kubani, *Russia* 59 K10 45 15N 38 11 E
Sława, *Poland* 55 G3 51 52N 16 2 E
Slawharad, *Belarus* 58 F6 53 27N 31 0 E
Sławno, *Poland* 54 D3 54 20N 16 41 E
Sławoborze, *Poland* 54 E2 53 55N 15 42 E
Sleaford, *U.K.* 20 D7 53 0N 0 24W
Sleaford B., *Australia* 127 E2 34 55 S 135 45 E
Sleat, Sd. of, *U.K.* 22 D3 57 5N 5 47W
Sleðbrjótur, *Iceland* 11 B12 65 34N 14 30W
Sleeper Is., *Canada* 139 C11 58 30N 81 0W
Sleepy Eye, *U.S.A.* 154 C7 44 18N 94 43W
Sleetmute, *U.S.A.* 144 F8 61 42N 157 10W
Sleman, *Indonesia* 85 D4 7 40 S 110 20 E
Slemon L., *Canada* 142 A5 63 13N 116 4W
Ślesin, *Poland* 55 F5 52 22N 18 14 E
Slide Mt., *U.S.A.* 151 E10 42 0N 74 25W
Slidell, *U.S.A.* 155 K10 30 17N 89 47W
Sliema, *Malta* 38 F8 35 55N 14 30 E
Slieve Aughty, *Ireland* 23 C3 53 4N 8 30W
Slieve Bloom, *Ireland* 23 C4 53 4N 7 40W
Slieve Donard, *U.K.* 23 B6 54 11N 5 55W
Slieve Gamph, *Ireland* 23 B3 54 6N 9 0W
Slieve Gullion, *U.K.* 23 B5 54 7N 6 26W
Slieve Mish, *Ireland* 23 D2 52 12N 9 50W
Slievenamon, *Ireland* 23 D4 52 25N 7 34W
Sligeach = Sligo, *Ireland* 23 B3 54 16N 8 28W
Sligo, *Ireland* 23 B3 54 16N 8 28W
Sligo, *U.S.A.* 150 E5 41 6N 79 29W
Sligo □, *Ireland* 23 B3 54 8N 8 42W
Sligo B., *Ireland* 23 B3 54 18N 8 40W
Slippery Rock, *U.S.A.* 150 E4 41 3N 80 3W
Slite, *Sweden* 17 G12 57 42N 18 48 E
Sliven, *Bulgaria* 51 D10 42 42N 26 19 E
Slivnitsa, *Bulgaria* 50 D7 42 50N 23 2 E
Sljeme, *Croatia* 45 C12 45 57N 15 58 E
Sloan, *U.S.A.* 161 K11 35 57N 115 13W
Sloansville, *U.S.A.* 151 D10 42 45N 74 22W
Slobodskoy, *Russia* 64 B3 58 40N 50 6 E
Slobozia, *Moldova* 53 D14 46 45N 29 42 E
Slobozia, *Argeş, Romania* 53 F10 44 30N 25 14 E
Slobozia, *Ialomiţa, Romania* 53 F12 44 34N 27 23 E
Slocan, *Canada* 142 D5 49 48N 117 28W
Slocomb, *U.S.A.* 152 D4 31 7N 85 36W
Słomniki, *Poland* 55 H7 50 16N 20 4 E
Slonim, *Belarus* 59 F3 53 4N 25 19 E
Slough, *U.K.* 21 F7 51 30N 0 36W
Slough □, *U.K.* 21 F7 51 30N 0 36W
Sloughhouse, *U.S.A.* 160 G5 38 26N 121 12W
Slovak Rep. ■, *Europe* 35 C13 48 30N 20 0 E
Slovakia = Slovak Rep. ■, *Europe* 35 C13 48 30N 20 0 E
Slovakian Ore Mts. = Slovenské Rudohorie, *Slovak Rep.* 35 C12 48 45N 20 0 E
Slovenia ■, *Europe* 45 C11 45 58N 14 30 E
Slovenija = Slovenia ■, *Europe* 45 C11 45 58N 14 30 E
Slovenj Gradec, *Slovenia* 45 B12 46 31N 15 5 E
Slovenska Bistrica, *Slovenia* 45 B12 46 24N 15 35 E
Slovenske Konjice, *Slovenia* 45 B12 46 20N 15 28 E
Slovenské Rudohorie, *Slovak Rep.* 35 C12 48 45N 20 0 E
Slovyansk, *Ukraine* 59 H9 48 55N 37 36 E
Słubice, *Poland* 55 F1 52 22N 14 35 E
Sluch →, *Ukraine* 59 G4 51 37N 26 38 E
Sluis, *Neths.* 24 C3 51 18N 3 23 E
Slŭnchev Bryag, *Bulgaria* 51 D11 42 40N 27 41 E
Slunj, *Croatia* 45 C12 45 6N 15 33 E
Słupca, *Poland* 55 F4 52 15N 17 52 E
Słupia →, *Poland* 54 D3 54 35N 16 51 E
Słupsk, *Poland* 54 D4 54 30N 17 3 E
Slurry, *S. Africa* 116 D4 25 49 S 25 42 E
Slutsk, *Belarus* 59 F4 53 2N 27 31 E
Slyne Hd., *Ireland* 23 C1 53 25N 10 10W
Slyudyanka, *Russia* 67 D11 51 40N 103 40 E
Småland, *Sweden* 17 G9 57 15N 15 25 E
Smålandsfarvandet, *Denmark* 17 J5 55 10N 11 20 E
Smålandsstenar, *Sweden* 17 G7 57 10N 13 25 E
Smalltree L., *Canada* 143 A8 61 0N 105 0W
Smallwood Res., *Canada* 141 B7 54 0N 64 0W
Smarhon, *Belarus* 58 E4 54 20N 26 24 E
Smarje, *Slovenia* 45 B12 46 15N 15 34 E
Smartt Syndicate Dam, *S. Africa* 116 E3 30 45 S 23 10 E
Smartville, *U.S.A.* 160 F5 39 13N 121 18W
Smeaton, *Canada* 143 C8 53 30N 104 49W
Smedby, *Sweden* 17 H10 56 41N 16 13 E
Smederevo, *Serbia, Yug.* 50 B4 44 40N 20 57 E
Smederevska Palanka, *Serbia, Yug.* 50 B4 44 22N 20 58 E
Smedjebacken, *Sweden* 16 D9 60 8N 15 25 E
Smela = Smila, *Ukraine* 59 H6 49 15N 31 58 E
Smerwick Harbour, *Ireland* 23 D1 52 12N 10 23W
Smethport, *U.S.A.* 150 E6 41 49N 78 27W
Smidovich, *Russia* 67 E14 48 36N 133 49 E
Śmigiel, *Poland* 55 F3 52 1N 16 32 E
Smila, *Ukraine* 59 H6 49 15N 31 58 E
Smilyan, *Bulgaria* 51 E8 41 29N 24 46 E
Smith, *Canada* 142 B6 55 10N 114 0W
Smith B., *U.S.A.* 144 A9 70 30N 154 20W
Smith Center, *U.S.A.* 154 F5 39 47N 98 47W
Smith I., *India* 95 H11 13 20N 93 4 E
Smith Sund, *Greenland* 10 B3 78 30N 74 0W
Smithburne →, *Australia* 126 B3 17 3 S 140 57 E
Smithers, *Canada* 142 C3 54 45N 127 10W
Smithfield, *S. Africa* 117 E4 30 9 S 26 30 E
Smithfield, *N.C., U.S.A.* 149 H6 35 31N 78 21W
Smithfield, *Utah, U.S.A.* 158 F8 41 50N 111 50W
Smiths, *U.S.A.* 152 C4 32 32N 85 6W
Smiths Falls, *Canada* 140 D4 44 55N 76 0W
Smithton, *Australia* 127 G4 40 53 S 145 6 E
Smithville, *Canada* 150 C5 43 6N 79 33W
Smithville, *Ga., U.S.A.* 152 D5 31 54N 84 15W
Smithville, *Mo., U.S.A.* 156 E2 39 23N 94 35W
Smithville, *Tex., U.S.A.* 155 K6 30 1N 97 10W
Smoky →, *Canada* 142 B5 56 10N 117 21W
Smoky Bay, *Australia* 127 E1 32 22 S 134 13 E
Smoky Hill →, *U.S.A.* 154 F6 39 4N 96 48W
Smoky Hills, *U.S.A.* 154 F5 39 15N 99 30W
Smoky Lake, *Canada* 142 C6 54 10N 112 30W
Smøla, *Norway* 14 E13 63 23N 8 3 E
Smolensk, *Russia* 58 E7 54 45N 32 5 E
Smolikas, Óros, *Greece* 50 F4 40 9N 20 58 E
Smolník, *Slovak Rep.* 35 C13 48 43N 20 44 E
Smolyan, *Bulgaria* 51 E8 41 36N 24 38 E
Smooth Rock Falls, *Canada* 140 C3 49 17N 81 37W
Smoothstone L., *Canada* 143 C7 54 40N 106 50W
Smorgon = Smarhon, *Belarus* 58 E4 54 20N 26 24 E
Smulţi, *Romania* 53 E12 45 57N 27 44 E
Smyadovo, *Bulgaria* 51 C11 43 2N 27 1 E
Smygehamn, *Sweden* 17 J7 55 21N 13 22 E
Smyrna = İzmir, *Turkey* 49 C9 38 25N 27 8 E
Smyrna, *Del., U.S.A.* 148 F8 39 18N 75 36W
Smyrna, *Ga., U.S.A.* 152 B5 33 53N 84 31W
Snæfell, *Iceland* 11 C11 64 48N 15 34W
Snaefell, *U.K.* 20 C3 54 16N 4 27W
Snæfellsjökull, *Iceland* 11 C3 64 49N 23 46W
Snæfellsnessýsla □, *Iceland* 11 C3 65 0N 23 0W
Snake →, *U.S.A.* 158 C4 46 12N 119 2W
Snake I., *Australia* 129 E7 38 47 S 146 33 E
Snake Range, *U.S.A.* 158 G6 39 0N 114 20W
Snake River Plain, *U.S.A.* 158 E7 42 50N 114 0W
Snasahögarna, *Sweden* 16 A6 63 13N 12 21 E
Snåsavatnet, *Norway* 14 D14 64 12N 12 0 E
Snedsted, *Denmark* 17 H2 56 55N 8 32 E
Sneek, *Neths.* 24 A5 53 2N 5 40 E
Sneeuberge, *S. Africa* 116 E3 31 46 S 24 20 E
Snejbjerg, *Denmark* 17 H2 56 8N 8 54 E
Snelling, *Calif., U.S.A.* 160 H6 37 31N 120 26W
Snelling, *S.C., U.S.A.* 152 B8 33 15N 81 27W
Snells Beach, *N.Z.* 130 C3 36 25 S 174 44 E
Snezhnoye, *Ukraine* 59 J10 48 0N 38 58 E
Sněžka, *Europe* 36 C8 50 41N 15 50 E
Snežnik, *Slovenia* 45 C11 45 36N 14 35 E
Śniadowo, *Poland* 55 E8 53 2N 22 0 E
Sniardwy, Jezioro, *Poland* 54 E8 53 48N 21 50 E
Śnieżka, *Europe* 34 A8 50 44N 15 44 E
Snigirevka = Snihurivka, *Ukraine* 59 J7 47 2N 32 49 E
Snihurivka, *Ukraine* 59 J7 47 2N 32 49 E
Snillfjord, *Norway* 18 A6 63 24N 9 30 E
Snina, *Slovak Rep.* 35 C15 48 58N 22 9 E
Snizort, L., *U.K.* 22 D2 57 33N 6 28W
Snøhetta, *Norway* 15 E13 62 19N 9 16 E
Snohomish, *U.S.A.* 160 C4 47 55N 122 6W
Snønuten, *Norway* 18 E3 59 31N 6 52 E
Snoul, *Cambodia* 87 F6 12 4N 106 26 E
Snow Hill, *U.S.A.* 148 F8 38 11N 75 24W
Snow Lake, *Canada* 143 C8 54 52N 100 3W
Snow Mt., *Calif., U.S.A.* 160 F4 39 23N 122 45W
Snow Mt., *Maine, U.S.A.* 151 A14 45 18N 70 48W
Snow Shoe, *U.S.A.* 150 E7 41 2N 77 57W
Snowbird L., *Canada* 143 A8 60 45N 103 0W
Snowdon, *U.K.* 20 D3 53 4N 4 5W
Snowdoun, *U.S.A.* 152 C3 32 15N 86 18W
Snowdrift →, *Canada* 143 A6 62 24N 110 44W
Snowflake, *U.S.A.* 159 J8 34 30N 110 5W
Snowshoe Pk., *U.S.A.* 158 B6 48 13N 115 41W
Snowtown, *Australia* 128 B3 33 46 S 138 14 E
Snowville, *U.S.A.* 158 F7 41 58N 112 43W
Snowy →, *Australia* 129 D8 37 46 S 148 30 E
Snowy Mt., *U.S.A.* 151 C10 43 42N 74 23W
Snowy Mts., *Australia* 129 D8 36 30 S 148 20 E
Snowy River Nat. Park, *Australia* 129 D7 37 15 S 147 29 E
Snug Corner, *Bahamas* 165 B5 22 33N 73 52W
Snyatyn, *Ukraine* 59 H3 48 27N 25 38 E
Snyder, *Okla., U.S.A.* 155 H5 34 40N 98 57W
Snyder, *Tex., U.S.A.* 155 J4 32 44N 100 55W
Soacha, *Colombia* 168 C3 4 35N 74 13W
Soahanina, *Madag.* 117 B7 18 42 S 44 13 E
Soalala, *Madag.* 117 B8 16 6 S 45 20 E
Soaloka, *Madag.* 117 B8 18 32 S 45 15 E
Soamanonga, *Madag.* 117 C7 23 52 S 44 47 E
Soan →, *Pakistan* 92 C4 33 1N 71 44 E
Soanierana-Ivongo, *Madag.* 117 B8 16 55 S 49 35 E
Soanindraniny, *Madag.* 117 B8 19 54 S 47 14 E
Şoarş, *Romania* 53 E9 45 56N 24 55 E
Soasiu, *Indonesia* 82 A3 0 40N 127 26 E
Soavina, *Madag.* 117 C8 20 23 S 46 56 E
Soavinandriana, *Madag.* 117 B8 19 9 S 46 45 E
Soba, *Nigeria* 113 C6 10 58N 8 4 E
Sobat, Nahr →, *Sudan* 107 F3 9 22N 31 33 E
Soběslav, *Czech Rep.* 34 B7 49 16N 14 45 E
Sobger →, *Indonesia* 83 B6 3 42 S 140 16 E
Sobhapur, *India* 92 H8 22 47N 78 17 E
Sobinka, *Russia* 58 E11 56 0N 40 0 E
Sobo-Yama, *Japan* 72 E3 32 51N 131 22 E
Sobótka, *Poland* 55 H3 50 54N 16 44 E
Sobra, *Croatia* 45 F14 42 44N 17 34 E
Sobradinho, Reprêsa de, *Brazil* 170 C3 9 30 S 42 0 E
Sobral, *Brazil* 170 B3 3 50 S 40 20W
Sobrance, *Slovak Rep.* 35 C15 48 45N 22 11 E
Sobreira Formosa, *Portugal* 42 F3 39 46N 7 51W
Soc Giang, *Vietnam* 76 F6 22 54N 106 1 E
Soc Trang, *Vietnam* 87 H5 9 37N 105 50 E
Soča →, *Europe* 34 E6 46 20N 13 40 E
Socastee, *U.S.A.* 149 J6 33 41N 79 1W
Sochaczew, *Poland* 55 F7 52 15N 20 13 E
Soch'e = Shache, *China* 65 D8 38 20N 77 10 E
Sochi, *Russia* 61 J4 43 35N 39 40 E
Social Circle, *U.S.A.* 152 B6 33 39N 83 43W
Société, Is. de la, *Pac. Oc.* 135 J12 17 0 S 151 0W
Society Hill, *U.S.A.* 152 C4 32 26N 85 27W
Society Is. = Société, Is. de la, *Pac. Oc.* 135 J12 17 0 S 151 0W
Socompa, Portezuelo de, *Chile* 174 A2 24 27 S 68 18W
Socorro, *Colombia* 168 B3 6 29N 73 16W
Socorro, *Phil.* 81 G5 9 37N 125 58 E
Socorro, *N. Mex., U.S.A.* 159 J10 34 4N 106 54W
Socorro, *Tex., U.S.A.* 159 L10 31 39N 106 18W
Socorro, I., *Mexico* 162 D2 18 45N 110 58W
Socotra, *Yemen* 99 D6 12 30N 54 0 E
Socovos, *Spain* 41 G3 38 20N 1 58W
Socuéllamos, *Spain* 41 F2 39 16N 2 47W
Soda L., *U.S.A.* 159 J5 35 10N 116 4W
Soda Plains, *India* 93 B8 35 30N 79 0 E
Soda Springs, *U.S.A.* 158 E8 42 39N 111 36W
Sodankylä, *Finland* 14 C22 67 29N 26 40 E
Soddy-Daisy, *U.S.A.* 149 H3 35 17N 85 10W
Söderala, *Sweden* 16 C10 61 17N 16 55 E
Söderbärke, *Sweden* 16 D9 60 5N 15 33 E
Söderfors, *Sweden* 16 D11 60 23N 17 25 E
Söderhamn, *Sweden* 16 C11 61 18N 17 10 E
Söderköping, *Sweden* 17 F10 58 31N 16 20 E
Södermanland, *Sweden* 15 G17 58 56N 16 55 E
Södermanlands län □, *Sweden* 16 E10 59 10N 16 30 E
Södertälje, *Sweden* 16 E11 59 12N 17 39 E
Sodiri, *Sudan* 107 E2 14 27N 29 0 E
Sodo, *Ethiopia* 107 F4 7 0N 37 41 E
Södra Dellen, *Sweden* 16 C10 61 48N 16 43 E
Södra Finnskoga, *Sweden* 16 D6 60 42N 12 34 E
Södra Sandby, *Sweden* 17 J7 55 43N 13 21 E
Södra Ulvön, *Sweden* 16 B12 62 59N 18 38 E
Södra Vi, *Sweden* 17 G9 57 45N 15 45 E
Sodražica, *Slovenia* 45 C11 45 45N 14 39 E
Sodus, *U.S.A.* 150 C7 43 14N 77 4W
Sodwana Bay Nat. Park, *S. Africa* 117 D5 27 35 S 32 43 E
Soe, *Indonesia* 82 C2 9 52 S 124 17 E
Soekmekaar, *S. Africa* 117 C4 23 30 S 29 55 E
Soest, *Germany* 30 D4 51 34N 8 7 E
Soest, *Neths.* 24 B5 52 9N 5 19 E
Sofádhes, *Greece* 48 B4 39 20N 22 4 E
Sofala □, *Mozam.* 117 B5 19 30 S 34 30 E
Sofara, *Mali* 112 C4 13 59N 4 9W
Sofia = Sofiya, *Bulgaria* 50 D7 42 45N 23 20 E
Sofia →, *Madag.* 117 B8 15 27 S 47 23 E
Sofievka, *Ukraine* 59 H7 48 6N 33 55 E
Sofikón, *Greece* 48 D5 37 47N 23 3 E
Sofiya, *Bulgaria* 50 D7 42 45N 23 20 E
Sofiya □, *Bulgaria* 50 D7 42 15N 23 20 E
Sōfu-Gan, *Japan* 71 K10 29 49N 140 21 E
Sogakofe, *Ghana* 113 D5 6 2N 0 39 E
Sogamoso, *Colombia* 168 B3 5 43N 72 56W
Soğār, *Iran* 97 E8 25 53N 58 6 E
Sögel, *Germany* 30 C3 52 50N 7 31 E
Sogeri, *Papua N. G.* 132 E4 9 26 S 147 35 E
Sogn og Fjordane □, *Norway* 18 C3 61 40N 6 45 E
Sogndalsfjøra, *Norway* 15 F12 61 14N 7 5 E
Søgne, *Norway* 15 G12 58 5N 7 48 E
Sognefjorden, *Norway* 15 F11 61 10N 5 50 E
Sogod, *Phil.* 81 F5 10 28N 124 59 E
Söğüt, *Bilecik, Turkey* 49 A12 40 2N 30 11 E
Söğüt, *Burdur, Turkey* 49 D11 37 2N 29 50 E
Söğüt Dağı, *Turkey* 49 D11 37 50N 29 55 E
Söğütköy, *Turkey* 49 E10 36 40N 28 8 E
Sŏgwipo, *S. Korea* 75 H14 33 13N 126 34 E
Soh, *Iran* 97 C6 33 26N 51 27 E
Sohâg, *Egypt* 106 B3 26 33N 31 43 E
Sohagpur, *India* 92 H8 22 42N 78 12 E
Sohano, *Papua N. G.* 132 C8 5 22 S 154 37 E
Sohela, *India* 94 D6 21 18N 83 24 E
Sŏhori, *N. Korea* 75 D15 40 7N 128 23 E
Soignies, *Belgium* 24 D4 50 35N 4 5 E
Soin, *Burkina Faso* 112 C4 12 47N 3 50W
Soira, *Eritrea* 107 E4 14 45N 39 30 E
Soissons, *France* 27 C10 49 25N 3 19 E
Sōja, *Japan* 72 C5 34 40N 133 45 E
Sojat, *India* 92 G5 25 55N 73 45 E
Sok →, *Russia* 60 D10 53 24N 50 8 E
Sokal, *Ukraine* 59 G3 50 31N 24 15 E
Söke, *Turkey* 49 D9 37 48N 27 28 E
Sokelo, *Dem. Rep. of the Congo* 119 D1 9 55 S 24 36 E
Sokh, *Uzbekistan* 65 D5 39 56N 71 9 E
Sokhós, *Greece* 50 F7 40 48N 23 22 E
Sokhumi, *Georgia* 61 J5 43 0N 41 0 E
Sokki, Oued In →, *Algeria* 111 C5 29 30N 3 42 E
Sokna, *Norway* 18 D6 60 16N 9 58 E
Sokndal, *Norway* 18 B7 62 57N 10 13 E
Soko Banja, *Serbia, Yug.* 50 C5 43 40N 21 51 E
Soko Islands, *China* 69 G10 22 10N 113 54 E
Sokodé, *Togo* 113 D5 9 0N 1 11 E
Sokol, *Russia* 58 C11 59 30N 40 5 E
Sokolac, *Bos.-H.* 52 G3 43 56N 18 48 E
Sokółka, *Poland* 54 E10 53 25N 23 30 E
Sokolo, *Ségou, Mali* 112 C3 14 53N 6 8W
Sokolo, *Sikasso, Mali* 112 C3 10 52N 6 59W
Sokolov, *Czech Rep.* 34 A5 50 12N 12 40 E
Sokołów Małpolski, *Poland* 55 H9 50 12N 22 7 E
Sokołów Podlaski, *Poland* 55 F9 52 25N 22 15 E
Sokoły, *Poland* 55 F9 52 59N 22 42 E
Sokoto, *Nigeria* 113 C6 13 2N 5 16 E
Sokoto □, *Nigeria* 113 C6 12 30N 6 0 E
Sokoto →, *Nigeria* 113 C5 11 20N 4 10 E
Sokuluk, *Kyrgyzstan* 65 B7 42 52N 74 18 E
Sol Iletsk, *Russia* 64 F5 51 10N 55 0 E
Sola, *Norway* 18 F2 58 53N 5 36 E
Sola, *Vanuatu* 133 C5 13 51 S 167 33 E
Sola →, *Poland* 55 H6 50 4N 19 15 E
Solai, *Kenya* 118 B4 0 2N 36 12 E
Solan, *India* 92 D7 30 55N 77 7 E
Solana, *Phil.* 80 C3 17 39N 121 41 E
Solander I., *N.Z.* 131 G1 46 34 S 166 54 E
Solano, *Phil.* 80 C3 16 31N 121 15 E
Solapur, *India* 94 F2 17 43N 75 56 E
Solca, *Romania* 53 C10 47 40N 25 50 E
Solda Gölü, *Turkey* 49 D11 37 33N 29 42 E
Soldăneşti, *Moldova* 53 C13 47 49N 28 48 E
Soldotna, *U.S.A.* 144 F10 60 29N 151 3W
Soléa, *Cyprus* 39 E9 35 5N 33 4 E
Solec Kujawski, *Poland* 55 E5 53 5N 18 14 E
Soledad, *Colombia* 168 A3 10 55N 74 46W
Soledad, *U.S.A.* 160 J5 36 26N 121 20W
Soledad, *Venezuela* 169 B5 8 10N 63 34W
Sølen, *Norway* 18 C8 61 53N 11 31 E
Solent, The, *U.K.* 21 G6 50 45N 1 25W
Solenzara, *France* 29 G13 41 53N 9 23 E
Solesmes, *France* 27 B10 50 10N 3 30 E
Solfonn, *Norway* 15 F12 60 2N 6 57 E
Solhan, *Turkey* 101 C9 38 57N 41 3 E
Sølheim, *Norway* 18 D2 60 53N 5 27 E
Soligalich, *Russia* 56 C7 59 5N 42 10 E
Soligorsk = Salihorsk, *Belarus* 59 F4 52 51N 27 27 E
Solihull, *U.K.* 21 E6 52 26N 1 47W
Solikamsk, *Russia* 64 B6 59 38N 56 50 E
Solila, *Madag.* 117 C8 21 25 S 46 37 E
Solimões = Amazonas →, *S. Amer.* 169 D7 0 5 S 50 0W
Solin, *Croatia* 45 E13 43 33N 16 30 E
Solingen, *Germany* 30 D3 51 10N 7 5 E
Sollebrunn, *Sweden* 17 F6 58 8N 12 32 E
Sollefteå, *Sweden* 16 A11 63 12N 17 20 E
Sollentuna, *Sweden* 16 E11 59 26N 17 56 E
Sóller, *Spain* 38 B3 39 46N 2 43 E
Sollerön, *Sweden* 16 D8 60 55N 14 37 E
Solling, *Germany* 30 D5 51 42N 9 38 E
Solnechnogorsk, *Russia* 58 D9 56 10N 36 57 E
Solo →, *Indonesia* 79 G15 6 47 S 112 22 E
Solofra, *Italy* 47 B7 40 50N 14 51 E
Sologne, *France* 27 E8 47 40N 1 45 E
Solok, *Indonesia* 84 C2 0 45 S 100 40 E
Sololá, *Guatemala* 164 D1 14 49N 91 10W
Solomon, N. Fork →, *U.S.A.* 154 F5 39 29N 98 26W
Solomon, S. Fork →, *U.S.A.* 154 F5 39 25N 99 12W
Solomon Is., *Papua N. G.* 132 D8 6 0 S 155 0 E
Solomon Is. ■, *Pac. Oc.* 133 L8 6 0 S 155 0 E
Solomon Sea, *Papua N. G.* 132 D6 7 0 S 150 0 E
Solon, *China* 69 B7 46 32N 121 10 E
Solon Springs, *U.S.A.* 154 B9 46 22N 91 49W
Solonópole, *Brazil* 170 C4 5 44 S 39 1W
Solor, *Indonesia* 82 C2 8 27 S 123 0 E
Solotcha, *Russia* 58 E10 54 48N 39 53 E
Solothurn, *Switz.* 32 B5 47 13N 7 32 E
Solothurn □, *Switz.* 32 B5 47 18N 7 40 E
Solsona, *Spain* 40 C6 42 0N 1 31 E
Solsvik, *Norway* 18 D1 60 26N 4 58 E
Solt, *Hungary* 52 D4 46 45N 19 1 E
Šolta, *Croatia* 45 E13 43 24N 16 15 E
Solṭānābād, *Khorāsān, Iran* 97 C8 34 13N 59 58 E
Solṭānābād, *Khorāsān, Iran* 97 B8 36 29N 58 5 E
Soltau, *Germany* 30 C5 52 59N 9 50 E
Soltsy, *Russia* 58 C6 58 10N 30 30 E
Solund, *Norway* 18 C1 61 5N 4 50 E
Solunska Glava, *Macedonia* 50 E5 41 44N 21 31 E
Solvang, *U.S.A.* 161 L6 34 36N 120 8W
Solvay, *U.S.A.* 151 C8 43 3N 76 13W
Sölvesborg, *Sweden* 17 H8 56 5N 14 35 E
Solvychegodsk, *Russia* 56 B8 61 21N 46 56 E
Solway Firth, *U.K.* 20 C4 54 49N 3 35W
Solwezi, *Zambia* 119 E2 12 11 S 26 21 E
Sōma, *Japan* 70 F10 37 40N 140 50 E
Soma, *Turkey* 49 B9 39 10N 27 35 E
Somabhula, *Zimbabwe* 117 B4 19 42 S 29 40 E
Somali Pen., *Africa* 104 F8 7 0N 46 0 E
Somali Rep. ■, *Africa* 120 C3 7 0N 47 0 E
Somalia = Somali Rep. ■, *Africa* 120 C3 7 0N 47 0 E
Sombe Dzong, *Bhutan* 90 B2 27 13N 89 8 E
Sombernon, *France* 27 E11 47 20N 4 40 E
Sombo, *Angola* 115 D4 8 42 S 20 59 E
Sombor, *Serbia, Yug.* 52 E4 45 46N 19 9 E
Sombra, *Canada* 150 D2 42 43N 82 29W
Sombrerete, *Mexico* 162 C4 23 40N 103 40W
Sombrero, *Anguilla* 165 C7 18 37N 63 30W
Sombrero Channel, *India* 95 L11 7 41N 93 35 E
Şomcuta Mare, *Romania* 53 C8 47 31N 23 28 E
Somdari, *India* 92 G5 25 47N 72 38 E
Somers, *U.S.A.* 158 B6 48 5N 114 13W
Somerset, *Bermuda* 9 a 32 17N 64 52W
Somerset, *Ky., U.S.A.* 148 G3 37 5N 84 36W
Somerset, *Mass., U.S.A.* 151 E13 41 47N 71 8W
Somerset, *Pa., U.S.A.* 150 F5 40 1N 79 5W
Somerset □, *U.K.* 21 F5 51 9N 3 0W
Somerset East, *S. Africa* 116 E4 32 42 S 25 35 E
Somerset I., *Bermuda* 9 a 32 17N 64 52W
Somerset I., *Canada* 138 A10 73 30N 93 0W
Somerset West, *S. Africa* 116 E2 34 8 S 18 50 E
Somersworth, *U.S.A.* 151 C14 43 16N 70 52W
Somerton, *U.S.A.* 159 K6 32 36N 114 43W
Somerville, *U.S.A.* 151 F10 40 35N 74 38W
Someş →, *Romania* 52 C7 47 49N 22 43 E
Someşul Mare →, *Romania* 53 C8 47 9N 23 55 E
Somme □, *France* 27 C9 49 57N 2 20 E
Somme →, *France* 27 B8 50 11N 1 38 E
Somme, B. de la, *France* 26 B8 50 14N 1 33 E
Sommen, *Jönköping, Sweden* 17 F8 58 12N 14 58 E
Sommen, *Östergötland, Sweden* 17 F9 58 0N 15 15 E
Sommepy-Tahure, *France* 27 C11 49 15N 4 31 E
Sömmerda, *Germany* 30 D7 51 9N 11 7 E
Sommesous, *France* 27 D11 48 44N 4 12 E
Sommières, *France* 29 E8 43 47N 4 6 E
Somnath, *India* 92 J4 20 53N 70 22 E
Somogy □, *Hungary* 52 D2 46 19N 17 30 E
Somogyszob, *Hungary* 52 D2 46 18N 17 20 E
Somosomo, *Fiji* 133 A3 16 47 S 179 58W
Somosomo Str., *Fiji* 133 A3 16 0 S 180 0 E
Somoto, *Nic.* 164 D2 13 28N 86 37W
Sompolno, *Poland* 55 F5 52 26N 18 30 E
Somport, Puerto de, *Spain* 40 C4 42 48N 0 31W
Somuncurá, Meseta de, *Argentina* 176 B3 41 30 S 67 0W
Somvarpet, *India* 95 H2 12 36N 75 52 E
Son, *Norway* 18 E7 59 32N 10 42 E
Son →, *India* 93 G11 25 42N 84 52 E
Son Ha, *Vietnam* 86 E7 15 3N 108 34 E
Son Hoa, *Vietnam* 86 F7 13 2N 108 58 E
Son La, *Vietnam* 76 G4 21 20N 103 50 E
Son Serra, *Spain* 38 B4 39 43N 3 13 E
Son Servera, *Spain* 38 B4 39 37N 3 21 E
Son Tay, *Vietnam* 76 G5 21 8N 105 30 E
Soná, *Panama* 164 E3 8 0N 81 20W
Sonamarg, *India* 93 B6 34 18N 75 21 E
Sonamukhi, *India* 93 H12 23 18N 87 27 E
Sonamura, *India* 90 D3 23 29N 91 15 E
Sonar →, *India* 93 G8 24 24N 79 56 E
Sŏnch'ŏn, *N. Korea* 75 E13 39 48N 124 55 E
Sondags →, *S. Africa* 116 E4 33 44 S 25 51 E
Sóndalo, *Italy* 44 B7 46 20N 10 19 E
Sondar, *India* 93 C6 33 28N 75 56 E
Søndeled, *Norway* 18 F6 58 46N 9 3 E
Sønder Felding, *Denmark* 17 J2 55 57N 8 47 E
Sønder Omme, *Denmark* 17 J2 55 50N 8 54 E
Sønderborg, *Denmark* 17 K3 54 55N 9 49 E
Sønderjyllands Amtskommune □, *Denmark* 17 J3 55 10N 9 10 E
Sondershausen, *Germany* 30 D6 51 22N 10 51 E
Søndre Strømfjord = Kangerlussuaq, *Greenland* 10 D5 66 59N 50 40W
Sóndrio, *Italy* 44 B6 46 10N 9 52 E
Sondur →, *India* 94 D6 20 40N 82 1 E
Sone, *Mozam.* 119 F3 17 23 S 34 55 E
Sonepur, *India* 94 D6 20 55N 83 50 E
Sonfim, *Brazil* 172 B4 6 0 S 67 52W
Song, *Nigeria* 113 D7 9 49N 12 39 E
Song, *Thailand* 86 C3 18 28N 100 11 E
Song Cau, *Vietnam* 86 F7 13 27N 109 18 E
Song-Köl, *Kyrgyzstan* 65 C7 41 50N 75 12 E
Song Xian, *China* 74 G7 34 12N 112 8 E
Songadh, *India* 94 D1 21 9N 73 33 E
Songan, *Indonesia* 79 J18 8 13 S 115 24 E
Songavatnet, *Norway* 18 E4 59 52N 7 32 E
Songch'ŏn, *N. Korea* 75 E14 39 12N 126 15 E
Songea, *Tanzania* 119 E4 10 40 S 35 40 E
Songeons, *France* 27 C8 49 32N 1 50 E
Songgang, *China* 69 F10 22 46N 113 50 E
Songhua Hu, *China* 75 C14 43 35N 126 50 E
Songhua Jiang →, *China* 69 B8 47 45N 132 30 E
Songimvelo Game Reserve, *S. Africa* 117 D5 25 50 S 31 2 E
Songjiang, *China* 77 B13 31 1N 121 12 E
Songjin, *N. Korea* 75 D15 40 40N 129 10 E
Songjŏng-ni, *S. Korea* 75 G14 35 8N 126 47 E
Songkan, *China* 76 C6 28 35N 106 52 E
Songkhla, *Thailand* 87 J3 7 13N 100 37 E
Songming, *China* 76 E4 25 12N 103 2 E
Songnim, *N. Korea* 75 E13 38 45N 125 39 E
Songo, *Angola* 115 D2 7 22 S 14 51 E
Songololo, *Dem. Rep. of the Congo* 115 D2 5 40 S 14 5 E
Songpan, *China* 76 A4 32 40N 103 30 E
Songtao, *China* 76 C7 28 11N 109 10 E
Songwe, *Dem. Rep. of the Congo* 118 C2 3 20 S 26 16 E
Songwe →, *Africa* 119 D3 9 44 S 33 58 E
Songxi, *China* 77 D12 27 31N 118 44 E
Songzi, *China* 77 B8 30 12N 111 45 E
Sonhat, *India* 93 H10 23 29N 82 31 E
Sonid Youqi, *China* 74 C7 42 45N 112 48 E
Sonipat, *India* 92 E7 29 0N 77 5 E
Sonkach, *India* 92 H7 22 59N 76 21 E
Sonkovo, *Russia* 58 D9 57 50N 37 5 E
Sonmiani, *Pakistan* 91 D2 25 25N 66 40 E
Sonmiani B., *Pakistan* 92 G2 25 15N 66 30 E
Sonnino, *Italy* 46 A6 41 25N 13 14 E
Sono →, *Minas Gerais, Brazil* 171 E2 17 2 S 45 32W

Su-no-Saki 285

Stadlandet, *Norway* **18 B2** 62 10N 5 10 E
Stadskanaal, *Neths.* **24 A6** 53 4N 6 55 E
Stadtallendorf, *Germany* **30 E5** 50 48N 9 1 E
Stadthagen, *Germany* **30 C5** 52 19N 9 13 E
Stadtlohn, *Germany* **30 D2** 51 59N 6 55 E
Stadtroda, *Germany* **30 E7** 50 52N 11 44 E
Stäfa, *Switz.* **33 B7** 47 14N 8 45 E
Stafafell, *Iceland* **11 C12** 64 25N 14 52W
Staffa, *U.K.* **22 E2** 56 27N 6 21W
Staffanstorp, *Sweden* **17 J7** 55 39N 13 13 E
Stafford, *U.K.* **20 E5** 52 49N 2 7W
Stafford, *U.S.A.* **155 G5** 37 58N 98 36W
Stafford, L., *U.S.A.* **153 F7** 29 20N 82 29W
Stafford Springs, *U.S.A.* **151 E12** 41 57N 72 18W
Staffordshire □, *U.K.* **20 E5** 52 53N 2 10W
Stagnone, *Italy* **46 E5** 37 53N 12 26 E
Staines, *U.K.* **21 F7** 51 26N 0 29W
Stainz, *Austria* **34 E8** 46 53N 15 17 E
Stakhanov, *Ukraine* **59 H10** 48 35N 38 40 E
Stalać, *Serbia, Yug.* **50 C5** 43 43N 21 28 E
Stalden, *Switz.* **32 D5** 46 14N 7 52 E
Stalingrad = Volgograd, *Russia* **61 F7** 48 40N 44 25 E
Staliniri = Tskhinvali, *Georgia* **61 J7** 42 14N 44 1 E
Stalino = Donetsk, *Ukraine* **59 J9** 48 0N 37 45 E
Stalinogorsk = Novomoskovsk, *Russia* **58 E10** 54 5N 38 15 E
Stallarholmen, *Sweden* **16 E11** 59 22N 17 12 E
Ställdalen, *Sweden* **16 E8** 59 56N 14 56 E
Stalowa Wola, *Poland* **55 H9** 50 34N 22 3 E
Stalybridge, *U.K.* **20 D5** 53 28N 2 3W
Stamford, *Australia* **126 C3** 21 15 S 143 46 E
Stamford, *U.K.* **21 E7** 52 39N 0 29W
Stamford, *Conn., U.S.A.* **151 E11** 41 3N 73 32W
Stamford, *N.Y., U.S.A.* **151 D10** 42 25N 74 38W
Stamford, *Tex., U.S.A.* **155 J5** 32 57N 99 48W
Stamnes, *Norway* **18 D2** 60 40N 5 45 E
Stamping Ground, *U.S.A.* **157 F12** 38 16N 84 41W
Stampriet, *Namibia* **116 C2** 24 20 S 18 28 E
Stamps, *U.S.A.* **155 J8** 33 22N 93 30W
Stanberry, *U.S.A.* **156 D2** 40 13N 94 35W
Stančevo = Kalipetrovo, *Bulgaria* **51 B11** 44 5N 27 14 E
Standerton, *S. Africa* **117 D4** 26 55 S 29 7 E
Standish, *U.S.A.* **148 D4** 43 59N 83 57W
Stanford, *S. Africa* **116 E2** 34 26 S 19 29 E
Stanford, *U.S.A.* **158 C8** 47 9N 110 13W
Stånga, *Sweden* **17 G12** 57 17N 18 29 E
Stange, *Norway* **18 D8** 60 43N 11 5 E
Stanger, *S. Africa* **117 D5** 29 27 S 31 14 E
Stangvik, *Norway* **18 B5** 62 55N 8 28 E
Stanhope, *Australia* **129 D6** 36 27 S 144 59 E
Stanhope, *U.S.A.* **156 B3** 42 17N 93 48W
Stanišić, *Serbia, Yug.* **52 E4** 45 56N 19 10 E
Stanislaus ➝, *U.S.A.* **160 H5** 37 40N 121 14W
Stanislav = Ivano-Frankivsk, *Ukraine* **59 H3** 48 40N 24 40 E
Stanisławów, *Poland* **55 F8** 52 18N 21 33 E
Stanley, *Australia* **127 G4** 40 46 S 145 19 E
Stanley, *Canada* **143 B8** 55 24N 104 22W
Stanley, *China* **69 G11** 22 13N 114 12 E
Stanley, *Falk. Is.* **9 f** 51 40 S 59 51W
Stanley, *U.K.* **20 C6** 54 53N 1 41W
Stanley, *Idaho, U.S.A.* **158 D6** 44 13N 114 56W
Stanley, *N. Dak., U.S.A.* **154 A3** 48 19N 102 23W
Stanley, *N.Y., U.S.A.* **150 D7** 42 48N 77 6W
Stanley Res., *India* **95 J3** 11 50N 77 40 E
Stanovoy Khrebet, *Russia* **67 D13** 55 0N 130 0 E
Stanovoy Ra. = Stanovoy Khrebet, *Russia* **67 D13** 55 0N 130 0 E
Stans, *Switz.* **33 C6** 46 58N 8 21 E
Stansmore Ra., *Australia* **124 D4** 21 23 S 128 33 E
Stanthorpe, *Australia* **127 D5** 28 36 S 151 59 E
Stanton, *Ky., U.S.A.* **157 G13** 37 54N 83 52W
Stanton, *Tex., U.S.A.* **155 J4** 32 8N 101 48W
Stanwood, *U.S.A.* **160 B4** 48 15N 122 23W
Staples, *U.S.A.* **154 B7** 46 21N 94 48W
Stąporków, *Poland* **55 G7** 51 9N 20 31 E
Star City, *Canada* **143 C8** 52 50N 104 20W
Star Harbour, *Solomon Is.* **133 N12** 10 47 S 162 19 E
Star Lake, *U.S.A.* **151 B9** 44 10N 75 2W
Stará L'ubovňa, *Slovak Rep.* **35 B13** 49 18N 20 42 E
Stara Moravica, *Serbia, Yug.* **52 E4** 45 50N 19 30 E
Stara Pazova, *Serbia, Yug.* **52 F5** 44 58N 20 10 E
Stara Planina, *Bulgaria* **50 C7** 43 15N 23 0 E
Stará Turá, *Slovak Rep.* **35 C10** 48 47N 17 42 E
Stara Zagora, *Bulgaria* **51 D9** 42 26N 25 39 E
Starachowice, *Poland* **55 G8** 51 3N 21 2 E
Staraya Russa, *Russia* **58 D6** 57 58N 31 23 E
Starbuck I., *Kiribati* **135 H12** 5 37 S 155 55W
Starchiojd, *Romania* **53 E11** 45 19N 26 11 E
Starcke Nat. Park, *Australia* **126 A4** 14 56 S 145 2 E
Stargard Szczeciński, *Poland* **54 E2** 53 20N 15 0 E
Stårheim, *Norway* **18 C2** 61 56N 5 40 E
Stari Bar, *Montenegro, Yug.* **50 D3** 42 7N 19 10 E
Stari Trg, *Slovenia* **45 C12** 45 29N 15 7 E
Staritsa, *Russia* **58 D8** 56 33N 34 55 E
Starke, *U.S.A.* **152 F7** 29 57N 82 7W
Starnberg, *Germany* **31 H7** 48 0N 11 21 E
Starnberger See, *Germany* **31 H7** 47 54N 11 19 E
Starobilsk, *Ukraine* **59 H10** 49 16N 39 0 E
Starodub, *Russia* **59 F7** 52 30N 32 50 E
Starogard Gdański, *Poland* **54 E5** 53 59N 18 30 E
Starokonstantinov = Starokonstyantyniv, *Ukraine* **59 H4** 49 48N 27 10 E
Starokonstyantyniv, *Ukraine* **59 H4** 49 48N 27 10 E
Starominskaya, *Russia* **59 J10** 46 33N 39 0 E
Staroshcherbinovskaya, *Russia* **59 J10** 46 40N 38 53 E
Starrs Mill, *U.S.A.* **152 B5** 33 19N 84 31W
Start Pt., *U.K.* **21 G4** 50 13N 3 39W
Stary Sącz, *Poland* **55 J7** 49 33N 20 35 E
Staryy Biryuzyak, *Russia* **61 H8** 44 46N 46 50 E
Staryy Chartoriysk, *Ukraine* **59 G3** 51 15N 25 54 E
Staryy Krym, *Ukraine* **59 K8** 45 3N 35 8 E
Staryy Oskol, *Russia* **59 G9** 51 19N 37 55 E
Stassfurt, *Germany* **30 D7** 51 51N 11 35 E
Staszów, *Poland* **55 H8** 50 33N 21 10 E
State Center, *U.S.A.* **156 B3** 42 1N 93 10W
State College, *U.S.A.* **150 F7** 40 48N 77 52W
Stateline, *U.S.A.* **160 G7** 38 57N 119 56W
Staten, I. = Estados, I. de Los, *Argentina* **176 D4** 54 40 S 64 30W
Staten I., *U.S.A.* **151 F10** 40 35N 74 9W
Statenville, *U.S.A.* **152 E6** 30 42N 83 2W
Statesboro, *U.S.A.* **152 C8** 32 27N 81 47W
Statesville, *U.S.A.* **149 H5** 35 47N 80 53W
Statham, *U.S.A.* **152 B6** 33 58N 83 35W
Stathelle, *Norway* **18 E6** 59 3N 9 41 E
Stauffer, *U.S.A.* **161 L7** 34 45N 119 3W
Staunton, *Ill., U.S.A.* **156 F7** 39 1N 89 47W
Staunton, *Va., U.S.A.* **148 F6** 38 9N 79 4W
Stavanger, *Norway* **15 G11** 58 57N 5 40 E
Stavelot, *Belgium* **24 D5** 50 23N 5 55 E
Stavern, *Norway* **15 G14** 59 0N 10 1 E
Stavoren, *Neths.* **24 B5** 52 53N 5 22 E
Stavropol, *Russia* **61 H6** 45 5N 42 0 E
Stavros, *Cyprus* **39 E8** 35 1N 32 38 E
Stavrós, *Ithákí, Greece* **39 C2** 38 27N 20 39 E
Stavrós, *Kríti, Greece* **39 E5** 35 12N 24 45 E
Stavrós, *Ákra, Greece* **39 E5** 35 26N 24 58 E
Stavroúpolis, *Greece* **51 E8** 41 12N 24 45 E
Stawell, *Australia* **128 D5** 37 5 S 142 47 E
Stawell ➝, *Australia* **126 C3** 20 20 S 142 55 E
Stawiski, *Poland* **54 E9** 53 22N 22 9 E
Stawiszyn, *Poland* **55 G5** 51 56N 18 4 E
Stayner, *Canada* **150 B4** 44 25N 80 5W
Stayton, *U.S.A.* **158 D2** 44 48N 122 48W
Steamboat Springs, *U.S.A.* **158 F10** 40 29N 106 50W
Steane, *Norway* **18 E5** 59 16N 8 33 E
Stebbins, *U.S.A.* **144 E7** 63 31N 162 17W
Steblevë, *Albania* **50 E4** 41 23N 20 33 E
Steckborn, *Switz.* **33 A7** 47 44N 8 59 E
Steele, *Ala., U.S.A.* **152 B3** 33 56N 86 12W
Steele, *N. Dak., U.S.A.* **154 B5** 46 51N 99 55W
Steelton, *U.S.A.* **150 F8** 40 14N 76 50W
Steelville, *U.S.A.* **156 G5** 37 58N 91 22W
Steen River, *Canada* **142 B5** 59 40N 117 12W
Steenkool = Bintuni, *Indonesia* **83 B4** 2 7 S 133 32 E
Steens Mt., *U.S.A.* **158 E4** 42 35N 118 40W
Steenstrup Gletscher, *Greenland* **10 B5** 75 15N 57 0W
Steenwijk, *Neths.* **24 B6** 52 47N 6 7 E
Steep Pt., *Australia* **125 E1** 26 8 S 113 8 E
Steep Rock, *Canada* **143 C9** 51 30N 98 48W
Ştefan Vodă, *Moldova* **53 D14** 46 27N 29 42 E
Ştefăneşti, *Romania* **53 C12** 47 44N 27 15 E
Stefanie L. = Chew Bahir, *Ethiopia* **107 G4** 4 40N 36 50 E
Stefanie Nat. Park, *Ethiopia* **107 G4** 4 55N 36 55 E
Stefansson Bay, *Antarctica* **7 C5** 67 20 S 59 8 E
Steffisburg, *Switz.* **32 C5** 46 47N 7 38 E
Stege, *Denmark* **17 K6** 54 59N 12 18 E
Ştei, *Romania* **52 D7** 46 32N 22 27 E
Steiermark □, *Austria* **34 D8** 47 26N 15 0 E
Steigerwald, *Germany* **31 F6** 49 44N 10 26 E
Steilacoom, *U.S.A.* **160 C4** 47 10N 122 36W
Steilrandberge, *Namibia* **116 B1** 17 45 S 13 20 E
Stein am Rhein, *Switz.* **33 A7** 47 39N 8 51 E
Steinbach, *Canada* **143 D9** 49 32N 96 40W
Steinfurt, *Germany* **30 C3** 52 9N 7 20 E
Steinhatchee, *U.S.A.* **152 F6** 29 40N 83 23W
Steinhausen, *Namibia* **116 C2** 21 49 S 18 20 E
Steinheim, *Germany* **30 D5** 51 51N 9 5 E
Steinhuder Meer, *Germany* **30 C5** 52 29N 9 21 E
Steinkjer, *Norway* **14 D14** 64 1N 11 31 E
Steinkopf, *S. Africa* **116 D2** 29 18 S 17 43 E
Steinshamn, *Norway* **18 B3** 62 47N 6 28 E
Stellarton, *Canada* **141 C7** 45 32N 62 30W
Stellenbosch, *S. Africa* **116 E2** 33 58 S 18 50 E
Stelvio, Paso dello, *Italy* **33 C10** 46 32N 10 27 E
Stenay, *France* **27 C12** 49 29N 5 12 E
Stendal, *Germany* **30 C7** 52 36N 11 53 E
Stende, *Latvia* **54 A9** 57 11N 22 33 E
Stenhamra, *Sweden* **16 E11** 59 20N 17 41 E
Stenón Ithákis, *Greece* **39 C2** 38 22N 20 39 E
Stenón Kerkiras, *Greece* **38 B10** 39 36N 20 5 E
Stenstorp, *Sweden* **17 F7** 58 17N 13 45 E
Stenungsund, *Sweden* **17 F5** 58 6N 11 50 E
Stenørnabhaigh = Stornoway, *U.K.* **22 C2** 58 13N 6 23W
Stepanakert = Xankändi, *Azerbaijan* **101 C12** 39 52N 46 49 E
Stepanavan, *Armenia* **61 K7** 41 1N 44 23 E
Stephens, C., *N.Z.* **131 A8** 40 42 S 173 58 E
Stephens Creek, *Australia* **128 A4** 31 50 S 141 30 E
Stephens I., *Canada* **142 C2** 54 10N 130 45W
Stephens I., *N.Z.* **131 A9** 40 40 S 174 1 E
Stephens L., *Canada* **143 B9** 56 32N 95 0W
Stephenville, *Canada* **141 C8** 48 31N 58 35W
Stephenville, *U.S.A.* **155 J5** 32 13N 98 12W
Stepnica, *Poland* **54 E1** 53 38N 14 36 E
Stepnoi = Elista, *Russia* **61 G7** 46 16N 44 14 E
Stepnoye, *Russia* **64 D8** 54 4N 60 26 E
Steppe, *Asia* **62 D9** 50 0N 50 0 E
Stereá Ellas □, *Greece* **48 C4** 38 50N 23 0 E
Sterkstroom, *S. Africa* **116 E4** 31 32 S 26 32 E
Sterling, *Alaska, U.S.A.* **144 F10** 60 32N 150 46W
Sterling, *Colo., U.S.A.* **154 E3** 40 37N 103 13W
Sterling, *Ga., U.S.A.* **152 D8** 31 16N 81 34W
Sterling, *Ill., U.S.A.* **156 C7** 41 48N 89 42W
Sterling, *Kans., U.S.A.* **154 F5** 38 13N 98 12W
Sterling City, *U.S.A.* **155 K4** 31 51N 101 0W
Sterling Heights, *U.S.A.* **157 B13** 42 35N 83 0W
Sterling Run, *U.S.A.* **150 E6** 41 25N 78 12W
Sterlitamak, *Russia* **64 E6** 53 40N 56 0 E
Sternberg, *Germany* **30 B7** 53 42N 11 50 E
Šternberk, *Czech Rep.* **35 B10** 49 45N 17 15 E
Stérnes, *Greece* **39 E5** 35 30N 24 9 E
Sterzing = Vipiteno, *Italy* **45 B8** 46 54N 11 26 E
Stettin = Szczecin, *Poland* **54 E1** 53 27N 14 27 E
Stettiner Haff, *Germany* **30 B10** 53 47N 14 15 E
Stettler, *Canada* **142 C6** 52 19N 112 40W
Steubenville, *U.S.A.* **150 F4** 40 22N 80 37W
Stevenage, *U.K.* **21 F7** 51 55N 0 13W
Stevens, *U.S.A.* **152 B1** 33 31N 89 34W
Stevens Point, *U.S.A.* **154 C10** 44 31N 89 34W
Stevens Pottery, *U.S.A.* **152 C6** 32 57N 83 17W
Stevens Village, *U.S.A.* **144 C10** 66 1N 149 6W
Stevenson, *U.S.A.* **160 E5** 45 42N 121 53W
Stevenson L., *Canada* **143 C9** 53 55N 96 0W
Stevensville, *U.S.A.* **158 C6** 46 30N 114 5W
Stevns Klint, *Denmark* **17 J6** 55 17N 12 28 E
Steward, *U.S.A.* **156 C7** 41 51N 89 1W
Stewardson, *U.S.A.* **157 E8** 39 16N 88 38W
Stewart, *Canada* **142 B3** 55 56N 129 57W
Stewart, *Ga., U.S.A.* **152 B6** 33 25N 83 52W
Stewart, *Nev., U.S.A.* **160 F7** 39 5N 119 46W
Stewart ➝, *Canada* **138 B6** 63 19N 139 26W
Stewart, C., *Australia* **126 A1** 11 57 S 134 56 E
Stewart, I., *Chile* **176 D2** 54 50 S 71 15W
Stewart I., *N.Z.* **131 G2** 46 58 S 167 54 E
Stewarts Point, *U.S.A.* **160 G3** 38 39N 123 24W
Stewartstown, *U.S.A.* **156 E2** 39 45N 94 30W
Stewartville, *U.S.A.* **154 D8** 43 51N 92 29W
Stewiacke, *Canada* **141 C7** 45 9N 63 22W
Steynsburg, *S. Africa* **116 E4** 31 15 S 25 49 E
Steyr, *Austria* **34 C7** 48 3N 14 25 E
Steyr ➝, *Austria* **34 C7** 48 3N 14 25 E
Steytlerville, *S. Africa* **116 E3** 33 17 S 24 19 E
Stia, *Italy* **45 E8** 43 48N 11 42 E
Stigler, *U.S.A.* **155 H7** 35 15N 95 8W
Stigliano, *Italy* **47 B9** 40 24N 16 14 E
Stigtomta, *Sweden* **17 F10** 58 47N 16 48 E
Stikine ➝, *Canada* **142 B2** 56 40N 132 30W
Stilfontein, *S. Africa* **116 D4** 26 51 S 26 50 E
Stilis, *Greece* **48 C4** 38 55N 22 47 E
Stillmore, *U.S.A.* **152 C7** 32 27N 82 13W
Stillwater, *Minn., U.S.A.* **154 C8** 45 3N 92 49W
Stillwater, *N.Y., U.S.A.* **151 D11** 42 55N 73 41W
Stillwater, *Okla., U.S.A.* **155 G6** 36 7N 97 4W
Stillwater Range, *U.S.A.* **158 G4** 39 50N 118 5W
Stillwater Reservoir, *U.S.A.* **151 C9** 43 54N 75 3W
Stilo, Pta., *Italy* **47 D9** 38 25N 16 35 E
Stilwell, *U.S.A.* **155 H7** 35 49N 94 38W
Štip, *Macedonia* **50 E6** 41 42N 22 10 E
Stíra, *Greece* **48 C6** 38 9N 24 14 E
Stirling, *Canada* **150 B7** 44 18N 77 33W
Stirling, *N.Z.* **131 G4** 46 14 S 169 49 E
Stirling, *U.K.* **22 E5** 56 8N 3 57W
Stirling □, *U.K.* **22 E4** 56 12N 4 18W
Stirling Ra., *Australia* **125 F2** 34 23 S 118 0 E
Stirling Range Nat. Park, *Australia* **125 F2** 34 26 S 118 20 E
Stittsville, *Canada* **151 A9** 45 15N 75 55W
Stjernøya, *Norway* **14 A20** 70 20N 22 40 E
Stjørdalshalsen, *Norway* **14 E14** 63 29N 10 51 E
Stock Island, *U.S.A.* **153 L8** 24 32N 81 34W
Stockach, *Germany* **31 H5** 47 50N 9 1 E
Stockaryd, *Sweden* **17 G8** 57 19N 14 36 E
Stockbridge, *Ga., U.S.A.* **152 B5** 33 33N 84 14W
Stockbridge, *Mich., U.S.A.* **157 B12** 42 27N 84 11W
Stockerau, *Austria* **35 C9** 48 24N 16 12 E
Stockholm, *Sweden* **16 E12** 59 20N 18 3 E
Stockholms län □, *Sweden* **16 E12** 59 30N 18 20 E
Stockhorn, *Switz.* **32 C5** 46 42N 7 33 E
Stockport, *U.K.* **20 D5** 53 25N 2 9W
Stocksbridge, *U.K.* **20 D6** 53 29N 1 35W
Stockton, *Calif., U.S.A.* **160 H5** 37 58N 121 17W
Stockton, *Ill., U.S.A.* **156 B6** 42 21N 90 1W
Stockton, *Kans., U.S.A.* **154 F5** 39 26N 99 16W
Stockton, *Mo., U.S.A.* **155 G8** 37 42N 93 48W
Stockton-on-Tees, *U.K.* **20 C6** 54 35N 1 19W
Stockton-on-Tees □, *U.K.* **20 C6** 54 35N 1 19W
Stockton Plateau, *U.S.A.* **155 K3** 30 30N 102 30W
Stoczek Łukowski, *Poland* **55 G8** 51 58N 21 58 E
Stöde, *Sweden* **16 B10** 62 28N 16 35 E
Stoeng Treng, *Cambodia* **86 F5** 13 31N 105 58 E
Stoer, Pt. of, *U.K.* **22 C3** 58 16N 5 23W
Stogovo, *Macedonia* **50 E4** 41 31N 20 38 E
Stoholm, *Denmark* **17 H3** 56 30N 9 8 E
Stoke, *N.Z.* **131 B8** 41 19 S 173 14 E
Stoke-on-Trent, *U.K.* **20 D5** 53 1N 2 11W
Stoke-on-Trent □, *U.K.* **20 D5** 53 1N 2 11W
Stokes Nat. Park, *Australia* **125 E2** 29 55 S 115 6 E
Stokes Pt., *Australia* **127 G3** 40 10 S 143 56 E
Stokes Ra., *Australia* **124 C5** 15 50 S 130 50 E
Stokkseyri, *Iceland* **11 D5** 63 50N 21 2W
Stokksnes, *Iceland* **11 C12** 64 14N 14 58W
Stokmarknes, *Norway* **14 B16** 68 34N 14 54 E
Stolac, *Bos.-H.* **50 C1** 43 5N 17 59 E
Stolberg, *Germany* **30 E2** 50 47N 6 13 E
Stolbovoy, Ostrov, *Russia* **67 B14** 74 44N 135 14 E
Stolbtsy = Stowbtsy, *Belarus* **58 F4** 53 30N 26 43 E
Stolin, *Belarus* **59 G4** 51 53N 26 50 E
Stöllet, *Sweden* **16 D7** 60 26N 13 15 E
Stolnici, *Romania* **53 F9** 44 31N 24 48 E
Stomion, *Greece* **39 C3** 38 21N 23 32 E
Ston, *Croatia* **45 F14** 42 51N 17 43 E
Stone, *U.K.* **20 E5** 52 55N 2 9W
Stone Mountain, *U.S.A.* **152 B5** 33 49N 84 10W
Stoneboro, *U.S.A.* **150 E4** 41 20N 80 7W
Stonehaven, *U.K.* **22 E6** 56 59N 2 12W
Stonehenge, *Australia* **126 C3** 24 22 S 143 17 E
Stonehenge, *U.K.* **21 F6** 51 9N 1 45W
Stonewall, *Canada* **143 C9** 50 10N 97 19W
Stongfjorden, *Norway* **18 C2** 61 26N 5 10 E
Stonington, *U.S.A.* **156 E7** 39 44N 89 12W
Stony L., *Man., Canada* **143 B9** 58 51N 98 40W
Stony L., *Ont., Canada* **150 B6** 44 30N 78 5W
Stony Point, *U.S.A.* **151 E11** 41 14N 73 59W
Stony Pt., *U.S.A.* **151 C8** 43 50N 76 18W
Stony Rapids, *Canada* **143 B7** 59 16N 105 50W
Stony River, *U.S.A.* **144 F8** 61 47N 156 35W
Stony Tunguska = Tunguska, Podkamennaya ➝, *Russia* **67 C10** 61 50N 90 13 E
Stonyford, *U.S.A.* **160 F4** 39 23N 122 33W
Stopnica, *Poland* **55 H7** 50 27N 20 57 E
Storå, *Sweden* **16 E9** 59 42N 15 6 E
Storå ➝, *Denmark* **17 H2** 56 20N 8 19 E
Stora Gla, *Sweden* **16 E6** 59 30N 12 30 E
Stora Le, *Sweden* **16 E5** 59 5N 11 55 E
Stora Lulevatten, *Sweden* **14 C18** 67 10N 19 30 E
Stora Sjöfallet, *Sweden* **14 C18** 67 29N 18 40 E
Storavan, *Sweden* **14 D18** 65 45N 18 10 E
Stord, *Norway* **15 G11** 59 52N 5 23 E
Stordal, *Norway* **18 B4** 62 23N 7 0 E
Store Bælt, *Denmark* **17 J4** 55 20N 11 0 E
Store Heddinge, *Denmark* **17 J6** 55 18N 12 23 E
Store Jukleggi, *Norway* **18 C5** 61 3N 8 12 E
Store Koldewey, *Greenland* **10 B9** 76 30N 19 0W
Store Sølnkletten, *Norway* **18 C7** 61 59N 10 16 E
Store Sotra, *Norway* **18 D1** 60 18N 5 4 E
Storebro, *Sweden* **17 G9** 57 35N 15 52 E
Storen, *Norway* **18 A7** 63 3N 10 18 E
Storerikvollen, *Norway* **18 A8** 63 7N 11 58 E
Storfjellseter, *Norway* **18 C7** 61 40N 10 30 E
Storfjorden, *Møre og Romsdal, Norway* **18 B3** 62 8N 6 33 E
Storfjorden, *Møre og Romsdal, Norway* **18 B3** 62 28N 6 35 E
Storfors, *Sweden* **16 E8** 59 32N 14 17 E
Stóridalur, *Iceland* **11 D7** 63 38N 19 57W
Stórinúpur, *Iceland* **11 C6** 64 3N 20 10W
Storli, *Norway* **18 B6** 62 42N 9 5 E
Storlien, *Sweden* **16 A6** 63 20N 12 5 E
Storm B., *Australia* **127 G4** 43 10 S 147 30 E
Storm Lake, *U.S.A.* **154 D7** 42 39N 95 13W
Stormberge, *S. Africa* **116 E4** 31 16 S 26 17 E
Stormsrivier, *S. Africa* **116 E3** 33 59 S 23 52 E
Stornoway, *U.K.* **22 C2** 58 13N 6 23W
Storo, *Italy* **44 C7** 45 51N 10 35 E
Storozhinets = Storozhynets, *Ukraine* **59 H3** 48 14N 25 45 E
Storozhynets, *Ukraine* **59 H3** 48 14N 25 45 E
Storrs, *U.S.A.* **151 E12** 41 49N 72 15W
Storsjøen, *Hedmark, Norway* **18 D8** 60 20N 11 40 E
Storsjøen, *Hedmark, Norway* **18 C8** 61 30N 11 14 E
Storsjön, *Gävleborg, Sweden* **16 D10** 60 35N 16 45 E
Storsjön, *Jämtland, Sweden* **16 B7** 62 48N 13 7 E
Storsjön, *Jämtland, Sweden* **16 A8** 63 9N 14 30 E
Storstrøms Amtskommune □, *Denmark* **17 J5** 54 50N 11 45 E
Storuman, *Sweden* **14 D17** 65 5N 17 10 E
Storuman, sjö, *Sweden* **14 D17** 65 13N 16 50 E
Storuvellir, *Iceland* **11 B9** 65 30N 17 29W
Storvätteshågna, *Sweden* **16 B6** 62 6N 12 30 E
Storvigelen, *Norway* **18 B9** 62 32N 12 2 E
Storvik, *Sweden* **16 D10** 60 35N 16 33 E
Storvreta, *Sweden* **16 E11** 59 58N 17 44 E
Story City, *U.S.A.* **156 B3** 42 11N 93 36W
Stouffville, *Canada* **150 C5** 43 58N 79 15W
Stoughton, *Canada* **143 D8** 49 40N 103 0W
Stoughton, *U.S.A.* **156 B8** 42 55N 89 13W
Stour ➝, *Dorset, U.K.* **21 G6** 50 43N 1 47W
Stour ➝, *Kent, U.K.* **21 F9** 51 18N 1 22 E
Stour ➝, *Suffolk, U.K.* **21 F9** 51 57N 1 4 E
Stourbridge, *U.K.* **21 E5** 52 28N 2 8W
Stout L., *Canada* **143 C10** 52 0N 94 40W
Stove Pipe Wells Village, *U.S.A.* **161 J9** 36 35N 117 11W
Støvring, *Denmark* **17 H3** 56 54N 9 50 E
Stow, *U.S.A.* **150 E3** 41 10N 81 27W
Stowbtsy, *Belarus* **58 F4** 53 30N 26 43 E
Stowmarket, *U.K.* **21 E9** 52 12N 1 0 E
Strabane, *U.K.* **23 B4** 54 50N 7 27W
Stracin, *Macedonia* **50 D6** 42 13N 22 2 E
Stradella, *Italy* **44 C6** 45 5N 9 18 E
Strahan, *Australia* **127 G4** 42 9 S 145 20 E
Strajitsa, *Bulgaria* **51 C9** 43 14N 25 58 E
Strakonice, *Czech Rep.* **34 B6** 49 15N 13 53 E
Straldzha, *Bulgaria* **51 D10** 42 35N 26 40 E
Stralsund, *Germany* **30 A9** 54 18N 13 4 E
Strand, *Norway* **18 E2** 59 3N 6 2 E
Strand, *S. Africa* **116 E2** 34 9 S 18 48 E
Stranda, *Møre og Romsdal, Norway* **15 E12** 62 19N 6 58 E
Stranda, *Nord-Trøndelag, Norway* **14 E14** 63 33N 10 14 E
Strandasýsla □, *Iceland* **11 B5** 65 45N 21 45W
Strandby, *Denmark* **17 G4** 57 30N 10 29 E
Strangford L., *U.K.* **23 B6** 54 30N 5 37W
Strängnäs, *Sweden* **16 E11** 59 23N 17 2 E
Stranraer, *U.K.* **22 G3** 54 54N 5 1W
Strasbourg, *Canada* **143 C8** 51 4N 104 55W
Strasbourg, *France* **27 D14** 48 35N 7 42 E
Strasburg, *Germany* **30 B9** 53 30N 13 43 E
Străşeni, *Moldova* **53 C13** 47 8N 28 36 E
Stråssa, *Sweden* **16 E9** 59 44N 15 12 E
Stratford, *N.S.W., Australia* **129 B9** 32 7 S 151 55 E
Stratford, *Vic., Australia* **129 D7** 37 59 S 147 7 E
Stratford, *Canada* **140 D3** 43 23N 81 0W
Stratford, *N.Z.* **130 F3** 39 20 S 174 19 E
Stratford, *Calif., U.S.A.* **160 J7** 36 11N 119 49W
Stratford, *Conn., U.S.A.* **151 E11** 41 12N 73 8W
Stratford, *Tex., U.S.A.* **155 G3** 36 20N 102 4W
Stratford-upon-Avon, *U.K.* **21 E6** 52 12N 1 42W
Strath Spey, *U.K.* **22 D5** 57 9N 3 49W
Strathalbyn, *Australia* **128 C3** 35 13 S 138 53 E
Strathaven, *U.K.* **22 F4** 55 40N 4 5W
Strathcona Prov. Park, *Canada* **142 D3** 49 38N 125 40W
Strathmore, *Canada* **142 C6** 51 5N 113 18W
Strathmore, *U.K.* **22 E5** 56 37N 3 7W
Strathmore, *U.K.* **22 C4** 58 22N 4 40W
Strathmore, *U.S.A.* **160 J7** 36 9N 119 4W
Strathnaver, *Canada* **142 C4** 53 20N 122 33W
Strathpeffer, *U.K.* **22 D4** 57 35N 4 32W
Strathroy, *Canada* **140 D3** 42 58N 81 38W
Strathy Pt., *U.K.* **22 C4** 58 36N 4 1W
Strattanville, *U.S.A.* **150 E5** 41 12N 79 19W
Stratton, *U.S.A.* **151 A14** 45 8N 70 26W
Stratton Mt., *U.S.A.* **151 C12** 43 4N 72 55W
Straubing, *Germany* **31 G8** 48 52N 12 34 E
Straumnes, *Iceland* **11 A3** 66 26N 23 8W
Strausberg, *Germany* **30 C9** 52 35N 13 54 E
Strawberry ➝, *U.S.A.* **158 F8** 40 10N 110 24W
Strawberry Point, *U.S.A.* **156 B5** 42 41N 91 32W
Strážnice, *Czech Rep.* **35 C10** 48 54N 17 19 E
Streaky B., *Australia* **127 E1** 32 48 S 134 13 E
Streaky Bay, *Australia* **127 E1** 32 51 S 134 18 E
Streator, *U.S.A.* **154 E10** 41 8N 88 50W
Středočeský □, *Czech Rep.* **34 B7** 49 55N 14 30 E
Streetsboro, *U.S.A.* **150 E3** 41 14N 81 21W
Streetsville, *Canada* **150 C5** 43 35N 79 42W
Strehaia, *Romania* **53 F8** 44 37N 23 10 E
Strelcha, *Bulgaria* **51 D8** 42 30N 24 19 E
Strelka, *Russia* **67 D10** 58 5N 93 3 E
Streng ➝, *Cambodia* **86 F4** 13 12N 103 37 E
Stresa, *Italy* **44 C5** 45 52N 8 28 E
Streymoy, *Færoe Is.* **14 E9** 62 8N 7 5W
Strezhevoy, *Russia* **66 C8** 60 42N 77 34 E
Stříbro, *Czech Rep.* **34 A6** 49 44N 13 0 E
Strickland ➝, *Papua N. G.* **132 D1** 7 35 S 141 36 E
Strimón ➝, *Greece* **50 F7** 40 46N 23 51 E
Strimonikós Kólpos, *Greece* **50 F7** 40 33N 24 0 E
Stroeder, *Argentina* **176 B4** 40 12 S 62 37W
Strofádhes, *Greece* **48 D3** 37 15N 21 0 E
Stroma, *U.K.* **22 C5** 58 41N 3 7W
Strómboli, *Italy* **47 D8** 38 47N 15 13 E
Stromeferry, *U.K.* **22 D3** 57 21N 5 33W
Strømmen, *Norway* **18 E7** 59 58N 10 59 E
Stromness, *U.K.* **22 C5** 58 58N 3 17W
Strömsbruk, *Sweden* **16 C11** 61 52N 17 18 E
Stromsburg, *U.S.A.* **154 E6** 41 7N 97 36W
Strömsnäsbruk, *Sweden* **17 H7** 56 35N 13 45 E
Strömstad, *Sweden* **17 F5** 58 56N 11 10 E
Strömsund, *Sweden* **14 E16** 63 51N 15 33 E
Stronghurst, *U.S.A.* **156 D6** 40 45N 90 55W
Strongilí, *Greece* **49 E11** 36 6N 29 42 E
Strόngoli, *Italy* **47 C10** 39 16N 17 3 E
Strongsville, *U.S.A.* **150 E3** 41 19N 81 50W
Stronie Śląskie, *Poland* **55 H3** 50 18N 16 53 E
Stronsay, *U.K.* **22 B6** 59 7N 2 35W
Stropkov, *Slovak Rep.* **35 B14** 49 13N 21 39 E
Stroud, *U.K.* **21 F5** 51 45N 2 13W
Stroud Road, *Australia* **129 B9** 32 18 S 151 57 E
Stroudsburg, *U.S.A.* **151 F9** 40 59N 75 12W
Stroumbi, *Cyprus* **39 F8** 34 53N 32 29 E
Struer, *Denmark* **17 H2** 56 30N 8 35 E
Struga, *Macedonia* **50 E4** 41 11N 20 44 E
Strugi Krasnyye, *Russia* **58 C5** 58 21N 29 1 E
Strumica, *Macedonia* **50 E6** 41 28N 22 41 E
Strumica ➝, *Europe* **50 E7** 41 20N 23 22 E
Struthers, *Canada* **140 C2** 48 41N 85 51W
Struthers, *U.S.A.* **150 E4** 41 4N 80 39W
Stryama, *Bulgaria* **51 D8** 42 16N 24 54 E
Stryker, *U.S.A.* **158 B6** 48 41N 114 46W
Stryków, *Poland* **55 G6** 51 55N 19 33 E
Stryn, *Norway* **18 C3** 61 54N 6 43 E
Stryy, *Ukraine* **59 H2** 49 16N 23 48 E
Strzegom, *Poland* **55 H3** 50 58N 16 20 E
Strzelce Krajeńskie, *Poland* **55 F2** 52 52N 15 33 E
Strzelce Opolskie, *Poland* **55 H5** 50 31N 18 18 E
Strzelecki Cr. ➝, *Australia* **127 D2** 29 37 S 139 59 E
Strzelin, *Poland* **55 H4** 50 46N 17 2 E
Strzelno, *Poland* **55 F5** 52 35N 18 9 E
Strzybnica, *Poland* **55 H5** 50 28N 18 48 E
Strzyżów, *Poland* **55 J8** 49 52N 21 47 E
Stuart, *Fla., U.S.A.* **149 M5** 27 12N 80 15W
Stuart, *Iowa, U.S.A.* **156 C2** 41 30N 94 19W
Stuart, *Nebr., U.S.A.* **154 D5** 42 36N 99 8W
Stuart ➝, *Canada* **142 C4** 54 0N 123 35W
Stuart Bluff Ra., *Australia* **124 D5** 22 50 S 131 52 E
Stuart I., *U.S.A.* **144 E7** 63 35N 162 30W
Stuart L., *Canada* **142 C4** 54 30N 124 30W
Stuart Mts., *N.Z.* **131 F2** 45 2 S 167 39 E
Stuart Ra., *Australia* **127 D1** 29 10 S 134 56 E
Stubbekøbing, *Denmark* **17 K6** 54 53N 12 9 E
Stuben, *Austria* **34 D3** 47 10N 10 8 E
Studen Kladenets, Yazovir, *Bulgaria* **51 E9** 41 37N 25 30 E
Studenka, *Czech Rep.* **35 B11** 49 44N 18 5 E
Studholme, *N.Z.* **131 E6** 44 42 S 171 9 E
Stugudal, *Norway* **18 B8** 62 53N 11 53 E
Stugun, *Sweden* **16 A9** 63 10N 15 40 E
Stühlingen, *Germany* **33 A6** 47 44N 8 26 E
Stuhr, *Germany* **30 B4** 53 5N 8 44 E
Stull L., *Canada* **140 B1** 54 24N 92 34W
Stung Treng = Stoeng Treng, *Cambodia* **86 F5** 13 31N 105 58 E
Stupart ➝, *Canada* **140 A1** 56 0N 93 25W
Stupava, *Slovak Rep.* **35 C10** 48 17N 17 2 E
Stupino, *Russia* **58 E10** 54 57N 38 2 E
Sturgeon B., *Canada* **143 C9** 52 0N 97 50W
Sturgeon Bay, *U.S.A.* **148 C2** 44 50N 87 23W
Sturgeon Falls, *Canada* **140 C4** 46 25N 79 57W
Sturgeon L., *Alta., Canada* **142 B5** 55 6N 117 32W
Sturgeon L., *Ont., Canada* **140 C1** 50 0N 90 45W
Sturgeon L., *Ont., Canada* **150 B6** 44 28N 78 43W
Sturgis, *Canada* **143 C8** 51 56N 102 36W
Sturgis, *Mich., U.S.A.* **157 C11** 41 48N 85 25W
Sturgis, *S. Dak., U.S.A.* **154 C3** 44 25N 103 31W
Sturkö, *Sweden* **17 H9** 56 5N 15 42 E
Štúrovo, *Slovak Rep.* **35 D11** 47 48N 18 41 E
Sturt Cr. ➝, *Australia* **124 C4** 19 8 S 127 50 E
Sturt Nat. Park, *Australia* **127 D3** 27 17 S 141 37 E
Sturts Meadows, *Australia* **128 A4** 31 18 S 141 42 E
Stutterheim, *S. Africa* **116 E4** 32 33 S 27 28 E
Stuttgart, *Germany* **31 G5** 48 48N 9 11 E
Stuttgart, *U.S.A.* **155 H9** 34 30N 91 33W
Stuyvesant, *U.S.A.* **151 D11** 42 23N 73 45W
Stykkishólmur, *Iceland* **11 B4** 65 2N 22 40W
Styria = Steiermark □, *Austria* **34 D8** 47 26N 15 0 E
Styrsö, *Sweden* **17 G5** 57 37N 11 46 E
Su-no-Saki, *Japan* **73 C11** 34 58N 139 45 E

286 Su Xian

Su Xian = Suzhou, China 74 H9 33 41N 116 59 E
Suakin, Sudan 106 D4 19 8N 37 20 E
Suan, N. Korea 75 E14 38 42N 126 22 E
Suapure →, Venezuela 168 B4 6 48N 67 1W
Suaqui, Mexico 162 B3 29 12N 109 41W
Suar, India 93 E8 29 2N 79 3 E
Suatá →, Venezuela 169 B4 7 52N 65 22W
Suau, Papua N. G. 132 F6 10 37 S 150 2 E
Suavanao, Solomon Is. 133 L10 7 35 S 158 47 E
Suba Talan, Malaysia 81 H1 6 22N 117 38 E
Subang, Indonesia 85 D3 6 34 S 107 45 E
Subankhata, India 90 B3 26 48N 91 25 E
Subansiri →, India 90 B4 26 48N 93 50 E
Subarnagiri, India 94 E6 19 50N 83 51 E
Subarnarekha →, India 93 H12 22 34N 87 24 E
Subayhah, Si. Arabia 96 D3 30 2N 38 50 E
Subcetate, Romania 52 E8 45 36N 23 0 E
Subi, Indonesia 85 B3 2 58N 108 50 E
Subiaco, Italy 45 G10 41 56N 13 5 E
Subotica, Serbia, Yug. 52 D4 46 6N 19 39 E
Suca, Ethiopia 107 F4 6 31N 39 14 E
Suceava, Romania 53 C11 47 38N 26 16 E
Suceava □, Romania 53 C10 47 37N 25 40 E
Suceava →, Romania 53 C11 47 32N 26 32 E
Sucesso, Brazil 170 B3 4 56 S 40 32W
Sucha-Beskidzka, Poland 55 J6 49 44N 19 35 E
Suchań, Poland 55 E2 53 18N 15 18 E
Suchan, Russia 70 C6 43 8N 133 9 E
Suchedniów, Poland 55 G7 51 3N 20 49 E
Suchitoto, El Salv. 164 D2 13 56N 89 0W
Suchou = Suzhou, China 77 B13 31 19N 120 38 E
Süchow = Xuzhou, China 75 G9 34 18N 117 10 E
Suchowola, Poland 54 E10 53 33N 23 3 E
Sucio →, Colombia 168 B2 7 27N 77 7W
Suck →, Ireland 23 C3 53 17N 8 3W
Suckling, Mt., Papua N. G. 132 E5 9 49 S 148 53 E
Sucre, Bolivia 173 D4 19 0 S 65 15W
Sucre, Colombia 168 B3 8 49N 74 44W
Sucre □, Colombia 168 B2 8 50N 75 40W
Sucre □, Venezuela 169 A5 10 25N 63 30W
Sucuaro, Colombia 168 C4 4 34N 68 50W
Sućuraj, Croatia 45 E14 43 10N 17 8 E
Sucuriju, Brazil 170 A2 1 39N 49 57W
Sucuriú →, Brazil 173 E7 20 47 S 51 38W
Sud, Pte. du, Canada 141 C7 49 3N 62 14W
Sud-Kivu □, Dem. Rep. of the Congo 118 C2 3 0 S 28 30 E
Sud Ouest, Pte., Mauritius 121 d 20 28 S 57 18 E
Sud-Ouest, Pte. du, Canada 141 C7 49 23N 63 36W
Suda →, Russia 58 C9 59 0N 37 40 E
Sudak, Ukraine 59 K8 44 51N 34 57 E
Sudan, U.S.A. 155 H3 34 4N 102 32W
Sudan ■, Africa 107 E3 15 0N 30 0 E
Sudbury, Canada 140 C3 46 30N 81 0W
Sudbury, U.K. 21 E8 52 2N 0 45 E
Sûdd, Sudan 107 F3 8 20N 30 0 E
Suddie, Guyana 169 B6 7 8N 58 29W
Süderbrarup, Germany 30 A5 54 38N 9 45 E
Süderlügum, Germany 30 A4 54 52N 8 54 E
Süderoogsand, Germany 30 A4 54 27N 8 28 E
Sudeten Mts. = Sudety, Europe 35 A9 50 20N 16 45 E
Sudety, Europe 35 A9 50 20N 16 45 E
Súðavík, Iceland 11 A3 66 2N 23 0W
Suður-múlasýsla □, Iceland 11 C12 65 0N 14 30W
Suður-þingeyjarsýsla □, Iceland 11 B9 65 30N 17 0W
Suðureyri, Iceland 11 A3 66 7N 23 32W
Suðuroy, Færoe Is. 14 F9 61 32N 6 50W
Sudi, Tanzania 119 E4 10 11 S 39 57 E
Sudirman, Pegunungan, Indonesia 83 B5 4 30 S 137 0 E
Suditi, Romania 53 F12 44 35N 27 38 E
Sudogda, Russia 60 C5 55 55N 40 50 E
Sudong, Pulau, Singapore 87 d 1 12N 103 43 E
Sudr, Egypt 106 B3 29 40N 32 42 E
Sudzha, Russia 59 G8 51 14N 35 17 E
Sue →, Sudan 107 F2 7 41N 28 3 E
Sueca, Spain 41 F4 39 12N 0 21W
Sŭedinenie, Bulgaria 51 D8 42 16N 24 33 E
Suemez I., U.S.A. 142 B2 55 15N 133 20W
Suez = El Suweis, Egypt 106 J8 29 58N 32 31 E
Suez, G. of = Suweis, Khalîg el, Egypt 106 J8 28 40N 33 0 E
Suez Canal = Suweis, Qanâ es, Egypt 106 H8 31 0N 32 20 E
Suffield, Canada 142 C6 50 12N 111 10W
Suffolk, U.S.A. 148 G7 36 44N 76 35W
Suffolk □, U.K. 21 E9 52 16N 1 0 E
Suga-no-Sen, Japan 72 B6 35 25N 134 25 E
Şugag, Romania 53 E8 45 47N 23 37 E
Sugar →, U.S.A. 156 B7 42 26N 89 12W
Sugar Cr. →, Ill., U.S.A. 156 D7 40 9N 89 38W
Sugar Cr. →, Ind., U.S.A. 157 E9 39 50N 87 23W
Sugar Hill, U.S.A. 152 A5 34 6N 84 2W
Sugar Loaf Pt., St. Helena 9 h 15 54 S 5 42W
Sugargrove, U.S.A. 150 E5 41 59N 79 21W
Sugarive →, India 93 F12 26 16N 86 24 E
Sugbai Passage, Phil. 81 J3 5 22N 120 33 E
Suğla Gölü, Turkey 100 D5 37 20N 32 0 E
Suguk = Salluit, Canada 139 B12 62 14N 75 38W
Sugun, China 65 D8 39 53N 76 47 E
Suhaia, Lacul, Romania 53 G10 43 45N 25 15 E
Şuḥār, Oman 97 E8 24 20N 56 40 E
Sühbaatar □, Mongolia 74 B8 45 30N 114 0 E
Suheli Par, India 95 J1 10 5N 72 17 E
Suhl, Germany 30 E6 50 36N 10 42 E
Suhr, Switz. 32 B6 47 22N 8 5 E
Şuhut, Turkey 49 C12 38 31N 30 32 E
Sui, Pakistan 92 E3 28 37N 69 19 E
Sui Xian, China 74 G8 34 25N 115 2 E
Suiá Missu →, Brazil 173 C7 11 13 S 53 15W
Šuica, Bos.-H. 52 G2 43 52N 17 11 E
Suichang, China 77 C12 28 29N 119 15 E
Suichuan, China 77 D10 26 20N 114 32 E
Suide, China 74 F6 37 30N 110 12 E
Suifenhe, China 75 B16 44 25N 131 10 E
Suihua, China 69 B7 46 32N 126 55 E
Suijiang, China 76 C4 28 40N 103 59 E
Suining, Hunan, China 77 D8 26 35N 110 10 E
Suining, Jiangsu, China 75 H9 33 56N 117 58 E
Suining, Sichuan, China 76 B5 30 26N 105 35 E
Suiping, China 74 H7 33 10N 113 59 E
Suippes, France 27 C11 49 8N 4 30 E
Suir →, Ireland 23 D4 52 16N 7 9W
Suisun City, U.S.A. 160 G4 38 15N 122 2W
Suita, Japan 73 C7 34 45N 135 32 E
Suixi, China 77 G8 21 19N 110 18 E
Suiyang, Guizhou, China 76 D6 27 58N 107 18 E
Suiyang, Heilongjiang, China 75 B16 44 30N 130 56 E
Suizhong, China 75 D11 40 21N 120 20 E
Suizhou, China 77 B9 31 42N 113 24 E
Sujangarh, India 92 F6 27 42N 74 31 E
Sukabumi, Indonesia 84 D3 6 56 S 106 50 E
Sukadana, Kalimantan, Indonesia 85 C4 1 10 S 110 0 E
Sukadana, Sumatera, Indonesia 84 D3 5 5 S 105 33 E
Sukagawa, Japan 71 F10 37 17N 140 23 E
Sukaraja, Indonesia 85 C4 2 28 S 110 25 E
Sukarnapura = Jayapura, Indonesia 83 B6 2 28 S 140 38 E
Sukawati, Indonesia 79 K18 8 35 S 115 17 E
Sukch'ŏn, N. Korea 75 E13 39 22N 125 35 E
Sukhindol, Bulgaria 51 C9 43 11N 25 10 E
Sukhinichi, Russia 58 E8 54 8N 35 10 E
Sukhona →, Russia 56 C6 61 15N 46 39 E
Sukhothai, Thailand 86 D2 17 1N 99 49 E
Sukhoy Log, Russia 64 C9 56 55N 62 1 E
Sukhumi = Sokhumi, Georgia 61 J5 43 0N 41 0 E
Sukkertoppen = Maniitsoq, Greenland 10 D5 65 26N 52 55W
Sukkur, Pakistan 91 D3 27 42N 68 54 E
Sukkur Barrage, Pakistan 92 F3 27 40N 68 50 E
Sukma, India 94 E5 18 24N 81 45 E
Sukovo, Serbia, Yug. 50 C6 43 4N 22 37 E
Sukri →, India 92 G4 25 4N 71 43 E
Sukumo, Japan 72 E4 32 56N 132 44 E
Sukunka →, Canada 142 B4 55 45N 121 15W
Sul, Canal do, Brazil 170 B2 0 10 S 48 30W
Sula, Norway 18 C1 61 7N 4 54 E
Sula →, Ukraine 59 H7 49 40N 32 41 E
Sula, Kepulauan, Indonesia 83 B3 1 45 S 125 0 E
Sulaco →, Honduras 164 C2 15 2N 87 44W
Sulaiman Range, Pakistan 92 D3 30 30N 69 50 E
Sulak →, Russia 61 J8 43 20N 47 34 E
Sūlār, Iran 97 D6 31 53N 51 54 E
Sulawesi □, Indonesia 82 B2 2 0 S 120 0 E
Sulawesi Sea = Celebes Sea, Indonesia 82 A2 3 0N 123 0 E
Sulawesi Selatan □, Indonesia 82 B1 2 30 S 120 0 E
Sulawesi Utara □, Indonesia 82 A2 1 0N 122 30 E
Suldalsosen, Norway 18 E3 59 29N 6 29 E
Sulechów, Poland 55 F2 52 5N 15 40 E
Sulęcin, Poland 55 F2 52 26N 15 10 E
Sulei, Solomon Is. 133 M10 8 3 S 159 34 E
Sulejów, Poland 55 G6 51 26N 19 53 E
Sulejówek, Poland 55 F8 52 13N 21 17 E
Süleymanlı, Turkey 49 C9 38 58N 27 47 E
Sulgen, Switz. 33 A8 47 33N 9 7 E
Sulima, S. Leone 112 D2 6 58N 11 32W
Sulina, Romania 53 E14 45 10N 29 40 E
Sulina, Braţul →, Romania 53 E14 45 10N 29 40 E
Sulingen, Germany 30 C4 52 41N 8 48 E
Suliţa, Romania 53 C11 47 39N 26 59 E
Sulitjelma, Norway 14 C17 67 9N 16 3 E
Sułkowice, Poland 55 J6 49 50N 19 49 E
Sullana, Peru 172 A1 4 52 S 80 39W
Süller, Turkey 49 C11 38 9N 29 29 E
Sullivan, Ill., U.S.A. 154 F10 39 36N 88 37W
Sullivan, Ind., U.S.A. 157 E9 39 6N 87 24W
Sullivan, Mo., U.S.A. 156 F5 38 13N 91 10W
Sullivan Bay, Canada 142 C3 50 55N 126 50W
Sullivan I. = Lanbi Kyun, Burma 87 G2 10 50N 98 20 E
Sully, U.S.A. 156 C4 41 34N 92 50W
Sully-sur-Loire, France 27 E9 47 45N 2 20 E
Sulmierzyce, Poland 55 G4 51 37N 17 32 E
Sulmona, Italy 45 F10 42 3N 13 55 E
Süloğlu, Turkey 51 E10 41 44N 26 53 E
Sulphur, La., U.S.A. 155 K8 30 14N 93 23W
Sulphur, Okla., U.S.A. 155 H6 34 31N 96 58W
Sulphur Pt., Canada 142 A6 60 56N 114 48W
Sulphur Springs, U.S.A. 155 J7 33 8N 95 36W
Sulsul, Ethiopia 120 C2 5 5N 44 50 E
Sultan, Canada 140 C3 47 36N 82 47W
Sultan, U.S.A. 160 C5 47 52N 121 49W
Sultan Dağları, Turkey 100 C4 38 20N 31 20 E
Sultan Kudarat, Phil. 81 H5 7 16N 124 18 E
Sultan Kudarat □, Phil. 81 H5 6 30N 124 10 E
Sultan Naga Dimaporo, Phil. 81 H4 7 55N 123 44 E
Sultan sa Barongis, Phil. 81 H5 6 45N 124 35 E
Sultanhisar, Turkey 49 D10 37 53N 28 9 E
Sultaniça, Turkey 51 F10 40 37N 26 8 E
Sultaniye, Turkey 51 F12 40 11N 28 12 E
Sultanpur, Mad. P., India 92 H8 23 9N 77 56 E
Sultanpur, Punjab, India 92 D6 31 13N 75 11 E
Sultanpur, Ut. P., India 93 F10 26 18N 82 4 E
Sulu □, Phil. 81 J3 5 30N 120 30 E
Sulu Arch., Phil. 81 J3 6 0N 121 0 E
Sulu Sea, E. Indies 81 G3 8 0N 120 0 E
Sülüklü, Turkey 100 C5 38 53N 32 20 E
Sülüktü, Kyrgyzstan 65 D4 39 56N 69 34 E
Sululta, Ethiopia 107 F4 9 10N 38 43 E
Suluova, Turkey 100 B6 40 46N 35 32 E
Suluq, Libya 108 B4 31 44N 20 14 E
Suluru, India 95 H5 13 42N 80 1 E
Sulütöbe, Kazakstan 65 A3 44 37N 66 3 E
Sulyukta = Sülüktü, Kyrgyzstan 65 D4 39 56N 69 34 E
Sulzbach, Germany 31 F3 49 18N 7 3 E
Sulzbach-Rosenberg, Germany 31 F7 49 30N 11 44 E
Sulzberg, Germany 33 A10 47 39N 10 39 E
Sulzberger Ice Shelf, Antarctica 7 D10 78 0 S 150 0 E
Sumalata, Indonesia 83 A2 1 0N 122 31 E
Sumampa, Argentina 174 B3 29 25 S 63 29W
Sumatera □, Indonesia 84 B2 0 40N 100 20 E
Sumatera Barat □, Indonesia 78 E2 1 0 S 101 0 E
Sumatera Utara □, Indonesia 78 D1 2 30N 98 0 E
Sumatra = Sumatera □, Indonesia 84 B2 0 40N 100 20 E
Sumatra, U.S.A. 152 E5 30 1N 84 59W
Sumba, Angola 115 D2 6 15 S 12 38 E
Sumba, Indonesia 82 C1 9 45 S 119 35 E
Sumba, Selat, Indonesia 82 C1 9 0 S 118 40 E
Sumbawa, Indonesia 85 D5 8 26 S 117 30 E
Sumbawa Besar, Indonesia 85 D5 8 30 S 117 26 E
Sumbe, Angola 115 E2 11 10 S 13 48 E
Sumbu Nat. Park, Zambia 119 D3 8 43 S 30 22 E
Sumburgh Hd., U.K. 22 B7 59 52N 1 17W
Sumdeo, India 93 D8 31 26N 78 44 E
Sumdo, China 93 B8 35 6N 78 41 E
Sumé, Brazil 170 C4 7 39 S 36 55W
Sumedang, Indonesia 85 D3 6 52 S 107 55 E
Sümeg, Hungary 52 D2 46 59N 17 20 E
Sumeih, Sudan 107 F2 9 50N 27 39 E
Šumen = Shumen, Bulgaria 51 C10 43 18N 26 55 E
Sumenep, Indonesia 85 D4 7 1 S 113 52 E
Sumgait = Sumqayıt, Azerbaijan 61 K9 40 34N 49 38 E
Sumisu-Jima, Japan 73 F12 31 27N 140 3 E
Sumiswald, Switz. 32 B5 47 2N 7 44 E
Summer L., U.S.A. 158 E3 42 50N 120 45W
Summerland, Canada 142 D5 49 32N 119 41W
Summerland Key, U.S.A. 153 L8 24 40N 81 27W
Summerside, Canada 141 C7 46 24N 63 47W
Summersville, U.S.A. 148 F5 38 17N 80 51W
Summerton, U.S.A. 152 B9 33 36N 80 20W
Summertown, U.S.A. 152 C7 32 45N 82 16W
Summerville, Ga., U.S.A. 149 H3 34 29N 85 21W
Summerville, S.C., U.S.A. 152 B9 33 1N 80 11W
Summit, U.S.A. 144 E10 63 20N 149 7W
Summit Lake, Canada 142 C4 54 20N 122 40W
Summit Peak, U.S.A. 159 H10 37 21N 106 42W
Sumner, N.Z. 131 D7 43 35 S 172 48 E
Sumner, Ill., U.S.A. 157 F9 38 42N 87 53W
Sumner, Iowa, U.S.A. 156 B4 42 51N 92 6W
Sumner, Wash., U.S.A. 160 C4 47 12N 122 14W
Sumner, L., N.Z. 131 C7 42 42 S 172 15 E
Sumoto, Japan 72 C6 34 21N 134 54 E
Sumpangbinangae, Indonesia 82 B1 4 24 S 119 36 E
Šumperk, Czech Rep. 35 B9 49 59N 16 59 E
Sumprabum, Burma 86 B6 26 33N 97 36 E
Sumqayıt, Azerbaijan 61 K9 40 34N 49 38 E
Sumsar, Kyrgyzstan 65 C5 41 18N 71 19 E
Sumter, U.S.A. 152 B9 33 55N 80 21W
Sumy, Ukraine 59 G8 50 57N 34 50 E
Sun City, S. Africa 116 D4 25 17 S 27 3 E
Sun City, Ariz., U.S.A. 159 K7 33 36N 112 17W
Sun City, Calif., U.S.A. 161 M9 33 42N 117 11W
Sun City Center, U.S.A. 153 H7 27 43N 82 18W
Sun Lakes, U.S.A. 159 K8 33 10N 111 52W
Sun Prairie, U.S.A. 156 A7 43 11N 89 13W
Sun Valley, U.S.A. 158 E6 43 42N 114 21W
Sunagawa, Japan 70 C10 43 29N 141 55 E
Sunan, N. Korea 75 E13 39 15N 125 40 E
Sunart, L., U.K. 22 E3 56 42N 5 43W
Sunburst, U.S.A. 158 B8 48 53N 111 55W
Sunbury, Australia 129 D6 37 35 S 144 44 E
Sunbury, U.S.A. 151 F8 40 52N 76 48W
Sunchales, Argentina 174 C3 30 58 S 61 35W
Suncho Corral, Argentina 174 B3 27 55 S 63 27W
Sunch'ŏn, S. Korea 75 G14 34 52N 127 31 E
Suncook, U.S.A. 151 C13 43 8N 71 27W
Sunda, Selat, Indonesia 84 D3 6 20 S 105 30 E
Sunda Is., Indonesia 62 K14 5 0 S 105 0 E
Sunda Str. = Sunda, Selat, Indonesia 84 D3 6 20 S 105 30 E
Sundance, Canada 143 B10 56 32N 94 4W
Sundance, U.S.A. 154 C2 44 24N 104 23W
Sundar Nagar, India 92 D7 31 32N 76 53 E
Sundarbans, Asia 90 E2 22 0N 89 0 E
Sundargarh, India 94 C7 22 4N 84 5 E
Sundays = Sondags →, S. Africa 116 E4 33 44 S 25 51 E
Sunderland, Canada 150 B5 44 16N 79 4W
Sunderland, U.K. 20 C6 54 55N 1 23W
Sundi Lutete, Dem. Rep. of the Congo 115 C2 4 34 S 14 14 E
Sundown Nat. Park, Australia 127 D5 28 49 S 151 38 E
Sundre, Canada 142 C6 51 49N 114 38W
Sunds, Denmark 17 H3 56 13N 9 1 E
Sundsvall, Sweden 16 B11 62 23N 17 17 E
Sundsvallsbukten, Sweden 16 B11 62 21N 17 25 E
Sung Hei, Vietnam 87 G6 10 20N 106 2 E
Sungai Acheh, Malaysia 87 c 5 8N 100 30 E
Sungai Kolok, Thailand 87 J3 6 2N 101 58 E
Sungai Lembing, Malaysia 87 L4 3 55N 103 3 E
Sungai Petani, Malaysia 87 K3 5 37N 100 30 E
Sungaigerong, Indonesia 84 C2 2 59 S 104 52 E
Sungailiat, Indonesia 84 C3 1 51 S 106 8 E
Sungaipenuh, Indonesia 84 C2 2 1 S 101 20 E
Sungaitiram, Indonesia 85 C5 0 45 S 117 8 E
Sungari = Songhua Jiang →, China 69 B8 47 45N 132 30 E
Sungguminasa, Indonesia 82 C1 5 17 S 119 30 E
Sunghua Chiang = Songhua Jiang →, China 69 B8 47 45N 132 30 E
Sungikai, Sudan 107 E2 12 20N 29 51 E
Sungu, Dem. Rep. of the Congo 114 C3 1 5 S 17 21 E
Sungurlu, Turkey 100 B6 40 12N 34 21 E
Sunja, Croatia 45 C13 45 21N 16 35 E
Sunland Park, U.S.A. 159 L10 31 50N 106 40W
Sunnansjö, Sweden 16 D8 60 13N 14 58 E
Sunndalsøra, Norway 15 E13 62 40N 8 33 E
Sunne, Sweden 16 E7 59 52N 13 5 E
Sunnemo, Sweden 16 E7 59 53N 13 44 E
Sunnfjord, Norway 18 C2 61 35N 5 45 E
Sunnmøre, Norway 18 B3 62 35N 6 30 E
Sunnyside, U.S.A. 158 C3 46 20N 120 0W
Sunnyvale, U.S.A. 160 H4 37 23N 122 2W
Sunset Beach, U.S.A. 145 J13 21 40N 158 3W
Suntar, Russia 67 C12 62 15N 117 30 E
Suntrana, U.S.A. 144 E10 63 52N 148 51W
Sunyani, Ghana 112 D4 7 21N 2 22W
Suō-Nada, Japan 72 D3 33 50N 131 30 E
Suomenselkä, Finland 14 E21 62 52N 24 0 E
Suomussalmi, Finland 14 D23 64 54N 29 10 E
Suoyarvi, Russia 58 A7 62 3N 32 20 E
Supai, U.S.A. 159 H7 36 15N 112 41W
Supamo →, Venezuela 169 B5 6 48N 61 50W
Supaul, India 93 F12 26 10N 86 40 E
Supe, Peru 172 C2 11 0 S 77 30W
Superior, Ariz., U.S.A. 159 K8 33 18N 111 6W
Superior, Mont., U.S.A. 158 C6 47 12N 114 53W
Superior, Nebr., U.S.A. 154 E5 40 1N 98 4W
Superior, Wis., U.S.A. 154 B8 46 44N 92 6W
Superior, L., N. Amer. 140 C2 47 0N 87 0W
Supetar, Croatia 45 E13 43 25N 16 32 E
Suphan Buri, Thailand 86 E3 14 14N 100 10 E
Suphan Dağı, Turkey 101 C10 38 54N 42 48 E
Supiori, Indonesia 83 B5 1 0 S 136 0 E
Supraśl, Poland 55 E10 53 13N 23 19 E
Supraśl →, Poland 55 E9 53 11N 22 57 E
Supung Shuiku, China 75 D13 40 35N 124 50 E
Sūq' Abs, Yemen 98 D3 16 0N 43 12 E
Sūq Suwayq, Si. Arabia 96 E3 24 23N 38 27 E
Suqian, China 75 H10 33 54N 118 8 E
Sūr, Lebanon 103 B4 33 19N 35 16 E
Sūr, Oman 99 B7 22 34N 59 32 E
Sur, C., Chile 172 b 27 12 S 109 26W
Sur, Pt., U.S.A. 160 J5 36 18N 121 54W
Sura →, Russia 60 C8 56 6N 46 0 E
Surab, Pakistan 91 C2 28 25N 66 15 E
Surabaja = Surabaya, Indonesia 85 D4 7 17 S 112 45 E
Surabaya, Indonesia 85 D4 7 17 S 112 45 E
Surahammar, Sweden 16 E10 59 43N 16 13 E
Suraia, Romania 53 E12 45 40N 27 25 E
Surakarta, Indonesia 85 D4 7 35 S 110 48 E
Surakhany, Azerbaijan 61 K10 40 25N 50 1 E
Šurany, Slovak Rep. 35 C11 48 6N 18 10 E
Surat, Australia 127 D4 27 10 S 149 6 E
Surat, India 94 D1 21 12N 72 55 E
Surat Thani, Thailand 87 H2 9 6N 99 20 E
Suratgarh, India 92 E5 29 18N 73 55 E
Suraż, Poland 55 F9 52 57N 22 57 E
Surazh, Belarus 58 E6 55 25N 30 44 E
Surazh, Russia 59 F7 53 5N 32 27 E
Surduc, Romania 53 C8 47 15N 23 25 E
Surduc Pasul, Romania 53 E8 45 21N 23 23 E
Surdulica, Serbia, Yug. 50 D6 42 41N 22 11 E
Surendranagar, India 92 H4 22 45N 71 40 E
Surf, U.S.A. 161 L6 34 41N 120 36W
Surfside, U.S.A. 153 K9 25 53N 80 8W
Surgana, India 94 D1 20 34N 73 37 E
Surgères, France 28 B3 46 7N 0 47W
Surgut, Russia 66 C8 61 14N 73 20 E
Sùria, Spain 40 D6 41 50N 1 45 E
Suriapet, India 94 F4 17 10N 79 40 E
Surigao, Phil. 81 G5 9 47N 125 29 E
Surigao del Norte □, Phil. 81 G5 10 0N 125 40 E
Surigao del Sur □, Phil. 81 G6 8 45N 126 0 E
Surigao Strait, Phil. 81 F5 10 15N 125 23 E
Surin, Thailand 86 E4 14 50N 103 34 E
Surin Nua, Ko, Thailand 87 H1 9 30N 97 55 E
Surinam ■, S. Amer. 169 C6 4 0N 56 0W
Suriname = Surinam ■, S. Amer. 169 C6 4 0N 56 0W
Suriname →, Surinam 169 B6 5 50N 55 15W
Surjagarh, India 94 E5 19 36N 80 25 E
Surkhandarya →, Uzbekistan 65 E3 37 12N 67 20 E
Surma →, Bangla. 90 C3 24 34N 91 14 E
Sūrmaq, Iran 97 D7 31 3N 52 48 E
Sürmene, Turkey 101 B9 41 0N 40 1 E
Surna →, Norway 18 B5 62 59N 8 40 E
Surnadalsøra, Norway 18 B5 62 58N 8 40 E
Surovikino, Russia 61 F6 48 32N 42 55 E
Surrency, U.S.A. 152 D7 31 44N 82 12W
Surrey □, U.K. 21 F7 51 15N 0 31W
Sursand, India 93 F11 26 39N 85 43 E
Sursar →, India 93 F12 26 14N 87 3 E
Sursee, Switz. 32 B6 47 11N 8 6 E
Sursk, Russia 60 D7 53 3N 45 40 E
Surskoye, Russia 60 C8 54 30N 46 44 E
Surt, Libya 108 B3 31 11N 16 39 E
Surt □, Libya 108 B3 30 0N 17 30 E
Surt, Al Hammadah al, Libya 108 C3 30 0N 17 50 E
Surt, Khalīj, Libya 108 B3 31 40N 18 30 E
Surtanahu, Pakistan 92 F4 26 22N 70 0 E
Surte, Sweden 17 G6 57 50N 12 1 E
Surtsey, Iceland 11 D6 63 20N 20 30W
Surubim, Brazil 170 C4 7 50 S 35 45W
Sürüç, Turkey 101 D8 36 58N 38 25 E
Surud Ad, Somali Rep. 120 B3 10 42N 47 9 E
Suruga-Wan, Japan 73 C10 34 45N 138 30 E
Surumu →, Brazil 169 C5 3 22N 60 19W
Susa, Italy 44 C4 45 8N 7 3 E
Suså →, Denmark 17 J5 55 12N 11 42 E
Sušac, Croatia 45 F13 42 46N 16 30 E
Susak, Croatia 45 D11 44 30N 14 18 E
Susaki, Japan 72 D5 33 22N 133 17 E
Susamyrtau, Khrebet = Suusamyr Kyrka Tooloru, Kyrgyzstan 65 B6 42 8N 73 15 E
Süsangerd, Iran 97 D6 31 35N 48 6 E
Susanville, U.S.A. 158 F3 40 25N 120 39W
Susch, Switz. 33 C10 46 46N 10 5 E
Suşehri, Turkey 101 B8 40 10N 38 6 E
Sušice, Czech Rep. 34 B6 49 17N 13 30 E
Susleni, Moldova 53 C13 47 25N 28 59 E
Susner, India 92 H7 23 57N 76 5 E
Susong, China 77 B11 30 10N 116 5 E
Susquehanna, U.S.A. 151 E9 41 57N 75 36W
Susquehanna →, U.S.A. 151 G8 39 33N 76 5W
Susques, Argentina 174 A2 23 35 S 66 25W
Sussex, Canada 141 C6 45 45N 65 37W
Sussex, U.S.A. 151 E10 41 13N 74 37W
Sussex, E. □, U.K. 21 G8 51 0N 0 20 E
Sussex, W. □, U.K. 21 G7 51 0N 0 30W
Sussex Inlet, Australia 129 C9 35 10 S 150 36 E
Sustut →, Canada 142 B3 56 20N 127 30W
Susuman, Russia 67 C15 62 47N 148 10 E
Susunu, Indonesia 83 B4 3 7 S 133 39 E
Susurluk, Turkey 49 B10 39 54N 28 8 E
Susuz, Turkey 101 B10 40 46N 43 8 E
Susz, Poland 54 E6 53 44N 19 20 E
Sütçüler, Turkey 100 D4 37 29N 30 57 E
Şuteşti, Romania 53 E12 45 13N 27 27 E
Sutherland, Australia 129 C9 34 2 S 151 4 E
Sutherland, S. Africa 116 E3 32 24 S 20 40 E
Sutherland, U.S.A. 154 E4 41 10N 101 8W
Sutherland Falls, N.Z. 131 E2 44 48 S 167 46 E
Sutherlin, U.S.A. 158 E2 43 23N 123 19W
Suthri, India 92 H3 23 3N 68 55 E
Sutlej →, Pakistan 91 C3 29 23N 71 3 E
Sutter, U.S.A. 160 F5 39 10N 121 45W
Sutter Creek, U.S.A. 160 G6 38 24N 120 48W
Sutton, Canada 151 A12 45 6N 72 37W
Sutton, N.Z. 131 F5 45 34 S 170 8 E
Sutton, Nebr., U.S.A. 154 E6 40 36N 97 52W
Sutton, W. Va., U.S.A. 148 F5 38 40N 80 43W
Sutton →, Canada 140 A3 55 15N 83 45W
Sutton Coldfield, U.K. 21 E6 52 35N 1 49W
Sutton in Ashfield, U.K. 20 D6 53 8N 1 16W
Sutton L., Canada 140 B3 54 15N 84 42W
Suttor →, Australia 126 C4 21 36 S 147 2 E
Suttsu, Japan 70 C10 42 48N 140 14 E
Sutwik I., U.S.A. 144 H8 56 34N 157 12W
Suusamyr, Kyrgyzstan 65 B6 42 12N 73 58 E
Suusamyr Kyrka Tooloru, Kyrgyzstan 65 B6 42 8N 73 15 E
Suva, Fiji 133 B2 18 6 S 178 30 E
Suva Gora, Macedonia 50 E5 41 45N 21 3 E
Suva Planina, Serbia, Yug. 50 C6 43 10N 22 5 E
Suva Reka, Kosovo, Yug. 50 D4 42 21N 20 50 E
Suvorov, Russia 58 E9 54 7N 36 30 E
Suvorov Is. = Suwarrow Is., Cook Is. 135 J11 15 0 S 163 0W
Suvorovo, Bulgaria 51 C11 43 20N 27 35 E
Suwa, Japan 73 A10 36 2N 138 8 E
Suwa-Ko, Japan 73 A10 36 3N 138 5 E
Suwałki, Poland 54 D9 54 8N 22 59 E
Suwana, Indonesia 79 K18 8 44 S 115 36 E
Suwanee, U.S.A. 152 A5 34 3N 84 4W
Suwannaphum, Thailand 86 E4 15 33N 103 47 E
Suwannee, U.S.A. 153 F6 29 20N 83 9W
Suwannee →, U.S.A. 149 L4 29 17N 83 10W
Suwannee Sd., U.S.A. 153 F6 29 20N 83 15W
Suwanose-Jima, Japan 71 K4 29 38N 129 43 E
Suwarrow Is., Cook Is. 135 J11 15 0 S 163 0W
Suwayq aş Şuqban, Iraq 96 D5 31 32N 46 7 E
Suweis, Khalîg el, Egypt 106 J8 28 40N 33 0 E
Suweis, Qanâ es, Egypt 106 H8 31 0N 32 20 E
Suwŏn, S. Korea 75 F14 37 17N 127 1 E
Suzak = Sosaq, Kazakstan 65 A4 44 9N 68 27 E
Suzaka, Japan 73 A10 36 39N 138 19 E
Suzdal, Russia 58 D11 56 29N 40 26 E
Suzhou, Anhui, China 74 H9 33 41N 116 59 E
Suzhou, Jiangsu, China 77 B13 31 19N 120 38 E
Suzu, Japan 71 F8 37 25N 137 17 E
Suzu-Misaki, Japan 71 F8 37 31N 137 21 E
Suzuka, Japan 73 C8 34 55N 136 36 E
Suzuka-Sammyaku, Japan 73 B8 35 5N 136 30 E
Suzzara, Italy 44 D7 44 59N 10 45 E
Svalbard, Arctic 6 B8 78 0N 17 0 E
Svalbarð, Norður-þingeyjarsýsla, Iceland 11 A11 66 12N 15 43W
Svalbarð, Suður-þingeyjarsýsla, Iceland 11 B8 65 45N 18 5W
Svalöv, Sweden 17 J7 55 57N 13 8 E
Svaneke, Denmark 17 J9 55 8N 15 8 E
Svängsta, Sweden 17 H8 56 16N 14 47 E
Svanskog, Sweden 16 E6 59 11N 12 33 E
Svappavaara, Sweden 14 C19 67 40N 21 3 E
Svärdsjö, Sweden 16 D9 60 45N 15 54 E
Svarstad, Norway 18 E6 59 27N 9 56 E
Svartå, Sweden 16 E8 59 8N 14 32 E
Svartárkot, Iceland 11 B9 65 20N 17 15W
Svartevatn, Norway 18 E3 59 10N 6 56 E
Svartisen, Norway 14 C15 66 40N 13 50 E
Svartvik, Sweden 16 B11 62 19N 17 24 E
Svatove, Ukraine 59 H10 49 22N 38 15 E
Svatovo = Svatove, Ukraine 59 H10 49 22N 38 15 E
Svatsum, Norway 18 C6 61 20N 9 50 E
Svay Chek, Cambodia 86 F4 13 48N 102 58 E
Svay Rieng, Cambodia 87 G5 11 9N 105 45 E
Svealand □, Sweden 16 D9 60 20N 15 0 E
Svedala, Sweden 17 J7 55 30N 13 15 E
Sveg, Sweden 16 B8 62 2N 14 21 E
Sveindal, Norway 18 F4 58 29N 7 30 E
Sveinseyri, Iceland 11 B3 65 38N 23 51W
Sveio, Norway 18 E2 59 33N 5 23 E
Svelgen, Norway 18 C2 61 46N 5 17 E
Svelvik, Norway 18 E7 59 37N 10 24 E
Svendborg, Denmark 17 J4 55 4N 10 35 E
Svene, Norway 18 E6 59 45N 9 31 E
Svenljunga, Sweden 17 G7 57 29N 13 5 E
Svenstavik, Sweden 16 B8 62 45N 14 26 E
Svenstrup, Denmark 17 H3 56 58N 9 50 E
Sverdlovsk = Yekaterinburg, Russia 64 C8 56 50N 60 30 E
Sverdlovsk, Ukraine 59 H10 48 5N 39 47 E
Sverdrup Is., Canada 6 B3 79 0N 97 0W
Svetac, Croatia 45 E12 43 3N 15 43 E
Sveti Nikola, Prokhad, Europe 50 C6 43 27N 22 6 E
Sveti Nikole, Macedonia 50 E5 41 51N 21 56 E
Sveti Rok, Croatia 45 D12 44 22N 15 39 E

Talikota 287

Svetlaya, *Russia* 70 A9 46 33N 138 18 E
Svetlogorsk = Svyetlahorsk, *Belarus* 59 F5 52 38N 29 46 E
Svetlograd, *Russia* 61 H6 45 25N 42 58 E
Svetlovodsk = Svitlovodsk, *Ukraine* 59 H7 49 2N 33 13 E
Svetlyy, *Russia* 64 F8 50 48N 60 51 E
Svidník, *Slovak Rep.* 35 B14 49 20N 21 37 E
Svignaskarð, *Iceland* 11 C5 64 40N 21 42W
Svilaja Planina, *Croatia* 45 E13 43 49N 16 31 E
Svilajnac, *Serbia, Yug.* 50 B5 44 15N 21 11 E
Svilengrad, *Bulgaria* 51 E10 41 49N 26 12 E
Svinafell, *Iceland* 11 D10 63 59N 16 51W
Svir →, *Russia* 58 B7 60 30N 32 48 E
Sviritsa, *Russia* 58 B7 60 29N 32 51 E
Svishtov, *Bulgaria* 51 C9 43 36N 25 23 E
Svislach, *Belarus* 59 F3 53 3N 24 2 E
Svitava →, *Czech Rep.* 35 B9 49 11N 16 37 E
Svitavy, *Czech Rep.* 35 B9 49 47N 16 28 E
Svitlovodsk, *Ukraine* 59 H7 49 2N 33 13 E
Svobodnyy, *Russia* 67 D13 51 20N 128 0 E
Svoge, *Bulgaria* 50 D7 42 59N 23 23 E
Svolvær, *Norway* 14 B16 68 15N 14 34 E
Svorkmo, *Norway* 18 A6 63 10N 9 46 E
Svoronáta, *Greece* 39 C2 38 7N 20 31 E
Svratka →, *Czech Rep.* 35 B9 49 11N 16 38 E
Svrljig, *Serbia, Yug.* 50 C6 43 25N 22 6 E
Svullrya, *Norway* 18 D9 60 25N 12 23 E
Svyetlahorsk, *Belarus* 59 F5 52 38N 29 46 E
Swa, *Burma* 90 F6 19 15N 96 17 E
Swa Tende, *Dem. Rep. of the Congo* 115 D3 7 9S 17 7 E
Swabian Alps = Schwäbische Alb, *Germany* 31 G5 48 20N 9 30 E
Swainsboro, *U.S.A.* 152 C7 32 36N 82 20W
Swakop →, *Namibia* 116 C2 22 38 S 14 36 E
Swakopmund, *Namibia* 116 C1 22 37 S 14 30 E
Swale →, *U.K.* 20 C6 54 5N 1 20W
Swamihalli, *India* 95 G3 14 52N 76 38 E
Swan →, *Australia* 125 F2 32 3 S 115 45 E
Swan →, *Canada* 143 C8 52 30N 100 45W
Swan Hill, *Australia* 128 C5 35 20 S 143 33 E
Swan Hills, *Canada* 142 C5 54 43N 115 24W
Swan Is. = Santanilla, Is., *Honduras* 164 C3 17 22N 83 57W
Swan L., *Canada* 143 C8 52 30N 100 40W
Swan Peak, *U.S.A.* 158 C7 47 43N 113 38W
Swan Ra., *U.S.A.* 158 C7 48 0N 113 45W
Swan Reach, *Australia* 128 C3 34 35 S 139 37 E
Swan River, *Canada* 143 C8 52 10N 101 16W
Swanage, *U.K.* 21 G6 50 36N 1 58W
Swansea, *N.S.W., Australia* 129 B9 33 3 S 151 35 E
Swansea, *Tas., Australia* 127 G4 42 8 S 148 4 E
Swansea, *Canada* 150 C5 43 38N 79 28W
Swansea, *U.K.* 21 F4 51 37N 3 57W
Swansea, *U.S.A.* 152 B8 33 44N 81 6W
Swansea □, *U.K.* 21 F3 51 38N 4 3W
Swanton, *U.S.A.* 157 C13 41 35N 83 53W
Swar →, *Pakistan* 93 B5 34 40N 72 5 E
Swartberge, *S. Africa* 116 E3 33 20 S 22 0 E
Swartmodder, *S. Africa* 116 D3 28 1 S 20 32 E
Swartnossob →, *Namibia* 116 C2 23 8 S 18 42 E
Swartruggens, *S. Africa* 116 D4 25 39 S 26 42 E
Swarzędz, *Poland* 55 F4 52 25N 17 4 E
Swastika, *Canada* 140 C3 48 7N 80 6W
Swatow = Shantou, *China* 77 F11 23 18N 116 40 E
Swaziland ■, *Africa* 117 D5 26 30 S 31 30 E
Sweden ■, *Europe* 15 G16 57 0N 15 0 E
Swedru, *Ghana* 113 D4 5 32N 0 41W
Sweet Home, *U.S.A.* 158 D2 44 24N 122 44W
Sweet Springs, *U.S.A.* 156 F3 38 58N 93 25W
Sweetgrass, *U.S.A.* 158 B8 48 59N 111 58W
Sweetwater, *Nev., U.S.A.* 160 G7 38 27N 119 9W
Sweetwater, *Tenn., U.S.A.* 149 H3 35 36N 84 28W
Sweetwater, *Tex., U.S.A.* 155 J4 32 28N 100 25W
Sweetwater →, *U.S.A.* 158 E10 42 31N 107 2W
Swellendam, *S. Africa* 116 E3 34 1 S 20 26 E
Swider →, *Poland* 55 F8 52 6N 21 14 E
Świdnica, *Poland* 55 H3 50 50N 16 30 E
Świdnik, *Poland* 55 G9 51 13N 22 39 E
Świdwin, *Poland* 54 E2 53 47N 15 49 E
Świebodzice, *Poland* 55 H3 50 51N 16 20 E
Świebodzin, *Poland* 55 F2 52 15N 15 31 E
Świecie, *Poland* 54 E5 53 25N 18 30 E
Świerzawa, *Poland* 55 G2 51 1N 15 54 E
Świętokrzyskie □, *Poland* 55 H7 50 45N 20 45 E
Świętokrzyskie, Góry, *Poland* 55 H7 51 0N 20 30 E
Swift Current, *Canada* 143 C7 50 20N 107 45W
Swiftcurrent →, *Canada* 143 C7 50 38N 107 44W
Swifts Creek, *Australia* 129 D7 37 17 S 147 44 E
Swilly, L., *Ireland* 23 A4 55 12N 7 33W
Swindon, *U.K.* 21 F6 51 34N 1 46W
Swindon □, *U.K.* 21 F6 51 34N 1 46W
Swinemünde = Świnoujście, *Poland* 54 E1 53 54N 14 16 E
Swinford, *Ireland* 23 C3 53 57N 8 58W
Świnoujście, *Poland* 54 E1 53 54N 14 16 E
Switzerland ■, *Europe* 32 D6 46 30N 8 0 E
Swords, *Ireland* 23 C5 53 28N 6 13W
Swoyerville, *U.S.A.* 151 E9 41 18N 75 53W
Syasstroy, *Russia* 58 B7 60 9N 32 33 E
Sycamore, *Ill., U.S.A.* 157 C8 41 59N 88 41W
Sycamore, *Ohio, U.S.A.* 157 D13 40 57N 83 10W
Sychevka, *Russia* 58 E8 55 59N 34 16 E
Syców, *Poland* 55 G4 51 19N 17 40 E
Sydenham →, *Canada* 150 D2 42 33N 82 25W
Sydney, *Australia* 129 B9 33 53 S 151 10 E
Sydney, *Canada* 141 C7 46 7N 60 7W
Sydney L., *Canada* 143 C10 50 41N 94 25W
Sydney Mines, *Canada* 141 C7 46 18N 60 15W
Sydprøven = Alluitsup Paa, *Greenland* 10 E6 60 30N 45 35W
Sydra, G. of = Surt, Khalīj, *Libya* 108 B3 31 40N 18 30 E
Syeverodonetsk, *Ukraine* 59 H10 48 58N 38 35 E
Syfteland, *Norway* 18 D2 60 14N 5 27 E
Syke, *Germany* 30 C4 52 55N 8 50 E
Sykesville, *U.S.A.* 150 E6 41 3N 78 50W
Sykkylven, *Norway* 18 B3 62 23N 6 35 E
Syktyvkar, *Russia* 56 B9 61 45N 50 40 E
Sylacauga, *U.S.A.* 152 B3 33 10N 86 15W
Sylarna, *Sweden* 14 E15 63 2N 12 13 E
Sylhet, *Bangla.* 90 C3 24 54N 91 52 E
Sylt, *Germany* 30 A4 54 54N 8 22 E
Sylte, *Norway* 18 B4 62 18N 7 17 E
Sylva →, *Russia* 64 B6 58 0N 56 54 E
Sylvan Beach, *U.S.A.* 151 C9 43 12N 75 44W
Sylvan Lake, *Canada* 142 C6 52 20N 114 3W
Sylvania, *Ga., U.S.A.* 152 B7 32 45N 81 38W
Sylvania, *Ohio, U.S.A.* 157 C13 41 43N 83 42W
Sylvester, *U.S.A.* 152 D6 31 32N 83 50W
Sym, *Russia* 66 C9 60 20N 88 18 E
Symón, *Mexico* 162 C4 24 42N 102 35W
Synelnykove, *Ukraine* 59 H8 48 25N 35 30 E
Synnfjell, *Norway* 18 C6 61 5N 9 46 E
Synnott Ra., *Australia* 124 C4 16 30 S 125 20 E
Syracuse, *Ind., U.S.A.* 157 C11 41 25N 85 45W
Syracuse, *Kans., U.S.A.* 155 G4 37 59N 101 45W
Syracuse, *N.Y., U.S.A.* 151 C8 43 3N 76 9W
Syracuse, *Nebr., U.S.A.* 154 E6 40 39N 96 11W
Syrdarya, *Uzbekistan* 65 C4 40 50N 68 40 E
Syrdarya →, *Kazakstan* 66 E7 46 3N 61 0 E
Syria ■, *Asia* 101 E8 35 0N 38 0 E
Syriam, *Burma* 90 G6 16 44N 96 19 E
Syrian Desert = Shām, Bādiyat ash, *Asia* 96 C3 32 0N 40 0 E
Sysert, *Russia* 64 C8 56 29N 60 49 E
Sysslebäck, *Sweden* 16 D6 60 44N 12 52 E
Syvde, *Norway* 18 B2 62 5N 5 44 E
Syzran, *Russia* 60 D9 53 12N 48 30 E
Szabolcs-Szatmár-Bereg □, *Hungary* 52 B6 48 2N 21 45 E
Szadek, *Poland* 55 G5 51 41N 18 59 E
Szamocin, *Poland* 55 E4 53 2N 17 7 E
Szamos →, *Hungary* 52 B7 48 7N 22 20 E
Szamotuły, *Poland* 55 F3 52 37N 16 33 E
Száraz →, *Hungary* 52 D6 46 10N 21 15 E
Szarvas, *Hungary* 52 D5 46 50N 20 38 E
Százhalombatta, *Hungary* 52 C3 47 20N 18 58 E
Szczawnica, *Poland* 55 J7 49 26N 20 30 E
Szczebrzeszyn, *Poland* 55 H9 50 42N 22 59 E
Szczecin, *Poland* 54 E1 53 27N 14 27 E
Szczecinek, *Poland* 54 E3 53 43N 16 41 E
Szczeciński, Zalew = Stettiner Haff, *Germany* 30 B10 53 47N 14 15 E
Szczekociny, *Poland* 55 H6 50 38N 19 48 E
Szczucin, *Poland* 55 H8 50 18N 21 4 E
Szczuczyn, *Poland* 54 E9 53 36N 22 19 E
Szczyrk, *Poland* 55 J6 49 43N 19 2 E
Szczytna, *Poland* 55 H3 50 25N 16 28 E
Szczytno, *Poland* 54 E7 53 33N 21 0 E
Szechwan = Sichuan □, *China* 76 B5 30 30N 103 0 E
Szécsény, *Hungary* 52 B4 48 7N 19 30 E
Szeged, *Hungary* 52 D5 46 16N 20 10 E
Szeghalom, *Hungary* 52 C6 47 1N 21 10 E
Székesfehérvár, *Hungary* 52 C3 47 15N 18 25 E
Szekszárd, *Hungary* 52 D3 46 22N 18 42 E
Szendrő, *Hungary* 52 B5 48 24N 20 41 E
Szentendre, *Hungary* 52 C4 47 39N 19 4 E
Szentes, *Hungary* 52 D5 46 39N 20 21 E
Szentgotthárd, *Hungary* 52 D1 46 58N 16 19 E
Szentlőrinc, *Hungary* 52 D3 46 3N 18 1 E
Szerencs, *Hungary* 52 B6 48 10N 21 12 E
Szigetszentmiklós, *Hungary* 52 C4 47 21N 19 3 E
Szigetvár, *Hungary* 52 D2 46 3N 17 46 E
Szikszó, *Hungary* 52 B5 48 12N 20 56 E
Szklarska Poreba, *Poland* 55 H2 50 50N 15 33 E
Szkwa →, *Poland* 55 E8 53 11N 21 43 E
Szlichtyngowa, *Poland* 55 G3 51 42N 16 15 E
Szob, *Hungary* 52 C3 47 48N 18 53 E
Szolnok, *Hungary* 52 C5 47 10N 20 15 E
Szombathely, *Hungary* 52 C1 47 14N 16 38 E
Szprotawa, *Poland* 55 G2 51 33N 15 35 E
Sztum, *Poland* 54 E6 53 55N 19 1 E
Sztutowo, *Poland* 54 D6 54 20N 19 15 E
Szubin, *Poland* 55 E4 53 1N 17 45 E
Szydłowiec, *Poland* 55 G7 51 15N 20 51 E
Szypliszki, *Poland* 54 D10 54 17N 23 2 E

T

Ta Khli Khok, *Thailand* 86 E3 15 18N 100 20 E
Ta Lai, *Vietnam* 87 G6 11 24N 107 23 E
Tab, *Hungary* 52 D3 46 44N 18 2 E
Tabacal, *Argentina* 174 A3 23 15 S 64 15W
Tabaco, *Phil.* 80 E4 13 22N 123 44 E
Tabagné, *Ivory C.* 112 D4 7 59N 3 4W
Ţābah, *Si. Arabia* 96 E4 26 55N 42 38 E
Tabajara, *Brazil* 173 B5 8 56 S 62 8W
Tabalo, *Papua N. G.* 132 A5 1 24 S 149 40 E
Tabalos, *Peru* 172 B2 6 26 S 76 37W
Tabanan, *Indonesia* 79 K18 8 32 S 115 8 E
Tabankort, *Niger* 113 B5 17 44N 0 20 E
Tabar I., *Papua N. G.* 132 B7 2 56 S 152 0 E
Tabar Is., *Papua N. G.* 132 B7 2 50 S 152 0 E
Tabarka, *Tunisia* 108 A1 36 56N 8 46 E
Ţabas, *Khorāsān, Iran* 97 C9 32 48N 60 12 E
Ţabas, *Khorāsān, Iran* 97 C8 33 35N 56 55 E
Tabasará, Serranía de, *Panama* 164 E3 8 35N 81 40W
Tabasco □, *Mexico* 163 D6 17 45N 93 30W
Tabāsīn, *Iran* 97 D8 31 12N 57 54 E
Tabatinga, *Brazil* 172 A4 4 16 S 69 56W
Tabatinga, Serra da, *Brazil* 170 D3 10 30 S 44 0W
Tabayin, *Burma* 90 D5 22 42N 95 20 E
Tabelbala, Kahal de, *Algeria* 111 C4 28 47N 2 0W
Tabelembila, *Algeria* 111 D5 24 43N 4 16 E
Taber, *Canada* 142 D6 49 47N 112 8W
Taberg, *Sweden* 17 G8 57 40N 14 6 E
Taberg, *U.S.A.* 151 C9 43 18N 75 37W
Tabi, *Angola* 115 D2 8 10 S 13 18 E
Tabira, *Brazil* 170 C4 7 35 S 37 33W
Tabla, *Niger* 113 C5 13 46N 3 1 E
Tablas I., *Phil.* 80 E4 12 25N 122 2 E
Tablas Strait, *Phil.* 80 E3 12 40N 121 48 E
Table, Pte. de la, *Réunion* 121 c 21 14 S 55 48 E
Table B. = Tafelbaai, *S. Africa* 116 E2 33 35 S 18 25 E
Table B., *Canada* 141 B8 53 40N 56 25W
Table C., *N.Z.* 130 F7 39 6 S 178 0 E
Table Grove, *U.S.A.* 156 D6 40 20N 90 27W
Table I., *Burma* 95 G11 14 12N 93 22 E
Table Mt., *S. Africa* 116 E2 34 0 S 18 22 E
Table Rock L., *U.S.A.* 155 G8 36 36N 93 19W
Tabletop, Mt., *Australia* 126 C4 23 24 S 147 11 E
Tabocal, *Brazil* 169 D6 2 42 S 57 40W
Tábor, *Czech Rep.* 34 B7 49 25N 14 39 E
Tabora, *Tanzania* 118 D3 5 2 S 32 50 E
Tabora □, *Tanzania* 118 D3 5 0 S 33 0 E
Taboshar, *Tajikistan* 65 C4 40 34N 69 38 E
Tabou, *Ivory C.* 112 E3 4 30N 7 20W
Tabrīz, *Iran* 101 C12 38 7N 46 20 E
Tabuaeran, *Kiribati* 135 G12 3 51N 159 22W
Tabubil, *Papua N. G.* 132 C1 5 20 S 141 15 E
Tabuenca, *Spain* 40 D3 41 42N 1 33W
Tabuk, *Phil.* 80 C3 17 24N 121 25 E
Tabūk, *Si. Arabia* 96 D3 28 23N 36 36 E
Tabwemasana, Mt., *Vanuatu* 133 E4 15 20 S 166 44 E
Täby, *Sweden* 16 E12 59 28N 18 4 E
Tacámbaro de Codallos, *Mexico* 162 D4 19 14N 101 28W
Tacarigua, Laguna de, *Venezuela* 168 A4 10 15N 65 50W
Tacheng, *China* 68 B3 46 40N 82 58 E
Tach'i, *Taiwan* 77 E13 24 46N 121 0 E
Tachia, *Taiwan* 77 E13 24 25N 120 28 E
Tachibana-Wan, *Japan* 72 E2 32 45N 130 7 E
Tachikawa, *Japan* 73 B11 35 42N 139 25 E
Tach'ing Shan = Daqing Shan, *China* 74 D6 40 40N 111 0 E
Táchira □, *Venezuela* 168 B3 8 7N 72 15W
Tachov, *Czech Rep.* 34 B5 49 47N 12 39 E
Tácina →, *Italy* 47 D9 38 57N 16 55 E
Tacloban, *Phil.* 81 F5 11 15N 124 58 E
Tacna, *Peru* 172 D3 18 0 S 70 20W
Tacna □, *Peru* 172 D3 17 40 S 70 20W
Tacoma, *U.S.A.* 160 C4 47 14N 122 26W
Tacuarembó, *Uruguay* 175 C4 31 45 S 56 0W
Tacurong, *Phil.* 81 H5 6 40N 124 41 E
Tacutu →, *Brazil* 169 C5 3 1N 60 29W
Tada-u, *Burma* 90 E5 21 49N 95 58 E
Tadahadi, *Solomon Is.* 133 N11 10 18 S 161 35 E
Tademaït, Plateau du, *Algeria* 111 C5 28 30N 2 30 E
Tadent, O. →, *Algeria* 111 D6 22 25N 6 40 E
Tadéra, *Niger* 111 D6 20 29N 8 18 E
Tadine, *N. Cal.* 133 U21 21 33 S 167 52 E
Tadio, L., *Ivory C.* 112 D3 5 10N 5 15W
Tadjerdjeri, O. →, *Algeria* 111 C6 26 0N 8 0 E
Tadjerouna, *Algeria* 111 B5 33 31N 2 3 E
Tadjettaret, O. →, *Algeria* 111 D6 21 20N 7 22 E
Tadjmout, *Laghouat, Algeria* 111 B5 33 52N 2 30 E
Tadjmout, *Saoura, Algeria* 111 C5 25 37N 3 48 E
Tadjoura, *Djibouti* 107 E5 11 50N 42 55 E
Tadjoura, Golfe de, *Djibouti* 107 E5 11 50N 43 0 E
Tadmor, *N.Z.* 131 B7 41 27 S 172 45 E
Tadotsu, *Japan* 72 C5 34 16N 133 45 E
Tadoule, L., *Canada* 143 B9 58 36N 98 20W
Tadoussac, *Canada* 141 C6 48 11N 69 42W
Tadpatri, *India* 95 G4 14 55N 78 1 E
Tadrés, Réserve Totale de Faune du, *Niger* 113 B6 16 0N 7 10 E
Tadzhikistan = Tajikistan ■, *Asia* 66 F8 38 30N 70 0 E
Taechŏn-ni, *S. Korea* 75 F14 36 21N 126 36 E
Taegu, *S. Korea* 75 G15 35 50N 128 37 E
Taegwan, *N. Korea* 75 D13 40 13N 125 12 E
Taejŏn, *S. Korea* 75 F14 36 20N 127 28 E
Taen, Ko, *Thailand* 87 b 9 22N 99 57 E
Tafalla, *Spain* 40 C3 42 30N 1 41W
Tafar, *Sudan* 107 F2 6 52N 28 15 E
Tafassasset, O. →, *Algeria* 111 D6 22 0N 9 57 E
Tafelbaai, *S. Africa* 116 E2 33 35 S 18 25 E
Tafelney, C., *Morocco* 110 B3 31 3N 9 51W
Tafermaar, *Indonesia* 83 C4 6 47 S 134 10 E
Taffermit, *Morocco* 110 C3 29 37N 9 15W
Tafí Viejo, *Argentina* 174 B2 26 43 S 65 17W
Tafīhān, *Iran* 97 D7 29 25N 52 39 E
Tafilalet, *Morocco* 110 B4 31 20N 4 45W
Tafiré, *Ivory C.* 112 D3 9 4N 5 4W
Tafjord, *Norway* 18 B4 62 14N 7 24 E
Tafnidilt, *Morocco* 110 C2 28 47N 10 58W
Tafo, *Ghana* 113 D4 6 15N 0 20W
Tafraoute, *Morocco* 110 C3 29 50N 8 58W
Tafresh, *Iran* 97 C6 34 45N 49 57 E
Taft, *Iran* 97 D7 31 45N 54 14 E
Taft, *Phil.* 81 F5 11 57N 125 30 E
Taft, *U.S.A.* 161 K7 35 8N 119 28W
Taftān, Kūh-e, *Iran* 97 D9 28 40N 61 0 E
Tafwap, *India* 95 L11 7 23N 93 43 E
Taga, *Samoa* 133 W23 13 46 S 172 28W
Taga Dzong, *Bhutan* 90 B2 27 5N 89 55 E
Tagana-an, *Phil.* 81 G5 9 42N 125 35 E
Taganrog, *Russia* 59 J10 47 12N 38 50 E
Taganrogskiy Zaliv, *Russia* 59 J10 47 0N 38 30 E
Tagânt, *Mauritania* 112 B2 18 20N 11 0W
Tagap Ga, *Burma* 90 B6 26 56N 96 13 E
Tagatay, *Phil.* 80 D3 14 6N 120 56 E
Tagauayan I., *Phil.* 81 F3 10 58N 121 13 E
Tagaung, *Burma* 90 D6 23 30N 96 2 E
Tagawa, *Japan* 72 D2 33 38N 130 51 E
Tagbilaran, *Phil.* 81 G5 9 39N 123 51 E
Tage, *Papua N. G.* 132 D2 6 19 S 143 20 E
Tàggia, *Italy* 44 E4 43 52N 7 51 E
Taghzout, *Morocco* 110 B4 33 30N 4 49W
Tagish, *Canada* 142 A2 60 19N 134 16W
Tagish L., *Canada* 142 A2 60 10N 134 20W
Tagkawayan, *Phil.* 80 E4 13 58N 122 32 E
Tagliacozzo, *Italy* 45 F10 42 4N 13 14 E
Tagliamento →, *Italy* 45 C10 45 38N 13 6 E
Tàglio di Po, *Italy* 45 D9 45 0N 12 12 E
Tagna, *Colombia* 168 D3 2 24 S 70 37W
Tago, *Phil.* 81 G6 9 2N 126 13 E
Tago, Mt., *Phil.* 81 G5 8 23N 125 5 E
Tagomago, *Spain* 38 C2 39 2N 1 39 E
Tagourāret, *Mauritania* 112 B3 17 45N 7 45W
Taguatinga, *Brazil* 171 D3 12 16 S 42 26W
Tagudin, *Phil.* 80 C3 16 56N 120 27 E
Taguenout Haggueret, *Mali* 111 D4 21 14N 0 48W
Tagula, *Papua N. G.* 132 F7 11 22 S 153 15 E
Tagula I., *Papua N. G.* 132 F7 11 30 S 153 30 E
Tagum, *Phil.* 81 H5 7 33N 125 53 E
Tagus = Tejo →, *Europe* 43 F2 38 40N 9 24W
Tahakopa, *N.Z.* 131 G4 46 30 S 169 23 E
Tahala, *Morocco* 110 B4 34 0N 4 28W
Tahan, Gunong, *Malaysia* 87 K4 4 34N 102 17 E
Tahānah-ye sūr Gol, *Afghan.* 91 C2 31 43N 67 53 E
Tahara, *Japan* 73 C9 34 40N 137 16 E
Tahat, *Algeria* 111 D6 23 18N 5 33 E
Tāherī, *Iran* 97 E7 27 43N 52 20 E
Tahiti, *Pac. Oc.* 133 S16 17 37 S 149 27W
Tahlab →, *Pakistan* 91 C1 28 9N 62 45 E
Tahlequah, *U.S.A.* 155 H7 35 55N 94 58W
Tahoe, L., *U.S.A.* 160 G6 39 6N 120 2W
Tahoe City, *U.S.A.* 160 F6 39 10N 120 9W
Tahoka, *U.S.A.* 155 J4 33 10N 101 48W
Taholah, *U.S.A.* 160 C2 47 21N 124 17W
Tahora, *N.Z.* 130 F3 39 2 S 174 49 E
Tahoua, *Niger* 113 C6 14 57N 5 16 E
Tahrūd, *Iran* 97 D8 29 26N 57 49 E
Tahsis, *Canada* 142 D3 49 55N 126 40W
Tahta, *Egypt* 106 B3 26 44N 31 32 E
Tahtaköprü, *Turkey* 51 G13 39 57N 29 39 E
Tahtalı Dağları, *Turkey* 100 C7 38 20N 36 0 E
Tahuamanu →, *Bolivia* 172 C4 11 6 S 67 36W
Tahulandang, *Indonesia* 82 A3 2 27N 125 23 E
Tahuna, *Indonesia* 82 A3 3 38N 125 30 E
Taï, *Ivory C.* 112 D3 5 55N 7 30W
Taï, Parc Nat. de, *Ivory C.* 112 D3 5 25N 7 5W
Tai Au Mun, *China* 69 G11 22 18N 114 17 E
Tai Hu, *China* 77 B12 31 5N 120 10 E
Tai Mo Shan, *China* 69 G11 22 25N 114 7 E
Tai O, *China* 69 G10 22 15N 113 52 E
Tai Pang Wan, *H.K.* 69 F11 22 33N 114 24 E
Tai Po, *China* 69 G11 22 27N 114 10 E
Tai Shan, *China* 75 F9 36 25N 117 20 E
Tai'an, *China* 75 F9 36 12N 117 8 E
Taiarapu, Presq. de, *Tahiti* 133 S16 17 47 S 149 14W
Taibei = T'aipei, *Taiwan* 77 E13 25 2N 121 30 E
Taibique, *Canary Is.* 9 e1 27 42N 17 58W
Taibus Qi, *China* 74 D8 41 54N 115 22 E
Taicang, *China* 77 B13 31 30N 121 5 E
T'aichung, *Taiwan* 77 E13 24 9N 120 37 E
Taieri →, *N.Z.* 131 G5 46 3 S 170 12 E
Taiga Madema, *Libya* 108 D3 23 46N 15 25 E
Taigu, *China* 74 F7 37 28N 112 30 E
Taihang Shan, *China* 74 G7 36 0N 113 30 E
Taihape, *N.Z.* 130 F4 39 41 S 175 48 E
Taihe, *Anhui, China* 74 H8 33 20N 115 42 E
Taihe, *Jiangxi, China* 77 D10 26 47N 114 52 E
Taihu, *China* 77 B11 30 22N 116 20 E
Taijiang, *China* 76 D7 26 39N 108 21 E
Taikang, *China* 74 G8 34 5N 114 50 E
Taikkyi, *Burma* 90 G6 17 20N 96 0 E
Tailem Bend, *Australia* 128 C3 35 12 S 139 29 E
Tailfingen, *Germany* 31 G5 48 15N 9 1 E
Tailuko, *Taiwan* 77 E13 24 9N 121 37 E
Taimyr Peninsula = Taymyr, Poluostrov, *Russia* 67 B11 75 0N 100 0 E
Tain, *U.K.* 22 D4 57 49N 4 4W
T'ainan, *Taiwan* 77 F13 23 0N 120 10 E
Taínaron, Ákra, *Greece* 48 E4 36 22N 22 27 E
Tainggyo, *Burma* 90 G5 18 49N 94 29 E
Taining, *China* 77 D11 26 54N 117 9 E
Taiobeiras, *Brazil* 171 E3 15 49 S 42 14W
Taipa, *China* 69 G10 22 10N 113 35 E
T'aipei, *Taiwan* 77 E13 25 2N 121 30 E
Taiping, *China* 77 B12 30 15N 118 6 E
Taiping, *Malaysia* 87 K3 4 51N 100 44 E
Taipingzhen, *China* 74 H6 33 35N 111 42 E
Taipu, *Brazil* 170 C4 5 37 S 35 36W
Tairbeart = Tarbert, *U.K.* 22 D2 57 54N 6 49W
Tairenpokpi, *India* 90 C4 24 39N 93 40 E
Tairua, *N.Z.* 130 D4 37 0 S 175 51 E
Taisha, *Japan* 72 B4 35 24N 132 40 E
Taishan, *China* 77 F9 22 14N 112 41 E
Taishun, *China* 77 D12 27 30N 119 42 E
Taita Hills, *Kenya* 118 C4 3 25 S 38 15 E
Taitao, C., *Chile* 176 C1 45 53 S 75 5W
Taitao, Pen. de, *Chile* 176 C2 46 30 S 75 0W
T'aitung, *Taiwan* 77 F13 22 43N 121 4 E
Taivalkoski, *Finland* 14 D23 65 33N 28 12 E
Taiwan ■, *Asia* 77 F13 23 30N 121 0 E
Taiwan Strait, *Asia* 77 E12 24 40N 120 0 E
Taixing, *China* 77 A13 32 11N 120 0 E
Taiyara, *Sudan* 107 E3 13 12N 30 47 E
Taïyetos Óros, *Greece* 48 D4 37 0N 22 23 E
Taiyiba, *Israel* 103 C4 32 36N 35 27 E
Taiyuan, *China* 74 F7 37 52N 112 33 E
Taizhong = T'aichung, *Taiwan* 77 E13 24 9N 120 37 E
Taizhou, *China* 77 A12 32 28N 119 55 E
Taizhou Liedao, *China* 77 C13 28 30N 121 55 E
Ta'izz, *Yemen* 98 D4 13 35N 44 2 E
Tājābād, *Iran* 97 D7 30 2N 54 24 E
Tajapuru, Furo do, *Brazil* 170 B1 1 50 S 50 25W
Tajarḥī, *Libya* 108 D2 24 21N 14 28 E
Tajikistan ■, *Asia* 66 F8 38 30N 70 0 E
Tajima, *Japan* 71 F9 37 12N 139 46 E
Tajimi, *Japan* 73 B9 35 19N 137 8 E
Tajo = Tejo →, *Europe* 43 F2 38 40N 9 24W
Tajrīsh, *Iran* 97 C6 35 48N 51 25 E
Tājūrā, *Libya* 108 B2 32 51N 13 21 E
Tak, *Thailand* 86 D2 16 52N 99 8 E
Takāb, *Iran* 101 D12 36 24N 47 7 E
Takachiho, *Japan* 72 E3 32 42N 131 18 E
Takachu, *Botswana* 116 C3 22 37 S 21 58 E
Takada, *Japan* 71 F9 37 7N 138 15 E
Takahagi, *Japan* 71 F10 36 43N 140 45 E
Takahashi, *Japan* 72 C5 34 51N 133 39 E
Takaka, *N.Z.* 131 A7 40 51 S 172 50 E
Takamaka, *Seychelles* 121 b 4 50 S 55 30 E
Takamatsu, *Japan* 72 C6 34 20N 134 5 E
Takanabe, *Japan* 72 E3 32 8N 131 30 E
Takaoka, *Japan* 73 A9 36 47N 137 0 E
Takapau, *N.Z.* 130 G5 40 2 S 176 21 E
Takapuna, *N.Z.* 130 C3 36 47 S 174 47 E
Takasago, *Japan* 72 C6 34 45N 134 48 E
Takasaki, *Japan* 73 A11 36 20N 139 0 E
Takatsuki, *Japan* 73 C7 34 51N 135 37 E
Takaungu, *Kenya* 118 C4 3 38 S 39 52 E
Takayama, *Japan* 73 A9 36 18N 137 11 E
Takayama-Bonchi, *Japan* 73 B9 36 0N 137 18 E
Take-Shima, *Japan* 71 J5 30 49N 130 26 E
Takefu, *Japan* 73 B8 35 50N 136 10 E
Takehara, *Japan* 72 C4 34 21N 132 55 E
Takeli, *Tajikistan* 65 C4 40 29N 69 26 E
Takengon, *Indonesia* 84 B1 4 45N 96 50 E
Takeo, *Japan* 72 D2 33 12N 130 1 E
Tåkern, *Sweden* 17 F8 58 22N 14 45 E
Tākestān, *Iran* 97 C6 36 0N 49 40 E
Taketa, *Japan* 72 E3 32 58N 131 24 E
Takev, *Cambodia* 87 G5 10 59N 104 47 E
Takh, *India* 93 C7 33 6N 77 32 E
Takhār □, *Afghan.* 91 A3 36 40N 70 0 E
Takht-Sulaiman, *Pakistan* 92 D3 31 40N 69 58 E
Taki, *Papua N. G.* 132 D8 6 29 S 155 52 E
Takikawa, *Japan* 70 C10 43 33N 141 54 E
Takla L., *Canada* 142 B3 55 15N 125 45W
Takla Landing, *Canada* 142 B3 55 30N 125 50W
Takla Makan = Taklamakan Shamo, *China* 68 C3 38 0N 83 0 E
Taklamakan Shamo, *China* 68 C3 38 0N 83 0 E
Takotna, *U.S.A.* 144 E8 62 59N 156 4W
Taku, *Japan* 72 D2 33 18N 130 3 E
Taku →, *Canada* 142 B2 58 30N 133 50W
Takua Thung, *Thailand* 87 a 8 24N 98 27 E
Takum, *India* 90 B4 27 47N 93 37 E
Takum, *Nigeria* 113 D6 7 18N 9 36 E
Takundi, *Dem. Rep. of the Congo* 115 C3 4 45 S 16 34 E
Takutu →, *Guyana* 169 C5 3 1N 60 29W
Tal Halāl, *Iran* 97 D7 28 54N 55 1 E
Tala, *Uruguay* 175 C4 34 21 S 55 46W
Talachyn, *Belarus* 58 E5 54 25N 29 42 E
Talacogan, *Phil.* 81 G5 8 32N 125 39 E
Talagang, *Pakistan* 92 C5 32 55N 72 25 E
Talagante, *Chile* 174 C1 33 40 S 70 50W
Talahouhait, *Algeria* 111 D5 24 52N 1 5 E
Talaimannar, *Sri Lanka* 95 K4 9 6N 79 43 E
Talaïnt, *Morocco* 110 C3 29 41N 9 40W
Talak, *Niger* 113 B6 18 0N 5 0 E
Talakag, *Phil.* 81 G5 8 16N 124 37 E
Talamanca, Cordillera de, *Cent. Amer.* 164 E3 9 20N 83 20W
Talant, *France* 27 E11 47 19N 4 58 E
Talara, *Peru* 172 A1 4 38 S 81 18W
Talas, *Kyrgyzstan* 66 E8 42 30N 72 13 E
Talas, *Turkey* 100 C6 38 41N 35 33 E
Talas →, *Kazakstan* 65 B5 44 0N 70 20 E
Talas Ala Too, *Kyrgyzstan* 65 B6 42 15N 72 0 E
Talasea, *Papua N. G.* 132 C6 5 20 S 150 2 E
Talasskiy Alatau = Talas Ala Too, *Kyrgyzstan* 65 B6 42 15N 72 0 E
Talâta, *Egypt* 103 E1 30 36N 32 20 E
Talata Mafara, *Nigeria* 113 C6 12 38N 6 4 E
Talaud, Kepulauan, *Indonesia* 82 A3 4 30N 126 50 E
Talaud Is. = Talaud, Kepulauan, *Indonesia* 82 A3 4 30N 126 50 E
Talavera de la Reina, *Spain* 42 F5 39 55N 4 46W
Talavera la Real, *Spain* 43 G4 38 53N 6 46W
Talawgyi, *Burma* 90 C6 25 4N 97 19 E
Talayan, *Phil.* 81 H5 6 52N 124 24 E
Talayuela, *Spain* 42 F5 39 59N 5 36W
Talbandh, *India* 93 H12 22 3N 86 20 E
Talbert, Sillon de, *France* 26 D3 48 53N 3 5W
Talbot, *Australia* 128 D5 37 10 S 143 44 E
Talbot, C., *Australia* 124 B4 13 48 S 126 43 E
Talbotton, *U.S.A.* 152 C5 32 41N 84 32W
Talbragar →, *Australia* 129 B8 32 12 S 148 37 E
Talca, *Chile* 174 D1 35 28 S 71 40W
Talcahuano, *Chile* 174 D1 36 40 S 73 10W
Talcher, *India* 94 D7 21 0N 85 18 E
Talcho, *Niger* 113 C5 14 44N 3 28 E
Taldy Kurgan = Taldyqorghan, *Kazakstan* 66 E8 45 10N 78 45 E
Taldy-Suu, *Kyrgyzstan* 65 B9 42 48N 78 26 E
Taldyqorghan, *Kazakstan* 66 E8 45 10N 78 45 E
Tālesh, *Iran* 97 B6 37 58N 48 58 E
Tālesh, Kūhhā-ye, *Iran* 97 B6 37 42N 48 55 E
Talgar = Talghar, *Kazakstan* 65 B8 43 19N 77 15 E
Talgar, Pik, *Kazakstan* 65 B8 43 5N 77 20 E
Talghar, *Kazakstan* 65 B8 43 19N 77 15 E
Talguharai, *Sudan* 106 D4 18 19N 35 56 E
Talguppa, *India* 95 G2 14 13N 74 56 E
Tali Post, *Sudan* 107 F3 5 55N 30 44 E
Taliabu, *Indonesia* 82 B2 1 50 S 125 0 E
Talibon, *Phil.* 81 F5 10 9N 124 20 E
Talibong, Ko, *Thailand* 87 J2 7 15N 99 23 E
Talihina, *U.S.A.* 155 H7 34 45N 95 3W
Talikota, *India* 95 F3 16 29N 76 17 E

Tetas, Pta. 289

Tatebayashi, *Japan* **73 A11** 36 15N 139 32 E
Tateshina-Yama, *Japan* **73 A10** 36 8N 138 11 E
Tateyama, *Japan* **73 C11** 35 0N 139 50 E
Tathlina L., *Canada* **142 A5** 60 33N 117 39W
Tathlīth, *Si. Arabia* **98 C3** 19 32N 43 30 E
Tathlīth, W. →, *Si. Arabia* **98 B4** 20 35N 44 20 E
Tathra, *Australia* **129 D8** 36 44 S 149 59 E
Tatinnai L., *Canada* **143 A9** 60 55N 97 40W
Tatitlek, *U.S.A.* **144 F11** 60 52N 146 41W
Tatkon, *Burma* **90 E6** 20 7N 96 13 E
Tatla L., *Canada* **142 C4** 52 0N 124 20W
Tatlısu, *Turkey* **51 F11** 40 24N 27 55 E
Tatnam, C., *Canada* **143 B10** 57 16N 91 0W
Tatra = Tatry, *Slovak Rep.* **35 B13** 49 20N 20 0 E
Tatry, *Slovak Rep.* **35 B13** 49 20N 20 0 E
Tatshenshini →, *Canada* **142 B1** 59 28N 137 45W
Tatsuno, *Hyōgo, Japan* **72 C6** 34 52N 134 33 E
Tatsuno, *Nagano, Japan* **73 B10** 35 58N 138 0 E
Tatta, *Pakistan* **91 D2** 24 42N 67 55 E
Tätti, *Kazakstan* **65 B6** 43 13N 73 18 E
Tatuī, *Brazil* **175 A6** 23 25 S 47 53W
Tatum, *U.S.A.* **155 J3** 33 16N 103 19W
Tat'ung = Datong, *China* **74 D7** 40 6N 113 18 E
Tatura, *Australia* **129 D6** 36 29 S 145 16 E
Tatvan, *Turkey* **101 C10** 38 31N 42 15 E
Ta'ū, *Amer. Samoa* **133 X25** 14 15 S 169 30W
Tau, *Norway* **18 E2** 59 3N 5 55 E
Tauá, *Brazil* **170 C3** 6 1 S 40 26W
Taubaté, *Brazil* **175 A6** 23 0 S 45 36W
Tauberbischofsheim, *Germany* **31 F5** 49 37N 9 39 E
Taucha, *Germany* **30 D8** 51 23N 12 29 E
Tauern, *Austria* **36 E7** 47 15N 12 40 E
Tauern-tunnel, *Austria* **34 D6** 47 0N 13 12 E
Taufikia, *Sudan* **107 F3** 9 24N 31 37 E
Taulé, *France* **26 D3** 48 37N 3 55W
Taumarunui, *N.Z.* **130 E4** 38 53 S 175 15 E
Taumaturgo, *Brazil* **172 B3** 8 54 S 72 51W
Taung, *S. Africa* **116 D3** 27 33 S 24 47 E
Taungdwingyi, *Burma* **90 E5** 20 1N 95 40 E
Taunggyi, *Burma* **90 E6** 20 50N 97 0 E
Taungtha, *Burma* **90 E5** 21 12N 95 25 E
Taungup, *Burma* **90 F5** 18 51N 94 14 E
Taungup Pass, *Burma* **90 F5** 18 40N 94 45 E
Taunsa, *Pakistan* **92 D4** 30 42N 70 39 E
Taunsa Barrage, *Pakistan* **92 D4** 30 42N 70 50 E
Taunton, *U.K.* **21 F4** 51 1N 3 5W
Taunton, *U.S.A.* **151 E13** 41 54N 71 6W
Taunus, *Germany* **31 E4** 50 13N 8 34 E
Taupo, *N.Z.* **130 E5** 38 41 S 176 7 E
Taupo, L., *N.Z.* **130 E4** 38 46 S 175 55 E
Tauragė, *Lithuania* **15 J20** 55 14N 22 16 E
Tauragė □, *Lithuania* **54 C9** 55 15N 22 17 E
Tauranga, *N.Z.* **130 D5** 37 42 S 176 11 E
Tauranga Harb., *N.Z.* **130 D5** 37 30 S 176 5 E
Taureau, Rés., *Canada* **140 C5** 46 46N 73 50W
Tauri →, *Papua N. G.* **132 E4** 8 8 S 146 8 E
Taurianova, *Italy* **47 D9** 38 21N 16 1 E
Taurus Mts. = Toros Dağları, *Turkey* **100 D5** 37 0N 32 30 E
Tauste, *Spain* **40 D3** 41 58N 1 18W
Tautira, *Tahiti* **133 S16** 17 44 S 149 9W
Tauz = Tovuz, *Azerbaijan* **61 K7** 41 0N 45 40 E
Tavaar, *Somali Rep.* **120 D3** 3 6N 46 1 E
Tavannes, *Switz.* **32 B4** 47 13N 7 12 E
Tavares, *U.S.A.* **153 G8** 28 48N 81 44W
Tavas, *Turkey* **49 D11** 37 34N 29 4 E
Tavda, *Russia* **66 D7** 58 7N 65 8 E
Tavda →, *Russia* **66 D7** 57 47N 67 18 E
Tavernes de la Valldigna, *Spain* **41 F4** 39 5N 0 13W
Tavernier, *U.S.A.* **153 K9** 25 1N 80 31W
Taveta, *Tanzania* **118 C4** 3 23 S 37 37 E
Taveuni, *Fiji* **133 A3** 16 51 S 179 58W
Taviano, *Italy* **47 C11** 39 59N 18 5 E
Tavignano →, *France* **29 F13** 42 7N 9 33 E
Tavildara, *Tajikistan* **65 D5** 38 41N 70 29 E
Tavira, *Portugal* **43 H3** 37 8N 7 40W
Tavistock, *Canada* **150 C4** 43 19N 80 50W
Tavistock, *U.K.* **21 G3** 50 33N 4 9W
Tavolara, *Italy* **46 B2** 40 54N 9 42 E
Távora →, *Portugal* **42 D3** 41 8N 7 35W
Tavoy = Dawei, *Burma* **86 E2** 14 2N 98 12 E
Tavşanlı, *Turkey* **49 B11** 39 32N 29 30 E
Tavua, *Fiji* **133 A1** 17 37 S 177 5 E
Tavuki, *Fiji* **133 B2** 19 7 S 178 8 E
Taw →, *U.K.* **21 F3** 51 4N 4 4W
Tawa →, *India* **92 H8** 22 48N 77 48 E
Tawa Tawa Mal Reef, *Papua N. G.* **132 F7** 11 3 S 152 55 E
Tawai, *India* **90 B6** 27 48N 96 47 E
Tawas City, *U.S.A.* **148 C4** 44 16N 83 31W
Tawau, *Malaysia* **85 B5** 4 20N 117 55 E
Taweisha, *Sudan* **107 E2** 12 19N 26 40 E
Tawi-Tawi □, *Phil.* **81 J3** 5 0N 120 0 E
Tawitawi, *Phil.* **79 B6** 5 10N 120 0 E
Tawitawi Group, *Phil.* **81 J3** 5 10N 120 15 E
Tawngche, *Burma* **90 B5** 26 34N 95 38 E
Tawu, *Taiwan* **77 F13** 22 30N 120 50 E
Tāwurghā', *Libya* **108 B3** 32 1N 15 2 E
Tāwurghā', Sabkhat, *Libya* **108 B3** 31 51N 15 15 E
Taxco de Alarcón, *Mexico* **163 D5** 18 33N 99 36W
Taxila, *Pakistan* **92 C5** 33 42N 72 52 E
Taxkorgan He →, *China* **65 E8** 37 45N 76 10 E
Taxkorgan Tajik Zizhixian, *China* **65 E7** 37 49N 75 14 E
Tay →, *U.K.* **22 E5** 56 37N 3 38W
Tay, Firth of, *U.K.* **22 E5** 56 25N 3 8W
Tay, L., *Australia* **125 F3** 32 55 S 120 48 E
Tay, L., *U.K.* **22 E4** 56 32N 4 8W
Tay Ninh, *Vietnam* **87 G6** 11 20N 106 5 E
Tayabamba, *Peru* **172 B2** 8 15 S 77 16W
Tayabas, *Phil.* **80 D3** 14 1N 121 35 E
Tayabas Bay, *Phil.* **80 E3** 13 45N 121 45 E
Tayandu, Kepulauan, *Indonesia* **83 C4** 5 30 S 132 15 E
Taylakova, *Russia* **66 D8** 59 13N 74 0 E
Taylakovy = Taylakova, *Russia* **66 D8** 59 13N 74 0 E
Taylor, *Canada* **142 B4** 56 13N 120 40W
Taylor, *Fla., U.S.A.* **152 E7** 30 26N 82 18W
Taylor, *Mich., U.S.A.* **157 B13** 42 14N 83 16W
Taylor, *Nebr., U.S.A.* **154 E5** 41 46N 99 23W
Taylor, *Pa., U.S.A.* **151 E9** 41 23N 75 43W
Taylor, *Tex., U.S.A.* **155 K6** 30 34N 97 25W
Taylor, Mt., *N.Z.* **131 D6** 43 30 S 171 20 E
Taylor, Mt., *U.S.A.* **159 J10** 35 14N 107 37W
Taylorsville, *U.S.A.* **157 F11** 38 2N 85 21W
Taylorsville L., *U.S.A.* **157 G11** 38 0N 85 15W
Taylorville, *U.S.A.* **156 E7** 39 33N 89 18W
Taymā, *Si. Arabia* **96 E3** 27 35N 38 45 E
Taymyr, Oz., *Russia* **67 B11** 74 20N 102 0 E
Taymyr, Poluostrov, *Russia* **67 B11** 75 0N 100 0 E
Tayport, *U.K.* **22 E6** 56 27N 2 52W
Tayshet, *Russia* **67 D10** 55 58N 98 1 E
Taytay, *Phil.* **81 F2** 10 45N 119 30 E
Taytay Bay, *Phil.* **81 F2** 10 55N 119 35 E
Tayug, *Phil.* **80 C3** 16 2N 120 45 E
Taz →, *Russia* **66 C8** 67 32N 78 40 E
Taza, *Morocco* **110 B4** 34 16N 4 6W
Tāzah Khurmātū, *Iraq* **101 E11** 35 18N 44 20 E
Tazawa-Ko, *Japan* **70 E10** 39 43N 140 40 E
Taze, *Burma* **90 D5** 22 57N 95 24 E
Tazenakht, *Morocco* **110 B3** 30 35N 7 12W
Tazerbo, *Libya* **108 C4** 25 45N 21 0 E
Tazin, *Canada* **143 B7** 59 48N 109 55W
Tazin L., *Canada* **143 B7** 59 44N 108 42W
Tazlina, *U.S.A.* **144 E11** 62 4N 146 27W
Tazoult, *Algeria* **111 A6** 35 29N 6 11 E
Tazovskiy, *Russia* **66 C8** 67 30N 78 44 E
Tbilisi, *Georgia* **61 K7** 41 43N 44 50 E
Tchad = Chad ■, *Africa* **109 F3** 15 0N 17 15 E
Tchad, L., *Chad* **109 F2** 13 30N 14 30 E
Tchaourou, *Benin* **113 D5** 8 58N 2 40 E
Tch'eng-tou = Chengdu, *China* **76 B5** 30 38N 104 2 E
Tchentlo L., *Canada* **142 B4** 55 15N 125 0W
Tchetti, *Benin* **113 D5** 7 50N 1 40 E
Tchibanga, *Gabon* **114 C2** 2 45 S 11 0 E
Tchien, *Liberia* **112 D3** 5 59N 8 15W
Tchin Tabaraden, *Niger* **113 B6** 15 58N 5 56 E
Tchingou, Massif de, *N. Cal.* **133 T19** 20 54 S 165 0 E
Tcholliré, *Cameroon* **114 A2** 8 24N 14 10 E
Tch'ong-k'ing = Chongqing, *China* **76 C6** 29 35N 106 25 E
Tczew, *Poland* **54 D5** 54 8N 18 50 E
Te Anau, *N.Z.* **131 F2** 45 25 S 167 43 E
Te Anau, L., *N.Z.* **131 F2** 45 15 S 167 45 E
Te Araroa, *N.Z.* **130 D7** 37 39 S 178 25 E
Te Aroha, *N.Z.* **130 D4** 37 32 S 175 44 E
Te Awamutu, *N.Z.* **130 E4** 38 1 S 175 20 E
Te Kaha, *N.Z.* **130 D6** 37 44 S 177 52 E
Te Karaka, *N.Z.* **130 E6** 38 26 S 177 53 E
Te Kauwhata, *N.Z.* **130 D4** 37 25 S 175 9 E
Te Kopuru, *N.Z.* **130 C2** 36 2 S 173 56 E
Te Kuiti, *N.Z.* **130 E4** 38 20 S 175 11 E
Te-n-Dghâmcha, Sebkhet, *Mauritania* **112 B1** 18 30N 15 55W
Te Puke, *N.Z.* **130 D5** 37 46 S 176 22 E
Te Teko, *N.Z.* **130 E5** 38 2 S 176 48 E
Te Waewae B., *N.Z.* **131 G2** 46 13 S 167 33 E
Tea →, *Brazil* **168 D4** 0 30 S 65 9W
Teaca, *Romania* **53 D9** 46 55N 24 30 E
Teague, *U.S.A.* **155 K6** 31 38N 96 17W
Teano, *Italy* **47 A7** 41 15N 14 4 E
Teapa, *Mexico* **163 D6** 18 35N 92 56W
Teba, *Spain* **43 J6** 36 59N 4 55W
Tebakang, *Malaysia* **78 D4** 1 6N 110 30 E
Teberau, *Malaysia* **84 B2** 1 32N 103 45 E
Teberda, *Russia* **61 J5** 43 30N 41 46 E
Teberu, *Malaysia* **87 d** 1 30N 103 42 E
Tébessa, *Algeria* **111 A6** 35 22N 8 8 E
Tebicuary →, *Paraguay* **174 B4** 26 36 S 58 16W
Tebingtinggi, *Riau, Indonesia* **84 B2** 1 0N 102 45 E
Tebingtinggi, *Sumatera Utara, Indonesia* **84 B1** 3 20N 99 9 E
Tébourba, *Tunisia* **108 A1** 36 49N 9 51 E
Téboursouk, *Tunisia* **108 A1** 36 29N 9 10 E
Tebulos, *Georgia* **61 J7** 42 36N 45 17 E
Tecate, *Mexico* **161 N10** 32 34N 116 38W
Tecer Dağları, *Turkey* **100 C7** 39 27N 37 27 E
Tech →, *France* **28 F7** 42 36N 3 3 E
Techa →, *Russia* **64 C9** 56 13N 62 58 E
Techiman, *Ghana* **112 D4** 7 35N 1 58W
Techirghiol, *Romania* **53 F13** 44 4N 28 32 E
Tecka, *Argentina* **176 B2** 43 29 S 70 48W
Tecomán, *Mexico* **162 D4** 18 55N 103 53W
Tecopa, *U.S.A.* **161 K10** 35 51N 116 13W
Tecoripa, *Mexico* **162 B3** 28 37N 109 57W
Tecuala, *Mexico* **162 C3** 22 23N 105 27W
Tecuci, *Romania* **53 E12** 45 51N 27 27 E
Tecumseh, *Canada* **150 D2** 42 19N 82 54W
Tecumseh, *Mich., U.S.A.* **157 B13** 42 0N 83 57W
Tecumseh, *Okla., U.S.A.* **155 H6** 35 15N 96 56W
Ted, *Somali Rep.* **120 D2** 4 24N 43 55 E
Tedjert, *Algeria* **111 D6** 21 23N 6 25 E
Tedzhen = Tejen, *Turkmenistan* **66 F7** 37 23N 60 31 E
Tees →, *U.K.* **20 C6** 54 37N 1 10W
Tees B., *U.K.* **20 C6** 54 40N 1 9W
Teeswater, *Canada* **150 C3** 43 59N 81 17W
Tefé, *Brazil* **169 D5** 3 25 S 64 50W
Tefé →, *Brazil* **169 D5** 3 35 S 64 47W
Tefenni, *Turkey* **49 D11** 37 18N 29 45 E
Tegal, *Indonesia* **85 D3** 6 52 S 109 8 E
Tegallalang, *Indonesia* **79 J18** 8 27 S 115 17 E
Tegalsari, *Indonesia* **79 J17** 8 25 S 114 8 E
Tegernsee, *Germany* **31 H7** 47 43N 11 46 E
Teggiano, *Italy* **47 B8** 40 23N 15 32 E
Tegid, L. = Bala, L., *U.K.* **20 E4** 52 53N 3 37W
Tegina, *Nigeria* **113 C6** 10 5N 6 11 E
Téglio, *Italy* **33 D10** 46 10N 10 4 E
Tegua, *Vanuatu* **133 C4** 13 15 S 166 37 E
Tegucigalpa, *Honduras* **164 D2** 14 5N 87 14W
Teguidda i-n-Tessoum, *Niger* **113 B6** 17 25N 6 37 E
Tehachapi, *U.S.A.* **161 K8** 35 8N 118 27W
Tehachapi Mts., *U.S.A.* **161 L8** 35 0N 118 30W
Tehamiyam, *Sudan* **106 D4** 18 20N 36 32 E
Tehilla, *Sudan* **106 D4** 17 42N 36 6 E
Téhini, *Ivory C.* **112 D4** 9 39N 3 40W
Tehoru, *Indonesia* **83 B3** 3 23 S 129 30 E
Tehrān, *Iran* **97 C6** 35 44N 51 30 E
Tehri, *India* **93 D8** 30 23N 78 29 E
Tehuacán, *Mexico* **163 D5** 18 30N 97 30W
Tehuantepec, *Mexico* **163 D5** 16 21N 95 13W
Tehuantepec, G. de, *Mexico* **163 D5** 15 50N 95 12W
Tehuantepec, Istmo de, *Mexico* **163 D6** 17 0N 94 30W
Teide, *Canary Is.* **9 e1** 28 15N 16 38W
Teifi →, *U.K.* **21 E3** 52 5N 4 41W
Teigebyen, *Norway* **18 D8** 60 12N 11 0 E
Teign →, *U.K.* **21 G4** 50 32N 3 32W
Teignmouth, *U.K.* **21 G4** 50 33N 3 31W
Teiuş, *Romania* **53 D8** 46 12N 23 40 E
Teixeira, *Brazil* **170 C4** 7 13 S 37 15W
Teixeira Pinto, *Guinea-Biss.* **112 C1** 12 3N 16 0W
Tejakula, *Indonesia* **79 J18** 8 8 S 115 20 E
Tejam, *India* **93 E9** 29 57N 80 11 E
Tejen, *Turkmenistan* **66 F7** 37 23N 60 31 E
Tejen →, *Turkmenistan* **97 B9** 37 24N 60 38 E
Tejo →, *Europe* **43 F2** 38 40N 9 24W
Tejon Pass, *U.S.A.* **161 L8** 34 49N 118 53W
Tekamah, *U.S.A.* **154 E6** 41 47N 96 13W
Tekapo →, *N.Z.* **131 E5** 44 13 S 170 21 E
Tekapo, L., *N.Z.* **131 D5** 43 53 S 170 33 E
Tekax, *Mexico* **163 C7** 20 11N 89 18W
Teke, *Kazakstan* **65 B4** 43 15N 68 10 E
Teke, *Turkey* **51 E13** 41 4N 29 39 E
Tekeli, *Kazakstan* **66 E8** 44 50N 79 0 E
Tekeze →, *Ethiopia* **107 E4** 14 20N 35 50 E
Tekija, *Serbia, Yug.* **50 B6** 44 42N 22 26 E
Tekirdağ, *Turkey* **51 F11** 40 58N 27 30 E
Tekirdağ □, *Turkey* **51 E11** 41 0N 27 0 E
Tekirova, *Turkey* **49 E12** 36 30N 30 32 E
Tekkali, *India* **94 E7** 18 37N 84 15 E
Tekke, *Turkey* **100 B7** 40 42N 36 12 E
Tekman, *Turkey* **101 C9** 39 38N 41 29 E
Tekoa, *U.S.A.* **158 C5** 47 14N 117 4W
Tekong Besar, Pulau, *Singapore* **87 d** 1 25N 104 3 E
Tekouiât, O. →, *Algeria* **111 D5** 22 25N 2 35 E
Tekro, *Chad* **109 E4** 19 32N 20 56 E
Teku, *Indonesia* **82 B2** 0 46 S 123 26 E
Tel →, *India* **94 D6** 20 50N 83 54 E
Tel Aviv-Yafo, *Israel* **103 C3** 32 4N 34 48 E
Tel Lakhish, *Israel* **103 D3** 31 34N 34 51 E
Tel Megiddo, *Israel* **103 C4** 32 35N 35 11 E
Tela, *Honduras* **164 C2** 15 40N 87 28W
Télagh, *Algeria* **111 B4** 34 51N 0 32W
Telanaipura = Jambi, *Indonesia* **84 C2** 1 38 S 103 30 E
Telavåg, *Norway* **18 D1** 60 15N 4 58 E
Telavi, *Georgia* **61 J7** 42 0N 45 30 E
Telč, *Czech Rep.* **34 B8** 49 11N 15 28 E
Telciu, *Romania* **53 C9** 47 25N 24 24 E
Telde, *Canary Is.* **9 e1** 27 59N 15 25W
Tele →, *Dem. Rep. of the Congo* **114 B4** 2 48N 23 54 E
Telefomin, *Papua N. G.* **132 C1** 5 10 S 141 31 E
Telegraph Creek, *Canada* **142 B2** 58 0N 131 10W
Telekhany = Tsyelyakhany, *Belarus* **59 F3** 52 30N 25 46 E
Telemark, *Norway* **15 G12** 59 15N 7 40 E
Telemark □, *Norway* **18 E5** 59 25N 8 30 E
Telén, *Argentina* **174 D2** 36 15 S 65 31W
Telen →, *Indonesia* **85 C5** 0 10 S 117 20 E
Teleneşti, *Moldova* **53 C13** 47 30N 28 22 E
Teleng, *Iran* **97 E9** 25 47N 61 3 E
Teleño, *Spain* **42 C4** 42 23N 6 22W
Teleorman □, *Romania* **53 G10** 44 0N 25 0 E
Teleorman →, *Romania* **53 G10** 43 52N 25 26 E
Teles Pires →, *Brazil* **173 B6** 7 21 S 58 3W
Telescope Pk., *U.S.A.* **161 J9** 36 10N 117 5W
Teletaye, *Mali* **113 B5** 16 31N 1 30 E
Telfer Mine, *Australia* **124 C3** 21 40 S 122 12 E
Telford, *U.K.* **21 E5** 52 40N 2 27W
Telford and Wrekin □, *U.K.* **20 E5** 52 45N 2 27W
Telfs, *Austria* **34 D4** 47 19N 11 4 E
Telida, *U.S.A.* **144 E9** 63 23N 153 16W
Télimélé, *Guinea* **112 C2** 10 54N 13 2W
Teljo, J., *Sudan* **107 E2** 14 42N 25 26 E
Telkwa, *Canada* **142 C3** 54 41N 127 5W
Tell City, *U.S.A.* **157 G10** 37 57N 86 46W
Teller, *U.S.A.* **144 D6** 65 16N 166 22W
Tellicherry, *India* **95 J2** 11 45N 75 30 E
Telluride, *U.S.A.* **159 H10** 37 56N 107 49W
Telok Datok, *Malaysia* **84 B2** 2 49N 101 31 E
Teloloapán, *Mexico* **163 D5** 18 21N 99 51W
Telpos Iz, *Russia* **56 B10** 63 16N 59 13 E
Telsen, *Argentina* **176 B3** 42 30 S 66 50W
Telšiai, *Lithuania* **15 H20** 55 59N 22 14 E
Telšiai □, *Lithuania* **54 C9** 55 59N 22 15 E
Teltow, *Germany* **30 C9** 52 24N 13 15 E
Teluk Anson = Teluk Intan, *Malaysia* **87 K3** 4 3N 101 0 E
Teluk Bahang, *Malaysia* **87 c** 5 28N 100 13 E
Teluk Betung = Tanjungkarang Telukbetung, *Indonesia* **84 D3** 5 20 S 105 10 E
Teluk Cenderawasih, *Indonesia* **83 B5** 2 30 S 135 20 E
Teluk Darvel, *Malaysia* **81 J2** 4 45N 118 30 E
Teluk Intan, *Malaysia* **87 K3** 4 3N 101 0 E
Teluk Kumbar, *Malaysia* **87 c** 5 18N 100 14 E
Telukbutun, *Indonesia* **85 B3** 4 13N 108 12 E
Telukdalem, *Indonesia* **84 B1** 0 33N 97 50 E
Tema, *Ghana* **113 D5** 5 41N 0 0W
Temanggung, *Indonesia* **85 D4** 7 18 S 110 10 E
Temasint, *Algeria* **111 D6** 23 18N 7 40 E
Temax, *Mexico* **163 C7** 21 10N 88 50W
Temba, *S. Africa* **117 D4** 25 20 S 28 17 E
Tembagapura, *Indonesia* **83 B5** 4 20 S 137 0 E
Tembe, *Dem. Rep. of the Congo* **118 C2** 0 16 S 28 14 E
Tembe Elephant Reserve, *S. Africa* **117 D5** 26 51 S 32 24 E
Tembesi, *Indonesia* **84 C2** 1 43 S 103 6 E
Tembilahan, *Indonesia* **84 C2** 0 19 S 103 9 E
Temblador, *Venezuela* **169 B5** 8 59N 62 44W
Tembleque, *Spain* **42 F7** 39 41N 3 30W
Temblor Range, *U.S.A.* **161 K7** 35 20N 119 50W
Teme →, *U.K.* **21 E5** 52 11N 2 13W
Temecula, *U.S.A.* **161 M9** 33 30N 117 9W
Temerloh, *Malaysia* **84 B2** 3 27N 102 25 E
Teminabuan, *Indonesia* **83 B4** 1 26 S 132 1 E
Temir, *Kazakstan* **57 E10** 49 1N 57 14 E
Temir, *Kazakstan* **65 B4** 42 49N 68 26 E
Temirlan, *Kazakstan* **65 B4** 42 36N 69 17 E
Temirtau, *Kazakstan* **66 D8** 50 5N 72 56 E
Temirtau, *Russia* **66 D9** 53 10N 87 30 E
Temiscamie →, *Canada* **141 B5** 50 59N 73 5W
Témiscaming, *Canada* **140 C4** 46 44N 79 5W
Témiscamingue, L., *Canada* **140 C4** 47 10N 79 25W
Temnikov, *Russia* **60 C6** 54 40N 43 11 E
Temo →, *Italy* **46 B1** 40 17N 8 28 E
Temora, *Australia* **129 C7** 34 30 S 147 30 E
Temosachic, *Mexico* **162 B3** 28 58N 107 50W
Tempe, *U.S.A.* **159 K8** 33 25N 111 56W
Témpio Pausánia, *Italy* **46 B2** 40 54N 9 6 E
Tempiute, *U.S.A.* **160 H11** 37 39N 115 38W
Temple, *U.S.A.* **155 K6** 31 6N 97 21W
Temple B., *Australia* **126 A3** 12 15 S 143 3 E
Temple Terrace, *U.S.A.* **153 G7** 28 2N 82 23W
Templemore, *Ireland* **23 D4** 52 47N 7 51W
Templeton, *U.S.A.* **160 K6** 35 33N 120 42W
Templeton →, *Australia* **126 C2** 21 0 S 138 40 E
Templin, *Germany* **30 B9** 53 7N 13 28 E
Tempoal, *Mexico* **163 C5** 21 31N 98 23W
Tempué, *Angola* **115 E3** 13 27 S 18 49 E
Temryuk, *Russia* **59 K9** 45 15N 37 24 E
Temska →, *Serbia, Yug.* **50 C6** 43 17N 22 33 E
Temuco, *Chile* **176 A2** 38 45 S 72 40W
Temuka, *N.Z.* **131 E6** 44 14 S 171 17 E
Ten Degree Channel, *India* **95 K11** 10 0N 92 30 E
Ten Thousand Is., *U.S.A.* **153 K8** 25 55N 81 45W
Tena, *Ecuador* **168 D2** 0 59 S 77 49W
Tenabo, *Mexico* **163 C6** 20 2N 90 12W
Tenaha, *U.S.A.* **155 K7** 31 57N 94 15W
Tenakee Springs, *U.S.A.* **142 B1** 57 47N 135 13W
Tenali, *India* **95 F5** 16 15N 80 35 E
Tenancingo, *Mexico* **163 D5** 19 0N 99 33W
Tenango, *Mexico* **163 D5** 19 7N 99 33W
Tenasserim, *Burma* **87 F2** 12 6N 99 3 E
Tenasserim □, *Burma* **86 F2** 14 0N 98 30 E
Tenby, *U.K.* **21 F3** 51 40N 4 42W
Tenda, Colle di, *France* **29 D11** 44 7N 7 36 E
Tendaho, *Ethiopia* **107 E5** 11 48N 40 54 E
Tende, *France* **29 D11** 44 5N 7 35 E
Tendelti, *Sudan* **107 E3** 13 1N 31 55 E
Tendjedi, Adrar, *Algeria* **111 D6** 23 41N 7 32 E
Tendrara, *Morocco* **111 B4** 33 3N 1 58W
Tendre, Mt., *Switz.* **32 C2** 46 35N 6 18 E
Tendrovskaya Kosa, *Ukraine* **59 J6** 46 16N 31 35 E
Tendukhera, *India* **93 H8** 23 24N 79 33 E
Tenebroûret, O. →, *Mauritania* **110 D1** 20 35N 16 0W
Teneida, *Egypt* **106 B2** 25 30N 29 19 E
Tenenkou, *Mali* **112 C4** 14 28N 4 55W
Tenente Marques →, *Brazil* **173 C6** 11 10 S 59 56W
Ténéré, *Niger* **113 B7** 19 0N 10 30 E
Ténéré, Erg du, *Niger* **109 E2** 17 35N 10 55 E
Tenerife, *Canary Is.* **9 e1** 28 15N 16 35W
Tenerife, Pico, *Canary Is.* **9 e1** 27 43N 18 1W
Ténès, *Algeria* **111 A5** 36 31N 1 14 E
Teng Xian, *Guangxi Zhuangzu, China* **77 F8** 23 21N 110 56 E
Teng Xian, *Shandong, China* **75 G9** 35 5N 117 10 E
Tengah □, *Indonesia* **82 B2** 1 30 S 121 0 E
Tengah, Kepulauan, *Indonesia* **85 D5** 7 5 S 118 15 E
Tengchong, *China* **76 E2** 25 0N 98 28 E
Tengchowfu = Penglai, *China* **75 F11** 37 48N 120 42 E
Tenggara □, *Indonesia* **82 B2** 3 50 S 122 0 E
Tenggarong, *Indonesia* **85 C5** 0 24 S 116 58 E
Tenggol, Pulau, *Malaysia* **87 K4** 4 48N 103 41 E
Tengiz, Ozero, *Kazakstan* **66 D7** 50 30N 69 0 E
Tenhult, *Sweden* **17 G8** 57 41N 14 20 E
Tenigerbad, *Switz.* **33 C7** 46 42N 8 57 E
Tenino, *U.S.A.* **160 D4** 46 51N 122 51W
Tenkasi, *India* **95 K3** 8 55N 77 20 E
Tenke, *Katanga, Dem. Rep. of the Congo* **119 E2** 11 22 S 26 40 E
Tenke, *Katanga, Dem. Rep. of the Congo* **119 E2** 10 32 S 26 7 E
Tenkodogo, *Burkina Faso* **113 C4** 11 54N 0 19W
Tenna →, *Italy* **45 E10** 43 14N 13 47 E
Tennant Creek, *Australia* **126 B1** 19 30 S 134 15 E
Tennessee □, *U.S.A.* **149 H2** 36 0N 86 30W
Tennessee →, *U.S.A.* **148 G1** 37 4N 88 34W
Tennille, *U.S.A.* **152 C7** 32 56N 82 48W
Teno, Pta. de, *Canary Is.* **9 e1** 28 21N 16 55W
Tenom, *Malaysia* **85 A5** 5 4N 115 57 E
Tenosique, *Mexico* **163 D6** 17 30N 91 24W
Tenri, *Japan* **73 C7** 34 39N 135 49 E
Tenryū, *Japan* **73 C9** 34 52N 137 49 E
Tenryū-Gawa →, *Japan* **73 B9** 35 39N 137 48 E
Tensift, Oued →, *Morocco* **110 B3** 32 3N 9 28W
Tentelomatinan, *Indonesia* **82 A2** 0 56N 121 48 E
Tentena, *Indonesia* **82 B2** 1 47 S 120 39 E
Tenterden, *U.K.* **21 F8** 51 4N 0 42 E
Tenterfield, *Australia* **127 D5** 29 0 S 152 0 E
Tenuaiur, Uad →, *W. Sahara* **110 D1** 21 36N 16 0W
Teo, *Spain* **42 C2** 42 45N 8 30W
Teófilo Otoni, *Brazil* **171 E3** 17 50 S 41 30W
Tepa, *Indonesia* **83 C3** 7 52 S 129 31 E
Tepalcatepec →, *Mexico* **162 D4** 18 35N 101 59W
Tepecik, *Bursa, Turkey* **51 F12** 40 7N 28 25 E
Tepecik, *Kütahya, Turkey* **49 B11** 39 32N 29 28 E
Tepehuanes, *Mexico* **162 B3** 25 21N 105 44W
Tepelenë, *Albania* **50 F4** 40 17N 20 2 E
Tepequem, Serra, *Brazil* **169 C5** 3 45N 61 45W
Tepetongo, *Mexico* **162 C4** 22 28N 103 9W
Tepic, *Mexico* **162 C4** 21 30N 104 54W
Teplá, *Czech Rep.* **34 B5** 49 59N 12 52 E
Teplice, *Czech Rep.* **34 A6** 50 40N 13 48 E
Teploklyuchenka, *Kyrgyzstan* **65 B9** 42 30N 78 30 E
Tepoca, C., *Mexico* **162 A2** 30 20N 112 25W
Tequila, *Mexico* **162 C4** 20 54N 103 47W
Ter →, *Spain* **40 C8** 42 2N 3 12 E
Ter Apel, *Neths.* **24 B7** 52 53N 7 5 E
Téra, *Niger* **113 C5** 14 0N 0 45 E
Tera →, *Spain* **42 D5** 41 54N 5 44W
Teraina, *Kiribati* **135 G11** 4 43N 160 25W
Terakeka, *Sudan* **107 F3** 5 26N 31 45 E
Téramo, *Italy* **45 F10** 42 39N 13 42 E
Terang, *Australia* **128 E5** 38 15 S 142 55 E
Terang, Teluk, *Indonesia* **79 K19** 8 44 S 116 0 E
Terawhiti, C., *N.Z.* **130 H3** 41 16 S 174 38 E
Terazit, Massif de, *Niger* **111 D6** 20 2N 8 30 E
Tercan, *Turkey* **101 C9** 39 47N 40 23 E
Terceira, *Azores* **9 d1** 38 43N 27 13W
Tercero →, *Argentina* **174 C3** 32 58 S 61 47W
Terdal, *India* **94 F2** 16 33N 75 3 E
Terebovlya, *Ukraine* **59 H3** 49 18N 25 44 E
Teregova, *Romania* **52 E7** 45 10N 22 16 E
Tereida, *Sudan* **107 E3** 10 35N 31 17 E
Terek →, *Russia* **61 J8** 44 0N 47 30 E
Terek-Say, *Kyrgyzstan* **65 C5** 41 30N 71 11 E
Terengganu □, *Malaysia* **84 B2** 4 55N 103 0 E
Terengözek, *Kazakstan* **65 A2** 45 3N 64 59 E
Terenos, *Brazil* **173 E7** 20 26 S 54 50W
Tereshka →, *Russia* **60 E8** 51 48N 46 26 E
Teresina, *Brazil* **170 C3** 5 9 S 42 45W
Teresinha, *Brazil* **169 C7** 0 58N 52 2W
Terespol, *Poland* **55 F10** 52 5N 23 37 E
Teressa, *India* **95 K11** 8 15N 93 10 E
Terewah, L., *Australia* **127 D4** 29 52 S 147 35 E
Terges →, *Portugal* **43 H3** 37 49N 7 41W
Tergnier, *France* **27 C10** 49 40N 3 17 E
Terhazza, *Mali* **110 D3** 23 38N 5 22W
Teridgerie Cr. →, *Australia* **129 A8** 30 25 S 148 50 E
Terlizzi, *Italy* **47 A9** 41 8N 16 32 E
Terme, *Turkey* **100 B7** 41 11N 37 0 E
Termez = Termiz, *Uzbekistan* **66 F7** 37 15N 67 15 E
Términi Imerese, *Italy* **46 E6** 37 59N 13 42 E
Términos, L. de, *Mexico* **163 D6** 18 35N 91 30W
Termiz, *Uzbekistan* **66 F7** 37 15N 67 15 E
Térmoli, *Italy* **45 F12** 42 0N 15 0 E
Ternate, *Indonesia* **82 A3** 0 45N 127 25 E
Terneuzen, *Neths.* **24 C3** 51 20N 3 50 E
Terney, *Russia* **67 E14** 45 3N 136 37 E
Terni, *Italy* **45 F9** 42 34N 12 37 E
Ternitz, *Austria* **34 D9** 47 43N 16 2 E
Ternopil, *Ukraine* **59 H3** 49 30N 25 40 E
Ternopol = Ternopil, *Ukraine* **59 H3** 49 30N 25 40 E
Terowie, *Australia* **128 B3** 33 8 S 138 55 E
Terpní, *Greece* **50 F7** 40 55N 23 26 E
Terra Bella, *U.S.A.* **161 K7** 35 58N 119 3W
Terra Nova Nat. Park, *Canada* **141 C9** 48 33N 53 55W
Terrace, *Canada* **142 C3** 54 30N 128 35W
Terrace Bay, *Canada* **140 C2** 48 47N 87 5W
Terracina, *Italy* **46 A6** 41 17N 13 15 E
Terralba, *Italy* **46 C1** 39 43N 8 39 E
Terranova = Ólbia, *Italy* **46 B2** 40 55N 9 31 E
Terrasini, *Italy* **46 D6** 38 10N 13 4 E
Terrassa, *Spain* **40 D7** 41 34N 2 1 E
Terrasson-la-Villedieu, *France* **28 C5** 45 8N 1 18 E
Terre Haute, *U.S.A.* **157 E9** 39 28N 87 25W
Terrebonne B., *U.S.A.* **155 L9** 29 5N 90 35W
Terrecht, *Mali* **111 D4** 20 10N 0 10W
Terrell, *U.S.A.* **155 J6** 32 44N 96 17W
Terrenceville, *Canada* **141 C9** 47 40N 54 44W
Terry, *U.S.A.* **154 B2** 46 47N 105 19W
Terryville, *U.S.A.* **151 E11** 41 41N 73 3W
Terschelling, *Neths.* **24 A5** 53 25N 5 20 E
Terskey Ala Too, *Kyrgyzstan* **65 C8** 41 50N 77 0 E
Terskey Alatau = Terskey Ala Too, *Kyrgyzstan* **65 C8** 41 50N 77 0 E
Tersko-Kumskiy Kanal →, *Russia* **61 H7** 44 32N 44 38 E
Tertenía, *Italy* **46 C2** 39 42N 9 34 E
Terter → = Tärtär →, *Azerbaijan* **61 K8** 40 26N 47 20 E
Teruel, *Spain* **40 E3** 40 22N 1 8W
Teruel □, *Spain* **40 E4** 40 48N 1 0W
Tervel, *Bulgaria* **51 C11** 43 45N 27 28 E
Tervola, *Finland* **14 C21** 66 6N 24 49 E
Teryaweyna L., *Australia* **128 B5** 32 18 S 143 22 E
Tešanj, *Bos.-H.* **52 F3** 44 38N 18 1 E
Teseney, *Eritrea* **107 D4** 15 5N 36 42 E
Tesha →, *Russia* **60 C6** 55 38N 42 9 E
Teshekpuk L., *U.S.A.* **144 A9** 70 35N 153 26W
Teshio, *Japan* **70 B10** 44 53N 141 44 E
Teshio-Gawa →, *Japan* **70 B10** 44 53N 141 45 E
Tešica, *Serbia, Yug.* **50 C5** 43 27N 21 45 E
Tesiyn Gol →, *Mongolia* **68 A4** 50 40N 93 20 E
Teslić, *Bos.-H.* **52 F2** 44 37N 17 54 E
Teslin, *Canada* **142 A2** 60 10N 132 43W
Teslin →, *Canada* **142 A2** 61 34N 134 35W
Teslin L., *Canada* **142 A2** 60 15N 132 57W
Tesouro, *Brazil* **173 D7** 16 4 S 53 34W
Tessalit, *Mali* **111 D5** 20 12N 1 0 E
Tessaoua, *Niger* **113 C6** 13 47N 7 56 E
Tessin, *Germany* **30 A8** 54 2N 12 26 E
Tessit, *Mali* **113 B5** 15 13N 0 18 E
Tessounfat, *Mali* **111 D5** 22 53N 0 32 E
Test →, *U.K.* **21 G6** 50 56N 1 29W
Testa del Gargano, *Italy* **45 G13** 41 50N 16 10 E
Testigos, Is. Las, *Venezuela* **165 D7** 11 23N 63 7W
Tét, *Hungary* **52 C2** 47 30N 17 33 E
Têt →, *France* **28 F7** 42 44N 3 2 E
Tetachuck L., *Canada* **142 C3** 53 18N 125 55W
Tetas, Pta., *Chile* **174 A1** 23 31 S 70 38W

Topusko 291

Tin Amzi, O. →, *Algeria* **111 D6** 18 20N 4 32 E
Tin Atanai, *Algeria* **111 C5** 25 52N 1 37 E
Tin Can Bay, *Australia* **127 D5** 25 56 S 153 0 E
Tin Ethisane, *Mali* **113 B4** 19 3N 0 52W
Tin Gornai, *Mali* **113 B4** 16 38N 0 38W
Tin Mt., *U.S.A.* **160 J9** 36 50N 117 10W
Tina →, *S. Africa* **117 E4** 31 18 S 29 13 E
Tîna, Khalîg el, *Egypt* **106 A3** 31 20N 32 42 E
Tinaca Pt., *Phil.* **81 J5** 5 30N 125 25 E
Tinaco, *Venezuela* **168 B4** 9 42N 68 26W
Tinafak, O. →, *Algeria* **111 C6** 27 10N 7 0 E
Tinajo, *Canary Is.* **9 e2** 29 4N 13 42W
Tinca, *Romania* **52 D6** 46 46N 21 58 E
Tindal, *Australia* **124 B5** 14 31 S 132 22 E
Tindivanam, *India* **95 H4** 12 15N 79 41 E
Tindouf, *Algeria* **110 C3** 27 42N 8 10W
Tinée →, *France* **29 E11** 43 55N 7 11 E
Tineo, *Spain* **42 B4** 43 21N 6 27W
Tinerhir, *Morocco* **110 B3** 31 29N 5 31W
Tinfouchi, *Algeria* **110 C3** 28 52N 5 49W
Ting Jiang →, *China* **77 E11** 24 45N 116 35 E
Tinggi, Pulau, *Malaysia* **87 L5** 2 18N 104 7 E
Tingkawk Sakan, *Burma* **90 B6** 26 4N 96 44 E
Tinglayan, *Phil.* **80 C3** 17 15N 121 9 E
Tinglev, *Denmark* **17 K3** 54 57N 9 13 E
Tingo Maria, *Peru* **172 B2** 9 10 S 75 54W
Tingrela, *Ivory C.* **112 C3** 10 27N 6 25W
Tingsryd, *Sweden* **17 H9** 56 31N 15 0 E
Tingstäde, *Sweden* **17 G12** 57 44N 18 37 E
Tingvoll, *Norway* **18 B5** 62 55N 8 12 E
Tingwon Group, *Papua N. G.* **132 B5** 2 37 S 149 42 E
Tinh Bien, *Vietnam* **87 G5** 10 36N 104 57 E
Tinharé, I. de, *Brazil* **171 D4** 13 30 S 38 58W
Tiniguiban, *Phil.* **81 F2** 11 22N 119 30 E
Tinjar →, *Malaysia* **85 B4** 4 14N 114 18 E
Tinn = Atrå, *Norway* **18 E5** 59 59N 8 45 E
Tinnevelly = Tirunelveli, *India* **95 K3** 8 45N 77 45 E
Tinnoset, *Norway* **18 E6** 59 43N 9 3 E
Tinnsjø, *Norway* **18 E5** 59 55N 8 54 E
Tinogasta, *Argentina* **174 B2** 28 5 S 67 32W
Tínos, *Greece* **49 D7** 37 33N 25 8 E
Tiñoso, C., *Spain* **41 H3** 37 32N 1 6W
Tinpahar, *India* **93 G12** 24 59N 87 44 E
Tinputz, *Papua N. G.* **132 C8** 5 33 S 155 0 E
Tinsukia, *India* **90 B5** 27 29N 95 20 E
Tinta, *Peru* **172 C3** 14 3 S 71 20W
Tintina, *Argentina* **174 B3** 27 2 S 62 45W
Tintinara, *Australia* **128 C4** 35 48 S 140 2 E
Tintioulé, *Guinea* **112 C3** 10 13N 9 12W
Tinto →, *Spain* **43 H4** 37 12N 6 55W
Tinui, *N.Z.* **130 G5** 40 52 S 176 5 E
Tinwald, *N.Z.* **131 D6** 43 55 S 171 43 E
Tioga, *N. Dak., U.S.A.* **154 A3** 48 23N 102 56W
Tioga, *Pa., U.S.A.* **150 E7** 41 55N 77 8W
Tioman, Pulau, *Malaysia* **87 L5** 2 50N 104 10 E
Tione di Trento, *Italy* **44 B7** 46 2N 10 43 E
Tionesta, *U.S.A.* **150 E5** 41 30N 79 28W
Tior, *Sudan* **107 F3** 6 26N 31 11 E
Tioulilin, *Algeria* **111 C4** 27 1N 0 2W
Tipp City, *U.S.A.* **157 E12** 39 58N 84 11W
Tippecanoe →, *U.S.A.* **157 D10** 40 30N 86 45W
Tipperary, *Ireland* **23 D3** 52 28N 8 10W
Tipperary □, *Ireland* **23 D4** 52 37N 7 55W
Tipton, *Calif., U.S.A.* **160 J7** 36 4N 119 19W
Tipton, *Ind., U.S.A.* **157 D10** 40 17N 86 2W
Tipton, *Iowa, U.S.A.* **156 C5** 41 46N 91 8W
Tipton, *Mo., U.S.A.* **156 F4** 38 39N 92 47W
Tipton Mt., *U.S.A.* **161 K12** 35 32N 114 12W
Tiptonville, *U.S.A.* **155 G10** 36 23N 89 29W
Tiptur, *India* **95 H3** 13 15N 76 26 E
Tiquié →, *Brazil* **168 C4** 0 5N 68 25W
Tiracambu, Serra do, *Brazil* **170 B2** 3 15 S 46 30W
Tirahart, O. →, *Algeria* **111 D5** 23 45N 3 10 E
Tīrān, *Iran* **97 C6** 32 45N 51 8 E
Tīrān, *Si. Arabia* **106 B3** 27 57N 34 32 E
Tiranë, *Albania* **50 E3** 41 18N 19 49 E
Tirano, *Italy* **44 B7** 46 13N 10 10 E
Tiraspol, *Moldova* **53 D14** 46 55N 29 35 E
Tiratimine, *Algeria* **111 C5** 25 56N 3 37 E
Tirau, *N.Z.* **130 D4** 37 58 S 175 46 E
Tirdout, *Mali* **113 B4** 16 7N 1 5W
Tire, *Turkey* **49 C9** 38 5N 27 45 E
Tirebolu, *Turkey* **101 B8** 40 58N 38 45 E
Tiree, *U.K.* **22 E2** 56 31N 6 55W
Tiree, Passage of, *U.K.* **22 E2** 56 30N 6 30W
Tîrgovişte = Târgovişte, *Romania* **53 F10** 44 55N 25 27 E
Tîrgu-Jiu = Târgu-Jiu, *Romania* **53 E8** 45 5N 23 19 E
Tîrgu Mureş = Târgu Mureş, *Romania* **53 D9** 46 31N 24 38 E
Tirich Mir, *Pakistan* **91 A3** 36 15N 71 55 E
Tiriolo, *Italy* **47 D9** 38 57N 16 30 E
Tiririca, Serra da, *Brazil* **171 E2** 17 6 S 47 6W
Tiriro, *Guinea* **112 C3** 10 27N 8 40W
Tiris, *W. Sahara* **110 D2** 23 10N 13 20W
Tirlyanskiy, *Russia* **64 D7** 54 14N 58 35 E
Tirna →, *India* **94 E3** 18 4N 76 57 E
Tírnavos, *Greece* **48 B4** 39 45N 22 18 E
Tirodi, *India* **94 D4** 21 40N 79 44 E
Tirol □, *Austria* **34 D3** 47 3N 10 43 E
Tiros, *Brazil* **171 E2** 19 0 S 45 58W
Tirrukkovil, *Sri Lanka* **95 L5** 7 7N 81 51 E
Tirschenreuth, *Germany* **31 F8** 49 53N 12 19 E
Tirso →, *Italy* **46 C1** 39 53N 8 32 E
Tirstrup, *Denmark* **17 H4** 56 18N 10 42 E
Tirthahalli, *India* **95 H2** 13 42N 75 14 E
Tirua Pt., *N.Z.* **130 E3** 38 25 S 174 40 E
Tiruchchendur, *India* **95 K4** 8 30N 78 11 E
Tiruchchirappalli, *India* **95 J4** 10 45N 78 45 E
Tirukkoyilur, *India* **95 J4** 11 57N 79 12 E
Tirumangalam, *India* **95 K3** 9 49N 77 58 E
Tirumayam, *India* **95 J4** 10 14N 78 45 E
Tirunelveli, *India* **95 K3** 8 45N 77 45 E
Tirupati, *India* **95 H4** 13 39N 79 25 E
Tiruppattur, *Tamil Nadu, India* **95 J4** 10 8N 78 37 E
Tiruppattur, *Tamil Nadu, India* **95 H4** 12 30N 78 30 E
Tiruppur, *India* **95 J3** 11 5N 77 22 E
Tirur, *India* **95 J2** 10 54N 75 55 E
Tiruttani, *India* **95 H4** 13 11N 79 58 E
Tirutturaippundi, *India* **95 J4** 10 32N 79 41 E
Tiruvadaimarudur, *India* **95 J4** 11 2N 79 27 E
Tiruvalla, *India* **95 K3** 9 23N 76 34 E
Tiruvallur, *India* **95 H4** 13 9N 79 57 E
Tiruvannamalai, *India* **95 H4** 12 15N 79 5 E
Tiruvettipuram, *India* **95 H4** 12 39N 79 33 E
Tiruvottiyur, *India* **95 H5** 13 10N 80 22 E
Tisa, *India* **92 C7** 32 50N 76 9 E
Tisa →, *Serbia, Yug.* **52 E5** 45 15N 20 17 E
Tisdale, *Canada* **143 C8** 52 50N 104 0W
Tishomingo, *U.S.A.* **155 H6** 34 14N 96 41W
Tisjön, *Sweden* **16 D7** 60 56N 13 0 E
Tisnaren, *Sweden* **17 F9** 58 58N 15 56 E
Tišnov, *Czech Rep.* **35 B9** 49 21N 16 25 E
Tisovec, *Slovak Rep.* **35 C12** 48 41N 19 56 E
Tissamaharama, *Sri Lanka* **95 L5** 6 17N 81 17 E
Tissemsilt, *Algeria* **111 A5** 35 35N 1 50 E
Tissint, *Morocco* **110 C3** 29 57N 7 16W
Tista →, *India* **90 C2** 25 23N 89 43 E
Tistedal, *Norway* **18 E8** 59 8N 11 27 E
Tisza = Tisa →, *Serbia, Yug.* **52 E5** 45 15N 20 17 E
Tiszaföldvár, *Hungary* **52 D5** 46 58N 20 14 E
Tiszafüred, *Hungary* **52 C5** 47 38N 20 50 E
Tiszalök, *Hungary* **52 B6** 48 1N 21 20 E
Tiszavasvári, *Hungary* **52 C6** 47 58N 21 18 E
Tit, *Ahaggar, Algeria* **111 D6** 23 0N 5 10 E
Tit, *Tademait, Algeria* **111 C5** 27 0N 1 29 E
Tit-Ary, *Russia* **67 B13** 71 55N 127 2 E
Titabar, *India* **90 B5** 26 36N 94 12 E
Titaguas, *Spain* **40 F3** 39 53N 1 6W
Titao, *Burkina Faso* **113 C4** 13 45N 2 5W
Titel, *Serbia, Yug.* **52 E5** 45 10N 20 18 E
Tithwal, *Pakistan* **93 B5** 34 21N 73 50 E
Titicaca, L., *S. Amer.* **172 D4** 15 30 S 69 30W
Titisee, *Germany* **31 H4** 47 54N 8 10 E
Tititira Hd., *N.Z.* **131 D4** 43 36 S 169 25 E
Titiwa, *Nigeria* **113 C7** 12 14N 12 53 E
Titlagarh, *India* **94 D6** 20 15N 83 11 E
Titlis, *Switz.* **33 C6** 46 46N 8 27 E
Tito, *Italy* **47 B8** 40 35N 15 40 E
Titograd = Podgorica, *Montenegro, Yug.* **50 D3** 42 30N 19 19 E
Titova Korenica, *Croatia* **45 D12** 44 45N 15 41 E
Titu, *Romania* **53 F10** 44 39N 25 32 E
Titule, *Dem. Rep. of the Congo* **118 B2** 3 15N 25 31 E
Titusville, *Fla., U.S.A.* **149 L5** 28 37N 80 49W
Titusville, *Pa., U.S.A.* **150 E5** 41 38N 79 41W
Tivaouane, *Senegal* **112 C1** 14 56N 16 45W
Tivat, *Montenegro, Yug.* **50 D2** 42 28N 18 43 E
Tiverton, *U.K.* **21 G4** 50 54N 3 29W
Tívoli, *Italy* **45 G9** 41 58N 12 45 E
Tiwī, *Oman* **99 B7** 22 45N 59 12 E
Tiyo, *Eritrea* **107 E5** 14 41N 40 15 E
Tiyo, Peg., *Indonesia* **83 B5** 4 0 S 135 30 E
Tizga, *Morocco* **110 B3** 32 1N 5 9W
Ti'zi N'Isli, *Morocco* **110 B3** 32 28N 5 47W
Tizi-Ouzou, *Algeria* **111 A5** 36 42N 4 3 E
Tizimín, *Mexico* **163 C7** 21 0N 88 1W
Tiznados →, *Venezuela* **168 B4** 8 16N 67 47W
Tiznap He →, *China* **65 D8** 38 23N 77 24 E
Tiznit, *Morocco* **110 C3** 29 48N 9 45W
Tjæreborg, *Denmark* **17 J2** 55 28N 8 36 E
Tjällmo, *Sweden* **17 F9** 58 43N 15 21 E
Tjeggelvas, *Sweden* **14 C17** 66 37N 17 45 E
Tjirebon = Cirebon, *Indonesia* **85 D3** 6 45 S 108 32 E
Tjluring, *Indonesia* **79 J17** 8 25 S 114 13 E
Tjøme, *Norway* **18 E7** 59 8N 10 26 E
Tjörn, *Sweden* **17 F5** 58 0N 11 35 E
Tkibuli = Tqibuli, *Georgia* **61 J6** 42 26N 43 0 E
Tkvarcheli = Tqvarcheli, *Georgia* **61 J5** 42 47N 41 42 E
Tlacotalpan, *Mexico* **163 D5** 18 37N 95 40W
Tlahualilo, *Mexico* **162 B4** 26 20N 103 30W
Tlaquepaque, *Mexico* **162 C4** 20 39N 103 19W
Tlaxcala, *Mexico* **163 D5** 19 20N 98 14W
Tlaxcala □, *Mexico* **163 D5** 19 30N 98 20W
Tlaxiaco, *Mexico* **163 D5** 17 18N 97 40W
Tlemcen, *Algeria* **111 B4** 34 52N 1 21W
Tleta Sidi Bouguedra, *Morocco* **110 B3** 32 16N 9 59W
Tłuszcz, *Poland* **55 F8** 52 25N 21 25 E
Tlyarata, *Russia* **61 J8** 42 9N 46 26 E
Tmassah, *Libya* **108 C3** 26 19N 15 51 E
Tnine d'Anglou, *Morocco* **110 C3** 29 50N 9 50W
To Bong, *Vietnam* **86 F7** 12 45N 109 16 E
To-Shima, *Japan* **73 C11** 34 31N 139 17 E
Toa Payoh, *Singapore* **87 d** 1 20N 103 51 E
Toad →, *Canada* **142 B4** 59 25N 124 57W
Toad River, *Canada* **142 B3** 58 51N 125 14W
Toamasina, *Madag.* **117 B8** 18 10 S 49 25 E
Toamasina □, *Madag.* **117 B8** 18 0 S 49 0 E
Toay, *Argentina* **174 D3** 36 43 S 64 38W
Toba, *China* **76 B1** 31 19N 97 42 E
Toba, *Japan* **73 C8** 34 30N 136 51 E
Toba, Danau, *Indonesia* **84 B1** 2 30N 97 30 E
Toba Kakar, *Pakistan* **91 C3** 31 30N 69 0 E
Toba Tek Singh, *Pakistan* **92 D5** 30 55N 72 25 E
Tobago, *Trin. & Tob.* **165 D7** 11 10N 60 30W
Tobarra, *Spain* **41 G3** 38 37N 1 44W
Tobelo, *Indonesia* **82 A3** 1 45N 127 56 E
Tobermory, *Canada* **140 C3** 45 12N 81 40W
Tobermory, *U.K.* **22 E2** 56 38N 6 5W
Tobi, *Pac. Oc.* **83 A4** 2 40N 131 10 E
Tobias Fornier, *Phil.* **81 F3** 10 30N 121 57 E
Tobin, *U.S.A.* **160 F5** 39 55N 121 19W
Tobin, L., *Australia* **124 D4** 21 45 S 125 49 E
Tobin L., *Canada* **143 C8** 53 35N 103 30W
Toblach = Dobbiaco, *Italy* **45 B9** 46 44N 12 14 E
Toboali, *Indonesia* **84 C3** 3 0 S 106 25 E
Tobol, *Kazakstan* **64 E9** 52 40N 62 39 E
Tobol →, *Russia* **66 D7** 58 10N 68 12 E
Toboli, *Indonesia* **82 B2** 0 38 S 120 5 E
Tobolsk, *Russia* **66 D7** 58 15N 68 10 E
Tobor, *Senegal* **112 C1** 12 40N 16 15W
Toboso, *Phil.* **81 F4** 10 43N 123 31 E
Tobruk = Tubruq, *Libya* **108 B4** 32 7N 23 55 E
Tobyhanna, *U.S.A.* **151 E9** 41 11N 75 25W
Tobyl = Tobol →, *Russia* **66 D7** 58 10N 68 12 E
Tocache Nuevo, *Peru* **172 B2** 8 9 S 76 26W
Tocantínia, *Brazil* **170 C2** 9 33 S 48 22W
Tocantinópolis, *Brazil* **170 C2** 6 20 S 47 25W
Tocantins □, *Brazil* **170 D2** 10 0 S 48 0W
Tocantins →, *Brazil* **170 B2** 1 45 S 49 10W
Toccoa, *U.S.A.* **149 H4** 34 35N 83 19W
Toce →, *Italy* **44 C5** 45 56N 8 29 E
Tochi →, *Pakistan* **92 C4** 32 49N 70 41 E
Tochigi, *Japan* **73 A11** 36 25N 139 45 E
Tochigi □, *Japan* **73 A11** 36 45N 139 45 E
Tocina, *Spain* **43 H5** 37 37N 5 44W
Töcksfors, *Sweden* **16 E5** 59 31N 11 52 E
Toco, *Chile* **172 E4** 22 5 S 69 35W
Toco, *Trin. & Tob.* **169 F10** 10 50N 60 4W
Toconao, *Chile* **174 A2** 23 11 S 68 1W
Tocopilla, *Chile* **174 A1** 22 5 S 70 10W
Tocumwal, *Australia* **129 C6** 35 51 S 145 31 E
Tocuyo →, *Venezuela* **168 A4** 11 3N 68 23W
Tocuyo de la Costa, *Venezuela* **168 A4** 11 2N 68 23W
Todal, *Norway* **18 B5** 62 49N 8 44 E
Todd →, *Australia* **126 C2** 24 52 S 135 48 E
Todeli, *Indonesia* **82 B2** 1 40 S 124 29 E
Todenyang, *Kenya* **118 B4** 4 35N 35 56 E
Todgarh, *India* **92 G5** 25 42N 73 58 E
Todi, *Italy* **45 F9** 42 47N 12 24 E
Tödi, *Switz.* **33 C7** 46 48N 8 55 E
Todos os Santos, B. de, *Brazil* **171 D4** 12 48 S 38 38W
Todos Santos, *Mexico* **162 C2** 23 27N 110 13W
Todtnau, *Germany* **31 H3** 47 49N 7 56 E
Toe Hd., *U.K.* **22 D1** 57 50N 7 8W
Toecé, *Burkina Faso* **113 C4** 11 50N 1 16W
Toetoes B., *N.Z.* **131 G3** 46 42 S 168 41 E
Tofield, *Canada* **142 C6** 53 25N 112 40W
Tofino, *Canada* **142 D3** 49 11N 125 55W
Tofte, *Norway* **18 E7** 59 30N 10 34 E
Tofua, *Tonga* **133 P13** 19 45 S 175 5W
Toga, *Vanuatu* **133 C4** 13 26 S 166 42 E
Tōgane, *Japan* **73 B12** 35 33N 140 22 E
Togba, *Mauritania* **112 B2** 17 26N 10 12W
Togbo, *C.A.R.* **114 A3** 6 0N 17 27 E
Toggenburg, *Switz.* **33 B8** 47 16N 9 9 E
Togiak, *U.S.A.* **144 G7** 59 4N 160 24W
Togian, Kepulauan, *Indonesia* **82 B2** 0 20 S 121 50 E
Togliatti, *Russia* **60 D9** 53 32N 49 24 E
Togo ■, *W. Afr.* **113 D5** 8 30N 1 35 E
Togtoh, *China* **74 D6** 40 15N 111 10 E
Toguzak →, *Kazakstan* **64 D9** 54 3N 62 44 E
Tohma →, *Turkey* **100 C7** 38 29N 38 23 E
Tōhoku □, *Japan* **70 E10** 39 50N 141 45 E
Töhöm, *Mongolia* **74 B5** 44 27N 108 2 E
Tohopekaliga, L., *U.S.A.* **153 G8** 28 12N 81 24W
Toi, *Japan* **73 C10** 34 54N 138 47 E
Toibalewe, *India* **95 J11** 10 32N 92 30 E
Toili, *Indonesia* **82 B2** 1 24 S 122 26 E
Toinya, *Sudan* **107 F2** 6 17N 29 46 E
Toiyabe Range, *U.S.A.* **158 G5** 39 30N 117 0W
Tojikiston = Tajikistan ■, *Asia* **66 F8** 38 30N 70 0 E
Tojo, *Indonesia* **82 B2** 1 20 S 121 15 E
Tōjō, *Japan* **72 C5** 34 53N 133 16 E
Tok, *U.S.A.* **144 E12** 63 20N 142 59W
Tok →, *Russia* **64 E4** 52 46N 52 22 E
Tok-do, *Japan* **71 F5** 37 15N 131 52 E
Toka, *Guyana* **169 C6** 3 58N 59 17W
Tokaanu, *N.Z.* **130 E4** 38 58 S 175 46 E
Tokachi-Dake, *Japan* **70 C11** 43 17N 142 5 E
Tokachi-Gawa →, *Japan* **70 C11** 42 44N 143 42 E
Tokai, *Japan* **73 B8** 35 2N 136 55 E
Tokaj, *Hungary* **52 B6** 48 8N 21 27 E
Tokala, *Indonesia* **82 B2** 1 30 S 121 40 E
Tōkamachi, *Japan* **73 A10** 37 8N 138 43 E
Tokanui, *N.Z.* **131 G3** 46 34 S 168 56 E
Tokar, *Sudan* **106 D4** 18 27N 37 56 E
Tokara-Rettō, *Japan* **71 K4** 29 37N 129 43 E
Tokarahi, *N.Z.* **131 E5** 44 56 S 170 39 E
Tokashiki-Shima, *Japan* **71 L3** 26 11N 127 21 E
Tokat, *Turkey* **100 B7** 40 22N 36 35 E
Tokat □, *Turkey* **57 F6** 40 15N 36 30 E
Tŏkch'ŏn, *N. Korea* **75 E14** 39 45N 126 18 E
Tokeland, *U.S.A.* **160 D3** 46 42N 123 59W
Tokelau Is., *Pac. Oc.* **134 H10** 9 0 S 171 45W
Toki, *Japan* **73 B9** 35 18N 137 8 E
Tokmak, *Kyrgyzstan* **66 E8** 42 49N 75 15 E
Tokmak, *Ukraine* **59 J8** 47 16N 35 42 E
Toko Ra., *Australia* **126 C2** 23 5 S 138 20 E
Tokomaru Bay, *N.Z.* **130 E7** 38 8 S 178 22 E
Tokoname, *Japan* **73 C8** 34 53N 136 51 E
Tokoro-Gawa →, *Japan* **70 B12** 44 7N 144 5 E
Tokoroa, *N.Z.* **130 E4** 38 13 S 175 50 E
Tokorozawa, *Japan* **73 B11** 35 47N 139 28 E
Toksook Bay, *U.S.A.* **144 F6** 60 32N 165 0W
Toktogul, *Kyrgyzstan* **65 C6** 41 50N 72 50 E
Toktogul Suu Saktagychy, *Kyrgyzstan* **65 C6** 41 48N 72 51 E
Toku, *Tonga* **133 P13** 18 10 S 174 11W
Tokuji, *Japan* **72 C3** 34 11N 131 42 E
Tokuno-Shima, *Japan* **71 L4** 27 56N 128 55 E
Tokushima, *Japan* **72 C6** 34 4N 134 34 E
Tokushima □, *Japan* **72 D6** 33 55N 134 0 E
Tokuyama, *Japan* **72 C3** 34 3N 131 50 E
Tōkyō, *Japan* **73 B11** 35 45N 139 45 E
Tōkyō □, *Japan* **73 B11** 35 40N 139 30 E
Tōkyō-Wan, *Japan* **73 B11** 35 25N 139 47 E
Tokzār, *Afghan.* **91 B2** 35 52N 66 26 E
Tolaga Bay, *N.Z.* **130 E7** 38 21 S 178 20 E
Tolbukhin = Dobrich, *Bulgaria* **51 C11** 43 37N 27 49 E
Tolé, *C.A.R.* **114 A3** 6 34N 16 1 E
Tôle Bī, *Kazakstan* **65 B6** 43 42N 73 46 E
Toledo, *Brazil* **175 A5** 24 44 S 53 45W
Toledo, *Phil.* **81 F4** 10 23N 123 38 E
Toledo, *Spain* **42 F6** 39 50N 4 2W
Toledo, *Ill., U.S.A.* **157 E8** 39 16N 88 15W
Toledo, *Iowa, U.S.A.* **156 C4** 42 0N 92 35W
Toledo, *Ohio, U.S.A.* **157 C13** 41 39N 83 33W
Toledo, *Oreg., U.S.A.* **158 D2** 44 37N 123 56W
Toledo, *Wash., U.S.A.* **158 C2** 46 26N 122 51W
Toledo, Montes de, *Spain* **43 F6** 39 33N 4 20W
Toledo Bend Reservoir, *U.S.A.* **155 K8** 31 11N 93 34W
Tolentino, *Italy* **45 E10** 43 12N 13 17 E
Tolfa, *Italy* **45 F8** 42 9N 11 56 E
Tolga, *Algeria* **111 B6** 34 40N 5 22 E
Tolga, *Australia* **126 B4** 17 15 S 145 29 E
Tolga, *Norway* **18 B8** 62 26N 11 1 E
Toliara, *Madag.* **117 C7** 23 21 S 43 40 E
Toliara □, *Madag.* **117 C8** 21 0 S 45 0 E
Tolima, *Colombia* **168 C2** 4 40N 75 19W
Tolima □, *Colombia* **168 C2** 3 45N 75 15W
Tolitoli, *Indonesia* **82 A2** 1 5N 120 50 E
Tolkmicko, *Poland* **54 D6** 54 19N 19 31 E
Tollarp, *Sweden* **17 J7** 55 55N 13 58 E
Tollensesee, *Germany* **30 B9** 53 30N 13 13 E
Tollhouse, *U.S.A.* **160 H7** 37 1N 119 24W
Tolmachevo, *Russia* **58 C5** 58 56N 29 51 E
Tolmezzo, *Italy* **45 B10** 46 24N 13 1 E
Tolmin, *Slovenia* **45 B10** 46 11N 13 45 E
Tolna, *Hungary* **52 D3** 46 25N 18 48 E
Tolna □, *Hungary* **52 D3** 46 30N 18 30 E
Tolo, *Dem. Rep. of the Congo* **114 C3** 2 55 S 18 34 E
Tolo, Teluk, *Indonesia* **82 B2** 2 20 S 122 10 E
Tolo Harbour, *China* **69 G11** 22 27N 114 12 E
Tolochin = Talachyn, *Belarus* **58 E5** 54 25N 29 42 E
Tolokiwa I., *Papua N. G.* **132 C4** 5 19 S 147 37 E
Tolong Bay, *Phil.* **81 G4** 9 20N 122 49 E
Tolono, *U.S.A.* **157 E8** 39 59N 88 16W
Tolosa, *Spain* **40 B2** 43 8N 2 5W
Tolox, *Spain* **43 J6** 36 41N 4 54W
Toltén, *Chile* **176 A2** 39 13 S 74 14W
Toluca, *Mexico* **163 D5** 19 20N 99 40W
Toluca, *U.S.A.* **156 C7** 41 0N 89 9W
Tolybay, *Kazakstan* **64 F9** 50 31N 62 19 E
Tom Burke, *S. Africa* **117 C4** 23 5 S 28 0 E
Tom Price, *Australia* **124 D2** 22 40 S 117 48 E
Toma, *Burkina Faso* **112 C4** 12 45N 2 53W
Tomah, *U.S.A.* **154 D9** 43 59N 90 30W
Tomahawk, *U.S.A.* **154 C10** 45 28N 89 44W
Tomai, *Moldova* **53 D13** 46 34N 28 19 E
Tomakomai, *Japan* **70 C10** 42 38N 141 36 E
Tomales, *U.S.A.* **160 G4** 38 15N 122 53W
Tomales B., *U.S.A.* **160 G3** 38 15N 123 58W
Tomanivi, *Fiji* **133 A2** 17 37 S 178 1 E
Tomar, *Portugal* **43 F2** 39 36N 8 25W
Tómaros, Óros, *Greece* **48 B2** 39 29N 20 48 E
Tomarza, *Turkey* **100 C6** 38 27N 35 48 E
Tomás Barrón, *Bolivia* **172 D4** 17 35 S 67 31W
Tomaszów Lubelski, *Poland* **55 H10** 50 27N 23 25 E
Tomaszów Mazowiecki, *Poland* **55 G7** 51 30N 20 2 E
Tomatlán, *Mexico* **162 D3** 19 56N 105 15W
Tombadonkéa, *Guinea* **112 C2** 11 0N 14 25W
Tombador, Serra do, *Brazil* **173 C6** 12 0 S 58 0W
Tombe, *Sudan* **107 F3** 5 53N 31 40 E
Tombel, *Cameroon* **114 B1** 4 45N 9 40 E
Tombigbee →, *U.S.A.* **149 K2** 31 8N 87 57W
Tomboco, *Angola* **115 D2** 6 48 S 13 18 E
Tombouctou, *Mali* **112 B4** 16 50N 3 0W
Tombstone, *U.S.A.* **159 L8** 31 43N 110 4W
Tombua, *Angola* **116 B1** 15 55 S 11 55 E
Tomé, *Chile* **174 D1** 36 36 S 72 57W
Tomé-Açu, *Brazil* **170 B2** 2 25 S 48 9W
Tomelilla, *Sweden* **17 J7** 55 33N 13 58 E
Tomelloso, *Spain* **43 F7** 39 10N 3 2W
Tömenaryk, *Kazakstan* **65 A3** 44 2N 67 1 E
Tomingley, *Australia* **129 B8** 32 26 S 148 16 E
Tomini, *Indonesia* **82 A2** 0 30N 120 30 E
Tomini, Teluk, *Indonesia* **82 B2** 0 10 S 121 0 E
Tominian, *Mali* **112 C4** 13 17N 4 35W
Tomiño, *Spain* **42 D2** 41 59N 8 46W
Tomintoul, *U.K.* **22 D5** 57 15N 3 23W
Tomioka, *Japan* **73 A10** 36 15N 138 54 E
Tomislavgrad, *Bos.-H.* **52 G2** 43 42N 17 13 E
Tomkinson Ranges, *Australia* **125 E4** 26 11 S 129 5 E
Tommot, *Russia* **67 D13** 59 4N 126 20 E
Tomnop Ta Suos, *Cambodia* **87 G5** 11 20N 104 15 E
Tomo, *Colombia* **168 C4** 2 38N 67 32W
Tomo →, *Colombia* **168 B4** 5 20N 67 48W
Tomobe, *Japan* **73 A12** 36 20N 140 20 E
Tomra, *Norway* **18 B3** 62 34N 6 56 E
Toms Place, *U.S.A.* **160 H8** 37 34N 118 41W
Toms River, *U.S.A.* **151 G10** 39 58N 74 12W
Tomsk, *Russia* **66 D9** 56 30N 85 5 E
Tomtabacken, *Sweden* **17 G8** 57 30N 14 30 E
Tona, *Spain* **40 D7** 41 51N 2 14 E
Tonalá, *Mexico* **163 D6** 16 8N 93 41W
Tonale, Passo del, *Italy* **44 B7** 46 16N 10 35 E
Tonami, *Japan* **73 A8** 36 40N 136 58 E
Tonantins, *Brazil* **168 D4** 2 45 S 67 45W
Tonasket, *U.S.A.* **158 B4** 48 42N 119 26W
Tonate, *Fr. Guiana* **169 C7** 5 0N 52 28W
Tonawanda, *U.S.A.* **150 D6** 43 1N 78 53W
Tonbo, *Burma* **90 F5** 18 31N 95 5 E
Tonbridge, *U.K.* **21 F8** 51 11N 0 17 E
Tonda, *Papua N. G.* **132 E1** 8 55 S 141 34 E
Tondabayashi, *Japan* **73 C7** 34 30N 135 36 E
Tondano, *Indonesia* **82 A2** 1 35N 124 54 E
Tondela, *Portugal* **42 E2** 40 31N 8 5W
Tønder, *Denmark* **17 K2** 54 58N 8 50 E
Tondi, *India* **95 K4** 9 45N 79 4 E
Tondi Kiwindi, *Niger* **113 C5** 14 28N 2 2 E
Tondibi, *Mali* **113 B4** 16 39N 0 14W
Tondoro, *Namibia* **116 B2** 17 45 S 18 50 E
Tone →, *Australia* **125 F2** 34 25 S 116 25 E
Tone-Gawa →, *Japan* **73 B12** 35 44N 140 51 E
Tonekābon, *Iran* **97 B6** 36 45N 51 12 E
Tong I., *Papua N. G.* **132 B4** 2 3 S 147 47 E
Tong Xian, *China* **74 E9** 39 55N 116 35 E
Tôngâ, *Sudan* **107 F3** 9 28N 31 3 E
Tonga ■, *Pac. Oc.* **133 P13** 19 50 S 174 30W
Tonga Trench, *Pac. Oc.* **134 J10** 18 0 S 173 0W
Tongaat, *S. Africa* **117 D5** 29 33 S 31 9 E
Tongala, *Australia* **129 D6** 36 14 S 144 56 E
Tong'an, *China* **77 E12** 24 37N 118 8 E
Tongareva, *Cook Is.* **135 H12** 9 0 S 158 0W
Tongariro Nat. Park, *N.Z.* **130 F4** 39 8 S 175 33 E
Tongass Nat. Forest, *U.S.A.* **144 H14** 56 30N 134 0W
Tongatapu, *Tonga* **133 Q14** 21 10 S 174 0W
Tongatapu Group, *Tonga* **133 Q13** 21 0 S 175 0W
Tongbai, *China* **77 A9** 32 20N 113 23 E
Tongcheng, *Anhui, China* **77 B11** 31 4N 116 56 E
Tongcheng, *Hubei, China* **77 C9** 29 15N 113 50 E
Tongchŏn-ni, *N. Korea* **75 E14** 39 50N 127 25 E
Tongchuan, *China* **74 G5** 35 6N 109 3 E
Tongdao, *China* **76 D7** 26 10N 109 42 E
Tongeren, *Belgium* **24 D5** 50 47N 5 28 E
Tonggu, *China* **77 C10** 28 31N 114 20 E
Tonggu Jiao, *China* **69 G10** 22 22N 113 37 E
Tongguan, *China* **74 G6** 34 40N 110 25 E
Tonghai, *China* **76 E4** 24 10N 102 53 E
Tonghua, *China* **75 D13** 41 42N 125 58 E
Tongjiang, *China* **76 B6** 31 58N 107 11 E
Tongjosŏn Man, *N. Korea* **75 E15** 39 30N 128 0 E
Tongkil, *Phil.* **81 H3** 6 4N 121 48 E
Tongking, G. of = Tonkin, G. of, *Asia* **68 E5** 20 0N 108 0 E
Tongliang, *China* **76 C6** 29 50N 106 3 E
Tongliao, *China* **75 C12** 43 38N 122 18 E
Tongling, *China* **77 B11** 30 55N 117 48 E
Tonglu, *China* **77 C12** 29 45N 119 37 E
Tongnae, *S. Korea* **75 G15** 35 12N 129 5 E
Tongnan = Anyue, *China* **76 B5** 30 9N 105 50 E
Tongoa, *Vanuatu* **133 F6** 16 54 S 168 34 E
Tongobory, *Madag.* **117 C7** 23 32 S 44 20 E
Tongoy, *Chile* **174 C1** 30 16 S 71 31W
Tongquil I., *Phil.* **81 H3** 6 2N 121 51 E
Tongren, *China* **76 D7** 27 43N 109 11 E
Tongres = Tongeren, *Belgium* **24 D5** 50 47N 5 28 E
Tongsa Dzong, *Bhutan* **90 B3** 27 31N 90 31 E
Tongue, *U.K.* **22 C4** 58 29N 4 25W
Tongue →, *U.S.A.* **154 B2** 46 25N 105 52W
Tongwei, *China* **74 G3** 35 0N 105 5 E
Tongxiang, *China* **77 B13** 30 39N 120 34 E
Tongxin, *China* **74 F3** 36 59N 105 58 E
Tongyang, *N. Korea* **75 E14** 39 9N 126 53 E
Tongyu, *China* **75 B12** 44 45N 123 4 E
Tongzi, *China* **76 C6** 28 9N 106 49 E
Tonica, *U.S.A.* **156 C7** 41 13N 89 4W
Tonj, *Sudan* **107 F2** 7 20N 28 44 E
Tonj →, *Sudan* **107 F2** 7 31N 28 55 E
Tonk, *India* **92 F6** 26 6N 75 54 E
Tonkawa, *U.S.A.* **155 G6** 36 41N 97 18W
Tonkin = Bac Phan, *Vietnam* **86 B5** 22 0N 105 0 E
Tonkin, G. of, *Asia* **68 E5** 20 0N 108 0 E
Tonle Sap, *Cambodia* **86 F4** 13 0N 104 0 E
Tonnay-Charente, *France* **28 C3** 45 56N 0 55W
Tonneins, *France* **28 D4** 44 23N 0 19 E
Tonnerre, *France* **27 E10** 47 51N 3 59 E
Tönning, *Germany* **30 A4** 54 19N 8 56 E
Tono, *Japan* **70 E10** 39 19N 141 32 E
Tonopah, *U.S.A.* **159 G5** 38 4N 117 14W
Tonoshō, *Japan* **72 C6** 34 29N 134 11 E
Tonosí, *Panama* **164 E3** 7 20N 80 20W
Tons →, *Haryana, India* **92 D7** 30 30N 77 39 E
Tons →, *Ut. P., India* **93 F10** 26 1N 83 33 E
Tønsberg, *Norway* **15 G14** 59 19N 10 25 E
Tonsina, *U.S.A.* **144 F11** 61 39N 145 11W
Tonstad, *Norway* **18 F3** 58 40N 6 45 E
Tonumea, *Tonga* **133 Q13** 20 30 S 174 30W
Tonya, *Turkey* **101 B8** 40 53N 39 16 E
Tonzang, *Burma* **90 D4** 23 36N 93 42 E
Tonzi, *Burma* **90 C5** 24 39N 94 57 E
Toobanna, *Australia* **126 B4** 18 42 S 146 9 E
Toodyay, *Australia* **125 F2** 31 34 S 116 28 E
Tooele, *U.S.A.* **158 F7** 40 32N 112 18W
Toompine, *Australia* **127 D3** 27 15 S 144 19 E
Toomsboro, *U.S.A.* **152 C6** 32 50N 83 5W
Toora, *Australia* **129 E7** 38 39 S 146 23 E
Toora-Khem, *Russia* **67 D10** 52 28N 96 17 E
Toowoomba, *Australia* **127 D5** 27 32 S 151 56 E
Top-ozero, *Russia* **56 A5** 65 35N 32 0 E
Top Springs, *Australia* **124 C5** 16 37 S 131 51 E
Topalu, *Romania* **53 F13** 44 31N 28 3 E
Topaz, *U.S.A.* **160 G7** 38 41N 119 30W
Topeka, *U.S.A.* **154 F7** 39 3N 95 40W
Topl'a →, *Slovak Rep.* **35 C14** 48 45N 21 45 E
Topley, *Canada* **142 C3** 54 49N 126 18W
Toplica →, *Serbia, Yug.* **50 C5** 43 15N 21 49 E
Toplița, *Romania* **53 D10** 46 55N 25 20 E
Topo, *Azores* **9 d1** 38 33N 27 45W
Topo, Pta. do, *Azores* **9 d1** 38 33N 27 48W
Topocalma, Pta., *Chile* **174 C1** 34 10 S 72 2W
Topock, *U.S.A.* **161 L12** 34 46N 114 29W
Topola, *Serbia, Yug.* **50 B4** 44 17N 20 41 E
Topolčani, *Macedonia* **50 E5** 41 14N 21 25 E
Topol'čany, *Slovak Rep.* **35 C11** 48 35N 18 12 E
Topolnitsa →, *Bulgaria* **51 D8** 42 11N 24 18 E
Topolobampo, *Mexico* **162 B3** 25 40N 109 4W
Topoloveni, *Romania* **53 F10** 44 49N 25 5 E
Topolovgrad, *Bulgaria* **51 D10** 42 5N 26 20 E
Topolvățu Mare, *Romania* **52 E6** 45 46N 21 41 E
Toppenish, *U.S.A.* **158 C3** 46 23N 120 19W
Topraisar, *Romania* **53 F13** 44 1N 28 27 E
Topusko, *Croatia* **45 C12** 45 18N 15 59 E

Two Hills 293

Trucial States = United Arab Emirates ■, Asia 97 F7 23 50N 54 0 E
Truckee, U.S.A. 160 F6 39 20N 120 11W
Trudfront, Russia 61 H8 45 56N 47 40 E
Trudovoye, Russia 70 C6 43 17N 132 5 E
Trujillo, Colombia 168 C2 4 10N 76 19W
Trujillo, Honduras 164 C2 16 0N 86 0W
Trujillo, Peru 172 B2 8 6 S 79 0W
Trujillo, Spain 43 F5 39 28N 5 55W
Trujillo, U.S.A. 155 H2 35 32N 104 42W
Trujillo, Venezuela 168 B3 9 22N 70 38W
Trujillo □, Venezuela 168 B3 9 25N 70 30W
Truk, Micronesia 134 G7 7 25N 151 46 E
Trumann, U.S.A. 155 H9 35 41N 90 31W
Trumansburg, U.S.A. 151 D8 42 33N 76 40W
Trumbull, Mt., U.S.A. 159 H7 36 25N 113 8W
Trŭn, Bulgaria 50 D6 42 51N 22 38 E
Trun, France 26 D7 48 50N 0 2 E
Trun, Switz. 33 C7 46 45N 8 59 E
Trundle, Australia 129 B7 32 53 S 147 35 E
Trung-Phan = Annam, Vietnam 86 E7 16 0N 108 0 E
Truro, Australia 128 C3 34 24 S 139 9 E
Truro, Canada 141 C7 45 21N 63 14W
Truro, U.K. 21 G2 50 16N 5 4W
Truskavets, Ukraine 59 H2 49 17N 23 30 E
Trŭstenik, Bulgaria 51 C8 43 31N 24 28 E
Trustrup, Denmark 17 H4 56 20N 10 46 E
Trutch, Canada 142 B4 57 44N 122 57W
Truth or Consequences, U.S.A. 159 K10 33 8N 107 15W
Trutnov, Czech Rep. 34 A8 50 37N 15 54 E
Truxton, U.S.A. 151 D8 42 45N 76 2W
Truyère →, France 28 D6 44 38N 2 34 E
Tryavna, Bulgaria 51 D9 42 54N 25 25 E
Tryonville, U.S.A. 150 E5 41 42N 79 48W
Trysilelva →, Norway 18 C9 61 2N 12 35 E
Trzcianka, Poland 55 E3 53 3N 16 25 E
Trzciel, Poland 55 F2 52 23N 15 50 E
Trzcińsko Zdrój, Poland 55 F1 52 58N 14 35 E
Trzebiatów, Poland 54 D2 54 3N 15 18 E
Trzebiez, Poland 54 E1 53 38N 14 31 E
Trzebnica, Poland 55 G4 51 20N 17 1 E
Trzemeszno, Poland 55 F4 52 33N 17 48 E
Tržič, Slovenia 45 B11 46 22N 14 18 E
Tsagan Aman, Russia 61 G8 47 34N 46 43 E
Tsakarisiánon, Greece 39 C2 38 10N 20 40 E
Tsala Apopka L., U.S.A. 153 G7 28 53N 82 19W
Tsamandás, Greece 48 B2 39 46N 20 21 E
Tsandi, Namibia 116 B1 17 42 S 14 50 E
Tsaratanana, Madag. 117 B8 16 47 S 47 39 E
Tsaratanana, Mt. de, Madag. 117 A8 14 0 S 49 0 E
Tsaratanana, Réserve de, Madag. 117 A8 13 57 S 48 52 E
Tsarevo = Michurin, Bulgaria 51 D11 42 9N 27 51 E
Tsarevo, Bulgaria 51 D9 42 28N 25 52 E
Tsaritsáni, Greece 48 B4 39 53N 22 14 E
Tsau, Botswana 116 C3 20 8 S 22 22 E
Tsavo East Nat. Park, Kenya 118 C4 2 44 S 38 47 E
Tsavo West Nat. Park, Kenya 118 C4 3 19 S 37 57 E
Tsebrykove, Ukraine 59 J6 47 9N 30 10 E
Tselinograd = Astana, Kazakstan 66 D8 51 10N 71 30 E
Tses, Namibia 116 D2 25 58 S 18 8 E
Tsetserleg, Mongolia 68 B5 47 36N 101 32 E
Tsévié, Togo 113 D5 6 25N 1 20 E
Tshabong, Botswana 116 D3 26 2 S 22 29 E
Tshabuta, Dem. Rep. of the Congo 115 D4 7 42 S 23 7 E
Tshane, Botswana 116 C3 24 5 S 21 54 E
Tshela, Dem. Rep. of the Congo 115 C2 4 57 S 13 4 E
Tshesebe, Botswana 117 C4 21 51 S 27 32 E
Tshibeke, Dem. Rep. of the Congo 118 C2 2 40 S 28 35 E
Tshibinda, Dem. Rep. of the Congo 118 C2 2 23 S 28 43 E
Tshikapa, Dem. Rep. of the Congo 115 D4 6 28 S 20 48 E
Tshilenge, Dem. Rep. of the Congo 118 D1 6 17 S 23 48 E
Tshindjambo, Dem. Rep. of the Congo 115 E4 10 52 S 22 43 E
Tshinota, Dem. Rep. of the Congo 115 D4 7 2 S 20 58 E
Tshinsenda, Dem. Rep. of the Congo 119 E2 12 20 S 28 0 E
Tshitadi, Dem. Rep. of the Congo 115 D4 6 46 S 21 43 E
Tshofa, Dem. Rep. of the Congo 118 D2 5 13 S 25 16 E
Tshuapa →, Dem. Rep. of the Congo 114 C4 0 14 S 20 42 E
Tshumbiri, Dem. Rep. of the Congo 114 C3 2 38 S 16 18 E
Tshwane, Botswana 116 C3 22 24 S 22 1 E
Tsigara, Botswana 116 C4 20 22 S 25 54 E
Tsihombe, Madag. 117 D8 25 10 S 45 41 E
Tsiigehtchic, Canada 138 B6 67 15N 134 0W
Tsimlyansk, Russia 61 G6 47 40N 42 6 E
Tsimlyansk Res. = Tsimlyanskoye Vdkhr., Russia 61 F6 48 0N 43 0 E
Tsimlyanskoye Vdkhr., Russia 61 F6 48 0N 43 0 E
Tsinan = Jinan, China 74 F9 36 38N 117 1 E
Tsineng, S. Africa 116 D3 27 5 S 23 5 E
Tsing Yi, China 69 G11 22 21N 114 6 E
Tsínga, Greece 51 E8 41 23N 24 44 E
Tsinghai = Qinghai □, China 68 C4 36 0N 98 0 E
Tsingtao = Qingdao, China 75 F11 36 5N 120 20 E
Tsingy de Bemaraha, Réserve Naturelle, Madag. 117 B8 18 35 S 45 25 E
Tsingy de Namoraka, Réserve de, Madag. 117 B8 16 29 S 45 25 E
Tsinjoarivo, Madag. 117 B8 19 37 S 47 40 E
Tsinjomitondraka, Madag. 117 B8 15 40 S 47 8 E
Tsiroanomandidy, Madag. 117 B8 18 46 S 46 2 E
Tsiteli-Tsqaro, Georgia 61 K8 41 33N 46 0 E
Tsitondroina, Madag. 117 C8 21 19 S 46 0 E
Tsitsikamma Nat. Park, S. Africa 116 E3 34 3 S 23 40 E
Tsivilsk, Russia 60 C8 55 50N 47 25 E
Tsivory, Madag. 117 C8 24 4 S 46 5 E
Tskhinvali, Georgia 61 J7 42 14N 44 1 E
Tsna →, Russia 60 C6 54 55N 41 58 E
Tsnori, Georgia 61 K7 41 40N 45 57 E
Tso Moriri, L., India 93 C8 32 50N 78 20 E
Tsobis, Namibia 116 B2 19 27 S 17 30 E
Tsodilo Hill, Botswana 116 B3 18 49 S 21 43 E
Tsogni, Gabon 114 C2 2 48 S 10 10 E
Tsogttsetsiy = Baruunsuu, Mongolia 74 C3 43 43N 105 35 E
Tsolo, S. Africa 117 E4 31 18 S 28 37 E
Tsomo, S. Africa 117 E4 32 0 S 27 42 E
Tsoukaládes, Greece 39 B2 38 41N 20 47 E
Tsu, Japan 73 C8 34 45N 136 25 E
Tsu L., Canada 142 A6 60 40N 111 52W
Tsubata, Japan 73 A8 36 40N 136 44 E
Tsuchiura, Japan 73 A12 36 5N 140 15 E
Tsuen Wan, H.K. 77 F10 22 22N 114 6 E
Tsugaru-Kaikyō, Japan 70 D10 41 35N 141 0 E
Tsukuba, Japan 73 A12 36 2N 140 4 E
Tsukumi, Japan 72 D3 33 4N 131 52 E
Tsukushi-Sanchi, Japan 72 D2 33 25N 130 30 E
Tsumeb, Namibia 116 B2 19 9 S 17 44 E
Tsumis, Namibia 116 C2 23 39 S 17 29 E
Tsuna, Japan 72 C6 34 28N 134 56 E
Tsuno-Shima, Japan 72 C2 34 21N 130 52 E
Tsuru, Japan 73 B10 35 31N 138 57 E
Tsuruga, Japan 73 B8 35 45N 136 2 E
Tsuruga-Wan, Japan 73 B8 35 50N 136 3 E
Tsurugi, Japan 73 A8 36 29N 136 37 E
Tsurugi-San, Japan 72 D6 33 51N 134 6 E
Tsurumi-Saki, Japan 72 E4 32 56N 132 5 E
Tsuruoka, Japan 70 E9 38 44N 139 50 E
Tsurusaki, Japan 72 D3 33 14N 131 41 E
Tsushima, Ehime, Japan 72 D4 33 7N 132 32 E
Tsushima, Gifu, Japan 73 B8 35 10N 136 43 E
Tsushima, Nagasaki, Japan 72 C1 34 20N 129 20 E
Tsuyama, Japan 72 B6 35 3N 134 0 E
Tsvetkovo, Ukraine 59 H6 49 8N 31 33 E
Tsyelyakhany, Belarus 59 F3 52 30N 25 46 E
Tu →, Burma 90 E6 21 50N 96 15 E
Tua, Dem. Rep. of the Congo 114 C3 3 38 S 16 38 E
Tua →, Papua N. G. 132 D3 6 30 S 144 28 E
Tua →, Portugal 42 D3 41 13N 7 26W
Tuaheni Pt., N.Z. 130 E7 38 43 S 178 4 E
Tuai, N.Z. 130 E6 38 47 S 177 10 E
Tuakau, N.Z. 130 D3 37 16 S 174 59 E
Tual, Indonesia 83 C4 5 38 S 132 44 E
Tuam, Ireland 23 C3 53 31N 8 51W
Tuamarina, N.Z. 131 B8 41 25 S 173 59 E
Tuamotu Arch. = Tuamotu Is., Pac. Oc. 135 J13 17 0 S 144 0W
Tuamotu Is., Pac. Oc. 135 J13 17 0 S 144 0W
Tuamotu Ridge, Pac. Oc. 135 K14 20 0 S 138 0W
Tuanfeng, China 77 B10 30 38N 114 52 E
Tuanxi, China 76 D6 27 28N 107 8 E
Tuao, Phil. 80 C3 17 55N 121 22 E
Tuapse, Russia 61 H4 44 5N 39 10 E
Tuas, Singapore 87 d 1 19N 103 39 E
Tuatapere, N.Z. 131 G2 46 8 S 167 41 E
Tuba City, U.S.A. 159 H8 36 8N 111 14W
Tuban, Indonesia 85 D4 6 54 S 112 3 E
Tubani, Botswana 116 C3 24 46 S 24 18 E
Tubarão, Brazil 175 B6 28 30 S 49 0W
Tūbās, West Bank 103 C4 32 20N 35 22 E
Tubas →, Namibia 116 C2 22 54 S 14 35 E
Tubau, Malaysia 85 B4 3 10N 113 40 E
Tubigon, Phil. 81 G4 9 57N 123 58 E
Tübingen, Germany 31 G5 48 31N 9 4 E
Tubod, Phil. 81 G4 8 3N 123 48 E
Tubou, Fiji 133 B3 18 13 S 178 48W
Tubruq, Libya 108 B4 32 7N 23 55 E
Tubruq □, Libya 108 B4 30 0N 24 0 E
Tubuai Is., Pac. Oc. 135 K13 25 0 S 150 0W
Tuburan, Basilan, Phil. 81 H4 6 39N 122 16 E
Tuburan, Cebu, Phil. 81 F4 10 44N 123 49 E
Tuc Trung, Vietnam 87 G6 11 1N 107 12 E
Tucacas, Venezuela 168 A4 10 48N 68 19W
Tucano, Brazil 170 D4 10 58 S 38 48W
T'uch'ang, Taiwan 77 E13 24 42N 121 25 E
Tuchodi →, Canada 142 B4 58 17N 123 42W
Tuchola, Poland 54 E4 53 33N 17 52 E
Tuchów, Poland 55 J8 49 54N 21 1 E
Tuckanarra, Australia 125 E2 27 7 S 118 5 E
Tucker, U.S.A. 152 B5 33 51N 84 13W
Tuckers Town, Bermuda 9 a 32 20N 64 42W
Tucson, U.S.A. 159 K8 32 13N 110 58W
Tucumán □, Argentina 174 B2 26 48 S 66 2W
Tucumcari, U.S.A. 155 H3 35 10N 103 44W
Tucunaré, Brazil 173 B6 5 18 S 55 51W
Tucupido, Venezuela 168 B4 9 17N 65 47W
Tucupita, Venezuela 169 B5 9 2N 62 3W
Tucuruí, Brazil 170 B2 3 42 S 49 44W
Tucuruí, Represa de, Brazil 170 B2 4 0 S 49 30W
Tuczno, Poland 55 E3 53 13N 16 10 E
Tuddal, Norway 18 E5 59 46N 8 49 E
Tudela, Spain 40 C3 42 4N 1 39W
Tudmur, Syria 101 E8 34 36N 38 15 E
Tudor, L., Canada 141 A6 55 50N 65 25W
Tudora, Romania 53 C11 47 31N 26 45 E
Tuella →, Portugal 42 D3 41 30N 7 12W
Tuen Mun, China 69 G10 22 24N 113 59 E
Tueré →, Brazil 170 B1 2 48 S 50 59W
Tufi, Papua N. G. 132 E5 9 8 S 149 19 E
Tufsingdalen, Norway 18 B8 62 18N 11 44 E
Tugela →, S. Africa 117 D5 29 14 S 31 30 E
Tugidak I., U.S.A. 144 H9 56 30N 154 40W
Tuguegarao, Phil. 80 C3 17 35N 121 42 E
Tugur, Russia 67 D14 53 44N 136 45 E
Tui, Spain 42 C2 42 3N 8 39W
Tuineje, Canary Is. 9 e2 28 19N 14 3W
Tukangbesi, Kepulauan, Indonesia 82 C2 6 0 S 124 0 E
Tukarak I., Canada 140 A4 56 15N 78 45W
Tukayyid, Iraq 96 D5 29 47N 45 36 E
Tûkh, Egypt 106 H7 30 21N 31 12 E
Tukituki →, N.Z. 130 F5 39 36 S 176 56 E
Tukkae, Ao, Thailand 87 a 7 51N 98 25 E
Tukobo, Ghana 112 D4 5 1N 2 47W
Tūkrah, Libya 108 B4 32 30N 20 37 E
Tuktoyaktuk, Canada 138 B6 69 27N 133 2W
Tukums, Latvia 15 H20 56 58N 23 10 E
Tukums □, Latvia 54 B10 56 55N 23 0 E
Tukuran, Phil. 81 H4 7 51N 123 34 E
Tukuyu, Tanzania 119 D3 9 17 S 33 35 E
Tula, Hidalgo, Mexico 163 C5 20 5N 99 20W
Tula, Tamaulipas, Mexico 163 C5 23 0N 99 40W
Tula, Nigeria 113 D7 9 51N 11 27 E
Tula, Russia 58 E9 54 13N 37 38 E
Tulagi, Solomon Is. 133 M11 9 5 S 160 10 E
Tulak, Afghan. 91 B1 33 55N 63 40 E
Tulancingo, Mexico 163 C5 20 5N 99 22W
Tulangbawang →, Indonesia 84 C3 4 24 S 105 52 E
Tulare, Serbia, Yug. 50 D5 42 48N 21 28 E
Tulare, U.S.A. 160 J7 36 13N 119 21W
Tulare Lake Bed, U.S.A. 160 K7 36 0N 119 48W
Tularosa, U.S.A. 159 K10 33 5N 106 1W
Tulbagh, S. Africa 116 E2 33 16 S 19 6 E
Tulcán, Ecuador 168 C2 0 48N 77 43W
Tulcea, Romania 53 E13 45 13N 28 46 E
Tulcea □, Romania 53 E13 45 0N 28 30 E
Tulchyn, Ukraine 59 H5 48 41N 28 49 E
Tūleh, Iran 97 C7 34 35N 52 33 E
Tulemalu L., Canada 143 A9 62 58N 99 25W
Tulgheş, Romania 53 D10 46 58N 25 45 E
Tuli, Zimbabwe 119 G2 21 58 S 29 13 E
Tulia, U.S.A. 155 H4 34 32N 101 46W
Tuliszków, Poland 55 F5 52 5N 18 18 E
Tulita, Canada 138 B7 64 57N 125 30W
Ţūlkarm, West Bank 103 C4 32 19N 35 2 E
Tulkibas, Kazakstan 65 B5 42 29N 70 17 E
Tulla, Ireland 23 D3 52 53N 8 46W
Tullahoma, U.S.A. 149 H2 35 22N 86 13W
Tullamore, Australia 129 B7 32 39 S 147 36 E
Tullamore, Ireland 23 C4 53 16N 7 31W
Tulle, France 28 C5 45 16N 1 46 E
Tulln, Austria 34 C9 48 20N 16 4 E
Tullow, Ireland 23 D5 52 49N 6 45W
Tullus, Sudan 107 E1 11 7N 24 31 E
Tully, Australia 126 B4 17 56 S 145 55 E
Tully, U.S.A. 151 D8 42 48N 76 7W
Ţulmaythah, Libya 108 B4 32 40N 20 55 E
Tulnici, Romania 53 E11 45 51N 26 38 E
Tulovo, Bulgaria 51 D9 42 33N 25 32 E
Tulsa, U.S.A. 155 G7 36 10N 95 55W
Tulsequah, Canada 142 B2 58 39N 133 35W
Tulu Milki, Ethiopia 107 F4 9 55N 38 20 E
Tulu Welel, Ethiopia 107 F3 8 56N 34 47 E
Tulua, Colombia 168 C2 4 6N 76 11W
Tulucești, Romania 53 E13 45 34N 28 2 E
Tuluksak, U.S.A. 144 F7 61 6N 160 58W
Tulun, Russia 67 D11 54 32N 100 35 E
Tulungagung, Indonesia 85 D4 8 5 S 111 54 E
Tuma, Russia 58 E11 55 10N 40 30 E
Tuma →, Nic. 164 D3 13 6N 84 35W
Tumaco, Colombia 168 C2 1 50N 78 45W
Tumaco, Ensenada, Colombia 168 C2 1 55N 78 45W
Tumatumari, Guyana 169 B6 5 20N 58 55W
Tumauini, Phil. 80 C3 17 17N 121 49 E
Tumba, Dem. Rep. of the Congo 114 C4 3 10 S 23 36 E
Tumba, Sweden 16 E11 59 12N 17 48 E
Tumba, L., Dem. Rep. of the Congo 114 C3 0 50 S 18 0 E
Tumbarumba, Australia 129 C8 35 44 S 148 0 E
Tumbaya, Argentina 174 A2 23 50 S 65 26W
Tumbes, Peru 172 A1 3 37 S 80 27W
Tumbes □, Peru 172 A1 3 50 S 80 30W
Tumbur, Sudan 107 G3 4 20N 31 34 E
Tumbwe, Dem. Rep. of the Congo 119 E2 11 25 S 27 15 E
Tumby Bay, Australia 128 C2 34 21 S 136 8 E
Tumd Youqi, China 74 D6 40 30N 110 30 E
Tumen, China 75 C15 43 0N 129 50 E
Tumen Jiang →, China 75 C16 42 20N 130 35 E
Tumeremo, Venezuela 169 B5 7 18N 61 30W
Tumiritinga, Brazil 171 E3 18 58 S 41 38W
Tumkur, India 95 H3 13 18N 77 6 E
Tump, Pakistan 91 D1 26 7N 62 16 E
Tumpat, Malaysia 87 J4 6 11N 102 10 E
Tumsar, India 94 D4 21 26N 79 45 E
Tumu, Ghana 112 C4 10 56N 1 56W
Tumucumaque, Serra, Brazil 169 C7 2 0N 55 0W
Tumupasa, Bolivia 172 C4 14 9 S 67 55W
Tumut, Australia 129 C8 35 16 S 148 13 E
Tumwater, U.S.A. 160 C4 47 1N 122 54W
Tuna, India 92 H4 22 59N 70 5 E
Tunadal, Sweden 16 B11 62 26N 17 22 E
Tunapuna, Trin. & Tob. 169 F9 10 38N 61 24W
Tunas de Zaza, Cuba 164 B4 21 39N 79 34W
Tunbridge Wells = Royal Tunbridge Wells, U.K. 21 F8 51 7N 0 16 E
Tunçbilek, Turkey 49 B11 39 37N 29 29 E
Tunceli, Turkey 101 C8 39 6N 39 31 E
Tuncurry, Australia 129 B10 32 17 S 152 29 E
Tundla, India 92 F8 27 12N 78 17 E
Tundubai, Sudan 106 D2 18 36N 28 35 E
Tunduru, Tanzania 119 E4 11 8 S 37 25 E
Tundzha →, Bulgaria 51 E10 41 40N 26 35 E
Tung Chung, China 69 G10 22 17N 113 57 E
Tung Lung Chau, China 69 G11 22 15N 114 17 E
Tunga →, India 95 G2 15 0N 75 50 E
Tunga Pass, India 90 A5 29 0N 94 14 E
Tungabhadra →, India 95 G4 15 57N 78 15 E
Tungabhadra Dam, India 95 G2 15 0N 75 50 E
Tungaru, Sudan 107 E3 10 9N 30 52 E
Tungawan, Phil. 81 H4 7 30N 122 20 E
Tungi, Bangla. 90 D3 23 53N 90 24 E
Tungla, Nic. 164 D3 13 24N 84 21W
Tungnafellsjökull, Iceland 11 C9 64 45N 17 55W
Tungsha Tao = Dongsha Dao, China 77 G11 20 45N 116 43 E
Tungshih, Taiwan 77 E13 24 12N 120 43 E
Tungsten, Canada 142 A3 61 57N 128 16W
Tungufell, Iceland 11 C6 64 17N 20 10W
Tungurahua □, Ecuador 168 D2 1 15 S 78 35W
Tunguska, Nizhnyaya →, Russia 67 C9 65 48N 88 4 E
Tunguska, Podkamennaya →, Russia 67 C10 61 50N 90 13 E
Tuni, India 94 F6 17 22N 82 36 E
Tunia, Colombia 168 C2 2 41N 76 31W
Tunica, U.S.A. 155 H9 34 41N 90 23W
Tunis, Tunisia 108 A2 36 50N 10 11 E
Tunis, Golfe de, Tunisia 108 A2 37 0N 10 30 E
Tunisia ■, Africa 108 B1 33 30N 9 10 E
Tunja, Colombia 168 B3 5 33N 73 25W
Tunkhannock, U.S.A. 151 E9 41 32N 75 57W
Tunliu, China 74 F7 36 13N 112 52 E
Tunnel Creek Nat. Park, Australia 124 C4 17 41 S 125 18 E
Tunnsjøen, Norway 14 D15 64 45N 13 25 E
Tunø, Denmark 17 J4 55 57N 10 27 E
Tuntutuliak, U.S.A. 144 F7 60 22N 162 38W
Tununak, U.S.A. 144 F6 60 37N 165 15W
Tunungayualok I., Canada 141 A7 56 0N 61 0W
Tununirusiq = Arctic Bay, Canada 139 A11 73 1N 85 7W
Tunuyán, Argentina 174 C2 33 35 S 69 0W
Tunuyán →, Argentina 174 C2 33 33 S 67 30W
Tuo Jiang →, China 76 C5 28 50N 105 35 E
Tuolumne, U.S.A. 160 H6 37 58N 120 15W
Tuolumne →, U.S.A. 160 H5 37 36N 121 13W
Tüp, Kyrgyzstan 65 B9 42 45N 78 20 E
Tūp Āghāj, Iran 101 D12 36 3N 47 50 E
Tupã, Brazil 175 A5 21 57 S 50 28W
Tupaciguara, Brazil 171 E2 18 35 S 48 42W
Tupelo, U.S.A. 149 H1 34 16N 88 43W
Tupik, Russia 58 E7 55 42N 33 22 E
Tupinambaranas, Brazil 169 D6 3 0 S 58 0W
Tupirama, Brazil 170 C2 8 58 S 48 12W
Tupiratins, Brazil 170 C2 8 23 S 48 8W
Tupiza, Bolivia 174 A2 21 30 S 65 40W
Tupižnica, Serbia, Yug. 50 C6 43 43N 22 10 E
Tupman, U.S.A. 161 K7 35 18N 119 21W
Tupper, Canada 142 B4 55 32N 120 1W
Tupper Lake, U.S.A. 151 B10 44 14N 74 28W
Tupungato, Cerro, S. Amer. 174 C2 33 15 S 69 50W
Tuquan, China 75 B11 45 18N 121 38 E
Túquerres, Colombia 168 C2 1 5N 77 37W
Tura, India 90 C3 25 30N 90 16 E
Tura, Russia 67 C11 64 20N 100 17 E
Turabah, Ḥā'il, Si. Arabia 96 D4 28 20N 43 15 E
Turabah, Makkah, Si. Arabia 98 B3 21 15N 41 34 E
Turagua, Serranía, Venezuela 169 B5 7 20N 64 35W
Turakina, N.Z. 130 G4 40 3 S 175 16 E
Turakina →, N.Z. 130 G4 40 5 S 175 8 E
Turakirae Hd., N.Z. 130 H3 41 26 S 174 56 E
Turakŭrghan, Uzbekistan 65 C5 41 0N 71 31 E
Turama →, Papua N. G. 132 D2 7 40 S 143 50 E
Tūrān, Iran 97 C8 35 39N 56 42 E
Turan, Russia 67 D10 51 55N 95 0 E
Turangi, N.Z. 130 E4 38 59 S 175 48 E
Turar Rysqulov, Kazakstan 65 B5 42 32N 70 20 E
Ţurayf, Si. Arabia 96 D3 31 41N 38 39 E
Turbaco, Colombia 168 A2 10 21N 75 25W
Turbacz, Poland 55 J7 49 30N 20 8 E
Turbat, Pakistan 91 D1 25 59N 63 4 E
Turbe, Bos.-H. 52 F2 44 15N 17 35 E
Turbenthal, Switz. 33 B7 47 27N 8 51 E
Turbeville, U.S.A. 152 B9 33 54N 80 1W
Turbo, Colombia 168 B2 8 6N 76 43W
Turčianske Teplice, Slovak Rep. 35 C11 48 52N 18 52 E
Turco, Bolivia 172 D4 18 10 S 68 11W
Turcoaia, Romania 53 E13 45 7N 28 11 E
Turda, Romania 53 D8 46 34N 23 47 E
Turek, Poland 55 F5 52 3N 18 30 E
Turfan = Turpan, China 68 B3 43 58N 89 10 E
Turfan Depression = Turpan Hami, China 62 E12 42 40N 89 25 E
Turgayskaya Stolovaya Strana, Asia 64 F8 51 0N 63 0 E
Turgeon →, Canada 140 C4 50 0N 78 56W
Tŭrgovishte, Bulgaria 51 C10 43 17N 26 38 E
Turgut, Turkey 49 D10 37 22N 28 4 E
Turgutlu, Turkey 49 C9 38 30N 27 43 E
Turgwe →, Zimbabwe 117 C5 21 31 S 32 15 E
Turhal, Turkey 100 B7 40 24N 36 5 E
Turia →, Spain 41 F4 39 27N 0 19W
Turiaçu, Brazil 170 B2 1 40 S 45 19W
Turiaçu →, Brazil 170 B2 1 36 S 45 19W
Turiec →, Slovak Rep. 35 B11 49 7N 18 55 E
Turin = Torino, Italy 44 C4 45 3N 7 40 E
Turinsk, Russia 64 B9 58 3N 63 42 E
Turkana, L., Africa 118 B4 3 30N 36 5 E
Türkeli, Turkey 51 F11 40 30N 27 30 E
Turkestan = Türkistan, Kazakstan 66 E7 43 17N 68 16 E
Turkestan Range, Asia 65 D4 39 35N 69 0 E
Túrkeve, Hungary 52 C5 47 6N 20 44 E
Turkey ■, Eurasia 100 C7 39 0N 36 0 E
Turkey →, U.S.A. 156 B5 42 43N 91 2W
Turkey Creek, Australia 124 C4 17 2 S 128 12 E
Turki, Russia 60 D6 52 0N 43 15 E
Türkistan, Kazakstan 66 E7 43 17N 68 16 E
Türkmenbashi, Turkmenistan 57 G9 40 5N 53 5 E
Turkmenistan ■, Asia 66 F6 39 0N 59 0 E
Türkmenli, Turkey 49 B8 39 45N 26 30 E
Türkoğlu, Turkey 100 D7 37 23N 36 50 E
Turks & Caicos Is. ■, W. Indies 165 B5 21 20N 71 20W
Turks Island Passage, W. Indies 165 B5 21 30N 71 30W
Turku, Finland 15 F20 60 30N 22 19 E
Turkwel →, Kenya 118 B4 3 6N 36 6 E
Turlock, U.S.A. 160 H6 37 30N 120 51W
Turnagain →, Canada 142 B3 59 12N 127 35W
Turnagain, C., N.Z. 130 G5 40 28 S 176 38 E
Turneffe Is., Belize 163 D7 17 20N 87 50W
Turner, U.S.A. 158 B9 48 51N 108 24W
Turner Pt., Australia 126 A1 11 47 S 133 32 E
Turner Valley, Canada 142 C6 50 40N 114 17W
Turners Falls, U.S.A. 151 D12 42 36N 72 33W
Turnhout, Belgium 24 C4 51 19N 4 57 E
Türnitz, Austria 34 D8 47 55N 15 29 E
Turnor L., Canada 143 B7 56 35N 108 35W
Turnov, Czech Rep. 34 A8 50 34N 15 10 E
Tŭrnovo = Veliko Tŭrnovo, Bulgaria 51 C9 43 5N 25 41 E
Turnu Măgurele, Romania 53 G9 43 46N 24 56 E
Turnu Roşu, P., Romania 53 E9 45 33N 24 17 E
Turobin, Poland 55 H9 50 50N 22 44 E
Tuross Head, Australia 129 D9 36 3 S 150 8 E
Turpan, China 68 B3 43 58N 89 10 E
Turpan Hami, China 62 E12 42 40N 89 25 E
Turrawan, Australia 129 A8 30 28 S 149 53 E
Turrës, Kala e, Albania 50 E3 41 10N 19 28 E
Turriff, U.K. 22 D6 57 32N 2 27W
Tursāq, Iraq 101 F11 33 27N 45 47 E
Tursi, Italy 47 B9 40 15N 16 28 E
Tursunzade, Tajikistan 65 D4 38 30N 68 14 E
Turtle Head I., Australia 126 A3 10 56 S 142 37 E
Turtle Is., Phil. 81 H2 6 7N 118 14 E
Turtle Is., S. Leone 112 D2 7 40N 13 0 E
Turtle L., Canada 143 C7 53 36N 108 38W
Turtle Lake, U.S.A. 154 B4 47 31N 100 53W
Turtleford, Canada 143 C7 53 23N 108 57W
Turua, N.Z. 130 D4 37 14 S 175 35 E
Turugart Shankou, Kyrgyzstan 65 C7 40 32N 75 24 E
Turukhansk, Russia 67 C9 65 21N 88 5 E
Turzovka, Slovak Rep. 35 B11 49 25N 18 35 E
Tuscaloosa, U.S.A. 149 J2 33 12N 87 34W
Tuscánia, Italy 45 F8 42 25N 11 52 E
Tuscany = Toscana □, Italy 44 E8 43 25N 11 0 E
Tuscarawas →, U.S.A. 150 F3 40 24N 81 25W
Tuscarora Mt., U.S.A. 150 F7 40 55N 77 55W
Tuscola, Ill., U.S.A. 157 E8 39 48N 88 17W
Tuscola, Tex., U.S.A. 155 J5 32 12N 99 48W
Tuscumbia, Ala., U.S.A. 149 H2 34 44N 87 42W
Tuscumbia, Mo., U.S.A. 156 F4 38 14N 92 28W
Tuskegee, U.S.A. 152 C4 32 25N 85 42W
Tustin, U.S.A. 161 M9 33 44N 117 49W
Tustna, Norway 18 A5 63 10N 8 5 E
Tuszyn, Poland 55 G6 51 36N 19 33 E
Tutak, Turkey 101 C10 39 31N 42 46 E
Tutayev, Russia 58 D10 57 53N 39 32 E
Tuticorin, India 95 K4 8 50N 78 12 E
Tutin, Serbia, Yug. 50 D4 42 58N 20 20 E
Tutóia, Brazil 170 B3 2 45 S 42 20W
Tutong, Brunei 85 B4 4 47N 114 40 E
Tutova →, Romania 53 D12 46 7N 27 30 E
Tutrakan, Bulgaria 51 B10 44 2N 26 40 E
Tuttle Creek L., U.S.A. 154 F6 39 22N 96 40W
Tuttlingen, Germany 31 H4 47 58N 8 48 E
Tutuala, E. Timor 82 C3 8 25 S 127 15 E
Tutuba, Vanuatu 133 E5 15 33 S 167 16 E
Tutubeia, Papua N. G. 132 E6 9 34 S 150 40 E
Tutuila, Amer. Samoa 133 X24 14 19 S 170 50W
Tutuko, Mt., N.Z. 131 E3 44 35 S 168 1 E
Tutun, Egypt 106 J7 29 9N 30 46 E
Tututepec, Mexico 163 D5 16 9N 97 38W
Tuva □, Russia 67 D10 51 30N 95 0 E
Tuvalu ■, Pac. Oc. 134 H9 8 0 S 178 0 E
Tuvuca, Fiji 133 A3 17 40 S 178 48W
Tuwal, Si. Arabia 98 B2 22 17N 39 6 E
Tuxer Alpen, Austria 34 D4 47 10N 11 45 E
Tuxpan, Mexico 163 C5 20 58N 97 23W
Tuxtla Gutiérrez, Mexico 163 D6 16 50N 93 10W
Tuy = Tui, Spain 42 C2 42 3N 8 39W
Tuy An, Vietnam 86 F7 13 17N 109 16 E
Tuy Duc, Vietnam 87 F6 12 15N 107 27 E
Tuy Hoa, Vietnam 86 F7 13 5N 109 10 E
Tuy Phong, Vietnam 87 G7 11 14N 108 43 E
Tuya L., Canada 142 B2 59 7N 130 35W
Tuyen Hoa, Vietnam 86 D6 17 50N 106 10 E
Tuyen Quang, Vietnam 76 G5 21 50N 105 10 E
Tuymazy, Russia 64 D4 54 36N 53 42 E
Tūysarkān, Iran 97 C6 34 33N 48 27 E
Tuz Gölü, Turkey 100 C5 38 42N 33 18 E
Ţūz Khurmātū, Iraq 101 E11 34 56N 44 38 E
Tuzi, Montenegro, Yug. 50 D3 42 22N 19 20 E
Tuzla, Bos.-H. 52 F3 44 34N 18 41 E
Tuzlov →, Russia 59 J10 47 17N 39 57 E
Tuzluca, Turkey 101 B10 40 3N 43 39 E
Tvååker, Sweden 17 G6 57 4N 12 25 E
Tvardiţa, Moldova 53 D13 46 9N 28 58 E
Tvedestrand, Norway 18 F5 58 38N 8 58 E
Tver, Russia 58 D8 56 55N 35 55 E
Tvrdošin, Slovak Rep. 35 B12 49 21N 19 35 E
Tvrdošovce, Slovak Rep. 35 C11 48 6N 18 4 E
Tvŭrditsa, Bulgaria 51 D9 42 42N 25 53 E
Twain, U.S.A. 160 E5 40 1N 121 3W
Twain Harte, U.S.A. 160 G6 38 2N 120 14W
Twann, Switz. 32 B4 47 6N 7 9 E
Twardogóra, Poland 55 G4 51 23N 17 28 E
Tweed, Canada 150 B7 44 29N 77 19W
Tweed →, U.K. 22 F6 55 45N 2 0W
Tweed Heads, Australia 127 D5 28 10 S 153 31 E
Tweedsmuir Prov. Park, Canada 142 C3 53 0N 126 20W
Twentynine Palms, U.S.A. 161 L10 34 8N 116 3W
Tweya, Dem. Rep. of the Congo 114 C3 0 54 S 18 58 E
Twillingate, Canada 141 C9 49 42N 54 45W
Twin Bridges, U.S.A. 158 D7 45 33N 112 20W
Twin City, U.S.A. 152 C7 32 35N 82 10W
Twin Falls, Canada 141 B7 53 30N 64 32W
Twin Falls, U.S.A. 158 E6 42 34N 114 28W
Twin Hills, U.S.A. 144 G8 59 23N 159 58W
Twin Lakes, U.S.A. 152 E6 30 43N 83 13W
Twin Valley, U.S.A. 154 B6 47 16N 96 16W
Twinnge, Burma 90 D6 23 10N 96 2 E
Twinsburg, U.S.A. 150 E3 41 18N 81 26W
Twistringen, Germany 30 C4 52 48N 8 37 E
Twitchell Reservoir, U.S.A. 161 L6 34 59N 120 19W
Two Boats Village, Ascension I. 9 g 7 56 S 14 22W
Two Harbors, U.S.A. 154 B9 47 2N 91 40W
Two Hills, Canada 142 C6 53 43N 111 52W

Varano, Lago di 295

Urgench = Urganch, *Uzbekistan* . 66 E7 41 40N 60 41 E
Ürgüp, *Turkey* 96 B2 38 38N 34 56 E
Urgut, *Uzbekistan* 65 D3 39 23N 67 15 E
Uri, *India* 93 B6 34 8N 74 2 E
Uri □, *Switz.* 33 C7 46 43N 8 35 E
Uribante →, *Venezuela* 168 B3 7 25N 71 50W
Uribe, *Colombia* 168 C3 3 13N 74 24W
Uribia, *Colombia* 168 A3 11 43N 72 16W
Uricani, *Romania* 52 E8 45 20N 23 9 E
Urimba, *Angola* 115 E3 10 56 S 16 32 E
Uriondo, *Bolivia* 174 A3 21 41 S 64 41W
Urique, *Mexico* 162 B3 27 13N 107 55W
Urique →, *Mexico* 162 B3 26 29N 107 58W
Urirotstock, *Switz.* 33 C7 46 52N 8 32 E
Urk, *Neths.* 24 B5 52 39N 5 36 E
Urla, *Turkey* 49 C8 38 20N 26 47 E
Urlaţi, *Romania* 53 F11 44 59N 26 15 E
Urmia = Orūmīyeh, *Iran* 101 D11 37 40N 45 0 E
Urmia, L. = Orūmīyeh,
Daryācheh-ye, *Iran* 101 D11 37 50N 45 30 E
Urnäsch, *Switz.* 33 B8 47 19N 9 17 E
Urner Alpen, *Switz.* 33 C7 46 45N 8 45 E
Uroševac, *Kosovo, Yug.* 50 D5 42 23N 21 10 E
Uroteppa, *Tajikistan* 65 D4 39 55N 69 1 E
Uroyan, Montanas de, *Puerto Rico* 165 d 18 12N 67 0W
Urrao, *Colombia* 168 B2 6 20N 76 11W
Urshult, *Sweden* 17 H8 56 31N 14 50 E
Uruaçu, *Brazil* 171 D2 14 30 S 49 10W
Uruana, *Brazil* 171 E2 15 30 S 49 41W
Uruapan, *Mexico* 162 D4 19 30N 102 0W
Uruará, *Brazil* 169 D7 3 42 S 53 51W
Uruará →, *Brazil* 169 D7 2 6 S 53 38W
Urubamba, *Peru* 172 C3 13 20 S 72 10W
Urubamba →, *Peru* 172 C3 10 43 S 73 48W
Urubaxi →, *Brazil* 169 D5 0 31 S 64 50W
Urubu →, *Brazil* 169 D6 2 55 S 58 25W
Uruçara, *Brazil* 169 D6 2 32 S 57 45W
Uruçuí, *Brazil* 170 C3 7 20 S 44 28W
Uruçuí, Serra do, *Brazil* 170 C3 9 0 S 44 45W
Uruçuí Prêto →, *Brazil* 170 C3 7 20 S 44 38W
Urucuia →, *Brazil* 171 E2 16 8 S 45 5W
Urucurituba, *Brazil* 169 D6 2 41 S 57 40W
Uruguai →, *Brazil* 175 B5 26 0 S 53 30W
Uruguaiana, *Brazil* 174 B4 29 50 S 57 0W
Uruguay ■, *S. Amer.* 174 C4 32 30 S 56 30W
Uruguay →, *S. Amer.* 174 C4 34 12 S 58 18W
Urumchi = Ürümqi, *China* 66 E9 43 45N 87 45 E
Ürümqi, *China* 66 E9 43 45N 87 45 E
Urup →, *Russia* 61 H5 45 0N 41 10 E
Urup, Ostrov, *Russia* 67 E16 46 0N 151 0 E
Urutaí, *Brazil* 171 E2 17 28 S 48 12W
Uryupinsk, *Russia* 60 E5 50 45N 41 58 E
Urzhum, *Russia* 60 B9 57 10N 49 56 E
Urziceni, *Romania* 53 F11 44 40N 26 42 E
Usa, *Japan* 72 D3 33 31N 131 21 E
Usa →, *Russia* 56 A10 66 16N 59 49 E
Uşak, *Turkey* 49 C11 38 43N 29 28 E
Uşak □, *Turkey* 49 C11 38 30N 29 0 E
Usakos, *Namibia* 116 C2 21 54 S 15 31 E
Usborne, Mt., *Falk. Is.* 9 f 51 40 S 59 55W
Ušće, *Serbia, Yug.* 50 C4 43 30N 20 39 E
Usedom, *Germany* 30 B10 53 55N 14 2 E
Useless Loop, *Australia* 125 E1 26 8 S 113 23 E
'Usfān, *Si. Arabia* 98 B2 21 58N 39 27 E
Ush-Tobe, *Kazakstan* 66 E8 45 16N 78 0 E
Ushakova, Ostrov, *Russia* 6 A12 82 0N 80 0 E
Ushant = Ouessant, Î. d', *France* . 26 D1 48 28N 5 6W
Usharal, *Kazakstan* 65 B5 43 53N 70 31 E
Ushashi, *Tanzania* 118 C3 1 59 S 33 57 E
Ushat, *Sudan* 107 F2 7 59N 29 28 E
'Ushayrah, *Si. Arabia* 106 C5 21 46N 40 42 E
Ushibuka, *Japan* 72 E2 32 11N 130 1 E
Ushuaia, *Argentina* 176 D3 54 50 S 68 23W
Ushumun, *Russia* 67 D13 52 47N 126 32 E
Usino, *Papua N. G.* 132 C3 5 32 S 145 23 E
Usk, *Canada* 142 C3 54 38N 128 26W
Usk →, *U.K.* 21 F5 51 33N 2 58W
Uska, *India* 93 F10 27 12N 83 7 E
Uskedal, *Norway* 18 E2 59 56N 5 53 E
Üsküdar, *Turkey* 51 F13 41 0N 29 5 E
Uslar, *Germany* 30 D5 51 39N 9 38 E
Usman, *Russia* 59 F10 52 5N 39 48 E
Usmat, *Uzbekistan* 65 D3 39 45N 67 38 E
Usoke, *Tanzania* 118 D3 5 8 S 32 24 E
Usolye, *Russia* 64 B6 59 28N 56 31 E
Usolye Sibirskoye, *Russia* 67 D11 52 48N 103 40 E
Usoro, *Nigeria* 113 D6 5 33N 6 11 E
Uspallata, P. de, *Argentina* 174 C2 32 37 S 69 22W
Uspenskiy, *Kazakstan* 66 E8 48 41N 72 43 E
Ussel, *France* 28 C6 45 32N 2 18 E
Usson-du-Poitou, *France* 28 B4 46 16N 0 31 E
Ussuri →, *Asia* 70 A7 48 27N 135 0 E
Ussuriysk, *Russia* 67 E14 43 48N 131 59 E
Ussurka, *Russia* 70 B6 45 12N 133 31 E
Ust-Aldan = Batamay, *Russia* 67 C13 63 30N 129 15 E
Ust-Amginskoye = Khandyga,
Russia 67 C14 62 42N 135 35 E
Ust-Bolsheretsk, *Russia* 67 D16 52 50N 156 15 E
Ust-Buzulukskaya, *Russia* 60 E6 50 8N 42 11 E
Ust-Chaun, *Russia* 67 C18 68 47N 170 30 E
Ust-Donetskiy, *Russia* 61 G5 47 35N 40 55 E
Ust-Ilimpeya = Yukta, *Russia* 67 C11 63 26N 105 42 E
Ust-Ilimsk, *Russia* 67 D11 58 3N 102 39 E
Ust-Ishim, *Russia* 66 D8 57 45N 71 10 E
Ust-Kamchatsk, *Russia* 67 D17 56 10N 162 28 E
Ust-Kamenogorsk = Öskemen,
Kazakstan 66 E9 50 0N 82 36 E
Ust-Khayryuzovo, *Russia* 67 D16 57 15N 156 45 E
Ust-Kut, *Russia* 67 D11 56 50N 105 42 E
Ust-Kuyga, *Russia* 67 B14 70 1N 135 43 E
Ust-Labinsk, *Russia* 61 H4 45 15N 39 41 E
Ust-Luga, *Russia* 58 C5 59 35N 28 20 E
Ust-Maya, *Russia* 67 C14 60 30N 134 28 E
Ust-Mil, *Russia* 67 D14 59 40N 133 11 E
Ust-Nera, *Russia* 67 C15 64 35N 143 15 E
Ust-Nyukzha, *Russia* 67 D13 56 34N 121 37 E
Ust-Olenek, *Russia* 67 B12 73 0N 120 5 E
Ust-Omchug, *Russia* 67 C15 61 9N 149 38 E
Ust-Port, *Russia* 66 C9 69 40N 84 26 E
Ust-Tsilma, *Russia* 56 A9 65 28N 52 11 E
Ust Urt = Ustyurt Plateau, *Asia* . 66 E6 44 0N 55 0 E
Ust-Usa, *Russia* 56 A10 66 2N 56 57 E
Ust-Vorkuta, *Russia* 56 A11 67 24N 64 0 E
Ustaoset, *Norway* 18 D5 60 30N 8 2 E
Ustaritz, *France* 28 E2 43 24N 1 27W
Uster, *Switz.* 33 B7 47 22N 8 43 E
Ústí nad Labem, *Czech Rep.* 34 A7 50 41N 14 3 E
Ústí nad Orlicí, *Czech Rep.* 35 B9 49 58N 16 24 E
Ústica, *Italy* 46 D6 38 42N 13 11 E
Ustinov = Izhevsk, *Russia* 64 C4 56 51N 53 14 E
Ustka, *Poland* 54 D3 54 35N 16 55 E
Ustroń, *Poland* 55 J5 49 43N 18 48 E
Ustrzyki Dolne, *Poland* 55 J9 49 27N 22 40 E
Ustupo, *Panama* 168 B2 9 27N 78 34W
Ustyurt Plateau, *Asia* 66 E6 44 0N 55 0 E
Ustyuzhna, *Russia* 58 C9 58 50N 36 32 E
Usu, *China* 68 B3 44 27N 84 40 E
Usuki, *Japan* 72 D3 33 8N 131 49 E
Usulután, *El Salv.* 164 D2 13 25N 88 28W
Usumacinta →, *Mexico* 163 D6 17 0N 91 0W
Usumbura = Bujumbura, *Burundi* 118 C2 3 16 S 29 18 E
Usure, *Tanzania* 118 C3 4 40 S 34 22 E
Usutuo →, *Mozam.* 117 D5 26 48 S 32 7 E
Usva, *Russia* 64 B6 58 41N 57 37 E
Uta, *Indonesia* 83 B5 4 33 S 136 0 E
Utah □, *U.S.A.* 158 G8 39 20N 111 30W
Utah L., *U.S.A.* 158 F8 40 10N 111 58W
Utansjö, *Sweden* 16 B11 62 46N 17 55 E
Utara, Selat, *Malaysia* 87 c 5 28N 100 20 E
Utarni, *India* 92 F4 26 5N 71 58 E
Utatlan, *Guatemala* 164 C1 15 2N 91 11W
Ute Creek →, *U.S.A.* 155 H3 35 21N 103 50W
Utebo, *Spain* 40 D3 41 43N 1 0W
Utemurat, *Uzbekistan* 65 B2 42 6N 65 42 E
Utena, *Lithuania* 15 J21 55 27N 25 40 E
Utete, *Tanzania* 118 D4 8 0 S 38 45 E
Uthai Thani, *Thailand* 86 E3 15 22N 100 3 E
Uthal, *Pakistan* 92 G2 25 44N 66 40 E
Utiariti, *Brazil* 173 C6 13 0 S 58 10W
Utica, *N.Y., U.S.A.* 151 C9 43 6N 75 14W
Utica, *Ohio, U.S.A.* 150 F2 40 14N 82 27W
Utiel, *Spain* 41 F3 39 37N 1 11W
Utikuma L., *Canada* 142 B5 55 50N 115 30W
Utinga, *Brazil* 171 D3 12 6 S 41 5W
Utkela, *India* 94 D6 20 6N 83 10 E
Utne, *Norway* 18 D3 60 25N 6 37 E
Utnur, *India* 94 E4 19 22N 78 46 E
Uto, *Japan* 72 E2 32 41N 130 40 E
Utö, *Sweden* 16 F12 58 56N 18 16 E
Utopia, *Australia* 126 C1 22 14 S 134 33 E
Utraula, *India* 93 F10 27 19N 82 25 E
Utrecht, *Neths.* 24 B5 52 5N 5 8 E
Utrecht, *S. Africa* 117 D5 27 38 S 30 20 E
Utrecht □, *Neths.* 24 B5 52 6N 5 7 E
Utrera, *Spain* 43 H5 37 12N 5 48W
Utsira, *Norway* 18 E1 59 19N 4 53 E
Utsjoki, *Finland* 14 B22 69 51N 26 59 E
Utsunomiya, *Japan* 73 A11 36 30N 139 50 E
Uttar Pradesh □, *India* 93 F9 27 0N 80 0 E
Uttaradit, *Thailand* 86 D3 17 36N 100 5 E
Uttaranchal □, *India* 93 D8 30 0N 79 30 E
Uttoxeter, *U.K.* 20 E6 52 54N 1 52W
Utuado, *Puerto Rico* 165 d 18 16N 66 42W
Utva →, *Kazakstan* 64 F4 51 28N 52 40 E
Uummannaq, *Greenland* 10 B4 77 0N 69 0W
Uummannarsuaq = Nunap Isua,
Greenland 10 F6 59 48N 43 55W
Uusikaarlepyy, *Finland* 14 E20 63 32N 22 31 E
Uusikaupunki, *Finland* 15 F19 60 47N 21 25 E
Uva, *Russia* 60 B11 56 59N 52 13 E
Uvá →, *Colombia* 168 C3 3 41N 70 3W
Uvac →, *Serbia, Yug.* 50 C3 43 35N 19 30 E
Uvalda, *U.S.A.* 152 C7 32 2N 82 31W
Uvalde, *U.S.A.* 155 L5 29 13N 99 47W
Uvarovo, *Russia* 60 E6 51 59N 42 14 E
Uvat, *Russia* 66 D7 59 5N 68 50 E
Uvdal, *Norway* 18 D5 60 17N 8 48 E
Uvelskiy, *Russia* 64 D8 54 26N 61 22 E
Uvinza, *Tanzania* 118 D3 5 5 S 30 24 E
Uvira, *Dem. Rep. of the Congo* 118 C2 3 22 S 29 3 E
Uvs Nuur, *Mongolia* 68 A4 50 20N 92 30 E
Uwa, *Japan* 72 D4 33 22N 132 31 E
'Uwairidh, Ḥarrat al, *Si. Arabia* 96 E3 26 50N 38 0 E
Uwajima, *Japan* 72 D4 33 10N 132 35 E
Uwanda Game Reserve, *Tanzania* 118 D3 7 46 S 32 0 E
Uweinat, Jebel, *Sudan* 106 C1 21 54N 24 58 E
Uwekuli, *Indonesia* 82 B2 1 25 S 121 6 E
Uxbridge, *Canada* 150 B5 44 6N 79 7W
Uxin Qi, *China* 74 E5 38 50N 109 5 E
Uxmal, *Mexico* 163 C7 20 22N 89 46W
Uyak, *U.S.A.* 144 H9 57 38N 154 0W
Uydzin, *Mongolia* 74 B4 44 9N 107 0 E
Uyo, *Nigeria* 113 D6 5 1N 7 53 E
Uyu →, *Burma* 90 C5 24 51N 94 57 E
Uyuk = Oyyq, *Kazakstan* 65 B5 43 36N 71 16 E
Üyüklü Tepe, *Turkey* 49 D9 37 5N 27 21 E
Uyûn Mûsa, *Egypt* 103 F1 29 53N 32 40 E
Uyuni, *Bolivia* 172 E4 20 28 S 66 47W
Uzbekistan ■, *Asia* 66 E7 41 30N 65 0 E
Uzen, *Kazakstan* 57 F9 43 29N 52 54 E
Uzen, Bolshoi →, *Kazakstan* 61 F9 49 6N 49 56 E
Uzen, Mal →, *Kazakstan* 61 F9 49 4N 49 44 E
Uzerche, *France* 28 C5 45 25N 1 34 E
Uzès, *France* 29 D8 44 1N 4 26 E
Uzgen = Özgön, *Kyrgyzstan* 65 C6 40 46N 73 18 E
Uzh →, *Ukraine* 59 G6 51 15N 30 12 E
Uzhgorod = Uzhhorod, *Ukraine* 59 H2 48 36N 22 18 E
Uzhhorod, *Ukraine* 59 H2 48 36N 22 18 E
Užice, *Serbia, Yug.* 50 C3 43 55N 19 50 E
Uzlovaya, *Russia* 58 F10 54 0N 38 5 E
Üzümlü, *Turkey* 49 E11 36 44N 29 14 E
Uzunköprü, *Turkey* 51 E10 41 16N 26 43 E
Uzunkuyu, *Turkey* 49 C8 38 17N 26 33 E
Uzwil, *Switz.* 33 B8 47 26N 9 9 E
Uzynaghash, *Kazakstan* 65 B8 43 35N 76 20 E
Uzynagash, *Kazakstan* 65 B8 43 13N 76 19 E

V

Vaal →, *S. Africa* 116 D3 29 4 S 23 38 E
Vaal Dam, *S. Africa* 117 D4 27 0 S 28 14 E
Vaalbos Nat. Park, *S. Africa* 116 D3 28 22 S 24 20 E
Vaalwater, *S. Africa* 117 C4 24 15 S 28 8 E
Vaasa, *Finland* 14 E19 63 6N 21 38 E
Vabkent, *Uzbekistan* 65 C2 40 1N 64 30 E
Vabre, *France* 28 E6 43 42N 2 24 E
Vác, *Hungary* 52 C4 47 49N 19 10 E
Vacaria, *Brazil* 175 B5 28 31 S 50 52W
Vacata, *Fiji* 133 A3 17 15 S 179 31W
Vacaville, *U.S.A.* 160 G5 38 21N 121 59W
Vaccarès, Étang de, *France* 29 E8 43 32N 4 34 E
Vach = Vakh →, *Russia* 66 C8 60 45N 76 45 E
Vache, Î. à, *Haiti* 165 C5 18 2N 73 35W
Väckelsång, *Sweden* 17 H8 56 37N 14 58 E
Vacoas, *Mauritius* 121 d 20 18 S 57 29 E
Vada, *India* 94 E1 19 39N 73 8 E
Väddö, *Sweden* 16 D12 60 0N 18 50 E
Väderstad, *Sweden* 17 F8 58 19N 14 55 E
Vadheim, *Norway* 18 C2 61 13N 5 49 E
Vadnagar, *India* 92 H5 23 47N 72 40 E
Vado Ligure, *Italy* 44 D5 44 17N 8 26 E
Vadodara, *India* 92 H5 22 20N 73 10 E
Vadret, Piz, *Switz.* 33 C9 46 51N 9 58 E
Vadsø, *Norway* 14 A23 70 3N 29 50 E
Vadstena, *Sweden* 17 F8 58 28N 14 54 E
Vaduj, *India* 94 F2 17 36N 74 27 E
Vaduz, *Liech.* 33 B9 47 8N 9 31 E
Værlandet, *Norway* 18 C1 61 18N 4 44 E
Værøy, *Norway* 14 C15 67 40N 12 40 E
Vagalat, *Albania* 38 B10 39 44N 20 8 E
Vågåmo, *Norway* 18 C6 61 52N 9 6 E
Vágar, *Færoe Is.* 14 E9 62 5N 7 15W
Vaggeryd, *Sweden* 17 G8 57 30N 14 10 E
Vaghena, *Solomon Is.* 133 L9 7 25 S 157 45 E
Vagney, *France* 27 D13 48 1N 6 43 E
Vagnhärad, *Sweden* 17 F11 58 57N 17 33 E
Vagos, *Portugal* 42 E2 40 33N 8 42W
Vågsfjorden, *Norway* 14 B17 68 50N 16 50 E
Váh →, *Slovak Rep.* 35 D11 47 43N 18 7 E
Vahsel B., *Antarctica* 7 D1 75 0 S 35 0W
Váï, *Greece* 39 E7 35 15N 26 18 E
Vaigach, *Russia* 66 B6 70 10N 59 0 E
Vaigai →, *India* 95 K4 9 15N 79 10 E
Vaiges, *France* 26 D6 48 2N 0 30W
Vaihingen, *Germany* 31 G4 48 54N 8 57 E
Vaijapur, *India* 94 E2 19 58N 74 45 E
Vaikam, *India* 95 K3 9 45N 76 25 E
Vail, *U.S.A.* 146 C5 39 40N 106 20W
Vailala →, *Papua N. G.* 132 D3 7 57 S 145 25 E
Vailly-sur-Aisne, *France* 27 C10 49 24N 3 31 E
Vaippar →, *India* 95 K4 9 0N 78 25 E
Vaisali →, *India* 93 F8 26 28N 78 53 E
Vaison-la-Romaine, *France* 29 D9 44 14N 5 4 E
Vaitogi, *Amer. Samoa* 133 X24 14 24 S 170 44W
Vajpur, *India* 94 D1 21 24N 73 17 E
Vakaga →, *C.A.R.* 114 A4 9 48N 21 32 E
Vakarai, *Sri Lanka* 95 K5 8 8N 81 26 E
Vakarel, *Bulgaria* 50 D7 42 35N 23 40 E
Vakfıkebir, *Turkey* 101 B8 41 2N 39 17 E
Vakh →, *Russia* 66 C8 60 45N 76 45 E
Vakhsh, *Tajikistan* 65 E4 37 43N 68 50 E
Vakhsh →, *Tajikistan* 65 E4 37 6N 68 18 E
Vakhtan, *Russia* 60 B8 57 53N 46 47 E
Vaksdal, *Norway* 18 D2 60 29N 5 45 E
Vakuta I., *Papua N. G.* 132 E6 8 51 S 151 10 E
Vál, *Hungary* 52 C3 47 22N 18 40 E
Val-de-Marne □, *France* 27 D9 48 45N 2 28 E
Val-d'Isère, *France* 29 C10 45 27N 6 59 E
Val-d'Oise □, *France* 27 C9 49 5N 2 10 E
Val-d'Or, *Canada* 140 C4 48 7N 77 47W
Val Marie, *Canada* 143 D7 49 15N 107 45W
Valaam, *Russia* 58 B6 61 22N 30 57 E
Valadares, *Portugal* 42 D2 41 5N 8 38W
Valahia, *Romania* 53 F9 44 35N 25 0 E
Valaichenai, *Sri Lanka* 95 L5 7 54N 81 32 E
Valais □, *Switz.* 32 D5 46 12N 7 45 E
Valais, Alpes du, *Switz.* 32 D5 46 5N 7 35 E
Valandovo, *Macedonia* 50 E6 41 19N 22 34 E
Valašské Meziříčí, *Czech Rep.* 35 B10 49 29N 17 59 E
Valáxa, *Greece* 48 C6 38 50N 24 29 E
Vålberg, *Sweden* 16 E7 59 23N 13 11 E
Valbo, *Sweden* 16 D10 60 40N 17 0 E
Valbondione, *Italy* 44 B7 46 2N 10 1 E
Vălcani, *Romania* 52 D5 46 0N 20 26 E
Vâlcea □, *Romania* 53 F9 45 0N 24 10 E
Valcheta, *Argentina* 176 B3 40 40 S 66 8W
Valdagno, *Italy* 45 C8 45 39N 11 18 E
Valdahon, *France* 27 E13 47 8N 6 21 E
Valday, *Russia* 58 D7 57 58N 33 9 E
Valdayskaya Vozvyshennost,
Russia 58 D7 57 0N 33 30 E
Valdeazogues →, *Spain* 43 G6 38 45N 4 55W
Valdecañas, Embalse de, *Spain* . . 42 F5 39 45N 5 25W
Valdemarsvik, *Sweden* 17 F10 58 14N 16 40 E
Valdemoro, *Spain* 42 E7 40 12N 3 40W
Valdepeñas, *Spain* 43 G7 38 43N 3 25W
Valderaduey →, *Spain* 42 D5 41 31N 5 42W
Valdérice, *Italy* 46 D5 38 4N 12 37 E
Valderrobres, *Spain* 40 E5 40 53N 0 9 E
Valdés, Pen., *Argentina* 176 B4 42 30 S 63 45W
Valdez, *Ecuador* 168 C2 1 15N 79 0W
Valdez, *U.S.A.* 144 F11 61 7N 146 16W
Valdivia, *Chile* 176 A2 39 50 S 73 14W
Valdivia, *Colombia* 168 B2 7 11N 75 27W
Valdobbiádene, *Italy* 45 C8 45 54N 12 0 E
Valdosta, *U.S.A.* 152 E6 30 50N 83 17W
Valdoviño, *Spain* 42 B2 43 36N 8 8W
Valdres, *Norway* 15 F13 61 5N 9 5 E
Vale, *Georgia* 61 K6 41 30N 42 58 E
Vale, *U.S.A.* 158 E5 43 59N 117 15W
Vale of Glamorgan □, *U.K.* 21 F4 51 28N 3 25W
Valea lui Mihai, *Romania* 52 C7 47 32N 22 11 E
Valea Mărului, *Romania* 53 E12 45 49N 27 42 E
Valemount, *Canada* 142 C5 52 50N 119 15W
Valença, *Brazil* 171 D4 13 20 S 39 5W
Valença, *Portugal* 42 C2 42 1N 8 34W
Valença do Piauí, *Brazil* 170 C3 6 20 S 41 45W
Valençay, *France* 27 E8 47 9N 1 34 E
Valence = Valence d'Agen, *France* 28 D4 44 6N 0 53 E
Valence, *France* 29 D8 44 57N 4 54 E
Valence d'Agen, *France* 28 D4 44 6N 0 53 E
Valencia, *Phil.* 81 H5 7 57N 125 3 E
Valencia, *Spain* 41 F4 39 27N 0 23W
Valencia, *Trin. & Tob.* 169 F9 10 39N 61 11W
Valencia, *U.S.A.* 159 J10 34 48N 106 43W
Valencia, *Venezuela* 168 A4 10 11N 68 0W
Valencia □, *Spain* 41 F4 39 20N 0 40W
Valencia, G. de, *Spain* 41 F5 39 30N 0 20 E
Valencia de Alcántara, *Spain* 43 F3 39 25N 7 14W
Valencia de Don Juan, *Spain* 42 C5 42 17N 5 31W
Valencia I., *Ireland* 23 E1 51 54N 10 22W
Valenciennes, *France* 27 B10 50 20N 3 34 E
Văleni, *Romania* 53 F9 44 15N 24 45 E
Vălenii de Munte, *Romania* 53 E11 45 11N 26 2 E
Valensole, *France* 29 E9 43 50N 5 59 E
Valentigney, *France* 27 E13 47 27N 6 51 E
Valentim, Sa. do, *Brazil* 170 C3 6 0 S 43 30W
Valentin, *Russia* 70 C7 43 8N 134 17 E
Valentine, *U.S.A.* 155 K2 30 35N 104 30W
Valenza, *Italy* 44 C5 45 1N 8 38 E
Våler, *Hedmark, Norway* 18 D8 60 41N 11 50 E
Våler, *Østfold, Norway* 18 E7 59 29N 10 51 E
Valera, *Venezuela* 168 B3 9 19N 70 37W
Valesdir, *Vanuatu* 133 F6 16 47 S 168 10 E
Valestrand, *Norway* 18 E2 59 40N 5 26 E
Valga, *Estonia* 15 H22 57 47N 26 2 E
Valguarnera Caropepe, *Italy* 47 E7 37 30N 14 23 E
Valier, *U.S.A.* 158 B7 48 18N 112 16W
Valinco, G. de, *France* 29 G12 41 40N 8 52 E
Valjevo, *Serbia, Yug.* 50 B3 44 18N 19 53 E
Valka, *Latvia* 15 H21 57 42N 25 57 E
Valkeakoski, *Finland* 15 F20 61 16N 24 2 E
Valkenswaard, *Neths.* 24 C5 51 21N 5 29 E
Vall de Uxó = La Vall d'Uixó,
Spain 40 F4 39 49N 0 15W
Valla, *Sweden* 16 E10 59 2N 16 20 E
Valladolid, *Mexico* 163 C7 20 40N 88 11W
Valladolid, *Spain* 42 D6 41 38N 4 43W
Valladolid □, *Spain* 42 D6 41 38N 4 43W
Vallata, *Italy* 47 A8 41 2N 15 15 E
Valldemossa, *Spain* 38 B3 39 43N 2 37 E
Valle, *Norway* 18 E4 59 13N 7 33 E
Valle d'Aosta □, *Italy* 44 C4 45 45N 7 15 E
Valle de Arán, *Spain* 40 C5 42 50N 0 55 E
Valle de la Pascua, *Venezuela* 168 B4 9 13N 66 0W
Valle de las Palmas, *Mexico* 161 N10 32 20N 116 43W
Valle de Santiago, *Mexico* 162 C4 20 25N 101 15W
Valle de Suchil, *Mexico* 162 C4 23 38N 103 55W
Valle de Zaragoza, *Mexico* 162 B3 27 28N 105 49W
Valle del Cauca □, *Colombia* 168 C2 3 45N 76 30W
Valle Fértil, Sierra del, *Argentina* 174 C2 30 20 S 68 0W
Valle Hermoso, *Mexico* 163 B5 25 35N 97 40W
Valledupar, *Colombia* 168 A3 10 29N 73 15W
Vallehermoso, *Canary Is.* 9 e1 28 10N 17 15W
Vallejo, *U.S.A.* 160 G4 38 7N 122 14W
Vallenar, *Chile* 174 B1 28 30 S 70 50W
Vallentuna, *Sweden* 16 E12 59 32N 18 5 E
Valleraugue, *France* 28 D7 44 6N 3 39 E
Vallet, *France* 26 E5 47 10N 1 15W
Valletta, *Malta* 38 F8 35 54N 14 31 E
Valley Center, *U.S.A.* 161 M9 33 13N 117 2W
Valley City, *U.S.A.* 154 B6 46 55N 98 0W
Valley Falls, *Oreg., U.S.A.* 158 E3 42 29N 120 17W
Valley Falls, *R.I., U.S.A.* 151 E13 41 54N 71 24W
Valley of the Kings, *Egypt* 110 B3 25 41N 32 34 E
Valley Springs, *U.S.A.* 160 G6 38 12N 120 50W
Valley Station, *U.S.A.* 157 F11 38 6N 85 52W
Valley View, *U.S.A.* 151 F8 40 39N 76 33W
Valley Wells, *U.S.A.* 161 K11 35 27N 115 46W
Valleyview, *Canada* 142 B5 55 5N 117 17W
Valli di Comácchio, *Italy* 45 D9 44 40N 12 15 E
Vallimanca, Arroyo, *Argentina* 174 D4 35 40 S 59 10W
Vallo della Lucánia, *Italy* 47 B8 40 14N 15 16 E
Vallon-Pont-d'Arc, *France* 29 D8 44 24N 4 24 E
Vallorbe, *Switz.* 32 C2 46 42N 6 20 E
Valls, *Spain* 40 D6 41 18N 1 15 E
Valmaseda = Balmaseda, *Spain* . . 40 B1 43 11N 3 12W
Valmeyer, *U.S.A.* 156 F6 38 18N 90 19W
Valmiera, *Latvia* 15 H21 57 37N 25 29 E
Valnera, *Spain* 42 B7 43 9N 3 40W
Valognes, *France* 26 C5 49 30N 1 28W
Valona = Vlorë, *Albania* 50 F3 40 32N 19 28 E
Valongo, *Portugal* 42 D2 41 8N 8 30W
Valozhyn, *Belarus* 58 E4 54 3N 26 30 E
Valpaços, *Portugal* 42 D3 41 36N 7 17W
Valparai, *India* 95 J3 10 22N 76 58 E
Valparaíso, *Chile* 174 C1 33 2 S 71 40W
Valparaíso, *Mexico* 162 C4 22 50N 103 32W
Valparaiso, *Fla., U.S.A.* 153 E3 30 29N 86 30W
Valparaiso, *Ind., U.S.A.* 157 C9 41 28N 87 4W
Valparaíso □, *Chile* 174 C1 33 2 S 71 40W
Valpovo, *Croatia* 52 E3 45 39N 18 25 E
Valpoy, *India* 95 G2 15 32N 74 8 E
Valréas, *France* 29 D9 44 24N 5 0 E
Vals, *Switz.* 33 C8 46 39N 9 11 E
Vals →, *S. Africa* 116 D4 27 23 S 26 30 E
Vals, Tanjung, *Indonesia* 83 C5 8 26 S 137 25 E
Vals-les-Bains, *France* 29 D8 44 42N 4 24 E
Valsad, *India* 94 D1 20 40N 72 58 E
Valsamáta, *Greece* 39 C2 38 10N 20 36 E
Valtellina, *Italy* 44 B6 46 11N 9 55 E
Valþjofsstaður, *Iceland* 11 B12 65 1N 14 59W
Valtí, *Greece* 39 C3 38 27N 21 7 E
Valuyki, *Russia* 59 G10 50 10N 38 5 E
Valverde, *Canary Is.* 9 e1 27 48N 17 55W
Valverde del Camino, *Spain* 43 H4 37 35N 6 47W
Valverde del Fresno, *Spain* 42 E4 40 15N 6 51W
Vama, *Romania* 53 C10 47 34N 25 42 E
Vambori, *India* 94 E2 19 17N 74 44 E
Vamdrup, *Denmark* 17 J3 55 25N 9 17 E
Vâmhus, *Sweden* 16 C8 61 7N 14 29 E
Vammala, *Finland* 15 F20 61 20N 22 54 E
Vámos, *Greece* 39 E5 35 24N 24 13 E
Vamsadhara →, *India* 94 E7 18 21N 84 8 E
Van, *Turkey* 101 C10 38 30N 43 20 E
Van, L. = Van Gölü, *Turkey* 101 C10 38 30N 43 0 E
Van Alstyne, *U.S.A.* 155 J6 33 25N 96 35W
Van Blommestein Meer, *Surinam* 169 C6 4 45N 55 5W
Van Buren, *Canada* 141 C6 47 10N 67 55W
Van Buren, *Ark., U.S.A.* 155 H7 35 26N 94 21W
Van Buren, *Maine, U.S.A.* 149 B11 47 10N 67 58W
Van Buren, *Mo., U.S.A.* 155 G9 37 0N 91 1W
Van Canh, *Vietnam* 86 F7 13 37N 109 0 E
Van Diemen, C., *N. Terr.,*
Australia 124 B5 11 9 S 130 24 E
Van Diemen, C., *Queens.,*
Australia 126 B2 16 30 S 139 46 E
Van Diemen G., *Australia* 124 B5 11 45 S 132 0 E
Van Gölü, *Turkey* 101 C10 38 30N 43 0 E
Van Horn, *U.S.A.* 155 K2 31 3N 104 50W
Van Horne, *U.S.A.* 156 B4 42 1N 92 4W
Van Meter, *U.S.A.* 156 C3 41 32N 93 57W
Van Ninh, *Vietnam* 86 F7 12 42N 109 14 E
Van Rees, Pegunungan, *Indonesia* 83 B5 2 35 S 138 15 E
Van Tivu, *India* 95 K4 8 51N 78 15 E
Van Wert, *U.S.A.* 157 D12 40 52N 84 35W
Van Yen, *Vietnam* 76 G5 21 4N 104 42 E
Vanadzor, *Armenia* 61 K7 40 48N 44 30 E
Vanavara, *Russia* 67 C11 60 22N 102 16 E
Vanceburg, *U.S.A.* 157 F13 38 36N 83 19W
Vancouver, *Canada* 142 D4 49 15N 123 10W
Vancouver, *U.S.A.* 160 E4 45 38N 122 40W
Vancouver, C., *Australia* 125 G2 35 2 S 118 11 E
Vancouver, Mt., *U.S.A.* 144 F13 60 20N 139 41W
Vancouver I., *Canada* 142 D3 49 50N 126 0W
Vandalia, *Ill., U.S.A.* 156 F7 38 58N 89 6W
Vandalia, *Mo., U.S.A.* 156 E5 39 19N 91 29W
Vandalia, *Ohio, U.S.A.* 157 E12 39 54N 84 12W
Vandavasi, *India* 95 H4 12 30N 79 30 E
Vandeloos B., *Sri Lanka* 95 L5 8 0N 81 45 E
Vandenburg, *U.S.A.* 161 L6 34 35N 120 33W
Vanderbijlpark, *S. Africa* 117 D4 26 42 S 27 54 E
Vandergrift, *U.S.A.* 150 F5 40 36N 79 34W
Vanderhoof, *Canada* 142 C4 54 0N 124 0W
Vanderkloof Dam, *S. Africa* 116 E3 30 4 S 24 40 E
Vanderlin I., *Australia* 126 B2 15 44 S 137 2 E
Vänern, *Sweden* 17 F7 58 47N 13 30 E
Vänersborg, *Sweden* 17 F6 58 26N 12 19 E
Vang, *Norway* 18 C5 61 7N 8 34 E
Vang Vieng, *Laos* 86 C4 18 58N 102 32 E
Vanga, *Kenya* 118 C4 4 35 S 39 12 E
Vangaindrano, *Madag.* 117 C8 23 21 S 47 36 E
Vangsnes, *Norway* 18 C3 61 9N 6 39 E
Vanguard, *Canada* 143 D7 49 55N 107 20W
Vangunu, *Solomon Is.* 133 M10 8 40 S 158 5 E
Vanimo, *Papua N. G.* 83 B6 2 42 S 141 21 E
Vanino, *Russia* 67 E15 48 50N 140 5 E
Vanivilasa Sagara, *India* 95 H3 13 45N 76 30 E
Vaniyambadi, *India* 95 H4 12 46N 78 44 E
Vanj, *Tajikistan* 65 D5 38 22N 71 27 E
Vânju Mare, *Romania* 52 F7 44 25N 22 52 E
Vanna, *Norway* 14 A18 70 6N 19 50 E
Vännäs, *Sweden* 14 E18 63 58N 19 48 E
Vannes, *France* 26 E4 47 40N 2 47W
Vanoise, *France* 29 C10 45 25N 6 40 E
Vanrhynsdorp, *S. Africa* 116 E2 31 36 S 18 44 E
Vansada, *India* 94 D1 20 47N 73 25 E
Vansbro, *Sweden* 16 D8 60 32N 14 15 E
Vanse, *Norway* 18 F3 58 6N 6 41 E
Vansittart B., *Australia* 124 B4 14 3 S 126 17 E
Vantaa, *Finland* 15 F21 60 18N 24 58 E
Vanua Balavu, *Fiji* 133 A3 17 12 S 178 55W
Vanua Lava, *Vanuatu* 133 C5 13 50 S 167 30 E
Vanua Levu, *Fiji* 133 A2 16 33 S 179 15 E
Vanua Vatu, *Fiji* 133 B3 18 22 S 179 15W
Vanuatu ■, *Pac. Oc.* 133 E6 15 0 S 168 0 E
Vanwyksvlei, *S. Africa* 116 E3 30 18 S 21 49 E
Vanzylsrus, *S. Africa* 116 D3 26 52 S 22 4 E
Vapnyarka, *Ukraine* 59 H5 48 32N 28 45 E
Var □, *France* 29 E10 43 27N 6 18 E
Var →, *France* 29 E11 43 39N 7 12 E
Vara, *Sweden* 17 F6 58 16N 12 55 E
Vara, Pico da, *Azores* 9 d3 37 48N 25 13W
Varada →, *India* 95 G2 15 0N 75 40 E
Varades, *France* 26 E5 47 25N 1 1W
Varáita →, *Italy* 44 D4 44 49N 7 53 E
Varaldsøy, *Norway* 18 D2 60 6N 5 59 E
Varallo, *Italy* 44 C5 45 49N 8 15 E
Varanasi, *India* 93 G10 25 22N 83 0 E
Varangerfjorden, *Norway* 14 A23 70 3N 29 25 E
Varangerhalvøya, *Norway* 14 A23 70 25N 29 30 E
Varano, Lago di, *Italy* 45 G12 41 53N 15 45 E

Volochanka 297

Vidzy, *Belarus* 15 J22 55 23N 26 37 E
Viechtach, *Germany* 31 F8 49 4N 12 53 E
Viedma, *Argentina* 176 B4 40 50 S 63 0W
Viedma, L., *Argentina* 176 C2 49 30 S 72 30W
Vieira do Minho, *Portugal* 42 D2 41 38N 8 8W
Vielha, *Spain* 40 C5 42 43N 0 44 E
Viella = Vielha, *Spain* 40 C5 42 43N 0 44 E
Vielsalm, *Belgium* 24 D5 50 17N 5 54 E
Vienenburg, *Germany* 30 D6 51 57N 10 34 E
Vieng Pou Kha, *Laos* 76 G3 20 41N 101 4 E
Vienna = Wien, *Austria* 35 C9 48 12N 16 22 E
Vienna, *Ga., U.S.A.* 152 C6 32 6N 83 47W
Vienna, *Ill., U.S.A.* 155 G10 37 25N 88 54W
Vienna, *Mo., U.S.A.* 156 F5 38 11N 91 57W
Vienne, *France* 29 C8 45 31N 4 53 E
Vienne □, *France* 28 B4 46 30N 0 42 E
Vienne →, *France* 26 E7 47 13N 0 5 E
Vientiane, *Laos* 86 D4 17 58N 102 36 E
Vientos, Paso de los, *Caribbean* 165 C5 20 0N 74 0W
Vieques, Isla de, *Puerto Rico* 165 d 18 8N 65 25W
Vierge Pt., *St. Lucia* 165 f 13 49N 60 53W
Viernheim, *Germany* 31 F4 49 31N 8 35 E
Viersen, *Germany* 30 D2 51 15N 6 23 E
Vierwaldstättersee, *Switz.* 33 C7 47 0N 8 30 E
Vierzon, *France* 27 E9 47 13N 2 5 E
Vieste, *Italy* 45 G13 41 53N 16 10 E
Vietnam ■, *Asia* 86 C6 19 0N 106 0 E
Vieux-Boucau-les-Bains, *France* 28 E2 43 48N 1 23W
Vieux Fort, *St. Lucia* 165 f 13 46N 60 58W
Vif, *France* 29 C9 45 5N 5 41 E
Viga, *Phil.* 80 E5 13 52N 124 18 E
Vigan, *Phil.* 80 C3 17 35N 120 28 E
Vigévano, *Italy* 44 C5 45 19N 8 51 E
Vigia, *Brazil* 170 B2 0 50 S 48 5W
Vigía Chico, *Mexico* 163 D7 19 46N 87 35W
Viglas, Ákra, *Greece* 39 A2 39 7N 20 50 E
Víglas, Ákra, *Greece* 38 F11 35 54N 27 51 E
Vignemalle, *France* 28 F3 42 47N 0 10W
Vigneulles-lès-Hattonchâtel, *France* 27 D12 48 59N 5 43 E
Vignola, *Italy* 44 D8 44 29N 11 1 E
Vigo, *Spain* 42 C2 42 12N 8 41W
Vigo, Ría de, *Spain* 42 C2 42 15N 8 45W
Vigrestad, *Norway* 18 F2 58 34N 5 42 E
Vigsø Bugt, *Denmark* 17 G2 57 8N 8 47 E
Vihiers, *France* 26 E6 47 10N 0 30W
Vihowa, *Pakistan* 92 D4 31 8N 70 30 E
Vihowa →, *Pakistan* 92 D4 31 8N 70 41 E
Vijayadurg, *India* 94 F1 16 30N 73 25 E
Vijayawada, *India* 94 F5 16 31N 80 39 E
Vijosë →, *Albania* 50 F3 40 37N 19 24 E
Vík, *Iceland* 11 D7 63 25N 19 1W
Vik, *Norway* 18 C3 61 21N 6 6 E
Vika, *Sweden* 16 D8 60 57N 14 28 E
Vikarabad, *India* 94 E3 17 20N 77 54 E
Vikarbyn, *Sweden* 16 D9 60 55N 15 1 E
Vike, *Norway* 18 D2 60 42N 5 35 E
Vikedal, *Norway* 18 E2 59 30N 5 55 E
Vikeke = Viqueque, *E. Timor* 82 C3 8 52 S 126 23 E
Vikeland, *Norway* 18 F4 58 5N 7 18 E
Viken, *Skåne, Sweden* 17 H6 56 9N 12 34 E
Viken, *Västra Götaland, Sweden* 17 F8 58 39N 14 20 E
Vikersund, *Norway* 18 E6 59 58N 9 59 E
Vikeså, *Norway* 18 F3 58 38N 6 3 E
Vikevåg, *Norway* 18 E2 59 5N 5 41 E
Viking, *Canada* 142 C6 53 7N 111 50W
Vikmanshyttan, *Sweden* 16 D9 60 18N 15 50 E
Vikna, *Norway* 14 D14 64 55N 10 58 E
Viksøyri, *Norway* 18 C3 61 4N 6 34 E
Vila Bela da Santissima Trindade, *Brazil* 173 C6 15 0 S 59 57W
Vila da Maganja, *Mozam.* 119 F4 17 18 S 37 30 E
Vila da Ribeira Brava, *C. Verde Is.* 9 j 16 32N 24 25W
Vila de João Belo = Xai-Xai, *Mozam.* 117 D5 25 6 S 33 31 E
Vila de Rei, *Portugal* 42 F2 39 41N 8 9W
Vila do Bispo, *Portugal* 43 H2 37 5N 8 53W
Vila do Conde, *Portugal* 42 D2 41 21N 8 45W
Vila do Porto, *Azores* 9 d4 36 56N 25 9W
Vila Franca de Xira, *Portugal* 43 G2 38 57N 8 59W
Vila Franca do Campo, *Azores* 9 d3 37 43N 25 26W
Vila Gamito, *Mozam.* 119 E3 14 12 S 33 0 E
Vila Gomes da Costa, *Mozam.* 117 C5 24 20 S 33 37 E
Vila Machado, *Mozam.* 119 F3 19 15 S 34 14 E
Vila Mouzinho, *Mozam.* 119 E3 14 48 S 34 25 E
Vila Nova de Famalicão, *Portugal* 42 D2 41 25N 8 32W
Vila Nova de Fos Côa, *Portugal* 42 D3 41 5N 7 9W
Vila Nova de Gaia, *Portugal* 42 D2 41 4N 8 40W
Vila Nova de Ourém, *Portugal* 42 F2 39 40N 8 35W
Vila Nova do Corvo, *Azores* 9 d2 39 40N 31 8W
Vila Pouca de Aguiar, *Portugal* 42 D3 41 30N 7 38W
Vila Real, *Portugal* 42 D3 41 17N 7 48W
Vila Real □, *Portugal* 42 D3 41 36N 7 35W
Vila-real de los Infantes, *Spain* 40 F4 39 55N 0 3W
Vila Real de Santo António, *Portugal* 43 H3 37 10N 7 28W
Vila Vasco da Gama, *Mozam.* 119 E3 14 54 S 32 14 E
Vila Velha, *Amapá, Brazil* 169 C7 3 13N 51 13W
Vila Velha, *Espírito Santo, Brazil* 171 F3 20 20 S 40 17W
Vila Viçosa, *Portugal* 43 G3 38 45N 7 27W
Vilafranca del Maestrat, *Spain* 40 E4 40 26N 0 16W
Vilafranca del Penedès, *Spain* 40 D6 41 21N 1 40 E
Vilagarcía de Arousa, *Spain* 42 C2 42 34N 8 46W
Vilaine →, *France* 26 E4 47 30N 2 27W
Vilakalaka, *Vanuatu* 133 E5 15 25 S 167 42 E
Vilanandro, Tanjona, *Madag.* 117 B7 16 11 S 44 27 E
Vilanculos, *Mozam.* 117 C6 22 1 S 35 17 E
Vilanova de Castelló, *Spain* 41 F4 39 5N 0 31W
Vilanova i la Geltrú, *Spain* 40 D6 41 13N 1 40 E
Vilar Formosa, *Portugal* 42 E4 40 38N 6 45W
Vilaseca, *Spain* 40 D6 41 7N 1 9 E
Vilaseca-Salou = Vilaseca, *Spain* 40 D6 41 7N 1 9 E
Vilbjerg, *Denmark* 17 H2 56 12N 8 46 E
Vilcabamba, Cordillera, *Peru* 172 C3 13 0 S 73 0W
Vilcanchos, *Peru* 172 C3 13 40 S 74 25W
Vilches, *Spain* 43 G7 38 12N 3 30W
Vileyka, *Belarus* 58 E4 54 30N 26 53 E
Vilhelmina, *Sweden* 14 D17 64 35N 16 39 E
Vilhena, *Brazil* 173 C5 12 40 S 60 5W
Viliga, *Russia* 67 C16 61 36N 156 56 E
Viliya →, *Lithuania* 15 J21 55 8N 24 16 E
Viljandi, *Estonia* 15 G21 58 28N 25 30 E
Vilkaviškis, *Lithuania* 54 D10 54 39N 23 2 E
Vilkija, *Lithuania* 54 C10 55 3N 23 35 E
Vil'kitskogo, Proliv, *Russia* 67 B11 78 0N 103 0 E
Vilkovo = Vylkove, *Ukraine* 59 K5 45 28N 29 32 E
Villa Abecia, *Bolivia* 174 A2 21 0 S 68 18W
Villa Ahumada, *Mexico* 162 A3 30 38N 106 30W
Villa Ana, *Argentina* 174 B4 28 28 S 59 40W
Villa Ángela, *Argentina* 174 B3 27 34 S 60 45W
Villa Bella, *Bolivia* 173 C4 10 25 S 65 22W
Villa Bens = Tarfaya, *Morocco* 110 C2 27 55N 12 55W
Villa Bruzual, *Venezuela* 168 C4 9 20N 69 6W
Villa Cañás, *Argentina* 174 C3 34 0 S 61 35W
Villa Cisneros = Dakhla, *W. Sahara* 110 D1 23 50N 15 53W
Villa Colón, *Argentina* 174 C2 31 38 S 68 20W
Villa Constitución, *Argentina* 174 C3 33 15 S 60 20W
Villa de Cura, *Venezuela* 168 A4 10 2N 67 29W
Villa de María, *Argentina* 174 B3 29 55 S 63 43W
Villa del Rio, *Spain* 43 H6 37 59N 4 17W
Villa del Rosario, *Venezuela* 168 A3 10 19N 72 19W
Villa Dolores, *Argentina* 174 C2 31 58 S 65 15W
Villa Frontera, *Mexico* 162 B4 26 56N 101 27W
Villa Grove, *U.S.A.* 157 E8 39 52N 88 10W
Villa Guillermina, *Argentina* 174 B4 28 15 S 59 29W
Villa Hayes, *Paraguay* 174 B4 25 5 S 57 20W
Villa Iris, *Argentina* 174 D3 38 12 S 63 12W
Villa Juárez, *Mexico* 162 B4 27 37N 100 44W
Villa María, *Argentina* 174 C3 32 20 S 63 10W
Villa Mazán, *Argentina* 174 B2 28 40 S 66 30W
Villa Minozzo, *Italy* 44 D7 44 22N 10 28 E
Villa Montes, *Bolivia* 174 A3 21 10 S 63 30W
Villa Ocampo, *Argentina* 174 B4 28 30 S 59 20W
Villa Ocampo, *Mexico* 162 B3 26 29N 105 30W
Villa Ojo de Agua, *Argentina* 174 B3 29 30 S 63 44W
Villa Rica, *U.S.A.* 152 B5 33 44N 84 55W
Villa San Giovanni, *Italy* 47 D8 38 13N 15 38 E
Villa San José, *Argentina* 174 C4 32 12 S 58 15W
Villa San Martín, *Argentina* 174 B3 28 15 S 64 9W
Villa Santina, *Italy* 45 B9 46 24N 12 55 E
Villa Unión, *Mexico* 162 C3 23 12N 106 14W
Villaba, *Phil.* 81 F5 11 13N 124 24 E
Villablino, *Spain* 42 C4 42 57N 6 19W
Villacarlos, *Spain* 38 B5 39 53N 4 17 E
Villacarriedo, *Spain* 42 B7 43 14N 3 48W
Villacarrillo, *Spain* 43 G7 38 7N 3 3W
Villacastín, *Spain* 42 E6 40 46N 4 25W
Villach, *Austria* 34 E6 46 37N 13 51 E
Villacidro, *Italy* 46 C1 39 27N 8 44 E
Villada, *Spain* 42 C6 42 15N 4 59W
Villadiego, *Spain* 42 C6 42 31N 4 1W
Villadóssola, *Italy* 44 B5 46 4N 8 16 E
Villafeliche, *Spain* 40 D3 41 10N 1 30W
Villafranca, *Spain* 40 C3 42 17N 1 46W
Villafranca de los Barros, *Spain* 43 G4 38 35N 6 18W
Villafranca de los Caballeros, *Spain* 43 F7 39 26N 3 21W
Villafranca del Cid = Vilafranca del Maestrat, *Spain* 40 E4 40 26N 0 16W
Villafranca del Panadés = Vilafranca del Penedès, *Spain* 40 D6 41 21N 1 40 E
Villafranca di Verona, *Italy* 44 C7 45 21N 10 50 E
Villafranca Tirrena, *Italy* 47 D8 38 20N 15 25 E
Villagrán, *Mexico* 163 C5 24 29N 99 29W
Villaguay, *Argentina* 174 C4 32 0 S 59 0W
Villaharta, *Spain* 43 G6 38 9N 4 54W
Villahermosa, *Mexico* 163 D6 17 59N 92 55W
Villahermosa, *Spain* 41 G2 38 46N 2 52W
Villaines-la-Juhel, *France* 26 D6 48 21N 0 20W
Villajoyosa, *Spain* 41 G4 38 30N 0 12W
Villalba, *Spain* 42 B3 43 26N 7 40W
Villalba de Guardo, *Spain* 42 C6 42 42N 4 49W
Villalón de Campos, *Spain* 42 C5 42 5N 5 4W
Villalpando, *Spain* 42 D5 41 51N 5 25W
Villaluenga, *Spain* 42 E7 40 2N 3 54W
Villamanán, *Spain* 42 C5 42 19N 5 35W
Villamartín, *Spain* 43 J5 36 52N 5 38W
Villamayor de Santiago, *Spain* 40 F2 39 50N 2 59W
Villamblard, *France* 28 C4 45 2N 0 32 E
Villanova Monteleone, *Italy* 46 B1 40 30N 8 28 E
Villanueva, *Colombia* 168 A3 10 37N 72 59W
Villanueva, *U.S.A.* 155 H2 35 16N 105 22W
Villanueva de Castellón = Vilanova de Castelló, *Spain* 41 F4 39 5N 0 31W
Villanueva de Córdoba, *Spain* 43 G6 38 20N 4 38W
Villanueva de la Fuente, *Spain* 41 G2 38 42N 2 42W
Villanueva de la Serena, *Spain* 43 G5 38 59N 5 50W
Villanueva de la Sierra, *Spain* 42 E4 40 12N 6 24W
Villanueva de los Castillejos, *Spain* 43 H3 37 30N 7 15W
Villanueva de los Infantes, *Spain* 43 G7 38 43N 3 1W
Villanueva del Arzobispo, *Spain* 41 G2 38 10N 3 0W
Villanueva del Fresno, *Spain* 43 G3 38 23N 7 10W
Villanueva y Geltrú = Vilanova i la Geltrú, *Spain* 40 D6 41 13N 1 40 E
Villaputzu, *Italy* 46 C2 39 26N 9 34 E
Villaquilambre, *Spain* 42 C5 42 39N 5 33W
Villar del Arzobispo, *Spain* 40 F4 39 44N 0 50W
Villar del Rey, *Spain* 43 F4 39 7N 6 50W
Villard-de-Lans, *France* 29 C9 45 3N 5 33 E
Villarramiel, *Spain* 42 C6 42 2N 4 55W
Villarreal = Vila-real de los Infantes, *Spain* 40 F4 39 55N 0 3W
Villarrica, *Chile* 176 A2 39 15 S 72 15W
Villarrica, *Paraguay* 174 B4 25 40 S 56 30W
Villarrobledo, *Spain* 41 F2 39 18N 2 36W
Villarroya de la Sierra, *Spain* 40 D3 41 27N 1 46W
Villarrubia de los Ojos, *Spain* 43 F7 39 14N 3 36W
Villars-les-Dombes, *France* 27 F12 46 0N 5 3 E
Villasayas, *Spain* 40 D2 41 24N 2 39W
Villaseca de los Gamitos = Villaseco de los Gamitos, *Spain* 42 D4 41 2N 6 7W
Villaseco de los Gamitos, *Spain* 42 D4 41 2N 6 7W
Villasimíus, *Italy* 46 C2 39 8N 9 31 E
Villastar, *Spain* 40 E3 40 17N 1 9W
Villatobas, *Spain* 42 F7 39 54N 3 20W
Villavicencio, *Argentina* 174 C2 32 28 S 69 0W
Villavicencio, *Colombia* 168 C3 4 9N 73 37W
Villaviciosa, *Spain* 42 B5 43 32N 5 27W
Villazón, *Bolivia* 174 A2 22 0 S 65 35W
Ville-Marie, *Canada* 140 C4 47 20N 79 30W
Ville Platte, *U.S.A.* 155 K8 30 41N 92 17W
Villedieu-les-Poêles, *France* 26 D5 48 50N 1 13W
Villefort, *France* 28 D7 44 28N 3 56 E
Villefranche-de-Lauragais, *France* 28 E5 43 25N 1 44 E
Villefranche-de-Rouergue, *France* 28 D6 44 21N 2 2 E
Villefranche-du-Périgord, *France* 28 D5 44 38N 1 5 E
Villefranche-sur-Saône, *France* 29 C8 45 59N 4 43 E
Villegrande, *Bolivia* 173 D5 18 30 S 64 10W
Villel, *Spain* 40 E3 40 14N 1 12W
Villemur-sur-Tarn, *France* 28 E5 43 51N 1 31 E
Villena, *Spain* 41 G4 38 39N 0 52W
Villenauxe-la-Grande, *France* 27 D10 48 35N 3 33 E
Villenave-d'Ornon, *France* 28 D3 44 46N 0 33W
Villeneuve, *Switz.* 32 D3 46 24N 6 56 E
Villeneuve-d'Ascq, *France* 27 B10 50 38N 3 9 E
Villeneuve-l'Archevêque, *France* 27 D10 48 14N 3 32 E
Villeneuve-lès-Avignon, *France* 29 E8 43 58N 4 49 E
Villeneuve-sur-Allier, *France* 27 F10 46 40N 3 13 E
Villeneuve-sur-Lot, *France* 28 D4 44 24N 0 42 E
Villeneuve-sur-Yonne, *France* 27 D10 48 5N 3 18 E
Villeréal, *France* 28 D4 44 38N 0 45 E
Villers-Bocage, *France* 26 C6 49 3N 0 40W
Villers-Cotterêts, *France* 27 C10 49 15N 3 4 E
Villers-sur-Mer, *France* 26 C6 49 21N 0 2W
Villersexel, *France* 27 E13 47 33N 6 26 E
Villerupt, *France* 27 C12 49 28N 5 55 E
Villeurbanne, *France* 29 C8 45 46N 4 55 E
Villiers, *S. Africa* 117 D4 27 2 S 28 36 E
Villingen-Schwenningen, *Germany* 31 G4 48 3N 8 26 E
Villisca, *U.S.A.* 156 D2 40 56N 94 59W
Villupuram, *India* 95 J4 11 59N 79 31 E
Vilna, *Canada* 142 C6 54 7N 111 55W
Vilnius, *Lithuania* 15 J21 54 38N 25 19 E
Vils, *Austria* 34 D3 47 33N 10 38 E
Vils →, *Bayern, Germany* 31 G9 48 37N 13 11 E
Vils →, *Bayern, Germany* 31 F7 49 10N 11 57 E
Vilsbiburg, *Germany* 31 G8 48 26N 12 22 E
Vilshofen, *Germany* 31 G9 48 37N 13 11 E
Vilusi, *Montenegro, Yug.* 50 D2 42 44N 18 34 E
Vilvoorde, *Belgium* 24 D4 50 56N 4 26 E
Vilyuy →, *Russia* 67 C13 64 24N 126 26 E
Vilyuysk, *Russia* 67 C13 63 40N 121 35 E
Vimianzo, *Spain* 42 B1 43 7N 9 2W
Vimioso, *Portugal* 42 D4 41 35N 6 31W
Vimmerby, *Sweden* 17 G9 57 40N 15 55 E
Vimoutiers, *France* 26 D7 48 57N 0 10 E
Vimperk, *Czech Rep.* 34 B6 49 3N 13 46 E
Vina →, *Cameroon* 114 A3 7 45N 15 36 E
Viña del Mar, *Chile* 174 C1 33 0 S 71 30W
Vinarós, *Spain* 40 E5 40 30N 0 27 E
Vincennes, *U.S.A.* 157 F9 38 41N 87 32W
Vincent, *U.S.A.* 161 L8 34 33N 118 11W
Vinces, *Ecuador* 168 D2 1 32 S 79 45W
Vinchina, *Argentina* 174 B2 28 45 S 68 15W
Vindelälven →, *Sweden* 14 E18 63 55N 19 50 E
Vindeln, *Sweden* 14 D18 64 12N 19 43 E
Vinderup, *Denmark* 17 H2 56 29N 8 45 E
Vindhya Ra., *India* 92 H7 22 50N 77 0 E
Vine Grove, *U.S.A.* 157 G11 37 49N 85 59W
Vineland, *U.S.A.* 148 F8 39 29N 75 2W
Vineuil, *France* 26 E8 47 35N 1 22 E
Vinga, *Romania* 52 D6 46 1N 21 14 E
Vingåker, *Sweden* 16 E9 59 2N 15 52 E
Vingelen, *Norway* 18 B7 62 25N 10 52 E
Vingnes, *Norway* 18 C7 61 7N 10 26 E
Vinh, *Vietnam* 86 C5 18 45N 105 38 E
Vinh Linh, *Vietnam* 86 D6 17 4N 107 2 E
Vinh Long, *Vietnam* 87 G5 10 16N 105 57 E
Vinh Yen, *Vietnam* 76 G5 21 21N 105 35 E
Vinhais, *Portugal* 42 D3 41 50N 7 5W
Vinica, *Croatia* 45 B13 46 20N 16 9 E
Vinica, *Macedonia* 50 E6 41 53N 22 30 E
Vinica, *Slovenia* 45 C12 45 28N 15 16 E
Vinita, *U.S.A.* 155 G7 36 39N 95 9W
Vinje, *Hordaland, Norway* 18 D3 60 48N 6 30 E
Vinje, *Sør-Trøndelag, Norway* 18 A5 63 12N 9 0 E
Vinje, *Telemark, Norway* 18 E4 59 37N 7 51 E
Vinkovci, *Croatia* 52 E3 45 19N 18 48 E
Vinnitsa = Vinnytsya, *Ukraine* 59 H5 49 15N 28 30 E
Vinnytsya, *Ukraine* 59 H5 49 15N 28 30 E
Vinslöv, *Sweden* 17 H7 56 7N 13 55 E
Vinstra, *Norway* 18 C6 61 37N 9 44 E
Vinstra →, *Norway* 18 C6 61 37N 9 44 E
Vintar, *Phil.* 80 B3 18 14N 120 39 E
Vintjärn, *Sweden* 16 D10 60 50N 16 4 E
Vinton, *Calif., U.S.A.* 160 F6 39 48N 120 10W
Vinton, *Iowa, U.S.A.* 156 B4 42 10N 92 1W
Vinton, *La., U.S.A.* 155 K8 30 11N 93 35W
Vinţu de Jos, *Romania* 53 D8 46 0N 23 30 E
Vinukonda, *India* 95 F4 16 4N 79 45 E
Viöl, *Germany* 30 A5 54 34N 9 11 E
Viola, *U.S.A.* 156 C6 41 12N 90 35W
Violet Town, *Australia* 129 D6 36 38 S 145 42 E
Vipava, *Slovenia* 45 C10 45 51N 13 58 E
Vipiteno, *Italy* 45 B8 46 54N 11 26 E
Viqueque, *E. Timor* 82 C3 8 52 S 126 23 E
Vir, *Croatia* 45 D12 44 17N 15 3 E
Vira, *Switz.* 33 D7 46 8N 8 50 E
Virac, *Phil.* 80 E5 13 30N 124 20 E
Virachei, *Cambodia* 86 F6 13 59N 106 49 E
Virago Sd., *Canada* 142 C2 54 0N 132 30W
Virajpet = Virarajendrapet, *India* 95 H2 12 10N 75 50 E
Viramgam, *India* 92 H5 23 5N 72 0 E
Viranşehir, *Turkey* 101 D8 37 13N 39 45 E
Virarajendrapet, *India* 95 H2 12 10N 75 50 E
Virawah, *Pakistan* 92 G4 24 31N 70 46 E
Virbalis, *Lithuania* 54 D9 54 39N 22 49 E
Virden, *Canada* 143 D8 49 50N 100 56W
Virden, *U.S.A.* 156 E7 39 30N 89 46W
Vire, *France* 26 D6 48 50N 0 53W
Vire →, *France* 26 C5 49 20N 1 7W
Virei, *Angola* 115 F2 15 43 S 12 52 E
Virgem da Lapa, *Brazil* 171 E3 16 49 S 42 21W
Vírgenes, C., *Argentina* 176 D3 52 19 S 68 21W
Virgin →, *U.S.A.* 159 H6 36 28N 114 21W
Virgin Gorda, *Br. Virgin Is.* 165 e 18 30N 64 26W
Virgin Is. (British) ■, *W. Indies* 165 e 18 30N 64 30W
Virgin Is. (U.S.) ■, *W. Indies* 165 e 18 20N 65 0W
Virginia, *S. Africa* 116 D4 28 8 S 26 55 E
Virginia, *Ill., U.S.A.* 156 E6 39 57N 90 13W
Virginia, *Minn., U.S.A.* 154 B8 47 31N 92 32W
Virginia □, *U.S.A.* 148 G7 37 30N 78 45W
Virginia Beach, *U.S.A.* 148 G8 36 51N 75 59W
Virginia City, *Mont., U.S.A.* 158 D8 45 18N 111 56W
Virginia City, *Nev., U.S.A.* 160 F7 39 19N 119 39W
Virginia Falls, *Canada* 142 A3 61 38N 125 42W
Virginiatown, *Canada* 140 C4 48 9N 79 36W
Virje, *Croatia* 45 B13 46 4N 16 59 E
Viroqua, *U.S.A.* 154 D9 43 34N 90 53W
Virovitica, *Croatia* 52 E2 45 51N 17 21 E
Virpazar, *Montenegro, Yug.* 50 D3 42 14N 19 6 E
Virpur, *India* 92 J4 21 51N 70 42 E
Virserum, *Sweden* 17 G9 57 20N 15 35 E
Virton, *Belgium* 24 E5 49 35N 5 32 E
Virú, *Peru* 172 B2 8 25 S 78 45W
Virudunagar, *India* 95 K3 9 30N 77 58 E
Virunga, Parc Nat. des, *Dem. Rep. of the Congo* 118 B2 0 5N 29 38 E
Vis, *Croatia* 45 E13 43 4N 16 10 E
Visalia, *U.S.A.* 160 J7 36 20N 119 18W
Visayan Sea, *Phil.* 81 F4 11 30N 123 30 E
Visby, *Sweden* 17 G12 57 37N 18 18 E
Viscount Melville Sd., *Canada* 6 B2 74 10N 108 0W
Visé, *Belgium* 24 D5 50 44N 5 41 E
Višegrad, *Bos.-H.* 52 G4 43 47N 19 17 E
Viseu, *Brazil* 170 B2 1 10 S 46 5W
Viseu, *Portugal* 42 E3 40 40N 7 55W
Viseu □, *Portugal* 42 E3 40 40N 7 55W
Vişeu de Sus, *Romania* 53 C9 47 45N 24 25 E
Vishakhapatnam, *India* 94 F6 17 45N 83 20 E
Vishera →, *Russia* 64 A6 59 55N 56 25 E
Vişina, *Romania* 53 G9 43 52N 24 27 E
Vişineşti, *Moldova* 53 D13 46 20N 28 27 E
Visingsö, *Sweden* 17 F8 58 2N 14 20 E
Viskafors, *Sweden* 17 G6 57 37N 12 50 E
Viskan →, *Sweden* 17 G6 57 14N 12 12 E
Viški Kanal, *Croatia* 45 E13 43 4N 16 5 E
Vislanda, *Sweden* 17 H8 56 46N 14 30 E
Visnagar, *India* 92 H5 23 45N 72 32 E
Višnja Gora, *Slovenia* 45 C11 45 58N 14 45 E
Viso, Mte., *Italy* 44 D4 44 38N 7 5 E
Viso del Marqués, *Spain* 43 G7 38 32N 3 34W
Visoko, *Bos.-H.* 52 G3 43 58N 18 10 E
Visokoi I., *Antarctica* 7 B1 56 43 S 27 15W
Visp, *Switz.* 32 D5 46 17N 7 52 E
Vispa →, *Switz.* 32 D5 46 9N 7 48 E
Vissefjärda, *Sweden* 17 H9 56 32N 15 35 E
Visselhövede, *Germany* 30 C5 52 59N 9 34 E
Vissenbjerg, *Denmark* 17 J4 55 23N 10 7 E
Vissoie, *Switz.* 32 D5 46 13N 7 36 E
Vista, *U.S.A.* 161 M9 33 12N 117 14W
Vistonikos, Ormos = Vistonís, Límni, *Greece* 51 E9 41 0N 25 7 E
Vistonís, Límni, *Greece* 51 E9 41 0N 25 7 E
Vistula = Wisła →, *Poland* 54 D5 54 22N 18 55 E
Vit →, *Bulgaria* 51 C8 43 30N 24 30 E
Vita, *India* 94 F2 17 17N 74 33 E
Vitanje, *Slovenia* 45 B12 46 25N 15 18 E
Vitebsk = Vitsyebsk, *Belarus* 58 E6 55 10N 30 15 E
Viterbo, *Italy* 45 F9 42 25N 12 6 E
Vitez, *Bos.-H.* 52 F2 44 10N 17 48 E
Viti Levu, *Fiji* 133 A1 17 30 S 177 30 E
Vitiaz Str., *Papua N. G.* 132 C4 5 40 S 147 10 E
Vitigudino, *Spain* 42 D4 41 1N 6 26W
Vitim, *Russia* 67 D12 59 28N 112 35 E
Vitim →, *Russia* 67 D12 59 26N 112 34 E
Vitina, *Bos.-H.* 45 E14 43 17N 17 29 E
Vitína, *Greece* 48 D4 37 40N 22 10 E
Vítkov, *Czech Rep.* 35 B10 49 46N 17 45 E
Vitória, *Espírito Santo, Brazil* 171 F3 20 20 S 40 22W
Vitoria, *Pará, Brazil* 169 D7 2 54 S 52 1W
Vitória da Conquista, *Brazil* 171 D3 14 51 S 40 51W
Vitória de São Antão, *Brazil* 170 C4 8 10 S 35 20W
Vitoria-Gasteiz, *Spain* 40 C2 42 50N 2 41W
Vitorino Friere, *Brazil* 170 B2 4 4 S 45 10W
Vitré, *France* 26 D5 48 8N 1 12W
Vitry-le-François, *France* 27 D11 48 43N 4 33 E
Vitry-sur-Seine, *France* 27 D9 48 47N 2 24 E
Vitsand, *Sweden* 16 D7 60 20N 13 0 E
Vitsi, Óros, *Greece* 50 F5 40 40N 21 25 E
Vitsyebsk, *Belarus* 58 E6 55 10N 30 15 E
Vittaryd, *Sweden* 17 H7 56 58N 13 57 E
Vitteaux, *France* 27 E11 47 24N 4 30 E
Vittel, *France* 27 D12 48 12N 5 57 E
Vittória, *Italy* 47 F7 36 57N 14 32 E
Vittório Véneto, *Italy* 45 C9 45 59N 12 18 E
Vittoriosa, *Malta* 38 F8 35 54N 14 31 E
Vittsjö, *Sweden* 17 H7 56 20N 13 40 E
Vitznau, *Switz.* 33 B6 47 1N 8 29 E
Viveiro, *Spain* 42 B3 43 39N 7 38W
Vivian, *U.S.A.* 155 J8 32 53N 93 59W
Viviers, *France* 29 D8 44 30N 4 40 E
Vivonne, *Australia* 128 C2 35 59 S 137 9 E
Vivonne, *France* 28 B4 46 25N 0 15 E
Vivonne B., *Australia* 128 C2 35 59 S 137 9 E
Viwa, *Fiji* 133 A1 17 10 S 177 58 E
Vizcaíno, Desierto de, *Mexico* 162 B2 27 40N 113 50W
Vizcaíno, Sierra, *Mexico* 162 B2 27 30N 114 0W
Vizcaya □, *Spain* 40 B2 43 15N 2 45W
Vize, *Turkey* 51 E11 41 34N 27 45 E
Vizianagaram, *India* 94 E6 18 6N 83 30 E
Vizille, *France* 29 C9 45 5N 5 46 E
Viziñada, *Croatia* 45 C10 45 20N 13 46 E
Viziru, *Romania* 53 E12 45 0N 27 43 E
Vizzini, *Italy* 47 E7 37 10N 14 45 E
Vlaardingen, *Neths.* 24 C4 51 55N 4 21 E
Vlădeasa, Vf., *Romania* 52 D7 46 47N 22 50 E
Vladičin Han, *Serbia, Yug.* 50 D6 42 42N 22 1 E
Vladikavkaz, *Russia* 61 J7 43 0N 44 35 E
Vladimir, *Russia* 58 D11 56 15N 40 30 E
Vladimir Volynskiy = Volodymyr-Volynskyy, *Ukraine* 59 G3 50 50N 24 18 E
Vladimirci, *Serbia, Yug.* 50 B3 44 36N 19 50 E
Vladimirovac, *Serbia, Yug.* 52 E5 45 1N 20 53 E
Vladimirovka, *Russia* 61 F8 48 27N 46 10 E
Vladimirovo, *Bulgaria* 50 C7 43 32N 23 22 E
Vladimirovskiy, *Kazakstan* 60 E10 50 51N 51 8 E
Vladislavovka, *Ukraine* 59 K8 45 12N 35 29 E
Vladivostok, *Russia* 67 E14 43 10N 131 53 E
Vlăhiţa, *Romania* 53 D10 46 21N 25 31 E
Vlakhiótis, *Greece* 48 E4 36 52N 22 42 E
Vlasenica, *Bos.-H.* 52 F3 44 11N 18 59 E
Vlašić, *Bos.-H.* 52 F2 44 19N 17 37 E
Vlašim, *Czech Rep.* 34 B7 49 40N 14 53 E
Vlasinsko Jezero, *Serbia, Yug.* 50 D6 42 44N 22 22 E
Vlasotince, *Serbia, Yug.* 50 D6 42 59N 22 7 E
Vlieland, *Neths.* 24 A4 53 16N 4 55 E
Vlissingen, *Neths.* 24 C3 51 26N 3 34 E
Vlorë, *Albania* 50 F3 40 32N 19 28 E
Vlorës, Gjiri i, *Albania* 50 F3 40 29N 19 27 E
Vltava →, *Czech Rep.* 34 A7 50 21N 14 30 E
Vo Dat, *Vietnam* 87 G6 11 9N 107 31 E
Vobarno, *Italy* 33 E11 45 39N 10 30 E
Voćin, *Croatia* 52 E2 45 37N 17 33 E
Vöcklabruck, *Austria* 34 C6 48 1N 13 39 E
Vodice, *Croatia* 45 E12 43 47N 15 47 E
Vodňany, *Czech Rep.* 34 B7 49 9N 14 11 E
Vodnjan, *Croatia* 45 D10 44 59N 13 52 E
Voe, *U.K.* 22 A7 60 21N 1 16W
Vogar, *Iceland* 11 D4 63 58N 22 22W
Vogel Pk., *Nigeria* 113 D7 8 24N 11 47 E
Vogelkop = Doberai, Jazirah, *Indonesia* 83 B4 1 25 S 133 0 E
Vogelsberg, *Germany* 30 E5 50 31N 9 12 E
Voghera, *Italy* 44 D6 44 59N 9 1 E
Vogorno, *Switz.* 33 D7 46 13N 8 52 E
Voh, *N. Cal.* 133 T18 20 58 S 164 42 E
Vohibinany, *Madag.* 117 B8 18 49 S 49 4 E
Vohilava, *Madag.* 117 C8 21 4 S 48 0 E
Vohimarina = Iharana, *Madag.* 117 A9 13 25 S 50 0 E
Vohimena, Tanjon' i, *Madag.* 117 D8 25 36 S 45 8 E
Vohipeno, *Madag.* 117 C8 22 22 S 47 51 E
Voi, *Kenya* 118 C4 3 25 S 38 32 E
Void-Vacon, *France* 27 D12 48 40N 5 36 E
Voineşti, *Iaşi, Romania* 53 C12 47 5N 27 27 E
Voineşti, *Prahova, Romania* 53 E10 45 5N 25 14 E
Voiotía □, *Greece* 48 C5 38 20N 23 0 E
Voiron, *France* 29 C9 45 22N 5 35 E
Voisey B., *Canada* 141 A7 56 15N 61 50W
Voitsberg, *Austria* 34 D8 47 3N 15 9 E
Vojens, *Denmark* 17 J3 55 16N 9 18 E
Vojmsjön, *Sweden* 14 D17 64 55N 16 40 E
Vojnić, *Croatia* 45 C12 45 19N 15 43 E
Vojnik, *Italy* 45 B12 46 18N 15 19 E
Vojvodina □, *Serbia, Yug.* 52 E5 45 20N 20 0 E
Vokeo I., *Papua N. G.* 132 B3 3 14 S 144 2 E
Vokhtoga, *Russia* 58 C11 58 46N 41 8 E
Volary, *Czech Rep.* 34 C6 48 54N 13 52 E
Volborg, *U.S.A.* 154 C2 45 51N 105 41W
Volcano, *U.S.A.* 145 D6 19 26N 155 14W
Volcano Is. = Kazan-Rettō, *Pac. Oc.* 134 E6 25 0N 141 0 E
Volcans, Parc Nat. des, *Rwanda* 118 C2 1 30 S 29 26 E
Volchansk = Vovchansk, *Ukraine* 59 G9 50 17N 36 58 E
Volchansk, *Russia* 64 B8 59 56N 60 4 E
Volchya →, *Ukraine* 59 H8 48 32N 36 0 E
Volda, *Norway* 15 E12 62 9N 6 5 E
Volga, *Russia* 58 C10 57 58N 38 16 E
Volga →, *Russia* 61 G9 46 0N 48 30 E
Volga Hts. = Privolzhskaya Vozvyshennost, *Russia* 60 E7 51 0N 46 0 E
Volgo-Baltiyskiy Kanal, *Russia* 58 B9 60 0N 38 0 E
Volgo-Donskoy Kanal, *Russia* 61 F7 48 40N 43 37 E
Volgodonsk, *Russia* 61 G6 47 33N 42 5 E
Volgograd, *Russia* 61 F7 48 40N 44 25 E
Volgogradskoye Vdkhr., *Russia* 60 E8 50 0N 45 20 E
Volgorechensk, *Russia* 60 B5 57 28N 41 14 E
Volímai, *Greece* 39 D2 37 52N 20 39 E
Volintiri, *Moldova* 53 D14 46 26N 29 37 E
Volissós, *Greece* 49 C7 38 29N 25 54 E
Volkach, *Germany* 31 F6 49 52N 10 14 E
Völkermarkt, *Austria* 34 E7 46 39N 14 39 E
Volkhov, *Russia* 58 C7 59 55N 32 15 E
Volkhov →, *Russia* 58 B7 60 8N 32 20 E
Völklingen, *Germany* 31 F2 49 15N 6 50 E
Volkovysk = Vawkavysk, *Belarus* 59 F3 53 9N 24 30 E
Volksrust, *S. Africa* 117 D4 27 24 S 29 53 E
Voll, *Norway* 18 B4 62 31N 7 27 E
Volnansk, *Ukraine* 59 H8 48 2N 35 29 E
Volnovakha, *Ukraine* 59 J9 47 35N 37 30 E
Volochanka, *Russia* 67 B10 71 0N 94 28 E

298 Volodarsk

Volodarsk, *Russia* **60 B6** 56 12N 43 15 E
Volodymyr-Volynskyy, *Ukraine* **59 G3** 50 50N 24 18 E
Vologda, *Russia* **58 C10** 59 10N 39 45 E
Volokolamsk, *Russia* **58 D8** 56 5N 35 57 E
Volokonovka, *Russia* **59 G9** 50 33N 37 52 E
Vólos, *Greece* **48 B4** 39 24N 22 59 E
Volosovo, *Russia* **58 C5** 59 27N 29 32 E
Volovets, *Ukraine* **59 H2** 48 43N 23 11 E
Volovo, *Russia* **58 F10** 53 35N 38 1 E
Volozhin = Valozhyn, *Belarus* **58 E4** 54 3N 26 30 E
Volsk, *Russia* **60 D8** 52 5N 47 22 E
Volta □, *Ghana* **113 D5** 7 0N 0 30 E
Volta →, *Ghana* **113 D5** 5 46N 0 41 E
Volta, L., *Ghana* **113 D5** 7 30N 0 0W
Volta Blanche = White Volta →, *Ghana* **113 D4** 9 10N 1 15W
Volta Redonda, *Brazil* **171 F3** 22 31 S 44 5W
Voltaire, C., *Australia* **124 B4** 14 16 S 125 35 E
Volterra, *Italy* **44 E7** 43 24N 10 51 E
Voltri, *Italy* **44 D5** 44 26N 8 45 E
Volturno →, *Italy* **46 A6** 41 1N 13 55 E
Volubilis, *Morocco* **110 B3** 34 2N 5 33W
Vólvi, L., *Greece* **50 F7** 40 40N 23 34 E
Volyně, *Czech Rep.* **34 B6** 49 10N 13 53 E
Volzhsk, *Russia* **60 C9** 55 57N 48 23 E
Volzhskiy, *Russia* **61 F7** 48 56N 44 46 E
Vomo, *Fiji* **133 A1** 17 30 S 177 15 E
Vonavona, *Solomon Is.* **133 M9** 8 15 S 157 5 E
Vondrozo, *Madag.* **117 C8** 22 49 S 47 20 E
Vónitsa, *Greece* **39 B2** 38 55N 20 53 E
Vopnafjörður, *Iceland* **11 B12** 65 45N 14 50W
Vorarlberg □, *Austria* **34 D2** 47 20N 10 0 E
Vóras Óros, *Greece* **50 F5** 40 57N 21 45 E
Voray-sur-l'Ognon, *France* **32 B2** 47 20N 6 1 E
Vorbasse, *Denmark* **17 J3** 55 39N 9 6 E
Vorchdorf, *Austria* **34 C6** 48 0N 13 55 E
Vorderrhein →, *Switz.* **33 C8** 46 49N 9 25 E
Vordingborg, *Denmark* **17 J5** 55 0N 11 54 E
Vorë, *Albania* **50 E3** 41 23N 19 40 E
Voreio Aigaio = Vórios Aiyaíon □, *Greece* **49 C7** 38 50N 25 30 E
Voreppe, *France* **29 C9** 45 18N 5 39 E
Vóriai Sporádhes, *Greece* **48 B5** 39 15N 23 30 E
Vórios Aiyaíon □, *Greece* **49 C7** 38 50N 25 30 E
Vórios Evvoïkos Kólpos, *Greece* **48 C5** 38 45N 23 15 E
Vorkuta, *Russia* **56 A11** 67 48N 64 20 E
Vorma →, *Norway* **18 D8** 60 9N 11 29 E
Vormsi, *Estonia* **15 G20** 59 1N 23 13 E
Vóroi, *Greece* **39 E5** 35 4N 24 49 E
Vorona →, *Russia* **60 E6** 51 22N 42 3 E
Voronezh, *Russia* **59 G10** 51 40N 39 10 E
Voronezh, *Ukraine* **59 G7** 51 47N 33 28 E
Voronezh →, *Russia* **59 G10** 51 32N 39 10 E
Vorontsovo-Aleksandrovskoye = Zelenokumsk, *Russia* **61 H6** 44 24N 44 0 E
Voroshilovgrad = Luhansk, *Ukraine* **59 H10** 48 38N 39 15 E
Voroshilovsk = Alchevsk, *Ukraine* **59 H10** 48 30N 38 45 E
Vorskla →, *Ukraine* **59 H8** 48 50N 34 10 E
Võrts Järv, *Estonia* **15 G22** 58 16N 26 3 E
Võru, *Estonia* **15 H22** 57 48N 26 54 E
Vosges, *France* **27 D14** 48 20N 7 10 E
Vosges □, *France* **27 D13** 48 12N 6 20 E
Voskopojë, *Albania* **50 F4** 40 35N 20 33 E
Voskresensk, *Russia* **58 E10** 55 19N 38 43 E
Voskresenskoye, *Russia* **60 B7** 56 51N 45 30 E
Voss, *Norway* **15 F12** 60 38N 6 26 E
Vostok I., *Kiribati* **135 J12** 10 5 S 152 23W
Votice, *Czech Rep.* **34 B7** 49 38N 14 39 E
Votkinsk, *Russia* **64 C4** 57 0N 53 55 E
Votkinskoye Vdkhr., *Russia* **64 C5** 57 22N 55 12 E
Votsuri-Shima, *Japan* **71 M1** 25 45N 123 29 E
Votuporanga, *Brazil* **171 F2** 20 24 S 49 59W
Vouga →, *Portugal* **42 E2** 40 41N 8 40W
Vouillé, *France* **26 F7** 46 38N 0 10 E
Voulou, *C.A.R.* **114 A4** 8 33N 22 36 E
Vouma →, *Cameroon* **114 B2** 3 19N 14 9 E
Vouvry, *Switz.* **32 D3** 46 21N 6 51 E
Voúxa, Ákra, *Greece* **39 E4** 35 37N 23 32 E
Vouzela, *Portugal* **42 E2** 40 43N 8 7W
Vouziers, *France* **27 C11** 49 22N 4 40 E
Vovchansk, *Ukraine* **59 G9** 50 17N 36 58 E
Vovodo →, *C.A.R.* **114 A4** 5 40N 24 21 E
Vozhe, Ozero, *Russia* **58 B10** 60 45N 39 0 E
Vozhega, *Russia* **58 B11** 60 29N 40 12 E
Voznesensk, *Ukraine* **59 J6** 47 35N 31 21 E
Voznesenye, *Russia* **58 B8** 61 0N 35 28 E
Vrå, *Denmark* **17 G3** 57 21N 9 56 E
Vráble, *Slovak Rep.* **35 C11** 48 15N 18 16 E
Vraćevšnica, *Serbia, Yug.* **50 B4** 44 2N 20 34 E
Vrådal, *Norway* **18 E5** 59 20N 8 25 E
Vrakhnéïka, *Greece* **48 C3** 38 10N 21 40 E
Vrancea □, *Romania* **53 E11** 45 50N 26 45 E
Vrancei, Munţii, *Romania* **53 E11** 46 0N 26 30 E
Vrang, *Tajikistan* **65 E6** 37 0N 72 22 E
Vrangelya, Ostrov, *Russia* **67 B19** 71 0N 180 0 E
Vranica, *Bos.-H.* **52 G2** 43 55N 17 50 E
Vranje, *Serbia, Yug.* **50 D5** 42 34N 21 54 E
Vranjska Banja, *Serbia, Yug.* **50 D6** 42 34N 22 1 E
Vranov nad Topľou, *Slovak Rep.* **35 C14** 48 53N 21 40 E
Vransko, *Slovenia* **45 B11** 46 17N 14 58 E
Vransko Jezero, *Croatia* **45 E12** 43 53N 15 34 E
Vrapčište, *Macedonia* **50 E4** 41 50N 20 53 E
Vratsa, *Bulgaria* **50 C7** 43 15N 23 30 E
Vråvatn, *Norway* **18 E5** 59 20N 8 8 E
Vrbas, *Serbia, Yug.* **52 E4** 45 40N 19 40 E
Vrbas →, *Bos.-H.* **52 E2** 45 8N 17 29 E
Vrbnik, *Croatia* **45 C11** 45 4N 14 40 E
Vrbovec, *Croatia* **45 C13** 45 53N 16 28 E
Vrbovsko, *Croatia* **45 C12** 45 24N 15 5 E
Vrchlabí, *Czech Rep.* **34 A8** 50 38N 15 37 E
Vrede, *S. Africa* **117 D4** 27 24 S 29 6 E
Vredefort, *S. Africa* **116 D4** 27 0 S 27 22 E
Vreden, *Germany* **30 C2** 52 2N 6 50 E
Vredenburg, *S. Africa* **116 E2** 32 56 S 18 0 E
Vredendal, *S. Africa* **116 E2** 31 41 S 18 35 E
Vretstorp, *Sweden* **16 E8** 59 1N 14 53 E
Vrgorac, *Croatia* **45 E14** 43 12N 17 20 E
Vrhnika, *Slovenia* **45 C11** 45 58N 14 15 E
Vriddhachalam, *India* **95 J4** 11 30N 79 20 E
Vridi, *Ivory C.* **112 D4** 5 15N 4 3W
Vrigstad, *Sweden* **17 G8** 57 22N 14 28 E
Vrin, *Switz.* **33 C8** 46 39N 9 6 E
Vrindavan, *India* **92 F7** 27 37N 77 40 E
Vríses, *Greece* **39 E5** 35 23N 24 13 E
Vrnograč, *Bos.-H.* **45 C12** 45 10N 15 57 E
Vrondádhes, *Greece* **49 C8** 38 25N 26 7 E
Vrpolje, *Croatia* **52 E3** 45 13N 18 24 E
Vršac, *Serbia, Yug.* **52 E6** 45 8N 21 20 E
Vrsacki Kanal, *Serbia, Yug.* **52 E5** 45 15N 21 0 E
Vrútky, *Slovak Rep.* **35 B11** 49 7N 18 55 E
Vryburg, *S. Africa* **116 D3** 26 55 S 24 45 E
Vryheid, *S. Africa* **117 D5** 27 45 S 30 47 E
Vsetín, *Czech Rep.* **35 B11** 49 20N 18 0 E
Vu Liet, *Vietnam* **86 C5** 18 43N 105 23 E
Vŭcha →, *Bulgaria* **51 D8** 42 10N 24 26 E
Vučitrn, *Kosovo, Yug.* **50 D4** 42 49N 20 59 E
Vukovar, *Croatia* **52 E3** 45 21N 18 59 E
Vulcan, *Canada* **142 C6** 50 25N 113 15W
Vulcan, *Romania* **53 E8** 45 23N 23 17 E
Vulcaneşti, *Moldova* **53 E13** 45 41N 28 18 E
Vulcano, *Italy* **47 D7** 38 24N 14 58 E
Vŭlchedruma, *Bulgaria* **50 C7** 43 42N 23 27 E
Vulkaneshty = Vulcaneşti, *Moldova* **53 E13** 45 41N 28 18 E
Vunduzi →, *Mozam.* **119 F3** 18 56 S 34 1 E
Vung Tau, *Vietnam* **87 G6** 10 21N 107 4 E
Vunidawa, *Fiji* **133 A2** 17 50 S 178 21 E
Vunisea, *Fiji* **133 B2** 19 3 S 178 10 E
Vuranggo, *Solomon Is.* **133 L9** 6 39 S 156 38 E
Vŭrbitsa, *Bulgaria* **51 D10** 42 59N 26 40 E
Vurshets, *Bulgaria* **50 C7** 43 13N 23 23 E
Vutcani, *Romania* **53 D12** 46 26N 27 59 E
Vuya, *Sudan* **107 F2** 5 21N 29 40 E
Vwaza Game Reserve, *Malawi* **119 E3** 10 58 S 33 25 E
Vyara, *India* **94 D1** 21 8N 73 28 E
Vyartsilya, *Russia* **58 A6** 62 8N 30 45 E
Vyatka = Kirov, *Russia* **64 B2** 58 35N 49 40 E
Vyatka →, *Russia* **60 C10** 55 37N 51 28 E
Vyatskiye Polyany, *Russia* **60 B10** 56 14N 51 5 E
Vyazemskiy, *Russia* **67 E14** 47 32N 134 45 E
Vyazma, *Russia* **58 E8** 55 10N 34 15 E
Vyazniki, *Russia* **60 B6** 56 10N 42 10 E
Vyborg, *Russia* **58 B5** 60 43N 28 47 E
Vychegda →, *Russia* **56 B8** 61 18N 46 36 E
Vychodné Beskydy, *Europe* **35 B15** 49 20N 22 0 E
Východočeský □, *Czech Rep.* **34 E8** 50 20N 15 45 E
Vyerkhnyadzvinsk, *Belarus* **58 E4** 55 45N 27 58 E
Vyg-ozero, *Russia* **56 B5** 63 47N 34 29 E
Vyksa, *Russia* **60 C6** 55 19N 42 11 E
Vylkove, *Ukraine* **59 K5** 45 28N 29 32 E
Vynohradiv, *Ukraine* **59 H2** 48 9N 23 2 E
Vypin, *India* **95 J3** 10 10N 76 15 E
Vyrnwy, L., *U.K.* **20 E4** 52 48N 3 31W
Vyshniy Volochek, *Russia* **58 D8** 57 30N 34 30 E
Vyshzha = imeni 26 Bakinskikh Komissarov, *Turkmenistan* **97 B7** 39 22N 54 10 E
Vyškov, *Czech Rep.* **35 B9** 49 17N 17 0 E
Vysoké Mýto, *Czech Rep.* **35 B9** 49 58N 16 10 E
Vysokovsk, *Russia* **58 D9** 56 22N 36 30 E
Vyšší Brod, *Czech Rep.* **34 C7** 48 37N 14 19 E
Vytegra, *Russia* **58 B9** 61 0N 36 27 E

W

W du Benin, Parc Nat. du, *Benin* **113 C5** 11 57N 2 43 E
W du Burkina Faso, Parc Nat. du, *Burkina Faso* **113 C4** 11 52N 2 50W
W du Niger, Parc Nat. du, *Niger* **113 C5** 13 31N 2 28 E
W.A.C. Bennett Dam, *Canada* **142 B4** 56 2N 122 6W
Wa, *Ghana* **112 C4** 10 7N 2 25W
Waal →, *Neths.* **24 C5** 51 37N 5 0 E
Waalwijk, *Neths.* **24 C5** 51 42N 5 4 E
Waar, *Indonesia* **83 B4** 2 5 S 134 23 E
Waat, *Sudan* **107 F3** 8 10N 32 7 E
Wabag, *Papua N. G.* **132 C2** 5 32 S 143 40 E
Wabana, *Canada* **141 C9** 47 40N 53 0W
Wabao, *N. Cal.* **133 U21** 21 36 S 167 57 E
Wabao, C., *N. Cal.* **133 U21** 21 35 S 167 53 E
Wabasca →, *Canada* **142 B5** 58 22N 115 20W
Wabasca-Desmarais, *Canada* **142 B6** 55 57N 113 56W
Wabash, *U.S.A.* **157 D11** 40 48N 85 49W
Wabash →, *U.S.A.* **157 G8** 37 48N 88 2W
Wabasso, *U.S.A.* **153 H9** 27 45N 80 26W
Wabawng, *Burma* **90 B6** 26 20N 97 25 E
Wabi →, *Ethiopia* **107 F5** 7 45N 40 50 E
Wabigoon L., *Canada* **143 D10** 49 44N 92 44W
Wabowden, *Canada* **143 C9** 54 55N 98 38W
Wąbrzeźno, *Poland* **55 E5** 53 16N 18 57 E
Wabu Hu, *China* **77 A11** 32 20N 116 50 E
Wabuda I., *Papua N. G.* **132 E2** 8 23 S 143 37 E
Wabuk Pt., *Canada* **140 A2** 55 20N 85 5W
Wabush, *Canada* **141 B6** 52 55N 66 52W
Waccasassa B., *U.S.A.* **153 F7** 29 10N 82 50W
Wąchock, *Poland* **55 G8** 51 4N 21 1 E
Wächtersbach, *Germany* **31 E5** 50 14N 9 17 E
Wacissa, *U.S.A.* **152 E6** 30 22N 83 59W
Waco, *U.S.A.* **155 K6** 31 33N 97 9W
Waconichi, L., *Canada* **140 B5** 50 8N 74 0W
Wad Ban Naqa, *Sudan* **107 D3** 16 32N 33 9 E
Wad Banda, *Sudan* **107 E2** 13 10N 27 56 E
Wad el Haddad, *Sudan* **107 E3** 13 50N 33 30 E
Wad en Nau, *Sudan* **107 E3** 14 10N 33 34 E
Wad Hamid, *Sudan* **107 D3** 16 30N 32 45 E
Wad Medanî, *Sudan* **107 E3** 14 28N 33 30 E
Wad Thana, *Pakistan* **91 D2** 27 22N 66 23 E
Wadai, *Africa* **104 E5** 12 0N 19 0 E
Wadayama, *Japan* **72 B6** 35 19N 134 52 E
Wadbilliga Nat. Park, *Australia* **129 D8** 36 25 S 149 35 E
Waddān, *Libya* **108 C3** 29 9N 16 10 E
Waddeneilanden, *Neths.* **24 A5** 53 20N 5 10 E
Waddenzee, *Neths.* **24 A5** 53 6N 5 10 E
Waddi, Chappal, *Nigeria* **113 D7** 7 2N 11 43W
Waddington, *U.S.A.* **151 B9** 44 52N 75 12W
Waddington, Mt., *Canada* **142 C3** 51 23N 125 15W
Waddy Pt., *Australia* **127 C5** 24 58 S 153 21 E
Wadebridge, *U.K.* **21 G3** 50 31N 4 51W
Wadena, *Canada* **143 C8** 51 57N 103 47W
Wadena, *U.S.A.* **154 B7** 46 26N 95 8W
Wädenswil, *Switz.* **33 B7** 47 14N 8 40 E
Wadern, *Germany* **31 F2** 49 32N 6 53 E
Wadeye, *Australia* **124 B4** 14 28 S 129 52 E
Wadgaon, *India* **94 E1** 18 44N 73 39 E
Wadhams, *Canada* **142 C3** 51 30N 127 30W
Wadi, *India* **94 F3** 17 4N 76 59 E
Wādī as Sīr, *Jordan* **103 D4** 31 56N 35 49 E
Wādī Banī Walīd, *Libya* **108 B2** 31 49N 14 0 E
Wadi Gemâl, *Egypt* **106 C4** 24 35N 35 10 E
Wadi Halfa, *Sudan* **106 C3** 21 53N 31 19 E
Wadian, *China* **77 A9** 32 42N 112 29 E
Wadlew, *Poland* **55 G6** 51 31N 19 23 E
Wadley, *Ala., U.S.A.* **152 B4** 33 7N 85 34W
Wadley, *Ga., U.S.A.* **152 C7** 32 52N 82 24W
Wadowice, *Poland* **55 J6** 49 52N 19 30 E
Wadsworth, *Nev., U.S.A.* **158 G4** 39 38N 119 17W
Wadsworth, *Ohio, U.S.A.* **150 E3** 41 2N 81 44W
Waegwan, *S. Korea* **75 G15** 35 59N 128 23 E
Waeplau, *Indonesia* **82 B3** 3 8 S 126 55 E
Wafangdian, *China* **75 E11** 39 38N 121 58 E
Wafania, *Dem. Rep. of the Congo* **114 C4** 1 23 S 20 22 E
Wafrah, *Si. Arabia* **96 D5** 28 33N 47 56 E
Wagener, *U.S.A.* **152 B8** 33 39N 81 22W
Wageningen, *Neths.* **24 C5** 51 58N 5 40 E
Wageningen, *Surinam* **169 B6** 5 50N 56 50W
Wager B., *Canada* **139 B11** 65 26N 88 40W
Wagga Wagga, *Australia* **129 C7** 35 7 S 147 24 E
Waghai, *India* **94 D1** 20 46N 73 29 E
Waghete, *Indonesia* **83 B5** 4 10 S 135 50 E
Wagin, *Australia* **125 F2** 33 17 S 117 25 E
Wagner, *U.S.A.* **154 D5** 43 5N 98 18W
Wagon Mound, *U.S.A.* **155 G2** 36 1N 104 42W
Wagoner, *U.S.A.* **155 H7** 35 58N 95 22W
Wagrowiec, *Poland* **55 F4** 52 48N 17 11 E
Wah, *Pakistan* **91 B4** 33 45N 72 40 E
Wahai, *Indonesia* **83 B3** 2 48 S 129 35 E
Waharoa, *N.Z.* **130 D4** 37 46 S 175 45 E
Wahiawa, *U.S.A.* **145 K13** 21 30N 158 2W
Wahiawa Reservoir, *U.S.A.* **145 K13** 21 30N 158 3W
Wâḥid, *Egypt* **103 E1** 30 48N 32 21 E
Wahnai, *Afghan.* **92 C1** 32 40N 65 50 E
Wahni, *Ethiopia* **107 E4** 12 40N 36 39 E
Wahoo, *U.S.A.* **154 E6** 41 13N 96 37W
Wahpeton, *U.S.A.* **154 B6** 46 16N 96 36W
Wahx, Ras il-, *Malta* **38 F7** 35 56N 14 20 E
Wai, *India* **94 F1** 17 56N 73 57 E
Waiai →, *N.Z.* **131 G2** 46 12 S 167 38 E
Waialee, *U.S.A.* **145 J13** 21 41N 158 1W
Waialua, *U.S.A.* **145 J13** 21 34N 158 8W
Waialua B., *U.S.A.* **145 J13** 21 35N 158 5W
Waianae, *U.S.A.* **145 K13** 21 27N 158 11W
Waianae Mts., *U.S.A.* **145 K13** 21 30N 158 10W
Waiapu →, *N.Z.* **130 D7** 37 47 S 178 29 E
Waiau, *N.Z.* **131 C8** 42 39 S 173 5 E
Waiau →, *N.Z.* **131 C8** 42 47 S 173 22 E
Waiawa →, *U.S.A.* **145 K14** 21 23N 157 59W
Waiawe Ganga →, *Sri Lanka* **95 L5** 6 15N 81 0 E
Waibeem, *Indonesia* **83 B4** 0 30 S 132 59 E
Waiblingen, *Germany* **31 G5** 48 49N 9 18 E
Waidhofen an der Thaya, *Austria* **34 C8** 48 49N 15 17 E
Waidhofen an der Ybbs, *Austria* **34 D7** 47 57N 14 46 E
Waigeo, *Indonesia* **83 B4** 0 20 S 130 40 E
Waihao →, *N.Z.* **131 E6** 44 52 S 171 11 E
Waihao Downs, *N.Z.* **131 E5** 44 48 S 170 55 E
Waiheke I., *N.Z.* **130 C4** 36 48 S 175 6 E
Waihi, *N.Z.* **130 D4** 37 23 S 175 52 E
Waihi Beach, *N.Z.* **130 D7** 37 25 S 175 57 E
Waihola, *N.Z.* **131 G5** 46 1 S 170 8 E
Waihola L., *N.Z.* **131 F5** 45 59 S 170 8 E
Waihou →, *N.Z.* **130 D4** 37 15 S 175 40 E
Waika, *Dem. Rep. of the Congo* **118 C2** 2 22 S 25 42 E
Waikabubak, *Indonesia* **82 C1** 9 45 S 119 25 E
Waikaia, *N.Z.* **131 F3** 45 44 S 168 51 E
Waikaka, *N.Z.* **131 F4** 45 55 S 169 1 E
Waikare, L., *N.Z.* **130 D4** 37 26 S 175 13 E
Waikareiti, L., *N.Z.* **130 E6** 38 43 S 177 10 E
Waikaremoana, *N.Z.* **130 E6** 38 42 S 177 12 E
Waikaremoana, L., *N.Z.* **130 E6** 38 49 S 177 9 E
Waikari, *N.Z.* **131 C7** 42 58 S 172 41 E
Waikato →, *N.Z.* **130 D3** 37 23 S 174 43 E
Waikelo, *Indonesia* **82 C1** 9 24 S 119 19 E
Waikerie, *Australia* **128 C4** 34 9 S 140 0 E
Waikiekie, *N.Z.* **130 B3** 35 57 S 174 16 E
Waikiki, *U.S.A.* **145 K14** 21 17N 157 50W
Waikokopu, *N.Z.* **130 F6** 39 3 S 177 52 E
Waikouaiti, *N.Z.* **131 F5** 45 36 S 170 41 E
Waikouaiti Downs, *N.Z.* **131 F5** 45 30 S 170 30 E
Wailingding Dao, *China* **69 G11** 22 6N 114 2 E
Wailua, *Hawaii, U.S.A.* **145 A2** 22 3N 159 20W
Wailua, *Hawaii, U.S.A.* **145 C5** 20 51N 156 8W
Wailuku, *U.S.A.* **145 C5** 20 53N 156 30W
Waimakariri →, *N.Z.* **131 D7** 43 24 S 172 42 E
Waimanalo, *U.S.A.* **145 K14** 21 21N 157 43W
Waimanalo B., *U.S.A.* **145 K14** 21 20N 157 40W
Waimanalo Beach, *U.S.A.* **145 K14** 21 21N 157 42W
Waimangaroa, *N.Z.* **131 B6** 41 43 S 171 46 E
Waimano →, *U.S.A.* **145 K14** 21 25N 157 58W
Waimarie, *N.Z.* **131 B6** 41 35 S 171 58 E
Waimate, *N.Z.* **131 E6** 44 45 S 171 3 E
Waimea, *Hawaii, U.S.A.* **145 B2** 21 58N 159 40W
Waimea, *Hawaii, U.S.A.* **145 J13** 21 39N 158 3W
Waimea B., *U.S.A.* **145 J13** 21 40N 158 5W
Waimea Plain, *N.Z.* **131 F3** 45 55 S 168 35 E
Wainganga →, *India* **94 E4** 18 50N 79 55 E
Waingapu, *Indonesia* **82 C2** 9 35 S 120 11 E
Waingmaw, *Burma* **90 C6** 25 21N 97 26 E
Waini →, *Guyana* **169 B6** 8 20N 59 50W
Wainuiomata, *N.Z.* **130 H3** 41 17 S 174 56 E
Wainwright, *Canada* **143 C6** 52 50N 110 50W
Wainwright, *U.S.A.* **144 A7** 70 38N 160 2W
Waiotapu, *N.Z.* **130 E5** 38 21 S 176 25 E
Waiouru, *N.Z.* **130 F4** 39 28 S 175 41 E
Waipa →, *N.Z.* **130 E4** 38 16 S 175 21 E
Waipahi, *N.Z.* **131 G4** 46 6 S 169 15 E
Waipahu, *U.S.A.* **145 K13** 21 23N 158 1W
Waipapa Pt., *N.Z.* **131 G3** 46 40 S 168 51 E
Waipara, *N.Z.* **131 D7** 43 3 S 172 46 E
Waipawa, *N.Z.* **130 F5** 39 56 S 176 38 E
Waipio Acres, *U.S.A.* **145 K13** 21 28N 158 1W
Waipio Peninsula, *U.S.A.* **145 K14** 21 20N 158 0W
Waipiro, *N.Z.* **130 E7** 38 2 S 178 22 E
Waipiro Bay, *N.Z.* **130 E7** 38 1 S 178 21 E
Waipu, *N.Z.* **130 B3** 35 59 S 174 29 E
Waipukurau, *N.Z.* **130 G5** 40 1 S 176 33 E
Wairakei, *N.Z.* **130 E5** 38 37 S 176 6 E
Wairarapa, L., *N.Z.* **130 H4** 41 14 S 175 15 E
Wairau →, *N.Z.* **131 B9** 41 32 S 174 7 E
Wairio, *N.Z.* **131 F3** 45 59 S 168 3 E
Wairoa, *N.Z.* **130 F6** 39 3 S 177 25 E
Wairoa →, *Hawke's Bay, N.Z.* **130 F6** 39 4 S 177 25 E
Wairoa →, *Northland, N.Z.* **130 C2** 36 5 S 173 59 E
Waïsisi, *Vanuatu* **133 J7** 19 32 S 169 22 E
Waita Reservoir, *U.S.A.* **145 B2** 21 55N 159 28W
Waitaki →, *N.Z.* **131 E6** 44 56 S 171 7 E
Waitaki Plains, *N.Z.* **131 E5** 44 22 S 170 0 E
Waitara, *N.Z.* **130 E3** 38 59 S 174 15 E
Waitara →, *N.Z.* **130 E3** 38 59 S 174 14 E
Waitoa, *N.Z.* **130 D4** 37 37 S 175 35 E
Waitotara, *N.Z.* **130 F3** 39 49 S 174 44 E
Waitotara →, *N.Z.* **130 F3** 39 51 S 174 41 E
Waitsburg, *U.S.A.* **158 C5** 46 16N 118 9W
Waiuku, *N.Z.* **130 D3** 37 15 S 174 45 E
Wajima, *Japan* **71 F8** 37 30N 137 0 E
Wajir, *Kenya* **118 B5** 1 42N 40 5 E
Waka, *Dem. Rep. of the Congo* **114 B4** 1 1N 20 13 E
Waka, *Ethiopia* **107 F4** 7 2N 37 20 E
Wakai, *Surinam* **169 B6** 5 18N 57 14W
Wakarusa, *U.S.A.* **157 C10** 41 32N 86 1W
Wakasa, *Japan* **72 B6** 35 20N 134 24 E
Wakasa-Wan, *Japan* **73 B7** 35 40N 135 30 E
Wakatipu, L., *N.Z.* **131 F3** 45 5 S 168 33 E
Wakaw, *Canada* **143 C7** 52 39N 105 44W
Wakaya, *Fiji* **133 A2** 17 37 S 179 0 E
Wakayama, *Japan* **73 C7** 34 15N 135 15 E
Wakayama □, *Japan* **73 D7** 33 50N 135 30 E
Wake, *Japan* **72 C6** 34 48N 134 8 E
Wake Forest, *U.S.A.* **149 H6** 35 59N 78 30W
Wake I., *Pac. Oc.* **134 F8** 19 18N 166 36 E
WaKeeney, *U.S.A.* **154 F5** 39 1N 99 53W
Wakefield, *Jamaica* **164 a** 18 26N 77 42W
Wakefield, *N.Z.* **131 B8** 41 24 S 173 5 E
Wakefield, *U.K.* **20 D6** 53 41N 1 29W
Wakefield, *Mass., U.S.A.* **151 D13** 42 30N 71 4W
Wakefield, *Mich., U.S.A.* **154 B10** 46 29N 89 56W
Wakema, *Burma* **90 G5** 16 30N 95 11 E
Waki, *Japan* **72 C6** 34 4N 134 9 E
Wakkanai, *Japan* **70 B10** 45 28N 141 35 E
Wakkerstroom, *S. Africa* **117 D5** 27 24 S 30 10 E
Wakool, *Australia* **128 C6** 35 28 S 144 23 E
Wakool →, *Australia* **128 C5** 35 5 S 143 33 E
Wakre, *Indonesia* **83 B4** 0 19 S 131 5 E
Waku, *Papua N. G.* **132 D5** 6 5 S 149 9 E
Wakuach, L., *Canada* **141 A6** 55 34N 67 32W
Wakulla, *U.S.A.* **152 E5** 30 14N 84 14W
Wakunai, *Papua N. G.* **132 C8** 5 52 S 155 13 E
Walamba, *Zambia* **119 E2** 13 30 S 28 42 E
Wałbrzych, *Poland* **55 H3** 50 45N 16 18 E
Walbury Hill, *U.K.* **21 F6** 51 21N 1 28W
Walcha, *Australia* **129 A9** 30 55 S 151 31 E
Walcheren, *Neths.* **24 C3** 51 30N 3 35 E
Walckenaer, Teluk, *Indonesia* **83 B5** 2 20 S 139 50 E
Walcott, *U.S.A.* **158 F10** 41 46N 106 51W
Wałcz, *Poland* **55 E3** 53 17N 16 27 E
Wald, *Switz.* **33 B7** 47 17N 8 56 E
Waldbröl, *Germany* **30 E3** 50 52N 7 37 E
Waldburg Ra., *Australia* **125 D2** 24 40 S 117 35 E
Waldeck, *Germany* **30 D5** 51 12N 9 4 E
Walden, *Colo., U.S.A.* **158 F10** 40 44N 106 17W
Walden, *N.Y., U.S.A.* **151 E10** 41 34N 74 11W
Waldenburg, *Switz.* **32 B5** 47 23N 7 45 E
Waldkirch, *Germany* **31 G3** 48 5N 7 58 E
Waldkirchen, *Germany* **31 G9** 48 43N 13 36 E
Waldkraiburg, *Germany* **31 G8** 48 11N 12 24 E
Waldo, *U.S.A.* **152 F7** 29 48N 82 10W
Waldport, *U.S.A.* **158 D1** 44 26N 124 4W
Waldron, *U.S.A.* **155 H7** 34 54N 94 5W
Waldviertel, *Austria* **34 C8** 48 30N 15 30 E
Walebing, *Australia* **125 F2** 30 41 S 116 13 E
Walembele, *Ghana* **112 C4** 10 30N 1 58W
Walensee, *Switz.* **33 B8** 47 7N 9 13 E
Walenstadt, *Switz.* **33 B8** 47 8N 9 19 E
Wales, *U.S.A.* **144 D5** 65 37N 168 5W
Wales □, *U.K.* **21 E3** 52 19N 4 43W
Walewale, *Ghana* **113 C4** 10 21N 0 50W
Walgett, *Australia* **127 E4** 30 0 S 148 5 E
Walgreen Coast, *Antarctica* **7 D15** 75 15 S 105 0W
Walhalla, *Australia* **129 D7** 37 56 S 146 29 E
Walis I., *Papua N. G.* **132 B2** 3 14 S 143 18 E
Walker, *Mich., U.S.A.* **157 B11** 42 58N 85 46W
Walker, *Minn., U.S.A.* **154 B7** 47 6N 94 35W
Walker, L., *Canada* **141 B6** 50 20N 67 11W
Walker L., *Canada* **143 C9** 54 42N 95 57W
Walker L., *U.S.A.* **158 G4** 38 42N 118 43W
Walkerston, *Australia* **126 K7** 21 11 S 149 8 E
Walkerton, *Canada* **140 D3** 44 10N 81 10W
Walkerton, *U.S.A.* **157 C10** 41 28N 86 29W
Wall, *U.S.A.* **154 D3** 44 0N 102 8W
Walla Walla, *Australia* **129 C7** 35 45 S 146 54 E
Walla Walla, *U.S.A.* **158 C4** 46 4N 118 20W
Wallace, *Idaho, U.S.A.* **158 C6** 47 28N 115 56W
Wallace, *N.C., U.S.A.* **149 H7** 34 44N 77 59W
Wallaceburg, *Canada* **140 D3** 42 34N 82 23W
Wallacetown, *N.Z.* **131 G3** 46 21 S 168 19 E
Wallachia = Valahia, *Romania* **53 F9** 44 35N 25 0 E
Wallal, *Australia* **127 D4** 26 32 S 146 7 E
Wallam Cr. →, *Australia* **127 D4** 28 40 S 147 20 E
Wallambin, L., *Australia* **125 F2** 30 57 S 117 35 E
Wallan, *Australia* **129 D6** 37 26 S 144 59 E
Wallangarra, *Australia* **127 D5** 28 56 S 151 58 E
Wallaroo, *Australia* **128 B2** 33 56 S 137 39 E
Walldürn, *Germany* **31 F5** 49 34N 9 22 E
Wallenhorst, *Germany* **30 C4** 52 21N 8 1 E
Wallenpaupack, L., *U.S.A.* **151 E9** 41 25N 75 15W
Wallerawang, *Australia* **129 B9** 33 25 S 150 4 E
Wallingford, *U.S.A.* **151 E12** 41 27N 72 50W
Wallis & Futuna, Is., *Pac. Oc.* **134 J10** 13 18 S 176 10W
Wallisellen, *Switz.* **33 B7** 47 25N 8 36 E
Wallowa, *U.S.A.* **158 D5** 45 34N 117 32W
Wallowa Mts., *U.S.A.* **158 D5** 45 20N 117 30W
Walls, *U.K.* **22 A7** 60 14N 1 33W
Walls of Jerusalem Nat. Park, *Australia* **127 G4** 41 56 S 146 15 E
Wallsend, *Australia* **129 B9** 32 55 S 151 40 E
Wallula, *U.S.A.* **158 C4** 46 5N 118 54W
Wallumbilla, *Australia* **127 D4** 26 33 S 149 9 E
Walmsley, L., *Canada* **143 A7** 63 25N 108 36W
Walney, I. of, *U.K.* **20 C4** 54 6N 3 15W
Walnut, *U.S.A.* **156 C7** 41 33N 89 36W
Walnut Creek, *U.S.A.* **160 H4** 37 54N 122 4W
Walnut Grove, *U.S.A.* **152 A3** 34 4N 86 18W
Walnut Hill, *U.S.A.* **153 E2** 30 53N 87 30W
Walnut Ridge, *U.S.A.* **155 G9** 36 4N 90 57W
Walpeup, *Australia* **128 C5** 35 7 S 142 2 E
Walpole, *Australia* **125 F2** 34 58 S 116 44 E
Walpole, *U.S.A.* **151 D13** 42 9N 71 15W
Wals, *Austria* **34 D5** 47 47N 12 58 E
Walsall, *U.K.* **21 E6** 52 35N 1 58W
Walsenburg, *U.S.A.* **155 G2** 37 38N 104 47W
Walsh, *U.S.A.* **155 G3** 37 23N 102 17W
Walsh →, *Australia* **126 B3** 16 31 S 143 42 E
Walsrode, *Germany* **30 C5** 52 51N 9 35 E
Waltair, *India* **94 F6** 17 44N 83 23 E
Walter F. George Reservoir, *U.S.A.* **152 D4** 31 38N 85 4W
Walterboro, *U.S.A.* **152 C9** 32 55N 80 40W
Walters, *U.S.A.* **155 H5** 34 22N 98 19W
Waltershausen, *Germany* **30 E6** 50 54N 10 33 E
Waltham, *U.S.A.* **151 D13** 42 23N 71 14W
Waltman, *U.S.A.* **158 E10** 43 4N 107 12W
Walton, *Ky., U.S.A.* **157 F12** 38 52N 84 37W
Walton, *N.Y., U.S.A.* **151 D9** 42 10N 75 8W
Walton-on-the-Naze, *U.K.* **21 F9** 51 51N 1 17 E
Waltonville, *U.S.A.* **156 F7** 38 13N 89 2W
Walu, *Burma* **90 B7** 26 28N 98 2 E
Walvis Bay, *Namibia* **116 C1** 23 0 S 14 28 E
Walvis Ridge, *Atl. Oc.* **8 J12** 26 0 S 5 0 E
Walvisbaai = Walvis Bay, *Namibia* **116 C1** 23 0 S 14 28 E
Walwa, *Australia* **129 C7** 35 59 S 147 44 E
Wamba, *Équateur, Dem. Rep. of the Congo* **114 C4** 1 37 S 22 30 E
Wamba, *Orientale, Dem. Rep. of the Congo* **118 B2** 2 10N 27 57 E
Wamba, *Kenya* **118 B4** 0 58N 37 19 E
Wamba, *Nigeria* **113 D6** 8 57N 8 42 E
Wamba →, *Dem. Rep. of the Congo* **115 C3** 3 56 S 17 12 E
Wamego, *U.S.A.* **154 F6** 39 12N 96 18W
Wamena, *Indonesia* **83 B5** 4 4 S 138 57 E
Wamsutter, *U.S.A.* **158 F9** 41 40N 107 58W
Wamulan, *Indonesia* **82 B3** 3 27 S 126 7 E
Wan Hat, *Burma* **90 E6** 20 14N 97 53 E
Wan Kinghao, *Burma* **90 E7** 21 34N 98 17 E
Wan Lai-kam, *Burma* **90 E7** 21 21N 98 22 E
Wan Tup, *Burma* **90 E7** 21 13N 98 42 E
Wan Xian, *China* **74 E8** 38 47N 115 7 E
Wana, *Pakistan* **91 B3** 32 20N 69 32 E
Wanaaring, *Australia* **127 D3** 29 38 S 144 9 E
Wanaka, *N.Z.* **131 E4** 44 42 S 169 9 E
Wanaka, L., *N.Z.* **131 E4** 44 33 S 169 7 E
Wan'an, *China* **77 D10** 26 26N 114 49 E
Wanapiri, *Indonesia* **83 B5** 4 30 S 135 59 E
Wanapitei L., *Canada* **140 C3** 46 45N 80 40W
Wanbi, *Australia* **128 C4** 34 46 S 140 17 E
Wandaik, *Guyana* **169 C6** 4 27N 59 35W
Wandel Sea = McKinley Sea, *Arctic* **10 A11** 82 0N 0 0W
Wandérama, *Ivory C.* **112 D4** 8 37N 4 25W
Wanderer, *Zimbabwe* **119 F3** 19 36 S 30 1 E
Wandhari, *Pakistan* **92 F2** 27 42N 66 48 E
Wanding, *China* **76 E2** 24 5N 98 4 E
Wandoan, *Australia* **127 D4** 26 5 S 149 55 E
Wanfu, *China* **75 D12** 40 8N 122 38 E
Wang →, *Thailand* **86 D2** 17 8N 99 2 E
Wang Kai, *Sudan* **107 F2** 9 3N 29 23 E
Wang Noi, *Thailand* **86 E3** 14 13N 100 44 E
Wang Saphung, *Thailand* **86 D3** 17 18N 101 46 E
Wang Thong, *Thailand* **86 D3** 16 50N 100 26 E
Wanga, *Dem. Rep. of the Congo* **118 B2** 2 58N 29 12 E
Wangal, *Indonesia* **83 C4** 6 8 S 134 9 E

Xili Shuiku 301

Wind →, *U.S.A.* 158 E9 43 12N 108 12W
Wind Point, *U.S.A.* 157 B9 42 47N 87 46W
Wind River Range, *U.S.A.* 158 E9 43 0N 109 30W
Windamere, L., *Australia* 129 B8 32 42 S 149 44 E
Windau = Ventspils, *Latvia* 15 H19 57 25N 21 32 E
Windber, *U.S.A.* 150 F6 40 14N 78 50W
Winder, *U.S.A.* 152 A6 34 0N 83 45W
Windermere, *U.K.* 20 C5 54 23N 2 55W
Windfall, *U.S.A.* 157 D11 40 22N 85 57W
Windhoek, *Namibia* 116 C2 22 35 S 17 4 E
Windisch, *Switz.* 32 B6 47 28N 8 14 E
Windischgarsten, *Austria* 34 D7 47 42N 14 21 E
Windom, *U.S.A.* 154 D7 43 52N 95 7W
Windorah, *Australia* 126 D3 25 24 S 142 36 E
Window Rock, *U.S.A.* 159 J9 35 41N 109 3W
Windrush →, *U.K.* 21 F6 51 43N 1 24W
Windsor, *Australia* 129 B9 33 37 S 150 50 E
Windsor, *N.S., Canada* 141 D7 44 59N 64 5W
Windsor, *Ont., Canada* 140 D3 42 18N 83 0W
Windsor, *N.Z.* 131 E5 44 59 S 170 49 E
Windsor, *U.K.* 21 F7 51 29N 0 36W
Windsor, *Colo., U.S.A.* 154 E2 40 29N 104 54W
Windsor, *Conn., U.S.A.* 151 E12 41 50N 72 39W
Windsor, *Ill., U.S.A.* 157 E8 39 26N 88 36W
Windsor, *Mo., U.S.A.* 156 F3 38 32N 93 31W
Windsor, *N.Y., U.S.A.* 151 D9 42 5N 75 37W
Windsor, *Vt., U.S.A.* 151 C12 43 29N 72 24W
Windsor & Maidenhead □, *U.K.* 21 F7 51 29N 0 40W
Windsorton, *S. Africa* 116 D3 28 16 S 24 44 E
Windward Is., *W. Indies* 165 D7 13 0N 61 0W
Windward Passage = Vientos, Paso de los, *Caribbean* 165 C5 20 0N 74 0W
Winefred L., *Canada* 143 B6 55 30N 110 30W
Winejok, *Sudan* 107 F2 9 1N 27 30 E
Winfield, *Iowa, U.S.A.* 156 C5 41 7N 91 26W
Winfield, *Kans., U.S.A.* 155 G6 37 15N 96 59W
Winfield, *Mo., U.S.A.* 156 F6 39 0N 90 44W
Wingate Mts., *Australia* 124 B5 14 25 S 130 40 E
Wingham, *Australia* 129 A10 31 48 S 152 22 E
Wingham, *Canada* 140 D3 43 55N 81 20W
Winisk, *Canada* 140 A2 55 20N 85 15W
Winisk →, *Canada* 140 A2 55 17N 85 5W
Winisk L., *Canada* 140 B2 52 55N 87 22W
Wink, *U.S.A.* 155 K3 31 45N 103 9W
Winkler, *Canada* 143 D9 49 10N 97 56W
Winklern, *Austria* 34 E5 46 52N 12 52 E
Winlock, *U.S.A.* 160 D4 46 30N 122 56W
Winneba, *Ghana* 113 D4 5 25N 0 36W
Winnebago, *U.S.A.* 156 B7 42 16N 89 15W
Winnebago, L., *U.S.A.* 148 D1 44 0N 88 26W
Winnecke Cr. →, *Australia* 124 C5 18 35 S 131 34 E
Winnemucca, *U.S.A.* 158 F5 40 58N 117 44W
Winnemucca L., *U.S.A.* 158 F4 40 7N 119 21W
Winnett, *U.S.A.* 158 C9 47 0N 108 21W
Winnfield, *U.S.A.* 155 K8 31 56N 92 38W
Winnibigoshish, L., *U.S.A.* 154 B7 47 27N 94 13W
Winnipeg, *Canada* 143 D9 49 54N 97 9W
Winnipeg →, *Canada* 143 C9 50 38N 96 19W
Winnipeg, L., *Canada* 143 C9 52 0N 97 0W
Winnipeg Beach, *Canada* 143 C9 50 30N 96 58W
Winnipegosis, *Canada* 143 C9 51 39N 99 55W
Winnipegosis L., *Canada* 143 C9 52 30N 100 0W
Winnipesaukee, L., *U.S.A.* 151 C13 43 38N 71 21W
Winnisquam L., *U.S.A.* 151 C13 43 33N 71 31W
Winnsboro, *La., U.S.A.* 155 J9 32 10N 91 43W
Winnsboro, *S.C., U.S.A.* 149 H5 34 23N 81 5W
Winnsboro, *Tex., U.S.A.* 155 J7 32 58N 95 17W
Winokapau, L., *Canada* 141 B7 53 15N 62 50W
Winona, *Minn., U.S.A.* 154 C9 44 3N 91 39W
Winona, *Miss., U.S.A.* 155 J10 33 29N 89 44W
Winooski, *U.S.A.* 151 B11 44 29N 73 11W
Winooski →, *U.S.A.* 151 B11 44 32N 73 17W
Winschoten, *Neths.* 24 A7 53 9N 7 3 E
Winsen, *Germany* 30 B6 53 22N 10 13 E
Winsford, *U.K.* 20 D5 53 12N 2 31W
Winslow, *Ariz., U.S.A.* 159 J8 35 2N 110 42W
Winslow, *Ind., U.S.A.* 157 F9 38 23N 87 13W
Winslow, *Wash., U.S.A.* 160 C4 47 38N 122 31W
Winsted, *U.S.A.* 151 E11 41 55N 73 4W
Winston-Salem, *U.S.A.* 149 G5 36 6N 80 15W
Winter Garden, *U.S.A.* 149 L5 28 34N 81 35W
Winter Haven, *U.S.A.* 149 M5 28 1N 81 44W
Winter Park, *U.S.A.* 149 L5 28 36N 81 20W
Winterberg, *Germany* 30 D4 51 11N 8 33 E
Winterhaven, *U.S.A.* 161 N12 32 47N 114 39W
Winters, *U.S.A.* 160 G5 38 32N 121 58W
Winterset, *U.S.A.* 156 C3 41 20N 94 1W
Wintersville, *U.S.A.* 150 F4 40 23N 80 42W
Winterswijk, *Neths.* 24 C6 51 58N 6 43 E
Winterthur, *Switz.* 33 B7 47 30N 8 44 E
Winthrop, *U.S.A.* 158 B3 48 28N 120 10W
Winton, *Australia* 126 C3 22 24 S 143 3 E
Winton, *N.Z.* 131 G3 46 8 S 168 20 E
Wintua, *Vanuatu* 133 F5 16 30 S 167 26 E
Wipper →, *Germany* 30 D7 51 16N 11 12 E
Wirraminna, *Australia* 128 A2 31 12 S 136 13 E
Wirrulla, *Australia* 127 E1 32 24 S 134 31 E
Wisbech, *U.K.* 21 E8 52 41N 0 9 E
Wisconsin □, *U.S.A.* 156 B7 44 45N 89 30W
Wisconsin →, *U.S.A.* 156 A5 43 0N 91 15W
Wisconsin Rapids, *U.S.A.* 154 C10 44 23N 89 49W
Wisdom, *U.S.A.* 158 D7 45 37N 113 27W
Wiseman, *U.S.A.* 144 C10 67 25N 150 6W
Wishaw, *U.K.* 22 F5 55 46N 3 54W
Wishek, *U.S.A.* 154 B5 46 16N 99 33W
Wisła, *Poland* 55 J5 49 38N 18 53 E
Wisła →, *Poland* 54 D5 54 22N 18 55 E
Wisłok →, *Poland* 55 H9 50 13N 22 32 E
Wisłoka →, *Poland* 55 H8 50 27N 21 23 E
Wismar, *Germany* 30 B7 53 54N 11 29 E
Wismar, *Guyana* 169 B6 5 59N 58 18W
Wisner, *U.S.A.* 154 E6 41 59N 96 55W
Wissant, *France* 27 B8 50 52N 1 40 E
Wissembourg, *France* 27 C14 49 2N 7 57 E
Wisznice, *Poland* 55 G10 51 48N 23 13 E
Witbank, *S. Africa* 117 D4 25 51 S 29 14 E
Witdraai, *S. Africa* 116 D3 26 58 S 20 48 E
Witham, *U.K.* 21 F8 51 48N 0 40 E
Witham →, *U.K.* 20 E7 52 59N 0 2W
Withernsea, *U.K.* 20 D8 53 44N 0 1 E
Withlacoochee →, *Fla., U.S.A.* 152 E6 30 24N 83 10W
Withlacoochee →, *Fla., U.S.A.* 153 G7 29 0N 82 45W
Witjira Nat. Park, *Australia* 127 D2 26 22 S 135 37 E
Witkowo, *Poland* 55 F4 52 26N 17 45 E
Witney, *U.K.* 21 F6 51 48N 1 28W
Witnica, *Poland* 55 F1 52 40N 14 54 E
Witnossob →, *Namibia* 116 D3 23 55 S 18 45 E
Wittdün, *Germany* 30 A4 54 38N 8 23 E
Witten, *Germany* 30 D3 51 26N 7 20 E
Wittenberge, *Germany* 30 B7 53 0N 11 45 E
Wittenburg, *Germany* 30 B7 53 31N 11 4 E
Wittenheim, *France* 27 E14 47 44N 7 20 E
Wittenoom, *Australia* 124 D2 22 15 S 118 20 E
Witti, Banjaran, *Malaysia* 85 A5 5 11N 116 29 E
Wittingen, *Germany* 30 C6 52 44N 10 44 E
Wittlich, *Germany* 31 F2 49 59N 6 53 E
Wittmund, *Germany* 30 B3 53 34N 7 46 E
Wittow, *Germany* 30 A9 54 38N 13 20 E
Wittstock, *Germany* 30 B8 53 10N 12 28 E
Witu Is., *Papua N. G.* 132 C5 4 50 S 149 25 E
Witvlei, *Namibia* 116 C2 22 23 S 18 32 E
Witzenhausen, *Germany* 30 D5 51 20N 9 51 E
Wixom, *U.S.A.* 157 B13 42 32N 83 32W
Wkra →, *Poland* 55 F7 52 27N 20 44 E
Władysławowo, *Poland* 54 D5 54 48N 18 25 E
Wleń, *Poland* 55 G2 51 2N 15 39 E
Wlingi, *Indonesia* 85 D4 8 5 S 112 25 E
Włocławek, *Poland* 55 F6 52 40N 19 3 E
Włodawa, *Poland* 55 G10 51 33N 23 31 E
Włoszczowa, *Poland* 55 H6 50 50N 19 55 E
Woburn, *U.S.A.* 151 D13 42 29N 71 9W
Wodian, *China* 74 H7 32 50N 112 35 E
Wodonga = Albury-Wodonga, *Australia* 129 D7 36 3 S 146 56 E
Wodonga, *Australia* 129 D7 36 5 S 146 50 E
Wodzisław Śląski, *Poland* 55 H5 50 1N 18 26 E
Wœrth, *France* 27 D14 48 57N 7 45 E
Wohlen, *Switz.* 33 B6 47 21N 8 17 E
Woinbogoin, *China* 76 A2 32 51N 98 39 E
Woinui, Selat, *Indonesia* 83 B4 1 10 S 134 36 E
Woippy, *France* 27 C13 49 10N 6 8 E
Woitape, *Papua N. G.* 132 E4 8 33 S 147 15 E
Wojcieszow, *Poland* 55 H2 50 58N 15 55 E
Wokam, *Indonesia* 83 C4 5 45 S 134 28 E
Wokha, *India* 90 B5 26 6N 94 16 E
Woking, *U.K.* 21 F7 51 19N 0 34W
Wokingham □, *U.K.* 21 F7 51 25N 0 51W
Woko Nat. Park, *Australia* 129 A9 31 46 S 151 49 E
Wolbrom, *Poland* 55 H6 50 24N 19 45 E
Wolcottville, *U.S.A.* 157 C11 41 32N 85 22W
Wołczyn, *Poland* 55 G5 51 1N 18 3 E
Woldegk, *Germany* 30 B9 53 27N 13 34 E
Wolf →, *Canada* 142 A2 60 17N 132 33W
Wolf, Volcán, *Ecuador* 172 a 0 2N 91 20W
Wolf Creek, *U.S.A.* 158 C7 47 0N 112 4W
Wolf L., *Canada* 142 A2 60 24N 131 40W
Wolf Point, *U.S.A.* 154 A2 48 5N 105 39W
Wolfe I., *Canada* 140 D4 44 7N 76 20W
Wolfeboro, *U.S.A.* 151 C13 43 35N 71 13W
Wolfen, *Germany* 30 D8 51 39N 12 15 E
Wolfenbüttel, *Germany* 30 C6 52 10N 10 33 E
Wolfratshausen, *Germany* 31 H7 47 54N 11 24 E
Wolfsberg, *Austria* 34 E7 46 50N 14 52 E
Wolfsburg, *Germany* 30 C6 52 25N 10 48 E
Wolfurt, *Austria* 33 B9 47 28N 9 45 E
Wolgast, *Germany* 30 A9 54 3N 13 44 E
Wolhusen, *Switz.* 32 B6 47 4N 8 4 E
Wolin, *Poland* 54 E1 53 50N 14 37 E
Wollaston, Is., *Chile* 176 E3 55 40 S 67 30W
Wollaston Forland, *Greenland* 10 C9 74 25N 19 40W
Wollaston L., *Canada* 143 B8 58 7N 103 10W
Wollaston Lake, *Canada* 143 B8 58 3N 103 33W
Wollaston Pen., *Canada* 138 B8 69 30N 115 0W
Wollemi Nat. Park, *Australia* 129 B9 33 0 S 150 30 E
Wollongong, *Australia* 129 C9 34 25 S 150 54 E
Wolmaransstad, *S. Africa* 116 D4 27 12 S 25 59 E
Wolmirstedt, *Germany* 30 C7 52 14N 11 37 E
Wołomin, *Poland* 55 F8 52 19N 21 15 E
Wołów, *Poland* 55 G3 51 20N 16 38 E
Wolseley, *Australia* 128 D4 36 23 S 140 54 E
Wolseley, *S. Africa* 116 E2 33 26 S 19 7 E
Wolsey, *U.S.A.* 154 C5 44 24N 98 28W
Wolstenholme, C., *Canada* 136 C12 62 35N 77 30W
Wolsztyn, *Poland* 55 F3 52 8N 16 5 E
Wolvega, *Neths.* 24 B6 52 52N 6 0 E
Wolverhampton, *U.K.* 21 E5 52 35N 2 7W
Wondai, *Australia* 127 D5 26 20 S 151 49 E
Wonenara, *Papua N. G.* 132 D3 6 48 S 145 53 E
Wonga Wongué, Parc Nat. de, *Gabon* 114 C1 0 29 S 9 25 E
Wongalarroo L., *Australia* 128 A6 31 32 S 144 0 E
Wongan Hills, *Australia* 125 F2 30 51 S 116 37 E
Wŏnju, *S. Korea* 75 F14 37 22N 127 58 E
Wonosari, *Indonesia* 85 D4 7 58 S 110 36 E
Wonosobo, *Indonesia* 85 D3 7 22 S 109 54 E
Wonowon, *Canada* 142 B4 56 44N 121 48W
Wŏnsan, *N. Korea* 75 E14 39 11N 127 27 E
Wonthaggi, *Australia* 129 E6 38 37 S 145 37 E
Wood Buffalo Nat. Park, *Canada* 142 B6 59 0N 113 41W
Wood Is., *Australia* 124 C3 16 24 S 123 19 E
Wood L., *Canada* 143 B8 55 17N 103 17W
Wood River, *U.S.A.* 156 F6 38 52N 90 5W
Woodah I., *Australia* 126 A2 13 27 S 136 10 E
Woodbine, *U.S.A.* 152 E8 30 58N 81 44W
Woodbourne, *U.S.A.* 151 E10 41 46N 74 36W
Woodbridge, *Canada* 150 C5 43 47N 79 36W
Woodbridge, *U.K.* 21 E9 52 6N 1 20 E
Woodburn, *U.S.A.* 158 D2 45 9N 122 51W
Woodbury, *U.S.A.* 152 C5 32 59N 84 35W
Woodenbong, *Australia* 127 D5 28 24 S 152 39 E
Woodend, *Australia* 128 D6 37 20 S 144 33 E
Woodford, *Australia* 127 D5 26 58 S 152 47 E
Woodfords, *U.S.A.* 160 G7 38 47N 119 50W
Woodlake, *U.S.A.* 160 J7 36 25N 119 6W
Woodland, *Calif., U.S.A.* 160 G5 38 41N 121 46W
Woodland, *Maine, U.S.A.* 149 C12 45 9N 67 25W
Woodland, *Pa., U.S.A.* 150 F6 40 59N 78 21W
Woodland, *Wash., U.S.A.* 160 E4 45 54N 122 45W
Woodland Caribou Prov. Park, *Canada* 143 C10 51 0N 94 45W
Woodlands, *Singapore* 87 d 1 27N 103 47 E
Woodlark I., *Papua N. G.* 132 E7 9 10 S 152 50 E
Woodridge, *Canada* 143 D9 49 20N 96 9W
Woodroffe, Mt., *Australia* 125 E5 26 20 S 131 45 E
Woods, L., *Australia* 126 B1 17 50 S 133 30 E
Woods, L. of the, *Canada* 143 D10 49 15N 94 45W
Woodside, *S. Austral., Australia* 128 C3 34 58 S 138 52 E
Woodside, *Vic., Australia* 129 E7 38 31 S 146 52 E
Woodson, *U.S.A.* 155 J5 33 1N 99 3W
Woodstock, *N.S.W., Australia* 129 B8 33 45 S 148 53 E
Woodstock, *Queens., Australia* 126 B4 19 35 S 146 50 E
Woodstock, *N.B., Canada* 141 C6 46 11N 67 37W
Woodstock, *Ont., Canada* 140 D3 43 10N 80 45W
Woodstock, *U.K.* 21 F6 51 51N 1 20W
Woodstock, *Ga., U.S.A.* 152 A5 34 6N 84 31W
Woodstock, *Ill., U.S.A.* 154 D10 42 19N 88 27W
Woodstock, *Vt., U.S.A.* 151 C12 43 37N 72 31W
Woodsville, *U.S.A.* 151 B13 44 9N 72 2W
Woodville, *N.Z.* 130 G4 40 20 S 175 53 E
Woodville, *Fla., U.S.A.* 152 E5 30 19N 84 15W
Woodville, *Ga., U.S.A.* 152 B6 33 40N 83 7W
Woodville, *Miss., U.S.A.* 155 K9 31 6N 91 18W
Woodville, *Ohio, U.S.A.* 157 C13 41 27N 83 22W
Woodville, *Tex., U.S.A.* 155 K7 30 47N 94 25W
Woodward, *U.S.A.* 155 G5 36 26N 99 24W
Woody, *U.S.A.* 161 K8 35 42N 118 50W
Woody →, *Canada* 143 C8 52 31N 100 51W
Woolamai, C., *Australia* 129 E6 38 30 S 145 23 E
Woolbrook, *Australia* 129 A9 30 56 S 151 25 E
Wooler, *U.K.* 20 B5 55 33N 2 1W
Woolgoolga, *Australia* 127 E5 30 6 S 153 11 E
Woomera, *Australia* 128 A2 31 5 S 136 50 E
Woonsocket, *R.I., U.S.A.* 151 E13 42 0N 71 31W
Woonsocket, *S. Dak., U.S.A.* 154 C5 44 3N 98 17W
Wooramel →, *Australia* 125 E1 25 47 S 114 10 E
Wooramel Roadhouse, *Australia* 125 E1 25 45 S 114 17 E
Wooster, *U.S.A.* 150 F3 40 48N 81 56W
Worb, *Switz.* 32 C5 46 56N 7 33 E
Worcester, *S. Africa* 116 E2 33 39 S 19 27 E
Worcester, *U.K.* 21 E5 52 11N 2 12W
Worcester, *Mass., U.S.A.* 151 D13 42 16N 71 48W
Worcester, *N.Y., U.S.A.* 151 D10 42 36N 74 45W
Worcestershire □, *U.K.* 21 E5 52 13N 2 10W
Worden, *U.S.A.* 156 F7 38 56N 89 50W
Wörgl, *Austria* 34 D5 47 29N 12 3 E
Workai, *Indonesia* 83 C4 6 40 S 134 40 E
Workington, *U.K.* 20 C4 54 39N 3 33W
Worksop, *U.K.* 20 D6 53 18N 1 7W
Workum, *Neths.* 24 B5 52 59N 5 26 E
Worland, *U.S.A.* 158 D10 44 1N 107 57W
Wormhout, *France* 27 B9 50 52N 2 28 E
Worms, *Germany* 31 F4 49 37N 8 21 E
Worsley, *Canada* 142 B5 56 31N 119 8W
Wörth, *Germany* 31 F8 49 1N 12 24 E
Wortham, *U.S.A.* 155 K6 31 47N 96 28W
Wörther See, *Austria* 34 E7 46 37N 14 10 E
Worthing, *Barbados* 165 g 13 5N 59 35W
Worthing, *U.K.* 21 G7 50 49N 0 21W
Worthington, *Ind., U.S.A.* 157 E10 39 7N 86 59W
Worthington, *Minn., U.S.A.* 154 D7 43 37N 95 36W
Worthington, *Ohio, U.S.A.* 157 D13 40 5N 83 1W
Worthington, *Pa., U.S.A.* 150 F5 40 50N 79 38W
Wosi, *Indonesia* 82 B3 0 15 S 128 0 E
Wosimi, *Indonesia* 83 B4 2 54 S 134 31 E
Wotu, *Indonesia* 82 B2 2 35 S 120 48 E
Wou-han = Wuhan, *China* 77 B10 30 31N 114 18 E
Wour, *Chad* 109 D3 21 14N 16 0 E
Wousi = Wuxi, *China* 77 B13 31 33N 120 18 E
Wowoni, *Indonesia* 82 B2 4 5 S 123 5 E
Woy Woy, *Australia* 129 B9 33 30 S 151 19 E
Wrangel I. = Vrangelya, Ostrov, *Russia* 67 B19 71 0N 180 0 E
Wrangell, *U.S.A.* 142 B2 56 28N 132 23W
Wrangell Mts., *U.S.A.* 144 F12 61 30N 142 0W
Wrath, C., *U.K.* 22 C3 58 38N 5 1W
Wray, *U.S.A.* 154 E3 40 5N 102 13W
Wrekin, The, *U.K.* 21 E5 52 41N 2 32W
Wrens, *U.S.A.* 152 B7 33 12N 82 23W
Wrexham, *U.K.* 20 D4 53 3N 3 0W
Wrexham □, *U.K.* 20 D5 53 1N 2 58W
Wriezen, *Germany* 30 C10 52 42N 14 7 E
Wright = Paranas, *Phil.* 81 F5 11 42N 125 2 E
Wright, *U.S.A.* 154 D2 43 47N 105 30W
Wright Pt., *Canada* 150 C3 43 48N 81 44W
Wrightmyo, *India* 95 J11 11 47N 92 43 E
Wrightson Mt., *U.S.A.* 159 L8 31 42N 110 51W
Wrightsville, *U.S.A.* 152 C7 32 44N 82 43W
Wrightwood, *U.S.A.* 161 L9 34 21N 117 38W
Wrigley, *Canada* 138 B7 63 16N 123 37W
Wrocław, *Poland* 55 G4 51 5N 17 5 E
Wronki, *Poland* 55 F3 52 41N 16 21 E
Września, *Poland* 55 F4 52 21N 17 36 E
Wschowa, *Poland* 55 G3 51 48N 16 20 E
Wu Jiang →, *China* 76 C6 29 40N 107 20 E
Wu Kau Tang, *China* 69 F11 22 30N 114 14 E
Wu'an, *China* 74 F8 36 40N 114 15 E
Wubin, *Australia* 125 F2 30 6 S 116 37 E
Wubu, *China* 74 F6 37 28N 110 42 E
Wuchang, *China* 75 B14 44 55N 127 5 E
Wucheng, *China* 74 F9 37 12N 116 20 E
Wuchuan, *Guangdong, China* 77 G8 21 33N 110 43 E
Wuchuan, *Guizhou, China* 76 C7 28 25N 108 3 E
Wuchuan, *Nei Monggol Zizhiqu, China* 74 D6 41 5N 111 28 E
Wuday'ah, *Si. Arabia* 98 C4 17 2N 47 7 E
Wudi, *China* 75 F9 37 40N 117 35 E
Wuding, *China* 76 E4 25 24N 102 21 E
Wuding He →, *China* 74 F6 37 2N 110 23 E
Wudinna, *Australia* 127 E2 33 0 S 135 22 E
Wudu, *China* 74 H3 33 22N 104 54 E
Wufeng, *China* 77 B8 30 12N 110 42 E
Wugang, *China* 77 D8 26 44N 110 35 E
Wugong Shan, *China* 77 D9 27 30N 114 0 E
Wuguishan, *China* 69 G9 22 25N 113 25 E
Wuhan, *China* 77 B10 30 31N 114 18 E
Wuhe, *China* 75 H9 33 10N 117 50 E
Wuhsi = Wuxi, *China* 77 B13 31 33N 120 18 E
Wuhu, *China* 77 B12 31 22N 118 21 E
Wujiang, *China* 77 B13 31 10N 120 38 E
Wukari, *Nigeria* 113 D6 7 51N 9 42 E
Wulajie, *China* 75 B14 44 6N 126 33 E
Wulanbulang, *China* 74 D6 41 5N 110 55 E
Wular L., *India* 93 B6 34 20N 74 30 E
Wulehe, *Ghana* 113 D5 8 39N 0 0W
Wulff Land, *Greenland* 10 A6 82 0N 49 0W
Wulian, *China* 75 G10 35 40N 119 12 E
Wuliang Shan, *China* 76 E3 24 30N 100 40 E
Wuliaru, *Indonesia* 83 C4 7 27 S 131 0 E
Wuling Shan, *China* 76 C7 30 0N 110 0 E
Wulong, *China* 76 C6 29 22N 107 43 E
Wuluk'omushih Ling, *China* 68 C3 36 25N 87 25 E
Wulumuchi = Ürümqi, *China* 66 E9 43 45N 87 45 E
Wum, *Cameroon* 113 D7 6 24N 10 2 E
Wuming, *China* 76 F7 23 12N 108 18 E
Wun Rog, *Sudan* 107 F2 9 0N 28 20 E
Wundowie, *Australia* 125 F2 31 47 S 116 23 E
Wuning, *China* 77 C10 29 17N 115 5 E
Wunna →, *India* 94 D4 20 18N 78 48 E
Wunnummin L., *Canada* 140 B2 52 55N 89 10W
Wunsiedel, *Germany* 31 E8 50 2N 12 0 E
Wunstorf, *Germany* 30 C5 52 25N 9 26 E
Wuntho, *Burma* 90 D5 23 55N 95 45 E
Wuping, *China* 77 E11 25 5N 116 5 E
Wuppertal, *Germany* 30 D3 51 16N 7 12 E
Wuppertal, *S. Africa* 116 E2 32 13 S 19 12 E
Wuqia, *China* 65 D7 39 40N 75 7 E
Wuqing, *China* 75 E9 39 23N 117 4 E
Würenlingen, *Switz.* 33 A6 47 32N 8 16 E
Wurtsboro, *U.S.A.* 151 E10 41 35N 74 29W
Würzburg, *Germany* 31 F5 49 46N 9 55 E
Wurzen, *Germany* 30 D8 51 22N 12 44 E
Wushan, *China* 74 G3 34 43N 104 53 E
Wushishi, *Nigeria* 113 D6 9 46N 6 7 E
Wusi, *Vanuatu* 133 E4 15 21 S 166 40 E
Wusuli Jiang = Ussuri →, *Asia* 70 A7 48 27N 135 0 E
Wutach →, *Germany* 31 H4 47 37N 8 15 E
Wutai, *China* 74 E7 38 40N 113 12 E
Wuting = Huimin, *China* 75 F9 37 27N 117 28 E
Wutong, *China* 77 E8 25 24N 110 4 E
Wutonghaolai, *China* 75 C11 42 50N 120 5 E
Wutongqiao, *China* 76 C4 29 22N 103 50 E
Wutung, *Papua N. G.* 132 B1 2 37 S 141 1 E
Wuwei, *Anhui, China* 77 B11 31 18N 117 54 E
Wuwei, *Gansu, China* 68 C5 37 57N 102 34 E
Wuxi, *Jiangsu, China* 77 B13 31 33N 120 18 E
Wuxi, *Sichuan, China* 76 B7 31 23N 109 35 E
Wuxiang, *China* 74 F7 36 49N 112 50 E
Wuxuan, *China* 76 F7 23 34N 109 38 E
Wuxue, *China* 77 C10 29 52N 115 30 E
Wuyang, *China* 74 H7 33 25N 113 35 E
Wuyi, *Hebei, China* 74 F8 37 46N 115 56 E
Wuyi, *Zhejiang, China* 77 C12 28 52N 119 50 E
Wuyi Shan, *China* 77 D11 27 0N 117 0 E
Wuyishan, *China* 77 D12 27 45N 118 0 E
Wuyo, *Nigeria* 113 C7 10 23N 11 50 E
Wuyuan, *Jiangxi, China* 77 C11 29 15N 117 50 E
Wuyuan, *Nei Monggol Zizhiqu, China* 74 D5 41 2N 108 20 E
Wuzhai, *China* 74 E6 38 54N 111 48 E
Wuzhi Shan, *China* 86 C7 18 45N 109 45 E
Wuzhong, *China* 74 E4 38 2N 106 12 E
Wuzhou, *China* 77 F8 23 30N 111 18 E
Wyaaba Cr. →, *Australia* 126 B3 16 27 S 141 35 E
Wyalkatchem, *Australia* 125 F2 31 8 S 117 22 E
Wyalusing, *U.S.A.* 151 E8 41 40N 76 16W
Wyandotte, *U.S.A.* 157 B13 42 12N 83 9W
Wyandra, *Australia* 127 D4 27 12 S 145 56 E
Wyangala, L., *Australia* 129 B8 33 54 S 149 0 E
Wyara, L., *Australia* 127 D3 28 42 S 144 14 E
Wycheproof, *Australia* 128 D5 36 5 S 143 17 E
Wye →, *U.K.* 21 F5 51 38N 2 40W
Wyemandoo, *Australia* 125 E2 28 28 S 118 29 E
Wyk, *Germany* 30 A4 54 41N 8 33 E
Wymondham, *U.K.* 21 E9 52 35N 1 7 E
Wymore, *U.S.A.* 154 E6 40 7N 96 40W
Wyndham, *Australia* 124 C4 15 33 S 128 3 E
Wyndham, *N.Z.* 131 G3 46 20 S 168 51 E
Wynne, *U.S.A.* 155 H9 35 14N 90 47W
Wynyard, *Australia* 127 G4 41 5 S 145 44 E
Wynyard, *Canada* 143 C8 51 45N 104 10W
Wyola L., *Australia* 125 E5 29 8 S 130 17 E
Wyoming, *Canada* 150 D2 42 57N 82 7W
Wyoming, *Ill., U.S.A.* 156 C7 41 4N 89 47W
Wyoming, *Iowa, U.S.A.* 156 B6 42 4N 91 0W
Wyoming, *Mich., U.S.A.* 157 B11 42 54N 85 42W
Wyoming □, *U.S.A.* 158 E10 43 0N 107 30W
Wyomissing, *U.S.A.* 151 F9 40 20N 75 59W
Wyong, *Australia* 129 B9 33 14 S 151 24 E
Wyperfeld Nat. Park, *Australia* 128 C4 35 35 S 141 42 E
Wyrzysk, *Poland* 55 E4 53 10N 17 17 E
Wyśmierzyce, *Poland* 55 G7 51 37N 20 50 E
Wysoka, *Poland* 55 E4 53 13N 17 2 E
Wysokie, *Poland* 55 H9 50 55N 22 40 E
Wysokie Mazowieckie, *Poland* 55 F9 52 55N 22 30 E
Wyszków, *Poland* 55 F8 52 36N 21 25 E
Wyszogród, *Poland* 55 F7 52 23N 20 9 E
Wytheville, *U.S.A.* 148 G5 36 57N 81 5W
Wyżyna Małopolska, *Poland* 55 H7 50 45N 20 0 E

X

Xa-Cassau, *Angola* 115 D4 9 5 S 20 15 E
Xa-Muteba, *Angola* 115 D3 9 34 S 17 50 E
Xaafuun, *Somali Rep.* 120 B4 10 25N 51 16 E
Xaçmaz, *Azerbaijan* 61 K9 41 31N 48 42 E
Xadded, *Somali Rep.* 120 C3 9 46N 48 2 E
Xaghra, *Malta* 38 E7 36 3N 14 16 E
Xai-Xai, *Mozam.* 117 D5 25 6 S 33 31 E
Xaidulla, *China* 65 E8 36 28N 77 59 E
Xainza, *China* 68 C3 30 58N 88 35 E
Xambioá, *Brazil* 170 C2 6 25 S 48 40W
Xangongo, *Angola* 116 B2 16 45 S 15 5 E
Xankändi, *Azerbaijan* 101 C12 39 52N 46 49 E
Xanlar, *Azerbaijan* 61 K8 40 37N 46 12 E
Xanten, *Germany* 30 D2 51 39N 6 26 E
Xánthi, *Greece* 51 E8 41 10N 24 58 E
Xánthi □, *Greece* 51 E8 41 10N 24 58 E
Xanthos, *Turkey* 49 E11 36 19N 29 18 E
Xanxerê, *Brazil* 175 B5 26 53 S 52 23W
Xapuri, *Brazil* 172 C4 10 35 S 68 35W
Xar Moron He →, *China* 75 C11 43 25N 120 35 E
Xarrë, *Albania* 38 B10 39 44N 20 3 E
Xátiva, *Spain* 41 G4 38 59N 0 32W
Xau, L., *Botswana* 116 C3 21 15 S 24 44 E
Xavantina, *Brazil* 175 A5 21 15 S 52 48W
Xenia, *U.S.A.* 157 E13 39 41N 83 56W
Xeropotamos →, *Cyprus* 39 F8 34 42N 32 33 E
Xertigny, *France* 27 D13 48 3N 6 24 E
Xewkija, *Malta* 38 E7 36 2N 14 15 E
Xhora, *S. Africa* 117 E4 31 55 S 28 38 E
Xhumo, *Botswana* 116 C3 21 7 S 24 35 E
Xi Jiang →, *China* 77 F9 22 5N 113 20 E
Xi Xian, *Henan, China* 77 A10 32 20N 114 43 E
Xi Xian, *Shanxi, China* 74 F6 36 41N 110 58 E
Xia Xian, *China* 74 G6 35 8N 111 12 E
Xiachengzi, *China* 75 B16 44 40N 130 18 E
Xiachuan Dao, *China* 77 G9 21 40N 112 40 E
Xiaguan, *China* 68 D5 25 32N 100 16 E
Xiajiang, *China* 77 D10 27 30N 115 10 E
Xiajin, *China* 74 F9 36 56N 116 0 E
Xiamen, *China* 77 E12 24 25N 118 4 E
Xi'an, *China* 74 G5 34 15N 109 0 E
Xian Xian, *China* 74 E9 38 12N 116 6 E
Xianfeng, *China* 76 C7 29 40N 109 8 E
Xiang Jiang →, *China* 77 C9 28 55N 112 50 E
Xiangcheng, *Henan, China* 74 H8 33 29N 114 52 E
Xiangcheng, *Henan, China* 74 H7 33 50N 113 27 E
Xiangcheng, *Sichuan, China* 76 C2 28 53N 99 47 E
Xiangdu, *China* 76 F6 23 13N 106 58 E
Xiangfan, *China* 77 A9 32 2N 112 8 E
Xianggang = Hong Kong □, *China* 77 F10 22 11N 114 14 E
Xianghuang Qi, *China* 74 C7 42 2N 113 50 E
Xiangning, *China* 74 G6 35 58N 110 50 E
Xiangquan, *China* 74 F7 36 30N 113 1 E
Xiangquan He = Sutlej →, *Pakistan* 91 C3 29 23N 71 3 E
Xiangshan, *China* 77 C13 29 29N 121 51 E
Xiangshui, *China* 75 G10 34 12N 119 33 E
Xiangtan, *China* 77 D9 27 51N 112 54 E
Xiangxiang, *China* 77 D9 27 43N 112 28 E
Xiangyin, *China* 77 C9 28 38N 112 54 E
Xiangyun, *China* 76 E3 25 34N 100 35 E
Xiangzhou, *China* 76 F7 23 58N 109 40 E
Xianju, *China* 77 C13 28 51N 120 44 E
Xianning, *China* 77 C10 29 51N 114 16 E
Xianshui He →, *China* 76 B3 30 10N 100 59 E
Xiantao, *China* 77 B9 30 25N 113 25 E
Xianyang, *China* 74 G5 34 20N 108 40 E
Xianyou, *China* 77 E12 25 22N 118 38 E
Xiao Hinggan Ling, *China* 69 B7 49 0N 127 0 E
Xiao Xian, *China* 74 G9 34 15N 116 55 E
Xiaofeng, *China* 77 B12 30 35N 119 32 E
Xiaogan, *China* 77 B9 30 52N 113 55 E
Xiaojin, *China* 76 B4 30 59N 102 21 E
Xiaolan, *China* 77 F9 22 38N 113 13 E
Xiaoshan, *China* 77 B13 30 12N 120 18 E
Xiaoyi, *China* 74 F6 37 8N 111 48 E
Xiapu, *China* 77 D12 26 54N 119 59 E
Xiawa, *China* 75 C11 42 35N 120 38 E
Xiayi, *China* 74 G9 34 15N 116 10 E
Xichang, *China* 76 D4 27 51N 102 19 E
Xichong, *China* 76 B5 30 57N 105 54 E
Xichou, *China* 76 E5 23 25N 104 42 E
Xichuan, *China* 74 H6 33 0N 111 30 E
Xide, *China* 76 C4 28 8N 102 19 E
Xiemahe, *China* 77 B8 31 38N 111 12 E
Xieng Khouang, *Laos* 86 C4 19 17N 103 25 E
Xifei He →, *China* 74 H9 32 45N 116 40 E
Xifeng, *Gansu, China* 74 G4 35 40N 107 40 E
Xifeng, *Guizhou, China* 76 D6 27 7N 106 42 E
Xifeng, *Liaoning, China* 75 C13 42 42N 124 45 E
Xifengzhen = Xifeng, *China* 74 G4 35 40N 107 40 E
Xigazê, *China* 68 D3 29 5N 88 45 E
Xihe, *China* 74 G3 34 2N 105 20 E
Xihua, *China* 74 H8 33 45N 114 30 E
Xilaganí, *Greece* 51 F9 40 58N 25 25 E
Xili Shuiku, *China* 69 F10 22 36N 113 57 E

302 Xiliao He

Xiliao He →, *China* **75 C12** 43 32N 123 35 E
Xilin, *China* **76 E5** 24 30N 105 6 E
Xilókastron, *Greece* **48 C4** 38 5N 22 38 E
Ximana, *Mozam.* **119 F3** 19 24 S 33 58 E
Xime, *Guinea-Biss.* **112 C2** 11 59N 14 57W
Ximeng, *China* **76 F2** 22 50N 99 27 E
Xin Jiang →, *China* **77 C11** 28 45N 116 35 E
Xin Xian = Xinzhou, *China* **74 E7** 38 22N 112 46 E
Xinavane, *Mozam.* **117 D5** 25 2 S 32 47 E
Xinbin, *China* **75 D13** 41 40N 125 2 E
Xincai, *China* **77 A10** 32 43N 114 58 E
Xinchang, *China* **77 C13** 29 28N 120 52 E
Xincheng, *Guangxi Zhuangzu, China* **76 E7** 24 5N 108 39 E
Xincheng, *Jiangxi, China* **77 D10** 26 48N 114 6 E
Xindu, *China* **76 B5** 30 50N 104 10 E
Xinfeng, *Guangdong, China* **77 E10** 24 5N 114 16 E
Xinfeng, *Jiangxi, China* **77 D11** 27 7N 116 11 E
Xinfeng, *Jiangxi, China* **77 E10** 25 27N 114 58 E
Xinfengjiang Skuiku, *China* **77 F10** 23 52N 114 30 E
Xing Xian, *China* **74 E6** 38 27N 111 7 E
Xing'an, *Guangxi Zhuangzu, China* **77 E8** 25 38N 110 40 E
Xingan, *Jiangxi, China* **77 D10** 27 46N 115 20 E
Xingcheng, *China* **75 D11** 40 40N 120 45 E
Xingguo, *China* **77 D10** 26 21N 115 21 E
Xinghe, *China* **74 D7** 40 55N 113 55 E
Xinghua, *China* **75 H10** 32 58N 119 48 E
Xinghua Wan, *China* **77 E12** 25 15N 119 20 E
Xinglong, *China* **75 D9** 40 25N 117 30 E
Xingning, *China* **77 E10** 24 3N 115 42 E
Xingping, *China* **74 G5** 34 20N 108 28 E
Xingren, *China* **76 E5** 25 24N 105 11 E
Xingshan, *China* **77 B8** 31 15N 110 45 E
Xingtai, *China* **74 F8** 37 3N 114 32 E
Xingu →, *Brazil* **169 D7** 1 30 S 51 53W
Xingwen, *China* **76 C5** 28 22N 104 50 E
Xingyang, *China* **74 G7** 34 45N 112 52 E
Xinhe, *China* **74 F8** 37 30N 115 15 E
Xinhua, *China* **77 D8** 27 42N 111 13 E
Xinhuang, *China* **76 D7** 27 21N 109 12 E
Xinhui, *China* **77 F9** 22 25N 113 0 E
Xining, *China* **68 C5** 36 34N 101 40 E
Xinjian, *China* **77 C10** 28 37N 115 46 E
Xinjiang, *China* **74 G6** 35 34N 111 11 E
Xinjiang Uygur Zizhiqu □, *China* **68 C3** 42 0N 86 0 E
Xinjie, *China* **76 D3** 26 48N 101 15 E
Xinjin = Pulandian, *China* **75 E11** 39 25N 121 58 E
Xinjin, *China* **76 B4** 30 24N 103 47 E
Xinkai He →, *China* **75 C12** 43 32N 123 35 E
Xinken, *China* **69 F10** 22 39N 113 36 E
Xinle, *China* **74 E8** 38 25N 114 40 E
Xinlitun, *China* **75 D12** 42 0N 122 8 E
Xinlong, *China* **76 B3** 30 57N 100 12 E
Xinmin, *China* **75 D12** 41 59N 122 50 E
Xinning, *China* **77 D8** 26 28N 110 50 E
Xinping, *China* **76 E3** 24 5N 101 59 E
Xinshao, *China* **77 D8** 27 21N 111 26 E
Xintai, *China* **75 G9** 35 55N 117 45 E
Xintian, *China* **77 E9** 25 55N 112 13 E
Xinwan, *China* **69 F10** 22 47N 113 40 E
Xinxian, *China* **77 B10** 31 36N 113 51 E
Xinxiang, *China* **74 G7** 35 18N 113 50 E
Xinxing, *China* **77 F9** 22 35N 112 15 E
Xinyang, *China* **77 A10** 32 6N 114 3 E
Xinye, *China* **77 A9** 32 30N 112 21 E
Xinyi, *China* **77 F8** 22 25N 111 0 E
Xinyu, *China* **77 D10** 27 49N 114 58 E
Xinzhan, *China* **75 C14** 43 50N 127 18 E
Xinzheng, *China* **74 G7** 34 20N 113 45 E
Xinzhou, *Hubei, China* **77 B10** 30 50N 114 48 E
Xinzhou, *Shanxi, China* **74 E7** 38 22N 112 46 E
Xinzo de Limia, *Spain* **42 C3** 42 3N 7 47W
Xiongyuecheng, *China* **75 D12** 40 12N 122 5 E
Xiping, *Henan, China* **74 H8** 33 22N 114 5 E
Xiping, *Henan, China* **74 H6** 33 25N 111 8 E
Xiping, *Zhejiang, China* **77 C12** 28 16N 119 29 E
Xique-Xique, *Brazil* **170 D3** 10 50 S 42 40W
Xiruá →, *Brazil* **172 B4** 6 3 S 67 50W
Xisha Qundao = Paracel Is., *S. China Sea* **78 A4** 15 50N 112 0 E
Xishui, *Guizhou, China* **76 C6** 28 19N 106 9 E
Xishui, *Hubei, China* **77 B10** 30 30N 115 15 E
Xitole, *Guinea-Biss.* **112 C2** 11 43N 14 50W
Xiu Shui →, *China* **77 C10** 29 13N 116 0 E
Xiuning, *China* **77 C12** 29 45N 118 10 E
Xiuren, *China* **77 E8** 24 27N 110 12 E
Xiushan, *China* **76 C7** 28 25N 108 57 E
Xiushui, *China* **77 C10** 29 2N 114 33 E
Xiuwen, *China* **76 D6** 26 49N 106 32 E
Xiuyan, *China* **75 D12** 40 18N 123 11 E
Xixia, *China* **74 H6** 33 25N 111 29 E
Xixiang, *China* **74 H4** 33 0N 107 44 E
Xiyang, *China* **74 F7** 37 38N 113 38 E
Xizang Zizhiqu □, *China* **68 C3** 32 0N 88 0 E
Xlendi, *Malta* **38 E6** 36 2N 14 13 E
Xu Jiang →, *China* **77 D11** 28 0N 116 25 E
Xuan Loc, *Vietnam* **87 G6** 10 56N 107 14 E
Xuan'en, *China* **76 C7** 30 0N 109 30 E
Xuanhan, *China* **76 B6** 31 18N 107 38 E
Xuanhua, *China* **74 D8** 40 40N 115 2 E
Xuanwei, *China* **76 C5** 26 15N 103 59 E
Xuanzhou, *China* **77 B12** 30 56N 118 43 E
Xuchang, *China* **74 G7** 34 2N 113 48 E
Xudat, *Azerbaijan* **61 K9** 41 38N 48 41 E
Xuddur = Oddur, *Somali Rep.* **120 D2** 4 11N 43 52 E
Xuefeng Shan, *China* **77 D8** 27 5N 110 35 E
Xuejiaping, *China* **77 B8** 31 39N 110 16 E
Xun Jiang →, *China* **77 F8** 23 35N 111 30 E
Xun Xian, *China* **74 G8** 35 42N 114 33 E
Xundian, *China* **76 E4** 25 36N 103 15 E
Xunwu, *China* **77 E10** 24 54N 115 37 E
Xunyang, *China* **74 H5** 32 48N 109 22 E
Xunyi, *China* **74 G5** 35 8N 108 20 E
Xupu, *China* **77 D8** 27 53N 110 32 E
Xúquer →, *Spain* **41 F4** 39 5N 0 10W
Xushui, *China* **74 E8** 39 2N 115 40 E
Xuwen, *China* **77 G8** 20 20N 110 10 E
Xuyen Moc, *Vietnam* **87 G6** 10 34N 107 25 E
Xuyong, *China* **76 C5** 28 10N 105 22 E
Xuzhou, *China* **75 G9** 34 18N 117 10 E
Xylophagou, *Cyprus* **39 F9** 34 54N 33 51 E

Y

Ya Xian, *China* **86 C7** 18 14N 109 29 E
Yaamba, *Australia* **126 C5** 23 8 S 150 22 E
Ya'an, *China* **76 C4** 29 58N 103 5 E
Yaapeet, *Australia* **128 C5** 35 45 S 142 3 E
Yabassi, *Cameroon* **113 E6** 4 30N 9 57 E
Yabelo, *Ethiopia* **107 G4** 4 50N 38 8 E
Yabelo Wildlife Reserve, *Ethiopia* **107 F4** 6 0N 37 50 E
Yablanitsa, *Bulgaria* **51 C8** 43 2N 24 5 E
Yablonovy Ra. = Yablonovyy Khrebet, *Russia* **67 D12** 53 0N 114 0 E
Yablonovyy Khrebet, *Russia* **67 D12** 53 0N 114 0 E
Yabrai Shan, *China* **74 E2** 39 40N 103 0 E
Yabrūd, *Syria* **103 B5** 33 58N 36 39 E
Yabucoa, *Puerto Rico* **165 d** 18 3N 65 53W
Yacheng, *China* **69 E5** 18 22N 109 6 E
Yackandandah, *Australia* **129 D7** 36 18 S 146 52 E
Yacuiba, *Bolivia* **174 A3** 22 0 S 63 43W
Yacuma →, *Bolivia* **173 C4** 13 38 S 65 23W
Yadgir, *India* **94 F3** 16 45N 77 5 E
Yadkin →, *U.S.A.* **149 H5** 35 29N 80 9W
Yadrin, *Russia* **60 C8** 55 57N 46 12 E
Yadua, *Fiji* **133 A2** 16 49 S 178 18 E
Yaeyama-Rettō, *Japan* **71 M1** 24 30N 123 40 E
Yafran, *Libya* **108 B2** 32 4N 12 31 E
Yafran □, *Libya* **108 B2** 32 0N 12 20 E
Yagaba, *Ghana* **113 C4** 10 14N 1 20W
Yagasa Cluster, *Fiji* **133 B3** 18 57 S 178 28W
Yağcılar, *Turkey* **49 B10** 39 25N 28 23 E
Yagodnoye, *Russia* **67 C15** 62 33N 149 40 E
Yagoua, *Cameroon* **109 F3** 10 20N 15 13 E
Yaguas →, *Peru* **168 D3** 2 45 S 70 10W
Yahila, *Orientale, Dem. Rep. of the Congo* **114 B4** 1 48N 23 37 E
Yahila, *Orientale, Dem. Rep. of the Congo* **118 B1** 0 13N 24 28 E
Yahk, *Canada* **142 D5** 49 6N 116 10W
Yahotyn, *Ukraine* **59 G6** 50 17N 31 46 E
Yahuma, *Dem. Rep. of the Congo* **114 B4** 1 0N 23 10 E
Yahyalı, *Turkey* **100 C6** 38 5N 35 2 E
Yaita, *Japan* **71 F9** 36 48N 139 56 E
Yaiza, *Canary Is.* **9 e2** 28 57N 13 46W
Yaizu, *Japan* **73 C10** 34 52N 138 20 E
Yajiang, *China* **76 B3** 30 2N 100 57 E
Yajua, *Nigeria* **113 C7** 11 27N 12 49 E
Yakage, *Japan* **72 C5** 34 37N 133 35 E
Yakamba, *Dem. Rep. of the Congo* **114 B3** 2 42N 19 38 E
Yakima, *U.S.A.* **158 C3** 46 36N 120 31W
Yakima →, *U.S.A.* **158 C3** 47 0N 120 30W
Yakkabag, *Uzbekistan* **65 D3** 38 55N 66 51 E
Yako, *Burkina Faso* **112 C4** 12 59N 2 15W
Yakobi I., *U.S.A.* **142 B1** 58 0N 136 30W
Yakoma, *Dem. Rep. of the Congo* **114 B4** 4 5N 22 27 E
Yakoruda, *Bulgaria* **50 D7** 42 1N 23 39 E
Yakossi, *C.A.R.* **114 A4** 5 37N 23 19 E
Yakovlevka, *Russia* **70 B6** 44 26N 133 28 E
Yakshur Bodya, *Russia* **64 C4** 57 11N 53 7 E
Yaku-Shima, *Japan* **71 J5** 30 20N 130 30 E
Yakumo, *Japan* **70 C10** 42 15N 140 16 E
Yakutat, *U.S.A.* **144 G13** 59 33N 139 44W
Yakutat B., *U.S.A.* **144 G12** 59 45N 140 45W
Yakutia = Sakha □, *Russia* **67 C13** 66 0N 130 0 E
Yakutsk, *Russia* **67 C13** 62 5N 129 50 E
Yala, *Thailand* **87 J3** 6 33N 101 18 E
Yalboroo, *Australia* **126 J6** 20 50 S 148 40 E
Yale, *U.S.A.* **150 C2** 43 8N 82 48W
Yalgoo, *Australia* **125 E2** 28 16 S 116 39 E
Yalgorup Nat. Park, *Australia* **125 D2** 24 34 S 115 2 E
Yali, *Dem. Rep. of the Congo* **114 B4** 0 4N 21 3 E
Yaligimba, *Dem. Rep. of the Congo* **114 B4** 2 13N 22 56 E
Yalikanda, *Dem. Rep. of the Congo* **114 B4** 0 23N 24 47 E
Yalinga, *C.A.R.* **114 A4** 6 33N 23 10 E
Yalkubul, Punta, *Mexico* **163 C7** 21 32N 88 37W
Yalleroi, *Australia* **126 C4** 24 3 S 145 42 E
Yalobusha →, *U.S.A.* **155 J9** 33 33N 90 10W
Yaloké, *C.A.R.* **114 A3** 5 19N 17 5 E
Yalong Jiang →, *China* **76 D3** 26 40N 101 55 E
Yalova, *Turkey* **51 F13** 40 41N 29 15 E
Yalta, *Ukraine* **59 K8** 44 30N 34 10 E
Yalu Jiang →, *China* **75 E13** 40 0N 124 22 E
Yalvaç, *Turkey* **100 C4** 38 17N 31 10 E
Yam Ha Melah = Dead Sea, *Asia* **103 D4** 31 30N 35 30 E
Yam Kinneret, *Israel* **103 C4** 32 45N 35 35 E
Yamada, *Japan* **72 D2** 33 33N 130 49 E
Yamaga, *Japan* **72 D2** 33 1N 130 41 E
Yamagata, *Japan* **70 E10** 38 15N 140 15 E
Yamagata □, *Japan* **70 E10** 38 30N 140 0 E
Yamagawa, *Japan* **72 F2** 31 12N 130 39 E
Yamaguchi, *Japan* **72 C3** 34 10N 131 32 E
Yamaguchi □, *Japan* **72 C3** 34 20N 131 40 E
Yamal, Poluostrov, *Russia* **66 B8** 71 0N 70 0 E
Yamal Pen. = Yamal, Poluostrov, *Russia* **66 B8** 71 0N 70 0 E
Yamanaka, *Japan* **73 A8** 36 15N 136 22 E
Yamanashi, *Japan* **73 B10** 35 41N 138 40 E
Yamanashi □, *Japan* **73 B10** 35 40N 138 40 E
Yamanie Falls Nat. Park, *Australia* **126 B4** 18 29 S 146 9 E
Yamantau, Gora, *Russia* **64 D7** 54 15N 58 6 E
Yamasaki, *Japan* **72 C6** 35 0N 134 32 E
Yamato, *Japan* **73 B11** 35 27N 139 25 E
Yamatotakada, *Japan* **73 C7** 34 31N 135 45 E
Yamba, *Australia* **127 D5** 29 26 S 153 23 E
Yambarran Ra., *Australia* **124 C5** 15 10 S 130 25 E
Yambata, *Dem. Rep. of the Congo* **114 B4** 2 26N 21 58 E
Yambéring, *Guinea* **112 C2** 11 50N 12 18 E
Yâmbiô, *Sudan* **107 G2** 4 35N 28 16 E
Yambol, *Bulgaria* **51 D10** 42 30N 26 30 E
Yamboyo, *Dem. Rep. of the Congo* **114 B4** 0 40N 22 18 E
Yambuya, *Dem. Rep. of the Congo* **114 B4** 1 17N 24 34 E
Yamdena, *Indonesia* **83 C4** 7 45 S 131 20 E
Yame, *Japan* **72 D2** 33 13N 130 35 E
Yamethin, *Burma* **90 E6** 20 29N 96 18 E
Yamma-Yamma, L., *Australia* **127 D3** 26 16 S 141 20 E
Yamoussoukro, *Ivory C.* **112 D3** 6 49N 5 17W
Yampa →, *U.S.A.* **158 F9** 40 32N 108 59W
Yampi Sd., *Australia* **124 C3** 16 8 S 123 38 E
Yampil, *Moldova* **59 H5** 48 15N 28 15 E
Yampol = Yampil, *Moldova* **59 H5** 48 15N 28 15 E
Yamrat, *Nigeria* **113 C6** 10 11N 9 55 E
Yamrukchal = Botev, *Bulgaria* **51 D8** 42 44N 24 52 E
Yamuna →, *India* **93 G9** 25 30N 81 53 E
Yamunanagar, *India* **92 D7** 30 7N 77 17 E
Yamzho Yumco, *China* **68 D4** 28 48N 90 35 E
Yan, *Nigeria* **113 C7** 10 5N 12 11 E
Yan Oya →, *Sri Lanka* **95 K5** 9 0N 81 10 E
Yana →, *Russia* **67 B14** 71 30N 136 0 E
Yanagawa, *Japan* **72 D2** 33 10N 130 24 E
Yanahara, *Japan* **72 C6** 34 58N 134 2 E
Yanai, *Japan* **72 D4** 33 58N 132 7 E
Yan'an, *China* **74 F5** 36 35N 109 26 E
Yanaul, *Russia* **64 C5** 56 25N 55 0 E
Yanbian, *China* **76 D3** 26 47N 101 31 E
Yanbu 'al Bahr, *Si. Arabia* **96 F3** 24 0N 38 5 E
Yanchang, *China* **74 F6** 36 43N 110 1 E
Yancheng, *Henan, China* **74 H8** 33 35N 114 0 E
Yancheng, *Jiangsu, China* **75 H11** 33 23N 120 8 E
Yanchep Beach, *Australia* **125 F2** 31 33 S 115 37 E
Yanchi, *China* **74 F4** 37 48N 107 20 E
Yanchuan, *China* **74 F6** 36 51N 110 10 E
Yanco, *Australia* **129 C7** 34 38 S 146 27 E
Yanco Cr. →, *Australia* **129 C6** 35 14 S 145 35 E
Yandé, Î., *N. Cal.* **133 T17** 20 3 S 163 49 E
Yandina, *Solomon Is.* **133 M10** 9 7 S 159 13 E
Yandja, *Dem. Rep. of the Congo* **114 C3** 1 41 S 17 43 E
Yandongi, *Dem. Rep. of the Congo* **114 B4** 2 51N 22 16 E
Yandoon, *Burma* **90 G5** 17 0N 95 40 E
Yanfeng, *China* **76 E3** 25 52N 101 8 E
Yanfolila, *Mali* **112 C3** 11 11N 8 9W
Yang Xian, *China* **74 H4** 33 15N 107 30 E
Yang-Yang, *Senegal* **112 B1** 15 30N 15 20W
Yangambi, *Dem. Rep. of the Congo* **118 B1** 0 47N 24 24 E
Yangbi, *China* **76 E2** 25 41N 99 58 E
Yangcheng, *China* **74 G7** 35 28N 112 22 E
Yangch'ü = Taiyuan, *China* **74 F7** 37 52N 112 33 E
Yangchun, *China* **77 F8** 22 11N 111 48 E
Yanggao, *China* **74 D7** 40 21N 113 55 E
Yanggu, *China* **74 F8** 36 8N 115 43 E
Yangi-Nishan, *Uzbekistan* **65 D2** 38 49N 65 47 E
Yangiabad, *Uzbekistan* **65 C5** 41 7N 70 6 E
Yangikishlak, *Uzbekistan* **65 C3** 40 25N 67 10 E
Yangirabad, *Uzbekistan* **65 C2** 40 2N 65 58 E
Yangiyer, *Uzbekistan* **65 C4** 40 16N 68 49 E
Yangiyul, *Uzbekistan* **65 C4** 41 0N 69 3 E
Yangjiang, *China* **77 G8** 21 50N 111 59 E
Yangliuqing, *China* **75 E9** 39 2N 117 5 E
Yangon = Rangoon, *Burma* **90 G6** 16 45N 96 20 E
Yangonde, *Dem. Rep. of the Congo* **114 B4** 0 3N 22 43 E
Yangping, *China* **77 B8** 31 12N 111 25 E
Yangpingguan, *China* **74 H4** 32 58N 106 5 E
Yangquan, *China* **74 F7** 37 58N 113 31 E
Yangshan, *China* **77 E9** 24 30N 112 40 E
Yangshuo, *China* **77 E8** 24 48N 110 29 E
Yangtse = Chang Jiang →, *China* **77 B13** 31 48N 121 10 E
Yangtze Kiang = Chang Jiang →, *China* **77 B13** 31 48N 121 10 E
Yangudi Rassa Nat. Park, *Ethiopia* **107 E5** 10 50N 40 42 E
Yangxin, *China* **77 C10** 29 50N 115 12 E
Yangyang, *S. Korea* **75 E15** 38 4N 128 38 E
Yangyuan, *China* **74 D8** 40 1N 114 10 E
Yangzhong, *China* **77 A12** 32 22N 119 22 E
Yangzhou, *China* **77 A12** 32 21N 119 26 E
Yanhe, *China* **76 C7** 28 31N 108 29 E
Yanji, *China* **75 C15** 42 59N 129 30 E
Yanjin, *China* **76 C5** 28 5N 104 18 E
Yanjing, *China* **76 C2** 29 7N 98 33 E
Yankari Nat. Park, *Nigeria* **113 D7** 9 50N 10 28 E
Yankton, *U.S.A.* **154 D6** 42 53N 97 23W
Yanonge, *Dem. Rep. of the Congo* **118 B1** 0 35N 24 38 E
Yanqi, *China* **68 B3** 42 5N 86 35 E
Yanqing, *China* **74 D8** 40 30N 115 58 E
Yanshan, *Hebei, China* **75 E9** 38 4N 117 22 E
Yanshan, *Jiangxi, China* **77 C11** 28 15N 117 41 E
Yanshan, *Yunnan, China* **76 F5** 23 35N 104 20 E
Yanshou, *China* **75 B15** 45 28N 128 22 E
Yantabulla, *Australia* **127 D4** 29 21 S 145 0 E
Yantai, *China* **75 F11** 37 34N 121 22 E
Yantian, *China* **69 F11** 22 35N 114 16 E
Yanting, *China* **76 B5** 31 11N 105 24 E
Yantra →, *Bulgaria* **51 C9** 43 40N 25 37 E
Yanuca, *Fiji* **133 B1** 18 24 S 178 0 E
Yanwa, *China* **76 D2** 27 35N 98 55 E
Yanykurgan = Zhangaqŭrghan, *Kazakstan* **65 B4** 43 50N 68 48 E
Yanyuan, *China* **76 D3** 27 25N 101 30 E
Yanzhou, *China* **74 G9** 35 35N 116 49 E
Yao, *Chad* **109 F3** 12 56N 17 33 E
Yao, *Japan* **73 C7** 34 32N 135 36 E
Yao Noi, Ko, *Thailand* **87 a** 8 7N 98 37 E
Yao Xian, *China* **74 G5** 34 55N 108 59 E
Yao Yai, Ko, *Thailand* **87 a** 8 0N 98 35 E
Yao'an, *China* **76 E3** 25 31N 101 18 E
Yaodu, *China* **76 A5** 32 45N 105 22 E
Yaoundé, *Cameroon* **113 E7** 3 50N 11 35 E
Yaowan, *China* **75 G10** 34 15N 118 3 E
Yap I., *Pac. Oc.* **134 G5** 9 30N 138 10 E
Yapehe, *Dem. Rep. of the Congo* **114 C4** 0 13 S 24 28 E
Yapen, *Indonesia* **83 B5** 1 50 S 136 0 E
Yapen, Selat, *Indonesia* **83 B5** 1 20 S 136 10 E
Yapero, *Indonesia* **83 B5** 4 59 S 137 11 E
Yappar →, *Australia* **126 B3** 18 22 S 141 16 E
Yaqaga, *Fiji* **133 A2** 16 35 S 178 36 E
Yaqui →, *Mexico* **162 B2** 27 37N 110 39W
Yar, *Russia* **64 B4** 58 14N 52 5 E
Yar-Sale, *Russia* **66 C8** 66 50N 70 50 E
Yaracuy □, *Venezuela* **168 A4** 10 20N 68 45W
Yaracuy →, *Venezuela* **168 A4** 10 33N 68 15W
Yaraka, *Australia* **126 C3** 24 53 S 144 3 E
Yaransk, *Russia* **60 B8** 57 22N 47 49 E
Yarbasan, *Turkey* **49 C10** 38 59N 28 49 E
Yardımcı Burnu, *Turkey* **49 E12** 36 13N 30 25 E
Yare →, *U.K.* **21 E9** 52 35N 1 38 E
Yaremcha, *Ukraine* **59 H3** 48 27N 24 33 E
Yarensk, *Russia* **56 B8** 62 11N 49 15 E
Yarfa, *Si. Arabia* **106 C4** 24 37N 38 35 E
Yarí →, *Colombia* **168 D3** 0 20 S 72 20W
Yarīm, *Yemen* **98 D4** 14 20N 44 22 E
Yaritagua, *Venezuela* **168 A4** 10 5N 69 8W
Yarkand = Shache, *China* **65 D8** 38 20N 77 10 E
Yarker, *Canada* **151 B8** 44 23N 76 46W
Yarkhun →, *Pakistan* **93 A5** 36 17N 72 30 E
Yarmouth, *Canada* **141 D6** 43 50N 66 7W
Yarmūk →, *Syria* **103 C4** 32 42N 35 40 E
Yaroslavl, *Russia* **58 D10** 57 35N 39 55 E
Yarqa, W. →, *Egypt* **103 F2** 30 0N 33 49 E
Yarra Ranges Nat. Park, *Australia* **129 D7** 37 40 S 146 3 E
Yarra Yarra Lakes, *Australia* **125 E2** 29 40 S 115 45 E
Yarram, *Australia* **129 E7** 38 29 S 146 39 E
Yarraman, *Australia* **127 D5** 26 50 S 152 0 E
Yarras, *Australia* **129 A10** 31 25 S 152 20 E
Yarrawonga, *Australia* **129 D7** 36 0 S 146 0 E
Yartsevo, *Sib., Russia* **67 C10** 60 20N 90 0 E
Yartsevo, *Smolensk, Russia* **58 E7** 55 6N 32 43 E
Yarumal, *Colombia* **168 B2** 6 58N 75 24W
Yasa, *Dem. Rep. of the Congo* **114 C4** 3 50 S 21 25 E
Yasawa, *Fiji* **133 A1** 16 47 S 177 31 E
Yasawa Group, *Fiji* **133 A1** 17 0 S 177 23 E
Yaselda, *Belarus* **59 F4** 52 7N 26 28 E
Yashbum, *Yemen* **98 D4** 14 19N 46 56 E
Yashi, *Nigeria* **113 C6** 12 23N 7 54 E
Yashikera, *Nigeria* **113 D5** 9 44N 3 29 E
Yashiro-Jima, *Japan* **72 D4** 33 55N 132 15 E
Yashkul, *Russia* **61 G7** 46 11N 45 21 E
Yasin, *Pakistan* **93 A5** 36 24N 73 23 E
Yasinovataya, *Ukraine* **59 H9** 48 7N 37 57 E
Yasinski, L., *Canada* **140 B4** 53 16N 77 35W
Yasinya, *Ukraine* **59 H3** 48 16N 24 21 E
Yasnyy, *Russia* **64 F7** 51 1N 59 58 E
Yasothon, *Thailand* **86 E5** 15 50N 104 10 E
Yass, *Australia* **129 C8** 34 49 S 148 54 E
Yasugi, *Japan* **72 B5** 35 26N 133 15 E
Yāsūj, *Iran* **97 D6** 30 31N 51 31 E
Yat, *Niger* **109 D2** 20 28N 13 27 E
Yata →, *Bolivia* **173 C4** 10 29 S 65 26W
Yata →, *C.A.R.* **114 A4** 10 23N 22 45 E
Yata-Ngaya, Réserve de Faune de la, *C.A.R.* **114 A4** 9 15N 23 25 E
Yatağan, *Turkey* **49 D10** 37 20N 28 10 E
Yatakala, *Niger* **113 C5** 14 50N 0 22 E
Yaté, *N. Cal.* **133 V20** 22 9 S 166 57 E
Yates Center, *U.S.A.* **155 G7** 37 53N 95 44W
Yates Pt., *N.Z.* **131 E2** 44 29 S 167 49 E
Yathkyed L., *Canada* **143 A9** 62 40N 98 0W
Yathong, *Australia* **129 B6** 32 37 S 145 33 E
Yatolemu, *Dem. Rep. of the Congo* **114 B4** 0 25N 24 35 E
Yatsuo, *Japan* **73 A9** 36 34N 137 8 E
Yatsushiro, *Japan* **72 E2** 32 30N 130 40 E
Yatsushiro-Kai, *Japan* **72 E2** 32 30N 130 25 E
Yatta Plateau, *Kenya* **118 C4** 2 0 S 38 0 E
Yatua →, *Venezuela* **168 C4** 1 30N 66 30W
Yauca, *Peru* **172 D3** 15 39 S 74 35W
Yauco, *Puerto Rico* **165 d** 18 2N 66 51W
Yauri, *Peru* **172 C3** 14 47 S 71 25W
Yauya, *Peru* **172 B2** 8 59 S 77 17W
Yauyos, *Peru* **172 C2** 12 19 S 75 50W
Yaval, *India* **94 D2** 21 10N 75 42 E
Yavan, *Tajikistan* **65 D4** 38 19N 69 2 E
Yavari →, *Peru* **172 A3** 4 21 S 70 2W
Yávaros, *Mexico* **162 B3** 26 42N 109 31W
Yavatmal, *India* **94 D4** 20 20N 78 15 E
Yavero →, *Peru* **172 C3** 12 6 S 72 57W
Yavne, *Israel* **103 D3** 31 52N 34 45 E
Yavoriv, *Ukraine* **59 H2** 49 55N 23 20 E
Yavorov = Yavoriv, *Ukraine* **59 H2** 49 55N 23 20 E
Yavuzeli, *Turkey* **100 D7** 37 18N 37 24 E
Yawatahama, *Japan* **72 D4** 33 27N 132 24 E
Yawnghwe, *Burma* **90 E6** 20 39N 96 56 E
Yawri B., *S. Leone* **112 D2** 8 22N 13 0W
Yaxi, *China* **76 D6** 27 33N 106 41 E
Yazagyo, *Burma* **90 D5** 23 30N 94 6 E
Yazd, *Iran* **97 D7** 31 55N 54 27 E
Yazd □, *Iran* **97 D7** 32 0N 55 0 E
Yazd-e Khvāst, *Iran* **97 D7** 31 31N 52 7 E
Yazdān, *Iran* **91 B1** 33 30N 60 50 E
Yazıköy, *Turkey* **49 E9** 36 40N 27 20 E
Yazman, *Pakistan* **92 E4** 29 8N 71 45 E
Yazoo →, *U.S.A.* **155 J9** 32 22N 90 54W
Yazoo City, *U.S.A.* **155 J9** 32 51N 90 25W
Ybbs, *Austria* **34 C8** 48 12N 15 4 E
Yding Skovhøj, *Denmark* **17 J3** 55 59N 9 46 E
Ye-ngan, *Burma* **90 E6** 21 9N 96 27 E
Ye-u, *Burma* **90 D5** 22 46N 95 26 E
Ye Xian = Laizhou, *China* **75 F10** 37 8N 119 57 E
Ye Xian, *China* **74 H7** 33 35N 113 25 E
Yea, *Australia* **129 D6** 37 14 S 145 26 E
Yebawmi, *Burma* **90 C5** 25 15N 95 45 E
Yebbi-Souma, *Chad* **109 D3** 21 7N 17 54 E
Yebyu, *Burma* **86 E2** 14 15N 98 13 E
Yecheng, *China* **65 E8** 37 54N 77 26 E
Yechŏn, *S. Korea* **75 F15** 36 39N 128 27 E
Yecla, *Spain* **41 G3** 38 35N 1 5W
Yécora, *Mexico* **162 B3** 28 20N 108 58W
Yedashe, *Burma* **90 F6** 19 10N 96 20 E
Yedintsy = Edineţ, *Moldova* **53 B12** 48 9N 27 18 E
Yedri, *Chad* **109 D3** 22 25N 17 30 E
Yedseram →, *Nigeria* **113 C7** 12 30N 14 5 E
Yefremov, *Russia* **58 F10** 53 8N 38 3 E
Yegguéba, *Niger* **109 E2** 19 59N 12 52 E
Yeghegnadzor, *Armenia* **101 C11** 39 44N 45 19 E
Yegorlyk →, *Russia* **61 G5** 46 35N 41 57 E
Yegorlykskaya, *Russia* **61 G5** 46 35N 40 35 E
Yegoryevsk, *Russia* **58 E10** 55 27N 38 55 E
Yegros, *Paraguay* **174 B4** 26 20 S 56 25W
Yehbuah, *Indonesia* **79 J17** 8 23 S 114 45 E
Yehuda, Midbar, *Israel* **103 D4** 31 35N 35 15 E
Yei, *Sudan* **107 G3** 4 9N 30 40 E
Yei, Nahr →, *Sudan* **107 F3** 6 15N 30 13 E
Yejmiadzin, *Armenia* **61 K7** 40 12N 44 19 E
Yekaterinburg, *Russia* **64 C8** 56 50N 60 30 E
Yekaterinodar = Krasnodar, *Russia* **61 H4** 45 5N 39 0 E
Yekumbe, *Dem. Rep. of the Congo* **114 C4** 1 2 S 23 27 E
Yelabuga, *Russia* **60 C11** 55 45N 52 4 E
Yelan, *Russia* **60 E6** 50 55N 43 43 E
Yelandur, *India* **95 H3** 12 6N 77 0 E
Yelarbon, *Australia* **127 D5** 28 33 S 150 38 E
Yelatma, *Russia* **60 C5** 55 0N 41 45 E
Yelcho, L., *Chile* **176 B2** 43 18 S 72 18W
Yelets, *Russia* **59 F10** 52 40N 38 30 E
Yélimané, *Mali* **112 B2** 15 9N 10 34W
Yelizavetgrad = Kirovohrad, *Ukraine* **59 H7** 48 35N 32 20 E
Yelizavetinka, *Russia* **64 F7** 51 46N 59 45 E
Yell, *U.K.* **22 A7** 60 35N 1 5W
Yell Sd., *U.K.* **22 A7** 60 33N 1 15W
Yellamanchilli = Elamanchili, *India* **94 F6** 17 33N 82 50 E
Yellandu, *India* **94 F5** 17 39N 80 23 E
Yellapur, *India* **95 G2** 14 58N 74 43 E
Yellareddi, *India* **94 E4** 18 12N 78 2 E
Yellow →, *U.S.A.* **153 E3** 30 30N 87 0W
Yellow Sea, *China* **75 G12** 35 0N 123 0 E
Yellowhead Pass, *Canada* **142 C5** 52 53N 118 25W
Yellowknife, *Canada* **142 A6** 62 27N 114 29W
Yellowknife →, *Canada* **142 A6** 62 31N 114 19W
Yellowstone →, *U.S.A.* **154 B3** 47 59N 103 59W
Yellowstone L., *U.S.A.* **158 D8** 44 27N 110 22W
Yellowstone Nat. Park, *U.S.A.* **158 D9** 44 40N 110 30W
Yelnya, *Russia* **58 E7** 54 35N 33 15 E
Yelsk, *Belarus* **59 G5** 51 50N 29 10 E
Yelwa, *Nigeria* **113 C5** 10 49N 4 41 E
Yemanzhelinsk, *Russia* **64 D8** 54 58N 61 18 E
Yemassee, *U.S.A.* **152 C9** 32 41N 80 51W
Yembongo, *Dem. Rep. of the Congo* **114 B3** 3 12N 19 2 E
Yemen ■, *Asia* **98 D4** 15 0N 44 0 E
Yen Bai, *Vietnam* **76 G5** 21 42N 104 52 E
Yenagoa, *Nigeria* **113 E6** 4 58N 6 16 E
Yenakiyeve, *Ukraine* **59 H10** 48 15N 38 15 E
Yenakiyevo = Yenakiyeve, *Ukraine* **59 H10** 48 15N 38 15 E
Yenangyat, *Burma* **90 E5** 21 6N 94 48 E
Yenangyaung, *Burma* **90 E5** 20 30N 95 0 E
Yenanma, *Burma* **90 F5** 19 46N 94 49 E
Yenbo = Yanbu 'al Bahr, *Si. Arabia* **96 F3** 24 0N 38 5 E
Yenda, *Australia* **129 C7** 34 13 S 146 14 E
Yende Millimou, *Guinea* **112 D2** 8 55N 10 10W
Yendéré, *Burkina Faso* **112 C4** 10 12N 4 59W
Yendi, *Ghana* **113 D4** 9 29N 0 1W
Yengisar, *China* **65 D8** 38 56N 76 9 E
Yengo, *Congo* **114 B3** 0 22N 15 29 E
Yengo Nat. Park, *Australia* **129 B9** 33 0 S 150 55 E
Yéni, *Niger* **113 C5** 13 30N 3 1 E
Yenice, *Ankara, Turkey* **100 C5** 39 14N 32 42 E
Yenice, *Aydın, Turkey* **49 D10** 37 49N 28 35 E
Yenice, *Çanakkale, Turkey* **49 B9** 39 55N 27 17 E
Yenice, *Edirne, Turkey* **51 F10** 40 42N 26 9 E
Yenice →, *Turkey* **100 D6** 37 37N 35 33 E
Yenifoça, *Turkey* **49 C8** 38 44N 26 51 E
Yenihisar, *Turkey* **49 D9** 37 22N 27 16 E
Yeniköy, *Bursa, Turkey* **51 F13** 40 31N 29 22 E
Yeniköy, *Çanakkale, Turkey* **49 B8** 39 55N 26 10 E
Yeniköy, *Kütahya, Turkey* **49 C11** 38 52N 29 17 E
Yenipazar, *Turkey* **49 D10** 37 49N 28 11 E
Yenisaía, *Greece* **51 E8** 41 1N 24 57 E
Yenişehir, *Turkey* **51 F13** 40 16N 29 38 E
Yenisey →, *Russia* **66 B9** 71 50N 82 40 E
Yeniseysk, *Russia* **67 D10** 58 27N 92 13 E
Yeniseyskiy Zaliv, *Russia* **66 B9** 72 20N 81 0 E
Yennádhi, *Greece* **38 E11** 36 2N 27 56 E
Yenne, *France* **29 C9** 45 43N 5 44 E
Yenotayevka, *Russia* **61 G8** 47 15N 47 0 E
Yenyuka, *Russia* **67 D13** 57 57N 121 15 E
Yeo →, *U.K.* **21 G5** 51 2N 2 49W
Yeo, L., *Australia* **125 E3** 28 0 S 124 30 E
Yeo I., *Canada* **150 A3** 45 24N 81 48W

Z

304 Zamora-Chinchipe

Zamora-Chinchipe □, *Ecuador* **168 D2** 4 15 S 78 50W
Zamość, *Poland* **55 H10** 50 43N 23 15 E
Zams, *Austria* **33 B11** 47 9N 10 35 E
Zamtang, *China* **76 A3** 32 26N 101 6 E
Zamuro, Sierra del, *Venezuela* **169 C5** 4 0N 62 30W
Zamzam, W. →, *Libya* **108 B2** 30 58N 14 48 E
Zan, *Ghana* **113 D4** 9 26N 0 17W
Zanaga, *Congo* **114 C2** 2 48 S 13 48 E
Záncara →, *Spain* **41 F1** 39 18N 3 18W
Zanderij, *Surinam* **169 B6** 5 20N 55 16W
Zandu, *Dem. Rep. of the Congo* **115 D3** 5 11 S 18 16 E
Zandvoort, *Neths.* **24 B4** 52 22N 4 32 E
Zanesville, *U.S.A.* **150 G2** 39 56N 82 1W
Zangābād, *Iran* **96 B5** 38 26N 46 44 E
Zangue →, *Mozam.* **119 F4** 17 50 S 35 21 E
Zanjān, *Iran* **97 B6** 36 40N 48 35 E
Zanjān □, *Iran* **97 B6** 37 20N 49 30 E
Zanjān →, *Iran* **97 B6** 37 8N 47 47 E
Zannone, *Italy* **46 B6** 40 58N 13 3 E
Zante = Zákinthos, *Greece* **39 D2** 37 47N 20 54 E
Zanthus, *Australia* **125 F3** 31 2 S 123 34 E
Zanzibar, *Tanzania* **118 D4** 6 12 S 39 12 E
Zanzūr, *Libya* **108 B2** 32 55N 13 1 E
Zaouatallaz, *Algeria* **111 D6** 24 52N 8 30 E
Zaouiet El-Kala = Bordj Omar Driss, *Algeria* **111 C6** 28 10N 6 40 E
Zaouiet Reggâne, *Algeria* **111 C5** 26 32N 0 3 E
Zaoyang, *China* **77 A9** 32 10N 112 45 E
Zaozhuang, *China* **75 G9** 34 50N 117 35 E
Zap Suyu = Zāb al Kabīr →, *Iraq* **101 D10** 36 1N 43 24 E
Zapadna Morava →, *Serbia, Yug.* **50 C5** 43 38N 21 30 E
Zapadnaya Dvina = Daugava →, *Latvia* **15 H21** 57 4N 24 3 E
Zapadnaya Dvina, *Russia* **58 D7** 56 15N 32 3 E
Západné Beskydy, *Europe* **35 B12** 49 30N 19 0 E
Zapadni Rodopi, *Bulgaria* **50 E7** 41 50N 24 0 E
Západočeský □, *Czech Rep.* **34 B6** 49 35N 13 0 E
Zapala, *Argentina* **176 A2** 39 0 S 70 5W
Zapaleri, Cerro, *Bolivia* **174 A2** 22 49 S 67 11W
Zapata, *U.S.A.* **155 M5** 26 55N 99 16W
Zapatón →, *Spain* **43 F4** 39 0N 6 49W
Zapiga, *Chile* **172 D4** 19 40 S 69 55W
Zapolyarnyy, *Russia* **56 A5** 69 26N 30 51 E
Zaporizhzhya, *Ukraine* **59 J8** 47 50N 35 10 E
Zaporozhye = Zaporizhzhya, *Ukraine* **59 J8** 47 50N 35 10 E
Zaqatala, *Azerbaijan* **61 K8** 41 38N 46 35 E
Zara, *Turkey* **100 C7** 39 58N 37 43 E
Zarafshon, *Uzbekistan* **65 C2** 41 34N 64 12 E
Zaragoza, *Colombia* **168 B3** 7 30N 74 52W
Zaragoza, *Coahuila, Mexico* **162 B4** 28 30N 101 0W
Zaragoza, *Nuevo León, Mexico* **163 C5** 24 0N 99 46W
Zaragoza, *Spain* **40 D4** 41 39N 0 53W
Zaragoza □, *Spain* **40 D4** 41 35N 1 0W
Zarand, *Kermān, Iran* **97 D8** 30 46N 56 34 E
Zarand, *Markazī, Iran* **97 C6** 35 18N 50 25 E
Zărandului, Munţii, *Romania* **52 D7** 46 14N 22 7 E
Zaranj, *Afghan.* **91 C1** 30 55N 61 55 E
Zarasai, *Lithuania* **15 J22** 55 40N 26 20 E
Zárate, *Argentina* **174 C4** 34 7 S 59 0W
Zarautz, *Spain* **40 B2** 43 17N 2 10W
Zaraysk, *Russia* **58 E10** 54 48N 38 53 E
Zaraza, *Venezuela* **169 B4** 9 21N 65 19W
Zarbdar, *Uzbekistan* **65 C4** 40 3N 68 10 E
Zard, Kūh-e, *Iran* **97 C6** 32 22N 50 4 E
Zāreh, *Iran* **97 C6** 35 7N 49 9 E
Zari, *Nigeria* **113 C7** 13 4N 12 45 E
Zaria, *Nigeria* **113 C6** 11 0N 7 40 E
Żarki, *Poland* **55 H6** 50 38N 19 23 E
Zárkon, *Greece* **48 B4** 39 38N 22 6 E
Zarneh, *Iran* **96 C5** 33 55N 46 10 E
Zărneşti, *Romania* **53 E10** 45 33N 25 18 E
Zarós, *Greece* **39 E5** 35 8N 24 54 E
Żarów, *Poland* **55 H3** 50 56N 16 29 E
Zarqā', Nahr az →, *Jordan* **103 C4** 32 10N 35 37 E
Zarrīn, *Iran* **97 C7** 32 46N 54 37 E
Zaruma, *Ecuador* **168 D2** 3 40 S 79 38W
Żary, *Poland* **55 G2** 51 37N 15 10 E
Zarza de Granadilla, *Spain* **42 E4** 40 14N 6 3W
Zarzaïtine, *Algeria* **111 C6** 28 15N 9 34 E
Zarzal, *Colombia* **168 C2** 4 24N 76 4W
Zarzis, *Tunisia* **108 B2** 33 31N 11 2 E
Zas, *Spain* **42 B2** 43 4N 8 53W
Zaskar →, *India* **93 B7** 34 13N 77 20 E
Zaskar Mts., *India* **93 C7** 33 15N 77 30 E
Zastron, *S. Africa* **116 E4** 30 18 S 27 7 E
Žatec, *Czech Rep.* **34 A6** 50 20N 13 32 E
Zaterechnyy, *Russia* **61 H7** 44 48N 45 11 E
Zator, *Poland* **55 J6** 49 59N 19 28 E
Zavala, *Bos.-H.* **50 D1** 42 50N 17 59 E
Zavāreh, *Iran* **97 C7** 33 29N 52 28 E
Zave, *Zimbabwe* **117 B5** 17 6 S 30 1 E
Zavérdhas, Kólpos, *Greece* **39 B2** 38 47N 20 51 E
Zavetnoye, *Russia* **61 G6** 47 13N 43 50 E
Zavidovići, *Bos.-H.* **52 F3** 44 27N 18 10 E
Zavitinsk, *Russia* **67 D13** 50 10N 129 20 E
Zavodovski, I., *Antarctica* **7 B1** 56 0 S 27 45W
Zavolzhsk, *Russia* **60 B6** 57 30N 42 0 E
Zavolzhye, *Russia* **60 B6** 56 37N 43 26 E
Zawadzkie, *Poland* **55 H5** 50 37N 18 28 E
Zawichost, *Poland* **55 H8** 50 48N 21 51 E
Zawidów, *Poland* **55 G2** 51 1N 15 1 E
Zawiercie, *Poland* **55 H6** 50 30N 19 24 E
Zāwiyat al Bayḑā = Al Bayḑā, *Libya* **108 B4** 32 50N 21 44 E
Zāwiyat Masūs, *Libya* **108 B4** 31 35N 21 1 E
Zâwyet Shammas, *Egypt* **106 A2** 31 30N 26 37 E
Zâwyet Um el Rakham, *Egypt* **106 A2** 31 18N 27 1 E
Zâwyet Ungeîla, *Egypt* **106 A2** 31 23N 26 42 E
Zāyā, *Iraq* **96 C5** 33 33N 44 13 E
Zāyandeh →, *Iran* **97 C7** 32 35N 52 0 E
Zaymah, *Si. Arabia* **98 B3** 21 37N 40 6 E
Zaysan, *Kazakstan* **66 E9** 47 28N 84 52 E
Zaysan, Oz., *Kazakstan* **66 E9** 48 0N 83 0 E
Zayü, *China* **76 C1** 28 48N 97 27 E
Zazafotsy, *Madag.* **117 C8** 21 11 S 46 21 E
Zāzamt, W. →, *Libya* **108 B2** 30 29N 14 30 E
Zazir, O. →, *Algeria* **111 D6** 22 0N 5 40 E
Zázrivá, *Slovak Rep.* **35 B12** 49 16N 19 7 E
Zbarazh, *Ukraine* **59 H3** 49 43N 25 44 E
Zbąszyń, *Poland* **55 F2** 52 14N 15 56 E
Zbąszynek, *Poland* **55 F2** 52 16N 15 51 E
Zblewo, *Poland* **54 E5** 53 56N 18 19 E
Žďár nad Sázavov, *Czech Rep.* **34 B8** 49 34N 15 57 E
Zdolbuniv, *Ukraine* **59 G4** 50 30N 26 15 E
Ždrelo, *Serbia, Yug.* **50 B5** 44 16N 21 28 E
Zduńska Wola, *Poland* **55 G5** 51 37N 18 59 E
Zduny, *Poland* **55 G4** 51 39N 17 21 E
Zearing, *U.S.A.* **156 B3** 42 10N 93 18W
Zēbāk, *Afghan.* **65 E5** 36 31N 71 20 E
Zeballos, *Canada* **142 D3** 49 59N 126 50W
Zebbug, *Malta* **38 F7** 35 52N 14 26 E
Zebbug, *Gozo, Malta* **38 E6** 36 4N 14 14 E
Zebediela, *S. Africa* **117 C4** 24 20 S 29 17 E
Zebila, *Ghana* **113 C4** 10 55N 0 30W
Zebulon, *U.S.A.* **152 B5** 33 6N 84 21W
Zeebrugge, *Belgium* **24 C3** 51 19N 3 12 E
Zeehan, *Australia* **127 G4** 41 52 S 145 25 E
Zeeland, *U.S.A.* **157 B10** 42 49N 86 1W
Zeeland □, *Neths.* **24 C3** 51 30N 3 50 E
Zeerust, *S. Africa* **116 D4** 25 31 S 26 4 E
Zefat, *Israel* **103 C4** 32 58N 35 29 E
Zegdou, *Algeria* **110 C4** 29 51N 4 45W
Zege, *Ethiopia* **107 E4** 11 43N 37 18 E
Zeggerene, Iracher, *Mali* **113 B5** 16 49N 2 16 E
Zégoua, *Mali* **112 C3** 10 32N 5 35W
Zehdenick, *Germany* **30 C9** 52 58N 13 20 E
Zeigler, *U.S.A.* **156 G7** 37 54N 89 3W
Zeil, Mt., *Australia* **124 D5** 23 30 S 132 23 E
Zeila, *Somali Rep.* **120 B2** 11 21N 43 30 E
Zeist, *Neths.* **24 B5** 52 5N 5 15 E
Zeitz, *Germany* **30 D8** 51 2N 12 7 E
Zejtun, *Malta* **38 F8** 35 51N 14 32 E
Żelechów, *Poland* **55 G8** 51 49N 21 54 E
Zelengora, *Bos.-H.* **50 C2** 43 22N 18 30 E
Zelenodolsk, *Russia* **60 C9** 55 55N 48 30 E
Zelenogorsk, *Russia* **58 B5** 60 12N 29 43 E
Zelenograd, *Russia* **58 D9** 56 1N 37 12 E
Zelenogradsk, *Russia* **15 J19** 54 53N 20 29 E
Zelenokumsk, *Russia* **61 H6** 44 24N 44 0 E
Železná Ruda, *Czech Rep.* **34 B6** 49 8N 13 15 E
Železnik, *Serbia, Yug.* **50 B4** 44 43N 20 23 E
Zelfana, *Algeria* **111 B5** 32 27N 4 15 E
Zelienople, *U.S.A.* **150 F4** 40 48N 80 8W
Želiezovce, *Slovak Rep.* **35 C11** 48 3N 18 40 E
Zelina, *Croatia* **45 C13** 45 57N 16 16 E
Zell, *Baden-W., Germany* **31 H3** 47 42N 7 52 E
Zell, *Rhld-Pfz., Germany* **31 E3** 50 1N 7 10 E
Zell am See, *Austria* **34 D5** 47 19N 12 47 E
Zella-Mehlis, *Germany* **30 E6** 50 39N 10 40 E
Zelów, *Poland* **55 G6** 51 28N 19 14 E
Zeltweg, *Austria* **34 D7** 47 11N 14 45 E
Zembra, I., *Tunisia* **108 A2** 37 5N 10 56 E
Zémio, *C.A.R.* **118 A2** 5 2N 25 5 E
Zemmora, *Algeria* **111 A5** 35 44N 0 51 E
Zemmur, *W. Sahara* **110 C2** 25 5N 12 0W
Zemongo, Réserve de Faune de, *C.A.R.* **114 A5** 6 45N 25 5 E
Zemoul, O. →, *Algeria* **110 C3** 29 15N 7 0W
Zempléni-hegység, *Hungary* **52 B6** 48 25N 21 25 E
Zemplínska šírava, *Slovak Rep.* **35 C15** 48 48N 22 0 E
Zemun, *Serbia, Yug.* **50 B4** 44 51N 20 25 E
Zendeh Jān, *Afghan.* **91 B1** 34 21N 61 45 E
Zengbé, *Cameroon* **113 D7** 5 46N 13 4 E
Zengcheng, *China* **77 F9** 23 13N 113 52 E
Zenica, *Bos.-H.* **52 F2** 44 10N 17 57 E
Zentsūji, *Japan* **72 C5** 34 14N 133 47 E
Zenza →, *Angola* **115 D2** 8 45 S 13 24 E
Zenza do Itombe, *Angola* **115 D2** 9 16 S 14 13 E
Žepče, *Bos.-H.* **52 F3** 44 28N 18 2 E
Zephyrhills, *U.S.A.* **153 G7** 28 14N 82 11W
Zepu, *China* **65 D8** 38 12N 77 18 E
Zeraf, Bahr ez →, *Sudan* **107 F3** 9 42N 30 52 E
Zeravshan, *Tajikistan* **65 D4** 39 10N 68 39 E
Zeravshan →, *Asia* **65 D1** 39 22N 63 45 E
Zeravshanskiy Khrebet, *Tajikistan* **65 D4** 39 20N 69 0 E
Zerbst, *Germany* **30 D8** 51 58N 12 5 E
Żerków, *Poland* **55 F4** 52 4N 17 32 E
Zermatt, *Switz.* **32 D5** 46 2N 7 46 E
Zernez, *Switz.* **33 C10** 46 42N 10 7 E
Zernograd, *Russia* **61 G5** 46 52N 40 19 E
Zerqan, *Albania* **50 E4** 41 27N 20 20 E
Zestaponi, *Georgia* **61 J6** 42 6N 43 0 E
Zetel, *Germany* **30 B3** 53 25N 7 58 E
Zeulenroda, *Germany* **30 E7** 50 39N 11 59 E
Zeven, *Germany* **30 B5** 53 17N 9 16 E
Zevenaar, *Neths.* **24 C6** 51 56N 6 5 E
Zévio, *Italy* **44 C8** 45 22N 11 8 E
Zeya, *Russia* **67 D13** 53 48N 127 14 E
Zeya →, *Russia* **67 D13** 51 42N 128 53 E
Zeytinbaği, *Turkey* **51 F12** 40 24N 28 47 E
Zeytindağ, *Turkey* **49 C9** 38 58N 27 4 E
Zghartā, *Lebanon* **103 A4** 34 21N 35 53 E
Zgierz, *Poland* **55 G6** 51 50N 19 27 E
Zgorzelec, *Poland* **55 G2** 51 10N 15 0 E
Zguriţa, *Moldova* **53 B13** 48 8N 28 1 E
Zhabasak, *Kazakstan* **64 F8** 50 22N 61 41 E
Zhabinka, *Belarus* **59 F3** 52 13N 24 2 E
Zhailma, *Kazakstan* **64 F8** 51 37N 61 33 E
Zhalanash, *Kazakstan* **65 B9** 43 3N 78 38 E
Zhambyl = Taraz, *Kazakstan* **66 E8** 42 54N 71 22 E
Zhanatas, *Kazakstan* **65 B4** 43 35N 69 35 E
Zhangaly, *Kazakstan* **61 G10** 47 1N 50 37 E
Zhangaqazaly, *Kazakstan* **66 E7** 45 48N 62 6 E
Zhangaqŭrghan, *Kazakstan* **65 B4** 43 50N 68 48 E
Zhangatas = Zhanatas, *Kazakstan* **65 B4** 43 35N 69 35 E
Zhangbei, *China* **74 D8** 41 10N 114 45 E
Zhangguangcai Ling, *China* **75 B15** 45 0N 129 0 E
Zhangjiabian, *China* **69 F9** 22 33N 113 28 E
Zhangjiakou, *China* **74 D8** 40 48N 114 55 E
Zhangping, *China* **77 E11** 25 17N 117 23 E
Zhangpu, *China* **77 E11** 24 8N 117 35 E
Zhangshu, *China* **77 C10** 28 4N 115 29 E
Zhangwu, *China* **75 C12** 42 43N 123 52 E
Zhangye, *China* **68 C5** 38 50N 100 23 E
Zhangzhou, *China* **77 E11** 24 30N 117 35 E
Zhanhua, *China* **75 F10** 37 40N 118 8 E
Zhanjiang, *China* **77 G8** 21 15N 110 20 E
Zhannetty, Ostrov, *Russia* **67 B16** 76 43N 158 0 E
Zhanyi, *China* **76 E4** 25 38N 103 48 E
Zhanyu, *China* **75 B12** 44 30N 122 30 E
Zhao Xian, *China* **74 F8** 37 43N 114 45 E
Zhao'an, *China* **77 F11** 23 41N 117 10 E
Zhaocheng, *China* **74 F6** 36 22N 111 38 E
Zhaojue, *China* **76 C4** 28 1N 102 49 E
Zhaoping, *China* **77 E8** 24 11N 110 48 E
Zhaoqing, *China* **77 F9** 23 0N 112 20 E
Zhaotong, *China* **76 D4** 27 20N 103 44 E
Zhaoyuan, *Heilongjiang, China* **75 B13** 45 27N 125 0 E
Zhaoyuan, *Shandong, China* **75 F11** 37 20N 120 23 E
Zharkovskiy, *Russia* **58 E7** 55 56N 32 19 E
Zhashkiv, *Ukraine* **59 H6** 49 15N 30 5 E
Zhashui, *China* **74 H5** 33 40N 109 8 E
Zhayyq →, *Kazakstan* **57 E9** 47 0N 51 48 E
Zhdanov = Mariupol, *Ukraine* **59 J9** 47 5N 37 31 E
Zhdanovo, *Kazakstan* **65 B5** 43 40N 71 6 E
Zhecheng, *China* **74 G8** 34 7N 115 20 E
Zhegao, *China* **77 B11** 31 46N 117 45 E
Zhejiang □, *China* **77 C13** 29 0N 120 0 E
Zheleznodorozhnyy, *Russia* **56 B9** 62 35N 50 55 E
Zheleznogorsk, *Russia* **59 F8** 52 22N 35 23 E
Zheleznogorsk-Ilimskiy, *Russia* **67 D11** 56 34N 104 8 E
Zheltyye Vody = Zhovti Vody, *Ukraine* **59 H7** 48 21N 33 31 E
Zhen'an, *China* **74 H5** 33 27N 109 9 E
Zhenba, *China* **76 A6** 32 34N 107 58 E
Zhenfeng, *China* **76 E5** 25 22N 105 40 E
Zheng'an, *China* **76 C6** 28 32N 107 27 E
Zhengding, *China* **74 E8** 38 8N 114 32 E
Zhenghe, *China* **77 D12** 27 20N 118 50 E
Zhengyang, *China* **77 A10** 32 37N 114 22 E
Zhengyangguan, *China* **77 A11** 32 30N 116 29 E
Zhengzhou, *China* **74 G7** 34 45N 113 34 E
Zhenhai, *China* **77 C13** 29 59N 121 42 E
Zhenjiang, *China* **77 A12** 32 11N 119 26 E
Zhenkang, *China* **76 F2** 23 58N 99 0 E
Zhenlai, *China* **75 B12** 45 50N 123 5 E
Zhenning, *China* **76 D5** 26 4N 105 45 E
Zhenping, *Henan, China* **74 H7** 33 10N 112 16 E
Zhenping, *Shaanxi, China* **76 B7** 31 59N 109 31 E
Zhenxiong, *China* **76 D5** 27 27N 104 50 E
Zhenyuan, *Gansu, China* **74 G4** 35 35N 107 30 E
Zhenyuan, *Guizhou, China* **76 D7** 27 4N 108 21 E
Zherdevka, *Russia* **60 E5** 51 56N 41 29 E
Zherong, *China* **77 D12** 27 15N 119 52 E
Zhetigen, *Kazakstan* **65 B8** 43 40N 77 6 E
Zhetiqara, *Kazakstan* **64 E8** 52 11N 61 12 E
Zhetisay, *Kazakstan* **65 C4** 40 46N 68 19 E
Zhezqazghan, *Kazakstan* **66 E7** 47 44N 67 40 E
Zhicheng, *China* **77 B8** 30 25N 111 27 E
Zhidan, *China* **74 F5** 36 48N 108 48 E
Zhigansk, *Russia* **67 C13** 66 48N 123 27 E
Zhigulevsk, *Russia* **60 D9** 53 28N 49 30 E
Zhijiang, *Hubei, China* **77 B8** 30 28N 111 45 E
Zhijiang, *Hunan, China* **76 D7** 27 27N 109 42 E
Zhijin, *China* **76 D5** 26 37N 105 45 E
Zhilinda, *Russia* **67 C12** 70 0N 114 20 E
Zhirnovsk, *Russia* **60 E7** 50 57N 44 49 E
Zhitomir = Zhytomyr, *Ukraine* **59 G5** 50 20N 28 40 E
Zhizdra, *Russia* **58 F8** 53 45N 34 40 E
Zhlobin, *Belarus* **59 F6** 52 55N 30 0 E
Zhmerinka = Zhmerynka, *Ukraine* **59 H5** 49 2N 28 2 E
Zhmerynka, *Ukraine* **59 H5** 49 2N 28 2 E
Zhob, *Pakistan* **91 C3** 31 20N 69 31 E
Zhob →, *Pakistan* **92 C3** 32 4N 69 50 E
Zhodino = Zhodzina, *Belarus* **58 E5** 54 5N 28 17 E
Zhodzina, *Belarus* **58 E5** 54 5N 28 17 E
Zhokhova, Ostrov, *Russia* **67 B16** 76 4N 152 40 E
Zhongdian, *China* **76 D2** 27 48N 99 42 E
Zhongdong, *China* **76 F6** 22 48N 107 47 E
Zhongdu, *China* **76 E7** 24 40N 109 40 E
Zhongning, *China* **74 F3** 37 29N 105 40 E
Zhongshan, *Guangdong, China* **77 F9** 22 26N 113 20 E
Zhongshan, *Guangxi Zhuangzu, China* **77 E8** 24 29N 111 18 E
Zhongshankong, *China* **69 F9** 22 35N 113 29 E
Zhongtiao Shan, *China* **74 G6** 35 0N 111 10 E
Zhongwei, *China* **74 F3** 37 30N 105 12 E
Zhongxiang, *China* **77 B9** 31 12N 112 34 E
Zhongyang, *China* **74 F6** 37 20N 111 11 E
Zhoucun, *China* **75 F9** 36 47N 117 48 E
Zhouning, *China* **77 D12** 27 12N 119 20 E
Zhoushan, *China* **77 B14** 30 1N 122 6 E
Zhoushan Dao, *China* **77 C14** 30 5N 122 10 E
Zhouzhi, *China* **74 G5** 34 10N 108 12 E
Zhovti Vody, *Ukraine* **59 H7** 48 21N 33 31 E
Zhovtneve, *Ukraine* **59 J7** 46 54N 32 3 E
Zhovtnevoye = Zhovtneve, *Ukraine* **59 J7** 46 54N 32 3 E
Zhu Jiang →, *China* **77 F9** 22 45N 113 37 E
Zhuanghe, *China* **75 E12** 39 40N 123 0 E
Zhŭantöbe, *Kazakstan* **65 A4** 44 46N 68 49 E
Zhucheng, *China* **75 G10** 36 0N 119 27 E
Zhugqu, *China* **74 H3** 33 40N 104 30 E
Zhuhai, *China* **77 F9** 22 17N 113 34 E
Zhuji, *China* **77 C13** 29 40N 120 10 E
Zhujiang Kou, *China* **69 G10** 22 20N 113 45 E
Zhukovka, *Russia* **58 F7** 53 35N 33 50 E
Zhumadian, *China* **74 H8** 32 59N 114 2 E
Zhuo Xian = Zhuozhou, *China* **74 E8** 39 28N 115 58 E
Zhuolu, *China* **74 D8** 40 20N 115 12 E
Zhuozhou, *China* **74 E8** 39 28N 115 58 E
Zhuozi, *China* **74 D7** 41 0N 112 25 E
Zhushan, *China* **77 A8** 32 15N 110 13 E
Zhuxi, *China* **76 A7** 32 25N 109 40 E
Zhuzhou, *China* **77 D9** 27 49N 113 12 E
Zhytomyr, *Ukraine* **59 G5** 50 20N 28 40 E
Zi Shui →, *China* **77 C9** 28 40N 112 40 E
Žiar nad Hronom, *Slovak Rep.* **35 C11** 48 35N 18 53 E
Zīārān, *Iran* **97 B6** 36 7N 50 32 E
Ziarat, *Pakistan* **92 D2** 30 25N 67 49 E
Zibo, *China* **75 F10** 36 47N 118 3 E
Zichang, *China* **74 F5** 37 18N 109 40 E
Zidarovo, *Bulgaria* **51 D11** 42 20N 27 24 E
Ziębice, *Poland* **55 H4** 50 37N 17 2 E
Zielona Góra, *Poland* **55 G2** 51 57N 15 31 E
Zierikzee, *Neths.* **24 C3** 51 40N 3 55 E
Ziesar, *Germany* **30 C8** 52 16N 12 17 E
Zifta, *Egypt* **106 H7** 30 43N 31 14 E
Zigey, *Chad* **109 F3** 14 43N 15 50 E
Zigon, *Burma* **90 F5** 18 20N 95 37 E
Zigong, *China* **76 C5** 29 15N 104 48 E
Ziguinchor, *Senegal* **112 C1** 12 35N 16 20W
Zihuatanejo, *Mexico* **162 D4** 17 38N 101 33W
Zijin, *China* **77 F10** 23 33N 115 8 E
Zile, *Turkey* **100 B6** 40 15N 35 52 E
Žilina, *Slovak Rep.* **35 B11** 49 12N 18 42 E
Žilinský □, *Slovak Rep.* **35 B12** 49 10N 19 0 E
Zillah, *Libya* **108 C3** 28 30N 17 33 E
Zillertaler Alpen, *Austria* **34 D4** 47 6N 11 45 E
Zima, *Russia* **67 D11** 54 0N 102 5 E
Zimane, Adrar in, *Algeria* **111 D5** 22 10N 4 30 E
Zimapán, *Mexico* **163 C5** 20 54N 99 20W
Zimba, *Zambia* **119 F2** 17 20 S 26 11 E
Zimbabwe, *Zimbabwe* **119 G3** 20 16 S 30 54 E
Zimbabwe ■, *Africa* **119 F3** 19 0 S 30 0 E
Zimi, *S. Leone* **112 D2** 7 20N 11 20W
Zimnicea, *Romania* **53 G10** 43 40N 25 22 E
Zimovniki, *Russia* **61 G6** 47 10N 42 25 E
Zina, *Cent. Amer.* **109 F2** 11 19N 14 54 E
Zinal, *Switz.* **32 D5** 46 8N 7 38 E
Zinave, Parque Nacional de, *Mozam.* **117 C5** 21 35 S 33 40 E
Zinder, *Niger* **113 C6** 13 48N 9 0 E
Zinga, *C.A.R.* **114 B3** 3 49N 18 34 E
Zinga, *Tanzania* **119 D4** 9 16 S 38 49 E
Zingst, *Germany* **30 A8** 54 26N 12 39 E
Ziniaré, *Burkina Faso* **113 C4** 12 35N 1 18W
Zinnowitz, *Germany* **30 A9** 54 4N 13 54 E
Zion, *U.S.A.* **157 B9** 42 27N 87 50W
Zion Nat. Park, *U.S.A.* **159 H7** 37 15N 113 5W
Zionsville, *U.S.A.* **157 E10** 39 57N 86 16W
Zipaquirá, *Colombia* **168 C3** 5 0N 74 0W
Zirbitzkogel, *Austria* **34 D7** 47 4N 14 34 E
Zirc, *Hungary* **52 C2** 47 17N 17 52 E
Žiri, *Slovenia* **45 B11** 46 5N 14 5 E
Žirje, *Croatia* **45 E12** 43 39N 15 42 E
Zirl, *Austria* **34 D4** 47 17N 11 14 E
Zirndorf, *Germany* **31 F6** 49 27N 10 57 E
Ziros, *Greece* **39 E7** 35 5N 26 8 E
Zirreh, Gowd-e, *Afghan.* **91 C1** 29 45N 62 0 E
Zisterdorf, *Austria* **35 C9** 48 33N 16 45 E
Zitácuaro, *Mexico* **162 D4** 19 28N 100 21W
Žitava →, *Slovak Rep.* **35 C11** 48 14N 18 21 E
Žitište, *Serbia, Yug.* **52 E5** 45 30N 20 32 E
Zitong, *China* **76 B5** 31 37N 105 10 E
Zítsa, *Greece* **48 B2** 39 47N 20 40 E
Zittau, *Germany* **30 E10** 50 53N 14 48 E
Zitundo, *Mozam.* **117 D5** 26 48 S 32 47 E
Živinice, *Bos.-H.* **52 F3** 44 27N 18 36 E
Ziwa Maghariba □, *Tanzania* **118 C3** 2 0 S 31 30 E
Ziway, L., *Ethiopia* **107 F4** 8 0N 38 50 E
Zixi, *China* **77 D11** 27 45N 117 4 E
Zixing, *China* **77 E9** 25 59N 113 21 E
Ziyang, *Shaanxi, China* **74 H5** 32 32N 108 31 E
Ziyang, *Sichuan, China* **76 B5** 30 6N 104 40 E
Ziyuan, *China* **77 D8** 26 2N 110 40 E
Ziyun, *China* **76 E6** 25 45N 106 5 E
Ziz, Oued →, *Morocco* **110 B4** 31 40N 4 15W
Zizhong, *China* **76 C5** 29 48N 104 47 E
Zlarin, *Croatia* **45 E12** 43 42N 15 49 E
Zlatar, *Croatia* **45 B13** 46 5N 16 3 E
Zlatar, *Serbia, Yug.* **50 C3** 43 25N 19 47 E
Zlataritsa, *Bulgaria* **51 C9** 43 2N 25 55 E
Zlaté Moravce, *Slovak Rep.* **35 C11** 48 23N 18 24 E
Zlatibor, *Serbia, Yug.* **50 C3** 43 45N 19 43 E
Zlatitsa, *Bulgaria* **51 D8** 42 41N 24 7 E
Zlatna, *Romania* **53 D8** 46 8N 23 11 E
Zlatna Panega, *Bulgaria* **51 C8** 43 5N 24 9 E
Zlatni Pyasŭtsi, *Bulgaria* **51 C12** 43 17N 28 3 E
Zlatograd, *Bulgaria* **51 E9** 41 22N 25 7 E
Zlatoust, *Russia* **64 D7** 55 10N 59 40 E
Zletovo, *Macedonia* **50 E6** 41 59N 22 17 E
Zlín, *Czech Rep.* **35 B10** 49 14N 17 40 E
Zlīţan, *Libya* **108 B2** 32 32N 14 35 E
Złocieniec, *Poland* **54 E3** 53 30N 16 1 E
Złoczew, *Poland* **55 G5** 51 24N 18 35 E
Zlot, *Serbia, Yug.* **50 B5** 44 1N 21 58 E
Złotoryja, *Poland* **55 G2** 51 8N 15 55 E
Złotów, *Poland* **54 E4** 53 22N 17 2 E
Zmeinogorsk, *Kazakstan* **66 D9** 51 10N 82 13 E
Żmigród, *Poland* **55 G3** 51 28N 16 53 E
Zmiyev, *Ukraine* **59 H9** 49 39N 36 27 E
Znamenka = Znamyanka, *Ukraine* **59 H7** 48 45N 32 30 E
Znamyanka, *Ukraine* **59 H7** 48 45N 32 30 E
Żnin, *Poland* **55 F4** 52 51N 17 44 E
Znojmo, *Czech Rep.* **34 C9** 48 50N 16 2 E
Zobeyrī, *Iran* **96 C5** 34 10N 46 40 E
Zobia, *Dem. Rep. of the Congo* **118 B2** 3 0N 25 59 E
Zoetermeer, *Neths.* **24 B4** 52 3N 4 30 E
Zofingen, *Switz.* **32 B5** 47 17N 7 56 E
Zogang, *China* **76 C1** 29 55N 97 42 E
Zogno, *Italy* **44 C6** 45 48N 9 40 E
Zogqên, *China* **76 A2** 32 13N 98 47 E
Zolfo Springs, *U.S.A.* **153 H8** 27 30N 81 48W
Zollikofen, *Switz.* **32 C4** 47 0N 7 28 E
Zollikon, *Switz.* **33 B7** 47 21N 8 34 E
Zolochev = Zolochiv, *Ukraine* **59 H3** 49 45N 24 51 E
Zolochiv, *Ukraine* **59 H3** 49 45N 24 51 E
Zolotonosha, *Ukraine* **59 H7** 49 39N 32 5 E
Zomba, *Malawi* **119 F4** 15 22 S 35 19 E
Zongo, *Dem. Rep. of the Congo* **114 B3** 4 20N 18 35 E
Zonguldak, *Turkey* **100 B4** 41 28N 31 50 E
Zongyang, *China* **77 B11** 30 42N 117 12 E
Zonqor Pt., *Malta* **38 F8** 35 52N 14 34 E
Zonza, *France* **29 G13** 41 45N 9 11 E
Zoo Baba, *Niger* **109 E2** 18 13N 13 2 E
Zorgo, *Burkina Faso* **113 C4** 12 15N 0 35W
Zorita, *Spain* **43 F5** 39 17N 5 39W
Zorleni, *Romania* **53 D12** 46 14N 27 44 E
Zornitsa, *Bulgaria* **51 D10** 42 23N 26 58 E
Zorritos, *Peru* **172 A1** 3 43 S 80 40W
Żory, *Poland* **55 H5** 50 3N 18 44 E
Zorzor, *Liberia* **112 D3** 7 46N 9 28W
Zossen, *Germany* **30 C9** 52 13N 13 27 E
Zou Xiang, *China* **74 G9** 35 30N 116 58 E
Zouan-Hounien, *Ivory C.* **112 D3** 6 55N 8 15W
Zouar, *Chad* **109 D3** 20 30N 16 32 E
Zouérate = Zouîrât, *Mauritania* **110 D2** 22 44N 12 21W
Zouîrât, *Mauritania* **110 D2** 22 44N 12 21W
Zouri, *Gabon* **114 C1** 1 1 S 8 53 E
Zourika, *Niger* **113 B6** 19 16N 7 52 E
Zourma, *Burkina Faso* **113 C4** 11 20N 0 50W
Zousfana, O. →, *Algeria* **111 B4** 31 28N 2 17W
Zoutkamp, *Neths.* **24 A6** 53 20N 6 18 E
Zrenjanin, *Serbia, Yug.* **52 E5** 45 22N 20 23 E
Zuarungu, *Ghana* **113 C4** 10 49N 0 46W
Zuba, *Nigeria* **113 D6** 9 11N 7 12 E
Zubayr, *Yemen* **98 D3** 15 3N 42 10 E
Zubtsov, *Russia* **58 D8** 56 10N 34 34 E
Zudáñez, *Bolivia* **173 D5** 19 6 S 64 44W
Zuénoula, *Ivory C.* **112 D3** 7 34N 6 3W
Zuera, *Spain* **40 D4** 41 51N 0 49W
Zuetina = Az Zuwaytīnah, *Libya* **108 B4** 30 58N 20 7 E
Ẕufār, *Oman* **99 C6** 17 40N 54 0 E
Zug, *Switz.* **33 B7** 47 10N 8 31 E
Zug, *W. Sahara* **110 D2** 21 36N 14 9W
Zug □, *Switz.* **33 B7** 47 9N 8 35 E
Zugdidi, *Georgia* **61 J5** 42 30N 41 55 E
Zugersee, *Switz.* **33 B7** 47 7N 8 35 E
Zugspitze, *Germany* **31 H6** 47 25N 10 59 E
Zuid-Holland □, *Neths.* **24 C4** 52 0N 4 35 E
Zuidbeveland, *Neths.* **24 C3** 51 30N 3 50 E
Zuidhorn, *Neths.* **24 A6** 53 15N 6 23 E
Zújar, *Spain* **43 H8** 37 34N 2 50W
Zújar →, *Spain* **43 G5** 39 1N 5 47W
Żukowo, *Poland* **54 D5** 54 21N 18 22 E
Zula, *Eritrea* **107 D4** 15 17N 39 40 E
Zulia □, *Venezuela* **168 B3** 10 0N 72 10W
Zülpich, *Germany* **30 E2** 50 41N 6 39 E
Zumaia, *Spain* **40 B2** 43 19N 2 15W
Zumárraga, *Spain* **40 B2** 43 5N 2 19W
Zumbo, *Mozam.* **119 F3** 15 35 S 30 26 E
Zummo, *Nigeria* **113 D7** 9 51N 12 59 E
Zumpango, *Mexico* **163 D5** 19 48N 99 6W
Zundi, *Angola* **115 E3** 10 28 S 16 48 E
Zungeru, *Nigeria* **113 D6** 9 48N 6 8 E
Zunhua, *China* **75 D9** 40 18N 117 58 E
Zuni, *U.S.A.* **159 J9** 35 4N 108 51W
Zunyi, *China* **76 D6** 27 42N 106 53 E
Zuo Jiang →, *China* **76 F6** 22 50N 108 6 E
Zuozhou, *China* **76 F6** 22 42N 107 27 E
Županja, *Croatia* **52 E3** 45 4N 18 43 E
Žur, *Kosovo, Yug.* **50 D4** 42 13N 20 34 E
Zura, *Russia* **64 C4** 57 36N 53 24 E
Zurbātīyah, *Iraq* **101 F12** 33 9N 46 3 E
Zürich, *Switz.* **33 B7** 47 22N 8 32 E
Zürich □, *Switz.* **33 B7** 47 26N 8 40 E
Zürichsee, *Switz.* **33 B7** 47 18N 8 40 E
Żuromin, *Poland* **55 E6** 53 4N 19 51 E
Zurrieq, *Malta* **38 F7** 35 50N 14 28 E
Zurzach, *Switz.* **33 A6** 47 35N 8 18 E
Žut, *Croatia* **45 E12** 43 52N 15 17 E
Zutphen, *Neths.* **24 B6** 52 9N 6 12 E
Zuurberg Nat. Park, *S. Africa* **116 E4** 33 12 S 25 32 E
Zuwārah, *Libya* **108 B2** 32 58N 12 1 E
Zuyevka, *Russia* **64 B3** 58 27N 51 10 E
Zūzan, *Iran* **97 C8** 34 22N 59 53 E
Žužemberk, *Slovenia* **45 C11** 45 52N 14 56 E
Zvenigorodka = Zvenyhorodka, *Ukraine* **59 H6** 49 4N 30 56 E
Zvenyhorodka, *Ukraine* **59 H6** 49 4N 30 56 E
Zverinogolovskoye, *Russia* **66 D7** 54 26N 64 50 E
Zvezdets, *Bulgaria* **51 D11** 42 6N 27 26 E
Zvishavane, *Zimbabwe* **119 G3** 20 17 S 30 2 E
Zvolen, *Slovak Rep.* **35 C12** 48 33N 19 10 E
Zvonce, *Serbia, Yug.* **50 D6** 42 57N 22 34 E
Zvornik, *Bos.-H.* **52 F4** 44 26N 19 5 E
Zwedru = Tchien, *Liberia* **112 D3** 5 59N 8 15W
Zweibrücken, *Germany* **31 F3** 49 15N 7 21 E
Zweisimmen, *Switz.* **32 C4** 46 33N 7 22 E
Zwenkau, *Germany* **30 D8** 51 13N 12 20 E
Zwettl, *Austria* **34 C8** 48 35N 15 9 E
Zwickau, *Germany* **30 E8** 50 44N 12 30 E
Zwierzyniec, *Poland* **55 H9** 50 36N 22 58 E
Zwiesel, *Germany* **31 F9** 49 1N 13 13 E
Zwoleń, *Poland* **55 G8** 51 21N 21 36 E
Zwolle, *Neths.* **24 B6** 52 31N 6 6 E
Zwolle, *U.S.A.* **155 K8** 31 38N 93 39W
Żychlin, *Poland* **55 F6** 52 15N 19 37 E
Żyrardów, *Poland* **55 F7** 52 3N 20 28 E
Zyryan, *Kazakstan* **66 E9** 49 43N 84 20 E
Zyryanka, *Russia* **67 C16** 65 45N 150 51 E
Zyryanovsk = Zyryan, *Kazakstan* **66 E9** 49 43N 84 20 E
Żywiec, *Poland* **55 J6** 49 42N 19 10 E

KEY TO EUROPEAN MAP PAGES

Large scale maps (>1:3 900 000)

Medium scale maps (1:4 000 000 – 1:9 900 000)

Small scale maps (<1:10 000 000)

Arctic Circle

11

14

19

22

22

20

23

24

26

28

42

40

38

ATLANTIC
OCEAN

8

WORLD COUNTRY INDEX